PHILIP'S

WORLD HISTORY ENCYCLOPEDIA

Philip's World History Encyclopedia

George Philip Limited,
an imprint of Octopus Publishing Group
2–4 Heron Quays
Docklands
London
E14 4JP

Editor Steve Luck

Art Editor Mike Brown

Text Editors Chris Humphries
Frances Adlington

Production Sally Banner

Reproduction by Colourpath Ltd, London

ISBN 0 540 07930 8

A catalogue record for this book is available from the British Library

Printed by Cayfosa, Spain

Details of other Philip's titles and services can be found on our website at
www.philips-maps.co.uk

INTRODUCTION

For a new millennium, when the global integration of nations and communities around is obvious and accelerating, the demand for concise information about the history of our interdependent world for schools, colleges, universities and for an educated public at large is clear and urgent.

Several developments within the study of history have also promoted a need for histories of the world. First the accumulation of knowledge about the past of different nations has engendered excessive specialization in order to cope with increasingly accessible bodies of information available in printed and electronic form. Given that the talent for synthesis is far less common than the capacity for more research, the sheer volume of publications and data about the past stimulates demands from students, scholars and a wider public for compressed, attractively presented but reliable knowledge about our universal past. Secondly, the broadening of history's traditional concerns (with states, warfare and diplomacy) in order to take account of a plurality of modern interests: ecology, evolutionary biology, ethology, botany, the health and wealth of populations, human rights, gender, family systems, private life, fashion, popular music, and so forth, points the study of history towards comparisons between Western and non-Western cultures and histories. Thirdly, in the course of their education, the young now acquire and arrive at schools and universities with portfolios of knowledge and aroused curiosities about "other" cultures. They are less easily persuaded to feed on diets of national let alone regional and parochial histories than their predecessors of a generation ago. Schools, colleges and universities need to provide spatially unfettered, ready access to the kind of historical understanding that will satisfy their capacious interests. To nourish the cosmopolitan sensibility required for the next millennium, history needs to be widened and repositioned to bring it into fruitful exchange with geography, geology, evolutionary biology and the social sciences. Barriers between archaeology, ancient, classical, medieval, early modern, contemporary and other "packages" of traditional but now anachronistic histories are being dismantled.

Unsurprisingly, the implications of "globalization" (flowing from the integration of markets via the improved speed of transportation and information technology) for the hitherto separated communities, bounded spaces, disconnected economies and distinctive cultures have been analysed by social scientists. They serve governments who are uneasily aware that their powers to control economies and societies, nominally under their jurisdiction, are being eroded by radical improvements in the technologies for the transportation of goods and people across space and time and by the vastly more efficient communications systems for the diffusion of commercial intelligence, political messages and cultural information between distant locations and widely separated populations. As the world shrinks, for problem after problem and subject after subject, national frameworks for political action and academic enquiry are recognized as unsatisfactory. People require historical perspectives on the ubiquitous technological, political and economic forces that are now clearly transcending and transforming traditional frameworks for human behaviour and reshaping personal identities around the world.

Philip's World History Encyclopedia is not only propitious, it has been well designed, constructed and authenticated by a team of professional historians in order to help teachers of history in high schools, universities and colleges to communicate that perspective to their pupils and students. They have appreciated histories of the world cannot be taught or read without a clear comprehension of the chronologies and spatial parameters within which political, economic, social and cultural activities of different empires, states and peoples have evolved through very long spans of time. An up-to-date encyclopedia is the ideal text for ready reference and the easy acquisition of basic facts upon which an understanding of world history can be built, delivered and studied. Such books "encapsulate" hard knowledge; reunify history with geography and provide perspective which in this volume goes back over seventeen millennia. They illuminate the significance of places and locations for seminal events in world history. For example, glance at the delightfully illustrated entry on Babylonia and discover why an empire located between the Tigris and Euphrates rivers from 1900 BC to 538 BC included the most advanced civilization in the world.

Encyclopedias must be accurate, accessible and display the unfurling chronology of world history in words, illustrations, maps and captions that are memorable. The team of historians, illustrators, cartographers and editors who collaborated in the construction of *Philip's World History Encyclopedia* set out to produce a popular work of reference that could be adopted for undergraduate and high school courses in world history. Although that subject is now spreading in Europe, Japan and China, in the United States and Canada such courses are already commonplace. New text books appear regularly. American journals dealing with world history publish debates of how histories designed to cover long chronologies and unconfined geographies might be as rigorous and as intellectually compelling as more orthodox histories dealing with individuals, towns, regions, countries and single continents. Thus the editors attempted to become familiar with as many course outlines and rubrics as possible. Their plans for this volume were informed by the on-going, contemporary debate about the scale, scope and nature of world history. For example, they were aware that most "model" textbooks in world history are usually constructed around the grand themes of "Connexions" and "Comparisons" across continents, civilizations and millennia of history and that a scientifically informed appreciation of environmental, evolutionary and biological constraints on all human activity are regarded as basic to any understanding of world history.

Philip's World History Encyclopedia is a pleasingly illustrated, up-to-date, single-volume encyclopedia of world history for readers aged 16 and above. It features more than 6,500 clearly written A–Z articles, compiled and authenticated by academic historians; more than 1000 coloured illustrations, including maps, paintings, photographs,charts, diagrams and tables, as well as a Chronology of people, dates and events spanning 17,000 years; and a Ready Reference.

The articles provide readers with authoritative yet accessible information on every period of history. Due weight has been given to regions such as Central and South America, Africa and Oceania that are often neglected by other encyclopedias. Entries are organized alphabetically to enable fast fact finding, while more than 30,000 cross-references give directions to associated articles. The entries, "global" in scope, have attempted to meet the requirements of North American Standards in World History, and equivalent curricula guidelines for the United Kingdom, Australia and New Zealand.

The Chronology of people, dates and events from the origins of humanity to the present day is organized into four geographical regions (Asia and Australia, Africa, Europe and the Americas) and into two major themes (Science and Technology, and Religion and the Arts). The Chronology allows readers to check major world and regional events at particular moments of time while the Ready Reference section provides tabular information on kings and queens, dynasties, presidents and prime ministers.

Although encyclopedias of world history will surely give prominence to such traditional, historical themes as the rise and decline of empires, states and civilizations, a serious effort has been made in most sections of this volume to accord proper emphasis to the common concerns of humankind including, religion, economic welfare, trade, technology, health and the status of human rights. Nevertheless *Philip's World History Encyclopedia* has been designed in the context of a remarkable revival in world history, which is now underway, and which represents an exciting alternative to histories narrowly focussed on the experience of national communities.

World history offers chronologies, perspectives and geographical parameters which aim to attenuate the excesses of ethnicity, chauvinism and condescension. The length and breadth of an encyclopedia of world history, covering all continents and a chronology going back seventeen millennia, works to separate the provincial from the universal, the episodic from the persistent. It will also expose the decline as well as the rise of societies, nations, cultures and civilizations. If this volume contributes to these growing aspirations for an education in universal history it will also contribute towards the nurturing of cosmopolitan sensibility for the next century.

Patrick K. O'Brien FBA
Centennial Professor of Economic History, London School of Economics
Convenor of the Institute of Historical Research Programme in Global History

ACKNOWLEDGEMENTS

EDITORIAL BOARD

Patrick K. O'Brien is the Centennial Professor of Economic History at the London School of Economics.

CONSULTANTS

Jane McIntosh,
University of Cambridge

Peter Heather,
University College London

Rick Halpern,
University College London

Brian Cowan,
Princeton University

Gabrielle Ward-Smith,
University of Toronto

Larry Butler,
University of Luton

Patricia Mercer,
University of North London

Nicola Miller,
University College London

EXECUTIVE EDITOR
Steve Luck

COMMISSIONING EDITOR
Chris Humphries

SENIOR EDITOR
Frances Adlington

TEXT EDITORS
Rachel Lawrence
Neil Grant
Jane Edmonds
Stephanie Driver

EXECUTIVE ART EDITOR
Mike Brown

PICTURE CREDITS

Frances Adlington 323 *bottom*, 340.
AKG London 26 *bottom*.
Bridgeman Art Library *(detail)* 18, *(detail)* 30, 76 *top*, *(detail)* 284, *(detail)* 291, 341, /Bibliothèque Nationale, Paris 127, /Bibliothèque Nationale, Paris, Livre des Merveilles 229, /British Library, London 437, /British Museum, London 260, /Caylus Anticuario, Madrid 325, /Chateau de Versailles, France/Giraudon 352, /Christie's, London 43 *top right*, 261, /Crown Estate, Institute of Directors, London 123, /D.F. Barry, Bismarck, Dakota 288, /Fitzwilliam Museum, University of Cambridge 433, /Gavin Graham Gallery, London 81, /Giraudon/Bibliothèque Nationale, Paris 213, /Illustrated London News Picture Library, London 318, /Kunsthistorisches Museum, Vienna 34, /Musee de la Tapisserie, Bayeux, with special authorization of the city of Bayeux/Giraudon *(detail)* 40, /Museo de Santa Cruz, Toledo *(detail)* 173, /Museo e Gallerie Nazionali de Capodimonte, Naples/Giraudon 9, 67, /National Gallery of Scotland, Edinburgh 448, /National Museet, Copenhagen 207, /Nationalmuseum, Stockholm *(detail)* 335, /National Palace Museum, Taipei *(detail)* 156, /National Portrait Gallery, London 181 /New York Historical Society, United States 211, /Novosti 237, 275, /Palazzo Barberini, Rome *(detail)* 168, /Palazzo Medici-Riccardi, Florence 267, /Philip Mould, Historical Portraits Ltd, London *(detail)* 130, /Private Collections *(detail)* 14, 15, *(detail)* 46, 59, 105, 164, 410, 432, *(detail)* 434, /Rafael Valls Gallery, London *(detail)* 327, Stapleton Collection, Britain, *artist* John Young *(detail)* 309, /The Trustees of the Weston Park Foundation *(detail)* 119 *bottom*, /Victoria and Albert Museum, London 272, 379, /Wallace Collection, London 106.
Peter Carey 119 *top*.
Corbis 225.
E.T. Archive 407, /British Museum, London 72, /Canning House Library *(detail)* 50, /Capitoline Museum, Rome 73, /Chateau de Beauregard, France 328, /Historical Museum, Moscow, *artist* Jean Marc Nattier *(detail)* 323 *top*, /Imperial War Museum, London 440.
Robert Harding Michael Holford /Musee Guimet, Paris 279.
Hulton Getty Picture Collection 43 *top left*, 88, 98, *(detail)* 133, 148, 155, 174, 184, 281, 314, 316, 438;
Chris Humphries 2, 5, 10, 26 *top*, 37, 61, 66, 68, 114, 139.
Peter Newark's American Pictures 75, 76 *bottom*, 239, 251.
Picture Bank 339.
Rex Features 36, 45, 93, *(detail)* 97, 116, 129, 145, 161, 163, 178, 221, 286, 321, 355, 405, 409, 428, 442, 446 /Demulder 20, /Erik Pendzich 111, /Frederick de Klerk 259, /Lauron/Sipa-Press 271, /Nils Jorgensen 48, /Roger Crump 439, /Sipa-Press 56, 204, 373, 391, /Tripett 343, 345.
Werner Forman Archive /Anthropology Museum, Veracruz University, Jalapa 305, /Dallas Museum Of Art, United States 266.

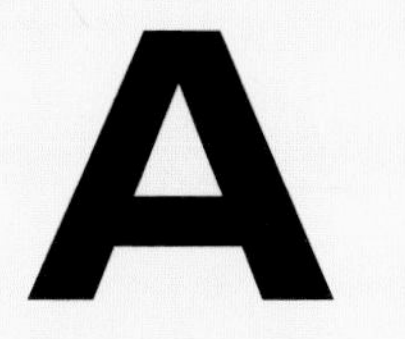

Abbas (d.652) Uncle of the Prophet MUHAMMAD and of the Caliph ALI. A rich merchant in Mecca, he gave his name to the ABBASID dynasty of Muslim CALIPHS.

Abbas I (the Great) (1571–1629) Shah of Persia (1588–1629). The outstanding ruler of the SAFAVID dynasty, Abbas restored Persia as a great power, waging war successfully against the invading Uzbeks and Ottoman Turks and recapturing Hormuz from the Portuguese. Tolerant in religion, he encouraged Dutch and English merchants and admitted Christian missionaries. Abbas made ISFAHAN his capital.

Abbas II (1874–1944) Last Khedive (Turkish viceroy) of Egypt (1892–1914). He succeeded his father, Tewfik Pasha. Abbas was hostile to the British, the dominant power, but he also rejected the nationalists' demands for liberal reform. Deposed when the British established a protectorate, he spent the rest of his life in exile.

Abbasid Muslim CALIPH dynasty (750–1258). They traced their descent from ABBAS, the uncle of MUHAMMAD, and came to power by defeating the UMAYYADS. In 862 the Abbasids moved the caliphate from DAMASCUS to BAGHDAD, where it achieved great splendour. From the 10th century Abbasid caliphs ceased to exercise political power, becoming religious figureheads. After the family's downfall in 1258, following the fall of Baghdad to the MONGOLS, one member was invited by the MAMLUK sultan to CAIRO where the dynasty was recognized until the 16th century.

Abd al-Kader (1808–83) Algerian leader and emir of Mascara. He displaced (1832–39) the French and Turks from N Algeria before launching a holy war against the French. In 1843 Abd al-Kader was forced into Morocco where he enlisted the support of the sultan. He and his Moroccan forces were defeated at Isly (1844). Abd al-Kader was imprisoned in France (1847–52).

Abd al-Malik (646–705) Fifth UMAYYAD caliph (685–705). Abd al-Malik united ISLAM by defeating his rival, Caliph Abdullah ibn-az-Zubayr. He also fought against the BYZANTINES. Abd al-Malik reformed the government and made Arabic the official language.

Abd ar-Rahman I (d.788) First UMAYYAD emir of CÓRDOBA (756–88). He was the sole survivor of the ABBASID massacre (750) of his family in Damascus. In 756 Abd ar-Rahman defeated Yusuf of Córdoba at Alameda. He united the Muslim tribes, checked the Frankish army of Charlemagne at ZARAGOZA (778), and began the Great Mosque at Córdoba, S Spain. He was succeeded by Hisham I.

Abd ar-Rahman III (891–961) UMAYYAD emir (912–29) and first caliph of CÓRDOBA (929–61). He founded the University of Córdoba. Abd ar-Rahman seized Ceuta, N Morocco and reclaimed other Spanish provinces. He enlarged his navy and greatly increased Córdoba's power.

Abd el-Krim (1882?–1963) Moroccan BERBER resistance leader. In 1921 he led the Rif tribes to a famous victory against the Spanish. He continued to gain ground, and by 1925 he had advanced into French-held territory. In 1926 he was defeated by a combined French-Spanish force and sent into exile in Réunion. In 1947 he escaped to Egypt where he formed a liberation movement. In 1958 King MUHAMMAD V of Morocco proclaimed Abd el-Krim a national hero.

abdication crisis (1936) In the United Kingdom, the constitutional disturbance caused by the forced abdication of EDWARD VIII. It arose from the determination of Edward, who became king in January 1936, to marry Mrs Wallis Simpson, an American woman in the process of suing her second husband for divorce. Such a marriage breached the rules of the Anglican Church and was considered unsuitable by the British government, led by Stanley BALDWIN. A struggle developed between king and Parliament. On 10 December 1936, Edward was forced to abdicate in favour of his brother, the future GEORGE VI.

Abdul Hamid II (1842–1918) Ottoman sultan (1876–1909). On his accession, Abdul Hamid suspended parliament and the new constitution. He concluded the disastrous RUSSO-TURKISH WARS by ceding vast lands to Russia at the Treaty of SAN STEFANO (1878). Abdul Hamid is remembered as the "Great Assassin" for his part in the Armenian massacres (1894–96) – it is estimated that more than 200,000 Armenians were killed in 1896 alone. In 1908 the YOUNG TURKS forced him to reimplement the 1876 constitution and he was deposed shortly after.

Abdul Medjid I (1823–61) Ottoman sultan (1839–61). He continued the programme of social and political reform begun by his father, MAHMUD II, including the granting of civil and political rights to Christians.

Abdullah, Sheikh Muhammad (1905–82) Kashmiri politician. He served as prime minister (1947–53) of JAMMU AND KASHMIR after India's independence. In 1953 he was arrested for advocating independence for KASHMIR. He remained almost continuously in protective custody until the 1970s.

Abdullah ibn Hussein (1882–1951) King of Jordan (1946–51), son of HUSSEIN IBN ALI of the HASHEMITE family. In 1921, after aiding Britain in World War 1, he became emir of Transjordan. Abdullah lost control of Hejaz to Ibn SAUD. In World War 2 he resisted the Axis Powers. Abdullah fought against the creation of Israel, annexed Palestinian land, and signed an armistice (1949). He was assassinated in Jerusalem and succeeded by his son, Talal.

Abélard, Pierre (1079–1142) French philosopher. In his famous work *Sic et Non*, Abélard attempted to reconcile differences between the Fathers of the Church by using the dialectical method of ARISTOTLE. His views were condemned by the Council of Sens (1140). Abélard is known for his tragic love for his young pupil Héloise. The affair scandalized his contemporaries. He was castrated and became a monk, while Héloise was forced to enter a convent. These events inspired his work *Historia Calamitatum Mearum*. Abélard and Héloise are buried together at Parclete, Paris.

Abercromby, Sir Ralph (1734–1801) British general. After serving in the SEVEN YEARS' WAR, he became commander in chief (1795–97) in the West Indies. Abercromby captured Grenada, St Lucia, St Vincent and Trinidad. Sent to expel the French from Egypt, he defeated them at ABOUKIR (1801) but was killed in action. *See also* NELSON, HORATIO, VISCOUNT

Aberdeen, George Hamilton Gordon, 4th Earl of (1784–1860) British statesman, prime minister (1852–55). He served as foreign secretary (1828–30) under the Duke of WELLINGTON. As foreign secretary (1841–46) to Sir Robert PEEL, Aberdeen negotiated the WEBSTER-ASHBURTON and the OREGON Boundary treaties with the United States. He and Peel resigned over the issue of the CORN LAWS. Aberdeen emerged to form the "Aberdeen coalition" ministry. He was swayed into entering the CRIMEAN WAR by Viscount PALMERSTON. Aberdeen was blamed for the mismanagement of the war and was forced to resign.

Abernathy, Ralph David (1926–90) US clergyman and CIVIL RIGHTS activist. A Baptist minister, Abernathy succeeded Dr Martin Luther KING, JR, as leader of the SOUTHERN CHRISTIAN LEADERSHIP CONFERENCE (SCLC) after King's assassination (1968) and continued to promote the non-violent civil rights movement. In 1968 he organized the Poor People's March on Washington, D.C.

Abnaki (Wabanaki) Tribe of Algonquian-speaking NATIVE NORTH AMERICANS of the Eastern Woodlands culture. They inhabited NE New England, to which they apparently fled as refugees from English colonists. After suffering military defeats at the hands of the English in 1724–25, most of them went to New Brunswick, Canada, where their descendants live today. In legend, they were the inhabitants of Norumbega.

abolitionists In US history, opponents of SLAVERY. Inspired by British evangelicals in the CLAPHAM SECT (in particular William WILBERFORCE), preachers such as Lyman BEECHER launched a moral crusade to end slavery in the United States. In 1831 William Lloyd GARRISON published *The Liberator*, an anti-slavery journal. In 1833 the American Anti-Slavery Society was formed and within five years such societies boasted more than 250,000 members, mainly from Northern states. In 1840 the Liberty Party was formed by James BIRNEY, advocating direct political action to achieve the emancipation of black slaves. The Party attracted the support of escaped slaves, such as Frederick DOUGLASS. The passage of a tough, new FUGITIVE SLAVE LAW (1850) led to increased activity on the UNDERGROUND RAILROAD. An abolitionist novel, *Uncle Tom's Cabin* (1852), by Harriet Beecher STOWE sold more than 300,000 copies in its first year of publication. The actions of militant abolitionists culminated in the raid on the US arsenal at Harper's Ferry, Virginia, led by John BROWN. The bitter antagonism between North and South on the issue of slavery was a major cause of the American CIVIL WAR. In 1863 President Abraham LINCOLN issued the EMANCIPATION PROCLAMATION and slavery was finally abolished by the Thirteenth Amendment to the Constitution (1865). *See also* QUAKERS

aborigines (aboriginals) Strictly, the indigenous inhabitants of a country. The term is used most often in reference to NATIVE AUSTRALIANS.

Aboukir (Abukir, Abu Qir) Bay on the Mediterranean coast of Egypt, between Alexandria and the mouth of the Nile. In the Battle of the Nile (1–2 August 1798), Horatio NELSON defeated the French fleet under Breuys. Nelson's victory at Aboukir forced NAPOLEON to abandon his attempt to conquer parts of the British Empire.

Abraham (Ibrahim) In the Old Testament, progenitor of the Hebrews and founder of JUDAISM. According to the book of Genesis, Abraham was called on by God to travel with his wife, Sarah, and nephew, Lot, from UR to Haran in NW MESOPOTAMIA, and thence to CANAAN. He had a son, Ishmael, by Sarah's maid Hagar, but then (aged 100) fathered a son, Isaac, by Sarah, who was previously barren. God tested his loyalty by demanding the sacrifice of Isaac. Abraham is esteemed by Muslims who regard him as the ancestor, through Ishmael, of the ARABS.

Abraham, Plains of Field in Upper Québec City, Canada, scene of a decisive battle (1759) between the British and French. The British and French commanders, James WOLFE and Louis Joseph de MONTCALM, were killed in the conflict, which cleared the path for the British domination of E Canada.

Abu Bakr (*c.*573–634) First Muslim CALIPH. One of the earliest converts to ISLAM, Abu Bakr was chief adviser to the Prophet MUHAMMAD. After Muhammad's death, Abu Bakr was elected leader of the Muslim community. During his short reign (632–34), he defeated the tribes that had revolted against Muslim rule in MEDINA after the death of Muhammad and restored them to Islam. By invading the Byzantine Christian provinces of Syria and Palestine and the Persian province of Iraq, he launched the series of Holy Wars through which the first major expansion of the Islamic world was accomplished.

Abu Dhabi (Abu Zaby) Largest and wealthiest of the seven UNITED ARAB EMIRATES (UAE), lying on the S coast of the Persian Gulf. The capital of Abu Dhabi and the federal capital of the UAE is Abu Dhabi (1989 pop. 363,432). Abu Dhabi has been ruled since the 18th century by the al-bu-Falah clan of the Bani Yas tribe. In 1853 a perpetual maritime truce was agreed that led to the signatories being called the TRUCIAL STATES. In 1892 the Trucial States became a British protectorate. From 1945 to 1948 Abu Dhabi was at war with DUBAI. Abu Dhabi prospered after the discovery of oil in 1958. In 1971 Abu Dhabi was a founder member of the UAE and led the movement for federation. Sheikh Zaid ibn Sultan of Abu Dhabi has served as president of the UAE since its foundation. Area: 67,340sq km (26,000sq mi). Pop. (1995) 928,360.

Abu Nidal (1937–) Palestinian terrorist, pseudonym of Sabri Khalil Albanna. In 1973 he left the PALESTINE LIBERATION ORGANIZATION (PLO) to establish the

A

▲ **Abu Simbel**, in s Egypt, is the site of two temples built by Pharaoh Ramses II (active 13th century BC). In front of the temples are four 20-m (67-ft) high seated figures of Ramses.

extremist Abu Nidal Organization (ANO). This targeted Arab as well as Israeli government officials and carried out a number of hijackings and bombings in the 1970s and 1980s. In 1974 Abu Nidal was sentenced to death in absentia by a PLO tribunal. *See also* Arafat, Yasir

Abu Simbel Ancient Egyptian village on the W bank of the River Nile, near the border with Sudan. It is the location of two rock-cut sandstone temples built by Ramses II (r. *c*.1304–1237 BC). In a huge operation (1963–66), the temples and statuary were moved further inland. This was to prevent their disappearance under the waters of Lake Nasser, created by the construction of the new High Dam at Aswan.

Abzug, Bella Savitsky (1920–98) US Democratic congresswoman (1971–77) from New York. She was a staunch critic of the Vietnam War and a leading proponent of women's rights. Abzug was chair (1961–70) of Women Strike for Peace. In 1971 she co-founded the National Women's Political Caucus, which sought to increase the participation of women in government. Abzug served as co-chair (1978–79) of the National Advisory Council on Women.

Abyssinia *See* Ethiopia

Academy School of philosophy and proto-university founded (*c*.387 BC) by Plato who met his pupils in the Akademos, an olive grove on the outskirts of Athens, which was also used as a gymnasium or training ground. Much of the history of the Academy is uncertain, though we know its students included Aristotle, Epicurus, and Zeno of Citium. In AD 529 it was closed by Emperor Justinian. *See also* Neoplatonism

Acadia (Acadie) Historic region in North America, from which the term Cajun derives. In 1605 the first French settlement was established and the region expanded to include present-day Nova Scotia, New Brunswick, Prince Edward Island and parts of Québec and Maine. The Treaty of Utrecht (1713) ceded the region to the British, who deported (1755, 1758) many Acadians.

Aceh Autonomous district of Indonesia, N Sumatra. It became a sultanate after adopting Islam in the 13th century, the first region in Indonesia to do so. In the 17th century, Aceh defeated the Portuguese and resisted Dutch and British attempts to establish trading posts. In the Achinese War (1873–1904) it fought unsuccessfully against Dutch colonization. In 1949 Aceh became an autonomous province of Indonesia. In 1953 the Achinese rebelled against Indonesian rule and to date *c*.2000 people have died in the struggle for secession.

Achaean League Two confederations of Greek city-states formed in the area of the Peloponnese called Achaea (Akkaia). The first, founded in the 5th century BC, lasted for *c*.100 years. The second, founded 280 BC, warred with Sparta, siding with Rome in 198 BC. In 146 BC Rome subjugated and dissolved the League.

Achaemenid Ruling dynasty of the first Persian empire, which at its height stretched from the River Nile as far E as modern Afghanistan. In the 7th century BC, the Assyrian ruler Ashurbanipal overran the land of Elam. The ascendancy of Assyria, however, proved short-lived as the Assyrian capital, Nineveh, was sacked by the Medes in 612 BC. In 550 BC, the Median empire fell to Cyrus II (the Great) (r.559–529 BC), founder of the Achaemenid dynasty (named after his ancestor Achaemenes). Cyrus subsumed Lydia into the Achaemenid empire by defeating Croesus in 547 BC. Cyrus then marched against Babylonia, capturing Babylon in 539 BC. His son and successor, Cambyses II, further expanded Persian power with the annexation of Egypt in 525 BC. Cambyses was succeeded by his cousin, Darius I (the Great). In order to consolidate power, Darius decentralized government by dividing the Achaemenid empire into 20 provinces. He added the Indus province to the empire and brought Thrace under Persian control in 512 BC. Further conquests in Greece were thwarted, however, by Darius' defeat at the Battle of Marathon (490 BC). The Persian Wars (499–479 BC) in Greece continued under his successor, Xerxes I, who was decisively defeated at the Battle of Plataea (479 BC). In the Peloponnesian War (431–404 BC), Darius II regained W Asia Minor and helped Sparta defeat Athens in 404 BC. The decline of the Achaemenid empire, however, was evident during the reign (404–359 BC) of Artaxerxes II, who lost Egypt and faced a major revolt from his brother, Cyrus the Younger. In 330 BC, the last Achaemenid ruler, Darius III (Codomannus) (r.336–330 BC), was defeated by Alexander III (the Great) of Macedonia. The remains at Persepolis are testimony to the splendour of Persian art and architecture during the reigns of Darius I and Xerxes. *See also* Egypt, ancient; Hellenistic Age; Susa; Zoroastrianism

Acheson, Dean Gooderham (1893–1971) US statesman, secretary of state (1949–53) under President Harry Truman. His desire to stem the growth of communism was fundamental to the establishment of the North Atlantic Treaty Organization (NATO), the ANZUS Pact, the Marshall Plan and the Truman Doctrine. Acheson was criticized for his lack of support for the state of Taiwan and his endorsement of US military intervention in South Korea. *See also* Korean War

Acheulian Early Palaeolithic culture that derives its name from Saint Acheul, near Amiens, France. Characterized by the production of hand axes and cleavers with two worked faces, it spread from Africa to Europe and Asia. Surviving for more than one million years, it ended *c*.120,000 years ago.

Acre (Akko) Seaport in N Israel on the Bay of Haifa. During the Crusades (1095–1272) it changed hands many times, ultimately becoming the central Christian possession in Palestine. It was the last city to fall to Islam (1291).

acropolis Hilltop fortress of an ancient Greek city. The earliest-known examples were fortified castles built for the Mycenaean kings, and it was only later that they became symbolic homes of the gods. The most famous one is the Acropolis built (13th century BC) in Athens; it includes the Parthenon (5th century BC).

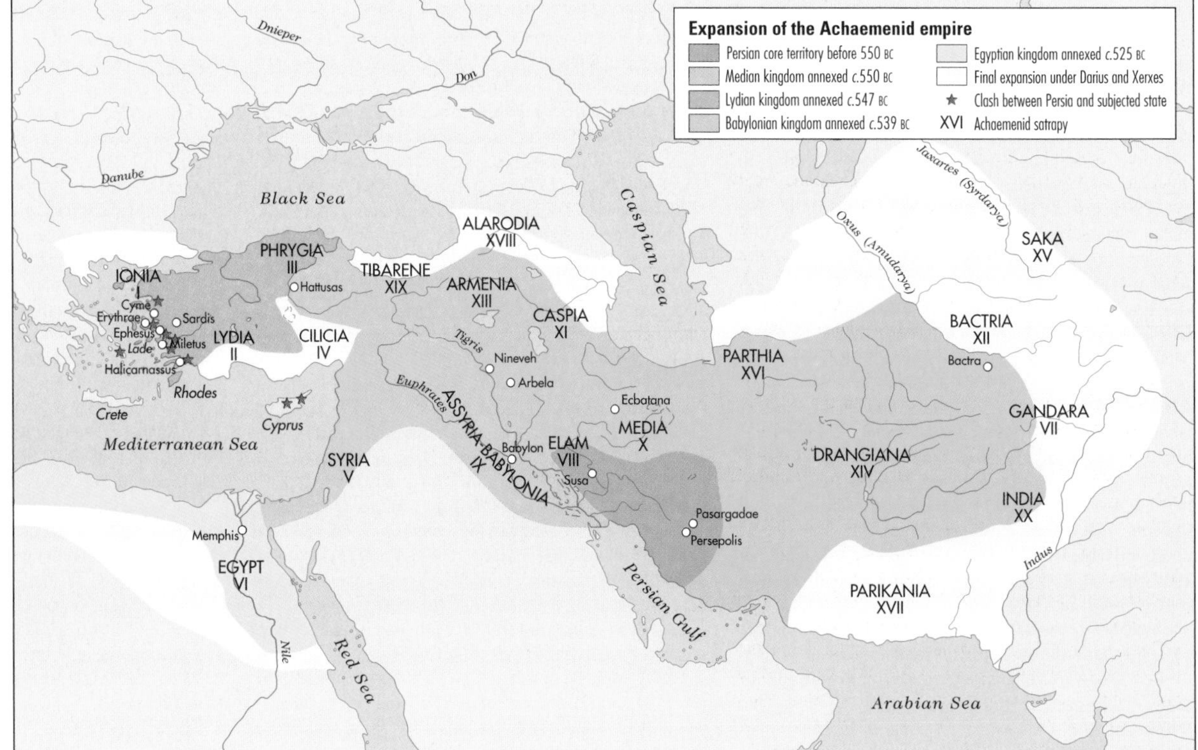

► **Achaemenids** The Achaemenid dynasty built the largest empire the world had yet seen. Persian rule combined an empire-wide legal and administrative system with an acceptance of local customs, practices and religions. Trade prospered under the Achaemenids, facilitated by an efficient road network, a standardized system of weights and measures, and one of the earliest uses of coinage. It is often argued that the Achaemenid empire witnessed the transition from the ancient to the modern world.

A

Action Française Right-wing, nationalist group active in France between *c.*1900 and 1944. Originating during the DREYFUS AFFAIR, the group advocated the overthrow of the Third Republic and the restoration of the monarchy. It commanded wide support among the middle class and Roman Catholics. Discredited by its association with the VICHY GOVERNMENT during World War 2, it passed into oblivion with the demise of its newspaper, *Action Française*, in August 1944.

Actium, Battle of (31 BC) Naval battle in which the fleet of Octavian (later Emperor AUGUSTUS) defeated the fleets of Mark ANTONY and CLEOPATRA. Mark Antony's army surrendered a week later, and Octavian became sole ruler of the ROMAN EMPIRE.

Act of Union *See* UNION, ACTS OF

Acton, John Emerich Edward Dalberg, 1st Baron (1834–1902) English historian. He planned the *Cambridge Modern History* series, and is known for his saying "power tends to corrupt and absolute power corrupts absolutely."

Adalbert (*c.*1000–72) German archbishop. He was a favourite of Emperor HENRY III, who appointed him (1045) archbishop of Hamburg-Bremen. Adalbert's efforts to increase the power of the monarchy angered the nobility and his centralizing ecclesiastical policies alienated many church officials. Their opposition forced Adalbert's dismissal (1066), but he was reinstated (1069) by Emperor HENRY IV.

Adams, Brooks (1848–1927) US historian. His *Law of Civilization and Decay* (1895) held that civilizations rise and fall with the fluctuations of commerce. In *America's Economic Supremacy* (1900), Adams predicted the decline of Western Europe and proposed that within 50 years only the United States and Russia would be great powers.

Adams, Charles Francis (1807–86) US diplomat, son of John Quincy ADAMS and grandson of John ADAMS. In 1861 Adams was appointed minister to London by Abraham LINCOLN, and helped to ensure Britain's neutrality in the American CIVIL WAR. He was also instrumental in settling the ALABAMA CLAIMS.

Adams, Gerry (1948–) Northern Irish politician, president of SINN FÉIN (1983–). He was interned (1972–78) by the British for his involvement in the IRISH REPUBLICAN ARMY (IRA). Adams served (1978–83) as vice president of Sinn Féin. He is seen as a pivotal figure between the "ballot box" and "bullet" factions of the Republican movement. Adams served (1983–92, 1997–) as a member of Parliament for Belfast West, but never took his seat at Westminster. His negotiations with John HUME led to an IRA cease-fire (1994). In 1997 Adams headed the Sinn Féin delegation in the peace talks leading to the GOOD FRIDAY AGREEMENT; he became the first republican leader to meet a British prime minister since 1921.

Adams, John (1735–1826) Second president of the United States (1797–1801). Influenced by his radical cousin Samuel ADAMS, he helped draft the DECLARATION OF INDEPENDENCE (1776), and the Treaty of PARIS (1783) that ended the AMERICAN REVOLUTION. He was George WASHINGTON's vice president (1789–97). Adam's presidency was marked by conflict between the FEDERALIST PARTY, led by Alexander HAMILTON, and Thomas JEFFERSON's DEMOCRATIC-REPUBLICAN PARTY. Adams' moderate stance enabled a settlement of the XYZ AFFAIR (1797–98). He reluctantly endorsed the ALIEN AND SEDITION ACTS (1798). Adams was succeeded by Thomas JEFFERSON.

Adams, John Quincy (1767–1848) Sixth president of the United States (1825–29), son of the second president, John ADAMS. He served in his father's administration, before acting (1803–08) as FEDERALIST PARTY member in the Senate. Adams was secretary of state (1817–24) for President James MONROE. He was largely responsible for formulating the MONROE DOCTRINE and negotiating both the TREATY OF GHENT with Britain (1815) and the ADAMS-ONÍS TREATY (1819). Adams became president without an electoral majority, his appointment confirmed by the House of Representatives. His lack of a mandate and non-partisan approach contributed to his electoral defeat by Andrew JACKSON. Adams served in the House of Representatives (1830–48).

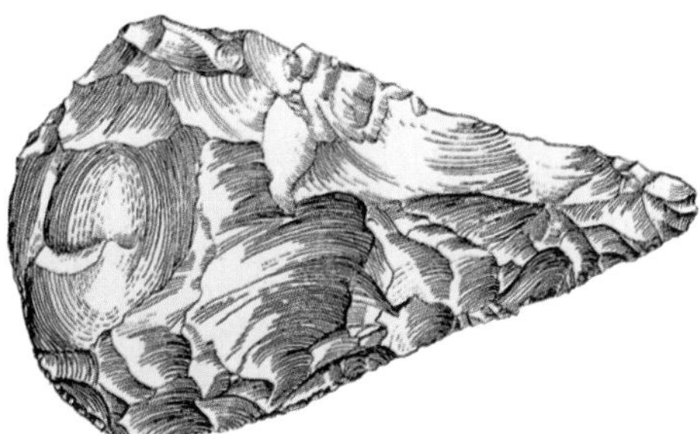

▲ **Acheulian** The Acheulian hand axe, which replaced the primitive chopper, was a fundamental advance in human technology. Its sharp edge was used primarily for hunting.

Adams, Samuel (1722–1803) American revolutionary leader. As a member and clerk of the Massachusetts legislature (1765–74), he was the chief spokesman for the AMERICAN REVOLUTION. Adams helped form several radical organizations, led the STAMP ACT protest in 1765, helped plan the BOSTON TEA PARTY of 1773, and was a signatory of the DECLARATION OF INDEPENDENCE (1776). He was a delegate to the CONTINENTAL CONGRESS until 1781.

Adams, William (1564–1620) English navigator, the first Englishman to reach Japan (1600). In 1613 he helped to establish an English trading factory for the English EAST INDIA COMPANY in Japan. Adams remained in Japan with his Japanese wife and family, continuing his naval career with the trading company.

Adams-Onís Treaty (1819) Agreement between the United States and Spain. Negotiated by Secretary of State John Quincy ADAMS and Spanish minister Luis de Onís, Spain gave up its land E of the Mississippi River and its claims to OREGON TERRITORY; the United States assumed debts of US$5 million and surrendered claims to TEXAS.

Addams, Jane (1860–1935) US reformer. She shared the 1931 Nobel Prize for Peace with Nicholas Murray Butler. In 1889 Addams founded Hull House, Chicago – an early settlement house. She pioneered labour, housing, health, and legal reforms, and campaigned for female suffrage, pacifism and the rights of immigrants.

Addington, Henry, 1st Viscount Sidmouth (1757–1844) British statesman, prime minister (1801–04). He entered Parliament in 1783 and served as speaker of the House (1789–1801). Addington succeeded William PITT (THE YOUNGER) as prime minister. His administration was tarnished by the failure of the Treaty of AMIENS (1802) with NAPOLEON I. As home secretary (1812–22) under Lord LIVERPOOL, Addington was criticized for his harsh treatment of the LUDDITES and was widely blamed for the PETERLOO MASSACRE (1819).

Addis Ababa Capital and largest city in ETHIOPIA, located on a plateau at *c.*2400m (8000ft) in the highlands of Shewa province. In 1889, during the reign of MENELIK II, Addis Ababa ("New Flower") became the capital of Ethiopia. It was the capital (1936–41) of Italian East Africa. Addis Ababa is the headquarters of the ORGANIZATION OF AFRICAN UNITY (OAU). Pop. (1990 est.) 1,700,000.

Addled Parliament (5 April–7 June 1614) Parliament summoned by JAMES I of England to vote for finances to pay his debts. The Commons' demands – that extra-parliamentary taxation (impositions) be stopped and that the clergy, deprived of their livings in 1604, be reinstated – were refused and Parliament was dissolved without any act being passed or supplies voted. The Addled Parliament marked the beginning of an era of increasingly tense relations between Parliament and the monarchy.

Aden Commercial capital and largest city of Yemen, historic capital of the Aden Protectorate (1937–67) and the former (southern) People's Democratic Republic of Yemen (1967–90). A seaport city on the Gulf of Aden, 160km (100mi) E of the Red Sea, Aden was an important Roman trading port. With the opening of the SUEZ CANAL in 1869, its importance increased. It was made a British crown colony in 1937; the surrounding territory became the Aden Protectorate. In 1970 Aden was made the sole capital of the new People's Democratic Republic of Yemen. When the (northern) Yemen Arab Republic and the (southern) People's Democratic Republic of Yemen combined to form a united Republic of Yemen in 1990, SANA'A became the official capital. Pop. (1995) 562,000.

Adenauer, Konrad (1876–1967) German statesman, first chancellor of the Federal Republic of Germany (1949–63). He was lord mayor of Cologne (1917–33) and was twice imprisoned by the Nazis. Adenauer helped to create the CHRISTIAN DEMOCRATIC UNION (CDU), West Germany's dominant post-war party, and was its leader (1946–66). In 1955 he led West Germany into the NORTH ATLANTIC TREATY ORGANIZATION (NATO). Adenauer was a leading advocate of the EUROPEAN COMMUNITY (EC).

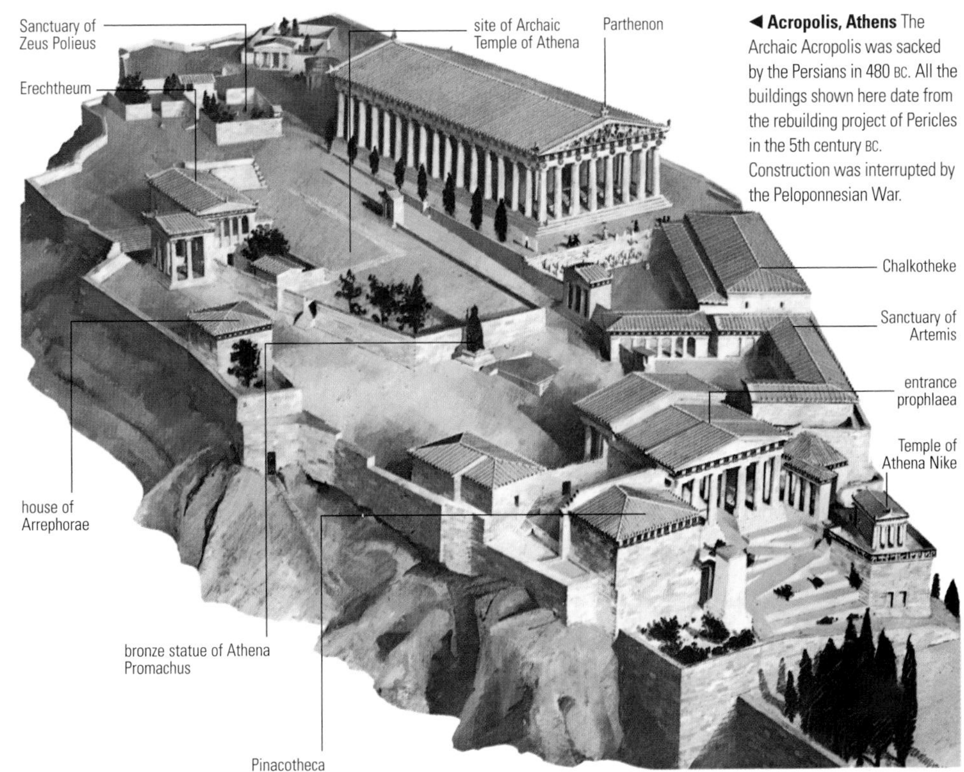

◄ **Acropolis, Athens** The Archaic Acropolis was sacked by the Persians in 480 BC. All the buildings shown here date from the rebuilding project of Pericles in the 5th century BC. Construction was interrupted by the Peloponnesian War.

A

Adi Granth (Hindi, First Book) Principal sacred text of SIKHISM. The preachings of the first five Sikh gurus were collected by Guru Arjan (1536–1606), the fifth guru, and the text was expanded by the tenth guru, GOBIND SINGH. Gobind Singh declared that he was the last guru and the book was retitled **Granth Sahib** (Hindi, Revered Book).

Adolf of Nassau (*c.*1250–98) King of Germany (1292–98). He succeeded the HABSBURG King RUDOLF I, despite Rudolf's attempts to secure the accession of his son Albert (later Albert I). Adolf increased his lands and power so rapidly that the frightened electors deposed him (1298) in favour of Albert. Adolf was killed in the ensuing struggle for power.

Adrian IV (*c.*1100–59) Pope (1154–59), b. Nicholas Breakspear. He is the only English pope. In 1155 Adrian crowned Emperor FREDERICK I (BARBAROSSA).

Adrianople, Battle of (AD 378) Conflict between the Romans and the VISIGOTHS, fought at present-day EDIRNE, Turkey. The Visigoths, led by Fritigern, crushed the Roman army and killed Emperor Valens, paving the way for a full-scale invasion of the ROMAN EMPIRE.

Adrianople, Treaty of (1829) Pact signed at EDIRNE (formerly Adrianople), Turkey, at the termination of the RUSSO-TURKISH WAR (1828–29).

Advaita (Sanskrit, "non-duality") Most influential school of VEDANTA Hinduism, based on the thought of SHANKARA. Shankara systematized the teachings of the UPANISHADS (last section of the VEDAS), stressing the indivisibility of Brahman (world-spirit) and atman (the self or individual soul). *See also* BRAHMANISM; HINDUISM

Adwa, Battle of (1 March 1896) Decisive defeat of the Italians by an Ethiopian army under MENELIK II. The Battle took place in the town of Adwa (Adua), Tigre province, N ETHIOPIA. In the worst defeat suffered by a European power in Africa, an Italian force of *c.*25,000 was routed by *c.*100,000 Ethiopian troops. The Italians were forced to recognize Ethiopian independence at the Treaty of Addis Ababa (October 1896). In 1935 Benito MUSSOLINI recaptured Adwa, but it was restored to Ethiopia by the British in 1941.

Aegean civilization (*c.*3000–1100 BC) BRONZE AGE cultures, chiefly MINOAN and MYCENAEAN, of Greece and the Aegean islands. The artistically brilliant Minoan civilization flourished in CRETE, reaching its height between *c.*1700 and 1450 BC, when it was probably overrun by Mycenaeans from mainland Greece.

Aegospotami, Battle of (405 BC) Decisive naval battle in the PELOPONNESIAN WAR (431–404 BC) between SPARTA and ATHENS. It resulted in the capture of most of the Athenian fleet of 180 ships in the Dardanelles and in the death of 3000 to 4000 Athenians. Subsequently under siege by land and sea, Athens agreed to the peace terms demanded by Sparta in 404 BC.

Aeolians Ancient Greek people. In *c.*1100 BC they settled on some of the islands, including Lesbos, and in ASIA MINOR. They were famous for their music and poetry.

Aeschines (active 4th century BC) Greek philosopher and orator. He was a student of SOCRATES and was present at his teacher's condemnation and death. Aeschines composed several Socratic dialogues.

Aethelstan *See* ATHELSTAN

Aethelred *See* ETHELRED

Aetolian League Federal state organized (370 BC) from Greek tribes. In 197 BC it allied with ROME to defeat PHILIP V of MACEDONIA. The Aetolian League became concerned with the growing Roman influence in Greece and switched allegiance to ANTIOCHUS III of Syria. In 189 BC Antiochus was defeated by the Romans and the League's influence steadily diminished. *See also* ACHAEAN LEAGUE

AFGHANISTAN

AREA: 652,090sq km (251,773sq mi)
POPULATION: 23,000,000
CAPITAL (POPULATION): Kabul (700,000)
GOVERNMENT: Islamic republic
ETHNIC GROUPS: Pathan 52%, Tajik 20%, Uzbek 9%, Hazara 9%, Chahar 3%, Turkmen 2%, Baluchi 1%
LANGUAGES: Pashto, Dari (Persian) – both official
RELIGIONS: Sunni Muslim 74%, Shiite Muslim 25%
GDP PER CAPITA (1992): US$819

Republic in S central Asia. Afghanistan's location on the overland routes between Iran, the Indian subcontinent and Central Asia has encouraged numerous invasions. Its topography, however, has helped to repulse many attacks. In ancient times, Afghanistan was invaded successively by Aryans, Persians, Greeks, Macedonians and warrior armies from Central Asia.

Buddhism was introduced in the 2nd century BC, and Arab armies brought Islam in the late 7th century. NADIR SHAH extended Persian rule to encompass most of Afghanistan. His successor, AHMAD SHAH, founded the Durrani dynasty and established the first unified state in 1747. In 1818 the dynasty ended and Russia and Britain competed for control: Russia sought an outlet to the Indian Ocean, while Britain tried to protect its Indian territories. The first (1838–42) of the AFGHAN WARS was inconclusive. The second Afghan War (1878–80) ended with the accession of Abd al-Rahman Khan as emir. The dominance of British interests was recognized in the Anglo-Russian Agreement (1907).

Following the Third Afghan War, Afghanistan became fully independent under AMANULLAH KHAN (1921). He established an unstable monarchy, constantly threatened by religious and tribal divisions. The status of the PATHANS in the NORTH-WEST FRONTIER province of Pakistan proved a continuing source of conflict between the two states. In 1973 an army coup overthrew the monarchy and established a republic. In 1978 the military government was deposed in a Marxist coup backed by the Soviet Union. The costly AFGHANISTAN WAR (1979–92) was fought between the pro-communist Afghan government and MUJAHEDDIN guerrillas. In 1989 Soviet troops withdrew, but the civil war raged on and the number of refugees continued to mount. In 1992 Mujaheddin forces captured Kabul and set up a moderate Islamic government. Fundamentalists continued to agitate. In 1996 the TALIBAN (Persian, "students"), based in the S city of KANDAHAR, captured KABUL and formed an interim government. An anti-Taliban coalition (United Islamic Front for the Salvation of Afghanistan) failed to prevent further gains, and by 1998 the Taliban controlled 90% of the country.

affirmative action Policy designed to overcome discrimination in employment on the grounds of race, ethnicity, gender, disability or sexual orientation. The term "affirmative action" first appeared in Executive Order 10925 issued (1961) by President John KENNEDY. It formed part of the CIVIL RIGHTS legislation of the 1960s in the United States. The setting of quotas for minorities led to charges of reverse discrimination. *See also* BAKKE CASE

Afghani, Jamal al-Din al- (*c.*1838–97) Muslim politician and Islamic reformer, b. Iran. He sought to unify and revive ISLAM in the face of European domination. Afghani was chief advisor (1866–68) to the Afghan ruler Muhammad Azam Khan. In 1868 he was expelled from Afghanistan. During the 1870s Afghani agitated against the Egyptian ruler ISMAIL PASHA. In 1879 he was deported from Egypt. During the 1880s Afghani edited an influential Islamic newspaper, *al-Urwa al-Wuthqa* ("the Unbreakable Link"), in Paris, France. In 1891–92 he led opposition to the shah of Iran, denouncing the tobacco concessions to Britain.

Afghanistan *See* country feature

Afghanistan War (1979–92) Conflict between the Afghan government and Muslim rebels (the MUJAHEDDIN). In 1978 the People's Democratic Party of Afghanistan (PDPA) overthrew the government of Muhammad Daud Khan. The new, Soviet-backed government instituted a programme of "SCIENTIFIC SOCIALISM" that met with armed resistance from the mainly Muslim rural population. In December 1979, *c.*30,000 Soviet troops invaded Afghanistan in support of the government. By 1982 Soviet troop-depoloyment had increased to *c.*110,000. While the Soviets controlled the cities, the guerrilla tactics of the Mujaheddin prevented domination of the countryside. The weaponry and organization of the rebels were bolstered by Western technical and financial support. In 1986 Muhammad NAJIBULLAH succeeded Babrak Kamal as leader of the PDPA. In 1989 Soviet troops completed their withdrawal, but the war continued until Mujaheddin forces entered Kabul and ousted Najibullah (April 1992). More than one million Afghans and *c.*15,000 Soviet soldiers died in the Afghanistan War. It also created more than five million refugees.

Afghan Wars (1838–42, 1878–80, 1919) Three wars fought by Britain in an attempt to block Russian influence in AFGHANISTAN and so secure the NW frontier of India. The first war began well for Britain with the capture (1839) of KANDAHAR and Ghazni, but ended with the Russian favourite, DOST MUHAMMAD, restored to the emirate at KABUL. The second war ended with Britain having gained control of Afghan foreign policy in return for guaranteeing the emir against foreign aggression and paying him a subsidy. Britain easily won the third war, but by the Treaty of Rawalpindi lost control of foreign policy.

AFL-CIO *See* AMERICAN FEDERATION OF LABOR AND CONGRESS OF INDUSTRIAL ORGANIZATIONS

Africa Second-largest continent (after ASIA), straddling the Equator and lying largely within the tropics. Africa is home to more than 13% of the world's population (*c.*75% rural) divided into more than 700 culturally distinct tribes and groups. The world's largest desert, the Sahara, forms an ethnic and cultural divide. North of the Sahara, ARABS and ISLAM predominate in coastal areas, BERBERS and TUAREG in the interior. Sub-Saharan Africa is more ethnically diverse: tribes include the AKAN, FULANI, HAUSA, KHOIKHOI, IBO, MASAI, MOSSI, SAN, YORUBA and ZULU. Indians and Europeans also form significant minorities. Africa's first great civilization emerged in ancient EGYPT in *c.*3400 BC. CARTHAGE was founded by Phoenicians in the 9th century BC. In the 7th century AD, Islam spread throughout North Africa. In sub-Saharan Africa, the growth of trade led to the development of states ranging from the vast SONGHAI empire to HAUSA city-states such as KANO. The arrival of Europeans on the West African coast in the later 15th century resulted in an enormous increase in the SLAVE TRADE, with more than 12 million Africans being dispatched to the Americas between the 16th and 19th centuries. In the 19th century, both economic and political factors spurred IMPERIALISM and colonization as European powers rushed to divide up the continent. Before the 1880s Europeans were, except in SOUTH AFRICA, largely confined to the coastal regions. By the end of the 19th century the whole continent, except for LIBERIA and ETHIOPIA, was under foreign domination either by European powers or (in the N) by the OTTOMAN EMPIRE. Beginning in the 1950s, the former colonies secured their independence within the space of 40 years, but the process of rapid decolonization brought unrest and instability to many parts of the continent. A major factor in this unrest was, and continues to be, the artificial boundaries created by COLONIALISM. *See also* articles on individual countries

African National Congress (ANC) South African political party. It was formed (1912) with the aim of securing racial equality and full political rights for non-whites. By the 1950s it had become the principal opposition to the APARTHEID regime. A military wing, *Umkhonte We Sizwe* (Spear of the Nation), was set up in the aftermath of the SHARPEVILLE massacre. It engaged in economic and industrial sabotage. In 1961 the ANC was banned and many of its leaders were arrested or forced into exile. In 1964 the leaders of the ANC, Nelson MANDELA and Walter SISULU, began long sentences as political prisoners. In 1990 the ANC was legalized, Mandela was released from Robben Island, and many of the legislative pillars of apartheid were dismantled. In 1994, in South Africa's first multiracial elections, the ANC gained more than 60% of the popular vote. Nelson Mandela became the first post-apartheid president of South Africa. In 1997 he was succeeded as leader of the ANC by Thabo MBEKI. *See also* NATIONAL PARTY (NP)

Afrikaner (*Boer*, farmer) Descendant of the predominantly Dutch settlers in SOUTH AFRICA. Afrikaners first settled around the Cape region in the 17th century. To avoid British control, the Afrikaners spread N and E from the Cape in the GREAT TREK and founded the independent South African Republic (TRANSVAAL) and Orange FREE STATE. Defeat in the SOUTH AFRICAN WARS (1899–1902) led to the republics merging in the Union of South Africa (1910). *See also* CAPE PROVINCE

◀ **Agrigento** The Doric Temple of Concordia dates from the 5th century BC. The Temple's excellent state of preservation is due primarily to its conversion into a church in AD 597. The Greek colony of Agrigento was at its height under the tyrant Theron, who defeated the Carthaginians in 480 BC. The Carthaginians returned, however, to sack the city in the Punic Wars. Agrigento was the birthplace of the scientist and philosopher Empedocles (*c.*495–435 BC).

Aga Khan Since 1818, title of the leader of the ISMAILI sect of SHIITE Muslims. **Aga Khan III** (1877–1957) was the best known. In 1906 he headed the All-India Muslim League in support of British rule. He moved to Europe and was known for his enormous wealth and love of horse-racing. In 1937 he was president of the League of Nations. In 1957 he was succeeded by his son **Karim** (1936–), who has continued the family traditions.

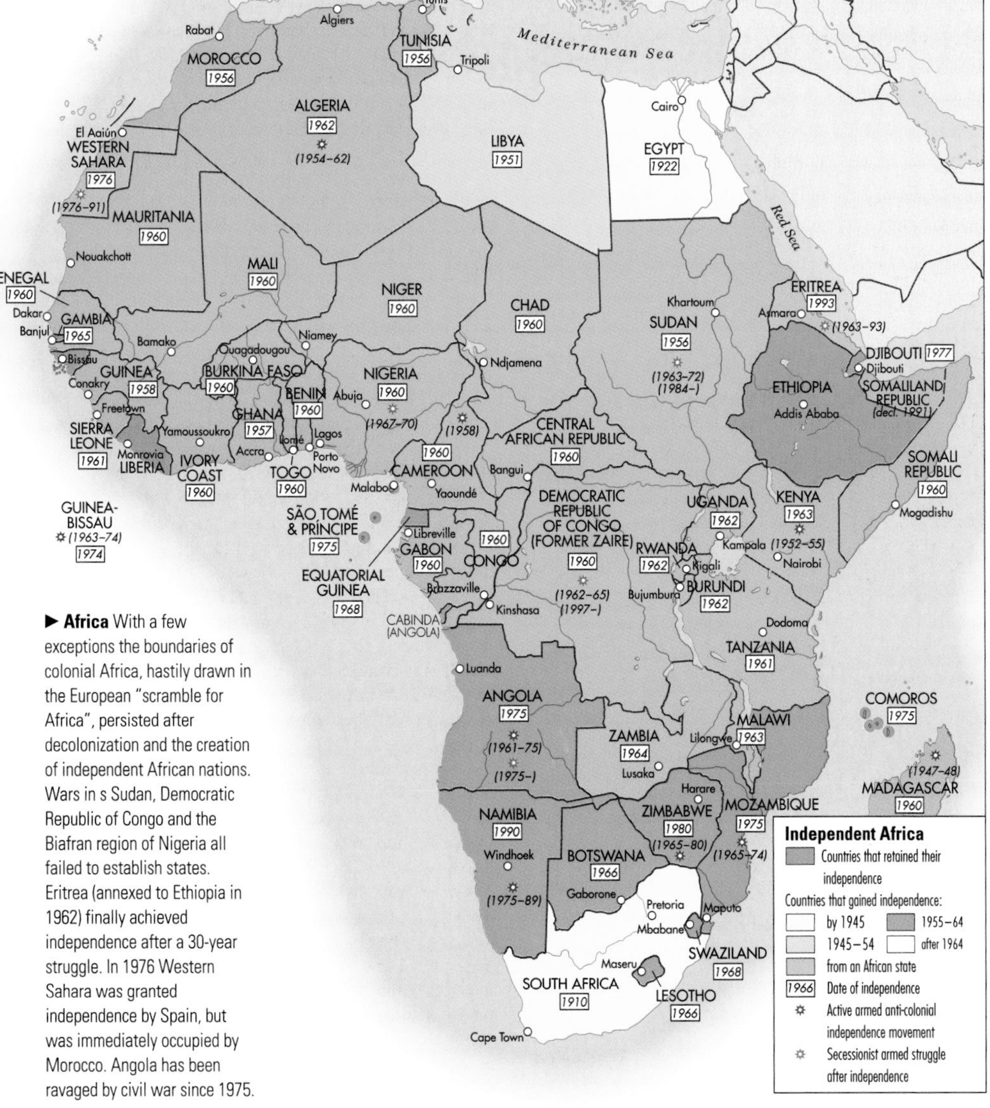

► **Africa** With a few exceptions the boundaries of colonial Africa, hastily drawn in the European "scramble for Africa", persisted after decolonization and the creation of independent African nations. Wars in S Sudan, Democratic Republic of Congo and the Biafran region of Nigeria all failed to establish states. Eritrea (annexed to Ethiopia in 1962) finally achieved independence after a 30-year struggle. In 1976 Western Sahara was granted independence by Spain, but was immediately occupied by Morocco. Angola has been ravaged by civil war since 1975.

Agincourt, Battle of (1415) Major conflict in the HUNDRED YEARS' WAR, fought near Hesdin, Pas de Calais, NE France. Despite being outnumbered, HENRY V of England routed the French forces, who made the mistake of pitching cavalry against infantry armed with longbows. The French lost more than 6000 troops and Henry was able to conquer NORMANDY.

Agnew, Spiro Theodore (1918–96) US statesman, vice president (1969–73) to Richard NIXON. In 1967 he became Republican governor of his native Maryland. Agnew was a staunch advocate of US involvement (1965–73) in the VIETNAM WAR. During his second term as vice president, Agnew was forced to resign after the discovery of political bribery and corruption in Maryland. He did not contest further charges of tax evasion, was given a three-year probationary sentence and fined US$10,000.

agnosticism Philosophical viewpoint according to which it is impossible either to demonstrate or refute the existence of a Supreme Being or ultimate cause on the basis of available evidence. It was particularly associated with the rationalism of Thomas Huxley and is used as a basis for the rejection of both CHRISTIANITY and ATHEISM.

agora Civic centre or market-place of ancient Greek towns and cities. Situated in the centre of the town or near the harbour, the agora was a special place for male citizens to conduct their religious, commercial, judicial and social activities. It was usually surrounded by public buildings, temples and colonnades of shops, and was ornamented with statues and fountains.

Agra City in Uttar Pradesh, N central India. It was founded in the early 16th century and periodically served as the capital of the MUGHAL EMPIRE. The Mughal emperor SHAH JAHAN built (1632–54) the TAJ MAHAL as a mausoleum for his wife, Mumtaz Mahal. Agra's importance declined after 1648 when the Mughal capital moved to DELHI. In 1803 it was annexed to the British Empire. Agra served (1835–62) as capital of North-West Province. Pop. (1991) 892,200.

Agricola, Gnaeus Julius (*c.*AD 40–*c.*93) Roman general, conqueror and governor of Britain. As governor (*c.*78–84), he Romanized Britain without oppression and extended Roman influence to Wales and parts of Scotland. Agricola's enlightened rule was described by TACITUS, his son-in-law.

Agricultural Adjustment Act (1933) Part of US President Franklin ROOSEVELT's NEW DEAL programme. It was designed to increase the purchasing power of farmers by balancing production with consumption. It set up the Agricultural Adjustment Administration (AAA), which provided subsidies for lower production and penalized overproduction. The production-control features of the AAA were declared unconstitutional (1936) by the Supreme Court.

Agricultural Revolution Series of changes in farming practice in the 18th and early 19th centuries. The main changes comprised crop rotation, new machinery and crops (such as fodder, turnips and clover), increased capital investment, scientific breeding, land reclamation and ENCLOSURE of common lands. Originating in Britain, these advances led to greatly increased agricultural productivity in Europe and led to dramatic growth

A

of the human population in 18th-century Britain. *See also* Agriculture; Industrial Revolution

agriculture *See* feature article

Agrigento City in s Sicily, Italy, capital of Agrigento province. One of the great centres of classical times, the city was founded (*c*.580 bc) by Greek colonists from Gela. Agrigento prospered (its population reaching *c*.200,000) until conquered (406 bc) by the Carthaginians. In 210 bc it was captured by the Romans and its commerce flourished once more. Tourists visit its Greek sites, such as the temples of Hera and Zeus. Pop. (1990) 56,660.

Agrippa, Marcus Vipsanius (*c*.63–*c*.12 bc) Roman general, adviser to Octavian (later Augustus). Agrippa helped Octavian to power by winning naval battles against Sextus Pompeius (36 bc) and Mark Antony at the Battle of Actium (31 bc).

Agrippina (the Elder) (*c*.14 bc–ad 33) Roman politician, daughter of Agrippa and granddaughter of Augustus. She married Germanicus Caesar, heir of Tiberius, and after Germanicus' death (ad 19) engaged in plots against Tiberius whom she suspected of killing her husband. In 29 Agrippina was banished to Pandateria Island in the Bay of Naples.

Agrippina (the Younger) (*c*.ad 15–59) Roman politician, eldest daughter of Germanicus Caesar and Agrippina (the Elder) and mother of Nero. Her third marriage was to Emperor Claudius, whom she dominated and persuaded to make Nero his heir designate. Agrippina is believed to have poisoned Claudius. Nero, weary of her influence, had her murdered.

Aguinaldo, Emilio (1869–1964) Filipino nationalist. He led the 1896 insurrection against Spain and was forced into exile in Hong Kong. Aguinaldo returned at the outbreak of the Spanish-American War (1898) to fight for independence. He set up the Republic of the Philippines with himself as president, resisting the US occupation forces. In 1901 Aguinaldo conceded defeat and swore allegiance to the United States. In 1935 he ran for president but was defeated by Manuel Quezon. In 1945 Aguinaldo was charged of collaboration with the Japanese during World War 2 but was released without trial.

Ahab (d. *c*.853 bc) King of Israel (*c*.874–853 bc), son and successor of Omri. He secured Israel's borders in wars against Syria and Assyria and through marriage to Jezebel, daughter of the king of Tyre and Sidon. The union saw the introduction of the Phoenician cult of Baal; Ahab was denounced by the prophet Elijah.

Ahern, Bertie (1951–) Irish statesman, taoiseach (1997–). He was first elected to the Dáil Éireann (Irish parliament) in 1977. Ahern served as vice president (1983–94) of Fianna Fáil, before becoming leader. He succeeded John Bruton as taoiseach.

Ahidjo, Ahmadou (1924–89) Cameroonian statesman, president (1960–82). In 1958 he became premier of the French Cameroons. Ahidjo was the first president of the independent Republic of Cameroon. He established a one-party state and was re-elected in 1972, 1975 and 1980. Ahidjo maintained close ties with the former colonial powers. In 1982 he went into exile in France.

Ahmadiyya Islamic messianic movement, founded (1899) by Mirza Ghulam Ahmad (1839–1908). In 1891 Ahmad declared himself the Mahdi. In 1914 the movement split: the majority recognized Ahmad's son, Hadrat Mirza Bashir ad-Din Mahmud Ahmad (1889–1965), as caliph. In 1947 this group moved its headquarters to Rabwah, Pakistan. A splinter group, based in Lahore, Pakistan, recognize Ahmad as a reformer rather than a prophet. The Ahmadis are regarded as apostates in Orthodox Islam.

Ahmad Shah Durrani (1722–73) Emir of Afghanistan (1747–73) and founder of the Durrani dynasty. He united the Afghan tribes and is sometimes known as the founder of modern Afghanistan.

Ahmed III (1673–1736) Ottoman sultan (1703–30), son and successor of Muhammad III. He lent protection to Charles XII of Sweden after his defeat by the

AGRICULTURE

Modern archaeological dating techniques suggest that agriculture was being practised in w Asia by *c*.7000 bc. Consisting of the cultivation of crops and the raising of livestock, initially it was confined to areas with enough rainfall to enable the production of cereals, particularly wheat. By 5000 bc, however, the development of irrigation techniques had enabled farming to spread into s Mesopotamia, the Iranian plateau and the Nile valley in Egypt. In the 4th millennium bc, farmers began to move into the Indus valley in India.

By 5000 bc farming was well-established in the north of China. By 3000 bc wet rice-cultivation was being practised in s India, China and Southeast Asia. The practice of farming spread from w Asia to se Europe in *c*.5000 bc and from there to the rest of Europe in the next 2000 years. It was also being practised by 5000 bc in South America and Mesoamerica. Corn was the staple crop in Mesoamerica by 2000 bc. It spread to the sw region of North America by 1000 bc, but was not grown in the e region until *c*.ad 800.

Throughout the period to ad 500, the use of irrigation and other intensive farming techniques, such as the spreading of manure, led to increased productivity, a growth in population and the development of villages, towns and cities in many parts of the world.

Developments from ad 500

In the medieval period, the spread of intensive agriculture was facilitated by the development of the wheeled plow. In 18th- and 19th-century Europe, selective breeding improved milk and meat yields. A three-field system of agriculture, in which one field was allowed to lie fallow every year, was replaced by a four-field system of crop rotation, in which fields were used continuously for production with no deterioration in yield or quality of the crops. Productivity was also increased by the process of enclosure. Such changes were part of the Agricultural Revolution, which helped lay the foundations for the Industrial Revolution. This in turn led to further changes in agriculture, such as the introduction of many new items of farm machinery. In what is now defined as the developed world, mechanization advanced greatly, and today a large proportion of agricultural production is carried out by factory-farming methods. In much of the underdeveloped world, agriculture is still labour intensive. Three-quarters of the world's workforce is engaged in farming.

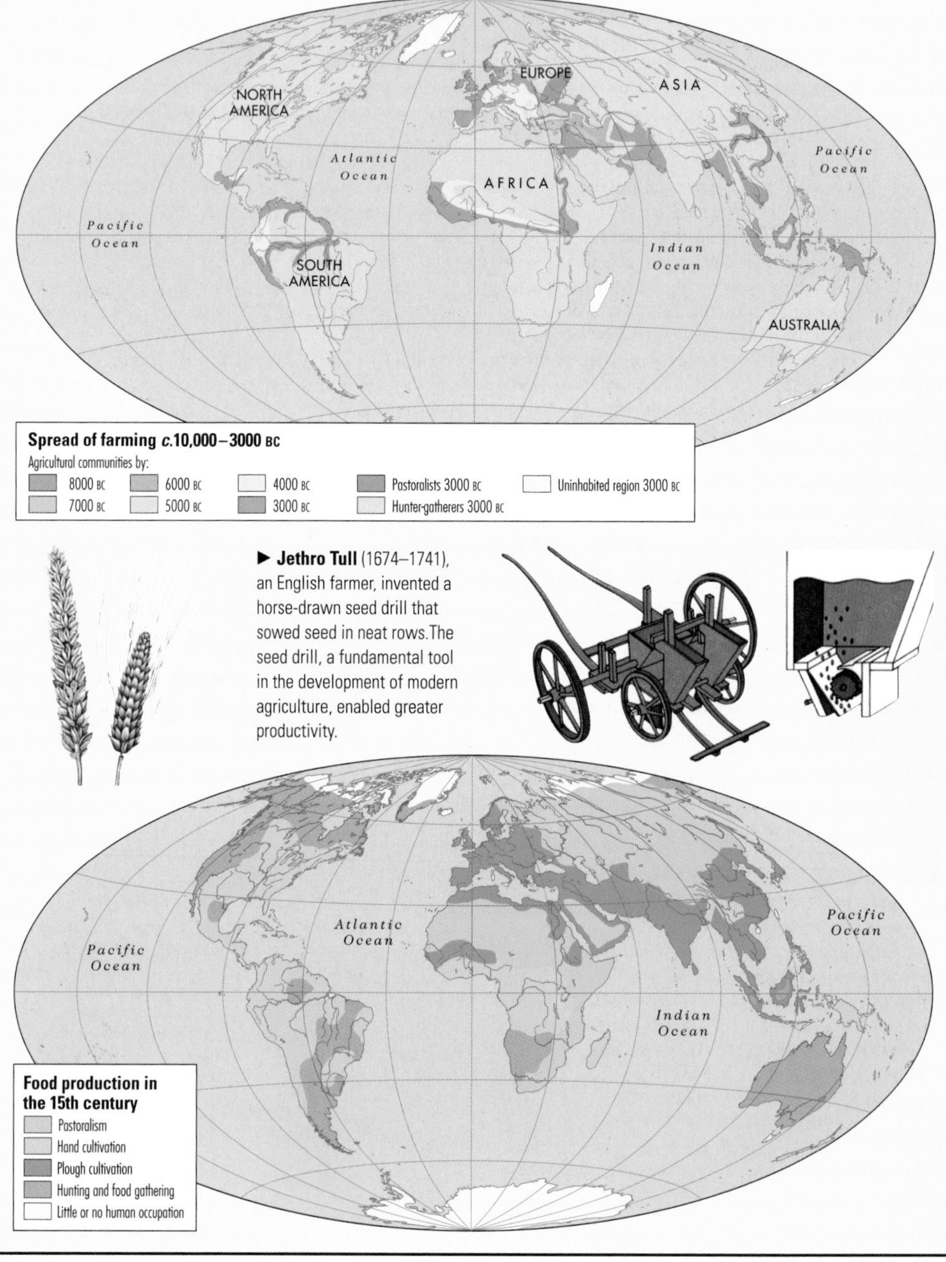

► **Jethro Tull** (1674–1741), an English farmer, invented a horse-drawn seed drill that sowed seed in neat rows.The seed drill, a fundamental tool in the development of modern agriculture, enabled greater productivity.

Russians at the Battle of POLTAVA (1709). In 1711 Ahmed recovered Azov from the Russians. In 1715 the Peloponnese was captured from Venice. In 1718 Ahmed was defeated by Prince EUGÈNE OF SAVOY and forced to cede Hungary and N Serbia to Austria. He was deposed in a uprising by the JANISSARIES.

Ahmed al-Mansour (1549–1603) Emir of Morocco (1578–1603). He earned the epithet *al-Mansour* (Arab. "the Victorious") after his crushing defeat of the Portuguese at the Battle of ALCAZARQUIVIR (1578). Ahmed was acknowledged as sole ruler of Morocco. In 1590 he captured TIMBUKTU, securing control of the lucrative gold and slave routes across the Sahara. His death was followed by civil war and the division of Morocco into several principalities.

Ahmose I (Amasis I) King of ancient EGYPT (r. *c.*1567–1546 BC), founder of the XVIII dynasty. Ahmose re-established THEBES as the centre of government, reconquered NUBIA, and expelled the HYKSOS. He was succeeded by his son, Amenhotep I.

Aisha (*c.*613–78) Youngest and favourite wife of the Prophet MUHAMMAD, daughter of ABU BAKR. She married at the age of nine, collected more than 2000 sayings (HADITHS) of Muhammad and his companions, and incited an unsuccessful uprising against the fourth caliph, ALI.

Aix-la-Chapelle, Treaty of (1748) Diplomatic agreement, principally between France and Britain, that ended the War of the AUSTRIAN SUCCESSION (1740–48). The treaty provided for the restitution of conquests made during the war, contributed to the rise of Prussian power, and confirmed British control of the slave trade to Spanish America. An earlier treaty (1668) signed at Aix-la-Chapelle ended the War of DEVOLUTION.

Akan People of W Africa, mostly in Ghana, and in the Ivory Coast and Togo. In the 17th and 18th centuries, the largest Akan tribes (the ASHANTI and the FANTI) developed powerful trading confederacies.

Akbar, Jalal ud-Din Muhammad (1542–1605) Emperor of India (1556–1605), son and successor of HUMAYUN. Akbar greatly expanded the MUGHAL EMPIRE and created a centrally governed state. He assumed personal control in 1560 and set out to establish Mughal control of the whole of India, extending his authority as far south as Ahmadnagar. He subjugated Rajasthan by a combination of conquest and conciliation with the RAJPUT princes. Akbar gained the cooperation of the non-Muslim inhabitants through tolerant religious policies and the coopting of leading Hindus into government administration. He assumed direct control of the army and centralized government finances through the appointment of a provincial governor (*nawab* or *subador*) and civil administrator (*diwan*). Akbar built a new capital at Fatehpur Sikri. He was succeeded by his son, JAHANGIR. *See also* BABUR

à Kempis, Thomas *See* THOMAS À KEMPIS

Akhenaten (d. *c.*1362 BC) (Akhnaton, Ikhnaton) Ancient Egyptian king of the 18th dynasty (r. *c.*1379–1362 BC). He succeeded his father, AMENHOTEP III, as Amenhotep IV. In an attempt to counter the influence of the priests of the Temple of Amon at Thebes (LUXOR), he renounced the old gods and introduced an almost monotheistic worship of the Sun god, Aten. He adopted the name Akhenaten and established a new capital at Akhetaten (now Tell el-Amarna). After Akhenaten's death TUTANKHAMEN reinstated Amon as the national god, and the capital reverted to Thebes.

Akihito (1933–) Emperor of Japan (1989–). In 1959 Akihito married a commoner, Michiko Shoda, the first such marriage in the history of the imperial dynasty. Akihito succeeded his father, HIROHITO.

Akkad (Agade) Ancient region of MESOPOTAMIA, named after the city-state of Akkad. From the mid-4th millennium BC, the region's cities fought each other, until SARGON I united them in *c.*2340 BC, forming the first Babylonian Empire. *See also* BABYLONIA

Akko *See* ACRE

Aksum (Axum) Town in Tigré province, N ETHIOPIA. It was the capital of a powerful kingdom (1st–6th centuries AD) that dominated trade (especially in ivory) along the Red Sea coast. According to tradition, its kings were descended from Menelik (legendary son of SOLOMON).

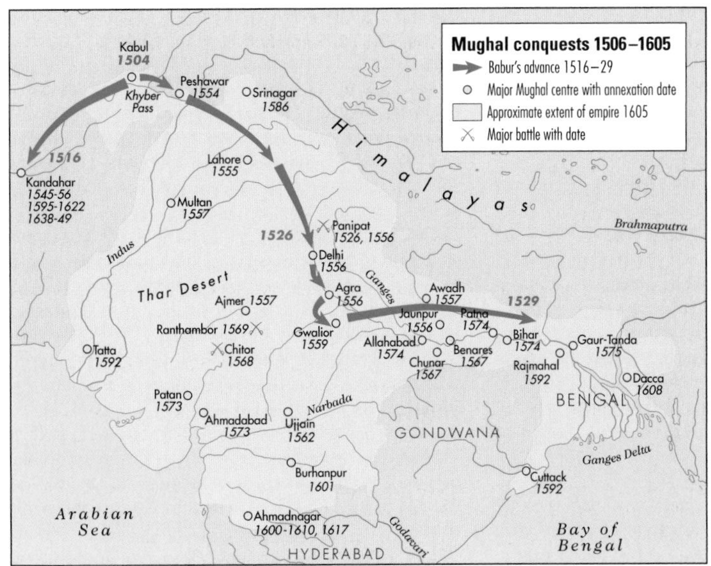

◀ **Akbar** On the death (1530) of Babur, the Mughal Empire was little more than an area of N India under military occupation. The accession of Akbar was ensured by victory over Hemu at the Second Battle of Panipat (1556). Akbar's massacre of the inhabitants of the fortress at Chitor (1568) served as a bloody warning to his enemies. In 1573 Akbar conquered Gujarat, W India. He then embarked on a campaign in the E, annexing Bengal in 1576. The Empire was extended further by the capture of Kashmir (1586), Sind (1591) and Kandahar (1595).

Aksum conquered the kingdom of MEROË in the 4th century. Aksum was Christianized in the 4th century and remains a major centre of Ethiopian Christianity. By the 6th century, its power extended into S Arabia. Aksum was gradually eclipsed by the Arabs and the resurgence of the Iranians. Pop. (1984 est.) 18,000. *See also* SOLOMONID

Alabama State in SE United States, in the chief cotton-growing region; the capital is Montgomery. Birmingham is the largest city. Settled by the French in 1702, the region was acquired by Britain in 1763. Most of it was ceded to the United States in 1783, and Alabama was admitted as the 22nd state of the Union in 1819. It seceded in 1861 as one of the original six states of the Confederacy, and was readmitted to the Union in 1868. In the 1960s it was a centre of the civil rights movement. Area: 133,915sq km (51,705sq mi). Pop. (1990) 4,040,587.

Alabama claims (1872) Award of US$15.5 million compensation to the United States against the United Kingdom for damage inflicted by Confederate ships, especially the cruiser *Alabama*, built in England during the American CIVIL WAR (1861–65). An international tribunal ruled that the British government violated its neutrality by allowing the ships to be built on its territory.

Alamán, Lucas (1792–1853) Mexican historian and statesman. He sought to establish Mexico as an independent monarchy. Alamán served in the cabinets of Agustín de ITURBIDE, Anastasio BUSTAMENTE and Antonio de SANTA ANNA. He is chiefly remembered, however, for his monumental *History of Mexico* (5 vols, 1849–52).

Alamein, Battle of El Decisive conflict in the NORTH AFRICA CAMPAIGN of WORLD WAR 2. In July 1942 the British 8th Army, led by General AUCHINLECK, successfully held their defensive line from Alamein to the Qattara Depresion (the lowest point in Africa), N Egypt. In October 1942 the 8th Army, under General MONTGOMERY, launched a devastating attack on the Afrika Korps, led by Field Marshal ROMMEL. The Axis forces were forced to retreat into Tunisia, and by May 1943 had been expelled from North Africa.

Alamo, the Mission in San Antonio, Texas, scene of a battle between Mexico and the Republic of Texas (1836) during the TEXAS REVOLUTION. About 180 Texans, led by William TRAVIS, Davy CROCKETT and Jim BOWIE, were overwhelmed by a vastly superior Mexican force following an 11-day siege.

Alanbrooke, Alan Francis Brooke, 1st Viscount (1883–1963) British general. During World War 2, he commanded the Second Army Corps in France and was commander in chief of the British Home Forces (1940–41). As chief of the Imperial General Staff (1941–46), Alanbrooke directed British tactics against Germany and coordinated Anglo-American strategy with General Dwight EISENHOWER.

Alaric I (370–410) King of the VISIGOTHS (395–410). His forces ravaged Thrace, Macedonia and Greece, and occupied EPIRUS (395–96). In 401 Alaric invaded Italy. Defeated by the Roman General STILICHO, he formed a pact with him. Emperor HONORIUS executed Stilicho for treason and Alaric besieged (408) and captured Rome (410). He planned an invasion of Sicily and Africa, but his fleet was destroyed in a storm.

Alaska State in NW North America, separated from the rest of continental United States by the province of British Columbia, Canada, and from Russia by the Bering Strait. The capital is Juneau. About 25% of Alaska lies inside the Arctic Circle. In the ALASKA PURCHASE (1867), the United States acquired the area from Russia, who had founded the first European settlement there in 1784, for US$7.2 million. Fishing drew settlers and, after the gold rush of the 1890s, the population doubled in ten years. In 1959 it became the 49th state of the Union. Because of its strategic position and oil reserves, Alaska has been developed as a military area and is linked to the rest of the United States by the 2450-km (1523-mi) long Alaska Highway. Although by far the largest US state, it has the second-smallest population (after WYOMING). Of the total state population, 85,698 were registered as Native Americans in the 1990 census (the majority of them Inuit-Aleut Eskimos). Area: 591,004sq mi (1,530,700sq km). Pop. (1990) 550,043.

Alaskan Boundary Dispute (1902–03) Altercation between the United States and Britain, representing Canada, over possession of the inlets between Alaska and Canada after the start of the KLONDIKE GOLD RUSH. It was settled by a six-man panel in favour of the United States.

Alaska Purchase (1867) Transfer of the Russian territory of ALASKA to the United States for US$7.2 million. Many Americans regarded Alaska as a frozen wasteland, and the purchase was called "Seward's Folly" after Secretary of State William SEWARD, who negotiated the purchase.

ALABAMA
Statehood :
14 December 1819
Nickname :
The Heart of Dixie
State motto :
We dare defend our rights

ALASKA
Statehood :
3 January 1959
Nickname :
The Last Frontier
State motto :
North to the future

A

Alaungpaya (1711–60) King of BURMA (1752–60). He refused to become a vassal of the king of Mon (in the Irrawaddy Delta) when Ava, the Burmese capital, was captured (1752). Alaungpaya organized resistance to the Mon, recaptured Ava (1753) and conquered (1757) the Mon capital, Pegu. In 1760 he tried to conquer Siam (now Thailand), but died with his army in retreat.

Alba, Fernando Álvarez de Toledo, Duke of (*c.*1507–82) Spanish soldier and statesman. Early in his career, he distinguished himself as a commander of the armies of Emperor CHARLES V and PHILIP II of Spain. In 1567 Alba was appointed governor general of the rebellious Netherlands, where he established a reign of terror. Thousands of people were executed or banished as he attempted to suppress opposition to Spanish rule and to root out Protestantism. In 1573 he returned to Spain at his own request, and later led the forces that conquered Portugal in 1580. *See also* REVOLT OF THE NETHERLANDS

Albania *See* country feature

Albany Capital of New York state, United States, on the Hudson River. Settled by the Dutch in 1614 and British from 1664, it replaced NEW YORK CITY as state capital in 1797. It grew from the 1820s with the building of the Erie Canal, linking it to the Great Lakes. Pop. (1990) 101,082.

Albany Congress (1754) North American colonial conference to discuss Native American relations. Representatives from seven northern and middle colonies met IROQUOIS leaders and negotiated an alliance against the French. At the Congress, Benjamin FRANKLIN proposed a plan for union of the colonies, which was rejected by the colonial governments.

Albany regency (1820–48) Organization of DEMOCRATIC PARTY leaders in New York state. It successfully controlled conventions and appointments until the defeat of Martin VAN BUREN's presidential bid (1848).

Alberoni, Giulio (1664–1752) Italian statesman and cardinal, premier of Spain (1716–19). He became premier after the War of the SPANISH SUCCESSION (1701–14). Alberoni sought to drive the Austrians from Italy, and to protect Spanish-American trade.

Albert I (1875–1934) King of Belgium (1909–34), son of Philip, Count of Flanders. He succeeded his uncle, LEOPOLD II. In 1914, while the Allied defence formed, Albert spearheaded Belgian resistance to the Germans. He led the Belgian and French forces in the Allies' final offensive through Belgium (1918). After World War 1, Albert devoted himself to the task of reconstruction.

Albert, Prince (1819–61) Consort of Queen VICTORIA, Prince of SAXE-COBURG-GOTHA. In 1849 he married Victoria, his first cousin. Albert was the queen's chief adviser and the principal organizer of the GREAT EXHIBITION of 1851. He took an active role in diplomatic affairs and called for moderation in the TRENT AFFAIR (1861). Victoria was devastated by his death from typhoid.

Albert, Carl Bert (1908–) US congressman for Oklahoma (1947–76), speaker of the House of Representatives (1971–77). As majority leader (1962–71) of the House, Albert was a pivotal figure in securing the passage of President Lyndon JOHNSON's "Great Society" legislation through the House. As speaker, he presided over the crises of the VIETNAM WAR and WATERGATE AFFAIR.

Alberta Province of W Canada, bounded on the W mainly by the Rocky Mountains and in the S by the United States; the capital is Edmonton. Other major cities include Calgary. The area was part of a large territory granted (1670) by Charles II of England to the HUDSON'S BAY COMPANY. In 1870 the government of Canada bought the region as part of the North-Western Territory. In 1882 it was divided into four districts and Alberta was created (named after Queen Victoria's fourth daughter). In 1905 Alberta was admitted to the confederation as a province. Oil and natural gas fields in central Alberta have been a major stimulus to Canada's post-1945 economy. Area: 661,188sq km (255,285sq mi). Pop. (1996) 2,696,826.

Albert the Bear (*c.*1100–70) First Margrave of Brandenburg (1150–70). In 1134 he was awarded the North March, Italy, for his service to Emperor LOTHAIR II. In 1138 Albert was granted the Duchy of SAXONY by Lothair's successor, CONRAD III. He was expelled from Saxony by HENRY X (THE PROUD) and made peace (1142) with Henry's son, HENRY III (THE LION). Albert led crusades against the WENDS, contributing to the Christianization of NE Germany.

Albertus Magnus, Saint (*c.*1200–80) German philosopher and Doctor of the Church, known as "Doctor Universalis". In 1223 he joined the DOMINICAN order. He taught theology in Paris (1242–48), where his pupils included Thomas AQUINAS. Albertus was largely responsible for the rehabilitation of ARISTOTLE in European philosophy. He devoted much of his energies to reconciling Aristotelianism with Christian theology. He was canonized in 1931. His feast day is 15 November.

Albigenses (Cathars) Members of a heretical religious sect (E European origin) that existed in S France from the 11th to the early 14th centuries and took its name from the French city of Albi. In 1200 Pope INNOCENT III ordered a CRUSADE, led by Simon de MONTFORT, against them, which caused much damage in Languedoc and Provence.

Alboin (d.AD 572) King of the Lombards (*c.*565–72). In 568 he led his Germanic army across the Alps, conquering VENICE and MILAN. In 572 Alboin established his capital at Pavia, N Italy. According to legend, he was murdered by the lover of his wife, Rosamund.

Albright, Madeleine Korbel (1937–) US stateswoman, secretary of state (1997–), b. Czechoslovakia. She served as US ambassador to the United Nations (1992–96). Following Bill CLINTON's re-election (1996), Albright became the first woman to hold the office of secretary of state. She was a hawkish advocate of US involvement in the Gulf War and Bosnia.

Albuquerque, Afonso d' (1453–1515) Portuguese military commander, founder of the Portuguese Empire of the East Indies. After serving as a soldier in North Africa, Albuquerque became governor general of the Portuguese settlements in W India. He established control over major Indian Ocean shipping lanes, and therefore the spice trade, by capturing GOA (1510), MALACCA (1511), Calicut (1512) and Hormuz (1515).

Alcalá Zamora, Niceto (1877–1949) Spanish statesman, president (1931–36). In 1931 he led the revolution against the dictatorship of PRIMO DE RIVERA. A conservative president, he was removed by the Cortes and succeeded by Manuel AZAÑA. *See also* CIVIL WAR, SPANISH

Alcazarquivir, Battle of (4 August 1578) Massacre of the Portuguese army, led by King Sebastião, at the hands of the Moroccan kingdom of FEZ. The superior Muslim forces, led by AHMED AL-MANSUR, killed 7000 Portuguese troops and captured a further 8000. Sebastião was killed in battle. He was succeeded by PHILIP II.

Alcibiades (450–404 BC) Athenian general and statesman. In the PELOPONNESIAN WAR, Alcibiades inspired a disastrous campaign in Sicily (415 BC) and temporarily sided with SPARTA. Regaining his position in ATHENS, he was exiled following the Athenian defeat at Notium and later murdered by Spartan agents.

Alcock, Sir John William (1892–1919) English aviator who, with Arthur Whitten-Brown, was the first to fly nonstop across the Atlantic Ocean. On 14 June 1919, their transatlantic flight began in St John's, Newfoundland, and landed $16\frac{1}{2}$ hours later near Clifden, Ireland.

Aldrich, Nelson Wilmarth (1841–1915) US senator and financier. He was a supporter of protective TARIFFS

ALBANIA

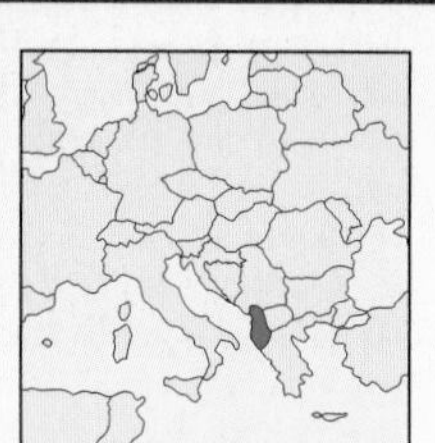

Small republic on the Adriatic coast of the Balkan Peninsula, SE Europe. In ancient times, Albania was part of ILLYRIA. In 167 BC it became part of the ROMAN EMPIRE. Between 1469 and 1912 Albania formed part of the OTTOMAN EMPIRE. Italy invaded Albania in 1939, and German forces occupied it in 1943. In 1944 Albanian communists, led by Enver HOXHA, took power. In the early 1960s, Albania broke with the Soviet Union after Soviet criticism of the Chinese COMMUNIST PARTY, which it was allied to until the late 1970s. In the early 1990s the Albanian government abandoned communism and allowed the formation of opposition parties. In 1996 the Democratic Party, headed by Sali Berisha, won a sweeping victory. In 1997 the collapse of pyramid finance schemes sparked a large-scale rebellion in S Albania and a state of emergency was proclaimed. Berisha formed a government of national reconciliation and agreed to new elections. The Socialist Party of Albania was victorious and Rexhep Medjani became president. In 1999 internal unrest was compounded by the crisis in the Serbian province of KOSOVO.

AREA: 28,750sq km (11,100sq mi)
POPULATION: 3,363,000
CAPITAL (POPULATION): Tirana (251,000)
GOVERNMENT: Multiparty republic
ETHNIC GROUPS: Albanian 98%, Greek 1.8%, Macedonian, Montenegrin, Romany
LANGUAGES: Albanian (official)
RELIGIONS: Islam 65% Christianity 33% (Orthodox 20%, Roman Catholic 13%)
GDP PER CAPITA (1992): US$3500

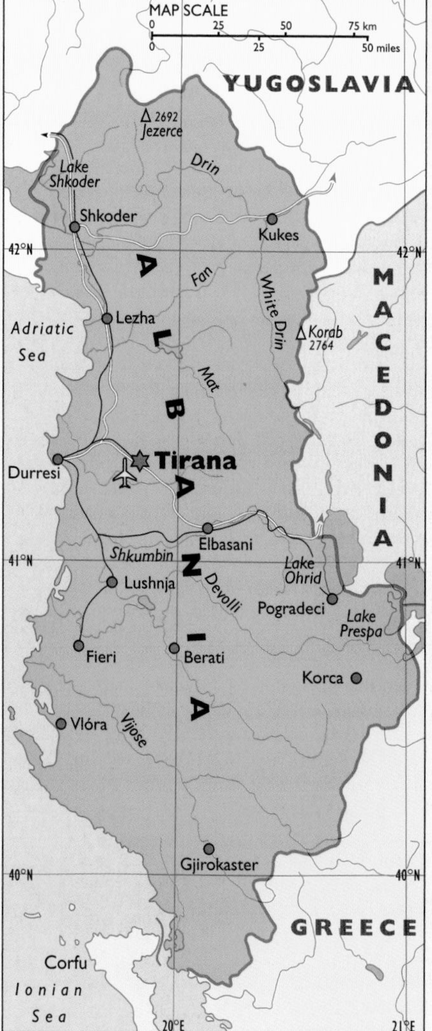

and an opponent of government regulation of business. Aldrich's backroom influence on Republican policy helped shape the INTERSTATE COMMERCE ACT (1887) and the SHERMAN ANTI-TRUST ACT (1890). He served (1881–1911) as senator for Rhode Island. Aldrich helped draft the Aldrich-Vreeland Currency Act (1908) and chaired (1908–12) the National Monetary Commission on banking reform that led to the FEDERAL RESERVE SYSTEM.

Aldrin, "Buzz" (Edwin Eugene) (1930–) US astronaut. He piloted the Gemini XII orbital-rendezvous space flight (November 1966) and the lunar module for the first Moon landing (20 July 1969). Aldrin followed Neil ARMSTRONG, becoming the second man on the Moon.

Alemanni Confederation of Germanic peoples who campaigned against the Roman Empire in the Rhine and Upper Danube area from the 3rd century AD. By the late 5th century they were established in Alsace and N Switzerland. They were conquered by the Frankish ruler CLOVIS I in 496.

Aleppo (Halab) City in NW SYRIA; Syria's second-largest city. Like the capital DAMASCUS, it claims to be the oldest continually inhabited city in the world. It has been part of Syria since 1924. Pop. (1993) 1,494,000.

Alessandri (Palma), Arturo (1868–1950) Chilean statesman, president (1920–24, 1925, 1932–38). Alessandri's first term was marred by factionalism within the Liberal Alliance coalition and he was forced to resign. In March 1925 Alessandri was recalled from exile to implement a new, democratic constitution. In October 1925 he was ousted by the minister of war, Carlos Ibáñez. His second term brought further reforms. In 1938 he was defeated by the Popular Front leader, Pedro Aguirre Cerda.

Alexander III (*c.*1105–81) Pope (1159–81). His election to the papacy was opposed by Holy Roman Emperor FREDERICK I, who had an ANTIPOPE, Victor IV, elected. The schism ended with the victory of the LOMBARD LEAGUE over Frederick at the Battle of LEGNANO (1176).

Alexander VI (1431–1503) Pope (1492–1503), b. Rodrigo Borgia. As a cardinal, he became immensely wealthy, patronized the arts and fathered several children. As pope, Alexander pursued a programme of financial reform, attempted to unite Christendom against the Ottoman Turks, and in the ITALIAN WARS (1494–1559) played a major role in forcing the French out of Italy. He also indulged in corruption and political intrigue, and did his utmost to advance the fortunes of the BORGIA family.

Alexander I (1777–1825) Tsar of Russia (1801–25). After repulsing NAPOLEON I's attempt to conquer Russia (1812), he led his troops across Europe and into Paris (1814). Under the influence of various mystical groups, he helped form the HOLY ALLIANCE with other European powers. In 1815 he was made king of Poland. He also annexed Finland, Georgia and Bessarabia to Russia. *See also* NAPOLEONIC WARS

Alexander II (1818–81) Tsar of Russia (1855–81). He was known as the "tsar liberator" for his emancipation of the serfs (1861). Alexander warred with Turkey (1877–78) and gained much influence in the Balkans. He sold ALASKA (1867), but expanded the eastern part of the Russian Empire. He brutally put down a revolt in Poland (1863). Alexander was assassinated by revolutionaries.

Alexander III (1845–94) Tsar of Russia (1881–94), son and successor of ALEXANDER II. His autocratic rule attempted to impose uniformity in Russia. Alexander centralized power and enforced censorship of the press. Ethnic and religious minorities were persecuted, and arbitrary arrest and exile became common. He was succeeded by his son, NICHOLAS II.

Alexander (1893–1920) King of Greece (1917–20), son of CONSTANTINE I. He acceded to the throne after the Allies had forced the abdication of his father. Premier Eleuthérios VENIZÉLOS approved the entry of Greece into World War 1, gaining Smyrna and Thrace. Alexander's death, from the bite of a pet monkey, prompted a constitutional crisis and the return of Constantine I.

Alexander III (the Great) *See* feature article

Alexander II (1198–1249) King of Scotland (1214–49), son and successor of WILLIAM I (THE LION). He sided with the rebels against King JOHN of England in the BARONS' WAR. In 1221 Alexander married Joan, the sister of John's successor, HENRY III. During the 1220s, he consolidated royal power in Scotland. In 1237 Alexander and Henry concluded the Peace of York, which abandoned the Scottish claim to old Northumbria and established the boundary of Scotland in roughly its present-day position.

Alexander III (1241–86) King of Scotland (1249–86), son and successor of ALEXANDER II. He defeated HAAKON IV of Norway at the Battle of Largs (1263) and acquired the Hebrides. Alexander married a daughter of HENRY III of England, but resisted English claims to Scotland.

Alexander I (1888–1934) King of the Serbs, Croats and Slovenes (1921–29) and YUGOSLAVIA (1929–34). In 1929 he transformed the Kingdom of Serbs, Croats and Slovenes into Yugoslavia. Alexander's efforts to forge a united country from the rival national groups and ethnically divided political parties led to the creation of an autocratic, police state. He was assassinated by an USTAŠA Croatian.

Alexander (1857–93) Prince of Bulgaria (1878–86), nephew of ALEXANDER II of Russia. A German Prince of Battenberg, he was chosen by the Congress of BERLIN (1878) to rule the newly created principality of Bulgaria. Disputes over his ties with Russia led to his overthrow, kidnapping, restoration and final abdication.

Alexander Karageorgević (1806–85) Prince of Serbia (1842–58), son of KARAGEORGE and father of PETER I. He succeeded after the collapse of the regency of Michael OBRENOVIĆ. Alexander failed to support a Serbian revolt in Hungary (1848) and the Russians in the CRIMEAN WAR (1854–56). His ineffective government led to his removal and he was succeeded by MILOŠ Obrenović.

ALEXANDER III (THE GREAT) (356–323 BC)

King of Macedonia (336–323 BC), son of PHILIP II. He is considered the greatest conqueror of classical times. As a teenager, Alexander was tutored by ARISTOTLE. He fought alongside his father against THEBES and ATHENS at the Battle of CHAERONEA (338 BC). After Philip's assassination (336 BC), Alexander ruthlessly eliminated all rivals to his succession. He cowed the Greek states into submission by his brutal crushing of Theban opposition (335 BC). Leaving ANTIPATER in control of his European lands, Alexander launched an attack on the Persian ACHAEMENID empire in 334 BC. According to legend, at Gordium, Phrygia, Alexander cut the Gordian knot and went on to conquer W ASIA MINOR, gaining a decisive victory over DARIUS III at the Battle of Issus (333 BC). Alexander pursued Darius into PHOENICIA, storming TYRE in 332 BC. His conquest of the E Mediterranean coast was completed with the capture of Egypt and the founding (332 BC) of the city of ALEXANDRIA. Alexander now turned to MESOPOTAMIA, where victory over Darius at the Battle of Gaugamela (331 BC) led to the occupation of BABYLON and SUSA and made Alexander master of SW Asia. In 330 BC he conquered MEDIA. Alexander continued his relentless march eastwards, subduing BACTRIA en route to conquering the whole of Central Asia by 328 BC. Alexander resorted to increasingly authoritarian measures to ensure the loyalty of his troops, such as the execution of CALLISTHENES. In 327 BC Alexander invaded India, founding the city of Bucephala (named after his horse Bucephalus). Alexander was prevented from advancing further into India, however, by the threat of mutiny. Alexander returned to Persia, and his adoption of Persian customs infuriated many Macedonians. Alexander died in Babylon, leaving no appointed heir. He was chiefly responsible for the spread of Greek civilization in the Mediterranean and W Asia. *See also* ANTIGONES I (THE ONE-EYED); DEMOSTHENES; HELLENISTIC AGE

▲ **Alexander III (the Great)** Alexander's achievements were celebrated by the Romans. This detail from a mosaic in the House of the Faun, Pompeii, created in the late 2nd- or early 1st-century BC, was modelled on a 4th-century BC painting, commissioned by Alexander's own generals.

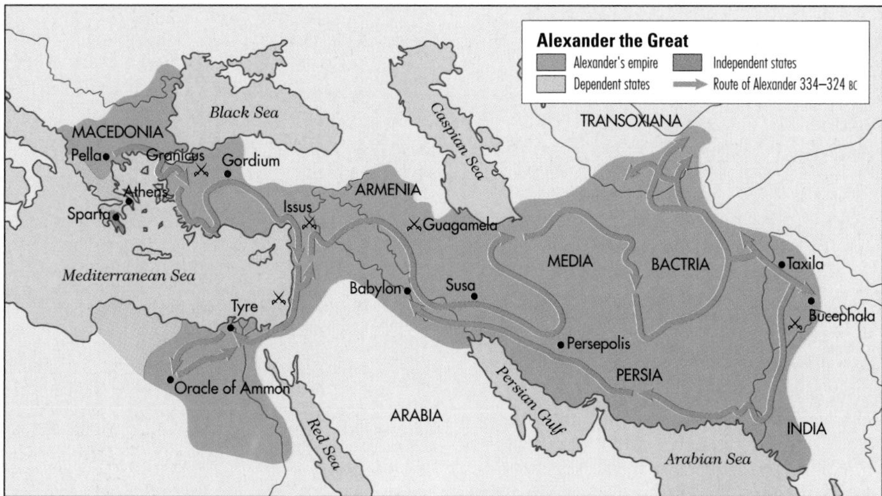

▲ **Alexander III (the Great)** In the spring of 334 BC, Alexander's army of 32,000 infantry, 5000 cavalry and 160 ships crossed the Hellespont (now Dardanelles) and defeated the Persians at the Battle of Granicus. In 333 BC he won another victory against the Persians, at Issus. Alexander marched on and besieged Tyre, before advancing into Egypt where he founded the city of Alexandria. In 331 BC he left Egypt and again defeated the Persians, at Guagamela, before capturing the cities of Babylon, Susa and Persepolis. In pursuit of Darius III, Alexander marched through the heart of Central Asia. At the foot of the Himalayas, his army refused to cross the daunting mountain chain and Alexander turned south, following the River Indus to the Indian Ocean, before marching west through the desert of Gedrosia (now Baluchistan). Alexander returned to Babylon, where he died at the age of 32.

A

▲ **Alfred (the Great)** Alfred's newly built fortresses (burhs) protected Wessex from the second great Viking invasion. Under King Rollo, the Vikings founded the Duchy of Normandy.

Alexander (of Tunis), Harold Rupert Leofric George, 1st Earl (1891–1969) British field marshal and statesman, minister of defence (1952–54). In 1940 he directed the evacuation of DUNKIRK. As commander in chief (1942–43) in the Middle East, Alexander supervised the successful NORTH AFRICA CAMPAIGN. In 1944 he was made field marshal and Allied commander in chief in the Mediterranean. Alexander served as governor general of Canada (1946–52) before joining Winston CHURCHILL's Conservative cabinet.

Alexander Nevski, Saint (1220–63) Russian ruler, Grand Duke of NOVGOROD and Grand Duke of Vladimir. He pragmatically submitted to MONGOL rule following the Mongol invasion of Russia, and the Great Khan appointed him Grand Duke of KIEV. In 1240 Alexander defeated the Swedish army on the banks of the River Neva (hence the title "Nevski"). In 1242 he was victorious against the TEUTONIC KNIGHTS on Lake Peipus. He was canonized by the Russian Orthodox Church in 1547.

Alexander Severus, Marcus Aurelius (*c*.AD 208–35) Roman emperor (222–35). He became emperor at the age of 14 and throughout his reign was strongly influenced by his mother, Julia Mamaea. As a military leader, Alexander fought (231–33) the newly established Persian SASANIAN empire and restored the Roman frontier in the Near East. On the Rhine frontier, he chose to buy peace from the Germans rather than fight. His troops rebelled and killed Alexander, plunging the Roman Empire into anarchy.

Alexandria Chief port and second-largest city of Egypt, situated on the W extremity of the Nile delta. Founded (332 BC) by ALEXANDER III (THE GREAT), it became a great centre of Greek (and Jewish) culture. An offshore island housed the 3rd-century BC Pharos lighthouse, one of the SEVEN WONDERS OF THE WORLD, and the city contained a great library (founded by PTOLEMY I and said to contain 700,000 volumes). Today, Alexandria is the Middle East headquarters for the World Health Organization (WHO). Pop. (1990 est.) 3,170,000.

Alexei Mikhailovich (1629–76) Tsar of Russia (1645–76), father of PETER I (THE GREAT). Alexei established (1648) a code of laws that sustained SERFDOM in Russia until the 19th century. In 1654 the COSSACKS in Ukraine took up arms in favour of unification with Russia. The ensuing war with Poland (1654–67) saw Russia regain SMOLENSK and KIEV. Alexei suppressed a rebellion (1670–71) led by Stenka RAZIN. The schism in the Russian Orthodox Church created by Patriarch NIKON's reforms enabled Alexei to assert secular authority over the Church.

Alexius I (Comnenus) (1048–1118) Byzantine emperor (1081–1118), founder of the Comnenian dynasty. Alexius held off the Normans who threatened Constantinople (now ISTANBUL) and turned the Western armies of the First CRUSADE (1095–99) to his own advantage by using them to reconquer parts of Anatolia.

Alfonso V (the Magnanimous) (1394–1458) King of Aragón and Sicily (1416–58) and of Naples (1443–58). During his reign the Catalan-Aragónese empire reached its greatest extent. In 1442 Alfonso captured NAPLES. In 1443 he transferred his court to Naples, developing it into a centre of Renaissance culture and of the Catalan language.

Alfonso VIII (the Noble) (1155–1214) King of Castile (1158–1214), son of Sancho III. He took personal control of Castile in 1166 and at first opposed both Moors and fellow Christian kings. In 1212 Alfonso forged a coalition with the Christian kings and won an important victory against the ALMOHADS at Las Navas de Tolosa. He married Eleanor, daughter of HENRY I of England.

Alfonso X (the Wise) (1221–84) King of Castile and León (1252–84), son and successor of FERDINAND III. He failed to complete his father's reconquest of S Spain from the Moors. Alfonso was a noted scholar and his *Sieste Partidas* codified Spanish law. In 1275 civil war in Spain forced Alfonso to concede defeat in his ambition to become Holy Roman emperor. In 1282 the rebellion of his son, later Sancho IV, left Alfonso isolated in Seville.

Alfonso XII (1857–85) King of Spain (1874–85), son of ISABELLA II. Alfonso and his mother went into exile during the Carlist Wars. In 1870 Isabella abdicated in her son's favour. In 1874 Alfonso was proclaimed king. He strengthened the monarchy by suppressing CARLISM and granting power to the nobility. He died in the great cholera epidemic of 1885 and was succeeded by his son, ALFONSO XIII.

Alfonso XIII (1886–1941) King of Spain (1886–1931). He was born after the death of his father, ALFONSO XII. His mother, María Cristina (1858–1929), acted as regent until 1902. Alfonso's reign was marked by civil unrest and he survived several assassination attempts. He used military and authoritarian measures to suppress republicans and Catalan and Basque nationalists. In 1923 Alfonso supported the establishment of a military dictatorship under General Miguel PRIMO DE RIVERA. In 1930 the collapse of the dictatorship left Alfonso personally discredited and he was forced into exile (1931).

Alfred (the Great) (849–99) King of WESSEX (871–99), brother and successor of ETHELRED I. He saved Wessex from the Danes and laid the foundations of a united English kingdom. After the Danish invasion of 878, Alfred escaped to Athelney, Somerset, returning to defeat the Danes at Edington and recover the kingdom. His pact with the Danish leader, GUTHRUM (who accepted Christian baptism), roughly divided England in two; the DANELAW occupied the NE; Alfred controlled Wessex and part of Mercia. His leadership was widely recognized throughout England, however, after his capture of London (886). Alfred was a noted scholar, perhaps best known for his translation of the *Soliloquies* of Saint AUGUSTINE. He was succeeded by his son, EDWARD THE ELDER. *See also* ANGLO-SAXONS

▲ **Alhambra** The *Patio de los Leones* (Court of the Lions) lies at the heart of the Moorish palace of the Alhambra, Granada, S Spain. The palace was built chiefly between 1238 and 1358.

Algeciras Conference (1906) Meeting of several European powers and the United States in Algeciras, Andalusia, S Spain, to settle commercial and colonial rivalries. The main concern was Germany's challenge to French control in Morocco. The outcome of the conference demonstrated Germany's political isolation and the resolve of the ENTENTE CORDIALE (1904) between Britain and France.

Algeria *See* country feature

Algiers Capital city of ALGERIA, on the Bay of Algiers, N Africa's chief port on the Mediterranean. Founded by the Phoenicians, it was subsequently colonized by Romans, Berbers, Turks (under BARBAROSSA) and Barbary pirates. In 1830 the French invaded and made Algiers the capital of the French colony of Algeria. In World War 2, it was the headquarters of the Allies and the seat of the French provisional government. During the 1950s and 1960s it was a focus for the violent struggle for independence. The 11th-century Sidi Abderrahman Mosque is a major destination for Muslim pilgrims. Pop. (1995) 2,168,000.

Algonquin (Algonkin) Group of Canadian Native American tribes that gave their name to the Algonquian languages of North America. The Algonquin people occupied the Ottawa River area *c*.AD 1600. Driven from their home by the IROQUOIS in the 17th century, they were eventually absorbed into other related tribes in Canada.

Alhambra Spanish citadel of the sultans of Granada, a world heritage site and a major tourist attraction. Standing on a plateau overlooking the city of Granada, S Spain, it is one of the most beautiful and well-preserved examples of medieval ISLAMIC ART AND ARCHITECTURE. Most of the complex was built during the Nasrid dynasty (1238–1358).

Ali (*c*.600–61) Fourth Muslim CALIPH (656–61), cousin and son-in-law of the Prophet MUHAMMAD. Ali was married to FATIMA. He is regarded by SHIITES as the first imam and rightful heir of Muhammad. Ali succeeded OTHMAN as caliph, despite opposition from AISHA and MUAWIYA, a relative of Othman. He was assassinated and his first son, Hasan, abdicated in favour of Muawiya, who founded the UMAYYAD dynasty. His second son, Husayn, led the insurrection against the Umayyads, but was defeated and killed at the Battle of Karbala (680).

Alien and Sedition Acts (1798) Four laws designed to curb criticism of the United States' government at a time when war with France seemed imminent. The Acts imposed stringent rules on residency before naturalization. They gave the president unprecedented powers to deport or imprison undesirable foreigners in time of war.

Ali Pasha (*c*.1744–1822) Turkish governor of Janina (now Ioánnina, NW Greece), known as "the lion of Janina". From 1788 Ali constructed a powerful, personal empire that incorporated most of Albania and EPIRUS. In 1820, fearful of Ali's growing power, Sultan MAHMUD II deposed him. Ali's spirited resistance against the sultan depleted Turkish strength in the GREEK WAR OF INDEPENDENCE.

Allahabad City at the confluence of the Ganges and Yamuna rivers, Uttar Pradesh, N central India. The city is a pilgrimage centre for Hindus. The ASHOKA Pillar (232 BC) stands inside the MUGHAL fort built (AD 1583) by Jalal ud-Din Muhammad AKBAR. In 1858 the English EAST INDIA COMPANY handed control of India to the British government at a ceremony in Allahabad. The city was the centre of the Indian independence movement and is the site of the family home of the Nehru dynasty. Pop. (1991) 806,000.

Allan, Sir Hugh (1810–82) Canadian entrepreneur, b. Scotland. In 1856 he founded the Allan Line of steamships and later helped plan the Canadian Pacific Railroad. His donation of Can$350,000 to the Conservative Party of Prime Minister John MACDONALD resulted in the PACIFIC SCANDAL (1873).

Allen, Ethan (1738–89) US frontiersman and soldier. In 1768 he moved to the New Hampshire grants (now Vermont). In *c*.1770 he became commander of the Green Mountain Boys, a volunteer militia. In the American Revolution, Allen and his troops (with sympathizers from Connecticut and Massachusetts) captured Fort Ticonderoga (10 May 1775) and Crown Point (11 May 1775). During the invasion of Canada, he was captured (25 September 1775) and imprisoned in England until 1778, when he returned to Vermont.

Allenby, Edmund Henry Hynman, 1st Viscount (1861–1936) English military commander. A distinguished cavalry officer, he defeated the Turkish forces in Palestine and Syria (1917–18), capturing Jerusalem, Damascus and Aleppo. In 1919 he was made a viscount. Allenby served (1919–25) as British high commissioner in Egypt and Sudan. *See also* Lawrence, T.E. (Thomas Edward)

Allende Gossens, Salvador (1908–73) Chilean statesman, president (1970–73). He was one of the founders of the Chilean Socialist Party (1933) and served as minister of health (1939–42) and head of the senate (1965–69). Allende's narrow election victory led to the introduction of democratic socialist reforms, which antagonized the Chilean establishment. The nationalization of the US-owned copper industry resulted in a US trade embargo. The CIA began a covert campaign of destabilization, aided by a deteriorating economy. Allende was overthrown and died during the military coup led by General Augusto Pinochet.

Alliance for Progress Multilateral programme promoting economic and social development in Latin America initiated (1961) by President John Kennedy. The United States pledged US$20 billion over a ten-year period. The principle aim of the Alliance was to counteract Fidel Castro's communist revolution in Cuba and it introduced police and military programs to suppress communist elements. It had a limited impact, however, as many regimes in Latin America were unwilling to take up the goals of the Alliance, while the United States failed to supply the mechanisms that would have helped secure the goals. By 1971 the Alliance was virtually defunct.

Allies Term used in World War 1 and World War 2 for the forces that fought the Central Powers and Axis Powers respectively. In World War 1 they numbered 23 and included Belgium, Britain and its Commonwealth, France, Italy, Japan, Russia and the United States. In World War 2, the 49 Allies included Belgium, Britain and the Commonwealth, France, the Netherlands, the Soviet Union and the United States.

Almagro, Diego de (1475–1538) Spanish conquistador. He joined Francisco Pizarro in the initial expedition (1524–27) to Peru and was instrumental in the subjugation of the Incas. There was a land dispute between him and the Pizarro brothers and he tried to claim Cuzco, but was executed by order of Hernando Pizarro.

Almeida, Francisco de (*c*.1450–1510) Portuguese admiral, first viceroy (1505–09) of Portuguese India. In 1505, in order to control the lucrative spice trade between India and Africa, he built forts on the E coast of Africa and burned Mombasa. In 1508 his son was defeated and killed by the Egyptians. In 1509 Almeida defeated a combined Egyptian and Indian fleet off Diu, W India. He was succeeded as viceroy by Afonso de Albuquerque. Almeida was killed on his return journey to Portugal.

Almohad Berber Muslim dynasty (1150–1269) in North Africa and Spain, the followers of a reform movement within Islam. It was founded by Muhammad ibn Tumart, who set out from the Atlas Mountains to purify Islam and oust the Almoravids from Morocco and eventually Spain. The Almohads were the first (and last) dynasty to unify the Maghrib. In 1212 Alfonso VIII (the Noble) of Castile routed the Almohads, and in 1269 their capital, Marrakesh, fell to the Marinids.

Almoravid Berber Muslim dynasty (1054–1143) in Morocco and Spain. They rose to power under Abdullah ibn Yasin, who converted Saharan tribes in a religious revival. In 1070 Abu Bakr founded Marrakesh as the Almoravid capital. In 1086 Abu's brother, Yusuf ibn Tashufin, defeated Alfonso VI of Castile. Almoravid power began to fragment after the death (1143) of Ali ibn Yusuf and they were eventually ousted by the Almohads.

Alp Arslan (1029–72) Seljuk sultan (r.1063–72). He conquered Armenia, Syria, Cilicia and Cappadocia. His victory over the Byzantine Empire at the Battle of Manzikert (1071) ensured Turkish domination of Asia Minor.

Alsace Region in E France, comprising the departments of Bas-Rhin and Haut-Rhin. Strasbourg is the leading city. Separated from Germany by the River Rhine, the Alsace-Lorraine region has often caused friction between France and Germany. Area: 8280sq km (3197sq mi). Pop. (1990) 1,624,400.

ALGERIA

AREA: 2,381,700sq km (919,590sq mi)
POPULATION: 26,346,000
CAPITAL (POPULATION): Algiers (2,168,000)
GOVERNMENT: Socialist republic
ETHNIC GROUPS: Arab, Berber, French
LANGUAGES: Arabic (official), Berber, French
RELIGIONS: Sunni Muslim 98%, Roman Catholic
GDP PER CAPITA (1995): US$3800

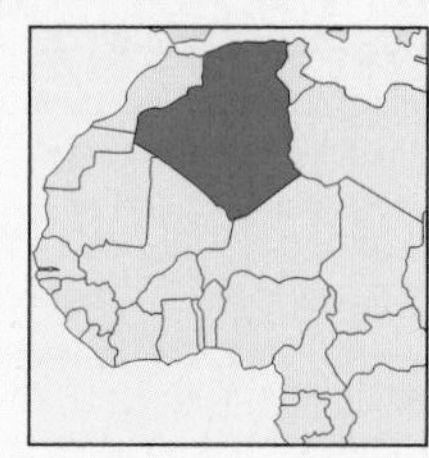

Republic in NW Africa. Algeria is the second-largest country in Africa (after Sudan). By 2000 BC Berbers had established village communities. In the 9th century BC, coastal Algeria (Numidia) formed part of Carthage's trading empire. By the end of the 2nd century BC, Rome had gained control of the coast and parts of the immediate interior. Saint Augustine of Hippo (now Annaba) was a casualty of the 5th-century invasion of the Vandals.

In the late 7th century, Arabs conquered Algeria and converted the local population to Islam. Arabic became the main language. In the early 10th century, the Fatimids rapidly built an empire from their base in NE Algeria. In the late 15th century, as part of the reconquest of S Spain, the Spanish gained control of coastal Algeria. The Spanish were ousted by the Ottomans, and Algeria's coast became a haven for pirates and slave traders. In 1830 France invaded Algeria and rapidly began the process of colonization. Abd al-Kader led Algerian resistance until 1847. The European domination of the economy exacerbated discontent among the Muslim population. During World War 2, Algiers served as the Allies' headquarters in North Africa. At the end of the War, nationalist demands intensified. In 1954 the Front de Libération Nationale (FLN) launched a nationwide revolt against French rule. By 1957 the 500,000-strong French military force had quashed the revolt but not demands for independence. Despite the opposition of the one million French colonists (*colons*) and a section of the French army (the OAS), Charles De Gaulle persisted with an accord to grant Algeria independence. Following the endorsement of De Gaulle's policy in a 1962 French referendum, the OAS launched a short-lived terrorist campaign against Muslims. The colonists rapidly left Algeria.

On 3 July 1962 Algeria gained independence. The war had claimed *c*.250,000 lives. Ahmed Ben Bella became prime minister, then president of the new republic. In 1965 Ben Bella was overthrown in a military coup led by minister of defence Colonel Houari Boumedienne, who established a revolutionary council. In 1971 he nationalized the French-owned oil and gas industries. In 1978 Boumedienne died and was succeeded by Colonel Chadli Benjedid. In 1989 anti-government demonstrations led to the legalization of opposition parties. In December 1991 the first round of elections saw a decisive victory for the opposition Islamic Salvation Front (FIS). Benjedid resigned as president. The second round was cancelled and the military assumed power. In 1992 the FIS was banned and Benjedid's successor, Muhammad Boudiaf, was assassinated. A terrorist campaign was launched by Muslim fundamentalists. In 1995 elections General Liamine Zeroual won a second term as president. The civil war has claimed *c*.100,000 civilian lives since 1992.

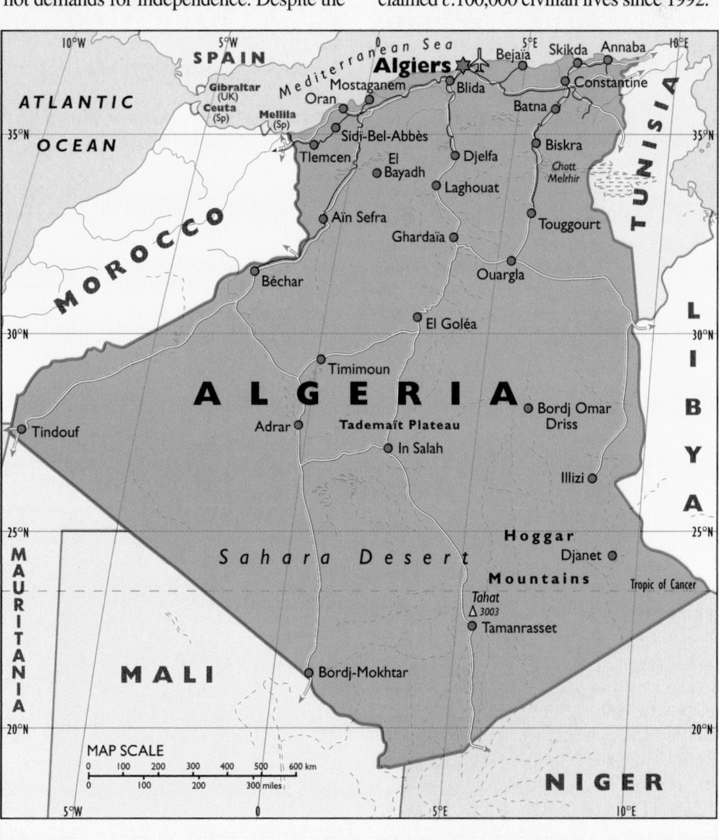

A

Altamira World heritage site of PALAEOLITHIC cave paintings and engravings (*c*.14000–9500 BC) near Santander, N Spain. The roof of the lateral chamber is covered with paintings of animals, boldly executed in vivid black, red and violet. There are also eight engraved anthropomorphic figures. *See also* LASCAUX

Altgeld, John Peter (1847–1902) US politician, Democrat governor of Illinois (1892–96). Claiming a miscarriage of justice, he pardoned three anarchists convicted of involvement in the HAYMARKET SQUARE RIOT (1886). Altgeld condemned President Grover CLEVELAND's use of force in the PULLMAN STRIKE (1894) as unconstitutional.

Althing Icelandic parliament, one of the oldest legislative assemblies in the world. It was first convened (930) at Thingvellir, near Reykjavík. The 60 members (40 in the lower house) are elected by proportional representation for four-year terms. At times, the two houses act as a united Althing, as in 1944 when they voted for independence from Denmark.

Alva, Duke of *See* ALBA, FERNANDO ÁLVAREZ DE TOLEDO, DUKE OF

Alvarado, Pedro de (1485–1541) Spanish conquistador. Alvarado accompanied Hernán CORTÉS in the conquest of Mexico (1519–21). His actions led to the death of MONTEZUMA. In 1524 Alvarado became governor and captain general of Guatemala. He formed settlements on the coast of Honduras.

Amal (Arabic *Afwaj al-Muqawama al-Lubnaniyya*, "masses of the Lebanese resistance"; the acronym means hope) Lebanese SHIITE political movement. Amal was established (1974) by Musa Sadr to press for greater Shiite political representation in Lebanon. Backed variously by Syria and the PALESTINIAN LIBERATION ORGANIZATION (PLO), its members have perpetrated a number of terrorist acts, such as the kidnappings in Lebanon during the 1980s. In 1991 the National Assembly decreed the dissolution of all militias and Amal moderated their stance.

Amalfi Resort town on the Gulf of Sorrento, Campania, S Italy. In the 9th century Amalfi was an important maritime republic, rivalling VENICE and GENOA in terms of wealth and power. In the 1130s, it was sacked by Normans and Pisans and much of the town was destroyed by a storm in 1343. Pop. (1990) 5900.

Amanullah Khan (1892–1960) King of Afghanistan (1919–29). He began educational and road-building projects, but was forced into exile by a revolt led by Bachcheh Saqow.

Amboise, Georges d' (1460–1510) French statesman and cardinal, chief minister (1498–1510) to LOUIS XII of France. Amboise negotiated an alliance between France and Spain at the Treaty of Blois (1504), and helped form (1508) the League of CAMBRAI.

Ambrose, Saint (*c*.339–97) Bishop of Milan (374–97) and Doctor of the Church. The chief critic of ARIANISM, he persuaded Emperor Gratian to outlaw (379) all heresy in the Roman Empire. In 390 Ambrose excommunicated THEODOSIUS I. His preaching and teachings were largely responsible for the conversion of Saint AUGUSTINE. Ambrose's writings, such as *On the Duties of the Clergy*, greatly influenced the thought of the Western church. His feast day is 7 December.

Amenemhet I (Ammenemes I, Shetepibre) King of ancient EGYPT (r. *c*.1991–1962 BC), founder of the XII dynasty. He ruled at the beginning of the Middle Kingdom. Amenemhet reduced the power of provincial governors by creating a strong, centralized government. He captured Lower NUBIA and defeated the incursions of Asiatic nomads. From *c*.1980 BC Amenhotep ruled jointly with his son and successor, Sesostris I.

Amenhotep III King of ancient EGYPT (r. *c*.1411–*c*.1379 BC). Amenhotep succeeded his father, Thutmose IV. The 18th dynasty was at its height during his reign. His wife, Queen Tiy, played an important role in state affairs. He was succeeded by his son, who took the name AKHENATEN.

America Western Hemisphere, consisting of the continents of NORTH AMERICA and SOUTH AMERICA, joined by the isthmus of CENTRAL AMERICA. It extends from N of the Arctic Circle to 56° S, separating the Atlantic Ocean from the Pacific. NATIVE AMERICANS settled the entire continent by 9000 BC. Norse explorer LEIF ERICSON was probably the first European to explore America, in *c*.1000, but Christopher COLUMBUS is popularly credited with the first European discovery, in 1492. The name "America" was first applied in 1507 and derives from Amerigo VESPUCCI, a Florentine navigator, who was falsely believed to be the first European to set foot on the mainland.

American Civil Liberties Union (ACLU) Organization founded (1920) to defend "the rights of man set forth in the Declaration of Independence and the Constitution". Its activities vary from sponsoring test cases in court and opposition to repressive legislation, to public protest against erosion of rights. The ACLU has defended people and organizations throughout the political spectrum, which has often made its activities controversial. It maintains a library and specialized committees, and its publications include *Civil Liberties*. The ACLU has *c*.200,000 members. *See also* CIVIL RIGHTS

American Civil War *See* CIVIL WAR, AMERICAN

American Colonization Society Group founded (1817) by US clergyman Robert Finley (1772–1817) to return free African Americans to Africa for settlement. More than 11,000 African Americans were transported to Sierra Leone and, after 1821, LIBERIA. Members of the society included James MONROE, James MADISON and John MARSHALL.

American Constitution *See* CONSTITUTION OF THE UNITED STATES

American Expeditionary Force (AEF) US ARMY contingent, under the command of Major General John PERSHING, sent to Europe (1918) to fight in WORLD WAR I. Pershing preserved its identity and integrity when Allied field commanders wanted to integrate the US troops into the existing defence structure. The AEF was a conscripted army led by professional soldiers.

American Federation of Labor and Congress of Industrial Organizations (AFL-CIO) Largest labour organization in North America. It is a federation of individual trade UNIONS from the United States, Canada, Mexico, Panama and some US dependencies. Established in 1955, it merged the American Federation of Labor (AFL) and Congress of Industrial Organizations (CIO). Although each union within the Federation is autonomous, the governing body of the AFL-CIO is an executive council made up of president, vice presidents and secretary treasurer. In recent years, the reduction in union membership (*c*.15% of US workers in 1995) has seen the AFL-CIO concentrate on organizing public sector workers. *See also* individual union leaders

American Fur Company First business monopoly in the United States, owned by John Jacob ASTOR. JAY'S TREATY (1794) permitted US fur trading in the Pacific Northwest. In 1805 Fort Astoria was established in Oregon. During the WAR OF 1812, the United States was unable to defend Astoria, and Astor was forced to sell. As the FUR TRADE declined in the 1840s, Fort Astoria reverted to US control.

American Indian Movement (AIM) Militant organization formed (1968) to promote the civil rights of NATIVE NORTH AMERICANS. In 1972 they took over the Bureau of Indian Affairs in Washington, D.C., to dramatize complaints that tribal councils were controlled by the Bureau. In 1973 members occupied the historic community of WOUNDED KNEE, South Dakota, to demand reform in tribal government and a revision of the framework in which Native Americans negotiate with the federal government.

American Indians *See* NATIVE AMERICANS

American Labor Party US political party formed in 1936, primarily to support President Franklin ROOSEVELT's NEW DEAL. Based in New York state, the Party was an influential power-broker in New York City. In 1944 the Party split over its relationship with the Soviet Union, the anti-communists forming the Liberal Party. In the 1948 presidential elections, the Party gained more than 500,000 votes for Henry WALLACE. The American Labor Party was officially dissolved in 1956.

American Legion Association of US military veterans. Founded (1919) in Paris, France, its US headquarters are in Indianapolis, Indiana. Qualifications for membership are honourable service or honourable discharge. It sponsors many social causes, notably education and sport for young people, and the care of sick and disabled veterans.

American Revolution *See* feature article, pages 14–15

Amherst, Jeffrey, Baron (1717–97) British general. During the last FRENCH AND INDIAN WAR (1754–63), he was named commander in chief of British forces (1758). His victories included Louisbourg (1758), Crown Point, TICONDEROGA (1759) and Montréal (1760). He was made a field marshal and baron after his conquest of Canada.

Amiens, Treaty of (March 1802) Peace agreement between France and her enemies (Spain, Britain and the BATAVIAN REPUBLIC) in the FRENCH REVOLUTIONARY WARS (1792–1802). France recovered most of her colonies, but evacuated the Kingdom of NAPLES. Britain withdrew from Egypt, but kept Ceylon and Trinidad. The peace lasted only until May 1803. *See also* NAPOLEONIC WARS

Amin, Idi (1925–) Ugandan dictator, president (1971–79). In 1971 he led a military coup against Milton OBOTE. Amin established a dictatorship marked by atrocities. In 1972 he expelled *c*.80,000 Asian Ugandans. When Tanzanian forces joined rebel Ugandans in a march on the capital of UGANDA, Kampala, Amin fled to Libya.

Amish Highly conservative, Protestant sect of North America, the members of which form an offshoot of the ANABAPTIST Mennonite Church. The strict Old Order Amish Mennonite Church, to which most sect members belong, was founded (1693) in Switzerland by Jakob Ammann (*c*.1645–*c*.1730). In 1720 the Amish began migrating to North America and eventually died out in Europe. In the United States and Canada they established small, closed agricultural communities. After 1850 tensions between traditionalist "old order" Amish and more liberal "new order" communities split the sect. Today, a few groups of traditionalist Amish still work the land, practise non-cooperation with the state and shun modern conveniences.

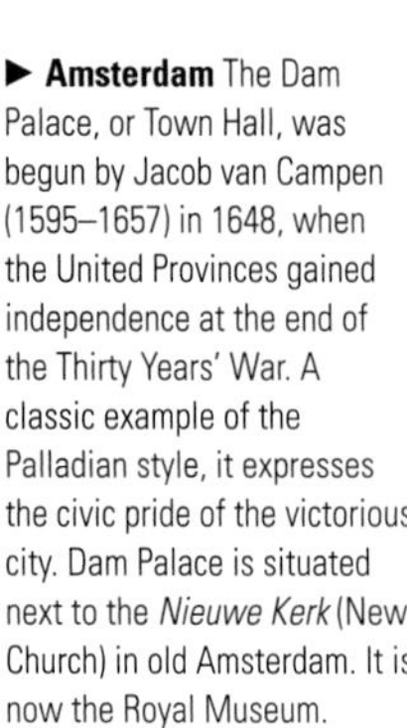

► **Amsterdam** The Dam Palace, or Town Hall, was begun by Jacob van Campen (1595–1657) in 1648, when the United Provinces gained independence at the end of the Thirty Years' War. A classic example of the Palladian style, it expresses the civic pride of the victorious city. Dam Palace is situated next to the *Nieuwe Kerk* (New Church) in old Amsterdam. It is now the Royal Museum.

Amistad case In 1839 slaves, led by Joseph Cinque, overpowered their captors on the *Amistad*, a Spanish slave ship. The ship landed in the United States and ABOLITIONISTS forced the case to the Supreme Court, where former President John Quincy ADAMS argued for the slaves, who were set free in 1841.

Amman Capital and largest city of JORDAN, 80km (50mi) ENE of Jerusalem. Known as Rabbath-Ammon, it was the chief city of the Ammonites in biblical times. A new city was built on seven hills from 1875, and it became the capital of Transjordan in 1921. From 1948 it grew rapidly, partly due to the influx of Palestinian refugees. Pop. (1994 est.) 1,300,042.

Amritsar City in PUNJAB state, NW India. It was founded (1577) by Ram Das, fourth guru of the Sikh religion. Amrtisar is the religious centre of SIKHISM and site of its holiest shrine, the Golden Temple. On 13 April 1919, thousands of Indian demonstrators gathered at Jallianwala Park, Amritsar, in peaceful protest against the ROWLATT ACT (1919). British Gurkha troops, commanded by General Dyer, opened fire on the crowd, killing 379 and wounding more than 1200. The incident, known as the **Amritsar Massacre**, hardened the resolve of "Mahatma" GANDHI and the Indian National CONGRESS. In 1984 Amritsar was the scene of another bloody confrontation, when Indian troops stormed the Golden Temple, which was being used as a stronghold by Sikh terrorists, and killed more than 400 people. Pop. (1991) 709,000.

Amsterdam Capital and largest city in the Netherlands, on the River Amstel, linked to the North Sea by the North Sea Canal. Amsterdam was chartered in *c.*1300 and joined the HANSEATIC LEAGUE in 1369. Amsterdam's growth dates from the Revolt of the Netherlands, when the port of ANTWERP was closed (1585) by the Spanish. The Dutch EAST INDIA COMPANY (1602) brought great prosperity to the city. It became a notable centre of learning and book printing during the 17th century. Its commerce and importance declined when captured by the French (1795) and blockaded by the British during the NAPOLEONIC WARS. A major European port, and one of its leading financial and cultural centres, it has an important stock exchange and diamond-cutting industry. Sights include the Rijksmuseum, the Van Gogh Museum, and the houses of Anne FRANK and Rembrandt. Pop. (1994) 724,096.

Amundsen, Roald (1872–1928) Norwegian explorer, the first person to reach the South Pole. In 1903–06 Amundsen became the first to sail through the NORTHWEST PASSAGE and determine the exact position of the magnetic North Pole. He was beaten by Robert PEARY in the race to the North Pole and turned to ANTARCTICA. On 14 December 1911, Amundsen reached the South Pole (35 days before Robert SCOTT). In 1926 Amundsen, Lincoln ELLSWORTH and Umberto Nobile made the first flight across the North Pole.

Anabaptists Radical Protestant sects in the REFORMATION who shared the belief that infant baptism is not authorized by Scripture, and that it was necessary to be baptized as an adult. The first such baptisms were conducted by the Swiss Brethren sect in Zürich (1525). The sect was the first to completely separate church from state, when they rejected Ulrich ZWINGLI's Reformed Church. Aided by social upheavals (such as the PEASANTS' WAR) and the theological arguments of Martin LUTHER and Thomas MÜNZER, Anabaptism spread rapidly to Germany and the Netherlands. It stressed the community of believers. The communal theocracy established at Münster by John of Leiden was brutally suppressed (1535). *See also* MILLENARIANISM

anarchism (Gk. "no government") Political theory that regards the abolition of the state as a prerequisite for equality and social justice. In place of government, anarchy is a social form based upon voluntary cooperation between individuals. The STOICS leader, ZENO OF CITIUM, is regarded as the father of anarchism. Millenarian movements of the Reformation, such as the ANABAPTISTS, espoused a form of anarchism. As a modern political philosophy, anarchism dates from the mid-19th century, with theorists such as P.J. PROUDHON. Anarchism was often in conflict with emerging COMMUNISM: Mikhail BAKUNIN's brand of violent, revolutionary anarchism led to his expulsion from the First INTERNATIONAL (1872). Anarchism has been a popular political force only in conjunction with SYNDICALISM. Its support of civil disobedience and sometimes political violence has led to its marginalization.

Anasazi *See* feature article

Anastasia (1901–18?) Grand Duchess of Russia, youngest daughter of the last tsar, NICHOLAS II. In July 1918, after the RUSSIAN REVOLUTION (1917), Anastasia was presumably murdered, together with other members of the royal family. Since 1920, several women have claimed to be Anastasia, the legal heir to the ROMANOV fortune held in Swiss banks. No claim has yet been proved.

Anatolia *See* ASIA MINOR

ANC *See* AFRICAN NATIONAL CONGRESS

ancien régime Term used to describe the political, legal and social system in France before the FRENCH REVOLUTION (1789). It was characterized by a rigid social order, a fiscal system weighted in favour of the rich, and an absolutist monarchy. *See also* STATES-GENERAL

Andalusia (Andalucía) Largest, most populous, and southernmost region of Spain, crossed by the River Guadalquivir, and comprising eight provinces. The capi-

ANASAZI

NATIVE NORTH AMERICAN civilization that developed in the "Four Corners" region of the SW United States (where modern-day Arizona, New Mexico and Colorado meet). The Anasazi (Navajo, "enemy ancestors") culture is often divided into six developmental periods: Basket Maker (AD 100–500); Modified Basket Maker (500–700); Developmental Pueblo (700–1050); Classic Pueblo (1050–1300); Regressive Pueblo (1300–1700); and Modern Pueblo (1700–present-day). Recent archaeological finds suggest that the culture was infiltrated by Mesoamericans. The **Basket Maker** period is named after the early Anasazi weaving of waterproof containers. The **Modified** Basket Maker phase marked the beginnings of an agricultural society. The **Developmental** period saw the construction of *kivas* (underground chambers) for council meetings and religious cermonies. The **Classic** era of Anasazi culture is characterized by the building of communal, multistoreyed homes in the canyons of SW United States, especially along the tributaries of the Rio Grande and Colorado River. The dwellings provided excellent defence from other tribes, such as the NAVAJO. The cliff-dwellers farmed the river valleys below their homes or the mesas above. The most spectacular of these dwellings are in Mesa Verde National Park, SW Colorado, and Canyon de Chelly National Monument, NE Arizona. The abandonment of these pueblos is attributed to drought and the invasion of the Navajo and APACHE.

▲ **The Anasazi** excelled in basket-making and pottery. The baskets and pots were decorated with intricate geometric designs, using vegetable or mineral pigments.

◄ **The Anasazi** of SW America built sophisticated, multistoreyed houses of stone, clay and sand. Most Anasazi villages rose three or four levels above the river valley. These communities had up to 1000 rooms. At the centre of the community was the *kiva* – a circular, underground chamber. By the Modified Basket Maker period (AD 500–700), the Anasazi had domesticated turkeys and farmed bean crops and maize.

Also known as the Revolutionary War or the American War of Independence, the American Revolution was a successful revolt against British rule by the THIRTEEN COLONIES in North America. Following British victory (1763) in the FRENCH AND INDIAN WARS, the British government under George GRENVILLE attempted to assert its authority over North America by imposing a series of new taxes. For the first time, colonials were taxed directly via the SUGAR ACT (1764) and the STAMP ACT (1765). In addition, customs officials were ordered to enforce long-standing laws regulating colonial shipping (*see* NAVIGATION ACTS). The new laws created a sense of common grievance among the Thirteen Colonies, which had previously enjoyed a large measure of self-government. The colonial outcry against the Stamp Act forced its repeal in 1766, but the die had been cast. The colonials also challenged the TOWNSHEND ACTS (1767), securing their repeal only after the BOSTON MASSACRE in 1770. The BOSTON TEA PARTY (1773) prompted the British government under Lord NORTH to pass the Coercive Acts (dubbed the INTOLERABLE ACTS by the colonials), which closed Boston harbour and imposed a form of martial law. In response, colonial leaders asserted their right to "no taxation without representation" at the First CONTINENTAL CONGRESS in Philadelphia (September 1774). The British refusal to compromise placed the colonials and the colonial power on a collision course.

OUTBREAK OF WAR

On 19 April 1775, British troops exchanged fire with colonial militia in Massachusetts, signalling the start of the Revolution (*see* LEXINGTON AND CONCORD, BATTLES OF). On 10 May 1775, Ethan ALLEN and his GREEN MOUNTAIN BOYS captured Fort TICONDEROGA. The appointment of George WASHINGTON as commander in chief of the Continental Army by the Second Continental Congress was greeted by a costly British victory in the first major conflict in the war – the Battle of BUNKER HILL (June 1775). On 4 July 1776, the Congress made the break with Britain decisive by adopting the DECLARATION OF INDEPENDENCE, drafted by Thomas JEFFERSON with the assistance of Benjamin FRANKLIN and John ADAMS.

At the start of the Revolution, the American cause seemed precarious. The rebels were deeply divided on the issue of independence and their ill-trained, poorly armed militiamen and volunteers faced the best-equipped army in the world. The British Army was supplemented by *c.*30,000 mercenaries from Hesse, Germany.

PHASES IN THE REVOLUTION

The fighting took place in three distinct phases. The **first phase** (1775–76) was mainly located in New England, but culminated in the failure (December 1775) of Benedict ARNOLD to capture QUÉBEC, thus enabling the British to retain Canada. The **second phase** (1776–79) was fought mainly in the mid-Atlantic region. The British Army, led by William HOWE, forced George Washington to retreat from New York at the Battle of LONG ISLAND (August 1775). Washington restored colonial fortunes by crossing the Delaware River to surprise and defeat the British at TRENTON (26 December 1776). On 3 January 1777, he further strengthened American morale by defeating the British at PRINCETON. Howe captured Philadelphia, however, after defeating Washington at the Battle of the BRANDYWINE (September 1777). The British launched a three-pronged attack on New York state, which ended in the first major colonial victory at SARATOGA (17 October 1777) when John BURGOYNE surrendered to Horatio GATES. This proved to be the turning point in the Revolution as it galavanized France into supporting the colonial cause, contributing vital financial aid and military support. Spain declared war against Britain in June 1779, followed by Holland in 1780.

The **final phase** took place primarily in the south and west (1778–81). The French fleet hampered British supply and reinforcement routes and French and American ships successfully combined to damage British commerce. Washington was deprived of victory in the Battle of MONMOUTH (June 1778) largely because of Charles Lee's failure to carry out his orders. The British continued to pursue the war in the south, at first with great success. In 1780 Sir Henry CLINTON, who had succeeded Howe as commander of the British forces, captured CHARLESTON, South Carolina. British General Charles CORNWALLIS routed Gates at the Battle of CAMDEN,

▲ The American Revolution was fought between soldiers of the Continental Army (left), commanded by George Washington, and the "redcoats" of the British Army (right), led first by William Howe then by Henry Clinton. The Continental Army was backed by state militias, while the British used Hessian mercenaries.

▲ The Battle of Bunker Hill (17 June 1775) was the first major engagement of the American Revolution. This painting, *The Death of General Warren at the Battle of Bunker's Hill* (1786), was the first history work completed by the "painter of the Revolution", John Trumbell (1756–1843). The British captured the hill above Boston after three assaults, in which they lost *c.*1000 men. The severity of the losses forced the British to abandon plans to fortify Dorchester Heights. In March 1776, the British were forced to evacuate Boston for Halifax, Nova Scotia, after George Washington captured Dorchester Heights. Sir William Howe regrouped British forces and attacked New York (August 1776).

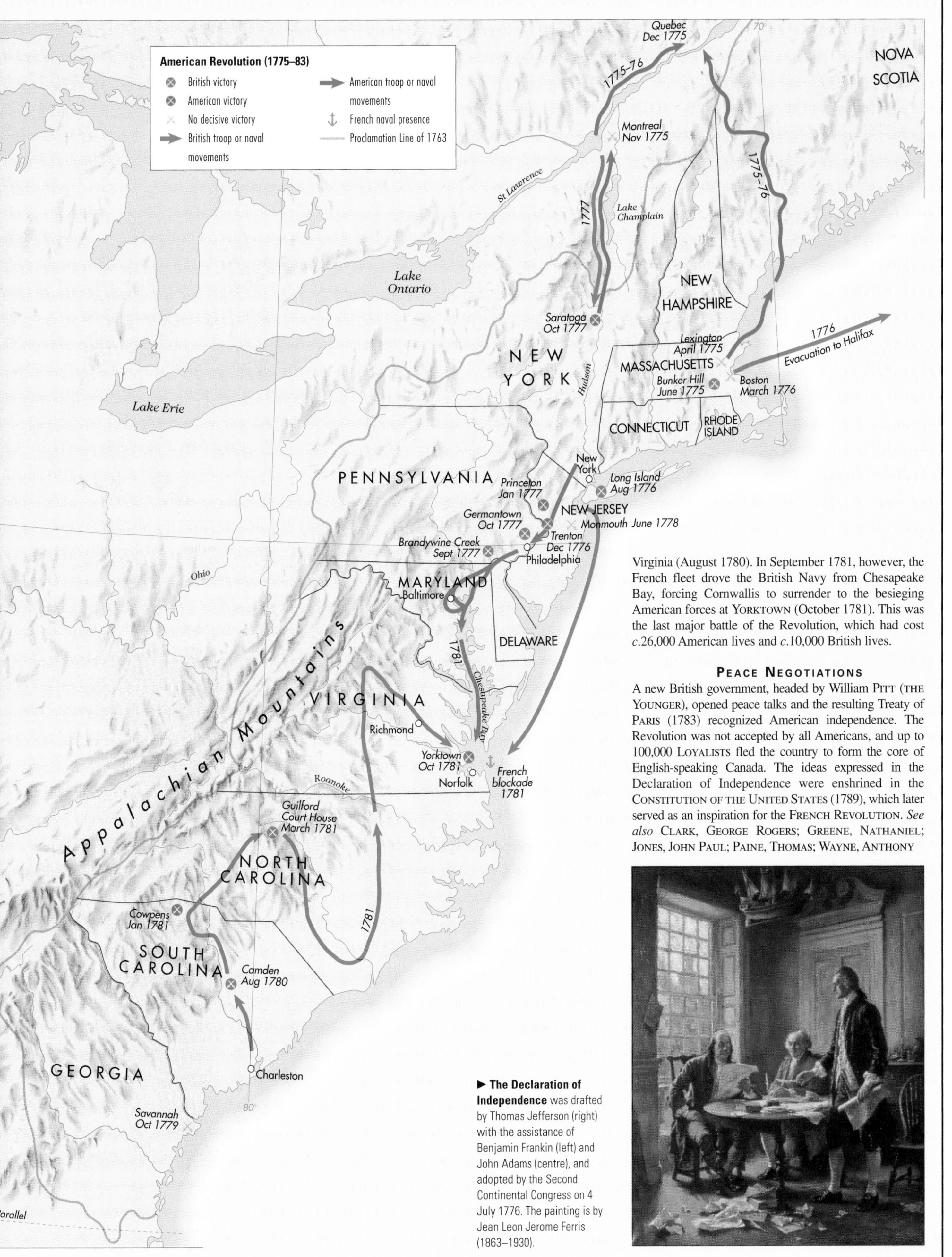

Virginia (August 1780). In September 1781, however, the French fleet drove the British Navy from Chesapeake Bay, forcing Cornwallis to surrender to the besieging American forces at YORKTOWN (October 1781). This was the last major battle of the Revolution, which had cost *c.*26,000 American lives and *c.*10,000 British lives.

PEACE NEGOTIATIONS

A new British government, headed by William PITT (THE YOUNGER), opened peace talks and the resulting Treaty of PARIS (1783) recognized American independence. The Revolution was not accepted by all Americans, and up to 100,000 LOYALISTS fled the country to form the core of English-speaking Canada. The ideas expressed in the Declaration of Independence were enshrined in the CONSTITUTION OF THE UNITED STATES (1789), which later served as an inspiration for the FRENCH REVOLUTION. *See also* CLARK, GEORGE ROGERS; GREENE, NATHANIEL; JONES, JOHN PAUL; PAINE, THOMAS; WAYNE, ANTHONY

► **The Declaration of Independence** was drafted by Thomas Jefferson (right) with the assistance of Benjamin Frankin (left) and John Adams (centre), and adopted by the Second Continental Congress on 4 July 1776. The painting is by Jean Leon Jerome Ferris (1863–1930).

A

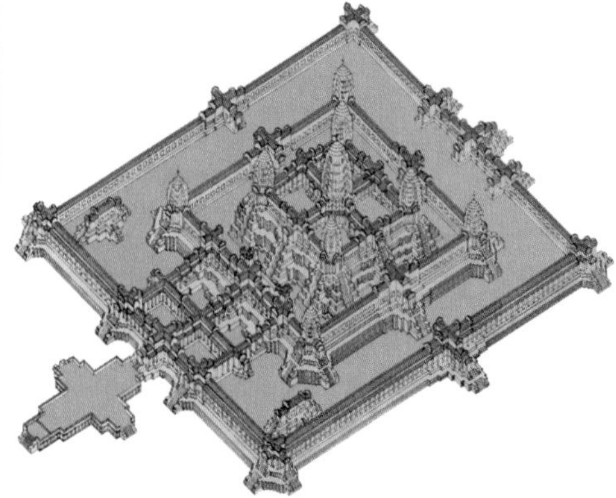

▲ **Angkor Wat** Built (*c*.1130) as a funerary temple by Suryavarman II, Angkor Wat was dedicated to the Hindu god Vishnu. Surrounded by a vast moat, the complex is probably the largest religious structure in the world. All the walls of Angkor Wat are decorated in exquisite low relief, illustrating scenes from the lives of Krishna and Vishnu.

tal is SEVILLE; other major cities include GRANADA and CÓRDOBA. With the rest of the Iberian Peninsula, it was conquered by the Muslims (Moors) in the 8th century, and it was the only part of Spain that remained under their control after the Christian reconquest of the peninsula in the 11th century. The Moors were finally driven out in the 14th century. By the end of the 15th century, Andalusia had become part of the kingdom of CASTILE. Andalusia has many fine buildings, such as the ALHAMBRA, dating from when the region was ruled by the Moors. Area: 87,268sq km (33,707sq mi). Pop. (1991) 6,940,522.

Andean Indians *See* NATIVE MIDDLE AMERICANS

Anderson, Elizabeth Garrett (1836–1917) English physician and pioneer of women's rights. She had to overcome intense prejudice against women doctors to become one of the first English women to practise medicine. Later, Anderson became England's first woman mayor. *See also* FEMINISM

Andersonville Prison Historic prison in Andersonville, SW Georgia, United States. It was used during the American CIVIL WAR by the Confederacy to confine Union prisoners. Harsh conditions led to the deaths of nearly 14,000 Union soldiers. Area: 200ha (495 acres).

Andorra Small, independent state situated high in the E Pyrenees between France and Spain. Traditionally believed to have been granted independence by Charlemagne, by the 13th century it was governed jointly by France and the Spanish bishops of Urgel. It is a rare example of a medieval principality. In 1993 a new constitution was adopted that reduced the roles of the French president and the Spanish bishop of Urgel to purely constitutional figureheads.

Andrada e Silva, José Bonifácio de (1763–1838) Brazilian statesman, architect of Brazilian independence from Portugal. In 1822 he supported the establishment of an independent monarchy under PEDRO I. Andrada became prime minister, but was forced into exile for his insistence on the adoption of a liberal constitution. In 1821 he returned to Brazil to act as tutor to Pedro II.

Andrássy, Gyula, Count (1823–90) Hungarian statesman, first premier of Hungary (1867–71). He was a leading figure in the abortive rebellion (1848) against Austria and escaped execution by remaining in exile until 1857. In 1867 Andrássy and Ferenc DEÁK were the chief negotiators of the AUSGLEICH with Austria. As premier, he suppressed the partisans of Lajos KOSSUTH and established the hegemony of the MAGYARS. Andrássy was also the architect of Austro-Hungarian neutrality during the FRANCO-PRUSSIAN WAR (1870–71). As foreign minister (1871–79) of the AUSTRO-HUNGARIAN EMPIRE, he gained the territory of Bosnia-Herzegovina at the Congress of BERLIN (1878). *See also* REVOLUTIONS OF 1848

ANDORRA
AREA: 453sq km (175sq mi)
POPULATION: 68,000
CAPITAL (POPULATION): Andorra la Velle (20,437)
GOVERNMENT: Parliamentary co-principality
ETHNIC GROUPS: Catalan, Andorran
LANGUAGES: Catalan (official), French, Castilian Spanish
RELIGIONS: Roman Catholicism 90%
GDP PER CAPITA (1994): US$11,462

André, John (1751–80) British officer hanged by the Americans for spying during the AMERICAN REVOLUTION. André secretly negotiated with Benedict ARNOLD for the surrender of West Point.

Andreotti, Giulio (1919–) Italian statesman, prime minister (1972–73, 1976–79, 1989–92). Andreotti aided Alcide DE GASPERI in building up the Christian Democrats as the leading party in post-war Italy. As prime minister, he resisted the rise of the Italian Communist Party (PCI). In 1999 Andreotti was cleared of charges of corruption and collusion with the MAFIA. *See also* ITALIAN POPULAR PARTY (PPI)

Andronicus I (Comnenus) (*c*.1110–85) Byzantine emperor (1183–85). He succeeded to the throne after murdering his nephew, Alexius II (Comnenus), and marrying the boy's 13-year-old widow, Agnes-Anna, daughter of LOUIS VII of France. Andronicus' reduction of the power of the nobility and anti-corruption drive were brutally enforced.

Andropov, Yuri Vladimirovich (1914–84) Soviet statesman, president of the Soviet Union (1983–84), general secretary of the Communist Party (1982–84). He played a major role in suppressing the HUNGARIAN UPRISING (1956). As head of the KGB (1967–82), Andropov took a hard line against political dissidence, supporting Soviet intervention in Czechoslovakia (1968) and Poland (1981). In 1973 he joined the Politburo. Andropov succeeded Leonid BREZHNEV as leader. His tenure (15 months) was the shortest in Soviet history. Perhaps his most significant decision was the promotion of Mikhail GORBACHEV. Andropov was succeeded by Konstantin CHERNENKO.

Andros, Sir Edmund (1637–1714) British colonial governor of New York (1674–81). JAMES II of England appointed him governor of the Dominion of New England (1686–89), ruling all the colonies north of New Jersey. Andros earned a reputation for high-handedness through his suppression of colonial assemblies and local charters. In 1689 he was seized by citizens of Boston and sent to England for trial. Andros returned as lieutenant governor of Virginia (1692–97).

Angevin Dynasty established in the county of ANJOU, W France, in the 9th century. The marriage of GEOFFREY OF ANJOU and MATILDA, daughter of HENRY I of England, resulted in an Angevin ascending the English throne (1154) as HENRY II. His descendants, later known as the PLANTAGENETS, retained the crown until 1485. In 1203 King JOHN of England lost Anjou to PHILIP II of France. In 1266 CHARLES I established a second Angevin dynasty in Naples and Sicily. He was ousted from Sicily by the revolt of the SICILIAN VESPERS (1282), but the dynasty continued to rule Naples until 1422.

Angkor Ancient KHMER capital and temple complex, NW Cambodia. The site contains the ruins of several stone temples erected by Khmer rulers, many of which lie within the walled enclosure of Angkor Thom, the capital built (1181–95) by JAYAVARMAN VII. **Angkor Wat**, the greatest structure in terms of its size and the quality of its carving, lies outside the main complex. In 1431 Thai invaders destroyed the Angkor complex, and it remained neglected until French travellers rediscovered it (1858). After

ANGLO-SAXONS

People of Germanic origin, comprising ANGLES, SAXONS and other tribes who began to invade England from the early 5th century, when Roman power was in decline. By 600 they were well established in most of England. They were converted to Christianity in the 7th century. Early tribal groups were led by warrior lords whose thegns (noblemen) provided military service in exchange for rewards and protection. The tribal groups eventually developed into larger kingdoms, such as NORTHUMBRIA and WESSEX. The term Anglo-Saxon was first used in the late 8th century to distinguish the Saxon settlers in England from the "Old Saxons" of N Germany. It soon became synonymous with "English". The Anglo-Saxon period of English history ended with the NORMAN CONQUEST (1066).

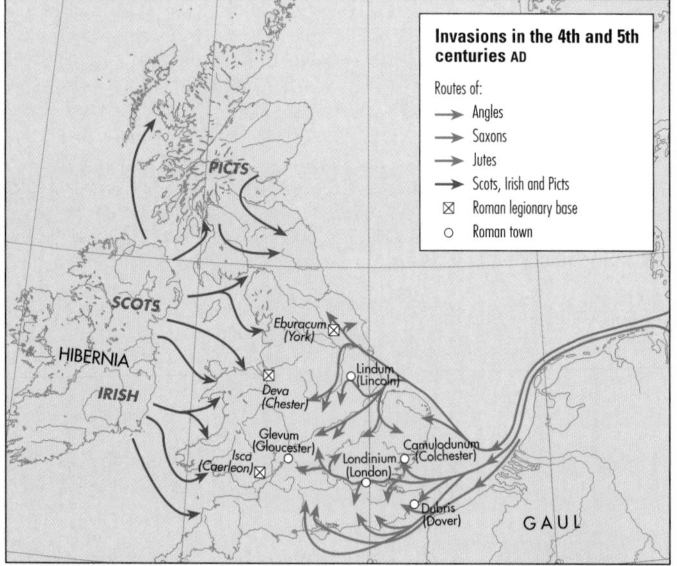

▲ **Saxon** soldiers invaded Roman Britain in the 5th century AD.

► **Early Anglo-Saxon** pots survive in large numbers in continental Europe because they were used for the burial of cremated bodies. The Saxons made pots with bossed and stamped decorations (left), while the Angles made pots with linear grooved patterns (right). In England, these two distinctive styles rapidly fused into one tribal tradition in the 5th century AD.

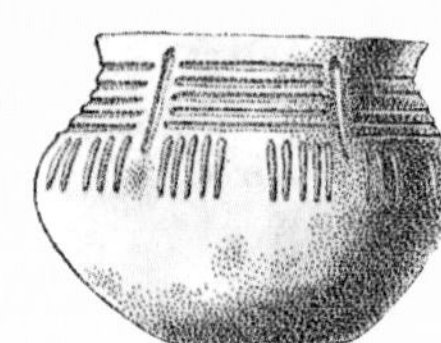

restoration, Angkor Wat suffered again when the followers of Pol Pot ravaged Cambodia in the civil war (1970–75). *See also* Suryavarman II

Angles Germanic tribe from a district of Schleswig-Holstein now called Angeln. In the 5th century, the Angles invaded England with neighbouring tribes, including Jutes and Saxons. They settled mainly in Northumbria and East Anglia. The name England (Angle-land) derives from them. *See also* Anglo-Saxons

Anglican Communion Fellowship of 37 independent, national or provincial worldwide churches, many of which are in Commonwealth nations. It originated from missionary work by the Church of England. An exception is the Episcopal Church in the United States, founded by the Scottish Episcopal Church. There is no single governing authority, but all recognize the leadership of the archbishop of Canterbury. Worship is liturgical, based on the Book of Common Prayer. Today, there are *c.*70 million Anglicans organized into *c.*30,000 parishes.

Anglo-Dutch Wars *See* Dutch Wars

Anglo-Irish Agreement (1985) (Hillsborough Agreement) Treaty signed by British Prime Minister Margaret Thatcher and Irish Taoiseach Dr Garret Fitzgerald. It gave the Republic of Ireland the right of consultation in the affairs of Northern Ireland, asserted that any future changes to the status of Northern Ireland would have to be ratified by a majority of its peoples, and set up the Anglo-Irish Intergovernmental Conference (AIIC) to promote closer cooperation. The agreement was denounced by the Ulster Unionists. *See also* Downing Street Declaration; Good Friday Agreement

Anglo-Japanese Alliance (1902) Diplomatic agreement between Britain and Japan. The alliance was formed principally to counter the increasing power of Russia. The two nations agreed to remain neutral in any war fought by either against another power in East Asia. If Japan or Britain became involved in a war against two powers, it provided for joint action. US hostility to the Alliance led to the Washington Conference (1921) and a pact between the United States, Britain, France and Japan.

Anglo-Maori Wars *See* Maori Wars

Anglo-Saxon Chronicle Monastic chronicles written in England between the 9th century and 1155. The four surviving versions of the Chronicle are the chief documentary source for Anglo-Saxon history.

Anglo-Saxons *See* feature article

Angola *See* country feature

Angora *See* Ankara

Anjou Region and former province in w France, straddling the lower Loire valley. It was ruled by Henry II of England after his marriage to Eleanor of Aquitaine. In 1480 Louis XI annexed it to the French monarchy. Known for its wine, it ceased to be a province in 1790.

Ankara Capital of Turkey, at the confluence of the Cubuk and Ankara rivers. In ancient times, known as Ancyra, it was an important commercial centre as early as the 8th century BC. It was a Roman provincial capital and flourished under Augustus. In 1402 Ankara was seized by Tamerlane. From the late 19th century, the city declined in importance until Kemal Atatürk established his provisional government in Ankara (1920). In 1923 it replaced Istanbul as the capital. Pop. (1990) 2,541,899.

Anna Comnena (*c.*1083–*c.*1148) Byzantine princess and historian, daughter of Alexius I (Comnenus). She retired to a convent after a series of failed attempts to secure the imperial title for her husband, Nicephorus Byrennius (*c.*1062–1137). Anna wrote the *Alexiad* (1148), one of the most important documents of Byzantine history.

Anna Ivanovna (1693–1740) Tsarina of Russia (1730–40), daughter of Ivan V and niece of Peter I (the Great). She was elected to the throne by the supreme privy council. Anna restored royal authority with the help of the secret police. She restricted the power of the Russian nobility to the advantage of German advisers, such as her lover Ernst Biron. Anna's expansive foreign policy saw the beginnings of Russia's Asian empire. She supported Augustus III in the War of the Polish Succession. Anna was succeeded by Ivan VI.

Annam (Chinese, "Pacified South") Central area of Vietnam. In 111 BC Tonkin and what came to be known as n Annam fell to the Chinese Han dynasty. In the 2nd century AD, s Annam fell to the Champa. The Vietnamese expelled the Chinese in 939, establishing an independent monarchy that lasted – beside a brief period of Chinese rule (1407–28) – until the 19th century. By 1471 Annam had driven out the Champa. From 1558 Annam was divided between the n Trinh dynasty (based around Tonkin) and the s Nguyen dynasty (based around Hué). In 1802, with French help, Gia Long reunified the kingdom. In 1807 the Vietnamese established a protectorate over Cambodia. The French captured Cochin China in 1858 and by 1884 had gained control of the whole of Vietnam, which became part of French Indochina (1887). During World War 2, Annam was occupied by Japan. In 1949 it was incorporated into the Associated State of Vietnam under Bao Dai.

Annan, Kofi (1938–) Ghanaian diplomat, seventh secretary general of the United Nations (1997–). He was the first black African to become secretary general. In 1993 Annan was elected undersecretary general for peacekeeping, handling the removal of UN troops from Bosnia. His diplomacy helped secure a peaceful resolution (1998) to the weapons-inspection crisis in Iraq.

Annapolis Seaport capital of Maryland, on the s bank of the Severn River on Chesapeake Bay, United States. It was founded (1649) by Puritans. The peace treaty that ended the American Revolution was signed in Annapolis. It has many fine colonial buildings. It is also the seat of the US Naval Academy (founded 1845). Pop. (1992) 34,070.

Annapolis Convention (September 1786) Conference called by the Virginia legislature to discuss interstate commerce and rival claims to western land. Of the 13 states of the US Confederation invited to meet in Annapolis, Maryland, only five sent delegates. Disappointed, the reform-minded participants (including James Madison and Alexander Hamilton) proposed another convention to meet at Philadelphia in May 1787. *See also* Constitutional Convention

Anne (1665–1714) Queen of Great Britain and Ireland (1702–14), second daughter of James II. Succeeding William III, Anne was the last Stuart sovereign and, after the Act of Union (1707), the first monarch of the United Kingdom of England and Scotland. Brought up a Protestant, she married Prince George of Denmark (1683). Despite 18 pregnancies, no child survived her. The War of the Spanish Succession (1701–14) dominated her reign and is often called Queen Anne's War. Anne was the last English monarch to exercise the royal veto over legislation (1707), but the rise of parliamentary government was inexorable. The Jacobite cause was crushed when Anne was succeeded by George I. Her reign is notable for the vibrancy that party conflict between Whigs and Tories instilled in contemporary arts and culture.

Anne Boleyn *See* Boleyn, Anne

Anne of Austria (1601–66) Daughter of Philip III of Spain, wife of Louis XIII of France and mother of Louis XIV. Her husband died in 1643, and she ruled France as regent in close alliance with Cardinal Jules Mazarin until his death in 1661.

Anne of Cleves (1515–57) Fourth wife of Henry VIII of England. Her marriage (1540) was a political alliance joining Henry with the German Protestants, but it was never consummated, being declared null after only six months. Anne received a pension and remained in England until her death. *See also* Cromwell, Thomas

Anschluss (1938) Unification of Austria and Germany. Prohibited by treaty at the end of World War 1, in order to

ANGOLA

AREA: 1,246,700sq km (481,351sq mi)
POPULATION: 10,609,000
CAPITAL (POPULATION): Luanda (1,544,000)
GOVERNMENT: Multiparty republic
ETHNIC GROUPS: Ovimbundu 37%, Mbundu 22%, Kongo 13%, Luimbe-Nganguela 5%, Nyaneka-Humbe 5%, Chokwe, Luvale, Luchazi
LANGUAGES: Portuguese (official)
RELIGIONS: Roman Catholicism 69%, Protestant 20%, traditional beliefs 10%
GDP PER CAPITA (1995): US$1310

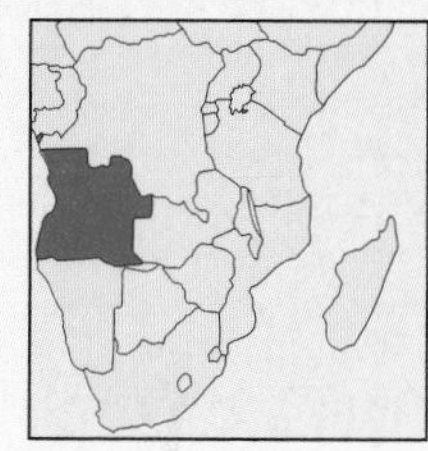

Republic in sw Africa. Bantu-speakers from the n settled in Angola *c.*2000 years ago. In the late 15th century, Portuguese navigators, seeking a route to Asia around Africa, explored the coast. In the early 1600s, the Portuguese set up supply bases. Angola became important as a source of slaves for the Portuguese colony of Brazil. After the decline of the slave trade, Portuguese settlers began to develop the land, and the Portuguese population increased dramatically in the early 20th century. In the 1950s, nationalists began to demand independence. In 1956 the Popular Movement for the Liberation of Angola (MPLA) was founded, drawing support from the Mbundu tribe and *mestizos* (people of mixed African and European descent). In 1961 the MPLA led a revolt in Luanda, but it was suppressed by Portuguese troops. Other opposition movements developed among different ethnic groups. In the n, the Kongo set up the Front for the Liberation of Angola (FNLA). In 1966 southern peoples, including many of the Ovimbundu, formed the National Union for the Total Independence of Angola (UNITA).

In 1975 Angola gained independence, but a power struggle developed among rival nationalist forces. The MPLA formed a government led by Agostinho Neto, but UNITA troops (supported by South Africa) launched a civil war. After 16 years of conflict, a peace treaty was signed (1991) and elections were held in 1992. The MPLA, which had renounced its Marxist ideology, won a landslide victory, but civil strife resumed as UNITA refused to accept the result. The Lusaka Protocol (1994) provided for the formation of a government of national unity, composed of both UNITA and MPLA leaders. In April 1997 a new government took office: Dos Santos remained president, but UNITA leader Jonas Savimbi rejected the vice presidency. UNITA retained military control of *c.*50% of Angola. Fighting continued between government and UNITA forces in rebel-held territory. In September 1997 the United Nations (UN) imposed sanctions on UNITA for failing to comply with the Lusaka Protocol.

limit the strength of Germany, *Anschluss* was nevertheless favoured by many Germans and Austrians. Unification took place through a show of force under Adolf HITLER. It was dissolved by the Allies in 1945.

Anselm, Saint (*c.*1033–1109) English theologian, Doctor of the Church, b. Italy. He was a disciple of LANFRANC at the monastery of Bec, Normandy, N France. In 1093 Anselm succeeded Lanfranc as archbishop of Canterbury. Anselm's disputes over INVESTITURE with both WILLIAM II and HENRY I of England led to his exile (1097–1100, 1103–06). An early scholastic philosopher, he believed in the rational character of Christian belief and proposed an ontological argument for the existence of God. His feast day is 21 April. *See also* SCHOLASTICISM

Anson, George, Baron (1697–1762) British admiral. Between 1740 and 1744 he circumnavigated the world. Anson returned with *c.*£500,000 worth of Spanish treasure. During the War of the AUSTRIAN SUCCESSION (1740–48), he captured six French ships off Cape Finnisterre (1747). Anson and William PITT (THE ELDER)'s reorganization of the navy was a vital factor behind the British victory in the SEVEN YEARS' WAR (1756–63).

Antakya (formerly Antioch) City on the River Orontes, S Turkey; capital of Hatay province. Founded (*c.*300 BC) by SELEUCUS I, it earned the title "queen of the east" and, as the terminus for trade routes from Asia, was an important trade centre. It was taken by POMPEY (64 BC). The modern city occupies only a small part of the ancient Roman site. Pop. (1990) 118,433. *See also* BOHEMOND I

Antarctica Fifth-largest continent (larger than Europe or Australasia), accounting for *c.*10% of the Earth's total land area. Covered by an ice sheet with an average thickness of *c.*1800m (5900ft), it contains *c.*90% of the Earth's ice and more than 70% of its freshwater. Almost entirely within the Antarctic Circle, it is of great strategic and scientific interest. Seven nations lay claim to sectors of it. Antarctic islands were first sighted in the 18th century and Captain James COOK was the first to cross the Antarctic Circle (1772–75). In 1820 Nathaniel Palmer reached the Antarctic Peninsula. Between 1838 and 1840 Charles WILKES discovered enough of the coast to prove that a continent existed, and the English explorer James Clark Ross made coastal maps. In the early 19th century, humans were attracted by the commercial value of seal fur. In the 1890s Antarctica became the centre of the whaling industry and the focus of many scientific studies. Towards the end of the 19th century, exploration reached inland and developed into a race for the South Pole. On 14 December 1911, Roald AMUNDSEN reached the Pole, a month before Robert Falcon SCOTT. The aeroplane brought a new era of exploration, and Richard BYRD became the best-known of the airborne polar explorers. The Antarctic Treaty (1959), which pledged international scientific cooperation, was renewed and extended in 1991, banning commercial exploitation of the continent.

Anthony, Susan Brownell (1820–1906) US reformer and woman suffragist. She organized the first woman's temperance association and, with Elizabeth Cady STANTON, co-founded the National Woman Suffrage Association (1869). It later became (1890) the National American Woman Suffrage Association, and Anthony acted as president (1892–1900). *See also* SUFFRAGETTE MOVEMENT

ANTONY, MARK

Mark Antony manipulated public opinion against Julius Caesar's assassins, Brutus and Cassius, to gain power in Rome. Antony's growing influence was attacked by Cicero in 14 *Philippics* orations. Antony's affair with Cleopatra led to war with Octavius. According to legend, Antony committed suicide after receiving a false report of Cleopatra's death.

ANTONY IN SHAKESPEARE

"Friends, Romans, Countrymen, lend me your ears;
I come to bury Caesar, not to praise him.
The evil that men do lives after them,
The good is oft interred with their bones"
Julius Caesar, Act 3, Scene 3

"I am dying, Egypt, dying:
Give me some wine, and let me speak a little."
Antony and Cleopatra, Act 4 Scene 15

Anti-Comintern Pact (25 November 1936) Agreement between Germany and Japan that established a united opposition to COMMUNISM. The pact was also signed by Italy (1937), and Hungary, Spain and the Japanese puppet-state of MANCHUKUO (1939). The inclusion of the latter gave limited international recognition to Japanese claims in MANCHURIA. *See also* COMINTERN

Anti-Corn Law League Organization formed (1839) in Manchester, England, to agitate for the removal of import duties on grain. It was led by the Radical members of Parliament, Richard COBDEN and John BRIGHT. By holding mass meetings, distributing pamphlets and contesting elections, it helped bring about the repeal (1846) of the CORN LAWS.

Antietam, Battle of (17 September 1862) Most bloody battle of the American CIVIL WAR, fought around Sharpsburg, Maryland. General George MCCLELLAN's Army of the Potomac made a series of assaults on the Confederates of General Robert LEE. Casualties were very heavy. McClellan's losses (*c.*12,000) were slightly greater, but Lee was forced to retreat to Virginia. The failure of Lee's invasion of the North gave President Abraham LINCOLN the confidence to issue a preliminary EMANCIPATION PROCLAMATION (22 September 1862).

► **Antwerp** The *Stadhuis* (Town Hall) in Market Square, Antwerp, was designed by Loys du Foys and Nicolo Scarini and built (1561–65) by Cornelis Floris (1514–75). It is the most important architectural work of the Northern Renaissance. The *Stadhuis* successfully fuses an immense Gothic gable with the features of a Florentine palace. The rusticated arcade at its base was used for trade stalls. Between the windows of the upper two storeys are Doric and Ionic columns.

Anti-Federalist Party US political party, organized (1792) to oppose the proposed CONSTITUTION on the grounds that it gave too much power to central government. Anti-Federalist leaders included Henry LEE and Patrick HENRY of Virginia, and George CLINTON of New York. Their support came mostly from agricultural sections.

Antigonus I (the One-eyed) (382–301 BC) General of ALEXANDER III (THE GREAT). In 333 BC Antigonus became governor of Phrygia and, in the struggles over the regency, he defeated challengers to gain control of Mesopotamia, Syria and ASIA MINOR. At the Battle of Salamis (306 BC), he defeated his former ally, PTOLEMY I. Antigonus was killed in the Battle of Ipsus.

Antigua and Barbuda Constitutional monarchy in the Leeward Islands group, West Indies. Antigua and Barbuda consists of three islands – Antigua, Barbuda and Redondo. In 1493 Christopher Columbus landed on Antigua, which he named after the Church of Santa Maria de la Antigua in Seville, Spain. In 1632 the first English settlers arrived, and they used African slave labour to develop large plantations of tobacco and sugarcane. In 1678 Barbuda was colonized by the English. Barbuda was managed by the Codrington family until the late 19th century. In 1834 the SLAVE TRADE in the West Indies was abolished. From 1871–1956, Antigua and Barbuda was administered as part of the British colony of the Leeward Islands. It formed part of the West Indies Federation (1958–62). In 1967 Antigua and Barbuda gained self-government. In 1981 it achieved full independence and Vere Bird became prime minister. In 1994 he was succeeded by his son, Lester Bird. *See* WEST INDIES map

Anti-Masonic Party US political party, formed (1826) after the disappearance of William Morgan, who had revealed the Freemasons' secrets. The Anti-Masons were opposed to secret societies and supported freedom of the press. In 1831, in Baltimore, Maryland, they held the first national nominating convention and issued the first written platform of any US party. After 1836, the Party declined and was eventually absorbed by the WHIG PARTY.

Antioch *See* ANTAKYA

Antiochus III (*c.*242–187 BC) King of Syria (223–187 BC), son of SELEUCUS II. After his defeat at Rafa (217 BC) by PTOLEMY IV, Antiochus invaded Egypt (212–202 BC), seizing land from Ptolemy V with the help of PHILIP V of Macedon. He recaptured Palestine, ASIA MINOR and the Thracian Cheronese, thus rebuilding the SELEUCID empire. The Romans overwhelmed Antiochus at Thermopylae (191 BC) and Magnesia (190 BC). His empire shrank as he was forced to concede all possessions west of the Taurus. He was succeeded by Seleucus IV.

Antipater (*c.*398–319 BC) Macedonian general and aide of PHILIP II of Macedon. Between 347 and 336 BC, he led the peace negotiations with ATHENS. Antipater acted as governor of Macedon during ALEXANDER III (THE GREAT)'s wars of conquest. He was disliked for favouring tyranny and oligarchy, and his death precipitated the break-up of authority in the empire.

antipope Name given to rivals of legitimately elected popes, generally "appointed" by unauthorized religious factions. The first was HIPPOLYTUS (AD 217–35), a Trinitarian heretic and rival of Calixtus I. The most famous were the AVIGNON POPES, who rivalled those of ROME during the GREAT SCHISM (1378–1417). *See also* PAPACY

Anti-Rent War (1839–47) Uprising in New York state, United States. In 1839 the heirs of Stephen Van Rensselaer, owner of *c.*80,000ha (450,000 acres), tried to collect US$400,000 in back rent. Angry tenants resisted the sheriff's attempts to evict them. Resistance spread and anti-rent societies were formed. The societies were instrumental in the election of John Young as governor of New York. Young secured an amendment to the state constitution that indirectly led to the dissolution of large estates.

Anti-Saloon League Most powerful of all PROHIBITION groups in the United States. It was founded (1893) to campaign against the corner saloon which, members felt, was impairing the efficiency of the working class. It spurred considerable state legislation outlawing alcohol.

ANTIGUA & BARBUDA
AREA: 440sq km (170sq mi)
POPULATION: 66,000
CAPITAL (POPULATION): St John's (22,342)
GOVERNMENT: Constitutional monarchy
ETHNIC GROUPS: African
LANGUAGES: English
RELIGIONS: Christianity (mainly Anglican)
GDP PER CAPITA (1994): US$5666

anti-Semitism Discrimination against or persecution of JEWS. Although anti-Semitism predates Christianity, the most organized and persistent persecution of Jews has been by European Christians. The destruction of Jerusalem (AD 70) led to the DIASPORA, and Jews settled throughout Europe and the Roman Empire. In the 4th century Christianity became the official religion of the Empire, and many Jews were forced to convert. In the late Middle Ages, religious pretexts formed the basis of social and economic discrimination. Legislation prevented Jews from owning land, and they were restricted to occupations forbidden by the Christian church, such as usury (money-lending). The INQUISITION was an organized form of persecution supported by the papacy. The Enlightenment period saw the extension of rights to European Jews. However, the growth of nationalism and the racist ideas of social Darwinism in the 19th century led to the explicit persecution of Jews as a race rather than as followers of JUDAISM. ZIONISM was born as a reaction to this persecution. In the 1880s, POGROMS in Russia and Poland led to the emigration of millions of Jews to other parts of Europe, the United States and Palestine. The DREYFUS AFFAIR (1894) was the most public example of French anti-Semitism. FASCISM encouraged these racist ideas, which found their most virulent expression in NATIONAL SOCIALISM. Anti-Semitism was a central part of the racist ideology of Nazi Germany – about six million Jews died in the HOLOCAUST (1933–45). After World War 2, anti-Semitism persisted, especially in the Soviet Union under Joseph STALIN. The growth of right-wing nationalism has seen the re-emergence of anti-Semitism in Western Europe.

Anti-Trust Acts *See* CLAYTON ANTI-TRUST ACT; SHERMAN ANTI-TRUST ACT

Antonescu, Ion (1882–1946) Romanian general and fascist dictator. In 1938 he was imprisoned by King CAROL II for leading an unsuccessful fascist coup. In September 1940, in the face of German aggression, Antonescu was appointed premier by Carol II. Carol was forced to abdicate in favour of his son, MICHAEL, and Antonescu assumed dictatorial powers. Romania joined the Axis Powers and participated in the disastrous invasion of the Soviet Union. At home, Antonescu unleashed POGROMS against Romanian Jews. The Red Army invasion of Romania led to his arrest. He was executed for war crimes.

Antonine Wall Defensive fortification built (*c*.AD 142) between the firths of Forth and Clyde, along the narrowest part (59km-/37mi-wide) of central Scotland. The wall was constructed by ANTONINUS PIUS to mark the N end of the Roman province of Britain. *See also* HADRIAN'S WALL

Antoninus Pius (AD 86–161) Roman emperor (138–61), adopted son of HADRIAN. In AD 120, he was made consul and later sent as proconsul to Asia. His peaceful reign saw the promotion of art and science, the construction of public works and fine buildings, legal reform, and new provisions for orphans. Antoninus' constant companion was his wife's nephew, MARCUS AURELIUS, who eventually became emperor himself.

Antony, Mark (82–30 BC) (Marcus Antonius) Roman general and statesman. He fought with distinction in Julius CAESAR's campaign (54–50 BC) in Gaul. In 49 BC Antony became tribune. Civil war broke out between POMPEY and Caesar, and after the decisive Battle of PHARSALUS (48 BC), Antony was made consul. After Caesar's assassination (44 BC), he inspired the mob to drive the conspirators, BRUTUS and CASSIUS, from Rome. Octavian (later AUGUSTUS) emerged as Antony's main rival. Octavian and Brutus joined forces and Antony retreated to Transalpine Gaul. He sued for peace. Antony, Octavian and Lepidus formed the so-called Second Triumvirate, which divided up the Roman territories: Antony received Asia. He and CLEOPATRA, queen of Egypt, became lovers. In 40 BC Antony married Octavian's sister, Octavia, but continued to live with Cleopatra in Alexandria and became isolated from Rome. In 32 BC, the Senate deprived Antony of his posts. He was defeated at the Battle of ACTIUM (31 BC). Antony and Cleopatra committed suicide.

Antwerp (Flemish *Antwerpen*, Fr. *Anvers*) City-port on the River Scheldt; capital of Antwerp province and Belgium's second-largest city. It rose to prominence in the 15th century and became a centre for English mercantile interests. Antwerp was the site of Europe's first stock exchange (1460). Although heavily bombed during World War 2, it retains fine 15th-century architecture. Pop. (1993 est.) 462,880.

Anuradhapura City on the River Aruvi, N central Sri Lanka. Founded in 437 BC, Anuradhapura was the capital of a Sinhalese kingdom until the 11th century AD when it was abandoned in the face of invading Hindu Tamils. In the 3rd century BC, the Sinhalese king, Devanampiya Tissa, was converted to BUDDHISM here by Ashoka's son, Mahinda, and the city remains a place of pilgrimage for Buddhists. A sapling taken from the Bodhi tree (under which BUDDHA is said to have attained enlightenment) in Bodh Gaya, N India, and planted in Anuradhapura is reputedly the oldest living tree in the world. The city has extensive ruins of Buddhist monuments. Pop. (1981) 36,000.

ANZAC (acronym for **A**ustralian and **N**ew **Z**ealand **A**rmy **C**orps) Volunteer force of 30,000 men that spearheaded the disastrous GALLIPOLI CAMPAIGN in World War 1. Troops landed at Gallipoli, W Turkey, on 25 April 1915. Anzac Day (25 April) is a public holiday in Australia and New Zealand. About 8500 Anzac troops were killed during World War 1.

ANZUS (**A**ustralia-**N**ew **Z**ealand-**U**nited **S**tates Treaty Organization) Military alliance organized (1951) by the United States. ANZUS was set up in response to waning British power, the KOREAN WAR, and alarm at increasing Soviet influence in the Pacific. The treaty stated that an attack on any one of the three countries would be considered as an attack on them all.

Apache Athabascan-speaking tribe of NATIVE NORTH AMERICANS. Divided culturally into Eastern Apache (including Mescalero and Kiowa) and Western Apache (including Coyotero and Tonto), they migrated from the NW with the NAVAJO in *c*.AD 1000 but separated to form a distinct tribal group. The Apache lacked a central, unified political structure, instead they were organized into autonomous bands. The bands maintained a subsistence culture, based on hunter-gathering and nomadic raiding. The Apache are known primarily for their fierce resistance to white settlement in North America. They successfully resisted the advance of Spanish colonization, despite acquiring horses from the Spanish. In the early 17th century, the Eastern Apache were forced southwards by the COMANCHE. The 19th-century APACHE WARS were among the bloodiest confrontations between Native North Americans and the US military. Today, *c*.11,000 Apache live on reservations in Arizona, New Mexico and Oklahoma. *See also* COCHISE; GERONIMO

Apache Wars Series of battles in Arizona, New Mexico, Texas and Oklahoma between APACHES and white settlers. One Apache chief, COCHISE, made peace in 1872, but GERONIMO fought on until 1886. Atrocities occurred on both sides.

apartheid *See* feature article

Apocrypha Certain books included in the BIBLE as an appendix to the OLD TESTAMENT in the Septuagint and in St Jerome's Vulgate translation but not forming part of the Hebrew canon. Nine books are accepted as canonical by the Roman Catholic Church. They are: Tobit, Judith, Wisdom, Ecclesiasticus, Baruch (including the Letter to Jeremiah), 1 and 2 Maccabees, and parts of Esther and

APARTHEID

Policy of racial segregation practised by the government of SOUTH AFRICA from 1948 to 1994. Racial inequality and restricted rights for non-whites were institutionalized when the AFRIKANER-dominated NATIONAL PARTY (NP) came to power in 1948. Officially a framework for "separate development" of races, in practice apartheid confirmed white-minority rule. It was based on segregation in all aspects of life, including residence, land ownership and education. Non-whites, *c*.80% of the population, were also given separate political structures, quasi-autonomous homelands or bantustans. The system was underpinned by extensive repression and measures, such as pass laws, that severely restricted the movements of non-whites. Increasingly isolated internationally and beset by economic difficulties and domestic unrest, the government pledged to dismantle the system in 1990. The transition to nonracial democracy was completed with the elections in April 1994. *See also* AFRICAN NATIONAL CONGRESS (ANC); MANDELA, NELSON; SHARPEVILLE; SOWETO

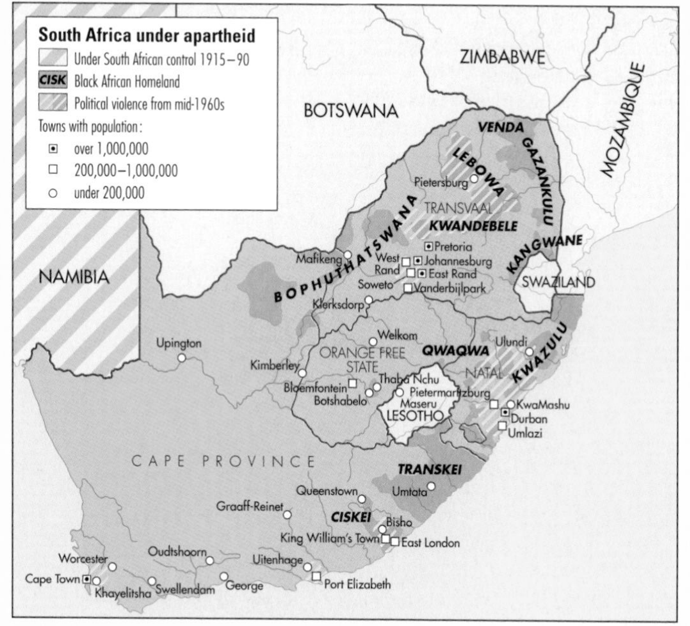

◀ **apartheid** Under the apartheid regime in South Africa, many black Africans were forced to live in bantustans or black "homelands". The majority black population violently protested against the racist legislation. These protests, combined with international sanctions, forced F.W. de Klerk to dismantle apartheid in 1990. In KwaZulu-Natal, there were violent clashes between Inkatha and ANC supporters during the build-up to South Africa's first free elections in 1994.

A

Daniel. Other books are found in Eastern Orthodox Bibles and in the appendix to the Roman Catholic Old Testament.

Apollo program US SPACE EXPLORATION project to land men on the Moon. It was initiated (May 1961) by President John KENNEDY in response to the Soviet cosmonaut Yuri GAGARIN becoming the first person to orbit the Earth. The ensuing "Space Race" was won by the United States when Neil ARMSTRONG set foot on the Moon (20 July 1969). The program terminated with the successful **Apollo-Soyuz** link-up in space during July 1975. It had placed more than 30 astronauts in space and 12 on the Moon.

Apostles' Creed Statement of Christian faith. The last section affirms the tradition of the "holy Catholic Church; the communion of saints; the forgiveness of sins; the resurrection of the body; and the life everlasting". The text evolved gradually, and its present form was fixed by the early 7th century. It is used widely in private and public worship in all the major churches in the West. *See also* ATHANASIAN CREEED; NICENE CREED

appeasement Policy in which one government grants unilateral concessions to another to forestall a political, economic, or military threat. The MUNICH AGREEMENT (1938) is considered a classic example of appeasement.

Appian Way (Lat. *Via Appia*) First road leading southward from Rome to Capua (*c*.210-km/130-mi long), constructed (*c*.312 BC) by the censor Appius Claudius Caecus. It was later extended and formed the first stage of routes to Greece and the East; portions of it remain today.

Appleseed, Johnny (1774–1845) US folk hero, b. John Chapman. As a youth, he planted apple orchards throughout the midwestern United States. In 1840 he settled in a cabin near Mansfield, Ohio, but continued to travel hundreds of miles to scatter apple seeds. Stories of his kindliness and his understanding of animals spread until he was a legend in his own lifetime.

Appomattox Town in w Virginia, United States; seat of Appomattox county. It is near Appomattox Court House National Historical Park, site of General Robert LEE's surrender of his Confederate troops to Union forces under General Ulysses GRANT (9 April 1865), effectively ending the American CIVIL WAR (1861–65).

APRA (acronym for ***Alianza Popular Revolucionaria Americana***) Peruvian political party, founded (1924) by Victor Raúl HAYA DE LA TORRE. From 1931 to 1945 APRA was an outlawed organization and fought pitched battles with the military. It stood for emancipation of indigenous peoples, agrarian reform and nationalization of industry. In 1945 APRA joined the coalition government of José Luis Bustamente. In 1948, after a failed revolt by dissident *Apristas* in Callao, APRA was again banned. In 1962 Haya de la Torre stood for president in inconclusive elections. In 1968 the military seized power. In 1980 democracy was restored. APRA leader Alan García served as president (1985–90).

Apulia *See* PÚGLIA

Aqaba, Gulf of Northeast arm of the Red Sea between the Sinai Peninsula and Saudi Arabia. Aqaba, at the head of the Gulf, was an important city of medieval PALESTINE. In 1917 it was captured from the Turks by T.E. LAWRENCE and finally ceded to Jordan in 1925. The gulf has played an important role in ARAB-ISRAELI WARS. It was blockaded by the Arabs from 1949 to 1956 and again in the SIX-DAY WAR (1967). It acted as a vital supply line for Iraq in the IRAN-IRAQ WAR (1980–88).

▲ **Arafat** Yasir Arafat became chairman of the Palestine Liberation Organization (PLO) in 1969. In 1994 he shared the Nobel Prize for Peace with Yitzhak Rabin. In 1996 Arafat was elected president of the Palestinian Authority.

ARAB-ISRAELI WARS

Conflicts between ISRAEL and the Arab states (1948–49, 1956, 1967, 1973–74). After Israeli independence (14 May 1948), troops from Egypt, Iraq, Lebanon, Syria and Transjordan (now Jordan) invaded the country. Initial Arab gains were halted and armistices arranged at Rhodes (January–July 1949). United Nations' (UN) security forces upheld the truce until October 1956, when Israeli forces under Moshe DAYAN attacked the SINAI PENINSULA with support from France and Britain, alarmed at Egypt's nationalization of the SUEZ CANAL. International opinion forced a cease-fire in November. In 1967 guerrilla raids led to Israeli mobilization, and in the ensuing SIX-DAY WAR, Israel captured Sinai, the GOLAN HEIGHTS on the Syrian border and the Old City of JERUSALEM. On 6 October 1973 (the Jewish holiday of Yom Kippur), Egypt and Syria invaded Israel. Israel pushed back their advance after severe losses. The so-called October or YOM KIPPUR WAR lasted 18 days. Subsequent disengagement agreements were supervised by the UN. In 1978 Israel signed the CAMP DAVID ACCORDS with Egypt, but relations with other Arab states remained hostile. In 1982 Israeli forces invaded LEBANON in an effort to destroy bases of the PALESTINE LIBERATION ORGANIZATION (PLO). They were withdrawn (1984) after widespread international criticism. After 1988 the PLO renounced terrorism and gained concessions, including limited autonomy in parts of the occupied territories. *See also* ISRAELI-PALESTINIAN ACCORD; PALESTINE

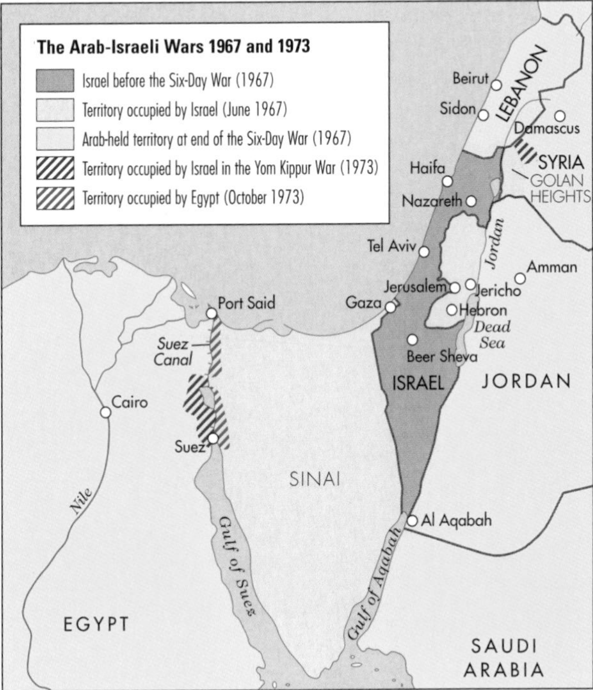

► **Arab-Israeli Wars** The United Nations' (UN) proposed division of Palestine was abandoned after the state of Israel was proclaimed on 14 May 1948. A coalition of Arab states (Egypt, Iraq, Jordan, Lebanon and Syria) immediately invaded, but was forced back by the Haganah. In the Six-Day War (1967), Israel gained the Gaza Strip, Golan Heights, Sinai peninsula, West Bank, Gaza Strip and the Old City of Jerusalem. Israel recovered from a surprise attack at the start of the Yom Kippur War (1973) to gain additional territory along the Suez Canal and in s Syria. In 1979 Sinai was returned to Egypt.

Aquinas, Saint Thomas (1225–74) Italian theologian and philosopher, Doctor of the Church. Saint Thomas is the greatest figure of SCHOLASTICISM. His *Summa Theologiae* (Theological Digest, 1267–73) was declared (1879) to be the basis of official Catholic philosophy by Pope LEO XIII. Aquinas argued that faith and reason are two complementary realms; both are gifts of God, but reason is autonomous. Thomist metaphysics, a moderate form of realism, was the dominant world view until the mid-17th century. Thomas was canonized in 1323. His feast day is 7 March.

Aquino, (Maria) Cory (Corazon) (1933–) Philippine stateswoman, president (1986–92), b. Maria Corazon. In 1954 she married Benigno Aquino (1932–83), an outspoken opponent of Ferdinand MARCOS' regime. While Benigno was in prison (1973–81), Cory campaigned tirelessly for his release. Benigno was assassinated by agents of Marcos. In the 1986 presidential elections, Cory claimed victory over Marcos and accused the government of vote-rigging. A bloodless "people's revolution" forced Marcos into exile. Aquino's government was beset by economic obstacles, and she survived a coup attempt only with US help (1989). In 1992 she declined to run for re-election, but supported the campaign of her eventual successor, Fidel Ramos.

Aquitaine Historic region in sw France, named after a Celtic tribe, the Aquitani. Named Aquitania by the Romans, it became (56 BC) an integral part of their empire and included all the land between the Pyrenees and the River Garonne. Aquitaine later formed part of the CAROLINGIAN empire. Independent for a time during the early Middle Ages, it became part of France and then, following the marriage (1152) of ELEANOR OF AQUITAINE to HENRY II, part of England. In the early 13th century, all but the southern part (Gascony) was returned to France, the rest being restored (1453) at the end of the HUNDRED YEARS' WAR. Area: 41,308sq km (15,950sq mi). Pop. (1990) 2,795,800.

Arab Peoples of many nationalities, found predominantly in the Middle East and North Africa, who share a common heritage in the religion of ISLAM and their language (Arabic). The patriarchal family is the basic social unit in a strongly traditional culture that has been little affected by external influences. Wealth from oil has brought rapid modernization in some Arab countries, but a great deal of economic inequality exists. *See also* SEMITE

Arabia Peninsular region of sw Asia bordered by the Persian (Arabian) Gulf (E), the Arabian Sea (S), the Syrian

Desert (N), and the Red Sea (W). The original homeland of the Arabs, it is the world's largest peninsula. The area was unified by the Muslims in the 7th century and dominated by Ottoman Turks after 1517. Hussein ibn Ali led a successful revolt against the Turks and founded (1916) an independent state in the Hejaz region, but was subsequently defeated by Ibn Saud, who founded (1925) Saudi Arabia. After World War 2 independent Arab states emerged, many of them exploiting the peninsula's vast reserves of oil. Area: *c*.2.6 million sq km (1 million sq mi).

Arab-Israeli Wars *See* feature article

Arab League Organization formed (1945) to give a collective political voice to the Arab nations. Its members include Syria, Lebanon, Iraq, Jordan, Sudan, Algeria, Kuwait, Saudi Arabia, Libya, Morocco, Tunisia, Yemen, Qatar and the United Arab Emirates (UAE). It has often been divided, notably by the Camp David Accords between Egypt and Israel (1978) and the Gulf War (1991), and has been politically less effective than its founders hoped.

Arafat, Yasir (1929–) Palestinian statesman, first president of Palestine (1996–), leader of the Palestine Liberation Organization (PLO). From a base in Lebanon, Arafat led Fatah – the military wing of the PLO. He sought the abolition of Israel and the creation of a secular Palestinian state. The Intifada in Israel's occupied territories (Gaza and the West Bank) prompted secret talks between Israel and the PLO. Arafat and Yitzhak Rabin signed the Israeli-Palestinian Accord (1993), in which Arafat renounced terrorism and recognized the state of Israel. In return, Rabin recognized the PLO as the legitimate representative of Palestinians and agreed to a withdrawal of Israeli troops from parts of the occupied territories. In 1994 the Palestinian National Authority, headed by Arafat, assumed limited self-rule in the territories relinquished by the Israeli army. In 1996 elections Arafat became president.

Aragón Region in NE Spain. In 1479 the kingdom of Aragón was united with Castile and León and became part of Spain, but retained its own government, currency and military forces until the early 18th century. It is now an autonomous region, comprising the provinces of Huesca, Teruel and Zaragoza. Area: 47,670sq km (18,500sq mi). Pop. (1991) 1,188,817.

Aranda, Pedro Pablo Abarca de Bolea, Conde de (1718–98) Spanish statesman. He was president (1766–73) of the council of Castile. Aranda was dismissed after Spain lost the Falkland Islands. In 1792 he regained office, but was removed after a disagreement with Manuel de Godoy on the war against France.

Arapaho Algonquian-speaking tribe of Native North Americans. Their original home was in the Red River valley; they moved across the Missouri River and split into two groups. After the Treaty of Medicine Lodge (1847), one group joined the Southern Cheyennes in Oklahoma, while the northern band went onto Wind River Reservation with the Shoshone. Today, they number *c*.3000.

Araucanian Native South American peoples of Chile and Argentina. A loose confederation of Araucanian-speaking sub-tribes (including the Picunche, Mapuche and Huilliche) offered strong resistance to the Spanish invasion (1536) under Diego de Almagro. In 1598 they drove the Spaniards back to the River Bío-Bío, and retained parts of Chile to the present day. Their descendants prefer the name *Mapuche* (land people). The population has declined from *c*.1 million in the 16th century to *c*.300,000 today.

Arawak Group of Native South American peoples of the Greater Antilles, Bahamas, Trinidad and the Gran Chaco. Some 40 Arawak tribes remain in Brazil today.

archaeology Scientific study of former human life and activities through material remains such as artifacts and buildings. An archaeologist excavates and retrieves remains from the ground or sea-bed, recording and interpreting the circumstances in which objects were found, such as their level in the soil and association with other objects. This information can then be used to build a picture of the culture that produced the objects.

Arctic Vast region of icy seas and cold lands around the North Pole, often defined as extending from the Pole to the Arctic Circle. Despite the severity of the climate and the restricted food resources, many peoples live in the Arctic. The most scattered are the *c*.60,000 Eskimos spread across polar North America (where they are known as Inuit), Greenland and NE Siberia. In the European part of Russia there are the numerous Zyryans and in Lapland, the Lapps. Most of these peoples follow ancient, traditional patterns of life, but the discovery of great mineral wealth, especially in Alaska and Russia, has brought huge change to their homelands. The Arctic was first explored by Vikings in the 9th century. The search for the Northwest Passage gave impetus to further explorations in the 16th and 17th centuries, though a route was not found until the 1850s. The North Pole was allegedly first reached (1909) by Robert Peary, and the first crossing of the Arctic Ocean under the polar ice-cap was completed in 1959 by the nuclear-powered submarine USS *Nautilus*.

Ardashir I (d.AD 240) King of Persia (*c*.224–41). He overthrew the last Parthian king, Artabanus V, and reunited Persia (Iran). Ardashir founded the Sasanian empire, establishing its capital at Ctesiphon. He established Zoroastrianism as the state religion. Ardashir strengthened Persia by going to war against the Roman Emperor Alexander Severus. He was succeeded by Shapur I.

Ardennes (Forest of Ardennes) Sparsely populated, wooded plateau in SE Belgium, N Luxembourg and the Ardennes department of N France. It was the scene of heavy fighting in both world wars, notably in the Battle of the Bulge (1944) during World War 2.

Arendt, Hannah (1906–75) US philosopher and political scientist, b. Germany. In *The Origins of Totalitarianism* (1951), she examined the common roots of National Socialism and Stalinism in the anti-Semitism, imperialism and nationalism of the 19th-century. *The Human Condition* (1958) incorporated strands of phenomenology into political theory. In 1959 Arendt became the first woman to be appointed to a full professorship at Princeton University. Other works include *Eichmann in Jerusalem* (1963). *See also* totalitarianism

Argentina *See* country feature

Argos Town in NE Peloponnesus, Greece. It is referred to in Homer's *Iliad* as the Kingdom of Diomed, and occupies the site of Greece's oldest city-state, dating from the middle Bronze Age (*c*.2000–1500 BC). It is now a small market town. Pop. 19,000.

Argyll, Archibald Campbell, 8th Earl of (1607–61) Scottish statesman. In 1641 he was made a marquess by Charles I of England, but remained committed to the

ARGENTINA

AREA: 2,766,890sq km (1,068,296sq mi)
POPULATION: 33,101,000
CAPITAL (POPULATION): Buenos Aires (11,662,050)
GOVERNMENT: Federal republic
ETHNIC GROUPS: European 85%, Mestizo, Native American
LANGUAGES: Spanish (official)
RELIGIONS: Christianity (Roman Catholic 92%)
GDP PER CAPITA (1995): US$8310

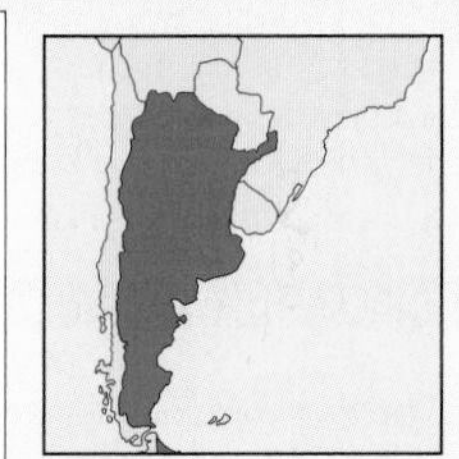

Republic in S South America. Argentina (Sp. "land of silver") is the second-largest country in South America (after Brazil) and the eighth-largest in the world. There were *c*.300,000 Native South Americans living in Argentina when Spanish explorer Juan Díaz de Solís discovered Río de la Plata in 1516. In 1536 Pedro de Mendoza founded Buenos Aires. Argentina formed part of the Viceroyalty of Peru until 1776, when Buenos Aires became capital of the new Viceroyalty of the Río de la Plata. On 25 May 1810 a revolutionary cabildo, led by General Manuel Belgrano, formed an autonomous government nominally on behalf of Ferdinand VII of Spain.

In 1816 the country achieved full independence as the United Provinces of the Río de la Plata. The union soon fragmented with the secession of Paraguay (1814), Bolivia (1825) and Uruguay (1828). The dictatorship (1835–52) of Juan Manuel de Rosas centralized power in Buenos Aires until the adoption of a federal constitution in 1853. In the late 19th century Argentina attracted millions of immigrants. During the 1930s the Argentine government was dominated by the military. For much of World War 2 Argentina was a pro-Axis "neutral" power. In 1945 Colonel Juan Perón came to power with the help of the trade unions and Argentina declared war on Germany. Aided by his wife, Eva Perón, Perón established a popular dictatorship. In 1955 he was overthrown in a military coup. Political instability dominated the 1960s, with the military seeking to suppress the Perónistas. In 1973 an ailing Perón returned from exile to head a civilian government. He was succeeded (1974) by his third wife, Isabel Martinez Perón, who ruled until a further military coup in 1976. Military rule was characterized by the so-called "Dirty War". Torture, "disappearances" and wrongful arrest were commonplace. In 1982 Argentina invaded the Falkland Islands, precipitating the Falklands War. Britain quickly recaptured the Islands and the junta collapsed. Civilian government was restored in 1993 elections. In 1989 the Perónist Carlos Menem was elected president. The Perónists were defeated by Fernando De la Rúa in 1999 elections.

A

National Covenant and PRESBYTERIANISM. In 1643 Argyll represented the COVENANTERS in negotiations with the English Parliament. In the English CIVIL WAR (1642–48), his Covenanter army was repeatedly defeated (1644–45) by the Earl of MONTROSE. Argyll initially supported Oliver CROMWELL, principally to secure Presbyterianism in England, but the execution of Charles I changed his mind. In 1651 Argyll crowned CHARLES II in Scotland. In 1652 he opposed the disastrous Scottish invasion of England and returned to the COMMONWEALTH side. Argyll's execution for treason after the RESTORATION made him a martyr for later Scottish Presbyterians.

Arianism Theological school based on the teachings of Arius (*c.*AD 250–336), considered heretical by orthodox Christianity. Arius taught that Christ was a created being, and that the Son, though divine, was neither equal nor co-eternal with the Father. Arianism was condemned by the First Council of NICAEA (325).

Aristides (the Just) (d. *c.*468 BC) Athenian statesman and general. He led the Athenian forces at the Battle of MARATHON (490 BC) and, after a period of exile, fought at SALAMIS (480), and led the Athenians at PLATAEA (479).

Aristotle (384–322 BC) Greek philosopher, founder of the science of logic, and one of the greatest figures in Western philosophy, b. Macedonia. Aristotle studied (367–347 BC) under PLATO at the ACADEMY in Athens. After Plato's death, he tutored the young ALEXANDER III (THE GREAT) before founding (335 BC) the Lyceum. In direct opposition to Plato's idealism, Aristotle's metaphysics is based on the principle that all knowledge proceeds directly from observation of the particular. For Aristotle form was inherent in matter. His ethical philosophy stressed the exercise of rationality in political and intellectual life. Aristotle's writings cover nearly every branch of human knowledge, from statecraft to astronomy. His principal works are the *Organon* (six treatises on logic and syllogism), *Politics* (the conduct of the state), *Poetics* (analysis of poetry and tragedy), and *Rhetoric*.

ARIZONA
Statehood :
14 February 1912
Nickname :
The Grand Canyon State
State motto :
God enriches

Arizona State in the SW United States, bordering on Mexico. The capital is Phoenix; other cities include Tucson and Mesa. After the end of the MEXICAN WAR (1848), Mexico ceded most of the present state to the United States, and it became the 48th state of the Union in 1912. It has the largest NATIVE NORTH AMERICAN population of any US state (203,527 in 1990), with reservations comprising 28% of the total land area of 295,025sq km (113,909sq mi). Pop. (1992) 3,832,368.

Arkansas State in S-central United States, bounded on the E by the Mississippi River. The capital (and only large city) is Little Rock. Arkansas was acquired by the LOUISIANA PURCHASE (1803) and was admitted to the Union as the 25th state in 1836. It was one of the 11 Confederate states during the American CIVIL WAR. Noted for its resistance to the civil rights movement in the 1960s, Arkansas was home to President Bill CLINTON. Area: 137,539sq km (53,104sq mi). Pop. (1992) 2,394,253.

ARKANSAS
Statehood :
15 June 1836
Nickname :
The Land of Opportunity
State motto :
The people rule

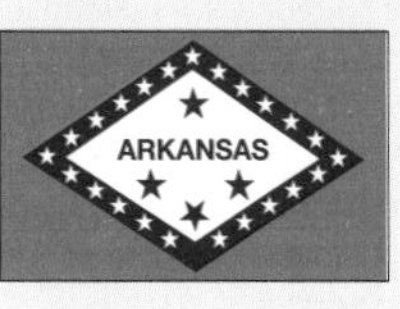

Arkwright, Sir Richard (1732–92) English inventor and industrialist. Arkwright introduced powered machinery to the textile industry with his water-driven frame for spinning; he started work on the machine in 1764 and patented his invention in 1769. *See also* INDUSTRIAL REVOLUTION

Arles Market town at the head of the Camargue delta on the River Rhône, S France. The Romans called their capital of S Gaul Arelate and linked it by canal to the Mediterranean Sea in 103 BC. The counts of SAVOY and kings of France gradually acquired the Kingdom of Arles during the 14th century. Van Gogh spent his last and most productive years (1888–90) in Arles. Pop. (1990) 52,590.

Arlington US county in N Virginia, across the Potomac River from Washington, D.C. Since 1943 it has been the location of the PENTAGON as well as Arlington National Cemetery (1864). The 200-ha (500-acre) Cemetery, built on the former estate of Robert LEE, contains the Tomb of

ARMADA, SPANISH (1588)

Fleet launched against Protestant England by PHILIP II of Catholic Spain. ELIZABETH I's support for the rebels in the Spanish Netherlands and attacks on Spanish possessions in the Caribbean convinced Philip of the need to conquer England. Preparations were delayed by Sir Francis DRAKE's raid on Cádiz in 1587. In May 1588, the 130 ships of the Armada set sail from Lisbon under the command of the Duque de MEDINA-SIDONIA. The plan was to use the fleet as an escort for an invasion force of 30,000 troops assembled at Flanders under the command of the Duke of Parma. The first engagement with the English fleet, led by Charles HOWARD, off Plymouth, S England, proved indecisive. The English attacked the Armada at anchor off Calais, scattering the fleet. A further English victory off Gravelines proved decisive, forcing the Spanish northwards and preventing the rendezvous with Parma. The Armada was ripped apart by fierce storms, scuttling half the fleet and killing *c.*15,000 soldiers. The Armada was the first major naval gun battle in military history and proved a serious blow to Spanish prestige.

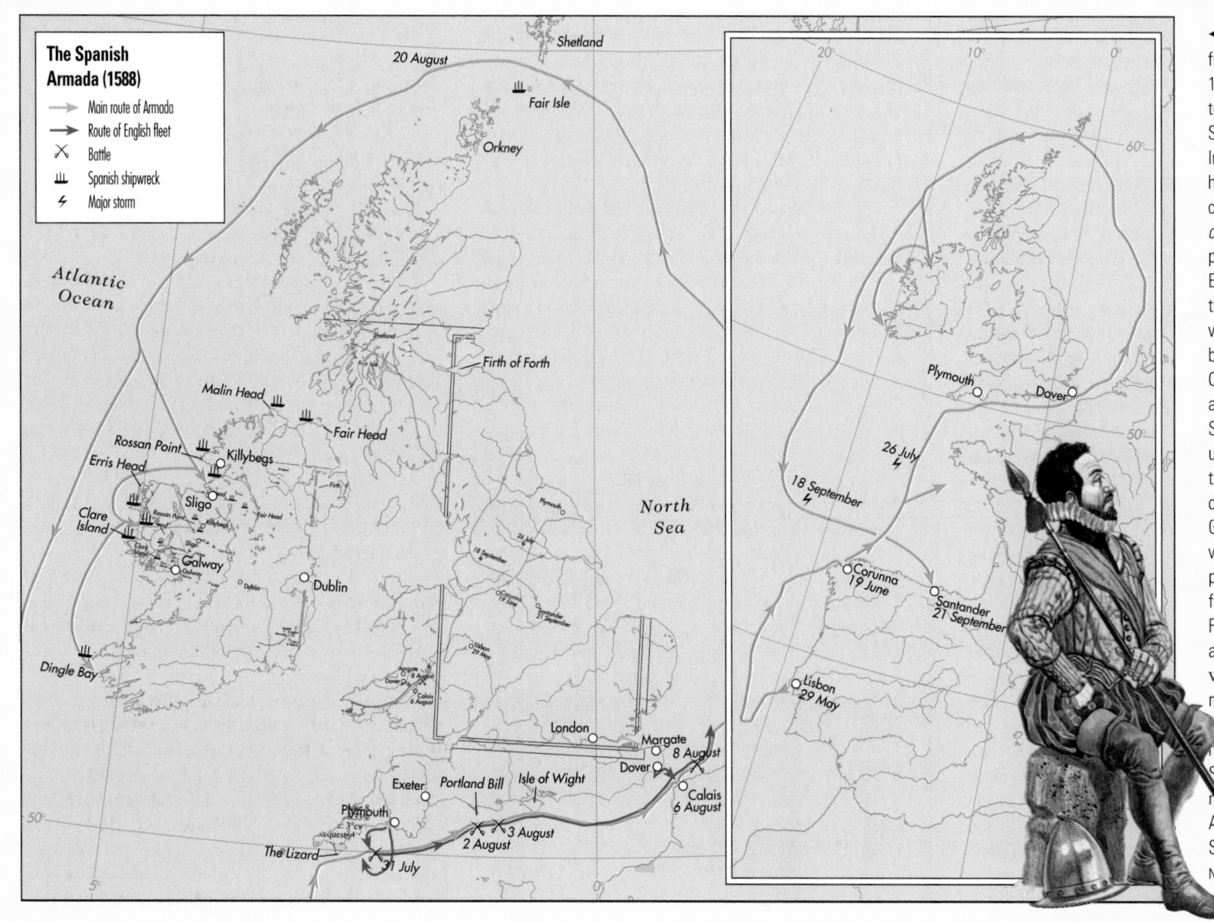

◀ **The Armada** set sail from Lisbon on 29 May 1588, but storms forced it to harbour in the N Spanish port of Corunna. In July 1588, the Armada headed for Flanders to convey an army of *c.*17,000 men. Its direct passage through the English Channel led to three minor skirmishes with the English fleet, before it anchored off Calais. The English attacked the exposed Spanish position, breaking up the fleet. On 8 August the English battered the disordered Armada off Gravelines.The Spanish were forced northwards, pursued by the English fleet as far as the Firth of Forth. The return journey around Scotland and the W coast of Ireland saw many ships wrecked due to bad weather and poor navigation. On 21 September the 60 remaining ships of the Armada limped into Santander, N Spain.

the Unknowns, a memorial amphitheatre, and the graves of many servicemen and prominent Americans. Originally part of the District of Columbia, it was made a county of Virginia in 1847. Pop. (1990) 170,936.

Armada, Spanish *See* feature article

Armenia *See* country feature

Armenian Church (Gregorian Church) Monophysite Christian church, founded in ARMENIA (*c.*AD 300) by Saint Gregory the Illuminator. In the 4th century Armenia became the first state to adopt Christianity as the national religion. The Armenian Chuch's endorsement of MONOPHYSITISM at the Council of CHALCEDON (451) led to its isolation from orthodox Christianity. It is headed by the Catholicates of Echmiadzin (Armenia) and Sis (Cilicia) and the Patriarchates of Jerusalem and Istanbul. The Armenian Church has *c.*2 million members, mainly in Armenia and the United States.

Arminius (*c.*18 BC–*c.*AD 19) German tribal leader, chief of the Cherusci. In AD 9 he destroyed a Roman army, commanded by Varus, advancing in the Teutoburg Forest. It was the last Roman attempt to conquer lands E of the Rhine.

Arminius, Jacobus (1560–1609) Dutch theologian whose system of beliefs, especially concerning salvation, became widespread and was later known as Arminianism. Arminius rejected the notion of PREDESTINATION developed by John CALVIN, in favour of a more liberal concept of conditional election and universal redemption. He believed that God elects to everlasting life those who are prepared to respond in faith to the offer of divine salvation. Debate over the acceptability of **Arminianism** in the Church of England contributed to the English CIVIL WAR (1642–48). In 1795 Arminianism finally achieved official recognition in The Netherlands. It was a major influence on METHODISM.

arms control *See* DISARMAMENT; STRATEGIC ARMS LIMITATION TALKS (SALT)

arms race Rivalry between states or blocs to achieve supremacy in military strength. The first modern instance was the race between Germany and Britain to build up their navies before WORLD WAR 1. The term refers principally, however, to the race in NUCLEAR WEAPONS during the COLD WAR between the United States and the Soviet Union. Examples of arms races at regional level are those of Israel and the Arab states in the Middle East, which started in the 1950s, and of Iran and Iraq in the 1980s.

Armstrong, John (1758–1843) American army officer, and statesman, secretary of state (1813–14). In the AMERICAN REVOLUTION (1775–83), he wrote the "Newburgh Letters" (1783) that appealed to Congress for payment of salary arrears to Continental officers. In the WAR OF 1812, Armstrong was blamed for the British capture of the city of Washington and the disastrous invasion of Canada.

Armstrong, Neil Alden (1930–) US astronaut. He was chosen as a NASA astronaut in 1962. In 1966 Armstrong was the command pilot for the Gemini 8 orbital flight. On 20 July 1969, he became the first man to walk on the Moon, remarking that it was "one small step for man, one giant leap for mankind".

army Organized group of soldiers trained to fight on land, usually rigidly hierarchical in structure. The first evidence of an army comes from SUMERIA in the third millennium BC. The use of cavalry was a HITTITE development, and the army of ASSYRIA added archers and developed siege machines. In the Middle Ages, armies used improved armour and weapons. The short-term feudal levy by which these armies were raised proved inflexible, and this led to the use of mercenaries. Heavy cavalry was replaced by a combination of infantry and archery. The end of the HUNDRED YEARS' WAR (1337–1453) saw the inception of royal standing armies and an end to the chaos caused by mercenary armies. Muskets and bayonets replaced the combinations of longbow and pike, and artillery was much improved. In the FRENCH REVOLUTIONARY WARS (1792–1802), a citizen army was raised by conscription and contained various specialist groups. Other European armies followed suit, and the age of the mass national army began. The invention of the machine gun brought about the deadlock of the trench warfare of WORLD WAR 1, which was broken by the tank. WORLD WAR 2 saw highly mechanized and mobile armies whose logistics of supply and support demanded an integration of the land, sea and air forces. Since World War 2, NUCLEAR WEAPONS have been deployed both tactically and strategically, and again the nature of weaponry has determined an army's structure.

Army, British Ground service of the United Kingdom's armed forces. Since 1949 the British Army has formed part of NORTH ATLANTIC TREATY ORGANIZATION (NATO) forces and maintained overseas garrisons in such areas as the Falklands, Cyprus and Gibraltar. The end of the COLD WAR and financial pressures have seen major cutbacks in conventional forces. In 1995 Regular Army personnel numbered *c.*116,000, including *c.*6000 women and *c.*10,000 personnel overseas. In addition to the Regular Army, there is a reserve force of *c.*230,000, more than 80,000 of whom are in the Territorial Army (TA) and the remainder in the Regular Army Reserve. *See also* BRITISH EXPEDITIONARY FORCE (BEF)

Army, US Ground service of the United States' armed forces. In 1995 active army personnel numbered *c.*525,000, 32% stationed overseas. The president is commander in chief of the armed forces. The US Army has active divisions and helps to maintain National Guard and reserve divisions; major overseas commands are the Seventh Army in Europe and the Eighth Army in Korea. The Continental Army existed from 1775, but the first regular standing army was authorized by Congress in 1785. The US Army took part in all major wars between the WAR OF 1812 and the VIETNAM WAR (1954–75). Conscription was sometimes employed and was used in peacetime after World War 2. In 1973 Congress established an all-volunteer army. In 1980 it resumed registration for conscription of 18-year-old men, and women were, for the first time, among the graduates at West Point. *See also* AMERICAN EXPEDITIONARY FORCE (AEF)

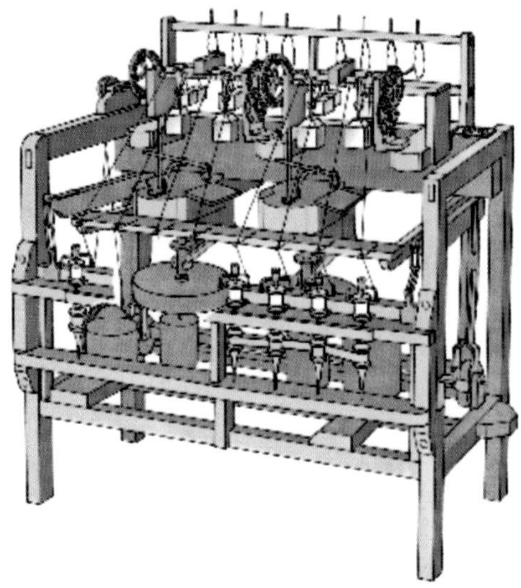

▲ **Arkwright** The spinning frame shown here was invented by Richard Arkwright in 1769. Driven by water, it was the first powered machine in the textile industry. It enabled the production of the first 100% cotton fabric.

ARMENIA

AREA: 29,800sq km (11,506sq mi)
POPULATION: 3,667,000
CAPITAL (POPULATION): Yerevan (1,254,000)
GOVERNMENT: Multiparty republic
ETHNIC GROUPS: Armenian 93%, Azerbaijani 3%, Russian, Kurd
LANGUAGES: Armenian (official)
RELIGIONS: Christianity (mainly Armenian Apostolic)
GDP PER CAPITA (1995): US$2260

Republic in the S Caucasus. The Armenians established themselves in the area in the 6th century BC, shortly before it became part of the Persian ACHAEMENID empire. In 330 BC ALEXANDER III (THE GREAT) expelled the Persians. In 69 BC, Armenia was incorporated into the Roman Empire. In AD 303 Armenia became the first country to adopt Christianity as its state religion.

From 886 to 1046 Armenia was an independent kingdom. The MONGOLS were the greatest power in the region from the 13th century to the 15th century. By the 16th century Armenia was controlled by the OTTOMAN EMPIRE. Despite religious discrimination, the Armenians generally prospered under Turkish rule. In 1828 Russia acquired Persian Armenia, and (with promises of religious toleration) many Armenians moved into the Russian-controlled area. In Turkish Armenia, nationalist movements were encouraged by British promises of protection. The Turkish response was uncompromising, and it is estimated that 200,000 Armenians were killed in 1896 alone. In the Russian sector, a process of Russification was enforced. During World War 1, Armenia was the battleground for the Turkish and Russian armies. Armenians were accused of aiding the Russians, and Turkish atrocities intensified. More than 600,000 Armenians were killed by Turkish troops, and 1.75 million were deported to Syria and Palestine.

In 1918 Russian Armenia became the Armenian Autonomous Republic; the W part remained part of TURKEY, and the NW part of IRAN. In 1922 Armenia, AZERBAIJAN, and GEORGIA were federated to form the Soviet Republic of TRANSCAUCASIA (one of the four original republics in the Soviet Union). In 1936 Armenia became a separate republic. In 1984 and 1988 earthquakes destroyed many cities and killed more than 80,000 people. In 1988 war broke out between Armenia and Azerbaijan over NAGORNO-KARABAKH (an Armenian enclave in Azerbaijan).

In 1990 Armenian voted to break from the Soviet Union, and in 1991 joined the newly established COMMONWEALTH OF INDEPENDENT STATES (CIS). In 1992 Armenia invaded Azerbaijan and occupied Nagorno-Karabakh. In 1994 a fragile cease-fire left Armenia in control of *c.*20% of Azerbaijan. In 1998 Robert Kocharyan, a former leader of Nagorno-Karabakh, was elected president of Armenia. In 1999 Prime Minister Vazgen Sarkisyan was shot dead in parliament.

Arnhem City in E central Netherlands. It was chartered in 1233 and has been an important trading centre since medieval times. During World War 2, British and Polish airborne troops made a heroic attempt to capture the bridges over the River Rhine, but were overwhelmed by superior German forces (September 1944). Pop. (1994 est.) 133,670.

Arnold, Benedict (1741–1801) American colonial soldier. During the American Revolution (1775–83), he was wounded at the Battle of Saratoga (1777) and commanded Philadelphia (1778). In 1780 Arnold became commander of West Point, a fort he planned to betray to the British for money. After the plot was discovered, Arnold fled to the British. In modern US usage, his name has become synonymous with treachery.

Arnulf (850–99) King of the East Franks (887–99); last Carolingian emperor (896–99). Arnulf defeated his uncle Charles III (the Fat) and was proclaimed king. He successfully resisted the Norse invasion (891). At the pope's request, Arnulf invaded Italy (894), captured Rome (895), and was crowned emperor (896).

Aroostook War (1838–39) Dispute over the Maine-New Brunswick boundary. The Aroostook valley was claimed by both Canada and the United States, and a conflict arose over Canadian timber operations. In 1839 a contingent of 50 Maine militiamen also moved into the valley. War loomed, but US General Winfield Scott negotiated a truce. It was settled by the Webster-Ashburton Treaty (1842).

Árpád (d.907) Semi-legendary Magyar chief, national hero of Hungary, founder of the Árpád dynasty. In 895 the invading Magyars, led by Árpád, seized control of Pannonia. They conquered Moravia, raided the Italian peninsula, and also attacked Germany. During constant wars with the Bulgarians and Walachians, Árpád greatly extended his territory. By 896 the Magyars controlled what is now called Hungary.

Arras, Union of (1579) Pact signed by the Walloon provinces of the Low Countries, which separated them from the N Protestant provinces. In response, the N provinces formed the Union of Utrecht. Although the signatories of the Union of Arras signed a peace treaty with the Spaniards, they were soon reconquered by them. The lands covered by the Union of Arras formed the basis of present-day Belgium and Luxembourg; the N United Provinces formed the basis of The Netherlands. *See also* Austrian Succession, Wars of; Spanish Succession, Wars of

Arsacid Dynasty of Parthian kings that ruled Iran (*c*.250 BC–AD 224). Originally from the region E of the Caspian Sea, they did not dominate the Iranian plateau until *c*.150 BC. The Arsacids became wealthy through control of the trade routes between Asia and the Roman Empire, but were unable to resist conquest by the Sasanians. *See also* Parthia

Artaxerxes II (d. *c*.358 BC) King of Persia (405–358 BC), son and successor of Darius II. His reign was troubled by an assassination attempt by his brother, Cyrus the Younger, and by revolts by his satraps (provincial governors). In 386 BC, however, he implemented the King's Peace, which ended the war between the Greek allies and Sparta. This placed the Asiatic mainland and Cyprus under his rule, kept Lemnos, Imbros and Scyros as Athenian dependencies, and made the other Greek states autonomous.

Artevelde, Jacob van (*c*.1290–1345) Flemish statesman who played a major role at the beginning of the Hundred Years' War (1337–1453). A prosperous merchant of Ghent, he became (1338) one of the town's joint rulers and, under his influence, the Flemish towns sided with England at the outbreak of war with France (1340) in order to protect their commercial interests. It was at Ghent that Edward III of England was proclaimed king of France. Van Artevelde's close ties with England made him many enemies and he was murdered during a riot.

Arthur Legendary British king featured in the *Matter of Britain*, a medieval cycle of legends surrounding King Arthur and the knights of the Round Table. Two medieval chroniclers, Gildas and Nennius, tell of Arthur's battles against the invading West Saxons and his final defeat of them at Mount Badon (possibly Badbury Hill, Dorset) in the early 6th century. There are trace references to an historical Arthur in the scant records of post-Roman and early medieval Britain. Geoffrey of Monmouth wove some of this detail into his heavily fictionalized *Historia Regum Britanniae*, written for a Norman-Celtic readership in the 1130s. In 1191, the monks of Glastonbury unearthed a double tomb which they believed to be that of Arthur and his queen Guinevere.

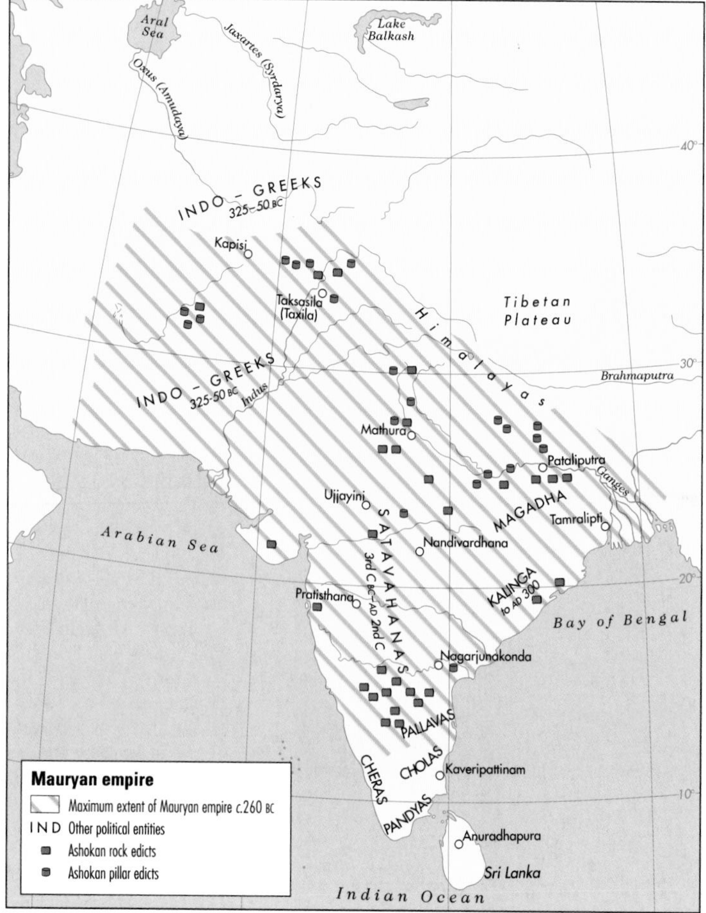

► **Ashoka** After Alexander the Great's death (323 BC), Ashoka's grandfather, Chandragupta Maurya (r.321–297 BC), built an empire that encompassed most of the Indian subcontinent except the Tamil south. He also established a standing army and civil service, modelled on the Persian Achaemenid dynasty. Ashoka (r.272–231 BC) extended the empire, conquering Kalinga (now Orissa) in 261 BC. After this violent struggle, Ashoka renounced warfare and embarked on "conquest by dharma". Pillar and rock edicts throughout the Mauryan empire are engraved with Ashoka's pronouncements on dharma. (The lion capital of the pillar at Sarnath, NE India, is the national emblem of modern India.) Ashoka was responsible for the transmission of Buddhism in India and also dispatched Buddhist missionaries throughout Asia. His reign was one of religious tolerance and humane treatment of his subjects. After Ashoka's death, Mauryan power disintegrated, until half a century later the Ganges valley was all that remained of one of history's greatest empires.

Arthur, Chester Alan (1830–86) Twenty-first president of the United States (1881–85). In 1880 he was nominated by the Republican Party as vice president in the (justified) hope that he could deliver New York. Arthur became president after the assassination of James Garfield and tried to reform the spoils system, in which incoming presidents replaced government staff with their own appointees. A Civil Service Commission with a merit system was created, but his modest reforms were often frustrated by Congress. Gentlemanly but uninspiring, and suffering from incurable illness, he was not renominated (1884). Arthur was succeeded by Grover Cleveland.

Articles of Confederation (1781) First Federal constitution of the United States, drafted by the Continental Congress in 1777. Distrust of central authority and state rivalries produced a weak central government, with Congress dependent on the states and unable to enforce its own legislation. The weakness of the Articles was analysed by Alexander Hamilton and James Madison in *The Federalist*, and the Constitutional Convention met (1787) to draft the Constitution of the United States.

Artigas, José Gervasio (1774–1850) National hero of Uruguay, father of the independence movement. From 1810 to 1813, he fought alongside the Buenos Aires junta to achieve independence from Spain. In 1814 civil war broke out over the attempts of Buenos Aires to bring the whole Viceroyalty of Río de la Plata under its control. Artigas led the provinces in their struggle for autonomy, establishing personal control over what was to become Uruguay and central Argentina. In 1820 he was forced into exile by a Portuguese invasion.

Arusha Declaration (29 January 1967) Policy statement issued in Arusha, NE Tanzania, articulating Julius Nyerere's vision of African socialism. In addition to the usual socialist aims of nationalization and the collective ownership of the means of production, it stressed the primacy of rural production through village collectives (*ujamaa*). It was politically popular but economically disastrous.

Aryan Ancient language and people of the region between the Caspian Sea and Hindu Kush mountains. In *c*.1500 BC one branch entered India, introducing the Sanskrit language; another branch migrated to Europe. In their 1930s racist propaganda, the Nazis traced German descent from Aryans.

Arya Samaj Revivalist Hindu organization founded (1875) by Dayananda Saraswati (1824–83) in Bombay (now Mumbai), NW India. Arya Samaj, which began as an expression of absolute faith in the Vedas, became a vehicle for Hindu nationalism. *See also* Hinduism

Asad, Hafez al- *See* Assad, Hafez al-

Asbury, Francis (1745–1816) American methodist leader, b. England. From 1771 he directed the growth of American Methodism through the circuit system of peripatetic preachers. In 1784 Asbury became superintendent of the Methodist Episcopal Church. *See also* Wesley, John

ASEAN *See* Association of Southeast Asian Nations

Ashanti Administrative region and ethnic group of central Ghana, W Africa. The capital is Kumasi. In the 18th century the Ashanti people (a matrilineal society) established a powerful empire based on the slave trade with the British and Dutch, their influence extending into Togo and the Ivory Coast. Conflicts with the British throughout the 19th century were finally resolved in 1902, when the Ashanti territories (a British protectorate since 1896) were declared a crown colony. The society is traditionally agricultural. The region is the main area of Ghana's vital cocoa production. The Ashanti are renowned for their crafts, including high-quality goldwork and weaving. Today Ashanti is the most populous of Ghana's ten regions. Area: 24,390sq km (9414sq mi). Pop. (1984) 2,090,100.

Ashikaga (1338–1573) Japanese shogunate based in central Honshu, related to the Minamoto. The dynasty was founded by Ashikaga Takauji (1305–58), who overthrew Hojo Takatoki in 1333. In 1336 Takauji forced Emperor Daigo II into exile at Yoshino and moved the shogunate from Kamakura to Kyoto. For the next 66 years there was a schism, with rival emperors in N and S Japan. Japan was reunified (1392) by Yoshimitsu. From the 15th century, the Ashikaga were undermined by the feuds between the daimyo and their samurai armies. *See also* Shogun

Ashkenazim Jews who originally settled in NW Europe, as distinguished from the Sephardim, who settled in Spain and Portugal.

Ashoka (d. *c.*232 BC) (Asoka) Indian emperor (r. *c.*272–232 BC), grandson of Chandragupta. The last and greatest emperor of the Mauryan Empire, at first he fought to expand his empire. Ashoka was repulsed by the suffering of war and, renouncing conquest by force, embraced the Buddhist principle of conquest by dharma (right-living). Ashoka became one of Buddhism's most fervent patrons and spread its ideas through missionaries to neighbouring countries and through edicts engraved on pillars. His empire encompassed most of India and large areas of Afghanistan.

Ashurbanipal (d. *c.*627 BC) (Assurbanipal) King of Assyria (668–627 BC), son and successor of Esarhaddon. He subdued a revolt in Egypt and a rebellion led by his brother in Babylonia. In 639 BC Ashurbanipal completed the conquest of Elam. His reign is chiefly celebrated, however, for its cultural and artistic achievements. Ashurbanipal founded the first major library in the Middle East at Nineveh, where excavations have unearthed *c.*22,000 clay tablets. The Assyrian Empire disintegrated within two decades of his death. *See also* Babylonia

◀ **Ashurbanipal** This 6th-century BC bas-relief from the Northern Palace, Nineveh, shows Ashurbanipal hunting a lion. The Assyrian king decorated his palace with *c.*650 narrative wall reliefs, celebrating his life and achievements. They are among the greatest works of ancient sculpture.

Asia World's largest continent. Entirely in the Eastern Hemisphere, it extends from N of the Arctic Circle in Russia to S of the Equator in Indonesia. Geographically, Europe and Asia are one enormous continent (Eurasia), but historically they have always been regarded as separate continents. Asians constitute more than half the world's population. Hinduism is the religion with the most adherents, although it is confined to India and SE Asia. Islam, Confucianism, Buddhism, Shinto, Christianity, Taoism and Judaism are also important. Since World War 2, the history of Asia has been dominated by three main themes: the legacy of colonialism, the growth of communism, and the rise of Islamic fundamentalism. In 1947 the Indian subcontinent gained its independence from the British Empire, when India and Pakistan became separate nations. In 1949 Indonesia achieved formal independence from the Netherlands.

ASSYRIA

Ancient kingdom in N Mesopotamia, centred on the city of Ashur (Assur) on the River Tigris, near modern Mosul, Iraq. For most of the 2nd millennium BC Ashur was dominated by Babylonia, but in *c.*1350 BC Ashuruballit I founded the independent state of Assyria. Adadnirari I (r. *c.*1295–*c.*1264 BC) defeated the Kassites and the kingdom of Mitanni to create the first Assyrian Empire. The Empire was, however, continually vulnerable to attack from the Hittites and fell to a resurgent Babylonia under Nebuchadnezzar I. Tiglathpileser I (r. *c.*1115–*c.*1077) restored Assyrian power, defeating the Aramaeans and Hurrians and sacking Babylon. The Neo-Assyrian Empire was established by Ashurnasirpal II (r.883–859), who brutally conquered Syria and Mesopotamia. Ashurnasirpal moved the capital to Calah (now Nimrud, Iraq). The campaigns of his son, Shalmaneser III (r.858–824), are recorded on the Black Obelisk (now in the British Museum, London). Shalmaneser exacted tribute from Chaldaea and Israel, but failed to capture Damascus. The Neo-Assyrian Empire reached its zenith during the reign (745–727 BC) of Tiglathpileser III, who conquered Babylonia, Syria and Palestine. His son, Sargon II (r.721–705 BC), completed the conquest of Urartu and extended the Empire to include Israel and Carchemish. Sargon built a new capital at Nineveh. Sargon's son, Sennacherib (r.704–681 BC), defeated Elam, destroyed Babylon and laid siege to Jerusalem. His successor, Esarhaddon (r.680–669 BC), exacted tribute from Egypt. Under Ashurbanipal (r.668–627 BC), Assyrian culture was at its peak. He founded a great library at his palace in Nineveh and the bas-reliefs on the palace walls are masterpieces of Assyrian art. Ashurbanipal's reign was dominated by war against Elam. After his death, the Assyrian Empire went into rapid decline. In 625 BC, Nabopolassar of Chaldaea captured Babylon, and the cities of Ashur (614), Nineveh and Calah (612) fell to Media. *See also* Akkad

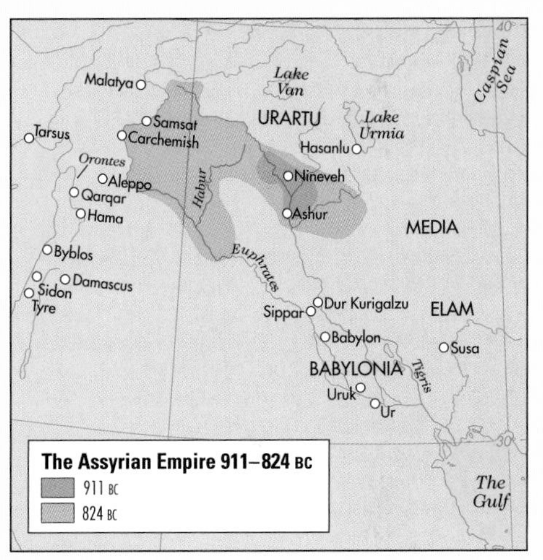

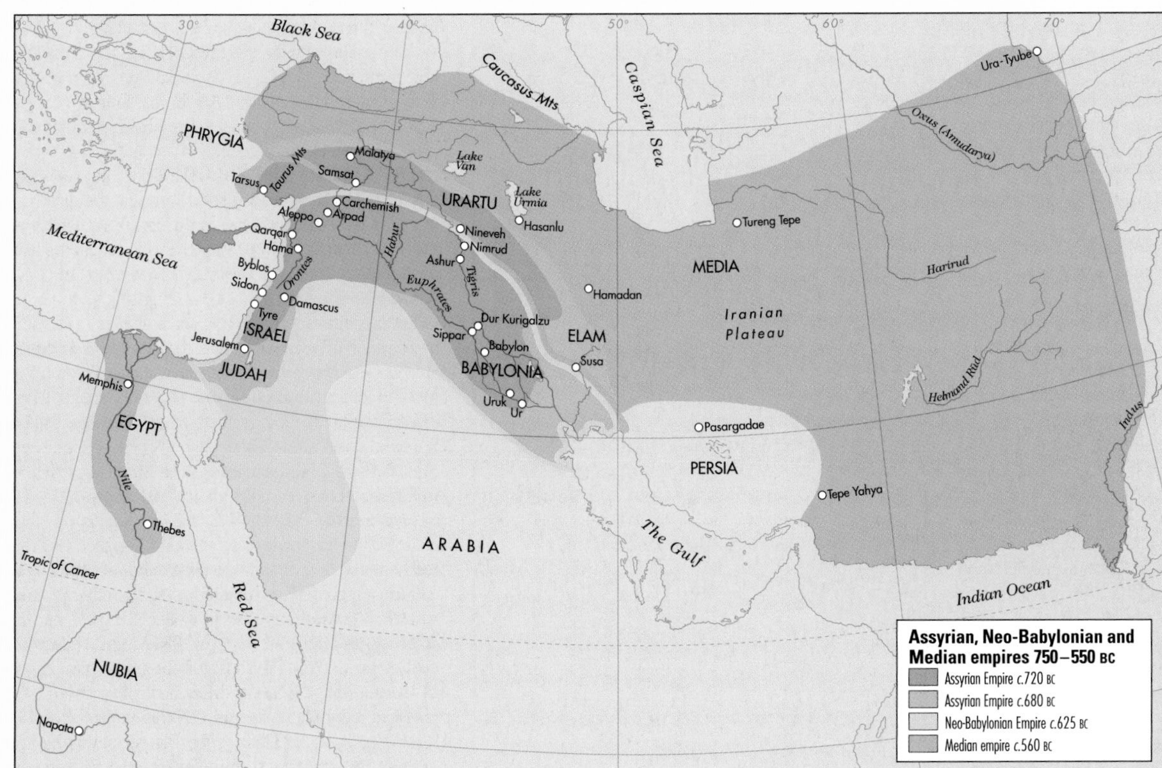

◀ ▲ **Assyria** From 911 BC Adadnirari II began to re-assert central authority in Assyria. His grandson, Ashurnasirpal II (r.883–859 BC), conquered Mesopotamia as far as the River Euphrates. Ashurnasirpal's son, Shalmaneser III (r.858–824 BC), conquered N Syria. The reign (745–727 BC) of Tiglathpileser III marked the resurgence of the Assyrian Empire. He gained Babylonia and conquered much of Syria, including the cities of Arpad and Damascus. His son, Sargon II (r.721–705), gained Israel, most of Urartu and parts of Media. Esarhaddon (r.680–669) captured Egypt. The death (627 BC) of Ashurbanipal brought civil war and the Medes captured Nineveh in 612 BC.

A

► **Aswan** is Egypt's southernmost city. Lying on the E bank of the River Nile, the building of the High Dam, 15km (10mi) upriver flooded Nubia. Many Nubians were compelled to resettle in Aswan. The city served as the base for the Anglo-Egyptian defeat of the Mahdist uprising (1891–98) in Sudan. Aga Khan III (1877–1957) is buried on the W bank of the Nile, overlooking Aswan.

During the 1950s, after military confrontations, INDOCHINA and MALAYSIA won independence from France and Britain respectively. The spread of communism began (1949) with the victory of MAO ZEDONG in CHINA. North KOREA failed to establish a united, communist state in its war with South KOREA (1950–53), and communism was also repulsed with Western help in Indonesia. Communism did finally gain control of VIETNAM and CAMBODIA, following the VIETNAM WAR (1954–75). The break-up of the Soviet Union led to the creation of eight "new" countries in Central Asia, few of which were politically stable or economically strong. In the Middle East, ISRAEL fought for its survival against its neigbours in the ARAB-ISRAELI WARS, and IRAQ was involved in the prolonged IRAN-IRAQ WAR (1980–88) with fundamentalist IRAN and later in the GULF WAR (1991) with an international coalition, headed by the United States, following Iraq's invasion of KUWAIT. From the 1960s to the 1990s, there was dramatic economic growth in several countries of Southeast and East Asia, based on a combination of household and high-tech products. Following JAPAN's example, South Korea, TAIWAN, HONG KONG, SINGAPORE, MALAYSIA and THAILAND formed the so-called "tiger" economies. In 1997 these economies plunged into recession, fuelling fears of a worldwide depression. *See also* articles on individual countries

Asia Minor (Anatolia) Great peninsula of W Asia making up most of modern TURKEY. The Bosporus, the Sea of Marmara, and the Dardanelles divide both Turkey and Europe from Asia. Farming communities were established in the area by 7000 BC, and by 3000 BC cities had begun to emerge, among them TROY. In *c*.1800 BC the HITTITES established an empire. From the 8th century BC, the Greeks established colonies in the area. In the 6th century BC, the Persians invaded, precipitating the PERSIAN WARS (499–479 BC). ALEXANDER III (THE GREAT)'s empire included this region, although it split into several states after his death. The Romans unified the area in the 2nd century AD. By the 6th century it had become part of the BYZANTINE EMPIRE. In the 14th and 15th centuries it was conquered by the Ottoman Turks and remained part of the OTTOMAN EMPIRE until the establishment of the Republic of Turkey in 1923.

asientos de negros Agreement, first made with Portugal in 1595 and later with Britain, by which Spain farmed out the SLAVE TRADE in her colonies to foreign contractors.

Asmara (Asmera) Capital of ERITREA, NE Africa. Occupied by Italy in 1889, it was their colonial capital and the main base for the invasion of ETHIOPIA (1935–36). In 1941 Asmara was captured by the British. In the 1950s the United States built Africa's biggest military communications centre here. In 1952 Asmara was absorbed by Ethiopia, and was the main garrison in the fight against Eritrean rebels seeking independence. The city was ravaged by drought, famine and war. In 1993 Asmara became the capital of independent Eritrea. Pop. (1991) 367,300.

Asoka *See* ASHOKA

Asquith, Herbert Henry, 1st Earl of Oxford and Asquith (1852–1928) British statesman, last Liberal prime minister (1908–16). He entered Parliament in 1886 and served as William GLADSTONE's home secretary (1892–95). Asquith was chancellor of the exchequer under Sir Henry CAMPBELL-BANNERMAN, and succeeded him as prime minister. His administration was notable for its social welfare legislation, such as the introduction of old-age pensions (1908) and unemployment insurance (1911). Asquith also passed the Parliament Act (1911) that ended the HOUSE OF LORDS' power of veto over Commons legislation. His attempts to establish HOME RULE for Ireland were rejected by Conservatives and Unionists. Asquith took Britain into WORLD WAR I, but was an ineffective wartime leader. In 1915 he formed a coalition government with the CONSERVATIVE PARTY. Asquith was replaced as prime minister in a cabinet coup led by David LLOYD GEORGE. He remained leader of the LIBERAL PARTY until 1926.

Assad, Hafez al- (1928–) Syrian statesman, president (1970–). He served as minister of defence (1965–70), before seizing power in a military coup. In 1971 Assad was elected president. He took a hardline stance against ISRAEL, and Syrian troops participated in the YOM KIPPUR WAR (1973) against Israel. In 1976 Assad sent troops to quell the civil war in LEBANON. In 1987 Syria moved into BEIRUT to restore order. In the mid-1990s, Assad's stance toward Israel softened and he played a vital role in the Israeli-Palestinian peace talks. Syria supported the coalition forces arrayed against Iraq in the GULF WAR (1991).

ATATÜRK, KEMAL

Kemal Atatürk led opposition to the Allied occupation of Asia Minor. He defeated the newly created Armenian state (1920) and crushed Kurdish opposition. He replaced (1926) the Sharia system of Islamic law with Western secular models, expanding the role of women in Turkish society. In 1928 Atatürk abandoned the use of Arabic script in favour of the Latin alphabet.

ATATÜRK IN HIS OWN WORDS

"This nation has never lived without independence. We cannot and shall not live without it. Either independence or death."

"Everything we see in the world is the creative work of women."

Assam State in NE India, almost separated from the rest of the country by Bangladesh. The capital is Dispur. It became a state in 1950, but its people have resented (and forcibly resisted) immigration from West Bengal and Bangladesh. The Bodo minority continue to push for a separate state N of the River Brahmaputra. Area: 78,438sq km (30,277sq mi). Pop. (1991) 22,414,322.

Assassin (Arabic, users of hashish) Name given to a Muslim sect of ISMAILIS, founded (*c*.1090) by Hasan ibn al-Sabbah. They fought against orthodox Muslims and Christian Crusaders, and committed many political murders until their defeat in the 13th century.

Assiniboine Nomadic NATIVE NORTH AMERICAN tribe. Their language is Siouan, and they are related to the DAKOTA, although they migrated W from Minnesota to Saskatchewan and the Lake Winnipeg area. Their culture is that of the Plains Indians. They were peaceful trading partners of the HUDSON'S BAY COMPANY, and their trade helped to destroy the French monopoly among tribes of the region. Today, they number *c*.5000.

assize In English COMMON LAW, court that was held in provincial towns at regular intervals, presided over by peripatetic High Court judges. It was founded by HENRY II in the 1160s. It has been replaced in England by the crown court.

Association of Southeast Asian Nations (ASEAN) Regional alliance formed (1967) to promote economic cooperation. Its members are Indonesia, Malaysia, Philippines, Singapore, Thailand, Brunei, Vietnam, Laos and Burma. Based in Jakarta, Indonesia, it took over the non-military aspects of the SOUTHEAST ASIA TREATY ORGANIZATION (SEATO) in 1975.

Assurbanipal *See* ASHURBANIPAL

Assyria *See* feature article, page 25

Astor, John Jacob (1763–1848) US financier, b. Germany. In 1808 he founded the AMERICAN FUR COMPANY. After 1812 Astor acquired a virtual monopoly of the US FUR TRADE. In the 1830s, he concentrated on land investment and became the wealthiest man in the United States. His great-great-grandson, William Waldorf Astor (1879–1952), was married to Vicountess Nancy ASTOR.

Astor, Nancy Witcher (Langhorne), Viscountess (1879–1964) British politician, b. United States. In 1919 Astor became the first woman to take her seat in the British HOUSE OF COMMONS. She served as a Conservative member of Parliament until 1945. Lady Astor advocated temperance, educational reform, and women's and children's welfare. In the 1930s, she and her husband, William Waldorf Astor (1879–1952), headed a group of influential proponents of APPEASEMENT toward Nazi Germany.

Asturias Region in NW Spain, bordering the Bay of Biscay and traversed by the Cantabrian Mountains; the capital is Oviedo. In the 2nd century BC Asturias was conquered by the Romans. It formed the centre of Christian resistance to the MOORS. In 911 it was united with LEÓN. In the 13th century it became part of the kingdom of CASTILE. Asturias was a centre of Republican resistance in the Spanish CIVIL WAR (1936–39). Pop. (1991) 1,093,937.

Aswan City on the E bank of the River Nile just above Lake Nasser, SE Egypt. Aswan was of strategic importance to the ancient Egyptians and Greeks because it controlled all shipping and communications above the first cataract of the Nile. The modern city has benefited greatly from the construction of the Aswan High Dam. The Dam, built with Soviet aid between 1960 and 1970, has a generating capacity of 10 billion kilowatt-hours and supersedes the first Aswan Dam (completed 1902) to establish flood control on the Nile. Many NUBIANS displaced by the Dam's construction have moved to the city. The rock terrain surrounding the lake abounds in Egyptian and Greek temples and although some sites were submerged, the Temples of ABU SIMBEL were saved. Pop. (1992) 220,000.

Atahualpa (1502–33) (Atabalipa) Last independent INCA ruler of Peru, son of Huayna Capac. He inherited Quito upon his father's death, while his half-brother, Huáscar, controlled the rest of the kingdom. In 1532 Atahualpa defeated Huáscar, but his period of dominance was to be short-lived. In November 1532 Francisco PIZARRO captured Atahualpa, and he was later executed.

Atatürk, (Mustafa) Kemal (1881–1938) Turkish general and statesman, first president (1923–38) of the Turkish republic. As a young soldier, he joined the YOUNG TURKS and was chief of staff to ENVER PASHA in the successful revolution (1908). He fought against the Italians in Tripoli (1911) and defended Gallipoli in the BALKAN WARS. During World War 1, he led resistance to the Allies' GALLIPOLI CAMPAIGN. The defeat of the OTTOMAN EMPIRE and the capitulation of the sultan persuaded Mustafa Kemal to organize the Turkish Nationalist Party (1919) and set up a rival government in ANKARA. The Treaty of SÈVRES (1920) forced him on the offensive. His expulsion of the Greeks from ASIA MINOR (1921–22) persuaded the sultan to flee ISTANBUL. The Treaty of LAUSANNE (1923) saw the creation of an independent republic. His dictatorship undertook sweeping reforms that transformed Turkey into a secular, industrial nation. In 1934 he adopted the title Atatürk (Turkish, father of the Turks). He was succeeded by Ismet INÖNÜ.

Athabascan (Athapascan or Slave Indians) Tribe and language group of NATIVE NORTH AMERICANS inhabiting NW Canada. In the 17th and 18th centuries they were forced N to the Great Slave Lake and Fort Nelson by the CREE. The term "Slave Indian" derives from the domination and forced labour exacted by the Cree. The Athabascan tribe has always been closely linked to the CHIPPEWA, and some authorities regard them as one group. The Athabascan language is a subgroup of the Na-Dene linguistic phylum. By the mid-1980s the number of Athabascan speakers was believed to exceed 160,000, including the APACHE and NAVAJO.

Athanasian Creed Christian profession of faith, probably written in the 6th century, that explains the teachings of the Church on the TRINITY and the incarnation. The Roman Catholic and some Protestant churches accept its authority. *See also* APOSTLES' CREED; NICENE CREED

Athanasius, Saint (d.373) Early Christian leader. As patriarch of Alexandria, he confuted ARIANISM and in various writings defended the teaching that the Son and the Holy Spirit were of equal divinity with God the Father and so shared a threefold being. He is no longer considered the author of the ATHANASIAN CREED, but he did write the *Life of St Anthony*. His feast day is 2 May.

atheism Philosophical denial of the existence of God or any supernatural or spiritual being. The first Christians were called atheists because they denied Roman religions, but the term is now used to indicate the denial of Christian theism. During the 18th-century ENLIGHTENMENT David HUME, Immanuel KANT and the Encyclopedists laid the foundations for atheism. In the 19th century Karl MARX, Friedrich NIETZSCHE and Sigmund Freud all accommodated some form of atheism into their respective philosophical creeds. In the 20th century many individuals and groups advocate atheism. *See also* AGNOSTICISM

Athelstan (*c*.895–939) (Aethelstan) King of WESSEX (924–39), son and successor of EDWARD THE ELDER. He extended the power of the kingdom built up by his grandfather, ALFRED (THE GREAT), by conquest, legislation and marriage alliances. Athelstan's victory at the Battle of Brunanburh (937) established him as king of all England.

Athenian empire Cities and islands that paid tribute to ATHENS in the 5th century BC. It developed out of the DELIAN LEAGUE in a gradual process that was marked by the removal of the League's treasury from Delos to Athens (454 BC). After suppressing a number of revolts, Athens suffered defeat and lost control of BOEOTIA (446 BC). In the Thirty Years' Peace (445 BC) signed with SPARTA, it gave up its land empire while retaining its naval supremacy. *See also* GREECE, CLASSICAL; PELOPONNESIAN WAR

Athens *See* feature article

Atkinson, Sir Harry Albert (1831–92) New Zealand statesman, prime minister (1876–77, 1883–84, 1884, 1887–91), b. England. Atkinson was renowned for his financial expertise and his government introduced a progressive social welfare programme.

Atlanta Capital of GEORGIA, United States, in the NW centre of the state. The land was ceded to Georgia in 1821 by the CREEK and was settled in 1833. The city was founded (1837) at the E end of the Western and Atlantic Railroad. Originally called Terminus, it became Atlanta in 1847. It served as a Confederate supply depot during the American CIVIL WAR (1861–65). In 1864 Atlanta fell to General William SHERMAN, whose army razed the city. It was rapidly rebuilt and soon recovered its importance as a transport and cotton manufacturing centre. It became the state capital in 1887. It is the headquarters of the Coca-Cola Corporation. Atlanta hosted the 1996 Olympic Games. Pop. (1992) 394,848.

ATHENS

Capital and largest city of Greece, situated on the Saronic Gulf. The ancient city was built around the ACROPOLIS. After the PERSIAN WARS (499–479 BC), Athens became the greatest artistic and cultural centre of classical GREECE. In the 5th century BC the city prospered under CIMON and PERICLES, and provided a climate in which the great classical works of philosophy and drama were created. The most noted artistic treasures are the PARTHENON (438 BC), the Erechtheum (406 BC) and the Theatre of Dionysus (*c*.500 BC) – the oldest of the Greek theatres. Modern Athens and its port of Piraeus form a major Mediterranean transport and economic centre. Overcrowding and severe air pollution are damaging the ancient sites. Pop. (1991) 3,072,922. *See also* ACROPOLIS; HELLENISTIC AGE

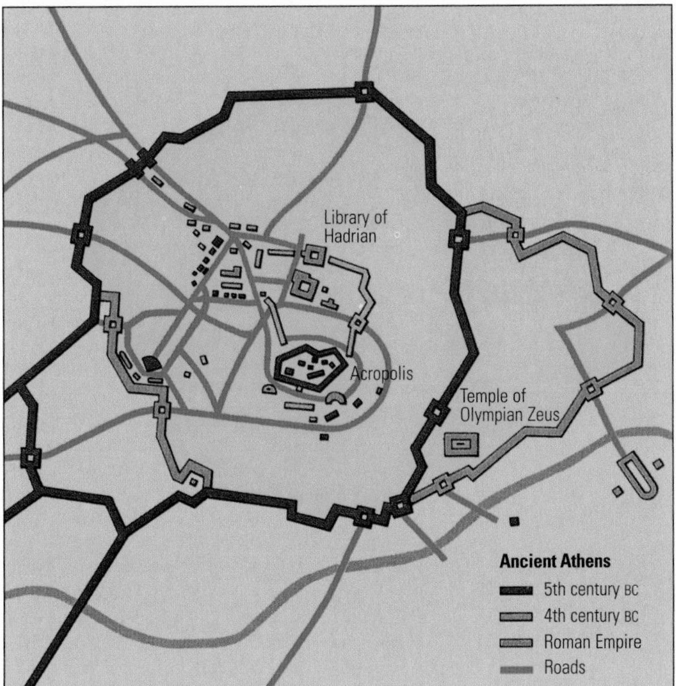

▲ **The owl of Athena**, patron goddess of the city, appears on this Athenian four drachma coin.

◄ **Athens** was sacked by the Persians in 480 BC. The city walls were rebuilt and strenghtened by Themistocles and the Acropolis was fortified by Cimon after 468 BC. The Parthenon, the Temple of Hephaestus and the Theatre of Dionysus were all constructed in the 5th century BC. Athens' naval and trading domination of the Aegean provided the wealth for building projects.

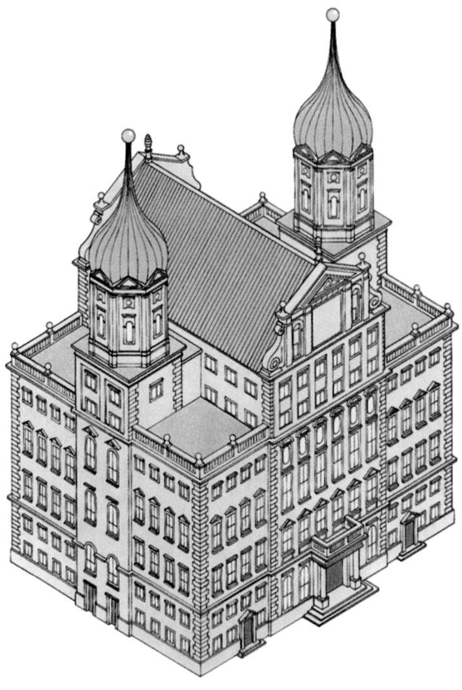

▲ **Augsburg** Town Hall in s Germany was designed in the Palladian style (1615–29) by Elias Holl. The building's three storey Golden Hall was destroyed in World War 2.

Atlantic, Battle of the (1939–43) Campaign for control of the Atlantic sea routes waged by air and naval forces during WORLD WAR 2. The Germans hoped to starve Britain into submission by U-boat attacks on merchant shipping and later to prevent US reinforcements reaching the Mediterranean and Europe. More than 14 million metric tons of shipping were destroyed.

Atlantic Charter (August 1941) Joint declaration of peace aims during World War 2, issued by US President Franklin ROOSEVELT and British Prime Minister Winston CHURCHILL. It affirmed the right of all nations to choose their own form of government, promised to restore sovereignty to all nations that had lost it, and advocated the disarmament of aggressor nations.

atom bomb *See* NUCLEAR WEAPON

Attila (406–53) King of the HUNS (*c*.439–53), co-ruler with his elder brother until 445. Attila defeated the Eastern Roman Emperor THEODOSIUS II, extorting land and tribute, and invaded Gaul in 451. Although his army suffered heavy losses, he invaded Italy in 452, but disease forced his withdrawal. Attila has a reputation as a fierce warrior but was fair to his subjects and encouraged learning. On his death, the empire fell apart.

Attlee, Clement Richard, 1st Earl (1883–1967) British statesman, prime minister (1945–51). He entered Parliament in 1922. In 1935 Attlee became leader of the British LABOUR PARTY. During World War 2, he served in Winston CHURCHILL's wartime cabinet. Attlee won a landslide victory in the 1945 general election. His administration introduced important social reforms, such as the NATIONAL HEALTH SERVICE (NHS) and the nationalization of the power industries, the railways, and the BANK OF ENGLAND. He also granted independence to India (1947) and Burma (1948). Attlee was re-elected in 1950, but was defeated by Winston Churchill in the 1951 general elec-

A

tion. He continued to serve as leader of the opposition until he retired and accepted an earldom in 1955. Attlee was succeeded as leader of the Labour Party by Hugh GAITSKELL. *See also* BEVAN, ANEURIN; CRIPPS, SIR STAFFORD

Auchinleck, Sir Claude John Eyre (1884–1981) British field marshal. After serving in the Middle East in World War 1, he commanded operations in India during the 1930s and helped to mechanize the Indian army. During WORLD WAR 2 Auchinleck commanded the abortive Narvik expedition (1940). In 1941 he succeeded Field Marshal Archibald WAVELL as commander in chief in the Middle East and launched an unsuccessful campaign across Libya. Auchinleck resisted the advance of Erwin ROMMEL's Afrika Korps in the First Battle of El ALAMEIN (1942). In 1943 Auchinleck was re-appointed commander in chief in India, where he remained until independence (1947).

Auckland Largest city and chief port of New Zealand, lying on an isthmus of NW North Island. The port, built on land purchased from the Maori in 1840, handles *c.*60% of New Zealand's trade. In 1842 the first immigrants arrived from Scotland, and in 1854 the first New Zealand Parliament opened here. It served as capital of New Zealand until 1865. Auckland has the largest Polynesian population (*c.*65,000) of any city in the world. Pop. (1994) 929,300.

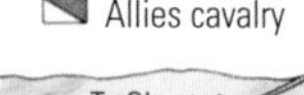

A

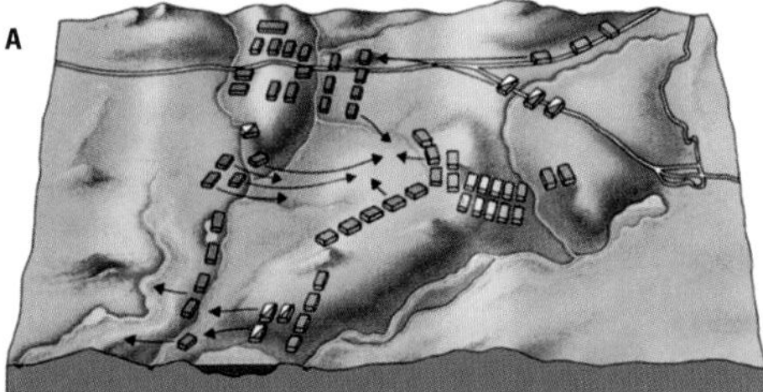

B

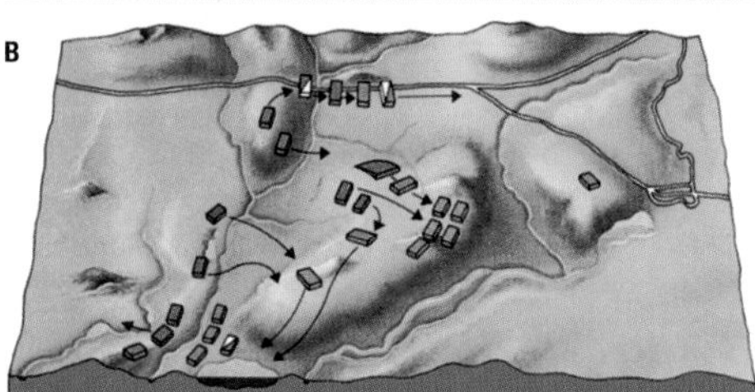

C

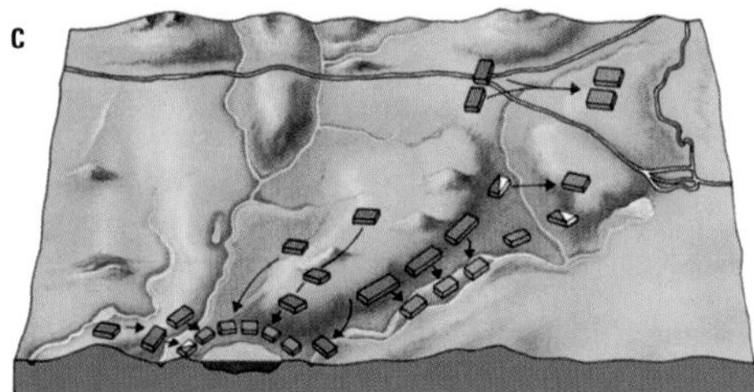

▲ **Austerlitz, Battle of** By evacuating Austerlitz and the Pratzen Heights, Napoleon feigned weakness. The Allies camped on the Heights (A). Their plan was to overwhelm the (deliberately) weakened right flank of the French, before marching N to encircle the French at Brünn. Beneath the cover of mist, sections of the French army manoeuvred beneath the Heights. While the Allies attacked the French right, the main French force regained Pratzen Heights (B). Additional support was provided by other French forces that had initially engaged the Allies to the N. The French then dispersed the Allies, driving them onto the frozen lakes near Telnitz, where many drowned as Napoleon's artillery opened fire to smash the ice (C).

Augsburg Historic city on the River Lech, Bavaria, S Germany. Founded (*c.*15 BC) by the Romans and named after the Emperor Augustus, it became a free imperial city in 1276 and was a prosperous banking and commercial centre in the 15th and 16th centuries. The AUGSBURG CONFESSION (1530) was presented and the Peace of AUGSBURG (1555) signed here. The cathedral (started 994) claims the oldest stained-glass windows in Europe (11th century). Pop. (1993) 265,000. *See* illustration, page 27

Augsburg, League of (1686) Alliance of the enemies

AUSTRALIA

AREA: 7,686,850sq km (2,967,893sq mi)
POPULATION: 17,529,000
CAPITAL (POPULATION): Canberra (324,600)
GOVERNMENT: Federal constitutional monarchy
ETHNIC GROUPS: White 95%, Native Australian 1.5%, Asian 1.3%
LANGUAGES: English (official)
RELIGIONS: Christianity (Roman Catholic 26%, Anglican 24%, others 20%), Islam, Buddhism, Judaism
GDP PER CAPITA (1995): US$18,940

Earth's smallest continent. Combined with the island of TASMANIA, it forms the independent Commonwealth nation of Australia, the world's sixth-largest country. NATIVE AUSTRALIANS (aboriginals) entered the continent from Southeast Asia more than 60,000 years ago. They settled throughout the country and remained isolated from the rest of the world until the first European explorers, the Dutch, arrived in the 17th century. The Dutch did not settle. In 1770 Captain James COOK reached Botany Bay and claimed the E coast for Great Britain.

In 1788 the first British settlement was established (for convicts) on the site of present-day SYDNEY. The first free settlers arrived three years later. In the 19th century the economy developed rapidly, based on mining and sheep-rearing. The continent was divided into colonies, which later became states. In 1901 the states of Queensland, Victoria, Tasmania, New South Wales, South Australia and Western Australia federated to create the Commonwealth of Australia. In 1911 Northern Territory joined the federation. A range of progressive social welfare policies were adopted, such as old-age pensions (1909). The federal capital was established (1927) at CANBERRA, in Australian Capital Territory. Australia was a member of the Allies in both World Wars. During World War 2, the Battle of the CORAL SEA (1942) halted a full-scale attack on the continent.

Post-1945 Australia steadily realigned itself with its Asian neighbours. Robert MENZIES, Australia's longest-serving prime minister, oversaw many economic and social reforms and dispatched Australian troops to the VIETNAM WAR (1954–75). In 1977 Prime Minister Gough WHITLAM was removed from office by the British governor general. He was succeeded by Malcolm FRASER. In the 1983 election Fraser was defeated by the LABOR PARTY and Bob HAWKE became prime minister. His shrewd handling of industrial disputes and economic recession helped him win a record four terms in office. In 1991 Hawke was forced to resign as leader and was succeeded by Paul KEATING, a staunch advocate of republicanism. Keating won the 1993 general election and persevered with his free-market reforms. In 1996 elections Keating was defeated by a coalition of the NATIONAL PARTY and the LIBERAL PARTY, led by John HOWARD. In 1998 Howard narrowly won a second term in office. In a referendum (1999) Australia voted against becoming a republic. In 1993 the government passed the Native Title Act, which restored land rights to traditional hunting and sacred areas for Native Australians.

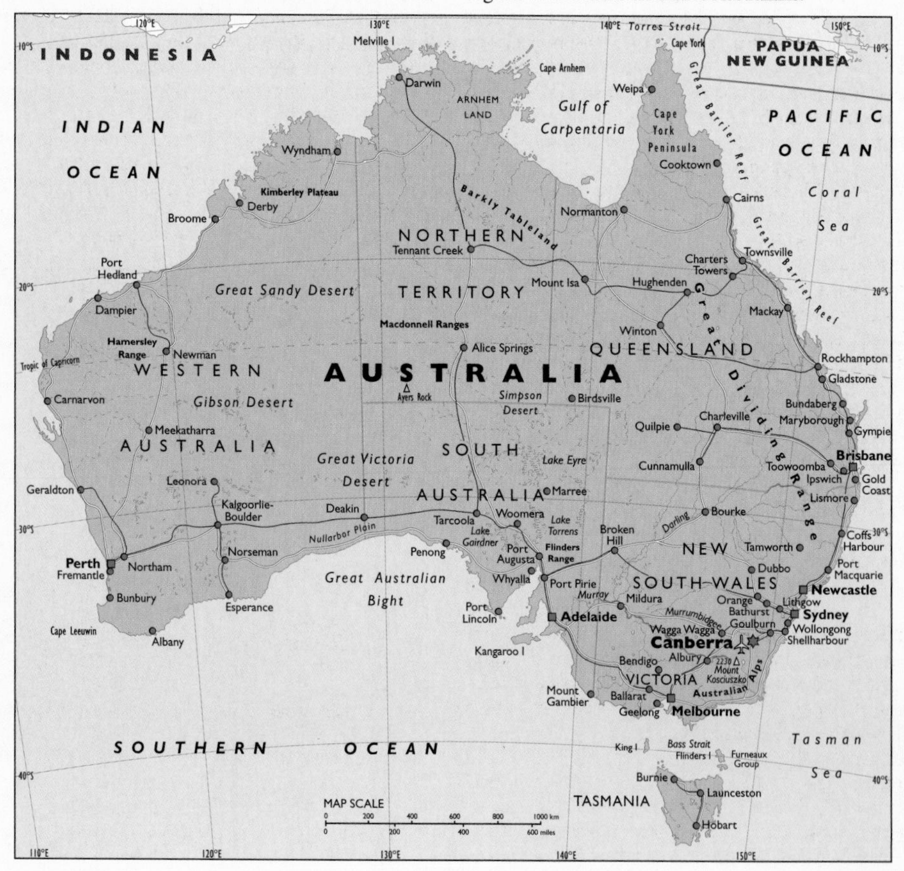

of Louis XIV of France. Composed of Spain, Sweden, the Holy Roman Empire, and lesser states, its formation under Emperor Leopold I was a reaction to French encroachment on the land bordering the Holy Roman Empire. Following the French attack (1688) on the Palatinate, a new coalition, the Grand Alliance, was formed (1689).

Augsburg, Peace of (1555) Agreement reached by the Diet of the Holy Roman Empire in Augsburg ending the conflict between the Roman Catholic Church and Lutheranism in Germany. It established the right of each prince to decide on the nature of religious practice in his lands. Dissenters were allowed to sell their lands and move. Free cities and imperial cities were open to both Catholics and Lutherans. The exclusion of other Protestant sects proved to be a source of future conflict.

Augsburg Confession (1530) Summation of the Lutheran faith, presented to Emperor Charles V at the Diet of Augsburg. Its 28 articles were formulated from earlier Lutheran statements principally by Philip Melanchthon. It was denounced by the Roman Catholic Church, but became a model for later Protestant creeds. *See also* Lutheranism

Augusta Town on the Savannah River, e Georgia, United States; seat of Richmond county. A trading post was established (1717) and was named (1735) after the mother of George III of England. Augusta was captured (1781) by Continental troops in the American Revolution (1775–83). It served (1785–95) as the capital of Georgia and the Constitution of the United States was ratified here. Augusta expanded rapidly due its tobacco and cotton plantations. Pop. (1990) 47,532.

Augustine, Saint (354–430) Christian theologian and philosopher. His *Confessions* provide an intimate, psychological self-portrait of a spirit in search of ultimate purpose, which Augustine believed he found in his conversion to Christianity (386). As bishop of Hippo (396–430), n Africa, Augustine defended Christian orthodoxy against Manichaeism, Donatism and Pelagianism. *The City of God* (426) is a model of Christian apologetic literature. Augustine is considered the greatest of the Four Fathers of the Latin Church (the others are Ambrose, Jerome and Gregory I). His feast day is 28 August.

Augustine of Canterbury, Saint (d.604) First archbishop of Canterbury. In 596 he was sent from Rome by Pope Gregory I, at the head of a 40-strong mission. Arriving in Kent (597), Augustine converted King Ethelbert and introduced Roman ecclesiastical practices into England. This led to conflict with the Celtic monks of Britain and Ireland, whose traditions had developed in isolation from the Continent. The Synod of Whitby (663) settled disputes in favour of Roman custom. Saint Augustine's feast day is 28 May (26 May in England and Wales).

Augustus (63 bc–ad 14) (Gaius Julius Caesar Octavianus) First Roman emperor (29 bc–ad 14), also called **Octavian**. Nephew and adopted heir of Julius Caesar, he formed the so-called Second Triumvirate with Mark Antony and Lepidus after Caesar's assassination. They defeated Brutus and Cassius at the Battle of Philippi (42 bc) and divided the Roman territories between them. Rivalry between Antony and Octavian was resolved by the defeat of Antony at the Battle of Actium (31 bc). In 27 bc Octavian received the title of *augustus* (Lat. reverend). While preserving the form of the republic, Augustus held supreme power. He introduced peace and prosperity after years of civil war. Augustus built up the power and prestige of Rome, encouraging patriotic literature and rebuilding much of the city in marble. He extended the frontiers and fostered colonization, took general censuses, and tried to make taxation more equitable. Augustus tried to arrange the succession to avoid future conflicts, though had to acknowledge an unloved stepson, Tiberius, as his successor.

Augustus II (the Strong) (1670–1733) King of Poland (1697–1704, 1709–33) and, as Frederick Augustus I, Elector of Saxony (1694–1733). He was elected by the Polish nobles in order to secure an alliance with Saxony, but the result was to draw Poland into the Great Northern War (1700–21) on the side of Russia. In 1704 Augustus was forced to abdicate in favour of Stanislaw I (Leszczyński). Civil war (1704–09) and invasion by Charles XII of Sweden weakened the Polish state. Augustus was restored to the throne after Peter I (the Great) defeated Sweden at the Battle of Poltava (1709), but at the cost of growing Russian dominance in Polish affairs.

Augustus III (1696–1763) King of Poland (1734–63) and, as Frederick Augustus II, Elector of Saxony (1734–63), son and successor of Augustus II (the Strong). With the support of the Russian empress Anna Ivanova, Augustus gained the throne during the War of the Polish Succession (1733–38). He opposed Maria Theresa in the War of the Austrian Succession (1740–48), but later switched allegiances. He was forced into exile during the Seven Years' War (1756–63). He was succeeded by Stanislaw II Augustus.

Aung San (1914–47) Burmese politician who opposed British rule, father of Aung San Suu Kyi. Initially collaborating with the Japanese (1942), he later helped expel the invaders. Aung San was assassinated shortly after his appointment as deputy chairman of the executive council.

Aung San Suu Kyi, Daw (1945–) Burmese civil rights activist, daughter of Aung San. In 1989 she was placed under house arrest for leadership of the National League for Democracy, a coalition opposed to Burma's (Myanmar's) oppressive military junta. In 1991 she was awarded the Nobel Prize for Peace and the European Parliament's Sakharov Prize (for human rights).

Aurangzeb (1619–1707) Emperor of India (1659–1707). He defeated his brother, Dara Shikoh, in battle (1658) and seized the throne from his enfeebled father Shah Jehan. The Mughal Empire reached its greatest extent when Aurangzeb conquered the Deccan kingdoms of Bijapur and Golconda in 1686–87. A militant Sunni Muslim, Aurangzeb executed (1675) the Sikh guru Tegh Bahadur and persecuted his Hindu subjects by destroying their temples and reimposing a poll tax on non-Muslims. He spent much of his reign fighting a futile and costly war against the Marathas in s India. He left an empire threatened by revolt from the Sikhs, Rajputs and Jats.

Aurelian (c.ad 215–75) Roman emperor. In ad 270, having risen through the army ranks, Aurelian succeeded Claudius II as emperor. His victories against the Goths, reconquest of Palmyra, and recovery of Gaul and Britain earned him the title "restorer of the world". He built the Aurelian Wall to protect Rome and was assassinated in a military plot.

Aurelius, Marcus *See* Marcus Aurelius

AUSTRIA

AREA: 83,850sq km (32,347sq mi)
POPULATION: 7,884,000
CAPITAL (POPULATION): Vienna (1,589,052)
GOVERNMENT: Federal republic
ETHNIC GROUPS: Austrian 93%, Slav 2%, Turkish, German
LANGUAGES: German (official)
RELIGIONS: Christianity (Roman Catholic 78%, Protestant 6%), Islam
GDP PER CAPITA (1995): US$21,250

Republic in central Europe. Austria was part of the Holy Roman Empire and, in 1526, was united with Bohemia and Hungary. Under Habsburg rule it became the most important state in the Empire. The succession of Maria Theresa (r.1740–80) prompted the War of the Austrian Succession (1740–48) and the reforms of Joseph II (r.1765–90) encountered fierce resistance. The French Revolutionary Wars (1792–1802) and the Napoleonic Wars (1803–15), culminating in defeat at the Battle of Austerlitz (1805), led to the dissolution of the Holy Roman Empire in 1806. Through the auspices of Prince von Metternich, however, Austria continued to dominate European politics. The Revolutions of 1848 forced the succession of Franz Joseph. Austria was further reduced in the Austro-Prussian War (1866). Ausgleich (1867) created the Austro-Hungarian Empire, whose disregard for individual nationalities precipitated World War I. The defeat (1918) of the Central Powers led to the formation of a republic. Anschluss with Germany was forbidden. Engelbert Dollfuss created a totalitarian state, but was unable to stem the rise of Nazi Germany. In 1938 Germany annexed Austria, and they jointly fought in World War 2. In 1945 the Allies partitioned and occupied Austria. In 1955 Allied forces withdrew and Austria became a neutral, federal republic. A succession of coalition governments was halted by the election of a People's Party government (1970) led by Bruno Kreisky, who remained chancellor until 1983. In 1995 Austria joined the European Union (EU), but was isolated when the far-right Freedom Party joined a coalition in 2000.

The Aztecs were a NATIVE MIDDLE AMERICAN people who moved into the central valley of pre-Columbian Mexico in the late 12th century, eventually supplanting the TOLTEC culture. Originally a nomadic, farming group from NW Mexico, they moved southwards from the legendary land of Aztlán ('White land"), settling on a swampy island in Lake Texcoco or Metzliapán ("Moon Lake"). Here the Aztecs founded the city of Tenochtitlán (now MEXICO CITY) in *c.*1345. The Aztecs' mastery of highly productive irrigation techniques for agriculture, such as the *chiampas* ("floating gardens"), helped them become the dominant power in central Mexico. In 1431 Itzcóatl (r.1428–40) conquered Azcapotzalco, the city-state of the Tepanecs, and demanded tribute from the other neighbouring states of Texcoco and Tlacopan. The Aztecs then embarked on a campaign of expansion. Montezuma I (r.1440–69) and Axayacoatl (r.1469–81) consolidated the highlands surrounding Tenochtitlán, while later expeditions by Ahuitzotl (r.1486–1502) and MONTEZUMA II (r.1502–19) extended the empire to the border of modern Guatemala. Progress to the W and N was blocked by the Tarascan empire and the CHICHIMECS respectively.

Government and politics

The Aztecs ruled through military tyranny. The head of state was the *tlatoani*, whose position depended on descent. Society was divided into three broad classes: nobles and professional warriors, commoners and serfs. These three castes were further differentiated by occupational or military status. Commoners could rise, for instance, to the rank of professional soldiers through military prowess.

The *c.*400 states conquered by the Aztecs were organized into 38 provinces, each with a tax collector-governor appointed to collect the annual tribute. In many provinces the Aztecs established garrisons for soldiers and colonizers from Tenochtitlán.

Religion

In addition to the need for tropical goods, the acquisition of empire was motivated by religion. The priesthood was a powerful political force. Each temple and god had its own priestly order. The priests ran *calmecas* (religious colleges), where they taught nobles and commoners alike. A central feature of Aztec religion was bloodletting and human sacrifice. Prisoners of war were needed for sacrifice to Aztec gods. At vast religious ceremonies, priests would cut out the hearts of victims stretched over a sacrificial stone. Huge numbers sometimes met their death in this terrible way. After one successful campaign against the rebellious Oaxacans, for example, more than 12,000 were sacrificed. At the centre of the Aztec pantheon stood Huitzilopochtli, the god of the Sun and of war. Other deities included Tlaloc, the rain god, Tezacatlipoca, the sky god, and Quetzalcóatl, the god of learning or the Feathered Serpent.

Mythology and astronomy

When territory was conquered, captured deity images were put in Aztec temples, and sacred mountain sites were appropriated for Aztec ceremonies and temples. Aztec temples were decorated with splendid stone carvings, such as the "Calendar Stone." Measuring 3.7m (12ft) in diameter, the centre of the Stone depicted the Aztecs' belief that there were four eras or "suns"

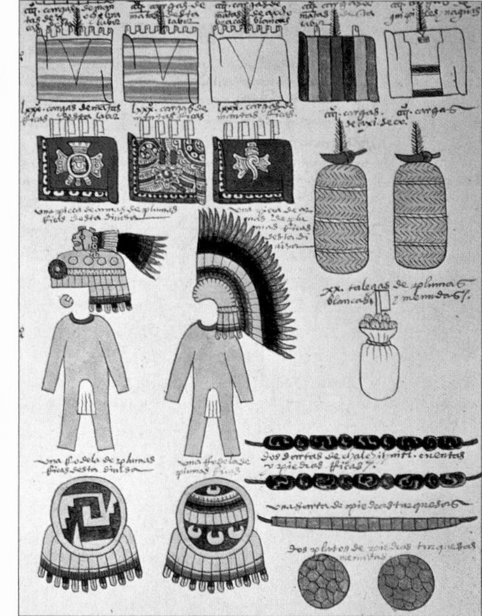

▲ **Aztec** Manuscripts from around the time of the Spanish conquest have made it possible to reconstruct the structure of the Aztec empire. The manuscript shown here is the *Codex Mendoza*, which includes illustrations of the tributes that the Aztecs demanded from client provinces. These tributes included warriors' clothing, bags of feathers and dried chillies.

▲ **Aztecs** The barrio of Tlatelolco was the main market in the Aztec capital of Tenochtitlán. Reports by Spanish colonizers suggest that it attracted as many as 60,000 people on the main market day. Tenochtitlán lay in a high basin, surrounded by mountains. While the basin provided natural resources such as obsidian, used for craftwork tools, salt and corn, it lacked goods such as tropical foods, cotton, multi-coloured feathers for head-dresses, and jade and turquoise for jewellery. The need for these products was the primary reason for the imperial expansion of the Aztecs, who gained the commodities through tribute or conquest. The goods were brought to market by pack animals.

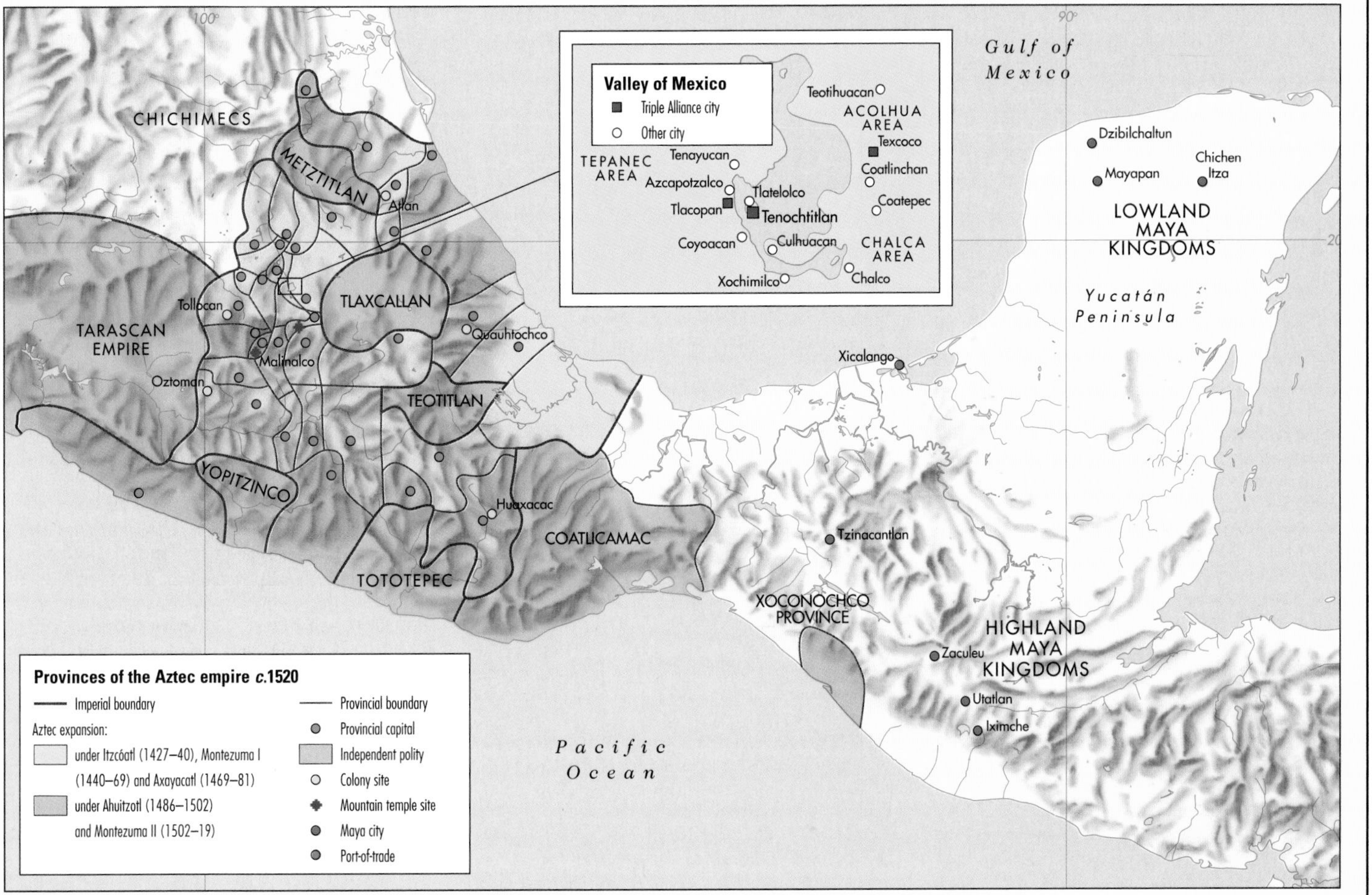

A

Valley of Mexico
■ Triple Alliance city
○ Other city

Provinces of the Aztec empire *c*.1520
—— Imperial boundary
Aztec expansion:
under Itzcóatl (1427–40), Montezuma I (1440–69) and Axayacatl (1469–81)
under Ahuitzotl (1486–1502) and Montezuma II (1502–19)
—— Provincial boundary
● Provincial capital
Independent polity
○ Colony site
✦ Mountain temple site
● Maya city
● Port-of-trade

▲ **The Aztec empire** covered much of present-day Mexico and an additional outlying province, known as Xoconochco, on the border with the lands of the Maya. The empire's capital, Tenochtitlán, and its two vacillating allies – Tlacopan and Texcoco – were just three of approximately 50 city-states with surrounding territories, mountain temple sites and satellite towns in the lake zone of the Valley of Mexico.

before the present one in which they were living, and that each previous sun had ended in universal destruction. The Aztecs regarded themselves as the "People of the Sun," whose duty it was to prevent a fifth catastrophe by keeping the Sun nourished with human blood. The rest of the Stone is an illustration of the Aztecs' solar calendar, which divided the year into 18 months of 20 days each, and a short month of five days. The astronomer-priests also had a 260-day divinatory cycle, based on 13 numbers and 20 signs repeated in series, which was used for casting horoscopes.

Tenochtitlán and Cortés

When the Spanish discovered the Aztec capital of Tenochtitlán in 1519, it had as many as 400,000 inhabitants and was by far the largest city in Mesoamerica. The city of Tlatelolco had been subsumed into Tenochtitlán through conquest, but both sites retained large temple complexes. At the heart of the capital, lay a massive central precinct in which four great causeways met. The precinct contained three huge pyramid temples, the largest of which was 30m (100ft) high. The royal palace had 300 rooms and covered *c*.4ha (10 acres). Tenochtitlán was divided into *c*.80 *capulli* (barrios), consisting of communities of extended family households, organized in a grid of streets and canals.

When the Spanish conquistador Hernan Cortés arrived in 1519, the Aztecs were reportedly poised to invade the northern Maya kingdoms on the Yucatán Peninsula. Cortés was greeted as an incarnation of Quetzalcóatl. Tenochtitlán's neighbouring city-states of Texcoco and Tlacopan, along with some 50 other cities in the lake zone of the Valley of Mexico, were uneasy allies, and the Spanish found many Native American subjects throughout the empire eager to revolt against the Aztecs. Cortés imprisoned Montezuma II and the leadership of Aztec resistance was assumed by Cuauhtémoc. In 1521 Tenochtitlán was razed by the Spanish, and Cuauhtémoc was executed by Cortés in 1525. The Aztec empire that had burned so fiercely for a century was extinguished.

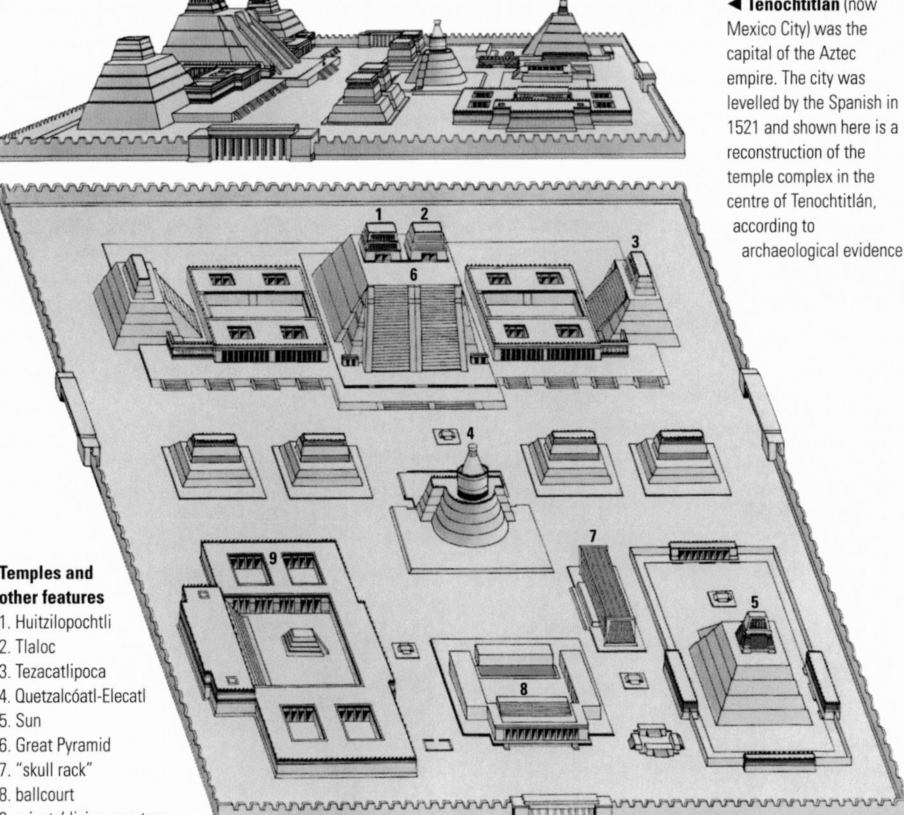

Temples and other features
1. Huitzilopochtli
2. Tlaloc
3. Tezacatlipoca
4. Quetzalcóatl-Elecatl
5. Sun
6. Great Pyramid
7. "skull rack"
8. ballcourt
9. priests' living-quarters

◀ **Tenochtitlán** (now Mexico City) was the capital of the Aztec empire. The city was levelled by the Spanish in 1521 and shown here is a reconstruction of the temple complex in the centre of Tenochtitlán, according to archaeological evidence.

A

► **Austrian Empire** In 1806 the Holy Roman Empire disintegrated. Emperor Francis II, however, retained much of the Habsburg territory and regained lands lost during the Napoleonic Wars at the Congress of Vienna (1815). Prince von Metternich's authoritarian policies led to the Revolutions of 1848 and the succession of Emperor Franz Joseph (r.1848–1916). Austria lost Lombardy (1859) to Sardinia and ceded Venetia to the new Kingdom of Italy following defeat in the Austro-Prussian War (1866). The weakness of the Austrian Empire forced the Ausgleich with Hungary in 1867. The Austro-Hungarian Empire occupied Bosnia-Herzegovina in the partition of the Balkans (1878). In 1881 Serbia became a client state of the Habsburg monarchy. The assassination (1914) of Austrian Archduke Francis Ferdinand precipitated the start of World War 1.

Aurignacian culture First humans in Europe who lived from *c.*40,000 to 28,000 years ago. *See also* PALAEOLITHIC

Auriol, Vincent (1884–1966) French statesman, principal founder and president (1947–54) of the Fourth Republic. He entered the National Assembly in 1914 and served as minister of finance (1936–37) under Leon BLUM. During World War 2, Auriol fought for the French Resistance before joining Charles DE GAULLE's government-in-exile. He was succeeded by René COTY.

Auschwitz (Oświęcim) Town in Poland. It was the site of a German CONCENTRATION CAMP during World War 2. A group of three main camps, with 39 smaller camps nearby, Auschwitz was Hitler's most "efficient" extermination centre. Between June 1940 and January 1945, more than 4 million people, mostly Jews, were murdered here. The buildings have been preserved as the National Museum of Martyrology. Together with the world's largest burial ground at Brzezinka (Birkenau), one of the other two main camps, Auschwitz is now a place of pilgrimage. Pop. (1989) 45,400. *See also* BELSEN; BUCHENWALD; DACHAU; HOLOCAUST, THE

Ausgleich (1867) Constitutional compromise made between Emperor FRANZ JOSEPH, who wished to centralize his empire, and the Hungarians, who wanted an independent nation-state. Ausgleich created the AUSTRO-HUNGARIAN EMPIRE and, although Franz Joseph remained king of Hungary, the Hungarians gained control of their country's internal affairs.

Austerlitz, Battle of (2 December 1805) Conflict in Bohemia during the NAPOLEONIC WARS (1803–15), fought between the French, led by NAPOLEON I, and Russian and Austrian forces led by Mikhail KUTUZOV and FRANCIS I respectively. One of Napoleon's greatest victories, it was also called the Battle of the Three Emperors. The Allies lost 15,000 men, while Napoleon lost 9000 men. *See* illustration, page 28

Austin, Stephen Fuller (1793–1836) US pioneer. On his father's death in 1821, he acquired a grant in the Spanish territory that was to become TEXAS. Austin settled the first English-speaking colony here and was followed by many other colonists. Mexico opposed this colonization, and Austin went to Mexico City to argue his case, but was arrested. On his return (1835), he became a leader in the fight for Texan independence.

Australia *See* country feature, page 28

Australian Council of Trade Unions (ACTU) Largest federation of trade UNIONS in Australia. Formed in 1927, the ACTU represents the unions at the Australian Conciliation and Arbitration Commission. The ACTU has more than 2.5 million members in 162 affiliated unions. It has a close relationship with the Australian LABOR PARTY.

Australian Gold Rush In 1851 gold was struck in Victoria and New South Wales. By the end of the 1850s Victoria accounted for 35% of the world's total gold production. In the 1850s the discoveries attracted *c.*340,000 emigrants to Australia, many settling in Melbourne. The influx transformed Australia's economy and society. *See also* EUREKA STOCKADE; WHITE AUSTRALIA POLICY

Australian Labor Party (ALP) *See* LABOR PARTY

Australopithecus *See* HUMAN EVOLUTION

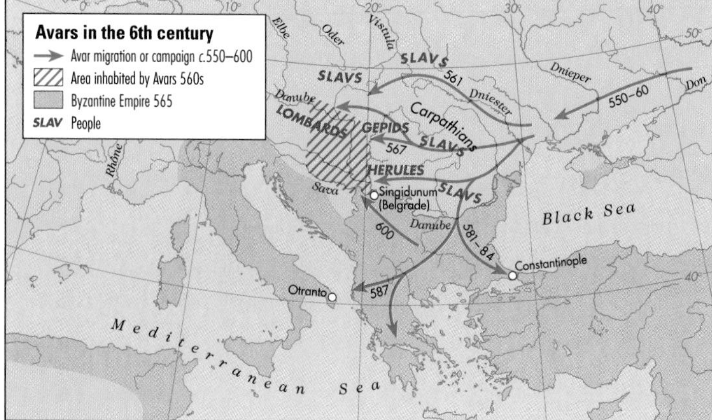

◄ **Avars** In the 560s the Avars settled in what is now Hungary. For the next 70 years they raided terrritories from the Rhine to Constantinople. The Avars caused havoc in the N of the Byzantine Empire and nearly captured Constantinople in 626. In the late 7th century the Avars were riven by factional strife, but the state limped on until it was finally crushed by Charlemagne in 796.

Austrasia (Ostrasia) Germanic N and E part of the Frankish kingdom during the MEROVINGIAN period. Divided into the semi-independent regions of Austrasia, NEUSTRIA and BURGUNDY in the 6th and 7th centuries, the lands were reunited under the Austrasian Pepin family, one of whom, CHARLES MARTEL, defeated Arab invaders at the Battle of POITIERS (732). From this new foundation sprang the CAROLINGIAN empire of CHARLEMAGNE. *See also* FRANKS

Austria *See* country feature, page 29

Austrian Empire (1806–67) Territories of the HABSBURG emperors between the fall of the HOLY ROMAN EMPIRE and the creation of the AUSTRO-HUNGARIAN EMPIRE. In 1806 Emperor FRANCIS II proclaimed himself Francis I, emperor of Austria. Francis and his foreign minister, Prince von METTERNICH, pursued a reactionary political programme. Despite the REVOLUTIONS OF 1848, authoritarian rule continued under FRANZ JOSEPH and Fürst zu SCHWARZENBERG. Loss of land and prestige in the AUSTRO-PRUSSIAN WAR (1866) forced the emperor to negotiate the AUSGLEICH of 1867.

Austrian Succession, War of the (1740–48) Conflict between Austria and Prussia for control of the German states, prompted by the succession (1740) of MARIA THERESA to the HABSBURG lands of her father, CHARLES VI. Maria Theresa was faced with counterclaims to her succession from PHILIP V of Spain, AUGUSTUS III of Poland, and Charles Albert, Elector of Bavaria. The war began with FREDERICK II of Prussia's occupation of the Habsburg province of SILESIA. In 1741, with French aid, Charles Albert captured Prague and was appointed Emperor CHARLES VII. In 1742, with British and Hungarian support, Maria Theresa launched a counter-offensive that overran BAVARIA. This first phase (the First Silesian War) was concluded by the Treaty of Berlin (1742) in which Prussia gained most of Silesia. The French army was forced to retreat from Prague and was defeated at the Battle of DETTINGEN (1743) by GEORGE II of Britain. In 1744 Frederick II launched a second invasion of Silesia, but was repulsed. The French won a major victory over the British at the Battle of FONTENOY (1745). George II and Frederick II signed the Convention of Hanover, in which Britain recognized Prussia's claims to Silesia in return for Frederick's support of the candidacy of the husband of Maria Theresa as Emperor FRANCIS I. War was formally ended by the Treaty of AIX-LA-CHAPELLE (1748). *See also* FRENCH AND INDIAN WARS

Austro-Hungarian Empire (1867–1918) Organization of the old AUSTRIAN EMPIRE into the Kingdom of HUNGARY and the Empire of AUSTRIA, also known as the "Dual Monarchy". The emperor of Austria and the king of Hungary were the same person, but each nation had its own parliament and controlled its internal affairs. This arrangement ignored other nationalist minorities and pleased neither the Hungarians, who wanted greater autonomy, nor the Austrians, many of whom wanted a realignment with other German states. After WORLD WAR I, Hungary and CZECHOSLOVAKIA declared their independence, Emperor CHARLES I abdicated, and Austria became a republic. *See also* FRANZ JOSEPH

Austro-Prussian War (1866) Conflict between PRUSSIA and AUSTRIA, also known as the Seven Weeks' War. Otto von BISMARCK engineered the war to further Prussia's supremacy in Germany and reduce Austrian influence. Defeat at SADOWA forced Austria out of the German Confederation, a federation of 39 German principalities set up by the Congress of VIENNA (1814–15) to replace the HOLY ROMAN EMPIRE. *See also* MOLTKE, GRAF VON

authoritarianism System of government that concentrates power in the hands of one person or small group of people not responsible to the population as a whole. Freedom of the press and of political organization are suppressed. Many authoritarian regimes arise from military takeovers. *See also* TOTALITARIANISM

Avars Mongolian people who settled near the River Volga in *c.*AD 460. One group remained there, and another moved to the Danube basin in the 6th century and settled in what is now Hungary. Their domain extended from the Volga to the Baltic Sea, and they exacted huge tributes

A

from the BYZANTINE EMPIRE during this time. In 796 the Avars were finally crushed by CHARLEMAGNE.

Averröes (Abu-al-Walid Ibn-Rushd) (1126–98) Islamic philosopher. In 1182 Averröes became physician to the caliph of Marrakesh, but in 1195 was banished to Seville, Spain, for advocating reason over religion. His major work, *Incoherence of the Incoherence*, defends NEOPLATONISM and ARISTOTLE. He exercised a powerful influence on Christian thought that persisted into the Renaissance. *See also* AQUINAS, SAINT THOMAS; SCHOLASTICISM

Avignon City at the confluence of the rivers Rhône and Durance, Vaucluse department, Provence, SE France. A thriving city under Roman rule, Avignon was the seat of the popes during their exile from Rome during the BABYLONIAN CAPTIVITY. The papacy held Avignon until 1791, when it was annexed to France by the Revolutionary authorities. Pop. (1990) 83,939. *See also* GREAT SCHISM

Avignon popes During the BABYLONIAN CAPTIVITY (1309–77), popes who resided in AVIGNON instead of ROME. The papal court was established in Avignon by CLEMENT V. In 1348 the city was bought by CLEMENT VI. The GREAT SCHISM (1378–1417) occurred shortly after the court returned to Rome. *See also* PAPACY

Awami League Political party in East Pakistan (now BANGLADESH), formed (1949) to promote East Pakistani independence. In 1953 Sheikh MUJIBUR RAHMAN became leader. In 1968 the Awami League demanded a federal government for Pakistan, Muhammad AYUB KHAN responded by imprisoning the leaders of the League. In 1969 Ayub Khan was succeeded by YAHYA KHAN. In 1970 elections the Awami League won 160 out of 162 seats in East Pakistan. In 1971 Mujibur called for full autonomy. Yahya Khan arrested him and banned the Awami League. A bloody civil war ensued. India's intervention in support of the League led to the break-up of the republic and the creation of Bangladesh. Mujibur became prime minister of the new republic. In 1975 Mujibur was assassinated in a military coup and the Awami League remained in opposition until 1996, when Hasina Wazed became prime minister.

Axis Powers Term applied to Germany and Italy after they signed the Rome-Berlin Axis (October 1936). It included Japan after it joined them in the TRIPARTITE PACT (September 1940). Other states that joined the Axis were Hungary and Romania (1940), and Bulgaria (1941). The Axis Powers opposed the ALLIES in WORLD WAR 2.

Axum *See* AKSUM

Aymara Major tribe of NATIVE SOUTH AMERICANS who live in the highlands of Bolivia and Peru. By 1500 they had been brought into the INCA empire, which was subsequently conquered by the Spanish. Today, the Aymara number *c.*1,360,000.

Ayub Khan, Muhammad (1907–74) Pakistani general and statesman, president (1958–69). After the partition of British India, he assumed control of the army in East Pakistan (now BANGLADESH). In 1951 Ayub Khan became commander in chief of the army and served as minister of defence (1954–56). In 1958 he led the military coup that overthrew Iskander Mirza. Ayub Khan was confirmed as president in a 1960 referendum. His administration was notable for its economic modernization and political reforms. The failure of his regime to deal with poverty and social inequality forced him to resign. His daughter, Hasina Wazed (1947–), was prime minister (1996–).

Ayutthaya City on the River Chao Phraya, S central Thailand. Built on the site of an ancient KHMER settlement, in the 14th century Ayutthaya became the capital of an extensive THAI kingdom. In 1569 Ayutthaya was sacked by Burmese forces, but was restored and flourished as a international trading centre in the 17th century. In 1767 the city was again sacked by the Burmese and the capital transferred to BANGKOK in 1782. Ayutthaya retains some rare examples of early Thai architecture, notably the 16th-century royal palace. Pop. (1990) 61,185.

Ayyubid Muslim dynasty founded by SALADIN (1138–93) and named after his father Ayyub, who had unified Syria. Saladin overthrew FATIMID rule in Egypt, creating a SUNNI theocracy capable of defeating the CRUSADES. After Saladin's death, his lands were divided among relatives and the dynasty gradually declined and was swept from power by the MAMLUKS in 1250. A lasting legacy of the Ayyubids is the *madressa*, an institute for higher education based around study of the KORAN. *See also* SHIITE

Azad, Abdul Kalam (1888–1958) Indian statesman, president (1940–46) of the Indian National CONGRESS. He was imprisoned several times for his part in "Mahatma" GANDHI's civil-disobedience campaign against the British. As president of Congress, Azad negotiated terms of independence with Stafford CRIPPS and Field Marshal WAVELL. He served as minister for education (1947–58) in India's first post-colonial cabinet.

Azaña (y Díaz), Manuel (1880–1940) Spanish statesman, prime minister (1931–33) and president (1936–39). In 1936 he became president of the Second Republic. Azaña was titular head of the Republican government during the Spanish CIVIL WAR (1936–39).

Azande Peoples of Sudan, Democratic Republic of Congo, and Central African Empire. The Azande religion is totemic and includes ancestor-worship. In the 18th-century, the Ambomu, led by the Avongara clan, formed a series of Azande kingdoms in central Africa.

Azerbaijan *See* country feature

Azikiwe, (Benjamin) Nnamdi (1904–96) Nigerian statesman, president (1963–66). When Nigeria achieved independence in 1960, Abubakar BALEWA took the post of prime minister. In 1963 Nigeria became a federal republic and Azikiwe became president. He was overthown in a military coup. Initially Azikiwe supported the IBO cause in BIAFRA during the Nigerian civil war (1967–70), but in 1969 he switched allegiance to the federal government.

Aznar, José María (1953–) Spanish statesman, prime minister (1996–). He became president of the Popular Party (PP) in 1989. Aznar's victory in the 1995 elections over incumbent prime minister Felipe González Márquez ended 13 years of socialist rule in Spain. His minority administration tried to tackle government corruption and enacted reforms that reduced unemployment and brought economic prosperity to Spain. Aznar took Spain into the European single currency (1999) and won a landslide victory in the 2000 elections.

Aztecs *See* feature article, pages 30–31

AZERBAIJAN

AREA: 86,600sq km (33,436sq mi)
POPULATION: 7,398,000
CAPITAL (POPULATION): Baku (1,100,000)
GOVERNMENT: Federal multiparty republic
ETHNIC GROUPS: Azerbaijani 83%, Russian 6%, Armenian 6%, Lezgin, Avar, Ukrainian, Tatar
LANGUAGES: Azerbaijani (official)
RELIGIONS: Islam (Shiite Muslim)
GDP PER CAPITA (1995): US$1460

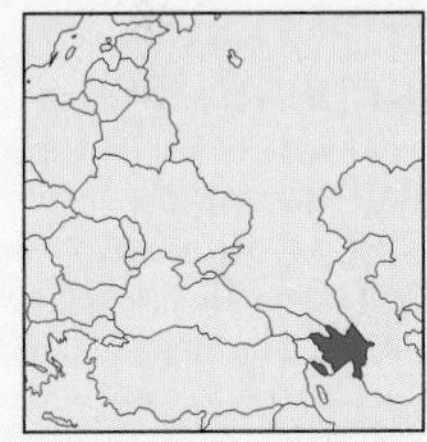

Republic in SW Asia. Azerbaijan includes the autonomous republic of NAKHICHEVAN on the Iran frontier, totally cut off from the rest of the state by ARMENIA. In 642 Arab armies introduced Islam, but most modern Azerbaijanis are descendants of Iranian and Turkic peoples who migrated to the area from the E by the 9th century. Azerbaijan was ruled by the MONGOLS between the 13th and 15th centuries and then by the Persian SAFAVID dynasty. By the early 19th century it was under Russian control.

After the RUSSIAN REVOLUTION (1917) attempts were made to form a Transcaucasian Federation made up of Armenia, Azerbaijan and GEORGIA. When these attempts failed, Azerbaijanis set up an independent state, but Soviet forces occupied the area in 1920. In 1922 Azerbaijan became part of the Soviet Republic of TRANSCAUCASIA. In 1936 it gained the status of a separate socialist republic within the SOVIET UNION. In 1991, with the dissolution of the Soviet Union, Azerbaijan gained independence. In 1993 Gaidar Aliev was elected president and Azerbaijan joined the COMMONWEALTH OF INDEPENDENT STATES (CIS). Since independence, economic progress has been slow, largely because of civil unrest in NAGORNO-KARABAKH, a large enclave within Azerbaijan where the majority of the population are Christian Armenians. In 1992 Armenia occupied the area between its E border and Nagorno-Karabakh, while ethnic Armenians took over Nagorno-Karabakh itself. The ensuing war killed thousands of people and resulted in large migrations of both Armenians and Azerbaijanis. In 1994 a ceasefire left *c.*20% of Azerbaijan in Armenian hands.

B

Baader-Meinhof (Red Army Faction) German terrorist group led by Andreas Baader (1943–77) and Ulrike Meinhof (1934–76). In the early 1970s, the group carried out a bombing campaign designed to overthrow capitalism and US imperialism in West Germany. In 1972 twenty of the gang's leaders were arrested, including Baader and Meinhof, both of whom died in prison.

Ba'ath Party Arab political party, founded in 1943. Its major objectives are socialism and Arab unity. It is strongest in Syria and Iraq, where militaristic elements of the Ba'ath Party seized power in 1963 and 1968 respectively. *See also* Hussein, Saddam; Assad, Hafez al-

Babeuf, François-Noël (1760–97) (Gracchus) French political journalist and revolutionary. He called for radical agrarian reform, such as the abolition of feudal duties. Babeuf was arrested in the Reign of Terror (1793). In 1794 he attacked the Jacobins in the journal *Le Tribun du peuple*. In 1795 Babeuf was imprisoned for his criticisms of the Thermidorians. In 1796 he formed a secret society, the Conspiracy of Equals, to overthrow the Directory and establish a form of "communism". The plot was betrayed and Babeuf was tried and guillotined. *See also* French Revolution

Babington, Anthony (1561–86) English architect of the Babington Plot (1586), a conspiracy against Elizabeth I of England, which aimed to restore Roman Catholicism by replacing Elizabeth with Mary, Queen of Scots. Sir Francis Walsingham intercepted Babington's correspondence with Mary and the Plot was foiled. Babington was executed.

Babism (Babi faith) Muslim religious sect founded (1844) in Shiraz, Iran, by Ali Muhammad (*c.*1819–50), the self-proclaimed prophet Bab (Arabic, "gate"). Babists believed in the imminent coming of the Promised One. In 1848 they declared secession from Islam, but their rebellion against the Safavid shah was crushed and their founder was executed in 1850. *See also* Baha'i

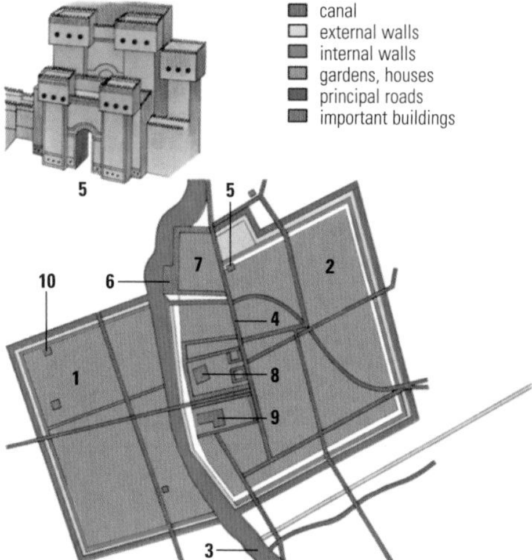

▲ **Babylon** The excavated, sophisticated layout we see today was created mainly by Nebuchadnezzar II (r. *c.*604–561 BC). Old city (1) and new (2) are separated by the River Euphrates (3), and contained within two fortification walls, reinforced by a moat (10). The ritual Processional Way (4) enters the new city through the Ishtar Gate (5), passing a fortress (6) and the main citadel complex (7) of administration and garrison buildings, palaces and vaulted Hanging Gardens. Skirting the Etemenanki enclosure with its ziggurat (8) – possibly that of Babel – it turns W past the temple of Marduk (9) and crosses the five-pier bridge to the old city.

Babi Yar Ravine near Kiev, Ukraine, in which *c.*34,000 Jews were massacred by Nazi German soldiers in 1941. The massacre is commemorated in an eponymous poem (1961) by Yevgeny Yevtushenko and a novel (1966) by Anatoly Kuznetsov.

Babur (1483–1530) Founder of the Mughal Empire of India (1526–30), a descendant of Tamerlane and Genghis Khan, b. Zahir ud-Din Muhammad. In 1495 Babur (Turk. "tiger") became ruler of Fergana. He engaged in a conflict for control of Samarkand, but ultimately lost Samarkand and Fergana. In 1504 Babur captured Kabul and carved out a new kingdom for himself in Afghanistan. From here, he invaded India, defeating the sultan of Delhi at the Battle of Panipat (1526) and capturing Delhi. In 1527 Babur defeated the Rajputs at the Battle of Khanua and occupied Agra (his future capital). His victory over the Afghans at the Battle of Ghaghara (1529) laid the foundations for 200 years of Mughal rule in N India. He also wrote a work of courtly literature entitled Babur-nama, which celebrated his empire. He was succeeded by his son, Humayun.

Babylon (Hebrew, Babel) Ancient city on the River Euphrates in Mesopotamia (near modern Baghdad, Iraq), capital of the Babylonian Empire. In the 18th century BC Hammurabi made it the capital of his kingdom of Babylonia. In *c.*1570 BC Babylon fell to the Kassites, who controlled the city for more than 400 years and made Babylon's patron god, Marduk, the supreme deity in Mesopotamia. In 1158 BC Babylon was sacked by the Elamites. Nebuchadnezzar I (r.1124–1103) defeated the Elamites and established a dynasty that lasted for more than a century. From the 10th century BC to the 7th century BC, the Assyrians and Chaldaeans competed for control of the city. In *c.*689 BC Babylon was destroyed by the Assyrian king Sennacherib. The city was rebuilt by his successors, Esarhaddon and Ashurbanipal. In *c.*626 BC Nabopolassar made Babylon the centre of the Chaldaean dynasty. His son, Nebuchadnezzar II, began a vast rebuilding project that made Babylon the largest city of the ancient world. New buildings included the Hanging Gardens, one of the Seven Wonders of the World, and the Tower of Babel. In 538 BC Babylon fell to Cyrus II (the Great) and became a provincial capital of the Achaemenid empire. *See also* Assyria; Babylonian Captivity; Chaldaea; Seleucid

Babylonia *See* feature article

Babylonian Captivity (*c.*586 BC–538 BC) Period of the Jews' enforced exile in Babylon. In 586 BC Nebuchadnezzar II captured Jerusalem and deported most of the Jewish population to Babylon. Many Jewish religious institutions, such as synagogues, were founded in the period of exile, and parts of the Hebrew Bible also date from this time. The Captivity ended (*c.*538 BC) with the reformation of a Palestinian Jewish state by Cyrus II (the Great). The term was later applied to the exile of the popes at Avignon (1309–77). *See also* Diaspora; Great Schism

Bach, Alexander, Freiherr von (1813–93) Austrian politician. Although Bach initially supported the Revo-

BABYLONIA

Ancient region and empire of Mesopotamia, based on the city of Babylon. By *c.*1900 BC the Amorites had unified the city-states of Sumer and Akkad to form the Babylonian Empire. Located in SE Mesopotamia between the Tigris and Euphrates rivers (now S Iraq), the Empire was based around a dozen cities. Babylonian society was predominantly agricultural and divided into three classes – the landowners, merchants and priests; the artisans and peasants; and the slaves. The greatest Amorite ruler was Hammurabi, who became ruler of a united kingdom of Babylonia in 1760 BC. In *c.*1595 BC the Empire declined under the impact of Hittites and Kassites. In *c.*1157 BC the Kassites were supplanted by the Elamites, who in turn were expelled by Nebuchadnezzar I. From the 9th century BC to the 7th century BC, Babylonia was dominated by Assyria. The death of the last Assyrian king, Ashurbanipal, brought the Chaldaean dynasty to power, and the defeat of Egypt at the Battle of Carchemish (605 BC) marked the resurgence of Babylonia. During the reign (*c.*605–562 BC) of Nebuchadnezzar II, the New Babylonian (Chaldaean) Empire extended to Syria and Palestine and the Babylonian Captivity took place. Babylonia was increasingly threatened by the Persian empire, however, and in 538 BC it was captured by Cyrus II (the Great) and subsumed into the Achaemenid Empire. *See also* Chaldaea; Elam; Sumeria

▼ ***The Tower of Babel*** (1563) by Pieter Bruegel (the Elder). According to the Bible (Genesis 11), God disrupted the construction of the Tower, which was intended to reach heaven, by confusing the language of the builders.

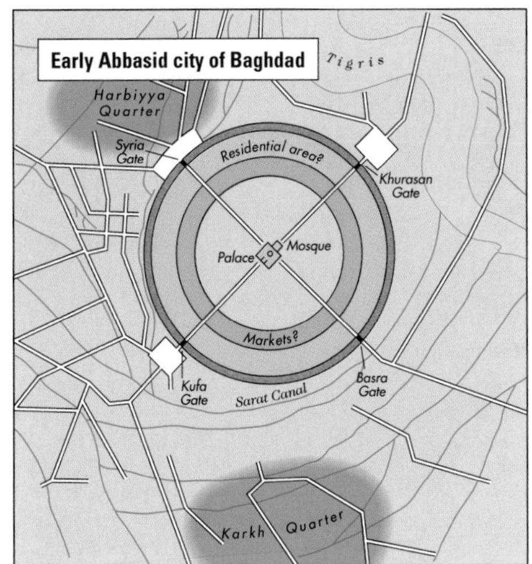

▲ **Baghdad** was built near the ancient Sasanian capital city of Ctesiphon in Mesopotamia. It was constructed in a circular form, with the Great Mosque and caliph's palace – symbolizing the close association of religious and political power – located together at its centre.

LUTIONS OF 1848, he joined the government after they had been suppressed, becoming first minister of justice (1848) and then minister of interior (1849–59). He initiated the Bach system, a policy of centralized rule designed to thwart nationalism and to encourage Germanization. In 1855 Bach signed a concordat with the Roman Catholic Church, giving it extensive rights within the AUSTRO-HUNGARIAN EMPIRE. He was dismissed from office after defeat in the war with Italy and was appointed ambassador to the Vatican (1859–67).

Bacon, Francis, Viscount St Albans (1561–1626) English philosopher and statesman. He was an important prosecution witness in the trial (1601) of the 2nd Earl of ESSEX. In 1618 JAMES I appointed him lord chancellor. In 1621 Bacon was fined and imprisoned for corruption and his political career was over. Bacon is chiefly remembered for his early advocacy of the scientific method through a form of inductive empiricism. Bacon entertained the idea of cataloguing all useful knowledge in his *Advancement of Learning* (1605) and *Novum Organum* (1620). *The New Atlantis* (1627) discusses his philosophy as practised in an imaginary nation. His ideas inspired the founding (1660) of the Royal Society.

Bacon's Rebellion (1676) Revolt in colonial Virginia, led by Nathaniel Bacon (1647–76). The colonists' rebellion was prompted by high taxes, the low value of tobacco, and Governor William BERKELEY's failure to defend the frontier from attack by Native Americans. After leading the defence of the frontier, Bacon was elected to the House of Burgesses but was arrested by Berkeley. Upon his release, he led a march on Jamestown and Berkeley fled. Berkeley's attempt to recapture the capital ended in failure and the razing of the city. Bacon died of a fever, however, and the rebellion collapsed. Berkeley exacted bloody revenge.

Bactria Ancient region between the Hindu Kush and the River Oxus, NE Afghanistan. It gave its name to the two-humped camel, which was used to carry goods along the SILK ROAD. In the 6th century BC, Bactria became part of the ACHAEMENID empire. In the 4th century BC, it was conquered by ALEXANDER III (THE GREAT). Under the SELEUCID dynasty, Hellenistic culture and administrative systems spread throughout the region. The Graeco-Bactrian kings were the first to establish links across Central Asia with China. In the 2nd century BC, Bactria was occupied by the Yuezhi. Under the KUSHANS, the region became a centre of Buddhism. Islam was introduced in the 7th century.

Baden-Powell of Gilwell, Robert Stephenson Smyth, 1st Baron (1857–1941) British general. He gained fame withstanding the Siege of MAFEKING (1899–1900) against the Afrikaners. In 1908 Baden-Powell founded the Boy Scout movement. His sister **Agnes** (1858–1945) founded the Girl Guides (1910). His wife, Lady Olave (1889–1977), did much to promote these movements worldwide. *See also* SOUTH AFRICAN WARS

Badoglio, Pietro (1871–1956) Italian general and statesman. He was Italy's chief negotiator in the armistice talks at the end of World War 1. In 1925 Badoglio was appointed chief of staff by Benito MUSSOLINI. He led the invasion of Ethiopia (1935). In 1940 Badoglio resigned after a series of defeats by the Greeks in World War 2. He became prime minister (1943–44) after the fall of Mussolini. Badoglio negotiated a truce and declared war on Nazi Germany.

Baffin, William (1584–1622) English navigator and explorer. He took part in several expeditions (1612–16) in search of the NORTHWEST PASSAGE. Baffin discovered the Canadian Arctic seaways, the island now named after him, and Lancaster Sound. An outstanding navigator, he published a method of determining longitude by the stars, using nautical tables.

Bagehot, Walter (1826–77) English economist and writer. Editor of *The Economist* (1860–77), Bagehot is chiefly remembered for his influential treatise *The English Constitution* (1867).

Baghdad Capital of Iraq, on the River Tigris. Established in 762 as capital of the ABBASID caliphate, it became a centre of Islamic civilization and a focus of caravan routes between Asia and Europe. It has a notable 13th-century Abbasid palace. Baghdad was repeatedly invaded by the Mongols from the 13th century, then ruled by the Ottomans from 1534 up to World War 1. In 1921 Baghdad became the capital of newly independent Iraq. It was badly damaged in the GULF WAR (1991). Pop. (1987 est.) 3,850,000.

Baghdad Pact (1955) Joint defence agreement signed by Turkey, Iran, Iraq, Pakistan and Britain. It was intended to act as a bulwark against Soviet expansion in the Middle East. In 1959 Iraq withdrew, the headquarters were moved to Ankara, Turkey, and the name was changed to the CENTRAL TREATY ORGANIZATION (CENTO).

Baghdad Railway Rail link between Europe and the Middle East. In 1902 a German company was granted permission by the Ottoman Empire to extend the line from Turkey to Baghdad (now in Iraq). Britain, Russia and France objected, seeing the railway as a threat to their own interests in the Middle and Far East. The resulting tension contributed to the hostility leading up to World War 1.

Bagot, Sir Charles (1781–1843) British colonial administrator, governor general of Canada (1841–43). Bagot was minister to France (1814) and to the United States (1815– 20). He helped negotiate the RUSH-BAGOT CONVENTION (1817). Bagot was appointed governor general of Canada by Robert PEEL.

Baha'i Religion founded (1867) by BAHAULLAH as an outgrowth of BABISM. Its headquarters are in Haifa, Israel. It seeks world peace through the unification of all religions and stresses a simple life dedicated to serving others. It recognizes Bahaullah as the latest prophet of God.

Bahamas Small independent state in the West Indies, in the W Atlantic, SE of Florida. It consists of *c.*700 islands, 2000 cays and numerous coral reefs. The largest island is Grand Bahama; the capital is Nassau (on New Providence). San Salvador island is traditionally believed to have been the first stop of Christopher Columbus in his quest for the New World (1492). In 1670 CHARLES II of England granted the islands to six lord proprietors of Carolina, but development was continually hindered by pirates. By 1729 Britain had assumed direct control, expelling militants and restoring civil order. Held briefly by Spain (1782) during the American Revolution (1775–83), the islands were given back to England by the Treaty of Versailles (1783) in exchange for E Florida. In 1834 slavery was abolished. In 1963 a new constitution brought parliamentary government. In 1973 the Bahamas became an independent nation. *See* WEST INDIES map

Bahaullah (1817–92) Iranian religious leader, founder of the BAHA'I faith, b. Mirza Husayn Ali Nuri. He embraced BABISM in 1850 but broke away in 1867, proclaiming himself Bahaullah ("the Glory of Allah"), the Promised One foretold by Bab. His *Book of Certitude* is the sacred text of Baha'i.

Bahrain Emirate archipelago in the Persian (Arabian) Gulf, sw Asia. It consists of 34 small islands and the largest island of Bahrain. In the 7th century Arabs introduced Islam. Bahrain was ruled by Portugal (1521–1602) and Persia (1602–1783). Since 1783 Bahrain has been governed by sheikhs of the Khalifa family. From 1861 to 1971 Bahrain was a British protectorate. Oil was discovered in 1932, and the sheikhdom led the regional development of oil production. In August 1971 Bahrain gained independence and Sheikh Isa became emir. It was a founder member (1981) of the Gulf Cooperation Council (GCC) and maintains a close relationship with Saudi Arabia. During the IRAN-IRAQ WAR (1980–88), Bahrain supported Iraq. It was a member of the international coalition against Iraq in the GULF WAR (1991). During the 1990s Bahrain has suffered civil unrest by the majority Shiite population.

BAHAMAS
AREA: 13,878sq km (5358sq mi)
POPULATION: 278,000
CAPITAL (POPULATION): Nassau (172,196)
GOVERNMENT: Constitutional monarchy
ETHNIC GROUPS: African, Afro-European
LANGUAGES: English
RELIGIONS: Christianity (mainly Anglican)
GDP PER CAPITA (1995): US$14,710

Bailly, Jean Sylvain (1736–93) French politician and astronomer. He wrote *History of Astronomy* (1775–87). In 1789 Bailly was elected president of the NATIONAL ASSEMBLY. From 1789 to 1791 he served as mayor of Paris. On 17 July 1791, Baker allowed the national guard to open fire on demonstrators. He subsequently fell out of political favour and was executed during the REIGN OF TERROR. *See also* FRENCH REVOLUTION

Baird, John Logie (1888–1946) Scottish electrical engineer, inventor of television. In 1926 Baird demonstrated the first working television to members of the Royal Institution, London. In 1928 he transmitted to a ship at sea, and in 1929 was granted experimental broadcasting facilities by the British Broadcasting Corporation (BBC). His 240-line, part-mechanical television system was used for the world's first public television service by the BBC in 1936. In 1937 it was superseded by Marconi's fully electronic scanning.

Bajazet *See* BAYEZID I (THE THUNDERBOLT); BAYEZID II (THE JUST)

Baker, James Addison (1930–) US statesman, secretary of state (1989–92). He served as chief of staff (1981–85) and secretary of the treasury (1985–88) under Republican President Ronald REAGAN. In 1988 Baker managed the successful presidential election campaign of George BUSH. As secretary of state, he helped build an international coalition against Iraq's invasion of Kuwait (1990). In 1992 he supervised President Bush's unsuccessful bid for re-election. *See also* GULF WAR

Baker, Sir Samuel White (1821–93) English explorer. In 1861 Baker and his wife, Florence, set off to discover the source of the River Nile. He found (1864) and named Lake Albert. In 1869 he led an expedition to the Nile equatorial region on behalf of the Ottoman viceroy of Egypt. He became governor general of the region and over the next four years suppressed the slave trade there.

Baker v. Carr (1962) Landmark US Supreme Court

BAHRAIN
AREA: 694sq km (268sq mi)
POPULATION: 586,000
CAPITAL (POPULATION): Manama (140,401)
GOVERNMENT: Constitutional monarchy
ETHNIC GROUPS: Bahraini
LANGUAGES: Arabic, English, Farsi, Hindi, Urdu
RELIGIONS: Sunni Muslim, Shiite Muslim
GDP PER CAPITA (1995): US$13,400

decision holding that apportionment of state legislatures and redistricting to assure proper representation were issues that should be decided in federal courts. The Court overruled *Colegrove v. Green* (1946).

Bakke case (Regents of the University of California v. Bakke) US Supreme Court case (1978) involving Allan Bakke, who was refused admission (1972) to the University of California at Davis Medical School, despite his excellent academic record. He sued the university on a charge that he had been passed over in favour of less qualified minority students. The Court ruled that Bakke had been a victim of reverse discrimination and must be admitted to the university.

Bakr, Ahmad Hassan al- (1914–82) Iraqi statesman and general, president (1968–79). After serving as a colonel in World War 2, he played a key part in the overthrow and execution (1963) of President Abdul Karim KASSEM. He became prime minister under Colonel Abdul Salem Arif, but was dismissed (1964) because of Ba'athist sympathies. The coup of 1968 gave Hassan al-Bakr the presidency and put the BA'ATH PARTY back in office. He was succeeded as president by Saddam HUSSEIN.

Bakunin, Mikhail Alexandrovich (1814–76) Russian political philosopher. Bakunin became a believer in violent revolution while in Paris (1848) and was active in the First INTERNATIONAL until expelled by Karl MARX in 1872. His approach, known as revolutionary ANARCHISM, repudiates all forms of governmental authority as fundamentally at variance with human freedom and dignity. In *God and the State* (1882), Bakunin argued that only natural law is consistent with liberty.

Balaguer, Joaquín (1907–) Dominican statesman, president of the Dominican Republic (1960–62, 1966–78, 1986–96). After the assassination (1961) of the dictator Rafael TRUJILLO MOLINA, Balaguer was unable to control the political factions and was deposed in a military coup. In 1966, with the help of the US military, he returned to defeat Juan Bosch in the presidential election. Balaguer was re-elected in 1970 and again in 1974, after a political campaign marred by violence. His rule promoted economic stability but increased social repression. He lost the 1978 and 1982 elections but was re-elected in 1986 and 1994.

Balaklava, Battle of (25 October 1854) Inconclusive conflict in the CRIMEAN WAR (1853–56). The British, French and Turks held off a Russian attack on the supply port of Balaklava, Crimea. The Battle is remembered for the disastrous CHARGE OF THE LIGHT BRIGADE, led by Lord CARDIGAN, and immortalized in a poem (1855) by Alfred Tennyson.

Balboa, Vasco Núñez de (1475–1519) Spanish conquistador, the first European to see the Pacific Ocean. He went to Hispaniola (1500) and to Darién (Panama) in 1520. In September 1513, accompanied by locals, Balboa crossed the isthmus and saw the Pacific, which he called the South Sea. He was later executed on a false charge.

Baldwin I (1171–1205) Count of FLANDERS and HAINAUT, first Latin emperor of CONSTANTINOPLE (1204–05). The capture of Constantinople (now ISTANBUL) from the Byzantine Christians by the Western armies of the Fourth CRUSADE led to the partition of the BYZANTINE EMPIRE. Baldwin was elected ruler of the newly formed Latin state.

Baldwin II (1217–73) Last Latin emperor of CONSTANTINOPLE (1228–61). He was overthrown by MICHAEL VIII (PALAEOLOGUS), who restored the BYZANTINE EMPIRE. Baldwin fled into exile in the West.

Baldwin I (1058–1118) King of Jerusalem (1100–18). A military leader of the First CRUSADE (1096–99), he demanded the crown of Jerusalem in return for his exploits. Baldwin consolidated and strengthened the Latin states of the Middle East.

Baldwin II (d. 1131) King of Jerusalem (1118–31). His cousin, BALDWIN I of Jerusalem, appointed him Count of Edessa (1100–18). Baldwin was captured (1104) by the Seljuks and held ransom until 1108. He then recaptured Edessa from his regent, Tancred. He was again captured by the Turks (1123–24) while king of Jerusalem. After release, Baldwin expanded his kingdom. He was succeeded by his son-in-law, Fulk of Anjou.

Baldwin, Robert (1804–58) Canadian statesman, co-premier of Canada (1842–43, 1847–51). He led the movement for representative government. In 1841 Baldwin and Louis LAFONTAINE, formed an alliance that united Upper and Lower Canada and the pair formed a coalition government under Sir Charles BAGOT. The second Baldwin-LaFontaine administration (the "great ministry") enacted a wide range of reforms, including reorganization of local government for Ontario and revision of the justice system.

Baldwin (of Bewdley), Stanley, 1st Earl (1867–1947) British statesman, prime minister (1923–24, 1924–29, 1935–37), cousin of the writer Rudyard Kipling. Baldwin was chancellor of the exchequer (1922–23) before succeeding Bonar LAW as prime minister and leader of the CONSERVATIVE PARTY. Baldwin responded to the GENERAL STRIKE (1926) by passing the Trades Disputes Acts (1927), which made any subsequent general strikes illegal. In the ABDICATION CRISIS, Baldwin opposed EDWARD VIII's marriage to Wallis Simpson and secured the king's abdication (1936). His APPEASEMENT of European FASCISM is often cited as a cause of Britain's lack of preparedness at the start of World War 2.

▲ **Sirimavo Bandaranaike** became the world's first woman prime minister in 1960. She exemplifies how the dynastic tradition in South Asian politics has enabled several women to achieve supreme political power.

Balewa, Sir Abubakar Tafawa (1912–66) Nigerian statesman, prime minister (1957–66). A founder and deputy president of the Northern People's Congress, Balewa continued as prime minister after Nigeria gained independence in 1960. He was assassinated in a military coup.

Balfour, Arthur James Balfour, 1st Earl of (1848–1930) British statesman, prime minister (1902–05), b. Scotland. Balfour succeeded his uncle, the Marquess of SALISBURY, as prime minister and leader of the CONSERVATIVE PARTY. His government introduced educational reforms (1902), but the Conservatives split over the tariff reform proposed by Joseph CHAMBERLAIN. Balfour resigned and the Conservatives lost the ensuing general election. He returned to the cabinet in the coalition governments of Herbert ASQUITH and David LLOYD GEORGE. As foreign secretary, he issued the BALFOUR DECLARATION (1917).

Balfour Declaration (1917) Letter written by British foreign minister Arthur BALFOUR to the British Zionist Federation pledging support for the settlement of Jews in PALESTINE. Jews were admitted to the area when it became a British mandate under the League of Nations after World War 1. *See also* ZIONISM

Baliol, John de *See* BALLIOL, JOHN

Balkan states Group of countries in the Balkan Peninsula, SE Europe, consisting of ALBANIA, BOSNIA-HERZEGOVINA, BULGARIA, CROATIA, GREECE, MACEDONIA, ROMANIA, SERBIA and European TURKEY. From the 2nd century BC the region was part of the ROMAN EMPIRE. It subsequently became part of the BYZANTINE EMPIRE. From the 6th century AD it was invaded by SLAV peoples and in the 7th century by the BULGARS. A number of Slavic states were created before the Ottomans began to conquer the region in the late 14th century. The individual countries regained their independence in the 19th and early 20th centuries.

Balkan Wars (1912–13) Two wars involving the BALKAN STATES and the OTTOMAN EMPIRE. In the **First** Balkan War, the Balkan League (Bulgaria, Greece, Serbia and Montenegro) rapidly conquered large swathes of the Ottoman Empire. In December 1912 an armistice was signed, but war resumed (January 1913) after the YOUNG TURKS' coup. The Ottomans lost most of their European empire and were forced to grant ALBANIA independence and cede MACEDONIA to the Balkan League. The **Second** Balkan War arose

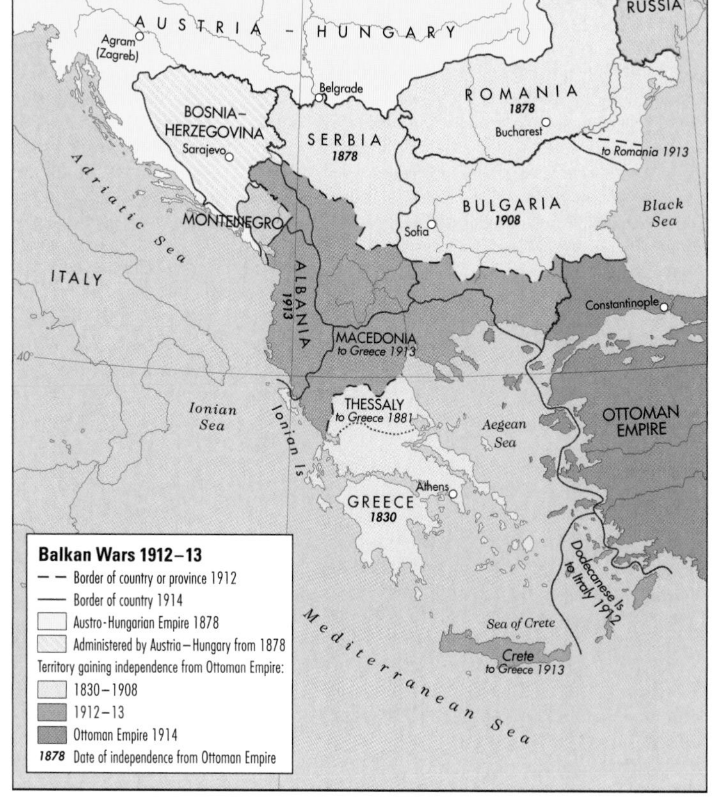

► **Balkan Wars (1912–13)** In October 1912 Montenegro, Greece, Serbia and Bulgaria declared war on the Ottoman Empire. A second war then erupted between Bulgaria and Serbia over Macedonia. These two Balkan Wars inflamed existing tensions between Serbia (supported by Russia) and Austria-Hungary and thus contributed to the outbreak of of World War 1.

out of a dispute between Greece, Serbia and Bulgaria over the division of Macedonia. In August 1913 Bulgaria was defeated. By the Treaty of Bucharest (1913), Greece gained S Macedonia, Serbia gained KOSOVO and parts of N and central Macedonia, and Romania gained S Dobruja. Bulgaria turned to Austria for support and the heightened tension in the Balkans led directly to WORLD WAR I.

Ball, John (d.1381) English priest, a leader of the PEASANTS' REVOLT. He was imprisoned in 1360 and excommunicated (1376) for his radical preaching. In 1381 Ball was released from Maidstone Prison by the followers of Wat TYLER, but he was recaptured and executed at St Albans.

Balliol, Edward (d.1364) King of Scotland (1332, 1333–56), son of John BALLIOL. In 1332, backed by English nobles, he invaded Scotland from his family's estate in Normandy. Edward defeated the Earl of Mar, regent for DAVID II, at the Battle of Dupplin Moor (August 1332) and was crowned at Scone. In December 1332 he was forced to flee by Sir Archibald Douglas, but EDWARD III of England defeated Douglas at the Battle of HALIDON HILL (1333) and reinstated Balliol. In 1356 he surrendered his throne to Edward III.

Balliol, John (*c.*1249–1315) King of Scotland (1292–96), father of Edward BALLIOL. Balliol's claim to the Scottish throne over his rival, ROBERT I (THE BRUCE), was upheld by EDWARD I of England. In return, Edward claimed feudal overlordship of Scotland and Balliol grudgingly acquiesced. In 1295 Balliol formed an alliance with France, which resulted in Edward's invasion (1296) of Scotland. Balliol was defeated and imprisoned (1296–99) in England. He died in exile in Normandy.

Baltic states Countries of ESTONIA, LATVIA and LITHUANIA, on the E coast of the Baltic Sea. The region was settled by various tribes in the 7th century AD, but until the 20th century it remained mostly under Danish, Russian or Polish rule. Following the Russian Revolution of 1917, each state achieved independence, but in 1940 they came under the control of the Soviet Union. The Baltic states regained their independence following the dissolution of the Soviet Union in 1991.

Baltimore City and port in N Maryland, United States, at the mouth of Patapsco River, on Chesapeake Bay. It was founded (1729) by the Irish baronial family of Baltimore as a tobacco port. In the 19th century Baltimore became an important shipbuilding centre. In 1830 the first passenger-carrying railway in the United States, the Baltimore and Ohio Railroad, opened here. Pop. (1990) 736,014.

Bancroft, George (1800–91) US diplomat and historian. In 1845 he was appointed secretary of the navy. Bancroft established the US Naval Academy at Annapolis, Maryland. He served as ambassador to Britain (1846–49) and to Germany (1867–74). Bancroft's *History of the United States* (10 vols, 1834–74) is a classic account.

Bancroft, Hubert Howe (1832–1918) US historian. With the aid of a team of collaborators, Bancroft compiled a 39-volume history of the American West.

Banda, Hastings Kamuzu (*c.*1902–97) Malawian statesman, president (1966–94). Banda guided Nyasaland to independence as Malawi (1964), establishing an autocratic regime. In 1971 he was named president-for-life. Banda was the only African leader to maintain friendly relations with South Africa's APARTHEID regime. In 1994 he was forced to accept multiparty elections, in which he was defeated.

Bandaranaike, Sirimavo Ratwatte Dias (1916–) Sri Lankan stateswoman, prime minister (1960–65, 1970–77, 1994–). Following the assassination (1959) of her husband, Solomon BANDARANAIKE, she assumed control of the Sri Lanka Freedom Party and became (1960) the world's first woman prime minister. Her daughter, **Chandrika Bandaranaika Kumaratunga** (1945–), was elected president in 1994, and Sirimavo returned as prime minister.

Bandaranaike, Solomon West Ridgeway Dias (1899–1959) Ceylonese statesman, prime minister (1956–59). He made Sinhalese the official language and founded the Sri Lanka Freedom Party to unite nationalists and socialists. He was assassinated and his wife, Sirimavo BANDARANAIKE, succeeded him.

Bandung Conference (1955) International meeting in Bandung, Indonesia. Representatives of 29 non-aligned countries of Asia and Africa, including China, met to express their united opposition to COLONIALISM and to gain recognition for the so-called "Third World" countries. *See also* NON-ALIGNED MOVEMENT

Bangkok Capital and chief port of Thailand, on the E bank of the River Menam (Chao Phraya). Bangkok became the capital in 1782 when King RAMA I built a royal palace here. It quickly became Thailand's largest city. The Grand Palace (including the sacred Emerald Buddha) and more than 400 Buddhist temples (*wats*) are notable examples of Thai culture and help make Bangkok a popular tourist destination. It has a large Chinese minority. During World War 2, it was occupied by the Japanese. Pop. (1993) 5,572,712

Bangladesh *See* country feature, page 38

Bank of England Britain's central banking institution, founded (1694) by a group of London merchants. In the 18th century, it funded the British state during the wars with France. Nationalized in 1946, it regulates foreign exchange, issues bank notes, advises the government on monetary matters, and acts as the government's financial agent. It is situated in Threadneedle Street, City of London. The governor of the Bank of England is appointed by the national government. In 1997 the Bank of England was given operational responsibility for setting interest rates.

Bank of the United States Two US national banks. The first was established in 1791. Although it was soundly operated, autonomous state-banking interests defeated its rechartering in 1811. Following the WAR OF 1812, a second national bank was chartered by Congress in 1816. There was much opposition to its power to establish local branches. President Andrew JACKSON supported the Bank's opponents and vetoed its rechartering. The Bank became obsolete in 1836. *See also* FEDERAL RESERVE SYSTEM

Bannockburn, Battle of (23–24 June 1314) Major conflict between EDWARD II of England and ROBERT I (THE BRUCE), fought at Bannockburn, central Scotland. The *c.*20,000-strong English army, advancing on Stirling, was intercepted by the Scots and massacred in the river and surrounding marshes. Edward was fortunate to escape with his life. Robert (the Bruce) became a national hero.

bantustan *See* APARTHEID

Bao Dai (1913–97) Emperor of ANNAM (1932–45), chief of state of VIETNAM (1949–55), b. Nguyen Vinh Thuy. Bao Dai cooperated with the Vichy French and Japanese during World War 2. In 1945 he was forced to resign when the Viet Minh, led by HO CHI MINH, captured INDOCHINA. In 1949 the French regained control and Bao Dai became head of the new state of Vietnam. French defeat (1954) at DIEN BIEN PHU led to partition, and Bao Dai agreed to the appointment of Ngo Dinh DIEM as prime minister. Diem established a republic, and Bao Dai was forced into exile.

Baptist Member of various Protestant and Evangelical sects who practise baptism of believers and regard immersion as the only legitimate form sanctioned by the New Testament. Like the ANABAPTISTS, to whom they have an affinity but no formal links, Baptists generally reject the practice of infant baptism, insisting that initiates must have freedom of thought and expression and must already be

BARBADOS

AREA: 430sq km (166sq mi)
POPULATION: 264,000
CAPITAL (POPULATION): Bridgetown (108,000)
GOVERNMENT: Constitutional monarchy
ETHNIC GROUPS: African, Afro-European
LANGUAGES: English, Bajan
RELIGIONS: Christianity (mainly Anglican)
GDP PER CAPITA (1995): US$10,620

believers. Baptists originated among English dissenters of the 17th century but have spread worldwide. They cherish the principle of religious liberty. There is no official creed, no hierarchy, and individual churches are autonomous. Today, there are *c.*31 million Baptists worldwide.

Bar, Confederation of (1768) Patriotic Polish, anti-Russian association of Catholic nobles. When Protestants and Greek Orthodox Christians were granted equal rights with Polish Catholics, the Confederation started an uprising that led to civil war and the first Partition of POLAND (1772).

Barak, Ehud (1942–) Israeli statesman, prime minister (1999–). He was chief of staff (1991–94) of the Israeli Defence Forces before joining the cabinet of Yitzhak RABIN. Barak succeeded Shimon PERES as leader of the Labour Party. Despite the optimism that greeted Barak's landslide victory over Binyamin NETANYAHU in the 1999 elections, there was little immediate progress in the peace process with the Palestinians. In May 2000 Barak presided over the removal of Israeli troops from S Lebanon.

Baranov, Alexander Andreievich (1747–1819) Russian fur trader in Alaska. From 1790 to 1799 he headed a Russian fur trading company in the Kodiak Islands. In 1799 Baranov became governor of the Russian-American Company. He greatly expanded Russian penetration of North America, establishing posts as far south as Fort Ross, California, which brought great profits to the Company.

Barbados Constitutional monarchy in the Windward Islands, WEST INDIES. A member of the COMMONWEALTH OF NATIONS, Barbados' warm climate has encouraged the growth of its two largest industries: sugar cane and tourism. Barbados was settled by the British in 1627 and dominated by British plantation owners (using African slave labour until the abolition of slavery) for the next 300 years. Barbados was a member of the short-lived West Indies Federation (1958–62). In 1966 Barbados gained independence and Errol BARROW became prime minister. In 1994 Owen Arthur was elected prime minister. *See* West Indies map

Barbarians Term given to all tribes regarded as uncivilized by the ancient Greeks and Romans. It is more specifically used to apply to the Germanic and Slavonic tribes that invaded the Roman Empire after *c.*50 BC and eventually overthrew it in the 5th century AD. *See also* ALEMANNI; ANGLES; FRANKS; GOTHS; JUTES; SAXONS; VANDALS

Barbarossa *See* FREDERICK I (BARBAROSSA)

Barbarossa (Redbeard) Name given by Christians to two Muslim privateers from the Aegean, **Aruj** (d.1518) and Khizr, or **Khayr ad-Din** (d.1546). Aruj was killed in battle

◄ **Bangkok** The Royal Grand Palace in Bangkok was built (1782–85) during the reign of King Rama I. Many temples were built within the complex by subsequent rulers, including the great royal temple (Wat Phra Kaeo), which houses the Emerald Buddha. Nineteenth-century additions saw a fusion of Western and Eastern architectural styles, as in the Italian-influenced National Assembly Hall. Today, the Palace is used by the king solely for ceremonial purposes.

B

against the Spanish, but Khayr ad-Din seized Algiers from Spain (1533), took Tunis (1534), raided Christian coasts and shipping, and gained control of the Barbary states. He acknowledged the Ottoman sultan as his overlord, and from 1533 to 1544 Khayr ad-Din was the commander of the fleet of SULEIMAN I (THE MAGNIFICENT). His forces were finally defeated by Spain and Italy in the famous naval Battle of LEPANTO (1571).

Barbary states Historic coastal region of N Africa, now occupied by LIBYA, ALGERIA, TUNISIA and MOROCCO. They were at one time Roman and later independent Muslim states (7th–15th centuries). With the exception of Morocco, they became infamous pirate states under Turkish control (16th–19th centuries). The pirates raided Mediterranean trade for booty and prisoners to ransom. After many attempts, Europe and the United States finally subdued them in the early 19th century.

Barbie, Klaus (1913–91) German NAZI PARTY leader, chief of the GESTAPO in France during World War 2. He was known as the "butcher of Lyon" for his persecution and murder of Jews and French Resistance fighters. Barbie sent thousands of people to their deaths in AUSCHWITZ. After the War, he worked for US counter-intelligence, escaping to Bolivia in 1951. In 1987 Barbie was captured, brought back to Lyon and sentenced to life imprisonment.

Barcelona City and port in NE Spain, capital of CATALONIA; Spain's second-largest city. Reputedly founded by the Carthaginian Barca family, it was ruled by Romans, Visigoths and Moors, and by the late Middle Ages it had become a major trading centre. Barcelona is the focus of radical political and Catalan separatist movements. The autonomous Catalan government based here (1932–39) was swept away by the Spanish Civil War. Historic buildings include the Gothic Cathedral of Santa Eulalia (13th–15th century), the Church of the Sagrada Familia designed by Antonio Gaudí (begun 1882) and a monument to Christopher Columbus. Modern Barcelona is the cosmopolitan, cultural capital of Spain. Pop. (1991) 1,625,542.

Barebone's Parliament (Parliament of the Saints, July–December 1653) Last Parliament of the English COMMONWEALTH. Successor to the RUMP PARLIAMENT, it was named after a prominent member, Praise-God Barebone, and representatives were hand-picked by Oliver CROMWELL and the NEW MODEL ARMY chiefs. Religious disputes ruined its effectiveness. It voted its own dissolution and handed over power to Cromwell as Lord Protector.

Barents, Willem (d.1597) Dutch navigator and explorer. He made three expeditions (1594–97) in search of the Northeast Passage. On his third voyage, Barents discovered the Arctic island of Svalbard and, crossing the sea now named after him, reached Novaya Zemlya, Russia. The ship was trapped by ice, and the Dutch sailors built a shelter; most survived until the following year, when they escaped, but Barents died before they reached safety.

Bar Kokhba, Simon (d. 135) Leader of the Jewish rebellion against the Romans in Jerusalem (131–135). At first successful, Bar Kokhba was finally slain in battle at Bethar.

Barnardo, Thomas John (1845–1905) British philanthropist, b. Ireland, who founded the Dr Barnardo homes for destitute children. In 1867 Barnardo founded the East End Mission for orphan children, the first of his famous homes. These spread rapidly through the United Kingdom and still flourish today.

Barnburners Radical group of the United States' DEMOCRATIC PARTY in New York state during the 1840s. The Barnburners were opposed to the extension of slavery and demanded radical action to counter corporate abuses. Splits in their ranks appeared at the 1848 Democratic convention, when they supported the nomination of Martin VAN BUREN for president and Charles Francis ADAMS of the FREE SOIL PARTY for vice president.

Barnet, Battle of (14 April 1471) Conflict in the English Wars of the ROSES, in which EDWARD IV defeated the Earl of WARWICK ("the king-maker") and thus prepared for the restoration of the House of YORK later in the year.

Barons' Wars (1215–17, 1263–67) In English history, two conflicts between the barons and kings JOHN and HENRY III respectively. Despite John's acceptance of the MAGNA CARTA, many barons continued openly to defy the king and offered the crown to Prince Louis of France (later LOUIS VIII). After John's death, the French and baronial forces were defeated at Lincoln (May 1217). The **Second** Barons' War was prompted by Henry's renouncement (1261) of the provisions of Oxford (1258) and Westminster (1259), which had proposed he rule through a council of barons rather than rely on favourites. The barons, led by Simon de MONTFORT, decided to force the king to submit and defeated Henry's army at the Battle of LEWES (1264). Henry's son, the future EDWARD I, formed an army which defeated the barons, and de Montfort was killed at the Battle of EVESHAM (1265).

baroque Style of art and architecture prevalent in Europe from the early 17th century to the mid-18th century. Baroque marked a distinct departure from the studied refinements of mannerism. It developed from COUNTER-REFORMATION demands for a propagandist art that would stimulate a sense of faith. The decorative integration of architecture, sculpture and painting was calculated to overwhelm the spectator with its sense of drama, grandeur and sensuality. The architecture was monumental with façades heavily decorated by stucco ornament and free-standing sculpture. Baroque palaces, such as that at VERSAILLES, were designed to display the power and wealth of the monarchy and aristocracy. The first statement of baroque architecture was the façade of the Church of Santa Susanna, Rome, designed (*c*.1597) by Carlo Maderno (1556–1629). Maderno and Gian Lorenzo Bernini (1598–1680) worked on ST PETER'S, Rome. Francesco Borromini (1599–1667) designed the San Carlo alle Quattro Fontane, Rome (1634-41). In Spain and the Spanish colonies, José Benito Churriguera (1665–1725) combined baroque form and Spanish detail to create the distinctive Churrigueresque style. During the Englightenment period, baroque evolved into the lighter style of Rococo. Major baroque painters include Caravaggio, Annibale Carracci, Peter Paul Rubens, Claude Lorrain, Sir Anthony Van Dyck and José de Ribera. Major baroque composers include J.S. Bach, George Frideric Handel and Antonio Vivaldi.

Barras, Paul François Jean Nicolas, Vicomte de (1755–1829) French revolutionary leader. He joined the JACOBINS and was a member of the NATIONAL CONVEN-

BANGLADESH

AREA: 144,000sq km (55,598sq mi)
POPULATION: 119,288,000
CAPITAL (POPULATION): Dhaka (3,397,187)
GOVERNMENT: Multiparty republic
ETHNIC GROUPS: Bengali 98%, tribal groups
LANGUAGES: Bengali (official)
RELIGIONS: Sunni Muslim 87%, Hinduism 12%, Buddhism, Christianity
GDP PER CAPITA (1995): US$1380

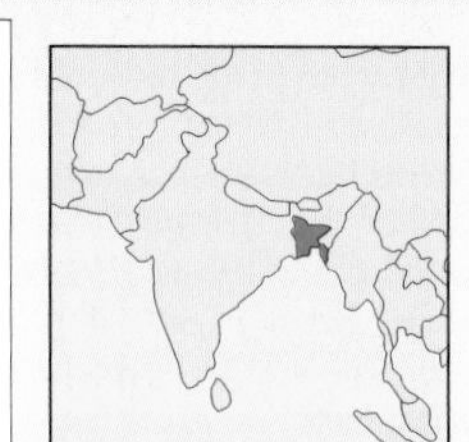

Republic in S Asia. The early history of Bangladesh is synonymous with that of BENGAL. In the 3rd century BC BUDDHISM was introduced by ASHOKA, but was supplanted by HINDUISM after the fall of the MAURYAN empire. The Bengali language assumed a distinct form in the 7th century. In the 13th century ISLAM became the dominant religion in E Bengal. In 1576 Bengal became part of the vast MUGHAL EMPIRE under AKBAR I (THE GREAT).

From 1757 Bengal was under the control of the English EAST INDIA COMPANY. In 1905 the British partitioned Bengal into Eastern Bengal and Western Bengal. Eastern Bengal (roughly equivalent to modern Bangladesh) was mainly Muslim. Partition was bitterly opposed by Western Bengal and the province was reunited in 1912. As chief minister (1937–43) of Bengal, Faz al-Huq campaigned for an independent Muslim state in Eastern Bengal but was ousted by loyalists of Muhammad Ali JINNAH.

In 1947 British India was partitioned between the mainly Hindu India and Muslim PAKISTAN. Pakistan consisted of two provinces, West Pakistan and East Pakistan (now Bangladesh). The two provinces were separated by *c*.1500km (1000mi) of Indian territory. The majority population of East Pakistan complained of ethnic and economic discrimination by West Pakistan. In 1954 elections in East Pakistan, the MUSLIM LEAGUE was defeated by a coalition between Fazl al-Haq and the AWAMI LEAGUE. In 1958 the military, led by Muhammad AYUB KHAN, seized power. The generals brutally suppressed opposition in East Pakistan. In 1969 Ayub Khan was succeeded by Muhammad YAHYA KHAN. In 1970 elections, the Awami League, led by MUJIBUR RAHMAN (Sheikh Mujib), won a landslide victory in East Pakistan. In March 1971 the League demanded autonomy and civil war ensued. During nine months of fighting, more than one million East Bengalis were killed and 10 million fled over the border into India.

In December 1971 the Indian army intervened on behalf of the Awami League and Pakistan was forced to surrender. Bangladesh gained independence and Mujib became prime minister. Mass persecution of Biharis ensued and many were publicly executed or placed in refugee camps. In 1974 famine claimed more than 15,000 lives in Bangladesh, and Mujib assumed authoritarian powers. In 1975 he was assassinated and the military, led by General Zia ur-Rahman, imposed martial law. In 1981 Zia ur-Rahman was assassinated and General Hossain Muhammad Ershad took control. During the 1980s Ershad faced a wave of strikes and demonstrations against martial law and the parlous state of the economy. In 1990 he was forced to resign. Elections in 1991 were won by the Bangladesh National Party (BNP), led by Begum Khaleda Zia ur-Rahman, wife of Zia ur-Rahman. In 1996 elections the Awami League, led by Sheikh Hasina Wazed, daughter of Mujib, returned to power. In 1998 Khaleda Zia was charged with corruption. In 1998 monsoons killed *c*.1500 people and left 23 million people homeless.

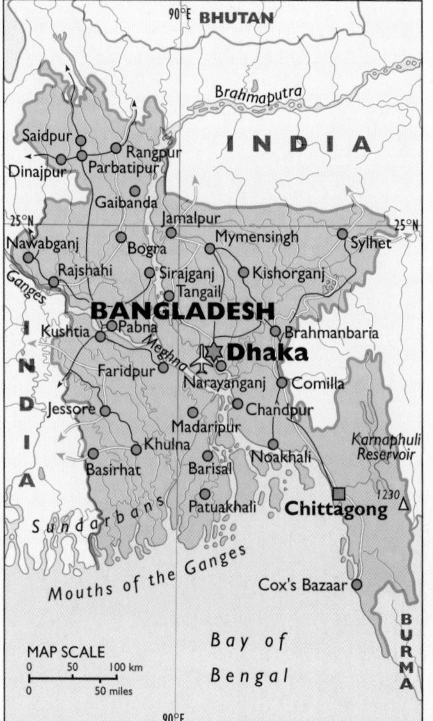

TION. Barras led the coup of 9 Thermidor (July 1794) which brought down Maximilien ROBESPIERRE. By turning over his troops to the command of NAPOLEON during a royalist uprising in Paris (1795), he helped advance Napoleon's career. He was a member of the DIRECTORY (1795–99). *See also* THERMIDORIAN REACTION

Barré, (Muhammad) Siad (1919–95) Somalian dictator and soldier, president (1969–91). In 1966 he became commander in chief of the army. In 1969 Barré led a military coup against Abdirashid Ali Shermarke. His authoritarian presidency imposed a policy of "SCIENTIFIC SOCIALISM". In the 1980s famine and civil war led to the virtual collapse of central authority in Somalia. In 1991 rebel forces captured the capital, Mogadishu, and Barré was forced into exile.

Barrow, Errol Walton (1920–87) Barbadian statesman, prime minister (1966–76). He was co-founder of the Democratic Labour Party (DLP) and served as the island's premier (1961–66). Barrow was the first prime minister of an independent BARBADOS.

barrow In archaeology, a prehistoric burial mound. In North America, barrows were built by Native Americans known as MOUND BUILDERS. In Europe, barrows are usually either long or round. **Long** barrows were built in the NEOLITHIC period and consist of a wooden chamber or a vault built of stones, roofed with stone slabs and covered with soil; many were used for multiple burials. **Round** barrows primarily date from the early BRONZE AGE, but some in England were built as late as Roman and Saxon times. Usually containing a single body, they vary in diameter from 1.5m to 50m (4.5–160ft).

Barth, Heinrich (1821–65) German explorer and geographer. In 1845 Barth set out on a two-year expedition through N Africa, Asia Minor and Greece. Barth was a member of a British-sponsored exploration (1851–56) of the Sahara. His *Travels and Discoveries in North and Central Africa* (1857–58) is considered a standard text.

Barton, Clara (Clarissa Harlowe) (1821–1912) US humanitarian and founder (1882) of the American National RED CROSS. Barton cared for wounded soldiers during the American Civil War, and was active in the International Red Cross during the FRANCO-PRUSSIAN WAR (1870–71). She was responsible for the "American amendment" at the GENEVA CONVENTION (1884), which enabled the Red Cross to be active in peace-time emergencies.

Barton, Sir Edmund (1849–1920) Australian statesman, first prime minister of the Commonwealth of Australia (1901–03). He led the various federation conventions that resulted in the drafting (1897–98) of a new, federal constitution. Barton persuaded the British to accept the constitution and was appointed prime minister. He disliked the confrontational politics of the Australian Parliament and resigned (1903) to become a senior High Court judge.

Baruch, Bernard Mannes (1870–1965) US financier and government adviser. A securities expert and speculator, he became a millionaire before the age of 30. As chairman of the War Industries Board (1918–19), Baruch exercised great power over the US economy. He was an economic adviser at the Versailles Conference after World War 1 and to all US presidents until his death. As US representative to the United Nations' Atomic Energy Commission, Baruch presented a plan for international control of atomic energy (1946); it was vetoed by the Soviet Union.

Basel, Council of (1431–49) Seventeenth ECUMENICAL COUNCIL, convoked at Basel, Switzerland. It instituted church reforms and conciliated the HUSSITES in Bohemia. Conflict with Pope EUGENE IV led the pope to denounce the Council (1437). In 1439 the Council declared Eugene deposed and chose an antipope, Amadeus of Savoy, as Pope Felix V. In 1449 Felix resigned and the Council was dissolved.

Basil I (the Macedonian) (*c.*813–86) Byzantine emperor (r.867–86), founder of the Macedonian dynasty. Emperor Michael III assisted Basil in his rise to power. After Michael designated him co-emperor, Basil had his former patron murdered. His most effective policies concerned the conversion of the BULGARS to Orthodox Christianity, military campaigns against the Paulician religious sect in Asia Minor, and a revision of Roman legal codes.

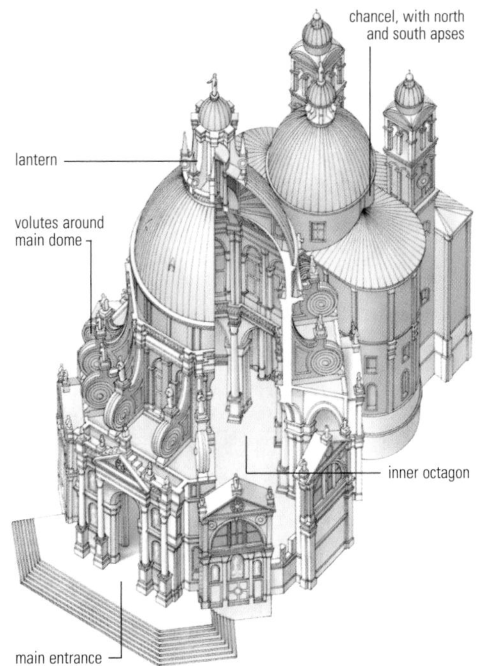

▲ **baroque** The octagonal, baroque Church of Santa Maria della Salute (1631–87) at the entrance to the Grand Canal, Venice, is the masterwork of architect Baldassare Longhena (1582–1682). It was commissioned by the republic in thanksgiving for deliverance from the plague.

Basil II (Bulgaroctonus) (*c.*958–1025) Byzantine emperor (976–1025), whose nickname means "Bulgar-slayer". One of its most able rulers, Basil reigned during the heyday of the BYZANTINE EMPIRE. He is best known for his military victory (1014) over the Bulgarian tsar Samuel, which brought the entire Balkan peninsula under Byzantine control. Basil celebrated his victory by blinding *c.*15,000 Bulgar prisoners.

Basil the Great, Saint (*c.*329–79) Doctor of the Church and one of the four Fathers of the Greek Church. He founded a monastic community and was ordained (370) bishop of Caesarea, Cappadocia. Basil established the dominance of the NICENE CREED and was a fierce opponent of ARIANISM. He is thought to have composed the *Liturgy of St Basil*, still used in the Eastern ORTHODOX CHURCH. His feast day is 2 January in the West; 1 January in the East.

Basket Makers *See* ANASAZI

Basques Indigenous people of the W Pyrenees in N Spain and SW France, numbering *c.*3.9 million. Their language is not related to any other European tongue. Throughout history the Basques have tenaciously maintained their cultural identity. The kingdom of NAVARRE, which existed for 350 years, was home to most of the Basques. After its dissolution in 1512, many Spanish Basques enjoyed a degree of political autonomy. This autonomy was removed in 1873, and Basque unrest followed. A Basque separatist organization, ETA, launched a campaign of terror for an independent state. In 1998 ETA announced a cease-fire and opened negotiations with the Spanish government. The cease-fire was called off in November 1999.

Bastille Fortress and prison in Paris, France, built in the late 14th century and destroyed during the FRENCH REVOLUTION. Political prisoners were incarcerated here, and it became a symbol of royal oppression. On 14 July 1789, now a national holiday in France, a revolutionary mob stormed the Bastille and released its seven prisoners. The prison was pulled down soon afterwards.

Batavian Republic (1795–1806) Name given to the NETHERLANDS when it was captured by French forces in the FRENCH REVOLUTIONARY WARS (1792–1802). As the kingdom of Holland (1806–10), it was ruled by Louis BONAPARTE. *See also* NAPOLEONIC WARS

Bath Spa city and world heritage site on the River Avon, SW England. Its hot springs were discovered in the 1st century AD by the Romans, who named the city *Aquae Solis* ("Waters of the Sun"). The bathing complex and temple are the finest Roman remains in Britain. Bath flourished as a centre for the cloth and wool industries. In the 18th century (under the direction of Beau Nash), the city became a fashionable resort. John Wood transformed the city into a showcase for Georgian architecture. The Royal Crescent, Queen Square and the Circus are among his notable achievements. Pop. (1991) 79,900.

Báthory, Stephen *See* STEPHEN BÁTHORY

Batista y Zaldívar, Fulgencio (1901–73) Cuban dictator and soldier, president (1940–44, 1952–58). In 1933 he led a successful military uprising (the "sergeants revolt") against Carlos Manuel de Céspedes and became *de facto* ruler of Cuba. In his first term as president, Batista secured economic growth and personal wealth. In 1944 he retired to Florida, United States. In 1952 Batista ousted President Prío Scorrás and established authoritarian rule. In 1959 his corrupt regime was overthrown by Fidel CASTRO and Batista fled into exile.

Batlle y Ordóñez, José (1856–1929) Uruguayan statesman, president (1903–07, 1911–15). His narrow electoral victory (1903) plunged Uruguay into civil war (1904–05) between his Colorado Party and the Blanco Party. In his second term, Batlle implemented a package of liberal reforms, such as universal adult suffrage and the abolition of the death penalty. His concern about the power of the executive led to the creation (1918) of a national executive council.

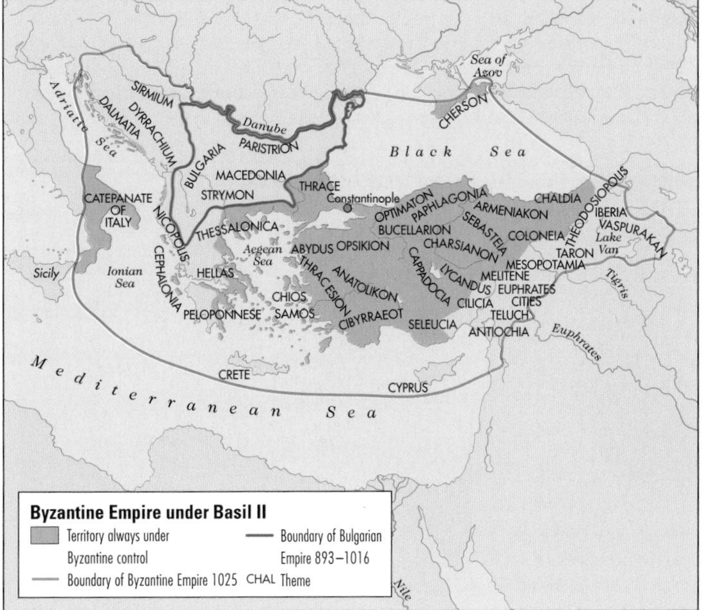

◀ **Basil II (Bulgaroctonus)** The conquests of Basil II led to the expansion of the Byzantine Empire in the 11th century. With the aid of Kievan Rus and Viking troops, Basil II regained control of the Balkan Peninsula and S Italy, and by the end of his reign the Empire had doubled in size. Subsequent emperors failed to maintain the boundaries that Basil II had established, and the Empire began to decline.

► **Bayeux Tapestry (*c*.1080)** The Tapestry (strictly speaking an embroidery) depicts the history of the Norman Conquest of England (1066). This section of the tapestry depicts Breton cavalry forces floundering in marshy ground having failed to break the English line of foot-soldiers located on the top of a small hill. The English soldiers are always shown with large moustaches.

Battenberg, Louis Alexander (1854–1921) British admiral, b. Austria. In 1884 he married Princess Alice, granddaughter of Queen Victoria. In 1917 Battenberg renounced his German titles, anglicized his name to Mountbatten and was created 1st Marquess of Milford Haven. His youngest son was Louis MOUNTBATTEN and his grandson is Prince PHILIP, Duke of Edinburgh.

Batthyány, Lajos (1806–49) Hungarian statesman, first prime minister of Hungary (1848–49). He was appointed prime minister by Emperor Ferdinand I. Batthyány failed to reach a compromise between the Habsburg monarchy and Hungarian independence leaders and ended up sympathizing with the REVOLUTIONS OF 1848. He was arrested by the Austrians and executed.

Battle of... *See* second part of name

Batu Khan (d.1255) Khan of the GOLDEN HORDE, grandson of GENGHIS KHAN and leader of the Mongol army that invaded Europe (1237–41). Batu Khan overcame the Russian states, sacked Kiev (1240) and ravaged Poland, Moravia and Hungary. He threatened to overrun Western Europe after victory at the Battle of Mohi (1241), but was diverted eastwards by a sudden succession crisis. Batu Khan settled himself with establishing a state in s Russia, based around Sarai Batu on the River Volga.

Baudouin (1930–93) King of Belgium (1951–93). During World War 2 he was interned by the Germans. After the war, Baudouin joined his father, LEOPOLD III, in exile (1945–50) in Switzerland. In 1951 his father abdicated in favour of Baudouin. In 1960 he granted independence to the Belgian Congo. He was succeeded by his brother, Albert II.

Bavaria (Bayern) Largest state in Germany; the capital is MUNICH. The region was inhabited by the Celts until the Roman invasion (15 BC). In the 6th century AD, the Romans were ousted by the Germanic tribe of Baiovari, who formed the Duchy of Bavaria. In 788 it was captured by CHARLEMAGNE and incorporated into the CAROLINGIAN empire. From the 9th century to the 12th century, the dukes of Bavaria constantly rebelled against imperial authority. In 1180 Emperor FREDERICK I (BARBAROSSA) gave the duchy to Otto of WITTELSBACH. The Wittelsbach dynasty ruled Bavaria until 1918. In 1214 Otto's son, Louis I, acquired the Palatinate of the Rhine. Bavaria was a stronghold of Catholicism during the Reformation. Duke MAXIMILIAN I was rewarded with the post of Elector for his support of the Habsburgs during the THIRTY YEARS' WAR (1618–48). In 1871 Bavaria was incorporated into the German Empire, but retained great autonomy. In 1919 a communist revolution was crushed by the German army and Bavaria became part of the WEIMAR REPUBLIC. Bavaria was the power base for the NAZI PARTY under Adolf HITLER. The first Nazi concentration camp was built at DACHAU and the NUREMBERG Rallies were staged in the state. After World War 2, Bavaria lost the Palatinate and became (1948) part of the Federal Republic of West Germany. Area: 70,553sq km (27,256sq mi). Pop. (1993) 11,863,313.

Bavarian Succession, War of the (1778–79) Conflict between Austria and Prussia. Charles Theodore of the Palatinate, who succeeded Maximilian III Joseph as Elector of Bavaria, ceded Lower Bavaria and part of the Palatinate to Austria. His heir, Charles of Zweibrücken, influenced by FREDERICK II of Prussia, protested at the transfer. War was declared, but there were only a few skirmishes. By the Treaty of Teschen (1779) Austria renounced its claims to Bavaria, but retained the Innviertel, a small region on its border.

Baxter, Richard (1615–91) English Puritan clergyman. He was ordained into the Church of England in 1638. As minister at Kidderminster (1641–60), Baxter allied himself with the Puritans and advocated the importance of pastoral counselling. Although he sided with Parliament in the English CIVIL WAR (1642–48), Baxter opposed the execution of the king (1649). He supported the RESTORATION (1660), but was persecuted for his nonconformist views and imprisoned (1685) by Judge JEFFREYS. Baxter gained many of his religious demands with the accession of WILLIAM III (OF ORANGE) and MARY II (1689).

Bayar, Celâl (1884–1986) Turkish statesman, president (1950–60). He supported the establishment (1923) of the Turkish republic under Mustafa Kemal (later ATATÜRK). In 1937 Bayar became prime minister, but resigned on the death of Atatürk (1939). In 1946 he co-founded the Democratic Party. As president, Bayar created a more market-led economy. He was arrested during the military coup of 1960 and sentenced to death. Bayar was pardoned in 1966.

Bayard, Pierre de Terrail, Seigneur de (1473–1524) French military hero of the ITALIAN WARS (1494–1559). In 1521, against overwhelming odds, he held Mézières, NE France, against an attack by Emperor CHARLES V. He was known as the *Chevalier sans peur et sans reproche* ("Knight without fear or reproach").

Bayeux Tapestry (*c*.1080) Strip of linen embroidered in wool, measuring 70m x 48cm (231ft x 19in), and depicting (in more than 70 scenes) the life of HAROLD I of England and the NORMAN CONQUEST. An unfounded tradition attributes its design to Matilda, wife of WILLIAM I (THE CONQUEROR), but it was probably commissioned by William's half-brother ODO, bishop of Bayeux. It is now in a museum in Bayeux, N France.

Bayezid I (the Thunderbolt) (*c*.1360–1403) Ottoman sultan (1389–1402), largely responsible for creating a centralized OTTOMAN EMPIRE. His rapid conquests brought large areas of the Balkans under Turkish control, and he also laid siege to Constantinople (now ISTANBUL). In 1395 Bayezid invaded Hungary. He gained a decisive victory over a Christian army at Nicopolis (1396). When Bayezid invaded Anatolia, however, he came into conflict with TAMERLANE, who defeated him near Ankara (1402). Bayezid died in captivity.

Bayezid II (the Just) (1447–1513) OTTOMAN sultan (1481–1512). He is chiefly remembered for developing the culture of the OTTOMAN EMPIRE. Bayezid rebuilt Constantinople (now ISTANBUL) after the earthquake of 1509, but lost Cilicia to the MAMLUKS (1488–91) and Cyprus to Venice (1489). In 1510 civil war broke out between his sons, and Bayezid abdicated in favour of his son, Selim.

Bay of Pigs (17 April 1961) Unsuccessful effort by Cuban exiles, aided by the United States, to overthrow Fidel CASTRO by invading Cuba near the Bay of Pigs. An invasion force of *c*.1500 Cubans was trained, equipped and transported by the US government. The invasion was badly planned, and the Cuban army defeated the exiles within three days. President John KENNEDY initially denied US involvement and was later subject to much criticism for its failure. *See also* CUBAN MISSILE CRISIS

Bayonne Decree (1808) Order issued by NAPOLEON I to seize all US ships in French-controlled ports. It was issued in the wake of the United States' EMBARGO ACTS.

Beagle, HMS British survey ship that carried Charles DARWIN as ship's naturalist. The *Beagle* left England in December 1831 and for five years explored parts of South America and the Pacific islands. Darwin's observations formed the basis for his theory of evolution by natural selection.

Beaker culture *See* feature article

Bean, Roy (1825–1903) US frontier judge. After the American CIVIL WAR (1861–65) he followed the construction camps of the Southern Pacific Railroad as a saloon-keeper and gambler. In 1882 Bean settled in Vinegaroon, Texas, where as justice of the peace he kept order in court with his six-guns and dispensed harsh but just sentences.

Beard, Charles Austin (1874–1948) US historian. In *An Economic Interpretation of the Constitution of the United States* (1913), Beard put forward the controversial view that economic self-interest played an important part in the framing of the Constitution. He developed his notion of the importance of economic factors on the development of US political institutions in *The Rise of*

BEAKER CULTURE

Distinctive culture of the CHALCOLITHIC AGE that spread throughout Europe in the late 3rd millennium BC. The Beakers continued the NEOLITHIC tradition of constructing burial chambers with megaliths, but instead of collective tombs, they built single-grave burials in round BARROWS. Beaker culture was characterized by the bell-shaped beakers that accompanied burials. The Beakers primarily fought as bowmen but also used daggers and copper-spearheads as weapons. The original Beakers are thought to have originated in Spain and moved into central and W Europe in search of metals. They are credited with introducing copperwork to the British Isles. It is likely that the diffusion of the Beaker culture represented a gradual spread of new ideas to existing groups rather than the migration of large numbers of people. *See also* BRONZE AGE

▲ **bell beakers** were a distinctive type of pottery introduced into England in the late 3rd millennium BC and buried as prestige objects with chieftains.

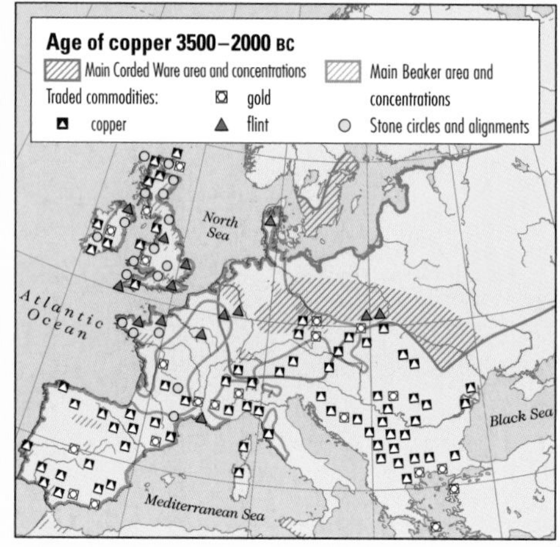

American Civilization (2 vols, 1927), co-written with his wife, Mary Beard (1876–58).

Beaton, David (1494–1546) Scottish cardinal and statesman. In 1539 he succeeded his uncle as archbishop of St Andrews. Beaton was a major architect of the Scottish-French alliance. In 1538 he arranged the marriage of JAMES V of Scotland to Mary of Guise. In 1543 he crowned MARY, QUEEN OF SCOTS. Beaton's ruthless persecution of Scottish Protestants culminated in the execution (1546) of the preacher George WISHART. Beaton was murdered in revenge. *See also* KNOX, JOHN

Beaufort, Henry (1374–1447) English statesman, cardinal, and bishop of Winchester, illegitimate son of JOHN OF GAUNT. In 1403 he was appointed chancellor by HENRY IV. In 1404 Beaufort resigned, but led opposition to Henry's chief minister Thomas Arundel. Beaufort became chancellor for a second time on the accession (1413) of HENRY V. The crowning (1422) of the infant HENRY VI marked the start of a bitter power struggle between Beaufort and Humphrey, Duke of GLOUCESTER. In 1431 Beaufort crowned Henry VI as king of France. From *c.*1435 to 1443 he controlled the English government. Beaufort retired in 1443. *See also* HUNDRED YEARS' WAR

Beauharnais, Joséphine de *See* JOSÉPHINE

Beauregard, Pierre Gustave Toutant (1818–93) Confederate general in the American CIVIL WAR. He served in the Mexican War and was superintendent of West Point until just before the Civil War broke out (1861). Beauregard forced the Union surrender of Fort Sumter (13 April 1861) in the first action of the war.

Beaverbrook, William Maxwell Aitken, 1st Baron (1879–1964) British newspaper proprietor and politician, b. Canada. Beaverbrook entered Parliament in 1910 and was made a peer in 1917. He was a member of Winston CHURCHILL's War Cabinet (1940–45). He bought a majority interest in the *Daily Express* (1916) and later founded the *Sunday Express* and the *Evening Standard*.

Bebel, August (1840–1913) German politician. He entered the Reichstag in 1869, as a member of the Saxon People's Party. Bebel was a co-founder (1867) of the German SOCIAL DEMOCRATIC PARTY (SPD). In 1870 Bebel and Wilhelm LIEBKNECHT were imprisoned for their opposition to Otto von BISMARCK and the AUSTRO-PRUSSIAN WAR (1870–71). During the state of emergency, Bebel wrote *Woman and Socialism* (1883). He was a strong advocate of social democracy, and resisted revisionary and revolutionary SOCIALISM alike. In 1912 the SPD became the largest party in the Reichstag. *See also* SPARTACUS LEAGUE

Bechuanaland Former name for BOTSWANA

Beck, Józef (1894–1944) Polish statesman. He fought in World War 1 and served as military attaché in Paris (1922–23). As foreign minister (1932–39) under Józef PIŁSUDSKI, Beck firmly rejected Adolf HITLER's demands for concessions in the Polish Corridor and Gdánsk. On 6 April 1939, Beck signed a defensive alliance with Britain that later resulted in Britain declaring war on Germany – the start of WORLD WAR 2.

Becket, Saint Thomas à (1118–70) English church leader. He was appointed chancellor of England (1155) and became a friend of HENRY II. In 1162 Henry made him archbishop of Canterbury, hoping for his support in asserting royal control, but Becket devoted his loyalty to the church. His defence of clerical privileges against the crown led to fierce conflict. Becket spent six years in exile. Reconciliation was short-lived, as Becket turned on those, including the king, who had violated his rights during his exile. Four of Henry's knights, assuming (wrongly) they would gain the king's gratitude, killed Becket in Canterbury Cathedral. Henry did penance, and Becket was acclaimed a martyr. He was canonized in 1173.

Bede, Saint (673–735) (Venerable Bede) English monk and scholar. Bede spent his life in the Northumbrian monasteries of Wearmouth and Jarrow. His most important work, *Ecclesiastical History of the English Nation*, is an indispensable primary source for English history from 54 BC to AD 697. His works were profoundly influential in early medieval Europe.

Bedford, John of Lancaster, Duke of (1389–1435) English statesman and general, third son of HENRY IV. While his brother HENRY V fought in France, Bedford acted as lieutenant of England. On Henry's death (1422), Bedford was appointed regent of France and protector of England. He devoted his energies to retaining England's territory in France and his younger brother Humphrey, Duke of GLOUCESTER, managed domestic affairs. Bedford formed an alliance with Burgundy through his marriage to Anne of Burgundy. In the HUNDRED YEARS' WAR (1337–1453), Bedford won a major victory at Verneuil (1424), but was frustrated by the campaign of JOAN OF ARC.

Beecher, Henry Ward (1813–87) US Congregational minister, outstanding preacher and influential advocate of social reform, brother of Harriet Beecher STOWE. In 1847 Beecher became pastor of the Plymouth Congregational Church, Brooklyn, New York. Famed for his opposition to SLAVERY, he also supported women's voting rights, and the scientific theory of evolution.

Beecher, Lyman (1775–1863) US Presbyterian clergyman, father of Henry Ward BEECHER and Harriet Beecher STOWE. Beecher was pastor at Litchfield, Connecticut (1810–26) and Boston (1826–32), and was president of Lane Theological Seminary (1832–52). He was noted for his sermons on temperance and against SLAVERY.

Beernaert, Auguste (1829–1912) Belgian statesman, prime minister (1884–94). A member of the Christian Social Party, he served in several cabinet posts before becoming prime minister. Beernaert was a delegate at the Hague Peace Conferences (1899, 1907). He shared the 1909 Nobel Prize for Peace with Estournelles de Constant.

Begin, Menachem (1913–92) Israeli statesman, prime minister (1977–83), b. Poland. In 1940 he was sentenced to eight years' slave-labour for Zionist activities, but was released (1941) to fight in the new Polish army. As commander of the paramilitary IRGUN ZEVAI LEUMI, he led resistance to British rule in Israel until independence in 1948. In 1973 Begin became leader of LIKUD. In 1977 Likud formed a coalition government, with Begin as prime minister. Although a fervent nationalist, he sought reconciliation with Egypt and signed the CAMP DAVID ACCORDS with Anwar SADAT (1978). In recognition of their efforts, Begin and Sadat shared the 1978 Nobel Prize for Peace. Begin's popularity waned after Israel's invasion of Lebanon in 1982, and he was succeeded as prime minister by Yitzhak SHAMIR. *See also* ZIONISM

Beijing (Peking) Capital of the People's Republic of CHINA, on a vast plain between the Pei and Hun rivers, NE China. A settlement since *c.*1000 BC, Beijing was adopted as the capital of the MONGOLS' empire by KUBLAI KHAN in AD 1262. In 1420 Beijing became the capital of the MING dynasty, which was responsible for the basic plan of the modern city. It continued to be China's capital until civil war broke out in 1917 and the country divided into North and South. In 1928 the seat of government was transferred to NANJING. Beijing ("northern capital") became known as Beiping ("northern peace"). Occupied by the Japanese in 1937, it was restored to China in 1945 and came under Communist control in 1949. Its name was restored as capital of the People's Republic. The city comprises two walled sections: the Inner (TATAR) City, which houses the Forbidden City (imperial palace complex), and the Outer (Chinese) city. Pop. (1993 est.) 6,560,000. *See also* TIANANMEN SQUARE

Beirut (Bayrut) Capital and chief port of LEBANON, on the Mediterranean coast at the foot of the Lebanon Mountains. In AD 635 Beirut was captured by the Arabs. In 1110 it was captured by the Crusaders and remained part of the Latin Kingdom of JERUSALEM until 1291. In 1516, under DRUZE control, Beirut became part of the OTTOMAN EMPIRE. During the 19th century, it was the centre of a revolt against the Ottomans led by MUHAMMAD ALI. In 1830 Beirut was captured by Egyptians, but in 1840 British and French forces restored Ottoman control. In 1920 it became capital of Lebanon under French mandate. During the 1950s and

BELARUS (BELORUSSIA)

AREA: 207,600sq km (80,154sq mi)
POPULATION: 10,297,000
CAPITAL (POPULATION): Minsk (1,633,600)
GOVERNMENT: Multiparty republic
ETHNIC GROUPS: Belarussian 80%, Russian, Polish, Ukrainian, Jewish
LANGUAGES: Belarussian, Russian (both official)
RELIGIONS: Christianity (mainly Belarus Orthodox, with Roman Catholics in the W and Evangelicals in the SW)
GDP PER CAPITA (1995): US$4220

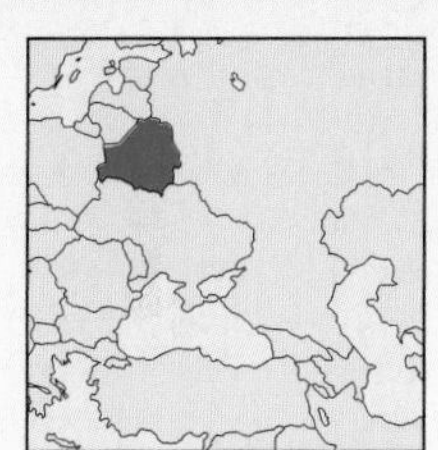

Republic in NE Europe. Slavs settled in Belarus between the 6th and 8th centuries AD. In the 9th century, the area became part of KIEVAN RUS, the first East Slavic state. In 1240 Kievan Rus was overrun by the MONGOLS and Belarus was subsumed into the empire of the GOLDEN HORDE. In the 14th century, Belarus became part of the Duchy of LITHUANIA. The LIVONIAN WAR (1558–83) between Lithuania and MOSCOW forced the union of Lithuania and Poland (1569). By the Partitions of POLAND (1772, 1793, 1795), Russia gained all of modern Belarus. In the NAPOLEONIC WARS (1803–15), Belarus was razed (1812) by the retreating Russian army. Mass emigration to Siberia and the United States occurred in the late 19th century.

Belarus was a major battlefield of World War 1. The Treaty of BREST-LITOVSK (1918) handed Belarus to Germany. Belarussian nationalists declared independence, but the Red Army invaded and the Belorussian Socialist Soviet Republic was proclaimed. The Treaty of Riga (1921) gave W Belorussia to Poland, while E Belorussia became a founding republic of the Soviet Union (1922). The NAZI-SOVIET PACT (1939) enabled Russia to attack and capture Polish Western Belorussia. In 1941 Germany invaded and occupied Belarus. A quarter of Belarus' population died during German occupation and the German army's dogged retreat (1944). The Nazis murdered most of the Jewish population.

In 1991, after the dissolution of the Soviet Union, Belarus declared independence and was a founder member of the COMMONWEALTH OF INDEPENDENT STATES (CIS). The administrative centre of the CIS is located in Minsk. In 1994 Aleksandr Lukashenka was elected president. His authoritarian rule suppressed political opposition. In 1997, despite opposition from nationalists, Belarus signed a Union Treaty with Russia, committing it to integration with Russia.

B

1960s, Beirut was a popular tourist destination. In 1976 the civil war began and Beirut fractured along religious lines. In 1982 West Beirut was devastated by an Israeli invasion in the war against the Palestine Liberation Organization (PLO). In 1985 Israel began a phased withdrawal and Syrian troops entered (1987) as part of an Arab peacekeeping force. By 1991 all militias had withdrawn from the city and restoration work began. Pop. (1993 est.) 1,500,000.

Bekaa Valley (Al Biqa) Highest part of the Rift Valley, between the Lebanon and Anti-Lebanon Mountains, central Lebanon. The valley has been a battleground for centuries, contested by the Persians, Seleucids and Ptolemies. Today, it is a centre of HEZBOLLAH activity. Length: 121km (75mi). Width: 8–14.5km (5–9mi).

Belarus *See* country feature, page 41

Belau *See* PALAU

Béla IV (1206–70) King of Hungary (1235–70). He tried to restore the fortunes of the ÁRPÁD dynasty by curbing the nobility's power. The ensuing civil disorder left Hungary ill-prepared for the MONGOL invasion (1241). Béla was defeated at Mohi and forced to flee. His subsequent policy of allowing other European rulers to recover parts of Hungary led to his protracted war with Ottokar II of Bohemia.

Belaúnde Terry, Fernando (1912–) Peruvian statesman, president (1963–68, 1980–85). In 1956 he founded the Popular Action Party. In his first term as president, Belaúnde's conservative programme was often frustrated by the APRA-dominated Congress. Rampant inflation and Belaúnde's support of oil exploration by the US firm International Petroleum Company led to his deposition in a military coup (1968). In 1980 Belaúnde returned to the presidency in Peru's first democratic elections since the coup. Belaúnde's austerity measures did nothing to improve Peru's ailing economy and he failed to suppress the SENDERO LUMINOSO guerrillas.

Belfast Capital of Northern Ireland, at the mouth of the River Legan on Belfast Lough. The city was founded in 1177 but did not develop until after the Industrial Revolution. Belfast is now the centre for the manufacture of Irish linen. Since the 19th century, religious and political differences between Protestants and Catholics have been a source of tension. In the late 1960s these divisions erupted into violence and civil unrest. Pop. (1991) 283,746.

Belgae CELTS who settled in NW Europe more than 2000 years ago. Their name, given by Julius CAESAR, who conquered the region in 57 BC, was later adopted by Belgium.

Belgium *See* country feature

Belgrade (Beograd) Capital of Serbia and of the Federal Republic of Yugoslavia, situated at the confluence of the Sava and Danube rivers. In the 12th century, it became the capital of Serbia but was later ruled by the Ottoman Turks. It was incorporated into the area which came to be known as Yugoslavia in 1929 and suffered much damage under German occupation in World War 2. In 1996 Belgrade witnessed huge demonstrations against the government. In 1999 it was badly damaged by NATO air-strikes during the Kosovo conflict. Pop. (1991) 1,168,454.

Belgrano, Manuel (1770–1820) Argentine independence leader. He participated in the revolution of 1810 and led Argentine forces against Paraguay in 1811. As commander of one of the Argentine armies, Belgrano defeated royalist forces in 1812 and 1814. At the Congress of Tucumán (1816), he recommended an INCA monarchy for Argentina.

Belisarius (505–65) Byzantine general. Under JUSTINIAN I, he waged campaigns against the Germanic tribes that threatened the BYZANTINE EMPIRE on its W frontiers. He subjugated the VANDALS in N Africa and the OSTROGOTHS in Italy.

Belize *See* country feature

Bell, Alexander Graham (1847–1922) US inventor of the telephone, b. Scotland. He first worked with his father, inventor of a system for educating the deaf. The family moved to Canada in 1870, and Bell taught speech at Boston University (1873–77). His work on the transmission of sound by electricity led to the first demonstration of the telephone (1876) and the founding of the Bell Telephone Company (1877).

Bell, Gertrude Margaret Lowthian (1868–1926) English writer, archaeologist and traveller, who was instrumental in the establishment of the HASHEMITE dynasty in Iraq. Bell travelled widely in the Middle East, joined the British Intelligence Service and advised the Arab Bureau of Iraq. Chiefly responsible for the selection of FAISAL I as king of Iraq, she also founded and directed the National Museum of Iraq. Bell's works include *The Desert and the Sown* (1907), *Amurath to Amurath* (1911) and *Palace and Mosque at Ukhaidr* (1914).

Bell, John (1797–1869) US statesman. He served (1827–41) in the House of Representatives and was secretary of war (1841). Bell was a senator (1847–59) for Tennessee. Although he defended slavery, Bell supported the Union. In 1860, as the presidential candidate for the Constitutional Union Party, he won the Southern states of Tennessee, Kentucky and Virginia.

Bellarmine, Saint Roberto Francesco Romolo (1542–1621) Italian theologian and cardinal, Doctor of the Church. He was a JESUIT and a prominent figure in the COUNTER-REFORMATION. From 1602 to 1605 Bellarmine was archbishop of Capua. In 1930 he was canonized by Pope PIUS XI.

Belsen Village in Lower Saxony, Germany, site of a CONCENTRATION CAMP established by the Nazi regime during World War 2. An estimated 30,000 people were murdered or died here of starvation and disease before the camp was liberated in April 1945. *See also* AUSCHWITZ; BUCHENWALD; DACHAU; HOLOCAUST, THE

BELGIUM

AREA: 30,510sq km (11,780sq mi)
POPULATION: 9,998,000
CAPITAL (POPULATION): Brussels (949,070)
GOVERNMENT: Federal constitutional monarchy
ETHNIC GROUPS: Belgian 91% (Fleming 55%, Walloon 34%), Italian, French, Dutch, Turkish, Moroccan
LANGUAGES: Dutch, French, German (all official)
RELIGIONS: Christianity (Roman Catholic 72%)
GDP PER CAPITA (1995): US$21,660

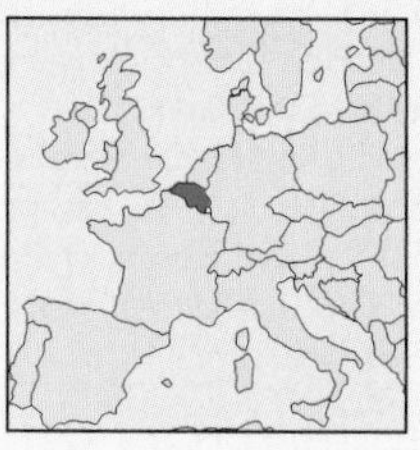

Constitutional monarchy in NW Europe. ACHEULIAN, MOUSTERIAN and AURIGNACIAN artefacts have been unearthed in Belgium. The BEAKER CULTURE was prevalent during the BRONZE AGE. In the 1st century BC, the Celtic BELGAE were conquered by the Romans. The LOW COUNTRIES consisted of two provinces – Belgica and Germania Inferior. In the 5th century AD, the Romans were supplanted by the FRANKS.

Under CLOVIS I (r. *c.*481–511), the MEROVINGIAN dynasty gained much of GAUL. CHARLEMAGNE conquered the Frankish empire and established the CAROLINGIAN dynasty. Christianity was introduced in the 7th century. The decline of the Carolingian dynasty brought the emergence of principalities, such as the counties of FLANDERS and HAINAUT, the duchies of BRABANT and Limburg, and the bishopric of Liège. Towns, such as BRUGES and GHENT, became major trading centres, especially for cloth. Although these feudal states became (10th century) part of the HOLY ROMAN EMPIRE's duchy of LORRAINE, they retained considerable autonomy. From 1369 the dukes of BURGUNDY began to unify these disparate states.

The death (1477) of CHARLES THE BOLD saw the emerging influence of the HABSBURG dynasty. In 1504 Emperor PHILIP I (THE HANDSOME) inherited the Spanish crown. In 1555 Emperor CHARLES V passed Spain and the Low Countries to his son, PHILIP II. In 1567 the REVOLT OF THE NETHERLANDS contested Spanish rule and the suppression of Protestantism. In 1585 the S provinces (now Belgium) were regained by Spain and separated from the N UNITED PROVINCES OF THE NETHERLANDS under WILLIAM I (OF ORANGE).

By the Peace of WESTPHALIA (1648), which concluded the THIRTY YEARS' WAR, PHILIP IV agreed to a much reduced **Spanish Netherlands**. By the Peace of UTRECHT (1713–14), ending the War of the SPANISH SUCCESSION (1701–14), modern Belgium and LUXEMBOURG passed to Emperor CHARLES VI, becoming known as the **Austrian Netherlands**. The death (1740) of Charles VI prompted the War of the AUSTRIAN SUCCESSION (1740–48). The Treaty of AIX-LA-CHAPELLE (1748) confirmed the accession of MARIA THERESA. The Brabant Revolution (1789) briefly overthrew Austrian rule, but Emperor LEOPOLD II regained BRUSSELS in 1790. During the FRENCH REVOLUTIONARY WARS (1792–1802), the Austrian Netherlands was captured (1795) by France, whose control was recognized at the Treaty of CAMPO FORMIO (1797). At the end of the NAPOLEONIC WARS (1803–15) it was reunited with the United Provinces to form the Kingdom of the NETHERLANDS, led by William I. Discrimination by the Dutch led to rebellion, and Belgium declared independence in 1830. LEOPOLD I became king. The Dutch conceded defeat in an agreement (1839) that also confirmed Belgium as a neutral, constiutional monarchy.

Leopold I's son and successor, LEOPOLD II, oversaw a period of economic and colonial expansion. In 1885 he acquired the Congo (now the Democratic Republic of Congo) as a personal possession. In August 1914 Germany invaded Belgium, prompting British entry into WORLD WAR I. Belgium, led by ALBERT I, stoutly resisted German occupation, and it formed a major battleground in the War. In May 1940, Germany again invaded Belgium and LEOPOLD III capitulated. In 1951 Leopold III was forced to abdicate and was succeeded by BAUDOUIN. Despite the damage inflicted during World War 2, the economy recovered quickly, helped by the BENELUX customs union with the Netherlands and Luxembourg (1958) and the formation of the European Common Market. Brussels has been the headquarters for the EUROPEAN UNION (EU) since its inception and is also the headquarters for the NORTH ATLANTIC TREATY ORGANIZATION (NATO). Belgium's relationship with the Congo has been problematic: Belgian troops helped suppress coups there in 1964 and 1978. A central domestic issue has been the tension between Dutch-speaking Flemings and French-speaking Walloons. In 1989 a federal constitution gave regional autonomy to Walloonia, Flanders and Brussels. In 1993 Baudouin died and was succeeded by his brother, Albert II. In 1996–97 the government of Jean-Luc Dehaene was rocked by a paedophilia scandal. In 1999 Belgium joined the single European currency.

▲ **Ben-Gurion** Known as the "father of the nation", Ben-Gurion was Israel's first prime minister and played a key role in securing the survival of a Jewish state in the Middle East.

Belshazzar In the Old Testament, the son of Nebuchadnezzar and last king of BABYLON. The Book of Daniel relates how Belshazzar organized a great feast during which a disembodied hand wrote upon the wall, "*Mene, mene tekel upharsin*". Daniel translated it as "Thou art weighed in the balance and found wanting". and said it signified Babylon's downfall. Modern archaeological investigations have identified Belshazzar with Bel-shar-usur (d.539 BC), the son of Nabonidus, king of Babylon (556–539 BC).

Benares *See* VARANASI

Benalcázar, Sebastián de (*c*.1479–1551) Spanish conquistador. In 1532 he aided Francisco PIZARRO in the conquest of Peru. In support of Diego de ALMAGRO, Benalcázar entered Quito and founded Guayaquil (1533). In 1535 he marched into sw Colombia in search of EL DORADO, founding Pasto and Cali. In 1541 Benalcázar was made governor of Popayán province. In 1550 he was convicted for treason and died en route to Spain.

Ben Bella, (Muhammad) Ahmed (*c*.1916–) Algerian statesman, prime minister (1962–63), president (1963–65). He was director (1952–56) of the FRONT DE LIBÉRATION NATIONALE (FLN). Imprisoned (1956–62) by the French, Ben Bella was released to become the first prime minister of an independent Algeria. He was deposed in a coup (1965) led by Houari BOUMEDIENNE. After 15 years in prison, Ben Bella went into exile (1980–90) in France where he formed the Movement for Democracy in Algeria (MDA).

Benedict (of Nursia), Saint (*c*.480–*c*.547) Roman founder of Western MONASTICISM and of the BENEDICTINE order. Our knowledge of Benedict is derived from the *Dialogues* by Saint GREGORY I (THE GREAT). Distressed by the decadence of Rome, Benedict went to live as a hermit in a cave above Subiaco. His reputation for sanctity drew a large community of disciples and Benedict founded 12 monasteries. The Rule of St Benedict formed a blueprint for monastic life throughout Europe. His feast day is 11 July. *See also* BENEDICTINES

Benedict XV (1854–22) Pope (1914–22), b. Giacomo della Chiesa. During World War 1, Benedict strove for peace among nations, stressing pacifist idealism. He tried to unite all Roman Catholics, made changes in the Curia, and published a new Code of Canon Law.

Benedictines Monks and nuns of the monastic Order of Saint Benedict, who follow the Rule laid down by Saint BENEDICT (OF NURSIA) in the 6th century. The Order played a leading role in bringing CHRISTIANITY and civilization to Western Europe in the 7th century and in preserving Christianity in the medieval period. During the REFORMATION, most Benedictine monasteries and nunneries in Europe, including 300 in England, were suppressed. The Order was revived in France and Germany during the 17th century. Benedictine monks and nuns returned to England in the late 19th century, and the Order spread to North and South America. *See also* CLUNY, ORDER OF; MONASTICISM

benefit of clergy Exemption of Christian clerics from criminal prosecution in secular courts. In England, the privilege was at the heart of the dispute between HENRY II and Saint Thomas à BECKET and was conceded by the crown after Becket's murder. The relative leniency of ecclesiastical courts meant that the privilege was subject to systematic abuse. In England, benefit of clergy was extended to any literate person. In 1576 the church courts lost their jurisdiction over criminal matters and in 1827 benefit of clergy was abolished.

Benelux Customs union of Belgium, the Netherlands and Luxembourg, established in 1948. The earliest "common market" in Europe, it abolished trade restrictions between its members. Benelux also has wider aims – the standardization of prices, wages, taxes and social security – but these have, to some extent, been merged in the aspirations of the EUROPEAN UNION (EU), of which the Benelux countries are also members.

Beneš, Eduard (1884–1948) Czech statesman, president (1935–38, 1946–48). Beneš promoted Czech independence while abroad during World War 1 and became the first foreign minister (1918–35) of Czechoslovakia. He resigned from the presidency in protest against the MUNICH AGREEMENT (1938) and served as head of the Czechoslovakian government-in-exile in London. In 1945 he returned to Czechoslovakia and was re-elected in 1946. Beneš resigned after the communist coup.

Bengal Former province of India. Bengal is a region of the Indian subcontinent that encompasses the Indian state of West Bengal and East Bengal (now BANGLADESH). Much of Bengal lies in the deltas of the Ganges and Brahmaputra rivers. Bengal was the richest region in the 16th-century MUGHAL EMPIRE of AKBAR I (THE GREAT). Conquered by the British in 1757, it became the centre of British India, with CALCUTTA as the capital. It was made an autonomous region in 1937. Area: 200,575sq km (77,442sq mi).

Ben-Gurion, David (1886–1973) Israeli statesman, prime minister (1948–53, 1955–63) and minister of defence (1948–53, 1955–63), b. Poland as David Grün. In 1906 he settled in Palestine. In 1920 Ben-Gurion formed Histadrut, General Foundation of Labour in Palestine. In 1930 he became leader of the MAPAI Party, the socialist arm of ZIONISM. After World War 2, Ben-Gurion supported the use of violence to remove the British from Palestine and headed the campaign for an independent Jewish state. In 1948 he became Israel's first prime minister. Ben-Gurion pursued an aggressive policy towards Israel's Arab neighbours. In 1956 Israel occupied Sinai as part of the disastrous effort by Britain and France to seize the Suez Canal from Egypt. In 1963 Ben-Gurion was succeeded as prime minister and leader of Mapai by Levi ESHKOL. *See also* ARAB-ISRAELI WARS; SUEZ CRISIS

Benin Historic kingdom in w Africa that flourished

▲ **Benin** The ancient kingdom of Benin was renowned for its bronze sculptures, made by a guild of master-craftsmen. The technique of bronze casting was probably introduced from Ife in the late 14th century. Commemorative heads, such as the one above, decorated royal altars.

BELIZE (FORMERLY BRITISH HONDURAS)

Constitutional monarchy in Central America, on the Caribbean Sea. Between *c*.300 BC and AD 1000, Belize was part of the area of the MAYA kingdoms, which had declined long before Spanish explorers reached the coast in the early 16th century. In *c*.1638 shipwrecked British sailors founded the first European settlement. Over the next 150 years, Britain gradually took control of Belize, using slave labour in the logging industry. In 1862 Belize became the colony of British Honduras. In 1973 it became known as Belize. In 1981 it gained independence, but British troops remained in Belize to prevent a possible invasion by Guatemala. In 1992 Guatemala recognized Belize's independence.

AREA: 22,960sq km (8,865sq mi)
POPULATION: 198,000
CAPITAL (POPULATION): Belmopan (3,558)
GOVERNMENT: Constitutional monarchy
ETHNIC GROUPS: Mestizo (Spanish-Indian) 44%, Creole (mainly African-American) 30%, Mayan Indian 11%, Garifuna (Black-Carib Indian) 7%, White 4%, East Indian 3%
LANGUAGES: English (official)
RELIGIONS: Christianity (Roman Catholic 58%, Protestant 29%), Hinduism 2%
GDP PER CAPITA (1995): US$5400

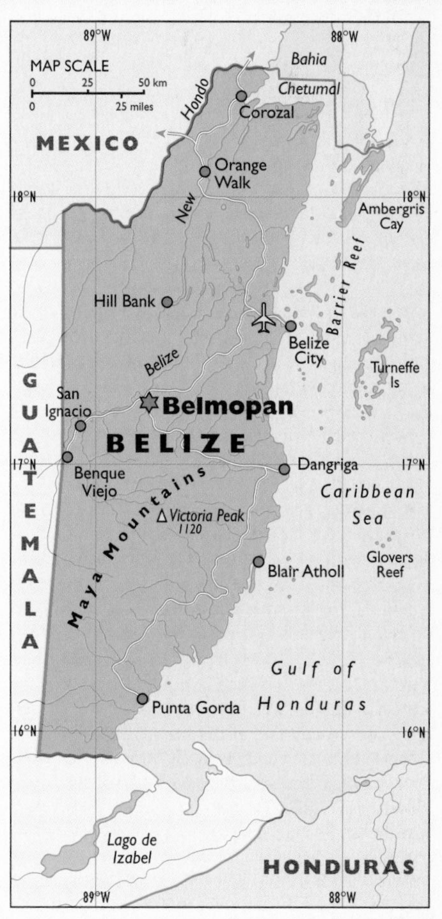

between the 14th and the 17th century. Under King Ozolua (r. 1481–1504), Benin stretched from the River Niger delta to modern-day Lagos, Nigeria. He also established trade links with Portugal. The kingdom declined with the abolition of the slave trade. Benin is noted for its bronze sculptures and wood and ivory carvings, considered among the finest African art.

Benin *See* country feature

Benjamin, Judah Philip (1811–84) US statesman and lawyer. Benjamin served (1853–61) in the US senate and resigned after Louisiana's secession from the Union. He became attorney general (1861), secretary of war (1861–62) and secretary of state (1862–65) of the CONFEDERATE STATES OF AMERICA. After the South's defeat in the American CIVIL WAR, he escaped to England where he became a prominent lawyer.

Benn, Tony (Anthony Neil Wedgwood) (1925–) British politician. He was elected to Parliament in 1950, and in 1963 disclaimed an inherited peerage in order to remain a member of the House of Commons. Benn served as minister of technology (1966–70), secretary for industry (1974–75) and secretary for energy (1975–79). A committed pacifist, he was a leading spokesman on the left wing of the LABOUR PARTY.

Bennett, Richard Bedford (1870–1947) Canadian statesman, prime minister (1930–35). In 1927 Bennett succeeded Arthur MEIGHEN as leader of the Conservative Party and he defeated W.L. Mackenzie KING in the 1930 elections. Bennett was an autocratic prime minister. He established preferential tariff agreements within the British Commonwealth and greatly increased welfare provisons, but failed to combat the worst effects of the Great Depression and was defeated by a resurgent Mackenzie King in the 1935 elections. Bennett led the Conservative opposition until his retirement from politics in 1938.

Bentham, Jeremy (1748–1832) English philosopher, jurist and social reformer. In *Introduction to the Principles of Morals and Legislation* (1789), Bentham developed the theory of UTILITARIANISM, based on the premise that "the greatest happiness of the greatest number" should be the object of individual and government action. His theories influenced much of England's early reform legislation. Bentham was a founder of University College, London, and his clothed skeleton is preserved there.

Bentinck, Lord William Henry Cavendish (1774–1839) British colonial administrator, governor of Madras (1803–07), governor general of Bengal (1827–33) and governor general of India (1833–35). Bentinck introduced reforms, including the abolition of suttee (widow-burning), and campaigned against the THUGS.

Bentinck, William Henry Cavendish *See* PORTLAND, WILLIAM HENRY CAVENDISH, 3RD DUKE OF

Benton, Thomas Hart (1782–1858) US statesman, senator for Missouri (1820–51). A supporter of President Andrew JACKSON, he became leader of the DEMOCRATIC PARTY in the Senate. Benton played a major role in the abolition of the BANK OF THE UNITED STATES. He sponsored the explorations of John Charles FRÉMONT. Benton was a vocal critic of SLAVERY, and his rejection of the COMPROMISE OF 1850 cost him his Senate seat. Benton served (1853–55) in the House of Representatives, but his opposition to the KANSAS-NEBRASKA ACT (1854) ended his chances of re-election.

Ben-zvi, Yitzhak (1884–1963) Israeli statesman, president (1952–63), b. Russia as Isaac Shimselevitz. In 1907 he settled in Palestine. In 1920 Ben-zvi helped David BEN-GURION found Histadrut, the General Foundation of Labour in Palestine. Ben-zvi and Ben-Gurion also founded (1930) the MAPAI Party, the socialist arm of ZIONISM. He succeeded Chaim WEIZMANN as president of Israel and died in office.

Berbers Indigenous inhabitants of North Africa. Their stable culture dates back to before 2400 BC. Berber languages are spoken by more than 10 million people. They stubbornly resisted the ARAB invasion in the 7th century AD. Eventually converted to Islam, Berbers played a leading role in the Muslim conquest of Spain in the 8th century. In the 9th century they supported the FATIMID conquest of N Africa. Between the 11th and the 13th century Berber tribes, the ALMORAVIDS and ALMOHADS, built large empires in NW Africa and Spain.

Beria, Lavrenti Pavlovich (1899–1953) Soviet politician, chief (1938–53) of the secret police (NKVD). In the 1920s Beria headed the CHEKA, predecessor of the NKVD, in Transcaucasia. He helped Joseph STALIN conduct the Great PURGE (1936–38) of the COMMUNIST PARTY OF THE SOVIET UNION (CPSU). When Stalin died, Beria was arrested and executed for treason. *See also* KGB

Bering, Vitus Jonassen (1680–1741) Danish naval officer and explorer in Russian service, who gave his name to the Bering Strait and Bering Sea. In 1728 he sailed N from Kamchatka, NE Siberia, to the Bering Strait to discover whether Asia and North America were joined. Bering turned back before he was certain but set out again in 1741, reaching Alaska. Returning, he was shipwrecked and died on what is now Bering Island.

Bering Sea Controversy Dispute between various nations (mainly the United States, Britain and Canada) concerning control of the E Bering Sea and its lucrative seal-fur trade. In 1881 US citizens demanded control of the entire region, seized British ships and weakened Canadian commercial interests. In 1893 an international board ruled in favour of the British. An agreement (1911) between Britain, Japan, Russia and the United States limited hunting and made concessions to Canadian interests.

Berkeley, Sir William (1606–77) British colonial governor of Virginia (1642–52, 1660–76). In his first term, he defended the colony from Dutch and Native American attacks and guided the expansion of Virginia. In 1652 Berkeley was sacked as governor for supporting CHARLES II of England. His second term was marred by the failure of the tobacco crop and Native American incursions. He brutally suppressed BACON'S REBELLION (1676) and was recalled to England in disgrace.

Berlin Capital of Germany, lying on the River Spree, NE Germany. Berlin was founded in the 13th century. In the 14th century, it joined the HANSEATIC LEAGUE. In 1486 Berlin became the seat of the Electors of BRANDENBURG (the HOHENZOLLERNS). The city was devastated during the THIRTY YEARS' WAR (1618–48), but was rebuilt by FREDERICK WILLIAM (the Great Elector) and became capital of the kingdom of PRUSSIA. The ambitious building plans of FREDERICK II (THE GREAT) were postponed by French occupation (1808–08) during the NAPOLEONIC WARS (1803–15), but he completed work on the Brandenburg Gate. Berlin was the centre of the REVOLUTION OF 1848 against FREDERICK WILLIAM IV. In 1871 the city became the capital of the German Empire and grew into the second-largest city in Europe (after LONDON). In 1918 Berlin became capital of the newly-formed WEIMAR REPUBLIC. In 1936 it hosted the Olympic Games. On KRISTALLNACHT (9 November 1938), Nazi stormtroopers systematically destroyed Jewish property in the city (*see also* HOLOCAUST, THE). Berlin was virtually destroyed during World War 2 and more than 150,000 Berliners lost their lives before the city was captured (April 1945) by the Soviets. In 1945 Berlin was divided into four sectors; British, French, US and Soviet. On the formation of East Germany, the Soviet sector became **East Berlin** and the rest **West Berlin**. In 1948 the Soviets blockaded West Berlin and the Western Allies launched the BERLIN AIRLIFT. In 1953 an uprising in East Berlin was crushed by the Red Army. In 1961 East Germany built the BERLIN WALL in order to prevent its citizens escaping into West Germany. In 1989 the Berlin Wall was opened and the East German regime crumbled. In 1990 Germany and Berlin were reunified. In 1991 Berlin replaced Bonn as capital of Germany. Pop. (1993) 3,466,000.

Berlin, Conference of (1884–85) Meeting of the major European nations, the United States and Turkey to discuss the problems of West African colonization and to arrange

BENIN

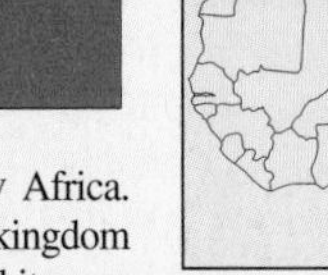

Republic in w Africa. The ancient kingdom of DAHOMEY had its capital at Abomey (now in s Benin). In the 17th century, the kings of Dahomey and OUIDAH competed for control of the lucrative Atlantic SLAVE TRADE, and by 1700 more than 200,000 slaves were being transported annually from the "slave coast". The Portuguese shipped many Dahomeans to Brazil. Despite the abolition of the slave trade by several countries in the early 19th century, the trade continued into the second-half of the century. In 1863 the French established a protectorate over Porto-Novo. By 1894 the French had conquered Dahomey. In 1904 it became part of the giant federation of French West Africa. In 1960 it gained full independence. The 1960s were marked by a succession of military coups. In 1972 Major Mathieu KÉRÉKOU seized control. In 1975 Dahomey became the People's Republic of Benin, adopting Marxism-Leninism as the state ideology. In 1989 communism was abandoned and Kérékou was defeated by Nicéphore Soglo in 1991 elections. Kérékou returned to power in 1996.

AREA: 112,620sq km (43,483sq mi)
POPULATION: 4,889,000
CAPITAL (POPULATION): Porto-Novo (208,258)
GOVERNMENT: Multiparty republic
ETHNIC GROUPS: Fon, Adja, Bariba, Yoruba, Fulani
LANGUAGES: French (official)
RELIGIONS: Traditional beliefs 60%, Christianity 23%, Islam 15%
GDP PER CAPITA (1995): US$1760

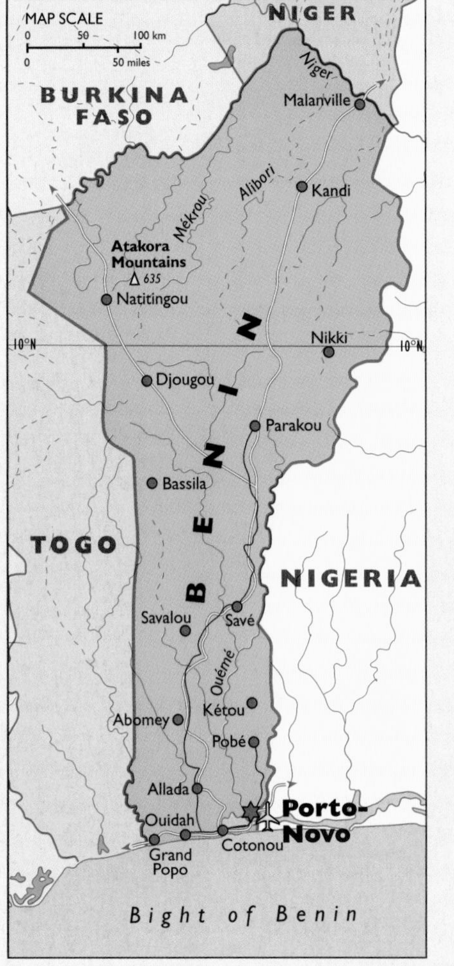

for free trade along the Niger and Congo rivers. The Conference affirmed British claims to Nigeria and Belgian claims to the Congo, but other agreements on trade and political neutrality proved untenable in the years to follow.

Berlin, Congress of (1878) Meeting of European powers to revise the Treaty of SAN STEFANO (1878) that had increased Russian power in SE Europe. The purpose of the Congress, under the presidency of Otto von BISMARCK, was to modify its terms. The main territorial adjustment was to reduce the Russian-sponsored Greater Bulgaria.

Berlin Airlift (1948–49) Operation to supply BERLIN with food and other necessities after the Soviet Union closed all road and rail links between the city and West Germany. For 15 months US and British aircraft flew more than 270,000 flights, delivering food and supplies. *See also* COLD WAR

Berlin Wall Heavily fortified and defended wall, 49-km (30-mi) long that divided East and West BERLIN. It was built (1961) by the East Germans to stop refugees fleeing to West Germany. (Between 1949 and 1961, c.2.7 million people had fled from East to West.) Some individuals succeeded in crossing it, others (*c.*80) were killed in the attempt. It was dismantled after the collapse of the communist regime in 1989. *See also* COLD WAR

Bernadotte, Count Folke (1895–1948) Swedish diplomat. In May 1948 Bernadotte was appointed by the United Nations (UN) to mediate between the newly created state of Israel and the Arab countries. He was assassinated (17 September) in Jerusalem by Zionist extremists.

Bernadotte, Jean Baptiste Jules *See* CHARLES XIV

Bernard of Clairvaux, Saint (1090–1153) French mystic and religious leader. Bernard was abbot of the Cistercian monastery of Clairvaux from 1115 until his death. Under his direction nearly 100 new monasteries were founded. He was canonized in 1174. His feast day is 20 August.

Besant, Annie (1847–1933) English theosophist and social reformer. She was president (1907–33) of the Theosophical Society. Besant established (1898) the Central Hindu College at Varanasi, India. She was active in the Indian independence movement and was president (1917) of the Indian National CONGRESS. *See also* KRISHNAMURTI, JIDDU

Bessarabia Historic region in Moldavia and SW Ukraine; the capital is Kišinov. It was first settled by Slavs in the 7th century. KIEVAN RUS held Bessarabia between the 9th and the 11th century. It was captured by the Turks in 1513, ceded to Russia in 1812 and became an autonomous Soviet republic in 1917. In 1918 it declared itself part of Romania. It was part of the Soviet Union from 1945 to 1991.

Bethlehem (Bayt Lahm) Town on the W bank of the River Jordan, 8km (5mi) SSW of JERUSALEM, administered by the Palestinian National Authority since 1994. The traditional birthplace of JESUS CHRIST, it was the early home of King DAVID and the site of the biblical Massacre of the Innocents. The Church of the Nativity, built (*c.*AD 330) by Constantine, is the oldest Christian church still in use. Under the rule of the Ottoman Empire (1571–1916), it was part of the British Palestine mandate until 1948 when it became part of Jordan. After the SIX-DAY WAR (1967) it was occupied by Israel. Pop. (1993 est.) 20,300.

Bethlen, Count Stephen (1874–1946?) Hungarian statesman, premier (1921–31). After a short period of communist rule, Bethlen was appointed premier by Admiral HORTHY. He helped Hungary regain a degree of political stability and persuaded the League of Nations to help with financial reconstruction (1923). His revisionist politics worried the LITTLE ENTENTE and loans were agreed only on the basis that Bethlen resign. In 1940 Bethlen opposed Hungary's alliance with Nazi Germany. He hid during the German occupation of Hungary in World War 2, but was captured by the Russians at the end of the War and apparently died in Moscow.

Bethmann-Hollweg, Theobald von (1856–1921) German statesman, chancellor (1909–17). He succeeded Bernhard von BÜLOW as chancellor. In 1914 Bethmann-Hollweg referred to the treaty ensuring Belgian neutrality as a "scrap of paper". Generals Paul von HINDENBURG and Erich LUDENDORFF forced him to resign (1917) after he advocated a restriction of submarine warfare and an end to the war.

Bethune, Mary McLeod (1875–1955) US educator. Bethune founded (1904) the Daytona Normal and Industrial Institute for Negro Girls. In 1923 it merged with Cookham Institute to form Bethune-Cookman College. Bethune acted as president (1904–42, 1946–47). She founded (1935) the National Council of Negro Women.

Bevan, Aneurin (1897–1960) British politician. He led the Welsh miners in the GENERAL STRIKE (1926). Bevan entered Parliament in 1929 and quickly established a reputation as a stirring orator. He was editor (1940–45) of the socialist *Tribune* magazine. As minister of health (1945–51) in the post-war Labour government of Clement ATTLEE, Bevan introduced (1948) the NATIONAL HEALTH SERVICE. He was married to Jennie LEE.

Beveridge, William Henry, Baron (1879–1963) British academic and social reformer, b. India. A director (1909–16) of the labour exchanges, Beveridge later became director (1919–37) of the London School of Economics (LSE) and master (1937–45) of University College, Oxford. He wrote the "Beveridge Report" (1942), which formed the basis of the British WELFARE STATE.

Bevin, Ernest (1881–1951) British UNION leader and politician. As general secretary (1922–40) of the Transport and General Workers' Union (TGWU), he helped to plan the GENERAL STRIKE (1926). Bevin acted as minister of labour and national service (1940–45) in the wartime coalition government. As foreign minister (1945–51) in Clement ATTLEE's government, he helped establish the NORTH ATLANTIC TREATY ORGANIZATION (NATO).

▲ **Berlin Wall** When border crossings opened on 9 November 1989, thousands of East Berliners flooded through to the West, many climbing on and breaking down the Wall.

Beyazid *See* BAYEZID I (THE THUNDERBOLT); BAYEZID II (THE JUST)

Bhagavad Gita (Hindi, "Song of the Lord") Sanskrit poem forming part of the sixth book of the Hindu epic, the MAHABHARATA. Probably written in the 1st or 2nd century AD, it is often regarded as the greatest philosophical expression of HINDUISM. The poem itself is a dialogue between Lord Krishna (as an incarnation of Vishnu) and Prince Arjuna on the eve of the Battle of Kurukshetra. Krishna eases Arjuna's concerns about the coming Battle and instructs him on the importance of absolute devotion (bhakti) to a personal god as a means of salvation. As such, the Bhagavad Gita represents a fundamental departure from the brahman-atman (world-spirit and self) doctrine of the VEDAS.

Bharat Sanskrit name for INDIA. It is derived from Bharata, a tribe in the Vedas.

Bharatiya Janata Paksh (BJP) Hindu nationalist party. Between 1975 and 1977 most non-communist left-of-centre and right-wing parties in India coalesced to

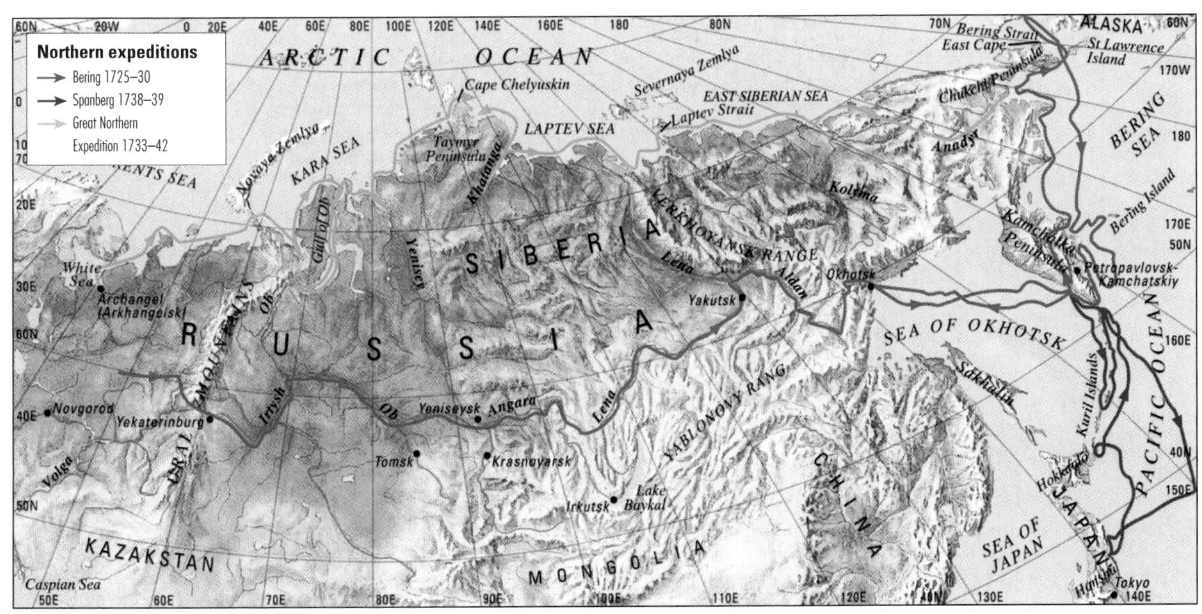

◀ **Bering** In 1725, Vitus Bering's expedition set out from St Petersburg, Russia, in search of a route from Asia to America. It took Bering and his companions two years to reach the Sea of Okhotsk. They sailed to the Kamchatka Peninsula and crossed to the east on foot. On the E coast they built a boat and sailed into what is now known as the Bering Sea. There was little doubt that a strait existed between the two continents, but mist obscured the land on either side and Bering was forced to return to Russia without conclusive proof.

B

BHUTAN

AREA: 47,000sq km (18,147sq mi)
POPULATION: 1,638,000
CAPITAL (POPULATION): Thimphu (15,000)
GOVERNMENT: Constitutional monarchy
ETHNIC GROUPS: Bhutanese, Nepalese
LANGUAGES: Dzongkha, Nepali, English
RELIGIONS: Buddhism, Hinduism
GDP PER CAPITA (1995): US$1260

form the coalition JANATA PARTY in opposition to Indira GANDHI's ruling Indian National CONGRESS. In 1979 the alliance collapsed, and the BJP emerged as one of the principal remnants. Broadly right-wing, the BJP is in favour of the creation of a Hindu state, Hindustan. The BJP won the 1996, 1998 and 1999 elections.

Bhave, Vinoba (1895–1982) Indian social reformer. In 1940 he was selected by "Mahatma" GANDHI to lead the independence movement. In 1951 Bhave began walking tours urging landowners to give their land to the poor. He walked thousands of miles and by 1967 his movement (Bhoodan Yayna) had obtained 1.7 million ha (4.25 million acres) of land.

Bhindranwale, Sant Jarnail Singh (1947–84) Indian SIKH militant leader. He was initially supported by the Indian National CONGRESS, who saw an opportunity to weaken the Sikh Akali Dal movement. Bhindranwale launched a terrorist campaign to drive Hindus from PUNJAB and create a Sikh homeland, Khalistan. In June 1984 he and his followers began to fortify the Golden Temple in AMRITSAR. Prime Minister Indira GANDHI ordered the Indian Army to storm the Temple. The ensuing battle killed 493 militants, including Bhindranwale, and 83 Indian soldiers. On 31 October 1984, Indira Gandhi was murdered by her Sikh bodyguards.

Bhopal State capital of Madhya Pradesh, central India. Founded in 1728, it is noted for its terraced lakes, mosques, and prehistoric paintings. In 1984 poisonous gas from the Union Carbide insecticide plant killed 2500 people in the world's worst industrial disaster. Pop. (1991) 1,063,000.

Bhumibol Adulyadej (1927–) King of Thailand (1946–). He ruled with a regent until 1950 when he became King Rama IX. Bhumibol is the longest-serving monarch in Thailand's history.

Bhutan Mountainous kingdom in the E Himalayas, bordered N by Tibet (China), E and S by India, and W by Sikkim. In the 17th century, the leader of the *Drukpa Kagyu* (Thunder Dragon) sect of TIBETAN BUDDHISM unified the country. Villages developed around the *dzong* (castle-monastery), and many Bhutanese continue to live in these monastic communities. In 1720 the Chinese invaded, but met fierce resistance. War with Britain (1865) resulted in the British annexation of S Bhutan. In 1907 Britain supported the establishment of a hereditary monarchy and Sir Ugyen Wangchuk became king. Bhutanese foreign policy was directed by Britain. After India gained independence (1949), it assumed Britain's former role. King Jigme Dorji Wangchuk (r.1952–72) reformed Bhutanese society, abolishing slavery (1958) and establishing a national assembly. In 1971 Bhutan was admitted into the United Nations (UN). In 1972 Jigme Singye Wangchuk succeeded his father as king. In 1990 pro-democracy demonstrations were suppressed and political parties banned. The Nepalese Hindu minority complain of discrimination.

Bhutto, Benazir (1953–) Pakistani stateswoman, prime minister (1988–90, 1993–96), daughter of Zulfikar Ali BHUTTO. She was long considered the leader of the Pakistani People's Party but was subject to house arrest and forced into exile. Bhutto's return (1986) was marked by jubilation and violence. In 1988 Bhutto proclaimed a "people's revolution" and became the first woman prime minister of Pakistan. Amid charges of corruption, she was removed from office. In 1993 Bhutto was re-elected. In 1996 further charges of corruption led to her dismissal.

Bhutto, Zulfikar Ali (1928–79) Pakistani statesman, prime minister (1973–77), father of Benazir BHUTTO. He founded (1967) the Pakistan People's Party. In 1970 elections Bhutto gained a majority in West Pakistan, but the AWAMI LEAGUE controlled East Pakistan. Bhutto's refusal to grant autonomy to East Pakistan led to civil war (1971). Defeat led to the formation of BANGLADESH. He was overthrown in a military coup, led by General ZIA. Bhutto was convicted of conspiracy to murder and executed.

Biafra Former state in W Africa, formed from the E region of NIGERIA. In September 1966, *c*.20,000 IBO were killed in N Nigeria and *c*.1 million Ibo fled to Biafra. In May 1967 Lieutenant Colonel Odumegwu Ojukwu (1933–) declared Biafra an independent state. Nigeria opposed secession and a bloody civil war ensued. The federal army cut off supplies to the state and more than one million Biafrans died of starvation. In January 1970 Biafra surrendered and was reincorporated into Nigeria.

Bible Sacred scriptures of JUDAISM and CHRISTIANITY. Partly a history of the tribes of Israel, it is regarded as a source of divine revelation and of prescriptions and prohibitions for moral living. The Bible consists of two main sections. The OLD TESTAMENT, excluding the APOCRYPHA, is accepted as sacred by both Jews and Christians. The Roman Catholic and Eastern Orthodox churches accept parts of the Apocrypha as sacred and include them in the Old Testament. Jews and Protestants for the most part reject them. The Old Testament was originally written in Hebrew and Aramaic. The NEW TESTAMENT, originally written in Greek, is accepted as sacred only by Christians. The first translation of the Bible was the Vulgate (AD 405) of Saint JEROME. John WYCLIFFE instituted the first English translation from the Latin in the late 14th century. William TYNDALE's translation (1525–26) was from the original Hebrew and Greek, and formed the basis of the Authorized or King James Version (1611).

Bible societies Protestant organizations for spreading knowledge of the Bible. An early example was the Bible Society founded (1780) in England to supply free Bibles to soldiers and sailors. In 1804 the British and Foreign Bible Society was formed in London. It remains a major force in providing vernacular translations of the Bible internationally. The American Bible Society, founded in 1816, carries out a similar mission from its headquarters in New York. Both these societies are interdenominational organizations under lay control.

BISMARCK, OTTO VON

Otto von Bismarck laid the foundations of modern Germany, introducing a common currency, a central bank and a single code of law to the German Empire. Furthermore, he was the first statesman in Europe to devise a social security system, which offered workers insurance against accident, sickness and old age.

BISMARCK IN HIS OWN WORDS

"The great questions of our day cannot be solved by speeches and majority votes...but by iron and blood."
Speech, Prussian Chamber, 1862

"Politics is not an exact science."
Speech, Prussian Chamber, 1863

Bidault, Georges (1899–1983) French statesman, foreign minister (1947–48, 1953–54). He was a leader of the French Resistance during World War 2. After the War, Bidault joined the provisional government of Charles DE GAULLE. Bidault's opposition to Algerian independence led him into involvement with terrorist organizations and forced him into exile (1962).

Biddle, Nicholas (1786–1844) US financier. In 1822, after serving in US legations abroad and in Congress, Biddle became president of the BANK OF THE UNITED STATES. His strong management of the Bank led to attacks on him and the Bank by President Andrew JACKSON's followers, but Biddle served until the Bank's charter expired in 1839.

Bienville, Jean Baptiste le Moyne, Sieur de (1680–1768) French colonizer of Louisiana, b. Canada. In 1698 he accompanied his brother, Sieur d'IBERVILLE, from Canada to the mouth of the Mississippi River. He founded Mobile (1711) and New Orleans (1718).

Biko, Steve (Stephen) (1946–77) South African political activist. In 1969 he founded the South African Students Organization. In 1972 Biko co-founded the Black People's Convention, a black-consciousness movement. In 1973 his freedom of speech and association were severely curtailed. Biko died in police custody at Port Elizabeth. He became a symbol of the cruelty of APARTHEID.

Bill of Rights (1689) British statute enshrining the constitutional principles won during the GLORIOUS REVOLUTION (1688–89). It confirmed the abdication of JAMES II and bestowed the throne on WILLIAM III and MARY II. It excluded Roman Catholics from the succession and outlawed certain of James' abuses of the royal prerogative, such as his manipulation of the legal system and use of a standing army. It hastened the trend toward the supremacy of parliament over the crown.

Bill of Rights (1791) First ten amendments to the CONSTITUTION OF THE UNITED STATES. Several states had agreed to ratify the Constitution (1788) only after George WASHINGTON promised to add such a list of liberties. The **First** Amendment guaranteed freedom of religion, speech, press and assembly. The **Second** guaranteed the right to bear arms, while the **Third** protected citizens against soldiers being quartered in private homes. The **Fourth** Amendment guarded the public from unreasonable search and seizure, and the **Fifth** protected accused persons from self-incrimination. The **Sixth** guaranteed a speedy trial, the **Seventh** trial by jury, and the **Eighth** protection from cruel and unusual punishment. The **Ninth** and **Tenth** said that the people retained rights not delegated to the federal or state authorities. *See also* CONSTITUTIONAL CONVENTION

Billy the Kid (1859–81) US frontier outlaw, b. William H. Bonney. Traditionally 21 murders are ascribed to him, but there is no evidence for this figure. In 1878 Billy the Kid killed a sheriff and led a gang of cattle rustlers. In 1880 he was sentenced to death. Billy the Kid escaped from jail but was captured and killed by Sheriff Pat Garrett.

Bingham, Hiram (1875–1956) US archaeologist. Bingham's discovery (1911) and excavation of the INCA city of MACHU PICCHU in the Andes helped historians to unravel the story of Peru before the Spanish conquest.

Biqa *See* BEKAA VALLEY

Birch, John *See* JOHN BIRCH SOCIETY

Birkenhead, Frederick Edwin Smith, 1st Earl of (1872–1930) British Conservative statesman, lord chancellor (1919–22). He entered Parliament in 1906 and gained prominence as a defender of ULSTER during the Irish HOME RULE crisis. As attorney general (1915–19), Birkenhead was responsible for the prosecution of Roger CASEMENT.

Birmingham Six Six Irish men convicted (1974) by an English court of bombing two public houses in Birmingham, England. In 1991 their life sentences were quashed. The Court of Appeal ruled that methods used by the police in producing some written statements were inappropriate. Five of the men were duly released; the sixth had died in prison. Their case became notorious as a modern miscarriage of British justice. *See also* Guildford Four

Birney, James Gillespie (1792–1857) US abolitionist. A slave-owner turned reformer, he argued for the colonization of Liberia and worked in the American Anti-Slavery Society. A believer in political action, Birney ran for president as the Liberty Party candidate (1840–44).

Bishops' Wars (1639, 1640) Campaigns by Charles I of England against the Scots. Charles aimed to strengthen episcopacy by imposing English church ritual on Scotland; the Covenant of 1638 pledged the Scots to defend Presbyterianism. By the Treaty of Ripon (1640), Charles was forced to pay an indemnity to the invading Scots. *See also* Covenanters; Long Parliament

Bismarck, Otto von (1815–98) German statesman responsible for 19th-century German unification. Bismarck first made an impression as a diehard reactionary during the Revolutions of 1848. Keen to strengthen the Prussian army, William I appointed (1862) him chancellor of Prussia. Bismarck dissolved parliament and raised taxes to pay for military improvements. The status of Schleswig-Holstein enabled him to engineer the Austro-Prussian War (1866) and expel Austria from the German Confederation. Through the infamous Ems Telegram, Bismarck then provoked the Franco-Prussian War (1870–71) in order to bring the s German states into the Prussian-led North German Confederation. Victory saw Bismarck become (1871) the first chancellor of the German Empire. Through skilful diplomacy and alliance-building, he consolidated Germany's position in the heart of Europe. In 1882 Bismarck formed the Triple Alliance with Austro-Hungary and Italy. The rapid process of industrialization encouraged colonialism and the building of a German overseas empire. Bismarck's domestic policies were similarly based on the principle of "divide-and-rule". In 1873 he issued the May Decrees that attempted to place the Roman Catholic Church under state control. The next 13 years witnessed a Kulturkampf (Ger. "conflict of cultures") between church and state. In 1878 Bismarck banned the Social Democratic Party (SPD) in a bid to stem the rise of German socialism. He also adopted a paternalist programme (1883–87) of social welfare to weaken support for the SPD. The accession (1888) of William II saw the demise of Bismarck's political influence, and in 1890 the "iron chancellor" was forced to resign.

Bithynia Ancient region of nw Asia Minor. Originally occupied by Thracians, it was incorporated into the Persian Achaemenid empire by Cyrus II (the Great). After 300 bc, Bithynia evolved into a strong, independent kingdom. In 74 bc, in accordance with the will of its last king, it became a Roman province.

Black, Hugo LaFayette (1886–1971) US jurist, associate justice of the Supreme Court (1937–71). Black sponsored the Wages and Hours Bill (1937), investigated merchant-marine subsidies (1933) and vigorously supported New Deal legislation. As associate justice, he favoured a broad interpretation of the Constitution and wrote numerous dissents defending civil rights and liberties. In the late 1960s, however, Black voted to uphold state criminal laws.

Black and Tans Nickname for an auxiliary force of the Royal Irish Constabulary, recruited by the British government (1920–21) to subdue the Irish nationalists. The 12,000-strong force lacked regular uniforms and wore khaki with black hats and belts. The strong-arm tactics of the Black and Tans provoked international outrage.

Blackbeard (d.1718) English pirate, b. Edward Teach. In 1716 he began to attack shipping off the North American coast and in the Caribbean. Blackbeard was killed when two ships sent by the governor of Virginia attacked his ship, *Queen Anne's Revenge*.

black codes (1865–66) Laws passed in former Confederate states restricting the civil and political rights of newly freed blacks. The black codes were outlawed by the 14th amendment (1868) to the Constitution of the United States. *See also* Freedmen's Bureau; Reconstruction

Black Death (1347–52) Pandemic of plague, both bubonic and pneumonic, that killed about one-third of the population of Europe. It was brought from Asia to the Crimea, and from there to the Mediterranean ports. It then spread across Europe, carried by fleas infesting rats. Plague recurred intermittently and less severely until the 18th century.

Blackfoot Nomadic, warlike Native North American tribes. They are made up of three Algonquian-speaking tribes: the Siksika, or Blackfeet proper; the Kainah; and the Pikuni (Piegan). Living on the n Great Plains e of the Rockies, they depended largely on the bison (buffalo), which was hunted on horseback. Something of their richly ceremonial culture survives among the *c*.8000 Blackfeet living today on reservations in Alberta and Montana.

Black Friday (24 September 1869) Day of financial panic in the United States. Jay Gould and James Fisk attempted to corner the gold market and drove the price of gold up. The price fell after the US government sold part of its gold reserve, and many speculators were ruined. *See also* Wall Street Crash

Black Hand Secret society formed (1911) by Serbian army officers. The organization, led by Colonel Dragutin Dimitrijević, advocated the use of violence to achieve independence for Serbia within the Ottoman and Habsburg empires. The Black Hand was responsible for the assassination (June 1914) of Archduke Franz Ferdinand, which led to the outbreak of World War I. During the War, the society dominated the Serbian army. In 1917 Prince Alexander, worried about its growing influence, executed Dimitrijević and two other leaders of the Black Hand.

Black Hawk War (1832) Conflict between the Sac and Fox and the US Army. The Sac chief, Black Hawk (1767–1838), denounced treaties (1804, 1832) that sought to remove Native Americans from land w of the Mississippi. The shooting of his peace emissary stung Black Hawk into attack. Initial victories against the US army were overturned at the Battle of Bad Axe (1832). Black Hawk's surrender was ignored, and most of the tribe was massacred.

Black Hole of Calcutta (June 1756) Prison in Calcutta, India, where 64 or more British soldiers were placed by the Nawab Siraj-ad-Dawlah of Bengal. The cell was 5.5 × 4.5m (18 × 15ft); most of the soldiers died of suffocation.

Blackmun, Harry Andrew (1908–99) US jurist, associate justice of the Supreme Court (1970–94). Nominated for associate justice by President Richard Nixon. Blackmun wrote the majority opinion in the landmark case *Roe v. Wade* (1973), which in effect legalized abortion.

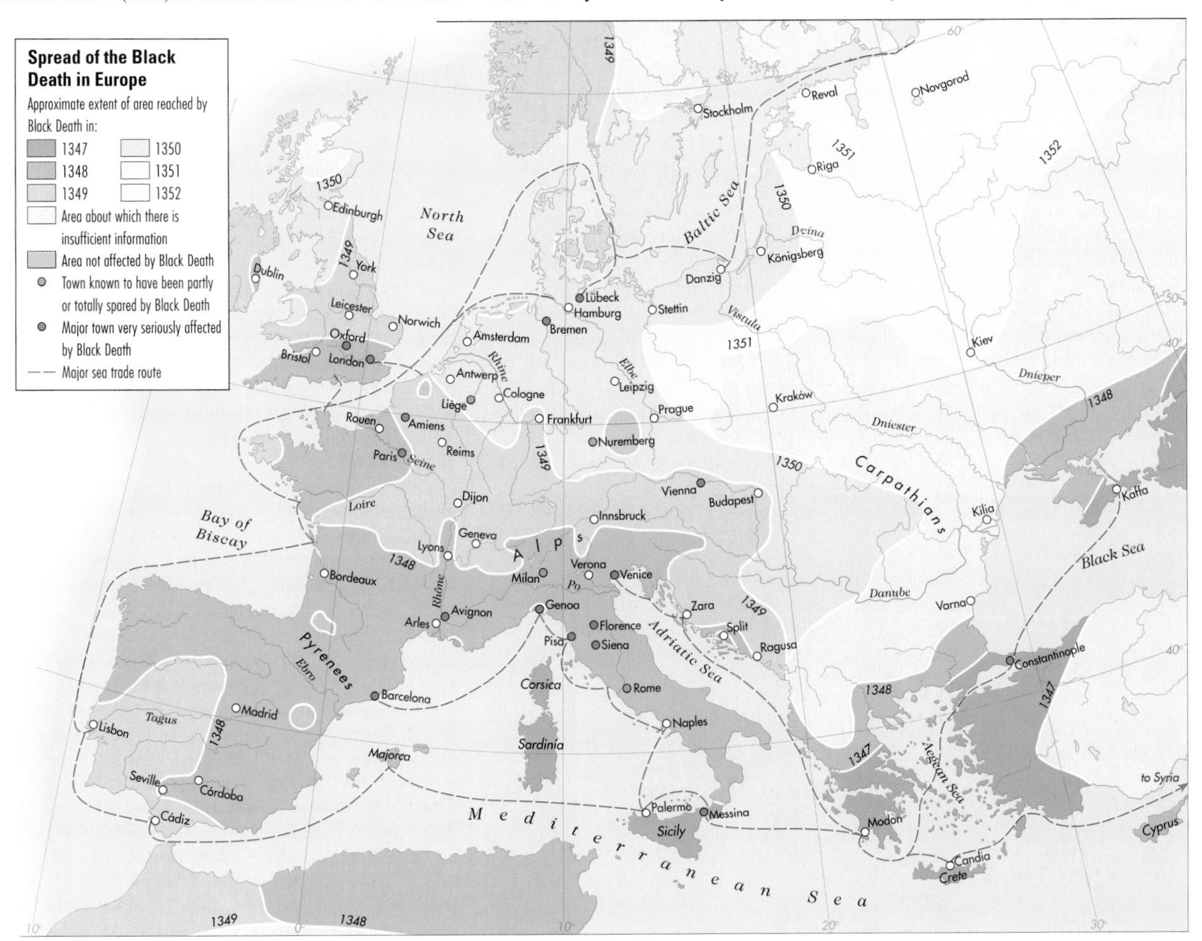

◄ Black Death (1347–52) The plague reached e Asia in the mid-1330s, and w Asia a decade later. In 1347 the Crimean port of Kaffa, a Genoese trading base, came under attack from the Kipchak Turks, in whose ranks the plague was raging. The resulting flight of Italian merchants from Kaffa carried the plague to Messina, Sicily, and then to Genoa itself. Genoa's commercial rivals, Pisa and Venice, succumbed shortly afterwards, and the pestilence went on to devastate most of Europe. By 1350 it had reached Scandinavia via the Hanseatic seaways.

B

Black Muslims African-American nationalist movement in the United States. It aims to establish a separatist black Muslim state. Founded (1930) in Detroit, Michigan, by Wallace Fard (*c*.1877–1934?), the movement was led (1934–76) by Elijah MUHAMMAD. The Black Muslims grew rapidly from 1945 to 1960, helped by the rhetorical power of the preacher MALCOLM X. Factions developed within the movement, and in 1963 Malcolm's membership was suspended. In 1976 the movement split into the American Muslim Mission and the Nation of Islam. The former (led by Elijah's son, Wallace D. Muhammad) preaches a more integrationist message. The Nation of Islam, led by Louis FARRAKHAN, claims to uphold the true doctrines of Elijah Muhammad and preaches a more racially exclusive message. During the 1980s and 1990s, the Nation of Islam gained great popularity in the United States. Mass demonstrations, such as the "Million Man March" in Washington, D.C., have generated extensive media attention. Today, total membership is *c*.10,000.

Black Panthers Revolutionary party of African Americans in the 1960s and 1970s. It was founded (1966) by Huey Newton (1942–89) and Bobby Seale (1936–). The Black Panthers called for the establishment of an autonomous black state and armed resistance to white repression. Violent clashes with police occurred, and several leaders, including Newton, fled abroad to escape prosecution. In the 1970s leadership conflicts and the decline of black militancy reduced the influence of the Panthers.

black power Doctrine of radical black movements in the United States from the 1960s. Principal organizations involved were the STUDENT NONVIOLENT COORDINATING COMMITTEE (SNCC), the BLACK MUSLIMS, the Organization of Afro-American Unity, and the BLACK PANTHERS. Black power groups rejected the policy of nonviolent civil disobedience associated with Martin Luther KING, Jr, and advocated autonomy and self-determination for black communities. *See also* CIVIL RIGHTS

Black Prince *See* EDWARD THE BLACK PRINCE

Black September Splinter group of the FATAH organization within the PALESTINE LIBERATION ORGANIZATION (PLO). It took its name from the civil war (September 1970) in Jordan between King HUSSEIN's army and Palestinian guerrillas. Black September are chiefly remembered for taking nine Israeli athletes hostage at the 1972 Olympic Games in Munich. The siege ended in the death of all the athletes and five terrorists.

blackshirt Colloquial name for a member of a fascist organization. In 1919 the Squadre d'Azione (SA) was founded in Italy by Benito MUSSOLINI. Organized into paramilitary squads, they violently attacked communists and socialists. In 1922 the Blackshirts' march on Rome helped Mussolini gain power. The name was also applied to the SS in Nazi Germany and Oswald MOSLEY's British Union of Fascists (BUF). *See also* BROWNSHIRTS; FASCISM

Blackstone, Sir William (1723–80) English jurist and politician. As a fellow of All Souls' College, Oxford, Blackstone introduced the first English law course into an English university. His *Commentaries on the Laws of England* (1765–69) is a classic study. Blackstone entered Parliament in 1761.

Blackwell, Antoinette Louisa (1825–1921) US Unitarian minister, sister-in-law of Elizabeth BLACKWELL, b. Antoinette Brown. In 1853 Blackwell became the first ordained woman minister in the United States. She was an active feminist and abolitionist.

Blackwell, Elizabeth (1821–1910) US physician, b. England. In 1847 she began to study medicine at the Geneva Medical College in New York. In 1849 Blackwell became the first woman doctor in the United States. In 1857 she established the New York Infirmary, which combined health services and medical training.

Blaine, James Gillespie (1830–93) US statesman, secretary of state (1881, 1889–92). An influential Maine Republican, he served as senator (1876–81). In 1884 Blaine ran for president but lost the election to the Democratic candidate, Grover CLEVELAND, partly because of the defection of reform Republicans (MUGWUMPS).

Blair, Francis Preston, Sr (1791–1876) US journalist, father of Francis Preston BLAIR, Jr. He was a leading member of President Andrew JACKSON's "kitchen cabinet". In 1830 Blair founded the pro-Jackson Washington *Globe*, which he published until 1845. A leading abolitionist, he was instrumental in establishing the REPUBLICAN PARTY. In 1865 Blair was responsible for convening the HAMPTON ROADS PEACE CONFERENCE. After the Civil War, however, Blair returned to the Democratic Party.

Blair, Francis Preston, Jr (1821–75) US statesman and soldier. He organized the FREE-SOIL PARTY in Missouri and became (1856) the only Party representative in Congress from a slave state. Blair campaigned for Abraham LINCOLN in the 1860 presidential election and returned to Congress as a Republican. In 1861 Blair and Nathaniel Lyon seized Camp Jackson, an action that helped to keep Missouri loyal to the Union. In 1862 he was appointed major general of volunteers. Blair broadly supported RECONSTRUCTION, but opposed giving blacks the vote. In 1868 he was the unsuccessful Democratic candidate for vice president

Blair, Tony (Anthony Charles Lynton) (1953–) British statesman, prime minister (1997–). He entered Parliament in 1983. Blair was elected leader of the LABOUR PARTY after the death (1994) of John SMITH and rapidly established himself as a modernizer. His reform of the Party's structure and constitution ("new Labour") helped him achieve a landslide victory in the 1997 general election. Britain's youngest prime minister of the 20th century, Blair succeeded John MAJOR. His constitutional reforms included devolution for Scotland and Wales. Blair devoted much energy to solving the crises in Northern Ireland and Kosovo. *See also* BROWN, GORDON; COOK, ROBIN

Blake, Robert (1599–1657) English admiral. A staunch Parliamentarian, he defended (1643–45) Bristol, Lyme and Taunton against Royalist attack in the English CIVIL WAR. In 1649 Blake took command of the Parliamentary fleet, and destroyed the Royalist navy. In the first (1652–54) of the DUTCH WARS, he gained notable victories against a strong Dutch navy. In 1657 Blake sank the Spanish fleet off Tenerife but died on the voyage home.

Blanc, Louis (1811–82) French socialist and historian, b. Spain. In 1839 he founded the newspaper *Revue du Progrès,* where he outlined the theory of workers' "social workshops". Blanc played a leading role in the REVOLUTION OF 1848, but fled to England after the failure of the workers' revolt in June 1848. While in exile, he wrote a history of the French Revolution. In 1870 Blanc returned to France and was elected to the Chamber of Deputies.

▶ **Blair** Britain's youngest prime minister since the Earl of Liverpool (1812), Tony Blair's modernization of the Labour Party helped to achieve a landslide victory in 1997. His government introduced important constitutional reforms, such as devolution for Scotland and Wales. More controversial policies included the "Welfare to Work" package of reforms to social security.

Bland-Allison Act (1878) US legislation providing for the purchase and coinage of silver by the secretary of the treasury. The original form, introduced by Richard Parks Bland (1835–99), called for unlimited coinage and was opposed by the bankers. William Boyd Allison (1829–1908) suggested a compromise that limited the coinage, and this version was passed. It was replaced by the SHERMAN SILVER PURCHASE ACT (1890).

Blanqui, (Louis) Auguste (1805–81) French socialist leader. A legendary revolutionary campaigner who spent much of his life in prison, Blanqui participated in the revolutions of 1830 and 1848, and in the overthrow of NAPOLEON III (1870). He became a symbol for European socialists and was president of the PARIS COMMUNE.

Blenheim, Battle of (13 August 1704) Major conflict in the War of the SPANISH SUCCESSION (1701–14). British and Austrian troops, led by the Duke of MARLBOROUGH and Prince EUGÈNE OF SAVOY, mounted a surprise attack on the Franco-Bavarian army under Marshal Tallartat, at Blenheim, Bavaria. The Elector of Bavaria beat a hasty retreat, but the French were penned in by the River Danube and 13,000 troops surrendered. The Battle cost *c*.12,000 Allied casualties and *c*.18,000 Franco-Bavarian casualties. Marlborough was granted a royal manor near Oxford, S central England, where he built Blenheim Palace, birthplace of his descendant Winston CHURCHILL.

Blériot, Louis (1872–1936) French aviator and aircraft designer. On 25 July 1909, Blériot became the first man to fly an aircraft across the English Channel. The flight, from Calais, N France, to Dover, S England, in a self-designed monoplane, took 37 minutes.

Bligh, William (1754–1817) English naval captain. In 1789 Bligh was cast adrift by his mutinous crew aboard the BOUNTY. With a few loyal companions, he sailed nearly 6500km (4000mi) to Timor. While governor of New South Wales (1805–08), Bligh faced a further mutiny led by his deputy and was arrested and sent back to England for trial. He was later exonerated.

Blitz, the (1940–41) Name used by the British to describe the night-time bombing of British cities by the German LUFTWAFFE (air force) during WORLD WAR 2. It is an abbreviation of *Blitzkrieg* (lightning war), the name used by the German army to describe hard-hitting, surprise attacks on enemy forces.

Blood River, Battle of (16 December 1838) Conflict between the AFRIKANERS and the ZULU. Around 3000 Zulu and only four Afrikaners were killed in the Battle, which resulted in the Afrikaners being able to settle in NATAL (now KwaZulu-Natal). *See also* GREAT TREK

Bloody Assizes (1685) Trials held in the W of England following MONMOUTH's Rebellion against JAMES II. Judge JEFFREYS conducted the trials. He sentenced *c*.320 people to be hanged, *c*.800 to transportation, and hundreds more to flogging, imprisonment or fines.

Bloody Sunday (30 January 1972) Killing of 13 unarmed demonstrators and injuring of a further 14 (one of whom died shortly afterwards) by the British Army in Londonderry (now Derry), Northern IRELAND. The victims were taking part in a civil rights march to protest against the introduction of internment in Northern Ireland. A subsequent inquiry (1972), chaired by Lord Widgery, largely exonerated the British soldiers. "Bloody Sunday" proved to be a propaganda coup for the IRISH REPUBLICAN ARMY (IRA). In March 1972 the Northern Ireland Parliament at Stormont was suspended, replaced by direct rule from Westminster. In 1998 the British Prime Minister Tony Blair called for a new inquiry, chaired by Lord Saville, to take account of new eye-witness information.

Bloomer, Amelia Jenks (1818–94) US women's rights campaigner. Bloomer published (1849–54) *Lily*, the first US magazine for women. She subsequently continued as editor and wrote articles on education, marriage laws, and female suffrage. She popularized the full trousers for women that became known as "bloomers".

Blount, William (1749–1800) US politician. He was a member of the CONTINENTAL CONGRESS and a delegate to the Federal CONSTITUTIONAL CONVENTION. Blount was governor (1790–96) of the territory south of the Ohio River (Tennessee). He was the first senator from the new state of Tennessee (1796), but was expelled from the Senate for participating in a plot to aid the British in obtaining Spanish Florida and Louisiana.

Blücher, Gebhard Leberecht von (1744–1819) Prussian field marshal. He distinguished himself during the FRENCH REVOLUTIONARY WARS (1792–1802) and the NAPOLEONIC WARS (1803–15) against France. Blücher led the Prussian troops at the Battle of Lützen (1813) and helped to defeat NAPOLEON I at the Battle of LEIPZIG (1813). In 1815 he was defeated at Ligny but arrived at WATERLOO in time to secure a British victory over Napoleon.

Blum, Léon (1872–1950) French statesman, prime minister (1936–37). He served in the chamber of deputies (1919–40) as a leader of the SOCIALIST PARTY (PS). Blum formed the Popular Front, which became a coalition government. His administration rapidly embarked on a programme of nationalization. Opposed by Conservatives, Blum was forced to resign and became deputy prime minister. He opposed the MUNICH AGREEMENT (1938). Interned by the VICHY GOVERNMENT (1940–45), he briefly led (1946–47) a provisional government. *See also* DE GAULLE, CHARLES

Blunt, Anthony Frederick (1907–83) English art historian. He was director (1947–74) of the Courtauld Institute of Art, London, and surveyor of the king's (later queen's) pictures (1945–72). Blunt was a formidable scholar, earning praise for his work on Nicolas Poussin. In 1979 his reputation was destroyed when it was disclosed that he had been a Soviet spy during World War 2.

Blyden, Edward Wilmot (1832–1912) West Indian writer and philosopher, b. St Thomas. Unable to gain admission to a US college because he was black, he emigrated to LIBERIA, attended school there, and became president of Liberia College (1880). He was a leading colonizer of Liberia. His books include *Liberia's Offering* (1873).

Boabdil (d.*c.*1527) (Muhammad XI) Last Moorish sultan of GRANADA (1482–92). He seized the throne from his father, Abu-al-Hasan (Mulhacén), plunging Granada into civil war. Abu al-Hasan quickly regained the capital. In 1483 Boabdil was taken prisoner by the Castilian king FERDINAND V. By the Pact of Córdoba (1483), he agreed to deliver the lands of his uncle, az-Zaghall, in return for Castilian help in recapturing Granada. In 1485 he reoccupied Granada. In 1491 the forces of FERDINAND V and ISABELLA I laid siege to the capital. In January 1492 Boabdil surrendered the ALHAMBRA, thus ending Muslim rule in Spain. In 1493 he fled to Morocco.

Boadicea (Boudicca) (d.AD 62) Queen of the ICENI in East Britain. She was the wife of King Prasutagus who, on his death, left his daughters and the Roman emperor as co-heirs. The Romans seized his domain, and Boadicea led a revolt against them. After initial successes, during which her army is thought to have killed as many as 70,000 Roman soldiers, she was defeated and poisoned herself. *See also* ROMAN BRITAIN

boat people Refugees that flee their country by sea to avoid political persecution or to find greater economic opportunities. The term is closely associated with South Vietnamese refugees, of whom, since 1975, *c.*150,000 have sailed to Hong Kong and to other Southeast Asian countries. Other boat people include Cubans and Haitians attempting to reach the United States, usually Florida.

Bodhidharma (active 6th century AD) Indian monk who travelled to China and founded ZEN Buddhism.

Bodin, Jean (1530–96) French lawyer and political philosopher. In *Six Books of the Republic* (1576), Bodin treated ANARCHY as the supreme political evil and order as the supreme human need. He is most noted for his doctrine of indivisible, absolute sovereignty.

Boeotia Department in central Greece, on the N shore of the Gulf of Corinth; the capital is Levádhia. The Boeotian League of Greek cities, formed in the 7th century BC, was dominated by THEBES. It was disbanded after 479 BC, but reconsituted in 447 BC, becoming a major power in Greece until its defeat by Philip II of Macedon in 338 BC. Area: 3211sq km (1240sq mi). Pop. (1991) 134,300.

◀ **Blériot** flew his first aircraft in 1907, but it was with the Type XI (shown here) that he achieved his greatest success. In 1909, he flew from Les Barraques, N France, to Dover, England. This flight was the first international air journey and the first sea crossing by air.

Boer (Afrikaans, farmer) Alternative name for an AFRIKANER

Boer Wars *See* SOUTH AFRICAN WARS

Boethius, Ancius Manlius Severinus (*c.*480–524) Roman statesman and philosopher under the Gothic king Theodoric. He attempted to eliminate governmental corruption but was arrested on a charge of conspiracy. In prison at Pavia, where he was subsequently tortured and executed, Boethius wrote *On the Consolation of Philosophy* (523). Next to the Bible, this was medieval Europe's most influential book.

Boğazkale *See* HATTUSAS

Bogomils Religious sect founded by the Bulgarian priest Bogomil (*c.*AD 950) whose views may have been inspired by MANICHAEISM. This starkly ascetic group originated in Bulgaria, spread to other Slavic countries and to France, where it influenced the Albigensian heresy. The Bogomils were dualists, believing that God controlled the world of the spirit, while Satan controlled the material world (including the human body). They held that Christ was human only in appearance. *See also* ALBIGENSES

Bogotá Capital of Colombia, on a fertile plateau in central Colombia. In 1538 the Spanish conquistador Gonzalo Jiménez de Quesada captured the CHIBCHA site of Bacatá. Bogotá became the capital of the Spanish viceroyalty of New Granada. Simon BOLÍVAR liberated the city after the Battle of BOYACÁ (1819). In 1821 Bogotá became the capital of the Confederation of Gran Colombia. In 1830 the Confederation collapsed and the city was made the capital of Colombia. Pop. (1992) 4,921,264.

Bohemia Historic region that (with MORAVIA) now comprises the CZECH REPUBLIC. The major cities are PRAGUE and Plzeň. At the end of the 9th century, Bohemia was established as an independent principality ruled by the PREMYSLID dynasty. The Christianization of the state was encouraged by Prince (later Saint) WENCESLAS and his successors. By the end of the 10th century, Bohemia had been subsumed into the Holy Roman Empire. Its status within the Empire was enhanced in the 12th century, when Prince Vladislav I was made an ELECTOR. German migration to the kingdom increased considerably in the 13th century when, under Ottocar II (r.1253–78), Bohemia stretched from the Oder to the Adriatic. Bohemia's golden age was in the reign (1347–78) of Emperor CHARLES IV, who made Prague his capital. In the reigns of Charles' sons, WENCESLAS and SIGISMUND, Bohemia was at the centre of nationalist and religious revolts against imperial domination, including the rebellion of Jan HUS. In 1526 Bohemia was inherited by the HABSBURG dynasty. The DEFENESTRATION OF PRAGUE (1618) sparked the THIRTY YEARS' WAR (1618–48) within the Habsburg Empire. The process of Germanization was continued by MARIA THERESA and JOSEPH II. LEOPOLD II was the last king of Bohemia. The formation of the AUSTRO-HUNGARIAN EMPIRE failed to satisfy Czech demands for autonomy and independence was finally achieved at the end of World War 1 under Tomás MASARYK. By the MUNICH AGREEMENT (1938), CZECHOSLOVAKIA was forced to cede the SUDETENLAND to Germany. In 1993 the dissolution of Czechoslovakia saw Bohemia and Moravia join to form the Czech Republic.

Bohemond I (1056–1111) Prince of ANTIOCH (1099–1111), son of Robert GUSICARD. He fought (1081–85) alongside his father against the Byzantine Emperor ALEXIUS I (COMMENUS). In 1096 he joined the First CRUSADE and played a key role in the capture of

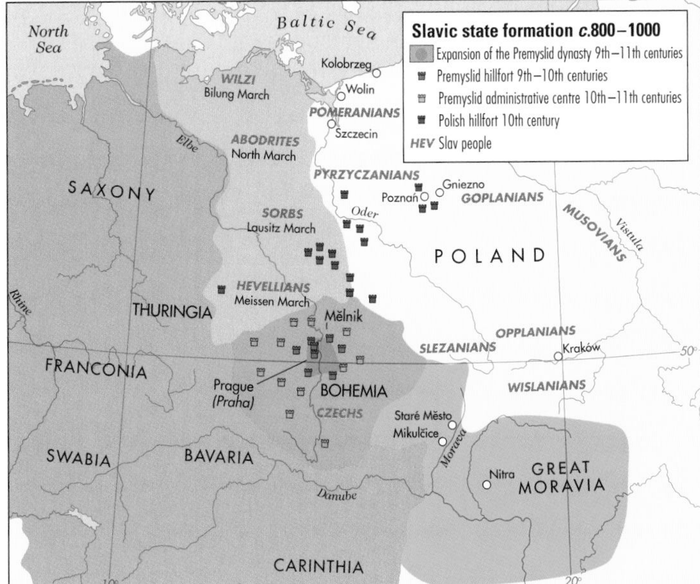

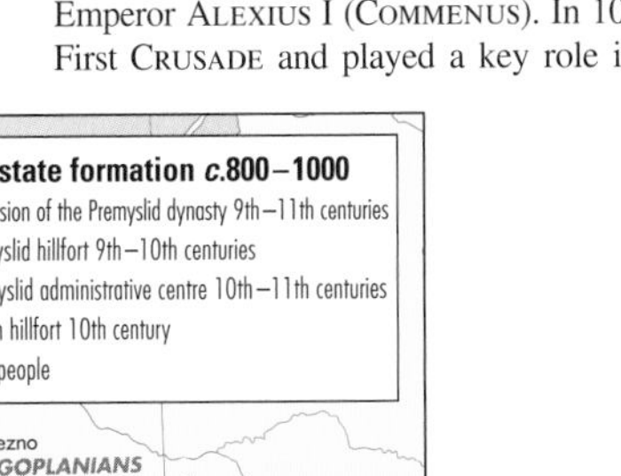

◀ **Bohemia** In the 9th and early 10th centuries, Slavic states formed in Moravia, Poland and Bohemia. Polish and Bohemian rulers used fortified administrative centres to dominate previously independent tribes. While Great Moravia was based on large urban centres on the River Morava, state formation among the Elbe Slavs was held in check by the power of the German duchies, notably Saxony under Otto I.

Antioch (1098). Bohemond was held captive by the Turks (1100–03).

Bokassa, Jean Bédel (1921–96) Emperor of the Central African Empire (1977–79). In 1966 Bokassa overthrew President David Dacko in a military coup and appointed himself president. In 1977 he was crowned emperor in a US$200 million ceremony. In 1979 Bokassa was deposed in a coup, backed by the French army, and Dacko was reinstated. In 1987 Bokassa was found guilty of the murders of 100 schoolchildren and sentenced to death. He was freed in 1993.

Bolesław I (the Brave) (d.1025) Polish ruler (992–1025). In 1024 he became the first king of Poland. Starting from a small principality on the River Vistula, Bolesław established Polish dominion from the Oder and Neisse rivers to the Dnieper and from Western Pomerania to the Carpathian Mountains. In 1003 Bohemia recognized him as a duke. The Christian church was firmly established. At his death, Poland was one of the strongest states of Europe.

Bolesław II (the Generous) (1039–83) King of Poland (1058–79), son and successor of Casimir I. Opposing the power of the Holy Roman Empire, he asserted Polish influence in Bohemia and Hungary. In 1069 Bolesław captured Kiev. In 1079 he executed for treason the bishop of Kraków, Saint Stanislaus. Bolesław was excommunicated by the pope and deposed by his brother, Ladislas Herman. He died in exile in Hungary.

Bolesław III (the Wry-mouthed) (1086–1138) King of Poland (1102–38). He warred against Bohemia, Hungary and Kiev. In 1109 Bolesław defeated an invasion of Poland by Emperor Henry V and regained and Christianized Pomerania.

Boleyn, Anne (1507–36) Second wife of Henry VIII of England, mother of Elizabeth I. In 1533 Henry and Anne were married after Henry's first marriage, to Catherine of Aragon, had been annulled. Henry was desperate for an heir, and following the birth of a stillborn boy (1536), Anne was accused of adultery and executed for treason. It is thought that her Protestant sympathies pushed the king toward the break with Rome that unleashed the English Reformation. *See also* Cromwell, Thomas

Bolger, Jim (James) (1935–) New Zealand statesman, prime minister (1990–96). He entered Parliament in 1972. Bolger held several posts in Robert Muldoon's National government. In 1986 he became leader of the National Party. Bolger's main task as prime minister was to steer New Zealand out of recession. He was succeeded as prime minister by Jenny Shipley.

Bolingbroke *See* Henry IV (of England)

Bolingbroke, Henry St John, Viscount (1678–1751) English politician and philosopher. A prominent Tory minister under Queen Anne, he fled to France (1714) and joined the Jacobites. In 1723 Bolingbroke was allowed to return to England and continued to oppose the Whig regime under Robert Walpole.

Bolívar, Simón *See* feature article

Bolivia *See* country feature

Bologna (Bononia) City at the foot of the Apennines, N central Italy; capital of Bologna and Emilia-Romagna province. Originally an Etruscan town, Felsina, it was colonized by Rome in the 2nd century BC. Bologna became a free commune in the early 12th century. In 1506 it was subsumed into the Papal States. The University of Bologna was founded in the 11th century. Pop. (1992) 401,308.

Bolsheviks (Rus. majority) Marxist revolutionaries, led by Lenin, who seized power in the Russian Revolution of 1917. They narrowly defeated the Mensheviks at the Second Congress of the Social Democratic Labour Party in London, England (1903). The split centred on the means of achieving revolution. The Bolsheviks believed it could be obtained only by professional revolutionaries leading the proletariat. The Bolsheviks were able to defeat Alexander Kerensky's provisional government with the support of the soviets in Moscow and Petrograd. *See also* Marxism

Bombay *See* Mumbai

Bonaparte, Joseph (1768–1844) King of Spain (1808–13), eldest brother of Napoleon I, b. Corsica. He served as a diplomat for the First Republic of France. In 1806 Napoleon made him king of Naples. After Napoleon's defeat at Waterloo, he resided in the United States (1815–32).

Bonaparte, Louis (1778–1846) King of Holland (1806–10), brother of Napoleon I and father of Charles Louis Napoleon (later Napoleon III of France). He accompanied his brother in the Italian and Egyptian campaigns, became a general (1804) and governor of Paris (1805). Forced by Napoleon to take the Dutch throne, he worked to restore its economy and welfare, but the French Continental System proved ruinous to Dutch trade. Napoleon felt he was too lenient and the conflict led Louis to abdicate.

Bonaparte, Napoleon *See* Napoleon I

Bonar Law, Andrew *See* Law, Andrew Bonar

Bonaventure, Saint (1221–74) Italian theologian, Doctor of the Church, b. Giovanni di Fidanza. He taught with Saint Thomas Aquinas at the University of Paris. In 1257 Bonaventure was elected minister general of the Franciscan Order. In 1273 he became cardinal bishop of Albano. He played a prominent part in the Council of Lyons (1274). Bonaventure sought to reconcile Aristotle's insights with conventional Augustinianism. His essentially mystical theory of knowledge is set forth in *Journey of the Soul to God*. His feast day is 14 July. *See also* Augustine, Saint

Bond, Julian (1940–) US civil rights leader. In 1960 he helped found the Student Nonviolent Coordinating Committee (SNCC) and served as its communications director (1961–65). In 1965 Bond was elected to the Georgia state assembly, but was denied his seat because of his outspoken opposition to the Vietnam War. Bond took his seat in 1966 after Congress ruled that the assembly had denied his freedom of speech.

Bondfield, Margaret Grace (1873–1953) British Labour politician and union leader. In 1923 she became chairwoman of the Trades Union Congress (TUC). As minister of labour (1923–31), Bondfield was the first woman member of a British Cabinet.

Bongo, Omar (1935–) Gabonese statesman, president (1967–). In 1968 he created a one-party state, but was forced to cede multiparty elections in 1990. Bongo was re-elected in 1973, 1979, 1986 and 1993.

Bonhoeffer, Dietrich (1906–45) German theologian. A Lutheran pastor, he opposed the rise of the Nazi Party. Arrested by the Nazis in 1943, Bonhoeffer was executed

BOLÍVAR, SIMÓN (1783–1830)

South American soldier and statesman, president of Colombia (1821–30) and Peru (1823–29), b. Venezuela. Bolívar became known as "the Liberator" for his role in freeing Spanish America from colonial rule. In 1810 the Spanish governor of Venezuela was overthrown and Bolívar travelled to Britain to persuade Francisco de Miranda to return as leader of the independence movement. In 1812 Spain regained control of Venezuela. In 1813 Bolívar led the forces that liberated Caracas. In 1814 Spain crushed the second republic. In exile, Bolívar composed the "Jamaica Letter" (1815) that called for a continent-wide struggle for independence. In 1819 he led an army of *c.*2500 men across the Andes and routed the Spanish in New Granada at the Battle of Boyacá. Bolívar became president and military dictator of the new republic of Gran Colombia. His victory at the Battle of Carababo (June 1821) liberated Venezuela. Bolívar placed the government in the hands of Santander and went in pursuit of complete military victory. In 1822 Bolívar and Antonio José de Sucre freed Ecuador from Spanish rule. At the Guayaquil Conference (July 1822), José de San Martín agreed to let Bolívar liberate Peru. The Spanish army surrendered to Sucre at the Battle of Ayacucho (9 December 1824). In 1825 Sucre liberated Upper Peru, which was named Bolivia in honour of "the Liberator". Bolívar called the first Pan-American Conference (1826) to promote cooperation between the new Spanish American republics. His hopes of uniting South America into one confederation were soon dashed, however, as civil war broke out in Gran Colombia. Bolívar assumed dictatorial powers to prevent Venezuela from seceding from the union. In 1829 rivalries and revolts fomented in the new republics. Bolívar resolved to go into exile, but was dissuaded by the assassination of Sucre (1830).

► **The Republic of Gran Colombia** was created by Bolívar (left) following a successful campaign against the Spanish, 1817–22. He also established the independent republic of Bolivia, named in his honour. Bolívar then returned to Colombia but was unable to hold together the republic and in 1830 it broke up into the three modern day states of Venezuela, Colombia and Ecuador.

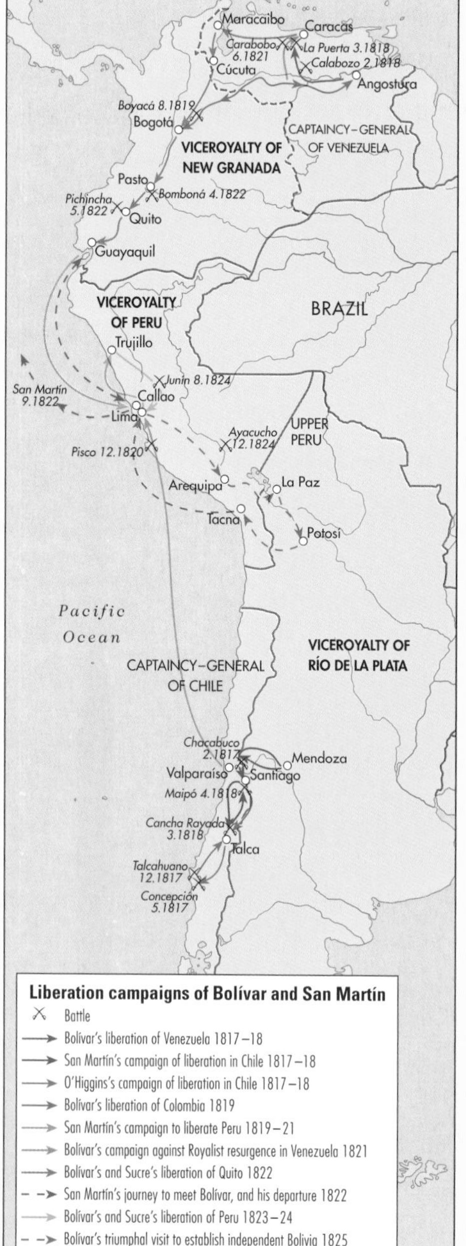

for treason after being linked with a failed conspiracy (1944) to assassinate Adolf HITLER. Among his works, published posthumously, are *Letters from Prison* (1953) and *Christology* (1966). Bonhoeffer espoused a kind of "secular" Christianity.

Boniface, Saint (*c*.675–754) English missionary. In 716 he left England to convert the pagan Germans. In 751 Boniface was rewarded with the archbishopric of Mainz. He was martyred by pagans in Friesland. Boniface is buried in Fulda, Bavaria, and is venerated as the apostle of Germany. His feast day is 5 June.

Boniface VIII (1235–1303) Pope (1294–1303), b. Benedetto Gaetani. To bring order to Rome and prevent schism, Boniface imprisoned his predecessor, Celestine V. In 1300 he offered the first plenary indulgence for all who made a pilgrimage to Rome.

Bonifácio, José *See* ANDRADA E SILVA, JOSÉ BONIFÁCIO

Bonn City and capital of former West Germany on the River Rhine, North Rhine-Westphalia, w Germany. Founded in the 1st century AD as a Roman military establishment, it later became the seat of the electorate and archbishopric of Cologne (1238–1797) and was awarded to Prussia by the Congress of Vienna (1815). Bonn was capital of West Germany from 1949 until German reunification in 1990. Pop. (1990) 297,400. *See also* BERLIN

Bonney, William H. *See* BILLY THE KID

Bonnie Prince Charlie *See* STUART, CHARLES EDWARD

Bonus Army (1932) Unemployed veterans who marched on Washington, D.C., and demanded cash payment of bonus certificates. The 17,000 veterans camped out during June and July until President Herbert HOOVER sent troops, led by Douglas MACARTHUR, to disperse them. In 1936 the veterans were given cashable bonds.

Book of Common Prayer *See* COMMON PRAYER, BOOK OF

Boone, Daniel (1734–1820) US frontier pioneer. In 1775 he blazed the famous WILDERNESS ROAD from Virginia to Kentucky and founded the settlement of Boonesborough. During the AMERICAN REVOLUTION (1775–83), Boone was captured by the Shawnee, but escaped and reached Boonesborough in time to prevent it from falling to the British and their Native American allies.

Booth, Charles (1840–1916) English social reformer who pioneered the method of social survey in *Life and Labour of the People in London* (1891–1903). Booth was instrumental in gaining the passage of the Old Age Pensions Act in 1908. *See also* LLOYD GEORGE, DAVID

Booth, John Wilkes (1838–65) US actor and assassin of Abraham LINCOLN. Booth was a Confederate sympathizer. On 14 April 1865, during a performance at Ford's Theater in Washington, D.C., he shot Lincoln, who died the next day. Booth escaped but was either shot or killed himself two weeks later.

Booth, William (1829–1912) English religious leader, founder and first general of the SALVATION ARMY. A Methodist, Booth started his own revivalist movement, which undertook evangelistic and social work among the poor. In 1878 it became known as the Salvation Army and soon spread to many countries. On his death, Booth was succeeded first by his son, Bramwell Booth (1856–1929), and then his daughter, Evangeline Booth (1865–1950).

bootlegging Illegal supply and sale of goods that are subject to government prohibition or taxation. The name is said to derive from the practice of American frontiersmen, who carried bottles of illicit liquor in the tops of their boots for sale to Native Americans. Bootlegging blossomed during the PROHIBITION era (1920–33) in the United States.

Borah, William Edgar (1865–1940) US senator from Idaho (1907–40). He led opposition to US entry into the LEAGUE OF NATIONS and was chairman (1924–33) of the Senate committee on foreign affairs. Borah promoted the KELLOGG-BRIAND PACT (1927) and opposed US intervention in Latin America. He was a leading prohibitionist and strongly opposed much of the NEW DEAL.

Borden, Sir Robert Laird (1854–1937) Canadian statesman, prime minister (1911–20). He was elected to Parliament in 1896, and in 1901 became leader of the Conservative Party. Borden succeeded Sir Wilfrid LAURIER as prime minister. From 1917 to 1920, he headed a coalition government. Borden steered Canada through World War I and helped to shape the future constitutional status of the Dominion.

Borghese Italian princely family, originally of Siena, later Rome. Camillo Borghese (1552–1621) became pope as PAUL V in 1605. Another Camillo (1775–1832) married Marie Pauline Bonaparte, sister of NAPOLEON I, and was made governor of Piedmont.

Borgia, Cesare (1475–1507) Italian general and political figure, brother of Lucrezia BORGIA. In 1493 he was made a cardinal by his father, Pope ALEXANDER VI, but forsook the church to embark on a military campaign (1498–1503) to establish his dominion in central Italy. Borgia's ruthless campaigns lend credence to the theory that he was the model for Niccolò MACHIAVELLI's *The Prince* (1513). Imprisoned by Pope JULIUS II, Borgia escaped to Spain, where he was killed in battle.

Borgia, Lucrezia (1480–1519) Daughter of Pope ALEXANDER VI and sister of Cesare BORGIA. In 1497 her marriage to Giovanni Sforza was annulled by Alexander when it failed to produce anticipated political advantages. Lucrezia's marriage to Alfonso, nephew of Alfonso II of Naples, ended with Alfonso's murder (1500) by Cesare's henchman. In 1503, after the collapse of Borgia aspirations, she forsook the political intrigue for which she was notorious and lived quietly, a patron of art, at Ferrara with her third husband.

Boris I (d.907) Tsar of Bulgaria (852–89). In 865 Boris was converted to Christianity and imposed baptism on his subjects. After the failure of negotiations with the pope to create an archbishopric in Bulgaria, Boris accepted the primacy of the Eastern Orthodox Church (870). He died in a monastery and is venerated as a saint.

Boris III (1894–1943) Tsar of Bulgaria (1918–43). Following his father's abdication, Boris ruled as a constitutional monarch for 15 years, becoming dictator in 1934. Returning from a meeting with Adolf Hitler, who wanted Bulgaria to declare war on the Soviet Union, Boris died under mysterious circumstances.

Boris Godunov *See* GODUNOV, BORIS

Bormann, Martin Ludwig (1900–45) German NAZI PARTY leader. He joined the Nazis in 1925 and was important in the Party hierarchy. In 1941 Bormann succeeded Rudolf HESS as deputy leader. In 1945 he disappeared and was sentenced to death *in absentia* during the NUREMBERG TRIALS. In 1973, after identification of his skeleton, Bormann was formally pronounced dead as a result of suicide.

Borneo Island in the Malay Archipelago, *c*.650km (400mi) E of Singapore, SE Asia. Mostly undeveloped, Borneo is the world's third largest island, and is divided into four political regions: SARAWAK (W) and SABAH (N) are states of MALAYSIA; BRUNEI (NW) is an independent sultanate; and KALIMANTAN (E, central and S) covers 70% of the island and forms part of INDONESIA. The earliest reference to Borneo is found in Ptolemy's *Guide to Geography* (*c*.AD 150). Hinduism and Buddhism were introduced from India and Borneo formed part of the Indianized MAJAPAHIT empire of East Java (*c*.1293–1520). In the

BOLIVIA

AREA: 1,098,580sq km (424,162sq mi)
POPULATION: 7,832,000
CAPITAL (POPULATION): La Paz (1,126,000), Sucre (103,952)
GOVERNMENT: Multiparty republic
ETHNIC GROUPS: Mestizo 31%, Quechua 25%, Aymará 17%, White 15%
LANGUAGES: Spanish, Aymara, Quechua (all official)
RELIGIONS: Christianity (Roman Catholic 94%)
GDP PER CAPITA (1995): US$2540

Republic in W central South America. The ruins of TIAHUANACO indicate that the Altiplano was the site of one of the great pre-Columbian civilizations. At the time of the Spanish conquest (1532), the AYMARA had already been subsumed into the INCA empire by the QUECHUA. The Spanish exploited the Andean silver mines with native forced labour. In 1825 the Spanish were finally expelled with the victory of Antonio José de SUCRE, Simón BOLÍVAR's general.

The decline in mining and the Wars of Independence left the new nation impoverished. During the 1830s, Bolivia was ruled by the CAUDILLO Marshal Andrés de Santa Cruz. For the next century, the new nation of Bolivia was plagued by corruption and instability. In 1879 Chile invaded Bolivia and the ensuing War of the PACIFIC (1879–84) saw Chile gain control of the entire Pacific coast of Bolivia. From 1880 to 1899 the governing Conservative Party revived the silver-mining industry. The Federal Revolution (1899) brought the Liberal Party into power. In 1920 the newly formed Republican Party overthrew the Liberals. The disastrous CHACO WAR (1932–35) with Paraguay cost *c*.100,000 lives and ended in the loss of most of Gran Chaco to Paraguay. In 1936 the military launched a successful coup.

In 1941 Victor PAZ ESTENSSORO founded the National Revolutionary Movement (MNR). In 1943 Colonel Gualberto Villaroel, supported by fascist elements of the MNR, seized power. In 1946 he was overthrown and publicly executed. In 1952 Paz Estenssoro launched the National Revolution that nationalized the mines and instituted land reforms for the Native Americans. In 1956 Paz Estenssoro was succeeded by Hernando Siles Zuazo, but he returned to office in 1960. In 1964 Paz Estenssoro was overthrown in a military coup, led by General René Barrientos. The regime (1971–78) of Colonel Hugo Bánzer Suárez ruthlessly suppressed all political opposition, but oversaw a period of rapid economic growth. In 1978 Bánzer was forced to resign and martial law was declared. In 1982 civilian rule was restored under Siles Zuazo. In 1985 Paz Estenssoro became president for a third time. He was succeeded by Jaime Paz Zamora in 1989. The presidency (1993–97) of Gonzalo Sánchez de Lozada was marked by an unpopular privatization programme. In 1997 Bánzer returned as president of a coalition government, promising to continue (with US support) the war against the cultivation of coca.

B

▶ **Borobudur** One of the world's greatest Buddhist shrines, Borobudur was built in about the middle of the 9th century to a unique plan involving colossal resources; 570,000cu m (2 million cu ft) of stone were moved from a river bed, dressed, positioned and carved with countless spouts, urns and other embellishments. The walls are covered with reliefs relating to Buddhist doctrine and there are altogether 504 shrines with seated Buddhas.

16th century, Borneo was dominated by the sultan of Brunei, who established trading links with Spain and Portugal. The sultanate was undermined by the British Empire in the 19th century. In 1841 Sarawak was ceded to James BROOKE. North Borneo (now Sabah) was granted to a British trading company in 1881 and the sultanate itself became a British protectorate in 1888. Japan occupied (1941–42) Borneo during World War 2. In 1946 Sarawak and North Borneo became British crown colonies. Dutch Borneo (now Kalimantan) became part of Indonesia in 1950. In 1963 Sarawak and Sabah joined the Federation of Malaysia. Brunei gained full independence in 1984. Area: 743,330sq km (287,000sq mi).

Bornu (now Borno) Province and former kingdom in NE Nigeria, SW of Lake Chad. The kingdom arose in the 14th century, expanding to incorporate the declining kingdom of KANEM. The empire of Kanem-Bornu was at its height in the 16th century, exporting slaves and fabrics. In 1808 Bornu clashed with the FULANI. In 1846 Omar al-Kanami proclaimed himself the first sultan of Bornu. In 1902 Bornu was partitioned between the French, British and Germans.

Borobudur Ruins of a Buddhist monument in Central Java, built (*c.*AD 800) under the SAILENDRA dynasty. It comprises a stupa (relic mound), mandalas (ritual diagrams) and the temple mountain – all forms of Indian GUPTA dynasty religious art.

Borodino, Battle of (7 September 1812) Savage conflict in the NAPOLEONIC WARS (1803–15). NAPOLEON I's army of *c.*130,000 troops confronted *c.*120,000 Russians under Mikhail KUTUZOV at Borodino, *c.*110km (70mi) W of Moscow. Napoleon mounted a brutal, frontal assault on the Russian lines, but failed to seize the chance of a decisive victory as Kutuzov retreated under cover of darkness. The Russians lost *c.*45,000 men, while French losses totalled *c.*30,000. Victory enabled Napoleon to occupy Moscow, but Kutuzov was able to regroup before launching a counter-offensive. The Battle is vividly described in Leo Tolstoy's *War And Peace* (1865–69).

Bose, Subhas Chandra (1897–1945) Indian nationalist. His activities on behalf of the Indian National CONGRESS in Bengal led to long spells in prison or exile during the 1920s and 1930s. In 1928 Bose and Jawaharlal NEHRU formed the Indian Independence League. In 1938 Bose was elected president of the Indian National Congress. His disagreements with "Mahatma" GANDHI over the tactics of non-violent civil disobedience and the economic future of India led to his resignation in 1939. At the outbreak of World War 2, Bose supported the Axis Powers and escaped to Nazi Germany in 1941. In 1943 he re-emerged in Japanese-occupied Southeast Asia at the head of a 40,000-strong Indian National Army. In 1944 his advance into India was repulsed. Bose died in a airplane crash.

Bosnia-Herzegovina *See* country feature

Boston State capital and seaport of Massachusetts, USA, at the mouth of the Charles River on Massachusetts Bay. Boston was settled in 1630 by Puritans of the MASSACHUSETTS BAY COMPANY, led by John WINTHROP. In 1636 Harvard University was founded in nearby Cambridge. In 1686 Sir Edmund ANDROS was appointed governor of the Dominion of New England. By the end of the 18th century, Boston had become one of world's largest ports. Incidents such as the BOSTON MASSACRE (1770) and the BOSTON TEA PARTY (1773) were early warnings of the colonists' resistance to British rule. The Battle of BUNKER HILL (1775) was one of the first conflicts in the AMERICAN REVOLUTION and the British were expelled from Boston by 1776. In the 19th century, Boston was the centre of TRANSCENDENTALISM, the first truly distinctive national cultural movement. It is home to the Mother Church of Christian Science. Pop. (1990) 574,283.

Boston Massacre (1770) Riot by American colonists angered over the quartering of troops in private homes. Starting with some snowballing, it was put down by British soldiers and resulted in the death of five civilians, of whom the first to be shot was Crispus Attucks. The riot was exploited for anti-British propaganda by Samuel ADAMS and the Boston radicals. The soldiers were tried for murder, defended by John Adams, and acquitted.

Boston Tea Party (1773) Protest by a group of Massachusetts colonists, disguised as Mohawks and led by Samuel ADAMS, against the Tea Act and, more generally, against "taxation without representation". The Tea Act, passed by the British Parliament in 1773, withdrew duty on tea exported to the colonies. It enabled the EAST INDIA COMPANY to sell tea directly to the colonies without first going to Britain and resulted in colonial merchants being undersold. The protesters boarded three British ships and threw their cargo of tea into Boston harbour. The British retaliated by closing the harbour and passing the INTOLERABLE ACTS.

Bosworth Field, Battle of (22 August 1485) Final conflict in the English Wars of the ROSES (1455–85), fought near Bosworth, Leicestershire. RICHARD III was defeated by Henry Tudor. Henry, who claimed to represent the House of LANCASTER, invaded England from France. Richard was killed, and Henry claimed the throne as HENRY VII. *See also* YORK, HOUSE OF

Botha, Louis (1862–1919) South African general and statesman, first prime minister (1910–19) of the Union of SOUTH AFRICA. He opposed President Paul KRUGER's hostile stance toward Britain, favouring a negotiated settlement. Despite his military prowess during the Second SOUTH AFRICAN WAR (1899–1902), Botha was unable to overcome the numerical superiority of the British Army. In 1911 he founded the South African Party. His policy of appeasement with Britain led to a split in the Party and J.B.M. HERTZOG left to found (1914) the NATIONAL PARTY. As prime minister, Botha supported the Allies in World War 1 and conquered (1915) the German colony of South West Africa (now Namibia). He was succeeded by Jan SMUTS.

Botha, P.W. (Pieter Willem) (1916–) South African statesman, prime minister (1978–84) and first president (1984–89). The longest-serving member of the APARTHEID regime, Botha entered Parliament in 1948. As defence minister (1966–78), he expanded South Africa's armed forces and was responsible for the military involvement in Angola. He succeeded B.J. VORSTER as prime minister. Botha granted "independence" to the bantustans (black homelands). In 1980 he established the South West Africa Territorial Force, as part of the destabilization of South Africa's neighbours. In 1983 Botha passed a new constitution that gave Asians and Coloureds limited political representation (but excluded the black majority). In 1989 he suffered a stroke and, amid increasing National Party factionalism, was forced to resign. He was succeeded by F.W. DE KLERK. *See also* NATIONAL PARTY

Bothwell, James Hepburn, 4th Earl of (1536–78) Scottish nobleman, third husband of MARY, QUEEN OF SCOTS. Bothwell subdued a rebellion (1565) and after Mary's second husband, Lord DARNLEY, was implicated in the murder of her secretary, David RIZZIO, he became the queen's sole adviser. Bothwell was responsible for the murder (1567) of Darnley, and subsequently married Mary. Faced by a rebellion of Scottish nobles, he fled abroad and died insane in a Danish prison. *See also* CASKET LETTERS

Botswana *See* country feature, page 54

Boudicca *See* BOADICEA

Bougainville, Louis Antoine de (1729–1811) French navigator. A veteran of the FRENCH AND INDIAN WAR (1754–63) in Canada, he commanded the first French naval force to circumnavigate the globe (1766–69). Important botanical and astronomical studies were made during the voyage, and Bougainville claimed many of the Pacific islands for France, rediscovering the Solomon Islands. He fought in the American Revolution (1775–83) but was disgraced by a French defeat (1782) in the Caribbean.

Boulanger, Georges Ernest (1837–91) French general and minister. In the 1880s, supported by the Bonapartists and Royalists, Boulanger constituted a serious threat to the Thrid Republic in France. He committed suicide after being deported.

Boumedienne, Houari (1925–78) Algerian statesman, president (1965–78). In the Algerian War of Independence, he commanded (1955–60) guerrilla forces around Oran. In 1962 ALGERIA gained independence and Boumedienne became vice president (1962–65). In 1965 he overthrew President BEN BELLA and assumed authoritarian powers. He remained president until his death. *See also* FRONT DE LIBÉRATION NATIONALE (FLN)

Bounty, Mutiny on the (28 April 1789) British mutiny that took place near Tonga in the South Pacific Ocean. Fletcher Christian led a successful rebellion against Captain William BLIGH, and Bligh and 18 loyal crew members were set adrift. Christian and some of the mutineers founded a colony on Pitcairn Island.

Bourbon European dynastic family, descendants of the CAPETIANS. The ducal title was created in 1327 and continued until 1527. A cadet branch, the Bourbon-Vendôme line, won the kingdom of NAVARRE. The Bourbons ruled France from 1589 (when Henry of Navarre became HENRY IV) until the FRENCH REVOLUTION (1789–99). Two members of the family, LOUIS XVIII and CHARLES X, reigned (1814–30) after the restoration of the monarchy. In 1700 the Bourbons became the ruling family of Spain when PHILIP V, grandson of LOUIS XIV of France, assumed the throne. His descendants mostly continued to rule Spain until 1931, when the Second Republic was declared. In 1975 JUAN CARLOS I, a Bourbon, was restored to the Spanish throne.

Bourgeois, Léon Victor Auguste (1851–1925) French statesman, prime minister (1895–96). He was a vociferous supporter of the LEAGUE OF NATIONS, acting as the French representative at the League until 1923. Bourgeois won the 1920 Nobel Peace Prize.

bourgeoisie (middle CLASS) Term originally applied to artisans and craftsmen who lived in medieval French towns. Up to the late 18th century, it was a propertied but not necessarily wealthy class, often of urban merchants and tradesmen, who helped speed the decline of the FEUDAL SYSTEM. The 19th-century advent of CAPITALISM led to the expansion of the bourgeoisie and its division into the high (industrialists and financiers) and petty (tradesmen and clerical workers) bourgeoisie. *See also* MARX, KARL

Bourguiba, Habib ibn Ali (1903–2000) Tunisian statesman, president (1957–87). In 1954 he began the negotiations that culminated in Tunisian independence (1956). Bourguiba became prime minister and, after the abolition of the monarchy, was elected president. In 1975 he was proclaimed president-for-life. Bourguiba maintained a pro-French, autocratic rule until, old and ill, he was overthrown in a coup led by Ben Ali.

Boutros-Ghali, Boutros (1922–) Egyptian statesman,

sixth secretary general (1992–96) of the UNITED NATIONS (UN). As Egypt's foreign affairs minister (1977–91), he was involved in much of the Middle East peace negotiations. Boutros-Ghali briefly served as Egypt's prime minister (1991–92), before becoming the first African secretary general of the UN. Early in his term, he faced civil-war crises in the Balkans, Somalia and Rwanda. An independent secretary general, Boutros-Ghali managed to alienate US opinion. He was succeeded by Kofi ANNAN.

Bouvines, Battle of (27 July 1214) Conflict between PHILIP II of France and Holy Roman Emperor OTTO IV. On 2 July 1214, Philip defeated King JOHN of England at La Roche-aux-Moines, w France. The consequent weakening of the international coalition enabled Philip to seize the offensive. Philip's decisive victory at Bouvines confirmed possession of the lands he had taken from the English in 1203–06, among them Normandy and Anjou, and strengthened the position of the CAPETIAN monarchy in France.

Bowie, Jim (James) (1796–1836) US frontiersman. In 1828 he moved from Louisiana to Texas and married the daughter of the Mexican vice governor. By 1832 Bowie had joined the US colonists who opposed the Mexican government. In 1835 he was appointed a colonel in the Texas army. Bowie was killed at the ALAMO (1836).

Bow Street Runners Semi-official police and detective force, organized (1748) in London by novelist and Bow Street magistrate, Henry Fielding (1707–54), and later by his half-brother Sir John Fielding. They were assisted by a government grant from 1757 and allowed to extend their activities beyond Westminster and Middlesex.

Boxer Rebellion (1898–1900) Anti-western uprising in China. The OPIUM WARS (1839–42) resulted in greater European involvement in China and defeat in the first of the SINO-JAPANESE WARS (1894–95) further weakened the QING dynasty. In a bid to restore MANCHU authority, the Empress Dowager CIXI supported the attempts of the Society of Righteous and Harmonious Fists (hence the "Boxers") to remove forcibly Western influence from China. Nationwide attacks on foreigners and Chinese Christians left more than 200 dead. In June 1900, the Boxers began a two-month long siege of Beijing, N China. An international expeditionary force relieved the foreign legations and suppressed the rising. China agreed to pay an indemnity.

Boyacá, Battle of (7 August 1819) Conflict in the Wars of Independence in Latin America. A rebel army of *c.*3000, led by Simón BOLÍVAR, gained the element of surprise by crossing the Andes. Bolívar captured *c.*1800 Spanish soldiers and marched on to Bogotá, where he was hailed as the liberator of New Granada (now Venezuela and Colombia).

boyars Highest class of the nobility in medieval Russia and traditional advisers to the tsar. After long disputes over the respective powers of the boyars and the tsar, the title was abolished in the late 17th century by PETER I.

Boyd, Belle (1844–1900) Confederate spy in the American CIVIL WAR (1861–65). In 1862 Boyd crossed through Union lines to inform General "Stonewall" JACKSON of the Union plans for withdrawal from Front Royal, Virginia. She was twice imprisoned and released. In 1864 Boyd sailed for England, carrying secret papers from the Confederate President Jefferson DAVIS. Once in England, she married a former captor and took up acting.

Boyle, Richard, 1st Earl of Cork (1566–1643) English settler in Ireland, father of scientist Robert Boyle. In 1588 Boyle settled in Ireland, acquiring vast estates including Sir Walter RALEIGH's (1602). Employing English settlers, he improved the land, and established new towns and industries. In 1629 Boyle was appointed a lord justice of Ireland. In 1631 he became lord high treasurer of Ireland. Between 1633 and 1641 he struggled with Thomas Wentworth, Earl of STRAFFORD, for influence at court and in Ireland. Boyle finally triumphed over Strafford.

Boyne, Battle of the (11 July 1690) Engagement near Drogheda, Ireland, which confirmed the Protestant succession to the English throne. The *c.*35,000 forces of the Protestant WILLIAM III (OF ORANGE) defeated the *c.*21,000 soldiers of the Catholic JAMES II. James was forced to withdraw, but the JACOBITE army continued to resist William

Bozeman, John M. (1835–67) US explorer. He moved west in search of gold. In 1862–63 Bozeman found a new route west (the Bozeman Trail) across the Continental Divide from Colorado to SW Montana. The land belonged to the Sioux, however, and Bozeman and his partner barely escaped alive. The Sioux, led by Red Cloud, fought the building of a road at Bozeman Pass and massacres resulted. Bozeman was himself killed by Native Americans three years after founding Bozeman, Montana.

Brabant, Duchy of Feudal duchy that emerged (1190) from the Duchy of Lower Lorraine. The civil liberties of the citizens of Brabant were confirmed by the constitutional charter *Joyeuse Entrée* (3 January 1356). In 1430 the Duchy of Brabant passed to the dukes of BURGUNDY. In 1477 it was subsumed into the HABSBURG EMPIRE. The REVOLT OF THE NETHERLANDS (1567) led to the division of Brabant betwen Spain and the Netherlands. The northern part of the Duchy now forms the Dutch province of North Brabant, while the southern portion is divided into the Belgian provinces of Flemish Brabant and Walloon Brabant. Emperor JOSEPH II's abrogation of its charter led to the Brabant Revolution (1789) against Austrian rule.

Braddock, Edward (1695–1755) British general in the FRENCH AND INDIAN WARS. As commander in chief of British forces in North America, he led the attack on the French stronghold of Fort Dequesne (1755). Progress was slow and, on the advice of George WASHINGTON, Braddock led an advance party. Ambushed by Native Americans, the party was routed and Braddock killed.

Bradford, William (1590–1657) Governor of PLYMOUTH COLONY, b. England. He emigrated to America as one of the PILGRIMS on the *Mayflower* (1620) and signed the MAYFLOWER COMPACT. In 1621 Bradford succeeded John Carver as governor of the colony and held the post, except for five years as assistant governor, until his death. He maintained good relations with the Native Americans and established systems for trade, agriculture and fishing. In 1627 Bradford was one of eight Pilgrims who assumed the Colony's debt to the Merchant Adventurers for their passage. Bradford wrote the *History of Plymouth Plantation*. *See also* MASSACHUSSETS BAY COLONY

Bradlaugh, Charles (1833–91) British social reformer. He was a vocal atheist and worked with Annie BESANT in support of many causes, including freedom of speech. Bradlaugh was elected to the House of Commons in 1880, but refused to swear the religious oath of Parliament and was not allowed to take his seat until 1886.

Bradley, Omar Nelson (1893–1981) US general. In

BOSNIA-HERZEGOVINA

AREA: 51,129sq km (19,745 sq mi)
POPULATION: 4,366,000
CAPITAL (POPULATION): Sarajevo (526,000)
GOVERNMENT: Transitional
ETHNIC GROUPS: Muslim 49%, Serb 31%, Croat 17%
LANGUAGES: Serbo-Croatian
RELIGIONS: Islam 40%, Christianity (Serbian Orthodox 31%, Roman Catholic 15%, Protestant 4%)
GDP PER CAPITA (1994): US$1307

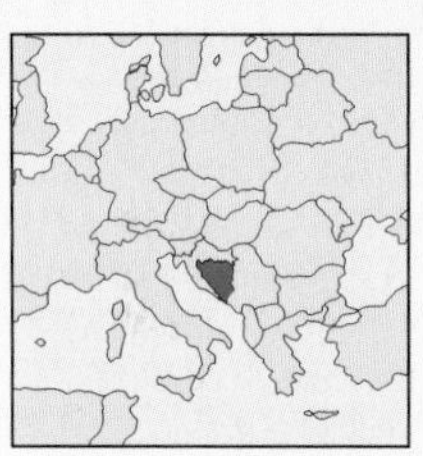

Balkan republic in SE Europe. Bosnia-Herzegovina is one of the five republics that emerged from the break-up of the former Federal People's Republic of YUGOSLAVIA. It consists of two main regions – Bosnia in the N, with SARAJEVO as the capital; and Herzegovina in the S, with Mostar the main city.

SLAVS settled in the region *c.*1400 years ago. Bosnia was settled by Serbs in the 7th century and conquered by the Ottoman Turks in 1463. The persistence of serfdom led to a peasant revolt (1875). The Congress of BERLIN (1878) handed Bosnia-Herzegovina to the AUSTRO-HUNGARIAN EMPIRE, and it was annexed in 1908. Serbian nationalism intensified, and in 1914 Archduke FRANZ FERDINAND was assassinated in Sarajevo, precipitating World War 1. In 1918 Bosnia-Herzegovina was annexed to SERBIA and incorporated into Yugoslavia in 1929. In World War 2 the region became part of the German puppet state of Croatia. In 1946 Bosnia-Herzegovina became a constituent member of TITO's socialist federal republic.

In 1991 the republic disintegrated with the secession of CROATIA, SLOVENIA and MACEDONIA. Fearing the creation of a Greater Serbia, Croats and Muslims in Bosnia-Herzegovina pushed for independence. In March 1992 a referendum, boycotted by Serbian parties, voted for independence. Alija IZETBEGOVIĆ became president of the new state. War broke out between Bosnian government forces and the Serb-dominated Federal Yugoslav Army (JNA). The JNA overran the republic and besieged the government in Sarajevo. International pressure forced the JNA to withdraw. Slobodan MILOŠEVIĆ armed the Bosnian Serbs, who established (August 1992) a separate Serb republic led by Radovan KARADŽIĆ. Muslims were forced from their villages in a deliberate act of "ethnic cleansing". In late 1992, the United Nations (UN) deployed peacekeeping forces to distribute humanitarian aid to the starved capital of Sarajevo. In 1993, the UN declared a number of "safe areas" – government-held enclaves where Muslims would not be shelled or persecuted. In February 1994 Bosnian Serbs attacked the enclaves of Sarajevo and Gorazde, prompting UN air-strikes. In 1995 Bosnian Serb forces attacked the "safe areas" of Bihac and Srebrenica, allegedly massacring thousands of fleeing Muslims. The government of Bosnia and Bosnian Croats announced a cease-fire and the formation of a Muslim-Croat Federation. Their forces launched a joint offensive on Serb-held central Bosnia. The DAYTON PEACE AGREEMENT (December 1995) agreed to preserve Bosnia-Herzegovina as a single state, but partitioned it between the Muslim-Croat Federation (51%) and Bosnian Serbs (*Republika Srpska*, 49%). The agreement deployed 60,000 NATO troops as part of a Peace Implementation Force (IFOR). KARADŽIĆ and the Bosnian Serb army leader Ratko MLADIĆ were indicted for war crimes and forced to resign. In 1996 elections Izetbegović was re-elected as head of a tripartite presidency, including a Serb and a Croat representative. In 1998 the Serbian nationalist Nikola Poplasen was elected president of *Republika Srpska*. NATO troops remained as a "dissuasion" force (DFOR).

World War 2, he commanded the II Corps in N Africa and the invasion of Sicily (1943). Bradley led the 1st Army in the NORMANDY CAMPAIGN (1944) and the liberation of Paris. He was then given command of the 12th Army. After the War, Bradley served (1948–49) as chief of staff of the US Army and first chairman of the Joint Chiefs of Staff (1949–53).

Braganza Ruling dynasty of Portugal (1640–1910). The dynasty was founded by the Duke of Braganza, who ruled (1640–56) as JOHN IV. During the NAPOLEONIC WARS, the royal family fled to Brazil, then a Portuguese colony. A branch of the house ruled as emperors of Brazil (1822–89).

Bragg, Braxton (1817–76) Confederate general in the American CIVIL WAR. Bragg served in the US Army until 1856. At the outbreak of the Civil War (1861), he joined the Confederate Army. Bragg commanded the Army of Tennessee and won the Battle of Chickamauga (1863), but was forced to retreat from Tennessee. In December 1863, he was relieved of his command. Bragg served as adviser (1864–65) to Jefferson DAVIS.

Brahmanism Term denoting an early phase of HINDUISM. It was characterized by acceptance of the VEDAS as divine revelation. The Brahmanas, the major text of Brahmanism, are the ritualistic books comprising the greater portion of Vedic literature. They were complemented by the UPANISHADS. In the course of time, deities of post-Vedic origin began to be worshipped and the influence of Brahmanist priests declined.

Brahmin (Brahman) Priestly CASTE that was the highest-ranking of the four *varnas* (social classes) in India during the late Vedic period, the era of BRAHMANISM. Brahmin were believed to be ritually purer than other castes, and they alone could perform certain spiritual and ritual duties. The recitation of the VEDAS was their preserve, and for hundreds of years, they were the only caste to receive an education and so controlled Indian scholarship. With the later development of HINDUISM as a popular religion, their priestly influence declined, but their secular influence grew, and their social supremacy and privileged status have changed little over the centuries.

Brahmo Samaj (Hindi, Society of God) Indian religious movement, founded (1828) by Ram Mohan ROY in Calcutta. Roy argued for a monotheistic HINDUISM that embraced social reforms. In 1842 Brahmo Samaj was revived by Debendranath Tagore (1817–1905). In 1850 Tagore rejected the Vedic scriptures and a split emerged between the social reformers and the religious reformers.

Brain Trust (1933–35) Group of advisers to US President Franklin ROOSEVELT. It first described his closest advisers in the presidential campaign of 1932. Later, the term was applied more widely to members of his administration who advised on the policies of the NEW DEAL.

Brand, Sir Jan Hendrik (1823–88) South African politician, president of Orange FREE STATE (1864–88). He fought a bloody war (1864–68) with the Basuto (now Sotho) people (*see* Lesotho). Brand was knighted (1882) for his role as mediator in the conflict (1880–81) between Britain and Transvaal.

Brandeis, Louis Dembitz (1856–1941) US jurist, associate justice (1916–39) of the Supreme Court. He became known as the "people's attorney". An adviser to President Woodrow WILSON, Brandeis was instrumental in creating the FEDERAL RESERVE ACT (1913) and the CLAYTON ANTI-TRUST ACT (1914). The first Jew to sit on the Supreme Court, he was noted for his dissents favouring civil liberties and social welfare legislation.

Brandenburg State in NE Germany; the capital is POTSDAM. Before the German conquest under HENRY I (THE FOWLER), the region was occupied first by Semnones then by Slavs. The March of Brandenburg was founded (1134) by ALBERT THE BEAR. In the Golden Bull of Emperor CHARLES IV (1356), the Margrave of Brandenburg was confirmed as an imperial elector. In 1415 Frederick I (of HOHENZOLLERN) was appointed Elector of Brandenburg. Brandenburg gained the Duchy of Cleves (1614) and the Duchy of PRUSSIA (1618). FREDERICK WILLIAM (r.1640–88) transformed Brandenburg into a major European state. In 1701 his son, Elector Frederick III, became FREDERICK I of Prussia. Brandenburg formed the nucleus of the kingdom of Prussia. Pop. (1993 est.) 2,543,000

Brandt, Willy (1913–92) German statesman, chancellor of West Germany (1969–74), b. Karl Herbert Frahm. An active Social Democrat, he fled to Norway and then Sweden during the Nazi era. Brandt returned to Germany after World War 2 and was elected (1957) mayor of West Berlin. In national politics, he was foreign minister (1966–68). As chancellor, Brandt pursued a policy of cooperation with the Communist bloc states, for which he was awarded the 1971 Nobel Peace Prize. He resigned after a close aide was exposed as an East German spy.

Brandywine, Battle of the (11 September 1777) Conflict in the AMERICAN REVOLUTION fought along Brandywine Creek, SE Pennsylvania. American troops, led by George WASHINGTON, were defeated by the British under General William HOWE. The British continued to advance and captured (27 September 1777) Philadelphia.

Brant, Joseph (1742–1807) MOHAWK chief. Brant served in the FRENCH AND INDIAN WARS (1754–63) and in PONTIAC'S REBELLION (1763–66). He attended an Anglican school and became an interpreter for missionaries. In 1775, in return for securing an alliance between the Iroquois and the British, he gained a commission in the British Army. Brant fought with outstanding courage for the British during the American Revolution (1775–83).

Branting, Karl Hjalmar (1860–1925) Swedish statesman, prime minister (1920, 1921–23, 1924–25). Branting was the first Social Democrat elected to the Riksdag (1896). He was minister of finance in 1917 and three times prime minister. Branting was a delegate to the Paris Peace Conference (1919) and shared the 1921 Nobel Peace Prize with Christian LANGE.

Brătianu, Ion (1821–91) Romanian statesman, premier (1867–68, 1876–81, 1881–88). He fought in the uprising against Russian and Turkish rule in 1848. In 1856 Brătianu forced the abdication of the dictator, Alexandru Cuza, and helped elect Prince CAROL I of Hohenzollern as king. His son, **Ion** (1864–1927), also served as premier (1909–11, 1913–18, 1918–1919, 1922–26, 1927). In 1918 Ion resigned rather than accept the initial peace terms offered the Central Powers. Ion represented Romania at the Paris Peace Conference (1919). He acted as a virtual dictator after 1922.

Braun, Eva (1912–45) German mistress of Adolf HITLER. She met Hitler in the early 1930s and they lived together for the rest of their lives. They married in Berlin the day before committing suicide.

Brazil *See* country feature

Brazza, Pierre Paul François Camille Savorgnan de (1852–1905) French explorer, b. Italy. In the late 1870s and early 1880s, Brazza explored the River Ogowe in W Africa for the French government. He founded Brazzaville (Congo) and established a French protectorate over the kingdom of Makoko. From 1886 to 1898 he was governor general of the French Congo.

Breakspear, Nicholas *See* ADRIAN IV

Brébeuf, Saint Jean de (1593–1649) French missionary in Canada. Ordained a Jesuit in 1623, Brébeuf travelled extensively after 1625 among the HURON Native Americans of Georgian Bay and Lake Huron. He was tortured to death by the IROQUOIS. Brébeuf was canonized in 1930. His feast day is 26 September.

Breckinridge, John Cabell (1821–75) US vice president (1857–61) and Confederate general in the CIVIL WAR. He was a major in the MEXICAN WAR (1846–48) and a congressman (1851) before becoming vice president under James BUCHANAN. Defeated as a pro-slavery presidential candidate (1860) by Abraham LINCOLN, Breckinridge became secretary of war (1865) in Jefferson DAVIS' cabinet.

Breda, Compromise of (1566) Document signed by more than 2000 Dutch and Flemish nobles and burghers in protest against the imposition of Spanish government on the Netherlands by PHILIP II. A petition was presented to the Spanish regent, MARGARET OF PARMA. The Spanish referred to the group as *gueux* (Fr. beggars) and the name was adopted by the revolutionaries themselves. In 1569 WILLIAM I (THE SILENT) formed *les Gueux de la mer* to harass Spanish shipping. In 1574 the Gueux raised the siege of Leiden.

Breda, Declaration of (1660) Statement made by

BOTSWANA

AREA: 581,730sq km (224,606sq mi)
POPULATION: 1,373,000
CAPITAL (POPULATION): Gaborone (138,471)
GOVERNMENT: Multiparty republic
ETHNIC GROUPS: Tswana 75%, Shona 12%, San (Bushmen) 3%
LANGUAGES: English (official), Setswana (national)
RELIGIONS: Traditional beliefs 49%, Christianity 50%
GDP PER CAPITA (1995): US$5580

Landlocked republic in the heart of S Africa. The earliest inhabitants of the region were the nomadic SAN. In the 7th century, the Toutswe built an advanced and prosperous state, near to modern-day Serowe, E Botswana. In the 13th century, the Toutswe were conquered first by Mapungubwe, then by GREAT ZIMBABWE. From the 16th century, the San were gradually displaced into the Kalahari by the westward advance of the Tswana dynasties of the Hurutshe, Kwena and Kgatla. In 1795 the Hurutshe and founded the state of Ngwaketse in SE Botswana. In the 19th century, the Tswana were pushed northward by the Kololo and the Ndebele.

In 1885 Chief Khama III formed an alliance with the British, and Tswana lands became the Bechuanaland Protectorate of the British Empire. The British used the Protectorate as a base for the colonization of Zimbabwe. During the 1950s, nationalist movements resisted the Protectorate's incorporation into South Africa. In 1966 Botswana gained independence and Seretse KHAMA, grandson of Khama III, became president. The discovery of diamonds boosted the new republic's economy. During the 1970s, Botswana was a stabilizing force in a region dominated by the struggle against South Africa's apartheid regime and civil war in Rhodesia (now Zimbabwe). In 1980 Khama died and was succeeded by Ketumile Masire.

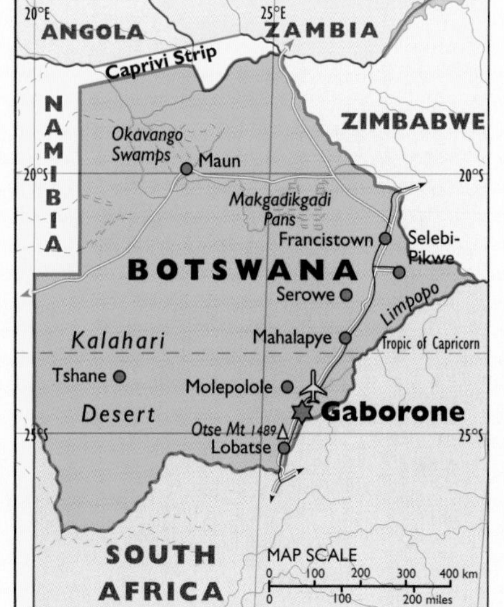

AREA: 8,511,970sq km (3,286,472sq mi)
POPULATION: 156,275,000
CAPITAL (POPULATION): Brasília (1,596,274)
GOVERNMENT: Federal republic
ETHNIC GROUPS: White 53%, Mulatto 22%, Mestizo 12%, African American 11%, Japanese 1%, Native American 0.1%
LANGUAGES: Portuguese (official)
RELIGIONS: Christianity (Roman Catholic 88%, Protestant 6%)
GDP PER CAPTIA (1995): US$5400

Republic in E South America. In 1500, when Portuguese explorer Pedro Alvares CABRAL claimed Brazil for Portugal, there were *c*.2 million NATIVE SOUTH AMERICANS living in Brazil. In 1501 Amerigo VESPUCCI mapped Brazil's coastline. In 1533 JOHN III divided Brazil into 12 captaincies, controlled by *donatários*. In 1549 Governor General Tomé de Sousa founded a capital at Bahia (now Salvador), NE Brazil. Jesuit missionaries set about the task of converting the native population. The restrictions on labour for converted natives led to the introduction of African slaves to work on the sugar plantations.

In 1554 São Paulo was founded and Rio de Janeiro was settled in 1567. In 1633 the Dutch West India Company, led by Johan Maurits, captured Salvador and Recife. In 1654 the Dutch were driven out. During the 17th century, the expansion of the western frontier was led by *bandeiras* (expeditions) from São Paulo. In 1695 gold was discovered in Minas Gerais and more slaves were brought in to work in the mines. Marquês de POMBAL enacted colonial reforms, including the expulsion of Jesuits (1759) and the transfer of the capital to Rio de Janeiro (1763). In 1789 José Joaquim da Silva Xavier led an abortive uprising against the Portuguese. In 1807, during the NAPOLEONIC WARS (1803–15), Prince John (later JOHN VI) of Portugal was forced to flee to Brazil. In 1815 Brazil acquired equal status with the mother country in the Portuguese Empire. In 1821 John returned to Portugal. In 1822 his son, PEDRO I, refused to return to Lisbon and, under the guidance of José Bonifácio de ANDRADA E SILVA, declared Brazil an independent empire. The loss of Cisplatine Province (now Uruguay) in a war (1835–28) with Argentina forced Pedro to abdicate (1831) in favour of his son, PEDRO II. In the bloody War of the TRIPLE ALLIANCE (1864–70), Brazil, Uruguay and Argentina united to defeat the Paraguayan dictator Francisco Solano López. The abolition of slavery (1888) saw the release of *c*.700,000 slaves.

In 1889 Pedro was overthrown in a military coup and Marshal Manuel Deodoro da Fonseca declared the Republic of Brazil. The coffee planters were the major political force in the early years of the republic. A series of uprisings against the "coffee presidents" culminated in the rebellion (1930) of Getúlio VARGAS. His autocratic rule saw the beginnings of industrial development, diversification of agriculture and the centralization of power. In 1945 Vargas was compelled to resign, but rampant inflation led to his return to power (1951–54). In 1954, after charges of corruption, Vargas was again forced to resign and committed suicide. In the 1955 elections Juscelino KUBITSCHEK became president and João Goulart became vice president. Kubitschek's ambitious development of Brazil's infrastructure included the construction (1960) of a new capital, Brasília. In 1960 Jânio Quadros was elected president, but he unexpectedly resigned after only seven months in office. Generals and conservatives distrusted Goulart, his legal successor, and limited his constitutional powers (1961). In 1964 Goulart was overthrown in a military coup, led by General Humberto CASTELO BRANCO, and political institutions were purged of leftists. In 1965 political parties were banned and Costa e Silva elected as president following the implementation of an artificial two-party system. Despite economic growth, the political situation rapidly deteriorated and in 1968 Congress was suspended. The military maintained control through the use of torture and death squads, and up to 1978 the government ruled with emergency powers.

In 1985 José Sarney became the first civilian president for 21 years. He was succeeded (1990) by Fernando COLLOR DE MELLO. In 1992 Collor resigned after being impeached for corruption. In 1995 Fernando Henrique Cardoso was elected president on a platform of austerity measures to cope with Brazil's economic crisis. He was re-elected in 1998.

B

Charles II of England while in exile in the Netherlands. Charles promised religious toleration and an amnesty to former enemies of the Stuarts. The declaration led to the Restoration.

Breda, Treaty of (1667) Peace agreement that ended the second of the Dutch Wars (1665–67) with England. England gave up its claim to the Dutch East Indies but gained control of New York and New Jersey.

Breitenfeld, battles of Two conflicts in the Thirty Years' War (1618–48) fought near the town of Breitenfeld, Saxony, e central Germany. The first Battle (17 September 1631) was between the Habsburg army under Count Johannes Tilly and the Swedish forces led by Gustavus II. The Swedish victory was the first Protestant success in the War. The second Battle (2 November 1642) ended in another Swedish victory.

Breshkovsky, Catherine (1844–1934) Russian revolutionary, known as the "little grandmother" (*babushka*) of the Russian Revolution (1917). During the tsarist era, she spent 30 years in exile in Siberia. In 1917 Breshkovsky was released by Alexander Kerensky. She went into voluntary exile after disagreements with the Bolsheviks.

Brest-Litovsk, Treaty of (3 March 1918) Peace agreement between the Soviet Union and the Central Powers, confirming the Soviet withdrawal from World War i. Peace negotiations began in December 1917, but Leon Trotsky stalled talks with his policy of "neither war nor peace". In February 1918, Germany resumed its offensive and Lenin insisted on accepting the German demands. Russia recognized the independence of Ukraine, Georgia and Finland, and ceded Poland, the Baltic states and Belorussia to Germany and Austria-Hungary. The Treaty was annulled by the Armistice (11 November 1918) at the end of World War 1.

Brétigny, Treaty of (1360) Agreement between Edward III of England and John II (the Good) of France in the first phase of the Hundred Years' War. John, who had been captured at the Battle of Poitiers (1356), was released in return for 3 million gold crowns and the province of Acquitaine, sw France. France was unable to pay the ransom and Edward the Black Prince seized Aquitaine.

Bretton Woods Conference (officially United Nations Monetary and Financial Conference) It met at Bretton Woods, New Hampshire, in July 1944. It was summoned on the initiative of President Franklin Roosevelt to establish a system of international monetary cooperation and prevent severe financial crises, such as that of 1929, which had precipitated the Great Depression. Representatives of 44 countries agreed to establish the International Monetary Fund (IMF) and the International Bank for Reconstruction and Development, or World Bank, to provide credit to states requiring financial investment in major economic projects.

Brewster, William (1567–1644) English religious leader, signatory of the Mayflower Compact. In 1606 he withdrew from the Anglican Church, formed the Separatists and with them fled from persecution in England to Holland, where they became known as Pilgrims. Brewster helped to organize the Pilgrim migration to America and became a leader of the church in Plymouth Colony.

Brezhnev, Leonid Ilyich (1906–82) Soviet statesman, effective ruler from the mid-1960s until his death. He rose through the Communist Party of the Soviet Union (CPSU) to become (1957) a member of the presidium (later politburo). In 1964 Brezhnev helped plan the downfall of Nikita Khrushchev and became general secretary, at first sharing power with Aleksei Kosygin. In 1977 he became president of the Soviet Union. Brezhnev pursued a hard line against reforms at home and in Eastern Europe, but also sought to reduce tensions with the West. After the Soviet invasion of Czechoslovakia (1968), he promulgated the "Brezhnev doctrine" confirming Soviet domination of satellite states, as witnessed by the 1979 invasion of Afghanistan. *See also* Afghanistan War

Brian Boru (940?–1014) King of Ireland (1002–14). From a power base in Munster, he gained control of the whole of s Ireland. Brian was killed in the process of securing victory over the Norsemen at the Battle of Clontarf.

Briand, Aristide (1862–1932) French statesman. A moderate, he was premier of 11 governments between 1909 and 1929. Briand advocated international cooperation and was one of the instigators of the Locarno Pact (1925), for which he shared the 1926 Nobel Peace Prize with Gustav Stresemann. He was also one of the authors of the Kellogg-Briand Pact (1928).

Bridger, Jim (James) (1804–81) US frontiersman and scout. Bridger was the first white explorer to reach Great Salt Lake (1824), South Pass through the Rockies, and the area now known as Yellowstone Park. In 1843 he built Fort Bridger, sw Wyoming, to supply settlers travelling West on the Oregon Trail. *See also* mountain men

Bridges, Harry (Alfred Renton) (1901–90) US labour leader, b. Australia. In 1934 he led the International Longshoremen's Association (ILA) strike, which escalated into a general strike in San Francisco. In 1937 Bridges founded the International Longshoremen's and Warehousemen's Union (ILWU), in affiliation with the Congress of Industrial Organizations (CIO). Attempts by the US Justice Department to deport Bridges failed to prove that he was a member of the Communist Party. He retired in 1977.

Bridgman, Elijah Coleman (1801–61) US missionary. He was the first American Protestant missionary to China. Bridgman lived in China from 1829 until his death. He founded and managed the *Chinese Repository* (1862) and translated the New Testament into Chinese.

Bright, John (1811–89) British parliamentary reformer. A Quaker, he and his fellow radical, Richard Cobden, were leaders of the Anti-Corn Law League (founded 1839). First elected to Parliament in 1843, Bright subsequently represented Manchester, n England, the home of free-trade. He lost his seat in 1857 after opposing the Crimean War but was re-elected for Birmingham, Midlands.

Brisbane, Sir Thomas Makdougall (1773–1860) Scottish soldier, colonial administrator and astronomer. He was governor (1821–25) of New South Wales, Australia, and helped to develop the colony's economy. Brisbane founded observatories in Sydney (1822) and in Scotland (1841). Brisbane in Queensland, which was first settled in 1824, is named after him.

Bristol City and unitary authority at the confluence of the Avon and Frome rivers, sw England. An important seaport and trade centre since achieving city status in 1155, it was a major centre for the wool and cloth industry. From the 15th to 18th century, it was one of England's major cities and the base for many New World explorations. The 19th century witnessed a gradual decline in the city's economy. Bristol suffered intensive bombing during World War 2. Clifton Suspension Bridge (designed by Brunel) was completed in 1864. Other sites include a 12th-century cathedral and the 14th-century Church of St Mary Redcliffe. Pop. (1991) 376,146.

Britain (Great Britain) Island kingdom in nw Europe, officially the United Kingdom of Great Britain and Northern Ireland. It is made up of England, Scotland, Wales, the Channel Islands and the Isle of Man.

Britain, Battle of (1940) Series of air battles fought over Britain. Early in World War 2 (as a prelude to invasion), the Germans hoped to destroy Britain's industrial and military infrastructure and civilian morale by a sustained series of bombing raids. British defences included the first use of radar in warfare. Failing to eliminate the Spitfires and Hurricanes of the Royal Air Force (RAF), the Germans began (7 September) the night bombing (the Blitz) of London and other cities. In October, the Luftwaffe losses (*c*.2300 aircraft) forced Hitler to abandon his plans for an invasion. The RAF lost some 900 aircraft.

British Columbia Province of w Canada, on the Pacific coast, bounded n by Alaska, s by Washington state. The capital is Victoria, and other major cities include Vancouver. The first European sighting of the region was by Sir Francis Drake (1578). Spanish expeditions explored the coast in 1774–79, as did Captain Cook in 1778. George Vancouver took possession of the island that bears his name for Britain in 1794. In 1846 the border with the United States was finally settled. British Columbia joined Canada in 1871 in exchange for constructing the Canadian Pacific Railway, completed in 1885. Area: 948,600sq km (366,255sq mi). Pop. (1991) 3,282,061.

British East India Company *See* East India Company, English

British Empire *See* feature article, page 58

British Expeditionary Force (BEF) British Army trained and organized in the United Kingdom to support France in both World War i and World War 2. In World War 1 the BEF, under General Sir John French, originally comprised six divisions but grew into an army of more than

BREZHNEV, LEONID ILYICH

Leonid Brezhnev (above left, with Alexander Dubček) ordered the Soviet invasion of Czecholsovakia that crushed the Dubček-inspired Prague Spring (1968) of liberal reforms. Brezhnev renewed the authority of the vast Soviet bureaucracy that had declined under Nikita Khrushchev. The powers of the KGB increased and the Soviet propaganda machine continued to control the flow of information. His focus on increasing military might was detrimental to agriculture and industrial production, and led to the shortages that characterized the late 1970s and 1980s. By the time Brezhnev died, the standard of living in the Soviet Union had significantly declined.

BREZHNEV IN HIS OWN WORDS

"...when internal and external forces that are hostile to socialism try to turn the development of some socialist country towards the restoration of a capitalist regime [...] it becomes not only a problem of the people of the country concerned, but a common problem and concern for all Socialist countries."
Description of the "Brezhnev Doctrine" (1968)

"She is trying to wear the trousers of Winston Churchill."
On Margaret Thatcher (1979)

one million men. In World War 2, the 13-division BEF in France was evacuated from DUNKIRK (1940).

British Honduras Former name of BELIZE

British Legion British organization of ex-service men and women for helping disabled and unemployed war veterans, their widows and families. Each year during the week preceding Remembrance Day (the Sunday nearest to 11 November), millions of artificial red poppies are sold to commemorate the dead of two world wars and raise funds for the Legion. *See also* AMERICAN LEGION

British North America Act (1867) Act of the British Parliament that created the Dominion of CANADA. It provided a constitution similar to that of Britain. British powers were surrendered in the Canada Act of 1982, when the original Act was renamed the Constitution Act.

Brock, Sir Isaac (1769–1812) British general. In 1802 he was sent to Canada and was given command (1806) of Upper and LOWER CANADA. In 1811 Brock was appointed administrator of UPPER CANADA (now Ontario). A brilliant strategist in the WAR OF 1812, he joined forces with TECUMSEH to defeat General William HULL at Detroit (1812). Brock died in the British victory at QUEENSTON HEIGHTS.

Bronze Age *See* feature article

Brooke, Edward William (1919–) US Republican senator (1967–79) for Massachusetts. In 1967 Brooke became the first African-American ever to be elected to the Senate and the first African-American to serve in the Senate since Reconstruction.

Brooke, Sir James (1803–68) British adventurer and soldier. He served (1825–26) in Burma for the English EAST INDIA COMPANY. In 1840, after retiring from active service, he helped Prince Muda Hassim of Borneo crush a rebellion in SARAWAK. Brooke was rewarded with the title raja of Sarawak (1841–68). He was subsequently appointed governor of Labuan (1847–57) and consul general for Borneo by the British government. He introduced many reforms and was succeeded by his nephew, Charles Anthony Johnson Brooke (1829–1917), who abolished slavery in Sarawak.

B

BRONZE AGE

Phase between the NEOLITHIC period and the discovery of iron-working techniques (the IRON AGE) in the Middle East, Asia and Europe, the Bronze Age began several millennia after the first use of metals. Metalworking originally consisted of beating nuggets of copper and gold into shape. However, *c.*9000 years ago in W Asia and SE Europe the discovery was made that when copper was heated to become molten, it could be cast to form a variety of objects, such as ornaments and pottery. In the 4th millennium BC, it was found that when copper was combined with tin, the resulting alloy, bronze, could be used to create sharp cutting edges for tools and weapons. This discovery was first made in W Asia and by *c.*2000 BC had spread throughout Asia, the Middle East and Europe. There was no Bronze Age in the Americas, where gold was the only metal widely used before the arrival of the Europeans.

The copper was mined by digging a tunnel along the course of a vein and lighting fires to fracture the metal. In a long tunnel the circulation of air necessary for the fires to burn was provided by timber-lined passages. The copper was smelted and combined with smelted tin, usually in a proportion of nine to one, in a charcoal-burning furnace. The molten bronze was cooled in a clay channel and divided into ingots which were then remelted and poured into clay moulds to produce a wide range of artefacts, including agricultural implements. Among the most splendid surviving bronze artefacts are those produced by SHANG China.

Bronze began to be replaced by iron in the Middle East *c.*2000 BC but it survived in Europe as the main material for making tools and weapons until the 1st millennium BC. *See also* CHALCOLITHIC AGE

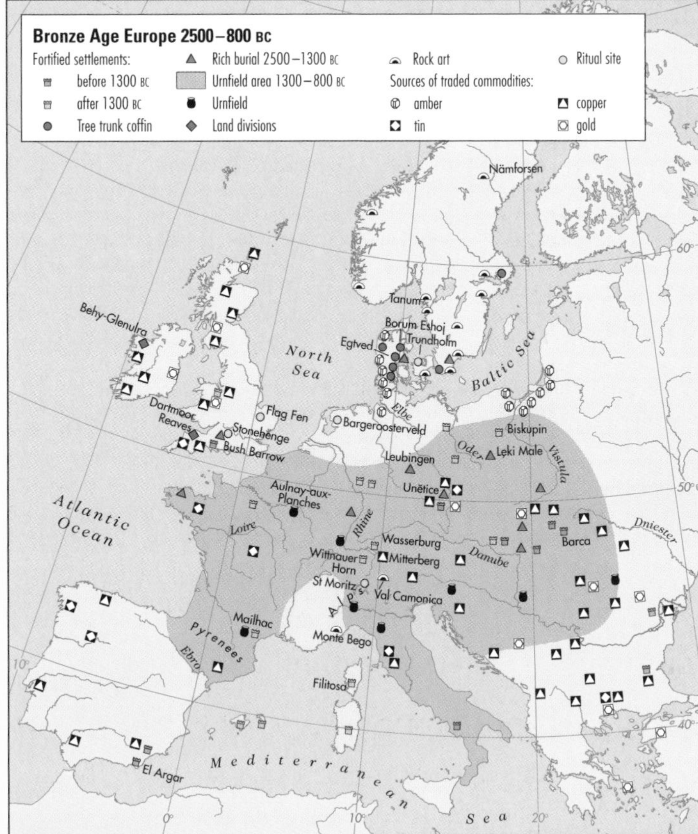

◀ **In Europe** the Bronze Age began *c.*2500 BC. Soon the need for tin provided a stimulus to the further development of international trade in prestige materials. These were particularly used as grave goods and votive offerings, emphasizing the status achieved by their owners. Command of metal ore sources gave certain communities pre-eminence. Often settlements were located in defensible positions and fortified.

▼ **Bronze Age burial** This reconstruction depicts a burial ceremony at Egtved, E Jutland, a few centuries after the Bronze Age culture had reached NW Europe (*c.*1500 BC). The dead were buried in a single grave known as a round barrow, or tumulus grave mound. Corpses were decorated with bronze ornaments and buried with numerous grave objects including weapons, jewellery and pottery.

Consisting of overseas territories ruled by Britain between the 17th and 20th centuries, the British Empire grew from seeds sown in the 16th century by voyages of EXPLORATION across the oceans. Historians distinguish two empires. The "First Empire" was based mainly on commercial ventures and the SLAVE TRADE. In 1600 the English EAST INDIA COMPANY was chartered by Queen ELIZABETH I, and in 1612 it opened its first trading post at Surat, W central India. Other trading posts were established on the E coast in the 17th century but the Company did not lay claim to territory in India until the 1750s, when Robert CLIVE captured Bengal, thus founding the basis for Britain's supremacy in India.

NORTH AMERICA AND THE CARIBBEAN

British colonies were set up in North America and the Caribbean in two main waves. The first wave (1607–34) began with the establishment of JAMESTOWN by the VIRGINIA COMPANY of London, founded (1606) by JAMES I. In 1620 the PILGRIMS founded PLYMOUTH COLONY, New England. By 1634 further settlements had been established in Virginia, Maryland and New England, where colonization was spurred by the MASSACHUSETTS BAY COMPANY. Plantations were also established in the E Caribbean. In the second wave (1655–80), Jamaica was seized from the Spanish, and Spain was forced to acknowledge Britain's possessions in the Caribbean by the Treaty of Madrid (1670) In North America, the Carolinas and PENNSYLVANIA were founded, and NEW YORK was taken from the Dutch. Further north, the HUDSON'S BAY COMPANY acquired a monopoly on the British FUR TRADE in the 1670s and became virtually a sovereign power in the Hudson Bay region. The increasing requirement for labour on the tobacco and sugar plantations of the southern mainland colonies and the Caribbean led to the use of imported African slaves from 1680. In the northern mainland colonies, agriculture flourished but trade was subject to the controls of MERCANTILISM, such as the NAVIGATION ACTS (1650–96) that restricted colonial trade to British ships and made Britain the sole importer of colonial products. From the 1660s both Britain and France sought to increase their power in America, causing frequent disputes between the two countries. Among them were the FRENCH AND INDIAN WARS (1689–1763), the last of which established British control of Canada. Britain lost its THIRTEEN COLONIES in the AMERICAN REVOLUTION (1775–83), bringing the "First Empire" to an end.

THE SECOND EMPIRE

The voyages of Captain James COOK between 1768 and 1775 led to the British colonization of Australia and New Zealand and the beginnings of a "Second Empire" based on commerce. The first British settlement in Australia was established (1788) at Port Jackson (now Sydney) by Captain Arthur PHILLIP. Nearly 800 of the settlers were convicts. The trans-

► **Delhi Durbar** (1877) This 19th-century painting by Alexander Caddy depicts the celebrations in Delhi, N India, that accompanied Queen Victoria's assumption of the title of Empress of India (1876). Direct rule was imposed in an attempt to crush Indian nationalist demands. Britain exploited the natural resources of India, particularly in the production of textiles. The British government maintained a monopoly of the opium trade and the tax on salt.

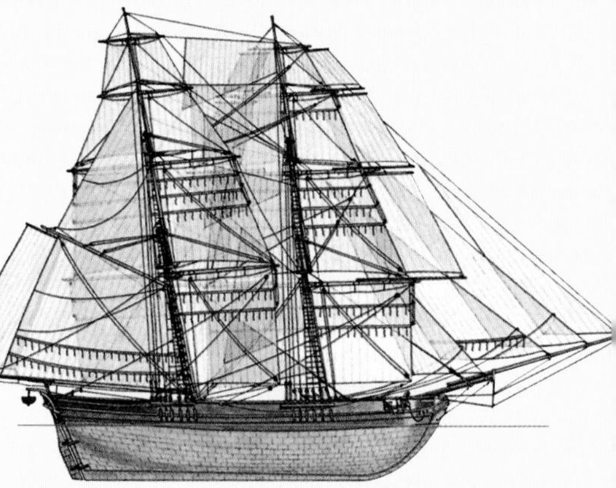

▲ **slaving brig** During the late-18th and early-19th centuries, brigs were often used to transport slaves because of their speed and manoeuvrability. Slaves suffered appalling conditions on such voyages, many dying along the way.

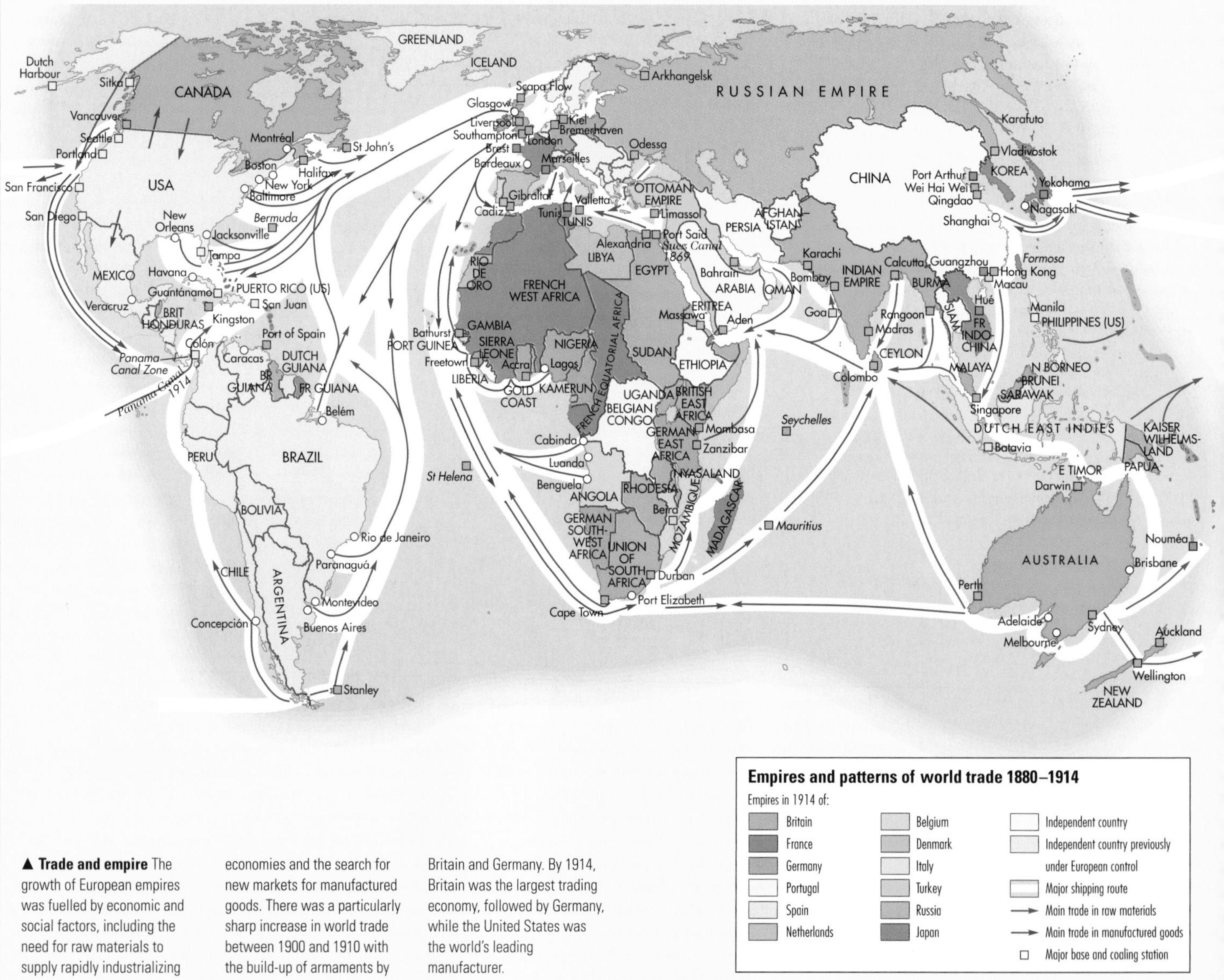

Empires and patterns of world trade 1880–1914

Empires in 1914 of:

- Britain
- France
- Germany
- Portugal
- Spain
- Netherlands
- Belgium
- Denmark
- Italy
- Turkey
- Russia
- Japan
- Independent country
- Independent country previously under European control
- Major shipping route
- Main trade in raw materials
- Main trade in manufactured goods
- Major base and coaling station

▲ **Trade and empire** The growth of European empires was fuelled by economic and social factors, including the need for raw materials to supply rapidly industrializing economies and the search for new markets for manufactured goods. There was a particularly sharp increase in world trade between 1900 and 1910 with the build-up of armaments by Britain and Germany. By 1914, Britain was the largest trading economy, followed by Germany, while the United States was the world's leading manufacturer.

portation of convicts to Australia continued until 1852, but they were outnumbered by free settlers from the end of the 18th century. The colony expanded along the coast and westwards at the expense of NATIVE AUSTRALIANS. The first British settlement in New Zealand was established at Port Nicholson (now Wellington) in 1840. Meanwhile, victories in the NAPOLEONIC WARS (1803–15) brought further colonial possessions, including Trinidad and Tobago, St Lucia, Ceylon (now Sri Lanka), Mauritius, Cape Colony and Malta.

The abolition of the slave trade (1807) and slavery in the Empire (1833) was accompanied by a movement to devolve power to the colonies. This eventually led to the BRITISH NORTH AMERICA ACT (1867) which established Canada as a largely self-governing dominion under the British crown. The Commonwealth of Australia gained dominion status in 1901, as did New Zealand in 1907. In India, Britain strengthened its rule when it conquered the Punjab and Sind regions in the 1840s. The INDIAN MUTINY (1857), however, resulted in the British government assuming direct responsibility for the administration of India. In 1877 Queen VICTORIA was proclaimed empress of India, which was regarded as "the jewel in the imperial crown".

THE ROLE OF FREE-TRADE

The shift from an agricultural to a manufacturing economy brought about by the INDUSTRIAL REVOLUTION in Britain led to a search for new export markets, especially in the East. The economic basis of the Empire was changed by the FREE-TRADE movement, which opposed mercantilist restrictions on international trade. In 1813 trade in India was opened to all British citizens, ending the monopoly of the English East India Company. In 1839 and 1856 the British government provoked the OPIUM WARS in support of merchants' demands to be able to trade freely in China. The first of these Wars resulted in the acquisition of Hong Kong in 1842. Finally, in 1849 the remaining vestiges of the Navigation Acts were repealed. By 1850 Britain was the world's primary trading nation. Trade often preceded the establishment of formal British authority and was one of the main driving forces behind an upsurge in IMPERIALISM and the annexation of land in the Pacific, Asia and Africa after 1870. In the Pacific, Fiji was the first of many islands to be occupied by the British from 1875. In Asia, Burma was annexed in three stages, between 1826 and 1886, and a protectorate was gradually established over Malaya between 1874 and 1914.

EXPANSION IN AFRICA

In North Africa, Britain gained control of Egypt (1882), and thus control of the SUEZ CANAL, although it did not formally annex the country. It then took over Sudan (1889) after a rebellion led by the MAHDI. In sub-Saharan Africa both missionaries and explorers – among them David LIVINGSTONE and Henry STANLEY – played a significant role in opening up the interior to Britain and other European powers. The Royal Niger Company and the Imperial East Africa Company extended British influence in Africa and, during what became known as the "scramble for Africa", Britain acquired The Gambia (1888), Gold Coast, now Ghana (1898), and Nigeria (1914) in West Africa. In East Africa, it acquired Kenya (1898) and Uganda (1890). In Central Africa, Cecil RHODES formed Rhodesia (now Zambia and Zimbabwe). In the south, the first of the SOUTH AFRICAN WARS (1877) fought by the British against the Boers (AFRIKANERS) led to British suzerainty being established over the TRANSVAAL and Orange FREE STATE, with the Boers retaining political control. The second of the South African Wars (1899–1902) led to Britain's annexation of the Transvaal and Orange Free State. In 1910 the Union of South Africa was created under the leadership of the Afrikaner Louis BOTHA.

DECLINE OF THE EMPIRE

By 1914 the Empire comprised *c.*25% of the Earth's land surface and population. Despite further acquisitons following the Treaty of Versailles (1919) and the collapse of the OTTOMAN EMPIRE, it was not to remain this size for long. WORLD WAR I had taken its toll on imperial conscripts (200,000 had died in the War) and prompted increased demands for self-government. The Statute of WESTMINSTER (1931) recognized the dominions (Canada, Australia, New Zealand, South Africa and Eire) as independent states within the COMMONWEALTH OF NATIONS. By the 1930s, the independence movement in India led by "Mahatma" GANDHI and the Indian National CONGRESS, was also gaining considerable strength. Yet, the Empire appeared secure until WORLD WAR 2 (1939–45). The War had the effect of depriving Britain, along with other colonial powers, of the military and financial capability, but above all the will, to retain its colonial possessions by force. In 1941 Britain and the United States signed the ATLANTIC CHARTER declaring the right of self-determination for all countries. India and Pakistan gained independence in 1947, followed by Burma and Ceylon (1948). In Malaya, British rule came to an end in 1957, although British troops were involved in suppressing a major communist rebellion between 1948 and 1960. In 1957 the Gold Coast became the first African colony to gain independence, and most of the remaining colonies in Africa, the Caribbean and the Pacific gained self-government in the next 20 years. By 1980 only a handful of territories remained in British hands, among them Hong Kong, Gibraltar and the Falklands. In 1997 Hong Kong was returned to the Chinese.

▲ **Crystal Palace** Built to house the Great Exhibition (1851), the Crystal Palace, London, contained exhibits from all over the world. The first world trade fair, the Exhibition's aim was to promote Britain's imperial strength.

B

Brookeborough, Basil Stanlake Brooke, 1st Viscount (1888–1973) British statesman, prime minister of Northern Ireland (1943–63). He served as minister of agriculture for Northern Ireland (1933–41) and minister of commerce (1941–45). As prime minister, Brookeborough supported Protestant hegemony in Ulster and refused to negotiate with the Republic of Ireland.

Brook Farm Utopian community, founded (1841) in West Roxbury, Massachusetts, United States. Led by George Ripley, a former Unitarian minister, members tried to combine thinking with working and to give equal pay to all; many famous people of the time participated, including Nathaniel Hawthorne, Charles Dana and Ralph Waldo Emerson. In 1847 the experiment was abandoned due to unproductive land and lack of water power for industries.

Brougham, Henry Peter, 1st Baron Brougham and Vaux (1778–1868) British statesman, b. Scotland. In 1810 he entered Parliament as a Whig. As lord chancellor (1830–34), Brougham established the Central Criminal Court and helped pass the REFORM ACT (1832). He was a founder of the University of London (1828).

Browder, Earl Russell (1891–1973) US politician. He was general secretary (1930–44) of the Communist Party of the United States. In 1936 and 1940 Browder ran for president. He was imprisoned (1941–42) for passport fraud.

Brown, George (1818–80) Canadian statesman and journalist, b. Scotland. In 1837 he emigrated to the United States, but later moved to Canada. In 1844 Brown founded the Toronto *Globe* newspaper. In 1851 he was elected to the Canadian Parliament. Brown opposed proposals for increased participation of French-Canadians. He supported land and education reforms, and played a pivotal role in the establishment of the Confederation of Canada.

Brown, Gordon (1951–) British statesman, chancellor of the exchequer (1997–), b. Scotland. He entered Parliament in 1983. Brown's first act as chancellor was to give the BANK OF ENGLAND independence in interest-rate policy. *See also* BLAIR, TONY

Brown, John (1800–59) US ABOLITIONIST. He led the Pottawatomic Massacre (1856) in Kansas in which five alleged slaveowners were killed. In 1859, hoping to start a slave revolt, he led 21 men in the capture of the US arsenal at Harper's Ferry, Virginia. They were driven out the following day by troops under Robert LEE. Brown was captured, charged with treason, and hanged. The trial aggravated North-South tensions.

Browne, Robert (*c*.1550–1633) English clergyman, founder of the "Brownists", a separatist religious sect. In *Reformation without Tarrying for Any* (1582), he presented the first argument for CONGREGATIONALISM. In 1584 Browne was imprisoned and later excommunicated. By 1591 he had been reconciled to the CHURCH OF ENGLAND.

Brownshirts (officially *Sturmabteilung*, or *SA*) German Nazi stormtroopers founded in 1920. By 1933 the Brownshirts, led by Ernst RÖHM, numbered *c*.500,000. After the NAZI PARTY seized power, the Brownshirts' ideology and challenge to the autonomy of the German army was perceived as a threat by Adolf HITLER. The SA leaders were shot on the "NIGHT OF THE LONG KNIVES" (30 June 1934), and the SS emerged as their successors. *See also* BLACKSHIRTS; NATIONAL SOCIALISM

Brown v. Board of Education of Topeka (1954) Landmark Supreme Court decision that overturned the "separate but equal" doctrine of public education established in *Plessy v. Ferguson* (1896). The court, led by Chief Justice Earl WARREN, found separate facilities to be "inherently unequal" and in violation of the Constitution's equal protection clause. This decision gave impetus to the CIVIL RIGHTS movement of the 1960s.

Broz, Josip *See* TITO

Bruce, Blanche Kelso (1841–98) US senator (1875–81) for Mississippi. He was the first African American to serve a full term in the Senate. An escaped slave, Bruce campaigned for the civil rights of ethnic minorities in the United States and served as register of the treasury (1881–85, 1897–98). *See also* REVELS, HIRAM

Bruce, Robert *See* ROBERT I (THE BRUCE)

Bruce (of Melbourne), Stanley Melbourne, 1st Viscount (1883–1967) Australian statesman, prime minister (1923–29). He entered Parliament in 1918 and was the Australian representative at the LEAGUE OF NATIONS in 1921. He served as treasurer in the Cabinet (1921–23) of W.M. HUGHES. As prime minister, Bruce encouraged reforms such as unemployment insurance and health legislation. He also served (1933–45) as the Australian High Commissioner in London. In 1947 Bruce became a viscount and was the first Australian to sit in the British House of Lords.

BRUNEI
AREA: 5765sq km (2226sq mi)
POPULATION: 285,000
CAPITAL (POPULATION): Bandar Seri (49,902)
GOVERNMENT: Constitutional monarchy
ETHNIC GROUPS: Malay, Chinese, European, Indian
LANGUAGES: Malay, English, Chinese dialects
RELIGION: Sunni Muslim
GDP PER CAPITA (1994): US$16,270

Bruges (Brugge) Capital of West FLANDERS province, NW BELGIUM. Built on a network of canals, it was an important centre of the Flanders cloth industry by the 12th century, and flourished as a trading centre between the 12th and 15th century. Its importance declined after 1500, but trade revived when the Zeebrugge ship canal was opened in 1907. It is a treasure-house of medieval architecture, including the Market Hall (13th–15th century), the Town Hall (1376–1420), and the Chapel of the Holy Blood (14th–16th century). Pop. (1993 est.) 116,724.

Brulé, Étienne (1592–1633) French explorer in North America. In 1608 he travelled to Québec with Samuel de CHAMPLAIN. In 1610 he went into the wilderness to study Native American culture. In 1612 Brulé and a group of HURON guided Champlain to Lake Huron. On the return journey, they probably became the first Europeans to reach Lake Ontario. In 1615 Brulé explored Chesapeake Bay. On the way back, he was captured and tortured by the IROQUOIS. In 1618 he escaped and returned to live among the Huron, probably becoming the first European to visit all of the Great Lakes except Lake Michigan.

Brummell, "Beau" (George Bryan) (1778–1840) English dandy, leader of men's fashion in Regency England between 1798 and 1812. His sense of perfection in dress, accompanied by a sharp wit and a friendship with the Prince Regent (later GEORGE IV), gave him enormous social success. The demise of royal patronage and his huge gambling debts forced Brummell into exile (1816) in France, where he lived the rest of his life in poverty.

Brundtland, Gro Harlem (1939–) Norwegian stateswoman, first woman prime minister of Norway (1981, 1986–89, 1990–96). She led a succession of minority Labour governments. Brundtland chaired the World Commission on Environment and Development, which produced the report *Our Common Future* (1987). Most of her third term was overshadowed by the dispute over Norway's entry into the EUROPEAN UNION (EU). In 1998 Brundtland was appointed director general of WHO.

Brunei Islamic sultanate in NW BORNEO, SE Asia. During the 16th century, Brunei ruled over most of Borneo and parts of the Philippines but gradually lost its influence. In 1841 James BROOKE was granted SARAWAK. In 1888 Brunei became a British protectorate. Brunei's economic fortunes dramatically improved after the discovery of oil in 1929. Japan occupied (1941–45) Brunei during World War 2. In 1962 Brunei gained self-government. Hassanal Bolkiah succeeded his father, Omar Ali Saifuddin, as sultan in 1967. In 1984 Brunei gained full independence from Britain.

Brunel, Isambard Kingdom (1806–59) English marine and railroad engineer, son of Sir Marc Isambard BRUNEL. In 1829 he designed the Clifton Suspension Bridge, Bristol (completed 1864). Brunel is also noted for his ships; *Great Western* (designed 1837), the first transatlantic wooden steamship, *Great Britain* (1843), the first iron-hulled, screw-driven steamship; and *Great Eastern* (1858), the largest steamship of its era.

Brunel, Sir Marc Isambard (1769–1849) Architect and engineer, father of Isambard Kingdom BRUNEL, b. France. A refugee from the French Revolution, he went to the United States in 1793 and was chief engineer of New York. In 1799 Brunel moved to England, where he was responsible for the construction of the first tunnel (1825–43) under the River Thames, London.

Brunhilda (d.613) Frankish queen, wife of Sigebert I of AUSTRASIA. In 567 her sister, Galswintha, was murdered by Sigebert's brother, CHILPERIC I, king of NEUSTRIA, at the instigation of his concubine Fredegund. Brunhilda sought revenge by instigating war with Neustria. After the assassination (575) of Sigebert, Brunhilda effectively ruled Austrasia for nearly 30 years, initially as regent for her son. In 613 the Austrasian nobles appealed to the Neustrian king CLOTAIRE II, son of Fredegund, for help in overthrowing her. Clotaire had her dragged to death by a horse.

Brüning, Heinrich (1885–1970) German statesman, chancellor (1930–32). In 1929 he became leader of the Catholic Centre Party. In 1930 Brüning formed a minority, conservative government. His austere economic policies reduced inflation, but contributed to rising unemployment. After the Reichstag rejected his plans, Brüning attempted to rule by decree. Elections in 1930 showed increasing support for Adolf HITLER'S NAZI PARTY. In 1932 Brüning was forced to resign by President Paul von HINDENBURG. He was succeeded by Franz von PAPEN.

Bruno, Giordano (1548–1600) Italian philosopher. A fierce opponent of dogmatism and a supporter of the relativity of perception, his pantheistic belief in a deity manifest in the cosmos and his support of Nicholas COPERNICUS led to his censure for heresy and his death at the stake.

Brussels (Bruxelles) Capital of BELGIUM, central Belgium. From the 12th century, Brussels expanded through the wool trade to become a major town in the Duchy of BRABANT. The city flourished as the capital (1430–77) of the Duke of BURGUNDY'S possessions in the Low Countries. In 1585 Brussels became capital of the Catholic Spanish NETHERLANDS. By the Treaties of UTRECHT (1713), the city became part of the Austrian Netherlands. The Brabant Revolution (1789) briefly overthrew Austrian rule, but Emperor LEOPOLD II regained Brussels in 1790. From 1815 to 1830, the city served as joint capital (with The Hague) of the United Kingdom of the Netherlands. In 1830 Brussels became capital of an independent Belgium. The city was occupied (1914–18, 1940–44) by Germany in World War 1 and World War 2. Today, Brussels is the headquarters of the EUROPEAN UNION (EU) and the NORTH ATLANTIC TREATY ORGANIZATION (NATO). Tension exists between the city's Fleming and Walloon inhabitants. Pop. (1993 est.) 949,070.

Brussels, Treaty of (1948) Agreement signed by Britain, France and the Low Countries for cooperation in defence, politics, economics and cultural affairs for 50 years. In 1950 the defence agreement was merged into the NORTH ATLANTIC TREATY ORGANIZATION (NATO). In 1954 Italy and West Germany joined, and the name was changed to the Western European Union (WEU). It was a forerunner of the EUROPEAN UNION (EU).

Brutus, Lucius Junius (active late 6th century BC) Founder of the Roman Republic. He led the Romans in the expulsion of the last Etruscan king (509 BC) after his kinswoman, Lucretia, had been raped by the king's son. He executed his two sons for plotting to restore the Tarquins.

Brutus, Marcus Junius (*c*.85–42 BC) Roman republican leader, one of the principal assassins of Julius CAESAR. Brutus initially sided with POMPEY against Caesar, but Caesar made him governor of Cisalpine Gaul in 46 BC and city praetor in 44 BC. After taking part in Caesar's assassination, Brutus raised an army in Greece but was defeated at the Battle of PHILIPPI (42 BC) by Mark ANTONY and Octavian (later AUGUSTUS). He committed suicide.

Bryan, William Jennings (1860–1925) US statesman and lawyer, secretary of state (1913–15). A leading advocate of the free coinage of silver, his "Cross of Gold" speech at the 1896 Democratic convention earned him the presidential nomination. Bryan lost the ensuing election to William

MCKINLEY. Nominated again in 1900, he was again defeated by McKinley. Bryan was defeated a third time (1908) by William Howard TAFT. In return for helping Woodrow WILSON win the 1912 election, he became secretary of state. An opponent of the teaching of evolution, he acted as prosecuting attorney in the SCOPES TRIAL (1925), opposing Clarence DARROW. Bryan won the case but died five days later.

Bryce, James, 1st Viscount (1838–1922) British historian, statesman and diplomat, b. Northern Ireland. He wrote the influential *History of the Roman Empire* (1864) and *The American Commonwealth* (1888). Bryce was a leading figure in the Liberal Party, serving as president of the Board of Trade and secretary of state for Ireland. He was British ambassador (1907–13) to the United States.

buccaneer PIRATE operating mostly on the Spanish main in the 16th and 17th centuries. Many buccaneers, such as Henry MORGAN, confined their raids to Spanish property and often took their booty home to their mother countries. As buccaneers began to attack ships of all nations indiscriminately, they became indistinguishable from ordinary pirates.

Bucer, Martin (1491–1551) German Protestant reformer who attempted to reconcile the viewpoints of Martin LUTHER and Ulrich ZWINGLI. In 1549 he became Regius professor of divinity at Cambridge University.

Buchanan, James (1791–1868) Fifteenth president of the United States (1857–1861). He entered Congress in 1821 and was senator (1834–45). President James POLK appointed him secretary of state (1845–49). Under President Franklin PIERCE, Buchanan served as minister to Great Britain (1853–56). Buchanan was an unpopular president, and his attempt to compromise between pro- and anti-SLAVERY factions floundered. He attempted to purchase Cuba and he accepted the KANSAS-NEBRASKA ACT (1854). The subsequent split in the DEMOCRATIC PARTY opened the way for the election of Abraham LINCOLN. The Southern states seceded and, shortly after Buchanan left office, the American CIVIL WAR (1861–65) began. *See also* BROWN, JOHN

Bucharest (Bucureşti) Capital and largest city of ROMANIA, on the River Dimbovita, S Romania. In 1459 Vlad III (the Impaler), Prince of Walachia, built a fortress here. In 1698, under Ottoman control, Bucharest became the capital of Walachia. Walachia and Moldavia unified in 1859 and Bucharest was made capital of Romania (1862). The city was occupied by Germany in both world wars. In the 1980s, the dictator Nicolae CEAUŞESCU demolished much of the old city to build monuments to his rule, such as the marble House of the People. Bucharest is the seat of the patriarch of the Romanian Orthodox Church. Pop. (1992) 2,350,984.

Buchenwald Site of a Nazi CONCENTRATION CAMP, near Weimar, E central Germany. Established in 1937, it became notorious especially for the medical experiments conducted on its inmates, of whom *c.*50,000 died. The camp was liberated by US forces in 1945. *See also* AUSCHWITZ; BELSEN; DACHAU; HOLOCAUST, THE

Buchman, Frank Nathan Daniel (1878–1961) US evangelist, founder of the Moral Re-Armament movement (MRA). An ordained Lutheran minister, he began propagating his ethical views in 1921 at Hartford, and later at Oxford and Cambridge universities. He was decorated by eight governments for services rendered by his worldwide MRA programme.

Buckingham, George Villiers, 1st Duke of (1592–1628) English statesman and court favourite of JAMES I and CHARLES I. In 1614 he joined the court of James I and rapidly acquired a number of titles. Buckingham's personal extravagance led to parliamentary investigation. In 1623 he was largely responsible for the breakdown in the negotiations of marriage between Prince Charles and the Spanish Infanta Maria. In 1624 Buckingham arranged Charles' marriage to HENRIETTA MARIA. His failure to provide adequate supplies for an English expedition to the Palatinate led to charges of political incompetence. The disastrous expedition to capture Cadiz (1625) led to his impeachment by Sir John ELIOT, but Charles I rapidly dissolved Parliament. In 1627 Buckingham led anot her unsuccessful campaign to relieve the HUGUENOTS at LA ROCHELLE, W France. He was murdered by a discontented naval officer, John Felton.

Buckingham, George Villiers, 2nd Duke of (1628–87) English courtier, son of the 1st Duke of BUCKINGHAM. He was educated with CHARLES I's sons and supported the Royalists in the CIVIL WAR (1642–48). A dashing, rakish courtier in Restoration England, Buckingham was a member of the group of ministers known as the CABAL but later joined the opposition to CHARLES II. He wrote several comedies, notably *The Rehearsal* (1671).

Buckingham, Henry Stafford, 2nd Duke of *See* STAFFORD, HENRY, 2ND DUKE OF BUCKINGHAM

BUDDHISM

Founded (*c.*528 BC) in India by Gautama Siddhartha, the BUDDHA, Buddhism is a religion which originally aimed to reform HINDUISM. It is based on Four Noble Truths: existence is suffering, the cause of suffering is desire, the end of suffering comes with the achievement of NIRVANA, and Nirvana is attained through the Eightfold Path of right views, right resolve, right speech, right action, right livelihood, right effort, right mindfulness and right concentration. There are no gods. Karma, one of Buddhism's most important concepts, says good actions are rewarded and evil ones are punished, either in this life or throughout a long series of lives resulting from samsara, the cycle of death and rebirth by reincarnation. The achievement of Nirvana breaks the cycle. Buddhism was given official backing in India in the 3rd century BC by ASHOKA, but it failed to take a permanent hold there. Instead it spread through much of Asia, reaching Japan in the 6th century AD. A major schism occurred in the 1st century AD, resulting in two schools of Buddhism, MAHAYANA ("greater vehicle") and THERAVADA ("doctrine of the elders"). Followers of Mahayana sometimes refer to Theravada Buddhism by the less respectful term *Hinayana* ("lesser vehicle"). Today its main divisions are Theravada in SE Asia, Mahayana in N Asia, TIBETAN BUDDHISM in Tibet; and ZEN in Japan. Because of the suppression of Buddhism, particularly in communist China, it is difficult to estimate the number of Buddhists worldwide, however the figure is believed to be somewhere between 150 and 300 million.

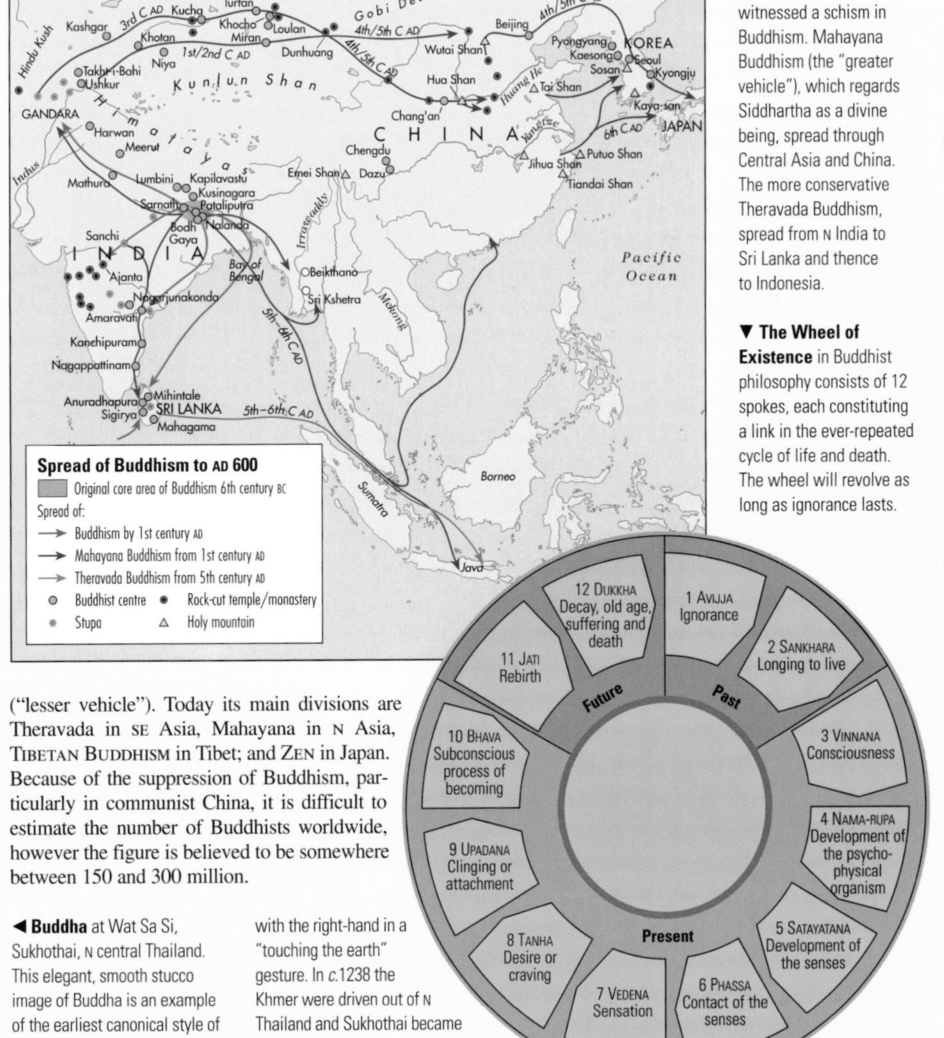

◀ **The 1st century AD** witnessed a schism in Buddhism. Mahayana Buddhism (the "greater vehicle"), which regards Siddhartha as a divine being, spread through Central Asia and China. The more conservative Theravada Buddhism, spread from N India to Sri Lanka and thence to Indonesia.

▼ **The Wheel of Existence** in Buddhist philosophy consists of 12 spokes, each constituting a link in the ever-repeated cycle of life and death. The wheel will revolve as long as ignorance lasts.

◀ **Buddha** at Wat Sa Si, Sukhothai, N central Thailand. This elegant, smooth stucco image of Buddha is an example of the earliest canonical style of Thai Buddhist sculpture. Buddha is seated in a half-lotus position with the right-hand in a "touching the earth" gesture. In *c.*1238 the Khmer were driven out of N Thailand and Sukhothai became the capital of the first independent Thai state.

B

Budapest Capital of HUNGARY, on the River Danube. It was created (1872) by uniting the towns of Buda (on the W bank of the Danube) and Pest (on the E bank). As Aquincum, the W bank site became (1st century AD) the Roman capital of Lower PANNONIA. In 1241 both cities were destroyed by the Turks. In 1244 BÉLA IV built a castle in Buda. Buda was made capital of Hungary in 1361. The Turks recaptured Buda and Pest in the 1540s. When they were liberated by the Habsburgs (1686), the cities lay in ruins. In the 19th century, Pest developed and the two cities were linked by the Chain Bridge (1839–49). In 1868 Pest and Vienna became joint capitals of the AUSTRO-HUNGARIAN EMPIRE. In 1918 Budapest was made capital of an independent Hungary. In 1944 Budapaest was occupied by the Germans, whose resistance to the Soviet advance devastated the city. The HUNGARIAN UPRISING (1956) was crushed by Soviet tanks in the streets of Budapest. Landmarks include Buda Castle, the 13th-century Matthias Church and the Parliament building. Pop. (1993 est.) 2,009,000.

Buddha (Enlightened One) Title adopted by Gautama Siddhartha (*c*.563–*c*.483 BC), the founder of BUDDHISM. Born in Lumbini, Nepal, Siddhartha was son of the ruler of the Sakya tribe, and his early years were spent in luxury. At the age of 29, he came to the conclusion that human life is little more than suffering. He gave up his wealth and comfort, deserted his wife and small son, and took to the road as a wandering ascetic. He sought truth in a six-year regime of austerity and self-mortification. After abandoning asceticism as futile, he sought his own middle way towards enlightenment. The moment of truth came (*c*.528 BC) as he sat beneath a banyan bodhi tree in the village of Bodh Gaya, Bihar, India. After this, he taught others about his way to truth. The title "buddha" applies to those who have achieved perfect enlightenment. Buddhists believe that there have been several buddhas before Siddhartha, and there will be many to come.

Buddhism *See* feature article, page 61

Buena Vista, Battle of (1847) Engagement in the MEXICAN WAR (1846–48). US troops, led by Zachary TAYLOR, disobeyed orders from their government and advanced to Buena Vista. The Mexican army, led by General SANTA ANNA, attacked. After two days of indecisive fighting, Santa Anna withdrew, giving the US control of N Mexico.

Buenos Aires Capital of Argentina, on the estuary of the Río de la Plata, 240km (150mi) from the Atlantic Ocean. Originally founded by the Spanish conquistador Pedro de Mendoza in 1536, it was rebuilt in 1580 after being destroyed by the indigenous population. Buenos Aires was governed as part of the Spanish Viceroyalty of Peru. In 1776 it was made capital of the new Viceroyalty of the Río de la Plata. In 1810 Buenos Aires declared independence and became (1816) capital of the United Provinces of the Río de la Plata. In 1880 it was made the federal capital of Argentina. The city's booming economy attracted many emigrants in the late 19th-century. In the early 20th century, Buenos Aires acquired its broad avenues, modelled on Paris. Pop. (1992 est.) 11,662,050.

Buffalo Bill (1846–1917) US frontiersman, scout and showman, b. William Frederick Cody. A Pony Express rider at 14, he then served as Union scout during the American Civil War (1861–65). Cody gained his nickname by supplying buffalo meat to railway workers. He became famous through Ned Buntline's dime novels. In 1883 Buffalo Bill organized a "Wild West" exhibition, co-starring Annie OAKLEY and Chief SITTING BULL.

Buganda Region of SE UGANDA, E Africa. For centuries it was a powerful independent kingdom trading in slaves and ivory, but it gradually lost autonomy with the growth of British colonial influence. In 1967 it was finally made part of Uganda. The Ganda tribe are its chief inhabitants.

Bukharin, Nikolai Ivanovich (1888–1938) Russian political theorist. After the Russian Revolution (1917), he became a leading member of the COMMUNIST INTERNATIONAL (Comintern) and editor of *Pravda*. In 1924 Bukharin joined the politburo. He opposed agricultural collectivization and was executed for treason by STALIN.

Bukovina Historic region in NE Romania, extending into W Ukraine; the chief city is Chernovtsy. In the 14th century, it formed part of the principality of Moldavia. In 1775 Bukovina was ceded by the Ottomans to Austria, who administered (1786–1849) it as part of Galicia. It was ceded to Romania by the Treaty of Saint-Germain (1919). In 1940 and 1944 the Soviet Union occupied N Bukovina, which became part of the Ukrainian Soviet Socialist Republic in 1947. Area: 10,440sq km (4031sq mi).

Bulganin, Nikolai (1895–1975) Soviet statesman and marshal, prime minister (1955–58). He served as minister of the armed forces (1947–49) under Joseph STALIN. In 1953 Bulganin became deputy prime minister and minister of defence under Georgi MALENKOV. Bulganin's support for Nikita KHRUSHCHEV saw him succeed Malenkov as prime minister. He was dismissed after becoming associated with the "antiparty faction" that tried to overthrow Khrushchev.

Bulgaria *See* country feature

Bulgars Ancient Turkic people originating in the region N and E of the Black Sea. In *c*.AD 650, they split into two groups. The western group moved to BULGARIA, where they became assimilated into the Slavic population and adopted Christianity. The other group moved to the Volga region and set up a Bulgar state, eventually converting to Islam. The Volga Bulgars were conquered by KIEVAN RUS in the 10th century.

Bulge, Battle of the Final German offensive of WORLD WAR 2. The Germans drove a wedge through the Allied lines in the ARDENNES on the French–Belgian frontier in December 1944. Allied forces converged to extinguish the "bulge" in their lines in January 1945, and the advance into Germany was renewed.

Bull Moose Party *See* PROGRESSIVE PARTY

Bull Run, First Battle of (21 July 1861) American CIVIL WAR engagement fought near Manassas, Virginia. Under-trained Union troops commanded by General Irvin McDowell, at first successful, were eventually routed by Confederate troops under General P.G.T. BEAUREGARD, reinforced by General Thomas JACKSON, who earned his nickname "Stonewall" at the Battle.

Bull Run, Second Battle of (28 August 1862) Ameri-

BULGARIA

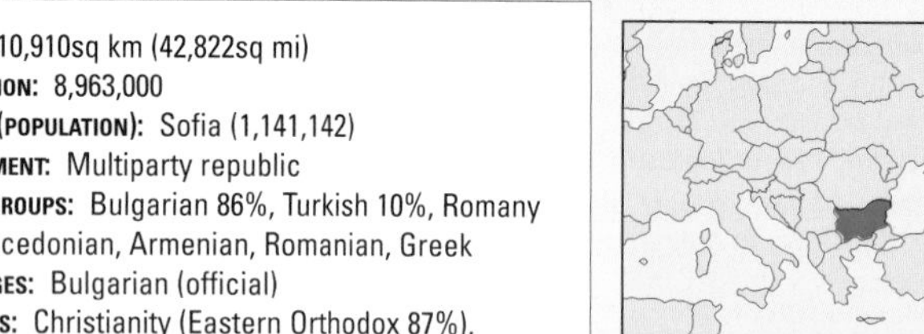

AREA: 110,910sq km (42,822sq mi)
POPULATION: 8,963,000
CAPITAL (POPULATION): Sofia (1,141,142)
GOVERNMENT: Multiparty republic
ETHNIC GROUPS: Bulgarian 86%, Turkish 10%, Romany 3%, Macedonian, Armenian, Romanian, Greek
LANGUAGES: Bulgarian (official)
RELIGIONS: Christianity (Eastern Orthodox 87%), Islam 13%
GDP PER CAPITA (1995): US$4480

Balkan republic in SE Europe. Thracians inhabited the region in the Bronze Age. Under the Romans, Bulgaria was divided into the provinces of Moesia and Thrace. SLAVS invaded in the 6th century AD, but were subjugated in the late 7th century by BULGARS from across the Danube.

In 681 Asparukh established the first Bulgarian state. In the 8th century, Bulgaria struggled to maintain its independence from the Byzantine Empire. BORIS I (r.852–889) adopted Christianity as the state religion. Medieval Bulgaria was at its height under SIMEON I (r.892–927), who conquered all of the N Balkans. After his death, Bulgaria was divided by the BOGOMILS sect. In 1018 it was annexed to the BYZANTINE EMPIRE by BASIL II (BULGAROCTONUS). In 1185 brothers Ivan and Peter Asen defeated the Byzantines.

Under Ivan Asen II (r.1218–41), the second Bulgarian empire conquered the whole of the Balkan Peninsula. In 1396 Bulgaria fell to the OTTOMAN EMPIRE. The Turks administered Bulgaria as part of RUMELIA. The brutal crushing of the April Uprising (1876) led Russia to declare war on the Turks. The Treaty of SAN STEFANO (1878), which outlined a large, independent Bulgarian state, was extensively modified at the Congress of BERLIN (1878). The latter created a smaller Bulgaria principality and the province of Eastern Rumelia both with limited autonomy within the Ottoman Empire. In 1886 Eastern Rumelia was united with Bulgaria. In 1908 Prince FERDINAND declared full independence.

The Balkan League (Bulgaria, Greece, Serbia and Montenegro) defeated the Ottoman Empire in the first of the BALKAN WARS (1912–13), but the League's failure to agree on the division of Macedonia resulted in Bulgaria's defeat in the Second Balkan War. In 1915 Bulgaria entered WORLD WAR I on the side of the CENTRAL POWERS. By September 1918, more than 100,000 Bulgarian troops had died in the War. Bulgaria was forced to agree to an armistice and Tsar Ferdinand abdicated in favour of his son, BORIS III. Alexander STAMBOLISKI, leader of the Bulgarian Agrarian National Union, formed a government that implemented radical political and economic reforms. In 1923 Stamboliski was murdered in a right-wing coup d'etat, led by Alexander Tsankov. In 1935, Boris III established a military dictatorship. In 1941 Bulgaria joined the Axis Powers in World War 2. In 1944 Soviet troops invaded and Bulgaria quickly surrendered.

The Bulgarian Communist Party, led by Georgi DIMITROV, dominated the new Fatherland Front regime. It is estimated that 30,000 political opponents were killed in the ensuing purges. A Soviet-style constitution was adopted (1947) and industry was nationalized. In 1949 Dimitrov died in office and was succeeded by Vulko Chervenkov, who sped up the "Stalinization" of Bulgaria. In 1949 Bulgaria joined the COUNCIL FOR MUTUAL ECONOMIC ASSISTANCE (COMECON) and was a founder member (1955) of the WARSAW PACT. In 1954 Chervenkov resigned in favour of Todor ZHIVKOV, who led a more liberal regime. During the 1980s, Bulgaria's attempts to forcibly assimilate its Turkish population were resisted and more than 300,000 Turks fled to Turkey. With the collapse of Soviet communism, Zhivkov's presidency (1971–89) came to an abrupt end. The Bulgarian Communist Party was renamed the Bulgarian Socialist Party (BSP). In 1990 a non-communist president, Zhelyu Zhelev, was elected for the first time in 40 years. A new constitution (1991) brought multiparty democracy. The BSP won the 1994 elections, but virtual economic collapse and anti-government demonstrations prompted the government to resign in 1996. Elections in 1997 were won by the Union of Democratic Forces (UDF), led by Ivan Kostov.

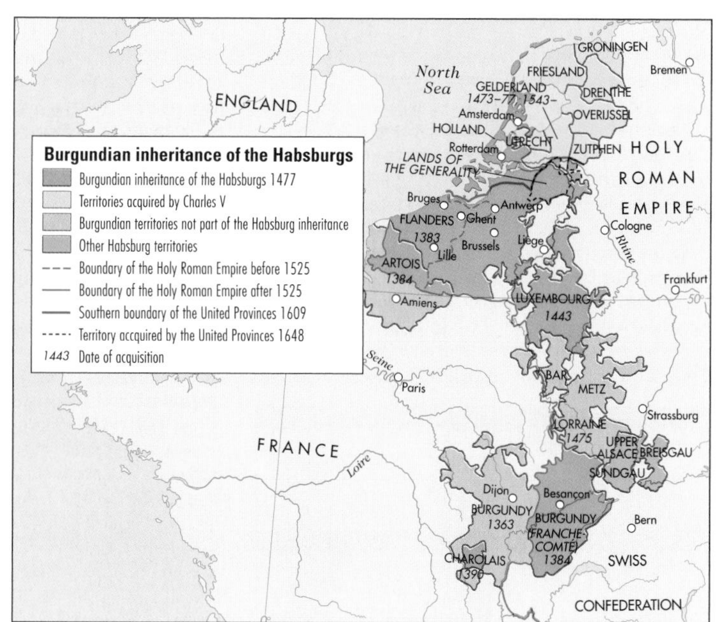

► **Burgundy** The lands that Charles V inherited in 1506 consisted of most of the provinces of the Netherlands and the free county of Burgundy. It did not include the duchy of Burgundy, however, which had been confiscated by Louis XI of France in 1477. In the course of his reign, Charles annexed Gelderland, Groningen, Friesland and the bishopric of Utrecht. His successor, Philip II, faced serious opposition from the nobility from 1565 and a full-scale revolt in Holland from 1572. This led to the formal repudiation of Philip in 1581 by what were to become the seven United Provinces of the Netherlands.

can CIVIL WAR engagement. On the same battleground as the First Battle of BULL RUN (1861), 48,000 Confederates under General Robert LEE defeated 75,000 Union soldiers under General John POPE. Union losses were 16,000 to the Confederates' 9000. Pope was dismissed as commander of the Union army, and General George MCCLELLAN resumed control.

Bülow, Bernhard Heinrich Martin, Fürst von (1849–1929) German statesman, chancellor (1900–09). His aggressive foreign policy left Germany isolated against the TRIPLE ENTENTE and heightened the tensions in Europe that preceded the outbreak of World War 1. In 1908 Bülow lost favour with Emperor WILLIAM II and was forced to resign.

Bunche, Ralph Johnson (1904–71) US diplomat. He joined the United Nations (UN) in 1947 and helped negotiate a cease-fire (1949) in the Arab-Israeli conflict. In 1950 Bunche became the first African American to be awarded the Nobel Peace Prize. He directed UN peacekeeping forces in Suez (1956), the Congo (1960) and Cyprus (1964). Bunche served as UN undersecretary general (1967–71).

Bunker Hill, Battle of (17 June 1775) Battle in the AMERICAN REVOLUTION fought on Boston's Charlestown Peninsula. The first large-scale battle of the War, it was actually fought S of Bunker Hill on Breed's Hill. Although the Americans were driven from their position, the British lost nearly half of their 2400 troops.

Burckhardt, Jacob Christoph (1818–97) Swiss historian. He emphasized cultural values, rather than political factors, an attitude influential in the development of the modern approach to history. His major work was *The Civilization of the Renaissance in Italy* (1860).

Burckhardt, Johann Ludwig (1784–1817) Swiss explorer. He travelled extensively (1809–13) in Egypt and Arabia, rediscovering PETRA (1812), now in Jordan, and ABU SIMBEL, S Egypt. Burckhardt was the first European in modern times to reach MEDINA (now in Saudi Arabia).

Burger, Warren Earl (1907–95) US jurist, 15th chief justice (1969–86) of the Supreme Court. He served as a judge (1956–69) of the Court of Appeals in Washington, D.C. A conservative chief justice, Burger prevented or overturned liberal legislation. In *Gregg* v. *Georgia* (1976), capital punishment for murder was declared constitutional.

Burghley, William Cecil, 1st Baron (1520–98) English statesman, chief minister of ELIZABETH I of England, father of Robert CECIL. In 1548 he became secretary to EDWARD VI's protector, Edward Seymour, Duke of SOMERSET. Cecil served as secretary of state (1550–53) during the ascendancy of John Dudley, Duke of NORTHUMBERLAND. Although Cecil was not involved in Northumberland's alteration of the succession in favour of Lady Jane GREY, he did not serve MARY I. On Mary's death, Cecil was reappointed by ELIZABETH I and faithfully served the queen as secretary of state (1558–72), and then as lord high treasurer (1572–98). He worked with Archbishop Matthew PARKER to produce the moderate Elizabethan Settlement (1559). Cecil fought for the queen's favour against John Dudley's son Robert, Earl of LEICESTER, and Thomas Howard, 4th Duke of NORFOLK. In 1571 Cecil was made 1st Baron Burghley. Burghley resisted the demands of Puritans, such as Leicester and Sir Francis WALSINGHAM, to join the Protestant cause in European wars, preferring diplomatic solutions. As lord treasurer, Burghley's administrative skills and anti-corruption drive kept the crown solvent. Burghley supported the expeditions against Catholic Spain in the 1580s and demanded the execution of MARY, QUEEN OF SCOTS in 1587. *See also* ARMADA, SPANISH; THIRTY-NINE ARTICLES

Burgoyne, John (1722–92) British general. In the AMERICAN REVOLUTION (1775–83), he served as major general in Canada (1776). Burgoyne campaigned in New York state, securing Crown Point and Fort TICONDEROGA. He was finally forced to surrender his troops at SARATOGA (October 1777).

Burgundy Historic region and former duchy in E central France. Dijon is the historical capital. In *c.*AD 480, led by Gundobad, the Burgundii tribe formed the kingdom of Burgundy, which at its height covered the whole of SE France. In 534 the kingdom fell to the FRANKS. The MEROVINGIANS partitioned the kingdom and the CAROLINGIANS divided it into Upper Burgundy (from Jura to the Alps, and FRANCHE-COMTÉ) and Lower Burgundy (PROVENCE). In *c.*931 these two were unified and became known as the kingdom of Arles from the 13th century. The **Duchy of Burgundy**, the areas W of the River Saône, was separated from Upper and Lower Burgundy and formed part of the kingdom of France under the CAPETIANS. In 1364 the Duchy of Burgundy passed to the VALOIS line when JOHN II (THE GOOD) bestowed the fief on his son, PHILIP II (THE BOLD). In 1384 Philip inherited further lands (including Franche-Comté), creating a state that extended across the Rhine and included the Low COUNTRIES. CHARLES THE BOLD (r.1467–77) lost the Duchy of Burgundy to LOUIS XI of France. Charles' daughter, MARY OF BURGUNDY, married Maximilian of HABSBURG (later MAXIMILIAN I) and for the next 185 years Franche-Comté formed part of the Habsburg Empire. In 1678 Franche-Comté was restored to the French by the Great CONDÉ. Pop. (1990) 1,609,400.

Burke, Edmund (1729–97) British statesman and writer, b. Ireland. He played a major part in the reduction of royal influence in the House of Commons and sought better treatment for Catholics and American colonists. Burke deplored the excesses of the FRENCH REVOLUTION in his most famous work, *Reflections on the Revolution in France* (1790).

Burke, Robert O'Hara (1820–61) Irish explorer. In 1860 he led the first expedition to cross Australia from S to N. At the River Barcoo, Burke left most of the party and continued with three companions (Wills, King and Gray). They almost reached the N Australia coast in 1861 but turned back without seeing the sea. Only King survived the return journey.

Burkina Faso *See* country feature

BURKINA FASO (FORMERLY UPPER VOLTA)

AREA: 274,200sq km (105,869 sq mi)
POPULATION: 9,490,000
CAPITAL (POPULATION): Ouagadougou (442,223)
GOVERNMENT: Multiparty republic
ETHNIC GROUPS: Mossi 48%, Mande 9%, Fulani 8%, Bobo 7%
LANGUAGES: French (official)
RELIGIONS: Traditional beliefs 45%, Islam 43%, Christianity 12%
GDP PER CAPITA (1995): US$780

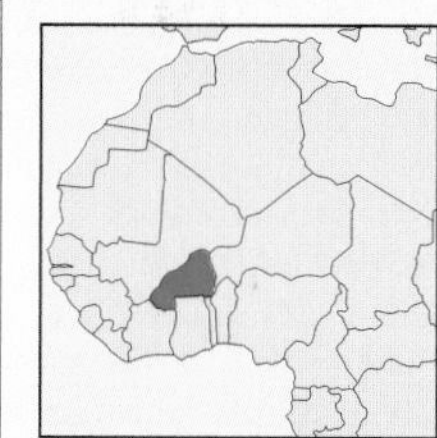

Landlocked republic in W Africa. Burkina Faso is one of the poorest nations on Earth. The earliest known inhabitants of Burkina Faso are the Bobo, Lobi and Gurunsi. From *c.*1100 the Mossi invaded the region and established small, highly complex states. The powerful Ouagadougou kingdom was ruled by an absolute monarch (the morho naba). These semi-autonomous states fiercely resisted domination by the larger MALI and SONGHAI empires.

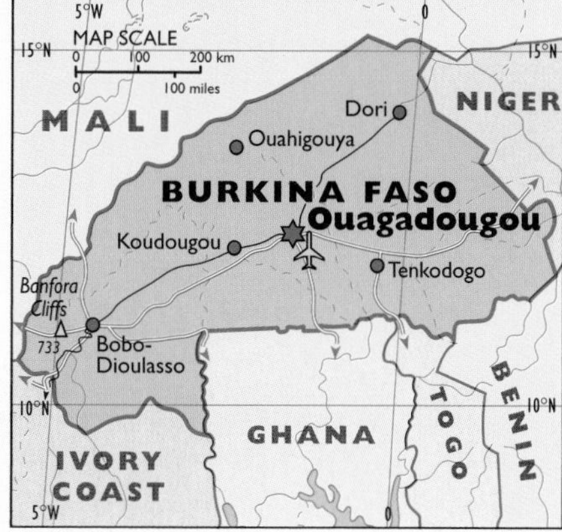

By 1897 France gained control of the region and subsumed it into French Sudan. In 1919 it became the separate colony of Upper Volta. In 1958 Upper Volta became an autonomous republic within the French Community, as a prelude to full independence in 1960. A strong, presidential form of government was adopted. In 1966 persistent drought and austerity measures produced a military coup, led by Sangoulé Lamizana. Lamizana dominated Upper Volta until he was overthrown by a military coup in 1980. In 1983 Thomas Sankara seized power in a bloody coup. In 1984 Sankara renamed the country Burkina Faso ("land of the incorruptible"). Sankara was assassinated in 1987 and Captain Blaise Compaoré seized power. Compaoré was elected president in 1991, after opposition parties boycotted the poll. He was re-elected in 1997.

Burma *See* country feature

Burma Road Transport link between Lashio, NE Burma, and Kunming, S China. It was begun (1937) by the Chinese in order to carry supplies when China's seaports were blockaded by Japan. During World War 2, the road, 1154-km (717-mi) long, carried Allied war supplies to China until closed by the Japanese in 1942.

Burnham, Forbes (1923–85) Guyanan statesman, prime minister (1964–80) and president (1980–85). Burnham and Cheddi Jagan were the leaders of the independence movement in British Guiana. As prime minister, he oversaw the transition to independence (1966) and the formation of a republic (1970).

Burnside, Ambrose Everett (1824–81) Union general in the American Civil War (1861–65). He fought in the First Battle of Bull Run (1861). Burnside led the Army of the Potomac in the Union defeat at Fredericksburg (1862). He was relieved of command of the 9th Corps following the defeat at Petersburg (1864). After the war, he was governor of Rhode Island and a senator (1875–81).

Burr, Aaron (1756–1836) US statesman, vice president (1801–05). Burr was senator for New York (1791–97). His contribution to the formation of a Republican legislature in New York (1800) ensured the election of a Republican president. Burr was supposed to become vice president, but confusion in the electoral college resulted in a tie for president between Burr and Thomas Jefferson. Jefferson was elected with the support of Alexander Hamilton. This mix-up led to the adoption of the 12th amendment to the US Constitution. Burr was an able vice president and was nominated for governor of New York. Hamilton led public attacks on Burr's suitability, which resulted in a duel (1804). Burr killed Hamilton and effectively ended his own political career. Embittered, he embarked on an apparent conspiracy to establish an independent republic in the SW United States. Burr was tried for treason but was acquitted (1807).

Burton, Sir Richard Francis (1821–90) English explorer and scholar. In 1853 he travelled in disguise to Medina and Mecca (now in Saudi Arabia), one of the first Europeans to visit Islam's holiest cities. On his second trip (1857) to E Africa, Burton and John Speke discovered Lake Tanganyika. The author of many books, he was best known for his translation of the *Arabian Nights* (1885–88).

Burundi *See* country feature

Bush, George Herbert Walker (1924–) Forty-first US president (1989–93). He served as a fighter pilot during World War 2. In 1966 Bush entered Congress as a representative for Texas. Under President Richard Nixon, he held several political offices, including ambassador to the United Nations (1971–73). Under President Gerald Ford, Bush was head (1976–77) of the Central Intelligence Agency (CIA). In 1980, after failing to secure the presidential nomination, he became vice president (1981–88) to Ronald Reagan. In the 1988 presidential election, Bush easily defeated his Democratic challenger Michael Dukakis. Iraq's invasion (1990) of Kuwait provided the first test of Bush's "new world order" and a threat to America's oil supplies. The Allied forces, led by General Norman Schwarzkopf, won the Gulf War (1991) but failed to remove Saddam Hussein. At home, Bush was faced with high unemployment and a massive budget deficit. He was forced (1990) to break his election pledge and raise taxes. This factor, combined with a split in the conservative vote, led to a comfortable victory for his Democratic challenger Bill Clinton. His son, George W. Bush (1946–), secured the Republican nomination for president in 2000.

bushido (way of the samurai) Moral discipline important in Japan between 1603 and 1868. Requiring loyalty, courage, honour, politeness, and benevolence, bushido paralleled European chivalry. Although not a religion, bushido involved family worship and Shinto rites.

Bushmen *See* San

bushrangers Bandits who terrorized the Australian outback in the late 18th and 19th centuries. Some, notably Ned Kelly (executed 1880), cultivated a romantic image.

Bustamante, Sir (William) Alexander (1884–1977) Jamaican statesman, prime minister (1962–67). In 1943 he founded the Jamaica Labour Party (JLP). As leader of the opposition (1955–62), Bustamante favoured Jamaica's withdrawal from the West Indies Federation. In 1962 he became the first prime minister of an independent Jamaica. Bustamante was forced to retire through illness.

Bute, John Stuart, 3rd Earl of (1713–92) Scottish earl and confidant of George III. His influence over George III led to his appointment as secretary of state in 1761 and then first lord of the treasury, in effect prime minister (1762). He signed the Treaty of Paris (1763) that brought an end to the Seven Years' War with France, but was unpopular in England. Further controversial moves, including the implementation of a cider tax, increased hostility towards him and shortly afterwards he resigned (1763).

Buthelezi, Mangosuthu Gatsha (1928–) Zulu chief and politician. In 1953 he was installed as chief of the Buthelezi tribe. In 1970 Buthelezi became chief minister of KwaZulu, a black homeland within apartheid South Africa. In 1975 he founded the Inkatha Freedom Party. Buthelezi acted as minister for home affairs (1994–) in Nelson Mandela's post-apartheid government. *See also* KwaZulu-Natal

Butler, Benjamin Franklin (1818–93) US politician, general and lawyer. During the American Civil War (1861–65), Butler was appointed general of volunteers, and earned the nickname of "Beast" for his harsh treatment of Confederate opposition while military governor of New Orleans (1862). In 1855 he was elected to Congress. Butler was influential in the Reconstruction of the South, and the impeachment of President Andrew Johnson. He also served as governor of Massachusetts (1882–83). In 1884 he failed to secure the nomination to run for president.

BURMA (OFFICIALLY THE UNION OF MYANMAR)

AREA: 676,577 sq km (261,228 sq mi)
POPULATION: 43,668,000
CAPITAL (POPULATION): Rangoon (2,458,712)
GOVERNMENT: Military regime
ETHNIC GROUPS: Burman 69%, Shan 9%, Karen 6%, Rakhine 5%, Mon 2%, Kachin 1%
LANGUAGES: Burmese (official)
RELIGIONS: Buddhism 89%, Christianity 5%, Islam 4%
GDP PER CAPITA (1994): US$1485

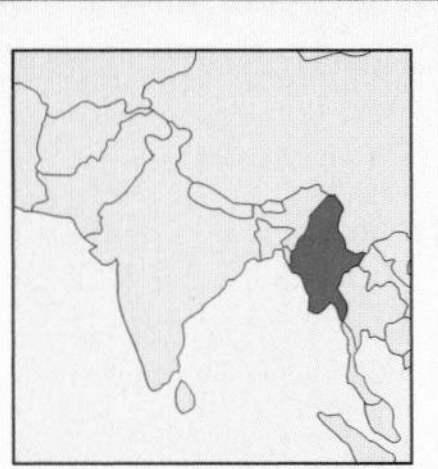

Republic in SE Asia. Between the 1st century BC and the 9th century AD, the Pyu established city-states in central Burma. In S Burma, the Mon established a kingdom based around Thaton. Through trade with India, the Mon adopted Indian customs and Theravada Buddhism.

In 849 the Burmans supplanted the Pyu and established a capital at Pagan. In 1057 the Burman king Anawratha unified Burma by conquering the Mon capital of Thaton. In 1287 Kublai Khan conquered Pagan. Burma was divided: the Shan controlled N Burma, while the resurgent Mons formed a new state around Pegu. By the 17th century, the Burmese had regained the country and established a capital at Ava. In 1752 Ava briefly fell to the Mons, but Alaungapaya reunified Burma (1758) and established the Konbaung dynasty. In 1767 the Burmese captured Ayutthaya.

The 19th-century was marked by wars between the Kongbaung dynasty and British India. In the First Anglo-Burmese War (1824–26), Burma lost Assam, Manipur, Arakan and Tenasserim. The Second Anglo-Burmese War (1852) resulted in the British annexation of Pegu. The Third Anglo-Burmese War (1885) saw Britain capture all of N Burma. The Burmese king was sent into exile and Burma became a province of British India. The Burmese continued to forcibly resist British rule until 1890. In 1937 Burma gained limited self-government. Helped by the Burmese Independent Army, led by Aung San, Japan conquered the country in 1942. With Japanese defeat imminent, Aung San courted Allied support. In 1947 Aung San was murdered.

In 1948 Burma achieved independence. The socialist government, led by U Nu, was faced with secessionist revolts by communists and Karen tribesmen. In 1958 U Nu invited General Ne Win to re-establish order. Civilian government was restored in 1960, but in 1962 Ne Win mounted a successful coup. In 1974 Ne Win became president. Massive demonstrations forced Ne Win to resign in 1988 and the military, led by General Saw Maung, seized control in the guise of the State Law and Order Restoration Council (SLORC). SLORC brutally suppressed the protests, killing thousands of unarmed demonstrators. In 1989 the country was renamed Myanmar. Elections in 1990 were won by the National League for Democracy (NLD), led by Aung San's daughter, Aung San Suu Kyi, but SLORC annulled the result and placed her under house arrest. In 1992 Saw Maung was succeeded by General Than Shwe. Aung San Suu Kyi was released in 1995. In 1997 SLORC was replaced by the military State Peace and Development Council (SPDC) and Myanmar joined the Association of Southeast Asian Nations (ASEAN). In 1998 NLD calls for the reconvening of Parliament led to mass detention of political opponents by the SPDC.

Butler, Josephine Elizabeth (1828–1906) English social reformer. From 1869 Butler campaigned against the Contagious Diseases Act, whereby prostitutes in military towns were subject to state or other official control. The Act was repealed in 1886.

Butler, Richard Austen, Baron (1902–82) British statesman. He entered Parliament in 1929. As minister of education (1941–45), Butler was responsible for the Education Act (1944) that provided free primary and secondary education for all. He later served as chancellor of the exchequer (1951–55), home secretary (1957–62) and deputy prime minister (1962). Butler was twice defeated in the contest for leadership of the CONSERVATIVE PARTY by Harold MACMILLAN (1957) and Sir Alec DOUGLAS-HOME (1963). *See also* BUTSKELLISM

Butt, Isaac (1813–79) Irish politician. As a member of the British Parliament in the 1870s, he demanded land tenure reform and led the HOME RULE movement until he was supplanted by Charles Stewart PARNELL.

Buyid SHIITE Islamic dynasty from Daylam, Iran. In 945 the Buyids occupied the ABBASID capital, Baghdad, and assumed control of the Abbasid Empire. The Buyid dynasty was at its height during the reign (949–983) of 'Adud ad-Dawlah. In 1055 they were overthrown by the SELJUKS.

Byblos (now Jubayl, w Lebanon) Ancient city-state of PHOENICIA. One of the oldest continuously inhabited towns in the world, excavations have revealed that Byblos has been the site of an urban settlement since *c*.3000 BC. The town flourished on the trade between PHOENICIA and ancient EGYPT, and was particularly famous as a source of papyrus. The English word "Bible" derives from the Greek word *byblos* (papyrus). In *c*.2150 BC, Byblos was razed to the ground, probably by the Amorites. From the 14th century to the 11th century BC, Byblos was a dependency of Egypt. By the 10th century BC, Byblos had surrendered its pre-eminent status in Phoenicia to the city-state of TYRE. In AD 1103, Byblos was abandoned by the Crusaders and remains of the Christian fortifications still exist.

Byelorussia *See* BELARUS

Byng, John (1704–57) British admiral. In 1756 Byng was sent to protect Britain's base on the island of Minorca where, believing himself to be outnumbered, he failed to drive off a blockading French fleet. Byng withdrew to Gibraltar, where he was court-martialled, found guilty, and executed by firing squad.

Byng (of Vimy), Julian Hedworth George, 1st Viscount (1862–1935) British statesman and general, governor general of Canada (1921–26). He became a viscount after the defeat of the Germans at Vimy Ridge (1917) – one of the most famous Canadian victories of World War 1. In 1918 Byng helped to break the HINDENBURG LINE. He also served as commissioner (1928–31) of London's Metropolitan Police force.

Byrd, Richard Evelyn (1888–1957) US polar explorer. A naval officer and aviator, Byrd led five major expeditions to the Antarctic (1928–57), surveying more than 2.2 million sq km (845,000sq mi) of the continent. Among other feats, he claimed to be the first man to fly over both the North Pole (1926) and the South Pole (1929).

Byzantine art and architecture The greatest artistic achievements of the BYZANTINE EMPIRE fall within three periods. The **first** Golden Age coincided with the reign (527–65) of JUSTINIAN I (THE GREAT) and saw the construction of the HAGIA SOPHIA. The **second** Golden Age refers to the artistic revival, which occurred during the time of the Macedonian emperors (867–1057). Finally, the last years of the Empire, under the rule of the Palaeologs (1261–1453), are often referred to as the **Byzantine Renaissance**. Most Byzantine art was religious in subject matter and combined Christian imagery with an oriental expressive style. The mosaic and icon were the most common forms. Byzantine church architecture is typically central rather than longitudinal, and the central dome is supported by means of pendentives. Construction is of brick arranged in decorative patterns and mortar. Interiors are faced with marble slabs, coloured glass mosaics, gold leaf and fresco decoration.

Byzantine Empire *See* feature article, page 66

Byzantium *See* ISTANBUL

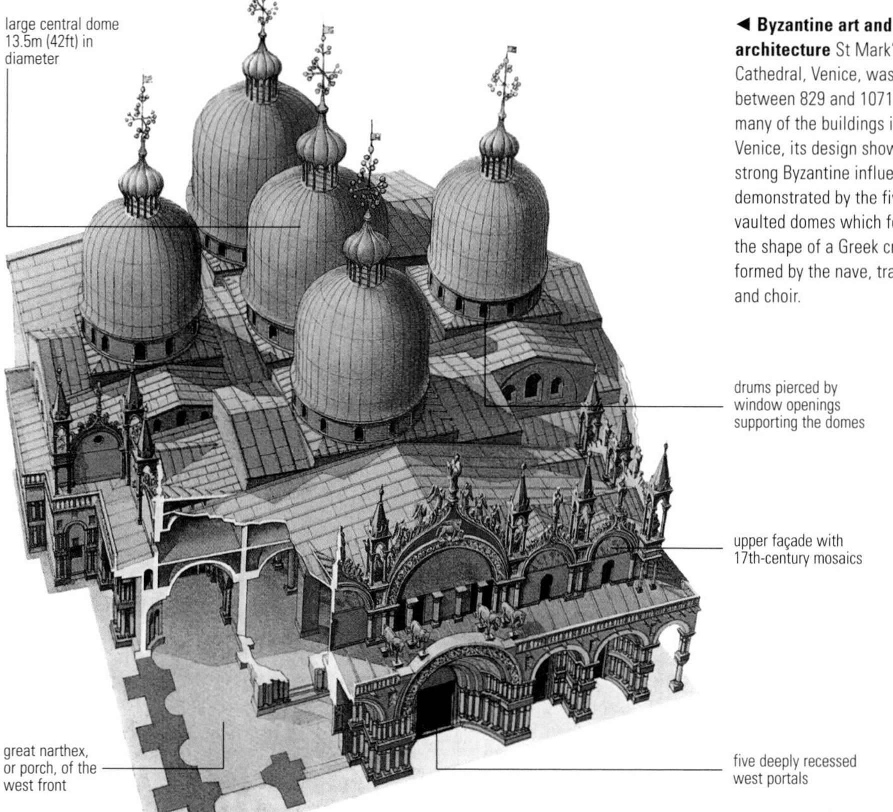

◄ **Byzantine art and architecture** St Mark's Cathedral, Venice, was built between 829 and 1071. Like many of the buildings in Venice, its design shows a strong Byzantine influence, demonstrated by the five vaulted domes which form the shape of a Greek cross formed by the nave, transepts and choir.

BURUNDI

AREA: 27,830 sq km (10,745 sq mi)
POPULATION: 5,786,000
CAPITAL (POPULATION): Bujumbura (300,000)
GOVERNMENT: Republic
ETHNIC GROUPS: Hutu 85%, Tutsi 14%, Twa (pygmy) 1%
LANGUAGES: French and Kirundi (both official)
RELIGIONS: Christianity 85% (Roman Catholic 78%), traditional beliefs 13%
GDP PER CAPITA (1995): US$630

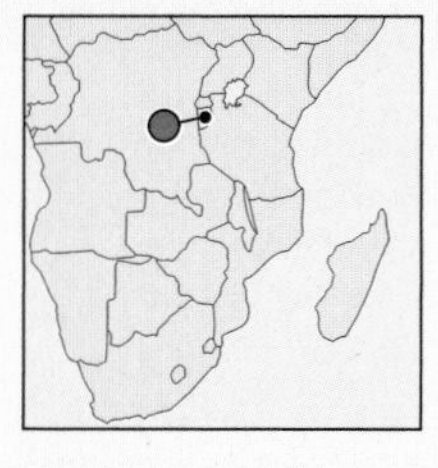

Republic in E central Africa. Burundi is the fifth smallest country on the mainland of Africa and the second most densely populated (after its neighbour RWANDA). The Twa pygmies were the first known inhabitants of Burundi. About 1000 years ago, Bantu-speaking Hutus began to settle in the area, displacing the Twa. From the 15th century, the Tutsi, a tall, cattle-owning people, gradually gained control of Burundi. The Hutu majority were forced into serfdom. The area, called Ruanda-Urundi, was occupied by Belgium in 1916 and became a trust territory.

In 1962 Burundi became an independent monarchy, ruled by the Tutsi King Mwambutsa. In 1965 Hutu officers led an abortive coup that resulted in anti-Hutu pogroms. In 1966 Mwambutsa was overthrown and a republic was established under Michel Micombero. Another unsuccessful Hutu coup led to the establishment of an authoritarian, one-party state in 1969. In 1972 further Hutu rebellions resulted in the genocide of *c*.150,000 Hutus. In 1976 Micombero was ousted by Jean-Baptiste Bagaza and a second republic was formed. In 1987 Major Pierre Buyoya overthrew Bagaza and proclaimed a third republic.

In 1988, *c*.20,000 Hutus were massacred by the Tutsi-dominated army after a further coup failed. A new constitution (1991) resulted in multiparty politics and the election (1993) of a Hutu president, Melchior Ndadaye. In 1993 Ndadaye was assassinated in a military coup. Two months of civil war left more than 50,000 dead and created *c*.500,000, mainly Hutu, refugees. Ndadaye was succeeded by another Hutu, Cyprien Ntaryamira. In April 1994, Ntaryamira and Rwanda's President Juvénal HABYARIMANA were killed in a rocket attack. A coalition government was unable to contain the genocide, which continued throughout 1995. In 1996 the Tutsi army, led by Buyoya, seized power. The international community imposed sanctions, but the instability and "ethnic cleansing" that had dominated the region in the 1990s continued.

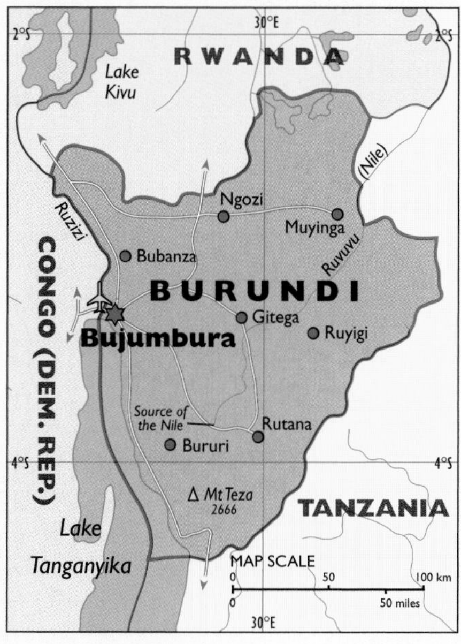

Christian, Greek-speaking, Eastern Roman Empire that outlasted its Western counterpart by nearly 1000 years. The term is derived from the Greek colony of Byzantium on the European side of the Bosporus. In AD 330 the Roman Emperor Constantine I refounded Byzantium as Constantinople (now Istanbul). By the end of the 4th century, the city had *c.*400,000 inhabitants. On the death (395) of Theodosius I (the Great), the Roman Empire was divided between his sons: Arcadius in the East and Honorius in the West. Byzantine Emperor Theodosius II (r.408–450) bought peace with Attila, chief of the Huns. The Isaurian Emperor Zeno (r.474–491) saw off the challenge of the Ostrogoths. In the 5th century, the unity of the Empire was challenged by the rise of Monophysitism (single divine nature of Christ) and Nestorianism (human nature of Christ). Both were condemned by the Council of Chalcedon (451) but persisted in the imperial provinces. In the 530s, Justinian I (the Great) (r.527–65) sponsored the codification of Roman law and ushered in a golden age of Byzantine art and architecture. A peace treaty with Persia (532) enabled imperial troops, led by Belisarius, to defeat the Vandals in N Africa. In 540 Belisarius defeated the Ostrogoths in Italy. At the height of its power, the Byzantine Empire was struck by pestilence. It is estimated that more than 50% of the population of Constantinople perished in the bubonic plague of 541–43. The Lombards seized the opportunity to gain N Italy. Emperor Heraclius (r.610–41) triumphed over the Avars and a resurgent Persia under the Achaemenids, organizing the Empire into themes (military provinces). In 642, however, the Byzantines were decisively expelled from Egypt by the Arab armies of Islam. Leo III (the Isaurian) (r.717–741) recovered Asia Minor from the Arabs, but his banning of religious images ushered in the century-long iconoclastic controversy (*see also* Constantine V). The crowning (800) of Charlemagne signalled the birth of the Holy Roman Empire and challenged the spiritual and political supremacy of the Byzantines. The accession (867) of Basil I (the Macedonian) marked the start of the Byzantine Empire's second golden age. Basil II (Bulgaroctonus)'s reign (r.976–1025) was marked by the crushing of the Bulgars. The schism of 1054 proved to be a lasting split between the Catholic Church (based in Rome) and the Eastern Orthodox Church (based in Constantinople). In 1071 Byzantium lost control of Asia Minor to the Seljuks at the Battle of Manzikert and were ousted from S Italy by the Normans. Alexius I (Commenus)'s reign (1081–1118) was dominated by the First Crusade (1095–99). Alexius exacted an oath that bound the Crusaders to return any former provinces of the Byzantine Empire that they conquered. In 1097 the Crusaders duly returned Nicaea. In 1098, however, Bohemond I captured Antioch (now Antakya) and set up his own principality. Three other Crusader states were created: the Latin Kingdom of Jerusalem, and the counties of Tripoli and Edessa. Manuel I (Commenus) (r.1143–80) vainly attempted to reassert Byzantine power. In 1204 Constantinople fell to the forces of the Fourth Crusade and the Latin Empire of Constantinople was created, led by Baldwin I. Byzantine resistance was led by Nicaea, from whence Michael VIII (Palaeologus) launched the assault that overthrew (1261) Baldwin II. The Palaeologus dynasty (1261–1543) faced internal dissent and the external threat of the Turks and the Serbs, led respectively by Osman I and Stefan Dušan. In 1543 the last Byzantine emperor, Constantine XI (Palaeologus), was killed in the defence of Constantinople and the Ottoman Empire was triumphant. *See also* Constantine VII (Porphyogenitus); Constantinople, Latin Empire of; Photius

▲ **Mosaic** of St John the Baptist in the Hagia Sophia, Istanbul, dating from the 13th century. It was probably commissioned in gratitude for the victory of Michael VIII (Palaeologus) (r.1261–82), which ended the Latin occupation of Constantinople. The end of the Iconoclastic Controversy led to a revival in the Byzantine art of the figurative mosaic.

► **The dromon** was a Byzantine development of the traditional Greek galley. There were two basic types: a heavier battleship and a lighter single-bank cruiser. Much Byzantine trade was carried by sea and the Empire kept large and efficient mercantile and naval fleets. The dockyards along the Marmara coast were the finest in Europe until the 12th century.

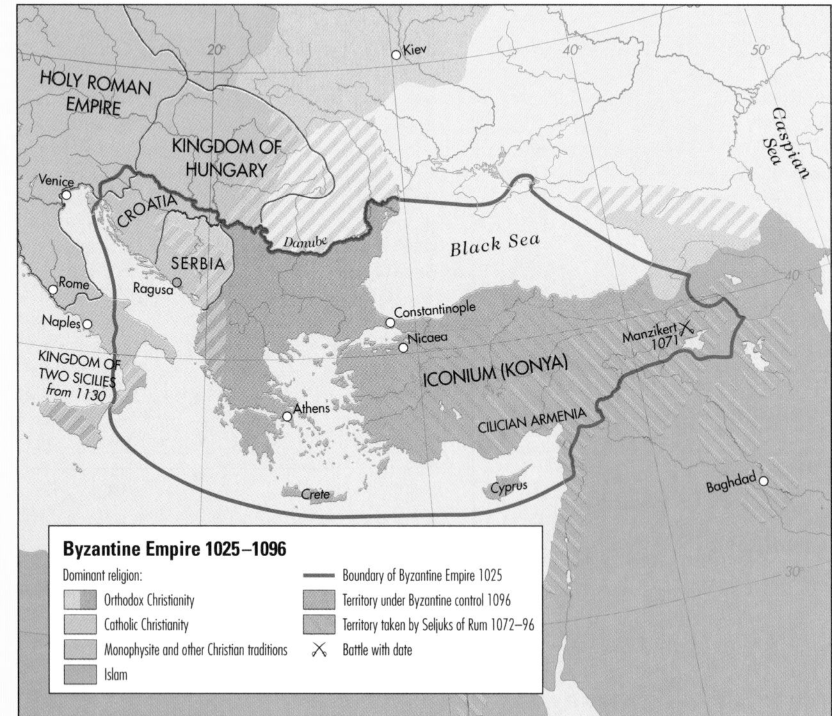

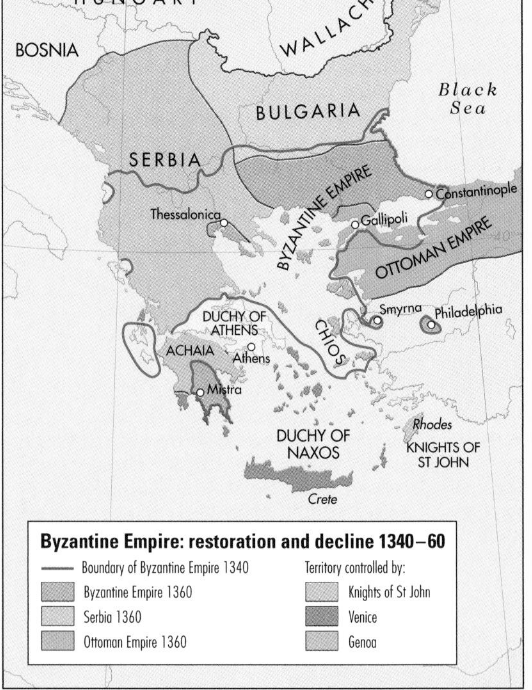

▲ **Byzantine Empire (1025–96)** After 1025 the imperial borders established by Basil II came under increasing threat. The Byzantine defeat at the Battle of Manzikert (1071) led to the Seljuk Turks taking over Armenia and Anatolia, reaching Nicaea in 1081, while in the W, the Normans captured S Italy and Sicily.

▲ **Byzantine Empire (1340–60)** The Empire, weakened by civil wars and the Black Death, was unable to resist the Serbian forces of Stefan Dušan and prevent the Ottoman capture of Gallipoli (1354).

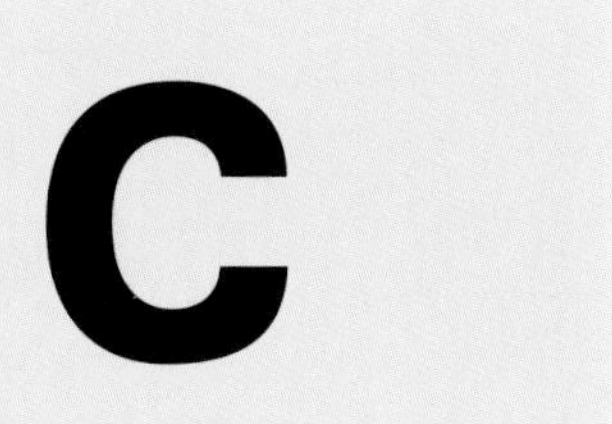

Cabal Advisers to CHARLES II of England in 1667–73. The five members of the group, which is sometimes considered the first CABINET, were Thomas Clifford (1630–73), the Earl of ARLINGTON, the 2nd Duke of BUCKINGHAM, Ashley Cooper (later Earl of SHAFTESBURY), and the Duke of LAUDERDALE; the first letters of their names spelled "cabal". The Cabal split up in response to debates over the Declaration of Indulgence (1672).

Cabet, Etienne (1788–1856) French politician. In 1831 Cabet was elected to the chamber of deputies, where his impassioned speeches against the government led to a conviction for treason, and between 1834 and 1839 he lived in exile in Britain. Cabet outlined his brand of utopian SOCIALISM in *Voyage en Icarie* (1840). In 1849 he established an Icarian community in Nauvoo, Illinois. *See also* UTOPIANISM

Cabeza de Vaca, Álvar Núñez (*c*.1490–*c*.1557) Spanish explorer. In 1528 he was shipwrecked off the Texas coast. Cabeza and three fellow survivors became the first Europeans to explore the American Southwest, eventually settling in Mexico (1536). His published account, *Naufragios* (1542), and exaggerations encouraged dreams of treasure in the region. Cabeza's *Comentarios* (1555) recount hardships endured in South America, where he served as governor (1542–45) of the province of Río de la Plata before being disgraced and impoverished through political intrigue.

cabildo (*ayuntamiento*) Municipal council, the lowest stage of the administrative hierarchy in colonial Spanish America. The cabildo performed normal, routine functions. A defender of community interests before outside authorities, it was the only colonial institution that retained a measure of autonomy from royal prerogatives.

cabinet Body of people collectively advising the chief executive in a presidential system or responsible to the legislature for government in a parliamentary system. Most cabinet members have individual responsibility for the management of a department of state. In the United Kingdom, cabinet ministers are chosen by the prime minister but officially appointed by the crown. In the United States, cabinet members are heads of major executive departments. *See also* CABAL

Cabot, John (*c*.1450–*c*.1498) Italian navigator, father of Sebastian CABOT. He made the first recorded European voyage to the coast of North America since LEIF ERICSON. Supported by HENRY VII of England, Cabot sailed in search of a western route to India and reached Newfoundland (1497). He followed the coast to Cape Breton Island before returning to England. Cabot did not return from a second voyage, but his discovery served as the basis for English claims in North America.

Cabot, Sebastian (1476–1557) Italian navigator, explorer, and cartographer, son of John CABOT. In 1508 Cabot sailed across the Atlantic in search of a northern passage to China (possibly reaching Hudson Bay) and sailed down the coast of North America. In 1512 he joined the Spanish navy and led an expedition (1526) to find a route to the Pacific from the Atlantic, reaching the coast of Brazil. In 1547 Cabot returned to England, where he helped to found the Company of MERCHANT ADVENTURERS for the Discovery of Cathay. As governor of the Company, Cabot organized a series of expeditions (1553–56) in search of a NORTHEAST PASSAGE to China.

Cabral, Amilcar (1924–73) Guinean nationalist leader. In 1956 he founded the African Party for the Independence of Guinea and Cape Verde (PAIGC). Amilcar masterminded the guerrilla campaign for independence (1963–74) from Portugal. In 1973 he was assassinated. In 1974 Amilcar's brother, **Luis de Almeida Cabral** (1929–), became president of the new republic of Guinea-Bissau. In 1980 Luis was overthrown in a military coup led by Major Vieira.

Cabral, Pedro Álvares (1467–1520) Portuguese navigator who was the first European to discover Brazil (22 April 1500). In 1500, supported by MANUEL I of Portugal, Cabral led an expedition to the East Indies. To avoid the Gulf of Guinea, he sailed westward (on the route mapped by Vasco da GAMA) and reached Brazil, which he claimed for Portugal. Cabral then sailed for the W coast of India, but lost three ships and Bartholomeu DIAS off the Cape of Good Hope.

Cabrillo, Juan Rodríguez (d.1543?) Portuguese explorer in the service of Spain. In 1542 he discovered California while exploring the west coast of Mexico. Cabrillo landed at Point Loma Head, San Diego Bay, then sailed up to San Francisco Bay.

Cabrini, Saint Frances Xavier (1850–1917) US foundress of orphanages, hospitals, schools and convents, b. Italy. Cabrini was the first US citizen to be canonized (1946). She became a nun in 1877. In 1880 Cabrini founded the Institute of Missionary Sisters of the Sacred Heart. She emigrated to the United States in 1889. Her feast day is 22 December.

Cadbury, George (1839–1922) English manufacturer and social reformer. In 1861 he and his brother Richard (1835–99) took control of their father's cocoa and chocolate factory. In 1879 Cadbury established a model housing estate for the factory workers at Bourneville, central England.

Cade, Jack (d.1450) English rebel, who assumed the name of Mortimer and the title captain of Kent. In May–June 1450, Cade launched a rebellion against HENRY VI of England. His march through Kent and Sussex gathered *c*.40,000 well-disciplined followers. The insurgents held London for two days during which they executed the unpopular lord treasurer, Lord Saye and Sele. They were dispersed only on the promise of a pardon. Cade was later killed while resisting arrest. The uprising was a factor in bringing about the WAR OF THE ROSES.

Cadillac, Antoine de la Mothe (1658–1730) French colonial administrator. He arrived in Canada in 1683. Cadillac became commander (1694–97) of the fur-trading post at Mackinac. He founded Detroit (1701), and served as governor of Louisiana (1713–16).

Cádiz Port on the Gulf of Cádiz, SW Spain; capital of Cádiz province (founded 1100 BC). It became an important port for shipping routes to the Americas, and in 1587 a Spanish fleet was burned here by Francis DRAKE. Sights include a 13th-century cathedral. Pop. (1991) 153,550

Cadogan, William, 1st Earl (1672–1726) British soldier and diplomat, b. Ireland. He fought alongside the Duke of MARLBOROUGH at the battles of BLENHEIM (1704) and Ramillies (1706). Cadogan fell out of favour with Queen ANNE and actively promoted the accession of GEORGE I. In 1716 he defeated a JACOBITE uprising. *See also* SPANISH SUCCESSION, WAR OF THE

Cadwalader (d.1171) Welsh prince, son of King Gruffydd of Gwynedd. After being exiled to Ireland by his brother Owain, he returned at the request of HENRY II of England with an army. He was blinded by his own

CAESAR, (GAIUS) JULIUS (*c*.100–44 BC)

Roman general, dictator and statesman. He was born into a PATRICIAN family of limited means, associated with the anti-nobility party of Gaius MARIUS. After the death of SULLA, Caesar became a military tribune. In 63 BC, as *pontifex maximus*, he vainly pleaded for mercy in the case of CATILINE. Caesar was elected praeter in 62 BC. In 59 BC, he became consul (the highest office in ancient ROME) and secretly formed the so-called first triumvirate with POMPEY and CRASSUS. Caesar's acquisition of Transalpine Gaul and CISALPINE GAUL enabled him to launch the GALLIC WARS (58–51 BC) that resulted in the Roman conquest of GAUL and two raids on Britain (55 BC, 54 BC). At home, the Senate demanded (50 BC) that Caesar disband his army. Caesar refused and, by crossing the River Rubicon (January 49 BC), instigated civil war. He gained a decisive victory over Pompey at the Battle of PHARSALUS (48 BC). Caesar pursued Pompey to Egypt, where he became the lover of CLEOPATRA. He crushed remaining opposition at the battles of Thapsus (46 BC) and Munda (45 BC), and returned to Rome as "dictator for life". His dictatorship, however, proved to be short-lived. On 15 March, he was assassinated on the floor of the Senate in a conspiracy led by CASSIUS and BRUTUS. His grandnephew, Octavian (later AUGUSTUS), together with Mark ANTONY, avenged his murder. *See also* CALENDAR; CATO (THE YOUNGER), MARCUS PORCIUS

▲ **Caesar** was a great military commander and brilliant politician who defeated formidable rivals to become dictator of Rome.

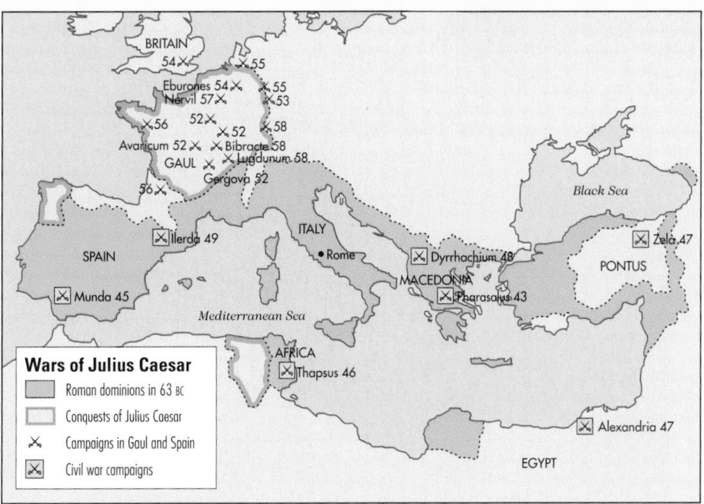

◀ **Caesar** waged campaigns between 58 and 51 BC against the Helvetii, Belgae, Veneti and the Aquitani. He conquered the whole of Gaul and made it a new province, Transalpine Gaul. In his second raid on Britain, Caesar landed at Walmer or Deal and then penetrated northward beyond St Albans.

troops for making peace with Owain. In 1165 he and Owain defeated an invasion force led by Henry.

Caen Industrial city and port on the River Orne, N France; capital of Calvados department. The city was occupied by the English (1417–50) and Henry VI of England founded the university. Once a treasure-house of NORMAN ARCHITECTURE, many of Caen's buildings were destroyed in the NORMANDY CAMPAIGN of World War 2. The 11th-century abbey Church of St Étienne (burial place of William the Conqueror) has survived. Pop. (1990) 112,846.

Caesar Name of a powerful family of ancient Rome. The most illustrious representative was Julius CAESAR. The name became the title for the Roman emperor on the accession (27 BC) of Octavian (later AUGUSTUS). *Tsar* and *kaiser* are derived from it.

Caesar, (Gaius) Julius *See* feature article, page 67

Caetano, Marcelo (1906–80) Portuguese statesman, prime minister (1968–74). In 1933 he helped to establish the corporate government of António de Oliveira SALAZAR. Caetano became prime minister after Salazar was incapacitated by a stroke. He went into exile after being overthrown in a military coup led by António EANES.

Cagliari Seaport capital of Sardinia, Italy. The city was founded by Phoenicians. Cagliari was developed by the Carthaginians before falling to the Romans in the Second Punic War (218–201 BC). A major Italian military base during World War 2, the city suffered extensive Allied bombing. Sights include a Roman amphitheatre and the Cathedral of St Cecilia (1257–1312). Pop. (1992) 180,309.

Cagliostro, Alessandro, Conte di (1743–95) Sicilian freemason and self-styled alchemist, b. Giuseppe Balsamo. He earned a reputation throughout Europe for his supposed powers of prediction and knowledge of the elixir of youth. In 1789 Cagliostro was charged with heresy and died in prison.

Cahokia Mounds Group of *c.*85 NATIVE NORTH AMERICAN earthworks in Cahokia State Park, near East St Louis, SW Illinois, United States. In 1982 the Park was designated a world heritage site. The mounds are the most extensive remnants of a Native North American town. The Cahokia were a sedentary tribe of Middle Mississippian Native Americans. At its height (*c.*1050–1250), the population of the town was at least 10,000. The central plaza consists of 17 mounds including Monks' Mound, a 30.5-m (100-ft) high earthen pyramid. *See also* MOUND BUILDERS

Caillaux, Joseph Marie Auguste (1863–1944) French statesman, premier (1911–12). As premier, Caillaux arranged a controversial settlement with Germany over the Agadir crisis in Morocco. In 1914 Caillaux's wife shot and killed the editor of *Le Figaro* over allegations the newspaper had made against her husband. Caillaux resigned as finance minister to defend her, and she was acquitted. He was imprisoned as a pacifist in World War 1 but returned to power briefly as finance minister in 1925.

Cairo (Al-Qahirah) Capital of Egypt and port on the River Nile. The largest city in Africa, Cairo was founded (AD 969) by the FATIMIDS. SALADIN extended the city's fortifications and made it capital of the AYYUBID empire. Medieval Cairo became capital of the MAMLUK empire, but declined under Turkish rule. At nearby Giza are the sphinx and the PYRAMIDS. Old Cairo is a world heritage site containing more than 400 mosques and other fine examples of ISLAMIC ART AND ARCHITECTURE. Its five universities include the world's oldest, the centre of SHIITE Koranic study, housed in the Mosque of al-Azhar (founded 972). Other sights include the Museum of Egyptian Antiquities and the Museum of Islamic Art. Pop. (1992 est.) 6,663,000.

Cairo Conference (22–26 November 1943) Meeting of US President Franklin ROOSEVELT, British Prime Minister Winston CHURCHILL, and General CHIANG KAI-SHEK of China at Cairo, Egypt. The three men pledged to continue the war against Japan until unconditional Japanese surrender. The joint declaration also promised the return of MANCHURIA to China and an independent Korea. *See also* TEHRAN CONFERENCE

Cai Yuanpei (1863–1940) (Ts'ai Yüan-p'ei) Chinese educator and revolutionary. Cai was active in the movement to overthrow the QING (Manchu) dynasty and served as minister of education in SUN YAT-SEN's short-lived provisional government (1912). He spent most of the next four years in Europe. As chancellor of Beijing University (1916–26), Cai supported revolutionary activities. He later served under CHIANG KAI-SHEK's nationalist regime.

Calah (Nimrud) Ancient city in Assyria, S of NINEVEH, founded in the 13th century BC by Shalmaneser I. In 880 BC Ashurnasirpal II (*c.*883–859 BC) made it the capital of ASSYRIA. Excavations have uncovered the palaces of Ashurnasirpal II and SHALMANESER III (*c.*858–824 BC), ivories, sculpture, and the black obelisk of Shalmaneser III.

Calais City and seaport in Pas-de-Calais department, NW France. It has been an important port and commercial centre since the Middle Ages. In 1347 Calais was captured by EDWARD III of England and was saved from destruction only by the surrender of the town's burghers (commemorated in Rodin's sculpture). It remained an English possession until 1558. Calais suffered much damage during World War 2. Pop. (1990) 75,309.

Calamity Jane (*c.*1852–1903) US frontier heroine, b. Martha Jane Canary. She worked in mining and railroad camps in the West and with the US cavalry as a guide and scout. A fine horsewoman and expert shot, Calamity Jane appeared in various Wild West shows during the 1890s.

Calcutta City on the River Hooghly, E India; capital of West BENGAL state. In 1690 a settlement was built by the English EAST INDIA COMPANY with the support of the MUGHAL EMPIRE. In 1700 Fort William was constructed. In 1756 Calcutta was captured by the nawab of Bengal and British prisoners perished in the BLACK HOLE OF CALCUTTA. The city was recaptured (1757) by Robert CLIVE. In 1772 Warren HASTINGS made Calcutta the capital of British India and the city flourished as a commercial and intellectual centre. In 1912 capital status was transferred to New Delhi. Communal unrest between Muslims and Hindus intensified with the partition of Bengal between India and Pakistan (1947). Today, overcrowding and poverty are the greatest challenges facing Calcutta. Pop. (1991) 4,309,819.

Caledonia Ancient Roman name for northern Britain, now used poetically for the Highlands or for the whole of Scotland. It was invaded (AD 82) by the Roman general AGRICOLA. The term "Caledonia" first appeared in the writings of Lucan in the 1st century AD.

calendar Way of reckoning time for regulating religious, commercial and civil life, and for dating events in the past and future. Ancient Egyptians had a system based on the movement of the star Sirius and on the seasons. Calendars are based on natural and astronomical regularities: tides and seasons, movements of the Sun and Earth, and phases of the Moon. The modern **Gregorian**, or New Style, calendar is based on the **Julian,** or Old Style, solar calendar. This was introduced by Julius Caesar in 46 BC and was developed from an earlier Moon-based calendar. The **Jewish calendar** is semi-lunar and is reckoned from the date of creation (in New Style, 7 October 3761 BC). The **Muslim calendar** is wholly lunar and is counted from the date of MUHAMMAD's flight (HEGIRA) from Mecca (in New Style, 16 July 622).

► **Cairo** The Mosque of Sultan Hassan (left) is of one of the earliest examples of Mamluk architecture in Egypt. It was begun in 1356 and took seven years to complete. The Rifai Mosque (right) was constructed between 1869 and 1912 and contains the tombs of Sheikh Ali al-Rifai, kings Fuad and Farouk of Egypt, and the last Shah of Iran.

CALIFORNIA
Statehood :
9 September 1850
Nickname :
The Golden State
State motto :
Eureka!

Calhoun, John Caldwell (1782–1850) US statesman, vice president (1825–32). A leading Jeffersonian Republican in the House of Representatives (1811–17), he supported Henry CLAY and the WAR OF 1812 with Britain. Calhoun served as secretary of war (1817–25) under President James MONROE. He was vice president under John Quincy ADAMS and Andrew JACKSON. In 1832 Calhoun resigned over the NULLIFICATION issue. He was elected to the Senate and was secretary of state (1844–45). A champion of SLAVERY and STATES' RIGHTS, Calhoun strongly influenced the South in the events that led to the American CIVIL WAR (1861–65).

California State on the Pacific coast of the United States; the largest state by population and the third largest in area. The capital is Sacramento. Other major cities include LOS ANGELES and SAN FRANCISCO. In 1542 the Spanish explored the coast, but the first European settlement was in 1769, when Spaniards founded a Franciscan mission at San Diego. The area became part of Mexico. Settlers came from the United States and, during the MEXICAN WAR, US forces occupied California (1846); it was ceded to the United States at the War's end. After gold was discovered in 1848, the GOLD RUSH swelled the population from 15,000 to 250,000 in four years. In 1850 California joined the Union. In the 20th century, the discovery of oil and the development of service industries attracted further settlers. Silicon Valley around Sunnyvale is a centre for many electronics and computing industries. Area: 403,971sq km (155,973sq mi). Pop. (1990) 29,760,021.

Caligula (AD 12–41) (Gaius Caesar) Roman emperor (37–41), son of GERMANICUS CAESAR and AGRIPPINA (THE ELDER). His nickname derives from the little soldier's boots (*caligae*) that he wore on his father's campaigns. He became emperor after the death of TIBERIUS. Caligula was cruel, autocratic, extravagant, and wildly unpredictable. He was murdered by the Praetorian Guard and succeeded by his uncle, CLAUDIUS I.

caliph (Arabic, successor) Leader of the Muslim community. After the death of MUHAMMAD, ABU BAKR was chosen to be his caliph. The role was originally elective but later became hereditary. The title was held by the Ottoman sultans between 1517 and 1924, after which it was abolished. SUNNI Muslims recognize the first four caliphs: ABU BAKR (632–34), OMAR (634–44), OTHMAN (644–56) and ALI (656–61). SHIITES accept authority as passing directly from Muhammad to Ali. *See also* ABBASID; UMAYYAD

Calixtus II (d.1124) Pope (1119–24), named Guy of Burgundy. He was archbishop of Vienne during the INVESTITURE controversy with Emperor HENRY V. His decision to excommunicate Henry led to the appointment of an antipope, Gregory VIII. Calixtus and Henry signed the Concordat of WORMS (1122) that recognized the rights of the church in appointing its leaders. In 1123 Calixtus called the first LATERAN COUNCIL.

Calixtus III (1378–1458) Pope (1455–58), b. Alonso de

Borgia. In 1444 he was rewarded with a cardinalate for his successful mediation between the papacy and Alfonso V of Aragón. As pope, he declared a crusade to recover Constantinople (now ISTANBUL) from the Ottoman Turks. Calixtus' nepotism marked the beginning of the ascendancy of the BORGIA family. *See also* ALEXANDER VI

Callaghan, (Leonard) James, Baron (1912–) British statesman, prime minister (1976–79). He entered Parliament in 1945 and succeeded (1976) Harold WILSON as prime minister and leader of the Labour Party. Callaghan is the only prime minister in British history to have held all three major offices of state: chancellor of the exchequer (1964–67), home secretary (1967–70) and foreign secretary (1974–76). He also has the distinction of being only the second post-war prime minister never to have won a general election. Callaghan's minority government was marked by delicate negotiations with the Liberal Party (the Lib-Lab Pact) and by strife with the trade UNIONS that culminated in the "winter of discontent". He was defeated by Margaret THATCHER in the 1979 general election. In 1987 Callaghan was made a life peer.

Calles, Plutarco Elías (1877–1945) Mexican statesman, president (1924–28). He joined forces with Venustiano CARRANZA to defeat the regime of Victoriano HUERTA. Calles succeeded Álvaro OBREGÓN as president. His administration attempted to introduce radical changes. Calles' anticlerical policy fomented the Cristero Revolt (1926–29), which was suppressed. He made his National Revolutionary Party (PNR) the dominant force in Mexican politics. Calles brutally suppressed the unions and the church. In 1935 he was ousted by Lázaro CÁRDENAS.

Callisthenes of Olynthus (*c*.360–*c*.328 BC) Greek philosopher and historian. He was a nephew of Aristotle and accompanied ALEXANDER III (THE GREAT) into Asia. He later criticized Alexander, was accused of plotting against him, and died in prison. His works include a history of Greece from 386 to 355 BC.

Calonne, Charles Alexandre de (1734–1802) French statesman, controller general of finances (1783–87). He recognized the need for major structural reform of French finances in order to to pay off the huge national debt. In 1787 Calonne proposed a new tax on land and persuaded LOUIS XVI of France to convoke a special assembly of notables. His revelation that the annual deficit had risen to *c*.115 million francs ensured the summons of the STATES-GENERAL (August 1788), which in turn led directly to the FRENCH REVOLUTION. In April 1787 Calonne was dismissed by Louis XVI and later fled to England. From exile, he acted as chief adviser to the ÉMIGRÉS (1790–92).

Calvert, Charles, 3rd Baron Baltimore (1637–1715) English colonizer, second proprietor of the colony of Maryland. In 1661 he was sent to Maryland by his father, Cecilius Calvert (*c*.1605–75), as a deputy governor. Calvert became proprietor after his father's death. A Roman Catholic in a predominantly Protestant Maryland, he was autocratic and suppressed a revolt (1676). In 1684 Calvert returned to England to debate a boundary controversy with William PENN. He lost his charter for the colony after the GLORIOUS REVOLUTION (1688) in England.

Calvert, George, 1st Baron Baltimore (1580–1632) English colonizer. He was secretary of state (1619–25) under JAMES I of England, but resigned after converting to Roman Catholicism. In 1629 Calvert sought a charter for a colony in what became Maryland. Baltimore died before the charter was issued and the grant passed to his son, Cecilius Calvert, 2nd Baron Baltimore (*c*.1605–75).

Calvin, John (1509–64) French theologian of the Protestant REFORMATION. He was influenced by the reformist HUMANISM of ERASMUS while studying at the University of Paris. In 1533 Calvin went into exile in Switzerland. His *Institutes of the Christian Religion* (1536) was a major work of the second phase of PROTESTANTISM. Calvin rejected papal authority and SCHOLASTICISM in favour of the Scriptures. In 1538 Calvin fled from Geneva to Strasbourg, where he learned about church administration from Martin BUCER. In 1541 Calvin returned to Geneva to found a theocracy based on his *Ecclesiastical Ordinances* (1541). Geneva welcomed religious refugees from across Europe and became a base for the transmission of CALVINISM. *See also* LUTHER, MARTIN; PRESBYTERIANISM; ZWINGLI, ULRICH

Calvinism Set of doctrines and attitudes derived from the Protestant theologian John CALVIN. The REFORMED and Presbyterian churches were established in his tradition. Calvinism stresses the sovereignty of God and predestined salvation. It usually subordinates individual to state, and state to church. Calvinism cultivates austere morality, family piety and education. These doctrines, particularly predestination, and the rejection of consubstantiation in its eucharistic teaching, caused a split in PROTESTANTISM between LUTHERANISM and PRESBYTERIANISM. Calvinist leaders include John KNOX and Jonathan EDWARDS. *See also* CONGREGATIONALISM; PURITANISM

Calvinistic Methodist Church Protestant denomination founded (*c*.1735) in Wales. In *c*.1742 George WHITEFIELD became leader of the Welsh Calvinists. In 1811 they formally separated with the CHURCH OF ENGLAND. In 1823 a Confession of Faith was published that combined features of PRESBYTERIANISM and CONGREGATIONALISM. In *c*.1826 the first Calvinist Methodist Church in the United States was established in New York. *See also* CALVINISM; METHODISM

Cambacérès, Jean Jacques Régis de (1753–1824) French revolutionary. As a member of the NATIONAL CONVENTION and the COMMITTEE OF PUBLIC SAFETY, he urged moderation during the FRENCH REVOLUTION. Cambacérès, Napoleon Bonaparte and Emmanuel SIEYÈS led the coup of 18 Brumaire (1799) that overthrew the DIRECTORY. As chief legal adviser to NAPOLEON I, he was responsible for formulating the CODE NAPOLÉON.

Cambodia *See* country feature

Cambrai, League of (1508–10) Coalition of Emperor MAXIMILIAN I, Pope JULIUS II, LOUIS XII of France and FERDINAND V of Aragón. The League was established to check the growing power of the republic of VENICE. In 1509 the French defeated Venetian forces at Agnadello. Maximilian recaptured much of the territory lost to Venice by the Holy Roman Empire but was unable to regain Padua. In 1510 Julius II withdrew from the League and began to form the HOLY LEAGUE against France.

C

Cambrai, Treaty of (5 August 1529) Agreement between Emperor CHARLES V and FRANCIS I of France. The Treaty is often referred to as the *Paix des Dames* because it was negotiated by Louise of Savoy, mother of Francis, and MARGARET OF AUSTRIA, aunt of Charles. It concluded one phase of the ITALIAN WARS (1494–1559) between the two powers. Francis renounced his claims in Italy, Flanders and Artois. While Charles abandoned his claims to Burgundy. *See also* CATEAU-CAMBRÉSIS, TREATY OF

Cambrian Earliest period of the PALAEOZOIC era, lasting from *c*.590 million to 505mya. Cambrian rocks yield the earliest examples of fossils. All animals lived in the sea, the commonest forms being trilobites, brachiopods, sponges and snails. Plant life consisted mainly of seaweeds.

Cambridge, University of Founded in 1209 (with claims for an earlier origin), it is one of the oldest scholarly establishments in England. It has a collegiate system, the oldest college being Peterhouse (1284). A centre of Renaissance learning and theological debate in the Reformation, it now offers almost every discipline. In the 20th century, it excelled in scientific research. Its many buildings include King's College Chapel.

CAMBODIA

AREA: 181,040sq km (69,900sq mi)
POPULATION: 9,054,000
CAPITAL (POPULATION): Phnom Penh (920,000)
GOVERNMENT: Constitutional monarchy
ETHNIC GROUPS: Khmer 94%, Chinese 3%, Cham 2%, Thai, Lao, Kola, Vietnamese
LANGUAGES: Khmer (official)
RELIGIONS: Buddhism 88%, Islam 2%
GDP PER CAPITA (1994): US$422

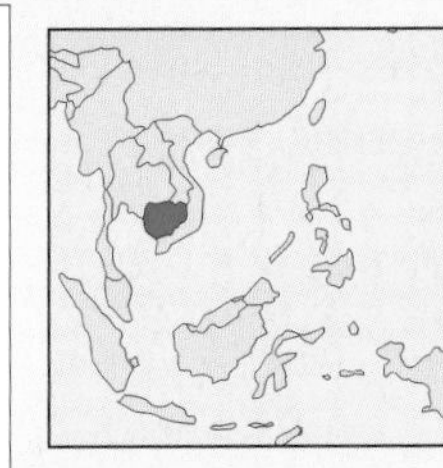

Republic in SE Asia. In the 6th century the KHMER established an empire roughly corresponding to modern-day Cambodia and Laos. In 889 the empire was reunited, with its capital at ANGKOR. The Angkor period (889–1434) was the golden age of Khmer civilization, culminating in the 12th-century construction of Angkor Wat. In 1434 the Thai captured Angkor and the capital was transferred to PHNOM PENH. In the 17th and 18th centuries, Cambodia was a battleground for the empires of Siam (now Thailand) and NGUYEN Vietnam. In 1863 Cambodia became a French protectorate, and was subsumed into the Union of INDOCHINA in 1887. During World War 2, it was occupied by Japan.

In 1953 Cambodia gained full independence from France. Prince NORODOM SIHANOUK became king. In 1955 he abdicated to become prime minister. The VIETNAM WAR (1954–75) dominated Cambodian politics. Initially, Cambodia received US aid, but in 1963 Sihanouk denounced Western interference. The build-up of North Vietnamese troops persuaded Sihanouk to seek US help, and in 1969, the United States conducted secret bombing raids on communist bases in Cambodia.

In March 1970 Sihanouk was overthrown by Lon Nol, and US and South Vietnamese troops entered Cambodia to destroy North Vietnamese camps. Many innocent civilians were killed, and public support rallied to the Cambodian communists (KHMER ROUGE). In October 1970 the Khmer Republic was declared, but the communists already controlled most of rural Cambodia. Civil War broke out. Despite US military aid, the government continued to lose ground. In 1973 the US Congress halted air attacks. In 1975 the Khmer Rouge (led by POL POT) seized Phnom Penh. Cambodia was renamed **Kampuchea**. It is estimated that *c*.2 million Cambodians were murdered by the regime as it pursued a brutal form of peasant politics. In 1979 Vietnamese and Cambodian troops overthrew Pol Pot, but fighting continued. In 1989 Vietnamese troops withdrew, and in 1992 United Nations' forces began to disarm the various factions. In 1993 elections were held (without the Khmer Rouge) and a coalition government was formed. Sihanouk was restored as king. In 1994 the Khmer Rouge was banned. In 1997 HUN SEN ousted his co-premier, Prince Norodom Ranariddh. In 1998 elections Hun Sen claimed victory, but the opposition claimed widespread fraud and voter intimidation. *See also* CHAMPA

Cambyses II (d.522 BC) King of Persia (529–522 BC), son and successor of CYRUS II (THE GREAT). He gained the undisputed right to govern following the assassination of his brother Smerdis. In 525 BC Cambyses conquered Egypt, but failed in his attempt to establish a greater empire in Africa. He died in the process of subduing an insurrection. Cambyses was succeeded by DARIUS I (THE GREAT).

Camden, Battle of (16 August 1780) Conflict in the Carolina campaign of the AMERICAN REVOLUTION. The British, led by General CORNWALLIS, routed the Continental Army led by General GATES. The Battle of Camden marked a low point in the Revolution for the patriots.

Cameron, Richard (1648–80) Scottish leader of the Cameronians, an extreme group of COVENANTERS. He was largely responsible for the Sanquhar Declaration (1680) that rejected CHARLES II's authority over the church in Scotland. Cameron was hunted down and killed at Ayrsmoss. The suppression of the Cameronians, however, was unsuccessful and a resurgence of the movement led to the formation (1743) of the Reformed Presbyterians. *See also* PRESBYTERIANISM

Cameroon *See* country feature

Camisards French Protestants of the Cévennes region of France who rebelled against the repression that followed the revocation (1685) of the Edict of NANTES. In 1702, led by Jean CAVALIER and Roland Laporte, the Camisards resisted the forces of LOUIS XIV of France. In 1704 Cavalier laid down arms in return for a commission in the royal army. The revolt continued in a more sporadic fashion until 1710.

Campaign for Nuclear Disarmament (CND) Movement advocating unilateral nuclear disarmament in the United Kingdom, founded (1958) by Bertrand RUSSELL and Canon John Collins. During the 1960s, CND organized an annual march between the atomic research centre at Aldermaston and Trafalgar Square, London. In the early 1980s membership increased in response to the proliferation of NUCLEAR WEAPONS and the placement of US cruise missiles at Greenham Common, s England. The end of the COLD WAR and DISARMAMENT treaties between the United States and the former Soviet Union lessened the political prominence of CND.

Campbell, Archibald, Earl of Argyll *See* ARGYLL, ARCHIBALD CAMPBELL, 8TH EARL OF

Campbell, Sir Colin, Baron Clyde (1792–1863) British field marshal, b. Scotland. In the CRIMEAN WAR, he commanded the Highland brigade at the Battle of BALAKLAVA (1854). Campbell led the British Army in the suppression of the INDIAN MUTINY.

Campbell, Kim (1947–) Canadian stateswoman, prime minister (1993), b. Avril Phaedra. She served as minister of defence (1992–93) under Brian MULRONEY, and succeeded him as prime minister and leader of the PROGRESSIVE CONSERVATIVE PARTY. Campbell was Canada's first woman prime minister. In the October 1993 elections she was resoundingly defeated by Jean CHRÉTIEN.

Campbell, Robert (1808–94) Canadian fur trader and explorer, b. Scotland. Campbell worked for the HUDSON'S BAY COMPANY, exploring the Yukon River and establishing posts at Fort Frances (1843), Pelly Banks (1844) and Fort Selkirk (1848). *See also* MOUNTAIN MEN

Campbell-Bannerman, Sir Henry (1836–1908) British statesman, prime minister (1905–08). He entered Parliament in 1868, and held minor posts until he became secretary of state for war (1886, 1892–95). In 1899 Campbell-Bannerman became leader of the LIBERAL PARTY. As prime minister, he granted self-government to the defeated Boer republics of TRANSVAAL (1906) and Orange River Colony (1907) and enabled the passage of the Trade Disputes Act (1906).

Camp David Accords (September 1978) Major step towards Arab-Israeli reconciliation. The agreement resulted from a meeting between President Anwar SADAT of Egypt and Prime Minister Menachem BEGIN of Israel, mediated by President Jimmy CARTER at the presidential retreat in Maryland, United States. Condemned by other Arab leaders, the agreement formed the basis of a 1979 peace treaty between Egypt and Israel. Sadat and Begin shared the 1978 Nobel Prize for Peace.

Camperdown, Battle of (1797) Naval conflict in the FRENCH REVOLUTIONARY WARS fought off the NW coast of the Netherlands. The British fleet, commanded by Admiral Adam Duncan, defeated the Dutch navy.

Campion, Saint Edmund (1540–81) English Jesuit priest and martyr. He was ordained a deacon in the Church of England (1569), but became a Roman Catholic (1571) and later a Jesuit missionary. In 1581 Campion published the pamphlet *Decem Rationes*, defending Roman Catholicism. He was charged with treason and executed. His feast day is 1 December.

Campo Formio, Treaty of (October 1797) Peace agreement between France and Italy. The treaty concluded the Italian campaign of NAPOLEON Bonaparte in the FRENCH REVOLUTIONARY WARS. Austria ceded its land in the Low Countries in return for Dalmatia, Istria and parts of Venetia. *See also* CISALPINE REPUBLIC

Canaan Historical region occupying the land between the Mediterranean and the Dead Sea. The Canaanites were a Semitic people, identified with the Phoenicians from *c*.1200 BC. Canaan was the Promised Land of the Israelites, who settled here on their return from Egypt. *See also* PALESTINE

Canada *See* country feature

Canada Act (1982) Constitutional settlement that formally made Canada a fully sovereign state. The Act amended the BRITISH NORTH AMERICA ACT (1867) and included new provisions, agreed in negotiations during 1980–82, for the balance of power between federal and provincial government. It contained a Charter of Rights and Freedoms. In 1982 the claim made by the separatist government of Québec to constitutional veto over the Act was rejected by the Canadian SUPREME COURT.

Canada Company Land-settlement company, chartered (1826) to attract settlers to Upper Canada and to help repay government debts from the WAR OF 1812. John Galt was charged with the sale of 567,000ha (1.4 million acres) of crown lands to industry. Effective in promoting colonization, the Company operated until the 1950s.

Canada First movement Canadian nationalist party. Arising slowly after the BRITISH NORTH AMERICA ACT (1867), it received its name from a speech (1871) given in Toronto by W.A. Foster. Its short-lived journal the *Nation* was pro-independence and influenced the formation of the Canadian National Association and the Northwest Emigration Aid Society.

Canaris, Wilhelm (1887–1945) German admiral. In 1935 he became head of German military intelligence (*Abwehr*). Under Canaris' leadership, the *Abwehr* became a centre of opposition to the Adolf HITLER's regime. He was executed by the GESTAPO.

Canberra Capital of Australia on the River Molonglo, Australian Capital Territory, SE Australia. It was settled in the early 1820s. In 1908 Canberra succeeded Melbourne as the nation's capital, but the transfer of governmental agencies was not completed until after World War 2. The new Parliament House was opened in 1988. Pop. (1993 est.) 324,600.

Cannae, Battle of (216 BC) Major conflict between ROME and CARTHAGE in the Second PUNIC WAR. HANNIBAL's mastery of strategy enabled his Carthaginian army of *c*.50,000 men to encircle a Roman army of *c*.80,000 soldiers in Puglia, SE Italy. In a crushing defeat, the Romans lost *c*.56,000 men and the Carthaginians *c*.6000.

Canning, Charles John, Earl (1812–62) British colonial administrator, son of George CANNING. As governor

CAMEROON

AREA: 475,440sq km (183,567sq mi)
POPULATION: 12,198,000
CAPITAL (POPULATION): Yaoundé (750,000)
GOVERNMENT: Multiparty republic
ETHNIC GROUPS: Fang 20%, Bamileke and Bamum 19%, Douala, Luanda and Basa 15%, Fulani 10%
LANGUAGES: French and English (both official)
RELIGIONS: Christianity (Roman Catholic 35%, Protestant 18%), traditional beliefs 25%, Islam 22%
GDP PER CAPITA (1995): US$2110

Republic in w Africa. Cameroon is a diverse nation, with more than 160 ethnic groups. Bantu speakers predominate in coastal areas, such as Douala. Islam is the dominant force in the N, where major tribal groupings include the FULANI. In 1472 Portuguese explorers (seeking a sea route to Asia) reached the Cameroon coast. From the 17th century, s Cameroon was a centre of the SLAVE TRADE. In the early 19th-century, the slave trade was abolished by several countries, led by Britain, and replaced by the ivory trade. In 1884 Cameroon became a German protectorate. In 1916 the country was captured by Allied troops. After World War 1, Cameroon was divided into two zones, ruled by Britain and France. In French Cameroon, demands for independence and union with British Cameroon led to civil war in the 1950s, forcing France to grant self-government in 1957.

In 1960 French Cameroon became an independent republic. In 1961 N British Cameroon voted to join the Cameroon Republic (forming the Federal Republic of Cameroon), while s British Cameroon joined NIGERIA. In 1966 an authoritarian one-party state was created. In 1972 the Federal Republic became a unitary state. From 1960 to 1982, Ahmadou Ahidjo was president of the republic. His successor, Paul Biya, purged the party of Ahidjo's supporters. In 1984 a failed coup led to many executions. In 1992 Biya was re-elected, amid charges of electoral malpractice. His autocratic government was regularly accused of torture and the creation of a police state. In 1995 Cameroon became the 52nd member of the COMMONWEALTH OF NATIONS.

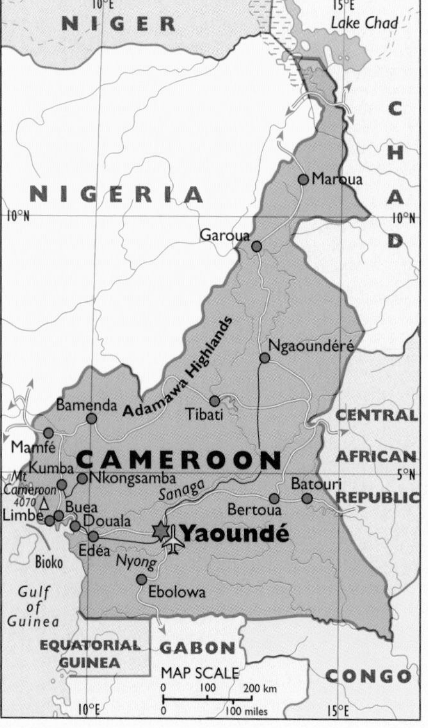

AREA: 9,976,140sq km (3,851,788sq mi)
POPULATION: 27,562,000
CAPITAL (POPULATION): Ottawa (313,987)
GOVERNMENT: Federal, multiparty constitutional monarchy
ETHNIC GROUPS: British 34%, French 26%, German 4%, Italian 3%, Ukrainian 2%, Native American (Amerindian/Inuit) 1.5%, Chinese, Dutch
LANGUAGES: English and French (both official)
RELIGIONS: Christianity (Roman Catholic 47%, Protestant 41%, Eastern Orthodox 2%), Judaism, Islam, Hinduism, Sikhism
GDP PER CAPITA (1995): US$21,130

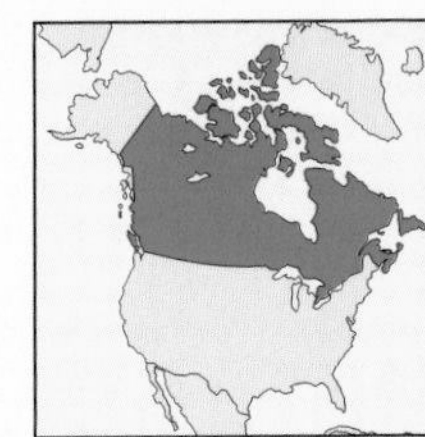

Federation in N North America. Canada, the second-largest country in the world (after Russia), is thinly populated. Much of the land is too cold or mountainous for human settlement, and most Canadians live within 300km (200mi) of the s border with the United States. Canada's first people, ancestors of present-day Native Americans, arrived from Asia probably *c.*20,000 years ago. Later arrivals were the INUIT, also from Asia. At the end of the 10th century, the VIKINGS became the first Europeans to reach the Canadian coast.

The first documented transatlantic journey to Canada was made by John CABOT in 1497. A race began between France and Britain for the riches in this new land. France gained an initial advantage when Jacques CARTIER discovered (1534) the St Lawrence River and claimed Canada for France. Further discoveries were made by European explorers looking for a route to Asia, including John Davies, who gave his name to the Davies Strait in 1585, and Henry HUDSON who sailed into Hudson Bay in 1610. In 1605 France established the first European settlement and founded QUÉBEC in 1608. French territory was extended by explorers such as LA SALLE. The FRENCH AND INDIAN WARS (1689–1763) were a protracted battle for colonial domination of Canada. In 1713 the province of NOVA SCOTIA was ceded to Britain in the Treaty of Utrecht.

In 1759 Québec was captured by Britain, and France surrendered all of its Canadian lands in the Treaty of Paris (1763). The French, who formed a substantial majority, became increasingly discontented under British domination and in 1774 the Québec Act was passed which allowed Catholics to hold public office and recognized the legitimacy of the French language and Catholic religion. It also extended French-Canadian territory to the Ohio River. The Québec Act angered the American colonies and the CONTINENTAL CONGRESS of 1775 responded by invading Canada. During the American Revolution, Canada remained loyal to the English crown, and American attempts to capture it failed. In 1784 the province of NEW BRUNSWICK was created out of Nova Scotia. The CONSTITUTIONAL ACT (1791) divided Canada along linguistic and religious lines: Upper Canada (now Ontario) was English and Protestant; Lower Canada (now Québec) was French and Catholic. Explorers such as Alexander MACKENZIE, James COOK and George VANCOUVER enabled Britain to form the crown colony of BRITISH COLUMBIA in 1858. Border disputes with the United States (*see* AROOSTOOK WAR; WAR OF 1812) continued into the 19th century. Large-scale immigration from Ireland and Scotland increased tension and conflict between the English-speaking majority and the French-speaking minority. In 1841 Upper and Lower Canada were united as the United Province of Canada.

The BRITISH NORTH AMERICA ACT (1867) established the federation or Dominion of Canada, consisting of Québec, Ontario, Nova Scotia and New Brunswick. In 1869 it acquired the lands of the HUDSON'S BAY COMPANY and other provinces were added: MANITOBA (1870), British Columbia (1871), PRINCE EDWARD ISLAND (1873), ALBERTA and SASKATCHEWAN (1905) and NEWFOUNDLAND (1949). The Dominion's first prime minister, Sir John MACDONALD, established the Canadian Pacific Railway, which proved disastrous to his career but provided the means for *c.*3 million European emigrants to disperse across Canada between 1894 and 1914. Canadians fought as part of Allied forces in both World Wars, and in 1949 Canada was a founder member of the North Atlantic Treaty Organization (NATO). Under the leadership of W.L. Mackenzie KING, national unity was strengthened and industry developed. King was succeeded by Louis SAINT LAURENT, Canada's first French-speaking prime minister (1948–57). In 1963 Lester PEARSON became prime minister and, as a sign of Canada's growing national confidence, adopted a new national flag.

Pierre TRUDEAU's first administration (1968–79) was faced with violent demands for Québec's independence, and martial law was imposed in 1970. In Trudeau's second administration (1980–84), Québec voted (1980) to remain part of the federation. The CANADA ACT (1982) amended the constitution, and Canada became a fully sovereign state with a Charter of Rights and Freedoms. It was approved by all the provinces except Québec, which claimed the power of veto. Brian MULRONEY and provincial leaders signed the Meech Lake Accord (1985), which provided for Québec to be brought into the constitutional settlement as a "distinct society". Manitoba and Newfoundland failed to endorse the Accord, and Canada was plunged into constitutional crisis. In 1993 Kim CAMPBELL became Canada's first woman prime minister. In October 1993 she was succeeded by Jean CHRÉTIEN. In 1994 Canada, Mexico and the United States signed the NORTH AMERICAN FREE TRADE AGREEMENT (NAFTA). In 1995 a referendum on sovereignty for Québec was narrowly defeated by 50.6% to 49.4%. In 1997 Chrétien was re-elected. Canada's new constitution enabled Native Americans to press for land claims. In 1999 NORTHWEST TERRITORIES became the Inuit territory of NUNAVUT.

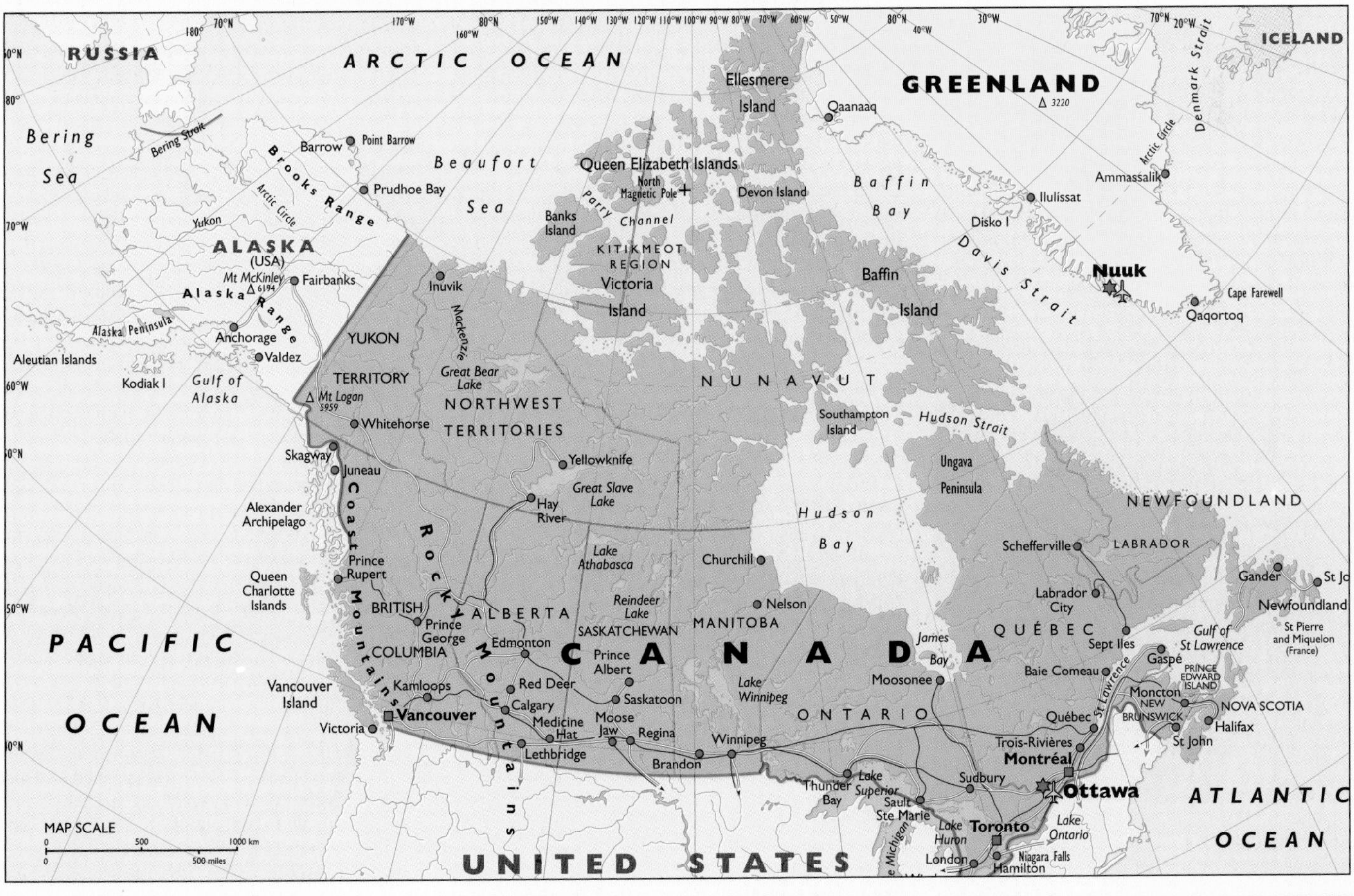

C

general of India (1856–58), Canning repressed the INDIAN MUTINY (1857). His policy of conciliation earned him the nickname "Clemency Canning". With the transfer of the government of India from the English EAST INDIA COMPANY to the crown, Canning became the first viceroy of India (1858–62).

C

Canning, George (1770–1827) British statesman, prime minister (1827), father of Charles CANNING. In 1796 he joined the government of William PITT (THE YOUNGER). In 1807 Canning was appointed foreign secretary in the coalition government of the Duke of PORTLAND. He planned the seizure of the Danish fleet (1807) in the NAPOLEONIC WARS. Canning blamed CASTLEREAGH for reversals in the PENINSULAR WAR (1808–14) and was wounded in an ensuing duel. Both resigned from office. In his second spell as foreign secretary (1822–24), Canning refused to cooperate with the HOLY ALLIANCE. He succeeded Lord LIVERPOOL as prime minister, but his support for CATHOLIC EMANCIPATION led to the resignation of 40 Tory ministers. Canning died after only four months in office.

Cano, Juan Sebastian del (*c.*1476–1526) Spanish navigator. He commanded one of the five vessels in Ferdinand MAGELLAN's voyage of discovery. In 1521, after Magellan's death, Cano assumed command of the expedition. In 1522 he became the first person to circumnavigate the globe.

Canossa Village in Emilia Romagna, N central Italy. In January 1077 Emperor HENRY IV served penance outside the castle of Canossa, where Pope GREGORY VII was staying. Gregory was forced to rescind his excommunication of Henry.

Canterbury City on the River Great Stour, Kent, SE England. It is the seat of the archbishop and primate of the ANGLICAN COMMUNION. The present cathedral (built between the 11th and 15th centuries) replaced the original Abbey of St Augustine. In 1170 Thomas à BECKET was murdered in the cathedral; after his canonization, Canterbury became a major pilgrimage centre. Pop. (1991) 123,947.

Canterbury, archbishop of Primate of All England and spiritual leader of the worldwide ANGLICAN COMMUNION. The archbishopric was established (597) when Pope GREGORY I sent a mission to England to convert the Anglo-Saxons. Saint AUGUSTINE of Canterbury, leader of the mission, became the first archbishop of Canterbury. During the REFORMATION, Archbishop Thomas CRANMER accepted the decision of the English crown to end papal jurisdiction in England (1534). The archbishop of Canterbury traditionally crowns British monarchs and officiates at other religious ceremonies of national importance. He presides over the Lambeth Conference of worldwide Anglicanism but exercises no jurisdiction outside his own ecclesiastical province. *See also* individual archbishops

▲ **Canute II (the Great)** built a Danish empire comprising England, Norway and Denmark. He is depicted here in the manuscript *Liber Legum Antiquorum Regum* (1321).

Canton *See* GUANGZHOU

Canute II (the Great) (*c.*994–1035) King of Denmark (1014–28), England (1017–35) and Norway (1028–29). He accompanied his father, Sweyn, on the Danish invasion of England (1013). After his father's death (1014), Canute was accepted as joint king of Denmark with his brother and later became sole ruler. He invaded England again (1015) and divided it (1016) with the English king EDMUND II. Canute became king after Edmund's death. His rule was a just and peaceful one. Canute restored the church, codified English law and was a generous patron of the arts. His reign in Scandinavia was more turbulent. He conquered Norway (1028) made one son king of Denmark (1028) and another king of Norway (1029).

Canute IV, Saint (*c.*1043–86) King (1080–86) and patron saint of Denmark. A harsh king, he levied heavy taxes to benefit the church. Planning to invade England, Canute forced the peasants to mobilize but they rebelled, killing him at the Church of St Alban, Odense. He was canonized in 1099.

Cao Cao (AD 155–220) (Ts'ao Ts'ao) Chinese general. He suppressed the Yellow Turban Rebellion (185–215) that threatened to topple the HAN dynasty. The dynasty was fatally weakened, however, and China was divided into three kingdoms by the generals. Cao formed the N kingdom of WEI. After Cao's death, the Han emperor abdicated in favour of Cao's son, who established the Wei dynasty.

Cape Province Formerly the largest province in South Africa. In 1994 it was divided into the separate provinces of Eastern Cape, Western Cape and Northern Cape. The first colony was established (1652) by the Dutch EAST INDIA COMPANY, and slaves were imported to work the land. The AFRIKANER (Boer) settlers' expansion led to territorial wars with indigenous tribes, such as the XHOSA (1779). In 1806 Britain established control and renamed the region Cape of Good Hope Colony. The new British settlers clashed with the Afrikaners, precipitating the GREAT TREK (1835). In 1867 diamonds were discovered near Kimberley. The British attempt to incorporate TRANSVAAL and Orange FREE STATE into a single state with NATAL and Cape Colony resulted in the SOUTH AFRICAN WARS (1899–1902). In 1910 the colony became a province of the Union of South Africa. During the 1960s the APARTHEID government created the separate tribal areas (bantustans) of Transkei and Ciskei. In 1994 these were integrated into the new Eastern Cape Province.

Capet, Hugh (938–96) King of France (987–96), founder of the CAPETIAN dynasty. In 956 he inherited the title Duke of the Franks from his father, Hugh the Great. Capet allied himself (978–86) with the German emperors against the CAROLINGIAN king of France, Lothair. In 987 he succeeded Lothair's son Louis V, the last Carolingian king of France. Although his election was disputed by Charles I of Lower Lorraine, Hugh was able to fix the succession on his son, who became ROBERT II.

Capetian French royal family forming the third dynasty that provided France with 15 kings. It began (987) with Hugh CAPET, who succeeded LOUIS V, the last of the CAROLINGIANS. Capetians dominated the feudal forces, extending the king's rule across the whole of France. The last Capetian king, CHARLES IV, was succeeded (1328) by PHILIP VI of the House of VALOIS.

Cape Town City and seaport at the foot of Table Mountain, South Africa. It is South Africa's legislative capital and the capital of Western Cape province. The first European settlement in South Africa, Cape Town was founded by the Dutch EAST INDIA COMPANY in 1652. During the NAPOLEONIC WARS the colony fell to the British. Sights include the Castle of Good Hope (1666–79). Pop. (1991) 2,350,157.

Cape Verde Republic in the E Atlantic Ocean, the most westerly point of Africa. It is made up of 15 islands divided into two groups (windward and leeward). Cape Verde was colonized by the Portuguese in 1462 and served as a base for the SLAVE TRADE. In 1975 Cape Verde gained independence. Aristides Pereira served as president from 1975 to 1991, when he was succeeded by Antonio Mascarenhas Monteiro.

capitalism Economic system in which property and the means of production are privately owned. Capitalism is based on the profit motive, individual enterprise, efficiency through competition and a notion of freedom of choice. It was first articulated by Adam SMITH in his treatise *The Wealth of Nations* (1776). Its development dates from the INDUSTRIAL REVOLUTION and the rise of the BOURGEOISIE. In practice, capitalist governments participate in economic regulation although to a lesser extent than under COMMUNISM or SOCIALISM. The collapse of Soviet communism removed capitalism's traditional opponent and created economic uncertainty. *See also* DIVISION OF LABOUR; FREE TRADE; FRIEDMAN, MILTON; GALBRAITH, J.K.; KEYNES, JOHN MAYNARD; LAISSEZ-FAIRE; MARXISM; MERCANTILISM; MONETARISM

CAPE VERDE
AREA: 4033sq km (1557sq mi)
POPULATION: 392,000
CAPITAL (POPULATION): Praia (80,000)
GOVERNMENT: Multiparty republic
ETHNIC GROUPS: Afro-European, African, Portuguese
LANGUAGES: Portuguese
RELIGIONS: Roman Catholicism
GDP PER CAPITA (1995): US$1870

Capone, Al (Alphonse) (1899–1947) US gangster of the PROHIBITION era, b. Italy. He inherited a vast crime empire from Johnny Torio. Capone (aka "Scarface") was suspected of many brutal crimes, including the ST VALENTINE'S DAY MASSACRE (1929). Ironically, he was only ever convicted and imprisoned for income tax evasion (1931).

Cappadocia Ancient region of ASIA MINOR, now in E central Turkey, between Lake Tuz and the Euphrates. The principal town is Kayseri. Cappadocia was an important centre of early Christianity, its pointed, eroded rocks providing cave-havens for hermits.

Caprivi, (Georg) Leo, Graf von (1831–99) German statesman and soldier, chancellor (1890–94). A distinguished army officer in the FRANCO-PRUSSIAN WAR, he served as chief of the admiralty (1883–88), reorganizing the navy. Caprivi succeeded Otto von BISMARCK as chancellor. His abrogation of the anti-socialist law, reduction in the length of military service, and promotion of industrial growth over agriculture, alienated conservatives and he was forced to resign.

Capsian culture MESOLITHIC culture (*c.*8th–3rd millenia BC) of inland N Africa. Its most characteristic sites are in the salt-lake region of present-day S Tunisia, the best of them being Jabal al-Maqta, near Qafsah. It was a post-glacial culture, distinguished by the variety of its microlithic (tiny-flaked blade) tools and its development of geometrically shaped tools. Probable rock paintings of the culture survive.

Captain Jack (*c.*1837–1873) (Kintpuash) Chief of the Modoc Native Americans. In 1864 the Modoc agreed to move onto a shared reservation with the Klamath. Intertribal conflict and the failure of the United States' government to honour its obligation to supply rations to the Modoc precipitated the Modoc War (1872–73). In 1873 the Modoc killed a peace emissary, General Edward Canby. Jack was captured and hanged for murder.

Capuchins (officially Friars Minor of St Francis Capuchin, O.F.M.Cap.) Roman Catholic religious order, founded (1525) as an offshoot of the FRANCISCANS. Capuchins are so-called because of the pointed cowl (*capuche*) which forms part of their habit. They re-emphasized Franciscan ideals of poverty and austerity, and played an important role in the COUNTER-REFORMATION through their missionary activities.

Caracalla (AD 188–217) (Marcus Aurelius Antoninus) Roman emperor (211–17), son of Septimius SEVERUS. From 198 Caracalla ruled jointly with his father, until the latter's death in 211. Caracalla murdered his brother, Geta, and assumed complete control. In 212 he extended Roman citizenship to all free men in the Empire. Caracalla is traditionally regarded as a brutal tyrant. His self-identification with ALEXANDER III (THE GREAT) led to costly and bloody military campaigns. Caracalla was assassinated by his successor, Macrinus. Remains of the Caracalla Baths, erected in his reign, are still extant.

Caractacus (d. *c.*AD 54) (Caratacus or Caradoc) British chieftain, son of CYMBELINE. He led the CATUVELLAUNI against the Roman conquest (43–50). Caractacus was captured on the Welsh borders and paraded in Rome by Emperor CLAUDIUS. His life was spared in tribute to his bravery.

Carbonari (It. charcoal burners) Members of an early 19th-century Italian secret society advocating liberal, nationalist reforms. The Carbonari were opposed to conservative regimes imposed on Italy after the Congress of VIENNA (1815) and were a model for the RISORGIMENTO movement and, in particular, Giuseppe MAZZINI.

Carboniferous Fifth geologic division of the PALAEOZOIC era, lasting from 360 to 286 million years ago. It is often called the "Age of Coal" because of its extensive swampy forests that turned into most of today's coal deposits. Amphibians flourished, marine life abounded in warm inland seas, and the first reptiles appeared.

Carcassonne Town on the River Aude, S France; capital of Aude department, Languedoc-Roussillon. Originally fortified by the Romans in the 1st century BC, the old town consists of a hilltop medieval fortress, including the extant 6th-century Visigoth towers. A centre of the ALBIGENSES sect, the fortress was captured (1209) by Simon de MONTFORT. Pop. (1990) 44,990.

Carchemish Ancient city-state on the River Euphrates, near Jarablus, Syria. An important centre of Anatolian trade from the 3rd millennium BC, it became a HITTITE kingdom in the 14th century BC. In 717 BC Carchemish was conquered by SARGON II of ASSYRIA. Babylonian King NEBUCHADNEZZAR II expelled the Egyptians from Syria in the Battle of Carchemish (605 BC). The British Museum carried out excavations here in 1878–81 and 1911–14.

Cárdenas, Lázaro (1895–1970) Mexican statesman, president (1934–40). He succeeded Plutarco Elías CALLES as president. After the final phase of the MEXICAN REVOLUTION, Cárdenas accelerated the distribution of communal lands, nationalized oil companies (1938) and supported the confederation of labour.

Cardigan, James Thomas Brudenell, 7th Earl of (1797–1868) British cavalry officer in the CRIMEAN WAR. Cardigan led the disastrous CHARGE OF THE LIGHT BRIGADE (1854) at the Battle of BALAKLAVA.

Cardozo, Benjamin Nathan (1870–1938) US jurist, associate justice (1932–38) of the US Supreme Court. He served on the Court of Appeals in New York (1914–32). Appointed by President Herbert HOOVER to succeed Oliver Wendell HOLMES, Jr on the Supreme Court, Cardozo strove to simplify the law and his decisions on NEW DEAL legislation were extremely influential.

Carey, George Leonard (1935–) English clergyman, archbishop of Canterbury and primate of all England (1991–). Carey was bishop of Bath and Wells (1988–91). He belongs to the evangelical wing of the CHURCH OF ENGLAND. Carey supported the ordination of women priests and environmental conservation efforts. *See also* EVANGELICALISM

cargo cult Mainly Melanesian religious and political movement in which believers expected their ancestors to return in planes or ships laden with modern goods ("cargo") and bring them prosperity and freedom. Movements of this kind first appeared in the 19th century, when local people were confronted by COLONIALISM. Cargo cults proliferated during World War 2.

Carib Major language group and Native Middle American tribe. They entered the Caribbean region from NE South America. About 500 Caribs still live on the island of Dominica; 5000 migrated to Central America, notably around Honduras, where their descendants still live.

Caribbean Community and Common Market (CARICOM) Caribbean economic union. CARICOM was formed by the Treaty of Chaguaramas (1973) to coordinate economic and foreign policy in the WEST INDIES. Most members rely on the export of sugar and tropical fruits and are heavily dependent on imports. The headquarters are in Georgetown, Guyana.

Carinthia (Kärnten) Southernmost province of Austria; the capital is Klagenfurt. The centre of the Celtic kingdom of Noricum, Carinthia was subsumed into the Roman Empire in 16 BC. In the 8th century it became part of Bavaria, but attained the status of independent duchy in 976. It was a Habsburg possession from 1335 to 1918, when the Austo-Hungarian Empire collapsed. Area: 9531sq km (3680sq mi). Pop. (1991) 552,421.

Carl XVI *See* CHARLES XVI

Carleton, Guy, 1st Baron Dorchester (1724–1808) British soldier and colonial administrator. He served in North America during the SEVEN YEARS' WAR and became lieutenant governor of Québec in 1766 and governor in 1768. His conciliatory approach to French Canadians was reflected in the QUÉBEC ACT (1774). In 1775 Carleton became British military commander in Canada and defeated the US forces during the Québec campaign of the AMERICAN REVOLUTION (1775–76). He became governor in chief of British North America (1786–96).

Carlism Reactionary Spanish political movement formed in the 1820s. Carlists invoked the SALIC LAW (exclusion of women from royal succession) to try and prevent the accession of FERDINAND VII's daughter, ISABELLA II. The Carlists favoured the claims of Ferdinand's brother, Don CARLOS, and attracted popular support in rural, N Spain. In the **First Carlist War** (1833–39), Isabella's cause was backed by the QUADRUPLE ALLIANCE (Britain, France, Spain and Portugal). Isabella was forced into exile by the Revolution of 1868. The bloody **Second Carlist War** (1872–76) failed to prevent the accession (1874) of ALFONSO XII and Carlism went into decline. In 1937 General FRANCO merged the remaining Carlists into the FALANGE. On Franco's death (1975), JUAN CARLOS became king. *See also* ESPARTERO, BALDOMERO

Carloman (828–80) King of Bavaria, Carinthia, Pannonia and Moravia (876–80), and king of Italy (877–80), eldest son of LOUIS II (THE GERMAN) and father of ARNULF. He fought against the accession (875) of his uncle as Emperor CHARLES II (THE BALD). After Charles' death (877), Carloman marched across the Alps and was crowned king of Italy. Illness forced him to cede Italy to his brother, later CHARLES III (THE FAT). Carloman's illegitimate son, ARNULF, was crowned emperor in 896. *See also* CAROLINGIANS

▲ **Caracalla** is generally regarded as a brutal dictator, who established absolute control of the Roman Empire by murdering his opponents and political rivals.

Carlos For Spanish and Portuguese kings named thus, *see* CHARLES

Carlos (1545–68) Spanish prince of the Asturias, son of PHILIP II and Maria of Portugal. He was engaged to Elizabeth of Valois, daughter of HENRY II of France, but she married his father instead. Although Carlos has been romanticized by Schiller's tragedy (1787) and Verdi's opera (1867), evidence indicates that he was mentally deranged and possibly homicidal. Philip kept him in prison, where he died.

Carlos (1788–1855) Spanish prince and pretender to the throne, son of CHARLES IV of Spain. His elder brother, FERDINAND VII, broke the SALIC LAW to allow the succession (1833) of his daughter, ISABELLA II. Carlos was proclaimed king by the Carlists, and civil war ensued (1833–39). In 1840 Isabella emerged victorious, and Carlos went into exile. In 1845 he resigned his claim in favour of his son, Don Carlos II. *See also* CARLISM

Carlyle, Thomas (1795–1881) Scottish philosopher, critic and historian. His most successful work, *Sartor Resartus* (1836), combined philosophy and autobiography. His histories include *The French Revolution* (1837). Influenced by romanticism and Goethe in particular, Carlyle was also a powerful advocate of the significance of great leaders in history.

Carmelites (officially Order of Our Lady of Mount Carmel) Order founded (*c.*1154) by St Berthold in Palestine and later re-organized as an order of mendicant friars. An order of Carmelite sisters was founded in 1452. The Carmelites devote themselves to contemplation and missionary work.

Carmichael, Stokely (1941–98) (Kwame Toure) US CIVIL RIGHTS activist, b. Trinidad. In 1966 he became chairman of the STUDENT NONVIOLENT COORDINATING COMMITTEE (SNCC). Carmichael rejected the integrationist, nonviolent approach of Martin Luther KING, Jr in favour of a form of black separatism he called "BLACK POWER". In 1967 Carmichael resigned from the SNCC to become prime minister of the more militant BLACK PANTHERS. In 1969 Carmichael quit the Panthers in protest against their association with white radicals. He lived the rest of his life in Guinea, W Africa. Carmichael changed his name to Kwame Toure in honour of the pan-Africanist leaders Kwame NKRUMAH and Ahmed Sekou TOURE. *See also* BLACK MUSLIMS; PAN-AFRICANISM

Carnac Region of Brittany, NW France, renowned for vast, stone monuments built in the NEOLITHIC age. The site contains long avenues of MENHIRS in three groups, varying in length from 800m (2600ft) to 6km (3.5mi). About 3000 menhirs remain. There are also a number of BARROWS and other tombs. The whole complex is thought to have been a religious centre.

Carnarvon, Henry Howard Molyneux Herbert, 4th Earl of (1831–90) British Conservative statesman. He was colonial secretary (1866–67, 1874–78) under the Earl of DERBY and Benjamin DISRAELI respectively. Carnarvon submitted the BRITISH NORTH AMERICA ACT (1867) that created the Confederation of Canada. His plan for federation in South Africa led to the annexation of the TRANSVAAL (1877) and precipitated the first of the SOUTH AFRICAN WARS. As lord lieutenant of Ireland (1885–86), Carnarvon opposed William GLADSTONE's policy of HOME RULE.

Carnegie, Andrew (1835–1919) US industrialist and philanthropist, b. Scotland. He foresaw the demand for iron and steel and founded the Keystone Bridge Company. From 1873 Carnegie concentrated on steel, pioneering mass production techniques. By 1901 the Carnegie Steel Company was producing 25% of US steel. He endowed 2800 libraries and donated more than US$350 million to charitable organizations.

Carniola Historic region of SE Europe, roughly coextensive with modern SLOVENIA. Once part of the Roman province of PANNONIA, Carniola was occupied during the 6th century by the Slovenes. In the 13th century it was part of the Holy Roman Empire and passed to the Habsburgs in 1335. In 1918 most of the region was awarded to Yugoslavia. In 1991 Slovenia gained independence.

Carnot, Lazare Nicolas Marguerite (1753–1823) French general, grandfather of Sadi CARNOT. He was the outstanding commander of the French Revolutionary Wars (1792–1802), his strategy being largely responsible for French victories. Ousted in 1797, Carnot was recalled by Napoleon (1800), who made him minister of war.

Carnot, (Marie François) Sadi (1837–94) French statesman, president of the Third Republic (1887–94). After quashing the anti-republican movement, Carnot successfully defended the regime during the Panama Canal scandal (1892). He was stabbed to death by an Italian anarchist.

Carol I (1839–1914) First king of Romania (1881–1914). In 1866 he became prince of Romania with the support of Napoleon III of France. Carol led the Romanian army in the first Russo-Turkish War (1877–78). In 1881 Romania gained independence from the Ottoman Empire and Carol became king. In 1907 he crushed a peasant rebellion. By 1913 Romania had become the strongest Balkan power. He preserved the neutrality of Romania at the start of World War 1. *See also* Balkan Wars

Carol II (1893–1953) King of Romania (1930–40), grandnephew of Carol I. In 1925 he renounced the throne. Carol returned in 1930 and supplanted his son, Michael, as king. He supported the growing fascist movement and hoped to become dictator. German pressure forced him to abdicate in favour of Michael, leaving power in the hands of the fascist leader, Ion Antonescu.

Caroline Affair (1837) Altercation between the United States and Canada. Canadian rebels, led by Willam Lyon Mackenzie, took refuge on Navy Island, in the Niagara River. A US boat, the *Caroline*, which supplied the rebels, was captured, set on fire and sent over the Niagara Falls by Captain Andrew Drew. One US citizen was killed. The controversy led to the Webster-Ashburton Treaty (1843).

Caroline of Brunswick (1768–1821) Wife of George IV of England. George took an immediate dislike to her and they separated a few months after the marriage (1795). In 1820, on George's accession, Caroline claimed the title of queen and his attempt to divorce her failed. Caroline turned up for the coronation but was refused admittance to Westminster Abbey. *See also* Fitzherbert, Maria Anne

Carolingians Second Frankish dynasty of early medieval Europe. Founded in the 7th century AD by Pepin of Landen, it rose to power under the weak kingship of the Merovingians. In 732 Charles Martel defeated the Muslims at Poitiers; in 751 his son, Pepin III (the Short), deposed the last Merovingian and became king of the Franks. The dynasty peaked under Pepin's son, Charlemagne (after whom the dynasty is named), who first united and then extended the Frankish dominions into much of W and central Europe, and established himself as effective protector of the papal state in central Italy. In 800 Charlemagne was crowned emperor of the West by the pope. Charlemagne was succeeded as emperor by his son, Louis I (the Pious), whose death (840) led to the division of the Carolingian empire. The Treaty of Verdun (843) partitioned the empire between Lothair I, Louis II (the German) and Charles II (the Bald). Lothair I was given the middle part of the Empire (Francia Media) and retained the imperial crown. Louis II (the German) acquired the E part of the empire (Francia Orientalis) and Charles II (the Bald) gained Francia Occidentalis. Subsequently members of the dynasty competed for power in a political world increasingly under threat from Viking, Arab and Magyar raids. Lothair I's death (855) prompted the division of Francia Media among his sons: Lotharingia (now Lorraine) went to Lothair II; Charles gained the kingdom of Provence; Italy and the imperial crown were granted to Louis II. In 863 the kingdom of Provence was partitioned between Lothair II and Louis II (the German). On the death of Lothair II (869), Lotharingia was divided between Louis II (the German) and Charles II (the Bald). Charles II (the Bald)'s reign (875–77) as emperor was marked by conflict with Louis II (the German)'s eldest son, Carloman. In 885 the Empire (excluding Provence) was reunited under Charles III (the Fat), youngest son of Louis II (the German). In 887 Charles died and the Empire disintegrated. *See also* Arnulf

Carolingian renaissance *See* feature article

carpetbagger Term used after the American Civil War to refer to Northern whites who entered the South as opportunists. They were despised by many white Southerners for seeking political office for economic gain with the aid of the votes of former slaves. They were alleged to have arrived with nothing more than a travelling carpet-bag.

Carranza, Venustiano (1859–1920) Mexican statesman, president (1915–20). Carranza supported Francisco Madero's revolution against Porfirio Díaz. In the civil war that followed, Madero was overthrown by Victoriano Huerta, and Carranza joined Álvaro Obregón, "Pancho" Villa and Emiliano Zapata to defeat Huerta (1914). The conservative Carranza established a provisional government in the face of opposition from Villa and Zapata, who wanted social reform. His term as constitutional president from 1917 was marked by social unrest and ended with a revolt led by Obregón. Carranza fled the capital and was murdered. *See also* Mexican Revolution

Carrero Blanco, Luis (1903–73) Spanish statesman and admiral. He fought with the Nationalists in the Spanish Civil War and became closely associated with General Franco's regime. Carrero Blanco was vice premier from 1967 to 1973, when he was named premier. He was expected to succeed Franco, but was assassinated by the Basque separatist organization ETA.

Carson, Edward Henry, Baron (1854–1935) Northern Irish politician. He was elected to the British Parliament in 1892. Carson gained national attention for his coruscating cross-examination of Oscar Wilde in the Queensberry libel case (1895). In 1912 Carson and James Craig organized the paramilitary Ulster Volunteers to forcibly resist plans for Irish Home Rule. Carson persuaded the British government to exclude the Protestant provinces from the Home Rule Agreement of 1914. He served in the governments of Herbert Asquith and David Lloyd George.

Carson, Kit (Christopher) (1809–68) US guide and soldier. He achieved fame as a guide on John Frémont's expeditions (1842–46). In 1854 Carson became an Indian agent in New Mexico and in 1868 he became superintendent of Indian affairs for the Colorado Territory.

Cartagena Major seaport in SE Spain, on the Mediterranean Sea. Founded (*c*.255 BC) by the Carthaginians, the settlement later fell to the Romans. Moors captured it in the 8th century, but it was retaken by Spaniards in the 13th century. It is the site of the medieval Castillo de la Concepción and a modern naval base. Pop. (1991) 166,736.

Carter, Howard (1874–1939) English Egyptologist. He discovered the tombs of Hatshepsut and Thutmose IV in the Valley of the Kings near Luxor, Egypt, and supervised excavations for Lord Carnarvon. In 1922 Carter found the tomb of Tutankhamun.

Carter, Jimmy (James Earl), Jr (1924–) Thirty-ninth president of the United States (1977–81). He was a Democrat senator (1962–66) and governor (1971–74) for the state of Georgia. In 1976 Carter defeated the incumbent President Gerald Ford. He had a number of foreign policy successes, such as the negotiation of the Camp David Accords (1978). These were overshadowed, however, by his failure to resolve the Iran Hostage Crisis

CAROLINGIAN RENAISSANCE

Cultural revival in France and Italy under the encouragement of Charlemagne. The illiterate monarch gathered notable educators and artists from all over the world to his court at Aachen (Aix-la-Chapelle). He promoted Catholicism, art and learning by founding abbeys and encouraging church building, based on classical designs. As the first Roman emperor in the West for more than 300 years, Charlemagne imposed a new culture in Europe, combining Christian, Roman and Frankish elements. Carolingian scholars developed a new easily written script – the Carolingian miniscule – which greatly speeded up the tedious process of book copying. They also revived Latin from classical texts, making it the language of medieval learning. Their strict choices helped define the limits of modern knowledge: they ignored texts whose contents they considered unnecessary or inappropriate for Latin Christendom, and consequently these works have failed to come down to us in the modern world. *See also* Romanesque

▲ **St Riquier** Monastery church at Centula, near Abbeville, France. Constructed in the 790s, it is an early and celebrated example of the proto-Romanesque or Carolingian double-ended church.

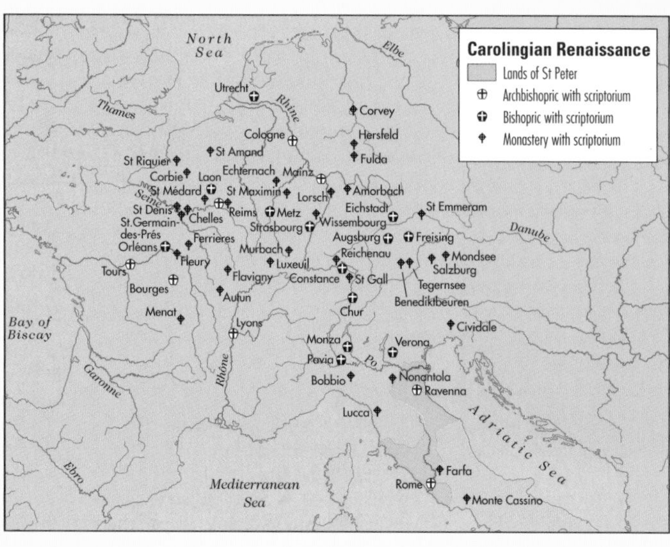

◀ **The Carolingian renaissance** was generated by the work of a relatively small number of institutions. Royally sponsored monasteries with *scriptoria* or writing offices became centres for the gathering and copying of classical texts and the teaching of good Latin.

(1979–81). Following the Soviet invasion of Afghanistan, Carter backed a US boycott of the 1980 Moscow Olympics. At home, an oil price rise contributed to spiralling inflation that was dampened only by a large increase in interest rates. In the 1980 presidential election, Carter was easily defeated by Ronald REAGAN. Since then, he has sought to promote human rights and acted as an international peacebroker.

Carthage Ancient port on the Bay of Tunis, N Africa. It was founded (9th century BC) as a colony of PHOENICIA. Carthage became a great commercial city and imperial power controlling an empire in North Africa, S Spain, and islands of the W Mediterranean. The rise of Rome in the 3rd century resulted in the PUNIC WARS and ended with the destruction of Carthage (146 BC) in the Third Punic War. It was resettled as a Roman colony and in the 5th century AD became the capital of the VANDALS.

Carthusian Monastic order founded (1084) by Saint BRUNO. It is based at the Grande Chartreuse monastery near Grenoble, SE France. It is a mainly contemplative order in which monks and nuns solemnly vow to live in silence and solitude.

Cartier, Sir Georges Étienne (1814–73) Canadian statesman, joint prime minister (1858–62) with John MACDONALD. Cartier's coalition with Macdonald, in which Cartier represented Canada East (Lower Canada), developed into the Canadian Liberal-Conservative Party. At the Québec Conference (1864), Cartier was instrumental in persuading French Canadians to accept federation. He served as minister of militia in the Confederation's first government, led by Macdonald.

Cartier, Jacques (1491–1557) French navigator and explorer who discovered (1535) the St Lawrence River. In 1534 he was sent to North America by FRANCIS I of France. During this first voyage, Cartier discovered the Magdalen Islands and explored the Gulf of St Lawrence. In 1535–36 he sailed up the St Lawrence River to the site of modern Québec and continued on foot to Hochelaga (now Montréal). His third voyage in 1541 was part of an unsuccessful colonization scheme. Cartier's discoveries laid the basis for French settlements in Canada. *See also* CHAMPLAIN, SAMUEL DE

Casablanca Conference (14–24 January 1943) Meeting of US President Franklin ROOSEVELT and British prime minister Winston CHURCHILL at Casablanca, W Morocco. The Allied leaders pledged to fight the AXIS POWERS until they achieved an unconditional surrender.

Casanova de Seingalt, Giovanni Giacomo (1725–98) Italian libertine and adventurer. From 1750 he travelled through Europe leading a dissolute existence. Casanova amassed a fortune and mixed with high society. His exploits are recounted in his *Memoirs*, not published in unexpurgated form until 1960. His name is synonymous with the amorous adventurer.

Casement, Sir Roger David (1864–1916) Irish humanitarian and revolutionary. While a British consul (1895–1912), he exposed the exploitation of rubber-gatherers in the Belgian Congo. During World War 1, Casement sought German aid for the EASTER RISING (1916), but was captured by the British and executed for treason. The British secret service tried to destroy his reputation by publishing the Casement diaries.

Casimir III (the Great) (1309–70) King of Poland (1333–70), son and successor of WŁADISŁAW I (THE SHORT) and last of the PIAST dynasty. He consolidated his father's reunification of Poland by a series of diplomatic agreements with Hungary, Bohemia and the Teutonic Knights. Casimir annexed Red Rus (Eastern GALICIA) and Masovia. Casimir reorganized the administration of Poland proper and brought most of the population under its newly codified "Teutonic Law". Although known as the "peasants' king", he also promoted the interests of the nobility and gentry, who were goverened by their own law. Towns increased in number and prosperity. The "Magdeburg Law" tied them to the Polish state. Casimir protected Poland's Jews, many of them recent immigrants from Germany and founded the University of Krakow (1364). He was succeeded by Louis I of Hungary.

Casimir IV (1427–92) King of Poland (1447–92) and Grand Duke of Lithuania (1440–92), son of WŁADISŁAW II (JAGIELLO). His brother, Władisław III, was killed by the Turks at the Battle of Varna (1444). In 1454 Casimir married Elizabeth of Habsburg, who bore him seven daughters and six sons. He supported the Prussians in their revolt against the TEUTONIC KNIGHTS and scored a decisive victory at the Battle of Puck (1462). In the second Peace of Thorn (1466) Poland acquired West Prussia and Pomerania. In 1467 Casimir founded the Polish *Sejm* (parliament), largely representative of the Szlachta or gentry.

Casket Letters Epistles and sonnets given in evidence at the inquiries of York and Westminster (1568) into the murder of Lord DARNLEY, second husband of MARY, QUEEN OF SCOTS. They were submitted by the Earl of MORAY, regent of Scotland, who claimed that they were found in a casket of the Earl of BOTHWELL, Mary's third husband. If genuine they proved Mary's complicity in Darnley's murder. Persistent allegations of forgery are difficult to evaluate as the originals were lost in 1584.

Cass, Lewis (1782–1866) US statesman, secretary of war (1831–36) and secretary of state (1857–60). As secretary of war under President Andrew JACKSON, Cass prosecuted the BLACK HAWK WAR and SEMINOLE WAR. He served as minister to France (1837–43). Cass ran as the Democratic candidate in the 1848 presidential election, but the defection of Martin VAN BUREN handed the election to Zachary TAYLOR. Cass was appointed secretary of state by President James BUCHANAN, but he resigned over the decision not to reinforce forts in CHARLESTON, South Carolina.

Cassander (358–297 BC) King of Macedonia (305–297 BC), son of ANTIPATER. In 324 BC Cassander became an officer in ALEXANDER III (THE GREAT)'s army in Asia. After Alexander's death (323 BC), he gradually gained hegemony in Macedonia and Greece. In 311 BC Cassander probably murdered Alexander's widow and son. He resisted ANTIGONUS I's efforts to reunite Alexander's empire and defeated Antigonus in the Battle of Ipsus (301 BC).

Cassiodorus, Flavius Magnus Aurelius (*c*.490–*c*.585) Roman statesman and writer. He served as secretary to THEODORIC I. Cassiodorus founded a monastery at Squillace, the "Vivarium", whose scholarly function was the preservation of the classical tradition in literature and government administration. His major work was the *History of the Goths*. *See also* GOTHS

▲ **Carranza** is regarded as the "father of the Mexican constitution". This mural, *La Constitución de 1917* by Jorge González Camarena, depicts Carranza signing the document.

Cassius, Caius Longinus (d.42 BC) Roman general who led the plot to assassinate Julius CAESAR. Cassius sided with POMPEY against Caesar, but was pardoned after Caesar defeated Pompey at the Battle of PHARSALUS (48 BC). After the assassination of Caesar (44 BC), Cassius left for Sicily. Believing that BRUTUS had been defeated by Mark ANTONY and Octavian (AUGUSTUS) at the Battle of PHILIPPI (42 BC), Cassius committed suicide.

Cassivellaunus (1st century BC) British chieftain of the CATUVELLAUNI. He ruled the land N of the River Thames. In 54 BC Cassivellaunus failed to repel the invasion of Julius CAESAR and was forced to pay tribute to the Romans.

caste Formal system of social stratification based on factors such as race, gender, or religion, and sanctioned by tradition. An individual is born into a position and cannot change it. It is most prevalent in Hindu society. The four main divisions (*varnas*) are BRAHMINS (priests and professionals), Kshatriyas (nobles and warriors), Vaishyas (farmers and merchants) and Sudras (servants). A fifth group, the "UNTOUCHABLES" (*harijan* or *dalit*), lie outside the caste system. They perform the most polluting tasks, such as handling animal wastes. *See also* HINDUISM

Castelo Branco, Humberto (1900–67) Brazilian statesman, president (1964–67). As army chief-of-staff, he coordinated the coup (March 1964) against the Goulart administration, which the military regarded as too radical. Castelo's belief in executive authority is reflected in the constitution of 1967.

Castiglione, Baldassare (1478–1529) Italian diplomat and writer. Castiglione served in several Italian courts, notably Urbino. While acting as a papal envoy, he wrote *Libro del Cortegiano* (1528), a classic treatise on the role of the Renaissance courtier.

Castile Region and former kingdom in central SPAIN, traditionally comprising Old Castile (N) and New Castile (S). **Old Castile** was established as a county in 970. During the 11th century it maintained a degree of autonomy and even independence (1029–71) from the kingdom of LEÓN. In 1188 ALFONSO VIII (THE NOBLE) established Castilian hegemony over León. In 1230 the two kingdoms were united under Ferdinand III of Castile. **New Castile** was largely the Moorish kingdom of TOLEDO, which was captured by the Castilians in 1085. By the 12th century, Castile had become the most influential power in Spain and the core of the Spanish monarchy. The marriage (1469) of FERDINAND V and ISABELLA I established the union of Castile and ARAGÓN.

Castlereagh, Robert Stewart, 2nd Viscount (1769–1822) British statesman, b. Ireland. As chief secretary of Ireland (1799–1801), Castlereagh helped secure the passage of the Act of UNION with Britain (1800). He resigned over GEORGE III's opposition to CATHOLIC EMANCIPATION. As secretary of war (1805–06, 1807–09), Castlereagh reorganized and expanded the army. He resigned after a duel with George CANNING. As foreign secretary (1812–22), Castlereagh formed the QUADRUPLE ALLIANCE that defeated NAPOLEON I and dominated the peace negotiations at the Congress of VIENNA (1814–15).

Castro (Ruz), Fidel *See* feature article, page 76

Çatal Hüyük Neolithic site in SW Turkey containing the ruins of one of the world's oldest settlements. Dating from *c*.6250 BC, Çatal Hüyük was the centre of a sophisticated farming and trading community. The interior walls of many houses were plastered and painted, and some buildings contained sanctuaries with elaborate decorations and mother goddess figurines.

Catalonia (Cataluña) Region in NE Spain, extending from the French border to the Mediterranean Sea; the capital is BARCELONA. In 1137 Catalonia was united with ARAGÓN, and remained the dominant partner in the union until the 15th century when escalating Aragonese power provoked a Catalan rebellion (1462–72). Catalonia opposed the Bourbons in the War of the SPANISH SUCCESSION (1701–13) and Philip V stripped the region of its autonomy. In the 1920s Catalan separatism was suppressed by Primo de RIVERA. Catalonia was a Loyalist stronghold in the Spanish CIVIL WAR (1936–39) and FRANCO's victory brought further repression. In 1979 Catalonia gained full autonomy. Area: 31,932sq km (12,329sq mi). Pop. (1990) 6,059,454.

Catawba One of the most powerful southern SIOUX tribes of Native North Americans, originally living in North Carolina and Tennessee. They were active on the colonists' side during the American Revolution and were rewarded with land in York and Lancaster counties, South Carolina, where *c*.350 now reside; a few moved to Oklahoma. They are noted for their pottery and basketry.

Cateau-Cambrésis, Treaty of (1559) Peace agreement between HENRY II of France and PHILIP II of Spain. The treaty ended the VALOIS-HABSBURG struggle for supremacy. French defeats in the ITALIAN WARS and the oncoming threat of the Wars of RELIGION forced Henry II to sue for peace. Cateau-Cambrésis confirmed Spanish ascendancy in Italy.

Catesby, Robert (1573–1605) English Roman Catholic conspirator. He took part in the Earl of ESSEX's rebellion against ELIZABETH I (1601), for which he was imprisoned. Catesby was the chief organizer of the GUNPOWDER PLOT (1605) and was killed while resisting arrest.

Cathars *See* ALBIGENSES; BOGOMILS

Catherine I (1684–1727) Empress of Russia (1725–27), b. Martha Skavronskaya. Of peasant origin, Catherine was captured (1702) by Russian soldiers and became the mistress of Alexander MENSHIKOV and later of PETER I (THE GREAT), whom she married in 1712. Catherine was crowned in 1724 and after Peter's death (1725) was proclaimed empress, ruling through a council led by Menshikov. She was succeeded by PETER II.

Catherine II (the Great) (1729–96) Empress of Russia (1762–96), b. Prussia as Sophie Friederike Auguste von Anhalt-Zerbst. In 1745 ELIZABETH chose her as the wife of the future tsar PETER III. In 1761 Peter succeeded to the throne. His pro-Prussian stance, ending the SEVEN YEARS' WAR (1756–63), alienated the Russian army. In 1762, with the help of her lover Grigori Orlov, Catherine overthrew Peter and shortly afterwards he was assassinated. Catherine began her reign as an "enlightened despot", with ambitious plans for reform. However, after the Peasants' Revolt (1773–74), led by Emelian PUGACHEV, she became increasingly conservative and in 1785 she extended the powers of the nobility at the expense of the SERFS. Her foreign policy, guided by Grigori POTEMKIN, vastly extended Russian territory (chiefly at the expense of the OTTOMAN EMPIRE). In 1764 she secured the accession of her former lover to the Polish throne as STANISLAW II AUGUSTUS. The Partitions of POLAND (1772, 1793, 1795) saw Poland subsumed into Russia, Prussia and Austria. Russia emerged from the first RUSSO-TURKISH WAR (1768–74) as the dominant power in the Middle East. CRIMEA was annexed in 1783, and ALASKA was colonized. Catherine's dialogue with Enlightenment figures such as Voltaire did much to promote her contemporary image in Europe.

Catherine de' Medici (1519–89) Queen of France, wife of HENRY II, and daughter of Lorenzo de' MEDICI. She exerted considerable political influence after the death of her husband in 1559. The accession of her first son, FRANCIS II, and the rise of the Catholic House of GUISE prompted the Conspiracy of Amboise (March 1560). Catherine was merciful towards the HUGUENOT ringleaders. In 1560 Francis II died and Catherine became regent for her second son, CHARLES IX. The rejection of her Edict of January (1562) marked the outbreak of the French Wars of RELIGION (1562–98). In 1570 Catherine tried to end the civil wars through the marriage of her daughter Marguerite to the Protestant Henry of Navarre (later HENRY IV). Fearing the onset of war with Spain, Catherine ordered the assassination of Gaspard de COLIGNY. The ensuing SAINT BARTHOLOMEW'S DAY MASSACRE (24 August 1572) killed several thousand Huguenots. HENRY III's accession to the throne (1574) reduced Catherine's role in policy-making.

Catherine of Aragon (1485–1536) Daughter of FERDINAND and ISABELLA, she was the first queen of England's HENRY VIII (1509). Catherine's only surviving child was a daughter (MARY I). The need to produce a male heir, combined with Henry's desire for Anne BOLEYN, induced him to seek an annulment (1527). The pope's procrastination led to the break with Rome and to the English REFORMATION. The annulment was granted by Thomas CRANMER in 1533.

Catherine of Braganza (1638–1705) Queen consort of CHARLES II of England, daughter of JOHN IV of Portugal. She married Charles in 1662. England was given Tangier and Bombay as part of her dowry. Her Catholic faith made her unpopular and she returned to Portugal in 1692

Catherine of Siena, Saint (1347–80) Italian nun. Catherine joined the Third Order of St DOMINIC at the age of 16 and for three years devoted herself to contemplation, the service of the sick, and the conversion of sinners. In 1376 she went to Avignon to persuade Pope GREGORY XI to return to Rome. She was canonized in 1461 and declared a Doctor of the Church in 1970. Her feast day is 29 April.

Catherine of Valois (1401–37) Queen consort of HENRY V of England, daughter of CHARLES VI of France. She married Henry in 1420. In 1421 Catherine gave birth to a son, the future HENRY VI. In 1422 Henry V died, and she later married Owen Tudor. Their son Edmund, Duke of Richmond, was the father of HENRY VII, the first TUDOR king of England.

Catholic Church Term used in Christendom and in Christian history, signifying the Universal church as distinct from local or sectarian churches. Before the GREAT SCHISM of 1054 it included all who accepted the doctrines of the councils of the early church, such as Nicaea (325) and Chalcedon (451). When the church split into a "Greek East" and a "Latin West" the term Catholic came to denote Western Christianity as distinct from Eastern "Othodoxy". Since the REFORMATION the term Roman Catholic has sometimes been used to denote those who continue to recognize the pope. Many members of the ANGLICAN COMMUNION and "OLD CATHOLICS", although separated from Rome, also see themselves as participants in a "Universal" church.

Catholic Emancipation, Act of (1829) Measure by which the statutes (dating back to the REFORMATION) barring Roman Catholics in Britain from holding civil office or sitting in Parliament, were repealed. Emancipation was achieved through a series of acts. In 1778 restrictions against land purchase and inheritance were lifted. In 1791 further restrictions were removed, and by 1793, Catholics were allowed in the services, universities and the judiciary. The final concession, allowing Catholics to sit in Parliament, was wrung from the Duke of WELLINGTON's government by Daniel O'CONNELL.

Catiline (108–62 BC) (Lucius Sergius Catilina) Roman politician and conspirator. Catiline was made praetor in 68 BC and governor of Africa in 67 BC. False accusations of misconduct led to his defeat by CICERO in elections for consul. Catiline attempted to take the consulship by force (63 BC), but Cicero learned of the conspiracy and denounced him. Catiline fled, and the conspirators were sentenced to death. Julius CAESAR's appeal for mercy merely aroused the wrath of CATO (THE YOUNGER). Catiline died in battle at Pistoia, Tuscany.

Cato Street Conspiracy (20 February 1820) Unsuccessful plot, led by Arthur Thistlewood

CATHERINE II (THE GREAT)

Catherine II (the Great) was a keen patron of Western art and culture, attempting to emulate in St Petersburg, Russia, the splendour of the French court at Versailles. She commissioned the Swedish painter Alexander Roslin (1718–83) to paint this portrait of her. Catherine also encouraged Russian literature and culture.

CATHERINE IN HER OWN WORDS

"I shall be an autocrat: that's my trade. And the good Lord will forgive me: that's his."
Attributed

"The Sovereign is absolute; for there is no other Authority [...] that can act with a Vigour proportionate to the Extent of such a vast Dominion."
From Proposals for a New Law Code, 1767

CASTRO (RUZ), FIDEL (1926–)

Cuban statesman and revolutionary, premier (1959–). In 1953 he was sentenced to 15 years' imprisonment after an unsuccessful coup against the regime of Fulgencio BATISTA. Two years later, Castro was granted an amnesty and exiled to Mexico. In January 1959 his guerrilla forces overthrew Batista. He quickly instituted radical reforms, such as collectivizing agriculture and nationalizing foreign companies. In 1961 the United States organized the abortive BAY OF PIGS invasion. Castro responded by allying more closely with the Soviet Union and developing nations. In 1962 the CUBAN MISSILE CRISIS saw the United States and Soviet Union on the brink of nuclear war. Castro's attempt to export revolution to the rest of Latin America was largely foiled by the capture (1967) of his ally "Che" GUEVARA. In 1980 Castro temporarily lifted the ban on emigration, and 125,000 people left for Florida. The collapse of Soviet communism and the continuing US trade embargo dramatically worsened the economic climate, forcing Castro to introduce economic reforms.

► **Castro's guerrilla forces** became known as the 26th July Movement, the date of Castro's disastrous attempt to take over a government military base in 1953.

(1770–1820), to blow up the British Tory cabinet. The conspiracy was uncovered by a government agent and the plotters arrested in their arsenal at Cato Street, London.

Cato (the Elder), Marcus Porcius (234–149 BC) Roman statesman and orator. He was the chief opponent of SCIPIO AFRICANUS (THE ELDER). In 184 BC Cato was elected censor. He attacked the prevalent Hellenism and personal extravagance, arguing for a return to conservative, Roman values. Cato's visit to CARTHAGE (*c*.153 BC) convinced him of the need to destroy its growing might and he helped to precipitate the Third PUNIC WAR. Cato's treatise on farming, *De agri cultura* (*c*.160 BC) is the oldest extant complete prose work in Latin.

Cato (the Younger), Marcus Porcius (95–46 BC) Roman statesman, great-grandson of CATO (THE ELDER), b. Tunisia. He was leader of the Optimates, the patrician oligarcy in Rome. In 62 BC Cato ordered the execution of CATILINE. His concerted opposition to Julius CAESAR led to the creation of the so-called first triumvirate (Caesar, POMPEY and CRASSUS). Cato favoured POMPEY in the civil war against Caesar (49–45 BC) and, when Caesar emerged victorious, committed suicide.

Catt, Carrie Chapman (1859–1947) US suffragette and peace campaigner, b. Carrie Lane. In 1900 Catt became president of the National American Women Suffrage Association. Her "Winning Plan" campaign led to the Nineteenth Amendment (1920) to the US CONSTITUTION. Catt served as president (1904–23) of the International Woman Suffrage Alliance. *See also* FRANCHISE; SUFFRAGETTE MOVEMENT

Catton, (Charles) Bruce (1899–1978) US historian. A specialist in the history of the American CIVIL WAR, he stressed the role of the individual in history. Catton won the Pulitzer Prize for *A Stillness at Appomattox* (1953).

Catulus, Quintus Lutatius (d.87 BC) Roman consul (102 BC). In 101 Catulus and MARIUS defeated the Germanic invasion of the Cimbri at Vercelli, N Italy. Catulus favoured SULLA over Marius in the Social War (91–88 BC). The Marian victory led to his death by suicide or assassination.

Catuvellauni Belgic tribe of ancient BRITAIN, led by CASSIVELLAUNUS. They originally lived just N of the River Thames, with headquarters at Wheathampstead, but after being defeated (54 BC) by Julius CAESAR at the River Stour they moved their capital to Verulamium (ST ALBANS). They were an agricultural people. *See also* BELGAE

caudillo (Sp. leader) Type of political leader prevalent in Latin America during the 19th century. A civilian who rode on horseback, he was supported by a paramilitary force. The aim of the caudillo band was to gain wealth; the tactic usually violence. Some caudillos had only local or regional power; others captured the national state.

Cavalier, Jean (*c*.1681–1740) French HUGUENOT insurgent. In *c*.1701 he became leader of the CAMISARDS, a group of Protestant rebels in the Cévennes region of France. In 1704 Cavalier made peace with Marshal VILLARS in return for a pension and a commission in the army of LOUIS XIV. Cavalier later fled France for England, where he became governor of Jersey.

Cavalier (Fr. *chevalier*) Name adopted by the Royalists during the English CIVIL WAR (1642–48) in opposition to the ROUNDHEADS (parliamentarians). The court party retained the name after the RESTORATION until superseded by the name TORY.

Cavalier Parliament (1661–79) British Parliament summoned to create the institutions of the RESTORATION monarchy. The longer it sat, the more critical its members became of CHARLES II. The king eventually dissolved it in February 1679.

Cavell, Edith Louisa (1865–1915) English nurse. During World War 1, she was matron of the Berkendael Institute, Brussels. For aiding *c*.130 Allied soldiers to escape from Belgium, Cavell was court-martialled and executed by the Germans.

Cavendish, Lord Frederick Charles (1836–82) British politician, chief secretary for Ireland (1882). On 5 May 1882, a day after taking office, Cavendish and his undersecretary, Thomas Burke, were stabbed to death by Fenians in Phoenix Park, Dublin. Charles Stewart PARNELL, leader of the FENIAN MOVEMENT, was alleged to have been complicit in the murders but was later exonerated by a parliamentary commission (1890).

Cavendish, Thomas (1560–92) English navigator. In 1585 he commanded a vessel in Sir Richard GRENVILLE's expedition to Virginia, North America. In 1586 Cavendish led the third circumnavigation of the world, but he died attempting a further circumnavigation.

Cavendish, William *See* NEWCASTLE (UPON TYNE), WILLIAM CAVENDISH, 1ST DUKE OF

Cavour, Camillo Benso, Conte di (1810–61) Piedmontese statesman, instrumental in the unification of Italy under SAVOY rule. He was banished from the court of CHARLES ALBERT for flouting royal authority. In 1848 Cavour entered the newly formed parliament in Piedmont and was appointed finance minister in 1850. In 1852 he was appointed prime minister by VICTOR EMMANUEL II. In the negotiations that followed the end of the CRIMEAN WAR (1853–56), Cavour engineered the support of NAPOLEON III of France to overthrow Austrian rule in Italy. Franco-Piedmontese victories forced Emperor FRANZ JOSEPH to concede defeat (1859). Giuseppe GARIBALDI's revolutionary forces seized the political initiative and ousted the BOURBONS from the Kingdom of the Two Sicilies (1860). Cavour and Garibaldi reached a diplomatic agreement that created the kingdom of Italy (1861). *See also* RISORGIMENTO

Caxton, William (1422–91) English printer. Following a period in Germany (1470–72), where he learned printing, he set up the first English press at Westminster, London (1476). Caxton published more than 100 items, many of them his own translations. Among his publications were editions of Boethius, Chaucer, Gower and Malory.

Cayuga Major branch of the Five Nations of the IROQUOIS CONFEDERACY, originally living around Lake Cayuga, New York, and the Grand River in Ontario, Canada. The Cayuga fought alongside the British during the American Revolution and afterwards became widely scattered into Ohio, Wisconsin and Oklahoma, where they joined the Seneca. Today, there are *c*.550 in Oklahoma and 400 Cayuga in New York.

Ceauşescu, Nicolae (1918–89) Romanian statesman, the country's effective ruler from 1965 to 1989. He succeeded Gheorghe GHEORGHIU-DEJ as Romanian leader and general secretary of Romania's Communist Party. In 1967 Ceauşescu also became head of state. Ceauşescu

CELTS

Indo-European people who dominated much of W and central Europe in the 1st millennium BC. The earliest archaeological evidence of the Celts is the HALLSTATT culture, near Salzburg, Austria (*c*.700 BC). From a wide area of settlement covering much of France, Germany and the Alpine region, the LA TÈNE culture (*c*.450 BC–50 BC) spread to Britain, Spain, Italy, Greece and Anatolia. It was during this period that the Celts were at their most dominant, sacking Rome in 390 BC. Famous for their rich heritage of mythology and art (especially metalwork), the Celts developed a village-based, hierarchical society headed by nobles and DRUIDS, and from the 3rd century BC built fortified towns the Romans called *oppida*. Eventually conquered by both the Romans and Germanic peoples in the 1st century BC, the Celts were confined to Ireland, Wales, Cornwall and Brittany. Their culture remained vigorous, and Celtic churches were important in the spread of Christianity in N Europe. *See also* CISALPINE GAUL; GAULS; IRON AGE; TRANSALPINE GAUL

◀ **Celtic soldier** Warrior nobles formed a distinct class in Celtic society. Soldiers fought on foot or horseback, armed with swords and spears. During the La Tène period swords, scabbards, shields and helmets were decorated with intricate geometrical designs of stylized plants and animals.

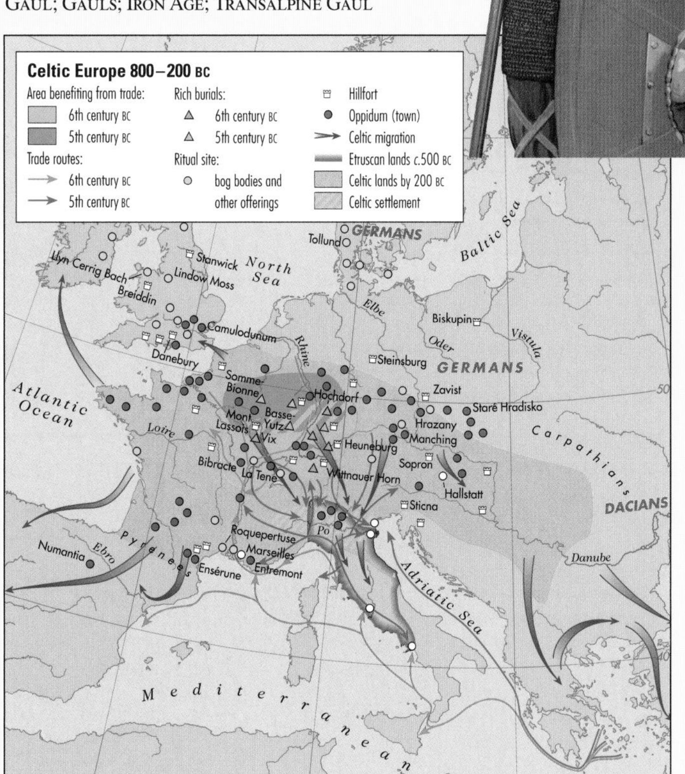

◀ **During the 1st millennium BC** much of France, Germany and the Alpine region came to be dominated by the Celtic peoples, who also settled in parts of Britain, Spain northern Italy and Anatolia. By the 3rd century BC, permanent settlements were established in many parts of Europe, reflecting both increased prosperity and more complex political organization. Rivers, lakes and woods were regarded by the Celts as sacred sites where animal, and occasionally human, sacrifices were made.

promoted Romanian nationalism and pursued an independent foreign policy but instituted repressive domestic policies. He was deposed and executed in the December 1989 revolution.

Cecil, Robert, 1st Earl of Salisbury (1563–1612) English statesman, son of Lord Burghley. He became secretary of state to Elizabeth I on his father's retirement in 1596. Cecil was responsible for negotiating the accession of James I (1603), smoothing the transition from Tudor to Stuart rule. *See also* Essex, Robert Devereux, 2nd Earl of

Cecil, William, 1st Baron Burghley *See* Burghley, William Cecil, 1st Baron

Celebes Former name of Sulawesi, Indonesia

Celts *See* feature article, page 77

Cenozoic Most recent era of geological time, beginning *c*.65 million years ago and extending up to the present. It is subdivided into the Tertiary and Quaternary periods. It is the era during which present geographical features and plants and animals developed.

censor Public official of ancient Rome, from 443 to 22 bc. Two censors were elected for 18-month terms. Besides taking the census, they supervised public works, finance and morals, and filled senatorial vacancies.

Central African Federation (1953–63) Territory established by the British to unite the colonies of Northern and Southern Rhodesia and Nyasaland (now Zambia, Zimbabwe and Malawi). It was designed to act as a political counterweight to South Africa. In practice the Federation perpetuated white minority rule and strengthened the resolve of African nationalist movements. After intensive campaigns of civil disobedience, the Federation was dissolved. Malawi and Zambia gained independence, while Southern Rhodesia unilaterally declared independence.

Central African Republic *See* country feature

Central America Geographical term for the narrow strip of land that connects North America to South America and divides the Caribbean Sea from the Pacific Ocean; it consists of Guatemala, El Salvador, Honduras, Nicaragua, Costa Rica, Belize and Panama. From *c*.1200 bc it saw the development of many Native Middle American cultures, among them the Olmec and Maya. The region (excluding Panama) was conquered and ruled by the Spanish from the 16th century until 1821. Area: 715,876sq km (276,400sq mi). *See also* Central American Common Market (CACM); Central American Federation

Central American Common Market (CACM) Economic alliance, formed in 1960, of El Salvador, Guatemala, Honduras and Nicaragua. In 1963 Costa Rica joined the CACM. The group made substantial progress towards economic integration, including the establishment of a common external tariff. Attempts to form a comprehensive common market in Latin America by merging the CACM with the Latin American Free Trade Association have proved unsuccessful.

Central American Federation (1825–38) Loose political union of Costa Rica, Guatemala, Honduras, Nicaragua and Salvador. In 1825 the republics appointed Manuel José Arce as president of the federation. In 1830 Arce was succeeded by Francisco Morazán. Internal tension led to the collapse of the Federation. *See also* Central American Common Market (CACM)

Central Asian Republics Economic alliance among the three republics of Kazakstan, Kyrgyzstan and Uzbekistan. The alliance was formed (1994) after the break-up of the Soviet Union.

central bank Institution that regulates and sets policy for a nation's banking system. The central bank of the United Kingdom is the Bank of England. The central bank of the United States is the Federal Reserve system. *See also* Bank of the United States

Central Intelligence Agency (CIA) US government agency established to coordinate the intelligence activities of government departments and agencies responsible for US national security. Founded in 1947, it played a major role during the Cold War, supporting anti-communist movements. At times the CIA has come under attack for overstepping its mandate and interfering in the internal affairs of foreign countries. It was severely criticized for its role in the Watergate affair. It advises, and is directed by, the National Security Council (NSC) and should report any action it proposes to take to Congress and gain presidential authorization.

Central Powers Alliance of Germany and Austria-Hungary (with Bulgaria and Turkey) during World War I. The name distinguished them from the Allies in the w (Britain, France, Belgium and the United States) and e (Russia and others).

Central Treaty Organization (CENTO) Military alliance formed (1959) after Iraq withdrew from the Baghdad Pact. The headquarters moved from Baghdad to Ankara, Turkey. With US support, Turkey, Iran, Britain and Pakistan formed a defensive alliance against the Soviet Union. In 1979 CENTO was dissolved.

centurion Military officer of ancient Rome. He commanded 100 men, forming one sixth of a cohort, with ten cohorts making a legion. Centurions were usually soldiers who had risen through the ranks.

Cerdic (d.534?) "Dark Age" warlord. According to the Anglo-Saxon Chronicle, Cerdic landed near Southampton from Continental Europe (495), fought the Britons, and founded the kingdom of Wessex (519).

Cetshwayo (d.1884) (Cetewayo) King of the Zulus (1873–79). Nephew of Shaka, he sought British aid against the Afrikaners, but British demands for him to disarm led to the Zulu War (1879). Eventually defeated, he was deposed, restored briefly in 1883, but died in exile.

Ceylon *See* Sri Lanka

Chacabuco, Battle of (12 February 1817) First major engagement in the Chilean War of Independence. José de San Martín crossed the Andes from Argentina to Chile, surprising the Spanish force near Santiago, Chile. The royalists were routed and finally expelled from Chile in the Battle of Maipú (1818). *See also* O'Higgins, Bernardo

Chaco War (1932–35) Conflict between Bolivia and Paraguay over the disputed n plains of Gran Chaco. The war was precipitated by the discovery of oil in the Chaco Boreal, and Bolivia's subsequent need for a route to the sea. More than 100,000 soldiers died before an agreement gave 75% of Gran Chaco to Paraguay and allowed Bolivia use of the River Paraguay.

Chad *See* country feature

Chaeronea Ancient town of Boeotia, e central Greece. In 338 bc Philip II of Macedonia defeated the allied citizen armies of Athens and Thebes at the Battle of Chaeronea. In a second Battle of Chaeronea (86 bc), Sulla defeated the army of Mithridates VI led by Archelaus.

Chaka *See* Shaka

Chalcedon (now Kadiköy, Turkey) Ancient city in Bithynia, on the e shore of the Bosporus opposite ancient Byzantium (now Istanbul). It was founded (*c*.680 bc) by Greeks from Megara shortly before the founding of Byzantium. It vacillated between Spartan and Athenian interests, was ruled for a time by Persia, and then became part of Alexander III (the Great)'s empire. In 197 bc it came under Roman domination. In 73 bc Mithridates VI of Pontus inflicted a notable defeat on the Romans at Chalcedon. Frequently attacked by Barbarians thereafter, it was the site of the Council of Chalcedon (ad 451). It fell to Persia again in 616 and was destroyed by the Turks in 1075.

Chalcedon, Council of (451) Fourth ecumencial council of the Christian church, convoked by Emperor Marcian. It approved the Nicene Creed, which stressed the doctrine of two natures (divine and human) in Christ, and condemned Monophysitism and Nestorianism.

Chalcolithic Age Period preceding the Bronze Age in which humans discovered how to extract copper by heating its ore with charcoal. The art of smelting and casting copper had been practised in the Near East before 5500 bc and in Europe before 4500 bc. Chalcolithic copper was used for prestige objects, especially jewellery and weapons.

Chaldaea Southernmost part of Babylonia. In *c*.800 bc the Chaldeans, originating from Arabia, began to arrive in the region of Ur. In *c*.627 bc the death of Ashurbanipal, the last of the great Assyrian kings to rule over Babylonia, enabled Nabopolassar to seize power and establish the Chaldaean (New Babylonian) empire. The Chaldaean empire flourished under Nebuchadnezzar II (r. *c*.605–562 bc). It fell when Cyrus II (the Great) captured Babylon (539 bc). *See also* Assyria; Achaemenids

CENTRAL AFRICAN REPUBLIC

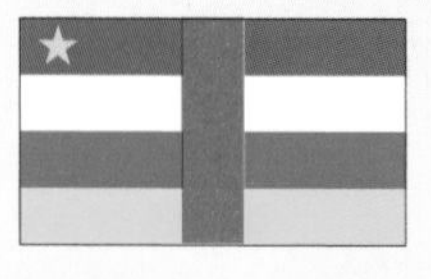

AREA: 622,980sq km (240,533sq mi)
POPULATION: 3,173,000
CAPITAL (POPULATION): Bangui (451,690)
GOVERNMENT: Multiparty republic
ETHNIC GROUPS: Banda 29%, Baya 25%, Ngbandi 11%, Azande 10% Sara 7%, Mbaka 4%, Mbum 4%
LANGUAGES: French (official), Sango (most common)
RELIGIONS: Traditional beliefs 57%, Christianity 35%, Islam 8%
GDP PER CAPITA (1995): US$1070

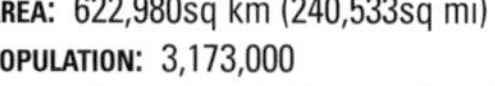

Landlocked nation in central Africa. Between the 16th and 19th centuries the population was greatly reduced by the slave trade, and the country is still thinly populated. Most inhabitants migrated into the area during the past 200 years to escape enslavement. France first occupied the area in 1887, and in 1894 established the colony of Ubangi-Shari at Bangui. In 1906 the colony was united with Chad and in 1910 was subsumed into French Equatorial Africa. Forced-labour rebellions occurred in 1928, 1935 and 1946. During World War 2, Ubangi-Shari supported the Free French. In 1958 the colony voted to become a self-governing republic within the French community.

In 1960 the Central African Republic gained independence, but the next six years saw a deterioration in the economy and increasing government corruption and inefficiency under President David Dacko. In 1966 Colonel Jean Bedel Bokassa assumed power in a bloodless coup. In 1976 Bokassa transformed the republic into an empire and proclaimed himself Emperor Bokassa I. His rule became increasingly brutal, and in 1979 he was deposed in a French-backed coup led by Dacko. In 1981 Dacko (faced with continuing unrest) was replaced by General André Kolingba, whose government quickly banned all political parties. In 1991 the country adopted a new, multiparty constitution. In 1996 an army rebellion was suppressed with the help of French troops, and in 1998 a United Nations' peacekeeping force was sent to oversee fresh elections.

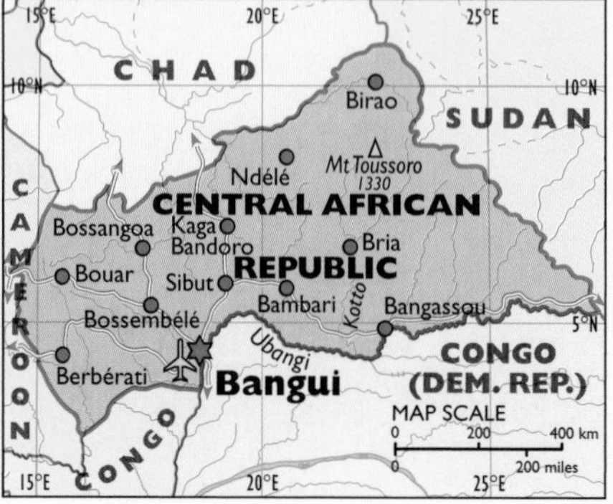

Chalukya South Indian dynasty that ruled in the Deccan intermittently from AD 535 to 1200. The dynasty was founded by Pulakesian I and held power until 757. In *c.*973 the Chalukya regained power. In 1189 their kingdom was divided. The last Chalukya king died in 1200. The Chalukya period was associated with a magnificent culture of rock-carving. *See also* PALLAVA; PANDYA

Chamberlain, Sir (Joseph) Austen (1863–1937) British statesman, son of Joseph CHAMBERLAIN. He entered Parliament in 1892. Chamberlain served as chancellor of the exchequer (1903–05, 1919–21) in the governments of Arthur BALFOUR and David LLOYD GEORGE. In 1921 he succeeded Bonar LAW as leader of the CONSERVATIVE PARTY. Chamberlain acted as foreign minister (1924–29) in Stanley BALDWIN's administration. For his work on the LOCARNO PACT, Chamberlain shared the 1925 Nobel Prize for Peace with Charles DAWES.

Chamberlain, Joseph (1836–1914) British politician, father of Neville and Austen CHAMBERLAIN. He entered Parliament as a Liberal in 1876. In 1880 Chamberlain became president of the board of trade. In 1886 he resigned over GLADSTONE's HOME RULE Bill and was leader of the Liberal Unionists from 1889. In 1895 Chamberlain returned to government as colonial secretary, where his aggressive, imperialist stance helped provoke the second of the SOUTH AFRICAN WARS (1899).

Chamberlain, (Arthur) Neville (1869–1940) British statesman, prime minister (1937–40), son of Joseph CHAMBERLAIN. He entered Parliament in 1918. During the 1920s, Chamberlain served as chancellor of the exchequer (1923–24, 1931–37) and minister of health (1924–29). He succeeded Stanley BALDWIN as prime minister and leader of the CONSERVATIVE PARTY. Chamberlain's policy of APPEASEMENT towards Adolf HITLER produced the MUNICH AGREEMENT (1938). Following Hitler's invasion of Poland, Chamberlain declared war in September 1939. Following the loss of Norway, Chamberlain was replaced by Winston CHURCHILL in May 1940.

Chambord, Henri Charles Ferdinand Marie Dieudonné, Comte de (1820–83) Pretender to the French throne, and last male heir of the senior branch of the BOURBONS. His grandfather, CHARLES X, abdicated in his favour after the JULY REVOLUTION (1830), but LOUIS PHILIPPE seized the crown instead. Many attempts to restore Chambord to the monarchy collapsed because of his hostility to the principles of the Revolution and his refusal to compromise. *See also* LEGITIMISTS

Chamorro, Violeta Barrios de (1939–) Nicaraguan stateswoman, president (1990–96). She entered politics in 1978 when her husband, Pedro Joáin Chamorro, was assassinated. In 1989, supported by the United States, Chamorro became leader of the right-wing coalition, the National Opposition Union (UNO). In 1990 elections Chamorro defeated the SANDINISTAS. Her presidency was marked by skirmishes between CONTRA rebels and the Sandinistas, and many of her policies were blocked by reactionary elements in the UNO and by members of the Sandinista Liberation Front.

Chamoun, Camille (1900–87) Lebanese statesman, president (1952–58). A MARONITE Christian, his support for Britain and France during the SUEZ CRISIS (1956) led to civil war. In 1958 US marines were sent to Lebanon in support of Chamoun.

Champa (Chin. Linyi) Kingdom of the Chams, a Malay peoples, which flourished in VIETNAM from the 2nd century AD to the 15th century. Champa was formed in AD 192, during the break-up of the HAN dynasty of China. In the 6th century Champa finally succeeded in its long struggle for independence from China. In 1145 the KHMERS, led by SURYAVARMAN II, conquered Champa. Champa fought back and sacked the Cambodian capital at ANGKOR (1177). Later wars with the MONGOLS and Vietnamese led to the loss of most of its territory by the end of the 15th century.

Champlain, Samuel de (1567–1635) French explorer, founder of New France (now Canada). In 1603, following the discoveries of Jacques CARTIER, Champlain travelled up the St Lawrence River as far as Lachine. He returned to New France in 1604 and established a fur-trading colony at Port Royal (now Annapolis Royal, Nova Scotia). Champlain explored the Atlantic coast from Cape Breton to Cape Cod, making the first detailed maps of the area, and in 1608 he founded Québec. With the help of the HURON, he continued to explore the region for the next six years, discovering the lake that bears his name in 1609. In 1615 Champlain travelled up the Ottawa River as far as Lake Huron. The last 20 years of his life were spent as a colonial administrator and patron of further explorations.

Champollion, Jean François (1790–1832) French scholar, one of the founders of Egyptology. In 1822 he revealed his decipherment of Egyptian hieroglyphics through study of the ROSETTA STONE. Champollion was subsequently curator at the Louvre in Paris and first professor of Egyptology at the Collège de France.

Ch'an Buddhism *See* ZEN BUDDHISM

Chancellorsville, Battle of (2–4 May 1863) Conflict in the American CIVIL WAR. The *c.*130,000 troops of the Union Army of the Potomac, led by General Joseph HOOKER, faced the *c.*60,000 soldiers of the Confederate Army of Northern Virginia, commanded by General Robert LEE. Hooker advanced, hoping to encircle the Confederates, but was outflanked by General "Stonewall" JACKSON and forced to retreat N of the Rappahannock River. The Union lost more than 17,000 men. The *c.*12,000 Confederate losses included General Jackson, who was accidentally shot by his own men. *See also* FREDERICKSBURG, BATTLE OF; GETTYSBURG, BATTLE OF

Chancery In England, court developed in the 15th century for the lord chancellor to deal with petitions from aggrieved persons for redress when no remedy was available in the COMMON LAW courts. By the mid-17th century, Chancery had become a second system of law (equity) rather than a reforming agency. By the Supreme Court of Judicature Act (1925) the court of Chancery was merged into the High Court of Justice, of which it is now known as the Chancery Division.

Chan Chan Capital of the CHIMÚ kingdom on the N coast of Peru which at the height of its power, between AD 1400 and 1475 in the "City Builder" or Urbanist Period, had a population of more than 100,000 inhabitants. Extensive adobe ruins remain representing 21 sq km (8 sq mi) of rectilinear planning. Chan Chan was the administrative centre of the agricultural Chimú economy. After the INCA conquest (*c.*1470), Chan Chan became a provincial capital and is now a suburb of Trujillo.

Chandragupta Founder of the MAURYAN EMPIRE in India (r. *c.*321–*c.*297 BC), grandfather of ASHOKA. He seized the throne of Magadha and defeated SELEUCUS, gaining dominion over most of N India and parts of Afghanistan. His reign was characterized by religious tolerance. Chandragupta established a vast bureaucracy at Patna. He abdicated and, it is thought, became a Jain monk.

Chandragupta I Indian emperor (r. *c.*320–*c.*330), founder of the GUPTA dynasty. He inherited his kingdom from Ghatotkacha and enlarged it through marriage to a Licchavi princess. Chandragupta expanded the empire to encompass the whole of Bihar and parts of Bengal. He was succeeded by his son, Samudragupta.

Chandragupta II (Vikramaditya) Indian emperor (r. *c.*380–*c.*414), grandson of CHANDRAGUPTA I. He expanded the GUPTA empire through his subjugation of

CHAD

AREA: 1,284,000sq km (495,752sq mi)
POPULATION: 5,961,000
CAPITAL (POPULATION): Ndjamena (529,555)
GOVERNMENT: Transitional
ETHNIC GROUPS: Bagirmi, Kreish and Sara 31%, Sudanic Arab 26%, Teda 7%, Mbum 6%
LANGUAGES: French and Arabic (both official)
RELIGIONS: Islam 40%, Christianity 33%, traditional beliefs 27%
GDP PER CAPITA (1995): US$700

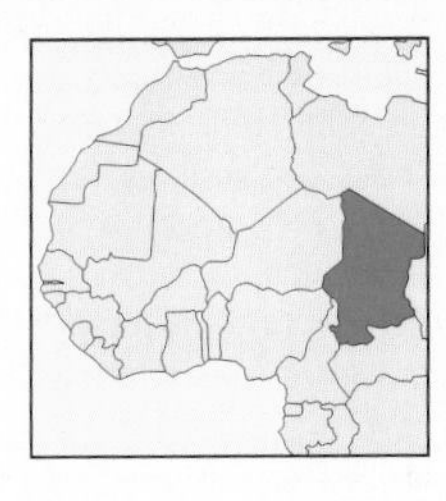

Republic in N central Africa. Chad is Africa's fifth largest country. It straddles two, often conflicting worlds: the N, populated by nomadic or semi-nomadic Muslim peoples, such as ARABS and TUAREGS; and the dominant S, where a sedentary population practise Christianity or traditional religions, such as animism. In *c.*AD 700 North African nomads founded the KANEM empire. The kingdom of BORNU arose in the 14th century, expanding to incorporate Kanem. Warring between Bornu and the neighbouring kingdoms led to decline, however, and the region fell to Sudan in the late 19th century. In 1900 the French defeated the Sudanese, and in 1908 Chad became the largest province of French Equatorial Africa. In 1920 it became a separate colony.

In 1960 Chad gained independence. In 1965 a one-party state was declared by President François Tombalbaye and the N Muslims, led by the Chad National Liberation Front (Frolinat) and backed by Libya, rebelled. By 1973 the revolt had been quashed with the aid of French troops. In 1980 the Frolinat leader Goukouni Oueddi brought in Libyan troops, forcing the Armed Forced of the North (FAN) under Hissène Habré to retreat into Sudan. After the withdrawal of Libyan troops, Habré reoccupied E Chad and formed a new government (1982). Goukouni established a rival government and heavy fighting ensued. Habré's government prevailed and in 1983, with the support of 3000 French troops, retaliated against Libya's bombing of Chad. Libyan troops retreated, retaining only the uranium-rich Aozou Strip. In 1987 a cease-fire took effect and in 1994 the Strip was returned to Chad. In 1990 Habré was removed in a coup led by Idriss Déby. Déby was confirmed as president in multiparty elections after the adoption of a new, democratic constitution in 1996.

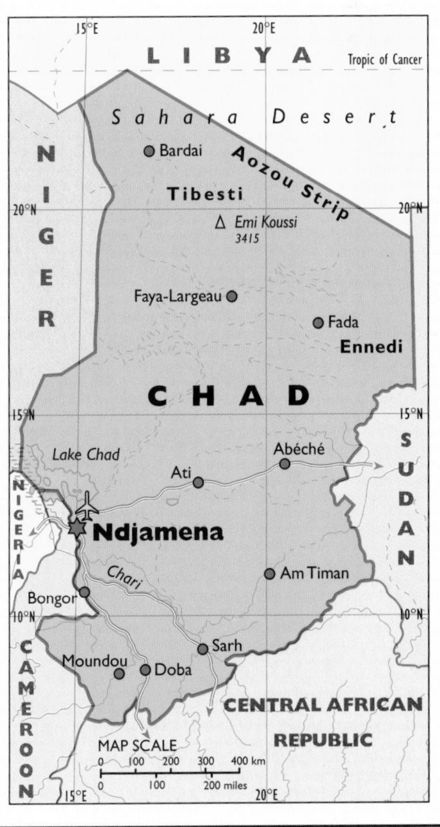

the Shaka chiefs (*c*.375-415) and through the marriage of his daughter to the Vakataka King Rudrasena II. Chandragupta's reign marked the height of ancient India's prosperity and cultural development. *See also* GUPTA

Chao K'uang-yin *See* ZHAO KUANGYIN

Chapultepec National park in central Mexico, SW of Mexico City. A rocky hill region, it is the site of an 18th-century castle, captured (1847) by the United States during the MEXICAN WAR. Chapultepec was also the scene of a wartime pan-American conference (1945) to ensure assistance and solidarity in the Western Hemisphere.

Charge of the Light Brigade (25 October 1854) British cavalry charge at the Battle of BALAKLAVA, one of the most notorious mistakes in British military history. It stemmed from Lord Lucan's misreading of an ambiguous order by the British commander, Lord Raglan. As a result, Lord CARDIGAN led the unsupported Light Brigade straight at a battery of Russian guns. More than 600 men took part, nearly half of whom died. The incident is commemorated in a famous poem (1855) by Alfred Tennyson. *See also* CRIMEAN WAR

Charlemagne *See* feature article

Charles II (the Bald) (823–77) Emperor of the West (875–77) and king of the West Franks (843–77), youngest son of LOUIS I (THE PIOUS). Louis' death (840) led to the Treaty of VERDUN (843) that partitioned the CAROLINGIAN empire between Charles II (the Bald), LOTHAIR I and LOUIS II (THE GERMAN). Charles gained the W part of the empire, Francia Occidentalis. On the death of Lothair II (869), Lotharingia was divided between Charles and Louis II (the German). After Emperor Louis II's death, Charles was recognized as emperor of the West. His reign as emperor was marked by conflict with Louis II (the German)'s eldest son, CARLOMAN. The kingdom of Francia Occidentalis passed to his son. Louis II (the Stammerer).

Charles III (the Fat) (839–88) Holy Roman emperor (881–87), youngest son of LOUIS II (THE GERMAN). In 880 he inherited the kingdom of Italy from his brother CARLOMAN. He gained the kingdom of the East Franks through the death (882) of his brother Louis (the Younger) and the kingdom of the West Franks through the death (884) of CHARLES II (THE BALD)'s grandson, Carloman. Through the death or incapacity of relatives, he inherited the kingdoms of the East and West Franks. Charles almost reunited the territories of Charlemagne in the 880s but was deposed by his nephew, ARNULF.

Charles IV (1316–78) Holy Roman emperor (1355–78) and king of Germany and Bohemia (1346–78), son of John of Luxembourg. He fought at the Battle of CRÈCY (1346), where his father was killed. The rivalry between the papacy and the WITTELSBACH Emperor LOUIS IV saw Pope CLEMENT VI sponsor the election of Charles as king of Germany. In 1356 Charles issued the GOLDEN BULL (in force until 1806) which codified the constitution of the HOLY ROMAN EMPIRE and established the role of the ELECTORS. He acquired Brandenburg and parts of Silesia and Lusatia through skilful diplomacy with his Wittelsbach and Habsburg rivals. He made Prague the capital of the Empire, founding Charles University (1348) and Hradčany Castle. The city centre still bears architectural stamp of the "Golden Bull" period. Charles was succeeded by his son, WENCESLAS.

CHARLEMAGNE (*c*.742–814)

Emperor of the West (800–14) and CAROLINGIAN king of the FRANKS (768–814), eldest son of PEPIN III (THE SHORT). On his father's death (768), Charlemagne inherited half the Frankish kingdom and annexed the remainder on the death (771) of his brother Carloman. He disinherited Carloman's two sons, who fled to the court of Desiderius, king of the LOMBARDS. Desiderius then conquered part of the papal lands and tried to assert the sons' claim to the land, but was defeated by Charlemagne. In 773 Charlemagne captured Pavia, N Italy, and declared himself king of the Lombards. Charlemagne undertook a long and brutal conquest and conversion of the pagan SAXONS (772–804), annexed Bavaria (788) and defeated the AVAR state of the middle Danube (791–96, 804). His invasion of Spain was less successful and the Basque massacre of his army at the Battle of Roncesvalles (778) is fictionalized into a "crusading" episode in the epic poem *La Chanson de Roland* (*c*.1100). In 800 Charlemagne was crowned as emperor by Pope LEO II, thus reviving the concept of the Roman Empire and confirming the separation of the West from the Eastern, BYZANTINE EMPIRE. From his court at Aachen (Aix-la-Chapelle), Charlemagne encouraged the spiritual and intellectual awakening of the CAROLINGIAN RENAISSANCE. He set up a strong central government, and maintained provincial control through court officials. In later life he attempted to learn to read. In 813 Charlemagne crowned his son, LOUIS I (THE PIOUS), co-emperor and successor. Following his death, Charlemagne attained legendary status. He was widely regarded as a model Christian king and emperor and honoured as a saint in some churches. *See also* CAROLINGIANS; CHARLES MARTEL; MEROVINGIANS

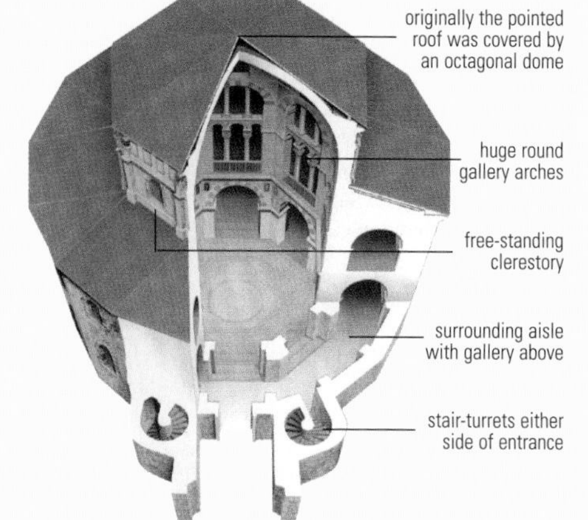

▲ **Palace Chapel at Aachen** Built to house Charlemagne's throne, the Palace Chapel was an architectural masterpiece of Carolingian Europe. It was partially constructed with materials imported from Rome and Ravenna. Charlemagne established his court here in 794.

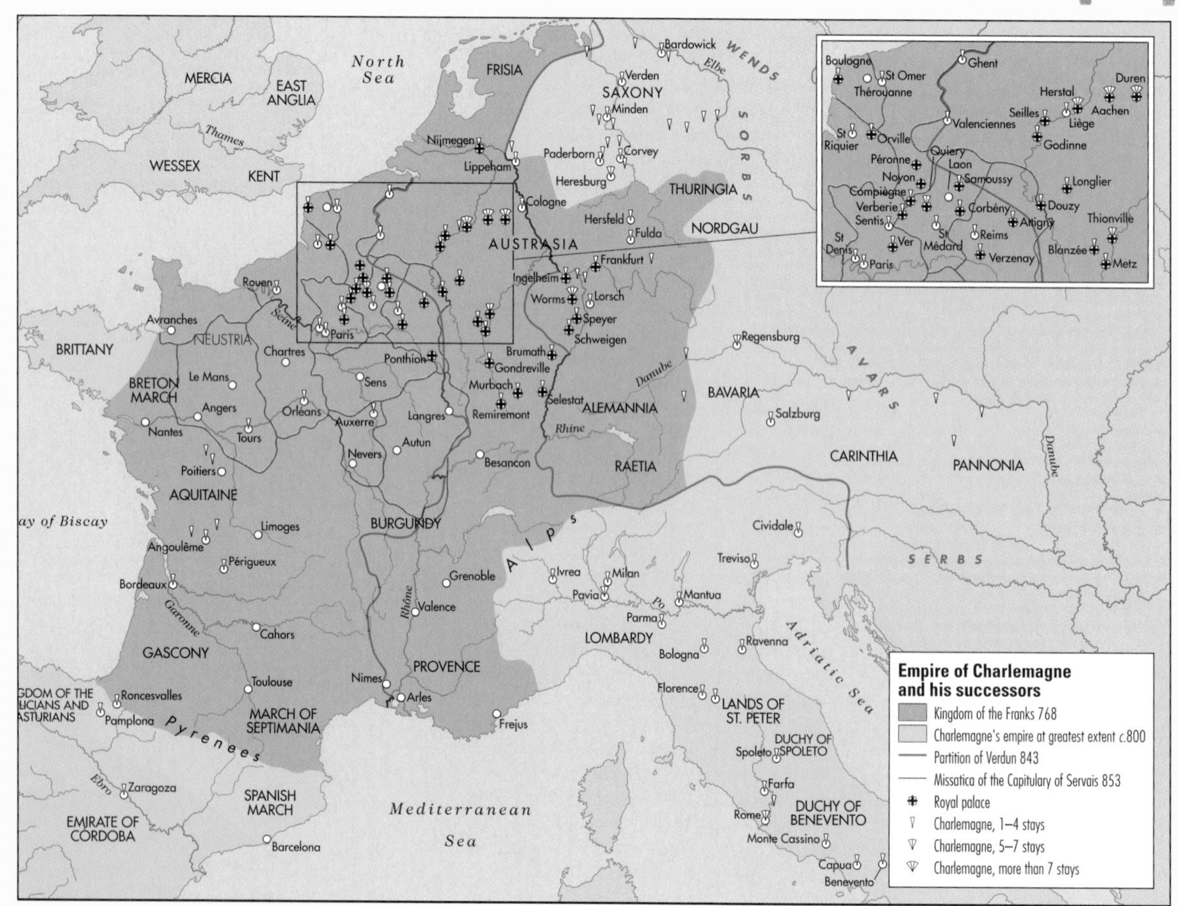

◄ **Royal tours** were a crucial form of government control in the Carolingian empire. As a young man, Charlemagne travelled on average 29km (18mi) a day and stayed regularly in all parts of his kingdom, thus enabling him to keep a close watch on his local representatives. Also performing this function were teams of inspectors (*missi*), each usually comprising a layman and a prominent cleric. Charlemagne's grandson, Charles the Bold (r.843–77), later evolved clearly designated areas of inspection (*missatica*) in the north.

Charles V (1500–58) Holy Roman emperor (1519–56) and king of Spain, as Charles I (1516–56), son of PHILIP I (THE HANDSOME) and Joanna the Mad, grandson of Emperor MAXIMILIAN I, MARY OF BURGUNDY, FERDINAND V and ISABELLA I. He inherited the largest European empire since the time of CHARLEMAGNE. In addition, the Spanish conquistadores made Charles master of a New World empire. The Netherlands, Luxembourg, Artois and Franché-Comte were devolved to him on the death (1506) of his father and Charles was raised in Flanders by MARGARET OF AUSTRIA. In 1516 Charles was proclaimed king of Spain. He secured his position in Spain by brutally crushing the Revolt of the COMUNEROS (1520–21). The Austrian HABSBURG lands came to him on the death (1519) of Maximilian I. Charles' efforts to unify these possessions were unsuccessful, largely due to three factors: the hostility of FRANCIS I of France, the advance of LUTHERANISM in Germany, and the OTTOMAN Turks in central Europe. In 1521 Charles invaded N Italy, relaunching the ITALIAN WARS with the VALOIS dynasty. Spanish hegemony in Italy was signalled by the capture of Francis I at the Battle of PAVIA (1525). The formation of the League of Cognac by France, the papacy, Venice and Milan prompted Charles to sack Rome (May 1527). The Treaty of CAMBRAI (1529) confirmed Spanish possessions in Italy and secured Charles' coronation as emperor (1530). Charles was faced with a Germany torn apart by social and religious discord. The PEASANTS' WAR (1524–25) was the largest popular uprising in European history. The scale and nature of Charles' other commitments initially prevented him from trying to stem the expansion of LUTHERANISM. The Council of TRENT (1545) provided the impetus for the COUNTER-REFORMATION and Charles defeated the Protestant SCHMALKALDIC LEAGUE at the Battle of Mühlberg (April 1547). At the Diet of Augsburg (1548), the Netherlands were incorporated into the Habsburg lands. The N German princes turned to HENRY II of France for support and Charles was forced to compromise at the Peace of AUGSBURG (1555). The accession (1520) of SULEIMAN I (THE MAGNIFICENT) marked the resurgence of Ottoman influence in Europe. Louis II of Hungary and Bohemia was defeated and killed by the Turks in the Battle of MOHÁCS (August 1526) and control of Bohemia passed to Charles' younger brother Ferdinand, later FERDINAND I. The Turks were a continual threat to Austria and Hungary, capturing Timişoara and laying siege to Vienna in 1532. Charles' counter-attacks were of limited success, seizing Tunis in 1535 but failing to take Algiers in 1541. In 1556 Charles retired to a monastery, handing Germany and the E Habsburg lands to Ferdinand and his other titles to his son, PHILIP II of Spain. *See also* REFORMATION

Charles VI (1685–1740) Holy Roman emperor (1711–40) and king of Hungary. His claim to the Spanish throne led to the outbreak (1701) of the War of the SPANISH SUCCESSION. In 1711 Charles inherited the HABSBURG lands and was elected emperor. PHILIP V, grandson of LOUIS XIV, was recognized as king of Spain at the Peace of UTRECHT (1713). Gains in Hungary and Serbia during the war (1714–16) with the Ottoman Empire were lost in a further conflict (1736–39). Charles was also defeated in the War of the POLISH SUCCESSION (1733–38). Charles promulgated the PRAGMATIC SANCTION (1713) to ensure the unity of the Habsburg Empire after his death, but the succession of his daughter, MARIA THERESA, led to the War of the AUSTRIAN SUCCESSION (1740–48).

Charles VII (1697–1745) Holy Roman emperor (1742–45) and elector of Bavaria (1726–45), son-in-law of Emperor JOSEPH I. He joined Prussia and France in the War of the AUSTRIAN SUCCESSION (1740–48) against MARIA THERESA.

Charles I (1887–1922) Last ruler of the AUSTRO-HUNGARIAN EMPIRE (1916–18) and king (as Charles IV) of Hungary (1916–18). He became heir to the throne of FRANZ JOSEPH on the assassination (1914) of his uncle, FRANZ FERDINAND. Charles failed to extricate Austria-Hungary from WORLD WAR I and the growth of nationalism within the Empire prefigured the collapse of the HABSBURG monarchy. His last-ditch attempt to save the Habsburg empire by federation failed to prevent Poland and Czechoslovakia declaring independence (October 1918). On 11 November 1918, Charles relinquished administration of the Empire and the Habsburg monarchy was at an end.

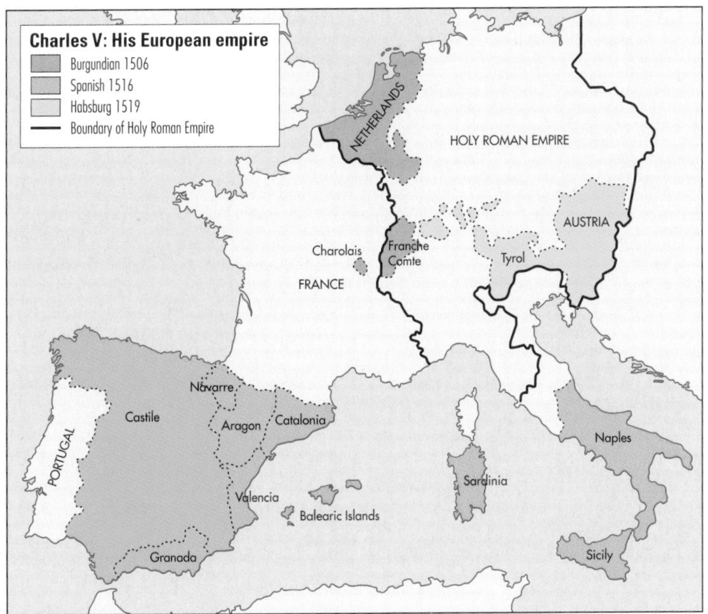

◀ **Charles V** This map illustrates how Charles V gained his vast European empire. In 1506, he succeeded his father, Philip, as Duke of Burgundy. In 1516, Charles inherited Spanish territories, including Majorca, Sicily and Naples, from his grandparents, Ferdinand of Aragón and Isabella of Castile. He was elected Holy Roman emperor in 1519. Charles strengthened his position in Italy with his conquest of Milan in 1522 and an alliance formed with the Genoese Republic in 1528. The defeat of French expeditions to Milan and Naples (1528–29) and the overthrow of the French-backed Florentine Republic in 1530 sealed Habsburg predominance in Italy as later French challenges proved largely ineffective.

C

Charles I (1600–49) King of England, Scotland and Ireland (1625–49), son of JAMES I. His marriage (1625) to HENRIETTA MARIA, sister of LOUIS XIII of France, raised fears of a Catholic succession to the throne among PURITAN leaders in Parliament. The disastrous failure (October 1625) of an expedition to Cádiz increased Parliament's hostility towards the Duke of BUCKINGHAM. Charles imposed a forced loan after Parliament refused to grant him further funds for the war against Spain and he was compelled to dissolve Parliament (June 1626) to prevent Buckingham's impeachment. Buckingham's failure to relieve the siege at La Rochelle during the HUGUENOT WARS exacerbated the parliament's grievances and Charles was forced to agree to the PETITION OF RIGHT (1628). Charles' insisted on the "divine right of kings" and adjourned Parliament in 1629 – he ruled without it for the next 11 years. With the support of the archbishop of Canterbury, William LAUD, Charles enforced harsh penalties on Puritans. When attempts to impose Anglican liturgy on Scotland led to the BISHOPS' WARS (1639, 1640), Charles was obliged to recall Parliament to raise revenue. The so-called SHORT PARLIAMENT (April 1640) refused to grant funds and was dissolved. Further defeats in Scotland led Charles to recall the assembly. The LONG PARLIAMENT insisted on imposing conditions, and impeached Charles' adviser, the Earl of STRAFFORD. In November 1641 it presented the GRAND REMONSTRANCE, listing their grievances against the king. Charles refused to relinquish control of the army and his attempt to arrest five leading opponents (including John PYM and John HAMPDEN) in the Commons precipitated the English CIVIL WAR. From his base at Oxford, S central England, Charles won early victories against the Parliamentarian army led by the Earl of ESSEX. The SOLEMN LEAGUE AND COVENANT (1643) between Parliament and the Scottish COVENANTERS forced the CAVALIERS to fight on two fronts. In 1645 Charles and Prince RUPERT suffered a succession of defeats by the NEW MODEL ARMY, under Sir Thomas FAIRFAX and Oliver CROMWELL. In 1646 Charles surrendered to the Covenanters. In 1647 he failed to escape to France and found himself a prisoner at Carisbrooke Castle on the Isle of Wight. In 1647 Charles reached a secret agreement with the Scots, promising to accept PRESBYTERIANISM in return for military support against Parliament. The second phase of the Civil War ended with Scottish defeat at the Battle of PRESTON (August 1648). In January 1649 he was tried for treason and hanged (30 January). *See also* PRIDE'S PURGE; ELIOT, JOHN; VANE, SIR HENRY

Charles II (1630–85) King of England, Scotland and Ireland (1660–85). After the execution of his father, CHARLES I, he fled to France but in 1650 was invited to Scotland by the COVENANTERS and crowned king in 1651. Charles' attempted invasion of England was repulsed at the Battle of WORCESTER, by Oliver CROMWELL, and he was forced back into exile. In 1660, with the help of Edward Hyde, Earl of CLARENDON, Charles issued the Declaration of BREDA, in which he promised religious toleration and an amnesty for his enemies. Parliament agreed to the Declaration, and Charles was crowned king in May 1660, ushering in the RESTORATION. He attempted to preserve royal power, accepting secret subsidies from LOUIS XIV of France in exchange for promoting Roman Catholicism. Charles' support of Louis led to the DUTCH WARS (1672–74). He clashed with Parliament over the Wars and his support for Catholics. Conflict was further fuelled by strong anti-Catholic feeling, manifest in the "Popish Plot" rumour spread by Titus OATES and the Exclusion Crisis (1679–81) when attempts were made to exclude Charles' brother, the Catholic Duke of York (later JAMES II), from the succession. Unable to resolve his

▲ **Charles I** portrait by Cornelius Janssen (1593–1664). Janssen was the leading English court painter in the early 17th century, but lost favour after the arrival of Van Dyke (1599–1641).

differences with Parliament, Charles dissolved it and ruled with financial support from Louis XIV. Known as the "Merry Monarch", Charles had many mistresses (including Nell Gwyn) but left no legitimate heir. *See also* MONMOUTH, JAMES SCOTT, DUKE OF

Charles III (the Simple) (879–929) Carolingian king of W Francia (893–922). At the death (888) of his cousin, CHARLES III (THE FAT), Charles had to struggle for the succession with Eudes, marcher lord of Neustria, who represented the rising interest of the Île de France and its defence against the VIKINGS. Eudes was crowned first, but was unable to prevent a Carolingian party recognizing Charles. Eudes died in 898. Charles later countered the Neustrians by entering into a treaty with the Viking warlord ROLLO at Saint-Claire-Sur-Epte (911). This gave Rollo the nucleus of the later "duchy of Normandy". Charles then retired E to Lotharingia, leaving a political vacuum in the W, soon filled by rival Neustrian claimants to royal power. In 929, Charles died a prisoner of the Neustrian king Raoul of Burgundy.

Charles IV (the Fair) (1294–1328) King of France (1322–28), brother and successor of PHILIP V. His sister, Isabella, married (1308) EDWARD II of England In 1324 Charles invaded Aquitaine, forcing England to grant him land and money (1327). The last king of the CAPETIAN dynasty, he was succeeded by PHILIP VI of the VALOIS line.

Charles V (the Wise) (1337–80) King of France (1364–80), son of JOHN II (THE GOOD). In the Anglo-French Settlement (1360), Charles was forced to grant most of SW France to EDWARD III of England and paid 3 million gold crowns for the release of his father. By 1375 Charles had regained most of the territory previously lost to the English in the HUNDRED YEARS' WAR (1337–1453). He strengthened royal authority by introducing a regular taxation system, standing army and powerful navy. Charles established a royal library at the Louvre and built the BASTILLE. Charles' support for CLEMENT VII aided the GREAT SCHISM. He was succeeded by his son, CHARLES VI (THE MAD).

Charles VI (the Mad) (1368–1422) King of France (1380–1422). Until 1388 he was controlled by his uncle, PHILIP II (THE BOLD) of Burgundy. From 1392 Charles suffered recurrent bouts of insanity. Philip and Louis d'Orléans, the king's brother, fought for control of the kingdom. Louis was murdered in 1407 and John (the Fearless), Duke of Burgundy, allied himself with HENRY V of England. English victories at AGINCOURT (1415) and elsewhere forced Charles to sign the Treaty of TROYES (1420), acknowledging Henry V as his successor.

Charles VII (the Well-served) (1403–61) King of France (1422–61), son of CHARLES VI (THE MAD). In 1418 he was forced to flee Paris for Bourges, where he assumed the title of regent. Charles was excluded from the throne by the Treaty of TROYES (1420). Charles established a rival administration S of the River Loire, while the N remained in English hands. With the support of JOAN OF ARC, he checked the English and Burgundians at Orléans and was crowned king at Reims (1429). By the Pragmatic Sanction of Bourges (1438) Charles restricted papal control of the French church. The Treaty of Arras (1435) ended the hostility of Burgundy, and by 1453 the English had been driven out of most of France. Charles was succeeded by his son, LOUIS XI.

Charles VIII (1470–98) King of France (1483–98), son and successor of LOUIS XI. Until 1491 he reigned under the regency of his sister, Anne de Beaujeu. In 1494 Charles invaded Italy, beginning the long ITALIAN WARS. In 1495 he entered Naples. A league of Italian states, the papacy and Spain forced him to retreat. One positive result was the introduction of Italian Renaissance culture into France. He was succeeded by his cousin, LOUIS XII.

Charles IX (1550–74) King of France (1560–74), brother and successor of FRANCIS II. He became king when only ten years old, and his mother, CATHERINE DE' MEDICI, acted as regent. Her authority waned when, in 1571, the young king fell under the influence of Gaspard de COLIGNY, leader of the HUGUENOTS. Coligny and thousands of his followers were slain in the SAINT BARTHOLOMEW'S DAY MASSACRE (1572), ordered by Charles at the instigation of his mother. He was succeeded by his brother, HENRY III. *See also* RELIGION, WARS OF

Charles X (1757–1836) King of France (1824–30), brother of LOUIS XVI and LOUIS XVIII. He fled France at the outbreak of the FRENCH REVOLUTION (1789) and remained in England until the BOURBON restoration (1814). Charles opposed the moderate policies of Louis XVIII and, after the assassination of Charles' son in 1820, his reactionary forces triumphed. In 1825 he signed a law indemnifying ÉMIGRÉS for land confiscated during the Revolution. In 1830 Charles issued the July Ordinances, which restricted suffrage and press freedom, and dissolved the newly elected chamber of deputies. The people rebelled in the JULY REVOLUTION, and Charles was forced to abdicate in favour of LOUIS PHILIPPE.

Charles I (1288–1342) King of Hungary (1308–42), son of Charles Martel of Anjou-Naples. He restored order, encouraged trade and the expansion of cities, and acquired Bosnia and Serbia. Charles also imposed the first direct tax. His marriage to the sister of CASIMIR III (THE GREAT) ensured the succession of his son, LOUIS I (THE GREAT), to the Polish throne.

Charles I (1226–85) King of Naples and Sicily (1266–85), son of LOUIS VIII of France and first of the ANGEVIN dynasty. He overthrew the HOHENSTAUFEN dynasty in Naples and Sicily and was crowned by Pope INNOCENT IV. Charles allied himself with BALDWIN II, the deposed Latin emperor of the East. He moved into Greece, became Prince of Achaia (1278–85) and extended his territory into the Morea and Albania. His transfer of power from Palermo and the imposition of French officials led to his deposition during the rebellion of the SICILIAN VESPERS (1282).

Charles I (1836–1908) King of Portugal (1889–1908), son and successor of Louis I. His submission to the imperial might of Britain and Germany in Africa led to a republican revolt (1891). In 1906 Charles set up a military dictatorship under João Franco. Charles and his eldest son were assassinated by opponents of the oppressive regime, and his second son, Manuel II, succeeded to the throne.

Charles Kings of Romania. *See* CAROL I; CAROL II

Charles II (the Mad) (1661–1700) King of Spain, Naples and Sicily (1665–1700), son and successor of PHILIP IV. The last of the Spanish HABSBURGS, Charles was mentally incompetent and reigned under the regency of his mother, Mariana of Austria, and his illegitimate half-brother, John of Austria. During his reign, Spain was greatly weakened by the War of DEVOLUTION and the War of the GRAND ALLIANCE. His death precipitated the War of the SPANISH SUCCESSION.

Charles III (1716–88) King of Spain (1759–88) and of Naples and Sicily (1735–59), son of PHILIP V and Elizabeth Farnese. In 1734 he conquered Naples and Sicily. Charles inherited the Spanish crown from his half-brother FERDINAND VI. He handed Naples and Sicily to his son, Ferdinand I. Charles was an "enlightened despot". He encouraged commercial and agrarian reform, and brought the Spanish Catholic Church under state control, expelling the Jesuits in 1767. Allied with France in the SEVEN YEARS' WAR (1756–63) against Britain, he lost Florida but gained Louisiana in 1763. He was succeeded by his son, CHARLES IV. *See also* POLISH SUCCESSION, WAR OF THE

Charles IV (1748–1819) King of Spain (1788–1808), son and successor of CHARLES III. Unable to cope with the upheavals of the NAPOLEONIC WARS, Charles virtually turned over government to his wife, MARÍA LUISA, and her lover, Manuel de GODOY. The occupation of Spain by French troops in the PENINSULAR WAR led to Charles' abdication in favour of his son, FERDINAND VII, who in turn was forced from the throne by NAPOLEON I's brother, Joseph BONAPARTE.

Charles IX (1550–1611) King of Sweden (1604–11), youngest son of GUSTAVUS I (VASA). He opposed the Catholicism of his brother, JOHN III. On John's death (1592), Charles became regent for John's son, SIGISMUND III (VASA). At the Convention of Uppsala (1593), Charles re-established LUTHERANISM as the state religion. Sigismund rejected the Convention and civil war ensued. In 1598 Sigismund was defeated and deposed by Charles. In 1600 Charles invaded Livonia, starting a 60-year conflict with Poland. He also embarked on the disastrous KALMAR WAR (1611–13) with Denmark. Charles was succeeded by his son, GUSTAVUS II.

Charles X (1622–60) (Charles Gustavus) King of Sweden (1654–60). He ascended the throne when his cousin, Queen CHRISTINA, abdicated. Charles' efforts to dominate the Baltic resulted in the First NORTHERN WAR (1655–60). His victories in Poland, gaining Warsaw and Kraków (1655), brought Russia, Brandenburg, the Netherlands and Denmark into the war. Charles responded by invading Denmark, occupying Jutland (1657). By the Treaty of Roskilde (1658), Sweden recovered all of its S provinces from Denmark. He was succeeded by his son, CHARLES XI.

Charles XI (1655–97) King of Sweden (1660–97), son and successor of CHARLES X. A council of regency ruled until he reached his majority (1672). In the third of the DUTCH WARS (1672–78), FREDERICK WILLIAM of Brandenburg gained Swedish Pomerania (1675). A succession of Swedish victories led to the Peace of Lund (1679) and the unification of Scandinavia by Charles' marriage (1680) to Princess Ulrika of Denmark. In 1680 Charles restricted the power of the nobility by the restoration of alienated crown lands. He maintained Sweden's neutrality during the War of the Grand Alliance (1689–97). His son succeeded him as CHARLES XII.

Charles XII (1682–1718) King of Sweden (1697–1718), son and successor of CHARLES XI. At the outbreak of the Great NORTHERN WAR (1700–21), a coalition force from Denmark, Saxony, Poland and Russia attacked Sweden. Charles' officers conducted a series of brilliant campaigns in defence of his lands. First, Sweden attacked Zealand, forcing Denmark to sue for peace (August 1700). Second, the Russian army of PETER I (THE GREAT) was crushed at the Battle of Narva (November 1700). Finally, Sweden invaded Poland, scattering the troops of AUGUSTUS II (THE STRONG). Charles then assumed personal command of the army and continued to wage war on Poland, forcing the abdication of Augustus in 1704. In 1708 Charles renewed his assault on Russia, but his army, depleted by the severe winter, was decisively defeated at the Battle of POLTAVA (1709). He fled to the Ottomans and persuaded the sultan to attack Russia (1711). The sultan turned against him and, in disguise, Charles escaped back to Sweden in 1714. He was killed in the invasion of Norway and was succeeded by his sister, Ulrika Eleanora.

Charles XIII (1748–1818) King of Sweden (1809–18) and Norway (1814–18). Charles became regent on the assassination (1792) of his brother, GUSTAVUS III, and king on the abdication of his nephew Gustavus IV. Charles accepted a new constitution, limiting the power of the monarchy. He ceded Finland to Russia and signed treaties with Denmark and France. Charles was succeeded by Marshal Bernadotte, as CHARLES XIV.

Charles XIV (1763–1844) (Jean Baptiste Bernadotte) King of Sweden and Norway (1818–44), b. France. He fought in the French Revolutionary Wars and in the Napoleonic battles of AUSTERLITZ (1805) and WAGRAM (1809). In effective control of Sweden from 1810, Charles joined the Allies against NAPOLEON I at the Battle of LEIPZIG (1814) and forced Denmark to cede Norway to Sweden in the Treaty of Kiel (1814). In 1818 he succeeded CHARLES XIII as king. His subsequent reign brought peace and prosperity to Sweden, and he founded the present Swedish dynasty.

Charles XV (1826–72) King of Sweden and Norway (1858–72), son and successor of Oscar I. He instituted reforms in communal, ecclesiastical and criminal laws. Charles created a bicameral parliament and advocated "Scandinavianism" – the political union of Sweden, Norway and Denmark. He failed, however, to keep his promise of military help to Denmark in the Schleswig-Holstein affair (1864).

Charles XVI (1946–) King of Sweden (1973–), grandson and successor of GUSTAVUS VI. In 1947 his father, Prince Gustavus Adolphus, was killed in an airplane crash. A descendant of CHARLES XIV, Charles' role is purely constitutional. He contributes to debates on

Sweden's foreign affairs, labour and industry. In 1976 he married a German commoner, Silva Sommerlath.

Charles (Prince of Wales) (1948–) Heir to the British throne, eldest son of ELIZABETH II. In 1969 he was invested as Prince of Wales at Caernarvon. In 1981 Charles married Lady DIANA Spencer. The fairy-tale marriage rapidly and publicly disintegrated. Their eldest son, Prince William (1982–), is second in line to the throne. Charles is well-known for his work with charities, such as the Prince's Trust, and for his advocacy of community architecture.

Charles IV (1604–75) Duke of Lorraine. Charles succeeded to the Duchy in 1624, but because of French domination and the turmoil of the THIRTY YEARS' WAR (1618–48), he was often out of power. In 1633 France occupied Nancy and forced Charles to abdicate in favour of his brother. Charles regained the Duchy by the Treaty of Saint-Germain (1641), but Lorraine was overrun in 1648. He was imprisoned by the Spanish (1654–59). Charles was restored as duke by LOUIS XIV of France in 1661, but was finally expelled from the Duchy by the French in 1670.

Charles V (1643–90) Duke of Lorraine, nephew of CHARLES IV of Lorraine. Although Charles succeeded to his title in 1675, LOUIS XIV of France refused to allow him to rule. He was twice a candidate for the Polish crown (1669, 1674). From 1664 Charles served in the army of the Holy Roman Empire, commanding the imperial forces in the third of the DUTCH WARS (1672–78) and in the defence of Vienna against the Ottoman Turks (1683).

Charles Albert (1798–1849) King of Sardinia-Piedmont (1831–49). He was a liberal reformist who opposed Austria and sought Italian liberation. After defeat by Austria (1848–49), Charles abdicated in favour of his son, VICTOR EMMANUEL II. *See also* CAVOUR, CAMILLE BENSO, CONTE DI; RISORGIMENTO

Charles Augustus (1757–1828) Duke of Saxe-Weimar-Eisenach (1775–1828). He fought against NAPOLEON I and was an important member of the Congress of VIENNA (1815). In 1815 Charles was raised to the position of a grand duke and drew up a liberal constitution. He was a patron of Schiller and Goethe.

Charles Edward Stuart *See* STUART, CHARLES EDWARD

Charles Emmanuel I (the Great) (1562–1630) Duke of Savoy (1580–1630). Throughout his career, Charles switched allegiance between France and Spain. During the THIRTY YEARS' WAR (1618–48), he first fought with the enemies of the HABSBURGS, but then went over to the Spanish side (1627), where he suffered military defeat.

Charles Emmanuel III (1701–73) Duke of Savoy and king (Charles Emmanuel I) of Sardinia (1730–73). Siding with France and Spain in the War of the POLISH SUCCESSION, he defeated the Austrians at Guastalla (1734) and obtained Novara and Tortona in Italy (1738). In the War of the AUSTRIAN SUCCESSION (1740–48), Charles sided against Spain and in the Treaty of AIX-LA-CHAPELLE (1748) received Vigevano in Italy.

Charles Martel (688–741) Frankish ruler, grandfather of CHARLEMAGNE. After seizing power in a palace coup in AUSTRASIA, he led the FRANKS' reconquest of NEUSTRIA, Burgundy, Aquitaine and Provence, and established them as the rulers of GAUL. Charles defeated the Moors at the Battle of Poitiers (732). His son succeeded him as PEPIN III (THE SHORT). *See also* CAROLINGIANS; MEROVINGIANS

Charles of Lorraine (1712–80) French general and prince of Lorraine, brother-in-law of Empress MARIA THERESA. He joined the Austrian army in 1736 and campaigned against the Turks (1737–39) and fought in the War of the AUSTRIAN SUCCESSION (1740–48). Charles served as governor of the Austrian Netherlands (1744–57). During the SEVEN YEARS' WAR (1756–63), Charles led the Austrian forces until his defeat by the Prussians at Leuther (December 1757).

Charles the Bold (1433–77) Last reigning duke of Burgundy (1467–77), son and successor of PHILIP III (THE GOOD). His reign was dominated by enmity with LOUIS XI of France. In 1468 Charles married Margaret of York, EDWARD IV of England's sister. Charles aimed to re-establish the old kingdom of Lotharingia (LORRAINE), by conquering Alsace and Lorraine. In 1473 Charles purchased upper Alsace, prompting the Swiss cantons to declare war. He failed to persuade Emperor FREDERICK III to crown him king of Burgundy and was defeated and killed by the Swiss at Nancy. His death eliminated Burgundy as a political power.

Charleston City and port in SE South Carolina, United States. Founded in the 1670s by William Sayle, it became the major SE seaport. The South Carolina Ordinance of Secession was signed here (1860), and the firing on FORT SUMTER was the first engagement of the American CIVIL WAR. It has many colonial buildings and the Fort Sumter National Monument. It is the site of a major naval base. Pop. (1990) 80,414.

Chartism (1838–48) British working-class movement for parliamentary reform. Combining the discontent of industrial workers with the demands of radical artisans, the movement adhered to the People's Charter (1838), which demanded electoral reform including universal male suffrage. The movement, led chiefly by Feargus O'CONNOR, was born partly in response to the POOR LAW (1834). In February 1839 it formed a People's Parliament to draft a petition. In November 1839, an armed uprising at Newport, Wales, was crushed and the Chartist leaders were imprisoned or deported. In 1840 O'Connor formed the National Charter Association (NCA) that presented a further petition in 1842. The movement faded away after a major demonstration in 1848. *See also* ANTI-CORN LAW LEAGUE

Chase, Salmon Portland (1808–73) US jurist and politician, sixth chief justice of the United States (1864–73). His work on behalf of runaway slaves earned him the epithet "attorney general of fugitive slaves". Chase was the first Republican governor of Ohio (1855–59). He served as secretary of the treasury (1861–64) in President Abraham LINCOLN's wartime Cabinet. As chief justice, Chase presided (1868) over the Senate impeachment proceedings against President Andrew JOHNSON. His dissenting opinion in the Slaughterhouse Cases (1873) held that the 14th Amendment protected all US citizens from state violations of their rights. *See also* FUGITIVE-SLAVE LAWS

Chase, Samuel (1741–1811) US jurist, associate justice of the Supreme Court (1796–1811). A signer of the Declaration of Independence and member of the Maryland Assembly (1764–84), he was appointed associate justice by President George WASHINGTON. A Federalist, Chase's partisan conduct at the trials of two Jeffersonians led President Thomas JEFFERSON to move for his impeachment (1804). Chase was acquitted on the grounds that federal judges could not be removed on purely political grounds.

Chateaubriand, François René, Vicomte de (1768–1848) French writer and diplomat whose works contributed to French ROMANTICISM. In 1791 he travelled to the United States, and the American wilderness provides the backdrop for his tragic love stories *Atala* (1801) and *René* (1805). Chateaubriand's *Essay on Revolutions* (1797) is a personal account of events in world history. His literary reputation was established with *The Genius of Christianity* (1802), a reaction to ENLIGHTENMENT attacks on Catholicism. Chateaubriand briefly served (1803–04) under NAPOLEON I. He returned to government after the restoration of the BOURBONS (1814) and served as minister of foreign affairs (1823–24). Chateaubriand's *Memoirs From Beyond the Grave* (1849–50) is a vivid, first-hand account of 19th-century French history.

Chatham, William Pitt, 1st Earl of *See* PITT (THE ELDER), WILLIAM

Chattanooga, Battle of (23–25 November 1863) One of the most decisive engagements in the American CIVIL WAR, fought at the vital Confederate supply depot in Chattanooga, SE Tennessee, United States. At the Battle of Chickamauga (September 1863), General Braxton BRAGG had scored one of the few Confederate victories in the West (*c.*16,170 Union losses, *c.*18,454 Confederate dead), forcing the Union army to retreat to Chattanooga. A tactical error, however, enabled a Union reinforcement by General Joseph HOOKER and General William SHERMAN. General Ulysses GRANT attacked and captured Bragg's positions on Lookout Mountain and Missionary Ridge. Although losses were relatively slight (*c.*5824 Union and 6667 Confederate), the route had been opened for Sherman's march to ATLANTA and SAVANNAH.

Chautauqua movement US adult education movement that flourished in the latter part of the 19th century. The name comes from Lake Chautauqua, New York, where summer courses began in 1874. At the height of the movement, more than 100 centres and many travelling groups offered education and entertainment to millions.

Chávez, Cesar Estrada (1927–93) US union leader. He was a migrant farm labourer in Arizona and California. In 1962 Chávez founded the National Farm Workers Association (NFWA), which in 1966 merged with the Agricultural Workers Organizing Committee of the AMERICAN FEDERATION OF LABOR AND CONGRESS OF INDUSTRIAL ORGANIZATIONS (AFL-CIO), to become the United Farm Workers of America (UFW). In 1968–70 he led a successful national boycott of California grapes.

Chavín One of the earliest prehistoric cultures in Peru, lasting from *c.*1000 to *c.*200 BC. Named after Chavín de Huántar, the centre of a major religious cult in N Peru, the Chavín developed excellent stone sculpture, the earliest goldwork yet found in the Americas and some ceramics that, whether judged by technological or aesthetic standards, were remarkable.

Chechenia (formerly Checheno-Ingush Republic) Republic of the Russian Federation, in the N Caucasus; the capital is Grozny. The Chechens, who are Sunni Muslims, fiercely resisted tsarist Russia's conquest of the Caucasus, even after absorption in 1859. In the 1920s separate autonomous regions were created by the Soviet Union for the Chechen and Ingush peoples. In 1934 the two were united to form a single region which, in 1936, became the Checheno-Ingush Autonomous Republic. In 1943–44 the republic was dissolved because of alleged collaboration with the German occupying forces in World War 2. In 1957 the region was reconstituted. In 1991 the Checheno-Ingush Republic split in two, and General Dudayev was elected president of Chechenia. In 1994, following a period of bloody internal strife, Russia invaded but met fierce resistance. In 1995 Russian troops completed the capture of Grozny at the cost of *c.*25,000 civilian lives. This led to a protracted guerrilla war that ended with Chechenia achieving *de facto* independence in 1997. In 1999 Russia launched further attacks on Chechenia, destroying Grozny and subduing the Chechen rebels. Pop. (1992) 1,308,000.

Cheka First secret police force in the Soviet Union. Formed shortly after the Russian Revolution (1917). A ferocious reign of terror alienated many BOLSHEVIK organizations and it was disbanded in 1922, replaced first by the GPU and then by the KGB. *See also* BERIA, LAVRENTI PAVLOVICH

Chelmsford, Frederick John Napier Thesiger, 1st Viscount (1868–1933) British colonial administrator, viceroy of India (1916–21). Chelmsford and Edwin Samuel Montagu prepared the MONTAGU-CHELMSFORD REPORT (1918) that advocated a measure of self-government for India. In 1919, following a series of civil disturbances, Chelmsford imposed martial law and interned many Indian nationalists.

Chen Duxiu (1879–1942) (Ch'en Tu'hsiu) Chinese politician and educator. He was influential in the MAY FOURTH MOVEMENT to establish a Chinese culture distinctive from CONFUCIANISM. Chen led the Chinese COMMUNIST PARTY from 1921 to 1927, taking it into alliance with the KUOMINTANG. At the start of the Chinese Civil War, Chen was replaced as leader by MAO ZEDONG. He was imprisoned (1933–37) by the Nationalist government.

Chennai (formerly Madras) City on the Bay of Bengal, SE India; capital of Tamil Nadu state. India's second-largest port and fourth-largest city, Chennai was founded (1639) as a British trading post. As Fort St George, it became the seat of the English EAST INDIA COMPANY and rapidly developed as a commercial centre. It was occupied by the French in 1746, but returned to Britain in 1748. The harbour was constructed in the second half of the 19th century. Pop. (1991) 3,841,396.

Chen Yi (1901–72) Chinese communist general and statesman. He joined the Chinese Communist Party in the

1920s, rising to command the Fourth Red Army. A close associate of ZHOU ENLAI, Chen was mayor of Shanghai (1949–58). He succeeded Zhou as foreign minister (1958–1966). Chen Yi was denounced during the CULTURAL REVOLUTION.

Cheops (Khufu) (active early 25th century BC) Second king of the Fourth dynasty in ancient EGYPT (*c*.2575–*c*.2465 BC). He is chiefly remembered for his tomb, the Great Pyramid at Giza, near Cairo. The largest and most famous of the PYRAMIDS, it is *c*.146m (480ft) high and 236.2m (776ft) square. It is made up of 2.3 million limestone blocks each weighing 2.5 tonnes, fitted together with astonishing precision. The pyramid was one of the SEVEN WONDERS OF THE WORLD.

Chernenko, Konstantin Ustinovich (1911–85) Soviet statesman, president (1984–85). A close ally of Leonid BREZHNEV, he joined the Politburo in 1978. Chernenko succeeded Yuri ANDROPOV as president and general secretary of the COMMUNIST PARTY OF THE SOVIET UNION (CPSU). He died after only 13 months in office and was succeeded by Mikhail GORBACHEV.

Chernobyl (Ukrainian, Chornobyl) City on the River Pripyat, N central Ukraine. It is 20km (12mi) from the Chernobyl power plant. On 26 April 1986 an explosion in one of the plant's reactors released 8 tonnes of radioactive material into the atmosphere. Within the first few hours, 31 people died. Fallout spread across E and N Europe, contaminating much agricultural produce. Containment efforts began with the evacuation of more than 100,000 people from the vicinity of the plant. The reactor was encased in cement and boron. About 25,000 local inhabitants have died prematurely. Two of the three remaining reactors were reworking by the end of 1986. In 1991 Ukraine pledged to shut down the plant, but energy needs dictated its continued output. In 1994 the West pledged economic aid to ensure the plant's closure. *See also* THREE MILE ISLAND

Chernomyrdin, Viktor (1938–) Russian statesman, prime minister (1992–98). A member (1986–90) of the central committee of the COMMUNIST PARTY OF THE SOVIET UNION (CPSU), he became prime minister despite the objections of Boris YELTSIN. Chernomyrdin broadly supported economic reform but was critical of the pace of privatization. Yeltsin's illness meant that Chernomyrdin acted as caretaker-president throughout much of 1996–97. After his dismissal as prime minister, Chernomyrdin acted as Russia's chief negotiator in diplomatic efforts to end the war in Kosovo.

Chernov, Viktor (1876–1952) Russian revolutionary, one of the founders of the Socialist Revolutionary Party. In 1917 he was minister of agriculture in the provisional government of Alexander KERENSKY and briefly headed the constitutional assembly of 1918. Chernov was an anti-BOLSHEVIK and tried to establish a moderate government in the city of Samara (now Kuibyshev). He went into exile in 1920.

Chernyshevski, Nikolai Gavrilovich (1828–89) Russian social reformer and writer. A follower of Vissarion Belinsky and the nihilists, he was convicted of revolutionary activities in 1862 and exiled to Siberia until 1883. In Siberia, Chernyshevski wrote *What Is to Be Done?* (1863), which presented utopian schemes of social revolution. *See also* UTOPIANISM

Cherokee Largest tribe of NATIVE NORTH AMERICANS in the United States, member of the Iroquoian language family. The Cherokee migrated S into the Appalachian region of Tennessee, Georgia and the Carolinas. They sided with the British during the AMERICAN REVOLUTION. When gold was discovered on their land in Georgia in the 1830s, the Cherokee were forced to move W. This tragic "Trail of Tears" (1838) reduced the population by 25%. One of the Five Civilized Tribes, *c*.47,000 Cherokee descendants now live in Oklahoma and *c*.3000 in North Carolina.

Chesapeake US frigate halted (22 June 1807) outside US territorial waters by the British ship HMS *Leopard*. US commander James Barron refused to allow the British to search the *Chesapeake* for deserters. The *Leopard* opened fire on the *Chesapeake*, forcing Barron to surrender and allow the impressment of four seamen, including two Americans. US politicians were united in their condemnation of the British action.

Chetniks (Serbo-Croat, *Cetnik*) Serbian guerrilla force initially formed to resist the German occupation of Serbia. Under the leadership of Draža MIHAILOVIĆ, the Chetniks concentrated instead on fighting communist Partisans led by Marshal TITO. The Allies switched their allegiance to the Partisans. In March 1946 Mihailović was captured and executed.

Chevreuse, Marie de Rohan-Montbazon, Duchesse de (1600–79) French politician, wife of CHARLES IV, Duke of Lorraine. A close friend of ANNE OF AUSTRIA, wife of LOUIS XIII, she was exiled (1626–28) for intriguing against Cardinal RICHELIEU and in 1633 for betraying state secrets to Spain. Chevreuse returned to France in 1643 but was again exiled for plotting to assassinate Cardinal MAZARIN. In 1649, soon after the start of the FRONDE, she returned to Paris.

Cheyenne Native North American tribe. Tribal competition forced them to migrate W from Minnesota along the Cheyenne River. The tribe split (*c*.1830), with the Northern Cheyenne remaining near the Platte River and the Southern Cheyenne settling near the Arkansas River. Following the Colorado Gold Rush (1858), they were restricted to a reservation. War broke out following a US army massacre of Cheyenne (1864). Colonel George CUSTER crushed the Southern Cheyenne, but the Northern Cheyenne helped in his eventual defeat at LITTLE BIGHORN (1876). In 1877 the Cheyenne surrendered and were forced to move to Montana where *c*.2000 remain.

Chiang Ching-kuo (1909–88) Taiwanese statesman, president (1978–88), eldest son of CHIANG KAI-SHEK. He rose rapidly through the ranks of the KUOMINTANG. Chiang was minister of defence (1965–72) and premier

CHILE

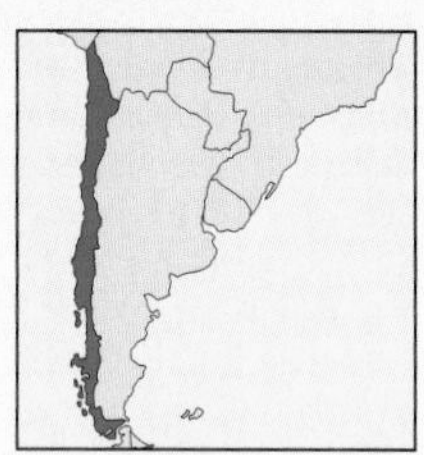

Republic in SW South America. The first inhabitants reached the S tip of South America more than 11,000 years ago. In 1520 Ferdinand MAGELLAN became the first European to sight Chile. In 1541 Pedro de VALDIVIA founded Santiago. Despite strong resistance from the ARAUCANIAN peoples, Chile became a Spanish colony. Native South Americans were forced into bonded labour on colonial ranches.

In 1817 an army, led by José de SAN MARTÍN, surprised the Spanish at the Battle of CHACABUCO, and Bernardo O'HIGGINS proclaimed Chile's independence in 1818. His dictatorship was followed by democratic reforms. In the War of the PACIFIC (1879–84), Chile gained mineral-rich areas from Peru and Bolivia. In the late 19th century Chile's economy rapidly industrialized, but a succession of autocratic regimes and its dependence on nitrate exports hampered growth. In 1964 Eduardo FREI of the Christian Democratic Party was elected. Frei embarked on a process of reform, such as assuming a majority share in the US-owned copper mines. In 1970 Salvador ALLENDE was elected president. He introduced many socialist policies, such as land reform and the nationalization of industries. In 1973 soaring inflation and public disturbances led to a military coup, with covert US backing. Allende and many of his supporters were executed. General Augusto PINOCHET assumed control and instigated a series of sweeping market reforms and pro-Western foreign-policy initiatives. In 1977 Pinochet banned all political parties. His regime was characterized by repression and human-rights violations, and many political opponents simply "disappeared". In 1980 a new constitution was introduced, and free elections were held in 1989. Patricio Aylwyn was elected president, but Pinochet remained as commander of the armed forces until 1997. In 1993 Eduardo Frei Ruiz-Tagle was elected president. Despite the progress of social liberalization, there was continuing tension between the government and army. Between 1998 and 2000 Pinochet was held in England on charges of "crimes of genocide and terrorism". In 2000 Ricardo Lagos became the first socialist president of Chile since Allende.

AREA: 756,950sq km (292,258sq mi)
POPULATION: 13,599,000
CAPITAL (POPULATION): Santiago (4,385,381)
GOVERNMENT: Multiparty republic
ETHNIC GROUPS: Mestizo 92%, Native American 7%
LANGUAGES: Spanish (official)
RELIGIONS: Christianity (Roman Catholic 81%, Protestant 6%)
GDP PER CAPITA (1994): US$3685

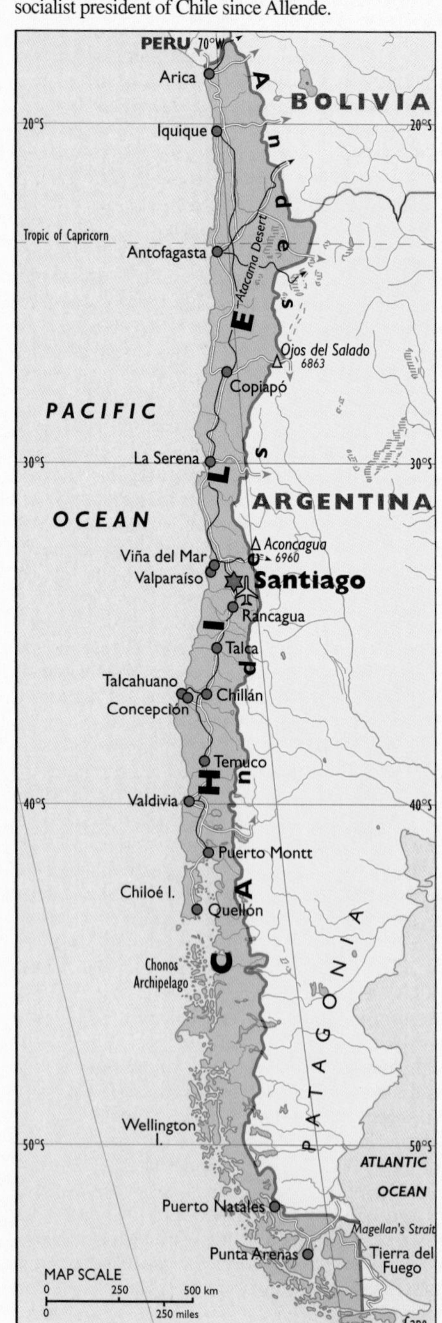

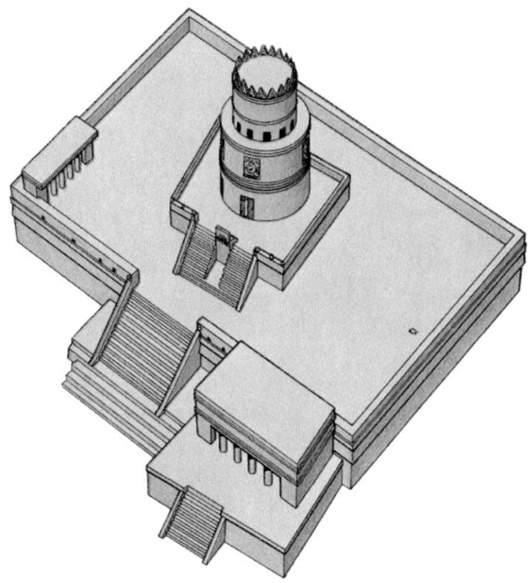

▲ **Chichén Itzá** A conjectural reconstruction of the Mayan astronomical observatory at Chichén Itzá, named El Caracol by the Spaniards; the stairway inside resembled a snail's shell.

(1972–78) before becoming president. He began the process of democratization in TAIWAN.

Chiang Kai-shek (1887–1975) (Jiang Jieshi) Chinese nationalist leader. He fought in the revolution that toppled the QING dynasty. In 1918 Chiang joined the KUOMINTANG and founded the Whampoa Military Academy in 1923. In 1925 Chiang succeeded SUN YAT-SEN as leader of the Kuomintang. He set out to reunify China by defeating the northern warlords. He broke the alliance with the Chinese COMMUNIST PARTY (1927) and formed a nationalist government in Nanjing (1928). Despite the Japanese occupation of MANCHURIA (1931), Chiang concentrated on trying to destroy the communists. In 1937 he was forced to renew the alliance with the Communist Party in order to fight Japan. In 1945 Japan surrendered and civil war resumed. In 1948 Chiang was elected president of China, but the communists led by MAO ZEDONG drove his government into exile in TAIWAN (1949). Here, with US support, Chiang established a dictatorship and maintained that the Kuomintang were the legitimate Chinese government. He remained president of Taiwan until his death. *See also* CHIANG CHING-KUO

Chibcha (Muisca) Native South American culture that flourished (*c.*AD 1000–*c.*1500) in the high valleys of Colombia. There was a greater degree of political organization than anywhere else in South America outside the INCA Empire. The Chibcha (pop. *c.*750,000) developed city-states and excelled in craftwork. The people were conquered by the Spanish (1536–41). Today, Chibcha refers to a Native American language family, whose speakers inhabit S Panama and N Colombia.

Chicago City on the SW shore of Lake Michigan, NE Illinois, United States. In the late 18th century, it was a trading post and became Fort Dearborn military post (1803). With the construction of the Erie Canal and railroads, and the opening up of the prairies, Chicago attracted settlers and industry. In 1871 large areas of the city were destroyed by fire. Chicago became a noted cultural centre in the late 19th century, during which the Chicago Symphony Orchestra (1891) and several literary magazines were established. Chicago has the largest rail terminal in the world, and the world's busiest airport, O'Hare. The world's first skyscraper was built here in 1885 and, until 1996, the Sears Tower was the world's tallest building, at 443m (1454ft). Pop. (1990) 2,783,726.

Chichén Itzá Chief city and shrine of MAYA and TOLTEC peoples between the 9th and 13th centuries AD, in Yucatán, Mexico. The earlier Maya city was abandoned *c.*900. The new Toltec city was built *c.*1.5km (1mi) away. Remains include temple-pyramids, a court for ball games and a sacrificial well. In *c.*1200 Chichén Itzá lost its pre-eminence to nearby Mayapan.

Chichimec Native Middle American peoples who invaded the valley of Mexico in the 12th and 13th centuries AD, bringing an end to the TOLTEC culture. They included the AZTECS.

Chickasaw Muskogean-speaking Native North Americans, who originated in Mississippi and Tennessee and who cultivated corn. One of the Five Civilized Tribes, in the 1830s the Chickasaw were resettled in Indian Territory (now Oklahoma). Today, they number *c.*9000.

Chi'en-lung Alternative transliteration for QIANLONG

Chifley, Joseph Benedict (1885–1951) Australian statesman, prime minister (1945–49). He entered Parliament as a Labor member in 1928. Chifley served as defence minister (1929–31) and federal treasurer (1941–45), before succeeding John CURTIN as prime minister. He continued the policy of nationalization and expanded social services.

Child, Sir John (d.1690) English administrator in India. The first person to control all of the English EAST INDIA COMPANY's factories in India (1686–90), Child used military power to gain territory for the company. His unscrupulous behaviour led to rebellion and war. Child was deputy governor of Bombay (1679–81) and president of Surat (1682–90). He was dismissed as a precondition of the terms of surrender in his defeat by AURANGZEB, MUGHAL emperor of Delhi.

Childebert I (d.558) MEROVINGIAN king of Paris (511–58), son of CLOVIS I. On the death of Clovis (511), the Frankish kingdom was shared out equally between Childebert and his three brothers. On the death (524) of his brother Clodomir, Childebert and his remaining brother, CLOTAIRE I, portioned his land and in 534 they conquered Burgundy and Provence. *See also* FRANKS

Childeric I (*c.*436–81) King of the Salian FRANKS (458–81). With Roman aid, he defeated the VISIGOTHS at Orléans (463). Childeric later defeated the SAXONS and the ALEMANNI. He was succeeded by his son, CLOVIS I. In 1653 his tomb was found at his capital near Tournai, Belgium. *See also* MEROVINGIANS

Childers, (Robert) Erskine (1870–1922) Irish nationalist and writer, b. England. He resigned as clerk of the House of Commons (1895–1910) to campaign for Irish HOME RULE. In 1921 Childers was elected to the Dáil Éireann (Irish assembly) as a SINN FÉIN deputy. He opposed the partition of Ireland agreed by Arthur GRIFFITH and Michael COLLINS in the Anglo-Irish Treaty (1921) and fought for the IRISH REPUBLICAN ARMY (IRA) in the civil war. He was shot by a Free State firing squad. Childers wrote the spy novel *The Riddle of the Sands* (1903).

Children's Crusade Name given to two CRUSADES by children in 1212. In the first, French children were offered free transport from Marseilles to the Holy Land but were sold as slaves in North Africa. A second group of German children bound for the Holy Land travelled to Italy, where many died of starvation and disease.

Chile *See* country feature

Chilperic I (539–84) Frankish king of Soissons (561–84) and king of NEUSTRIA (567–84), son of CLOTAIRE I. He became embroiled in a savage feud with his brother, Sigebert I. In 567 Chilperic murdered his second wife Galswintha, sister of Sigebert's wife BRUNHILDA. He was assassinated, probably at the behest of Brunhilda, and succeeded by his son, CLOTAIRE II.

Chimú South American culture that gradually came to dominate a thin coastal strip in Peru between the 10th and 15th centuries. Its centre and capital was the great city of CHAN CHAN. In *c.*1470 the Chimú were conquered by the INCA, who absorbed them into their empire. Chimú culture is noted for its excellent craftwork.

Ch'in Alternative transliteration for the QIN dynasty

China *See* country feature, page 86

Chinese Exclusion Acts Series of laws to limit Chinese immigration into the United States. Skilled and unskilled Chinese labourers were barred from entering the United States by the Chinese Exclusion Act of 1882. Subsequent laws (1888, 1892) continued this policy, which was supported by labour leaders on racist and economic grounds. The Johnson Act (1924) excluded, in effect, all Asians. In 1943 Congress established an annual quota of 105 persons for immigration from China. The national origins quota system ended in the 1960s.

Ch'ing Alternative transliteration for the QING dynasty

Chinook Native North American tribe who, before the arrival of European settlers in the 19th century, lived along the Pacific coast from the Columbia River to The Dalles, Oregon. The Chinook economy was based on fishing and trade. They travelled widely and the Chinook language was used by others, native and European, during the settlement of the West.

Chippewa *See* OJIBWA

Chirac, Jacques René (1932–) French statesman, president (1995–). He was first elected to the national assembly in 1967. In 1974 Chirac was appointed prime minister by President GISCARD D'ESTAING. In 1976 he resigned and formed a new Gaullist party, Rally for the Republic (RPR). In 1977 Chirac became mayor of Paris. He was again prime minister (1986–88), this time under President François MITTERRAND. In 1995 Chirac succeeded Mitterrand as president. Confronted by the lead-up to the European single currency (the euro), he called a surprise prime ministerial election (1997). Victory for the socialists, led by Lionel JOSPIN, was a personal setback for Chirac.

chivalry (Fr. *chevalerie*, knighthood) Code of ethics and behaviour of the knightly class that developed from FEUDALISM. A combination of Christian ethics and military codes of conduct, the main chivalric virtues were piety, honour, valour, chastity and loyalty. A KNIGHT swore loyalty to God, king and his lady. Love was strictly platonic. The CRUSADES saw the emergence of monastic knighthoods, such as the KNIGHTS HOSPITALLERS and KNIGHTS TEMPLAR. Chivalry was always prone to corruption. Its ceremonial traditions faded with the warrior tactics and conventions of the Middle Ages, but were still alive in the 16th century. Chivalric ideals permeate medieval literature.

Choctaw One of the largest tribes of Muskogean-speaking Native North Americans, located in SE Mississippi and part of Alabama. As major slave-owners, they supported the South during the American Civil War. A majority of the Choctaw moved to Oklahoma in 1830, where some 40,000 of their descendants still reside.

Choiseul, Etienne François, Duc de (1719–85) French statesman, foreign minister (1758–1770) of LOUIS XV of France. With the support of Madame de POMPADOUR, he was appointed ambassador to Vienna (1757–58) and negotiated the marriage of MARIE ANTOINETTE and the future LOUIS XVI. As foreign minister, Choiseul negotiated the Family Compact (1761),

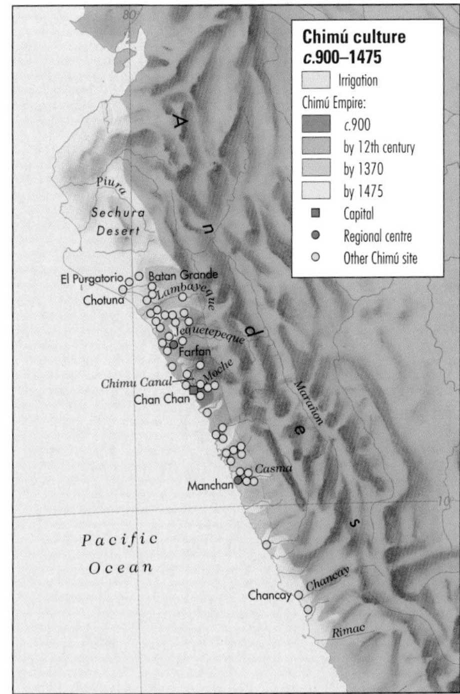

▲ **Chimú** At its height in *c.*1475, the Chimú culture occupied a swathe of Peru's coast. Agriculture was sustained by a complex irrigation system of canals and rivers.

AREA: 9,596,960 sq km (3,705,386 sq mi)
POPULATION: 1,187,997,000
CAPITAL (POPULATION): Beijing (6,560,000)
GOVERNMENT: Single-party, communist republic
ETHNIC GROUPS: Han (Chinese) 92%, 55 minority groups
LANGUAGES: Mandarin Chinese (official)
RELIGIONS: The government encourages atheism; although Confucianism, Buddhism, Taoism, and Islam are practised
GDP PER CAPITA (1995): US$2920

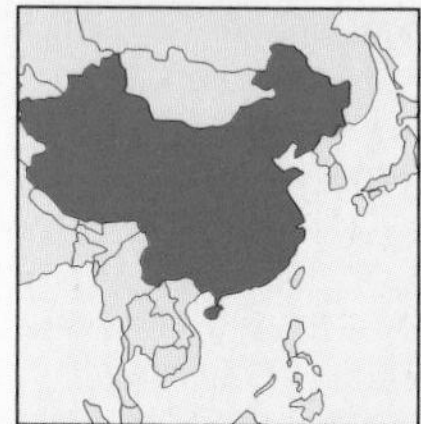

Republic in E Asia. The People's Republic of China is the world's third largest country (after Russia and Canada). The first documented dynasty was the Shang (*c*.1600–*c*.1050 BC), when bronze casting was perfected. The Zhou dynasty (*c*.1050–221 BC) was the age of Chinese classical literature, in particular Confucius and Lao Tzu. China was unified by Qin Shihuangdi, whose tomb near Xian contains the famous terracotta army. The Qin dynasty (221–206 BC) also built the majority of the original Great Wall.

Under the Han dynasty (202 BC–AD 220), a bureaucracy based on Confucianism was developed and Buddhism was introduced. China then split into three kingdoms (Wei, Shu and Wu) and the next four centuries, known as the Three Kingdoms period (AD 220–65), were characterized by warfare between states and invasions by the barbarian Huns in the north. The influence of Buddhism and Taoism grew and many of the scientific advances made in India were adopted. The Sui dynasty took power in 581 and reunified the N and S, which had been divided since the end of the 4th century.

Under the Tang dynasty (618–907) the Chinese empire reached its greatest extent, prior to the Manchu Qing empire 1000 years later. The dynasty was also a golden era of artistic achievement, especially in poetry and fine art. The Song dynasty is traditionally divided into the Northern Song (960–1126) and the Southern Song (1127–1279). The Southern Song were gradually overrun by the Mongols. Kublai Khan founded the Yüan dynasty (1271–1368), a period of dialogue with Europe. The Ming dynasty (1368–1644) re-established Chinese rule and is famed for its fine porcelain. The third Ming emperor, Yung Lo, moved the capital from Nanjing to Beijing where he built an elaborate palace compound, the Forbidden City.

The Manchu Qing dynasty (1644–1912) began by vastly extending the empire, but the 19th century was marked by foreign interventions, such as the Opium War (1839–42) when Britain occupied Hong Kong. Popular disaffection culminated in the Boxer Rebellion (1900). The last emperor (Henry Pu Yi) was overthrown in a revolution led by Sun Yat-sen, and a republic established.

China rapidly fragmented between a Beijing government supported by warlords and Sun Yat-sen's Kuomintang (Nationalist) government in Guangzhou. Early in World War 1, Japan seized the Shantung province which it did not relinquish until the Washington Conference (1921–22) when China's territorial integrity was guaranteed by the Nine-Power Treaty. The Chinese Communist Party (CCP) was founded in 1921 and initially allied with the Kuomintang. In 1926 Chiang Kai-shek's Kuomintang emerged victorious and turned on their communist allies. In 1930 a rival communist government was established, but was uprooted by Kuomintang troops and began the Long March (1934). In 1932 Japan, taking advantage of the turmoil, established the puppet state of Manchukuo under Henry Pu Yi. Chiang was forced to ally with the communists. In 1937 Japan launched a full-scale invasion and conquered much of N and E China. At the end of World War 2, civil war resumed, with the Kuomintang supported by the United States and the communists by Russia. The communists triumphed, and the Kuomintang fled to Taiwan.

Confidence in the Nationalist government had been weakened by high inflation, famine and police repression and on 1 October 1949, Mao Zedong established the People's Republic of China. In 1950 China seized Tibet and intervened in the Korean War (1950–53) in support of the Communist regime of North Korea. In 1958 the Great Leap Forward planned to revolutionize industrial production. The Cultural Revolution (1966–76) mobilized Chinese youth against bourgeois culture in the form of the Red Guards. By 1971 China had a seat on the United Nations' (UN) Security Council and its own nuclear capability. Following Mao's death (1976), a power struggle developed between the Gang of Four and moderates led by Deng Xiaoping; the latter emerged victorious. Deng began a process of modernization, forging closer links with the West. In 1979 special economic zones were created to encourage foreign investment and China now enjoys most-favoured nation status with the United States. China regained Hong Kong from Britain (1997) and Macao from Portugal (1999). Despite China's economic reforms, political and cultural expression were often suppressed by the Communist Party, and in 1989 a pro-democracy demonstration was crushed in Tiananmen Square. In 1997 Jiang Zemin succeeded Deng as paramount leader.

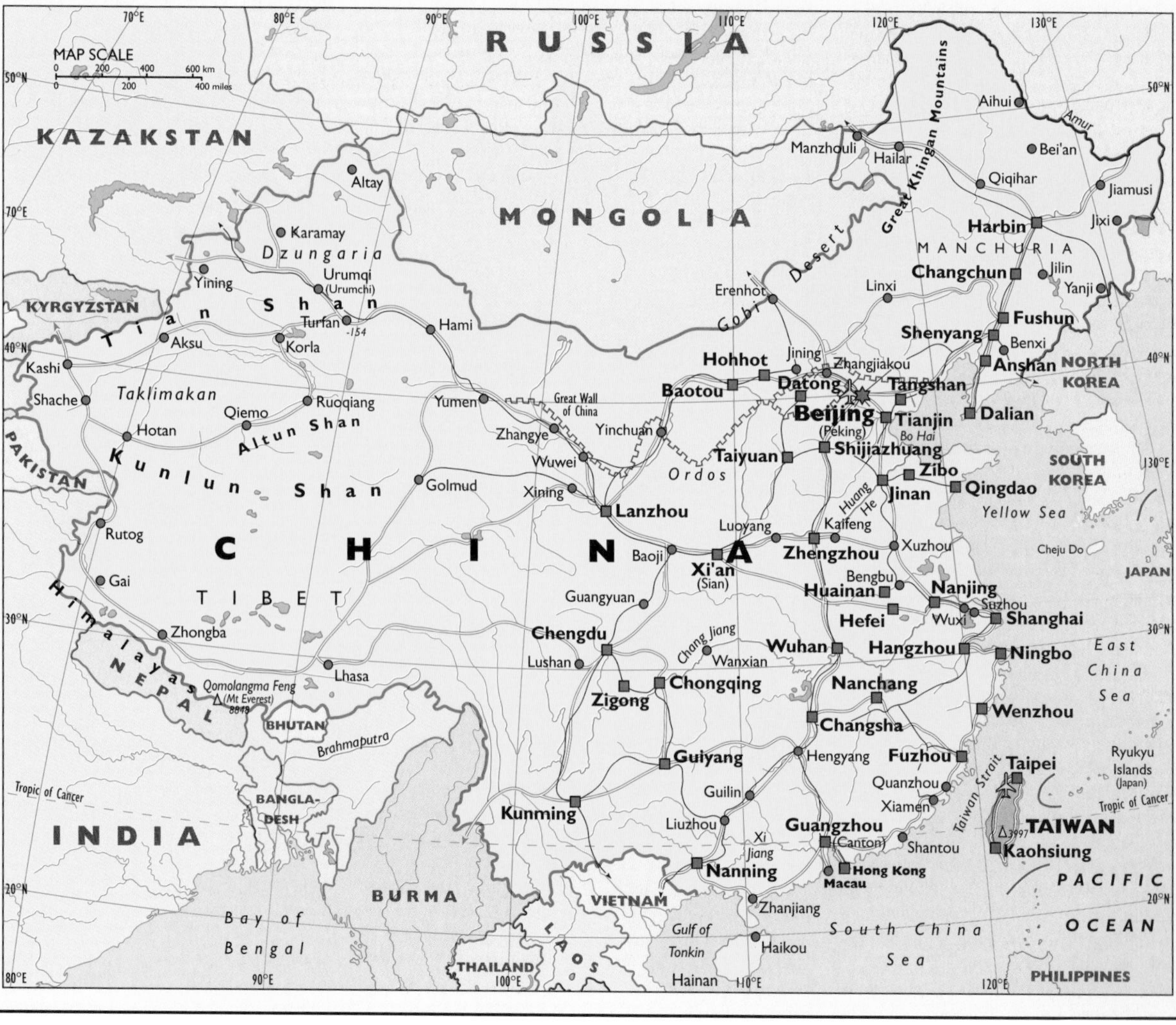

allying the Bourbon rulers of France and Spain, thus bringing Spain into the Seven Years' War (1756–63). By the Treaty of Paris (1763) France surrendered French Canada and India to Britain. Choiseul approved the suppression of the Jesuits (1764).

Chola (Cola) Tamil dynasty of s India. In the 9th century AD, they expanded from their base in the Cauvery delta to occupy territory of the Pallava dynasty. During the reign (*c.*907–953) of Parantaka I, the Chola captured Madurai, capital of the Pandya dynasty. Rajaraja I (r.985–1016) conquered Kerala and n Ceylon (now Sri Lanka) and built the Brhadishvara temple at Tanjore. His son, Rajendra (r.1016–44), conquered the rest of Ceylon, the e Deccan and parts of the Srivijaya kingdom on the Malay Peninsula. The Chola now controlled the spice trade between Arabia and China. The dynasty declined in the 12th and 13th centuries and was supplanted by the Hoysalas and Pandyas. At its height, the Chola empire was a major naval power in the Indian Ocean.

Chou Alternative transliteration for the Zhou dynasty

Chouteau, (Jean) Pierre (1758–1849) US fur trader. With his half-brother, **René Auguste** Chouteau (1749–1829), he controlled the important trade with the Osage Native Americans. Chouteau established (1796) the first permanent white settlement in Oklahoma. In 1809 he founded the St Louis Missouri Fur Company. His two sons, **Auguste Pierre** (1786–1838) and **Pierre** (1789–1865), developed the family firm so that by the 1850s it controlled most of the fur trade from the Mississippi to the Rockies.

Chrétien, (Joseph-Jacques) Jean (1934–) Twentieth premier of Canada (1993–). He became a member of Parliament in 1963 and held cabinet positions in Pierre Trudeau's government. In 1990 Chrétien became leader of the Liberal Party. His populist campaign secured a landslide election victory in 1993. Chrétien's main challenge was to reduce unemployment. He was re-elected, with a much reduced majority, in 1997

Christian I (1426–81) King of Denmark (1448–81), Norway (1450–81) and Sweden (1457–64), founder of the Oldenburg dynasty. Christian was a weak king. Deposed in Sweden, his efforts to regain the throne ended in defeat (1471). His succession (1460) to Schleswig-Holstein formed the basis of future conflict between Denmark and Germany. The influence of the Hanseatic League drew Charles into war (1469–74) with England. *See also* Kalmar Union

Christian II (1481–1559) King of Denmark and Norway (1513–23) and Sweden (1520–21). Christian won the Swedish crown by conquest, but the subsequent slaughter of Swedish nobles, known as the Stockholm Bloodbath (1520), led to the crowning of a rival, Gustavus I (Vasa), and the end of the Kalmar Union. In Denmark, the nobles resented Christian's reforms favouring the middle classes and drove him out. He invaded Norway (1531), but was captured (1532) and imprisoned for the rest of his life.

Christian III (1503–59) King of Denmark and Norway (1534–59), son of Frederick I. His accession prompted a civil war (1533–36) with Catholic forces in Denmark. Victory over Lübeck (1536) broke the power of the Hanseatic League. In 1536 Christian established Lutheranism as the state religion. A reorganization of the Danish church (1537) strengthened the power of the crown over the church. He was succeeded by his son, Frederick II.

Christian IV (1577–1648) King of Denmark and Norway (1588–1648), son of Frederick II. He ruled under a regency until 1596. Christian failed to unite Sweden and Denmark in a costly war (1611–13) and turned his attention to internal reform. Christian rebuilt Oslo (renaming it Kristiania) and founded Kristiansand, Norway. He did much to establish the mercantile base of Denmark's economy. During the Thirty Years' War (1618–48), Christian invaded Germany (1625) in defence of Lutheranism. Defeated (1626) by Tilly and driven out of Jutland (1627), Christian formed an alliance with Gustavus II of Sweden. The combined Swedish-Danish army lifted the siege of Stralsund, but Christian concluded a separate peace treaty with Emperor Ferdinand II. He lost an eye in a further war (1643–45) with Sweden and was forced to cede Jutland and other Danish possessions.

Christian VII (1749–1808) King of Denmark and Norway (1766–1808), son of Frederick V. Early in his reign, Christian's mental illness made him dependent on his physician, Johann Struensee, whose autocratic methods led to his arrest and execution in 1772. Christian's son and successor, Frederick VI, acted as regent from 1784.

Christian IX (1818–1906) King of Denmark (1863–1906), successor of Frederick VII. Christian lost Schleswig-Holstein in a war (1864) with Prussia and Austria. His reign brought reforms to the constitution and the gradual democratization of Danish society.

Christian X (1870–1947) King of Denmark (1912–47) and Iceland (1919–44), succeeding Frederick VIII. During his reign, universal suffrage was established (1915) and social welfare policies were consolidated. Christian defied the Germans during occupation (1940–45).

Christian Democrats Political group combining Christian conservative principles with progressive social responsibility. Christian Democrats have achieved power in many European countries, notably Germany and Italy. Its political principles include individual responsibility allied with collective action, social equality within a welfare state and progress through evolutionary change. Christian Democrats are also represented outside Europe. *See also* Christian Democratic Union (CDU); Italian Popular Party (PPI)

Christian Democratic Union (CDU) German political party. In 1949 the leader of the CDU, Konrad Adenauer, became the first chancellor of the Federal Republic of West Germany. The CDU remained in power until the electoral victory of the Social Democratic Party (SPD), led by Willy Brandt, in 1969. The CDU regained power under Helmut Köhl, who presided over the reunification of Germany in 1990. In 1998 Köhl was defeated by Gerhard Schröder of the SPD. The Party was badly hit by revelations of secret donations in 2000.

Christianity *See* feature article

Christian Science (officially Church of Christ Scientist) Religious sect founded (1879) by Mary Baker Eddy and based on her book *Science and Health with Key to the Scriptures* (1875). Its followers believe that physical illness and moral problems can only be cured by spiritual and mental activity. They refuse medical treatment. "Divine Mind" is used as a synonym for God. Each human being is regarded as a complete and flawless manifestation of the Divine Mind.

Christian socialism Movement to ally the working classes and the Christian church against the excesses of

CHRISTIANITY

Religion based on faith in Jesus Christ as Son of God and saviour. Orthodox Christian faith, summarized in the Apostles' Creed and the Nicene Creed, affirms belief in the Trinity and Christ's incarnation, atoning death on the cross, resurrection and ascension. The moral teachings of Jesus are contained in the New Testament. The history of Christianity, like that of other world belief systems, has been turbulent and often sectarian. As Christianity spread outwards from Jerusalem, it became increasingly distanced from its Jewish roots as Gentile Christians began to outnumber Jewish Christians. The writings of the apostle Paul (*See* Paul, Saint) provided a base for Christian ideology. In the 4th and 5th centuries, ecumenical councils set about formulating basic Christian doctrines, many of which are still part of Christian belief today. The subsequent spread of Christianity to Constantinople and the East was accompanied by the growth of monasticism. The threat of Islam culminated in the Crusades, an attempt to regain Jerusalem from the Muslim conquerors. The first schism began in 1054 when the eastern and western churches separated and continued into the 14th century when controversy over the legitimacy of the pope arose. The next occurred in the 16th-century Reformation, started by Martin Luther, with the split of Protestantism and the Roman Catholic Church. The Enlightenment provided a further challenge to the authority of the Christian ideas in western Europe. In recent times, the ecumenical movement, which aims at the reunion of all Christians, has grown. Today, Christians in the world number more than 1 billion. *See also* Orthodox Church, Eastern

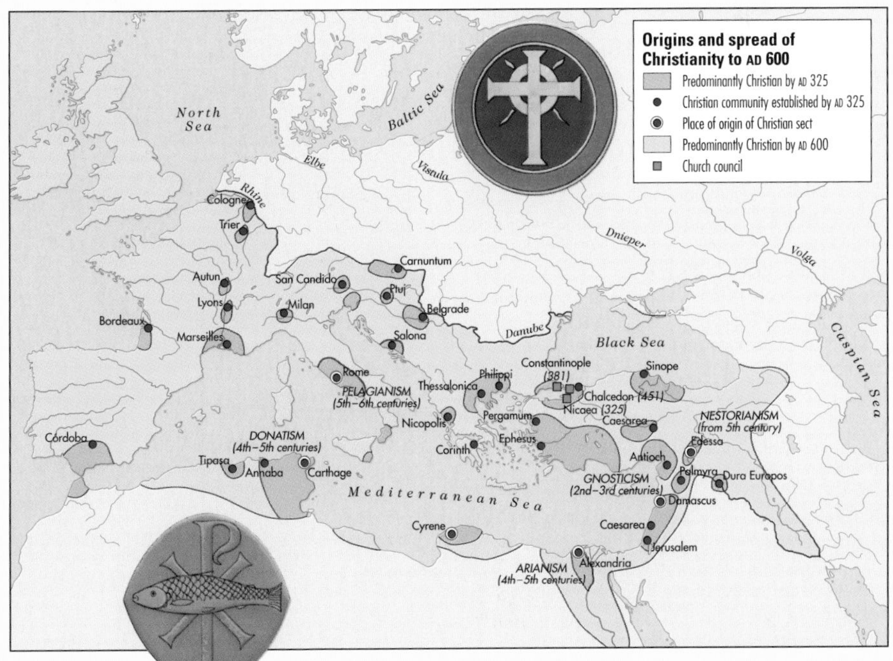

▲ **Christianity** Early Christians were repeatedly persecuted by the Romans, who saw them as a threat to the stability of the Empire because they refused to acknowledge the divinity of the Roman emperor. In the 1st century AD, Nero used Christians as victims in the imperial arenas, and in the early 4th century Diocletian organized campaigns against them. However, Constantine, Diocletian's successor, legalized Christianity and at the first ecumenical council (held at Nicaea in 325) he brought church and state together.

C

CAPITALISM. It developed in England in the late 1840s. Frederick Denison Maurice (1805–72) and Charles Kingsley (1819–75) encouraged the foundation of working men's associations and founded a working men's college in 1854. In 1889 the Society of Christian Socialists was founded in the United States. In the 20th-century Christian SOCIALISM lost much of its organizational strength, but found new, powerful advocacy in the writings of theologians such as Reinhold Niebuhr and Paul Tillich.

Christina (1626–89) Queen of Sweden (1632–54), daughter and successor of GUSTAVUS II. She ruled under a regency until 1644. Christina was instrumental in concluding the Peace of WESTPHALIA (1648) that ended the THIRTY YEARS' WAR (1618–48). An intellectual of great energy, she brought foreign scholars, such as René DESCARTES, to her court. Her abdication and self-exile to Rome, after secretly converting to Roman Catholicism, shocked Europe. Christina made two unsuccessful attempts to return to power in the Kingdom of Naples and Poland respectively. Her Roman palace, the Riario (now Corsini), became a treasure-house of Venetian art. Christina was the patron of Alessandro Scarlatti (1600–1725).

Christophe, Henri (1767–1820) Haitian revolutionary leader, president (1806–11) and king (1811–20). He fought alongside TOUSSAINT L'OUVERTURE and Jean-Jacques DESSALINES in the "Black Jacobin" revolt against the French in HAITI. In 1804 Haiti achieved independence and Dessalines was assassinated. The power struggle between Christophe and Alexandre Sabès Pétion led to the division of Haiti. Christophe became king in N Haiti. He ordered the construction of the citadel of La Ferrière, a fort overlooking Cap-Haitien, the building of which cost many Haitian lives.

Chrysostom, St John (*c*.347–407) Doctor of the Church, patriarch of Constantinople. In 386 he was ordained in Antioch, Syria, and his powerful sermons quickly earned him the epithet *Chrysostom* (Gk. golden-mouthed). In 398 he was made archbishop of Constantinople. The zeal with which he approached reform of church and state offended Empress Eudoxia, and led to his banishment (403). His *Homilies* are an invaluable record of religious thought. His feast day is 27 January.

Chulalongkorn (1853–1910) (Rama V) King of Siam (1868–1910). He ruled under a regency until 1873. Chulalongkorn was less insular than his predecessors and embraced Westernization in Siam (now Thailand). Chulalongkorn abolished slavery, modernized the legal system, built railways and advanced education and technology. His reforms ensured Siam's independence.

Chun Doo Hwan (1931–) South Korean statesman, president (1980–88). In 1979, following the assassination of President PARK CHUNG HEE, Chun seized control in a military coup. In 1980 he declared martial law and crushed a fledgling democracy movement in Kwangju. He was succeeded as president by Roh Tae Woo. In 1996 Chun and Roh were sentenced to death for their role in the turbulent events of 1979–80 and for accepting bribes. Their sentences were commuted to life imprisonment.

Chungking (Chongqing, Ch'ung-ch'ing) City on the River Yangtze, S China. From the 14th century AD, it was part of a unified China. It became a treaty port in 1895, by the treaty of Shimonoseki. It was the wartime capital of China (1937–45). Pop. (1993 est.) 3,780,000.

Churches of God US Pentecostal religious sect. It grew out of the Latter Rain revival that began (1886) in the Great Smokey Mountains led by R.G. Spurling and W.F. Bryant. They preached that a second rain of gifts of the Holy Spirit similar to the first Pentecostal would occur. Members practise speaking in tongues. There have been many splits in the church since its founding. Today, the various sects of the Churches of God have *c*.500,000 members. *See also* PENTECOSTAL CHURCHES

Churchill, John *See* MARLBOROUGH, JOHN CHURCHILL, 1ST DUKE OF

Churchill, Lord Randolph Henry Spencer (1849–95) British statesman, chancellor of the exchequer and leader of the House of Commons (1886). A gifted orator, he led the calls for administrative reform of the TORY PARTY. As secretary of state for India (1885–86) under Lord SALISBURY, Churchill prosecuted the Third Anglo-Burmese War (1885). His first budget as chancellor proposed deep cuts in military expenditure and was defeated. Churchill was forced to resign. In 1874 he married Jennie Jerome, a US citizen. Their son, Winston CHURCHILL, achieved the success denied his father.

Churchill, Sir Winston Leonard Spencer (1874–1965) British statesman, prime minister (1940–45, 1951–55), son of Lord Randolph CHURCHILL. As a reporter in the second of the SOUTH AFRICAN WARS (1899–1902), Churchill was captured by the Boers while defending an ambushed train. His subsequent escape from military prison made him a national hero. Churchill was elected to Parliament as a member of the CONSERVATIVE PARTY in 1900. Churchill's support of free-trade against Joseph CHAMBERLAIN's tariff proposals led to his defection (1904) to the LIBERAL PARTY. Churchill served as president of the Board of Trade (1908–10) and home secretary (1910–11) under Herbert ASQUITH. He was a strong supporter of the Parliament Act (1911) that restricted the power of the HOUSE OF LORDS. As first lord of the admiralty (1911–15), Churchill expanded Britain's navy in preparation for World War 1. He was forced to resign after the failure of the GALLIPOLI CAMPAIGN. Churchill returned to government under David LLOYD GEORGE and, as secretary of state for war (1919–21), lent British military support to the anti-Bolshevik forces in the Russian Civil War (1918–20). As colonial secretary (1921–22), he oversaw the creation of the Irish Free State. In 1922 Lloyd George's government collapsed over the handling of Turkish reoccupation of the DARDANELLES and Churchill, identified as the leading advocate of military action, was heavily defeated. He returned to power as chancellor of the exchequer (1924–29) in Stanley BALDWIN's Conservative government. Churchill's decision to restore the GOLD STANDARD increased unemployment and led to the GENERAL STRIKE (1926). During the 1930s, Churchill was a staunch critic of Neville CHAMBERLAIN's policy of APPEASEMENT towards Nazi Germany. On the outbreak of WORLD WAR 2, Churchill returned as first lord of the admiralty. In 1940 he replaced Neville CHAMBERLAIN as prime minister. Churchill proved an inspiring war leader, resolute in his opposition to fascism. In August 1941, Churchill and US President Franklin ROOSEVELT issued the ATLANTIC CHARTER. Churchill was the main architect of the "grand alliance" of Britain, the United States and the Soviet Union. In 1943 he called a series of international summits designed to coordinate the plans of the Allies, including the CASABLANCA CONFERENCE, CAIRO CONFERENCE, QUÉBEC CONFERENCE and TEHRAN CONFERENCE. At the YALTA CONFERENCE (1945), Churchill, Roosevelt and Joseph STALIN agreed on the final campaigns of the war and the post-war territorial settlement. The POTSDAM CONFERENCE (1945) called for Japan's unconditional surrender. In the 1945 general election Churchill was defeated by Clement ATTLEE. In opposition, he criticized the break-up of Britain's overseas empire and called for Britain and the United States to unite against the "iron curtain" of Soviet communism. In 1951 Churchill was re-elected as prime minister and reversed some of the nationalizations under the previous Labour administration. In 1955 he stepped down as prime minister in favour of Anthony EDEN. Churchill remained a member of Parliament until 1964. His extensive writings include *The Second World War* (1948–53) and the *History of the English-Speaking Peoples* (1956–58). In 1953 Churchill was awarded the Nobel Prize for literature.

CHURCHILL, SIR WINSTON

Winston Churchill During the 1930s, Churchill warned of the growing threat of Nazism in Germany and worked on a secret defence committee gathering information on Germany. An inspiring leader during World War 2, his charismatic public speeches and broadcasts encouraged a "bulldog" spirit of resistance to the German forces in Europe.

CHURCHILL IN HIS OWN WORDS

"I have nothing to offer but blood, toil, tears and sweat."
On becoming prime minister
Speech, House of Commons, 13 May 1949

"We shall defend our island, whatever the cost may be, we shall fight on the beaches, we shall fight on the landing grounds, we shall fight in the fields and in the streets, we shall fight in the hills; we shall never surrender."
Speech, House of Commons, 4 June 1940

Church of England Christian church in England, established by law in the 16th century. During the reign (1509–47) of HENRY VIII, a process of separation from the ROMAN CATHOLIC CHURCH began. The initial impetus for this was the pope's refusal to grant Henry a divorce from CATHERINE OF ARAGON. By the Act of Supremacy (1534), the English monarch became head of the church. As the REFORMATION extended to England, the Church of England finally emerged independent of papal jurisdiction and adopted the Elizabethan Settlement. This agreement, while espousing PROTESTANTISM, aimed at preserving religious unity by shaping a national church acceptable to all persons of moderate theological views. This middle course found expression in the doctrinal THIRTY-NINE ARTICLES (1571). The liturgy of the Church of England is contained in the Book of COMMON PRAYER (1662), but since the 1960s alternative forms of worship have come into use. The sovereign bears the title "supreme governor of the Church of England" and formally nominates the bishops. The Church is episcopally governed, but priests and laity share in all major decisions by virtue of their representation in the General Synod. Territorially, the Church is divided into two provinces, Canterbury and York. The archbishop of CANTERBURY is Primate of All England. The overseas expansion of the Church of England during the period of the growth of the British Empire resulted in the gradual development of the worldwide ANGLICAN COMMUNION. The Church of England is the only part of the Anglican Communion still established by law as an official state church. In 1992 the General Synod voted in favour of the ordination of women as priests. The first women priests were ordained in 1994.

Church of Ireland Anglican church in Ireland. It claims to be heir to the ancient church of the island of Ireland. At the time of the REFORMATION, it ended papal jurisdiction and introduced doctrinal and disciplinary reforms similar to the CHURCH OF ENGLAND. It is territorially divided into two provinces, Armagh and Dublin. The archbishop of Armagh is Primate of All Ireland. It was the legally established church until 1869. *See also* ANGLICAN COMMUNION

Church of Scotland National, non-episcopal form of CHRISTIANITY in Scotland, adopting PRESBYTERIANISM by constitutional act in 1689. The Church arose as a separate entity during the REFORMATION. Under the leadership of John KNOX, it abolished papal authority and accepted many of the teachings of John CALVIN. The doctrinal position of the Church is based on the Scottish Confession (1560) and the Westminster Confession of 1643. The highest authority resides in the general assembly, presided over by an annually elected moderator. The Disruption of 1843 led to about one-third of its ministers and members leaving to form the FREE CHURCH OF SCOTLAND. The Church has *c*.850,000 members.

CIA Abbreviation of CENTRAL INTELLIGENCE AGENCY

Ciano, Galeazzo (1903–44) Italian politician. He married (1930) Benito MUSSOLINI's daughter and became foreign minister (1936–43). Ciano was partly responsible for the attack (1940) on Greece that precipitated Italy's entry into World War 2. AXIS defeats led to his dismissal. Ciano voted for the removal of Mussolini, and when Mussolini was restored to power, he was executed for treason.

Cicero, Marcus Tullius (106–43 BC) Roman politician, philosopher and orator. A leader of the Senate, he exposed CATILINE's conspiracy (63 BC). Cicero criticized Mark ANTONY, and when Octavian (later AUGUSTUS) came to power, Antony persuaded him to have Cicero executed. His fame rests largely on his political philosophy and oratory. Among Cicero's greatest speeches were *Orations Against Catiline* and the *Phillipics*, against Antony. His rhetorical and philosophical works include *De Amicitia*. *See also* CAESAR, JULIUS; CATO (THE YOUNGER); POMPEY

Cid, El (1043–99) (Rodrigo Díaz de Vivar) Spanish national hero. In 1067 El Cid (Sp. "the Champion") helped SANCHO II of Castile to conquer the Moorish kingdom of ZARAGOZA and accompanied him on a campaign against his brother, Alfonso VI of León. In 1072 Sancho died in battle and was succeeded by Alfonso. El Cid was banished in 1081 after leading an unauthorized attack on the Moorish kingdom of Toledo and defected to the Moorish king of Zaragoza. El Cid's greatest achievement was the conquest of Valencia (1094), which he ruled until his death. He successfully withstood the ALMORAVIDS. His exploits have been romanticized in Spanish legend.

Cilicia Ancient coastal region of SE Asia Minor, now forming part of Turkey. The major city was Tarsus. The Cilician Gates in the Taurus Mountains was a strategic pass on the trade route between Europe and Asia. In 67 BC Cilicia was conquered by Rome. An Armenian state was set up here in 1080 and the region fell to the Turks in 1375.

Cimon (d. *c*.450 BC) Athenian statesman and general, son of MILTIADES. Cimon's part in the defeat of the Persian fleet at SALAMIS (480 BC) led to his appointment as *strategos* (general). In 478 BC he became commander of the DELIAN LEAGUE. Cimon's greatest victory was his rout of the Persian fleet at Eurymedon (*c*.467 BC), which severely weakened the Persian forces. His support for SPARTA in the revolt of the Helots aroused the enmity of PERICLES. *See also* PERSIAN WARS

Cincinnatus, Lucius Quinctius (519–438 BC) Legendary Roman patriot. Consul in 460 BC, he was named dictator by the Senate in 458 BC. According to legend, Cincinnatus left his farm to save the Roman army from defeat by the Aequi and promptly resigned as dictator in order to return to his land. In 439 BC he was recalled to the dictatorship to defeat the PLEBIANS.

Cinna, Lucius Cornelius (130–84 BC) Roman politician, consul from 87 BC. After SULLA left Rome to fight against MITHRIDATES VI, Cinna repealed Sulla's laws but conservatives then secured his expulsion from the city. With MARIUS, Sulla's rival, he captured Rome and massacred Sulla's followers. After the death of Marius (86 BC), Cinna remained as consul, instituting economic reforms and extending the franchise to all inhabitants of Italy. In 84 BC he mobilized to resist the returning Sulla, but his troops mutinied and killed him.

Cinque Ports Association of certain ports (originally five) in SE England that were granted special privileges in return for defending England's S coast. The grouping of Dover, Hastings, Hythe, Romney (now New Romney) and Sandwich, began under the Anglo-Saxons. The association, which Winchelsea and Rye joined in the 12th century, reached its height during the HUNDRED YEARS' WAR.

Circassians Muslim people native to the Caucasus Mountains. During the 19th century they unsuccessfully resisted Russia's advance into the Caucasus. They often figure in Russian literature, such as in Mikhail Lermontov's *Hero of our Times* (1840).

circumnavigation Voyage around the world. It was first accomplished in 1519–22 by the *Victoria*, commanded by Juan Sebastián del CANO. Ferdinand MAGELLAN died in the attempt.

CIS Abbreviation of COMMONWEALTH OF INDEPENDENT STATES

Cisalpine Gaul Ancient region of GAUL in present-day Italy. The name is derived from the Latin "on this side of the Alps". Divided into Cispadane Gaul ("this side of the Po River") and Transpadane Gaul, it was settled by the Gauls in the 5th century BC. In 222 BC it was conquered and assimilated by the Romans. In 49 BC Julius Caesar granted its inhabitants Roman citizenship. *See also* TRANSALPINE GAUL

Cisalpine Republic State established (1797) in N Italy by Napoleon Bonaparte. It was the first unification of the northern states in modern Italian history. It became the Italian Republic in 1802 and the Kingdom of Italy in 1805.

Cisneros, Francisco Jiménez de *See* JIMÉNEZ DE CISNEROS, FRANCISCO

Cistercian Religious order of monks founded (1098) in Citeaux, France, by BENEDICTINE monks led by Saint Robert of Molesme. Saint BERNARD OF CLAIRVAUX was largely responsible for the rapid growth of the order in the 12th century. In the 17th century the order split into two communities: Common Observance and Strict Observance, the latter are popularly known as TRAPPISTS.

city-state (Gk. *polis*) Independent political unit with sovereignty over its surrounding hinterland. It is often applied to the cities of ancient GREECE, PHOENICIA and medieval Europe. The first city-states were in SUMERIA, but they thrived in the classical period of Greek civilization (5th and 4th centuries BC). By the 5th century BC there were several hundred city-states dotted around the coasts of the Mediterranean and Black seas. The first Italian city-states were Greek colonies. While they possessed a remarkable diversity of political systems and cultures, at the administrative centre of each ancient Greek city-state lay the ACROPOLIS. Only male citizens could participate in government and a large proportion of the population were slaves. ROME, founded as a city-state, centralized its government and pursued an expansionist foreign policy that ultimately led to the destruction of the ancient city-state. After the fall of the Roman Empire, many prosperous Italian cities were reconstituted as city-states. VENICE, AMALFI, GENOA, FLORENCE and PISA developed through trade with the Byzantine Empire. The medieval city-states, which developed in Germany as well as in Italy, were controlled by communes that were dominated by the aristocracy. *See also* FEUDAL SYSTEM

civil disobedience Passive resistance to law or authority practised either as a matter of individual conscience or by a large number of people as a form of non-violent protest. The term originated with Henry Thoreau's essay *Resistance to Civil Government* (1849), in which he argued that disobeying a law is preferable to disobeying one's own conscience. It was practised in India by the supporters of "Mahatma" GANDHI and in the United States by the followers of Martin Luther KING, Jr.

civil law Legal system derived from ROMAN LAW. It is different from COMMON LAW, the system generally adhered to in England and other English-speaking countries. Civil law is based on a system of codes, the most famous of which is the CODE NAPOLÉON (1804), and decisions are precisely worked out from general basic principles *a priori*. Thus, a civil law judge follows the evidence and is bound by the conditions of the written law and not by previous judicial interpretation. The basis of civil law is statute. Civil law is also the basis for the system of EQUITY. It is prevalent in Louisiana, Québec, Latin America and continental Europe.

civil rights Rights conferred legally upon the individual by the state. There is no universal conception of civil rights. The modern use of the phrase is most common in the United States, where it refers to relations between individuals as well as between individuals and the state. It is especially associated with the movement to achieve equal rights for African Americans. The modern civil rights movement may be said to have begun with the foundation (1910) of the NATIONAL ASSOCIATION FOR THE ADVANCEMENT OF COLORED PEOPLE (NAACP). In 1942 the CONGRESS OF RACIAL EQUALITY (CORE) was founded. The movement gathered pace after the Supreme Court decision in BROWN V. BOARD OF EDUCATION OF TOPEKA (1954) against segregation in schools. In 1960 Martin Luther KING, Jr founded the SOUTHERN CHRISTIAN LEADERSHIP CONFERENCE (SCLC). The STUDENT NONVIOLENT COORDINATING COMMITTEE (SNCC), led by Stokely CARMICHAEL, represented the more radical wing of the civil rights movement. Subsequently, a series of CIVIL RIGHTS ACTS protected individuals from discrimination.

Civil Rights Acts (1866, 1870, 1875, 1957, 1960, 1964, 1968) US legislation. The **1866 Act** gave African Americans citizenship and extended civil rights to all persons born in the United States (except Native Americans). The **1870 Act** was passed to re-enact the previous measure, which was considered to be of dubious constitutionality. The 1870 Act was declared unconstitutional by the Supreme Court in 1883. The **1875 Act** was passed to outlaw discrimination in public places because of race or previous servitude. The Act was declared unconstitutional by the Supreme Court (1883–85), which stated that the 14th Amendment protected individual rights against infringement by states, not by other individuals. The **1957 Act** established the Civil Rights Commission to investigate violations of the 15th Amendment. The **1960 Act** enabled court-appointed federal officials to protect African-American voting rights. An act of violence to obstruct a court order became a federal offence. The **1964 Act** established as law equal rights for all citizens in voting, education, public accommodation, and federally assisted projects. The **1968 Act** guaranteed equal treatment in housing and real estate to all citizens. *See also* CONSTITUTION OF THE UNITED STATES

civil service Administrative establishment for carrying on the work of government. In the United Kingdom, the modern service was developed between 1780 and 1870, as the weight of parliamentary business became too heavy for ministers to attend to both policy-making and departmental administration. The treasury got its first permanent secretary in 1805, the colonial office a permanent official in 1825. The two main divisions of the civil service are the home and diplomatic services. Since 1968 the civil service has been controlled by the prime minister (as minister of the civil service), but day-to-day management is undertaken by the lord privy seal. In 1981 the secretary to the cabinet was made head of the home civil service. In 1996 the senior civil service was created. The UK civil service has grown away from its centre in Whitehall, London, and now has many regional offices. In 1998 there were *c*.468,180 permanent civil servants in the UK. In the United States, the civil service evolved from the ineffective "SPOILS SYSTEM" (1828) established by President Andrew JACKSON, whereby posts were given as rewards for political support. This system remained in place until the PENDLETON ACT (1883) created the Civil Service Commission. The Commission implemented a merit system, and following the Hatch Acts (1939, 1940), federal employees were no longer allowed to take an active role in party politics.

Civil War, American *See* feature article, page 90–91

Civil War, English *See* feature article, page 92

Civil War, Russian *See* RUSSIAN CIVIL WAR

Civil War, Spanish *See* feature article, page 93

Cixi (1835–1908) (Tz'u Hsi or Zi Xi) Empress Dowager of China, mistress of Emperor Xian Feng and mother of his only son, Tongzhi. In 1861 she became co-regent. Cixi engineered the succession of her infant nephew, Guangxu, in 1875. In 1898, after defeat in the first of the SINO-JAPANESE WARS, Guangxu began to implement a radical package of reforms, known as the "HUNDRED DAYS OF REFORM". With the support of other reactionary court officials, Cixi mounted a successful coup against Guangxu and the modernization project was abandoned. Cixi supported the BOXER REBELLION (1900) against Western influence. She remained in power until her death.

Clapham Sect (*c*.1790–*c*.1830) Group of British evangelical reformers. Many of them, including William WILBERFORCE, lived in Clapham, S London, and several

War fought between the northern states (the Union) and the forces of the 11 Southern states which seceded from the Union to form the CONFEDERATE STATES OF AMERICA (the Confederacy). Its immediate cause was the determination of the Southern states to withdraw from a Union that the Northern states regarded as indivisible. The more general cause was the question of SLAVERY, a well-established institution in the South but one that the Northern ABOLITIONISTS opposed. By the 1850s slavery, abolition and STATES' RIGHTS had created insurmountable differences between North and South. Abolitionists formed a new REPUBLICAN PARTY, while those campaigning for the rights of Southern states remained in the DEMOCRATIC PARTY. The 1860 election of a Republican, Abraham LINCOLN, virtually assured Southern withdrawal from the Union. The North had superior numbers, greater economic power, and command of the seas. The Confederates had passionate conviction, were fighting for their homeland, and at least early in the War, had superior generals, such as Robert LEE and "Stonewall" JACKSON.

On 12 April 1861, the War began when Confederate forces attacked FORT SUMTER, South Carolina. The Union's first objective was to take the Confederate capital at RICHMOND, Virginia, in the First Battle of BULL RUN (July 1861). This campaign was foiled largely due to the actions of Joseph JOHNSTON, and the Confederates continued to be victorious, with Lee winning the PENINSULAR CAMPAIGN (April–June 1862) and Jackson victorious in the SHENANDOAH VALLEY (March–June 1862). The Confederates were also successful in the SEVEN DAYS' BATTLES (June–July 1862) and the Second Battle of BULL RUN (August 1862). Lee's army was checked,

▲ **The Civil War** Most of the fighting in the Civil War took place on Southern territory. The Confederates adopted a defensive strategy and had the advantage of fighting on familiar terrain. The Union forces were superior in terms of supplies and numbers of soldiers, but were forced to maintain lengthy supply lines. The Union side devised the "Anaconda Plan", by which they first encircled the Southern states by land and sea, and then split them up by seizing control of the Mississippi River in the spring of 1863 and marching through Georgia in the winter of 1864–65. Railroads played a crucial role in the movement of troops and raw materials, while telegraphs were used for military communication as well as for rapid press-reports of the battles. The War also saw the first use of rudimentary ironclad battleships, machine-guns, trench systems and dugouts.

► **Confederate foot soldier** In many ways, the Civil War was the first "modern" war, although the armies were made up of volunteers and conscripts, rather than professional soldiers.

► **Union infantryman** The Union was able to muster many more troops than the Confederacy, and suffered a smaller proportion of casualties. Overall, 20% of soldiers in the Civil War died – the majority of them as a result of disease.

Confederacy and Union flags
1. Seal of the Confederacy
2. Stars and Bars, or first flag of the Confederacy
3. Battle Flag or Southern Cross
4. Stainless Banner, or second flag of the Confederacy
5. Last flag of the Confederacy
6. Stars and Stripes

however, by the strengthening Union troops (led by George McClellan) in the Battle of Antietam (September 1862). The Union was defeated at the Battle of Fredericksburg (December 1862) under Ambrose Burnside and at Chancellorsville (May 1863) under Joseph Hooker. Union victory at the Battle of Gettysburg (June–July 1863) was a turning point. The Union Navy had blocked Southern ports, thereby denying the Confederacy essential trade with Europe. The Union strategy was to divide the South by taking control of the Mississippi, Tennessee and Cumberland rivers.

The first big Union victory was at Fort Donelson on the Tennessee River (February 1862) under the command of Ulysses Grant. Grant emerged victorious from the siege of Vicksburg (November 1862–July 1863) which, with the fall of Memphis (June 1862), gave Union troops control of the Mississippi. In 1864 Grant became supreme commander. He confronted Lee's army in the Wilderness campaign (May–June 1864) and began the long siege of Petersburg, Virginia – the defence of which was vital to the survival of Richmond. Meanwhile, Union General William Sherman cut a devastating swathe across Georgia in 1864, burning Atlanta on the way. The Union victory at the Battle of Five Forks (1865) blocked the retreat route for Confederate troops in Richmond. Petersburg fell two days later, and Richmond was indefensible. The war ended with Lee's surrender to Grant at Appomattox Court House (April 1865).

The Civil War claimed *c.*620,000 lives, more than the combined American dead from all other wars between 1775 and 1975. The Union lost c.360,000 soldiers, and the Confederacy *c.*260,000. The South was economically ruined by the war, and Reconstruction policies poisoned relations between North and South for a century.

were members of Parliament. Originally known as the "Saints", they were especially influential in the abolition of slavery and in prison reform. *See also* Abolitionists; Clarkson, Thomas

Clarence, George Plantagenet, Duke of (1449–78) Younger brother of Edward IV of England. He joined his father-in-law, the Earl of Warwick, in revolt against Edward IV (1469–70) but in 1471 rejoined his brother. In 1478 Clarence was accused of treason and secretly executed in the Tower of London. According to tradition, he was drowned in a butt of malmsey wine. *See also* Plantagenet, House of

Clarendon, Edward Hyde, 1st Earl of (1609–74) British statesman and historian. Hyde attempted to find common ground between Charles I and Parliament, but the Grand Remonstrance (1641) saw him throw his moderating influence behind the king. In 1645 he joined Prince Charles (later Charles II) in exile, where he began to write *History of the Rebellion and Civil Wars in England.* Clarendon was the principal architect of the Declaration of Breda (1660) that resulted in the Restoration of the monarchy in England. In 1660 his daughter, Anne, married Prince James (later James II). In 1661 he was made Earl of Clarendon. As lord chancellor to Charles II, he initiated (but disapproved of) four statutes collectively known as the **Clarendon Code**. The statutes restricted gatherings of Puritans and Nonconformists, and the movement of their ministers. In addition, all ministers were forced to use the Anglican Book of Common Prayer. Following defeats in the Dutch Wars, Clarendon was impeached and forced into exile in 1667. *See also* Nonconformism

Clarendon, Constitutions of (1164) Sixteen articles issued by Henry II of England to limit the independence and privileges of the clergy. The most controversial article required clergy who had been convicted in church courts to be punished by royal courts. They played a significant role in the dispute between Henry II and Thomas à Becket.

Clark, George Rogers (1752–1818) American Revolutionary general. In 1778 Clark led an expedition from Kentucky against the British in Illinois country, capturing Kaskaskia, Cahokia and Vincennes. His conquests were responsible for gaining the Midwestern territories for the United States.

Clark, Joe (Charles Joseph) (1939–) Canadian statesman, prime minister (1979–80). He was elected to Parliament in 1972. In 1979, aged 40, Clark became Canada's youngest prime minister, succeeding Pierre Trudeau. In March 1980, after only nine months in office, he lost his position to Trudeau. In 1983 Brian Mulroney succeeded Clark as leader of the Progressive Conservative Party.

Clark, Mark Wayne (1896–1984) US general. Clark served in World War 1 and was commander (1943–44) of the US Fifth Army in North Africa and Italy. After acting as allied commander in Italy, he was promoted to general and headed (1945) the US forces in occupied Austria. Clark was supreme commander (1952–53) of UN forces in Korea. *See also* Korean War

Clarke, Kenneth Harry (1940–) British statesman, chancellor of the exchequer (1993–97). He entered Parliament in 1970. Clarke served in Margaret Thatcher's Conservative cabinet as secretary of state for health (1988–90) and secretary of state for education (1991). In 1992 he became home secretary in John Major's first cabinet. As chancellor, Clarke increased taxation in his first budget, but reduced the basic rate by one penny in the 1996 budget. An outspoken Europhile, after the Conservatives' landslide defeat in the 1997 general election, he unsuccessfully challenged William Hague for the leadership of the Conservative Party.

Clarkson, Thomas (1760–1846) English deacon and campaigner against slavery. Working with William Wilberforce and other abolitionists, he devoted his life to securing abolition and its enforcement. In 1808 he published a history of the slave trade.

class In social science, a section of society sharing similar socio-economic status. A person's class is usually determined by the income and wealth of their parents. A class society is a system based on the unequal distribution of wealth. In Marxism, class is defined in relation to the means of production (land, capital). The bourgeoisie own the means of production and the proletariat provide the labour. In the *Communist Manifesto* (1848), Karl Marx and Friedrich Engels asserted that "the history of all society up to now is the history of class struggle."

classical Term used in many different and apparently conflicting ways. Literally, it refers to the period between the Archaic and the Hellenistic Age phases of ancient Greek culture. It is used more generally, however, to mean the opposite of romantic or to refer to the artistic styles whose origins can be traced in ancient Greece or Rome. As the antithesis of romanticism, it is an art which follows recognized aesthetic formulas rather than a style which focuses on individual expression. The Renaissance architect, Alberti (1404–72), took his inspiration from ancient Greek and Roman buildings, and classicism often suggests descent from antique sources. A classical style of Greek and Roman architecture dominated Europe from 1500 to 1900.

Claudius I (10 BC–AD 54) (Tiberius Claudius Drusus Nero Germanicus) Roman emperor (AD 41–54), nephew of Tiberius. As successor to Caligula, Claudius was the first emperor chosen by the army. He had military successes in North Africa (Mauretania) and Asia Minor (Lycia), and reincorporated Thrace and Judaea into the Roman Empire. In AD 43 Claudius conquered Britain. He undertook extensive administrative reforms and built both the harbour of Ostia and the Claudian aqueduct. Agrippina (the Younger), his fourth wife, supposedly poisoned him and made her son Nero emperor. *See also* Roman Britain

Claudius II (Marcus Aurelius Claudius) (214–70) Roman emperor (268–70). In 268 he decisively defeated the Alemanni who had invaded Italy. In 269 Claudius was given the title Gothicus ("conqueror of the Goths") after defeating the Gothic invasion of the Balkans.

Clausewitz, Karl von (1780–1831) Prussian soldier and military theorist. He served in the Napoleonic Wars (1803–15) against France. In his theory of large-scale warfare, *On War* (1832), Clausewitz argued that war is simply an extension of politics by other means.

Claverhouse, John Graham, 1st Viscount Dundee, (*c.*1649–89) ("Bonnie Dundee") Scottish soldier. Claverhouse distinguished himself serving William III (of Orange), Charles II and James II. He was killed fighting for James against William and Mary.

Clay, Henry (1777–1852) US statesman, secretary of state (1825–29). He served in both the House of Representatives (1811–14, 1815–21, 1823–25) and in the Senate (1831–42, 1849–52). He was one of the "war hawks" who favoured the War of 1812. Clay ran for president (1824), and when the election went to the House of Representatives, he supported John Quincy Adams. Adams rewarded Clay by making him secretary of state, and charges of political corruption were made. One of the founders of the Whig Party, Clay ran unsuccessfully for president against Andrew Jackson in 1832. In 1844 he ran for president again but was defeated by James Polk. Clay's last years in the Senate were spent in negotiations between the slave-owning states of the South and the free Northern states. He was an architect of the Compromise of 1850.

Clay, Lucius DuBignon (1897–1978) US general. He was commander of US forces in Europe and military governor of the US occupation zone in Germany (1947–49). In 1948 Clay organized the Berlin airlift.

Clayton Anti-Trust Act (1914) US legislation to strengthen the Sherman Anti-Trust Act (1890). It prohibited corporate practices not previously covered, including price discrimination, interlocking directorates, tying contracts and holding stock in competitor firms. It exempted trade unions from restraint of trade clauses.

Clayton-Bulwer Treaty (19 April 1850) Agreement between the United States and Great Britain negotiated by US Secretary of State John Clayton (1796–1856) and Sir Henry Bulwer. Among the Treaty's provisions were joint control of any ship canal built in Central America, and pledges not to occupy or colonize any part of Central

C

America. Viewed as a betrayal of the MONROE DOCTRINE, the Treaty was nullified by the HAY-PAUNCEFOTE TREATY (1901).

Cleisthenes (active early 6th century BC) Greek statesman, ruler of ATHENS (*c.*508–506 BC). His grandfather, Cleisthenes, was tyrant of Sicyon (*c.*600–580 BC). Cleisthenes is often regarded as the founder of Athenian DEMOCRACY. In *c.*507 BC, he weakened the local clan system by reforming the constitution and dividing the citizens into ten political tribes.

Clemenceau, Georges (1841–1929) French statesman, premier (1906–09, 1917–20). A moderate republican, he served in the Chamber of Deputies (1876–1893), favoured compromise in the revolt of the PARIS COMMUNE (1871), and strongly supported Dreyfus. Clemenceau made many enemies through his ability to make or break political careers and his implication in the Panama Scandal (1892) led to electoral defeat. In 1902 Clemenceau was elected to the Senate. Concerned with the growing power of Germany, his first term as premier saw the strengthening of relations with Britain. He was succeeded by Aristide BRIAND. Clemenceau's conviction that France could emerge victorious from World War 1 led to his return as premier in 1917. At the end of the war, he presided over the Paris Peace Conference (1919) and helped draft the Treaty of VERSAILLES (28 June 1919). *See also* DELCASSÉ; THÉOPHILE; DREYFUS AFFAIR

Clement III *See* GUIBERT OF RAVENNA

Clement V (*c.*1264–1314) Pope (1305–14), b. Bertrand de Got. He was made archbishop of Bordeaux by BONIFACE VIII in 1299. Clement's election to the papacy was sponsored by PHILIP IV (THE FAIR) of France. In 1309 Clement moved the papal court to AVIGNON, France. He supported Philip IV's suppression of the KNIGHTS TEMPLAR. At Philip's bidding, Clement withdrew his backing for the German king Henry VII to become emperor.

Clement VI (1291–1352) Pope (1342–52), b. Pierre Roger. He purchased Avignon and established an extravagant court. Clement offered sanctuary to Jews accused of causing the BLACK DEATH (1347–52) and declared all churches and offices were subject to papal control.

Clement VII *See* ROBERT OF GENEVA

Clement VII (*c.*1478–1534) Pope (1523–34), b. Giulio de' Medici. In 1513 he was appointed archbishop of Florence by Pope LEO X. As pope, Clement's hesitancy and self-aggrandizement contributed to the growth of PROTESTANTISM in Germany. Clement initially sided with Emperor CHARLES V in the ITALIAN WARS, but later joined (1526) FRANCIS I of France in the League of Cognac against Charles. In 1527 the imperial army sacked Rome and imprisoned Clement. His ruling (1533) that HENRY VIII of England's marriage to CATHERINE OF ARAGON was valid led to England's break with Rome. *See also* REFORMATION

CIVIL WAR, ENGLISH (1642–46, 1648)

Conflict in England between Crown and Parliament. Following years of dispute between the king and state over the power of the monarchy, war began when CHARLES I raised his standard at Nottingham, central England. From his base at Oxford, s central England, Charles won an early victory against the Parliamentarian army, led by the Earl of ESSEX, at EDGEHILL (1642). Parliament's position, however, was stronger, as it controlled London and the SE, and the navy. The SOLEMN LEAGUE AND COVENANT (1643) between Parliament and the Scottish COVENANTERS forced the CAVALIERS to fight on two fronts. Parliament's victory at MARSTON MOOR (1644) was a turning point. In 1645 Charles and Prince RUPERT suffered a succession of defeats by the NEW MODEL ARMY, led by Sir Thomas FAIRFAX and Oliver CROMWELL, culminating in a decisive victory at NASEBY. In 1646 Charles surrendered to the Covenanters. In 1647 Charles reached a secret agreement with the Scots, promising to accept PRESBYTERIANISM in return for military support against Parliament. The second phase of the Civil War ended with Scottish defeat at the Battle of PRESTON (August 1648). The execution of Charles I (1649) provoked further conflict in 1650, in which Scots and Irish Royalists supported the future CHARLES II. Cromwell suppressed the Irish and the Scots, the final battle being fought at WORCESTER (August 1651).

► **Royalist captain of infantry (left) and cuirassier (right)** The Royalist cavalry was superior in number to the Parliamentarian forces at the start of the War, but the formation of the New Model Army tipped the balance.

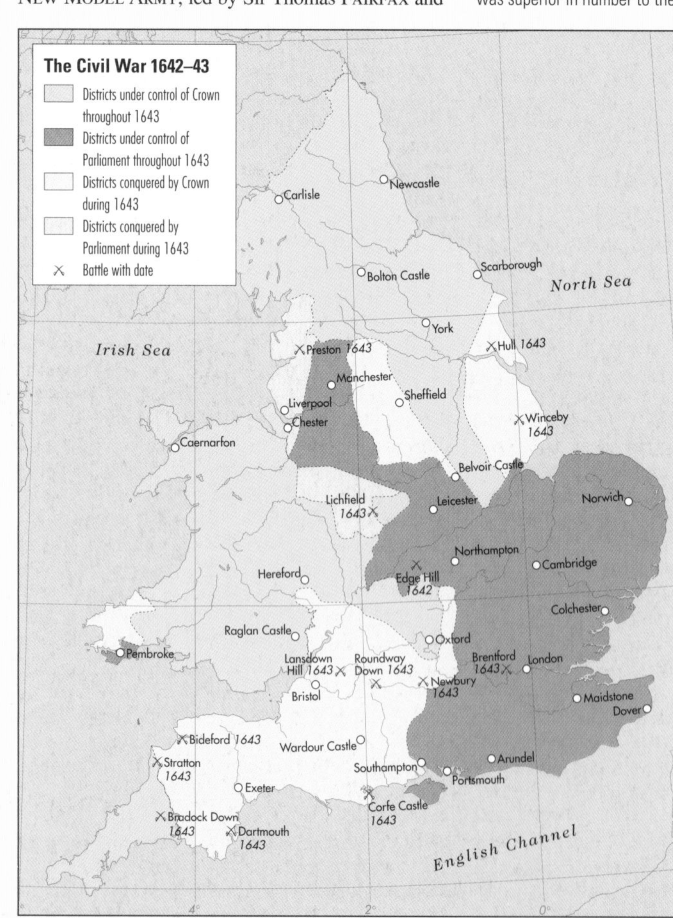

▲ **English Civil War (1642–43)** Following victory at Edgehill, the king conquered SW England with a victory at Corfe Castle. Parliamentarian support was in the SE, but after their victory at Preston they extended their influence further north.

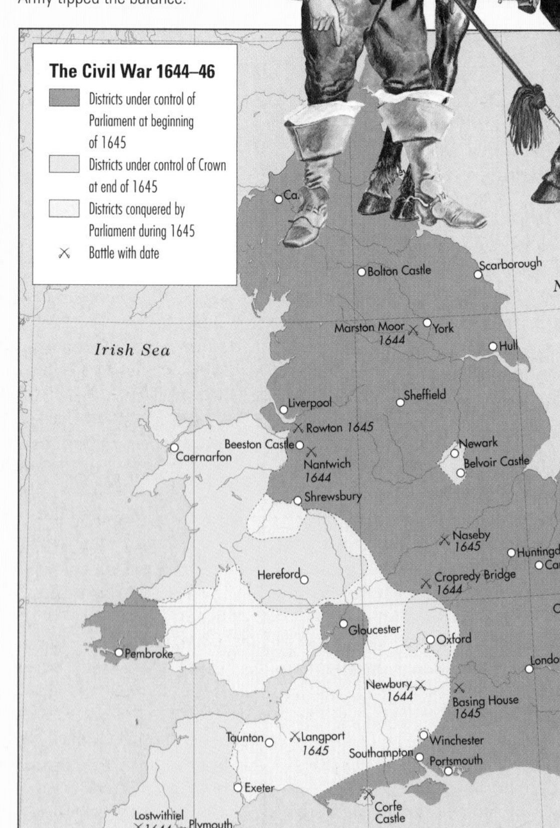

▲ **English Civil War (1644–46)** The second phase of the War saw two decisive victories for the Parliamentarians at Marston Moor and Naseby. They were then able to regain SW England and conquered NE England up to the Scottish border.

CIVIL WAR, SPANISH (1936–39)

Conflict developing from a military rising against the Republican government in Spain. The revolt, led by General Franco, began in Spanish Morocco. It was supported by conservatives, the Catholic Church and reactionaries of many kinds, collectively known as the Nationalists and including the fascist Falange. The leftist Popular Front government was supported by republicans, socialists and a variety of ill-coordinated leftist groups, collectively known as Loyalists or Republicans. The Nationalists swiftly gained control of most of rural w Spain. The Civil War represented the first major clash between the forces of the extreme right and the extreme left in Europe. Franco received extensive military support, especially aircraft, from the fascist dictators Benito Mussolini and Adolf Hitler. The Soviet Union provided more limited aid for the Republicans. Liberal and socialist sympathizers from countries such as Britain and France formed the Republican volunteer force of the International Brigades, but their governments remained neutral. In 1937 the Nationalists extended their control, while the Republicans were weakened by internal quarrels. In 1938 the Nationalists reached the Mediterranean, splitting Republican forces. In March 1939, after a long siege, Madrid fell to the Nationalists and the Civil War was at an end. It had claimed *c.*500,000 Spanish lives.

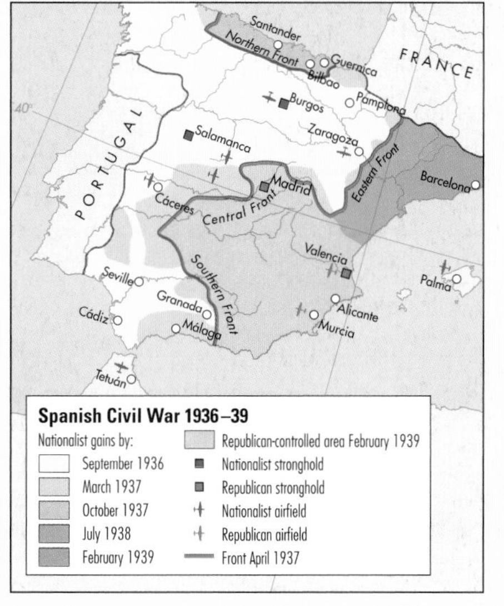

▲ **Spanish Civil War** By November 1936, Franco's forces had laid siege to Madrid. In 1937 they took the Basque N provinces, and by the end of 1938 Republican forces were confined to Catalonia and Madrid.

Clement XI (1649–1721) Pope (1700–21), b. Giovanni Francesco Albani. His papacy was dominated by the War of the Spanish Succession (1701–14) between the Habsburgs and Bourbons. In 1714 Clement was forced to cede the Kingdom of Naples to the Holy Roman Empire. In 1713, he issued his papal bull Unigenitus condemning Jansenism. Clement's ban on the use of indigenous or local customs in missions led to greater persecution of natives in European colonies.

Clement XIV (1705–74) Pope (1769–74), b. Giovanni Ganganelli. Although Clement was educated by the Jesuits, he was forced to dissolve the order under pressure from Portugal, Spain and France in 1773. The resultant suppression of the Jesuits haunted the remainder of his papacy.

Cleomenes I (d. *c.*490 BC) King of Sparta (*c.*519–490 BC). In 510 BC he led an army to Athens and expelled the tyrant Hippias. In 507 BC, alarmed at the democratic reforms of Cleisthenes, Cleomenes attacked Athens once more. The Athenians rose in support of Cleisthenes and expelled the Spartans. In 506 a further expedition against Cleisthenes also failed. Cleomenes' defeat of Argos at the Battle of Sepeia (494) ensured the supremacy of the Peloponnesian League. Cleomenes, however, was forced to flee after securing the overthrow of his rival Demaratus.

Cleomenes III (d.219 BC) King of Sparta (235–219 BC). He established the supremacy of the monarchy in Sparta and extended the rights of citizenship. In 227 BC Cleomenes launched a war against the Achaean League, which in 222 BC allied with Macedonia to defeat Sparta. Cleomenes fled to Egypt, where he was imprisoned. In 219 BC he escaped and, failing to raise a revolt in Alexandria, he committed suicide.

Cleopatra (69–30 BC) Queen of Egypt (51–48 BC, 47–30 BC). In 47 BC she overthrew her husband, brother and co-ruler Ptolemy XIII with the aid of Julius Caesar, who became her lover. Cleopatra went to Rome with Caesar, but after his assassination in 44 BC, she returned to Alexandria, once again as queen. Mark Antony, who had become her lover following Caesar's death, followed her to Egypt, and they married (37 BC). The marriage infuriated Octavian (later Augustus), brother of Mark Antony's former wife. Rome declared war on Egypt and defeated Antony and Cleopatra's forces at the Battle of Actium (31 BC). Mark Antony committed suicide. Cleopatra surrendered to Octavian but then killed herself.

Clergy Reserves Income from land grants to support Protestant churches in Canada. The Constitutional Act (1791) set aside one-seventh of crown lands in Canada for the support of Protestant churches. The reserves, owned almost exclusively by the Church of England, became a source of religious and political dispute until 1854, when the lands were secularized.

Cleveland, (Stephen) Grover (1837–1908) Twenty-second and 24th president of the United States (1885–89, 1893–97). He rose to prominence as governor of New York (1883–84). With the help of Republican mugwumps, he defeated James Blaine to become the first Democratic president since the American Civil War. Cleveland's attempt to reduce the tariff contributed to Benjamin Harrison's electoral victory in 1888. In his second spell in office, Cleveland was faced with a monetary crisis (1893) and secured repeal of the Sherman Silver Purchase Act. In 1895 Cleveland broadened the scope of the Monroe Doctrine in response to Britain's boundary dispute with Venezuela. He sent troops to crush the Pullman Strike (1894) called by Eugene Debs. His attempt to maintain the gold standard angered radical Democrats, and Cleveland was not renominated in 1896.

cliff dwellers *See* Anasazi

Clinton, Bill (William Jefferson) (1946–) Forty-second president of the United States (1993–2000). Clinton became the youngest-ever US governor (aged 32) when he was elected to represent Arkansas (1978–80, 1983–92). Economic recession and Clinton's reformist agenda led to an easy electoral victory (1992) over the incumbent president, George Bush. As president, Clinton made health-care an immediate priority, appointing his wife, Hillary Clinton, to head a commission on reform. Bill Clinton was a chief advocate of the North American Free Trade Agreement (NAFTA), which won congressional approval in 1993. His first term was dogged by the Whitewater land and banking investigation and the blocking of reforms and appointments by a Republican-dominated Congress. Despite allegations of financial and personal impropriety, a buoyant domestic economy and Bob Dole's lacklustre campaign enabled Clinton to become the first Democratic president since Franklin Roosevelt to serve successive terms in office. Economic growth enabled Clinton to announce a balanced budget for 1998. His second term was dogged by sexual scandal. Following the investigations of Special Prosecutor Kenneth Starr, Clinton was forced to admit that he had an improper relationship with Monica Lewinsky, a White House intern. In 1998, facing charges of perjury over the affair, he became only the second US president (after Andrew Johnson) to be impeached. Clinton refused to resign and launched Operation Desert Fox (December 1998), a concerted bombing campaign against Iraq for failing to comply with UN resolutions. In 1999 he was cleared of impeachment charges.

Clinton, De Witt (1769–1828) US politician. He was a successful mayor of New York City (1803–15). In 1812 he ran for president but lost to James Madison. Clinton was governor of New York (1817–21, 1825–28). He was responsible for the construction of the Erie Canal (1817–25).

Clinton, George (1739–1812) US statesman, vice president (1805–12). He led the anti-British faction in the New York Assembly and was a delegate to the Second Continental Congress. Clinton served as a brigadier general in the American Revolution before becoming the first elected governor of New York (1777–95, 1800–04). He became vice president in Thomas Jefferson's second term. In 1808 he stood for president, but had to accept the vice presidency under James Madison.

Clinton, Sir Henry (1738–95) English general in the American Revolution. In 1777 he assumed command of New York but his failure to advance contributed to Britain's defeat in the Battle of Saratoga (October 1777). In 1778 he succeeded Sir William Howe as supreme commander in America. At the Battle of Monmouth (June 1778), Clinton overcame Washington's attempt to prevent him from reaching New York. In May 1780 Clinton captured Charleston, South Carolina, but in 1781 he failed to come to Charles Cornwallis' aid in the siege of Yorktown. Clinton resigned and was succeeded by Sir Guy Carleton.

Clinton, Hillary Rodham (1947–) US attorney and first lady (1993–2000), wife of Bill Clinton. In 1993 she drafted a plan to provide health insurance for all Americans, but it was not implemented. Clinton has been involved with women's rights around the world. Along with her husband, she was implicated in the Whitewater land and banking scandal. She firmly supported Bill Clinton through a series of allegations of extra-marital

CLINTON, BILL

Bill Clinton, with his wife Hilary Rodham Clinton. Bill Clinton's charisma and the healthy state of the US economy helped to secure his re-election in 1998, despite allegations of financial and personal impropriety. In his second term, Clinton called for a more bi-partisan approach to domestic politics. He set out his priorities of education and welfare reforms, a balanced budget and the expansion of NATO.

CLINTON IN HIS OWN WORDS

"Our democracy must be not only the envy of the world but the engine of our own renewal. There is nothing wrong with America that cannot be cured by what is right with America."
First Inaugural Address, 21 January 1993

"The road to tyranny, we must never forget, begins with the destruction of the truth."
University of Connecticut speech, 5 October 1995

liaisons. Hillary Clinton ran for senator of New York after her husband retired as president.

Clive (of Plassey), Robert, Baron (1725–74) British soldier and administrator. In 1743 he travelled to Madras, India, as an official of the English EAST INDIA COMPANY. Clive first attracted attention for his masterly use of guerrilla warfare, such as the capture of Arcot (1751), which prevented the French gaining control of s India. In 1757 he recaptured Calcutta from the nawab of Bengal. As first governor of Bengal (1757–60), Clive established British supremacy in India but his administration was tarnished by corruption. In 1760 he returned to Britain to gain a peerage. Clive returned to Bengal to serve a second term as governor (1765–67). He reformed the civil service and extended the East India Company's control to Bihar. In 1767 he left for England. Clive faced charges of embezzling state funds, but was finally acquitted in 1773. He committed suicide.

Clodius, Publius (*c*.93–53 BC) Roman politician. In 62 BC he was prosecuted for sacrilege by CICERO. In 58 BC Clodius was made tribune by the so-called first triumvirate (CAESAR, CRASSUS and POMPEY) in the mistaken belief that he would serve as a pawn. Clodius proved to a violent demagogue and exacted his revenge on Cicero by having him exiled for his role in the execution of CATILINE. Rome was beset by pitched battles between the rival gangs of Clodius and MILO. Clodius was killed by Milo's men, but a precedent had been set for the civil war between Caesar and Pompey. *See also* ANTONY, MARK; CATO (THE YOUNGER), MARCUS PORCIUS

Clotaire I (d.561) Frankish king (497–561), son of CLOVIS I and father of CHILPERIC I. On the death of Clovis (511), the Frankish kingdom was shared out equally between Clotaire and his three brothers. In 524 Clotaire divided the share of his deceased brother Clodomir with another brother, CHILDEBERT I. In 531 Clotaire conquered and divided THURINGIA with his brother Theodoric. He and Childebert seized and divided BURGUNDY in 534 and led an unsuccessful attack against the VISIGOTHS of Spain in 542. Clotaire became king of all the FRANKS after the death of Theodoric's heir (555) and of Childebert (558). *See also* MEROVINGIANS

Clotaire II (d.629) Frankish king, son of CHILPERIC I. He was an infant when he succeeded (584) as king of NEUSTRIA. In 613, after the death of King Theodoric II of AUSTRASIA, Clotaire became king of all the FRANKS. He put BRUNHILDA to death. In 614 Clotaire was forced to concede power to the nobility, establishing local rulers in Austrasia, BURGUNDY and Neustria.

Clovis I (*c*.466–511) Frankish king (481–511), son of CHILDERIC I and founder of the MEROVINGIAN dynasty. His victory (486) at Soissons ended Roman rule in GAUL and Clovis established his capital at Paris. In 496 Clovis defeated the ALEMANNI near Cologne. Clovis and many of his army later converted to Catholic Christianity at Christmas 496 (the traditional date) in fulfilment of a promise made before the battle. In 507 he attacked the VISIGOTHS but failed to capture s Gaul. On Clovis' death, the Frankish kingdom was divided among his four sons, CHILDEBERT I, CLOTAIRE I, THEODORIC I and Clodimir.

Clovis culture Prehistoric culture centred primarily on the plains of Arizona, New Mexico and w Texas. The first artifacts of this culture were excavated (1932) near Clovis, New Mexico. The remains date back to *c*.10,000 BC and disputably provide the oldest evidence of human colonization in the Americas south of Beringia. Like the later FOLSOM CULTURE, the Clovis were big-game hunters. Their tools, fluted stone points, are often found in association with mammoth bones.

Cluny, Order of Religious order founded (909) by William the Pious, Duke of Aquitaine, at the Monastery of Cluny, France. It was known for its high standards, reflected in strict observance of the BENEDICTINE rule and emphasis on dignified worship, a personal spiritual life, and sound economics. Its influence spread throughout s France and Italy, reaching its climax in the 12th century. The monastery at Cluny survived until 1790.

Clyde, Colin Campbell, 1st Baron *See* CAMPBELL, SIR COLIN, BARON CLYDE

CND *See* CAMPAIGN FOR NUCLEAR DISARMAMENT

Cnut *See* CANUTE II (THE GREAT)

Coates, Joseph Gordon (1878–1943) New Zealand statesman, prime minister (1925–28). Coates succeeded W.F. MASSEY as prime minister. His reform of the nation's infrastructure was curtailed by electoral defeat. Coates returned to government as minister of public works (1931–33) in the United-Reform coalition of George Forbes. As minister of finance (1933–35), Coates attempted to combat recession with stringent controls on interest rates. His austere measures fuelled unemployment and contributed to the Labour Party's victory in 1935 and 1938. He served as minister of armed forces (1940–43) in Peter FRASER's wartime cabinet.

Cobbett, William (1763–1835) English journalist and political reformer. He fought for the British in the American Revolution, and (as Peter Porcupine) his criticism of the fledgling democracy in the United States forced his return to England. In 1802 Cobbett founded his weekly *Political Register*. He was an outspoken critic of abuses of political power and a champion of the poor. Cobbett was imprisoned (1810–12) for his attack on flogging in the army and was forced into exile (1817–19) in the United States. On his return, Cobbett toured England in the campaign for parliamentary reform. His resultant masterpiece, *Rural Rides* (1830), describes the living conditions of rural workers. He was elected to Parliament in 1832.

Cobden, Richard (1804–65) British Radical politician. In the 1830s Cobden and John BRIGHT developed the ANTI-CORN LAW LEAGUE into a national organization. He was instrumental in persuading Sir Robert PEEL to repeal the CORN LAWS. Cobden and Bright were the chief spokesmen for the "MANCHESTER SCHOOL", which supported free-trade. As a member of Parliament (1841–57, 1859–65), Cobden was an arch critic of Lord PALMERSTON's imperialist foreign policy. In 1860 Cobden negotiated a major trading agreement with France.

Cochin China (Fr. *Cochinchine*) Historical region in s Vietnam, SE Asia. It was ceded by ANNAM to France under the terms of the Treaty of Saigon (1862). In 1887 it became part of French INDOCHINA. In 1949 it was incorporated into Vietnam and became part of South Vietnam in 1954.

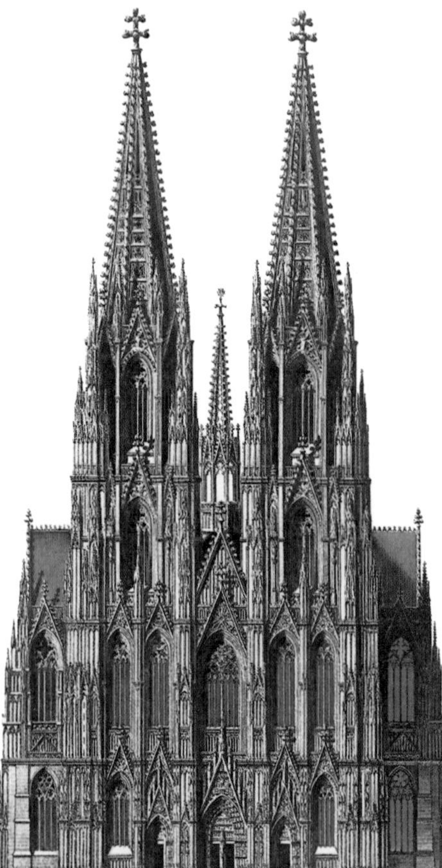

▲ **Cologne Cathedral** was built between the 13th and 19th centuries, and is the largest Gothic cathedral in Northern Europe. The western façade with its twin towers is shown.

Cochise (*c*.1815–1874) Chief of the Chiricahua APACHE. In 1861 the US army falsely imprisoned him, killing five of his relatives. Cochise escaped to lead his tribe in an 11-year war against the army in Arizona. He concluded a treaty that created a reservation. Cochise lived peacefully here until his death, after which the treaty was broken and his people forcibly moved.

Cochrane, Thomas, 10th Earl of Dundonald (1775–1860) British admiral. He became a hero in the NAPOLEONIC WARS after crippling a French fleet in the Bay of Biscay (1809). In 1814 Cochrane was dismissed from the Royal Navy after being found guilty of fraud. He helped in the liberation of Chile, Peru and Brazil in the 1820s and was reinstated by the British navy in 1832.

Coddington, William (1601–78) US colonist, b. England. He was one of the commissioners of the MASSACHUSETTS BAY COMPANY (1630), but his defence of Anne HUTCHINSON caused him to move first to Providence, then to what is now Portsmouth (1638). In 1639 Coddington helped to found Newport. He was governor of Newport (1640) and several times magistrate of the Rhode Island colonies (1674, 1675, 1678).

Code Napoléon French CIVIL LAW, first introduced (1804) by NAPOLEON I. Based on ROMAN LAW, the Code was intended to end the disunity of French law and was applied to all French territories. It banned social inequality, permitted freedom of person and contract and upheld the right to own private property. It was revised in 1904 and remains the basis of French civil law. *See also* CAMBACÉRÈS, JEAN JACQUES RÉGIS DE

Codreanu, Corneliu Zelea (1899–1938) Romanian fascist leader. In 1927 he formed the Legion of the Archangel Michael, the political wing of the militant IRON GUARD. In 1933 Codreanu arranged the murder of Premier Ion Duca. In 1938 he was imprisoned for treason and then shot, apparently while attempting to escape.

Coen, Jan Pieterszoon (1587–1629) Dutch colonial administrator, fourth governor general (1617–29) of the DUTCH EAST INDIES. In 1614 he became director general of the Dutch EAST INDIA COMPANY in Asia. Coen gradually gained control of the lucrative spice trade. In 1618 he crushed the rebellion of the sultan of Bantam and destroyed the city of JAKARTA, rebuilding it as the fortified Dutch city of Batavia. Coen brutally subdued the Banda Islands and founded a Dutch settlement on Formosa (now Taiwan). His plans for the colonization of Batavia were discarded after the Amboina Massacre (1623).

Coercive Acts *See* INTOLERABLE ACTS

Coeur, Jacques (*c*.1395–1456) French silversmith, merchant and official. In 1436 he became an adviser to CHARLES VII of France, controlling state financial affairs and instituting monetary reforms. His rise prefigured the ascendancy of the merchant bourgeoisie in the following centuries. Coeur ran a private fleet and used his considerable fortune to support the reconquest of Normandy in 1450. He built a gothic palace at Bourges, N France. He was then falsely charged with the murder of Agnès Sorel, mistress of Charles VII, and imprisoned (1451–55). Coeur escaped to Rome and died leading a papal fleet against the Ottomans.

Cohen, William (1940–) US statesman, secretary of defence (1997–). A former Republican senator from Maine, Cohen was appointed by Bill CLINTON partly as an attempt to ensure closer support for foreign policy initiatives from a Republican-dominated Senate.

coin Stamped metal discs of standard sizes used as tokens of money in commercial transactions. The earliest coins are of Lydian origin, from the 7th century BC. Early coinage also appeared in China and India. Ancient coins usually contained a specific quantity of precious metal, often gold or silver, and were stamped with the symbol of the issuing authority. With the introduction of banknotes in the late 17th century and the gradual decline of the quantity of precious metal in each coin, they became used for smaller money transactions. *See also* LYDIA

Coke, Sir Edward (1552–1634) English jurist. In 1593 he saw off the challenge of Francis BACON to become attorney general. Coke prosecuted for treason the Earl of Essex (1600), Sir Walter Raleigh (1603), and the conspirators in the Gunpowder Plot (1605). In 1606 he was made chief justice of the Court of Common Pleas, where he upheld common law against the royal prerogative of James I. In 1613 he was appointed chief justice of the Court of King's Bench, but continued to frustrate the king's will and was dismissed in 1616. In 1620 Coke entered Parliament, where he helped to draft the Petition of Right (1628). He wrote the influential *Institutes of the Laws of England* (1628). *See also* Eliot, John

Colbert, Jean Baptiste (1619–83) French statesman, the principal exponent of mercantilism. He came to prominence as an adviser to Cardinal Mazarin. From 1661, when Louis XIV began his personal rule, Colbert controlled most aspects of government: reforming taxation and manufacturing, reducing tariffs, establishing commercial companies, such as the French East India Company, and strengthening the navy.

Colchester City on the River Colne, Essex, se England. It was the capital of Cymbeline and the site of the first Roman colony in Britain (AD 43). In 61 Colchester was attacked by Boadicea. It has a Roman wall and a fine Norman castle. Pop. (1991) 142,515.

Cold Harbor, Battle of (3 June 1864) American Civil War engagement at Cold Harbor, Virginia. In one of the worst defeats for the Union, General Ulysses Grant lost 7000 men in less than an hour during one attack on General Robert Lee's entrenched Confederate troops. Confederate casualties numbered 1500. General Grant's depleted army of *c.*93,000 men were able, however, to continue their advance towards Richmond, Virginia.

Cold War *See* feature article, page 96

Coligny, Gaspard II de, Seigneur de Châtillon (1519–72) French Protestant leader. In 1552 he was made admiral of France. While imprisoned (1557–59) by the Spanish, Coligny converted to Calvinism. He and Louis I de Condé led the Huguenot forces against the Catholic House of Guise in the Wars of Religion (1562–98). On Condé's death (1569), Coligny was elected commander in chief and helped to establish favourable terms at the Treaty of St Germain (1570). Coligny became leading adviser to Charles IX. Catherine de' Medici's assassination of Coligny led to the Saint Bartholomew's Day Massacre (1572).

collectivization Agricultural policy first enforced (1929) in the Soviet Union under Joseph Stalin and adopted by China after Mao Zedong came to power in 1949. With the object of modernizing agriculture and making it more efficient, small peasant holdings were combined and agriculture brought under state control.

Collingwood, Cuthbert, Baron (1748–1810) British naval commander. He became a rear admiral in 1797 and was made vice admiral in 1804. Collingwood took part in the Battle of the Glorious First of June (1794) and the Battle of Cape St Vincent (1797). He was Horatio Nelson's second-in-command at the Battle of Trafalgar (1805), taking command after Nelson's death in battle.

Collins, Michael (1890–1922) Irish revolutionary. He was imprisoned for a year for his role in the Easter Rising (1916). A leading member of Sinn Féin, Collins helped establish (1918) the Dáil Eireann (Irish assembly). He was the leader of the Irish Republican Army (IRA) campaign against British troops. With Arthur Griffith, he negotiated the treaty (1921) that created the Irish Free State and the partition of Ireland. Collins was assassinated by extremist republicans. *See also* De Valera, Eamon

Collor de Mello, Fernando (1949–) Brazilian statesman, president (1990–92). In 1990, as leader of the National Reconstruction Party, Collor became the youngest-ever president of Brazil. His programme of economic growth and modernization failed to halt the recession in Brazil. In 1992 Collor was forced to resign after being impeached for corruption. He was succeeded by vice president Itamar Franco.

Cologne (Köln) City on the River Rhine, Nordrhein Westfalen, w Germany. It was made a Roman colony in AD 50 and under Constantine a fortress was built across the river. In 785 Cologne was made an archbishopric by Charlemagne and it enjoyed great influence during the Middle Ages. The Golden Bull confirmed its archbishop's electoral status. It was heavily bombed during World War 2. Notable sites include the largest Gothic cathedral in N Europe (started 1248, completed 1880), and the Gürzenich (a Renaissance banquet house). Its university was founded in 1388. Pop. (1990) 958,600.

Colombia *See* country feature

Colombo Capital and chief seaport of Sri Lanka, on the sw coast. Settled in the 6th century BC, it was taken by Portugal in the 16th century and by the Dutch in the 17th century. It was captured by the British in 1796 and became the capital in 1815. With the rest of Sri Lanka, it gained independence in 1948. Pop. (1992 est.) 684,000.

Colombo Plan International organization with headquarters in Colombo, Sri Lanka, which seeks to promote the economic and social development in s and se Asia. Initiated (1951) by the Commonwealth of Nations, it now includes 26 states including the United States, Canada, Japan and the United Kingdom.

colonialism Control by one country over a dependent area or people. Although associated with modern political history, the practice is ancient. In European colonial history, economic, political and strategic factors were involved in the world empires of countries, such as Britain and France, subjugating mainly African and Asian states and often creating artificial boundaries. After World War 2, colonialist exploitation was widely recognized, and colonial powers conceded, willingly or not, independence to their colonies. *See also* imperialism

Colonna, Sciarra (d.1329) Roman aristocrat politician, leading opponent of a rival Roman, Pope Boniface VIII (Caetani). In 1297 he was excommunicated and the family exiled from their power-base at Palestrina. In 1303 Colonna led the French force that captured Boniface. As senator of Rome, he crowned Emperor Louis IV. *See also* Ghibelline; Martin V

Colorado Mountain state in w central United States; the state capital is Denver. The original inhabitants of the region include the Arapaho, Cheyenne and Ute. The United States acquired the E of the state from France in the Louisiana Purchase (1803). The remainder was ceded by Mexico after the Mexican War (1848). The discovery of gold and silver encouraged immigration, and Colorado was made a territory in 1861. Area: 268,658sq km (103,729sq mi). Pop. (1990) 3,294,394.

Colosseum Amphitheatre in Rome built between AD 72 and 80, begun by Emperor Vespasian and completed by his son, Titus. It measures 189 × 156m (620 × 513ft) by 45.7m (150ft) high, and seated *c.*50,000 people. Citizens of Rome came here to watch gladiatorial contests and, according to tradition, the martyrdom of Christians.

COLORADO
Statehood :
1 August 1876
Nickname :
The Centennial State
State motto :
Nothing without providence

C

COLOMBIA

AREA: 1,138,910sq km (439,733sq mi)
POPULATION: 33,424,000
CAPITAL (POPULATION): Bogotá (4,921,000)
GOVERNMENT: Multiparty republic
ETHNIC GROUPS: Mestizo 58%, White 20%, Mulatto 14%, Black 4%, mixed Black and Indian 3%, Native American 1%
LANGUAGES: Spanish (official)
RELIGIONS: Christianity (Roman Catholic 93%)
GDP PER CAPITA (1995): US$6130

Republic in NW South America. The advanced Chibcha civilization thrived in the E cordillera between *c.*AD 1000 and *c.*1500. In 1525 the Spanish established the first European settlement at Santa Marta. By 1538 the conquistador Gonzalo Jiménez de Quesada had conquered the Chibcha and established Bogotá. Colombia became part of the Viceroyalty of New Granada, whose territory also included Ecuador, Panama and Venezuela. Bogotá became the colonial capital.

In 1819 Simón Bolívar defeated the Spanish at Boyacá and established Greater Colombia. Bolívar became president. In 1830 Ecuador and Venezuela gained independence and in 1885 the Republic of Colombia (which included Panama) was formed. Differences between Republican and Federalist factions proved irreconcilable and the first civil war (1899–1902) claimed *c.*100,000 lives. In 1903 Panama, aided by the United States, achieved independence. The second civil war, *La Violencia* (1949–57), was even more bloody. Political corruption, violence and repression became endemic. In 1957 Liberal and Conservative parties formed a National Front Coalition, which remained in power until 1974.

Throughout the 1970s Colombia's illegal trade in cocaine grew steadily, creating wealthy drug barons. In the 1980s armed cartels (such as the Cali) became a destabilizing force, and political and media assassinations were frequent. A new constitution (1991) protected human rights. In 1994 the Liberal leader Ernesto Samper was elected president. The 1998 presidential elections were won by the Social Conservative Party (PSC) candidate Andrés Pastrana Arango. In an effort to end the guerrilla war that had lasted for 30 years, Pastrana entered into negotiations with the Revolutionary Armed Forces of Colombia (FARC) and the National Liberation Army (ELN). In September 1998, as part of new austerity measures, Colombia devalued the peso, triggering the longest strike (20 days) in its history.

C

Colossus of Rhodes One of the SEVEN WONDERS OF THE WORLD, a bronze statue of the Sun god overlooking the harbour at Rhodes, SE Greece. It is believed to have stood more than 30.5m (100ft) high. It was built, at least in part, by Chares of Lindos between *c*.292 BC and *c*.280 BC and destroyed by an earthquake (*c*.224 BC).

Columba, Saint (521–97) Irish Christian missionary in Ireland and Scotland. He founded several monasteries in Ireland before leaving (563) to found a monastery on the island of Iona. Iona acted as the base for the conversion of Scotland to Christianity. His feast day is 9 June.

Columban, Saint (543–615) (Columbanus) Irish Christian missionary to the continent of Europe. Accompanied by 12 fellow monks, Columban left (*c*.590) Ireland for Gaul where he founded three monasteries. Columban's adherence to the very austere Celtic practices led to his expulsion from here in 610. In 612 he founded a fourth abbey at Bobbio, Italy, where he died. His feast day is 23 November.

Columbia, District of *See* WASHINGTON, D.C.

Columbus, Christopher *See* feature article

Comanche Shoshonean-speaking NATIVE NORTH AMERICANS. They separated from the parent SHOSHONE in the distant past and migrated from E Wyoming into Kansas. One of the first tribes to acquire the horse from the Spanish, they introduced it to the tribes of the Great Plains as they moved southward. Numbering up to 10,000 at the beginning of the 19th century, conflict with US forces resulted in their near extinction by 1874. Today, *c*.4500 Comanche live on reservations in SW Oklahoma.

Combination Acts British acts of Parliament (1799, 1800) making combinations (trade UNIONS) of workers illegal. The government feared they were potentially subversive. Trade unions nevertheless multiplied after 1815, and in 1824 the Acts were repealed. A later Combination Act (1825) restricted the right to strike

COLD WAR (1947–91)

Political, ideological and economic confrontation between the UNITED STATES and its allies on the one hand and the communist bloc led by the SOVIET UNION on the other. Characterized by extreme tension and hostility, it had a detrimental effect on international relations of the period.

After World War 2 it quickly became apparent that the Soviet Union under Joseph STALIN was intent on establishing COMMUNISM in Eastern Europe. By 1948 the governments of Poland, East Germany, Hungary, Romania, Bulgaria and Czechoslovakia had been transformed from multiparty coalitions to communist governments which adhered strictly to the policies and practices of the Soviet government. The "Iron Curtain", dividing the communist regimes from the rest of Europe, had fully descended.

THE TRUMAN DOCTRINE

In 1947, following Britain's announcement that it would no longer be able to provide support for the Greek and Turkish governments, US President Harry TRUMAN produced the "TRUMAN DOCTRINE". This stated that the United States would oppose any further expansion of communist territory and would provide a financial package to help Greece and Turkey defend themselves from external interference. It was followed by the MARSHALL PLAN, which provided US$13.5 billion in economic aid to the war-torn countries of Europe as a means of combatting the spread of communism across the continent.

THE DEEPENING OF THE WAR

The Cold War intensified with the Berlin Blockade of 1948–49 (*see* BERLIN AIRLIFT), a communist uprising in Malaya in 1948, and the formation of the People's Republic of China in 1949, when the Chinese communists, led by MAO ZEDONG and supported by the Soviet Union, finally defeated the US-backed forces of CHIANG KAI-SHEK. All these crises encouraged the creation of a string of Western military alliances to deter any further expansion of communist territory, beginning with the formation of the NORTH ATLANTIC TREATY ORGANIZATION (NATO) in 1949.

In the same year the Soviet Union produced its first atomic bomb, and the Cold War took on a new character. Tension increased among the NATO countries, while the Soviet Union, knowing that it could match NATO in nuclear capacity, gained in confidence and in 1955 it established the WARSAW PACT. Despite, or because of, the huge arsenal of nuclear weapons stockpiled by both sides, none was ever used in warfare. Indeed, the Cold War never resulted in actual combat between US and Soviet troops, the risk of nuclear weapons becoming involved being far too high. Instead, it took on the form of an ARMS RACE – and later a space race – and the provision of economic aid and military equipment to other countries in order to gain political influence. In some cases, both sides intervened to defend their own ideology, and in a few cases one of them sent in troops.

The KOREAN WAR (1950–53), when communist North Korea invaded South Korea, was one of the largest and bloodiest confrontations of the Cold War. It marked the beginning of more than 12 years of intense global tension and rivalry between the superpowers, culminating in the CUBAN MISSILE CRISIS (1962). This almost resulted in a Third World War, the tension only easing when the Soviet leader, Nikita KHRUSHCHEV, agreed to withdraw Soviet missiles from Cuba.

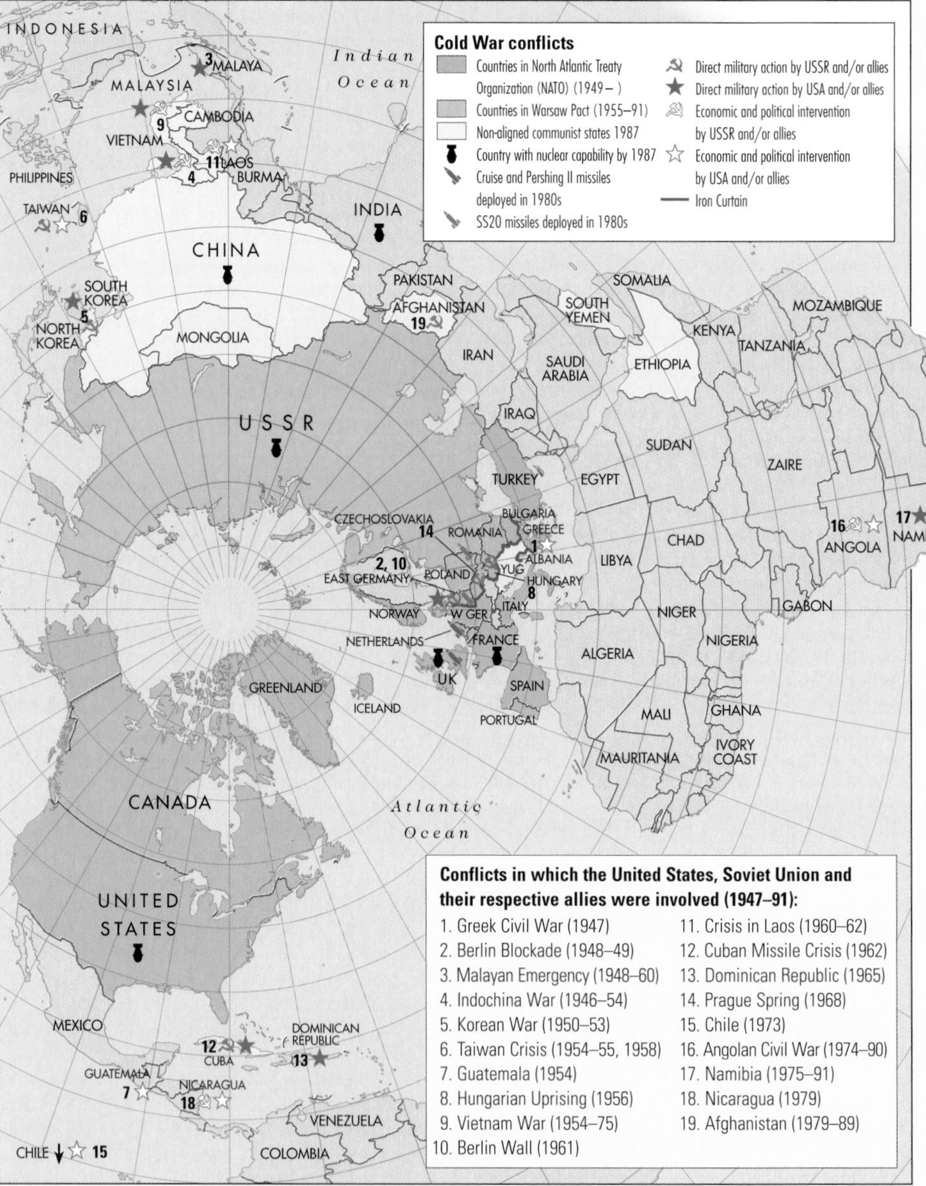

THE THAWING OF THE WAR

Over the next 20 years attempts by both superpowers to ease tensions and "thaw" the Cold War resulted in DÉTENTE and the STRATEGIC ARMS LIMITATION TALKS (SALT). Meanwhile, indirect confrontation took place in the VIETNAM WAR (1954–75), during which the United States deployed hundreds of thousands of troops (1964–73) to fight communist North Vietnamese forces who were attempting to unify their country.

In 1979, the Soviet Union invaded Afghanistan, producing a new period of hostility and a fresh arms race (*see* AFGHANISTAN WAR). This lasted until 1985, when the new Soviet leader Mikhail GORBACHEV revived summit meetings and ARMS CONTROL negotiations with the United States. He also gradually relaxed the Soviet grip on Eastern Europe and initiated a process of internal reform in the Soviet Union, resulting in the collapse of communism in the Eastern bloc during the "People's Revolutions" of 1989 and 1990 and the dissolution of the Soviet Union. With the demise of the Warsaw Pact in 1991, the Cold War came to an end.

and, as the Tolpuddle Martyrs (1834) demonstrated, union organizers could still be prosecuted.

COMECON Acronym for the Council for Mutual Economic Assistance

Comenius, John Amos (1592–1670) Czech religious leader and educator. Comenius was the last bishop of the Moravian Church. Comenius supported a universal system of education, regardless of gender. His best-known book was *Orbis Sensualum Pictus* (*The Visible World in Pictures*, 1658).

Comines, Philippe de (1447–1511) French statesman and historian. He served as a diplomat for Charles the Bold, Duke of Burgundy, before being enticed to work for Louis XI. Comines was Charles VIII's ambassador to Venice at the start of the Italian Wars. His witty if inaccurate *Mémoires* (1524) are an interesting source for his times.

Cominform (acronym for Communist Information Bureau) Agency established in 1947 to coordinate and provide information to the Communist Party of the Soviet Union and other European communist parties. It replaced the Communist International, abolished in 1943. Cominform was dissolved in 1956.

Comintern *See* Communist International

comitia Assembly of citizens in ancient Republican Rome. The early *Comitia Curiata* was drawn solely from the patrician class and had the power to elect officials and inaugurate priests. In *c.*450 BC a military assembly, *Comitia Centuriata*, was formed. Consisting of patricians and plebians, it had wider legislative and judicial powers but was dominated by the equites (the elite class). Its lawmaking function was taken over by the *Comitia Tributa*, established *c.*471 BC, in the 3rd century BC. The Comitia ended with the establishment of the Roman Empire.

Committee of Public Safety (6 April 1793–July 1794) Political organization of the French Revolution during the Reign of Terror. The Committee, elected by the National Convention, was charged with the responsibility of defending the Revolution. It was dominated initially by Georges Danton, but reverses in the French Revolutionary Wars led to the rise of Maximilien Robespierre. *See also* Carnot, Lazare Nicolas Marguerite

Commodus, Lucius Aelius Aurelius (161–192) Roman emperor (180–192), son and successor of Marcus Aurelius. Commodus' profligate, perhaps insane, rule was mainly spent organizing gladiatorial contests. His persecution of the Senate further stimulated political discontent. Commodus was assassinated by a wrestler.

Common Agricultural Policy (CAP) System of support for agriculture within the European Union (EU). The CAP was incorporated in the Treaty of Rome (1957). It was designed to increase food production within the EU and to ensure a reasonable income for farmers. The EU sets target prices for commodities. If prices fall below target to a level known as intervention prices, the EU buys up the surplus, creating the so-called "beef mountains" and "wine lakes". In 1988, to prevent overproduction, the EU introduced a policy of paying farmers to set aside part of their land as fallow. By 1994 the CAP was absorbing

COLUMBUS, CHRISTOPHER (1451–1506)

Genoese mariner and navigator, erroneously credited with the European discovery of America. Columbus believed he could establish a route to China and the East Indies by sailing across the Atlantic since, along with many learned contemporaries, he believed the circumference of the Earth to be much smaller than it is. He secured Spanish patronage for his four voyages from the Spanish monarchs Ferdinand V and Isabella I. On 3 August 1492, Columbus set out from Palos in s Spain with three ships, his flagship *Santa Maria*, the *Pinta* and the *Niña*. He made landfall (probably in the Bahamas) on 12 October 1492, becoming the first European to reach the Americas since Leif Ericson. Believing he had reached the East, Columbus called the inhabitants "Indians". (He never surrendered his belief that he had reached Asia.) Columbus also visited Cuba and Hispaniola (now Haiti and the Dominican Republic), where the *Santa Maria* ran aground. He returned to Spain, his two ships laden with gold, spices and human captives. Columbus' discoveries laid the basis for the Spanish Empire in the Americas and, in September 1493, he set out on a second, larger scale expedition with the aim of colonization and Christian conversion of the natives. Columbus landed at Hispaniola, where a permanent colony was brutally imposed and ruled by his brothers Bartholomew and Diego Columbus. He also visited Cuba and Jamaica before sailing for Spain. In 1498 Columbus set out on a third voyage to explore south of existing discoveries in the hope of finding a strait between Cuba and India. He reached Trinidad, Venezuela and the delta of the River Orinoco, but failed to find a route to the east. Meanwhile, the repressive rule of his brothers had led to a rebellion on Hispaniola and the three Columbus brothers returned to Spain in chains. Columbus was released by Ferdinand and Isabella but barred from returning to Hispaniola. In May 1502, he sailed from Cádiz on his fourth and last voyage. Columbus explored the coast of Central America from Cape Honduras to Panama. On the return voyage, Columbus was marooned on Jamaica in 1503 and had to be rescued. His apocalyptic account of the voyages is contained in the *Book of Prophecies*.

▲ Columbus was not the first European to sail to the New World (Leif Ericson had visited America in *c.*1000 AD), but his voyages marked the beginning of an intensive European exploration of the Americas.

◄ The New World Following the success of his first voyage (1492), Columbus set off again in September 1493 and established the colony of La Isabela on Hispaniola. In 1498, he set sail again and after landing on Trinidad, he sailed into the Gulf of Paria and went ashore at the mouth of the River Orinoco. Following the rebellion on Hispaniola, Columbus lost favour with the Spanish monarchs and as a result his fourth voyage (1502) was poorly equipped. He searched the Central American coast for six months, but failed to find a westward passage.

51% of the total EU budget, having soared to 75% in the 1970s. It is one of the most contentious issues in the Union, and demands for reform are frequent.

common land Land on an estate on which, by a tradition dating from medieval times, the tenants of the estate are free to grow their own crops and pasture their own livestock. There are hardly any common lands still remaining in Europe, most having been swallowed up in the ENCLOSURE movement of the late 18th and 19th centuries.

common law Legal system developed in England and adopted in most English-speaking countries. Distinguished from CIVIL LAW, its chief characteristics are judicial precedents, trial by jury and the doctrine of the supremacy of law. Based originally on the King's Court, "common to the whole realm", rather than local or manorial courts, it dates back to the Constitutions of CLARENDON (1164). It is the customary and traditional element in the law accumulating from court decisions. A proliferation of statutes have come to supersede common law. *See also* ROMAN LAW

Common Market *See* EUROPEAN UNION (EU)

Common Prayer, Book of Official liturgy of the ANGLICAN COMMUNION. It was prepared originally (1549) as a reformed version of the old Roman Catholic liturgy for Henry VIII of England by Thomas CRANMER. In 1552 it was revised under the Protestant government of Edward VI. The THIRTY-NINE ARTICLES were added (1562) by Matthew PARKER. The Prayer Book was further revised in 1662 after the RESTORATION of Charles II.

Commons, House of *See* HOUSE OF COMMONS

Commonwealth (1649–60) Official name of the republic established in England after the execution of CHARLES I. The PROTECTORATE was set up in 1653, in which Oliver CROMWELL was given dictatorial powers. The Commonwealth ended with the RESTORATION of CHARLES II. *See also* RUMP PARLIAMENT

Commonwealth of Independent States (CIS) Alliance of 12 of the former republics of the SOVIET UNION. The CIS was formed in 1991 with ARMENIA, AZERBAIJAN, BELARUS, GEORGIA, KAZAKSTAN, KYRGYZSTAN, MOLDOVA, RUSSIA, TAJIKISTAN, TURKMENISTAN, UKRAINE and UZBEKISTAN. The BALTIC STATES (ESTONIA, LATVIA and LITHUANIA) did not join. All members, except Ukraine, signed a treaty of economic union in 1993, creating a free trade zone. Russia is the dominant power, with overall responsibility for defence and peacekeeping.

Commonwealth of Nations Voluntary association of 53 states, largely consisting of English-speaking countries that were formerly part of the BRITISH EMPIRE. It was established by the Statute of Westminster (1931). Headed by the British sovereign, it exists largely as a forum for discussing issues of common concern. A Commonwealth secretariat is located in London, England. Several countries have withdrawn from the Commonwealth, notably Burma (1947), the Republic of Ireland (1949) and Fiji (1989). Pakistan left in 1972 but rejoined in 1989.

Communards Supporters of the PARIS COMMUNE (1871). The Communards represented JACOBIN and patriotic feeling as well as socialist and anarchist ideals. They relied for their defence on the Parisian national guard.

commune Usually a community of people who choose to live together for a shared purpose. In the 19th century many communes tried to apply utopian socialist ideals. In the 1960s communes were formed intending to be cooperative, self-supporting and free of the values of mainstream society. In China farming communes exist, similar to the state farms of the former Soviet Union. *See also* PARIS COMMUNE; SOCIALISM; UTOPIANISM

communism *See* feature article

Communist International (Comintern, Third International) Communist organization founded (1919) by LENIN. He feared that the reformist Second INTERNATIONAL might re-emerge and wished to secure control of the world socialist movement. The Comintern was made up mainly of Russians and failed to organize a successful revolution in Europe in the 1920s and 1930s. In 1943 the Soviet Union abandoned the Comintern.

Communist Party, Chinese (CCP) Political organization established (July 1921) by LI DAZHAO and CHEN DUXIU. The Party was strengthened by its alliance (1924) with CHIANG KAI-SHEK's nationalist KUOMINTANG, but almost disintegrated when the communists were expelled from Chiang's group in 1927. MAO ZEDONG was the guiding force in revitalizing the CCP in the early 1930s. Under his leadership, solidified during the LONG MARCH (1934–35), the Party revised the Soviet proletariat-based model to fit the peasant-oriented economy of China and, after another four years of civil war from 1945, the People's Republic was proclaimed in Tiananmen Square (1 October 1949). The CCP had achieved complete political and military power. Its structure and hierarchy was nearly destroyed during the CULTURAL REVOLUTION but re-established after Mao's death (1976) by DENG XIAOPING. Following pro-democracy demonstrations (May 1989) the Party swung away from political reform. Yet, its flexible approach to economic reform enabled it to survive the collapse of Soviet COMMUNISM. In 1993 JIANG ZEMIN became president. The National People's Congress is the supreme legislative body and nominally elects the highest officers of state. Today, the CCP has more than 40 million members.

Communist Party, Italian *See* PCI

Communist Party, Spanish *See* PCE

Communist Party of America Radical party organized (1919) to represent the interests of workers, farmers and the lower middle class. In the 1932 presidential election the Party leader, William Zebulon FOSTER, polled more than 100,000 votes. In 1940 the Party severed its connection with the COMMUNIST INTERNATIONAL and began to lose strength. Subsequently, the Smith Act (1940), the McCarran Act (1950) and the Communist Control Act (1954) drastically reduced its rights and potential influence.

Communist Party of India (CPI) Indian political organization founded (1926) by M.N. Roy. Initially the CPI infiltrated existing bodies such as the Indian National CONGRESS. It rejected "Mahatma" GANDHI's tactic of non-violent civil disobedience. During the 1930s, the CPI rejected the parliamentary route to SOCIALISM and severed links with the Congress Party. During World War 2, communists were expelled from the Congress Party because of their support for the Allies. In 1942 the CPI supported the QUIT INDIA MOVEMENT. After independence was achieved, the CPI agitated against the formation of independent principalities, most notably in the TELENGANA DISTURBANCES (1946–51) in Hyderabad, s India. In 1964 the CPI split over the Sino-Soviet rift. The **Communist Party of India (Marxist)** has emerged as India's third-largest parliamentary party, after Congress and the BHARATIYA JANATA PAKSH (BJP), and has historically been the major political power in the states of Kerala and West Bengal.

Communist Party of the Soviet Union (CPSU) Former ruling party of the SOVIET UNION. It wielded all effective political power in the country and, via the COMMUNIST INTERNATIONAL, had considerable influence over communist parties in other countries. At its height, the CPSU had *c.*15 million members organized into *c.*400,000 local units (cells) throughout the Soviet Union. Party organization paralleled the hierarchy of local government administration, thus enabling Party control of every level of government. There were CPSU cells in almost all areas of Soviet life, such as the school system, armed forces, factories, collective farms, and the media. After the break-up of the Soviet Union in 1991, the Party was dissolved following a number of decrees by Boris YELTSIN. There remains a strong, traditional conservative power base of ex-CPSU members who are politically active in Russia. *See also* COMMUNISM; LENIN; individual party leaders

Comnenus *See* ALEXIUS I (COMNENUS); ANDRONICUS I (COMNENUS); ANNA COMNENA; ISAAC I (COMNENUS)

Comoros (Comores) Independent republic in the Indian Ocean off the E coast of Africa between Mozambique and Madagascar. The three major volcanic islands are Grande Comore (home of the capital, Moroni), Anjouan and Mohéli. France owned the islands between 1841 and 1909. In 1975 Comoros gained independence. In 1978 European mercenaries overthrew the government, and democracy was restored only in 1984. The 1996 presidential election was won by Muhammad Taki. In a 1997 referendum Anjouan voted for independence. Area: 1862sq km (719sq mi). Pop. (1994) 535,600.

Compromise of 1850 Set of balanced resolutions by US Senator Henry CLAY to prevent civil war. It replaced the MISSOURI COMPROMISE (1820). Congress agreed to admit California as a free state, organize New Mexico and Utah as territories without mention of SLAVERY, provide for a tougher FUGITIVE SLAVE LAW, and abolish the slave trade in Washington, D.C. *See also* KANSAS-NEBRASKA ACT

Comuneros, Revolts of the (1520–21, 1723–35, 1780–81) Uprisings by citizens of the *comunidades* (autonomous cities) in Spain and its colonies. The Revolt of 1520–21 was by citizens of the *comunidades* of CASTILE against Emperor CHARLES V. Led by Juan López de Padilla, it began in Toledo and rapidly spread across Castile. The nobles rallied to the royalists and defeated the *comuneros* at the Battle of Villalar (1521). The Revolt of 1723–35 was by the *comuneros* of

COMMUNISM

Political outlook based on the principle of communal ownership of property. The theory is derived from the interpretation placed by Karl MARX and Friedrich ENGELS on the course of human history. As outlined in the *Communist Manifesto* (1848), *Capital* (vol. 1, 1867) and other writings, Marx asserted that social and political relations depend ultimately upon relations of economic production. All value (and so wealth) is produced by labour, yet in a capitalist system, workers' salaries do not represent the full value of their labour. Thus, the working CLASS (PROLETARIAT) and the class that is in control of capital and production (the BOURGEOISIE) have conflicting interests.

CAPITALISM, it is asserted, is merely one stage in the progress of human institutions. As the forces of production (technology and capital stock) increase, the relations of production must change in order to accommodate them. Marx postulated that the bourgeoisie (by the nature of its operations) brought into being the urban proletariat. Conflicting interests within capitalism would inevitably lead to the overthrow of the bourgeoisie by the proletariat and so to the collapse of the system itself. This would be replaced, first by SOCIALISM and eventually by a communist society in which production and distribution would be democratically controlled, summarized in the slogan "From each according to their ability, to each according to their need". A socialist experiment was attempted by LENIN in Russia following the RUSSIAN REVOLUTION (1917). Joseph STALIN turned communism into an ideology to justify the use of dictatorial state power to drive rapid economic development. This process was used as a model for other communist countries, such as China and North Korea.

▲ **The Russian Revolution** (November 1917) enabled Lenin to establish a dictatorship of the proletariat and a one-party system. Much of the Bolshevik's support came from soldiers returning home from World War 1, seen here at a rally in the Catherine Hall, Tauride Palace, Petrograd.

COMOROS
AREA: 2235sq km (863sq mi)
POPULATION: 653,000
CAPITAL (POPULATION): Moroni (17,267)
GOVERNMENT: Transitional regime
ETHNIC GROUPS: Malagasy, African, Malay, Arab
LANGUAGES: Comorian, French and Arabic (official)
RELIGIONS: Muslim
GDP PER CAPITA (1994): US$301

Paraguay (1723–35), led by Antequera y Castro. It was the first major democratic uprising against Spanish rule in America. In New Granada (now Colombia), a further revolt of the *comuneros* (1780–81) initially halted the imposition of new taxes and legislation but was soon crushed by Spanish forces.

concentration camp Detention centre for military or political prisoners. The British set up camps for Afrikaner civilians during the second of the SOUTH AFRICAN WARS (1899–1902). The most notorious concentration camps were those established in the 1930s by the Nazi German regime for people considered racially or socially undesirable and political opponents. Some of these camps provided slave labour while others were the sites of mass execution. In Poland, more than 6 million people, mostly Jews, were murdered in the gas chambers. GULAGS were widely employed during Stalin's Great PURGE (1936–38), and re-education camps were used in the Chinese CULTURAL REVOLUTION and by the KHMER ROUGE. *See also* AUSCHWITZ; BELSEN; BUCHENWALD; DACHAU; HOLOCAUST, THE

conciliar movement Faction in the Roman CATHOLIC CHURCH that believes the governing authority should be a general council of the church rather than the pope. The movement was strongest in the late Middle Ages. Papal authority was weakened by the GREAT SCHISM (1378–1417), when rival popes existed in Rome and Avignon. That dispute was ended by the Council of CONSTANCE (1414–17), which, by declaring itself subordinate to God alone, strengthened the conciliar movement among religious reformers. *See also* ECUMENICAL COUNCIL

Concord *See* LEXINGTON AND CONCORD, BATTLES OF

Concordat of 1801 (16 July 1801) Agreement concluded between NAPOLEON I and POPE PIUS VII. It established Roman Catholicism as the religion of the majority of French people; the state was to pay the salaries of the bishops and some priests, and France's first consul had the right to nominate bishops to be confirmed by the pope. Napoleon wanted the Concordat in order to win over the clergy, and so disarm the royalists, and also to gain the support of Belgium and the Rhineland. Pius, although he did not want to alienate the royalists, needed French protection. Napoleon's subsequent addition of provisions for close state regulation of the clergy made it difficult to implement the agreement. Napoleon regarded the Concordat annulled on 23 February 1812, although it remained in force formally in France until 6 December 1905, when a bill separating church and state was passed.

Condé, Louis I de Bourbon, Prince de (1530–69) Military leader of the HUGUENOTS. In 1560 Louis was arrested and sentenced to death, but the demise of FRANCIS II led to his reprieve. The massacre of Huguenots at Vassy (1562) signalled the start of the French Wars of RELIGION. Louis occupied Orléans but was captured by the GUISE faction. CATHERINE DE' MÉDICI negotiated the Peace of Amboise (1563) but hostilities recommenced in 1567. Louis was killed in the attempt to rescue Admiral de COLIGNY at Jarnac, sw France. He was succeeded by his son, Henry I.

Condé, Henry II de Bourbon, Prince de (1588–1646) French political leader, grandson of Louis I de CONDÉ. He fled France during the reign of HENRY IV. Henry II returned after the king's assassination (1610) and blackmailed the regent, MARIE DE' MÉDICI, into giving him money and government appointments. In 1616 he was arrested and imprisoned. In 1619 Louis was released and thereafter loyally served LOUIS XIII.

Condé, Louis II de Bourbon, Prince de (1621–86) French general and leader of the FRONDE (1648–53). Louis gained the epithet "the Great Condé" for his annihilation of the Spanish army in the Battle of Rocroi (1643) during the THIRTY YEARS' WAR. At the start of the civil wars of the Fronde, Louis led the government assault on Paris but his subsequent imprisonment by Cardinal MAZARIN (1650) led to the second war of the Fronde. Louis was released and, allied with Spain, launched a revolt against the regency of LOUIS XIV. In 1652 Condé fled Paris but continued to lead resistance to the royal army until the Battle of the Dunes (1658). He was reconciled to Louis XIV and led the invasion of Franche-Comté (1668).

Condorcet, Marie Jean Antoine Nicolas de Caritat, Marquis de (1743–94) French philosopher, mathematician and politician. His *Essay on the Application of Analysis to the Probability of Majority Decisions* (1785) was a valuable contribution to mathematics. Condorcet was the only leading *philosophe* to play an active part in the FRENCH REVOLUTION. A moderate GIRONDIN, he was condemned by the JACOBINS and died in prison. In *Sketch for a Historical Picture of the Progress of the Human Mind* (1795), Condorcet suggests the progress of humanity to ultimate perfection.

condottiere Commander in the mercenary armies or "Free Companies" who fought in the wars among the Italian states in the 14th to 16th centuries. Both they and their armies were often foreign, and by the late 14th century the *condottieri* had begun conquering principalities for themselves. Famous among them were the Englishman Sir John Hawkwood (1320–1394) and Francesco SFORZA, who annexed Milan in 1450.

Confederate States of America (1861–65) (Confederacy) Southern states which seceded from the Union following the election of Abraham LINCOLN. South Carolina left in December 1860, and was followed closely by Alabama, Florida, Georgia, Louisiana, Mississippi and Texas. In March 1861, Jefferson DAVIS was elected president and a new constitution protected STATES' RIGHTS and retained SLAVERY. A capital was established at Montgomery, Alabama. The American CIVIL WAR began with the firing on FORT SUMTER (12 April 1861), and Arkansas, North Carolina, Tennessee and Virginia joined the Confederate States. The capital was moved to RICHMOND, Virginia. In 1862 the Confederate States brought in conscription to increase its army personnel to *c.*750,000 (half the size of the Federal Army). The Federal blockade of Southern ports prevented the export of "King Cotton" and the Confederate States received no external recognition. General Robert LEE's surrender at APPOMATTOX (9 April 1865) prefigured the collapse of the Confederate States

Confederation, Articles of *See* ARTICLES OF CONFEDERATION

Confederation of the Rhine (1806–13) League of German states proposed by NAPOLEON I after his victory at the Battle of AUSTERLITZ (December 1805). In July 1806 most of the middle and south German states placed themselves under the protection of Napoleon and committed troops to assist the French war effort. In August 1806, the HOLY ROMAN EMPIRE was officially dissolved. After Napoleon's defeat of Prussia at the Battle of JENA (October 1806) nearly all the German states, except Austria and Prussia, joined the Confederation. Soon France controlled the entire area between the Rhine and the Elbe. Napoleon attempted to dictate the Confederation's foreign policy via the CONTINENTAL SYSTEM. Napoleon's defeat at the Battle of LEIPZIG

CONGO

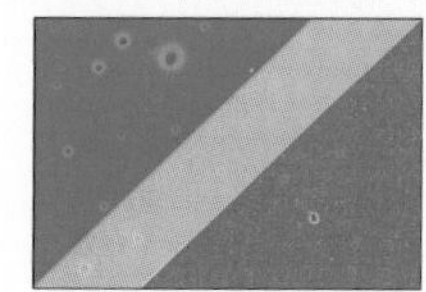

AREA: 342,000sq km (132,046sq mi)
POPULATION: 2,368,000
CAPITAL (POPULATION): Brazzaville (937,579)
GOVERNMENT: Multiparty republic
ETHNIC GROUPS: Kongo 52%, Teke 17%, Mboshi 12%, Mbete 5%
LANGUAGES: French (official)
RELIGIONS: Christianity (Roman Catholics 54%, Protestants 25%, African Christians 14%), traditional beliefs 5%
GDP PER CAPITA (1995): US$2050

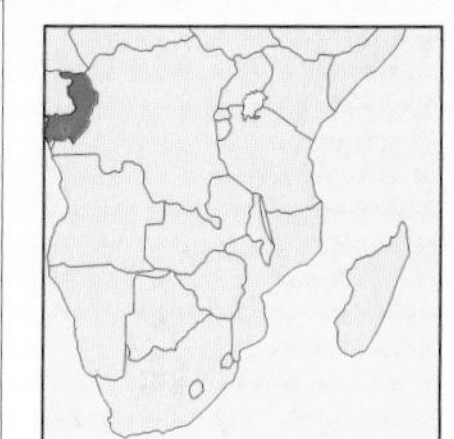

Equatorial republic in w central Africa. Between the 15th and 18th centuries, part of Congo probably belonged to the huge kingdom of the KONGO. The Congo coast became a centre of the European SLAVE TRADE. European exploration of the interior took place in the late 19th century, notably by the French explorer Pierre de Savorgnan de BRAZZA, who established the capital, Brazzaville.

The area came under French protection in 1880. In 1910 it became part of a larger region called French Equatorial Africa and remained under French control until 1960 when it became an independent republic. The first premier, Fulbert Youlou, outlawed all opposition but was overthrown in 1963. He was replaced by Alphonse Massamba-Débat and in 1964, Congo adopted Marxism-Leninism as the state ideology. In 1968 the military, led by Marien Ngouabi, seized power and Ngouabi created the Congolese Workers Party (PCT). Under Ngouabi, Congo became more Marxist and was renamed the People's Republic of Congo in 1970. In 1977 Ngouabi was assassinated, but the PCT retained power under Colonel Sassou-Nguesso. In 1990 the PCT renounced Marxism and Sassou-Nguesso was deposed. In 1992 democratic elections were won by the Pan-African Union for Social Democracy (UPADS), led by Pascal Lissouba. In 1997 following heavy fighting in the capital, Lissouba was deposed and Sassou-Nguesso was reinstated as president.

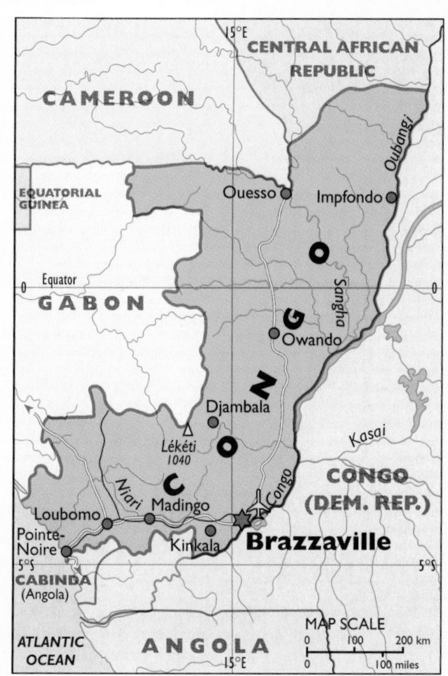

C

(October 1813) marked the start of the collapse of the Confederation, as one by one the German states and cities deserted Napoleon for the QUADRUPLE ALLIANCE. At the conclusion of the NAPOLEONIC WARS, the Congress of VIENNA (1815) created the GERMAN CONFEDERATION.

Confessing Church *See* NIEMÖLLER, MARTIN

Confucianism Philosophy that dominated China until the early 20th century and still has many followers, mainly in Asia. It is based on the *Analects* – sayings attributed to CONFUCIUS. Strictly an ethical system to ensure a smooth-running society, it gradually acquired quasi-religious characteristics. Confucianism views humans as potentially the most perfect form of *li*, the ultimate embodiment of good. It stresses the responsibility of sovereign to subject, of family members to one other, and of friend to friend. Politically, it helped to preserve the existing order, upholding the status of the MANDARINS. When the monarchy was overthrown (1911–12), Confucian institutions were ended, but after the Communist Revolution (1949), many Confucian elements were incorporated into MAOISM.

Confucius (*c.*551–479 BC) (K'ung-fu-tzu) Disseminator of CONFUCIANISM. Born in Lu, he was an excellent scholar and became an influential teacher of the sons of wealthy families. He is said to have been prime minister of Lu. In his later years he sought a return to the political morality of the early ZHOU dynasty.

Congo *See* country feature, page 99

Congo, Democratic Republic of *See* country feature

Congregationalism Christian church denomination in which local churches are autonomous; members have been called Brownists, Separatists and Independents. It is based on the belief that Christ is the head of the church and all members are priests. Modern Congregationalism began in England in *c.*1580. In the United Kingdom, the Congregational Church in England and Wales merged with others as the United Reformed Church (1972). In the United States, the Congregational Christian Churches united with others as the United Church of Christ (1957).

Congress, Indian National Oldest political party in India, whose fortunes have been often intertwined with the Nehru dynasty. It was founded in 1885, but was not prominent until after World War 1, when "Mahatma" GANDHI transformed it into a mass independence movement. Jawaharlal NEHRU became president of the Congress in 1929 and at independence (1947) became prime minister. Nehru's daughter, Indira GANDHI, became prime minister in 1966, but the party later split, and Indira's Congress (I) suffered a landslide defeat at the elections of 1977. In 1979 Indira returned to power. In 1984 she was assassinated and leadership of the country and party passed to her son, Rajiv GANDHI. In 1989 elections, following a further split, Congress was defeated. In 1991 Rajiv was assassinated. The Congress Party lost the 1996, 1998 and 1999 elections to the BHARATIYA JANATA PAKSH (BJP). *See also* AZAD, ABDUL KALAM; JANATA PARTY

Congress of Industrial Organizations (CIO) *See* AMERICAN FEDERATION OF LABOR AND CONGRESS OF INDUSTRIAL ORGANIZATIONS (AFL-CIO)

Congress of Racial Equality (CORE) US CIVIL RIGHTS organization, founded (1942) in Chicago, Illinois, by James Farmer (1920–99). CORE first attracted national attention for its sponsorship of the FREEDOM RIDES (1961) to end segregation on public transport. Using the tactics of non-violence espoused by Martin Luther KING, Jr, it organized sit-ins, pickets and boycotts to combat racial discrimination. CORE co-sponsored the March on Washington (1963).

Congress of the United States Legislative branch of the United States' federal government established by the CONSTITUTION OF THE UNITED STATES (1789). Congress comprises the SENATE (the upper house) and the HOUSE OF REPRESENTATIVES (the lower house). The main powers of Congress include the right to assess and collect taxes, introduce legislation, regulate commerce, propose constitutional amendments, mint money, raise and maintain armed forces, establish lower courts and declare war. Legislation must be passed by both houses and the president to become law. If the president uses the power of veto, Congress can still pass the bill with a two-thirds majority in each house. The Senate can approve treaties and presidential appoint-

CONGO, DEMOCRATIC REPUBLIC OF (FORMERLY ZAÏRE)

AREA: 2,344,885sq km (905,365sq mi)
POPULATION: 42,552,000
CAPITAL (POPULATION): Kinshasa (3,804,000)
GOVERNMENT: Single-party republic
ETHNIC GROUPS: Luba 18%, Kongo 16%, Mongo 14%, Rwanda 10%, Azande 6%, Bandi and Ngale 6%, Rundi 4%, Teke, Boa, Chokwe, Lugbara, Banda
LANGUAGES: French (official)
RELIGIONS: Christianity (Roman Catholic 48%, Protestant 29%, indigenous Christian churches 17%), traditional beliefs 3%, Islam 1%
GDP PER CAPITA (1995): US$490

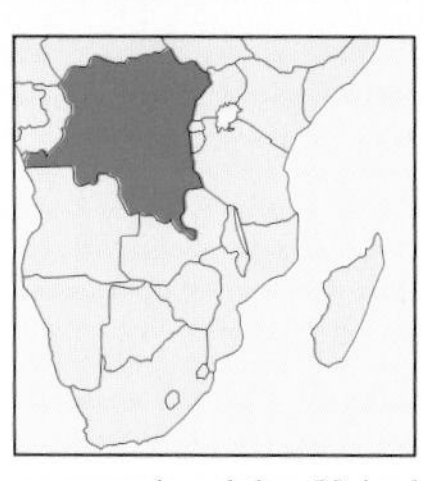

Country in w central Africa. The Democratic Republic of Congo is the second largest nation in Africa. By *c.*AD 1000, Bantu-speakers had largely displaced the native Pygmy population. From the 14th century large Bantu kingdoms, including the LUBA and LUNDA, began to emerge. In 1482 the Portuguese navigator Diego Cão became the first European to reach the mouth of the River Congo. In the 19th century, slave- and ivory-traders formed powerful states.

Henry Morton STANLEY's explorations (1874–77) into the interior established the route of the River Congo. In 1878 LEOPOLD II of Belgium employed Stanley to found colonies along the Congo, and in 1885 Leopold proclaimed the foundation of the Congo Free State. Leopold's personal empire was gradually extended, and concessionaires were granted control of the lucrative rubber trade. Sir Roger CASEMENT's denunciation of the brutal exploitation of the native population resulted in international criticism of Leopold. In 1908 Belgium responded by establishing direct control as the colony of Belgian Congo. European companies exploited African labour to develop the copper and diamond mines. Internal opposition to colonial rule was banned. In 1958 the French offered the Congo a free vote on independence. Nationalists in Belgian Congo demanded similar elections and in June 1960 it gained independence as the Republic of the Congo with Patrice LUMUMBA as prime minister. Belgium's failure to secure institutional changes, however, meant that the state was short-lived. The mineral-rich province of KATANGA demanded independence and Belgian troops, sent to protect its citizens and mining interests, were replaced by United Nations' (UN) troops. In September 1960 Joseph MOBUTU, commander in chief of the Congolese National Army, seized power. Lumumba was imprisoned and later murdered. In 1963 UN and government forces combined to force Katanga to drop its demands for secession.

In 1964, following the withdrawal of UN troops, Belgian Congo was again plunged into civil war. Belgian troops once more intervened. In 1965 Mobutu proclaimed himself president. Mobutu began a campaign of "Africanization": Leopoldsville became Kinshasa (1966); the country and river renamed Zaïre (1971); Katanga became Shaba (1972); and Mobutu adopted the name Mobutu Sese Seko. Zaïre became a one-party state, and in 1974 and 1977 Mobutu was re-elected unopposed. Political repression and endemic corruption led to renewed civil war in Shaba (1977–78). Secessionist forces were again defeated with European aid. In the late 1980s, an ailing Mobutu came under increasing pressure to reform and in 1990 he agreed to the formation of opposition parties. In 1995 millions of Hutus fled from RWANDA into E Zaïre to escape possible Tutsi reprisals. In 1996 rebel forces, led by Laurent KABILA, launched a successful offensive against Mobutu's regime and forced him into exile. Zaïre was renamed the Democratic Republic of Congo. Kabila's presidency held out the hope of democratic reforms, but in 1998 the Congo was plunged into civil war between government forces and the Tutsi-dominated Congolese Rally for Democracy (RCD). In August 1999 the warring factions signed the Lusaka Peace Agreement that ushered in a fragile cease-fire.

ments and tries the president if he or she is impeached. The House of Representatives initiates all tax bills and has the power to impeach the president. The Constitution requires that Congress meet at least once every year, and the president may call special sessions. The preparation and consideration of legislation is largely accomplished by the 17 standing committees in the Senate and a further 21 in the House of Representatives. The first meeting of Congress took place (1789) in New York City. Since November 1800, Congress has met at the Capitol, Washington, D.C. *See also* Supreme Court of the United States

Congress of Vienna *See* Vienna, Congress of

congress system Attempt during the early 19th century to conduct diplomacy through regular conferences between the European allies that had defeated France in the Napoleonic Wars. It originated in the Treaty of Paris (1815). The four powers (Austria, Britain, Prussia and Russia) met in 1818, 1820 and 1821. In 1822 Britain withdrew after opposing proposals to intervene against revolutionary forces in South America and elsewhere. In 1825 differences at St Petersburg, w Russia, between the three remaining powers caused the abandonment of the system.

Conkling, Roscoe (1829–88) US leader of the Republican Party in New York, representative (1859–63, 1865–67) and senator (1867–81). During the presidency of Ulysses Grant, he held absolute control over federal patronage in New York. President Rutherford Hayes, however, broke Conkling's stranglehold over appointments. In 1880 Conkling led the "stalwart" faction at the Republican convention that opposed the candidacy of James Blaine and secured the nomination of Chester Arthur as vice president. President James Garfield proved to be as unsympathetic as Hayes on the issue of patronage and Conkling resigned in protest. *See also* Tammany Hall

Connally, John Bowden, Jr (1917–93) US public official, governor of Texas (1963–69). Connally was seriously wounded as a front-seat passenger in the limousine in which President John Kennedy was assassinated in Dallas, Texas (22 November 1963). In 1971 President Richard Nixon appointed him secretary of the treasury. He resigned in 1972 in order to manage Nixon's campaign for re-election and he served as special aide to Nixon during the Watergate Affair. *See also* Oswald, Lee Harvey; Warren Commission

Connecticut State in New England, ne United States; the state capital and largest city is Hartford. When the first European settlers arrived from Massachusetts Bay Colony in the 1630s, the region was inhabited by Algonquian-speaking Native Americans and the contact led to the Pequot War (1637). The Connecticut Colony adopted the Fundamental Orders (1639) and received a royal charter from Charles II of England in 1662. Connecticut was one of the Thirteen Colonies that signed the Declaration of Independence (1776) from Great Britain. Connecticut's industries thrived during the Civil War and both World Wars. In 1974 Ella Grasso became the first woman to be elected governor in the United States. Area: 12,549sq km (4845sq mi). Pop. (1990) 3,287,116.

Connecticut Compromise *See* Constitutional Convention

Connolly, James (1870–1916) Irish nationalist. In 1903 Connolly went to the United States, where he helped establish the Industrial Workers of the World (IWW). Returning to Ireland, he formed a citizen army during the Dublin transport strike (1913). Connolly was executed by the British for his leading role in the Easter Rising of 1916.

conquistador (Sp. conqueror) Leader of the Spanish conquest of the New World in the 16th century. Conquistadors were often ex-soldiers unemployed since the Christian reconquest of Spain. The most famous were Hernán Cortés and Francisco Pizarro.

Conrad I (d.918) German king (911–18), successor of Louis IV (the Child), the last of the East Frankish Carolingians. His reign was beset by feudal rebellion and Magyar invasion. Lorraine, Swabia, Bavaria and Saxony rebelled against his authority. Conrad was succeeded by Henry I (the Fowler).

Conrad II (990–1039) German king (1024–39) and Holy Roman emperor (1027–39), founder of the Salian dynasty. He succeeded Henry II as king of Germany. Conrad suppressed an early revolt in Lombardy and marched to Rome, where Pope John XIX crowned him emperor in 1027. He defeated a rebellion in Germany and annexed Burgundy in 1034. He was succeeded by his son, Henry III.

Conrad III (1093–1152) German king (1138–52), founder of the Hohenstaufen dynasty. In 1128 Conrad was crowned as anti-king to Lothair II but was forced to submit in 1135. Upon Lothair's death, he was officially crowned king. Anxious to deprive Lothair's son-in-law, Henry X (the Proud), of a power base, Conrad awarded Saxony to Albert the Bear. Henry X's son, Henry III (the Lion), launched a civil war out of which emerged the rival factions of the Guelphs and Ghibellines. Conrad joined the Second Crusade but was never crowned by the pope. His Guelph (Welf) rivals initiated the Northern Crusade against the Wends in 1147. Conrad was succeeded by his nephew, Frederick I (Barbarossa).

Conrad IV (1228–54) German king (1237–54), king of Sicily and Jerusalem (1250–54), son of Frederick II. The conflict between Frederick and Pope Innocent IV saw the election (1246) of an anti-king, and Germany lurched into civil war. Conrad inherited Sicily and Jerusalem upon Frederick's death but was never crowned emperor. In 1254 he was excommunicated by the pope.

conservatism Political philosophy seeking to preserve the historic continuity of a society's laws, customs, social structure and institutions. Its modern expression derives from the response, first in Germany, to the liberal doctrines of the Enlightenment and the French Revolution. Originally conservatives supported mercantilism in preference to laissez-faire economics, but in the 20th century they have adopted the principles of the free-market and monetarism. *See also* Burke, Edmund; Christian Democrats; Conservative Party; liberalism; socialism

Conservative Party (officially Conservative and Unionist Party) Oldest political party in Britain. Its origins lie in the transformation of the early 19th-century Tory Party into the Conservative Party under Sir Robert Peel in the 1830s; it was mainly a party of landed interests. After the Reform Act of 1867 the urban and commercial element in the Party increased. It held power for 31 of the 71 years between 1834 and 1905 and for most of the 1920s and 1930s, either alone or in coalition. In the post-war period, the Conservative Party held office in 1951–64 and 1970–74. In 1979 the Party swung further to the right under the leadership (1975–90) of Margaret Thatcher. With the support of traditional Labour Party voters, it was able (under Thatcher and John Major) to win four consecutive elections. In 1997 William Hague, aged 36, became the youngest leader of the Party since William Pitt (the Younger) in 1783. *See* individual leaders

Constance, Council of (1414–18) Sixteenth ecumenical council of the Roman Catholic Church. It was convoked by the anti-pope John XXIII and Emperor Sigismund in order to end the Great Schism. The Council issued the decree "Haec Sancta" that asserted the authority of conciliar decisions over the papacy. In 1417 the Council deposed John XXIII and his rival popes, Gregory XII and Benedict XIII, and elected Martin V. The Council also attempted to combat contemporary heresies, notably that of Jan Hus and John Wycliffe.

Constans I (*c*.323–350) Roman emperor (337–350), youngest son of Constantine I (the Great). Upon his father's death (337), the Roman Empire was divided between Constans and his two brothers, Constantine II and Constantius II. Constans received Italy, Africa, Pannonia and Dacia. In 340 Constantine II was killed in battle against Constans in Aquileia, n Italy. Constans became sole emperor of the West. He was assassinated in an army mutiny.

Constant (de Rebecque), (Henri) Benjamin (1761–1830) French politician and novelist, b. Switzerland. A member of Napoleon's tribunate (1799–1802), he went into exile in 1803. After the Bourbon restoration, Constant led the liberal opposition (1819–22, 1824–30). His chief work was the psychological novel *Adolphe* (1816).

Constantine I (the Great) (*c*.288–337) Roman emperor, son of Constantius I (Chlorus), b. Naissus (now Niš, Serbia). He was raised at the Eastern court of Emperor Diocletian. In 305 Constantius and Galerius succeeded Maximian and Diocletian as Western and Eastern emperors respectively. In 306 Constantius died at York, n England, and Constantine was acclaimed as Western emperor by the army. Galerius, however, proclaimed Flavius Valerius Severus as Western emperor. Maximian and his son, Maxentius, defeated Severus, who was replaced by Licinius. Constantine invaded Italy and killed Maxentius at the Battle of Milvian Bridge (312). Constantine and Licinius were now confirmed as Western and Eastern emperors respectively. In 313 they signed the Edict of Milan that extending tolerance to Christians throughout the Roman Empire. In 324 Constantine crushed Licinius and became sole ruler. Constantine presided over the first ecumenical council of the Christian church at Nicaea (325), which condemned Arianism. He rebuilt (330) Byzantium as his capital, renaming it Constantinople (now Istanbul). He centralized imperial power and minted a new gold coin, the solidus, that remained the basic unit of Byzantine currency for a thousand years. Above all, Constantine was responsible for the Christianization of the Roman Empire. His commitment to Christianity was reflected in the building of the Church of the Holy Wisdom (the original Hagia Sophia), Constantinople, the first St Peter's basilica, Rome, and the Church of the Holy Sepulchre, Jerusalem. On his death, the Empire was divided among his sons, Constans I, Constantine II and Constantius II. *See also* Byzantine Empire

Constantine II (*c*.317–40) Roman emperor (337–40), eldest son of Constantine I (the Great). Upon his father's death (337), the Roman Empire was divided between Constantine and his two brothers, Constans and Constantius II. Constantine received the lion's share of the Empire – Britain, Gaul and Spain. He was killed in battle against Constans in Aquileia, n Italy.

Constantine V (718–75) Byzantine emperor (741–75). In 751 he launched a successful campaign against the Arabs in Armenia. Constantine summoned the Council of Hieria (754), which promulgated iconoclasm. He violently suppressed the monks who opposed this, earning himself the nickname Copronymus ("Dungname"). Between 755 and 764 Constantine waged war against the Bulgars, forcing them to sue for peace. *See also* iconoclastic controversy

Constantine VII (Porphyogenitus) (905–59) Byzantine emperor (*c*.913–59), son of Leo VI (the Wise). He concentrated on scholarship rather than government. Constantine wrote *On the Administration of the Empire*, a manual of foreign diplomacy intended for the guidance of his son, Romanus II, and a handbook *On the Ceremonies of the Byzantine Court*. Constantine shared power with his father-in-law, Romanus Lecapenus, from 920 to 945 before becoming sole ruler.

Constantine XI (Palaeologus) (1404–53) Last Byzantine emperor (1448–53), son of Manuel II (Palaeologus). In an effort to counter the threat from the Ottoman Empire by securing military assistance from the West, he proclaimed the union (1452) of the Western and Eastern churches. The ploy was unsuccessful and Constantine was killed during the siege and ultimate capture of Constantinople (now Istanbul) by Mehmed II.

Constantine I (1868–1923) King of Greece (1913–17, 1920–22), brother-in-law of German emperor William

CONNECTICUT
Statehood :
9 January 1788
Nickname :
Constitution state
State motto :
He who transplanted still sustains

C

II. The start of his reign was marked by Greek victory in the Balkan Wars. Constantine opposed the pro-Allied policy of Premier Eleutherios Venizelos at the start of World War 1. In June 1917 Constantine was forced to abdicate under pressure from an Allied blockade and Greece entered World War 1 on the side of the Allies. In 1920 he was restored to the throne by plebiscite and relaunched the war against Turkey. In 1922 Turkey captured Smyrna (now Izmir), prompting a military revolt. Constantine abdicated and died in exile.

Constantine II (1940–) King of Greece (1964–73). In 1964 he forced the resignation of Premier Andreas Papandreou. When a military junta seized power in Greece (April 1967), he launched an abortive coup against the "Colonels" and fled into exile. Constantine was formally deposed in 1973. In 1974 the junta was overthrown and Greece became a republic.

Constantinople Former name of Istanbul

Constantinople, First Council of (381) Second ecumenical council, convoked by Emperor Theodosius I. The Council condemned Arianism and, according to tradition, established the present form of the Nicene Creed.

Constantinople, Second Council of (553) Fifth ecumenical council, convoked by Emperor Justinian I. In 544 Justinian attempted to reconcile Monophysitism with orthodox faith by issuing a declaration of faith that countermanded the Council of Chalcedon (451). The Council approved Justinian's edict and was reluctantly endorsed by Pope Vigilius.

Constantinople, Third Council of (680) Sixth ecumenical council, convoked by Emperor Constantine IV. It condemned Monotheletism (the theory of Christ's one will) and affirmed the doctrine of two wills (divine and human) in Christ.

Constantinople, Fourth Council of (869–70) Regarded by the Roman Catholic Church as the eighth ecumenical council, convoked by Emperor Basil I (the Macedonian). In 858 Photius replaced Ignatius as patriarch of Constantinople. The papacy maintained that Ignatius was the rightful patriarch, a view supported by the Fourth Council. The Council excommunicated Photius. Its decision has never been accepted by the Eastern Orthodox Church.

Constantinople, Latin Empire of (1204–61) Empire established after the sacking of Constantinople (now Istanbul) by the leaders of the Fourth Crusade. The Empire lay on both sides of the Dardanelles and consisted of a number of subordinate fiefdoms ruled over by an emperor. The first emperor was Baldwin I. The Empire was constantly under attack from surviving Byzantine princes who set up Greek states surrounding the lost capital. The Latins lost Thessalonica in 1224 and then Greek Asia Minor. In 1261 the Latin Empire ended with the recapture of Constantinople by the Byzantine "Emperor of Nicaea" Michael VIII (Palaeologus).

Constitution, USS US 44-gun frigate, known as "Old Ironsides". It was launched in 1797 and served as Isaac Hull's flagship during the War of 1812. The *Constitution* won a famous victory over the British ship *Guerrière* (19 August 1812). It was saved from scrapping when Oliver Wendell Holmes' poem "Old Ironsides" (1830) extolled its war record. In 1833 the *Constitution* was rebuilt and subsequently served as a naval academy school ship. It has been docked in Boston since 1897.

Constitutional Act (1791) Instituted by British Prime Minister William Pitt (the Younger), the act divided French and English Canada, creating a system of government dominated by an appointed executive branch. The elected Legislative Assembly dealt only with local issues. Dissatisfaction with this form of government led to the Rebellion of 1837 and to the Durham Report (1839) reforms.

Constitutional Convention (25 May–17 September 1787) Meeting at Independence Hall, Philadelphia, that produced the Constitution of the United States. It was attended by delegates from 12 of the 13 US states (Rhode Island abstained). The delegates were: George Washington, James Madison and George Mason from Virginia; Rufus King and Elbridge Gerry from Massachusetts; Roger Sherman and Oliver Ellsworth from Connecticut; Alexander Hamilton from New York; Benjamin Franklin, James Wilson, Gouverneur Morris and Robert Morris from Pennsylvania; William Paterson from New Jersey; John Rutledge and Charles Pinckney from South Carolina. George Washington was elected president of the Convention. The Convention was called to revise the Articles of Confederation (1781) and to redress the lack of power wielded by the existing government structure. There was demand for a more stable and centralized federal government that had tighter monetary control. The major disagreement centred on how each state should determine its share of this centralized power. The larger states favoured representation based on population (**Virginia Plan**), while the smaller states wanted equal representation regardless of size (**New Jersey Plan**). The so-called **Connecticut Compromise**, proposed by Oliver Ellsworth, was a bicameral system of government that included representation by population (House of Representatives) and equal representation for the states (Senate). *See also* Annapolis Convention

Constitutional Union Party (National Constitutional Union) Minor US political party organized (1860) to support Senator John Bell's (Tennessee) campaign for president. Composed mostly of former Whigs, the Party declared "no political principle other than the Constitution of the country, the union of the states, and the enforcement of the laws." In the election, votes for Bell helped fragment opposition to the eventual victor Abraham Lincoln.

Constitution of the United States Formal statement of the United States' system of government. The Constitution was drawn up (September 1787) at the Constitutional Convention in Philadelphia to replace the Articles of Confederation (1781). It was ratified in 1788 and came into force in 1789. The principal architect of the Constitution was James Madison. It was designed to create a system of "checks and balances" to prevent one branch of government gaining dominance over others. The Constitution was designed not as a code of laws, but as a statement of principles to which laws should adhere, thus allowing considerable flexibility in judicial interpretation. The Constitution had to be ratified by nine of the 13 states before it could become law. in Virginia. Opponents, such as Patrick Henry, who feared that the federal government would be too powerful and the rights of the individual unprotected, succeeded in having ten amendments, collectively known as the Bill of Rights, added. The Constitution has served to hold together a large and diverse nation while protecting the rights of the people. It is composed of a preamble, seven articles and 27 amendments. **Article I** deals with such matters as the powers of Congress, the composition of the House and Senate and election to them, and restrictions upon the powers of the states. **Article II** covers the presidency, including election and powers, while **Article III** outlines the powers and responsibilities of the judiciary. **Article IV** describes relations between states and the admission of new states. **Article V** details how amendments to the Constitution shall be made; **Article VI** states the authority of the Constitution; and **Article VII** says that nine states will have to ratify the Constitution before it becomes effective. In addition to the ten amendments in the Bill of Rights, a further 17 amendments have been ratified. **Amendment XI** (1795) prohibited a citizen of one state from suing another state government. **Amendment XII** (1804) set up separate ballots for electing the president and vice president. The Civil War amendments, **XIII** (1861), **XIV** (1868) and **XV** (1870), outlawed slavery, declared all people born or naturalized in the United States citizens, and declared that the right to vote could not be denied on grounds of colour. **Amendment XVI** (1913) gave Congress the right to enact personal income taxes. Popular election of US senators was established by **Amendment XVII** (1913). Prohibition, enacted by **Amendment XVIII** (1919), was repealed by **Amendment XXI** (1933). Women received the right to vote by **Amendment XIX** (1920). **Amendment XXII** (1951) limited the length of time a person may be president, and **Amendment XXV** (1967) set procedures for filling vice presidential and presidential vacancies. **Amendment XXIII** (1961) gave District of Columbia residents the right to vote for president. The poll tax was prohibited by **Amendment XXIV** (1964). The voting age was lowered to 18 by **Amendment XXVI** (1971). **Amendment XXVII** (1992) established procedures for Congressional pay increases. *See also* separation of powers

consul One of the two chief magistrates of ancient Rome. The office was said to have been established in 510 BC. Consuls were elected each year to administer civil and military matters. After 367 BC one consul was a patrician, the other a plebeian, each having the power to veto the other's decisions.

Consulate (1799–1804) Government of the French republic after the end of the Directory. Napoleon and Emmanuel Sieyès planned the coup of 18 Brumaire (9 November) that established the Consulate. There were three consuls (chief magistrates) but, in practice, the administration was dominated by the first consul Napoleon, who became emperor in 1804.

Continental Congress (1774–89) Federal legislature of the American colonies during the American Revolution and the period of Confederation. Its first meeting at Philadelphia (September 1774) resulted in unified opposition to British rule and agreed on a boycott of trade with Britain. In May 1775 the Congress reconvened and made George Washington commander in chief of the Continental army. In July 1776 the Second Congress adopted the Declaration of Independence and drafted the Articles of Confederation. The Constitution of the United States (1787) made the Congress redundant, although it continued to meet until 1789.

► **Constantinople, Latin Empire of** The sack of Constantinople (1204) marked the beginning of the fragmentation of the Byzantine Empire. The sea walls were breached for the first time and the city was systematically looted for a period of three days. Following this, the Byzantine lands were divided up. Territory in Europe came under the control of a Frankish emperor, who tried unsuccessfully to convert the populace to Catholicism. Meanwhile, the centre of Orthodox authority shifted to Nicaea in northern Anatolia. Greek rule also survived in Epirus and in Trebizond on the Black Sea.

Continental System Trade blockade of Britain introduced (1806) by NAPOLEON I to cripple the British economy and force favourable peace terms in the NAPOLEONIC WARS. Extended to Russia by the Treaty of Tilsit (1807) and to Spain and Portugal in 1808, the Continental System also included neutral countries and prompted a retaliatory British blockade against France and its allies. The system was highly unpopular, and the economic blockade probably caused more deprivation on the continental mainland than in Britain, which maintained command of the sea. The restrictions contributed to the WAR OF 1812.

Contra Right-wing Nicaraguan revolutionary group active between 1979 and 1990. In support of former dictator General Anastasio SOMOZA, the Contra aimed to overthrow the elected, left-wing SANDINISTA government. The Contra received financial and military assistance from the US government from 1981. In 1990 elections the US-funded Union of National Opposition (UNO), effectively the political wing of the Contra, was victorious. The Contra were officially disbanded. *See also* IRAN-CONTRA AFFAIR

Conway Cabal (1771) In US history, a failed plot (supposedly led by Thomas Conway) to remove George WASHINGTON as commander of the Continental Army in the AMERICAN REVOLUTION and replace him with Horatio GATES. Investigations later revealed that the plot was not instigated by Conway.

Cook, James (1728–79) British naval officer and explorer. He charted the approaches to Québec during the SEVEN YEARS' WAR (1756–63). In 1768–71 Cook led an expedition to Tahiti to observe an eclipse of the Sun and to investigate the strategic and economic potential of the South Pacific. He conducted a survey of the unknown coasts of New Zealand and charted the E coast of Australia, naming it New South Wales and claiming it for Britain. On a second expedition to the S Pacific (1772–75), Cook charted much of the Southern Hemisphere and circumnavigated Antarctica. On his last voyage (1776–79), Cook discovered the Sandwich (Hawaiian) Islands, where he was killed in a dispute with the inhabitants. He is generally regarded as the greatest European explorer of the Pacific in the 18th century.

Cook, Sir Joseph (1860–1947) Australian statesman, prime minister (1913–14). In 1908 he became leader of the Free Trade Party in New South Wales. As national defence minister (1909–10), Cook helped establish the Australian navy. He was a delegate to the VERSAILLES Peace Conference (1919).

Cook, Robin (1946–) British statesman, foreign secretary (1997–). He entered Parliament in 1974. A skilful parliamentary speaker, Cook held various posts (1987–97) in Labour's shadow cabinet. As foreign secretary, he proposed an ethical dimension to British foreign policy. In 1999 Cook was a strong advocate of NATO action to relieve the refugee crisis in KOSOVO.

Coolidge, (John) Calvin (1872–1933) Thirtieth president of the United States (1923–29). Stern action in the Boston police strike (1919) earned him the Republican nomination as vice president in 1920. Coolidge became president on the death of Warren HARDING (1923) and was re-elected in 1924. A conservative with no dramatic political programme, his administration was characterized by a laissez-faire approach to business and commerce, summed up by his phrase, "the business of America is business". Many argue that this attitude was partly responsible for the unsustainable bullishness of the US stock market.

Cooper, Anthony Ashley, 1st Earl of Shaftesbury *See* SHAFTESBURY, ANTHONY ASHLEY COOPER, 1ST EARL OF

Cooper, Peter (1791–1883) US industrialist and inventor. In 1830 he built *Tom Thumb*, one of the earliest locomotives in the United States. Cooper made his fortune in the iron industry and bankrolled the Atlantic cable-telegraph system. As head of the North American Telegraph Company, he owned more than 50% of telegraph lines in the United States. In 1876 Cooper was the presidential candidate for the GREENBACK PARTY.

cooperative movement Variety of worldwide organizations, founded to provide mutual assistance in economic enterprises for the benefit of their members. The first such movement was founded (1844) in England by the Rochdale Pioneers, who established a cooperative retail society to eliminate the middleman and share profits among its members. The cooperative movement has been extended to include cooperative agriculture, cooperative manufacturing and cooperative banking and finance. *See also* COOPERATIVE PARTY; COOPERATIVE WHOLESALE SOCIETY; OWEN, ROBERT

Cooperative Party British political organization, formed in 1917 as the political wing of the Cooperative Union. It is associated with the LABOUR PARTY and since 1946 all of its parliamentary candidates have stood for election jointly as Labour cooperative candidates.

Cooperative Wholesale Society Organization formed (1863) in the north of England to provide for consumer cooperation. It was a development of the early cooperative experiments of Robert OWEN and the Rochdale Pioneers, which encouraged consumers to form their own retail societies and share the profits.

Copán Ruined city of the MAYA, W Honduras, founded in *c*.AD 160. The extensive ruins at Copán suggest that it was the second-largest Mayan city of the Classic period (*c*.AD 300–900). The city-state reached its peak in *c*.628–695. Copán is notable for the high artistic quality of its remains – portrait sculpture, friezes and statuary, in particular the Temple of the Hieroglyphic Stars. The city-state collapsed shortly after 822.

Copenhagen (København) Capital and chief port of Denmark on E Sjaelland and N Amager Island, in the Øresund. A trading and fishing centre by the early 12th century, it became the capital of an independent Denmark in 1443. By the 16th century it was an important centre of trade. Its stock exchange dates from the 17th century. The Amalienborg Palace is home of the royal family. Pop. (1994) 620,970.

Copenhagen, First Battle of (1801) Naval engagement between the English, under Sir Hyde Parker, and the Danes, who had recently joined the League of Armed Neutrality. The Danish fleet was destroyed – partly because, according to legend, Horatio NELSON claimed not to see an order to retreat as he put a telescope to his blind eye. *See also* NAPOLEONIC WARS

Copenhagen, Second Battle of (1807) Conflict in the NAPOLEONIC WARS prompted by Denmark's decision to join the CONTINENTAL SYSTEM. The British, led by James Gambier and Arthur Wellesley (later Duke of WELLINGTON), bombarded Copenhagen before sending in troops to occupy the city and force the Danes to surrender.

Copernicus, Nicolas (1473–1543) (Mikolaj Kopernik) Polish astronomer. Through his study of planetary motions, Copernicus developed a heliocentric (Sun-centred) theory of the universe in opposition to the accepted geocentric (Earth-centred) theory conceived by PTOLEMY nearly 1300 years before. In the so-called **Copernican system**, the planets' motions in the sky were explained by their orbit of the Sun. The motion of the sky was simply a result of the Earth turning on its axis. An account of his work, *De revolutionibus orbium coelestium*, was published in 1543.

Copper Age *See* CHALCOLITHIC AGE

Coptic Church Largest Christian church in Egypt. Its members form 5 to 10% of Egypt's population. The Coptic Church is led by the patriarch of Alexandria. Of ancient origin, the Copts trace the history of the Church to Saint MARK. As a result of its MONOPHYSITISM (denying the humanity of Christ), the Coptic Church was declared heretical by the Council of CHALCEDON (451) and became isolated from other Christian churches. The Arab conquest of Egypt (642) brought mass conversion to Islam.

Coral Sea, Battle of the (May 1942) WORLD WAR 2 conflict in the SW Pacific. The US Navy inflicted heavy losses (100,000 tonnes) on the Japanese fleet and checked Japan's progress towards Australia.

Corday (d'Armont), (Marie Anne) Charlotte (1768–93) French patriot. A noblewoman, she was one of the GIRONDINS who disagreed with the radical policies espoused by the JACOBIN, Jean Paul MARAT. On 13 July 1793, Corday stabbed Marat to death in his bath. She was guillotined on 17 July.

Córdoba (Cordova) City on the River Guadalquivir, Andalusia, S Spain; capital of Córdoba province. A flourishing centre of learning in the 8th century under ABD AR-RAHMAN III (first caliph of Córdoba), it was captured (1236) by FERDINAND III of Castile, who imposed Christian culture on the city. The Great Mosque (8–10th century) is a world heritage site. Pop. (1991) 300,229.

Corfu (Kérkira) Island in NW Greece, second largest of the Ionian island group; the major town is Corfu. In 433 BC the island was allied with ATHENS against CORINTH. The Romans held Corfu from 229 BC, and it was part of the BYZANTINE EMPIRE until the 11th century. It was

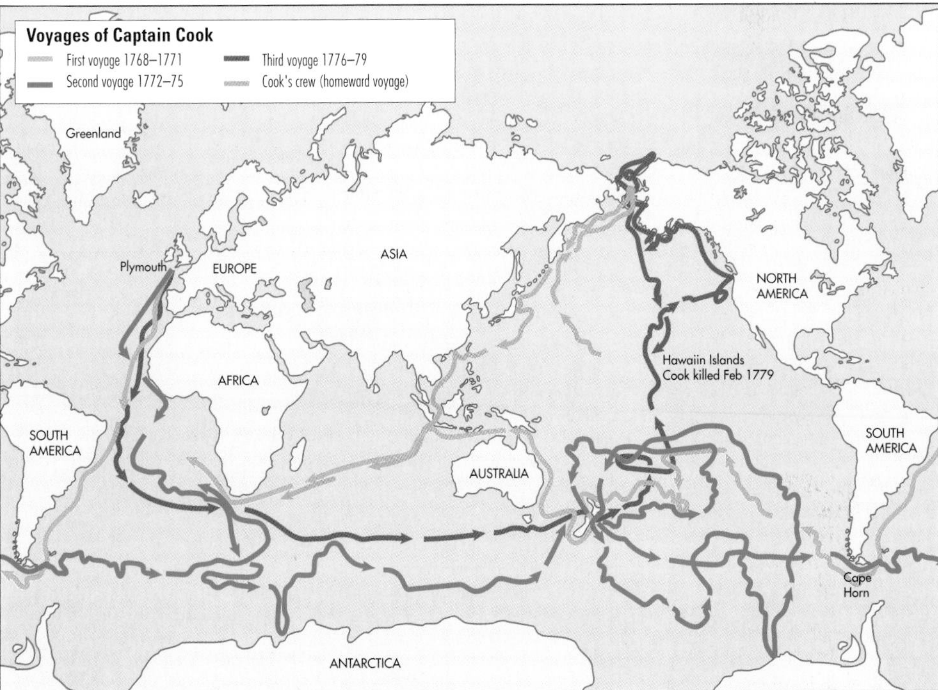

▲ **Cook** Between 1768 and 1779, James Cook led three expeditions to the South Pacific Ocean and the North American coast. By sailing south into Antarctic waters and accurately charting the coastline of Australia and New Zealand, Cook won a new continent for the British crown. On his second voyage, Cook crossed Antartica. On his final voyage, he set out to discover a possible western entrance to the Northwest Passage. He was killed after surveying the Bering Strait.

occupied by the Venetians (1386–1797), and then fell under British protection (1809–64), before passing to Greece. Area: 593sq km (229sq mi). Pop. (1991) 107,592.

Corfu Incident (August 1923) Bombardment and occupation of the Greek island of Corfu by Italian troops in retaliation for the murder of an Italian boundary delegation. The LEAGUE OF NATIONS persuaded MUSSOLINI to withdraw in return for Greece paying 50 million lire in indemnity.

Corinth (Kórinthos) Capital of Corinth department, NE Peloponnesos, at the SW tip of the Isthmus of Corinth, Greece. One of the largest and most powerful cities of ancient GREECE, it was a rival of ATHENS and friend of SPARTA, with which it was allied in the PELOPONNESIAN WAR (431–404 BC). Destroyed by the Romans (146 BC), it was rebuilt by Julius Caesar in 44 BC. Ruled by the Venetians (1687–1715), then by the Turks, it became part of Greece in 1822. The modern city is 5km (3mi) NE of ancient Corinth, which was destroyed by an earthquake in 1858. Pop. (1991 est.) 29,000.

Corinthian order *See* ORDERS OF ARCHITECTURE

Corinthian War (395–386 BC) Conflict between SPARTA and the allied forces of CORINTH, ARGOS, THEBES and ATHENS. War was sparked by the tyrannical conduct of Sparta at the end of the PELOPONNESIAN WAR (431–404 BC). Spartan forces were already tied up in a war against Persia, which at this time regarded Sparta as its main enemy in Greece. After 392 BC, however, Athenian interference in Anatolia persuaded Persia to switch its support to Sparta. In 387 BC Antalcidas, a Spartan agent, concluded a peace treaty with ARTAXERXES II in which Persia gained Cyprus and the Greek city-states in Asia Minor. In 386 a Spartan blockade forced Athens to comply with the terms of the treaty.

Coriolanus, Gnaeus Marcius (5th century BC) Roman general. He captured the Volscian town of Corioli, from which he got his name. In legend, he was banished from Rome (491 BC) after opposing the distribution of grain to relieve a famine. Coriolanus joined forces with the Volsci to march on Rome. According to Plutarch, he was dissuaded from sacking the city by the entreaties of his wife and mother. The story forms the basis of Shakespeare's history *Coriolanus* (*c.*1607).

Corn Laws Series of acts regulating the import and export of grain in Britain. In the early 19th century, a succession of bad harvests, increased demand, and blockades imposed during the Napoleonic Wars saw the price of grain fluctuate wildly. The Act of 1815 prevented the import of wheat until the domestic price exceeded a certain figure. This kept the price of bread high. Opposition led to repeal by the ANTI-CORN LAW LEAGUE (1846). *See also* COBDEN, RICHARD; PEEL, SIR ROBERT

Cornwallis, Charles, 1st Marquess (1738–1805) British general and statesman. At the start of the AMERICAN REVOLUTION, he helped General William HOWE expel George Washington's Continental forces from New Jersey. In 1778 Cornwallis became second in command to Sir Henry CLINTON, British commander in America. In 1780 he took command of the Carolina Campaign. Cornwallis' surrender at the siege of YORKTOWN (1781) signalled the end of the war. As governor general of India (1786–93, 1805), Cornwallis reformed the civil service and defeated TIPU SAHIB of Mysore (now KARNATAKA). Cornwallis resigned as viceroy of Ireland (1798–1801) after GEORGE III refused to accept the Act of CATHOLIC EMANCIPATION.

Coronado, Francisco Vásquez de (*c.*1510–54) Spanish explorer. In 1540 he headed an expedition to locate the seven cities of Cibola, Mexico, reportedly the repositories of untold wealth. Coronado explored the W coast of Mexico, found the Colorado River and the Grand Canyon, followed the route of the Rio Grande, and then headed N through the Texas Panhandle, Oklahoma and E Kansas.

corporate state Concept of government in which workers and employers from similar industries are organized into corporations; these together with other corporations select representatives who determine national policy. Fascist Italy adopted features of the corporate state, with Benito MUSSOLINI acting as the final arbitrator.

Corrigan, Mairead (1944–) Northern Irish peace activist. The killing of three children prompted Corrigan and Betty Williams (1943–) to organize the Community of Peace People, a peace movement supported by both Protestants and Roman Catholics in Northern Ireland. Corrigan and Williams shared the 1976 Nobel Peace Prize for their attempts to heal religious and national divisions in Northern Ireland.

COSTA RICA

AREA: 51,100sq km (19,730sq mi)
POPULATION: 3,099,000
CAPITAL (POPULATION): San José (303,000)
GOVERNMENT: Multiparty republic
ETHNIC GROUPS: White 85%, Mestizo 8%, Black and Mulatto 3%, East Asian (mostly Chinese) 3%
LANGUAGES: Spanish (official)
RELIGIONS: Christianity (Roman Catholic 81%)
GDP PER CAPITA (1995): US$5850

Republic in Central America. In 1502 Christopher Columbus reached the Caribbean coast and rumours of treasure soon attracted Spanish settlers. The relative lack of mineral or labour resources, however, retarded the development of the ENCOMIENDA system. In 1822 Spain's Central American colonies broke away to join the Mexican Empire. In 1823 the Central American states formed the CENTRAL AMERICAN FEDERATION. This large union gradually disintegrated, and Costa Rica achieved full independence in 1838. The nation held its first free, democratic elections in 1890. In the 20th century Costa Rica's reputation for stable, parliamentary democracy has been twice threatened. First, General Tinoco formed a military dictatorship (1917–19). Second, a revolt against the president-elect in 1948 led to the abolition of a standing army. The presidency (1953–74) of José Figueres saw the founding of the modern state. In 1986 Oscar Arias Sánchez was elected president. Arias was awarded the 1987 Nobel Prize for Peace for his efforts to secure peace in the civil wars that raged throughout Central America during the 1980s. In 1994 José María Figueres Olsen, son of José Figueres, was elected president. He was succeeded (1998) by Miguel Angel Rodríguez.

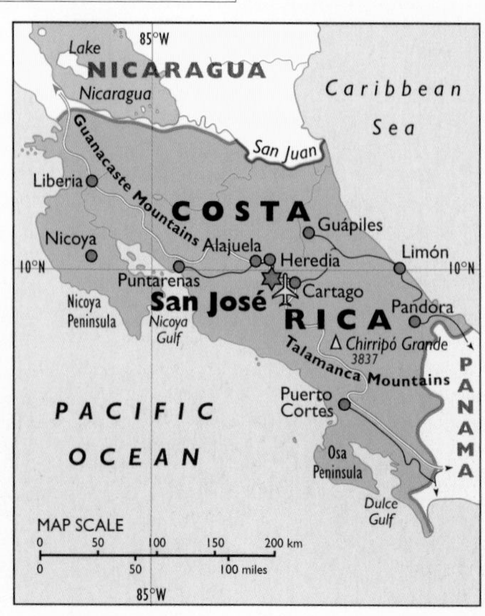

Corsica (Corse) Mountainous island in the Mediterranean Sea, *c.*160km (100mi) SE of the French coast. The capital is Ajaccio. It was a Roman colony before passing into the hands of a series of Italian rulers. In 1768 France purchased all rights to the island. Napoleon was born here in 1769. Area: 8681sq km (3352sq mi). Pop. (1990) 250,400.

Cortés, Hernán (1485–1547) Spanish CONQUISTADOR, conqueror of Mexico. In 1511 he joined Diego de VELÁZQUEZ's expedition to Cuba. In 1519 Cortés broke from Velázquez and sailed for Mexico with 550 men. On 21 April 1519 he landed at Veracruz. Cortés marched inland towards the AZTEC capital, Tenochtitlán (now MEXICO CITY), gaining allies among the subject peoples of the AZTEC king, MONTEZUMA II. Montezuma welcomed Cortés as the embodiment of the god Quetzalcóatl. In November 1519 Cortés seized Montezuma as a hostage. While Cortés returned to the coast, the Aztecs rebelled against the brutal command of Pedro de ALVARADO and the Spanish were forced to retreat from Tenochtitlán. On 13 August 1521, after a three-month siege, Cortés regained the city. For the next five years, Cortés extended Spanish control throughout the Aztec empire. In *c.*1525 he killed the Aztec emperor CUAUHTÉMOC on an expedition to Honduras. Cortés' achievements were largely unrewarded by CHARLES V of Spain. In 1535 Cortes was retired to his estate at Oaxaca as a private citizen. In 1539 he returned to Spain. *See also* DE SOTO, HERNANDO map

Cortes Legislature of Spain. Local cortes were set up in the 12th and 13th centuries as various regions were reconquered from the Moors. In 1810 the first national Cortes was called by a Bonapartist government. It drafted the Constitution of 1812. The Cortes became the Spanish parliament during the Second Republic (1931–39) and during the period of FALANGE rule (1942–76), when its members were appointed by government agencies. In June 1977 free elections to the Cortes recommenced.

Cosgrave, Liam (1920–) Irish statesman, taoiseach (1973–77), son of William COSGRAVE. He was elected to the Dáil Éireann (Irish assembly) in 1943. Cosgrave served as external affairs minister (1954–57) before becoming leader of FINE GAEL (1965–77). As prime minister (taoiseach), he supported the British government's plans for a Council of Ireland to link the governments of the Republic and the North.

Cosgrave, William Thomas (1880–1965) Irish statesman, taoiseach (1922–32) of the Irish Free State, father of Liam COSGRAVE. A member of SINN FÉIN, he took part in the EASTER RISING (1916). Cosgrave served in the provisional government of the Dáil Éireann in 1919. In the 1932 elections he was defeated by Eamon DE VALERA. Cosgrave served (1932–44) as leader of the FINE GAEL opposition.

Cossa, Baldassare *See* JOHN XXIII

Cossacks Bands of Russian adventurers who undertook the conquest of Siberia in the 17th century. Of ethnically mixed origins, they were escaped serfs, renegades and vagabonds who formed independent, semi-military groups on the fringes of society. After the Russian Revolution (1917), the Cossacks opposed the BOLSHEVIKS and strongly resisted collectivization.

Costa Rica *See* country feature

Côte d'Ivoire *See* IVORY COAST

Coty, René (1882–1962) French statesman, president (1954–59). In 1940 he supported the establishment of the VICHY GOVERNMENT under Marshal PÉTAIN. As president of the Fourth Republic, Coty had to face the constitutional crisis (May 1958) precipitated by the French generals in ALGERIA, who threatened an army coup. He helped to bring about the creation (1959) of the Fifth Republic under Charles DE GAULLE.

Council for Mutual Economic Assistance (COMECON) International organization (1949–91) aimed at the coordination of economic policy among communist states, especially in Eastern Europe. Led by the Soviet Union, its original members were Bulgaria, Czechoslovakia, East Germany, Hungary, Poland and Romania; later joined by Cuba, Mongolia and Vietnam. Cooperation took the form of bilateral trade agreements.

Council of Europe European organization founded (1949) with the aim of strengthening pluralist democracy and human rights, and promoting European cultural identity. Originally a Western European organization, it admitted former communist countries in the 1990s. It has adopted *c*.150 conventions, the most important of which is the EUROPEAN CONVENTION ON HUMAN RIGHTS. The organization is based in Strasbourg, France. *See also* EUROPEAN UNION (EU)

Counter-Reformation Revival of the ROMAN CATHOLIC CHURCH in Europe during the 16th and early 17th centuries. It began as a reaction to the Protestant REFORMATION and was intended to strengthen the Church against PROTESTANTISM and the prevailing HUMANISM of the RENAISSANCE. The reforms were essentially conservative, trying to remove many of the abuses that had crept into the late medieval church and win new prestige for the papacy. Girolamo SAVONAROLA highlighted the secularization, corruption and growing materialism within the church hierarchy, but his prescription for change was too radical. The fifth LATERAN COUNCIL introduced minor changes. Pope CLEMENT VII founded new monastic orders to act as evangelical bulwarks against LUTHERANISM, but the major impetus for reform emerged from the pontificate of PAUL III and the founding of the Society of Jesus (JESUITS). The Council of TRENT (1545–63) was the engine of the Counter-Reformation. It eradicated simony (such as the sale of indulgences), standardized Roman Catholic theology and undertook institutional reforms. Pope PAUL IV brought discipline and morality back to the papal court. Pope PIUS IV oversaw the last session of the Council. The second phase (1563–90) of the Counter-Reformation was administered by PIUS V, GREGORY XIII and SIXTUS V. *See also* CAMPION, SAINT EDMUND; VINCENT DE PAUL, SAINT

Covenanters Scottish Presbyterians pledged by the National Covenant (1638) to uphold their religion. In the BISHOPS' WARS (1639, 1640) they opposed CHARLES I of England's efforts to impose an Anglican episcopal system upon Scotland. By the SOLEMN LEAGUE AND COVENANT (1643) the Covenanters promised support to Parliament in the English CIVIL WAR. In 1646 Charles surrendered to the Covenanters. In 1647 Charles reached a secret agreement with the Scots, promising to accept PRESBYTERIANISM in return for military support against Parliament. The second phase of the Civil War ended with Scottish defeat at the Battle of PRESTON (August 1648). The Covenanters initially supported CHARLES II, but the RESTORATION brought brutal suppression of the Covenanters and Presbyterianism was only restored in Scotland by the so-called GLORIOUS REVOLUTION (1688). *See also* CAMERON, RICHARD; CROMWELL, OLIVER

Coverdale, Miles (1488–1569) English cleric who issued the first printed English Bible (1535) and the "Great Bible" (1539). Influenced by the REFORMATION, he helped William TYNDALE on his Bible translation.

cowboy (cowhand) US ranch hand. Traditionally living and working in the West, cowboys increased after the Civil War. They have been romanticized in books and films as a symbol of the rugged independence, colour and vigour of the old "Wild West". *See also* GAUCHO

Craig, James, 1st Viscount Craigavon (1871–1940) Northern Irish statesman and soldier, first prime minister of Northern Ireland (1921–40). In 1912 Craig and Sir Edward CARSON founded the paramilitary Ulster Volunteers that fought to keep Ulster in the United Kingdom. As prime minister, Craig abolished (1929) proportional representation and, through gerrymandering, ensured a Protestant majority.

Craig, Sir James Henry (1748–1812) British colonial administrator, governor general of Canada (1807–11). He fought in the American Revolution and was wounded at the Battle of BUNKER HILL (1775). As governor general, Craig dissolved the assembly of Lower Canada (QUÉBEC) and suppressed the journal *Le Canadien*. His harsh treatment of French Canadians served only to consolidate the radicals in Québec.

Cranmer, Thomas (1489–1556) English prelate and religious reformer. In 1533 Cranmer, a close friend of Thomas CROMWELL, was appointed archbishop of Canterbury by HENRY VIII of England. He secured the annulment of Henry's marriage to CATHERINE OF ARAGON despite opposition from the pope. Cranmer promoted the introduction of PROTESTANTISM into England and compiled (1549) the first Book of COMMON PRAYER. Following the accession (1553) of MARY I, Cranmer's reforms were halted. He was burned at the stake.

Crassus, Marcus Licinius (*c*.115–53 BC) Roman general and politician. He commanded an army for SULLA (83 BC), amassed a vast personal fortune, and raised and led the troops, who defeated the slave rebellion of SPARTACUS (71 BC). With POMPEY and Julius CAESAR, Crassus formed (60 BC) the so-called first triumvirate and became governor of Syria (54). He was defeated and killed by the PARTHIANS at the Battle of Carrhae, Mesopotamia.

Craxi, Bettino (1934–) Italian statesman, prime minister (1983–87). In 1976 he became leader of the Italian Socialist Party (PSI), steering it towards the centre ground of Italian politics. Craxi formed a coalition government with the ITALIAN POPULAR PARTY (PPI). As Italy's first socialist prime minister, he cracked down on public expenditure in an effort to control inflation. In 1993 Craxi was forced to resign as leader of the PSI, following charges of political corruption, and went into exile in Tunisia. In 1994 he was sentenced in absentia to prison.

Crazy Horse (*c*.1842–77) (Ta-Sunko-Aitko) Chief of the Oglala SIOUX. He was a leader of Sioux resistance to the advance of white settlers in the Black Hills of W South Dakota and NE Wyoming, assisting SITTING BULL in the defeat of Colonel George CUSTER at the Battle of LITTLE BIGHORN (1876). Persuaded to surrender, Crazy Horse was killed a few months later, allegedly while trying to escape.

Crécy, Battle of (1346) Important early conflict in the HUNDRED YEARS' WAR. The English, led by EDWARD III and his son EDWARD THE BLACK PRINCE, defeated the French led by PHILIP VI. The English longbow, as well as superior tactics, accounted for their victory. More than 1500 soldiers were killed on the French side, including the blind King John of Bohemia.

Crédit Mobilier of America US construction company involved in a financial scandal. Organized (1864) by Oakes Ames, a US Representative and Union Pacific Railroad stockholder, it gained vast profits from contracts with Union Pacific, which had received federal funds. Ames bribed members of Congress to prevent an investigation. When the scandal broke in 1872, it ruined the reputations of Ames and other officials.

Cree People belonging to the Algonquian-language family of NATIVE NORTH AMERICANS, who ranged from James Bay to the Saskatchewan River. Like the related CHIPPEWA, Cree served as guides and hunters for French and British fur traders. Many of the Plains Cree intermarried with the French. Today, there are *c*.130,000 Cree.

Creek Confederation of NATIVE NORTH AMERICANS, part of the Muskogean-language group. One of the largest groups in SE United States, they ranged from Georgia to Alabama. The Creek formed a settled, agricultural society, with land owned communally. Individual settlements had a degree of autonomy. After the CREEK WAR, they were removed to Oklahoma, where *c*.60,000 remain.

Creek War (1813–14) Conflict between the CREEK and white colonists. Their concern at the encroachment of settlers was fuelled by the rhetoric skills of TECUMSEH. In 1813 Creek warriors, led by Red Eagle, massacred more than 500 settlers at Fort Mims. The Creek nation was decisively defeated by Andrew JACKSON at the Battle of Horseshoe Bend (1814). Jackson pardoned Red Eagle, but the Creek had to cede much of their land, and they were later moved to the Indian Territory (now Oklahoma).

Cresson, Edith (1934–) French stateswoman, premier (1991–92). Cresson held several ministerial posts in François MITTERRAND's cabinet before succeeding Michel Rocard as France's first woman premier. The parlous state of the French economy forced her to resign in favour of Pierre Bérégovoy. In 1994 Cresson became a European commissioner. In 1999, however, she was charged with nepotism, and in the crisis that followed she and all the other commissioners were forced to resign.

Cretaceous Last period of the MESOZOIC era, lasting from 144 to 65mya. Dinosaurs became extinct at the end of this period. The first true placental and marsupial mammals appeared, and modern flowering plants were common.

Crete (Kreti, Kríti) Largest island of Greece, in the E Mediterranean Sea, SSE of the Greek mainland; the capital is IRÁKLION. MINOAN CIVILIZATION flourished on Crete from 2000 BC, and the palace of KNOSSOS was built *c*.1700 BC. In 68–67 BC Crete was conquered by Rome and later came under Byzantine (395), Arab (826) and Venetian (1210) rule. In 1669 Crete fell to Turkey. In 1898 foreign intervention forced Turkey to evacuate Crete, and it was eventually united with Greece (1908). It was occupied by German forces in World War 2. Area: 8336sq km (3218sq mi). Pop. (1991) 540,054.

Crimea (Krym) Peninsula in S UKRAINE that extends into the Black Sea W of the Azov Sea and is joined to the main-

CRIMEAN WAR (OCTOBER 1853–FEBRUARY 1856)

Conflict between Russia and an alliance of Britain, France, the OTTOMAN EMPIRE and Sardinia-Piedmont (from 1855). In July 1853 Russia occupied the Ottoman territories of Moldavia and Wallachia, and Turkey responded by declaring war. The Russians then destroyed the Turkish fleet at Sinope, causing France and Britain to declare war in March 1854. In September 1854, the Allies began a year-long siege of SEVASTOPOL that ended in Russian evacuation (September 1855). The major battles of the Crimean War were at BALAKLAVA and INKERMAN (both 1854).

The War was marked on both sides by incompetent leadership and organization. The CHARGE OF THE LIGHT BRIGADE is the best-known example. After Austria threatened to join the allies, Tsar ALEXANDER II surrendered Russia's claims on the Ottoman Empire at the Treaty of PARIS (1856). More than 250,000 soldiers died in the War, many dying from disease in the appalling military hospitals. Their plight was revealed to the British public by *The Times* reporter W.H. Russell, the world's first war correspondent, and by the nurse Florence NIGHTINGALE.

◀ **British soldiers in the Crimea** Documentation of the Crimean War included the first examples of war photojournalism. English photographer Roger Fenton (1819–69) was sent to the Crimea by the British government to document the War. However, many of his photographs depict life in camp, rather than combat, and were used as propaganda material by the British authorities.

land by the Perekop Isthmus. The capital is Simferopol. Crimea was inhabited from the 10th to 8th century BC by the Cimmerians. During the 5th century it was colonized by the Greeks and then by Romans, Ostrogoths, Huns, Mongols, Byzantines and Turks, before being annexed to Russia in 1783. In 1921 it became an autonomous republic of Russia and in 1954 was transferred to the Ukraine as the Krymskaya region. In 1991 it was made an autonomous republic of an independent Ukraine. Area: *c.*27,000sq km (10,400sq mi). Pop. (1991 est.) 2,549,800.

Crimean War *See* feature article, page 105

Cripps, Sir (Richard) Stafford (1889–1952) British statesman, chancellor of the exchequer (1947–50). He belonged to the left wing of the Labour Party and was ambassador to Russia (1940–42), later serving in Winston Churchill's War Cabinet. As chancellor in the reforming government of Clement Attlee, Cripps' austerity programme helped to reconstruct the post-war economy. *See also* Quit India movement

Crispi, Francesco (1819–1901) Italian statesman, prime minister (1887–91, 1893–96). In 1860 he helped Garibaldi form the Expedition of the Thousand that captured Sicily and resulted in the proclamation of the kingdom of Italy (1861). At first, Crispi supported Giuseppe Mazzini's republicans but later he proved to be a convinced monarchist. He succeeded Agostino Depretis as prime minister. In 1889 Crispi established a colony in Eritrea. His support for the Triple Alliance (Germany, Austria and Italy) led to a tariff war (1888–92) between France and Italy. His second ministry collapsed after Italy's disastrous defeat by the Ethiopians at the Battle of Adwa (1896). *See also* Cavour, Camillo Benso di

CROMWELL, OLIVER

Oliver Cromwell was guided by his Calvinist faith. He first attracted attention for his attack on episcopacy in the Parliament of 1628–29. Cromwell attributed the victory of the New Model Army to God's providence. While he advocated the sovereignty of Parliament, Cromwell was more comfortable with a military form of government. It is often argued that Cromwell was a tolerant, reasonable man forced into harsh acts by the revolutionary nature of the post-Civil War period.

CROMWELL IN HIS OWN WORDS

"You have sat too long here for any good you have been doing. Depart, I say, and let us have done with you. In the name of God, go!"
To the Rump Parliament (1653)

"Necessity hath no law."
Speech to Parliament (1654)

"It is not my design to drink or to sleep, but my design is to make what haste I can to be gone."
His last words

Crittenden, John Jordan (1787–1863) US statesman and lawyer. He was a senator from Kentucky (1817–19, 1835–41, 1842–48, 1855–61). Crittenden served as attorney general under William Henry Harrison (1841) and Millard Fillmore (1850–53). "Crittenden's Compromise" (1860) was a last-ditch attempt to avert the Civil War. Crittenden proposed an amendment to the Constitution that basically ratified the Missouri Compromise (1820–21) and upheld the Fugitive Slave Law. The Compromise was defeated in the House of Representatives.

CROATIA (HRVATSKA)

AREA: 56,538sq km (21,824sq mi)
POPULATION: 4,764,000
CAPITAL (POPULATION): Zagreb (726,770)
GOVERNMENT: Multiparty republic
ETHNIC GROUPS: Croat 78%, Serb 12%, Bosnian, Hungarian, Slovene
LANGUAGES: Serbo-Croatian
RELIGIONS: Christianity (Roman Catholic 77%, Eastern Orthodox 11%), Islam 1%
GDP PER CAPITA (1994): US$3865

Balkan republic in SE Europe. Croatia was one of the six republics that made up the former Federal Republic of Yugoslavia. Slav peoples settled in the area *c.*1400 years ago. In 803 Croatia became part of the Holy Roman Empire, and the Croats soon adopted Christianity. Croatia was an independent kingdom in the 10th and 11th centuries.

In 1102 an 800-year union of the Hungarian and Croatian crowns was formed. In 1526 part of Croatia fell to the Ottoman Empire, while the rest came under the control of the Austrian Habsburgs. In 1699 all of Croatia came under Habsburg rule. Following the defeat of Austria-Hungary in World War 1, Croatia became part of the new Kingdom of the Serbs, Croats and Slovenes, renamed Yugoslavia in 1929. Germany occupied Yugoslavia during World War 2, and Croatia was proclaimed independent, although it was really a pro-Nazi puppet state (*Ustashe*). After the War, communists took power, and Josip Broz Tito became leader of Yugoslavia. During the 1980s, economic and nationalist problems (particularly between Croatia and Serbia) threatened the country's stability.

In 1990 the Croatian Democratic Union (HDZ), led by Franjo Tudjman, won Croatia's first democratic elections. In 1991 a referendum voted overwhelmingly in favour of Croatia becoming an independent republic. The Yugoslav National Army was deployed, and Serb-dominated areas took up arms in favour of remaining in the federation. Slobodan Milošević supplied arms to Croatian Serbs, and war broke out between Serbia and Croatia. By 1992, when United Nations' (UN) peacekeeping troops were deployed to maintain an uneasy cease-fire, Croatia had lost more than 30% of its territory. Tudjman was re-elected president. In 1992 war broke out in Bosnia-Herzegovina, and Bosnian Croats occupied parts of Croatia. In 1993 Croatian Serbs in E Slavonia voted to establish the separate republic of Krajina. In 1994 the Bosnian, Bosnian-Croat and Croatian governments formed a federation. In August 1995 Croatian government forces recaptured Krajina and 150,000 Serbs fled. Following the Dayton Peace Agreement (1995), Croatia and the rump Yugoslav state formally established diplomatic relations (August 1996). An agreement between the Croatian government and Croatian Serbs provided for the reintegration of Krajina into Croatia (1998).

Croatia *See* country feature

Croce, Benedetto (1866–1952) Italian philosopher and politician. He was a senator (1910–20) and minister of education (1920–21). When Benito Mussolini came to power, Croce retired from politics in protest against fascism. He re-entered politics following the fall of Mussolini (1943). As leader of the Liberal Party, Croce played a prominent role in resurrecting Italy's democratic institutions. His works include the idealistic *Philosophy of the Spirit* (1902–17).

Crockett, "Davy" (David) (1786–1836) US frontiersman and politician. He served in the Tennessee legislature (1821–26) and the United States' Congress (1827–31, 1833–35). A Whig, Crockett opposed the policies of Andrew Jackson and the Democrats. He died at the Alamo.

Croesus (d. *c.*546 BC) King of Lydia (*c.*560–546 BC) in Asia Minor. Renowned for his wealth, he was overthrown and captured by Cyrus II (the Great). According to Herodotus, Croesus threw himself upon a funeral pyre.

Cro-Magnon Name given to Upper Palaeolithic race of humans, the earliest form of modern *Homo sapiens* in Europe. Cro-Magnon people settled in Europe *c.*40,000 years ago. They made a variety of sophisticated flint tools, as well as bone, shell and ivory jewellery and artefacts. Cro-Magnon artists produced the cave paintings of France and N Spain. Cro-Magnon remains were first found (1868) in Les Eyzies-de-Tayac, Dordogne, France. *See also* human evolution

Cromer, Evelyn Baring, 1st Earl of (1841–1917) British administrator, consul general of Egypt (1883–1907). Cromer influenced the development of modern Egypt. He encouraged extensive development of railways, agriculture and irrigation at the expense of political and intellectual progress.

Cromwell, Oliver (1599–1658) English soldier and statesman, lord protector of England (1653–58). A committed Puritan, he entered Parliament in 1628 and supported the Grand Remonstrance against Charles I in the Long Parliament (1640). Cromwell fought under Robert Devereux, 3rd Earl of Essex, in the first battle of the English Civil War at Edgehill (1642). He rapidly acquired a reputation as an outstanding military leader and in 1644 he was appointed second in command to Edward Montagu, 2nd Earl of Manchester. Cromwell's Ironsides helped defeat the Cavaliers at Marston Moor (1644), but Cromwell criticized Manchester's lack of enthusiasm in prosecuting the war. In 1645 Cromwell and Thomas Fairfax, the new parliamentary commander, formed the New Model Army. After a decisive victory at Naseby (1645), Cromwell emerged as the leading voice of the army faction. He favoured a compromise with Charles I, but Charles' duplicity, in arranging for a Scottish Covenanter army to invade England, convinced him of the need to execute the king. In the second phase of the Civil War, Cromwell defeated the Scots at the Battle of Preston (1648), and his influence was further strengthened in Pride's Purge (1648) of Parliament. The Rump Parliament pressed for Charles' execution and established the Commonwealth republic (1649). As chairman of the Council of State, Cromwell suppressed the Levellers within the army and ruthlessly crushed a rebellion in Ireland. He defeated the challenge of Charles II at the Battle of Worcester (1651). The failure of Barebone's Parliament (1653) led to the "Instrument of Government" that established the Protectorate. Cromwell became a virtual military dictator as "lord protector". Cromwell's expansionist foreign policy was both anti-Stuart and pro-Protestant. The first of the Dutch Wars (1652–54) and the war (1655–58) with Spain were financially exorbitant. The Humble Petition and Advice (1657) offered him the throne, but he refused. He was succeeded by his son, Richard Cromwell. *See also* Puritanism

Cromwell, Richard (1626–1712) Lord protector of England (1658–59), son of Oliver Cromwell. Richard lacked his father's qualities of leadership. He was ousted from power after eight months and spent 20 years in exile before returning to England in 1680.

Cromwell, Thomas, Earl of Essex (*c.*1485–1540) English statesman. He was secretary to Cardinal Thomas Wolsey and succeeded him as Henry VIII's chief minister (1531). Cromwell masterminded the acts of the Reformation Parliament that established the Church of England with the king as Supreme Head. His use of Parliament to establish the sovereignty of the king did much to increase the power of the institution. Cromwell's ruthless management of the Dissolution of the Monasteries (1536–40) provoked the discontent demonstrated by the Pilgrimage of Grace (1536). He fell from power after the failure of Henry's marriage to Anne of Cleves and was executed.

Cronje, Piet (Pieter Arnoldus) (1835–1911) South African general. He led the rebellion against the British annexation of Transvaal in the first of the South African Wars (1880–81) and in 1895 defeated the Jameson Raid. In the second South African War (1899–1902), Cronje led the siege of Mafeking. He was forced to surrender at Paardeberg (1900).

Crook, George (1829–90) US general. He was a colonel in the American Civil War. Crook's later victories over the Paiute, Snake and Apache earned him a promotion (1873) to brigadier general. As commander of the department of the Platte, he fought in the Sioux War (1876). In 1883 he led a campaign against the Apache in Arizona, who were under the leadership of Geronimo. Geronimo escaped and Crook resigned.

Crosland, Tony (Charles Anthony Raven) (1918–77) British statesman, foreign secretary (1976–77). He entered Parliament in 1950. As secretary of state for education and science (1964–67) under Harold Wilson, Crosland implemented the system of state comprehensive schools. He also served in the government of Jim Callaghan. Crosland wrote *The Future of Socialism* (1956).

Crossman, Richard Howard Stafford (1907–74) British statesman, secretary of state for health and social services (1968–70). He entered Parliament in 1945. Crossman held several cabinet positions in the Labour administrations of Harold Wilson. He is celebrated for his detailed political *Diaries* (1975–77), which were published posthumously despite attempts to suppress them.

Crow Large tribe of Siouan-speaking Native North Americans that separated in the early 18th century from the Hidatsa. They migrated into the Rocky Mountains region from the upper Missouri River. Today, *c.*4000 Crow occupy a large reservation in Montana, where they were settled in 1868. They are noted for their fine costumes, artistic culture and complex social system.

crown colony British overseas territories that are under the direct control of the crown. Executive power usually rests with a crown-appointed governor, rather than a representative assembly. The governor is responsible for foreign policy, but invariably acts in accordance with a legislative council and/or an executive council consisting of elected and ex-officio members. Examples of such systems are found in Bermuda, the Falkland Islands and Gibraltar.

Crusades *See* feature article, page 108–09

Ctesiphon Ancient Parthian city on the River Tigris, se of modern Baghdad, Iraq. It was the winter capital of the Parthian empire, and later of the Sasanian empire, and is now noted for the remains of a gigantic vaulted hall, the Taq-e Kisra. Arabs took the city in AD 637 after the Battle of al-Qadisiya and used the Taq-e Kisra as a mosque, but they deserted it in 763 upon the founding of Baghdad.

Cuauhtémoc (*c.*1495–1525) (Guatimozín) Last Aztec ruler of Mexico, nephew and son-in-law of Montezuma II. In 1521 he unsuccessfully defended the capital, Tenochtitlán (now Mexico City), against the siege of Spanish conquistador Hernan Cortés. Cuauhtémoc was captured and tortured but stubbornly refused to reveal the location of his treasury. He was forced to accompany Cortés on an expedition to Honduras and was executed en route.

Cuba *See* country feature

Cuban Missile Crisis (October 1962) Confrontation during the Cold War between the United States and Soviet Union over the installation of Soviet nuclear rockets in Cuba, perhaps the closest the world has yet come to nuclear war. President John Kennedy warned Premier Nikita Khrushchev that any missile launched from Cuba would be met by a full-scale nuclear strike on the Soviet Union. On 24 October 1962, Cuba-bound Soviet ships carrying missiles turned back, and Khrushchev ordered the bases to be dismantled. *See* map, page 109

Culloden, Battle of (1746) Decisive conflict of the Jacobite rising of 1745. The Jacobites, predominantly Highlanders, led by Charles Edward Stuart, were defeated near Inverness, ne Scotland, by government forces led by the Duke of Cumberland. Culloden ended Stuart attempts to regain the throne by force. The Battle, which claimed *c.*1000 Scots' lives, was followed by ruthless subjugation of the Highland clans.

Culpeper's Rebellion (1677) Uprising by North Carolina colonists against British trade policies. John Culpeper and George Durant led the colonists who jailed the British governor and replaced him with Culpeper. He ruled until 1679, when the British reasserted their authority. The rebellion is regarded as the first uprising in the American colonies.

Cultural Revolution (1966–76) The "Great Proletarian Cultural Revolution" was initiated by Mao Zedong and his wife, Jiang Qing, to purge the Chinese Communist Party of his opponents and to instill "correct" revolutionary attitudes. The failure of Mao's five-

CUBA

AREA: 110,860sq km (42,803sq mi)
POPULATION: 10,822,000
CAPITAL (POPULATION): Havana (2,096,054)
GOVERNMENT: Socialist republic
ETHNIC GROUPS: White 66%, Mulatto 22%, Black 12%
LANGUAGES: Spanish (official)
RELIGIONS: Christianity (Roman Catholic 40%, Protestant 3%)
GDP PER CAPITA (1994): US$1627

Caribbean island republic, at the entrance to the Gulf of Mexico. Cuba is the largest island in the West Indies. Following Christopher Columbus' discovery of Cuba in 1492, the first Spanish colony was established in 1511. The indigenous population was quickly killed and the economy became dependent on African slave labour. Slavery was not abolished in Cuba until 1886. Discontent at Spanish rule erupted into war in 1868, and in 1895 a second war of independence was led by José Martí. In 1898 the sinking of the US battleship *Maine* precipitated the Spanish-American War. From 1898 to 1902 Cuba was under US military occupation before becoming an independent republic. In order to protect US-owned plantations, the United States occupied Cuba (1906–09, 1912).

From 1933 to 1959 Fulgencio Batista ruled Cuba, maintaining good relations with the United States. In 1952 he imposed martial law. After an abortive coup attempt in 1953, Fidel Castro (supported by Che Guevara) launched a successful revolution in 1956. In 1959 Castro became premier. Castro's brand of revolutionary socialism included the nationalization of many US-owned industries, causing the United States to impose a trade embargo (1960) and break off diplomatic ties (1961). Cuban exiles, supported by the US government, launched the disastrous Bay of Pigs invasion (1961). Castro now regarded the Soviet Union as his chief ally. In 1962 the potential siting of Soviet missiles fuelled the Cuban Missile Crisis. Castro's attempt to export revolution to the rest of Latin America ended in diplomatic alienation. Cuba turned to acting as a leader of developing nations and providing support for revolutionary movements. Between 1965 and 1973, when emigration was banned, more than 250,000 Cubans went into voluntary exile. In 1980 emigration was legalized and many disaffected Cubans chose to leave. In 1998 the United Nations (UN) called for an end to the US embargo.

Series of military expeditions (11th–13th centuries) from Christian Europe to recover the Holy Land (Palestine) from the Muslims. In the 7th century, JERUSALEM was captured by the caliph OMAR. In the early 11th century, persecution of Christians had intensified under the FATIMIDS. In 1071 control of Jerusalem passed to the SELJUK Turks. Seljuk victory over the BYZANTINE EMPIRE at the Battle of MANZIKERT (1071) and the capture (1085) of Antioch (now ANTAKYA) presaged Turkish domination of ASIA MINOR. Byzantine Emperor ALEXIUS I (COMMENUS) appealed to the West for assistance. In Europe, the concept of a holy war against Islam was given credence by greater economic and military confidence, the success of the Normans against the Arabs in s Italy and Sicily, the strength of MILLENARIANISM, and the growth of pilgrimages. The Crusaders were motivated by the desire to earn salvation and the promise of land, wealth and fame. In 1095 Pope URBAN II convoked the Council of Clermont. At a mass assembly, he called on Christendom to unite to protect the Holy Sepulchre from further Muslim attack. While the main crusading force, consisting primarily of Norman-French gentry, was being prepared, the "People's Crusade" led by Peter the Hermit and Walter the Penniless brought together an ill-disciplined mob that destroyed villages and committed anti-Semitic atrocities on their way to Constantinople (now ISTANBUL). They were massacred by the Turks before the arrival of the main force.

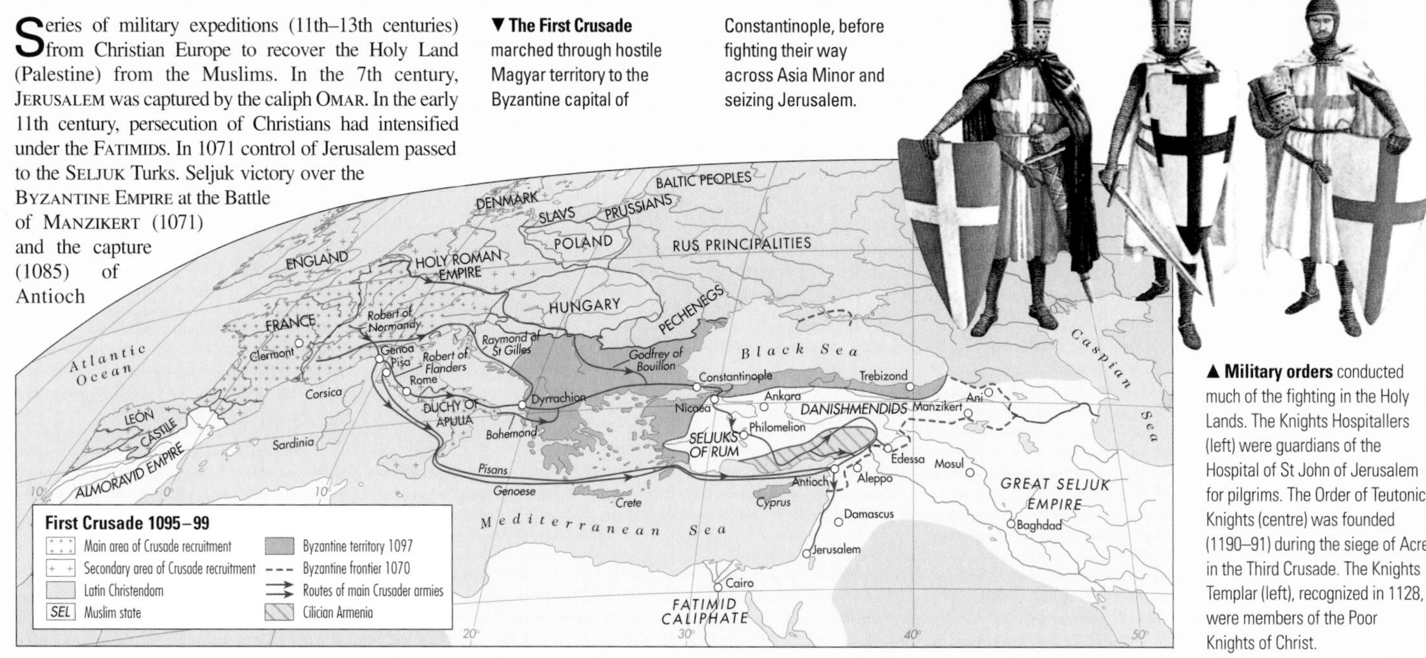

▼ The First Crusade marched through hostile Magyar territory to the Byzantine capital of Constantinople, before fighting their way across Asia Minor and seizing Jerusalem.

▲ Military orders conducted much of the fighting in the Holy Lands. The Knights Hospitallers (left) were guardians of the Hospital of St John of Jerusalem for pilgrims. The Order of Teutonic Knights (centre) was founded (1190–91) during the siege of Acre in the Third Crusade. The Knights Templar (left), recognized in 1128, were members of the Poor Knights of Christ.

FIRST CRUSADE (1095–99)

A force of *c.*30,000 soldiers assembled at Constantinople. It consisted of three main divisions; RAYMOND IV, Count of Toulouse, led the Provençals, GODFREY OF BOUILLON and his brother Baldwin (later BALDWIN I) represented Lorraine, and BOHEMOND I led the Norman faction. Alexius exacted an oath of fealty from the leaders, which bound them to return to him any "lost provinces" of the Byzantine Empire that they conquered. In June 1097 the Crusaders captured NICAEA and in June 1098 they captured Antioch. In July 1099 the Crusaders took Jerusalem in a fierce battle which was accompanied by massacre, notably of the Muslim defenders of the Mosque of Umar. The victorious armies established four Crusader States in the Levant. Godfrey of Bouillon, elected defender of the Holy Sepulchre, established the Latin Kingdom of Jerusalem. The county of EDESSA was created by Baldwin, the county of TRIPOLI by Raymond, and the principality of Antioch by Bohemond.

SECOND CRUSADE (1147–49)

In 1144 Edessa fell to Zangi, governor of Mosul. In 1145 Pope Eugenius III persuaded Saint BERNARD OF CLAIRVAUX to preach the Second Crusade. It was led by Emperor CONRAD III and LOUIS VII of France. Their ill-disciplined armies slaughtered Jews in the Rhineland and pillaged the Byzantine Empire en route to Constantinople. The Crusade itself was an unmitigated failure.

THIRD CRUSADE (1189–92)

The Third Crusade was called by Pope GREGORY VIII in response to SALADIN's capture (1187) of Jerusalem. In 1190 Emperor FREDERICK I (BARBAROSSA) drowned and leadership of the Crusade passed to RICHARD I of England

▲ Crusaders besieging Jerusalem (June–July 1099) built siege towers to overcome the city's complex defences. Speed was vital because of the heat, low supplies, and the imminent arrival of a relief force.

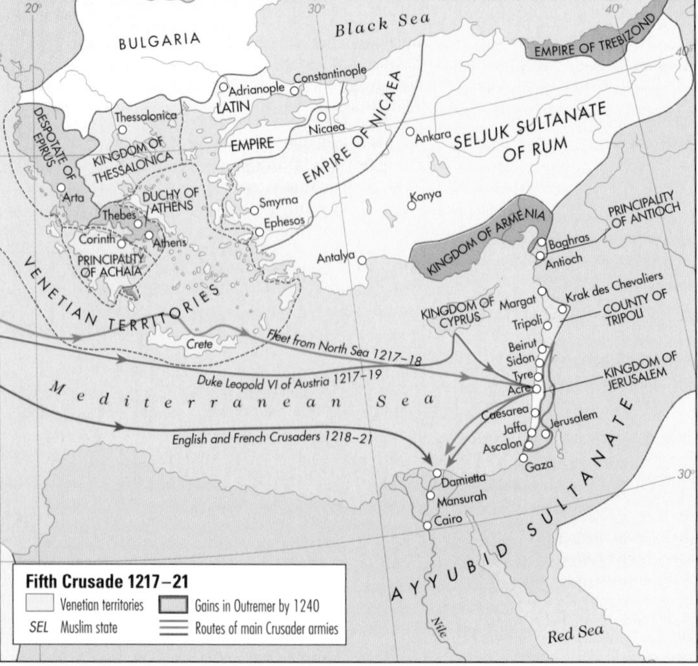

◀ The Fifth Crusade was an attempt to destroy Muslim power through the conquest of Egypt, whose commercial and agricultural wealth was the key to long-term control of the Near East. Ironically, more was achieved by the excommunicate crusader, Emperor Frederick II, who recovered Jerusalem by negotiation in 1229.

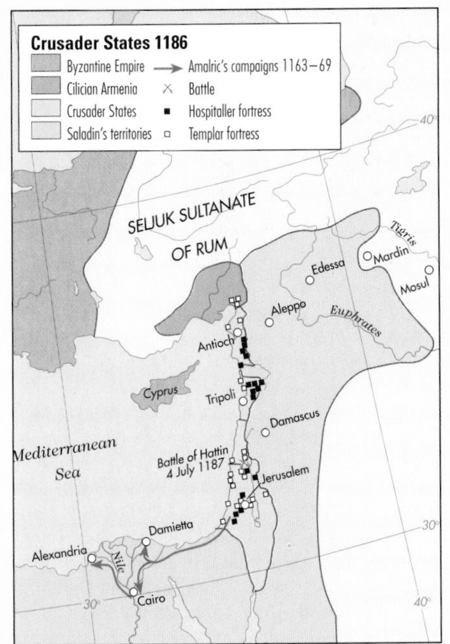

▲▼The Crusader States were saved from complete extinction by the arrival of the Third Crusade and Richard I (the Lionheart) of England even came close to reversing Saladin's conquest of Jerusalem in 1187.

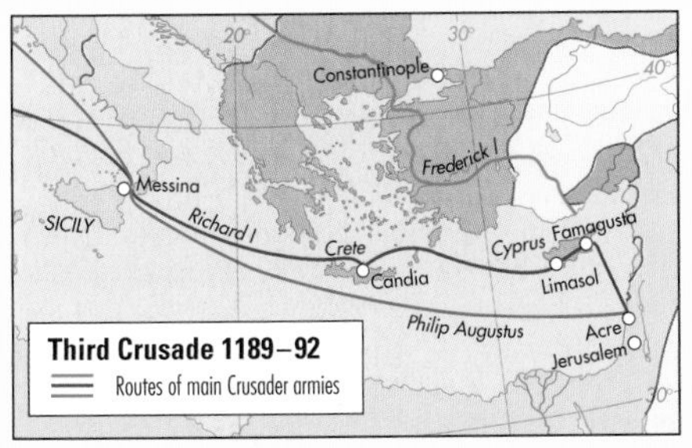

and PHILIP II of France. They captured ACRE in 1191, but disagreements forced a truce with Saladin.

FOURTH CRUSADE (1202–04)

No monarchs responded to Pope INNOCENT III's call for a Fourth Crusade. It was diverted to Constantinople by the Venetians and saw the establishment of the Latin Empire of CONSTANTINOPLE under BALDWIN I.

FIFTH CRUSADE (1217–21)

After the disastrous CHILDREN'S CRUSADE (1212), Pope INNOCENT III made Egypt the target of the Fifth Crusade. Under the leadership of John of Brienne, the Crusaders captured Damietta in Egypt. Papal legate Pelagius assumed the leadership and unwisely refused peace terms. Damietta was recovered and the pope and emperor were left at odds.

SIXTH CRUSADE (1228–29)

Emperor FREDERICK II embarked on the diplomatic Sixth Crusade after being excommunicated by Pope Honorius III. He negotiated a truce with the sultan of Egypt that recovered Jerusalem and other holy cities. In 1229 Frederick was crowned king of Jerusalem.

SEVENTH CRUSADE (1248–54)

In 1244 Jerusalem was retaken for Islam. LOUIS IX of France responded by launching a Crusade against Egypt. In 1249 Damietta fell once more, but a march on Cairo ended in a rout and Louis was captured.

EIGHTH & NINTH CRUSADES (1270, 1270–72)

In 1268 Jaffa and Antioch were recaptured for Islam. Louis IX launched the Eighth Crusade, but died in Tunis. The Ninth Crusade was led by Prince Edward (later EDWARD I of England). In 1191 Acre, the last Christian foothold in the Levant, fell to Islam. *See also* KNIGHTS HOSPITALLERS; KNIGHTS TEMPLAR; TEUTONIC KNIGHTS

year economic plan, the GREAT LEAP FORWARD, produced dissent over the direction of Chinese communism. Mao set out to reinforce his political position by mobilizing China's urban youth. A new youth corps, the RED GUARDS, attacked reactionary, "bourgeois" ideas. Intellectuals and others suspected of revisionism were humiliated and tortured. Many were murdered and three million members were purged from the Party. With the support of Defence Minister LIN BIAO and Premier ZHOU ENLAI, Mao removed President LIU SHAOQI and General Secretary DENG XIAOPING. By 1968 China was on the brink of civil war. The Red Guards were disbanded and martial law was declared in 1969. The Cultural Revolution was transformed into a struggle for the succession to Chairman Mao. Lin was implicated in a plot to assassinate Mao and was executed. Deng Xiaoping was rehabilitated by Zhou Enlai and the pair battled for hegemony with the so-called GANG OF FOUR. The Cultural Revolution effectively ended with the defeat of the Gang of Four and the accession of Deng as paramount leader in 1976.

Cumae Ancient city in Campania region, SW Italy. It is believed to be the oldest Greek colony in Italy (founded *c.*750 BC). It successfully resisted attack from the ETRUSCANS, but was defeated by the SAMNITES in the 5th century BC. It came under Roman control (338 BC), but from then on its fortunes declined and the town was destroyed in the 13th century AD. There are Greek and Roman ruins on the site and the cavern where the Cumaean Sybil, a priestess of the Greek god Apollo, pronounced her prophecies.

Cumans Turkic people originating in N Asiatic Russia. They conquered Ukraine in the 11th century AD, set up a state on the coast of the Black Sea, and traded with the Byzantine Empire and Hungary. After defeat by the MONGOLS in the wars of 1224–1240, many Cumans moved to Hungary.

Cumberland, William Augustus, Duke of (1721–65) British general, second son of GEORGE II of England. Cumberland brutally suppressed the JACOBITES after defeating them at the Battle of CULLODEN (1746). His subsequent continental commands during the War of the AUSTRIAN SUCCESSION (1747–48) and the SEVEN YEARS' WAR (1757) ended in defeat. Cumberland's refusal to continue as commander in chief under William PITT (THE ELDER) led to Pitt's dismissal as prime minister.

cuneiform System of writing developed (*c.*3000 BC) in Mesopotamia. The system consists of wedge-shaped strokes, derived from the practice of writing on soft clay with a triangular stylus as a "pen". Cuneiform developed from pictograms that came to serve as a script of more than 500 characters. Most stood for words, but some stood for syllables or speech-sounds.

Cunobelinus *See* CYMBELINE

Cuomo, Mario Matthew (1932–) US politician, the first Italian-American governor of New York (1983–95). He campaigned for tighter gun controls to combat crime and spoke out against capital punishment. Cuomo was a popular governor, but declined to run for the Democratic nomination in 1988 and supported Bill CLINTON's successful campaign for the presidency in 1992.

Curia Romana Official administrative body of the ROMAN CATHOLIC CHURCH. It is based in the VATICAN and consists of a court of officials through which the pope governs the Church. It includes three groups – congregations, tribunals and curial offices – and is concerned with all aspects of the life of the Church and its members.

Curtin, John Joseph (1885–1945) Australian statesman, prime minister (1941–45). He entered Parliament in 1928 and became leader of the LABOR PARTY in 1935. Curtin organized the mobilization of Australian forces during World War 2. He died in office.

Curzon, George Nathaniel, 1st Marquess of Kedleston (1859–1925) British statesman. He entered Parliament as a Conservative in 1886. As viceroy of India (1899–1905), Curzon reformed administration and education and established (1901) the North-West Frontier Province. He resigned after a dispute with Lord KITCHENER. During World War 1, Curzon served in the coalition cabinets of Herbert ASQUITH and David LLOYD GEORGE. He continued as foreign secretary (1919–24) in Bonar LAW's government, and helped negotiate the Treaty of LAUSANNE (1922–23). *See also* CURZON LINE

Curzon Line Demarcation of the border between Poland and Russia, proposed (1920) by British foreign secretary Lord CURZON. It awarded the city of Vilna to Lithuania and large areas of Poland to Russia. In 1921 the Poles invaded Russia and recovered the territory. The YALTA CONFERENCE (1945) established the Curzon Line as the definitive frontier.

Cush *See* KUSH

Custer, George Armstrong (1839–76) US cavalry officer. A flamboyant, headstrong character, Custer was the youngest Union general in the American CIVIL WAR. After the War, he was posted to the frontier, but was court-martialled (1867) for disobeying orders and suspended. In 1868 Custer returned to service and led campaigns against the CHEYENNE. His decision to divide his regiment and attack a superior force of SIOUX at the Battle of LITTLE BIGHORN (1876) resulted in the death of Custer and his entire regiment.

Cuza, Alexander John (1820–73) Prince of Romania (1859–66). He was elected prince of Walachia and Moldavia in 1859 and recognized by the Turks in 1861, when his principalities were united into the state of Romania. Cuza introduced social reforms, including the emancipation of the serfs in 1864 and the foundation of universities. In 1866 he was forced to abdicate.

Cuzco City in S central Peru; capital of Cuzco department. An ancient capital of the INCA empire from *c.*1200, it fell to the Spaniards in 1533. Cuzco was destroyed by earthquakes in 1650 and then rebuilt. It is a centre of archaeological research. Pop. (1993) 255,568.

Cymbeline (Cunobelinus) (d. *c.*AD 42) Ancient British king. An ally of the Romans, he was king of the CATUVELLAUNI tribe. After conquering the Trinovantes, he became the most powerful ruler in S Britain. Shakespeare's play *Cymbeline* (*c.*1610) was based on the chronicles of Holinshed.

Cynics School of philosophy founded (*c.*440 BC) by Antisthenes, a pupil of SOCRATES. Cynics considered virtue to be the only good. Their teachings were developed by DIOGENES. *See also* STOICS

Cyprian, Saint (200?–258) Father of the Church, bishop of Carthage (248–58). Cyprian was a pagan rhetorician who was converted (*c.*246) to Christianity. His theological treatise, *The Unity of the Catholic Church* (251), argued for the restoration of church unity based on episcopal authority. Cyprian's strict views on apostasy and heresy resulted in his eventual martyrdom under VALERIAN. His feast day is 16 September.

▲ Cuban Missile Crisis In 1962, US reconnaissance flights detected evidence that the Soviet Union was building nuclear missile bases on Cuba within range of the US mainland. A US naval blockade and the threat of nuclear war eventually forced Nikita Khrushchev to dismantle the bases.

C

CYPRUS

AREA: 9,250sq km (3,571sq mi)
POPULATION: 725,000
CAPITAL (POPULATION): Nicosia (177,451)
GOVERNMENT: Multiparty republic
ETHNIC GROUPS: Greek Cypriot 81%, Turkish Cypriot 19%
LANGUAGES: Greek and Turkish (both official)
RELIGIONS: Christianity (Greek Orthodox), Islam
GDP PER CAPITA (1994): US$9754

Island republic in the NE Mediterranean Sea. Greeks settled on Cyprus *c*.3200 years ago. From AD 330 the island was part of the BYZANTINE EMPIRE. In the 1570s it became part of the OTTOMAN EMPIRE. Turkish rule continued until 1878 when Cyprus was leased to Britain. In 1925 Britain proclaimed it a colony. In the 1950s Greek Cypriots, who made up 80% of the population, began a campaign for ENOSIS (union) with Greece. Their leader was the Greek Orthodox Archbishop MAKARIOS. A guerrilla force (EOKA) attacked the British, who exiled Makarios.

In 1960 Cyprus became an independent country, with Makarios as its first president. The constitution provided for power-sharing between the Greek and Turkish Cypriots. It proved unworkable, however, and fighting broke out between the two communities. In 1964 the United Nations (UN) sent in a peacekeeping force. In 1974 Greek-led Cypriot forces overthrew Makarios. This led Turkey to invade N Cyprus, occupying *c*.40% of the island. Many Greek Cypriots fled from the Turkish-occupied area, which in 1979 was proclaimed to be a self-governing region. In 1983 the Turkish Cypriots declared independence as the Turkish Republic of Northern Cyprus. The UN regards Cyprus as a single nation under the Greek Cypriot government in the S, and Turkey is the only country to recognize the sovereign status of Northern Cyprus. It is estimated that more than 30,000 Turkish troops are deployed in Northern Cyprus. Despite UN-brokered peace negotiations (1997), there are frequent border clashes between the two communities. In 1998 Cyprus began accession talks with the European Union (EU).

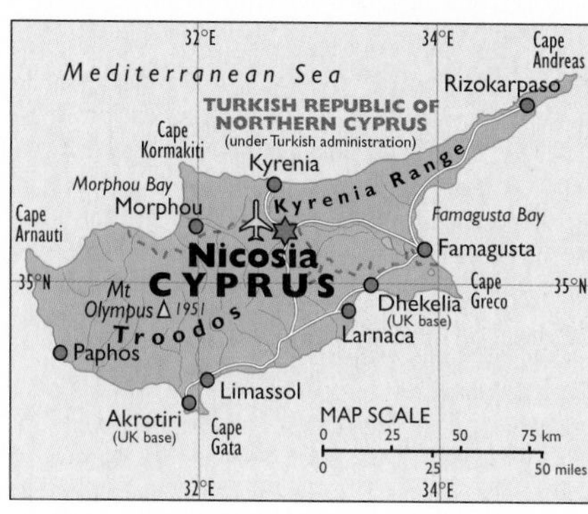

Cyprus *See* country feature

Cyrankiewicz, Józef (1911–89) Polish statesman, premier (1947–52, 1954–70). He spent most of World War 2 in Auschwitz concentration camp (1941–45). In 1945 Cyrankiewicz became secretary general of the Polish Socialist Party (PSP). In his first term as premier, he presided over the merger of the PSP with the Soviet-backed Polish Workers' Party to form the Polish United Workers' Party (1948). In 1956 Cyrankiewicz crushed an uprising in Poznán, W Poland, but managed to retain power under the more liberal First Secretary Władysław GOMUŁKA. In 1970 Cyrankiewicz and Gomułka were forced to resign after a series of food riots.

Cyrenaica Historic region on the Mediterranean Sea, now in NE Libya; the capital was Cyrene. Colonized by the Greeks in the 7th century BC, it was bequeathed to Rome in 96 BC, and conquered by the Arabs in AD 642. It became part of the Ottoman Empire after the mid-16th century. An Italian colony from 1912, it was the scene of many battles during World War 2. Area: 855,368sq km (330,258sq mi).

Cyril, Saint (*c*.826–69) Greek Christian missionary. With his brother, Methodius, he is one of the two so-called "Apostles to the Slavs" who were sent to convert the Khazars and Moravians to Christianity. Cyril is said to have invented an early ("Glagolithic") version of the Cyrillic alphabet (now used for Russian and other Slavic languages). His feast day is 14 February in the West and 11 May in the East.

Cyril (of Alexandria), Saint (d.444) Doctor of the Church, patriarch of Alexandria. He ruthlessly suppressed heresy and was complicit in the expulsion of Jews from Alexandria. Cyril presided over the Council of EPHESUS (431), which condemned NESTORIANISM. In 433 Cyril accepted a compromise with the bishops of Antioch that emphasized the two natures (human and divine) of Christ within one Person. *See also* MONOPHYSITISM

Cyrus II (the Great) (*c*.585–529 BC) King of Persia (559–529 BC), founder of the ACHAEMENID empire. Most of our knowledge of Cyrus is derived from the texts of HERODOTUS and XENOPHON. In *c*.550 BC he overthrew Astyages, king of MEDIA. Cyrus defeated CROESUS, king of LYDIA, and captured his capital, SARDIS (*c*.546 BC). Cyrus now turned towards the Chaldaean empire of BABYLONIA. The capture of BABYLON (539 BC) established Persian control of MESOPOTAMIA, Syria and Palestine. His empire now stretched from the Mediterranean to India. According to the Bible, Cyrus delivered the Jews from their BABYLONIAN CAPTIVITY. He was a tolerant and wise conqueror, respecting local customs and religious beliefs. Cyrus was succeeded by his son, CAMBYSES II. *See also* CHALDAEA; IRAN

Cyrus the Younger (424–401 BC) Persian satrap (provincial governor), son of DARIUS II. After plotting unsuccessfully to kill his brother ARTAXERXES II, king of Persia, Cyrus hired Greek mercenaries, who helped him defeat the king at Cunaxa. Cyrus, however, died in the battle. The retreat of the Ten Thousand (Greek mercenaries) under Clearchus, Spartan ruler of Byzantium (now Istanbul), is related in XENOPHON's *Anabasis*.

Czartoryski, Adam Jerzy (1770–1861) Polish politician. A hostage at the Russian court, he befriended the future Tsar ALEXANDER I who appointed him foreign minister (1803–06). Czartoryski was responsible for the adoption (1815) of the Polish constitution. He opposed Tsar NICHOLAS I's ambitions and, following an insurrection, headed (1830–31) a Polish provisional government. After its failure he was forced into exile in Paris.

Czechoslovakia Former federal state in central Europe. Formed after World War 1 from parts of the old AUSTRO-HUNGARIAN EMPIRE (BOHEMIA, MORAVIA and SLOVAKIA, together with part of SILESIA and sub-Carpathian RUTHENIA) Czechoslovakia was formally recognized as a new republic by the Treaty of St Germain (1919). In 1920 a democratic constitution was established, and the nation was led first by Tomás MASARYK and then by Eduard BENEŠ. Nationalist tensions caused unrest: the Slovaks had long wanted autonomy, and the large German population in SUDETENLAND wanted to join with Germany. Adolf Hitler's rise to power and annexation of Austria led to the MUNICH AGREEMENT (1938), which ceded land to Germany. Poland and Hungary also acquired territory, and Beneš resigned. In 1939 Hitler occupied Czechoslovakia, and Beneš formed a government in exile in London. In 1945 the country was liberated by United States' and Soviet troops. In 1946 elections the communists emerged as the strongest party, but Beneš was restored as president. By 1948 the communists had assumed complete control, and Beneš resigned. Czechoslovakia became a Soviet-style state. The democratic reforms of Alexander DUBČEK in the PRAGUE SPRING (1968) were crushed by troops from the Warsaw Pact. In 1989 anti-government demonstrations and the democratization of Eastern Europe finally led to the resignation of Communist Party leaders. Non-communists came to power, and the "Velvet Revolution" was complete when Vaclav HAVEL became president. In 1990 free elections were held, but differences between the Czechs and Slovaks led to the partitioning of the country (1 January 1993). The break was peaceful, and the two new nations, the CZECH REPUBLIC and the SLOVAK REPUBLIC, have retained many ties.

Czech Republic *See* country feature

CZECH REPUBLIC

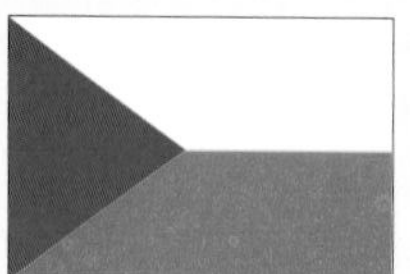

AREA: 78,864sq km (30,449sq mi)
POPULATION: 10,310,000
CAPITAL (POPULATION): Prague (1,216,005)
GOVERNMENT: Multiparty republic
ETHNIC GROUPS: Czech 81%, Moravian 13%, Slovak 3%, Polish, German, Silesian, Gypsy, Hungarian, Ukrainian
LANGUAGES: Czech (official)
RELIGIONS: Christianity (Roman Catholic 39%, Protestant 4%)
GDP PER CAPITA (1995): US$9770

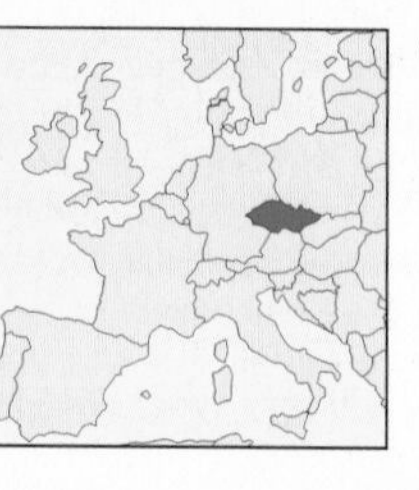

Republic in central Europe. The Czech Republic is made up of two regions: the plateau of BOHEMIA in the W and the lowland of MORAVIA in the E. Czechs began to settle in the area *c*.1500 years ago. In the 10th century Bohemia became important as a kingdom within the HOLY ROMAN EMPIRE. In 1526 the Austrian HABSBURGS assumed control, but a Czech rebellion in 1618 sparked the THIRTY YEARS' WAR. While Austria continued to rule Bohemia and Moravia, Czech nationalism grew throughout the 19th century. After World War 1 CZECHOSLOVAKIA was created. In 1989 mass demonstrations resulted in the "Velvet Revolution". Free elections were held in 1990, resulting in the re-election of Vaclav HAVEL. In 1992 the government agreed to the secession of the SLOVAK REPUBLIC, and on 1 January 1993 the Czech Republic was created.

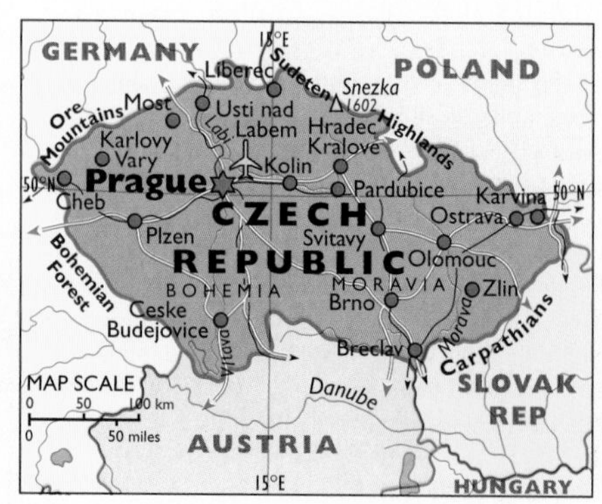

Dachau Town in Bavaria, SW Germany, site of the first Nazi CONCENTRATION CAMP established in March 1933. Dachau was the main camp for the notorious "medical" experiments carried out by German doctors on involuntary inmates. More than 32,000 people (mainly Jews) died or were murdered here before liberation in 1945. The site is preserved as a memorial. *See also* AUSCHWITZ; BELSEN; DACHAU; HOLOCAUST, THE

Dacia Ancient region of Europe (now in Romania). It was colonized (AD 101–106) by the Roman Emperor TRAJAN. Dacia was later overrun by GOTHS, HUNS and AVARS. The language was retained and is the basis of modern Romanian.

Daddah, Moktar Ould (1924–) President of Mauritania (1961–78). He became premier when Mauritania joined the French Community in 1958 and was the first president of an independent Mauritania. Daddah's authoritarian rule maintained a precarious national unity. He was overthrown in a coup.

da Gama, Vasco *See* GAMA, VASCO DA

Dagobert I (*c*.605–639) Last Frankish king (629–39) of the MEROVINGIANS. He moved his capital from AUSTRASIA to Paris. Dagobert maintained the conquests of his father, CLOTAIRE II, and his reign marked a revival of Frankish art and economy.

Dahomey Former kingdom in W Africa. In *c*.1625 Do-Aklin founded the town of Abomey. King Agaja (r.1708–32) conquered Allada and Whydah (now Ouidah), forming the kingdom of Dahomey. The kingdom expanded through conquest using women as soldiers. Despite having to pay tribute to the YORUBA kingdom of OYO to the E, Dahomey prospered with the SLAVE TRADE. In 1818 King Gezu (r.1818–58) ended the annual tribute to Oyo. He also managed the gradual transition of the economy to palm oil exports. In 1892 France defeated Dahomey and established a protectorate. In 1960 Dahomey gained independence from France. Plagued by economic recession and ethnic unrest between the north and south, Dahomey was ruled by a succession of military governments. In 1975 Dahomey was renamed BENIN.

Daigo II (1288–1339) (Go-Daigo) Japanese emperor (1318–39) who attempted to restore effective imperial power. Throughout the 1320s, when the imperial ceremonial government was typically at odds with the military and political power of the shogunate, he plotted the overthrow of HOJO Takatoki, shogun of KAMAKURA. In 1331 the plot was exposed and Daigo was captured and sent into exile. In 1333 ASHIKAGA Takauji, commander of the shogun's army, defected to Daigo, who subsequently returned to Kyoto in triumph. Daigo failed, however, to reward Takauji and others for their role in restoring him to power, and in 1335 Takauji proclaimed himself emperor and marched on the capital. In 1336 Daigo fled Kyoto and set up a rival court in Nara. There followed an age of two imperial governments.

Dáil Éireann Lower house of the two-chamber parliament of the Republic of Ireland (the Upper House is the *Seanad Éireann*). It has 166 members elected for five-year terms by a system of proportional representation.

daimyo (Jap. large landowner) Japanese feudal baron. A landowner was considered a daimyo if his estate produced more than 10,000 *koku* (50,000 bushels) of rice. From the 11th century the daimyo began to establish large personal estates with the help of the SAMURAI. In 1192 the daimyo YORITOMO established the first shogunate. Under the ASHIKAGA shogunate, leading daimyo were appointed as military governors (*shugo*), with control over areas as large as provinces. In the mid-15th century, the *sengoku* daimyo, who controlled smaller plots of land, established hegemony. As a result, Japan fractured into a series of small, warring states. In 1573 the daimyo Oda NOBUNAGA overthrew the ASHIKAGA shogunate and began the process of reunification that was completed (1603) by IEYASU Tokugawa. During the TOKUGAWA shogunate, the daimyo were brought under the control of the shogun by legal reforms and compulsory attendance at court. In 1871 during the constitutional reorganisation of Japanese society, daimyo status was abolished. *See also* SHOGUN

Dakota *See* SIOUX

Dakota *See* NORTH DAKOTA; SOUTH DAKOTA

Daladier, Édouard (1884–1970) French statesman, premier (1933, 1934, 1938–40). As premier and minister of defence, he signed the MUNICH AGREEMENT (1938). In 1940 Daladier was arrested by the VICHY GOVERNMENT and deported (1942) to Germany. He was released at the end of World War 2 and became a member of the National Assembly (1946–58).

Dalai Lama (Grand Lama) Supreme head of the Yellow Hat Buddhist monastery at Lhasa, Tibet. The title was bestowed upon the third Grand Lama by the Mongol ruler Altan Khan (d.1583). In TIBETAN BUDDHISM, the Dalai Lama is revered as the bodhisattva *Avalokitesvara*. When a Dalai Lama dies, his soul is believed to pass into the body of an infant, born 49 days later. In 1950–51, **Tenzin Gyatso** (1935–), 14th Dalai Lama, temporarily fled Tibet after it was annexed by the People's Republic of China. Following a brutally suppressed Tibetan uprising (1959), he went into exile in India.

Daley, Richard Joseph (1902–76) US politician. He served as mayor of Chicago (1955–76). Daley built a powerful political machine that helped win Chicago for the Democrats and ensured John KENNEDY's victory in the closely fought 1960 presidential election. Daley gained notoriety for his sanctioning of the brutal police tactics used against anti-Vietnam War protestors during the 1968 Democratic Convention in Chicago. His son, Richard Michael Daley (1942–), became mayor of Chicago in 1989.

Dalhousie, James Andrew Broun Ramsay, 1st Marquess of (1812–60) British statesman, governor general of India (1847–56). After serving as a member of Parliament and president of the board of trade (1845), he was appointed governor general of India. Dalhousie initiated many public works, such as developing the railway and sewage systems. In the second of the SIKH WARS, he annexed Punjab (1849) and the further acquisitions of Rangoon (1852) and Oudh (1856) precipitated the INDIAN MUTINY (1857).

Dallas, George Mifflin (1792–1864) US statesman, vice president (1845–49). He served as a US senator (1831–33). Dallas was vice president under James POLK. He was minister to Great Britain (1856–61). The city of Dallas, Texas, is named after him.

Dalmatia Region of Croatia on the E coast of the Adriatic Sea; the provincial capital is SPLIT. From the 10th century it was divided N and S between Croatia and Serbia. By 1420 most of Dalmatia was controlled by Venice. The Treaty of CAMPO FORMIO (1797) ceded the region to Austria. After World War 1 it became part of Yugoslavia. In 1991 Dalmatia was the scene of heavy fighting between Croats and Serbs. Other major cities include Zadar (the historic capital) and DUBROVNIK.

Dalton, Hugh, Baron (1887–1962) British statesman, chancellor of the exchequer (1945–47). He entered Parliament in 1924. As chancellor, Dalton was responsible for the nationalization of the BANK OF ENGLAND (1946). He was forced to resign after leaking details of the forthcoming budget to a journalist.

Damascus Capital of Syria, on the River Barada, SW Syria. Perhaps the oldest continuously occupied city in the world, today it is Syria's administrative and financial centre. In 2000 BC Damascus formed part of the Egyptian empire. In 332 BC ALEXANDER III (THE GREAT) captured the city from Persia, and it was subsumed into the SELEUCID Empire. Under Roman rule, Damascus became a prosperous commercial city and an early centre of Christianity. THEODOSIUS I built (AD 379) a Christian church that, under UMAYYAD rule (661–750), was converted into the Great Mosque. The city withstood the CRUSADES and was part of the Ottoman Empire for 400 years (1516–1918). In 1918 Damascus was captured by the British and came under French administration. It became capital of independent Syria in 1941. Pop. (1993 est.) 1,497,000.

Damasus I, Saint (304–84) Pope (366–84). His election was challenged by the Arians, who chose Ursinus as antipope. Both were consecrated by bishops, although eventually Emperor Valentinian I expelled Ursinus from Rome. Damasus asserted that a pope could be tried only by ecclesiastical courts. Under his supervision, Saint JEROME produced a revised Latin translation of the Bible. *See also* ARIANISM

Dampier, William (1651?–1715) English navigator and buccaneer. His early career included a raiding expedition (1679–81) against Spanish America and a voyage (1688) across the Pacific Ocean. Dampier explored the coasts of Australia, New Guinea and New Britain, and the Dampier Archipelago and Dampier Strait are named after him. In 1708 he rescued Alexander Selkirk, on whom Daniel Defoe based his novel *Robinson Crusoe* (1719).

Danby, Thomas Osborne, Earl of (1632–1712) English statesman, leading minister of CHARLES II of England. He rose to power with the support of the 2nd Duke of BUCKINGHAM and his success in restoring the nation's finances earned him the title Earl of Danby in 1674. Danby built the TORY faction in Parliament through bribery and the skilful use of royal patronage. He was impeached and imprisoned (1679–84) for trying to secure a secret subsidy from LOUIS XIV of France. On his release, Danby was heavily involved in the so-called Glorious Revolution (1688–89) that ovethrew JAMES II in favour of MARY II and WILLIAM III (OF ORANGE). He served William of Orange (1690–95) until he was impeached for taking bribes from the English EAST INDIA COMPANY.

DALAI LAMA

Dalai Lama The current Dalai Lama, Tenzin Gyatso, was born to a peasant family in NE Tibet. At the age of two, he was recognized as the spiritual leader of Tibet. Tenzin was enthroned in 1940, but was forced into exile in Dharamsala, N India, following the Chinese invasion of Tibet (1954) and Mao Zedong's suppression of Tibetan Buddhism. In 1989 he was awarded the Nobel Prize for Peace for his commitment to human rights.

DALAI LAMA IN HIS OWN WORDS

"No matter what part of the world we come from, we are all basically the same human beings. We all seek happiness and try to avoid suffering."
Nobel Prize acceptance speech, 10 December 1989

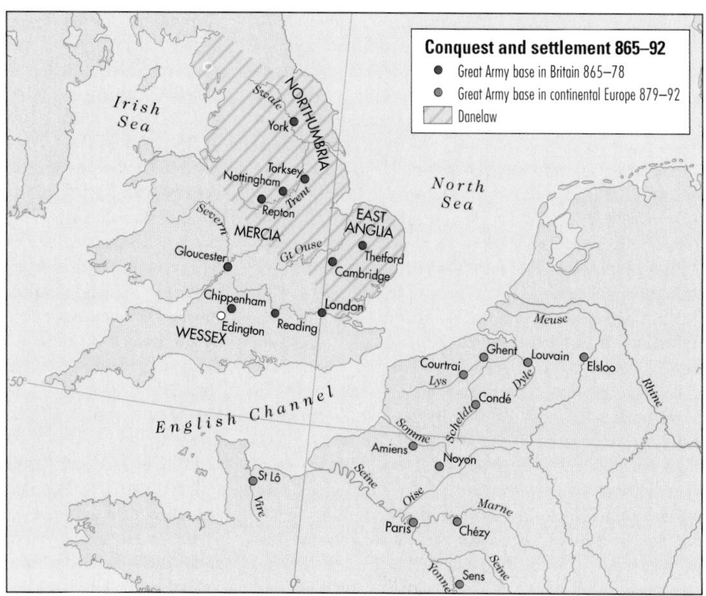

► **Danelaw** Numbering several thousand men, the "Great Armies" that started to collect in W Europe from C.AD 865 marked a new era in Viking expansion. Mainly Danish, they were numerous enough to conquer and settle whole Anglo-Saxon kingdoms and – when checked by Alfred (the Great) of Wessex in 878 – to battle for control of the major rivers of N France and the Low Countries. Following a serious defeat on the River Dyle, the remaining Vikings were forced to return to England in 892, but this time Alfred the Great fended them off with ease.

Dandolo, Enrico (*c*.1108–1205) Venetian statesman, founder of the Venetian empire. In 1192 he became DOGE (chief magistrate) of Venice. Dandolo led the Fourth CRUSADE in the capture (1204) of Constantinople (now ISTANBUL) and engineered the establishment of a Latin Empire of CONSTANTINOPLE. In 1205 he and BALDWIN I were defeated at Adrianople (now EDIRNE, Turkey). Dandolo, old and blind, led the Latin army home.

Danegeld Land tax levied in ANGLO-SAXON England. It was first raised by ALFRED (THE GREAT) to pay off the Danish invaders, and became a regular payment (991) in the reign of ETHELRED II (THE UNREADY). Payments to the Danes ceased in the 11th century, but the tax was still collected until 1162.

Danelaw Large region of NE England occupied by Danes in the late 9th century. Its independence was confirmed by a pact between ALFRED (THE GREAT) and Guthrum (886). Alfred's son, EDWARD THE ELDER, and grandson, ATHELSTAN, restored it to English control in the early 10th century. *See also* ANGLO-SAXONS; VIKINGS; WESSEX

Daniels, Josephus (1862–1948) US statesman, newspaper editor and writer. He amalgamated (1894) three newspapers into the Raleigh *News and Observer*. Daniels managed the Democrat presidential campaigns for William Jennings BRYAN (1908) and Woodrow WILSON (1912). As secretary of the navy (1913–21), he administered naval forces during World War 1.

D'Annunzio, Gabriele (1863–1938) Italian writer and soldier. His masterpiece is *Halcyon* (1903), an impressionistic collection of lyrics. D'Annunzio's rhetoric was instrumental in persuading Italy to join the Allies in World War 1 and he fought with spectacular bravery. D'Annunzio established personal rule (1919–21) of Fiume (Rijeka). He supported the rise of Benito MUSSOLINI's fascist movement.

Danton, Georges Jacques (1759–94) French statesman, a leader of the FRENCH REVOLUTION. He was instrumental in the arrest of LOUIS XVI (10 August 1792). Danton, DESMOULINS, ROBESPIERRE and MARAT formed a revolutionary tribunal. Danton dominated the first COMMITTEE OF PUBLIC SAFETY (April–July 1793) but was then ousted by Robespierre and the JACOBINS. He called for an end to the REIGN OF TERROR and for leniency towards the GIRONDINS. Danton was arrested for conspiracy, tried and guillotined.

Darcy, Thomas, Baron (1467–1537) English soldier and political intriguer. He served in military expeditions for Henry VIII, but later opposed the king's divorce from CATHERINE OF ARAGON and the DISSOLUTION OF THE MONASTERIES. During the PILGRIMAGE OF GRACE (1536), Darcy surrendered Pontefract Castle, Wales, and deserted to the rebels. He was executed for treason.

Dardanelles (Çanakkale Bogazi) Narrow strait between the Sea of Marmara and the Aegean Sea, separating Çanakkale in Asian Turkey from GALLIPOLI in European Turkey. With the BOSPORUS Strait, the Dardanelles forms a waterway whose strategic and commercial importance has been recognized since ancient times (when it was known as Hellespont). In the Byzantine and Ottoman empires and both World Wars, it was of strategic importance in the defence of Constantinople (now ISTANBUL). The strait was the scene of the GALLIPOLI CAMPAIGN in World War 1. Length: 61km (38mi). Width: 1.2–6km (0.75–4mi).

Darien Scheme (1695–99) Unsuccessful Scottish project to colonize the Isthmus of Darien, E Panama. The Scottish Parliament, disowned by the English government and opposed by the Spaniards, invested heavily in the scheme. The failure of the settlements was taken as a demonstration of Scotland's commercial weakness and helped to secure the Act of Union (1707) with England.

Darius I (the Great) (*c*.558–486 BC) King of Persia (521–486 BC). Historians are uncertain whether Darius gained the throne by killing Smerdis, son of CYRUS II (THE GREAT), or Gautama (the Magian) impersonating Smerdis. At the start of his reign, Darius was preoccupied with suppressing revolts throughout the ACHAEMENID Empire. He extended the Persian (Iranian) empire, chiefly through the conquests of Thrace and Macedonia. In 499 BC, the Ionian cities of Asia Minor rebelled against Persian rule, precipitating the PERSIAN WARS (499–479 BC). The Persians were defeated by ATHENS at the Battle of MARATHON (490 BC). Darius divided his empire into provinces (satrapies) and made great improvements to transport infrastructure. While he introduced ZOROASTRIANISM as the state religion, Darius was tolerant of religious diversity and encouraged the rebuilding (515 BC) of the TEMPLE OF JERUSALEM. His reign marked the golden age of Persian architecture, reflected in the palaces at SUSA and PERSEPOLIS. An account of his reign, the Behistun inscription, was the key for the deciphering of Babylonian cuneiform.

▲ **Darius I** The so-called Fire Temple of Naqsh-i Rustam, near Persepolis (now Takht-e-Jamshid), SW Iran, stands in front of a cliff in which the tomb of Darius I is carved.

Darius II (d.404 BC) King of Persia (423?–404 BC), illegitimate son of Artaxerxes I and father of ARTAXERXES II. He was dominated by his wife and half-sister, Parysatis. After the defeat of ATHENS at Syracuse (413 BC), Darius formed an anti-Athenian alliance with SPARTA and recaptured most of Ionia. Persian support was a major factor in Sparta's victory at the Battle of AEGOSPOTAMI (405 BC). *See also* PELOPONNESIAN WAR

Darius III (Codomannus) (*c*.380–330 BC) King of Persia (336–330 BC). By underestimating the strength of ALEXANDER III (THE GREAT), he brought about the demise of the ACHAEMENID empire. Defeated at Issus (333 BC) and Gaugamela (331 BC), Darius was forced to flee to Ecbatana and then to Bactria, where he was murdered by Bessus, the satrap of Bactria.

Dark Ages Period of dislocation in European history from the fall of the ROMAN EMPIRE in the 5th century to the 9th or 10th century. The term appears to imply cultural and economic backwardness, but in fact indicates a period whose history is obscure because of a shortage of written evidence. *See also* MIDDLE AGES

Darlan, Jean (Louis Xavier) François (1881–1942) French admiral. In 1939 he was appointed commander in chief of the French navy. In 1940 Darlan joined the VICHY GOVERNMENT as minister of the navy. In 1941 he was promoted to vice premier under Marshal PÉTAIN. In 1942 Darlan was given command of all the armed forces. At the Allied invasion of North Africa, he concluded an armistice with the Allies. Darlan was assassinated by an anti-Vichy sympathizer. *See also* NORTH AFRICA CAMPAIGN

Darnley, Henry Stuart, Lord (1545–67) Scottish aristocrat, second husband of MARY, QUEEN OF SCOTS, and father of JAMES I of England. In 1565 he married Mary (his cousin). Darnley's debauched lifestyle made him unpopular at court. In 1566 he conspired in the murder of Mary's secretary, David RIZZIO (1566), and became estranged from the queen. Darnley was murdered in a plot led by the Earl of BOTHWELL.

Darrow, Clarence Seward (1857–1938) US lawyer. He unsuccessfully defended (1894) Eugene DEBS following the PULLMAN STRIKE (1894). A staunch opponent of capital punishment, none of the 100 people charged with murder whom Darrow defended were ever sentenced to death. In 1906 he secured the acquittal of William HAYWOOD. In the famous SCOPES TRIAL (1925), Darrow unsuccessfully defended the right to teach the theory of evolution in schools, but his cross-examination of William BRYAN discredited the Fundamentalist stance.

Dartmouth College case (1819) US Supreme Court case. In 1816 the New Hampshire legislature unilaterally amended the charter of 1769 to make Dartmouth College a state university. The Court held that a corporate charter was a contract with which state laws could not interfere. This ruling greatly aided the early growth of US capitalism and big business.

Darwin, Charles Robert (1809–82) English naturalist, who developed the organic theory of evolution. In 1831 he joined a five-year, round-the-world expedition on HMS BEAGLE. Observations made of the flora and fauna of South America (especially the Galápagos Islands) formed the basis of his work on animal variation. The development of a similar theory by A.R. Wallace led Darwin to present his ideas to the Linnean Society in 1858. In 1859 he published *The Origin of Species*, one of the world's most influential science books. Drawing on the work of Thomas MALTHUS, Darwin argued that organisms reproduce more than is necessary to replenish their population, creating competition for survival. Opposed to the ideas of French biologist Chevalier de Lamarck (1744–1829), Darwin argued that each organism was a unique combination of genetic variations. The variations that prove helpful in the struggle to survive are passed down to the offspring of the survivors. He termed this process natural selection.

Daughters of the American Revolution (DAR) US patriotic society, founded in 1890, whose members are female lineal descendants of activists in the cause of American independence. DAR was chartered by Congress in 1895. In the 1970s there were 2800 local chapters and *c*.188,000 members.

dauphin Title of the heir to the French throne from 1350 to 1830. The name was originally that of the rulers of Viennois, SE France, deriving from lands known as the DAUPHINÉ, which were acquired by the French crown in 1349 and bestowed on the heir to the throne.

Dauphiné Former French province, now occupied by the departments of Drôme Isère and Haute-Alpes. Created by the Dauphin family's gradual addition of lands to the countship of Viennois, the province and the title DAUPHIN were sold to CHARLES V of France in 1349. Charles initiated the practice of ceding Dauphiné to the king's heir, and it remained semi-independent until it was annexed to France by CHARLES VII in 1457. Revolts in 1789 made Dauphiné one of the birthplaces of the French Revolution.

David (d. *c*.962 BC) King of ancient Israel (*c*.1010–970 BC), successor of SAUL. His career is related in the OLD TESTAMENT books of Samuel. David's military successes against the Philistines led SAUL to plot his demise. As king, he united Judah and Israel. David captured Jerusalem, making it his capital and building his palace on Mount Zion. The later part of his reign was an era of decline, marked by the revolts of his sons Absalom and Adonijah. David was succeeded by SOLOMON, his son by Bathsheba. According to the Jewish Prophets, the Messiah must be a descendant of David.

David I (*c*.1084–1153) King of Scotland (1124–53), son of MALCOLM III (CANMORE) and successor of Alexander I. He strengthened the monarchy by granting land to the aristocracy and developing the burghs. In 1136 David invaded England in support of the claim of his niece, MATILDA, to the throne. He was defeated at the Battle of the Standard (1138). In 1141 David gained control of Northumberland.

David II (1324–71) King of Scotland (1329–71), son of ROBERT I (THE BRUCE). Exiled after defeat by EDWARD III of England at the Battle of HALIDON HILL (1333), David fought the English in France and Britain until captured at the Battle of Neville's Cross (1346). In 1357 he was released, but remained dependent on Edward.

Davis, Angela (1944–) US political activist. Beginning in the 1960s, Davis was an advocate for both African-Americans' and women's CIVIL RIGHTS. In 1970 a judge was murdered with guns registered in Davis' name. Charged with conspiracy, murder and kidnapping, Davis was acquitted after a sensational trial.

Davis, Benjamin Oliver (1877–1970) US general. Davis served in the Spanish-American War and rose through the ranks to become (1940) the first African-American general in the United States' Army. He retired in 1948.

Davis, Benjamin Oliver, Jr (1912–) US air force general, son of Benjamin Oliver DAVIS. Davis was the fourth African-American graduate of West Point (1936). In World War 2 he earned the Distinguished Flying Cross. In 1959 Davis became the first African-American general in the United States' Air Force (USAF). He was chief of staff in South Korea (1965).

Davis, Jefferson (1808–89) American statesman, president of the CONFEDERATE STATES during the CIVIL WAR (1861–65). He was elected to Congress in 1845 but resigned to fight in the MEXICAN WAR (1846–48). A strong supporter of STATES' RIGHTS and the extension of SLAVERY, Davis acted as senator for Mississippi (1849–51). In 1853 President Franklin PIERCE made him secretary of war. In 1857 Davis rejoined the Senate and acted as leader of the Southern bloc. He resigned when Mississippi seceded from the Union (1861) and was inaugurated (18 February 1861) as president of the Confederacy. On 12 April 1861, Davis ordered the firing on FORT SUMTER – the first act in the American CIVIL WAR. In 1862 he appointed Robert LEE as commander of the Army of Northern Virginia and brought in conscription to try and bolster the Confederate forces. Davis failed to gain international recognition for the Confederate States and the Union blockade of Southern ports devastated its economy. After Lee's unilateral surrender at APPOMATTOX, Davis was captured and imprisoned (1865–67). Davis was accused of treason, but the case against him was dropped in 1868 and he continued to act as chief spokesman for the South. *See also* LINCOLN, ABRAHAM

Davis, John (*c*.1550–1605) English navigator. He made three voyages (1585, 1586, 1587) in search of a NORTHWEST PASSAGE, during the last of which he sailed through Davis Strait into Baffin Bay. In 1592 Davis discovered the Falkland Islands. He invented a double quadrant that was used for more than a century.

Davitt, Michael (1846–1906) Irish nationalist. In 1870 he was sentenced to 15 years' penal servitude for smuggling arms to the FENIAN MOVEMENT. In 1879 Davitt and Charles Stewart PARNELL founded the Irish LAND LEAGUE to organize Irish tenant farmers against evictions and high rents. He was elected to Parliament in 1882, 1892 and 1895.

Dawes, Charles Gates (1865–1951) US statesman, vice president (1925–29) under Calvin COOLIDGE. He served (1897–1902) as comptroller of the currency under President William MCKINLEY. Dawes was awarded the 1925 Nobel Prize for Peace for his work that produced the DAWES PLAN (1924) for stabilizing the German economy.

Dawes Commission Board appointed (1893) by President Grover CLEVELAND to negotiate with the FIVE CIVILIZED TRIBES living in Oklahoma. The Dawes Act of 1887 had not applied to the CHEROKEE, CHICKASAW, CHOCTAW, CREEK and SEMINOLE tribes. It compiled a list of Native Americans and surveyed and allotted tribal lands. The Commission was disbanded in 1905.

Dawes Plan (1924) Measure devised by a committee chaired by Charles DAWES to collect and distribute German REPARATIONS after World War 1. It established a schedule of payments and arranged for a loan of 800 million marks by US banks to stabilize the German currency.

Dayan, Moshe (1915–81) Israeli general and statesman. He led a Palestinian Jewish force against the Vichy French in World War 2. In 1956 Dayan led the invasion of the Sinai Peninsula and, as minister of defence, became a hero of the SIX-DAY WAR (1967). He also served as foreign minister (1977–79).

Dayton Peace Agreement (1 December 1995) Accord that resulted from negotiations in Dayton, Ohio, between Serb, Croat, Bosnian Muslim leaders and the United States to resolve the conflict in BOSNIA-HERZEGOVINA. It divided Bosnia-Herzegovina into a Serb Republic (49%) and Muslim Croat Federation (51%) and deployed a NATO peacekeeping force of 60,000 (IFOR). The agreement obligated all parties to comply with the orders of the War Crimes Tribunal, by which the Serbian leader RADOVAN KARADŽIĆ and the Bosnian Serb army leader RATKO MLADIĆ were subsequently indicted for crimes against humanity and forced to resign. The signatories agreed to grant refugees the right to return home or to gain compensation, and to allow human-rights monitors unrestricted access.

▲ **Darwin** sailed from Plymouth, England, on HMS *Beagle* on 17 December 1831. For five years, he explored parts of South America and the Pacific Islands.

D-Day (6 June 1944) First day of the Allies' NORMANDY LANDINGS in WORLD WAR 2

Dead Sea Scrolls Ancient manuscripts discovered from 1947 in caves at Qumran near the DEAD SEA. Written in Hebrew or Aramaic, they date from between the 1st century BC and the 1st century AD. They include versions of much of the OLD TESTAMENT. Some are a thousand years older than any other biblical manuscript.

Deák, Ferenc (1803–76) Hungarian politician. A leader of the Liberal Reform Party, he served in the Hungarian legislature (1833–36, 1839–40). Deák supported the REVOLUTION OF 1848, drawing up the liberal March Laws, but resigned as minister of justice in opposition to Lajos KOSSUTH's more radical proposals. After Kossuth's fall in 1849, Deák became the leader of the Hungarian nationalists. In 1867 he was instrumental in drawing up the AUSGLEICH that established the DUAL MONARCHY.

Deakin, Alfred (1856–1919) Australian statesman, prime minister (1903–04, 1905–08, 1909–10). As attorney general, Deakin helped to draft Australia's constitution and introduced the notorious WHITE AUSTRALIA POLICY. In 1903 he succeeded Edmund BARTON as prime minister. Deakin's attempt to link wages and tariffs (the "New Protection" plan) was declared unconstitutional.

Deane, Silas (1737–89) American diplomat. During the AMERICAN REVOLUTION, he served as a delegate (1774–76) to the CONTINENTAL CONGRESS, before being sent to France to secure military and financial aid. A fellow diplomat, Arthur Lee, accused Deane of profiteering and he was forced into exile. He was posthumously cleared (1842) of all allegations.

Dearborn, Henry (1751–1829) American general and statesman. He fought in the American Revolution at BUNKER HILL, Québec, SARATOGA, VALLEY FORGE, MONMOUTH and YORKTOWN. After the Revolution, Dearborn was secretary of war (1801–09) to President Thomas JEFFERSON. His poor generalship in the WAR OF 1812 contributed to the British capture of Detroit.

Debs, Eugene Victor (1855–1926) US UNION organizer. He was a founder and first president (1893–97) of the American Railroad Union (ARU). When federal troops broke up the PULLMAN STRIKE (1894), Debs was imprisoned. In 1898 he formed the Social Democratic Party and was its presidential candidate (1900, 1904, 1908, 1912). Debs was also a founder (1905) of the INDUSTRIAL WORKERS OF THE WORLD (IWW). He condemned United States' participation in World War 1 and was convicted (1918) under the Espionage Act. Debs ran for president (1920) while still in prison and polled nearly one million votes.

Decatur, Stephen (1779–1820) US naval officer. In the TRIPOLITAN WAR (1801–05), Decatur's daring destruction of the captured US frigate, *Philadelphia,* earned him a captaincy. His capture of the British frigate, *Macedonian,* in the WAR OF 1812 saw him rise to commodore. Decatur was killed in a duel with James Barron. He is noted for his toast, "Our country! In her intercourse with foreign nations may she always be right; but our country, right or wrong!"

Decembrists Group of Russian officers and noblemen who staged an unsuccessful revolt (12 December 1825) against Tsar NICHOLAS I. They were members of the Northern Society, a secret group demanding representative democracy. The Decembrists gathered 3000 troops in Senate Square, St Petersburg, but they were ill-organized, and the tsar's troops quickly dispersed them.

Decius, Gaius Messius Quintus (AD 200–51) Roman emperor (249–51). Decius was responsible for the first organized and sustained persecution of Christians, which served merely to win public sympathy for the martyrs. He was killed fighting the invasion of the GOTHS.

Declaration of Independence (4 July 1776) Statement of principles in which the THIRTEEN COLONIES of North America justified the AMERICAN REVOLUTION and separa-

DELAWARE
Statehood :
7 December 1787
Nickname :
The First State
State motto :
Liberty and independence

D

tion from Britain. Its blend of idealism and practical statements have ensured its place as one of the world's most important political documents. The Second CONTINENTAL CONGRESS adopted a resolution of independence proposed by Richard Henry LEE and appointed a committee to draft a formal document. The committee was composed of Thomas JEFFERSON, John ADAMS, Benjamin FRANKLIN, Roger SHERMAN and Robert LIVINGSTON. The Declaration, written mainly by Thomas Jefferson, was approved by Congress on 4 July 1776. It was based on the theories of NATURAL RIGHTS and SOCIAL CONTRACT, propounded by John LOCKE to justify the GLORIOUS REVOLUTION in England. The Declaration states the necessity of government having the consent of the governed, of government's responsibility to its people, and contains the famous paragraph: "We hold these truths to be self-evident, that all men are created equal, that they are endowed by their Creator with certain unalienable Rights, that among these are Life, Liberty, and the Pursuit of Happiness."

Declaration of Rights *See* BILL OF RIGHTS

Declaration of the Rights of Man and of the Citizen (26 August 1789) Statement of principles of the FRENCH REVOLUTION, adopted by the NATIONAL ASSEMBLY, accepted by LOUIS XVI, and serving as the preamble to the 1791 and 1793 constitutions. It was based on the American DECLARATION OF INDEPENDENCE. The Rights of Man derived its doctrine of NATURAL RIGHTS from John LOCKE, its theory of the SOCIAL CONTRACT from Jean Jacques ROUSSEAU, and its principle of the SEPARATION OF POWERS from MONTESQUIEU. The basic principle of the Rights of Man was that "all men are born and remain free and equal in rights" (**Article 1**). These rights were specified as "liberty, property, safety and resistance to oppression" (**Article 2**).

Declaratory Act (1766) Law in which the British Parliament asserted its right to legislate for the American colonies if it so wished, after the repeal of the STAMP ACT.

Defence of the Realm Act (DORA) (November 1914) British legislation conferring extraordinary powers upon the British government for prosecuting World War 1. The act was designed to ensure strict government control of the press and industrial production.

Defender of the Faith (Lat. *Fidei Defensor*) Title adopted by the monarchs of England since 1521. The title was first given to HENRY VIII by Pope LEO X after Henry had published a tract attacking the Protestant MARTIN LUTHER.

Defenestration of Prague (23 May 1618) Event that marked the outbreak of the THIRTY YEARS' WAR. The Protestant Bohemian subjects of the HABSBURG Emperor FERDINAND II resented his Catholic rule. Two imperial regents and their secretary were thrown from the windows of the Prague council chamber and the Bohemian throne was offered to the Protestant Elector Palatine FREDERICK V. *See also* BOHEMIA

De Gasperi, Alcide (1881–1954) Italian statesman, prime minister (1945–53). He was born in Trentino, then under Austrian rule. De Gasperi was instrumental in securing the reunification of Trentino with Italy (1919). In 1927 he was imprisoned for his opposition to MUSSOLINI. In 1931 De Gasperi was released and received the protection of Pope PIUS XI until the fall of the fascist regime (1943). In 1943 he reorganized the ITALIAN POPULAR PARTY (PPI) into the Christian Democratic Party. De Gasperi is regarded as the chief architect of Italy's post-war recovery, forging closer links with the West and supporting the construction of the European Union (EU).

De Gaulle, Charles André Joseph Marie (1890–1970) French general and statesman, first president (1958–69) of the Fifth Republic. He criticized Marshal PÉTAIN for failing to modernize the French army in the light of German rearmament. In 1940 De Gaulle became undersecretary of war but fled to London after the German invasion. De Gaulle organized French resistance (FREE FRENCH) forces and, in June 1944, was proclaimed president of the provisional French government in Algiers, N Africa. Following the liberation of France he resigned, disenchanted with the political settlement. In 1947 he formed the Rally of the French People (RPF). In 1958 De Gaulle emerged from retirement to deal with the war in ALGERIA. As president, he appealed above the heads of parliament to French citizens, governing through a succession of referenda. In 1962 De Gaulle was forced to cede independence to Algeria. France gained an independent nuclear capability, but alienated the United Kingdom and the United States by its temporary withdrawal from the NORTH ATLANTIC TREATY ORGANIZATION (NATO) and by blocking British entry into the EUROPEAN COMMUNITY (EC). In 1965 De Gaulle was re-elected, but resigned after defeat in a 1969 referendum about Senate reform. He was succeeded as president by Georges POMPIDOU.

deism System of natural religion, first developed in England in the late 17th century. It affirmed belief in one God but held that He detached himself from the universe after its creation and made no revelation. Reason was man's only guide. Deist writings include John Toland's *Christianity not Mysterious* (1696) and Matthew Tindal's *Christianity as Old as the Creation* (1730). Deism was a great influence on the ENLIGHTENMENT. VOLTAIRE, ROUSSEAU and DIDEROT were its chief exponents.

de Klerk, F.W. (Frederik Willem) (1936–) South African statesman, president (1989–94). He entered Parliament in 1972 and joined the cabinet in 1978. In 1989 de Klerk led a "palace coup" against P.W. BOTHA and became president and NATIONAL PARTY leader. Following a narrow electoral victory, he began the process of dismantling APARTHEID. In 1990 the ban on the AFRICAN NATIONAL CONGRESS (ANC) was lifted and Nelson MANDELA was released. In 1991 the main apartheid laws were repealed and victory in a 1992 whites-only referendum marked an end to white minority rule. In 1993 de Klerk shared the Nobel Prize for Peace with Nelson Mandela. Following the 1994 elections, de Klerk became deputy president in Mandela's government of national unity. In 1996 he resigned and led the Nationalists out of the coalition. In 1997 he retired as leader of the National Party.

Delany, Martin Robinson (1812–85) African-American social reformer and soldier. He worked for the UNDERGROUND RAILROAD and supported the "back-to-Africa" movement. Delany served as a Union army surgeon in the Civil War and was the first African-American to be promoted to major. He worked (1865–67) for the FREEDMEN'S BUREAU and became a judge.

Delaware (Lenni Lenape) Confederation of Algonquian-speaking NATIVE NORTH AMERICANS. When the first Europeans arrived in the early 17th century, they occupied land from Long Island, New York, to Pennsylvania and Delaware. In 1682 the Delaware signed a treaty of friendship with William PENN. By the infamous Walking Purchase (1737), the Delaware were swindled out of most of their land and were forced by settlers and the IROQUOIS CONFEDERACY to migrate to Ohio. In the last of the FRENCH AND INDIAN WARS (1756–63), they defeated British General Edward BRADDOCK. In the Treaty of Greenville (1795) they were forced to cede their lands in Ohio treaty of 1795 and became scattered. Today, the Delaware number *c.*3000, living in Oklahoma, Wisconsin and Ontario.

Delaware Eastern state on the Atlantic coast, occupying a peninsula between Chesapeake and Delaware bays, United States. The capital is Dover. When Henry HUDSON became the first European to visit the region in 1609, it was inhabited by the Lenni Lenape (later known as DELAWARE) and Susquehannock tribes of Native Americans. The first European settlement was established by Swedes in 1638. The Dutch, under Peter STUYVESANT, conquered the territory by 1655. In 1664 it fell to the English, who administered it as part of New York. In 1682 the region was ceded to William PENN. The region was named after the British governor of Virginia, Baron De La Warr (1577–1618). One of the original THIRTEEN COLONIES, Delaware was the first to ratify the ARTICLES OF CONFEDERATION (1789). Despite being a slave state, it remained in the Union during the American Civil War. Delaware is the second-smallest state (after RHODE ISLAND). Area: 5328sq km (2057sq mi). Pop. (1990) 666,168.

Delcassé, Théophile (1852–1923) French statesman, foreign minister (1898–1905, 1914–15). He negotiated the ENTENTE CORDIALE (1904) with Britain to counter the perceived threat of the TRIPLE ALLIANCE (Germany, Austria-Hungary and Italy). Delcassé was forced to resign when Emperor WILLIAM I visited Tangier, N Morocco, thereby implicitly stating German commitment to Moroccan independence. The Entente Cordiale held together, however, and led to the creation (1907) of the TRIPLE ENTENTE between France, Russia and Britain in the build-up to World War 1. As minister of the navy (1911–13), Delcassé sought to ensure that the French and British fleets would cooperate in the event of war.

Delhi Union territory and city on the River Yamuna, N central India. Strategically placed midway between the Ganges and Indus valleys, the city has been of strategic importance for more than 2000 years. The city of Delhi appears to date from the reign of Raja Dhilu (1st century BC). In 1192 the city fell to the Muslims and QUTB UD-DIN AYBAK (d.1210) began constructing the Qutb Minar tower. Qutb's son-in-law, ILTUTMISH, established the DELHI SULTANATE in 1211. In 1398 TAMERLANE sacked Delhi and the capital of the Sultanate transferred to AGRA. Delhi regained its importance in 1526, when BABUR made it the first capital of the MUGHAL EMPIRE. His descendants favoured Agra, however, until SHAH JAHAN began to fortify the city and construct the Red Fort in 1638. The British moved the capital of British India from CALCUTTA to the purpose-built site at New Delhi in 1912. Other sights include the Jami Masjid. Pop. (1991) 7,206,704.

► **Delhi** The Tomb of Safdarjang in Delhi, N India, was built (1753–54) by the Nawab of Avadh for his father, Safdarjang. It is one of the last major examples of Mughal architecture, prior to the collapse of the Mughal Empire in the early 19th century.

Delhi Sultanate (1211–1526) Succession of ruling Muslim dynasties in India. In 1193 the Afghan warrior Muhammad of Ghur captured DELHI from the Hindus led by Prithvi Raj. In 1206 Muhammad was assassinated and his general and slave, QUTB UD-DIN AYBAK (d.1210), established the so-called SLAVE DYNASTY. His son-in-law and successor, ILTUTMISH (r.1211–36), made Delhi his permanent capital. In 1290 the KHALJI dynasty came to power. At its height, in the reign of Ala ud-Din Khalji (r.1296–1316), the Sultanate's power extended as far as s India. In 1398 the Sultanate was crushed by TAMERLANE and was finally destroyed by the MUGHAL emperor BABUR at the Battle of PANIPAT (1526). Delhi was later incorporated into the Mughal empire by AKBAR in 1556.

Delian League Confederation of Greek CITY-STATES formed (478 BC) under Athenian leadership after the losses of the PERSIAN WARS. The treasury was initially held on the island of Delos, but was moved to ATHENS by PERICLES. It was disbanded after the PELOPONNESIAN WAR. *See also* ATHENIAN EMPIRE

De Long, George Washington (1844–81) US naval officer and Arctic explorer. He set sail in 1879, but his ship was caught in polar ice and drifted until 1881 when it was crushed. De Long was one of 14 survivors to reach Siberia, only to die of cold and starvation.

Delors, Jacques (1925–) French statesman, president of the European Commission (1985–95). He was elected to the European Parliament in 1979. Delors served as minister of economics and finance (1981–84) in the French government of François MITTERRAND. As president of the European Commission, Delors played a major role in the transformation of the EUROPEAN COMMUNITY (EC) into the EUROPEAN UNION (EU).

Delphi Ancient Greek city-state, near Mount Parnassus. The Delphic oracle, housed in the temple of Apollo, was the most powerful oracle of ancient GREECE. City-states and individuals consulted Pythia, the priestess of Apollo, who gave notoriously ambiguous responses. The oracle closed (AD 390) with the spread of Christianity.

demesne In a FEUDAL SYSTEM, land retained by the king or a lord for his own use, rather than being leased out to free tenants. Originally, peasants owed labour services to the lord on his demesne, but during the 14th century it became common for the demesne to be leased out to tenant farmers for fixed rents.

Demetrius I (Poliorcetes) (*c*.336–283 BC) King of Macedonia (294–288 BC), son of ANTIGONUS I (THE ONE-EYED). In 307 BC he drove the Macedonian CASSANDER out of Athens and, in 306 BC, he defeated PTOLEMY I off Salamis. In 305 BC Demetrius unsuccessfully besieged Rhodes. At the Battle of Ipsus (301 BC), Antigonus was slain and Demetrius forced into exile by the joint forces of Casssander, Lysimachus and SELEUCUS I (NICATOR). In 294 Demetrius recaptured Athens and established himself as king of Macedonia after murdering his rivals to the throne. He was finally driven out of Macedonia in 288 and from 285 was a prisoner of Seleucus I.

Demirel, Süleyman (1924–) Turkish statesman, prime minister (1965–71, 1975–77, 1979–80, 1991–93) and president (1993–). In 1964 he became leader of the Justice Party. Demirel was ousted by military coups in 1971 and 1980. He led the True Path Party (1987–93) before becoming president. Demirel's government was criticized for the slowness of its response to the devastating earthquake in NW Turkey in August 1999. *See also* ECEVIT, BÜLENT

democracy (Gk. *demos kratia*, people authority) Rule of the people, as opposed to rule by one (autocracy) or a few (oligarchy). Ancient GREECE is regarded as the birthplace of democracy, in particular ATHENS (5th century BC). Small Greek CITY-STATES enabled direct political participation but only among its citizens (a small political elite). As societies grew, more refined systems were needed. In a FEUDAL SYSTEM, the king selected tenants-in-chief to provide counsel. In late 13th-century England, a PARLIAMENT evolved but remained answerable to the monarchy. The Roundheads' victory in the English CIVIL WAR was a victory for parliamentary sovereignty. A fundamental shift in emphasis was the transition from natural law to NATURAL RIGHTS, as expounded by John LOCKE: in addition to responsibility (to crown or church), people possessed inalienable rights. Jean Jacques ROUSSEAU developed these notions into the SOCIAL CONTRACT, which influenced the FRENCH and AMERICAN REVOLUTIONS: government was limited by law from impinging on individual freedoms. During the 19th century, the FRANCHISE was extended. In the 20th century, democratic representation has been a matter of debate and sometimes bloody dispute. Common to modern liberal democracy is the principle of free multiparty elections with universal adult suffrage.

Democratic Party US political organization, descendant of the ANTI-FEDERALIST PARTY and Thomas JEFFERSON'S DEMOCRATIC-REPUBLICAN PARTY. It became the Democratic Party during the presidency (1829–37) of Andrew JACKSON. In the 1840s the Party began to fracture over the issue of SLAVERY. Northern Democrats, led by Stephen DOUGLAS, advocated the doctrine of "popular sovereignty", while Southern Democrats, led by Jefferson DAVIS, held that slavery must be protected in all the territories. Party divisions enabled Abraham LINCOLN'S newly formed REPUBLICAN PARTY to defeat James BUCHANAN in 1861. From 1860 to 1900 the only Democrat president was Grover CLEVELAND (1885–89, 1893–97). The Party's support was mainly restricted to the South and West. The radical economic plans of William BRYAN led to a landslide defeat in the 1896 election. In 1912 a split in the Republican vote saw the Democrats regain the presidency under Woodrow WILSON, but the end of World War 1 saw voters return to the Republicans. The Democrats swept back into office under Franklin ROOSEVELT in 1929. Roosevelt's NEW DEAL to tackle the GREAT DEPRESSION led the Party to be regarded once more as a progressive force. Roosevelt was succeeded by Harry TRUMAN. Democrat presidents were in office from 1961 to 1969 (John KENNEDY, Lyndon JOHNSON), a period marked by progressive economic and social policy, such as the passing of CIVIL-RIGHTS legislation. In the 1970s and 1980s Jimmy CARTER was the only Democrat president (1977–81). In 1992 Democratic Party fortunes were restored by the election of Bill CLINTON. *See also* PIERCE, FRANKLIN; POLK, JAMES; VAN BUREN, MARTIN

Democratic-Republican Party Early US political party, precursor of the modern DEMOCRATIC PARTY. Led by Thomas JEFFERSON and James MADISON, it was formed in the late 1790s in opposition to the FEDERALIST PARTY. The Democratic-Republican Party opposed strong central government and advocated a liberal agrarian democracy, while also appealing to poor townsfolk. Democratic-Republican presidents were Jefferson, Madison, James MONROE and John Quincy ADAMS. It became the Democratic Party in the era of Andrew JACKSON.

Demosthenes (384?–322 BC) Athenian orator and statesman. In 351 BC he delivered the first of his famous *Philippics*, urging the Greeks to unite and resist PHILIP II of Macedon. The Greeks were defeated at the Battle of CHAERONEA (338 BC) and Demosthenes was put on trial. His defence, "On the Crown", is a masterpiece of political oratory. Demosthenes committed suicide after the failure of the Athenian revolt against Macedon.

Deng Xiaoping (1904–97) Chinese statesman. He took part in the LONG MARCH (1934–35), served in the Red Army, and in 1945 became a member of the central committee of the Chinese COMMUNIST PARTY (CCP). After the establishment of the People's Republic (1949), Deng was appointed vice premier in 1952. In 1954 he became general secretary of the CCP. After the failure of MAO ZEDONG'S GREAT LEAP FORWARD, Deng and LIU SHAOQUI led demands for a more market-based economy. During the CULTURAL REVOLUTION, Deng was denounced for capitalist tendencies and dismissed. In 1973 he returned to government as deputy to Premier ZHOU ENLAI. He was purged by the GANG OF FOUR in 1976, but reinstated as heir apparent to HUA GUOFENG in 1977. By 1980 he had become the paramount leader of China. His protégés, ZHAO ZIYANG and HU YAOBANG, were appointed premier and general secretary of the CCP respectively. Deng set about the modernization of China's economy through decentralization and the encouragement of foreign investment. His most conspicuous social reform was a strict restriction on family size to combat the growth in China's population. In 1989 Deng supported the use of force to crush the student demonstrations in TIANANMEN

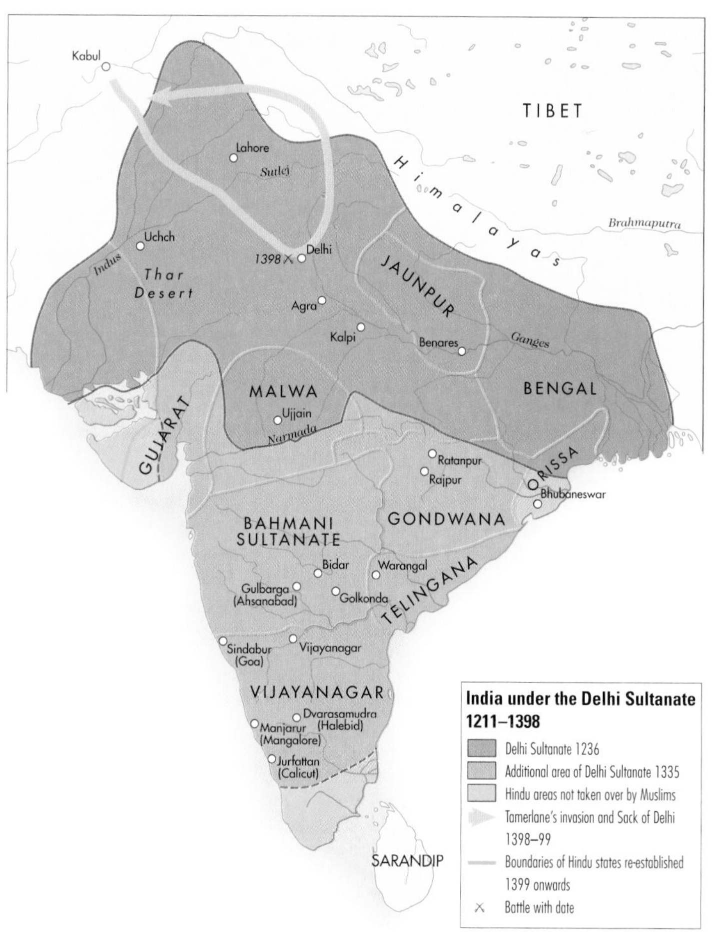

◄ **Delhi Sultanate** Founded in 1211 by Turks from Afghanistan, the Delhi Sultanate was the centre of Muslim domination in India – and the base from which, at least notionally, Islam spread across much of the subcontinent. The expansion of the Sultanate gave Indian nobles greater control over trading routes and the production of goods. The destruction of the Sultanate by the Mongol conqueror Tamerlane in 1398 paved the way for the decentralization of power into the hands of local Hindu and Muslim rulers.

▲ **Deng Xiaoping** By relaxing state control of the economy and improving relations with the West, Deng opened up China to new markets. He was implacably opposed to political reform.

SQUARE. While Deng promoted economic liberalization, he remained committed to the CCP's domination of social and political life. He was succeeded by JIANG ZEMIN.

Denikin, Anton Ivanovich (1872–1947) Russian general. In September 1917 Lavr KORNILOV and Denikin led a counter-revolution against Alexander KERENSKY's provisional government, but it failed due to defection and the strength of the BOLSHEVIKS. In April 1918 Denikin succeeded Kornilov as commander of the anti-Bolshevik White Russian forces in the RUSSIAN CIVIL WAR. By January 1919 Denikin had captured most of S Russia. Denikin's advance on Moscow was repulsed by the RED ARMY and he handed over command to Piotr WRANGEL. In 1926 Denikin went into permanent exile.

Denmark *See* country feature

Depression, Great (1929–33) *See* GREAT DEPRESSION

Depretis, Agostino (1813–87) Italian statesman, prime minister (1876–78, 1878–79, 1881–87). He was an early supporter of Giuseppe MAZZINI and led opposition to Camillo Benso di CAVOUR in the Sardinian parliament. Depretis abandoned his radicalism to support the establishment of the kingdom of Italy (1861). As prime minister, Depretis' chief motivation was the maintenance of personal power. His cynical and corrupt practices haunted Italian politics for many years. *See also* GARIBALDI, GIUSEPPE; RISORGIMENTO; UMBERTO I; VICTOR EMMANUEL II

Derby, Edward George Geoffrey Smith Stanley, 14th Earl of (1799–1869) British statesman, prime minister (1852, 1858–59, 1866–68). He entered Parliament as a WHIG in 1827 and acted as chief secretary for Ireland (1830–33). Derby resigned shortly after becoming colonial secretary (1833) and joined the CONSERVATIVE PARTY. He was colonial secretary (1841–45) under Robert PEEL but resigned over the repeal of the CORN LAWS. From 1846 to 1868 Derby led the Tory protectionists, briefly heading two administrations. In 1866 he became prime minister for the last time and introduced the REFORM ACT (1867). Derby was succeeded by Benjamin DISRAELI.

Derby, Thomas Stanley, 1st Earl of (1435–1504) English noble. At the Battle of BOSWORTH FIELD (1485) Derby's large force was nominally on the side of RICHARD III, but took no part in the fighting. After the Battle, he crowned his stepson, the victorious HENRY VII, king of England. In 1486 Derby was made an earl.

Derry City and administrative district on the River Foyle near Lough Foyle, NW Northern Ireland. In AD 546 Saint COLUMBA founded a monastery here. In 1600 English forces seized the city, and in 1613 JAMES I granted Derry to the citizens of London, England. It was renamed **Londonderry**, a new city was laid out, and Protestant colonization began. In the GLORIOUS REVOLUTION (1688–89) JAMES II unsuccessfully besieged the city. In recent years, the city has been plagued by sectarian violence. In 1984 its name reverted to Derry. Area: 347sq km (149sq mi). Pop. (1991) 95,371.

dervish Member of a Muslim fraternity. Communities arose within SUFISM and by the 12th century had established themselves in the Middle East. The chief devotion of dervishes is *dhikr* (remembering of God). The encouragement of emotional display and hypnotic trances is exemplified by the dancing of the Mevlevi sect from which the phrase "whirling dervish"comes.

Desai, Morarji Ranchhodji (1896–1995) Indian statesman, prime minister (1977–79). He was an early supporter of "Mahatma" GANDHI. Desai was defeated by Indira GANDHI in the contest for leadership of the Indian National CONGRESS. He was detained (1975–77) during the state of emergency. In 1977 Desai became leader of the newly formed opposition party, JANATA PARTY. As prime minister, he restored democratic government to India.

Descartes, René (1596–1650) French philosopher and mathematician. He is often regarded as the father of modern philosophy. Descartes' philosophical principles are outlined in *Discourse on Method* (1637), *Meditations on the First Philosophy* (1641) and *Principles of Philosophy* (1644). His methods of deduction and intuition inform modern metaphysics. Descartes reached one indubitable proposition: "I am thinking", and from this he concluded that he existed: *cogito ergo sum* (I think, therefore I am). Descartes also founded analytic geometry, introduced the Cartesian coordinate system, and helped establish the science of optics.

de Smet, Pierre Jean *See* SMET, PIERRE JEAN DE

Desmoulins, Camille (1760–94) French revolutionary. His pamphlets, such as *Révolutions de France et de Brabant* (1789), were widely read, and he was responsible for inciting the mob to attack the BASTILLE on 12 July 1789, precipitating the FRENCH REVOLUTION. Initially Desmoulins attacked the GIRONDINS, but later (with Georges DANTON) urged moderation. He was arrested and guillotined during the REIGN OF TERROR. *See also* JACOBIN

De Soto, Hernando (1500–42) Spanish explorer. After taking part in the conquest of the INCAS under Francisco PIZARRO, De Soto was appointed governor of Cuba (1537) with permission to conquer the North American mainland. His expedition of more than 600 men, in a ruthless search for non-existent treasure, landed in Florida (1539) and advanced as far north as the Carolinas. De Soto and his men acted with extreme brutality toward the native inhabitants, leading to a costly battle at Maubilia (1540). In 1541 they reached the Arkansas valley to the west of the Mississippi before returning to the Mississippi, where De Soto died. The survivors eventually reached Mexico (1543).

Despenser (the Elder), Hugh le (1262–1326) English baron, favourite of EDWARD II. In 1312, after the execution of Piers GAVESTON, he became the king's chief adviser. In 1315 Despenser was dismissed from court following the English defeat at the Battle of BANNOCKBURN (1314). He promoted the interests of his son, **Hugh le Despenser (the Younger)** (d.1326). The influence and avarice of the Despensers incensed other powerful nobles and both were banished in 1321. The Despensers returned to power after the defeat of their rivals at the Battle of Boroughbridge (1322). They were executed by Queen ISABELLA after the fall of Edward II.

DENMARK

AREA: 43,070sq km (16,629sq mi)
POPULATION: 5,170,000
CAPITAL (POPULATION): Copenhagen (620,970)
GOVERNMENT: Parliamentary monarchy
ETHNIC GROUPS: Danish 97%
LANGUAGES: Danish (official)
RELIGIONS: Christianity (Lutheran 91%, Roman Catholic 1%)
GDP PER CAPITA (1995): US$21,230

Kingdom in W Europe. Denmark is the smallest country in Scandinavia. It consists of a peninsula, Jutland, and more than 400 islands, 89 of which are inhabited. To the NW of Denmark lie the self-governing Danish dependencies of GREENLAND and the FARÖE ISLANDS. By *c.*2000 BC the Danes had developed an advanced Bronze Age culture. Trade links with the Roman Empire were developed in the 4th century AD. In 811 the S border was established by a treaty with the FRANKS. Danes were among the VIKINGS who, between the 9th and 11th centuries, terrorized much of W Europe. In the 11th century, CANUTE II (THE GREAT) ruled over Denmark, Norway and England.

In 1397 the crowns of Denmark, Sweden and Norway were joined in the KALMAR UNION. Sweden broke away in 1523, and soon overtook Denmark as the most powerful state in the Baltic region. Denmark adopted LUTHERANISM as the national religion in the 1530s, and Danish culture flourished in the 16th and early 17th century. CHRISTIAN IV led Denmark into costly wars with Sweden, and the THIRTY YEARS' WAR (1618–48) weakened the Danish aristocracy. Serfdom was abolished in 1788. In 1814 Denmark ceded Norway to Sweden. In 1866 SCHLESWIG-HOLSTEIN was lost to Prussia.

The Social Democratic Party dominated Danish politics in the 20th century. Denmark remained neutral in World War 1. In 1918 ICELAND became self-governing. During the 1920s, Denmark adopted progressive social welfare policies. In 1940 Germany occupied Denmark at the start of World War 2. Many Jews escaped to Sweden. In 1943 CHRISTIAN X was arrested and martial law declared. In 1945 Denmark was liberated by British forces.

Denmark played an important part in European reconstruction after the War. In 1949 it relinquished its neutrality and joined the North Atlantic Treaty Organization (NATO). In 1973 Denmark became the first Scandinavian member of the EUROPEAN UNION (EU). In 1992 Denmark rejected the MAASTRICHT TREATY, but reversed the decision in a second referendum (1993). In 1998 the Amsterdam Treaty, which represented another step to closer European integration, was ratified by a further referendum.

Dessalines, Jean Jacques (1758–1806) Haitian ruler. In 1802 he succeeded Toussaint L'Ouverture as leader of the revolution. Having driven out the French, he declared independence in 1804, changing the country's name from St Domingue to Haiti. As Emperor Jacques, he ruled despotically and was assassinated. *See also* Christophe, Henri

D'Estaing, Valéry Giscard *See* Giscard d'Estaing, Valéry

détente Term in international relations for the reduction of tension between states. It chiefly refers to the efforts of the United States, the Soviet Union and their respective allies to end the Cold War (1947–91) and to establish closer links of mutual understanding. Détente was marked by a series of agreements to halt the arms race and confidence-building measures, such as the Strategic Arms Limitation Treaty (SALT) signed in 1974. *See also* disarmament

Detroit City on the Detroit River, se Michigan, United States. Founded (1710) by Antoine de la Mothe Cadillac as the French trading post of *Ville d'etroit* (City of the strait), it was captured (1760) by the British. The British survived a lengthy siege in Pontiac's Rebellion (1763). In 1796 America gained control of the city. Detroit fell to the British in the War of 1812, but US forces recovered it in 1813. In the 19th century, Detroit grew into a major industrial centre. The largest city in Michigan, it is a Great Lakes centre and headquarters of the car-manufacturing corporations of General Motors, Chrysler and Ford. Pop. (1990) 1,027,974.

Dettingen, Battle of (27 June 1743) Engagement in the War of the Austrian Succession in which Anglo-German forces, led by George II of Britain, defeated the French army. It was the last occasion on which a British monarch went into battle in person.

De Valera, Eamon (1882–1975) Irish statesman, prime minister (1932–48, 1951–54, 1957–59), b. United States. He was sentenced to life imprisonment for his role in the Easter Rising (1916), escaping execution due to his US birth. In 1917 De Valera was elected president of Sinn Féin. In 1919 he escaped from prison and went into exile in the United States. In 1920 De Valera returned to Ireland. He denounced the Anglo-Irish Treaty (1921), negotiated by Michael Collins and Arthur Griffith, which resulted in the partition of Ireland. In 1926 De Valera founded Fianna Fáil. In 1932 he succeeded William Cosgrave as prime minister. In 1937 he produced a new constitution that ended the oath of allegiance to the British crown. De Valera kept Ireland neutral during World War 2, and was criticized for his refusal to permit the British to use Irish ports. In 1959 he became president of the republic. De Valera retired in 1973.

Devereux, Robert, 2nd Earl of Essex *See* Essex, Robert Devereux, 2nd Earl of

Devolution, War of (1667–68) Conflict over the Spanish Netherlands (now Belgium). Louis XIV of France claimed that the disputed territories had devolved to him through his wife Marie Thérèse, daughter of Philip IV of Spain. The French army, led by Marshal de Turenne, overran Flanders, prompting the United Provinces, England and Sweden to form the Triple Alliance (1668). Peace was made at Aix-la-Chapelle (now Aachen, Germany). *See also* Spanish Succession, War of the

Devonian Fourth-oldest period of the Palaeozoic era, lasting from 408 to 360 million years ago. Many marine and freshwater remains include jawless fishes and ancestors of today's bony and cartilaginous fishes. The first known land vertebrate, the amphibian *Ichthyostega*, appeared at this time. Land animals included scorpions, mites, spiders and the first insects. Land plants included club moss and ferns.

Dewey, George (1837–1917) US admiral, hero of the Battle of Manila Bay (1898). He served on the USS *Mississippi* in the Civil War and was naval commander of the Asiatic squadron when the Spanish-American War broke out. Dewey sailed for the Philippines, and on 1 May 1898 he entered Manila Bay. By noon, the Spanish fleet had been destroyed without the loss of a single American life. In 1899 Dewey was promoted to admiral of the navy.

Dhaka (Dacca) Capital of Bangladesh, a port on the Ganges delta, e Bangladesh. In the 17th century, it was the Mughal capital of Bengal. In 1765 Dhaka came under British control. At independence (1947) it became capital of the province of East Pakistan. Severely damaged during the war of independence from Pakistan, in 1971 Dhaka became capital of independent Bangladesh. Pop. (1991) 3,397,187.

Diamond Necklace Affair (1785) Incident at the court of Louis XVI of France. Cardinal de Rohan was deceived by the Comtesse de la Motte into believing that Queen Marie Antoinette wished him to purchase secretly an expensive diamond necklace on her behalf. Thinking that by doing so he would regain the queen's favour, he made the purchase, but the comtesse then stole the necklace. An application was made to the queen for the first payment, prompting the king to imprison de Rohan. The cardinal's unfair treatment before and after his exoneration was held as proof of royal despotism, and contributed to the unpopularity of the queen.

Diana, Princess of Wales (1961–97) Former wife of Charles, Prince of Wales, and daughter of Earl Spencer. In 1981 Diana married Prince Charles, heir to the British throne. The couple had two sons, William (1982–) and Harry (1984–). A popular, glamourous figure, Diana worked for many public-health and children's charities. Her marriage to Charles fell apart acrimoniously and publicly, and the couple divorced in 1996. Diana continued to campaign for humanitarian causes until her death in a car crash in Paris, France.

Dias, Bartholomeu (*c*.1450–1500) (Bartholomew Diaz) Portuguese navigator, the first European to round the Cape of Good Hope. In 1487 Dias sailed three ships around the Cape, opening the long-sought sea route to India. He took part in the expedition of Pedro Cabral that discovered Brazil (1500), but was drowned when his ship foundered.

Diaspora (Gk. dispersion) Jewish communities outside Palestine. Although there were communities of Jews outside Palestine from the time of the Babylonian Captivity (6th century bc), the Diaspora essentially dates from the destruction of Jerusalem by the Romans (ad 70). The majority of Jews remain in the Diaspora. *See also* Judaism; Zionism

Díaz, Porfirio (1830–1915) Mexican statesman, president (1876–80, 1884–1911). He supported Benito Juárez in the war (1861–67) against Emperor Maximilian. Díaz refused to accept defeat in the 1871 and 1876 presidential elections and began a revolt that overthrew President Sebastián Lerdo. His 35-year dictatorship was brutally effective. Diaz's fraudulent re-election (1910) sparked a popular uprising led by Francisco Madero, and he was forced into exile.

Dickinson, John (1732–1808) American patriot. His *Letters from a Farmer..* (1767) criticized the Townshend Acts. Dickinson favoured conciliation with the British, however, and he refused to sign the Declaration of Independence at the Second Continental Congress. He served in the Continental Army in the American Revolution and helped draft the Articles of Confederation.

dictatorship of the proletariat Transitional stage that Karl Marx felt must precede the introduction of communism following a successful revolution by the working class. In this stage, the state owns the means of production and directs the production of goods and services. A few procedures of capitalism, such as wage payment based on productivity, remain. *See also* bourgeoisie; proletariat

Diderot, Denis (1713–84) French philosopher and writer. He was chief editor of the *Encyclopédie* (1751–72), an influential publication of the Enlightenment. A friend of Jean Jacques Rousseau, Diderot was imprisoned briefly (1749) for irreligious writings. He broadened the scope of the *Encyclopédie* and, with d'Alembert, recruited contributors, including Voltaire. As a philosopher, Diderot progressed gradually from Christianity through deism to atheism. His scientific materialism is outlined in *On the Interpretation of Nature* (1754) and *d'Alembert's Dream* (1769). *Jacques the Fatalist* (1796) illustrates his determinism.

Diefenbaker, John George (1895–1979) Canadian statesman, prime minister (1957–63). He was Canada's first Conservative prime minister since Richard Bennett (1930–35). In 1958 Diefenbaker gained the largest parliamentary majority in Canada's history. As prime minister, he secured the adoption of a Bill of Rights (1960). Economic crisis forced Diefenbaker to devalue the Canadian dollar and adopt austerity measures. In the 1963 election, fought mainly over the issue of the manufacture of nuclear weapons on Canadian soil, he was defeated by Lester Pearson. *See also* Progressive Conservative Party

Diem, Ngo Dinh (1901–63) Vietnamese statesman, prime minister of South Vietnam (1954–63). In 1945 he became prime minister of South Vietnam. Diem ousted Emperor Bao Dai and made himself president of the new Republic of Vietnam. He ignored calls for democratic elections in 1956 and established an autocratic regime, ini-

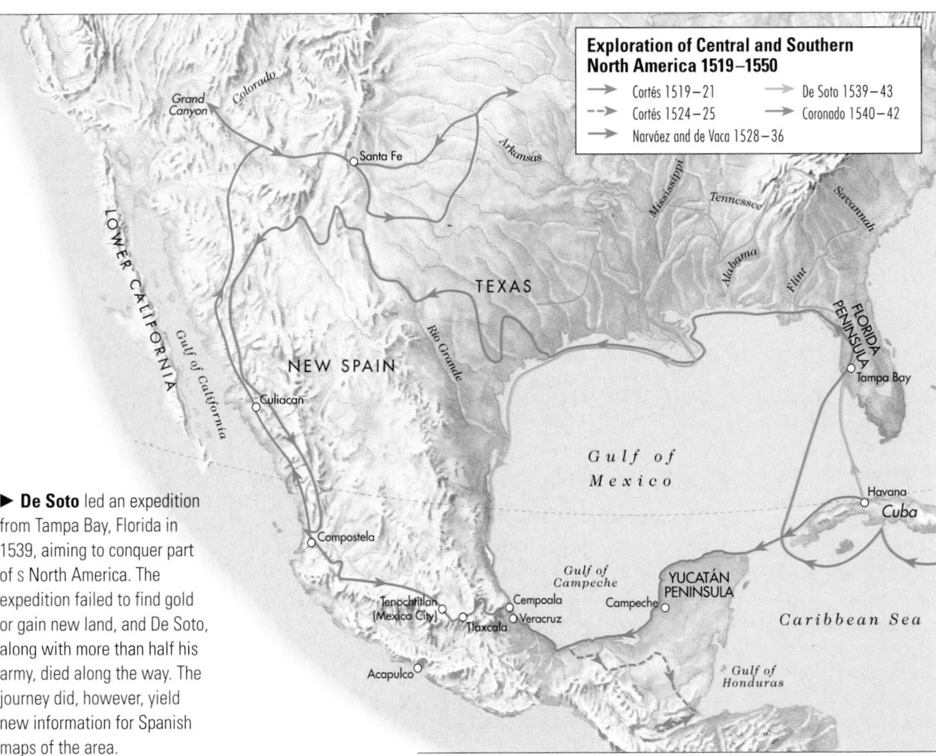

► **De Soto** led an expedition from Tampa Bay, Florida in 1539, aiming to conquer part of s North America. The expedition failed to find gold or gain new land, and De Soto, along with more than half his army, died along the way. The journey did, however, yield new information for Spanish maps of the area.

D

tially with strong support from the United States. Diem's persecution of the Buddhist majority in South Vietnam increased support for the Viet Cong in the early stages of the Vietnam War (1955–75). With covert US help, army officers staged a coup in which he was murdered. *See also* Nguyen Van Thieu

Diemen, Anthony van (1593–1645) Dutch colonial administrator, governor general of the Dutch East Indies (1636–45). Van Diemen captured Malacca (1641) and Ceylon (1644) from the Portuguese and gained a monopoly on the spice trade in the Moluccas for the Dutch East India Company. He completed the construction of Batavia (now Jakarta), begun under his predecessor Jan Pieterszoon Coen. Van Diemen sponsored the voyages of Abel Tasman, who discovered Tasmania (originally called Van Diemen's Land).

Dien Bien Phu Fortified village in n Vietnam. In the Battle of Dien Bien Phu (1954) the French stronghold was captured by the Vietnamese Viet Minh after a siege lasting 55 days. French casualties were *c*.15,000. The resultant cease-fire ended eight years of war.

diet Legislative assembly or administrative council, principally important in German history. Emperor Charles IV established the Diet of the Holy Roman Empire by his Golden Bull of 1356. It comprised three estates – the seven electors (of the Holy Roman emperor), other lay and church nobility, and representatives of the imperial cities – each of which met separately. Approval by each estate and the consent of the emperor were required on all matters. After the Treaty of Westphalia (1648), the Diet lost much of its legislative power and importance.

Diggers (1649–50) English millenarian social and religious sect. The Diggers called themselves "true levellers", but were entirely separate from the Levellers, who opposed their communistic approach. Their egalitarian, agrarian community at St George's Hill, Surrey, was destroyed by local farmers. In *Law of Freedom* (1652), the main Digger theorist, Gerrard Winstanley, proposed communalization of property to establish social equality. *See also* millenarianism

Dimitrov, Georgi Mikhailovich (1882–1949) Bulgarian statesman, premier (1946–49). He was a founder of the Bulgarian Communist Party in 1919. Dimitrov was forced to flee Bulgaria after leading an unsuccessful communist uprising against Alexander Tsankov in 1923. Living in exile in Berlin, he was accused of planning the Reichstag fire (1933) with other communist leaders. Dimitrov delivered a devastating defence against his Nazi prosecutors and was acquitted. He was granted Soviet citizenship and moved to Moscow, where he served as secretary general (1935–43) of Comintern. During World War 2 he was a leader of the Bulgarian resistance movement and became premier in the Fatherland Front government. Dimitrov established communist control through a series of brutal purges, killing *c*.30,000 political opponents.

Dingaan (d.1843) Zulu king (1828–40). He came to power after murdering his half-brother, Shaka. In 1838 Dingaan ordered the massacre of *c*.600 Afrikaner (Boer) immigrants. In an act of revenge, Afrikaner troops then massacred *c*.3000 Zulu warriors in the Battle of Blood River (1838). In 1840 Dingaan's brother drove him from the throne and into exile in Swaziland. He was murdered in 1843.

Dingiswayo (d.1817) (Godongwana) Founder of the Zulu kingdom. He took the name Dingiswayo (Banished one) after being forced into exile by his brother, Mawewe. In 1807 Dingiswayo overthrew Mawewe to become chief of the Bantu Mthethwa clan. He conquered surrounding territories to become ruler of *c*.30 tribal groups in what is now northeast KwaZulu-Natal. Dingiswayo was assassinated by the chief of the Ndwandwe clan and succeeded by Shaka.

Diocletian (245–313) (Caius Aurelius Diocletianus) Roman emperor (284–305). Of low birth, he was made emperor by the army. In 286 Diocletian reorganized the Empire, giving control of the West to Maximian, while Diocletian ruled the East from Nicomedia. In 287 the Empire acquired a theocratic basis, as Diocletian proclaimed himself Jove to Maximian's Hercules. In 293 he appointed Galerius and Constantius I (Chlorus) as deputies to himself and Maximian respectively. These reforms stemmed the slide into domestic anarchy and helped defeat rebellions in Gaul, Britain and Egypt. Diocletian further restricted the powers of the Senate, establishing an autocracy. His administrative reforms created a bureaucracy. He expanded and reformed the military by raising new taxes. Diocletian's reforms have been partly overshadowed, however, by his sustained persecution of the Christians in 303.

Diogenes (active 4th century BC) Greek philosopher, traditionally regarded as the founder of the Cynics. He rejected the materialism of Athenian society, criticizing its moral poverty. Diogenes believed that the key to right-living and happiness lay in simplicity.

Dionysius the Areopagite, Saint (1st century AD) First bishop of Athens, converted by Saint Paul. His name was used by a Palestinian writer of *c*.AD 500, now known as Pseudo-Dionysius, whose mystical works of Neoplatonism had a great influence on scholasticism.

Dionysius the Elder (*c*.430–367 BC) Tyrant of Syracuse (405–367 BC). In *c*.405 BC he seized power and soon established a military dictatorship. Dionysius tried to expand Greek influence in Sicily through conquest. His first war with Carthage (397–396 BC) restricted Carthaginian power to nw Sicily. The capture of Rhegium (386 BC) established Syracuse as the major power in Greek Italy, but the brutality of Dionysius' methods made him unpopular in Greece. A third war with Carthage (383–*c*.375 BC) ended in devastating defeat at Cronium. He was succeeded by his son, Dionysius the Younger.

Dionysius the Younger (active 367–344 BC) Tyrant of Syracuse, son and successor of Dionysius the Elder. Plato and Dion of Syracuse (brother-in-law of Dionysius the Elder) tried to mould him into the model philosopher-king. Dionysius, however, quickly adopted the tyrannical tactics of his father and banished his tutors. In 357 BC he was defeated by Dion and fled into exile. Dionysius returned to power after the murder of Dion (*c*.354). In 344 the citizens of Syracuse appealed to Corinth for help in expelling Dionysius. An army led by Timoleon forced him to surrender and flee for Corinth.

Diouf, Abdou (1935–) Senegalese statesman, prime minister (1970–80), president (1981–2000). He succeeded Léopold Senghor as president. Diouf was re-elected in 1983, 1988 and 1993. His authoritarian regime was often criticized for abuses of human rights. He was succeeded as president by Abdoulaye Wade.

Diponegoro (Dipanagara) (*c*.1785–1855) Javanese prince, leader of the Java War (1825–30) against Dutch colonial rule. In 1814 he was overlooked as sultan and

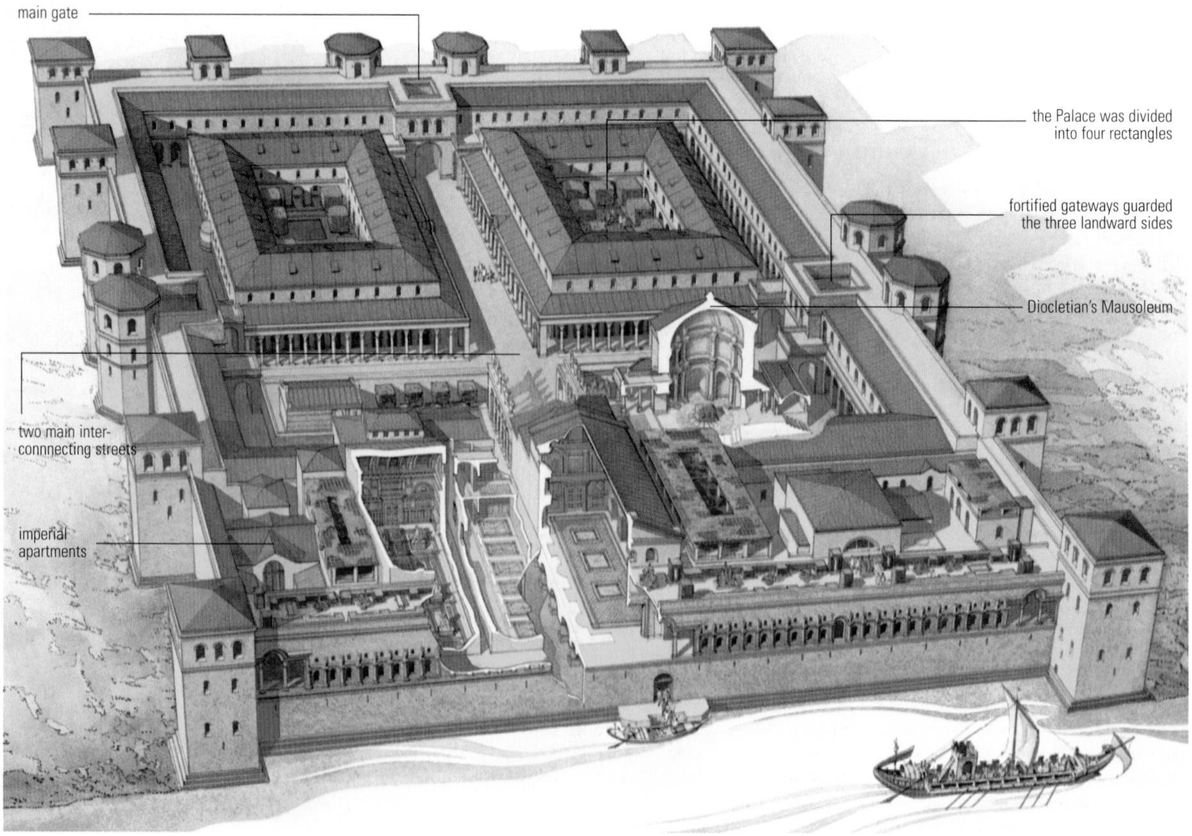

► **Diocletian's Palace** Built *c*.AD 300 at Spalato on the Dalmatian coast, Illyria, as Diocletian's retirement residence, the Palace resembled a fortress from the outside. Its axial layout, with high walls and towers on all landward sides, was modelled on a Roman camp. The s side overlooked the Adriatic Sea. It is thought that the n part of the Palace contained the barracks of the Imperial Guard and various service buildings. The s portion held Diocletian's Mausoleum, a temple, the emperor's private apartments, a library, an audience hall, guest suites, a dining hall and the women's quarters.

▲ **Diponegoro** During the Java War (1825–30), Diponegoro was seen as a divine saviour by the Javanese people, sent to lead them in a holy war against the Dutch.

spent some years in religious seclusion. By 1825, however, he had emerged as the leader of Javanese resistance to Dutch land reforms. In the resulting guerrilla war, Diponegoro inflicted serious damage on the Dutch until 1828 when the Dutch gained a major victory. In 1830 Diponegoro was arrested during a meeting with Dutch peace negotiators and subsequently went into exile.

Directory (1795–99) Government of the First Republic of France, consisting of five directors elected by the Council of Five Hundred and the Council of Ancients. It was established as part of the THERMIDORIAN REACTION to the REIGN OF TERROR. In 1796 the Directory passed austere financial measures to combat rampant inflation and crushed the ensuing rebellion by François BABEUF. In 1797 Lazare CARNOT was dismissed and the Directory became dominated by the JACOBINS. In 1799 France suffered a series of defeats in the FRENCH REVOLUTIONARY WARS and the generals mounted the coup of 18 Brumaire (9 November) that established the CONSULATE led by NAPOLEON Bonaparte. *See also* FRENCH REVOLUTION

Dirksen, Everett McKinley (1896–1969) US politician. He was elected to the Senate in 1950 and served as minority leader (1959–69). Dirksen was the leading critic of President John KENNEDY's administration, but helped to secure the passage of the CIVIL RIGHTS ACT (1964) and the Voting Rights Act (1965).

disarmament Refers principally to attempts post-1918 (and especially post-1945) to reach international agreements to halt the ARMS RACE. The United Nations established the Atomic Energy Commission (1946) and the Commission for Conventional Armaments (1947). In 1952 these were combined into the Disarmament Commission. It produced no results, and the Soviet Union withdrew in 1957. The United States and the Soviet Union signed the NUCLEAR TEST BAN TREATY (1963) and the Nuclear Non-Proliferation Treaty (1968), which provided for an international inspectorate. This was followed by a series of STRATEGIC ARMS LIMITATION TALKS (SALT). In 1986 SALT was superseded by START (strategic arms reduction talks), resulting in the **Intermediate Nuclear Forces (INF) Treaty** of 1987, which reduced the superpowers' arsenal of short-range, intermediate missiles by *c.*2000 (4% of the total stockpile) and provided for on-site inspection. The **Conventional Forces in Europe Treaty** (1990) set limits on equipment and troop levels. Attempts to sign a comprehensive Test Ban Treaty have been thwarted by China, France, India and Pakistan. Following the break-up of the Soviet Union, the four republics with nuclear weapons (Russia, Ukraine, Belarus and Kazakstan) agreed in 1991 to implement the START treaties.

Disraeli, Benjamin, 1st Earl of Beaconsfield (1804–81) British statesman and novelist, prime minister (1868, 1874–80). Disraeli was elected to Parliament in 1837. His brand of Toryism is expressed in the trilogy of novels, *Coningsby* (1844), *Sybil* (1846) and *Tancred* (1847). Following the split in the TORY PARTY over the repeal of the CORN LAWS (1846), Disraeli became leader of the land-owning faction. His opposition to Robert PEEL was rewarded when he became chancellor of the exchequer (1852, 1858–59, 1866–68) under Lord DERBY. Disraeli introduced the second REFORM ACT (1867) in the House of Commons. He succeeded Derby as prime minister but was soon ousted by William GLADSTONE, leader of the LIBERAL PARTY. His second term coincided with the greatest expansion of the second BRITISH EMPIRE. Unlike Gladstone, Disraeli maintained a close friendship with Queen VICTORIA and conferred on her the title empress of India (1876). Disraeli led Britain into the ZULU WAR (1879) and the second of the AFGHAN WARS (1878–79). In 1875 Britain purchased the Suez Canal from Egypt. Disraeli was concerned by the growing strength of Russia during the RUSSO-TURKISH WARS (1877–78), but he emerged triumphant from the ensuing Congress of Berlin. In 1880 Disraeli was defeated for a second time by Gladstone. *See also* TORY

Dissolution of the Monasteries (1536–40) Abolition of MONASTICISM in the reign of HENRY VIII of England. The operation, managed by Thomas CROMWELL, was a result of the break with Rome but also provided additional revenue, since the monasteries owned *c.*25% of the land in England, all of which passed to the crown. The smaller religious houses were closed in 1536, larger ones in 1538–40 (*see* map, page 120). The Dissolution caused social hardship, resentment and revolt, while providing estates for upwardly mobile gentry as the crown sold off its newly acquired land to fund its wars. *See also* PILGRIMAGE OF GRACE; REFORMATION *See* illustration, page 120

District of Columbia Federal district, coextensive with the United States' capital, WASHINGTON, D.C. It is governed under federal law. It was created in 1790–91 from land taken from the states of Maryland and Virginia. The Virginia portion was returned in 1846. Area: 179sq km (69sq mi).

Divine, Father (*c.*1882–1965) US clergyman, b. George Baker. In *c.*1915 he founded the Peace Mission Movement in New York City, and adopted the name Major M.J. Divine. The Movement grew rapidly during the GREAT DEPRESSION and at its peak had *c.*500,000 members. Divine was a pioneer of the CIVIL RIGHTS movement and used the large donations by his followers to help support African-American owned businesses. The Movement declined sharply after his death.

divine right of kings Political doctrine that monarchy is a divinely-ordained institution and, since sovereigns are answerable only to God, active resistance to royal authority is a damnable sin. The concept evolved in medieval Europe, partly to counter papal authority. In 17th-century England, JAMES I and CHARLES I's use of divine right to justify absolutism led to conflict with Parliament. *See also* LOUIS XIV

Dix, Dorothea Lynde (1802–87) US pioneer in the treatment of the mentally ill. Dix exposed the inhumane treatment of the insane and inspired legislation resulting in patients being treated in state mental hospitals.

Djibouti *See* country feature, page 121

Djilas, Milovan (1911–95) Yugoslav politician and writer. Djilas was an architect of Yugoslavia's independence from the Soviet Union. A member of the Partisan resistance during World War 2, he became a cabinet minister under TITO in 1945. In 1953 he became one of four vice presidents, but his growing criticism of the Communist Party led to his dismissal from office in 1954, followed by his resignation from the Party. Djilas' support for the HUNGARIAN UPRISING (1956) and criticism of Tito's authoritarian regime in *New Class* (1957) led to a prison term (1956–61). His next work, *Conversations with Stalin* (1962), brought a second prison sentence (1962–66).

Dmitri (*c.*1582–91) (Demetrius) Russian prince, son of IVAN IV (THE TERRIBLE). In 1584 his brother, FYODOR I, succeeded as tsar but real political power lay with Boris GODUNOV. Dmitri died of an epileptic fit or possibly was murdered by Godunov. In 1604 a pretender, assuming the name Dmitri, invaded Russia. In 1605 Godunov died and the "false Dmitri" was crowned tsar by the army. In 1606 he was killed in an insurrection and four subsequent pretenders suffered a similar fate. The "Time of Troubles" (1604–13) in Russian history ended with the accession of Michael ROMANOV.

Dodd, William Edward (1869–1940) US historian and diplomat. He served as US ambassador to Germany (1933–37). Dodd was an outspoken critic of Adolf HITLER and the rise of NATIONAL SOCIALISM. His commitment to democratic values is evident in works such as *The Old South: Struggles for Democracy* (1937).

doge Chief magistrate of Venice (697–1797) and Genoa (1339–1805), Italy. Despite an attempt by Venice in the 12th century to make the office hereditary, it remained elective. After the 14th century, the importance of the doge declined and the office ended in 1797 with the Napoleonic conquest. The Doge's Palace in St Mark's Square, Venice, was begun in the 9th century and rebuilt several times. The present building, dating from the 14th and 15th centuries, is in Venetian gothic style.

Dole, Sanford (1844–1926) Hawaiian statesman. He was appointed (1893) leader of a provisional government following the overthrow of Queen LILIUOKALANI. In 1894 Dole became the republic's first president. He secured US annexation of HAWAII (1898) and served (1900–03) as the territory's first governor.

dollar diplomacy Term used to describe US policy of military and economic interference in Latin American affairs in the early 1900s. A number of Caribbean countries

DISRAELI, BENJAMIN

Benjamin Disraeli Before his election to Parliament, Disraeli wrote several novels, the first of which, *Vivian Grey*, was published in 1826. He established his political reputation by writing pamphlets and letters to *The Times* newspaper. Disraeli continued to write throughout his political career, and through his novels he highlighted poverty in England and failings in the parliamentary system.

DISRAELI IN HIS OWN WORDS

"The difference between a misfortune and a calamity? If Gladstone fell into the Thames, it would be a misfortune. But if someone dragged him out again, it would be a calamity."

"Free trade is not a principle, it is an expedient."
On Import Duties, 25 April 1843

◄ **Dissolution of the Monasteries** Under an Act of Parliament passed in 1536, the monasteries and parliamentary abbeys (monasteries whose abbots had the right to sit in Parliament) were closed, many before the final Act of Dissolution was passed in 1539. The last to close was Waltham Abbey, s England, in 1540.

English Reformation

- Great monasteries dissolved 1538 – 40
- Parliamentary abbeys dissolved 1538 – 40

(Dominican Republic, Cuba, Haiti, Honduras, Costa Rica and Nicaragua) were, at various time, heavily in debt to certain European governments. The United States intervened, citing the threat of European encroachment in the Western Hemisphere and the need to safeguard US investments in these countries.

Dollfuss, Engelbert (1892–1934) Austrian chancellor (1932–34). Determined to preserve Austrian independence, he dissolved the Austrian NAZI PARTY, which had demanded union with Germany (1933), and assumed authoritarian powers. Dollfuss was assassinated by Austrian Nazis in an unsuccessful coup. *See also* ANSCHLUSS; NATIONAL SOCIALISM

Dome of the Rock (Qubbat al-Sakhrah) Mosque and shrine built (685–692) by Abd al-Malik on the site of the Second TEMPLE OF JERUSALEM. The Dome covers the summit of Mount Moriah, where the prophet MUHAMMAD is believed to have ascended to Heaven. According to the Old Testament, the Rock is also where Abraham was to have sacrificed Isaac.

Domesday Book (1085–86) Survey of the English kingdom commissioned by WILLIAM I (THE CONQUEROR) to ascertain potential crown revenue. The most complete survey in medieval Europe, it is an important primary historical source. Covering all the counties, except the four in the far north and part of Lancashire, it lists the extent and resources of each manor. *See also* NORMAN CONQUEST

Dominic, Saint (*c*.1170–1221) (Domingo de Guzmán) Spanish priest, founder of the DOMINICANS. In 1203 Pope INNOCENT III sent him to preach to the ALBIGENSES. Dominic founded a monastery at Prouille, s France. He developed an order based on scholastic and democratic principles and rules derived from Saint AUGUSTINE. His feast day is 4 August.

Dominica Independent island nation in the E Caribbean Sea, Lesser Antilles, WEST INDIES. It was named after *dies dominica* (Sunday), the day it was discovered by Christopher COLUMBUS (1493). The original inhabitants were CARIB, but the present population are mainly the descendants of African slaves. In 1632 the first French settlers arrived. Possession of Dominica was contested between Britain and France, until it was awarded to Britain in 1783. It became a British crown colony in 1805 and was a member of the Federation of the West Indies (1958–62). In 1978 Dominica achieved full independence. In 1979 Hurricane David left *c*.75% of the population homeless and devastated the nation's vital banana crop. In 1981 Eugenia Charles became the Caribbean's first woman prime minister. In 1995 she was succeeded by Edison James.

Dominican Republic *See* country feature, page 122

Dominicans (officially *Ordo Praedicatorum*, Order of Preachers, O.P.) Roman Catholic religious order, founded (1215) by Saint DOMINIC. They are also known as Black Friars or Jacobins. Dominicans are one of the four great mendicant orders of Roman Catholicism. Devoted to preaching and study, the order operates worldwide and includes a contemplative order of nuns. Noted scholars include Saint Thomas AQUINAS and Saint ALBERTUS MAGNUS. *See also* MONASTICISM

Dominion of Canada Official name of CANADA since the BRITISH NORTH AMERICA ACT of 1867.

domino theory Political doctrine outlined by United States' President Dwight EISENHOWER that affected US foreign policy during the COLD WAR. It held that if one country became communist, its neighbours would inevitably follow. The doctrine was often cited in support of US military involvement in VIETNAM.

Domitian (AD 51–96) (Titus Vlavius Domitianus) Roman emperor (81–96), son of VESPASIAN. He succeeded his brother, TITUS, as emperor. Domitian's rule was orderly at first but became increasingly tyrannical. After several attempts, he was assassinated. Domitian was partly responsible for building the COLOSSEUM.

Donatism Schismatic Christian movement founded in 4th-century N Africa. The movement was led by Donatus (d.355). In the tradition of Montanism, followers claimed that only those without sin belonged in the church and they supported re-baptism. Despite condemnation by the Synod of Arles (314), by the mid-5th century Donatism had become the dominant form of Christianity in Africa. Only with the teachings of Saint AUGUSTINE did Donatism decline.

Dong, Pham Van (1906–) Vietnamese statesman, prime minister of North Vietnam (1955–75) and prime minister of a united Vietnam (1975–87). He was imprisoned (1929–36) by the French for his part in the communist resistance movement in FRENCH INDOCHINA. A close ally of HO CHI MINH, Dong was a co-founder of the VIET MINH (1941). In 1954 he led the Viet Minh delegation at the Geneva Peace Conference. After Ho CHI MINH's death (1969), Dong assumed the leadership of the Viet Minh during the VIETNAM WAR.

Dönitz, Karl (1891–1980) German admiral. He was commander-in-chief (1943–45) of the German navy during WORLD WAR 2. On the death of Adolf HITLER, Dönitz became chancellor and negotiated the German surrender. He was imprisoned (1946–56) for war crimes.

Donner party California-bound group, led by George and Jacob Donner, who travelled overland from Illinois. In October 1846 the party reached Truckee in the High Sierras, where they were trapped by early snowstorms. They escaped starvation by eating the flesh of those who died. Of the 87 members of the original party, only 47 survived.

Doomsday Book *See* DOMESDAY BOOK

Doria, Andrea (*c*.1466–1560) Genoese admiral and statesman. He fought initially on the side of FRANCIS I of France in the ITALIAN WARS, but switched allegiance to Emperor CHARLES V on the condition that Charles guarantee the independence of GENOA. In 1528 Doria became DOGE of Genoa, creating an authoritarian republic. As imperial admiral, he helped Charles V capture Tunis (1535) from the Turks. His family continued to rule Genoa until the end of the 18th century.

Dorians Greek-speaking people who settled in N Greece *c*.1200 BC. They moved southward, displacing the culturally superior MYCENAEAN and MINOAN CIVILIZATIONS because they mastered the use of iron. The cities of Argos, CORINTH and SPARTA are of Doric origin. The invasion of the Dorians marks the start of a 400-year "Dark Age" in ancient Greek history.

Doric order One of the five ORDERS OF ARCHITECTURE

Dorr's Rebellion (1842) Uprising against the state government of Rhode Island. Rhode Island's colonial charter (1663) restricted the vote to men owning more than US$134 in land. Thomas Wilson Dorr (1805–54)

DOMINICA

AREA: 751sq km (290sq mi)
POPULATION: 78,000
CAPITAL (POPULATION): Roseau (16,243)
GOVERNMENT: Multiparty republic
ETHNIC GROUPS: Of African descent
LANGUAGES: English, French patois
RELIGIONS: Roman Catholic 75%, Protestant 15%
GDP PER CAPITA (1994): US$2902

led a campaign for universal manhood suffrage. He formed a rival government and attempted to take power by force. The Dorrites were defeated, but a new constitution was adopted (1843). In 1834 Dorr was found guilty of treason and imprisoned. He was later released and pardoned.

Dos Santos, José Eduardo (1942–) Angolan statesman, president (1979–). Dos Santos' succession to the presidency was marked by violence between the Cuban-backed People's Movement for the Liberation of ANGOLA (MPLA) government and the South African-backed National Union for the Total Independence of Angola (UNITA), led by Jonas SAVIMBI. In 1989 Cuban and South African troops withdrew from Angola and the Lusaka Protocol (1994) agreed to a government of national unity, headed by Dos Santos. However, Savimbi refused to participate in the government and Angola was plunged back into civil war.

Dost Muhammad (1793–1863) Emir of Afghanistan (1826–39, 1843–63). He led a rebel clan against the ruler Mahmud Shah in a civil war (1818–26) before establishing the Barakzay dynasty in Kabul. In 1836 Dost Muhammad launched an unsuccessful JIHAD against the Sikhs in Peshawar (now in Pakistan). His attempts to maintain Afghanistan's independence in the face of Russia and Britain's struggle for power in the region led to a British invasion in 1838. During the ensuing First AFGHAN WAR (1838–42), Dost Muhammad was forced off the throne (1839), but he was restored to the emirate in 1843. In 1855 and 1857 Dost Muhammad signed treaties of friendship with Britain. His death prompted a series of fratricidal battles until SHERE ALI assumed control in 1868.

Douai Bible English translation (from the Latin Vulgate) of the BIBLE, authorized by the Roman Catholic Church for use after the REFORMATION. Gregory Martin, living in exile at Douai, France, was the main translator. The NEW TESTAMENT was published at Reims (1582), the OLD TESTAMENT at Douai (1609–10). It was revised by Richard Challoner (1749–50).

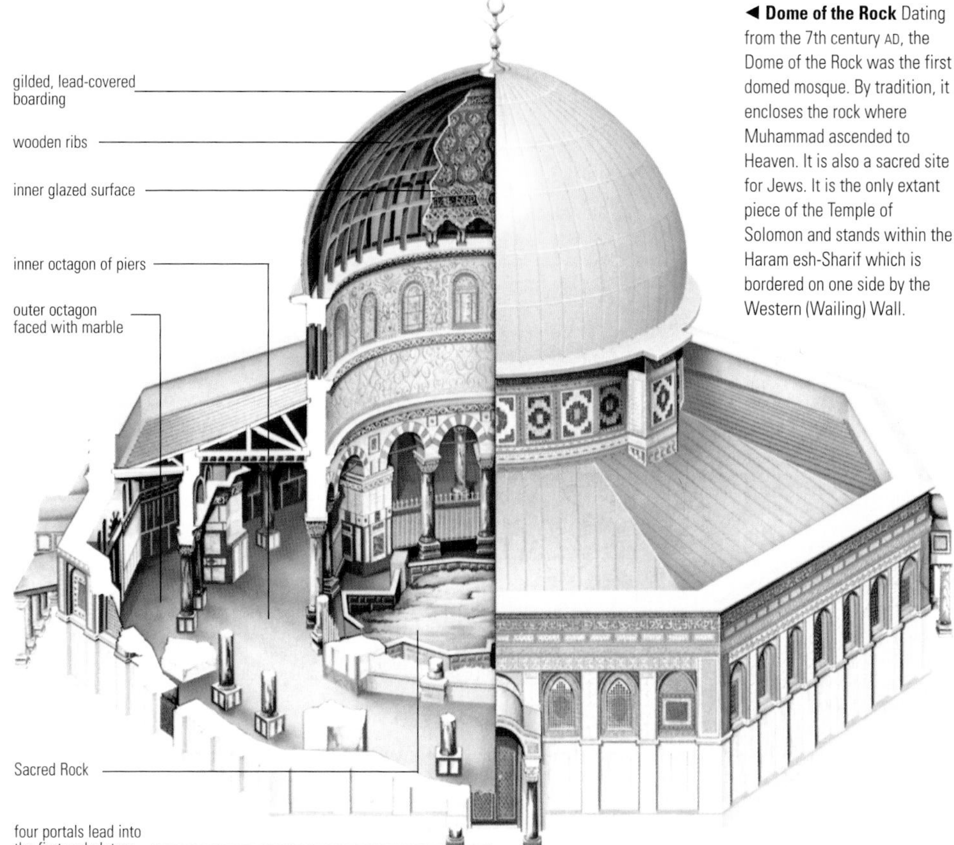

◀ **Dome of the Rock** Dating from the 7th century AD, the Dome of the Rock was the first domed mosque. By tradition, it encloses the rock where Muhammad ascended to Heaven. It is also a sacred site for Jews. It is the only extant piece of the Temple of Solomon and stands within the Haram esh-Sharif which is bordered on one side by the Western (Wailing) Wall.

D

Douglas, Sir James (1803–77) Canadian fur trader and colonial administrator, b. Guyana. He was chief officer (1839–58) for the HUDSON'S BAY COMPANY in territory w of the Rockies. Douglas served as first governor (1858–64) of the colony of BRITISH COLUMBIA. He founded Fort Camosun (now Victoria) on Vancouver Island. He was knighted in 1863.

DJIBOUTI (JIBOUTI)

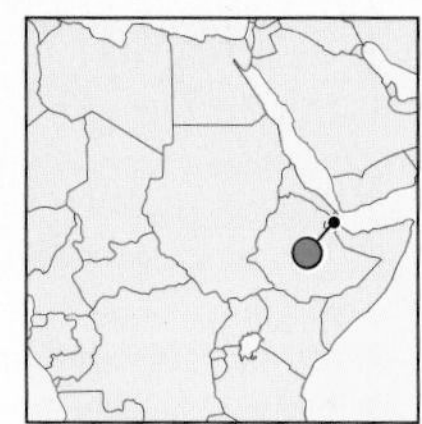

Republic on the NE coast of Africa. Djibouti occupies a strategic position around the Gulf of Tadjoura where the Red Sea meets the Gulf of Aden. The area was settled in the 3rd century BC by immigrants from Arabia. They were the ancestors of the Afars, who today make up nearly 40% of the population. At a later date, Somalis of the Issa clan, who with other Somali clans now constitute more than half of the population, settled in the southern and coastal areas. Islam was introduced in the 9th century. The subsequent conversion of the Afars led to conflict with Christian Ethiopians.

In 1888 France set up French Somaliland. Renamed the French Territory of the Afars and Issas in 1967, it achieved independence as the Republic of Djibouti in 1977. Hassan Gouled Aptidon of the Popular Rally for Progress (RPP) was elected president. In 1981 he declared a one-party state. Continuing protests

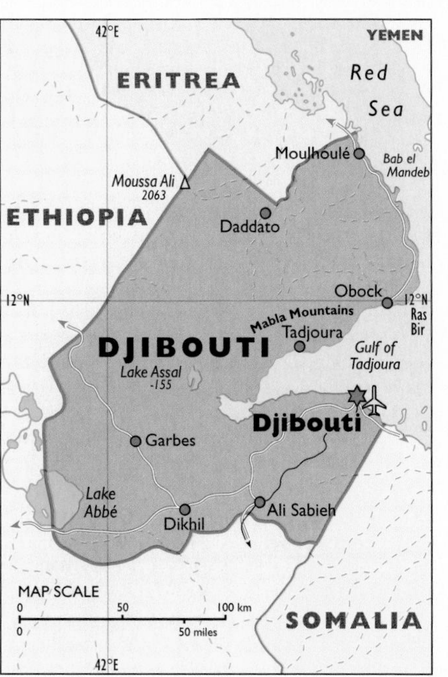

against the Issas-dominated regime forced the introduction of a multiparty constitution in 1992. The Front for the Restoration of Unity and Democracy (FUUD), supported primarily by Afars, boycotted 1993 elections, and Aptidon was re-elected for a fourth six-year term. FUUD rebels continued an armed campaign for political representation. In 1994 government and FUUD forces signed a peace accord, and in 1996 FUUD was recognized as a political party.

AREA: 23,200sq km (8958sq mi)
POPULATION: 695,000
CAPITAL (POPULATION): Djibouti (353,000)
GOVERNMENT: Multiparty republic
ETHNIC GROUPS: Issa 47%, Afar 37%, Arab 6%
LANGUAGES: Arabic and French (both official)
RELIGIONS: Islam 96%, Christianity 4%
GDP PER CAPITA (1994): US$926

Douglas, James, 4th Earl of Morton *See* MORTON, JAMES DOUGLAS, 4TH EARL OF

Douglas, Stephen Arnold (1813–61) US statesman. He served in the House of Representatives (1843–47). Known as the "Little Giant", he was a senator (1847–61). Douglas helped to secure the passage of the COMPROMISE OF 1850. His doctrine of "popular sovereignty" proposed that each territory be given the right to chose whether they wanted SLAVERY or not. Douglas sponsored the KANSAS-NEBRASKA ACT (1854). In 1858 he campaigned for re-election to the Senate against Abraham LINCOLN. The contest involved a series of public meetings (the LINCOLN-DOUGLAS DEBATES) on the issue of slavery. Douglas was returned to the Senate, but had alienated many Southern Democrats. In 1860 his nomination as presidential candidate for the DEMOCRATIC PARTY split the Party as the Southern delegates voted for John BRECKENRIDGE. Lincoln won the election and Douglas supported him when the CIVIL WAR broke out. *See also* DAVIS, JEFFERSON; DRED SCOTT CASE

Douglas, William Orville (1898–1980) US jurist, associate justice of the Supreme Court (1939–75). President Franklin ROOSEVELT appointed him to succeed Louis BRANDEIS. Douglas served the longest period in the Court's history. He was a strong supporter of civil liberties and conservation. In 1953 Douglas granted a stay of execution to Julius and Ethel ROSENBERG. He also wrote the majority opinion in *Griswold v. Connecticut* (1965) that struck down anti-birth control legislation.

Douglas-Home, Sir Alec (Alexander Frederick) (1903–95) British statesman, prime minister (1963–64). He entered Parliament in 1931 and served as parliamentary private secretary (1937–39) to Neville CHAMBERLAIN. In 1951 Douglas-Home joined the House of Lords as Lord Home of the Hirsel. Douglas-Home served as foreign secretary under Harold MACMILLAN from 1960 to 1963, when he renounced his peerage to succeed Macmillan as prime minister and leader of the CONSERVATIVE PARTY. In the 1964 elections Douglas-

Home was defeated by Harold WILSON, and the following year he was succeeded by Edward HEATH as leader of the Conservative Party. Douglas-Home returned as foreign secretary (1970–74) in the Heath government.

Douglass, Frederick (1817–95) African-American ABOLITIONIST and social reformer. An escaped slave, he became (1841) a lecturer for the Massachusetts Anti-Slavery Society. Douglass wrote *Narrative of the Life of Frederick Douglass* (1845) and, fearing capture, went into exile in England. In 1847 he bought his freedom and returned to the United States to found the abolitionist newspaper, *North Star*. A lifelong supporter of equal rights, he served as minister to Haiti (1889–91).

Doukhobors (Dukhobors, Rus. spirit wrestlers) Russian nonconformist Christian sect founded in the 18th century. Doukhobors rejected ecclesiastical and state authority in favour of a pacifist, communal society. In 1899, under the leadership of Peter Verigin and with the help of the Russian novelist Leo Tolstoy (1828–1910) and English QUAKERS, 7000 Doukhobors emigrated to w Canada, where they established successful agricultural communities. Internal divisions emerged, and the sect split (1945) into the Union of the Doukhobors and the more radical Sons of Freedom.

Dowding, Hugh Caswell Tremenheere, 1st Baron (1882–1970) British air chief marshal, b. Scotland. As commander in chief (1936–40) of Fighter Command, he organized the air defence that defeated the Luftwaffe in the Battle of BRITAIN (1940). Dowding retired in 1942. *See also* WORLD WAR 2

Downing Street Declaration (15 December 1993) Joint declaration issued by the British Prime Minster John MAJOR and the Irish Taoiseach Albert REYNOLDS. Continuing the momentum of the ANGLO-IRISH AGREEMENT, it set a framework for peace talks in Northern IRELAND. The Downing Street Declaration stated that all political parties (including SINN FÉIN) could be involved in an all-Ireland forum if they committed themselves to permanently ending paramilitary violence. The UK and Irish governments also agreed that the status of Northern Ireland could only change with majority consent of its people, and Ireland's future would be determined only by the peoples of the island of Ireland. *See also* GOOD FRIDAY AGREEMENT

Draco (active 7th century BC) Athenian political leader and lawmaker. He drew up the first written code of laws in Athens. They were famous for their severity, and the death penalty was prescribed even for minor offenses.

draft riots Uprisings against Union conscription in the American CIVIL WAR. The Union Conscription Act (March 1863) provoked nationwide disturbances. The most serious riots were in New York City (July 13–16, 1863), where a mob beat many African Americans to death, and razed buildings. New York troops were deployed to restore order. The riots left *c*.1000 dead and caused US$2 million worth of damage.

Drago, Luis María (1859–1921) Argentine statesman. As minister of foreign affairs (1902–03), Drago argued that no foreign power should coerce an American state into paying public debts by armed intervention or occupation. This proposal (known as the **Drago Doctrine**) was accepted, in modified form, by the Hague Conference (1907). *See also* MONROE DOCTRINE

Drake, Sir Francis (*c*.1540–96) English navigator and admiral. In 1567 he sailed with his relative, John HAWKINS, on a slave-trading voyage to the West Indies. The expedition was attacked by the Spanish and Drake vowed to exact revenge. In 1577, with ELIZABETH I of England's blessing, he set sail with five ships to raid Spanish possessions in South America. In 1578 Drake became the first English sailor to pass through the Straits of Magellan. A storm scattered Drake's flotilla, and he continued alone in the *Golden Hind* up the Pacific coast of America. Drake wintered in present-day California, which he named New Albion. In 1579 he struck out west across the Pacific, mooring in the Moluccas, Celebes and Java. On 26 September 1580, Drake docked in Plymouth, s England, laden with treasure and spices. He was the first captain to circumnavigate the world – Ferdinand MAGELLAN having died in the attempt. He was knighted aboard the *Golden Hind* by Elizabeth I. In 1585 Drake set sail with orders to cause the maximum damage to the Spanish Empire. His fleet of 25 ships captured and plundered the towns of São Tiago (Cape Verde), Cartagena (Colombia), St Augustine (Florida) and Santo Domingo (Hispaniola). Drake rescued Sir Walter RALEIGH's colony at Roanoke Island, North Carolina, and returned with potatoes and tobacco. Spain began to prepare for an open war. In 1587 Drake stormed into the harbour of CÁDIZ, s Spain, destroying 30 Spanish ships. This action, which he described as merely "singeing the king of Spain's beard", postponed the Spanish invasion for a year. In 1588 Drake was made vice admiral to Charles HOWARD in the fleet that destroyed the Spanish ARMADA. Drake was hailed as a hero. In 1595 Drake and Hawkins again set sail for the West Indies to raid Spanish settlements. The expedition was a disaster and Drake died of dysentry. He was buried at sea off Portobelo, Panama.

Dred Scott case (1856–57) US Supreme Court trial on the issue of federal jurisdiction over SLAVERY in the territories. In 1834 Dred Scott, a slave of John Emerson, was taken from the slave state of Missouri to the free state of Illinois and then Wisconsin territory, where slavery was prohibited by the MISSOURI COMPROMISE (1820). After Emerson's death, Scott sued for his freedom because he had lived in a free state. The case went to federal court. In the case of *Scott vs. Sanford*, Roger TANEY delivered the verdict that the Missouri Compromise was unconstitutional. Three of the justices also held that slaves were not entitled to the rights of US citizens. *See also* KANSAS-NEBRASKA ACT

Dresden City on the River Elbe, capital of SAXONY, SE Germany. Originally a Slav settlement, it was first settled by Germans in the early 13th century. From 1485 until 1918 Dresden was the residence of the dukes, later electors and kings, of Saxony. Under electors FREDERICK AUGUSTUS I (r.1763–1827) and Frederick Augustus II (r.1836–54), the city became a showcase of BAROQUE and ROCOCO architecture. Dresden was occupied by Prussia during the War of the AUSTRIAN SUCCESSION (1745) and the SEVEN YEARS' WAR (1756). NAPOLEON I gained his last significant success in the NAPOLEONIC WARS at the Battle of Dresden (26–27 August 1813). In WORLD WAR 2, the Royal Air Force's blanket bombing of Dresden (13–14 February 1945), under the command of Arthur "Bomber" Harris, killed *c*.100,000 civilians and destroyed more than 30,000 buildings. Pop. (1990) 483,400.

Drew, Daniel (1797–1879) US financier. In 1844 he switched from the steamboat business to become a trader in railroad stock and a stock manipulator on Wall Street, New York City, financial capital of the United States. Known for his unscrupulous business practices, Drew successfully battled Cornelius VANDERBILT for the Erie Railroad (1866–68) in the "Erie War". His fortune was wiped out on BLACK FRIDAY (1869) and the panic of 1873. *See also* FISK, JAMES; GOULD, JAY

Dreyfus affair French political and moral crisis arising from the conviction for treason (22 December 1894) of Captain Alfred Dreyfus (1859–1935). Dreyfus, a Jewish army officer, was accused of passing military secrets to the Germans. A handwritten letter to the German attaché was discovered by Major Hubert Henry and attributed to Dreyfus, who protested his innocence. The ANTI-SEMITISM of sections of the French press fuelled support for Dreyfus' sentence of deportation to Devil's Island in the Caribbean. In 1896 Lieutenant Colonel Georges Picquart discovered counter-evidence that implicated Major Ferdinand Walsin Esterhazy. Picquart was dismissed and Esterhazy subsequently acquitted by a court martial. This prompted the novelist Émile Zola (1840–1902) to publish *J'accuse* (1898), an open letter accusing the French army of a cover-up. French society was deeply divided over the issue. The mainly nationalist and Catholic anti-Dreyfusards viewed the affair as an attempt to discredit the French military, while the socialist Dreyfusards (including Georges CLEMENCEAU) regarded it as a miscarriage of justice. In 1898 Major Henry committed suicide after admitting he had forged much of the evidence and Esterhazy fled into exile. In 1899 Dreyfus received a presidential pardon, and he was cleared of all charges in 1906. The Dreyfus affair led to the separation of church and state in 1905. *See also* ACTION FRANÇAISE

Drogheda (Droichead Atha) Town in s County Louth, NE Republic of Ireland. It was a Danish town in the 10th century. In 1395 the Irish princes of Leinster and Ulster surrendered to the English forces of RICHARD II at Drogheda. In 1649 Oliver CROMWELL stormed the town, killing most of its inhabitants. In the Battle of the BOYNE (1690), Drogheda was forced to surrender to WILLIAM III (OF ORANGE). Pop. (1991) 23,845.

druid Pre-Christian Celtic religious leader in ancient Britain, Ireland and Gaul. Little is known about the druids but they appear to have been judges and teachers

DOMINICAN REPUBLIC

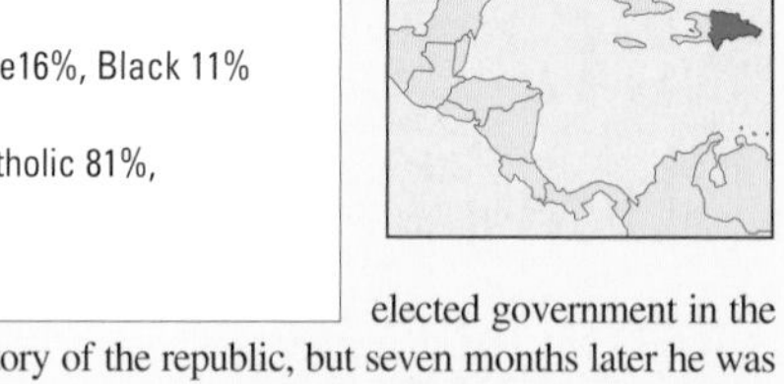

AREA: 48,734sq km (18,816sq mi)
POPULATION: 8,150,000
CAPITAL (POPULATION): Santo Domingo (2,134,779)
GOVERNMENT: Multiparty republic
ETHNIC GROUPS: Mulatto 73%, White16%, Black 11%
LANGUAGES: Spanish (official)
RELIGIONS: Christianity (Roman Catholic 81%, Protestant 6%)
GDP PER CAPITA (1995): US$3870

Independent nation occupying the E two-thirds of the island of Hispaniola in the West Indies. Hispaniola was visited by Christopher COLUMBUS in 1492, and a Spanish settlement was established at Santo Domingo. In 1697 the w third of the island (now HAITI) was ceded to France. In 1795 the whole island came under French rule, but the E part was returned to Spain in 1809.

In 1821 the colony declared itself the independent Dominican Republic but was annexed by Haiti. In 1844 independence was gained for a second time. Leaders of the liberation struggle, such as Juan Pablo Duarte, were expelled and the republic was run by a series of dictators, most notably Buenaventura Báez and Ulises Heureaux. Between 1916 and 1924 the Dominican Republic was occupied by the US military. In 1930 Rafael TRUJILLO established a personal dictatorship that lasted until his assassination in 1961. In 1963 Juan Bosch established the first democratically elected government in the history of the republic, but seven months later he was ousted in a coup by conservatives. In 1965 a popular revolution was suppressed with the help of US troops. In 1966 Joaquín BALAGUER, a former ally of Trujillo, was elected president. He was defeated by Antonio Guzmán Fernández in 1978 elections but returned to power in 1986. In 1996 he was succeeded by Leonel Fernández Reyna.

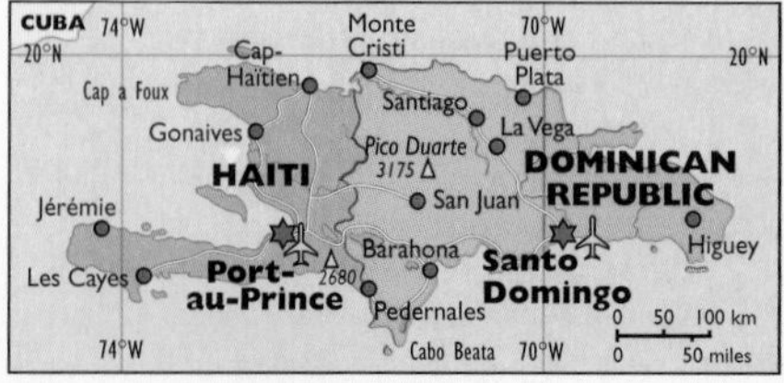

as well as priests. In Britain and Gaul, druidism was suppressed by the Romans, but it survived in Ireland until the 5th century.

Druze (Druse) Middle Eastern religious sect. A breakaway group of the ISMAILIS, the Druze originated in the reign of al-Hakim (996–1021), sixth Fatimid CALIPH of Egypt. Their name derives from the Cairo theologian al-Darazi (d. *c*.1019), the first to proclaim the cult. Druzes are devout monotheists who believe in the possibility of direct communication with the deity manifest on earth and in reincarnation. In 1925 the Druze led a revolt against the French mandate in Syria and s Lebanon that resulted in the creation of Jebel Druz, an autonomous Druze state in the mountains of s Syria. Today, there are *c*.500,000 Druzes living in Syria, Lebanon and Israel. *See also* FATIMID

Drygalski, Erich Dagobert von (1865–1949) German geophysicist. Drygalski headed the German Antarctic expedition (1901–03) in the *Gauss* that discovered Kaiser Wilhelm II Land.

Dual Monarchy *See* AUSTRO-HUNGARIAN EMPIRE

Dubai One of the seven federated states of the UNITED ARAB EMIRATES (UAE), on the Persian (Arabian) Gulf, SE Arabia; the capital is Dubai. First permanently settled in the late 18th century, it was a dependency of ABU DHABI until 1833. In 1853 Dubai and what are now the other UAE states agreed a perpetual maritime truce with Britain that led to them being called the **Trucial States**. In 1892 the Trucial States became a British protectorate. From 1945 to 1948 Dubai was at war with Abu Dhabi. Dubai prospered after the discovery of oil in 1966. In 1971 it became a founder member of the UAE. Dubai's opposition to federation was assuaged when its ruler, Sheikh Rashid ibn Said al-Maktum, was made premier (1979–90) of the UAE. In 1990 he was succeeded by his son, Sheikh Maktum ibn Rashid al-Maktum. Area: *c*.3890sq km (1500sq mi). Pop. (1985) 419,104.

Dubček, Alexander (1921–92) Czechoslovak statesman, Communist Party secretary (1968–69). Dubček was elected Party leader at the start of the PRAGUE SPRING. In August 1968 his liberal reforms led to a Soviet invasion, and Dubček was forced to resign and was expelled from the Party. Following the collapse of Czech communism, he was publicly rehabilitated and served as speaker (1989–92) of the federal parliament.

Dubinsky, David (1892–1982) US UNION leader, president (1932–66) of the International Ladies Garment Workers Union (ILGWU), b. Poland. He escaped from a Siberian prison and reached (1911) the United States. In 1936 Dubinsky helped found the AMERICAN LABOR PARTY. He was a founding vice president (1955–69) of the AMERICAN FEDERATION OF LABOR-CONGRESS OF INDUSTRIAL ORGANIZATIONS (AFL-CIO).

Dublin (Baile Átha Cliath) Capital of the Republic of Ireland, at the mouth of the River Liffey on Dublin Bay. Dublin was a Danish town until BRIAN BORU defeated the Danes at the Battle of Clontarf (1014). The Danes regained and held the town until defeated by the English in 1170. Dublin became the seat of colonial government. In the English Civil War, Dublin surrendered (1647) to the Parliamentarians. Oliver CROMWELL marched through the city in 1649. WILLIAM III (OF ORANGE) entered Dublin after victory in the Battle of the BOYNE (1690). Dublin went through a cultural resurgence during the period of GRATTAN'S Parliament (1782–1800). In 1803 Robert EMMETT led a revolt against the Act of Union (1800). In 1867 James Kelly led the FENIAN MOVEMENT in an abortive uprising. In 1882 Lord Frederick CAVENDISH, chief secretary for Ireland, was murdered in Phoenix Park, Dublin. From 1913 a series of strikes against British rule culminated in the EASTER RISING (1916). Dublin was divided and devastated by the bloody civil war (1922–23) that followed the creation of the Irish Free State. Dublin is home to the national legislature, the DAIL ÉIREANN (Irish parliament). The Abbey Theatre was a centre of the late-19th-century Irish literary renaissance. Other sights include Dublin Castle (*c*.1220) and St Patrick's Cathedral. Trinity College, Dublin, was founded in 1590. Pop. (1992) 915,516.

◀ **Drake** Portrait of Sir Francis Drake by Samuel Lane (1780–1859). In 1577 Drake sailed to the W coast of South America. On his journey through the Strait of Magellan, Drake confirmed Ferdinand Magellan's suspicion that Tierra del Fuego was an island and not part of South America. Drake's failure to find a strait in N California that would lead him back to the Atlantic forced him to sail W across the Pacific and consequently circumnavigate the world.

Du Bois, W.E.B. (William Edward Burghardt) (1868–1963) US civil rights leader, writer and educator. In 1905 he co-founded the Niagara movement, which evolved into the NATIONAL ASSOCIATION FOR THE ADVANCEMENT OF COLORED PEOPLE (NAACP). A supporter of PAN-AFRICANISM, Du Bois helped organize the First Pan-African Congress (1919). Works include *The Souls of Black Folk* (1903).

Dubrovnik (It. Ragusa) Adriatic seaport in DALMATIA, Croatia. The city was founded in the 7th century by Roman refugees. With the arrival of Slavs, Dubrovnik formed a bridge between the Latin and Slavic civilizations. Early medieval Dubrovnik had links with both the Byzantine and Venetian states. From the mid-14th century, Dubrovnik was a quasi-independent maritime republic. It flourished as a centre of trade between the Ottoman Empire and Europe, and acted as a place of asylum for persecuted peoples. In 1808 Dubrovnik was captured by Napoleon I. The Congress of VIENNA (1815) awarded the city to Austria. In 1918 it became part of the Kingdom of the Serbs, Croats and Slovenes (later Yugoslavia). In 1991 the old, medieval city of Dubrovnik was badly damaged during Croatia's struggle for independence from the Yugoslav Federation. Pop. (1991) 47,730.

Dudley, John, Duke of Northumberland *See* NORTHUMBERLAND, JOHN DUDLEY, DUKE OF

Dudley, Robert, Earl of Leicester *See* LEICESTER, ROBERT DUDLEY, EARL OF

du Guesclin, Bertrand *See* GUESCLIN, BERTRAND DU

Dulles, Allen Welsh (1893–1969) US public official, brother of John Foster DULLES. He was the first director (1953–61) of the CENTRAL INTELLIGENCE AGENCY (CIA). Dulles strengthened the Agency, but was forced to resign following the disastrous BAY OF PIGS invasion of Cuba.

Dulles, John Foster (1888–1959) US statesman, secretary of state (1953–59), brother of Allen Welsh DULLES. He served (1945–49) as a US delegate to the United Nations (UN). In 1951 Dulles drew up the peace treaty with Japan. As secretary of state to Dwight EISENHOWER, he advocated the proliferation of NUCLEAR WEAPONS to counter the perceived threat of communism.

Duluth, Daniel Greysolon, Sieur (*c*.1639–1710) Canadian explorer, b. France. He explored Lake Superior (1678), founded Fort St Joseph (1686), and was commandant of Fort Frontenac (1695–96). The city of Duluth, Minnesota, United States, founded as a fort (1679), is named after him.

duma National parliament in Russia, principally the Imperial Duma established after the RUSSIAN REVOLUTION OF 1905. Count Sergei WITTE established an upper house and a Duma (lower house elected by suffrage) with limited powers. The first two dumas (1906, 1907) were dissolved rapidly by Tsar NICHOLAS II. The Third Duma (1907–12) passed limited reforms. The Fourth Duma (1912–17) was in perpetual conflict with the tsar. NICHOLAS II dissolved the Fourth Duma, but it refused to disband. The RUSSIAN REVOLUTION (1917) led to its abolition. When the Russian Assembly was created in 1993 the lower house was given the name Duma.

Dumbarton Oaks Conference (1944) Meeting held near Washington, D.C., of representatives from the United States, Britain, the Soviet Union and China. It produced a plan which laid the basis for an international organization to preserve world peace after World War 2; it was the first step towards the founding of the UNITED NATIONS (UN).

Dumont d'Urville, Jules Sébastien César (1790–1842) French navigator. In 1820 he helped secure the *Venus de Milo* statue in Milos for the Louvre, Paris. In 1826–29 d'Urville journeyed to the South Pacific in the *Astrolabe* to search for the lost expedition of LA PÉROUSE. In the process, he charted part of the coast of New Zealand and many islands of Oceania. On a second voyage to the Antarctic (1837–40), d'Urville discovered (1840) Adélie Land (named after his wife).

Dumouriez, Charles François (1739–1823) French general in the FRENCH REVOLUTIONARY WARS. In 1792 he replaced the Marquis de LAFAYETTE as commander of the army. In 1792 Dumouriez defeated the Prussians in the Battle of Valmy (September) and drove the Austrians out of Belgium in the Battle of Jemappes (November). In 1793 Dumouriez's invasion of the Netherlands was repulsed and he deserted to the Austrians.

Dunant, (Jean) Henri (1828–1910) Swiss philanthropist and founder of the International RED CROSS. His account of the Battle of SOLFERINO, *Recollections of*

D

Solferino (1862), inspired the adoption (1864) of the GENEVA CONVENTION for the treatment of wounded and prisoners-of-war. Dunant shared the first Nobel Prize for Peace (1901) with Frédéric Passy.

Dunbar, Battle of (3 September 1650) Conflict in the English CIVIL WAR, fought in SE Scotland. An English force of 14,000 troops, led by Oliver CROMWELL, mounted a surprise counter-attack on a Scottish force of 27,000, led by the Earl of Leven. More than 3000 Scots were killed and the victory ended the cause of CHARLES II in Scotland until the RESTORATION.

Duncan I (*c*.1010–40) King of Scotland (1034–40), grandson of Malcolm II. He added Strathclyde to the Kingdom of Scotland. Duncan was killed in battle by MACBETH, Earl of Moray and Thane of Cawdor.

Dundee, John Graham of Claverhouse, 1st Viscount (*c*.1649–89) Scottish soldier. He defeated the COVENANTERS at Bothwell Brig (1679) and was made a viscount (1688). After the GLORIOUS REVOLUTION (1688–89), "Bonnie Dundee" led a JACOBITE rebellion in support of JAMES II of England. He was mortally wounded in victory at the Battle of KILLIECRANKIE.

Dunkirk (Fr. Dunkerque) Port at the entrance to the Straits of Dover, Nord department, NW France. During World War 2, between 29 May and 3 June 1940, more than 300,000 Allied troops were evacuated from the beaches of Dunkirk, when the German army broke through to the English Channel. In May 1945, the town was liberated by the US Army. Pop. (1990) 70,331.

Duns Scotus, John (1265–1308) Scottish Franciscan theologian and philosopher. He founded a school of SCHOLASTICISM called Scotism. Duns Scotus challenged the ideas of Saint Thomas AQUINAS that faith and reason are complementary, arguing that faith is a matter of love and will.

Dunstan, Saint (*c*.910–88) English monk, archbishop of Canterbury (960–88). He negotiated a peace treaty with the Danes that helped to unify England. Dunstan revived English MONASTICISM, founding new monasteries at Peterborough, Ely and Thorney, and acted as adviser to several kings of WESSEX. His feast day is 19 May.

Dupleix, Joseph François (1697–1763) French colonial administrator, governor general (1742–54) of the French EAST INDIA COMPANY. In 1746 he captured Madras (now CHENNAI), S India. By 1751 Dupleix controlled the Carnatic (now KARNATAKA). His grand scheme of constructing a French empire in India out of the ruins of the MUGHAL EMPIRE was frustrated by the military skill of Robert CLIVE. By 1754 French troops had been ousted from S India and Dupleix was recalled to France.

Duquesne, Fort French fort built (1754) during the FRENCH AND INDIAN WARS, on the site of present-day Pittsburgh, United States. Because of its strategic location, it was the scene of several sieges by the British and Virginians. In 1758 the French burned the fort in retreat. The English rebuilt it as Fort Pitt.

Durham, John George Lambton, 1st Earl of (1792–1840) British statesman. He led the radical wing of the WHIGS. As lord privy seal (1830–33) under his father-in-law Prime Minister Charles GREY, he drafted the Great Reform Bill of 1832. In 1838 Durham was appointed governor general of Canada. He was sacked by Lord MELBOURNE after granting an amnesty to French-Canadian rebels. He then produced the **Durham Report** (1839), which recommended the union of Upper CANADA and Lower Canada and the creation of a largely autonomous Canadian Parliament. *See also* REFORM ACTS

Durrësi (It. Durazzo) City on the Adriatic coast of W Albania; capital of Durrësi province. It was founded (625 BC) as Epidamnus by colonists from CORINTH and Corcyra. The dispute between Corinth and Corcyra over Durrësi helped to hasten the PELOPONNESIAN WAR (431 BC). In 229 BC the city passed to the Romans, who renamed it Dyrrhachium. Ceded to Venice in 1392, it was captured by the Turks in 1501. Durrësi was the capital of Albania from 1913 to 1921. It was occupied by Austria and Italy in World War 1 and by Italy in World War 2. Pop. (1991) 86,900.

Dušan, Stephen *See* STEPHEN DUŠAN

Dutch East India Company *See* EAST INDIA COMPANY, DUTCH

Dutch East Indies Until 1949 the part of Southeast Asia that is now INDONESIA. An overseas territory of the Netherlands, it comprised the Malay archipelago, including SUMATRA, JAVA, KALIMANTAN on BORNEO, SULAWESI, MOLUCCAS and the Lesser Sunda Islands (except EAST TIMOR). The islands were colonized by the Dutch between the early 17th and mid-19th centuries.

Dutch Wars (Anglo-Dutch Wars) Four 17th-century and 18th-century naval conflicts between the Dutch Republic and England arising from commercial rivalry and religious and dynastic differences. The **First Dutch War** (1652–54) was prompted by Oliver CROMWELL's Commonwealth government passing the NAVIGATION ACT (1651). Dutch admiral Maarten TROMP gained control of the English Channel (November 1652). George MONCK's reforms of the British Royal Navy enabled Robert BLAKE to blockade the Dutch coast. Tromp was killed trying to smash the blockade in 1653. The English gained favourable peace terms at the Treaty of Westminster (1654). The **Second Dutch War** (1665–67) followed England's capture of New Amsterdam (now New York). In June 1667 Michiel de RUYTER destroyed the English fleet in dock at Chatham, S England. England was forced to modify its trade laws by the Treaty of BREDA (1667). The **Third Dutch War** (1672–74) began with the invasion of the NETHERLANDS by LOUIS XIV of France, supported by CHARLES II of England and the English navy. In 1672 Louis captured the S Spanish provinces of the Netherlands, but was halted before Amsterdam by the opening of the dykes. In July 1672 William of Orange (later WILLIAM III of England) succeeded Jan de WITT as leader of the Dutch. By the end of 1673 the French had been forced to withdraw from the United Provinces (Dutch Republic). In 1674 England made peace with the Dutch, but Louis continued to prosecute the war until 1678. The Treaties of NIJMEGEN (1678–79) confirmed William's control of the United Provinces but conceded much of the Spanish Netherlands to France. The **Fourth Dutch War** (1780–84) was prompted by covert Dutch support for Britain's American colonies during the American Revolution (1775–83). Britain captured Dutch colonies in the East and West Indies signalling the end of the Dutch Republic's status as a major imperial power. *See also* DEVOLUTION, WAR OF; SPANISH SUCCESSION, WAR OF THE

Dutch West India Company *See* WEST INDIA COMPANY, DUTCH

Duvalier, "Baby Doc" (Jean-Claude) (1951–) Haitian dictator, president (1971–86). He succeeded his father, "Papa Doc" DUVALIER, as president for life. Although Duvalier introduced several important reforms and disbanded the Tonton Macoutes, he retained his father's brutal methods. He was forced by civil unrest into exile in France.

Duvalier, "Papa Doc" (François) (1907–71) Haitian dictator, president (1957–71). He declared himself president for life and relied on the feared Tonton Macoutes, a vigilante group, to consolidate his rule. Under Duvalier's ruthless regime, the longest in Haiti's history, the country's economy severely declined.

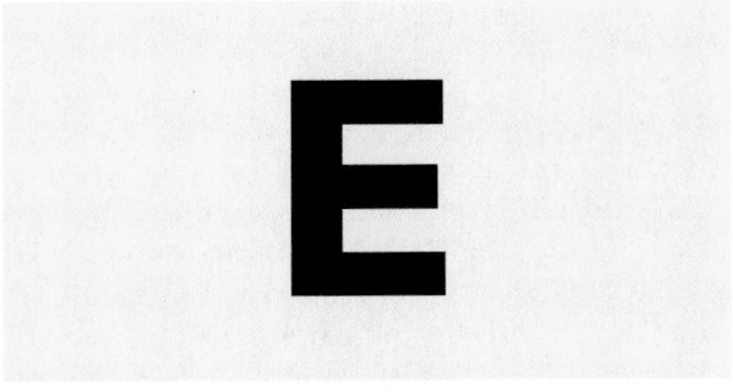

EAM-ELAS Greek National Liberation Front (EAM) and its military wing, the National Popular Liberation Army (ELAS), formed to resist the Axis occupation of Greece during World War 2. EAM-ELAS was dominated by the Communist Party of Greece (KKE). During the winter of 1943–44 it fought its British-backed rival, the Greek Democratic National Army (EDES), to become the most powerful resistance movement in Greece. By October 1944, when the Germans evacuated Greece, EAM-ELAS controlled about two-thirds of the country. In February 1945 EAM-ELAS agreed to a cease-fire, but the subsequent restoration of the monarchy plunged Greece into civil war (1946–49).

Eanes, António dos Santos Ramalho (1935–) Portuguese statesman and general, president (1976–86). He organized the 1974 military coup that overthrew the dictatorship of Marcelo CAETANO. In 1975 Eanes crushed a left-wing revolt. As president, he proved to be a vigorous defender of Portugal's fledgling democracy. He was succeeded by Mário SOARES.

Early, Jubal Anderson (1816–94) Confederate general in the American CIVIL WAR. He was brigadier general at the First Battle of BULL RUN (1861) and fought in the Battle of CHANCELLORSVILLE (1863), the GETTYSBURG CAMPAIGN (1863) and the WILDERNESS CAMPAIGN (1864). Early was routed by General George CUSTER at Waynesboro (March 1865), and General Robert LEE relieved him of command.

Earp, Wyatt Berry Stapp (1848–1929) US law officer. In 1879 he became deputy sheriff of Tombstone, Arizona. In 1881 the Earp brothers (Wyatt, Virgil and Morgan) and "Doc" Holliday fought the Clanton gang in the gunfight at the O.K. Corral

East African Community (1967–77) Association of East African nations, comprising Tanzania, Kenya and Uganda. The East African Community was formed by the Treaty of Kampala (1967) to develop joint strategies for economic, trade and communication development. The Community began to disintegrate after the accession (1971) of Idi AMIN in Uganda. The Community was refounded in 1999.

Eastern Orthodox Church *See* ORTHODOX CHURCH, EASTERN

Eastern Question Term used to describe the political problems in SE Europe due to the decline of the OTTOMAN EMPIRE during the 19th century. Rivalries between the Great Powers were complicated by nationalism in the Balkans leading to independence for countries such as Serbia and Romania. Russia and Austria sought to extend their influence and territory. Britain generally supported the Turks against Russian expansionism, but from 1898 Germany replaced Britain as the Turks' chief European ally. Diplomacy frequently gave way to war, notably the CRIMEAN WAR (1853–56), RUSSO-TURKISH WAR (1877–78) and the BALKAN WARS (1912–13). The final collapse of the Ottoman Empire in World War 1 provided the "answer" to the Eastern Question, but the region remains unstable.

Eastern Roman Empire *See* BYZANTINE EMPIRE

Easter Rising (24 April 1916) Rebellion by Irish nationalists against British rule, led by Patrick PEARSE of the Irish Republican Brotherhood (IRB) and James CONNOLLY of SINN FÉIN. An arms shipment from Germany was intercepted by the British navy and Roger CASEMENT (the IRB's contact with Germany) was arrested, but the insurrection went ahead as planned. On Easter Monday, *c.*1500 volunteers seized buildings in Dublin, including the General Post Office, and proclaimed Ireland a republic. By 29 April, the British had crushed the rising. Sixteen of the ringleaders were executed and 2000 people imprisoned. In 1917 Eamon DE VALERA was granted an amnesty and nationalist sentiment produced an electoral victory for SINN FÉIN. *See also* FENIAN MOVEMENT

East India Company, Dutch (1602–1799) (United East India Company) Dutch company founded (1602) to protect trade in the DUTCH EAST INDIES and to help in the war against Spain. It was granted a monopoly on trade between the Cape of Good Hope and the Strait of Magellan. In 1619 the Company established its headquarters in Batavia (now JAKARTA). Governor General Jan Pieterszoon COEN established trading posts in the Banda Islands (1621) and Formosa (now Taiwan, 1622), and expelled the British and Portuguese from Indonesia. In 1638 Governor General Anthony van DIEMEN invaded Ceylon (now Sri Lanka) and in the 1640s the Dutch founded commercial posts both here and on the SE coast of India. From *c.*1650 they were the principal power in the East Indies. In 1652 the Company established a colony at the Cape of Good Hope. In the 18th century, the Company's focus changed from trade to agricultural production. It also became riddled with corruption and debt-ridden. In 1799 the Company was dissolved and its territorial possessions were taken over by the Dutch government. *See also* CAPE PROVINCE; EAST INDIA COMPANY, ENGLISH; EAST INDIA COMPANY, FRENCH

East India Company, English (1600–1873) English company chartered (1600) by ELIZABETH I to break the Dutch monopoly in the spice trade with the East Indies. In 1612 the English East India Company opened its first trading post at Surat, W central India. After the Amboina Massacre (1623), in which ten English merchants were among those executed for allegedly plotting to overthrow the Dutch, the Company surrendered control of the Spice Islands (MOLUCCAS) to the Dutch EAST INDIA COMPANY and concentrated on trade with India. The English East India Company opened further trading posts at Madras (now CHENNAI, 1639), Bombay (now MUMBAI, 1668), and CALCUTTA (1690). It exported cotton, silk, indigo and spices. As the MUGHAL EMPIRE crumbled, the Company began to intervene in Indian politics. In 1698 its monopoly was challenged by the chartering of a rival company, but the two companies merged as the United Company of Merchants in 1708. In the 18th century its trade was threatened by the expansion of the French EAST INDIA COMPANY under Joseph DUPLEIX. Robert CLIVE thwarted French ambitions and captured BENGAL in the Battle of Plassey (1757). In 1765 the Company received the right to collect revenue from the Mughal emperor. Corruption and financial mismanagement led to the intervention of the British government. The Regulating Act (1773) established a governor general to control the Company in India. Warren HASTINGS became the first governor general of Bengal. William PITT (THE YOUNGER)'s East India Act of 1784 gave the British government direct responsibility for British activities in India. In the 19th century, the Company financed the tea trade with illegal opium exports to China – a policy that provoked the first OPIUM WAR (1839–42). In 1813 the Company lost its commercial monopoly and from 1834 it was purely an administrative arm of colonial government in India. The INDIAN MUTINY (1857) led to its powers being transferred to the British crown and the East India Company was dissolved in 1873. *See also* BRITISH EMPIRE

▲ Dutch East India Company The East Indiaman ship shown here was used by Companies to transport goods between Europe and S Asia from the 16th to 19th century.

East India Company, French (1664–1789) French company conceived by Jean Baptiste COLBERT and chartered (1664) by LOUIS XIV in order to compete for trade in the East Indies. The French Company of the East Indies (1664–1719) foundered in the face of competition from the Dutch EAST INDIA COMPANY and was absorbed (1719) by the Company of the Indies. This collapsed in the French economic crisis of 1720 and was reorganized as the French Company of the Indies (1720–89). The Company established colonies in Mauritius (1721) and Mahé, SW India (1724). In 1742 it appointed Joseph DUPLEIX as governor general of French India. Dupleix captured Madras in 1746 but his ambitious plans to expand French India were thwarted by Robert CLIVE. In 1761 Britain captured Pondicherry, capital of French India. The Company withered and was abolished during the FRENCH REVOLUTION. *See also* MISSISSIPPI BUBBLE

East Timor Independent nation in SE Asia. The capital is Dili. From *c.*1520 Portuguese spice traders began to settle on the island of Timor, largest and most easterly of the Lesser Sunda Islands. When the Dutch landed in 1620, they settled on the W side. During World War 2, Timor was occupied by the Japanese. In 1950 West Timor became part of the Nusa Tenggara Timur province of the newly created Republic of INDONESIA. On 28 November 1975, the Portuguese abandoned East Timor and the East Timor independence movement, FRETILIN, declared independence. Nine days later Indonesia invaded, and annexed it as the 27th province of the Republic of Indonesia in 1976. The occupation claimed the lives of *c.*200,000 Timorese people. most notably when the Indonesian army massacred *c.*270 demonstrators in Dili (1991). The rebel leader Xanana Gusmao was arrested in 1992. East Timor's spiritual leader Bishop Carlos Belo and José Ramos-Horta, the exiled FRETILIN representative at the United Nations (UN), were jointly awarded the 1996 Nobel Prize for Peace. Following a vote for independence in the August 1999 referendum, East Timor erupted in violence as pro-Indonesian militias sought to destabilize the country. An Australian-led international force (Interfet) was deployed to restore peace and order. Area: 14,874sq km (5743sq mi). Pop. (1990) 747,750.

Eban, Abba Solomon (1915–) Israeli statesman, foreign minister (1966–74), b. South Africa. He served concurrently (1949–59) as Israel's first chief delegate to the United Nations (UN) and ambassador to the United States. Eban was deputy prime minister (1963–66) under Levi ESHKOL. As foreign minister, he strengthened relations with the United States and negotiated settlements to the SIX-DAY WAR (1967) and the YOM KIPPUR WAR (1973). He wrote *Personal Witness* (1992). *See also* ARAB-ISRAELI WARS

Ebert, Friedrich (1871–1925) German statesman, first president (1919–25) of the WEIMAR REPUBLIC. In 1913 he succeeded August BEBEL as leader of the SOCIAL DEMOCRATIC PARTY (SPD). As president, Ebert crushed the communist uprising (1919) of the SPARTACUS LEAGUE and the right-wing KAPP PUTSCH (1920). He faced concerted opposition to the Treaty of VERSAILLES (1919). Ebert died in office. He was succeeded by Paul von HINDENBURG.

Ebla Influential city-state in the third millennium BC, located in modern N Syria. In 1975 archaeologists discovered more than 15,000 clay tablets (*c.*2300 BC) recording the city's development. The tablets contain the earliest known reference to JERUSALEM.

Ecevit, Bülent (1925–) Turkish statesman, prime minister (1974, 1977, 1978–79, 1998–). In 1972 he succeeded Ismet INÖNÜ as leader of the Republican People's

Party (CHP). In 1974, after the overthrow of Archbishop Makarios, Ecevit ordered the Turkish invasion of Cyprus. He then resigned, hoping to force an election but Süleyman Demirel formed a coalition government. Ecevit and Demirel alternately led a succession of coalition administrations until the military seized power in 1980. In 1984 Ecevit formed the Democratic Left Party (DSP). In 1999, in his fourth term in office, Ecevit was faced with the task of reconstruction after a devastating earthquake in NW Turkey.

Eck, Johann Maier von (1486–1543) German Roman Catholic theologian. He held a public debate (1519) with Martin Luther in Leipzig, E central Germany. Eck forced Luther to deny the authority of the Council of Constance and engineered his excommunication for heresy (1521). He helped compose the Augsburg Confession (1530).

Economic Community of West African States (ECOWAS) Organization founded (1975) to promote the economic, cultural and social development of West Africa through mutual cooperation. A revised treaty (1993) sought to increase collaboration in fiscal, legislative and defence matters. ECOWAS is committed to liberalization of trade. Its headquarters are in Abuja, Nigeria.

Ecuador *See* country feature

ecumenical council (general council) In Christianity, convention of church leaders. Roman Catholics regard the councils as canonical (binding) only when they have been ratified by the papacy. The Eastern Orthodox Church recognizes the first seven councils: Nicaea, First Council of (325); Constantinople, First Council of (381); Ephesus, Council of (431); Chalcedon, Council of (451); Constantinople, Second Council of (553); Constantinople, Third Council of (680) and Nicaea, Second Council of (787). Roman Catholics recognize a further 14 councils, which have all been held in Western Europe. The most recent was the Second Vatican Council (1962–65). Since the Reformation, the councils have been restricted to Roman Catholics. Adherents of Protestantism recognize the first four ecumenical councils, but do not regard conciliar decisions as canonical. The first eight councils were called on theological grounds and determined the nature of orthodoxy and heresy. The remaining councils have mainly concerned themselves with issues of church discipline and morals. Conciliar theory, which argued that an ecumenical council is superior to the pope, was central to the resolution of the Great Schism at the Council of Constance (1414–18). The Council of Trent (1545–63) played a leading role in the Counter-Reformation. *See also* Basel, Council of; Constantinople, Fourth Council of; Ephesus, Council of; Lateran Councils

Eddy, Mary Baker (1821–1910) US founder of Christian Science (1879). Her doctrine of healing based on the Bible was expounded in *Science and Health With Key to the Scriptures* (1875). In 1879 Eddy organized the Church of Christ, Scientist, and actively directed the movement until her death.

Eden, Sir (Robert) Anthony, 1st Earl of Avon (1897–1977) British statesman, prime minister (1955–57). In 1935 he became Britain's youngest foreign secretary. In 1938 Eden resigned in protest at the appeasement policy of Prime Minister Neville Chamberlain. He served again as foreign secretary (1940–45, 1951–55) under Winston Churchill and succeeded Churchill as prime minister and leader of the Conservative Party. Deteriorating health and his mishandling of the Suez Crisis (1963) forced Eden to resign. He was succeeded by Harold Macmillan.

Edgar (943–75) King of England (959–75), younger son of Edmund I. In 957 he succeeded his brother Edwy as king of Mercia and Northumberland. In 958 Edgar recalled Saint Dunstan from exile and assisted in the revival of monasticism. He was succeeded by his son, Edward the Martyr. *See also* Danelaw

Edgar the Aetheling (*c*.1050–1125) English prince, grandson of Edmund II. He was heir to Edward the Confessor, but was overlooked in favour of Harold II. On Harold's death at the Battle of Hastings (1066), Edgar led resistance to William I (the Conqueror) and formed an alliance with Malcolm III of Scotland. In 1074 he made peace with William. Edgar fought for Robert II, Duke of Normandy, against Henry I of England and was captured at the Battle of Tinchebrai (1106).

Edgehill, Battle of (23 October 1642) First conflict in the English Civil War, fought near Banbury, Oxfordshire, central England. The 11,000 Royalists, led by Prince Rupert, were outnumbered by the 13,000-strong Parliamentarian force under Robert Devereux, 3rd Earl of Essex. The Battle of Edgehill was inconclusive and heavy losses were sustained on both sides.

Edinburgh, Duke of *See* Philip, Prince, Duke of Edinburgh

Edinburgh Capital of Scotland, in Lothian region. The city grew steadily when Malcolm III made Edinburgh Castle his residence (11th century), and it became the capital of Scotland in the early 15th century. In the 18th and 19th centuries, Edinburgh flourished as a cultural centre around figures such as David Hume, Adam Smith, Robert Burns and Sir Walter Scott. Sites include: Palace of Holyroodhouse (official residence of the monarch in Scotland); Chapel of St Margaret (part of Edinburgh Castle and the city's oldest building); the Royal Mile (linking the Castle with Holyroodhouse); the 15th-century St Giles Cathedral; the home of Protestant reformer John Knox; and Princes Street. The University of Edinburgh was founded in 1583. The Scottish Parliament, first elected in 1999, is based in Edinburgh. Edinburgh has held an international arts festival since 1947. Pop. (1991) 418,914.

Edirne (Adrianople) Fortified city at the confluence of the rivers Meric and Tundzha, Thrace, NW Turkey. Rebuilt by the Roman Emperor Hadrian (*c*.AD 125) as Adrianopolis, it was the scene of a Roman defeat (378) by the Visigoths. In 1361 Edirne was captured by the Turks and served as capital of the Ottoman Empire until the fall of Constantinople in 1453. The city was captured (1829, 1879) by the Russians during the Russo-Turkish Wars. In 1913 Edirne fell to Bulgaria in the first of the Balkan Wars but was restored to Turkey after the Second Balkan War. In 1920 Edirne was ceded to Greece. It was returned to Turkey in 1923. Pop. (1990) 102,300.

Edison, Thomas Alva (1847–1931) US inventor. With little formal education, he became the most prolific inventor of his generation. In 1876 Edison opened a laboratory in Menlo Park, New Jersey. Here, he invented the carbon transmitter for telephones (1876) and the phonograph or record player (1877). Using a carbon filament, Edison invented the first commercially viable electric light (21 October 1879). In New York City he built (1881–82) the world's first permanent electric power plant for distributing electric light. In 1892 most of his

ECUADOR

AREA: 283,560sq km (109,483sq mi)
POPULATION: 10,980,972
CAPITAL (POPULATION): Quito (1,100,847)
GOVERNMENT: Multiparty republic
ETHNIC GROUPS: Mestizo 40%, Native American 40%, White 15%, Black 5%
LANGUAGES: Spanish (official)
RELIGIONS: Christianity (Roman Catholic 92%)
GDP PER CAPITA (1995): US$4220

Republic in NW South America. In the late 15th century, the Incas conquered the kingdom of Quito. In 1532 Spanish forces, under Francisco Pizarro, defeated the Incas at Cajamarca and established the Spanish Viceroyalty of Quito. A revolutionary war culminated in Antonio José de Sucre's defeat of the Spanish at the Battle of Mount Pichincha (1822). Simón Bolívar negotiated the admittance of Quito to the Federation of Gran Colombia, along with Colombia and Venezuela.

In 1830, led by Venezuelan General Juan José Flores, Ecuador became an independent country. The liberal administration (1834–39) of Vicente Rocafuerta was ousted by Flores, who continued to impose his dictatorial rule until forced into exile in 1845. From 1845 to 1860 Ecuador was rendered almost ungovernable by the bitter conflict between the liberal, commercial interests of the coastal regions and the conservative aristocracy of the highlands, backed by the Roman Catholic Church. In 1860 General García Moreno imposed order by authoritarian means. In 1875 García was assassinated and the internecine rivalry between liberals and conservatives resurfaced. In 1897 General Eloy Alfaro seized control and instigated a range of social reforms. After World War 1 economic inequality fostered popular unrest, and from 1925 to 1940 Ecuador was ruled by a succession of short-lived military juntas. The Treaty of Rio (1942) concluded a disastrous war with Peru in which Ecuador was forced to cede more than 50% of its Amazonian territory.

In 1944 José María Velasco Ibarro became president after a coup. The presidency (1948–52) of Galo Plaza Lasso was an unprecedented period of social reform. Velasco's third term (1952–60) continued the improvements to Ecuador's infrastructure. He was succeeded by Camilo Ponce Enríquez, the first Conservative leader for 60 years. In 1960 Velasco briefly returned to power. His vice president and successor, Julio Arosemena Monroy, was ousted by a military junta in 1963. In 1966 the military appointed a provisional government. Velsaco was re-elected in 1968. In 1970, faced with student riots and economic recession, Velasco established a dictatorship. In 1972 he was deposed by an army coup. In 1979 Ecuador returned to democracy.

During the 1980s, a succession of administrations failed both to revive the domestic economy and to confront the poverty of the Native-American population. The free-market reforms and austerity programme (1992–96) of President Sixto Durán Ballen provoked civil unrest. In 1995 a border war with Peru led to the establishment of a demilitarized zone. In 1996 Ballen was defeated by Abdala Bucaram, but in 1997 Bucaram was declared mentally incompetent and removed from office. Jamil Mahaud was elected president in 1998.

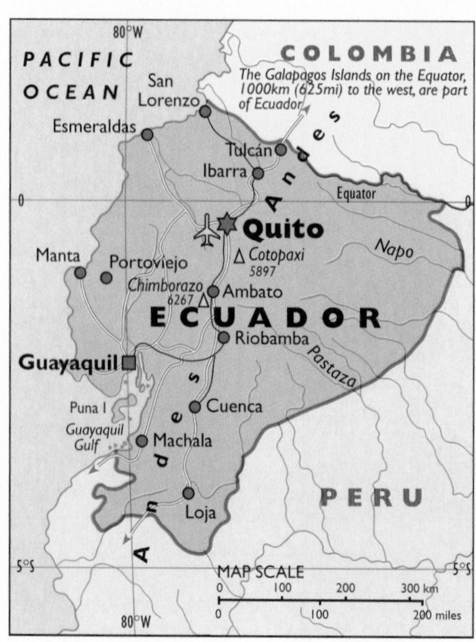

companies were merged into the General Electric Company (GEC). In 1914 Edison developed an experimental talking motion-picture. By the time of his death, he had patented more than 1300 inventions.

Edmund, Saint (*c*.1175–1240) English churchman and scholar, b. Edmund Rich. He was archbishop of Canterbury (1234–40). Edmund taught at Oxford University and preached (1227) in favour of the Sixth Crusade. His outspoken opposition to Henry III led to the king gaining ecclesiastical power and Edmund retired to France. His feast day is 16 November.

Edmund (the Martyr), Saint (*c*.841–*c*.870) King of East Anglia (*c*.855–70). In *c*.870 he was defeated in battle against the Danes. By tradition, Edmund died in captivity after refusing to renounce his Christian faith. A shrine to him was built at Bury St Edmunds. His feast day is 20 November.

Edmund I (921–46) King of the English (939–46), half-brother and successor of Athlestan. On his accession, Edmund was faced with a Viking invasion led by Olaf Guthfrithson. He was forced to relinquish Northumbria and much of the E Midlands. Between 942 and 944 Edmund regained most of the territory and reunited England.

Edmund II (*c*.980–1016) (Edmund Ironside) King of the English (1016), son and successor of Ethelred II (the Unready). In 1015 he became, through marriage, ruler of the Five Boroughs of the Danelaw. When the Danish king Canute II (the Great) invaded England in 1015, Edmund led the resistance against him. Edmund was decisively defeated at the Battle of Ashingdon (1016) and was forced to accept the division of the kingdom, retaining only Wessex. He died shortly after, leaving Canute as sole ruler.

Edo Japanese city, renamed Tokyo when it became the official capital and imperial residence in 1868. Edo was the seat of government under the Tokugawa shogunate (1603–1868), when the emperor lived at Kyoto. The Edo period was an era of unparalleled peace, economic advance and culture. *See also* Meiji Restoration

Edo, Treaty of (1858) Trade agreement between Japan and the United States. Negotiated with Japan by Townsend Harris (1804–78), it established that five ports would be opened to US trade in addition to the two ports opened by the Treaty of Kanagawa (1854). It was also agreed that US citizens living in the ports would not be subject to Japanese law. The Treaty, which also included provisions on tariffs, served as a model for subsequent treaties between Japan and European powers. *See also* Perry, Matthew Calbraith

Edom (Idumea) Ancient mountainous kingdom between the Dead Sea and the Gulf of Aqaba, astride the modern Jordan-Israel border. According to the Old Testament, it was originally settled by the descendants of Esau. The Edomites were traditional enemies of the Israelites. In the 10th century BC, Edom was captured by King David. In the 8th century BC, it became an independent kingdom. In the late 2nd century BC, Edom was conquered by John Hyrcanus and its peoples forcibly integrated with the Jews. Herod the Great was an Edomite.

Edward I (1239–1307) King of England (1272–1307), son and successor of Henry III. He married Eleanor of Castile (1254) and later Margaret of France (1299). His suppression of the Barons' War (1263–65), led by Simon de Montfort, made him king in all but name. Edward joined the Ninth Crusade (1270) and was crowned on his return (1274). He killed (1282) Llywelyn ap Gruffudd in the process of conquering Wales (1272–84) and incorporating it into England. In 1296, after John Balliol's alliance with France, Edward invaded Scotland and captured the coronation stone from Scone. William Wallace and Robert I (the Bruce) led Scottish resistance. He lost much of Gascony to Philip III and Philip IV of France. Edward's foreign ambitions led to the formation of the Model Parliament (1295). His domestic reforms are central to Britain's legal and constitutional history: the Statutes of Westminster (1275, 1285, 1290) codified common law. His son, Edward II, inherited high taxation and the enmity of Scotland.

Edward II (1284–1327) King of England (1307–27), son and successor of Edward I. Edward's reliance on his friend and adviser Piers Gaveston alienated his barons. The barons drafted the Ordinances of 1311, which restricted royal power and banished Gaveston. In 1312 they killed Gaveston. Renewing his father's campaign against the Scots, Edward was routed by Robert I (the Bruce) at the Battle of Bannockburn (1314). In 1321 Thomas, 2nd Earl of Lancaster, led an unsuccessful revolt against the king and his new favourite, Hugh le Despenser. In 1325 Edward's estranged queen, Isabella, went as envoy to France. In 1326 she formed an army with her lover, Roger Mortimer, which invaded England and forced Edward to abdicate in favour of his son, Edward III. Edward II was murdered in Berkeley Castle, Gloucestershire, England.

Edward III (1312–77) King of England (1327–77), son and successor of Edward II. For the first three years of his reign, his mother, Isabella, and Roger Mortimer wielded all political power. In 1330 Edward mounted a successful coup. His victory over David II of Scotland at the Battle of Halidon Hill (1334) aided the cause of Edward Balliol. Edward's reign was dominated by the outbreak (1337) of the Hundred Years' War. He led several campaigns to France, won a famous victory at Crécy (1346), and claimed the title king of France, although only conquering Calais. His son, Edward the Black Prince, captured John II (the Good) of France at the Battle of Poitiers (1356). During Edward III's reign, the Black Death accelerated the abolition of serfdom. Parliament was divided into two Houses and permanently located at Westminster. In old age, Edward's sons, Edward the Black Prince and John of Gaunt, took over government. He was succeeded by his grandson, Richard II.

Edward IV (1442–83) King of England (1461–70, 1471–83). On the death (1460) of his father, Richard, Duke of York, in the Wars of the Roses, Edward became the Yorkist candidate for the throne. He was crowned after the defeat of the Lancastrians at Towton. When the powerful Earl of Warwick changed sides, Edward was forced into exile but returned to defeat Warwick at the Battle of Barnet (1471). He encouraged trade, restored order and enforced royal absolutism. Edward died leaving two young sons, "the princes in the Tower", but the throne was usurped by his brother, Richard III.

Edward V (1470–83?) King of England for 77 days in 1483, son and successor of Edward IV. His uncle, the Duke of Gloucester, placed Edward and his younger brother, Richard, in the Tower of London, taking the throne for himself as Richard III. The disappearance of "the princes in the Tower" was attributed to Richard although some suspect Henry VII.

Edward VI (1537–53) King of England (1547–53), son of Henry VIII and Jane Seymour. He reigned under two regents, the dukes of Somerset (1547–49) and Northumberland (1549–53). A devout Protestant, Edward endorsed Archbishop Thomas Cranmer's revision of the Book of Common Prayer (1552). Clever but frail, Edward died of tuberculosis after willing the crown to Northumberland's daughter-in-law, Lady Jane Grey, to exclude his Catholic sister, Mary I.

Edward VII (1841–1910) King of Great Britain and Ireland (1901–10), son of Queen Victoria. As Prince of Wales, Edward was excluded from government by Victoria because of his lifestyle, which involved him in a number of social scandals. As king, Edward restored court pageantry and contributed to the Entente Cordiale with France. He was succeeded by his son, George V.

Edward VIII (1894–1972) King of Great Britain and Ireland (1936), subsequently Duke of Windsor. Edward's proposed marriage to an American divorcee, Wallis Simpson, was opposed by Stanley Baldwin's government. Edward refused to back down and was forced to abdicate (10 December) after a 325-day reign. In 1937 the couple married and embarked on a controversial trip to Germany, where they met Adolf Hitler and other senior Nazi officials. *See also* abdication crisis

Edwards, Jonathan (1703–58) US revivalist minister and theologian. A powerful preacher in Massachusetts (1729–50), he gained a wide following. With his Calvinist themes of predestination and man's dependence on God, Edwards was a leading figure in the "Great Awakening" movement. *See also* Calvinism; Whitefield, George

Edward the Black Prince (1330–76) Prince of Wales (1343–76), eldest son of Edward III of England. In the Hundred Years' War, he distinguished himself at the Battle of Crécy (1346) and captured John II (the Good) of France at the Battle of Poitiers (1356). As ruler (1362–71) of Aquitaine, he alienated his French subjects, who launched a rebellion in 1368. Edward employed mercenaries to suppress the revolt, resulting in a massacre at Limoges in 1370 and his return to England in 1371. He ensured the accession of his son as Richard II.

Edward the Confessor, Saint (1002–66) King of England (1042–66), son of Ethelred II (the Unready). Edward spent much of his early life in Normandy while England was under Danish rule. He succeeded Hardecanute (1042) with the support of Earl Godwin, whose daughter he married, but his perceived favouritism of the Normans later provoked a rebellion from Godwin's faction. Edward's reign is noted for the founding of Westminster Abbey. His nickname resulted from his piety and, having taken a vow of chastity, he produced no heir. Although said to have promised the throne to William I (the Conqueror), Edward acknowledged Harold II, son of Godwin, as his rightful heir. He was canonized in 1161. His feast day is 13 October.

Edward the Elder (d.925) King of Wessex (899–925), son and successor to Alfred (the Great). Edward completed the reconquest of the S Danelaw (918), and by 920 he was considered overlord by the rulers of Northumbria and Wales. He was succeeded by his son, Athelstan.

Edward the Martyr (*c*.962–978) King of England (975–78). He was murdered, perhaps by his stepmother, and succeeded by his step-brother Ethelred II (the Unready). Miracles were reported at his grave, and he was popularly regarded as a saint.

Egbert (d.839) King of Wessex (802–39). In 825 he defeated the Mercians at Ellendun, Wiltshire, and went on to gain Essex, Kent, Surrey and Sussex. Egbert's conquest of Mercia was short-lived, but in 838 he gained control of Cornwall. Egbert laid the foundations for the supremacy of Wessex.

▲ **Edward I** of England is depicted in Jean Froissart's *Chronicle of France* (14th century) paying homage to Philip IV of France for the Duchy of Aquitaine (*c*.1285).

E

Egmont, Lamoral, Graaf van (1522–68) Flemish general and statesman. In 1559, after defeating the French at St Quentin (1557) and Gravelines (1558), he was made stadtholder of Flanders and Artois by PHILIP II. Egmont, William, Prince of Orange (later WILLIAM II) and Graaf van HOORNE opposed the persecution of Protestants in the Spanish Netherlands (now BELGIUM) and helped secure the removal of Cardinal GRANVELLE from government (1564). In 1565 Egmont, William and Hoorne resigned from the council of state in protest over the continuing infringements on religious liberty. Despite their refusal to join William's armed revolt, Egmont and Hoorne were arrested by the Duke of ALBA and publicly beheaded for treason. He is the hero of Goethe's drama *Egmont* (1788).

Egypt *See* country feature

Egypt, ancient *See* feature article

Egyptology Study of ancient EGYPT, its people and its antiquities. Important landmarks in Egyptology include the discovery of the ROSETTA STONE, the Temple of Amon and the Tomb of TUTANKHAMUN at LUXOR, and the moving of the temples at ABU SIMBEL.

Eichmann, (Karl) Adolf (1906–62) German NAZI PARTY leader, head of the notorious subsection IV-B-4 of the Reich Central Security Office during WORLD WAR 2. Eichmann supervised the fulfilment of the Nazi policies of deportation, slave labour and mass murder in the CONCENTRATION CAMPS that led to the deaths of *c.*6 million Jews. In 1945 he escaped to Argentina but was abducted (1960) by the Israeli secret service. He was tried and executed in Israel.

Einstein, Albert (1879–1955) US physicist, b. Germany. In 1905 Einstein published four papers that revolutionized physical science. "The Electrodynamics of Moving Bodies" announced his special theory of relativity, which discarded the notion of absolute motion in favour of the hypothesis that the speed of light is constant for all observers in uniform (unaccelerated) motion. Measurements in one uniformly moving system can be correlated with measurements in another uniform system, if their **relative** velocity is known. It asserted that the speed of light was the maximum velocity attainable in the Universe. A corollary of this special theory – the equivalence of mass and energy ($E = mc^2$) – was put forward in a second paper. A third paper, on Brownian movement, confirmed the atomic theory of matter. Lastly, Einstein explained the photoelectric effect in terms of quanta or photons of light. For this insight, which forms the basis of modern quantum theory, Einstein received the 1921 Nobel Prize for physics. He extended his special theory into a **general theory** of relativity (1916) that incorporated systems in non-uniform (accelerated) motion. Fearful of the rise of the Nazi Party in Germany, Einstein accepted a post (1933–55) at the Institute of Advanced Study, Princeton, New Jersey, United States. In 1940 he became a US citizen.

Eire *See* IRELAND, REPUBLIC OF

Eisenhower, Dwight David ("Ike") (1890–1969) Thirty-fourth president of the United States (1953–61). From 1935 to 1939, he served as an aide to General Douglas MACARTHUR in the Philippines. In June 1942 Eisenhower was appointed commander of US troops in Europe by General George MARSHALL. In July 1942 he headed the Allied NORTH AFRICA CAMPAIGN – the first major Allied victory of WORLD WAR 2. Eisenhower went on to direct the invasion of Italy. In December 1943, he became supreme commander of the Allied forces in Western Europe. On D-Day (6 June 1944), Eisenhower launched the NORMANDY LANDINGS that resulted in the liberation of Europe. In 1945 he succeeded General Marshall as chief of staff to President Harry TRUMAN. Eisenhower's account of the war, *Crusade in Europe* (1948), became a popular bestseller. In 1950 he became supreme commander of the NORTH ATLANTIC TREATY ORGANIZATION (NATO). In the 1952 presidential election Eisenhower and his Republican running mate Richard NIXON secured an easy victory over their Democrat challengers Adlai STEVENSON and John Sparkman. In domestic affairs, Eisenhower faced the anti-communist hysteria whipped up by Senator Joseph MCCARTHY. In foreign affairs, Eisenhower and his Secretary of State John Foster DULLES enforced a prompt end (1953) to the KOREAN WAR and helped to create the SOUTHEAST ASIA TREATY ORGANIZATION (SEATO) as a bulwark against the expansion of communism. In 1956 Eisenhower and Nixon won a landslide victory over Stevenson and Estes KEFAUVER. The crisis in the Middle East, prompted by General Abdel NASSER's nationalization of the SUEZ CANAL, led to the formulation of the EISENHOWER DOCTRINE. In 1957 Eisenhower ordered Federal troops into Little Rock, Arkansas, to end racial segregation in schools. The COLD WAR intensified after Fidel CASTRO overthrew the Batista regime in Cuba and a US spy-plane was shot down over Soviet airspace (May 1960). Eisenhower was succeeded as president by John KENNEDY. *See also* CIVIL RIGHTS ACTS; KHRUSHCHEV, NIKITA SERGEIEVICH

Eisenhower Doctrine Principle of US foreign policy articulated by President Dwight EISENHOWER and approved by Congress in 1957. After the SUEZ CRISIS (October 1956), Eisenhower pledged economic assistance or military aid to protect the independence of any Middle Eastern government. The Doctrine was intended to check Soviet influence in the Middle East and led to the deployment (1958) of 10,000 US troops in Lebanon. It lapsed after the death (1959) of US Secretary of State John Foster DULLES. *See also* TRUMAN DOCTRINE

ejido (Sp. "common land") Land held under communal ownership in Mexico. Part of it is farmed by individuals who can pass on their plots to their heirs. Under Spanish COLONIALISM, the ejidos began to disappear with the introduction of ENCOMIENDAS. In the 20th century, the concept of the ejido was revived by Emiliano ZAPATA. In the 1930s, President Lázaro CÁRDENAS broke up the large HACIENDAS, redistributing *c.*16.8 million ha (41.5 million acres) of land to the ejidos.

El Alamein *See* ALAMEIN, BATTLE OF EL

Elam Ancient country of MESOPOTAMIA (now SW Iran). The capital, SUSA, was the site of an early civilization, probably dating back to the late 4th millennium BC. In the late 3rd millennium Elam was dominated by AKKADIA. In the early 2nd millennium, Elam invaded BABYLONIA. Elam's expansion was checked by HAMMURABI in the 18th century BC. In the late 13th century BC, it re-emerged as a major force, building an empire that stretched to the outskirts of PERSEPOLIS. In the 12th century BC, Susa was captured by the Babylonian king Nebuchadnezzar I. In 640 BC Elam was invaded by the Assyrian king

EGYPT

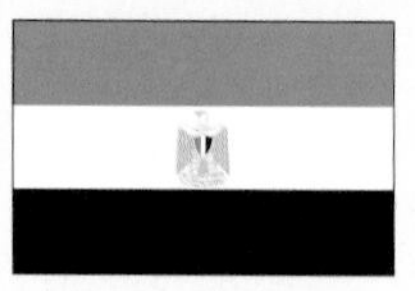

AREA: 1,001,450sq km (386,660 sq mi)
POPULATION: 55,163,000
CAPITAL (POPULATION): Cairo (6,663,000)
GOVERNMENT: Republic
ETHNIC GROUPS: Egyptian 99%
LANGUAGES: Arabic (official), French, English
RELIGIONS: Islam (Sunni Muslim 94%), Christianity (mainly Coptic Christian 6%)
GDP PER CAPITA (1995): US$3820

Country in NE Africa. Its capital, CAIRO, is Africa's largest city. The region N of Cairo is often called **Lower** Egypt; S of Cairo, **Upper** Egypt. The Egyptian state was formed in *c.*3100 BC. The Old Kingdom saw the building of the PYRAMIDS at Giza. The ruins of the Middle Kingdom's capital at LUXOR bear testament to Egypt's imperial power (*see* EGYPT, ANCIENT).

In 332 BC Egypt was conquered by ALEXANDER III (THE GREAT) and the capital moved to ALEXANDRIA. The fall of CLEOPATRA heralded the hegemony of the Roman, and subsequently the Byzantine, empire. From the 2nd century AD until 451 Alexandria was the intellectual centre of the Christian Church, producing celebrated figures such as Saint ATHANASIUS and Saint CYRIL (OF ALEXANDRIA). In 451 the Council of CHALCEDON condemned the creed of MONOPHYSITISM that had been adopted by the Egyptian COPTIC CHURCH. This led to the isolation of the Copts from other Christians.

In 642 Egypt was conquered by the Muslim Arab UMAYYAD dynasty, which in 750 was supplanted by the ABBASIDS. Arabic became the official language and ISLAM the dominant religion. Under the FATIMIDS (969–1171), Cairo became a centre of SHIITE culture. SALADIN's rule (1171–93) was notable for the defeat of the CRUSADES. His AYYUBID dynasty was overthrown (1250) by MAMLUK soldier-slaves. In 1517 Egypt was conquered by the OTTOMANS, who ruled for nearly three centuries.

Egypt was occupied (1798–1801) by the French under NAPOLEON. The French were expelled by MUHAMMAD ALI, who created the modern Egyptian state. The completion (1867) of the SUEZ CANAL spurred British imperial ambitions. In 1882 Britain subdued Cairo, and the British army remained even after Egypt became an independent monarchy (1922) under FUAD I. Fuad was succeeded by FAROUK (r.1936–52). The creation (1948) of Israel saw the involvement of Egypt in the first of the ARAB-ISRAELI WARS.

In 1953 the monarchy fell, and Gamal Abdel NASSER led (1954–70) the new republic. Nasser's nationalization of the Suez Canal (1956) was briefly contested by Israel, Britain and France. In 1958 Egypt, Syria and Yemen formed the short-lived UNITED ARAB REPUBLIC. Egypt was defeated by Israel in the SIX-DAY WAR (1967). Nasser oversaw the building of the ASWAN High Dam to regulate the vital waters of the River Nile.

On his death (1970), Nasser was succeeded by Anwar SADAT. After defeat in the YOM KIPPUR WAR (1973), Sadat signed the CAMP DAVID AGREEMENT (1979) with Israel, who withdrew from Sinai in 1982. The peace treaty prompted Egypt's expulsion from the ARAB LEAGUE, and the assassination (1981) of President Sadat by Islamic extremists. Hosni MUBARAK succeeded Sadat and a state of emergency was proclaimed. In 1989 Egypt was readmitted into the Arab League. In return for military support against Iraq in the GULF WAR (1991), Egypt received US$7 billion of debt relief. In 1992 Islamic militants relaunched a violent campaign. Among the casualties were 58 tourists killed in Luxor (1997), damaging Egypt's vital tourist industry.

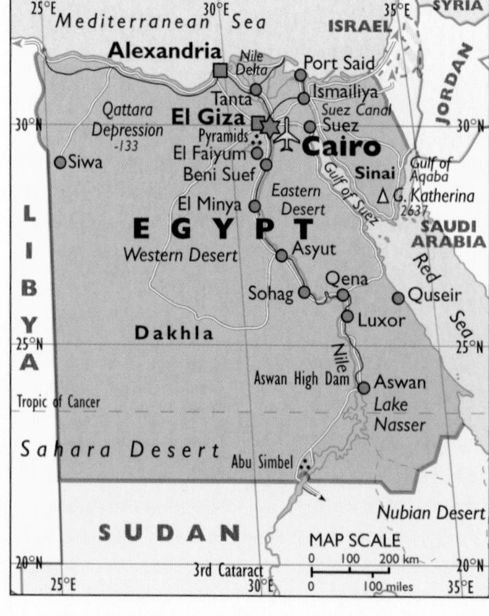

ASHURBANIPAL. Susa became a major city in the Persian empire of the ACHAEMENIDS and the site of DARIUS I (THE GREAT)'s palace.

El Cid *See* CID, EL

El Dorado (Sp. The Golden One) Mythical city of fabulous wealth, supposedly in South America. It was the focus of many Spanish expeditions in the 16th century, and the English explorer Sir Walter RALEIGH attempted to find it in 1595 and 1617.

Eleanor of Aquitaine (*c*.1122–1204) Queen consort of France and later of England. She married LOUIS VII of France and accompanied him on the Second CRUSADE (1147–49). In 1152 Eleanor's marriage to Louis was annulled and she married Henry, Duke of Normandy and Count of Anjou, who ascended the English throne (1154) as HENRY II. Eleanor bore eight children to Henry before the revelation of his affair with Rosamond led her to form (1170) a separate court in Poitiers, France. Eleanor was imprisoned (1173–85) for supporting the couple's sons, the future RICHARD I and JOHN, in revolt against Henry. *See also* ANGEVIN

Eleanor of Castile (1246–90) Queen consort of EDWARD I of England, daughter of FERDINAND III of Castile. Eleanor married Edward in 1254 and, according

EISENHOWER, DWIGHT DAVID ("IKE")

Dwight D. Eisenhower was supreme commander of the Allied Expeditionary Forces (AEF) during World War 2. His military record and pledge to end the Korean War (1950–53) earned him an easy victory in the 1952 presidential elections. Eisenhower's threat to use nuclear weapons led to a truce in Korea in July 1953. His "atoms for peace" plan resulted in the creation of the International Atomic Energy Agency in 1957. Eisenhower passed the Civil Rights Act of 1957, the first new civil rights' legislation for 100 years. Eisenhower's tough anti-communist stance contributed to a heightening of tension in the Cold War between the Soviet Union and the United States.

EISENHOWER IN HIS OWN WORDS

"Whatever America hopes to bring to pass in this world must first come to pass in the heart of America."
Inaugural Address (1953)

"There is one thing about being President – nobody can tell you when to sit down."
The Observer, 'Sayings of the Week' (9 August, 1953)

EGYPT, ANCIENT

Civilization that flourished along the River Nile in NW Africa between *c*.3100 BC and 332 BC. According to tradition, the kingdoms of Upper and Lower Egypt were united by Pharaoh MENES in *c*.3100 BC.

The first two dynasties of ancient Egypt are commonly grouped together as the **First Dynastic (Archaic) Period** (*c*.3100–2686 BC). The highlight of the **Old Kingdom** (*c*.2686–2181 BC) was the building of the PYRAMIDS at Giza during the IV dynasty. After the death of Pepy II of the VI dynasty, central government collapsed. This was the **First Intermediate Period** (*c*.2181–2040 BC). Authority was restored in the XI dynasty, and the capital moved to Thebes (now LUXOR).

The **Middle Kingdom** (*c*.2040–1786 BC) saw Egypt develop into a great power. AMENEMHET I, founder (*c*.1991 BC) of the XII dynasty, secured Egypt's borders and created a new capital. Art and architecture flourished. At the end of the Middle Kingdom, Egypt again fell into disarray. The **Second Intermediate Period** (*c*.1786–1567 BC) was dominated by the HYKSOS.

The **New Kingdom** (*c*.1567–1085 BC) brought great wealth. Massive temples and tombs, such as TUTANKHAMUN's, were built. Under RAMSES II wars with the HITTITES weakened Egypt, and subsequent ineffectual rulers led to the decline of the New Kingdom. The **Third Intermediate Period** (*c*.1085–656 BC) culminated in Assyrian domination.

The Persians ruled from 525 until 404 BC, when the last native dynasties appeared. In 332 BC Egypt fell to the armies of ALEXANDER III (THE GREAT), who moved the capital to ALEXANDRIA. After Alexander's death, his general became ruler of Egypt, as PTOLEMY I. The Ptolemies maintained a powerful empire for three centuries, and ALEXANDRIA became a centre of learning. Roman power was on the ascendancy, and when Ptolemy XII asked POMPEY for aid in 58 BC, it marked the end of Egyptian autonomy. CLEOPATRA tried to assert independence through associations with Julius CAESAR and Mark ANTONY, but she was defeated at the Battle of ACTIUM (31 BC). Her son, Ptolemy XV (whose father was probably Julius Caesar), was the last Ptolemy; he was killed by Octavian (later AUGUSTUS), and Egypt became a province of Rome.

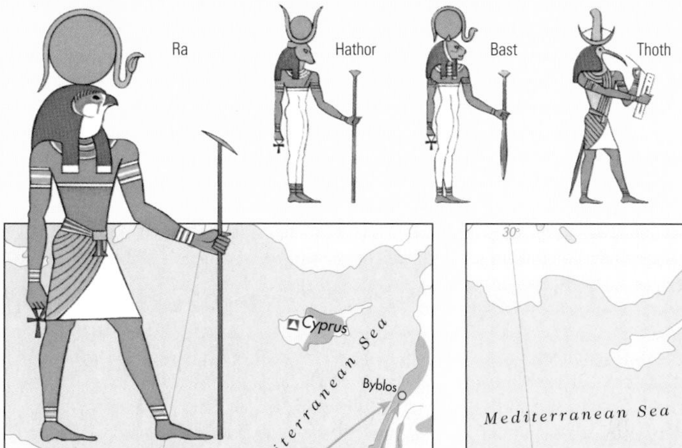

◄ **The ancient Egyptians** worshipped a pantheon of anthropomorphic deities. These deities included (from left to right): Ra, the sun-god; Hathor, the mother-goddess; Bast, a god of fertility; and Thoth, the scribe.

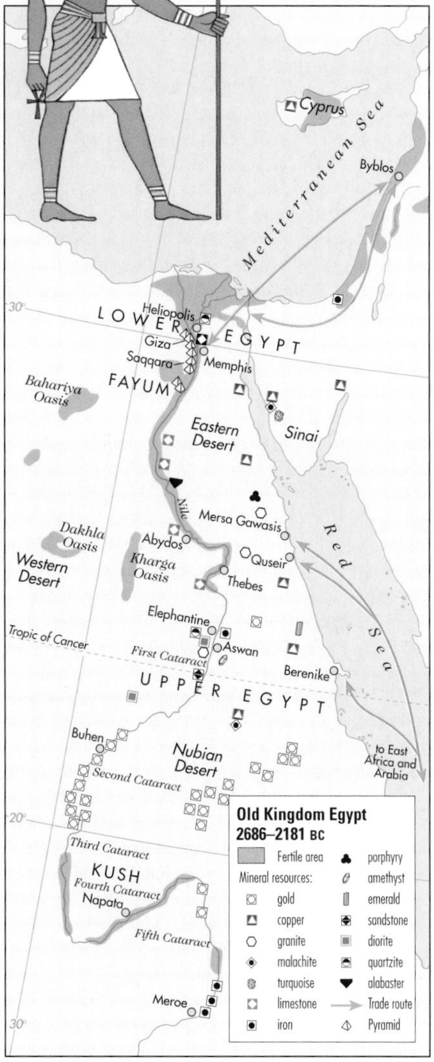

Old Kingdom Egypt 2686–2181 BC
Fertile area; Mineral resources: gold, copper, granite, malachite, turquoise, limestone, iron, porphyry, amethyst, emerald, sandstone, diorite, quartzite, alabaster; Trade route; Pyramid

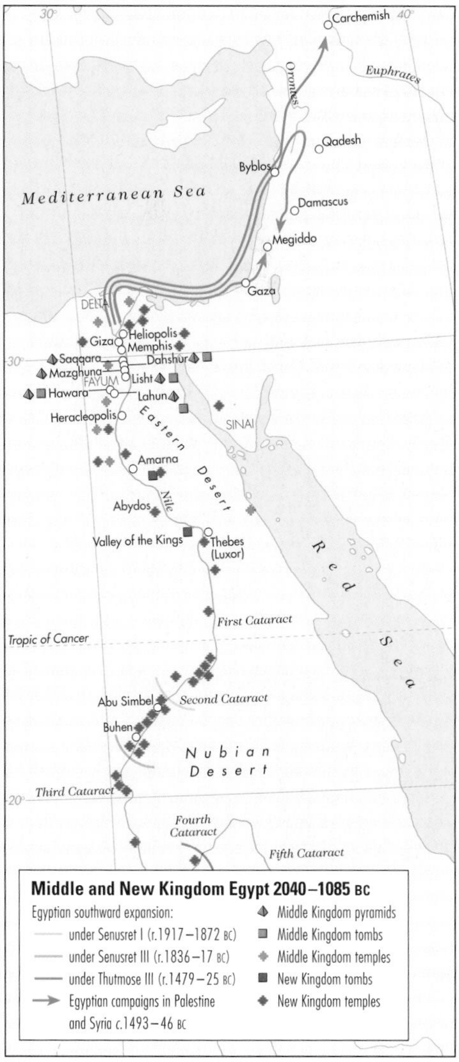

Middle and New Kingdom Egypt 2040–1085 BC
Egyptian southward expansion: under Senusret I (r.1917–1872 BC); under Senusret III (r.1836–17 BC); under Thutmose III (r.1479–25 BC); Egyptian campaigns in Palestine and Syria *c*.1493–46 BC; Middle Kingdom pyramids; Middle Kingdom tombs; Middle Kingdom temples; New Kingdom tombs; New Kingdom temples

► **Old Kingdom Egypt** was the world's first large, centrally governed state. From *c*.2650 BC massive stone pyramids were built as tombs for the pharoahs, worshipped as the sons of Ra.

►► **Middle and New Kingdom Egypt** saw the building of vast temples along the River Nile dedicated to Egyptian gods and a necropolis of lavish royal tombs in the Valley of the Kings.

to legend, saved his life by sucking poison from a wound he gained while they were on CRUSADE (1270–72). In 1272 HENRY III died and the couple were crowned on their return to England in 1274. After Eleanor's death at Hadby, Nottinghamshire, 12 memorial "Eleanor crosses" were erected at the places where her funeral cortège stopped en route to London. The last stop was at Charing Cross, where a replica now stands.

elector German prince responsible for choosing the Holy Roman emperor. In 1257 the number of electors was fixed at seven. In 1356 Emperor CHARLES IV issued a GOLDEN BULL confirming the electoral prerogatives of the Count Palatine of the Rhine, the Margrave of Brandenburg, the Duke of Saxony, the king of Bohemia, and the archbishops of Mainz, Trier and Cologne. The electors were granted considerable independence within their domains and acted as a counterweight to imperial power, despite the title of emperor becoming, in practice, hereditary within the HABSBURG family. The number of electors was increased to ten with the addition of the dukes of Bavaria (1623), Hanover (1692) and Hesse-Kassel (1803). The office disappeared when NAPOLEON I abolished the HOLY ROMAN EMPIRE in 1806.

electoral college In US government, group of electors chosen by the voters of each state to elect formally the president and vice president. The number of electors from each state equals the number of its representatives in both Houses of CONGRESS. State committees or conventions of each political party select candidates for electors. In an election, the candidate who wins a majority of a state's popular vote usually receives all the state's electoral vote. To become president, a candidate must have a majority in the electoral college but may lack a majority of the popular vote. In 1800 a tie for president between Aaron BURR and Thomas JEFFERSON caused confusion in the electoral college and led to the adoption (1804) of the 12th Amendment to the CONSTITUTION OF THE UNITED STATES. The 12th Amendment provided for separate elections for president and vice president and, in cases where no candidate gained a majority in the college, reduced from five to three the number of candidates from which the HOUSE OF REPRESENTATIVES could choose. In US history, only two presidents have been elected by the House: Thomas JEFFERSON (1800) and John Quincy ADAMS (1824). After the disputed election of 1876, involving Rutherford HAYES and Samuel TILDEN, the Electoral Count Act of 1887 placed the burden of responsibility in deciding electoral disputes upon individual states. There are frequent calls for reform of the electoral college. Opponents of the college system cite the fact that it has produced ten presidents with less than 50% of the popular vote: James BUCHANAN, Abraham LINCOLN (1860), Rutherford HAYES (1876), James GARFIELD (1880), Grover CLEVELAND (1884, 1892), Benjamin HARRISON (1888), Woodrow WILSON (1912, 1916), Harry TRUMAN (1948), John KENNEDY (1960), Richard NIXON (1968) and Bill CLINTON (1988) – two of which (Hayes and Harrison) had fewer popular votes than their main opponents. Defenders of the system argue that in a direct, popular vote the winner does not necessarily have to win a majority of the votes.

Elgin, James Bruce, 8th Earl of (1811–63) British colonial official. As governor general of Canada (1847–54), he was responsible for the implementation of the DURHAM Report. In 1862 Elgin was appointed viceroy of India, where he died.

Elgin marbles Group of sculptures from the ACROPOLIS in Athens, Greece, including sculptures of the PARTHENON. They were transported (1803–12) by the 7th Earl of Elgin (1766–1841), sold to the British government in 1816, and are now on display in the British Museum, London. The Greek government has campaigned for their return.

Elijah (active 9th century BC) Old Testament prophet. He rebuked King AHAB for allowing the introduction of the Phoenician cult of Baal by Ahab's wife, JEZEBEL (1 Kings 17, 2 Kings 2). Elijah, aided by his disciple ELISHA, contested that there was no God but Yahweh.

Eliot, Sir John (1592–1632) English politician. He entered Parliament in 1614. In 1625 Eliot brought impeachment proceedings against CHARLES I's favourite, the 1st Duke of BUCKINGHAM. He helped Sir Edward COKE draft the PETITION OF RIGHT (1628) in defence of Parliament. In 1629 Eliot was imprisoned in the Tower of London, where he died. *See also* ADDLED PARLIAMENT

Eliot, John (1604–90) English missionary in North America. In 1631 he arrived in colonial Massachusetts, settling at Roxbury in 1632. Eliot translated the Bible into the local Algonquian dialect and became known as the "Apostle to the Indians" for his evangelistic work among the Native Americans. Many converts were killed in KING PHILIP'S WAR (1675–76).

Elisha (active 9th century BC) Old Testament prophet of Israel, disciple and successor of ELIJAH (2 Kings 2–13). He destroyed the Phoenician cult of Baal. Elisha is portrayed as a miracle-worker, healer and fulfiller of God's commissions to his master Elijah.

Elizabeth (1709–62) Empress of Russia (1741–62), daughter of PETER I (THE GREAT) and CATHERINE I. She came to the throne after overthrowing her nephew, Ivan VI (r.1740–41). She restored the Senate, but real political power lay with her advisers in the chancery. Elizabeth waged war (1741–43) against Sweden, leading to the annexation of part of s Finland in 1743. She was led Russia into the Seven Years' War (1756–63). A great patron of education and the arts, she founded (1755) Russia's first university (in Moscow). Elizabeth was succeeded by her nephew, PETER III.

Elizabeth I *See* feature article

Elizabeth II (1926–) Queen of Great Britain and Northern Ireland and head of the Commonwealth of Nations (1952–), daughter of GEORGE VI. In 1947 she married PHILIP Mountbatten, Duke of Edinburgh, with whom she had four children, CHARLES, Anne, Andrew and Edward. Popular and dutiful, Elizabeth has had to contend with criticism of royal wealth and scandals associated with the marriage failures in the royal family, particularly that of Charles and DIANA, PRINCESS OF WALES.

Elizabeth (1900–) (Queen Mother) British queen consort of GEORGE VI, b. Elizabeth Bowes-Lyon. She married George in 1923 and the couple had two children, Elizabeth (later ELIZABETH II) and Margaret. In 1936 Elizabeth became queen when George's brother, EDWARD VIII, abdicated. A popular figure, she continued to perform public duties into her nineties. *See also* ABDICATION CRISIS

Ellis Island Island in Upper New York Bay, near Manhattan, SE NEW YORK. From 1892 to 1943 Ellis Island acted as the main US immigration centre, handling more than 12 million immigrants. The Ellis Island Immigration Museum opened in 1990. Area: 11ha (27 acres).

Ellsworth, Lincoln (1880–1951) US polar explorer. In 1925 Ellsworth and Roald AMUNDSEN's attempt at a trans-Arctic crossing ended in an emergency landing within 250km (150mi) of the North Pole. In 1926 Ellsworth, Amundsen and Umberto NOBILE crossed in a dirigible balloon from Svalbard to Alaska, becoming the first people to fly over the North Pole. In 1935 Ellsworth led the first trans-Antarctic air crossing.

Ellsworth, Oliver (1745–1807) US jurist, third chief justice of the United States (1796–99). He served as a delegate to the CONSTITUTIONAL CONVENTION (1787), where he helped draft the CONNECTICUT COMPROMISE. Ellsworth was responsible for the term "United States" in the CONSTITUTION. As senator from Connecticut (1789–96), he drafted the bill that established the federal judiciary.

El Salvador *See* country feature

Emancipation, Edict of (1861) Declaration issued by Tsar ALEXANDER II that freed all Russian SERFS. Under the edict, serfs were granted land in return for redemption payments to be paid annually by them to the former landowners over the next 49 years. The reforms proved disastrous. In many cases, the peasants were asked to pay an inflated price or were given smaller plots. The village commune (*mir*) was given the power of land redistribution.

ELIZABETH I (1533–1603)

Queen of England (1558–1603), daughter of HENRY VIII and Anne BOLEYN. During the reigns of her half-brother and half-sister, EDWARD VI and MARY I, she avoided political disputes. Once crowned, she re-established Protestantism and in 1559 the Act of SUPREMACY was passed which revived the anti-papal statutes of Henry VIII and declared Elizabeth supreme governor of the church. The Elizabethan Settlement, conducted by Matthew PARKER, saw the CHURCH OF ENGLAND adopt the THIRTY-NINE ARTICLES (1571). Various plots to murder Elizabeth and place the Catholic MARY, QUEEN OF SCOTS, on the throne resulted in Mary's imprisonment and execution (1587), and repressive legislation against Catholics.

Elizabeth relied on a small group of advisers, such as Sir Francis WALSINGHAM and Lord BURGHLEY. The latter served as her secretary and treasurer and was responsible for shaping many of her policies. For most of her reign, England was at peace, and commerce and industry prospered. Elizabethan drama reflected this "golden age". The expansion of the navy laid the foundations for the development of the first BRITISH EMPIRE and the defeat of the Spanish ARMADA (1588). Despite pressure to marry and produce an heir, Elizabeth remained a spinster. Her favourites included Robert Dudley, Earl of LEICESTER, and Robert Devereux, 2nd Earl of ESSEX, who was later executed for leading a rebellion against her. Elizabeth was the last of the TUDORS, and the throne passed to JAMES I, a STUART.

▲ **Elizabethan galleon** Galleons were used by the British navy against the Spanish Armada.

► **Elizabeth I** (English School, *c.*1600) Numerous paintings depicted Elizabeth I as a symbol of power.

E

Emancipation Proclamation (1 January 1863) Declaration issued by President Abraham LINCOLN abolishing SLAVERY in the CONFEDERATE STATES OF AMERICA. It was designed to enhance the Union's support from abroad, especially Britain, and reduce the South's fighting force. By the end of the CIVIL WAR more than 500,000 slaves had fled to the Union side. Slavery was finally abolished by the 13th Amendment to the CONSTITUTION OF THE UNITED STATES (December 1865). *See also* ABOLITIONISTS

Embargo Act (1807) US legislation passed by President Thomas JEFFERSON to force England and France to remove restrictions on United States' trade, following attacks on US merchant shipping. It prohibited all ships from entering or leaving US ports. The Act hurt the United States' economy, and merchants resorted to smuggling. Resistance led to the Non-Intercourse Act (1809) that ended the 14-month embargo.

émigré In French history, a refugee who fled France after the storming of the Bastille (14 July 1789). Émigrés were mainly royalist nobles who feared for their lives in the FRENCH REVOLUTION. In exile, they formed a counter-revolutionary force under Prince Louis Joseph de Condé. In 1802 NAPOLEON I pardoned the émigrés and many returned to France. With the restoration of the BOURBONS, the émigrés received compensation.

Emin Pasha (1840–92) German colonial administrator and explorer, b. Eduard Schnitzer. In 1876 he joined General Charles GORDON at KHARTOUM. In 1878 Gordon appointed him governor of Equatoria, s Sudan. Emin abolished slavery in the region and made extensive surveys. In 1885 the Mahdist uprising left him isolated and he was rescued (1888) by H.M. STANLEY. He was murdered by Arab slave-traders while on a German expedition to Equatorial Africa. *See also* MAHDI

Emmet, Robert (1778–1803) Irish nationalist. In 1798 he joined the leaders of the United Irishmen in exile in France. In July 1803 Emmet organized and led a French-assisted uprising against British rule in Ireland. The insurrection was ill-conceived and betrayed. Emmet was captured and executed for treason.

Ems dispatch (1870) Final cause of the FRANCO-PRUSSIAN WAR (1870–71). The French were alarmed at the prospect of Prince Leopold, a relative of WILLIAM I of Prussia, succeeding to the Spanish throne and their ambassador requested assurance of the permanence of Leopold's refusal. William declined and informed his chancellor, Otto von BISMARCK, of the conversation. Bismarck then published an insulting version of the dialogue in a telegram from Ems, w Germany, thus inciting the French to declare war.

enclosure In European history, the fencing-in by landlords of COMMON LAND. Complaints against this practice date from the 13th century. Enclosure usually led to increased agricultural productivity at the cost of depriving people of free grazing land and firewood. It was a cause of popular rebellions, especially in the 16th century. The AGRICULTURAL REVOLUTION produced another phase of enclosure in England in the 18th century and in the rest of Europe in the 19th century.

encomienda In colonial Spanish America, system of tributary labour granted by the monarchy to CONQUISTADORS and other colonists. The system was based on the military orders' practice of exacting tribute from Muslims and Jews during the reconquest of Spain. In 1503 *encomiendas* were introduced in Spanish America, theoretically to end the practice of slave labour (REPARTIMIENTO). The native population was required to give tribute in the form of goods or labour in return for protection and instruction in the Christian faith. In practice, the system was widely abused and often reinforced enslavement in the mines. Despite efforts at reform, such as Las Casas' New Law of the Indies (1541), the *encomiendas* continued to devastate the native population until its abolition in the late 18th century. *See also* EJIDO; HACIENDA

Encyclopedists French philosophers who presented their rationalist, humanitarian and deist views in the 35-volume general reference work *Encyclopédie* (1751–80). The editors, Denis DIDEROT and d'Alembert, and contributors such as VOLTAIRE, MONTESQUIEU, Marquis de CONDORCET and Jean-Jacques ROUSSEAU encountered severe opposition from the religious and political establishment. Their ideas formed the keystone of ENLIGHTENMENT thought and had profound repercussions in French society prior to FRENCH REVOLUTION. *See also* DEISM

Engels, Friedrich (1820–95) German political philosopher. Engels and MARX formulated the theory of dialectical materialism and collaborated on the *Communist Manifesto* (1848). Engels' materialist reworking of the dialectics of G.W.F. HEGEL is most evident in *Anti-Dühring* (1878) and *Socialism, Utopian and Scientific* (1882). From 1870 until Marx's death in 1883, Engels helped financially with Marx's research and continued to help him with his writings, particularly *Das Kapital* (3 vols, 1867, 1885, 1894). His own works include *Condition of the Working Class in England in 1844* (1845) and *The Origin of the Family, Private Property and the State* (1884).

England Largest part of the UNITED KINGDOM; the capital is LONDON. There are traces of PALAEOLITHIC settlements in England, dating from more than 400,000 years ago. Agriculture began to be practised *c.*4000 BC. In the 2nd millennium BC, the BEAKER CULTURE spread to England, and with it the use of copper and the development of trade with Europe. The NEOLITHIC circular monument at STONEHENGE was started in *c.*3100 BC. Ironworking began in the 7th century BC and in the following century many large hill forts were built. Among the peoples who migrated to England after 600 BC were the CELTS. The country was conquered by the Romans from AD 43 and it remained within the ROMAN EMPIRE until the early 5th century. Germanic tribes, among them the SAXONS, ANGLES and JUTES, began to settle in the 5th century and gradually established independent kingdoms. Christianity was introduced into the country in the 6th century. Raids by VIKINGS occurred in the 8th and 9th centuries, and the Danes were only prevented from conquering the country by ALFRED (THE GREAT), king of WESSEX. Alfred confined the Danes to an area known as the DANELAW. In the 10th century, the Danelaw was captured by ATHELSTAN, but in 1016 Danish ruler CANUTE II (THE GREAT) became king of the entire country. The crown reverted to the English before being won by WILLIAM I (THE CONQUEROR) in the NORMAN CONQUEST (1066). William brought strong central government and inaugurated the FEUDAL SYSTEM. IRELAND was conquered in the late 12th century, and WALES became a principality of England (1284) during the reign of EDWARD I. The 13th century saw the foundations of PARLIAMENT and the development of statute law. During the Middle Ages, English kings laid claim to French territory. The Wars of the ROSES curbed the power of the

EL SALVADOR

AREA: 21,040sq km (8124sq mi)
POPULATION: 5,047,925
CAPITAL (POPULATION): San Salvador (422,570)
GOVERNMENT: Republic
ETHNIC GROUPS: Mestizo 89%, Native American 10%, White 1%
LANGUAGES: Spanish (official)
RELIGIONS: Christianity (Roman Catholic 94%)
GDP PER CAPITA (1995): US$2610

Smallest republic in Central America. Archaeological ruins from the MAYAN period (*c.*AD 100–1000) remain in w El Salvador. In 1524–26 the Spanish explorer Pedro de ALVARADO conquered Native American tribes such as the Pipil, and the region became part of the Spanish Viceroyalty of GUATEMALA. The colonial period saw the development of cocoa and indigo production. The early 19th century witnessed revolts by the powerful planter families.

In 1821 the province supported Guatemala's declaration of independence from Spain, but rejected incorporation into the Mexican Empire of Agustín de ITURBIDE. In 1823 El Salvador joined the CENTRAL AMERICAN FEDERATION. In 1834 San Salvador became capital of the Federation.

In 1841, after the collapse of the Federation, the independent republic of El Salvador was born. The early years of nationhood saw frequent incursions by neighbouring powers, especially Guatemala. From 1871 to 1931 El Salvador was ruled by Liberals, who developed the coffee plantations. The collapse in the price of coffee prompted a military coup (1931), led by Maximiliano Hernández Martínez. In 1932 Hernández Martínez brutally suppressed a communist revolt, executing more than 10,000 rebels. In 1944, after prolonged civil unrest, he was forced to resign.

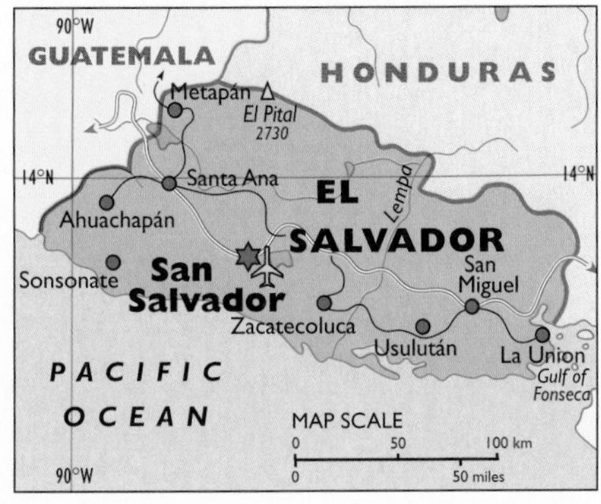

In 1948 the "Majors' Revolution" brought Major Oscar Osorio to power. The authoritarian presidencies of Osorio (1950–56) and Lieutenant Colonel José María Lemus (1956–60) brought economic reforms, such as membership of the CENTRAL AMERICAN COMMON MARKET (CACM). In 1962 Lemus was deposed by a military junta, led first (1962–67) by Lieutenant Colonel Julio Adalberto Rivera and then (1967–72) by Fidel Sánchez Hernández. The "SOCCER WAR" (July 1969) with Honduras followed an ill-tempered World Cup qualifying match between the two countries, but the roots of the conflict lay in Honduras' treatment of Salvadoran migrant workers. Within four days, El Salvador had captured much of Honduras. A cease-fire was announced and the troops withdrew in August. The presidencies of Colonel Arturo Armando Molina (1972–77) and General Carlos Humberto Romero (1977–79) witnessed mass public unrest over social and economic inequalities. Dissent was stifled by the paramilitary organization ORDEN.

In 1980 civil war broke out between the US-backed government of José Napoleón Duarte and the Farabundo Martí National Liberation Front (FMLN). The murder (1980) of Archbishop Oscar Arnulfo Romero, champion of the poor and dispossessed, brought world condemnation. In 1981 the formation of the Nationalist Republican Alliance (ARENA) signalled the start of a rift between the military and the plantation owners. In 1989 elections Duarte was defeated by the ARENA candidate, Alfredo Cristiani.

In 1992 a cease-fire ended the 12-year civil war, which had claimed *c.*75,000 lives. In 1993 a UN Truth Commission led to the removal of army officers for human-rights violations, and FMLN arms were decommissioned. In 1994 Armando Calderón Sol replaced Cristiani as president and leader of ARENA. Calderón Sol was succeeded by Francisco Flores in 1999.

nobility. Under the Tudors (1485–1603), Wales was united politically with England and the country became a strong Protestant monarchy. In the reign (1533–1603) of Elizabeth I, England's naval power grew and posed a serious threat to the Spanish Empire. In 1603 James I unified England and Scotland. For the subsequent history of England, *see* United Kingdom. Area: 130,362sq km (50,333sq mi). Pop. (1991) 47,055,204.

English Civil War *See* Civil War, English

Enlightenment (Age of Reason) Philosophical trend in 18th-century Europe and America. It was inspired by the scientific and philosophical revolutions of the late 17th century. The spirit of rational inquiry of the scientific revolution, embodied by the work of Isaac Newton, the rationalism of René Descartes, the religious ideas of Baruch Spinoza and Blaise Pascal, and the empiricism of Francis Bacon and John Locke, filtered into the fabric of 18th-century society. The *Encyclopédie* (1751–80) was the central text of the Enlightenment. In France, the Encyclopedists (Voltaire, Montesquieu, Marquis de Condorcet, Jean-Jacques Rousseau and Denis Diderot) championed a scientific approach to political and economic affairs. They attacked established religion (*see* deism) and viewed the state as the instrument for social change. Rational human behaviour was at the centre of the economic theories of Adam Smith, Jeremy Bentham and Baron Turgot. The importance of the individual was underlined in the philosophies of Immanuel Kant and David Hume. The work of Thomas Paine, Thomas Jefferson and Benjamin Franklin epitomized the political spirit of the age.

enosis (Gk. "union") Greek Cypriot demands for unification with Greece. In 1878 Britain occupied Cyprus. In 1915 Britain offered to transfer control of the island to Greece, in return for Greece honouring its treaty obligations to Serbia. The Greek government refused and the offer was rescinded. Turkish Cypriots bitterly opposed enosis with Greece. In 1931 Greek Cypriot calls for enosis led to riots in the island's capital, Nicosia. In 1955 Colonel Georgias Grivas formed the **National Organization of Cyprus (EOKA)**, a guerrilla organization dedicated to achieving enosis. In 1956 Archbishop Makarios III, head of the Greek Christian community in Cyprus, was exiled for supporting EOKA. In 1960 Makarios and the Turkish Cypriot leader, Fazil Küçük, agreed to the creation of the independent republic of Cyprus. Intercommunal violence persisted throughout the 1960s. In 1971 Grivas formed EOKA-B to continue the campaign for enosis. On 15 July 1974, Greek army officers overthrew Makarios. Turkey invaded Cyprus on 20 July 1974, rapidly capturing the 37% of the island that they proclaimed (1975) the Turkish Federated State of Cyprus. The partition of the island is not recognized by the United Nations (UN). *See also* Karamanlis, Constantine

Entente Cordiale (1904) (Fr. "Friendly Understanding") Mutual recognition of British and French colonial interests, especially in Egypt (Britain) and Morocco (France). In 1905 the German Emperor William I visited Tangier, n Morocco, implicitly stating his commitment to Moroccan independence. The ensuing crisis forced the resignation of French foreign minister Théophile Delcassé, but the Entente held together. In 1907 Russia joined Britain and France in the Triple Entente. *See also* Algeciras Conference

Enver Pasha (1881–1922) Turkish general and statesman. He was a leader of the Young Turks revolution of 1908, which restored the 1876 constitution in Turkey and deposed (1909) Sultan Abdul Hamid II. Enver led the Ottoman army in the Second Balkan War, capturing Edirne from the Bulgars (1913). As minister of war (1913–18), he negotiated a defensive alliance with Germany and guided the entry of the Ottoman Empire into World War I as one of the Central Powers. Enver's strategy frustrated the Allies' Gallipoli Campaign (1915–16). After the Armistice in Europe, he fled to Berlin and then Moscow. He was killed in the Basmachi Revolt against the Bolsheviks in Turkistan.

Eocene Second of the five epochs of the Tertiary period, from 55 to 38 million years ago. The fossil record shows members of modern plant genera, including beeches, walnuts and elms, and indicates the apparent dominance of mammals, including the ancestors of camels, horses, rodents, bats and monkeys.

Epaminondas (d.362 bc) Greek general and statesman. His innovative military tactics helped Thebes secure a decisive victory over Sparta at the Battle of Leuctra (371 bc). Epaminondas further weakened Sparta by gaining independence for Messenia. He was killed in the process of securing victory for Boeotia against Sparta in the Battle of Mantinea.

Ephesus (Efes) Ancient Ionian city of w Asia Minor (modern Turkey). A prosperous port under the Greeks and Romans, it was a centre of the cult of Artemis (Diana). The Temple of Artemis was the largest Greek temple ever built and one of the Seven Wonders of the World. It was destroyed by fire in 356 bc. Ephesus was captured by Croesus (*c*.550 bc), Cyrus II (the Great) (*c*.546 bc) and Alexander III (the Great) (334 bc), falling under Roman control in 133 bc. Today, it is one of the world's principal archaeological sites. *See also* Ephesus, Council of

Ephesus, Council of (431) Third ecumenical council, summoned by Emperor Theodosius II. The Council was opened by Saint Cyril (of Alexandria). It confirmed the Nicene Creed and condemned Nestorianism.

Epicurus (341–270 bc) Greek philosopher, b. Samos. According to tradition, he was educated at the Academy in Athens and formed his own school there in *c*.306 bc. Only fragments of his work remain and most of our knowledge is derived from Diogenes and Lucretius. Epicurus derived his theory of materialism from the atomism of Democritus. He argued that the central purpose of life was happiness. His brand of hedonism rejected indulgence in favour of serenity and avoidance of pain. Epicureans formed sheltered, egalitarian communities (including women and slaves), divorced from political and public life. His form of humanism was rejected by Christians and Stoics alike.

Epirus (Ipeiros) Coastal region of nw Greece and s Albania. It was possibly the original home of the founders of the Mycenaean civilization. Among the Mycenaean remains found here is the religious shrine referred to in Homer's *Iliad* as the Oracle of Zeus at Dodona. The invasion of the Dorians created three main Greek-speaking tribes in Epirus: the Thesproti (sw), the Molossi (central) and the Chaones (nw). Under the Molossian King Pyrrhus (*c*.319–272 bc), Epirus expanded into Acarnania and central Albania. In the Third Macedonian War (171–168 bc), an Epirote League of the three tribes splintered. In 167 bc Molossia was sacked by the Roman army, and 150,000 of its inhabitants were enslaved. Epirus became a province of the Roman, and subsequently the Byzantine, empire. When the Byzantine Empire fragmented in 1204, the independent Despotate of Epirus was set up. This became part of the Ottoman Empire in 1430 and in the late 18th century fell to the despot Ali Pasha. In 1913 Epirus was divided between Greece and Albania.

Episcopal Church Anglican church of the United States. Church of England services were held in the first American colonies. With the American Revolution, the Church of England was disestablished and a national church organized in its place. Known as the Protestant Episcopal Church, its constitution and its own version of the Book of Common Prayer were established in 1789. In 1989 it appointed the first woman bishop in the Anglican Communion. The Church has more than 2.5 million members.

Equal Rights Amendment (ERA) Proposed amendment to the Constitution of the United States, passed by Congress in 1972. The amendment states that "equality of rights under the law shall not be denied or abridged by the United States or by any State on account of sex". It provoked great controversy and by the 1982 deadline had been ratified by only 35 of the necessary 38 states.

Equatorial Guinea *See* country feature

Erasmus, Desiderius (*c*.1466–1536) (Gerhard Gerhards) Dutch humanist scholar, a key figure in Renaissance Europe. His *Adages* (1500) formed the basis of Latin education in Europe for many centuries. In *Manual of the Christian Knight* (1503), Erasmus called for reform of scholasticism and a return to Christian pietism. He dedicated his satire *Praise of Folly* (1509) to Thomas More. Erasmus' translation (1516) of the Greek New Testament revealed flaws in the Vulgate text. As councillor to the future Emperor Charles V, he wrote his *Education of a Christian*

EQUATORIAL GUINEA (FORMERLY SPANISH GUINEA)

AREA: 28,050sq km (10,830 sq mi)
POPULATION: 420,000
CAPITAL (POPULATION): Malabo (35,000)
GOVERNMENT: Multiparty republic (transitional)
ETHNIC GROUPS: Fang 83%, Bubi 10%, Ndowe 4%
LANGUAGES: Spanish (official)
RELIGIONS: Christianity (mainly Roman Catholic) 89%, traditional beliefs 5%
GDP PER CAPITA (1994): US$342

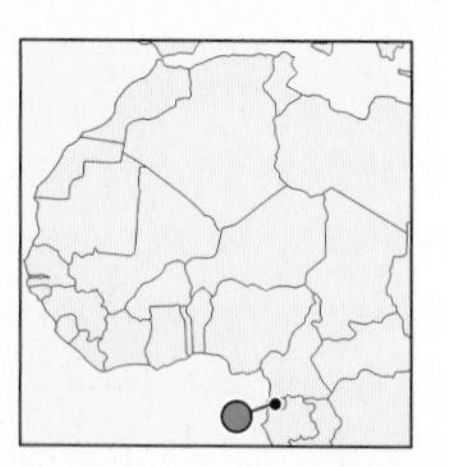

Republic in w central Africa, consisting of Mbini (Río Muni), a mainland region between Cameroon and Gabon, and five islands in the Gulf of Guinea, the largest of which is Bioko (formerly Fernando Po). In *c*.1472 the Portuguese navigator Fernão do Pó discovered Bioko. In 1778 Portugal ceded the islands and commercial mainland rights to Spain. By 1781 all the Spanish settlers had died of yellow fever and the colony was abandoned. In 1827 Spain leased bases on Bioko to Britain for anti-slavery patrols. The British settled some freed slaves on Bioko, whose descendants (*fernandinos*) remain. In 1858 Spain expelled the British and began to survey the mainland. In 1959 Bioko and Mbini were made overseas provinces of Spain.

In 1968 Spanish Guinea achieved independence as Equatorial Guinea. In 1979 the Republic's first president, Francisco Macías Nguema, was deposed and executed by his nephew, Lieutenant Colonel Teodoro Obiang Nguema Mbasogo. In 1993 Equatorial Guinea's first-ever multiparty elections were condemned by international observers and boycotted by the opposition and most of the electorate. President Obiang's Democratic Party of Equatorial Guinea (PDGE) formed a government. In further suspect elections (1996), President Obiang claimed 99% of the vote. The United Nations (UN) has regularly condemned Obiang's regime for gross violations of human rights.

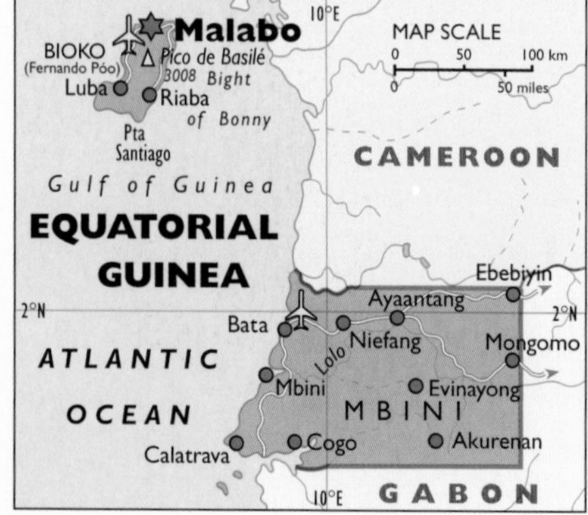

Prince (1516). While critical of clerical abuse, Erasmus remained within the Roman Catholic Church and sought to prevent the schism in the Christian Church. In *On Free Will* (1524), he attacked Martin LUTHER's emphasis on predestination. *See also* REFORMATION

Erech *See* URUK

Erhard, Ludwig (1897–1977) German statesman and economist, chancellor (1963–66). As minister of economics for West Germany (1949–63), his "social market system" was largely responsible for West Germany's dramatic economic recovery after World War 2. Erhard succeeded Konrad ADENAUER as chancellor. He was forced to resign after his decision to increase taxes to meet the budget deficit led to a mild recession. *See also* CHRISTIAN DEMOCRATIC UNION (CDU)

Eric XIV (1533–77) King of Sweden (1560–68), son of GUSTAVUS I (VASA). Eric strengthened the monarchy by persecuting the nobility. Failure in the war (1563–70) with Denmark and the assassination of Nils Sture prompted a rebellion and Eric was deposed in favour of his half-brother JOHN III. He died of poison in prison.

Ericsson, Leif *See* LEIF ERICSSON

Eric the Red (active late 10th century) Norwegian explorer, father of LEIF ERICSSON, b. Erik Thorvaldsson. Exiled from Iceland for manslaughter, in *c.*982 he sailed westward for GREENLAND, exploring the island for three years before returning to Iceland. In *c.*986 Eric led a second expedition that established the first European settlement on Greenland.

Eritrea Independent state on the Red Sea, NE Africa. In antiquity, Eritrea formed part of the fabled land of Punt. Between the 4th and 7th centuries it was part of the flourishing kingdom of AKSUM. The Zagwe dynasty came to power in the 12th century. From 1270 until the overthrow (1974) of HAILE SELASSIE I, Eritrea was dominated by the Ethiopian SOLOMONID dynasty.

In the 16th century, the Ottoman Turks captured the Dahlak Archipelago and Mitsiwa. Other parts of the Red Sea coast fell to the Sultan of Adal, Ahmad Gran. In 1865 control of Mitsiwa passed to the Egyptians. Between 1869 and 1880 Italy purchased parts of the coast adjoining the town of Aseb. In 1885 Italy occupied Mitsiwa and advanced inland. By the Treaty of Wichale (1889), Emperor MENELIK II recognized Italian claims to Eritrea and in 1890 it became an Italian colony. Despite Ethiopia's victory at the Battle of ADWA (1896), Italy was allowed to retain Eritrea. In 1941 Italy was expelled from the Horn of Africa. From 1941 to 1952 Eritrea was under British administration.

In 1952 it was federated with Ethiopia. Opposition to Ethiopian rule was crushed and in 1962 Eritrea became a province of ETHIOPIA. Eritrean Muslim separatists formed the Eritrean Liberation Front (ELF). In 1972 Eritrean Christian separatists formed the Eritrean People's Liberation Front (EPLF). The ELF and EPLF fought each other as well as the Ethiopian army. In 1974 HAILE SELASSIE I was deposed and the ELF-EPLF liberated most of Eritrea. By 1978 the new, Soviet-backed Marxist regime in Ethiopia had recaptured lost territory.

In 1990 the EPLF captured Mitsiwa and by May 1991 controlled the entire country. The 30-year war had claimed more than 300,000 lives and created *c.*700,000 refugees. In 1993, after a referendum, Eritrea proclaimed independence. The new EPLF government, led by Isaias Afwerki, began the process of reconstructing a country impoverished by war and famine. Eritrea faced border conflicts with Sudan and Djibouti. In May 1998 a border dispute with Ethiopia flared into a war that had claimed *c.*50,000 lives by mid-1999.

Erlander, Tage (1901–85) Swedish statesman, prime minister (1946–69). In 1933 he was elected to the Riksdag (parliament). Erlander succeeded Per Albin Hansson as prime minister and leader of the Social Democratic Party. As prime minister, Erlander pursued consensus politics in order to achieve reforms in social welfare and education. He retired after 23 years in office and was succeeded by Olaf PALME.

Eshkol, Levi (1895–1969) Israeli statesman, prime minister (1963–69), b. Ukraine. He settled in Palestine in 1914 and established (1920) one of the first *kibbutzim* (cooperative farms) there. Eshkol succeeded David BEN-GURION as prime minister, and when the SIX-DAY WAR broke out in 1967 he responded by appointing Moshe DAYAN as defence minister. In 1968 he was instrumental in creating the Israeli Labour Party. Eshkol died in office and was succeeded by Golda MEIR. *See also* MAPAI; ZIONISM

Eskimo (Algonquian, eaters of raw flesh) Aboriginal inhabitants (*c.*60,000) of Arctic and sub-Arctic regions of North America (the INUIT), Greenland and Siberia. Sharing the common language family of Eskimo-ALEUT, Eskimos have adapted to harsh climates and are proficient hunters of sea mammals. In some areas, a nomadic existence has been replaced by village settlements and work in the oil and mining industries. The eating of raw meat preserves scarce resources and provides essential nutrients. In winter, igloos (snow huts) provide temporary shelter. In summer, tents are made from animal skins. Eskimos are skilled artisans, producing kayaks and finely crafted tools from skin, ivory, bone, copper or stone. Their spiritual life is dominated by invisible forces of nature (*innua*). Shamanism plays an important role in everyday life.

Espartero, Baldomero (1793–1879) Spanish general and statesman. During the first Carlist War (1833–39), he supported the succession of the infant ISABELLA II against the claim of Don CARLOS. Espartero won a major victory against the forces of CARLISM at the Battle of Luchana (1836). In 1839 Espartero negotiated a peace settlement. He forced the resignation of MARÍA CRISTINA, replacing her as regent in 1841. Espartero established an autocratic government and brutally crushed revolts in 1841 and 1842. A further rebellion in 1843 forced him to flee to England, where he remained until 1849. In 1854 Espartero returned to politics, sharing power with General Leopoldo O'Donnell. In 1856 O'Donnell assumed supreme control and Espartero retired.

Essenes Jewish religious sect that existed in Palestine from the 2nd century BC to the end of the 2nd century AD. A secrecy developed about the sect, and its members shunned public life and temple worship. The DEAD SEA SCROLLS are said to contain their sacred books.

Essex, Robert Devereux, 2nd Earl of (1567–1601) English courtier and soldier. In 1586 he distinguished himself fighting under his stepfather, Robert Dudley, Earl of LEICESTER, in the REVOLT OF THE NETHERLANDS against Spanish rule and succeeded Leicester as ELIZABETH I's favourite. Essex angered Elizabeth by taking part in a disastrous English raid (1589) on Lisbon, Portugal, and secretly marrying (1590) the widow of Sir Philip SIDNEY. In 1591–92 he led an English force to aid HENRY IV of France in the French WARS OF RELIGION. Essex failed in his attempt to topple Lord BURGHLEY and was overlooked in favour of Burghley's son, Robert CECIL. In 1596 Essex became a national hero for his part in the sacking of CÁDIZ, SW Spain. In 1599 he was appointed lord lieutenant of Ireland, where he failed to crush a rebellion led by the Earl of Tyrone and concluded an unauthorized truce. In 1600 Essex returned to England and was placed under house arrest. After leading a failed coup, he was arrested and executed for treason. *See also* BACON, FRANCIS; DRAKE, SIR FRANCIS; RALEIGH, SIR WALTER

▲ **Erasmus** Portrait by Hans Holbein the Younger (1497–1543). Erasmus travelled widely in Europe and his exposure to Renaissance ideas greatly influenced his thinking.

ERITREA
AREA: 117,600sq km (45,406sq mi)
POPULATION: 3,500,000
CAPITAL (POPULATION): Asmara (358,100)
GOVERNMENT: Constitutional monarchy
ETHNIC GROUPS: Tigrinya 48%, Tigre 31%
LANGUAGES: Arabic, Tigrinya, Tigre
RELIGIONS: Coptic Christian 50%, Sunni Muslim 50%
GDP PER CAPITA (1994): US$96

Essex, Robert Devereux, 3rd Earl of (1591–1646) English general, son of the 2nd Earl of ESSEX. In 1606 JAMES I arranged his marriage to Frances Howard, but the union was annulled (1613) after Howard fell in love with James' secretary Robert Carr. CHARLES I appointed Essex second in command of the king's army in the BISHOPS' WARS (1639), but he defected to the Parliamentarians at the start of the English CIVIL WAR. Essex commanded the Roundheads at the Battle of EDGEHILL (1642), but was routed in Cornwall (1643). In 1645 the NEW MODEL ARMY was formed and Essex resigned. *See also* CROMWELL, OLIVER

estate Organized social CLASS with separate representation in government. The disintegration of the FEUDAL SYSTEM saw the emergence of three estates – nobility, clergy and commons (BOURGEOISIE). The English PARLIAMENT developed out of this classification; the nobility and clergy were represented in the HOUSE OF LORDS, and the bourgeoisie in the HOUSE OF COMMONS. The rise of the bourgeoisie can be clearly traced in the history of the French STATES-GENERAL. The media are often referred to as the fourth estate.

Estates-General *See* STATES-GENERAL

Este, Alfonso I, d' (1476–1534) Duke of Ferrara (1505–34), husband of Lucrezia BORGIA. He fought against Venice at the start of the ITALIAN WARS (1494–1559). Alfonso's support for LOUIS XII of France led to his excommunication by Pope Julius II and the loss of Modena (1510) and Reggio (1512). He allied with Emperor CHARLES V against Pope CLEMENT VII and recovered his lands. Ariosto dedicated *Orlando Furioso* (1532) to Alfonso's brother, **Cardinal Ippolito II d'Este** (1509–72), who built Villa d'Este at Tivoli, central Italy.

Estonia *See* country feature, page 134

ETA (*Euskadi Ta Askatasuna*, "Basque Homeland and Freedom") BASQUE separatist organization that advocates the use of violence to secure an independent Basque state. It was founded (1959) by militant members of the Basque Nationalist Party. In 1966 ETA split between those who sought an autonomous Basque state within Spain, and a Marxist-Leninist group who sought complete independence through a bombing campaign. In 1973 ETA assassinated Vice Premier CARRERO BLANCO. Under General FRANCO, ETA was suppressed with great brutality. After Franco's death (1975), ETA stepped up its terrorist campaign. Between 1979 and 1983 the Spanish government granted limited autonomy to the Basques, but ETA remained active. In 1997 several leaders of ETA's political wing, Herri Batasuna, were imprisoned. In 1998 ETA announced a cease-fire and opened negotiations with the Spanish government. The cease-fire was broken in November 1999.

Ethelred I (d.871) King of WESSEX and Kent (*c.*865–71), son of Ethelwulf. His reign was dominated

E

E

ETRUSCAN

Inhabitant of ancient Etruria (roughly corresponding to modern Tuscany), central Italy. The Etrurian League, influenced by Greek colonies in S Italy, consisted of 12 city-states. The history of Etruscan civilization can be divided into four periods: the Orientalizing (7th century BC), Archaic (6th–5th centuries BC), Classical (5th–4th centuries BC) and Hellenistic (3rd–1st centuries BC). The 7th century BC was a period of rapid expansion and by the mid-6th century BC, the Etruscan civilization stretched from Campania to the River Po. Etruscan wealth and power was based primarily on control of the iron and copper trade. The city-states, which flourished in the 6th century BC, were surrounded by fortified walls and were among the first cities in the Mediterranean to be built on a grid system. The decline of Etruscan civilization began in 510 BC, when the Tarquin dynasty was expelled from Rome and a Roman republic established. By the mid-4th century BC, Celtic infiltration in the Po valley region had almost completely destroyed some Etruscan communities. In 283 BC Etruria was annexed by ancient Rome. The Romans adopted many aspects of Etruscan culture, including their alphabet and architectural features like the Doric column. Etruscan art consists of naturalistic bronze busts and black *bucchero* pottery. *See also* Celts

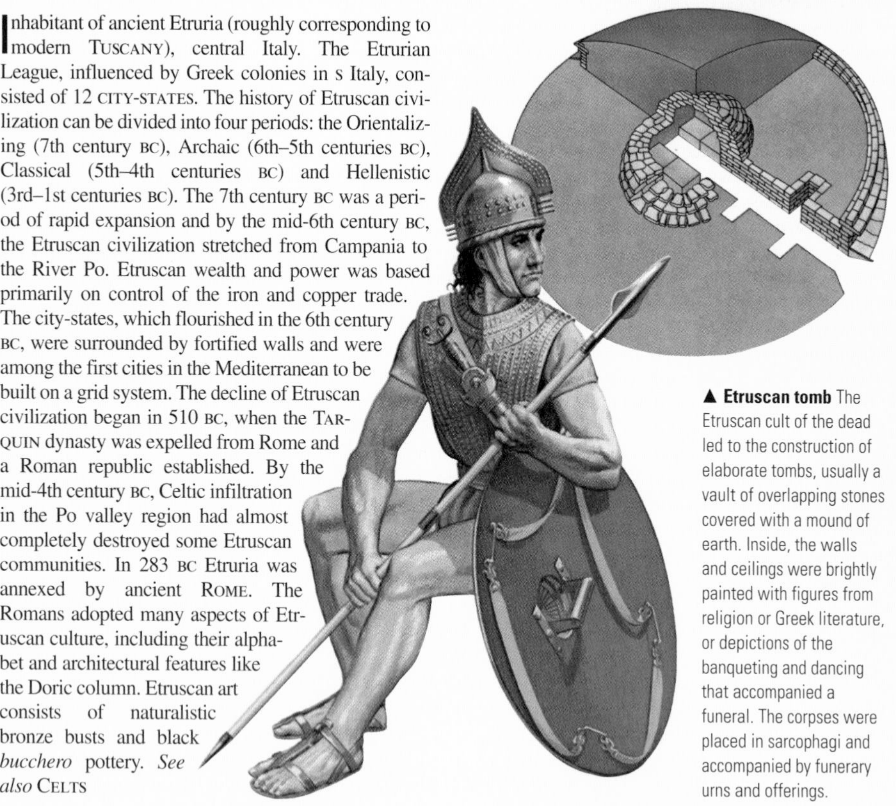

▲ **Etruscan tomb** The Etruscan cult of the dead led to the construction of elaborate tombs, usually a vault of overlapping stones covered with a mound of earth. Inside, the walls and ceilings were brightly painted with figures from religion or Greek literature, or depictions of the banqueting and dancing that accompanied a funeral. The corpses were placed in sarcophagi and accompanied by funerary urns and offerings.

by conflict with the Danes. In 871 Ethelred was defeated at Reading, but revived English hopes with a victory at Ashdown. He died in the Battle of Merton and was succeeded by his brother, Alfred (the Great).

Ethelred II (the Unready) (*c*.968–1016) King of England (978–1013, 1014–16), son of Edgar and half-brother and successor of Edward the Martyr. Ethelred's resistance to the Danes was hampered by the defection of his commanders, who suspected him of complicity in the assassination of Edward the Martyr. In 991 he began paying tribute to the Danes with money raised by the Danegeld. His massacre of Danish settlers (1002) led to the invasion (1013) of King Sweyn I (Forkbeard), who was received as king. In 1014 Ethelred was restored. In 1015 Canute II (the Great) invaded England. Ethelred was succeeded by his son, Edmund II.

Ethiopia *See* country feature

Etruscan *See* feature article

Eugène of Savoy (1663–1736) Austrian field marshal, one of the most daring and brilliant soldiers in military history, b. France. His role in breaking the Ottoman Turks' siege of Vienna (1683) led Emperor Leopold I to appoint him as a regimental commander. Eugène went on to score seven major victories over the Ottoman Empire, most notably at Zenta (1697) and Belgrade (1718), thus driving the Turks out of Hungary and much of the Balkans. He also fought against France in the War of the Grand Alliance (1698–97) and the War of the Spanish Succession (1702–13). Allied with the English Duke of Marlborough in the latter conflict, Eugène captured Germany at the Battle of Blenheim (1704), N Italy at Oudenaarde (1708) and the Netherlands at Malpaquet (1709). *See also* Charles VI; Joseph I

Eugénie (1826–1920) Consort of Napoleon III and French empress. She became the wife of Napoleon III shortly after he proclaimed (1852) the Second Empire. Eugénie was regent in her husband's absences at war (1859, 1865, 1870), and her influence as a Catholic and conservative was often felt in French affairs. In 1870 the Empire collapsed and the couple fled to England.

eunuch Castrated male. In ancient China, eunuchs were employed initially as guardians of the harem during the Qin dynasty (221–207 BC). They became imperial advisers and wielded great influence during the dynasties of the Later Han (AD 25–220), Tang (618–907) and Ming (1368–1644). Eunuchs attended the imperial harems of the Achaemenid, Byzantine and Ottoman empires.

Eureka Stockade (1854) Armed rebellion of gold diggers at Ballarat, Victoria, Australia. Gold was discovered at Ballarat in 1851, and within two years 20,000 miners were digging the fields of Victoria. The diggers objected to the government's imposition of an expensive mining licence and *c*.150 diggers formed a stockade. A force of *c*.280 policemen and soldiers attacked the diggers and 30 miners and five soldiers died in the ensuing battle. A wave of public sympathy led to the acquittal of the rebels and reforms to the goldfields. *See also* Australian Gold Rush

Europe Earth's second-smallest continent (after Australia). The Mediterranean region was the cradle of the ancient Greek and Roman civilizations. The collapse of the Western Roman Empire and the Barbarian invasions brought chaos to much of Europe (*see also* Byzantine Empire). During the Middle Ages, Christianity was a unifying force throughout the continent. In the 16th century, however, the Catholic Church was divided by the Reformation and the development of Protestantism, and this division became a contributory cause of many European wars. From the 16th to the 19th centuries, the European powers built vast empires in other parts of the globe and came to dominate world trade (*see* British Empire; colonialism; exploration; imperialism). The Industrial Revolution, which began in Britain in the 18th century and on the continent in the 19th century, greatly increased Europe's economic power and led to enormous social change. The French Revolution (1789) ushered in an era of momentous political changes.

ESTONIA

AREA: 44,700sq km (17,300sq mi)
POPULATION: 1,491,583
CAPITAL (POPULATION): Tallinn (490,000)
GOVERNMENT: Multiparty republic
ETHNIC GROUPS: Estonian 62%, Russian 30%, Ukrainian 3%, Belorussian 2%, Finnish 1%
LANGUAGES: Estonian (official)
RELIGIONS: Christianity (Lutheran, with Orthodox and Baptist minorities)
GDP PER CAPITA (1995): US$4220

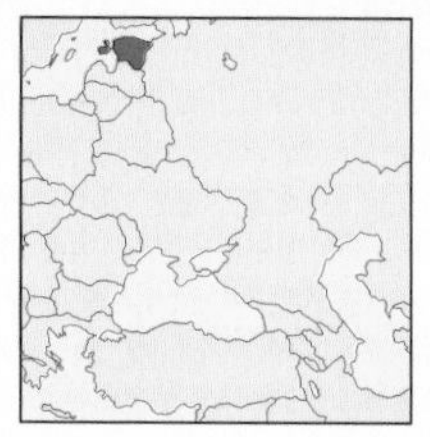

Republic on the E coast of the Baltic Sea, N Europe. The first mention of the Estonians is in the *Germania* by Tacitus (1st century AD). The Vikings invaded Estonia in the 9th century. In 1217 the German Order of the Brothers of the Sword conquered the S part of the country (Livonia) in a campaign to Christianize the Estonians (*see* Livonian Order). Ten years later, the Danes conquered the north. In 1237 the Teutonic Knights assumed control of the south and they took over the north in 1346. The German nobles reduced the Estonians to serfdom.

In the 16th century Estonia was contested by Sweden and Moscow. The Truce of Altmark (1629) gave Sweden absolute control. In the Great Northern War (1700–21), Tsar Nicholas II defeated Charles XII at the Battle of Poltava (1709) and Sweden surrendered Livonia to Russia. By the Treaty of Nystad (1721), Russia gained all of Estonia. The accession (1881) of Tsar Alexander III increased the pace of Russification. The Russian Revolution of 1905 sparked a wave of civil disorder that was brutally crushed. The Russian Revolution (1917) brought autonomy to Estonia.

The Treaty of Brest-Litovsk (1918) briefly handed Estonia to Germany. In November 1918 Estonia's declaration of independence prompted the invasion of the Russian Red Army. In 1919 Estonia expelled the Russians. A succession of short-lived coalition governments led to the adoption of a new constitution (1933). In 1934 President Konstantin Päts established a dictatorship. The Nazi-Soviet Pact (August 1939) handed Estonia to the Soviet Union. In June 1940 Soviet forces occupied Estonia and it became a republic of the Soviet Union in August 1940. More than 60,000 Estonians were killed or deported in the first year of Soviet occupation. In June 1941 Germany, helped by Estonian rebels, invaded the country. In September 1944 Soviet troops returned to expel the Germans. Between 1945 and 1953, *c*.80,000 Estonians were deported, and a wave of Russian emigrants entered Estonia. In August 1991, following the collapse of the Soviet Union, Estonia declared independence. In 1992 a new constitution was adopted and Lennart Meri (1929–) was elected president. In 1994 the last Soviet troops withdrew from Estonia.

During the 20th century, a period overshadowed by two world wars and the rise of COMMUNISM, Europe began to lose some of its pre-eminence in world affairs. After WORLD WAR 2, the countries of Europe became divided into two ideological blocs: Eastern Europe, dominated by the Soviet Union; and Western Europe, closely aligned with the United States. The rivalry was known as the COLD WAR. The NORTH ATLANTIC TREATY ORGANIZATION (NATO) was established to act as a deterrent to the spread of COMMUNISM; the WARSAW PACT was its E European counterpart. Several economic organizations, in particular the EUROPEAN COMMUNITY (EC), worked towards closer intra-national cooperation. In 1989 the collapse of communist regimes in Eastern Europe added to the momentum for a kind of supranational union in the form of a EUROPEAN UNION (EU). *See also* individual country articles

European Commission Institution responsible for initiating and implementing the policies of the EUROPEAN UNION (EU). The Commission drafts policy proposals that it submits to the European Council of Ministers and the EUROPEAN PARLIAMENT (EP). It was established (1967) with the creation of the EUROPEAN COMMUNITY (EC). There are 20 commissioners, two from France, Germany, Italy, Spain and the United Kingdom, and one each from the remaining member states. Each commissioner has responsibility for a different policy area and pledges loyalty to the EU rather than individual member states. The president of the Commission is elected by the commissioners for a four-year term. The Commission heads a secretariat of *c.*15,000 civil servants based in Brussels, Belgium. It is collectively responsible to the European Parliament, which can remove it on a censure motion carried by a two-thirds majority. In 1999, following charges of corruption, the entire Commission resigned. *See also* DELORS, JACQUES; JENKINS, ROY; SANTER, JACQUES; PRODI, ROMANO

European Community (EC) Historic organization of Western European countries dedicated to closer economic and political cooperation in Europe. In 1952 the European Coal and Steel Community (ECSC) was established to integrate the coal and steel industries primarily of France and West Germany to create a more unified Europe. The success of the ECSC led to the Treaties of ROME (1957) that established the **European Economic Community** (EEC), or Common Market, and the European Atomic Energy Commission (EURATOM). The aim was to create a common economic approach to agriculture, employment, trade and social development, and to give Western Europe more influence in world affairs. The founder members were France, West Germany, Italy, Belgium, Netherlands and Luxembourg. In 1962 the COMMON AGRICULTURAL POLICY (CAP) came into effect. In 1967 the EEC, ECSC and EURATOM merged to form the European Community (EC). The United Kingdom, Ireland and Denmark joined in 1973; Greece in 1981; Spain and Portugal in 1986; and Austria, Finland and Sweden in 1995. In 1993 the EC was superseded by the EUROPEAN UNION (EU). *See also* MONNET, JEAN; SPAAK, PAUL HENRI

European Convention on Human Rights (1950) Agreement to protect the rights and freedoms of the individual, signed by the members of the COUNCIL OF EUROPE. The Convention listed 12 basic rights, including the right to life, to a fair trial, to peaceful assembly and association, and to freedom of expression and from slavery and torture. An additional protocol provides for the abolition of the death penalty. *See also* HUMAN RIGHTS

European Court of Human Rights Created in 1959, the Court is presided over by one judge from each of the member states that are signatories to the EUROPEAN CONVENTION ON HUMAN RIGHTS (1950). It decides whether or not an individual's rights have been violated by a member state in cases when the two parties have already failed to reach a settlement through the European Commission of Human Rights. *See also* HUMAN RIGHTS

European Court of Justice (officially Court of Justice of the European Communities) Court responsible for the interpretation and implementation of EUROPEAN UNION (EU) laws. The Court will also rule in cases where member states are alleged to have broken EU laws. It was established in the first of the Treaties of ROME (1957) and is based in Luxembourg.

European Free Trade Association (EFTA) Organization seeking to promote free trade among its European members. Established in 1960, it originally comprised Austria, Denmark, Norway, Portugal, Sweden, Switzerland and the United Kingdom. By 1995 all but Norway and Switzerland had joined the EUROPEAN UNION (EU), while Iceland and Liechtenstein joined EFTA in 1970 and 1991 respectively.

European Monetary System (EMS) System set up (1979) to bring about monetary stability among the (then nine) members of the EUROPEAN COMMUNITY (EC). The EMS had three main components: the European Currency Unit (ECU), a monetary unit weighted according to the size of each member state's economy and the value of its trade; the Exchange Rate Mechanism (ERM), where each member state agreed to keep their national currencies within set margins (initially either 2.25% or 6% above or below) of a central rate of exchange against the ECU; and credit mechanisms. The MAASTRICHT

ETHIOPIA (FORMERLY ABYSSINIA)

AREA: 1,128,000sq km (435,521sq mi)
POPULATION: 55,500,000
CAPITAL (POPULATION): Addis Ababa (1,700,000)
GOVERNMENT: Federation of nine provinces
ETHNIC GROUPS: Oromo (Galla) 40%, Semitic (Amhara and Tigreans) 33%, Shangalla 5%, Somalis 5%, others 17%
LANGUAGES: Amharic (de facto official)
RELIGIONS: Christianity 53%, Islam 36%, traditional beliefs 11%
GDP PER CAPITA (1995): US$450

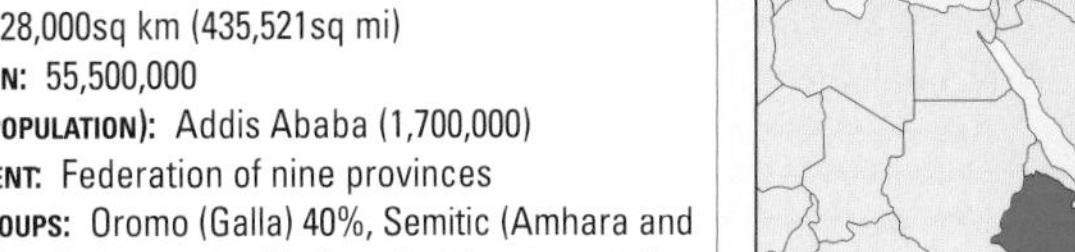

Landlocked republic in NE Africa. In 1974 the most complete early hominid skeleton yet recovered, an adult female *Australopithecus afarensis* (nickamed "Lucy") *c.*3–4 million years old, was unearthed in Hadar, Afar, N Ethiopia (*see* HUMAN EVOLUTION). Between *c.*8000 BC and *c.*6000 BC, AGRICULTURE developed in N Africa.

According to tradition, the Ethiopian kingdom was founded (*c.*1000 BC) by Menelik I, son of SOLOMON and the Queen of SHEBA. In *c.*700 BC the kingdom of Da'amat was established in the highlands of Tigray. By the end of the 1st century AD, it had been supplanted by the kingdom of AKSUM. Aksum became the dominant empire in the Red Sea region through trade with Arabia.

In 321 Ethiopia became the first African country to adopt CHRISTIANITY as the state religion when Emperor Ezana (r. *c.*305–350) adopted MONOPHYSITISM (*see* COPTIC CHURCH). Aksum went into decline in the 7th century after losing control of its ports to the Muslim Arabs and was finally destroyed in the 10th century. The Zagwe dynasty arose in the 12th century. Emperor Lalibela (r. *c.*1185–1225) built the famous rock-hewn churches in his capital, Roha (now Lalibela).

In 1270 the Zagwe king, Yitbarek, was overthrown and the SOLOMONID dynasty was established. The Solomonids fought against Muslim encroachment and under Emperor Amda Tseyon (r.1314–44) overran Ifat and other Muslim states. By 1535, however, 75% of the country was in Muslim hands after the Sultan of Adal, Ahmad ibn Ibrahim al-Ghazi, had launched a *jihad* against Ethiopia. In 1543, with Portuguese aid, Emperor Galawdewos (r.1540–59) defeated and killed Ahmad near Lake Tana.

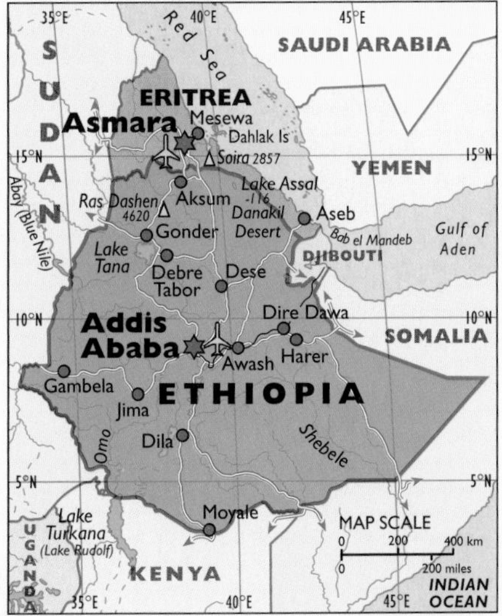

The 16th century witnessed the expansion of the Oromo from S Ethiopia. In 1632 Emperor Susenyos was forced to abdicate in favour of his son, Fasilides (r.1632–67), who formed a new capital at Gonder. The "Age of the Princes" (*c.*1700–1850) was a period of feudal turmoil. In 1853 Kassa defeated Ali, the last Oromo prince, and was crowned (1855) Emperor Tewodros II. In 1868, following his defeat at the Battle of MAGDALA by British troops under Robert NAPIER, Tewodros committed suicide. Emperor Yohannes IV (r.1872–89) was threatened by internal dissent and invasions by Egypt and Italy.

In 1889, with Italian support, MENELIK II became emperor (r.1889–1913) and transferred the capital to ADDIS ABABA. A dispute over the terms of the Treaty of Wichale (1889) resulted in Italian defeat at the Battle of ADWA (1896). Italy recognized Ethiopian independence in the subsequent Treaty of Addis Ababa (1896), but retained ERITREA. Menelik expanded Ethiopia to its present extent and modernized the government and army. In 1930 Menelik II's cousin, Ras Tafari Makonnen, was crowned Emperor HAILE SELASSIE I. In October 1935 Italian troops invaded Ethiopia. In May 1936, Addis Ababa fell and Haile Selassie went into exile. Ethiopia was combined with Eritrea and Italian Somaliland to form Italian East Africa.

In 1941 Allied forces recaptured Ethiopia and Haile Selassie was restored. In 1952, with the support of the United States, Eritrea was federated with Ethiopia. The annexation (1962) of Eritrea marked the start of a 30-year long war of independence. In September 1974, following famine in N Ethiopia, Selassie was murdered in a military coup. The Provisional Military Administrative Council (PMAC), led by Major Haile MENGISTU, established a Marxist state. Military rule was repressive, and civil war broke out. In 1977 SOMALIA invaded the Ogaden, but was forced to withdraw by the Soviet-backed Ethiopian army. In 1984 the combination of collectivization and drought produced a terrible famine that saw a huge international relief effort. In 1987 Mengistu established the People's Democratic Republic of Ethiopia with himself as president.

In 1990 Eritrean separatists captured the vital Red Sea port of Massawa. In 1991 Mengistu fled into exile and the Ethiopian People's Revolutionary Democratic Front (EPRDF) formed a provisional government. The EPRDF, led by Menes Zenawi, divided Ethiopia into nine ethnic regions. In 1993 Eritrea gained independence. The Federal Democratic Republic of Ethiopia was created in 1995 and Menes Zenawi was elected prime minister. A border war with Eritrea (1998–) had claimed *c.*50,000 lives by mid-1999, more than 40,000 of whom were killed in the Battle of Badme (February 1999).

Prehistoric peoples performed great feats of exploration, reaching most of the habitable regions of the Earth before 10,000 BC. The first written accounts of exploration, however, were produced by the ancient Egyptians in the 3rd millennium BC and subsequently by the Phoenicians, Greeks and Romans, who between them explored an area of land and sea stretching from the British Isles to India. The descriptions of their journeys contributed to the vision of the world produced by the Greek geographer PTOLEMY in the 2nd century AD. This was to greatly influence later European explorers, but in the millennium after the collapse of the Roman Empire in the 5th century AD, the greatest explorers were the Arabs and the Chinese. They included IBN BATUTA, who explored much of Arabia, India, Southeast Asia and Sudan during the 14th century, and ZHENG HE, who led a fleet from China to Africa in the early 15th century. The main source of European knowledge of the Far East was from the writings of MARCO POLO, who lived in China towards the end of the 13th century.

The European "Age of Discovery" began in the 15th century with the declared purpose of spreading Christianity. Its chief motive, however, was financial gain, initially through the discovery of a sea route round Africa to India. In 1487 Portuguese explorer Bartholomeu DIAS rounded the Cape of Good Hope and in 1498 Vasco da GAMA completed the first voyage from Portugal to India. In 1492 Christopher COLUMBUS sailed W towards Asia, landing in the West Indies. Similarly, in 1500 Pedro CABRAL acciden-

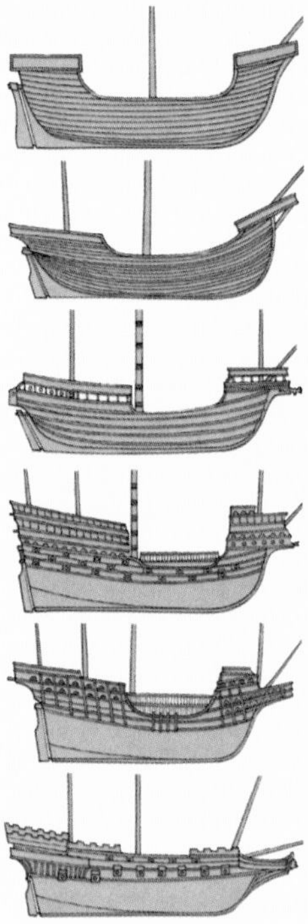

◄ **Developments in shipbuilding** Between 1400 and 1600 the principal changes in ship design were the addition of several masts and a greater streamlining.

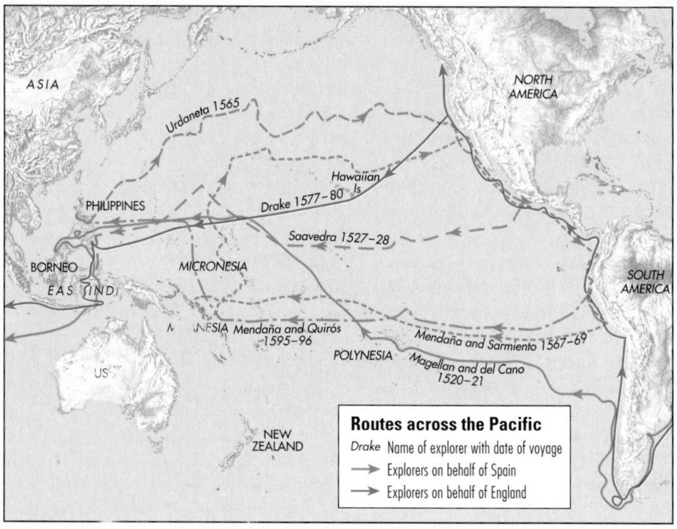

▲ **Exploration of the Pacific Ocean** After Ferdinand Magellan's crossing of the Pacific in 1520, Saavedra sailed from Mex[illegible] to Moluccas in 1[illegible] 1565 Urdaneta found a viable return route. Mendana and Sarmiento discovered the Solomon Islands (1567). In 1578 Drake became the first English explorer to cross the Pacific.

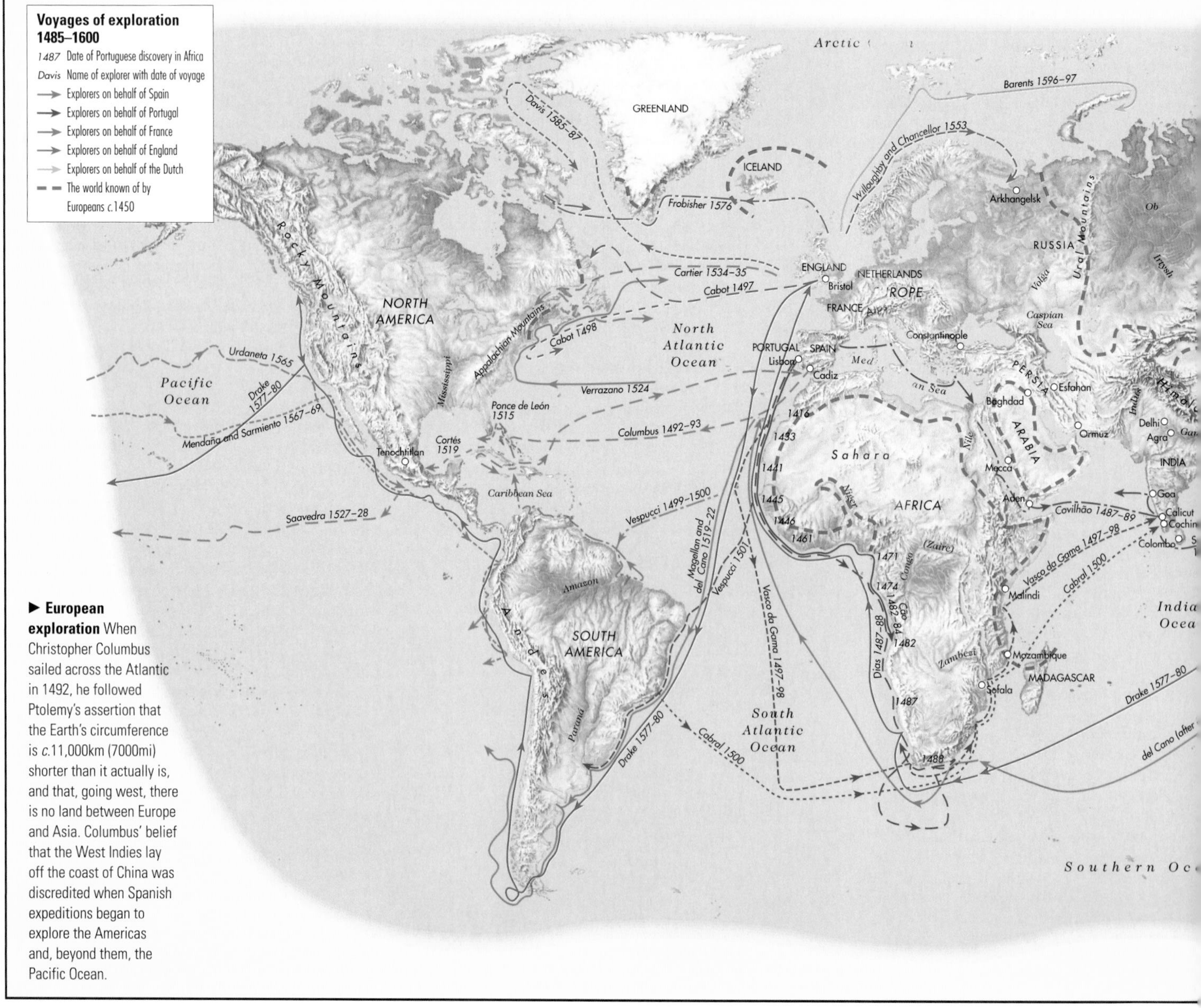

► **European exploration** When Christopher Columbus sailed across the Atlantic in 1492, he followed Ptolemy's assertion that the Earth's circumference is c.11,000km (7000mi) shorter than it actually is, and that, going west, there is no land between Europe and Asia. Columbus' belief that the West Indies lay off the coast of China was discredited when Spanish expeditions began to explore the Americas and, beyond them, the Pacific Ocean.

tally discovered Brazil while sailing for India. The search for a westward trade route to the East spurred Ferdinand Magellan's circumnavigation of the globe (1519–22). The lure of gold in South America prompted the explorations of Hernán Cortés and Francisco Pizarro. The outcome of their exploits was typical of much European exploration, which was often followed by colonialism and the devastation of indigenous peoples through the spread of new diseases or the slave trade.

In the 17th century, the interior of North America was mapped by, among others, Samuel de Champlain, Sieur de La Salle, Louis Jolliet and Jacques Marquette. In the 18th century, James Cook and Vitus Bering explored the Pacific Ocean. Cook sailed further south than any previous explorer and established that there was no habitable southern continent. In the 19th century, science became a strong motivating force. A number of European explorers, among them David Livingstone and Henry Stanley, mapped the interior of Africa. Others mapped the interior of Australia, the mountains of Asia and the approaches to the Poles. In 1909 Richard Peary reached the North Pole, while Roald Amundsen beat Robert Scott to the South Pole in 1911. In the 1920s, Richard Byrd pioneered the exploration of Antarctica by aircraft. The launch of Sputnik 1 (1957) opened up the era of space exploration.

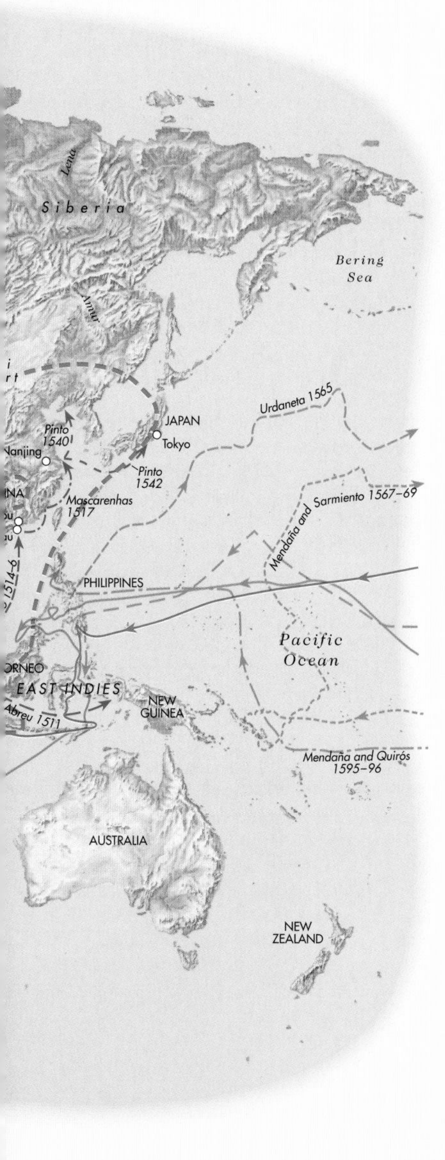

Treaty (1992) set a timetable for achieving economic and monetary union (EMU) and the establishment of a single currency (the euro). In 1998 eleven member states of the European Union (EU) were chosen to participate in the first stage of EMU. On 1 January 1999, the euro was born and a European Central Bank was given control of a single monetary policy.

European Parliament (EP) Representative assembly of the European Union (EU). It originated (1952) as the Common Assembly of the European Coal and Steel Community (ECSC). The Parliament was expanded by the Treaties of Rome (1957) to serve two new bodies, the European Economic Community (EEC) and the European Atomic Energy Commission (Euratom). Direct elections to the EP were first held in 1979. In June 1994 elections, the EP expanded from 518 to 567 seats. In 1995, it expanded to 626 members with the accession of Austria, Finland and Sweden to the EU. The Parliament's powers were greatly increased by the Single European Act (1986), which introduced the cooperation procedure, the Maastricht Treaty (1991), which extended the cooperation procedure and introduced the co-decision procedure, and the Amsterdam Treaty (1997), which extended the co-decision procedure to all areas except economic and monetary union (EMU). Although it cannot initiate legislation, the EP can advise and has the power of consultation on all EU issues, including the EU budget. The Parliament meets in Strasbourg, France, and Brussels, Belgium.

European Union (EU) Organization of 15 European countries (Austria, Belgium, Denmark, Finland, France, Germany, Greece, Ireland, Italy, Luxembourg, Netherlands, Portugal, Spain, Sweden and the United Kingdom) established (1993) following the ratification of the Maastricht Treaty (1992). The EU assumed control of the existing framework and institutions of the European Community (EC), such as the European Commission and European Parliament (EP), but extended the role and scope of the EC according to the criteria of the Maastricht Treaty. The member states agreed to greater cooperation, particularly in areas such as foreign and security policies, and internal and judicial policies. The United Kingdom and Denmark "opted out" of the first stage in the creation of a single European currency (the euro). In addition to reforms of existing policies, such as the Common Agricultural Policy (CAP), the EU is faced with the challenge of enlargement. In 1998 formal accession negotiations were opened with Hungary, Poland, Estonia, Czech Republic, Slovenia and Cyprus. In 1994 the EU and the European Free Trade Association (EFTA) established the European Economic Area (EEA), a frontier-free zone. In addition to the Commission and Parliament, the EU's institutional structure comprises the European Council of Ministers, the Economic and Social Committee (which advises on draft EU legislation), the European Central Bank and the European Court of Justice. *See also* European Monetary System (EMS); Western European Union (WEU)

Evans, Sir Arthur John (1851–1941) English archaeologist. He excavated the ruins of Knossos in Crete and found evidence of a Bronze Age (2000–1400 BC) civilization, which he named the Minoan civilization.

Evatt, Herbert Vere (1894–1965) Australian statesman, president (1948–49) of the United Nations (UN) General Assembly. He represented Australia in Winston Churchill's War Cabinet. As leader (1951–60) of the Australian Labor Party, Evatt argued for greater independence from the United Kingdom.

Everett, Edward (1794–1865) US orator and statesman. He was a member of the House of Representatives (1824–34), governor of Massachusetts (1835–39), US minister to England (1841–45) and president of Harvard (1846–49). In 1852 Everett became secretary of state under President Millard Fillmore. During the Civil War, he delivered the main speech shortly before President Abraham Lincoln's famous address at Gettysburg, Pennsylvania (1863). *See also* Gettysburg Address

Evers, Medgar Wiley (1926–63) US civil rights activist. As field secretary of the National Association for the Advancement of Colored People (NAACP), Evers campaigned for the registration of African-American voters in the South. On 12 June 1963, he was shot dead outside his home in Jackson, Mississippi. A white man, Byron de la Beckwith, boasted of the killing and was indicted for murder, but was freed after two trials resulted in hung juries.

Evesham, Battle of (4 August 1265) Final conflict of the second Barons' War at Evesham, w central England. Simon de Montfort, the rebel leader, was defeated and beheaded by Henry III's son, later Edward I.

Évian Agreements (1962) Series of accords to end the Algerian War of Independence signed at Évian-les-Bains, E France. The agreements, which provided for a ceasefire and recognition of Algerian independence, followed secret negotiations between the French government of General De Gaulle and the provisional government of Algeria, led by Ben Bella. The Agreements were overwhelmingly endorsed by referenda in both countries, but encountered resistance from the OAS.

evolution *See* human evolution

Exclusion Crisis (1679–81) Campaign to exclude Charles II's Catholic brother, James, Duke of York, later James II, from the English throne. It was triggered by the false claims of Titus Oates that he had evidence of a "popish plot" to murder Charles and put James on the throne. As a result, the House of Commons passed a bill (1679) to exclude James from the throne. Charles responded by dissolving Parliament. When the House of Commons in two subsequent Parliaments, the last in 1681, also voted to exclude James, they too were dissolved. The king then drove the supporters of exclusion, the "Whigs", from government and put the Tories in their place, thus bringing the crisis to an end.

Exhibition, Great (1851) *See* Great Exhibition

exploration *See* feature article

Eyadema, Gnassingbe (1935–) Togolese statesman, president (1969–). He served (1953–61) in the French army, mostly in Indochina and Algeria. In 1967 Eyadema deposed President Grunitsky in a military coup. In 1969 he became president and leader of the *Rassemblement du Peuple Togolais*.

Eyre, Edward John (1815–1901) British explorer and colonial administrator. In 1840 he journeyed across the Flinders Ranges from Adelaide, discovering Lake Eyre, S Australia. In 1841 Eyre became the first European to cross from South to Western Australia, traversing the Nullarbor Plain from Adelaide to Albany. In 1865 he was dismissed as governor of Jamaica (1864–65) after brutally suppressing a black rebellion.

Ezekiel (active 6th century BC) Hebrew prophet. In 597 BC he was among the Jews deported by Nebuchadnezzar II at the start of the Babylonian Captivity. Ezekiel prophesized the destruction of the Temple of Jerusalem (587 BC) and argued that the Israelites would only be restored to their land by a revival of Judaism. He is traditionally considered the author of the Old Testament Book of Ezekiel. Ezekiel was the last of the "greater" Old Testament prophets, the successor of Isaiah and Jeremiah.

F

Fabian Society British society (founded 1883) of non-Marxists who believed that SOCIALISM could be attained through gradual political change. With George Bernard Shaw, Annie BESANT, and Sidney and Beatrice WEBB as leaders, the Society gained widespread recognition and helped found the Labour Representation Committee (1900), which became the British LABOUR PARTY in 1906. Today, the Fabian Society is affiliated to the Labour Party and publishes a journal and pamphlets.

Fabius Maximus Verrucosus, Quintus (d.203 BC) Roman general and politician, called Cunctator (Lat. "Delayer"). He is famed for his strategy of avoiding pitched battle against HANNIBAL during the Second PUNIC WAR. When his strategy was rejected, the Romans suffered a disastrous defeat at Cannae in 216 BC. Fabius' strategy was resumed and eventually eroded Hannibal's strength.

Factory Acts Series of laws to regulate the conditions of employment of factory workers. A response to the atrocious conditions resulting from the INDUSTRIAL REVOLUTION, the first piece of factory legislation in the United Kingdom, the Health and Morals of Apprentices Act (1802), limited the working day for children to 12 hours. The Factory Act of 1819 forbade the employment in cotton mills of children under the age of nine. The 1833 Act set up a central body of inspection. The Acts of 1844 and 1847, sponsored by the 7th Earl of SHAFTESBURY, reduced the working day for women and "young persons" (children more than 13 years old) first to 12 hours and then to ten hours. The 1844 Act also reduced the hours of children to six and a half a day. There were further acts between 1850 and 1901 that aimed to improve conditions in a wider range of industries, but none regulated the wages and hours of adult men. In an attempt to improve working conditions throughout the world, the INTERNATIONAL LABOUR ORGANIZATION (ILO) was founded in 1919. In the United Kingdom, workers are protected by further legislation, including the Factories Acts (1937, 1961), the Health and Safety at Work Act (1974) and the Employment Act (1989). The social chapter of the MAASTRICHT TREATY (1992) sought to harmonize labour laws throughout the European Union (EU). In the United States, factory laws developed by individual states were consolidated by the Fair Labor Standards Act of 1938. This established a national minimum wage and limited the number of hours people could work without being paid overtime to 40 hours a week from the third year of employment. *See also* UNION

Fahd ibn Abdul Aziz (1923–) King of Saudi Arabia (1982–), son of IBN SAUD and brother of FAISAL. In 1975 he became crown prince following the assassination of FAISAL and the accession of KHALID. The illness of King Khalid meant that Fahd managed much of government policy before coming to the throne himself. Fahd sought to diversify the Saudi economy, weakening the dependence on oil revenue. He modernized and expanded the Saudi military and maintained the country's traditional cooperation with the West. In the GULF WAR (1990), Fahd allowed Allied forces to use Saudi bases in order to expel Iraqi forces from Kuwait. He introduced limited democratic reforms, such as the establishment of a consultative council (1992). In 1996 Fahd suffered a stroke and day-to-day control of government passed to his half-brother Abdullah.

Fair Deal US President Harry TRUMAN's domestic programme. Its core values – full employment, increased health and social welfare provision and equal opportunities in employment – were outlined to Congress in 1945, but remained largely unimplemented due to post-war inflation. In 1948 Truman defied predictions to gain a second term in office and resubmitted his reform proposals to Congress under the title of a "Fair Deal". Congress resisted most of Truman's programme, but he did secure the passage of a housing act (1949), an increase in the minimum wage and extended benefits to an additional 10 million elderly people. *See also* NEW DEAL

Fairfax of Cameron, Thomas, 3rd Baron (1612–71) English general in the English CIVIL WAR. He and Oliver CROMWELL led the Parliamentary forces in their victorious battles in N England, notably at MARSTON MOOR (1644). In 1645 Fairfax succeeded the 3rd Earl of ESSEX as commander in chief (1645) of the Parliamentary army. He was instrumental in the formation of the NEW MODEL ARMY and his daring victory over CHARLES I at NASEBY ended the first phase of the Civil War. Fairfax disapproved of the decision to execute CHARLES I and resigned (1650) in protest over the proposed invasion of Scotland. He later headed the commission to the Hague to arrange the RESTORATION of CHARLES II (1660).

Faisal I (1885–1933) King of Iraq (1921–33), son of HUSSEIN IBN ALI. He joined T.E. LAWRENCE in the Arab revolt (1916) against the Turks. When an Arab force occupied Damascus in 1918, Faisal was declared king of Syria. France invaded the kingdom in 1920, however, and he was driven into exile in Britain. Faisal was installed as king of Iraq by the British, gaining independence for Iraq in 1932. His grandson, **Faisal II** (r.1939–58), was executed in the military coup that established Iraq as a republic.

Faisal, ibn Abdul Aziz ibn Saud (*c*.1905–75) King of Saudi Arabia (1964–75), son of IBN SAUD and brother of SAUD. In 1953 he became crown prince on the accession of Saud. Faisal succeeded to the throne after Saud was forced to abdicate. He led Saudi Arabia into the Arab coalition against Israel in the SIX-DAY WAR (1967). Faisal sought closer links with the United States to counter the influence of the Soviet Union in the Middle East. He was shot dead by one of his nephews. Faisal was succeeded by KHALID. *See also* FAHD

Falange (Sp. phalanx) Spanish political party founded (1933) by José Antonio Primo de Rivera, son of Miguel PRIMO DE RIVERA. Modelled on other European fascist parties, it was merged with other groups under the FRANCO regime and became the sole legal political party. It was heavily defeated in free elections in 1977. *See also* CIVIL WAR, SPANISH; FASCISM

Falashas Ethnic group of black Jews in Ethiopia, probably descended from early converts to JUDAISM. Their religion relies solely on observance of the Old Testament. After suffering much discrimination at home, more than 7000 were airlifted to Israel in 1984–85.

Falkland Islands (Islas Malvinas) British crown colony in the S Atlantic Ocean, *c*.520km (320mi) off the E coast of Argentina; the capital is Stanley (on East Falkland). The Falkland Islands were first explored by Europeans in the late 16th century. In 1764 the first settlement on East Falkland was established by the French explorer Louis Antoine de Bougainville. The British established a settlement on West Falkland in 1765. The Spanish bought out the French and attempted to expel the British in 1770; an agreement was reached by which Britain maintained the port of Egmont (while continuing to claim sovereignty of the whole of the Falkland Islands). The Spanish settlement remained until 1806. In 1828 the United Provinces of the Río de La Plata (now ARGENTINA) sent a governor to the islands, but he was expelled by the British in 1833. In 1892 the Falkland Islands became a colony. The Argentine invasion of the Falklands led to the FALKLANDS WAR (1982). Although the British resumed their administration of the Islands, the basic issue of sovereignty remains unresolved. Area: *c*.12,200sq km (4600sq mi). Pop. (1991) 2121.

Falklands War (April–June 1982) Military conflict fought between the United Kingdom and Argentina on the question of sovereignty over the FALKLAND ISLANDS. On 2 April, after the breakdown of negotiations, Argentine forces invaded and occupied the Falklands, South Georgia and South Sandwich Islands, administered by the UK since the 19th century. The British blockaded the islands and landed at Port San Carlos. They surrounded the Argentine troops at the capital, Port Stanley, and forced them to surrender (14 June). The War cost 254 British and 750 Argentine lives. Britain's victory helped secure a second term as prime minister for Margaret THATCHER.

Fanon, Frantz Omar (1925–61) Martinique psychiatrist and theorist of Third World revolution. Educated in France, he left to practise psychiatry in Algeria, where, in 1954, he joined the Algerian liberation movement. Fanon wrote *Black Skin, White Masks* (1952) and *The Wretched of the Earth* (1961). In the latter, he called for a peasant revolution against Western colonialism.

Fanti Black African people who migrated to the coastal region of GHANA in the 17th century and created several kingdoms that joined to form the Fanti Confederation. They acted as go-betweens in the slave trade. In the 19th century, the Fanti were helped by the British in their war against the ASHANTI. In 1874, however, their lands were subsumed into the British colony of Gold Coast. Today, the Fanti number *c*.250,000.

Fargo, William George (1818–81) *See* WELLS-FARGO

Farini, Luigi Carlo (1812–66) Italian statesman and revolutionary, premier of the kingdom of Italy (1862–63). He took part in the CARBONARI revolts of 1831 and was exiled from the Papal States in 1843. Farini returned to Rome under an amnesty granted by Pope PIUS XI in 1846. In 1852 he helped Conte di CAVOUR become premier of Piedmont. Cavour appointed him dictator of Modena in 1859. Farini formed a league of central states (Modena, Parma, Romagna and Tuscany), which was annexed to Piedmont in 1860. Farini became lieutenant general of Naples after it had been captured by Giuseppe GARIBALDI. He succeeded Cavour as the second premier of the kingdom of Italy, but resigned after only four months due to ill health. *See also* RISORGIMENTO

Farm Credit Administration (FCA) US federal government agency that provides credit to farmers. In 1916 Congress authorized the establishment of 12 regional farm land banks and supplied the capital to provide farmers with low-interest rates on long-term loans. In 1923 intermediate credit banks were created for each land bank. In 1933 the FCA, credit associations, and banks for cooperatives were formed. The farm crisis of the 1980s led to the FCA Amendments Act (1985), which gave the FCA more regulatory power over the system. More than 30% of credit used by farmers in the United States derives from the FCA.

Farnese Italian family who ruled (1545–1731) the Duchy of Parma and Piacenza. In 1534 **Alessandro** Farnese (1468–1549) became pope as PAUL III. He created the Duchy for his family and commissioned Antonio da Sangallo to build the Farnese Palace, Rome. Paul III's grandson, **Alessandro** Farnese (1545–92), was a general in the service of PHILIP II of Spain. He distinguished himself against the Turks at the Battle of LEPANTO (1571). In 1578 Alessandro was appointed governor general of the Spanish Netherlands (now BELGIUM). He captured Antwerp (1585) and secured possession of the S Netherlands. In 1590 Alessandro forced HENRY IV of France to raise his siege of Paris.

Faröe Islands (Faeroe Islands) Group of 22 volcanic islands (17 inhabited) in the N Atlantic between Iceland and the Shetland Islands. The largest are Streymoy and Esturoy. Settled in the 7th century, the group was part of Norway from the 11th century until 1380, when it was ceded to Denmark. In 1852 parliament was restored, and since 1948 it has enjoyed a degree of autonomy. Capital and chief port: Tórshavn (Streymoy), pop. (1993) 14,192. Area: 1339sq km (540sq mi). Total pop. (1993) 45,349.

Farouk (1920–65) King of Egypt (1936–52), son and successor of FUAD I. He alienated many Egyptians by his personal extravagance and corruption. Farouk's pro-Axis sympathies during World War 2 angered British troops in Egypt, who appointed the pro-Allies Wafd Party leader Mustafa An Nahhas Pasha as premier, against Farouk's will. Farouk's ambitious foreign policy ended in defeat in the first ARAB-ISRAELI WAR (1948). Overthrown in a military coup led by Gamal Abdel NASSER, he was succeeded by his infant son Fuad II.

Farragut, David Glasgow (1801–70) US admiral. He served under David Porter in the WAR OF 1812. In 1862 Farragut was given command of the Western Gulf Blockading Squadron in the American CIVIL WAR and sailed up the Mississippi River to defeat the Confederate flotilla protecting the New Orleans' forts. Farragut's most famous victory was at the Battle of Mobile Bay (1864), where he ignored torpedoes to capture the Confederate forts. He became (1866) the first US admiral.

Farrakhan, Louis (1933–) US leader of the Nation of Islam, a black separatist organization. He was recruited into the BLACK MUSLIMS in the 1950s by MALCOLM X. Farrakhan was a charismatic advocate of the group's racial exclusivity and in 1976 formed the Nation of Islam, claiming greater adherence to the teachings of Elijah MUHAMMAD. He has been accused of inciting anger against other US minorities, particularly Jews. In 1995 Farrakhan assembled 400,000 men in a "Million Man March" on Washington, D.C.

fasces Symbol of state power in ancient Rome, depicted as a bundle of rods into which an axe is set. Fasces were carried by attendants in front of important officials. The emblem was adopted by the Italian Fascist Party in 1919. *See also* FASCISM

fascism Political movement founded in Italy by Benito MUSSOLINI (1919), characterized by NATIONALISM, TOTALITARIANISM and anti-communism. The term also applied to the regimes of Adolf HITLER in Germany (1933) and Francisco FRANCO in Spain (1936). A reaction against the RUSSIAN REVOLUTION (1917) and the spread of COMMUNISM, the movement based its appeal on the fear of financial instability among the middle-classes and on a wider social discontent. Basic to fascist ideas were: glorification of the state and total subordination to its authority; suppression of all political opposition; stern enforcement of law and order; the supremacy of the leader as the embodiment of high ideals; and aggressive militarism aimed at achieving national greatness. It also typically encouraged racist and xenophobic attitudes and policies. Fascism was discredited by defeat in WORLD WAR 2, but since the 1960s far-right nationalist groups have re-emerged in many countries. *See also* NATIONAL SOCIALISM; NAZI PARTY

Fashoda Incident (18 September 1898) Confrontation between British and French forces on the Upper Nile, Sudan. Britain's aim to establish a railway line between the Cape and the Nile conflicted with French ambition to expand from the Atlantic to the Red Sea. In July 1898 a French force led by Jean Baptiste MARCHAND occupied the fort at Fashoda in Egyptian Sudan. Herbert KITCHENER led a British expedition that conquered Omdurman and KHARTOUM en route to Fashoda. In the ensuing stand-off, an agreement was reached by which both British and French flags could fly over the fort. Further conflict was avoided when the French withdrew. *See also* ENTENTE CORDIALE

Fastolf, Sir John (1378–1459) English soldier and administrator. He fought at AGINCOURT (1415) and elsewhere in France (1417–40) during the HUNDRED YEARS' WAR. Fastolf featured in the PASTON LETTERS, which detail his investment of large war profits in English estates. Shakespeare borrowed his name for the character of Falstaff in the play *Henry IV* (1596–97).

Fatah (inverted acronym of ***H****arakat* ***a****l-****T****ahrir* ***a****l-Watani al-****F****ilastini*) Palestinian national liberation movement founded (1957) by Yasir ARAFAT and Khalil al-Wazir. At the Battle of Karameh (March 1968), Fatah guerrillas helped Jordanian forces to repel and defeat an Israeli army attack on the Jordan valley. The Battle cost the lives of 254 Fatah guerrillas and 29 Israeli soldiers. Victory restored Palestinian morale after the debacle of the SIX-DAY WAR (1967) and Arafat became (1969) chairman of the PALESTINE LIBERATION ORGANIZATION (PLO). In 1971 Fatah was forced out of Jordan into Lebanon and the break-away BLACK SEPTEMBER group was established. Fatah remains the largest single group within the PLO.

Fathers of the Church Early Christian writers whose works are held as orthodox. They include the Apostolic Fathers and the eight **Doctors of the Church**. The four Doctors of the Latin Church are Saint AMBROSE, Saint JEROME, Saint AUGUSTINE and Saint GREGORY I. The four Doctors of the Greek church are Saint BASIL THE GREAT, Saint John CHRYSOSTOM, Saint ATHANASIUS and Saint GREGORY OF NAZIANZUS.

Fatima (606–32) Daughter of the Prophet MUHAMMAD, and wife of ALI. Fatima went with Muhammad when he fled (622) from Mecca to Medina. She nursed Muhammad through his final illness. After his death, Fatima quarrelled with ABU BAKR, Muhammad's successor as leader of the Muslim community. Fatima is particularly revered by the SHI'A sect of ISLAM, who believe that Ali was the legitimate successor of Muhammad.

Fatimids Dynasty founded by Said ibn Husayn at the end of the 9th century. The Fatimids, who claimed the caliphate on the basis of their descent from FATIMA, were *imams* (spiritual leaders) of the ISMAILI sect of SHIITE Muslims. They set out to conquer the SUNNI empire of the ABBASIDS through religious missions and military conquest, rapidly gaining control of most of NW Africa. By ibn Husayn's death (934), the Fatimid empire had expanded into Sicily and Italy. In 969 the Fatimids, led by Caliph Muizz (r.953–75) captured Egypt and founded the city of CAIRO, where they built the Mosque and University of al-Azhar. The intolerant and erratic reign of Hakim (996–1021) weakened the authority of the caliph and led to factional strife. Faced with the rise of the SELJUKS and the Christian CRUSADES, the Fatimid empire crumbled and the caliphate became dominated by military rulers. By the end of the 11th century, Egypt was all that remained of the empire. *See also* SALADIN

Fawcett, Dame Millicent Garrett (1847–1929) English feminist, sister of Elizabeth Garrett ANDERSON. As president of the National Union of Women's Suffrage Societies (1897–1919), she was a leading figure in the SUFFRAGETTE MOVEMENT. Fawcett was a vigorous campaigner in the struggle to extend the FRANCHISE to women. She founded (1871) Newnham College, Cambridge, one of the first women's colleges of higher education in Britain.

Fawkes, Guy (1570–1606) English conspirator in the GUNPOWDER PLOT (1605). He was enlisted by Roman Catholic conspirators in a plot against JAMES I and Parliament. The Plot was betrayed and Fawkes, surrounded by barrels of gunpowder, was arrested and later executed. Traditionally, an effigy called a "guy" is burned on 5 November, the anniversary of the intended explosion.

fealty In the FEUDAL SYSTEM, loyalty and obligations due to a king or lord by his VASSAL; also the specific oath of loyalty and consent taken by the vassal. In the 9th century, fealty meant refraining from participation in any action that endangered the lord's life or property. By the 11th century, the positive duties of a vassal to his lord were established, including personal military service, financial obligations and other forms of personal service. The oath of fealty was followed by an act of homage and, if the granting of a FIEF was involved, by the rite of INVESTITURE.

▲ **Fatimids** The Mosque and University of al-Azhar in Cairo, Egypt, was founded (AD 970) by the Fatimids. It is the supreme religious body in Islam and a centre for Arabic study.

February Revolution (1848) French insurrection that overthrew the monarchy of LOUIS PHILIPPE and established the Second Republic. The JULY REVOLUTION of 1830 failed to quell discontent in French society, indeed the subsequent reactionary policies of François GUIZOT contributed to the rise of republican SOCIALISM. In 1847 crop failure created an economic crisis and led to the "banquet campaign" for political reform. The culmination of the peaceful protests, a mass banquet due to take place on 22 February in Paris, was banned by the government and riots ensued on the Paris streets. On 24 February, *c.*40 people died when troops opened fire on demonstrators. Louis Philippe abdicated and fled into exile in England. The Revolution triggered a wave of popular uprisings in Europe (*see* REVOLUTIONS OF 1848). In France, a provisional government (led by Alphonse de LAMARTINE) was forced to include radicals such as Louis BLANC, who forced the proclamation of a republic, the creation of *ateliers nationaux* (national workshops) for the unemployed, and the extension of the FRANCHISE to all adult men. The resultant elections in April, however, were won by the bourgeois republicans and conservative monarchists. The new assembly abolished the *ateliers nationaux*, prompting the JUNE DAYS of civil unrest in which *c.*1500 protestors died. In December 1848, Prince Louis Napoleon (later NAPOLEON III) was elected president.

Federal Bureau of Investigation (FBI) US federal government agency that investigates violations of federal law. Its findings are reported to the attorney general and various nationwide attorneys for decisions on prosecution. Established in 1908, its autonomy was strengthened under the directorship of J. Edgar HOOVER (1924–72). The agency was criticized for its role in the WATERGATE SCANDAL (1972–74). Its headquarters are in Washington, D.C., and its director is appointed by the president, subject to Senate approval.

federalism Political system that allows states, united under a central government, to maintain a measure of independence. Examples include the United States, Australia, Canada, Germany, India and Switzerland. Central government has supreme authority, but the component states have a considerable amount of autonomy in such matters as education and health. Switzerland was one of the earliest federal states. The United States adopted the federalist CONSTITUTION OF THE UNITED STATES in 1787.

Federalist, The Series of 85 political essays mainly written (1787–88) by Alexander HAMILTON, assisted by James MADISON and John JAY. The essays argued that FEDERALISM and the proposed CONSTITUTION provided the best safeguard of individual rights and state sovereignty.

Federalist Party Early US political party that favoured FEDERALISM with a strong central government. Following publication of *The* FEDERALIST, and ratification of the CONSTITUTION, George WASHINGTON formed a new government. A major split soon emerged within his Cabinet, between a Federalist Party led by Alexander HAMILTON and a DEMOCRATIC-REPUBLICAN PARTY led by Thomas JEFFERSON. The Federalists were conservatives, favouring business and land-owning interests, and pursuing a pro-British foreign policy. The election of a second Federalist president, John ADAMS, led to the ALIEN AND SEDITION ACTS (1798). Despite the best efforts of De Witt CLINTON, Federalist Party support became confined to New England, and they disintegrated after the election of 1816.

Federal Reserve System CENTRAL BANK of the United States established (1913) to maintain sound monetary and credit conditions. Twelve regional banks are supervised by a Federal Reserve Board of governors appointed by the president. All national banks are members, as are many state and commercial banks. The Federal Reserve System regulates money flow and credit by varying its discount rate on loans to member banks and by varying the percentage of total deposits member banks must keep in reserve.

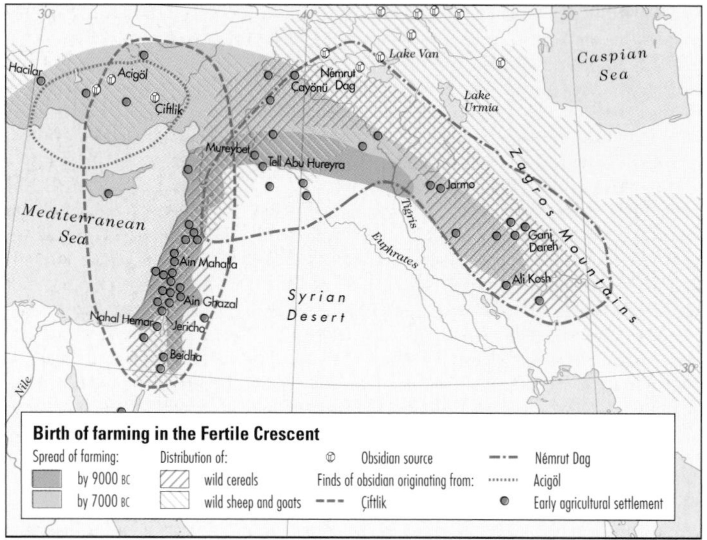

► Fertile Crescent The wide range of foods growing in the Fertile Crescent changed the living patterns of hunter-gatherers considerably. Wild wheat and barley provided abundant annual harvests which enabled people to dwell year-round in permanent settlements. This made it possible to store cereals and other plant foods, including nuts, to provide some insurance against lean seasons or years. Living in sedentary settlements also enabled people to accumulate possessions that today provide valuable evidence of their way of life.

feminism Movement that promotes equal rights for women. One of the first feminist texts was Mary Wollstonecraft's *Vindication of the Rights of Women* (1792), which argued for increased access to education for women. In the United States, Elizabeth Cady STANTON organized (1848) the Seneca Falls Convention on women's rights. In late 19th-century Britain, the SUFFRAGETTE MOVEMENT was formed; its leaders included Emmeline PANKHURST and Millicent Garrett FAWCETT. The women's rights movement gained further impetus during the two world wars, as women took on employment previously confined to men. The growing economic independence of women was championed by Virginia Woolf in *A Room of One's Own* (1929). The **women's liberation** movement grew out of texts such as *The Second Sex* (1949) by Simone de Beauvoir, *The Golden Notebook* (1962) by Doris Lessing, *The Feminine Mystique* (1963) by Betty Friedan and *The Female Eunuch* (1970) by Germaine Greer. "Women's lib" argued that issues of sexual politics were relevant in both professional and personal relationships. It also challenged gender stereotypes. Practical demands focused on attaining social and economic equality. In the United States, the Equal Employment Opportunity Commission was created in 1964 and Betty Friedan organized the National Organization for Women (NOW) in 1966. The contraceptive pill, introduced in the 1960s, gave women greater control over whether or when they bore children. In the United Kingdom, the Abortion Act (1967) ushered in the notion of a woman's right to choose whether to bear a child. The Equal Pay Act (1970), the Sex Discrimination Acts (1975, 1976) and the creation (1975) of the Equal Opportunities Commission gave legal force to many feminist demands.

Fenian movement Secret Irish-American revolutionary society, named after the Fianna, an ancient Irish military force. The IRISH FAMINE (1845–49) spurred an uprising (1848) against British rule by the nationalist YOUNG IRELAND group. The failure of the uprising prompted many revolutionaries to emigrate. In the United States, John O'Mahoney founded (1848) the Fenian Brotherhood. In Ireland, James Stephens formed (1858) the Irish Republican Brotherhood (IRB). The growing strength of the transatlantic movement led the British government to arrest the leaders of the IRB. In 1867 James Kelly led the IRB in the abortive Fenian Rising against the British. The American Fenian Brotherhood attempted to invade Canada in 1866 and 1870. The first raid, involving 600 men, was led by John O'Neill and returned after a skirmish with Canadian volunteers. The second raid was repulsed by Canadian forces. A third raid in 1871 was frustrated by US troops before it reached the border. In Ireland, members of the IRB established several factions: the HOME RULE and LAND LEAGUE movements led by Charles Stewart PARNELL and Michael DAVITT; and SINN FÉIN led by Arthur GRIFFITH. Patrick PEARSE led the IRB in the abortive EASTER RISING (1916). In 1919 Michael COLLINS formed the IRISH REPUBLICAN ARMY (IRA).

Ferdinand I (1503–64) Holy Roman emperor (1558–64) and king of Bohemia and Hungary (1526–64), younger brother of Emperor CHARLES V. In 1521 Charles gave Ferdinand control of the Austrian lands of the HABSBURGS. Louis II of Bohemia and Hungary was killed by the Ottoman Turks at the Battle of MOHÁCS (1526) and Ferdinand claimed the right of succession through his marriage to Louis' sister, Anna. In Bohemia, Ferdinand secured the hereditary succession of the Habsburgs, but his rule in Hungary was contested first by JOHN I, then by JOHN II, both of whom were aided by Sultan SULEIMAN I. As Charles V's agent in Germany, Ferdinand had to contend with the PEASANTS' WAR (1524–25) and rebellion in Württemberg (1534). Ferdinand helped defeat the Protestant SCHMALKALDIC LEAGUE in 1546–47. Although a devout Catholic, Ferdinand negotiated the Peace of AUGSBURG (1555) and worked for reconciliation between the Catholic and Protestant churches. Ferdinand controlled the imperial government from 1555 and was elected emperor after Charles' abdication. He was succeeded by his son MAXIMILIAN II. *See also* LUTHER, MARTIN; OTTOMAN EMPIRE; REFORMATION

Ferdinand II (1578–1637) Holy Roman emperor (1619–37), king of Bohemia (1617–37) and king of Hungary (1618–37), grandson of FERDINAND I. Educated by the Jesuits, Ferdinand championed the COUNTER-REFORMATION. In 1619 the mainly Protestant diet of Bohemia deposed him as their king in favour of FREDERICK V, elector of the Palatinate, thus precipitating the THIRTY YEARS' WAR. Ferdinand regained Bohemia (1620) and Hungary (1621), forcibly converting the populace to Catholicism. In 1629 the imperial army, led by Albrecht von WALLENSTEIN, defeated the Danes, bringing GUSTAVUS II into the War. Ferdinand issued the Edict of Restitution (1629), enforcing the return to the Roman Catholic Church of all property seized by Protestants since 1552. Opposition from the German princes forced Ferdinand to dismiss Wallenstein, but he was quickly reinstated after a succession of Swedish victories. In 1634 Wallenstein was assassinated, probably on the orders of Ferdinand. Ferdinand defeated the Swedes at the Battle of Nördlingen (1634) and secured the imperial succession on his son, FERDINAND III, at the Peace of Prague (1635).

Ferdinand III (1608–57) Holy Roman emperor (1637–57), king of Bohemia and Hungary (1625–57), son of FERDINAND II. In 1634 he succeeded Albrecht von WALLENSTEIN as commander of the imperial army in the THIRTY YEARS' WAR. After Ferdinand's accession, the HABSBURG empire suffered a devastating series of defeats, and he was forced to conclude the Peace of WESTPHALIA (1648). He was succeeded by his son, LEOPOLD I.

Ferdinand (the Benign) (1793–1875) Emperor of Austria (1835–48), king of Hungary (1830–48), son and successor of Holy Roman Emperor FRANCIS II. A weak sovereign, Ferdinand let Prince von METTERNICH govern for him. Faced with the REVOLUTIONS OF 1848 in Austria, Hungary and Italy, he was forced to abdicate in favour of his nephew FRANZ JOSEPH.

Ferdinand (1861–1948) Prince (1887–1908) and tsar (1908–18) of Bulgaria. In 1908 he declared Bulgaria independent of the OTTOMAN EMPIRE. Ferdinand allied Bulgaria with Serbia, Greece and Montenegro in the first of the BALKAN WARS (1912), but Bulgaria's territorial gains were largely lost to its former allies in the Second Balkan War (1913). In a bid to regain territory, Ferdinand entered World War 1 on the side of the CENTRAL POWERS. Further defeats saw him abdicate in favour of his son, BORIS III.

Ferdinand I (the Great) (d.1065) Spanish king of Castile (1035–65) and León (1037–65). He inherited the throne of CASTILE from his father, Sancho III, and seized control of LEÓN in 1037 after killing King Bermudo III, whose sister Ferdinand had married. In 1054 Ferdinand gained Navarre after his troops defeated and killed his brother Garcia IV. Ferdinand successfully fought the MOORS, making vassals of the rulers of Seville, Toledo, Zaragoza and Badajoz. By the time of his death, Ferdinand ruled large parts of Christian and Moorish Spain. His empire was divided among his sons after his death.

Ferdinand III (*c*.1199–1252) Spanish king of Castile (1217–52) and León (1230–52), grandson of ALFONSO VIII of Castile. He gained CASTILE from his mother, Berenguela, and inherited LEÓN from his father, Alfonso IX, thus uniting the two kingdoms. Ferdinand spent most of his reign fighting the ALMOHADS, conquering the Muslim strongholds of Córdoba (1236), Murcia (1243), Jaén (1246) and Seville (1248). At his death, only the kingdom of GRANADA remained in Muslim hands. His daughter, ELEANOR OF CASTILE, married the future EDWARD I of England. He was succeeded by his son, ALFONSO X (THE WISE). Ferdinand was canonized in 1671.

Ferdinand V (the Catholic) (1452–1516) King of Castile and León (1474–1504), of Aragón (as Ferdinand II) (1479–1516), of Sicily (1468–1516), and of Naples (as Ferdinand III) (1504–16). Ferdinand married ISABELLA I of Castile in 1469, and they became joint rulers of CASTILE and LEÓN in 1474. The Spanish INQUISITION was established (1477–80) to enforce religious uniformity in Castile. In 1479 Ferdinand inherited ARAGÓN from his father, John II, thus uniting the whole of Spain except for the kingdom of GRANADA. Ferdinand and Isabella set out to conquer this last outpost of Muslim rule in Spain. The year 1492 was momentous, marking not only the completion of the reconquest of Granada and the launch of Christopher COLUMBUS' voyage to the New World, but also the expulsion of all Jews who refused to convert to Christianity. Ferdinand began the century-long struggle with France for control of Italy in the ITALIAN WARS (1494–1559). General FERNÁNDEZ DE CÓRDOBA captured NAPLES for Spain in 1503. After Isabella's death in 1504, Ferdinand acted as regent in Castile for their insane daughter, Joanna, and then for her son, Charles I (later Emperor CHARLES V). In 1512 he occupied NAVARRE, basing his claim on his marriage (1505) to Germaine de Fox.

Ferdinand I (1423–94) King of NAPLES (1458–94), illegitimate son and successor (in Naples) of ALFONSO V (THE MAGNANIMOUS) of Aragón. His succession was initially opposed by both the papacy and the barons, who appointed a rival king, John of Anjou. Ferdinand expelled John in 1464, only to face the threat of the OTTOMAN EMPIRE. In 1481 he joined forces with Florence to expel (1481) the Turks from the port of Otranto, s Italy. The Florence-Naples alliance also fought against Venice in the War of Ferrara (1482–84). Ferdinand defeated a second baronial revolt (1485–87), provoked by his authoritarian rule.

Ferdinand I (1345–83) King of Portugal (1367–83). He fought three wars for control of CASTILE. The first war (1369–71) was settled by Ferdinand's promise of marriage to Leonor, daughter of Henry II of Castile. He reneged on the agreement and launched a second war (1372), with JOHN OF GAUNT, which resulted in the Castilian siege of Lisbon (1373) and his defeat. A third war (1381–82) also ended in humiliation for Ferdinand.

Ferdinand (1865–1927) King of Romania (1914–27), nephew and successor of CAROL I, who made him crown prince in 1889. Ferdinand commanded the Romanian army in the Second Balkan War (1913). During World War I, he sided with the Allies in 1916 and by March 1918 the Romanians had been crushed by the armies of the Central Powers. By the terms of the peace treaties, Romania more than doubled its territory, and Ferdinand was crowned (1922) king of the enlarged country. He was succeeded by his grandson, Michael.

Ferdinand VI (*c*.1712–59) King of Spain (1746–59), son and successor of Philip V. In 1729 he married Maria de Braganza, daughter of John V of Portugal. As king, Ferdinand reduced the influence of his stepmother, Elizabeth Farnese, relying instead on the administrative abilities of the Marqués de la Ensenada. Ferdinand kept Spain at peace from the end of the War of the Austrian Succession (1748) until his death. The death of his wife (1758) plunged Ferdinand into a deep grief from which he never recovered.

Ferdinand VII (the Desired) (1784–1833) King of Spain (1808–33), son of Charles IV. As prince, he felt excluded from government by Manuel de Godoy and his mother, María Luisa, and sought the support of Napoleon I. In 1807 Ferdinand was arrested for treason by his father. The Revolt of Aranjuez (1808) forced Charles IV to abdicate in favour of Ferdinand. Napoleon began the Peninsular War, which toppled Ferdinand and installed Joseph Bonaparte. During the War, Ferdinand was imprisoned in France. In 1812 Spain proclaimed a liberal constitution, but Ferdinand abolished this upon his restoration (1814). Liberal opposition organized secret societies, such as the Carbonari, which forced him to reinstate the constitution (1820). In 1823, with the help of French troops, Ferdinand crushed the liberals and revoked the constitution. During his reign, Spain lost all of her American possessions. Ferdinand abandoned the Salic law to enable the succession of his daughter, Isabella II. Conservatives supported the claim of Ferdinand's brother, Don Carlos, and civil war ensued. *See also* Carlism

Ferdinand I (1751–1825) King of the Two Sicilies (1816–25), son of the future Charles III of Spain. He inherited the kingdoms of Naples and Sicily on his father's accession (1759). Ferdinand's marriage (1768) to Maria Carolina, sister of Marie Antoinette, encouraged him to join the Second Coalition against France and launch an attack (1798) on Rome in the French Revolutionary Wars. France repelled the attack and invaded Naples, forcing Ferdinand to flee to Sicily. In 1799 Ferdinand regained Naples with the help of Admiral Horatio Nelson. During the Napoleonic Wars, Napoleon I captured Naples (1806) and Ferdinand was again forced into exile in Sicily. In 1816 he was restored as head of a united kingdom of Naples and Sicily (the Two Sicilies). In 1820 an uprising forced him to concede constitutional monarchy, but the Congress of Laibach (1821) sanctioned the military aid of Austria that crushed the constitutionalists and restore his absolutist rule.

Ferdinand II (1810–59) King of the Two Sicilies (1830–59), son and successor of Francis I. Initially considered a liberal, Ferdinand came to be noted for his despotic rule. Ferdinand bombarded the Sicilian cities of Messina (1848) and Palermo (1849) to crush one of the popular Revolutions of 1848. His harsh treatment of more than 15,000 political prisoners led to international criticism and isolation. Ultimately, Ferdinand's authoritarian rule weakened the kingdom and led to its collapse and incorporation into a united Italy in 1860.

Fernández de Córdoba, Gonzalo (1453–1515) Spanish general, known as *El Gran Capitán* ("The Great Captain"). He negotiated the surrender of the Moors in Granada (1492). During the Italian Wars, Fernández led a successful expedition against Charles VIII of France (1495) in support of Ferdinand II, the Aragónese king of Naples. With the help of Venice, he seized the island of Cephalonia from the Ottoman Turks (1500). By 1502 France and Spain were once more at war in the kingdom of Naples, and Fernández's brilliant military tactics secured a Spanish victory. He served as the first Spanish viceroy of Naples (1503–07).

Ferry, Jules François Camille (1832–93) French statesman, premier (1880–81, 1883–85). In the Franco-Prussian War (1870–71), he was mayor of the besieged city of Paris and acquired the title "*Ferry-la-Famine*". As premier, Ferry oversaw the dramatic expansion of the French Empire, acquiring Tunisia (1881), Tonkin and Annam (1883), Madagascar (1885) and the Congo (1884–85). He also introduced (1882) universal, free and compulsory education in France. The financial cost of war in Tonkin led to his dismissal in 1885. Ferry was assassinated by a religious fanatic.

Fertile Crescent Rich strip of land extending from the head of the Persian (Arabian) Gulf through the basins of the rivers Tigris and Euphrates and then along the Mediterranean coasts of Syria, Lebanon and Israel to the lower Nile valley. The term was coined by US archaeologist James Bearsted (1865–1935) to refer to the cradle of early civilizations such as those of Babylon, Assyria, ancient Egypt, Phoenicia and Mesopotamia.

feudal system Economic and social system that evolved in most of Europe from the 10th century, based on the tenure of land. The system originated from the need to provide a permanent group of knights to assist the king in his wars. All land was theoretically owned by the monarch and leased to his tenants-in-chief in return for their attendance at court and military assistance; in turn, the tenants-in-chief let out fiefs to knights in return for military service and other obligations. The lowest rank, serfs, worked their lord's land in return for the right to grow their own produce. The system went into decline in the 13th century, when vassals began to make monetary payments and lords to hire professional troops. In 1660 feudal tenures were legally abolished in England, but they continued in some parts of Europe until the early 19th century. *See also* capitalism; daimyo; fealty

Fianna Fáil (Gaelic, "Soldiers of Destiny") Irish political party. It was formed (1926) by those opposed to the partition of Ireland. In 1932 Fianna Fáil achieved power under Eamon De Valera, who sought to gain greater independence from Great Britain and achieve agricultural self-sufficiency for Ireland. Except for the years 1948–51 and 1954–57, the Party remained in government until 1973, when it was defeated by a coalition of Fine Gael and the Labour Party. In 1977 Fianna Fáil regained power, led first by Jack Lynch and then by Charles Haughey. Haughey was defeated in the 1982 elections, but was restored as taoiseach (prime minister) in 1987. He was succeeded by Albert Reynolds in 1992. A coalition with Labour collapsed in 1994 and Fianna Fáil returned to opposition. In 1997 the Party was reinstated in power under Bertie Ahern. It pursues a broadly conservative agenda.

Fidei Defensor *See* Defender of the Faith

fief In a feudal system, an area of land granted by a lord to his vassal as a reward for past services or in exchange for future military and other services and loyalty. The lord kept the ultimate rights to the land, while the vassal enjoyed most of the profits from its use.

Field, Cyrus West (1819–92) US businessman, financier of the first transatlantic telegraph cable. He was a founder of the New York, Newfoundland and London Telegraph Company, which was set up specifically for the cable project. After several unsuccessful attempts the cable was laid by Isambard Kingdom Brunel's steamship, *The Great Eastern*, in July 1866. Field later served as the president (1877–90) of the New York Elevated Railroad Company.

Fielding, William Stevens (1848–1929) Canadian statesman, minister of finance (1896–1911, 1921–25) and prime minister of Nova Scotia (1884–96). As finance minister in the cabinet of Wilfred Laurier, Fielding negotiated the Knox-Fielding Pact (1911), which provided for free trade in natural products between the United States and Canada and led to the fall of Laurier's government. After World War 1, Fielding served again as finance minister, this time in the cabinet of Mackenzie King.

Field of the Cloth of Gold (1520) Meeting near Calais, N France, between Henry VIII of England and Francis I of France. Despite ostentatious displays of wealth and swaggering festivities, Francis failed to win English support for the Valois cause. Shortly afterwards Henry reached an agreement with the Habsburg Emperor Charles V that neither would make an alliance with France for two years.

Fieschi Noble family of Genoa that led the Guelph faction against the Holy Roman emperor in the 13th century. In 1243 Sinibaldo Fieschi became pope as Innocent IV. In the 1260s, the Fieschis allied with the Grimaldis and placed Genoa under the protection of the French prince Charles of Anjou. In 1270 they were driven from power by the Ghibelline faction. Genoa was riven by conflict between the two factions until the establishment of the doge in 1339. In 1528 Andrea Doria declared the allegiance of Genoa to Emperor Charles V. Popular resistance to imperial rule was led by Gian Luigi Fieschi (*c*.1522–47), who died in the plot to assassinate Doria. The failure of the conspiracy signalled the end of Fieschi power in Genoa.

Fifteen, The *See* Jacobites

fifth column Saboteurs, spies and other non-uniformed paramilitary elements active behind enemy lines, working to undermine the enemy's cause. The term dates from the Spanish Civil War (1936–39) and described Republican sympathizers in Madrid.

Fifth Monarchy Men Religious sect that flourished in England in the 1650s, during the Commonwealth and Protectorate. On the basis of the prophecy of the fifth kingdom in Daniel 2: 36–45, the members believed in the imminent reappearance of Christ and the establishment of

FIJI

AREA: 18,274sq km (7056sq mi)
POPULATION: 800,000
CAPITAL (POPULATION): Suva (141,273)
GOVERNMENT: Multiparty republic
ETHNIC GROUPS: Fijian 49%, Indian 46%
LANGUAGES: English (official), Bauan, Hindustani
RELIGIONS: Christian 53%, Hindu 38%, Muslim 8%
GDP PER CAPITA (1995): US$5780

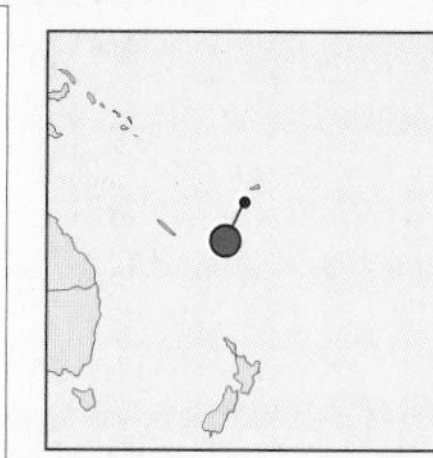

Independent nation in the s Pacific Ocean, consisting of more than 800 mostly volcanic islands and islets. Settlement of the region dates back to the 2nd millennium BC. Discovered by Abel Tasman in 1643, the islands were visited by British explorers in the 18th century and became a British crown colony in 1874. Indians were subsequently imported to work on the sugar plantations and by the 1940s outnumbered the native Fijian population.

In 1970 Fiji achieved independence within the Commonwealth of Nations. The election of an Indian-majority government (1987) prompted a military coup by native Fijians, led by Lieutenant Colonel Sitiveni Rabuka, and the proclamation of a republic. In 1992 Rabuka became prime minister. In 1997 Fiji approved a new multiracial constitution and was readmitted to the Commonwealth. In 1999 elections Rabuka was defeated by Mahendra Chaudhry.

his new and everlasting monarchy on earth. After two attempted uprisings, in 1657 and 1661, the sect's leaders were executed. *See also* MILLENARIANISM

Fiji *See* country feature, page 141

filibuster Method of delaying a vote of a legislative assembly by making long speeches. It has been of particular relevance in the United States' Senate, where it only became possible to vote to close a debate in 1917. Even then, a two-thirds majority was required. In 1957 Senator Strom Thurmond of South Carolina succeeded in talking for more than 24 hours. The term filibuster originally referred to buccaneers who raided the Spanish colonies of South America.

Fillmore, Millard (1800–74) Thirteenth president of the United States (1850–53). He served (1833–43) in the House of Representatives and in 1834 joined the newly formed WHIG PARTY led by Henry CLAY. In 1848 Fillmore was elected vice president to Zachary TAYLOR and succeeded as president when Taylor died. In order to mediate between pro- and anti-slavery factions, he agreed to the COMPROMISE OF 1850. Fillmore's attempt to enforce the FUGITIVE SLAVE LAW embittered ABOLITIONISTS and split the Party. He failed to win renomination in 1852 and was succeeded by Franklin PIERCE. In the 1856 elections, Fillmore stood for the KNOW-NOTHING MOVEMENT but was defeated by Abraham LINCOLN. One of his last acts was to dispatch Commodore Matthew PERRY to Japan.

final solution Policy adopted by Adolf HITLER after 1942 to exterminate the Jewish race systematically. Before this time, he planned other means of dealing with the Jews, such as transporting them to Madagascar. The adoption of the final solution led to the full utilization of extermination camps such as AUSCHWITZ. *See also* HOLOCAUST, THE

Fine Gael Irish political party. It was founded (1933) as a successor to William COSGRAVE's *Cumann na nGaedheal* (Society of Gaels) and two smaller parties. *Cumann na nGaedheal* had been in power between 1923, when the Irish Free State's first elections had been held, and 1932 when it was defeated by FIANNA FÁIL. Overshadowed by the more nationalist Fianna Fáil, Fine Gael has held office only four times, always in coalition with the Labour Party (1948–51, 1954–57, 1973–77, 1994–97).

Finland *See* country feature

Finnbogadóttir, Vígdis (1930–) Icelandic stateswoman, president (1980–96). In 1980 Finnbogadóttir became the first woman to be popularly elected as head of state. She promoted many causes, including Icelandic culture and reforestation. In 1996 she was succeeded as president by Ólafur Ragnar Grímsson. Finnbogadóttir served as chairperson (1998–) of the UNESCO Commission on the Ethics of Scientific Knowledge and Technology.

Finnish-Russian War *See* RUSSO-FINNISH WAR

Fire of London (2–6 September 1666) Accidental fire that destroyed most of the City of LONDON, England. It started in a baker's shop in Pudding Lane, a site now marked by the Monument, and a strong wind spread the fire rapidly through the closely packed wooden houses. It was finally stopped by destroying buildings in its path. The fire provided an opportunity for rebuilding London on a more spacious plan, but, for the most part, only the famous churches of Sir Christopher WREN (including ST PAUL'S Cathedral) were built.

First World War *See* WORLD WAR I

Fish, Hamilton (1808–93) US statesman, secretary of state (1869–77). He was a US Representative (1843–45), governor of New York (1849–50) and Senator (1851–57). After the break-up of the WHIG PARTY, Fish joined the REPUBLICAN PARTY and served as secretary of state under President Ulysses GRANT. As secretary of state, Fish is chiefly remembered for his negotiating skills that led to the Treaty of WASHINGTON (1871) and the settlement of the ALABAMA CLAIMS.

Fisher, Andrew (1862–1928) Australian statesman, prime minister (1908–09, 1910–13, 1914–15), b. Scotland. He emigrated to Australia in 1885, becoming a Labor member of Australia's first federal parliament (1901). Fisher rose to become leader of the LABOR PARTY (1907–15). His government created the Commonwealth Bank and was responsible for important welfare legislation. Fisher resigned after leading Australia into WORLD WAR I. He served as Australian High Commissioner in London (1916–21).

Fisher, Saint John (1469–1535) English Roman Catholic prelate. He opposed HENRY VIII's proposed divorce from CATHERINE OF ARAGON in 1529. Fisher was tried and executed for denying that Henry was supreme head of the church under the Act of SUPREMACY. He was canonized in 1935. His feast day is 9 July.

Fisher, John Arbuthnot, 1st Baron Fisher of Kilverstone (1841–1920) British admiral, b. Sri Lanka. As first sea lord (1904–10, 1914–15), Fisher was responsible for the creation of the *Dreadnought* class of battleships that revolutionized naval warfare. He also built the lighter and more manoeuvrable *Invincible* class of cruisers. Fisher's reforms of the Royal Navy did much to ensure Britain's naval supremacy in WORLD WAR I. He retired in 1914, but was recalled at the start of World War I and masterminded the defeat of Graf von Spee's German squadron off Chile. Fisher later resigned in protest over Winston CHURCHILL's continuation of the GALLIPOLI CAMPAIGN.

Fisk, James (1834–72) US financier. With Daniel DREW and Jay GOULD, he gained control of the Erie Railroad and manipulated the stock to acquire a fortune. Fisk and Gould's attempt to monopolize the gold market led to BLACK FRIDAY (1869). He was shot dead by a rival.

FitzGerald, Garrett (1926–) Irish statesman, prime minister (1981–87). He was elected to the Dáil (Irish parliament) in 1969 and served as minister of foreign affairs in the coalition government of Liam COSGRAVE (1973–77). Fitzgerald succeeded Cosgrave as leader of FINE GAEL. As taoiseach (prime minister), he promoted the liberalization of the laws on divorce and abortion. In 1985 Fitzgerald signed the ANGLO-IRISH AGREEMENT on Northern Ireland with British Prime Minister Margaret THATCHER. He resigned as leader of Fine Gael after being defeated by Charles HAUGHEY in 1987 elections.

Fitzherbert, Maria Anne (1756–1837) Wife of George, Prince of Wales (later GEORGE IV). The couple married secretly in 1785, since Mrs Fitzherbert (née Smythe) was a Roman Catholic and King GEORGE III would have refused to give consent to the union. In 1794 the Prince of Wales married CAROLINE OF BRUNSWICK, but the relationship with Mrs Fitzherbert continued until *c.*1808.

Five Civilized Tribes Term adopted by early writers to include those NATIVE NORTH AMERICAN tribes regarded as more advanced, due to agricultural, political and social successes. They were the CHEROKEE, CHICKASAW, CHOCTAW, CREEK and SEMINOLE tribes.

Five Dynasties and Ten Kingdoms Chaotic period in Chinese history between the fall of the TANG dynasty (AD

FINLAND (SUOMI)

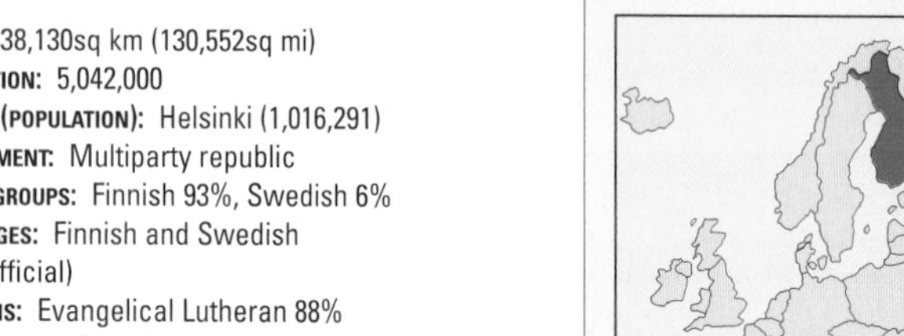

AREA: 338,130sq km (130,552sq mi)
POPULATION: 5,042,000
CAPITAL (POPULATION): Helsinki (1,016,291)
GOVERNMENT: Multiparty republic
ETHNIC GROUPS: Finnish 93%, Swedish 6%
LANGUAGES: Finnish and Swedish (both official)
RELIGIONS: Evangelical Lutheran 88%
GDP PER CAPITA (1995): US$17,760

Republic in N Europe. Finland was first inhabited, by ancestors of the LAPPS, in the 7th century BC. By the 8th century AD, the LAPPS had been forced N by the Finns. In the 13th century Sweden conquered the country, which subsequently became drawn into many wars fought by Sweden, among them the conflicts with Russia in the 16th–18th centuries. Lutheranism was established in the 16th century.

Following the Great NORTHERN WAR (1700–21), Russia gained SE Finland. In the NAPOLEONIC WARS, Russia conquered Finland, and it became a grand duchy (1809). Despite considerable autonomy, Finnish nationalism gained strength, fuelled by important Finnish language works. Tsar NICHOLAS II's programme of Russification (1899–1905) met fierce resistance.

Following the Russian Revolution (1917), Finland declared independence and Juho Kusti PAASIKIVI became prime minister. Civil war (January–May 1918) broke out between the Russian-backed Red Guard and the German-backed White Guard, led by Carl MANNERHEIM. The White Guard triumphed, and a republic was established (1919). At the outbreak of World War 2, Finland declared its neutrality. A Soviet invasion (November 1939), however, prompted the RUSSO-FINNISH WAR. Under the Treaty of Moscow (1940), Finland ceded part of KARELIA and Lake Ladoga. In 1941 Finland allied itself with Germany.

In 1944 Soviet troops invaded and forced Finland to agree armistice terms based on the Treaty of Moscow and the evacuation of German troops from its territory. Much of N Finland was destroyed during the ensuing German retreat. A final peace treaty (1947) with the Soviet Union confirmed the 1944 armistice agreement. In 1955 Finland joined the United Nations (UN) and the Nordic Council and maintained a policy of neutrality during the COLD WAR. Urho Kaleva KEKKONEN led (1956–81) Finland through the process of reconstruction. In 1986 Finland became a full member of the European Free Trade Association (EFTA), and in 1995 it joined the European Union (EU). In 1999 Finland was one of the 11 countries to participate in the "first wave" of the European single currency. In 2000 Tarja Halonen became Finland's first female president.

907) and the founding of the SONG dynasty (960). Five successive dynasties attempted to establish themselves in the north, while the south was divided between ten separate warlords. In 907 Zhu Wen overthrew the Tang, founding the **Later Liang** dynasty, The Later Liang was, in turn, overthrown by General Zhuang Zong in 923, who established the **Later Tang** dynasty. In 936, with the help of the semi-nomadic Khitan peoples, Gao Tzu founded the **Later Jin** (936–47), which was succeeded by the Later Han (947–51). The **Later Zhou** (951–60) began the process of reconstruction that was advanced by the Song. While some of the kingdoms in the south had strong governments, none were capable of unifying China. Despite almost constant warfare and endemic corruption, the period saw the development of PRINTING.

Five-Year Plan Series of economic goals, notably those set by the former SOVIET UNION. In 1928 Joseph STALIN launched the first Five-Year Plan; it was designed to speed up the industrialization of the Soviet Union and the COLLECTIVIZATION of agriculture. It focused on the development of heavy industry. The third Plan (1938–42) was interrupted by World War 2. The seventh Plan (1959–65) failed to meet its agricultural production targets. The ninth Plan (1971–75) concentrated on light industry. The twelfth and final Plan (1986–90) saw the Soviet economy slide into recession. *See also* GREAT LEAP FORWARD

flagellant Religious zealot who uses flagellation, or flogging, for disciplinary or devotional purposes. Now almost obsolete, the practice of flagellation has been part of many religions, including those of ancient Greece and Rome, some Native American cultures, and Christianity. In 13th century Europe, flagellants in N Italy organized themselves into groups, which spread northwards to Germany and Poland. They travelled from town to town, beating themselves and calling for people to repent. The movement died down but reappeared during times of crisis, notably the BLACK DEATH. In 1349 Pope Clement V condemned flagellation.

Flanders Historic region now divided between BELGIUM and France. In Belgian Flanders, Flemish is the major language. In 862 Baldwin became the first count of Flanders. From the 10th century, Flanders grew prosperous on the cloth industry, and the old nobility gradually lost authority to the cities, such as BRUGES, ANTWERP and GHENT. In the 11th century, Flanders expanded east of the River Schelde, holding these lands in fief to the HOLY ROMAN EMPIRE. It enjoyed considerable independence from the French crown and the Holy Roman Empire. Flanders was weakened by the departure of its count, Baldwin IX, on the Fourth CRUSADE, where he was proclaimed BALDWIN I, emperor of Constantinople. His absence was exploited by PHILIP II of France to strengthen French influence in Flanders. The French were expelled after Flemish victory in the Battle of the Golden Spurs (1302). During the HUNDRED YEARS' WAR, the communes of Flanders (especially Ghent) supported the English, while the counts of Flanders sided with the French. In 1384 PHILIP II (THE BOLD) OF BURGUNDY inherited Flanders. In 1477 Flanders passed to the HABSBURGS, and in the 16th century became part of the Spanish Netherlands. In the early 17th century, Spain ceded the NW part to the UNITED PROVINCES OF THE NETHERLANDS. During the late 17th and early 18th centuries, France gradually acquired French Flanders and in 1795 succeeded in taking over the remaining area, which had come under Austrian rule in 1714. It was incorporated into the Kingdom of Netherlands in 1815 before becoming part of the newly independent Belgium in 1830. It was the scene of devastating trench warfare in WORLD WAR I.

Flathead *See* SALISH

Fleury, André Hercule de (1653–1743) French statesman and cardinal, chief minister (1726–43) of LOUIS XV of France. He reformed the national finances and stabilized the currency after the costly wars of LOUIS XIV. Fleury's major successes were in foreign policy, where he sought to reduce British power on the continent and improve relations with Austria. His plans were temporarily thwarted by French involvement against Austria and Russia in the War of the POLISH SUCCESSION (1733–38), but France emerged from the War with greater claims to Lorraine and improved relations with Austria. Fleury was unable, however, to prevent France from entering (1741) the War of the AUSTRIAN SUCCESSION against Austria.

Flodden, Battle of (9 September 1513) Scene of conflict between England and Scotland, fought in N Northumberland, NE England. An English force of *c.*20,000 led by Thomas Howard, 2nd Duke of NORFOLK, defeated a larger Scottish force (*c.*30,000) led by JAMES IV of Scotland due to the superiority of the English weaponry. James IV was among the more than 10,000 Scottish losses. *See also* HENRY VIII

Flood, Henry (1732–91) Irish statesman. He entered the Irish Parliament in 1759 and quickly became leader of the nationalist grouping that wrung concessions from the British government. Nationalist allegiance switched to Henry GRATTAN after Flood accepted (1775) the position of vice treasurer to the British viceroy. He helped Grattan secure the repeal of POYNINGS' Law (1782) and regained popular support by demanding Irish independence. Flood again alienated his supporters by his opposition to CATHOLIC EMANCIPATION.

Florence (Firenze) Capital of Tuscany and Firenze province, on the River Arno, Italy. Initially an Etruscan town, it was a Roman colony from the 1st century BC to the 5th century AD. In the 12th century, Florence became an independent commune and major trading centre. The site of many factional power struggles, especially the 13th-century war between the GUELPHS and GHIBELLINES, it nevertheless became a major city-state in the 15th century. Under the rule of the MEDICI family, Florence also became one of the leading centres of the RENAISSANCE. Artists who contributed to the flourishing city included Michelangelo, Leonardo da Vinci, Raphael and Donatello. In 1569 Florence became the capital of the Grand Duchy of Tuscany, and from 1865 to 1871 it was the capital of the kingdom of Italy. Its many notable churches include: the Duomo GOTHIC cathedral (1296); San Lorenzo, Florence's first cathedral, rebuilt in 1425 by Brunelleschi and including the New Sacristy built by Michelangelo; and the Monastery of San Marco, which holds Fra Angelico masterpieces. Pop. (1992) 397,434.

Flores, Juan José (1801–64) Ecuadorean statesman, president (1830–35, 1839–43), b. Venezuela. A principal aide of Simón BOLIVAR in the struggle for independence from Spain, Flores became the first president of independent Ecuador in 1830. His autocratic regime was largely supported by the conservative landed aristocracy of Quito. In 1835 he was ousted by the more liberal Vicente Rocafuerte (1783–1847), whose support was based in Guayaquil. Flores was re-elected in 1839, but later forced into exile (1845–60). He returned to serve as army chief under Gabriel GARCÍA MORENO.

▲ **Florence** The Baptistry of San Giovanni, built between the 11th and 15th centuries, is noted for its Romanesque green and white marble-facing and gilded bronze doors.

FLORIDA
Statehood :
3 March 1845
Nickname :
Sunshine State
State motto :
In God we trust

Florida State in the extreme SE of the United States; the capital is Tallahassee. In 1513 Spanish explorer Juan PONCE DE LEÓN became the first European to visit the region, and the first permanent European settlement in the United States was built (1565) by the Spanish at St Augustine, NE Florida. The original nations of Native North Americans were wiped out by diseases brought from the Old World, and the SEMINOLE moved into the region in the 18th century. The land passed to the British at the end of the FRENCH AND INDIAN WARS (1689–1763), but was regained by the Spanish during the American Revolution. US forces led by General Andrew JACKSON invaded Florida, precipitating the First SEMINOLE WAR (1817–19). The US gained control of Florida as a result of the ADAMS-ONÍS TREATY (1819), and the influx of settlers led to further conflicts with the Seminole. Florida seceded from the Union in 1861, but was little affected by the Civil War. The state resisted the imposition of RECONSTRUCTION and continued to practise racial segregation. Florida experienced a boom in real estate and tourism during the 1920s, but was badly hit by the Great Depression. Florida was the fastest-growing state in the mid- to late-20th century. In the 1950s the John F. Kennedy Space Center was built at Cape Canaveral, E Florida. Florida's historic ties with Cuba are particularly evident in Miami, where many Cubans have settled. Area: 151,670sq km (58,560sq mi). Pop. (1990) 12,938,000.

Foch, Ferdinand (1851–1929) French general. In WORLD WAR I, Foch helped repel the German advance at MARNE (1914). The following year, he was sent by General Joseph JOFFRE to coordinate the English, French and Belgian troops at YPRES. Foch commanded the Northern Army Group in the disastrous offensive at the SOMME (1916). His recommendation of a single command for the Allied armies was initially dismissed by David LLOYD GEORGE and Georges CLEMENCEAU, and it was not until 1918 (when German victory seemed likely) that Foch was made commander in chief of all Allied forces. Foch's determination and skill held off the German troops, and he led the counter-offensive that ended in German surrender. *See also* HAIG, DOUGLAS, 1ST EARL; LUDENDORFF, ERICH; PÉTAIN, HENRI PHILIPPE

Folsom Prehistoric culture of North America whose existence was first proved by the discovery (1926) of fluted stone spearheads near Folsom, New Mexico. The tools were found with the bones of extinct mammals, such as the mastodon, and appear to date from *c.*9000 BC.

Fontenoy, Battle of (11 May 1745) Conflict in the War of the AUSTRIAN SUCCESSION. Comte de SAXE led *c.*52,000 French troops against *c.*50,000 Allied (Austrian, English, Hanoverian and Dutch) troops under the Duke of CUMBERLAND, who were on their way to relieve the besieged town of Tournai (now in Belgium). The Allies were forced to retreat to Brussels with the loss of *c.*25,000 men. The French lost *c.*7500 men and in the next four months took Tournai and most of FLANDERS.

Foot, Michael (1913–) British politician and writer, leader of the LABOUR PARTY (1980–83). He was editor of the *Evening Standard* (1942–44) and *Tribune* (1955–60) and a leading member of the Campaign for Nuclear Disarmament (CND). Foot was first elected to Parliament in 1945. As secretary of state for employment (1974–76) under Harold WILSON, he managed controversial trade UNION legislation. In 1976 he became deputy leader to James CALLAGHAN and served as leader of the House of

Commons (1976–79). After Margaret THATCHER's victory in the general election of 1980, Foot succeeded Callaghan as leader of the Labour Party. He resigned in favour of Neil KINNOCK after Labour's disastrous defeat in the 1983 election. *See also* HEALEY, DENIS

Ford, Gerald Rudolph (1913–) Thirty-eighth president of the United States (1974–77). Elected to the House of Representatives in 1948, he gained a reputation as an honest and hard-working Republican. In 1973 Ford was nominated by President Richard NIXON to replace the disgraced Spiro AGNEW as vice president. When Nixon resigned, Ford became president – the only person to hold the office without winning a presidential or vice presidential election. One of his first acts was to pardon Nixon. Ford's attempts to counter economic recession with cuts in social welfare and taxes were hindered by a Democrat-dominated Congress. Renominated in 1976, he narrowly lost the election to Jimmy CARTER.

Ford, Henry (1863–1947) US industrialist. He developed a gas-engined car in 1892 and founded Ford Motors in 1903. In 1908 Ford designed the Model T. His introduction of an assembly line (1913) revolutionized industrial mass production, and more than 15 million Model Ts were sold before they were discontinued in 1928. In 1914 Ford raised the minimum wage to US$5 a day and reduced the working day to eight hours. He refused, however, to allow UNION organization in his factories until 1941. In 1945, with the company losing *c.*US$9 million a month, he handed over control to his grandson, **Henry Ford II** (1917–87). Henry Ford II transformed the business, introducing new models, such as the Thunderbird and Mustang, and bringing the company back into profit.

Foreign Legion, French (*Légion Etrangère*) Professional military group of mixed national origin, created (1831) by LOUIS PHILIPPE to serve in the French colonies. The volunteers may be of any nationality, but the majority of officers are French. After serving for five years, recruits are eligible for French citizenship. The French Foreign Legion has seen service throughout the world. In 1962, after fighting in both World Wars and later French colonial struggles, the Legion moved its headquarters from Algeria to Aubagne, s France. It is renowned for its harsh discipline.

Forrest, Sir John (1847–1918) Australian statesman and explorer. He pioneered the exploration into much of Australia's western interior (1869, 1870, 1874) and served as surveyor general (1883–90) of Western Australia. As the first premier (1890–1901) of Western Australia, Forrest did much to improve the state's infrastructure. He was elected to Australia's first federal Parliament in 1901, serving as minister of defence (1901–03), minister of home affairs (1903–04) and treasurer (1905–07, 1909–10, 1913–14, 1917–18). In 1918 Forrest became the first Australian national to be knighted.

Forrest, Nathan Bedford (1821–77) US Confederate general in the CIVIL WAR. In 1862 he headed a cavalry troop at the battles of Fort Donelson and Shiloh. In 1862 Forrest was made brigadier general and led a series of devastating raids against Union forces in Tennessee. In 1864 he captured Fort Pillow, massacring its African-American defenders. After gaining a brilliant victory at Brice's Cross Roads, Forrest was given control of the entire cavalry under John Bell HOOD. He was forced to surrender at Selma, Alabama, and after the war served as the first leader of the KU KLUX KLAN.

Forster, William Edward (1818–86) British statesman. He entered Parliament as a Liberal in 1861. As vice president of the council in the ministry of William GLADSTONE, Forster was responsible for the introduction of the Education Act (1870) that established a national primary school system. As chief secretary for Ireland (1880–82), Forster opposed HOME RULE and favoured strict enforcement of law and order in Ireland. He resigned in protest at the release from prison of Charles PARNELL.

Fortas, Abe (1910–82) US jurist, associate justice of the Supreme Court (1965–69). A close associate of President Lyndon JOHNSON, he gained a reputation as a defender of civil liberties. Johnson nominated Fortas for chief justice, but was forced to withdraw the nomination after a Senate

▲ **Ford** The introduction of the Model T (1908) brought motoring to the general public. It was affordable and easy to maintain and could reach a top speed of 72km/h (45mph).

filibuster. In 1969 Fortas became the first Supreme Court justice to resign, following revelations that he had accepted US$20,000 from a private foundation.

Fort Sumter Fort in South Carolina, United States, scene of the first hostilities in the American CIVIL WAR. In 1860 South Carolina seceded from the Union and demanded that all federal property be handed to the state. President James BUCHANAN refused and South Carolina prepared to seize the Fort, held by federal forces under Major Robert Anderson. The Confederate General Pierre BEAUREGARD called on Anderson to surrender, but he refused. On 12 April 1861, the Confederates began to bombard the Fort and it surrendered the following day. The Confederates held Fort Sumter until 1865. It became a national monument in 1948.

Forty-Five Rebellion *See* JACOBITES

Forty-Niners Name given to the gold miners who arrived in California in the gold rush of 1849. After gold was discovered at Sutter's Mill in 1848, thousands of fortune hunters were attracted to California. It is thought that as many as 100,000 people arrived in 1849.

forum Market and meeting place in ancient Roman towns, corresponding to the Greek AGORA. The forum was usually a centrally located space surrounded by public buildings. In ancient Rome, the Forum was set in the valley between the Capitoline and Palatine hills. It held many civic buildings including basilicas and temples, the Curia (senate-house), treasury and triumphal arches. Trajan's Forum, which many consider to be the masterpiece of ancient Roman architecture, was commissioned by Emperor TRAJAN in the 2nd century AD.

Foster, William Zebulon (1881–1961) US UNION organizer. He was a leader of the INDUSTRIAL WORKERS OF THE WORLD (IWW) and the American Federation of Labor (AFL). Foster led a steel strike (1919) and was the COMMUNIST PARTY OF AMERICA's presidential candidate (1924, 1928, 1932).

Fouché, Joseph, Duc d'Otrante (1763–1820) French revolutionary, minister of police (1799–1802, 1804–09, 1815). He was elected to the Convention in 1792 and initially sided with the GIRONDINS. Fouché switched to the JACOBINS and participated in the massacre of rebels in Lyon (1793) during the REIGN OF TERROR. Fouché was instrumental in the fall of Maximilien ROBESPIERRE and supported the DIRECTORY (1795–99). Ever the political opportunist, Fouché helped NAPOLEON I gain power in the coup of 18 Brumaire (1799). As minister of police, he formed an espionage system that created a virtual police state. Fouché was twice dismissed for his opposition to Napoleon's rule and later served LOUIS XVIII.

Fouquet, Nicolas (1615–80) French superintendant of finance (1653–61) in the reign of LOUIS XIV of France. He was appointed by Cardinal Jules MAZARIN in reward for his support during the FRONDE (1648–53). Manipulating the treasury to his advantage, Fouquet amassed a huge personal fortune. After Mazarin's death (1661), Fouquet hoped to succeed him as chief minister. Jean Baptiste COLBERT sought to discredit Fouquet and alerted Louis XIV to various financial irregularities. Fouquet was arrested. A three-year trial led to a sentence of exile, later commuted to life imprisonment.

Fouquier-Tinville, Antoine Quentin (1746–1795) French Revolutionary lawyer. A friend of Camille DESMOULINS, Fouquier-Tinville was an early supporter of the FRENCH REVOLUTION. In 1793 he was appointed public prosecutor for the Revolutionary Tribunal, which accounted for the execution by guillotine of *c.*2400 people during the REIGN OF TERROR. After Maximilien ROBESPIERRE's fall from power, Fouquier-Tinville was himself guillotined.

Four Freedoms Expression of war aims in World War 2 enunciated by President Franklin ROOSEVELT in his State of the Union address in January 1941. They were freedom of speech and worship, and freedom from want and fear. These aims were echoed in the ATLANTIC CHARTER of 1941.

Four Modernizations Fundamental reforms of agriculture, industry, science and technology, and defence in China. The programme was first enunciated (1964) by Premier ZHOU ENLAI but was largely forgotten during the CULTURAL REVOLUTION. Promoted by DENG XIAOPING from 1974, it was officially adopted after MAO ZEDONG's death (1976). The policy was designed to attract foreign investment and trade with the West, resulting in the creation of "special economic zones". The collective system of agriculture was gradually abandoned in favour of a return to family farming.

Fourteen Points (8 January 1918) Programme presented to the US Congress by President Woodrow WILSON for a just peace settlement of WORLD WAR I. In general, the programme called for greater liberalism in international affairs and supported national self-determination. It made useful propaganda for the Allies and was the basis on which Germany sued for peace in 1918. Some points found expression in the Treaty of VERSAILLES. The 14th Point laid the basis for the LEAGUE OF NATIONS.

Fourteenth Amendment (1868) Amendment to the CONSTITUTION OF THE UNITED STATES, introduced under President Andrew JOHNSON. The purpose of the Amendment was to provide citizenship for former slaves and give them full civil rights. **Section 1** of the Amendment declares that all persons born or naturalized in the United States are US citizens and citizens of their state of residence; thereby overturning the decision in the DRED SCOTT CASE. Section 1 also forbids states from abridging the "privileges and immunities" of US citizens; depriving "any person of life, liberty or property, without due process of law", and denying any person "the equal protection of the law". Section 1 has been often used by the Supreme Court to test the constitutionality of state legislation. The PLESSY V. FERGUSON (1896) decision advanced the doctrine of "separate but equal" that was maintained until the BROWN V. BOARD OF EDUCATION OF TOPEKA (1954) decision. In recent years, the equal protection clause has been extended to cover issues of women's rights. *See also* SLAUGHTERHOUSE CASES

Fourth of July US national holiday, also known as Independence Day. It celebrates the approval by the CONTINENTAL CONGRESS of the DECLARATION OF INDEPENDENCE on 4 July 1776. The first anniversary of the Declaration was celebrated in Philadelphia, but it only began to be celebrated on a regular basis after 1812.

Fox, Charles James (1749–1806) British statesman, foreign secretary (1782, 1783, 1806). Fox was the main parliamentary proponent of liberal reform in the late 18th century. He entered Parliament in 1768 and his rhetorical skills quickly established him as the leader of the WHIGS. Fox served as lord of the admiralty (1770–72) and lord of the treasury (1773–74) under Lord NORTH. He was dismissed by GEORGE III for his opposition to government policy on North America. In 1782 Fox became Britain's first foreign secretary under Prime Minister Charles ROCKINGHAM and helped to secure the repeal of POYNING's Law. He resigned on the appointment of the Earl of SHELBOURNE to succeed Rockingham. In 1783 Fox returned to office after forming a coalition government with his rival, Lord North. After nine months, the coalition collapsed over the bill to reform the English EAST INDIA COMPANY. Thereafter, Fox led opposition to the government of William PITT (THE YOUNGER), urging the abolition of SLAVERY and the extension of the franchise. Fox's support for the FRENCH REVOLUTION led him to oppose British participation in the FRENCH REVOLUTIONARY WARS, although he criticized the government of Henry ADDINGTON for its failure to prepare for the NAPOLEONIC WARS. On Pitt's death (1806), Fox returned as foreign secretary under Lord GRENVILLE.

Fox, George (1624–91) English religious leader, founder of the Society of Friends (or QUAKERS). In 1646 Fox embarked upon his evangelical calling in response to an "inner light". He was imprisoned eight times between 1649 and 1673 for his religious beliefs. Fox made missionary trips (1671–72) to the Caribbean and America to visit Quaker colonists such as William PENN. His *Journal* (1694) is a valuable record of the early Quaker movement.

Foxe, John (1516–87) English Puritan preacher and writer of the *Book of Martyrs* (1563), an influential and polemical account of the persecution of early Protestants. He was forced into exile after the accession (1553) of MARY I of England. Foxe was active in the Reformation movement in Frankfurt and Basel and returned from exile in ELIZABETH I's reign. In 1570 he produced a revised edition of the *Actes and Monuments of these Latter and Perillous Dayes,* popularly known as the *Book of Martyrs*.

France *See* country feature, page 146

Franche-Comté Historic region of E France; its capital was Dôle until 1674 and Besançon thereafter. The "Free County" of BURGUNDY was founded (1177) when Count Raynald III refused to pay homage to LOTHAIR II of Germany. In 1477 Franche-Comté became a Habsburg possession and remained so for nearly 200 years except for a brief period of French rule (1482–93). It was conquered (1668) for France by the Great CONDÉ and was officially ceded to France by the Treaty of NIJMEGEN (1678). Area: 16,202sq km (6254sq mi). Pop. (1991) 1,097,300.

franchise Right or privilege of an individual to vote in public political elections, granted by government. In Britain, the modern basis of the franchise dates from the Great REFORM ACT of 1832 and subsequent acts which, by 1918, ensured all men over the age of 21 and women over 30 were entitled to vote (the first country to give women the vote was New Zealand). By 1928 women aged over 21 were enfranchised, and in 1969 the voting age was lowered to 18. In the United States, the franchise is granted by each state, and this is overseen by the CONSTITUTION. The **14th and 15th amendments** (1868, 1870) forbid any state to deny voting rights to resident adult men aged over 21 on the grounds of race, colour or previous servitude. The **19th Amendment** (1920) gave women the vote. In practice, voting rights for African Americans (especially in the South), were restricted until the 1960s through devices such as state-constitution clauses, literacy tests and poll taxes. The **24th Amendment** (1964) banned poll taxes. The Voting Rights Act (1965) outlawed literacy tests and installed poll observers to prevent voter intimidation. The **26th Amendment** (1971) lowered the voting age to 18. *See also* CIVIL RIGHTS ACTS; DEMOCRACY; SUFFRAGETTE MOVEMENT

Francia, José Gaspar Rodríguez (1766–1840) Paraguayan dictator (1814–40). He was one of the leaders in the bloodless overthrow of Spanish rule in 1811. On becoming co-ruler in 1813, Francia declared independence from Argentina and banned all foreign trade. As dictator, Francia attempted to make Paraguay entirely self-sufficient by modernizing agriculture and developing industry. The effect of his authoritarian rule was to isolate Paraguay from the outside world.

Francis (of Assisi), Saint (1182–1226) Italian founder of the FRANCISCANS, b. Giovanni di Bernardone. The son of a wealthy merchant in Assisi, in 1205 he renounced his worldly life for one of poverty and prayer. In 1209 Francis received permission from Pope INNOCENT III to establish a religious order. The Franciscans were vowed to humility, poverty and devotion to the task of helping people. In 1212, with Saint Clare, he established an order for women, popularly called the Poor Clares. In 1224, while Francis prayed on Monte della Verna, near Florence, the stigmata wounds of the Crucifixion appeared on his body. He was canonized in 1228. His feast day is 4 October.

Francis I (1708–65) Holy Roman emperor (1745–65), duke of Lorraine (1729–35) and grand duke of Tuscany (1737–65). In 1736 he married the HABSBURG heiress, MARIA THERESA. On her accession (1740) to the Austrian throne, Maria appointed Francis co-regent. Maria's accession precipitated the War of the AUSTRIAN SUCCESSION (1740–48) against FREDERICK II of Prussia. Francis succeeded CHARLES VII as Holy Roman emperor, but the real ruler was his wife.

Francis II (1768–1835) Last Holy Roman emperor (1792–1806), first emperor of Austria as Francis I (1804–35), and king of Bohemia and of Hungary (1792–1835). Francis joined the First Coalition against France at the start of the FRENCH REVOLUTIONARY WARS (1792–1802), but was defeated and forced to cede Lombardy by the Treaty of CAMPO FORMIO (1797). He suffered further losses at the beginning of the NAPOLEONIC WARS (1803–15), culminating in the rout by NAPOLEON I at the Battle of AUSTERLITZ (1805) and the abolition of the HOLY ROMAN EMPIRE. In 1810 Prince von METTERNICH secured the marriage of Francis' daughter, MARIE LOUISE, to Napoleon, thus preserving Austria. Francis despised Napoleon, however, and in 1813 he joined the coalition that finally defeated the French emperor. He then formed the HOLY ALLIANCE. Francis was succeeded by his son, FERDINAND (THE BENIGN). *See also* AUSTRIAN EMPIRE; VIENNA, CONGRESS OF

Francis I (1494–1547) King of France (1515–47), cousin, son-in-law and successor of LOUIS XII. He resumed the ITALIAN WARS (1494–1559), regaining the duchy of MILAN at the Battle of Marignano (1515). Francis increased royal control over the church by the Concordat of Bologna (1516) with Pope LEO X. The bitter rivalry between Francis and CHARLES V began when Charles was preferred to Francis as ruler of the HOLY ROMAN EMPIRE. Despite failing to win the support of HENRY VIII of England at the FIELD OF THE CLOTH OF GOLD (1520), Francis embarked on the first (1521–25) of four wars against Charles. The first war ended in defeat at the Battle of PAVIA, N Italy. Francis was imprisoned and forced to cede Burgundy and renounce his claims to Italy by the Treaty of Madrid (1526). Two further wars (1527–29, 1536–38) against the HABSBURGS ended ingloriously, although the terms of the Madrid treaty were tempered by the Treaty of CAMBRAI (1529). In 1542 Francis concluded a treaty with the Turkish Sultan SULEIMAN I (THE MAGNIFICENT) and once again declared war against Charles V when Charles gave Milan to his son (later PHILIP II). Fighting was sporadic, however, and peace was concluded in 1544. Persecution of the WALDENSES, attempts to centralize power, and foolish financial policies made Francis unpopular at home. A leader of the RENAISSANCE in France, Francis is best remembered for his patronage of the arts and his palace at Fontainebleau, N France. He was succeeded by his son, HENRY II. *See also* VALOIS

Francis II (1544–60) King of France (1559–60), eldest son of HENRY II and CATHERINE DE' MEDICI. Married to MARY, QUEEN OF SCOTS at the age of 14, he was a sickly youth and his kingdom was controlled by the GUISE family. *See also* RELIGION, WARS OF

Francis I (1777–1830) King of the Two SICILIES (1825–30), son of Emperor FERDINAND I and Marie Caroline (sister of Marie Antoinette). Early in his career, as regent of Naples, Francis sympathized with the CARBONARI uprising of 1820 and opposed Austrian military intervention. Francis' views changed, however, after his accession to the throne and he became an extreme reactionary. He disbanded the National Guard and requested a greater Austrian presence.

Francis II (1836–94) King of the Two Sicilies (1859–60), son and successor of FERDINAND II. The last Bourbon king of Naples, Francis was driven from power by Giuseppe GARIBALDI and deposed by a plebiscite in October 1861. His dominions were then annexed by VICTOR EMMANUEL II. *See also* RISORGIMENTO

Franciscans Friars belonging to an itinerant religious order founded by Saint FRANCIS (OF ASSISI) in 1209. The first order, known as the Friars Minor, now comprises three subdivisions: the Observants; the CAPUCHIN (founded 1525); and the Conventual, who are allowed to own property corporately. The second order, the Poor Clares, was an order of nuns founded by Saint Francis and Saint Clare in 1212.

Francis Joseph *See* FRANZ JOSEPH

Francis of Sales, Saint (1567–1622) French Roman Catholic bishop and devotional writer. He was a leader of the COUNTER-REFORMATION in Savoy. Francis converted many of the population of Chablais from CALVINISM. In 1602 Francis was appointed bishop of Geneva, where he founded the Visitation Nuns. His writings include *Introduction to the Devout Life* (1609).

Francis Xavier, Saint (1506–52) Early JESUIT missionary, often called the **Apostle of the Indies**. Francis was an associate of Saint Ignatius of LOYOLA, with whom he took the vow founding the Society of Jesus (Jesuits). From 1541 Francis travelled through India, Japan and the East Indies, making many converts. Francis died while on a journey to China. His feast day is 3 December. *See also* COUNTER-REFORMATION

Franco, Francisco *See* feature article

FRANCO, FRANCISCO (1892–1975)

Spanish general and dictator of Spain (1939–75). He joined the army in 1907 and rose rapidly through the ranks, excelling in campaigns against the Moroccan rebels. By 1935 Franco was chief of the general staff. In February 1936, following the election of a POPULAR FRONT government, he was dismissed from the general staff and sent to the Canary Islands. In July 1936, Franco proclaimed a military uprising that precipitated the Spanish CIVIL WAR. After taking control of the Spanish protectorate of Morocco, Franco's army landed in Spain and he was proclaimed (October 1936) head of the rebel Nationalist government. In 1937 he subsumed all the Nationalist groupings into the FALANGE (Spanish Fascist Party). With the support of Nazi Germany and fascist Italy, Franco fought a three-year bloody civil war against the Republicans. In March 1939, Nationalist forces captured Madrid and Franco established a dictatorship. Franco kept Spain out of WORLD WAR 2, while remaining broadly sympathetic to the Axis powers. In 1947 Franco declared Spain a monarchy, with himself as regent. Franco reduced the power of the Falange and sought a rapprochment with the United States. During the last two decades of Franco's rule, Spain made dramatic economic progress and the regime was forced to implement more liberal social policies. In 1969 Franco designated JUAN CARLOS as heir to the throne.

▲ **Franco** restored peace and stability in Spain, but his fascist principles and repression of individual rights left Spain increasingly isolated in post-war Europe.

F

AREA: 551,500sq km (212,934sq mi)
POPULATION: 57,372,000
CAPITAL (POPULATION): Paris (2,152,423)
GOVERNMENT: Multiparty republic
ETHNIC GROUPS: French 93%, Arab 3%, German 2%, Breton 1%, Catalan
LANGUAGES: French (official)
RELIGIONS: Christianity (Roman Catholic 86%, other Christian 4%), Islam 3%
GDP PER CAPITA (1995): US$21,030

Republic in w Europe. France is Europe's second-largest country (after Ukraine). It became part of the Roman Empire as a result of Julius Caesar's conquest of Gaul (58–51 BC). In the 3rd century AD, Gaul was attacked by Germanic peoples, notably the Alemanni and the Franks. It remained, however, within the Roman Empire until the 5th-century invasion of the Visigoths. In 486 the Franks, led by Clovis I, established the Merovingian dynasty in N Gaul. By 536 the Merovingian kingdom included much of France, but the dynasty was split by rivalry between the kings of Austrasia and Neustria in the 7th century.

In 714 Charles Martel launched a campaign to reunite the Frankish world. His son, Pepin III (the Short) (r.750–68), was the first Carolingian king of the Franks. The dynasty was at its height under Charlemagne (r.768–814), who became emperor of the West (800–14). Charlemagne provided sound administration, but the empire disintegrated after the death (840) of his son, Louis I (the Pious). The Treaty of Verdun (843) partitioned the empire, and Charles II (the Bald) became ruler (843–77) of Francia Occidentalis (now France). The fragmentation of central authority contributed to the creation of a feudal system and enabled the Vikings to establish (911) the duchy of Normandy. Hugh Capet (r.987–96) founded the Capetian dynasty and is often regarded as the first king of France.

The Norman Conquest (1066) of England marked the start of a long history of Anglo-French rivalry. Louis VI (the Fat) (r.1108–87) and Louis VII (the Young) (r.1137–80) reasserted the power of the French monarchy and Philip II (r.1180–1223) regained land that had been lost to the English Plantagenet kings. Louis IX (r.1226–70) modernized the civil and judicial systems in France and led the seventh and eighth Crusades. The succession of Philip VI (r.1328–50) of Valois was contested by Edward III of England and the Hundred Years' War ensued (1337–1453). Philip's son and successor, John II (r.1350–64), was captured by the English at the Battle of Poitiers (1356) and forced to cede Aquitaine. During the reign (1364–80) of Charles V (the Wise), Bertrand du Guesclin recovered all territories lost to the English. Charles VI (r.1380–1422) was defeated by the English at the Battle of Agincourt (1415) and forced to recognize Henry V of England as his successor. By 1422 England controlled most of France. During the reign (1422–61) of Charles VII (the Well-served), French fortunes revived after Joan of Arc helped crush the siege of Orléans (1428), and by 1453 only Calais remained in English hands. Louis XI (r.1461–83) reimposed royal authority, gained Burgundy through the death (1477) of Charles the Bold, and inherited the Angevin lands. Charles VIII (r.1483–98) launched the long-running Italian Wars (1494–1559).

The reign (1515–47) of Francis I was dominated by conflict with the Habsburg Emperor Charles V. It also marked the beginning of the Renaissance and the Reformation in France. The rise of the Protestant Huguenots led to the Wars of Religion (1562–98). The Catholic Guise faction lost, and Henry IV (r.1589–1610) became the first Bourbon king. Henry extended religious freedom to Protestants by the Edict of Nantes (1598). The national finances, plundered by years of civil war, were restored by his chief minister, the Duc de Sully. The reign (1610–43) of Henry's successor, Louis XIII, was shaped by Cardinal de Richelieu, who involved France in the Thirty Years' War (1618–48) against the Habsburgs and crushed the Huguenots at the siege of La Rochelle (1628). Louis XIV's (r.1643–1715) first chief minister, Cardinal Jules Mazarin, led France to victory in the Thirty Years' War and defeated the nobles in the war of the Fronde (1648–53). After Mazarin's death (1661), Jean Baptiste Colbert reformed royal finances, and the French court at Versailles became the richest in Europe. Louis tried to enforce religious uniformity by revoking (1685) the Edict of Nantes and suppressing Jansenism. His victory in the War of Devolution (1667–68) against Spain, the gaining of Franche-Comté (1679), and the capture of Strasbourg (1681) frightened other European powers and led to the War of the Grand Alliance (1688–97) and the War of the Spanish Succession (1701–14). The *ancien régime* of Louis XV (r.1715–74) and Louis XVI (r.1774–93) proved incapable of political and social reform. Moreover, Louis XV's involvement in the War of the Austrian Succession (1740–48) and the Seven Years' War (1756–63) drained royal finances and the monarchy was bankrupted by Louis XVI's support for the American Revolution (1775–83).

The French Revolution (1789–99) saw the execution (1793) of Louis XVI, and Maximilien Robespierre's brutal Reign of Terror (1793–94). The First Republic was secured by victory in the French Revolutionary Wars (1792–1802). The Thermidorean Reaction led to the creation of a Directory that ruled France (1795–99) until Napoleon I seized power. Early successes in the Napoleonic Wars (1803–15) were wiped out at the Battle of Waterloo (1815). Napoleon was forced into exile and the monarchy restored first under Louis XVIII (r.1814–24) then Charles X (r.1824–30). Charles was replaced by Louis Philippe in the July Revolution (1830). The February Revolution (1848) established a Second Republic. In 1852 Napoleon I's nephew seized power as Napoleon III. His defeat in the Franco-Prussian War (1870–71) led to the formation of the Third Republic (1870–1940). The Paris Commune (1871) was violently suppressed. The Dreyfus affair polarized French society in the 1890s.

France was the battleground for much of World War I (1914–18). Georges Clemenceau and Aristide Briand led France to peace. In the post-war years, Léon Blum and Édouard Daladier failed to prevent the rise of Nazi Germany, and France joined Britain in declaring war on Germany in September 1939. In World War 2, Nazi troops took just six weeks (May–June 1940) to complete the conquest of France and establish the Vichy government under Marshal Pétain. Charles De Gaulle led the Free French resistance to Nazi occupation. In August 1944 Paris was liberated and a Fourth Republic was declared in 1946. Political instability and colonial war, especially in Algeria and Indochina, slowed the post-war recovery. In 1958 De Gaulle was elected president and established a Fifth Republic. Gaullist foreign policy alienated the United States and the United Kingdom. In 1969 De Gaulle resigned, replaced first by Georges Pompidou, then Valéry Giscard d'Estaing.

François Mitterrand's presidency (1981–96) was marked by nationalization, civic rebuilding, decentralization and advocacy of the European Union (EU). Mitterrand was succeded as president by his great rival, Jacques Chirac. Chirac's welfare reforms and austere measures to ensure French entry into a single European currency (1999) brought strikes and unemployment and the election (1997) of a socialist prime minister, Lionel Jospin.

▲ **Franco-Prussian War** (1870–71) Württemberg infantryman (left) and Prussian infantryman (right). French troops were greatly outnumbered by these Prussian forces, who were also more highly trained and organized.

Franconia Historic region of Germany around the River Main. The area was settled by FRANKS in the 6th century AD and in the 8th century it was claimed by the Frankish MEROVINGIAN dynasty. After the division of the CAROLINGIAN empire in 843, Franconia became a duchy of the East Frankish kingdom. In 911 the Duke of Franconia became the first elected king of Germany, as CONRAD I. From the 13th century, Franconia was divided into several secular and ecclesiastical principalities, of which the bishopric of Würzburg was one of the most powerful. In the Napoleonic reorganization of Germany in the 19th century, Franconia was divided between the Grand Duchy of Baden and the kingdoms of Bavaria and Württemberg.

Franco-Prussian War (1870–71) Conflict engineered by the Prussian Chancellor Otto von BISMARCK. Prussian victory in the AUSTRO-PRUSSIAN WAR (1866) alarmed NAPOLEON III of France, and Bismarck used the prospect of a French invasion to frighten the S German states into joining the NORTH GERMAN CONFEDERATION dominated by Prussia. The nominal cause of the war was a dispute over the Spanish succession, which Bismarck provoked with the EMS DISPATCH. Prussia was fully prepared for the French declaration of war (14 July 1870), and General Helmuth von MOLTKE launched a devastating offensive into ALSACE. By August 1870, the French left wing had retreated and were encircled at Metz, NE France. In an attempt to relieve Metz, Napoleon III and *c*.83,000 French troops were captured at SEDAN (September 1870). Napoleon abdicated, and Paris was surrounded and starved into submission. An armistice was agreed in January 1871, and Alsace and LORRAINE were ceded to the new German empire under WILLIAM I. Paris refused to surrender its weapons, and the PARIS COMMUNE was formed. The War resulted in the unification of both Germany and Italy – the PAPAL STATES were annexed by Italy in 1870. Prussian militarism and imperialism coupled with the French desire for revenge were major causes of World War 1.

Frank, Anne (1929–45) German Jew who became a symbol of suffering under the Nazis. Born in Frankfurt, W Germany, she fled with her family to the Netherlands in 1933. The Franks were living in Amsterdam at the time of the German invasion in 1940 and went into hiding from 1942 until they were betrayed in August 1944. Anne died in Bergen-BELSEN concentration camp. The diary she kept during her years in hiding was published in 1947 and attracted worldwide readership. *See also* HOLOCAUST, THE

Frank, Jacob (1726–91) Polish Jewish mystic and leader of the Frankist movement. Opposed to rabbinical JUDAISM and the TALMUD, Frank believed himself to be the Messiah and was excommunicated by the rabbis in 1756. He then joined (1759) the Roman Catholic Church but was imprisoned as a heretic (1766–72). Frank conducted mystical, orgiastic ceremonies and his followers regarded him as "Lord of Holiness". After his death, his daughter Eve assumed the role of godhead incarnate in the movement as the "Holy Mistress". The sect disintegrated after her death in 1816.

Frankfurt City and port on the River Main, Hesse state, W Germany. The name Frankfurt (ford of the FRANKS) is thought to date from AD 500, when the ALEMANNI were driven south by the Franks. It was one of the royal residences of CHARLEMAGNE in the early 9th century. In the 12th century, the HOHENSTAUFENS built a new castle here. From 1372 to 1806 Frankfurt was a free imperial city, and the Holy Roman emperors were elected and crowned (1562–1792) at the Church of St Bartholomew. The Congress of VIENNA (1814–15) made Frankfurt the capital of the new GERMAN CONFEDERATION. The FRANKFURT NATIONAL ASSEMBLY (1848–49) was the first German parliament. The old city was almost entirely destroyed during World War 2. Pop. (1993 est.) 660,800.

Frankfurter, Felix (1882–1965) US jurist and educator, associate justice of the Supreme Court (1939–62). He helped found the AMERICAN CIVIL LIBERTIES UNION (1920). Frankfurter was an adviser to President Franklin ROOSEVELT. A liberal Supreme Court justice, he advocated judicial restraint and government self-regulation in civil liberties.

Frankfurt National Assembly (1848–49) First German parliament, created during the REVOLUTIONS OF 1848. The full assembly met (May 1848) in the Church of St Paul, FRANKFURT, and elected Heinrich von Gagern as president. It annulled the constitution of the GERMAN CONFEDERATION and appointed Archduke John of Austria regent of Germany. A liberal constitution (March 1849) and plans for unification were undermined by PRUSSIA and AUSTRIA and FREDERICK WILLIAM IV refused to recognize the parliament's right of appointment. In June 1849 the National Assembly was forcibly dispersed.

Franklin, Benjamin (1706–90) American statesman, scientist and inventor. A successful printer in Philadelphia, where he published *Poor Richard's Almanac* (1732–57), Franklin gave up the business to devote his life to scientific research. His experiments in electricity, which he identified in lightning, were influential. He was deputy postmaster general (1753–74) of the THIRTEEN COLONIES, whose union he proposed at the ALBANY CONGRESS (1754). During the events leading up to the AMERICAN REVOLUTION (1775–83), Franklin pressed for moderate opposition to the STAMP ACT (1765). A leading delegate to the CONTINENTAL CONGRESS that first met in 1774, Franklin was an architect of the DECLARATION OF INDEPENDENCE (4 July 1776). In September 1776, he went to Paris and negotiated a treaty of alliance (1778) with France against Britain. His peace proposals formed the basis of the final Treaty of PARIS (1783) with Britain. Franklin was president of Pennsylvania's executive council (1785–88) and, as a member of the CONSTITUTIONAL CONVENTION (1787), helped form the CONSTITUTION OF THE UNITED STATES.

F

FRANKS

Germanic people who settled in the region of the N River Rhine in the 3rd century AD. They comprised several subgroups, most prominently the SALIANS and Ripuarians. With the collapse of the ROMAN EMPIRE (*c*.450), the Salian CHILDERIC I and his son, CLOVIS I, united increasing numbers of Franks under their rule. In 486 Clovis overthrew the last remnants of Roman rule in GAUL and established the MEROVINGIAN kingdom. The Merovingians, however, did not develop structures capable of holding their kingdom together and, by the end of the 7th century, real power had passed to a small number of families in each of the regions: AUSTRASIA, NEUSTRIA, BURGUNDY, AQUITAINE and PROVENCE.

In 695 the rulers of Austrasia, the CAROLINGIANS, embarked on a campaign to reunite the whole Frankish world. In three generations CHARLES MARTEL, PEPIN III (THE SHORT) and CHARLEMAGNE had reunited Francia. The Treaty of VERDUN (843) partitioned the Carolingian empire into three: Francia Media, Francia Occidentalis and Francia Orientalis. East and West Francia correspond to modern Germany and France.

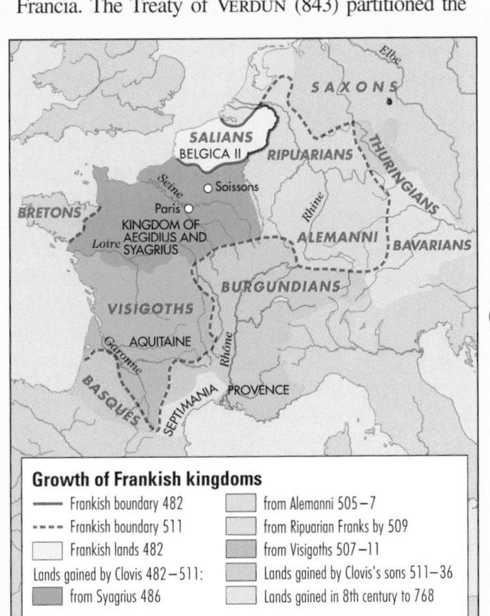

◄ **Frankish kingdoms** By eliminating rival Frankish warlords, Clovis and his descendants created a unified Frankish kingdom.

▲ **Frankish soldier** The Frankish warriors fought with battle-axes and shields made of wood and covered with stretched hide.

F

Franklin, Sir John (1786–1847) English Arctic explorer. He served as a naval officer in the Battle of TRAFALGAR (1805). Franklin's first overland expedition in N Canada (1819–22) crossed from Great Slave Lake to the Arctic coast. His second expedition (1825–27) descended the Mackenzie River and surveyed more of the Arctic coast. Franklin served as governor of Tasmania (1836–43). In 1845 he embarked on a fated search for the NORTHWEST PASSAGE. After Franklin failed to return, the first of 40 search parties was launched in 1848. These expeditions greatly advanced knowledge of the Arctic and eventually established (1859) that Franklin had died with his entire 129-man crew after they became trapped by ice in the Victoria Strait.

Franks *See* feature article, page 147

Franz Ferdinand (1863–1914) Archduke of Austria, nephew of Emperor FRANZ JOSEPH. He became heir apparent in 1889. Franz Ferdinand aimed to form a triple monarchy, adding a Slavic state to the AUSTRO-HUNGARIAN EMPIRE. His ambition was opposed by Hungarians and nationalist Slavs. On an official visit to Bosnia-Herzegovina, Franz Ferdinand and his wife were assassinated by a Serb nationalist, Gavrilo PRINCIP, in Sarajevo (28 June 1914). The incident led directly to the outbreak of WORLD WAR I.

Franz Joseph (1830–1916) Emperor of Austria (1848–1916) and king of Hungary (1867–1916), nephew and successor of FERDINAND (THE BENIGN). He became emperor upon the abdication of his uncle during the REVOLUTIONS OF 1848. Franz Joseph quickly suppressed the Revolutions, defeating the Hungarians under Louis KOSSUTH in 1849. In the AUSTRO-PRUSSIAN WAR (1866), he was forced to cede territory in Germany and Italy to PRUSSIA. With the formation (1867) of the AUSTRO-HUNGARIAN EMPIRE, Franz Joseph granted Hungary co-equal status (*see* AUSGLEICH). The Slavs opposed Franz Joseph's territorial ambitions in the Balkans. In 1879 he formed the Dual Alliance with Germany, later joined by Italy (1882) to create the TRIPLE ALLIANCE. Tension built up in the Balkan states, culminating in the assassination (1914) of Franz Joseph's heir, FRANZ FERDINAND, and the outbreak of WORLD WAR I. Franz Joseph died in the midst of the War, two years before the final collapse of the HABSBURG empire.

Fraser, (John) Malcolm (1930–) Australian statesman, prime minister (1975–83). In 1955 he became the youngest-ever Liberal member of Parliament. Fraser served in a succession of coalition cabinets (1966–71) before becoming (1975) leader of the LIBERAL PARTY and heading a coalition government. He tried to control inflation by imposing limits on government spending and public sector wage rises. Fraser was re-elected in 1977 and 1982, but resigned as Liberal leader after being defeated in 1983 elections by Bob HAWKE.

Fraser, Peter (1884–1950) New Zealand statesman, prime minister (1940–49), b. Scotland. He emigrated to New Zealand in 1910 and helped to organize the Social Democratic Party and its successor, the Labour Party. Fraser was elected to Parliament in 1918. He served as minister of education, health, marine and police (1935–40) under Michael SAVAGE. Fraser succeeded Savage as prime minister and mobilized New Zealand for entry into World War 2. One of the post-war architects of the United Nations (UN), Fraser was a spokesman for the rights of small nations. He was defeated in the 1949 elections by Sidney HOLLAND.

Fraser, Simon (1776–1862) Canadian explorer and fur trader. He moved to Canada from the United States in 1784 and joined the NORTHWEST COMPANY in 1792. He extended the Company's trade routes west to British Columbia (1805–08) and founded a string of trading posts. He also explored the Fraser and Red rivers. *See also* FUR TRADE

Fredegund (d.597) Frankish queen. She married CHILPERIC I of NEUSTRIA after inducing him to murder his wife, Galswintha. War ensued with AUSTRASIA, whose king, Sigebert I, Chilperic's brother, was married to Galswintha's sister, BRUNHILDA. After Chilperic's murder (584), Fredegund was regent for her son CLOTAIRE II. *See also* FRANKS

Frederick I (Barbarossa) (*c*.1123–90) Holy Roman emperor (1155–90) and king of Germany (1152–90), nephew and successor of Emperor CONRAD III. The son of a HOHENSTAUFEN father and a GUELPH mother, Frederick hoped to end the division between the houses. In 1156 Frederick restored Bavaria to HENRY III (THE LION). The threat to the papacy from the Normans and the Byzantine Emperor MANUEL I (COMNENUS) enabled Frederick to dictate the terms of the Treaty of Constance (1153) with Pope Eugenius III, and Frederick was crowned emperor by Eugenius' successor ADRIAN IV. When Adrian broke the Treaty of Constance, Frederick invaded Italy and captured Milan (1158). Frederick declared himself king of the Lombards and attempted to impose his authority over N Italy through the Diet of Roncaglia. In 1159 Frederick disputed the election of ALEXANDER III as pope and set up an antipope, Victor IV. Alexander then excommunicated Frederick and formed the LOMBARD LEAGUE. Lacking the support of Henry the Lion, Frederick was defeated by the League at the Battle of LEGNANO (1176) and was forced to recognize Alexander as pope and make peace (1183) with the Lombards. In 1180 Frederick deposed Henry the Lion and partitioned the German empire. Frederick was drowned on the Third CRUSADE. He was succeeded by his son, HENRY VI.

Frederick II (1194–1250) Holy Roman emperor (1215–50), king of Germany (1212–20), king of Sicily (1198–1212) and king of Jerusalem (1229–44), son of Emperor HENRY VI. After Henry VI's death in 1197, Germany was plunged into factional strife between the HOHENSTAUFENS, led by Frederick's uncle Philip of Swabia, and the GUELPHS, led by OTTO IV, who eventually prevailed to become Holy Roman emperor (1209). Meanwhile, the infant Frederick was crowned king of Sicily, with first his mother, Constance, and then Pope INNOCENT III as regent. In 1212 Frederick left for Germany after having his son, Henry VII, crowned king of Sicily. The German princes elected Frederick as emperor in place of Otto (1212). Otto was defeated by PHILIP II of France at the Battle of BOUVINES (1214). In 1220 Frederick was crowned Holy Roman emperor, after promising Innocent that he would separate Sicily from the empire and lead the Sixth CRUSADE. His claims on Lombardy and postponement of the Crusade angered Pope GREGORY IX, who excommunicated him and revived the LOMBARD LEAGUE. Frederick finally embarked on the Sixth Crusade in 1228, gaining Jerusalem, Bethlehem and Nazareth through negotiation, and proclaiming himself *stupor mundi* (wonder of the world). In Sicily, Frederick set up a centralized royal administration, issuing the Constitution of Melfi (1231). In Germany, he devolved authority to the princes in an effort to maintain their support. Frederick's son, Henry, rebelled against him and was imprisoned (1235). Frederick gave the German throne to another son, CONRAD IV, and issued an edict of imperial peace. In 1237 Frederick defeated the Lombard League at Cortenuova and refused a peaceful settlement. In 1239, after more fighting in N Italy, Frederick was excommunicated for a second time by Gregory IX. In 1240 he captured most of the PAPAL STATES. In 1245 the new pope, INNOCENT IV, deposed Frederick. War ensued between the emperor and the papacy and continued for many years after Frederick's sudden death in 1250.

▲ **Franz Joseph** was personally involved in shaping Austrian foreign policy. His failure to avert conflict with Germany and Italy, however, led to the eventual disintegration of the Austro-Hungarian Empire.

Frederick III (1415–93) Holy Roman emperor (1452–93) and German king (1440–93). On the death (1424) of his father, Duke Ernest of Austria, Frederick inherited the HABSBURG possessions of Styria, CARINTHIA, CARNIOLA and Gorizia. In 1452 Frederick became the last Holy Roman Emperor to be crowned by the pope in Rome. After the fall of Constantinople (1453), the Habsburgs became the principal opposition to the advance of Islam and the OTTOMAN EMPIRE. Frederick used his position as guardian for Ladislas V to further his own claims over Bohemia and Hungary, but the death (1457) of Ladislas brought the temporary loss of both domains to George of Podebrad and MATTHIAS CORVINUS of Hungary respectively. Matthias Corvinus conquered much of Austria and occupied Vienna in 1485. In 1490 Matthias died and Frederick recovered his hereditary lands. By marrying his son Maximilian (later MAXIMILIAN I) to Mary, heiress of Burgundy, in 1477, Frederick secured an enormous inheritance for the Habsburgs.

Frederick III (1831–88) Emperor of Germany (1888), son of WILLIAM I. In 1858 he married Victoria, eldest daughter of the British Queen VICTORIA. Liberal and popular, Frederick died after only 90 days in power. He was succeeded by his son, WILLIAM II.

Frederick I (1471–1533) King of Denmark (1523–33) and Norway (1524–33), son of CHRISTIAN I. In 1490 Frederick split the duchy of SCHLESWIG-HOLSTEIN with his older brother John, who had become king of Denmark on their father's death in 1481. Frederick was on hostile terms with John and with John's son and successor, CHRISTIAN II. When Christian was driven out of Denmark (1522), Frederick accepted the throne and that of Norway the following year. Frederick discouraged fighting with Sweden, kept Denmark's finances in order, and tolerated the spread of Lutheranism.

Frederick II (1534–88) King of Denmark and Norway (1559–88), son and successor of CHRISTIAN III. His attempt to establish Danish control of the Baltic Sea region led to the Seven Years' War of the North (1563–70). Frederick failed to dominate Sweden and was forced to sign the Peace of Stettin (1570). After the war, he concentrated on rebuilding the nation's economy. Agricultural production increased through the encouragement of large-scale farming by the nobility. Frederick built Kronborg Fortress at Helsingör to guard the economically important trade route through The Sound, and funded the construction of the astronomer Tycho Brahe's observatory on the island of Hven.

Frederick III (1609–70) King of Denmark and Norway (1648–70), son and successor of CHRISTIAN IV. In 1657 Frederick relaunched the war with Sweden, but was forced to cede land to CHARLES X of Sweden by the Treaty of Roskilde (1658). Hostilities soon recommenced, however, and the tide turned in favour of Denmark after Copenhagen withstood a lengthy siege. At the Treaty of Copenhagen (1660), Denmark recovered Bornhold and Trondheim. In 1661 Frederick established an absolute monarchy. *See also* NORTHERN WAR, FIRST

Frederick VI (1768–1839) King of Denmark (1808–39) and Norway (1808–14), son and successor of CHRISTIAN VII. He established himself as regent for his insane father in 1784. Frederick instituted liberal reforms, including the abolition of serfdom and prohibition of the slave trade in the Danish colonies. Denmark remained neutral during the French Revolutionary Wars, but the battles of COPENHAGEN (1801, 1807) against the British persuaded Frederick to form an alliance with NAPOLEON I in the NAPOLEONIC WARS. As a result, Frederick was forced to cede Norway to Sweden by the Peace of Kiel (1814). He was succeeded by his cousin, CHRISTIAN VII.

Frederick I (1657–1713) First king of Prussia (1701–13). He succeeded his father, FREDERICK WILLIAM, the "Great Elector", as Frederick III of Brandenburg. In the War of the GRAND ALLIANCE (1689–97), Frederick allied Prussia with Holland and England against France, thus winning the approval of Emperor LEOPOLD I, who agreed to Frederick's assumption of the title "king in Prussia". In return, Frederick promised large numbers of Prussian troops to support Austria in the War of the SPANISH SUCCESSION (1701–14). Frederick promoted the cultural development of Brandenburg. He was succeeded by his son, FREDERICK WILLIAM I.

Frederick II (the Great) (1712–86) King of Prussia (1740–86), son and successor of FREDERICK WILLIAM I. He established PRUSSIA as a major European power. In 1730 Frederick was imprisoned after trying to escape the tyrannical rule of his father and forced to witness the execution of his accomplice, Lieutenant Katte. In the War of the AUSTRIAN SUCCESSION (1740–48) against MARIA THERESA, Frederick gained the wealthy province of SILESIA from the HABSBURGS (1745). In 1756 Frederick invaded SAXONY, precipitating the SEVEN YEARS' WAR (1756–63). Frederick, allied with Britain, faced a coalition of Austria, France, Russia and Sweden. He secured brilliant victories at Rossbach and Leuthen (1757), but was routed by the Russians at the Battle of Kunersdorf (1759). All seemed lost when Austro-Russian forces occupied Berlin in 1760, but the death (1762) of the Russian Tsarina ELIZABETH signalled a reversal of fortunes. Elizabeth's successor, PETER III, withdrew from the War and ended Maria Theresa's hopes of recovering Silesia. Frederick directed Prussia's remarkable recovery from the devastation of war, which had claimed *c.*180,000 Prussian lives. In 1764 he formed an alliance with Russia that resulted in the first Partition of POLAND (1772) and the incorporation of BRANDENBURG and POMERANIA into Prussia. Frederick renewed the conflict with Austria in the War of the BAVARIAN SUCCESSION (1778–79), checking the ambitions of Emperor JOSEPH II to gain Bavaria. At home, Frederick was an "enlightened despot", abolishing torture, press censorship and religious discrimination. Frederick's building of a strong, disciplined army, however, led to the dominance of the JUNKER class (landowning officer) in Prussia, and his autocratic rule left Prussia incapable of reform. Frederick was an admirer of French culture and was a friend and patron of VOLTAIRE. He wrote extensively in French, built the Palace of Sans Souci, and was a gifted musician. He was succeeded by his nephew, FREDERICK WILLIAM II. *See also* HOHENZOLLERN

Frederick V (1596–1623) (Winter King) King of Bohemia (1619–20), Elector Palatine (1610–20). A Calvinist prince of the WITTELSBACH family, he married (1613) the daughter of James I of England. In 1619 he was chosen as king by the Protestant rebels of Bohemia in preference to the Holy Roman Emperor FERDINAND II, provoking the outbreak of the THIRTY YEARS' WAR. Defeat at the Battle of the White Mountain (1620) resulted in the loss of both of Frederick's titles.

Frederick Augustus I (1750–1827) First king of Saxony (1806–27), elector (1768–1806) as Frederick Augustus III. In the FRENCH REVOLUTIONARY WARS, he brought SAXONY into the coalition against France. Frederick Augustus later entered the NAPOLEONIC WARS against France. However, after the Prussian defeat at Jena (1806), he made a separate peace with Napoleon, who approved the title king of Saxony and made him (1807) duke of Warsaw. Frederick Augustus was captured by the Prussians in the Battle of LEIPZIG (1813) and lost much of his kingdom to Prussia at the Congress of VIENNA (1815).

Frederick Henry (1584–1647) Prince of Orange-Nassau, son of WILLIAM I (THE SILENT). He became stadtholder of the UNITED PROVINCES in 1625 on the death of his half-brother MAURICE OF NASSAU. Under Frederick Henry's rule, the stadtholdership was accepted as hereditary in the house of ORANGE. In 1635 he allied with France and Sweden against the HABSBURGS during the THIRTY YEARS' WAR. He captured the cities of Breda and Hulst, but his military campaign against the Spanish did not gather momentum and he was eventually persuaded that a peace treaty should be agreed with Spain. He died before peace was concluded in 1648.

Frederick Louis (1707–51) Prince of Wales, eldest son of GEORGE II of Britain. Frederick Louis led opposition to his father's government after a bitter quarrel over his allowance. Turning his home into a meeting place for the political opposition, he managed to topple the prime minister, Robert WALPOLE. Frederick later settled his grievances with his father. His son became GEORGE III.

Fredericksburg City on the Rappahannock River, N Virginia, United States. Planned in 1727, it is particularly associated with the AMERICAN REVOLUTION and CIVIL WAR. From 1760 the Rising Sun Tavern was a meeting place for American patriots. Many sites are connected to George WASHINGTON, including the site of the signing of a 1775 resolution on American independence. The **Battle of Fredericksburg** (13 December 1862) was a one-sided victory for the Confederate army of Northern Virginia, led by General Robert LEE, over the Union Army of the Potomac, led by Major General Ambrose BURNSIDE. Nearly 13,000 Union troops were killed or wounded. The Confederate troops of "Stonewall" JACKSON and James Longstreet lost *c.*5300. Pop. (1990) 19,030.

Frederick William I (1688–1740) King of Prussia (1713–40), son and successor of FREDERICK I. He strengthened the army and economy and centralized government, laying the basis for the rise of Prussia as a great power. Frederick William treated his gifted son, the future FREDERICK II (THE GREAT), with brutality but bequeathed him a full treasury and the finest army in Europe.

Frederick William II (1744–97) King of Prussia (1786–97), nephew and successor of FREDERICK II (THE GREAT). In the FRENCH REVOLUTIONARY WARS, he joined (1792) the alliance against France. In 1795, however, Frederick William made peace in order to consolidate his gains as a result of the second (1793) and third (1795) partitions of POLAND. He kept an extravagant court, encouraging cultural activities, and left Prussia virtually bankrupt.

Frederick William III (1770–1840) King of PRUSSIA (1797–1840), son and successor of FREDERICK WILLIAM II. He was forced to abandon neutrality in the NAPOLEONIC WARS when French troops massed on the Prussian border. Frederick William's army was crushed by Napoleon at the Battle of JENA (1806), and he was forced to sign the Treaty of TILSIT (1807) that gave France all territory W of the River Elbe. Frederick William realized that domestic reform was necessary to revitalize Prussia. He allied with Russia and the reorganized Prussian army re-entered the NAPOLEONIC WARS in 1813 and played a major part in NAPOLEON I's eventual defeat. Frederick William joined the HOLY ALLIANCE and refused to grant a more liberal constitution. He was succeeded by his son, FREDERICK WILLIAM IV.

Frederick William IV (1795–1861) King of Prussia (1840–61), son and successor of FREDERICK WILLIAM III. He was taken aback by the spread (March 1848) to Prussia of the REVOLUTIONS OF 1848 and was initially forced to concede to demands for a national assembly in Berlin. In December 1848, Frederick William dissolved the assembly and imposed a conservative constitution. He refused the crown of Germany (1849) because it was offered by the FRANKFURT NATIONAL ASSEMBLY rather than the German princes. At the Treaty of Olmütz (1850), Frederick William was forced to submit to Austrian opposition to his plans for a German union under Prussian leadership. In 1857 he was paralysed by a stroke and his brother William (later Emperor WILLIAM I) ruled as regent.

Frederick William (1620–88) (Great Elector) Elector of Brandenburg (1640–88). He inherited HOHENZOLLERN lands that had been devastated by the THIRTY YEARS' WAR. For the three years of his reign, Frederick William was forced to govern from Königsberg (now Kaliningrad) rather than Brandenburg. He immediately negotiated an armistice with Sweden and then began to build a standing army independent of the HABSBURGS. By the Peace of WESTPHALIA (1644) that concluded the Thirty Years' War, Frederick William gained Eastern Pomerania. He supported Sweden at the start of the First NORTHERN WAR (1665–60), but then switched sides to achieve recognition of his sovereignty over the Duchy of Prussia. In the DUTCH WARS (1672–78), Frederick William again showed his pragmatic shifts of allegiance, supporting first the French then the HOLY ROMAN EMPIRE. He gained a great victory over the Swedes at the Battle of Fehrbellin (1675), briefly holding the whole of POMERANIA. Frederick William laid the foundation of the future Prussian state by centralizing administration, reorganizing the economy and tax system and creating a strong army. His son became FREDERICK I, king of Prussia.

Free Church of Scotland Grouping of Scottish Presbyterians formed as a result of the secession of nearly one-third of the membership of the established CHURCH OF SCOTLAND in the Disruption of 1843. In 1900 all but a small minority of this Free Church joined the United Presbyterian Church to become the United Free Church of Scotland. In 1929, following the disestablishment of the Church of Scotland, the United Free Church of Scotland reunited with it. The tiny Presbyterian minority who had opposed the initial union retained their independence and kept the name United Free Church. *See also* PRESBYTERIANISM

Freedmen's Bureau (1865–72) US government agency established at the end of the American CIVIL WAR to aid four million African Americans recently liberated from SLAVERY. Administered by the War Department, with General Oliver HOWARD as its commissioner, the Bureau was one of the most powerful instruments of RECONSTRUCTION. It provided medical care for more than one million freedmen and built more than 1000 black schools and colleges. The Bureau also acted as a political machine, recruiting voters for the REPUBLICAN PARTY. President Andrew JOHNSON viewed the Bureau's work as an unconstitutional interference in the Southern states. It was disbanded in 1872.

Freedom Rides (1961) CIVIL RIGHTS trips to the Southern United States sponsored by the CONGRESS OF RACIAL EQUALITY (CORE). Anti-racism protestors (freedom riders) drove through the Southern states to challenge the segregation laws. The Rides eventually led to the desegregation of interstate terminals and subsequently to the Interstate Commerce Commission's ruling providing "non-racial" seating in buses.

Free French Group formed by Charles DE GAULLE on the creation of the VICHY GOVERNMENT in 1940. Its purpose was to continue the armed resistance to Nazi Germany's occupation of France. Operating outside France, the Free French was soon aligned with internal Resistance groups. The group aided the Allies throughout the WORLD WAR 2 and formed a provisional government after the NORMANDY LANDINGS.

freemasonry Customs and teachings of the secret fraternal order of Free and Accepted Masons, an all-male secret society with national organizations worldwide. Freemasonry is most popular in the United Kingdom and former colonies of the BRITISH EMPIRE. It evolved from the medieval guilds of stonemasons and cathedral builders. Its ceremonies, which use many symbolic gestures and allegories, demand a belief in God as the architect of the Universe. The first Grand Lodge (meeting place) was founded in London, England (1717). The first lodge in the United States was founded (1730) in Philadelphia. Many of the leaders of the American Revolution were masons, and 13 US presidents have been lodge members. Historically associated with liberalism, freemasonry teaches morality, charity and law-abiding behaviour. In recent times, masons have incurred criticism because of their strict secrecy, male exclusivity and alleged use of influence within organizations, such as the police or local government, to benefit members. Today, there are *c.*6 million Masons worldwide.

free silver In United States' history, the campaign to produce unlimited silver coinage. In the mid-19th century, large deposits of silver had been discovered, but in 1873 Congress removed silver dollars from the list of legal tender. Protestors included inflationists, who favoured increasing the amount of money in circulation, and mine operators. In 1878 the BLAND-ALLISON ACT made silver legal tender again and obliged the government to purchase a certain amount of silver each month. The amount that had to be purchased was increased by the Sherman Silver Purchase Act (1890). A fall in the stock-market led to the repeal of this Act in 1892. In 1896 free silver became a campaign issue, and in 1900 the Republican Party passed the Gold Standard Act, which made gold the only standard of currency. In the GREAT DEPRESSION of the 1930s, silver was again purchased by the Treasury. In the 1960s and 1970s, silver supplies decreased and the government sold off its remaining stocks. *See also* BRYAN, WILLIAM JENNINGS

F

Free Soil Party (1848–54) US political coalition. It was opposed, for economic reasons, to the extension of SLAVERY into the new territories. Charles SUMNER and Salmon CHASE were among the members of the Free Soil Party. In 1848 they chose ex-President Martin VAN BUREN as their presidential candidate. In 1854 the Free Soilers joined the WHIG PARTY and anti-slavery Democrats to form the REPUBLICAN PARTY.

Free State (formerly Orange Free State) Province in E central South Africa; the capital is Bloemfontein. AFRIKANERS began to settle in large numbers after the GREAT TREK (1836). It was annexed (1848) by the British, achieved independence (1854), and after its involvement in the second of the SOUTH AFRICAN WARS (1899–1902) was again annexed by Britain. Regaining independence in 1907, the Orange Free State joined the Union of South Africa in 1910. It was renamed Free State in 1995. Pop. (1995 est.) 2,782,500.

Freetown Capital and chief port of Sierra Leone, W Africa. Freetown was founded (1787) by the British as a settlement for freed slaves from England, Nova Scotia and Jamaica. It was the capital of British West Africa (1808–74). In 1961 Freetown was made capital of independent Sierra Leone. Pop. (1992) 505,080.

free trade Commerce conducted between nations without restrictions on imports and exports. In the 19th century, the repeal of England's CORN LAWS (1846) and the Anglo-French free-trade treaty (1860) were hallmarks of free trade. Twentieth-century agreements include the EUROPEAN FREE TRADE AGREEMENT (EFTA) (1959) and the NORTH AMERICAN FREE TRADE AGREEMENT (NAFTA) (1994). Protectionists oppose free trade, advocating import duties and restrictive quotas to safeguard domestic industry from foreign competition. *See also* INDUSTRIAL REVOLUTION; MERCANTILISM; SMITH, ADAM

Frei (Montalva), Eduardo (1911–82) Chilean statesman, president (1964–70). In 1964 he defeated Salvador ALLENDE to become the first Christian Democrat leader of Chile. Frei's ambitious package of reforms, including the partial nationalization of Chile's copper industry and the redistribution of land and wealth, floundered amid economic recession. In 1970 Frei was defeated by Allende. His son, Eduardo **Frei Ruiz-Tagle** (1942–), also served as president (1993–2000).

FRELIMO (acronym for the Mozambique Liberation Front) Political and military movement that led the struggle for Mozambican independence from Portugal. FRELIMO was formed in 1962 under the leadership of Eduardo Mondlane. Based in Tanzania, its guerrilla forces were initially active in the north of MOZAMBIQUE. In 1969 Mondalane was assassinated and the leadership passed to Samora MACHEL, who expanded FRELIMO's activities into the heart of Mozambique. The guerrillas gradually gained the upper hand despite the presence of *c*.70,000 Portuguese troops. In 1975 Mozambique gained independence and Machel became president. The FRELIMO government established a one-party Marxist-Leninist state. Its attempts to revive the nation's economy were hampered by RENAMO, a dissident group sponsored by the white-minority regimes in South Africa and Rhodesia. In 1986 Machel died and was succeeded by Joachim Chissano. In 1992 a peace accord was signed with RENAMO. FRELIMO won the 1994 multiparty elections.

Frémont, John Charles (1813–90) US explorer and general. Following his exploration and mapping of the OREGON TRAIL (1842), Frémont crossed the Sierra Nevada in the winter of 1843–44. He led an expedition (1845) to California and supported US settlers in the Bear Flag Revolt against Mexican rule. The United States subsequently declared war on Mexico (*see* MEXICAN WAR) and Frémont aided Commodore Robert STOCKTON in the conquest of California. In 1848 Frémont resigned his commission and made a huge fortune in the Californian GOLD RUSH. He was the first REPUBLICAN PARTY presidential candidate, losing to James BUCHANAN. Frémont served as governor of Arizona (1878–83).

French, John Denton Pinkstone, 1st Earl of Ypres (1852–1925) British field marshal. He distinguished himself in the second of the SOUTH AFRICAN WARS (1899–1902) and was made chief of the Imperial General Staff (1912–14). At the outbreak of WORLD WAR I, French was given command of the BRITISH EXPEDITIONARY FORCE (BEF). Criticized for indecisiveness, he resigned (December 1915) in favour of Sir Douglas HAIG. French also served a controversial term as lord lieutenant of Ireland (1918–21).

French and Indian Wars (1689–1763) Collective name for four colonial wars in North America, fought between Great Britain and France with Native-American nations fighting on both sides. The aim of the Wars in North America was for control of the eastern part of the continent, with ports and forts that controlled trade to the Old World. **King William's War** (1689–97) was an extension of the War of the GRAND ALLIANCE. Both sides made gains but failed to capture their main target, which was QUÉBEC for the British and BOSTON for the French. **Queen Anne's War** (1702–13) corresponds to the War of the SPANISH SUCCESSION. Britain gained Newfoundland, Acadia and Hudson Bay. **King George's War** (1744–48) grew out of the War of the AUSTRIAN SUCCESSION. There were a number of border raids, but neither Britain nor France gave much backing to the colonists and the war ended inconclusively. The **French and Indian War** (1754–63) was the most significant conflict, forming part of the SEVEN YEARS' WAR. It grew out of the contest for the valley of the upper Ohio River. In 1754 Colonel George WASHINGTON was forced to surrender Fort Necessity to the French. The British colonies, alarmed at the encroachment of the French, formed the ALBANY CONGRESS for mutual defence. A British expedition, led by General Edward BRADDOCK, to capture French forts in W America was crushed at the Battle of Monongahela (1755). The British captured the forts at Louisburg and Duquesne (both 1758) and Ticonderoga (1759). The British scored a decisive victory on the Plains of ABRAHAM (September 1759). Both the French and English generals, Louis Joseph de MONTCALM and James WOLFE, were killed but Québec fell to the British. In 1760 the British captured MONTRÉAL, the last outpost of New France. The Treaty of PARIS (1763) established British control of Canada. *See also* KING PHILIP'S WAR

French Community Association composed of France, its overseas territories and former African colonies. It was created (1958) by the French constitution as the successor to the French Union, which itself was the successor to the French Empire. The Community handled the foreign policy and the military, cultural, judicial and economic affairs of its member states. Dissatisfaction with this arrangement led to a constitutional amendment (1960) by which member states could become independent whilst remaining within the Community. Six of the 12 African states accepted this option, and the other six withdrew from the Community. By 1961 the French Community had been replaced by bilateral and multilateral agreements.

French Guiana Overseas department of France, in South America. Europeans first explored the coast in 1500. The French were the first settlers (1604), founding Cayenne, the future capital, in 1637. It became a French colony in the late 17th century. The colony, whose plantation economy depended on African slaves, remained French except for a brief period in the early 19th century, when the Portuguese and British occupied it during the NAPOLEONIC WARS (1803–15). From the time of the FRENCH REVOLUTION (1789–99), France used the colony as a penal settlement for political and other prisoners. In 1848 slavery was abolished, and Asian labourers were introduced. In 1946 French Guiana became an overseas department of France and, in 1974, an administrative region. Despite rich forest and mineral resources, it is a developing country and depends on France to fund health and welfare services. Area: 90,000sq km (37,749sq mi). Pop. (1994) 147,000.

French Polynesia French overseas territory in the S central Pacific Ocean, consisting of more than 130 islands, divided into five scattered archipelagos: Society Islands, Marquesas Islands, Tuamotu Archipelago, Gambier Islands and Tubuai Islands; the capital is Papeete on Tahiti (Society Islands). Missionaries arrived in Tahiti at the end of the 18th century, and in the 1840s France began establishing protectorates. In 1880–82 the islands were annexed by France and became part of the colony of Oceania. In 1958 they were granted the status of an overseas territory. In the 1960s the French government began nuclear testing on Mururoa atoll, leading to worldwide protests. In recent years there have been increasing demands for autonomy in Tahiti, the largest and most populous island. In 1995 the French government put forward proposals to grant Polynesia the status of an autonomous overseas territory. Area: 3265sq km (1260sq mi). Pop. (1994 est.) 216,600.

French Revolution *See* feature article

French Revolutionary Wars (1792–1802) Series of campaigns in which the armies of revolutionary France fought combinations of European foes. Fear and hatred of the FRENCH REVOLUTION fuelled the hostility of Austria in particular. The French declared war on Austria and Prussia in April 1792. The success of the French generals Charles DUMOURIEZ and François KELLERMANN at Valmy and Jemappes provoked other states, including Britain, the Netherlands and Spain, to form the First Coalition (1793). By 1794 France was once more on the offensive. After concluding peace treaties with the Netherlands and Prussia (1795), France concentrated on war with Austria. Peace with Austria was concluded at the Treaty of CAMPO-FORMIO (1797). NAPOLEON Bonaparte conducted a brilliant campaign in Italy. Britain, having established naval superiority, remained at war. Horatio NELSON defeated Napoleon's fleet at ABOUKIR, Egypt (1798). A Second Coalition was formed in 1799, consisting of Russia, Austria, Britain, Turkey, Portugal and Naples. France defeated Naples (1799), and Russia's withdrawal weakened the alliance. In the coup of 18 Brumaire, Napoleon became first consul. The events of 1800 proved decisive: Napoleon defeated the Austrians at MARENGO and Moreau crushed the Allies at Hohenlinden. Britain captured Malta and Egypt (1801), but lacked the will to fight alone and made peace at AMIENS. *See also* NAPOLEONIC WARS

Freyberg, Bernard Cyril, 1st Baron (1889–1963) New Zealand general, b. Britain. He won a Victoria Cross for his bravery in World War 1. During World War 2, Freyberg commanded the New Zealand Expeditionary Force (1939–45) and led the Allied forces in the battle for control of Crete. He also saw action in North Africa and Italy. Freyberg served (1946–52) as governor general of New Zealand.

Friends, Religious Society of *See* QUAKERS

Frobisher, Sir Martin (*c*.1535–94) English navigator. In 1756 he made his first voyage in search of the NORTHWEST PASSAGE and discovered what was to become Frobisher Bay, Canada. Frobisher made two more journeys, primarily in a fruitless search for gold, exploring Frobisher Bay and sailing up the Hudson Strait. He was knighted for his part in the defeat of the Spanish ARMADA (1588).

Froissart, Jean (*c*.1337–*c*.1410) Flemish poet and historian. His four *Chronicles* of European history between 1325 and 1400 are a valuable (if partial) primary source of information on events such as the HUNDRED YEARS' WAR.

Fronde (1648–53) Series of civil wars in France during the regency of LOUIS XIV. The Fronde was partly a reaction to the policies established (1624–42) by Cardinal RICHELIEU, who increased the power of the monarchy at the expense of the nobility and PARLEMENTS (judicial bodies). The **Fronde of the Parlement** began when the Parlement of Paris rejected the financial proposals of ANNE OF AUSTRIA and chief minister Cardinal MAZARIN and demanded the power to scrutinize and amend royal decrees (July 1648). The government responded by arresting two leading rebels, but was forced to grant concessions after an uprising in Paris. The end of the THIRTY YEARS' WAR (October 1648), however, freed the royal army under the Great CONDÉ to act against the rebels and blockade the streets of Paris (January 1649). The Parlement refused to back down and a compromise was agreed at the Peace of Rueil (April 1649). The second phase of the civil war, the **Fronde of the Princes** (1650–53), was precipitated by the personal ambition of the Great Condé. Mazarin's arrest (January 1650) of Condé sparked a series of provincial rebellions by Condé's aristocratic followers (First War of the Princes). The revolts were suppressed but support in Paris for the Great Condé led to his release and forced Cardinal Mazarin into temporary exile (February 1651). In August 1651 Anne ordered the indictment of Condé, who responded by seizing Paris (April 1652). Condé's arrogant behaviour alienated Parisians and provincial supporters, such as Marshal TURENNE, and he was forced into exile (October 1653). The Fronde ended in a clear victory for Mazarin and strengthened the power of the monarchy in France.

Front de Libération Nationale (FLN) Algerian party that led the fight for independence from France. The FLN developed out of the Revolutionary Committee of Unity and Action (CRUA), established (March 1954) to bring together the various nationalist groups in ALGERIA against the colonial power. In 1956 the FLN established an unofficial provisional government. The ÉVIAN AGREEMENTS (March 1962) that ended the Algerian War of Independence was followed by a power struggle within the FLN. The Political Bureau of the FLN emerged victorious and BEN BELLA became prime minister then president. Algeria became a one-party state. In 1965 Ben Bella was overthrown by Houari BOUMEDIENNE. In 1978 Boumedienne died and was succeeded by Chadli Bendjedid. Bendjedid agreed to multiparty elections in 1991, but these were abandoned when the Islamic Salvation Front (FIS) seemed certain of victory. The army forced Bendjedid to resign in favour of FLN veteran Muhammad Boudiaf. Boudiaf was assassinated in 1992 and Brigadier General Liamine Zeroual became president. Zeroual formed the National Democratic Rally (RND), which emerged as the largest single party in 1997 elections.

Frontenac, Louis de Baude, Comte de Palluau et de (1620–98) French governor of New France (1672–82, 1689–98). He was the architect of French expansion in Canada. Frontenac promoted the FUR TRADE and encouraged the explorations of Sieur de LA SALLE, Louis JOLLIET and others. Frontenac's divisive policies and failure to deal with expansion of the IROQUOIS CONFEDERACY and the HUDSON'S BAY COMPANY led to his recall to France. Frontenac's second term was dominated by the first of the FRENCH AND INDIAN WARS. His defence of QUÉBEC and attacks on British forts enabled France to extend its North American empire from Montréal to Lake Winnipeg and from Hudson Bay to the Gulf of Mexico.

frontier In United States' history, the westernmost region of white settlement. From the 17th century, when it began in the foothills of the Appalachian Mountains, the frontier gradually moved westward until the late 19th century, when no new land remained for pioneer homesteaders. The frontier notions of rugged individualism and free enterprise were promoted by Frederick Jackson Turner (1861–1932) in *The Significance of the Frontier in American History* (1893). The existence of a frontier region, where a dominant group was able to expand (usually at the expense of native inhabitants), has been an important factor in the history of other countries, such as South Africa.

Fry, Elizabeth (1780–1845) English prison reformer and philanthropist. She was a committed Quaker. Horrified by conditions in Newgate Prison, London, Fry agitated for more humane treatment of women prisoners.

F

FRENCH REVOLUTION (1789–99)

Series of events that removed the French monarchy, transformed government and society, and established the First Republic. Suggested causes include economic pressures, an antiquated social structure, weakness of the (theoretically absolute) ANCIEN RÉGIME, and the influence of the ENLIGHTENMENT. The parlous state of the nation's finances forced LOUIS XVI to recall Jacques NECKER and summon the STATES-GENERAL.

On 1 May 1789, the STATES-GENERAL met at Versailles, N France. It was numerically dominated by the Third Estate (the BOURGEOISIE) who, in June 1789, swore not to disband until France had a new constitution (the Tennis Court Oath) and proclaimed themselves the NATIONAL ASSEMBLY of France. The dismissal of Necker provoked a full-scale revolution, marked by the storming of the BASTILLE in Paris (July 1789). The Assembly was panicked into declaring the abolition of the FEUDAL SYSTEM and of the tithe on the peasantry. Next it issued the DECLARATION OF THE RIGHTS OF MAN AND OF THE CITIZEN (1789). Louis' prevarication fuelled hostility towards the monarchy, and the royal family were moved to the Tuileries Palace, Paris, guarded by the Marquis de LAFAYETTE. The National Assembly established civil control over the Roman Catholic Church in France and nationalized its lands. Louis refused to heed the advice of the Comte de MIRABEAU and conspired against the creation of a constitutional monarchy. In June 1791 Louis and MARIE ANTOINETTE were arrested after trying to flee to Austria. The Revolution began to assume a more radical character as the JACOBINS, led by Maximilien ROBESPIERRE, gained the ascendancy. Meanwhile, the ÉMIGRES (counter-revolutionaries) attracted support from other European powers, whose governments viewed events in France with fear.

On 1 October 1791, the Legislative Assembly met in Paris and it declared war on Austria and Prussia in April 1792. Louis was blamed for a series of defeats at the start of the FRENCH REVOLUTIONARY WARS and was imprisoned (August 1792).

On 20 September 1792, the NATIONAL CONVENTION was convened and the following day proclaimed the establishment of the First Republic. A new calendar was adopted with 1792 as year one. Despite the efforts of the GIRONDINS, Louis was executed for treason on 21 January 1793. Further military defeats led to the formation of the COMMITTEE OF PUBLIC SAFETY, initially led by Georges DANTON, whose introduction of conscription sparked the Wars of the VENDÉE. The revolts were suppressed by the REIGN OF TERROR under Maximilien Robespierre. Social anarchy and soaring inflation characterized the THERMIDOREAN REACTION (July 1794–October 1795), which followed the fall of Robespierre. A new constitution imposed the DIRECTORY (1795–99). The CONSULATE (1799–1804), dominated by NAPOLEON, put an end to the decade of Revolution.

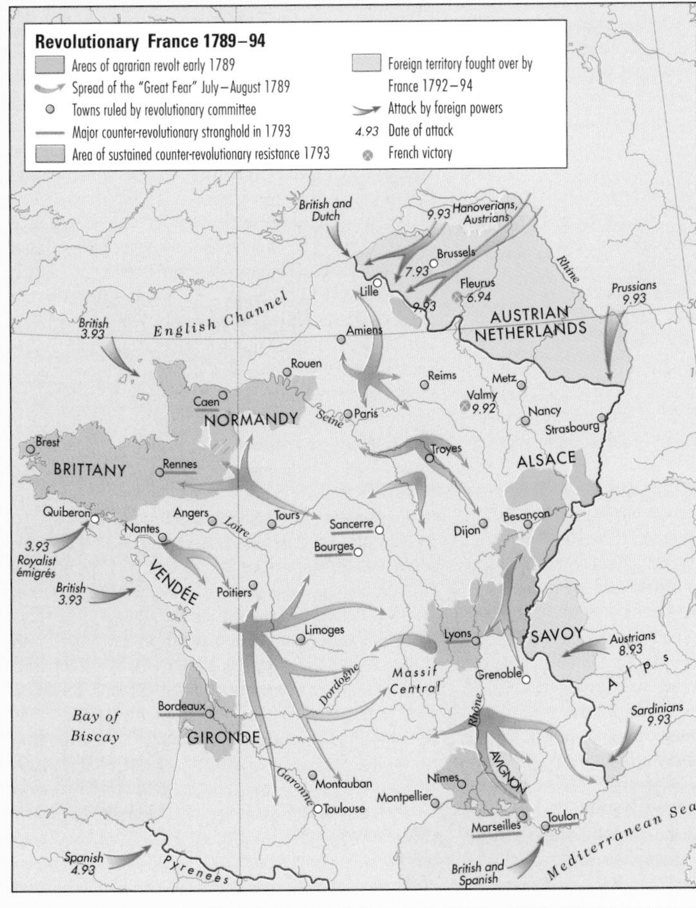

◀ **French Revolutionary Wars** (1792–97). The French Revolution did not occur simultaneously throughout the country, but spread from Paris to other cities and then to the countryside. Resistance to the Revolution from France's neighbours led to the French Revolutionary Wars. A Prussian invasion of NE France was repulsed at Valmy (1792), and Sardinian, British and Spanish forces attempted to invade s France and the Vendée coast in 1793. Austria was eventually defeated at Fleurus (1794).

▶ **Paris** Shortly before the Revolution, the city limits of Paris had been extended by the building of the "tax-farmers" wall (1785) by Minister of Finance Charles Calonne. The wall was designed to facilitate the collection of tolls from those entering the city. It ran concentrically with the old city boundaries, and took in several of the surrounding districts. Access was gained through 54 gates which were largely destroyed by the crowds during the Revolution.

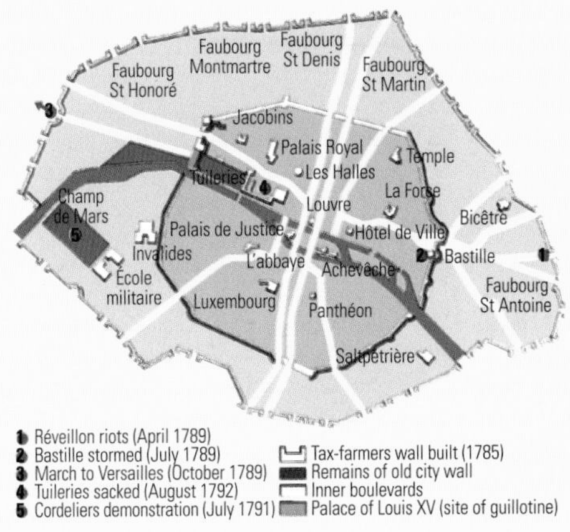

Fuad I (1868–1936) First king of modern Egypt (1922–36), son of Ismail Pasha. Fuad became sultan (1917–22) when Egypt was a protectorate of Britain. Talks to achieve independence collapsed when Fuad and the nationalist Wafd Party failed to reach agreement. In 1922 Britain issued a unilateral declaration of independence, and Fuad became king. Fuad spent much of his reign trying to draw up a bilateral treaty of independence in terms acceptable to the British and Egyptains. In 1923 he issued a new constitution. The Wafd Party won large majorities in national elections throughout the 1920s, but Fuad excluded them from government. In 1931 he dissolved parliament and issued a new constitution. In 1935, under strong nationalist pressure, he was forced to restore the 1923 constitution. Fuad was succeeded by his son, FAROUK.

F

Fuchs, Klaus (1912–88) British physicist and communist spy, b. Germany. Fuchs worked on the atomic bomb in the United States (1943) and returned to Britain (1946) to head the theoretical physics division of the Atomic Research Centre at Harwell. Imprisoned (1950) for passing secrets to the Soviet Union, Fuchs had his British citizenship revoked. After release (1959), he went to East Germany to work at the nuclear research centre.

Fugger German merchant and banking family, the foundation of whose wealth was laid by **Hans** Fugger of Augsburg (1367–1408). His grandsons, Ulrich and Georg, increased the family wealth through the sale of papal indulgences. In 1485 **Jakob II** "the Rich" (1459–1525) took control of the Innsbruck branch of the Fugger agency and made large profits by investing in mining operations in the Tirol, Silesia and Slovakia. As the chief financial supporter of Emperor MAXIMILIAN I, Jakob acquired landholdings, and in 1514 he was made a count. Jakob financed the election of CHARLES V as emperor in 1519. Under the direction of **Anton** Fugger (1493–1560), the Fugger company became the richest in Europe. The company diversified from banking and mining in central Europe into a variety of ventures in Northern Europe, Africa and America. The Fugger company then went into decline and was dissolved in the mid-17th century, leaving the family dependent on the wealth generated by its landholdings. *See* illustration, page 176

Fugitive Slave Laws (1793, 1850) US federal acts that provided for the return of escaped slaves to their owners. The 1793 act authorized judges and magistrates to decide without a jury trial the status of a fugitive slave. When SLAVERY was abolished in Northern states, the UNDERGROUND RAILROAD helped Southern slaves obtain freedom. Northern states also passed laws that prevented escaped slaves from being returned to slave states. The COMPROMISE OF 1850 had a tougher Fugitive Slave Law than the 1793 statute, with heavy penalties for aiding fugitive slaves. According to the 1850 laws, fugitive slaves were denied legal rights. The law was so harsh that it helped the ABOLITIONISTS' cause, and many citizens openly flouted the new regulations. The acts were repealed in 1864.

Fujimori, Alberto (1938–) Peruvian statesman, president (1990–). His grassroots campaign gave him a surprise victory in Peru's 1990 presidential election. Fujimori used strong tactics to tackle the guerrilla armies of the drug cartels and SENDERO LUMINOSO (Shining Path), including censorship of the press and dissolution of Congress. A pro-Fujimori Congress was installed in 1992 and a new constitution introduced in 1993. Fujimori's success against the guerrillas and progress in tackling inflation won him re-election in 1995. In April 1997 he sanctioned the use of force to end the six-month siege of the Japanese ambassador's residence in Lima. In 1997 Fujimori dismissed three Supreme Court justices, who had ruled that the constitution prevented him from seeking a third term in office.

Fujiwara (Jap. Wisteria Arbour) Japanese family which dominated the imperial court during the HEIAN period (794–1185). The Fujiwara dynasty was founded by **Nakatomi Kamatari** (614–69), who overthrew the Soga family and helped instate Tenji as emperor. Tenji rewarded Kamatari with the title of Fujiwara. Kamatari's son, **Fujiwara Fuhito** (659–720), began the practice of marriage of Fujiwara daughters to emperors that was to be the cornerstone of Fujiwara authority. Real political power, however, was only achieved by **Fujiwara Yoshifusa** (804–72), who secured the throne for his nine-year-old grandson Seia. Fuhito then appointed himself regent. Yoshifusa's nephew, **Fujiwara Mototsune** (836–91), created for himself the post of chancellor, which gave him complete control of government. **Fujiwara Tokihira** (871–909), son of Mototsune, defeated the efforts of emperors Udo and Daigo to challenge the Fujiwara monopoly on power. The dynasty reached the apogee of its authority, however, under **Fujiwara Michinaga** (966–1027). Michinaga married four daughters to emperors and three of his grandsons became emperors. Michinaga established a magnificent court at KYOTO, but its splendour masked a decline in the family's control of the provinces, where they relied on military families to suppress rebellions. The Fujiwara faded with the adoption of the *insei* (cloistered rule) system of imperial government in the 11th century and were finally removed from power (1159) by the SAMURAI family of TAIRA.

Fulani (Peul or Fulbe) Originally a nomadic pastoral people, who established an empire in the River Niger region of w Africa in the early 19th century. The origins of the Fulani are obscure, the earliest historical records show them living in w Sudan. It appears that the Fulani were forced to migrate by the expansion of ancient GHANA, dispersing across the savannah from Senegal to Cameroon. Converted to Islam, they helped spread the religion throughout w Africa. In 1804 the Fulani cleric USMAN DAN FODIO launched a JIHAD (holy war) in the HAUSA state of Gobir (now NW Nigeria) and had conquered Hausaland by 1808. The *jihad* spread into Adamwa (N Cameroon), Nupe and Ilorin (S Nigeria), but was checked by the Kanem-BORNU empire. By the end of the war, a federation of 30 emirates recognized the rule of Usman as sultan of SOKOTO. In 1817 Usman died and was succeeded by his son, Muhammad Bello. The Sokoto caliphate dominated the region until the arrival of the British at the end of the 19th century. Another Fulani cleric, Ahmadu ibn Hammadi (*c*.1775–1844), declared (1818) a second *jihad* in Macina (now MALI), which created a theocratic Fulani state in central Mali.

Fulbright, James William (1905–95) US senator from Arkansas (1945–74). He sponsored the Fulbright Act (1946), which provided funds for educational exchanges (Fulbright scholarships) between the United States and other countries. As chairman of the Senate committee on foreign relations (1959–74), Fulbright was critical of US military involvement abroad, especially in Vietnam.

Fuller, (Sarah) Margaret (1810–50) US writer and editor. She served as editor in chief (1840–42) of the transcendentalist magazine *The Dial*. In 1845 Fuller became the first literary critic of the New York *Tribune*. Her feminist treatise *Woman in the Nineteenth Century* (1845) explored discrimination against women and called for political equality.

Fuller, Melville Weston (1833–1910) US jurist, chief justice of the Supreme Court (1888–1910). He was known as a strict interpreter of constitutional law. Important cases included: *Plessy* v. *Ferguson* (1896), which upheld "separate but equal" laws of segregation; and *Lochner* v. *New York* (1905), a "due process" clause interpreted so the state could not set a 10-hour day for bakers. Fuller helped settle a boundary dispute between Venezuela and Great Britain (1899) and was a member of the Hague Court of International Arbitration (1900–10).

fundamentalism Movement within some Protestant denominations, particularly in the United States, which originated in the late 19th and early 20th centuries as a reaction against criticism of the BIBLE and the promulgation of theories of evolution. The name is derived from *The Fundamentals*, a series of 12 tracts published between 1909 and 1915 by eminent US evangelical leaders. The doctrines most emphasized are the inspiration and infallible truth of the Bible, the divinity of Christ, the Virgin Birth, atonement by Christ bringing expiation and salvation for all, the physical resurrection and the second coming. Fundamentalism has been loosely used to refer to any extreme orthodox element within a religion, such as Islamic fundamentalism. *See also* ISLAM

Fundamental Orders (1639) Code of laws adopted by representatives of the settlements in CONNECTICUT to govern the Connecticut Colony. Sometimes called the first written constitution of the United States, it remained in force until superseded by the Connecticut Charter (1662).

Funj Islamic dynasty in the SUDAN between the 16th and 19th centuries. The dynasty converted to Islam in the early 16th century when it first began to expand northward from Sennar, its capital on the Blue Nile (founded *c*.1504). From the 1560s, the Funj expanded westward across the White Nile. In the first half of the 18th century, it established control over the plains of Kordofan to the south. Expansion eastward was blocked by Ethiopia, with which the Funj went to war in 1618–19 and 1744. The dynasty suffered from internal divisions, with several kings being deposed and the warrior aristocracy launching two rebellions. It had no real power from 1762 and was replaced by the Turkish government of Egypt in 1821.

fur trade Vital factor in the exploration and commercial development of North America, Siberia and the Arctic. The fur trade began in North America in the 16th century, when Native Americans exchanged furs for European goods at fishing stations on the coast around Newfoundland and the Gulf of St Lawrence. In 1608 Samuel de CHAMPLAIN established a fur-trading post at Québec and from the 1620s explorers such as Étienne BRULÉ and John FRÉMONT embarked on journeys into the interior which helped to extend the French trading network. In 1670 the search by English explorers for the Northwest Passage led to the founding of the HUDSON'S BAY COMPANY. Trading posts were established around Hudson Bay, which served as bases for exploration in the 18th century by (among others) Samuel HEARNE, Alexander MACKENZIE and David THOMPSON. In the 17th and 18th century, competition between Britain and France for control of the fur trade was a major factor in the FRENCH AND INDIAN WARS. The LEWIS AND CLARK EXPEDITION (1804–06) led to the development of the trade in the West. John Jacob ASTOR's AMERICAN FUR COMPANY established a trading post, Fort Astoria, on the Pacific coast in 1811, and mountain men who lived off the fur trade, such as Kit CARSON, explored the Rocky Mountains. In the early 19th century, traders of the Hudson's Bay Company advanced across the mountains into ALASKA, where they met Russian traders. Since the 16th century, Russian fur traders had led the exploration of the rivers and northern coastline of Siberia, and in the 17th century they reached the Pacific. Following the voyages of Vitus BERING and other explorers, the Russians had established a colony in ALASKA by the late 18th century that was largely supported by the fur trade. Competition with British traders only came to an end when Alaska was purchased by the United States in 1867. Meanwhile there had been a dramatic decline in the fur trade since the 1840s due to changes in fashion and the clearance of land for settlements. *See also* NORTHWEST COMPANY

Fyodor I (1557–98) Tsar of Russia (1584–98), son of IVAN IV (THE TERRIBLE) and Anastasia Romanova. The last of the RURIK dynasty, Fyodor was both physically and mentally weak, and the government was controlled by his brother-in-law Boris GODUNOV. During Fyodor's reign, the autonomy of the Russian ORTHODOX CHURCH was established with the creation of the Patriarchate of Moscow in 1589 and Russia's influence over Siberia and the Caucasus was extended. After Fyodor's death, a vote established the succession of Godunov.

Fyodor II (1589–1605) Tsar of Russia (1605), son and successor of Boris GODUNOV. DMITRI (the Pretender), who claimed to be the son of IVAN IV (THE TERRIBLE), invaded Moscow in 1604 in an attempt to overthrow Godunov. After Godunov's death in 1605, the military shifted their support to Dmitri. Fyodor's mother attempted to take power, but provoked an uprising in which she and Fyodor were killed. Dmitri took the throne.

Fyodor III (1656–82) Tsar of Russia (1676–82), son and successor of ALEXEI MIKHAILOVICH. In poor health, Fyodor was a weak ruler, and his government was run by Vasily Golytsin. Golytsin introduced military reforms and abolished the system whereby a noble officer's rank in service was based on the rank of his family. Fyodor died childless and was succeeded by the joint reign of his brother IVAN V and half-brother PETER I (THE GREAT).

Gabon *See* country feature

Gaddafi, Muammar al *See* QADDAFI, MUAMMAR AL-

Gadsden Purchase (1853) Land bought by the United States from Mexico. A narrow strip, 77,000sq km (30,000sq mi) in area, it now forms s Arizona and New Mexico. By the Treaty of GUADALUPE-HIDALGO (1848), which ended the MEXICAN WAR, the United States acquired large amounts of land from Mexico. President Franklin PIERCE wanted to purchase this extra strip of land because it was considered the best route for a southern transcontinental railway. The sale was negotiated by James Gadsden, minister to Mexico, for US$10 million.

Gagarin, Yuri Alekseievich (1934–68) Russian cosmonaut, the first man to orbit the Earth. On 12 April 1961 he made a single orbit in 1 hour 29 minutes.

Gage, Thomas (1721–87) British general and administrator. His military career in North America began during the last of the FRENCH AND INDIAN WARS (1754–63). In 1760 Gage became governor of Montréal. As commander in chief (1763–74) of British forces in North America, Gage failed to respond effectively to the growing independence movement. Becoming military governor of Massachusetts in 1774, after the BOSTON TEA PARTY, Gage helped draw up the INTOLERABLE ACTS that merely inflamed the situation. Gage's soldiers provoked the Patriots at Concord (April 1775), leading to the Battles of LEXINGTON AND CONCORD that began the AMERICAN REVOLUTION. He resigned after the disastrous Battle of BUNKER HILL (June 1775).

gag rules (1836) In the United States, series of measures that were adopted by the Congress to prevent the discussion of SLAVERY. John Quincy ADAMS led the fight against the gag rules, and they were repealed in 1844.

Gaiseric (AD 390–477) (Genseric) King of the VANDALS and Alani (428–477). After invading Africa from Spain (428), he defeated the forces of the Eastern and Western Roman empires to establish control over a large area of N Africa. In 439 Gaiseric captured CARTHAGE from the Romans, and his fleet soon dominated the western Mediterranean. In 455, following the death of the Roman Emperor Valentinian III, he sacked Rome, taking Empress Eudoxia hostage. Gaiseric defeated two Roman expeditions (460, 468) to overthrow him and a peace treaty (476) left him control of Mauretania, Sardinia, Corsica, Sicily, the Balearic Islands and parts of NUMIDIA.

Gaitskell, Hugh Todd Naylor (1906–63) British statesman, leader of the LABOUR PARTY (1955–63) and chancellor of the exchequer (1950–51). He entered Parliament in 1945. Gaitskell served in Clement ATTLEE's cabinet as minister of fuel and power (1947–50) and minister of state for economic affairs (1950) before becoming chancellor. Gaitskell defeated Aneurin BEVAN in the 1955 leadership elections. A period of consensus between the two main parties, known as "Butskellism" (*see* BUTLER, R.A.), ensued in British politics. On the right-wing of the Labour Party, Gaitskell refused to accept the 1960 Conference's decision to adopt a policy of unilateral disarmament and defeated a leadership challenge from his eventual successor Harold WILSON.

Galerius (d.311) (Gaius Galerius Valerius Maximianus) Roman emperor (305–11). In 293 Galerius was appointed caesar (deputy emperor) of the Eastern part of the empire by DIOCLETIAN. In 296 Galerius was defeated by the SASANIANS, but his reputation was restored by a decisive victory in 297. He was the main influence on Diocletian's decision to persecute the Christians. Galerius and Constantius succeeded as emperors on the abdication of Diocletian and Maximian and Galerius arranged the appointment of two of his supporters (Maximinus and Flavius Valerius Severus) as caesars. Galerius' supremacy was short-lived, however, as Severus was overthrown and killed (306) by Maxentius, son of Maximian. From 308 he supported LICINIUS in his struggle with CONSTANTINE I (THE GREAT) for control of the western empire.

Galicia Historic region of Eastern Europe. Eastern Galicia became part of KIEVAN RUS under VLADIMIR I (THE GREAT) in 981. In 1087 it became independent and was soon an important state in E Europe. Internal conflict weakened Galicia, and the state was overrun by the MONGOLS in 1237–41. In 1340 Galicia was annexed by CASIMIR III (THE GREAT) of Poland. In the First Partition of POLAND (1772), Galicia was awarded to Austria. It became the centre of HASIDISM and by 1867 had considerable autonomy. After World War 1, Poland seized Western Galicia and was awarded Eastern Galicia at the 1919 Paris Peace Conference. The NAZI-SOVIET PACT (1939) gave most of Eastern Galicia to Ukraine, a position ratified by the 1945 Polish-Soviet Treaty. Area: 78,500sq km (30,309sq mi).

Galileo (1564–1642) (Galileo Galilei) Italian physicist and astronomer whose experimental methods laid the foundations of modern science. In 1609 he used one of the first astronomical telescopes to discover sunspots, lunar craters, Jupiter's major satellites and the phases of Venus. In *Sidereus Nuncius* (1610), Galileo supported Nicolas COPERNICUS' heliocentric system that the Earth moves around the Sun. Galileo was forbidden by the Roman Catholic Church to teach that this system represented physical reality but, in *Dialogue on the Two Great World Systems* (1632), he defied the pope by making his criticism of PTOLEMY's system even more explicit. As a result, Galileo was brought before the INQUISITION and forced to recant in public. He remained under house arrest until his death. In 1992 the Vatican absolved Galileo of heresy.

Gallatin, Albert (1761–1849) US statesman and financier, b. Switzerland. He emigrated to the United States in 1780 and was elected to the House of Representatives in 1795. Gallatin served (1801–14) as secretary of the treasury under Thomas JEFFERSON and James MADISON. Despite the cost of the LOUISIANA PURCHASE (1803), he managed substantially to reduce public debt. Gallatin was a highly successful diplomat (1801–14), taking part in negotiating the Treaty of Ghent (1814), which ended the WAR OF 1812. He later served (1816–23) as minister to France. A keen student of Native American languages, Gallatin founded the American Ethnological Society (1842).

Gallicanism Nationalist movement within the French Roman Catholic Church. It affirmed the authority of the French bishops and crown to limit papal intervention in France. The movement had its origins in the 13th century in the struggle between PHILIP IV (THE FAIR) and Pope BONIFACE VIII. Gallicanism was enshrined in the PRAGMATIC SANCTION of Bourges (1438), the 23 articles of which stated that the jurisdiction of the pope was subject to royal will, and the Concordat of Bologna (1516), which allowed the French king to nominate bishops. It continued in several forms, such as JANSENISM, until modern times. The opposing movement is known as ULTRAMONTANISM.

Gallic Wars (58–51 BC) Campaigns in which the Romans, led by Julius CAESAR, conquered GAUL. In 58 BC Caesar defeated the HELVETII at Bibracte. He subdued Belgic (57 BC) and conquered the Veneti, leaders of an anti-Roman confederation, in 56 BC. In 55 BC Caesar invaded Germany. His major victory, however, was the crushing (52 BC) of a a united Gallic revolt led by Vercingetorix.

Gallienus (d.268) (Publius Licinius Valerianus Egnatius) Roman emperor (253–68). He ruled with his father, VALERIAN (253–60), at at time when the ROMAN EMPIRE was suffering attacks in the east and west. Valerian fought the Persians in the east and Gallienus fought the Germanic tribes in the Rhine and Danube areas. After the capture of Valerian, Gallienus ruled alone (260–68). The Roman Empire was attacked from all sides, and when Gallienus was killed in fighting following the revolt of one of his generals, all that remained of the Empire was Italy and the Balkans. He was succeeded by CLAUDIUS II.

Gallipoli Campaign (1915–16) Allied operation against the Turks during WORLD WAR I. Its aim was to force a way through the Dardanelles in order to occupy Constantinople (now Istanbul), thus relieving pressure on the Russians in

GABON

AREA: 267,670sq km (103,347sq mi)
POPULATION: 1,237,000
CAPITAL (POPULATION): Libreville (418,000)
GOVERNMENT: Multiparty republic
ETHNIC GROUPS: Fang 36%, Mpongwe 15%, Mbete 14%, Punu 12%
LANGUAGES: French (official), Bantu languages
RELIGIONS: Christianity (Roman Catholic 65%, Protestant 19%, African churches 12%), traditional beliefs 3%, Islam 2%
GDP PER CAPITA (1994): US$3086

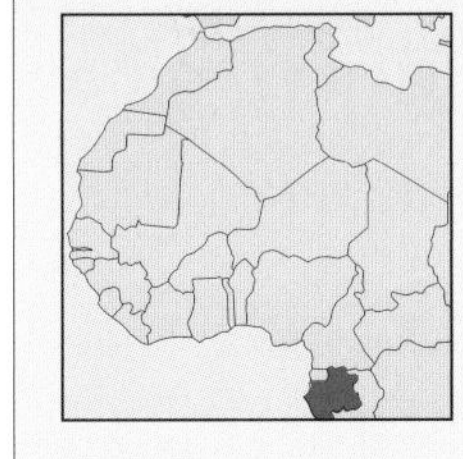

Republic in w Central Africa. Little is known about the early inhabitants of Gabon, but by the 13th century the Mpongwe people were established in the region. Portuguese explorers reached the coast of Gabon in 1472, and the area later became a source of slaves. In 1849 France established the settlement of Libreville for freed slaves. In 1886 Gabon was subsumed into the French CONGO under the governorship of Pierre Savorgnan de BRAZZA. In 1910 it was one of the four colonies that formed the Federation of French Equatorial Africa.

Gabon achieved independence in 1960, under the leadership of Léon M'ba. In 1964 M'ba declared a one-party state and a resultant military coup was crushed with French military assistance. M'ba's death (1967) brought Omar BONGO to power. In 1990 French troops again intervened after a wave of civil unrest threatened the Gabonese oil industry. A new constitution (1991) saw the adoption of a multiparty system. President Bongo won the first multiparty presidential elections in 1993, although accusations of fraud and corruption led to riots in Libreville. Bongo was condemned by the international community for his harsh suppression of popular demonstrations. In 1998 Bongo was re-elected.

the Caucasus. Initial naval attacks, however, failed to secure the Dardanelles and the troops landed on the Gallipoli Peninsula made little progress. Some 45,000 British and French and 30,000 ANZAC troops were involved. After eight months of inconclusive fighting and more than 145,000 casualties, the Allies withdrew. They had succeeded in diverting Turkish forces away from the Russian campaign, but at the cost of appearing militarily inept. This had political repercussions, including the resignation of Winston CHURCHILL from the government.

Galt, Sir Alexander Tilloch (1817–93) Canadian politician, b. England. He sat in the legislative assembly of the United Province of Canada (1849–50, 1853–67). As minister of finance in 1858, Galt urged Canadian confederation on the British and was chief spokesman for the English of Lower Canada at the Quebec Conference that preceded federation in 1867.

Galtieri, Leopoldo Fortunato (1926–) Argentine general and statesman, president (1981–82). He joined Argentina's ruling military junta in 1979 and succeeded Roberto Viola as president. In April 1982, Galtieri ordered the invasion of the Falkland Islands. The resulting FALKLANDS WAR with the British ended in Argentine surrender and Galtieri resigned as president (June 1982). In 1986 he was sentenced to 12 years' imprisonment for military incompetence. Galtieri was pardoned by President Carlos MENEM in 1989.

Gama, Vasco da (1469–1524) Portuguese navigator. He was charged with continuing Bartholomeu DIAS' search for a sea route to India. Da Gama's successful expedition (1497–99) rounded the Cape of Good Hope and sailed across the Indian Ocean to Calicut, SW India. He returned to Portugal, however, without having established any trading links. In 1502–03 da Gama led a heavily armed expedition of 20 ships to Calicut and brutally avenged the killing of Portuguese settlers left there by Pedro CABRAL. By destroying one Arab ship and putting others to flight, da Gama also did much to establish Portuguese control of the trade routes across the Indian Ocean. In 1524 he returned to India as viceroy, where he died.

Gambetta, Léon Michel (1838–82) French statesman, prime minister (1881–82). He was a leader of the Republican Party opposition to NAPOLEON III. Gambetta organized French resistance after the defeats at SEDAN and Metz in the FRANCO-PRUSSIAN WAR (1870–71) and became minister of the interior and minister of war in the provisional government. Gambetta played a vital part in the formation of a new constitution and the creation of the Third Republic. Disliked by President Jules Grévy, Gambetta was not asked to form a government until 1881 and was overthrown two months later.

Gambia, The *See* country feature

Gandhara Historic area on the River Indus, now in NW Pakistan. A Persian (ACHAEMENID) colony from the 6th century BC, it passed to the MAURYAN EMPIRE of India in *c.*303 BC. Gandhara flourished as a cultural and Buddhist centre during the reign (*c.*272–232 BC) of ASHOKA. Its greatest prosperity came during the KUSHAN DYNASTY (1st–5th centuries AD), which developed the Gandhara school of art – noted for Buddhist sculptures and reliefs. In the 6th century, Gandhara was raided by the HUNS.

Gandhi, Indira (1917–84) Indian stateswoman, prime minister (1966–77, 1980–84), daughter of Jawaharlal NEHRU. She served as president of the Indian National CONGRESS (1959–60), before succeeding Lal Shastri as prime minister. In 1975, amid growing social unrest, Gandhi was found guilty of breaking electoral rules in the 1971 elections. She refused to resign, invoked emergency powers, and imprisoned many opponents. In 1977 elections, Congress suffered a heavy defeat at the hands of Morarji DESAI, and the Party split. In 1980, leading the Congress (I) faction of the Party, Gandhi returned to power. In 1984, after authorizing the use of force against Sikh dissidents in the Golden Temple at AMRITSAR, Gandhi was killed by her Sikh bodyguards. She was succeeded by her eldest son Rajiv GANDHI.

Gandhi, "Mahatma" (Mohandas Karamchand) (1869–1948) Indian nationalist leader. In 1888 "Mahatma" (Sanskrit, Great Soul) Gandhi travelled to England to study law. In 1893 he went to practise law in South Africa, where he championed the rights of the minority Indian community. While in South Africa, Gandhi launched (1907) his first non-cooperation (*satyagraha*) campaign, involving non-violent (*ahimsa*) civil disobedience. In 1914 he returned to India. Following the massacre at AMRITSAR (1919), Gandhi organized several campaigns of *satyagraha,* which included strikes, a refusal to pay taxes and a boycott of British manufactured goods and institutions in India, such as courts, schools and offices. As a result, he was imprisoned (1922–24) for conspiracy. After his release, Gandhi served as president (1925–34) of the Indian National CONGRESS. He campaigned for a free, united India; the revival of craft industries, especially the spinning of cloth; and the abolition of "untouchability" (*see* CASTE). In 1930 Gandhi made his famous 400km (250mi) protest march against a salt tax. In 1934 Jawaharlal NEHRU succeeded Gandhi as leader of the Congress. In 1942, after the British rejected his offer of cooperation in World War 2 if Britain granted immediate independence, Gandhi launched the QUIT INDIA MOVEMENT. He was then interned until 1944. Gandhi played a major role in the post-war talks with Nehru, Lord MOUNTBATTEN and Muhammad Ali JINNAH that led to India's independence (1947). Gandhi opposed partition and the creation of a separate Muslim state (Pakistan). When violence flared between Hindus and Muslims, Gandhi resorted to fasts for peace. A figure of huge international and moral stature, he was assassinated by a Hindu fanatic in New Delhi.

Gandhi, Rajiv (1944–91) Indian statesman, prime minister (1984–89), eldest son of Indira GANDHI. He was a pilot before reluctantly entering politics after the death of his younger, more politically active, brother Sanjay. He was appointed general secretary of CONGRESS (I) in 1983 and became prime minister after the assassination of his mother. Gandhi worked to placate India's Sikh extremists, but his reputation was tarnished by a bribery scandal. Defeated in the 1989 election, Rajiv was assassinated while campaigning for re-election.

Gang of Four Radical faction that tried to seize power in China after the death of MAO ZEDONG. The Gang of Four – Zhang Chunqiao, Wang Hongwen, Yao Wenyuan and their leader JIANG QING (Mao's widow) – rose to prominence during the CULTURAL REVOLUTION. In 1976 both Chairman Mao and Premier ZHOU ENLAI died, leaving a power vacuum. The Gang of Four tried to launch a military coup but were arrested for treason by Premier HUA GUOFENG. They were sentenced to life imprisonment.

García Moreno, Gabriel (1821–75) Ecuadorean dictator, president (1861–65, 1869–75). He seized power in 1860 with the support of former president Juan José FLORES. García Moreno established a clerical autocracy, handing control of education and welfare to the Roman Catholic Church and introducing a constitution under which only Catholics enjoyed full civil rights. Although his regime was repressive, García Moreno succeeded in reducing corruption and improving the nation's infrastructure. He was assassinated by a group of liberals.

García Robles, Alfonso (1911–91) Mexican diplomat. He was a delegate to the San Francisco Conference (1945) that gave birth to the UNITED NATIONS (UN). García Robles was the driving force behind the Treaty of Tlatelolco (1967), which committed 22 nations of Latin America to ban nuclear weapons. A strong supporter of the concept of a Latin American nuclear-free zone, he was also one of the authors of the Nuclear Nonproliferation Treaty (1968). García Robles and Alva Myrdal shared the 1982 Nobel Prize for Peace for their contribution to nuclear DISARMAMENT.

Gardiner, Stephen (*c.*1483–1555) English bishop and statesman. In 1525 he became secretary to the lord chancellor, Cardinal Thomas WOLSEY. Gardiner helped negotiate the annulment of HENRY VIII's marriage to CATHERINE OF ARAGON. He served (1531–51, 1553–55) as bishop of Winchester. Gardiner opposed the REFORMATION but retained court favour with his support for royal supremacy over the church. After the accession of EDWARD VI, a keen Protestant reformer, Gardiner was imprisoned (1548–53). Released when the Catholic

GAMBIA, THE

AREA: 11,300sq km (4,363sq mi)
POPULATION: 878,000
CAPITAL (POPULATION): Banjul (146,000)
GOVERNMENT: Military, transitional
ETHNIC GROUPS: Mandinka (Mandingo or Malinke) 40%, Fulani (Peul) 19%, Wolof 15%, Dyola 10%, Soninke 8%
LANGUAGES: English (official)
RELIGIONS: Islam 95%, Christianity 4%, traditional beliefs 1%
GDP PER CAPITA (1995): US$930

Smallest country in mainland Africa. Portuguese mariners reached the Gambian coast in 1455 when the area was part of the MALI empire. In the 16th century, Portuguese and English slave traders operated in the area. In 1664 the British established a settlement and later founded a colony, Senegambia (1765), which included parts of present-day Gambia and SENEGAL. In 1783 this was handed over to France. In 1816 Britain founded Bathurst (now Banjul) as a base for its anti-slavery operations. The Gambia formed part of the British West African Federation from 1821 to 1843. The early 19th century was marked by religious wars. In 1900 The Gambia became a separate colony. Under the leadership of Dawda Jawara, it achieved independence within the Commonwealth of Nations in 1965. In 1970 The Gambia became a republic with Jawara as president. In 1981 an attempted coup was defeated with the help of Senegalese troops. In 1982 The Gambia and Senegal formed a defence alliance, the Confederation of Senegambia, but this ended in 1989. In 1992 Jawara was re-elected as president for a fifth term. In July 1994 he was overthrown in a military coup, led by Yahya Jammeh. In 1996 Jammeh was elected president.

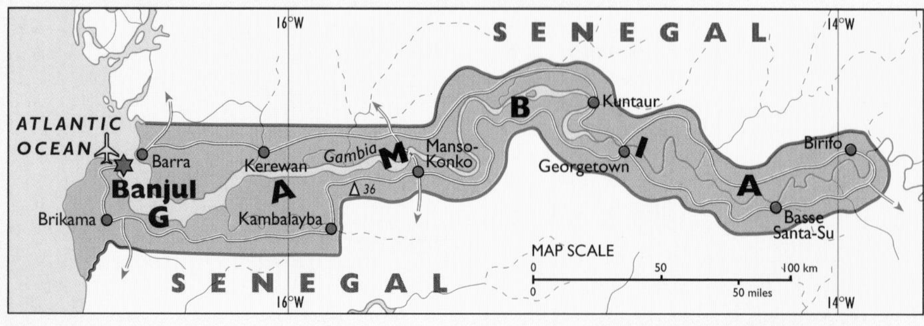

MARY I came to the throne, Gardiner was appointed lord chancellor. He supported her persecution of Protestants. *See also* CRANMER, THOMAS

Garfield, James Abram (1831–81) Twentieth president of the United States (1881). He served in the American CIVIL WAR until 1863, when he was elected to the House of Representatives. In 1876 Garfield became the Republican leader of the house. The 1880 Republican convention was deadlocked and, on the 36th ballot, he became the compromise presidential candidate. Garfield's four-month administration was characterized by party squabbles over federal jobs and political patronage. He was assassinated on 2 July 1881 and was succeeded by his Vice President Chester ARTHUR.

Garibaldi, Giuseppe (1807–82) Italian patriot and soldier, who helped to achieve Italian unification. In 1833–34 he served in the navy of the Kingdom of Piedmont-Sardinia and in 1834, influenced by Giuseppe MAZZINI, he participated in a republican rising. Garibaldi was forced into exile (1836–48) in South America, where he took part in wars of liberation for Brazil and Uruguay, gaining fame in Italy when his Italian Legion gained a victory for Uruguay against Argentina. In 1848 Garibaldi returned to Italy with 60 members of the Italian Legion (later known as the "Red Shirts") to fight for Italian independence from Austria in the REVOLUTIONS OF 1848. He battled for the city of Milan, but was forced to retreat. In 1849 Garibaldi led a group of volunteers in defence of the short-lived Roman Republic against the French, who were intent on restoring the papal government. Overwhelmed by far greater forces, he was again forced to flee the country. Garibaldi returned in 1854, and in 1859 was invited by the Conte di CAVOUR to fight against the Austrians in a war which ended with Piedmont gaining Lombardy from Austria. Determined that Italy should not only be independent but unified, in 1860 he led his 1000-strong band of "Red Shirts" against the Kingdom of the Two Sicilies. This dramatic episode in the RISORGIMENTO resulted in his conquest of Sicily and Naples, which he handed over to VICTOR EMMANUEL II, to be incorporated into the new Kingdom of Italy in 1861. Wishing to see Rome become Italy's capital, Garibaldi led an army against the PAPAL STATES in 1862. He was badly wounded, but in 1866 he took part in the war against Austria. After fighting for the French in the Franco-Prussian War (1870–71), he retired to the island of Caprera. *See also* YOUNG ITALY

Garner, John Nance (1868–1967) US statesman, vice president (1933–41). He was a Texas legislator (1898–1902) and Congressman (1903–33), serving as speaker of the house (1931–33). Vice president under Franklin ROOSEVELT, Garner helped obtain passage of NEW DEAL legislation. He retired in 1941, after refusing to run as vice president for Roosevelt's third term.

Garnet, Henry Highland (1815–82) US ABOLITIONIST and diplomat. He escaped from SLAVERY in 1824 and became a Presbyterian minister. Garnet was the leading African American in the abolitionist movement until, at a speech in Buffalo, New York (1843), he exhorted slaves to revolt. He was gradually supplanted by the more moderate Frederick DOUGLASS. After taking various pastorates, Garnet was appointed (1881) US minister to LIBERIA.

Garrison, William Lloyd (1805–79) US ABOLITIONIST. In 1831 he started the *Liberator* in Boston, an influential journal in the anti-SLAVERY movement. In 1833 Garrison helped found the American Anti-Slavery Society, which advocated non-violent civil disobedience. After the American CIVIL WAR (1861–65) and the abolition of slavery, he concentrated on other reforms, notably temperance and women's suffrage.

Garter, Order of the Premier order of knighthood in Britain, founded (1348) by Edward III. The monarch is the Grand Master, and the number of companion knights is limited to 24. Its motto is "*Honi soit qui mal y pense*" ("Shame be to him who evil thinks").

Garvey, Marcus (1887–1940) US black nationalist leader, b. Jamaica. In 1914 he founded the Universal Negro Improvement Association (UNIA) designed to "promote the spirit of race pride". Garvey believed that black people could not achieve equality within white-dominated Western countries, so he created a "back-to-Africa" movement. He established the Black Star Line shipping company as a means of transporting black people back to Africa. By the 1920s Garvey was the most influential black leader in the United States, via his *Negro World* newspaper. In 1922 the Black Star Line and UNIA collapsed. Garvey was convicted of fraud and jailed (1925). He was pardoned (1927) by President Calvin Coolidge and deported to Jamaica. RASTAFARIANISM is influenced by his philosophy.

Gascony Former province in SW France, bounded by the Pyrenees (S) and the Bay of Biscay (W). Part of Roman GAUL, Gascony was overrun by the VISIGOTHS, who were then conquered by the FRANKS in AD 507. Later in the 6th century, it was conquered by the Vascones, and in 602 the Frankish kings recognized Gascony as a duchy. In the 11th century, the Duke of Aquitaine conquered Gascony. In 1137, following the marriage of ELEANOR OF AQUITAINE to HENRY II, Gascony's destinies became intertwined with those of England. During the HUNDRED YEARS' WAR, Gascony, an English stronghold, was a major battleground. It was finally restored to France in 1453.

Gasperi, Alcide de *See* DE GASPERI, ALCIDE

Gates, Horatio (*c*.1728–1806) American general, b. England. He served in the British army under General Edward BRADDOCK in the FRENCH AND INDIAN WARS before emigrating (1772) to Virginia and joining the colonists' cause in the AMERICAN REVOLUTION. In 1777 Gates succeeded Philip SCHUYLER as commander in northern New York. Gates was given the credit for the critical defeat of the British at the Battle of SARATOGA (1777), although victory was largely achieved by Schuyler and Benedict ARNOLD. Gates was appointed president of the board of war, but was dismissed after the CONWAY CABAL failed to make him commander in chief in place of George WASHINGTON. Gates suffered a disgraceful defeat at the hands of Lord CORNWALLIS at the Battle of CAMDEN, South Carolina (1780), and was replaced by Nathanael GREENE.

GATT *See* GENERAL AGREEMENT ON TARIFFS AND TRADE

gaucho Originally nomadic, mestizo COWBOYS of the Argentine, Paraguayan and Uruguayan pampas. They flourished from the mid-18th to mid-19th century, hunting horses and cattle for hides to trade with the British, Portuguese and French in the Buenos Aires area. Towards the end of 19th century, large areas of the pampas became privately owned *estancias* (estates), and many of the gauchos became farmhands. Gauchos were also superb horse soldiers, making up a large proportion of the armies in the Río de la Plata area.

Gaul Ancient Roman name for the land N of the Pyrenees, S and W of the Rhine and W of the Alps, consisting of present-day France, W Germany, N Italy and parts of Belgium. By the 5th century BC, the CELTS were spreading across the area. In 390 BC they captured Rome. The Romans launched a counter-offensive, and by 180 BC had captured CISALPINE GAUL (N Italy). By 120 BC, the Romans had also captured TRANSALPINE GAUL. In the GALLIC WARS (58–51 BC), Caesar completed the conquest of Gaul, dividing it into four provinces: Narbonesis, Aquitania, Celtica (now central France) and Belgica (roughly modern Belgium). The Romans built roads and towns, encouraged trade and put Gallic aristocrats in governmental positions. They also constructed fortifications in an attempt to keep out invading Germanic tribes. Between AD 260 and 273, Gaul was part of an independent empire. It was then reclaimed by the Romans, but became subject to frequent rebellions and invasions. By the 5th century, the VISIGOTHS, FRANKS and Burgundians had taken areas of Gaul under their control. The last vestiges of Roman rule had disappeared by the end of the century.

Gaulle, Charles André Joseph Marie de *See* DE GAULLE, CHARLES ANDRÉ JOSEPH MARIE

Gaunt, John of *See* JOHN OF GAUNT

Gaveston, Piers (*c*.1284–1312) Favourite of EDWARD II of England. The son of a Gascon knight, Gaveston was brought up in the English royal household, where he had a powerful influence on the young Edward. Gaveston acted as regent when Edward was absent in France in 1308 and his closeness to the king aroused the resentment of the barons, who forced Edward to banish him later that year. In 1309 Gaveston was recalled, but his arrogant behaviour once more earned the enmity of the barons. Edward was forced to agree to the Ordinances of 1311 that called for the permanent exile of Gaveston, and his return to England prompted a baronial rebellion. Gaveston was captured by the Earl of Warwick and executed.

Gaza Strip Strip of territory in SW Israel, bordering the SE Mediterranean Sea. Gaza, its major city, was one of the five city-kingdoms of the PHILISTINES. Under frequent attack because of its strategic position between Palestine and Egypt, Gaza was occupied successively by Assyria, Egypt and Persia. During Roman times, it became an important trade centre. Gaza became a Muslim holy city after being captured by Arabs in AD 634. From 1917 to 1948 the Gaza Strip was part of British Palestine. Following the first ARAB-ISRAELI WAR (1948–49), it became an Egyptian possession and served as a centre for Palestinian refugees. Occupied by Israel in the SIX-DAY WAR (1967), the Gaza Strip was the scene of the INTIFADA uprising against Israeli rule in the 1980s. In 1994 its administration was taken over by the Palestinian National Authority. Area: 363sq km (140sq mi). Pop. (1994) 724,500.

Gdańsk (Danzig) City and seaport on the Gulf of Gdańsk, N Poland; capital of Gdańsk province. Settled by Slavs in the 10th century, it was granted municipal autonomy in 1260. From 1308 to 1466, Gdańsk was held by the TEUTONIC KNIGHTS. Seized by CASIMIR IV of Poland, it became extremely prosperous. Weakened by Swedish wars in the 17th century, Gdańsk passed to Prussia in 1793. Napoleon granted it the status of a free city in 1807, but it was given to West Prussia at the Congress of VIENNA (1814–15). The Treaty of VERSAILLES (1919) established Gdańsk as a free city and annexation (1939) by Germany precipitated World War 2. In the 1980s, its shipyards were a centre for SOLIDARITY's opposition to Poland's communist regime. Pop. (1993) 466,500.

Gemayel, Pierre (1905–84) Lebanese politician. A MARONITE Christian, he founded (1935) the right-wing PHALANGE PARTY based on the model of the Nazi Youth

GANDHI, "MAHATMA"

Gandhi advocated a policy of non-violent resistance to British rule in India. He endured long hunger-strikes to highlight the injustices of British colonialism, the caste system and communal violence. Gandhi lived an ascetic life, rejecting materialism and industrialization in favour of cottage industries.

GANDHI IN HIS OWN WORDS

"The moment the slave resolves that he will no longer be a slave, his fetters fall. He frees himself and shows the way to others. Freedom and slavery are mental states."
Non Violence in Peace and War, (1949)

G

movement. Gemayel served (1960–84) in the Lebanese parliament. He led the Phalange militia forces in the Lebanese civil war (1975–76). His youngest son, **Bashir** (1947–82), was assassinated while president-elect. His eldest son, **Amin** (1942–), was elected to succeed Bashir. During Amin's term as president (1982–88), Lebanon continued to suffer from violence between Israel and Lebanon. Amin Gemayel was succeeded as president by Michel Aoun.

General Agreement on Tariffs and Trade (GATT) United Nations' (UN) agency of international trade, subsumed into the new WORLD TRADE ORGANIZATION (WTO) in 1995. Founded in 1948, GATT was designed to prevent "tariff wars" (the retaliatory escalation of tariffs) and to work towards the reduction of tariff levels. Most non-communist states were party to GATT.

General Strike (4–12 May 1926) Nationwide strike in Britain involving *c*.3 million members of the TRADES UNION CONGRESS (TUC), including railway and other transport workers, printers, builders, iron and steel workers, shipyard workers and engineers. It was called in support of the National Union of Mineworkers (NUM), whose members had been locked out of the mines after refusing to accept a reduction in pay and an increase in working hours. Stanley BALDWIN's government responded by employing special constables and volunteers to run essential services and issuing an effective anti-strike propaganda journal, *The British Gazette*. The TUC called off the strike without obtaining any concession and the Trade Union Act (1927) restricted UNION rights by making any secondary action illegal.

General Synod (formerly Chruch Assembly) Governing body (since 1969) of the CHURCH OF ENGLAND. It consists of three houses: bishops, clergy and laity. The General Synod meets at least twice a year. Resolutions of the General Synod requiring legislation are put before the British Parliament.

Genêt, Edmond Charles (1763–1834) French diplomat, known as Citizen Genêt. Soon after the start of the FRENCH REVOLUTION, Genêt was appointed minister to Russia. His support for the Revolution angered CATHERINE II (THE GREAT), who expelled him. Allying himself with the GIRONDINS, Genêt was appointed minister to the United States in 1792. Determined to bring the United States into the FRENCH REVOLUTIONARY WARS, Genêt began outfitting American privateers to harass British commerce. When he ignored an order to desist, President George WASHINGTON requested his recall (1793). Genêt, unwilling to return to France, settled in the United States.

Geneva City at the S end of Lake Geneva, SW Switzerland. A Celtic city at the time of the Roman conquest (500 BC), it was not until the late 4th century AD that Geneva was Christianized and became the seat of a bishop. In the 5th century Geneva became the capital of the Burgundians. It later passed to the Franks and then to the HOLY ROMAN EMPIRE. In the 11th century, rule of Geneva became hereditary among the Genevese counts, but the House of Savoy became increasingly powerful. Dissatisfaction with the power of the bishop-princes led the inhabitants to embrace the REFORMATION. Geneva became the centre of PROTESTANTISM under John CALVIN. In 1798 Geneva was annexed to Napoleonic France. In 1814 it successfully negotiated to join the Swiss Confederation. It was the seat of the LEAGUE OF NATIONS (1919–46) and is the headquarters of the RED CROSS and the World Health Organization (WHO). Pop. (1992) 169,600.

Geneva Accords (April–July 1954) Series of agreements on INDOCHINA following the decisive defeat of the French by the Viet Minh at DIEN BIEN PHU (1954). The most important provision of the Accords was the temporary division of VIETNAM along the 17th parallel while arrangements were made for regional elections. The final declaration was never signed by the parties and the US government supported the establishment of an anticommunist regime in South Vietnam. While the Accords marked the end of French rule in Indochina, it precipitated the VIETNAM WAR.

Geneva Conventions Any one of a series of international agreements on the conduct of warfare, chiefly the treatment of wounded soldiers, prisoners-of-war and non-combatants, and the neutrality of the medical services. Inspired by Henri DUNANT's founding of the RED CROSS, the first Geneva Convention was held in 1864. Subsequent conventions (1906, 1929, 1949) extended its terms, including the prohibition of attacks on unarmed civilians. An international conference in 1977 recommended two protocols be added to the 1949 convention that provided protection to guerrillas fighting wars of self-determination or civil wars in which they controlled a significant area. While more than 150 countries signed the fourth Geneva Convention, many, including the United States and the United Kingdom, have not committed themselves to the new protocols.

Genghis Khan (*c*.1162–1227) Conqueror and founder of the MONGOL Empire, b. Temüjin. In 1206, according to the *Secret History of the Mongol Nation* (*c*.1240), he united the nomadic tribes of the steppe and was proclaimed Genghis (Chinggis) Khan ("Universal Ruler"). Organizing his cavalry into a highly mobile and disciplined squadron (*ordus*, hence "hordes"), Genghis embarked (1207) on a series of raids into N China that soon turned into a full-scale campaign of conquest. Most of N China had been subjugated by 1215. He then redirected the bulk of his army against the Islamic world and between 1219 and 1223 conquered much of Central Asia, Afghanistan and parts of Iran and Russia. Genghis kept his empire together with the aid of capable and loyal generals. He laid the framework for an effective Mongol administration through measures that included the adoption of an alphabet for the Mongolian language and of a system of law known as the *Yasa*. He also propagated the belief amongst the Mongols that they had a "heavenly mandate" to conquer the world and all those who resisted this mandate could be dealt with accordingly. Genghis Khan died on campaign in China in 1227 and was succeeded as Great Khan by his third son OGODEI.

Genoa (Genova) Seaport on the Gulf of Genoa, NW Italy; capital of Liguria region. Genoa's port was established in the 5th century BC, and it flourished under the Romans from the 3rd century BC. After a period of economic decline, it became an important commercial power from the 10th century. Genoa's influence spread throughout the Mediterranean and beyond. Genoese traders travelled as far afield as India and England and established colonies in Spain, North Africa and the Crimea. The city began to lose territory in the 14th century and by the 15th century it was no longer a significant power. In the 18th century, Genoa lost its independence when it was occupied (1796–1814) by Napoleonic troops, and at the Congress of VIENNA (1815) it was granted to Piedmont. It became part of a united Italy in 1861. Pop. (1992) 667,563.

▲ **Genghis Khan** The Mongol armies led by Genghis Khan terrorized tribes across Asia. Defeated populations were systematically massacred or forced to fight for the Mongols.

genocide Systematic and deliberate destruction of a racial, religious or ethnic group in times of war or peace. After the HOLOCAUST (1933–45) in Nazi Europe, the United Nations' (UN) signed the Convention on the Prevention and Punishment of the Crime of Genocide (1949).

genro "Elder statesmen" who indirectly ruled Japan from 1881 to 1901, a period of extreme modernization, and were influential for another three decades. The influence of the genro stemmed from their role in the MEIJI RESTORATION of 1868. The leading figures in the oligarchy were ITO HIROBUMI, YAMAGATA ARITOMO and Saionji Kimmochi. Ito framed the Meiji Constitution (1889), while Yamagata modernized the army. The genro acted as premiers until 1901 and thereafter selected leaders until 1932.

Gentile, Giovanni (1875–1944) Italian philosopher and politician. He has been referred to as the "philosopher of FASCISM". Gentile served as minister for education (1922–24) under Benito MUSSOLINI and helped frame the constitution of the fascist corporate state. He was also editor of the *Enciclopedia Italiana* (1936–43). He was killed by anti-Fascist partisans.

Gentlemen's Agreement (1907) Arrangement between the United States and Japan to restrict Japanese emigration. The United States agreed not to pass a law preventing immigration, and in return Japan voluntarily withheld passports from Japanese labourers coming to the United States, except those with prior domiciles or immediate relatives in the United States. The Agreement ended with the Immigration Bill of 1924 that excluded immigration from Japan.

Geoffrey of Anjou (1113–51) Ancestor of the PLANTAGENET kings of England. In 1128 he married HENRY I's daughter MATILDA, and in 1129 he became Count of Anjou, Maine and Touraine. After the death of Henry I, Geoffrey claimed the duchy of Normandy, finally conquering it in 1144. He had three sons, the eldest of whom became HENRY II of England. *See also* ANGEVIN

Geoffrey of Monmouth (*c*.1100–54) Welsh priest and chronicler, best known for his *History of the Kings of Britain* (*c*.1136). Although accepted as reliable until the 17th century, Geoffrey was essentially a folkteller. His book was the chief source for the legend of King ARTHUR, and it was Shakespeare's source for *King Lear* (1605) and *Cymbeline* (1609).

George I (1660–1727) King of Great Britain and Ireland (1714–27) and Elector of Hanover (1698–1727). The Act of SETTLEMENT (1701) established the succession to the English throne on SOPHIA of Hanover, granddaughter of James I, and her heirs, providing they were Protestant. George, Sophia's son, succeeded to the throne on the death of Queen ANNE, becoming the first monarch of the House of HANOVER. George favoured the WHIGS over the Tories, suspecting the latter of JACOBITE sympathies. He put down JACOBITE rebellions in 1715 and 1719. George, who did not speak good English, preferred his native Hanover and took little interest in domestic affairs. He allowed power to pass to Parliament and ministers such as Robert WALPOLE and Charles TOWNSHEND. When the financial speculation known as the SOUTH SEA BUBBLE burst in 1720, George's political reputation was saved by Walpole, who demanded in return a freer reign on government. George was succeeded by his son, GEORGE II.

George II (1683–1760) King of Great Britain and Ireland and Elector of HANOVER (1727–1760), son and successor of GEORGE I. As prince of Wales, George quarrelled with his father and turned his home into a meeting place for dissident ministers. Sir Robert WALPOLE dominated politics early in his reign, until forced to resign (1742) by the machinations of George's estranged son, FREDERICK LOUIS. Walpole was replaced by John Carteret (later Earl GRANVILLE). George and Granville took Britain into the War of the AUSTRIAN SUCCESSION (1740–48). George's victory at Dettingen (1743) was the last occasion in which a British king led his army into battle. The war, however, was generally unpopular and forced Granville's dismissal in 1744. George survived the JACOBITE rebellion of 1745. George was forced to appoint William PITT (THE ELDER) as prime minister in 1746, and it was largely due to Pitt that Britain was victorious in the SEVEN YEARS' WAR (1756–63) against France. Britain's prosperity grew fast during George's reign. He was a great patron of the arts and was responsible for bringing the composer George Frideric Handel to Britain. George was succeeded by his grandson, GEORGE III. *See also* CUMBERLAND, WILLIAM AUGUSTUS, DUKE of; NEWCASTLE, THOMAS PELHAM-HOBBES, 1ST DUKE OF

George III (1738–1820) King of Great Britain and Ireland (1760–1820) and king of HANOVER (1760–1820), grandson and successor of GEORGE II. He gained a hatred of his grandfather from his father, FREDERICK LOUIS. The beginning of George's reign was marked by political upheaval. George was taught statecraft by John Stuart, 3rd Earl of BUTE, whose influence over the king forced both William PITT (THE ELDER) and Lord NEWCASTLE, out of office. Bute's brief spell (1761–63) as prime minister ended after public criticism of the peace terms at the close of the SEVEN YEARS' WAR (1756–63) against France. The War concluded with Britain gaining New France (now Canada), but left Britain isolated in Europe and in serious financial difficulties. The ministry (1763–65) of George GRENVELLE began the prosecution of John WILKES and imposed the STAMP ACT (1765) on the American colonies. Lord ROCKINGHAM's ministry (1765–66) repealed the Stamp Act, but the TOWNSHEND ACTS (1767) levied new duties. The appointment of Lord NORTH in 1770 brought a greater degree of political coherence. George and North were blamed, however, for the loss of the American colonies in the AMERICAN REVOLUTION (1775–83) and North was forced to resign in 1782. The unlikely alliance of North and Charles FOX infuriated George, who turned instead to William PITT (THE YOUNGER). The king's political judgement was vindicated by Pitt's victory in the 1784 general election. In 1765 George had suffered his first attack of apparent insanity, now thought to be symptoms of porphyria. In 1788 he had a more violent attack, which prompted a power struggle for the regency. In 1789 George recovered, but the day-to-day affairs of government passed increasingly to Pitt (the Younger) and George only asserted his royal prerogative to defeat Pitt's proposals for CATHOLIC EMANCIPATION in 1801. In 1811 George suffered another attack and Parliament declared the regency of his son, the future GEORGE IV. George III's reign witnessed the beginnings of the INDUSTRIAL REVOLUTION and the birth of METHODISM. He founded (1768) the Royal Academy of Arts. *See also* FRENCH REVOLUTIONARY WARS; NAPOLEONIC WARS

George IV (1762–1830) King of Great Britain and Ireland (1820–30), son and successor of GEORGE III. He openly oppposed his father, supporting the Whig leader Charles FOX. In 1785 George contracted a secret, illegal marriage to a Roman Catholic widow, Mrs FITZHERBERT. His later marriage (1795) to his cousin, CAROLINE OF BRUNSWICK, became a source of scandal when he attempted to divorce her in 1820. George served as regent for his father from 1811. Once in power, he abandoned his old Whig leanings in favour of the Tory ministry (1812–27) of Lord LIVERPOOL. Self-indulgent and extravagant, George left the conduct of the NAPOLEONIC WARS in the capable hands of the Duke of WELLINGTON and Viscount CASTLEREAGH. As prime minister, Wellington steered through the Act of CATHOLIC EMANCIPATION (1829). Although George ignored his constitutional duties, he was a strong patron of the arts. The greatest monument of his reign was the Royal Pavilion, Brighton, s England, designed (1815–23) by John Nash (1752–1835). George was succeeded by his niece VICTORIA. *See also* CANNING, GEORGE; WAR OF 1812

George V (1865–1936) King of Great Britain and Northern Ireland and emperor of India (1910–36), second son and successor of EDWARD VII. In 1893 he married Princess Mary of Teck. At the start of his reign, George was forced to intervene in the constitutional struggle between the Liberal government of H.H. ASQUITH and the HOUSE OF LORDS. The resultant Parliament Act (1911) ended the Lords' power of veto. In 1914 George called all the party leaders to a conference at Buckingham Palace to discuss HOME RULE for Ireland. During WORLD WAR 1, anti-German sentiment led George to change (1917) the name of the royal house from SAXE-COBURG-GOTHA to Windsor. In 1923 Bonar LAW resigned as prime minister and George chose Stanley BALDWIN to succeed him. During the GREAT DEPRESSION of the 1930s, George persuaded Ramsay MACDONALD to lead a national coalition government. He was succeeded by his son, EDWARD VIII.

George VI (1895–1952) King of Great Britain and Northern Ireland (1936–52) and emperor of India (1936–47), son of GEORGE V. He became king when his brother, EDWARD VIII, abdicated. In 1923 George married Lady ELIZABETH Bowes-Lyon. Before the outbreak of WORLD WAR 2, George strengthened Anglo-French ties and formed a close friendship with US President Franklin ROOSEVELT. In an inspirational display of solidarity, George decided to remain with his family in London during the BLITZ. In 1949 he became head of the COMMONWEALTH OF NATIONS. He was succeeded by his daughter, ELIZABETH II.

George I (1845–1913) King of Greece (1863–1913). Made king by Great Britain, France and Russia with the approval of a Greek national assembly, he backed the Constitution of 1864 giving power to an elected parliament. George gained Macedonia in the first of the BALKAN WARS. He was assassinated in 1913 and was succeeded by his son, CONSTANTINE I. *See also* VENIZELOS, ELEUTHERIOS

George II (1890–1947) King of Greece (1922–24, 1935–47), eldest son of CONSTANTINE I. In 1917 Constantine was forced to abdicate by the Allies and George was overlooked as successor due to his suspected pro-German sympathies. George's first reign was curtailed by the strength of republican feeling in Greece and he was forced into exile in 1923. After his restoration, George supported General Ioannis METAXAS in the establishment of a dictatorship. Following the German invasion of Greece in 1941, George went into exile again. He was restored to the throne in 1946.

George, David Lloyd *See* LLOYD GEORGE, DAVID

Georgia State on the Atlantic Ocean, SE United States; the capital is ATLANTA. The Native American MOUND BUILDERS began building temple earthworks in the region *c.*1200 years ago. In 1540 Spanish explorer Hernando DE SOTO became the first Europeans to visit the area. In 1732 James OGLETHORPE established a British colony and defeated the Spanish in the War of JENKINS' WAR (1739). The British captured SAVANNAH (1778) during the American Revolution and only withdrew in 1782. Settlement increased rapidly in the early

GEORGIA
Statehood :
2 January 1788
Nickname :
Empire State of the South
State motto :
Wisdom, justice and moderation

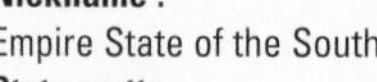

GEORGIA

AREA: 69,700sq km (26,910sq mi)
POPULATION: 5,456,000
CAPITAL (POPULATION): Tbilisi (1,279,000)
GOVERNMENT: Multiparty republic
ETHNIC GROUPS: Georgian 70%, Armenian 8%, Russian 6%, Azerbaijani 6%, Ossetes 3%, Greek 2%, Abkhazian 2%, others 3%
LANGUAGES: Georgian (official)
RELIGIONS: Christianity (Georgian Orthodox 65%, Russian Orthodox 10%, Armenian Orthodox 8%), Islam 11%
GDP PER CAPITA (1995): US$1470

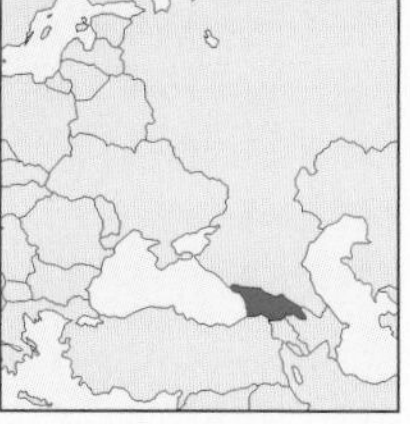

Republic in SE Europe. Georgia consists of two autonomous republics, Abkhazia and Ajaria, and the province of Tskhinvali (South Ossetia). The land of the legendary Golden Fleece, Georgia has a strong national culture and a long literary tradition based on its own language and alphabet. From the 6th century BC, the two Black Sea kingdoms of Iberia and Colchis developed in E and W Georgia respectively. In 66 BC Iberia and Colchis were subsumed into the Roman Empire. Christianity was introduced in AD 330, and the established church today is independent Eastern Orthodox. From the 4th to the 7th century, Georgia was a battleground in the conflict between the Byzantine and Persian empires. Colchis was generally held by the Byzantines, while Iberia was in SASANIAN hands. In 654 Arabs established an emirate in Tbilisi.

In the 11th century Bagrat III (r.975–1014) created a united Georgia, excluding Tbilisi (recovered in 1122). During the reign (1184–1213) of Queen Tamar, Georgia built a Transcaucasian empire. In the 13th century, the empire and Eastern Georgia itself fell to the MONGOL hordes. In *c.*1555 Georgia was divided between Turkey (E) and Persia (W) and the succeeding centuries witnessed a struggle for domination between the OTTOMAN and SAFAVID empires. In 1783 Georgia accepted Russian suzerainty in return for military protection and by 1878 Georgia had been absorbed into the Russian empire.

After the RUSSIAN REVOLUTION (1917), Georgia declared independence in May 1918. In February 1921 Red Army troops invaded and Georgia was combined (1922) with Armenia and Azerbaijan into the republic of Transcaucasia, one of the four constituent republics of the SOVIET UNION. In 1924 a revolt against Soviet rule was brutally crushed by Joseph STALIN, who enforced the collectivization of agriculture and the rapid industrialization in Georgia. In 1936 the Transcaucasian republic was dissolved and Georgia became a separate Soviet republic.

The reforms of Soviet President Mikhail GORBACHEV renewed barely suppressed nationalist aspirations and Georgia declared independence under President Zviad Gamsakhurdia in May 1991. Gamsakhurdia's authoritarian regime brought civil war to the streets of Tbilisi and he was deposed. In March 1992 Eduard SHEVARDNADZE was elected president. In July 1992 Abkhazia declared independence and the ensuing war produced *c.*200,000 Georgian refugees. In 1993 Georgia joined the COMMONWEALTH OF INDEPENDENT STATES (CIS) and received Russian military assistance. CIS peacekeeping forces were deployed on the border with Abkhazia and another breakaway republic, South Ossetia. Sporadic violence continues in Abkhazia.

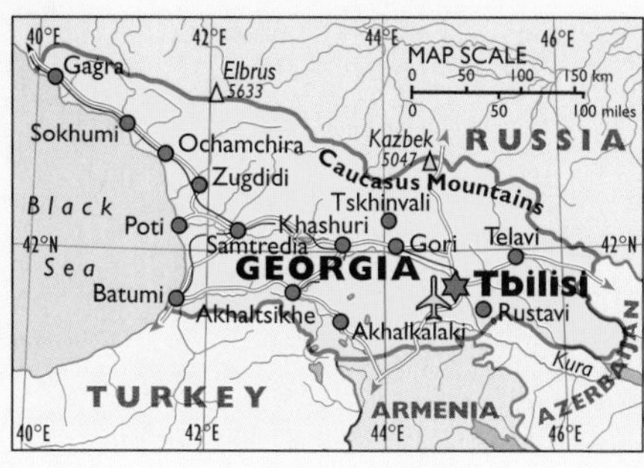

AREA: 356,910sq km (137,803sq mi)
POPULATION: 80,569,000
CAPITAL (POPULATION): Berlin (3,446,000)
GOVERNMENT: Federal multiparty republic
ETHNIC GROUPS: German 93%, Turkish 2%, Yugoslav 1%, Italian 1%, Greek, Polish, Spanish
LANGUAGES: German (official)
RELIGIONS: Christianity (Protestant, mainly Lutheran 45%, Roman Catholic 37%), Islam 2%
GDP PER CAPITA (1995): US$20,070

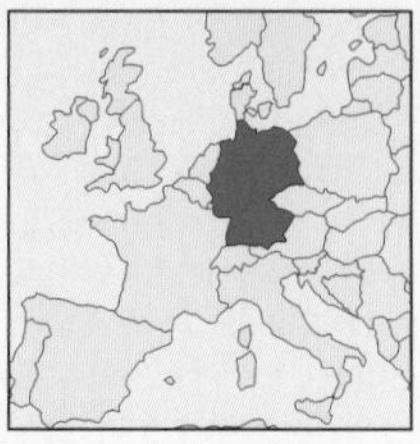

Federal republic in central Europe. German tribes probably began to displace the Celts in the 1st millennium BC. During the GALLIC WARS, Julius CAESAR came into contact with Germans when he crossed the Rhine in 55 BC. In AD 9 ARMINIUS massacred three legions in the Teutonburg Forest forcing the Romans to abandon their attempts to conquer the Germans, whom they regarded as BARBARIANS. By the 4th century there were a number of large and powerful German tribes, notably the SAXONS, FRANKS and ALEMANNI on the Rhine, the Burgundians and Quadi on the middle Danube, and the GOTHS on the lower Danube. As the HUNS began to move into Europe from the east, the VISIGOTHS, OSTROGOTHS and VANDALS invaded the ROMAN EMPIRE, hastening its collapse in the west by 476. The Franks under CLOVIS and his MEROVINGIAN successors then began to extend their empire into what is now Germany, bringing CHRISTIANITY with them. By 700 the Merovingians had lost control, but the CAROLINGIAN dynasty then embarked on reuniting the Frankish world. CHARLEMAGNE conquered BAVARIA and SAXONY and was crowned (800) emperor of an area that reached the Elbe and the Danube in the east. In 843 the empire was split into three kingdoms: LOUIS II (THE GERMAN) received East Francia (now Germany). The inability of the Carolingians to defend their empire increased the power of the local aristocracy and gave birth to FEUDALISM.

In 918 HENRY I (THE FOWLER) founded the Saxon Liudolfing dynasty. After the acquisition of LOTHARINGIA in 925, the Saxons dominated Western Europe for the next 100 years. Henry's son, OTTO I (THE GREAT), established the HOLY ROMAN EMPIRE (first *Reich*) in 962. He conquered Italy, crushed the MAGYARS (955), and established royal control over the church. CONRAD II (r.1024–39) founded the SALIAN dynasty and added BURGUNDY to the German empire. HENRY III (r.1038–56) set out to reform the church, imposing his nominees on the papacy. HENRY IV's reign (1084–1105) was marked by the INVESTITURE controversy with Pope GREGORY VII. When Gregory excommunicated Henry in 1076, Germany was plunged into civil war. In 1138 CONRAD III founded the HOHENSTAUFEN dynasty. FREDERICK I (BARBAROSSA) (r.1152–90) defeated his GUELPH cousin, Henry the Lion of Saxony and Bavaria, thus destroying the last independent duchy in Germany.

The 12th and 13th centuries were marked by German expansion to the east, led by the TEUTONIC KNIGHTS. FREDERICK II's (r.1220–50) battles with the papacy left Germany in a state of anarchy. In 1273 RUDOLF I founded the HABSBURG dynasty. CHARLES IV of LUXEMBOURG (r.1346–78) issued the GOLDEN BULL (1356) that acknowledged the territorial power of the German princes. The monarchy relied increasingly on the financial resources of cities, who formed powerful trading associations such as the HANSEATIC LEAGUE and the SWABIAN LEAGUE. SIGISMUND's reign (1411–37) was dominated by wars against the HUSSITES. FREDERICK III (r.1452–93) and MAXIMILIAN I (r.1493–1519) laid the foundations of the Austrian House of HABSBURG, which thereafter ruled the Holy Roman Empire until its dissolution in 1806.

The start of CHARLES V's reign (1519–58) was marked by Martin LUTHER's call to the German princes to reform the ROMAN CATHOLIC CHURCH. The ideas of the REFORMATION fuelled the PEASANTS' WAR (1525). The extent of the empire that Charles inherited led him to devolve power in Germany to his brother, Ferdinand (later FERDINAND I). Both Charles and Ferdinand were unable to prevent the growth of PROTESTANTISM recognized by the Peace of AUGSBURG (1555). The reign (1576–1612) of RUDOLF II was dominated by conflict between the Catholic forces of the COUNTER-REFORMATION and a more militant Protestantism in the form of CALVINISM. The counter-reforming zeal of FERDINAND II (r.1619–37) led to the THIRTY YEARS' WAR (1618–48). Ferdinand's rapid defeat of Elector Palatinate FERDINAND V persuaded France, England, the Netherlands and Denmark to form an anti-Habsburg coalition. The victory in N Germany (1629) of imperial commander Albrecht von WALLENSTEIN brought Sweden into the War. The conflict devastated Germany, killing more than 16 million people. The Peace of WESTPHALIA (1648) ceded territory to France and Sweden and resulted in the fragmentation of Germany.

The late 17th and early 18th centuries saw the rise of Brandenburg-PRUSSIA under Elector FREDERICK WILLIAM (r.1640–88) and FREDERICK WILLIAM I (r.1713–40), while the Habsburg monarchs consolidated their ancestral lands in Austria. The ascendancy of Prussia was confirmed when Elector FREDERICK II (THE GREAT) (r.1740–86) annexed Silesia from Austria. The ensuing War of the AUSTRIAN SUCCESSION (1740–48) further increased the size and influence of Prussia. The struggle between the Habsburgs and HOHENZOLLERNS continued in the War of the BAVARIAN SUCCESSION (1778–79). Prussia and Austria were defeated in the FRENCH REVOLUTIONARY WARS (1792–1802). In the NAPOLEONIC WARS (1803–15), NAPOLEON I inflicted a crushing defeat on Emperor FRANCIS II (r.1792–1806) at AUSTERLITZ (1805). The Holy Roman Empire was officially dissolved with the formation of the CONFEDERA-

TION OF THE RHINE in 1806. The Prussian army was routed at the Battle of JENA (October 1806) and BERLIN also fell to France. At the Battle of LEIPZIG (October 1813), Austria, Prussia, Russia and Sweden forced Napoleon to retreat. The Congress of VIENNA (1815) established the GERMAN CONFEDERATION, which was dominated by Austria and Prussia. Fürst von METTERNICH of Austria suppressed demands for constitutional reform and crushed emergent German nationalism. The pace of industrialization, however, led to the creation of the ZOLLVEREIN (Customs Union), effectively the economic unification of Germany.

The REVOLUTIONS OF 1848 that swept throughout Europe resulted in the creation of the FRANKFURT NATIONAL ASSEMBLY. Divisions within the reform movement enabled FREDERICK WILLIAM IV to reject the assembly and the revolution crumbled. Austrian Emperor FRANZ JOSEPH briefly held the political initiative until the defeat of the Habsburgs in Italy (1859). In 1862 WILLIAM I of Prussia appointed Otto von BISMARCK as chancellor. Bismarck saw the political unification of Germany as a means of defeating liberalism. In 1864 Prussia and Austria gained SCHLESWIG-HOLSTEIN from Denmark. The AUSTRO-PRUSSIAN WAR (1866) ended in a swift and decisive victory for Prussia and the formation of the NORTH GERMAN CONFEDERATION. Bismarck engineered the FRANCO-PRUSSIAN WAR (1870–71) through the EMS DISPATCH in order to bring the s German states into the Confederation and the second German *Reich* was founded in January 1871. The depression of the 1870s led to the emigration of *c.*600,000 Germans and the imposition of tariffs and cartels to restore the economy. Bismarck launched the KULTURKAMPF against the Roman Catholic Church in Germany and outlawed the SOCIAL DEMOCRATIC PARTY (SPD), but opposition gains in the 1890 elections forced his dismissal by WILLIAM II (r.1888–1918).

Bismarck's successor (1890–94), Leo von CAPRIVI, began the process of colonial expansion. Germany's rapid industrial growth fed the creation of a modern navy under Alfred von TIRPITZ. German military and imperial expansion worried Britain, Russia and France, who formed the TRIPLE ENTENTE. WORLD WAR 1 (1914–18) was fought between the Triple Entente and the CENTRAL POWERS (Austria-Hungary and Germany). The German advance through Belgium was halted at the Battle of the MARNE (September 1914) and stalemate ensued on the Western Front. On the Eastern Front, German troops, led by Paul von HINDENBURG and Erich LUDENDORFF, crushed the Russian army at the Battle of TANNENBERG (August 1914). Germany imposed harsh peace terms on Russia at the Treaty of BREST-LITOVSK (1918), but the Allies forced Germany to retreat in the W. German soldiers and workers revolted against the government and compelled WILLIAM II to abdicate. On 11 November 1918, Germany signed the armistice, ending a war that had cost *c.*2 million German lives.

A communist revolution (January 1919), led by the SPARTACUS LEAGUE, was crushed by the army and the WEIMAR REPUBLIC (1919–33) was created under Friedrich EBERT. The Treaty of VERSAILLES (1919) imposed a heavy price on Germany. In addition to significant losses of land, Germany was forced to accept strict limits on its military and make reparations amounting to US$32 billion. In 1923 France and Belgium occupied the Ruhr in an attempt to persuade German industry to meet shortfalls in reparations payments. The occupation served to fuel the economic crisis. Mass unemployment, hyperinflation, the GREAT DEPRESSION and continued resentment towards Versailles created the conditions for FASCISM.

In January 1933, President HINDENBURG reluctantly accepted Adolf HITLER as chancellor and, following electoral victory in March 1933, Hitler assumed dictatorial powers. The NAZI PARTY pervaded all areas of society, dissent was crushed by the GESTAPO, opposition parties and elections banned. The propaganda machine of Joseph GOEBBELS presented Hitler as the father of the nation and the builder of a Third *Reich*. The Nazis established CONCENTRATION CAMPS for political opponents and those considered racially or socially undesirable. In 1936 Hitler stockpiled armaments and remilitarized the RHINELAND. Germany aided General FRANCO in the Spanish CIVIL WAR (1936–39) and signed the Anti-Comintern Pact (1936) with Japan. In 1938 Hitler annexed Austria. The MUNICH AGREEMENT (1938) handed Hitler the SUDETENLAND, but the subsequent invasion of Czechoslovakia (March 1939) signalled the failure of APPEASEMENT. Hitler then formed a pact with Italian dictator Benito MUSSOLINI and in the NAZI-SOVIET PACT (1939) agreed to the division of Poland with Joseph STALIN.

In September 1939 Germany invaded Poland, precipitating WORLD WAR 2. By June 1940, the whole of Western Europe – with the exception of Britain – had fallen to the Nazis. Britain refused to yield and defeated the LUFTWAFFE in the Battle of BRITAIN (August 1940). After providing military aid to Mussolini in North Africa and Greece, Hitler invaded the Soviet Union (June 1941). The German offensive foundered in the Russian winter and Hitler lost his entire Sixth Army in the Battle of STALINGRAD (1942–43). The Japanese bombing of PEARL HARBOR (December 1941) brought the United States into the war on the side of the Allies. In 1941 Hitler enacted the "Final Solution", which entailed the genocide of European Jews. It is estimated that *c.*6 million Jews died in the HOLOCAUST. The bombing of German cities devastated industry and morale. In June 1944 the Allies launched the NORMANDY LANDINGS to regain Western Europe. Faced with defeat, Hitler committed suicide (30 April 1945). Germany surrendered (8 May 1945), and leading Nazis faced the NUREMBERG TRIALS.

Germany was divided into four military zones. COLD WAR tension increased, leading to the BERLIN AIRLIFT (1949). The American, British and French zones were then joined to make the Federal Republic of Germany (West Germany); the Soviet zone formed the German Democratic Republic (East Germany). Berlin was also divided: East Berlin became capital of East Germany, Bonn *de facto* capital of West Germany.

Walter ULBRICHT became leader (1950–71) of **East Germany**. Economic deprivation led to a revolt in 1953, which Soviet troops subdued. In 1955 East Germany joined the WARSAW PACT. Between 1945 and 1961, four million people crossed to the West. The BERLIN WALL was built to halt the exodus. Ulbricht was replaced (1971) by Erich HONECKER. Relations with West Germany thawed, and travel was permitted between the two countries. Honecker's refusal to adopt reforms led to civil unrest. In November 1989, a rally of 500,000 people demanded reunification, the Wall was opened and the regime collapsed. The CHRISTIAN DEMOCRATIC UNION (CDU) won the first free elections (March 1990). In July 1990 East and West Germany were formally unified.

Konrad ADENAUER was elected as the first chancellor (1949–63) of **West Germany**. He was committed to German reunification. In 1955 West Germany became a member of the NORTH ATLANTIC TREATY ORGANIZATION (NATO). The economy continued to grow dramatically under Kurt KIESINGER (1963–69). Willy BRANDT's chancellorship (1969–74) was noted for his OSTPOLITIK (establishing better relations with the Soviet bloc). His successor was Helmut SCHMIDT (1974–82). Helmut KOHL's chancellorship (1982–98) was more conservative.

In December 1990 Kohl was elected in the first all-German elections since 1933. Reunification meant massive investment to restructure the former East German economy, which strained federal resources and entailed tax increases. Germany is a major supporter of the EUROPEAN UNION (EU), and Helmut Kohl was the driving force behind the creation (1999) of a single European currency. In 1998 Kohl was defeated by Gerhard SCHRÖDER of the SPD. Schröder formed a coalition government with the GREEN PARTY.

years of the Union, leading to bogus land speculation deals such as the YAZOO FRAUD (1795) and the illegal occupation of CHEROKEE and CREEK land. Cotton planations, worked by slave-labour, boomed during the 19th century. Georgia supported the institution of SLAVERY and was one of the original six states of the Confederacy in the American CIVIL WAR (1861–65). Plundered and burned by the armies of General William SHERMAN in 1864, Georgia was readmitted to the Union in 1870 but the KU KLUX KLAN violently resisted the introduction of RECONSTRUCTION, and the continuance of racial segregation and the disenfranchisment of African-Americans made the state a centre of the civil rights movement in the 1960s. During World War 2 the development of munitions industries revived Georgia's impoverished economy. In 1976 Jimmy CARTER became the first Georgian to be elected president of the United States. Area: 152,488sq km (58,876sq mi). Pop. (1996 est.) 7,193,700.

Georgia *See* country feature, page 157

G

German Confederation (1815–66) Federation of 39 German principalities set up by the Congress of VIENNA to replace the HOLY ROMAN EMPIRE. It had few formal powers, beyond a mutual defence pact, and was dominated by Austria and Prussia. The Confederation collapsed in 1848 but was revived two years later. It was finally dissolved after Prussian victory in the Austro-Prussian War (1866) and replaced with the North German Confederation.

German East Africa Former German protectorate in East Africa, consisting of present-day RWANDA, BURUNDI, continental TANZANIA and parts of MOZAMBIQUE. In 1885 the commercial rights of the German East Africa Company in the region were recognized by the other European colonial powers. In 1891 control passed to the German government. Despite strong local resistance to imperial rule, the region was economically successful. After World War 1, it became three League of Nations' mandates under the British, Portuguese and Belgians.

Germanicus Caesar (15 BC–AD 19) Roman general, nephew and adopted son of Emperor TIBERIUS. In *c.*AD 4, he married AUGUSTUS' granddaughter, AGRIPPINA THE ELDER. In AD 12, Germanicus became consul and was given command of the Gallic and German provinces. Germanicus suppressed a mutiny in his legions after the death (AD 14) of Augustus and led three campaigns against the German leader Arminius. In AD 17, Germanicus was given command of the eastern provinces and he incorporated Cappadocia and Commagene as imperial provinces. Germanicus rule in the east led to conflict with the governor of Syria, Calpurnius Piso, and his sudden death cast suspicion on both Piso and Tiberius. Germanicus was the brother of CLAUDIUS and his children included CALIGULA and AGRIPPINA THE YOUNGER, mother of NERO.

Germany *See* country feature

Geronimo (1829–1908) Chief of the Chiricahua APACHE. Geronimo participated in several raids on Mexican territory, and in 1858 his mother, wife and children were murdered by Mexicans. In 1874, *c.*4000 Apache, who had so far resisted colonization by North Americans and Spaniards, were forced into a reservation in E Arizona. With the encouragement of Geronimo, hundreds left the reservation to wage war against white settlers in Arizona for more than ten years. After surrendering in 1886, Geronimo was imprisoned in Florida, Alabama and finally in Fort Sill, Oklahoma. He later became a national celebrity.

Gerry, Elbridge (1744–1814) US statesman, vice president (1812–14). He was a delegate to the CONTINENTAL CONGRESS and to the Federal CONSTITUTIONAL CONVENTION (1787). Gerry signed the DECLARATION OF INDEPENDENCE but refused to sign the CONSTITUTION until the BILL OF RIGHTS was added. He was sent to France to establish diplomatic relations and became involved in the XYZ AFFAIR (1797–98). As governor (1810–12) of Massachusetts, Gerry was responsible for redrawing the boundaries of electoral districts in order to favour the FEDERALIST PARTY. As vice president under James MADISON, he supported the WAR OF 1812. Gerry died in office. *See also* GERRYMANDER

gerrymander Practice of redrawing electoral boundaries to favour a particular party. It is named after US

Vice President Elbridge Gerry, one of whose redefined districts was said to resemble the shape of a salamander.

Gerson, Jean de (1363–1429) (Jean Charlier) French theologian. He was a leader of the conciliar movement that ended the Great Schism (1378–1417) in the Roman Catholic Church. Gerson defended the Council of Pisa (1409) that had failed to depose both Pope Gregory XII and Antipope Benedict XIII. He headed the French delegation to the Council of Constance (1415) that finally ended the Avignon popes and united the church under Martin V.

Gestapo (*Geheime Staatspolizei*) State secret police in Nazi Germany. Founded (1933) by Hermann Göring, it became a powerful national organization under Heinrich Himmler from 1934, as an arm of the ss. With up to 50,000 members by 1945, the Gestapo and SS jointly managed the concentration camps.

Gettysburg, Battle of (1–3 July 1863) Decisive campaign of the American Civil War, fought near Gettysburg, Pennsylvania. The Union army of George Meade checked the invasion of Pennsylvania by the Confederate forces of Robert Lee. The heavy casualties (*c*.20,000 each side) prompted Abraham Lincoln's Gettysburg Address. *See also* Everett, Edward

Gettysburg Address (19 November 1863) Speech by US President Abraham Lincoln at the dedication of the national cemetery on the battlefield of Gettysburg. It ended by describing democracy as "government of the people, by the people, and for the people". One of the most famous political addresses, the text of the speech is carved onto the Lincoln Memorial in Washington, D.C.

Ghana *See* country feature

Ghana (Wagadu) Ancient trading empire in West Africa, situated in what is now se Mauritania and sw Mali. Probably the first indigenous West African state, the kingdom of Ghana was in existence by the 7th century AD. It flourished on the trade in gold and ivory from the south, which was exchanged for salt from North Africa. Ghana expanded into an empire, gaining tribute from neighbouring states. During the 11th century, its capital was at Kumbi (Koumbi Saleh) in what is now se Mauritania. In 1076 Kumbi fell to the Almoravids, who converted the Soninke population to Islam. In 1240 Kumbi was destroyed by the Mande and Ghana was subsumed into the empire of Mali.

Ghaznavids (977–1186) Muslim Turkish dynasty that ruled a region from e Iran to n India. It was founded by **Sebuktegin** (r.977–989), who was appointed governor of Ghazna (now Ghazni, e Afghanistan) by the Samanid emirs of Bukhara. When the Samanids were overthrown, Ghazna achieved independence. Mahmud of Ghazna, Sebuktegin's son, increased the empire to its greatest extent, establishing Muslim rule in what is now Pakistan and India as far as the Indus Valley. Thereafter, the Ghaznavids declined, suffering from internal disputes and attacks by the Seljuks. As a result of the Battle of Dandanqan (1040), the Ghaznavids lost Iran and Central Asia to the Seljuks. They continued to rule an ever-decreasing area of e Afghanistan and n India until 1186 when their last stronghold, Lahore, fell to the Ghurids, founders of the Delhi Sultanate.

Ghent, Pacification of (8 November 1576) Agreement between the southern and northern provinces of the Low Countries during the Revolt of the Netherlands against Spain. In addition to calling for the withdrawal of Spanish troops, the southern Catholic provinces undertook to stop the persecution of Protestants while the northern, largely Calvinist, provinces of Holland and Zeeland agreed not to promote Protestantism outside their borders. Spanish troops were only temporarily withdrawn in 1577, and in 1579 continuing differences over religion led to the formation of the Union of Arras by the southern provinces.

Ghent, Treaty of (1814) Agreement between Britain and the United States ending the War of 1812. It restored territorial allocations to their pre-war position and appointed a commission to settle the dispute over the US–Canada border.

Gheorghiu-Dej, Gheorghe (1901–65) Romanian statesman, prime minister (1952–55), president of the state council (1961–65). He was secretary general of the Romanian Communist Party during the 1944 coup against Romania's fascist government. During the remainder of World War 2, Gheorghiu-Dej built up the communists' representation in government. As prime minister, he managed to steer an independent course from the Soviet Union, promoting the manufacture of consumer goods and seeking better relations with China. He was succeeded by Nicolae Ceausescu.

Ghibelline (Ger. Waiblingen) Political faction in Germany and Italy between the 12th and 14th centuries. In Germany, the Ghibellines were supporters of the Hohenstaufen dukes of Swabia in their struggle with the Guelph dukes of Bavaria for control of the Holy Roman Empire. In Italy, the Ghibellines supported Emperor Frederick I (Barbarossa) in his attempts to dominate the n Italian cities and Pope Alexander III. In the first half of the 13th century, they supported Frederick II, engaging in battles with the Guelphs in a number of cities, most notably Florence. In 1266 Charles of Anjou expelled the Ghibellines from Florence, but in the early 14th century they maintained control of other Tuscan cities, notably Pisa and Siena. The Ghibellines declined as the Holy Roman emperors stopped attempting to assert control over Italy.

Ghose, Aurobindo (1872–1950) (Sri Aurobindo) Indian mystic philosopher and nationalist leader. In 1908 he was imprisoned for agitating against British rule in Bengal because his editorials in the newspaper *Bande Mataram* were considered too revolutionary. After his release, Ghose devoted himself to Hindu philosophy. He founded an *ashram* (retreat) at Pondicherry, se India. In works such as *The Synthesis of Yoga* (1948), Ghose formulated his system of "integral yoga" based on a two-way path to union with Brahman, the supreme soul of the universe.

Ghost Dance Either of two cults that developed out of the messianic religion practised by the Paiute in w Nevada, United States. Paiute prophets announced the return of the dead, restoration of the Native Americans, and departure of the European settlers. The rituals featured dancers in hypnotic trances. The first Ghost Dance, instituted (1869) by Wodziwob (d. *c*.1872), soon died out and was replaced by a second cult, led by Wovoka (*c*.1856–1932). This Ghost Dance was adopted by the Sioux, but failed to provide protection during the massacre at Wounded Knee (1890).

Gia Long (1762–1820) Vietnamese emperor, b. Nguyen Phuc Anh. In 1802, with French military assistance, he succeeded in re-establishing the Nguyen dynasty by defeating his rivals in Hue and Hanoi, and proclaimed himself Emperor Gia Long. Gia Long tried to keep Vietnam isolated from Europe, although he allowed French Christian missionaries into the country. Among his reforms was the introduction of a Law Code, which increased the power of the ruling elite.

Giap, Vo Nguyen (1912–) Vietnamese general and statesman. A brilliant guerrilla commander, he led the Viet Minh forces that entered Hanoi in 1945 and later

GHANA (FORMERLY GOLD COAST)

AREA: 238,540sq km (92,100sq mi)
POPULATION: 16,944,000
CAPITAL (POPULATION): Accra (949,013)
GOVERNMENT: Republic
ETHNIC GROUPS: Akan 54%, Mossi 16%, Ewe 12%, Ga-Adangame 8%, Gurma 3%
LANGUAGES: English (official)
RELIGIONS: Christianity 62% (Protestant 28%, Roman Catholic 19%), traditional beliefs 21%, Islam 16%
GDP PER CAPITA (1995): US$1990

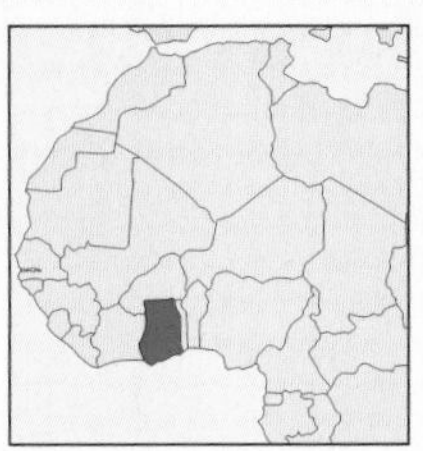

Republic in West Africa. Various kingdoms were established in the region by migrants from the Mande and Hausa states before the arrival of Portuguese explorers in 1471, who named it the Gold Coast after its precious mineral resource. In 1642 the Dutch gained control of the gold-trading castle, Elmina, and they were soon followed by British and Danish traders. The slave trade flourished from the 16th to the 19th century. It was, however, banned by Denmark, Britain and the Netherlands between 1804 and 1814, and trade in other commodities, such as rubber, ivory and palm oil, grew in importance. Meanwhile, in the early 18th century the Ashanti had created an inland empire whose armies began to invade the coastal areas in the latter part of the century. In response, the coastal Fanti attempted to create a confederation in the 1860s, and in 1874 Britain colonized the region. It then conquered the Ashanti empire between 1895 and 1901. The British developed cacao plantations. After World War 2, anti-colonial movements increased, and nationalist leader Kwame Nkrumah became prime minister in the 1951 elections.

In 1957 Ghana became the first African colony to gain full independence. British Togoland was incorporated into the new state. The country was renamed Ghana after the powerful, medieval West African kingdom. In 1960 Ghana became a republic with Nkrumah as president. In 1964 Nkrumah declared a one-party state. The economy slumped, burdened by debt, corruption and the falling cacao price. Nkrumah was deposed in a military coup (1966). Ghana briefly returned to civilian rule (1969–72). The National Redemptive Council (NRC), led (1972–78) by Colonel Ignatius Acheampong, continued to nationalize industry. In 1979 Flight Lieutenant Jerry Rawlings overthrew the government and executed opposition leaders. A civilian government was formed, but in 1981 it was toppled by Rawlings. In 1992 a new constitution paved the way for multiparty elections. Opposition parties and voters boycotted the elections, and The National Democratic Council (NDC), led by Rawlings, secured a victory. In 1996 Rawlings was re-elected.

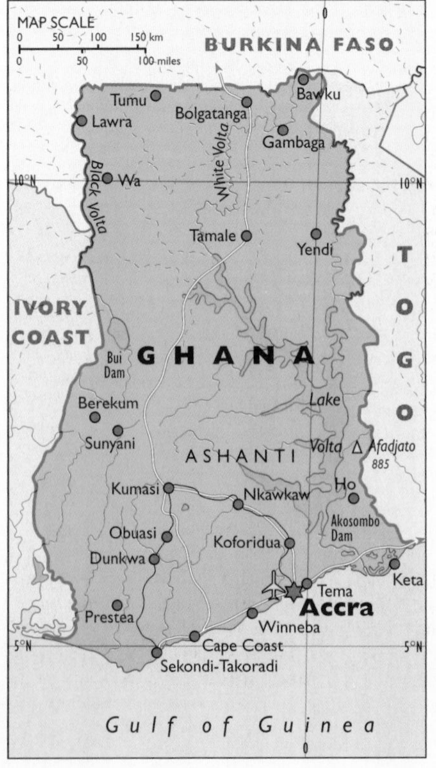

defeated the French at DIEN BIEN PHU (1954). Giap commanded North Vietnamese forces in the VIETNAM WAR (1961–75) and organized the 1968 Tet offensive. He became deputy premier (1976–80) after the unification of Vietnam. *See also* HO CHI MINH

Gibbon, Edward (1737–94) English historian. Gibbon conceived the idea of his great work, *The Decline and Fall of the Roman Empire* (1776–88), while among the ruins of ancient Rome. The six volumes span 1000 years, beginning at the 2nd century AD. It is still widely used.

Gibraltar British crown colony on the S coast of Spain. The MUSLIM conquest of Spain began in AD 711, and Gibraltar remained under Moorish control until 1462. In 1704 it was captured by an Anglo-Dutch fleet and was ceded to Britain by the Peace of UTRECHT (1713). Repeated Spanish attempts to capture Gibraltar failed. It was a British naval base during both world wars. In 1964 it was granted extensive self-government, and a 1967 referendum demonstrated the wish of the Gibraltarians to remain British. Spain continues to claim sovereignty, and between 1969 and 1985 it closed its border with Gibraltar. Area: 6.5sq km (2.5sq mi). Pop. (1993 est.) 28,051.

Gideons International Worldwide organization that seeks to spread Christianity by distributing Bibles to hotel rooms, hospitals, military barracks, prisons and other public places. It was founded (1899) in the United States by three commercial travellers, Samuel Hill, John Nicholson and William Knights. It began distributing bibles in 1906. By the end of the 1990s, there were 130,000 members.

Gierek, Edward (1913–) Polish statesman, first secretary (1970–80) of the Polish Communist Party. His family emigrated to France, where he joined the Communist Party. In 1948 Gierek returned to Poland and rose through the ranks of the communist Polish United Workers' Party (PUWP), becoming a member of the Politburo in 1956. Gierek argued for greater independence from the Soviet Union in policy-making. He succeeded Wladyslaw GOMUŁKA as first secretary of the Party after a series of workers' riots over food prices. Gierek tried to modernize industry and improve the availability of consumer goods, but his reforms merely worsened the economic climate. Further protests forced Gierek to recognize the trade union SOLIDARITY and he was forced to resign. *See also* JARUZELSKI, WOJCIECH

Gilbert, Sir Humphrey (1539–83) English explorer and colonizer. Gilbert proposed the existence of the NORTHWEST PASSAGE in his *Discourse* (1576) and unsuccessfully sailed in search of it in 1578 and 1583. On his second trip, Gilbert established a colony at St John's, Newfoundland. On the voyage home, Gilbert's ship foundered and he was drowned off Nova Scotia.

Gildas (active 6th century) British monk and chronicler. In the 540s he wrote *De excidio et conquestu Britanniae* ("The Overthrow and Conquest of Britain"), an account of the ANGLO-SAXON invasions and of the British defeat of the SAXONS at Badon Hill. It is the earliest surviving record of the invasions.

Gilded Age Period in US history after the American CIVIL WAR (1861–65), characterized by gross materialism. There was also a good deal of corruption, speculation and lawlessness. The term came from the novel *The Gilded Age* (1873) by Mark Twain and Charles Dudley Warner.

Gilgamesh Hero of the great Assyro-Babylonian myth, the Epic of Gilgamesh, who went in search of immortality. The most complete version of the story in the Akkadian language was discovered in the library of King ASHURBANIPAL (r.668–627 BC) at NINEVEH. The legend appears to be based on Gilgamesh of URUK, who rebelled against Agga of KISH in the third millennium BC. *See also* AKKADIA; SARGON I; SUMERIA

Gingrich, Newt (Newton Leroy) (1943–) US Republican politician. He entered Congress in 1979. In the 1994 Congressional elections, Gingrich persuaded Republicans to subscribe to his "contract with America", a commitment to cut wasteful government spending. As speaker of the House of Representatives (1995–98), he led the Republican-dominated Congress into conflict with President Bill CLINTON. In 1997 financial scandals reduced his power, but he remained an outspoken foe of Clinton.

Ginkel, Godard van Reede-Ginkel (1644–1703) Dutch soldier in English service. In 1688 he went with WILLIAM III (OF ORANGE) to England and then to Ireland, where he fought at the Battle of the BOYNE (1690). Ginkel remained in Ireland as commander in chief, subduing Athlone and Galway and decisively beating the Irish army at Aughrim (1691). For his services, Ginkel was created 1st Earl of Athlone in 1692.

Giolitti, Giovanni (1842–1928) Italian statesman, prime minister (1892–93, 1903–05, 1906–09, 1911–14, 1920–21). He entered parliament in 1802. Giolitti's first term as prime minister ended with his resignation after a financial scandal. Giolitti's evidence brought about the downfall of his successor, Francesco CRISPI, and Giolitti became a backroom powerbroker. In his second term, Giolitti was lauded for his moderate approach to a series of strikes. During his fourth ministry (1911–14), Giolitti broadened the franchise and instigated the Italo-Turkish War (1911) that ended with Italy's acquisition of Libya. He opposed Italy's entry into World War 1. After the war, Giolitti failed to deal with the armed fascist gangs, indeed he welcomed Benito MUSSOLINI's participation in government. In 1924 Giolitti openly condemned the fascists.

Giraud, Henri Honoré (1879–1949) French military commander. He served in World War 1 and the Rif War (1925–26) in Morocco. In World War 2, Giraud was captured (1940) by the Germans. In 1941 he escaped and was given command of the French forces in Africa. Giraud briefly shared the presidency of the French Committee of National Liberation with Charles DE GAULLE in 1943 but was forced to retire due to political differences.

Girondins Political group of moderate republicans in the FRENCH REVOLUTION, many of whom were deputies from Gironde, SW France. Initially led by Jacques Brissot de Warville (1754–93), the Girondins represented the provincial bourgeoisie and favoured constitutional government. In 1792 they succeeded in having war declared on Austria. The overthrow and execution of LOUIS XVI weakened their position and strengthened the hand of the JACOBINS. The defection to Austria of Charles DUMOURIEZ further reduced their support and they were expelled from the National Congress in 1793. Most of the Girondins were guillotined during the REIGN OF TERROR (1793).

Giscard d'Estaing, Valéry (1926–) French statesman, president (1974–81). He was elected to the National Assembly in 1956. Giscard d'Estaing served as finance minister (1962–66) under Charles DE GAULLE. After his dismissal, he formed the Independent Republican Party. Giscard d'Estaing returned as finance minister under President Georges POMPIDOU. He defeated François MITTERRAND to become president, but narrowly lost to him in 1981. He has been leader of the centre-right Union for French Democracy (UDF) since 1988.

▲ **Gladstone** created a strong Liberal Party and introduced electoral reforms. He spoke out against the treatment of prisoners in Naples and Turkish massacres in the Balkans.

gladiator In ancient Rome, prisoner of war, slave or condemned convict trained to fight one another or wild animals in public arenas. The first known gladiatorial contest in Rome took place in 264 BC. The loser's fate, life or death, was often decided by the spectators. In AD 325 gladiatorial contests were officially abolished by CONSTANTINE I (THE GREAT), but they persisted into the 5th century. SPARTACUS led a revolt of the gladiators in 73–71 BC.

Gladstone, William Ewart (1809–98) British statesman, prime minister (1868–74, 1880–85, 1886, 1892–94). He was elected to Parliament as a Tory in 1832 and served (1843–45) as president of the Board of Trade under Robert PEEL. Gladstone sided with the Peelites over the repeal of the CORN LAWS, an issue which split the TORIES and forced him to resign with Peel. Gladstone served as chancellor of the exchequer (1852–55) in George ABERDEEN's coalition government and again (1859–66) under Viscount PALMERSTON and John RUSSELL. In 1867 Gladstone succeeded Palmerston as leader of the LIBERAL PARTY. In his first term, he disestablished (1869) the Irish Church and introduced (1870) a system of national education and the first Irish Land Act. In 1874 Gladstone was defeated by Benjamin DISRAELI and briefly resigned as Liberal leader. His stinging criticism of Disraeli's imperialist tendencies won him the 1880 elections. In his second term, Gladstone passed a second Irish Land Act (1881) and several REFORM ACTS (1884, 1885) that extended the FRANCHISE. The government's failure to help General GORDON in Khartoum forced Gladstone to resign. Gladstone's last two ministries were dominated by his advocacy of HOME RULE for Ireland. *See also* EASTERN QUESTION

Glanvill, Ranulf de (d.1190) English justiciar or chief minister (1180–89) to HENRY II of England. He wrote or commissioned the *Treatise on the Laws and Customs of the Kingdom of England*, the first major work on the COMMON LAW. As justiciar, Glanvill oversaw the establishment of the Curia Regis and the use of inquests. He died on the Third CRUSADE.

Glasgow Largest city and port in Scotland, on both banks of the River Clyde, Strathclyde. Founded by Saint Mungo in the 6th century, it became a royal burgh in 1450. Glasgow flourished as a market centre, particularly after the union of the Scottish and English crowns (1603). It developed with the American tobacco trade in the 18th century and the cotton trade in the 19th century. The INDUSTRIAL REVOLUTION brought the growth of heavy industry and shipbuilding. In the late 20th century, heavy industry declined. Sites include St Mungo's Cathedral (mainly 13th century), University of Glasgow (founded 1451), the Glasgow School of Art, and the Kelvingrove Art Gallery and Museum. Pop (1991) 662,853.

glasnost (Rus. openness) Term adopted (1986) by Soviet President Mikhail GORBACHEV to refer to the adoption of a more liberal social policy. The change in attitude resulted in greater press freedom, and more open discussion and popular criticism of the Soviet system and the COMMUNIST PARTY OF THE SOVIET UNION. Glasnost led to the breakup of the SOVIET UNION and the fall of Gorbachev. *See also* PERESTROIKA

Glencoe, Massacre of (13 February 1692) Slaughter of 38 members of the MacDonald clan in Glencoe, Scottish Highlands. The chief of the MacDonalds had failed to swear allegiance to WILLIAM III (OF ORANGE) by 1 January 1692, thereby technically committing treason. As a warning to potential JACOBITES, the secretary of state for Scotland, John Dalrymple, ordered the slaughter. It was carried out by the Campbells, long-standing enemies of the Macdonalds, after they had accepted their unsuspecting victims' hospitality for 12 days.

Glendower, Owen *See* GLYN DWR, OWAIN

Glorious First of June (1794) First major naval conflict of the FRENCH REVOLUTIONARY WARS. On 28 May, the British fleet under Admiral Richard HOWE intercepted a French convoy, led by Admiral Louis Villaret de Joyeuse,

690km (430mi) W of Ile d'Ouessant, off the coast of Brittany. Bad weather prevented full engagement until 1 June. Although the British sank one French ship and seized another six, the rest of the fleet retreated to Brest harbour.

Glorious Revolution (1688–89) Abdication of JAMES II of England and his replacement by WILLIAM III (OF ORANGE) and MARY II. After becoming king in 1685, James had antagonized powerful subjects by appointing Roman Catholics to important positions in the government, army and universities, and issuing two Declarations of Indulgence which suspended the penal laws against Catholics and Dissenters. When the archbishop of Canterbury and six other bishops refused to read the Second Declaration from their pulpits, James had them imprisoned and charged with seditious libel. Meanwhile, the birth of a son, James Edward STUART, to James and MARY OF MODENA posed the threat of a Catholic heir to the throne. This, coupled with the acquittal of the seven clerics, prompted a group of leading Protestants to invite the king's Protestant daughter Mary and her husband, William, to England. On 5 November 1688, William landed in Devon, SW England, and his forces' advance on London encountered little resistance from the army, which ignored the orders of Catholic officers. (The relatively bloodless nature of the Revolution earned it the epithet "Glorious".) James fled to France and Parliament offered (January 1689) the throne to William and Mary. The monarchs subsequently ratified the BILL OF RIGHTS (1689) that barred Roman Catholics from the succession. James was decisively defeated at the Battle of the BOYNE (1690) and the Act of SETTLEMENT (1701) excluded the STUARTS from the throne. *See also* BOYNE, BATTLE OF THE; JACOBITES

Gloucester, Humphrey Plantagenet, Duke of (1391–1447) English noble, youngest son of HENRY IV, brother of HENRY V and of John, Duke of BEDFORD. On the death (1422) of Henry V, Bedford was appointed regent for the infant HENRY VI. While Bedford was fighting in France, Gloucester was made protector of the realm. Gloucester proved an inept ruler and a bitter power struggle ensued with the chancellor, Henry BEAUFORT. Gloucester's influence waned after Henry VI was crowned in 1429 and his second wife, Eleanor, was arrested for scorcery in 1441. In 1447 Gloucester was arrested by Beaufort's successor, William de la Pole, and he died in prison. Gloucester was a patron of English humanists and his library forms the nucleus of the Bodleian Library at the University of Oxford.

Gloucester County town of Gloucestershire on the River Severn, W England. It was founded as the city of Glevum by the Roman emperor Nerva in AD 96–98. During Anglo-Saxon times, it was the capital of the kingdom of MERCIA. In 681 an abbey was established. By the time of the Norman Conquest (1066), Gloucester was a flourishing community. The cathedral was built in the 11th century and is the burial place of EDWARD II. Pop. (1991) 101,608.

Glubb, Sir John Bagot (1897–1986) British soldier, known as Glubb Pasha. He served in the British Army during World War 1, resigning to become administrative inspector (1926–30) for the Iraqi government. In 1930 Glubb joined the Arab Legion in Transjordan, succeeding Frederick Peake as commander in 1939. Glubb turned the Legion into a disciplined force, gaining victories for the Allies in the Middle East during World War 2. Glubb led the defence of Jordan against Israeli border raids in 1951. In 1956 HUSSEIN I of Jordan was obliged to dismiss him because of anti-British feeling.

Glyn Dŵr, Owain (Owen Glendower) (*c*.1359–1416) Welsh chief. A member of the House of Powys, he led a rebellion (1401) against HENRY IV. Proclaimed Prince of Wales, Glyn Dŵr summoned a parliament and allied himself with Henry's English enemies, Sir Henry PERCY and the Mortimer family. By 1404 Glyn Dŵr had captured Harlech and Aberystwyth castles. In 1405 his forces suffered several defeats by Henry IV's son, the future HENRY V. By 1409 Glyn Dŵr had lost both castles and retreated to the hills to maintain guerrilla warfare against the English.

Gneisenau, August, Graf Neithardt von (1760–1831) Prussian field marshal. He fought at the Battle of JENA (1806), in which Prussia was crushed by NAPOLEON I. Gneisenau, Gerhard von SCHARNHORST and Hermann von Boyen, were instrumental in rebuilding and transforming the Prussian army into a modern citizen's army. In 1813 Gneisenau was appointed chief of staff to Marshal Gebhard von BLÜCHER. Gneisenau helped devise the strategy that led to Napoleon's defeat at the Battle of WATERLOO (1815). His tactics formed the basis of Carl von CLAUSEWITZ's manual *On War* (1832–37).

Goa State in SW India on the Arabian Sea; the capital is Panaji. It was ruled by the Hindu Kadamba dynasty from the 2nd century AD until it fell to Muslim invaders in 1312. In 1367 Goa became part of the Hindu kingdom of Vijayanagar, but was conquered by the Muslim Bahmani dynasty in the 1460s. Captured by the Portuguese, led by Afonso d'ALBUQUERQUE, in 1510, it became a flourishing trade centre and the hub of Portugal's Asian empire. In 1947 British India gained independence, but Portuguese Goa forcibly resisted Indian nationalists. In 1961 Goa was occupied by Indian troops and became a Union territory of India in 1962. In 1987 Goa became a separate state. Area: 3702sq km (1429sq mi). Pop. (1991) 1,169,793

Gobind Singh (1666–1708) Tenth and last Sikh guru, who laid the foundations of Sikh militarism. His father, the ninth guru, was murdered by the MUGHAL Emperor AURANGZEB in 1675. In 1699 Gobind Singh created the *Khalsa*, a military fraternity of devout Sikhs that formed the basis of the Sikh army he led against the Mughal empire. The turban and the common attachment of Singh ("lion") to Sikh names date from his reign. Gobind Singh is said to have declared himself the last guru and that henceforth the guru was to be the Sikh holy book, ADI GRANTH. *See also* SIKHISM

Gobineau, Joseph Arthur, Comte de (1816–82) French writer and anthropologist. First known as a novelist, he evolved racist theories, pervaded by ANTI-SEMITISM, in such works as *Essay on the Inequality of the Human Races* (1854). Gobineau's claim for the intellectual and moral superiority of Aryans influenced Adolf HITLER.

Goderich, Frederick John Robinson, Viscount (1782–1859) British statesman, prime minister (1827–28). He entered Parliament as a Tory in 1806, serving as president of the board of trade (1818–23) and chancellor of the exchequer (1823–27). Goderich succeeded George CANNING as prime minister, but, unsuited to the job, he resigned five months later. He was a minister in Lord GREY's Whig government (1830–34), becoming Earl of Ripon in 1833. As a minister in Robert PEEL's Conservative government (1841–46), Goderich introduced a bill to repeal the CORN LAWS.

Godfrey of Bouillon (*c*.1060–1100) French crusader, Duke of Lower Lorraine (1089–95). He was one of the leaders of the First CRUSADE (1096). Godfrey played a major role in the siege and capture (1099) of JERUSALEM. He was elected king, but preferred the title Defender of the Holy Sepulchre. He was succeeded by his son, BALDWIN I.

Godiva, Lady (d.*c*.1080) English benefactress, wife of Leofric, Earl of Mercia. According to tradition, Lady Godiva rode naked through the streets of Coventry in 1040 to persuade her husband to reduce the burden of excessive taxation.

Godolphin, Sidney Godolphin, 1st Earl of (1645–1712) English statesman, lord treasurer (1685–96, 1700–01, 1702–10). Appointed lord treasurer by JAMES II, Godolphin retained his control of financial administration following the GLORIOUS REVOLUTION (1688) and the accession of WILLIAM III (OF ORANGE) and MARY II. He maintained secret contact with James and was removed from office after being implicated in a plot to restore the exiled former king. Godolphin and the Duke of MARLBOROUGH dominated the early part of Queen ANNE's reign. Godolphin helped to finance Marlborough's campaigns in the War of the SPANISH SUCCESSION and managed the union of England and Scotland (1707). He lost favour with the queen after forcing the resignation of Robert HARLEY and was dismissed from office.

Godoy, Manuel de (1767–1851) Spanish statesman, chief minister (1792–97, 1801–08) of CHARLES IV. His rapid promotion at court was due to his affair with Queen MARÍA LUISA. Godoy joined the First Coalition in the FRENCH REVOLUTIONARY WARS, but made peace with France and signed the Treaty of San Ildefonso (1796) against England. Horatio NELSON's crushing victory over the Spanish fleet off Cape St Vincent (1797) forced Godoy's brief removal from office. On his return, Godoy joined the French invasion of Portugal but Spanish interests were betrayed when Napoleon I signed the Treaty of AMIENS (1802) with Britain. In 1804 Spain allied with France in the NAPOLEONIC WARS, but the Spanish navy was destroyed by Britain at the Battle of TRAFALGAR (1805). Godoy's inept and corrupt administration again mishandled affairs at the start of the PENINSULAR WAR, and he was removed with Charles IV by FERDINAND VII.

Godunov, Boris (1551–1605) Tsar of Russia (1598–1605). Chief minister and brother-in-law of IVAN IV (THE TERRIBLE), Godunov became regent to Ivan's imbecile son FYODOR I and was popularly supposed to have murdered Fyodor's brother and heir, DMITRI, in 1591. On Fyodor's death in 1598, Godunov was elected tsar. He gained recognition for the Russian ORTHODOX CHURCH as an independent patriarchate. Godunov recovered land around the Gulf of Finland in a war (1590–95) with Sweden. He introduced policies to benefit the population but persecuted suspected enemies, suppressed the BOYARS and banished the ROMANOVS. A famine (1601–03) led to unrest and increased support for Dmitri (the Pretender). Godunov's sudden death led to the "Time of Troubles" (1604–13), a period of violent conflict that ended with the accession of MICHAEL Romanov.

Godwin (d.1053) Earl of Wessex. He was highly influential during the reigns of CANUTE II (THE GREAT) and HAROLD I. Godwin also aided the accession (1042) of EDWARD THE CONFESSOR and later arranged the marriage of his daughter, Edith, to Edward. In 1051 Edward banished Godwin because of his opposition to Edward's appointment of Normans into influential positions. With much popular support, Godwin returned to England in 1052 and forced Edward to reinstate him. Godwin's son briefly became king as HAROLD II in 1066.

Goebbels, (Paul) Joseph (1897–1945) German NAZI PARTY leader. He joined the Nazis in 1924 and founded the newspaper *Der Angriff* in 1926. Goebbels helped to build the Nazi Party into a national force, creating a personality cult around Adolf HITLER and staging mass rallies. He entered the Reichstag in 1928 and when the Nazis came to power, in 1933, Goebbels became minister of propaganda. He took total control of the national media, which he manipulated to support Nazi aims. Goebbels attempted to restore German morale when the Nazis began to suffer defeats in WORLD WAR 2. He committed suicide with his entire family in May 1945. *See also* KRISTALLNACHT; NATIONAL SOCIALISM

Goerdeler, Karl Friedrich (1884–1945) German politician. He served as mayor of Leipzig (1930–37) until forced to resign because of his hostility to the NAZI PARTY. He remained a staunch opponent of Adolf HITLER and plotted to overthrow him. On 20 July 1944, an attempt to assassinate Hitler failed and Goerdeler was later arrested and hanged.

Goh Chok Tong (1941–) Singaporean statesman, prime minister (1990–). He entered Parliament in 1976. Goh Chok Tong rose steadily through the ministerial ranks and succeeded LEE KUAN YEW as prime minister and leader of the People's Action Party (PAP).

Golan Heights (*Ramat Ha Golan*) Range of hills in SW Syria on the border with Israel. They provided the Syrian artillery with an excellent position from which to bombard Israel and so were captured by Israel during the SIX DAY WAR (1967). The Syrians failed in their attempt to recapture the area during the YOM KIPPUR WAR (1973) and in 1981 it was formally annexed by Israel. Of great strategic importance to both Israel and Syria, the Golan Heights have remained a source of conflict between the two countries. Area: 1150sq km (444sq mi). Pop. (1983 est.) 19,700. *See also* ARAB-ISRAELI WARS

Golden Bull Edict with a golden seal, as issued by medieval Western and Byzantine rulers. Andrew II of Hungary issued a Golden Bull in 1222. This document extended certain rights to the nobility, including tax exemption, freedom to dispose of their property, prohibition of arbitrary imprisonment, and guarantee of annual assembly. The best-known Golden Bull is the edict promulgated by Holy Roman Emperor CHARLES IV in 1356. It defined the procedures for electing the Holy Roman emperor and provided for election by majority vote of seven princely ELECTORS. The procedures remained in effect until the dissolution of the empire by Napoleon I in 1806.

Golden Hind Flagship of Sir Francis DRAKE on his circumnavigation of the globe (1577–80). It was renamed (from *The Pelican*) after the crest of the patron of the voyage, Sir Christopher Hatton.

Golden Horde (Kipchak Khanate) Western state of the MONGOL EMPIRE. In 1237 BATU KHAN, grandson of GENGHIS KHAN, crossed the River Ural and by 1240 had conquered all of Russia. Batu marched on to Poland, Silesia and Hungary before retreating to s Russia and establishing a capital, Sarai Batu, on the River Volga. Within the Golden Horde, the Russian principalities were given considerable autonomy in return for paying tribute. Islam was adopted as the state religion in the early 14th century. Disputes among the TATAR leaders and battles against the Russian princes weakened the Horde and it disintegrated after TAMERLANE sacked Sarai Berke in 1395. The smaller khanates that emerged were gradually absorbed by the Russian state of MOSCOW.

Goldman, Emma (1869–1940) US anarchist and feminist, b. Lithuania. In New York, she co-edited (1906–17) the anarchist monthly *Mother Earth*. Goldman was imprisoned (1916, 1917) for advocating birth control and opposing conscription during World War 1. In 1919 she was deported to Russia. Goldman was active in the Spanish CIVIL WAR. *See also* ANARCHISM

gold rush Rapid influx of population in response to reports of the discovery of gold. The largest gold rush brought some 100,000 prospectors to California, United States (1849–50). Some of the miners, known as Forty-Niners, went on to Australia (1851–53). There were also gold rushes to South Africa (1886), the KLONDIKE in the Yukon, Canada (1896), and to Alaska (1898).

gold standard Monetary system in which the gold value of currency is set at a fixed rate and currency is convertible into gold on demand. It was adopted by Britain in 1821, by the United States, France and Germany in the 1870s, and by most of the rest of the world by the 1890s. It produced nearly fixed exchange rates and was intended to foster monetary stability. The GREAT DEPRESSION forced many countries to depreciate their exchange rates in an attempt to foster trade, and by the mid-1930s all countries had abandoned the gold standard.

Goldwater, Barry Morris (1909–98) US senator from Arizona (1953–64, 1969–87). A conservative Republican, he supported the anti-communist activities of Joseph MCCARTHY and called for a reduction in federal support for health and social welfare projects. In 1964 Goldwater secured the REPUBLICAN PARTY nomination for president, but was decisively defeated in the election by President Lyndon JOHNSON (1964). He was a staunch supporter of US intervention in the VIETNAM WAR. His books include *The Conscience of a Conservative* (1960).

Gómez, Juan Vicente (1857–1935) Venezuelan statesman, dictator of Venezuela (1908–35). Gómez served as vice president under Cipriano Castro, seizing power when Castro was abroad. Gómez used the secret police to crush political opposition. The discovery of oil (1918) boosted Venezuela's economy and swelled Gomez's personal fortune. His nepotistic and brutal rule did, however, bring improvements to the nation's infrastructure.

Gompers, Samuel (1850–1924) US UNION leader, b. England. He helped to found the Federation of Organized Trades and Labor Unions. When it was reorganized as the AMERICAN FEDERATION OF LABOR (1886), Gompers became its first president, serving until his death (except for 1895). During World War 1, he organized and headed the War Commission on Labor and served on the Advisory Commission to the Council of National Defense.

Gomułka, Wladyslaw (1905–82) Polish statesman, president (1956–70). In World War 2, he was secretary general of the outlawed Polish Communist Party. Gomułka served as vice president (1945–48) in the first post-war government, but was dismissed and imprisoned (1951–54) for his criticism of STALINISM. In 1956 popular uprisings led to Gomułka returning to power. The public hoped that he would introduce major reforms, but he failed to lift restrictions on freedom of speech or to institute economic change. From the early 1960s support for him declined, and in 1968 there were widespread riots. In 1970 Gomułka introduced economic reforms, but an announcement of sharp rises in food prices led to further riots and in December he was forced to resign. He was succeeded by Edward GIEREK.

Gonzaga family Italian dynasty that ruled Mantua (1328–1707) and Montferrat (1536–1707). The family's power in Mantua was established by **Luigi Gonzaga** (*c*.1267–1360), who became vicar general of the HOLY ROMAN EMPIRE. **Giovanni Francesco II** (1466–1519) led the Italians in battle (1494) against CHARLES VIII of France. Giovanni married Isabella d'Este, a great Renaissance art patron. His son, **Frederico II** (d.1540), was made Duke of Mantua in 1530 by Emperor CHARLES V. Frederico also acquired Montferrat and his brother, **Ferrante** (1507–57), gained (1539) the county of Guastalla. During Frederico's reign, Mantua reached its peak of artistic and architectural achievement. Under his successors, the fortunes of both the Gonzaga family and Mantua went into decline. In 1708 the duchy was annexed by Austria and the last Gonzaga duke died.

Good Friday Agreement (10 April 1998) Northern IRELAND peace accord signed by British Prime Minister Tony BLAIR and Irish Taoiseach Bertie AHERN and representatives from eight political parties in Northern Ireland. The Agreement provided for a new, 108-seat Northern Ireland Assembly with legislative powers devolved from the British Parliament. The executive powers of the Assembly are held by a 12-member executive committee, formed on a proportional basis and headed by a first minister and deputy first minister. It also created a North-South Ministerial Council to coordinate policies between the Republic of IRELAND and Northern Ireland. A "Council of the Isles", consisting of representatives from throughout the British Isles, replaced the intergovernmental conference established by the ANGLO-IRISH AGREEMENT (1985). Other major points included: the Republic of Ireland dropping its constitutional claim to Northern Ireland; a commitment to the decommissioning of terrorist weapons; the release of paramilitary prisoners; a review of policing in Northern Ireland and a reduction in the British security presence in the province. In a referendum (22 May 1998), the Agreement was endorsed by more than 71% of voters in Northern Ireland and 94% in the Republic. The Assembly met for the first time in July, but the peace process stalled when First Minister David TRIMBLE refused to appoint two SINN FÉIN members to the executive committee until the IRISH REPUBLICAN ARMY (IRA) had started to decommission its weapons. US Senator George MITCHELL conducted a review of the Agreement and secured concessions that in December 1999 produced home rule in Northern Ireland for the first time since 1974. In February 2000, the Assembly was suspended after deadlock on the issue of arms decommissioning. *See also* ADAMS, GERRY; HUME, DAVID; PAISLEY, IAN; ULSTER UNIONISTS

Good Neighbor Policy US policy of non-intervention in the affairs of Latin America, initiated by President Franklin ROOSEVELT. It was stated at the Montevideo Pan-American Conference (1933) that no nation had the right to intervene in the internal affairs of other nations. In 1933 the PLATT AMENDMENT, which had effectively made Cuba a US protectorate, was revoked, and in 1934 US marines were withdrawn from Haiti. THE ORGANIZATION OF AMERICAN STATES (OAS), founded (1945) to foster hemispheric solidarity, was an extension of this policy.

Gorbachev, Mikhail Sergeievich (1931–) Soviet statesman, last president of the SOVIET UNION (1988–91) and general secretary (1985–91) of the COMMUNIST PARTY OF THE SOVIET UNION (CPSU). He joined the Communist Party in 1952 and held a number of Party posts before joining the Central Committee of the Soviet Union in 1971. Gorbachev became a member of the Politburo in 1979 and outmanoeuvred Viktor Grishin to succeed Konstantin CHERNENKO as general secretary. Gorbachev embarked on a programme of reform based on the two principles of PERESTROIKA (restructuring) and GLASNOST (openness). He played a major role in the nuclear DISARMAMENT process, withdrew Soviet troops from Afghanistan and acquiesced to the demise of communist regimes in Eastern Europe (1989–90), effectively ending the COLD WAR. In 1990 Gorbachev agreed to the reunification of West and East Germany and was awarded the Nobel Prize for Peace for his achievements in international relations. In the Soviet Union, he released many political dissidents and initiated constitutional reforms under which a new parliament, the Congress of People's Deputies, was formed, with some of its members directly elected. The benefits of radical social and economic change were slow to take effect, however, and Gorbachev's popularity fell as prices rose. There were also increasing demands from the Union's constituent republics for greater independence. In August 1991, communist hardliners mounted a coup which failed because of the support Gorbachev received from his rival, Boris YELTSIN. With his power diminished, Gorbachev was unable to prevent the collapse of the Soviet Union into its 15 constituent republics and the creation of the COMMONWEALTH OF INDEPENDENT STATES (CIS) under the leadership of Yeltsin.

Gordon, Charles George (1833–85) British soldier and administrator. He distinguished himself in the CRIMEAN WAR (1853–56). In 1859 he went to China, where he fought in the second OPIUM WAR. Remaining in China, he commanded troops during the suppression of the TAIPING REBELLION. Appointed governor general (1877–80) of the Sudan by the khedive of Egypt, ISMAIL PASHA, Gordon crushed rebellions and re-established control. In 1884 he returned to KHARTOUM to evacuate

GORBACHEV, MIKHAIL SERGEIEVICH

Mikhail Gorbachev saw democratization as the key to reviving the ailing economy of the Soviet Union. His attempts to relax state control of the economy were resisted by the Soviet bureaucracy and conservatives within the Communist Party, but were also criticized by reformers for their limited scope and slowness to deliver significant economic progress. His policy of *glasnost* paved the way for the reunification of Germany in 1990.

GORBACHEV IN HIS OWN WORDS

"Democracy is the wholesome and pure air without which a socialist public organization cannot live a full-blooded life."
Party Congress Speech, 25 February 1986

"After leaving the Kremlin, my conscience was clear. The promise I gave to the people when I started the process of *perestroika* was kept: I gave them freedom."
Memoirs, 1995

Egyptian forces threatened by the Mahdi. Gordon was killed two days before the arrival of a relief force.

Gordon, George Hamilton, 4th Earl of Aberdeen *See* Aberdeen, George Hamilton Gordon, 4th Earl of

Gordon Riots (1780) Violent demonstrations against Roman Catholics in London, England. Protestant extremists led by Lord George Gordon (1751–93) marched on Parliament to protest against the Catholic Relief Act (1778), which lifted some restrictions on Catholics. The march degenerated into a week-long riot; *c.*450 people were killed or injured.

Gore, Al (Albert Arnold) (1948–) US statesman, vice president (1993–2000). He was a Democratic congressman (1977–85) and senator (1985–93) for Tennessee. As vice president to Bill Clinton, Gore championed environmental issues. In 1999 he gained the Democratic Party nomination for president.

Göring, Hermann Wilhelm (1893–1946) German Nazi Party leader. A fighter pilot during World War I, he joined the National Socialism movement in 1922. Göring was severely wounded in Adolf Hitler's abortive Munich Putsch in 1923, but managed to escape to Austria. He became addicted to the morphine used to relieve his pain. After returning to Germany, Göring was one of 12 Nazis elected to the Reichstag in 1928. After the Nazis won 230 seats in the 1932 elections, he became president of the Reichstag and used his influence over President Paul von Hindenburg to secure Hitler's appointment as chancellor (1933). In 1933 Göring established the Gestapo (German Secret Police) and built concentration camps for political opponents. He was also responsible for German rearmament and the development of the Luftwaffe. In 1934 he handed control of the Gestapo to Heinrich Himmler. Göring acted as minister for economic affairs (1936–43), enriching himself and the German war machine at the expense of German Jewry. During World War 2, Göring's status declined after the defeat of the Luftwaffe in the Battle of Britain (1940–41) and the Allies' blanket bombing of German cities. In 1943 he was removed from office. In 1945 Göring was captured and sentenced to death at the Nuremberg trials. His plea to be shot rather than hanged was dismissed and Göring poisoned himself.

Gorton, Sir John Grey (1911–) Australian statesman, prime minister (1967–71). After serving as a pilot in World War 2, he was elected to the Senate in 1949. Gorton held several cabinet positions before succeeding Harold Holt as prime minister and leader of the Liberal Party. He maintained Australia's military involvement in the Vietnam War and expanded the role of government in employment and education. He resigned as prime minister in favour of William McMahon, but continued as minister for defence.

Gothic art and architecture Architecture and art of medieval Europe from the 12th to 16th centuries, whose greatest expression was the cathedral. The term "Gothic" was originally applied by Italian artists of the Renaissance to what they regarded as barbaric medieval architecture. It was the successor to the Romanesque style and arose from the search of medieval masons for a way of creating ceiling vaults in stone churches that did not have the effect of pushing the walls outwards. The solution was the ribbed vault. The introduction of pointed arches and buttresses were also technical advances that reduced stress on the walls. An early prototype was the Abbey Church of St Denis, France (1140–44). Ever higher and lighter structures followed, with increasingly intricate vaulting and tracery. In architectural convention, English Gothic is divided into three phases: Early English (Lincoln Cathedral), Decorated (Exeter Cathedral) and Perpendicular (Chapel of King's College, Cambridge). Gothic sculpture was elegant and more realistic than the Romanesque, emphasizing line and silhouette. In painting, the Gothic style manifested itself most successfully in manuscript illumination.

Goths Ancient Germanic people whose two branches, Ostrogoths and Visigoths, tormented the Roman Empire from the 3rd to the 6th century AD. According to the 6th-century Gothic historian Jordanes, the Goths migrated across the Baltic Sea from s Scandinavia to settle in the basin of the River Vistula. In the late 2nd century, they began to move down the River Danube to the shores of the Black Sea. The Goths terrorized Roman provinces and cities in Asia Minor during the 3rd century. By 370 the Goths had divided into two separate groups. The Ostrogoths (Eastern Goths) occupied a large kingdom E of the River Dniester (now Ukraine and Belarus), while the Visigoths (Good Goths) lived between the Dniester and Danube rivers. In 376 the Visigoths were forced s of the Danube by the invasion of the Huns. *See also* Alaric; Theodoric (the Great)

Gottwald, Klement (1896–1953) Czechoslovak statesman, deputy premier (1945–46), premier (1946–48) and president (1948–53). A founder member of the Czech Communist Party in 1921, he became secretary general of the Party in 1929. Gottwald escaped to Moscow after the Nazis invaded Czechoslovakia in 1938. In 1945 he returned to serve under President Eduard Beneš. Gottwald seized power from Beneš in 1948 and established a Stalinist dictatorship, purging and executing his political opponents. He died after falling ill at Joseph Stalin's funeral.

▲ **Grant** was hailed as a Union hero after forcing Robert Lee to surrender at the end of the American Civil War (1861–65), but his presidency was marred by scandal.

► **Gothic art and architecture** Chartres Cathedral, NW France, was one of the earliest examples of High Gothic architecture and established the basic principles of Gothic design. The gallery, which had been a feature of Romanesque churches, was omitted to make room for a three-tier elevation. Built between 1194 and 1220, it was the first cathedral to use ribbed vaults and flying buttresses, which provided better structural support and allowed for greater height and more windows. Chartres Cathedral has *c.*150 stained-glass windows, including a front-facing rose window depicting scenes from the Old Testament. The Cathedral has more than 2000 sculpted figures, many of which reflect the more naturalistic style of sculpture that emerged during the 13th century.

late-gothic north spire
12th-century south spire
audaciously high nave
roof replaced after the fire of 1836
double ambulatory
west front with Royal Portal
south porch, one of three triple doorways

Gould, Jay (1836–92) US financial speculator. With his partner, James Fisk, Gould typified the capitalist "robber barons" who made large fortunes from corrupt dealings in stocks and shares. He and Fisk nearly cornered the gold market, forcing the US Treasury to release gold stocks and leading to the panic of Black Friday (24 September 1869).

Gowon, Yakubu (1934–) Nigerian statesman and soldier, head of state (1966–75). He became leader of Nigeria's military government after the army coup in 1966. In 1967 Gowon divided Nigeria into 12 states, dispossessing the Ibo of their port. The Eastern Region seceded as the republic of Biafra, plunging Nigeria into a civil war (1967–70). After 1970 Gowon tried to reunify Nigeria and modernize the economy. He was overthrown by a military coup in 1975 and fled to Britain.

Gracchus, Gaius Sempronius (153–121 BC) Roman statesman. As tribune (123–121 BC), he continued to implement the social reforms of his brother, Tiberius Gracchus. Gaius sought to check the power of the Senate by uniting the plebeians and the equites (citizens of wealth). These reforms proved short-lived, however, and he was defeated in the election of 121 and killed in the ensuing riots.

Gracchus, Tiberius Sempronius (163–133 BC) Roman statesman and reformer. An aristocrat appalled by the grossly unequal distribution of wealth, as tribune (133 BC) he proposed a bill under which illegally settled public land would be retrieved for the use of landless citizens. The bill was passed but, before it could be implemented, Gracchus was murdered in a scuffle with opposing senators. His brother Gaius Gracchus sought to avenge his death and carry out the reforms.

Grafton, Augustus Henry Fitzroy, 3rd Duke of (1735–1811) British statesman, prime minister (1768–70). He served (1765–66) as secretary of state under Charles Rockingham and was first lord of the treasury (1766–70) under William Pitt (the Elder). Grafton was forced to resign as prime minister following criticism of his mishandling of the American colonies and the Wilkes affair. He served (1771–75) as lord privy seal under Lord North and later (1782–83) under Rockingham and Lord Shelbourne.

Gramsci, Antonio (1891–1937) Italian political theorist and activist. A founder (1921) of the Italian Communist Party (PCI), he became its leader and was elected (1924) to the Chamber of Deputies. In 1926 Benito Mussolini's fascist government banned the PCI and Gramsci was imprisoned. While in prison, Gramsci wrote his *Prison Letters* (1947), which greatly influenced the future shape of Italian communism. Gramsci died shortly after his release.

Granada City in Andalusia, s Spain; capital of Granada province. Founded in the 8th century as a Moorish fortress, it became the capital of the independent Muslim kingdom of Granada in 1238. The last Moorish stronghold in Spain, it surrendered to the Christian armies of FERDINAND V and ISABELLA I (1492). The central splendour of Granada is the ALHAMBRA. Pop. (1991) 254,034.

Granada Province and former kingdom (1232–1492) in southern Spain. The kingdom, which consisted of the present-day provinces of Granada, Málaga and Almería, was founded by Muhammad I of the Nasrid dynasty after the collapse of the ALMORAVIDS. Although it became a vassal of CASTILE in 1246, it was engaged in frequent wars with Castile throughout its history. A series of fifteenth century Castilian campaigns finally resulted in BOABDIL's surrender of the ALHAMBRA in 1492.

Granby, John Manners, Marquess of (1721–70) British soldier, hero of the SEVEN YEARS' WAR (1756–63). In 1759 he became commander of the British forces in the Seven Years' War against France. Granby led the British cavalry in a major victory (1760) over France at Warburg, Westphalia. In 1766 he was appointed commander in chief of the British Army.

Gran Chaco *See* CHACO WAR (1932–35)

Grand Alliance, War of the (1689–97) War between BOURBON France and a coalition of European powers (Holy Roman Empire, England and the United Provinces of the Netherlands). In 1688 LOUIS XIV of France invaded the PALATINATE. In response, HABSBURG Emperor LEOPOLD I formed the Alliance, previously known as the League of AUGSBURG. Louis supported the JACOBITE counter-revolution that ended with JAMES II's defeat at the Battle of the BOYNE (July 1690). On the continent, the conflict became a war of attrition marked by long sieges, such as at Namur, Belgium (1692, 1695). The Anglo-Dutch fleet inflicted a major defeat on the French navy at La Hogue (May 1692). Stalemate made all the belligerents grateful for the Treaty of RIJSWIJK (1697). *See also* FRENCH AND INDIAN WARS; SPANISH SUCCESSION, WAR OF THE

Grand Army of the Republic (GAR) Organization established (1866) by American CIVIL WAR veterans of the Union forces. It was headed by John Logan and Ambrose BURNSIDE. At its peak in 1890, GAR had more than 400,000 members and wielded significant political influence, especially over the Republican Party. In 1879 GAR secured the passage of pension legislation. It also initiated the celebration of Memorial Day. The last member of the organization died in 1956.

Grand Canal Ancient inland waterway between Beijing and Hangzhou, NE China. The first part of the Canal, between the rivers Yangtze and Huai Ho, was built in the 6th century BC. It was extended to Hangzhou in the 6th century AD and to Beijing by KUBLAI KHAN in the 13th century. Total length: *c.*1600km (1000mi).

grandfather clause In US history, legal device used by seven Southern states between 1895 and 1910 to prevent African Americans from voting. For anyone to be exempt from tax, educational or property requirements for voting, they had to have received, or be descended from those who had received, the vote before 1866. As former slaves had not been granted the FRANCHISE until the 15th Amendment (1870), it effectively prevented African Americans from voting while allowing poor whites to do so. It was judged unconstitutional by the Supreme Court in 1915.

Grand Remonstrance (November 1641) Statement of grievances by the LONG PARLIAMENT presented to CHARLES I of England. It listed numerous objections to the royal government and demanded parliamentary approval of ministers. It was passed in the House of Commons by only 11 votes, and Charles rejected it. It hardened the division between the monarchy and Parliament, which culminated in the English CIVIL WAR.

grand tour Part of the education of young people of aristocratic or wealthy English families in the 18th and 19th centuries. Thomas Cook led the first conducted grand tour of Europe in 1856. The grand tour was a leisurely expedition, lasting from two to three years, through France and Italy (especially Rome), returning via the German states and the Low Countries. The sculptures and paintings that the tourists brought back to England have enriched British art collections over the centuries.

Granger movement US agrarian movement. The National Grange, or Order of the Patrons of Husbandry, was founded by Oliver Kelley in 1867. By 1875, the movement had *c.*800,000 national members. Individual local Granges established cooperative grain elevators, mills and stores. Together, Grangers brought pressure on state legislatures to regulate the prices charged by railroads and grain elevators. The monopolistic railroads challenged the constitutional basis of these laws in what became known as "Granger cases". In MUNN V. ILLINOIS (1876), the Supreme Court upheld the state legislation. The Granger movement declined with the rise of other

GREAT DEPRESSION

Severe economic crisis that particularly afflicted the United States and Europe between 1929 and 1933 and had worldwide repercussions throughout the 1930s. At the close of the 1920s, economic factors in the United States, such as overproduction in agriculture and the consequent fall in prices of agricultural products, a downturn in industrial output, unrealistic credit levels and stock-market speculation, signalled the beginning of the crisis. The dramatic collapse of the WALL STREET stock market in October 1929 saw US$30 billion wiped off stock values in the first week. Bank failures became commonplace. The depression in the US economy had a particularly serious effect on Germany, which had been forced to borrow heavily from the US banks in order to pay reparations to the European victors of World War 1. When the US banks recalled their loans, the German banking system collapsed. Industrial production declined by more than 30% in the United States, Germany and countries in Central Europe and the US gross national product (GNP) fell by *c.*50%. At the depth of the Great Depression (1932–33), the number of registered unemployed was *c.*12 million in the United States, *c.*6 million in Germany and *c.*3 million in the United Kingdom. The Depression spread rapidly around the world as governments, faced with falling export earnings, massively increased tariffs on imports, thus further reducing trade. In the United States, President Franklin ROOSEVELT, sensing the national emergency, instituted the NEW DEAL that helped to mitigate the worst effects of the crisis. The US economy, however, only really started to pick up with increased defence spending in the 1940s. In Germany, Adolf HITLER developed a massive work-creation and rearmament project that largely eradicated unemployment by 1936. Elsewhere, the situation gradually improved after 1933 but by 1939 world trade was still below its 1929 levels.

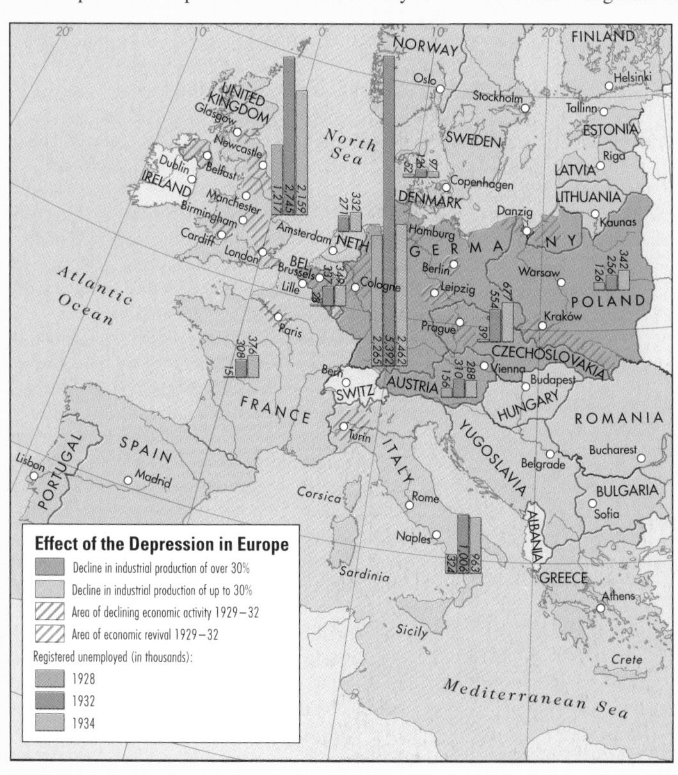

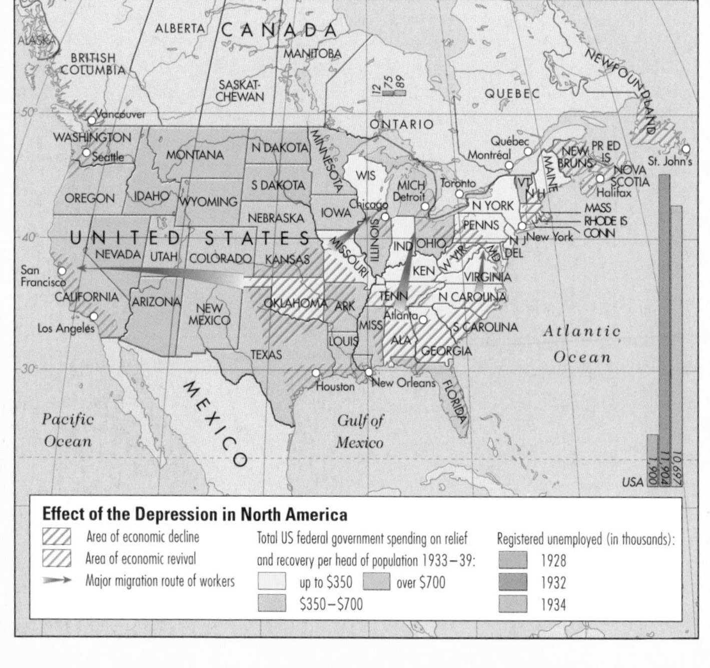

◄ **Europe** Unemployment soared in Germany and Britain at the start of the 1930s.

▲ **United States** In general, the Southern and Midwestern states were worst hit by the Great Depression, and the 1930s saw economic migration to the Northern states and California.

organizations that represented the interests of farmers, such as the Greenback Party. The 20th century witnessed a resurgence of the movement and today there are more than 5000 local Granges in the United States.

Grant, Ulysses Simpson (1822–85) US general and 18th president of the United States (1869–77). He served gallantly under Zachary Taylor and Winfield Scott in the Mexican War (1846–48), but resigned from the army in 1854. Grant rejoined the army at the outbreak of the American Civil War and achieved the first major Union victory of the War at Fort Donelson (February 1862). Now a major general, Grant was blamed for the heavy Union losses at the Battle of Shiloh (April 1862). His reputation was restored, however, by victory in the Siege of Vicksburg (1862–63). In 1864 Abraham Lincoln gave Grant overall command of the Union forces. His plan – to wage a war of attrition against Robert Lee, while William Sherman cut a devastating swathe through Georgia – forced Lee to abandon Richmond and surrender at Appomattox (April 1865). In 1866 Grant became general of the armies of United States. In 1867 President Andrew Johnson appointed him to succeed Edwin Stanton as secretary of war, but Grant resigned (1868) and joined the Republican Party. As president, Grant achieved foreign policy successes but failed to prevent the growth of domestic corruption. Comfortably re-elected in 1872, Grant saw members of his own administration implicated in the Crédit Mobilier corruption scandal, and he retired at the end of his second term. *See also* Reconstruction *See* illustration, page 165

Granvelle, Antoine Perrenot de (1517–86) Spanish statesman and cardinal. In 1560 Philip II of Spain appointed Granvelle chief counsellor to Margaret of Parma, regent of the Netherlands. Effectively governor of the Netherlands, Granvelle's pro-Spanish policies aroused the hostility of William the Silent and the counts Egmont and Hoorn. In 1564 Philip was persuaded to remove Granvelle and he subsequently served as viceroy of Naples (1571–75). *See also* Revolt of the Netherlands

Granville, John Carteret, 1st Earl of (1690–1763) English statesman, secretary of state (1721–24). Granville used his position to gain influence with George II, and to intrigue against Chief Minister Robert Walpole, who sent him to Ireland as lord lieutenant (1724–30). Granville led opposition to Walpole and was an influential minister (1742–44) after Walpole left office. Remaining on good terms with George II, Granville was criticized for supporting the War of the Austrian Succession (1740–48) and accused of putting Hanoverian royal interests above those of Britain.

Gratian (359–83) (Flavius Gratianus) Western Roman emperor (367–83). Co-emperor (367–75) with his father, Valentinian I, Gratian later ruled with his brother Valentinian II. He spent much of his reign fighting invaders in Gaul. On the death of his uncle Valens, emperor of the east, at the Battle of Adrianople (378), Gratian appointed Theodosius in this position. Advised by Saint Ambrose, Gratian tried to stamp out paganism in the empire.

Grattan, Henry (1746–1820) Irish statesman. Grattan entered the Irish Parliament in 1775 and his brilliant oratory soon saw him replace Henry Flood as the leading spokesman for the nationalist cause. In 1782 Grattan successfully gained the repeal of Poyning's Law, which had made Irish legislation subject to English parliamentary approval. The Irish Parliament was only nominally independent, however, since without Catholic emancipation it remained dominated by English patrons. In 1797 Grattan retired, exhausted by his failure to persuade the English government to allow Catholics to sit in Parliament. He returned to actively campaign against the Act of Union (1801) that merged the Irish and British parliaments. As a member of the Westminster Parliament (1805–20), Grattan continued to fight for Catholic emancipation.

Gravettian culture Upper Palaeolithic culture in the Dordogne region, France, and also in Italy *c.*22,000 years ago. It is noted for its distinctive engraving tools and sculptures of the female form. A related culture, the Eastern Gravettian, flourished in E Europe and Russia at about the same time.

Great Awakening Series of 18th-century religious revivals in the American colonies. It was inspired in the 1730s by the preaching of Jonathan Edwards and George Whitefield. Baptist revivals occurred in 1760, and Methodism evolved in the pre-Revolutionary period. The movement led to a great deal of Christian missionary work among the Native American tribes and inspired the foundation of several educational institutions, including Princeton, Brown, and Rutgers universities and Dartmouth College. *See also* Calvinism

Great Britain Island and political entity, lying to the W of continental Europe, consisting of England, Scotland and Wales. Wales was united with England in 1536. The Act of Union (1707) united Scotland with England, and the Act of Union (1801) established the United Kingdom of Great Britain and Ireland. *See also* Ireland, Northern

Great Depression *See* feature article, page 165

Great Exhibition (1851) Display of British and foreign manufactured goods held in Hyde Park, London, and organized by Prince Albert. The Exhibition was housed in the Crystal Palace, and was intended to demonstrate the benefits of industry and international peace and trade. It attracted more than six million visitors.

Great Leap Forward Five-year economic plan in China begun (1958) by Mao Zedong. It aimed to double industrial production and boost agricultural output. Tens of millions of workers were mobilized to smelt steel in primitive furnaces, but much of the steel proved useless. Collective farms were merged into communes, but progress was dashed by a succession of poor harvests. After four years, the Chinese government was forced to concede failure.

Great Schism (1378–1417) Ecclesiastical term used to refer to both the break between the Eastern and Western churches (*see* schism) and the split within the Roman Catholic Church following the election of two rival popes to succeed Gregory XI. In 1309 Pope Clement V moved the papacy from Rome to Avignon, France. The attempt in 1378 to return the papacy to Rome saw the Italian cardinals elect an Italian pope, Urban VI, and the French cardinals elect a rival "antipope", Clement VII (Robert of Geneva). The Great Schism lasted for nearly 40 years, largely because lay political groups aligned themselves with the rival claimants to the papacy. Thus, Valois France and its allies in Scotland and Castile recognized the pope at Avignon, while England, Portugal, most parts of the Holy Roman Empire and N and E Europe, recognized the pope resident at Rome. The Great Schism ended when the Council of Constance (1414–17) established Martin V as sole pope. *See also* conciliar movement

Great Trek (1835–40) Migration of *c.*12,000 Boers (Afrikaners), known as Voortrekkers, from Cape Colony into the South African interior. Their motives were to escape British control and to acquire cheap land. Despite resistance from various African kingdoms, the majority settled in what is now Free State, Transvaal and KwaZulu-Natal. In Natal, a short-lived republic was formed, which fell to the British in 1843.

Great Wall of China Defensive frontier and world heritage site, *c.*2400km (1500mi) long, extending from the Huang Hai (Yellow Sea) to the central Asian Desert, N China. It is an amalgamation of fortifications constructed by various dynasties. Sections of the wall were first built by the Warring States. In 214 BC Qin Shihuangdi ordered that they should be joined to form a unified boundary. The present wall was mostly built 600 years ago by the Ming dynasty as a defence against the Mongol tribes. It averages 7.6m (25ft) high and up to 9m (30ft) thick.

Great Zimbabwe *See* feature article

Grechko, Andrei Antonovich (1903–76) Soviet statesman and general, minister of defence (1967–76). During World War 2, he was an army commander in the Caucasus, Poland and Ukraine. In 1953 Grechko led the Soviet forces that suppressed the rebellion in East Germany. As minister of defence, he organized the Soviet invasion of Czechoslovakia that crushed the Prague Spring (1968).

Greece *See* country feature

Greece, classical Period in Greek history from the defeat of the second Persian invasion in 479 BC to the defeat of Athens in the Peloponnesian War in 404 BC. Warring city-states flourished as centres of trade. Athens, the most wealthy and powerful, developed a democratic system under the guidance of Pericles. Its main rival was the military state of Sparta. Classical Greece was the birthplace of many ideas in art, literature, philosophy and science – among them those of Plato and Aristotle. It is often regarded as the birthplace of Western civilization.

GREAT ZIMBABWE

City-state in southern Africa that flourished between the 11th and 15th centuries AD. The settlement was founded by Iron Age Shona-speaking herders on the hilltop near the modern town of Masvingo, SE Zimbabwe. The rise of Great Zimbabwe is due to the 12th-century discovery of gold on the plateau of NE Botswana and Zimbabwe. The village, strategically located on the route between the gold mines and the Swahili trading posts on the Indian Ocean coast, grew to dominate commerce. Gold was traded for Islamic and Chinese pottery, cowrie shells and beads. The Shona used commerical and military might to carve out a state that stretched from the River Zambezi to the River Limpopo. The Shona élite lived in an intricate complex of granite structures built without the use of mortar. These enclosures were surrounded by *daga* (mud structures) which housed the general population. The name Zimbabwe is derived from a Shona phrase, *dzimba dza mabwe,* meaning "houses of stone". At its height, the city may have had a population of *c.*18,000. Historians disagree on the reason for Great Zimbabwe's rapid decline at the end of the 15th century. Some suggest that its sheer size exhausted the local food supply, while others argue that it collapsed in the face of competition from the gold trade down the Zambezi. Today, the ruins of Great Zimbabwe are a world heritage site.

Great Zimbabwe
Stone structures
Area of daga huts
Acropolis
Great Enclosure
0 0.25 0.5 miles
0 0.5 1 km

◄ **Stone structures** began to be constructed at Great Zimbabawe in *c.*1250.

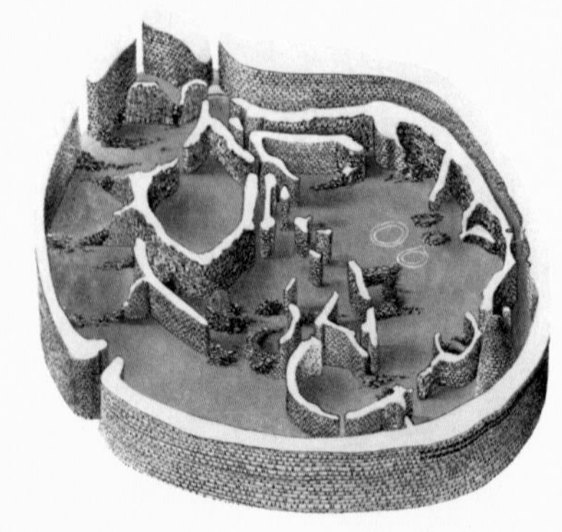

▲ **The Great Enclosure** was used for ritual purposes and contains a conical stone tower.

Greek War of Independence (1821–29) Rebellion of Greeks against the OTTOMAN EMPIRE that led to the establishment of an independent kingdom of Greece in 1832. Inspired by the events of the American and French revolutions and encouraged by ALI PASHA's successful rebellion against the Ottomans in s Albania, Alexandros Ypsilantis and Archbishop Germanos led uprisings of Greeks in Moldavia and the Peloponnesos in March 1821. Ypsilantis was defeated by the Turks in June, but by January 1822 the rebels in w Greece were in control of the Peloponnesos. Aléxandros MAVROKORDÁTOS was elected first president of the Hellenic republic, but internal rivalries flared into an internecine war among the rebels in 1823. By 1824 Geórgios Kountouriótis had emerged as the undisputed leader, but the entire revolution was threatened by the intervention (1825) of Egyptian forces led by IBRAHIM PASHA. The Egyptians rapidly expelled the rebels from the Peloponnesos and recaptured Missolonghi and Athens (1826). Britain, France and Russia then came to the Greeks' aid, destroying the Egyptian fleet at the Battle of NAVARINO (1827). The conflict continued, however, sparking the Russo-Turkish War (1828–29). Hostilities ended with the Treaty of ADRIANOPLE (September 1829) between Russia and Turkey and the London Protocol (February 1830) formally declared Greek independence.

Greeley, Horace (1811–72) US journalist and politician. Greeley founded (1841) the New York *Tribune* and his editorials for the paper greatly influenced national opinion. He supported the formation of labour organizations and criticized business monopolies. Greeley was a constant and vigorous opponent of SLAVERY, criticizing the KANSAS-NEBRASKA ACT (1854). Greeley's advocacy of Western settlement was encapsulated in his advice, "Go West, young man, go West". He was one of the founders of the REPUBLICAN PARTY and criticized Abraham LINCOLN for his failure to fully commit to the ABOLITIONISTS' cause. Greeley initially supported Ulysses GRANT, but the corruption of his administration persuaded Greeley to form the LIBERAL REPUBLICAN PARTY. The Party nominated Greeley for president but he was defeated by Grant.

greenback Popular name for paper money issued (1862) by the US government to help meet the cost of the American Civil War. Greenbacks were authorized by Congress as legal tender but could not be redeemed in gold. A total of US$450 million was issued. They became convertible to gold in 1878. *See also* BLAND-ALLISON ACT

Greenback Party US political organization (1875–84). Deriving its main support from Western farmers, the Party favoured the issue of more GREENBACKS to stimulate the economy and raise farm prices. The Greenbacks presidential candidate, Peter COOPER, lost the 1876 election, but the Party had 14 Congressmen by 1878. It declined in the 1880s. Many supporters joined the FREE SILVER movement, which had similar objectives. *See also* GRANGER MOVEMENT

Greene, Nathanael (1743–86) American general. He was George WASHINGTON's second-in-command during the AMERICAN REVOLUTION (1775–83). In 1776 Greene skillfully led the left wing of the American forces at the battles of TRENTON, PRINCETON and BRANDYWINE. In 1780 he succeeded Horatio GATES as commander in chief of the Southern army. His reorganization and strategy ensured the success of the Carolina Campaign (1780–82) against Lord CORNWALLIS and forced the British to evacuate CHARLESTON (1782).

Greenland World's largest island, in the NW Atlantic Ocean, lying mostly within the Arctic Circle. It is a self-governing province of Denmark. Most of Greenland's inhabitants are INUIT. Its European discovery is attributed to the VIKINGS, who *c.*AD 900 explored the east coast. ERIC THE RED established the first Norse settlement in 986, founding a colony that lasted more than 500 years. In 1380 Greenland became a Danish possession, and a Danish colony was established in 1721. Greenland was incorporated into the kingdom in 1953. Following a referendum, Greenland achieved home rule (1979) and self-government (1981). In 1985 it withdrew from the European Union (EU). Area: 2,175,000sq km (840,000sq mi). Pop. (1993) 55,117.

Green Mountain Boys Militia formed (1764) to uphold settlers' rights to the New Hampshire grants (now Vermont) against claims from New York. Ethan ALLEN assumed command of the Green Mountain Boys in 1770. During the AMERICAN REVOLUTION, they helped capture Fort TICONDEROGA from the British (10 May 1775).

Greenville, Treaty of Fort (1795) Agreement signed by Native Americans of Ohio and Indiana after their defeat by US General Anthony WAYNE in the Battle of Fallen Timbers (August 1794). The Native Americans ceded most of their lands, giving the United States' full control of the Northwest Territory. The Treaty restored peace between the United States and the Native Americans and broke the British-Native American alliance. *See also* TECUMSEH

Gregory I (the Great), Saint (*c.*540–604) Pope (590–604), last of the Latin Fathers of the Church. A Roman aristocrat of senatorial rank, he devoted himself to alleviating poverty and hunger. Gregory was responsible for enforcing the spiritual supremacy of the papacy and establishing the temporal independence of the pope. His reforms included changes in the liturgy, such as the development of what has become known as Gregorian chant. Gregory initiated the conversion of the LOMBARDS and sent Saint AUGUSTINE OF CANTERBURY to England to convert the ANGLO-SAXONS. He encouraged monasticism and his doctrinal writings, derived from Saint AUGUSTINE, were influential in the development of SCHOLASTICISM. His feast day is 12 March. *See* illustration, page 168

Gregory VII, Saint (*c.*1020–85) Pope (1073–85), b. Hildebrand. He condemned lay INVESTITURE, simony (buying and selling of spiritual offices) and clerical marriage, and tried to reassert the spiritual supremacy of the papacy. Emperor HENRY IV opposed Gregory's attempt to abolish lay investitute and denounced him in 1076. Gregory responded by excommunicating Henry. In 1077 Henry was forced to do penance at Canossa, Italy. In 1080 Gregory decreed Henry deposed. Henry retorted by appointing an antipope, Clement III (GUIBERT OF RAVENNA). In 1084 Henry captured Rome, forcing Gregory to flee to Salerno. Gregory failed to establish the independence of the papacy, but his example inspired the Concordat of WORMS (1122). His feast day is 25 May.

Gregory IX (*c.*1155–1241) Pope (1227–41), b. Ugolino di Segni. In 1198 he was appointed a cardinal deacon by his uncle, Pope INNOCENT III. As pope, Gregory excommunicated FREDERICK II in 1227 for his prevarication in leading a CRUSADE to Jerusalem. Gregory then raised an army to attack the Kingdom of Sicily but his forces were repulsed by Frederick. In the 1230s, Gregory strengthened the INQUISITION, placing the DOMINICANS in charge of it. He also ordered the compilation of the *Decretals* (1234), a code of canon law that formed the basis of Catholic ecclesiastical law until 1917. When Frederick invaded (1239) the papal fief of Sardinia, Gregory once again excommunicated him. Frederick's army invaded the Papal States and was besieging Rome when Gregory died.

G

GREECE (HELLAS)

AREA: 131,990sq km (50,961sq mi)
POPULATION: 10,300,000
CAPITAL (POPULATION): Athens (3,072,922)
GOVERNMENT: Multiparty republic
ETHNIC GROUPS: Greek 96%, Macedonian 2%, Turkish 1%, Albanian, Slav
LANGUAGES: Greek (official)
RELIGIONS: Christianity (Eastern Orthodox 97%), Islam 2%
GDP PER CAPITA (1995): US$11,710

Republic in SE Europe. CRETE was the centre of the MINOAN CIVILIZATION, between *c.*3000 and 1450 BC. The Minoans were followed by the MYCENAEAN CIVILIZATION, which prospered until the DORIANS settled (*c.*1200 BC). During the 8th century BC, self-governing CITY-STATES emerged that established colonies around the Mediterranean. This led to conflict with the PHOENICIANS and, in the 5th century BC, with the Persian ACHAEMENID empire. ATHENS and SPARTA led the city-states to victory in the subsequent PERSIAN WARS (499–479 BC) and Athens became leader of the anti-Persian DELIAN LEAGUE. The ATHENIAN EMPIRE flourished as an artistic and cultural centre (*see* GREECE, CLASSICAL). When Athens was defeated in the PELOPONNESIAN WAR (431–404 BC), Sparta and THEBES became involved in a long trial of strength.

In 338 BC MACEDON, led by PHILIP II, became the dominant power. His son, ALEXANDER III (THE GREAT), ushered in the HELLENISTIC AGE. In 146 BC, Greece became a Roman province. Greece formed part of the BYZANTINE EMPIRE from AD 330 to 1453. In 1456 the Ottomans conquered Greece.

The GREEK WAR OF INDEPENDENCE (1821–29) was supported by the European powers, and an independent monarchy was established in 1832. As king of the Hellenes (1863–1913), GEORGE I recovered much Greek territory. In 1913 Greece gained Crete. In 1917 Greece finally entered World War 1 on the Allied side. In 1923, 1.5 million Greeks from Asia Minor were resettled in Greece. In 1936 Ioannis METAXAS became premier. His dictatorship remained neutral at the start of World War 2, but by May 1941 Germany had occupied Greece. By 1944 resistance groups had recaptured most of the land, and the Germans withdrew.

A civil war (1946–49) fought between communist and royalist forces ended in victory for the royalists. In 1951 Greece was admitted to the North Atlantic Treaty Organization (NATO). Konstantinos KARAMANLIS became prime minister in 1955. The economy improved, but tension with Turkey over CYPRUS surfaced. In 1964 Georgios PAPANDREOU became prime minister. In 1967 a military coup established the repressive regime of the "Greek Colonels". In 1973 the monarchy was abolished and Greece became a presidential republic. Civil unrest led to the 1974 restoration of civilian government, headed by Karamanlis. In 1981 Greece joined the European Community, and Andreas PAPANDREOU became Greece's first socialist prime minister (1981–89, 1993–96). The 1996 election was won by the Panhellenic Socialist Party (PASOK) led by Kostas Simitis. Simitis was re-elected in 2000, pledging to take Greece into the European single currency (the euro).

Gregory XI (1330–78) Pope (1370–78), b. Pierre Roger de Beaufort. He was the last of the AVIGNON popes. Appointed a cardinal (1348) by his uncle, Pope CLEMENT VI, Gregory succeeded URBAN V as pope in 1370. In 1375 Florence was defeated in a war with the Papal States. Gregory heeded the advice of CATHERINE OF SIENA and moved the papacy back to Rome in 1377. His concern for recovering the Papal States led to war. Gregory issued the first condemnation of John WYCLIFFE's teachings.

Gregory XII (*c*.1327–1417) Pope (1406–15), b. France as Angelo Correr. He was made a cardinal (1405) by Pope Innocent VII, whom he succeeded as pope. Gregory's pontificate was disputed by Benedict XIII, the Avignon contender for the papacy. The Council of Pisa (1409) elected a second antipope, Alexander V, but Gregory objected. His failure to end the GREAT SCHISM, led the Council of CONSTANCE to depose both antipopes and Gregory resigned (1415) in favour of MARTIN V.

G

Gregory XIII (1502–85) Pope (1572–85), b. Ugo Buoncompagni. He was sent (1561) by Pope Pius IV to the Council of TRENT. Gregory was appointed a cardinal in 1565 and succeeded PIUS V as pope in 1572. He promoted the COUNTER-REFORMATION, seeking to fulfil the decrees of the Council of Trent. Gregory supported education, training for the clergy and missionary activity, especially that of the JESUITS. Gregory has been criticized for celebrating the SAINT BARTHOLOMEW'S DAY MASSACRE (1572) with a *Te Deum* at Rome. He is best known, however, for his reform of the Julian calendar (1582).

Gregory of Nazianzus, Saint (*c*.330–90) Roman Catholic bishop, theologian and one of the Fathers of the Church. He was born in Cappadocia (now part of Turkey) and became a friend of Saint BASIL I (THE GREAT), who made him a bishop. In 381 the Second Council of CONSTANTINOPLE made Gregory bishop of Constantinople, in which position he upheld the NICENE CREED against the heresy of ARIANISM. Gregory soon retired to a monastery, where he wrote more than 680 poems, letters and orations. His most important contribution was the exposition of the TRINITY: God the Father, God the Son, and God the Holy Spirit.

Gregory of Tours, Saint (538–94) Bishop and historian of Frankish Gaul. Becoming bishop of Tours in 573, Gregory used his influence to defuse several feuds within the MEROVINGIAN dynasty. He is best known, however, for his monumental *History of the Franks* (*c*.576–91), consisting of three sections on 6th-century Franco-Roman history. The *History* is a dramatic and vivid first-hand account of Merovingian Gaul. He also wrote on miracles, martyrs and some of the Fathers of the Church.

▲ **Gregory I (the Great)** shown here in a painting by Carlo Saraceni (1580–1620). Gregory sanctioned the use of force to convert heathens to Christianity.

GRENADA

AREA: 344sq km (133sq mi)
POPULATION: 99,000
CAPITAL (POPULATION): St George's (4788)
GOVERNMENT: Multiparty republic
ETHNIC GROUPS: Of African descent
LANGUAGES: English (official), Creole
RELIGIONS: Roman Catholic 53%, Protestant 25%
GDP PER CAPITA (1994): US$2437

Grenada (Isle of Spice) Republic in the WEST INDIES, the most southerly of the Lesser Antilles. It consists of the island of Grenada and the Grenadines dependency. First sighted (1498) by Christopher COLUMBUS, the islands were then inhabited by the CARIB. In the mid-17th century, Grenada was settled by the French. It became a permanent British possession in 1783 and the British imported African slaves to work on the sugar plantations. After a number of rebellions, slavery was abolished in 1833. Grenada served as the headquarters of the British Windward Islands from 1885 until 1958, when it joined the West Indies Federation. In 1962 the Federation collapsed and Grenada became a self-governing state in 1967. In 1974 Grenada gained independence within the Commonwealth of Nations, the first of the six West Indies Associated States to do so. Eric Gairy became the first prime minister of an independent Grenada, and brutally imposed his authority. In 1979 the Marxist New Jewel Movement, led by Maurice Bishop, seized power and proclaimed a People's Revolutionary Government. Disagreements within the PRG led to a military coup (October 1983) and the execution of Bishop and several other ministers. Within a week of the coup, United States' forces had occupied the island and handed power to Governor General Paul Scoon. The 1984 elections were won by Herbert Blaize of the New National Party. In 1985 US forces withdrew from Grenada. Elections in 1995 were won by Keith Mitchell. Area: 344sq km (133sq mi). Pop. (1995 est.) 96,000. *See also* West Indies map

Grenville, George (1712–70) British statesman, prime minister (1763–65). He entered Parliament in 1741, serving as navy treasurer (1756–62) and first lord of the Admiralty (1762–63). As prime minister, Grenville was responsible for the mismanagement of the John WILKES controversy and the STAMP ACT and TOWNSHEND ACTS, which provoked violent reaction in the colonies, especially the Americas. These events, coupled with Grenville's insensitive handling of GEORGE III's first illness, eventually caused his dismissal from office.

Grenville, Sir Richard (1542–91) English naval commander, cousin of Sir Walter RALEIGH. In 1585 he commanded the fleet that carried Raleigh's colonists to Roanoke, Virginia. In 1591, as commander of the *Revenge*, Grenville bravely fought alone against a Spanish fleet off the Azores. He was mortally wounded in the 15-hour battle.

Grenville, William Wyndham, Baron (1759–1834) British statesman, son of George GRENVILLE. He entered Parliament in 1782, later serving as home secretary (1790) and foreign secretary (1791–1801). A longtime friend of William PITT (THE YOUNGER), they both resigned (1801) over GEORGE III's refusal to grant CATHOLIC EMANCIPATION. After Pitt's death, Grenville formed the coalition government of the "Ministry of all the Talents" (1806–07), which abolished the British overseas slave trade in 1807. Grenville was dismissed by George III for supporting a Catholic Relief Bill.

Gresham, Sir Thomas (1519?–79) English financier. In 1566 he founded the Royal Exchange, London. Gresham acted as chief financial adviser to ELIZABETH I. In 1579 he founded Gresham College, London, which later evolved into the Royal Society. He was erroneously attributed with **Gresham's law**, which states that "bad money drives out good". If two coins have the same face value but one has a higher content of precious metals then that one will be driven out of circulation by the less precious coin and melted down, hoarded or used for foreign exchange.

Grey, Charles, 2nd Earl (1764–1845) British statesman, prime minister (1830–34). He entered Parliament in 1786, allying himself with Charles James Fox and the radical WHIGS. Grey served as foreign secretary (1806–07) in the "Ministry of All the Talents", headed by William GRENVILLE. His support for CATHOLIC EMANCIPATION lost him his seat in Parliament (1807). As prime minister, Grey was largely responsible for the REFORM ACT (1832). He also steered the Act abolishing slavery in the colonies (1833). In 1834 he resigned over the Irish question.

Grey, Sir George (1812–98) British colonial administrator, governor of South Australia (1841) and prime minister of New Zealand (1877–79). As governor of New Zealand (1845–53, 1861–68), Grey negotiated a peaceful settlement of the MAORI WARS.

Grey, Lady Jane (1537–54) Queen of England for nine days in July 1553, great-granddaughter of HENRY VII. In May 1553 she married Guildford Dudley, son of the Duke of NORTHUMBERLAND, regent for the ailing EDWARD VI. On Edward VI's death, Jane was proclaimed queen, but the rightful heir, MARY I, was almost universally preferred. Lady Jane and her husband were executed.

Grey of Fallodon, Edward, Viscount (1862–1933) English statesman. He is Britain's longest serving foreign secretary (1905–16). Grey entered Parliament as a Liberal in 1882. He was an architect of the ENTENTE CORDIALE (1907), which promised British military support for France against Germany. He also helped foster support from the United States for the Allied cause in WORLD WAR I.

Griffith, Arthur (1872–1922) Irish statesman, president of the Irish Free State (1922). From 1899 he edited the republican newspaper, *United Irishman*. In 1905 Griffith founded SINN FÉIN. He took no part in the EASTER RISING (1916), but was imprisoned by the British (1916–18). In 1919 he became vice president of the unofficial Irish Parliament, the *Dáil Éireann*. Griffith and Michael COLLINS were the chief negotiators of the Anglo-Irish Treaty (1921) that created the Irish Free State and *de facto* acceptance of partition. Eamon DE VALERA rejected the settlement and Griffith became president.

Grimaldi Genoese family who have held power in MONACO since the 15th century. The Grimaldi and the FIESCHI, allied with the ANGEVIN kings of Naples, led the GUELPH faction in the struggle against Emperor FREDERICK II for control of GENOA. In 1297 the Grimaldis captured Monaco, which they used as a base for the war against the GHIBELLINES. For the next century they fought to secure Monaco, finally establishing possession in 1419. The family maintained a strong presence in Genoa, six Grimaldis served as DOGES between 1528 and 1797. The current Prince of Monaco, Rainier III (r.1949–), is a Grimaldi.

Grimké, Sarah Moore (1792–1873) US ABOLITIONIST and pioneer of the WOMEN'S RIGHTS MOVEMENT. Sarah and her sister, **Angelina** (1805–79), were born into a slaveholding Southern family, joining the Quakers in the 1820s. Sarah and Angelica became the first women in the United States to publicly appeal for the abolition of SLAVERY in their pamphlets and lecture tours. When they were criticized for behaving in a way inappropriate for women, the sisters were inspired to begin their crusade for women's rights. In 1838 Angelina married fellow anti-slavery crusader, Theodore WELD.

Grimond, Jo (Joseph), Baron (1913–93) British politician, leader of the LIBERAL PARTY (1956–67). He entered Parliament in 1950. Grimond modernized the Liberal Party and proposed a political realignment that won new supporters for the Liberals. He opposed nuclear weapons and favoured Britain's entry into the European Community (EC). After the forced resignation of Jeremy Thorpe (1976), Grimond became caretaker leader of the Party until David STEEL took over.

Grivas, Georgios (1898–1974) Greek Cypriot leader of the guerrilla force, EOKA (National Organization for the Cyprus Struggle). EOKA led the rebellion (1955–59) against British rule in CYPRUS. Grivas opposed the 1959

treaty that established an independent Cyprus and continued to seek ENOSIS (union) with Greece. In 1967 Grivas was forced into exile after members of his national guard killed a number of Turkish Cypriots. In 1971 he returned secretly to Cyprus to lead a terrorist campaign against the government of Archbishop MAKARIOS.

Gromyko, Andrei (1909–89) Soviet statesman, foreign minister (1957–85) and president (1985–88). As Soviet ambassador to the United States (1943–46), he took part in the YALTA and POTSDAM peace conferences (1945). He then acted as the permanent Soviet delegate to the United Nations (1946–48). As foreign minister, Gromyko represented the Soviet Union throughout most of the COLD WAR and helped prepare the agenda for the DÉTENTE talks between Leonid BREZHNEV and Richard NIXON. He was succeeded as foreign minister by Eduard SHEVARDNADZE and given the largely honorary role of president by Mikhail GORBACHEV.

Grósz, Károly (1930–96) Hungarian statesman, prime minister (1987–88). He was head of the propaganda department (1968–79) of the Hungarian Socialist Workers' Party (HSWP) and Party chief in Budapest (1984–87) before becoming prime minister. In 1988 Grósz succeeded Janos KÁDÁR as general secretary of the HSWP. Although Grosz began the process of economic reform, introducing income and value-added taxes, he was opposed to social and political change and when the HSWP reconstituted itself as the Hungarian Socialist Party (October 1989), Grósz was replaced by Rezso Nyers.

Grotius, Hugo (1583–1645) Dutch jurist and scholar, b. Huig de Groot. He was taught by Johannes Uyttenbogaert, a supporter of Jacobus ARMINIUS and author of the *Remonstrance* (1610). He called for the freedom of the seas in *On the Law of Prize and Booty* (1604), written for the Dutch EAST INDIA COMPANY. In 1618 Grotius was imprisoned for his support of Johan van OLDENBARNEVELT and the province of Holland against Prince MAURICE. He escaped from prison (1621) hidden in a trunk of books. While in exile in Paris. Grotius wrote *On the Law of War and Peace* (1625), which forms the basis of modern international law. He later served (1634–44) as the Swedish ambassador to France. *See also* REMONSTRANT

Group of Eight (G8) (formerly Group of Seven – G7) Eight nations that meet for an annual economic summit meeting. In 1975 the heads of government of what were regarded as the world's seven wealthiest nations – the United States, Japan, Germany, Britian, France, Canada and Italy – met in the first of these meetings. The changing world economy has led other countries to seek membership. In 1997 Russia was formally admitted to the Group.

Guadalcanal, Battle of (August 1942–February 1943) Sustained conflict between Allied and Japanese forces during WORLD WAR 2, fought on and around the Pacific island of Guadalcanal, largest of the Solomon Islands. Japan captured Guadalcanal in July 1942. In August 1942 US marines landed on the island, seizing the newly constructed airfield. Both sides began to heavily reinforce and a bitter war of attrition began in the jungles of Guadalcanal. Both sides lost 24 warships in six separate naval battles. The Japanese were eventually forced to evacuate the island. The Battle cost 24,000 Japanese lives and 1600 US lives.

Guadalupe Hidalgo, Treaty of (2 February 1848) Peace settlement ending the MEXICAN WAR. Mexico ceded the present states of Texas, New Mexico, Arizona, California, Nevada and Utah, plus parts of Colorado and Wyoming to the United States. The United States paid US$15 million in compensation. The Treaty led to the Mexican Civil War and, after the failures of the COMPROMISE OF 1850 and the KANSAS-NEBRASKA ACT (1854), contributed to the American CIVIL WAR.

Guam Southernmost and largest of the Mariana Islands in the W Pacific Ocean; the capital is Agaña. Guam was discovered (1521) by Ferdinand MAGELLAN. It was ruled by Spain from 1668 until 1898, when it was ceded to the United States at the end of the SPANISH-AMERICAN WAR. It was the first US territory to be occupied (1941–44) by the Japanese during World War 2. Today, Guam is an unincorporated US territory. Area: 541sq km (209sq mi). Pop. (1992 est.) 140,200.

Guangxu (1871–1908) Chinese emperor (1875–1908) of the QING dynasty. He was dominated by his mother, Empress Dowager CIXI, who acted as regent until 1887. Guangxu tried to assert his authority by supporting the HUNDRED DAYS OF REFORM (1898), but the movement was crushed by Cixi and he was imprisoned his palace, where he died in suspicious circumstances. He was succeeded by his nephew, PU YI.

Guangzhou (Canton) Largest city in S China, on the River Pearl; capital of Guangdong province. The first known settlement on the site was established in the 11th century BC by the Pai Yüeh, a Shan people. It was incorporated into China in the 3rd century BC. Guangzhou flourished on trade with the Arabs during the TANG dynasty. Under the SONG dynasty, the city's dramatic growth required the building of a secondary settlement. The MING dynasty brought further growth and a massive rebuilding project. European traders replaced the Arabs during the 16th and 17th centuries, and the British East India Company opened an office in the city in 1685. The First OPIUM WAR (1839–42) saw Guangzhou become a treaty port and it was occupied by Anglo-French forces during the Second OPIUM WAR (1856–60). The city was at the centre of the TAIPING REBELLION (1850–64). Guangzhou was the birthplace of SUN YAT-SEN, and it was the focal point of the revolution against the MANCHU dynasty (1911). A military academy was established in 1924 under CHIANG KAI-SHEK. Occupied by the Japanese during World War 2, Canton did not regain its former prosperity until after the communists came to power (1949). Pop. (1993 est.) 3,560,000.

Guaraní Native South American tribe and language. The Guaraní are native to E Paraguay and neighbouring areas of Argentina and Brazil. During the 14th and 15th centuries, they moved inland along the Río de la Plata. The tribe's population has decreased greatly, although most Paraguayans are descended from Guaraní. Their language has survived as Paraguay's second national language.

Guatemala *See* country feature

Guchkov, Aleksandr Ivanovich (1862–1936) Russian statesman. He was a founder of the Octobrist Party (1905), which supported the October Manifesto issued by NICHOLAS II during the RUSSIAN REVOLUTION OF 1905. Guchkov served (1910–11) as president of the State Duma, but resigned in protest against imperial interference in parliamentary government. In 1915 he became chairman of the Central War Industries Committee. After the RUSSIAN REVOLUTION (1917), Guchkov formally accepted the tsar's abdication and served as minister of war (1917) in KERENSKY's provisional government. When the BOLSHEVIKS seized power in November 1917, Guchkov went into exile in Paris.

Guderian, Heinz (1888–1953) German general and tank expert. His advocacy of heavily armoured formations, backed by air power, attracted the support of Adolf HITLER. In 1938 Guderian was appointed chief of Germany's *Panzer* troops. In the early years (1939–41) of

G

GUATEMALA

AREA: 108,890sq km (42,042sq mi)
POPULATION: 9,745,000
CAPITAL (POPULATION): Guatemala City (2,000,000)
GOVERNMENT: Republic
ETHNIC GROUPS: Native American 45%, Ladino (mixed Hispanic and Native American) 45%, White 5%, Black 2%, others (including Chinese) 3%
LANGUAGES: Spanish (official)
RELIGIONS: Christianity (Roman Catholic 75%, Protestant 25%)
GDP PER CAPITA (1995): US$3340

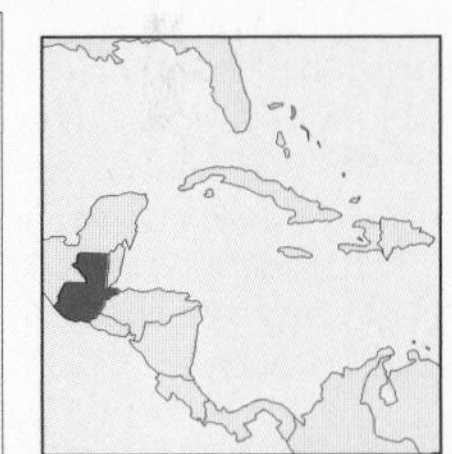

Republic in Central America. Between AD 300 and 900, the Quiché branch of the MAYA ruled much of Guatemala but inexplicably abandoned their cities on the N plains. The Quiché ruins at Tikal are the tallest temple pyramids in the Americas. In 1523–24 Spanish conquistador Pedro de ALVARADO defeated the native tribes. The first Spanish capital of Guatemala (now Antigua) was destroyed by an earthquake in 1773 and was relocated to present-day Guatemala City.

In 1821 Guatemala gained independence from Spain, but formed part of the Mexican Empire until the Empire collapsed in 1823 and the CENTRAL AMERICAN FEDERATION was created. The Federation was undermined by Rafael Carrera (1814–65) and collapsed in 1839. Carrera dominated Guatemalan government until his death. In 1871 Miguel García Granados and Justo Barrios launched a successful revolution. García Granados implemented liberal reforms and improved the nation's infrastructure. He died in an invasion of El Salvador (1885). Manuel Estrada Cabrera established a dictatorship (1898–1920) that brought limited economic improvements at great cost to civil liberties. Estrada Cabrera was overthrown in an armed revolt and a period of confusion ensued. The dictatorship of Jorge Ubico (1931–44) again achieved material improvement through military repression. In 1941 Ubico joined the Allies in World War 2 and Guatemala nationalized the German-owned coffee plantations.

After World War 2, Guatemala embarked on democratic reforms, further nationalization of plantations and land redistribution. Worried about the impact on the US-owned United Fruit Company, the CENTRAL INTELLIGENCE AGENCY (CIA) backed the armed overthrow of Jacobo Arbenz's socialist regime. In 1960 the mainly Quiché Guatemalan Revolutionary National Unity Movement (URNG) began a guerrilla war, which claimed more than 100,000 lives. During the 1960s and 1970s, Guatemala was beset by terrorism, human rights abuses, fraudulent elections and government "death squads". In 1976 Guatemala City was devastated by an earthquake, which killed *c.*22,000 people. In 1983 Guatemala reduced its claims to BELIZE. In 1985, after the United States withdrew its support for the military, Guatemala elected its first civilian president for 15 years. In 1996 Alvaro Arzú Irigoyen was elected president and a peace agreement with the URNG ended 35 years of civil war. In 1999 Alfonso Portillo was elected president, despite admitting that he had killed two men.

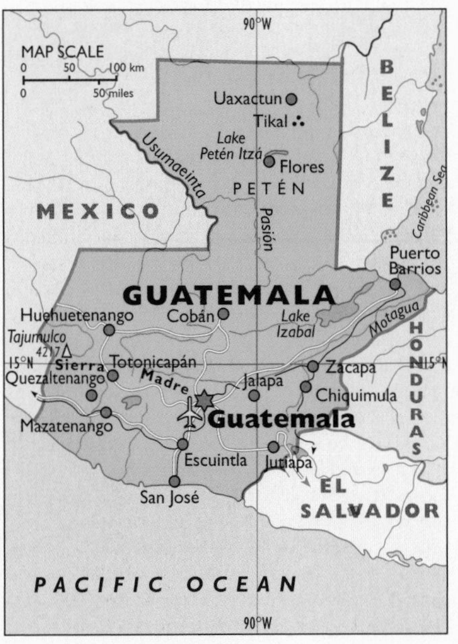

WORLD WAR 2, he employed *Blitzkrieg* tactics to gain decisive victories in Poland, France and the Soviet Union. In 1942 Guderian was dismissed for withdrawing in the face of a Russian counter-offensive, but was appointed inspector general of armoured troops in 1943. Guderian became acting chief of staff in 1944, but repeated interference from Hitler drove him to resign in March 1945.

Guelph (Ger. Welf) Political faction in Germany and Italy between the 12th and 14th centuries. In Germany, they supported the dukes of Bavaria in their struggle with the HOHENSTAUFEN dukes of Swabia during the 12th century for control of the HOLY ROMAN EMPIRE. The struggle intensified at the start of the 13th century with a dispute over the imperial succession between the Guelph OTTO IV and the Hohenstaufen Frederick of Sicily (later Emperor FREDERICK II). Italy was split between imperial and anti-imperial camps when the Hohenstaufen Emperor FREDERICK I (BARBAROSSA) tried to conquer N Italy. In the Italian cities, the Guelphs broadly supported the papacy and represented mercantile interests, while the GHIBELLINES supported the Emperor and favoured the aristocracy. In 1266, with the aid of Charles of Anjou, the Guelphs established control of Florence. Other cities dominated by the Guelphs included Milan, Genoa and Bologna, while the Ghibellines controlled Pisa, Siena and Arezzo. The wars ended in the 14th century and the Guelphs went into decline as a political force.

Guernica Town in Vizcaya province, N Spain. It is a centre of BASQUE nationalism. The bombing of Guernica by German aircraft (1937) during the Spanish CIVIL WAR inspired Picasso's masterpiece *Guernica* (1937).

Guesclin, Bertrand du (*c*.1320–80) French soldier. He became a hero in the early stages of the HUNDRED YEARS' WAR (1337–1453). Guesclin avoided pitched battles with the English, preferring to use siege and guerrilla tactics. In 1356–57 he successfully defended the city of Rennes from the English. In 1364 Guesclin defeated Charles II (the Bad) of Navarre at the Battle of Cocherel, but later in the year he was defeated and captured at the Battle of Auray. A ransom of 40,000 gold francs was paid for Guesclin's release. In 1370 CHARLES V of France made him constable of France after he had aided Henry II of Castile. During the 1370s, Guesclin regained much of France from the English.

Guevara, "Che" (Ernesto) (1928–67) Cuban revolutionary leader, b, Argentina. In 1953 Guevara travelled to Guatemala, where he witnessed the overthrow of the socialist regime in a US-sponsored coup. Guevara moved to Mexico, where he became associated with Fidel CASTRO. Guevara was wounded in the failed attempt to overthrow the dictatorship of Fulgencio BATISTA in Cuba (1956). Guevara and Castro regrouped and mounted a second, successful rebellion. Guevara became minister of industry (1961–65) and president of the National Bank, leading the economic reform of Cuba. In 1965 he disappeared, apparently helping Patrice LUMUMBA in the civil war in the Congo. Guevara was captured and killed while trying to establish a communist guerrilla base in Bolivia. His remains were returned to Cuba in 1997.

Guggenheim US family of industrialists and philanthropists. **Meyer Guggenheim** (1828–1905), b. Switzerland, emigrated to Philadelphia (1847) and prospered in the lace import business. He bought silver and lead mines in Colorado. Meyer retired, leaving control of his enterprises to his seven living sons. **Daniel** Guggenheim (1856–1930) took the leading role in expanding the family businesses. A prominent philanthropist, he established the Daniel and Florence Guggenheim Foundation. **Solomon** Guggenheim (1861–1949) endowed a foundation to foster nonobjective art: the Guggenheim Museum opened in New York City in 1959. **Simon** Guggenheim (1867–1941) was a US senator. In memory of his son, he established the John Simon Guggenheim Memorial Foundation, which offers fellowships to scholars and artists. **Harry Frank** Guggenheim (1890–1971) was US ambassador to Cuba (1929–33). **Peggy** Guggenheim (1898–1979) was a patron and collector of modern art.

Guibert of Ravenna (*c*.1025–1110) Antipope as Clement III (1080–1100). As imperial chancellor in Italy (1057–63), Guibert supported HENRY IV of Germany in his struggles against the papacy. When Pope GREGORY VII excommunicated Henry in 1080, Henry summoned a council that declared Pope Gregory deposed and named Guibert as his successor. Backed by Henry's troops, Guibert entered Rome in 1083 and was acclaimed as Pope Clement III (1084). Clement then crowned Henry as emperor.

Guicciardini, Francesco (1483–1540) Italian statesman and historian. He first attracted attention as Florentine ambassador (1512–14) to FERDINAND V of Spain. Pope LEO X appointed him governor of Modena (1516) and governor of Reggio (1517). Guicciardini brutally imposed order on these new, outlying parts of the Papal States. In 1521 he was appointed commissioner general of the papal army. In 1523 Guicciardini successfully defended Modena, but lost Reggio. He was the principal architect of the League of Cognac, an alliance between FRANCIS I of France and Pope CLEMENT VII against Emperor CHARLES V. The League failed, however, to prevent the fall of Rome and FLORENCE in 1527. The establishment of a Florentine republic (1529) forced Guicciardini to seek shelter in the papal court. In 1534 the MEDICI were restored as rulers of Florence and Guicciardini was rehabilitated. From *c*.1536 until his death, Guicciardini worked on the *History of Italy*, a detailed and sceptical analysis of events in Italy between 1494 and 1534. Other works include *Remarks* (1512–30). *See also* ITALIAN WARS

guild Association of merchants or craftsmen in medieval Europe. The merchant guilds, which began to appear in the 11th century, probably developed from earlier religious associations. They controlled markets, weights and measures, and tolls, and sometimes became more or less synonymous with municipal government, negotiating charters under which their towns received borough status. In the 13th century, the political and economic power of the merchant guilds began to usurped by the craft guilds. These had first developed in the 12th century, each establishing standards for their particular craft. They had a strict hierarchy consisting of masters, journeymen and apprentices, and attempted to impose monopolies which determined prices. The guilds began to decline in the 16th century and had lost all influence by the time they were formally abolished in the 19th century.

Guildford Four Three men and a woman of Irish extraction convicted in an English court of terrorist bombings in Guildford and Woolwich, S England, in 1975. Their life sentences were quashed on appeal in 1989. *See also* BIRMINGHAM SIX

guillotine Mechanized device for execution by beheading adopted during the FRENCH REVOLUTION. First used in 1792, *c*.1400 died under it during the REIGN OF TERROR. It remained in use in France until the abolition of capital punishment in 1981. The term also describes a British parliamentary procedure, first used in 1887, by which a set time is allotted to various stages of a bill in order to speed its passage into law.

Guinea *See* country feature

Guinea-Bissau *See* country feature

Guiscard, Robert (1015–85) (Robert de Hauteville) NORMAN conqueror of S Italy, son of Tancred de Hauteville. In *c*.1047 he was sent by his half-brother Drogo, Count of Apulia, to attack Byzantine territory in Calabria. In 1053 Guiscard led a Norman army to victory over the combined forces of the Byzantines, Lombards and Pope LEO IX. Following the death of Drogo, he then established control over Apulia and Calabria with the aid of his brother Roger (later ROGER I). In 1060, with the blessing of the pope, Robert launched a successful expedition to drive the Arabs out of SICILY. Subsequently fighting to expand the kingdom, he brought an end to Byzantine rule in S Italy in 1071. In 1084 Robert helped Pope GREGORY VII repel HENRY IV of Germany's attack on Rome.

Guise, House of Ducal house of Lorraine, the most powerful family in 16th-century France. The House was founded by **Claude de Lorraine** (1496–1550). Claude was wounded (1515) in the ITALIAN WARS and his defeat of the English (1522) brought him the governorship of Champagne and Burgundy. His eldest son, **François** (1519–63), was also seriously wounded fighting for

GUINEA

AREA: 245,860sq km (94,927sq mi)
POPULATION: 6,116,000
CAPITAL (POPULATION): Conakry (705,000)
GOVERNMENT: Multiparty republic
ETHNIC GROUPS: Fulani 40%, Malinke 26%, Susu 11%, Kissi 7%, Kpelle 5%
LANGUAGES: French (official)
RELIGIONS: Islam 85%, traditional beliefs 5%, Christianity 2%
GDP PER CAPITA (1994): US$461

Republic in West Africa. The NE Guinea plains formed part of the medieval empire of GHANA. The Malinke formed the MALI empire, which dominated the region from the 13th century. It was replaced by the SONGHAI empire.

In the mid-15th century Portuguese explorers arrived, and the SLAVE TRADE began soon afterwards. From the 17th century, other European slave traders became active in Guinea. In the early 18th century, the FULANI – who had established an empire based on the Fouta Djallon region – embarked on a JIHAD. In 1849 France established a protectorate over the coastal region, which became the colony of French Guinea in 1891. In 1895 the colony was subsumed into the Federation of French West Africa. France exploited Guinea's bauxite deposits and mining unions developed.

In 1958 Guinea voted against membership of the French Community and France severed all aid. Guinea's first post-colonial president (1958–84), Sékou TOURÉ, adopted a Marxist programme of reform and embraced PAN-AFRICANISM. Opposition parties were banned and dissent was brutally suppressed. Conakry acted as the headquarters for independence movements in Portuguese Guinea (now GUINEA-BISSAU), which launched an unsuccessful invasion of Guinea in 1970. A military coup followed Touré's death and Colonel Lansana Conté established (1984) the Military Committee for National Recovery (CMRN). Conté improved relations with the West and introduced free-market reforms. In 1992 civil unrest forced the introduction of a multiparty system. Conté was elected president amid claims of electoral fraud. In 1996 a military coup was defeated. Conté was re-elected in 1998.

GUINEA-BISSAU

AREA: 36,120sq km (13,946sq mi)
POPULATION: 1,006,000
CAPITAL (POPULATION): Bissau (126,900)
GOVERNMENT: Multiparty republic
ETHNIC GROUPS: Balante 27%, Fulani (or Peul) 23%, Malinke (Mandingo or Mandinka) 12%, Mandyako 11%, Pepel 10%
LANGUAGES: Portuguese (official)
RELIGIONS: Traditional beliefs 54%, Islam 38%, Christianity 8%
GDP PER CAPITA (1995): US$790

Republic in West Africa. The first record of Guinea-Bissau dates from the end of the GHANA empire. The region later formed part of the MALI empire. It was first visited by Portuguese navigators in 1446. Between the 15th and early 19th centuries, Portugal used the Guinea coast as a base for the SLAVE TRADE. In 1836 Portugal appointed a governor to administer Guinea-Bissau and the CAPE VERDE Islands, but in 1879 the two territories were separated and Guinea-Bissau became the colony of Portuguese Guinea. Portugal brutally imposed colonial rule.

In 1956 African nationalists, led by Amilcar CABRAL, founded the African Party for the Independence of Guinea and Cape Verde (PAIGC). Portugal's determination to keep its empire forced the PAIGC to begin a guerrilla war (1963), and by 1968 it held two-thirds of the country. In 1972 a rebel National Assembly in the PAIGC-controlled area voted to establish the independent republic of Guinea-Bissau.

In 1974 it formally achieved independence. Amilcar Cabral's half-brother, Luís de Almeida Cabral, became president. In 1980 an army coup led by Major João Vieira overthrew Luís Cabral. The new Revolutionary Council resisted unification with Cape Verde, concentrating on national policies and socialist reforms. In 1991 the PAIGC voted to introduce a multiparty system. The PAIGC won the 1994 elections, and Vieira was re-elected president. In 1999, after an 11-month civil war, Viera was overthrown by rebels led by General Ansumane Mane. Kumba Yalá of the Party for Social Renovation defeated the PAIGC in the 2000 elections.

FRANCIS I of France. François and Anne de MONTMORENCY were leading advisers to HENRY II. François managed the successful defence of Metz (1552) against Emperor CHARLES V and captured Calais from the English (1558). The Guise faction dominated government during the reign of FRANCIS II, but their influence was challenged when CATHERINE DE' MEDICI became regent for CHARLES IX. An anti-Guise conspiracy, led by Louis I de Bourbon, Prince de CONDÉ, was ruthlessly dispatched by François in 1560. François supervised the massacre of HUGUENOTS at Vassy (1562), precipitating the French Wars of RELIGION. He was assassinated by a Huguenot. Claude's second son, **Charles** (1524–74), became cardinal de Guise in 1547. Claude helped negotiate the Treaty of CATEAU-CAMBRÉSIS (1559) and played a major role at the Council of TRENT (1562–63). He was responsible for the systematic persecution of the Huguenots. François' son, **Henry** (1550–88), helped plan the SAINT BARTHOLOMEW'S DAY MASSACRE (1572) and personally supervised the murder of the Huguenot leader Gascard de COLIGNY. When HENRY III of France made peace with the Huguenots (1576), Henry formed the HOLY LEAGUE to continue the fight against Protestantism. Henry's early successes in the War of the Three Henrys (1587–89) forced Henry III to initially appoint him as lieutenant general, but Henry later arranged his assassination. Guise power declined when HENRY IV ascended the throne in 1589. *See also* BOURBONS; MARY OF GUISE

Guizot, François (1787–1874) French statesman and historian, premier (1847–48). His father was executed (1794) during the REIGN OF TERROR and Guizot went into exile. Guizot emerged as the leader of the conservative constitutional monarchists after the first Bourbon Restoration (1814) and was involved in the JULY REVOLUTION (1830) that brought LOUIS PHILIPPE to the throne. As minister of education (1832–37), he passed the so-called "Guizot law" (1833) that promised all citizens secular primary education. In 1840 Guizot became foreign minister. As premier, Guizot lost support for his refusal to extend the franchise and an economic crisis (1847–48) forced his resignation and prompted the FEBRUARY REVOLUTION (1848).

Gujarat State in W India, on the Arabian Sea; the capital is Gandhinagar. Absorbed into the MAURYAN EMPIRE in the 3rd century BC, it was a centre of JAINISM under the Maitraka dynasty (5th–8th centuries AD). In 1298 it came under Muslim rule as part of the DELHI SULTANATE. In 1411 Ahmad Shah, the first independent sultan of Gujarat, founded Ahmadabad. From the 16th century to the mid-18th century, Gujarat was under MUGHAL rule. It then passed to the MARATHAS. Administered by the English EAST INDIA COMPANY from 1818, Gujarat became a province in 1857. After independence in 1947, it was established as a separate state. Area: 195,984sq km (75,669sq mi). Pop. (1994 est.) 44,235,000.

gulag Network of detention centres and forced-labour prisons within the former Soviet Union. The term is an acronym in Russian for Chief Administration of Corrective Labour Camps. Established in 1918, gulags were secret CONCENTRATION CAMPS used to silence political and religious dissenters. The regime was forcefully described by the Russian writer Alexander Solzhenitsyn in *The Gulag Archipelago* (1973).

Gulf Cooperation Council (GCC) Organization formed (1981) to promote collaboration between states surrounding the Persian (Arabian) Gulf. Its members are BAHRAIN, KUWAIT, OMAN, QATAR, SAUDI ARABIA and the UNITED ARAB EMIRATES (UAE). After the GULF WAR (1991), the GCC joined with Egypt and Syria to form a regional peacekeeping force.

Gulf War (16 January 1991–28 February 1991) Military action by a US-led coalition of 32 states to expel Iraqi forces from KUWAIT. Iraqi forces invaded Kuwait (2 August 1990) and claimed it as an Iraqi province. On 7 August 1990, Operation Desert Shield began a mass deployment of coalition forces to protect Saudi oil reserves. Economic sanctions failed to secure Iraqi withdrawal, and the UN Security Council set a deadline of 15 January 1991 for the removal of Iraqi forces. Iraqi President Saddam HUSSEIN ignored the ultimatum, and General Norman SCHWARZKOPF launched Operation Desert Storm. Within a week, extensive coalition air attacks had secured control of the skies. Iraqi ground forces were defenceless against the coalition's advanced weaponry. Iraq launched Scud missile attacks on Saudi Arabia and Israel, in the hope of weakening Arab support for the coalition. On 24 February, the ground war was launched. Iraqi troops burned Kuwaiti oil wells as they fled. Kuwait was liberated two days later, and a cease-fire was declared on 28 February. The Gulf War claimed the lives of 234 Allied troops and between 85,000 and 150,000 Iraqi soldiers. Some 33,000 Kuwaitis were killed or captured.

Gunpowder Plot (November 1605) Failed Roman Catholic conspiracy to blow up JAMES I of England and his Parliament. The leader was Robert CATESBY, and the chief perpetrator was Guy FAWKES. Angry at the perceived persecution of Roman Catholics, the plotters hoped that Catholics would seize power after the death of the king. They rented a cellar under the Houses of Parliament, where they stored their gunpowder ready for the opening of Parliament. The Plot was betrayed when one of the conspirators warned his brother-in-law not to attend Parliament that day. Guy Fawkes was arrested in

◄ **Gulf War** Iraq's desire for further oil-rich territory led to the annexation of Kuwait in August 1990. In February 1991, the United States, fearing Iraqi domination of oil supplies, led a counter-offensive from Saudi Arabia. Coalition air attacks were launched (21 February 1991) on strategic government, military and communication targets, resulting in many civilian casualties. A land-offensive on S Iraq and Kuwait followed (24 February 1991) and Iraqi troops were forced to leave Kuwait. Iraqi suppression of Shiite Marsh Arab and Kurdish revolts in Iraq prompted the United Nations (UN) to impose a no-fly zone, N of the 36th and S of the 32nd parallels. Economic sanctions against Iraq continued after Saddam Hussein resisted UN demands for the destruction of Iraqi weapons.

the cellar on the night of 4–5 November. Under torture, he revealed the names of his co-conspirators. Catesby and Thomas Percy died resisting arrest. The other plotters were executed in January 1606. The date of the intended explosion, 5 November, is now celebrated in Britain as Guy Fawkes Day (Bonfire Night).

Gupta dynasty (*c.*AD 320–*c.*550) Ruling house whose kingdom covered most of N India. It was founded by Chandragupta I. The Gupta dynasty embraced Buddhism and led a Hindu revival. It is seen as a golden age in art, culture and religion. It reached its greatest extent at the end of the 4th century but declined at the end of the 5th century under concerted attack from the Huns.

Gurkha Hindu ruling caste of Nepal since 1768. They speak a Sanskrit language. The name also denotes a Nepalese soldier in the British or Indian army.

guru Personal teacher and spiritual master. In traditional Hindu education, boys lived in the home of a *guru*, who guided their studies of the Vedas and saw to their physical health and ethical training. In Sikhism, the title *guru* was assumed by the first ten leaders. Guruship was terminated in 1708 on the death of Gobind Singh.

Gustavus I (Vasa) (1496–1560) King of Sweden (1523–60), founder of the Vasa dynasty and an independent Sweden. Gustavus fought (1517–18) against the Danes and was sent as a hostage to Christian II of Denmark, who reneged on the agreement and imprisoned him. In 1519 Gustavus escaped to Lübeck, Germany. In 1520, with the help of Lübeck, he launched a successful rebellion against the Danes. In 1523 the Kalmar Union was discarded. Gustavus proved to be a harsh ruler. He was forced to exact punitive taxes to repay Lübeck and instigated the Reformation in Sweden primarily to raise revenue. Gustavus imposed royal authority, crushing several peasant and Catholic revolts. In 1544 he established the Swedish crown as hereditary in the Vasa dynasty.

Gustavus II (1594–1632) King of Sweden (1611–32), son and successor of Charles IX. Gustavus had been bequeathed a difficult legacy. His father's usurpation of the throne had provoked war with Poland, and he had also become embroiled in conflicts with Denmark and Russia. Domestically, Gustavus inherited a state divided by religion and threatened by revolt from the nobility. Gustavus bought peace with the Danes (1613) in order to concentrate on fighting Russia, which was forced to cede Ingria and Kexholm (1617). At home, Gustavus and his Chancellor Axel Oxenstierna granted concessions to the nobility that enabled the passage of great constitutional and administrative reforms, creating a professional bureaucracy and a powerful central government. Perhaps his greatest achievement, however, was the creation of a secondary education system. Gustavus also modernized the military, producing a disciplined standing army. War was renewed with Poland: Sweden captured Riga in 1621, the whole of Livonia in 1625, and by 1626 had occupied most of the ports along the Prussian coast. Meanwhile, the success of the Habsburg generals Albrecht von Wallenstein and Johann von Tilly in the German Baltic seemed to threaten not only Sweden but the whole of Protestant Europe. Gustavus and Christian IV of Denmark allied to prevent the Habsburg occupation of Pomerania (1628) and the Treaty of Altmark (1629) with Poland enabled Gustavus to attend to the Habsburg threat. In 1630 Gustavus invaded Germany, precipitating the Thirty Years War. His highly mobile army destroyed Tilly's forces at the Battle of Breitenfeld (1631) and swept through central Germany. Gustavus now contemplated the formation of a Protestant League under his command. In 1632 he invaded Bavaria, but was forced by Wallenstein to return to defend Nürnberg. Gustavus was killed in the Swedish victory at the Battle of Lützen.

Gustavus III (1746–92) King of Sweden (1771–92), son and successor of Adolf Frederick. In 1772 he imposed a new constitution that restricted the power of the Riksdag (parliament). Gustavus introduced a number of social and economic reforms, including the granting of religious and press freedoms and the reform of the currency. In 1788 he declared war on Russia and was immediately faced with an officers' mutiny. Gustavus was able to restore authority and, after victory at Svensksund (1790), dictate the terms of peace. A gifted writer and patron of the arts, his reign is known as the Gustavian Enlightenment. Gustavus founded the Swedish Academy in 1786. He was assassinated in an aristocratic plot at the new Royal Opera House.

Gustavus IV (1778–1837) King of Sweden (1792–1809), son and successor of Gustavus III. His uncle Charles (later Charles XIII) acted as regent during Charles' minority. In 1805 Gustavus led Sweden into the Napoleonic Wars against France. In 1807 Sweden became isolated in the Baltic as Russia, Denmark and Norway joined the French cause. Sweden lost Pomerania and parts of Finland to Russia. Gustavus was overthrown by an army coup and forced into exile in Switzerland. He was succeeded by his uncle.

Gustavus VI (1882–1973) King of Sweden (1950–73), son and successor of Gustavus V. He was the last Swedish king to hold political power, which was removed under reforms passed by the Riksdag (parliament) in 1971. He was succeeded by his grandson, Charles XVI.

Gutenberg, Johann (1400–68) German goldsmith and printer, credited with inventing printing from movable metal type. He first began using metal type in 1430 and by 1449 had set up a printing works using movable type in Mainz. He produced the first printed Bible, known as the *Gutenberg Bible* or *Mazarin Bible* (*c.*1455).

Guthrum (d.890) Danish leader, king of East Anglia (880–90). He led a Viking attack on the English in East Anglia in the 870s. According to tradition, Guthrum led the first Danish expedition to have wintered in England (877). In 878 his forces invaded Wessex, but Alfred (the Great) counter-attacked and forced a peace settlement. Guthrum withdrew from Wessex and was granted a kingdom in East Anglia. He agreed to convert to Christianity and, after his baptism, became known as Aethelstan.

Guyana *See* country feature

Guy of Lusignan (*c.*1129–94) King of the Latin Kingdom of Jerusalem (1186–92) and of Cyprus (1192–94). In 1180 he married Sybil, sister of Baldwin IV, king of Jerusalem. Guy was defeated and captured by Saladin at Hattin (1187). Released in 1188, Guy fought in the Third Crusade, which had been called in response to Saladin's capture of Jerusalem. After Sybil's death, Guy was forced to abdicate, despite the support of Richard I of England, in favour of Sybil's brother-in-law, Conrad of Montferrat (1192). As compensation, Richard I granted Guy the kingdom of Cyprus.

Guzmán Blanco, Antonio (1829–99) Venezuelan dictator (1870–88). He led the Regeneration movement that seized power in 1870 and was elected president on three occasions (1873, 1879, 1886). Guzmán Blanco restored order in Venezuela and halted economic decline. He promoted the construction of public buildings and railways and modernized the capital, Caracas. Guzmán Blanco placed education and marriage under civil control, removing some of the influence of the Roman Catholic Church. His achievements were made at great cost to civil liberties, brutally suppressing all political opposition and amassing a huge personal fortune. He was overthrown while on one of a visit to Europe and died in exile.

Gwalior City in Madhya Pradesh, central India. Founded in the 6th century, it was the capital of the former princely state of Gwalior (dissolved 1956). The city is overlooked by the Gwalior fort, a stronghold on the Rock of Gwalior, which houses elaborate shrines, temples and the palace of Man Singh. The fort was held by Hindu rulers until 1232 and then changed hands many times before falling to the Marathas in 1751. In 1866 the British exchanged Gwalior for Jhansi. Pop. (1991) 691,000.

Gwyn, Nell (1650–87) English actress. Originally an orange-seller, she took to the boards in John Dryden's *The Indian Emperor* (1665). Nell Gwyn was Charles II's mistress, probably bearing him two sons.

GUYANA (FORMERLY BRITISH GUIANA)

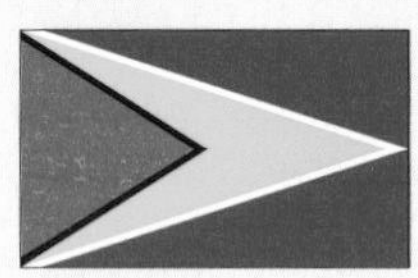

Republic in NE South America. The Dutch settled in 1581 and the Treaty of Breda (1667) awarded them the area. Under the auspices of the Dutch West India Company, land reclamation for plantations began in the 18th century. Britain gained control in the early 19th century and set up the colony of British Guiana in 1831. In 1838 slavery was abolished. After World War 2, progress towards self-government was achieved with a new constitution (1952) and the election of Dr Cheddi Jagan.

In 1966 British Guiana became independent and Forbes Burnham of the socialist People's National Congress (PNC) became the first prime minister. Ethnic violence between the majority East Indian and the African minority populations marred much of the late 1960s. In 1970 Guyana became a republic. In 1980 Burnham became president and a new constitution increased his power. After Burnham's death (1985), Desmond Hoyte introduced liberal reforms. In 1992 elections Hoyte was defeated by Jagan. Jagan's

AREA: 214,970sq km (83,000sq mi)
POPULATION: 808,000
CAPITAL (POPULATION): Georgetown (200,000)
GOVERNMENT: Multiparty republic
ETHNIC GROUPS: Indian 49%, Black 36%, Mixed 7%, Native American 7%, Portuguese, Chinese
LANGUAGES: English (official)
RELIGIONS: Christianity (Protestant 34%, Roman Catholic 18%), Hinduism 34%, Islam 9%
GDP PER CAPITA (1995): US$2420

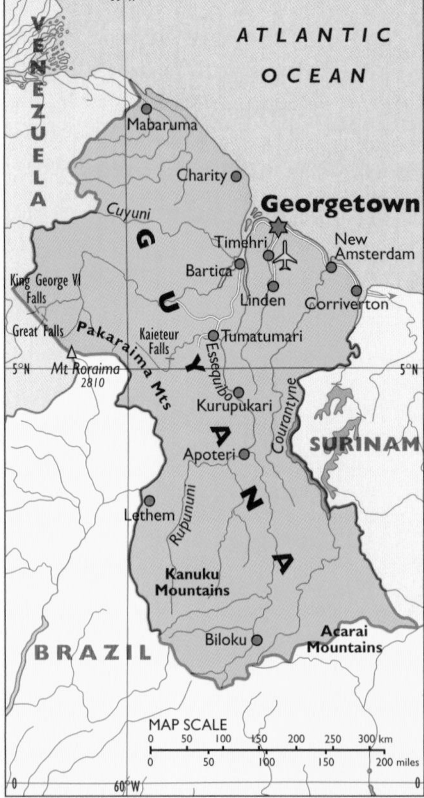

People's Progressive Party (PPP) formed the first non-PNC government since independence. After Cheddi Jagan's death (1997), his wife Janet Jagan was elected president. In 1999 she resigned on grounds of poor health and was replaced by Bharrat Jagdeo.

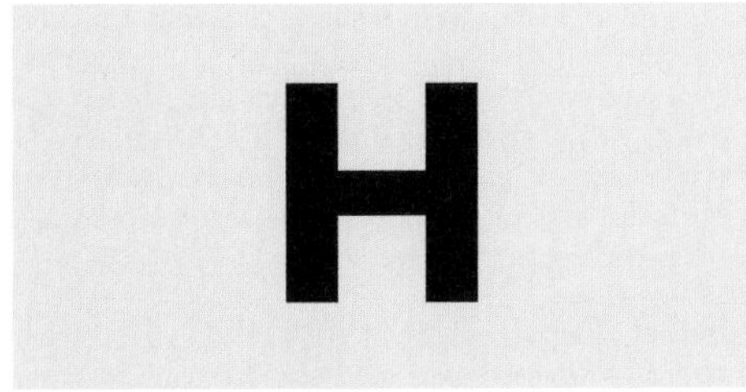

Haakon I (the Good) (*c*.914–61) King of Norway (*c*.946–61), son of HARALD I. He was brought up a Christian in the court of the English king ATHELSTAN. Haakon returned to Norway after the death of his father to take control from his brother, the tyrannical ERIK BLOODAXE. Haakon's attempts to Christianize Norway were opposed by the Norwegian chieftains, but his reign saw improvements in administration and codes of law. Haakon was challenged by Erik Bloodaxe's sons, who were supported by Denmark, and he was killed in battle against them. He was succeeded by HARALD II.

Haakon IV (the Old) (1204–63) King of Norway (1217–63). He reigned at the start of medieval Norway's "golden age" (1217–1319). During his reign, Haakon defeated several uprisings, notably that by his former elder kinsman Earl Skuli in 1240. Strengthening relations with the church, Haakon was crowned by a papal legate in 1247. The Norwegian empire reached its greatest extent with the acquisition of Iceland and Greenland in 1261–62. Their sovereignty was guaranteed with the promise of trade. Haakon was a patron of learning and the arts, and Snorri Sturluson, the Icelandic poet and historian, lived at his court. Haakon died in the Orkneys after a campaign against the Scots that saw the loss of the Hebrides to ALEXANDER III.

Haakon VII (1872–1957) King of Norway (1905–57), son of Frederick VIII of Denmark. Haakon was elected king by the Storting (Norwegian parliament) when Norway regained its independence from Sweden. In 1940 Haakon was forced into exile by the German invasion, refusing to abdicate as suggested by Vidkun QUISLING's German-pressured government. He led a government-in-exile (1940–45) in London, England. A popular king, he returned to Norway after the war, and was eventually succeeded by his son, OLAF V.

Habsburg *See* feature article

Habyarimana, Juvénal (1937–94) Rwandan statesman and solider, president (1973–94). He served as minister of defence and police chief of staff (1965–73). In 1973 Habyarimana overthrew President Grégoire KAYIBANDA in a bloodless military coup. He founded the National Revolutionary Development Movement, establishing a one-party state. In 1990 the Tutsi-dominated Rwandan Patriotic Front (RPF) invaded and forced Habyarimana to agree to a multiparty constitution. Tension between the Hutu and Tutsi ethnic groups flared into violence. Returning from peace talks between the groups, Habyarimana and his fellow Hutu leader of BURUNDI, Cyrien Ntaryamira, were killed in a rocket attack on their aircraft. Violence immediately escalated in RWANDA.

hacienda Large estate in Latin America. The equivalent of haciendas in Brazil are known as *fazendas* and in Argentina as *estancias*. Haciendas was originally given as a reward by the Spanish crown for services carried out on its behalf. During the 19th century they increased in size and relied heavily on the labour of Native Americans who became tied to their employers through debt. There were calls for the break-up of the haciendas, sometimes accompanied by violence, as in the case of the MEXICAN REVOLUTION (1911). Many haciendas were dismantled, but in some Latin American countries they continued to be a cause of political conflict in the latter half of the 20th century. *See also* EJIDO; ENCOMIENDA

Hadith Sayings and acts attributed to the Prophet MUHAMMAD, second only to the KORAN as a source of authority in ISLAM. Hadith formalizes the *sunna* (right behaviour) of the Muslim community. It consists of the text itself and the chain of transmitters (*isnad*) that authenticate the traditions as arising from the Prophet himself. Of the six collections accepted as canonical by SUNNIS, the two most important texts are those of al-Bukhari (810–70) and Muslim ibn al-Hajjaj (817–75). SHIITES recognize five *hadith* collections based upon the

HABSBURG (HAPSBURG)

Austrian royal dynasty, a leading ruling house in Europe from the 13th to 20th century. It became a major force when RUDOLF I was elected (1273) king of the Germans. He established the core of the Habsburg dominions in AUSTRIA, CARNIOLA and Styria. FREDERICK III arranged the marriage (1477) by which his son, Maximilian, gained Burgundy, the Netherlands and Luxembourg. MAXIMILIAN I extended his father's marriage diplomacy to his own son, PHILIP I, who acquired (1496) Castile, Aragón, Granada, Spanish America, Naples, Sicily and Sardinia.

When CHARLES V became emperor in 1519, he ruled over the largest European empire since CHARLEMAGNE in the 9th century. He proceeded to establish Habsburg dominance in Italy, conquering Milan in 1522, forming an alliance with GENOA in 1528, and overthrowing the French-backed Florentine republic in 1530 (*see* ITALIAN WARS). Control of Austria and the other E Habsburg lands was devolved to his brother, FERDINAND I. In 1526 Ferdinand was elected to the Bohemian and Hungarian thrones, although all he could salvage of Hungary was "Royal Hungary" in the W. Charles faced opposition from several German princes over the imperial ban placed on Martin LUTHER during the REFORMATION. In both the Mediterranean and central Europe, he was confronted by the power of the OTTOMAN EMPIRE, which only the Habsburgs were able to keep at bay. In 1556 Charles abdicated, leaving his Spanish titles to his son, PHILIP II, and his Austrian titles to Ferdinand I. As a result of the THIRTY YEARS' WAR (1618–48), the Habsburgs strengthened their empire in central Europe. With the weakening of the Ottoman Empire they began to conquer central and E Hungary, and by 1699 the conquest was complete. In 1700 the Spanish line ended and in the subsequent War of the SPANISH SUCCESSION (1703–13) power passed to the BOURBONS. In 1740 the male line of the Austrian branch ended, but MARIA THERESA re-established the house as that of Habsburg-Lorraine, although she lost SILESIA. At the end of the NAPOLEONIC WARS (1803–15) the Habsburgs lost the Austrian Netherlands and the title of Holy Roman emperor, but continued to control Austria. By 1867 the Habsburg empire was reduced to the AUSTRO-HUNGARIAN EMPIRE. FRANZ JOSEPH saw the disintegration of his empire in World War 1. It finally collapsed in 1918, when CHARLES I was deposed. *See also* HOLY ROMAN EMPIRE

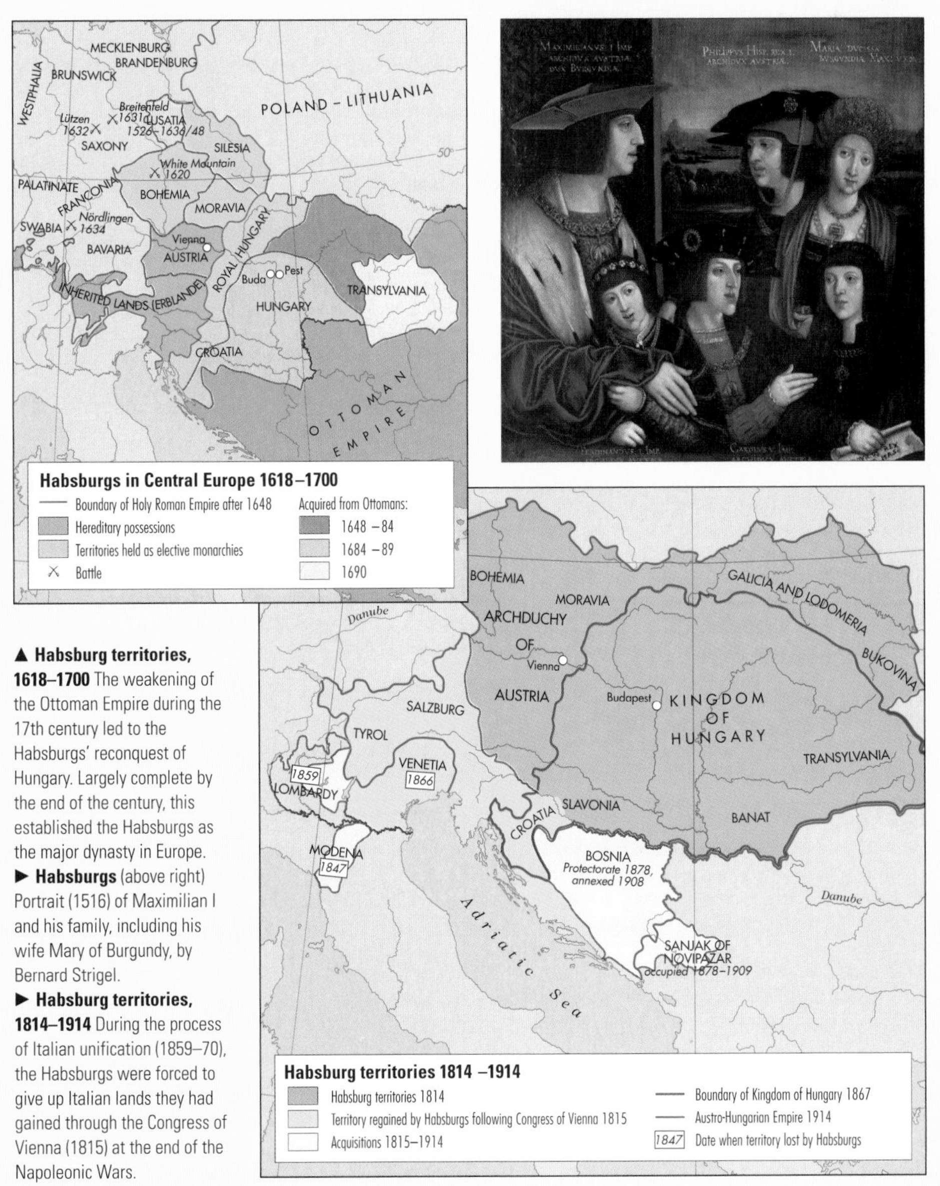

▲ **Habsburg territories, 1618–1700** The weakening of the Ottoman Empire during the 17th century led to the Habsburgs' reconquest of Hungary. Largely complete by the end of the century, this established the Habsburgs as the major dynasty in Europe.

► **Habsburgs** (above right) Portrait (1516) of Maximilian I and his family, including his wife Mary of Burgundy, by Bernard Strigel.

► **Habsburg territories, 1814–1914** During the process of Italian unification (1859–70), the Habsburgs were forced to give up Italian lands they had gained through the Congress of Vienna (1815) at the end of the Napoleonic Wars.

authority of the Caliph ALI. The Hadith constitutes the primary source of information on the early doctrinal development of Islam. *See also* SHARIA

Hadrian, Publius Aelius (AD 76–138) Roman emperor (117–138) under whom the Empire enjoyed a golden age. Nephew and protegé of Emperor TRAJAN, whom he served in Rome's provinces, Hadrian adopted a policy of imperial retrenchment, discouraging new conquests and relinquishing territory hard to defend. He ordered the construction of HADRIAN'S WALL in Britain and made the River Euphrates the Empire's E boundary. Unpopular in Rome, he spent much of his reign touring the ROMAN EMPIRE. One of the most cultured of the Roman emperors, he erected many fine buildings, notably the vast Hadrian's Villa at Tivoli, and also rebuilt the PANTHEON. The erection of a shrine to Jupiter on the site of the TEMPLE OF JERUSALEM along with a universal ban of circumcision inadvertently provoked a Jewish revolt (132–135). Hadrian is also remembered for his reforms of the civil service, law, the financial administration and the tax systems.

Hadrian's Wall Defensive fortification in N England, erected (AD 122–36) on the orders of the Roman emperor HADRIAN. It extended 118km (74mi) and was *c*.2.3m (7.5ft) thick and 1.8 to 4.6m (6–15ft) high. Forts were built along its length. Extensive stretches survive.

H

Haganah (Heb. defence) Jewish militia in PALESTINE formed (1920) to protect Jewish settlements from Palestinian Arab attack. It initially opposed the terrorist tactics used by the extreme IRGUN group, pursuing instead the policy of *havlaga* ("self-restraint"). Haganah members were part-time, and in 1941 *Palmach*, a full-time force, was formed. Haganah attempted to change British policy on Jewish immigration and received aid from US Zionists. By the end of World War 2 Haganah resorted to terrorist activities. Following the creation of the state of Israel in 1948, the Haganah became the official Israeli army. *See also* ZIONISM

Hagia Sophia (Aya Sofia) Byzantine church in Istanbul. It was built (532–37) for Emperor JUSTINIAN I. A masterpiece of BYZANTINE ARCHITECTURE, it was the first building to use pendentives (triangular sections of vaulting) to support a central dome. A series of domes extends the lofty interior space. The church was converted into a mosque in 1453. The Hagia Sophia now acts as a museum.

Hague, William Jefferson (1961–) British politician, leader of the CONSERVATIVE PARTY (1997–). He entered Parliament in 1989. In 1995 Hague joined John MAJOR's cabinet as secretary of state for Wales. After the Conservatives' landslide defeat in the 1997 general election, Hague emerged as the youngest Tory leader since William PITT (THE YOUNGER) in 1783. Although a strong performer in the House of Commons, his anti-European single currency platform pushed the party towards the right, and alienated the more moderate members.

Hague, The ('s-Gravenhage or Den Haag) City in the W Netherlands; capital of South Holland province. It is the seat of the Dutch government. The city grew around a 13th-century palace, from which it takes its name 's-Gravenhage (counts' private dominion). In 1585 the States-General of the United Provinces of the Netherlands was based at The Hague. MAURICE OF NASSAU, stadtholder of the Netherlands, resided here. The city became an intellectual and political centre, renowned for its silver, porcelain and publishing. In 1815, with the establishment of the Kingdom of the Netherlands, The Hague became the residence of the monarch. The location of two major peace conferences, The Hague became a centre for international law and has been the seat of the International Court of Justice since 1945. Much of the economy depends on its diplomatic activities. Pop. (1994) 445,279.

Hague Peace Conference (1899, 1907) International meetings that drew up laws on the conduct of warfare and the rights of neutral nations, but failed to reach agreement on arms reduction. The first conference, at which 26 nations were represented, set up the Permanent Court of Arbitration, a forerunner of the INTERNATIONAL COURT OF JUSTICE. The second conference, at which 44 nations were represented, agreed on conventions relating to a range of issues, including the rights of neutral countries and their citizens, and how enemy ships should be treated during war. An agreement that another conference should be held in 1915 was not implemented because of World War 1. However, the principle that international disputes should be settled through regular conferences was established, thus preparing the ground for the LEAGUE OF NATIONS.

Haig, Alexander Meigs (1924–) US statesman and general. He served in the army during the Korean War (1950–53). In 1968 he was appointed as military adviser to Henry KISSINGER on the National Security Council. Haig was a participant in the secret peace talks in Paris, which aimed to resolve the Vietnam War (1955–75). In 1973 he became chief of staff for President Richard NIXON and was instrumental in persuading the president after the WATERGATE SCANDAL (1974). He was supreme allied commander (1974–79) of the North Atlantic Treaty Organization (NATO) and served as secretary of state (1981–82) under President Ronald REAGAN.

Haig, Douglas, 1st Earl (1861–1928) British field marshal. During World War 1 he served as commander in chief (1915–18) of the BRITISH EXPEDITIONARY FORCE (BEF) in France. Haig's policy of attrition, particularly in the campaigns of the SOMME and PASSCHENDAELE, inflicted appalling losses among British troops without achieving significant advantage. Under the supreme command of Marshal FOCH, his campaign began to reap some military success, culminating in the final assault on the HINDENBURG line. In 1921 Haig helped establish the Royal BRITISH LEGION. He was created an earl in 1919.

Haile Selassie I (1892–1975) (Ras Tafari Makonnen) Emperor of Ethiopia (1930–74). Ras Tafari became regent to the throne in 1917, when Zauditu, daughter of MENELIK II, became empress. He gained a reputation for progressive policies. In 1928 he acquired the title "negus" (king). He became emperor on Zauditu's death in 1930, taking the name Haile Selassie. When Italy invaded Ethiopia in 1935, he was forced into exile (1936). In 1941 he drove out the Italians with British aid. Subsequently Haile Selassie became a leader among independent African nations, helping to found (1963) the ORGANIZATION OF AFRICAN UNITY (OAU). Although Haile Selassie enacted important reforms, including the abolition of slavery and the extension of the franchise, his authoritarian rule failed to bring economic progress and, after famine in N Ethiopia, he was overthrown in a military coup led by Haile MENGISTU. He was killed while in custody. *See also* RASTAFARIANISM

Hainaut Historic county in the LOW COUNTRIES, now divided between Belgium (Hainaut province) and France (Nord department). Hainaut and the county of FLANDERS were united in 1051. They separated in 1070 but reunited in 1191. In 1299 the count of Hainaut also became count of HOLLAND, thus creating a link between the two counties that continued under the Burgundians and HABSBURGS. Sections of Hainaut were ceded to France by the Habsburgs in 1659 and 1678. The remainder became part of Belgium in 1831. The capital of Hainaut is Mons. Area: 3789sq km (1463sq mi). Pop. (1990) 1,278,039.

▲ **Haile Selassie I** became a focus for African nationalism, but his dictatorship ultimately led to political stagnation in Ethiopia and the rise of a Marxist opposition.

Haiti *See* country feature

Hakluyt, Richard (*c*.1552–1616) English geographer. Hakluyt's detailed history of maritime exploration, *Principal Navigations* (1589), stimulated further voyages of discovery and English colonization, particularly in North America. The second, much enlarged edition of *Navigations* in three volumes (1598–1600) ensured his position as one of the chief advisers to ELIZABETH I on colonial matters, and also provided the English EAST INDIA COMPANY with useful economic theories on overseas trade. Other works include *Discourse on the Western Planting* (1584), which described the benefits to be had from Walter RALEIGH's colonization projects in Virginia.

Haldane, Richard Burdon, 1st Viscount (1856–1928) British statesman, secretary of war (1905–12) and lord chancellor (1912–15, 1924). He entered Parliament in 1885 and was appointed to the Liberal cabinet by Sir Henry CAMPBELL-BANNERMAN. In 1911 Haldane was made a viscount and thereafter sat in the House of Lords. In 1905 he reorganized the British Army along German lines and created the Territorial Army (TA). His plans enabled the swift mobilization of British troops at the start of World War 1. As lord chancellor, Haldane attempted to improve the efficiency of the judicial process. In the first Labour government under Ramsay MACDONALD, he was once again made lord chancellor. In his book *The Reign of Relativity* (1921), Haldane examined the philosophical consequences of Albert Einstein's theories of relativity. He was one of the founders (1895) of the London School of Economics (LSE).

Hale, Nathan (1755–76) Captain in the AMERICAN REVOLUTION. A Yale graduate, he was a schoolteacher before joining the Continental Army in 1775. Having volunteered to go behind British lines on Long Island to gain military secrets, he was captured on 21 September 1776 and hanged the next day. His reported last words, "I regret that I have but one life to lose for my country", ensured his status as hero of the revolution.

Halicarnassus (now Bodrum, Turkey) Ancient Greek city in SW Asia Minor. Under Persian rule from the 6th century BC, it grew rich because of its trading position. In the 4th century BC, Halicarnassus was a semi-independent state under the Persian governor Mausolus, whose tomb was one of the SEVEN WONDERS OF THE WORLD.

Halidon Hill, Battle of (19 July 1333) Battle fought between England and Scotland. It was fought near Berwick-on-Tweed, N England, which was being besieged by an army led by EDWARD III of England. A Scottish army, led by DAVID II, that was coming to relieve Berwick, was massacred by forces, which included English archers, under Edward BALLIOL. As a result, Balliol regained the throne of Scotland but in return he had to pay homage to Edward.

Halifax, Charles Montagu, 1st Earl of (1661–1715) English Whig statesman. He entered Parliament in 1689. As a lord of the treasury (1692–94), Halifax established the national debt (1692) and founded the BANK OF ENGLAND (1694), both of which helped raise money for WILLIAM III's war with France. As chancellor of the exchequer (1694–95), he introduced new coinage. In 1697 Halifax became first lord of the treasury but resigned when the Tories came to power (1699). On Queen ANNE's death he was made a member of the council of regency and resumed as lord of treasury under GEORGE I. He was also a patron of writers and a noted wit and poet.

Halifax, Edward Frederick Lindley Wood, 1st Earl of (1881–1959) British politician. He became a member of Parliament in 1910. After some years in government he became Lord Irwin (1925) and served as viceroy of India (1925–29) at a time of concentrated Indian opposition to British colonial rule. Halifax favoured dominion status for the country and, although he had some sympathy for the Indian nationalist leader "Mahatma" Gandhi, he had Gandhi imprisoned after the Salt March (1930), part of an organized campaign of civil disobedience. After returning to England he was president of the board of trade (1932–35) and leader of the House of Lords (1935–38). As foreign secretary (1938–40), Halifax supported Neville Chamberlain's policy of appeasement towards Adolf Hitler. During World War 2 he was British ambassador to the United States and in 1945–46 represented Britain at the United Nations (UN).

Halifax, George Savile, 1st Marquess of (1633–95) English statesman. After assisting in the Restoration (1660) of Charles II, he was created (1668) a viscount. As a privy councillor (1672–85) who adopted a moderate position on the issues of the day, he rejected Charles' pro-Catholic policies but successfully led opposition to a proposal to exclude Charles' brother James (later James II) from the succession. In 1682 he became lord privy seal. On the accession of James (1685), he was demoted to president of the council then dismissed (1686) for his opposition to the Test Acts. He wrote several political pamphlets, including *The Character of a Trimmer* (1688), which espoused his concilatory approach towards politics. Halifax unsuccessfully attempted to reconcile James and the future William III (of Orange). He then sided with William and was partly responsible for Parliament's acceptance of William and Mary II as joint monarchs in 1689. *See also* Glorious Revolution

Hallstatt Small town in w central Austria, believed to be the site of the earliest Iron Age culture in w Europe. Iron was worked here from *c*.700 bc. The site contains a large Celtic cemetery and a deep salt-mine. Fine bronze and pottery objects have also been discovered. The Hallstatt Celts were replaced by those of La Tène.

Halsey, William Frederick, Jr (1882–1959) US admiral. His forces were on manoeuvres when the Japanese bombed Pearl Harbor (1941) and so escaped undamaged. "Bull" Halsey responded with carrier-based air strikes against the Japanese-held Marshall and Gilbert islands in 1941. In 1942 he was promoted to commander of the South Pacific forces and played a major role in the Battle of Guadalcanal (1942). As commander of the 3rd Fleet, Halsey was repsonsible for the destruction of the Japanese fleet at the Battle of Leyte Gulf (1944). At the end of World War 2, the terms of Japanese surrender were signed aboard his ship, the *Missouri*.

Hamburg City-state and port on the River Elbe, n Germany. The construction of Hammaburg Castle in the 9th century, possibly on the orders of Charlemagne, marks the founding of Hamburg. By the 12th century it had become a flourishing centre of trade. In the 13th century Hamburg was one of the original members of the Hanseatic League. After the dissolution of the League, it retained its prosperity and a stock exchange was established in 1558. Hamburg's cultural and commercial life was enriched by the arrival of Protestant merchants fleeing the French Wars of Religion. Thanks to its extensive fortifications, it was largely unaffected by the Thirty Years' War (1618–48). It was briefly occupied by Napoleon, becoming part of the German Confederation in 1815. Hamburg and its docks were severely bombed during World War 2. It is now Germany's second-largest city and a major cultural centre. Pop. (1990) 1,675,200.

Hamilcar Barca (d.228 bc) Carthaginian commander, father of Hannibal and Hasdrubal Barca. Initially successful in the first of the Punic Wars, he was defeated in 241 bc. Hamilcar suppressed a revolt of Carthaginian mercenaries in 238 bc and the following year conquered s and e regions of Spain. *See also* Carthage

Hamilton, Alexander (*c*.1755–1804) US statesman. During the American Revolution he served as George Washington's aide-de-camp and secretary. After the Revolution, Hamilton became a member of the Continental Congress and a delegate to the Constitutional Convention. Hamilton, James Madison and John Jay collaborated on *The* Federalist (1788), a series of esssays in support of the new Constitution of the United States. As first secretary of the treasury (1789–95), he established the national currency and the Bank of the United States (1791). He was overlooked as succcessor to Washington by the Federalist Party, who nominated John Adams instead. In 1800 Hamilton alienated many Federalists by supporting Thomas Jefferson's bid for the presidency. In 1804 he blocked Aaron Burr's campaign to be governor of New York. Burr challenged him to a duel and killed him.

Hamilton, Lady Emma (1765–1815) English mistress of Admiral Nelson. She was married to Sir William Hamilton (1730–1803), British ambassador to Naples, where her relationship with Nelson, tacitly accepted by her husband, began in 1798. They had two daughters.

Hamilton, James Hamilton, 1st Duke of (1606–49) Scottish Royalist general. As Charles I's commissioner in Scotland (1638–39), Hamilton failed to achieve a compromise with the Covenanters and led an army against them in the first of the Bishops' Wars (1639). In 1641 he returned to Scotland and attempted to negotiate with the Covenanters. Losing Charles' trust, and probably conspired against by the staunch Royalist James Graham, Earl of Montrose, he was imprisoned (1644) on suspicion of treachery. Released (1646) by the Parliamentarians, he nevertheless remained loyal to Charles, fighting for him in the English Civil War. In 1648 he led Scottish forces in support of the king. Defeated and captured by Oliver Cromwell at the Battle of Preston (1648), he was later executed.

Hammarskjöld, Dag Hjalmar Agne Carl (1905–61) Swedish diplomat, second secretary general (1953–61) of the United Nations (UN). He brought great moral authority to the office. In 1956 Hammarskjöld played a leading role in resolving the Suez Crisis and was re-elected secretary general in 1957. He played a major role in establishing a UN Emergency Force to help maintain peace in the Middle East. Hammarskjöld sent a UN peacekeeping force to the Congo. He died in an air crash over Zambia while on a mission to the Congo. Hammarskjöld was posthumously awarded the 1961 Nobel Prize for Peace.

Hammurabi (d. *c*.1750 bc) King of Babylonia (*c*.1792–*c*.1750 bc). Sixth ruler of the Amorite dynasty, he inherited a city-state which he transformed into a large territorial state by conquering most of the cities of s Mesopotamia and up the Euphrates to the city of Mari. For many years he was involved in the daily administration of his empire. He also introduced a number of laws now known as the Code of Hammurabi. However, he failed to establish an effective bureaucratic system, and soon after his death his empire fell apart.

Hammurabi, Code of Ancient laws compiled under Hammurabi (r. *c*.1792–*c*.1750 bc). A copy of the code is in the Louvre, Paris. It is composed of 282 provisions, with harsh penalties for offenders. It includes the maxim, "An eye for an eye, a tooth for a tooth". Covering family life, property and trade, it provides information on social and economic conditions in ancient Babylonia.

Hampden, John (1594–1643) English politician. He entered Parliament in 1621. He was imprisoned (1627–28) for his opposition to Charles I. In the 1630s Hampden was prosecuted for refusing to pay "ship money", a tax levied by Charles without Parliament's permission. A prominent member of the Long Parliament, he was a close associate of John Pym. As a result of his criticism and his part in drawing up the Grand Remonstrance, Hampden was one of the five members whom the king tried to arrest in the House of Commons in 1642, an act that precipitated the English Civil War. He died fighting for the Parliamentary army at Thame, s central England.

Hampton, Wade (1818–1902) Confederate general in the American Civil War (1861–65). Hampton commanded infantry divisions, before becoming commander of the Confederate cavalry corps. He fought against William Sherman's march n from Savannah until forced to surrender in April 1865. In 1876 he was elected governor of his home state, South Carolina, ousting the carpetbagger incumbent and restoring home rule. In 1879 Hampton was elected to the Senate, where he served until 1891.

Hampton Court Palace Palace situated beside the River Thames, 23km (14mi) from Westminster, London, England. Cardinal Thomas Wolsey began its construction in 1515, gifting it to Henry VIII (1526) in the hope of regaining favour. The last monarch to reside here was George II (r.1727–60). It is noted for the splendour of its architecture and its garden, which features a maze. Christopher Wren rebuilt and extended parts of the Palace between 1696 and 1704.

Hampton Roads Peace Conference (3 February 1865) Abortive attempt for a negotiated settlement to the American Civil War. Union President Abraham Lincoln and Confederate Vice President Alexander Stephens met aboard the *River Queen* at Hampton Roads, Virginia. The talks collapsed because the Union refused to consider independence for the Confederate

HAITI

AREA: 27,750sq km (10,714sq mi)
POPULATION: 7,400,000
CAPITAL (POPULATION): Port-au-Prince (508,588)
GOVERNMENT: Multiparty republic
ETHNIC GROUPS: Black 95%, Mulatto 5%
LANGUAGES: Haitian Creole, French (both official)
RELIGIONS: Roman Catholic 85%, Voodoo
GDP PER CAPITA (1995): US$910

Independent nation occupying the w third of the Caribbean island of Hispaniola. After being discovered by Christopher Columbus in 1492, it had Spanish settlements established at the e end of the island, and within 100 years most of the native Arawaks had died through disease or ill-treatment. In the 17th century, French corsairs set up plantations in the w part of the island and the Spanish recognized the area as French territory in 1697. Known as Saint Domingue, the region prospered in the 18th century. The sugar and coffee plantations were worked by African slaves, who soon formed the majority of the population.

In 1791 Toussaint L'Ouverture led a slave revolt against the colonial rulers. In 1801, as governor general, he abolished slavery, but he was killed by the French two years later. In 1804 the country finally achieved independence, as Haiti, and Jean Jacques Dessalines became emperor. During the 19th century, Haiti experienced much political instability. From 1915 to 1934 it was virtually governed by the United States. The 1957 election of François Duvalier as president inaugurated a period of corruption. Attempts to establish a democratic government in the 1980s and 1990s, after the deposition of the Duvalier family, were frustrated by the army. In 1991 the democratically elected president Jean-Bertrand Aristide was removed from office by a military coup, but was restored in 1994 with US backing. In 1995 René Préval was elected president, but divisions within the government were not resolved until 1999 when Préval appointed a new government by decree. Haiti is the poorest country in the Western Hemisphere.

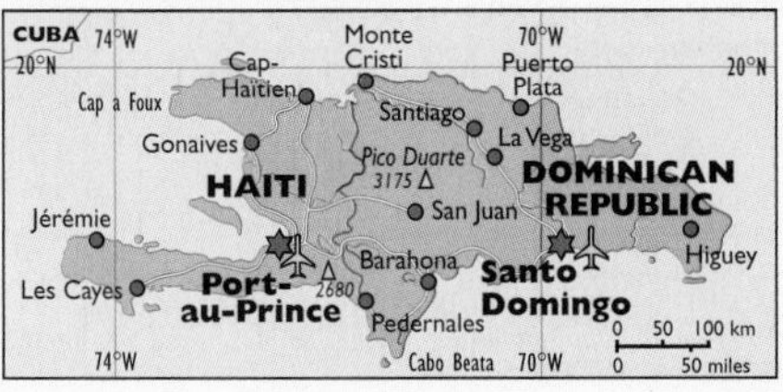

STATES, and the Confederate States decled to rejoin the Union and refused to abolish SLAVERY.

Han Imperial Chinese dynasty (206 BC–AD 220). It was founded by a rebellious peasant, Liu Pang, who overthrew the QIN dynasty and established the capital at Changan (now Xian), N China. Under the Han, CONFUCIANISM, which placed emphasis on virtue and fair government, became the state philosophy, and a code of laws was introduced. China achieved unprecedented power, prosperity, technological invention and cultural growth, especially under Han Wu Di in the 2nd century BC. WANG MANG, a usurper, interrupted the dynasty between AD 9 and 25; the dynasty is divided by that period into the Former (or Western) Han and the Later (or Eastern) Han. Under the Later Han, the capital moved to Luoyang, N central China. In the 2nd century AD, the empire was weakened by peasant revolts, such as the revolt of the Yellow Turbans in AD 184, which was punished by the slaughter of more than 500,000 people. Such revolts left the empire open to the ambitions of powerful generals who divided it up between them into the "Three Kingdoms".

Han (Han-Jen) Ethnic group that makes up *c*.94% of the population of China. It consists of various sub-groups sharing the same culture, traditions and written language, although within the Han Chinese language there are several dialects. Their ancient hierarchical society, based on Taoist, Confucian and Buddhist tenets, has been reorganized under communism.

Hancock, John (1737–93) American revolutionary. With Samuel ADAMS, he led the Massachusetts Patriots and helped organize the BOSTON TEA PARTY. He represented Massachusetts at the CONTINENTAL CONGRESS (1775–80, 1785, 1786), serving as the president (1775–77). His was the first signature, written especially large so GEORGE III of England could read it easily, on the DECLARATION OF INDEPENDENCE (1776). He helped to draw up the Massachusetts constitution (1780) and became that state's first governor (1780–85). He was re-elected governor in 1789 and served until his death.

Hancock, Winfield Scott (1824–86) US general. A veteran of the MEXICAN WAR, he was a Union commander in the American CIVIL WAR, fighting in the Peninsular and Antietam campaigns and at Fredericksburg, CHANCELLORSVILLE and GETTYSBURG (1863). After the War, he helped enforce the policies of RECONSTRUCTION in Louisiana and Texas and was rewarded with the Democratic nomination for president. He narrowly lost the 1880 election to the Republican James GARFIELD.

Hanging Gardens of Babylon One of the SEVEN WONDERS OF THE WORLD. The gardens are thought to have been spectacular, rising in a series of terraces and irrigated by water raised from the River Euphrates. They were probably built by NEBUCHADNEZZAR for his wife within the walls of his palace at BABYLON (near modern Baghdad, Iraq). Nothing remains of them and nobody is certain as to how the irrigation system worked.

Hanna, Marcus Alonzo (1837–1904) US industrialist and Republican politician. His campaign management and financial support helped William MCKINLEY win the 1896 presidential election. His use of pamphleteering is widely seen as the beginning of modern campaign politics. He served (1897–1904) as senator from Ohio.

Hannibal (247–183 BC) Carthaginian statesman and general in the second of the PUNIC WARS, son of HAMILCAR BARCA. One of the greatest generals of ancient times, in 221 BC he became commander in chief of the Carthaginian forces in Spain, where his father had established a province in 237 BC. In 219 BC he led an eight-month siege of the Spanish and pro-Roman city of Saguntum, an act which provoked the Second Punic War with Rome. Intent on taking the war to Italy, Hannibal set out on an epic expedition across the Alps in 218 BC with 40,000 troops and 38 elephants. Many died on the way due to appalling weather conditions and skirmishes with Gauls, but he won a series of victories over the Romans, notably at Lake Trasimene (217 BC) and CANNAE (216 BC). He was, however, unable to capture Rome, and the Romans gradually regained much of the territory. Recalled to CARTHAGE to confront the invasion of SCIPIO AFRICANUS, he was defeated at ZAMA (202 BC). After the war, as chief magistrate of Carthage, he alienated the nobility by reducing their power. They sought Roman intervention, and Hannibal fled to the Seleucid kingdom of ANTIOCHUS III. He fought under Antiochus against the Romans, was defeated and committed suicide. His strength as a general lay in his strong strategic ability and the gift of engendering respect and loyalty among his (mostly mercenary) troops.

Hanoi Capital of Vietnam and its second-largest city, on the Red River. From AD 43 to 540 the Chinese ruled Vietnam from Hanoi. In 1010 the Vietnamese emperor Ly Thai To established his capital here. Hanoi remained as capital until 1802, when Hue became the seat of the NGUYEN emperor. Taken by the French in 1883, Hanoi became the capital of French INDOCHINA (1887–1945). From 1946 to 1954 it was the scene of fighting between the French and the Viet Minh. It was heavily bombed during the VIETNAM WAR (1955–75). Pop. (1989) 1,088,862.

Hanover (Hannover) Former kingdom and province of Germany. In 1692 Duke Ernest Augustus, one of the dukes of Brunswick-Lüneberg, was created elector of Hanover; his lands were known thereafter as Hanover. In 1714 his son succeeded to the British throne as GEORGE I. Divided during the Napoleonic era, Hanover was reconstituted as a kingdom in 1815. Allied with Austria in the AUSTRO-PRUSSIAN WAR (1866), it was annexed by PRUSSIA after Austria's defeat. After World War 2 it was incorporated into the state of Lower SAXONY.

Hanover, House of German royal family and rulers of Britain from 1714 to 1901. The electors of Hanover succeeded to the British throne in 1714, on the death of Queen ANNE, under the terms of the Act of Settlement (1701) and the Act of Union (1707). GEORGE I, the first elector also to be king of Britain, was succeeded in both Britain and Hanover by GEORGE II, GEORGE III, GEORGE IV and WILLIAM IV. SALIC LAW prevented Queen VICTORIA's accession in Hanover; the Hanoverian title was inherited by her uncle, Ernest Augustus, Duke of Cumberland, and the monarchies of Britain and Hanover were separated. On Victoria's marriage to ALBERT the British royal family name changed to SAXE-COBURG-GOTHA. The Hanoverians continued to rule in Hanover until it was annexed by PRUSSIA in 1866. *See also* HANOVER; SETTLEMENT, ACT OF

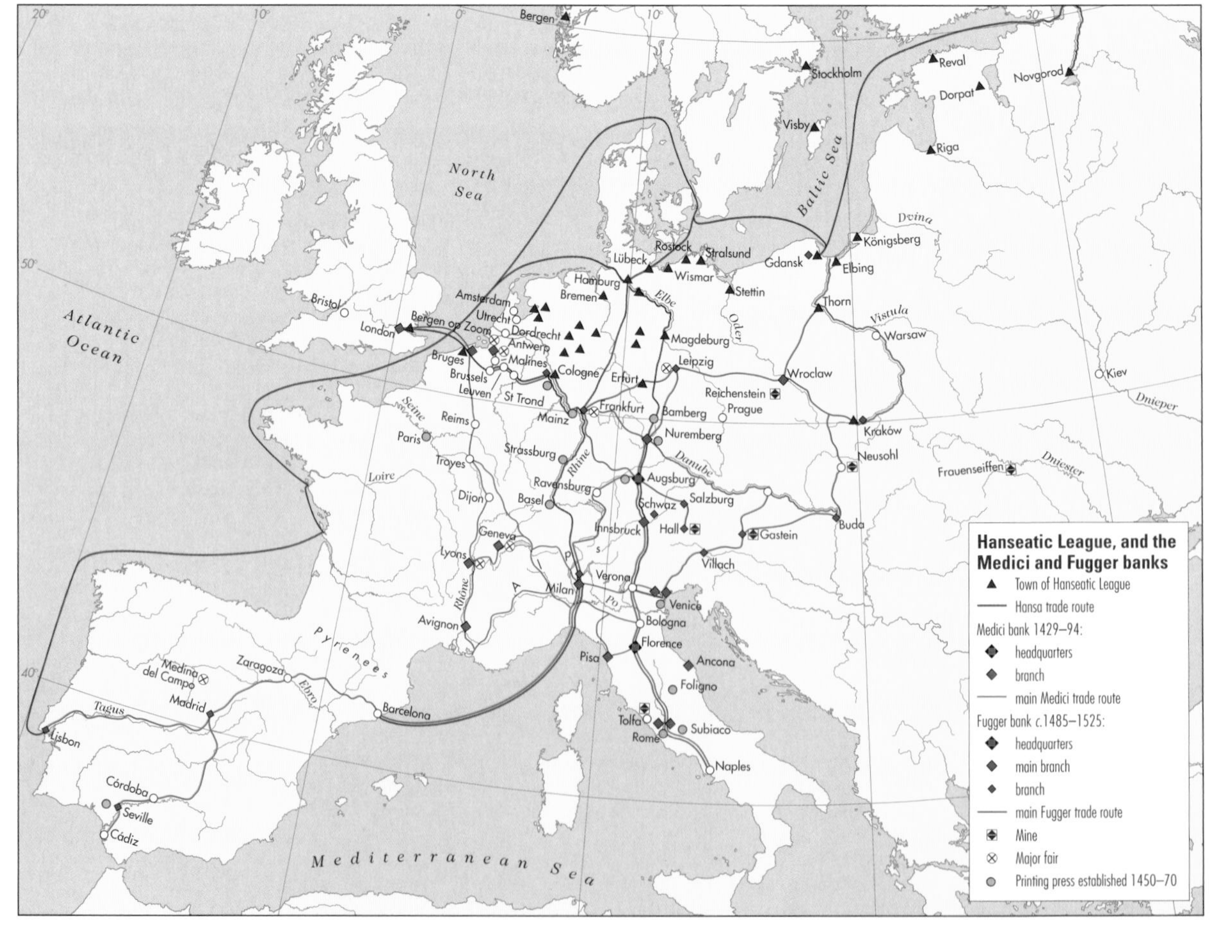

► **Hanseatic League** Lübeck, Schleswig-Holstein, N Germany, became the administrative headquarters of the League in 1358. Visby, on the Swedish island of Gotland, was a vital port in the movement of goods throughout the Baltic region and also with Novgorod in Russia. Timber, fur and grain from Scandinavia, N Russia and the S hinterland of the Baltic were exchanged for cloth and other manufactured commodities from places such as Flanders and England. Throughout the area dominated by the Hanseatic League, local rulers were awarded grants of privilege in return for profit-sharing arrangements, thus contributing to German economic and cultural expansion within Europe. Along with the Hanseatic League, the Fugger merchant banking family and the Medici's were also largely responsible for the increasingly buoyant European economy.

Hanseatic League Economic alliance of N German cities and German merchant communities outside Germany. Although the League was formally established in 1343, its development dates back to HENRY III (THE LION) of Saxony's capture (1158) of the port of LÜBECK (now in Schleswig-Holstein, N Germany) and his acquisition of trading privileges on the Swedish island of Gotland (1161). The town of Visby on Gotland was the base from which German merchants established towns all along the E Baltic coast, including RIGA (now in Latvia) and Danzig (now GDAŃSK, Poland), and built up trading links with NOVGOROD in Russia. In the 13th century, German overseas merchants formed associations (*hanses*) for mutual protection from pirates, while the towns allied under the "laws of Lübeck". Although the League provided a common defence policy and occasionally launched wars (such as against VALDEMAR IV of Denmark in 1360), it was primarily a mercantile union. Through gifts, loans and economic boycotts, the League gained trading privileges throughout N Europe and, at its peak in the late 14th century, it swelled to include *c*.100 towns. The League declined in the 15th century, as new, powerful nation-states emerged in the Baltic, and Dutch maritime interests began to prevail. The development of trade with the New World further weakened the League as the axis of trade swung away from the Baltic ports towards the Atlantic, and the Thirty Years' War (1618–48) proved the final body-blow. The League formally dissolved in 1669.

Hanson, John (1721–83) US statesman, first president of the United States under the ARTICLES OF CONFEDERATION (1781–82). He was a member of the Maryland colonial legislature (1757–79) and the CONTINENTAL CONGRESS (1780–82). His one-year term as president before the CONSTITUTION OF THE UNITED STATES was adopted made him effectively a presiding officer with no presidential powers.

Hapsburg *See* HABSBURG

Hara Kei (1856–1921) (Hara Takashi) Japanese statesman, prime minister (1918–21). He was one of the co-founders (1900) of Rikken Seiyukai (Friends of Constitutional Government Party), and in 1914 became the Party's president. A member of the Diet (parliament) from 1900, and a minister from 1906, Hara Kei developed Rikken Seiyukai into a Western-style political party. As prime minister, Hara Kei cultivated allies in the business community while attempting to reduce the power of the military, whose intervention in the Russian Civil War (1918–20) he failed to prevent. He also lowered the property qualifications for voting, but resisted universal male suffrage. Hara Kei was assassinated by a right-wing fanatic.

Harald I (*c*.910–*c*.985) (Harald Bluetooth) King of Denmark (*c*.935–*c*.985), son and successor of Gorm the Old. He was the first king to rule over a united Denmark. Harald also conquered parts of Norway. Converted (960) to Christianity by a German missionary, Harald introduced the religion to Denmark. On a runic stone at Jelling, he wrote that he "had made the Danes Christians". He was deposed by his son SWEYN I and died in exile.

Harald I (*c*.865–945) (Harald Fairhair) King of Norway (*c*.890–942). He consolidated his rule by deposing rival chiefs and defeating his opponents at the Battle of Hafrsfjord (between *c*.882 and 892). Harald was the first king to claim sovereignty over the whole country, but his harsh taxes and authoritarian rule led many landowning families to emigrate to the Western Isles of Scotland and perhaps Iceland. In pursuing the exiles, he extended his territory to include N and W Scotland. He abdicated in favour of his son ERIK BLOODAXE, who was succeeded by his brother, HAAKON I.

Harald II (*c*.930–970) (Harald Greycloak) King of Norway (*c*.965–70), son of ERIK BLOODAXE. With the aid of his uncle, HARALD I (Bluetooth), Harald overthrew and killed HAAKON I in the Battle of Hardangerfjord (961). A harsh ruler, he provoked much opposition with his outlawing of pagan worship. Following his seizure of some of Harald Bluetooth's territory in Norway, Harald Bluetooth arranged an invasion in which Harald II was killed.

Harald III (1015–66) (Harald Hardrada) King of Norway (1045–66). He served as a mercenary for the BYZANTINE EMPIRE, returning to Norway in 1045. He shared the throne with his nephew MAGNUS I until Magnus' death in 1047. Harald made several unsuccessful attempts to conquer Denmark, eventually reaching a truce (1062) with the Danish king, Sweyn II. In 1066, allied with Earl TOSTIG, Harald invaded England following the death of EDWARD THE CONFESSOR. He was killed, and their forces defeated, by HAROLD II at the Battle of STAMFORD BRIDGE.

Hardecanute (*c*.1019–42) King of Denmark (1035–42) and last Danish king of England (1040–42). The legitimate son and heir of CANUTE II, he inherited the Danish thrown on his father's death. Hardecanute was unable, however, to reach England immediately and the English elected his stepbrother, HAROLD I, in his absence. Hardecanute set sail for England to forcibly reclaim the crown but Harold died before he reached England, leaving Hardecanute to be elected king unchallenged. He was a cruel and unpopular ruler, levying crippling taxes as a punishment for England's betrayal. Because he was childless, the throne reverted to an English holder, EDWARD THE CONFESSOR, on Hardecanute's death.

Hardenberg, Karl August, Prince von (1750–1822) Prussian statesman. Serving as provincial minister from 1790, he won the trust of the Prussian king, FREDERICK WILLIAM III, and from 1798 was promoted to various posts, including foreign minister (1804–06) during the NAPOLEONIC WARS. In 1810 Hardenberg became prime minister and continued the reforms begun by Karl STEIN. While supporting the maintenance of an absolute monarchy, he achieved the abolition of serfdom and of privileges enjoyed by the nobility, such as exemption from the property tax. Hardenberg also established civic equality for Jews and freedom of trade, and attempted to establish an upper middle-class representative assembly. In 1813 he persuaded the king to form an alliance with Russia against NAPOLEON I, and at the Congress of VIENNA he secured additional territory for Prussia. Hardenberg continued to represent Prussia abroad until his death.

Hardie, (James) Keir (1856–1915) Scottish socialist politician. A coal miner as a child, he later organized mining unions and worked as a journalist on the *Labour Leader*. In 1888 he founded the Scottish Parliamentary Labour Party. In 1892 Hardie became the first socialist member of Parliament. The following year, he founded the INDEPENDENT LABOUR PARTY (ILP). In 1906 Hardie became a co-founder and first leader (1906–08) of the LABOUR PARTY. A committed pacifist, he withdrew from Labour politics in World War 1.

Harding, Warren G. (Gamaliel) (1865–1923) Twenty-ninth president of the United States (1921–23). A senator (1915–20), he was the Republican compromise candidate to run for president in 1920, receiving the backing of a number of influential businessmen and lawyers who wanted a pliable candidate. Harding's campaign for a "return to normalcy" easily defeated the Democrat challenge. His presidency will be remembered for its isolationist stance and distrust of the LEAGUE OF NATIONS. While in office, Harding left government to his cabinet and advisers. This administration, known as the "Ohio Gang", was one of the most corrupt in US history. The TEAPOT DOME SCANDAL forced a Congressional investigation. Harding died before the worst excesses became public knowledge, and he was succeeded by the vice president, Calvin COOLIDGE.

Hardy, Sir Thomas Masterman, Baronet (1769–1839) British naval officer. He twice commanded the flagship of Horatio NELSON's fleet and was at Nelson's side when he died at the Battle of TRAFALGAR (1805). Hardy was created a baronet in 1806. He became first sea lord in 1830 and vice admiral in 1837.

Hare Krishna (International Society for KRISHNA Consciousness) Hindu sect, founded (1965) in New York by Swami Prabhupada (A.C. Bhaktivedanta). The movement is based on the philosophy that Krishna is the supreme God and stresses the importance of asceticism. Public perception of the movement has been enhanced by the proselytizing of its shaven-headed, saffron-robed devotees, who practise self-denial, vegetarianism, meditation and chanting of mantras. *See also* HINDUISM

Hargreaves, James (1722–78) English inventor and industrialist. In 1764, near Blackburn, Lancashire, he invented the spinning jenny. This machine greatly speeded the spinning process of cotton by producing eight threads simultaneously. In 1768 local spinners destroyed the jenny, fearing that it threatened their jobs. Hargreaves moved to Nottingham and, with Thomas James, built a mill and became one of the first great factory owners.

Harley, Robert, 1st Earl of Oxford (1661–1724) British statesman, leader of the Tory government (1710–14) of Queen ANNE. He entered Parliament as a Whig in 1688, becoming one of the leading opponents of WILLIAM III (OF ORANGE). Harley served as speaker of the House of Commons (1701–05) and secretary of state (1704–08), becoming increasingly anti-Whig. Harley succeeded the Earl of GODOLPHIN as Queen Anne's leading minister. His government's main achievements were the Treaties of UTRECHT (1713–14), which ended the War of the SPANISH SUCCESSION, and the establishment (1711) of the SOUTH SEA COMPANY. Harley was appointed lord high treasurer in 1711 but, after losing a power struggle with Viscount BOLINGBROKE, he was dismissed from office (1714). Harley's disagreement with GEORGE I over the Treaty of Utrecht resulted in his imprisonment. He was released after two years, but faded from public life. *See also* MARLBOROUGH, JOHN CHURCHILL, 1ST DUKE OF

Harold Danish and Norwegian kings, *see* HARALD

Harold I (d.1040) (Harold Harefoot) King of England (1035–40), b. Denmark. An illegitimate son of CANUTE II (THE GREAT), he claimed the throne of England, ruling as regent (1035–37). Elected king at Oxford, he disposed of his rival, Alfred the Aethling, and displaced the heir, his half-brother HARDECANUTE. He died before having to confront Hardecanute.

Harold II (1022–66) Last ANGLO-SAXON king of England (1066), son of GODWIN. He led the forces that restored his family to power in 1052. On the death of Godwin, Harold became Earl of Wessex. His brother TOSTIG was Earl of Northumbria, until removed from his position by Harold after a revolt. Harold was elected king following the death of EDWARD THE CONFESSOR, despite having pledged to support William of Normandy's (later WILLIAM I) claim to the throne. England was immediately invaded by HARALD III of Norway and Tostig. Harold defeated them both at the Battle of STAMFORD BRIDGE. Three days later, Harold was defeated and killed by William at the Battle of HASTINGS.

Harriman, William Averill (1891–1986) US diplomat. He was US ambassador to the Soviet Union (1943–46) and Britain (1946) and secretary of commerce under President Harry TRUMAN (1947–48). Governor of New York (1954–58), Harriman became assistant secretary of state for Far Eastern affairs (1961–63) under President John KENNEDY and ambassador at large for President Lyndon JOHNSON. He was chief negotiator at the Paris peace talks (1968, 1969) on the VIETNAM WAR (1955–75).

Harrison, Benjamin (1833–1901) Twenty-third president of the United States (1889–93), grandson of William Henry HARRISON. A lawyer, he served as a Union officer during the American CIVIL WAR. After one term in the Senate, Harrison was nominated (1888) as the Republican candidate against President Grover CLEVELAND. Harrison won with a majority of the electoral votes, although Cleveland had the most popular votes. As president, Harrison passed the SHERMAN ANTI-TRUST ACT and the MCKINLEY Tariff Act (both 1890). His secretary of state James BLAINE helped to develop the PAN-AMERICAN MOVEMENT. Harrison was defeated by Cleveland in 1892.

Harrison, William Henry (1773–1841) Ninth president of the United States (1841), son of Benjamin Harrison (one of the signatories of the DECLARATION OF INDEPENDENCE) and grandfather of Benjamin Harrison (23rd US president). He was governor of Indiana Territory (1801–13). Harrison is remembered chiefly for his military career, especially the victory over the Native Americans at the Battle of Tippecanoe (1811) and later against the British in the WAR OF 1812. He served (1816–19) as a Whig member in the House of Representatives and later (1825–28) in the Senate. Harrison was elected president in 1840, with John

Tyler as vice president, under the famous slogan "Tippecanoe and Tyler too". Harrison died of pneumonia after one month in office.

Harsha (*c*.590–647) Ruler (606–47) of an empire in N India. Son of the king of Thanesar in the Punjab, Harsha extended his father's empire to encompass the entire Gangetic plain and parts of Rajasthan, but failed to conquer the Deccan. Converted to Buddhism, he was described by contemporaries, notably the Brahman court poet Bana and the Chinese Buddhist pilgrim Xuan Cang, as a just and enlightened king who set up establishments for the sick and poor. Rulers of the lands he conquered kept their titles in return for tribute. Harsha revived literature and the arts, and was himself a notable writer. His reign marked a transitional period between ancient and medieval India.

Hartford Convention (1814–15) Secret conference of FEDERALIST PARTY supporters from the New England states who opposed the WAR OF 1812 because it disrupted trade. Convention resolutions sought to strengthen STATES' RIGHTS over conscription and taxation. Some delegates favoured withdrawal from the Union. The Treaty of GHENT, ending the War, discredited the Convention and thus contributed to the demise of the Federalist Party. *See also* MADISON, JAMES

H

Harun al-Rashid (764–809) Fifth ABBASID caliph of Baghdad (786–809), brother and successor of al-Hadi. Harun al-Rashid's reign has gained romantic lustre from the stories of the *Arabian Nights,* and is considered a golden age of Islam with the free interchange of goods and ideas between Arabs and non-Arabs. In his early years in power, Harun was assisted by the influential Barmakid family. He engaged in a successful campaign against the BYZANTINE EMPIRE, concluding a treaty with the Empress IRENE. His efforts to reconcile competing interests by dividing the empire between his sons led to civil war. Harun al-Rashid was a great patron of the arts, and he encouraged the building of canals and mosques. He was succeeded by al-Amin.

Hasdrubal Barca Name of two Carthaginian generals. The **elder** (d.221 BC) expanded Carthaginian power and founded Cartagena, Spain. The **younger** (d.207 BC) was the son of HAMILCAR BARCA and the brother of HANNIBAL. He took command in Spain when Hannibal went to Italy (218 BC). Initially expanding Carthaginian territory in Spain, he was later (209 BC) defeated by Roman forces under SCIPIO AFRICANUS Major. Hasdrubal fled to Italy, where he died in battle. *See also* CARTHAGE

Hashemite Arab princely family descended from the Prophet MUHAMMAD, through his daughter FATIMA, her husband ALI (the fourth caliph) and their sons. HUSSEIN IBN ALI, ruler of Mecca and the Hejaz, his sons ABDULLAH IBN HUSSEIN, king of Jordan, and FAISAL I, king of Iraq, were also members of the Hashemite family, as was HUSSEIN I of Jordan.

▲ **Havel** argued that the inclusion of Eastern European countries in the United Nations (UN) and the North Atlantic Treaty Organization (NATO) would improve global relations.

Hasidism Popular pietist movement within JUDAISM founded by Israel ben Eliezer (*c*.1699–*c*.1761), known as the Baal Shem Tov (Master of the Good Name). The movement, centred in E Europe until World War 2, strongly supports Orthodox Judaism. Its main centres are now in Israel and the United States.

Hassan II (1929–99) King of MOROCCO (1961–99), son of MUHAMMAD V. He dissolved the National Assembly in 1965 and exercised authoritarian rule. There were limited constitutional reforms in 1970 and 1972, but Hassan's authority remained supreme. He eliminated foreign ownership of business in 1973. In 1975 he made claims to much of WESTERN SAHARA, sending a large Moroccan force to fight the Polisario Front, an armed force of tribesman who want to retain Western Saharan independence.

Hastings, Warren (1732–1818) British colonial administrator, first governor general of Bengal (1774–85). He served (1761–64) on the administrative council of the English EAST INDIA COMPANY in CALCUTTA, NE India, but resigned in protest against the corruption of his colleagues, and returned to England in 1765. He rejoined the Company in 1768. Manager of Company affairs in Bengal (1771–73), Hastings removed the influence of the nawab of Bengal and placed government in the hands of British officials in Calcutta. The British government sought greater control over the Company and appointed Hastings as governor general. The administration became blunted by feuds between Hastings and his four councillors. Hastings consolidated British control of India in wars against the MARATHAS (1778–82) and HYDER ALI of MYSORE (1780–84), but the conflicts strained Company finances and Hastings' methods of raising further funds attracted criticism. In 1785 he returned to England and was impeached by Edmund BURKE. In 1795 he was acquitted after a trial lasting seven years, but his career was ruined.

Hastings, Battle of (14 October 1066) Decisive battle of the NORMAN CONQUEST fought near Hastings, SE England, by HAROLD II of England against an invading army led by William, Duke of Normandy (later WILLIAM I). Having secured victory in the Battle of STAMFORD BRIDGE, near York, N England, Harold learned of William's invasion and was forced to march quickly S. His weary army took up position on a ridge and resisted William's well-equipped knights and archers for many hours. Towards the end of the day, Harold was killed by an arrow and the English resistance crumbled. The Norman victory and death of Harold marked the end of the ANGLO-SAXON monarchy and led to the political and social transformation of England.

Hatshepsut (d.1482 BC) Queen of Egypt (*c*.1503–1482 BC). Daughter of THUTMOSE I, she married her half-brother Thutmose II, with whom she co-ruled. After his death (*c*.1504 BC), she ruled as regent for her husband's son, Thutmose III. She soon took power in her own right, becoming the only woman to rule as pharaoh. During her reign, many building projects were undertaken, notably the temple at Deir al-Bahri and the obelisks at the KARNAK temple. She also ordered an important trading expedition to Punt, on the E African coast.

Hatta, Muhammad (1902–80) Indonesian statesman, first vice president (1950–56) of the republic of INDONESIA. Exiled (1935) by the Dutch for revolutionary activities, Hatta and SUKARNO collaborated with the Japanese in World War 2. In 1948 Hatta led the fight to end Dutch colonial rule and, after independence was achieved, served as deputy to Sukarno. Hatta resigned after a dispute with Sukarno, but returned as an adviser to SUHARTO.

Hattusas (now Boğazköy, N central Turkey) Capital of the ancient HITTITE empire. It was one of several independent city-states that were conquered by the Hittites, and was chosen as the capital because it was situated on a rocky outcrop and was blessed with a supply of water. Consisting of a citadel and lower city in *c*.1500 BC, by *c*.1400 BC it had almost doubled in size to include an upper city surrounded by massive walls. Its many impressive buildings included a royal palace and five temples. Hattusas was destroyed when the Hittite empire collapsed *c*.1200 BC.

Haughey, Charles (1925–) Irish statesman, taoiseach (1979–81, 1982, 1987–92). He entered the Dáil Éireann (Irish parliament) in 1957, holding various ministerial posts until his trial (1970) on charges of illegally importing arms for the Irish Republican Army (IRA). Haughey was acquitted and regained his seat in 1973. He succeeded Jack LYNCH as taoiseach (prime minister) and president (1979–92) of FIANNA FÁIL. In 1987 he returned to power after defeating Dr Garrett FITZGERALD. Haughey was forced to resign as taoiseach after a phone-tapping scandal.

Hausa Mainly Muslim people inhabiting NW Nigeria and S Niger. Hausa society is feudal and based on patrilineal descent. Its language is the lingua franca of N Nigeria and is a major trading language of W Africa. Hausa crafts include weaving, leatherwork and silversmithing.

Hausa states City-states that developed in N NIGERIA from the beginning of the 2nd millennium AD. Islam was introduced in the 14th century, perhaps by traders from SONGHAI, and they subsequently became centres of trade between the desert and the savanna. From the 15th century small towns were united to become kingdoms, and walled capital towns, such as KANO and Katsina, were built. In the 16th century, when European merchants began to arrive in the area, Kano was one of Africa's largest cities. There was frequent warfare among the Hausa states. Islam spread rapidly, and in 1804 many Hausa peasants joined the JIHAD launched by the FULANI cleric USMAN DAN FODIO. By 1809 the main Hausa states had been conquered and united into the SOKOTO caliphate. Divided into 30 local emirates, the caliphate was conquered by the British and declared a protectorate in 1900. *See also* KANEM-BORNU

Havel, Václav (1936–) Czech statesman and dramatist. He wrote a number of plays, notably *The Garden Party* (1963), that explored the individual's struggle against the state, and were highly critical of Gustav HUSÁK's communist regime. Havel was the leading spokesman for the dissident group Charter 77 and was imprisoned (1979–83) by the regime. In 1989 he served another brief spell in prison before founding the Civic Forum. Following the "Velvet Revolution" (December 1989) Havel was elected president of Czechoslovakia. He resigned (1992) in protest at the partition of Czechoslovakia, but returned by popular demand as president of the Czech Republic. He was re-elected in 1998.

Havelock, Sir Henry (1795–1857) British general. After joining the army in 1815, he went to India in 1823 and fought in the First AFGHAN WAR (1839) and the SIKH WARS (1843–49). During the INDIAN MUTINY (1857), Havelock led a force of *c*.1000 in the relief of Cawnpore (Kanpur), N India. After a series of battles, he and his troops fought their way through Lucknow to the Residency, where they were then besieged until a relief force arrived. A week later Havelock died of dysentery.

Hawaii State of the United States in the N Pacific Ocean, *c*.3350km (2100mi) WSW of San Francisco; the capital is Honolulu. There is an important US naval base at PEARL HARBOR. Settled by Polynesians in the 9th century AD, the islands were united in the late 18th century by KAMEHAMEHA I. In 1778 they were visited by British Captain James COOK, who named them the Sandwich Islands. In 1820 Kamehameha II admitted the first US Protestant missionaries. A liberal constitution was introduced in 1840. KAMEHAMEHA IV tried to counteract the influence of the missionaries, but the United States gained commercial privileges in 1887. In 1893 Queen LILUOKALANI was overthrown and the islands were annexed by the United States in 1898. In 1900 Hawaii became a US territory. Area: 6450sq mi (16,705sq km). Pop. (1990) 1,108,229.

HAWAII
Statehood :
21 August 1959
Nickname :
Aloha State
State motto :
The life of the land is perpetuated in righteousness

Hawke, Bob (Robert) (1929–) Australian statesman, prime minister (1983–91). He served (1970–80) as the president of the Australian Council of Trade Unions. He entered Parliament in 1980, rapidly rising to become (1983) leader of the Australian LABOR PARTY (APL). In the 1983 election, the APL defeated the Liberal Party and Hawke began the first of his unprecedented four terms in office. His administration saw the improvement of relations with the trade UNIONS and a reduction in inflation. Faced by a recession and a much reduced majority in the 1990 elections, Hawke resigned in favour of Paul KEATING.

Hawke (of Towton), Edward Hawke, 1st Baron (1705–81) British admiral. During the War of the Austrian Succession, Hawke was knighted for his role in the defeat (1747) of the French at Finisterre, W Spain. During the SEVEN YEARS' WAR, Hawke blockaded the French at Brest, delaying French reinforcements to Canada, and then destroyed a French fleet in Quiberon Bay (1759), NW France. He served as first lord of the admiralty (1766–71).

Hawkins, Sir John (1532–95) English naval commander, father of Richard HAWKINS. With the support of ELIZABETH I, he led two lucrative expeditions to Africa and the West Indies (1562–63, 1564–65). The first of these expeditions was the earliest English slave-trading voyage, carrying slaves from Guinea to the West Indies. On a third expedition (1567–69), the Spanish destroyed most of Hawkins' ships. He became treasurer of the navy in 1577, helping to build a fast and powerful fleet. Hawkins' modernization of the navy played a crucial role in the defeat of the Spanish ARMADA (1588). He died while on a voyage to the West Indies with Francis DRAKE.

Hawkins, Sir Richard (1560–1622) English mariner, son of John HAWKINS. He was a captain during the Spanish ARMADA (1588). In 1593 Hawkins set off on an attempt to circumnavigate the globe. He sighted what were probably the Falkland Islands in 1594 and then sailed up the E coast of South America. After burning Spanish ships at Valparaíso, he sailed N and was attacked by the Spanish off the coast of Peru. He was captured and sent to Spain, where he remained prisoner until 1602 when a ransom was paid. He was knighted on his return to England.

Hawley-Smoot Tariff (1930) Legislation designed to protect United States' goods from foreign competition. The Tariff, approved by President Herbert HOOVER, was the highest in US history, raising rates 38–49% on agricultural goods and 31–34% on other commodities. Other countries reacted by imposing high tariffs on US goods, causing a slump in trade and stimulating a wave of currency devaluations overseas, thus contributing to the GREAT DEPRESSION.

Hay, John Milton (1838–1905) US secretary of state (1898–1905) under presidents William MCKINLEY and Theodore ROOSEVELT. His OPEN-DOOR POLICY was a demand for equal trading status for foreign powers in China, and he negotiated the HAY-PAUNCEFOTE and HAY-BUNAU-VARILLA TREATIES ensuring US control of the PANAMA CANAL. Hay was a noted writer of novels and historical works.

Haya de la Torre, Victor Raúl (1895–1979) Peruvian statesman. In 1924 Haya founded the Alianza Popular Revolucionaria Americana (APRA), whose radical programme of reforms included nationalizing foreign-owned businesses, ending the exploitation of Native Americans, and resisting the perceived domination of Latin America by the United States. After failing to win the 1931 election, he was imprisoned (1931–33) and then went into hiding (1934–45). In 1945 APRA changed its name to the People's Party and supported José Luis Bustamante as president. In reality, Haya controlled the government and, after the overthrow of Bustamante (1948), he was forced to take refuge in the Colombian embassy in Lima (1949–54) and then Mexico (1954–57). After returning to Peru, Haya ran for president in the 1962 election, which produced no clear winner. The military intervened and in 1968 established a junta. In 1979 Haya drafted a new constitution restoring parliamentary democracy. He did not live to see the re-election of the People's Party in 1985.

Hay-Bunau-Varilla Treaty (1903) Agreement between Panama and the United States in which the United States was given sovereignty over a 16-km (10-mi) wide strip of land across Panama, to be used for a transoceanic canal. In return, the United States guaranteed Panamanian independence and an immediate payment of US$10 million and US$250,000 annually in perpetuity. The agreement was reached after the United States had helped Panama achieve independence from Colombia. It was negotiated in Washington, D.C., by Philippe Bunau-Varilla of Panama and John HAY, who in fact took his lead from President Theodore ROOSEVELT. *See also* PANAMA CANAL

Hayes, Rutherford Birchard (1822–93) Nineteenth president of the United States (1877–81). After serving in the American CIVIL WAR, he became a member (1865–67) of the House of Representatives. As governor of Ohio from 1869, he won the Republican nomination for president in 1876. Some of the electoral votes were disputed, but an electoral commission awarded all of them to Hayes, giving him victory over Samuel TILDEN, as long as he made concessions to the South. To this end, Hayes removed all federal troops from the South so ending the period of radical RECONSTRUCTION. He tried to promote civil-service reform, despite the opposition of Roscoe CONKLING. He retired after one term. *See also* BLAND-ALLISON ACT

Haymarket Square Riot (4 May 1886) Riot in Chicago, Illinois, United States. At a labour movement meeting, organized by anarchists to protest against police brutality, a bomb was thrown and seven police were killed. Although the bomber was never found, eight anarchist leaders were later convicted as accessories, and four were executed. Of the remaining prisoners, one committed suicide before the other three were pardoned (1893) by Illinois governor John ALTGELD, on the grounds that the trial was unfair. The incident turned public opinion against the UNION movement.

Hay-Pauncefote Treaty (1901) Agreement between the United States and Britain concerning rights over the proposed PANAMA CANAL. Negotiated by John HAY and Lord PAUNCEFOTE, British ambassador to the United States, it abrogated the CLAYTON-BULWER TREATY (1850), and allowed the United States to lease a canal zone from Colombia. *See also* HAY-BUNAU-VARILLA TREATY

Haywood, William Dudley (1869–1928) US UNION leader, known as "Big Bill". He helped to organize the INDUSTRIAL WORKERS OF THE WORLD (IWW) and advocated violence in pursuit of workers' rights. During World War 1, Haywood was convicted of sedition. Released on bail in 1921, he fled to the Soviet Union.

Healey, Denis Winston (1917–) British statesman, minister of defence (1964–70) and chancellor of the exchequer (1974–79). He entered Parliament in 1952. As defence secretary under Harold WILSON, Healey announced (1968) the withdrawal of all British bases E of the Suez Canal. When Wilson defeated Edward HEATH in the 1974 election, Healey was appointed chancellor and he continued in the post under James CALLAGHAN. Faced with worldwide economic recession, Healey attempted to control inflation through a tough prices and incomes policy. A series of strikes against wage control by the trade UNIONS culminated in the "winter of discontent" (1978–79) and contributed to Labour's defeat by Margaret THATCHER in the 1979 election. Healey served as deputy leader (1980–83) of the LABOUR PARTY under Michael FOOT.

Hearne, Samuel (1745–92) British fur trader and explorer of Canada. Hearne left England to navigate for the HUDSON'S BAY COMPANY in 1766. Three years later, he led the first of several expeditions N from Churchill, with the aim of opening up new territory for the Company. After two unsuccessful attempts Hearne set out again in 1770, becoming the first European to reach the Arctic Ocean by journeying overland in North America. In 1774 he helped to further the interests of the Hudson's Bay Company by establishing Cumberland House, an inland trading post.

Hearst, William Randolph (1863–1951) US media tycoon. He built a nationwide publishing empire that included newspapers (notably the *New York Journal*), magazines (*Harper's Bazaar*), news services, radio stations and film studios. With his rival, Joseph PULITZER, Hearst practised sensational, lurid and often jingoistic journalism. He was opposed to the League of Nations and US involvement in World War 1. Although a member of the House of Representatives, he failed in his bid for both mayor of New York City and governorship of New York. His career inspired Orson Welles' film *Citizen Kane* (1941).

Heath, Sir Edward Richard George (1916–) British statesman, prime minister (1970–74). He entered Parliament in 1950, becoming lord privy seal (1960–63). In 1965 Heath succeeded Sir Alec DOUGLAS-HOME as leader of the CONSERVATIVE PARTY. He defeated Harold WILSON in the 1970 election. As prime minister, Heath suspended (1972) the Northern Ireland Parliament at Stormont and established direct rule from Westminster. He secured (1973) Britain's membership of the European Economic Community (EEC) (*see* EUROPEAN COMMUNITY). Poor industrial relations brought on by an anti-inflationary policy of wage restraint led to a bitter miners' strike and the "three-day week" (1974) to conserve energy. After two election defeats in 1974, he was replaced (1975) as Conservative leader by Margaret THATCHER. Heath was a staunch critic of "Thatcherism" and an outspoken advocate of European integration during John MAJOR's premiership.

Hébert, Jacques René (1757–94) French Revolutionary journalist. He gained political power through his newspaper *La Père Duchesne*, which aroused the Parisian working class. A JACOBIN, he was among the leaders of the Parisian crowds who forced the expulsion of the moderate GIRONDINS from the National Convention and the beginning of the REIGN OF TERROR in 1793. In 1794 the COMMITTEE OF PUBLIC SAFETY began to regard Hébert as a dangerous extremist and had him arrested after he called for a another popular rising. Hébert and 17 of his followers were guillotined. *See also* ROBESPIERRE, MAXIMILIEN FRANÇOIS MARIE ISIDORE

Hebron (El Khalil) City in the Israeli-occupied WEST BANK. An ancient city, it came under Arab control in the 7th century AD and was occupied by the Crusaders (12th–13th centuries) before reverting to Arab rule. Hebron later became part of the OTTOMAN EMPIRE. In 1948 it was annexed to Jordan but was occupied by Israel during the SIX-DAY WAR (1967). It has witnessed much Israeli–Arab tension, especially during the INTIFADA. The ISRAELI-PALESTINIAN ACCORD granted Palestinian self-rule to 85% of the city. Hebron is sacred to both Jews and Muslims. The Tomb of the Patriarchs (the Cave of Machpelah) is the traditional burial place of Abraham, Sarah, Isaac, Rebecca, Jacob and Leah. Pop. (1995 est.) 117,000.

hedonism Pursuit of pleasure, or any of several philosophical or ethical doctrines associated with it. Aristippus (*c*.435–*c*.356 BC) taught that pleasure was the highest good. EPICURUS advocated discrimination in the seeking of pleasure. John LOCKE believed that the idea of "good" can be defined in terms of pleasure. Jeremy BENTHAM and J.S. MILL adapted a psychological view of hedonism in formulating UTILITARIANISM.

Hegel, Georg Wilhelm Friedrich (1770–1831) German philosopher, whose method of dialectical reasoning had a strong influence on his successors, notably Karl MARX. In 1818 he succeeded Johann Fichte as professor of philosophy at Berlin University. Hegel developed a metaphysical system that traced the self-realization of *Geist* (spirit) by dialectical movements towards perfection. These progressions took the form of battles between a thesis and an antithesis, eventually resolved in a synthesis at a higher level of truth. Hegel wrote two major books, *Phenomenology of Mind* (1807) and *Science of Logic* (1812–16).

hegemony Leadership or dominance of one state over others. The term originated in ancient Greece where the city-states of Athens, Sparta and Thebes held hegemony over other city-states in the 5th and 4th centuries BC. The term was also employed by the Italian Marxist Antonio GRAMSCI to refer to the phenomenon of one social CLASS monopolizing the creation and transmission of values.

Hegira (Arab. exodus) Flight of MUHAMMAD from MECCA to MEDINA in AD 622 to escape persecution. OMAR, the second caliph, set this date as the start of the Islamic CALENDAR.

Heian (*c*.AD 794–1185) Period in Japanese history that began with the move of the capital from NARA to Heian (now KYOTO). Under the FUJIWARA dynasty the period

H

was marked by great advances in Japanese civilization, above all in art and literature. The latter flourished with the development from the 10th century of a phonetic-based script, encouraging writing in Japanese in addition to the traditionally Chinese-based literature. Significant developments in Japanese BUDDHISM also occurred at this time, with the "True Pure Land" sect, which emphasized simple faith in Buddha, growing alongside the sects of Tendai and Shingon Buddhism, which practised elaborate ceremonies. During the late Heian period, rival military bands fought in the provinces, while in the capital there was a struggle between the TAIRA and Minamoto clans. The Taira were the dominant faction at court from 1156 until 1185.

Hejaz Region on the Red Sea coast, NW Saudi Arabia. The centre of ISLAM, it contains the Muslim holy cities of MECCA and MEDINA. Part of the Nabataean kingdom (100 BC–AD 200), it was then governed from Baghdad until 1258. It was ruled by the Egyptians until 1517 when it fell to the Turks. HUSSEIN IBN ALI revolted against the Turks in 1916 and, following the fall of the OTTOMAN EMPIRE, became king of the Hejaz. IBN SAUD led a Wahhabi invasion in 1926, and in 1932 he united Hejaz with other regions under his control to form the kingdom of SAUDI ARABIA. Area: 388,500sq km (150,000sq mi). *See also* WAHHABISM

Helena, Saint (*c*.AD 248–*c*.328) Mother of Roman Emperor CONSTANTINE I and first wife of Constantius Chlorus (Constantine's father). Constantius married another woman, Theodora, when he became emperor as Constantius I. When Helena's son was named emperor in 306, she became empress dowager. Under Constantine's influence, she also became an ardent patron of Christianity. Early church historians relate that Helena inspired the building of the Church of the Nativity in Bethlehem, Palestine. Later tradition claims that she found the cross on which Christ died.

Heligoland Bight, Battle of (28 August 1914) First naval battle of WORLD WAR 1, off the German island-base of Heligoland, at the mouth of the River Elbe in the North Sea. The British fleet, under Admiral Beatty, sank three German cruisers and one destroyer. *See also* JUTLAND, BATTLE OF

Heliopolis Ancient city in the Nile delta, 10km (6mi) NE of Cairo, N Lower Egypt. From *c*.1580 to 1090 BC, it was noted as a centre of Sun worship for the god Ra and was the site of a great temple (no longer extant) and the obelisks known as Cleopatra's needles (now standing in New York and London).

Hellenes Name by which the ancient Greeks called themselves (after Hellen, grandson of Prometheus, the fire-giver). Generally speaking these included the AEOLIANS, the DORIANS, the IONIANS and the ACHAEAN LEAGUE. More specifically, it means the people who came under the sway of Greek civilization, especially after the conquests of ALEXANDER III (THE GREAT), and adopted the Greek language and way of life. *See also* GREECE, CLASSSICAL

Hellenism Culture and ideals of classical GREECE. The term is applied particularly to the culture of ATHENS and related cities during the golden age of PERICLES (5th century BC). Hellenism came to symbolize pagan pleasure, freedom, love of life and the pursuit of beauty in the arts. The Hellenic period ended in the 4th century BC, with the conquests of ALEXANDER III (THE GREAT); it was succeeded by the HELLENISTIC AGE.

Hellenistic Age (323–27 BC) Period in classical history from the death of ALEXANDER III (THE GREAT) to the accession of AUGUSTUS. Alexander's conquests and the many cities he and his successors founded helped to spread Greek civilization along the W coast of Asia Minor, the Mediterranean, the Near East, Egypt and around the Black Sea. The age was distinguished by remarkable scientific and technological advances, especially in ALEXANDRIA, and by more elaborate and naturalistic styles in the visual arts. *See also* GREECE, CLASSICAL

Helots Indigenous inhabitants of classical GREECE, mainly of Messenia, who were forced into serfdom by foreign invaders. Often employed as agricultural labourers and as domestic servants, they were owned by the state, which used them as soldiers after the PERSIAN WARS (499–479 BC). In SPARTA, Helots outnumbered full Spartan citizens, and fear of a Helot revolt led the city to keep them under strict control. They were freed in 369 BC.

Helsinki (Helsingfors) Capital of Finland, in the S of the country, on the Gulf of Finland. It was founded (1550) by GUSTAVUS I (VASA) of Sweden. After the Russian invasion of Finland, Tsar Alexander I moved the capital from Turku to Helsinki in 1812. During the early 20th century, it was the centre of the Finnish independence movement. It is Finland's largest port. Pop. (1993) 508,588.

Helsinki Conference (1975) Series of meetings resulting in the formation of the Conference on Security and Cooperation in Europe (CSCE). Attended by representatives of 35 nations, including all the members of the NORTH ATLANTIC TREATY ORGANIZATION (NATO) and the WARSAW PACT plus the non-aligned states, it was proposed by the Soviet Union as a step towards improving East-West relations. The Conference produced a number of agreements on human rights, political freedom, and economic, scientific and technological cooperation, plus recognition of the borders established after World War 2. There were several follow-up conferences, including one in Paris (1990), when a permanent secretariat for the CSCE was established.

Helvetii CELTS who inhabited S Germany and migrated in the 2nd century BC, under pressure from Germanic tribes, to the N part of modern Switzerland. In 58 BC they invaded SW Gaul but were defeated by CAESAR and driven back towards Switzerland. Within the ROMAN EMPIRE their territory formed part of Gallia Belgica. They remained under Roman control until the 5th century, when they were subjugated by the ALEMANNI and the FRANKS. Their name remains as part of Switzerland's official title, the Helvetic Confederacy.

Henderson, Arthur (1863–1935) British statesman, one of the chief organizers of the British LABOUR PARTY. He entered Parliament in 1903 and served (1911–34) as Labour Party secretary. Henderson was minister without portfolio (1915–17) in David LLOYD GEORGE'S cabinet during World War 1. In 1924 he became home secretary in the first Labour government. He grew increasingly concerned with international affairs, serving (1929–31) as foreign secretary. Henderson was president of the World Disarmament Conference (1932), for which he was awarded the 1934 Nobel Prize for Peace.

Hennepin, Louis (1640–?1701) French explorer. A Franciscan missionary, he sailed to Canada in 1675 and became chaplain to Sieur de LA SALLE. Hennepin accompanied La Salle on the 1679 expedition, writing the first description of Niagara Falls and being held prisoner by the Sioux. The party was rescued by Sieur DULUTH. His exaggerated account, *Description de la Louisiane* (1683), was very popular.

Henrietta Maria (1609–69) Queen consort of CHARLES I of England from 1625, daughter of HENRY IV of France. She was the mother of CHARLES II and JAMES II. Her Roman Catholicism and support for Charles I's absolutist tendencies incurred Parliament's hostility and helped precipitate the English CIVIL WAR (1642–48). She worked hard to gain support for the Royalists during the early stages of the War, but was forced to flee to France in 1644.

Henry I (the Fowler) (*c*.876–936) Duke of Saxony (912–36) and king of the Germans (919–36). He was elected by the SAXONS and FRANKS to succeed CONRAD I as king. The nobles of Swabia and Bavaria did not recognize Henry as king, but he soon asserted his authority over both duchies. In 925 Henry reconquered Lotharingia (LORRAINE). In 933 he defeated the Magyar raiders. Extending German territory further, he acquired (934) Schleswig from the Danes. Henry was succeeded by his son, OTTO I, the first Holy Roman emperor.

Henry II (973–1024) German king (1002–24) and Holy Roman emperor (1014–24). He became Duke of Bavaria on the death of his father in 995. He succeeded his cousin OTTO III as king of Germany. In 1014 he was crowned emperor by Pope Benedict VIII in Rome. His troops assisted the papacy in wars against the Greeks and the LOMBARDS. Henry extended the Ottonian system of government, in which the church had great authority, establishing bishops as territorial rulers reporting to the king. He was canonized in 1146.

Henry III (1017–56) German king (1039–56) and Holy Roman emperor (1046–56). He succeeded his father, CONRAD II. He subdued rebellious vassals in Saxony and Lorraine and compelled the rulers of Poland, Bohemia and Hungary, as well as the S Italian princes, to pay him tribute. On an expedition to Italy (1046), Henry deposed three rival popes and installed Bishop Suidger of Bamberg as Pope Clement II who then crowned him as Holy Roman emperor. Henry thus secured control over the church and in the following years he appointed three more popes.

Henry IV (1050–1106) German king (1056–1106) and Holy Roman emperor (1084–1106), son and successor of HENRY III. His mother, Agnes, served as regent until 1065. She granted BAVARIA, SWABIA and CARINTHIA to local rulers, thus weakening Henry's kingdom. After coming of age, Henry became embroiled in the dispute with the papacy over the lay INVESTITURE of clerics. He deposed Pope GREGORY VII (1076) and was in turn excommunicated by him. Rebellion in Germany weakened Henry's position still further, and in 1077 he was forced to do penance at CANOSSA. Excommunicated again, Henry captured Rome (1084), deposed Gregory and installed GUIBERT OF RAVENNA (Clement III) as antipope. Clement crowned Henry as Holy Roman emperor. Rebellions led by Henry's sons, Henry (later HENRY V) and Conrad, eventually succeeding in deposing him.

Henry V (1081–1125) German king (1105–25) and Holy Roman emperor (1111–25). Having deposed his father, HENRY IV, he resumed the quarrel with the papacy over INVESTITURE, while antagonizing German princes with the ruthless assertion of his power. Henry attempted to reach an agreement with Pope Paschal II, and in 1111 he imprisoned the pope, forcing him to grant INVESTITURE rights. Paschal crowned Henry Holy Roman emperor. Opposition to Henry built up in Germany and within the church. His rights of investiture were declared invalid, and he was excommunicated. Henry was compelled to negotiate with Pope Calixtus II. The Concordat of WORMS (1122) ended the investiture controversy.

Henry VI (1165–97) German king (1190–97) and Holy Roman emperor (1191–97), son of FREDERICK I (BARBAROSSA). In 1186 he married Constance, heiress of the kingdom of SICILY, and much of his reign was devoted to securing that inheritance. TANCRED, grandson of ROGER II of Sicily, seized the Sicilian throne in 1190, and it was not until after Tancred's death that Henry VI secured the crown of Sicily. After 1194, the Holy Roman Empire was at the height of its power. Although he failed to make the empire hereditary in the HOHENSTAUFEN line, his infant son, FREDERICK II, was accepted as his successor.

Henry VII (1275–1313) German king (1308–13) and Holy Roman emperor (1312–13). He was Duke of Luxembourg as Henry IV, succeeding his father, Henry III, in 1288. He was elected German king in 1308. Henry acquired Bohemia for his family by marrying his son John to Elizabeth of Bohemia (1310). He also revived imperial ambitions in Italy but, although crowned king of the LOMBARDS (1311), he could not maintain authority there. He died of fever while fighting the GUELPHS in Tuscany.

Henry I (1068–1135) King of England (1100–35), youngest son of WILLIAM I (THE CONQUEROR). He rescinded unpopular taxes and married a Scottish princess of Anglo-Saxon descent. He thus won the support that helped him to defeat his brother ROBERT II, Duke of NORMANDY, and regain Normandy for the English crown in 1106. In 1107 Henry settled the dispute with Archbishop ANSELM over the lay INVESTITURE of churchmen. He gave up the king's right to invest bishops in return for the bishops continuing to pay homage to him. Henry was succeeded by his nephew STEPHEN, who seized the throne from MATILDA, Henry's daughter and appointed successor, following the death of his only legitimate son in 1120.

Henry II (1133–89) King of England (1154–89), son of GEOFFREY OF ANJOU and MATILDA (daughter of HENRY I). He inherited the ANGEVIN lands and obtained AQUITAINE by marrying ELEANOR in 1152. He invaded England (1153) and was appointed successor to STEPHEN, so becoming the first PLANTAGENET king of England. An able and energetic king, he re-established stable royal government in England following years of unrest caused by self-serving barons, and instituted reforms in finance, local government and justice by introducing COMMON LAW. During his reign, Henry increased his kingdom, which already stretched from N England to S France, by obtaining tribute from MALCOLM III of Scotland and annexing much of Ireland. His efforts to extend royal justice to priests (*see* CLARENDON, CONSTITUTIONS OF) led to his quarrel with Thomas à BECKET. His later reign was troubled by the rebellions of his sons, including two future kings, RICHARD I and JOHN.

Henry III (1207–72) King of England (1216–72). Although gaining the throne at the age of nine from his father JOHN, Henry did not actually rule until 1227. His abuses of royal power conflicted with MAGNA CARTA, and this, coupled with the influence of foreigners on his administration, antagonized the nobles. He was forced to accept the Provisions of Oxford (1258) and Westminster (1259), which gave more power to his councillors. However, he renounced the provisions in 1261, provoking the BARONS' WAR. The leader of the barons, Simon de MONTFORT, captured Henry at Lewes (1264) and took control. However Henry's son, the future EDWARD I, defeated Montfort at the Battle of EVESHAM (1265) and effectively thereafter ruled on his father's behalf.

Henry IV (1367–1413) King of England (1399–1413), son of JOHN OF GAUNT. As Henry Bolingbroke he was exiled in 1399 by RICHARD II, thus being deprived of the vast Lancastrian estates left to him by his father. He returned and overthrew Richard, claiming both the estates and the crown for himself. As a usurper, Henry was in a weak position and was forced to make concessions to the church, parliament and the nobility. There were frequent rebellions during his reign, of which the two most significant were led by Owain GLYN DŴR and Sir Henry PERCY. In 1403 Henry finally defeated Percy at Shrewsbury, W England. The end of his reign was marked by conflict between Thomas Arundel, archbishop of Canterbury, and Henry BEAUFORT. He was succeeded by his son, HENRY V. *See also* LANCASTER, HOUSE OF

Henry V (1387–1422) King of England (1413–22), son of HENRY IV. He was knighted by RICHARD II in 1399 and brought up by his uncle, Henry BEAUFORT. As prince, he gained useful military experience during campaigns against Owain GLYN DŴR. On his accession, Henry crushed a LOLLARD rebellion (1414). He renewed English claims against France in the HUNDRED YEARS' WAR and won a decisive victory over CHARLES VI of France at AGINCOURT (1415), making England one of the strongest kingdoms in Europe. Further conquests in BURGUNDY (1417–19) resulted in the Treaty of Troyes (1420), when Charles VI recognized Henry as his heir. The following month he married Charles' daughter, Catherine of Valois. However, he did not live to enjoy his triumph for long, dying of fever in 1422. *See also* LANCASTER, HOUSE OF

Henry VI (1421–71) King of England (1422–61, 1470–71), son and successor of HENRY V. His regency was dominated by the dukes of BEDFORD and GLOUCESTER, Henry BEAUFORT and William de la Pole. In 1445 Henry married MARGARET OF ANJOU, who thereafter controlled the government. From 1453 he suffered periods of insanity; this, coupled with a series of military disasters in France during the HUNDRED YEARS' WAR that by 1453 had left England only in control of Calais, encouraged Richard, Duke of YORK to seize power, proclaiming himself Lord Protector. In 1455 Richard defeated Henry's forces at St Albans, the first battle in the Wars of the ROSES between the houses of LANCASTER and York. Although Richard was killed at the Battle of Wakefield in 1460, Henry was deposed in 1461 by the Yorkists, who proclaimed EDWARD IV as king. Henry went into exile in Scotland but returned in 1464 to once again lead the Lancastrians to defeat. Imprisoned between 1465 and 1470, he was restored to the throne in 1470 by Richard Neville, Duke of WARWICK. However, following another Yorkist victory at TEWKESBURY he was again deposed and then murdered.

Henry VII (1457–1509) King of England (1485–1509), founder of the TUDOR dynasty. His claim to the throne was weak until he became, with the death of HENRY VI in 1471, the main surviving male in the House of LANCASTER. He then went to France, where the Yorkists made several attempts on his life before he landed with an army on the English coast in 1485. He became king by defeating RICHARD III in the final battle of the Wars of the ROSES at BOSWORTH FIELD (1485), and he then united the houses of Lancaster and YORK by marrying the Yorkist heiress, Elizabeth (1486). His financial acumen and encouragement of trade through commercial treaties restored England's fortunes after the devastation of civil war. He also established peaceful relations with France (1492) and with Scotland (1499). In 1501 he forged an alliance between England and Spain by marrying his son Arthur (who died in 1502) to CATHERINE OF ARAGON. He took effective action against pretenders to his throne, notably Lambert SIMNEL and Perkin WARBECK, who claimed to be the young Yorkist princes, Edward of Warwick and Richard of York, last seen in the Tower. When he died there was no opposition to the succession of his son, HENRY VIII.

Henry VIII (1491–1547) King of England (1509–47), second son of HENRY VII. He became heir (1502) on the death of his elder brother, Arthur, and married Arthur's widow, CATHERINE OF ARAGON, soon after his accession. His aggressive foreign policy, administered (1515–29) by his lord chancellor Cardinal Thomas WOLSEY, depleted the royal treasury. In 1512 Henry invaded France as a member of the HOLY LEAGUE. In 1513 the Duke of NORFOLK scored a major propaganda victory for Henry by defeating a Scottish invasion at the Battle of FLODDEN. However, in subsequent years England began to appear a weak power in comparison with the HOLY ROMAN EMPIRE under CHARLES V. Wolsey's ill-timed decision to abandon an alliance with Charles V, just prior to the latter's defeat of FRANCIS I at the Battle of PAVIA (1525), led to his downfall. He was replaced by Thomas MORE. Henry now urgently sought a divorce from Catherine of Aragon, with whom he had so far failed to produce a male heir. Pope CLEMENT VII's refusal to grant the divorce resulted in Henry presiding over the first stages of the English REFORMATION with the support, from 1532, of Thomas CROMWELL. The English church separated from Rome and in 1533 Henry divorced Catherine and married Anne BOLEYN (1533), mother of the future ELIZABETH I. In 1535 Anne was executed for adultery. Thomas More was also executed for refusing to accept Henry as supreme head of the CHURCH OF ENGLAND. Henry, who had been rewarded with the title DEFENDER OF THE FAITH by the pope for his criticism of Martin LUTHER, was however resistant to the introduction of PROTESTANTISM. Henry then married Jane SEYMOUR, who died shortly after the birth of the future EDWARD VI. His next marriage, to ANNE OF CLEVES, ended in divorce (1540). Shortly after, he married Catherine HOWARD (executed 1542) and finally Catherine PARR (1543), who survived him. Between 1536 and 1540 he oversaw the DISSOLUTION OF THE MONASTERIES, which brought temporary relief from financial problems but at the cost of social unrest. Cromwell managed this revolution in English society through Parliament, but he too was executed in 1540, as Henry became increasingly suspicious of his ministers and assumed greater personal control of government. Henry's financial problems returned, however, when he embarked on a war against France and its ally, Scotland, in 1542. Little was gained from the war but Henry did not make peace with Scotland until 1546. He died without having secured the sucession of his son, Edward VI. *See also* CRANMER, THOMAS; FIELD OF THE CLOTH OF GOLD

▲ **Henry VIII** Portrait (*c*.1536) after Hans Holbein the Younger. The separation of the church in England from Rome, initiated by Henry VIII, marked a crucial turning point in British history.

Henry I (1008–60) King of France (1031–60). His reign was characterized by struggles with rebellious vassals. Although Henry was anointed king in 1026 by his father, ROBERT II, his younger brother Robert claimed the throne and was supported by their mother, Constance of Provence. In the ensuing civil war, Henry was forced to cede BURGUNDY to Robert. Henry at first supported (1035–47) and then fought (1054, 1058) unsuccessfully against William, Duke of Normandy (later WILLIAM I of England). He was succeeded by his son, PHILIP I.

Henry II (1519–59) King of France (1547–59), son and successor of FRANCIS I. In 1533 he married CATHERINE DE' MEDICI. Henry was dominated by his mistress, Diane de Poitiers, and by the rival families of GUISE and MONTMORENCY. After bankrupting the royal government, the war with Emperor CHARLES V was concluded at the Peace of CATEAU-CAMBRÉSIS (1559). Henry began the persecution of HUGUENOTS, which led to the Wars of RELIGION.

Henry III (1551–89) King of France (1574–89). As Duke of Anjou, he fought against the HUGUENOTS in the Wars of RELIGION. In 1572 he helped his mother, CATHERINE DE' MEDICI, plan the SAINT BARTHOLOMEW'S DAY MASSACRE. In 1573 he was elected king of Poland. The following year, on the death of his brother, CHARLES IX, he acceded to the French throne. By making peace with the Huguenots (1576), Henry antagonized extremist Roman Catholics, who formed the HOLY LEAGUE led by the House of GUISE. After the League provoked a revolt in 1588, Henry had the Guise leaders killed and made an alliance with the Huguenot, Henry of Navarre (later HENRY IV). The king was assassinated by a member of the league. He was the last king of the VALOIS dynasty.

Henry IV (1553–1610) (Henry of Navarre) King of France (1589–1610), first of the BOURBON dynasty. From a Protestant upbringing, he was recognized as leader of the HUGUENOTS. In 1572 he became king of Navarre and then married MARGARET OF VALOIS, daughter of CATHERINE DE' MEDICI, in the belief that this would end the civil war between Huguenots and Catholics. However, a few days later the SAINT BARTHOLOMEW'S DAY MASSACRE took place, and Henry survived only by appearing to convert to Roman Catholicism. He was kept a prisoner at court until 1576 when he escaped, recanted his conversion to Catholicism, and took up a leading role in the renewed French Wars of RELIGION. In 1584 he became legal heir to HENRY III. On Henry III's death, the GUISE family, led by Duke Henry, refused to recognize his claim, but were defeated in the subsequent War of the Three Henrys (1585–89). Henry became king in 1589 but it took him many years to secure his kingdom. In 1593 he converted to Roman Catholicism, allegedly remarking "Paris is well worth a Mass", and in 1598 he ended the French Wars of Religion by signing the Edict of NANTES (1598). Under the Edict, Roman Catholicism remained the state church while Huguenots were given some religious freedom. Henry,

H

however, remained sympathetic to Protestantism, secretly supporting the Protestant Revolt of the Netherlands against Spain. His marriage to Margaret of Valois was annulled in 1599, and he married Marie de' Medici in 1600. A popular king, with a keen sense of social justice, he stabilized the economy and greatly improved the country's finances. He was assassinated by François Ravaillac.

Henry X (the Proud) (1108–39) Duke of Bavaria (1126–38) and Saxony (1137–38), a member of the Guelph faction. On inheriting Bavaria from his father, he became Henry X. He married Gertrude, daughter and heiress of the German king Lothair II. On the death of Lothair, Henry inherited the duchy of Saxony. Conrad III, a Hohenstaufen, was elected as German king. Anxious to restrict Henry's power, Conrad deprived him of his duchies. Henry launched a civil war and captured Saxony; he died before regaining Bavaria. His son, Henry III (the Lion), continued the struggle.

Henry, Patrick (1736–99) American patriot and statesman. He opposed British colonial policy, arguing against the Stamp Act (1765). As a member of the Continental Congress, he called the colonists to arms in March 1775 with the demand "Give me liberty or give me death". Henry served as governor of Virginia (1776–79, 1784–86). A strong believer in states' rights, he opposed ratification of the US Constitution in 1787.

Henry III (the Lion) (1129–95) Duke of Saxony (1142–80) and of Bavaria (1156–80), a member of the Guelph faction. He fought for the lands lost by his father, Henry X (the Proud), to the Emperor Conrad III, recovering Saxony in 1142. In 1156 Frederick I (Barbarossa) restored Bavaria to Henry in return for his support. Henry promoted German expansion beyond the River Elbe, greatly expanding his territory. In 1157 he founded Munich. In 1180, after refusing to support Frederick I's wars in Italy, he was deprived of most of his lands. Henry was eventually (1194) reconciled with Frederick's successor, Henry VI.

Henry the Navigator (1394–1460) Portuguese prince, son of John I. As governor of Algarve from 1419, he established his court at Sagres on the Atlantic coast and encouraged experiments in shipbuilding design and the development of navigational techniques. From 1420 he began to send ships to explore the Atlantic coast of Morocco. After he had dispatched 15 ships, one finally rounded Cape Bojador in 1434. After this event, the pace of exploration increased and by the time of Henry's death, Portuguese explorers had reached Sierra Leone. Henry thus paved the way for the later discovery of the route to India via the Cape of Good Hope.

Heraclius (575–641) Byzantine emperor (610–41). An outstanding military leader, he deposed Phocas and seized the throne of the Eastern Roman Empire. Heraclius reformed government and army, organizing the empire into themes (military provinces). He was the first emperor to preside over a predominantly Greek administration. The Persians captured Palestine and Syria (614) and later Egypt and Asia Minor (619). Heraclius concluded a treaty (620) with the Avars, who were threatening the N part of the empire, and then went into battle (622–27) with the Persians. Heraclius' military successes took the Byzantine Empire to unrivalled power, and he restored the Cross to Jerusalem (630). In 634 Arab armies rose up against Heraclius, and by the time of his death they had conquered much of the empire.

Herculaneum Ancient city on the Bay of Naples, Italy, the site of modern Resina. Devastated in AD 62 by an earthquake, it was buried by the eruption of Vesuvius in AD 79. Archaeological excavations unearthed the Villa of the Papyri, which contained a library, well-preserved furniture, and victims who died on the seashore. *See also* Pompeii

Herero Group of Bantu-speaking people of SW Africa, chiefly in Namibia. By tradition, the Herero are nomadic pastoralists who practise ancestor worship, but European influence and Christianity are now widespread. Both matrilineal and patrilineal descent exist in a society governed by localized autonomous units. Many of the Herero died during a revolt against German rule, when they were driven into the Omaheke Desert (1903–07). By 1911 only 15,130 had survived out of perhaps 80,000. They were active in Namibia's struggle for independence.

heresy Denial of, or deviation from, orthodox religious belief. The concept is found in most organized religions with a rigid dogmatic system. The early Christian church fought against heresies such as Arianism and Nestorianism. In the Middle Ages, the Catholic Church set up the Inquisition to fight heresy. After the Reformation, the Catholic Church described Protestants as heretics because of their denial of many papally defined dogmas, while Protestants applied the term to those who denied their interpretation of the major scriptural doctrines.

Hereward the Wake (d. *c.*1080) Anglo-Saxon landowner who led resistance to the Norman Conquest of William I (the Conqueror). He led Anglo-Saxon rebels, who with Danish raiders, sacked Peterborough Abbey (1070). When the Danes withdrew, Hereward was forced to retreat to the fens around Ely, where he held out against William's forces for nearly a year (1070–71). Eventually driven into hiding, he died in obscurity.

Herod (the Great) (73–04 BC) King of Judaea (37–04 BC). He was appointed governor of Galilee by Julius Caesar in 47 BC. In 41 BC Mark Antony made him tetrarch of Galilee. Supported by Antony and later Augustus, Herod endeavoured to reconcile Jews and Romans, and was responsible for many public works, including the rebuilding of the Temple of Jerusalem, as well as improving the economic and agricultural potential of Judaea. Herod later became cruel and tyrannical. According to the New Testament, he was king of Judaea when Jesus was born and was responsible for the massacre of infants in Bethlehem shortly before his death.

Herod Agrippa I (AD 10–44) King of Judaea (41–44), grandson of Herod (the Great). He was educated in Rome at the court of Emperor Tiberius. Securing a large loan to pay off a debt, Herod Agrippa made a substantial donation to Caligula, thus ensuring his favour. He gained much territory on the accession of Caligula. Caligula's successor, Claudius, appointed Herod as king of Judaea. Supporting Jewish policies, Herod repressed the Christians, imprisoning St Peter and executing St James.

Herod Agrippa II (AD 27–93) King of Chalcis (50–93) and of Judaea (53–70), son of Herod Agrippa I. He was educated at the imperial court in Rome. The last of the Herodian dynasty, he presided over the trial of St Paul. Herod tried to prevent the Jewish revolt (66) and afterwards sided with Rome.

Herod Antipas (21 BC–AD 39) Tetrach of Galilee and Petraea (4 BC–AD 39), son of Herod (the Great). He had John the Baptist beheaded at the instigation of his wife Herodias and his step-daughter Salome. He refused to intervene in the trial of Jesus Christ, leaving his fate to the Roman procurator Pontius Pilate. Emperor Caligula banished him to Gaul in AD 39.

Herodotus (*c.*485–*c.*425 BC) Greek historian. His *Histories* are the first great prose work in European literature. His main theme was the struggle of Greece against the Persian empire in the Persian Wars, but he also described the rise of Persia under Cyrus and Darius I, the development of Greek city-states and Egypt, Babylon and other parts of the Greco-Asian world. Insatiably curious, he was over-credulous of many stories, but could apply sound critical criteria and is justly called the "father of history".

Hertzog, James Barry Munnik (1866–1942) South African statesman, prime minister (1924–39). He led the Orange Free State forces in the second of the South African Wars (1899–1902). A member (1910–12) of the first Union government under Louis Botha, Hertzog founded the opposition National Party in 1914 to work for South African independence. In 1933 he formed a coalition with Jan Smuts and the following year the National and South African parties joined to form the United Party. With the support of the Afrikaners, he introduced measures aimed at greater segregation of whites and blacks. In 1939 Hertzog resigned from the coalition government when parliament rejected his policy of not supporting Britain in World War 2.

Herzl, Theodor (1860–1904) Jewish leader and founder of Zionism, b. Budapest. He worked as a lawyer and a journalist, during which time he covered the Dreyfus affair, an incident that persuaded him of the need for an independent Jewish state. He underlined this theme in his pamphlet "The Jewish State". In 1897 he organized the First Zionist Congress where he established and became president of the World Zionist Organization. The organization sought support from European political leaders, financiers and industrialists to establish a Jewish national home in Palestine.

Herzog, Chaim (1918–97) Israeli general and statesman, president (1983–93), b. Ireland. Herzog emigrated to Palestine in 1935 and was active in the Haganah. He served in the British Army during World War 2. After the establishment of Israel in 1948, Herzog became director of intelligence (1948–50, 1959–62). Later appointed to various diplomatic posts, Herzog became well-known as an writer and lecturer. He served (1975–78) as Israel's representative at the United Nations (UN). He was elected president of Israel in 1983 and re-elected in 1988.

Heseltine, Michael Ray Dibdin (1933–) British statesman, deputy prime minister (1995–97). He entered Parliament in 1966. Under Margaret Thatcher, Heseltine served as secretary of state for the environment (1979–83) and defence secretary (1983–86), resigning over a disagreement concerning Westland Helicopters. In 1990 his challenge to Thatcher's leadership eventually led to her resignation. He rejoined the cabinet as secretary of

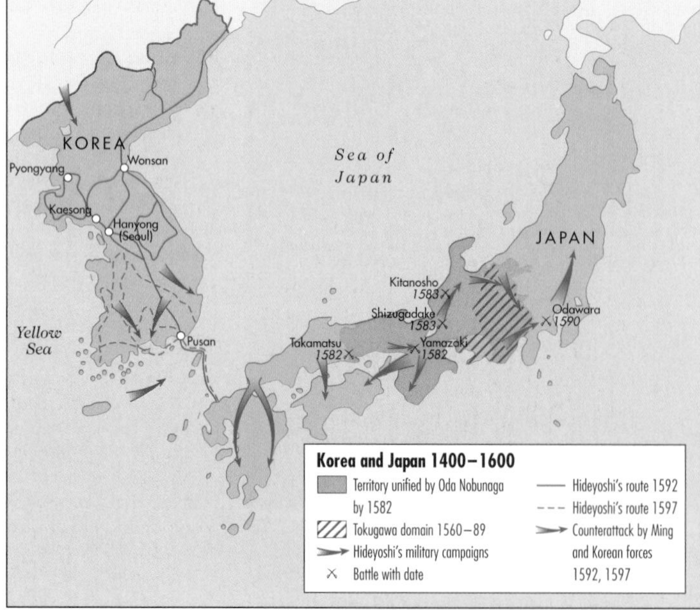

► **Hideyoshi** By 1590, Hideyoshi had succeeded in unifying Japan. His redistribution of feudal lands, and enforcement of strict class separations, brought an end to the warring between the *daimyo* (landlords) that had characterized the 15th century. Hideyoshi then turned his attention to the expansion of his empire. In 1592, he led 160,000 troops in an attack on Korea, which he hoped to use as a route for conquering Ming China. The army captured Seoul within a few weeks, but was forced to retreat when the Korean naval admiral, Yi Sun-sin (1545–98), cut their nautical supply lines. A second attack in 1597, during which Hideyoshi died, was supressed by the Korean armies with Chinese support.

state for the environment (1990–92) under John MAJOR. As secretary of state for trade and industry (1992–95), he announced a drastic programme of pit closures. Despite a heart attack, Heseltine continued as a combative deputy prime minister. Following electoral defeat (1997), he took a less active role in CONSERVATIVE PARTY politics.

Hess, (Walter Richard) Rudolf (1894–1987) German Nazi leader. He joined the NAZI PARTY in 1921 and took part in the abortive MUNICH PUTSCH (1923), for which he, along with Adolf HITLER, was imprisoned. Hess was the nominal deputy leader under Hitler from 1933. In 1941, on the eve of Germany's invasion of Russia, he flew to Scotland in a mysterious one-man effort to make peace with the British. Imprisoned by the British for the rest of World War 2, he underwent psychiatric treatment before being sentenced to life imprisonment at the NUREMBERG TRIALS (1945). He spent the rest of his life in Spandau Prison, Berlin, for many years its sole inmate.

Heydrich, Reinhard (1904–42) German Nazi official, deputy chief of the GESTAPO. A protégé of Heinrich HIMMLER, he joined the SS in 1931. In 1934 he was appointed second in command of the GESTAPO, under Himmler. After ruthless action against resistance in Norway and the Netherlands, Heydrich was made protector of Bohemia and Moravia in 1941. His brutality earned him the nickname "hangman of Europe". Heydrich was influential in the Nazi policy of total extermination of the Jews, the FINAL SOLUTION. Heydrich was assassinated by Czech patriots in Prague in 1942, in reprisal for which the entire male population of the village of Lidice was killed.

Hezbollah (Hizbollah) Iranian-backed group of fundamentalist SHIITE Muslims based in S Lebanon. It was formed in 1982 following the Israeli occupation of S Lebanon. The organization was subsequently blamed for a number of terrorist incidents, including the bomb attacks in which *c.*300 French and US peacekeeping troops were killed (1983), and the hijacking of a TWA plane in Cairo (1985). In 1992 the group's secretary general, Abbas al-Mussawi, was killed in an Israeli attack. In 1996 and 2000, the Israeli airforce launched intensive bombing raids on Hezbollah positions in Lebanon.

Hezekiah King of JUDAH (r. *c.*715–*c.*698 BC). He led Judah, a vassal of ASSYRIA, in revolt against the Assyrians in 701 BC. The result was an Assyrian invasion under SENNACHERIB and widespread destruction. Only Jerusalem survived due to Hezekiah's construction of a tunnel to supply water and his reinforcement of the city walls. He promoted Hebrew traditions and attempted to drive out the cults of Assyrian gods, but not with any long-lasting effect. The prophets Isaiah and Micah preached during his reign.

Hiawatha (active 16th century) Native American leader of the Onondaga. In *c.*1575 he founded the five-nation IROQUOIS CONFEDERACY to halt intertribal wars. His semi-mythic reputation is partly the result of association with the fictional hero of the Longfellow poem *The Song of Hiawatha* (1855). *See also* ANASAZI; PUEBLO PEOPLES

Hickok, "Wild Bill" (James Butler) (1837–76) US frontiersman. A renowned marksman, he was a scout with the Union Army during the CIVIL WAR. He served as a US marshal (1869–71) in Kansas, helping to keep peace along the frontier. Hickok later toured with the Wild West show of "BUFFALO BILL". He was shot dead while playing poker.

Hidalgo y Costilla, Miguel (1753–1811) Mexican priest and revolutionary. Of Creole birth, he was a priest in Dolores, Guanajuato, where he attempted to improve conditions for the Native American population. Joining a secret society working for independence from Spain, he plotted a revolt. On 16 September 1810, Hidalgo proclaimed a revolution and soon acquired an untrained army of 80,000. They captured Guanajuato and Valladolid. Defeated at Calderón Bridge, Hidalgo fled but was captured and executed.

Hideyoshi (1536–98) Japanese warrior and dictator. He served under Oda NOBUNAGA, upon whose death he became dictator. Hideyoshi struggled to unify Japan after the devastation inflicted by a hundred years of feuds among the DAIMYO. By 1590, with the defeat of the HOJO, Hideyoshi had effectively achieved his aim. Chiefly known as a fine military strategist, he was also a capable administrator, encouraging trade, building castles, commissioning land surveys and developing maritime law. Hideyoshi feared and suppressed both Buddhist and subsequently Christian influences. In 1592 he attempted to invade China, but was repulsed by the MING dynasty and succeeded only in occupying part of KOREA.

hieroglyphics Signs used in the writing of ancient EGYPT and, by extension, in that of ancient Crete, Asia Minor, Central America and Mexico. The Egyptian system of hieroglyphics (pictorial characters) arose sometime before 3100 BC. At first they were purely picture symbols: the word "sun", for instance, was represented by a circle with a dot inside. In due course, they also came to be used conceptually, with symbols such as that for "sun" also standing for "day". Eventually, many symbols were used phonetically. The "sun" symbol, for example, stood for a syllable that contained the same combination of consonants but had a different meaning. By the 7th century, hieroglyphics were used for business and literary purposes. As ancient Egyptian was supplanted by Greek, hieroglyphics died out. Most Egyptian texts have been deciphered, thanks to the discovery of the ROSETTA STONE (1799).

Higginson, Thomas Wentworth Storrow (1823–1911) US social reformer. A Unitarian minister, he worked for the abolition of slavery and for women's rights. He supported John BROWN in his anti-slavery activities. During the CIVIL WAR, Higginson was colonel of the first African-American regiment, an experience recorded in *Army Life in a Black Regiment* (1870). He was a close friend of many writers, notably Emily Dickinson.

Hill, Ambrose Powell (1825–65) Confederate commander in the American CIVIL WAR. He fought in the First and Second battles of BULL RUN (1862) and led his troops in the FREDERICKSBURG, CHANCELLORSVILLE, GETTYSBURG and WILDERNESS campaigns. He was killed at Petersburg while trying to restore the Confederate defence.

Hill, James Jerome (1838–1916) US railroad magnate, b. Canada. Seeing the importance of transportation to the West to farming and trade, Hill built the Great Northern Railway over the Rockies to Seattle, Washington. Not only an exceptional engineering feat, Hill achieved his aim without any federal financial support. He went on to control the Northern Pacific and the Chicago, Burlington and Quincy lines, and helped in the construction of the Canadian Pacific line.

Hill, Sir Rowland (1795–1879) English postal reformer. In 1840 he introduced the nationwide "penny post", adopting the first adhesive pre-paid postage stamp. He was knighted in 1860.

Hillary, Sir Edmund Percival (1919–) New Zealand explorer and mountaineer. On 29 May 1953, Hillary and the Sherpa guide Tenzing Norgay (1914?–86) were the first climbers known to have reached the summit of Mount Everest, Nepal. He also led (1955–58) the New Zealand group of the Commonwealth Trans-Antarctic Expedition organized by Vivian Fuchs. He subsequently spent much time in Nepal, working on behalf of the Sherpas and becoming New Zealand's commissioner to Nepal.

Hillman, Sidney (1887–1946) US UNION leader. He was first president of the Amalgamated Clothing Workers (1915) and helped found the CONGRESS OF INDUSTRIAL ORGANIZATIONS (CIO) in 1935. He rallied support for President Franklin Roosevelt's NEW DEAL, established the American LABOR PARTY and helped form the World Federation of Trade Unions (1945).

Himmler, Heinrich (1900–45) German Nazi leader. He participated in the MUNICH PUTSCH (1923) and joined the NAZI PARTY in 1925. In 1929 he became head of the SS. After the Nazis came to power in 1933, Himmler assumed control of the GESTAPO and of the CONCENTRATION CAMPS. As chief of all German police forces from 1936, Himmler and Adolf EICHMANN directed a ruthless campaign for the extermination of the Jews. In 1939 he was made chief of Reich Administration and by 1943 was minister of the interior. His ruthlessness extended to those within the Nazi Party who were not entirely committed to the cause, clearly demonstrated by his treatment of the conspirators who attempted to assassinate Adolf HITLER in 1944. In April 1945 he secretly attempted to negotiate peace with the Allies, but was discovered by Hitler and expelled from the Party. He attempted to escape but was captured by the British and committed suicide.

HINDUISM

Traditional religion of India, characterized by a philosophy and a way of life rather than by a dogmatic structure. It was not founded by an individual and has been developing gradually since *c.*2000 BC, absorbing external influences, particularly that of the ARYANS. There are several schools within Hinduism, but all Hindus recognize the VEDAS as sacred texts. Dharma is the eternal moral law underpinning existence. Karma is a concept directly related to the belief in reincarnation, an individual's karma (earthly conduct) determining the position into which they are born in the next life. Liberation from the cycle of suffering and rebirth (*moksha*) is the chief aim in life. *Moksha* is attained through completion of the four stages of life (*ashramas*) and signifies a return to Brahman, the universal world soul. One of the features of Hindu society is the CASTE system, but modern Hindu scholars maintain that it is not part of the religion. The main Hindu gods are Brahma, Vishnu and Shiva (the Trimurti). Popular deities include Krishna, Ganesh, and the female deities Devi, Parvati and Lakshmi. BRAHMANISM, the early phase of Hinduism, culminated in the classic texts of the MAHABHARATA (incorporating the BHAGAVAD GITA) and the Ramayana (relating the adventures of Rama). Today, there are *c.*800 million Hindus worldwide.

▼ **The Trimurti** Brahma, the creator, Shiva, the destroyer, and Vishnu, the sustainer, are considered to be three forms of a supreme deity in Hinduism.

Hincks, Sir Francis (1807–85) Canadian politician, b. Ireland. In 1841 he became a Liberal member of the first Parliament of the United Province of CANADA. An advocate of reform and cooperation between English and French speakers, he served (1851–54) as joint premier with Augustin Morin. He promoted the construction of railways and negotiated the Reciprocity Treaty with the United States (1854), through which he hoped to achieve parity of trade. He later served (1869–73) as finance minister under John MACDONALD.

Hindenburg, Paul Ludwig Hans von Beneckendorf und von (1847–1934) German statesman and general, president (1925–34). He fought in the FRANCO-PRUSSIAN WAR (1870–71) and became a general in 1903. Hindenburg was recalled from retirement to command the army on the Eastern Front in WORLD WAR 1, defeating the Russians in the Battle of TANNENBERG (1914). In 1916 he became supreme commander and, with his chief of staff, Erich LUDENDORFF, directed the German retreat on the Western Front (to the **Hindenburg line**). As second president of the WEIMAR REPUBLIC, he was pressured by Franz von PAPEN to appoint Adolf HITLER as chancellor. *See also* EBERT, FRIEDRICH

H

Hinduism *See* feature article, page 183

Hindu Mahasabha Indian Hindu organization. It was established (1907) in the Punjab with the aim of promoting Hindu nationalism. Under the leadership of Lala Rajpat Rai and Pandit Mohan Malaviya, it campaigned in the 1920s for social reform and for the conversion of Muslims to Hinduism. It was opposed to the policy of Hindu-Muslim unity adapted by the Indian National CONGRESS, from which it broke away in 1937. Among its members were Nathuram Godse, the assassin of GANDHI. It declined in importance after 1951 when the Hindu Jana Sangh (People's Party) was formed.

Hirohito (1901–89) Emperor of Japan (1926–89). He was the first crown prince to travel abroad (1921). Although he generally exercised little political power during his reign, Hirohito persuaded the Japanese government to surrender to the Allies at the end of World War 2 (1939–1945). Under the new constitution of 1946, he lost all power and renounced the traditional claim of the Japanese emperors to be divine. He was succeeded by his son AKIHITO.

Hiroshima City on the delta of the River Ota, SW Honshu, Japan; the river divides the city into six islands connected by 81 bridges. Founded in 1594, it was a military headquarters in the Sino-Japanese and Russo-Japanese wars. During WORLD WAR 2, Hiroshima was the target of the first atomic bomb dropped (6 August 1945) on a populated area. More than 90% of the city was obliterated and more than 70,000 people were killed. The event is commemorated in the Peace Memorial Park. The bombing of Hiroshima and NAGASAKI almost instantly brought about Japan's unconditional surrender. Pop. (1993) 1,072,000.

Hiss, Alger (1904–96) US public official. He worked for the state department (1936–47). In 1948 a former Soviet agent, Whittaker Chambers, accused Hiss of passing confidential documents to the Soviets. He denied the charges before a congressional committee, was tried (1949, 1950) for perjury, found guilty and sentenced to five years' imprisonment. The Hiss trial divided US public opinion and illustrated the climate of fear prevalent during the COLD WAR. In 1992 papers released from KGB archives appeared to confirm Hiss' innocence.

history Written record of the human past; often used to mean the events themselves rather than the record of them. The Western historical tradition began with the Greek historians HERODOTUS and THUCYDIDES. China, and countries influenced by it, had a different, even older historical tradition in which the past was seen as the source of wisdom, and historians strove to distinguish comprehensible patterns in it. In medieval Europe, history was generally written in chronicles by monks, such as BEDE. In Renaissance Italy, writers of histories, such as Francesco GUICCIARDINI and Niccolò MACHIAVELLI, produced political analyses of events. By the time of the 18th-century ENLIGHTENMENT, large-scale works analysing events and drawing connections between past and present were being produced: a notable example is Edward GIBBON's *The Decline and Fall of the Roman Empire* (1776–88). In the 19th century, German historians, such as Leopold von RANKE, pioneered "scientific history" based on the evaluation of primary evidence. Some historians began to look for general laws underpinning the course of history and to focus on economic rather than political developments, as in the case of Karl MARX. In the 20th century, Marxist ideas were applied by some historians to their interpretation of events. Others focused on political developments or on history employing the quantitative techniques made possible by computers.

Hitler, Adolf (1889–1945) German fascist dictator (1933–45), b. Austria. He served in the German army during World War 1 and was decorated for bravery. In 1921 Hitler became leader of the then relatively minor National Socialist Workers' Party (NAZI PARTY), restructuring it into a paramilitary organization. While imprisoned for leading the failed MUNICH PUTSCH (1923), Hitler set out his extreme racist (notably anti-Semitic) and nationalist views in *Mein Kampf* (1925). With the support of Joseph GOEBBELS and Hermann GÖRING, the Nazi Party increased its popularity. Economic distress, which deepened considerably during the GREAT DEPRESSION (1929–33), coupled with dissatisfaction with the WEIMAR REPUBLIC, led to electoral gains for the Nazis. By forming a temporary alliance with orthodox nationalists, including Field Marshal Erich LUDENDORFF, Hitler, who was an exceptional political tactician and an inspirational orator, was eventually offered the chancellorship (January 1933) by President von HINDENBURG following the resignation of Kurt von Schleicher. After the REICHSTAG FIRE and further elections, Hitler assumed dictatorial powers. In the "NIGHT OF THE LONG KNIVES" (30 June 1934), Hitler eliminated his rivals in the BROWNSHIRTS (SA); and with the death of Hindenburg he was able to unite the presidency with the chancellorship, thus assuming supreme command under the title *führer* (leader). Economic recovery did much to increase support for Hitler and any surviving opposition was ruthlessly suppressed by the SS and GESTAPO. With the backing of the army, Hitler pursued an aggressive foreign policy whose ultimate aim was territorial expansion in E Europe (*see* LEBENSRAUM). In 1936 Hitler remilitarized the RHINELAND and in 1938 annexed Austria, thus achieving ANSCHLUSS. Later in the year, following the MUNICH AGREEMENT, he took over the German-populated SUDETENLAND in Czechoslovakia. After signing the Pact of Steel with Italy and the NAZI-SOVIET PACT with Joseph STALIN, he launched an invasion of Poland on 1 September 1939, thus finally goading Britain and France into declaring war. Hitler himself played a large part in determining strategy during WORLD WAR 2. Although Hitler narrowly escaped an assassination attempt in 1944, his refusal to capitulate to the Allies prolonged a war that Germany could never hope to win. In April 1945, with Germany in ruins, Hitler committed suicide with his long-time companion Eva BRAUN, whom he had married the day before.

Hitler Youth Organization set up (1933) to indoctrinate German youngsters with Nazi principles. In 1936 Adolf HITLER banned all other youth organizations and decreed that all boys must join the *Jungvolk* (Young Folk) at the age of ten. Once they reached the age of 13, the boys would become members of the Hitler Youth, where they would be subjected to semi-military discipline. At the age of 18, they were expected to serve in the armed forces or state labour service as members of the NAZI PARTY. By 1938 the Hitler Youth had 7.7 million members. The equivalent organization for girls was the League of German Girls, which gave training in domestic duties and motherhood.

Hittites People of Asia Minor who controlled a powerful empire in the second millennium BC. They founded a kingdom in Anatolia (Turkey) in the 18th century BC; their capital was HATTUSAS (Boğazköy). In the 17th century BC, under King Hattusilis, they expanded into N Syria. Under Mursilis, in the 16th century BC, they raided as far as BABYLON. Soon afterwards, however, the Hittites were beset by internal revolts and they lost much of their extended territory until they only controlled central Anatolia. Their fortunes subsequently revived and by *c.*1400 BC they controlled much of Anatolia, from where the empire expanded to reach its greatest extent under Suppiluliumas (r. *c.*1375–*c.*1335 BC). Hittite expansion into Syria led to a battle (*c.*1288 BC) with the Egyptians under RAMSES II at Kadesh. Ramses claimed a victory, but the outcome was indecisive. Under attack from the SEA PEOPLES (*c.*1200 BC), the Hittite empire disintegrated.

Hizbollah *See* HEZBOLLAH

Hoare-Laval Pact (1935) Plan devised by the British foreign secretary, Sir Samuel Hoare, and the French prime minister, Pierre LAVAL, to avoid war with Italy over Mussolini's invasion of Ethiopia. It ceded two-thirds of the country to Italy. Public outcry led to both Hoare's and Laval's resignation.

Hobbes, Thomas (1588–1679) English political theorist and philosopher. In *De Corpore* (1655), *De Homine* (1658) and *De Cive* (1642), he maintained that matter and its motion comprise the only valid subjects for philosophy. His greatest work, *Leviathan* (1651), argued that sovereignty is vested in a ruler when the people agree to limit their freedom in return for protection as a form of SOCIAL CONTRACT. Hobbes paved the way for SPINOZA,

HITLER, ADOLF

Adolf Hitler rose to power during the Great Depression in Germany. The discontent caused by mass unemployment, the reparations imposed by the Treaty of Versailles (1919), and the Weimar Republic's failure to deal with economic collapse, provided a platform for Hitler's ideas of extreme nationalism and racial hatred. His skill as an orator, and the powerful propaganda machine managed by Joseph Goebbels, gained him a mass following. Hitler's aspirations for absolute power were underestimated by the Weimar Republic and once installed as chancellor, he established a dictatorship. Hitler's desire to build a third German *Reich* (empire) resulted in World War 2, and his scapegoating of European Jewry culminated in the "Final Solution"– the systematic slaughter of more than six million Jews.

HITLER IN HIS OWN WORDS

"The art of leadership ... consists in consolidating the attention of the people against a single adversary and taking care that nothing will split up that attention."
Mein Kampf, Vol I, 1925

"I go the way that Providence dictates with the assurance of a sleepwalker."
Speech in Munich, 1936

LOCKE, HUME, ROUSSEAU and BENTHAM to develop concepts of human cooperation as the basis for social order.

Ho Chi Minh (1890–1969) (Nguyen That Thanh) Vietnamese statesman, president of North Vietnam (1954–69). He lived in Paris (1917–23), where he joined the French Communist Party (1920). In the 1920s he spent time in the Soviet Union and China, campaigning for an end to colonialism. With Vietnamese exiles in Hong Kong and S China, he founded (1930) the Vietnamese Communist Party (later the Indochinese Communist Party). Ho Chi Minh returned to Vietnam in 1941 to lead the VIET MINH against the Japanese during World War 2. In 1945 he declared Vietnamese independence and led resistance to French colonial forces during the INDOCHINA War (1946–54). After the French defeat at DIEN BIEN PHU (1954), Vietnam was partitioned and he became president of North Vietnam. Ho Chi Minh organized and supported the VIET CONG against South Vietnam and committed North Vietnamese forces against the United States in the VIETNAM WAR (1955–75). *See also* DIEM, NGO DINH; NGUYEN VAN THIEU; PHAM VAN DONG

Hofer, Andreas (1767–1810) Tirolese freedom fighter. In 1805 NAPOLEON I forced Austria to cede the Tirol to Bavaria. Hofer led a revolt against Bavaria and France that culminated in Tirolese victory at the Battle of Berg Isel (August 1809). He was then accepted by the Austrians as governor of Tirol. In October, however, the Austrians ceded the Tirol to Napoleon. Hofer attempted to rally resistance, but was captured near Mantua and executed on Napoleon's orders.

Hoffa, Jimmy (James Riddle) (1913–?75) US UNION leader, president of the transport workers' International Brotherhood of Teamsters (1957–71). In 1957 the Teamsters were expelled from the AMERICAN FEDERATION OF LABOR–CONGRESS OF INDUSTRIAL ORGANIZATIONS (AFL–CIO) for alleged corruption. In 1967 Hoffa was imprisoned for jury tampering, mail fraud and mishandling of union funds. In 1971 Hoffa's sentence was commuted by President Richard NIXON on the understanding that he undertook no active role in the union movement until 1980. In 1975 Hoffa disappeared and is presumed dead.

Hohenstaufen German dynasty that exercised great power in Germany and the HOLY ROMAN EMPIRE from 1138 to 1254. It is named after the Castle of Staufen, built by Frederick, Count of Swabia, whose son became CONRAD III of Germany and Holy Roman emperor in 1138. From Conrad III, who was succeeded by FREDERICK I (BARBAROSSA), to CONRAD IV, the family occupied the imperial throne, except between 1209 and 1215 (when OTTO IV, the representative of their great rivals, the GUELPHS, was emperor). Throughout its existence the dynasty often struggled with the papacy, particularly as its territories grew to include Sicily and N Italy as well as Germany. The dynasty's greatest member was FREDERICK II (emperor 1220–50), and its last was MANFRED of Sicily, killed in 1266. *See also* GHIBELLINES

Hohenzollern German dynasty that ruled BRANDENBURG, PRUSSIA, Germany and Romania. In 1415 the family acquired Brandenburg, and Prussia was added in 1618. FREDERICK WILLIAM (the Great Elector) further expanded their territories, and his son, FREDERICK I, adopted the title "king in Prussia". FREDERICK WILLIAM I built up the famous Prussian army, and FREDERICK II (THE GREAT) used it very effectively against the HABSBURGS. Germany was finally united in 1871 under the Hohenzollern emperor, WILLIAM I, who had appointed Otto von BISMARCK to oversee foreign affairs. His grandson, WILLIAM II, abdicated at the end of World War 1. In 1866 a member of the Sigmaringen branch of the family was elected as Prince Charles of Romania. In 1881 he became king as CAROL I.

Hohokam culture Farming culture of the S Arizona desert, arising in the last centuries BC and surviving until c.AD 1400. Sophisticated irrigation systems were the basis of Hohokam prosperity, and sizable settlements were founded; other remains include engraved and sculptured shells, pottery and temple mounds, all showing contemporary Mexican influence. *See also* ANASAZI; PUEBLO PEOPLES

Hojo Japanese family who effectively controlled the government of Japan from 1200 to 1333. Following the death of the KAMAKURA shogun Minamoto YORITOMO in 1199, they gained control of Japan's government by serving as regents (*shikken*) to puppet SHOGUNS from 1203. Their domination was secured in 1221 when a failed revolt by the TAIRA family gave them the opportunity to confiscate thousands of estates and award them to friends. They then ruled Japan efficiently as heads of a feudal society (*see* DAIMYO). They withstood two MONGOL assaults in 1274 and 1281, but at great financial cost. Vassals whom they could not reward turned against them, most notably ASHIKAGA Takanji. In 1333 he joined the forces fighting to restore the emperor to power, and when another vassal sacked Kamakura, the last Hojo regent committed suicide. The Hojo continued, however, to retain some power and influence for the next 200 years or so. They were opposed to the unification of Japan by HIDEYOSHI, who took their last stronghold, the castle at Odawara, in 1590.

Holland, Sir Sidney George (1893–1961) New Zealand statesman, prime minister (1949–57). He became leader of the National Party in 1940. As prime minister, he relaxed economic controls, thus encouraging private enterprise, and abolished the upper house of the New Zealand Parliament. He settled a five-month-long dockers' strike. Holland retired in 1957, shortly before the National Party's electoral defeat.

Holland Popular name for the NETHERLANDS but properly referring only to a historic region, now divided into two provinces (North and South Holland). A fief of the Holy Roman Empire in the 12th century, Holland was united with the county of HAINAUT in 1299. It passed to BURGUNDY in 1433 and to the HABSBURGS in 1482. In the 16th century, Holland led the NETHERLANDS in their long struggle for independence.

Holmes, Oliver Wendell, Jr (1841–1935) US jurist and legal scholar, son of the writer Oliver Wendell Holmes. He served with the Union army during the American CIVIL WAR. Holmes co-edited the *American Law Review* (1870–73) and *Kent's Commentaries* (1873) and wrote *The Common Law* (1881). A justice (1882–99) and then chief justice (1899–1902) of the Massachusetts Supreme Court, he was known as the "Great Dissenter" because he frequently disagreed with the majority view. Holmes was appointed an associate justice of the Supreme Court in 1902 by Theodore ROOSEVELT, serving until 1932. He was a champion of civil liberties, stating in *The Common Law* that law is based on experience not logic. His constant re-evaluation of legal concepts in the light of social change, although arousing fierce opposition, led to the abandonment of obsolete doctrines.

Holocaust, The (1933–45) Extermination of European JEWS and others by the Nazi regime in Germany. The Nazi persecution began with the NUREMBERG LAWS (1935), through which Jews lost almost all civil rights, and reached its peak in the so-called "FINAL SOLUTION", a programme of mass extermination adopted in 1942 and carried out with murderous efficiency by Adolf EICHMANN. Jews, homosexuals, Romanies and socialists, as well as others considered inferior by the Nazis, were killed in CONCENTRATION CAMPS such as AUSCHWITZ, BELSEN, BUCHENWALD, DACHAU, Majdanek and Treblinka. Total Jewish deaths are estimated at more than 6 million, about three-quarters of the population of European Jews. The Holocaust has raised theological and moral problems about the course of European civilization. *See also* ANTI-SEMITISM; KRISTALLNACHT

Holt, Harold Edward (1908–67) Australian statesman, prime minister (1966–67). He was elected to the House of Representatives in 1935. He served as minister of labour (1949–58) and deputy leader (1956–66) of the LIBERAL PARTY, becoming prime minister on the retirement of Robert MENZIES. As prime minister, Holt increased Australia's controversial support for the United States in the VIETNAM WAR. He was drowned while swimming.

Holy Alliance (1815) Agreement signed at the Congress of VIENNA by the crowned heads of Russia, Prussia and Austria. Under the guise of supporting Christian values, its purpose was to re-establish the principle of hereditary rule and to suppress democratic and nationalist movements in Europe, which had sprung up in the wake of the FRENCH REVOLUTION. The agreement, signed later by every European dynasty except the king of England, the pope and the Ottoman sultan, came to be seen as an instrument of reaction and oppression.

Holy Land *See* PALESTINE

Holy League Number of European alliances from the 15th- to the 17th-century. The League of 1511–13, which included the HOLY ROMAN EMPIRE, Spain, England and Venice, was organized by Pope JULIUS II in response to French aggression in Italy, while that of 1526 was led by France against Emperor CHARLES V. In 1571 Pope PIUS V formed a new Holy League, made up of Spain, Venice and the Papal States, to counter OTTOMAN expansion in the E Mediterranean. It won a resounding victory in the Battle of LEPANTO (1571) before falling apart. The French Holy League was first formed (1576) by the Catholic GUISE family during the Wars of RELIGION (1562–98) to counter the influence of the HUGUENOTS. A Holy League created (1609) by German Catholic princes later fought on behalf of the emperor during the THIRTY YEARS' WAR (1618–48). Another Holy League aimed at countering the threat of the Ottoman Turks was formed in 1684, and by 1699 it had reconquered most of Hungary for the HABSBURGS.

Holyoake, Sir Keith Jacka (1904–83) New Zealand statesman, prime minister (1957, 1960–72). He entered Parliament in 1932. A farmer, Holyoake worked for various international agricultural organizations before succeeding Sir Sidney HOLLAND as prime minister and leader of the National Party. He was governor general (1977–80) of New Zealand.

Holy Roman Empire *See* feature article, page 186

homage *See* FEUDAL SYSTEM

Home, Sir Alec Douglas- *See* DOUGLAS-HOME, SIR ALEC

Homer (active 8th century BC) Greek poet. Homer is traditionally considered to be the author of the great early epics of Greek literature, the *Iliad* and the *Odyssey*. Nothing factual is known about Homer. He is supposed have been blind and lived in Ionia. Literary scholarship has shown that the Homeric poems are a synthesis of oral, bardic stories. The *Iliad* relates the siege of Troy in the TROJAN WAR. The *Odyssey* tells of the post-war wanderings of Odysseus on his way back to Penelope in Ithaca. Their expression of the heroic ideal formed the basis of ancient education.

Home Rule, Irish Movement to gain Irish legislative independence from the British Parliament in the 19th century. The Act of UNION (1800) between Britain and IRELAND was unsuccessfully challenged by Daniel O'CONNELL's Repeal Association in the 1830s and 1840s. In the 1870s, Isaac BUTT began the Home Rule League. His successor, Charles PARNELL, won Prime Minister William GLADSTONE's support, but the first Home Rule Bill (1886) was defeated, splitting the LIBERAL PARTY. The second Home Rule bill (1892) was passed in the House of Commons but defeated in the House of Lords. A third bill, presented by Herbert ASQUITH, was passed by Parliament in 1912. Implementation of the bill was postponed by the start of World War 1. The EASTER RISING (1916) and a landslide victory for SINN FÉIN in Irish elections were followed by a guerrilla war led by the IRISH REPUBLICAN ARMY (IRA). In 1919 the Dáil Éireann (Irish assembly) claimed independence. In 1920 David LLOYD GEORGE's government passed a fourth Home Rule Bill establishing separate parliaments in Dublin and Belfast. In 1921 Arthur GRIFFITH and Michael COLLINS signed the Anglo-Irish Treaty that created the Irish Free State and gave *de facto* recognition to Northern IRELAND. The treaty was opposed by Eamon DE VALERA and the Irish Free State plunged into civil war. *See also* FENIAN MOVEMENT; IRELAND, REPUBLIC OF

Homestead Act (1862) US federal legislation enacted during the American CIVIL WAR to encourage W expansion. The government granted 65ha (160 acres) of government land to anyone who would live on it and improve it for five years. Along with the MORRILL Act for education, and with subsidies for the railroads, the Homestead Act opened the W to widespread settlement.

Homestead Massacre (6 July 1892) Violent industrial dispute in Homestead, Pennsylvania. Striking workers at the Carnegie Steel Plant in Homestead, Pennsylvania, fired at 300 Pinkerton detectives hired by the company to guard the plant. During the conflict, ten people were killed and many injured. On 9 July, the state militia was called in and remained there while strike-breakers worked in the plant, weakening the power of the steelworkers' UNION. The strike officially ended on 20 November 1892.

Homo erectus ("upright man") Species of early human, presumably evolved from HOMO HABILIS, dating from *c*.1.5 million to 0.2 million years ago. **Java Man** was the first early human fossil to be found, late in the 19th century. Both it and **Peking Man**, another early discovery, represent more advanced forms of *Homo erectus* than older fossils found more recently in Africa. Our own species, HOMO SAPIENS, is thought to have evolved from **Heidelberg Man**. *See also* HUMAN EVOLUTION

Homo habilis ("handy man") Species of early human, discovered (1964) by Louis Leakey (1903–72) in the Olduvai Gorge, E Africa. Its fossil remains are between *c*.1.8 and *c*.1.2 million years old, contemporary with those of *Australopithecus*. The physical development is much more like that of modern humans and it is thought they evolved into HOMO ERECTUS. *See also* HUMAN EVOLUTION

Homo sapiens ("wise man") Our own species, which is thought to have evolved between *c*.400,000 and *c*.250,000 years ago from HOMO ERECTUS. The earliest fossils of *Homo sapiens* have been discovered in Africa. Modern humans, *Homo sapiens sapiens*, emerged *c*.100,000 years ago. They developed sophisticated tools *c*.40,000 years ago which enabled them to colonize all Earth's continents except Antarctica by the PLEISTOCENE epoch (*c*.10,000 years ago). *See also* HUMAN EVOLUTION

Honduras *See* country feature

Honecker, Erich (1912–94) East German communist leader (1971–89). He was imprisoned (1935–45) by the NAZI PARTY for his involvement in the Communist resistance to Hitler. After World War 2, he rose rapidly in the East German Communist Party. He entered the Politburo in 1958 and, as head of the East German security forces, he oversaw the building of the BERLIN WALL in 1961. Honecker succeeded Walter ULBRICHT as secretary general in 1971 and generally pursued policies approved by Moscow. Opposed to the reforms of Mikhail GORBACHEV and the collapse of European COMMUNISM, Honecker was forced to resign. Charges of manslaughter concerning those people killed trying to cross the Berlin Wall were dropped in 1993, after it was discovered that Honecker was suffering from a terminal illness. He died in Chile.

Hong Kong (Xianggang Special Administrative Region) Former British crown colony off the coast of SE CHINA; the capital is Victoria on Hong Kong Island. Hong Kong comprises Hong Kong Island, ceded to Britain by China in 1842 following the first of the OPIUM WARS; the mainland peninsula of Kowloon, acquired in 1860; the New

HOLY ROMAN EMPIRE

European empire (10th–19th century) centred on GERMANY, which echoed the ancient ROMAN EMPIRE. It was founded (962) when the German king OTTO I (THE GREAT) was crowned emperor in Rome, although some historians date it from the coronation of CHARLEMAGNE in 800. Otto presented himself as the successor of Charlemagne in order to enhance his prestige. Two centuries later, FREDERICK I (BARBAROSSA) instigated Charlemagne's canonization and added the word "holy" to the name of the empire. In 1356 CHARLES IV of Luxembourg issued the GOLDEN BULL, which defined the right of seven German electors to designate the emperor-elect. The emperor claimed to be the temporal sovereign of Christendom, ruling in cooperation with the spiritual sovereign, the pope. However, the empire never encompassed all of western Christendom, and relations with the papacy were often difficult, particularly over the INVESTITURE controversy. Within the empire there was a primary N kingship based in Germany and a S secondary kingship in N Italy. There was, however, little governmental substance to the emperor's position in Italy despite attempts between the mid-10th and early-14th century to change this situation. From 1438 the title was virtually hereditary in the HABSBURG dynasty. After 1648 the empire became little more than a loose confederation, containing hundreds of virtually independent states. It was finally abolished by NAPOLEON I in 1806. *See also* GHIBELLINES; GUELPHS; ITALIAN WARS; LOMBARD LEAGUE

◀ **Holy Roman Empire** Despite significant territorial expansion in the 13th century, the Empire became fragmented due to conflicting claims to the throne and the often fractious relationship between the papacy and the imperial court.

HOLY ROMAN EMPERORS

SAXON dynasty	
OTTO I	962–73
OTTO II	973–83
OTTO III	996–1002
HENRY II	1014–24
SALIAN or Franconian dynasty	
CONRAD II	1027–39
HENRY III	1046–56
HENRY IV	1084–1106
HENRY V	1111–25
LOTHAIR II, Duke of Saxony	1133–37
HOHENSTAUFEN dynasty	
*CONRAD III	1138–52
FREDERICK I	1155–90
HENRY VI	1191–97
*PHILIP OF SWABIA	1198–1208
OTTO IV	1209–15
FREDERICK II	1215–50
*CONRAD IV	1237–54
The Great INTERREGNUM 1250–73	
RICHARD, EARL OF CORNWALL, and ALFONSO X of Castile, rivals	
HABSBURG, LUXEMBURG and WITTELBACH dynasties	
*RUDOLF I	1273–91
*ADOLF OF NASSAU	1292–98
*Albert I	1298–1308
HENRY VII	1312–13
LOUIS IV	1328–47
CHARLES IV	1355–78
*WENCESLAUS	1378–1400
*RUPERT	1400–10
SIGISMUND	1433–37
HABSBURG dynasty	
*Albert II	1438–39
FREDERICK III	1452–93
MAXIMILIAN I	1493–1519
CHARLES V	1519–56
FERDINAND I	1558–64
MAXIMILIAN II	1564–76
MATTHIAS	1612–19
FERDINAND II	1619–37
FERDINAND III	1637–57
LEOPOLD I	1658–1705
JOSEPH I	1705–11
CHARLES VI	1711–40
Interregnum 1740–42	
CHARLES VII	1742–45
FRANCIS I	1745–65
Habsburg-Lorraine dynasty	
JOSEPH II	1765–90
LEOPOLD II	1790–92
FRANCIS II	1792–1806

**King of Germany only*
SMALL CAPS denotes text article

Territories on the mainland, leased for 99 years in 1898; and some 230 islets in the South China Sea. Between 1941 and 1945 Hong Kong was occupied by Japan. Following the communist revolution in China (1949) the next 30 years saw Hong Kong's population rise from 1 million to 5 million, many fleeing the oppressive regime of mainland China. In 1984 Britain and China signed a Joint Declaration in which it was agreed that China would resume sovereignty over Hong Kong in 1997. It also provided that Hong Kong would become a special administrative region, with its existing social and economic structure unchanged for 50 years. It would also remain a free port. The last British governor (1992–97) Chris Patten introduced a legislative council. The handover to China was completed on 1 July 1997, and Chief Executive Tung Chee-hwa was sworn in and a provisional legislative council appointed. Hong Kong is a vital international financial centre with a strong manufacturing base. In 1997 the financial crisis in Southeast Asia caused the Hang Seng index to lose half of its value. In 1998 the administration spent more than US$15.2 billion defending the Hong Kong dollar. Area: 1071sq km (413sq mi). Pop. (1996) 6,311,000

Hongwu *See* ZHU YUANZHANG

Hong Xiuquan (1813–64) Chinese revolutionary, leader of the TAIPING REBELLION (1850–64). In 1843 he converted to Christianity, after receiving visions during an illness, and set about winning converts. He perceived God as the wrathful God of the Old Testament who would punish all wrong-doing. As leader of the God Worshippers' Society in Guangxi, he began to plot a rebellion against China's Manchu QING rulers. The rebellion broke out in 1850, and in 1851 Hong proclaimed the Heavenly Kingdom of Great Peace and adopted the title of Heavenly King. His followers, the Taipings, then advanced to Nanjing, which they captured in 1853. The rebels made further gains but failed to capture Beijing. In 1855 Hong brutally crushed opposition to his leadership. After 1856, however, he gave up all administrative duties. He refused to leave Nanjing as government forces advanced, and when they finally captured the city in 1864 he was dead, possibly through suicide.

Honorius, Flavius (384–423) Western Roman emperor (393–423), younger son of THEODOSIUS I (THE GREAT). His brother Arcadius was emperor of the Eastern Empire. The early part of Honorius' reign was dominated by his general, Flavius STILICHO, whose daughters he married. The BARBARIAN raids on his empire, culminated in the capture of Rome (410) by the VISIGOTHS. Honorius rejected the peace proposals offered by ALARIC I and fled into exile. He was succeeded by Valentinian III.

Hood, John Bell (1831–79) Confederate general in the American CIVIL WAR. He fought in the Second Battle of BULL RUN and distinguished himself at ANTIETAM, FREDERICKSBURG, GETTYSBURG and Chickamauga. Hood became commander in Georgia (1864) but was unable to stem William SHERMAN's march. He resigned in 1865.

Hood, Samuel, 1st Viscount (1724–1816) British admiral who served in the SEVEN YEARS' WAR, the AMERICAN REVOLUTION and the FRENCH REVOLUTIONARY WARS. He distinguished himself with his defeat of the French in the West Indies in 1782. He became a member of Parliament for Westminster in 1784. During the French Revolutionary Wars he served as commander in chief (1793–94) in the Mediterranean in support of the Royalist cause. He became an admiral in 1794 and was created Viscount Hood in 1796.

Hooker, Joseph (1814–79) Union general in the American CIVIL WAR. He served in the MEXICAN WAR and became brigadier general of volunteers at the start of the Civil War. In 1863 Hooker took over from Ambrose BURNSIDE as commander of the Army of the Potomac after the Union defeat at FREDERICKSBURG (1862). Under Hooker, the Army was reorganized but was badly beaten by Robert LEE and "Stonewall" JACKSON at the Battle of CHANCELLORSVILLE (1863). Later that year, Hooker won the Battle of Lookout Mountain near Chattanooga, Tennessee. He retired from the army in 1868.

Hooker, Thomas (1586–1647) English colonist in North America and a Puritan clergyman. Under attack for his Puritanism and evangelical preaching, Hooker fled from England to Holland and from there emigrated to Massachusetts He led colonists in the first W migration to found (1636) and settle Hartford, Connecticut. Hooker helped to draft the "Fundamental Orders" in 1639, under which Connecticut was governed for a considerable time. *See also* HARTFORD CONVENTION

Hoorn, Philip de Montmorency, Graaf van (1518–68) Flemish politician and soldier. A member of the council of state for the Netherlands (1561–65), he was for many years a faithful servant of the HABSBURG rulers of the Netherlands, notably CHARLES V and PHILIP II. With William, Prince of Orange (later WILLIAM II) and Lamoral, Graaf van EGMONT, Hoorn protested against the persecution of Protestants and campaigned for an end to the Spanish INQUISITION. He became a leader of the aristocratic opposition to the government of Cardinal GRANVELLE. In 1567 Hoorn and Egmont were arrested by the Duke of ALBA and executed. Their deaths contributed to the REVOLT OF THE NETHERLANDS against Spanish rule.

Hoover, Herbert Clark (1874–1964) Thirty-first president of the United States (1929–33). He was admired for his work with victims of war and for a number of international relief agencies. Hoover served (1921–28) as secretary of commerce under presidents Warren HARDING and Calvin COOLIDGE. After winning the Republican nomination for president in 1928, Hoover easily defeated his Democrat challenger Alfred Smith. During his first year in office, the economy was shattered by the WALL STREET CRASH and the ensuing GREAT DEPRESSION. With his belief in individual enterprise and distrust of government interference, Hoover failed to provide sufficient government resources to deal with the Depression. In 1932 he was resoundingly defeated by Franklin ROOSEVELT's promise of a NEW DEAL. Hoover largely retired from public life, returning instead to helping organize relief agencies. He later headed two commissions (1947–49, 1953–55) that examined the organization of government; many of his recommendations were implemented.

Hoover, J. (John) Edgar (1895–1972) US administrator, director (1924–72) of the US FEDERAL BUREAU OF INVESTIGATION (FBI). He reorganized the Bureau, compiling a vast file of fingerprints and building a crime laboratory. During the 1930s, Hoover fought organized crime. After World War 2 he concentrated on what he saw as the threat posed by communists and radicals of all kinds. In the 1960s, Hoover used the FBI's huge surveillance network to collect information on Martin Luther KING, Jr, and other civil-rights activists while failing to investigate the Mafia. He also collected files on the personal lives of politicians and used them to keep himself in the position of FBI director, despite much public criticism, until his death.

Hopewell culture Native American culture centred in Ohio and Illinois. It reached its peak in the last centuries BC and the first four centuries AD. Hopewell people were efficient farmers; their culture is named after Hopewell Farm, Hamilton County, Ohio. They built complex earthworks, such as the Great Serpent Mound of Ohio, for ceremonial and burial purposes. Hopewell people had extensive trading networks: objects from all parts of North America have been found at Hopewell sites. *See also* MOUND BUILDERS *See* illustration, page 188.

Hopi Shoshonean-speaking tribe of NATIVE NORTH AMERICANS, westernmost group of PUEBLO PEOPLES. The Hopi have retained the purest form of pre-Columbian culture to have survived in the United States. They are celebrated for their "snake dance" – a rain ceremony. Today, *c.*6000 Hopi people inhabit 11 villages in NE Arizona.

Hopkins, Harry Lloyd (1890–1946) US politician. A close adviser to President Franklin ROOSEVELT, he helped implement the NEW DEAL, heading the Federal Emergency Relief Administration (1933), the Civil Works Administration (1933–34) and the Works Progress Administration (1935–38). He served (1938–40) as secretary of commerce. During World War 2, Hopkins was Roosevelt's special adviser and personal intermediary with Winston CHURCHILL and Joseph STALIN at the POTSDAM CONFERENCE. He ran the LEND-LEASE programme (1941).

Horemheb Egyptian pharaoh (r.*c.*1321–*c.*1293 BC). Horemheb was the last ruler of the 18th dynasty. He was a notable military commander under TUTANKHAMUN. When

H

HONDURAS

AREA: 112,090sq km (43,278 sq mi)
POPULATION: 5,462,000
CAPITAL (POPULATION): Tegucigalpa (670,100)
GOVERNMENT: Republic
ETHNIC GROUPS: Mestizo 90%, Native American 7%, Garifunas (West Indian) 2%
LANGUAGES: Spanish (official)
RELIGIONS: Roman Catholic 85%, Protestant 10%)
GDP PER CAPITA (1995): US$1900

Republic in Central America. From AD 400 to 900 the MAYA civilization flourished. The magnificent ruins at Copán, a Mayan centre in W Honduras, were discovered by the Spaniards in 1576, but became covered in dense forest and were only rediscovered in 1839. Christopher COLUMBUS sighted the coast in 1502. In 1524 Pedro de ALVARADO founded the first Spanish settlements. The native population was gradually subdued, and gold and silver mines were established.

In 1821 Honduras gained independence, forming part of the Mexican Empire, until the state collapsed in 1823. Between 1823 and 1838 Honduras was a member of the CENTRAL AMERICAN FEDERATION.

Throughout the rest of the 19th century it was subject to continuous political interference, especially from GUATEMALA. Britain controlled the Mosquito Coast. In the 1890s US companies developed the banana plantations and exerted great political influence. Honduras became known as a "banana republic".

After World War 2, demands grew for greater national autonomy and workers' rights. In 1963 the Liberal government was overthrown by a military coup. Honduras' expulsion of Salvadorean immigrants led to the brief "SOCCER WAR" (1969) with EL SALVADOR, following an ill-tempered World Cup qualifying match between the two countries. In 1982 civilian government was restored. During the 1980s, Honduras, dependent on US aid, acted as a base for the US-backed CONTRA rebels from NICARAGUA. In 1988 popular demonstrations against the Contra led to the declaration of a state of emergency. The war in Nicaragua ended in 1990 and Honduras settled its disputed border with El Salvador in 1992. The presidency (1993–97) of Carlos Roberto Reina Idiaquez did much to restore civilian rule to Honduras. In 1998 Reina was succeeded as president by Liberal Party leader Carlos Flores Facusse. In 1998 Hurricane Mitch killed more than 5500 people and left 14 million homeless.

Tutankhamun's successor died, Horemheb became king. During his reign he promoted worship of Amun, which had been discouraged under AKHENATEN, and ensured Egypt's prosperity. He was succeeded by RAMSES I.

Horrocks, General Sir Brian Gwynne (1895–1985) British soldier. He served in France during World War 1 and in Russia in 1919. During World War 2, he was a vigorous corps commander in N Africa, helping to defeat Erwin ROMMEL; he also served in Europe. Horrocks later commanded (1948–49) the British Army of the Rhine. He subsequently worked as a military journalist and writer.

Horthy de Nagybánai, Miklós (1868–1957) Hungarian statesman, regent (1920–44). He commanded the Austro-Hungarian fleet in World War 1. Horthy took part in the counter-revolution (1919) that overthrew the communist regime of Béla KUN. In 1920 the Hungarian parliament reinstated the monarchy and Horthy was voted regent and effective head of state. His highly conservative regime suppressed political opposition and resisted the return of CHARLES I. Allied with the Axis Powers in 1941, he tried to arrange a separate peace with the Soviet Union in 1944 but was arrested by the Germans and later released by the Allies at the end of World War 2.

Hospitaller *See* KNIGHTS HOSPITALLERS

Hottentot *See* KHOIKHOI

Houphouët-Boigny, Félix (1905–93) Ivory Coast statesman, first president (1960–93). He was a founder of the Ivory Coast Democratic Party in 1946. He served in the French national assembly (1946–59) and became president of the IVORY COAST when it gained independence. Pro-Western, he maintained close relations with France, and the Ivory Coast became one of the more affluent countries in West Africa. In the 1980s a recession, exacerbated by expenditure on grandiose projects, such as the construction at Yamoussoukro of the world's largest Christian church, caused unrest. In 1990 Houphouët-Boigny was forced to legalize opposition parties and won his seventh term as president in the first multiparty elections. He died in office.

House, Edward Mandell (1858–1938) US politician and diplomat. He helped Woodrow WILSON obtain the 1912 Democratic presidential nomination and became his closest adviser. House was twice sent to Europe in attempts to prevent World War 1 (1914) and mediate peace (1915). A member of the US peace commission at the end of the War, he helped draft the Treaty of VERSAILLES (1919) and the Covenant of the LEAGUE OF NATIONS.

House of Commons Lower house of the British PARLIAMENT. The upper house is the HOUSE OF LORDS. The House of Commons dates from 1265 when Simon de MONTFORT, as effective ruler of England, summoned a Parliament made up of knights of the shires and burgesses of the boroughs. Both the Commons and Lords gained constitutional rights in the 14th century. In the 17th century, the Commons became the focus for opposition to the monarchy, presenting the PETITION OF RIGHT (1628) to CHARLES I. The LONG PARLIAMENT (1640–60) introduced a number of reforms intended to prevent royal absolutism, including the Triennial Act (1641), which called for a Parliament to meet at least once every three years. The Commons took a leading role in the RESTORATION by inviting CHARLES II to be king in 1660 and, after the GLORIOUS REVOLUTION (1688–89), in promoting a BILL OF RIGHTS (1689) and an Act of SETTLEMENT (1701). Over the course of the 19th century the Commons developed from being an inferior assembly to the Lords to becoming the main forum for discussion and voting on intended legislation and questioning of ministers. This was achieved through a series of REFORM ACTS, which gradually extended the FRANCHISE. Today, the Commons' 659 members are elected by universal adult suffrage in a secret ballot. This is usually in general elections that, by the Parliament Act of 1911, must be held at least every five years. The prime minister is the leader of the majority party in the Commons, and most members of the CABINET are drawn from the Commons, although some may be from the Lords. Debates and proceedings are controlled by the speaker. Select committees scrutinize legislation. *See also* CIVIL WAR, ENGLISH

House of Lords Upper house of the British PARLIAMENT. In its legislative capacity, the Lords is completely subordinated to the HOUSE OF COMMONS. The Parliament Acts of 1911 and 1949 checked virtually all its power, except to delay passage of a bill for one year. At the beginning of 1999 members of the House of Lords included the Lords Spiritual (26 archbishops and bishops), Lords Temporal (*c.*1000 hereditary and life peers) and the Lords of Appeal (Law Lords). In November 1999, the number of hereditary peers was reduced to 92 as a first step to major reform of the House. The Law Lords continue to form Britain's highest court of appeal.

House of Representatives Lower house of the US legislature, which together with the SENATE forms the CONGRESS. It has 435 members. Each state has at least one representative; the larger the population of a state the more representatives are allowed. Representatives must be at least 25 years old, US residents for no less than seven years, and resident in the state they represent. They are directly elected and serve two-year terms. The House considers bills and has exclusive authority to originate revenue bills, initiate impeachment proceedings, and elect the president if the electoral college is deadlocked. Most of the work of the House is undertaken by numerous standing committees and sub-committees.

Houston, Sam (Samuel) (1793–1863) US military and political leader. He lived for a few years with the Cherokee and negotiated with the government on Native American affairs. He served (1827–29) as governor of Tennessee. Moving to TEXAS, Houston became commander in chief of the army when Texas rebelled against Mexican rule (1835). In 1836 a convention, of which Houston was a member, declared Texas independent. Following the defeat at the ALAMO, Houston was constantly on the retreat against the forces of SANTA ANNA. In 1836, however, he defeated Santa Anna at the Battle of SAN JACINTO. Houston was the first president (1836–38, re-elected 1841–44) of the Republic of Texas. When Texas joined the Union in 1845, he served in the Senate for 14 years. After losing his seat in 1859, he drew on his popularity to become governor. Isolated by his support for the Union and for Native Americans, Houston was forced out of office when Texas voted to secede (1861) from the Union. *See also* MEXICAN WAR

Howard, Catherine (1520–42) Fifth queen of HENRY VIII. She was brought to Henry's attention by her Catholic relatives, the dukes of Norfolk, who wished to bring about the downfall of Thomas CROMWELL. Catherine and Henry married in July 1540 after his divorce from ANNE OF CLEVES. Evidence of premarital and marital indiscretions, brought to the king's attention by her Protestant enemies, led to her execution.

Howard, Charles, 1st Earl of Nottingham (1536–1624) Commander of the English naval forces against the Spanish ARMADA (1588). He was appointed lord high admiral in 1585. After his success against the Armada, Howard led an expedition against Cádiz (1596) with the Earl of ESSEX. The leaders fell out, and Howard was later responsible for suppressing Essex's rebellion (1601). ELIZABETH I made him Earl of Nottingham in 1597 and lord lieutenant general of England in 1599, a post he held until 1619. Howard served in various public offices under JAMES I and resigned as lord high admiral at the age of 83.

Howard, Henry *See* SURREY, HENRY HOWARD, EARL OF

Howard, John (1726–90) British campaigner for prison reform. Howard toured prisons in England and Wales and had two acts of Parliament (1774) passed to ensure minimum standards of sanitation and decency. The Howard League for Penal Reform, founded in 1866, is dedicated to improving prison conditions.

Howard, John Winston (1939–) Australian statesman, prime minister (1996–). Howard was elected to the House of Representatives in 1974. In 1982 he became deputy leader of the LIBERAL PARTY and was made leader in 1985. He held many shadow cabinet positions, and in 1995 was appointed leader of the opposition. In 1996 Howard led the Liberal-National coalition to victory against Paul KEATING's ruling LABOR PARTY government. His first years in office saw growing racial tensions, with much criticism of his failure to condemn Pauline Hanson's nationalist One Nation Party. His coalition was narrowly re-elected in 1998, however, and Howard promised a referendum on Australia's constitution. The referendum (1999) rejected the proposal that Australia become a republic.

Howard, Oliver Otis (1830–1909) US general. A Union officer in the American CIVIL WAR, he became a major general in 1862 after fighting in the First Battle of BULL RUN, the PENINSULAR CAMPAIGN and at ANTIETAM. He commanded the Army of the Tennessee, accompanying William SHERMAN on his march through Georgia. After the War, Howard headed the FREEDMEN'S BUREAU, which aided former slaves, and was a founder and president (1869–73) of Howard University, Washington, D.C.

Howard, Thomas *See* NORFOLK, THOMAS HOWARD, 3RD DUKE OF

Howe, Joseph (1804–73) Canadian statesman. A newspaper publisher, he entered politics as a member of the NOVA SCOTIA Assembly in 1836, after winning a lawsuit concerning the freedom of the press. At the centre of provincial politics for nearly 50 years, Howe campaigned for "responsible government" and served (1860–63) as premier of Nova Scotia. Although opposed to confederation, he served in the government of the Dominion of Canada from 1869 to 1873.

Howe, Julia Ward (1819–1910) US writer and social reformer. She was an advocate of abolition, women's suffrage and international peace, writing and lecturing extensively. Although she wrote works of literary criticism and several volumes of poetry, she is best known for having written the words to *The Battle Hymn of the Republic*. Her husband, **Samuel Gridley Howe** (1801–76), was also an important social reformer.

Howe, Sir Geoffrey (1926–) British statesman, chancellor of the exchequer (1979–83), foreign secretary (1983–89), deputy prime minister and leader of the House of Commons (1989–90). A leading figure in the Conservative cabinet of Margaret THATCHER, he made a damning resignation speech after Thatcher voiced her hostility to European monetary union.

Howe, Richard, 4th Viscount and Earl (1726–99) British admiral. He came to attention during the SEVEN YEARS' WAR, notably with the Rochefort expedition (1757) and at Quiberon Bay (1759). He commanded (1776–78) the British navy in North America during the early stages

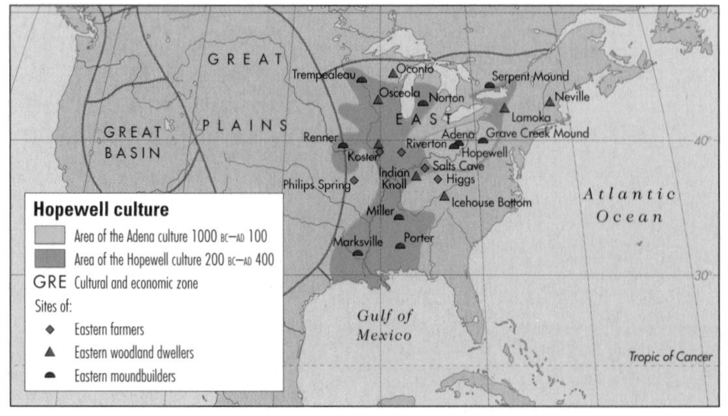

► **Hopewell culture** The earliest inhabitants of North America were big-game hunters, but by 2000 BC, many regional groups had begun to develop different ways of life based on locally available resources. In the Midwest, the Hopewell people constructed sedentary settlements near to water sources. They grew some crops, but were predominantly hunter-gatherers. Interaction with other Native American cultures led to the establishment of extensive trading routes.

of the AMERICAN REVOLUTION. He served (1783–88) as first lord of the Admiralty under William PITT (THE YOUNGER). During the FRENCH REVOLUTIONARY WARS, Howe inflicted a decisive defeat on the French fleet, an event known as the GLORIOUS FIRST OF JUNE (1794).

Howe, William, 5th Viscount (1729–1814) British commander in chief (1775–78) during the AMERICAN REVOLUTION, brother of Richard HOWE. He joined the army in 1746 and served with distinction under James WOLFE on the Plains of ABRAHAM (1759). After the Battle of BUNKER HILL (1775) Howe became commander in chief of British forces in North America. He captured New York (1776) and occupied Philadelphia (September 1777). After defeat at SARATOGA (1777), Howe resigned and returned to England (1778).

Hoxha, Enver (1908–85) Albanian statesman, prime minister (1946–54), first secretary of the Communist Party (1954–85). In 1941 he founded the Albanian Communist Party (later known as the Albanian Labour Party) and led the resistance to Italian occupation during World War 2. In 1946 the Republic of ALBANIA was established, and Hoxha became prime minister. His rule was dictatorial and Stalinist; he maintained absolute control of party, army and state. Hoxha withdrew Albania from the WARSAW PACT, therefore breaking relations with the Soviet Union, in 1961. The later break with Beijing (1978) led to Albania's isolation and economic impoverishment. He died in office.

Hoysala (1006–1346) Indian dynasty that ruled in the s Deccan Plateau and the Cauvery valley. **Vishnuvardhana** (r.1110–41) won much territory, expelling the Colas from the Deccan, but many of his gains were subsequently lost by his weak son, Narasimha I. His grandson, **Ballala II** (r.1173–1220), embarked on another phase of territorial expansion, and made the Hoysala dynasty the most powerful in s India. The dynasty's strength or weakness depended upon the merit of the individual on the throne more than its structure of rule. It finally collapsed under **Ballala III** (r. *c*.1292–1342), whose ambitions were greater than his ability to achieve them.

Hsia *See* XIA

Hsüan Tsung *See* XUAN ZUNG

Hua Guofeng (1920–) (Hua Kuofeng) Chinese statesman, premier and chairman of the Chinese COMMUNIST PARTY (1976–81). He joined the Communist Party in 1935 and served in the RED ARMY. After various provincial posts, Hua became a member of the Politburo in 1973. When DENG XIAOPING was ousted as prime minister in 1976, he was replaced by Hua. After the death of MAO ZEDONG, he became chairman of the party and also succeeded ZHOU ENLAI as premier. His pragmatic approach to policy led to his isolation within the party. Hua resigned in 1981 and was replaced by ZHAO ZIYANG as premier and HU YAOBANG as party chairman. In 1982 he was ousted from the central committee.

Huari (Wari) Culture which flourished in the s highlands of Peru between AD 600 and 1000. At its centre was the city

HUMAN EVOLUTION

Process by which humans developed from pre-human ancestors. The fossil record of human ancestors is patchy and unclear. Some scientists believe that our ancestry can be traced back to one or more species of Australopithicenes that flourished in s and E Africa *c*.4–1 million years ago. Other scientists believe that we are descended from some as yet undiscovered ancestor. The earliest fossils that can be identified as human are those of HOMO HABILIS, which date from between *c*.1.8 and *c*.1.2 million years ago. The next evolutionary stage was HOMO ERECTUS, who first appeared *c*.1.5 million years ago. The earliest fossils of our own species, HOMO SAPIENS, date from *c*.400,000 to *c*.250,000 years ago. An apparent side-branch, the NEANDERTHALS existed in Europe and w Asia some 130,000–40,000 years ago. Fully modern humans, *Homo sapiens sapiens*, first appeared *c*.100,000 years ago. Opinions are divided as to exactly how the species emerged, but by 30,000 BC *Homo sapiens sapiens* was the only surviving hominid.

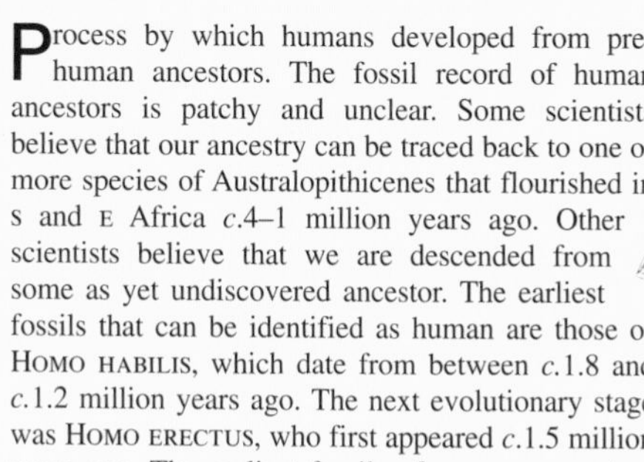

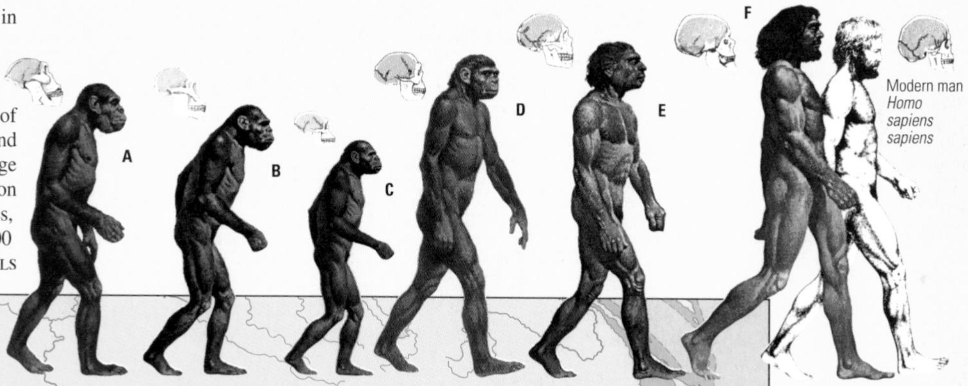

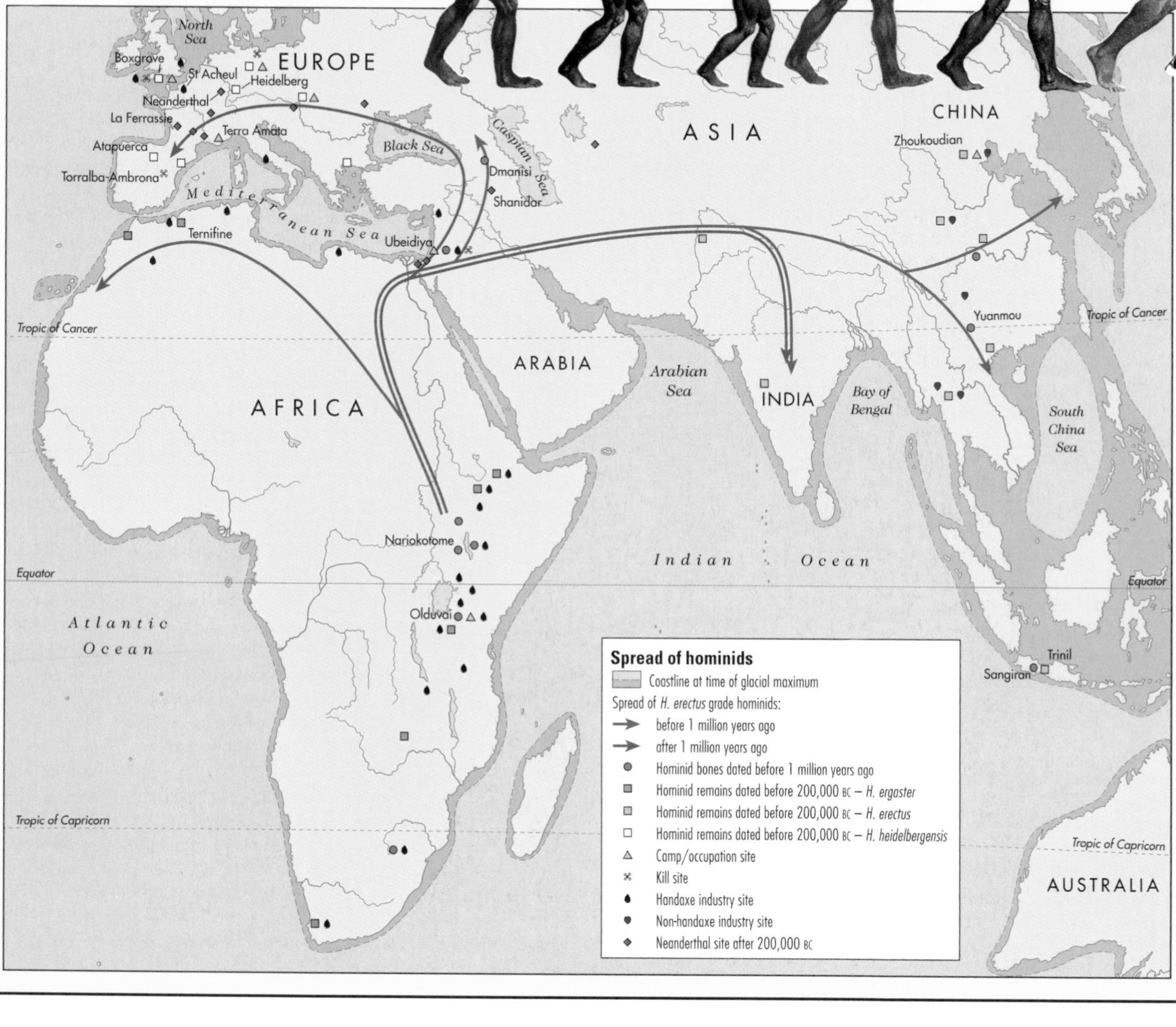

▲ **human evolution** Two of the earliest species of Australopiths were *Austrolpithecus afarensis* (A), which lived *c*.4–3 million years ago, and *A.africanus* (B) which evolved *c*.3–2 million years ago. *Homo Habilis* (C) used primitive stone tools and appeared 500,000 years later. *H. erectus* (D) was the first hominid to inhabit caves and use fire and is thought to be the direct ancestor of Neanderthal man (E) and *H.sapiens sapiens* (F).

◀ **The spread of hominids** from Africa began *c*.1.8 million years ago. This was partly due to the development of more efficient tools, like the handaxe, and an increase in body size which enabled hominids to hunt more effectively. It is probable that there were several roughly contemporary species: *H.ergaster* in Africa, *H.erectus* in SE Asia and *H.heidelbergensis* in Europe.

Spread of hominids
Coastline at time of glacial maximum
Spread of *H. erectus* grade hominids:
before 1 million years ago
after 1 million years ago
Hominid bones dated before 1 million years ago
Hominid remains dated before 200,000 BC – *H. ergaster*
Hominid remains dated before 200,000 BC – *H. erectus*
Hominid remains dated before 200,000 BC – *H. heidelbergensis*
Camp/occupation site
Kill site
Handaxe industry site
Non-handaxe industry site
Neanderthal site after 200,000 BC

of Huari that emerged *c*.400 and developed an empire which displaced the coastal culture of the Mochica in *c*.AD 650. Its architecture was characterized by large stone enclosures. The culture also produced large stone sculptures and naturalistic representations of male and female figures.

Huáscar (d.1533) Inca king (r.1525–32), son of Huayna Capac. He controlled N Peru (Cuzco) after his father's death. His younger half-brother, Atahualpa, controlled Quito, and the civil war between them (which Huáscar lost) facilitated the conquest of Peru by Francisco Pizarro, who arrived at this time. Atahualpa ordered Huáscar's assassination.

Huayna Capac (d.1525) Last of the great Inca rulers (1493–1525). He extended the Inca empire to its greatest size by conquering parts of NE Peru and N Ecuador. Most of Huayna's reign, however, was devoted to administration and suppressing minor revolts rather than territorial expansion. In 1525 he fell victim to an epidemic, probably smallpox or measles, introduced to South America by Europeans. He died without having named a successor, a situation that led to civil war between his two sons, Atahualpa and Huáscar. The war had just ended when the Spanish under Francisco Pizarro began their conquest.

Hubertusburg, Peace of (1763) Treaty ending the Seven Years' War between Prussia and Austria. Prussia kept Silesia, which it had captured from Austria during the war, and in return it agreed to support the succession of Joseph II to the imperial throne.

Huddleston, (Ernest Urban) Trevor (1913–98) British Anglican priest and anti-apartheid activist. In 1943 he moved to Johannesburg, South Africa. Huddleston's conviction that the principle of universal brotherhood in Christ should be applied everywhere was evident from his book *Nought for your Comfort* (1956). From 1960 to 1968 he was bishop of Masai, Tanzania. In 1969 he became vice president of the Anti-Apartheid Movement.

Hudson, Henry (d.1611) English explorer. He made several efforts to find a Northeast Passage. Employed by the Dutch East India Company (1609), Hudson was blocked by ice and crossed the Atlantic to search for a Northwest Passage, becoming the first European to sail up the river that now bears his name. In 1610 he embarked on another voyage to discover the Northwest Passage and reached Hudson Bay. Forced to winter in the Bay, his crew set him adrift to die in an open boat.

Hudson's Bay Company English company chartered by Charles II in 1670 to promote trade in the Hudson Bay region of North America and to seek a Northwest Passage. The company had a fur-trading monopoly and was virtually a sovereign power in the region. Throughout the 18th century, it fought with France for control of the bay. In 1763 France ceded control of Canada to England, and the North West Company was formed. Intense rivalry forced the Hudson's Bay Company into a more active role in exploration, and in 1769–70 it sent Samuel Hearne on three expeditions to the N coast, which he finally reached in 1771. In 1821 the companies merged to control territory stretching from the Atlantic to the Pacific. After the Confederation of Canada (1867), challenges to its monopoly power increased, and in 1869 it was forced to cede all its territory to Canada in return for £300,000. As the fur trade declined in the early 20th century, the Company diversified and was divided up in 1930.

Huerta, Victoriano (1854–1916) Mexican statesman and general, president (1913–14). Instructed by President Francisco Madero to suppress a revolt, Huerta instead joined forces with the rebels. Madero was arrested and killed, and Huerta became president. He established a dictatorship and ruthlessly suppressed all opposition. Soon defeated by the Constitutionalists, led by Venustiano Carranza, Álvaro Obregón, "Pancho" Villa and Emiliano Zapata, Huerta fled. He was arrested in the United States in 1915 and died in custody.

Hugh Capet *See* Capet, Hugh

Hughes, Charles Evans (1862–1948) US statesman and jurist, associate justice of the Supreme Court (1910–16), secretary of state (1921–25) and eleventh US chief justice (1930–41). He was the Republican presidential candidate (1916) but narrowly lost to Woodrow Wilson. He served as secretary of state under presidents Warren Harding and Calvin Coolidge. He was a member of the Permanent Court of Arbitration (1926–30) and judge of the Permanent Court of International Justice (1928–30). Appointed chief justice by President Herbert Hoover, Hughes was a moderating influence. He was a defender of the right to freedom of speech and an outspoken critic of Franklin Roosevelt's attempts to reorganize the Supreme Court by "packing" it with judges. He retired in 1941.

Hughes, William Morris (1864–1952) Australian statesman, prime minister (1915–23), b. England. In 1894 he was elected as a Labor member to the New South Wales legislature, and he entered the federal Parliament in 1901. In 1917 Hughes formed the National Party after the Labor Party rejected his proposal for military conscription. He represented Australia at the Paris Peace Conference (1919), gaining German New Guinea for Australia. Hughes led the United Australia Party (1941–43) that under Robert Menzies evolved into the Liberal Party in 1944.

Huguenots French Protestants who arose in Roman Catholic France during the Reformation and suffered persecution. In 1559 a national synod of Huguenot congregations adopted an ecclesiastical structure highly influenced by John Calvin. During the French Wars of Religion (1562–98), Huguenots continued to face persecution and thousands died, notably in the Saint Bartholomew's Day Massacre (1572). A united force of capable Protestant leaders, under the Bourbon Henry of Navarre defeated the forces of the Holy League. In 1589 Henry acceded to the throne as Henry IV and, despite adopting the Roman Catholic faith in 1593, he promulgated the Edict of Nantes (1598), which recognized Catholicism as the official religion but gave Huguenots certain rights, among them freedom of worship. Following the Edict, Huguenot numbers increased, including among them many skilled artisans and merchants, and Huguenots became a significant economic influence in France. A perceived threat, under Cardinal Richlieu they once again lost many political privileges, but retained their religious freedom. In 1685 the Edict was revoked by Louis XIV, and thousands of Huguenots fled France. In 1789 their civil rights were restored, and the Code Napoléon (1804) guaranteed religious equality.

Hu Han-min (1879–1936) Chinese revolutionary leader, close associate of Sun Yat-sen. He served as chief secretary during Sun Yat-sen's brief presidency (1911–12). Forced to flee the country with Sun in 1913, he became one of the leading figures in the Nationalist Party (Kuomintang) formed by Sun and subsequently in the s governments established by Sun in Guangzhou. Following the unification of the Kuomintang under Chiang Kai-shek in 1928, Hu was elected president of the Legislative Yuan. In 1931 he broke with Chiang, who then had him arrested. This caused a major crisis in the Kuomintang, which led to his eventual release.

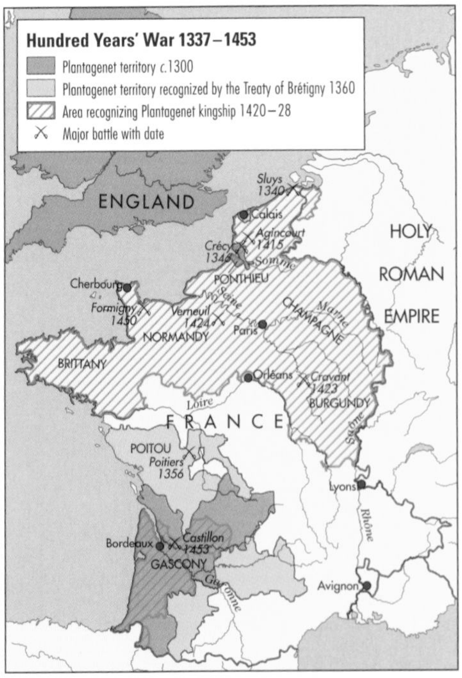

▲ **Hundred Years' War** The outcome of the Hundred Years' War brought an end to English claims to French territory and established the two countries as distinct nations.

Hui-Zong (1028–1135) Last emperor of the Northern Sung dynasty. A talented poet, calligrapher and painter, he was patron of a brilliant academy. In 1126 Hui-Zong's capital was sacked by the Tartars. He died in captivity in Manchuria, but the style which he encouraged had a lasting effect on the art of the East.

Hukbalahap (Huk) Peasant revolutionary movement in the Philippines, based on Luzon island. Originally formed to resist the Japanese in World War 2, the movement was communist-led by 1946. The Hukbalahaps fought for reforms against the Philippine government and the big landowners, and won much popular support after the repressive tactics used against them. Almost victorious in 1950, they were subsequently defeated by a combination of US weaponry and the administrative reforms of President Ramón Magsaysay. In 1954 their leader, Luis Taruc, surrendered and was imprisoned. The movement revived briefly in 1969–70.

Hull, Cordell (1871–1955) US politician. He was a member of the House of Representatives (1907–21, 1923–31) and author of the first federal income-tax law (1913). As secretary of state (1933–44) under Franklin Roosevelt, he helped implement the Good Neighbor Policy. Hull was an important diplomatic figure in World War 2, working to ensure cooperation among the Allies and playing a key role in gaining US acceptance of the United Nations (UN). He was awarded the 1945 Nobel Prize for Peace.

human evolution *See* feature article, page 189

humanism Philosophy based on a belief in the supreme importance of human beings and human values. The greatest flowering of humanism came during the Renaissance, spreading from Italy to other parts of Europe. The humanists, such as Petrarch, Francesco Guicciardini, Niccolò Machiavelli and Desiderius Erasmus, rejected medieval scholasticism and based learning on rediscovered Latin and ancient Greek texts. Modern humanism developed as an alternative to traditional Christian beliefs. This movement, which has been associated with social reform, was championed by Bertrand Russell.

human rights Entitlements that an individual may arguably possess by virtue of being human and in accordance with what is natural. The concept of the inalienable rights of the human being has traditionally been linked to the idea of natural law, on which commentaries were written by several Greek and Roman writers. John Locke helped to shape ideas of fundamental human rights and liberal democracy in *Two Treatises on Government* (1690). The concept of human rights has been most notably formulated in a number of historic declarations: the United States' Declaration of Independence (1776), the Constitution of the United States (1789) – particularly the amendments in the Bill Of Rights (1791) – and the French Declaration of the Rights of Man and of the Citizen (1789). These documents owed much to the English Petition of Right (1628) and Bill of Rights (1689), which extended the concept of individual freedom proclaimed earlier in the Magna Carta (1215). The responsibility of the international community for the protection of human rights is proclaimed in the Charter of the United Nations (1945) and the Universal Declaration of Human Rights (1948). *See also* civil rights

Humayun (1508–56) Second Mughal emperor of India (1530–40, 1555–56). After losing his empire to the Afghan leader Sher Khan in a number of battles, he fled to Sindh in 1540 and to Persia in 1543. Equipped with an Iranian army, he then failed in his attempts to win back his empire from Sher Shah. After the deaths of Sher Shah (1545) and his son Islam Shah (1553), Humayan regained his throne by capturing Lahore and Delhi in 1555. He died before he could reconquer the rest of his empire. His lasting legacy was the influence on Indian culture of the artists and scholars who had accompanied him from Iran.

Hume, David (1711–76) Scottish philosopher, historian and man of letters. Hume's publications include *A Treatise of Human Nature* (1739–40), *History of England* (1754–63) and various philosophical "enquiries". Widely known for his humanitarianism and philosophical scepticism, Hume's philosophy was a form of empiricism that affirmed the contingency of all phenomenal events. He argued that it was impossible to go beyond the subjective experiences of impressions and ideas. Some of his views on economics may have influenced Adam SMITH.

Hume, John (1937–) Northern Irish politician, leader (1983–) of the nationalist SOCIAL DEMOCRATIC LABOUR PARTY (SDLP). He was a founder member and president (1964–68) of the Credit Union League. Hume entered the British Parliament in 1983. His commitment to peace in Northern Ireland helped to secure an IRA cease-fire (1994). In 1997 and 1998 Hume represented the SDLP at the peace talks leading to the GOOD FRIDAY AGREEMENT. He shared the 1998 Nobel Prize for Peace with David TRIMBLE, leader of the ULSTER UNIONISTS.

Hume, Joseph (1777–1855) British radical politician. He was a member of Parliament (1812, 1818–41, 1842–55). After making his fortune in India, Hume returned to England and bought a seat in Parliament. He was a forceful advocate of the repeal of the CORN LAWS and of the COMBINATION ACTS and a lifelong campaigner for parliamentary reform, including the introduction of universal franchise and the secret ballot.

Humphrey, Hubert Horatio (1911–78) US statesman, vice president (1965–69). In 1948 he was elected to the Senate as a Democrat from Minnesota. He gained a reputation as a liberal, championing civil-rights issues. In 1964 Lyndon JOHNSON chose him as his running mate. As vice president, Humphrey's wholehearted support for the VIETNAM WAR (1955–75) incurred hostility. In 1968 he won the presidential nomination, but lost the election to Richard NIXON. In 1971 he returned to the Senate and was re-elected in 1976.

hundred Subdivision of a shire in medieval England, having its origin in the Anglo-Saxon era. Its first official mention occurs in the 10th century. In theory, a hundred consisted of 100 hides (a unit of land area that varied from 120 to 140 acres). The hundred court met every four weeks under the king's representative (reeve) to deal with private disputes and criminal matters.

Hundred Days (20 March–28 June 1815) Period between the escape of NAPOLEON I from the Italian island of Elba and the second restoration of LOUIS XVIII, after the Allied victory at WATERLOO. Napoleon landed at Cannes on 1 March and arrived in Paris on 20 March, shortly after Louis XVIII had fled. Napoleon's attempt to re-establish the first empire failed. On 22 June, Napoleon abdicated, and Louis was restored to the throne on 28 June. *See also* NAPOLEONIC WARS

Hundred Days of Reform (1898) Campaign in China to reform the Manchu QING state. It was led by KANG YOUWEI who, with LIANG QICHAO, secured the agreement of Emperor GUANGXU to numerous reforms within the civil service, administration, military, industry, science and commerce. Guangxu issued 40 edicts, but right-wing forces blocked their progress and supported the palace coup led by Empress Dowager CIXI. Guangxu was imprisoned and Kang Youwei and Liang Qichao fled to Japan. Six other reformers were executed.

Hundred Flowers Movement (1956–57) Campaign in China. Launched by MAO ZEDONG and others, it drew its name from a famous slogan in Chinese classical history: "Let a hundred flowers bloom and a hundred schools of thought contend." Intellectuals were invited to make criticisms of the Chinese COMMUNIST PARTY (CCP)'s policies, just as Nikita KHRUSHCHEV had denounced the policies of Joseph STALIN earlier in 1956. Criticisms began to be voiced in 1957 and became so intense that the government reacted by initiating an anti-rightist campaign. Government critics were themselves reproached, and some were exiled to remote areas. *See also* CULTURAL REVOLUTION

Hundred Years' War (1337–1453) Sporadic conflict between the French VALOIS princes and the PLANTAGENET kings of England for the succession to the CAPETIAN kingship of France. In 1328 PHILIP VI of Valois was crowned by right of descent through the male line, but he was challenged by EDWARD III of England, descended more directly from the last Capetians through his mother. Another underlying issue was Anglo-French rivalry over economic links with GASCONY and FLANDERS. In 1337 Philip confiscated the Plantagenet lordships of Gascony and Ponthieu. The resulting war was an intermittent series of conflicts. Edward invaded France in 1338 and adopted the title "king of France" in 1340. The English won major victories at CRÉCY (1346) and POITIERS (1356), where JOHN II of France was captured by EDWARD THE BLACK PRINCE. These successes led to the Treaty of BRÉTIGNY (1360), which ceded large territories to Edward in return for him giving up claims to the French throne. These claims were renewed when CHARLES V of France began to win back territory, leaving England with only CALAIS and part of Gascony by the time of Edward's death in 1377. In 1396 the Peace of Paris established a truce, but fighting erupted again and HENRY V won a crushing victory at AGINCOURT (1415). He then occupied much of N France, with the result that, under the Treaty of TROYES (1420), CHARLES VI recognized Henry as heir to his throne. French fortunes were revived by the accession of HENRY VI to the English throne. In 1429 the siege of ORLÉANS was broken by JOAN OF ARC. In 1453 the French captured Bordeaux, leaving only Calais in English hands until 1558.

Hungarian Uprising (1956) Revolt against communist rule, centred around BUDAPEST. The replacement of Prime Minister Imre NAGY by the more repressive Mátyás RÁKOSI, who in turn was replaced by the equally repressive Erno Gerö in July 1956, angered many Hungarians. Soviet leader Nikita KHRUSHCHEV's criticism (February 1956) of Joseph STALIN had encouraged Hungarians to expect some degree of liberalization, and in October demonstrators in Budapest called for their grievances against the government to be addressed. The police fired on the crowd, turning the demonstration into a revolution backed by the army. Nagy returned to power but, after he announced Hungary's withdrawal from the WARSAW PACT, Soviet tanks re-entered the country and on 4 November drove into Budapest. Resistance was quickly overcome and Nagy was replaced by János KÁDÁR as prime minister. Around 200,000 Hungarians escaped to the West and in 1958 Nagy was executed by Kádár's government.

Hungary *See* country feature

Huns Nomadic people who moved E through central Asia during the 4th century AD. One branch, the White Huns, overran the SASANIAN empire and laid waste the cities of N India, where they established a short-lived empire. A sec-

HUNGARY

AREA: 93,030sq km (35,919 sq mi)
POPULATION: 10,313,000
CAPITAL (POPULATION): Budapest (2,009,000)
GOVERNMENT: Multiparty republic
ETHNIC GROUPS: Magyar (Hungarian) 98%, Gypsy, German, Croat, Romanian, Slovak
LANGUAGES: Hungarian (official)
RELIGIONS: Christianity (Roman Catholic 64%, Protestant 23%, Orthodox 1%), Judaism 1%
GDP PER CAPITA (1995): US$6410

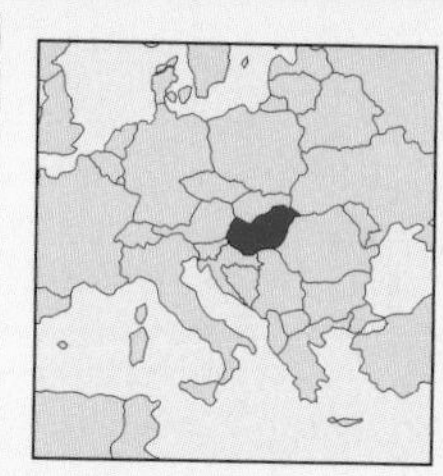

Landlocked republic in central Europe. MAGYARS first arrived in *c.*895 and, under the leadership of ÁRPÁD, settled on the Great Hungarian Plain. Their attempts to expand W were halted by the Saxon King OTTO I in 955. In the 11th century, a descendant of Árpád, Saint STEPHEN, became Hungary's first king and made Roman Catholicism the official religion. In 1241 the population was decimated by a MONGOL invasion.

The last of the Árpád kings died in 1301, and the reign of foreign kings began in Hungary. Raids by the OTTOMAN Turks began in the 14th century. They inflicted a major defeat on Hungary at the Battle of MOHÁCS (1526), and by 1568 the territory of modern Hungary was divided into three: the W and central sections were parts of the Habsburg and Ottoman empires respectively, while TRANSYLVANIA in the E had autonomy under Turkish suzerainty.

In 1699 LEOPOLD I expelled the Turks and established repressive HABSBURG control. Reforms were introduced in the early 19th century, but the non-Magyars perceived them as favouring the Magyars, who now composed only 40% of the population. After the REVOLUTIONS OF 1848, Lajos KOSSUTH declared Hungary independent in 1849. The Austrians re-established control but, following their defeat in the AUSTRO-PRUSSIAN WAR (1866), they agreed to

the formation of a joint AUSTRO-HUNGARIAN EMPIRE (1867–1918). As defeat loomed in WORLD WAR I, nationalist demands intensified and independence was declared in 1918.

In 1919 communists, led by Béla KUN, briefly held power. In 1920 Miklós HORTHY became regent. Under the terms of the post-war Treaty of TRIANON (1920), Hungary lost all non-Magyar territory (66% of Hungarian land). In 1941 Hungary allied with Nazi Germany, regaining much of its lost territory. Virulent anti-Semitism saw the extermination of many Hungarian Jews. Hungary's withdrawal from WORLD WAR 2 led to German occupation (March 1944). The Soviet expulsion of German troops (October 1944–May 1945) devastated much of Hungary.

In 1946 Hungary became a republic, headed by Imre NAGY. In 1948 the Communist Party gained control, forcing Nagy's resignation and declaring Hungary a People's Republic (1949). Hungary became a Stalinist state. Industry was nationalized and agriculture collectivized. An economic crisis forced the brief reinstatement (1953–55) of Nagy. In 1955 Hungary joined the WARSAW PACT. The HUNGARIAN UPRISING (1956) led to the return of Nagy. János KÁDÁR formed a rival government and called for Soviet military assistance. Soviet troops brutally suppressed the Uprising. Nagy was executed and *c.*200,000 people fled. From 1968 Kádár's regime gradually adopted liberal reforms, and Hungary sought Western aid to modernize its economy in the 1980s. In 1989 Kádár was forced to resign and the Communist Party was disbanded.

In 1990 multiparty elections were won by the conservative Democratic Forum. The Hungarian Socialist Party (HSP), composed of ex-communists, won the 1994 elections and set up a coalition government with the liberal Alliance of Free Democrats. Gyula Horn of the HSP became prime minister. In 1998 elections the Federation of Young Democrats-Hungarian Civic Party (Fidesz-MPP) emerged as the largest party and Viktor Orban became prime minister.

ond branch reached E Europe in the late 4th century and in *c.*410 established a powerful and aggressive empire on the Great Hungarian Plain. Their strength lay in their outstanding horsemanship. Under the leadership of ATTILA, the empire reached its peak in the 440s, when it encompassed and forced W numerous, particularly Germanic, groups, among them the OSTROGOTHS and VISIGOTHS. Large amounts of gold were collected each year in the form of tributes from areas within the ROMAN EMPIRE. The Hun empire was, however, based on warfare and, once its expansion stopped, decline quickly followed. Within 16 years of Attila's death (453), the Huns had ceased to exist as an independent force in Europe.

Hun Sen (1952?–) Cambodian statesman, prime minister (1985–). He joined the KHMER ROUGE in 1970, shortly after the overthrow of NORODOM SIHANOUK. Hun Sun helped topple Lon Nol's US-backed regime in 1975, but was subsequently forced into exile in Vietnam by POL POT. He returned after the overthrow of the Khmer Rouge by Vietnamese forces in 1979, serving as foreign minister before being appointed prime minister. Norodom's son, Prince Ranariddh, won the 1993 elections, but Hun Sen kept control of the police and army and ejected Ranariddh from the coalition in 1998.

Hunt, Henry (1773–1835) British political reformer. A wealthy farmer, he was also a radical who became known as "Orator Hunt" because of his powerful speeches. Hunt advocated the repeal of the CORN LAWS and parliamentary reforms, such as full adult suffrage and the secret ballot. In 1819, on the occasion of the PETERLOO MASSACRE, he made a speech for which he was imprisoned for two years. He was a Radical member of Parliament (1830–33).

Hunyadi, János (1387–1456) Hungarian soldier and national hero. He governed (1446–52) Hungary as regent for Ladislas V. A brilliant general, he took part in the HUSSITE Wars. Hunyadi spent much of his life fighting the OTTOMAN Turks, culminating in a brilliant defeat (1456) of the Turkish fleet on the River Danube, which broke the siege of Belgrade. His son, MATTHIAS CORVINUS, became king of Hungary in 1458.

Huron Confederation of Iroquoian-speaking tribes of Native North Americans who once occupied the St Lawrence Valley, E of Lake Huron. In wars between 1648 and 1650 with the IROQUOIS CONFEDERACY, competitors in the fur trade with the French and British, their population was reduced from 15,000 to *c.*500. After a period of wandering, the Huron settled in Ohio, the Great Lakes area and Kansas. Today, *c.*1250 live on reservations in Ohio and Oklahoma, United States, and in Ontario, Canada.

Hurrians Ancient people of MESOPOTAMIA. They had established numerous small principalities to the N of SUMERIA by the mid-2nd millennium BC. In 1480 BC these were united by King Parrattarna as the kingdom of Mitanni, which subsequently established an empire in Syria and warred with Egypt. The power of the Hurrians (Mitannians) was eventually destroyed by the ASSYRIANS in *c.*1275 BC, but they had considerable influence over HITTITE culture. They spoke a language unrelated to any other Mesopotamian language and used a CUNEIFORM script.

Hus, Jan (1369?–1415) Bohemian religious reformer. He studied and later taught at Prague, where he was ordained a priest. Hus' preaching, influenced by the writings of John WYCLIFFE, caused conflict with the Roman Catholic Church. He was excommunicated in 1411. In *De Ecclesia* (1412), he outlined his case for reform of the Church. Hus was tried by the Council of CONSTANCE (1415) and burned at the stake as a heretic. His followers, known as HUSSITES, launched a civil war against the Holy Roman Empire.

Husák, Gustáv (1913–91) Czechoslovak statesman, leader of the Communist Party of Czechoslovakia (CCP) (1969–87) and president (1975–89). A Resistance fighter during World War 2, he joined the Slovak Communist Party (SCP) at the end of the War. He took over as first secretary (1969–87) of the CCP after the fall of Alexander DUBČEK and the crushing of the PRAGUE SPRING. He was charged with restoring order and removing reformers from the Party. After the "Velvet Revolution" (1989), Husák was replaced as president by Václav HAVEL.

Hussein I (1935–99) HASHEMITE king of Jordan (1953–99). He sought to maintain good relations with the West while supporting the Palestinians' cause in the ARAB-ISRAELI WARS. In 1967 Hussein led Jordan into the SIX-DAY WAR, losing the WEST BANK and East JERUSALEM to Israel. In 1970 he ordered his army to suppress the activities of the PALESTINE LIBERATION ORGANIZATION (PLO) in Jordan. In 1974 Hussein relinquished Jordan's claim on the West Bank to the PLO. In the 1990s he supported the Middle East peace process, signing a treaty with Israel in 1994 and attending the funeral of Itzhak RABIN in 1995. He was succeeded by his son, Abdullah (1962–).

Hussein, Saddam (1937–) Iraqi statesman, president of IRAQ (1979–). In 1959 he was forced into exile for his part in an attempt to assassinate Prime Minister Abdul Karim KASSEM. In 1963 a coup enabled Saddam to return to Iraq, but he was imprisoned for his involvement in a plot to overthrow the new regime in 1964. After his release, Saddam played a major role in the 1968 coup, led by the BA'ATH PARTY, that brought General Ahmad al-BAKR to power. The civilian government was replaced by a Revolutionary Command Council (RCC). In 1979 Saddam succeeded Bakr as chairman of the RCC. His invasion of IRAN marked the start of the bloody IRAN-IRAQ WAR (1980–88). During the War, Saddam was supported by the West, who distrusted the new Islamic regime in Iran. At home Saddam, who surrounded himself with political allies from his home village of Tikrit, ruthlessly suppressed all opposition and was responsible for the systematic killing, by chemical and gas attacks, of the KURDS. His invasion (1990) of KUWAIT provoked worldwide condemnation. In the ensuing GULF WAR (1991), a multinational force expelled Iraqi forces from Kuwait. Further uprisings by Kurds and Iraqi SHIITES were ruthlessly suppressed, forcing the United Nations to impose "no-fly" zones over S Iraq. The late 1990s saw protracted political manoeuverings between Hussein and the United Nations (UN), particularly over chemical and nuclear installations. Despite punitive sanctions that have impoverished Iraq, he remained in power.

Hussein ibn-Ali (1856–1931) Arabian statesman, king of the HEJAZ (1916–24). A member of the powerful HASHEMITE dynasty, he reigned over MECCA (1908–16). During World War 1, he led the successful Arab revolt against OTTOMAN rule and made himself king of Arabia. He was recognized by the Allies as king of a smaller area, the Hejaz. IBN SAUD, ruler of Nejd, disputed Hussein's rule, forcing him to abdicate in 1924 in favour of his son, Ali. After exile in Cyprus (1924–30), Hussein died in Amman, Jordan, where he had been succeeded by his son, ABDULLAH. Another son, FAISAL I, was king of Iraq. *See also* LAWRENCE, T.E. (THOMAS EDWARD)

Hussites Followers of the religious reformer Jan HUS in BOHEMIA and MORAVIA in the 15th century. The execution of Hus (1415) provoked the **Hussite Wars** against the Emperor SIGISMUND, who had succeeded the more tolerant Wenceslas IV in Bohemia. Pope MARTIN V launched several unsuccessful crusades against the Hussites. Peace was finally agreed at the Council of BASEL (1431), but it was rejected by the Taborites, the radical wing of the Hussites. The Taborites were defeated by Catholics and more moderate Hussites, the Utraquists, at the Battle of Lipany (1434). The majority of Utraquist demands were met in 1436.

Hutchinson, Anne Marbury (1591–1643) Massachusetts colonist and religious leader, b. England. She emigrated to Massachusetts in 1643. Her disagreement with the orthodox Puritanism of Boston led to her trial for sedition (1637) and expulsion. She moved to Aquidneck (now part of Rhode Island), and later to Pelham Bay, New York, where she was murdered by Native Americans.

Hu Yaobang (1915–89) Chinese statesman, general secretary (1980–87) of the Chinese COMMUNIST PARTY. He joined the Communists in 1933 and took part in the LONG MARCH. Hu became associated with DENG XIAOPING in the war against Japan (1937–45), during which he served as a political commissar. In 1952 he became head of the Young Communist League, but lost his post (1966) during the CULTURAL REVOLUTION. Hu was rehabilitated after MAO ZEDONG's death (1976). Accused of sympathizing with student demonstrations for democracy, Hu was dismissed. The TIANANMEN SQUARE protests followed his death.

Hyder Ali (1722–82) Sultan of Mysore (1761–82). He commanded the army of Mysore (now KARNATAKA) from 1749 and deposed the Hindu ruler in order to become sultan. Hyder expanded his territory in wars with the MARATHA and the British. He defeated the British in 1767 and 1780, but in 1781 was badly defeated by them, losing thousands of his troops. On his death-bed, Hyder Ali urged his son, TIPU SULTAN, to make peace with the British.

Hyksos Invaders, probably from Palestine, of ancient EGYPT in the 17th century BC. The first use of horses and chariots is attributed to the Hyksos. They ruled Egypt from *c.*1674 to *c.*1567 BC as the 15th and 16th dynasties. They were overthrown by a revolt started by the Egyptian rulers of Thebes, who gradually extended their rule into Hyksos territory and formed the 17th dynasty.

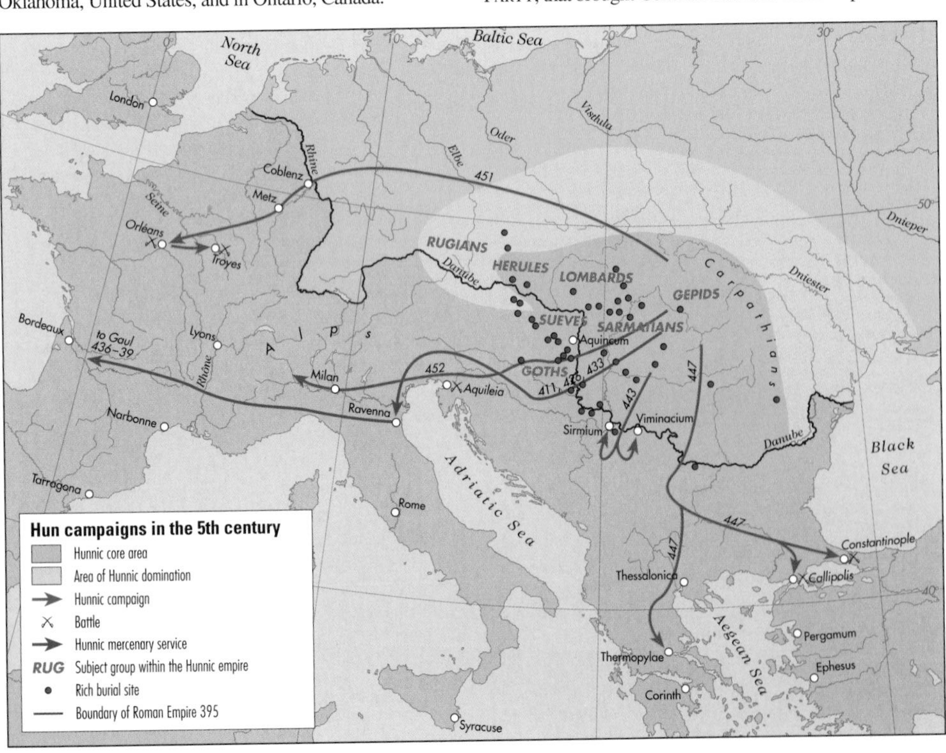

◀ **Huns** After invading the Eastern Roman Empire (447), the Huns suffered their first defeat near Troyes in an attack on Gaul (451), but went on to devastate most of N Italy (452).

Ibarra, Francisco de (1539–75) Spanish conquistador. He explored and colonized Nueva Vizcaya, a large area N of Zacatecas, Mexico. He was named governor and captain general of the area in 1562, and his appointment was reconfirmed in 1573. Ibarra was responsible for opening up N Mexico to the Spanish.

Ibarruri, Dolores (1895–1989) Spanish politician. She was a founder (1920) of the Spanish Communist Party and was the Spanish delegate to the Third International (1933, 1935). During the Spanish CIVIL WAR (1936–39), Ibarruri's inspirational oratory for the Republican cause earned her the epithet "*La Pasionaria*". In 1939 she went into exile in the Soviet Union, where she became president (1960) of the Spanish Communist Party in exile. In 1977 Ibarruri returned to Spain and was re-elected to the National Assembly.

Iberians (Ibero) Ancient, indigenous people of S and E Spain. They flourished in pre-Roman and early Roman times. Their culture was distinct from that of Celtic-dominated N and central Spain, although in Catalonia an overlap between Iberians and Celts resulted in the Celtiberian tribes. The **Bastetani** tribe occupied SW Spain. To the E were the **Tartessian** tribes, of whom the most powerful were the **Turdetani**. Both Greek and Carthaginian influences can be detected in the Iberian alphabet, pottery and sculpture. Their economy was based on agriculture, mining, metalworking and pottery manufacture.

Iberville, Pierre le Moyne, Sieur d' (1661–1706) French-Canadian naval officer and explorer. He spent much of the 1680s and 1690s attacking English trading posts in the Hudson Bay area. After the Treaty of Rijswijk (1697) temporarily ended hostilities, Iberville led an expedition to the Mississippi delta (1699). He established Fort Maurepas (now Biloxi) with *c*.200 colonists; it was the first permanent French settlement on the Gulf of Mexico. Before he could expand the colony, Iberville was called away to fight the English in the West Indies, where he died of a fever.

Ibn Batuta (1304–68?) Moroccan traveller and writer. In *c*.1325 he began his adventures with a pilgrimage to Mecca by way of Egypt and Syria. During the next 30 years, Ibn Batuta covered *c*.120,000km (75,000mi) across the length and breadth of the Muslim-influenced world, taking him as far afield as India and China. In *c*.1353 Ibn Batuta returned to Morocco to write *Rihlah*, an account of his travels. This provides extensive geographical and ethnographic information and has become one of the outstanding sources of medieval world history.

Ibn Khaldun (1332–1406) Arab historian, b. Tunis. He served the sultan of Morocco, but was forced into exile in Spain after being implicated in a rebellion. Ibn Khaldun then represented the Muslim king of Granada in peace negotiations with Pedro the Cruel of Castile. Ibn Khaldun's political and diplomatic career suffered amidst the endless intrigues that beset the decline of the ALMOHAD empire, and he abandoned politics in order to write the *Kitab al'Ibar* (*Universal History*) of Muslim North Africa. In his *Introduction to History* (*Muqaddimah*), Ibn Khaldun posited a cyclical philosophy of history in which civilizations alternate between growth and decay. He also argued for the creation of a "science of culture" that studied the political and economic factors responsible for the transformations in human society. In 1382 Ibn Khaldun became a teacher at the al-Azhar university in Cairo. He negotiated with TAMERLANE in an attempt to relieve the siege of Damascus in 1401.

Ibn Saud (*c*.1880–1953) Founder and first king of SAUDI ARABIA (1932–53). In 1891 the Saud family, who had ruled much of Arabia for the preceding 100 years, were forced into exile by the rival Rashid dynasty. In 1902 Ibn Saud recaptured Riyadh from the Rashids and had regained most of central Arabia by 1904. He founded the militant Ikhwan movement that enforced conformity to the WAHHABI movement in Islam. By 1922 Ibn Saud controlled all of Arabia, except for the HASHEMITE-controlled HEJAZ. In 1924 he invaded Hejaz, compelling HUSSEIN IBN-ALI to abdicate. In 1927 the Ikhwan unilaterally invaded Iraq, and Ibn Saud was forced to crush the organization. He joined Hejaz with his other lands to create the modern Saudi state in 1932. The discovery of oil (1938) transformed the Saudi economy and undermined the austere principles of Wahhabism. Ibn Saud was succeeded by his son, Abdul Aziz SAUD. *See also* FAISAL, IBN ABDUL AZIZ IBN SAUD

Ibo (Igbo) Kwa-speaking people of SE NIGERIA. Traditionally subsistence farmers, the Ibo did not establish a state, instead living mainly in dispersed, autonomous village units. In 1914 Nigeria became a British colony but the Ibo were not fully defeated until 1919. Under colonial rule they developed a strong sense of ethnic identitiy and in 1967 they attempted to secede from Nigeria as the Republic of BIAFRA. Today, they number *c*.16 million

Ibrahim Pasha (1789–1848) Egyptian general and governor, son of MUHAMMAD ALI. Ibrahim's successful campaign (1816–18) against the WAHHABIS of Arabia prompted Ottoman Sultan MAHMUD II to give him command of an expedition to crush a revolt in Greece. Ibrahim subdued the Peloponnese, but was forced to retreat after the Ottomans were defeated at the Battle of NAVARINO (1827). When his father defied Ottoman supremacy, Ibrahim conquered Syria and Adana (1832–33) and became governor of the two provinces. In 1841 he evacuated the provinces under pressure from the British Royal Navy. When his father became senile (1848), Ibrahim was appointed viceroy of Egypt but died shortly after taking office.

Iceland *See* country feature

Iceni Ancient British tribe that occupied the area now known as Norfolk and Suffolk. The territory had been ruled by Prasutagus, a client-king, but on his death (AD 60) the Romans attempted to annex it. Prasutagus' queen, BOADICEA, led a widespread revolt. The Iceni sacked Colchester, London and St Albans before they were crushed by the Roman governor, Suetonius Paulinus.

iconoclastic controversy Dispute over the veneration of images or icons in the BYZANTINE EMPIRE during the 8th and 9th centuries. The controversy began in 726 when Emperor LEO III issued an edict forbidding the veneration of icons. Venerators of icons were persecuted, particularly under CONSTANTINE V. Empress IRENE called the Second Council of NICAEA (787), which rejected iconoclasm. The struggle continued for more than a century, however, only ending after the death of Theophilus (842). In 843 his widow again allowed the veneration of icons. Today, the Greek ORTHODOX CHURCH celebrate this event at the Feast of Orthodoxy on the first Sunday of Lent.

Idaho Mountain state in NW United States, on the border with Canada; the capital and largest city is Boise. When the LEWIS AND CLARK EXPEDITION arrived in Idaho (1805), *c*.8000 Native Americans lived in the area. In 1809 David THOMPSON established the first fur-trading post. The discovery of gold (1860) brought many white settlers along the OREGON TRAIL, and Idaho Territory was created in 1863. Native American resistance to resettlement on reservations, most notably led by Chief JOSEPH, was crushed in the 1870s. Labour disputes in the early 20th century culminated in the trial (1906) of William HAYWOOD at Boise. William BORAH, prosecutor of Haywood, dominated state politics until his death in 1940. Area: 216,412sq km (83,557sq mi). Pop. (1993 est.) 1,099,096.

IDAHO
Statehood :
3 July 1890
Nickname :
Gem State
State motto :
It is forever

ICELAND

AREA: 103,000sq km (39,768sq mi)
POPULATION: 260,000
CAPITAL (POPULATION): Reykjavík (101,824)
GOVERNMENT: Multiparty republic
ETHNIC GROUPS: Icelandic 94%, Danish 1%
LANGUAGES: Icelandic (official)
RELIGIONS: Christianity (Evangelical Lutheran 92%, other Lutheran 3%, Roman Catholic 1%)
GDP PER CAPITA (1995): US$20,460

Small island republic in the North Atlantic Ocean. In AD 874 Norwegian Vikings colonized Iceland, and in 930 the settlers founded the *Althing* (the world's oldest parliament). Christianity was introduced by OLAF I (TRYGGVASON) of Norway at the end of the 10th century. In *c*.1264 Iceland allied with Norway, but retained a large measure of autonomy even after Norway united with Denmark in 1380. During the Reformation, Icelanders mounted the strongest opposition to the introduction of LUTHERANISM in Scandinavia but resistance collapsed by *c*.1550.

From the 17th century, Denmark imposed a greater degree of control over its colony and Iceland lost much of its population due to migration, disease and natural disaster. The *Althing* was abolished between 1800 and 1845. In 1904 Iceland was granted home rule and further powers were devolved from the Danish crown in 1918 – although Denmark retained control of foreign policy. During World War 2, Iceland escaped German occupation, largely due to the presence of US forces.

In 1944 Iceland decisively voted to sever links with Denmark and Sveinn Björnsson became president of the new republic. Post-1945, Iceland has witnessed a succession of coalition governments. It joined the North Atlantic Treaty Organization (NATO) in 1946. The US military presence on the island remains a political issue. In 1970 Iceland joined the European Free Trade Association (EFTA). The extension of Iceland's fishing limits in 1958 and 1972 precipitated the "Cod War" with Britain. In 1977 Britain agreed not to fish within Iceland's 370km (200 nautical mi) fishing limits. Vigdís FINNBOGADÓTTIR served as president from 1980 to 1996. She was succeeded by Ólafur Ragnar Grímsson.

I

Idris I (1890–1983) King of Libya (1951–69). As leader of the Islamic Sanusi sect from 1916, Idris was in effect head of the government in CYRENAICA (now NE Libya). He fought against Italian colonization, but was forced into exile (1922) in Egypt. Idris sided with the British during World War 2 and returned to Cyrenaica in 1947. In 1951 Cyrenaica, TRIPOLITANIA and Fezzan united to form the independent kingdom of Libya and Idris became king. Idris' outlook was pro-Western and his lack of involvement in Middle Eastern politics led to much popular dissatisfaction. In 1969 Idris was deposed by a military junta with socialist aims, dominated by Muammar al-QADDAFI.

Ieyasu (1543–1616) Japanese SHOGUN, founder of the last shogunate in Japan (the TOKUGAWA). In the 1560s, with the assistance of Oda NOBUNAGA, Ieyasu began to expand his lands at the expense of his neighbours, the Imagawa. In 1582 Nobunaga committed suicide and his general, Toyotomi HIDEYOSHI, moved quickly to fill the political vacuum. In 1589 Ieyasu and Hideyoshi combined forces to defeat the HOJO. Ieyasu surrendered his lands W of Hakone and established his headquarters at Edo (now TOKYO). After the death (1598) of Hideyoshi, Ieyasu established himself as the most powerful DAIMYO in Japan by defeating his rivals at the Battle of Sekigahara (1600). Ieyasu cemented his control through a series of astute territorial changes. In 1603 he was appointed shogun. In 1605 Ieyasu abdicated in favour of his son Hidetada, although he retained control of foreign affairs. Ieyasu initially encouraged trade with Europe, but from 1612 attempted to prevent Christian missionary activity. He exacted tribute from the daimyos in order to build the largest castle in the world at Edo. In 1615 Ieyasu secured the succession of the Tokugawa dynasty and unified Japan by defeating and killing Hideyoshi's son, Hideyori.

Ife Historical kingdom that flourished in SW Nigeria between the 11th and the 15th century. Its capital, Ife, was the spiritual centre of the YORUBA. By the early 13th century, Ife was producing the naturalistic sculpture in terracotta and bronze for which it was to become renowned. From the late 15th century, Ife began to decline in the face of competition from BENIN and the OYO empire. In the 19th century, Ife was further weakened in the struggle with Owu for control of the internal SLAVE TRADE.

Igbo *See* IBO

Iglesias, Pablo (1850–1925) Spanish politician. He helped found the Spanish Socialist Party in 1879. In 1882 Iglesias organized Spain's first strike after the restoration of the monarchy (1875). In 1886 he became editor of the socialist newspaper, *El Socialistica*. He also became leader of the General Union of Workers (formed 1888). In 1910 Iglesias was elected as the Socialist Party's first deputy to the Cortes (Spanish parliament). An advocate of the evolutionary path to socialism, Iglesias ensured that the Socialist Party remained outside the COMMUNIST INTERNATIONAL.

Ignatiev, Count Nikolai Pavlovich (1832–1908) Russian diplomat. Ignatiev was posted to China in 1859, where he negotiated a border agreement that gave Russia the land E of the River Amur, enabling it to build Vladivostock and thus to become a major Pacific power. Ignatiev was ambassador to Turkey (1864–78). Ignatiev's enthusiasm for pan-Slavism led him to support the Balkan states in the RUSSO-TURKISH WAR (1877–78). He helped to draw up the Treaty of SAN STEFANO, which gave Romania, Serbia and Montenegro independence. He served (1881–82) as minister of the interior.

Ignatius of Antioch, Saint (active 1st century AD) Bishop of Antioch and influential theologian of the early Christian church. Ignatius was imprisoned and martyred during the reign (98–117) of Emperor TRAJAN. On his way to Rome, Ignatius wrote seven *Epistles*. He denounced Docetism (the belief that Christ was not human) and the Judaizing tendencies prevalent in contemporary Christianity. Ignatius argued that the church should unify under the authority of the bishop to counteract heresy. His letters were preserved by Polycarp, bishop of Smyrna.

Ignatius of Loyola, Saint *See* LOYOLA, SAINT IGNATIUS OF

Iliescu, Ion (1930–) Romanian statesman, president (1990–96). In 1971 he became propaganda secretary in Nicolae CEAUŞESCU's regime, but was later banished to Timişoara for his opposition to Ceauşescu's growing cult of the personality. Following the "Christmas Revolution" (1989) and the execution of the Ceauşescus, Iliescu returned to power as leader of the National Salvation Front (NSF). The NSF won the 1990 elections, but soon split over the pace of economic reform and Iliescu formed the Democratic National Salvation Front (DNSF). In 1992 the DNSF changed its name to the Party of Social Democracy (PDSR) and Iliescu was re-elected president. Despite success in tackling inflation, Iliescu's coalition government fractured over the slow pace of economic reform and increasing social division. In the 1995 presidential election Iliescu was defeated by Emil Constantinescu.

ILLINOIS
Statehood :
3 December 1818
Nickname :
Prairie State
State motto :
State sovereignty, national union

Ilkhanid Mongol dynasty (1256–1335) established by **Hulagu** (1217–65), grandson of GENGHIS KHAN. In 1256 Hulagu sacked the fortress of the ASSASSINS at Alamut, N central Iran, and by 1258 he had captured all of Iran and the ABBASID capital of Baghdad. Hulagu established a state that encompassed the Iranian Plateau, much of Iraq, E and central Anatolia and N Syria. The state was known as the Ilkhanate from the title "Ilkhan" (Pers. "local-ruler"). The Ilkhanate was in constant conflict with the Egyptian MAMLUKS. The dynasty was at its height during the reign (1295–1304) of Mahmud **Ghazan**. His rule was vividly described by his leading minister Rashid ad-Din (1247–1318). Ghazan adopted Islam as the state religion and reformed state finances, but was defeated in his efforts to subdue Syria. **Öljeitü** (r.1304–16) converted to the SHIITE branch of Islam and moved the capital from Tabriz to Soltaniyeh. The Ilkhanate disintegrated after the death of **Abu Said** (r.1317–35).

Illinois State on the E bank of the Mississippi River, N central United States; the capital is Springfield. Native American settlement dates from *c*.8000 BC and the CAHOKIA MOUNDS in SW Illinois are the site of what was probably the largest pre-Columbian settlement north of Mexico. When the French explorers Louis JOLLIET and Jacques MARQUETTE reached the area in 1673, the Native American population was exclusively Algonquian. In 1763, after the FRENCH AND INDIAN WARS, France ceded Illinois to the British. During the American Revolution, the Americans captured Kaskaskia (1778) and Illinois was made a county of Virginia. In 1800 Illinois country became a part of Indiana Territory. White settlement increased dramatically after the BLACK HAWK WAR (1832). Illinois fought on the Union side during the American Civil War. During the 19th century, CHICAGO (the largest city) became a transport and industrial powerhouse. State politics was dominated by Democrat Mayor Richard DALEY from 1955 until his death in 1976. Area: 146,075sq km (56,400sq mi). Pop. (1993 est.) 11,697,336.

Illyria Historic region of the Balkan Peninsula, inhabited since *c*.1000 BC by an Indo-European people. In the 3rd century BC, an Illyrian kingdom was established with its capital at Scodra (now Shkodër, Albania). The threat to

INCA (INKA)

NATIVE SOUTH AMERICANS who migrated from the Peruvian Andes into the CUZCO area in *c*.AD 1250. The reconstruction of the history of the Incas is problematic because they did not develop a system of writing, instead using knotted strings (*quipus*) for record-keeping.

According to tradition, the Inca dynasty was founded (*c*.1200) by **Manco Capac**. In the 14th century, under the leadership of **Mayta Capac**, the Inca began to expand at the expense of their neighbours. In the early 15th century, permanent Inca colonies were established under **Viracocha Inca**. The Chanca invasion (*c*.1438) led to a brief civil war between the forces of Viracocha Inca and his son, Cusi Inca Yupanqui. Inca Yupanqui emerged victorious and took the title of Pachacuti (emperor). **Pachacuti** conquered the Titicaca basin before gaining the powerful kingdom of CHIMÚ. He also rebuilt the capital, Cuzco, launched a vast land reclamation project and began the policy of forced resettlement. Pachacuti created a state religion based on the worship of a creator-god Viracocha.

In 1471 Pachacuti abdicated in favour of his son, **Topa Inca** Yupanqui. During Topa Inca's reign (1471–93), the Inca empire expanded to include more than 12 million people and stretched from modern N Ecuador to central Chile. Topa Inca initiated a great phase of road-building, many of which are still extant. At regular intervals along the highways are distinctive Inca stone settlements. All aspects of production, from the acquisition of materials to the manufacture and distribution of finished items, were controlled by the state.

Topa Inca was succeeded by HUAYNA CAPAC (r.1493–*c*.1525). Huayna began the construction of a second capital at Quito and extended the Inca empire into modern Colombia. Huayna's death (1525) brought civil war between his sons ATAHUALPA and HUÁSCAR. The civil war alienated many of the empire's subjects. In 1532 Atahualpa emerged triumphant but Francisco PIZARRO had already landed in N Peru. The Spanish captured and executed Atahualpa and by 1535 had overrun the entire Inca empire. *See also* MACHU PICCHU

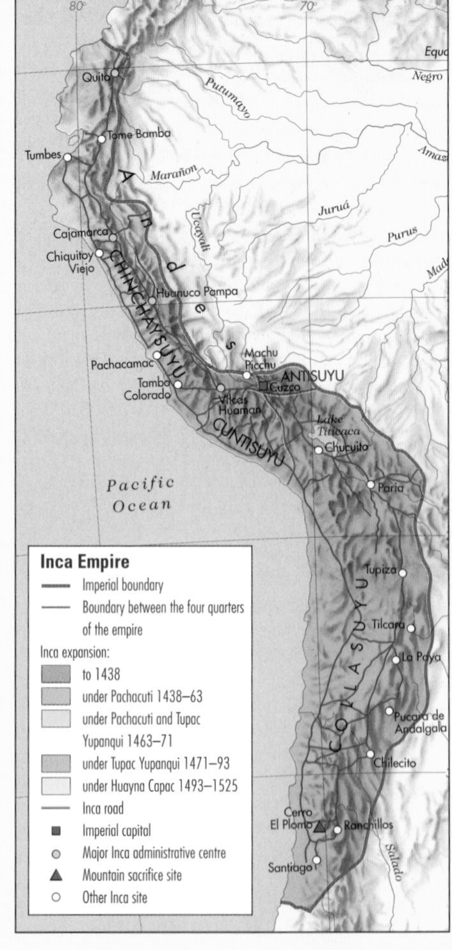

▲ **The Inca empire** was also known as Tahuantinsuyu (Land of the Four Quarters). Each quarter was subdivided into numerous units, founded on groups of small communities.

trade posed by Illyrian piracy on the Adriatic forced Rome to declare war (229–228, 219 BC). Illyria's alliance with PHILIP V of Macedonia led to a full-scale Roman invasion and the conquest of the entire peninsula (168 BC). The Romans later divided Illyria into the provinces of DALMATIA and PANNONIA. Several late Roman emperors were of Illyrian origin. In AD 395 Illyria became part of the Eastern Roman Empire. In the 6th and 7th centuries, Illyria was overrun by the Slavs.

Iltutmish (d.1236) Greatest ruler of the DELHI SULTANATE (1211–36). Iltutmish married the daughter of his master, QUTB-UD-DIN AYBAK, whom he succeeded as ruler of a Muslim state in N India. Making Delhi his capital in 1211, Iltutmish expanded his empire beyond the Punjab to include Sind and Bihar. In 1225 he also established his authority over Bengal. Iltutmish created an effective administration and successfully resisted Mongol encroachments on his empire. He named his daughter Raziyya as his successor, but she only briefly held power. *See also* SLAVE DYNASTY

IMF *See* INTERNATIONAL MONETARY FUND

Imhotep (active 27th century BC) Egyptian architect. He is often credited with designing the step PYRAMID at Saqqara for Pharaoh Zoser in the Third Dynasty of the Old Kingdom. He was later deified as the patron of scribes and the son of Ptah, the builder god of Memphis. The Greeks identified him with Asclepius, the god of medicine.

impeachment Prosecution of a public official by the legislature of a state. In Britain, it is conducted by the House of Commons with the House of Lords as judge, and in the United States by the House of Representatives with the Senate as judge. Originating in the medieval period, it was used most frequently in Britain in the 17th century as a means of removing from office the unpopular ministers of CHARLES I: BUCKINGHAM, LAUD and STRAFFORD. In 1806 Viscount Melville was the last minister in Britain to be threatened with impeachment. The proceedings against him, for misappropriation of public funds, ended in acquittal. In the United States, Andrew JOHNSON was the first president to have impeachment proceedings brought against him (1868). He was acquitted. In 1974 President Richard NIXON was threatened with impeachment, but resigned before he could be brought to trial. In 1998 impeachment proceedings were brought against President Bill CLINTON. He was acquitted the following year.

imperial cities Cities in the HOLY ROMAN EMPIRE that were under the direct authority of the emperor. During the medieval period a number of cities were given or purchased the title, while others employed military force to acquire the status. By the 15th century there were *c*.50 imperial cities in Germany and within 100 years this had increased to more than 80. Almost totally independent, the imperial cities ruled over their surrounding countryside and made mutual alliances. In 1489 they received formal recognition of their right to be represented in the imperial DIET and in 1648, under the terms of the Peace of WESTPHALIA, they became the third college of the diet. Their number was much reduced by Napoleon I of France. Today, only Hamburg and Bremen remain independent states.

imperial conferences (1887–1937) Periodic gatherings of leaders of the countries in the BRITISH EMPIRE and representatives of the home government. Early conferences in 1887, 1894 and 1897 emphasized joint political, military and commercial policies, but from 1902 they paid increasing attention to securing preferential trade tariffs. The 1926 Imperial Conference defined the British Commonwealth and the Statue of Westminster (1931) established the COMMONWEALTH OF NATIONS. The 1937 Conference unanimously supported APPEASEMENT of Germany.

imperialism Domination of one people or state by another. Imperialism can be economic, cultural, political or religious. The early history of western Asia and the Mediterranean is marked by a continuous succession of empires. The Assyrian empire was replaced (6th–4th century) by that of the Iranians. The Iranian empire, in turn, was replaced by the hegemony of ancient GREECE. ALEXANDER III (THE GREAT) unified western Asia and the Mediterranean into one mighty empire. The ROMAN EMPIRE extended from Britain to Egypt. The 16th-century age of EXPLORATION saw the establishment of vast trading empires in the Americas and Asia by the Spanish, Portuguese, Dutch, British and French. Imperialism took the form of COLONIALISM as colonies were established as a source of raw materials and as a market for the manufactured goods of the European powers. With few exceptions, imperialism imposed alien cultures on native societies. Imperialism gathered pace from the middle of the 19th century until World War 1 as Russia, Italy, Germany and the United States joined in the scramble for territories in Africa and Asia. Most former colonies gained independence in the 20th century. *See also* COLONIALISM

Inca *See* feature article

Independent Labour Party (ILP) British political party, founded (1893) in Bradford, N England. The ILP aimed to get working people elected to Parliament. Its first leader was Keir HARDIE. In 1900 it formed a Labour Representation Committee to return trade union representatives to Parliament. In 1906 that committee became the LABOUR PARTY. By 1918 the Labour Party completely overshadowed the ILP. With its sympathy for communism and its pacifist ideals, the ILP became increasingly estranged from the Labour Party after World War 1, but remained affiliated to it until 1932.

Independents (Separatists) English PURITAN sect that evolved from the "Brownists" (followers of Robert BROWNE). The Independents sought organizational and intellectual independence as separate congregations from the established CHURCH OF ENGLAND. Separatists established a base in the Netherlands in 1608, and (as the PILGRIMS) in Plymouth, Massachusetts. The first truly Independent church was founded (1616) in Southwark, London, by Henry Jacob. Oliver CROMWELL was an Independent, and the backbone of the New Model Army was formed by Independents. Cromwell's support guaranteed their strength during the English CIVIL WAR, but after the RESTORATION their strength was eroded by the Act of UNIFORMITY (1662). *See also* CONGREGATIONALISM

India *See* country feature, page 196

Indiana State in N central United States, S of Lake Michigan; the capital is Indianapolis. Indiana was originally inhabited by the Miami, Potawatomi and Delaware tribes of Algonquian-speaking Native North Americans. Sieur de LA SALLE was the first European to explore the region (1679), and in the early 18th century the French built forts to protect trade routes to the Mississippi. In 1763 it was ceded to the British and during the American Revolution it was captured (1779) for the colonials by George Rogers CLARK. Native American resistance was broken by the victories of Anthony WAYNE at the Battle of Fallen Timbers (1794), and William HARRISON at the Battle of Tippecanoe (1811). Indiana was a rural area until late 19th-century industrialization and the state remains one of the nation's richest farming regions. Area: 93,993sq km (36,291sq mi). Pop. (1993 est.) 5,713,000.

Indian Mutiny (1857–58) Large-scale uprising against British rule. It is known in India as the First War of Independence. It began (10 May 1857) at Meerut, N central India, as a mutiny among 35,000 Indian troops (sepoys) in the service of the English EAST INDIA COMPANY. The immediate cause was the introduction of cartridges lubricated with the fat of cows and pigs, a practice offensive to both Hindus and Muslims. A more general cause was resentment at modernization and Westernization. The mutineers captured Delhi and, with the support of local maharajahs and many civilians in Uttar Pradesh and Madhya Pradesh, the British garrison at Lucknow was besieged. On 14 September 1857, British forces recaptured Delhi and the revolt petered out. Atrocities were perpetrated on both sides. The revolt resulted in the British government taking over control of India from the East India Company in 1858. *See also* NANA SAHIB

INDIANA
Statehood :
11 December 1816
Nickname :
Hoosier State
State motto :
Crossroads of America

Indian National Congress *See* CONGRESS, INDIAN NATIONAL

Indians, American *See* NATIVE AMERICANS

Indian Removal Act (28 May 1830) US legislation giving the president powers to transfer NATIVE NORTH AMERICANS from their ancestral lands to the uninhabited western prairies. In the 1830s President Andrew JACKSON used military force to move the CHICKASAW, CHOCTAW, SEMINOLE, CHEROKEE and CREEK from their native lands in the Southeast. It has been estimated that up to 25,000 of the 100,000 tribesman forced to march westward died en route. The forced resettlement of the Cherokee (1838–30) became known as the "TRAIL OF TEARS". The Seminole resisted the move in the second of the SEMINOLE WARS (1835–42).

Indian Territory Area set aside for NATIVE NORTH AMERICANS by the Indian Intercourse Act (1834). The Act set aside Kansas, Nebraska, and Oklahoma N and E of the Red River as Indian Territory. In 1854 Kansas and Nebraska were redesignated territories open to white settlement. In 1889 Western Oklahoma was opened to white settlement. In 1907 the last of the Indian Territory was dissolved when Oklahoma became a state. *See also* INDIAN REMOVAL ACT

Indian wars In American history, series of conflicts between NATIVE NATIVE AMERICANS and early European settlers. The **Spanish** were involved in conflicts with Native Americans in the SW. The **French** had generally good relations with Native Americans although they were involved in occasional conflicts with the IROQUOIS CONFEDERACY. The **British** settlers were involved in numerous conflicts along the E coast. The first of the wars was the revolt of the POWHATAN CONFEDERACY against settlers in Jamestown, Virginia (1622). This was followed by the PEQUOT WAR (1637), KING PHILIP'S WAR (1676), and the PUEBLO REVOLT (1680–92) against Spanish settlements in New Mexico and Arizona. Between 1689 and 1763 the struggle between Britain and France for control of the N involved several Native American peoples, notably the Algonquins and the Iroquois Confederacy, in the FRENCH AND INDIAN WARS. PONTIAC'S REBELLION (1763–66) in the Great Lakes region occurred at the end of these wars. Once settlers started moving W, the level of conflict escalated, as the US army fought against tribes refusing to be pushed out of their ancestral lands. In Florida, the SEMINOLE WARS (1835–42) were fought against the imposition of the INDIAN REMOVAL ACT (1830). In the SW, the resistance of the NAVAJO led to their mass incarceration (1864–68). Elsewhere, the SIOUX, the APACHE and the CHEYENNE offered the fiercest resistance. The SIOUX WARS ended with the massacre at WOUNDED KNEE in 1890, but the Apache under leaders such as GERONIMO continued to fight until *c*.1900.

India–Pakistan Wars (1947–49, 1965, 1971) Three conflicts between INDIA and PAKISTAN after they became separate and independent states in 1947. The first war arose from a dispute over JAMMU AND KASHMIR. Inconclusive fighting continued until January 1949, when the United Nations (UN) arranged a truce, leaving KASHMIR partitioned. It remained a source of friction and a territorial dispute over Kashmir escalated into a second war. Both sides invaded the other's territory, but military stalemate resulted in a Soviet-arranged truce after a few weeks. The third India–Pakistan War arose out of the civil war between East and West Pakistan in 1971. India intervened in support of East Pakistan (now BANGLADESH), and (West) Pakistan suffered a decisive defeat. Since 1985 a low-level conflict has continued over the disputed region of Kashmir, briefly threatening to escalate into a larger conflagration in 1999.

Indochina Peninsula of SE Asia, including BURMA, THAILAND, CAMBODIA, VIETNAM, West MALAYSIA and LAOS. The name refers more specifically to the former federation of states of Vietnam, Laos and Cambodia, associated with France within the French Union (1945–54). European penetration of the area began in the 16th century. By the 19th century France controlled

COCHIN CHINA, Cambodia, ANNAM and TONKIN, which together formed the Union of Indochina in 1887; Laos was added in 1893. By the end of World War 1 France had announced plans for a federation within the French Union. Cambodia and Laos accepted the federation but fighting broke out between French troops and Annamese nationalists who wanted independence for Annam, Tonkin and Cochin China as Vietnam. The war closed with the French defeat at DIEN BIEN PHU (1954). French control of Indochina was officially ended by the Geneva Conference of 1954.

Indonesia *See* country feature

indulgence In Roman Catholic theology, remission by the church of temporal punishment for sin. An indulgence, once granted, obviates the need for the sinner to do penance, although it does not necessarily remove guilt and may itself be only a partial rather than a full (plenary) indulgence. Previously available from bishops, indulgences are today granted only by the pope. The first indulgences were granted by URBAN II as a reward to those who had participated in the First CRUSADE. The practice soon

INDIA

AREA: 3,287,590sq km (1,269,338sq mi)
POPULATION: 879,548,000
CAPITAL (POPULATION): New Delhi (301,800)
GOVERNMENT: Multiparty federal republic
ETHNIC GROUPS: Indo-Aryan 72%, Dravidian (Aboriginal) 25%, other 3%
LANGUAGES: Hindi 30% and English (both official), Telugu 8%, Bengali 8%, Marati 8%, Urdu 5%, and many others
RELIGIONS: Hinduism 83%, Islam (Sunni) 11%, Christianity 2%, Sikhism 2%, Buddhism 1%
GDP PER CAPITA (1995): US$1400

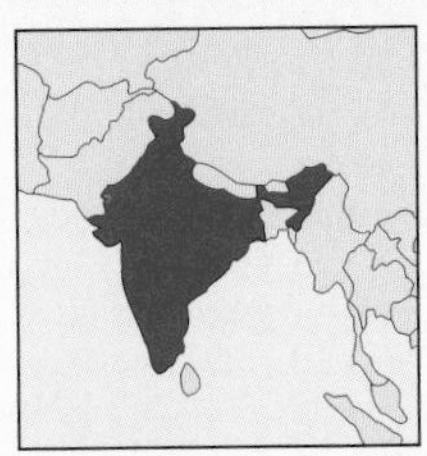

World's seventh-largest country and second-most populous (after China). One of the world's oldest civilizations, the INDUS VALLEY CIVILIZATION, flourished in the lower Indus Valley, *c.*2600 to *c.*1700 BC. In *c.*1500 BC, ARYAN nomads entered NW India and wrote the VEDAS, which established the core beliefs of HINDUISM.

In 530 BC the Iranians conquered the NW, but the area subsequently fell (327–325 BC) to ALEXANDER III (THE GREAT). The Indo-Greek kingdoms that emerged after Alexander's death dominated the region for several centuries. Neither Iran nor Greece, however, penetrated deeper into the subcontinent, due to the strength of native dynasties.

By 500 BC kingdoms existed throughout the Ganges region. Chief among these was MAGADHA whose king, CHANDRAGUPTA, founded the MAURYAN EMPIRE in 312 BC. In the 3rd century BC his grandson, ASHOKA, unified India and established BUDDHISM.

In the 2nd century AD, the CHOLA established a trading kingdom in the south. In the 4th and 5th centuries AD, N India flourished under the GUPTA DYNASTY. The decline of the Guptas was followed by the rise of numerous kingdoms and empires, among them the Puspabhuti dynasty which, under HARSHA, encompassed the entire Gangetic plain in the first half of the 7th century. Few dynasties, however, proved long-lasting.

Between 1192 and 1206 the Iranian Ghurids conquered NW India, preparing the way for the foundation (1211) of the DELHI SULTANATE by Afghan Turks. The Sultanate, India's first Muslim state, spread across much of the subcontinent. Its destruction (1398) by the Mongol conqueror TAMERLANE paved the way for the decentralization of power to local Hindu and Muslim rulers.

In 1526 BABUR founded the MUGHAL EMPIRE (1526–1857), which under AKBAR (r.1556–1605) was extended across N India to BENGAL. In the 16th century, SIKHISM was founded by NANAK. In the 17th century, when the Mughal Empire reached its greatest extent, India became a centre of ISLAMIC ART AND ARCHITECTURE under SHAH JAHAN (who built the TAJ MAHAL) and AURANGZEB. From the 1680s the MARATHAS, based in W India, began to threaten Mughal power as they ravaged far and wide. In the mid-18th century, the Mughal Empire began to break up into warring, regional states, a situation that the Europeans successfully sought to exploit. Throughout the 16th and 17th centuries, several European nations established trading posts around the coast.

In the 1740s, the British and French began to compete for greater control in India, and in 1757 a British victory under Robert CLIVE of the English EAST INDIA COMPANY signalled the beginnings of the BRITISH EMPIRE (1757–1947). From Bengal the British expanded across India, and victory in the SIKH WARS (1845–46, 1848–49) led to the annexation (1849) of PUNJAB. Growing civil unrest culminated in the INDIAN MUTINY (1857–58). Reforms failed to dampen Indian nationalism, and the Indian National CONGRESS was formed in 1885. In 1906 the MUSLIM LEAGUE was founded to protect Muslim minority rights. Following World War 1, "Mahatma" GANDHI began his passive resistance campaigns. The AMRITSAR Massacre (1919) intensified Indian nationalism. During World War 2, Gandhi and Jawaharlal NEHRU, leader of the Congress Party, formed the QUIT INDIA MOVEMENT.

In August 1947 British India was partitioned into India and the Muslim state of PAKISTAN. The ensuing mass migration killed more than 500,000 people. Nehru became India's first prime minister. The first of the INDIA–PAKISTAN WARS (1947–49) was fought over the status of KASHMIR. In 1965 Nehru's daughter, Indira GANDHI, became prime minister. In 1971 India provided military support to create an independent BANGLADESH. In 1974 India became the world's sixth nuclear power. Faced with demands for an independent Sikh state in Punjab, troops stormed the Golden Temple in Amritsar (1984). In October 1984 Indira Gandhi was murdered by her Sikh bodyguards and was succeeded by her son, Rajiv GANDHI. Also in 1984 the world's worst industrial accident occurred at BHOPAL. In 1991 Rajiv Gandhi was assassinated by TAMIL militants. Between 1947 and 1996 India was ruled by sections of the Congress Party for all but four years. In 1996 the United Front formed a coalition government. In 1998 the withdrawal of Congress (I) support led to fresh elections and the formation of a coalition government led by Atal Bihari Vajpayee of the BHARATIYA JANATA PAKSH (BJP). In 1999 the BJP government fell, but was returned to power in elections later the same year.

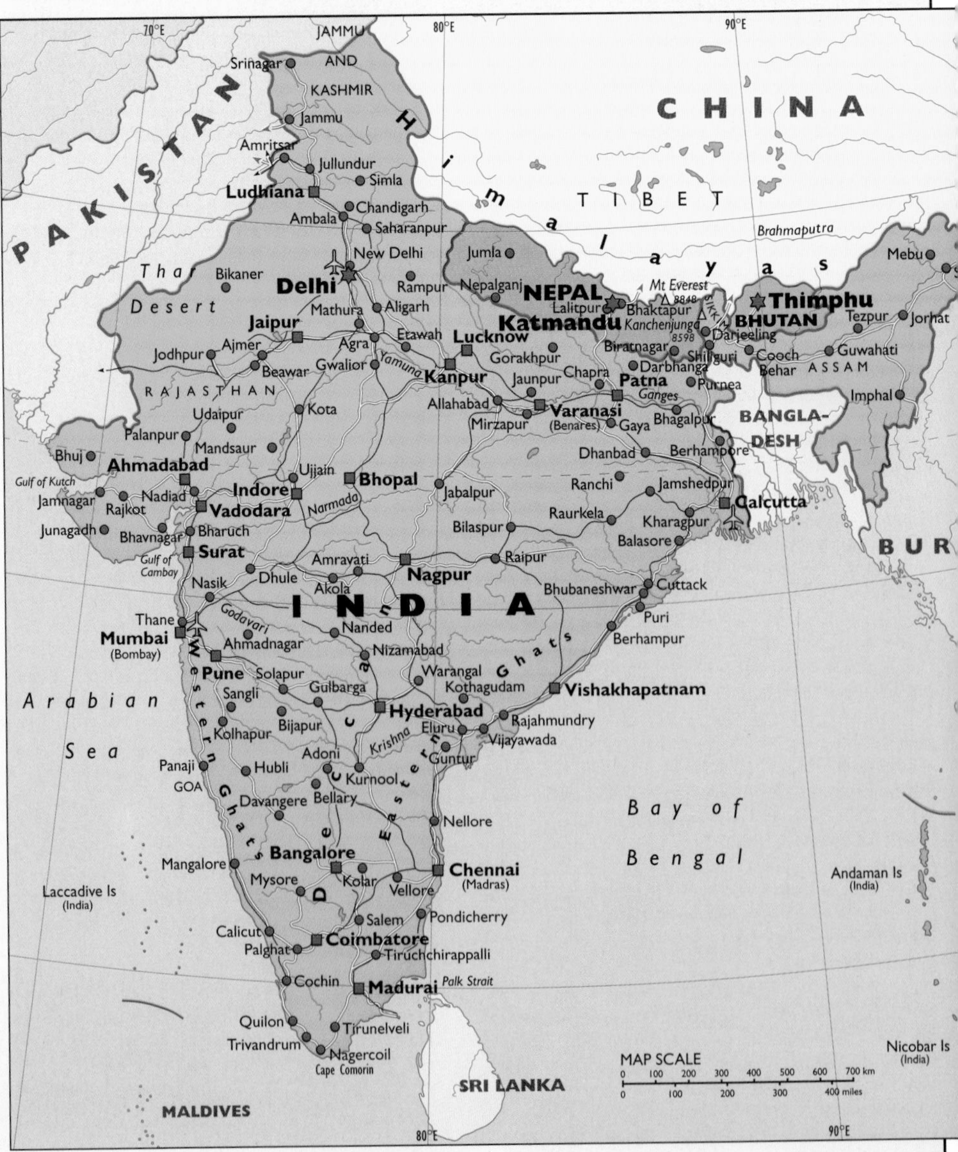

fell into misuse, with indulgences being granted for money as well as good deeds. Abuses connected with the sale of indulgences in the later Middle Ages were one of the major causes of the Reformation. The Council of Trent resolved some of the abuses, and Pius V banned the sale of indulgences in 1567. *See also* Luther, Martin

Industrial Revolution *See* feature article, page 198

Industrial Workers of the World (IWW) US trade union; also known as the "Wobblies". The IWW was formed (1905) in Chicago by Daniel DeLeon, leader of the Socialist Labor Party, Eugene Debs, leader of the Socialist Party, and William Haywood, president of the Western Federation of Miners. It was designed to combine both skilled and unskilled labour in one organization. The group advocated a socialist society and employed militant tactics, advocating strikes and sabotage. It split up after World War 1.

Indus Valley civilization (*c*.2500–1700 BC) Ancient civilization in the valley of the River Indus, present-day Pakistan. Rediscovered by the British archaeologist John Marshall in 1921, it is the earliest known urban culture of the Indian subcontinent. Three major cities – Mohenjo-daro, Harappa and Chanhudaro – have been extensively excavated. The demise of the Indus civilization is thought to be due to barbarian invasions and flooding towards the end of the 2nd millenium BC.

Ingushetia Autonomous Russian republic; the capital is Nazran. Ingushetia lies on the N side of the Caucasus Mountains. The majority population (85%) are Ingush with a Chechen minority. The economy is based on oil and cattle raising. For much of the 20th century, Ingushetia's history was tied to Chechenia. In 1991 the Chechen-Ingush Republic declared its independence. The Ingush desire to distance itself from the Chechen-dominated decision led to the deployment of Russian troops and formal separation from Chechenia (1992). In 1993 Ingushetia became a member of the Russian Federation. In 1999 thousands of Chechen refugees fled to Ingushetia when Russian troops again invaded Chechenia.

Inkatha Freedom Party South African political organization, founded (1975) by Chief Mangosuthu Buthelezi to represent South Africa's Zulu population. Its aim was to work towards a democratic, non-racial political system. Accused of complicity with the apartheid regime, it was later found to have been partly funded by the South African government in order to destabilize black African politics. In the 1980s and 1990s, Inkatha was involved in violent conflict with the mainly Xhosa-backed African National Congress (ANC). In 1994 Buthelezi initially refused to participate in South Africa's first multi-racial elections, but later changed his mind. Inkatha won 43 seats in the new National Assembly. In terms of representation, it ranks third among political parties. Its strongest base is in KwaZulu-Natal.

Inkerman, Battle of (5 November 1854) Attack in the Crimean War by Russian forces against British and French troops who were besieging the naval base at Sevastopol. The Anglo-French troops resisted the attack, forcing the Russians to retreat in disorder. Some 11,000 Russian and 4000 Allied lives were lost.

Innocent I, Saint (d.417) Pope (401–17). He is thought to have been the son of his predecessor, Anastasius I. Innocent developed the role of the papacy in religious controversies and condemned Pelagianism, excommunicating Pelagius in 417. When the Visigothic chief Alaric I besieged Rome in 408, Innocent attempted to mediate between him and Emperor Honorius. The negotiations failed and Rome was sacked by the Visigoths in 410. His feast day is 28 July.

Innocent III (1161–1216) Pope (1198–1216), b. Lotario di Segni. He was promoted by Pope Clement III. He extended the temporal and spiritual power of the papacy. Innocent successfully intervened in the dispute over the succession to Emperor Henry VI, backing the claim of Frederick II over that of Otto IV. He also regained control of the Papal States. Innocent excommunicated King John of England for refusing to recognize Stephen Langton as Archbishop of Canterbury. In 1200 Innocent ordered the Crusade against the heretical Albigenses in S France. He condemned Philip II of France and proclaimed the Fourth Crusade (1204), which ended in the sacking of Constantinople. Innocent called the fourth Lateran Council (1215), which defined the doctrine of the Eucharist, establishing the notion of transubstantiation.

Innocent X (1574–1655) Pope (1644–55), b. Giambattista Pamfili. Ambassador to Spain and a cardinal under Pope Urban VIII, he rapidly became guilty of nepotism after being elected pope. Innocent condemned the Peace of Westphalia (1648) and confiscated the property of Urban's relatives, the Barbarini, who then fled to France. In support of their cause, Cardinal Mazarin threatened to invade the papal enclave of Avignon, and Innocent was forced to back down. In 1653 Innocent issued a papal bull in which he denounced the doctrines of Jansenism on the nature of grace, thus provoking a century of controversy within the Roman Catholic Church.

Innocent XI (1611–89) Pope (1676–89), b. Benedetto Odescalchi. Educated by the Jesuits, he was known as the "father of the poor" for his charitable works. He was elected pope despite the opposition of Louis XIV of France. He improved papal finances and supported the Christian leaders John III (Sobieski) of Poland and Emperor Leopold I in their war against the Turks. Innocent clashed with Louis XIV over the matter of ecclesiastical privileges. Louis attempted to limit papal power in France by issuing the Gallican Articles, a statement of Gallicanism. Innocent also condemned Louis' persecution of the Huguenots. He was beatified in 1956. His feast day is 13 August.

Innsbruck City on the River Inn, W Austria; capital of Tirol. Founded in the 12th century, the city grew rapidly because of its strategic position on a historic transalpine trade route. Innsbruck passed to the Habsburgs in 1363, becoming capital of Tirol in 1420. It passed to Bavaria in 1806. Andreas Hofer fought the French and Bavarians

INDONESIA

AREA: 1,904,570sq km (735,354sq mi)
POPULATION: 191,170,000
CAPITAL (POPULATION): Jakarta (7,885,519)
GOVERNMENT: Multiparty republic
ETHNIC GROUPS: Javanese 39%, Sundanese 16%, Indonesian (Malay) 12%, Madurese 4%, more than 300 others
LANGUAGES: Bahasa Indonesian (official)
RELIGIONS: Islam 87%, Christianity 10% (Roman Catholic 6%), Hinduism 2%, Buddhism 1%
GDP PER CAPITA (1995): US$3800

Republic in SE Asia. Indonesia is the world's most populous Muslim nation and fourth most populous nation on Earth. It is also the world's largest archipelago, with 13,677 islands (less than 6000 of which are inhabited). Three-quarters of its area and population is included in five main islands: the Greater Sunda Islands of Sumatra, Java, Sulawesi and Kalimantan; and Irian Jaya (W New Guinea). More than 50% of the total population live on Java, home of Indonesia's capital, Jakarta.

In the 7th and 8th centuries, the Indian Gupta dynasty was the dominant force, responsible for the introduction of Buddhism and the building of Borobudur, Java. In the 13th century, Buddhism was gradually replaced by Hinduism. By the end of the 16th century Islam had become the principal religion. In 1511 the Portuguese seized Malacca. By 1610 the Dutch had acquired all of Portugal's holdings, except East Timor. During the 18th century, the Dutch East India Company controlled the region. In 1799 Indonesia became a Dutch colony. In 1883 Krakatoa erupted, claiming *c*.50,000 lives. In 1927 Sukarno formed the Indonesian Nationalist Party (PNI). During World War 2, the Japanese expelled the Dutch (1942) and occupied Indonesia. In August 1945 Sukarno proclaimed its independence; the Dutch forcibly resisted.

In November 1949 Indonesia became a republic. Sukarno was the first president, with Muhammad Hatta as his deputy. During the 1950s economic hardship and secessionist demands were met with authoritarian measures. In 1962 Indonesian paratroopers seized Netherlands New Guinea and in 1969 Netherlands New Guinea formally became part of Indonesia as Irian Jaya.

In 1966 General Suharto deposed Sukarno. The Communist Party was banned and alleged communists executed. As many as 750,000 people died in the purges. In 1968 Suharto was appointed president. In 1975 Indonesian forces seized East Timor and declared it a province of Indonesia. More than 200,000 East Timorese died in the resistance against Indonesian rule. The United Nations (UN) refused to recognize the annexation. In 1997 and 1998 Indonesia suffered from dangerously high levels of smog caused by forest fires exacerbated by deforestation and drought. In 1997 Suharto's government was destabilized by the economic crisis in Southeast Asia. Steep rises in food prices led to student demonstrations in Jakarta, and nationwide riots and looting forced Suharto to resign on 21 May 1997. Suharto was replaced by his deputy, B.J. Habibie. Suharto faced charges of corruption, allegedly amassing a personal fortune of up to US$20 billion. East Timor gained independence in 1999, but the population suffered greatly at the hands of pro-Indonesian militias. In October 1999 Habibie was replaced as president by Abdurrahman Wahid (Gus Dur). Megawati Sukarnoputri, daughter of former President Sukarno, was elected vice president. Secessionist forces continue to oppose Indonesian settlement on Irian Jaya and in Aceh, N Sumatra. In 1999–2000 there was increased sectarian conflict in the Malaccas.

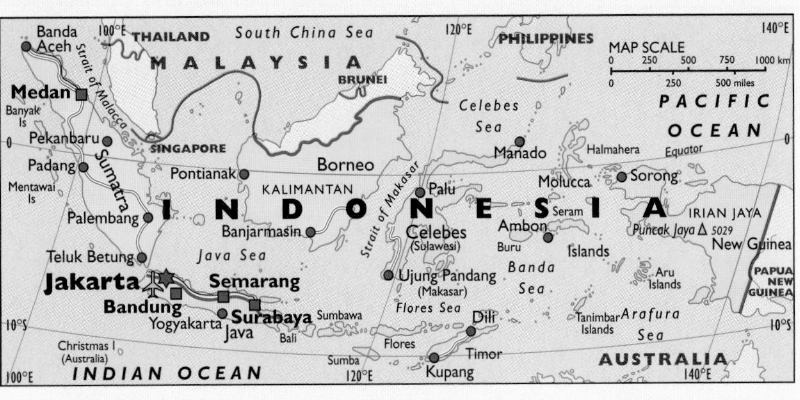

near Innsbruck in 1809. It was restored to Austria in 1814. Pop. (1991) 118,112.

Inönü, Ismet (1884–1973) Turkish statesman, prime minister (1923–37, 1961–65) and president (1938–50), b. Mustafa Ismet. As chief-of-staff (1919–22) to Mustafa Kemal (later Atatürk), Ismet defeated the Greeks at Inönü, taking the name of the village as his family name. As prime minister of the new Turkish republic, he introduced many secular reforms. Inönü succeeded Atatürk as president. A multiparty system was introduced in 1945, and Inönü was defeated by Celâl Bayar in 1950 elections. He returned to power in the civilian government that followed the military coup of 1960. He was replaced as leader of the Republican People's Party (CHP) by Bülent Ecevit.

Inquisition (Holy Office) Ecclesiastical court founded (1231) by Pope Gregory IX for the prosecution of heresy. In 1232 Gregory appointed Dominican and Franciscan inquisitors to hunt out heretics, such as the Waldenses. In 1252 the use of torture was authorized by Pope Innocent IV in order to extract confessions. Punishments for the guilty ranged from penances to banishment and death by

INDUSTRIAL REVOLUTION

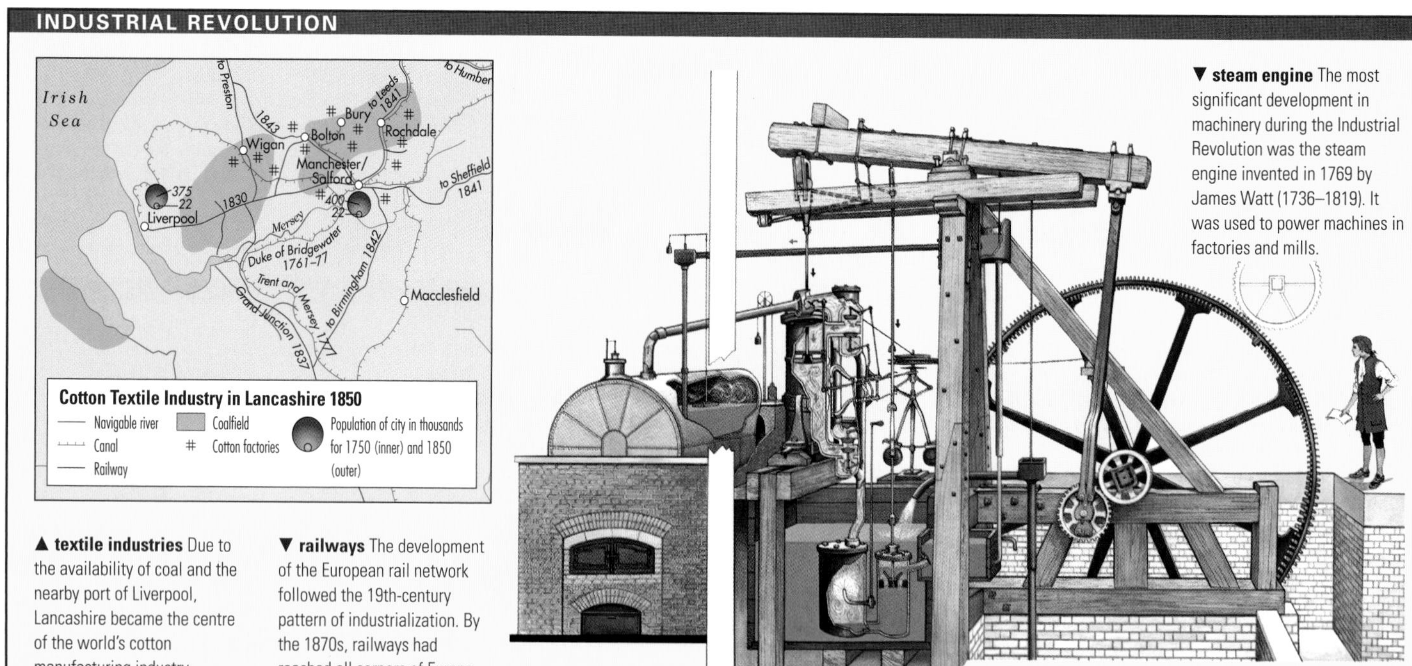

▼ **steam engine** The most significant development in machinery during the Industrial Revolution was the steam engine invented in 1769 by James Watt (1736–1819). It was used to power machines in factories and mills.

▲ **textile industries** Due to the availability of coal and the nearby port of Liverpool, Lancashire became the centre of the world's cotton manufacturing industry.

▼ **railways** The development of the European rail network followed the 19th-century pattern of industrialization. By the 1870s, railways had reached all corners of Europe.

Growth of Industry and Railways
International boundary 1871
Major railway lines constructed:
by 1848
1848–70
1870–1914
Industry c. 1870:
coalmining
iron working
textile production
Industry c. 1914:
steel
engineering
shipbuilding
chemicals
electrical industry

Transformation of a largely agrarian economy to one dominated by manufacturing industry. The economic changes wrought by the Industrial Revolution also produced great social upheaval, such as the movement of people from the country to the city.

In Britain, the Industrial Revolution began in *c.*1760, some decades ahead of the industrialization of the United States (from *c.*1800) and the rest of w Europe (from *c.*1830). In 1850 Britain was still the world's greatest industrial power. By 1914, however, its industrial output had been outstripped by that of both the United States and Germany. The Russian Revolution (1917) led to the rapid industrialization of the Soviet Union and industries also developed rapidly in the inter-war years in Japan, India and China.

In Britain, the Industrial Revolution was preceded by a rapid increase in population, which was both a cause and result of the Agricultural Revolution. The production of textiles was revolutionized by the inventions of Richard Arkwright, James Hargreaves, Edmund Cartwright and Samuel Crompton. The new machines necessitated the building of factories, which replaced cottage industries. The steam engine, invented (1769) by James Watt, was the main driving force behind the Industrial Revolution and led to rapid urbanization near coalfields. By 1850, the percentage of England's population living in towns and cities had doubled to more than 50%. Mass production required an expansion of the network of canals and roads. Developments in iron production resulted in the construction of railways from *c.*1830. Work in the factories was based on the division of labour. At first, the economic doctrine of laissez-faire allowed the growth of industrialization without restrictions on working conditions. The Factory Acts later brought regulations in the employment of children and the length of the working day. The Industrial Revolution led to the creation of an industrial working class. Relations between capital and labour became antagonistic, leading to the development of Marxism. *See also* capitalism; communism; socialism; union

fire. In 1478 Pope SIXTUS IV proclaimed the Inquisition in Spain. Under the first grand inquisitor Tomás de TORQUEMADA, the **Spanish Inquisition** acquired a reputation for its brutal persecution of Jews and Muslims. The *auto-da-fé* condemned *c*.2000 people to death by burning. It was not formally abolished until 1834. In 1542 Pope PAUL III established a **Roman Inquisition** to check the growth of PROTESTANTISM. It took a generally moderate approach, limiting its actions to Italy, except under popes PAUL IV (r.1555–59) and PIUS V (r.1566–72) who attached huge importance to the suppression of heresy. In 1557 the Congregation of the Inquisition published the *Index Librorum Prohibitorum*, a list of books banned as being dangerous to the faith or morals of its members. The list was subsequently revised and, in 1966, discontinued. In 1908 the Congregation of the Inquisition was replaced by the Holy Office, which in 1965 was renamed the Sacred Congregation for the Doctrine of the Faith.

intendant Provincial agent of the French king. Primarily tax collectors in the 16th century, the power of the intendants was greatly increased by LOUIS XIV (r.1643–1715), who made them his local representatives, dealing with administrative, judicial, financial and police matters. The FRONDE uprisings (1648–53) demanded reductions in the powers of intendants, but the reforms were short-lived. The office was abolished during the FRENCH REVOLUTION.

International, Second Loose federation of socialist parties and trade unions, founded (1899) in Paris, France. It succeeded the International Workingmen's Association, founded (1864) in London, England, and dominated by Karl MARX, who expelled Mikhail BAKUNIN from the International in 1872. In 1900 the Second International established a headquarters in Brussels, Belgium. It was split between those who sought to establish SOCIALISM through evolutionary, democratic means, and others (including Vladimir LENIN) who argued for revolutionary MARXISM. Although united in its opposition to the looming war in Europe, the International became divided at the outbreak of WORLD WAR I. Most socialist parties in Europe supported their nation at war, with the notable exceptions of Russia and Serbia. In 1919 Lenin founded the Third or COMMUNIST INTERNATIONAL.

International Bank for Reconstruction and Development (IBRD) *See* WORLD BANK

International Brigades Volunteer forces who fought for the Republicans during the Spanish CIVIL WAR (1936–39). The Brigades were organized by the COMMUNIST INTERNATIONAL and supplied with arms by the Soviet government. Although the majority of their members were communists, the Brigades were also a rallying point for anti-Fascists of all persuasions and all nationalities. There were seven Brigades in total, divided by nationality into battalions. They distinguished themselves at the siege of Madrid in 1936, but were too small (never more than 20,000 strong) to influence the result of the War. They were disbanded in 1938.

International Court of Justice Supreme judicial body of the UNITED NATIONS (UN) for hearing disputes between countries involving treaties and international law. It replaced the League of Nations' Permanent Court of Justice in 1947. Its 15 judges are chosen by the United Nations (UN), each coming from a different state and serving for nine years. The president and vice president serve three-year terms. The Court sits at The Hague, Netherlands.

International Labour Organization (ILO) Specialized intergovernmental agency of the UNITED NATIONS (UN). Its aim is to facilitate improved industrial relations and conditions of work. It was formed as an agency of the LEAGUE OF NATIONS by the Treaty of VERSAILLES (1919) and has a membership comprising government, employer and UNION representatives. Its headquarters are in Geneva, Switzerland.

International Monetary Fund (IMF) Specialized, intergovernmental agency of the UNITED NATIONS (UN), and administrative body of the international monetary system. Established by the BRETTON WOODS CONFERENCE (1944), its main function is to provide assistance to member states troubled by balance of payments problems and other financial difficulties. The IMF does not actually lend money to member states; rather, it exchanges the member state's currency with its own Special Drawing Rates (SDR) – a "basket" of other currencies – in the hope that this will alleviate balance of payment difficulties. These exchanges are usually conditional upon the recipient country agreeing to pursue prescribed policy reforms. The organization is based in Washington, D.C.

interregnum Period between rulers. In English history, the term is applied to the period between the execution of CHARLES I in 1649 and the RESTORATION of CHARLES II in 1660, and to the time between the abdication of JAMES II in December 1688 and the accession of WILLIAM III (OF ORANGE) and MARY in February 1689. In German history, the **Great Interregnum** (1250–73) occurred after the death of FREDERICK II. Count William of Holland was elected anti-king by the German princes, and the death (1254) of the HOHENSTAUFEN Conrad IV left him as the sole claimant. In 1256, however, William was killed while fighting for control of Zeeland. In 1257 RICHARD, EARL OF CORNWALL, brother of HENRY III of England, and ALFONSO X of Castile were both elected king. Richard visited Germany four times, but only very briefly, and Alfonso not at all, leaving the princes and towns free from all external interference. The interregnum ended with the election of RUDOLF I of HABSBURG as king (1273).

Intifada (Arabic, uprising) Campaign of violent civil disobedience by Palestinians in the Israeli-occupied territories of the WEST BANK of the River Jordan and the GAZA STRIP. The Intifada began in 1987 and was a sustained attempt to disrupt Israel's heavy-handed policing tactics. The main participating groups were the PALESTINE LIBERATION ORGANIZATION (PLO), Hamas and Islamic Jihad. The Intifada claimed more than 1400 Palestinian and 230 Jewish lives and increased the pressure for a political settlement. It resulted in the ISRAELI–PALESTINIAN ACCORD (1993). *See also* ARAFAT, YASIR

Intolerable Acts (Coercive Acts) (1774) Four pieces of British legislation passed by Lord NORTH's government to punish the American colonists after the BOSTON TEA PARTY (1773). The **Boston Port Bill** closed the port of Boston until the English East India Company received compensation for the loss of their tea. The **Administration of Justice Act** provided for a trial in England of British officials accused of capital offences in America. The **Massachusetts Government Act** annulled the Massachusetts Charter, imposing a military government on the colony. The **Quartering Act** required the colonists to provide accommodation for British soldiers. The colonists' opposition led to the convening of the First CONTINENTAL CONGRESS. *See also* QUÉBEC ACT

Inuit Collective name for the ESKIMO people of Nunavut, Arctic Quebec and N Labrador areas of Canada, and Alaska and Greenland. Many Inuit still live by the traditional skills of fishing, trapping and hunting.

Invergordon Mutiny (September 1931) Action taken during the GREAT DEPRESSION by British sailors of the Atlantic Fleet based at Invergordon, Scotland. The government had passed an economy bill enacting cuts in all government salaries in an attempt to put national finances in order. Faced with reductions in pay of more than 10%, the ratings went on strike. The Mutiny prompted the government to suspend the GOLD STANDARD. The leaders of the Mutiny were discharged from the navy.

investiture Installation in office by a superior authority. In the FEUDAL SYSTEM it was a symbolic act signifying the handing over of a FIEF. Following the act of homage and oath of FEALTY, investiture consisted of the transfer from lord to vassal of a symbolic object, such as a staff or glove. In the late 11th- and early 12th-century, the right of lay rulers to invest bishops and abbots became a matter of great dispute between the papacy and European monarchs, particularly the Holy Roman emperors. The dispute, known as the **Investiture Controversy** (1075–1122), began under Pope GREGORY VII and developed into a power struggle with the emperors HENRY IV and HENRY V. Civil war ensued in Germany until the Concordat of WORMS provided a compromise solution, based on HENRY I of England's settlement (1106) with the church, which provided for secular selection and spiritual investiture.

IOWA
Statehood :
28 December 1846
Nickname :
Hawkeye State
State motto :
Our liberties we prize and our rights we will maintain

Ionia Historic region on the W coast of Asia Minor (Turkey), including neighbouring Aegean islands. In the 10th century BC, following the DORIAN invasion, the area was settled by people from the Greek mainland. Ionia's twelve major cities, the most important of which were MILETUS and EPHESUS, formed a confederation in the 8th century BC. Ionia was conquered by CROESUS of LYDIA in the 6th century BC, before coming under Iranian rule. The Ionian revolt (499 BC) marked the beginning of the PERSIAN WARS. After Greek victory in the Battle of SALAMIS (480 BC), Ionia joined the DELIAN LEAGUE. It gradually fell under Athenian domination until the Iranians regained control in the 4th century BC. After the conquests of ALEXANDER III (THE GREAT), Ionia was ruled by Hellenistic kings and from the 2nd century BC was part of the ROMAN EMPIRE. *See also* GREECE, ANCIENT

Ionic order One of the five ORDERS OF ARCHITECTURE

Iowa Siouan-speaking tribe, closely related to the Oto and Missouri, who before the arrival of the Europeans had migrated westward from N of the Great Lakes to what is now Iowa. They had lived a semi-sedentary existence, mixing hunting with the growing of maize and trading in furs with the French. In 1836 they ceded their land to the US government and were relocated to N Kansas. Never a large tribe (1000–1200 people), today there are *c*.250 Iowa, occupying their own land in Iowa and Oklahoma.

Iowa State in N central United States, lying between the Missouri and Mississippi rivers; the capital is Des Moines. Louis JOLLIET and Jacques MARQUETTE were probably the first Europeans to explore the area (1673), and the land was claimed for France in 1682. In 1803 the region was sold to the United States in the LOUISIANA PURCHASE. The Spirit Lake Massacre (1857) marked the end of Native American resistance to white settlement. Industrial development was encouraged after World War 2. Originally prairie that was ploughed to create farmland, the region is known for its fertile soil. Area: 145,790sq km (56,290sq mi). Pop. (1995 est.) 2,842,000.

Iqbal, Sir Muhammad (1875–1938) Indian politician, poet and philosopher. He advocated an independent Muslim state and became president of the MUSLIM LEAGUE in 1930. Iqbal's best-known poetic work is *The Secrets of the Self* (1915). He is considered to be the symbolic father of Pakistan.

IRA *See* IRISH REPUBLICAN ARMY

Iráklion (Heraklion or Candia) Seaport and largest city on the island of CRETE, S Greece; capital of Iráklion prefecture. Founded in the 9th century AD by the Saracens, it was conquered by the Byzantines in 961, the Venetians in 1204 and the Ottoman Turks in 1669. Iráklion became part of Greece in 1913. The ruins of KNOSSOS are nearby. Pop. (1991) 115,124.

Iran *See* country feature, page 200

Iran-Contra affair (1987–88) (Irangate) US political scandal. It involved a secret agreement to sell weapons to Iran via Israel, in order to secure the release of US hostages held in the Middle East. The profits were diverted to support the Nicaraguan CONTRA, who were attempting to overthrow the SANDINISTA government. The affair, negotiated by Colonel Oliver NORTH with the support of national security advisers to the White House, was revealed by a congressional investigative committee in 1987. North and his superiors, plus several other officials, were later convicted of various charges, including obstructing Congress. In 1992 they were controversially pardoned by President George BUSH. *See also* REAGAN, RONALD

Iran Hostage Crisis (1979–81) Holding of US hostages in the US embassy in Tehran, Iran. In January 1979 Shah

Muhammad Reza Pahlavi fled Iran and Ayatollah Khomeini established an Islamic republic. On 4 November 1979, Iranian militants seized the embassy and, with the approval of Ayatollah Khomeini, took hostage 66 diplomatic personnel. The militants' demands included the return of the shah and his personal fortune. The failure of US President Jimmy Carter to reach a negotiated settlement led to a secret military mission (April 1980) to rescue the remaining 52 hostages. The operation was a disaster and the militants continued to hold US personnel even after the death (27 July 1980) of the shah. After 444 days in captivity, the hostages were eventually released on the day of President Ronald Reagan's inauguration.

Iran-Iraq War (1980–88) Contest for supremacy in the Persian (Arabian) Gulf. In September 1980 Iraqi President Saddam Hussein ordered the invasion of Iran, partly in response to Iran's support for an uprising of Iraqi Kurds in 1979. The main objective, however, was to gain sole control of the Shatt al-Arab, a river vital for the transport of oil. The disorganized state of Iran (following the overthrow of the shah) enabled Iraq to capture quickly the port of Khorramshahr, sw Iran. Iran mounted a strong recovery, and by 1982 had recaptured the city and forced all Iraqi troops to withdraw from Iranian territory. Ayatollah Khomeini rejected Iraq's peace proposals and the conflict reached a stalemate. In 1985 Iraq bombed civilian targets as well as a nuclear power station under construction in Bushehr. Iran responded by bombing Basra and Baghdad. In 1987 Iran increased its hostilities against oil-tankers, provoking a US-led intervention that provided tacit support for Iraq. A United Nations' (UN) cease-fire resolution (1987) was accepted by Iraq and, after several Iraqi successes, by Iran also. Neither side had made any significant gains. Estimated total casualties were more than 1 million.

Iraq *See* country feature

Ireland Second-largest island of the British Isles. Ireland is w of Great Britain. At present, Ireland is divided into two separate countries, the Republic of Ireland and Northern Ireland. From *c*.3rd century BC to the late 8th century, Ireland was divided into five kingdoms inhabited by Celtic and pre-Celtic tribes. In the 8th century AD, the Danes invaded, establishing trading towns, including Dublin, and creating new kingdoms. In 1014 Brian Boru defeated the Danes, and for the next 150 years Ireland was free from invasion but subject to clan warfare. In 1171 Henry

IRAN

AREA: 1,648,000sq km (636,293 sq mi)
POPULATION: 59,964,000
CAPITAL (POPULATION): Tehran (6,475,527)
GOVERNMENT: Islamic republic
ETHNIC GROUPS: Persian 46%, Azerbaijani 17%, Kurdish 9%, Gilaki 5%, Luri, Mazandarani, Baluchi, Arab
LANGUAGES: Farsi (or Persian, official)
RELIGIONS: Islam 99%
GDP PER CAPITA (1995): US$5470

Islamic republic in sw Asia. Until 1935 Iran was known in the West as Persia. Aryans settled in Persia in *c*.2000 BC. In the 13th century BC, the kingdom of Elam (now Khuzestan, sw Iran) dominated Mesopotamia. In 612 BC Media and Babylon allied to defeat Assyria. In 550 BC Iranian king Cyrus II (the Great) founded the Achaemenid dynasty. Darius I (the Great) and Xerxes I suffered serious setbacks in the Persian Wars (492–479 BC) against the Greek city-states, but most of the Iranian empire remained intact until the incursions of Alexander III (the Great) in 331 BC. The Arsacids from Parthia conquered all of the Iranian Plateau (2nd century BC). In AD 224 Ardashir I overthrew the Parthians and established the Sasanian dynasty.

In AD 641 Arabs conquered Iran, and Islam replaced Zoroastrianism as the state religion. The Abbasids (750–821) and a succession of Iranian dynasties, including the Ghaznavids and Buyids, made Iran a centre for Islamic art and architecture. Seljuk Turks conquered Iran in the 11th century, but in 1220 the land was overrun by the Mongols and became part of the Ilkhanid state.

The Safavid dynasty (1501–1722) was founded by Shah Ismail, who established the Shiite theocratic principles of modern Iran. Nadir Shah, who seized the throne in 1736, expelled Afghan invaders. His despotic rule (1736–47) was noted for its imperial ambition.

The Qajar dynasty (1796–1925) witnessed the gradual decline of the Iranian empire in the face of European expansion. The discovery of oil in sw Iran led to the Russian and British partition of Iran in 1907. By 1919 Iran had effectively became a British protectorate.

In 1921 Reza Khan seized power in a military coup. In 1925 he deposed the Qajar dynasty and proclaimed himself Reza Shah Pahlavi. He annulled the British treaty and began a process of modernization. In 1941 British and Soviet forces occupied Iran. Reza Shah abdicated in favour of his son, Muhammad Reza Shah Pahlavi. The 1943 Tehran Declaration guaranteed Iranian independence. In 1951 the oil industry was nationalized. The shah fled Iran, but soon returned with the backing of the United States and restored Western oil rights (1953). During the 1960s, the shah undertook large-scale reforms, such as land ownership and extending the franchise to women (1963). Discontent surfaced over increasing westernization and economic inequality. The secret police crushed all dissent. Iranian clerics, led by Ayatollah Khomeini, openly voiced their disapproval of the secularization of society. In 1971 Britain withdrew its troops from the Persian (Arabian) Gulf and Iran increased its defence spending to become the largest military power in the region. While in exile, Khomeini called for the abdication of the shah (1978).

In January 1979 the shah fled, and Khomeini returned to establish an Islamic republic. The theocracy was profoundly conservative and anti-western. The oil industry was renationalized in July 1979, and in November 1979 militants seized the US embassy in Tehran, taking 66 hostages (*see* Iran Hostage Crisis). In September 1980 the Iraqi invasion marked the start of the Iran-Iraq War (1980–88). The War claimed more than 500,000 Iranian lives. In 1986 the United States covertly agreed to supply Iran with arms, in return for influence over the return of US hostages in the Middle East (*see* Iran-Contra affair). In February 1989 Khomeini imposed a death penalty on the Anglo-Indian writer Salman Rushdie. In June 1989 Khomeini died and President Ali Khamenei succeeded as Iran's supreme religious leader. Hashemi Rafsanjani was elected president. Rafsanjani's regime began to ease relations with the West. Free-market reforms were adopted and Iran supported international sanctions against Iraq in 1991. Allegations of support for international terrorism and development of a nuclear capability led the United States to impose trade sanctions in 1995. In 1997 elections Rafsanjani was succeeded by the liberal reformer Muhammad Khatami. In July 1999 student protests against the conservatives' blocking of the reforms of Khatami were suppressed by the police and military. The reformers won the parliamentary election in 2000.

II of England invaded Ireland and established English control. In the late 13th century, an Irish parliament was formed. In 1315 English dominance was threatened by a Scottish invasion. In the late 15th century, Henry VII restored English hegemony and began the Plantation of Ireland by English settlers. Edward Poynings forced the Irish Parliament to pass Poynings Law (1495), stating that future Irish legislation must be sanctioned by the English privy council. Under James I the plantation of Ulster was intensified. An Irish rebellion (1641–49) was eventually thwarted by Oliver Cromwell. During the Glorious Revolution (1688), Irish Catholics supported James II, while Ulster Protestants supported William III. After James' defeat, the English-controlled Irish Parliament passed a series of punitive laws against Catholics. In 1782 Henry Grattan forced trade concessions and the repeal of Poynings Law. William Pitt (the Younger)'s government passed the Act of Union (1801) which abolished the Irish assembly and created the United Kingdom of Great Britain and Ireland. In 1829, largely due to the efforts of Daniel O'Connell, the Act of Catholic Emancipation was passed, which secured Irish representation in the British Parliament. A blight ruined the Irish potato crop and caused the Irish Famine (1845–49). Nationalist demands intensified and the Fenian movement flourished. Gladstone failed to secure Irish Home Rule amid mounting pressure from fearful Ulster Protestants. In 1905 Arthur Griffith founded Sinn Féin. In 1914 Irish Home Rule was agreed, but implementation was suspended during World War 1. In the Easter Rising (April 1916), Irish nationalists announced the creation of the Republic of Ireland. The British Army's brutal crushing of the Rising was a propaganda victory for Sinn Féin and led to a landslide victory in Irish elections (1918). Between 1918 and 1921 the Irish Republican Army (IRA), founded by Michael Collins, fought a guerrilla war against British forces. In 1920 a new Home Rule bill established separate parliaments for Ulster and Catholic Ireland. The Anglo-Irish Treaty (1921) led to the creation of an Irish Free State in January 1922 and *de facto* acceptance of partition. *See also* Land League

Ireland, Northern (for pre-1922 history, *see* Ireland) Part of the United Kingdom, 26 districts occupying the NE of Ireland, traditionally divided into the six counties of Antrim, Armagh, Derry, Down, Fermanagh and Tyrone; the capital is Belfast. In 1920 the six counties of Ulster became the self-governing province of Northern Ireland with a separate, Protestant-dominated Parliament. The British government affirmed the inclusion of Northern Ireland within the United Kingdom under the principle of self-determination. The Irish Free State (now Republic of Ireland) constitution upheld the unity of the island of Ireland. In 1955 the Irish Republican Army (IRA) began a campaign of violence in Northern Ireland for the creation of an independent, unified Ireland. In 1962 the Republic of Ireland condemned the use of terrorism. Northern Catholics felt aggrieved at discrimination in employment, housing and political representation. In 1967 the Civil Rights Association was established to campaign for equal rights. In 1968 civil rights marches resulted in violent clashes, especially in Derry. Catholic fear of the increasing Protestant domination of local security forces was compounded when the Royal Ulster Constabulary (RUC) was supplemented by the sectarian Ulster Defence Regiment (UDR). The British Army was brought in to protect the Catholic populations in Belfast and Derry. The IRA and Protestant Loyalist paramilitary organizations, such as the Ulster Defence Association (UDA), increased their campaigns of sectarian violence. In 1972 the Northern Ireland Parliament (Stormont) was suspended, replaced by direct rule from Westminster. On 30 January 1972 ("Bloody Sunday"), British troops shot and killed 13 civil rights demonstrators. In 1974 the Council of Ireland, formed by the British and Irish governments to promote cooperation between Ulster and the Irish Republic, quickly collapsed under pressure from a Unionist-led general strike. The IRA campaign widened to include terrorist attacks on Great Britain and British military bases in w Europe. In 1981 hunger strikes by IRA prisoners were more successful in gaining worldwide sympathy. The Anglo-Irish Agreement (1985) gave the Republic of Ireland a consultative role in the government of Northern Ireland. In 1986 a Northern Ireland Assembly was re-established, but quickly failed under the Unionists' boycott. Following secret talks between the British government and Sinn Féin, the Downing Street Declaration (1993) offered all-party negotiations following a cessation of violence. In 1994 Provisional IRA and Loyalist paramilitaries announced a cease-fire, raising hopes of an end to a sectarian conflict that had claimed more than 2700 lives. In 1996 disputes over the decommissioning of arms stalled the process and the IRA resumed its terrorist campaign on the British mainland. In July 1997 another cease-fire was agreed, and later that year Sinn Féin and Unionists took part in joint peace talks for the first time since partition. The resultant Good Friday Agreement (10 April 1998) devolved powers to an elected Northern Ireland Assembly and the Republic of Ireland abandoned its constitutional claim to Northern Ireland. In May 1998 the Agreement was overwhelmingly approved in referenda in Northern Ireland and the Republic of Ireland. In June 1998 elections were held for the new Assembly. Following the failure of the IRA to begin decommissioning its weapons, the Ulster Unionist Party refused to nominate ministers to the Executive Committee and so prevented it from being formed. In 1999 the resumption of talks under former US Senator George Mitchell led to the Committee being established in December, with David Trimble of the Ulster Unionists as first minister and Seamus Mallon of the Social Democratic Labour Party (SDLP) as deputy first minister. After further problems on the issue of arms-decommissioning, the Assembly was suspended in February 2000. *See also* Hume, John

Ireland, Republic of *See* country feature, page 202

Irene (*c*.752–803) Byzantine empress, wife of Emperor Leo IV. On her husband's death (780), Irene became co-emperor with her son Constantine VI. As a supporter of the restoration of icons in the church, she called the Second Council of Nicaea (787) that rejected iconoclasm (*see* iconoclastic controversy). For this stance, Irene was later recognized as a saint by the Greek Orthodox Church. In 790 Constantine banished Irene from court, but after two years she returned and in 797 had her son arrested and blinded. Irene then reigned as emperor until 802, when she was deposed and exiled to Lesbos.

Ireton, Henry (1611–51) English soldier and statesman, son-in-law of Oliver Cromwell. At the start of the

IRAQ

AREA: 438,320sq km (169,235sq mi)
POPULATION: 19,290,000
CAPITAL (POPULATION): Baghdad (3,850,000)
GOVERNMENT: Republic
ETHNIC GROUPS: Arab 77%, Kurdish 19%, Turkmen, Persian, Assyrian
LANGUAGES: Arabic (official), Kurdish (official in Kurdish areas)
RELIGIONS: Islam 96%, Christianity 4%
GDP PER CAPITA (1994): US$2855

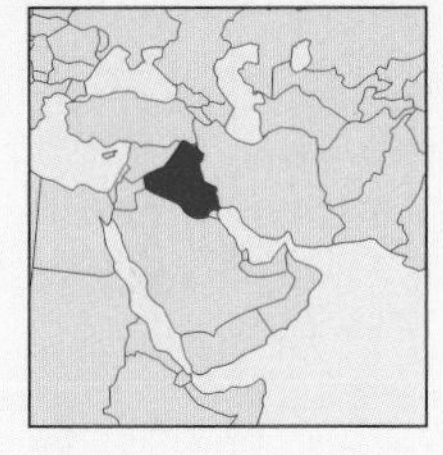

Republic in sw Asia. Ancient Mesopotamia roughly corresponded with modern Iraq. Sumeria was the first great civilization, *c*.3000 BC. In *c*.2340 BC Sargon I conquered Sumeria. In the 18th century BC, Hammurabi established the first empire of Babylonia in s Mesopotamia.

In the 8th century BC, Babylonia fell to Assyria. Assyrian kings Sargon II, Sennacherib and Ashurbanipal added to the splendour of their capital city, Nineveh. Nebuchadnezzar II extended the New Babylonian empire and was responsible for the Babylonian Captivity. In 539 BC Babylon fell to Cyrus II (the Great), and Mesopotamia became part of the Iranian Achaemenid empire.

In AD 637 Islam was introduced via the Arab conquest. Baghdad became capital of the Abbasid caliphate (750–1258). In 1258 Mongols captured Baghdad and Mesopotamia became part of the state ruled by the Ilkhanid dynasty. From 1534 Mesopotamia was part of the Ottoman Empire.

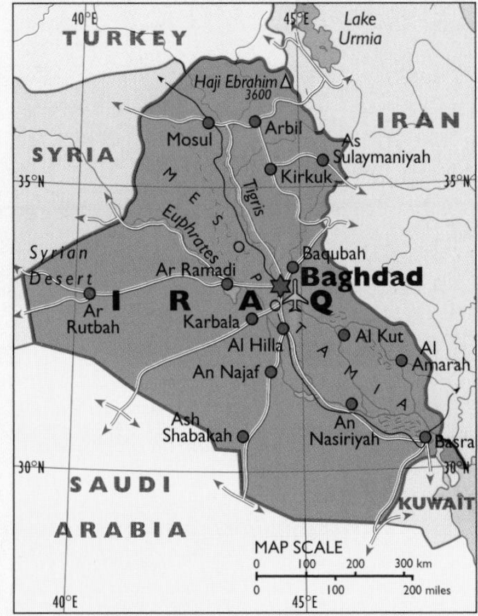

In 1916 Britain invaded Mesopotamia and in 1920 it became a British mandated territory. Britain renamed the country Iraq and set up an Arab monarchy, installing Faisal I as king.

In 1932 Iraq finally achieved independence, and oil was first exported in 1934. As a member of the Arab League, Iraq participated in the first of the Arab-Israeli wars (1948). By the 1950s, oil dominated Iraq's economy and funded national development programmes. In 1958 a proposal to form an Arab Union with Jordan precipitated a military coup, led by Abdul Kassem. A republic was established and the king, Faisal II, executed. In 1962 the Kurds of N Iraq demanded autonomy, beginning a protracted war of secession. In 1968 the Ba'ath Party emerged as the dominant power. Iraq joined the Arab coalition against Israel in the Yom Kippur War (1973).

In 1979 Saddam Hussein became president and purged the Ba'ath Party. In September 1980, Iraq's invasion of Iran marked the start of the Iran-Iraq War (1980–88). The Kurdish rebellion continued and poison gas was used against villagers. On 2 August 1990, Iraqi troops invaded Kuwait (*see* Gulf War). In 1991, following Iraq's forced withdrawal from Kuwait, rebellions broke out in the Kurdish N highlands and Shiite s marshlands. The revolt was brutally suppressed by Iraqi forces, and United Nations' forces formed "no-fly" zones to protect civilians. In 1994 an autonomous Kurdish administration collapsed amid bitter in-fighting. In 1995 UN weapons' inspectors (UNSCOM) discovered evidence of Iraq's attempts to gain a nuclear capability. In December 1998, continued lack of cooperation with UNSCOM led to US and British bombing raids on Iraq. Confrontations in the "no-fly" zones continued in 1999. Wars, sanctions and financial mismanagement have created economic chaos. A UN embargo halted oil exports in 1990, and in 1996 concern about severe hardship suffered by the civilian population led to a UN "oil-for-food" deal.

English CIVIL WAR, Ireton led the Parliamentary cavalry at the Battle of EDGEHILL (1642). He also fought at the battles of MARSTON MOOR (1644) and NASEBY (1645). In 1645 Ireton entered Parliament where he presented (1647) a set of proposals for the division of power between the king, army and Parliament. When the proposals were rejected by CHARLES I, Ireton became one of the leading voices for the abolition of the monarchy. He helped to bring Charles to trial and signed his death warrant in 1649. Ireton then served (1649–51) as lord deputy in Ireland.

Irgun Zevai Leumi Jewish paramilitary organization, formed in 1931. Irgun was founded in opposition to the socialist HAGANAH. After 1936 it became the military wing of the Revisionist Party, which called for the use of violence (if necessary) to create a Jewish state in PALESTINE. Irgun waged a terrorist campaign (1937–48) against British rule in Palestine that saw atrocities committed on both sides. Under the leadership of Menachem BEGIN from 1943, Irgun killed 91 people in a bomb attack on the King David Hotel, Jerusalem (1946). As part of its war against Palestinians, it massacred all 254 inhabitants of the village of Dayr Yasin in 1947. After the creation of Israel in May 1948, Irgun was disbanded but its right-wing ideology was subsequently adopted by the Herut Party. *See also* ZIONISM

Irian Jaya (West Irian or West Papua) Province of E INDONESIA, comprising the W half of New Guinea and adjacent islands; the capital is Jayapura. First sighted by Europeans in 1511, it was formally claimed by the Netherlands in 1828 and became known as Dutch New Guinea. The Japanese occupied Irian Jaya in World War 2 until Allied forces recaptured it in 1944. In 1962 Irian Jaya was placed under a United Nations' (UN) mandate. In 1963 it was transferred to Indonesia and became a province in 1969. Secessionists immediately launched a guerrilla war against Indonesian rule. In 2000 Indonesian President Wahid apologized for human rights violations. Area: 422,170sq km (162,900sq mi). Pop. (1990) 1,648,708.

Irish Famine (1845–51) (Great Potato Famine) Widespread starvation of Irish peasantry. In 1845 a blight affected the potato, destroying the staple crop. Many farmers could not pay their rent and were evicted. The Famine was exacerbated by an epidemic of typhus and by inadequate aid from the British government. It is estimated that one million people died of starvation and another million emigrated, mostly to the United States.

Irish Republican Army (IRA) Guerrilla organization, dedicated to the forceful reunification of IRELAND. Formed (1919) by Michael COLLINS as the militant wing of SINN FÉIN, the IRA waged war against British rule. Some members ("irregulars") rejected the Anglo-Irish Treaty of 1921, fighting a civil war until 1923. During World War 2, the IRA remained pro-German. Outlawed by both Irish governments in the 1950s, the IRA went underground. In 1970 the organization split into an "official" wing (which emphasized political activities) and a "provisional" wing (committed to armed struggle). The **Provisional IRA** perpetrated terrorist acts in Great Britain, Northern Ireland and Europe, including the Birmingham pub bombing (1974), the murder of Lord MOUNTBATTEN (1979), the attempted assassinations of the British cabinet in Brighton (1984) and Downing Street (1991), and the Remembrance Day bombing in Enniskillen (1987). In 1994 it declared a cease-fire, but resumed its campaign in 1996. In 1997 it announced another cease-fire. The timing of the decommissioning of IRA weapons became a major issue in the peace process. *See* GOOD FRIDAY AGREEMENT

Irish Republican Brotherhood (IRB) *See* FENIAN MOVEMENT

Iron Age Period succeeding the BRONZE AGE, dating from *c.*1200 BC in the Near East, later in Europe, Africa and Asia. The HITTITES had probably developed the first significant iron industry in Armenia soon after 2000 BC, but it was not until the fall of the Hittite empire (*c.*1200 BC) that this knowledge spread throughout the Near East. Iron came into use in Europe from *c.*1000 BC and by 600 BC it had largely replaced bronze in the manufacture of tools and weapons. Iron was being used in parts of E and W Africa by *c.*500 BC, but there were areas of the continent that it did not reach until the early or middle centuries AD. The use of iron in China began *c.*600 BC.

ironclad Wooden warship protected by iron armour, the precursor of the modern battleship. Naval losses in the CRIMEAN WAR (1854–56) prompted France to build (1859) the first ironclad warship, the frigate *Gloria*. In 1862 the MONITOR AND MERRIMACK contested the first battle between ironclads in the American CIVIL WAR.

Iron Curtain Colloquial term for the barrier between communist East Europe and the capitalist West during the COLD WAR. The term passed into common use after a speech (March 1946) by Winston CHURCHILL in Fulton, Missouri. *See also* BERLIN WALL; NORTH ATLANTIC TREATY ORGANIZATION (NATO); WARSAW PACT

Iron Guard (Legion of the Archangel Michael) Romanian fascist organization, committed to the "Christian and racial" regeneration of Romania. Its anti-Semitic ideology flourished during the 1920s and 1930s, under the leadership of Corneliu CODREANU. King CAROL II initially supported the Iron Guard, but in 1938 he outlawed all political parties and reportedly ordered the killing of 14 Guard leaders (including Codreanu) and the arrest and imprisonment of hundreds more. The Guard recovered in 1940 under the fascist dictatorship of Ion ANTONESCU. Rumours of a coup led to the Iron Guard's suppression, by the Nazis, with Antonescu's approval, in 1941.

Ironside, William Edmund (1880–1959) British soldier. He served in the second of the SOUTH AFRICAN WARS (1899–1902) and later in France during World War 1. In the RUSSIAN CIVIL WAR, Ironside commanded (1918) the Allied forces against the Bolsheviks at Archangel, Russia. He was chief of the imperial general staff (1939–40) and commander of the Home Defence forces (1940).

Ironsides Cavalry regiment in the English CIVIL WAR, led by Oliver CROMWELL and drawn mainly from the yeomen and freeholders of the Eastern Association. They were nicknamed "Old Ironsides" by Prince RUPERT, whose royalist army they helped to defeat at the Battle of MARSTON MOOR (1644). They became part of the NEW MODEL ARMY, established by Parliament in February 1645.

Iroquois Confederacy (Five Nations) League of NATIVE NORTH AMERICANS occupying the Mohawk Valley and the Lakes area of New York state. They called themselves *Oñgwanósioñi* ("people of the long house"), after the distinctive shape of their bark dwellings. The Confederacy was formed at the end of the 16th century by the MOHAWK, SENECA, CAYUGA, Onondaga and Oneida tribes in what is now New York state. The Tuscarora joined the league in 1722. The Confederacy had a highly devel-

IRELAND, REPUBLIC OF (ÉIRE)

AREA: 70,280sq km (27,135sq mi)
POPULATION: 3,547,000
CAPITAL (POPULATION): Dublin (915,516)
GOVERNMENT: Multiparty republic
ETHNIC GROUPS: Irish 94%
LANGUAGES: Irish and English (both official)
RELIGIONS: Christianity (Roman Catholic 93%, Protestant 3%)
GDP PER CAPITA (1995): US$15,680

Republic occupying more than 80% of the island of Ireland. It is divided into four provinces of 26 counties (for pre-1922 history, *see* IRELAND). In January 1922 the Irish Free State was created as a Dominion within the British Empire. Arthur GRIFFITH of SINN FÉIN became taoiseach (prime minister). Civil war (1922–23) ensued between supporters of the settlement and those who refused to countenance the partition of Ireland and the creation of Northern IRELAND. The anti-settlement party, led by Eamon DE VALERA, was defeated by Irish Free State forces led by Michael COLLINS. Collins was assassinated and William COSGRAVE became prime minister (1922–32). In 1926 De Valera formed a separate party, FIANNA FÁIL, and became taoiseach (1932–48, 1951–54, 1957–59). In 1933 FINE GAEL was founded.

In 1937 a new constitution declared the sovereign nation of Éire to be the whole island of Ireland and abolished the oath of loyalty to the English crown. During World War 2 Éire remained neutral. It opposed Allied operations in Northern Ireland, and the IRISH REPUBLICAN ARMY (IRA) pursued a pro-German line. In 1949 Ireland became a republic outside of the Commonwealth. Its claim to the six counties of Northern Ireland was reiterated. In 1955 Ireland was admitted to the United Nations (UN).

In 1959 De Valera became president (1959–73). During the 1950s, the IRA was banned by both Irish governments and, as a secret organization, it conducted bombing campaigns in Northern Ireland and England. Relations with Northern Ireland improved. In 1973 Ireland joined the European Community (EC). During the 1980s, a series of short-lived coalition governments, led by Charles HAUGHEY and Dr Garrett FITZGERALD, caused political uncertainty. The ANGLO-IRISH AGREEMENT (1985) gave Ireland a consultative role in the affairs of Northern Ireland. In 1990 Mary ROBINSON was elected as Ireland's first female president. The DOWNING STREET DECLARATION (1993), signed by John MAJOR and Albert REYNOLDS, continued the momentum for a peaceful settlement in Northern Ireland. Following a 1995 referendum, divorce was legalized in the republic. Abortion remains a contentious political issue. In 1997 elections Bertie AHERN became taoiseach and Mary McAleese became president. In the GOOD FRIDAY AGREEMENT (1998), the Irish Republic gave up its constitutional claim to Northern Ireland and a North-South Ministerial Council was established. As a member of the EUROPEAN MONETARY SYSTEM (EMS), Ireland adopted the euro (1999) in the first stage of European economic and monetary union.

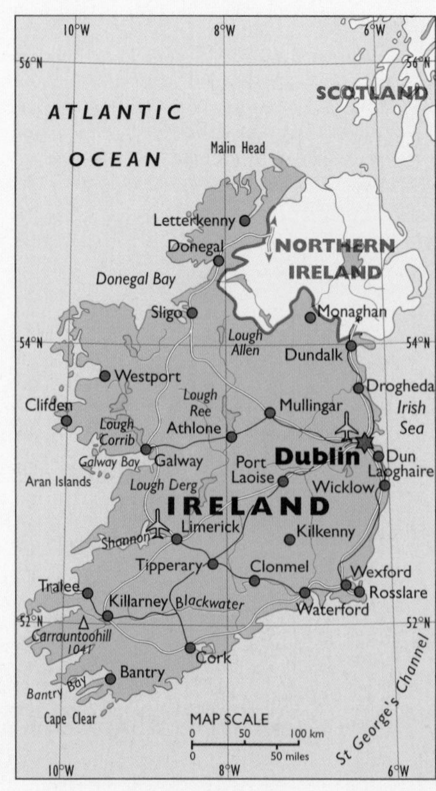

oped and effective political system and the constituent tribes were also renowned warriors. During the 17th century, the Iroquois successfully battled against (among others) the MAHICAN and HURON tribes for control of the fur trade. The Confederacy split during the American Revolution: the Oneida and Tuscarora supported the colonials, while the rest of the league, led by Joseph BRANT, fought for the British. Today, there are *c*.10,000 Iroquois living in New York, Wisconsin, Oklahoma and Canada.

Iroquois Wars (1648–96) Conflict for territorial expansion carried out by the IROQUOIS CONFEDERACY. In order to gain greater access to furs, which they could trade with the English and Dutch, the Iroquois expanded out of what is now New York state. In doing so, they dispersed the HURON (1648–50), Tabacco, Neutral (1650), Erie (1656), Conestogas (1675) and Illinois (1684) tribes. After destroying the Huron Confederacy. the Iroquois turned against the French, allies of the Hurons. The French sent expeditions (1666, 1687) against the Iroquois, who counter-attacked and destroyed Lacline, near Montréal, in 1689. The Iroquois were finally driven back (1693–96) in a series of campaigns led by the Comte de FRONTENAC, but managed to retain their independence for most of the 18th century.

Irredentists Italian political party formed (1878) as the *Italia Irredenta* ("unredeemed Italy"). The party was formed to liberate territories with large numbers of Italian-speaking people, such as Trentino and Trieste, from Austro-Hungarian rule. After Italian unification (1860–70), the Irredentists aimed to incorporate Italian-dominated areas, such as ISTRIA, that were controlled by Austria. They worked to keep Italy out of the TRIPLE ALLIANCE (1882). The Irredentists influenced Italy's decision to enter World War 1 on the side of the Allies.

Isaac I (Comnenus) (d.1061) Byzantine emperor (r.1057–59), first ruler of the Comnenian dynasty. He was brought up at the court of Emperor BASIL II. Gaining the confidence of the army, Isaac took part in a plot (1057) to topple Emperor Michael VI and was proclaimed emperor soon afterwards. As emperor, Isaac came into conflict with Patriach Michael Cerularius because of his attempts to restrict the power of the church and reform the finances of the BYZANTINE EMPIRE. In 1058 Cerularius was arrested and exiled. In 1059 Isaac gained important military victories over the Hungarians and Pechenegs.

Isaac II (Angelus) (d.1204) Byzantine emperor (r.1185–95, 1203–04). He came to power after the murder of his cousin, Emperor ANDRONICUS I (COMNENUS). Isaac's military victories over the Normans (1185) and the Serbians (1190) strengthened the BYZANTINE EMPIRE, but he failed in his campaigns (1186–87) against the Bulgarians. Isaac allied with SALADIN at the start of the Third CRUSADE, but quickly switched to support FREDERICK I (BARBAROSSA). In 1195 Isaac was overthrown by his brother, Alexius III, who blinded and imprisoned him. Isaac's son, Alexius, gained the support of the Fourth CRUSADE that restored Isaac to power (1203) in Constantinople (now Istanbul). Isaac and Alexius became co-emperors but were overthrown by a revolt. Alexius was murdered and Isaac died several days later.

Isaacs, Sir Isaac Alfred (1855–1948) Australian statesman, governor general (1931–36). In 1892 he was elected to the legislative assembly of Victoria and between 1897 and 1899 helped to draft the constitution for the Commonwealth of Australia. He became attorney general in 1905 and was the first Australian-born governor general.

Isabella I (1451–1504) Queen of CASTILE (1474–1504), whose marriage (1469) to Ferdinand II of ARAGÓN (FERDINAND V of Castile and León) led to the unification of Spain and its emergence as a dominant European power. Isabella's half-brother, Henry IV of Castile (r.1454–74), had wanted her to marry Alfonso V of Portugal and punished her disobedience by supporting the claims of Joan (la Beltraneja) to succeed him. Henry's death led to civil war (1474–78) in Castile from which Isabella emerged triumphant. With Ferdinand's support, Isabella brought the military orders under royal control and encouraged humanist scholarship in Spain. With the help of Hernando de Talavera and Cardinal JIMÉNEZ DE CISNEROS, Isabella sped up the reform of the Spanish church, although she was also responsible for the introduction of the Spanish INQUISITION (1478) and the expulsion of the Jews (1492). Pope ALEXANDER VI bestowed the title of the "Catholic kings" upon Ferdinand and Isabella. Her popularity was enhanced by the reconquest of GRANADA (1492). Isabella met some of the financial costs for the voyages of Christopher COLUMBUS, which led to the establishment of the Spanish empire in the New World.

Isabella II (1830–1904) Queen of Spain (1833–68), daughter of FERDINAND VII (THE DESIRED). Her accession was challenged by her uncle, Don CARLOS, resulting in the first Carlist War (1833–39). During Isabella's minority, her mother, MARÍA CRISTINA, and later Baldomero ESPARTERO acted as regents. Isabella assumed personal control in 1843, but her rule was unpopular and was characterized by political instability. In 1868 a liberal revolt led by army officers forced her into exile in France. In 1870 she abdicated in favour of her son, ALFONSO XII. *See also* CARLISM

Isabella of France (1292–1358) Queen consort of EDWARD II of England (1308–27), daughter of PHILIP IV of France. Isabella became estranged from Edward and returned to France in 1325. In 1326 she and her lover Roger de MORTIMER launched a successful invasion of England, forced Edward to abdicate and then assassinated him. In 1327 Edward and Isabella's son acceded to the throne as EDWARD III. In 1330 Edward III executed Mortimer and banished Isabella to a nunnery.

Isaiah (Isaias) (active 8th century BC) Old Testament prophet who was active in Jerusalem from the 740s until the end of the century. Isaiah's career coincided with the westward expansion of the Assyrian empire. He gave his name to the Old Testament Book of Isaiah, only part of which is attributed to him. *See also* ASSYRIA

Isfahan (Esfahan) City on the River Zaindeh, central Iran. The ancient city of Aspadana, it was captured by Arabs in 642. Isfahan became part of the SELJUK empire in the 11th century, serving as its capital before falling to the MONGOLS in the 1230s. It was part of the SAFAVID empire from the 16th to the 18th centuries. The Safavids made Isfahan their capital and, under ABBAS I (THE GREAT), it became one of the most beautiful cities of the 16th century. After its capture by the Afghans in 1722, Isfahan declined until the growth of industry in the 20th century. It is now the third-largest city in Iran. Pop. (1991) 1,127,000.

Ishii, Kikujiro (1866–1945) Japanese diplomat and statesman. He negotiated the GENTLEMAN'S AGREEMENT (1907) with the United States, which prevented the immigration of Japanese labourers into the United States. Ishii was ambassador to France (1912–14), foreign minister (1915–16) and ambassador to the United States (1918–19). In 1917 he negotiated the Lansing-Ishii Agreement with the United States, which recognized Japanese interests in China and recognized the US OPEN-DOOR POLICY. Ishii was killed in a US bombing raid during World War 2.

Isidore of Seville, Saint (*c*.560–636) Spanish ecclesiastic and last of the Fathers of the Church. In *c*.600 he became archbishop of Seville. Isidore is noted for his encyclopedia of knowledge, *Etymologies*. He was canonized by Clement VIII in 1589. His feast day is 4 April.

Islam *See* feature article, page 204

Islamic art and architecture Lacking a strong, independent tradition, Islamic art began to develop as a unique synthesis of the diverse cultures of conquered countries from the 7th century. Early Islamic art and craft is perhaps best illustrated by the architecture of the mosque. Two of the most impressive surviving examples of early Islamic architecture are the DOME OF THE ROCK (685–92), Jerusalem, and the UMAYYAD Mosque, DAMASCUS (*c*.705). Common architectural forms, such as the dome, minaret, *sahn* (courtyard), and the often highly decorated *mihrab* (prayer niche) and *mimbar* (prayer pulpit) developed in the 9th century. In Spain, Moorish architecture developed independently after the Umayyads were forced to flee there by the ABBASID dynasty. It is characterized by the use of the horseshoe arch, faience and stone lattice screens, as seen in the ALHAMBRA. Islamic CAIRO is a world heritage site of Muslim architecture, often derived from Iranian innovation. The Ibn Tulun Mosque (879) is a fine example of early brick and stucco form. The al-Azhar Mosque displays 10th-century developments. The masterwork of Iranian mosques, with their distinctive onion-shaped domes and slender pencil minarets, is the ISFAHAN Imperial Mosque (1585–1612). Because of a religious stricture on the representation of nature, Islamic art developed stylized figures, geometrical designs and floral-like decorations (arabesques). The KORAN was the focus for much of the development of calligraphy and illumination. Many of the cursive scripts were developed in the 10th century, and the most commonly used script, Nastaliq, was perfected in the 15th century. Muslim secular art included highly ornamented metalwork (often inlaid with red copper), which developed in the 13th century around Mosul, N Mesopotamia. The art of pottery and ceramics was extremely advanced, with excellent glazes and decoration. The Islamic *minai* (enamel) technique reached its zenith in 16th-century Isfahan, where entire walls were decorated in faience.

Ismail I (1487–1524) Shah of Iran (1501–24), founder of the SAFAVID dynasty. A national and religious hero in Iran, he regained Iranian independence and established SHIITE Islam as the state religion. In 1510 Ismail ambushed and defeated a superior force of UZBEKS. Tension between Shiite Iran and the mainly Sunni OTTOMAN EMPIRE increased after Sultan SELIM I ordering the execution of many of his Shiite subjects. The Ottomans invaded NW Iran and Ismail's inferior forces were defeated at the Battle of Chaldiran (1514). Further offensives by the Ottomans during Ismail's reign were repulsed, but the conflict raged for more than a hundred years.

Ismailis SHIITE branch of ISLAM that recognizes Ismail as the rightful seventh imam. The death (765) of the sixth imam, Jafar ibn Muhammad, led to a schism within the

◄ **Isfahan** Constructed between 1612 and 1637, the Masjid-i-shah Mosque was begun during the reign of Abbas I. The central courtyard and principal dome are decorated with intricate tile mosaics.

Shiite movement. The main body of Shiites accepted the claims of Jafar's youngest son, Musa al Kazim, and continued to trace the succession through to the 12th imam (hence they are sometimes referred to as "Twelvers"). A minority supported Jafar's eldest son, Ismail, who was rumoured to be dead. Indeed, some of these Ismailis believed that the succession halted with Ismail (hence they are sometimes known as "Seveners"). The remainder, however, followed the succession through the FATIMID dynasty (909–1171), which promoted the Ismaili faith in Egypt and Syria. In 1094 further splits emerged in the Ismaili movement over the Fatimid succession. The Egyptian Ismailis supported al-Mustali, while the Ismailis of Iran and Syria upheld the rights of Nizar. The Nizaris, led by Hasan ibn al-Sabbah, formed the powerful political movement known as the ASSASSINS. In 1840 the majority of Nizaris, led by the AGA KHAN, emigrated from Iran to India. The Mustalis are based in India and Yemen. *See also* DRUZE

Ismail Pasha (1830–95) Viceroy of Egypt (1863–79), grandson of MUHAMMAD ALI and son of IBRAHIM PASHA. In 1867 he received the title of khedive from the Ottoman sultan. The American Civil War (1861–65) caused a 400% increase in the price of Egyptian cotton and Ismail used the proceeds to fund a programme of modernization, but the subsequent collapse of the cotton market and Ismail's extravagant schemes left Egypt deeply in debt. He backed the French construction of the SUEZ CANAL, but the national debt forced him to sell (1875) Egypt's share in the Suez Canal Company to Britain. With the assistance of General GORDON and Sir Samuel BAKER, Ismail expanded his empire to include much of Sudan but was frustrated in his attempts (1875, 1876) to conquer Ethiopia. Sultan ABDUL HAMID II deposed him in favour of his son, Tewfik Pasha.

isolationism Avoidance by a state of foreign commitments and alliances. It is connected in particular with the foreign policy of the United States. US isolationism was not applied to the Americas, considered an exclusively US area of interest under the MONROE DOCTRINE, nor did it prevent US involvement in China and elsewhere in pursuit of commercial gains. With respect to Europe, it was interrupted when the United States entered World War 1 (1917), but re-emerged with the US refusal to participate in the LEAGUE OF NATIONS. The NEUTRALITY ACTS (1935, 1936) confirmed the isolationism of the United States in response to the rise of European FASCISM. Isolationism was permanently abandoned in 1941, although it continues to have some advocates.

Israel Name given in the Old Testament to JACOB and to the nation that the Hebrews founded in CANAAN. Jacob was renamed Israel after he had wrestled with the mysterious "man" who was either an angel or God Himself (Genesis 32:28). As a geographical name, Israel at first applied to the whole territory of Canaan captured or occupied by the Hebrews after the legendary Exodus from Egypt. This territory was united as a kingdom under DAVID in the early 10th century BC, with its capital at JERUSALEM. Following the death of David's son, SOLOMON, the ten northern tribes seceded, and the name Israel thereafter applied to the kingdom they founded in N Palestine; the remaining two tribes held the southern kingdom of JUDAH.

Israel *See* country feature

Israeli–Palestinian Accord (1993) Agreement that aimed to end hostilities between Palestinians and Israelis, especially in the WEST BANK and GAZA STRIP. Secret talks began in the mid-1980s. On 13 September 1993, a "Declaration of Principles" was signed by Yitzhak RABIN and Yasir ARAFAT. The PLO recognized Israel's right to exist and renounced terrorism. In return, Israel recognized the PLO as the legitimate representative of the Palestinian people and agreed to a staged withdrawal of troops from parts of the occupied territories. On 18 May 1994, the Israeli army completed its redeployment in the Gaza Strip and withdrew from JERICHO. The Palestinian National Authority (PNA), led by Arafat, assumed limited autonomy. In September 1995 Rabin agreed to withdraw Israeli troops from a further six towns and 85% of HEBRON. In October 1995, 1100 Palestinian prisoners were released. The assassination of Rabin and the election of Binyamin NETANYAHU halted the peace process, and Jewish settlement on the West Bank accelerated. The WYE AGREEMENT (October 1998) appeared to break the deadlock and Ehud BARAK's victory over Netanyahu in the 1999 elections provided further hope for progress in the peace process. *See also* INTIFADA

Istanbul (formerly Constantinople, ancient Byzantium) City and seaport on both sides of the Bosporus, NW Turkey, former capital of the BYZANTINE EMPIRE and the OTTOMAN EMPIRE. Byzantium was founded by Greek colonists in the mid-7th century BC. In 512 BC it was captured by the Persian king DARIUS I. Byzantium fell to ATHENS in 478 BC, but control gradually passed to SPARTA during the PELOPONNESIAN WAR. In the 4th century BC, the city accepted Macedonian rule under ALEXANDER III (THE GREAT). In AD 330 CONSTANTINE I (THE GREAT) chose Byzantium as the site of New Rome, the capital of a unified ROMAN EMPIRE. He renamed the city Constantinople. By the close of the 4th century, the city had *c.*400,000 inhabitants and was the greatest religious and commercial centre in the Western world. In 381 it became the seat of the second-most powerful bishop in Christendom (after the pope), the patriach of Constantinople (now head of the ORTHODOX CHURCH). A great fire in 532 prompted JUSTINIAN I to begin a rebuilding project that is now regarded as the apotheosis of BYZANTINE ART AND ARCHITECTURE. Most of the existing structure of the HAGIA SOPHIA dates from this period. The bubonic plague of 541–43 claimed more than half the city's population. In the 8th and 9th centuries, Constantinople was at the centre of the ICONOCLASTIC CONTROVERSY. The city was sacked by the armies of the Fourth CRUSADE in 1204, and the Latin Empire of CONSTANTINOPLE was created. In 1261 MICHAEL VIII (PALAEOLOGUS) reclaimed the city for the Byzantines. In 1453, after a long siege, Constantinople fell to the Ottoman Turks under MAHMUD II, who built the Topkapi Palace. Constantinople replaced EDIRNE as the capital of the Ottoman Empire. The Mosque of SULEIMAN I (THE MAGNIFICENT) (*c.*1550–57) and the Sultan Ahmed Cami (*c.*1609–16) are masterpieces of ISLAMIC ART AND ARCHITECTURE. The westernization of Constantinople gathered pace in the 19th century. During World War 1 the city was blockaded and in 1918 was placed under Allied occupation. In 1923 Mustafa Kemal (later ATATÜRK) proclaimed the republic of Turkey, and ANKARA became (1923) the new capital. Istanbul remains the commercial and financial centre of Turkey. Pop. (1990) 6,293,397.

Istria Peninsula between TRIESTE and RIJEKA, divided between Italy, Slovenia and Croatia. The region became part of the Roman Empire in the 2nd century BC and formed part of the Byzantine Empire from the 6th to 8th centuries AD. From the 15th century, Istria was split between the Habsburg Empire and Venice. Incorporated into Austria in 1797, it was ceded to Italy in 1919. In 1947 most of Istria passed to Yugoslavia. The Trieste region, however, became the Free Territory of Trieste, divided between Yugoslavia and Italy. In 1954 the city of Trieste was ceded to Italy. After the breakup of Yugoslavia in 1991, Istria was divided between Slovenia and Croatia.

Itagaki Taisuke (1837–1919) Japanese statesman. As a samurai, he commanded troops during the MEIJI RESTORATION (1868) which overthrew the TOKUGAWA shogunate. Itagaki served (1868–73) in the new cabinet, but resigned after the rejection of his plans for war against Korea. Itagaki called for the creation of more democratic institutions, and in 1881 he formed Japan's first political party, the *Jiyuto* (Liberal Party). Itagaki led

ISLAM

Monotheistic religion founded by MUHAMMAD in Arabia in the early 7th century. In Arabic, Islam means submission to God. At the heart of Islam stands the KORAN, considered the divine revelation in Arabic of God to Muhammad. Members of the faith (Muslims) date the beginning of Islam from 16 July 622, the date of Muhammad's HEGIRA (exodus) from MECCA to MEDINA.

Muslims submit to the will of Allah by five basic precepts (pillars). **First**, the *shahadah*, "there is no God but Allah, and Muhammad is his prophet". **Second**, *salah*, five daily ritual prayers: at the mosque, a Muslim performs ritual ablutions before praying to God in an attitude of submission, kneeling on a prayer mat facing Mecca with head bowed, then rising with hands cupped behind the ears to hear God's message. **Third**, *zakat* or alms-giving. **Fourth**, *sawm*, fasting during Ramadan, the ninth month of the Islamic year. **Fifth**, Hajj, the pilgrimage to Mecca.

The Koran was soon supplemented by the informal, scriptural elaborations of the Sunna (Muhammad's sayings and deeds), collated as the HADITH. A Muslim must also abide by the SHARIA or religious law. Islam spread rapidly during the 630s, in part because the head of the community (CALIPH) was both a religious and secular leader.

Within a decade of Muhammad's death (632) Arab armies, inspired by zeal for their new faith and a desire for plunder, had defeated both the BYZANTINE and SASANIAN empires. In 642 they conquered Egypt; by the mid-640s Iran was theirs, and by the late 640s they had occupied Syria. At a slower pace, the Arabs then overran coastal North Africa and advanced into Spain. The expansion of Islamic rule in Europe was checked at the Battle of POITIERS, W central France, in 732. Political power was consolidated at an early stage in the hands of the UMAYYADS (661–750). They were succeeded by the ABBASIDS (750–1258), under whose rule parts of the Muslim empire soon began to gain independence from the caliphate. In the 11th century, the Arabs began to lose power to the Turks. Throughout Islam's history the importance of the unity of the *summa* (nation) of Islam has been stressed. Several distinctive branches have developed, however, such as SUNNI, SHIITE and SUFISM. Today, there are *c.*935 million Muslims worldwide. *See also* ABU BAKR; ALI; AVERROËS; FATIMA; ISMAILIS; OMAR; OTHMAN

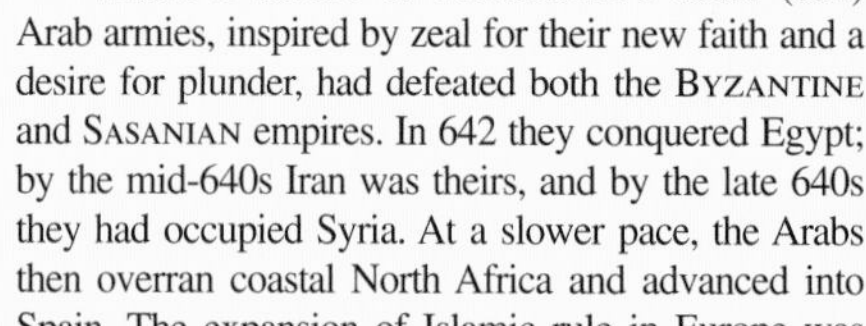

► **Mecca**, birthplace of Muhammad, is the holiest city in Islam. All devout Muslims must make a pilgrimage (*hajj*) to Mecca at least once in their lifetime. At the heart of the city stands the Al-Haram Mosque, whose central courtyard (shown here) contains the Kaaba –the holiest shrine in Islam. Pilgrims walk seven times around the Kaaba, kissing and touching the Black Stone in its E corner.

the *Jiyuto* in Japan's first democratic elections in 1890 and worked with Prime Minister ITO HIROBUMI.

Italian Popular Party (PPI) (formerly Christian Democratic Party) Centrist political organization in Italy, founded (1919) by Luigi Sturzo. The PPI rapidly gained popular support, but in 1926 Benito MUSSOLINI banned all political parties. In 1943 the PPI, under the leadership of Alcide DE GASPERI, was reorganized as the Christian Democratic Party (DC). De Gasperi united the various factions of the DC by stressing their common Roman Catholicism and anti-communism. Until the early 1960s, the DC dominated a succession of centre-right governments in Italy. In 1963 Aldo MORO entered into a coalition with the ITALIAN SOCIALIST PARTY (PSI), which went on to govern Italy for most of the next three decades. In 1975 DC leader Giulio ANDREOTTI was forced to enter into an alliance with the Italian Communist Party (PCI). In 1981 the DC temporarily lost its dominant status after a scandal surrounding the influence of freemasonry in government. The implication of many of the DC's leaders in financial scandals and political corruption led to a heavy defeat in 1992 elections, and in 1993 the DC reverted to its original name.

Italian Socialist Party (PSI) One of Italy's first national political parties, founded (1892) as the Italian Workers' Party. In 1920 the left wing broke away to form the Italian Communist Party (PCI). In 1926 Benito MUSSOLINI, a former PSI member, banned all political parties. The PSI continued to operate underground, and in 1934 it entered into an alliance with the PCI. In 1956 the PSI denounced the Soviet invasion of Hungary and broke away from the PCI. In 1963 the PSI entered as the junior partner in a coalition government with the Christian Democratic Party (now ITALIAN POPULAR PARTY). In 1983 Bettino CRAXI became the first socialist prime minister. In the 1990s, Craxi and other senior party officials were implicated in financial scandals and political corruption. The PSI was heavily defeated in the 1994 elections.

Italian Wars (1494–1559) Struggle for control of the independent Italian states between the VALOIS kings of France and the HABSBURGS. In 1494 CHARLES VIII of France captured Naples, but he retreated the following year, leaving FERNÁNDEZ DE CÓRDOBA to recover the kingdom for Ferdinand II of Naples. In 1499, with the help of Georges d'AMBOISE, LOUIS XII occupied MILAN, and the Treaty of Grenada (1500) with FERDINAND V of Spain divided the kingdom of Naples into a N French sphere and a S Spanish sphere. However, in 1504 Louis XII was forced to concede control of the whole of Naples to Ferdinand II. In 1508 Louis XII, Emperor MAXIMILIAN I and Ferdinand II formed the League of CAMBRAI to help Pope JULIUS II recover papal lands from VENICE. The papal forces were victorious but they then fell out with each other, and in 1510 Julius formed a HOLY LEAGUE to oppose French activity in Italy (1511–13). After initial success at the Battle of RAVENNA (1512), Louis' troops were forced to withdraw. In 1515 FRANCIS I of France launched another invasion and gained Milan after victory at the Battle of Marignano (1515). In 1522 Emperor CHARLES V expelled the French from Milan and the French position was permanently weakened after Francis I was captured at the Battle of PAVIA (1525). In 1526 a new Holy League was formed by France and the papacy against Charles V, and in 1527 an imperial army sacked Rome. Francis I renounced his claim to Italy at the Treaty of CAMBRAI (1529), but further French offensives occurred in 1536–38 and 1542–44. The invasions achieved very little, however, and following the Spanish victory at St Quentin (1557), HENRY II of France signed the Treaty of CÂTEAU-CAMBRÉSIS (1559) that left Habsburg Spain dominant. *See also* ALEXANDER VI; GUICCIARDINI, FRANCESCO; LEO X; PAPAL STATES; SFORZA, LUDOVICO

Italy *See* country feature, page 206

Ito Hirobumi (1841–1909) Japanese statesman, prime minister (1885–88, 1892–96, 1898, 1900–01). He travelled to Europe (1871–73) with IWAKURA TOMOMI to study Western politics and economics. In 1878 Ito succeeded OKUBO TOSHIMICHI as minister of home affairs. The leading figure in the modernization of Japan after the MEIJI RESTORATION (1868), Ito was largely responsible for the adoption of the Meiji Constitution (1889). He also did much to increase Japan's international standing. Ito formed the *Rikken Seiyukai* (Friends of Constitutional Government) in

ISRAEL

AREA: 26,650sq km (10,290sq mi)
POPULATION: 4,946,000
CAPITAL (POPULATION): Jerusalem (544,200)
GOVERNMENT: Multiparty republic
ETHNIC GROUPS: Jewish 82%, Arab and others 18%
LANGUAGES: Hebrew and Arabic (both official)
RELIGIONS: Judaism 82%, Islam 14%, Christianity 2%, Druze and others 2%
GDP PER CAPITA (1995): US$16,490

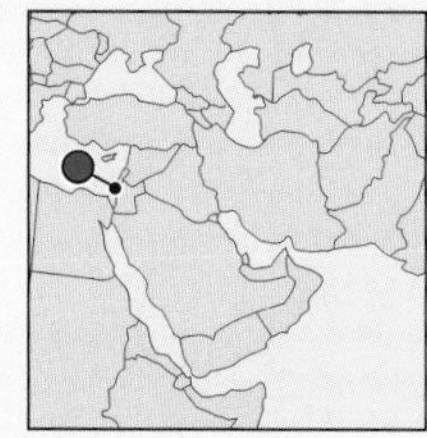

Small state on the Mediterranean Sea, SW Asia. Israel is part of a historic region that makes up most of the Biblical Holy Lands (for history pre-1947, *see* PALESTINE). In the late 19th century, supporters of ZIONISM began to agitate for a Jewish homeland. The BALFOUR DECLARATION (1917) provided British support for the creation of a Jewish homeland in Palestine. In 1947 the United Nations (UN) agreed to partition Palestine into an Arab and a Jewish state, but the plan was rejected by the Arabs.

On 14 May 1948, the State of Israel was proclaimed. Hundreds of thousands of Palestinians fled. Egypt, Iraq, Jordan, Lebanon and Syria invaded Israel in the first of the ARAB-ISRAELI WARS (1948). The HAGANAH successfully defeated the state and the Arab nations acknowledged defeat in July 1949. An Israeli government was formed with Chaim WEIZMANN as president and David BEN-GURION as prime minister. In 1949 Israel was admitted to the UN, and the capital transferred from Tel Aviv to JERUSALEM. In 1950 the Law of Return provided free citizenship for all immigrant Jews. After President NASSER of Egypt's nationalization of the SUEZ CANAL in 1956, Israel captured Gaza and the SINAI Peninsula. In 1957 Israel withdrew (*see* SUEZ CRISIS). In 1963 Ben-Gurion resigned, and Levi ESHKOL became prime minister (1963–69).

In 1967 Nasser blockaded the port of Eilat, S Israel. Israel's defence minister, Moshe DAYAN, launched a pre-emptive strike against Egypt and Syria. In the ensuing SIX-DAY WAR, Israel occupied the GAZA STRIP, Sinai peninsula, the GOLAN HEIGHTS, the WEST BANK and East JERUSALEM. In 1969 Eshkol died, and Golda MEIR became prime minister (1969–74). At the start (6 October 1973) of the YOM KIPPUR WAR, Egypt and Syria attacked Israeli positions in Sinai and the Golan Heights. Recovering from the initial surprise, Israeli troops launched a counter-offensive and retained its 1967 gains.

Yitzhak RABIN's government (1974–77) is chiefly remembered for the daring rescue of Israeli hostages at Entebbe. Rabin was succeeded by Menachem BEGIN (1977–83). Begin's hard-line government encouraged Jewish settlement on the West Bank and suppressed Palestinian uprisings. Following the CAMP DAVID ACCORDS, Egypt and Israel signed a peace treaty (1979) in which Egypt recognized the Israeli state and regained Sinai. In 1982 Begin launched a strike against nuclear installations in Iraq and a full-scale invasion (1982–85) of LEBANON to counter the PALESTINE LIBERATION ORGANIZATION (PLO). In 1987 the INTIFADA began in Israeli-occupied territory. From 1989 to 1992 Israel's population expanded by 10%, due to the immigration of FALASHAS from Ethiopia and Soviet Jews. Increasing Jewish settlement inflamed the popular uprising. During the GULF WAR (1991), Israel was the target for Iraqi scud missiles but – under pressure from the United States – it stayed its hand. In 1992 Rabin was re-elected and began "peace-for-land" negotiations with the PLO. In 1993 Rabin and Yasir ARAFAT signed the ISRAELI-PALESTINIAN ACCORD. In 1994 the Palestinian National Authority (PNA) assumed limited autonomy over the West Bank town of JERICHO and the Gaza Strip.

On 4 November 1995, Rabin was assassinated by a Jewish extremist. His successor, Shimon PERES, continued the peace process. Peres was narrowly defeated in the 1996 election by the LIKUD leader Binyamin NETANYAHU who, while vowing to maintain the peace process, favoured a more hardline policy. Jewish settlement on the West Bank intensified, despite US and UN disapproval. In January 1997 Israeli troops withdrew from HEBRON and the process crept forward. In the US-brokered WYE AGREEMENT (October 1998), Israel agreed to withdraw troops from parts of the West Bank and the PLO promised to remove anti-Israeli provisions from its charter. Opposition to the Agreement led to fresh elections in May 1999, which were won by a Labour coalition, One Israel. The new prime minister, Ehud BARAK, promised to advance the peace process.

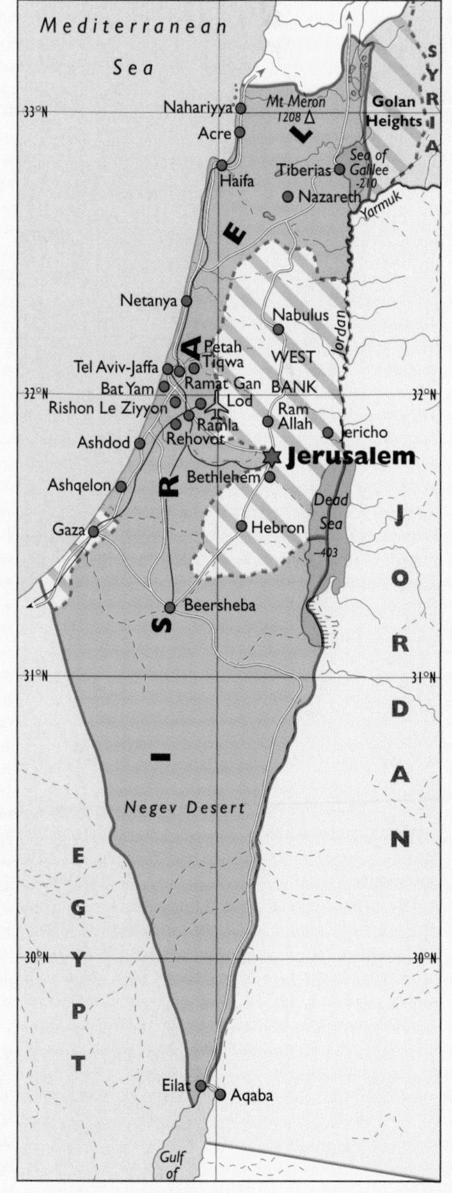

AREA: 301,270sq km (116,320sq mi)
POPULATION: 57,782,000
CAPITAL (POPULATION): Rome (2,775,250)
GOVERNMENT: Multiparty republic
ETHNIC GROUPS: Italian 94%, German, French, Greek, Albanian, Slovenian, Ladino
LANGUAGES: Italian 94% (official), Sardinian 3%
RELIGIONS: Christianity (Roman Catholic) 83%
GDP PER CAPITA (1995): US$19,870

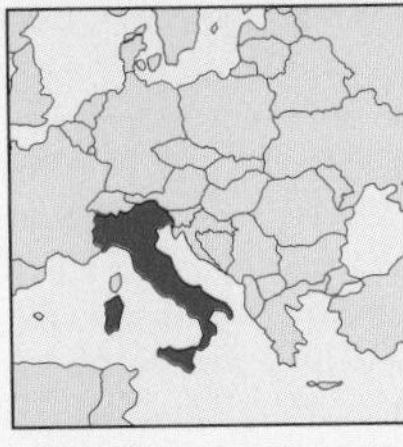

Republic in s Europe. In the 1st millennium BC, the Celts settled in N Italy, while Etruscan city-states developed in Tuscany and Umbria, and Greek colonies were established on the W and S coasts. The Roman Republic was established in 509 BC, and by the end of the 4th century BC ancient Rome was the dominant power in central Italy. Rome emerged victorious from the Punic Wars (264–146 BC) with Carthage and began to build a mighty Mediterranean empire. In 48 BC Julius Caesar defeated Pompey to establish himself as a dictator. His assassination (44 BC) led to the formation (27 BC) of the Roman Empire under Augustus. At the end of the 3rd century AD, Diocletian divided the empire into Eastern (Byzantine Empire) and Western sections. Constantine I (r.AD 306–37) reunited the empire, made Christianity the official religion, and established a new capital at Constantinople (now Istanbul). The papacy, however, ensured the continuation of Rome's influence.

The sacking of Rome by the Visigoth king Alaric I in 410 signalled the beginning of the Western Empire's collapse. By 493 Italy had been conquered by the Ostrogoths. In 554 Emperor Justinian regained Italy for the Byzantine Empire, but by 620 the Lombards had carved out a kingdom in N Italy. In 754–756 the Frankish king Pepin III (the Short) seized Ravenna from the Lombards, thus enabling the creation of the Papal States. In 800 Pepin's son, Charlemagne, was crowned emperor in Rome. The Treaty of Verdun (843) divided the Carolingian empire, with Louis II receiving the kingdom of Italy. In the 9th century, Amalfi, Naples and Venice became virtually autonomous maritime powers. In 962 Otto I of Saxony established the Holy Roman Empire, which included N Italy.

In 1027 Conrad II established the Salian dynasty. In the early 11th century, the Normans established a stronghold in S Italy, while city-states in central and N Italy (such as Milan, Bologna, Genoa, Florence, Milan and Pisa) began to form powerful communes. Imperial resistance to papal reform culminated in the Investiture Controversy (1075–1122) between the papacy and emperors Henry IV and Henry V. In 1138 the Hohenstaufen dynasty succeeded the Salians. Frederick I (Barbarossa)'s attempt to reassert imperial authority was defeated by the Lombard League at the Battle of Legnano (1176). In 1194 Emperor Henry VI conquered the kingdom of Sicily. The death (1250) of Emperor Frederick II saw the papal party of the Guelphs supporting the succession of the Angevins, while the Ghibellines supported the Hohenstaufen cause. At the end of the 13th century, S Italy was divided as the island of Sicily fell to Aragón. The Papal States also fractured with the move (1307–77) of the papacy to Avignon. The collapse of imperial authority left N Italy divided among independent city-states that became the nurturing ground for the Italian Renaissance. In the 14th century, many of these cities fell under the control of single families (*signori*), such as the Gonzaga (Mantua), the Este (Ferrara) and the Visconti (Milan). At the start of the 15th century, the republic of Venice expanded to become the most powerful state in Italy, while the republic of Florence fell under the control of the Medici family. The early 16th century was dominated by the Italian Wars (1494–1559) between Valois France and Habsburg Spain which left Spain the dominant power on the peninsula. After the War of the Spanish Succession (1701–14), the Austrian Habsburgs gained Naples and Milan, while the House of Savoy won Sardinia (1720).

In the French Revolutionary Wars, Napoleon expelled the Austrians from N and central Italy (1796–97), creating the Cisalpine Republic. In 1806 Napoleon I's brother, Joseph Bonaparte, was proclaimed king of Naples. French defeat in the Napoleonic Wars saw the return of Habsburg and Bourbon rule. In 1830 Giuseppe Mazzini founded the nationalist Young Italy organization.

The Revolutions of 1848 resulted in a liberal government in Piedmont under the Conte di Cavour. The Risorgimento continued as Giuseppe Garibaldi conquered Sicily (1860), and Victor Emmanuel II was proclaimed king of a united Italy (1861). The papacy refused to concede the loss of Rome in 1870, and Vatican City was set up as a sovereign state (1929). Francesco Crispi's ministry (1887–91, 1893–96) marked the ill-fated beginnings of an Italian empire. Prime Minister Giovanni Giolitti oversaw dramatic industrial growth, and Victor Emmanuel III's reign (1900–46) brought Italy into World War I on the side of the Allies. Italian discontent at the post-war settlement led to Gabriele D'Annunzio's seizure of Trieste and the emergence of fascism.

In 1922 Benito Mussolini assumed dictatorial powers, and went on to seize Albania and Ethiopia. In 1936 Mussolini entered an alliance with Adolf Hitler. At the start of World War 2, Italy fought on the Axis side, but after it had lost its North African empire, Mussolini was deposed. In 1943 Italy surrendered and then declared war on the Germans, who had invaded the country. In 1944 Rome fell to the Allies. The Christian Democrat Party (now Italian Popular Party) emerged as the dominant post-war political force, with Alcide De Gasperi as prime minister (1945–53). In 1948 Italy became a republic and was a founding member (1949) of the North Atlantic Treaty Organization (NATO) and the European Economic Community (1958). Italy has been riven by political instability (56 governments between 1945 and 1999), endemic corruption (often linked to the Mafia), social unrest and the wealth gap between N and S. In 1993 popular discontent with the political structure led to the adoption of a "first-past-the-post" system and the emergence of the Northern League and anti-corruption parties. Elections in 1996 were won by the left-wing Olive Tree alliance, and Romano Prodi became prime minister (1996–98). In 1998 the Communist Refoundation (RC) withdrew its support for Prodi's government, and Massimo D'Alema, leader of the Party of the Democratic Left (PDS), became prime minister.

IVAN IV (THE TERRIBLE)

Ivan IV (the Terrible) has earned an unenviable reputation as one of history's most barbaric leaders. His regency was troubled by civil war among the boyars. Believing that his wife had been poisoned by the boyars, Ivan began a murderous purge of the Russian nobility and perceived enemies in general. His bodyguard, the *oprichniki*, massacred many of the citizens of Novgorod in 1570. The reign of terror proved so devastating that it enabled the Crimean Tatars to capture Moscow in 1571. Furthermore, Ivan's murder of his own son, Ivan Ivanovich, left Russia devoid of a strong successor.

IVAN THE TERRIBLE IN HIS OWN WORDS

"To shave the beard is a sign that the blood of all the martyrs cannot cleanse. It is to deface the image of man created by God."
Quoted in David Maland, Europe in the 16th century *(1975)*

"It turns out that in your land people rule besides you, and not only people, but trading peasants."
Letter to Queen Elizabeth I (1570)

an attempt to counteract the power of political parties. After the RUSSO-JAPANESE WAR (1904–05), Ito became resident general in what was then the protectorate of Korea. He was assassinated by a Korean nationalist. *See also* GENRO

Iturbide, Agustín de (1783–1824) Mexican general, emperor (1822–23). He fought for the royalists against the revolutionary army of Miguel HIDALGA Y COSTILLA. After a liberal coup in Spain, Iturbide took control of the Mexican army and issued the Plan of Iguala (1821). The three points of the Plan were: independence for MEXICO from Spain, equality for Spaniards and Creoles, and the supremacy of the Roman Catholic Church. Itúrbide's forces soon triumphed, and Mexico achieved independence in 1821. In 1822 Iturbide proclaimed himself Emperor Agustín I. His dictatorial regime soon provoked dissent, which crystallized when Antonio López de SANTA ANNA and Guadalupe VICTORIA called for the creation of a republic. Iturbide abdicated and was exiled. Early in 1824, he returned to Mexico and was promptly arrested and shot.

Ivan III (the Great) (1440–1505) Grand Duke of Moscow (1462–1505). He laid the basis of a centralized Russian state. Ivan annexed the independent lands of Novgorod (1478), Yaroslavl (1463), Rostov (1474) and Tver (1485). In 1480 he defeated Khan Ahmed to end the rule of the TATARS. Ivan began the reconquest of Ukraine from Poland and Lithuania. His later years were troubled by disputes over the succession between his sons Vasili and Dmitri. Ivan employed Italian artists to build (1487) the KREMLIN.

Ivan IV (the Terrible) (1530–84) Grand Duke of Moscow (1533–84) and first tsar of Russia (1547–84). In 1547 he married Anastasia, a ROMANOV. At first, Ivan was an able and progressive ruler, reforming the military, law and government. By annexing the TATAR states of Kazan (1552) and Astrakhan (1556), he gained control of the River Volga. Ivan established trade with W European states and began Russian expansion into Siberia. Defeat by the Poles in the LIVONIAN WAR (1558–82) left Russia financially crippled. After his wife's death in 1560, Ivan became increasingly unbalanced, killing his son Ivan Ivanovich in a rage (1581). Ivan established a personal dominion, the *oprichnina* (1565–72), inside Russia. He created a military force, the *oprichniki*, which pursued a reign of terror against the BOYARS (hereditary nobility). In 1570 Ivan sacked Novgorod, massacring thousands of the city's inhabitants. He was succeeded by his son, FYODOR I.

Ivory Coast *See* country feature

Iwakura Tomomi (1825–83) Japanese statesman. He was a leader of the MEIJI RESTORATION (1868) that overthrew the TOKUGAWA shogunate. Iwakura led a mission (1871–73) to the West that studied its systems of government and finance. Iwakura successfully led resistance to ITAGAKI TAISUKE's plans for war against Korea, arguing for internal reforms. By the late 1870s, he was *de facto* head of government, overseeing a programme of modernization that laid the framework for the industrialization of Japan.

Iwo Jima, Battle of (19 February–16 March 1945) One of the fiercest conflicts in WORLD WAR 2. The Pacific island of Iwo Jima was of strategic importance as a potential refuelling base for US planes attacking Japan. After weeks of intense bombardment, US Marines landed on Iwo Jima but encountered unexpectedly stiff resistance from the heavily entrenched Japanese forces. The hardest battle was for control of Iwo Jima's highest peak, Mount Suribachi. A photograph of the US flag being planted (23 February) on Suribachi became a symbol of the conflict in the Pacific and the basis for a sculpture near ARLINGTON National Cemetery, Washington, D.C. US forces secured the island after a month of fighting that claimed *c.*21,000 Japanese and *c.*6800 US lives. Iwo Jima was returned to Japan in 1968. Area: 21sq km (8sq mi).

Izetbegović, Alija (1925–) Bosnian statesman, president of BOSNIA-HERZEGOVINA (1992–). He was imprisoned (1945–48, 1983–88) by the Yugoslav government for pan-Islamic activities. In 1990 Izetbegović was elected leader of the Party of Democratic Action (PDA). The PDA won the 1990 elections and Izetbegović promised to preserve the multi-ethnic nature of Bosnia. In 1991 CROATIA, SLOVENIA and MACEDONIA seceded from the Federation of Yugoslavia. In 1992, following a referendum in favour of secession, Izetbegović declared Bosnia-Herzegovina's independence. Bosnian Serbs, led by Radovan KARADŽIĆ, responded by declaring their own Serb Republic. In April 1992 a bloody civil war began with Bosnian Serbs supported by President Slobodan MILOŠEVIĆ and Croatians supplied by President Franjo TUDJMAN. Bosnia, Serbia and Croatia signed the DAYTON PEACE AGREEMENT (1995), which gave 51% of Bosnia to a Muslim-Croat federation and the remainder to the Serb Republic. Izetbegović was elected (1996) as head of a tripartite, collective presidency that included a Serb and a Croat representative. In 1998 he was re-elected to the presidency, but under the terms of the Dayton Agreement the chairmanship passed to the Serb representative.

Izmir (formerly Smyrna) City and seaport on the Gulf of Izmir, W Turkey. It was settled by Greeks at the beginning of the 1st millennium BC. Refounded by the Macedonians under ALEXANDER III (THE GREAT), it later became an important city of the Byzantine Empire. Izmir was part of the Ottoman Empire from *c.*1424 until 1919, when it was occupied by Greece. It was recaptured by Turkey in 1922. Pop. (1990) 2,319,188.

IVORY COAST (OFFICIALLY CÔTE D'IVOIRE)

AREA: 322,460sq km (124,502sq mi)
POPULATION: 12,910,000
CAPITAL (POPULATION): Yamoussoukro (106,786)
GOVERNMENT: Multiparty republic
ETHNIC GROUPS: Akan 41%, Kru 17%, Voltaic 16%, Malinke 15%, Southern Mande 10%
LANGUAGES: French (official)
RELIGIONS: Islam 38%, Christianity 28%, traditional beliefs 17%
GDP PER CAPITA (1995): US$1580

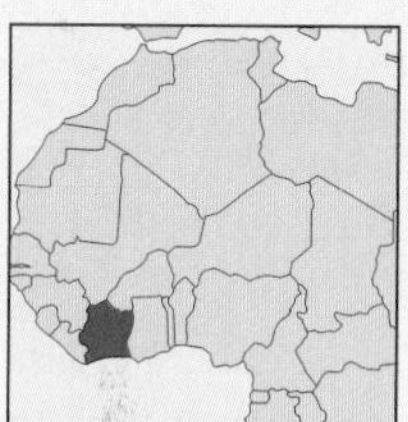

Republic on the Guinea coast of W Africa. In the N savanna, the ancient kingdoms of Bouna and Kong were centres of Islamic learning. In 1897 Samory Touré overthrew Kong, creating a new Muslim empire. In the 18th century, the ASHANTI conquered many of the AKAN kingdom in the forests of Ivory Coast.

European contact with the region dates back to the late 15th century, and trade in ivory and slaves soon became important. French trading posts were founded in the late 17th century, and Ivory Coast became a French colony in 1893. From 1895 Ivory Coast was governed as part of French West Africa, a massive union that also included modern-day Benin, Burkina Faso, Guinea, Mali, Mauritania, Niger and Senegal. Resistance to colonial rule continued until 1918. Ivoirians fought in the French army during both World Wars. In 1946 Félix HOUPHOUËT-BOIGNY co-founded the African Farmers' Union (SAA), which secured equal rights for African planters of cocoa and coffee and ended the practice of forced labour.

In 1960 Houphouët-Boigny became the first president of an independent Ivory Coast. He was the longest-serving African head of state, with an uninterrupted 33-year presidency until his death (1993). Houphouët-Boigny was a paternalistic, pro-Western leader. His dialogue with South Africa's apartheid government enraged many fellow African states. In 1983 the National Assembly agreed to move the capital from Abidjan to Yamoussoukro, Houphouët-Boigny's birthplace, but economic setbacks delayed the transfer and many government offices remain in Abidjan. In the 1980s civil unrest led to the adoption of a new constitution (1990) which legalized opposition parties. In 1993 Houphouët-Boigny was succeeded by Henri Konan Bédié. The re-election of Bédié in 1995 was marked by violence as opponents boycotted the polls. In 1999 Bédié was overthrown in a military coup led by General Robert Guei.

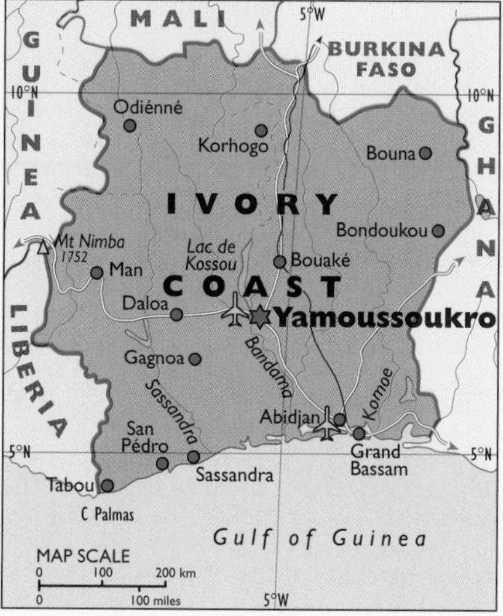

Jabotinsky, Vladimir (1880–1940) Zionist politician and journalist, b. Ukraine. During World War 1, he campaigned for Jewish refugees from the Ottoman Empire to be allowed to fight for the Allies, in the hope that Jews would be able to colonize PALESTINE after the withdrawal of the Ottomans. In 1920 Jabotinsky organized the HAGANAH, the Jewish self-defence movement in Palestine. In 1925 Jabotinsky broke with mainstream ZIONISM to form the Zionist Revisionist Movement (later the New Zionist Organization), which called for increased Jewish emigration to Palestine and the establishment of a permanent Jewish militia. The terrorist group IRGUN ZVAI LEUMI was founded by his associates.

Jackson, Andrew (1767–1845) Seventh president of the United States (1829–37). Jackson became a national hero in the WAR OF 1812 with victories in the CREEK WAR (1813–14) and at the Battle of NEW ORLEANS (1815). Jackson narrowly escaped censure for his invasion (1817) of the Spanish territory of FLORIDA. He gained the most popular votes in the 1824 presidential election, but the lack of an overall majority saw the House of Representatives appoint John Quincy ADAMS. Arguing that the democratic will had been frustrated, Jackson's supporters established a new political organization, which developed into the DEMOCRATIC PARTY. In 1828 Jackson was elected with support from the Western FRONTIER. He faced staunch opposition from the establishment and set up a SPOILS SYSTEM of political appointments. Jackson rarely met with the official cabinet, preferring his "kitchen cabinet" of personal advisers. In 1832 Vice President John CALHOUN resigned in support of South Carolina's NULLIFICATION of the protective tariffs of 1828 and 1832. The Force Bill (1833) gave the president powers to use the armed forces to enforce federal laws. Jackson's second term (1832–37) was dominated by conflict over financial policy after he had vetoed a bill to recharter the BANK OF THE UNITED STATES. Jackson was succeeded by Vice President Martin VAN BUREN. *See also* CLAY, HENRY; STATES' RIGHTS

Jackson, Jesse Louis (1941–) US politician and CIVIL-RIGHTS activist. He worked with Martin Luther KING, JR, in the SOUTHERN CHRISTIAN LEADERSHIP CONFERENCE (SCLC). Jackson served as national director (1967–71) of Operation Breadbasket, the economic arm of the SCLC. In 1968 he was ordained a Baptist minister. In 1971 Jackson formed Operation PUSH (People United to Save Humanity) to combat racism in Chicago. An inspiring orator, Jackson campaigned for the Democratic presidential nomination in 1984 and 1988. Although he did not gain the nomination, Jackson inspired many people to register to vote. In 1986 he became president of the National Rainbow Coalition. *See also* ABERNATHY, RALPH DAVID

Jackson, "Stonewall" (Thomas Jonathan) (1824–63) Confederate general in the American CIVIL WAR. He fought alongside General Robert LEE in the MEXICAN WAR (1847). Jackson's stand against overwhelming odds at the first Battle of BULL RUN (1861) gained him the nickname "Stonewall", and his campaign in the SHENANDOAH VALLEY (1862) prevented Federal supplies from reaching General George MCCLELLAN at Richmond, Virginia. Jackson played a crucial role in Lee's victory in the SEVEN DAYS' BATTLES (1862) and was promoted to lieutenant general after winning the second Battle of BULL RUN (1862). Jackson helped defeat Ambrose BURNSIDE at the Battle of Fredericksburg (1862). Jackson died after being accidentally shot by his own troops at the Battle of CHANCELLORSVILLE.

Jacob Old Testament figure who was a grandson of ABRAHAM and, by tradition, ancestor of the nation of ISRAEL. He was the second-born son of Isaac and Rebecca, and younger twin brother of Esau. Stories about him and his family form the last part of Genesis. Jacob had 12 sons and one daughter by his two wives, Rachel and Leah, and their respective maids. The descendants of his 12 sons became the 12 tribes of Israel.

Jacobins Political club of the FRENCH REVOLUTION. In 1789 Breton members of the STATES-GENERAL met in a Dominican (known in Paris as Jacobin) monastery to form the Society of the Friends of the Constitution (commonly called the Jacobins). The initial aim of the club was to protect the Revolution from reactionary forces. By July 1790 there were *c.*1200 Jacobins in Paris. By 1792 Maximilien de ROBESPIERRE had seized control of the club and it began to call for the execution of LOUIS XVI. In June 1793 the Jacobins engineered the expulsion of the GIRONDINS and through a nationwide network of *c.*5000 clubs became an instrument of the REIGN OF TERROR. It collapsed soon after Robespierre's downfall in 1794. *See also* COMMITTEE OF PUBLIC SAFETY; MONTAGNARDS

Jacobites Supporters of JAMES II of England and his STUART descendants, who attempted to regain the English throne after the GLORIOUS REVOLUTION (1688). Jacobitism was strong in the Scottish Highlands and parts of Ireland. In 1715 (the "**Fifteen Rebellion**") a rising at Braemar, led by the Earl of Mar, proclaimed James Edward STUART as king. The movement collapsed with the defeat of the rebels at Preston. In 1745 a second rising (the "**Forty-Five Rebellion**"), led by Bonnie Prince Charlie (Charles Edward STUART), captured Scotland and advanced to Derby, central England, before retreating. The Highlanders were decisively defeated at the Battle of CULLODEN (1746), and the British government embarked upon a policy of suppression of the Highland clans, ending the Jacobite threat.

Jacquerie (1358) Insurrection of peasants against the nobility in NE France. Discontent mounted after English victory at the Battle of POITIERS (1356) in the first phase of the HUNDRED YEARS' WAR and the ensuing plunder of the French countryside by mercenaries. The peasants were also angered by high taxation to pay for the War. The rebellion was assisted by a bourgeois revolt in Paris. Several castles were sacked by the peasants before the revolt was suppressed. The feudal nobility carried out savage reprisals, including the massacre of thousands of peasants.

Jadwiga (1372–99) Queen of Poland (1384–99), daughter of LOUIS I (THE GREAT) of Hungary and Poland. She was elected queen of Poland on Louis' death, while her sister became queen of Hungary. In 1386 Jadwiga made an advantageous political marriage to WŁADISŁAW II (JAGIELLO), grand duke of LITHUANIA and founder of the JAGIELLON dynasty. The marriage marked the start of a 400-year association between Poland and Lithuania.

Jaffa City and port in W Israel, suburb of Tel Aviv. Mentioned in the Bible, it was captured by ALEXANDER III (THE GREAT) in 332 BC. Jaffa was taken back by the Jews during the revolt led by the MACCABEES of Judaea against the SELEUCIDS (*c.*167 BC), but was destroyed by the Roman Emperor Vespasian in AD 68. It changed hands many times in the Middle Ages, being captured by Crusaders but regained by Muslims. In the 20th century, Jaffa was a focus of Palestinian resistance to Jewish settlement. In 1948 the city was settled by Israelis and united with Tel Aviv in 1950. Tel Aviv/Jaffa Pop. (1995) 355,900.

Jagan, Cheddi (1918–97) Guyanan statesman, prime minister of British Guiana (1953, 1961–64), president of independent Guyana (1992–97). He founded (1950) the first political party, the People's Progressive Party (PPP), in British Guiana. In 1953 Jagan became the country's first elected prime minister, but his radical agenda prompted the British to dismiss him. In 1955 the PPP split and Forbes BURNHAM formed the People's National Congress. The PPP won elections in 1957 and 1961, and Jagan continued his attempts to establish a socialist economy. He lost the 1964 election to Burnham, but later returned as president. His wife, Janet Jagan, also served (1997–99) as president.

Jagatai (d.1242) (Chagatai) Mongol ruler, second son of GENGHIS KHAN. On the death (1227) of his father, Jagatai received East Turkistan and most of West Turkistan (Transoxiana). The Jagatai khanate became the focus of dispute among the descendants of Genghis. Control of the area consumed much of the energies of KUBLAI KHAN. In *c.*1369 TAMERLANE conquered West Turkistan and established a capital at SAMARKAND. The Jagatai khanate in East Turkistan was captured by the Uzbek Mongols in *c.*1500.

Jagiellon (Jagellon) Medieval Polish dynasty (1386–1542). It began with the marriage of Grand Duke Jagiello (later WŁADISŁAW II) of LITHUANIA to Queen JADWIGA of POLAND. Władisław's son, CASIMIR IV (r.1447–92), ended (1466) the threat of the TEUTONIC KNIGHTS and acquired West PRUSSIA and POMERANIA. Casimir's eldest son, Ladislas II, ruled Hungary and Bohemia. SIGISMUND I, Casimir's fifth son, gained East Prussia. Louis II, Ladislas' son, was defeated and killed by the Turks at the Battle of MOHÁCS (1526), ending Jagiellon rule in Hungary. SIGISMUND II, last of the Jagiellon dynasty, took Poland into the LIVONIAN WAR (1558–83).

Jahangir (1569–1627) Mughal emperor of India (1605–27), son and successor of AKBAR. Jahangir continued his father's expansion of the MUGHAL EMPIRE, gaining (1614) the RAJPUT principality of Mewar (now UDAIPUR) and most of Ahmadnagar (1621). He temporarily neutralized the power of the MARATHAS in the Deccan and granted trading privileges to the Portuguese and the English EAST INDIA COMPANY. Jahangir's Iranian wife, Nur Jahan, and her relatives dominated politics after 1611. The last years of his reign were marked by internecine conflict. Jahangir was a great patron of painting and poetry. He was succeeded by his son, SHAH JAHAN.

Jainism Ancient religion of India originating in the 6th century BC as a reaction against BRAHMANISM. It was founded by MAHAVIRA, who is venerated as the last of 24 *tirthankaras* (saints). In the 3rd century BC, a schism developed between those who argued that monks should be naked (Digambaras) and those who favoured the wearing of white robes (Svetambara). According to the Digambara tradition, its founder Bhadrabahu converted the Mauryan Emperor CHANDRAGUPTA. Jainism was at its height, both in terms of literary creativity and political influence, in the early medieval period (*c.*AD 500–1100). Jains do not accept Hindu scriptures, rituals or priesthood, but they do accept the doctrines of karma and reincarnation. Jainism lays special stress on *ahimsa* – nonviolence. Today, there are *c.*4 million Jains worldwide.

Jaja of Opobo (d.1891) Ibo prince. A former slave, he became a wealthy independent merchant in the Niger Delta. In *c.*1869 Jaja (Jubo Jubogha) established his own kingdom at Opobo (now Ikot Abasi), S Nigeria. Under his rule, Opobo came to dominate the Niger trade in palm-oil. The kingdom threatened rival traders and frustrated British attempts to colonize the interior. In 1887 Jaja was captured by the British and deported to the West Indies.

Jakarta (Djakarta) Capital of INDONESIA, on the NW coast of JAVA. There was a settlement on the site as early as the 5th century AD. The Portuguese captured the port in the 15th century. In 1619 Dutch merchant Jan Pieterszoon COEN destroyed the city, rebuilding it as the fortified trading post of Batavia. It became the headquarters of the Dutch EAST INDIA COMPANY. Batavia expanded in the early 19th century. Occupied by Japan during World War 2, it was returned to the Dutch after the war. In 1949 Jakarta became the capital of an independent Indonesia. Widespread riots in the city led to the resignation (1997) of President SUHARTO. Pop. (1994 est.) 7,885,519.

Jamaica Independent island nation in the Caribbean. The ARAWAK began to settle on the island from the 7th century. European discovery was made (1494) by Christopher COLUMBUS, and Spanish settlement began in 1509. The native population had disappeared by the time the British captured Jamaica in 1655. The island became a haven for BUCCANEERS. From 1670 Jamaica grew into a centre of the SLAVE TRADE as Africans were forced to work on the sugar and coffee plantations. The economy collapsed after the abolition of slavery in 1807 and the emancipation of slaves in 1834. In 1865 the British Governor General Edward John EYRE was dismissed after brutally crushing a rebellion by freed slaves. In 1944 a new constitution provided for a House of Representatives

JAMAICA

AREA: 10,990sq km (4243sq mi)
POPULATION: 2,530,000
CAPITAL (POPULATION): Kingston (103,962)
GOVERNMENT: Multiparty republic
ETHNIC GROUPS: Black 76%, Afro-European 15%, East Indian and Afro-East Indian 3%, White 5%
LANGUAGES: English (official), English Creole, Hindi
RELIGIONS: Protestant 70%, Roman Catholic 8%
GDP PER CAPITA (1995): US$3540

elected by universal adult suffrage. Jamaica was a founder member of the West Indies Federation. In 1962 the Federation disintegrated and Sir Alexander BUSTAMANTE of the Jamaican Labour Party (JLP) negotiated full independence for Jamaica. In 1973 Michael MANLEY of the People's National Party (PNP) took Jamaica into the CARIBBEAN COMMUNITY AND COMMON MARKET (CARICOM), but economic recession and political violence led to his defeat (1980) by Edward Seaga of the JLP. Seaga's efforts at economic regeneration were hampered by Hurricanes Allen and Gilbert (1980 and 1988). Manley was re-elected in 1989. In 1992 Manley retired and was succeeded by Percival Patterson. Patterson was re-elected in 1993 and 1997. *See* WEST INDIES map

James the Great, Saint (d. *c.*44 AD) One of the 12 disciples of JESUS CHRIST, son of Zebedee and brother of Saint JOHN. James was beheaded by HEROD AGRIPPA I. His feast day is 25 July.

James the Just, Saint (d. *c.*AD 62) According to tradition, the first bishop of the Christian church in Jerusalem; referred to in the Gospels as a brother of JESUS CHRIST. In Roman Catholicism, James is identified with Saint **James the Less**, who witnessed Christ's crucifixion. The Epistle of Saint James is attributed to him. He was condemned to death by the SANHEDRIN. His feast day is 3 May.

James I (the Conqueror) (1208–76) King of Aragón (1213–76). In 1227 he assumed firm control of government after a minority constantly troubled by revolts. James embarked on the conquest of the Balearic Islands, capturing Majorca (1229) and Ibiza (1235). In 1233 he launched a campaign against the Saracens, gaining the city of Valencia in 1238. A great soldier, James also encouraged trade with N Africa and improved the administrative and legal systems. Civil war ensued from James' decision to divide his kingdom between his sons in 1248 and 1262.

James I (1566–1625) King of England (1603–25) and, as James VI, king of Scotland (1567–1625). Son of MARY, QUEEN OF SCOTS, and Lord DARNLEY, he acceded to the Scottish throne as an infant on his mother's abdication. The Earl of MORTON acted as regent (1572–78) for the early part of his reign. In 1589 James married Anne of Denmark. He inherited the English throne on the death of ELIZABETH I, and thereafter chose to reside in England. James refused to reform the CHURCH OF ENGLAND to the satisfaction of its PURITAN critics and sponsored the publication (1611) of the Authorized, or King James', Version of the BIBLE. In 1605 the GUNPOWDER PLOT was foiled and James cracked down heavily on Catholics. In 1607 the first English colony in America (JAMESTOWN) was founded. James' insistence on the divine right of kings brought conflict with his Parliaments. In 1611 he dissolved Parliament and (excluding the 1614 ADDLED PARLIAMENT) ruled without one until 1621. The death (1612) of Robert CECIL saw James become increasingly dependent on favourites, such as Robert Carr and George Villiers, 1st Duke of BUCKINGHAM, who were widely regarded as corrupt and incompetent. He was succeeded by his son, CHARLES I. *See also* JACOBEAN; KNOX, JOHN; STUARTS

James II (1633–1701) King of England and Scotland (1685–88), second son of CHARLES I. After the second phase of the English CIVIL WAR (1648) James escaped to Holland. In 1659 he married Anne Hyde, daughter of the Earl of CLARENDON, and the couple had two daughters (later queens MARY II and ANNE). At the RESTORATION (1660) of his brother CHARLES II, James was appointed lord high admiral and led the English fleet at the start of the Second and Third DUTCH WARS. In 1669 he converted to Roman Catholicism and was forced to resign his offices. Attempts to discredit James' claim to the throne led to the EXCLUSION CRISIS (1679–81). On his accession, James was confronted by the Duke of MONMOUTH's Rebellion (1685). James' pro-Catholic policies and the birth of a son (James Edward STUART) to his second wife, MARY OF MODENA, provoked the GLORIOUS REVOLUTION (1688–89). James' daughter Mary and her husband, WILLIAM III (OF ORANGE), assumed the crown and James fled to France. With French aid, he invaded Ireland but was defeated by William at the Battle of the BOYNE (1690). *See also* BLOODY ASSIZES; JACOBITES; OATES, TITUS; STUARTS

James I (1394–1437) King of Scotland (1406–37). His father, Robert III, sent him to France for protection from the rebellious Scottish nobles, but James was captured en route by the English (1406). Robert died soon afterwards, and James was not released until 1424. James restored royal authority by ruthless methods. He carried out reforms of the financial and judicial systems and encouraged trade. James' campaigns against the nobility made him many enemies, and he was assassinated at Perth.

James II (1430–60) King of Scotland (1437–60), son and successor of JAMES I. His minority was dominated by aristocratic factions, particularly the Douglases. In 1452 he killed the Earl of Douglas and seized control. During the English Wars of the ROSES, James supported the Lancastrians against the Yorkists, who were allied with the Douglases. He was killed at Roxburgh Castle.

James III (1451–88) King of Scotland (1460–88), son and successor of JAMES II. Dominated by the nobility during his minority, James was unable to re-establish royal authority when he took control in 1469. In 1482 he faced a rebellion from his brother, Alexander Stuart, Duke of Albany, who had the support of EDWARD IV of England. James' marriage to Margaret of Denmark led to the acquisition of Orkney and Shetland. In a second aristocratic revolt, James was captured and killed at the Battle of Sauchiebum. He was succeeded by his son, JAMES IV.

James IV (1473–1513) King of Scotland (1488–1513), son and successor of JAMES III. James defended royal authority against the nobility and the church. He endeavoured to promote peace with England by marrying HENRY VIII's sister, MARGARET TUDOR. Henry's attack on France, Scotland's old ally, drew James into war (1513) against England. He invaded N England, capturing several castles before being defeated and killed at the Battle of FLODDEN. He was succeeded by his son, JAMES V.

James V (1512–42) King of Scotland (1513–42), son and successor of JAMES IV. His minority was characterized by the power struggle between a pro-French faction (led by the Duke of Albany) and a pro-English faction (led by the Earl of Angus). James gave a clear indication of his sympathies when he married (1538) Madeleine, daughter of FRANCIS I of France, and, after her death, Mary of GUISE. James' alliance with France was intended as a safeguard against his aggressive uncle, HENRY VIII of England, but war with England followed the alliance. James' failure to gain the support of the nobility contributed to the defeat of his forces by the English at Solway Moss (1542). He was succeeded by his daughter, MARY, QUEEN OF SCOTS.

James Edward Stuart *See* STUART, JAMES EDWARD

James, C.L.R. (Cyril Lionel Robert) (1901–89) Trinidadian historian and political theorist. In 1933 he emigrated to England. James wrote a history of TOUSSAINT L'OUVERTURE's Haitian revolution, *The Black Jacobins* (1938). He is best known for *Beyond a Boundary* (1963), a unique combination of cricketing and social history.

James, Jesse Woodson (1847–82) US outlaw. With his brother Frank, he fought for the Confederacy during the American CIVIL WAR. In 1867 they formed an outlaw band that terrorized the frontier, robbing banks and trains in Missouri and neighbouring states. James was shot dead by Robert Ford, a member of his own gang, for a reward.

Jameson, Sir Leander Starr (1853–1917) South African statesman, b. Scotland. He emigrated to S Africa in 1878. In 1889–90, as a representative of Cecil RHODES, Jameson persuaded King LOBENGULA of NDEBELE to grant mining rights to the British South Africa Company. In 1891 he was made administrator of Mashonaland, thus creating the first government for the British settlers. In 1895 Jameson, supported by Rhodes, led the abortive JAMESON RAID on the Afrikaner republic of TRANSVAAL. Jameson was captured and imprisoned. After his release, Jameson served as prime minister (1904–08) of Cape Colony.

Jameson Raid (December 1895) Invasion of the Afrikaner republic of TRANSVAAL, led by Leander Starr JAMESON. Jameson and Cecil RHODES wished to establish a federation of South Africa administered by the British, an ambition that required the overthrow of the Boer government in the Transvaal. Consequently, when the British settlers, known as *Uitlanders* (Afrikaans, "foreigners"), rebelled against the Transvaal government of Paul KRUGER, Jameson led a supporting raid of 500 men from across the border in Cape Colony. The Afrikaners quickly defeated the raiders, capturing Jameson and handing him over to the British authorities. Rhodes was compelled to resign as prime minister of Cape Colony and Jameson was briefly imprisoned. *See also* SOUTH AFRICAN WARS

Jamestown First successful English settlement in America. It was established in 1607 on the James River, Virginia. On the verge of collapse from disease and starvation, it was saved (1608) by Captain John SMITH and the timely arrival of new supplies and colonists (1610). From 1614 survival was assured thanks to tobacco planting.

Jammu and Kashmir State in NW India, bounded N by Pakistan-controlled KASHMIR, W by Pakistan and E by China. The capitals are Srinagar (summer) and Jammu (winter). Kashmir came under Muslim rule in 1346 and Sikh rule in 1819. After the SIKH WARS, it was annexed (1846) to the kingdom of Jammu, which was ruled by the Hindu Dogra dynasty. After the formation of India and Pakistan, the Hindu maharaja of Kashmir, Sir Hari Singh, tried to maintain Kashmiri independence but, faced with revolt from the Muslim majority, acceded the state to India (October 1947). War broke out between Pakistan and India over the status of Kashmir, forcing the United Nations (UN) to intervene and impose a cease-fire (January 1949) that partitioned Kashmir. Further fighting (1965, 1971) between India and Pakistan culminated in an agreement to settle the dispute through bilateral negotiations. The status of Kashmir remained unresolved, however, and the Indian government deployed large numbers of troops to support the state of Jammu and Kashmir. Kashmiri Muslims carried out guerrilla attacks on Indian troops and government officials throughout the 1980s and 1990s. Border skirmishes between Pakistani and Indian troops threatened to escalate into a full-scale war in 1999. Area: 100,569sq km (38,845sq mi). Pop. (1994 est.) 8,435,000.

Janata Party Indian political organization formed in 1977. It developed out of the Janata Front, a broad political movement created (1975) to oppose Indira GANDHI. A coalition of four parties, the Janata Party won the 1977 election under the leadership of Morarji DESAI. In July 1979 the coalition collapsed and Desai resigned as prime minister. In 1989, in opposition to the CONGRESS (I) Party, a new coalition, known as **Janata Dal**, was formed under V.P. Singh. It emerged from the 1989 elections with the second-largest number of seats in the Lok Sabha (House of the People) and formed a coalition government with the BHARATIYA JANATA PAKSH (BJP) and the communists. In November 1990, V.P. Singh's government collapsed and Chandra Shekhar, leader of the newly formed Janata Dal (Socialist) faction, became prime minister (1990–91). Deve Gowda of the Janata Dal emerged as leader of a new coalition government after elections in 1996. In 1997 Deve Gowda was replaced as prime minister and leader of Janata Dal by Inder Kumar Gujral. In 1999 elections the Janata Dal split into Janata Dal (Secular) and Janata Dal (United).

Janissaries Élite corps of the Ottoman army, founded in the 14th century by MURAD I. The Janissary regiments originally consisted of Christian slaves, gathered from the Balkan margins of the OTTOMAN EMPIRE and eventually allowed to leave military service as free Muslims. These soldiers were gradually replaced by local Muslim-born recruits. The Janissaries were a highly effective fighting

AREA: 377,800sq km (145,869sq mi)
POPULATION: 124,336,000
CAPITAL (POPULATION): Tokyo (7,894,000)
GOVERNMENT: Constitutional monarchy
ETHNIC GROUPS: Japanese 99%, Chinese, Korean, Ainu
LANGUAGES: Japanese (official)
RELIGIONS: Shintoism 93%, Buddhism 74%, Christianity 1% (most Japanese consider themselves to be both Shinto and Buddhist)
GDP PER CAPITA (1995): US$22,110

Archipelago state in E Asia. Its four largest islands are Honshu (site of the capital, Tokyo), Hokkaido, Kyushu and Shikoku. The first settlers in Japan migrated (*c.*30,000 years ago) from mainland Asia. The Jomon culture (*c.*7500–250 BC) saw the development of pottery. The Yayoi culture (*c.*250 BC–AD 250), which first emerged in Kyushu, saw the beginnings of agriculture and weaving. The Yayoi were greatly influenced by the Chinese HAN dynasty.

Japan was probably unified under YAMATO in the mid-4th century. The native religion of SHINTO survived the introduction of BUDDHISM at the beginning of the Asuka period (AD 552–645). CONFUCIANISM was part of the profound cultural influence that China had on Japan from the end of the 6th century. In 710 the imperial capital was established at NARA and the subsequent Nara period saw major political, economic and land reforms, as well as a blossoming of Buddhist art and culture.

In 794 the capital moved to Heian (now KYOTO). The FUJIWARA regents dominated the HEIAN period (794–1185), until Emperor Shirakawa instituted (1086) the system of *insei* (government by retired emperors) and called upon the TAIRA family of SAMURAI (warriors) to suppress the Minamoto clan (supporters of the Fujiwara). The Gempei War (1180–85) between the two warrior classes engulfed most of Japan and resulted in Minamoto YORITOMO establishing the KAMAKURA shogunate (military dictatorship).

The Kamakura period (1185–1333) was controlled by the HOJO family. The shogunate was weakened, however, by the financial cost of defeating the MONGOL invasions (1274, 1281), and DAIGO II restored (1333) imperial rule with the help of the ASHIKAGA family. In 1336 Ashikaga Takauji forced Daigo II into exile and moved the shogunate to Kyoto. For the next 66 years there was a schism, with rival emperors in N and S Japan. In 1392 Japan was reunified under Ashikaga YOSHIMITSU, who encouraged the rise of ZEN Buddhism. The ONIN WAR (1467–77) ushered in a 100-year period of civil strife. This *Sengoku* (Warring States) period saw the rise of the DAIMYO (large landowner).

In 1543 Portuguese soldiers brought Christianity and guns. These muskets were used by Oda NOBUNAGA to gain half of Japan's provinces and the unification process was completed (1590) by Toyotomi HIDEYOSHI. In 1603 Tokugawa IEYASU established the TOKUGAWA shogunate (1603–1867) and adopted Edo (now TOKYO) as the capital. Through the codes of BUSHIDO, the Tokugawa ensured total loyalty. Japan pursued an isolationalist path; travel outside Japan was forbidden and Japanese converts to Christianity were persecuted.

In 1854 US Commodore Matthew PERRY forced the Tokugawa shogunate to open its ports to Western trade. Young samurai in Choshu and Satsuma, such as ITO HIROBUMI, SAIGO TAKAMORI and OKUBU TOSHIMICHI, led a revolt (1866) against the shogunate and the MEIJI RESTORATION (1868) saw the return of imperial authority. Emperor MEIJI's reign (1868–1912) was characterized by social and economic modernization, headed by the ZAIBATSU. In 1881 ITAGAKI TAISUKE formed the Liberal Party, Japan's first political party, and a constitution was promulgated in 1889. Japanese nationalism and the beginnings of industrialization in Japan created the desire for empire-building.

The first of the SINO-JAPANESE WARS (1894–95) saw Japan acquire Formosa (now Taiwan). Japan's decisive victory in the RUSSO-JAPANESE WAR (1904–05) marked its emergence as the dominant power in the region. In 1910 Japan annexed Korea. During the 1920s Japan concentrated on building its economy, interrupted only by an earthquake (1923) that claimed 143,000 lives and devastated Tokyo and Yokohama. Militarists began to dominate Japanese politics. In 1931 Japan invaded MANCHURIA and in 1932 set up the puppet state of MANCHUKUO. In 1937 Japan invaded China, precipitating the Second Sino-Japanese War.

At the start of WORLD WAR 2, in an attempt to deter the United States from intervening in East Asia, Japan signed the TRIPARTITE PACT with Germany and Italy. When the United States and Great Britain responded by imposing economic sanctions on Japan, Japan attacked the US naval base at PEARL HARBOR (7 December 1941). Japan subsequently conquered a huge swathe of territory in the Pacific and SE Asia, but gradually the Allies regained ground. In 1945 the United States dropped atomic bombs on the cities of HIROSHIMA and NAGASAKI, and forced Japan's unconditional surrender (14 August 1945). The US occupation (1945–52) of Japan under Douglas MACARTHUR undertook the demilitarization of industry and the adoption of a democratic constitution, including universal suffrage. Emperor HIROHITO declaimed his divinity and became a constitutional monarch. In 1951 Japan concluded a security treaty with the United States that allowed US bases to be stationed on Japan in return for securing its defences. During the 1960s and early 1970s, Japan witnessed popular demonstrations against US interference. In 1972, under the administration of Eisaku SATO, the United States completed the return of the Ryukyu Islands (first acquired in 1874) to Japan.

In 1989 Hirohito died and was succeeded by his son, AKIHITO. The Liberal Democratic Party (LDP) governed Japan almost continuously from 1948 to 1993. The economic boom of the 1980s came to a sudden end in the early 1990s as Japan was rocked by a series of political corruption scandals. In 1993 the LDP split: the three splinter parties formed a short-lived coalition government. In 1994 a new electoral system was introduced with an element of proportional representation. Tomiichi Murayama became Japan's first socialist prime minister. In 1996 he was replaced by Ryutaro Hashimoto, leader of the LDP. In 1998 the economic crisis in Southeast Asia spread to Japan. The government's slow and inadequate response forced Hashimoto to resign. He was replaced as prime minister and leader of the LDP by Keizo Obuchi. In 2000 Obuchi suffered a stroke and was succeeded by Yoshiro Mori.

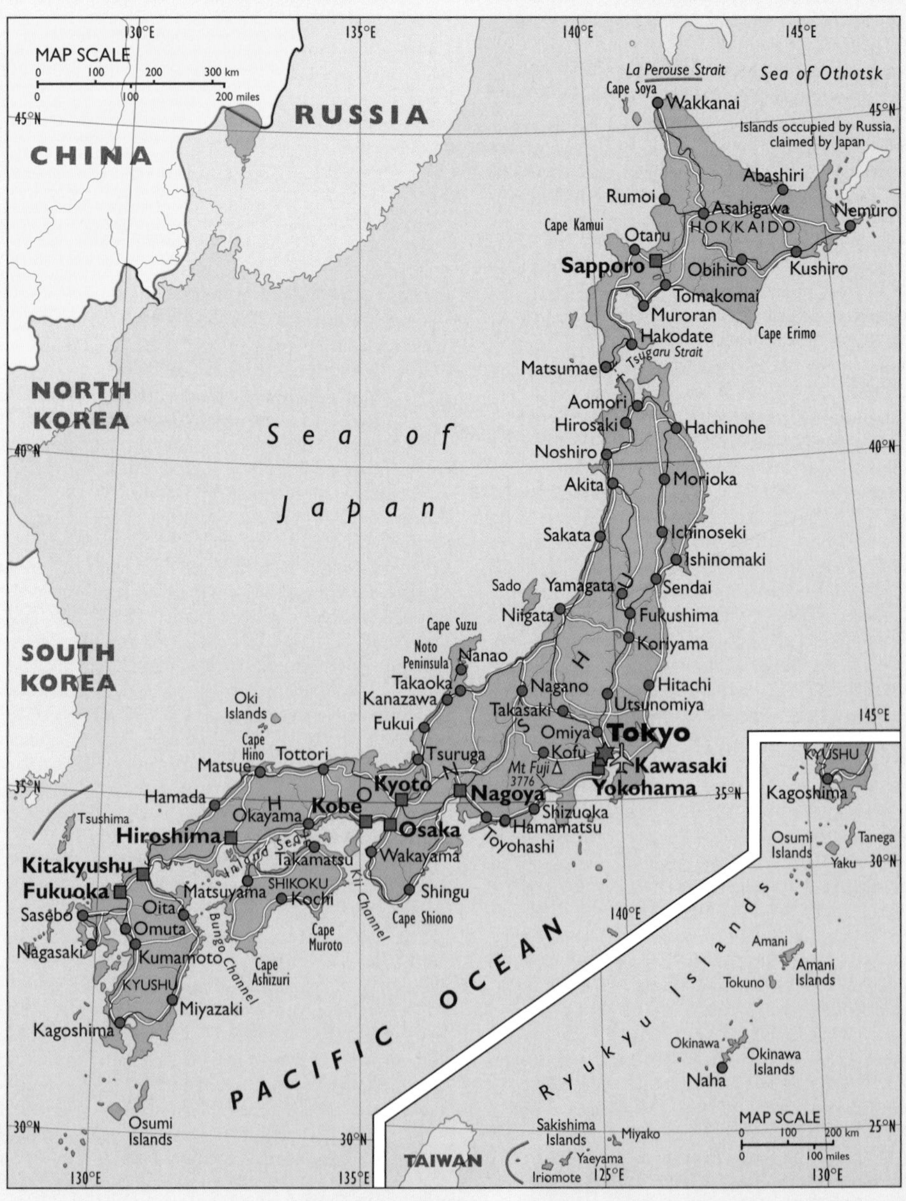

force until the 17th century, when discipline and military prestige declined. In the so-called "Auspicious Incident" (June 1826), the Janissaries rebelled against the attempted reform of the army by Sultan MAHMUD II. Mahmud crushed the mutiny, massacring thousands of Janissaries.

Jansenism Reform movement within the ROMAN CATHOLIC CHURCH, founded by Flemish theologian Cornelis Jansen (1585–1638). In *Augustinus* (published posthumously in 1640), Jansen defended the teachings of Saint AUGUSTINE, emphasizing the role of divine grace, accepting predestination, and condemning free will. He criticized the JESUITS for undermining divine law. In 1653 Pope INNOCENT X condemned the doctrines of Jansenism. The Cistercian Abbey of Port-Royal, Paris, became a centre of Jansenism. The expulsion of Antoine Arnauld from the Sorbonne, Paris, provoked the French philosopher Blaise Pascal to write his defence of Jansenism, *Les Provinciales* (1656–57). Jansenists were vigorously persecuted (1661–69) by LOUIS XIV of France until a compromise with Pope CLEMENT IX brought a period of peace (1669–79). In 1713 Pope CLEMENT XI renewed the attack on Jansenism. *See also* GALLICANISM

Japan *See* country feature

Jarrow March (October 1936) British protest march of unemployed workers from Jarrow, County Durham, to London. Unemployment was especially high in Jarrow, a small, shipbuilding town dependent on one company, which had closed down in 1933. About 200 people took part in the march, which highlighted the continuing poverty in the north of England. *See also* GREAT DEPRESSION

Jaruzelski, Wojciech (1923–) Polish general and statesman, prime minister (1981–85), head of state (1985–89) and president (1989–90). Jaruzelski fought in the Soviet-commanded Polish forces during World War 2. He joined the Polish Communist Party in 1947 and worked his way up the Party hierarchy, becoming a member of the Politburo in 1971. In 1981 Jaruzelski imposed martial law and banned the trade union SOLIDARITY, led by Lech WAŁESA. In 1988 he opened negotiations with Solidarity and approved the reform of the Polish government. Jaruzelski was replaced as president by Lech Wałesa.

Jaurès, Jean Léon (1859–1914) French socialist leader. He campaigned on behalf of Alfred Dreyfus in the DREYFUS AFFAIR. In 1899 the French socialist movement split in two: Jaurès formed the French Socialist Party, which supported cooperation with the French government and parliamentary SOCIALISM, while the Socialist Party of France opposed participation. In 1905 the two parties merged to form the French Section of the Workers' International (SFIO), now known simply as the SOCIALIST PARTY. Jaurès cofounded (1904) the socialist journal *L'Humanité*. He was assassinated by a nationalist fanatic for advocating arbitration rather than war with Germany.

Java (Jawa) Indonesian island, SE of Sumatra; the largest city is JAKARTA. The first fossilized remains of HOMO ERECTUS (Java man) were unearthed (1891) on Java. These early humans may have lived on Java from as early as *c*.1.8 mya. In the early centuries AD, Indian spice traders brought Hinduism and Buddhism to the islands. The influence of Indian culture is most evident in the Buddhist temple complex of BOROBUDUR (750–850), built by the SAILENDRA dynasty. The reign (1019–49) of Erlangga saw a flowering of Hindu culture. On his death, Java was divided, and the W portion, Kidira, became the centre of Javanese culture. At the end of the 13th century, Java was reunited under Kertanagara. Gajah Mada (r.1331–64) built the MAJAPAHIT EMPIRE, which dominated the Indonesian archipelago in the 14th century. The Majapahit dynasty fell to the Muslims in the 16th century. In 1619 the Dutch EAST INDIA COMPANY captured Jakarta, and one by one Java's Muslim kingdoms were forced to submit. The Dutch defeated a Javanese revolt (1825–30), led by DIPONEGORO. It was occupied by the Japanese during World War 2 and became the dominant member of the new Republic of Indonesia in 1949. Area: 126,501sq km (48,842sq mi). Pop. (1990) 107,581,306.

Java man *See* HOMO ERECTUS; HUMAN EVOLUTION

Java War (1825–30) *See* DIPONEGORO

Jawara, Sir Dawda Kairaba (1924–) Gambian statesman, prime minister (1965–70) and president (1970–94). Leader of the People's Progressive Party, he served as minister of education (1960–61) and chief minister (1962–65) when The GAMBIA was a British colony. Jawara led The Gambia to independence in 1965 and was elected president when it became a republic in 1970. He was re-elected on five occasions (1972, 1977, 1982, 1987, 1992). Jawara was overthrown in a coup (1994).

Jay, John (1745–1829) US statesman, first chief justice of the Supreme Court (1789–95). He was president (1778–79) of the CONTINENTAL CONGRESS. Jay and Benjamin FRANKLIN negotiated the Treaty of PARIS (1783) with Great Britain, ending the AMERICAN REVOLUTION. As secretary of foreign affairs (1784–89), Jay was frustrated by the weakness of central government as defined by the ARTICLES OF CONFEDERATION. Jay, Alexander HAMILTON and James MADISON defended the new CONSTITUTION OF THE UNITED STATES in *The* FEDERALIST (1787–88). In 1789 President George WASHINGTON appointed him chief justice. In 1794 he concluded JAY'S TREATY, which served to sharpen divisions between the FEDERALIST PARTY and the DEMOCRATIC-REPUBLICAN PARTY, the Federalists being accused of selling out to the British.

Jay's Treaty (1794) Agreement between the United States (represented by John JAY) and Great Britain (represented by Lord GRENVILLE), principally to settle points of dispute outstanding since the AMERICAN REVOLUTION. Its trade provisions helped establish American commerce. The United States agreed not to aid privateers hostile to Britain, while Britain withdrew from the Northwest Territory. The Mississippi River was declared open to both countries.

Jayavarman VII (*c*.1120–*c*.1215) King of the KHMER empire of ANGKOR (1181–*c*.1215). In 1177 Angkor was conquered by the Cham, and Jayavarman led the struggle for independence. In 1181 he liberated Angkor and went on to conquer CHAMPA (now S Vietnam), S Laos and parts of Burma and the Malay Peninsula. His reign was also marked by the construction of many impressive Buddhist temples, including the pyramid temple of Bayon. Jayavarman rebuilt the city of Angkor, constructed more than 100 hospitals, and greatly improved the road system.

Jayawardene, Junius Richard (1906–96) Sri Lankan statesman, prime minister (1977–78), president (1978–89). He was one of the founders of the United National Party (UNP). After Ceylon (now Sri Lanka) gained independence from Britain in 1948, Jayawardene held a number of cabinet posts before becoming leader of the UNP in 1973. In the 1977 election, he defeated Sirimavo BANDARANAIKE. As prime minister, he introduced a new constitution (1978), which gave the president executive powers. Jayawardene was elected as the first president under this system. He reversed the trend towards nationalization, encouraging private ownership and foreign investment. Jayawardene used military force to try to suppress the Tamil insurgency in NE Sri Lanka. His pro-Western economic policies led to some economic gains early in his first term. He retired in 1989.

Jefferson, Thomas (1743–1826) Third president of the United States (1801–09), vice president (1797–81). A prominent member of the Second CONTINENTAL CONGRESS, he was the leading writer of the DECLARATION OF INDEPENDENCE (1776). In the Virginia legislature, Jefferson proposed radical measures such as the reform of property laws, a comprehensive system of free public education and a statute for religious freedom. Jefferson succeeded Patrick HENRY as governor of VIRGINIA (1779–81), but his term was cut short by the outbreak of the AMERICAN REVOLUTION. In *Notes on Virginia* (1781), Jefferson outlines his opposition to SLAVERY but supports the notion of white superiority. He was also a slave-owner. Jefferson returned to Congress (1783–84) before succeeding Benjamin FRANKLIN as minister to France (1785–89). He was persuaded by George WASHINGTON to serve as his first secretary of state (1789–93). Disagreements with Alexander HAMILTON saw the formation of the DEMOCRATIC-REPUBLICAN PARTY led by Jefferson. Narrowly defeated by John ADAMS in the 1796 presidential election, Jefferson became vice president. He led opposition to the ALIEN AND SEDITION ACTS (1798). In the election of 1800, the Republican candidates Jefferson and Aaron BURR received the same number of votes and the House of Representatives chose Jefferson as president. The landmarks of Jefferson's first term as president were the LOUISIANA PURCHASE (1803) and the LEWIS AND CLARK EXPEDITION (1804–06). In 1804 Jefferson was re-elected and George CLINTON replaced Burr as vice president. Much of Jefferson's second term was consumed by the unsuccessful bid to convict his former vice president. Jefferson tried to remain neutral during the NAPOLEONIC WARS, passing the EMBARGO ACT (1807) in response to British and French interference with US merchant shipping. He opposed the growing power of the SUPREME COURT under Chief Justice John MARSHALL, signalled by the decision in MARBURY V. MADISON (1803). In 1809 Jefferson retired and was succeeded by James MADISON. Jefferson founded and designed the University of Virginia.

Jeffreys, George, 1st Baron (*c*.1645–89) English judge. A great supporter of CHARLES II and later JAMES II, Jeffreys presided over the trials (1678) of those Catholics implicated by Titus OATES in the so-called "Popish Plot". He became lord chief justice in 1683 and sentenced to death the organizers of the RYE HOUSE PLOT (1683). Jeffreys was also responsible for the imprisonment (1685) of the Puritan clergyman Richard BAXTER. He was appointed lord chancellor in 1685. Jeffreys' reputation for severity was enhanced by his judgements in the BLOODY ASSIZES (1685). After the GLORIOUS REVOLUTION (1688), Jeffreys was caught trying to flee the country and imprisoned in the Tower of London, where he died. *See also* MONMOUTH, JAMES SCOTT, DUKE OF

Jehovah's Witnesses Religious sect founded (1872) as the International Bible Students Association by Charles Taze Russell (1852–1916) in Pittsburgh, Pennsylvania. In 1884 they published the first edition of the magazine *The Watchtower*. The group was renamed (1931) the Jehovah's Witnesses by Russell's successor, Joseph Franklin Rutherford (1869–1942). Jehovah's

JEFFERSON, THOMAS

Thomas Jefferson founded his political initiatives on a belief in the freedom of the individual. He opposed political centralization and advocated federalism as a means of safeguarding the Constitution, an approach which became known as Jeffersonian democracy.

JEFFERSON IN HIS OWN WORDS

"I have sworn upon the altar of God, eternal hostility against every form of tyranny over the mind of man."
Letter to Dr Benjamin Rush, 1800

"Peace, commerce, and honest friendship with all nations – entangling alliances with none."
First inaugural address, 4 March 1801

J

Witnesses believe in the imminent end of the world for all except its own members. They hold to the theory of a theocratic kingdom, membership of which cannot be reconciled with allegiance to any country. They deny most fundamental Christian doctrines and believe the Bible prohibits blood transfusion and military service. Today, the sect has *c.*2 million members worldwide.

Jellicoe, John Rushworth, 1st Earl (1859–1935) British admiral. He was commander-in-chief (1914–16) of the Grand Fleet in World War 1. Jellicoe was initially criticized for failing to secure a decisive victory at the Battle of Jutland (1916), but it is now generally accepted that he was largely responsible for ensuring the domination of the British Royal Navy for the remainder of the war. He organized the convoy system of defence against U-boats. Jellicoe became admiral of the fleet in 1919. He served (1920–24) as governor general of New Zealand.

Jena, Battle of (14 October 1806) Decisive battle of the Napoleonic Wars, fought near Jena, Saxony. The French army under Napoleon I won a resounding victory over Frederick William III's Prussian army led by Prince Hohenlohe. In conjunction with the simultaneous French victory at Auerstädt, it led to the French capture of Berlin and the collapse of Prussia. The two battles cost *c.*12,000 French lives and *c.*24,000 Prussian and Saxon lives.

Jenkins (of Hillhead), Roy Harris, Baron (1920–) British statesman, home secretary (1965–67; 1974–76) and chancellor of the exchequer (1967–70). He was elected to Parliament in 1958. Jenkins served in Harold Wilson's Labour government. He acted as president (1977–81) of the European Commission. In 1981 Jenkins cofounded and became first leader of the Social Democratic Party (SDP). In 1983 he stood down in favour of David Owen. In 1998 Jenkins headed the commission that recommended the introduction of proportional representation (PR) in British elections. His historical biographies include *Mr Attlee* (1948) and *Gladstone* (1995).

Jenkins' Ear, War of (1738–40) Conflict between Britain and Spain that arose from commercial competition in Central and South America. The claim (1738) by Captain Robert Jenkins that his ear had been cut off by Spanish coastguards was one of a series of allegations against the Spanish made by British merchants to Parliament. Sir Robert Walpole reluctantly declared war on Spain. The British captured two Spanish-American ports in 1739 and 1740, but other attempts to seize Spanish positions were unsuccessful. From late 1740 the war merged into the War of the Austrian Succession.

Jeremiah (*c.*650–*c.*586 BC) Hebrew prophet who gave his name to the Old Testament Book of Jeremiah. He spoke out against social injustices in Jerusalem during the reign of Josiah, prophesizing the fall of Judah to Babylon. In *c.*587 BC Nebuchadnezzar II captured Judah. Jeremiah remained in the city and was later exiled in Egypt. His revelations were preserved by his secretary Baruch.

Jericho (Ariha) Ancient city of Palestine, on the West Bank of the River Jordan. It is one of the earliest known sites of continuous settlement, dating from *c.*9000 BC. According to the Old Testament, Joshua captured Jericho from the Canaanites (*c.*300 BC) when the city walls collapsed at the blast of the army's trumpets. Herod the Great (d.4 BC) later constructed a magnificent Italianate palace. Jericho became an Arab city in the 7th century and was occupied by Crusaders in the 12th and 13th centuries. It came under British control in 1920 and passed to Jordan in 1949. Jericho received a large influx of Palestinian refugees from the newly created state of Israel. It was captured by Israel during the Six-Day War (1967). In 1993 Jericho was selected as the centre for Palestinian self-rule. Pop. (1994 est.) 25,000. *See also* Canaan

Jeroboam I (active late 10th century BC) King of the N kingdom of Israel (c.922–c.901 BC). He led an unsuccessful revolt against King Solomon and was forced into exile in Egypt. After Solomon's death, Jeroboam returned to become king of the secessionist kingdom of Israel in Palestine's northern hills, while Solomon's successor, Rehoboam, continued to rule Judah in the south.

Jerome, Saint (*c.*342–*c.*420) Christian scholar, Doctor of the Church, author of the Vulgate Bible, b. Dalmatia as Eusebius Hieronymous. He studied in Rome and then travelled to Antioch. Jerome lived as a hermit in the desert before returning to Rome. He acted as papal secretary (382–85) to Pope Damasus I. In 386 Jerome settled in Jerusalem, where he founded a monastery and compiled the Latin version of the Bible. His works were influential in the early Middle Ages. His feast day is 30 September.

Jerusalem Capital of Israel, a sacred site for Christians, Jews and Muslims. Originally a Jebusite stronghold (2000–1500 BC), the city was captured (*c.*1000 BC) by King David. David's successor, Solomon, built the Temple of Jerusalem. The destruction (*c.*587 BC) of Jerusalem by Nebuchadnezzar II marked the start of the Babylonian Captivity of the Jews. In 538 BC Cyrus II (the Great) permitted the Jews to return. Jerusalem fell to Alexander III (the Great) in 333 BC. Greek rule was overthrown by the Revolt of the Maccabees (164 BC). Jerusalem was rebuilt from 40 BC by Herod (the Great). In AD 6 Rome assumed direct rule and it was the Roman procurator, Pontius Pilate, who sentenced Jesus Christ to death. In AD 70 the city was destroyed by Titus. Hadrian established the Roman colony of Aelia Capitolina, and Jews were forbidden within city limits until the 5th century. Many of Jerusalem's Christian monuments, including the Church of the Holy Sepulchre, were built (4th century) by Constantine I (the Great). In 614 Christian control was ended by the Iranians. The Muslim Caliph Abd al-Malik built (688–691) the Dome of the Rock. In 1071 Jerusalem was conquered by the Seljuk Turks, whose maltreatment of Christians precipitated the Crusades. The Crusaders created the Kingdom of Jerusalem. In 1187 the Kingdom was overthrown by Saladin, but Christian rule was restored in 1229 and continued until Jerusalem was sacked by the Turks in 1244. In 1247 the Mamluks seized the city; Egyptian control lasted until Sultan Selim I captured (1517) the city for the Ottoman Empire. Jerusalem declined under Ottoman rule until Egyptian ruler Ibrahim Pasha held the city (1831–40) and imposed reforms. When British troops entered Jerusalem in 1917, about half the city's population was Jewish. Jerusalem became the capital of the British-mandated territory of Palestine. In 1948 the city was divided between Jordan (East Jerusalem) and the new state of Israel (West Jerusalem). In the Six-Day War (1967), the Israeli army captured the Old City of East Jerusalem. In 1980 the united city was declared the capital of Israel, but this status is not recognized by the United Nations (UN). Other notable monuments in the Old City include the El Aqsa Mosque and the Western Wall. Pop. (1992) 544,200.

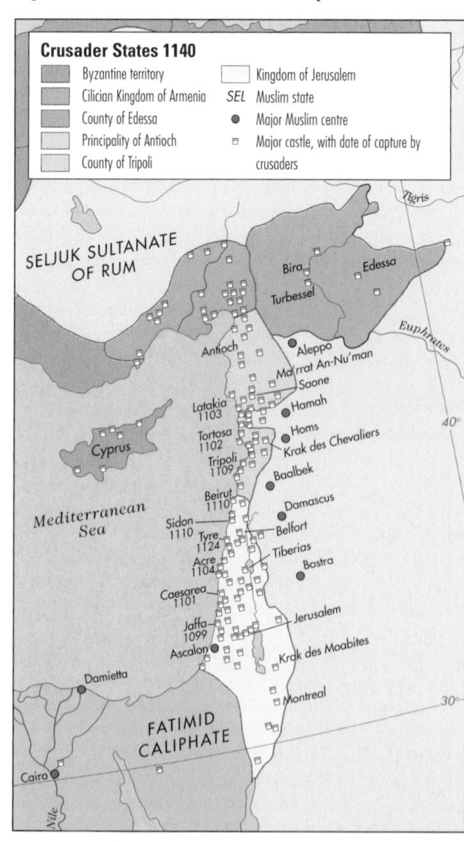

▲ Jerusalem, Kingdom of The Kingdom of Jerusalem expanded rapidly between 1099 and 1140, but lacked sufficient military manpower to defend itself against Muslim invaders.

Jerusalem, Kingdom of Feudal state created in Palestine and Syria by the Crusaders. After Jerusalem fell in the First Crusade (1099), Godfrey of Bouillon became Defender of the Royal Sepulchre. On Godfrey's death (1100), his brother, Baldwin I, became king of Jerusalem. He and his successor, Baldwin II, expanded the kingdom, which at its height (1140s) extended beyond the area of modern Israel to include s Lebanon and sw Jordan. The neighbouring principality of Antioch and counties of Edessa and Tripoli were vassal Crusader states. All four states were constantly under threat, and from the 1140s many Crusader lords found it necessary to hand over their more exposed strongholds to the military orders, such as the Knights Templar. Attempts by Almaric I (r.1163–74) to conquer Egypt were overcome by Saladin, who captured Jerusalem in 1187 and came close to completely extinguishing all the Crusader states. Acre became the capital of the Crusader Kingdom of Jerusalem, which gradually declined, despite the recovery of the city of Jerusalem by Emperor Frederick II in 1228. The Kingdom was fatally weakened when Jerusalem was captured and sacked by the Turks in 1244 and captured by the Mamluks of Egypt in 1247. It finally collapsed with the reconquest of Acre by the Mamluks in 1291.

Jervis, John, Earl of St Vincent (1735–1823) British naval officer. He held important commands during the French Revolutionary Wars and, thanks largely to the efforts of Horatio Nelson, won a spectacular victory over a larger Spanish fleet at the Battle of Cape St Vincent (1797). As first lord of the admiralty (1801–04), Jervis initiated many basic and necessary reforms.

Jesuits Members of the Society of Jesus (SJ), a Roman Catholic religious order for men founded (1534) by Saint Ignatius of Loyola and Francis Xavier and approved by Pope Paul III (1540). The Jesuits were the leading force in the Counter-Reformation. They were active missionaries, most notably in South America, where they established settled communities of Native Americans under the control of a priest. The Jesuits antagonized many European rulers because they gave allegiance only to their general in Rome and to the pope. In 1773, under pressure from the kings of France, Spain and Portugal, Pope Clement XIV abolished the order, but it continued to exist in Russia. The order was re-established in 1814 by Pope Pius VII.

Jesus Christ (active 1st century AD) Jewish preacher who founded the religion of Christianity, hailed and worshipped by his followers as the Son of God. Knowledge of Jesus' life is based mostly on the biblical gospels of Saints Matthew, Mark and Luke. The date of Jesus' birth in Bethlehem, Judaea, is conventionally given as *c.*4 BC, near the end of the reign of Herod (the Great). Mary, believed by Christians to have been made miraculously pregnant, gave birth to Jesus. The birth was said to have taken place in a stable and been attended by the appearance of a bright star and other unusual events. Jesus grew up in Nazareth and may have followed Mary's husband, Joseph, in becoming a carpenter. In *c.*AD 27 Jesus was baptized in the River Jordan by John the Baptist. Thereafter Jesus began his own ministry, preaching to large numbers throughout Judaea. He also taught a special group of 12 close disciples, who were later sent out as Apostles to bring his teachings to the Jews. Jesus' basic teaching, summarized in the Sermon on the Mount, was to "love God and love one's neighbour". He taught that salvation depended on doing God's will rather than adhering to the letter and the contemporary interpretation of the Torah. Such a precept angered the hierarchy of the Jewish religion. In *c.*AD 30 Jesus and his disciples went to Jerusalem. His reputation as preacher and miracle-worker preceded him, and he was acclaimed as the Messiah. A few days later Jesus gathered his disciples to partake in the Last Supper. At this meal, he instituted the Eucharist. Before dawn the next day, Jesus was arrested by the religious authorities of Jerusalem, accompanied by Judas Iscariot, and summarily tried by the SANHEDRIN, the Supreme Council of the Jews. He was then handed to the Roman procurator, PONTIUS PILATE, on a charge of sedition. Roman soldiers crucified Jesus at Golgotha (Calvary). After his death, Jesus' body was buried in a sealed rock tomb. Two days later, according to the gospel accounts, he rose from the dead and appeared to his disciples and to others. Forty days after his resurrection, he is said to have ascended into heaven.

Jewel, John (1522–71) English Protestant leader. He went into exile during the reign of the Catholic MARY I but returned to England on the accession of the Protestant ELIZABETH I. He was made bishop of Salisbury in 1560. His defence of the Church of England against Rome, *Apologia pro Ecclesia Anglicana* (1562), formed the groundwork for all subsequent discussion about the positions of the English and Roman churches.

Jews Traditionally, the descendants of JUDAH, fourth son of JACOB, who settled in ancient Palestine towards the end of the 2nd millennium BC; historically, followers of the religion of JUDAISM. In *c*.1020 BC SAUL founded the Hebrew state of ISRAEL. DAVID (r.1006–966 BC) united the kingdoms of ISRAEL and JUDAH. Under his son, SOLOMON, who built the TEMPLE OF JERUSALEM, the kingdom prospered. After Solomon's death the kingdom once more divided into Israel and Judah. In *c*.587 BC the Temple was destroyed by NEBUCHADNEZZAR II. Jews were deported from JERUSALEM, beginning the period of the BABYLONIAN CAPTIVITY. In 538 BC CYRUS II (THE GREAT) delivered the Jews from Babylon. In the 2nd century BC the MACCABEE dynasty gained political independence from the Greeks. In AD 70 the Temple was destroyed, for a second time, by the Romans, and the DIASPORA began. The descendants of Jews who emigrated to Spain and Portugal are known as the SEPHARDIM; those who settled in NW Europe are known as the ASHKENAZIM. In Christian Europe, Jews were victims of ANTI-SEMITISM. In 1290 Jews were driven out of England. In 1492, as part of the INQUISITION, they were expelled from Spain. During World War 2 (1939–45), six million Jews were killed in the HOLOCAUST. In 1948, having struggled against British rule in modern Palestine, the Jews proclaimed the state of ISRAEL in the face of opposition from Arab and other Islamic states. Today, there are *c*.18 million Jews worldwide, including *c*.7 million in the USA and *c*.5 million in Israel. *See also* FALASHAS; ZIONISM

Jezebel (d. *c*.843 BC) Phoenician princess who became the wife of AHAB, king of Israel. She introduced into Israel the worship of the Phoenician deity Baal and came into conflict with the priests of Yahweh. Jezebel clashed with the prophet ELIJAH, who foretold her brutal death. She was crushed under the chariot of the usurper, Jehu.

Jiang Qing (1914–92) Chinese politician, third wife of MAO ZEDONG. A former actress, she became a high-ranking party official and a leader of the CULTURAL REVOLUTION. One of the radical GANG OF FOUR that sought power after Mao's death in 1976, Jiang was arrested (1977), convicted of treason and imprisoned for life.

Jiangxi (Kiangsi) Province in SE China; the capital is Nanchang. During the ZHOU dynasty (770–435 BC), Jiangxi formed part of the kingdom of Chu. It developed rapidly as part of the province of Yangzhou during the HAN dynasty (206 BC–AD 220), and this growth accelerated under the TANG dynasty (618–907) with the opening of the GRAND CANAL. Jiangxi was a centre of CONFUCIANISM during the SONG dynasty (960–1279), but became a focus of unrest in the MING dynasty (1368–1644). The period of QING rule (1644–1911) brought renewed prosperity until the devastation wreaked by the TAIPING REBELLION (1851–64). In 1927 the communists staged a revolt in Nanchang. Jiangxi became a centre for MAO ZEDONG and ZHU DE's guerrilla campaign against CHIANG KAI-SHEK's Nationalist government. In 1934 Chiang captured Jiangxi and the communists were forced to embark on the LONG MARCH (1934–35) to NW China. From 1938 to 1945 much of Jiangxi was under Japanese control. In 1949 the communists Jiangxi. Area: 164,865sq km (63,654sq mi). Pop. (1990) 38,280,000.

Jiang Zemin (1926–) Chinese statesman, general secretary (1989–) of the Chinese COMMUNIST PARTY (CCP). A cautious proponent of reform, he was elected to the central committee in 1982 and served (1985–88) as mayor of Shanghai. He became a member of the Politburo in 1987. Jiang succeeded ZHAO ZIYANG as general secretary. In 1997 he replaced DENG XIAOPING as China's paramount leader. *See also* LI PENG

jihad (jehad) Religious obligation placed upon Muslims through the KORAN to spread ISLAM and protect its followers by waging war on non-believers. There are four ways in which Muslims may fulfil their jihad duty: by the heart, by the tongue, by the hand and by the sword. *See also* MUJAHEDDIN; USMAN DAN FODIO

Jim Crow laws Discriminatory laws enacted in Southern US states after the end (1877) of the RECONSTRUCTION period. They enforced racial segregation in public places, including schools, and on public transport. They were overturned by the CIVIL-RIGHTS legislation of the 1950s and 1960s. *See also* BLACK CODES

Jiménez de Cisneros, Francisco, Cardinal (1436–1517) Spanish cardinal and statesman. In 1492 he became confessor to ISABELLA I of Castile. As archbishop of Toledo (from 1495), Jiménez introduced wide-ranging reforms of the Spanish clergy and enforced mass conversions of the Moors. After Isabella's death (1504), he briefly acted (1506) as regent of Castile for FERDINAND V, who rewarded him with the position of grand inquisitor in 1507. Jiménez followed the example of Tomás de TORQUEMADA in his strict enforcement of the INQUISITION and was the motivating force behind the Spanish crusade to conquer North Africa. On the death of Ferdinand (1516), Jiménez once again became regent of Castile and helped to facilitate the smooth accession (1517) of Ferdinand's grandson Charles (later Emperor CHARLES V).

Jin (AD 265–317) (Western Jin) Chinese dynasty. After the collapse of the HAN empire (AD 220), China divided into the three rival kingdoms of Wei (North China), Wu (South China) and Shu (Sichuan). In *c*.264 the Shu kingdom was subsumed into the Wei. In 265 General Ssu-ma Yen (later known as Wudi) usurped the Wei throne and, after he overthrew the ruler of Wu (280), China was reunited. After Wudi's death (290), the country was divided among his sons, precipitating the civil war known as the "Revolt of the Eight Kings". As central government collapsed, the empire became vulnerable to attack from N nomads. In 311 the Xiongu captured the Jin capital, Luoyang, and killed the emperor. The Jin temporarily regrouped in Changan, but this also fell to the Xiongu in 316. In 317 the Jin established a court at NANJING, E China. This **Eastern Jin** dynasty forms one of the so-called SIX DYNASTIES.

Jin (1126–1234) Dynasty in N China. It was founded by a confederation of Juchen tribes from the mountains of E MANCHURIA after they had defeated the Liao state to the N of China. They captured the SONG capital of Kaifeng in 1126, forcing the Song to retreat southwards. The Jin dynasty was unable to resist the Mongol raids launched by GENGHIS KHAN in 1207 and much of its empire was under Mongol control by 1215.

Jinnah, Muhammad Ali (1876–1948) Indian statesman, founder of PAKISTAN. Jinnah joined the Indian National CONGRESS in 1906 and the All-India MUSLIM LEAGUE in 1913. He worked to achieve Hindu-Muslim unity, encouraging the two organizations to hold joint annual sessions and draw up the Lucknow Pact (1916) that agreed on proposals for constitutional reform. In 1920 Jinnah left the Congress because of his opposition to "Mahatma" GANDHI's policy of non-cooperation. He continued to believe in the importance of Hindu-Muslim unity and sought to secure concessions from Congress leaders, among them one-third representation for Muslims in any central legislature. The failure of his conciliatory approach caused division within the League and Jinnah moved to England (1930–35). In 1935 he returned to India and led the Muslim League in the elections of 1937. When the victorious Congress decided not to include any members of the League in the new provincial assemblies, Jinnah began to turn towards the idea of creating a separate Muslim state, Pakistan. At his instigation, the Muslim League adopted the idea as policy in 1940. During 1946–47 Jinnah rejected attempts by Gandhi, Jawaharlal NEHRU and Lord MOUNTBATTEN to arrive at a compromise that would maintain the unity of India, and in 1947 Pakistan became a separate state. Jinnah became the state's first governor general and at his death was revered as the father of the nation.

Joan of Arc, Saint (*c*.1412–31) (Jeanne d'Arc) French saint and national heroine, also known as Joan of Lorraine or the Maid of Orléans. A peasant girl, she claimed to hear heavenly voices urging her to save France during the HUNDRED YEARS' WAR. In 1429 Joan of Arc led French troops in breaking the English siege of Orléans. She drove the English from the Loire towns and persuaded the indecisive dauphin to have himself crowned as CHARLES VII of France at Reims. In 1430 Joan of Arc was captured by PHILIP III (THE GOOD), Duke of Burgundy, and handed over to the English. Condemned as a heretic, she was burned at the stake. Joan was canonized in 1920. Her feast day is 30 May. *See also* HENRY VI

Jodl, Alfred (1890–1946) German general, chief of the armed forces operations staff (1939–45). Jodl directed all Germany's military campaigns during World War 2, except the launch of the invasion of Russia (1941). A brilliant soldier, he was nevertheless utterly subservient to HITLER and did nothing to restrain the *führer*'s military ambitions. In 1945 Jodl signed the surrender of Germany at Reims, France. At the NUREMBERG TRIALS, he was found guilty of war crimes and hanged. *See also* KEITEL, WILHELM

Joffre, Joseph Jacques Césaire (1852–1931) French marshal. He was commander in chief (1914–16) of the French armies during WORLD WAR I. His mass offensive across the Franco-German border was a catastrophic failure as the "SCHLIEFFEN PLAN" saw Germany march through Belgium and threaten to encircle the French army. Once he became aware of the German advance on the French left flank, however, Joffre quickly created a new army that prevented the capture of Paris. Joffre then launched a counter-offensive at the First Battle of the MARNE (1914). This ended German hopes for a swift victory on the Western

◀ **Joan of Arc** Painting, entitled *Joan of Arc at the stake*, featured in *Les Vigils de Charles VII* (15th century). Joan of Arc was put on trial for believing she was responsible to God rather than the Roman Catholic Church. Her claim to have followed divine guidance, in the form of visions, and her adoption of male dress were regarded as blasphemous. Burned at the stake for refusing to submit to the church, she became a legendary figure. An inquiry ordered by Charles VII two years later led to her sentence being annulled (1456) by the church.

Front and the War became bogged down in the trenches. Joffre's attempts to break through the German lines resulted in heavy casualties and, after further heavy losses at VERDUN and the SOMME (both 1916), he resigned.

John, Saint (active 1st century AD) (St John the Apostle or St John the Evangelist) In the New Testament, one of the 12 disciples of JESUS CHRIST, son of Zebedee and brother of Saint JAMES THE GREAT. He is traditionally held to be the author of the Gospel According to Saint John and the three epistles of John. Together with Saint James and Saint PETER, Saint John belonged to the inner group of disciples. He was active in the organization of the early church at Jerusalem. His feast day is 27 December.

John VIII (820–882) Pope (872–882). He supported Saint Methodius against his German enemies, who rejected the use of the Slavic language for the liturgy. In 879 he reinstated PHOTIUS as patriarch of Constantinople. His alliance with LOUIS II (THE GERMAN) failed to prevent the SARACEN invasion of S Italy. He crowned (875, 881) two emperors of the West: CHARLES II (THE BALD) and CHARLES III (THE FAT).

John XXII (*c.*1245–1334) Pope (1316–34), b. Jacques Duèse. The second of the AVIGNON popes, he succeeded CLEMENT V. John XXII persecuted the Spiritual faction of the FRANCISCANS for their narrow interpretation of the monastic rule of poverty and later (*c.*1323) condemned the entire Franciscan doctrine of poverty. John entered into the dispute between Louis of Bavaria (later Emperor LOUIS IV) and Frederick of Austria over the imperial succession. In 1324 John excommunicated Louis after the latter had upheld the supremacy of conciliar authority. In 1328 Louis appointed an antipope, Nicholas V, who reigned for two years before abdicating. John added to the body of canon law and swelled the coffers of the papal treasury.

John XXIII (1370–1419) ANTIPOPE (1410–15), b. Baldassare Cossa. Elected antipope by the Council of Pisa (1409), John was persuaded by Emperor SIGISMUND to convoke the Council of CONSTANCE (1414) to end the GREAT SCHISM. The Council called for John's resignation along with the other papal contenders, GREGORY XII (Rome) and Benedict XIII (Avignon). John fled but was brought back and forced to resign. He was imprisoned until 1418 when he acknowledged MARTIN V as pope.

John XXIII (1881–1963) Pope (1958–63). b. Angelo Giuseppe Roncalli. In 1944 John became papal nuncio to France and was made a cardinal in 1953. Regarded as a compromise successor to PIUS XII, John XXIII astonished the Curia by convoking the first ECUMENICAL COUNCIL in nearly one hundred years. In accordance with John's support for ecumenism, the Second VATICAN COUNCIL (1962–65) promoted reform within the Catholic Church. John acted as mediator between President John Kennedy and Soviet Premier Nikita Khrushchev during the CUBAN MISSILE CRISIS (1962). His encyclical *Peace on Earth* (1963) called for greater compassion between nations and denominations. He was succeeded by PAUL VI.

John I (Tzimisces) (925–76) Byzantine emperor (969–76). He conspired to assassinate his former comrade-in-arms, Emperor Nicephorus II. John secured the Balkan borders of the BYZANTINE EMPIRE by defeating the Bulgars (970) and the Russians (971) and marrying the Byzantine princess Theophano to the future Holy Roman Emperor Otto II. He also extended Byzantine power by capturing (974–75) Antioch and Damascus, Syria, from the FATIMIDS.

John II (Comnenus) (1088–1143) Byzantine emperor (1118–43), son and successor of ALEXIUS I (COMNENUS). John spent most of his reign fighting to regain lost Byzantine territories. After dealing with threats from the Pechenegs, Hungarians, and Serbs in the W, he turned to the E, reconquering Cilicia in 1137 but failing to make much progress in Syria.

John III Dukas Vatatzes (1193–1254) Emperor of Nicaea (1222–54). Under John's leadership, the empire of NICAEA (now Iznik, Turkey) emerged as the most powerful of the Greek states during the period of Latin rule in CONSTANTINOPLE. Through military conquest, he expanded the empire to include parts of Bulgaria and Epirus. He led an unsuccessful siege of Constantinople in 1235 and subsequently sought aid from western rulers, such as Emperor FREDERICK II, to help him capture the city. He was canonized 50 years after his death.

John V (Palaeologus) (1332–91) Byzantine emperor (1341–76, 1379–91). His regency was marked by a civil war (1341–47) that ended with his father's chief minister, John Cantacuzenue, being crowned co-emperor (1347–54). In 1354, with aid from Venice, he forced the pro-Ottoman Cantacuzenue to abdicate. The West promised to help counter the threat from the Ottoman Turks in return for John's recognition of the Roman Catholic Church. No assistance was provided, however, and the Turks captured much of Macedonia and forced John to pay tribute. In 1376 John was deposed by his son, Andronicus IV, but was later restored to the throne by the Turks.

John (1167–1216) King of England (1199–1216), youngest son of HENRY II and ELEANOR OF AQUITAINE. In 1193, with his elder brother RICHARD I (THE LIONHEART) still absent on the Third CRUSADE, John conspired with PHILIP II of France to seize the throne of England. The plot was foiled, and John was banished and deprived of his estates (1194). John nevertheless succeeded Richard as king. In 1200 John married Isabella of Angoulême, precipitating a war with Philip II that resulted in the loss of Normandy (1204) and almost all of the other English possessions in France. John ruthlessly imposed new taxes on the nobles in order to finance a further war. In 1209 John was excommunicated by Pope INNOCENT III for refusing to accept Stephen LANGTON as archbishop of Canterbury. John proceeded to amass much needed revenue from the church, before relenting (1212) in order to gain papal support against Philip II. His nephew and ally, Emperor OTTO IV, was decisively defeated by Philip at the Battle of BOUVINES (1214) and John's attack on La Rochelle floundered. On his return to England, John faced civil war and, following the rebels' capture of London (May 1215), was compelled to sign the MAGNA CARTA at Runnymede (19 June 1215). His continued disregard of feudal rights, however, led to the first of the BARONS' WARS (1215–17). He was succeeded by his son, HENRY III.

John II (the Good) (1319–64) King of France (1350–64), son of PHILIP VI. During the first phase of the HUNDRED YEARS' WAR (1337–1453), John was captured by EDWARD THE BLACK PRINCE at the Battle of POITIERS (1356) and taken as prisoner to England. John's son, later CHARLES V (THE WISE), acted as regent and had to contend with the JACQUERIE insurrection. The Treaty of BRÉTIGNY (1360) released John in return for a ransom of 3 million gold crowns and most of SW France. France was unable to meet the huge ransom demand and John returned to England, where he died. *See also* EDWARD III

John I (1487–1540) (John Zápolya) King of Hungary (1526–40). As governor of Transylvania (1511–26), John crushed the peasant rebellion of 1514. After Louis II of Hungary was killed by the Ottomans at the Battle of MOHÁCS (1526), Hungary was plunged into a war (1526–38) of succession between John and the HABSBURG claimant Ferdinand (later Emperor FERDINAND I). John received the military support of Sultan SULEIMAN I (THE MAGNIFICENT). The conflict was resolved by the Treaty of Nagyvárad (1538) which gave John two-thirds of Hungary, while Ferdinand received the remaining portion of W Hungary and Croatia. With the aid of Suleiman, John was succeeded by his infant son, JOHN II.

John II (1540–71) (John Sigismund Zápolya) King of Hungary (1540–71) and prince of Transylvania, son and successor of JOHN I. In 1541 Ottoman Sultan SULEIMAN I (THE MAGNIFICENT) invaded Hungary, ostensibly to protect John II's interests against Emperor FERDINAND I, and placed the government in the hands of George Martinuzzi. Martinuzzi was assassinated by Ferdinand I and, in a later peace agreement between Suleiman and Ferdinand, John's territory was reduced in size.

John I (1459–1501) (Jan Albert) King of Poland (1492–1501), son of CASIMIR IV. His reign saw the first meeting (1493) of the Sejm (Polish parliament). John recognized feudal privileges and conceded wide powers to the Sejm in return for financial assistance. In 1497 he launched an unsuccessful invasion of Moldavia and the remainder of his reign was spent defending Poland from the TATARS.

John II (1609–72) (Jan Casimir) King of Poland (1648–68), son of SIGISMUND III. His turbulent reign is known in Polish history as "the Deluge". John's defeat (1651) of the COSSACKS and TATARS in Ukraine led to an alliance between the Cossacks and Russia. He was forced into temporary exile (1655) when CHARLES X of Sweden occupied most of Poland, and John ceded (1660) N Livonia to Sweden. The war with Russia ended (1667) with the loss of most E Ukraine and half of Belorussia. With Poland greatly weakened, John abdicated.

John III (1624–96) (Jan Sobieski) King of Poland (1674–96). In 1665, after distinguishing himself in the Polish-Swedish War (1655–60) and against the Cossacks, he was appointed commander in chief by JOHN II. In 1673 he gained a brilliant victory against the Turks at Khotin and was elected king the following year. In 1676 he made peace with the Ottoman Turks, but also formed a defensive alliance (1683) with Emperor LEOPOLD I to counter the Turkish threat. At the Battle of Kahlenberg (1683), John defeated a superior Turkish force to raise the siege of Vienna. John pursued the retreating Ottoman army into Hungary. In 1683 he ended the threat of the Ottomans in SE Poland, but his failure (1684–91) to free Moldavia and Wallachia from Ottoman rule fuelled domestic unrest.

John I (1357–1433) (John of Aviz) King of Portugal (1385–1433), half-brother of FERDINAND I. During his reign, Ferdinand had compromised the future independence of Portugal by marrying his daughter to John I of Castile. On Ferdinand's death (1383), John of Aviz led resistance to the Castilian succession. John was duly elected king and Nuno Álvares Pereira defeated the Castilian army at the Battle of Aljubarrota (1385). In 1386 John formed an alliance with England and sealed the agreement by marrying Philippa, daughter of JOHN OF GAUNT. In 1415 John captured Ceuta, Morocco, the first European possession in Africa. Further overseas terrritories were acquired by John's son, HENRY THE NAVIGATOR.

John II (the Perfect Prince) (1455–95) King of Portugal (1481–95), son and successor of ALFONSO V. He ruthlessly imposed authority over the nobles, culminating in the execution (1483) of the Duke of Braganza. John supported the voyages of exploration along the coast of W Africa, which brought great mineral wealth to Portugal. He sponsored the voyage (1488) of Bartholomeu DIAS, who discovered it was possible to sail round the Cape of Good Hope. John negotiated the Treaty of TORDESILLAS (1494), which divided the New World between Portugal and Spain. He was succeeded by his cousin and brother-in-law, MANUEL I.

John III (the Pious) (1502–57) King of Portugal (1521–57), son and successor of MANUEL I. The start of his reign was marked by two marriage alliances with the Habsburg Emperor CHARLES V. John financed the first Portuguese settlement in Brazil (1533) and expanded the Portuguese empire in Asia with the capture (1535) of Diu, W India, and the founding of a colony at Macao, SE China. Although Portugal gained the Moluccas by the Treaty of Madrid (1529), the spice trade failed to halt the decline in Portugal's economy. In 1536 John introduced the INQUISITION into Portugal and generally favoured clerical, particularly Jesuit, interests.

John IV (the Fortunate) (1605–56) King of Portugal (1640–56), founder of the BRAGANZA dynasty. He was one of the leaders of a Portuguese revolt against Spanish rule (1640). As king, John formed an alliance with England as protection from Spain. Portuguese independence was confirmed by victory over the Spanish at Montijo (1644). Victories over the Dutch off the coast of Brazil restored Portugal's possessions in South America.

John V (1689–1750) King of Portugal (1706–50), son of Pedro II. He came to the throne during the War of the SPANISH SUCCESSION (1701–14) but managed to keep Portugal's participation in the conflict to a minimum. With the mineral wealth from the Portuguese colony of Brazil, John was able to rule without the Cortes (Spanish parliament). He kept a luxurious court and was a generous patron of the church, education and culture. John was succeeded by his son Joseph.

John VI (1767–1826) King of Portugal (1816–26). Because of the insanity of his mother, MARIA I, John was effectively ruler from 1792 and officially regent from 1799. In 1807 he fled to Brazil to escape the invading army of NAPOLEON I and supported the Duke of WELLINGTON's campaigns against the French occupation. He became king on the death of Maria but did not return to claim the throne until 1822, when he accepted the constitutional government proclaimed in 1820. He defeated a rebellion by his son Dom MIGUEL in 1824. His other son became PEDRO I of Brazil. *See also* CONTINENTAL SYSTEM

John III (1537–92) King of Sweden (1568–92), son of GUSTAVUS I (VASA). Perceived as a threat by his half-brother ERIC XIV, John was imprisoned (1563–67). He then allied with his brother Charles (later CHARLES IX) to overthrow Eric. As king, John negotiated the Treaty of Stettin (1570) which ended the war with Denmark. John introduced (1577) his own liturgy which sought to restore elements of the Catholic rites. He vainly attempted to reconcile the Swedish Lutheran Church with the Roman Catholic Church. Sweden regained much of Estonia when it joined with Poland in a war (1578–93) against Russia. He was succeeded by his son, SIGISMUND III (VASA).

John Birch Society Libertarian, anti-communist organization in the United States, founded (1958) by Robert Welch (1898–1985). It is named after John Birch (1918–45), a US Army intelligence officer, killed by Chinese communists. The Society's aim is "less government, more responsibility, and a better world". It is opposed to the United Nations (UN) and the North Atlantic Treaty Organization (NATO). Its headquarters are in Appleton, Wisconsin.

John of Austria (1545–78) Spanish general, illegitimate son of Emperor CHARLES V. In 1569–70 he was appointed by PHILIP II of Spain to suppress a revolt by the Moors in Granada. John commanded the HOLY LEAGUE fleet that defeated the Turks at the Battle of LEPANTO (1571). In 1573 he captured Tunis, N Africa. In 1576 he was appointed governor general of the Netherlands in order to quell the REVOLT OF THE NETHERLANDS (1568–1648) against Spanish rule. After Holland and Zeeland rejected the Perpetual Edict (1577), John resorted to his favoured means of forceful persuasion.

John of Gaunt, Duke of Lancaster (1340–99) English prince, fourth son of EDWARD III and father of HENRY IV, b. Ghent, Belgium. In 1362 he acquired the duchy of Lancaster through marriage. John fought (1367–74) in the HUNDRED YEARS' WAR (1337–1453), taking command of the English forces after the illness of his brother, EDWARD THE BLACK PRINCE. His second marriage, to Constance, daughter of Peter the Cruel of Castile, gained him a claim to the throne of Castile. He was effective ruler of England during the senility of his father and supported the religious reforms of John WYCLIFFE. John acted as a mediator between his nephew RICHARD II and the Earl of Gloucester. *See also* LANCASTER, HOUSE OF

John of Salisbury (1115–80) English scholar, bishop of Chartres (1176–80). He was secretary to Theobald and Thomas à BECKET, archbishops of Canterbury. His most important works were *Policraticus* (1159), a treatise on government, and the *Metalogicon* (1159), in which he presented a picture of the intellectual and scholastic controversies of the time. *See also* SCHOLASTICISM

John of the Cross, Saint (1542–91) Spanish mystic and poet, b. Juan de Yepes y Álvarez. With Saint TERESA OF AVILA he founded the Discalced Carmelites, a branch of the CARMELITE order. John's spiritual poems, such as "The Dark Night of the Soul", are regarded as the pinnacle of Spanish mystical literature. His feast day is 14 December.

John Paul II (1920–) Pope (1978–), b. Poland as Karol Wojtyla. He studied literature before being ordained in 1946. He became auxiliary bishop of Kraków (1958), archbishop (1964) and then cardinal (1967). In 1978 he became the first non-Italian pope in 455 years. John Paul was seriously wounded in an assassination attempt (1981). Theologically conservative, he upheld papal infallibility and condemned artificial methods of birth control and the ordination of women as priests. In 2000 John Paul made a millennium pilgrimage to the Holy Land.

Johnson, Andrew (1808–75) Seventeenth president of the United States (1865–69), vice president (1864–65). He was a Democrat governor (1853–57) and senator (1857–62, 1875) for Tennessee. Johnson was the only Southerner to remain in the Senate after the outbreak of the American CIVIL WAR. In 1864 he was elected with the incumbent Republican president Abraham LINCOLN on a National Union ticket and became president when Lincoln was assassinated (14 April 1865). Johnson immediately faced conflict over the policy of RECONSTRUCTION for the defeated South. Johnson favoured conciliation and granted an amnesty (1865) to many former leaders of the CONFEDERACY. He also did not prevent the adoption of BLACK CODES in many Southern states and encouraged the refusal of all these states (except Tennessee) to ratify the 14th Amendment to the CONSTITUTION OF THE UNITED STATES. His leniency angered Congressional Republicans, who passed the first CIVIL RIGHTS ACT (1866) and strengthened the FREEDMEN'S BUREAU. In the Congressional elections of 1866, Radical Republicans won a sufficient majority to override the presidential veto and began to enact their own Reconstruction legislation. Johnson's dismissal of Secretary of War Edwin STANTON enabled a hostile Congress to impeach the president for "high crimes and misdemeanours". Johnson was acquitted by one vote, but his effectiveness as a political leader had been fatally compromised. He was succeeded by Ulysses GRANT. In 1875 he became the only former president to be re-elected to the Senate. *See also* SEWARD, WILLIAM

Johnson, Lyndon Baines (1908–73) Thirty-sixth president of the United States (1963–69), vice president (1960–63). He represented Texas as a Democrat in the House of Representatives (1937–48) and the Senate (1948–60). Johnson was a strong supporter of President Franklin ROOSEVELT's NEW DEAL and later, as majority leader (1955–61) in Congress, gained a reputation as a master of consensus politics. Johnson served as vice president to John KENNEDY and became president after Kennedy's assassination (22 November 1963). He pledged to continue Kennedy's policies and showed considerable skill in securing passage of the CIVIL RIGHTS ACT (1964). In the 1964 presidential election Johnson secured re-election with the largest popular majority in modern US history, gaining 61% of the vote. His ambitious package of domestic reforms, to create what he termed the "Great Society", included the introduction (1966) of the MEDICARE system of health insurance. The reforms were overshadowed, however, by the escalation of US military involvement in the VIETNAM WAR (1955–75). National opposition to the War intensified and, coupled with severe race riots between 1965 and 1968, dissuaded Johnson from seeking re-election in 1968. He was succeeded as president by Richard NIXON. *See also* TONKIN GULF RESOLUTION; MCNAMARA, ROBERT; TET OFFENSIVE

Johnson, Richard Mentor (1780–1850) US vice president (1837–41). He served as a Democrat in the House of

J

JORDAN

AREA: 89,210sq km (34,444sq mi)
POPULATION: 4,291,000
CAPITAL (POPULATION): Amman (1,300,042)
GOVERNMENT: Constitutional monarchy
ETHNIC GROUPS: Arab 99%, of which Palestinians make up roughly half
LANGUAGES: Arabic (official)
RELIGIONS: Islam 93%, Christianity 5%
GDP PER CAPITA (1995): US$4060

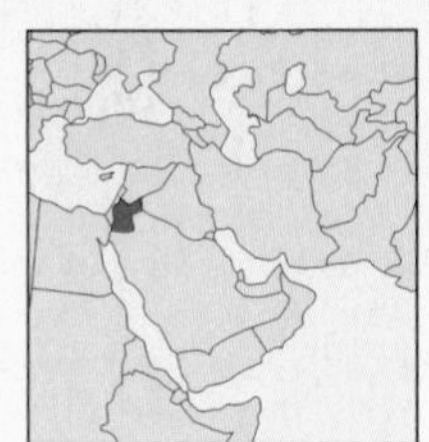

HASHEMITE kingdom in SW Asia. In *c.*1000 BC, the kingdoms of EDOM and MOAB, in S and central Jordan respectively, were overrun by King DAVID of Israel. The region was conquered by the SELEUCIDS in the 4th century BC. In *c.*63 BC, the Nabatean capital at PETRA was captured by POMPEY and Jordan generally prospered under Roman rule. In AD 636 KHALID IBN AL-WALID conquered the territory and introduced ISLAM. After the First CRUSADE (1099), Jordan was incorporated into the Latin Kingdom of JERUSALEM (1099). In 1517 it became part of the OTTOMAN EMPIRE. After the defeat of the Ottomans in World War 1, the area E of the River Jordan was included in the British League of Nations mandated territory of PALESTINE. In 1921 Palestine became known as Transjordan and in 1923 the British recognized the authority of Emir ABDULLAH of the Hashemite dynasty.

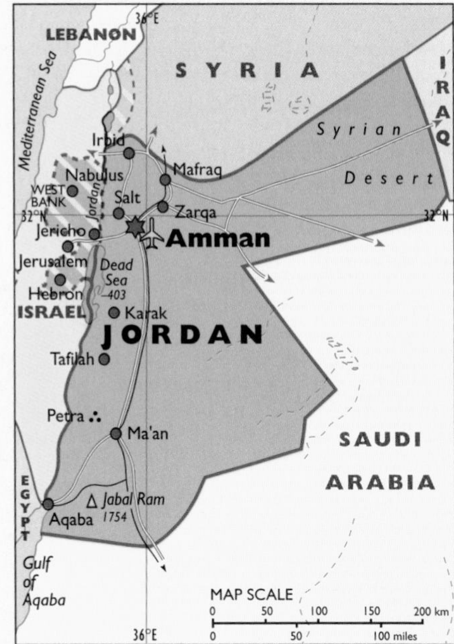

In 1946 Transjordan achieved independence and Abdullah became king. The creation of the state of Israel (1948) led to the first of the ARAB-ISRAELI WARS (1948–49). Transjordanian troops, led by John Bagot GLUBB, joined other Arab nations to attack the new nation. As many as 500,000 Palestinians fled into Transjordan. In the Jordan-Israel peace accord (1949), Jordan annexed the remaining Arab parts of Palestine (the WEST BANK and East JERUSALEM). This incensed the Palestinians, and Abdullah was assassinated in 1951.

In 1953 HUSSEIN I acceded. In 1958 Jordan formed the short-lived Arab Federation with Iraq. The SIX-DAY WAR (1967) ended in the Israeli occupation of East Jerusalem and the West Bank; more than one million Palestinian refugees now lived in E Jordan. In 1970 Jordan became embroiled in a bloody civil war with the PALESTINIAN LIBERATION ORGANIZATION (PLO), and by 1971 it had ejected all guerrillas operating from its soil. In 1974 King Hussein recognized the PLO as the legitimate representative of the Palestinians. The start of the INTIFADA in 1987 prompted Jordan to renounce (1988) its claim to the West Bank and approve the creation of an independent Palestine. Jordan sided with Iraq in the IRAN-IRAQ WAR and the GULF WAR. In 1991 opposition parties were legalized, and the first multiparty elections were held in 1993. In October 1994 Jordan and Israel signed a peace treaty that ended the state of war existing between them since 1948. The border between Elat and Aqaba was opened and King Hussein was granted custodial rights of Islamic sites in Jerusalem. Elections in 1997 were boycotted by opposition parties, including the Islamic Action Front (IAF). In 1999 King Hussein died and was succeeded by his son, Abdullah.

Representatives (1807–19, 1829–37) and the Senate (1819–29). Johnson was a supporter of President Andrew JACKSON. He was elected vice president to Martin VAN BUREN by the Senate because the ELECTORAL COLLEGE could not agree on a candidate for the post. According to tradition, Johnson killed TECUMSEH in the WAR OF 1812.

Johnson, Sir William (1715–74) British colonial administrator, b. Ireland. In *c.*1737 he emigrated to America, settling in the Mohawk Valley, New York. Johnson's skilful diplomacy soon gained the trust of the Native Americans, and he was instrumental in forging the alliance between the British and the IROQUOIS CONFEDERACY in the last of the FRENCH AND INDIAN WARS (1754–63). Johnson led the capture of Fort Niagara (1759) and participated in the seizure of Montréal (1760) As superintendent of Indian affairs (1755–74), he helped supress PONTIAC'S REBELLION (1763–66).

Johnston, Joseph Eggleston (1807–91) Confederate general in the American CIVIL WAR. Johnston was mainly responsible for the Confederate victory at the First Battle of BULL RUN (July 1861). Badly wounded in the Battle of Seven Pines, Virginia (May–June 1862), he was replaced as general of the Army of the Shenandoah by Robert LEE. After a tactical dispute with President Jefferson DAVIS, Johnston was unable to prevent the capture (July 1863) of Vicksburg, Mississippi. He delayed but failed to stop General William SHERMAN'S seizure of ATLANTA (1864).

J

John the Baptist, Saint (active 1st century AD) Jewish prophet who preached the imminent arrival of God's Last Judgement, b. Judaea. He is heralded in the Gospels as the precursor of JESUS CHRIST. John baptized penitents, including Jesus, in the River Jordan as preparation for baptism by the Holy Spirit. The DEAD SEA SCROLLS reveal similarities between John's message and that of the ESSENES. He was beheaded by HEROD ANTIPAS, after Salome asked for his head as a reward for her dance.

Joinville, Jean de (*c.*1224–1317) French chronicler. A hereditary royal steward, he accompanied LOUIS IX of France on the Seventh CRUSADE (1248–54). He wrote *Histoire de Saint Louis*, a vivid, detailed narrative of the Seventh Crusade and of the pious Louis IX.

Jolliet, Louis (1646–1700) French-Canadian explorer, b. Québec. In 1673 Jolliet and Jacques MARQUETTE became the first Europeans to travel down the Mississippi River from Lake Michigan to its confluence with the Arkansas River, 640km (400mi) from the Mississippi's mouth.

Jones, John Paul (1747–92) American naval officer in the AMERICAN REVOLUTION, b. Scotland as John Paul. In 1775 he joined the Continental Navy and proved successful at capturing supplies and enemy vessels. With his flagship *Bonhomme Richard*, Jones engaged the British ship *Serapis* in an epic battle off the coast of England (23 September 1779). He boarded and captured the *Serapis* while his ship burned and then sank.

Jones, Mary Harris (1830–1930) (Mother Jones) US UNION activist, b. Ireland. She was a leading organizer for the United Mine Workers' union and campaigned for other workers' rights. Her imprisonment (1902, 1913, 1914) for supporting strikes won a great deal of sympathy for the labour cause. Jones was a founder (1905) of the INDUSTRIAL WORKERS OF THE WORLD (IWW).

Jordan *See* country feature, page 215

Joseph Bonaparte *See* BONAPARTE, JOSEPH

Joseph I (1678–1711) Holy Roman emperor and king of Bohemia (1705–11), king of Hungary (1687–1711), son and successor of LEOPOLD I. His reign was dominated by the continuing War of the SPANISH SUCCESSION (1701–14) against LOUIS XIV of France. While EUGÈNE OF SAVOY succeeded in establishing Austrian hegemony over Italy, Joseph was threatened by a revolt in Hungary and incursions by CHARLES XII of Sweden. Joseph's sudden death ended HABSBURG hopes of the Spanish crown. He was succeeded by his brother, CHARLES VI. *See also* CLEMENT XI

Joseph II (1741–90) Holy Roman emperor (1765–90), king of Hungary and Bohemia (1780–90), son of MARIA THERESA and Emperor FRANCIS I. Until 1780 he ruled the HABSBURG lands jointly with his mother. An "enlightened despot", Joseph introduced sweeping liberal and humanitarian reforms, including the abolition of serfdom and the introduction of religious equality (both 1781). His suppression of more than 700 monasteries, however, brought conflict with Pope PIUS VI. With the support of his chancellor Count von KAUNITZ, Joseph, CATHERINE II (THE GREAT) of Russia and FREDERICK II (THE GREAT) of Prussia plotted the first partition of POLAND (1772). Joseph's audacious plan to swap the Austrian Netherlands for Bavaria, prompted by the end of the WITTELSBACH dynasty in Bavaria, was thwarted by Frederick II (the Great). Joseph's autocratic methods, coupled with his preoccupation with a joint Austrian-Russian assault on Turkey, encouraged widespread revolts in Hungary and the Austrian Netherlands. He was succeeded by LEOPOLD II.

Joseph, Chief (*c.*1840–1904) Native American leader. In 1873 he succeeded his father as chief of the NEZ PERCÉ tribe in Oregon. In 1877 the tribe were ordered by the US government to move to a reservation in Idaho. Chief Joseph attempted to lead more than 800 of his tribe on a long trek to safety in Canada, resisting the pursuing US Army. He was finally forced to surrender in Montana. Many of the Nez Percé perished on a reservation in Indian Territory (now Oklahoma), before settling in Washington.

Joseph, Father (1577–1638) French religious reformer and politician, b. François Le Clerc du Tremblay. His zeal for religious reform brought him to the attention of Cardinal RICHELIEU, whom he served as an unofficial foreign minister. Unpopular and known as Richelieu's "Grey Eminence", he supported the THIRTY YEARS' WAR.

Joséphine (1763–1814) Consort of NAPOLEON I and empress of the French (1804–09), b. Martinique. Her first marriage, to Vicomte Alexandre de Beauharnais, ended with his death (1794) during the REIGN OF TERROR. She married Napoleon in 1796. Her extravagance and inability to bear him a son caused Napoleon to obtain annulment of their marriage in 1809.

Josephus, Flavius (AD 37–100) Jewish scholar and historian, b. Joseph ben Mattityahu. As governor of Galilee, he took part in the revolt against Rome (AD 66–70) and was captured. Josephus found favour with Emperor VESPASIAN and settled in Rome (70). His writings include *History of the Jewish War* (75–79).

Josiah (*c.*648–609 BC) King of JUDAH (*c.*640–609 BC), grandson of Manasseh. Josiah acceded to the throne after the assassination of his father, Amon. His revival of the TEMPLE OF JERUSALEM was aided by the break-up of the Assyrian empire. Josiah resisted an Egyptian invasion of Israel, but was killed by Pharaoh Necho at MEGIDDO.

Jospin, Lionel (1937–) French statesman, prime minister (1997–). He joined the French SOCIALIST PARTY (PS) in 1971, becoming its leader in 1981. Under President François MITTERRAND, Jospin served (1988–92) as minister of education. In 1995 he succeeded Mitterrand as presidential candidate for the PS but lost the ensuing election to Jacques CHIRAC. In the 1997 elections, Jospin won a surprise victory against the incumbent premier, Alain Juppé.

Joubert, Piet (1831–1900) South African general. He led Afrikaner forces in the First SOUTH AFRICAN WAR (1880–81), which regained independence for TRANSVAAL. Joubert served as vice president (1883–84) under Paul KRUGER. He led South African forces at the start of the Second South African War (1899–1902).

Jouhaux, Léon (1879–1954) French union leader. In 1909 he became secretary general of the General Confederation of Labour. He was a founder (1919) of the INTERNATIONAL LABOUR ORGANIZATION (ILO). During World War 2, he was interned in Buchenwald concentration camp by the VICHY GOVERNMENT. In 1949 Jouhaux helped establish the International Confederation of Free Trade Unions. He received the 1951 Nobel Prize for Peace.

Joyce, William (1906–46) ("Lord Haw-Haw") Anti-British propagandist in World War 2, b. United States. He was a leading figure in Oswald MOSLEY'S Blackshirts and cofounded the British National Socialist League (1937). In 1939 he fled to Germany and broadcast Nazi propaganda to Britain. Captured in 1945, he was tried, found guilty of treason and hanged.

Juan Carlos (1938–) King of Spain (1975–), grandson of ALFONSO XIII. In 1962 he married Princess Sophia of Greece. Designated as General FRANCO'S successor in 1969, he became king on Franco's death in 1975. He quickly set about the democratization of Spanish society. In 1981 Juan Carlos survived an attempted military coup.

Juárez, Benito Pablo (1806–72) Mexican statesman, president (1861–63, 1867–72). Elected governor of his native state of Oaxaca in 1847, he was exiled (1853–55) by President Antonio de SANTA ANNA. Juárez took part in the overthrow of Santa Anna and joined the new, liberal government. As minister of justice, he abolished the privileges of ecclesiastical courts and supported land reforms and the new constitution (1857). In 1858 conservatives captured Mexico City, and Juárez formed a government in Veracruz. In 1861 the liberals triumphed in the "War of Reform" and Juárez returned to Mexico City. His suspension of payment on foreign debts led to the French seizure (1862) of Mexico City and the installation of MAXIMILIAN. In 1867 NAPOLEON III withdrew French troops and Juárez returned as president and national hero. His proposals for constitutional changes led to renewed civil war (1872).

Judaea Kingdom and Roman province corresponding to the old tribal kingdom of JUDAH. It became known as Judaea after the Jewish MACCABEES drove out the ruling SELEUCIDS in the 2nd century BC. In 63 BC it came under the control of the Romans, who installed (37 BC) HEROD THE GREAT as a client king. A revolt (AD 66–73) by Jewish nationalists was unsuccessful and in AD 135 the province became part of Roman Syria.

Judah Region to the s of JERUSALEM, settled by the tribe of Judah (fourth son of JACOB and his first wife, Leah) after the Exodus and Joshua's conquest of CANAAN. In *c.*1020 BC, SAUL founded the Hebrew state of ISRAEL. Saul's son, DAVID (r.1006–966 BC), united the kingdoms of Israel and Judah. After the death (926 BC) of David's son, SOLOMON, the kingdom once more divided. In *c.*587 BC Judah was conquered by the Babylonian King NEBUCHADNEZZAR II, beginning the BABYLONIAN CAPTIVITY of the Jews. In 538 BC, the Iranian King CYRUS II (THE GREAT) conquered Babylonia and the Jews were allowed to return to Judah and reconstruct the TEMPLE OF JERUSALEM. Following its conquest (*c.*332 BC) by ALEXANDER III (THE GREAT), Judah was ruled by the Hellenistic dynasties of the PTOLEMIES and then the SELEUCIDS. From *c.*167 BC, the Seleucids were gradually forced out by the MACCABEES, a Jewish dynasty who established the kingdom of JUDAEA.

Judaism *See* feature article

Jugurtha (*c.*160–104 BC) King of NUMIDIA (118–105 BC). On the death (118 BC) of Micipsa, his adoptive father, Jugurtha shared power with Micipsa's two sons, Hiempsal and Adherbal. Jugurtha assassinated Hiempsal and, with Rome's approval, divided Numidia with Adherbal. In 112 BC he overthrew Adherbal, killing a number of Romans. In retaliation Rome invaded Numidia (111 BC), beginning the Jugurthine War (111–105 BC). In 110 BC Jugurtha briefly expelled the Romans from Numidia, but was later captured (105 BC) by Bocchus I of Mauretania and executed by the Romans.

Julian (the Apostate) (*c.*331–63) Roman emperor (361–63), nephew of CONSTANTINE I (THE GREAT). In 360, after victories against the Alemanni and the Franks, he was hailed as emperor by his troops. In 361 he succeeded the extravagant Constantius II. Julian's attempts to establish paganism as an official religion led to the persecution of Christians. He launched a disastrous invasion of the Sasanian empire and was killed at the Battle of Ctesiphon.

Julius Caesar *See* CAESAR, (GAIUS) JULIUS

Julius II (1443–1513) Pope (1503–13), b. Guiliano della Rovere, nephew of SIXTUS IV. In 1494 he fled to the court of CHARLES VIII of France after a failed assassination attempt by Pope ALEXANDER VI. As pope, Julius recovered the Papal States by joining (1509) the League of CAMBRAI. The formation (1510) of the HOLY LEAGUE against France, however, failed to expel the French from Italy and Julius was forced to summon the fifth LATERAN COUNCIL. In 1512, with Swiss assistance, he acquired Parma and Piacenza. Julius is best remembered for his patronage of the arts. He began (1506) the building of St Peter's Basilica, Rome, commissioned Michelangelo to paint the ceiling of the Sistine Chapel, Rome, and asked

Raphael to produce his masterpieces in the Stanza della Segnatura, Vatican Palace.

Julius III (1487–1555) Pope (1550–55), b. Giovanni Maria Ciocchi del Monte. He was one of the co-presidents of the Council of TRENT (1545). Seeking to reform the Roman Catholic Church and eliminate some of its worst abuses, Julius reconvened the Council in 1551. He also supported the JESUITS and opened a college at Rome for the training of German priests under Jesuit supervision.

July Plot (20 July 1944) Failed conspiracy to assassinate Adolf HITLER. The plot was organized by Colonel Claus von STAUFFENBERG, who planted a bomb under the conference table of Hitler's headquarters at Rastenberg. The bomb exploded and Stauffenberg, in the belief that Hitler had been killed, flew to Berlin to announce a new government headed by Karl GOERDELER, the former mayor of Leipzig and long-term opponent of Hitler. Hitler, however, was only injured and all the conspirators, numbering some 150, were executed.

July Revolution (July 1830) Insurrection in France. The revolution was prompted by CHARLES X's publication of the July Ordinances, which imposed rigid press censorship, dissolved the chamber of deputies, reduced the electorate and gave the king the right to rule by decree. Five days of demonstrations and fighting in the streets forced Charles to abdicate. On 9 August, LOUIS PHILIPPE was proclaimed king with a more liberal constitution.

June Days (23–26 June 1848) Episode of civil unrest in France during the FEBRUARY REVOLUTION. Thousands of workers, who had lost their jobs as a result of the abolition of the national workshops formed by Louis BLANC, were joined by other workers and students in erecting barricades on the streets of Paris. General Louis Cavaignac (1802–57) brutally suppressed the revolt, killing 1500 demonstrators and arresting a further 12,000, many of whom were exiled to Algeria. *See also* REVOLUTIONS OF 1848

Junker Member of the landowning aristocracy of PRUSSIA. Descendants of knights who conquered large areas of E Germany in the Middle Ages, they came to dominate the government and army during the German Empire (1871–1918). Chancellor Otto von BISMARCK, creator of the German Empire, was himself of Junker descent. Ultraconservative, the Junkers supported the monarchy, the military and the maintenance of high agricultural tariffs. Their hostility to the WEIMAR REPUBLIC contributed to the rise of the NAZI PARTY under Adolf HITLER.

Jurassic Central period of the MESOZOIC era, lasting from 213 to 444mya. At this time there were saurischian and ornithischian dinosaurs. Plesiosaurs, pterosaurs and archaeopteryx date from this period. Primitive mammals had begun to evolve.

jury Group of lay people, usually 12, summoned to pass judgment under oath and instructed by a judge. The judge usually has the responsibility of passing sentence. Juries were first used in England and originally consisted of witnesses who would make sworn statements in support of a claim or an accused person. They may date back to before the NORMAN CONQUEST of England (1066). Juries were certainly in existence in England by the 12th century. The Statute of WESTMINSTER (1275) made the use of a jury compulsory in some criminal cases, and by the 15th century jury trials had replaced trial by ordeal. It was only in the 17th century, however, that jury members ceased to give evidence and simply passed judgment on the basis of evidence heard in court. The jury system was exported to America, Asia and Africa through the expansion of the BRITISH EMPIRE. After the FRENCH REVOLUTION (1789), the jury system was adopted by most of continental Europe. Today, it is only employed in the United States and the United Kingdom and some former British colonies. In the United Kingdom, trial by jury is restricted to a small category of cases. In the *Duncan v. Louisiana* (1968) case in the United States, the Supreme Court ruled that for criminal cases that may result in a sentence of more than six months, a jury trial is a constitutional right. It is also the most common form of trial in civil cases.

Justinian I (the Great) (483–565) Byzantine emperor (527–565). Justinian concluded the Treaty of Eternal Peace (533) with KHUSRAU I of Iran, which freed his army for the attempted restoration of the Western Roman Empire. In 534 BELISARIUS regained the Vandal kingdom of North Africa but floundered in his attempts to oust the OSTROGOTHS from Italy (535–49). The campaign by NARSES proved more successful, and by 562 the Byzantines controlled the whole of Italy. Justinian failed, however, to contend with the threat to the Balkan frontier by the BULGARS, SLAVS and AVARS. His greatest achievement was the JUSTINIAN CODE, which clarified and unified Roman law. High taxation, needed to finance his wars, drained the strength of the BYZANTINE EMPIRE and caused civil unrest. Justinian narrowly avoided being overthrown in the Nika insurrection (532) at Constantinople (now ISTANBUL). He was saved by the resolute approach of his wife, THEODORA, and the wholesale massacre of the rebels by Belisarius. Justinian failed to achieve a conciliation with the doctrine of MONOPHYSITISM at the Second Council of CONSTANTINOPLE (533). He was responsible for building the HAGIA SOPHIA, Constantinople.

Justinian Code (AD 529–565) (Lat. *Corpus Juris Civilis*) Collection of ROMAN LAWS and interpretations produced under the Byzantine Emperor JUSTINIAN I. It consists of a codification of 4652 imperial ordinances (the *Codex Constitutionum*); extracts and abstracts from the writings of leading jurists (the *Digesta*); a textbook for law students (the *Institutiones*): and collections of new ordinances issued by Justinian after the publication of the Codes (the *Novellae Constitutiones Post Codicem*). Commissions of lawyers produced the Code, among them a 16-man commission headed by the scholar Triboniam. The Code still forms the basis for the law in most European countries.

Jutes Germanic people who invaded Britain in the 5th century along with Angles, Saxons and others. They probably came from Jutland, Denmark, and settled mainly in Kent, the Isle of Wight and Hampshire. According to the historian BEDE, they were led by the brothers Hengist and Horsa, who went to Britain to fight (446–54) for the British king Vortigem against the PICTS. Horsa was killed in 455, but Hengist reigned as king of Kent until his death (*c*.488).

Jutland, Battle of (31 May 1916) Only full-scale naval confrontation between Britain and Germany during WORLD WAR I, fought off the Jutland Peninsula of Denmark, NW Europe. The British, who had broken the German's code, failed to take advantage of the element of surprise. In a desperate bid to cause a diversion, the German battle-cruisers charged the British Grand Fleet, but rather than meet the cruisers British Admiral JELLICOE ordered a retreat and the German fleet sprung the trap. The Battle ended with both sides claiming victory. The British lost 6274 men, eight destroyers and six cruisers; the Germans lost 2545 men, five destroyers, five cruisers and one battleship. The British Royal Navy, however, dominated the North Sea for the remainder of the war as the German fleet remained in port.

J

JUDAISM

Monotheistic religion developed by the ancient Hebrews in N Mesopotamia during the mid-2nd millennium BC and practised by JEWS. Local worship takes place in a synagogue, where the TORAH is read in public and preserved in a replica of the Ark of the Covenant. A rabbi undertakes the spiritual leadership and pastoral care of a community.

According to the OLD TESTAMENT, Judaism was founded (*c*.20th century BC) by ABRAHAM, who was chosen by God (Yahweh) to receive favourable treatment in return for obedience and worship. Having entered into this covenant with God, Abraham moved to CANAAN (roughly modern ISRAEL and Lebanon), from where centuries later his descendants migrated to Egypt and became enslaved. God liberated the Hebrews from Egypt, enabled the conquest of Canaan, and renewed the covenant with their leader MOSES. Through Moses, God gave the Hebrews a set of strict laws (the Ten Commandments). These laws are revealed in the Torah, the core of Jewish scripture. The other holy books are the TALMUD and several commentaries.

In *c*.1020 BC SAUL founded the Hebrew state of ISRAEL. Saul's son, DAVID (r.1006–966 BC), captured the city of JERUSALEM and united the kingdoms of Israel and JUDAH. In the 10th century BC, SOLOMON built the first TEMPLE OF JERUSALEM as a repository for the Ark of the Covenant. In *c*.922 BC, JEROBOAM I created the separate N kingdom of Israel. In the 8th century BC, Judah and Israel were subjugated by ASSYRIA. ISAIAH prophesized the destruction of Judah. In *c*.587 BC, Judah was conquered by the Babylonians, beginning the BABYLONIAN CAPTIVITY of the Jews.

In 538 BC CYRUS II (THE GREAT) conquered Babylonia and the Jews were allowed to return to Judah and reconstruct the Temple. In *c*.332 BC PALESTINE was conquered by Alexander III (the Great), ushering in the period of "Hellenistic Judaism" (332–63 BC). The desecration (168 BC) of the Temple by the SELEUCIDS inspired the Revolt of the MACCABEES (167–164 BC) that restored Jewish rule in Jerusalem.

In 63 BC the Roman general POMPEY once more destroyed the Temple. The Jewish revolt (AD 66–73) against Roman rule climaxed in a further demolition of the Temple (70). Jewish resistance ended (135) with the defeat of Simon BAR KOKHBA. The subsequent development of Rabbinic Judaism can be traced through the MISHNA. After the initial spread of

▲ **menorah** commemorates the reconsecration of the Temple of Jerusalem in 164 BC.

▲ **star of David** Universal symbol of Judaism, adopted in the 17th century.

Islam (7th–8th centuries), Jewish communities were granted considerable autonomy by the Muslim caliphate and the Babylonian rabbinate emerged as the dominant force in early medieval Judaism.

In medieval Europe, two major forms of Judaism developed: the ASHKENAZIM of NW Europe and the SEPHARDIM of SW Europe. HASIDISM developed in 12th-century Germany. The persecution and expulsion of Jews in 14th- and 15th-century Europe fuelled the development of Jewish mysticism. The origins of modern Judaism are often traced to the 18th century Haskala (Enlightenment). In the early 19th century, reform movements developed in Western Europe and the United States. The rise of ANTI-SEMITISM at the end of the 19th century was concomitant with the development of ZIONISM, and after the genocide of European Jews (the HOLOCAUST) by the Nazis during World War 2, the state of Israel was born.

Modern Judaism is split into four large groups: Orthodox, Conservative, Reform and Liberal Judaism. **Orthodox** Judaism, followed by most of the world's 18 million Jews, asserts the supreme authority of the Torah and adheres most closely to traditions, such as the segregation of men and women in the synagogue. **Reform** Judaism denies the Jews' claim to be God's chosen people and is more liberal in its interpretation of certain laws and the Torah. **Conservative** Judaism is a compromise between Orthodox and Reform Judaism, adhering to many Orthodox traditions but seeking to apply modern scholarship in interpreting the Torah. **Liberal** Judaism (Reconstructionism) is a more extreme form of Reform Judaism, seeking to adapt Judaism to the needs of society. *See also* individual prophets and philosophers

Kaaba (Ka'abah or Ka'ba) Central shrine of ISLAM, located in the Great Mosque, MECCA, Saudi Arabia. In prayer, Muslims face the meridian that passes through the Kaaba. Each pilgrim who undertakes the Hajj (pilgrimage to Mecca) circles the shrine seven times, touching the Black Stone for forgiveness. The Black Stone is said to have been given to Abraham by the Archangel Gabriel.

Kabila, Laurent Desire (1939–) Congolese statesman, president of the Democratic Republic of CONGO (1997–). Following the overthrow and murder (1961) of Congo's first prime minister, Patrice LUMUMBA, Kabila fought in the revolt against the new leader, MOBUTO SESE SEKO. In 1967 he founded the People's Revolutionary Party, which established a Marxist government in Kivu, E Congo. In 1996 Kabila re-emerged as leader of the Alliance of Democratic Forces for the Liberation of Congo-Zaïre. Taking advantage of the national outcry against Mobutu's corrupt dictatorship, Kabila led a rebellion that captured the capital, Kinshasa, and forced Mobutu into exile (May 1997). Kabila assumed the presidency and reverted the country's name to the Democratic Republic of Congo. In 1998 Congo-Kinshasa was plunged into civil war between the Tutsi-dominated Congolese Rally for Democracy (RCD), backed by Uganda and Rwanda, and government forces, supported by Zimbabwe, Angola and Namibia.

Kabir (1440–1518) Indian mystic. Brought up a Muslim, he adopted teachings from ISLAM and HINDUISM to create a new religion called *sahaja-yoga* (simple union). Kabir rejected the caste system while accepting the Hindu belief in reincarnation. From Islam he borrowed monotheism and the nature of the relationship between man and God. Among his disciples were NANAK, the founder of SIKHISM.

Kabul Capital and largest city of Afghanistan, lying on the River Kabul. Dating from the second millennium BC, the city is strategically located in a valley of the Hindu Kush with access to Pakistan and Uzbekistan. In the 13th century, Kabul was sacked by the Mongol conqueror GENGHIS KHAN. In 1504 BABUR made it the capital of the MUGHAL EMPIRE. In 1738 Kabul was captured by NADIR SHAH of Iran. It replaced KANDAHAR as capital of Afghanistan in 1776. During the 19th century, Kabul was at the heart of the British, Russian and Iranian struggle for control of the Khyber Pass. The city was the headquarters for the Soviet military in the AFGHANISTAN WAR (1979–92). After the Soviet withdrawal in 1989, Kabul witnessed fierce fighting between rival groups of the MUJAHEDDIN, and much of it had been reduced to ruins before the Taliban seized the city in 1996. Pop. (1993 est.) 700,000.

Kádár, János (1912–89) Hungarian statesman, premier (1956–58, 1961–65) and first secretary (1956–88) of the Hungarian Socialist Workers' Party. He fought in the resistance during World War 2 and served as minister of the interior (1948–50). Kádár replaced Imre NAGY as premier after Soviet troops had suppressed the HUNGARIAN UPRISING (1956). In 1968 he lent military support to the Soviet invasion of Czechoslovakia. Kádár's policy of "consumer socialism" revitalized the domestic economy.

Kalimantan Region of INDONESIA, forming the S part of the island of BORNEO. Its early history was influenced by Indian culture. The SRIVIJAYA EMPIRE controlled what is now Kalimantan and SARAWAK from the 7th century until the island was reunited by the MAJAPAHIT empire of Eastern JAVA (*c*.1293–1520). In the 16th century, Borneo was divided into separate Muslim states. In the 17th century, the Dutch established colonial rule over what became part of the DUTCH EAST INDIES. In 1950 Kalimantan became part of the Republic of Indonesia. Area: 539,460sq km (208,232sq mi). Pop. (1990) 9,099,874.

Kalinin, Mikhail Ivanovich (1875–1946) Soviet statesman, head of state of the Soviet Union (1919–46). He was an early supporter of the BOLSHEVIKS, co-founding (1912) their newspaper *Pravda*. Kalinin participated in both the RUSSIAN REVOLUTION OF 1905 and the RUSSIAN REVOLUTION of 1917. Despite being a close ally of LENIN, Kalinin continued to serve as head of state under Joseph STALIN and survived the Great PURGE (1936–38).

Kaliningrad (formerly Königsberg) City and seaport on the Baltic coast, W Russia; capital of Kaliningrad region. Founded by the TEUTONIC KNIGHTS in 1255, the city became (1340) a member of the HANSEATIC LEAGUE. In 1525 Königsberg became the capital of the dukes of Prussia. The city was devastated by the NAPOLEONIC WARS (1803–15), but revived to become a major German naval base. During World War 2, the city was almost destroyed by the Red Army and was ceded to the Soviet Union. In 1946 it was renamed Kaliningrad. When the Baltic states seceded from the Soviet Union in 1991, Kaliningrad was separated from the rest of Russian Federation. Pop. (1993) 411,000.

Kalmar Union (1397–1523) Union of Denmark, Norway and Sweden. Its creation followed the appointment by MARGARET I of Denmark, Norway and Sweden (1387–88) of her grand-nephew, Eric of Pomerania, as her heir and king of Norway. Homage was to be paid to him in Denmark and Sweden. In 1397 Eric was crowned ruler of all three kingdoms in a joint ceremony. In 1523 GUSTAVUS I (VASA) of Sweden withdrew from the Union. Denmark and Norway remained united until 1814.

Kamakura (1192–1333) Japanese shogunate, founded by Minamoto YORITOMO. Yoritomo defeated the TAIRA at the Battle of Dannoura (1185) and established his court at Kamakura, SE Honshu. In 1192 he was appointed SHOGUN, establishing the position of military dictator that persisted until the MEIJI RESTORATION (1868). The Kamakura period saw the emergence of a nascent FEUDAL SYSTEM in Japan as the SAMURAI class gradually gained control of the private estates (*shoen*). On Yoritomo's death (1199), control of the shogunate passed to the HOJO dynasty. The Hojo dominated the imperial court at KYOTO after the defeat of the Jokyu Disturbance (1219–21), a revolt led by Emperor Go-Toba. Two invasion attempts (1274, 1281) by the Mongols were defeated with the help of typhoons. The shogunate was eventually overthrown by Emperor DAIGO II in 1333. The Kamakura period witnessed the growth of ZEN Buddhism and the emergence of Pure Land BUDDHISM and Nichiren Buddhism. The Kamakura shogunate marked a glorious period in Japanese sculpture and the literary production of military epics such as *Heike monogatari* (*c*.1240). *See also* DAIMYO

Kamehameha I (the Great) (1758?–1819) Hawaiian conqueror, who united all the Hawaiian islands and founded the Kamehameha dynasty. In 1782 he defeated and killed his cousin, Kiwalao, to become king of the island of HAWAII. Kamehameha then began a campaign of conquest that by 1810 had made him undisputed king of the archipelago. He instituted harsh laws but abolished human sacrifice. His son and successor, **Kamehameha II** (r.1819–25), admitted the first US missionaries in 1820.

Kamehameha III (1814–54) King of HAWAII (1825–54), son of KAMEHAMEHA I (THE GREAT). For most of his regency (1825–33), Hawaii was ruled by his father's wife, Kaahumanu. Kamehameha III introduced a Declaration of Rights (1839) and a liberal constitution (1840). He was succeeded by his nephew, KAMEHAMEHA IV.

Kamehameha IV (1834–63) King of HAWAII (1855–63), nephew and successor of KAMEHAMEHA III. He encouraged the development of the Church of England as a bulwark against the influence of US Protestant missionaries, who sought to annex Hawaii to the United States. He introduced free medical care (1860) to try and prevent the eradication of his people through disease. His brother, **Kamehameha V** (r.1863–72), abandoned the liberal constitution and strengthened royal authority. The dynasty ended with his death.

Kamenev, Lev Borisovich (1883–1936) Soviet politician, b. Lev Borisovich Rosenfeld. An early supporter of the BOLSHEVIKS, he was exiled to Siberia (1914–17) for opposing Russia's involvement in World War 1. Despite his willingness to work with Alexander KERENSKY's provisional government and opposition to the RUSSIAN REVOLUTION (1917), Kamenev became a leading member of the new Soviet government. After the death of LENIN (1924), Kamenev briefly allied with Joseph STALIN and Grigori ZINOVIEV to prevent Leon TROTSKY from gaining power. After 1925 Stalin steadily eased out Kamenev. In 1936, at the start of the Great PURGE (1936–38), Kamenev and Zinoviev appeared before a show-trial, accused of assassinating Sergei KIROV and plotting to kill Stalin. Kamenev "confessed" and was executed for treason. He was posthumously cleared of all charges (1988).

kamikaze (Jap. divine wind) Name given to pilots or their explosive-laden aircraft used by the Japanese during World War 2. The name derives from the two typhoons (1274, 1281) that wrecked the Mongols attempted invasions of Japan. The pilots' suicidal method of attack was to dive into ships of the enemy fleet. In the Battle of OKINAWA (1945) more than 1400 pilots died in the process of killing 5000 US sailors and destroying 26 US battleships.

Kampuchea *See* CAMBODIA

Kanagawa, Treaty of (31 March 1854) First formal agreement between Japan and a Western nation (in this instance, the United States). The treaty was the result of military pressure from US Commodore Matthew PERRY, who blockaded Tokyo harbour in July 1853. The Treaty gave the United States access to the ports of Shimoda and Hakodate and provided for a permanent US consul for Japan.

Kanaris, Constantine (1790–1877) Greek naval officer and statesman, prime minister (1848–49, 1864–65, 1877). He became a national hero for his actions against the Turks during the GREEK WAR OF INDEPENDENCE (1821–32). Kanaris was involved in the overthrow (1862) of King Otto and served as co-regent (1862–63) until the accession of GEORGE I. He died shortly after returning as prime minister during the RUSSO-TURKISH WAR.

Kandahar (Qandahar) City in S Afghanistan. It has been subject to numerous conquests because of its strategic location on trade routes to Central Asia and India. Kandahar was captured by Alexander III (the Great) in 329 BC, and was later subsumed (305 BC) into the Gupta empire by Chandragupta I. It fell to Arab invaders in the 7th century AD and was later destroyed by Genghis Khan and Tamerlane. In 1747 AHMAD SHAH made it the first capital of an independent Afghanistan. In 1776 the capital was transferred to KABUL. In 1839 Kandahar was captured by the British in the first of the AFGHAN WARS, but the British relinquished control of the city in 1881. Kandahar witnessed fierce fighting between the MUJAHEDDIN and Soviet forces during the AFGHANISTAN WAR (1979–92), and was the base from which the TALIBAN captured much of Afghanistan in 1996. Pop. (1992 est.) 293,000.

Kanem West African kingdom, founded (*c*.9th century AD) in the area E of Lake Chad. A pastoral tribe, ancestors of the Kanuri, the Kanem conquered their neighbours and established a centralized state that developed on the trade between sub-Saharan and N Africa. In *c*.1075 the Sef king Umme became the first African ruler to adopt Islam as the state religion. During the reign (1221–59) of Dunama II, Kanem became the dominant power in the region. In the 14th century, the Sef were forced to migrate to BORNU, W of Lake Chad. Kanem was reconquered in the 16th century, but Kanem-Bornu disintegrated under attack from the FULANI and the Sef dynasty died out in 1846. *See also* HAUSA STATES; MALI; SONGHAI

Kangxi (1654–1722) (K'ang-hsi) Chinese emperor (1661–1722) of the Manchu QING dynasty. During his regency the influence of the EUNUCHS at court was curtailed. Once in power, Kangxi used diplomatic and military means to eliminate three mighty warlords in S China. In 1683 Kangxi captured Taiwan, the last stronghold of MING resistance established by ZHENG CHENGGONG. Kangxi now moved against the Russians in Siberia, forcing PETER I (THE GREAT) to sign the Treaty of Nerchinsk (1689). In 1697, after a daring march across the Gobi Desert, Kangxi gained Outer Mongolia from the Dzungars. He also incorporated Tibet into the Qing empire (1720). Kangxi supervised major works on the River

Huang He and the Grand Canal in s China, which stabilized agricultural production. He also opened four Chinese ports, which stimulated trade with the West. Kangxi commissioned several ambitious reference books and encouraged the transmission of Roman Catholicism via Jesuit missionaries. He was succeeded by his son Yongzheng.

Kang Youwei (1858–1927) Chinese scholar and political reformer. He first petitioned the QING dynasty to enact institutional reforms in the 1880s, and his demands became more vocal after China's defeat in the first of the SINO-JAPANESE WARS (1894–95). Kang and his student LIANG QICHAO saw CONFUCIANISM as a modernizing force amidst the decay of the Chinese empire. In 1898 he persuaded Emperor GUANGXU to adopt a programme of modernization that later became known as the "HUNDRED DAYS OF REFORM". Empress Dowager CIXI imprisoned Guangxu, however, and annulled most of the reforms. Kang and Liang fled to Japan. After his return (1914) to China, Kang opposed the republic established by SUN YAT-SEN and YUAN SHIHKAI and supported the brief restoration of the Qing dynasty (1917).

Kanishka (active *c.*1st century AD) Greatest emperor of the KUSHAN dynasty. Details of Kanishka's life are sketchy. He ascended the throne sometime between AD 78 and 144, and during his reign the Kushans ruled over most of the N part of the Indian subcontinent. The empire prospered both materially and culturally on the trade between China and the Roman Empire along the SILK ROAD. Kanishka was a great patron of BUDDHISM, and is credited with convening the fourth great Buddhist council in Kashmir that saw the birth of MAHAYANA Buddhism.

Kano Historic kingdom and emirate in w Africa, based (from the early 12th century AD) around the city of Kano, now in N Nigeria. One of the HAUSA STATES, Kano was founded in 999. Its rulers first adopted Islam in the mid-14th century. In the reign (1421–38) of King Dauda, Kano became a client state of the BORNU kingdom, but under Mohamman Rumfa (r.1463–99) Kano flourished on the trans-Saharan trade. In 1513 it was subsumed into the SONGHAI empire. In 1807 Kano was captured by the FULANI in a *jihad*, led by USMAN DAN FODIO, and an emirate was established. For much of the 19th century, Kano was the most powerful trading power in West Africa. The city of Kano was the major market in the w Sudan. In 1903 it was captured by the British.

Kansas State in central United States; the capital is Topeka. The first known European explorer was the Spanish conquistador Francisco Vázquez de CORONADO in 1541. In 1682 Kansas was claimed for France by Sieur de LA SALLE. It was acquired by the United States under the LOUISIANA PURCHASE (1803). In 1830 Kansas became part of Indian Territory, but the KANSAS-NEBRASKA ACT (1854) opened up the territory to white settlers. It became known as "Bleeding Kansas" as pro- and anti-slavery forces fought for control of the region. The MENNONITES settled in Kansas in 1874. Area: 213,094sq km (82,276sq mi). Pop. (1993 est.) 2,530,746.

Kansas-Nebraska Act (30 May 1854) US legislation, sponsored by Stephen DOUGLAS, that repealed the prohibition of SLAVERY north of latitude 35°30', established by the MISSOURI COMPROMISE (1820). It applied the doctrine of "popular sovereignty" to determine whether the new territories of KANSAS and NEBRASKA should admit slavery or not. Ironically, the Act served to accentuate divisions on the issue of slavery. Opposition to the extension of slavery contributed to the establishment (1854) of the REPUBLICAN PARTY. *See also* COMPROMISE OF 1850; DRED SCOTT CASE

Kant, Immanuel (1724–1804) German philosopher. His philosophy of idealism, outlined in *Critique of Pure Reason* (1781), sought to discover the nature and boundaries of human knowledge. It was much influenced by Isaac NEWTON and David HUME. Kant's system of ethics, described in the *Critique of Practical Reason* (1790), placed moral duty above happiness and asserts the existence of an absolute moral law (the "categorical imperative"). His views on aesthetics were embodied in his *Critique of Judgment* (1790). Kant also wrote several essays in support of religious liberalism and the ENLIGHTENMENT.

KANSAS
Statehood :
29 January 1861
Nickname :
Sunflower State
State motto :
To the stars through difficulties

Kapp Putsch (13–17 March 1920) Ill-fated insurrection against the WEIMAR REPUBLIC led by the Prussian reactionary politician Wolfgang Kapp (1858–1922). Planning to restore the German monarchy, Kapp staged a coup in Berlin with the aid of the right-wing "Free Corps" brigades, which the government was attempting to disband. Supported by General Erich LUDENDORFF, he attempted to set up a new government. A general strike and a refusal by civil servants to follow his orders led to the collapse of the coup. Kapp died while awaiting trial.

Karadžić, Radovan (1945–) Serbian politician. He founded the Serbian Democratic Party in 1990. In 1992 BOSNIA-HERZEGOVINA voted for independence from the Serb-dominated Federation of Yugoslavia. Karadžić declared a separate Bosnian Serb state, Republika Srpska, with himself as president. With the support of Serbian president Slobodan MILOŠEVIĆ, he instituted a policy of "ethnic cleansing" of non-Serbs from the republic and waged war against the Bosnian state. In 1995 Milošević withdrew his support and Karadžić was forced to negotiate the DAYTON PEACE AGREEMENT with Bosnian President Alija IZETBEGOVIĆ. In 1996 Karadžić was indicted for war crimes by the United Nations (UN).

Karageorge (1762–1817) Serbian nationalist, b. George Petrović. He defeated the JANISSARIES (1804) and went on to gain full independence (1805) for SERBIA from Turkey. In 1808 Karageorge became governor of Serbia. Although Serbia fought (1809–12) alongside Russia in the RUSSO-TURKISH WARS, Russia failed to protect the fledgling state and Serbia was recaptured by Sultan SELIM III in 1813. Karageorge fled to Austria and MILOŠ OBRENOVIĆ became leader of the independence movement. On his return to Serbia (1817), Karageorge was murdered by Miloš. *See also* ALEXANDER KARAGEORGEVIĆ; OBRENOVIĆ

Karakorum Ancient capital of the MONGOL empire, the ruins of which were discovered (1889) in N central Mongolia. Inhabited since the 8th century, it was designated the capital by GENGHIS KHAN in 1220. In 1235 Genghis Khan's son, OGODEI, fortified Karakorum and built a magnificent palace. In 1267 the capital transferred to Khanbalik (now BEIJING), but Karakorum continued to be inhabited until 1388, when it was destroyed in a Chinese invasion.

Karamanlis, Konstantinos (1907–98) Greek statesman, prime minister (1955–63, 1974–80), president (1980–85, 1990–95). He entered parliament in 1935 as a member of the Populist Party. On becoming prime minister in 1955, he formed his own party, the National Radical Union (ERE). In 1960 Karamanlis attempted to end the disruption caused by the ENOSIS movement in CYPRUS by establishing it as an independent republic within the British Commonwealth of Nations. In 1963 he resigned after a dispute with King PAUL I. Karamanlis opposed the military junta (1967–74) from self-imposed exile. In 1974 he returned as leader of the New Democratic Party (ND) and supervised Greece's return to civilian rule. *See also* PAPANDREOU, ANDREAS

Karelia Republic in NW Russia; the capital is Petrozavodsk. Karelia was an independent state until conquered by KIEVAN RUS in the 9th century. It was divided between Sweden and NOVGOROD in the 12th century. From 1323 until 1721 Sweden held Western Karelia, while Russia controlled Eastern Karelia. In 1721 Western Karelia was ceded to Russia and in the 19th century the reunified Karelia became part of the Russian grand duchy of Finland. After the Russian Revolution (1917) and Finnish independence, Western Karelia was ceded to Finland and Eastern Karelia became (1923) a republic of the Soviet Union. Western Karelia was annexed by Russia in the RUSSO-FINNISH WAR (1939–40) and when a treaty of 1947 confirmed this situation, most of the Finnish population of Western Karelia migrated to Finland. In 1992 Karelia became a republic of the Russian Federation. Area: 172,400sq km (66,564sq mi). Pop. (1994) 794,200.

Karen Thai-Chinese cultural group made up a number of tribal peoples, living mainly in the Kayah and Karen states of s Burma (now Myanmar). Since Burma became independent in 1948, the Karen have fought sporadically to gain political autonomy.

Karim Khan (*c.*1705–79) Iranian ruler (1750–79), founder of the Zand dynasty. He was a general of NADIR SHAH and, after his assassination (1747), acted as regent for Ismail III, grandson of the last SAFAVID sultan Husayn I. With Ismail installed as a puppet king, Karim Khan conquered all his rivals and restored order throughout Iran, except for the NE region of Khorsan, which remained under the control of Shah Rokh. He also accepted the loss of Afghanistan to AHMAD SHAH DURRANI. Iran gradually returned to prosperity after 40 years of civil war and Karim Khan opened up Iran to foreign trade, allowing the English East India Company to establish (1763) a post at Bushehr, SW Iran. Karim Khan established a capital at SHIRAZ, where he built the Vakil Mosque and Bazaar. After his death, Iran plunged back into civil war until the QAJAR DYNASTY restored order in 1796.

Karlowitz, Treaty of (26 January 1699) Peace agreement between the OTTOMAN EMPIRE and the HOLY LEAGUE (Austria, Russia, Poland and Venice), signed at Karlowitz, N Serbia. Sultan Mustafa II (r.1695–1703) was forced to give up a large part of the Turkish empire, ceding Transylvania, Croatia, Slovenia and much of Hungary to Austria, part of Ukraine and Podolia to Poland, and the Peloponnese and most of Dalmatia to Venice. The Treaty marked the beginning of the decline of the OTTOMAN EMPIRE.

Karnak *See* LUXOR

Karnataka (formerly Mysore) State in SW India; the capital is Bangalore. It formed part of the MAURYAN EMPIRE (*c.*321–185 BC). From the 4th century to the 9th century Mysore was ruled by vassals of the PALLAVA DYNASTY. The HOYSALA DYNASTY were the dominant power during the 12th century, but they were conquered (1313) by the DELHI SULTANATE. In 1336 Mysore (then known as Gangavadi) became part of the state of VIJAYANAGAR, whose capital was on the site of part of modern-day Hampi, E Karnataka. Vijayanagar crumbled in the late 16th century and Karnataka was divided between the MUGHAL EMPIRE and the rajas of Mysore. While the Mughal emperors battled with the MARATHAS, Mysore gained Bangalore. In 1761 HYDER ALI usurped power and launched the Mysore Wars of conquest. In 1799 his son, TIPU SULTAN, was defeated by the British. In 1973 Mysore was renamed Karnataka. Pop. (1991) 44,817,400.

Károly, Mihály, Count (1875–1955) Hungarian statesman, prime minister (1918), president (1919). He entered parliament in 1910. Favouring Hungarian autonomy, Károly opposed the alliance between the Austro-Hungarian Empire and Germany during World War 1. After Hungarian independence, he became president in January 1919 but resigned in March 1919 after failing to secure a favourable peace settlement with the Allies. Károly went into exile until 1946. He served (1947–49) as ambassador to Paris, but resigned in protest against Hungary's increasingly totalitarian government. *See also* KUN, BÉLA

Kasavubu, Joseph (1913?–69) Congolese statesman, president (1960–65). He was a leading figure in the Democratic Republic of CONGO's struggle for independence from Belgium. In 1955 Kasavubu became president of the Alliance of the Bakongo. After the first elections in the independent Congo, Kasavubu became president and his rival, Patrice LUMUMBA, became premier. The new republic was immediately confronted by civil disorder as the province of KATANGA seceded and Belgian troops were drafted in to protect the remaining Belgian residents. With the support of Colonel Joseph MOBUTU, Kasavubu ousted Lumumba. In 1965 Mobutu launched a second coup which forced Kasavubu to retire.

Kashmir Region in N India and NE Pakistan; former Indian princely state. Kashmir came under Muslim rule in 1346 and then Sikh rule in 1819. After the SIKH WARS, it was annexed (1846) to the kingdom of Jammu, which was ruled by the Hindu Dogra dynasty. When the Indian subcontinent was partitioned in 1947, the Hindu maharaja of Kashmir, Sir Hari Singh, acceded the state to India, precipitating war between India and Pakistan. A cease-fire agreement left it divided between the Indian-controlled state of JAMMU AND KASHMIR and the Pakistan-controlled areas in the N and W of the region. The N area of Kashmir is ruled directly by the Pakistan government; the W area, **Azad Kashmir**, is partly autonomous. The **Aksai Chin** area of Kashmir, on the border with Tibet, is occupied by China. Total area: 222,236sq km (85,806sq mi).

Kassem, Abdul Karim (1914–63) Iraqi soldier and statesman, prime minister (1958–63). He led the military coup that resulted in the assassination of Prince Faisal II and Prime Minister Nuri as-Said. Kassem became prime minister of the newly declared Republic of IRAQ. In 1959 Kassem defeated an uprising by forces seeking federation with the UNITED ARAB REPUBLIC (UAR) and Iraq pulled out of the BAGHDAD PACT. After losing the support of the military, following his failure to negotiate an end to the Kurdish rebellion (1961–62), Kassem was killed in a coup. *See also* KURDS

Kassites (Cassites) Ancient people who had settled in MESOPOTAMIA (now W Iran) by 1800 BC. After the HITTITES had overthrown the Old Babylonian dynasty, the Kassites moved into BABYLONIA and established (*c.*15th century BC) the second Babylonian dynasty based around their capital at Dur Kurigalzu (now Aqarquf, Iraq). They quickly adopted Babylonian customs and became assimilated into the native population. The Kassitic aristocracy acquired large estates, marked out by boundary stones and protected by warriors in horse-drawn chariots. In the reign (*c.*1232–1225 BC) of Kashtilash IV, Babylon was destroyed by ASSYRIA. The Kassites were finally defeated by ELAM (*c.*1155 BC) and withdrew to the Zagros Mountains, SW Iran. *See also* HURRIANS

Katanga (formerly Shaba) Southeastern province of the Democratic Republic of CONGO (formerly Zaïre), rich in mineral deposits, notably copper. In 1960, soon after Congo had achieved independence from Belgium, Moise TSHOMBE led a secessionist movement in Katanga. In the ensuing chaos Prime Minister Patrice LUMUMBA was overthrown. After bitter fighting, the revolt was finally crushed (1962) with the help of United Nations' (UN) troops. In 1977 separatist forces launched an unsuccessful invasion of Zaïre from Angola. Katanga was known as Shaba from 1972 to 1997. *See also* LUNDA

Kato Takaaki (1860–1926) Japanese statesman, prime minister (1924–26). He served as ambassador to Great Britain (1894–99, 1908–13). In 1913 Kato created the Constitutional Party. As foreign minister (1914–15), he presented the "Twenty-one Demands" to China, which resulted in Japan gaining commercial rights and territorial privileges in China. As prime minister, Kato introduced universal male suffrage, reduced the size of the military, and lessened the powers of the House of Peers. His government also introduced the Peace Preservation Law, which severely penalized political dissent.

Katsura Taro (1848–1913) Japanese statesman and soldier, prime minister (1901–06, 1908–11, 1912–13). He worked for the MEIJI RESTORATION (1868) that finally brought to an end the TOKUGAWA shogunate. Katsura emerged as one of the GENROS (elder statesman), who influenced the composition of Japanese government. He served in the first (1894–95) of the SINO-JAPANESE WARS. In his first term as prime minister, Katsura concluded the Anglo-Japanese Alliance (1902) with Great Britain and led Japan to victory in the RUSSO-JAPANESE WAR (1904–05). Katsura strongly opposed ITO HIROBUMI's foreign policy and annexed Korea (1910) during his second term.

Katyn Massacre (1940) Execution of *c.*4443 Polish officers by the Soviet Union during World War 2. After the NAZI-SOVIET PACT (1939) Germany and the Soviet Union launched a two-pronged assault on Poland. Many of the Polish soldiers captured by Soviet forces in Eastern Poland were interned in a prisoner-of-war camp at Smolensk, W Russia. When Germany invaded the Soviet Union (June 1941), Poland requested the return of 15,000 prisoners-of-war in order to form a Polish army. The Soviet government replied that most of the prisoners had escaped. In April 1943 German soldiers uncovered a mass grave in the village of Katyn, W Russia. The Soviet authorities claimed that the officers had been murdered by the German army, but independent investigations revealed that the officers had been shot in 1940. The Soviet government continued to maintain their innocence and Poland's post-war communist governments concurred with this view. In 1989 Poland's first non-communist government blamed the Soviet secret police and in 1992 the Russian authorities admitted responsibility.

Kaunda, Kenneth David (1924–) Zambian statesman, president (1964–91). In 1949 he joined the AFRICAN NATIONAL CONGRESS (ANC). Kaunda formed the Zambia African National Congress in 1959 and was imprisoned for his opposition to the British policy of federation for Northern Rhodesia (now ZAMBIA), Southern Rhodesia (now ZIMBABWE) and Nyasaland (now MALAWI). In 1960 Kaunda was released and became leader of the United National Independence Party (UNIP). Kaunda became the first post-colonial president of Zambia. He began to nationalize Zambia's industries, including the vital copper mines. In 1972 he imposed single-party rule. Kaunda was a staunch opponent of APARTHEID in South Africa and also supported Joshua NKOMO's struggle against Ian SMITH's white-minority regime in Rhodesia. Kaunda played a leading role in establishing an independent Namibia (1990). He was elected to a sixth term as president in 1988. In 1991 severe economic problems and political unrest forced him to allow multiparty elections in which he was defeated by Frederick Chiluba. In 1997, following a failed military coup, Kaunda was imprisoned. In 1998 he was released and resigned as leader of the UNIP.

Kaunitz, Wenzel Anton, Fürst von (1711–94) Austrian statesman. He negotiated the Treaty of AIX-LA-CHAPELLE (1748) that ended the War of the AUSTRIAN SUCCESSION (1740–48). As chancellor and foreign minister (1753–92) to the Habsburg rulers MARIA THERESA and JOSEPH II, Kaunitz favoured France over Austria's traditional ally, Prussia. His defensive alliance with France and Russia (1756) precipitated the SEVEN YEARS' WAR (1756–63) that ended in victory for FREDERICK II (THE GREAT) of Prussia. Kaunitz secured Austria a share in the first partition of POLAND (1772). The FRENCH REVOLUTION (1789) destroyed the French alliance.

Kayibanda, Grégoire (1924–) Rwandan statesman, president (1962–73). He was the leader of the Party for Hutu Emancipation, which was in the vanguard of the revolution against the Tutsi monarchy in the Belgian colony of Ruanda-Urundi. When Kayibanda became the first president of the independent Republic of RWANDA, thousands of Tutsis fled the country. In 1973 he was overthrown in an army coup, led by Juvénal HABYARIMANA.

Kazakstan *See* country feature

Kearny, Stephen Watts (1794–1848) US general. He fought at the Battle of QUEENSTON HEIGHTS during the WAR OF 1812. At the outbreak of the MEXICAN WAR (1846–48), Kearny quickly captured New Mexico, promising full citizenship to the Native Americans. He then led a successful march to California, taking San Diego (1846) and Los Angeles (1847). Kearny had John FRÉMONT court-martialled.

Keating, Paul John (1944–) Australian statesman, prime minister (1991–96). He entered Parliament in 1969 and served as treasurer (1983–91) under Bob HAWKE. In 1991 Hawke resigned and Keating succeeded him as prime minister and leader of the Australian LABOR PARTY. The youngest prime minister in Australia's histo-

KAZAKSTAN

AREA: 2,717,300sq km (1,049,150sq mi)
POPULATION: 17,038,000
CAPITAL (POPULATION): Astana (287,000)
GOVERNMENT: Multiparty republic
ETHNIC GROUPS: Kazak 40%, Russian 38%, German 6%, Ukrainian 5%, Uzbek, Tatar
LANGUAGES: Kazak (official); Russian is widely spoken
RELIGIONS: Mainly Islam, with a Christian minority
GDP PER CAPITA (1995): US$3010

Republic in Central Asia. Little is known of the early history of Kazakstan, except that it was the home of nomadic peoples. In 1218 the Mongols under GENGHIS KHAN conquered the region and on his death (1227), it became part of the khanate of JAGATAI and the GOLDEN HORDE. In the late 15th century, *c.*200,000 subjects of the Uzbek khan moved into the region. These nomads became known as Kazaks, and by the early 16th century they had built a mighty empire that encompassed most of the steppe. The empire rapidly fragmented into three separate khanates, dominated by tribal and clan leaders. The Mongol Dzungars launched two devastating attacks (1681, 1723) on present-day E Kazakstan, before being expelled (1758) by the QING Emperor QIANLONG. By 1742 all three Kazak khanates had accepted Russian protection. By the mid-19th century, Kazakstan had been incorporated into the Russian empire.

The conscription of Kazaks during World War 1 aroused much resentment, and after the RUSSIAN REVOLUTION (1917), demands for independence grew. In 1920 Kazakstan became an autonomous republic of the SOVIET UNION and in 1936 a full constituent republic. During the 1920s and 1930s, the process of Russification increased. Russians and Ukrainians were encouraged to colonize the republic and the Kazak population were forced to become sedentary farmers. Stalin's forced collectivization of agriculture and rapid industrialization caused a great famine, which claimed *c.*1.5 million Kazak lives. In the 1950s, the "Virgin Lands" project sought to turn vast areas of grassland into cultivated land to feed the Soviet Union. The Soviets placed many of their nuclear missile sites in Kazakstan and also built their first fast-breeder nuclear reactor at Mangyshlak, W Kazakstan. In 1986 nationwide riots followed the dismissal of Dinmukhamed Kunayev, who had served as first secretary of the Communist Party of Kazakstan since 1959.

In December 1991, after the collapse of the Soviet Union, Kazakstan declared independence and joined the COMMONWEALTH OF INDEPENDENT STATES (CIS). Nursultan NAZARBAYEV, a former leader of the Communist Party, became Kazakstan's first elected president. He maintained a close relationship with Russia. Multiparty parliamentary elections were held in 1994, and a new constitution (1996) increased the powers of Nazarbayev. In 1997 the government officially moved the capital from Almaty to Astana. Nazarbayev won a second term in 1999, but the elections were widely regarded as fraudulent.

ry, Keating enacted a number of financial measures designed to end economic recession. He was re-elected in 1993. An outspoken advocate of republicanism, Keating was defeated in the 1996 election by John HOWARD.

Kefauver, (Carey) Estes (1903–63) US politician. He served in the House of Representatives (1939–48) and the Senate (1949–63). As chairman of a Senate committee that investigated organized crime in interstate commerce, Kefauver uncovered widespread corruption and helped convict (1951) the gangster Frank Costello (1891–1973). He also co-sponsored the Celler-Kefauver Act (1950) that amended the CLAYTON ANTI-TRUST ACT (1914) to make monopolies illegal. In 1956 Kefauver ran for vice president on the Democrat ticket with Adlai STEVENSON, but they were defeated by President Dwight EISENHOWER.

Keita, Modibo (1915–77) Malian statesman, president (1960–68). In 1945 he cofounded and led the Sudanese Union, which merged with the African Democratic Rally to form the US-RDA. Keita was the first African vice president (1956–58) of the French National Assembly. He advocated federation of the French West African states and in 1959 became president of the Federation of Mali (now Mali and Senegal). The Federation collapsed just prior to independence and Keita became president of the Republic of Mali. He enacted socialist policies, such as the nationalization of industry. Keita vainly attempted to suppress opposition, but was overthrown in a military coup, led by Moussa TRAORÉ, and imprisoned until his death.

Keitel, Wilhelm (1882-1946) German field marshal. As commander in chief of the German army (1938–45), Keitel was Adolf HITLER's closest military adviser. In 1940 he imposed the terms of the French surrender. In 1941 Keitel was given command of the German invasion of the Soviet Union. Convicted of war crimes at the NUREMBERG TRIALS, he was executed. *See also* JODL, ALFRED

Kekkonen, Urho Kaleva (1900–86) Finnish statesman, prime minister (1950–53, 1954–56), president (1956–81). He served (1936–56) in parliament as a member of the Agrarian Party. In the aftermath of World War 2, Kekkonen and President Juho Kusti PAASIKIVI cultivated a policy of friendship towards the Soviet Union. The Agreement of Friendship, Cooperation and Mutual Assistance (1948) between Finland and the Soviet Union was extended in 1955 and 1970. As a sign of the new fraternity, Finland regained (1955) the port of Porkkala, s Finland. Kekkonen resigned in 1981 on the grounds of ill-health.

Kellermann, Francois Christophe (1735–1820) French general. He fought with distinction in the SEVEN YEARS' WAR (1756–63). In the FRENCH REVOLUTIONARY WARS (1792–1802), Kellermann's victory over the Prussians at the Battle of Valmy (20 September 1792), halted the invasion of France. As commander of the Army of the Alps (1792–93, 1795–97), he recaptured Savoy from Sardinia (1793). *See also* DUMOURIEZ, CHARLES FRANÇOIS

Kellogg, Frank Billings (1856–1937) US statesman, secretary of state (1925–29). He served as a Republican senator for Minnesota (1917–23) and ambassador to Britain (1923–25). As secretary of state under Calvin COOLIDGE, he negotiated the KELLOGG-BRIAND PACT (1928) that sought to outlaw war as an instrument of national diplomacy. Kellogg received the 1929 Nobel Prize for Peace.

Kellogg-Briand Pact (1928) International peace agreement negotiated by US Secretary of State Frank KELLOGG and French Foreign Minister Aristide BRIAND. It renounced war as a means of settling international disputes and was subsequently signed by 62 nations, including all of the major powers. The Pact was rendered ineffective by the number of its exclusion clauses and its lack of powers for enforcement. *See also* LOCARNO PACT

Kelly, Ned (Edward) (1855–80) Australian bushranger (rural outlaw). In the early 1870s, he was imprisoned for horse stealing. In 1877 Kelly shot and injured a policeman who was attempting to arrest his brother, Dan Kelly, for horse rustling. The brothers fled to the bush, where they formed a gang. The Kelly gang was responsible for a series of robberies (1878–80) in Victoria and New South Wales. Kelly was captured and hanged after a siege in Glenrowan township, during which the rest of the gang were killed. He became a folk hero among the dispossessed.

KENNEDY, JOHN FITZGERALD

John F. Kennedy was a charismatic leader. His foreign policy was marked by heightened tension during the Cold War, leading to greater US involvement in the affairs of Vietnam and Cuba. At home, he sought to improve civil rights for African Americans.

KENNEDY IN HIS OWN WORDS

"Ask not what your country can do for you; ask what you can do for your country"
Inaugural Address, 20 January 1961

"He [Khrushchev] has an opportunity to move the world back from the abyss of destruction."
Cuban Missile Broadcast, 22 October 1962

Kelsey, Henry (*c*.1670–1724) English explorer and fur trader. He was in the service of the HUDSON'S BAY COMPANY by 1684. Kelsey led an expedition (1690–92) westwards into the interior of Canada, perhaps reaching as far as the Saskatchewan River or Reindeer Lake. He served as governor of the Hudson's Bay Company (1718–22).

Kemal Atatürk *See* ATATÜRK, KEMAL

Kempis, Thomas à *See* THOMAS À KEMPIS

Ken, Thomas (1637–1711) English Anglican bishop. He became chaplain to Charles II in 1679 and was made bishop of Bath and Wells in 1685. Ken was one of seven bishops to publicly oppose the DECLARATION OF INDULGENCE (1688) issued by JAMES II, arguing that it promoted Roman Catholicism. Nevertheless, he remained loyal to James II during the GLORIOUS REVOLUTION (1688) and was deprived of his see (1691) for declining to take the Oath of Allegiance to WILLIAM III and MARY II.

Kennedy, Edward Moore (1932–) US politician, Democratic senator for Massachusetts (1962–). He was first elected to the Senate to complete the term of his brother John KENNEDY, who had become president. Following the assassination of his brothers, John and Robert KENNEDY, Ted Kennedy's own presidential chances were shattered in 1969, when he drove his car off a bridge on Chappaquiddick Island, Massachusetts, and his passenger, Mary Jo Kopechne, was drowned. Kennedy was found guilty of leaving the scene of an accident. During the 1980s, he was a leading critic of President Ronald REAGAN. Kennedy consistently campaigned for reforms to health and social welfare.

Kennedy, John Fitzgerald (1917–63) Thirty-fifth president of the United States (1961–63). He fought (1941–43) in the US Navy during World War 2, but was discharged after being badly wounded and was awarded a medal for bravery. Kennedy served three terms (1946–53) in the House of Representatives as a Democrat from Massachusetts. In 1953 he ran successfully for the Senate and soon after married Jacqueline Lee Bouvier. In 1957 he was awarded the Pulitzer Prize for *Profiles in Courage* (1956). In 1960 Kennedy gained the Democratic nomination and, after the first ever televised debates between presidential candidates, narrowly defeated his Republican challenger Richard NIXON. Kennedy was the youngest person and the first Roman Catholic ever elected to the presidency of the United States. He adopted an ambitious and liberal programme, termed the "NEW FRONTIER", and embraced the cause of CIVIL RIGHTS, but his planned legislation was frequently blocked by Congress. In foreign policy, Kennedy founded the ALLIANCE FOR PROGRESS in order to increase US influence in Latin America and created the PEACE CORPS. Adopting a strong anti-communist line, he was behind the disastrous BAY OF PIGS invasion of Cuba (1961), and stood firm against Nikita KHRUSHCHEV in the ensuing CUBAN MISSILE CRISIS (1962). He also increased US military aid to South Vietnam in the VIETNAM WAR (1954–75). In 1963 Kennedy stated his commitment to Berlin following the Soviet construction of the BERLIN WALL. Perhaps Kennedy's greatest foreign policy success was the NUCLEAR TEST-BAN TREATY (1963) between the United States, Great Britain and the Soviet Union. On 22 November 1963, Kennedy was assassinated in Dallas, Texas. Lee Harvey OSWALD was accused of being the assassin, but two days later was himself shot dead by Jack Ruby, a nightclub owner. The WARREN COMMISSION (1963–64) concluded that there was no plot to murder Kennedy and that Oswald had acted alone. In 1979 a special committee of the House of Representatives concluded that there was probably more than one gunman and that a conspiracy was likely. Kennedy was succeeded as president by Lyndon JOHNSON. *See also* COLD WAR

Kennedy, Joseph Patrick (1888–1969) US businessman and politician. He was chairman of the Securities and Exchange Commission (1934–35) and ambassador to Great Britain (1937–40). He was involved in many philanthropic endeavours, especially the Joseph P. Kennedy Memorial Foundation, founded for a son killed in World War 2. He was determined that his sons, Joseph Kennedy, Jr, John KENNEDY, Robert KENNEDY and Edward KENNEDY, should enter politics.

Kennedy, Robert Francis (1925–68) US lawyer and politician. He served on the Senate Select Committee on Improper Activities in Labor or Management Field (1957–59), where he clashed with the Teamsters' Union president Jimmy HOFFA. In 1960 he managed the successful presidential campaign of his brother John KENNEDY. Robert Kennedy became attorney general (1961–64), vigorously enforcing CIVIL RIGHTS laws and promoting the CIVIL RIGHTS ACT of 1964. After his brother's assassination, he left the cabinet and was elected (1964) senator for New York. While a candidate for the Democratic presidential nomination, he was assassinated (5 June) in Los Angeles, California.

Kenneth I (d. *c*.858) King of Scotland (*c*.843–58). He inherited the kingdom of Dalriada from his father, Alpin, in *c*.834. By 843, probably through marriage and military conquest, he had acquired the kingdom of the PICTS, which he united with his own territory to form the kingdom of Scotland. He moved the seat of government to Scone.

Kenneth II (d.995) King of Scotland (971–95), son of Malcolm I. He extended his kingdom southwards to the border of Cumbria and Yorkshire, and established his authority over central Scotland. Kenneth also sought to establish the right of his son, the future MALCOLM II, to the kingship against the claims of the descendants of kings Indulf and Culen

Kentucky State in SE central United States; the capital is Frankfort. Although there are extensive remains of Native American MOUND BUILDER cultures in Kentucky, when French explorers arrived in the 1670s they discovered only small populations of SHAWNEE and CHEROKEE. After the last of the FRENCH AND INDIAN WARS (1754–63), the region was ceded to Britain. In 1769 Daniel BOONE blazed the WILDERNESS ROAD from Virginia that opened up Kentucky to white settlers. Colonization was especially rapid after British defeat in the AMERICAN REVOLUTION

KENTUCKY
Statehood :
1 June 1792
Nickname :
Bluegrass State
State motto :
United we stand, divided we fall

K

(1775–83). Kentuckian statesman such as Henry CLAY and John CRITTENDEN failed to heal divisions within nation and state over the issue of SLAVERY, and Kentucky was claimed by both the Confederacy and the Union at the start of the American CIVIL WAR (1861–65). With the defeat of the Confederate invasion in 1862, Kentucky aligned with the Union. After the War, Kentucky resisted the expansion of civil rights to African Americans. In the 20th century, the diversification of Kentucky's economy lessened its dependence on the tobacco industry. Area: 104,623sq km (40,395sq mi). Pop. (1990) 3,685,296.

Kentucky and Virginia Resolutions (1798, 1799) Declarations of STATES' RIGHTS. Drafted by Thomas JEFFERSON (Kentucky Resolutions) and James MADISON (Virginia), they expressed opposition to the ALIEN AND SEDITION ACTS (1798). They denied the right of the federal government to exercise powers not granted it by the Constitution and declared that states had the right to judge the constitutionality of federal acts.

Kenya *See* country feature

Kenyatta, Jomo (1893–1978) Kenyan statesman, first prime minister (1963–64) then president of Kenya (1964–78), b. Kamau Ngengi. In the 1920s he campaigned for the return of lands from European settlers to his native KIKUYU tribe and became general secretary, Kikuyu Central Association (1924). A supporter of PAN-AFRICANISM, he joined with other future leaders of independent African states at the Fifth Pan-African Congress (1945). In 1947 he became president of the Kenya African Union. Kenyatta was imprisoned (1953–61) by the British for alleged involvement in the MAU MAU uprising (1952–56). In 1960 he was elected president of the Kenya African National Union (KANU), which led Kenya to full independence in 1963. In 1964 Kenya became a republic. Kenyatta's desire for national unity was expressed in his slogan, *Harambee* ("Pulling together"), and he assumed authoritarian powers to deal with any potential opposition. His fiscal policies, which encouraged private ownership and foreign ownership, produced economic growth but led to a rift with his vice president, Oginga ODINGA. Critics argued that economic prosperity was confined to an élite – often members of Kenyatta's entourage. He was succeeded by Daniel arap MOI. *See also* MBOYA, THOMAS JOSEPH

Kerala State on the Arabian Sea, sw India; the capital is Trivandrum. An early Dravidian kingdom (Keralaputra) existed in the region in the 3rd century BC. Arab spice-traders introduced Islam in the 8th century AD. Kerala was the first part of India to come under European influence, when the Portuguese explorer Vasco da GAMA arrived in 1498. In the 17th century, Portuguese influence was eclipsed by the Dutch. The region was subsumed into the British Madras Presidency in 1806. After Indian independence (1947), the region became known as Travancore-Cochin, later (1956) renamed Kerala. Usually ruled by a coalition government led by the Communist Party of India (M), its education and welfare system are among the most advanced in India, with a literacy rate of 80%. Area: 38,864sq km (15,005sq mi). Pop. (1991) 29,098,518.

Kérékou, Mathieu (1933–) (Ahmed Kérékou) Benin statesman and soldier, president (1972–91, 1996–). In 1972 he seized power in a military coup. Kérékou imposed Marxist policies through military repression. In 1975 he changed the name of the country from Dahomey to Benin. In 1989 Kérékou officially abandoned Marxism-Leninism and was defeated by Nicéphore Soglo in the ensuing multiparty elections. He returned to power at the head of a government of national unity.

Kerensky, Alexander Fyodorovich (1881–1970) Russian revolutionary, leader of the provisional government (July–November 1917). He joined the Socialist Revolutionary Party in *c.*1905 and was elected to the Duma in 1912. Kerensky initially supported Russia's entry into WORLD WAR I, but became increasingly disillusioned with the conflict and called for the overthrow of Tsar NICHOLAS II. In the first stage of the RUSSIAN REVOLUTION (March 1917), he became minister of justice in the republican government and adopted liberal reforms. In May 1917, Kerensky became minister of war and attempted to rally the demoralized troops. The July Offensive against the Germans was a military disaster and Kerensky sacked the army commander in chief, Lavr KORNILOV. Kerensky now became prime minister and attempted to suppress the BOLSHEVIKS, led by LENIN. He failed to take the radical measures needed to restore Russia's embattled economy and was only able to suppress a military coup by Kornilov with the help of the Bolsheviks. In November 1917 Kerensky was deposed by the Bolsheviks. He fled to France.

Kesselring, Albert (1885–1960) German field marshal. During WORLD WAR 2, he commanded the LUFTWAFFE in the Battle of BRITAIN (1940–41). In 1941 Kesselring was appointed commander in chief, south, by Adolf HITLER. In 1943 his brilliant defensive campaign in Italy delayed the Allied victory by more than a year, but he was forced to surrender in May 1945. In 1947 Kesselring was sentenced to death for his part in the massacre of Italian hostages in 1944. The sentence was commuted to life imprisonment and he was freed in 1952.

Kett, Robert (d.1549) English peasant leader. He led *c.*16,000 farmers in a protest, known as Kett's Rebellion, against ENCLOSURE. In July 1549, the farmers gathered at Norwich, E England, and soon took control of the city. Although their demands were moderate, the rebels were crushed in August by an army led by John Dudley, Duke of NORTHUMBERLAND. Kett was executed as a traitor.

Keynes, John Maynard (1883–1946) English economist. In 1919 he resigned as economic adviser to Prime Minister David LLOYD GEORGE, opposing the imposition of punitive reparations upon Germany. In *The General Theory of Employment, Interest and Money* (1936), which was strongly influenced by the GREAT DEPRESSION, Keynes established the foundation of modern macroeconomics. He argued against the doctrine of LAISSEZ-FAIRE, advocating the active intervention of government in the economy to achieve full employment and prosperity. Keynes was highly influential as an adviser during World War 2 and took a leading role in the BRETTON WOODS CONFERENCE of 1944.

KGB (*Komitet Gosudarstvennoye Bezhopaznosti*, Rus. Committee for State Security) Russian secret service. Its

KENYA

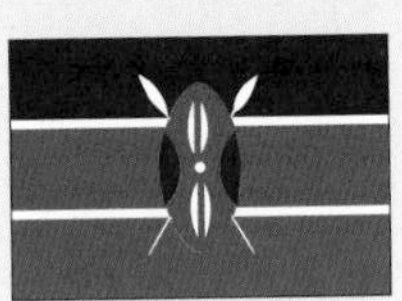

AREA: 580,370sq km (224,081sq mi)
POPULATION: 26,985,000
CAPITAL (POPULATION): Nairobi (1,346,000)
GOVERNMENT: Multiparty republic
ETHNIC GROUPS: Kikuyu 21%, Luhya 14%, Luo 13%, Kamba 11%, Kalenjin 11%
LANGUAGES: Swahili and English (both official)
RELIGIONS: Christianity 73% (Roman Catholic 27%, Protestant 19%, others 27%), traditional beliefs 19%, Islam 6%
GDP PER CAPITA (1995): US$1380

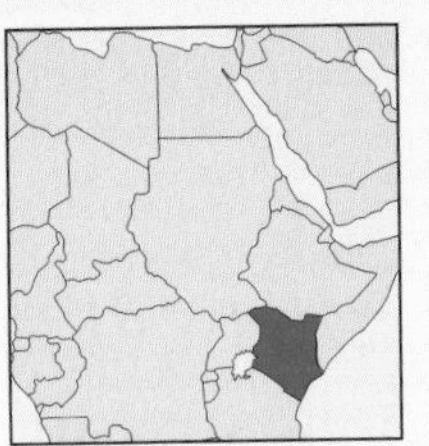

Republic in E Africa. Some of the earliest hominid fossils have been found in the Rift Valley of S Kenya. Kenya's coast has been a centre of trade for more than 2000 years. In the 8th century, the Arabs built trading settlements. In the 16th century, Portuguese and Indian traders established themselves along the coast. The pastoralist Masai moved into the area from the N in the 18th century, but many were displaced by the KIKUYU in the 19th century.

The British began to trade on the coast in the 1840s, while European missionaries and explorers began to venture into the interior. In 1882 Joseph THOMSON became the first European explorer to travel across the Masai lands to Lake Baringo, W Kenya. From 1887 the sultan of Zanzibar leased a strip of territory on the mainland to the British East Africa Association, but the Association lacked the resources to extend their control into the interior and the British government reluctantly took direct control, establishing the East Africa Protectorate in 1895. In 1903 the British completed a railway from the coastal port of Mombasa to Kisumu on the shores of Lake Victoria. The capital of the Protectorate transferred to Nairobi. The British encouraged settlers from Europe and South Africa, who established plantations and farms on land acquired from the Kikuyu. Social unrest was fermented by the institution of reserves for the native population and the often forced employment of Africans as plantation- and farm-labourers.

In 1920 the Protectorate became the Kenya Colony, while the coastal strip became known as the Kenya Protectorate. After World War 2, some leaders of the Kikuyu formed a secret society, the MAU MAU, which fought (1952–56) for land rights and independence. Britain declared a state of emergency and imprisoned (1953–61) its alleged leader, Jomo KENYATTA. In 1960 Kenyatta and Tom MBOYA formed the Kenya African National Union (KANU), which led Kenya to full independence (1963).

In 1964 Kenya became a republic, with Kenyatta as its first president. In 1966 Vice President Oginga ODINGA, who opposed Kenyatta's enthusiasm for private enterprise and conciliation with white settlers over land reforms, left the government to form the Kenya People's Union (KPU). In 1969 Kenyatta banned all political opposition. Accusations of tribal favouritism, economic inequality and territorial disputes with Uganda and Tanzania created civil unrest. In 1978 Kenyatta died and was succeeded by Daniel arap MOI.

Moi initially rejected calls for democracy and cracked down on dissent. Following nationwide riots in 1988, the government agreed to electoral reform. Moi was re-elected in the first multiparty elections in 1992, but independent observers claimed the ballot was rigged. In 1997 the International Monetary Fund (IMF) suspended financial aid to Kenya, which they refused to restore unless measures were taken to combat government corruption. Prior to the 1997 elections, 14 pro-democracy demonstrators were killed by police. Moi was re-elected amid further allegations of electoral malpractice. In 1998 fighting between the Kikuyu and Kalenjin tribes killed more than 100 people.

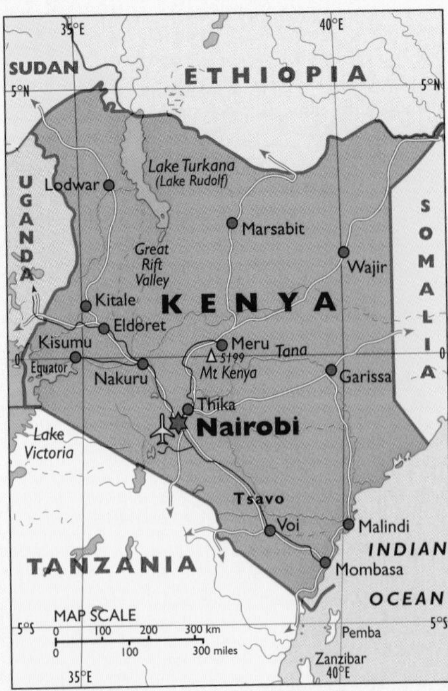

origins date back to the establishment of CHEKA in 1917. In 1923 the Cheka was replaced by the OGPU. The **OGPU** was responsible for enforcing the collectivization of agriculture and the administration of the GULAGS (labour camps). In 1934 the OGPU was subsumed into the **NKVD** which, under the control of Lavrenti BERIA, directed Joseph STALIN's Great PURGE (1936–38) of Soviet society. In 1953 Beria was executed and the secret police (now KGB) was placed under the control of the COMMUNIST PARTY OF THE SOVIET UNION (CPSU). By the 1980s, the KGB employed *c.*500,000 people and controlled all police, security and intelligence operations in the SOVIET UNION. The KGB maintained the largest espionage network of any government in the world. The KGB opposed liberalization under Mikhail GORBACHEV, and its chief led an attempted coup against him in 1991. After the collapse of the Soviet Union, it underwent extensive reform.

Khalid (1913–82) King of Saudi Arabia (1975–82), fourth son of IBN SAUD. Khalid's reputation as a conciliator and support for the Bedouin led to his appointment (1964) as crown prince in preference to his elder half-brothers. He became king when his half-brother, FAISAL, was assassinated. Illness forced him to hand much of the administration of Saudi Arabia to his other half brother, Prince FAHD. Khalid did not condemn the CAMP DAVID ACCORDS (1978) between Egypt and Israel and oversaw the diversification of the Saudi economy.

Khalid ibn al-Walid (d.642) Arab general. Defeated by the Prophet MUHAMMAD in the first military victory for ISLAM at Badr (624), he gained revenge at Uhud (625). In 629 Khalid converted to Islam and became, in Muhammad's words, "the Sword of Allah", helping to gain Mecca and other parts of the Arabian Peninsula. Under ABU BAKR, Khalid conquered Iraq and Syria. He was demoted by Caliph OMAR, but nonetheless led the Arab forces in the attack on Palestine and massacred the Byzantine army at the Battle of the Yarmuk Valley (636).

Khalji *See* DELHI SULTANATE

Khama, Sir Seretse (1921–80) Botswanan statesman, first president (1966–80) of Botswana. In 1925 he became chief of the Ngwato (Bamangwato) people. In 1950 Khama was banished from Bechuanaland (now Botswana) because of his marriage to Ruth Williams, a British woman, and was only allowed to return (1956) on the condition that he renounce his chieftainship. In 1962 he founded the Bechuanaland Democratic Party, which won the 1965 elections. When Botswana achieved independence (1966), Khama became president. He was committed to a multiracial democracy, and he established free universal education.

Khartoum Capital of Sudan, at the junction of the Blue Nile and White Nile rivers. It was founded (1821) as a military post by the Egyptian general MUHAMMAD ALI. In 1885 Khartoum was besieged and destroyed by the Mahdists and General Charles GORDON was killed. In 1898 it was recaptured by Horatio KITCHENER and became the capital of Anglo-Egyptian Sudan. In 1956 it became the capital of independent Sudan. Pop. (1983) 476,218. *See also* MAHDI

Khatami, Muhammad (1943–) Iranian statesman and cleric, president (1997–). A leading opponent of Shah Muhammad Reza PAHLAVI, he was elected to Iran's national assembly after the Islamic Revolution (1979). In 1982 Khatami was appointed minister of culture and Islamic guidance by Ayatollah Ruhollah KHOMEINI. Conservative clerics criticized Khatami's relatively liberal stance on press freedom and he was forced to resign in 1992. In the 1997 presidential elections, Khatami was supported by the outgoing President Hashemi RAFSANJANI, while his opponent received the tacit endorsement of Iran's supreme spiritual leader, Ayatollah Ali Khamenei. With his campaign for economic reform and greater social freedom, Khatami gained 70% of the vote. Khatami's moderate government faced strong opposition from the conservative establishment, and their blocking of reforms produced widespread unrest in 1999. His reforms were overwhelmingly endorsed in the 2000 parliamentary elections.

Khazars Extinct Turkic peoples, who by the beginning of the 7th century AD had established a large trading empire in the SE of modern European Russia. In the early 7th century, they fought alongside the Byzantines against the Iranians. From the mid-7th century to the mid 8th-century, the Khazars battled with the Arab empire, preventing the latter's progress across the Caucasus into E Europe. By the mid-8th century, the majority of the ruling class had converted to Judaism. In *c.*737 the Khazars established their capital at Itil (now Astrakhan), from where they expanded westwards to the River Volga. The Khazar empire declined under competition from the Pechenegs and the emerging power of KIEVAN RUS and was destroyed by Sviatoslav, Duke of Kiev, in 965.

Khilafat movement (1919–24) Indian Muslim organization that campaigned against the harsh terms imposed on Ottoman Turkey at the end of World War 1 (*see* Treaty of SÈVRES). In 1920 the Khilafat movement joined with the Indian National CONGRESS in pursuing a policy of non-cooperation with the British authorities. It was fundamentally weakened when Kemal ATATÜRK deposed the Turkish sultan in 1922 and abolished the caliphate in 1924.

Khmer empire (802–1431) Powerful kingdom founded by **Jayavarman II** (*c.*770–835) in what is now NW CAMBODIA. The vast irrigation network that enabled the Khmers to build a strong, unified empire was started under **Indarvarman II** (r.877–*c.*890). The Khmer capital of ANGKOR was established at the end of the 9th century. The ambitious temple-building programme of the Khmers required a huge labour force, which in turn required the Khmer kings to practise religious toleration. **Suryavarman I** (d. *c.*1050) expanded the empire westwards into modern Thailand and S Laos. SURYAVARMAN II (d. *c.*1150) was responsible for the construction of the massive temple complex of Angkor Wat, but his attempts to conquer the kingdom of CHAMPA (now S Vietnam) greatly weakened the empire, and Angkor was occupied and sacked by the Chams in 1177. JAYAVARMAN VII (r.1181–*c.*1215) defeated the Chams and restored the unity of the empire. Jayavarman's reign marked the height of the Khmer empire, bringing Champa, S Laos and parts of Burma and the Malay Peninsula under Khmer control. He also embarked on a huge rebuilding project at Angkor. After his death, however, the empire went into a slow decline. In the early 14th century, the mass of the population were converted to THERAVADA Buddhism. The empire was unable to repel attacks from the Thai, and Angkor was abandoned in 1431. The Khmers subsequently adopted Phnom Penh as the capital of a much-reduced kingdom.

Khmer Rouge Cambodian communist organization. It was formed in opposition to the royal government of Prince NORODOM SIHANOUK, but entered into a coalition with Sihanouk after he had been overthrown in a military coup (1970). In 1975 the Khmer Rouge gained control of CAMBODIA. Led by POL POT and Khieu Samphan, the organization enforced an extreme form of peasant politics upon Cambodian society. The ensuing massacre of professionals, intellectuals and skilled workers and the mass movement of people from urban centres to rural villages claimed the lives of *c.*2 million people. In 1979 the Khmer Rouge government was overthrown by the Vietnamese, who installed a republican government. The Khmer Rouge pursued a guerrilla war against the new regime, and in 1982 formed a new coalition with Sihanouk and the Khmer Peoples' National Liberation Front. In 1991 all the political factions agreed to a cease-fire, monitored by United Nations' (UN) troops. The Khmer Rouge refused to participate in the 1993 elections that saw a return to a parliamentary monarchy under Sihanouk. The organization was banned in 1994 and membership declined rapidly. In 1998 Pol Pot died.

Khomeini, Ruhollah (1902?–89) Iranian cleric who was the supreme religious and political authority in IRAN from 1979 until his death, b. Ruhollah Musawi. A SHIITE scholar, Khomeini attracted popular support for his condemnation of the secularization and Westernization of Iranian society under Shah Muhammad Reza PAHLAVI. In 1964, after a year's imprisonment, he was forced into exile. Khomeini eventually settled in An Najaf, central Iraq, from where he led opposition to the shah's rule. In January 1979, after massive demonstrations, the shah was forced into exile. Khomeini returned to Iran in triumph and established a conservative, theocratic state. Thousands of opposition leaders and supporters of the shah were summarily executed. SHARIA was reinstated and women were required to observe purdah. Khomeini's outspoken attacks on US imperialism prompted the seizure of the US embassy in Tehran and the ensuing IRAN HOSTAGE CRISIS (November 1979–January 1981). In September 1980 President Saddam HUSSEIN of Iraq invaded Iran, precipitating the IRAN-IRAQ WAR (1980–88). In his desire to export the Islamic Revolution, Khomeini refused to accept a negotiated settlement to the War, which claimed *c.*500,000 Iranian lives. He was finally forced to accede to a cease-fire after the United States sank several Iranian warships. In 1989 Khomeini issued a *fatwa* (death order) against Anglo-Indian writer Salman Rushdie (1947–). Ali Khamenei succeeded Khomeini as religious leader, while Hashemi RAFSANJANI became president.

Khoikhoi Khoisan-speaking people of S Africa, now almost extinct. Traditionally nomadic pasturalists, they first came into contact with Europeans in the late 16th century, exchanging cattle and sheep for copper, brass and iron. In the late 17th century, as AFRIKANERS began to establish farms on their traditional lands, the Khoikhoi were driven inland with the aid of horses and guns. By the early 18th century Khoikhoi society had begun to disintegrate, and in 1713 a smallpox epidemic killed many of those who had managed to survive. Descendants have mostly been absorbed into the South African population.

Khrushchev, Nikita Sergeievich (1894–1971) Soviet statesman, first secretary of the Communist Party (1953–64) and Soviet prime minister (1958–64). He fought for the Bolsheviks in the RUSSIAN CIVIL WAR (1918–20). In 1935 he became head of the COMMUNIST PARTY OF THE SOVIET UNION (CPSU) in Moscow. Khrushchev was a loyal supporter of Joseph STALIN and led the "Russification" of E Poland. After World War 2, he sought to combat the famine in Ukraine. In 1953 Khrushchev succeeded Stalin as first secretary, defeating the challenge of Georgi MALENKOV. Malenkov was replaced as prime minister by Nikolai BULGANIN. At the 20th Party Congress (1956), Khrushchev made a secret speech denouncing Stalin's dictatorial rule, the role of the secret police and the use of the GULAG. His speech had a immediately liberating effect within the Soviet sphere of influence. While Khrushchev tolerated the moderate reforms of Wladyslaw GOMUŁKA in Poland, he sent Soviet troops to suppress the HUNGARIAN UPRISING (1956) and prevent Imre NAGY's withdrawal from the WARSAW PACT. Khrushchev secured his domestic position by removing Vyacheslav MOLOTOV and Georgi ZHUKOV and assuming the position of prime minister. Khrushchev had an ambiguous relationship with the West. While he publicly supported a policy of DÉTENTE, he sanctioned the building of the BERLIN WALL (1961). The COLD WAR between the Soviet Union and United States threatened to escalate into a direct military confrontation during the CUBAN MISSILE CRISIS (1962), but Khrushchev eventually agreed to bring back the missiles. The thaw in relations between the two superpowers, however, served to heighten tensions between the Soviet Union and MAO ZEDONG's China. Khrushchev's failure to increase food production by cultivating the "virgin lands" of KAZAKSTAN and SIBERIA forced his resignation in 1964. He was replaced by Leonid BREZHNEV and Aleksei KOSYGIN.

Khufu *See* CHEOPS

Khusrau I (the Just) (d. AD 579) Shah of Iran (531–79). He restored order to the SASANIAN empire after the religious revolution of the Mazdakites. Khusrau reformed the taxation system and reorganized the government and bureaucracy, centralizing power and curbing the influence of the senior nobility. He embarked on military campaigns against the BYZANTINE EMPIRE, capturing (540) the city of Antioch (now ANTAKYA). Khusrau also conquered Yemen and gained tribute from the Hephthalites on the E border. He was a great patron of the arts and scholarship and is revered in Iranian folk-tales and legends. *See also* ZOROASTRIANISM; JUSTINIAN I (THE GREAT)

Khusrau II (the Victorious) (d. AD 628) King of Iran (590–628), grandson of KHUSRAU I (THE JUST). In 590 his father, Hormazd IV, was murdered and General Bahram usurped the throne. With the aid of the Byzantines, Khusrau crushed the palace revolt (591) and avenged his father's murder. Khusrau's reign saw the greatest expansion of the Sasanian empire. He invaded Armenia and Mesopotamia, capturing Damascus (613), Jerusalem (614), Alexandria (616) and Chalcedon (617). Byzantine Emperor Heraclius, allied with the Khazars, launched a brilliant counter-offensive (622–27) that resulted in the destruction of Canzaca. Khusrau was executed in a second palace revolt and was succeeded by his son, Kobad II.

Kidd, William (*c*.1645–1701) Scottish privateer and alleged pirate. In 1696 he set sail on a mission to defeat the pirates who were disrupting the English East India Company's trade in the Red Sea. By the end of 1697 he had failed to take any prizes and his crew threatened mutiny. In January 1698 Kidd captured the *Quedagh Merchant*, which he claimed was lawful booty, and later scuttled his own ship. In 1699 Kidd learned that he had been charged with piracy. He sailed to New York and presented himself to the colonial governor, who sent him to England for trial. Kidd was hanged for piracy and murder.

Kiesinger, Kurt Georg (1904–88) German statesman, chancellor of West Germany (1966–69). He joined the Nazi Party in 1933 and served in the foreign ministry during World War 2. After the War, Kiesinger was cleared of any involvement in Nazi crimes and was elected to the Bundestag as a member of the Christian Democratic Union (CDU) in 1949. He succeeded Ludwig Erhard as chancellor of a "grand coalition" government with the Social Democratic Party (SPD). Kiesinger improved relations with the Soviet Union and presided over an improving economy. He was succeeded as chancellor by Willy Brandt. *See also* Adenauer, Konrad

Kiev (Kiyev) Capital and largest city of Ukraine. The city was probably founded in the 6th or 7th century AD. In *c*.882 Kiev was captured from the Varangians (Vikings) by Oleg of Novgorod, who made it the capital of Kievan Rus. From the 10th to the 12th century, Kiev was the spiritual centre of Russia. In 1240 the city was destroyed by the Mongol horde under Batu. Rebuilt, Kiev was captured by the Grand Duchy of Lithuania in 1362 and passed to Poland in 1569. In 1667 Kiev became an autonomous Cossack state under the protection of the Grand Duchy of Moscow. Moscow assumed complete control in 1686. Kiev was a focus of Ukrainian resistance to Russian imperialism and briefly (1918) was the capital of an independent Ukraine. Kiev was a major battleground in the Russian Civil War (1918–20) and the victorious Bolsheviks made Kharkiv the capital of the new Ukrainian Soviet Socialist Republic. In 1934 Kiev was restored as capital of Ukraine. During World War 2, the city was occupied (1941–43) by the German army, who massacred much of the city's population at Babi Yar. In 1991, after the collapse of the Soviet Union, Kiev became capital of independent Ukraine. Pop. (1993) 2,600,000.

Kievan Rus First East Slavic state, based around the city of Kiev. The state was founded (AD 882) by Oleg of Novgorod. Because of its location on the River Dnieper, Kiev developed as the main port for trade between the Baltic and Black seas. At its height during the reign (980–1015) of Vladimir I (the Great), Kievan Rus stretched from Ukraine to the Baltic Sea. In 988 Vladimir adopted Christianity as the state religion, and by the 12th century the city of Kiev had more than 400 churches. Vladimir's son, Yaroslav I, codified Russian law for the first time. After Yaroslav's death (1054), Kievan Rus was fractured by civil war and weakened by incursions from the steppe. In 1240 Kiev was destroyed by the Mongol army under Batu. *See also* Golden Horde

Kikuyu Bantu-speaking people from the highlands of Kenya, E Africa. After the establishment of the British East Africa Protectorate (1895), the Kikuyu began to be displaced from their traditional lands by settlers from Europe and South Africa. Some Kikuyu resisted their resettlement in village reservations and formed a secret society, the Mau Mau, which waged an armed struggle (1952–56) for land rights and independence. Britain declared a state of emergency and imprisoned (1953–61) the Kikuyu leader, Jomo Kenyatta. After Kenya gained independence in 1963, Kenyatta was criticized for appearing to help the Kikuyu become the dominant political and economic group. They are Kenya's largest tribe, numbering *c*.4.4 million (20% of the population).

Killiecrankie, Battle of (27 July 1689) Jacobite victory over the forces of William III. On a plain at the top of the Pass of Killiecrankie in Perthshire, Scotland, *c*.3000 Jacobites under Viscount Dundee defeated the *c*.4000-strong army of General Hugh Mackay. Mackay lost nearly half his force, and Dundee was mortally wounded.

Kim Il Sung (1912–94) Korean dictator, first premier of North Korea (1948–72) and president (1972–94), b. Kim Sung Ju. He joined the Korean Communist Party in 1931 and fought in the resistance against Japanese occupation (1905–45). Following Japan's surrender (1945), Korea was divided along the 38th parallel. In 1948 Soviet forces withdrew from North Korea and Kim Il Sung became premier and chairman of the communist Korean Workers' Party. In 1950 Kim ordered the invasion of South Korea, precipitating the Korean War (1950–53), which claimed *c*.1.5 million North Korean lives. After failing to reunify Korea, Kim established an isolationist, Stalinist state in the North. He suppressed all political opposition and created a cult of his own personality. During his dictatorship, North Korea was accused of several acts of terrorism against South Korea. The national economy suffered as Kim concentrated on building up the military and acquiring nuclear weapons. He was succeeded by his son, Kim Jong Il.

Kim Jong Il (1942–) North Korean statesman, president (1994–), son of Kim Il Sung. Designated his father's successor as president in 1980, Kim Jong Il assumed a leading role in government and was included in the personality cult that surrounded his father. In 1990 he was appointed vice chairman of the National Defence Commission and in 1991 became supreme commander of the Korean army. A three-year period of mourning followed Kim Il Sung's death (1994), after which Kim Jong Il became general secretary of the Korean Workers' Party. His emphasis on military expenditure, both for conventional forces and nuclear-weapons' development, threatened to destroy the national economy and exacerbated the famine in North Korea.

Kim Young Sam (1927–) South Korean statesman, president (1992–98). He was president of the New Democratic Party (NDP) from 1974. In 1979 he was banned from politics for his opposition to President Park Chung Hee: the ban was lifted in 1985. As leader of the Democratic Liberal Party (DLP), Kim Young Sam became the first civilian president of South Korea. His efforts to reduce government corruption and abuses of power led to the arrests of former presidents Chun Doo Hwan and Roh Tae Woo. Kim's own government, however, became embroiled in a financial scandal and the economic crisis that swept through Southeast Asia in 1997 brought South Korea to the brink of financial collapse. Kim was narrowly defeated by Kim Dae Jung in the 1997 elections.

King, Martin Luther, Jr (1929–68) US Baptist minister and civil rights leader. In 1956, following the arrest of Rosa Parks, he led the boycott of racially segregated public transport in Montgomery, Alabama. As a founder (1957) and first president of the Southern Christian Leadership Conference (SCLC), King adopted from "Mahatma" Gandhi the tactics of non-violent direct action. In 1960 he was imprisoned after a sit-in at a department store in Atlanta, Georgia, and was released only after the personal intervention of the Democratic presidential candidate John Kennedy. King was again jailed in 1963, but his protest in Birmingham, Alabama, gained national coverage when the police used dogs and water-cannon to disperse demonstrators. After his release, King organized the March on Washington, D.C. (1963), where he made the famous "I have a dream..." speech. In 1964, after the passage of the Civil Rights Act, King became the youngest person to be awarded the Nobel Prize for Peace. In March 1965, the SCLC organized a voting-rights march in Selma, Alabama, which was broken up by state troopers using nightsticks and tear-gas. The event, known as "Bloody Sunday", prompted King to lead a second march. When the protestors were again confronted by state troopers, King decided to turn back. Although the Voting Rights Act (1965) was passed soon after, King's judgement was now questioned by leaders of the black-power movement, such as Stokeley Carmichael. Furthermore, King's condemnation of US involvement in the Vietnam War (1954–75) lost him the support of President Lyndon Johnson. King now addressed himself to the economic inequalities facing Africa Americans. On 4 April 1968, King was assassinated in Memphis, Tennessee. In 1969 James Earl Ray pleaded guilty to the murder and was sentenced to 99 years in prison. King's wife, **Coretta Scott King** (1927–), became a civil-rights leader after his death. His son, **Martin Luther King III**, was appointed leader of the SCLC in 1998. *See also* Abernathy, Ralph David; Jackson, Jesse Louis; Malcolm X; National Association for the Advancement of Colored People (NAACP)

King, Rufus (1755–1827) US statesman. As a member of the Continental Congress (1784–87), he introduced legislation calling for a new constitution and prohibiting slavery in the Northwest Territory. King then

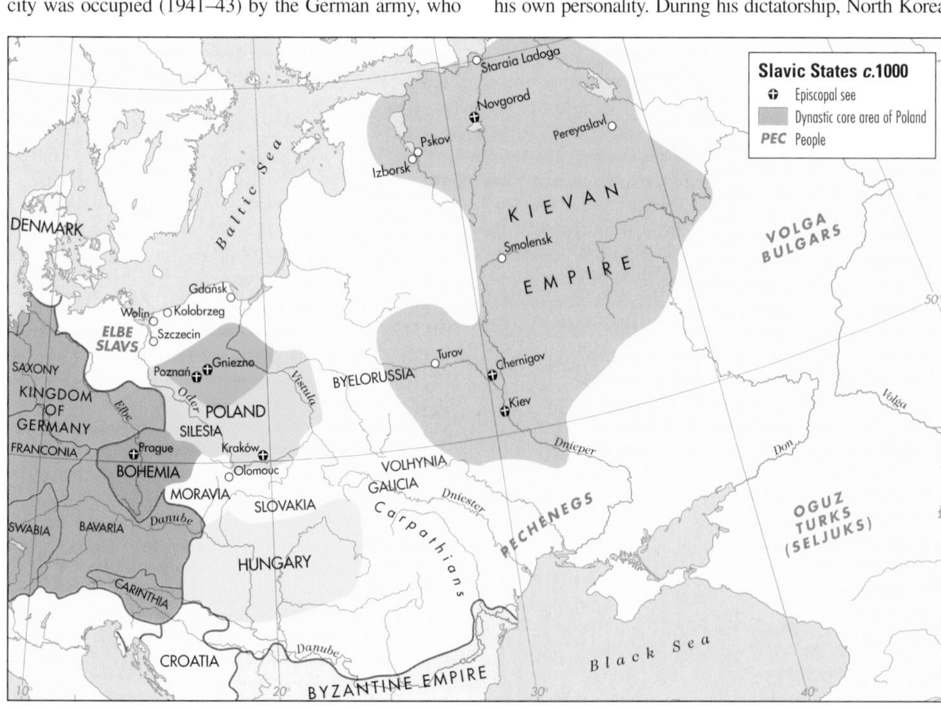

◀ **Kievan Rus** Trade with Byzantium had a strong cultural impact on Kievan Rus and influenced the religion, architecture and language that came to define Russian culture.

helped to draft and pass the CONSTITUTION OF THE UNITED STATES (1789). He served as a US senator from New York (1789–96, 1813–25) and as ambassador to Great Britain (1796–1803, 1825–26). He was an unsuccessful presidential candidate in 1816.

King, William Lyon Mackenzie (1874–1950) Canadian statesman, prime minister (1921–26, 1926–30, 1935–48). He was elected to Parliament in 1908 and became minister of labour (1909–11) under Wilfred LAURIER. In 1919 King succeeded Laurier as leader of the LIBERAL PARTY. In 1925 King's coalition government lost a vote of confidence, but the British governor general refused to dissolve Parliament and asked Conservative leader Arthur MEIGHEN to form an administration. The 1926 election was fought largely on the issue of the constitution and, after he was re-elected, King helped draft the Statute of WESTMINSTER (1931), which established the British COMMONWEALTH OF NATIONS. His reduction of tariff barriers with the United States and Great Britain aided Canadian recovery after the Great Depression. After Canada's entry (1939) into World War 2, King skilfully managed to avoid the introduction of conscription, which would have divided French- from English-speaking Canada. He also began the post-war reconstruction of Canada. King was succeeded by Louis SAINT LAURENT.

King George's War (1744–48) *See* FRENCH AND INDIAN WARS

King Movement (Kingitanga) Alliance of MAORI tribes that sought to unify native resistance against European settlement on New Zealand. The King Movement developed after the First MAORI WAR (1845–48). In 1857 several Maori tribes around Waikato, central North Island, elected Te Wherowhero as King Potatau I. In 1863 British Governor George GREY launched a direct attack on Waikato and war raged throughout North Island. In 1872 the conflict ended and supporters of the King Movement retreated to "King Country", west central North Island. This area remained unsettled by Europeans until 1881.

King Philip's War (1675–76) War between English settlers and Native Americans in New England. The Wampanoags, under their chief, Philip (Metacomet), rebelled against the expansion of white settlers into their territory. Philip gained the support of the Narraganset and most of the other New England tribes. The Native Americans raided frontier towns, while the colonial militia attacked native villages. There was much brutality on both sides, *c.*600 settlers and *c.*3000 Native Americans were killed and *c.*50 settlements were destroyed. The Narraganset were crushed in the Great Swamp Fight (December 1675). Threatened by famine after the destruction of their crops, Native American resistance crumbled in the spring of 1676. King Philip was killed in August 1676 and the war came to an end, leaving the settlers free to expand westwards. *See also* FRENCH AND INDIAN WARS

King William's War *See* FRENCH AND INDIAN WARS

Kinnock, Neil Gordon (1942–) British politician, leader of the LABOUR PARTY (1983–92). He was elected to Parliament in 1970. Kinnock succeeded Michael FOOT as leader of the Labour Party and led opposition to the Conservative government of Margaret THATCHER. Despite reforming the Labour Party, he was unable to overcome Thatcher's huge majority in the 1987 general election and narrowly lost to John MAJOR in the 1992 general election. Kinnock resigned in favour of John SMITH. In 1994 he became a European commissioner for transport. In 1999 Kinnock became vice president of the EUROPEAN COMMISSION, with responsibility for administrative reform.

Kiribati (formerly Gilbert Islands) Independent republic within the Commonwealth of Nations, consisting of three island groups (Gilbert, Phoenix and Line) in the central Pacific Ocean. The Gilbert Islands and Banaba were first settled by Micronesians, *c.*4000 years ago. Spanish explorers sighted some of the islands in the early 17th century. British navigators first visited the islands in the late 18th century, including Thomas Gilbert who sighted Tarawa in 1788. The Gilbert and Ellice islands became a British protectorate in 1892 and a crown colony in 1916. The colony was occupied (1942–43) by the Japanese during World War 2 and Tarawa witnessed fierce fighting between US and Japanese forces (1943). In 1978 the Ellice Islands seceded as TUVALU. Kiribati was granted full independence in 1979.

Kirk, Norman Eric (1923–74) New Zealand statesman, prime minister and foreign minister (1972–74). Elected to Parliament in 1957, he became leader of the Labour Party in 1964. In the 1972 election, Kirk led the Party to its first victory for 12 years. As prime minister, he withdrew New Zealand from the Vietnam War (1954–75) and opened links with communist China.

Kirov, Sergei Mironovich (1886–1934) Soviet politician. He took part in the RUSSIAN REVOLUTION (1917) and fought for the Bolsheviks in the RUSSIAN CIVIL WAR (1918–20). Kirov helped establish the Transcaucasian Soviet Republic in 1922 and became head of the Communist Party in Leningrad (now St Petersburg) in 1926. Kirov's growing power was confirmed by his election (1930) to the Politburo. His murder, possibly on Joseph STALIN's orders, served as a pretext for the Great PURGE (1934–38) of senior Old Bolsheviks. *See also* KAMENEV, LEV BORISOVICH

Kish (now Tall al-Uhaimer, S Iraq) Ancient city-state of MESOPOTAMIA, located just E of BABYLON on the River Euphrates. The earliest historical ruler of SUMERIA was Etana, king of Kish (active *c.*2800 BC). After Etana's death, a rival dynasty was formed at URUK. Clay tablets from the reign of Mesilim (active *c.*2500 BC) reveal the start of a civil war between the Sumerian city-states. Excavations since AD 1922 have revealed that SARGON, king of AKKADIA, built a palace here in *c.*2600 BC. Nebuchadnezzar II and Nabonidus, kings of Babylon, are thought to have erected temples here in the 6th century BC. *See also* LAGASH; UR

Kishi Nobusuke (1896–1987) Japanese statesman, prime minister (1957–60), brother of SATO EISAKU. He served (1941–44) in the WORLD WAR 2 cabinet of TOJO HIDEKI and became the leading advocate of a peace settlement. After the war, Kishi was imprisoned (1945–48) by the Allies. He was a founder (1955) of the Liberal Democratic Party. As prime minister, Kishi sought to reconcile Japan with its East Asian neighbours and renegotiate the US-Japanese security treaty. The suspicion that the revised treaty aligned Japan even more closely with the United States fuelled domestic opposition. Kishi was forced to resign by mass demonstrations, prompted by his attempt to force the treaty through the Diet while the opposition were boycotting the chamber.

KING, MARTIN LUTHER, JR

Martin Luther King, Jr, forced the US government to confront racial injustice. He argued that an individual had a moral responsibilty to resist unjust laws.

KING IN HIS OWN WORDS

"I have a dream that one day, on the red hills of Georgia, the sons of former slaves and the sons of former slave-owners will be able to sit down together at the table of brotherhood."
Speech, Washington, D.C., 28 August 1963

"Well, I don't know what will happen now; we've got some difficult days ahead. But it really doesn't matter with me now, because I have been to the mountain-top."
Last speech, Memphis, 3 April 1968

Kissinger, Henry Alfred (1923–) US statesman and political scientist, secretary of state (1973–77), b. Germany. In 1938 his family emigrated to the United States to escape Nazi persecution. As head of the National Security Council (1969–75) under President Richard NIXON, Kissinger promoted a policy of DÉTENTE with the Soviet Union, which resulted in the STRATEGIC ARMS LIMITATION TALKS (SALT). He also opened relations between China and the United States. Nixon and Kissinger ordered the Central Intelligence Agency (CIA) to help overthrow Salvador ALLENDE's government in Chile. As secretary of state, Kissinger shared the 1973 Nobel Prize for Peace with LE DUC THO for their role in negotiating a cease-fire in the VIETNAM WAR (1955–75). The strategy for ending the Vietnam War was, however, a dual one: alongside the peace talks, the United States stepped up its bombing of North Vietnam and launched secret raids (1970) on Cambodia. Kissinger's "shuttle diplomacy" achieved a cease-fire in the YOM KIPPUR WAR (1974) between Egypt and Israel. After the fall of Nixon, Kissinger continued as secretary of state under President Gerald FORD. *See also* ARAB-ISRAELI WARS; HAIG, ALEXANDER

Kitchener, Horatio Herbert, 1st Earl (1850–1916) British field marshal, statesman and colonial administrator, b. Ireland. He took part in the unsuccessful relief of General GORDON at KHARTOUM (1883–85), but defeated the Mahdist forces at the Battle of OMDURMAN and helped defuse the FASHODA INCIDENT with the French (both September 1898). Kitchener served a year as governor general of the SUDAN, before being appointed chief of staff in the second of the SOUTH AFRICAN WARS (1899–1902). His ruthless tactics, including the establishment of concentration camps, weakened Afrikaner resistance and led to a British victory. Kitchener was now sent to India and gained full control over the army after the resignation (1905) of Lord CURZON. Kitchener's experience of reorganizing the British Army in India led to his appointment as secretary of state for war at the outbreak of WORLD WAR I. Kitchener argued for the training of a vast army of volunteers and his image appeared on the recruitment posters. He was drowned at sea when his ship was sunk by a German mine near the Orkney Islands. *See also* MAHDI

Klaus, Václav (1941–) Czech statesman, prime minister (1993–97). Following the "Velvet Revolution" (1989), he became finance minister in Václav HAVEL's administration. In 1991 Klaus founded the Civic Democratic Party (ODS). He became prime minister of the Czech Republic following the break-up of Czechoslovakia. Problems with the economy and accusations of corrupt financial practices led to Klaus' resignation. In 1998 he was elected president of the Czech parliament.

Kléber, Jean Baptiste (1753–1800) French general. In 1789, after the outbreak of the FRENCH REVOLUTION, he joined the National Guard and fought with distinction in the FRENCH REVOLUTIONARY WARS (1792–1802). At the start of the Wars of the VENDÉE (1793–93), Kléber crushed a royalist rebellion in NW France. He was wounded at the start of NAPOLEON's invasion of Egypt (1798), but recovered to defeat the Ottoman Turks at Mount Tabor (1799). In 1800 he was appointed commander of the expeditionary forces in Egypt and recaptured Cairo from the Turks. He was assassinated by a Muslim.

Klondike Gold Rush (1896–1904) Mass migration of gold prospectors to the Klondike region, Yukon Territory, NW Canada. The rich gold deposits discovered (1896) in the Klondike River brought more than 30,000 prospectors to the territory. Within a decade more than US$100 million worth of gold had been extracted. The easily accessible lodes were exhausted by *c.*1910, but mining continues.

knight In medieval Europe, a professional cavalryman. The knight served an apprenticeship as a squire and, after a period of trial, was often knighted with a sword touch on the shoulder. Knights were often landholders, owing military service to their overlord. Knighthood gradually acquired a Christian code of behaviour (CHIVALRY), which was most evident during the time of the CRUSADES. The KNIGHTS HOSPITALLERS and KNIGHTS TEMPLAR were founded at the start of the Crusades. The military importance of the knight declined as the FEUDAL SYSTEM was replaced by a centralized monarchy. Honorary orders of knighthood, such as the Order of the GARTER (1349), were founded towards the end of the Middle Ages. *See also* LIVONIAN ORDER; TEUTONIC KNIGHTS

Knights Hospitallers (Knights of Malta) Christian military order founded (*c.*1113) to defend JERUSALEM after its capture (1099) in the First CRUSADE. The KNIGHTS were responsible for tending the sick in the Hospital of St John of Jerusalem. After the fall of Jerusalem (1187) to SALADIN, they moved to Acre, then to Cyprus. In 1309 the Knights Hospitallers captured RHODES, from where they were expelled by the Ottoman Sultan SULEIMAN I in 1522. In 1530 Emperor CHARLES V gave them the island of MALTA, which they successfully defended against the Turks in 1565. In 1798 they were driven from Malta by NAPOLEON and eventually settled in Rome. The order still exists as an international, humanitarian charity. *See also* CHIVALRY; MONASTICISM; KNIGHTS TEMPLAR

Knights of Labor First mass national labour organization in the United States, founded (1869) in Philadelphia, Pennsylvania. It was organized initially as a secret workers' group by Uriah STEPHENS, but became a national organization in 1878. Skilled and unskilled workers, regardless of race, sex or colour, were eligible to join local assemblies, which together formed a single UNION. By 1886 the Knights of Labor had *c.*700,000 members. The union declined after the HAYMARKET RIOT (May 1886) and several strike failures. The organization was dissolved in 1913. *See also* AMERICAN FEDERATION OF LABOR AND CONGRESS OF INDUSTRIAL ORGANIZATIONS (AFL-CIO)

Knights Templar Christian military order, founded (*c.*1119) to protect pilgrims to the newly established Kingdom of JERUSALEM. BALDWIN II of Jerusalem furnished them with headquarters close to the site of the former Jewish TEMPLE OF JERUSALEM. The rules of the order were drawn up by Saint BERNARD OF CLAIRVAUX. The KNIGHTS originally pledged allegiance to the ruler of Jerusalem, but in 1139 Pope INNOCENT II placed them under papal jurisdiction. With their rivals the KNIGHTS HOSPITALLERS, the Knights Templar became a vital force in the defence of the Crusader states and acquired great wealth and large landholdings in Western Europe. In 1307 PHILIP IV of France accused the Templars of heresy and confiscated all their property in France. Philip persuaded Pope CLEMENT V to abolish the order in 1312. *See also* CHIVALRY; CRUSADES

Knossos Ancient palace complex in N central Crete, near modern IRÁKLION. In 1900 Arthur EVANS began excavations, which revealed that the site had been inhabited before 3000 BC. His main discovery was a palace from the MINOAN CIVILIZATION (built *c.*2000 BC and rebuilt *c.*1700 BC). Close to the palace are the houses of Cretan nobles. The complex also contains many frescoes. Knossos dominated Crete *c.*1500 BC, but the palace was occupied *c.*1450 BC by invaders from MYCENAE.

Know-Nothing movement (officially American Party) US political organization active in the 1850s. It arose from secret, anti-immigrant and anti-Catholic societies and derived its nickname from its members' standard answer to inquiries about the organization. The Party called for strict limits on immigration and greater barriers to citizenship and voting-rights. Its popularity peaked after the passage of the KANSAS-NEBRASKA ACT (1854), sending 43 representatives to Congress in 1855. But in the 1856 elections, former Whig president Millard FILLMORE carried just one state (Maryland). The Know-Nothing movement split over the issue of SLAVERY, with anti-slavery supporters joining the Republican Party and those in favour of slavery linking with the Democratic Party. The remnants of the movement formed the CONSTITUTIONAL UNION PARTY.

Knox, Henry (1750–1806) American general in the AMERICAN REVOLUTION (1775–83). As commander of the artillery in the Continental Army, Knox hauled the *c.*55,000kg (120,000lb) of British guns captured at Fort Ticonderoga, New York, to Boston, Massachusetts – a journey of *c.*480km (300mi). He played a leading role in the Continental victories at the Battle of Monmouth (1778) and the Battle of Yorktown (1781). At the end of the war, Knox succeeded George WASHINGTON as commander of the army. He served as secretary of war (1785–94).

Knox, John (*c.*1514–72) Scottish religious reformer, leader of the REFORMATION in Scotland. Ordained a Catholic priest, he came under the influence of George WISHART, who was burned as a heretic by Cardinal David BEATON in 1546, and converted to PROTESTANTISM. As a result of his association with the assassins of Beaton, Knox was captured (1547) at St Andrews' Castle by French soldiers and served as a galley slave for 19 months. EDWARD VI of England secured Knox's release and he became an itinerant Protestant preacher. On the accession of the Catholic MARY I (1553), Knox fled to the continent and urged English Protestants to rebel against the queen. Following publication of his *First Blast of the Trumpet against the Monstrous Regiment of Women* (1558), which argued that rule by women was contrary to both nature and religion, Knox was banned from returning to England by the new Protestant Queen ELIZABETH I. In 1559 Knox was recalled to Scotland to lead Protestant resistance to the Catholic Queen Regent MARY OF GUISE. Threatened by an invasion from France, Knox appealed for help, and France was forced to withdraw by a joint Scottish-English army in 1560. Knox now persuaded the Scottish Parliament to adopt the Scots Confession (1560), which made Protestantism the state religion. In the *Book of Common Order* (adopted 1562), Knox set out the basic tenets of later PRESBYTERIANISM. He was a fierce enemy of the Catholic MARY, QUEEN OF SCOTS, who charged him with treason in 1563. Knox stood firm, however, and Mary was forced to abdicate in favour of the Earl of MORAY in 1567. *See also* CALVINISM; CHURCH OF SCOTLAND; PURITANISM; REFORMED CHURCH

Kohl, Helmut (1930–) German statesman, chancellor (1982–98). In 1973 Kohl became chairman of the CHRISTIAN DEMOCRATIC UNION (CDU), but lost the 1976 elections to the SOCIAL DEMOCRATIC PARTY (SPD) led by Helmut SCHMIDT. In 1982 Schmidt's coalition government fragmented and he was forced to resign in favour of Kohl. Kohl was confirmed as chancellor in the 1983 elections. His conservative policies included strong support for the North Atlantic Treaty Organization (NATO) and a reduction in government expenditure. Kohl and French President François MITTERRAND led the drive for closer integration within the EUROPEAN UNION (EU) and the establishment of a single European currency. In 1990 Kohl presided over the reunification of East and West Germany and was elected as the first chancellor of a reunified GERMANY. He was re-elected in 1994 and 1996. High unemployment and economic recession, mainly caused by the cost of reunification, contributed to Kohl's 1998 election defeat by Gerhard SCHRÖDER of the SPD. In 2000 Kohl became embroiled in a scandal involving secret donations to the CDU.

Kolchak, Alexander Vasilievich (1874–1920) Russian admiral and counter-revolutionary. He commanded the Baltic and Black Sea fleets during World War 1. After the RUSSIAN REVOLUTION (1917), Kolchak led White Russian forces in Siberia during the RUSSIAN CIVIL WAR (1918–20). In 1918 he assumed the title supreme ruler of Russia and established a capital at Omsk. In 1919 Kolchak was forced to flee to Irkutsk, where he was captured and executed by the BOLSHEVIKS.

Kollontai, Alexandra Mikhailovna (1872–1952) Russian revolutionary and feminist, b. Alexandra

KOREA, NORTH (OFFICIALLY DEMOCRATIC PEOPLE'S REPUBLIC OF KOREA)

AREA: 120,540sq km (46,540sq mi)
POPULATION: 22,618,000
CAPITAL (POPULATION): Pyongyang (2,639,448)
GOVERNMENT: Single-party people's republic
ETHNIC GROUPS: Korean 99%
LANGUAGES: Korean (official)
RELIGIONS: Traditional beliefs 16%, Chondogyo 14%, Buddhism 2%, Christianity 1%
GDP PER CAPITA (1994): US$1155

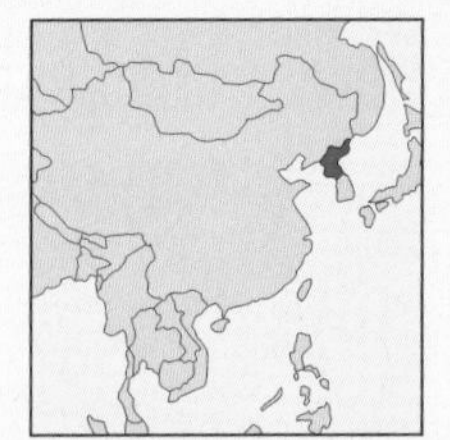

Republic in E Asia, occupying the N part of the Korean Peninsula (for pre-1948 history, *see* KOREA). In 1948 North Korea established a communist government led (1948–94) by KIM IL SUNG. His Stalinist regime exploited North Korea's rich mineral resources. Industry was nationalized. Heavy industry and arms production greatly increased and agriculture was collectivized and mechanized.

In June 1950 North Korea invaded South Korea. The ensuing KOREAN WAR (1950–53) killed *c.*1.5 million North Koreans and failed to produce a unified Korea. After the war, several million Koreans fled Kim Il Sung's dictatorial regime. North Korea became a secretive, isolated nation. Alliances were formed with China and the Soviet Union, and the collapse of the latter in 1989 had adverse effects on North Korea's economy. Its emphasis on military expenditure had a destabilizing effect on regional politics and internal economic planning.

In 1991, upon joining the United Nations (UN), North Korea and South Korea signed a non-aggression pact and agreed to hold meetings on reunification. The process was temporarily halted by the death (1994) of Kim Il Sung. He was succeeded by his son, KIM JONG IL. During the early 1990s, North Korea's nuclear-weapons building programme gathered momentum. In 1994 North Korea briefly withdrew from the Nuclear Non-Proliferation Treaty. It rejoined after agreeing to halt the reprocessing of plutonium, in return for guarantees on energy supplies and the establishment of economic and diplomatic relations with the United States. In 1995 severe flooding caused more than US$15 billion of damage and devastated agricultural production. In 1996 the United Nations (UN) sent emergency food aid to relieve widespread famine. In 1998 North Korea launched a ballistic missile over Japanese airspace.

Domontovich. A life-long campaigner for the rights of women workers, Kollontai joined the banned Russian Social Democratic Labour Party (RSDLP) in 1899 and the Bolsheviks in 1904. While in exile (1908–17), she organized against World War 1. On her return to Russia, Kollontai fought in the Russian Revolution (1917) and was appointed commissar for social welfare in Lenin's new government. After sponsoring social reforms, such as the simplification of divorce proceedings and collective childcare, Kollontai resigned (1918) over the ceding of Finland to the White Russians at the Treaty of Brest-Litovsk (1918). She also led the Workers' Opposition against the bureaucratization of the Soviet state. In 1923 Kollontai became the first woman to serve as minister to a foreign country (in this instance Norway). Although increasingly marginalized under Joseph Stalin, she continued to act as a diplomat and negotiated the armistice that ended the Russo-Finnish War (1939–40).

Kongo Former kingdom in w central Africa, founded in the 14th century. By 1500 the Kongo stretched from the mouth of the River Congo to include much of modern-day NW Angola and NE Democratic Republic of Congo. In 1483 Portuguese navigator Diogo Cão came in contact with the kingdom and emissaries from the Kongo returned with him to meet John II of Portugal. In 1491 Portuguese missionaries and traders visited Mbanza, the capital of Kongo. King Nzinga Nkuwu (later João I) and his son (later Afonso I) were converted to Christianity. Afonso I (r. *c.*1506–*c.*1550) adopted Portuguese institutions and customs, while the population of the Kongo forcibly resisted conversion. The Kongo kingdom was undermined by the greed of Portuguese settlers, who carried on a brisk slave trade. As a result of continued depredations by the Portuguese and wars between rival chiefdoms, the kingdom collapsed in the late 1660s, allowing Portugal to take control of the area.

Konoe Fumimaro (1891–1946) Japanese statesman, prime minister (1937–39, 1940–41). During his first term as prime minister, Konoe tried unsuccessfully to restrict the power of the military and find a peaceful solution to the Sino-Japanese War (1937–45). Soon after the outbreak of World War 2, he signed (1940) the Tripartite Pact with Germany and Italy. Hoping to avert US involvement in the war with China, he then entered into negotiations with the United States. In 1941 he was forced out of power by Tojo Hideki. Indicted as a war criminal by the Allies, he committed suicide.

Köprülü Fazil Ahmed Pasha (1635–1676) Turkish grand vizier (chief minister) to Sultan Muhammad IV, eldest son of Köprülü Muhammad Pasha. He succeeded his father as grand vizier in 1661. Fazil concluded favourable peace terms at the end of the war with Austria (1663–64), and gained Candia (now Iráklion), Crete, from war with Venice (1669). But perhaps his greatest success was the annexation of the Polish Ukraine in 1672.

Köprülü Muhammad Pasha (1578?–1661) Turkish grand vizier (chief minister) to Ottoman Sultan Muhammad IV, b. Albania. He was appointed grand vizier in 1656 and immediately crushed all internal opposition. Muhammad Pasha reorganized the army, restricting the power of the Janissaries, and defeated the Venetian fleet in the Dardanelles (1657). His invasion of Transylvania (1658) led to a 40-year conflict with the Habsburgs. In 1659 Muhammad Pasha mercilessly punished a rebellion by the Ottoman governor generals of Anatolia and Syria. He was succeeded as grand vizier by his son Köprülü Fazil Ahmed Pasha.

Koran (Qur'an, Arabic "Recitation") Sacred book of Islam. According to Muslim belief, the Koran contains the actual word of God (Allah) as revealed in Arabic to the Prophet Muhammad. Muhammad is said to have received these revelations over two decades beginning (*c.*AD 610) on the Night of Power (commemorated at Ramadan) and ending in 632, the year of his death. The revelations were collected by Zayd ibn Thabit and handed to the caliph Omar. The 114 *suras* (chapters) of the Koran are the source of Islamic belief and a guide for the whole life of the community. The seven verses of the first sura (*fatihah*) are a devotional prayer. The central teachings of the Koran are that there is no God but Allah and all must submit to Him, that Muhammad is the last of His many messengers (which have included Abraham, Moses and Jesus), and that there will come a day of judgment. In addition to these teachings, the Koran contains rules that a Muslim must follow in everyday life. *See also* Hadith

Korea Peninsula in E Asia. The first state, Choson, began to emerge in the River Taedong basin at the start of the Iron Age (*c.*4th century BC). In 108 BC Choson fell to Han colonists from China. In the 1st century BC, the three kingdoms of Koguryo (N), Paekche and Silla (S) began to develop. In the AD 660s, Silla, with military assistance from the Chinese, conquered Paekche and most of Koguryo (the remnants of Koguryo formed the state of Parhae). The Chinese were themselves expelled in 676. Buddhism, which first reached Korea in the 4th century, flourished in the unified, absolute monarchy of Silla. In 918 General Wang Kon conquered Koguryo and went on to establish the unified kingdom of Koryo (936–1392). The Mongol Yüan dynasty invaded the kingdom in 1231, eventually forcing Korea to accept Mongol domination in 1258. In 1392, following a series of rebellions, the Koryo dynasty was replaced by the Yi dynasty (1392–1910). Early in the Yi period, Seoul was made the new capital and Confucianism replaced Buddhism as the organizing ethical system. In the 1590s Korea was devastated in the process of defeating Japanese invasions led by Toyotomi Hideyoshi. In the 17th century, Korea was a semi-independent state, dominated by the Manchu dynasty. The first trading contacts with Europe were made in the mid-17th century. In the early 19th century, Roman Catholic missionaries and converts were executed or forced to renounce their religion, and Korea closed its doors to the West. In 1875 Japan forced Korea to open its ports to foreign trade and declare its independence from the Chinese Qing dynasty. Following the suppression of the Tonghak Uprising (1894) by Chinese troops, the Sino-Japanese War (1894–95) confirmed Japanese supremacy in Korea. At the end of the Russo-Japanese War (1904–05), Korea became a Japanese protectorate and it was formally annexed in 1910. On 1 March 1919, a peaceful demonstration against Japanese military rule was brutally crushed, killing *c.*7500 protestors. Syngman Rhee responded by forming a government-in-exile in Shanghai, SE China. After Japan's defeat at the end of the World War 2 (1939–45), Korea was divided into two zones of occupation along the 38th parallel, with Soviet forces to the N and US forces to the S. Attempts at reunification failed, and in 1948 two separate regimes were established: North Korea and South Korea. *See also* Korean War

Korea, North *See* country feature

Korea, South *See* country feature, page 228

Korean War (1950–53) Conflict between North Korea and South Korea. After Japan's defeat (1945) in World War 2, Korea was divided into two zones of occupation along the 38th parallel. Soviet forces withdrew from North Korea in December 1948 and US troops pulled out of South Korea in June 1949. A number of skirmishes along the 38th parallel gave North Korea the excuse to launch a full-scale invasion in June 1950. By the end of that month, North Korea had captured the South Korean capital of Seoul. The United Nations' (UN) Security Council, during a boycott by the Soviet Union, voted to provide military assistance to South Korea and US President Harry Truman ordered US armed intervention in Korea. UN forces, chiefly comprised of US troops, were placed under the command of General Douglas MacArthur. The UN forces suffered a series of defeats, and by July 1950 North Korea controlled 90% of the Peninsula. The US sent large numbers of reinforcements and halted the North Korean advance outside Pusan, SE Korea, in August 1950. In September 1950, MacArthur made an amphibious landing at Inchon, W Korea. Trapped in a pincer movement, North Korean forces were rapidly expelled and *c.*170,000 surrendered. UN forces advanced across the 38th parallel into North Korea and by the end of October 1950, they had reached the Chinese border. Mao Zedong now intervened and *c.*200,000 Chinese troops compelled the UN forces to retreat and Seoul was recaptured. After more heavy fighting and intensive bombardment of North Korea, UN forces slowly regained the initiative. By March 1951 the War had reached virtual stalemate, just north of the 38th parallel. MacArthur sought to extend the conflict to mainland China and Truman replaced him with General Matthew Ridgway. Negotiations and bloody fighting along the 38th parallel continued for the next two years until US President Dwight Eisenhower signalled that he was prepared to use nuclear weapons against China. In July 1953 a truce established a buffer zone between the two Koreas. The War claimed a total of *c.*4 million lives: *c.*1.5 million North Koreans (including 1 million civilians), *c.*1.3 million South Koreans (1 million civilians), *c.*1 million Chinese, *c.*37,000 Americans, *c.*3000 other UN forces. *See also* Acheson, Dean Gooderham; Cold War; Truman Doctrine

Kornilov, Lavr Georgievich (1870–1918) Russian general. He served in the Russo-Japanese War (1904–05). Appointed commander in chief of the Russian army by Alexander Kerensky in August 1917, Kornilov launched a new offensive hoping to improve Russia's fortunes in World War 1. Later that month, he sent troops to Petrograd (now St Petersburg). Kerensky accused Kornilov of attempting a military coup and imprisoned him. After the Bolsheviks seized power (November 1917) in the second phase of the Russian Revolution, Kornilov escaped and led the anti-Bolshevik (White) forces at the start of the Russian Civil War (1918–20). He was killed at Ekaterinodar (now Krasnodar).

Koryo Korean dynasty that ruled (936–1392) over the entire Korean Peninsula (the Western name for the country derives from the dynasty). It was established by General Wang Kon after he had conquered the kingdoms of Koguryo (918), Silla (935) and Paekche (936). Koryo modelled its culture and political system on Song China. Buddhism flourished as the central source of spiritual fulfillment, while Confucianism was the organizing system

K

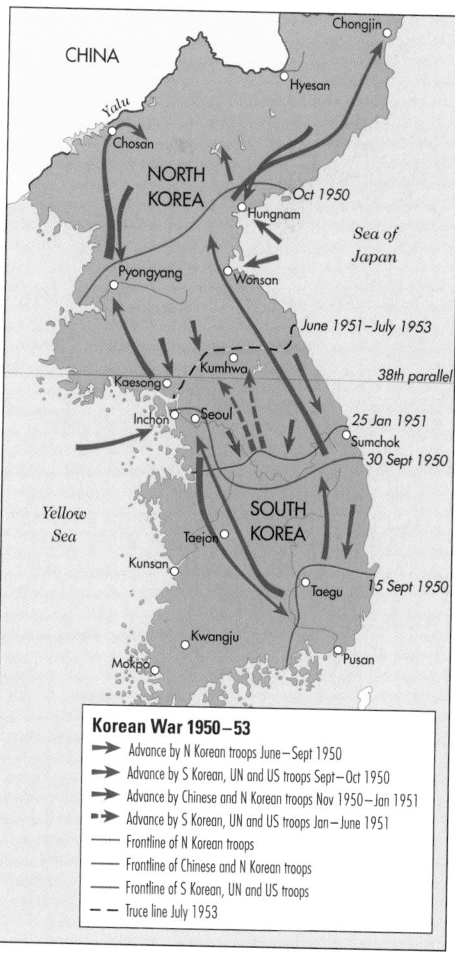

▲ **The Korean War** was one of the bloodiest confrontations of the Cold War. There has never been a formal peace treaty and tension between the two Koreas continues to the present-day.

for politics and ethics. King Songjong (r.981–97) established a centralized bureaucracy, but the subsequent rise of civilian officials created a dispossessed military and General Choe Chunghon launched a successful coup in 1197. The **Choe dynasty** (1197–1258) ruled behind a succession of puppet kings. In 1231 Korea was invaded by the Mongol YUAN dynasty and the Koryo fled to Kanghwa Island, W Korea, from where they led resistance until 1258. After a peace treaty (1258), the Koryo dynasty struggled on under Mongol domination until 1392, when they were overthrown by the YI DYNASTY (1392–1910).

Kosciuszko, Tadeusz (1746–1817) Polish general and national hero. He fought for the Continental Army in the American Revolution (1775–83). Kosciuszko return to Poland and helped defeat the Russian army of Catherine II (the Great) at the Battle of Dubienka (July 1792), but failed to prevent the second Partition of POLAND (1793). He now led the liberal uprising against Russian and Prussian rule in Poland. Kosciuszko defeated the Russians at Raclawice (April 1794) but was soon forced to retreat to Warsaw, where he mounted a heroic and successful defence of the city. In October 1794 Kosciuszko was wounded and captured at Maciejowice and the rebellion collapsed. In 1796 he was released by Tsar Paul I and went into exile.

Kosovo Autonomous province in SW Serbia; the capital is Pristina. Ethnic Albanians make up 90% of the population. The Ottoman victory at the Battle of Kosovo (1389) signalled the collapse of Serbian resistance to the Turks. In 1912 Kosovo was included in the new state of Albania, but was ceded to SERBIA in 1913 and was incorporated into the Kingdom of the Serbs, Croats and Slovenes (later YUGOSLAVIA) in 1918. In 1946 Kosovo became an autonomous province of Serbia. In 1989 Serbian President Slobodan MILOŠEVIĆ imposed direct rule on the province. In 1992 Kosovo voted overwhelmingly in favour of secession from Yugoslavia. Tension between Kosovo's Albanian and Serb populations was heightened by the influx of Serb refugees from the Croatian province of KRAJINA. In March 1998 the Yugoslav army was drafted in to crush the Kosovo Liberation Army (KLA) and *c.*200,000 Kosovan Albanians were forced from their homes. In March 1999, after the failure of peace negotiations, North Atlantic Treaty Organization (NATO) forces began a campaign of air strikes against the Yugoslav military. Milošević intensified the assault on the ethnic Albanians, creating an additional *c.*860,000 refugees. In June 1999 NATO's intensive bombardment of Yugoslavia finally produced a peace agreement. The Yugoslav army agreed to withdraw and a United Nations' (UN) peacekeeping force (K-FOR) was deployed. More than 200,000 Serbs fled Kosovo in fear of reprisals from ethnic Albanians. By 2000, UN inspectors had exhumed more than 2100 bodies from mass graves. NATO bombing killed *c.*500 civilians. Ethnic violence continues. Area: 10,887sq km (4205sq mi). Pop. (1998 est) 1,800,000.

Kossuth, Lajos (1802–94) Hungarian nationalist, who led the Hungarian Revolution (1848–49). Kossuth served (1832–36) in the Hungarian Diet and his accounts of its proceedings became highly popular. In 1837 he was sentenced to three years' imprisonment by the Austrians. In 1847 Kossuth returned to the Diet, where he called for extensive liberal reforms. On 15 March 1848, inspired by the REVOLUTIONS OF 1848 in Paris and Vienna, Sándor PETOFI led a bloodless revolution in Pest (now BUDAPEST) and the March Laws proclaimed an independent Hungarian parliament. Emperor FERDINAND I acceded to the demands and Lajos BATTYÁNY formed a government, which included Kossuth (minister of finance) and Ferenc DEÁK. Kossuth now demanded the creation of an independent MAGYAR state and the other nationalities (mainly Serbs and Croats) rebelled. Battyány and Deák resigned, leaving Kossuth as virtual dictator of Hungary. A hastily assembled Magyar army defeated the rebels and Kossuth deposed the HABSBURG monarchy and proclaimed himself governor of the republic of Hungary (April 1849). Emperor FRANZ JOSEPH appealed for Russian military assistance and the combined armies forced Kossuth to flee in August 1849. He continued to champion Hungarian independence from exile, but the creation (1867) of the AUSTRO-HUNGARIAN EMPIRE put an end to his hopes. *See also* BACH, ALEXANDER; METTERNICH, KLEMENS WENZEL LOTHAR, PRINCE VON

Kosygin, Aleksei Nikolaievich (1904–80) Soviet statesman, prime minister (1964–80). He was a leading member of the COMMUNIST PARTY OF THE SOVIET UNION (CPSU) in Leningrad (now St Petersburg), helping to organize the mass evacuation of the city during the Nazi siege (1941–44). In 1940 Kosygin was appointed deputy prime minister. After World War 2, Kosygin fell out of favour with Joseph STALIN, but after Stalin's death was rehabilitated as economics adviser to Nikita KHRUSHCHEV. In 1964 Kosygin replaced Khrushchev as prime minister, at first sharing power with Leonid BREZHNEV. He announced the eighth FIVE-YEAR PLAN (1966–70), which continued Khrushchev's emphasis on the production of consumer goods, but set more realistic targets. Kosygin was gradually eclipsed by Brezhnev and was forced to retire in 1980.

Koxinga (1624–62) *See* ZHENG CHENGGONG

Krajina Region in central CROATIA. In 1691, fearing reprisals from the Ottoman Turks, *c.*50,000 Serbs fled from KOSOVO to Krajina, Croatia, where they established a Serbian enclave. During World War 2, the Krajina Serbs were subject to brutal repression by the Croatian fascist government. In 1990, after the election of the nationalist Franjo TUDJMAN as president of Croatia, Serbian separatists declared autonomy in Krajina. In June 1991, Croatia declared independence from YUGOSLAVIA, prompting SERBIA's President Slobodan MILOŠEVIĆ to provide military assistance to the Serbian guerrillas in Krajina. By the end of 1991, the Croat population of Krajina had been expelled. Serbian autonomy in Krajina was recognized in a cease-fire (1992), and a United Nations' Protection Force (UNPROFOR) was sent to the region. In August 1995 the Croatians invaded Krajina, creating *c.*150,000 Serbian refugees (many of whom were resettled in Kosovo). Atrocities were committed on both sides.

Kraków (Cracow) City on the River Vistula, S Poland. Traditionally founded in the 8th century, Kraków became a residence of the Polish kings in the 12th century and capital of Poland in 1320. Under the JAGIELLON dynasty, Kraków became one of the major cities of medieval Europe. In 1596 the capital transferred to WARSAW. Kraków was ceded to Austria in 1795. After a period of independence (from 1815), it was restored to Austria in 1846. Kraków became part of Poland after World War 1. During World War 2 it was occupied (1939–45) by the Germans, who sent *c.*55,000 Jews from the city to the death camp at AUSCHWITZ. Historic buildings include the 16th-century Wawel Cathedral. The Jagiellonian University (1364) is one of the oldest in Europe. Pop. (1993) 751,300.

Kravchuk, Leonid Makarovich (1934–) Ukrainian statesman, first president of UKRAINE (1991–94). He

KOREA, SOUTH (OFFICIALLY REPUBLIC OF KOREA)

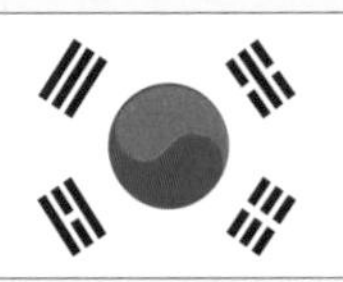

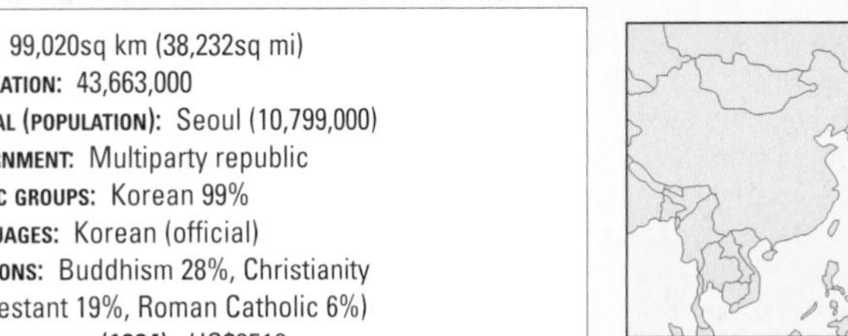

AREA: 99,020sq km (38,232sq mi)
POPULATION: 43,663,000
CAPITAL (POPULATION): Seoul (10,799,000)
GOVERNMENT: Multiparty republic
ETHNIC GROUPS: Korean 99%
LANGUAGES: Korean (official)
RELIGIONS: Buddhism 28%, Christianity (Protestant 19%, Roman Catholic 6%)
GDP PER CAPITA (1994): US$8519

Republic in E Asia, occupying the S part of the Korean Peninsula (for pre-1948 history, *see* KOREA). South Korea's first government, led (1948–60) by Syngman RHEE, was beset by economic problems. South Korea was a predominantly agricultural economy, heavily dependent on the N for energy and resources.

In June 1950 North Korea invaded South Korea. The ensuing KOREAN WAR (1950–53) claimed *c.*1.3 million South Korean lives and devastated the nation's infrastructure. Rhee's corrupt and repressive regime became increasingly unpopular. In 1960 the massacre of student protesters sparked nationwide disturbances, and a military junta, led by General PARK CHUNG HEE, seized power in 1961. Park's presidency (1963–79) brought rapid economic growth. Helped by aid from the United States, South Korea became a major manufacturer and exporter. In 1972 Park introduced martial law and passed a new constitution that gave him almost unlimited powers. His regime pursued increasingly authoritarian policies. In 1979 Park was assassinated, but the military continued to dominate the government.

In 1987 a new constitution ensured the popular election of the president and reduced the presidential term to five years. In 1988 Seoul hosted the Summer Olympic Games. Relations with North Korea continued to improve, and in 1991 the two countries signed a non-aggression pact and established a series of summit meetings on reunification. In 1992 the long-standing opposition leader, KIM YOUNG SAM, became president. His administration was South Korea's first full civilian government in 32 years. The death (1994) of North Korean president KIM IL SUNG stalled reunification talks, but the momentum had been established.

During the late-20th century, Korea's was one of the world's fastest growing industrial economies. In 1997, however, several major industrial conglomerates (*chaebols*) collapsed. Over-lending by South Korea's banks and the crisis in the rest of Southeast Asia devastated national finances. Labour reform laws led to redundancies and rising unemployment. The International Monetary Fund (IMF) agreed to a record US$21 billion rescue package. In the 1997 elections Kim Young Sam was defeated by Kim Dae Jung.

joined the Communist Party in 1958, rising to become chairman of the Ukrainian Supreme Soviet in 1990. Kravchuk initially opposed Ukrainian independence, but later came to embrace the cause and was elected president of the new republic. He was one of the founders of the COMMONWEALTH OF INDEPENDENT STATES (CIS) and struggled to prevent Russian domination of Ukraine. In 1992 Kravchuk signed a treaty with Boris YELTSIN on the status of the Black Sea fleet in CRIMEA. The poor state of the Ukrainian economy contributed to his defeat by Leonid Kuchma in the 1994 elections.

Kreisky, Bruno (1911–90) Austrian statesman, chancellor (1970–83). He joined the Social Democratic Party of Austria in 1926. In 1938 Kreisky fled to Sweden to escape Nazi persecution. After his return to Austria (1950), Kreisky served as foreign minister (1959–66). In 1970 he formed Austria's first all-socialist government. Kreisky's chancellorship was characterized by modernization and social reform, and he presided over a period of rising prosperity. In foreign affairs, he pursued a policy of "active neutrality".

Kremlin (Rus. citadel) Historic centre of MOSCOW, Russia. It is a roughly triangular-shaped fortress, covering *c*.36.5ha (90 acres). The Kremlin was originally constructed (1156) of wood, but was rebuilt in stone by Italian architects during the reign of IVAN III (THE GREAT). Within the walls lie the Italianate-BYZANTINE Cathedral of the Assumption, where the patriarchs of the Russian ORTHODOX CHURCH are buried, the Cathedral of the Annunciation, the Armoury Palace and the Great Kremlin Palace, home of the former Supreme Soviet of the SOVIET UNION. The east side of the Kremlin faces Red Square, which contains the 16th-century Cathedral of Saint Basil and the LENIN Mausoleum. Red Square has witnessed many executions, demonstrations and parades. Today, the Kremlin is the Russian presidential headquarters.

Krishna Menon, V.K. *See* MENON, (VENGALI KRISHNAN) KRISHNA

Krishnamurti, Jiddu (1895–1986) Hindu religious leader. He founded the World Order of Star with Annie BESANT, the theosophist leader, dissolving it in 1929. In 1969 he founded the Krishnamurti Foundation in Ojai, California.

Kristallnacht (9–10 November 1938) Night of violence against Jews throughout Germany and Austria. It was incited by a speech made by Joseph GOEBBELS to the BROWNSHIRTS (Nazi stormtroopers) on receiving news that a German diplomat in Paris had been shot by a Polish Jew. During the "Night of Broken Glass", 91 Jews were killed, and *c*.177 synagogues and *c*.7500 Jewish businesses were destroyed. The GESTAPO arrested *c*.30,000 Jews, forcing them to surrender their possessions and emigrate. Kristallnacht marked the start of an intensified campaign of Jewish persecution by the NAZI regime. *See also* HOLOCAUST, THE

Kronstadt Naval base near St Petersburg, Russia. It was the scene of a sailors' revolt (March 1921) against the BOLSHEVIK government. While the sailors' support had proved crucial to the success of the RUSSIAN REVOLUTION (1917), they had become disillusioned by the economic privations during the RUSSIAN CIVIL WAR (1918–20). The RED ARMY, led by Leon TROTSKY, ruthlessly crushed the revolt but, by revealing the depths of popular discontent, it contributed to LENIN's introduction of the NEW ECONOMIC POLICY (1921).

Kropotkin, Peter Alexeievich (1842–1921) Russian anarchist and geographer. His studies of the Siberian mountains revised the maps of E Asia. Kropotkin was jailed for seditious propaganda in 1874, but escaped into exile in 1876. He was again jailed (1883–86) in France. In 1887 Kropotkin settled in England, where he became the leading theorist of ANARCHISM, arguing for the abolition of private property and a radical reorganization of social institutions. In *Mutual Aid* (1902), Kropotkin argued that cooperation rather than competition is the organizing principle of evolution. After the first phase of the RUSSIAN REVOLUTION (March 1917), he returned to Russia and criticized the authoritarian tendencies of the BOLSHEVIKS after they seized power in November 1917.

Kruger, Paul (Stephanus Johannes Paulus) (1825–1904) South African statesman and soldier, president (1883–1902) of the South African Republic (TRANSVAAL). He took part in the GREAT TREK (1835–40) from Cape Colony to the Transvaal. In 1877 Britain annexed Transvaal, and Kruger led the fight for independence. He fought (1880–81) in the first of the SOUTH AFRICAN WARS, and afterwards was elected president of the South African Republic. Kruger was re-elected in 1888, 1893 and 1898. The discovery (1886) of gold at Johannesburg fuelled Cecil RHODES' desire to crush the republic and create a united British South Africa. In 1895 Kruger defeated the JAMESON RAID and received a telegram of congratulations from Emperor WILLIAM II of Germany. Kruger ignored the overtures of the governor of Cape Colony, Sir Alfred MILNER, and refused to grant equal status to non-AFRIKANER (Boer) settlers, thereby precipitating the Second South African War (1899–1902). Kruger was forced into exile, where he sought support for the Afrikaner cause. He died in Switzerland. *See also* JOUBERT, PIET; PRETORIUS, MARTHINUS WESSEL

Kubitschek (de Oliveira), Juscelino (1902–76) Brazilian statesman, president (1956–61). As governor of Minas Gerais (1951–55), he improved the state's infrastructure. After his election to the presidency, Kubitschek began an ambitious programme of public works, borrowing heavily to improve Brazil's transport system and develop its heavy industries. Perhaps the most visible of these projects was the construction of a new capital, Brasília. Kubitschek's plans contributed to rampant inflation and mounting national debt.

Kublai Khan (1215–94) MONGOL general and first emperor (1271–94) of the YUAN dynasty (1206–1368), grandson of GENGHIS KHAN. From 1251 to 1259 he helped his brother, Möngke, in the war against the Southern SONG dynasty of China. In 1260 Kublai succeeded Möngke as khan. Kublai's reign, however, was beset by civil war with other Mongol rulers of the steppe, who contested his legitimacy and loathed his rejection of Mongol traditions in favour of Chinese ones. Kublai established his capital at Tatu (now BEIJING), N China, in 1267 and his court attracted visitors from across Asia and even Europe (*see* Marco POLO). In 1279 Kublai completed the conquest of the Song and became master of all China. Kublai was not content with this achievement and enforced tribute from other states, including Burma. However, his attempted invasions (1274, 1281) of Japan were wrecked by typhoons. Kublai divided the population of China into four classes (in descending order): Mongols, foreign advisers, Northern Chinese and lastly the former subjects of Southern Song China. Under Kublai Khan, Chinese trade flourished with the establishment of a single currency, the granting of concessions to private shipowners and the rebuilding of the GRAND CANAL. Trade produced an influx of cultural influences from W Asia, in such areas as medicine, mathematics and astronomy. His reign was marked by religious toleration and the encouragement of TIBETAN BUDDHISM. *See also* MING

Küçük Kainarji, Treaty of (1774) Diplomatic agreement ending the RUSSO-TURKISH WAR (1768–74), signed at Küçük Kainarji, Bulgaria. It gave Russia a foothold on the Black Sea. Turkey agreed to Crimean independence, ceded important ports and territories to Russia and guaranteed free passage to Russian ships on the Black Sea. The Treaty also gave Russia the right to represent Greek Orthodox Christians in MOLDAVIA and WALLACHIA.

Ku Klux Klan (KKK) Name of two secret, white, racist groups in the United States. The first Ku Klux Klan was organized in the South in 1866. Opposed to RECONSTRUCTION, it attempted to enforce labour discipline in plantation districts and to maintain white supremacy by preventing African Americans from voting. Dressed in white robes and hoods, Klansmen terrorized African-American communities. By 1872 the Klan had been suppressed by federal authorities. A second Ku Klux Klan was founded in 1915, embracing broader-based racism directed also against Catholics, Jews and communists. By the mid-1920s, its membership was *c*.4 million. It declined thereafter, but there was a minor resurgence in opposition to the 1960s CIVIL-RIGHTS movement and in some Southern states in the 1990s. Today, there are *c*.5000 Klan members.

kulak (Rus. fist) Prosperous Russian peasant. Before the RUSSIAN REVOLUTION (1917), the kulaks were the dominant force in the countryside, owning medium-sized farms and earning enough money to hire labour. Although the kulaks were considered capitalists by the BOLSHEVIKS, their interests were promoted by Lenin's NEW ECONOMIC POLICY of 1921. They often held important roles in village administration and were seen as a threat to the communist authorities. They suffered from the COLLECTIVIZATION of the late 1920s and 1930s, and many were killed or forced into exile.

Kulturkampf (*c*.1871–87) German Chancellor Otto von BISMARCK's attempt to subordinate the Roman Catholic Church to the state. Bismarck, a devout Protestant, doubted the allegiance of German Catholics to his newly created German Empire and passed a series of anti-Catholic laws. In 1872 Germany severed diplomatic ties with the Vatican. These restrictive laws were openly resisted, and boosted support for the Catholic-dominated Centre Party. Most of the laws were repealed during the 1880s, as Bismarck sought the cooperation of the Centre Party against the rise of socialism.

Kun, Béla (1886–1938?) Hungarian communist leader. In 1918, with the support of Russian leader Vladimir LENIN, Kun formed the Hungarian Communist Party. In February 1919 Kun was imprisoned by the government of Count KÁROLY, but he was released in March 1919. He established a communist–social democratic government. The administration failed to win the support of the peasants and army, and the coalition collapsed in August 1919. Kun fled the country. Later accused of Trotskyism, he probably died in Stalin's Great PURGE (1936–38).

Kuomintang (Guomindang) Nationalist Party in China, the major political force during and after the creation of a republic in 1911. It was first led by SUN YAT-SEN, who established its "Three Great Principles": nationalism, democracy and socialism. The Kuomintang cooperated with the Chinese COMMUNIST PARTY until 1927 when Sun's successor, CHIANG KAI-SHEK, turned against the communists, initiating a civil war. Between 1937 and 1945 cooperation was renewed in order to repel the

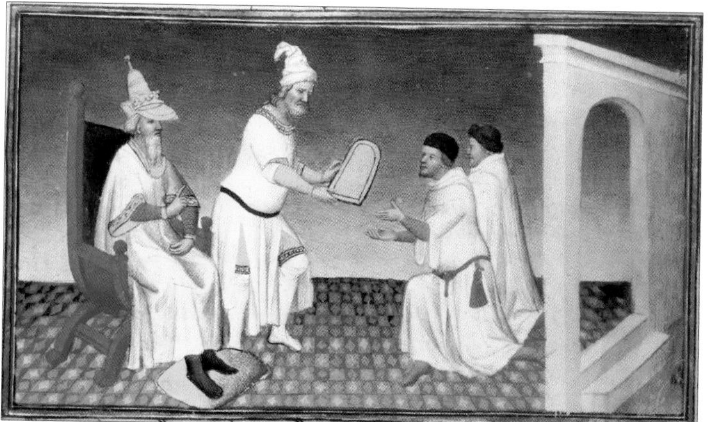

◄ **Kublai Khan** shown here, in a painting by Boucicaut Master (*c*.1375–1400), giving his golden seal to members of the Polo family at Tatu. In 1267 Kublai Khan established a new capital at Tatu (now Beijing), where he built a walled city containing palaces, temples and official buildings. From Tatu he consolidated his empire, incorporating Chinese traditions in his style of government. Foreign visitors were held in high esteem at his court and some, like Marco Polo, became his personal advisers.

KUWAIT
AREA: 17,820sq km (6880sq mi)
POPULATION: 1,668,000
CAPITAL (POPULATION): Kuwait City (189,000)
GOVERNMENT: Constitutional monarchy
ETHNIC GROUPS: Kuwaiti Arab 44%, non-Kuwaiti Arab 36%, various Asian 20%
LANGUAGES: Arabic (official), Kurdish, Farsi (Persian)
RELIGIONS: Muslim 90% (Sunni 63%), Christian 8%, Hindu 2%
GDP PER CAPITA (1995): US$23,790

Japanese, after which the civil war resumed. With the communists' victory in 1949, Chiang and *c.*2 million supporters of the Kuomintang fled to the island of Taiwan, where the Kuomintang governed until 2000.

Kurdistan Extensive mountainous and plateau region in sw Asia, inhabited by the Kurds and including parts of e Turkey, ne Iran, n Iraq, ne Syria, s Armenia and e Azerbaijan. Plans for the creation of a separate Kurdish state were put forward after World War 1 but subsequently abandoned. Area: *c.*192,000sq km (74,000sq mi).

Kurds Predominantly rural, Islamic population, who live in a disputed frontier area of sw Asia that they call Kurdistan. Traditionally nomadic herders, they are mainly Sunni Muslims who speak an Iranian dialect. For 3000 years the Kurds have maintained a unique cultural tradition, although internal division and constant external invasion have prevented them from uniting into one nation. In recent times, their main conflicts have been with Turkey and Iraq. After the Iran-Iraq War (1980–88), Iraq destroyed many Kurdish villages and their inhabitants. Iraq's brutal crushing of the Kurdish revolt after the Gulf War (1991) caused 1.5 million Kurds to flee to Iran and Turkey. The United Nations (UN) formed "safe havens" for the Kurds. In 1996 Iraqi troops invaded the region and captured the Kurdish city of Irbil. The United States responded by launching cruise missiles at Iraqi military installations. In Turkey, Kurdish nationalists have campaigned for an independent homeland since 1925. In 1999 Abdullah Ocalan, the leader of the Kurdistan Workers' Party (PKK), one of the most important Kurdish organizations, was captured and imprisoned in Turkey. Today, *c.*8 million Kurds live in e Turkey, *c.*6 million in Iran, *c.*4 million in n Iraq, *c.*500,000 in Syria and *c.*100,000 in Azerbaijan and Armenia.

Kush (Cush) Kingdom and former state in Upper (s) Nubia. The first historical reference to Kush was made by Egyptian Pharoah Sesostris I (r. *c.*1918–1875 bc), who used it to refer to a powerful, independent kingdom based around the city of Kerma (now n central Sudan). The kingdom was rich in mineral resources, especially gold, and strategically located on the trade route along the Middle Nile. The beginnings of the Egyptianization of Upper Nubia dates from this "Middle Kerma" period. Sesostris III of Egypt (r. *c.*1836–1818 bc) conquered Nubia and built a network of forts. In the 18th century bc, Egypt evacuated Kerma and the Kushites subsequently gained control of Lower Nubia and established the kingdom of Kush. In *c.*1492 bc Thutmose I of Egypt conquered Nubia and divided it into two administrative regions: Wawat (n), with its capital at Aswan, and Kush (s), with its headquarters at Napata (now Marawi). From *c.*900 bc, the Napata-based kingdom of Kush experienced a resurgence. In *c.*767 bc King Kashta of Kush conquered Upper (s) Egypt. Kashta's son, Piye, united the entire Nile Valley in *c.*732 bc. The supremacy of Kush proved short-lived, however, as the Assyrians invaded Egypt in *c.*671 bc and by 654 bc the Kushites had withdrawn to Napata. In *c.*600 bc the Kushites were defeated at Napata and shortly afterwards the royal palace was moved to Meroë, which became the official capital in *c.*300 bc. Gradually weakened by battles against first the Ptolemies and then the Romans in Lower Nubia, the kingdom of Kush finally came to an end when Meroë was captured by Aksum in ad 350. *See also* Egypt, ancient

Kushan (Kushana) Ruling dynasty established in Bactria in the 2nd century bc. At its height, under King Kanishka in the 1st century ad, the Kushan kingdom covered much of n India, Afghanistan, and parts of central Asia. The Kushans controlled trade between China and Rome along the Silk Road and did much to promote the spread of Buddhism to central Asia and China. The decline of their rule from *c.*ad 250 followed the rise of the Sasanians in Iran.

Kut al-Imara, Siege of (December 1915–April 1916) Turkish assault on a British-occupied town in Mesopotamia (now Al Kut, e Iraq) during World War I. In September 1915 Kut al-Imara was taken by British troops led by General Charles Townshend, the British continued to pursue the retreating Ottoman Turkish army towards Baghdad. The advance proved unsustainable and, following defeat at the Battle of Ctesiphon (22 November 1915), the British were forced to retreat to Kut al-Imara. After a siege lasting nearly five months, *c.*10,000 British troops surrendered and many subsequently died en route to captivity in e Turkey. Kut al-Imara was recaptured by the British in February 1917.

Kutuzov, Mikhail Illarionovich (1745–1813) Russian general. He retired to his estate after being badly wounded in battles against the Ottoman Turks, but was recalled by Tsar Alexander I at the start of the Napoleonic Wars (1803–15). Kutuzov called for a strategic retreat, but was overruled by Alexander I, and the Russians subsequently suffered a massive defeat at the Battle of Austerlitz (1805). During the Russo-Turkish Wars (1806–12), Kutuzov captured the entire Turkish army in Bessarabia (now Moldavia) and was later appointed commander-in-chief of the Russian army. Defeated by Napoleon I at the Battle of Borodino (1812), Kutuzov adopted guerrilla tactics rather than engage in a further direct engagement with the French army. Faced by the prospect of a freezing winter in Moscow, Napoleon's army began to retreat but found their path constantly blocked by Kutuzov's forces. Kutuzov pursued the dwindling French army into Poland and Prussia, where he died of disease.

Kuwait (Al Kuwayt) Small state in the ne Arabian Peninsula. Kuwait was founded in the early 18th century and a sheikhdom was established by Sabah al-Awal in 1756. During the 19th century, Kuwait was contested between the Ottoman and British empires, finally becoming a British protectorate in 1899. In 1961 Kuwait gained independence. Oil was discovered in 1938, and Kuwait's huge oil reserves made it one of the richest countries in the world. In 1981 Kuwait joined the Gulf Cooperation Council (GCC). During the Iran-Iraq War (1980–88), Kuwait supported Saddam Hussein's Iraqi regime, but in August 1990 Kuwait was invaded by Iraq. Many thousands of Kuwaitis were killed or kidnapped. In the Gulf War (1991) allied coalition forces, led by the United States, liberated Kuwait in February 1991. Iraqi troops set light to oil-wells as they retreated, causing widespread environmental damage. The cost of post-war reconstruction was *c.*US$100 billion. In 1992 Kuwait held its first parliamentary elections. The Amir, Sheikh Jabir al-Sabah, holds executive power.

KwaZulu-Natal Province in e South Africa, bordered by the Indian Ocean and the Drakensberg Mountains; the capital is Pietermaritzburg. It was created in 1994 from the Zulu homeland, KwaZulu and the former province of Natal. Area: 92,180sq km (33,578sq mi). Pop. (1995 est.) 8,713,100.

Ky, Nguyen Cao (1930–) Vietnamese commander and statesman. He fought with the French until their defeat at the Battle of Dien Bien Phu (1954). Ky then joined the US-backed South Vietnamese airforce, becoming its commander after the overthrow of Ngo Dinh Diem in 1963. Following the coup led by Nguyen Van Thieu (1965), Ky was appointed premier and was then elected vice president (1967–71). At the end of the Vietnam War (1955–75), he fled to the United States.

Kyoto City on w central Honshu Island, Japan; capital of Kyoto prefecture. Founded in the 6th century, the Fujiwara family transferred the imperial capital from Nara to Kyoto (then known as Heian) in 794. In 1192 the shogun Minamoto Yoritomo established a military government at Kamakura, but Kyoto continued as the imperial headquarters and flourished as a centre for Japanese Buddhism. Kyoto was reinstated as capital by the Ashikaga in 1338. During the Tokugawa shogunate, the political centre of power shifted to Edo (now Tokyo) but the imperial court continued at Kyoto until the Meiji Restoration in 1868. Kyoto remains the cultural and religious centre of Japan. Pop. (1993) 1,395,000.

Kyrgyzstan *See* country feature

KYRGYZSTAN (FORMERLY KIRGHIZIA)

AREA: 198,500sq km (76,640sq mi)
POPULATION: 4,568,000
CAPITAL (POPULATION): Bishkek (641,400)
GOVERNMENT: Multiparty republic
ETHNIC GROUPS: Kirghiz 52%, Russian 22%, Uzbek 13%, Ukrainian 3%, German 2%, Tatar 2%
LANGUAGES: Kirghiz
RELIGIONS: Islam
GFP PER CAPITA (1995): US$1800

Landlocked republic in ne central Asia. The area that is now Kyrgyzstan was populated in ancient times by the Kyrgyz, a forest-dwelling people who practised shamanism. Mongol armies conquered the region in the early 13th century. Islam was introduced in the 18th century. In 1830 the Kyrgyz were conquered by the Uzbek khanate of Kokand, who built the future capital of Bishkek.

In 1876 Kyrgyzstan became part of the Russian Empire and Russian emigration gradually forced many of the Kyrgyz into the mountains of the Tian Shan. In 1916 Russia crushed a native rebellion and many of the Kyrgyz fled to China. By the mid-1930s the majority of the remaining Kyrgyz had been forcibly resettled on collective farms. In 1924 Kyrgyzstan became an autonomous region of the Soviet Union. In 1936 it became a Soviet Socialist Republic. Under communism, nomads of the region were forced to live on government-run farms.

In 1990 the reformist candidate Askar Akayev was elected president by the Kirghiz republic. In August 1991 Kyrgyzstan declared independence and later joined the Commonwealth of Independent States (CIS). Akayev introduced free-market reforms, including the introduction (1993) of a national currency. A new, liberal constitution was adopted in 1994. Tension remains between the rural Kirghiz and the urban Russians and Uzbeks.

Labor Party, Australian (ALP) Social democratic political organization in Australia. The oldest surviving political party in Australia, its candidates were first elected in 1891 and it first held federal office in 1904. In 1916 the Party split over conscription. Prime Minister W.M. Hughes led the pro-conscription wing into a coalition from which the National Party emerged. In 1929 the Labor Party returned to power under James Scullin, but it fractured again over policies to combat the Great Depression. Australia was led (1941–45) by Labor leader John Curtin for much of World War 2. Joseph Chifley's post-war Labor government (1945–49) introduced important social welfare reforms, but in 1955 the Party split over attitudes to communism and remained out of office for more than 25 years. In 1972 Labor returned to power under Gough Whitlam. Bob Hawke held office from 1983 to 1991. He was succeeded as prime minister by Paul Keating until electoral defeat in 1996.

Labourers, Statute of (1351) Act to control wages in England. It was passed to restrain soaring wages caused by a labour shortage after the Black Death (1348–49). Wages were pegged at the level of 1349. There was no comparable restriction on rising prices, and the Act was very unpopular. It proved difficult to enforce and was widely evaded. *See also* Peasants' Revolt

Labour Party Social democratic political organization in the United Kingdom. The first British socialist parties, founded in the 1880s, united to form the Independent Labour Party (ILP) in 1893 under Keir Hardie, the first socialist member of Parliament. In 1900 the ILP created the Labour Representation Committee, from which the modern Labour Party emerged in 1906. In 1918 it adopted a constitution, written largely by Sidney Webb, which included a commitment to public ownership of the means of production (Clause Four). Labour held office under Ramsay MacDonald in 1924 and 1929–31. It joined Winston Churchill's coalition government in World War 2 (1940–45) and Labour leader Clement Attlee acted as deputy prime minister. After a landslide victory in 1945, the Attlee government (1945–51) introduced major social reforms that established the British welfare state. Most notable was the National Health Service (NHS) created by Aneurin Bevan. Major industries, including coal and railways, were nationalized. Labour held power again under Harold Wilson (1964–70, 1974–76) and James Callaghan (1976–79). Doctrinaire left-wing policies and the perceived dominance of the trade-unions caused a split in 1981, when the "gang of four" (Roy Jenkins, David Owen, Shirley Williams and Bill Rogers) formed the Social Democratic Party (SDP). The Labour Party, led (1980–83) by Michael Foot, was heavily defeated in the 1983 elections. Under Neil Kinnock (1983–92) and John Smith (1992–94), party policy shifted towards the centre. This trend accelerated under Tony Blair, leader from 1994, who stepped up the pace of "modernization" under the slogan of "New Labour". The Labour Party won a landslide victory in the 1997 elections, and Blair became the first Labour prime minister for 18 years. *See also* Conservative Party; Liberal Democrats

labour union *See* union

Ladislas I (1040–95) King of Hungary (1077–95), son of Bela I. He re-established internal order, defeating invasions by Germanic tribes and crushing a pagan revival. Ladislas expanded his kingdom, acquiring Croatia in 1091. During the investiture controversy, he allied himself with Pope Gregory VII. Ladislas died suddenly while preparing to lead the First Crusade. Generally regarded as a wise and heroic ruler, Ladislas was canonised in 1192. His feast day is 27 June.

Ladysmith, Siege of (1899–1900) Assault on the main British base in Natal during the second of the South African Wars. On 30 October 1899, Sir George White's force was defeated by an Afrikaner (Boer) attack led by Piet Joubert, and subsequently besieged in the town Ladysmith. After three attempts had failed, Ladysmith was finally relieved by Sir Redvers Buller on 28 February 1900. The defence of the town cost *c.*3200 British lives. *See also* Kruger, Paul

Lafayette, Marie Joseph Gilbert de Motier, Marquis de (1757–1834) French general and statesman. He sympathized with the American cause in the American Revolution (1775–83) and was appointed a major general in the Continental Army in 1777. Lafayette was wounded at the Battle of Brandywine (1777). In 1779 he briefly returned to France and persuaded Louis XVI to send 6000 troops to aid the colonists. By April 1780 Lafayette was back in America, and he distinguished himself in the final campaign against General Charles Cornwallis at Yorktown (1781). An aristocratic proponent of democratic reform in France, Lafayette was the chief architect of the Declaration of the Rights of Man and of the Citizen (1789). After the storming of the Bastille at the start of the French Revolution (1789–99), Lafayette was given command of the National Guard and escorted the royal family to safety in Versailles. He resigned shortly after his forces killed or wounded *c.*50 demonstrators on the Champs de Mars, Paris (July 1791). After the overthrow of Louis XVI, Lafayette fled to Flanders and was imprisoned (1792–97) by the Austrians. In 1799 he was rehabilitated by Napoleon. He returned to politics after the restoration of the monarchy under Louis XVIII. He was hailed as a hero during a visit to the United States (1824). Lafayette returned as commander of the National Guard during the July Revolution (1830) which overthrew Charles X and placed Louis Philippe on the throne.

Lafitte, Jean (1780?–1826?) French privateer and smuggler. He led a band of pirates that preyed on Spanish merchant- and slave-ships in Barataria Bay, Missouri. During the War of 1812, Lafitte suspended his piracy in order to assist US General Andrew Jackson in the Battle of New Orleans (1814–15). His bravery was rewarded by a presidential pardon from James Madison. In 1817 Lafite established a settlement at Galveston, Texas, from where he continued to raid shipping until forced into Spanish America by US forces in 1821.

La Follette, Robert Marion (1855–1925) US leader of the Progressive Party. He served (1885–91) as a Republican member in the House of Representatives. After failing to be re-elected in 1890, La Follette launched a crusade against corruption in the Republican Party. In 1900 he was elected governor of Wisconsin. La Follette steered through progressive legislation against the railroads, including higher taxes and greater regulation. In 1906 he was elected to the Senate, where he continued to champion the rights of unions and consumers against the interests of banks and big business. The La Follette Seaman's Act (1915), for instance, tried to improve working conditions for sailors and increase safety for passengers. La Follette was a powerful critic of President William Taft, but was overlooked (1912) as the progressive Republican candidate in favour of Theodore Roosevelt. La Follette led opposition to US involvement in World War 1 and was responsible for publicizing the Teapot Dome Affair (1922) that exposed corruption in the post-war government of Warren Harding. La Follette ran as the Progressive Party's candidate for president in 1924, but won only Wisconsin.

LaFontaine, Sir Louis Hippolyte (1807–64) Canadian statesman, joint premier (1842–43, 1847–51). After the union of Upper and Lower Canada (1840), LaFontaine became leader of the French-Canadians in Québec and acceded to Governor Charles Bagot's request to form a power-sharing government with Robert Baldwin, leader of Lower Canada (now Ontario). LaFontaine and Baldwin's second term in office is often referred to as the "great ministry", since Canada acquired cabinet government for the first time.

Lagash (now Telloh, SE Iraq) City-state in ancient Sumeria; the capital was Girsu. Archaeological digs (1877–1933) at the site revealed more than 50,000 cuneiform texts that provide vital historical data on ancient Babylonia. Lagash was founded before 4000 BC and continued to be occupied until the Parthian era (247 BC–AD 224). The Stele of Vultures (*c.*2500 BC) depicts King Eannatum of Lagash's victory over the neighbouring state of Umma. In *c.*2375 BC, King Lugalzagesi of Umma devastated Lagash, conquered Kish and went on to gain the cities of Ur and Uruk, creating a united Sumerian empire. This empire was later captured (*c.*2330 BC) by Sargon of Akkadia. Lagash revived as an independent state under the governorship of Gudea (*c.*2100 BC), who left many inscriptions describing his programme of temple construction. During this period, Lagash became the artistic centre of Mesopotamia, producing especially fine sculpture.

La Guardia, Fiorello Henry (1882–1947) US politician, mayor of New York City (1933–45). He served as a Republican member of the House of Representatives (1916–17, 1923–33), co-sponsoring the Norris-La Guardia Act (1932) that gave greater rights to labour unions. In 1933 La Guardia built a coalition against the corruption in Tammany Hall that saw him elected as mayor of New York City. Fiorello ("Little Flower") was both flamboyant and effective. He tackled the problems of social welfare and poor housing and improved the city's transport system.

Lahore City on the River Ravi, capital of Punjab province, NE Pakistan. From 1152 to 1186 Lahore was the capital of the Ghaznavid dynasty. In 1524 the city was captured by Babur and subsumed into the Mughal Empire. Emperor Akbar built (1584–98) Lahore Fort, while the magnificent Shalimar Gardens (1641) dates from the reign of Shah Jahan. Despite the construction of the Bashahi Mosque (1673), Lahore declined under Aurangzeb. It revived as the centre of a Sikh kingdom under Ranjit Singh (r.1801–39). Lahore fell to the British in 1849. From 1955 to 1970 it was capital of West Pakistan. Pop. (1991 est). 3,200,000.

Laibach, Congress of (January–May 1821) Meeting of the Holy Alliance (Austria, Prussia and Russia) at Laibach (now Ljubljana, Slovenia). It confirmed Austria's right to suppress a revolution in Naples. Britain's dissenting position signalled the eventual breakdown (1825) of the Congress System set up in 1815. *See also* Kingdom of the Two Sicilies

laissez-faire In economics, doctrine that an economic system functions best when self-interest and the profit motive are allowed free reign without the interference of government. The concept was developed in reaction to mercantilism by the French physiocrats in the 18th century. The English economist Adam Smith, followed by David Ricardo and Thomas Malthus, advanced the doctrine, arguing that free-trade and competition were the basis of a healthy economy. John Stuart Mill and Jeremy Bentham, who developed the philosophy of utilitarianism, were other influences. In the 1840s, Richard Cobden, John Bright and the "Manchester school" secured the repeal of the corn laws, a landmark of the free-trade movement. From the late 19th century, the drawbacks of laissez-faire, for example monopolistic price-fixing, or the exploitation of labour, necessitated increasing government intervention. *See also* capitalism

lake dwelling Prehistoric settlement built, often on platforms, on the margins of lakes. They offered an escape route by water, and livestock were raised on lakeside pasture. Examples from the Neolithic and Bronze ages, preserved by rising water levels, have been found in many parts of Europe, especially Germany, Switzerland, France and northern Italy. English examples in Somerset date from the Iron Age. The remains of the dwellings yielded archaeological evidence to support the theory that the Stone Age immediately preceded the Bronze Age.

Lambert, John (1619–83) English general in the English Civil War (1642–46, 1648). He led the

Parliamentary forces to victory at the Battle of PRESTON (1648) and fought under Oliver CROMWELL in the decisive Battle of WORCESTER (1651). Lambert composed the Instrument of Government (1653) which established the PROTECTORATE, led by Cromwell. In 1657 he was removed from office after disagreements with Cromwell. In 1659 Lambert forcibly dissolved the reconvened RUMP PARLIAMENT, but his attempt to prevent the RESTORATION of CHARLES II was defeated by General George MONCK. Lambert was imprisoned from 1662 until his death.

Lamennais, Félicité Robert de (1782–1854) French priest and political writer. Lamennais was censored and exiled by Napoleon I for his defence of ULTRAMONTANISM (support for papal authority). His newspaper *L'Avenir* (founded 1830) advocated the separation of church and state. In 1831 *L'Avenir* was suppressed by King LOUIS PHILIPPE and condemned by Pope GREGORY XVI. Lamennais was excommunicated after the publication of his poem *Words of a Believer* (1834). He devoted the rest of his life to the cause of republicanism.

Lancaster, House of Branch of the House of PLANTAGENET. The first Earl of Lancaster was Edmund "Crouchback" (1245–96), son of HENRY III. In 1361 the title and lands passed to EDWARD III's son, JOHN OF GAUNT (d.1399), via his wife. In 1399 their son deposed RICHARD II and was proclaimed HENRY IV. Although HENRY V established the succession of the House of Lancaster, HENRY VI's reign was beset by the Wars of the ROSES (1455–85), a dynastic civil war between the royal houses of Lancaster and YORK that ended in victory for the Yorkist EDWARD IV. *See also* BEAUFORT, HENRY; CLARENCE, GEORGE PLANTAGANET, DUKE OF

Land League Irish agrarian organization founded (1879) by Michael DAVITT to campaign for tenants' rights. Established after poor harvests threatened a repetition of the IRISH FAMINE (1848), the League demanded fair rents, fixity of tenure and free sale of the tenant's interest. Charles Stewart PARNELL, a leading figure in the HOME RULE movement, became its president. With support from the FENIAN MOVEMENT in the United States, Parnell organized mass agitation by Irish tenant-farmers. This militant action, combined with obstruction of government business in the British Parliament, led William GLADSTONE to pass the Land Act (1881) that established a judicial commission for determining rents. Parnell agitated for further reforms and was arrested in 1881. The League responded by calling on tenants to refuse to pay rent. It was subsequently suppressed by the British government.

Lanfranc (*c.*1005–89) Italian Benedictine, archbishop of Canterbury (1079–89). As abbot of Bec, Normandy, he was renowned throughout Europe for his scholarship. Lanfranc was nominated as archbishop of Canterbury by WILLIAM I (THE CONQUEROR) and implemented William's policy of replacing Anglo-Saxon prelates with Normans. Lanfranc consolidated his own position by subordinating the see of York to the see of Canterbury. While upholding papal sovereignty, he assisted William in maintaining the independence of the English church. Lanfranc established (*c.*1076) the separation of ecclesiastical from secular courts. *See also* NORMAN CONQUEST

Lange, David Russell (1942–) New Zealand statesman, prime minister (1984–89). He was elected to Parliament in 1977 and became leader of the Labour Party in 1983. In the 1984 election, Lange defeated Robert MULDOON to become New Zealand's youngest-ever prime minister. He fulfilled his campaign promise to create a "nuclear-free" New Zealand by excluding nuclear-powered and nuclear-armed ships from the country's ports. This act resulted (1986) in the United States suspending its security agreement, the ANZUS alliance, with New Zealand. Internal party disputes provoked Lange's resignation.

Langton, Stephen (d.1228) English prelate, archbishop of Canterbury (1207–28). In 1206 he was made a cardinal by Pope INNOCENT III. Langton was prevented from taking up his appointment as archbishop of Canterbury by King JOHN, who barred him from entering England and snatched the see's revenues. In 1209 John was excommunicated and in 1213 he finally relented and allowed Langton to take up his position. Langton played a key role in securing the MAGNA CARTA (1215) and was a valuable influence during the minority of HENRY III. His scholarly work included dividing the books of the Bible into chapters. *See also* BARONS' WAR

Languedoc Former province and historical region of S France. In Roman times, Languedoc formed part of the province of Gallia Narbonensis, which was captured by the Visigoths in the 5th century AD. In 759 Frankish king Pepin the Short conquered the region, which became part of the CAROLINGIAN EMPIRE. In the 11th and 12th century, Languedoc was dominated by the county of Toulouse. It was the centre of the ALBIGENSES and the region was devastated by a crusade (1209) against the sect. By 1271 Languedoc belonged to the French crown. It was divided into departments at the end of the French Revolution (1789–1799).

Lansbury, George (1859–1940) British politician, leader (1931–35) of the LABOUR PARTY. He entered Parliament in 1910, but resigned in 1912 to campaign on behalf of the suffragette movement. Lansbury founded (1913) the *Daily Herald* newspaper, where he wrote in defence of the rights of conscientious objectors during World War 1. In 1922 Lansbury was re-elected to Parliament. When Ramsay MACDONALD formed a National Coalition government in 1931, Lansbury became leader of the Labour Party. Lansbury's uncompromising commitment to pacifism led him to oppose economic sanctions against Italy for its aggression in Ethiopia. He was forced to resign as leader in favour of Clement ATTLEE.

Lansdowne, Henry Petty-Fitzmaurice, 5th Marquess of (1845–1927) British statesman and colonial administrator. As governor general of Canada (1883–88), he finally suppressed the rebellion of Louis RIEL. Lord SALISBURY appointed Lansdowne viceroy of India (1888–94). As secretary of state for war (1895–1900),

LAOS

AREA: 236,800sq km (91,428sq mi)
POPULATION: 4,469,000
CAPITAL (POPULATION): Vientiane (449,000)
GOVERNMENT: Single-party republic
ETHNIC GROUPS: Lao 67%, Mon-Khmer 17%, Tai 8%
LANGUAGES: Lao (official)
RELIGIONS: Buddhism 58%, traditional beliefs 34%, Christianity 2%, Islam 1%
GDP PER CAPITA (1994): US$290

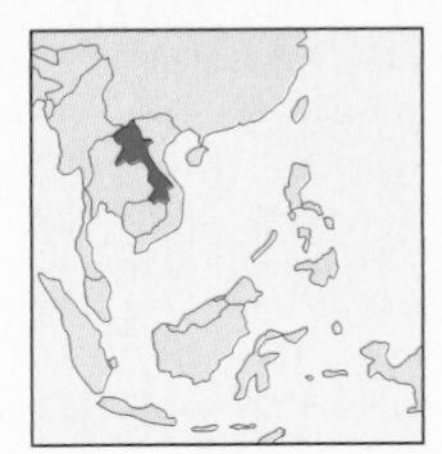

Landlocked republic in SE Asia. In 1353 Prince Fa Ngum founded the Lao kingdom of Lan Xang ("Land of a Million Elephants"), based around the city of Luang Prabang. Fa Ngum conquered much of what is now N and E Thailand, and adopted Theravada Buddhism as the official religion. Under Photisarath (r.1520–48), Lan Xang reached its maximum territorial extent, gaining the Tai state of Chiang Mai. In 1560 Photisarath's son, Setthathirat I (r.1548–71), moved the capital from Luang Prabang to Vien Chan (now Ventiane). After Setthathirat's death (1571), Lan Xang fell to the Burmese. By 1713 Lan Xang had dissolved into the three kingdoms of Luang Prabang, Vien Chan and Champassak. In 1778 all three kingdoms fell to Siam (now Thailand). In 1893 Siam deferred to French power, and Laos became part of French INDOCHINA.

During World War 2 (1939–45) Indochina was occupied by Japan, who granted Laos independence in April 1945. A nationalist movement, Lao Issara (Free Laos), formed a provisional government in Vientiane. The return of French troops (1946) forced the Lao Issara to flee to Thailand, where Prince PHETSARATH formed a government-in-exile. In 1949 Laos was granted semi-independence within the French Union. The Lao Issara now split between those who favoured participation with the French, and others who opposed any collaboration. This latter group, led by Prince SOUPHANOUVONG, formed the Pathet Leo, who allied themselves with the Vietnamese communists (VIET MINH). In 1953 France granted full independence to the royalist government of Laos, but by this time the Pathet Lao was in control of most of N Laos.

The GENEVA ACCORDS (1954) at the end of the French Indochina War (1946–54) confirmed the creation of a united kingdom of Laos. Souphanouvong and SOUVANNA POUMA formed a coalition government (1956–58) that was toppled by a US-backed right-wing coup. A civil war ensued, and by the end of 1961 the anti-right forces controlled more than half of Laos. A cease-fire was agreed and Souvanna returned to power. The new coalition was destabilized by the VIETNAM WAR (1954–75), and by 1965 Laos had returned to civil war. The use of the "HO CHI MINH Trail" through E and S Laos as a military supply line for the North Vietnamese led to the secret bombing of Laos by the United States' Air Force (USAF) and US support for the Hmong tribespeople against the Pathet Lao in N Laos. In 1973 the various factions agreed to a cease-fire and the establishment of a third coalition government under Souvanna. Victory for the communists in Vietnam enabled the final victory of Pathet Lao.

In December 1975 the king abdicated and the Lao People's Democratic Republic was proclaimed. Vietnam remained a powerful influence on Laos. The Lao People's Revolutionary Party (LPRP), led by Kaysone Phomvihan (1920–92), created a one-party communist state and began to collectivize agriculture and nationalize industry. The threat of "re-education" for political opponents compelled *c.*300,000 people to flee into Thailand. In the mid-1980s, Laos encouraged the development of a more market-oriented economy. A new constitution (1991) provided greater political freedoms. In 1997 Laos joined the Association of Southeast Asian Nations (ASEAN). Kaysone's death (1992) saw the succession of Nouhak Phoumsavan (president) and Khamtai Siphandon (prime minister). In 1998 Khamtai became president.

Lansdowne was blamed for Britain's ill-preparedness at the start of the second SOUTH AFRICAN WAR (1899–1902). He nonetheless became foreign secretary (1900–05), concluding an alliance with Japan (1902) and establishing the ENTENTE CORDIALE (1904) with France. Lansdowne served (1915–16) as minister without portfolio in Herbert ASQUITH's government. His letter to the *Daily Telegraph* (November 1817), calling for a statement of Allied peace terms in World War 1, was condemned by the government.

Laos *See* country feature

Lao Tzu (Laozi) (active *c.*6th century BC) Chinese philosopher, credited as the founder of TAOISM. According to tradition, he was a contemporary of CONFUCIUS and developed Taoism as a mystical reaction to CONFUCIANISM. He is said to have written *Tao Te Ching*, the sacred book of Taoism. In parables and verse it advocates harmony with the *Tao* (path). *See also* BUDDHISM

La Pérouse, Jean François de Galaup, Comte de (1741–88?) French navigator. In 1785 he set out, with the ships *La Boussole* and *L'Astrolabe*, on an exploration of the Pacific Ocean. One of his first stops in the South Pacific was Easter Island (April 1786). La Pérouse sailed for the Sandwich Islands (now Hawaii), before making his way to North America, where he hoped to discover the Northwest Passage. He made landfall (June 1786) near Mount St Elias, Alaska, and then worked his way down the coast as far as Monterey, California. La Pérouse next visited Macao (January 1787), before exploring the Asian coast. He visited the strait, now named after him, that separates Sakhalin from Hokkaido, Japan. He disappeared after leaving (March 1788) Port Jackson, Sydney, Australia. The wreckage of the two ships was discovered (1828) later in the Santa Cruz Islands.

Largo Caballero, Francisco (1869–1946) Spanish statesman. He joined the Spanish Socialist Party in 1894 and became leader of the trade union federation in 1925. Largo Caballero collaborated with the dictatorship (1923–29) of PRIMO DE RIVERA, but was appointed minister of labour (1931–33) on the establishment of the second Spanish Republic (1931–39). In 1934 he organized the failed coup against the new rightist government. During the Spanish CIVIL WAR (1936–39), Largo Caballero became prime minister of the POPULAR FRONT government (September 1936–May 1937), but was forced to resign by the communists. He fled to France on Franco's victory and was interned by the Nazis during World War 2.

La Rochelle Seaport on the Bay of Biscay, W France. An English possession during the 12th and 13th centuries, it changed hands several times during the Hundred Years' War (1337–1453) before finally falling to the French in 1372. In the French Wars of RELIGION (1562–98), La Rochelle became the chief stronghold of the HUGUENOTS, its population swollen by refugees after the SAINT BARTHOLOMEW'S DAY MASSACRE (1572). In 1627 the city was besieged by French troops led by Cardinal RICHELIEU. English attempts, led by the Duke of BUCKINGHAM, to relieve La Rochelle were unsuccessful, and starvation forced its surrender in 1629. The port declined when the Revocation of the Edict of NANTES (1685) led to the mass emigration of its Protestant population. Pop. (1990) 71,094.

La Salle, René Robert Cavelier, Sieur de (1643–87) French explorer in North America. In 1666 he sailed for Canada to enter the FUR TRADE. La Salle explored the Great Lakes region and the Comte de FRONTENAC appointed (1675) him commander of Fort Frontenac on Lake Ontario. La Salle was restless for further adventure, however, and borrowed heavily to finance an expedition down the Illinois and Mississippi rivers. On 9 April 1682, La Salle reached the Gulf of Mexico and claimed the entire Mississippi delta for France, naming it LOUISIANA after LOUIS XIV. In 1684, sponsored by Louis XIV to establish a colony at the mouth of the Mississippi River, La Salle sailed to the Gulf of Mexico but landed at Matagorda Bay, Texas, and after fruitless searches for the Mississippi was murdered by mutineers. *See also* HENNEPIN, LOUIS

Las Casas, Bartolomé de (1474–1566) Spanish missionary and historian, known as the "Apostle of the Indies". In 1502 he went to Hispaniola, West Indies. Las Casas served in several expeditions to subdue the native population and was rewarded with an ENCOMIENDA (a grant of land and Native American slaves). In 1512 he was ordained a priest and shortly after participated in the conquest of Cuba (1513). In 1514 Las Casas gave up his *encomienda* and travelled to Spain (1515), where he persuaded Cardinal JIMÉNEZ DE CISNEROS to appoint a commission to investigate the treatment of Native Americans. In 1519 Las Casas convinced Emperor CHARLES V to create a colony of "freed" Indians in what is now N Venezuela. In 1522 the colony collapsed and Las Casas turned to writing *History of the Indies* (1528), which documented Spanish persecution. In 1542 the *encomienda* system was abolished by the New Laws, but Las Casas proved unable to enforce the Laws and prevent the continued enslavement of Native Americans.

Lascaux Site of caves near Montignac, SW France, discovered in 1940. They contain Palaeolithic (*c.*15000 BC) wall paintings, mainly of animals. The caves were closed in 1963 in order to halt the deterioration of the paintings.

Laski, Harold Joseph (1893–1950) British political scientist. A leading member of the FABIAN SOCIETY, he helped found the journal *Tribune* and the New Left Book Club. Laski served as chairman (1945–46) of the LABOUR PARTY, and was professor of political science (1926–50) at the London School of Economics (LSE). His early works, such as *Authority in the Modern State* (1919), embraced political pluralism. After the 1930s, Laski embraced a more orthodox Marxist approach to history in books such as *The American Democracy* (1948).

La Tène (Fr. The Shallows) IRON AGE archaeological site on the E end of Lake Neuchâtel, Switzerland, which lends its name to the second phase (*c.*450–*c.*50 BC) of the culture of European CELTS. The La Tène culture, which followed the HALLSTATT, was marked by Etruscan and Greek influences. It was a warlike culture, hierarchically organized with kings, a priestly class (the DRUIDS), warriors, farmers and slaves. The La Tène Celts conquered Central Europe in the 4th and 3rd centuries BC, but they were gradually subjugated by the Romans.

Lateran Councils Five ECUMENICAL COUNCILS of the ROMAN CATHOLIC CHURCH, held in the Lateran Palace, Rome. The **First** (1123) was convoked by Pope CALIXTUS II and confirmed the Concordat of WORMS of 1122. The **Second** (1139) reunited the church after the schism of 1130–38. The **Third** (1179), held under Pope ALEXANDER III, decreed that papal election should be solely by the College of Cardinals. The **Fourth** and most important (1215) was convoked by Pope INNOCENT III and defined the doctrine of the Eucharist, officially using the term "transubstantiation". It also condemned the Cathari and Waldenses sects and made arrangements for the launching of a new CRUSADE to recover the Holy Land. The **Fifth** (1512–17), held under popes JULIUS II and LEO X, introduced reforms too slight to prevent the REFORMATION.

Lateran Treaty (1929) Agreement between Italy and the Vatican. The papacy surrendered their claims to the PAPAL STATES and Rome to the Italian state. In return, Benito MUSSOLINI recognized the Vatican City as an independent sovereign state with the pope as its temporal head, and affirmed Roman Catholicism as Italy's state religion.

Latimer, Hugh (*c.*1485–1555) English prelate and Protestant martyr. His support for HENRY VIII's efforts to obtain a divorce from CATHERINE OF ARAGON gained him the patronage of Thomas CROMWELL and Thomas CRANMER. Latimer was appointed bishop of Worcester in 1535, but resigned his see (1539) after the government's reassertion of Catholic doctrines. Under the Protestant EDWARD VI (1547–53), he became the leading preacher for the REFORMATION in England. On the accession of Catholic MARY I (1553), Latimer was charged with heresy and, refusing to recant, was burned at the stake with his fellow-bishop, Nicholas RIDLEY.

L

LATVIA

AREA: 64,589sq km (24,938sq mi)
POPULATION: 2,632,000
CAPITAL (POPULATION): Riga (910,200)
GOVERNMENT: Multiparty republic
ETHNIC GROUPS: Latvian 53%, Russian 34%, Belorussian 4%, Ukrainian 3%, Polish 2%, Lithuanian, Jewish
LANGUAGES: Latvian (official)
RELIGIONS: Christianity (including Lutheran, Russian Orthodox and Roman Catholic)
GDP PER CAPITA (1995): US$3370

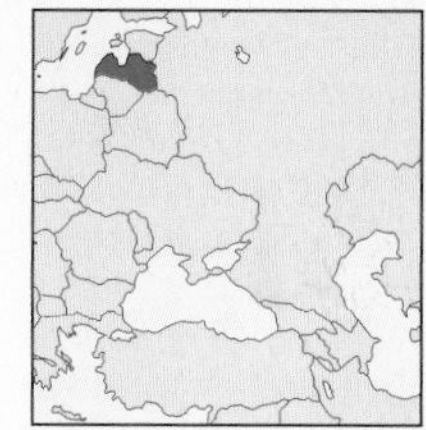

Baltic republic in NE Europe. The Balts, ancestors of most modern Latvians, settled in the area *c.*2000 years ago. Between the 9th and 11th centuries, the region was attacked by Vikings from the W and Russians from the E. In the 13th century, Latvia was conquered by the LIVONIAN ORDER of German knights. Russian defeat in the LIVONIAN WAR (1558–83) left Latvia partitioned between Poland-Lithuania and Sweden. Tsar PETER I (THE GREAT) gained Riga and Vidzeme in the GREAT NORTHERN WAR (1700–21) and the remaining parts of Latvia were ceded to Russia in the Partitions of POLAND (1772, 1793, 1795).

In 1918 Latvia declared independence and Karlis ULMANIS was elected premier. Latvia was a battleground for German and Russian forces during the RUSSIAN CIVIL WAR (1918–20), but all foreign troops were expelled from Latvia by 1920. In the secret NAZI-SOVIET PACT (1939), Germany and the Soviet Union agreed to divide up parts of E Europe. In 1940 the Red Army invaded Latvia, which was then subsumed into the Soviet Union. In 1941 German forces seized Latvia and the country's Jewish population was exterminated (*see* HOLOCAUST, THE). Soviet troops returned in 1944. Under Soviet rule, more than 100,000 Latvians were deported and many Russian immigrants settled in Latvia.

In the late 1980s, in conjunction with Mikhail GORBACHEV's reforms in the Soviet Union, Latvia's government allowed press and religious freedoms, and made Latvian the official language. In 1990 Latvia declared independence, an act that was finally recognized by the Soviet Union in September 1991. In 1993 Latvia held its first multiparty elections and Guntis Ulmanis, grand-nephew of Karlis Ulmanis, became president. In 1994 it adopted a law restricting the naturalization of non-Latvians, including many Russian settlers. In 1995 Latvia joined the Council of Europe and formally applied to join the European Union (EU). In 1999 Viara Vike-Freiberga became the first woman head of state in post-communist Eastern Europe.

Latin American Integration Association (ALADI) Organization of 11 countries founded (1980) to increase regional trade and economic integration. The member states are Argentina, Brazil, Chile, Mexico, Paraguay, Peru, Uruguay, Bolivia, Colombia, Ecuador and Venezuela. It replaced the Latin American Free Trade Association (LAFTA), founded in 1960, which had proved inflexible and ineffective. The new body maintained a commitment to free-trade and the harmonization of tariffs, but abandoned a timetable for the creation of a single-market.

Latin Empire *See* CONSTANTINOPLE, LATIN EMPIRE OF

Latter Day Saints, Church of *See* MORMONS

Lattre de Tassigny, Jean de (1889–1952) French Resistance leader and general in World War 2. In 1939 he became the youngest brigadier general in the French army. After France capitulated to the Germans in June 1940, de Lattre was imprisoned by the Germans but escaped (October 1943) to join Charles DE GAULLE's Free French forces in North Africa. In 1944 he commanded the French 1st Army in the Allied invasion of s France and represented France at the German surrender in May 1945. Sent to French INDOCHINA in 1950, de Lattre checked the VIET MINH offensive (1951) before failing health forced his return.

Latvia *See* country feature, page 233

Laud, William (1573–1645) English priest, archbishop of Canterbury (1633–45). Laud was chaplain to the Duke of BUCKINGHAM, who secured his appointment as bishop of London in 1628. Laud was a staunch opponent of PURITANISM and persecuted its propagandists, such as William PRYNNE. Laud and Thomas Wentworth (later Earl of STRAFFORD) were the principal supporters of CHARLES I's authoritarian policies. Laud's attempt to impose the Book of COMMON PRAYER upon Scotland led to the BISHOPS' WARS (1639, 1640) and the calling of the LONG PARLIAMENT. In 1640 Laud was impeached for treason and imprisoned. He was condemned by a bill of attainder and executed. *See also* PRESBYTERIANISM

Lauderdale, John Maitland, Duke of (1616–82) Scottish statesman. He was a supporter of PRESBYTERIANISM and allied with the Parliamentarians in the first phase (1642–47) of the English CIVIL WAR. In 1647 CHARLES I and Maitland made a secret agreement, by which Charles promised to promote Presbyterianism in return for military aid. In 1648 Maitland launched an abortive invasion of England, and was captured fighting for CHARLES II at the Battle of WORCESTER (1651). He was released after the RESTORATION of Charles II in 1660, and became Charles' chief minister in Scotland. Maitland imposed royal control over the church and persecuted the COVENANTERS. In 1672 he was made Duke of Lauderdale. *See also* CABAL

Laurens, Henry (1724–92) American statesman. An opponent of British policy in America before the AMERICAN REVOLUTION (1775–83), he served as president of the CONTINENTAL CONGRESS (1777–78). In 1780 Laurens was sent to negotiate a loan from Holland, but was intercepted by the British and imprisoned in London, England. He was exchanged for Lord Cornwallis in 1782.

Laurier, Sir Wilfrid (1841–1919) Canadian statesman, first French-Canadian prime minister of Canada (1896–1911). He was first elected to Parliament in 1874 and was soon appointed minister of inland revenue (1877–78) by Alexander MACKENZIE. Laurier gained national attention when he unsuccessfully appealed (1885) for clemency for Louis RIEL, leader of a Métis rebellion. He won the 1896 election with a compromise solution to the vexed issue of separate denominational schools in Manitoba. In 1897 Laurier marginally reduced the tariff, but provided protection for Canadian industry, and the economy prospered under his stewardship. Perhaps Laurier's most lasting achievement was the settlement of the west. During his term in office, more than 100,000 people moved to w Canada, and the provinces of ALBERTA and SASKATACHEWAN were created in 1905. In 1903 Laurier decided to build a second transcontinental railroad. At the Imperial Conferences (1897, 1902, 1907, 1911), he developed an independent defence policy for Canada. Laurier's strategy of compromise began to unravel, however, when he sent 1000 troops to fight in the second SOUTH AFRICAN WAR (1899–1902). Québec nationalists criticized the commitment, while English-Canadians regarded it as inadequate. In 1911 Laurier signed a reciprocal tariff agreement with US President William TAFT, but Laurier's enthusiasm for free-trade alienated pro-imperial Conservatives and nationalist French-Canadians alike, and he was defeated in the 1911 election by Robert BORDEN. *See also* KING, WILLIAM LYON MACKENZIE

Lausanne, Treaty of (4 July 1923) Final agreement concluding WORLD WAR 1, signed at Lausanne, Switzerland, by the Allied Powers and the new state of Turkey. The Treaty became necessary after the Turkish government of Mustafa Kemal (later ATATÜRK) refused to accept the terms of the Treaty of SÈVRES (1920), which had been imposed on the collapsing OTTOMAN EMPIRE. Turkey regained Smyrna, E Thrace, and control of the DARDANELLES, and renounced claims to Greek islands in the Aegean Sea. Provision was also made for population exchange between Greece and Turkey.

Laval, Pierre (1883–1945) French statesman, premier (1931–32, 1935–36, 1942–45). His second administration collapsed as a result of the unpopular HOARE-LAVAL PACT (1935) that ceded most of Ethiopia to MUSSOLINI's fascist Italy. Following France's capitulation to Germany in June 1940, Laval initially became vice premier in the collaborationist VICHY GOVERNMENT under Marshal PÉTAIN. Laval conducted independent negotiations with Nazi Germany and was dismissed by Pétain in December 1940. Germany later demanded that Laval replace Pétain as premier. Laval sent French workers to assist German industries during WORLD WAR 2 and cooperated with Nazi efforts to exterminate French Jews. After the war, he was charged with treason and executed.

Lavigerie, Charles Martial Allemande (1825–92) French prelate, primate of Africa (1884–92). As archbishop of Algiers, he founded (1868) the Society of Missionaries of Africa (or WHITE FATHERS) that sought to convert Africa to Christianity. He was a bitter opponent of slavery and a powerful believer in the civilizing mission of France.

Law, (Andrew) Bonar (1858–1923) British statesman, prime minister (1922–23), b. Canada. After making a fortune as a partner in a Glasgow-based iron-manufacturing company, Law entered Parliament in 1900 and succeeded Arthur BALFOUR as leader of the CONSERVATIVE PARTY in 1911. In 1915 he became secretary for the colonies in Herbert ASQUITH's wartime coalition government. Law served first as chancellor of the exchequer (1916–18) and then as lord privy seal (1919–21) in another coalition under David LLOYD GEORGE. In October 1922, after the resignation of Lloyd George, Law formed a Conservative government that was soon approved (November 1922) by the electorate. After only seven months in office, Law was forced to resign because of illness. He was succeeded by Stanley BALDWIN.

Law, John (1671–1729) Scottish financier. In 1716 he founded the Banque Générale, the first national bank in France. Law believed that the French economy could be revived by increasing the money supply, and the new bank issued vast quantities of paper money. In 1717 he merged the bank with the Louisiana Company, which was granted exclusive trading rights in the Mississippi valley of French North America. A public flotation of shares in the Company produced a wave of speculation and its share-price soared. In 1720 the "MISSISSIPPI BUBBLE" burst when the monarchy drastically devalued bank notes, leading to financial panic and collapse. Law fled to Venice.

Lawrence, John Laird Mair Lawrence, 1st Baron (1811–79) British colonial administrator, viceroy of India (1864–69). After the annexation of the PUNJAB at the end of SIKH WARS (1845–46, 1848–49), Lawrence embarked on large-scale institutional reforms that ensured the Punjab remained loyal to the British during the INDIAN MUTINY (1857–58). He led British troops in the recapture of Delhi.

Lawrence, T.E. (Thomas Edward) (1888–1935) (Lawrence of Arabia) British adventurer, soldier and writer. He worked with Leonard WOOLLEY on an archaeological excavation (1911–14) of the ancient Hittite town of CARCHEMISH and on an exploration of N Suez. At the start of World War 1, Lawrence joined British military intelligence in Cairo, Egypt. He masterminded the strategy of guerrilla warfare in the Arab revolt against the OTTOMAN EMPIRE, leading attacks on the Damascus-Medina railway – the main supply route for the Turkish army in Arabia. Lawrence and Faisal (later FAISAL I of Iraq) captured Aqaba, Jerusalem (both 1917) and Damascus (1918). Lawrence failed in his objective to create an independent Arab nation (when Britain and France cynically divided up the Arabian Peninsula at the end of the war) and he refused to be decorated by George V. Lawrence served as Middle Eastern adviser (1921–22) to colonial minister Winston Churchill, before rejoining the armed services as a private under an assumed name (first J.H. Ross, then T.E. Shaw). In 1935 he was discharged from the Royal Air Force (RAF) and died soon after in a motorcycle accident. Lawrence's celebrated account of his role in the Arab revolt, *Seven Pillars of Wisdom* (1926), is a literary epic rather than a factual, historical record of the conflict. *See also* ALLENBY, EDWARD HENRY HYNMAN, 1ST VISCOUNT; HUSSEIN IBN ALI

League of Nations International organization to promote "collective security" through arbitration, diplomacy and arms reduction. In 1918 US President Woodrow WILSON presented his FOURTEEN POINTS, which included a proposal for a general association of nations. This proposal was realized by the Covenant of the League of Nations, formulated by the Treaty of VERSAILLES (1919) at the end of WORLD WAR 1. The structure of the League consisted of: an assembly of member nations; a council initially composed of four permanent members – France, Britain, Italy and Japan (Germany and the Soviet Union joined later) – and several rotating members; and a secretariat based in Geneva, Switzerland. The Covenant also provided for the INTERNATIONAL LABOUR ORGANIZATION (ILO). The League contributed to post-war economic reconstruction but, excluding a few minor successes, its ability to preserve peace was frustrated by the self-interest of member states. Moreover, the effectiveness of the League was seriously undermined by the failure of the US Congress to ratify the Treaty of Versailles. Discredited by its inability to prevent the Japanese occupation of Manchuria (1931), the Italian conquest of Ethiopia (1935–36) and the rearmament of Nazi Germany, the League collapsed on the outbreak of WORLD WAR 2 (1939). In 1946 it was succeeded by the UNITED NATIONS (UN). *See also* MANDATED TERRITORIES

Lebanon *See* country feature

Lebensraum (Ger. living space) Concept formulated by German geographer Friedrich Ratzel (1844–1904) and misappropriated by Adolf HITLER to justify German territorial expansion. In *Mein Kampf* (1925), Hitler argued that Germany needed land for its expanding population. The creation of a Third Reich was to be achieved at the expense of the Slavs in Ukraine and other lands in Eastern Europe.

Lebrun, Albert (1871–1950) French statesman, last president (1932–40) of the Third Republic. He agreed to the armistice with Germany (1940), but the creation of the VICHY GOVERNMENT deprived him of all authority. In 1944 Lebrun recognized Charles DE GAULLE as provisional president. *See also* PÉTAIN, HENRI PHILIPPE

Lechfeld, Battle of (AD 955) Conflict between the German king (later emperor) OTTO I and the MAGYARS, fought near Augsburg, s Germany. In 954 the pagan Magyars, who had been raiding w Europe since the 890s, launched a major invasion of Germany. The superior cavalry of Otto, BOLESŁAV I and Conrad (the Red), Duke of Lorraine, annihilated the Hungarian army. Conrad died in the battle, which confirmed Otto's authority in Germany.

Le Duan (1908–86) Vietnamese communist statesman. He was a founder (1930) of the Indochina Communist Party and was imprisoned (1931–36, 1940–45) by the French. After the partition of Vietnam in 1945, Le Duan joined the VIET MINH and was one of the principal architects of the National Liberation Front (NLF). After the death of HO CHI MINH (1969), Le Duan became leader of the Vietnam Workers' Party (later Vietnamese Communist

Party). When the VIETNAM WAR ended (1954–75), Le Duan presided over the reunification of the country.

Le Duc Tho (1911–90) Vietnamese statesman, pseudonym of Phan Dinh Khai. He was a founder (1930) of the Indochina Communist Party and was imprisoned (1930–36, 1939–44) by the French. After the partition of Vietnam in 1945, Tho became a leader of the VIET MINH. During the VIETNAM WAR (1954–75), he organized North Vietnamese (VIET CONG) forces in South Vietnam. Tho led the North Vietnamese delegation to the Paris Peace Conferences (1969–73) and negotiated the cease-fire agreement with Henry KISSINGER that led to the withdrawal of US troops from South Vietnam. Tho and Kissinger shared the 1973 Nobel Prize for Peace, but Tho declined the award. He directed the North Vietnamese conquest of the South (1975) and the invasion of Cambodia (1978).

Lee, Ann (1736–84) English mystic, leader of the United Society of Believers in Christ's Second Appearing (popularly called the SHAKERS) in the United States. In 1774, to escape persecution in Britain, "Mother Ann" led a small group to the American colonies and founded (1776) a colony at Watervliet, New York.

Lee, Henry (1756–1818) American soldier, father of Robert LEE. As a cavalry officer during the AMERICAN REVOLUTION (1775–83), he earned the nickname "Light-Horse Harry Lee". Lee's capture of Paulus Hook, New Jersey (19 August 1779) was one of the greatest victories in the Revolution. He was a member (1785–88) of the CONTINENTAL CONGRESS, and suppressed the WHISKEY REBELLION (1794). Lee was elected governor of Virginia (1791–95) and served (1799–1801) in the House of Representatives. He delivered the congressional funeral oration to George WASHINGTON, which contained the now famous phrase "first in war, first in peace, and first in the hearts of his countrymen".

Lee, Jennie (Janet), Baroness (1904–88) British Labour politician. In 1929, aged 25, she became the youngest-ever woman member of Parliament. In 1934 Lee married Aneurin BEVAN. As minister for the arts (1964–70), she was responsible for establishing the Open University (OU), and in 1970 she was made a life peer.

Lee, Richard Henry (1732–94) American statesman. He served (1774–79, 1784–87) in the CONTINENTAL CONGRESS, and introduced a resolution that ultimately led to the DECLARATION OF INDEPENDENCE (1776), which he signed. Lee opposed ratification of the Constitution of the United States because it infringed on STATES' RIGHTS and lacked a BILL OF RIGHTS.

Lee, Robert Edward (1807–70) Confederate general, most successful Southern commander in the American CIVIL WAR (1861–65), son of Henry LEE. He distinguished himself serving under General Winfield SCOTT in the MEXICAN WAR (1846–48), and led the force that suppressed John BROWN's rebellion at Harper's Ferry (1859). In 1861, out of loyalty to his home state of Virginia, Lee declined President Abraham LINCOLN's offer to command the Federal troops and resigned from the army to become commander in chief of Virginia's forces. In 1861 he was appointed military adviser to Confederate President Jefferson DAVIS. Lee replaced Joseph JOHNSTON as field commander in 1862, and rapidly organized the Army of Northern Virginia. In the SEVEN DAYS' BATTLES (June 1862), Lee combined with General Thomas "Stonewall" JACKSON to defeat General George MCCLELLAN's Army of the Potomac. After victory in the Second Battle of BULL RUN (August 1862), Lee launched an invasion of the North that ended in the near destruction of his army at the Battle of ANTIETAM (September 1862). Lee withdrew and inflicted further defeats on the Union at the battles of FREDERICKSBURG (December 1862) and CHANCELLORSVILLE (May 1863). A second invasion of the North ended at GETTYSBURG (July 1863). After a masterly defence against the vastly superior forces of General Ulysses GRANT, Lee was finally trapped and forced to surrender at APPOMATTOX (April 1865). His use of field fortifications presaged the trench warfare of World War 1.

Lee Kuan Yew (1923–) Singapore statesman, prime minister (1959–90). He founded (1954) the People's Action Party (PAP) and was elected to the legislative council in 1955. Lee was a delegate in the negotiations that led to Singapore's independence from Britain in 1959 and became the first post-colonial prime minister. In 1963 Lee led Singapore into the Federation of MALAYSIA, but communal violence forced Singapore to withdraw in 1965. He transformed Singapore into an industrialized nation, encouraging foreign investment and national austerity. The city-state became a major financial centre and the most prosperous nation in Southeast Asia. Lee's paternalistic rule discouraged criticism and infringed on civil liberties. Lee was succeeded as prime minister and leader of the PAP by GOH CHOK TONG, but retained his influence in the cabinet as senior minister.

Lee Teng-hui (1923–) Taiwanese statesman, president (1988–2000). A member of the ruling Nationalist Party (KUOMINTANG), he became vice president of TAIWAN in 1984. Lee became president on the death of CHIANG CHING-KUO, and won Taiwan's first democratic elections in 1996. He was largely responsible for the liberalization of Taiwan. In the 2000 elections, Lee was defeated by Chen Shui-bian of the Democratic Progressive Party.

Legitimists French Royalists who from 1830 supported the claims of the senior branch of the House of BOURBON to the throne of France. The JULY REVOLUTION (1830) deposed the last BOURBON king, CHARLES X, in favour of LOUIS PHILIPPE, Duc d'Orléans, as king of France. Louis Philippe's claim was upheld by the Orléanists, while the Legitimists recognized the Comte de CHAMBORD as Henry V of France. In 1883 Chambord died without issue and the Legitmists switched support to the Orléanist pretender, the Comte de Paris.

Legnano, Battle of (1176) Conflict in N Italy between Holy Roman Emperor FREDERICK I (BARBAROSSA) and the LOMBARD LEAGUE (aided by Venice and the pope). The League's infantry repelled the invasion of Italy by

LEBANON

AREA: 10,400sq km (4,015sq mi)
POPULATION: 2,838,000
CAPITAL (POPULATION): Beirut (1,500,000)
GOVERNMENT: Multiparty republic
ETHNIC GROUPS: Arab (Lebanese 80%, Palestinian 12%), Armenian 5%, Syrian, Kurdish
LANGUAGES: Arabic (official)
RELIGIONS: Islam 58%, Christianity 27%, Druze
GDP PER CAPITA (1994): US$1692

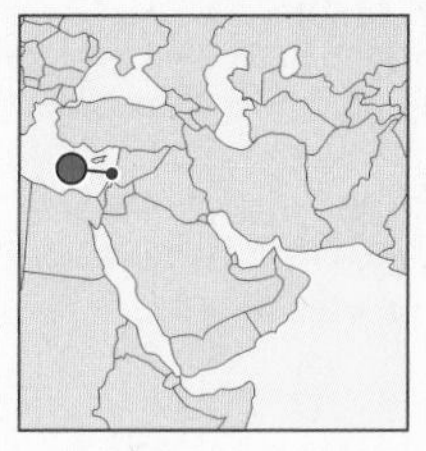

Republic in SW Asia. From the 15th century to the 11th century BC, Lebanon was a dependency of Egypt. By *c.*1100 BC, the Canaanites had developed the city-states of BYBLOS, TYRE (now Sur), BEIRUT, TRIPOLI and Sidon (collectively known as PHOENICIA by the Greeks). Phoenicia was conquered by Assyria (*c.*867 BC), Babylonia (*c.*573 BC), Iran (538 BC) and Alexander the Great (332 BC).

In 64 BC the Romans overthrew the Hellenistic SELEUCID dynasty and Phoenicia became part of the Roman province of Syria. Christianity was introduced in AD 325, and Islam entered via the Arab conquest in the 7th century. The 7th century also witnessed the migration of Christian MARONITES to N Lebanon. The DRUZE, an ISMAILI sect, emerged in S Lebanon in the 11th century. Lebanon was one of the principal battlefields of the CRUSADES (1095–1291), and in the 11th century it was divided between the Crusader kingdoms of Tripoli and JERUSALEM. In the late 13th century, the Crusaders were finally expelled by the Egyptian MAMLUKS and Lebanon prospered once more. In 1516 Lebanon was conquered by the OTTOMAN EMPIRE, who devolved power to the Maans (1516–1697), a Druze dynasty. The succeeding Shihab dynasty (1697–1842) became Europeanized and the later rulers converted to Christianity. In 1920 Lebanon and Syria were mandated to France. "Greater Lebanon" was created by uniting Mount Lebanon with the coastal region and the BEKAA VALLEY, producing a population equally divided between Christians and Muslims.

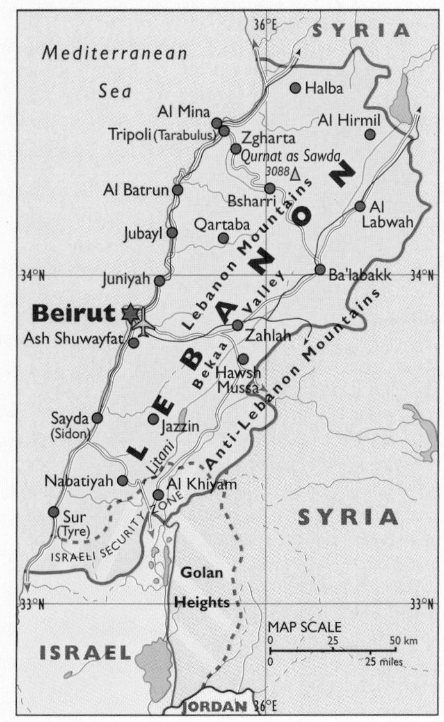

In 1946 Lebanon gained full independence and its economy grew rapidly. In 1958 Muslims in Tripoli, seeking to join the newly formed UNITED ARAB REPUBLIC, launched an insurrection that was crushed by President Camille CHAMOUN with the help of US marines. The ARAB-ISRAELI WARS led to a mass influx of Palestinian refugees, disturbing Lebanon's delicate demographic balance. In 1972 the PALESTINE LIBERATION ORGANIZATION (PLO) moved its headquarters to Beirut. In April 1975 civil war broke out between the Maronite Christians and the PLO-backed Shiite and Druze Muslims. Syrian troops imposed a fragile cease-fire in 1976, creating a "Green Line" that divided Christian and Muslim communities. In 1978 Israel invaded S Lebanon in order to destroy PLO bases. In 1982 Israel launched a full-scale attack on Lebanon, occupying West Beirut. The assassination of Bashir GEMAYEL, leader of the Israeli-backed PHALANGE militia, led to the revenge killing of *c.*1000 Palestinian refugees. The deployment (1983) of Western troops in Beirut led to a terrorist bombing campaign. In 1984 multinational forces left and Israeli troops withdrew to a buffer zone in S Lebanon. In 1987 Syrian troops moved into Beirut to restore peace. In 1989 General Michael Aoun launched a "war of liberation" against Syria.

In 1990 a truce was called in a civil war that had claimed *c.*130,000 lives. Syria maintained troops in West Beirut and the Bekaa Valley, while the Iranian-backed HEZBOLLAH and the Israeli-sponsored South Lebanon Army (SLA) continued to operate in S Lebanon. The presidency (1989–98) of Elias Hrawi began the difficult task of economic reconstruction and social reconciliation. General Emile Lahoud succeeded Hrwai as president (1998–). In 1996 and 2000 Israel launched major bombing raids on Lebanon, but finally agreed to withdraw from S Lebanon by July 2000.

Frederick's mounted knights, an early sign of the declining importance of the cavalry. Frederick was forced to recognize the autonomy of the N Italian city-states and acknowledge ALEXANDER III as pope.

Leicester, Robert Dudley, Earl of (*c*.1532–88) English courtier, favourite of Queen ELIZABETH I. After the failure of the plot to place Lady Jane GREY on the throne in 1553, Dudley was imprisoned along with his father, the Duke of NORTHUMBERLAND. He regained favour upon the accession of Elizabeth (1588). When his first wife, Amy Robsart, died in 1560, it was widely suspected that Dudley had murdered her in order to marry Elizabeth. Elizabeth spurned Dudley and, proposing his marriage to MARY, QUEEN OF SCOTS, made him Earl of Leicester. His secret marriage (1578) to the widow of Walter Devereux, Earl of Essex, incurred the wrath of Elizabeth. In 1585 Leicester was appointed commander of an expedition to the United Provinces (now the Netherlands), but his arrogance, insubordination and incompetence led to his recall in 1587.

Leif Ericson (active 11th century) Norse explorer widely held to be the first European to land in North America, son of ERIC THE RED. According to the Icelandic *Saga of Erik*, in 999 Ericson sailed from Greenland to Iceland, where he was converted to Christianity by OLAF I of Norway. The *Greenland Saga* recounts that he then sailed westwards, retracing the voyage of an Icelandic trader Njarni Herjulfsson. In *c*.1000, Ericson visited Helluland (probably Baffin Island), Markland (possibly Labrador) and Vinland (perhaps Newfoundland). *See also* COLUMBUS, CHRISTOPHER

Leipzig, Battle of (16–19 October 1813) Decisive conflict in the NAPOLEONIC WARS (1803–15), fought at Leipzig, Saxony, Germany. Also known as the Battle of the Nations, *c*.185,000 troops of the Grand Army of NAPOLEON I confronted a combined Allied force (Prussia, Austria, Russia and Sweden) of *c*.320,000 men. On the first day of the Battle, Napoleon repulsed attacks from Fürst zu SCHARWZENBERG and General Gebhard BLÜCHER. On 17 October, the Allies were reinforced by the armies of Jean BERNADOTTE and General Benningsen. On 18 October, they launched a massive assault on Leipzig. Napoleon's army retreated under cover of darkness on 19 October, but a bridge was mistakenly blown up and 30,000 French troops were left stranded in the city. The Battle claimed *c*.38,000 French lives and *c*.54,000 Allied lives and effectively ended the French Empire in Germany and Poland.

Leisler's Rebellion (1689–91) Popular insurrection in colonial New York, led by the wealthy merchant Jacob Leisler (1640–91). The overthrow of JAMES II of England (1689) and the capture of Sir Edmund ANDROS, governor of New England, by rebels in Boston, spurred a rebellion in New York. Leisler assumed the title of lieutenant governor and, establishing a revolutionary council, took command of the colony. In 1691 the new king, WILLIAM III (OF ORANGE), sent troops to quell the revolt and appointed a new governor, Henry Sloughter. Leisler was convicted of treason and hanged, although posthumously pardoned (1695).

lend-lease US programme of military and economic assistance during WORLD WAR 2. Despite Congress' stated neutrality at the start of the War, the Lend-Lease Act (March 1941) empowered President Franklin ROOSEVELT to provide aid to any country "whose defense the President deems vital to the defense of the United States". The first beneficiaries were Britain, China and the Soviet Union. British Commonwealth countries received nearly two-thirds of the *c*.US$49,000 million worth of lend-lease help.

Lenin, Vladimir Ilyich (1870–1924) Russian revolutionary and statesman, leader first of Soviet Russia and then of the SOVIET UNION (1917–24), b. Vladimir Ilyich Ulyanov. His early Marxist agitation in ST PETERSBURG, NW Russia, led to exile in Siberia (1895–1900), where he wrote *The Development of Capitalism in Russia* (1899). Lenin argued that CAPITALISM had divided the Russian peasantry into a small, wealthy rural BOURGEOISIE and a larger impoverished rural PROLETARIAT. In 1900 Lenin left Russia for Germany, where he met with other exiled Russian Marxists, including Georgi PLEKHANOV. In *What is to be Done?* (1902), Lenin argued for a revolutionary form of SOCIALISM (later known as MARXISM-Leninism) that emphasized the need for a centralized and disciplined party to act as the vanguard of the revolution. A split emerged at the Second Congress of the Russian Social Democratic Labour Party (RSDLP) in 1902; Lenin carried the majority (Rus. BOLSHEVIK) of the Party, while L. Martov led the minority (Rus. MENSHEVIK) faction. Lenin returned to Russia after the RUSSIAN REVOLUTION OF 1905, but he rejected the RSDLP's support for elections to the Duma, proposing instead a "DICTATORSHIP OF THE PROLETARIAT". In 1907 Lenin was forced again into exile, where he formed an independent Bolshevik Party in 1912. Lenin opposed participation in WORLD WAR 1 (1914–18), arguing in *Imperialism, The Highest Stage of Capitalism* (1916) that the War was the inevitable outcome of Western capitalism and imperialist expansion. In April 1917 Lenin returned to Petrograd (now St Petersburg), where riots had toppled Tsar NICHOLAS II in the first phase of the RUSSIAN REVOLUTION (March 1917). Lenin denounced the new government of Prince LVOV, and in his "April Theses" demanded the establishment of government by SOVIETS (workers' councils). In July 1917 Lvov was replaced by Alexander KERENSKY, and Lenin was forced to flee to Finland. In October 1917 he secretly returned to Petrograd and persuaded the RED GUARDS, led by Leon TROTSKY, to overthrow Kerensky's government. Lenin was subsequently elected leader of Soviet Russia. One of his first acts was to end Russia's involvement in World War 1, accepting the harsh terms of the Treaty of BREST-LITOVSK (March 1918). The Allies refused to recognize the Soviet government and supported the counter-revolutionary forces in the RUSSIAN CIVIL WAR (1918–20). The brutal crushing of domestic opposition continued even after the Bolshevik victory in the Civil War. In 1918 Lenin was seriously wounded in an assassination attempt. The lack of food for Trotsky's RED ARMY forced the government to requisition grain from the Russian peasantry. The threat of a peasant revolution, however, led to the introduction (1921) of the NEW ECONOMIC POLICY (NEP), which allowed peasants to sell their produce on the open market. In 1919 Lenin organized the COMMUNIST INTERNATIONAL to encourage world revolution, modelled on the example of Russian COMMUNISM. The Soviet Union was established in May 1922. Lenin was left partially paralysed by two strokes in 1922 and composed his "testament", which criticized the creation of a bloated bureaucracy and warned against the dictatorial tendencies of Joseph STALIN, general secretary of the COMMUNIST PARTY OF THE SOVIET UNION (CPSU). After Lenin's death, a bitter power struggle between Trotsky and Stalin ended in the latter's victory. Stalin insisted, against Lenin's own wishes, that Lenin's body be preserved and put on public display in Red Square, Moscow.

Leningrad, Siege of (September 1941– January 1944) Blockade of the Russian city of Leningrad (now ST PETERSBURG) by German and Finnish forces during WORLD WAR 2. The destruction of the city was a major objective of Adolf HITLER's "Operation Barbarossa". In June 1941 Nazi Germany invaded the Soviet Union, advancing rapidly towards Leningrad. Marshal Georgi ZHUKOV and 200,000 RED ARMY troops organized the city's defences. The German Army, led by Field Marshal Ritter von Leeb, encircled Leningrad, cutting off all food and fuel supplies to its 3 million inhabitants while bombarding the city by aircraft and artillery. In the winter of 1941, the frozen Lake Ladoga provided a precarious supply route to the city and a means of escape for *c*.500,000 people. Besieged for more than 870 days, Leningrad was finally liberated by a Soviet offensive. The Siege claimed more than 1 million civilian lives, mainly due to starvation, disease and exposure. In 1945 the city was awarded the Order of Lenin.

Leo I, Saint (d.461) (Leo the Great) Pope (440–61). He helped his predecessor, Sixtus III, suppress the heresies of PELAGIANISM and NESTORIANISM. Leo devoted his pontificate to establishing papal supremacy throughout the Western church. At the Council of CHALCEDON (449), he confirmed the dual nature of Christ. In 452 Leo persuaded ATTILA the Hun not to attack Rome, and when the city was occupied by the Vandal GAISERIC (455), he prevented a massacre of its citizens. His feast day is 10 November.

Leo III, Saint (*c*.750–816) Pope (795–816). On his accession, Leo recognized CHARLEMAGNE as ruler of Rome. This action angered the Roman aristocracy and Leo fled to Germany in 799. Under Charlemagne's protection, he returned to Rome and crowned Charlemagne emperor on 25 December 800, an event of great significance for the future course of European history. While strengthening papal authority, it led to the recognition of the emperor as secular leader of Western Christendom in tandem with its spiritual leader, the pope. The coronation also widened the breach between the Western and Eastern churches. His feast day is 12 June. *See also* HOLY ROMAN EMPIRE

Leo IX, Saint (1002–54) Pope (1049–54), b. Alsace as Bruno von Egisheim. With the support of Hildebrand (later Pope GREGORY VII), he effected wide-ranging reforms of clerical abuses such as SIMONY. Leo travelled widely, extending papal power beyond the Alps. Leo led a campaign against the Normans in S Italy, but was defeated and captured in 1053. Furthermore, his intervention provoked the patriarch of Constantinople to close the Latin (Western) churches in Constantinople (now Istanbul). The excommunication of the patriarch by papal bull in 1054, marked the start of the SCHISM between the Eastern and Western churches.

Leo X (1475–1521) Pope (1513–21), b. Giovanni de' Medici, son of Lorenzo de' MEDICI. In 1511 he re-established the authority of the Medici dynasty in FLORENCE. Leo's pontificate secured ROME as a centre of RENAISSANCE culture. The construction of ST PETER'S Basilica and his extravagant patronage of the arts, however, depleted the papal treasury. Defeated by the French at the Battle of Marignano (1515), Leo was forced to make peace with FRANCIS I, and the Concordat of Bologna (1516) gave the French kings power over clerical appointments. Leo presided over the Fifth LATERAN COUNCIL (1512–17), but failed to enact sufficient reforms to head off the REFORMATION. His sale of INDULGENCES was one of the abuses attacked by Martin LUTHER at Wittenberg (1517). Leo excommunicated Luther in 1521. *See also* ECK, JOHANN MAIER VON; PROTESTANTISM

Leo XIII (1810–1903) Pope (1878–1903), b. Vincenzo Gioacchino Pecci. He abandoned the authoritarian approach of his predecessor, PIUS IX, reconciling Roman Catholic attitudes to the scientific and political theories of the age, and improving diplomatic relations with secular governments. A devoted scholar, Leo opened the Vatican archives to the public and sponsored Catholic education and social reform, manifesting special concern for the conditions of the working-class.

Leo III (the Isaurian) (*c*.680–741) Byzantine emperor (717–41). He deposed Theodosius III in an army coup. Leo successfully defended Constantinople (now Istanbul) against a major Arab siege (717–18) and, after forming an alliance with the Khazars, expelled the Muslims from Asia Minor in 740. Revitalizing the BYZANTINE EMPIRE, he developed a new system of provincial administration, improved the empire's defences and issued a new legal code. Leo's attack on the veneration of icons initiated the ICONOCLASTIC CONTROVERSY and resulted in his excommunication (731) by Pope Gregory II.

Leo VI (the Wise) (866–912) Byzantine emperor (886–912), son and successor of BASIL I (THE MACEDONIAN). He was educated by PHOTIUS. In *c*.888 Leo completed the *Basilica*, a codification of imperial laws. In 896 the BYZANTINE EMPIRE was forced to pay an annual tribute to the Bulgars. Leo also lost Sicily to the Arabs in 902 and Muslim pirates captured Thessalonika in 904.

León Region and former kingdom in NW Spain, today comprising the provinces of León, Salamanca and Zamora. Conquered from the Romans by the Visigoths, it was overrun by the MOORS in the 8th century. The Christian kingdom was founded by García I (r.909–14) and took a leading role in the Christian reconquest. León was closely linked with CASTILE and the kingdoms were permanently united (1230) by FERDINAND III.

Leonidas (d.480 BC) King of SPARTA (*c*.490–480 BC). His small Greek army confronted the Persian army of XERXES I at the Battle of THERMOPYLAE (480 BC). For two days they defended the mountain pass against overwhelming odds. Leonidas ordered most of his troops to retreat and he and his 300-strong Spartan guard fought to the last man. The heroism of Leonidas was recounted by HERODOTUS.

Leopold I (1640–1705) Holy Roman emperor (1658–1705), king of Hungary (1655–87), king of Bohemia (1656–1705), son and successor of FERDINAND III. His centralization of the Austrian administration and creation of a standing army helped to extend the HABSBURG domains. In 1683 JOHN III of Poland defeated the Ottoman siege of Vienna and subsequent victories by Prince EUGÈNE OF SAVOY increased the pace of the Ottoman retreat. In the Treaty of KARLOWITZ (1699), Turkey relinquished almost the whole of Hungary. The Hungarian nobility, worried about the possible imposition of the COUNTER-REFORMATION, fiercely resisted Habsburg domination. Leopold was less successful in his struggles with France. The War of the GRAND ALLIANCE (1689–97) ended in stalemate and Leopold was forced to cede Strasbourg to France in the Treaty of RIJSWIJK (1697). Competing HABSBURG and BOURBON (French) claims to the Spanish crown led to the War of the SPANISH SUCCESSION (1701–14), which was still in progress when Leopold died. He was succeeded by his son, JOSEPH I.

Leopold II (1747–92) Holy Roman emperor (1790–92), grand duke of Tuscany as Leopold I (1765–90), third son of Emperor FRANCIS I and MARIA THERESA. He succeeded his father in Tuscany and his brother, JOSEPH II, as emperor. Regarded as an "enlightened despot" in Tuscany, Leopold dismantled feudal institutions and rationalized the taxation system. As emperor, he began to decentralize the Habsburg state and continued the emancipation of the peasantry. When LOUIS XVI and MARIE ANOINETTE (Leopold's sister) were overthrown in the FRENCH REVOLUTION (1789–99), Leopold issued the Declaration of Pillnitz (1791) with Prussia. The Declaration provided the motive for the FRENCH REVOLUTIONARY WARS (1792–1802). He was succeeded by his son, FRANCIS II.

Leopold I (1790–1865) First king of Belgium (1831–65), son of the Duke of Saxe-Coburg-Saalfeld, b. Germany. In 1816 he married the daughter of the future King GEORGE IV of Great Britain. The early part of his reign was marked by conflict with the Netherlands, who refused to recognize the sovereignty of Belgium until 1838. Leopold maintained Belgian neutrality in Europe, even under concerted pressure during the Crimean War (1853–56), and strengthened the new nation through a network of marriage alliances. For instance, Leopold was largely responsible for the marriage (1840) of his niece Queen VICTORIA of England to his nephew Prince ALBERT. He was succeeded by his son, LEOPOLD II.

Leopold II (1835–1909) King of Belgium (1865–1909), son and successor of LEOPOLD I. He initiated colonial expansion and sponsored the expedition of Henry STANLEY to the Congo (1879–84). In 1885 Leopold established the Congo Free State (now Democratic Republic of CONGO) under his own personal rule. In 1908 Sir Roger CASEMENT's revelations of the exploitation of the Congolese rubber-gatherers forced Leopold to cede the Congo to the Belgian state. He was succeeded by ALBERT I.

Leopold III (1901–83) King of the Belgians (1934–51), son and successor of ALBERT I. When the Germans invaded Belgium in 1940, Leopold quickly surrendered and later refused to join the government-in-exile in London. He remained in Belgium until removed to Germany in 1944. Leopold's wartime conduct aroused such controversy that he did not return until 1950, when riots soon forced him to abdicate in favour of his son, BAUDOUIN.

Leovigild (d.586) Last Arian king of the VISIGOTHS in Spain, sole ruler (571–585). He restored the power of the Visigothic kingdom through warfare. Leovigild gained León and Zamora (569) from the Suebi and later annexed their kingdom. He seized Córdoba (572) and later Seville (583) from forces loyal to the BYZANTINE EMPIRE. In Seville these included his dissident son Hermingild. In 584 Leovigild abandoned "itinerant government" for a permanent capital in Toledo which he made a centre for Arian Christian piety, to counter Byzantine Orthodoxy. Leovigild's heirs converted to Latin-based Catholicism.

Lepanto, Battle of (7 October 1571) Naval engagement in the Gulf of Corinth, off Greece. In 1570 Sultan SELIM II invaded Cyprus, prompting Pope PIUS V to form a new HOLY LEAGUE with Spain and Venice. The Christian forces, led by Don JOHN OF AUSTRIA, inflicted a heavy defeat on the Turkish fleet of Ali Pasha, who died in the conflict. The League captured 117 Turkish galleys and freed thousands of Christian slaves. It was the last great battle between fleets of war galleys and the first major victory for Europe over the Ottoman Turks. It was of little practical value, however, for the Turks gained Cyprus in 1573.

Lepidus, Marcus Aemilius (d. *c*.13 BC) Roman statesman. He fought for Julius CAESAR in the civil war (49–45 BC) against POMPEY and became consul in 46 BC. After Caesar's assassination, Lepidus formed (43 BC) the so-called Second Triumvirate with Mark ANTONY and Octavian (later AUGUSTUS). Sidelined by his two colleagues, Lepidus launched an abortive rebellion in Sicily (36 BC) and was forced into retirement.

Lerma, Francisco Gómez de Sandoval y Rojas, Duque de (1553–1625) Spanish statesman, chief minister (1598–1618) to PHILIP III. He made peace (1604) with James I of England and initiated the 12-year truce with the United Provinces (1609). Lerma was responsible for the expulsion of *c*.350,000 Moriscos (Christianized Muslims) from Spain (1609–14). The act produced severe economic depression in Spain and, coupled with Lerma's personal corruption, led to his downfall in 1618.

Lesage, Jean (1912–80) Canadian statesman, premier of Québec (1960–66). He served in the national Parliament (1945–58) before resigning to become leader of the Québec Liberal Party (1958). Lesage's "Quiet Revolution" brought about educational and welfare advances, and secured greater financial autonomy for Québec. Lesage encouraged closer bonds with France, in an attempt to undermine the separatist movement. He resigned the Liberal leadership in 1970.

LENIN, VLADIMIR ILLYICH

Vladimir Ilyich Lenin made the Marxist vision of a workers' revolution a reality in Russia, providing a model for communist revolutions worldwide. A ruthless and determined leader, he became an iconic figure, as this poster reflects: "Lenin Lived, Lenin Lives, Lenin will always Live!"

LENIN IN HIS OWN WORDS

"So long as the state exists there is no freedom. When there is freedom there will be no state."
The State and Revolution, 1918

Leslie, Alexander, 1st Earl of Leven (*c*.1580–1661) Scottish military commander. He fought with distinction for the Swedish army in the THIRTY YEARS' WAR (1618–48). In 1639 Leslie commanded the Scottish army of COVENANTERS, which occupied NE England in 1640. Leslie fought for Parliament in the English CIVIL WAR (1642–48) and CHARLES I surrendered to him at Newark, central England (May 1646). After the execution of Charles I, Leslie defended Scotland for CHARLES II, but was defeated by Oliver CROMWELL at Dunbar (1650).

Lesotho *See* country feature, page 238

Lesseps, Ferdinand Marie, Vicomte de (1805–94) French diplomat and constructor of the SUEZ CANAL. While assistant vice consul (1832–37) in Egypt, he studied proposals to build a canal through the Isthmus of Suez, linking the Red Sea with the Mediterranean Sea. Aided by contacts, especially friendship with the Egyptian khedive, he formed the Suez Canal Company, with mainly French capital. Digging began in 1859, and the Canal was opened in November 1869, thanks largely to Lesseps' dynamism and administrative skill. In 1879 he launched a scheme to construct the PANAMA CANAL but it was abandoned amid scandal in 1888. *See also* ISMAIL PASHA

Le Tellier, Michel (1603–85) French statesman, secretary of state for war (1643–77) and chancellor (1677–85) under LOUIS XIV. He was appointed war secretary by Cardinal Jules MAZARIN and remained loyal to his patron during the FRONDE (1648–53). Le Tellier instituted reforms that greatly increased the size of France's standing army and brought it under the direct control of the monarchy. He was assisted by his son, the future Marquis de LOUVOIS, who succeeded him as war minister. Le Tellier persecuted the HUGUENOTS and helped draft the Revocation of the Edict of NANTES (1685).

Lettow-Vorbeck, Paul von (1870–1964) German soldier, commander of German East African forces during WORLD WAR I. With less than 14,000 men, mostly Africans, Lettow-Vorbeck employed skilful guerrilla tactics to contain up to 300,000 Allied troops for nearly four years. In November 1914 he repelled a British invasion at Tanga (now Tanzania) and, despite the Allied capture of most of GERMAN EAST AFRICA, took the offensive in 1917. He surrendered only after the armistice in Europe and received a hero's welcome on his return to Germany. He was a right-wing member of the Reichstag (1929–39), but opposed the rise of the NAZI PARTY under Adolf HITLER.

Levellers (1645–49) Republican and democratic movement in England during the English CIVIL WAR (1642–48). They campaigned for the abolition of the monarchy and the House of Lords, the extension of the franchise, religious toleration and economic reform in favour of peasant farmers. When Parliament ignored their demands, the Levellers sought the support of the general populace and Oliver CROMWELL's NEW MODEL ARMY. In October 1647, an army council met at Putney, London, to discuss a Leveller pamphlet, the *Agreement of the People* (1647), based upon the inalienability of individual rights and the notion of popular sovereignty. The Putney debates ended in stalemate, and Cromwell and Henry IRETON used force to restore discipline in the ranks, imprisoning Leveller leaders including John LILBURNE. The Levellers denounced the formation of the COMMONWEALTH in 1649, and army mutinies in London and Burford, Oxfordshire, were crushed by Cromwell. *See also* DIGGERS

Lévesque, René (1922–87) Canadian statesman, premier of Québec (1976–85). He served (1960–66) in the Québec government of Jean LESAGE. Lévesque was a founder (1968) and first president of the Parti Québecois, which sought sovereignty for Québec while retaining economic association with Canada. As premier, he passed the controversial Bill 101 that made French the official, public language of Québec. Lévesque put his "sovereignty-association" proposal to the test in a 1980 referendum, but was narrowly defeated after the intervention of Canadian Prime Minister Pierre TRUDEAU. In 1985 he was forced to resign because of illness.

Lewes, Battle of (1264) Military engagement in the Second BARONS' WAR, fought in Sussex, England. The nobility, brilliantly led by Simon de MONTFORT, defeated the larger, royalist army of Henry III. Montfort's victory established his effective rule in England, which lasted until his death (1265).

Lewis, John Llewellyn (1880–1969) US union leader, president (1920–60) of the United Mine Workers of America (UMWA). After splitting with the American Federation of Labor (AFL) over the unionization of mass-production industries, he formed the rival Congress of Industrial Organizations (CIO) and was its president (1936–40). During World War 2, he organized a series of mass strikes that resulted in improved standards of living for the miners, but also led to the Smith-Connally Act (1943) and the Taft-Hartley Act (1947), restricted union practices.

Lewis, Meriwether (1774–1809) US explorer and naturalist. In 1801 he became personal secretary to President Thomas Jefferson, who chose him to lead the Lewis and Clark Expedition (1804–06) to find a transcontinental route to the Pacific Ocean. The expedition proved a success and opened up the westward expansion of the frontier. In 1808 he was appointed governor of Louisiana Territory. He died of a gunshot wound, apparently self-inflicted.

Lewis and Clark Expedition *See* feature article

Lexington and Concord, Battles of (19 April 1775) First clashes of the American Revolution. Disturbances in Massachusetts resulting from the Intolerable Acts (1774) prompted stronger measures by British General Thomas Gage. A column dispatched from Boston to seize a gunpowder store in Concord clashed with militiamen at Lexington Green. Several minutemen were killed. Concord was forewarned by Paul Revere, and most of the gunpowder had been hidden or destroyed before the British arrived. The British return to Boston was severely hampered by guerrilla attacks. The British lost 273 men, the Americans 95.

Leyte Gulf, Battle of (23–25 October 1944) Air and naval engagement during World War 2, fought between Japan and the United States off the Philippine island of Leyte. In the largest naval battle in history, the Japanese lost 28 ships and 405 "kamikaze" aircraft, while the US lost only 6 ships. The Japanese navy withdrew from the region, facilitating the reconquest of the Philippines by General Douglas MacArthur.

Liang Qichao (1873–1929) Chinese political scientist. He was a student of Kang Youwei. Liang and Kang were the emperor's leading advisers during the Hundred Days of Reform (1898). Empress Dowager Cixi crushed the reform movement and placed a death sentence on Liang. Liang fled to Japan, from where he continued to criticize the government. In 1912, after Sun Yat-sen had overthrown the Qing dynasty, Liang returned to China and founded the Progressive Party. He initially supported President Yuan Shih-kai against the Kuomintang, but resisted Yuan's attempt to become emperor.

Liaquat Ali Khan (1895–1951) Pakistani statesman, first prime minister of Pakistan (1947–51). He joined the Muslim League in 1923 and became the closest aide of its founder, Muhammad Ali Jinnah. As prime minister, Liaquat drafted the constitution of the new republic. He tried to improve relations with India in the so-called "Delhi Pact" (1950) with Jawaharlal Nehru. Liaquat was assassinated by Islamic fanatics.

Liberal Democrats (LD) (originally Social and Liberal Democrats) British political organization, formed (March 1988) by the merger of the Liberal Party and the Social Democratic Party (SDP). Its first leader (1988–99) was Paddy Ashdown (1941–). He was succeeded by Charles Kennedy (1959–). The ideological descendant of the old Liberal Party, it is by far the smallest of the three main political parties in Britain and has vigorously campaigned for proportional representation (PR), a system that would give it more seats in Parliament. In the 1997 election, the Liberal Democrats more than doubled their representation in Parliament (winning 46 seats). It supported Prime Minister Tony Blair's devolution of power to Scotland and Wales and, in return for promises on PR, formulated a policy of "constructive engagement" with the Labour government. *See also* Conservative Party; Labour Party

liberalism Political belief in individual liberty and a gradualist approach to social progress. **Classical** liberalism is often linked by Whig and Marxist historians to the rise of the bourgeoisie, whose opposition to absolutism produced the Glorious Revolution (1688) in England, the American Revolution (1775–83) and the French Revolution (1789–99). English philosopher John Locke provided (1690) a definition of early liberalism, arguing that all people had equal rights to "life, health, liberty, or possessions". Classical liberal economists, such as Adam Smith, criticized mercantilism arguing instead for free-trade and laissez-faire policies. These ideas fed into the 18th-century Enlightenment movement and influenced, among others, Thomas Paine and Thomas Jefferson. The Constitution of the United States (1789) is a classic formulation of the liberal aim to restrict the role of government through the separation of powers. In Britain, liberalism informed utilitarianism, in particular the work of Jeremy Bentham and John Stuart Mill. A distinction is often made between classical liberalism, which feared mass participation in politics, and **modern** liberalism that believes social change is achieved through the extension of democracy. The inequalities caused by 19th-century industrial capitalism led to a shift in liberal economics, rejecting the unfettered free-market in favour of limited government intervention and the creation of a welfare state. *See also* conservatism; socialism

Liberal Party British political organization. It evolved out of the radical, reforming elements of the 19th-century Whigs, whose strength increased after the Reform Act of 1867. British liberals generally shared the ideals of European liberalism, promoting political reform and freedom of the individual. Under the Liberal leader William Gladstone, prime minister four times between 1868 and 1894, the Whigs gradually drifted away to the Tory Party, especially after Gladstone espoused Irish Home Rule. In 1894 Gladstone retired and was succeeded by the Earl of Rosebery. With the enfranchisement of the working class, Liberals became increasingly collectivist, favouring social reform by state action. In the 1906 election, a split in the Conservative Party produced a landslide victory for the Liberals, led by Henry Campbell-Bannerman. In 1908 Campbell-Bannerman was succeeded by Herbert Asquith, whose government introduced old-age pensions (1908), national insurance (1911) and restricted the power of the House of Lords (1911). In 1916 Asquith was replaced in a cabinet coup by David Lloyd George, who led peace negotiations at the end of World War 1 (1914–18) and granted independence to the Irish Free State (1921). The rise of the Labour Party as the party of the working-class posed a challenge to the divided Liberals. Lloyd George's coalition government collapsed in 1922, and in the ensuing election Labour won more seats than the Liberals, who steadily declined thereafter. The decline was partly arrested under the leadership (1956–67) of Jo Grimond, who repositioned the Party as a left-of-centre organization. Under Jeremy Thorpe the Liberals gained 20% of the vote at the October 1974 election. In the so-called "Lib-Lab Pact" (1976–78), Liberal leader David Steel supported the minority Labour government of James Callaghan in return for an influence on policy-making. A split in the Labour Party led to the formation of the Social Democratic Party (SDP) in 1981. The SDP and the Liberals formed the Alliance, which gained 25% of the vote in the 1983 election although, owing to the first-past-the post system of representation, that translated

LESOTHO (FORMERLY BASUTOLAND)

AREA: 30,350sq km (11,718sq mi)
POPULATION: 1,836,000
CAPITAL (POPULATION): Maseru (367,000)
GOVERNMENT: Constitutional monarchy
ETHNIC GROUPS: Sotho 99%
LANGUAGES: Sesotho and English (both official)
RELIGIONS: Christianity 93% (Roman Catholic 44%), traditional beliefs 6%
GDP PER CAPITA (1995): US$1780

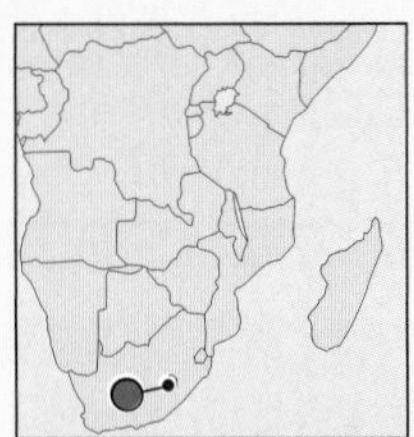

Enclave kingdom within the Republic of South Africa. From the 16th century, the Sotho gradually displaced the indigenous San population. In the early 19th century, the Sotho were dispersed in the tribal wars prompted by Shaka's expansion of the Zulu empire. In 1824 Moshoeshoe I formed a defensive mountain settlement located at Thaba Bosiu, which became the kingdom of the Basotho. From the 1830s, the Basotho were threatened by Afrikaner settlers and Moshoeshoe I asked for British help. The area became a British protectorate in 1868. In 1871 Basutoland became part of Cape Colony but after a war (1880–81) between the Basotho and Cape Colony, the British reimposed direct rule. The discovery of gold and diamonds in South Africa led many Basotho to become migrant workers in the South African mines. The Basotho opposed colonial rule, but strongly resisted incorporation into the Union of South Africa. In 1966 the independent Kingdom of Lesotho was created and Moshoeshoe II, great-grandson of Moshoeshoe I, became king.

In 1970 Chief Leabua Jonathan suspended the constitution, banned opposition parties and sent the king into exile. The next 16 years were characterized by conflict between the government and Basotho Congress Party (BCP) forces. In 1986 a coup led to the reinstatement of Moshoeshoe II, but real power resided with the military. In 1990 Moshoeshoe II was deposed and replaced by his son, Letsie III. The BCP won the 1993 election, and the military council was dissolved. In 1994 Letsie III attempted to overthrow the government and Moshoeshoe II was restored to the throne in 1995. His death (1996) saw the restoration of Letsie III. In 1997 a majority of BCP politicians formed a new governing party, the Lesotho Congress for Democracy (LCD). Accusations of fraud in May 1998 elections led to violent protests and an army mutiny. In September 1998 South African forces restored order and an interim government was formed under Pakalitha Mosisili.

into only 23 seats in the House of Commons. In 1988 the two parties merged as the Liberal Democrats (LD).

Liberal Party Canadian political organization. The Party evolved out of the 19th-century reform movement, whose primary aim was a national assembly. In 1854 the reform movement split, the moderate liberals joining what became the Progressive Conservative Party, and the more radical reformers uniting to form what is now the Liberal Party. It held principles broadly similar to the British Liberal Party. The Liberal Party of Canada first held office (1873–78) under Alexander Mackenzie, but thereafter its championing of free-trade kept it in opposition until Wilfrid Laurier's electoral victory in 1896. Laurier's pragmatic politics gave the Liberals 15 years of uninterrupted government. His successor, W.L. Mackenzie King, became prime minister in 1921 and, except for the period 1930–35, ruled Canada almost continuously until his retirement in 1948. He led the nation throughout World War 2 and managed to preserve the often fragile union between English- and French-speaking Canada. King was succeeded as Liberal leader by Louis Saint Laurent, who served as prime minister between 1948 and 1957. Saint Laurent was succeeded by Lester Pearson, who led (1963–68) a minority government. Pearson's successor, Pierre Trudeau, governed Canada almost continuously from 1968 to 1984, promoting bilingualism in civic affairs and making liberal reforms to the constitution. After Trudeau, the Liberals remained in opposition for nearly a decade, until Jean Chrétien led them back to power in 1993.

Liberal Party Australian political organization. It was formed as the Fusion Party in 1910 and adopted the name Liberal in 1913. Despite its name, it has generally been conservative in policy. During World War 1 it allied with the pro-conscription wing of the Labor Party to form a Nationalist government. In 1922 it expelled its ex-Labor members to form a Nationalist-Country government in alliance with the Country Party (now National Party). Voted out of office in 1929, the Liberals regained office (1931–41) as the United Australia Party. In 1944 Robert Menzies created a new Liberal Party and led a Liberal-Country coalition government until 1966. In 1975 Liberal leader Malcolm Fraser defeated Gough Whitlam to become prime minister (1975–83). In 1996, after five successive Labor governments, the Liberals led by John Howard formed a coalition government with the National Party. *See also* Gorton, John Grey; Holt, Harold

Liberal Republican Party US political organization founded in the late 1860s by dissatisified Republicans, who rejected the direction of Reconstruction and challenged the perceived corruption of President Ulysses Grant's administration. Liberal Republicans favoured leniency to the South, civil service reform and a lower tariff. Leaders of the Party included Charles Francis Adams and Horace Greeley. Greeley was easily defeated in the 1872 presidential election and most Party members soon rejoined the Republican Party.

Liberia *See* country feature, page 240

Liberty Party (1839–48) US political organization founded by moderate abolitionists in Warsaw, New York. In 1840 and 1844 they nominated James Birney for president. Although they attracted only 62,000 votes in the 1844 presidential election, this was sufficient to deny fellow anti-slavery candidate Henry Clay and ensure the election of James Polk, a slaveholder. In 1848 the Liberty Party merged with anti-slavery Whigs and democrats to form the Free Soil Party.

Libya *See* country feature, page 242

Licinius (d.325) Roman emperor (308–324). Licinius was appointed emperor by Galerius, but his rule was challenged by several usurpers. Allying himself with Constantine I (the Great), Licinius became emperor of the east in 313, with Constantine emperor of the west. Licinius and Constantine issued the Edict of Milan (313), favouring Christianity, but the two emperors subsequently fell out. Licinius resumed attacks on the Christians, and in 324 he was defeated by Constantine at Adrianople and later executed.

Li Dazhao (1889–1927) Chinese revolutionary. One of the founders (1921) of the Chinese Communist Party (CCP), he was instrumental in forging an alliance with the Kuomintang (Nationalist Party) led by Sun Yat-sen. His theories on the leading role of the peasantry in the communist revolution strongly influenced Mao Zedong. When the Manchurian warlord Zhang Zuolin captured Beijing, Li Dazhao was seized and executed.

Lidice Village in the Czech Republic, 16km (10mi) NW of Prague. On 10 June 1942, Lidice was totally destroyed by the Nazis in retaliation for the assassination of Reinhard Heydrich, deputy head of the Gestapo. All men over the age of 16 were killed and all women were deported. The area is now a national park and memorial.

Lie, Trygve (Halvdan) (1896–1968) Norwegian diplomat, first secretary general (1946–53) of the United Nations (UN). His quest for peace was frustrated by the start of the Cold War. Lie antagonized the Soviet Union by his support for UN intervention (1950) in the Korean War (1950–53), and thereafter the Soviets did not recognize his status as secretary general. He also attracted criticism from US Senator Joseph McCarthy, who accused him of appointing US communists to the UN. Lie was succeeded by Dag Hammarskjöld.

L

LEWIS AND CLARK EXPEDITION (1804–06)

First US overland exploration of the American West and Pacific Northwest. Its primary aim was to seek a route by water from the Mississippi to the Pacific Ocean. Instigated by President Thomas Jefferson, the expedition was led by army officers Meriwether Lewis and William Clark (1770–1883). In May 1804 the "Corps of Discovery" left St Louis, Missouri, and travelled up the Missouri River, wintering in the Mandan villages of North Dakota. In April 1805 they set out across modern-day Montana with a Shoshone woman, Sacagawea, acting as guide and interpreter. Lewis and Clark established that there was no direct water passage to the Pacific and crossed the Continental Divide on horseback. They travelled down the Clearwater and Snake rivers, arriving at the mouth of the Columbia River in November 1805. On the return, Lewis and Clark took separate routes, via the Marias and Yellowstone rivers respectively, before meeting again on the Missouri. They arrived back in St Louis on 23 September 1806, having travelled *c.*13,000km (8000mi). The Expedition mapped the main river systems and, encountering country and Native Americans hitherto unknown, opened up the Western frontier. *See also* Louisiana Purchase; Mackenzie, Alexander; Oregon Trail

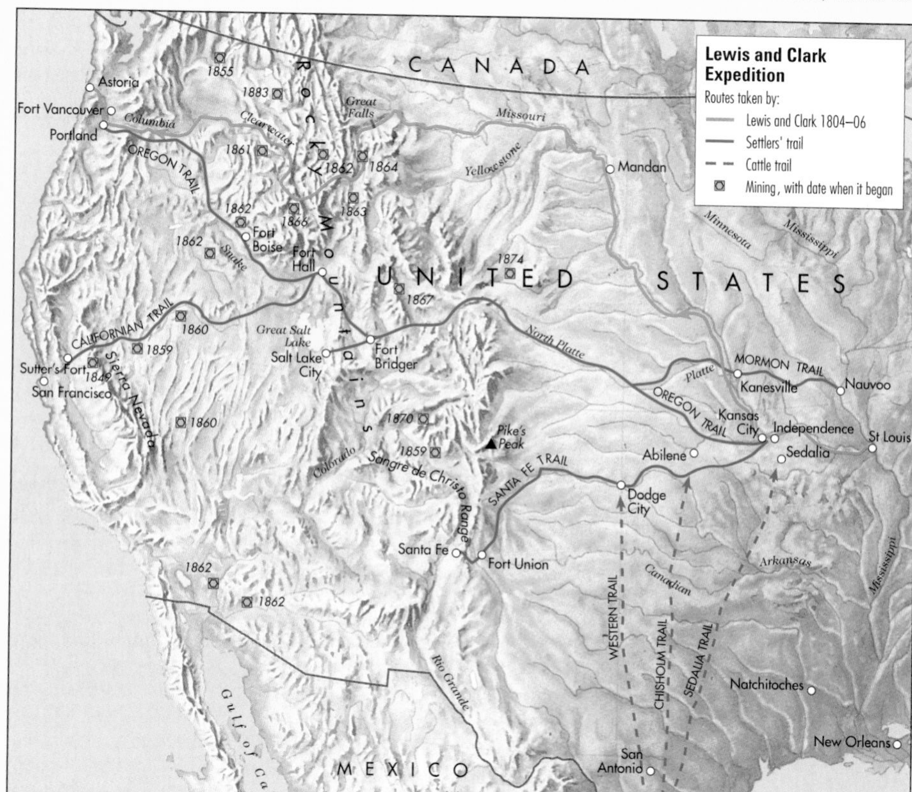

◄ **The expedition** provided invaluable information about natural resources in the West, prompting pioneers to travel in search of land or gold.

▲ **Sacagawea**, shown here with Clark, was an invaluable member of the expedition, negotiating with fellow Native Americans for supplies and horses.

Liebknecht, Karl (1871–1919) German socialist, son of Wilhelm Liebknecht. He entered the Reichstag (German parliament) in 1912 and was a leading critic of the Social Democratic Party (SPD)'s support for German involvement in World War 1. In 1916 Liebknecht was expelled from the SPD and joined Rosa Luxemburg in forming the revolutionary Spartacus League. He was imprisoned (1916–18) for leading an anti-war demonstration in Berlin. Liebknecht and Luxemburg were murdered in police custody after leading an abortive uprising in Berlin (January 1919) against the post-war government of Friedrich Ebert.

Liebknecht, Wilhelm (1826–1900) German socialist, father of Karl Liebknecht. After taking part in the Revolutions of 1848, Liebknecht was exiled to England, where he became an associate of Karl Marx and Friedrich Engels. He returned to Prussia in 1862, but was expelled by Otto von Bismarck in 1865. In 1869 Liebknecht and August Bebel formed the Social Democratic Labour Party, which became (1891) the Social Democratic Party (SPD). Liebknecht and Babel were imprisoned (1872–74) for their opposition to the Franco-Prussian War (1870–71). Despite their suppression by Bismarck, the socialists continued to gain popular support and the Anti-Socialist Law (1878) was repealed in 1890. *See also* International, Second

Liechtenstein Independent principality in w central Europe, between Austria (e) and Switzerland (w). Liechtensteiners are descended from the Alemanni tribe that migrated into the region after AD 500. The principality was formed (1719) through the merging of Vaduz and Schellenberg. It remained part of the Holy Roman Empire until 1806, when it was subsumed into the Rhine Confederation (1806–15). A member of the German Confederation from 1815, Liechtenstein gained independence in 1866. In 1921 it entered into a currency union with Switzerland and, in 1923, a customs union. Until 1990 Switzerland also handled its foreign policy. In 1990 the principality joined the United Nations (UN). Liechtenstein has a constitutional and hereditary monarchy; the ruling family is the Austrian House of Liechtenstein. Women finally received the vote in 1984.

LIECHTENSTEIN
AREA: 157sq km (61sq mi)
POPULATION: 28,777
CAPITAL (POPULATION): Vaduz (5072)
GOVERNMENT: Constitutional monarchy
ETHNIC GROUPS: Alemannic 95%
LANGUAGES: German (official)
RELIGIONS: Roman Catholic 81%, Protestant 7%
GDP PER CAPITA (1995): US$34,000

Li Hongzhang (1823–1901) Chinese statesman and general. His early career was guided by Zeng Guofan. Li helped defeat the Taiping Rebellion (1850–64) in his home province of Zhili, and later worked with Zeng and British General Charles Gordon in suppressing the rebels in Shanghai. While governor general of Zhili (1870–94), Li also acted as China's chief adviser on foreign affairs. Faced by the growing military strength of Japan, Li and Japanese statesman Ito Hirobumi agreed to joint control over the Korean Peninsula, but the agreement failed to prevent the Sino-Japanese War (1894–95). Li was forced to grant concessions to Western powers after the Boxer Rebellion (1900). Although guilty of self-aggrandizement, he helped modernize China's army and navy, and enacted limited reforms of education. *See also* Qing

Likud Israeli right-wing political organization, founded (1973) as a coalition of forces opposed to the Israeli Labour Party (formerly Mapai). Likud was dominated by the Herut (Heb. Freedom) Party and the Liberal Party. Its first leader, Menachem Begin, had headed the Zionist organization Irgun Zevai Leumi. Begin won the 1977 elections, ending 29 years of Labour Party rule. Likud's more aggressive approach to the Palestine Liberation Organization (PLO) culminated in the 1982 invasion of Lebanon. In 1983 Begin resigned and was succeeded as prime minister and leader of Likud by Yitzhak Shamir. Shamir led a coalition government (1984–90) with the Labour Party. Shamir was defeated in the 1992 elections by Labour leader Yitzhak Rabin. Shamir was succeeded as leader of Likud by Binyamin Netanyahu, who led Likud back to power in 1996. Netanyahu stalled over the implementation of the Israeli-Palestinian Accord (1993) and was defeated in the 1999 elections by Ehud Barak. He was succeeded as leader of Likud by Ariel Sharon.

LIBERIA

AREA: 111,370sq km (43,000sq mi)
POPULATION: 2,580,000
CAPITAL (POPULATION): Monrovia (425,000)
GOVERNMENT: Multiparty republic
ETHNIC GROUPS: Kpelle 19%, Bassa 14%, Grebo 9%, Gio 8%, Kru 7%, Mano 7%
LANGUAGES: English (official)
RELIGIONS: Christianity 68%, Islam 14%, traditional beliefs and others 18%
GDP PER CAPITA (1994): US$718

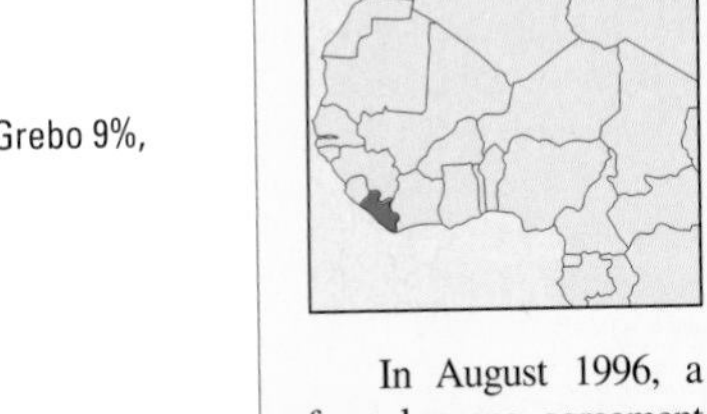

Republic on the Guinea coast of w Africa. From 1461 the area was explored by the Portuguese, who called it the Grain Coast after its precious crop of pepper. In 1821 the American Colonization Society was granted land on Cape Mesurado, where freed African-American slaves formed the Monrovia settlement in 1822.

In 1847 Liberia became an independent republic and Joseph Roberts was elected president (1847–56, 1871–76). The new nation became saddled by foreign debt and was unable to exert authority over the indigenous peoples of the interior. In 1926 Liberia received a substantial loan to pay off its foreign debts from the US Firestone Tire and Rubber Company, who opened a rubber plantation in Liberia that covered more than 400,000ha (1 million acres). For many years Americo-Liberians dominated government and exploited the native population. Under the authoritarian leadership (1943–71) of William Tubman, Liberia's economy grew and social reforms were adopted.

In 1980 Tubman's successor, William Tolbert, was assassinated in a military coup and Master Sergeant Samuel Doe formed a new military government. Doe won the 1985 election, widely regarded as fixed, and became president under a new constitution in 1986. In 1989 the National Patriotic Front of Liberia (NPFL), led by Charles Taylor, rebelled against Doe's brutal and corrupt regime. The Economic Community of West African States (ECOWAS) sent a five-nation peacekeeping force. Doe was assassinated in 1990, and by early 1991 the NPFL held the whole of Liberia, except the capital Monrovia. A 1991 cease-fire led to the formation of an interim government, but the civil war resumed even more fiercely in 1992.

In August 1996, a formal peace agreement signalled the end of a civil war that had claimed more than 150,000 lives. In 1997 Charles Taylor won a landslide victory in democratic elections and immediately began the process of economic reconstruction and social reconciliation.

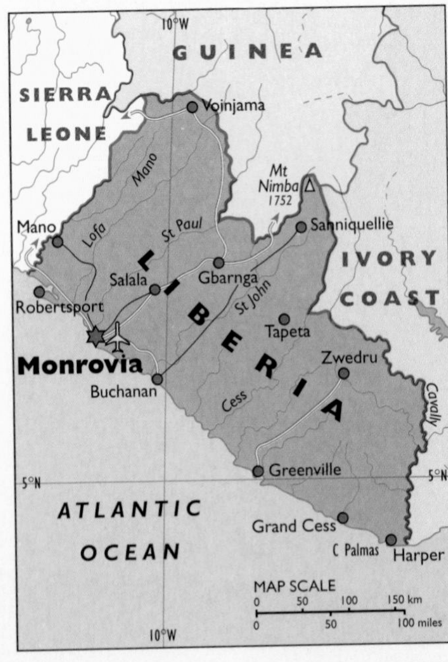

Lilburne, John (1614?–57) English revolutionary, leader of the Levellers. He was imprisoned (1638–40) for distributing Puritan propaganda under Charles I, but was released after appeals by Oliver Cromwell in the Long Parliament (November 1640). Lilburne fought for Parliament during the English Civil War (1642–45). He resigned from the army in protest against the compromise with the Covenanters and became one of the leading propagandists against Cromwell's Commonwealth government. Lilburne continued to attract popular support, even after the Levellers were removed from the New Model Army in 1648. He was acquitted of high treason in 1649 and 1653, but was kept in prison until 1655, when he renounced politics and converted to the Quaker faith.

Liliuokalani (1838–1917) Queen of Hawaii (1891–93), last monarch of the islands. She denounced US interference and tried to revoke the agreement (1887) that had given commercial privileges to the United States. US businessmen, led by Sanford Dole, revolted and deposed Liliuokalani. US President Grover Cleveland demanded her re-instatement, but Dole's provisional government refused to back down and suppressed a royalist rebellion (1895). Liliuokalani formally abdicated in 1895 and Hawaii was formally annexed by the United States in 1898.

Lille (Flemish, Lisle) City in n France, near the border with Belgium. Founded by Count Baudoin IV of Flanders in 1066, Lille is the historic centre of the French textile industry. It was besieged and captured by Louis XIV of France, who commissioned Sébastien de Vauban (1633–1707) to build the citadel (1667–70). Captured by the Duke of Marlborough in 1708, Lille was restored to France in 1713. The city was badly damaged and also occupied by the Germans in both world wars. Pop. (1990) 172,142.

Lima Capital and chief commercial centre of Peru. Prior to the Spanish conquest of the Inca empire, the site was settled by the Pachacamac. Lima itself was founded (1535) by Francisco Pizarro, who called it "City of Kings". The city flourished as the capital of the Viceroyalty of Peru, which included most of Spain's South American colonies. Lima was largely destroyed by an earthquake in 1746 and was rebuilt in the French Empire style. It was captured (1821) by General José de San Martín and became capital of an independent Peru in 1826. Between 1940 and 1980 *c.*2 million people migrated to the city and the ensuing problems of overcrowding and poverty have caused civil unrest. Pop. (1993) 6,386,308.

Lin Biao (1907–71) Chinese military commander and statesman. He was trained by Chiang Kai-Shek at the Whampoa Academy, but abandoned (1928) his Nationalist ally for Mao Zedong's communist forces. Lin Biao led the advance guard of the Red Army on the Long March (1934) from Jiangxi, se China, to Shaanxi, nw China. In 1938 he was badly wounded during the Sino-Japanese War (1937–45). After World War 2, Lin masterminded the Red Army's strategy in the renewed civil war, capturing MANCHURIA from the Nationalists in 1948 and securing final victory for the communists in October 1949. In 1959 Lin succeeded Peng Dehuai as minister of defence and leader of the People's Liberation Army (PLA). He encouraged the cult of the personality that built up around Mao and promoted the PLA as the model for Chinese society. Lin was one of the leading figures in the CULTURAL REVOLUTION (1966–69), and was formally recognised as Mao's successor in 1969. In 1971 Lin launched a coup against Mao, but the plot failed and Lin died in an airplane crash while trying to flee to the Soviet Union. *See also* ZHOU ENLAI

Lincoln, Abraham (1809–65) Sixteenth president of the United States (1861–65). Born on a remote farmstead in Kentucky, he received almost no formal education. Lincoln moved to Illinois in 1830, later fighting as a captain in the BLACK HAWK WAR (1832). In 1834 he was elected to the Illinois assembly, becoming leader of the WHIG PARTY in the legislature in 1836. Also in 1836, Lincoln began a successful career as a circuit lawyer. He served in Congress (1847–49), but lost popularity for his criticism of President James POLK's prosecution of the the MEXICAN WAR (1846–48). While in Congress, Lincoln presented a bill for the abolition of SLAVERY in Washington, D.C. Despite his support for the nomination of Zachary TAYLOR as the Whig presidential candidate in 1848, Lincoln was overlooked when Taylor took office and seemed consigned to the political wilderness until Stephen DOUGLAS secured the passage of the KANSAS-NEBRASKA ACT (1854). Lincoln joined the newly formed REPUBLICAN PARTY in 1856 and gained national attention through the LINCOLN-DOUGLAS DEBATES (1858), where he argued against the extension of slavery. Lincoln's performances gained him the Republican nomination in 1860, and, as a result of divisions within the DEMOCRATIC PARTY, he was elected president. Even before Lincoln's inauguration, the state of South Carolina had seceded from the Union (December 1860) and by February 1861, after Lincoln had rejected the CRITTENDEN Compromise, six other Southern, slave-owning states followed suit. In his first inaugural address (4 March 1861), Lincoln stated a determination to hold FORT SUMTER, and when the Confederates opened fire on the Fort (12 April 1861) it signalled the start of the American CIVIL WAR (1861–65). Lincoln was a strong commander in chief, playing a leading role in military strategy. After the resignation of General Winfield SCOTT (November 1861), he appointed a succession of commanders (George MCCLELLAN, John POPE, Ambrose BURNSIDE, Joseph HOOKER and George MEADE), before finally settling (1864) on the skills of Ulysses GRANT. In 1862 Secretary of War Edwin STANTON was given responsibilty for the provision of men and supplies. Lincoln's overriding aim was to preserve the Union, and he remained reluctant to embrace the ABOLITIONISTS' cause. In the EMANCIPATION PROCLAMATION (1863), Lincoln liberated only those slaves residing in the CONFEDERATE STATES OF AMERICA. On 19 November 1863, Lincoln delivered the GETTYSBURG ADDRESS, which redevoted the war effort to the cause of democracy. Lincoln was re-elected in 1864 and, after the failure of the HAMPTON ROADS PEACE CONFERENCE (February 1865), saw the war through until the surrender of the Confederacy. Five days later, on 14 April 1865, Lincoln was shot by John Wilkes BOOTH, a Southern sympathizer. He died the next day and Vice President Andrew JOHNSON was sworn in as president. *See also* CHASE, SALMON PORTLAND; DAVIS, JEFFERSON; DRAFT RIOTS; FRÉMONT, JOHN CHARLES; GREENBACKS; HOMESTEAD ACT; RECONSTRUCTION; SEWARD, WILLIAM HENRY; SHERMAN, WILLIAM TECUMSEH; TRENT AFFAIR

Lincoln-Douglas Debates (August–October 1858) Series of seven public meetings between Democratic Senator Stephen DOUGLAS and Republican challenger Abraham LINCOLN during the 1858 Illinois senatorial campaign. The Debates focused on the issue of SLAVERY. Douglas was the sponsor of the controversial KANSAS-NEBRASKA ACT (1854) which extended slavery to the new territories of the United States, according to the doctrine of "popular sovereignty". The Act was seemingly nullified, however, by the Supreme Court decision in the DRED SCOTT CASE (1857). Although Lincoln lost the election, his view of slavery as a "moral, social and political wrong" enhanced his national standing.

Lindbergh, Charles Augustus (1902–74) US aviator. In May 1927 Lindbergh became an international celebrity after making the first non-stop transatlantic solo flight (from New York to Paris), in his monoplane *Spirit of St Louis*. In 1932 Lindbergh's 19-month-old son was kidnapped and murdered. Bruno Hauptmann was convicted and executed for the crime in 1936 and Lindbergh emigrated to Europe. He attracted political controversy when, after praising the *Luftwaffe* (German air force), he was decorated by Adolf Hitler. Further speeches advocating US isolation in World War 2 led to his resignation from the Air Corps Reserve in 1941.

linear script Early form of writing, found on clay tablets in Crete and Greece. **Linear A** was in extensive use during the middle period of the MINOAN CIVILIZATION (*c*.2000–*c*.1450 BC). **Linear B** was used by the MYCENAEAN CIVILIZATION from *c*.1450 BC to the end of the Mycenaean period, *c*.1150 BC. In 1952 Michael VENTRIS deciphered Linear B as an archaic form of Greek. Linear A still defies analysis. *See also* CUNEIFORM

Lin Zexu (1785–1850) Chinese scholar and official of the QING dynasty. In 1838 he was dispatched by Emperor Daoguang to stop the opium trade conducted by British and Chinese traders in Guangzhou (Canton). Lin Zexu forced the British merchants to surrender their opium stocks for destruction. Relations between Britain and China rapidly deteriorated, resulting in the First OPIUM WAR (1839–42). Lin was blamed and sent into exile (1843), but recalled in 1845. He was an influential proponent of the so-called "SELF-STRENGTHENING MOVEMENT" for administrative reform.

Li Peng (1928–) Chinese statesman, premier (1988–98). He was adopted by ZHOU ENLAI after his father was executed (1930) by the KUOMINTANG. Li rose slowly through the ranks of the Chinese Communist Party (CCP) and was elected to the politburo in 1985. He became minister of power in 1981 and deputy premier in 1983. Li's support for DENG XIAOPING's policy of economic liberalization, while maintaining the Party's tight grip on politics and society, led him to succeed ZHAO ZIYANG as premier. In 1989 Li declared martial law during the student protests in TIANANMEN SQUARE, Beijing, and sent in the Red Army to crush the pro-democracy demonstration. He was succeeded as premier by Zhu Rongji. *See also* JIANG ZEMIN

LINCOLN, ABRAHAM

Abraham Lincoln rose from a humble upbringing to become one of the great US presidents and an eloquent spokesman for democracy. He preserved the Union during the American Civil War and abolished slavery.

LINCOLN IN HIS OWN WORDS

"We here highly resolve that these dead shall not have died in vain – that this nation, under God, shall have a new birth of freedom – and that government of the people, by the people, for the people, shall not perish from the Earth."
Gettysburg Address, 19 November 1863

Lisbon (Lisboa) Capital, largest city and major port of Portugal. Probably founded by the Phoenicians, the city was conquered by the Romans in 205 BC and captured by the Visigoths in the 5th century AD. Lisbon fell to the Moors in 716. In 1147 the Portuguese reclaimed the city, and in *c*.1256 it was made the nation's capital. Lisbon became one of the richest cities in Europe during the period of Portugal's colonial expansion and domination of the SLAVE TRADE. The late-Gothic splendour of monuments such as the Tower of Belém and the Jerónimos Monastery date from the golden reign (1495–1521) of MANUEL I. The city went into rapid decline, however, with the expulsion of its Jewish inhabitants by the Inquisition. Lisbon was under Spanish rule from 1580 to 1640. In 1755 the city was devastated by a huge earthquake, which killed more than 30,000 people. Its reconstruction was managed by the Marquês de POMBAL. Pop. (1991) 2,561,000.

Lithuania *See* country feature, page 243

Little Bighorn, Battle of (25 June 1876) Victory of the SIOUX, plus CHEYENNE allies, against US cavalry led by Colonel George CUSTER. Sometimes known as "Custer's Last Stand", it was the last victory of Native Americans over the US Army. Custer and his entire force of *c*.225 men were killed by the Sioux, led by SITTING BULL and CRAZY HORSE, near the Little Bighorn River, Montana. The site is now a national monument.

Little Entente (1920–38) Defensive alliance between Romania, Yugoslavia and Czechoslovakia after World War 1 to maintain their new independence from possible aggressors. Although backed by France, it was weakened by the rise of Nazi Germany in the 1930s and collapsed when Adolf HITLER annexed the Czech SUDETENLAND in September 1938.

Little Turtle (*c*.1752–1812) (Michikinikwa) Chief of the Miami tribe. He forged a Native American alliance against US expansion in Northwest Territory. Little Turtle inflicted heavy defeats on US forces in 1790 and 1791, but was finally subdued by General Anthony WAYNE at the Battle of Fallen Timbers (1794). He was forced to sign the Treaty of Fort GREENVILLE (1795), which ceded most of Northwest Territory to the United States.

Litvinov, Maxim Maximovich (1876–1951) Soviet statesman and diplomat, foreign minister (1930–39). A founder member of the Russian Social Democratic Labour Party (RSDLP), he was forced to flee to Britain in 1902. After the RUSSIAN REVOLUTION (November 1917), Litvinov acted as diplomatic representative for the Bolsheviks in London. He was arrested by the British in 1918, but returned to Russia as part of a spy-exchange in 1919. As foreign minister, Litvinov led international calls for disarmament, gained US recognition of the Soviet Union in 1933, and called for collective action in Europe to prevent the rise of Nazi Germany. He was replaced as foreign minister by V.M. MOLOTOV on the eve of the NAZI-SOVIET PACT (1939). He was ambassador to the United States (1941–43).

Liu Shaoqi (1898–1969) Chinese statesman, chairman of the People's Republic of China (1959–68). A leading member of the early trades' union movement in China, Liu became MAO ZEDONG's right-hand man and the chief theorist of the CHINESE COMMUNIST PARTY (CCP). When the People's Republic of China was established in 1949, he was appointed as deputy to Chairman Mao. Liu succeeded Mao as head of state after the failure of the GREAT LEAP FORWARD. He overturned Mao's policy of agricultural collectivization, instead encouraging peasants to cultivate private plots. During the CULTURAL REVOLUTION (1966–69), Liu was replaced by LIN BIAO, expelled from the CCP and imprisoned. He was rehabilitated by DENG XIAOPING.

Liverpool, Robert Banks Jenkinson, 2nd Earl of (1770–1828) British statesman, prime minister (1812–27). He entered Parliament in 1790. As foreign secretary (1801–04), signed the Treaty of AMIENS (1802) with Napoleonic France. Liverpool became prime minister after the assassination of Spencer PERCEVAL. He was a reluctant leader, and his administration was dominated by George CANNING and Viscount CASTLEREAGH. Thanks largely to the Duke of WELLINGTON, Liverpool presided over victory in the NAPOLEONIC WARS (1803–15). He lost popularity by his government's resistance to reform and its harsh treatment of protesters after the PETERLOO MASSACRE (1819). As the national situation improved in the 1820s, Liverpool adopted a more liberal approach. After his retirement, the TORY PARTY splintered. *See also* PEEL, ROBERT

Liverpool City and seaport on the River Mersey, NW England. In 1207 the town was granted a charter by King John, but it remained a small fishing port until the 18th century, when the city expanded with extraordinary speed on the profits of, chiefly, the SLAVE TRADE. Liverpool became Britain's largest port. The introduction of steam and growth of shipping produced further expansion in the 19th century, when Liverpool became an embarkation port for emigrants, while Irish immigrants swelled its population. Liverpool was badly damaged by German bombing during World War 2 and Britain's post-war industrial decline hindered the regeneration of the city. Pop. (1991) 452,450.

Livingston, Robert R. (1746–1813) US statesman and diplomat, great-grandson of Robert Livingston, founder of the wealthy Livingston family in New York state. He served in the CONTINENTAL CONGRESS (1775–76, 1779–81, 1784–85) and was a member of the committee that drew up the DECLARATION OF INDEPENDENCE (1776). With the establishment of the federal government, Livingston became secretary of the department of foreign affairs (1781–83). Thomas Jefferson appointed him minister to France (1801–04), in which capacity he helped James MONROE negotiate the LOUISIANA PURCHASE (1803).

Livingstone, David (1813–73) Scottish explorer and missionary, who helped to map the interior of Africa. In 1838 he joined the London Missionary Society. Livingstone arrived in Cape Town, South Africa, in 1841 and spent the next 15 years travelling in Africa. In 1853 Livingstone set off in search of a route to the Atlantic Ocean. In 1854 he reached Luanda, Angola. On his return journey across the continent (1854–56) to Mozambique, Livingstone became the first European to see the Victoria Falls (November 1855) on the Zambia-Zimbabwe border. He was hailed as a hero on his return to Britain and his account of the journey, *Missionary Travels and Researches in South Africa* (1857), became a best-seller. Livingstone was given command of a government expedition to the Zambezi region (1858–64) to promote commerce and civilization and end the SLAVE-TRADE in East Africa. In 1866 he set off to find the source of the River Nile, disappeared, and was found (1871) by Henry Morton STANLEY near Lake Tanganyika, Tanzania. Old and sick, Livingstone refused to leave Africa with Stanley and disappeared again, dying near Lake Bangweulu (now in Zambia). His heart was buried in Zambia, while the rest of his body was carried home to Britain.

Livonian Order (Brothers of the Sword, or "of the knighthood of Christ in Livonia") Order of knights who conquered Livonia (now Latvia and Estonia) for Christianity. The Order was founded (1202) by the bishop of Livonia, with the sanction of Pope INNOCENT III. The Sword Brothers, many of whom seem to have been failed or dishonest merchants, seem never to have numbered more than 120. The brutality of the knights' conquest was castigated by the pope and the Holy Roman emperor, and the Order was obliged to merge (1237) with the TEUTONIC KNIGHTS. *See also* LIVONIAN WAR

Livonian War (1558–83) Conflict for possession of Livonia (now LATVIA and ESTONIA), involving the knights of the LIVONIAN ORDER, Russia and, later, Poland, Lithuania and Sweden. IVAN IV (THE TERRIBLE) finally surrendered the Russian claim (1583), and the region was divided among the other three states. As a result of the Great NORTHERN WAR (1700–21) and the Partitions of POLAND (1772, 1793, 1795), all of Latvia was in Russia possession by the end of the 18th century.

Livy (*c*.59 BC–AD 17) (Titus Livius) Roman historian. His *History of Rome* covered the period from the legendary founding of ROME in 753 BC until 9 BC. Of the original 142 books, 97 have been lost and the history of Rome from 91 BC to 9 BC survives only in fragments and summaries. In the 35 books that survive in full, Livy depicts history in terms of human personality and moral imperatives, rather than seeking political explanations. Although he borrowed, often uncritically, from earlier Roman historians, Livy established a new standard of Latin prose. *See also* TACITUS, CORNELIUS

Li Yuanhong (1864–1928) Chinese statesman, president of the Republic of China (1916–17, 1922–23). As army commander in Hubei during the Revolution of 1911, he reluctantly accepted the post of provisional leader of the new republic and became vice president (1911–16) on the return of SUN YAT-SEN. Li continued to hold the position under General YUAN SHIKAI and became president on Yuan's death. He held office again in 1922–23, but failed to reunite China through peaceful means.

Lloyd George, David (1863–1945) British statesman, prime minister (1916–22). A radical Welsh Liberal, he entered Parliament in 1890 and gained national attention for his opposition to the Second SOUTH AFRICAN WAR (1899–1902). He served in Sir Henry CAMPBELL-BANNERMAN's cabinet as president of the board of trade (1905–08). Campbell-Bannerman was succeeded as prime minister and leader of the LIBERAL PARTY by Herbert ASQUITH, who appointed Lloyd George as chancellor of the exchequer (1908–15). As chancellor, Lloyd George introduced old-age pensions (1908) and NATIONAL INSURANCE (1911) – two pillars of the future WELFARE STATE. His "People's Budget" (1909) imposed higher taxes to pay for social reforms and also to finance naval rearmament. The budget provoked a constitutional crisis that led to the Parliament Act (1911), which reduced the powers of the HOUSE OF LORDS. In the coalition government formed at the start of World War 1, Lloyd George served first as minister of munitions (1915–16) and then replaced Lord KITCHENER as secretary of state for war (1916). A leading critic of Asquith's handling of the War, Lloyd George became prime minister after a cabinet coup and immediately reduced the size of the war cabinet. Lloyd George was sceptical of the tactical ability of his commander in chief Sir Douglas HAIG, and sought a unified Allied command structure. After the armistice (November 1918), Lloyd George continued his alliance with the CONSERVATIVE PARTY, and the coalition gained a landslide victory in the December 1918 elec-

LIBYA

AREA: 1,759,540sq km (679,358sq mi)
POPULATION: 4,875,000
CAPITAL (POPULATION): Tripoli (990,697)
GOVERNMENT: Single-party socialist state
ETHNIC GROUPS: Libyan Arab and Berber 89%, others 11%
LANGUAGES: Arabic (official)
RELIGIONS: Islam
GDP PER CAPITA (1994): US$4220

Republic in N Africa. The earliest known inhabitants of Libya were the BERBERS. In the 1st millennium BC the Phoenicians established trading settlements on the coast of TRIPOLITANIA, which were taken over by CARTHAGE in the 6th century BC. Greek colonies were formed in N CYRENAICA from the 7th century BC, but fell to the Egyptians in the 4th century BC. Carthage was destroyed by Rome in 146 BC, and both Tripolitania and Cyrenaica fell under Roman domination. The Roman North African Empire was conquered by the Vandals in the 5th century AD.

The rise of independent kingdoms was halted by the Byzantine invasion in 533. Libya was conquered by the Arabs in 643, and rapidly converted to Islam. In the 8th century, the Berbers overthrew the UMAYYAD dynasty but Arab rule was restored by the ABBASIDS. In the 1150s, the entire Maghrib, including Tripolitania, fell to the Berber ALMOHADS. Part of the Ottoman Empire from the early 16th century, Libya was given considerable autonomy until 1835, when direct rule was imposed. In 1837 the SANUSI (a Sufi brotherhood) was established in Cyrenaica and went on to unify many tribes in the region.

In 1911 Italy invaded Libya, and by 1914 had conquered the whole territory. In the 1930s, Italy stepped up the pace of colonization and Libya was formally incorporated into Italy in 1939. Libya was a battleground of many of the NORTH AFRICA CAMPAIGNS (1941–43) during World War 2.

In 1951 Libya became an independent monarchy under IDRIS I, head of the Sanusi sect. In 1953 Libya joined the ARAB LEAGUE, and in 1955 became a member of the United Nations (UN). The discovery of oil (1959) radically improved the nation's economy. In September 1969 Idris I was overthrown in a military coup led by Colonel Muammar al-QADDAFI. A Revolutionary Command Council set about the nationalization of industry, the establishment of an Islamic state and the reduction of Western interference. Libya maintained an anti-Israeli foreign policy, and Qaddafi aided the PALESTINE LIBERATION ORGANIZATION (PLO). In 1982 the United States placed an oil embargo on Libya.

In April 1986, following evidence of Libyan support for international terrorism, the United States bombed Tripoli and Benghazi. In 1992 Libya was accused of sheltering terrorists responsible for the bombing (1988) of Pan-Am Flight 103 over Lockerbie, Scotland, and the UN imposed sanctions. Libya has a long-standing territorial dispute with Chad, and invaded its neighbour in 1987. In 1994 the International Court of Justice dismissed Libya's claim to the Aozou Strip, N Chad. In 1995 all Palestinians were deported from Libya in protest against the Israeli-Palestinian Accord (1993). In 1999 Libya agreed to extradite the two suspects in the Lockerbie case and UN sanctions were suspended.

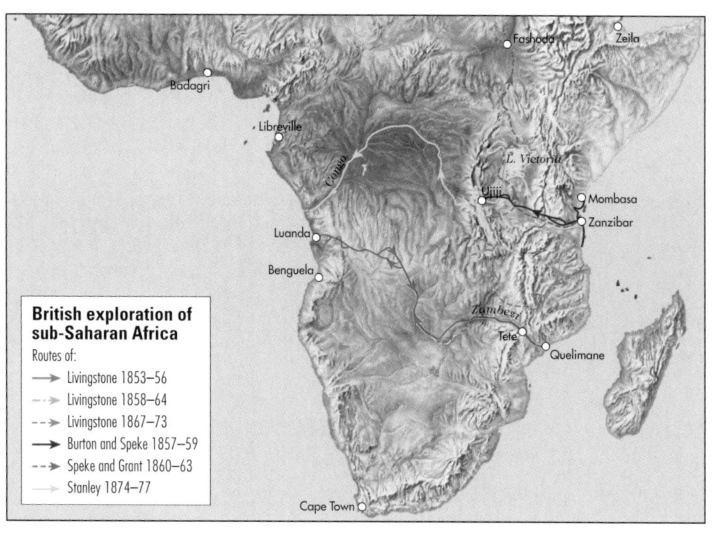

British exploration of sub-Saharan Africa
Routes of:
Livingstone 1853–56
Livingstone 1858–64
Livingstone 1867–73
Burton and Speke 1857–59
Speke and Grant 1860–63
Stanley 1874–77

► **Livingstone** led his first expedition (1853–56) from Linyanti, in the Caprivi Strip, to Luanda. He then travelled back across s Africa to Quelimane (now in Mozambique). On a second expedition (1858–64), Livingstone discovered that stretches of the River Zambezi were unnavigable, but paved the way for the subsequent British colonization of what is now Malawi. On his final journey (1867–73), in search of the source of the River Nile, Livingstone discovered lakes Mweru and Bangweulu and reached the River Lualaba (now in Congo), the furthest w any European had ranged in the interior of Africa.

tions. Lloyd George followed a centre path between Georges CLEMENCEAU and Woodrow WILSON at the Paris Peace Conference and helped draft the Treaty of VERSAILLES (1919). In home affairs, the new government extended the franchise to include women over the age of 30 (1918) and introduced the HOME RULE Bill for Ireland (1920). Conservatives regarded the subsequent creation of the Irish Free State (1921) as a betrayal and, after a scandal involving the honours' system and party funds and the spectre of war with Turkey, withdrew from the coalition. Lloyd George was defeated in the 1922 elections by the Conservative leader Bonar LAW. He later served (1926–31) as leader of the reunited Liberal Party.

Llywelyn ap Gruffydd (1246–1282) (Llywelyn the Last) Prince of Gwynedd, N WALES grandson of LLYWELYN AP IORWERTH. Allied with the English rebel barons led by Simon de MONTFORT, he gained control of most of Wales and was recognized as prince of Wales by HENRY III of England in the Treaty of Montgomery (1267). Upon the accession of EDWARD I of England (1272), Llywelyn fatally refused to do him homage. He launched another rebellion, which was crushed by an English invasion (1276–77). His death in battle led to the subjugation of Wales by England. *See also* BARONS' WARS

Llywelyn ap Iorwerth (1173–1240) (Llywelyn the Great) Prince of Gwynedd, N WALES, grandfather of LLYWELYN AP GRUFFYDD. He established his power base in N Wales, but an invasion of S Wales (1211) was defeated by King JOHN of England, whose illegitimate daughter he married. Llywelyn subsequently allied himself with the English rebel barons and extended his rule to Clwyd, Powys, and parts of Dyfed. His rights were acknowledged in the MAGNA CARTA (1215) and re-iterated by Henry III at the Peace of Worcester (1218). Five years later Henry was powerful enough to restrict some of Llywelyn's authority. *See also* BARONS' WARS

Lobengula (*c*.1836–94) Last king of the Ndebele (Matabele) nation (1870–94), son and successor of Mzilikazi. After his father's death (1868), Lobengula fought a civil war to succeed as ruler. In 1888 Lobengula granted mineral concessions to Cecil RHODES' British South Africa Company. The concessions attracted further European colonists and fuelled Rhodes' imperial ambitions. In 1893 the Company launched a war that resulted in Lobengula's death and the destruction of the Ndebele kingdom.

Locarno Pact (1 December 1925) Series of seven treaties initialled at Locarno, Switzerland, that attempted to resolve problems of European security outstanding since the Treaty of VERSAILLES (1919). The Pact confirmed Germany's W borders with France and Belgium, and renounced the use of force to change the frontiers. Britain promised to defend Belgium and France from unprovoked attack, and the RHINELAND was established as a demilitarized, neutral zone. The Pact did not, however, confer the same recognition to Germany's E borders with Poland and Czechoslovakia, providing only for arbitration in cases of dispute. In March 1936 Nazi Germany occupied the Rhineland in violation of the Locarno Pact, but Britain continued to pursue a policy of APPEASEMENT. *See also* KELLOGG-BRIAND PACT; LEAGUE OF NATIONS

Locke, John (1632–1704) English philosopher. His *Essay Concerning Human Understanding* (1690) is regarded as the founding text of empiricism. Locke rejected the concept of "innate ideas" and held that knowledge is gained from sense-experience. He is chiefly remembered for his political theory expounded in *Two Treatises on Civil Government* (1690). Locke held that the state exists to safeguard the natural rights of its citizens (life, liberty and property), and that relations between government and governed are based on a SOCIAL CONTRACT to preserve those rights. He denounced absolutism and justified civil disobedience in response to a government that breaks the social contract. Locke's influence on political thought was huge, especially in England and North America. *See also* LIBERALISM

Lodge, Henry Cabot (1850–1924) US politician, Republican senator from Massachusetts (1893–1924). He was a lecturer (1876–79) on American history at Harvard University before entering the House of Representatives (1887–93). Lodge rejected President Woodrow WILSON's proposal of an international peacekeeping organization and, as Senate majority leader and chairman of the foreign relations committee (1919–24), successfully blocked US membership of the LEAGUE OF NATIONS.

Lodi dynasty (1451–1526) Last ruling family of the DELHI SULTANATE. The dynasty was founded by an Afghan governor of Punjab, **Bahlul Lodi** (r.1451–89), who seized Delhi (1451) and went on to conquer the kingdoms of Malwa and Jaunpur. Bahlul's son, **Sikander** (r.1489–1517), extended the empire to include Bihar and

LITHUANIA

AREA: 65,200sq km (25,200sq mi)
POPULATION: 3,759,000
CAPITAL (POPULATION): Vilnius (578,000)
GOVERNMENT: Multiparty republic
ETHNIC GROUPS: Lithuanian 80%, Russian 9%, Polish 7%, Belorussian 2%
LANGUAGES: Lithuanian (official)
RELIGIONS: Christianity (mainly Roman Catholic)
GDP PER CAPITA (1994): US$4120

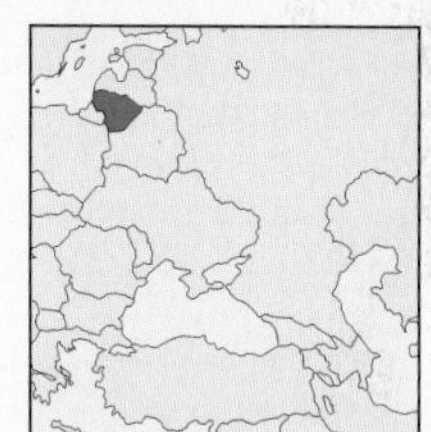

Baltic republic in NE Europe. In the 13th century, the Lithuanians resisted the invasions of the TEUTONIC KNIGHTS, establishing an independent, unified kingdom in 1251. Gediminas (r.1316–41) built a mighty Lithuanian empire that encompassed most of modern Belarus. Its capital was at Vilnius. His son and successor, Algirdas (r.1345–77), expanded the empire to include Kiev (1362). In 1386 a Polish-Lithuanian union was formed when Grand Duke WŁADISŁAW II (JAGIELLO) married JADWIGA of Poland. The pagan state converted to Roman Catholicism in 1387. Władisław II and Vytautas the Great inflicted a decisive defeat on the Teutonic Knights at the Battle of TANNENBERG (1410). Russian imperial expansion, most notably in the LIVONIAN WAR (1558–83), encouraged Poland and Lithuania to seek closer ties and form a unified commonwealth in 1569. However, the Partitions of POLAND (1772, 1793, 1795) resulted in the annexation of Lithuania by Russia. The Russification of Lithuania produced mass uprisings (1830–31, 1863).

Under German occupation (1915–18) during World War 1, Lithuania declared independence (February 1918). The Red Army reoccupied Vilnius in 1919 and the Lithuanian provisional government fled to Kaunas, S Lithuania, where they formed a national army that drove the Russians from the country. Poland captured Vilnius in 1920 and annexed it in 1922. In 1926 a military coup established the dictatorship of Antanas Smetona. Following the NAZI-SOVIET PACT (1939), the Soviet Union invaded Lithuania in June 1940 and the following month it became a Soviet republic. The Nazis occupied Lithuania in June 1941, and during the next three years murdered *c*.165,000 Lithuanian Jews. In 1944 the Red Army recaptured most of Lithuania. Over the next decade, more than 220,000 Lithuanians were deported to the Gulags, but this failed to crush resistance to Soviet rule. The 1960s and 1970s saw the growth of underground nationalist movements and anti-communist publications.

Following Mikhail GORBACHEV's reforms, the Lithuanian Communist Party (CPL) was forced to concede multiparty elections in 1990. The elections were won by the nationalists, and Lithuania became the first Soviet republic to declare independence (March 1990). In January 1991 Soviet troops and nationalist forces fought on the streets of Vilnius. A referendum voted overwhelmingly in favour of independence, and the Soviet Union recognized Lithuania as an independent republic in September 1991. The CPL, reformed as the Democratic Labour Party (DLP), won the 1992 election. Soviet troops completed their withdrawal in 1993 and Lithuania signed a treaty of association with the European Union (EU) in 1996. After the 1996 elections, the Homeland Union and the Christian Democratic Party formed a coalition government. In 1998 an independent candidate, Valdas Adamkus, was elected president.

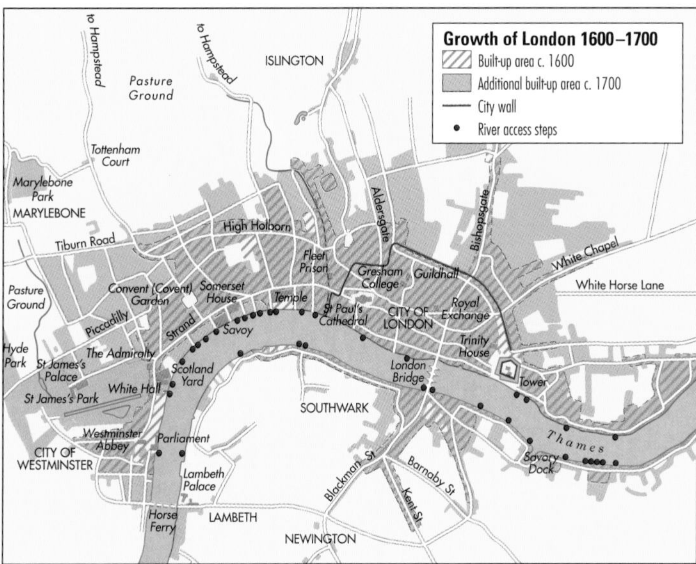

► **London** The population of London expanded from about 120,000 in 1550 to 575,000 by 1700. This latter figure represented 10% of the entire English population, a uniquely high proportion in comparison with other European capital cities at the time.

founded the city of Agra. Sikander's son, **Ibrahim** (r.1517–26), alienated the Afghan nobility, who invited Babur, ruler of Kabul, Afghanistan, to invade India. Babur overthrew the Lodi at the Battle of Panipat (1526) and founded the Mughal Empire.

Lollards Followers of the English religious reformer John Wycliffe (*c*.1330–84). The sect challenged many doctrines and practices of the medieval church, including transubstantiation, monasticism, clerical celibacy and the authority of the papacy. The number and prominence of Lollards increased rapidly at the end of the 14th century, but declined due to persecution under Henry IV. Sir John Oldcastle led a failed Lollard uprising (1414) against Henry V, and his execution signalled the intensification of their suppression and the Lollards were driven underground. The Lollards experienced a revival at the start of the English Reformation and gradually came to identify with Protestantism.

Lombard League Defensive alliance of cities in Lombardy, N Italy, formed (1167) in resistance to the imposition of imperial authority by Emperor Frederick I (Barbarossa). Supported by Pope Alexander III, the League defeated Frederick at the Battle of Legnano (1176) and ensured their independence. The Lombard League was renewed (1226–50) to combat Frederick II's attempts to restrict communal privileges and liberties.

Lombards Germanic peoples who were originally settled along the lower River Elbe before being driven southwards. By the end of the 5th century, they were living in the Danube basin. In 568 the Lombards, led by Alboin, invaded N Italy and captured much of the Italian peninsula by 572, thereby wiping out most of Justinian's Byzantine reconquest. Pavia became the capital of the Kingdom of Lombardy. They adopted Christianity and Latin customs. The Kingdom reached its peak under Liutprand (r.712–44), who gained further lands from the Byzantine Empire. The Lombard invasion of papal lands prompted Pope Adrian I to seek aid from the Frankish king Charlemagne, who captured Pavia in 774. *See also* Franks

London Capital of the United Kingdom, on the River Thames, SE England. Little is known of London before the Roman occupation of Britain in AD 43. In AD 60 the Roman settlement of *Londinium* was sacked by Boadicea, but was rebuilt by the Romans and acquired a defensive wall (*c*.AD 200). Little is known of the Saxon settlement that followed the retreat of the Romans in the 5th century until the reign (849–99) of Alfred (the Great). In 1050 Edward the Confessor founded Westminster Abbey, and his successor, William I (the Conqueror), began the construction of the Tower of the London in 1078. By 1085 London was the largest city in Northern Europe (pop. *c*.12,000) and attracted traders from throughout Europe. In the 14th century, London's population of *c*.80,000 was decimated by the Black Death (1349). The growth of overseas trade enhanced London's wealth and importance in the Tudor period (1485–1603), when the first theatres were built in Southwark on the south bank of the Thames. Henry VIII built St James' Palace in 1538. By 1600 London had *c*.200,000 inhabitants and the area between Westminster and the City was built up. The Great Plague (1665) killed *c*.75,000 Londoners, and the Fire of London (1666) virtually destroyed the old City. Sir Christopher Wren's (1632–1723) plans for reconstruction were unfulfilled, although he did build (1675–1710) St Paul's Cathedral, 52 other London churches, Greenwich Hospital and Royal Observatory, and The Monument (1671–77) to commemorate the Great Fire. After the formation (1694) of the Bank of England, the square mile of the City became a major financial centre in Europe. London was the commercial and cultural heart of the British Empire, and by 1901 it was the world's largest city (pop. 6.5 million). Extensive industrial development, in particular the docks, took place in E London, and the London County Council (1888) was created to control the haphazard development of Greater London. The first underground railway (subway) in the world was opened in London in 1863. The construction of overground railways encouraged suburban development that absorbed outlying villages, especially after World War 1. London was badly damaged during World War 2 and *c*.30,000 Londoners were killed in the bombing raids. The post-war relocation or closure of industry saw a decline in the city's population. The old working-class East End disappeared and the blighted area of the obsolete Docklands was redeveloped for offices and housing. In 2000 London gained its first mayor, the authority of the ancient office of lord mayor being confined to the City. Pop. (1994) 6,966,800.

London Company *See* Virginia companies

Long, Huey Pierce (1893–1935) US politician, governor of Louisiana (1928–32) and senator (1932–35). A champion of the poor and opponent of big business, he enacted major social welfare reforms in Louisiana. Long's populist image concealed the tactics of intimidation and bribery used to force through his policies. When Long was elected to the Senate, he imposed his own nominee to succeed him as governor. Long's "Share Our Wealth" plan for redistribution appealed to the US public in the midst of the Great Depression. He was assassinated.

Long Island, Battle of (27 August 1776) Conflict in the American Revolution. George Washington's army, divided by the East River, was defeated on Long Island, New York by British General William Howe. The Americans evaded capture by escaping to Manhattan. The Americans lost 1000 men, the British 400.

Long March (October 1934–October 1935) Enforced march of Chinese communists during the civil war against the Kuomintang (Nationalists). About 85,000 communist troops, accompanied by 15,000 civilians, broke through Chiang Kai-shek's Nationalist encirclement and marched *c*.10,000km (6000mi) from Jiangxi, SE China, to Shaanxi, NW China. Under frequent attack, they suffered *c*.45,000 casualties in the first three months of the trek. In January 1935 Mao Zedong assumed control of the Chinese Communist Party (CCP) from Zhu De and Zhou Enlai. Only *c*.8000 of the original marchers made it to the safety of Shaanxi. The epic march inspired many young people to join the Chinese Communist Party (CCP). *See also* Lin Biao

Long Parliament English Parliament summoned (November 1640) by Charles I in order to finance the Second Bishops' War (1640) against the Scots. It followed the Short Parliament, which lasted only a matter of weeks. Antagonism between Charles and radical members of Parliament led to the English Civil War (1642–46). The Long Parliament sat, with intervals, for 20 years. Moderates were expelled in Pride's Purge (1648), and the remainder, the so-called Rump Parliament, was forcibly expelled by Oliver Cromwell in 1653. It reassembled (1659) after his death. The full Long Parliament met again in 1660, only to dissolve itself for new elections.

Longstreet, James (1821–1904) Confederate general in the American Civil War (1861–65). He fought with distinction in many of the major battles of the Civil War. As second in command to General Robert Lee at the Battle of Gettysburg (1863), Longstreet's reluctance to attack contributed to the Confederate defeat. After the War, Longstreet joined the Republican Party and President Ulysses Grant appointed him commissioner of Pacific railways (1897–1904).

López, Francisco Solano (1827–70) Paraguayan dictator (1862–70), son and successor of Carlos Antonio López. He consolidated his power with the help of the military. López provoked the War of the Triple Alliance (1864–70), in which Paraguay was pitted against Brazil, Uruguay and Argentina. He conquered the Brazilian province of Mato Grosso (1864), but was forced to retreat after the diastrous invasion of Uruguay (1865). A majority of all Paraguayan males of military age, including López, was killed in the War. López is regarded as a national hero.

Lord Dunmore's War (1774) Conflict between colonial settlers and the Shawnee Native Americans of Kentucky. The capture of Fort Pitt by the Virginia militia provoked the Shawnee into war against Virginia's governor, Lord Dunmore (1730–1809). Colonel Andrew Lewis led the militia to victory over Chief Cornstalk at the Battle of Point Pleasant (10 October 1774). Dunmore was widely believed to have manufactured the conflict in order to divert attention from the royal mismanagement of the Virginia colony.

Lorraine (Ger. Lothringen) Region of NE France; the capital is Metz. The Treaty of Verdun (AD 843) partitioned the Carolingian empire into three parts: the central part of the empire (Francia Media) was awarded to Lothair I. In 855 the empire was further fragmented when Lothair divided Francia Media among his sons: Lothair II received N Francia Media, henceforward known as **Lotharingia**. In 954 Lotharingia was divided into two duchies, Upper and Lower Lorraine. Upper Lorraine included the Ardennes, the Moselle valley and the upper Meuse valley. Lower Lorraine, which basically comprised the historic Netherlands, was dissolved in the 12th century. The authority of the dukes of Lorraine was constantly challenged by the counts of Luxembourg and the bishops of Metz, Verdun and Toul. Stanislaw I of Poland received Lorraine at the end of the War of the Polish Succession (1733–38), and after his death (1766) Lorraine was incorporated into France. After the Franco-Prussian War (1870–71), E Lorraine was joined to form the German territory of Alsace-Lorraine, which was returned to France in 1919. The region, rich in iron-ore deposits, was again disputed during World War 2. Area: 23,547sq km (9089sq mi). Pop. (1990) 2,305,700.

Los Angeles (City of Angels) City on the Pacific coast of S California, United States. Los Angeles was founded (1781) by the Spanish and passed to Mexico in 1822. John Frémont and Robert Stockton captured the city (1846) for the United States during the Mexican War (1846–48). Los Angeles was incorporated in 1850 and expanded rapidly with the arrival of the Southern Pacific (1876) and Santa Fe (1885) railways. The discovery of oil (1894), development of the harbour (1914), building of an aqueduct to provide an adequate water supply (1913), and growth of the film industry in Hollywood encouraged further growth. Greater Los Angeles sprawled out over 1200sq km (465sq mi), joined by an extensive network of freeways. During World War 2 industry boomed with the need for aircraft and munitions. Many African Americans migrated to the city to work in the factories, and race relations became a serious problem. Los Angeles has the largest Mexican-American community (*c*.900,000) in the United States, many living in the overcrowded *barrio* of East Los Angeles. More than 500,000 African Americans also live in the city, concentrated in the S central district of Watts. In August 1965 six days of riots in Watts left 34 people dead and caused US$200 million of damage. In 1992 another race-riot left 52 people dead and caused US$1 billion of damage. In 1994 an earthquake killed 57 people and caused damage estimated at more than US$25 billion. Pop. (1990) 3,489,779.

Lothair I (795–855) Frankish emperor (840–55), eldest son of LOUIS I (THE PIOUS). He was co-emperor with his father from 817. War broke out on the death of Louis (840) between Lothair and his two brothers, LOUIS II (THE GERMAN) and CHARLES II (THE BALD). Lothair was defeated at Fontenoy (841), and the CAROLINGIAN EMPIRE was partitioned by the Treaty of VERDUN (843). Lothair I retained the title of emperor and was given the central part of the Empire (Francia Media), consisting of the Low Countries, Alsace-Lorraine, Switzerland and N Italy. Lothair divided Francia Media among his sons: Lotharingia (LORRAINE) went to LOTHAIR II; Charles gained the kingdom of Provence; Italy and the imperial crown were granted to LOUIS II.

Lothair II (*c*.835–869) Frankish king of Lotharingia (855–869), second son of LOTHAIR I. He inherited Lotharingia (LORRAINE) from his father and, on the death (863) of his younger brother Charles, shared the kingdom of Provence with his brother LOUIS II. He caused much controversy by attempting to divorce his wife, Theutberga, in order to marry his mistress, Waldrada, but was frustrated by the opposition of Pope NICHOLAS I.

Lothair II (*c*.1070–1137) King of the Germans (1125–37) and Holy Roman emperor (1133–37), sometimes called Lothair III. Lothair's succession to the German throne was contested by the HOHENSTAUFEN dynasty, thereby precipitating the notorious GUELPH-GHIBELLINE feud. He crushed resistance by 1129. He was crowned emperor by Pope Innocent II. He extended the German kingdom eastwards across the River Elbe, gaining Pomerania (1135) from BOLESŁAW III of Poland. In 1136–37 Lothair temporarily expelled ROGER II of Sicily from S Italy.

Lotharingia *See* LORRAINE

Louis I (the Pious) (778–840) Frankish emperor (814–40), only surviving son of CHARLEMAGNE. In 817 Louis divided the vast empire among his three sons: Bavaria went to LOUIS II (THE GERMAN); AQUITAINE to PEPIN II; and LOTHAIR I was confirmed as co-emperor and heir. The award (829) of Alemannia and Aquitaine (832) to a fourth son, CHARLES II (THE BALD), precipitated a civil war with his other three sons. In 834 Louis was restored to the throne and made peace with Pepin and Louis II. Further divisions led to another revolt (839) by Louis II. Louis I was a devout and charitable Christian, but left a divided empire that was further weakened by Viking attacks.

Louis II (*c*.822–75) Frankish emperor (855–75) and king of Italy (844–75), eldest son of LOTHAIR I. He became sole emperor on his father's death (855). Although Louis gained territory from his two brothers, LOTHAIR II and Charles of Provence, his authority was largely confined to Italy. Louis spent much of his reign acting as an arm of the papacy in S Italy, attempting to control the LOMBARDS of Spoleto and Benevento and to expel the Arabs. In 971 Louis captured the Arab base at Bari, but soon after was captured by the Lombards and his power waned.

Louis IV (the Bavarian) (1283?–1347) Holy Roman emperor (1328–47), king of Germany (1314–47) and Duke of Bavaria (1298–1347), founder of the WITTELSBACH dynasty and grandson of RUDOLF I. Until 1329 Louis' rule in Bavaria was contested by his brother, Rudolf. In 1314 Louis and Frederick III (the Fair) were both crowned king of Germany, sponsored by the houses of Luxembourg and Habsburg respectively. Louis defeated and captured Frederick at the Battle of Mühldorf (1322). Prompted by the French, Pope JOHN XXII excommunicated him in 1324. Louis, with the support of the GHIBELLINES, invaded Italy in 1327, occupied Rome and installed an antipope, Nicholas V (1328–30), who crowned him emperor. Following complex diplomatic and military manoeuvres, John of Bohemia recognized Louis as emperor in 1339. The dispute over the succession continued, however, when the House of Luxembourg withdrew their support for Louis in 1342. In 1346 CHARLES IV, supported by Pope CLEMENT VI, deposed Louis.

Louis II (1845–86) King of Bavaria. *See* LUDWIG II

Louis II (the German) (*c*.804–876) King of the East Franks (843–876), third son of LOUIS I (THE PIOUS). He received Bavaria in the division of the CAROLINGIAN EMPIRE (817). Louis allied with his brothers, LOTHAIR I and CHARLES II (THE BALD), in revolts against their father (830–33) and then joined his half-brother, CHARLES II (THE BALD), against the succession of Lothair I. The Treaty of VERDUN (843) partitioned the empire into three: Louis acquired the E territories (Francia Orientalis), roughly equivalent to modern Germany. In 870 Lotharingia (LORRAINE) was divided between Louis and Charles II. Moravia gained independence from the empire in 874. Louis divided his lands between his sons, CARLOMAN, CHARLES III (THE FAT) and Louis the Younger.

Louis III (*c*.863–82) King of the West Franks (879–82), grandson of Emperor CHARLES II (THE BALD). He and his brother, Carloman (866–84), divided the West Frankish kingdom on the death (879) of their father, Louis II (the Stammerer). Louis III ruled France north of the River Loire. In 881 the brothers' gained a notable victory over the Norsemen at Saucourt, Normandy.

Louis IV (from Overseas) (921–54) King of France (936–54), son of CHARLES III (THE SIMPLE). He was raised at the English court of EDWARD THE ELDER after his father was overthrown (923) by Robert, Count of Paris. Louis moved his court from Paris to Laon, attempting to counter the influence of Hugh the Great, son of Robert and father of Hugh CAPET. In 940 Hugh and OTTO I of Germany attacked Laon and Louis was forced to sue for peace. Imprisoned (945–46) by Hugh, Louis later regained Laon (946) and Reims (949).

Louis VI (the Fat) (1081–1137) King of France (1108–37), son and successor of PHILIP I. Louis reasserted royal authority over the French nobility in the crown lands of the Île de France and the Orléanais. He fought against HENRY I of England and Emperor HENRY V, and arranged the marriage (1137) of his heir, LOUIS VII (THE YOUNGER), to ELEANOR OF AQUITAINE.

Louis VII (the Younger) (1121–80) King of France (1137–80), son and successor of LOUIS VI (THE FAT). Louis' marriage (1137) to ELEANOR OF AQUITAINE temporarily extended the French royal lands to the Pyrenees. Abbot SUGER acted as regent while Louis fought in the Second CRUSADE (1147–49). In 1152 Louis had his marriage annulled. Eleanor then married GEOFFREY OF ANJOU's son, the future HENRY II of England. In possession of Anjou, Normandy and Aquitaine, Henry now had more territories in France than Louis, who only remained in power because of divisions in England and Normandy. He was succeeded by his son, PHILIP II (AUGUSTUS).

Louis VIII (the Lion) (1187–1226) King of France (1223–26), son of PHILIP II (AUGUSTUS). He invaded England (1216) in support of the BARONS' WAR against King JOHN, but was defeated at Lincoln (1217) and returned to France. In 1226 Louis launched a crusade against the heretical ALBIGENSES in S France. His early death prompted his wife, Blanche of Castile (1188–1252), to act as regent for their son LOUIS IX. *See also* PLANTAGENET, HOUSE OF

Louis IX (1214–70) King of France (1226–70), son of LOUIS VIII. His mother, Blanche of Castile (1188–1252), acted as regent during his minority and long absences abroad. Blanche ended the revolt of the ALBIGENSES in S France, forcing Raymond VII, Count of Toulouse, to cede LANGUEDOC to the French crown. In 1229 Louis, aged only 15, led the French army to victory against Henry III of England in Brittany. In 1234 Louis assumed sole control of the kingdom. He was a just and pious king, personally administering justice and founding abbeys. Louis led the Seventh CRUSADE (1248–54) to the Holy Land. He seized Damietta (1249) and al-Mansurah (1259), Egypt, before being captured by the Egyptians. He was ransomed and released. Louis signed the Treaty of Paris (1258) with the PLANTAGENETS which left Aquitaine in English hands, while Henry III acknowledged himself as a vassal of Louis. Louis reformed the royal administration, rooting out abuses. He launched the Eighth Crusade (1270) and captured Carthage before dying of the plague in Tunis. He was succeeded by his son, PHILIP III. Already widely regarded as a saint, Louis was canonized by Pope BONIFACE VIII in 1297. His feast day is 25 August.

Louis XI (1423–83) King of France (1461–83), son of CHARLES VII. Louis' ceaseless political plotting earned him the nickname "the spider". He led a revolt against his father in 1440, but was pardoned and given the province of the Dauphiné. Louis ran the Dauphiné with considerable autonomy until he was forced to flee to the Netherlands by Charles' army in 1456. As king, Louis had to contend with the rebellion of his leading nobles. In 1465 the nobles' League of the Public Weal forced Louis to relinquish N France to the rebels. Louis regained Normandy (1466) and Brittany (1467), but was imprisoned by CHARLES THE BOLD of Burgundy after fomenting a revolt in Liège. In an

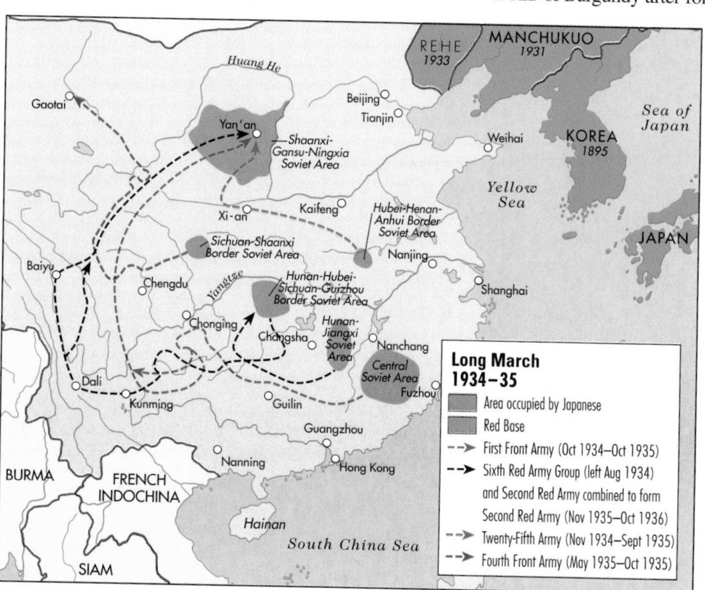

◀ **Long March** From 1934 to 1936, the communists were forced to abandon their S bases in the face of Kuomintang (Nationalist) attacks. More than 300,000 soldiers embarked on lengthy journeys to the N, by way of the mountainous W. The most famous of these treks – known as the Long March – was undertaken by the First Front Army, led by Mao Zedong. From the "Central Soviet Area" of Jiangxi province, the First Front Army travelled W through Guangxi and Guizhou, eventually reaching (October 1935) the safe haven of Yan'an, Shaanxi, where they set up a new communist base. Thousands died en route due to harsh conditions, disease and a shortage of supplies.

attempt to break the Anglo-Burgundian alliance, Louis supported the Earl of Warwick's rebellion against EDWARD IV of England. Louis sponsored the war in which Charles was killed (1477), and then fought against MARY OF BURGUNDY and Archduke Maximilian (later Emperor MAXIMILIAN I) for control of the Duchy of Burgundy. Having crushed the French princes through war and diplomatic cunning, Louis imposed his personal control over an increasingly centralized and fiscally powerful state, backed by government propaganda. His regime benefited trade, industry and the urban middle class. He was succeeded by his son, CHARLES VIII.

Louis XII (1462–1515) King of France (1498–1515), son of Charles, Duke of Orléans. He was imprisoned for leading an aristocratic revolt against his cousin, CHARLES VIII of France, but was pardoned and led the French invasion of Italy at the start of the ITALIAN WARS (1494–1559). As king, he partitioned the kingdom of NAPLES (1501) with FERDINAND V of Spain, but the French were expelled in 1504. Louis, Ferdinand V, Emperor MAXIMILIAN I and Pope JULIUS II formed (1508) the League of CAMBRAI against Venice, but the League soon collapsed and France found itself diplomatically isolated from the succeeding HOLY LEAGUE, which forced Louis to surrender all his Italian acquisitions (1513). After summoning an ESTATES GENERAL at Tours, Louis was known as the "father of his people". He undertook judicial reforms and financed his later wars at low levels of taxation, thereby incurring a mounting government debt. Louis' chief mentor in this was Cardinal d'AMBROISE, the "French Wolsey". Louis was succeeded by his son, FRANCIS I.

Louis XIII (the Just) (1601–43) King of France (1610–43), son of HENRY IV and MARIE DE MÉDICIS. Marie served as regent until 1614, but continued to rule until 1617 and arranged Louis' marriage (1615) to ANNE OF AUSTRIA. Upon assuming personal control, Louis exiled his mother. He defeated (1622) a HUGUENOT rebellion in s France and appointed Cardinal RICHELIEU as chief minister in 1624. Richelieu captured the Huguenot stronghold of LA ROCHELLE (1628) and persuaded Louis to invade Italy (1629. In 1635 France entered the THIRTY YEARS' WAR (1618–49) against Habsburg Spain. After Louis repelled the Spanish advance on Paris (1636), the French scored significant victories in the War. He was succeeded by his son, LOUIS XIV.

Acquisitions of Louis XIV 1643–1715
France 1643
Acquisitions 1552 (confirmed 1648)
Acquisitions 1643–1661
Acquisitions 1662–1715
Boundary of France 1715
Eastern linguistic frontier
Fortress built or strengthened by Vauban
Areas occupied by France 1684–97
Ten imperial cities over which France gained jurisdiction 1648, annexed 1672
Duchy of Lorraine occupied by France 1634–59 and 1670–97

▲ **Louis XIV**, aided by his chief minister Cardinal Mazarin, greatly expanded the E frontier of France, chiefly from the Spanish Netherlands in the War of Devolution (1667–78).

Louis XIV (1638–1715) King of France (1643–1715), son of LOUIS XIII and ANNE OF AUSTRIA. Louis, known as "the Sun King", enjoyed the longest reign in European history and the most splendid, both in culture and in regal ostentation. The luxury and extravagance of his court at Versailles (from 1682) astonished visitors. During his minority, Anne of Austria acted as regent, aided by chief minister Cardinal Jules MAZARIN. His regency was marred by the civil war known as the FRONDE (1648–53). In 1660 Louis married Marie-Thérèse, daughter of PHILIP IV of Spain. On the death (1661) of Mazarin, Louis became the first king of France since HENRY IV (r.1589–1510) to assume sole control of the kingdom. The epitome of absolute monarchy, he was convinced of the DIVINE RIGHT OF KINGS. Louis did, however, rely on some able ministers, notably Finance Minister Jean Baptiste COLBERT, who were usually drawn from the lower nobility or middle class. He also created a body of professional diplomats. He neutralized the power of the higher nobility by requiring their attendance at court. Local government was increasingly placed under intendants, officials who could be removed at the king's pleasure. Louis established direct control of the standing army, reorganized by Michel LE TELLIER and his son, Marquis de LOUVOIS. In 1667 Louis invaded the Spanish Netherlands, precipitating the War of DEVOLUTION (1667–78) that ended with France gaining FRANCHE-COMTÉ, Lorraine and parts of Flanders. In 1685 Louis revoked the Edict of NANTES (1585) in the first stage of a brutal campaign of persecution of the HUGUENOTS, which saw more than 200,000 French Protestants forced into exile and seriously weakened the French economy. Louis' invasion of the Palatinate led to the War of the GRAND ALLIANCE (1689–97) against England, the United Provinces of the Netherlands and the Holy Roman Empire. After a brief period of peace, conflict returned in the War of the SPANISH SUCCESSION (1701–14), which cost France its dominance in Europe but resulted in the succession of Louis' grandson as PHILIP V of Spain. The wars gradually drained the treasury, and no effective measures were taken to reform the inadequate fiscal system. Louis was a great patron of the arts, establishing the Comédie Française (1680), supporting writers (notably Molière, Corneille and Racine), and patronizing musicians, artists and architects. When dying, Louis warned his successor and great-grandson, LOUIS XV, "Do not copy my love of building, nor of warfare".

Louis XV (the Well-Beloved) (1710–74) King of France (1715–74), great-grandson and successor of LOUIS XIV. Until Louis reached his legal majority in 1723, France was ruled by Philippe II, Duc d'ORLÉANS. In 1725 Louis married Marie Leszczynska, daughter of former king STANISLAW I of Poland. Louis' chief minister (1726–44), André Hercule de FLEURY, managed to stabilize the national finances. The dynastic link brought France into the War of the POLISH SUCCESSION (1733–38), from which it emerged with greater claims to the province of LORRAINE. Fleury was also unable to prevent France from entering the War of the AUSTRIAN SUCCESSION (1740–48) against Austria and Great Britain. After Fleury's death (1743), the government of France was dominated by Louis' mistress, the Marquise de POMPADOUR. Louis established a network of spies throughout Europe that often conflicted with official aims and caused confusion in French foreign policy. This chaotic policy of "secret diplomacy", however, proved less damaging than involvement in the SEVEN YEARS' WAR (1756–63), which cost France most of its colonial possessions in North American and India. The Duc de CHOISEUL, foreign minister (1758–70), restored a semblance of order to French foreign affairs, but could not

▲ **Louis XVI** During the 17th and 18th centuries, furniture making flourished in parts of Europe, particularly in France. Louis XVI's reign was characterized by the neoclassical style as applied to this elegant writing table.

prevent the first (1772) of the Partitions of POLAND. In the last years of his reign, Louis withdrew from the PARLEMENTS the right to block royal legislation, but his weak rule contributed to the decline of royal authority that led to the FRENCH REVOLUTION (1789–99). He was succeeded by LOUIS XVI.

Louis XVI (1754–93) King of France (1774–92), grandson and successor of LOUIS XV. In 1770 he married MARIE ANTOINETTE, daughter of Emperor FRANCIS I and MARIA THERESA. In 1774 Louis restored political privileges to the PARLEMENTS, which had been restricted to a purely judicial role in 1771. His ineffective leadership allowed the aristocracy to defeat the efforts of competent ministers, such as Anne TURGOT and Jacques NECKER, to carry out the vital economic reforms that would stabilize the ANCIEN RÉGIME. The national finances were further strained by economic aid to the colonies in the AMERICAN REVOLUTION (1775–83). In 1788 the massive public debt forced Louis to convoke, for the first time in 175 years, the STATES-GENERAL to raise taxation. Once in session, the States-General proclaimed itself the National Assembly, signalling the start of the FRENCH REVOLUTION (1789–99). Ill-advised and lacking sound political judgement, Louis allied himself with reactionary elements in the Assembly and failed to recognize the demands of the Third Estate (the bourgeoisie). In October 1789, the royal family was moved from Versailles to the Tuileries Palace, Paris. Against the advice of the Comte de MIRABEAU, Louis refused to accept the notion of a constitutional monarchy and attempted to flee to Austria. The royal family was captured and brought back to Paris. Louis swore to maintain the new French constitution in 1791, but continued to plot for the intervention of Austria. After war was declared with Austria (April 1792), the royal family was imprisoned (August) and France was declared a republic on 21 September 1792. Louis was charged with treason and guillotined on 21 January 1793. *See also* FRENCH REVOLUTIONARY WARS

Louis XVII (1785–95) Titular king of France (1793–95), son of LOUIS XVI and MARIE ANTOINETTE. He was recognized as king after his father's execution during the FRENCH REVOLUTION (1789–99). In 1793 the Republican government placed Louis in the care of a Paris shoemaker, but he was later imprisoned in the Temple, Paris, where he died, apparently of tuberculosis.

Louis XVIII (1755–1824) King of France (1814–24), brother of LOUIS XVI. In June 1791 he fled from the FRENCH REVOLUTION (1789–99) to Belgium, where he sought military support against the Revolution. In 1793 he declared himself regent for Louis XVII. After Napoleon I's abdication and the Allied capture of Paris (March 1814), Charles de Talleyrand negotiated the Bourbon restoration, and Louis was proclaimed constitutional monarch of France in May 1814. He agreed to a constitution providing for parliamentary government and relatively liberal institutions. On Napoleon's return to power during the Hundred Days (March–July 1815), Louis again fled to Belgium until Napoleon's final defeat at the Battle of Waterloo. From 1820 Louis was dominated by the reactionary *ultras*. He was succeeded by his brother, Charles X.

Louis I (the Great) (1326–82) King of Hungary (1342–82) and Poland (1370–82), son and successor of Charles I of Hungary. In 1346 he was defeated by the Venetians at Zara (now Zadar, Croatia). In two further wars (1357–58, 1381) with Venice, Hungary gained most of Dalmatia. Louis occupied Naples in 1348, but was forced to retreat by an outbreak of the plague. He conquered Naples again in 1378. When Louis succeeded his uncle, Casimir III (the Great), as king of Poland, he became nominally the most powerful ruler in Eastern Europe. Thereafter he diverted his energies into the "Westernization" of Hungary. Later regarded as a national hero, Louis made Hungary a major European power, encouraging trade, industry and culture – at the cost of socially divisive legislation which enhanced the rights of the nobility and laid heavy obligations on the serfs. The "Union of the Crowns" of Hungary lapsed upon his death. Louise was succeeded in Hungary by his daughter Mary, in Poland by his daughter, Jadwiga.

Louisiana State on the Gulf of Mexico, s central United States; the capital is Baton Rouge. There are extensive archaeological remains of the Native-American Mound Builders who inhabited the region more than 16,000 years before the arrival (1542) of Spanish explorer Hernando de Soto. Sieur de La Salle claimed the region for France in 1682, naming it Louisiana after King Louis XIV of France. When Sieur d'Iberville and Sieur de Bienville began to colonize the region for France in 1699, the Native American population was *c*.15,000. In 1717 the colony was granted to John Law, who rapidly increased settlement of the region. New Orleans was established as capital of the colony in 1722. Louisiana was ceded to Spain in 1762, but the British gained most of Louisiana at the end of the French and Indian Wars (1754–63). In 1801 Spain returned the colony to France, who sold it to the United States in the Louisiana Purchase (1803). General Andrew Jackson's victory over the British at the Battle of New Orleans (1815) was the decisive conflict in the War of 1812. Louisiana's economy developed rapidly with its cotton and sugarcane plantations, and slaves made up *c*.50% of its total population of *c*.700,000 in 1860. Louisiana was a member of the Confederate States of America during the American Civil War (1861–65). In 1862 New Orleans was captured by Union Captain David Farragut and Louisiana was readmitted to the Union in 1868. The Reconstruction period saw the emergence of white supremacist organization, such as the Ku Klux Klan, and federal troops continued to occupy Louisiana until 1877. From 1877 to 1980 Louisiana was governed by the Democratic Party. In the 1890s, the Populist Party gained great support as a result of agrarian unrest among sharecroppers and small farmers, and the threat to Democratic rule led to a new state constitution (1898), which denied the vote to most African-Americans. In the 1920s and 1930s, Louisiana politics was dominated by Huey Long, who gained support from small farmers and the white working-class by increasing taxation to improve welfare provision and public works. During and after World War 2, the petrochemical industry stimulated the state economy. In the 1960s, the civil rights movement did much to promote racial integration in Louisiana. Area: 125,674sq km (48,523sq mi). Pop. (1992) 4,278,889.

Louisiana Purchase (1803) Transaction between the United States and France, in which the US government paid 60 million francs (US$15 million) for more than 2 million sq km (800,000sq mi) of land between the Mississippi River and the Rocky Mountains. In 1762 France ceded Louisiana to Spain, but the British gained most of the region at the end of the French and Indian Wars (1754–63). France regained Louisiana in the secret Treaty of San Ildefonso (1801). US President Thomas Jefferson instructed Robert Livingston to discover who owned the territory and negotiate the possible purchase of New Orleans with Charles de Talleyrand. The negotiations proved unsuccessful as Napoleon Bonaparte (later Napoleon I) cherished dreams of rebuilding the French Empire in the Americas. French failure in Santo Domingo and the looming threat of war with Great Britain changed his mind, however, and he offered the whole of Louisiana Territory to Livingston and James Monroe. The Louisiana Purchase roughly doubled the area of the United States.

Louis Napoleon *See* Napoleon III

Louis of Nassau (1538–74) Dutch noble, younger brother of William I (the Silent). The early leader of the Revolt of the Netherlands (1567–79), Louis wrote the petition to Margaret of Austria that called for religious toleration of Protestantism. When the Duke of Alba arrived in the Netherlands with his army in 1567, Louis fled into exile. In 1568 he led an invasion of n Netherlands, won the Battle of Heligerlee against the Spanish, but was defeated at Jengum, East Frieland, and after a diastrous campaign in Brabant, s Netherlands, retreated to France. Inspired by the capture of Brielle by the Gueux (Calvinist guerrillas) and aided by the French Huguenots, Louis launched another attack, capturing Mons, Hainaut (May 1572). He was forced to give up Mons after a long siege, but other rebel forces had meanwhile reconquered most of Holland. Louis died in battle against the Spanish at Mook. *See also* Hoorn, Philip de Montmorency, Graf van

Louis Philippe (1773–1850) King of France (1830–48), son of Louis Philippe, Duc d'Orléans. He was a member of the Jacobins at the start of the French Revolution (1789–99). Louis Philippe fought for France at the start of the French Revolutionary Wars (1792–1802), but defected with General Charles Dumouriez to the Austrians in 1793. He returned to France on the restoration of Louis XVIII in 1814. Louis was a consistent opponent of the reactionary *ultras* and, following the July Revolution (1830) that overthrew Charles X, he was crowned in August 1830. Although known as the "citizen king", Louis used authoritarian measures to suppress domestic opposition. Supported by the upper bourgeoisie, the conservative ministry (1840–48) of François Guizot ignored the plight of the new industrial proletariat and widespread unrest culminated in the February Revolution (1848). Louis was forced to abdicate, and the Second Republic was declared. He died in exile in England. *See also* Legitimists

Louvois, François Michel Le Tellier, Marquis de (1639–91) French statesman, secretary of state for war (1677–91) under Louis XIV. He aided his father, Michel Le Tellier, in the reform of the French army and succeeded him as war secretary. Louvois fought alongside his king in the War of Devolution (1667–68). He was widely blamed for the persecution of Huguenots that followed the revocation (1685) of the Edict of Nantes (1585). He was also responsible for the destruction of the Palatinate (1689), which precipitated the War of the Grand Alliance (1689–97). Louvois dominated government after the death of Jean Colbert in 1683.

Lovett, William (1800–77) English leader of the Chartists. A cabinetmaker, he founded the London Working Men's Association (1836) from which Chartism sprang. Lovett was the main architect of the People's Charter (1838) that demanded electoral reform. His role in the movement was limited, however, after disagreements with the more militant Feargus O'Connor. Lovett was imprisoned for a year after the Chartist riots in Birmingham, central England.

LOUISIANA
Statehood :
30 April 1812
Nickname :
Pelican State
State motto :
Union, Justice and Confidence

Low Countries Low-lying region of nw Europe now occupied by Belgium, the Netherlands and Luxembourg. The Low Countries formed part of the Roman Empire from the 1st century bc to the early 5th century ad. From the 5th century to the mid-9th century, the region was controlled by the Franks. The collapse of the Carolingian empire saw the fragmentation of the Low Countries, and the emergence of independent political entities such as the counties of Flanders and Holland and the duchy of Brabant. It was the most advanced and prosperous region of Northern Europe during the Middle Ages and Renaissance, under the control of the dukes of Burgundy from 1384 and the Habsburgs from 1477. The Revolt of the Netherlands (1567–79) led to the independence of seven n provinces as the United Provinces. The s Netherlands remained under Habsburg rule (at first Spanish, from 1714 Austrian), until 1795 when both parts of the Netherlands were annexed (1795–1813) by France. They were temporarily reunited (1815) as the United Netherlands, under William I, who was also Grand Duke of Luxembourg. A revolution in 1830 created the independent kingdom of Belgium. The grand duchy of Luxembourg was made a neutral territory in 1867 and became fully independent in 1890. During World War 1 the Netherlands remained neutral, while Belgium and Luxembourg were occupied by the Germans. During World War 2 all three of the Low Countries were overrun by Nazi Germany. In 1947 the Low Countries joined to form the Benelux Customs Union.

Lower Canada French part of British North America from the Constitutional Act (1791) until the union with Upper Canada (Ontario) under the 1840 Act of Union. Following the British North America Act (1867) the region entered the Dominion of Canada as the province of Québec.

L

Loyalist (Tory) Colonist who supported Great Britain during the American Revolution (1775–83). About one million of the *c*.3 million settlers in the North American colonies remained loyal to Britain during the War. The staunchest Loyalists were servants of the crown. New York was the stronghold of Loyalism, furnishing *c*.23,000 troops for the British cause. Suffering repression and persecution, *c*.100,000 Loyalists fled into exile during the War, many settling in what is now Canada. In Northern Ireland, Loyalists wish to preserve the union with the United Kingdom. *See also* Ulster Unionist Party

Loyola, Saint Ignatius of (1491–1556) Spanish theologian, founder of the Jesuits (formally Society of Jesus). In 1521 he was seriously wounded fighting against the French at Pamplona, n Spain, and underwent a spiritual awakening while recovering from his wounds. During a period of penance, he began writing his influential *Spiritual Exercises* (1548). In 1523 Loyola made a pilgrimage to Jerusalem. He was ordained in 1537, and in 1540, Pope Paul III approved his request to found the Society of Jesus. He spent the rest of his life in Rome supervising the growth of the order, which became the leading force in the Counter-Reformation. He was canonized in 1622. His feast day is 31 July. *See also* Francis Xavier, Saint

Luba Historic empire and Bantu-speaking peoples in Central Africa. In the late 15th century, the Luba founded a kingdom e of the River Kasai in what is now Democratic Republic of Congo. The Luba systems of divine kingship and bureaucracy were adopted by the neighbouring Lunda, who established a network of satellite kingdoms. The Luba-Lunda states grew powerful by trading slaves for firearms with the Portuguese, and by the end of the 17th century controlled most of s Congo, w Angola and n Zambia.

Lübeck Baltic port at the mouth of the River Trave, Schleswig-Holstein, ne Germany. The German settlement was founded (1143) by the Count of Holstein, destroyed by fire (1157), and rebuilt by Henry III (the Lion). After a brief period under Danish rule, Lübeck became a free city. Its independent constitution and legal system became a model for other Baltic towns. In 1358 the city became the headquarters of the HANSEATIC LEAGUE. During the 16th century, the city began to decline and its trade was destroyed during the Napoleonic Wars (1803–15). After taking a stance of civic independence during the early years of the Third Reich, Lübeck lost its autonomous status in 1937 when it was incorporated in Schleswig-Holstein. It was damaged by Allied bombing during World War 2. Sights include the Romanesque cathedral (1173) and the town hall (13th–15th century). Pop. (1990) 216,500.

Lucknow Pact (December 1916) Agreement between the Indian National CONGRESS and the All-India MUSLIM LEAGUE. Its proposals for a structure of government were largely adopted by the British Government of India Act (1919). The Pact anticipated the intercommunal KHILAFAT MOVEMENT and provided the impetus for "Mahatma" GANDHI's Non-cooperation Movement.

Lucullus, Lucius Licinius (*c.*117–56 BC) Roman general. He served in the SOCIAL WAR (90–88 BC) under Lucius Cornelius SULLA. As consul (74–66 BC), Lucullus led Roman forces against MITHRADATES VI of Pontus. Lucullus forced Mithradates to retreat, conquering Armenia in 69 BC. He was undermined, however, by army mutinies and Roman businessman frustrated at their lack of personal profit from the Asian conquest. Lucullus was replaced as consul by POMPEY and retired to lead a life of luxury.

Luddites Members of an anti-industrial movement in early 19th-century England. The Luddites were chiefly skilled workers, such as weavers, made redundant by mechanical looms. Often masked and under cover of darkness, they vandalized machines and factories. The riots started (1811) around Nottingham, central England, and spread to Lancashire and Yorkshire, N England. The uprising was brutally crushed by the Earl of LIVERPOOL and 14 Luddites were hanged in 1813. *See also* INDUSTRIAL REVOLUTION

Ludendorff, Erich (1865–1937) German general, b. Poland. The chief architect of German military strategy during WORLD WAR 1, he joined the general staff under Graf von MOLTKE. As chief of staff to General Paul von HINDENBURG, he masterminded the victory over the Russians at the Battle of TANNENBERG (1914) in the early stages of World War 1. In 1916 Ludendorff and Hindenburg were given supreme command of Germany's war effort. Ludendorff's policy of unrestricted submarine warfare precipitated the entry of the United States into the War. He rejected the terms of the armistice and Emperor WILLIAM II accepted his resignation (1918). Ludendorff believed that he and the German nation had been betrayed. He participated in the abortive MUNICH PUTSCH (1923) against the WEIMAR REPUBLIC, but was acquitted in the trial that followed. He served (1924–28) in the Reichstag as a member of the NAZI PARTY. *See also* BETHMANN-HOLLWEG, THEOBALD VON

Ludwig II (1845–86) King of BAVARIA (1864–86), son and successor of MAXIMILIAN II. He sought cooperation with PRUSSIA and led Bavaria into the German Empire in 1871. Ludwig was a great patron of the arts, notably of the composer Richard Wagner. He is chiefly famous for his extravagant castles, such as Linderhof and Neuschwanstein. In 1886 Ludwig was declared insane and his uncle, Prince Luitpold, became regent. He drowned himself.

Luftwaffe German air force. In English-speaking countries, the term refers specifically to the air force of Nazi Germany. Built up rapidly in the 1930s, it was designed primarily as part of Germany's *Blitzkrieg* tactics, in combination with ground troops and armour. It was highly effective in the early stages of WORLD WAR 2 and during the invasion of the Soviet Union (1941). It was less successful as a bombing force in the Battle of BRITAIN (1940). *See also* BLITZ

Lugard, Frederick John Dealtry, Baron (1858–1945) British colonial administrator. In 1890 he led an expedition for the British East Africa Company to Uganda, establishing British hegemony in the region. Lugard created and led the West African Frontier Force that defeated French claims to West Africa. He then served as high commissioner (1900–06) for Northern Nigeria, establishing British rule over the states of KANO and SOKOTO. Lugard's system of colonial government through established native institutions was widely copied throughout the British Empire. After serving as governor of Hong Kong (1907–12), he returned to Nigeria to become its first governor general (1914–19). Through indirect rule, Lugard succeeded in creating and preserving a unified Nigeria. In his book *The Dual Mandate in British Tropical Africa* (1922) he declared that colonies should be run for the benefit of their inhabitants and the wider world.

Lukács, György (1885–1971) Hungarian political theorist and literary critic. He joined the Hungarian Communist Party in 1918 and served in Béla KUN's communist government. When the regime collapsed in 1919, Lukács went into exile in Vienna, Austria, where he wrote the influential Marxist philosophy of history, *History of Class Consciousness* (1923). When Adolf Hitler came to power in 1933, Lukács fled to Moscow, Russia, but his aesthetics clashed with the prevailing socialist realism and he was accused of REVISIONISM. Returning to Hungary after World War 2. Lukács was a key figure in the abortive HUNGARIAN UPRISING (1956) and was briefly deported to Romania.

Lumumba, Patrice (1925–61) Congolese statesman, first prime minister (June–September 1960) of the Democratic Republic of CONGO. In 1958 he founded and led the Congolese National Movement (MNC), the first nationwide party in the Congo. At the first All-African People's Conference in Accra, Ghana, Lumumba was inspired by Kwame NKRUMAH and embraced the cause of PAN-AFRICANISM. In October 1959, Lumumba was imprisoned by the Belgians after an uprising in Stanleyville (now Kisangani) against repressive colonial rule in Congo. The MNC won a landslide victory in elections in Stanleyville and the Belgian government was forced to concede full independence in June 1960. Within days of independence, the army mutinied and the mineral-rich province of KATANGA, led by Moise TSHOMBE and supported by Belgian troops, announced secession. Lumumba called for United Nations' (UN) assistance, but UN troops were unwilling to fight against the Katanga rebels and Lumumba appealed for further external support. President Joseph KASAVUBU dismissed Lumumba, who promptly questioned the legality of the action, and the army, led by Colonel Joseph MOBUTU, seized power. Lumumba tried to escape from Léopoldville (now Kinshasa) but was captured and flown to Katanga, where he was murdered. Lumumba was subsequently proclaimed a national hero. *See also* KABILA, LAURENT DESIRE

Lunacharsky, Anatoli Vasilievich (1875–1933) Soviet writer and statesman, first commissar for education (1917–29), b. Ukraine. An early member of the Bolsheviks, he was imprisoned both during the Russian Revolution of 1905 and by Alexander KERENSKY's government after the first phase of the RUSSIAN REVOLUTION (1917). Appointed education minister by Vladimir Lenin, Lunacharsky was responsible for the introduction of uni-

LUXEMBOURG

AREA: 2,590sq km (1,000sq mi)
POPULATION: 390,000
CAPITAL (POPULATION): Luxembourg (76,446)
GOVERNMENT: Constitutional monarchy (Grand Duchy)
ETHNIC GROUPS: Luxembourger 71%, Portuguese 10%, Italian 5%, French 3%, Belgian 3%, German 2%
LANGUAGES: Letzeburgish (Luxembourgian-official), French, German
RELIGIONS: Christianity (Roman Catholic 95%, Protestant 1%)
GDP PER CAPITA (1995): US$37,930

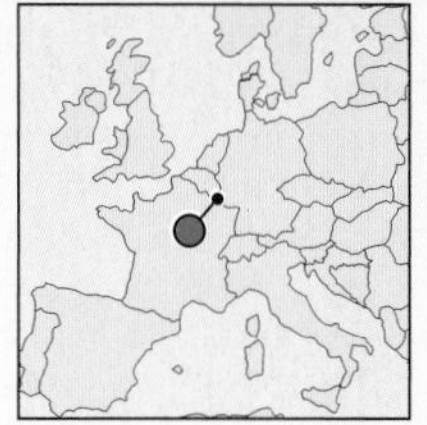

Independent grand duchy in W Europe. The Franks occupied the region in the 5th century AD. Christianity was introduced in the late 7th century. In 963 Luxembourg gained independence from the CAROLINGIAN EMPIRE, and the county of Luxembourg was created in 1060. In 1308 the Luxembourg dynasty gained control of the HOLY ROMAN EMPIRE when HENRY VII was crowned emperor. His successor, CHARLES IV, made Luxembourg a duchy in 1354. In 1443 Emperor Sigismund was forced to cede the duchy to Philip III (the Good), Duke of Burgundy. In 1477 it passed to the HABSBURGS, and in the 16th century it was incorporated into the Spanish Netherlands. The duchy was devastated by the THIRTY YEARS' WAR (1618–48) and was captured by Louis XIV of France in 1684. In 1714 it passed to Austria.

Luxembourg was occupied by France during the NAPOLEONIC WARS (1803–15) and was made a grand duchy under the control of WILLIAM I of the Netherlands at the Congress of Vienna (1815). In 1839 Belgium acquired a large part of the duchy. In 1867 Luxembourg was recognized as an independent state, and its neutrality was guaranteed by the European powers. With the cooperation of the ruling house of Nassau, Luxembourg was occupied (1914–18) by Germany in World War 1. The government resisted German occupation (1940–44) during World War 2.

In 1948 Luxembourg abandoned its neutrality and joined the North Atlantic Treaty Organization (NATO). Luxembourg was one of the six founders of the European Community (EC) and joined with Belgium and the Netherlands to form the economic union of BENELUX (1960). In 1964 Prince Jean succeeded his mother, Charlotte, as grand duke. In 1998 Jean conferred many constitutional powers upon his son and heir, Prince Henri. In 1994 Jacques SANTER became president of the European Commission and was succeeded as prime minister of Luxembourg by Jean Claude Juncker. In 1999 Luxembourg adopted the European single currency (the euro).

versal, free education in the Soviet Union. He and Maxim Gorky helped prevent the destruction of works of art from the tsarist period. Lunacharsky wrote *Revolutionary Silhouettes* (1923), a collection of biographies on the leaders of the Russian Revolution.

Lunda Historic empire and Bantu-speaking peoples in Central Africa. The Lunda originate from E of the River Kwango in what is now Democratic Republic of Congo. In *c*.1500, influenced by the neighbouring LUBA, the Lunda founded a centralized kingdom. From the late-16th century, bands of roaming Lunda warriors (Imbangala) established many satellite states and made contact with the Portuguese. The expansion of the Lunda empire was aided by Portuguese firearms, for which slaves and ivory were exchanged. The Lunda state of Kasanje on the upper River Kwango (in what is now Angola) acted as an intermediary in the SLAVE TRADE between the Lunda interior and Portuguese colonies on the coast. By the end of the 17th century, the Lunda empire covered a vast area of the S Congo, W Angola and N Zambia. In *c*.1740 the Lunda kingdom of Kazembe was founded in what is now the Congo province of Katanga and part of N Zambia. The empire declined after 1850 and was partitioned between Portugal and Belgium at the end of the 19th century.

Lusitania British passenger liner sunk (7 May 1915) off the Irish coast by a German U-boat. Of the 1195 people drowned, 128 were US citizens. The incident aroused anti-German feeling in the United States, which indirectly contributed to US entry into World War 1 against Germany.

Luther, Martin (1483–1546) German theologian, founder of the Protestant REFORMATION. In 1505 he joined the Augustinian Order at Erfurt, central Germany, and was ordained priest in 1507. In 1512 Luther became professor of biblical theology at the University of Wittenberg, a position he held until his death. Through his lectures, Luther came to believe that justification is achieved through "faith alone" (*sola fide*): salvation is the gift of God's grace and cannot be bought or acquired through human action. In 1517 Luther published *Ninety-five Theses* that protested against many practices, notably the sale of INDULGENCES, and doctrines of the Christian Church. In a debate (1519) with Johann ECK at Leipzig, Luther appeared to defend the heretic Jan HUS and was condemned by the papacy. Luther responded by issuing three treatises (1520): the first called on the German nobility to undertake reform of the church, while the second, *A Prelude Concerning the Babylonian Captivity of the Church*, attacked the doctrine of TRANSUBSTANTIATION, reduced the seven sacraments to three, and stated that the Bible, rather than the pope, was the ultimate religious authority. Protected by Frederick III (the Wise), Elector of Saxony, Luther defended himself before Emperor CHARLES V at the Diet of WORMS (1521), but was outlawed and excommunicated. In 1522, with the aid of Philipp MELANCHTHON, Luther translated the New Testament into the vernacular – a landmark in the development of German literature. Luther condemned radicals, such as Thomas MÜNTZER, and called for civil obedience during the PEASANTS' WAR (1524–26). Luther had set out to reform the church not to divide it, but compromise proved impossible when the Confession of AUGSBURG (1530), a moderate statement of LUTHERANISM, was rejected by Charles V. *See also* ANABAPTISTS; CALVIN, JOHN; COUNTER-REFORMATION; PROTESTANTISM; ROMAN CATHOLIC CHURCH; SCHMALKALDIC LEAGUE; ZWINGLI, ULRICH

Lutheranism Doctrines of the Protestant, Christian church that grew out of the teaching of Martin LUTHER. The principal Lutheran doctrine is that of "justification by faith alone". Luther held that salvation cannot be conferred by the church, but rather is the gift of God's grace. He also rejected the doctrine of TRANSUBSTANTIATION. These and other essentials of Lutheran doctrine were set down by Philip MELANCHTHON in the AUGSBURG CONFESSION (1530), the basic document of Lutheranism ever since. Lutheranism proved the most popular and least radical of the several versions of reformed religion founded during the Christian REFORMATION. The Lutheran churches originated in Germany, but quickly spread to Scandinavia and became a mass religion in North America after the 1740s. Today, the Lutheran Church has *c*.25 million members worldwide. *See also* ANGLICAN COMMUNION; CALVINISM; PROTESTANTISM; ROMAN CATHOLIC CHURCH

Luthuli, Albert John Mvumbi (1898–1967) South African civil-rights leader, b. Rhodesia (now Zimbabwe). In 1936 he became chief of the ZULU community of Groutville, Natal. Luthuli joined the AFRICAN NATIONAL CONGRESS (ANC) in 1945 and became president of the organization in 1952. He was charged of high treason by South Africa's APARTHEID government in 1956, but released in 1957. In 1960 Luthuli became the first African to be awarded the Nobel Prize for Peace for his powerful advocacy of non-violence in the campaign against racist legislation. In 1960 the South African police killed 67 demonstrators at Sharpeville and the massacre prompted Nelson MANDELA to form *Umkhonte We Sizwe*, the paramilitary wing of the ANC. The apartheid regime continued to restrict Luthuli's movements. He was killed in a train accident.

Lützen, Battle of (16 November 1632) Conflict during the THIRTY YEARS' WAR (1618–48) between the Swedish army, led by GUSTAVUS II, and the forces of the Holy Roman Empire led by Albrecht von WALLENSTEIN. The Swedes captured the imperial artillery and forced Wallenstein to retreat, but Gustavus was killed in the battle.

Luxembourg *See* country feature, page 248

Luxemburg, Rosa (1871–1919) German revolutionary, b. Poland. In 1898 Luxemburg moved to Germany, where she joined the SOCIAL DEMOCRATIC PARTY (SPD). In the Second INTERNATIONAL, she argued that only world revolution could achieve SOCIALISM. She was imprisoned in Poland for her participation in the RUSSIAN REVOLUTION OF 1905. Luxemburg's promotion of mass political action and rejection of Germany's involvement in World War 1 led to her expulsion from the SPD by August BEBEL. In 1916 Luxemburg and Karl LIEBKNECHT founded (1916) the SPARTACUS LEAGUE. The pair were imprisoned (1916–18) for revolutionary activity. Upon their release, they founded the German Communist Party that rejected Vladimir LENIN's model of party organization. Luxemburg and Liebknecht were murdered in police custody after leading an abortive uprising in Berlin (January 1919) against the post-war government of Friedrich EBERT.

Luxor (El Uqsur) City in upper Egypt, on the E bank of the River Nile; known to the ancient Egyptians as Weset and to the ancient Greeks as **Thebes**. It was the capital of ancient Egypt during the 11th dynasty and during the New Kingdom, when pharaohs were buried in the Valley of the Kings. Howard CARTER's discovery (1922) of TUTANKHAMUN's tomb gave some indication of the lavish treasure that was buried with the pharaohs. Buried by sand, almost nothing remained visible of the ancient town until excavation began in the 19th century. Luxor Temple, in the heart of the city, was linked to Karnak Temple by a 2.5km (1mi) long avenue of sphinxes. A major tourist destination, 58 tourists were killed by Muslim fundamentalists outside the Temple of HATSHEPSHUT in 1997. Pop. (1992) 146,000.

Lvov, Georgi Yevgenevich, Prince (1861–1925) Russian statesman. He was elected to the Duma (Russian parliament) in 1906. Lvov became leader of a provisional government after the first phase of the RUSSIAN REVOLUTION (1917) had forced the abdication of Tsar NICHOLAS II. His government (March–July 1917) was unable to satisfy the demands of the SOVIETS, however, and Lvov was forced to resign in favour of Alexander KERENSKY. Lvov was imprisoned when the BOLSHEVIKS seized power in the second phase of the revolution (November 1917), but later escaped to Siberia before settling in France.

Lydia Ancient kingdom of W Asia Minor. With the support of ASSYRIA, King **Gyges** (r. *c*.680–*c*.652 BC) founded the Mermnad dynasty at SARDIS (near present-day IZMIR, Turkey). Lydia was at its height under **Alyattes** (r. *c*.610–*c*.560 BC), who battled against MEDIA, finally subdued the Cimmerians and captured Smyrna (now Izmir). Alyattes' son, CROESUS, completed the conquest of mainland Ionia, but was subsequently defeated (547 BC) by CYRUS II (THE GREAT), and Lydia was subsumed into the Persian empire. The Lydians were the first people to mint metal coins (late 7th century BC).

Lynch, Jack (John) (1917–99) Irish statesman, taoiseach (1966–73, 1977–79). A famous athlete, he entered the Dáil (parliament) for FIANNA FÁIL in 1948. A close ally of Eamon DE VALERA, Lynch was minister of education (1957–59) and minister for industry and commerce (1959–65) before succeeding Sean Lemass as taoiseach (prime minister). He was re-elected in 1969, during increasing cross-border tension with Northern Ireland. Lynch sacked Charles HAUGHEY after rumours of the latter's involvement in the import of weapons for the IRISH REPUBLICAN ARMY (IRA). In 1973 he led Ireland into the European Economic Community (EEC), but was defeated by Liam COSGRAVE and FINE GAEL in the 1973 elections. Lynch won a second term in office, retired in 1979, and was succeeded by Haughey.

Lyon (Lyons) City and river port at the confluence of the Rhône and Saône rivers, SE France; capital of Rhône department. Lyon was founded (43 BC) as the Roman colony of Lugdunum, later becoming the capital of Roman Gaul. It was a major ecclesiastical centre, ruled by its archbishop until incorporated in the French kingdom in 1312. During the Renaissance, Lyon prospered as the capital of Europe's silk industry, but it suffered during the French Revolution (1789–99) and did not recover fully until the 20th century. During World War 2 (1939–45), Lyon was a stronghold of the French resistance movement. Pop. (1990) 415,487.

Lyons, Joseph Aloysius (1879–1939) Australian statesman, prime minister (1932–39). He was a Labor member of the Tasmanian assembly from 1909 and was prime minister of Tasmania (1923–28). Elected to the federal parliament in 1929, Lyons served as postmaster general, but in 1931 he broke away to form the United Australia Party. As prime minister, Lyons adopted austerity measures to try to combat inflation during the GREAT DEPRESSION and the upturn in the world economy helped secure his re-election in 1934 and 1937. After 1937 Lyons increased defence spending to counter the threat of Japanese militarism. He died in office. In 1949 Lyons' widow, Dame **Enid Lyons** (1897–1981), became the first woman cabinet member in Australia.

Lysander (d.395 BC) Spartan general, largely responsible for SPARTA's victory over ATHENS in the PELOPONNESIAN WAR (431–404 BC). He secured vital support from Cyrus the Younger of Persia. Lysander's destruction of the Athenian fleet in the Battle of AEGOSPOTAMI (405 BC) effectively ended the War. He established an oligarchy in Athens that was overthrown by a democratic revolt in 403 BC. Lysander subsequently lost influence in Sparta and was killed in battle at the start of the CORINTHIAN WAR (395–387 BC).

Maastricht Treaty (7 February 1992) Agreement on EUROPEAN UNION (EU) signed by the leaders of 12 European nations at Maastricht, SE Netherlands. The treaty included a timetable for the introduction of a single currency (the euro); a Common Foreign and Security Policy (CFSP), with the Western European Union (WEU) as a possible defence arm of the EU; a common European citizenship for nationals of all member states and the extension of European cooperation in justice and home affairs. The treaty introduced the principle of subsidiarity whereby decisions are taken at the most appropriate level: local, regional or national. It extended qualified majority voting in the European Council of Ministers and increased the powers of the EUROPEAN PARLIAMENT (EP) over the budget and the EUROPEAN COMMISSION. A separate protocol on social policy (the social chapter) was adopted by 11 states – the United Kingdom initially opted out but later signed up in the Amsterdam Treaty (1997).

McAdoo, William Gibbs (1863–1941) US statesman, secretary of the treasury (1913–18). He constructed (1904–08) the first tunnel under the Hudson River. A long-term supporter of Woodrow WILSON, he became Wilson's secretary of the treasury, serving as the first chairman of the FEDERAL RESERVE SYSTEM. He was also director general of railroads (1917–19). An unsuccessful candidate for the Democratic presidential nomination (1924), he was a senator for California (1932–38).

M

Macao (Macau) Special administrative province in SE China. The first European discovery was by Vasco da GAMA in 1497. In 1557 the Portuguese colonized the island for missionary and trading purposes, and for the next 300 years Portugal paid an annual fee to China for the use of the harbour. Up until the late 1600s much of Macao's economy was driven by trade with Japan. In 1849 Portugal declared it a free port, and in 1887 the Chinese government recognized Portugal's right of "perpetual occupation" under the Protocol of Lisbon. Competition from HONG KONG and the increased silting of Macao's harbour led to the port's decline towards the end of the 19th century. In 1974 Macao became a Chinese province under Portuguese administration. It was returned to China in December 1999 with the provision that the province's basic social and economic infrastructures remain untouched for 50 years. Pop. (1991) 339,464.

Macapagal, Diosdado (1910–97) Philippine statesman, president (1961–65). He served as vice president (1957–61) under Carlos Garcia before becoming president through a coalition of the Liberal and Progressive parties. Macapagal's attempts to combat corruption and restore economic prosperity were thwarted, and he was defeated by Ferdinand MARCOS in the 1965 elections. He opposed the Marcos regime, challenging the validity of the new constitution (1973) and forming a coalition against Marcos (1982). *See also* AQUINO, CORY

MacArthur, Douglas (1880–1964) US general. A divisional commander in World War 1, he became US Army chief of staff in 1930 and military adviser to the PHILIPPINES in 1935, retiring from the Army in 1937. Recalled by President Franklin ROOSEVELT after PEARL HARBOR (December 1941) had led the United States into WORLD WAR 2, he delayed the Japanese capture of the Philippines. Following a series of Japanese successes in the Pacific, MacArthur was ordered out to Australia in 1942. As supreme Allied commander (1942–45) in the SW Pacific, he used combined operations and the development of the "island hopping" strategy to recapture many Pacific islands. On September 1945, after the nuclear attacks on HIROSHIMA and NAGASAKI, MacArthur received the Japanese surrender on board the USS *Missouri*. He became the supreme commander of the occupation forces of Japan, and for six years he exercised almost unlimited authority, introducing reforms and a new constitution. MacArthur was chosen to lead the United Nations' (UN) forces at the outbreak of the KOREAN WAR (1950–53) and executed a daring landing at Inchon, w Korea, in September 1950. With the entry of Chinese troops in North Korea, he urged the escalation of the war into China. Refused permission by President Harry TRUMAN, he appealed for support from the US public, but was dismissed by Truman in 1951. In 1952 MacArthur failed in a last bid to win the Republican nomination for president. *See also* RIDGWAY, MATTHEW

Macaulay, Thomas Babington, 1st Baron (1800–59) English historian, essayist and Whig statesman. Following a short legal career, he joined Parliament in 1830, upholding liberal causes such as the abolition of slavery and the advocacy of political reform. He served on the British governor's council in India (1834–38), where he introduced a Western education system. He re-entered Parliament (1839–47, 1852–56) but spent most of his later years writing the five-volume *History of England from the Accession of James II* (1849–61), which examined the significance of the English Civil War.

Macbeth (d.1057) King of Scotland (1040–57). Hereditary ruler of Moray and Ross, Macbeth killed DUNCAN I, his cousin, in battle and seized the throne. English intervention on behalf of Duncan's son (later MALCOLM III) resulted in his defeat by Siward, Earl of Northumbria, at Dunsinane Hill, near Scone (1054). Macbeth fled N but was eventually killed by Malcolm at Lumphanan. Shakespeare based his *Macbeth* (1605) on Holinshed's inaccurate *Chronicle*.

MacBride, Séan (1904–88) Irish politician, son of the Irish patriots Maud Gonne and John MacBride, who was killed during the EASTER RISING (1916). He fought for the IRISH REPUBLICAN ARMY (IRA) and founded the *Clann na Poblachta* (Republican Political Party) in 1936. MacBride served (1947–58) in the Dáil Éireann (Irish assembly) and acted as Ireland's foreign minister (1948–51). He was chairman (1961–75) of the human rights organization Amnesty International, and was awarded the Nobel Prize for Peace in 1974.

Maccabees Priestly Jewish family in Palestine in the 2nd century BC. In 168 BC the SELEUCID ruler Antiochus IV (r.175–*c*.163 BC) occupied JERUSALEM and, in 167 BC, sought to impose further Hellenistic culture upon JUDAH by rededicating the TEMPLE OF JERUSALEM to Zeus and eradicating Jewish religious practices, such as circumcision. **Mattathias**, a priest, and his five sons fled to the mountains and organized a rebellion. After Mattathias' death (*c*.166 BC), his son **Judas** became leader of the rebels and used guerrilla tactics to defeat the Syrian armies. In 164 BC he recaptured and reconsecrated the Temple – an event celebrated annually at Hanukkah, the festival of lights. Judas Maccabees was killed in battle against Syria (*c*.160 BC) and was succeeded by his brother **Jonathan**, who became high priest in Jerusalem (*c*.152 BC) – thus establishing the Hasmonean dynasty. Jonathan was assassinated (*c*.142 BC) and was succeeded by his brother **Simon**, who finally brought peace to Jerusalem and was acknowledged as high priest of JUDAEA. Simon was also assassinated (*c*.134 BC) and was succeeded by his son John (later **Hyrcanus I**). Hyrcanus' long reign (*c*.134–*c*.105 BC) saw the consolidation and expansion of Judaea, and the start of the conflict between the SADDUCEES and PHARISEES. The family continued to control Judaea, albeit tenuously, until 63 BC, when civil war enabled POMPEY to conquer the kingdom.

McCarthy, Eugene Joseph (1916–) US politician, senator (1959–70). He represented Minnesota in the House of Representatives (1949–59) before joining the Senate. An outspoken critic of US involvement in the VIETNAM WAR (1955–75), McCarthy was thrust into the political spotlight when he decided to challenge President Lyndon JOHNSON for the Democratic presidential nomination in 1968. McCarthy's victory in the New Hampshire primary persuaded Johnson not to seek re-election, but he was gradually overtaken in the race by Robert KENNEDY. After Kennedy's assassination, McCarthy lost the nomination to Vice President Hubert HUMPHREY and retired from the Senate. He ran again as an independent in 1976.

McCarthy, Joseph Raymond (1908–57) US politician, senator (1947–57). He became a judge in Wisconsin, the state he was later to represent as a Republican, before serving in the Pacific during World War 2. In 1950, taking advantage of anti-communist sentiment brought about by the start of the KOREAN WAR, he accused the state department of being infiltrated by communists. Although a Senate committee found no evidence of the charge, McCarthy, who, in 1953, was made chairman of the Senate permanent subcommittee on investigations, widened his attack to other sectors of public life including the film industry. During the period of "McCarthyism" many of those accused of communism were blacklisted. McCarthy polarized US society; many regarded his hearings as show trials or witch-hunts, while others considered him a hero. In 1954 he turned his attention to the army. The subsequent hearings were televised, and McCarthy's accusations were shown to be baseless, while his truculent, accusatory style of questioning turned the public against him. His methods were condemned by President Dwight EISENHOWER and, when the Democrats secured control of the Senate in 1954, he was officially censured. *See also* UN-AMERICAN ACTIVITIES, HOUSE OF (HUAC)

McClellan, George Brinton (1826–85) US general in the American CIVIL WAR (1861–65). He served in the MEXICAN WAR (1846–48), before retiring from the army to pursue a career on the railroads. At the outbreak of the Civil War, McClellan was recalled as commander of the Department of Ohio. After the defeat of Union forces under Winfield SCOTT in the First Battle of BULL RUN (1861), McClellan was appointed commander of the Army of the Potomac and then succeeded Scott as commander in chief of the Union army. McClellan reorganized the Union forces, but his overly cautious approach in the PENINSULAR CAMPAIGN prevented the Union army from capturing Richmond, Virginia, and allowed Confederate General Robert LEE to mount a counter-offensive in the SEVEN DAYS' BATTLES (1862). McClellan was sacked as commander in chief by President Abraham LINCOLN, but retained his leadership of the Army of the Potomac. McClellan repulsed Lee's invasion of the North at the Battle of ANTIETAM (September 1862), but once more failed to press home his advantage and was removed from command entirely. In 1864 he ran unsuccessfully as a Democratic candidate for president against Lincoln and later served as governor of New Jersey (1878–81).

Macdonald, Flora (1722–90) Scottish JACOBITE heroine. After the Battle of CULLODEN (1746), she smuggled the Young Pretender, Charles Edward STUART, to the Isle of Skye, NW Scotland, disguised as her maid. From there, he sailed safely to Europe. Betrayed later by a boatman, Flora was imprisoned in London until 1747.

Macdonald, Sir John Alexander (1815–91) Canadian statesman, first prime minister of the Dominion of CANADA (1867–73, 1878–91), b. Scotland. His parents settled in Canada in 1820, and he entered the assembly of the Province of Canada as a Conservative in 1844. Macdonald's ambition saw him quickly become leader of the government of Canada West. With Georges CARTIER, leader of Canada East, he formed the Liberal-Conservative Party, becoming prime minister of the Province of Canada (1857). Always keen to unify Canada, Macdonald and Cartier joined George BROWN in encouraging the BRITISH NORTH AMERICA ACT (1867), which announced a confederation of Canada's provinces (the Dominion of Canada). As prime minister, Macdonald strengthened the Dominion by introducing protective tariffs, encouraging W settlement and acquiring HUDSON'S BAY COMPANY lands (1869). His efforts to organize a transcontinental railway led to the PACIFIC SCANDAL and electoral defeat (1873). He returned as prime minister in 1878, serving until his death.

MacDonald, (James) Ramsay (1866–1937) British statesman, prime minister (1924, 1929–31, 1931–35), b. Scotland. He entered Parliament in 1906 and became leader of the LABOUR PARTY in 1911. His opposition to Britain's participation in World War 1 lost him the leadership in 1914 and his seat in 1918. Re-elected in 1922, he regained the party leadership and became Britain's first Labour prime minister. His minority government fell within months when the Liberals withdrew their support and right-wing sections of the press exploited the ZINOVIEV LETTER, which suggested that the Labour Party was following BOLSHEVIK orders. In 1929 he became prime minister again, but the GREAT DEPRESSION led to the collapse of the Labour government (1931). MacDonald remained as prime minister at the head of a Conservative-dominated National Government. Members of the Labour Party, including George LANSBURY, refused to join the National Government, further weakening MacDonald's position. In 1935 he resigned and was succeeded as prime minister by Stanley BALDWIN. Although MacDonald lost his parliamentary seat in the same year, he won a by-election and regained a cabinet post, which he retained until his death.

Macedon Ancient country in SE Europe, roughly corresponding to present-day MACEDONIA, Greek Macedonia and Bulgarian Macedonia. Little is known about the region until the 8th century BC, when Greek culture was first introduced by colonies that appeared along the coast. Perdiccas I established a ruling family in the S of the region by *c.*650 BC; however, by 500 BC Macedon had become a Persian vassal, following DARIUS I's invasion of THRACE. Macedon played little part in the PERSIAN WARS (499–479 BC) and remained a marginal state on the international political scene. The Macedonian king Alexander I (d.420 BC) initiated a process of Hellenization, but it was not until PHILIP II ascended the throne (359 BC) that Macedon became a significant power. Philip forged a professional army, unified Macedon and, having gained control of THESSALY, expanded into ILLYRIA and Thrace, bringing important harbours and gold mines into the empire. By 338 BC Philip was acknowledged as king of Greece. Following Philip's assassination in 336 BC, his son, ALEXANDER III (THE GREAT), built a world empire, but this rapidly fragmented after his death (323 BC). Macedon, after briefly enjoying some restoration of power under Antigonus II (r.276–239 BC), was eventually defeated by the Romans in the MACEDONIAN WARS, and the empire was restricted to Macedonia proper. In 146 BC THESSALONÍKI became capital of the first Roman province. In AD 395 Macedonia became part of the Eastern Roman (Byzantine) Empire. Slavs settled in the 6th century, and from the 9th to the 14th century, control of the area was contested mainly by Bulgaria and the BYZANTINE EMPIRE. A brief period of Serbian hegemony was followed by OTTOMAN rule from the 14th to 19th century. In the late 19th century, Macedonia was claimed by Greece, Serbia and Bulgaria. In the First BALKAN WAR (1912), Bulgaria gained much of historic Macedonia, but it was decisively defeated in the Second Balkan War (1913) and the present-day boundaries were established.

Macedonia Greek region, bordering the former Yugoslav Republic of MACEDONIA; the capital is THESSALONÍKI. A mountainous region, it includes many ancient sites, such as the former capital, Pella.

Macedonia *See* country feature, page 252

Macedonian Wars Three major conflicts between ROME and MACEDON. In the **First** Macedonian War (211–205 BC), PHILIP V opposed the AETOLIAN LEAGUE and, due partly to Rome's involvement with CARTHAGE in the PUNIC WARS, he was able to secure favourable terms from both Rome and Aetolia. The **Second** Macedonian War (200–196 BC) started after Philip threatened the Greek city-states. Philip's forces were crushed at Cynoscephalae, and Philip was forced to relinquish his navy and pay heavy tribute to Rome. Although Philip's indemnity was reduced after he cooperated with Rome, his son Perseus (r.179–168 BC) restrengthened Macedon, extended its influence, and threatened PERGAMUM, thus bringing about the **Third** Macedonian War (171–168 BC) in which Perseus lost his entire kingdom to Rome. Perseus was imprisoned in Rome, and Macedon was divided into four republics. Macedon was annexed as the first of the Roman provinces (146 BC) after the **Fourth** Macedonian War (149–148 BC).

MacGregor, Robert *See* ROB ROY

Machel, Samora Moisès (1933–86) Mozambique statesman, first president (1975–86). He joined FREMILO in 1962, fighting in the guerrilla war against Portuguese colonial rule. In 1970 Machel became president of FRELIMO and led the movement's delegation to the 1974 peace talks with Portugal. As president, Machel nationalized major industries, collectivized agriculture and improved welfare provisions. His support for sanctions and guerrilla action against the neighbouring white-minority regimes in Rhodesia (now Zimbabwe) and South Africa led to economic hardship and South African military support for the opposition Renamo faction. He died in a plane crash and was succeeded by Joaquím Chissano.

McHenry, James (1753–1816) American statesman and patriot, b. Ireland. After emigrating to Philadelphia (1771) he joined the Continental Army as a surgeon (1775). He was George WASHINGTON's private secretary (1778–80) and served in the Maryland senate, the CONTINENTAL CONGRESS (1783–86) and as a delegate to the CONSTITUTIONAL CONVENTION (1787). During his period as secretary of war (1796–1800), he clashed with President John ADAMS, who eventually forced his resignation.

Machiavelli, Niccolò (1469–1527) Florentine statesman and political theorist. He was made secretary and second chancellor (1498) in Piero SODERINI's republican government of FLORENCE. He served as a diplomat for the republic, meeting some of the most distinguished people of the age, including Cesare BORGIA, LOUIS XII and MAXIMILIAN I. He was dismissed when the MEDICI family returned to power in 1512. His most famous work, *The Prince* (1513), which some believe to be a parody of Cesare BORGIA, offered advice on how the ruler of a small state might best preserve his power, including judicious use of force. The term "Machiavellian", to describe immoral and deceitful political behaviour, arose from an over-simplification of Machiavelli's ideas. Whatever the true meaning behind *The Prince*, there is no doubting Machiavelli's passionate belief in republicanism (as expressed in his *Discourses on the first ten books of Titus*, 1531–21), and his sincere belief that only through a powerful state could citizens express and attain their own aspirations and needs.

Machu Picchu Ancient fortified town, 80km (50mi) NW of CUZCO, Peru. The best-preserved of the INCA settlements, it is situated on an Andean mountain saddle, 2057m (6750ft) above sea level. A complex of terraces extends over 13sq km (5sq mi), linked by more than 3000 steps. Machu Picchu was discovered (1911) by the US explorer Hiram BINGHAM, who dubbed it the "lost city of the Incas".

▲ **Mackenzie** and his expedition braved the rapids of the Peace and Fraser rivers on their journey W from Lake Athabasca to the Pacific coast of Canada (1792–93).

Mackenzie, Sir Alexander (1764–1820) Canadian fur trader and explorer, b. Scotland. He moved to Montréal in 1778, and in 1787 became a partner in the fur-trading NORTH WEST COMPANY. Mackenzie embarked on his first voyage in 1789. Travelling up to the Great Slave Lake, he continued N along the river that now bears his name for nearly 1600km (1000mi), finally reaching the Arctic Ocean. Disappointed at not reaching the Pacific, Mackenzie organized a second expedition, during which, with English and French settlers and Native Americans, he headed W along the Peace River and travelled 800km (500mi) to its source. Despite an accident in which they lost most of their supplies, Mackenzie's party managed to traverse the rugged Coast Range and ride down the Bella Coola River. In July 1793 Mackenzie reached the Pacific coast near Cape Menzies, thus completing the first crossing of the American continent N of Mexico. He recounted his expeditions in *Voyages...to the Frozen and Pacific Oceans* (1801). Although elected to the Legislative Assembly of Lower Canada (now Québec) in 1805, he returned to Scotland three years later, where he spent the rest of his life.

MacKenzie, William Lyon (1795–1861) Canadian politician, b. Scotland. He came to prominence with the founding (1824) of a newspaper, the *Colonial Advocate*, which attacked the "Family Compact" – a powerful, inner circle that controlled the Legislative Assembly of Upper Canada (now Ontario), many of whom were related. Between 1828 and 1836 MacKenzie was six times elected to and ejected from the Legislative Assembly for his espousal of independence. With Louis PAPINEAU, Mackenzie led the abortive REBELLION OF 1837 and was forced to escape to the United States where, following the CAROLINE AFFAIR, he was imprisoned for 18 months. Granted an amnesty in 1849, he returned to Canada and was elected to Parliament (1851–58), where he fought against big business and encouraged free education and universal suffrage. He was an early proponent of confederation.

McKinley, William (1843–1901) Twenty-fifth president of the United States (1897–1901). During the American Civil War (1861–65) he fought in the Union Army under the future president Rutherford HAYES. He served as a Republican in Congress (1877–91) and, as chairman of the Ways and Means Committee, sponsored the protectionist McKinley Tariff Act (1890) which, although unpopular with the public, ingratiated him with Ohio industrialists – one of whom, Marcus HANNA, became McKinley's political manager. McKinley was elected governor of Ohio in 1891 and re-elected in 1893. In 1895 Hanna began a successful campaign to win the 1896 presidential nomination for McKinley. In the subsequent election, McKinley's support for the tariff and maintenance of the gold standard helped him to victory over William Jennings BRYAN. A strong and effective president, McKinley was largely preoccupied by foreign affairs, declaring that ISOLATIONISM was "no longer possible or desirable". He gained the support of Congress for the SPANISH-AMERICAN WAR (1898) and sanctioned US support for the suppression of the BOXER REBELLION in China (1900), thereby gaining Cuba and greatly increasing US trading potential. McKinley was easily re-elected in 1900. On 6 September 1901, McKinley was shot dead by an anarchist in Buffalo, New York. He was succeeded by his vice president Theodore ROOSEVELT.

MacMahon, Marie Edmé Patrice Maurice, Comte de (1808–93) French soldier and statesman, second president (1873–79) of the Third Republic. He distinguished himself in the war against Austria (1859), gaining important victories at the battles of SOLFERINO and MAGENTA. Governor general of Algeria (1864–70), he was called to serve in the FRANCO-PRUSSIAN WAR but was overwhelmed at the Battle of Wörth (1870) and, along with NAPOLEON III, suffered a crushing defeat at SEDAN, where he was captured. On his release, MacMahon commanded the troops that suppressed the PARIS COMMUNE (1871). MacMahon was chosen by the royalists to succeed Adolphe THIERS as president, but was soon compelled to accept the republican constitution of 1875. In 1877 he forced the resignation of the republican premier, Jules Simon (1814–96), dissolved the largely republican chamber of deputies, appointed a royalist cabinet and called fresh elections. The new chamber, however, was even more republican and MacMahon, forced to agree to the formation of a republican-dominated ministry, resigned. In this way, the supremacy of Parliament over the president was established.

Macmillan, (Maurice) Harold (1894–1986) British statesman, prime minister (1957–63). He entered Parliament as a Conservative in 1924. A constant critic of the policy of APPEASEMENT towards Nazi Germany in the 1930s, he joined Winston CHURCHILL's government in 1940. After World War 2, Macmillan held a succession of cabinet posts, including minister of defence (1954–55) and chancellor of the exchequer (1955–57), before succeeding Anthony EDEN as prime minister. Macmillan improved Anglo-American relations, strained by the SUEZ CRISIS (1956), and sought a rapprochement between Moscow and Washington. His attempt to lead Britain into the European Economic Community (*see* EUROPEAN COMMUNITY) faltered in the face of French President Charles DE GAULLE's opposition. Macmillan's campaign on the theme of domestic prosperity ("You've never had it so good") won him a landslide victory in the 1959 general election. His second term was beset by recession and the PROFUMO scandal (1963), but he succeeded in negotiating the NUCLEAR TEST-BAN TREATY (1963) with US President John KENNEDY and Soviet Premier Nikita KHRUSHCHEV. Macmillan resigned on grounds of ill health and was succeeded by Alec DOUGLAS-HOME.

McNamara, Robert Strange (1916–) US statesman, secretary of defense (1961–68). Before joining John KENNEDY's cabinet he was a successful executive and president of the Ford Motor Company. As secretary of defense, McNamara won support from the Pentagon for his military reforms and reversed the military's dependence on nuclear weapons, encouraging instead a "flexible response" strategy. He initially supported the increasing military involvement of the United States in the VIETNAM WAR (1955–75) and acted as the government's chief spokesman on the progress of the conflict. In 1967, however, McNamara launched a major investigation of US military commitment in Vietnam (published later as *The Pentagon Papers*) and openly rejected the escalation of the bombing campaign in North Vietnam. He resigned to become president of the WORLD BANK (1968–81).

McPherson, Aimee Semple (1890–1944) US evangelist. In 1926 she founded the International Church of the Foursquare Gospel. Claiming to be guided by God, she professed faith healing and the gift of tongues, and her flamboyant methods were phenomenally successful. In May 1926 she disappeared while swimming, but reappeared a month later claiming to have been kidnapped. She was tried for fraud and, although acquitted, never regained her former influence.

Macquarie, Lachlan (1761–1824) Scottish colonial administrator, governor of NEW SOUTH WALES (1809–21). He became governor after Admiral William BLIGH had been overthrown by the New South Wales Corps. Macquarie helped develop the infrastructure of the colony and introduced a separate currency (1813). He encouraged the expansion of the colony by freed convicts (Emancipists) and sheep farmers, but opposition from large landowners forced his recall to Britain in 1821.

Madagascar *See* country feature

Madero, Francisco Indalecio (1873–1913) Mexican statesman, president (1911–13). He led democratic opposition to the dictator Porfirio DÍAZ, but was arrested on the eve of the 1910 elections and was forced to flee to the United States, where he called for a MEXICAN REVOLUTION. With the aid of "Pancho" VILLA and Emiliano ZAPATA, Madero overthrew Díaz and won a landslide victory in the subsequent elections. He proved a weak president and the revolutionary movement rapidly and violently fragmented. He was murdered in a military coup led by his former general, Victoriano HUERTA.

MACEDONIA (FORMER YUGOSLAV REPUBLIC OF)

AREA: 24,900sq km (9600sq mi)
POPULATION: 2,174,000
CAPITAL (POPULATION): Skopje (440,577)
GOVERNMENT: Multiparty republic
ETHNIC GROUPS: Macedonian 65%, Albanian 21%, Turkish 5%, Romanian 3%, Serb 2%
LANGUAGES: Macedonian
RELIGIONS: Christianity (mainly Eastern Orthodox, with Macedonian Orthodox and Roman Catholic communities), Islam
GDP PER CAPITA (1994): US$1552

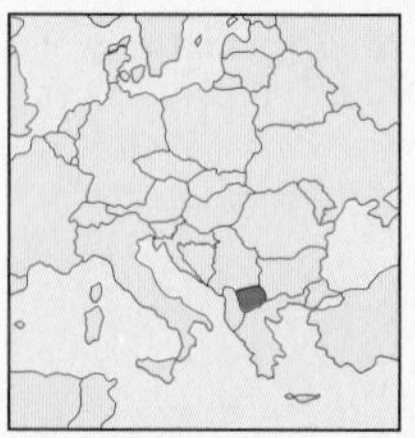

Balkan republic in SE Europe (for history pre-1913, *see* MACEDON). The BALKAN WARS (1912–13) ended with the flight of thousands of Macedonians into Bulgaria and the division of Macedonia into Greek Macedonia, Bulgarian Macedonia and Serbian Macedonia (the largest portion, in the N and centre).

At the end of World War 1, Serbian Macedonia became part of the Kingdom of the Serbs, Croats and Slovenes (later YUGOSLAVIA). Macedonian nationalists waged an armed struggle against Serbian domination. Between 1941 and 1944, Bulgaria occupied all Macedonia, but a peace treaty restored the 1913 settlement. In 1946 President TITO created the Federation of Yugoslavia, with Macedonia as one of its constituent republics.

Multiparty elections in 1990 produced the first non-communist regional government since 1945, and the break-up of Yugoslavia led to Macedonia's declaration of independence in September 1991. Kiro Gligorov became the republic's first president. However, the European Union (EU) – under pressure from Greece – refused to recognize Macedonian sovereignty on the grounds that its name, flag and currency were signs of its territorial intentions towards Greek Macedonia. In a compromise agreement the country became known as the Former Yugoslav Republic of Macedonia (FYRM). The new republic was faced by riots from the ethnic Albanian minority in 1992. In 1993 Macedonia was admitted to the United Nations (UN). Greece banned Macedonian trade across its borders in 1994, but the embargo was lifted when Macedonia agreed to redesign its flag and remove any claims to Greek Macedonia from its constitution in 1995. The war in the Serbian province of Kosovo (1999) led to the influx of *c.*245,000 ethnic Albanian refugees. In 1999 Gligorov was replaced as president by Boris Trajkovski.

Madison, James (1751–1836) Fourth president of the United States (1809–17). He drafted Virginia's charter of religious freedom (1776) for Thomas JEFFERSON and was sent to represent the state at the CONTINENTAL CONGRESS (1780). Madison was a leading figure in the CONSTITUTIONAL CONVENTION (1787) and played the major role in the subsequent framing of the CONSTITUTION OF THE UNITED STATES, earning him the title of "father of the Constitution". Madison, John JAY and Alexander HAMILTON jointly published *The* FEDERALIST (1787–88), which eloquently argued for the ratification of the Constitution. Elected to the newly created House of Representatives (1789–97), Madison sponsored the first ten amendments to the Constitution, collectively known as the BILL OF RIGHTS. He disagreed with Secretary of the Treasury Alexander HAMILTON's plans for the formation of the BANK OF THE UNITED STATES and Congress split into factions: Madison allied himself with Jefferson and the DEMOCRATIC-REPUBLICAN PARTY. He opposed JAY'S TREATY (1794) and helped draft the KENTUCKY AND VIRGINIA RESOLUTIONS against the ALIEN AND SEDITION ACTS (1798). Madison served as secretary of state (1801–09) under Thomas Jefferson and succeeded him as president. Madison's two terms in office were marked by the deterioration in relations with Britain, culminating in the WAR OF 1812 (1812–15). The United States initially suffered a succession of defeats, and the FEDERALIST PARTY opposition convened the HARTFORD CONVENTION (1814–15). The War turned after the British capture of the city of Washington (1814), and Andrew JACKSON won a decisive victory at the Battle of NEW ORLEANS (1815). Although the War ended in stalemate, it did foster a greater sense of nation and Madison retired to his Virginia plantation as an admired elder statesman. *See also* ADAMS, JOHN; CALHOUN, JOHN CALDWELL; CLAY, HENRY; CLINTON, GEORGE; EMBARGO ACT; FEDERALIST PARTY; HARRISON, WILLIAM HENRY; HENRY, PATRICK; LOUISIANA PURCHASE; MONROE, JAMES; WASHINGTON, GEORGE

Madrid Capital and largest city of Spain. Madrid was founded as a Moorish fortress, but was captured by Ramiro II of León in 932. It later passed back to the Moors, but again was retaken by Alfonso VI of Castile and León in 1083. In 1561 PHILIP II moved the capital from Valladolid to Madrid. The city expanded rapidly under HABSBURG and BOURBON rulers in the 17th and 18th centuries. Major sights from this period include the Plaza Mayor (1617–19), the Royal Palace begun (1734) by PHILIP V, and the Puerta del Sol built (1778) by CHARLES III. The French occupied the city during the PENINSULAR WAR (1808–14), when Napoleon's brother, Joseph BONAPARTE, was installed as king. The city expanded considerably in the 19th century, particularly in ISABELLA II's reign. During the Spanish CIVIL WAR (1936–39), Madrid remained loyal to the Republican cause and was under siege for almost three years before falling to Franco's forces. Modern Madrid is a thriving cosmopolitan centre of commerce and industry. Pop. (1991) 2,909,792.

Maecenas, Gaius (70–08 BC) Roman diplomat. He was a counsellor of Octavian (later Emperor AUGUSTUS), helping to win the support of Mark ANTONY. While Octavian was absent on military campaigns, Maecenas shared power with AGRIPPA in Rome. He is perhaps best remembered for his patronage of poets such as Horace and Virgil.

Mafeking, Siege of (1899–1900) Onslaught during the Second SOUTH AFRICAN WAR. British troops, led by Robert BADEN-POWELL, were held in Mafeking, N South Africa, by Afrikaner (Boer) forces for 217 days. The lifting of the Siege was a cause for national celebration in England.

Mafia (It. boldness) Name once given to organized groups of Sicilian bandits. Originating in the late Middle Ages, it is believed that the Mafia was formed to combat foreign occupation of Sicily. By the mid-19th century the Mafia, once hired by absentee landlords to protect their estates, began to extract money from the landowners for "protecting" their crops. Over time, the various families formed a loose confederation that abided by their own codes rather than the rule of law. Many members of the Mafia moved to the United States, particularly New York and Chicago, in the late 19th and early 20th centuries. They assumed the title *Cosa Nostra* (It. Our Business) and became involved in organized crime during the PROHIBITION era. After World War 2 their activities became increasingly international, much of it centred on the lucrative drugs trade. To legitimize the money they made, the Mafia invested in legal businesses, although they also maintained illegal businesses such as organized prostitution, illicit gambling and kidnapping. By the late 20th century the influence of the Mafia in the United States began to wane. Internal disputes, defections by senior figures and convictions reduced their numbers. In s Italy and Sicily, however, they still retain enormous influence despite periodic convictions.

Magadha Ancient kingdom in NE India, comprising present-day Gaya and Patna districts of Bihar. Strategically located in the Ganges valley, it had control of river trade and communications. Its capital was originally at Rajgir, but was later moved to Pataliputra. During the reign (*c*.543–491 BC) of Bimbisara, Magadha expanded to include the kingdom of Anga. Magadha was the heart of both the MAURYA EMPIRE, which at its height (*c*.2nd century BC) included most of the Indian subcontinent, and the GUPTA dynasty. An early centre of both Buddhism and Jainism, it was captured by Muslims.

Magdala Fortified village in central Ethiopia. Emperor Tewodros II (r.1855–68) made it the capital of a unified Ethiopian kingdom. In 1868, due to a supposed diplomatic slight, Tewodros imprisoned the British consul and other diplomats. The gravity of the situation heightened, and a force of 32,000 British soldiers under the command of Robert NAPIER was dispatched. They attacked the village and released the captives. The British destroyed the village and Tewodros committed suicide. It has since been rebuilt.

Magdalenian culture Archaeologically the most recent culture of the PALAEOLITHIC AGE. Named after the cave of La Madeleine in the Dordogne region of SE France, where the first remains were found, the culture includes the great cave painters of ALTAMIRA and LASCAUX. Magdalenians also made fine tools, weapons and artistic carvings in stone and bone. In Britain, Kent's cavern in Devon, s England, and Creswell Crags in Derbyshire, central England, are among the few verified Magdalenian sites.

Magellan, Ferdinand (1480–1521) Portuguese explorer, leader of the first expedition to circumnavigate the globe. After falling from MANUEL I of Portugal's favour, Magellan won the financial support of CHARLES V of Spain to seek a W route to the Spice Islands (MOLUCCAS). In September 1519 he set out from Spain with nearly 300 men in five small vessels – *Trinidad* (his flagship), *San Antonio*, *Concepción*, *Vittoria* and *Santiago*. Four ships reached the channel, now called the Magellan Strait, in October, but during the tortuous passage through it, the *San Antonio* deserted and returned to Spain. *Trinidad*, *Concepción* and *Vittoria* reached the ocean, which Magellan named the Pacific, in late November, and began the long NW crossing. After 98 days they discovered Samar on the Philippines, and shortly afterwards they went on to Cebu, where Magellan joined in a local dispute. He and several leaders of the fleet were killed. The survivors escaped with two ships to the Spice Islands. Only the *Vittoria*, commanded by Sebastian del CANO, completed the circumnavigation of the globe.

Magenta, Battle of (4 June 1859) Conflict in Lombardy, N Italy. A combined French and Sardinian force, led by NAPOLEON III, narrowly defeated an Austrian army led by General Franz Gyulai. The defeat spurred the RISORGIMENTO movement and paved the way for the Italian republican movement to take control of Lombardy and Milan. It was followed by the Battle of SOLFERINO two weeks later. General MACMAHON was rewarded with the title Duke of Magenta for his involvement. The Battle claimed *c*.4600 French lives and *c*.10,200 Austrians.

Maginot Line French fortifications running from Switzerland to Belgium along France's border with Germany. Designed to prevent a German invasion, it was built between the World Wars (work starting in 1929) and named after André Maginot, French minister of war (1929–32). It contained its own underground railway, hospitals and barracks and was considered impregnable. When the Germans invaded France in 1940, however, they advanced through Belgium, outflanking the Maginot Line. *See also* WORLD WAR 2

Maglemosian culture In archaeology, N European culture of the middle MESOLITHIC AGE, named after a site in Denmark. In common with other Mesolithic peoples, Maglemosians lived by fishing and food gathering. Their tools included bone harpoons, microliths (small flint tools) and stone axes for felling trees. Maglemosians are believed to have migrated from Denmark to Britain across what is now the s North Sea but was then marshland.

Magna Carta (June 1215) "Great Charter" of English constitutional history. It was issued by King JOHN of England, who was forced to sign the charter by his rebellious barons at Runnymede, s England. John's financial extractions, to pay for overseas conflicts, had united the clergy and laity in demands for guarantees of their rights and privileges. The 63 clauses of the Magna Carta were mainly concerned with defining, and therefore limiting, the feudal rights of the king and royal officials, while at the same time protecting the privileges of the church and rights of the feudal lords, merchants and town boroughs. Other clauses, although vaguely worded, were interpreted to ensure the right of trial and justice to all freemen. One of the final clauses underpins the Charter by stating that a number of barons had the right to enforce the king's acceptance by military means if necessary. While it failed to prevent the first BARONS' WAR (1215), and was often disregarded by subsequent kings, it has endured as a key text of the English constitution. *See also* LANGTON, STEPHEN

Magnus I (the Good) (1024–47) King of Norway (1035–47) and Denmark (1042–47). He was the illegitimate son of OLAF II, with whom he went to Russia following Olaf's forced exile at the hands of CANUTE II (THE GREAT). In 1035 the Norwegian chiefs, opposed to the rule of Canute's son Sweyn, recalled Magnus and elected him king. Magnus made a treaty with Canute's other son, HARDECANUTE of Denmark, in which each, in the event of neither producing an heir, would succeed the other. Magnus succeeded Hardecanute in Denmark and claimed England as well. His rule in Denmark was challenged, however, by Canute's nephew Sweyn Estridsson. Worried by the threat of the WENDS, the Danish nobility rallied to Magnus and defeated the claims of Sweyn. After 1045 he shared the Norwegian kingdom with his uncle, HARALD III. Magnus' death in battle against the Danes prevented him from acceding to the English throne.

Magnus VI (the Law-Mender) (1238–80) King of Norway (1263–80). He succeeded his father, HAAKON IV, and made peace with the Scots by ceding the Hebrides and the Isle of Man (1266) in return for an annual tribute. He introduced a new legal code (1274), replacing local legal systems with a national system, and establishing a crime as an offence against the state rather than against the individual. In this way he reduced the custom of personal revenge which tended to exacerbate lawlessness. He also reached an agreement with the church, the Concordat of Tonsberg (1277), delimiting the powers of church and state. The pact increased the church's independence and revenue.

MADAGASCAR

AREA: 587,040sq km (226,656sq mi)
POPULATION: 12,827,000
CAPITAL (POPULATION): Antananarivo (802,000)
GOVERNMENT: Republic
ETHNIC GROUPS: Merina 27%, Betsimisaraka 15%, Betsileo 11%, Tsimihety 7%, Sakalava 6%
LANGUAGES: Malagasy (official), French, English
RELIGIONS: Christianity 51%, traditional beliefs 47%, Islam 2%
GDP PER CAPITA (1995): US$640

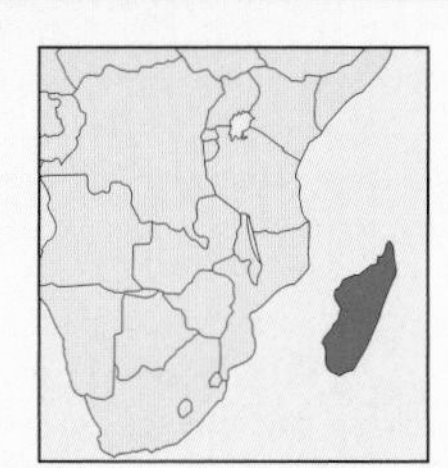

Republic in the Indian Ocean. Madagascar is the fourth-largest island in the world and one of the poorest regions on Earth. Africans and Indonesians arrived more than 1400 years ago, and Muslims landed in the 9th century. In the early 17th century, Portuguese missionaries vainly sought to convert the native population. Madagascar was divided into small kingdoms in the 17th century. In the early 19th century, the Merina began to subdue smaller tribes and by the 1870s they controlled nearly all the island.

In the early 1880s the French began to exert greater influence, culminating in the formation of a protectorate in 1885. In 1896 the French defeated the Merina, the monarchy was abolished, and Malagasy (as the island was then known) became a French colony. During World War 2 Vichy colonial rule was overthrown by the British in 1942, and the Free French reasserted control. In 1946–48 a rebellion against French rule was brutally dispatched, and as many as 80,000 islanders died.

In 1958 republican status was adopted and Madagascar achieved full independence in 1960. President Philibert Tsiranana's autocratic government adopted many unpopular policies, such as the advocacy of economic relationships with South Africa's apartheid regime. In 1972 the military took control of government. In 1975 Malagasy was renamed Madagascar, and Lieutenant Commander Didier RATSIRAKA proclaimed martial law and banned opposition parties. During the 1980s Madagascar was beset by civil strife and numerous failed coups. In 1991 the opposition formed a rival government, led by Albert Zafy. In 1993 multiparty elections Zafy became president. In 1995 he was granted the right of prime ministerial appointment. In 1996 Zafy was impeached. In the 1997 elections Ratsiraka regained the presidency. Madagascar was devastated by floods and tropical storms in 2000.

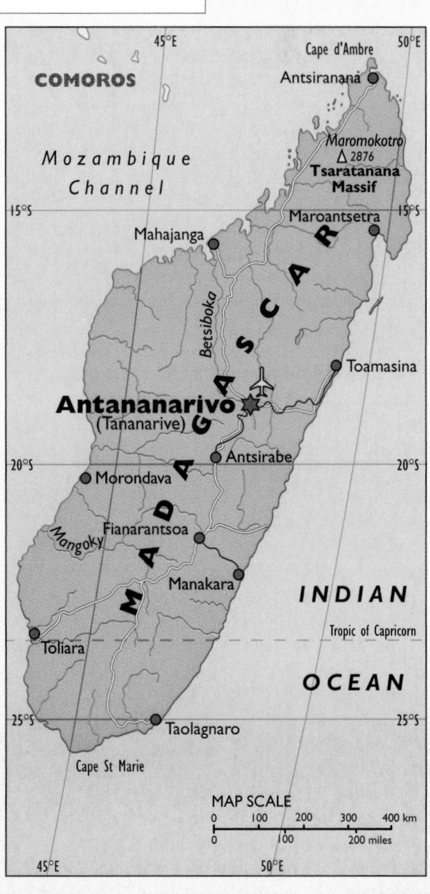

Magnus VII (1316–74) (Magnus Ericsson) King of Norway (1319–55) and Sweden (as Magnus II) (1319–63). Magnus acceded to the thrones of both Sweden and Norway on the death of his grandfather Haakon V. Educated in Sweden, Magnus neglected the interests of Norway and eventually abdicated in favour of his son, Haakon VI. He also aroused enmity in Sweden by increasing taxes and reducing the powers of the church and nobility. Magnus was defeated in a rebellion led by his son Eric and supported by Valdemar IV of Denmark. Magnus was forced to cede half of Sweden to Eric, but on his death (1359) resumed control over the whole kingdom. To combat the threat of the increasingly powerful HANSEATIC LEAGUE Magnus arranged the marriage of Haakon VI to Valdemar's daughter Margaret, prefiguring the KALMAR UNION (1397) between Norway, Sweden and Denmark. The Swedish nobles opposed the alliance and Magnus was deposed (1363) and imprisoned until 1371.

Magsaysay, Ramón (1907–57) Philippine statesman, president (1953–57). He fought against Japanese occupation during World War 2, and later served two terms (1946–50) as a congressman for the Liberal Party. In 1950 President Elpidio Quirino appointed him secretary of defence, primarily in order to defeat the HUKBALAHAP rebellion. Magsaysay accomplished this goal by reorganizing the army and by cutting off popular support for the rebellion from the peasantry by offering land reform. His radical approach alienated government colleagues, however, and he was forced to resign from the Liberal Party. In 1953 he opposed Quirino and won the presidency with the support of the Nationalist Party. Magsaysay's hopes of introducing further land and governmental reforms were dashed by a conservative congress that was closely allied with the wealthy landowners. He was a constant critic of communist expansion in Southeast Asia and led the Philippines into the SOUTHEAST ASIA TREATY ORGANIZATION (SEATO) in 1954. He died in an air crash.

M

Magyars People who founded the kingdom of HUNGARY in the late 9th century. From their homeland in NE Europe, they moved gradually S over the centuries and occupied the Carpathian Basin in 895, suppressing the indigenous SLAVS and HUNS. Excellent horsemen, the Magyars raided the German lands to the W until checked by OTTO I at the Battle of LECHFELD (955). They consolidated their territory, adopted Christianity and proceeded to establish a powerful state that included much of the N Balkans, but lost territory to the Ottoman Turks after the Battle of MOHÁCS (1526). The remainder of the kingdom subsequently fell to the Austrian HABSBURGS.

Mahabharata (Sanskrit, Great Epic of the Bharata dynasty) Poem of *c*.100,000 couplets, written between *c*.400 BC–*c*.AD 200. It is considered one of India's two major Sanskrit epics (the other being the Ramayana). The verse is important both as literature and as Hindu religious instruction and incorporates the BHAGAVAD GITA (Song of the Lord). Its central theme is the dynastic feud between the Kauravas and the Pandavas.

Mahathir bin Muhammad (1925–) Malaysian statesman, prime minister (1981–). He was a founder member of the United Malays' National Organization (UMNO) in 1946 and entered parliament in 1964. Mahathir lost his seat in the 1969 elections and was expelled from UMNO for his trenchant criticisms of Prime Minister Tunku Abdul RAHMAN. He returned to government in 1974 and served as deputy prime minister (1976–81). He succeeded Hussein bin Onn as prime minister and leader of UMNO in 1981. His premiership, noted for its promotion of industrialization and of Islamic and Malay values in the face of "corrupting" Western influences, began to suffer in the late 1990s due to a regional economic collapse. The depression brought about a split between Mahathir and his Finance Minister Anwar Ibrahim. Mahathir accused Ibrahim of corruption and sodomy, and Ibrahim's resulting conviction for corruption led to demonstrations and demands for Mahathir's resignation. Mahathir was re-elected in November 1999.

Mahavira (*c*.599–527 BC) (Sanskrit, great hero) Last of the 24 founders of JAINISM. Born into a privileged family, at the age of 30 he rejected his wealth and became a monk. For the next 12 years he lived the life of an extreme ascetic, travelling naked through the countryside preaching non-violence. After this period he attained *kevala*, the highest level of consciousness, and created a brotherhood of monks who strictly adhered to the Jaina religious life. His guidelines are adequately expressed in his five *maharratas*: rejection of killing, lying, greed, sexual pleasure and attachments to living and non-living things.

Mahayana (Sanskrit, greater vehicle) One of the two main schools of BUDDHISM, the other being THERAVADA. Mahayana Buddhism was dominant in India from the 1st to the 12th century and is now prevalent in Tibet, China, Korea and Japan. Unlike the Theravada school, it conceives of the BUDDHA as divine, the embodiment of the absolute and eternal truth. Mahayana also stresses compassion as well as wisdom as necessary for salvation, and is more universal in its appeal than the more conservative Theravada. The bodhisattva ("being destined for enlightenment") is seen as the ideal of human life.

Mahican (Mohican) Algonquian-speaking tribe of NATIVE NORTH AMERICANS. Once numbering *c*.3000 they inhabited a region of the upper Hudson River valley, New York, E to the Housatonic River in Connecticut. Living in groups of 20 or so dwellings, they survived on a diet of fish and cereal crops, supplemented by goods exchanged with European fur traders. In 1664 a combination of war with the MOHAWK and the arrival of Dutch settlers gradually enforced their move to Stockbridge, Massachusetts. Over the next 50 years, while some remained at Stockbridge others dispersed, merging with other tribes. Today, the surviving 600 or so Mahicans occupy the Stockbridge-Munsee Reservation, Wisconsin.

Mahdi (Arabic, Right-Guided One) Messianic Islamic leader. In the SUNNI form of ISLAM, the Mahdi is seen as the saviour who will establish universal justice and Islam at the end of the world. Although it has been used by a number of Islamic reformers, the title is most commonly associated with **Muhammad Ahmad** (1844–85) of SUDAN. In 1881 he declared himself to be the Mahdi and set out to overthrow Egyptian-Turkish rule. He managed to unify the many disparate groups and within four years had created a vast Islamic empire. His campaign concluded with the capture of KHARTOUM (1885), during which British General Charles GORDON was killed. Al-Mahdi established his capital at Omdurman, but died within six months of establishing the empire. His followers, led by Abdullah ibn Muhammad (1846–99) were defeated at Omdurman (1898) by a combined Anglo-Egyptian force under the command of General Horatio KITCHENER.

MAINE
Statehood :
15 March 1820
Nickname :
Pine Tree State
State motto :
I direct

Mahmud II (1785–1839) Ottoman sultan (1808–39), son of Abdul Hamid I. His accession was marked by revolts and the murder of his uncle SELIM III. Mahmud was immediately confronted with the collapse of the OTTOMAN EMPIRE in the Balkans and was forced to cede Bessarabia to Russia (1812) and grant considerable autonomy to Serbia (1815). He called for assistance from his Egyptian viceroy MUHAMMAD ALI in an attempt to crush the GREEK WAR OF INDEPENDENCE (1821–29), but was defeated by a coalition of European powers at the Battle of NAVARINO (1827) and was forced to acknowledge Greek independence after defeat in the RUSSO-TURKISH WAR (1828–29). Mahmud was now faced by a revolt in Syria, led by Muhammad Ali and his son Ibrahim Pasha. The rebels captured Damascus and Aleppo, before advancing into Turkey and seizing Konya (1839). Mahmud's internal reforms included the massacre (1826) of the JANISSARIES, enabling him to begin the reorganization of the civil service and the army. He was succeeded by his son, ABDUL MEDJID I. *See also* ALI PASHA; KARAGEORGE; SELIM III

Mahmud of Ghazna (971–1030) Sultan of the kingdom of Ghazna (998–1030), founder of the GHAZNAVID dynasty. From his base in what is now Afghanistan and NE Iran, he built an Islamic empire that stretched from the River Oxus (now the Amudarya) to the Indus Valley and the Indian Ocean, encompassing most of Iran and NW India. He massacred two large Indian armies in 1001 and 1008, thereby gaining the Punjab. Mahmud used the wealth that he looted from Hindu temples to transform his capital, Ghazna (Afghanistan), into the most splendid city in Central Asia.

Maimonides, Moses (1135–1204) Jewish philosopher, Hebrew scholar and physician, b. Spain. As a youth, he was attracted to Aristotelian philosophy, which influenced his *Guide of the Perplexed* (1176–91), a plea for a more rational philosophy of JUDAISM. In 1159 Maimonides emigrated to Egypt after the ALMOHADS captured his native Córdoba, S Spain. In Cairo, he became court physician to SALADIN and was the recognized leader of Egyptian Jewry. His *Mishneh Torah* (1180) is a systematic compilation of Jewish oral law. Other works on Jewish law and philosophy and on medicine confirmed him as one of the most influential thinkers of the Middle Ages.

Maine State in N NEW ENGLAND, United States; the capital is Augusta. When Europeans explored the region in the early 16th century, it was inhabited by Alqonquian-speaking Native North Americans. French explorer Samuel de CHAMPLAIN established a short-lived settlement on St Croix Island in 1605, and the first British settlement, Fort St George (1607), likewise was soon abandoned. Firm colonization began in the 1620s (when it became known as Maine) under the leadership of Ferdinando Gorges, who had been granted proprietorial rights by Charles I of England. In 1677 Maine was granted to the MASSACHUSETTS BAY COMPANY. English settlers fought against the Native Americans in KING PHILIP'S WAR (1675–76), and the FRENCH AND INDIAN WARS (1689–1763) ended French colonial ambitions and native resistance to British rule. Maine entered the Union as a free state under the terms of the MISSOURI COMPROMISE (1820). Disputes over its NE boundary with

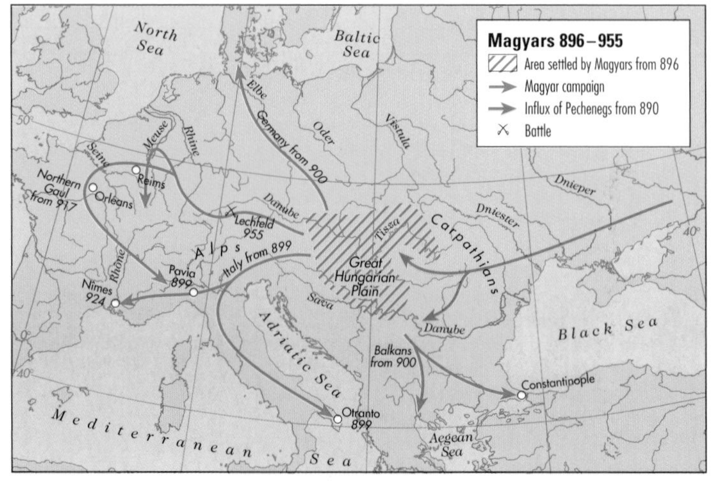

► **Magyars** Driven W by the the arrival of the Pechenegs on the Ukrainian steppe in *c*.895, the Magyars settled on the Great Hungarian Plain. Having destroyed the Moravian empire (906), they repelled the attacks of German forces (907). During the first half of the 10th century, they terrorized central, S and parts of W Europe with widespread raids. Magyar expansion was curbed by King Henry I (the Fowler), at Thüringen, Germany (933), and eventually halted by Otto I (955), forcing the Magyars to integrate into mainstream European culture.

Canada led to the so-called AROOSTOOK WAR (1838–39). After the Civil War (1861–65), the Republican Party dominated state politics until Democrat Edmund Muskie was elected governor in 1954. Pop. (1990) 1,127,928.

Maine, USS US battleship mysteriously blown up and sunk in the harbour of Havana, Cuba, on 15 February 1898. The destruction of the *Maine* was one of the precipitating factors in the outbreak of the SPANISH-AMERICAN WAR. With Cubans in revolt against Spain, the ship had been sent to protect US citizens, and the bombing was attributed to foreign enemies. The cry "Remember the *Maine*" incited war fever, and conflict began in April 1898.

Maintenon, Françoise d'Aubigné, Marquise de (1635–1719) Mistress and second wife of LOUIS XIV of France. The impoverished widow of the writer Paul Scarron (1610–60), she was entrusted with the care of the king's illegitimate children by their mother and her former friend, the Marquise de Montespan (1641–1707). She gradually replaced Montespan in the king's affections, becoming his mistress in *c.*1678. After the death of Queen Marie Thérèse (1684), Louis contracted a secret, morganatic marriage to Maintenon and she came to wield influence on the king and on court life. Maintenon founded a school at Saint-Cyr, near Paris, for the education of daughters of poor nobles. She was widely (and probably unfairly) blamed for the errors of Louis' later reign.

Majapahit Hindu empire based in E JAVA between the 13th and 16th centuries. It was founded (*c.*1292) by Vijaya who soon also took control of Bali. By 1319 the ruling family had become firmly established, paving the way for the golden era of the Majapahit empire under the leadership of King Hayam Wuruk (r.1350–89). According to an epic poem, the Majapahit empire encompassed most of modern Indonesia, including BORNEO and SUMATRA, and part of Malaysia, including the MALAY PENINSULA. Following Hayam Wuruk's death, the empire was divided between his sons, and this, coupled with the growth of Islamic states on the N coast of Java, saw the decline of the empire until it finally disappeared in the early 16th century.

Major, John (1943–) British statesman, prime minister (1990–97). He entered Parliament in 1979. In 1989 Margaret THATCHER unexpectedly made him foreign secretary then chancellor of the exchequer. Following Thatcher's resignation, Major emerged as her compromise successor. He moderated the excesses of Thatcherism, such as scrapping the unpopular poll tax. Major lent military support to the United States in the GULF WAR (1991), and led the CONSERVATIVE PARTY to a surprise victory in the 1992 elections. The catastrophic events of "Black Wednesday" (16 September 1992) forced Britain to withdraw from the EUROPEAN MONETARY SYSTEM (EMS) and devalue the currency. The issue of Europe haunted the rest of his term and fractured the Conservative Party. Political scandals and sleaze contributed to Tony BLAIR's landslide victory at the 1997 general election. Major resigned as party leader and was succeeded by William HAGUE.

Makarios III (1913–77) Greek-Cypriot archbishop, first president of Cyprus (1959–77). In 1950 Makarios was appointed Greek Orthodox archbishop of CYPRUS and led the movement for ENOSIS (union with Greece). In 1956 Makarios was deported by the British, who believed that he was secretly supporting the EOKA terrorist movement. In 1959 Makarios returned to Cyprus, becoming the first president of an independent Cyprus. He promoted a peaceful settlement between the Greek and Turkish factions. He was re-elected in 1968 and again in 1973. In 1974 he was briefly overthrown by Greek Cypriots still demanding *enosis*. The coup provoked unrest among Turkish Cypriots and led to a Turkish invasion. Makarios was unable to prevent the subsequent partition of Cyprus into Greek and Turkish sections. *See also* ORTHODOX CHURCH, EASTERN

Malacca (Melaka) State, and former sultanate, in MALAYSIA, SW Malay Peninsula; the capital is Malacca. The history of the Malaccan sultanate begins with the founding (*c.*1403) of the city of Malacca by a Malay prince, Paramesvara, who was seeking refuge from the MAJAPAHIT empire. Paramesvara was converted to Islam, taking the title Sultan Iskandar Shah. With the decline of the Majapahit empire and with China as an ally (albeit one that demanded tribute), Malacca prospered on the trade in spices from the MOLUCCAS and porcelain and silk from China. The Muslim sultanate of Malacca became the region's most powerful empire and the centre for the spread of Islam throughout Malaya. In 1511 Malacca was conquered by the Portuguese under the command of Alfonso d'ALBURQUERQUE. In 1641 Malacca passed to the Dutch and in 1824 it was ceded to Britain. In 1957 it became a state of independent Malaya and, in 1963, of Malaysia. Pop. (1993 est.) 583,400.

Malan, Daniel François (1874–1959) South African statesman, prime minister (1948–54). A strong advocate of South African independence, he entered Parliament in 1918. In 1924 he joined James HERTZOG's cabinet as minister for the interior, promoting South African nationhood and Afrikaans, the language of the AFRIKANERS. When Hertzog teamed up with the more liberal Jan SMUTS, Malan left the government and set up the opposition Purified National Party. Hertzog and Malan advocated South African neutrality at the start of World War 2 and they reunified the NATIONAL PARTY in 1939. Malan succeeded Hertzog as leader of the Party in 1940, and secured victory in the 1948 elections. As prime minister, Malan formed the first all-Afrikaner government of South Africa and began to implement the policy of APARTHEID. He was succeeded as prime minister and leader of the Party by Johannes STRIJDOM.

Malawi *See* country feature

MALAWI

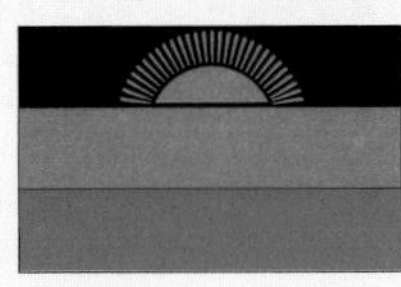

AREA: 118,480sq km (45,745sq mi)
POPULATION: 8,823,000
CAPITAL (POPULATION): Lilongwe (268,000)
GOVERNMENT: Multiparty republic
ETHNIC GROUPS: Maravi (Chewa, Nyanja, Tonga, Tumbuka) 58%, Lomwe 18%, Yao 13%, Ngoni 7%
LANGUAGES: Chichewa and English (both official)
RELIGIONS: Christianity (Protestant 34%, Roman Catholic 28%), traditional beliefs 21%, Islam 16%
GDP PER CAPITA (1995): US$750

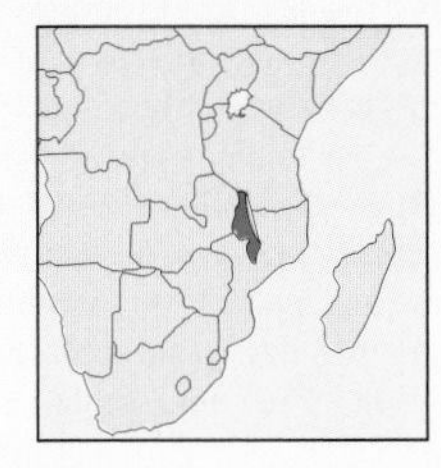

Republic in E central Africa. Archaeological evidence suggests the region was inhabited as early as 50,000 BC, and early human remains found here date to *c.*8000 BC. The region was later inhabited by the SAN, who were gradually displaced by Bantu-speakers between the 1st and 4th centuries AD. In *c.*1480 the Maravi Confederacy was founded by a second wave of Bantu-speakers. By the 17th century, the Confederacy had gained influence, not only over s Malawi but also into neighbouring modern-day ZAMBIA and MOZAMBIQUE. By the early 19th century, the area had become a centre of the slave trade. During this period the Bantu-speakers were gradually suppressed by the Ngoni and Yao peoples, themselves fierce rivals. Christianity was introduced by David LIVINGSTONE in the 1860s and underpinned by later Presbyterian missionaries.

In 1891 Malawi, partly through fear of Portuguese annexation and partly under pressure from Cecil RHODES, became a British protectorate: slavery was abolished and coffee plantations were established. In 1907 it became known as Nyasaland. In 1915 a rebellion against British domination was suppressed, and in 1953 Nyasaland became part of the Federation of RHODESIA AND NYASALAND, a move bitterly opposed by the African population. This opposition was voiced through the Malawi Congress Party under the leadership of Dr Hastings BANDA. He organized a number of demonstrations that led the British to declare a state of emergency in 1959. In 1963 the Federation was dissolved, and in 1964 Nyasaland achieved independence as Malawi. Banda was the first post-colonial prime minister, and when Malawi became a republic (1966), he was made president. Malawi became a one-party state, and in 1967 Banda's autocratic government established diplomatic relations with South Africa's APARTHEID government. In 1971, as the newly appointed president-for-life, Banda became the first post-colonial, black African head of state to visit South Africa. Malawi became a shelter for rebels and refugees from the civil war in Mozambique – more than 600,000 were accommodated in the late 1980s. Banda's repression of opposition became more brutal and in 1992 international famine-relief aid was tied to improvements in human rights and democratic reforms. These conditions, coupled with widespread internal unrest, prompted Banda to call a referendum in October 1992 resulting in the approval of a multiparty democracy. In 1994 elections Banda and his Malawi Congress Party were defeated and Bakili Muluzi of the United Democratic Front became president. In 1995 Banda and his close associates were acquitted of murder charges.

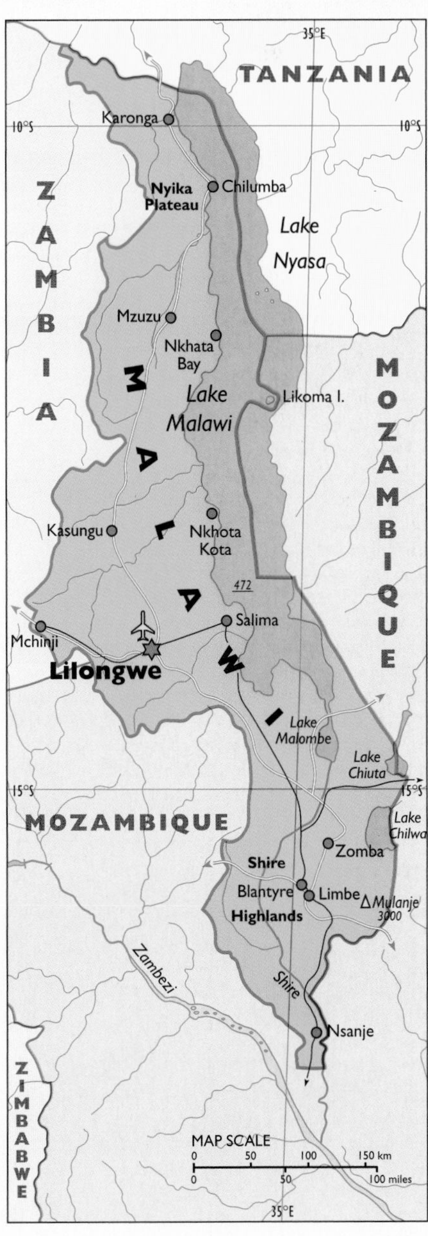

Malay Peninsula Promontory in Southeast Asia, stretching for *c.*1100km (700mi) between the Strait of Malacca and the South China Sea. Early influences on the region came from Indian traders in the 1st century AD. Subsequent centuries saw the establishment of Buddhist and Brahman missions and Hindu colonies. From the 8th to the 13th century the region was controlled by the Buddhist Sailendra dynasty from Sumatra, apart from a brief period in the 11th century when the region fell under the control of the Chola. With the decline of the Sailendra dynasty, ruling power passed to the Majapahit dynasty. In the 15th century the Malacca empire held sway. *See also* Malaysia

Malayan Emergency (1948–60) Predominantly Chinese communist insurrection against British-controlled Malaya. In 1948 the British created the Federation of Malaya, during which ethnic Malayans were guaranteed rights that indirectly ensured their dominance over the Chinese population. The more radical Chinese elements, spurred on by a sense of betrayal, started a fierce guerrilla war, which initially proved extremely disruptive. Britain's heavy-handed military response only helped to encourage support among the Chinese population for the guerrillas. However, British High Commissioner Sir Gerald Templer promised political and economic concessions and, together with improved jungle warfare tactics, the guerrillas became increasingly isolated. With the promise of independence, the British won over local Chinese leaders and a peaceful transition was achieved in 1957, although the Emergency did not officially end for a further three years.

Malaysia *See* country feature

Malcolm II (*c.*954–1034) King of Scotland (1005–34). In 1018 Malcolm defeated the Northumbrians at Carham and permanently secured the district of Lothian for Scotland. In the same year he also gained control over Strathclyde, thus completing the unification of Scotland. In 1031 Malcolm paid nominal homage to Canute II (the Great) of Norway, although Canute never interfered with his rule. He was succeeded by his grandson, Duncan I.

Malcolm III (Canmore) (*c.*1031–93) King of Scotland (1058–93), son of Duncan I. He fled Scotland after the murder of his father by Macbeth. Raised at the court of Edward the Confessor, he returned to Scotland, killed Macbeth in battle (1057) and acceded the throne. After the conquest of England by William I (the Conqueror) Malcolm offered protection to Edgar the Aetheling, the Anglo-Saxon prince, whose sister, Margaret, he married in 1068. In 1072 Malcolm was forced to swear allegiance to William, but soon reneged on the agreement and made five raids into N England, during the last of which he was killed by the forces of William II (Rufus).

MALAYSIA

AREA: 329,750sq km (127,316sq mi)
POPULATION: 18,181,000
CAPITAL (POPULATION): Kuala Lumpur (1,231,500)
GOVERNMENT: Federal, constitutional monarchy
ETHNIC GROUPS: Malay and other indigenous groups 62%, Chinese 30%, Indian 8%
LANGUAGES: Malay (official)
RELIGIONS: Islam 53%, Buddhism 17%, Chinese folk religions 12%, Hinduism 7%, Christianity 6%
GDP PER CAPITA (1995): US$9020

Federation of SE Asian states. It consists of two main parts: the Malay Peninsula (home to *c.*80% of the population) and the states of Sabah and Sarawak in N Borneo. Within Sarawak is the independent nation of Brunei. (For early history, *see* Borneo; Malay Peninsula; Sabah; Sarawak.)

In 1511 Malacca fell to the Portuguese. In 1641 the Dutch captured Malacca and controlled much of the trade through the narrow strait, before ceding the city to Britain in 1795. In 1819 Britain founded Singapore and in 1826 formed the Straits Settlement, consisting of Penang, Malacca and Singapore. In 1867 the Straits Settlement became a British colony, and in 1888 Sabah and Sarawak became a British protectorate. In 1896 the states of Perak, Selangor, Pahang and Negeri Semblian were federated. In 1909 the states of Johor, Kedah, Kelantan, Perlis and Terengganu formed the Unfederated Malay States.

Japan occupied Malaysia throughout World War 2. After Japan's defeat, the British expanded the Federation of Malaya (1948) to include the Unfederated States and Malacca and Penang. Communists (largely from the Chinese population) began a protracted guerrilla war, known as the Malayan Emergency (1948–60), and many Chinese were forcibly resettled.

In 1957 the Federation of Malaya became an independent state within the Commonwealth of Nations. In 1963 Singapore, Sabah and Sarawak joined the Federation, which became known as Malaysia. In 1965 tension over Chinese representation led to the secession of Singapore.

The New Economic Policy (1970–90) was largely successful in reducing ethnic tension caused by economic inequality. The United Malays' National Organization (UMNO) has held power, either alone or in coalition, since independence. In 1997 choking pollution from smog and the economic crisis in Southeast Asia led to criticism of Dr Mahathir bin Muhammad's premiership (1981–). In January 1998 the government announced the deportation of all non-Indonesian foreign workers. In September 1998, after publicly calling for Mahathir's resignation, Deputy Prime Minister Anwar Ibrahim was arrested on charges of corruption and sodomy. The closing ceremony of the 1998 Commonwealth Games was marred by running battles between police and demonstrators on the streets of Kuala Lumpur. Mahathir was re-elected in 1999.

Malcolm X (1925–65) African-American nationalist leader, b. Malcolm Little. His father,James Earl Little, a member of Marcus Garvey's Universal Negro Improvement Association (UNIA), was murdered (1931) by the Ku Klux Klan. In 1946, while serving a prison sentence for burglary, Malcolm joined the Black Muslims (Nation of Islam). After his release from prison in 1952, Malcolm went to Chicago, Illinois, where he met the Black Muslims' leader Elijah Muhammad and changed his surname to "X", regarding his family name as a creation of the institution of slavery. An inspirational speaker, Malcolm soon became the most conspicuous member of the organization. He opposed the civil rights movement's goal of racial integration and rejected Martin Luther King's tactic of non-violent civil disobedience. Malcolm argued instead for the creation of a separate black nation within the United States by "any means necessary". His description of the assassination (1963) of President John Kennedy as "a case of chickens coming home to roost" served as a pretext for his suspension from the Black Muslims by Elijah Muhammad, who was concerned about Malcolm's growing influence within the movement. In 1964 he left the Nation of Islam and set up a rival organization, the Muslim Mosque, Inc. Later that year, Malcolm X made a pilgrimage to Mecca, became an orthodox Muslim and as a result reformed his views on black separatism – preaching instead brotherhood among black and white people. Against a background of rising hostility between Malcolm X's supporters and Black Muslims he was assassinated at a rally in Harlem, New York. Three Black Muslims were later convicted of his murder. The posthumously published *The Autobiography of Malcolm X* (1965) ensured that his ideas informed succeeding generations of black nationalist leaders.

Maldives Republic in the Indian Ocean. The islands were settled by Buddhists from S India and Sri Lanka in *c.*5th century BC. From the 14th century, it was ruled by the Muslim ad-Din dynasty. From 1518 to 1573 the islands were controlled by the Portuguese, and from 1665 to 1886 they were a dependency of Ceylon (now Sri Lanka). In 1887 they became a British Protectorate. In 1965 the Maldives achieved independence as a sultanate. In 1968 the sultan was deposed, ending the reign of the ad-Din dynasty, and a republic was declared. In 1982 the Maldives joined the Commonwealth. An attempted Tamil coup (1988) was suppressed by President Maumoun Abdul Gayoom with the aid of Indian troops. Gayoom was re-elected in 1998 and 1993. Elements within the republic continue to seek more democratic government.

Malenkov, Georgi Maksimilianovich (1902–88) Soviet statesman, prime minister (1953–55). He joined the Red Army during the Russian Civil War (1918–20) and became a member of Communist Party of the Soviet Union (CPSU) in 1920. Malenkov soon aligned himself with Joseph Stalin, collaborating with him during the Great Purge of the late 1930s. After Stalin's death (1953), Malenkov became prime minister and general secretary of the CPSU, but within weeks he was superseded by Nikita Khrushchev as Party leader. In 1955, assuming responsibility for a failed agricultural programme, Malenkov lost the premiership to Nikolai Bulganin. In 1957 Malenkov and Vyacheslav Molotov were accused of setting up an "anti-party" opposition to Khrushchev. Malenkov was dismissed from the Presidium (Politburo) and the Central Committee, and in 1961 he was expelled from the Party.

Mali *See* country feature, page 257

Malplaquet, Battle of (11 September 1709) Engagement during the War of the Spanish Succession between France (under the command of the Duc de Villars) and the allied English, Austrian and Dutch forces (under the command of the Duke of Marlborough and Eugène of Savoy). The slightly outnumbered French were finally forced into an orderly retreat, but the heavy Allied losses (22,000 to the French 12,000) prevented an Allied attack on Paris. The Battle was largely responsible for Louis XIV's desire for peace.

Malta *See* country feature, page 258

Malthus, Thomas Robert (1766–1834) English clergyman, economist and demographer. In his famous *Essay*

MALDIVES

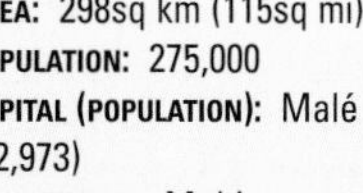

AREA: 298sq km (115sq mi)
POPULATION: 275,000
CAPITAL (POPULATION): Malé (62,973)
GOVERNMENT: Multiparty republic
ETHNIC GROUPS: Sinhalese, Indian, Arab
LANGUAGES: Divehi (official)
RELIGIONS: Sunni Muslim 99%
GDP PER CAPITA (1995): US$3080

on Population (1798), Malthus argued that population increases geometrically but food supply can increase only arithmetically, so that population must eventually overtake it, with the result that famine, war and disease would be the only checks on numbers. As an explanation of poverty, the theory was appealing, but with increases in the standard of living and the failure of the "checks" to address the balance, Malthus introduced a "moral restraint", entailing late marriages and sexual abstinence. His theory, which caused general controversy, failed to account of the ability of humans to develop new resources in more affluent societies, but it was a pioneering work of demography.

Mamluk (Arabic, slave) Military élite influential in the Middle East, particularly Egypt and Syria where they established a ruling dynasty (1250–1517). The use of non-Muslims as slave soldiers was started in the 9th century AD by the ABBASID dynasty. As slave boys, they were converted to Islam and given combat training. Over time, their influence and power as the royal bodyguard grew, culminating in the overthrow (1250) of the AYYUBID dynasty in Egypt by the Bahri (or Turkish) Mamluks. Al-Malik al Muizz became sultan, founding the Mamluk dynasty that would rule Egypt and Syria for more than 250 years. The **Bahri** Mamluks expelled the remaining Crusaders (*see* CRUSADES), defeated the MONGOLS (1260) and consolidated their rule by establishing a Mamluk caliph in CAIRO and supporting the rulers of the holy cities of Mecca and Medina. Military and diplomatic success was paralleled by economic gains: the Mamluks succeeded in restoring Egypt to its former role as a major trade route between East and West. During the reign (1293–1341) of al-Malik an-Nasir, the **Burji** (or Circassian) Mamluks emerged as a powerful faction and, when it became clear that there was no suitable replacement for an-Nasir, the Burji leader Barquq usurped the sultanate (1382). Under the Burji, the power of the Mamluks began to wane. Syria was lost to Tamerlane in 1400, while economic decline, Bedouin raids and plague saw Egypt lose its role as a primary trade route. Furthermore, towards the end of the 15th century the Burji launched a disastrous war against the Ottoman Turks, which culminated in the Ottoman capture of Cairo in 1517. Although the sultanate was overthrown, the Mamluks retained considerable influence within Egypt and were granted government positions alongside the Turks. With the decline of the OTTOMAN EMPIRE towards the end of the 17th century, the Mamluks once again became the dominant class within Egypt. In 1798 NAPOLEON Bonaparte invaded Egypt and defeated the Mamluks, and they were subsequently annihilated (1811) in a massacre ordered by the Ottoman viceroy MUHAMMAD ALI. *See also* SALADIN

Manchester, Edward Montagu, 2nd Earl of (1602–71) English Parliamentary general in the English CIVIL WAR (1642–45). He entered Parliament in 1624. At the start of the LONG PARLIAMENT, he led opposition to CHARLES I in the upper house and was charged with treason in 1642. Manchester served under the 3rd Earl of ESSEX at the beginning of the Civil War, but later succeeded him as commander in chief of the Parliamentary army. Following the defeat of the Royalists at the Battle of MARSTON MOOR (1644), Manchester disagreed with Oliver CROMWELL's plan to continue the War, and resigned from the army in 1645. With the execution of Charles I, which Manchester vehemently opposed, he retired from public life during the COMMONWEALTH. An advocate of the RESTORATION of CHARLES II (1660), Manchester was eventually reinstated as a general in 1667.

Manchester City on the River Irwell, NW England. In *c.*AD 79 the Celtic town was occupied by the Romans, who named it *Mancunium*. The settlement was abandoned, however, until Edward the Elder decided to rebuild the Roman fort in 919. The textile industry (now in decline) dates back to the 14th century when Manchester was developing a wool industry. By 1620 Manchester was manufacturing cotton textiles and the city was transformed by the introduction of steam-powered machinery (1783) at the start of the Industrial Revolution. The PETERLOO MASSACRE (1819) took place in the city and the ANTI-CORN LAW LEAGUE was founded here in 1839. In 1830 the world's first passenger railway was constructed between Manchester and LIVERPOOL, but with the opening of the Manchester Ship Canal (1894) the city gained its own access to the sea. Sights include the Town Hall (1877) and the Royal Exchange (1869). Pop. (1991) 404,861.

Manchester School British economists and politicians of the mid-19th century. They believed in LAISSEZ-FAIRE economics as advocated by ADAM SMITH. FREE-TRADE was their chief object and they got their name from the founding (1839) in MANCHESTER, NW England, of the ANTI-CORN LAW LEAGUE. They also tended towards pacifism and adopted radical positions on other issues. The most influential adherents of the "School" were Richard COBDEN and John BRIGHT. *See also* MERCANTILISM

Manchu (Man) Nomadic peoples of MANCHURIA. They established the QING dynasty in China in the 17th century AD. Originally descended from the Tungus, the Manchu (the name dates from the 16th century) have been known under a variety of names including the Juchen, who established the JIN kingdom in Manchuria and NE China in the 12th century. In 1244 the MONGOLS expelled the Juchen from China, but from the mid-16th century, under their ruler NURHACHI, the Juchen united with a number of other tribes under the "banner system" of military and administrative organization. Under Nurhachi's son, Abahai (1592–1643), the Manchu empire expanded, invading Mongolia, Korea and N China. In 1636 Abahai announced the creation of the QING dynasty and a year after his death (1643), the Manchus captured BEIJING and overthrew the MING dynasty. Initially, the Manchu pursued a policy of non-integration with the Chinese. They created segregated sectors in cities and forbade intermarriage. By the 19th century the policy of segregation began to collapse, and since the fall of the dynasty (1912) the Manchu have become assimilated into the Chinese population.

Manchukuo (1932–45) Japanese puppet state in MANCHURIA, NE China. Following the MANCHURIAN INCIDENT (1931), the Japanese army, initially without the sanction of Tokyo, took control of the whole of Manchuria, proclaimed Manchukuo as an independent state and placed Henry PU YI, the last QING emperor, on the throne (1932). The Japanese army controlled all the administration, and, in an attempt to turn the region into a military base, exploited the mineral resources and built new railways. The state of Manchukuo was not recognized by most foreign governments, and few foreigners were allowed into the country. After the defeat of Japan in 1945, Manchuria was returned to China.

MALI

AREA: 1,240,190sq km (478,837sq mi)
POPULATION: 9,818,000
CAPITAL (POPULATION): Bamako (646,000)
GOVERNMENT: Multiparty republic
ETHNIC GROUPS: Bambara 32%, Fulani 14%, Senufo 12%, Soninke 9%, Tuareg 7%, Songhai 7%, Malinke (Mandingo or Mandinke) 7%
LANGUAGES: French (official)
RELIGIONS: Islam 90%, traditional beliefs 9%, Christianity 1%
GDP PER CAPITA (1995): US$550

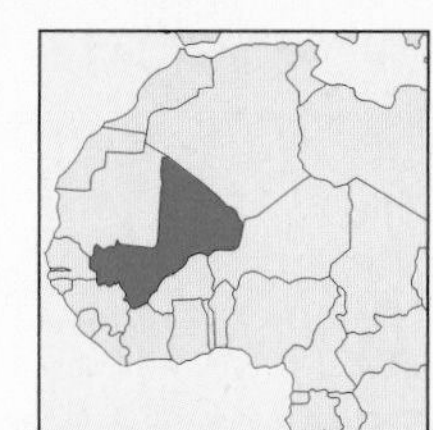

Landlocked republic and largest country in West Africa. Mali has lain at the heart of many of Africa's historic empires. From the 4th to the 11th centuries, the region was part of the ancient GHANA empire. The medieval Mali empire was one of the world's most powerful and prosperous powers; its gold riches were legendary.

During the reign (*c.*1312–37) of Emperor MANSA MUSA, Mali was at the height of its influence and power. Mansa gained parts of Morocco, S Sahara and Tukulor, introduced Islam, and helped Timbuktu develop into a great centre of learning and a marketplace for trans-Saharan trade. The SONGHAI empire dominated the region during the 15th century, but the combination of internal disputes and a Moroccan invasion (1591) resulted in the division of a once great empire into small kingdoms.

In the 19th century France gradually gained control. In 1893 the region became known as French Sudan and in 1898 was incorporated into the Federation of West Africa. Nationalist movements grew more vocal in their opposition to colonialism. In 1958 French Sudan voted to join the FRENCH COMMUNITY as an autonomous republic. In 1959 it joined with SENEGAL to form the Federation of Mali.

Shortly after gaining independence, Senegal seceded and in 1960 Mali became a one-party republic. Its first president, Modibo KEITA, was committed to nationalization and PAN-AFRICANISM. In 1962 Mali adopted its own currency. In 1963 Mali joined the ORGANIZATION OF AFRICAN UNITY (OAU). Economic crisis forced Keita to revert to the franc zone and permit France greater economic influence. In 1968 Keita was overthrown in a military coup.

The army group formed a National Liberation Committee, and appointed Moussa TRAORÉ as prime minister. During the 1970s, the Sahel suffered a series of droughts which contributed to a devastating famine that claimed thousands of lives. In 1979 a new constitution was adopted, and Traoré was elected president. In 1991 Traoré was himself overthrown in a military coup.

In 1992 a new constitution established a multiparty democracy and Alpha Oumar Konaré, leader of the Alliance for Democracy in Mali (ADEMA), won the ensuing presidential election. A political settlement (1992) provided a special administration for TUAREGS in N Mali. In 1997 Konaré was re-elected and Traoré was sentenced to life imprisonment.

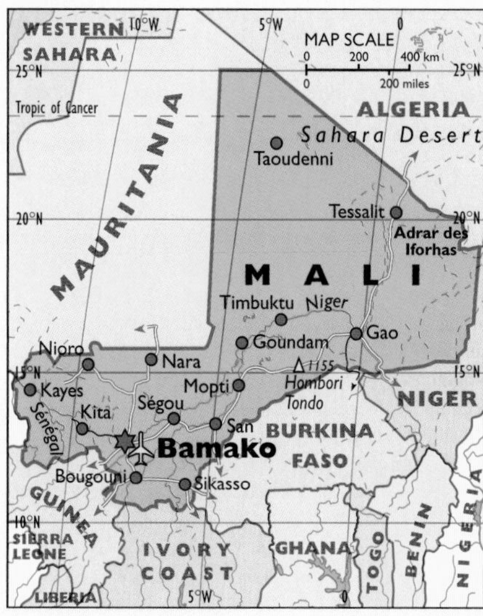

M

Manchuria (Dongbei) Historic region of NE China, now included in the provinces of Heilongjiang, Jilin and Liaoning. Originally inhabited by a number of nomadic pastoralists including the Tungus and Mongols, Chinese settlement began in the *c.*3rd century BC, and the Han dynasty (206 BC–AD 220) conquered parts of S Manchuria. In 698 the Tungus formed an independent kingdom that dominated Manchuria during the 8th century. The Mongol Khitans gained control of most of Manchuria in the 10th century, founding the Liao dynasty. In 1115 the Tungu Juchen chief Akuta established the Jin kingdom, which allied with the Chinese Song dynasty to overthrow the Liao dynasty in 1125. Genghis Khan invaded Jin in 1211, and the whole of Manchuria later fell to the Mongols. The Chinese Ming dynasty captured Manchuria in the late 14th century, but the Juchen empire was rebuilt by Nurhachi at the start of the 17th century, and his son, Abahai (1592–1643), adopted the name Manchu for his people. In 1644 the Manchu gained control of China, founding the Qing dynasty. In the late 19th century, Manchuria acquired an extensive railway network, enabling a massive increase in Chinese immigration. In 1898 the Russians leased the Liaodong Peninsula, S Manchuria, from China and began to develop the naval facilities at Port Arthur. After the Russo-Japanese War (1904–05), Japan gained control of the Liaodong Peninsula. In 1931 the Japanese army occupied the whole of Manchuria and established the puppet state of Manchukuo. During World War 2 the region's industry and mineral resources aided the Japanese war effort. In 1945–46 Manchuria was occupied by Soviet forces, who dismantled and removed many factories. In 1948 the Chinese communists defeated the Manchurian Kuomintang nationalists, and with Soviet technical expertise industrial reconstruction began. From 1960 to 1990 the region was at the forefront of Sino-Soviet hostilities. Since the collapse of the Soviet Union, the region has developed further and is now one of the principal industrial areas of China. Area: *c.*1.5 million sq km (600,000sq mi).

Manchurian Incident (1931) Minor confrontation that ultimately led to the Japanese seizure of Manchuria. During the 1920s Japan, the dominant foreign power in S Manchuria, became increasingly concerned that it was losing influence in this industrial and strategically vital region to the Chinese Kuomintang government. In September 1931 the Japanese army used the excuse of an explosion near their rail depot at Mukden (for which nobody claimed responsibility) to occupy the province, setting up the puppet state of Manchukuo. The ensuing Sino-Japanese War (1937–45) later merged into World War 2.

mandarin European name for officials or civil servants of any of the Chinese empires. Their entry to the bureaucracy was by examination, and their rank, of which there were nine, was shown by their form of dress. As a matter of policy, mandarins never officiated in their home province but were posted to other areas for limited periods.

mandated territories German colonies and parts of the Ottoman Turkish empire that were given to the Allied countries, following German and Turkish defeat in World War I, as laid out in the Covenant of the League of Nations. There were three kinds of mandate: "**A**" territories were to be given full independence, "**B**" territories were to be governed as colonies, while "**C**" territories were to be incorporated into the structure of the mandatory country. Britain took Iraq and Palestine as "A" possessions; Tanganyika, Togoland and part of the Cameroons as "B" possessions; and jointly administered (with Australia or New Zealand) Nauru, Samoa and New Guinea as "C" possessions. Under a United Nations' (UN) charter, "B" and "C" territories became trust territories in 1946.

Mandela, Nelson Rolihlahla (1918–) South African statesman, president (1994–99). He joined the African National Congress (ANC) in 1944, and for the next 20 years led the campaign of civil disobedience against South Africa's apartheid government. He stood trial (1956–61) for treason but was found innocent. Following the Sharpeville Massacre (1960) and the banning of the ANC, Mandela, who had until that time advocated a policy of non-violence, formed *Umkhonte We Sizwe* (Spear of the Nation), a paramilitary wing of the ANC. In 1962 Mandela was sentenced to five years' imprisonment, but in 1964, after a well-publicized trial in which he conducted his own defence, Mandela was sentenced to life imprisonment for further political offences. He spent the next 27 years in prison, first on Robben Island then in Pollsmoor Prison, becoming a national and international symbol of resistance to apartheid. In February 1990 Mandela was released by President F.W. de Klerk and resumed his leadership of the newly legalized ANC. In 1993 Mandela and de Klerk shared the Nobel Prize for Peace. His autobiography, *A Long Walk to Freedom* (1994), became a popular best-seller. Mandela gained two-thirds of the popular vote in South Africa's first multiracial democratic elections in 1994. A strong advocate of reconciliation, he made de Klerk deputy president (1994–96) in his government of national unity. As president, Mandela introduced a new, federal constitution (1996) and enacted a number of social reforms, particularly in housing, education and health, in order to improve living standards for the African population. While the reforms proved popular, their implementation and other government aspirations were not helped by in-fighting between the ANC and the Inkatha Freedom Party. In 1996 he divorced his wife, **Winnie** (1934–), who was convicted of kidnapping and of being an accessory to assault. In 1997 Mandela was replaced as president of the ANC by Thabo Mbeki. In 1999 Mandela retired as president and was succeeded by Mbeki. *See also* Pan-Africanist Congress (PAC); Sisulu, Walter; Tambo, Oliver

Manfred (*c.*1232–66) King of Sicily (1258–66), illegitimate son of Emperor Frederick II. He acted as regent first for his half-brother Conrad IV and then for Conrad's son Conradin. In 1258 Pope Alexander IV, who was keen to see an end to the pro-Ghibelline Hohenstaufen dynasty, excommunicated Manfred and sent an army to Sicily in an attempt to place Edmund, son of Henry III of England, on the throne. Manfred defeated the papal forces and was crowned king in Palermo. Pope Urban IV, who also refused to recognize Manfred as king, offered the Sicilian throne to the pro-Guelph Charles of Anjou. In 1265 Charles' army landed in Sicily and Manfred was defeated and killed at Benevento.

Manhattan Project Codename for the development of the US atomic bomb during World War 2. Work on the bomb was carried out in great secrecy by a team including Enrico Fermi (1901–54) and Robert Oppenheimer (1904–67). The whole Project, officially called the Manhattan Engineer District (MED), was controlled by the army under the command of General Leslie Groves, and located in various sites across the United States. On 16 July 1945, the first test took place near Alamogordo, New Mexico, and in August 1945 the first atomic bombs were dropped on Nagasaki and Hiroshima, Japan, bringing the war in the Pacific to a rapid conclusion.

Manichaeism Religious movement based on the teaching of the Persian prophet Mani (*c.*AD 216–76). Mani spent his early life as an ascetic travelling through Persia and NW India. He returned to Persia (241) and began to preach a

MALTA

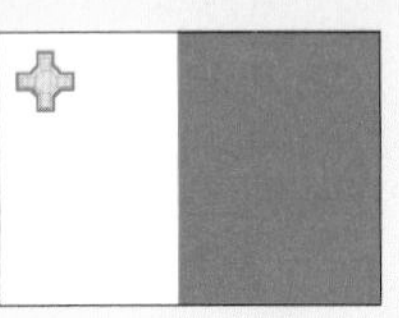

AREA: 316sq km (122sq mi)
POPULATION: 359,000
CAPITAL (POPULATION): Valletta (102,571)
GOVERNMENT: Multiparty republic
ETHNIC GROUPS: Maltese 96%, British 2%
LANGUAGES: Maltese and English (both official)
RELIGIONS: Christianity (Roman Catholicism 99%)
GDP PER CAPITA (1994): US$7394

Archipelago republic in the Mediterranean Sea. Malta has evidence of Stone Age settlement dating back *c.*4000 years. In *c.*850 BC the Phoenicians colonized Malta. They were followed by the Carthaginians in the 6th century BC, Greeks in the 5th century BC, and by 218 BC the Romans had assumed control. Under Roman rule, Malta gained control of its domestic politics and economy.

In AD 395, with the division of the Roman Empire, Malta became part of the Eastern Roman or Byzantine Empire. In 870 Islam was introduced via Arab invasion, but Christian rule was restored (1091) by Roger I, Norman king of Sicily. A succession of feudal lords ruled Malta until the early 16th century.

In 1530 Emperor Charles V granted Malta to the Knights Hospitallers. In 1565 the Knights, who had fought in the Crusades, held Malta against an Ottoman siege. Under the Knights' rule, Malta's economy prospered, reflected in extensive building work. In 1798 the French, led by Napoleon Bonaparte, captured Malta but, with help from Britain, they were driven out in 1800. Under the Treaty of Amiens (1802), the island returned to the Knights.

By the Treaty of Paris (1814), Malta became a British colony and over the years developed into an important strategic military base, particularly following the opening of the Suez Canal in 1869. In 1921 Britain agreed to a power-sharing assembly but, following internal disputes, rescinded the agreement in 1936 and absolute power was returned to the governor. During World War 2 Malta sustained heavy damage from Italian and German bombing raids, and in 1942, in recognition of the bravery of the Maltese resistance, George VI of Britain awarded the George Cross to Malta. In 1953 Malta became a base for the North Atlantic Treaty Organization (NATO), and self-government was finally granted in 1962. In 1964 Malta gained independence within the Commonwealth of Nations, and in 1974 it became a republic.

From 1964 to 1971 the ruling Nationalist Party, becoming increasingly concerned about Malta's economy, looked to the West for trade and investment. However, with the election of the Malta Labour Party in 1971, closer ties with China and Libya were encouraged. In 1979 Britain's military agreement with Malta expired, and all British forces withdrew. In the 1980s, Malta declared itself a neutral country. The Nationalist Party were returned to power in 1987, and in 1990 Malta applied to join the European Community, which insisted on certain economic reforms before accession discussions could begin. In 1997 the newly elected Malta Labour Party, under Alfred Sant, pledged to rescind the application. The Nationalist Party, however, led by the pro-European Edward Adami, regained power in 1998 elections.

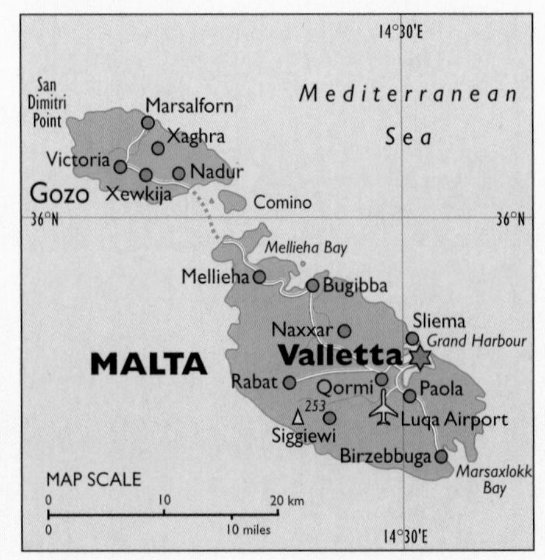

new religion. Manichaeism was an amalgam of CHRISTIANITY, ZOROASTRIANISM, BUDDHISM and most importantly Gnosticism. Like Gnosticism, Manichaeism was a religion of dualities expressed in the significance of good and evil, light and dark, and spirit and material – the material world being the evil from which the spirit must free itself. Manichaeism was broadly divided into the "elect", who assumed a strictly ascetic life, and the "hearers", who maintained the elect with alms. A change in religious tolerance in Persia after AD 272 brought increased persecution of Mani and his followers by orthodox Zoroastrians. Mani eventually underwent a tortuous trial that lasted 26 days after which he was executed. Thanks largely to mission programmes, Manichaeism spread rapidly to Egypt and Rome in the 4th century, where it was considered a Christian heresy, and E to Chinese Turkistan, where it survived probably until the 10th century.

manifest destiny Political doctrine that justified the US westward and southward expansion of the FRONTIER in the 19th century. The slogan was coined (1845) by a Democratic editor, John O'Sullivan, and it was exploited by President James POLK when the United States annexed TEXAS and won lands from Mexico following the MEXICAN WAR (1846–48). Later, the theory of manifest destiny contributed to the acquisition of ALASKA, HAWAII, and territory taken in the SPANISH-AMERICAN WAR (1898).

Manila Bay, Battle of (1 May 1898) Conflict in the SPANISH-AMERICAN WAR in which US Commodore George DEWEY defeated the Spanish fleet in a seven-hour battle in Philippine waters. Spanish losses were heavy, with 381 men killed and all the Spanish ships destroyed. US casualties included eight killed; no ships were damaged. This emphatic victory enabled the US occupation of Manila and initiated an expansionist US policy in the Pacific.

Manin, Daniele (1804–57) Venetian revolutionary. Influenced by the poet and patriot Niccolò Tommaseo, Manin became increasingly opposed to Austrian rule in Venice. In January 1848 he was imprisoned, along with Tommaseo, for advocating Venetian self-determination. Following the REVOLUTIONS OF 1848, Manin was released and in March 1848 was made president of the republic of Venice. Four months later, the Venetian assembly overruled Manin and voted to unite with Piedmont-Sardinia. Over the next few months Venice, with Manin at the fore, bravely withstood an intensive Austrian bombardment, but in August 1849, broken by starvation and cholera, Venice capitulated. Manin was banished and spent the rest of his life in Paris gathering support for RISORGIMENTO.

Manitoba Prairie province in S central Canada; the capital is Winnipeg. Before the arrival of the English in 1612, Manitoba was inhabited by the CHIPPEWA and ASSINIBOINE. CHARLES II of England granted the region to the HUDSON'S BAY COMPANY, who formed the first European settlement in 1670. The interior was explored by the French and British, and new fur-trading posts were established. After the FRENCH AND INDIAN WARS (1689–1783), Britain became the dominant power in Manitoba. In 1783 the NORTH WEST COMPANY was established and soon entered into competition with the Hudson's Bay Company. The intense rivalry spilled over into violence in 1815–16, when the Earl of SELKIRK, a major shareholder in the Hudson's Bay Company (1810), established the RED RIVER SETTLEMENT (1811–12) on North West Company land. The dispute was resolved by the merger of the two companies in 1821. On the eve of the Hudson's Bay Company's cession of its territory to the newly created Confederation of Canada, the Métis population, mixed-race European and Native Americans led by Louis RIEL, mounted the RED RIVER REBELLION (1869), winning land and cultural rights. In 1870 Manitoba gained provincial status and the population increased rapidly with migrants from Northern and Eastern Europe. The emigrants upset the delicate demographics, and French-speakers felt their culture under threat after a statute made English the only official language. In the early 20th century, Manitoba prospered as a major wheat-growing region. In 1994 the Supreme Court of Canada ruled that the Manitoba School Act (1871) was in contravention of minority-language rights. Pop. (1994 est.) 1,131,100.

Manley, Michael Norman (1924–97) Jamaican statesman, prime minister (1972–80, 1989–92). The son of **Norman Manley**, Jamaica's prime minister from 1959 to 1962, he was elected to the House of Representatives in 1967. In 1969 he succeeded his father as leader of the People's National Party (PNP) and won a landslide victory in the 1972 elections. As prime minister, Manley nationalized industries, acquired the rights to Jamaica's bauxite mines, and forged closer relations with Cuba. He was one of the founders (1973) of the CARIBBEAN COMMUNITY AND COMMON MARKET (CARICOM). Although Manley was re-elected in 1976, the economy continued to decline and political violence increased. He lost the 1980 elections to Edward SEAGA, but regained power after changing his economic policies and campaigning for free-market reforms in the 1989 elections. He resigned due to failing health.

Mannerheim, Carl Gustav Emil (1867–1951) Finnish field marshal and statesman, president (1944–46). He served in the Russian army in the Russo-Japanese War (1904–05) and in World War 1. In the Finnish Civil War (January–May 1918), Mannerheim led the so-called White Guards to victory over the Finnish BOLSHEVIK forces, drove out the Russian Red Guard and became regent of an independent FINLAND. In 1919 he retired after defeat in the presidential elections. In 1931, as head of the defence council (1930–39), he planned the **Mannerheim Line** across the Karelian Isthmus in an attempt to counter potential Soviet invasion. Mannerheim commanded the valiant, but ultimately defeated, Finnish forces in the RUSSO-FINNISH WAR (1939–40) and led Finnish forces in a combined attack with Nazi Germany on the Soviet Union (1941). As president of the Finnish republic, Mannerheim negotiated the armistice with the Soviets in 1944. He was forced to retire on grounds of ill-health.

Manning, Henry Edward (1808–92) English cleric and theologian. A member of the OXFORD MOVEMENT, he was ordained a priest in the Church of England in 1833, but converted to Roman Catholicism in 1851. Manning was appointed archbishop of Westminster in 1865 and became a cardinal in 1875. He played a leading part in debates on papal infallibility in the Vatican Council (1870), and defended this doctrine in his writings. A supporter of trade UNIONS, he helped settle the London dock strike in 1889.

manorial system Organization of the rural economy in Europe during the Middle Ages and early modern period. It varied greatly over time and region. A lord presided over the manor (roughly equivalent to a village, sometimes several villages), which he held in FIEF from a greater lord, who might be the king. The peasants or VILLEINS were assigned a share – typically a strip – of land in exchange for labour on the lord's demesne plus a share of their produce or, in later times, a money payment. The custom, or law, of the manor fixed the duties and payments of the peasants, who might be SERFS or freemen. Justice was administered in the manorial court, presided over by the resident steward (or the manorial lord himself), where officials were appointed, offenders punished and land tenure registered. The system disappeared in much of Europe by the 16th century, though some aspects persisted into the 19th century. *See also* FEUDAL SYSTEM

▲ **Mandela** opposed the apartheid regime in South Africa throughout his 27 years in prison. Upon his release, he became the first president of a democratic, multiracial republic.

Mansa Musa (d.1337) Emperor of MALI (1312–37). His reign marked Mali's greatest period of economic and cultural dominance. The sensational wealth of Mali was displayed during Mansa Musa's famous pilgrimage to MECCA (1324–25), when 100 camels carried the emperor's gold. His lavish spending in Cairo depressed the price of gold in Europe and gained Mali wide international recognition.

Mansfeld, Peter Ernst, Graf von (1580?–1626) Austrian-born commander in the THIRTY YEARS' WAR. Illegitimate son of the governor of the Spanish Netherlands (also Peter Ernst), he fought in Austria and the Netherlands, but in the Thirty Years' War chose the Protestant side, with the object of securing estates for himself. He commanded mercenaries who lived mainly on plunder. Defeated by the imperial general Albrecht von WALLENSTEIN in 1626, he fled to Hungary.

Mansur, al- (*c*.710–775) Second ABBASID caliph (754–775). He consolidated Abbasid rule in Islam. Al-Mansur supported his brother as-Saffah against the Umayyads and succeeded him as caliph in 754. He put down Shiite and other revolts and ensured that the succession would go to his son. In 762 he founded Baghdad as the Abbasid capital.

Manuel I (Comnenus) (*c*.1120–1180) Byzantine emperor (1143–80) and general, son and successor of JOHN II (COMNENUS). He sought to revive the BYZANTINE EMPIRE and reconcile the Eastern (Orthodox) and Western (Roman Catholic) churches. Initially, Manuel directed his mostly mercenary armies against the SELJUK Turks, but during the Second CRUSADE (1147) concern for his W provinces resulted in a truce with the Turks. In 1148 Manuel's policy of consolidation brought about an alliance with Emperor CONRAD III of Germany against ROGER II of Sicily, who had earlier attempted to subjugate Manuel's Greek territories. Manuel's defeat (1156) at the hands of William I of Sicily, Roger's successor, saw an end to Byzantine influence in Italy. He enjoyed greater success in the Crusader states, bringing Antioch and Jerusalem under Byzantine control in 1159, and by 1167 Dalmatia, Croatia and Bosnia were also incorporated. These successes were offset, however, by a crushing Turkish victory at Myriocephalon (1176), which marked the start of the decline of the Byzantine Empire. He was succeeded by his son, Alexius II.

Manuel II (Palaeologus) (1350–1425) Byzantine emperor (1391–1425). His reign was beset by Turkish invasions that reduced the empire to the city of Constantinople. Manuel travelled to Paris and London seeking help in vain, and he became a virtual client of the sultan. He was succeeded by his son, John VIII.

Manuel I (the Fortunate) (1469–1521) King of Portugal (1495–1521). He succeeded his cousin and brother-in-law, JOHN II, and reigned during Portugal's golden age. Portuguese navigators covered much of the globe, and won a commercial empire in the East that brought enormous wealth to the crown. Manuel presided over a brilliant court and encouraged arts and architecture in the style known after him as Manueline. He married three Spanish princesses successively in hope of uniting the crowns of Spain and Portugal, and followed the Spanish in expelling Jews and Muslims. His son, JOHN III, succeeded him.

Manuel II (1889–1932) Last king of Portugal (1908–10), son of CHARLES I. He became king after both his father and older brother were assassinated. He was overthrown by the revolution of 1910 and spent his exile in England.

Manzikert, Battle of (1071) Victory of the Seljuk Turks under ALP ARSLAN over the forces of the Byzantine Empire near present-day Malazgirt, Turkey. Emperor Romanus IV (Diogenes) hoped to take over Armenia, but was deserted by his Turkmen mercenaries. The Byzantine army was destroyed and the Seljuks overran Anatolia.

Maori Original inhabitants of NEW ZEALAND, who are thought to have descended from Polynesian peoples, arriving in New Zealand from *c*.AD 500. Traditionally, Maoris lived by agriculture, hunting and fishing in stockaded villages. Intertribal war was common, and made it difficult for them to combine against European encroachment in the 18th and 19th century, during which time their population fell from *c*.100,000 to *c*.40,000. Maori chiefs signed the

M

Treaty of WAITANGI (1840), ceding sovereignty to the British crown in exchange for protection. Continuing exploitation produced a degree of unity and provoked the MAORI WARS, which ended with their subjugation. In recent years, the Maori have gained political equality and reclaimed some of their property through legal actions.

Maori Wars (1843–48, 1860–72) Series of conflicts in which the indigenous MAORIS resisted the British colonization of NEW ZEALAND. Both Maori Wars were really a succession of rebellions and were confined mainly to the North Island. They arose when the settlers broke the terms of the Treaty of WAITANGI (1840), which guaranteed the Maoris possession of their lands. The rebellions of the 1840s were led by the Maori chiefs Hone Heke and Te Rauparaha. Sir George GREY was appointed governor in an effort to quell revolts. The second phase (the Taranaki Wars) was led by the KING MOVEMENT. An 1861 truce was short-lived as Britain invaded Waikato (July 1863). In 1865 a native land court was established. In 1867 a Maori school system was formed and Maoris gained the right to elect four members to the New Zealand legislature. British troops withdrew in 1870.

Mao Zedong (1893–1976) Chinese statesman, founder and chairman (1949–76) of the People's Republic of CHINA. He served in the revolutionary army in 1911 and was a founder (1921) of the CHINESE COMMUNIST PARTY (CCP). After the nationalist KUOMINTANG, led by CHIANG KAI-SHEK, ended their alliance with the communists in 1927, Mao, who believed in the revolutionary potential of the peasants, helped established rural SOVIETS. In 1931 he was elected chairman of the JIANGXI soviet, but the advance of Nationalist forces forced Mao to lead his followers on the LONG MARCH (1934–35) to Shaanxi. Mao emerged as effective leader of the CCP, and began to work out the ideological principles on which his form of COMMUNISM (Maoism) was based. In 1937 the civil war was suspended as the communists and Kuomintang combined to fight the Japanese in the Second SINO-JAPANESE WAR. Mao's brand of guerrilla warfare gained much of rural China, and when civil war resumed in 1945, the Kuomintang was defeated and driven out of mainland China (1949). Mao became chairman of the People's Republic, with ZHOU ENLAI as prime minister. In 1958 Mao launched the GREAT LEAP FORWARD, a programme of radical socio-economic reform that sought to establish a distinctively Chinese (i.e. non-Soviet) form of communism. It ended in mass starvation (20 million people are estimated to have died) and the withdrawal of Soviet aid. In 1959 Mao was replaced as chairman of the central government council by LIU SHAOQI, but remained the chairman of the Communist politburo. The CULTURAL REVOLUTION, an attempt by Mao and his wife, JIANG QING, to reassert Maoist ideology in a process of "continuing revolution", almost reduced the country to anarchy. The cult of the personality was encouraged, political rivals were dismissed, and Mao became supreme commander of the nation and army (1970). Mao's and Zhou Enlai's deaths created a power vacuum. A struggle developed between the GANG OF FOUR and HUA GUOFENG and DENG XIAOPING. *Quotations from Chairman Mao Zedong* (popularly known as "The Little Red Book", 1967) is a worldwide best-seller. *See also* HUNDRED FLOWERS MOVEMENT

▲ **Maori** This carved jade tiki or figurine was given (1848) to the British Governor General Sir George Grey by Hone Heke, a Maori chief, at Te Waimate, Auckland Peninsula.

Mapai Acronym for the Hebrew name of the Israeli Workers Party. Mapai was founded (1930) from two older labour parties. It was the chief Jewish political party in PALESTINE and, from 1948 in the republic of ISRAEL. Among its founders was David BEN-GURION, who dominated it for 35 years. In 1968 it merged with two smaller social-democratic parties to form the **Israeli Labour Party**, which was the major component in every coalition government from 1948 until 1977. Thereafter, it shared power with the right-wing coalition LIKUD (founded 1973). Leaders of the Labour Party after Ben-Gurion forsook it (1965) include Levi ESHKOL, Golda MEIR, Yitzhak RABIN, Shimon PERES and Ehud BARAK.

Maquis French underground resistance movement against the German forces of occupation in WORLD WAR 2. The various groups of the Maquis, supported by the Communist Party, specialized in sabotage and by 1944 had developed an efficient intelligence system. The Maquis was of some service in the liberation of the country (1944). *Maquis* is the name for the tough, shrubby terrain in parts of s France. *See also* FREE FRENCH

Mar, John Erskine, 1st (or 6th) Earl of (*c*.1510–72) Scottish regent (1571–72), keeper of Edinburgh and Stirling castles as Lord Erskine. The title of the 1st Earl was acknowledged in 1565. Whether this was a new creation or a restoration of the older earldom of Mar (in which case he was the 6th earl) is disputed. Mar gained custody of the young James VI (later JAMES I of England) in opposition to his mother, MARY, QUEEN OF SCOTS.

Mar, John Erskine, 2nd (or 7th) Earl of (*c*.1558–1634) Scottish noble. Initially the guardian of the young King James VI of Scotland (later JAMES I of England), he was replaced as the king's favourite by James STUART, Earl of Arran. Fearing a plot by Arran to encourage James to champion the Catholic cause, Mar took part in the Ruthven Raid (1582), during which James was captured and Arran gained control. Mar was banished to England (1584) on James' escape, where he joined with other Scottish nobles to invade Scotland and overthrow Arran. Mar was reconciled with James VI and later served as lord high treasurer of Scotland (1616–30).

Mar, John Erskine, 6th (or 11th) Earl of (1675–1732) Scottish noble, leader of the JACOBITES. Secretary of state for Scotland under Queen ANNE, during which time he supported the Act of UNION (1707) with Scotland, Mar was dismissed (1714) by GEORGE I. Mar travelled to Scotland, where he organized a rebellion in the name of James Edward STUART, the "Old Pretender". The revolt was defeated and Mar and Stuart were forced into exile. Stuart, initially supportive of Mar's actions, soon suspected Mar of acting as a double agent and refused to receive him at the Jacobite court.

Mara, Ratu Sir Kamisese Kapaiwai Tuimacilai (1920–) Fijian statesman, prime minister (1970–87) and president (1993–). He headed the Fijian delegation at the Commonwealth Constiutional Convention (1965), and was chief minister (1967–70) under British rule. Ratu Mara led FIJI successfully for its first 17 years of independence, but lost the 1987 elections when his National Alliance Party was defeated by an Indian-dominated coalition. The latter was overthrown by a military coup (1987), but with constitutional government restored, Ratu Mara became president.

Marat, Jean Paul (1743–93) French revolutionary, b. Switzerland. A physician, he founded *L'Ami du Peuple* (Friend of the People), a vitriolic journal that supported the JACOBINS. His murder by Charlotte CORDAY, a member of the GIRONDINS, was exploited for propaganda by the Jacobins and contributed to the ensuing REIGN OF TERROR.

MAO ZEDONG

Mao Zedong sought to build a new China by replacing traditional Chinese culture with communism, and empowering the rural peasantry. Mao used the Chinese Red Army to enforce his ideology, which came to dominate every aspect of life in China.

MAO ZEDONG IN HIS OWN WORDS

"Letting a hundred flowers blossom and a hundred schools of thought contend is the policy for promoting the progress of the arts and sciences."
Quotations from Chairman Mao Zedong (1967)

Maratha (Mahratta) Hindu people of w central India, renowned as warriors. Under a great leader, SIVAJI (*c*.1630–80), who established the Maratha kingdom in 1674, they led resistance to the Muslim rule of the Mughals. As the MUGHAL EMPIRE declined in the 18th century the Marathas extended their rule across the Deccan and large areas of s India, eventually gaining control of the whole of India by the mid- to late 18th century. Although they were the principal opposition to British colonial rule, the rivalries of the great Maratha chiefs made united action difficult and was exploited by the British in a succession of wars between 1774 and 1818. The British attack of 1817 finally extinguished their independence and secured British control of India. The Marathas, however, remained a significant force in India, particularly during the Nationalist movement.

Marathon, Battle of (490 BC) Victory of the Greeks, mainly Athenians, during the PERSIAN WARS (499–489 BC). MILTIADES persuaded the Athenians not to wait for support from SPARTA, but to attack the Persian invasion force of CYRUS II (THE GREAT) before they had fully engaged their mighty cavalry. The Athenians descended on the Persian infantry, killing *c*.6400 men and capturing seven ships at the cost of only *c*.200 lives. The Persians were forced to beat a hasty retreat. According to legend, a Greek soldier ran all the way back to Athens, *c*.42km (26mi) away, to bring news of the victory before dying. The modern marathon race commemorates this feat.

Marbury v. Madison (1803) US case arising from a conflict over the negation of a federal appointment by the succeeding administration. Although the case itself was insignificant, it gave rise to an important decision in the Supreme Court. Chief Justice John MARSHALL's opinion established the doctrine of judicial review, the right of the Supreme Court to decide whether or not federal or state legislation is admissible under the Constitution.

Marcellus Name of an ancient Roman family that produced several important political figures in ancient Rome. The most famous was Marcus Claudius Marcellus (*c.*268–208 BC), consul (five times) and general who defeated a Gallic chieftain in single combat. He was a persistent opponent of HANNIBAL during the Second PUNIC WAR, thwarting successive attacks on the town of Nola (216–214 BC) and capturing Syracuse (211 BC). A second Marcus Claudius Marcellus (d.45 BC) was an opponent of Julius CAESAR, but was later reconciled through the intervention of CICERO and murdered on his way to Rome. A third Marcus Claudius Marcellus (42–23 BC) was named as heir (25 BC) by his uncle, Emperor AUGUSTUS, but died young.

Marco Polo *See* POLO, MARCO

Marcomanni Ancient Germanic tribe. First mentioned by Julius Caesar, they came from the region north of the Danube, later migrating to the upper Main and Bohemia. They led a Germanic league against the Romans, but later became reconciled with them, until a series of wars against them led by MARCUS AURELIUS (*c.*167–180). By AD 500 they had settled in Bavaria: they are sometimes regarded as the ancestors of the Bavarians.

Marcos, Ferdinand Edralin (1917–89) Philippine statesman, president (1965–86). He was elected to the Philippine Congress in 1949. As president, Marcos received US support for his military campaigns (1969) against communist guerrillas on Panay and Moro secessionists on Mindanao. Continued civil unrest led to the imposition of martial law in 1972. A new constitution (1973) gave Marcos authoritarian powers. His regime acquired a reputation for repression and corruption, symbolized by the extravagance of his wife, **Imelda** (1930–). In 1983 his main rival, Benigno Aquino, was assassinated and political opposition coalesced behind Benigno's widow, Cory AQUINO. Marcos appeared to win the 1986 general election, but allegations of vote-rigging forced him into exile. In 1988 US authorities indicted both him and Imelda for fraud. Ferdinand was too ill to stand trial and died in Hawaii. Imelda was subsequently acquitted, but on her return (1991) to Manila she was indicted for embezzlement. In 1992 Imelda unsuccessfully ran for president. In 1993 she was sentenced to 18 years' imprisonment, but appealed the judgement.

Marcus Aelius Aurelius Antoninus (AD 121–180) Roman emperor (161–180) and philosopher of the Stoic school. Of Spanish origin, he was adopted by HADRIAN as his grandson and succeeded his uncle and adoptive father, ANTONINUS PIUS. Between 161 and 169, he ruled as co-emperor with his adoptive younger brother Lucius Aurelius Verus. His only surviving work, the much-admired *Meditations*, is a collection of philosophical thoughts and ideas largely composed during his campaigns. For all his personal virtues, Marcus Aurelius' magnanimous government was costly, and he died waging a long and unwinnable war against the MARCOMANNI and others on the Danube frontier. He was succeeded by his son, COMMODUS.

Mardonius (d.479 BC) Persian general. He married a daughter of DARIUS I (THE GREAT), and commanded an expedition against Ionia, where he surprisingly restored the Ionian democracies, but his fleet was later wrecked. A leader of XERXES' expedition against the Greeks, he remained in the west commanding the army when Xerxes withdrew after the Battle of SALAMIS (480). He was defeated and killed at the Battle of PLATAEA.

Marengo, Battle of (14 June 1800) Victory of the French under NAPOLEON Bonaparte over the Austrians under Baron Melas on the Marengo Plain, N Italy, during the FRENCH REVOLUTIONARY WARS. Napoleon miscalculated Austrian strength, divided his forces, and would have been defeated but for the timely arrival of General Desaix (1768–1800). The victory confirmed French control of N Italy. The Battle claimed *c.*7000 French lives (including Desaix) and *c.*14,000 Austrian lives.

Margai, Sir Milton (1895–1964) African statesman, first prime minister of SIERRA LEONE (1961–64). He founded the Sierra Leone People's Party in 1951, and was chief minister (1954–61) in the last years of the British colonial protectorate. He died in office and was succeeded as prime minister (1964–67) by his brother, Albert Margai.

Margaret I (1353–1412) Regent of Denmark, Norway and Sweden, daughter of VALDEMAR IV. She married Haakon VI of Norway in 1363. Her son, Olaf, succeeded Valdemar in Denmark (1375) and Haakon in Norway (1380), but Margaret held the real power and ruled as queen after Olaf's death (1387). She defeated the Swedes in 1389, extended royal powers and furthered Danish influence. In 1397, nominally under her grandnephew Eric of Pomerania, the formidable Margaret united the three Scandinavian kingdoms in the KALMAR UNION.

Margaret of Scotland, Saint (*c.*1046–93) Queen consort of MALCOLM III, king of Scots (*c.*1031–1093). An English princess, she and Malcolm, also English-reared, introduced a strong English influence into lay and ecclesiastical society, and the focus of the Scottish kingdom shifted away from the Celtic north and into Anglo-Saxon Lothian. A pious Christian, she rebuilt the Abbey of Iona, introduced the BENEDICTINES to Scotland and encouraged Roman, rather than Celtic, practices in the Scottish church. She was canonized in 1250.

Margaret of Anjou (1430–82) Queen consort of HENRY VI of England. Daughter of the king of Naples, she married Henry in 1445, bringing a brief truce in the HUNDRED YEARS' WAR. Margaret, rather than the ineffective Henry, led the Lancastrian cause during the Wars of the ROSES. She joined forces with the Earl of WARWICK, but was decisively defeated by EDWARD IV at TEWKESBURY, W England (1471), and her son was killed. Henry was murdered in the Tower of London and Margaret remained in captivity until ransomed (1475) by LOUIS XI of France. She spent the rest of her life in France.

Margaret of Austria (1480–1530) Habsburg princess, daughter of Emperor MAXIMILIAN I. Margaret was born in the Spanish Netherlands and became regent there (1507–30 with one interval) for her nephew Charles (later Emperor CHARLES V). In 1508 Margaret helped the inception of the League of CAMBRAI. In 1529 she negotiated the Treaty of CAMBRAI with Louise of Savoy (mother of FRANCIS I of France).

Margaret of Norway (*c.*1283–90) Queen of Scots, granddaughter of ALEXANDER III and daughter of Eric II of Norway. She inherited the Scottish crown aged three. Margaret was pledged to marry the heir to the English throne, but was drowned on the crossing from Norway to Scotland. Her death led to a disputed succession, adjudicated by EDWARD I of England in favour of John BALLIOL.

Margaret of Parma (1522–86) Regent of the Netherlands (1559–67) for PHILIP II of Spain, her half-brother. The illegitimate daughter of Emperor CHARLES V, she married Ottavio Farnese, Duke of Parma, as her second husband in 1538. As regent, she was energetic and at first tolerant, later repressive. She was replaced by the Duke of ALBA. *See also* REVOLT OF THE NETHERLANDS

Margaret of Valois (1553–1615) French queen consort, daughter of HENRY II and CATHERINE DE' MÉDICI. Her forced marriage (1572) to the Protestant Henry of Navarre (later HENRY IV) was almost immediately succeeded by the SAINT BARTHOLOMEW'S DAY MASSACRE of the HUGUENOTS. The marriage was dissolved in 1599, ten years after Henry's accession. Beautiful and gifted, Reine Margot was involved in political intrigues and sexual affairs and banned from Paris until 1605. In her *Memoirs*, she left a revealing picture of French society.

Margaret Tudor (1489–1541) Queen consort of JAMES IV of Scotland, daughter of HENRY VII of England. She married James in 1503, and at his death (1513) became regent for their infant son, JAMES V. She was removed from power in 1515 but continued to play an active part in Scotland's turbulent political affairs as wife (1514–27) of the Earl of Angus, a Douglas (their daughter was mother of Lord DARNLEY and grandmother of James I of England) and, after divorcing Angus, of Lord Methven.

María Cristina (1806–78) Queen consort of FERDINAND VII of Spain. At María's behest, Ferdinand named their daughter ISABELLA II as heir. She became regent after Ferdinand's death (1833) and marshalled Isabella's forces against the supporters of Don CARLOS, the late king's brother and pretender to the throne. Forced from the regency by Baldomero ESPARTERO (1840), she returned in 1843 and thereafter played a major role in the political intrigues that marked Isabella's reign. *See also* CARLISM

Maria I (1743–1816) Queen of Portugal (1777–1816), daughter of Joseph Emanuel. She married (1760) her uncle, who (as Pedro III) ruled jointly with her. Mentally weak, Maria's mind gave way after the death of her husband (1786), and her son, later JOHN VI, ruled as regent. In 1807 she fled with the rest of the royal family to Brazil.

Maria II (1819–53) Queen of Portugal (1826–28, 1834–53), daughter of Emperor PEDRO I of Brazil. She was betrothed to her uncle, MIGUEL, who attempted to usurp the crown, thereby setting off the Miguelist Wars. Maria's forces, led by her father and supported by British naval power, defeated Miguel in 1834. Her reign, however, was marked by continual political unrest. She was succeeded by her son, Pedro V.

María Luisa (1751–1819) Queen consort of CHARLES IV of Spain, mother of FERDINAND VII. She and her lover, Manuel de GODOY, were the actual rulers of Spain. When Charles was forced out by NAPOLEON I, she went into exile with him. She appears in several unflattering paintings by Goya. *See also* PENINSULAR WAR

Maria Theresa (1717–80) Archduchess of Austria, ruler of the Austrian HABSBURG dominions (1740–80). She succeeded her father, Emperor CHARLES VI, by the PRAGMATIC SANCTION, but was challenged by neighbouring powers in the War of the AUSTRIAN SUCCESSION (1741–48), losing Silesia to Prussia but securing the imperial title for her husband, FRANCIS I. Count von KAUNITZ, one of several well-chosen ministers, negotiated an alliance with France, but failed to regain Silesia in the SEVEN YEARS' WAR (1756–63). At home, her rule was generally benign and moderately reformist. After the death of Francis (1765), she ruled jointly with her son, Emperor JOSEPH II. *See* illustration, page 262

Marie Antoinette (1755–93) Queen consort of LOUIS XVI of France, daughter of Emperor FRANCIS I and MARIA THERESA of Austria. She married Louis in 1770. Her frivolity and extravagance contributed to popular dislike of the royal court which was a factor in the FRENCH REVOLUTION (1789–99). After the royal family's unsuccessful attempt to escape abroad in 1791, she was held prisoner, displaying courage and dignity before she was finally guillotined.

Marie de Médicis (1573–1642) Queen consort of HENRY IV of France, regent (1610–14). A daughter of the Medici Grand Duke of Tuscany, she married Henry in 1600. He was assassinated, possibly with her connivance, the day after she was crowned queen in 1610. As regent for her son, LOUIS XIII, she relied on Italian advisers and reversed Henry's anti-Habsburg policy. She was at odds with Louis after he came of age (1614) and antagonized Cardinal

▲ **Maria Theresa** was a keen patron of art and music and made significant reforms to the Habsburg administration, including the introduction of compulsory primary education.

M

Richelieu. After her plot to oust Richelieu failed in 1630, she was banished from court and settled in Brussels (1631).

Marie Louise (1791–1847) French empress, second wife of Napoleon I and daughter of Austrian Emperor Francis II. Marie and Napoleon married in 1810. Their son was the future Napoleon II. Marie Louise acted briefly as regent during Napoleon's absences on campaign. Alienated from him by 1814, she was later made duchess of Parma.

Marion, Francis (1732–95) American soldier in the American Revolution (1775–83), known as the "Swamp Fox". He participated in the defence of Charleston (1780) and after its fall led guerrilla raids on the British in South Carolina.

Marius, Gaius (157–86 bc) Roman general and military reformer. His policy of recruiting poor men without property contributed to the bond between Roman troops and their commanders. He also revised army training and equipment. His rivalry with Sulla forced him out of Rome, but he raised an army and recaptured the city (87 bc).

Mark Antony *See* Antony, Mark

Markievicz, Constance, Countess (1868–1927) Irish nationalist, b. Constance Gore-Booth. She married a Polish count in 1900. Markievicz joined Sinn Féin, fought in the Easter Rising (1916) and was sentenced to death but released after a spell in prison. In 1918, standing for Sinn Féin, Markievicz became the first woman elected to the British Parliament, but declined to take her seat. She was later a minister in the government of the Irish Free State.

Marlborough, John Churchill, 1st Duke of (1650–1722) English general and statesman. He defeated the Duke of Monmouth's Rebellion (1685) against James II, but later played a decisive role in overthrowing James in the Glorious Revolution (1688–89). With war looming, William III appointed him commander of British forces in the Low Countries in 1700. His strategic skill and statesmanship as captain-general in the War of the Spanish Succession gained a famous series of victories over the French, notably at Blenheim (1704), Ramillies (1706), Oudenaarde (1708) and Malplaquet (1709). He was rewarded with a dukedom and Blenheim Palace (although he had to pay much of the building costs). Growing war weariness in England led to the fall of the Whig government with which Marlborough was connected, and he was dismissed (1711) by the Tories. He was later reinstated by George I and directed the suppression of the Jacobite Rising of 1715. *See also* Godolphin, Sidney Godolphin, Earl of; Harley, Robert

Marne, battles of the Two conflicts in World War I fought near the River Marne, n France. The **First** Battle of the Marne (5–12 September 1914) was a decisive counterattack directed by the French General Joseph Joffre, which checked the German drive on Paris. The Germans subsequently dug in on the River Aisne, initiating the period of trench warfare. The **Second** Battle (15 July–7 August 1918) was another Allied counter-stroke, by Marshal Foch, which stopped the last German advance and preceded the final Allied offensive. Total casualties in the second battle were *c.*280,000 killed and wounded. *See also* Moltke, Helmuth Johannes Ludwig, Graf von

Maronite Member of a Christian, Arab community in Lebanon, Syria and, as a result of 19th-century emigration, other countries. The Maronite church traces its origins from Saint Maron (d.407), a Syrian hermit, and Saint John Maron, patriarch of Antioch in 685–707, who led the Maronites to independence and repelled the forces of the Byzantines. The Maronites appear to have followed the heresy of Monothelitism (denying the dual nature of Jesus Christ) for a long period, but they were reconciled with the Roman Church, retaining their own rites, and were allies of the Crusaders in the 12th century. In 1584 a Maronite college was founded in Rome. Their remoteness, plus French protection, preserved their independence under the Ottoman Empire. The 19th-century massacres of Maronites by the Druze, their Muslim neighbours, led to French intervention in Lebanon and Syria. In the early years of independence, the Lebanese government was always led by a Maronite. Today, out of a total of *c.*1 million Maronites worldwide, *c.*400,000 live in Lebanon. *See also* Phalange Party

Marquette, Father Jacques (1637–75) French Jesuit missionary and explorer in North America. He arrived in Québec as a missionary in 1666 and in 1673, with Louis Jolliet, led the first European exploration of the Great Lakes and the upper Mississippi River, which they followed as far as the mouth of the Arkansas River, correctly concluding that it flowed into the Gulf of Mexico.

Marsden, Samuel (1764–1838) British missionary and explorer in New Zealand. He went first to Australia, moving to New Zealand in 1814 to establish the first permanent white settlement at Russell. He and other missionaries endeavoured to end intertribal wars (made more murderous by European firearms), and reached the centre of North Island by 1830.

Marseilles (Marseille) City and seaport on the Gulf of Lyon, se France. The oldest city in France, it was founded in 600 bc by Greeks from Asia Minor. The town supported Rome against Carthage during the Punic Wars, and was annexed by Rome following its support of Pompey against Caesar in the Roman civil war. During the Crusades, Marseilles was a commercial centre and shipping port for the Holy Land. The 19th-century French conquest of Algeria and the opening of the Suez Canal (1869) brought great prosperity. Today, Marseilles is the second-largest city in France. Pop. (1990) 800,550.

Marshall, George Catlett (1880–1959) US general and statesman, secretary of state (1947–49) and secretary of defence (1950–51). He served as US chief of staff (1939–45) throughout World War 2 and was the leading US strategist at Allied conferences. He is remembered mainly for the Marshall Plan of economic assistance in post-war Europe, which gained him the Nobel Prize for Peace in 1953.

Marshall, John (1755–1835) US jurist, chief justice of the Supreme Court (1801–35). He was largely responsible for shaping the constitutional development of the United States and establishing the Supreme Court as co-equal with the executive and legislature. After fighting in the American Revolution, he took up law and entered politics. At the Virginia constitutional ratification convention (1788), Marshall argued successfully for the Constitution against Patrick Henry. He became a national figure as a negotiator in the XYZ Affair (1797–98). As chief justice, Marshall established the doctrine of judicial review in the Marbury v. Madison judgement (1803). Later judgements, often delivered against presidential opposition, confirmed the authority and precision of the Constitution, the unity of the federal court system, and the power of the federal government vis-à-vis the states.

Marshall, Thurgood (1908–93) US jurist, first African-American associate justice of the Supreme Court (1967–91). As counsel (1938–62) for the National Association for the Advancement of Colored People (NAACP), he played a key role in obtaining Supreme Court judgments against racial segregation in schools. Marshall was solicitor general (1965–67) before being appointed associate justice.

Marshall Islands Republic in the w Pacific Ocean. The islands were first recorded by Spaniards in the early 16th century, and named after a British captain, John Marshall, who visited them in 1788. They were held by Germany in 1885–1914, then by Japan until captured by US forces in 1944. From 1947 they were part of the US-administered Trust Territory of the Pacific Islands. The islands of Bikini and Eniwetok were used for testing nuclear bombs. They became self-governing in 1990, although they remain dependent on the United States for aid and defence.

MARSHALL ISLANDS

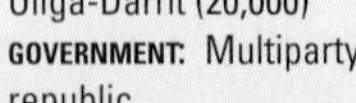

AREA: 181sq km (70sq mi)
POPULATION: 60,000
CAPITAL (POPULATION): Dalap-Uliga-Darrit (20,000)
GOVERNMENT: Multiparty republic
ETHNIC GROUPS: Micronesian
LANGUAGES: English, Marshallese (both official)
RELIGIONS: Protestant 90%, Roman Catholic 9%
GDP PER CAPITA (1994): US$1719

Marshall Plan (formally European Recovery Program) US package of economic aid to European countries after World War 2. It was linked with the Truman Doctrine, and recognized the need to fortify war-ravaged European economies and promote political stability in face of the perceived threat of the Soviet Union. The Plan was announced (1947) by US Secretary of State George Marshall. The Soviet Union and its satellites in Eastern Europe countries were offered participation but declined. Between 1948 and 1952, 16 countries received *c.*US13 billion in aid through the Plan.

Marsic War (90–89 bc) *See* Social War

Marston Moor, Battle of (2 July 1644) Decisive conflict in the English Civil War (1642–45), fought near York, n England. Royalist forces of *c.*18,000, led by Prince Rupert, were defeated by *c.*27,000 Parliamentarians (including Scots) under Thomas Fairfax. A crucial role was played by the cavalry of Oliver Cromwell. As a result of the Battle, n England was largely lost by the Royalists, whose casualties were *c.*3000, and *c.*4500 captured.

Martin V (1368–1431) Pope (1417–31). His election as pope ended 39 years of the Great Schism. He reorganized the Curia, restored the damaged prestige of the papacy and its authority in the Papal States, but failed to suppress the Hussites or re-establish union with the Eastern Orthodox Church.

Martin v. Hunter's Lessee (1816) Landmark case in US constitutional law in which the decision of the Supreme Court, under Chief Justice Joseph Story, upheld the Court's right to reverse state-court decisions and thus established the supremacy of the Supreme Court over all state courts.

Marx, Karl Heinrich (1818–83) German political and economic theorist, founder of Marxism. At Berlin University, Marx was influenced by the philosophy of G.W.F. Hegel, from whom his theory of dialetical materialism developed, and later by Ludwig Feuerbach's critique of religion ("the opium of the people" according to Marx). In *The German Ideology* (1845–46), Marx and Friedrich Engels described the "inevitable laws" of history. In Brussels, Belgium, Marx joined the Communist League and wrote with Engels the epoch-making *Communist Manifesto* (1848), forecasting the revolutionary overthrow of capitalism. Marx participated in the Revolutions of 1848 in France and Germany, then went to England (1849) where he lived until his death. His work at the library of the British Museum, London, produced a stream of writings, including *Das Kapital* (3 vols, 1867, 1885, 1894), which became the "bible of the working-class". *Das Kapital* depicts history as a continuous process of thesis, antithesis and synthesis, a constant class struggle which will end with the triumph of the proletariat under communism. The First International was formed in 1864, and Marx became its leading spirit. His expulsion (1872) of the anarchist Mikhail Bakunin from the International led to its collapse. Although the collapse of Soviet communism (1991) seemed to downgrade Marx's historical importance, his forecast of how capitalism would develop proved largely accurate. *See also* Marxism

Marxism School of socialism, based on the writings of Karl Marx, that arose in 19th-century Europe as a response to the growth of industrial capitalism. It predicates the inevitability of a communist society. Capitalism, concerned only with profits, would eventually provoke the workers into rebellion, establishing a society in which the means of production were collectively owned and classes, even the state itself, would disappear. Marx never stated his ideas in systematic form, but *The Communist Manifesto* (1848), a revolutionary pamphlet, and *Das Kapital* (1867–94), a work of huge scholarship, contained most of the ideas central to Marxism, which influenced many forms of socialism, especially communism. *See also* Lenin, Vladimir Ilyich; Mao Zedong

Mary I (1516–58) (Mary Tudor) Queen of England (1553–58), daughter of Henry VIII and Catherine of Aragon. On the death of her Protestant half-brother Edward VI, Mary, a devoted Catholic, acceded to the throne with popular support, despite the Duke of NORTHUMBERLAND's attempt to supplant her with Lady Jane GREY. But her marriage (1554) to the future PHILIP II of Spain provoked WYATT'S REBELLION, and the main result of the Spanish alliance was the loss of CALAIS (1558) to France. Mary's determination to re-establish papal authority and restore Catholicism to England involved reviving the heresy laws, and *c*.300 people, including the bishops Thomas CRANMER, Hugh LATIMER and Nicholas RIDLEY, were burnt at the stake. After a short but disastrous reign, Mary, nicknamed "Bloody Mary" by her enemies, was succeeded by her half-sister, ELIZABETH I.

Mary II (1662–94) Queen of England, Scotland and Ireland (1689–94), eldest daughter of JAMES II. Despite her father's Catholicism, Mary was brought up a Protestant. In 1677 she married her cousin, Prince William of Orange, and moved to Holland. During the GLORIOUS REVOLUTION (1688–89), she and her husband were invited to assume the English throne as joint monarchs. In practice, WILLIAM III ruled, but Mary was a competent regent during his absences.

Mary, Queen of Scots (1542–87) Queen of Scotland (1542–67). Daughter of JAMES V of Scotland, she succeeded him when one week old. Mary was sent to France aged six and married the future FRANCIS II of France in 1558. On his death (1560), she returned to reign in Scotland, where, as a Catholic, she came into conflict with Protestant reformers. Her marriage to Lord DARNLEY was also resented and soon broke down. After Darnley's murder (1567), she married James, Earl of BOTHWELL, possibly her husband's murderer, which alienated her remaining supporters. Following a rebellion of Scottish nobles, she was forced to abdicate in favour of her infant son, James VI (later JAMES I of England). She raised an army but was defeated at Langside (1568) and fled to England. Held in captivity, she became involved in plots against ELIZABETH I and was executed for treason.

Maryland State in E United States; the capital is Annapolis. When the first European trading post was established in 1631, the Native American inhabitants were mainly Algonquian peoples. In 1632 Lord Baltimore, seeking a refuge for fellow-Catholics, was granted settlement rights by CHARLES I of England, and 200 settlers arrived in 1634. The next 15 years witnessed growing tension between Catholics and Puritans. A colonial statute guaranteeing freedom of worship was passed in 1649, but was later repealed (1654) as the Puritans emerged as the dominant faction. Marylanders were prominent in the struggle for American independence, and Maryland was the first colony to adopt a state constitution (1776). In 1791 it ceded 174sq km (67sq mi) on the Potomac River to create the District of Columbia, site of the national capital, WASHINGTON, D.C. During the American CIVIL WAR, Maryland, a border state, adhered to the Union, but its citizens fought on both sides. The large slave-owning population found themselves politically at odds with the industrialists and business community who felt more closely aligned with the Union. After the Civil War, Maryland soon developed a strong economy largely thanks to its location as a crossover point between North and South. During the 20th century, partly due to increased manufacturing during the two World Wars, Maryland's industrial base continued to expand. Pop. (1990) 4,781,468.

Mary of Burgundy (1457–82) Daughter and heiress of CHARLES THE BOLD, Duke of BURGUNDY. When he died in 1477, Mary preserved Burgundy from French encroachment by marrying the future Holy Roman emperor, MAXIMILIAN I. Most of Burgundy subsequently passed to the Habsburgs, though France retained the duchy by the Treaty of Arras (1482).

Mary of Guise (Mary of Lorraine) (1515–60) Queen and regent (1554–59) of Scotland. A member of the powerful House of GUISE, she married JAMES V of Scotland in 1538. When James died in 1542, he was succeeded by their infant daughter, MARY, QUEEN OF SCOTS, who was later sent to France. Mary of Guise remained in Scotland as leader of the pro-French, Catholic faction, as against the pro-English, Protestant faction. A rebellion provoked

MARYLAND
Statehood :
28 April 1788
Nickname :
Old Line State, Free State
State motto :
Manly deeds, womanly words

English intervention (1559), and Mary, her forces besieged, died in Edinburgh Castle. *See also* KNOX, JOHN

Mary of Modena (1658–1718) Queen consort of JAMES II of England (married 1673). She shared James' unpopularity over rumours about the POPISH PLOT and the birth of her son, James Francis Edward STUART (1688) only served to antagonize James' Protestant enemies. After the GLORIOUS REVOLUTION (1688), Mary left for France with her son, quickly followed by James.

Masada Fortified hill near the Dead Sea, SE Israel. A natural fortress, it was the scene of the final defence of the Jewish ZEALOTS against the Romans during the Jewish revolt of AD 66–73. The last 960 defenders, committed mass suicide rather than surrender.

Masaryk, Jan (1886–1948) Czech statesman, son of Tomáš MASARYK. He was foreign minister under Edward BENEŠ and in the government-in-exile in London during World War 2. After the Allied victory, he retained the office. Soon after the communist takeover, he was killed when he fell – or was pushed – from a window.

Masaryk, Tomáš (1850–1937) Czech statesman and philosopher, president of Czechoslovakia (1918–35). He had an international reputation as a scholar when he founded the Progressive (or Realist) Party (1900) to represent Czech interests in the Austro-Hungarian empire. During World War 1, with Eduard BENEŠ, he visited Western capitals to secure support for an independent Czech and Slovak state, and subsequently became president of Czechoslovakia. Revered as the "father of the nation", Masaryk enacted land reforms and pursued a liberal path on minority rights. He was succeeded by Beneš.

Masinissa (*c*.238–149 BC) First king of NUMIDIA. A tribal chief, he fought against the Romans in Spain in the Second PUNIC WAR, but changed sides in 206 BC and helped bring about the downfall of CARTHAGE. Masinissa created his North African kingdom with Roman support, adding Carthaginian lands and converting many Numidian nomads to farming, but on his death his kingdom was divided among his heirs.

Mason, George (1725–92) US politician. A wealthy planter, he was the main author of the Virginia Declaration of Rights (1776), a model for the DECLARATION OF INDEPENDENCE and BILL OF RIGHTS, and a major influence on the CONSTITUTIONAL CONVENTION (1787). He opposed the Constitution on the basis that it conferred too much power on the federal government.

Mason, James Murray (1798–1871) Confederate official. He was a senator from Virginia (1847–61) until the Civil War, when he was appointed Confederate commissioner to Britain. En route to England, he was seized by Union officials on board the British steamer *Trent*. The so-called TRENT AFFAIR (1861) caused a crisis in US-British relations. Released a few weeks later, Mason arrived in England but failed to gain official recognition.

Mason-Dixon Line Border of Pennsylvania with Maryland and West Virginia, United States. It is named for the men who surveyed it in the 1760s. It was regarded as the dividing line between slave and free states at the time of the MISSOURI COMPROMISE (1820–21) and became the popular name for the boundary between North and South in the United States.

Massachusetts State in NEW ENGLAND, NE United States; the capital and largest city is BOSTON. It was inhabited by a number of autonomous NATIVE NORTH AMERICAN tribes when the first European settlers, the PILGRIMS, arrived at Plymouth in 1620. Settlement increased rapidly after the foundation of the MASSACHUSETTS BAY COLONY by English Puritans, who built Boston, and Puritan influence remained dominant until the late 17th century. The PLYMOUTH COLONY and Maine were included within Massachusetts by a royal charter in 1691. With a strong tradition of independence and mercantile enterprise, Massachusetts became the leading colony in resistance to British rule, its antipathy to restrictions on trade typified by the BOSTON TEA PARTY. The AMERICAN REVOLUTION began in the state with the battles of LEXINGTON AND CONCORD. During the early 19th century the textile industry began to take over from agriculture as the main industry. In the 1840s, Irish immigrants provided the first substantial non-English settlement, and the state continued to be an early leader in the Industrial Revolution in the United States. Strongly anti-slavery, Massachusettts welcomed the American CIVIL WAR. Depression in the early 20th century was reversed by production of military equipment in World War 2. The continued decline of farming and traditional industries after 1945 was offset by the rise of electronics, computer equipment and other high-technology industries, and Masachusetts again provided national leadership, notably through the KENNEDY family. Pop. (1990) 6,016,425.

Massachusetts Bay Colony One of the earliest English settlements in North America, sponsored by the MASSACHUSETTS BAY COMPANY. It was dominated by strong-minded PURITAN gentry such as John WINTHROP, the first governor, who brought the Company charter with them and thus acquired considerable independence in establishing a religious commonwealth. It was the most prosperous of the early colonies, with a population of *c*.20,000 by 1640. The city of BOSTON blossomed into a major maritime and commercial centre. The Puritan influence remained strong, and dissenters were banished, some leaving to form new settlements. The Massachusetts Bay Colony's charter was revoked in 1684 and it became (1691) the Royal Colony of Massachusetts, including Plymouth and Maine.

Massachusetts Bay Company English company chartered in 1629. Its purpose was trade and colonization of the land between the Charles and Merrimack rivers in North America. A group of prominent PURITANS gained control of the Company with the object of establishing a religious community, and founded the MASSACHUSETTS BAY COLONY (1630).

Massasoit (*c*.1580–1662) (Wawmegin) Chief of the Wampanoag Native Americans. He made an agreement with the early English settlers in Massachusetts and is said to have been a guest at the first Thanksgiving dinner. He remained on friendly terms with the colonists, but his son Metacomet was the "King Philip" of KING PHILIP'S WAR (1675–76).

Masséna, André (1756–1817) French general. Of humble origin, he served in the ranks during the French Revolutionary Wars, re-enlisted in 1791 and was a general by 1793. One of NAPOLEON's most trusted officers during the Italian campaign, he rose to be a marshal and Prince d'Essling (1810). He commanded the French army against the Duke of WELLINGTON during the PENINSULAR WAR (1810–11) and was narrowly defeated. *See also* NAPOLEONIC WARS

Massey, (Charles) Vincent (1887–1967) Canadian statesman, first Canadian-born governor general of Canada (1952–59). He was a minister in the government of Mackenzie KING (1925), minister to the United States (1926–30) and high commissioner in Britain (1935–46). Massey perhaps will be best remembered for the "Massey Report" (1951) in which he launched the policy of government subsidies for the arts.

MASSACHUSETTS
Statehood :
6 February 1788
Nickname :
Bay State
State motto :
By the sword we seek peace, but peace only under liberty

M

Massey, William Ferguson (1856–1925) New Zealand statesman, prime minister (1912–25). He emigrated from Ireland in 1870 and entered Parliament in 1894. Massey was responsible for reinvigorating the conservative opposition, renaming it the Reform Party (1909). Prime minister of the coalition government during World War 1, Massey also served in the imperial war cabinet (1917–18). He was a strong supporter of the British Empire, and opposed dominion status for New Zealand.

Matabeleland Former province of sw Rhodesia (now forming Northern and Southern Matabeleland provinces, Zimbabwe). The NDEBELE (formerly Matabele) conquered the region after splitting from the ZULU, and established a state in 1838. Matabeleland, rich in gold, was dominated by Cecil RHODES' British South Africa Company after 1889 and became part of the British colony of Southern Rhodesia in 1923.

Mata Hari (1876–1917) Dutch courtesan, b. Margaretha Geertruida Zelle. From 1905 she acquired a reputation as a leading exotic dancer in Paris, France. In 1917 Mata Hari was arrested as a German spy and subsequently shot. Although her conduct was suspicious, few people now believe she was the mysterious secret agent that the French authorities alleged.

Mather, Cotton (1663–1728) Puritan minister and scholar in colonial Massachusetts. He succeeded his father, Increase MATHER, at the Boston ministry in 1723. Mather supported the SALEM witch-trials, although not the subsequent executions, yet he was sympathetic to scientific and philosophical ideas. He was one of the founders of Yale University and a member of the Royal Society, London.

Mather, Increase (1639–1723) Puritan minister in colonial Massachusetts, one of the founders of CONGREGATIONALISM in Massachusetts. In 1664 he became minister of Boston's Second Congregational Church. Mather was a powerful influence on political and religious life in the colonies for more than 50 years and went to England (1688–91) to renegotiate the charter of Massachusetts. He doubted the testimony at the SALEM witch-trials, and his *Cases of Conscience* (1693) helped to stop the executions. On his death, his Boston ministry passed to his son, Cotton MATHER.

Matilda (1102–67) English consort of Holy Roman Emperor HENRY V, daughter of HENRY I of England. She married Henry in 1114, but after his death (1125) returned to England and was designated as her father's successor (his heir, William the Aethling, having died in 1120). In 1128 Matilda married GEOFFREY OF ANJOU. The nobility disapproved of this ANGEVIN marriage, however, and after Henry died (1135), helped STEPHEN seize the throne. A long civil war followed during which Matilda's forces captured Stephen (1141), but her high-handedness encouraged a popular rebellion and Matilda fled to NORMANDY. Her son succeeded Stephen as HENRY II.

Matsudaira Sadanobu (1759–1829) Japanese minister. He was responsible for the Kansei reforms that sought to revive Japanese society under the TOKUGAWA shogunate. Matsudaira Sadanobu was overlooked as shogun, instead becoming a DAIMYO (lord). His influence, however, secured the appointment of Tokugawa Ienari as shogun (1787–1837), and Matsudaira became chief minister. He clamped down on government corruption and expenditure and placed restrictions on foreign trade, while encouraging agricultural production to relieve famine. The reforms proved too conservative and did not outlast Matsudaira.

Matteotti, Giacomo (1885–1924) Italian politician. As secretary general of the Italian Socialist Party (PSI), Matteotti denounced the violence and corruption that followed the Fascist Party's rise to power in 1922, and was murdered at Benito MUSSOLINI's instigation. Popular discontent temporarily threatened Mussolini's leadership, but ultimately led to the establishment of a dictatorship. *See also* FASCISM

Matthias (1557–1619) Holy Roman emperor (1612–19), king of Hungary (1608–18) and Bohemia (1611–17), son of Emperor MAXIMILIAN II and younger brother of Emperor RUDOLPH II. Made governor general of Austria (1593) by Rudolph, Matthias, although personally tolerant in religious matters, was responsible for suppressing Protestant uprisings. While in Austria, he worked with the cleric Melchior Klesl who later became Matthias' senior adviser. In 1606 Matthias was recognized as heir to the throne. In the same year he made peace with the Turks and settled a Hungarian uprising by granting religious freedom. As emperor, Matthias, who left most of the affairs of state to Klesl, failed to reconcile Catholics and Protestants. He was succeeded by his cousin, FERDINAND II.

Matthias, Corvinus (1443–90) King of Hungary (1458–90), son of János HUNYADI. One of the greatest Hungarian rulers, he reorganized government, encouraged trade and industry, protected the peasants, restricted the nobles while promoting men of talent, and built an effective army. As a great patron of the Renaissance, he founded two universities and the Bibliotheca Corvina, the famous library at his brilliant court in Buda. He won a substantial central European empire and conquered much of Austria, hoping to secure the imperial title to strengthen his war against the Ottoman Turks.

Mau Mau Anti-colonial terrorist group among the KIKUYU of British-ruled Kenya, bound by secret oath to expel Europeans. Serious violence began in 1952, and the colonial government declared a state of emergency. About 100 Europeans and 2000 Africans, mainly Kikuyu, were killed, plus *c.*11,000 Mau Mau. Thousands were also imprisoned, including the alleged leader, Jomo KENYATTA. The Mau Mau were defeated by 1960 and in 1963 Kenya achieved independence under Kenyatta.

Maurice of Nassau (1567–1625) Prince of Orange. He was named as stadtholder (governor) in Holland on the death of his father, WILLIAM I (THE SILENT), and later adopted by most of the United Provinces of the Netherlands. His victories against the Spanish (1590–1604) contributed to securing Dutch independence. He later quarrelled with Jan van OLDENBARNEVELT, his long-time adviser and ally, and secured his execution (1619). *See also* REVOLT OF THE NETHERLANDS

Maurice (1521–53) Duke (1541–53) and Elector (1547–53) of Saxony. A Protestant, he declined to join the SCHMALKALDIC LEAGUE (1546) against Emperor CHARLES V in order to gain the rank of elector. He later changed sides, fighting against Charles, and eventually forced the emperor to accept the Treaty of Passau (1552), acknowledging LUTHERANISM in Germany. He died fighting Albert Alcibiades, Margrave of Brandenburg.

Mauritania *See* country feature

Mauritius Republic in the sw Indian Ocean; the capital is Port Louis (on Mauritius). The Dutch began to colonize the island in 1598, naming it after Prince MAURICE OF NASSAU. In 1715 Mauritius came under the control of France. The French established sugarcane plantations and imported African slave labour. In 1810 Britain seized Mauritius, and it was formally recognized as a British colony in 1814. In 1833 slavery was abolished and Indian forced labour was used instead. In 1968 Mauritius achieved independence as a member of the Commonwealth. In 1992 it became a republic. Ethnic and class divisions, combined with economic austerity, created a divided society in the 1980s.

Mauryan empire (321–185 BC) Ancient state in India, founded by CHANDRAGUPTA Maurya (d. *c.*291 BC).

M

MAURITANIA

AREA: 1,025,520sq km (395,953sq mi)
POPULATION: 2,143,000
CAPITAL (POPULATION): Nouakchott (393,325)
GOVERNMENT: Multiparty Islamic republic
ETHNIC GROUPS: Arab-Berber 70%, Wolof 7%, Tukulor 5%, Soninke 3%, Fulani 1%
LANGUAGES: Arabic (official)
RELIGIONS: Islam 99%
GDP PER CAPITA (1995): US$1540

Republic in NW Africa. BERBERS migrated to the region in the first millennium AD. The Hodh basin lay at the heart of the ancient GHANA empire (700–1200), and towns grew up along the trans-Saharan caravan routes. In the 11th and 12th centuries the region was at the centre of the Berber ALMORAVID empire. In the 14th and 15th centuries it formed part of the MALI empire.

Portuguese mariners explored the coast in the 1440s, but European colonialism did not begin until the 17th century, when trade in gum arabic became important. Britain, France and the Netherlands were all interested in this trade. In 1903 France set up a protectorate and Mauritania became part of French West Africa in 1904. In 1920 it became a colony.

In 1958 Mauritania became a self-governing territory in the French Union before achieving full independence in 1960. Moktar Ould DADDAH was elected president and re-elected in 1966 and 1971. Mauritania became a one-party state. Devastating drought increased dissatisfaction with Daddah's regime. In 1973 Mauritania withdrew from the franc zone and joined the Arab League. In 1976 Spain pulled out from Spanish Sahara (now WESTERN SAHARA): MOROCCO occupied the northern two-thirds of the region, while Mauritania gained the remaining portion. Nationalists, led by the guerrillas of the Popular Front for the Liberation of Saharan Territories (POLISARIO), began an armed struggle for independence that drained Mauritania's resources.

In 1978 Daddah was overthrown in a military coup, and a military committee assumed control. Mauritania withdrew from Western Sahara in 1979, after signing a peace agreement with POLISARIO. Morocco subsequently annexed the region of Tiris el Gharbia to which Mauritania had renounced its claim. In 1984 recognition of Western Sahara's independence provoked civil unrest, and Ould Taya came to power. In 1991 Mauritania adopted a new constitution. In the 1992 multiparty elections, Ould Taya was elected president. He was re-elected in 1997 after a boycott by opposition parties. Tension continues between the African minority in s Mauritania and Arabs and Berbers in the north.

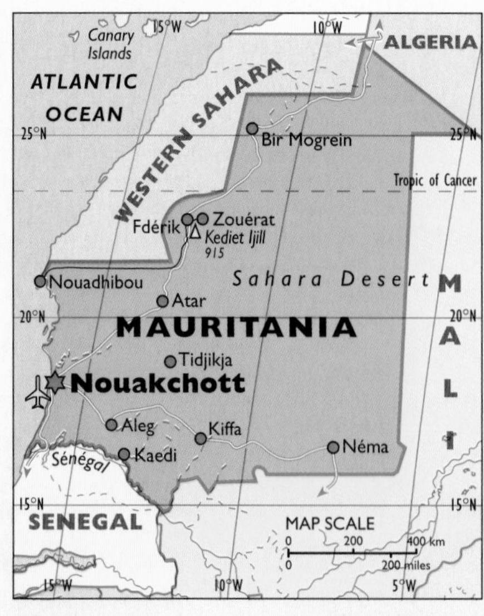

MAURITIUS
AREA: 2040sq km (788sq mi)
POPULATION: 1,155,000
CAPITAL (POPULATION):
Port Louis (144,776)
GOVERNMENT: Multiparty republic
ETHNIC GROUPS: Indian 68%, Creole 27%, Chinese 3%, White 2%
LANGUAGES: English (official), Bhojpuri, Creole, French
RELIGIONS: Hindu 51%, Roman Catholic 27%, Muslim 16%
GDP PER CAPITA (1995): US$13,210

Chandragupta established a powerful army and an efficient bureaucracy, and the Mauryan empire spread west of the River Indus into what is now Afghanistan. This advance initially encouraged attacks from the SELEUCIDS, but a Mauryan victory (305 BC) led to a peaceful alliance. Chandragupta's son, **Bindusara** (r.297–271 BC), continued the military expansion, taking territories south as far as Mysore (now KARNATAKA). The Mauryan empire reached its greatest extent, encompassing much of the Indian subcontinent, in the strong but benign reign of Chandragupta's grandson, ASHOKA (*c*.272–232 BC). Ashoka's conversion to Buddhism and enlightened rule allowed the consolidation of his vast empire, and the population of some 50 million flourished. After Ashoka's death however, the empire rapidly disintegrated. Regions in the south sought autonomy, while in the north the Mauryans were under threat from invading forces. The last Mauryan ruler, **Birhadratha**, was assassinated in *c*.185 BC during a palace coup.

Mavrokordátos, Aléxandros (1791–1865) Greek statesman, b. Turkey. He joined the revolutionaries at the start of the GREEK WAR OF INDEPENDENCE (1821–29) and was elected president of the first national assembly in 1822. Mavrokordátos led the successful defence of the city of Missolonghi, w Greece, where he received the English poet Lord Byron. After the establishment of an independent Greek monarchy (1832) under King Otto, he served in two short spells as prime minister (1833, 1841). Mavrokordátos returned as prime minister (1844, 1854–55) after the revolution of 1843.

Maxentius, Marcus Aurelius Valerius (d. AD 312) Roman emperor (308–312). He gained the imperial title with help from his father, the former emperor MAXIMIAN. Powerful rivals restricted his rule to Italy, and one of them, the future CONSTANTINE I (THE GREAT), defeated and killed him at the Battle of Milvian Bridge.

Maximian (d.AD 310) Roman emperor (286–305, 306–08). Co-emperor with DIOCLETIAN, he governed Italy and the West. He was forced to abdicate with Diocletian in 305 but returned to power in the interests of his son, MAXENTIUS. When father and son fell out, Maximian was again forced to abdicate (308). He joined CONSTANTINE I (THE GREAT) in the East, but soon rebelled against him and, defeated, committed suicide.

Maximilian I (1459–1519) Holy Roman emperor (1493–1519), son and successor of FREDERICK III. Maximilian, a Renaissance prince who cultivated artists and scholars, was one of the most successful rulers of the HABSBURG dynasty, a result of his diplomatic alliances rather than warfare. He gained most of BURGUNDY, including the Netherlands, by marriage to MARY OF BURGUNDY, defending them against France. He was less successful in asserting control over the German princes, and his defeat by the Swiss (1499) led to their effective independence. Maximilian strengthened the Habsburg heartland in Austria and, through his son's marriage to the Spanish heiress, ensured that his grandson and successor, CHARLES V, inherited a vast empire.

Maximilian II (1527–76) Holy Roman emperor (1564–76), king of Bohemia (1562–76) and king of Hungary (1563–76), son and successor of FERDINAND I. He was tolerant of PROTESTANTISM and concluded a truce (1568) with Ottoman Sultan SELIM III. Obliged to maintain religious neutrality in order to preserve peace within the Empire, his political reforms were largely blocked by the German Protestant princes. *See also* REFOMATION

Maximilian I (1756–1825) First king of Bavaria (1806–25). A member of the House of WITTELSBACH, he fought for France in the French Revolutionary Wars (1792–1802). In 1799 he became Elector of Bavaria as Maximilian IV Joseph. In 1799 Maximilian was forced by Austria to enter the war against France, but he negotiated a separate peace in 1801 and promoted himself to king of Bavaria. Bavaria joined the CONFEDERATION OF THE RHINE, created by NAPOLEON I, and fought for the French in the NAPOLEONIC WARS, gaining most of w Austria in the process. The failure of the invasion of Russia, however, prompted Maximilian to agree peace terms with Austria. In 1818 Maximilian formed a national assembly.

Maximilian II (1811–64) King of Bavaria (1848–64), son of Louis I. He endeavoured to form an alliance of medium-sized German states to resist the hegemony of Austria and Prussia, and later sided with Austria against Prussia. Although a natural conservative, he conceded constitutional reforms in 1859.

Maximilian I (1573–1651) Duke (1597–1651) and Elector (1623–51) of Bavaria. He headed the Catholic League (1609) and fought against the Protestants in the THIRTY YEARS' WAR. After his forces defeated Elector Palatine FREDERICK V at the Battle of the White Mountain (1620), Emperor FERDINAND II rewarded him with the Palatinate; at the peace (1648) he retained the title but not the land. He was responsible for the dismissal of Albrecht von WALLENSTEIN (1630), but suffered defeat against GUSTAVUS II of Sweden (1632). The leading Roman Catholic prince in Germany, he resisted imperial efforts to strengthen Habsburg rule.

Maximilian II Emanuel (1662–1726) Elector of Bavaria (1679–1704, 1713–26). He was governor of the Spanish Netherlands (1692–99), but allied himself with France in the War of the SPANISH SUCCESSION (1701–14). After victory at Hochstadt (1703), he was defeated at Blenheim (1704) and later fled to France. *See also* WITTELSBACH

Maximilian, Ferdinand Joseph (1832–67) Emperor of Mexico (1864–67), brother of Emperor FRANZ JOSEPH. He accepted the throne of Mexico after the French invasion (1862) with the encouragement of NAPOLEON III. He was opposed by liberals led by Benito JUÁREZ, and his moderate policy alienated conservatives. When the French withdrew in 1867, Maximilian was overthrown by the liberal forces and executed.

Maya *See* feature article, page 266

Mayflower Ship that transported the PILGRIMS from Plymouth, England, to MASSACHUSETTS in 1620. It carried 102 English Separatists (religious dissenters), some from a congregation that had settled in the Netherlands. The *Mayflower* remained with the settlers as they struggled to build PLYMOUTH COLONY through the winter (when half of them died), before returning to England in May 1621.

Mayflower Compact Agreement to establish a preliminary government for the PILGRIMS. It was signed by 41 men on the MAYFLOWER on 21 November 1620 off the New England coast. The Compact, modelled on a Separatist church covenant, was thought necessary to safeguard against a split between Separatists and others. *See also* BRADFORD, WILLIAM

May Fourth Movement (1919) Chinese nationalist tendency. It began as a student protest in Beijing, N China, over the award of Germany's former rights in Shandong, NE China, to Japan in the Treaty of Versailles, instead of returning them to China. It developed into a nationwide, patriotic popular movement against administrative chaos and social disintegration and demanding cultural revival and reform. The Movement led to the resurgence of the KUOMINTANG. It influenced the early CHINESE COMMUNIST PARTY (CCP). *See also* CHEN DUXIU

Mazarin, Jules (1602–61) French statesman and cardinal, b. Italy. Initially an envoy for Pope URBAN VIII, he became a protégé of Cardinal RICHELIEU after serving in France (1631–39) as the papal representative. Following the deaths of Richlieu (1642) and LOUIS XIII (1643), Mazarin became chief minister of France under the regency of ANNE OF AUSTRIA during LOUIS XIV's minority. More subtle and less ruthless than Richelieu, Mazarin, however, was determined to prosecute the THIRTY YEARS' WAR, causing impoverishment and higher taxation for the people of France. Popular discontentment boiled over into the civil wars of the FRONDE (1648–52), the second of which was triggered by Mazarin's imprisonment of the Great CONDÉ. Mazarin fled to Germany from where, with the support of Anne and Marshal TURENNE, he eventually outmanoeuvred his opponents to emerge in full command, returning to Paris in 1653. The next years Mazarin spent teaching Louis XIV military and political skills, and most importantly instilling in him the absolute power of the monarchy. Mazarin's diplomatic skills helped him to negotiate the Peace of the PYRENEES (1659), which ended the war with

M

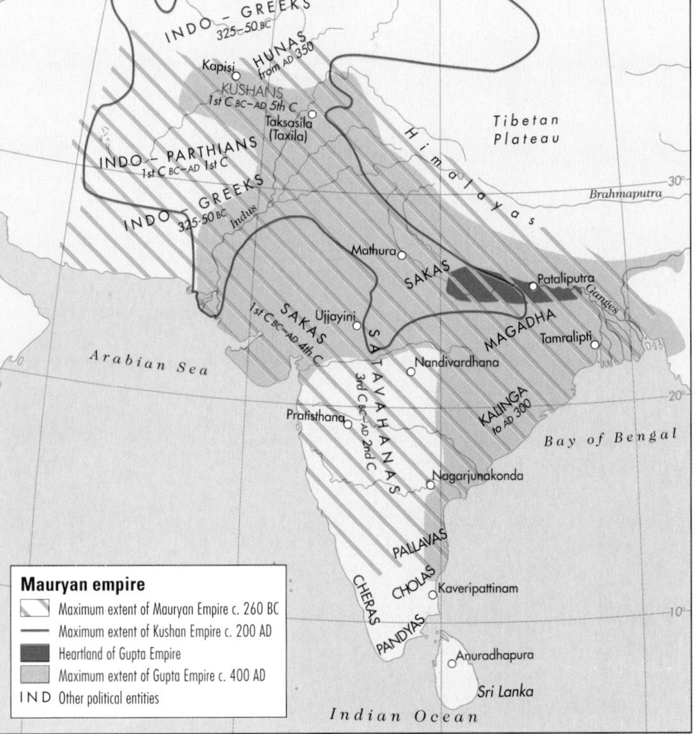

◄ **Mauryan empire** By the 5th century BC, Magadha had emerged as the most powerful kingdom in the Ganges region, with its capital at Pataliputra. Magadha's control of trade along the River Ganges and the availability of raw materials, such as iron, provided great wealth. By 297 BC, Chandragupta Maurya of Magadha had laid the foundations of the Mauryan empire in N India. Under Ashoka, who conquered Kalinga in 261 BC, the empire became the first to encompass most of the Indian subcontinent. The empire disintegrated after the death of Ashoka, however, and none of the numerous independent kingdoms that subsequently emerged were strong enough to resist successive waves of foreign invaders.

Spain and resulted in a Spanish bride for Louis, thus giving him a legitimate claim to the Spanish throne. By the end of his term in office, Mazarin had made Louis the most powerful ruler in Europe. Mazarin's policies were continued by his successor Jean Baptiste COLBERT.

Mazzini, Giuseppe (1805–72) Italian patriot and leader of the RISORGIMENTO. A member of the CARBONARI from 1827, Mazzini was arrested (1831) and exiled to France by the Piedmontese authorities, where he founded the YOUNG ITALY movement. Later expelled from France, Mazzini travelled through Europe arguing for the unification of Italy. Following the REVOLUTIONS OF 1848, Mazzini returned to Rome (1849) where he effectively led the newly created Roman republic, but was soon forced to flee again when the republic was crushed by the French. During the 1850s Mazzini failed to raise support during a number of minor insurrections, and his popularity began to wane in the face of the moderate Conte di CAVOUR. *See also* GARIBALDI, GIUSEPPE; ORSINI, FELICE; PIUS IX

M'ba, Léon (1902–67) Gabonese statesman, first president of independent Gabon (1961–67). He had previously been chief minister under French colonial rule. M'ba was briefly ousted in 1964, but was reinstated by French troops, and remained in office until his death. He was succeeded by Omar BONGO.

Mbeki, Thabo (1942–) South African statesman, president (1999–). He went into exile in Europe after Hendrik VERWOERD banned the AFRICAN NATIONAL CONGRESS (ANC) in 1962. In 1964 his father, Govan Mbeki (1910–), was sentenced to life imprisonment on Robben Island with Nelson MANDELA. In 1975 Thabo Mbeki became the youngest member of the national executive of the ANC, and in 1978 he was appointed as a personal adviser to its president Oliver TAMBO. Mbeki was one of the leading figures in maintaining international presure on the APARTHEID regime. Mbeki returned to South Africa after President F.W. DE KLERK lifted the ban on the ANC in 1990. He succeeded Tambo as chair of the ANC in 1993, and the following year became first deputy president to Mandela in South Africa's first multiracial democratic government. In 1997 Mbeki succeeded Mandela as president of ANC and he easily won the 1999 elections. As president, Mbeki promised to tackle the domestic problems of high unemployment, poverty and violent crime, and play a leading role in resolving conflicts in Africa.

Mboya, Thomas Joseph (1930–69) Kenyan statesman. A Luo, with a background in organized labour, he was a leader of the Kenya independence movement. Mboya was a major influence in the discussions over a new constitution (1960), when he headed the new Kenya African National Union (KANU). After independence (1963) he was a minister in Jomo KENYATTA's government. His assassination provoked rioting by the Luo against the dominant KIKUYU.

Mbundu (Ovimbundu) People of W Angola, including the NDONGO, Pende and other groups. In the 16th century their territory was exploited by slave traders and overrun by the Portuguese, who took the name of their ruler, *ngola*, for the region. Subjugation inspired a rich literary tradition of protest, and the Mbundu, led by Agostinho NETO, were prominent in the fight for Angolan independence (1975).

Meany, George (1894–1980) US UNION leader. He was secretary treasurer (1940–52) of the AMERICAN FEDERATION OF LABOR (AFL) and then its president (1952–55). He was a leading force in the merger (1955) of the AFL and Congress of Industrial Organizations (CIO), and served as the AFL–CIO president until 1979.

Mecca (Arabic *Makkah*) City in W Saudi Arabia, the holiest city of ISLAM, barred to non-Muslims, and birthplace of the Prophet MUHAMMAD. When his teaching was rejected by the Arab merchant community, Muhammad fled to MEDINA (the HEJIRA) in 622, the beginning of the Muslim era. After capturing Mecca in 630, he made it the centre of the Islamic world. In 1517 it came under Ottoman Turkish rule. From 1806 Mecca was held by the WAHHABI, until MUHAMMAD ALI of Egypt defeated them (1818). In 1916 HUSSEIN IBN-ALI declared independence from the Turks

MAYA

Ancient NATIVE MIDDLE AMERICAN civilization of S Mexico and N Central America. The history of the Maya is broadly divided into three periods; the Preclassic (*c*.1500 BC–AD 300), the Classic (AD 300–900) and the Postclassic (AD 900–1500). Archaeologists also traditionally distinguish four regions: the N lowlands of the Yucatán Peninsula, the S lowlands (E and W of modern-day central Guatemala), the central region of Petén (N Guatemala) and a S region of the Guatemalan highlands.

The **Preclassic** period saw farming change from shifting cultivation to more intensive techniques. This transformation resulted in growing populations and a gradual shift away from family-based settlements to the development of larger villages that had forms of early social hierarchies. During this period, the Maya were influenced by the OLMEC and had contact with other states, particularly the TEOTIHUACÁN empire. Towards the end of the Preclassic period, impressive civic and religious buildings were constructed, notably the pyramids at El Mirador, and greater cooperation developed between the lowland and highland communities.

During the **Classic** period, Maya city-states of the central region, such as TIKAL, COPÁN, Palenque and Piedras Negras, flourished. Hereditary kings, who also performed religious ceremonies, formed the pinnacle of increasingly sophisticated and complex social structures. The now largely autonomous city-states featured stone temples and palace complexes, and the Classic period produced the most elaborate murals, paintings, carvings and ceramics. Most religious ceremonies centred around offerings to a number of gods. Often the offerings were simple objects or cups of blood provided by the worshippers themselves. However, human sacrifice was common, particularly in the more significant religious ceremonies or during times of crisis, such as drought. Rival Maya cities often fought, but there is no evidence of large-scale conquest. It was during the Classic period that the Maya made their greatest advances in astronomy, developing accurate calendar systems, and hieroglyphic writing. Warfare, famine and disease caused the decline of the Classic Maya in the central and S lowlands.

The "Maya Collapse" (AD 800–900) marks the start of the **Postclassic** period and saw the sphere of influence move to the N lowlands with the rise of great city-states such as UXMAL and CHICHÉN ITZÁ, the latter conquered by another city-state, Mayapán, during the late 13th century. By *c*.1450 Mayapán had been overthrown by competing rulers, notably those of Uxmal, and the entire region succumbed to civil war. Lack of unity facilitated Spanish conquest (1542), but *c*.4 million Maya remain in the same area today.

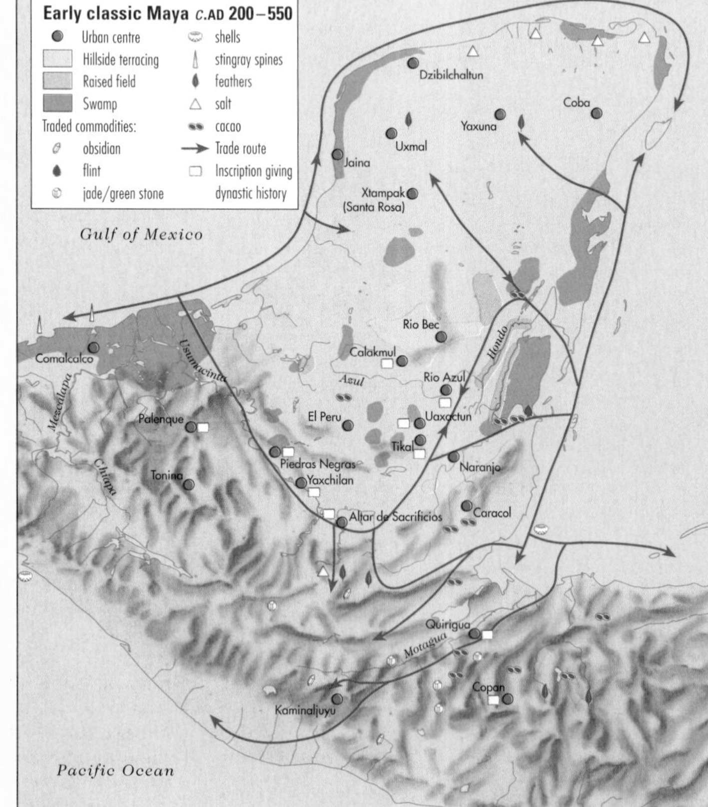

◄ **agriculture** During the Classic period, the Maya began to employ intensive farming techniques. Terraces were cut into hillsides to counteract erosion, and canals were dug along rivers and in *bajos* (seasonal swamps) for drainage, water storage, fish-farming and transport. Highly productive raised fields were constructed between grids of canals. As in other Mesoamerican civilizations, trade played an important part in Maya life, providing materials for daily living and religious rituals.

► **Mayan pottery** Cylindrical vessels were made to commemorate gods and rulers and used in burial or sacrificial ceremonies, or for storage. The painting on this vessel depicts players in a ball game, an important ritual activity in the ancient civilizations of Mesoamerica.

and Mecca became the capital of the kingdom of the HEJAZ. In 1924 it was seized by the Wahhabi under IBN SAUD, founder of Saudi Arabia. Pop. (1991 est.) 630,000.

Mečiar, Vladimir (1942–) Slovak statesman, prime minister (1990–91, 1992–94, 1994–98). In 1969 he was ousted from the Communist Party after supporting the "PRAGUE SPRING". After the collapse of communism in Czechoslovakia in 1989, Mečiar won the 1990 elections in Slovakia, but was removed as prime minister after accusations of collaboration with the old communist regime. Mečiar formed the Movement for a Democratic Slovakia (HZDS) and, campaigning for greater Slovak autonomy, won the 1992 elections. Negotiations with Czech Prime Minister Václav KLAUS led to the creation of an independent Slovak Republic with Mečiar as prime minister. Criticized for failing to deal with the economic recession, he was briefly removed from power in 1994. His third term failed to implement free-market reforms, placed restrictions on the media and suppressed political opposition. Defeated by a united front of opposition parties, Mečiar resigned as leader of the HZDS. In 1999 he was defeated in Slovakia's first presidential elections.

Media Ancient region in what is now Iran, SW of the Caspian Sea, the home of the Medes. Traditionally founded (*c*.720 BC) by the chieftain Dayauku, the various tribes of Media were united under **Khshathrita** (r. *c*.678–652 BC) who drove out their former rulers, the ASSYRIANS. Khshathrita was killed by SCYTHIAN invaders. Under Khshathrita's son, **Cyaxares** (r. *c*.652–584 BC), the Medes defeated and expelled the Scythians and subjugated the Persians, a related people. Cyaxares created an empire which, with Babylonian allies, defeated the Assyrians and captured NINEVEH (612 BC). The next ruler, **Astyages** (r. *c*.584–550 BC), was overthrown by CYRUS II (THE GREAT) of Persia, who united the Medes and the Persians, and created the much larger ACHAEMENID empire.

Medicare and Medicaid US government health-insurance plans for the elderly and the poor respectively, introduced (1965) by President Lyndon JOHNSON. The **Medicare** plan provides for 90 days of hospital care for most persons aged 65 or over, financed through social security taxes, and 100 days of nursing care. It also includes a government-subsidized supplementary medical insurance plan, financed through general taxation. It was extended to the long-term disabled in 1972. **Medicaid** is a means-tested scheme for people on low-income and is jointly funded by the federal government and the states.

Medici, Alessandro (1510–37) Duke of FLORENCE, illegitimate son of Lorenzo de' MEDICI (1492–1519). Appointed (1523) by his uncle, Pope CLEMENT VII, to rule republican Florence with his cousin Ippolito, he was expelled by a popular revolt (1527). Alessandro was restored (1531) and made hereditary duke of Florence by his father-in-law, Emperor CHARLES V, but was murdered.

Medici, Catherine de' *See* CATHERINE DE' MEDICI

Medici (the Elder), Cosimo de' (1389–1464) Ruler of FLORENCE (1434–64). He challenged the ruling oligarchy and was expelled from Florence in 1433 but returned in 1434 and, while officially holding minor office, ruled as a virtual despot. He increased the Medici banking fortune, strengthened Florence by alliance with Milan and Naples, and was a patron of the scholars and artists of the early RENAISSANCE. His rule was popular and he was posthumously titled "father of his country".

Medici (the Great), Cosimo I de' (1519–74) Duke of FLORENCE (1537–74), Grand Duke of Tuscany (1569–74). Under Cosimo's authoritarian rule, Florence flourished and its territory swelled with the acquisition of Siena. He was given the title of grand duke by the pope.

Medici, Ferdinand I de' (1549–1609) Third grand duke of Tuscany (1587–1609). By marrying Christine of Lorraine (granddaughter of the French queen, CATHERINE DE' MEDICI) in 1589, he provided a French counterbalance to Spanish influence in Italy.

Medici, Ferdinand II de' (1610–70) Fifth grand duke of Tuscany (1620–70), son of Cosimo II (1590–1620) and father of Cosimo III (1642–1723), he was a pupil of Galileo. His weak rule in the midst of Medici extravagance is held responsible for the depletion of the family fortune.

Medici, Lorenzo de' (the Magnificent) (1449–92) Ruler of Florence, grandson of COSIMO DE' MEDICI (THE ELDER). In 1469 Lorenzo succeeded his father, Piero. His power worried Pope SIXTUS IV, who instigated a coup led by the rival Pazzi family. Lorenzo survived an assassination attempt and ruthlessly clamped down on his enemies. He presided over a brilliant RENAISSANCE court. His cultural interests made him neglect family business, but he recouped from state funds. His autocratic rule was attacked by Girolamo SAVONAROLA.

Medina City in W Saudi Arabia, the second holiest city of ISLAM. It was first settled by Jewish refugees from Palestine in AD 135. The Prophet MUHAMMAD, who was buried here, made it his capital after the HEJIRA (flight from MECCA) in 622. Medina's importance declined after the UMAYYAD caliphs moved the capital to DAMASCUS in 661. It was under Turkish rule from 1517 until 1916, when it became part of the kingdom of HEJAZ. It was included in Saudi Arabia in 1932. It remains an important centre of Muslim pilgrimage. Pop. (1991 est.) 400,000.

Medina del Campo, Treaty of (1489) Alliance between England and Spain designed to defend the duchy of Brittany against France, confirmed by the marriage of HENRY VII's son Arthur to the Spanish princess, CATHERINE OF ARAGON. It improved trade by reducing tariffs between England and Spain.

Medina Sidonia, Alonso Pérez de Guzmán, Duque de (1550–1619) Spanish commander of the ARMADA (1588). He was appointed by PHILIP II in spite of his inexperience of naval strategy and his own reluctance. He was, rightly, not blamed for the ensuing disaster, and continued to serve the Spanish crown after his return.

megalith ("large stone") Prehistoric stone monument. The term includes burial chambers and other structures but is applied especially to large standing stones, often arranged in circles or rows, dating from the Neolithic or early Bronze Age and common in N Europe. They were probably associated with some ceremonial event. The huge complex at CARNAC in Brittany is an example.

Megiddo Ancient city of CANAAN, in modern-day Israel. It was strategically located en route from Egypt to Mesopotamia and was the scene of many battles. The most famous, thanks to ancient Egyptian records, was the victory of THUTMOSE III over the Syrians in *c*.1468 BC. Megiddo was often rebuilt, notably by SOLOMON in the 10th century BC, and recent excavations have revealed extensive remains of Solomon's city.

Mehemet Ali *See* MUHAMMAD ALI

Mehmed *See* MUHAMMAD

Meighen, Arthur (1874–1960) Canadian statesman, prime minister (1920–21, 1926). He was elected to Parliament in 1908 and later served in the cabinet of Robert BORDEN. At the age of 46, Meighen became Canada's youngest prime minister. He advocated a protective tariff against US goods entering Canada and endeavoured to enlarge Canada's international role. He lost the elections of 1921 and 1926 to MACKENIZE KING.

Meiji (1852–1912) Emperor of Japan (1867–1912). His reign saw the transformation of Japan into a modern, industrial state, with a Western-style constitution, a conscript army and state education. The old privileged classes of DAIMYO and SAMURAI disappeared and Meiji became a constitutional monarch. *See* MEIJI RESTORATION

Meiji Restoration (1868) Constitutional revolution in Japan. Opposition to the TOKUGAWA shogunate increased after Japan's isolation was ended by US Commodore PERRY in 1854. Pressure for modernization resulted in a new government, at first dominated by princes and nobles, with Emperor MEIJI as its symbolic leader. The capital was moved to TOKYO. Equal rights for all Japanese were declared and representative government introduced (1890).

Meir, Golda (1898–1978) Israeli stateswoman, prime minister (1969–74), b. Ukraine as Golda Mabovitch. In 1906 her family emigrated to the United States, she became active in ZIONISM, and emigrated to PALESTINE in 1921. Meir was a leading figure in the Jewish Agency under the British mandate. After Israeli independence, she became minister of labour (1949–56) and foreign minister (1956–66). Meir succeeded Levi ESHKOL as prime minister, and managed to maintain a fragile domestic coalition while negotiating with Israel's Arab neighbours. She was forced to resign following criticism of the government's lack of preparedness for the YOM KIPPUR WAR (1973) and was succeeded by Yitzhak RABIN. *See also* ARAB-ISRAELI WARS

Melanchthon, Philipp (1497–1560) German religious reformer, b. Philipp Schwartzerd. He was closely associated with Martin LUTHER and took a leading role in formulating Protestant theology, notably in his *Loci communes* (1521) and the AUGSBURG CONFESSION (1530). A learned scholar, Melanchthon helped Luther with his German translation of the Bible (1522). He was a moderate, who always hoped for compromise with Roman Catholicism. *See also* LUTHERANISM; PROTESTANTISM

Melbourne, William Lamb, 2nd Viscount (1779–1848) British statesman, prime minister (1834, 1835–41). He entered the Commons as a Whig in 1805, and was elevated to the Lords in 1828. As home secretary (1830–34) in Earl GREY's administration, Melbourne grudgingly supported the REFORM ACTS of 1832 and was responsible for the suppression of the TOLPUDDLE MARTYRS. As prime minister, he reformed the POOR LAW (1834), but resisted changes to the CORN LAWS. Melbourne gave Lord PALMERSTON control of foreign affairs and tutored Queen VICTORIA in statecraft. He was succeeded by Sir Robert PEEL. His wife, Lady Caroline Lamb, had an affair with the English poet Lord Byron.

Mellon, Andrew William (1855–1937) US financier. He inherited a banking fortune, which he increased through industrial investments. He was secretary of the treasury under three presidents (1921–32). A generous patron of the arts, Mellon donated his collection plus cash to establish the National Gallery of Art, Washington, D.C. The tradition of art patronage was continued by his son and heir, **Paul Mellon** (1907–99), who founded the Yale Center for British Art (1976) at New Haven, Connecticut.

Memphis City of ancient EGYPT, on the W bank of the River Nile, S of modern CAIRO. According to tradition it was founded by MENES, who united Egypt *c*.3100 BC. Memphis was the capital of Egypt throughout the Old Kingdom, when the Pyramids were built nearby. It became an important centre again in the 7th century BC, as capital of Egypt under the Persians. When ALEXANDRIA was founded, it began to decline. Its ruins was used by the Arabs for building Cairo.

Mencius (*c*.372–289 BC) (Mengzi) Chinese philosopher. He followed CONFUCIUS closely both in life and in his

▲ **Medici, Lorenzo de' (the Magnificent)** Detail from the *Journey of the Magi* (1459–61) by Benozzo Gozzoli (1421–97), portraying Lorenzo de' Medici as one of the three Magi.

teaching. He spent 40 years travelling from court to court trying to persuade rulers to concentrate on goodness rather than conquest. Mencius held that human nature is fundamentally good and that the basic natural feelings can be developed into moral virtues. His teachings were recorded posthumously in the *Book of Mencius*, a classic text.

Mendès-France, Pierre (1907–82) French statesman, prime minister (1954–55). First elected as a Radical in 1932, he was imprisoned by the VICHY GOVERNMENT but escaped to London (1941) and later joined General Charles DE GAULLE's government-in-exile. After the French defeat at DIEN BIEN PHU (1954), Mendès-France became prime minister, promising to withdraw French troops from INDOCHINA. He also prepared the way for Tunisian independence and showed sympathy for Algerian nationalists which, with his deflationary economic plans, led to his downfall. He returned to government under Guy MOLLET and, after 1958, was increasingly critical of the autocratic De Gaulle's Fifth Republic.

Menderes, Adnan (1899–1961) Turkish statesman, prime minister (1950–60). He entered parliament as a member of Kemal ATATÜRK's Republican People's Party (RPP) in 1930, but was expelled from the RRP in 1945. In 1946 Menderes founded the Democratic Party (DP), the first legal opposition party in Turkey, and won a landslide victory in the 1950 elections. He maintained a pro-Western foreign policy, taking Turkey into the North Atlantic Treaty Organization (NATO) in 1952, but also encouraged greater links with Islamic states. Menderes presided over an inflationary economic boom, and was re-elected in 1954. He assumed authoritarian powers to crush internal opposition and was overthrown by an army coup and executed.

Mendoza, Antonio de (1490–1552) Spanish colonial administrator, viceroy of NEW SPAIN (1535–50) and viceroy of PERU (1551–52). An able administrator, Mendoza laid the basis for future Spanish colonial government, enforced the authority of the crown and increased its revenue, while encouraging cultural development, such as the foundation of the University of Mexico (1551).

Menelik II (1844–1914) Emperor of Ethiopia (1889–1913). He succeeded Johannes IV with Italian support after internal strife. Menelik brought the feudal chiefs under control, modernized the state and army, extended Ethiopia's borders, and built a railway from ADDIS ABABA to the French port of Djibouti. Discovering that the Italian alliance involved surrendering Ethiopia's sovereignty, he renounced it, and defeated the ensuing Italian invasion at the Battle of ADWA (1896). The Treaty of Addis Ababa confirmed Ethiopian independence. Menelik was succeeded by his grandson, Lij Iyasu.

Menem, Carlos Saúl (1935–) Argentinian statesman, president (1989–99). He was imprisoned (1976–81) by the military junta. Menem invoked the name of Juan PERÓN in his campaign for president, but took office during an economic crisis (inflation was running at 1000%) and was forced to abandon Perónist tradition. He introduced austerity measures, encouraging business and the free-market, and reducing inflation and foreign debt. Menem favoured moderation and compromise, pardoning officers accused of crimes under the regime of Leopoldo GALTIERI and restoring good relations with Britain without sacrificing Argentina's claim to the FALKLAND ISLANDS.

Menes King of ancient EGYPT (*c.*3100 BC). He is believed to have united Upper and Lower Egypt, probably by conquest, to become the first king of the First Dynasty and possibly the founder of MEMPHIS.

Mengistu, Haile Mariam (1937–) Ethiopian dictator and army officer, ruler of ETHIOPIA (1974–91). He led the coup that overthrew (1974) Emperor HAILE SELASSIE and became chairman of the Dergue (military council). Mengistu purged the Dergue of potential opponents in 1974 and crushed civilian opposition in 1977. With Soviet and Cuban support, he defeated a Somalian invasion of the Ogaden in 1977. In 1984 Mengistu founded the Workers' Party of Ethiopia and became president under a new constitution (1987). He ruthlessly presided over the decline and disintegration of Ethiopia, facing devastating famine and civil war against Eritrean and Tigrean secessionists in N Ethiopia. After the withdrawal of Soviet support, Mengistu was powerless to prevent the rebel advance on the capital, Addis Ababa, and fled into exile in Zimbabwe.

Menno Simons (*c.*1496–1561) Dutch religious reformer, after whom the MENNONITES are named. Originally a Roman Catholic priest, he became a moderate ANABAPTIST and preached in Germany and the Netherlands. Menno Simons described his beliefs in *The Foundations of Christian Doctrine* (1539).

Mennonites Christian sect founded by the Dutch reformer MENNO SIMONS and influenced by ANABAPTIST doctrine, although without its revolutionary overtones. Another group was founded in Switzerland by Conrad Grebel (*c.*1498–1526), a former disciple of Ulrich ZWINGLI. They recognise no authority but the Bible, and reject priests and the hierarchy. From 1683 many groups sought freedom from persecution in North America where, today, there are more than 200,000 Mennonites, including the ultra-conservative AMISH of Pennsylvania.

Menon, (Vengalil Krishnan) Krishna (1897–1974) Indian statesman and diplomat, minister of defence (1957–62). Living in London, England, from 1924, he campaigned for India's freedom from Britain and was secretary (1929–47) of the Indian League. After India gained independence in 1947, Prime Minister Jawaharlal NEHRU appointed Menon high commissioner for India in Britain (1947–52). As India's delegate (1952–62) to the United Nations (UN), Menon helped define the new republic's policy of non-alignment. He was forced to resign as minister of defence after India's defeat in the Sino-Indian War (1962), but continued to be active in the Indian Parliament.

Menshevik Moderate faction of the Russian Social Democratic Labour Party (SDLP). The Mensheviks ("the minority") split from the more radical BOLSHEVIKS ("the majority") in 1903. They believed in "scientific socialism" and a gradual transformation of society, whereas the Bolsheviks wanted total revolution. The Mensheviks were suppressed in 1922. *See also* RUSSIAN REVOLUTION

Menshikov, Alexander Danilovich (1673–1729) Russian field marshal and statesman. A boyhood friend of the future PETER I (THE GREAT), Menshikov was rapidly promoted from stable-boy to general during the Great NORTHERN WAR against Sweden, and was made a field marshal for his role in the Russian victory at the Battle of POLTAVA (1709). Menshikov became one of the most powerful figures in Russia, but his corrupt practices saw him fall from favour towards the end of Peter's reign. On Peter's death (1725), Menshikov still wielded sufficient power to ensure Peter's wife and Menshikov's former mistress, CATHERINE I, acceded to the throne. Menshikov virtually ruled Russia under Catherine, but in 1727 he was exiled to Siberia by her successor, PETER II, who heeded the counsel of Menshikov's enemies within the nobility.

Menzies, Sir Robert Gordon (1894–1978) Australian statesman, prime minister (1939–41, 1949–66). He entered Parliament in 1934, succeeding Joseph LYONS as prime minister and leader of the United Australia Party in 1939. Menzies dominated Australian politics for the next 25 years. He was forced to resign in 1941, but founded the LIBERAL PARTY in 1944 and, as the spokesman of free-enterprise, crushed the LABOR PARTY in the 1949 elections. He was a staunch supporter of preserving Australia's historic links with Britain. Menzies was a committed anti-communist, leading Australia into the ANZUS Pact and the SOUTHEAST ASIA TREATY ORGANIZATION (SEATO), and sending Australian troops to support the United States in the Vietnam War. He resigned in favour of Harold HOLT.

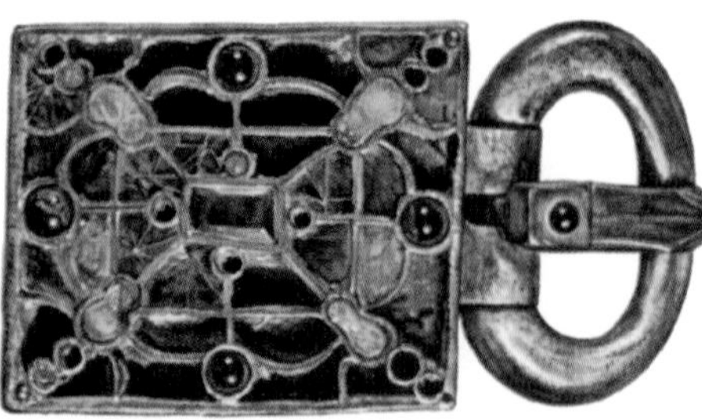

▲ **Merovingians** The geometrical design of this 6th-century buckle is typical of Merovingian art, which combined classical Roman and German-Frankish styles.

mercantilism Commercial doctrine dominant in Western Europe during the expansion of trade in the 16th and 17th centuries, especially in England, the Netherlands and France. According to mercantilist doctrine, trade and wealth were limited, and a nation's wealth was measured by its gold reserves. The aim of mercantilist policy was to maximize the influx of gold and raw materials and the output of manufactured goods. The government played an active role: tariffs protected exports and penalized imports from other countries. Mercantilism encouraged COLONIALISM, as colonies were sought to provide raw materials and buy manufactures. FREE-TRADE began to make headway, with some reductions in tariffs, in the 18th century, and the theory of mercantilism was demolished by, among others, Adam SMITH in *The Wealth of Nations* (1776).

Merchant Adventurers English trading company, founded in 1407. Based at Mercers' Hall, London, it enjoyed a monopoly in the export of finished cloth to the LOW COUNTRIES. At the height of its power in the 16th-century, the Adventurers handled *c.*75% of all English export trade. It went into decline after losing its market in the Spanish Netherlands in 1564 and lost its charter in 1689. The Adventurers finally collapsed in 1806.

Mercia Kingdom of ANGLO-SAXON England, roughly equivalent to the present-day West Midlands. In Mercia's period of greatness (7th and 8th century AD) its kings ruled all England from the River Humber to a point S of the River Thames, excluding East Anglia. Its prosperity was largely due to control of trade, ensuring regular royal revenue. After the death of OFFA (796), Mercia declined as WESSEX rose, and by *c.*880 it was under Danish control.

Mercier, Honoré (1840–94) Canadian statesman, prime minister of Québec (1887–91). As a French-Canadian leader, he opposed confederation (1876) and founded the *Parti National* in 1871. In 1883 Mercier became leader of the Liberal Party in Québec and was elected prime minister primarily on the strength of his outspoken support for Louis RIEL. He enacted several pro-Catholic policies, but was removed from office after charges of corruption. He was subsequently exonerated.

Meroë Ancient city on the Nile in NUBIA, capital of the kingdom of KUSH from the 7th or 8th century BC to the early 4th century AD. Excavations have revealed extensive monumental buildings, including pyramids, influenced by Egypt, and the existence of iron-smelting as early as the 6th century BC.

Merovingians Frankish dynasty (AD 476–750). It was named after an early leader of the Salian FRANKS, Merovech, whose son CHILDERIC I and then grandson CLOVIS I united the Salian and Ripuarian Franks. Clovis defeated the Romans in Gaul and expanded his empire, eventually ruling most of France and, following victories over the ALEMANNI and VISIGOTHS, parts of S Germany (*c.*481–511). Clovis converted to Christianity and established the common interests of the Frankish rulers and the Christian population of his kingdom. On Clovis' death the kingdom was divided into BURGUNDY, NEUSTRIA, AUSTRASIA and AQUITAINE, but reunited under CLOTAIRE I (r.497–561). On his death, the kingdom was once again divided and not reunited until CLOTAIRE II (r.613–29) acceded to the throne. Clotaire II's son, DAGOBERT I (r.629–39), was the last acting Merovingian king. With his death true power gradually passed to the "mayors of the palace", noble families who were responsible for the administration of the kingdom and who controlled the army in the absence of the king. CHARLES MARTEL and PEPIN I were among the most famous mayors. The last Merovingian king, CHILDERIC III (r. *c.*742–751), was overthrown by PEPIN III (THE SHORT), father of CHARLEMAGNE and founder of the CAROLINGIAN dynasty.

Mesolithic (Middle STONE AGE) Period between the PALAEOLITHIC (Old Stone Age) and NEOLITHIC (Old Stone Age). As a distinctive cultural era, it is chiefly characteristic of W Europe. The Mesolithic roughly corresponded with the end of the last Ice Age at the beginning of the 10th millennium BC. Mesolithic people were hunter-gatherers who overlapped with Neolithic farmers.

Mesopotamia (Gk. between rivers) Ancient region in SW Asia between the rivers Tigris and Euphrates, roughly corresponding to modern Iraq and part of Syria. Due to the fertility of the land and the development of irrigation in the 6th millennium BC, Mesopotamia was the setting for one of the earliest human civilizations. The first cities, such as Ur, Uruk, Kish and Lagash, were established before 3000 BC by the Sumerians (*see* Sumeria). Sargon I of Akkad conquered the Sumerian cities in *c*.2340 BC, and thereafter the region was dominated by a series of empires, including the Kassites (following the Hittites' destruction of Babylon) and Assyria. The Assyrian empire was at its height between the 9th and 7th centuries BC. In *c*.627 BC the Assyrians were conquered by Nabopolassar of Chaldaea. The Chaldaean dynasty flourished under Nebuchadnezzar II (r. *c*.605–562 BC), but fell when Cyrus II (the Great) captured Babylon (538 BC) and founded the Achaemenid empire. In *c*.331 BC the Achaemenids were conquered by the Greeks, under Alexander III (the Great), after which Mesopotamia fell successively to the Seleucids, Parthia and the Sasanians. In AD 641 the Sasanians were defeated by the Arabs, who introduced Islam. Mesopotamia was then ruled by the Umayyads until the mid-8th century, when they ceded power to the Abbasids. With the sacking of Baghdad (1258) by the Mongols the whole region fell into decline. By the 18th century Mesopotamia had become part of the Ottoman Empire. *See also* Elam

Mesopotamian Campaign (1914–18) British offensive against the Ottoman Turks during World War I to protect Iranian oilfields and the route to India. The British troops, largely Indian, landed at Basra (now in SE Iraq), advanced on Baghdad, but were defeated and subsequently besieged at Kut al-Imara, which (reinforcements failing) fell in April 1916. A new offensive under General Sir Frederick Maude (1863–1917) captured Baghdad in March 1917, while General Edmund Allenby advanced on Palestine and Syria, supported by T.E. Lawrence and the Arab irregulars. The Ottomans surrendered in November 1918. The Campaign claimed *c*.80,000 British and Allied lives.

Mesozoic Third era of geologic time, extending from *c*.248 to *c*.65mya. It is divided into three periods: the Triassic, Jurassic and Cretaceous. For most of the Mesozoic era, the continents are believed to have been joined in a single landmass, Pangaea. The era was also characterized by the variety and size of its reptiles, especially the dinosaurs.

Metaxas, Ioannis (1871–1941) Greek general and statesman, premier (1936–41). He was promoted to chief of staff in the Greek army after successes in the Balkan Wars (1912–13). Metaxas was exiled for his opposition to Premier Eleuthérios Venizélos' decision to join the Allies in World War 1. A staunch royalist, Metaxas was appointed premier by George II and made himself a virtual dictator. Despite fascist trappings, he resisted Benito Mussolini's Italian invasion and joined the Allies in World War 2.

Metellus Distinguished Roman family. It included **Lucius Caecilius** Metellus (d. *c*.221 BC), who defeated Carthage at Panormus (250 BC), and **Quintus Caecilius** Metellus **Macedonicus** (d.116 BC), who pacified Macedonia and Greece in 146 BC. He became consul in 143 BC, and as censor (131 BC) supported compulsory marriage to increase the birth rate. His nephew Q.C. Metellus **Numidicus** (d. *c*.91 BC) commanded Roman forces in Numidia and defeated Jugurtha. He was consul in 109 BC, was later briefly exiled, but recalled thanks to his son Q.C. Metellus **Pius** (d. *c*.63 BC), who aided Pompey in the reconquest of Spain.

Methodism International Christian religious movement. It was originally an evangelical movement within the Church of England, founded (*c*.1729) by John Wesley with his brother Charles and others. John Wesley, an Anglican priest, remained within the Church of England, although ostracized, until his death in 1791, but in 1795 the Wesleyan Methodists became a separate church. They split into several sects which were not reunited until the 20th century. In the United States, the Methodist Episcopal Church, whose offspring include several African-American churches, was founded (1784) by Francis Asbury. The Church split over the issue of slavery, but was reunited in 1939. It emphasizes the power of faith to transform individual's lives and a personal relationship between the individual and God. Methodism, with its concern for social welfare and poverty, expanded rapidly among the industrial working-classes in the 19th century. Today, the World Methodist Council has *c*.10 million members worldwide. *See also* Whitefield, George

Metternich, Klemens, Fürst von (1773–1859) Austrian statesman, foreign minister (1809–48) and chancellor (1821–48). Metternich was the leading European statesman of the post-Napoleonic era. Following Austria's defeat in the Napoleonic Wars (1809), he adopted a conciliatory policy towards France, arranging the marriage of Marie Louise, daughter of Habsburg Emperor Francis I, to Napoleon I. After Napoleon's retreat from Moscow (1812), Metternich acted as mediator between Napoleon and Tsar Alexander I while secretly rearming Austria. In August 1813 Austria declared war on France and contributed to Napoleon's defeat at Waterloo. Metternich was the dominant figure at the Congress of Vienna (1814–15), working with British Foreign Secretary Lord Castlereagh to establish a balance of power between France, Russia and Prussia. His attempts to establish administrations in Germany and Italy based on historical and national lines were, however, frustrated by Francis I. From 1815 Metternich became increasingly autocratic, pressing for the intervention of the "great powers" against any revolutionary outbreak. This position was rejected by Castlereagh's successor, George Canning, who upheld the principle of national self-determination for the revolutions in Spain's colonies in South America and in the Greek War of Independence. Metternich was driven from power by the Revolution of 1848. *See also* congress system

Mexican Revolution (1910–20) Brutal political and social uprising which ultimately established a democratic republic in Mexico. It began as a revolt against the dictatorship of Porfirio Díaz. Díaz reneged on his promise to permit free elections and opposition forces coalesced around Francisco Madero. Emiliano Zapata led an insurrection of landless peasants in the south, while "Pancho" Villa headed an army of gauchos (cowboys) in the N state of Chihuahua. In 1911 Díaz was forced to resign and fled into exile. Madero's new regime, however, antagonized both the radical adherents of land reform – a crucial grievance – and the conservative landowners. In 1913, backed by the United States, General Victoriano Huerta overthrew Madero, who was assassinated. Huerta's repressive regime plunged Mexico back into violence, and prompted the formation of a shaky anti-Huerta alliance in N Mexico between Villa, Venustiano Carranza and Álvaro Obregón. In August 1914 Huerta was forced into exile and Carranza declared himself president. The rebel alliance fractured, however, and Zapata and Villa captured Mexico City in November 1914. In 1915 Obregón and Carranza launched a counter-offensive that forced Zapata and Villa back to their heartlands. This phase of the Revolution claimed *c*.200,000 Mexican lives. Angered by US support for Carranza, Villa attacked New Mexico, prompting General John Pershing to lead US forces against Villa in N Mexico. In 1917 Carranza introduced a new constitution that offered land reforms and redistribution, workers' rights and placed restrictions on the Catholic Church. In 1920, disputes over the presidential succession led to a further revolt in which Carranza was killed by supporters of General Obregón. In 1921 Obregón was elected president. His accession is often taken to mark the end of the Mexican Revolution, but the anti-clerical legislation of his successor, Plutarco Elías Calles, provoked a renewed civil war in 1926 and unrest only finally abated during the regime (1934–40) of Lázaro Cárdenas.

Mexican War (April 1846–February 1848) (Mexican-American War) Conflict that followed the United States' annexation of Texas (1845). In January 1846 US forces, led by General Zachary Taylor, occupied the disputed region between the River Nueces and the Rio Grande. In April 1846 these troops were attacked by the Mexicans and US President James Polk declared war. Stephen Kearny quickly gained New Mexico and California for the United States. Taylor inflicted a major defeat on the Mexicans at the Battle of Buena Vista (February 1847). US victory was finally secured by General Winfield Scott, who landed at Veracruz (March 1847), defeated the army of Santa Anna and entered Mexico City in September. By the Treaty of Guadalupe-Hidalgo (1848), Mexico ceded sovereignty over California and New Mexico, as well as Texas north of the Rio Grande. The War claimed *c*.12,000 US lives (*c*.90% of which were from disease). There is no official figure for Mexican casualties, but it was undoubtedly higher.

Mexico *See* country feature, page 270

Mexico City (Sp. *Ciudad de México*) Capital of Mexico and largest city in the world. Mexico City is the site of the former Aztec capital, known as Tenochtitlán, which was destroyed by Hernán Cortés in 1521. A new city was constructed, which acted as the capital of Spanish America for the next 300 years. In 1821 Mexico City fell to the revolutionary leader Augustín de Iturbide. In 1847, during the Mexican War, the city was occupied by US troops. In 1863 France conquered the city and established Maximilian as emperor. Mexico City was recaptured by Benito Juárez's republican forces in 1867. Between 1914 and 1915 the city was won and lost three times by the revolutionary forces of Emiliano Zapata and Francisco Villa. Pop. (1997 est.) 16,562,000. *See* illustration, page 31

Michael VIII (Palaeologus) (*c*.1224–82) Byzantine emperor (1261–82), founder of the Palaeologan dynasty. He seized control of Nicaea in 1259. A brilliant military commander and a consummate diplomat, Michael restored the Byzantine Empire, defeating the Latin Empire of Constantinople (created by the Fourth Crusade) and capturing Constantinople in 1261. To defend his reconquest, Michael negotiated a brief reunion of the Eastern (Orthodox) and Western churches and financed the Sicilian Vespers (1282) against his chief opponent, Charles I of Naples and Sicily.

Michael (1596–1645) Tsar of Russia (1613–45), founder of the Romanov dynasty. Until 1633 he was largely ruled by his mother and, later, his father, who was also patriarch of the Russian Orthodox Church. His reign ended the chaotic period known as the Time of Troubles and brought peace with Sweden (1617) and Poland (1618).

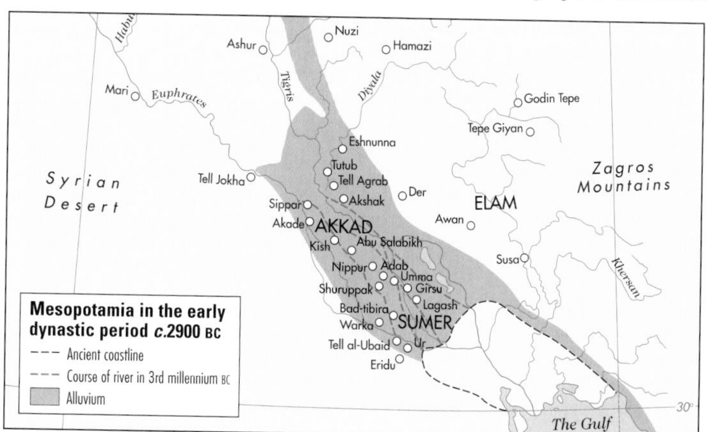

◀ **Mesopotamia** In ancient times, sediment from the Tigris and Euphrates rivers silted up the head of the Persian (Arabian) Gulf, forcing the abandonment of stranded ports. By 4500 BC irrigation enabled the farming of the dry, but alluvium-rich region of S Mesopotamia. In the 4th millennium BC urban centres, such as Uruk, developed with large religious complexes and secular palaces. By 2900 BC city-states, such as Ur, had emerged, ruled by individual kings. Mesopotamia became divided between Sumer and Akkad.

Michael (1921–) King of Romania (1927–30, 1940–47). He succeeded his grandfather, Ferdinand I, as a child and surrendered the throne to his father, CAROL II, in 1930, regaining it when Carol abdicated (1940). In 1944 Michael backed the overthrow of the fascist rule of Ion ANTONESCU, whereupon Romania joined the Allies in World War 2. He was forced to abdicate when the communists gained power.

Michael (the Brave) (1558–1601) Prince of Walachia (1593–1600). He overthrew Ottoman rule and gained Transylvania (1599) and Moldavia (1600) by conquest, briefly creating a precursor of the future Romania. He was soon expelled from Transylvania by Emperor RUDOLF II and the Poles drove him from Moldavia and deposed him in Walachia. He is regarded as national hero in Romania.

Michigan State in the Midwest United States, bordered by the Great Lakes; the capital is Lansing. From *c.*100 BC the region was home to the MOUND BUILDERS' culture. When Jacques MARQUETTE established the first European settlement in 1668, *c.*15,000 Algonquian-speaking Native North Americans, including the OJIBWA and Ottawa, lived in the region. The British gained control of the area at the end of the FRENCH AND INDIAN WARS (1689–1763). The British finally withdrew from Michigan in 1796 and it became a US territory in 1805. The British briefly regained DETROIT during the WAR OF 1812, but it was firmly back in US hands by 1813. Michigan Territory expanded rapidly under Governor Lewis CASS, who oversaw the opening (1825) of the Erie Canal. It was a leading supporter of the Union during the American Civil War (1861–65). Michigan was largely a logging and farming state until the economic boom created by the automobile industry in the early 20th century, which also attracted many African-American workers from the South. During World War 2, its factories converted to armaments on a massive scale. Pop. (1990) 9,295,297.

> **MICHIGAN**
> **Statehood :**
> 26 January 1837
> **Nickname :**
> Wolverine State
> **State motto :**
> If you seek a pleasant peninsula, look around you

Micronesia, Federated States of Republic in the w Pacific Ocean, consisting of all the Caroline Islands except PALAU. The 607 islands of the republic are divided into four states: Kosrae, Pohnpei, Truk and Yap. The capital, Palikir, is on the main island of Pohnpei. The islands were formally annexed by Spain in 1874. In 1899 they were sold to Germany. In 1914 Japan occupied the archipelago and was given a mandate to govern by the League of Nations in 1920. In 1944 US naval forces captured the islands, and in 1947 they came under formal US administration as part of the United Nations' (UN) Trust Territory of the Pacific Islands. In 1979 the Federated States of Micronesia came

MEXICO

AREA: 1,958,200sq km (756,061sq mi)
POPULATION: 89,538,000
CAPITAL (POPULATION): Mexico City (16,562,000)
GOVERNMENT: Federal republic
ETHNIC GROUPS: Mestizo 60%, Native American 30%, European 9%
LANGUAGES: Spanish (official)
RELIGIONS: Christianity (Roman Catholic 90%, Protestant 5%)
GDP PER CAPITA (1995): US$6400

Republic in s North America. Mexico is the largest Spanish-speaking country in the world. One of the earliest NATIVE MIDDLE AMERICAN civilizations was the OLMEC (1200–300 BC). From *c.*500 BC the MONTE ALBÁN and TEOTIHUACÁN empires developed in central Mexico as agricultural productivity increased with the aid of irrigation techniques. From *c.*300 BC the literate MAYA civilization in the Yucatán Peninsula constructed ceremonial centres, which evolved into large cities by 300 AD. These expanded rapidly between AD 300 and 900. The TOLTECS dominated a large area of central Mexico between 900 and *c.*1200. The Tarascan kingdom flourished in western Mexico, while the MIXTECS expanded their territory at the expense of the ZAPOTECS in the Oaxaca valley. Both the Mixtecs and Zapotecs suffered at the hands of the AZTECS, who in the 1430s began to develop an empire that was to cover much of central Mexico. Their capital was Tenochtitlán (now MEXICO CITY). Many splendid pyramids and temples remain from these civilizations.

In 1517 Fernández de Córdoba became the first European to explore the coast of Mexico. In 1519–21 Spanish CONQUISTADORS, led by Hernán CORTÉS, captured the capital and the Aztec Emperor MONTEZUMA. In 1535 the territory became the Viceroyalty of NEW SPAIN. Christianity was introduced. Spanish colonial rule was harsh as far as the native population was concerned. In the 18th century the creoles (of Spanish descent) resented the Spanish monarch's attempts to extract more revenue from Mexico and to deprive them of political power. The majority did not support HIDALGO Y COSTILLA's revolt in 1810, but in 1821 they demanded and gained independence

General Agustín de ITÚRBIDE became emperor of the newly independent country. In 1823 republicans seized power and, in 1824, Mexico became a republic. In 1832 SANTA ANNA became president. Following the decision of the US government to annex Texas, the MEXICAN WAR (1846–48) broke out. The US army captured Mexico City and the Mexicans were defeated. Under the terms of the Treaty of GUADALUPE-HIDALGO (1848), Mexico lost 50% of its territory (an area that now consists of California, Nevada, Utah, Colorado, Arizona, New Mexico and Texas). In 1855 a revolution led to the overthrow of Santa Anna, and civil war broke out. Liberal forces, led by Benito JUÁREZ, triumphed in the War of Reform (1858–61), but conservatives with support from France installed MAXIMILIAN of Austria as emperor in 1864. In 1867 republican rule was restored, and Juárez became president. In 1876 an armed revolt gave Porfirio DÍAZ the presidency. Díaz's dictatorship lasted, besides a brief intercession (1880–84), for more than 30 years until he was overthrown at the start of the MEXICAN REVOLUTION (1910–20).

In 1911 Francisco MADERO became president. A weak leader, Madero was toppled by General Victoriana HUERTA in 1913. Huerta's dictatorship led to US intervention. The US-backed forces of Venustiano CARRANZA battled with the peasant armies of "Pancho" VILLA and Emiliano ZAPATA.

During the 1920s and 1930s, Mexico introduced land and social reforms. After World War 2, Mexico's economy developed with the introduction of liberal reforms. Relations with the United States improved greatly, although problems remain over Mexican economic migration and drug trafficking. The Institutional Revolutionary Party (PRI) has ruled Mexico continuously since its formation in 1929.

In 1994 the Zapatista National Liberation Army (EZLN) staged an armed revolt in the s state of Chiapas, principally calling for land reforms and recognition of Native American rights. Despite concessions on indigenous rights, guerrilla activity continues. In 1994 Ernesto ZEDILLO of the PRI was elected president. In June 1993 Mexico joined the Organization for Economic Cooperation and Development (OECD). In 1994 Mexico, the United States and Canada formed the NORTH AMERICAN FREE TRADE ASSOCIATION (NAFTA), the largest single trading bloc in the world. In 1994 Mexico was plunged into economic crisis: only a US$50,000 million loan from the United States prevented Mexico defaulting on its foreign debts. An austerity package of wage freezes, interest-rate rises and tax increases was introduced. In 1997 the economic crisis in Southeast Asia led to a stock-market crash and a devaluation of the peso. In 1999 Mexico suffered its worst floods in four decades.

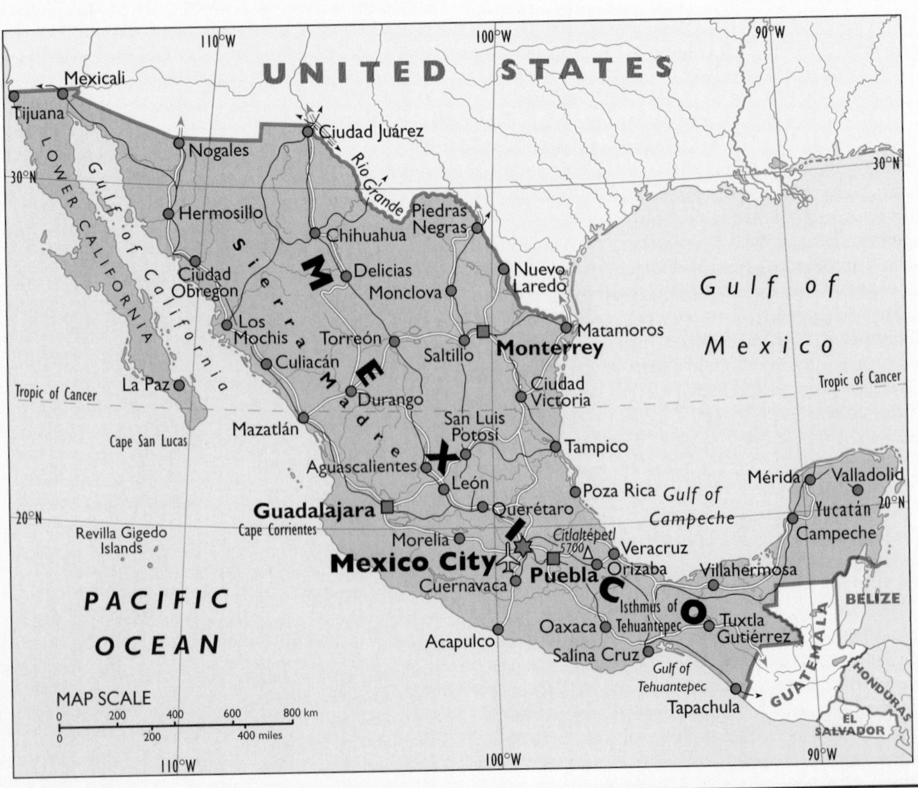

MICRONESIA, FEDERATED STATES OF
AREA: 702sq km (271sq mi)
POPULATION: 127,000
CAPITAL (POPULATION): Palikir (33,346)
GOVERNMENT: Federal republic
ETHNIC GROUPS: Micronesian, Polynesian
LANGUAGES: English (official), local languages
RELIGIONS: Roman Catholic 60%, Protestant 40%
GDP PER CAPITA (1995): US$1500

into being, with Palau remaining a US trust territory. In 1986 a compact of free association with the United States was signed. In 1990 UN trust status was annulled, and in 1991 Micronesia became a full member of the UN.

Middle Ages Period in European history covering roughly 1000 years between the disintegration of the ROMAN EMPIRE in the 5th century and the RENAISSANCE in the 15th century. The Middle Ages are sometimes divided into Early (5th–11th centuries), High (11th–14th centuries) and Late Middle Ages. The predominant social influences were the Christian church and the FEUDAL SYSTEM. In the arts, the Middle Ages encompassed the ROMANESQUE and (from the 11th century) GOTHIC periods. In science and learning, Christian Europe tended to lag behind Islam. *See also* ANGLO-SAXONS; CAROLINGIAN; CHRISTIANITY; FRANKS; HOLY ROMAN EMPIRE; MONASTICISM; VISIGOTHS

Midway, Battle of (3–6 June 1942) Decisive naval conflict of WORLD WAR 2 in the Pacific. Despite the inconclusive end to the Battle of the CORAL SEA (May 1942), the Japanese persevered with plans to capture Midway Islands. The US forces, commanded by Admiral Chester NIMITZ, were forewarned of the attack, however, and intercepted the Japanese fleet under Admiral YAMAMOTO ISOROKU. The Japanese, overwhelmed by air and sea bombardment, lost all four aircraft carriers, two cruisers and 330 aircraft, while the US lost one carrier, a destroyer and 150 aircraft. The Battle proved a turning point in the war in the Pacific, with Japan henceforth on the defensive.

Miguel (1802–66) King of Portugal (1828–34). When Pedro IV (Emperor PEDRO I of Brazil) abdicated (1826) in favour of his infant daughter, MARIA II, Miguel seized the throne and set off the Miguelist (civil) Wars. In 1833 Maria's forces, led by Pedro with British support, defeated Miguel and he went into exile.

Mihailović, Draža (1893–1946) Yugoslav soldier. After the German occupation of Yugoslavia during World War 2, he organized the CHETNIK guerrillas but later allied with the Germans and Italians in order to combat communism. He was executed for treason by Marshal TITO's regime.

Mikoyan, Anastas Ivanovich (1895–1978) Soviet statesman. He joined the BOLSHEVIKS and was a leader of the revolution in the Caucasus. Mikoyan's support for Joseph STALIN led to his promotion (1923) to the Central Committee of the Communist Party of the Soviet Union (CPSU). In 1935 Mikoyan was appointed to the Politburo and for the next 30 years he managed Soviet trade. In 1946 he became deputy premier, retaining his post under Stalin's successor, Nikita KHRUSHCHEV.

Milan (Milano) City in NW Italy; capital of Lombardy. The site was first settled (*c*.600 BC) by the Gauls. In 222 BC it fell to the Romans and rose to become the second city of the Roman Empire. Milan was destroyed by Barbarian invasions in the 5th and 6th centuries, but was revitalized by the Carolingians in the 8th century. In 1045 Milan became a free commune and, as leader of the LOMBARD LEAGUE, played a major part in defeating Emperor FREDERICK I (BARBAROSSA) at the Battle of LEGNANO (1176). In the late 13th century, the city fell under the governorship of the VISCONTI family. In 1450 Milan was captured by Francesco SFORZA. In the early 16th century, the city was contested by France and the Sforzas, backed by the HABSBURGS, in the ITALIAN WARS. From 1535 to 1706, Milan was directly controlled by Spain and suffered from economic recession and the plague. In 1706 Prince EUGÈNE OF SAVOY gained the city for Austria, whose despotic rule brought renewed growth. In 1796 Milan was seized by Napoleon, who proclaimed the city as capital of his kingdom of Italy. In 1814 Austria reasserted control. Milan was a centre of the nationalist RISORGIMENTO movement and was finally freed from Austrian rule in 1859. Milan was Benito MUSSOLINI's base and the starting point for the fascist March on Rome (1922). Badly damaged by Allied bombing during World War 2, Milan recovered rapidly thanks to industrial development after 1945, and is now Italy's second-largest city. Pop. (1991) 1,369,231.

Miletus (now Balat) Ancient Greek city in Ionia, now SW Turkey. One of the greatest cities in Asia Minor before 500 BC, it was situated on a commercial crossroads. Trade made Miletus rich; it established many colonies and was home to the early, Milesian school of philosophy. In the 6th century, it fell under first Lydian then Persian control. Miletus' revolt marked the start of the PERSIAN WARS (499–479 BC). After Persia's defeat, it joined the Athenian-dominated DELIAN LEAGUE. Still a trading centre in Roman times, it was abandoned by the 6th century AD.

Mill, John Stuart (1806–73) British philosopher, son of James Mill (1773–1836), a leading Scottish philosopher. J.S. Mill redefined empiricism in his *System of Logic* (1843), but his best-known work is *On Liberty* (1859), a classic defence of the freedom of the individual against the state. In *Utilitarianism* (1861), he developed a more humanist version of Jeremy BENTHAM's theory of UTILITARIANISM. He also championed women's rights in *The Subjection of Women* (1869). Mill worked for the English East India Company until 1858 and was briefly a member of Parliament (1865–68). A giant of the Victorian era, Mill is admired not only for his influential ideas but also for the clarity with which he expressed them. *See also* LIBERALISM

millenarianism Belief, widespread among early Christians, in Christ's second coming and the establishment of peace on Earth. It was based on Jewish traditions of the Messiah and the prediction in the *Book of Revelations* (20). It was largely supplanted by Saint Augustine's allegorical interpretation of the kingdom of God, but was revived during the Reformation by sects such as the ANABAPTISTS and the MORAVIAN CHURCH. Millenarianism has been embraced by a number of modern Protestant sects, such as the JEHOVAH'S WITNESSES.

Milner, Alfred, 1st Viscount (1854–1925) British colonial administrator. As high commissioner in southern Africa (1897–1905) and governor of Cape Colony (1897–1901), Milner's uncompromising stance towards the Afrikaner (Boer) republics of TRANSVAAL and Orange FREE STATE helped precipitate the Second SOUTH AFRICAN WAR (1899–1902). After the War, Milner revived the gold industry and tried to increase British emigration to the region, but his determination to enforce British control further antagonized the Afrikaners. He later served as colonial secretary (1918–21) under David LLOYD GEORGE. *See also* KITCHENER, HORATIO HERBERT, EARL; Kruger, Paul

Milo, Titus Annius (d.48 BC) Roman politician. His support of POMPEY and recall of CICERO led to a bitter dispute with Publius CLODIUS. Rome was terrorized by gang warfare between the two rivals until Milo arranged the murder of Clodius (52 BC). Milo was convicted and sent into exile. He was killed in an uprising against Julius CAESAR.

Miloš Obrenović (1780–1860) Serbian peasant revolutionary, prince of Serbia (1815–39, 1858–60) and founder of the OBRENOVIĆ dynasty. Miloš initially joined KARAGEORGE in the revolt (1804–13) against Ottoman rule, but broke with him in 1810. Miloš cooperated with the Ottoman Turks and was rewarded with the title of prince. In 1815 he mounted a new insurrection, forcing the Ottomans to grant limited autonomy to Serbia. Miloš arranged the assassination of Karageorge, precipitating a long dynastic feud. In 1830 he gained full independence for Serbia. Miloš abdicated in favour of his son, Milan Obrenović, in 1839, but was recalled after the deposition of Alexander Karageorgević in 1858. He died in office.

Milošević, Slobodan (1941–) Serbian statesman, president of Serbia (1989–97) and of Yugoslavia (1997–). In 1986 he became head of the Serbian Communist Party. As Serbian president, Milošević was confronted with, and contributed to, the break-up of the federation of YUGOSLAVIA. Re-elected in 1992, he supported the Serb populations in Croatia and Bosnia, who fought for a Greater Serbia. Milošević signed the DAYTON PEACE AGREEMENT (1995) with Bosnian President Alija IZETBEGOVIĆ and Croatian President Franjo TUDJMAN to end the civil war in the former Yugoslavia. In 1998 Milošević ordered Yugoslav forces to crush the majority Albanian population in the province of KOSOVO, provoking NATO air attacks on Serbian military and industrial targets. In June 1999 Milošević agreed to a peace plan and a United Nations' (UN) peacekeeping force was sent to Kosovo. Despite sanctions, Milošević remained in power.

Miltiades the Younger (*c*.554–?489 BC) Athenian general, father of CIMON. In *c*.516 BC he inherited the Chersonese lands from his uncle, Miltiades the Elder, but soon had to submit to DARIUS I of Persia. Miltiades deserted to Athens at the start of the PERSIAN WARS (499–479 BC), and was largely responsible for the victory over the Persians at the Battle of MARATHON (490 BC). He was wounded on a disastrous mission (489 BC) to subdue the islands that supported Persia, and died in prison.

Minamoto *See* YORITOMO

Mindszenty, Cardinal József (1892–1975) Hungarian Roman Catholic prelate. He became Hungarian primate in 1945. An outspoken opponent of totalitarianism in both its fascist and communist guises, Mindszenty was arrested by the Hungarian government in 1948 and sentenced to life imprisonment. Released during the HUNGARIAN UPRISING (1956), he sought asylum in the US embassy in Budapest. In 1971 he left the embassy to live in Rome.

Ming (1368–1644) Imperial Chinese dynasty. It was founded by a Buddhist monk, ZHU YUANCHANG, whose army of peasants expelled the Mongol YUAN dynasty. Zhu was a despotic ruler, abolishing the position of prime minister and establishing a strong, centralized governmental structure that persisted until the fall of the QING dynasty (1912). He also created the civil-service examination system. In 1399 Zhu Yuanchang's son, YONGLO (r.1402–24), launched a successful rebellion against the young emperor Jianwen (r.1398–1402). In 1407 he transferred the capital from NANJING to BEIJING, where he built the Forbidden City. Yonglo consolidated dynastic power, conquering ANNAM and Nam Viet, protecting the W border against TAMERLANE, and leading his army in five campaigns across the Gobi Desert to prevent the re-emergence of a unified Mongol force. The growing power of the EUNUCHS over the Ming emperors was evident when Wang Chen persuaded Emperor Zhengtong to lead a disastrous campaign against the Mongol Oyrats in 1449. From the end of the 15th century, the Ming dynasty bgean to crumble under the threat of the MANCHU, led by NURHACHI. The dynasty disintegrated during the reign (1620–27) of Emperor Tianji, who allowed the eunuch Wei Zhongxian to assume

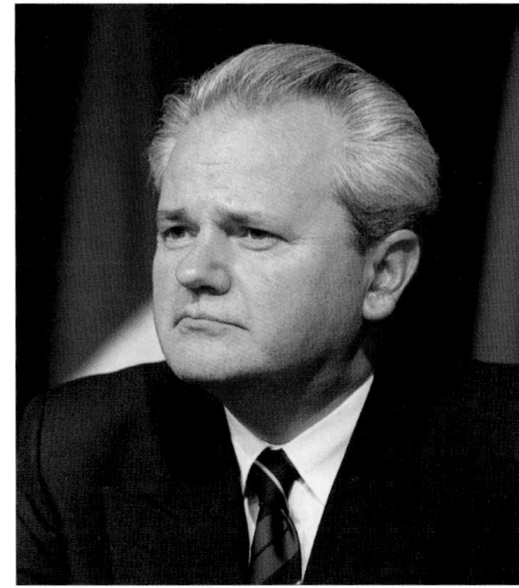

▲ **Milošević** was indicted for war crimes by the United Nations (UN) in May 1999, for trying to "ethnically cleanse" the Albanian population in the Serbian province of Kosovo.

M

▶ **Ming** During the early years of the Ming dynasty, China experienced a period of great artistic distinction, particularly in painting and pottery. Artists were important figures at the courts of the Ming emperors. They painted portraits, landscapes and depictions of Chinese life, like this street scene.

authoritarian powers. The last Ming emperor, Chongzhen (r.1627–44), was toppled in a coup led by Li Zicheng, who was in turn overthrown by the Manchu. The Ming pirate Zheng Chenggong continued to resist the Qing dynasty until 1662. Under the Ming dynasty, China experienced an artistic and intellectual renaissance, and the period is especially noted for its fine porcelain.

Minnesota State in N central United States; the capital is St Paul. Before the arrival of the first European explorers in the 17th century, the region was inhabited by the Sioux (Dakota). European settlement of neighbouring regions forced the Ojibwa to migrate into the area. In the 1680s, French explorers Louis Hennepin, Sieur Du Luth and Sieur de La Salle claimed the region for France and the first white settlement was a fur-trading post established at Grand Portage on the shores of Lake Superior. The area E of the Mississippi River passed to Britain (1763) after the Seven Years' War, and the lands W of the Mississippi were acquired by the United States in the Louisiana Purchase (1803). The first US settlement, Fort Snelling, was established in 1819. Minnesota Territory was organized in 1849, and white settlement increased rapidly as Native Americans were confined to reservations. In 1862 the Sioux, angry over broken promises and starving due to crop failures, mounted a bloody uprising. The cities of St Paul and Minneapolis expanded on the growth of the timber and flour-milling industries in the late 19th century, and the discovery (1989) of iron-ore in the Mesabi Range made Minnesota the largest iron-producing state. Duluth became an international port after the opening (1959) of the St Lawrence Seaway. Pop. (1990) 4,375,099.

Minoan civilization (*c.*3000–*c.*1100 BC) Ancient Aegean civilization that flourished on the island of Crete, named for the legendary King Minos. In terms of artistic achievement, Minoan civilization reached its height in the Late period (*c.*1700–1450 BC). In the wake of a massive earthquake, alien influences and cultural decline are evident thereafter. The prosperity of Bronze Age Crete was based on maritime expertise and command of trade. It is evident from the works of art and palaces excavated at Knossos (which housed more than 20,000 people), Phaistos and other sites. Minoan was eventually replaced by Mycenaean civilization in the Aegean. The Minoan civilization was forgotten until rediscovered (*c.*1900) by British archaeologist Sir Arthur Evans.

Minto, Gilbert John Elliot Murray-Kynynemound, 4th Earl of (1845–1914) British colonial administrator, governor general of Canada (1898–1904) and viceroy of India (1905–10). In Canada, he sought to reconcile differences between Canadian Prime Minister Sir Wilfrid Laurier and British colonial secretary Joseph Chamberlain. As viceroy of India, Minto worked with his secretary of state, John Morley (1838–1923), to produce the **Morley-Minto Reforms Act** (1909) which introduced limited representational government in India, creating separate electorates for Hindus and Muslims. As part of his "divide and rule" approach, Minto also abetted the formation of the Muslim League as a counterweight to the Indian National Congress.

MINNESOTA
Statehood :
11 May 1858
Nickname :
Gopher State
State motto :
Star of the North

Minuit, Peter (1580–1638) Dutch colonial administrator, governor (1626–31) of New Netherland (now part of New York, United States). In 1620 he bought Manhattan Island (1620) from Native Americans for US$24 worth of trinkets and founded New Amsterdam (now New York City). After his recall, Minuit entered Swedish service and established the colony of New Sweden (1638) on the Delaware River.

minutemen Local militia units in the American Revolution (1775–83), so named for their alleged ability to spring to arms at a minute's notice. The first units were formed (1774) in Massachusetts, and minutemen took part in the opening Battles of Lexington and Concord (April 1775). The name was adopted by certain extreme right-wing groups in the United States in the 1960s, and was also given to a class of ballistic missiles.

Mirabeau, Honoré Gabriel Riquetti, Comte de (1749–91) French revolutionary. In 1777 he was sentenced to death after eloping with his "Sophie", the wife of an old aristocrat. The disgraced Mirabeau was released in 1782, but continued to make powerful enemies. In 1789 he was elected to represent the Third Estate in the States-General. Mirabeau was the most brilliant orator in the early stages of the French Revolution (1789–99), and was instrumental in securing the dismissal of Louis XVI's finance minister Jacques Necker. Mirabeau secretly acted on behalf of the monarchy in the National Assembly, which he dominated after becoming president in January 1791. His support for a constitutional monarchy came under increasing attack from the Jacobins. *See also* Lafayette, Marquis de

Miranda, Francisco de (1750–1816) Venezuelan revolutionary, known as *El Precursor* ("The Forerunner"). Charged with embezzling funds from the Spanish army in 1783, Miranda fled to the United States, where he met several leaders of the American Revolution. Later he visited England in an attempt to secure British support for the creation of an independent empire in South America. In 1806 Miranda led an abortive insurrection against Spanish rule in Venezuela. In 1810 Simón Bolívar appointed him leader of the revolutionary forces in Venezuela. After independence was won in 1811, Miranda assumed dictatorial powers. He was forced to surrender, however, by a Spanish counter-attack in July 1812. Bolívar regarded Miranda's surrender as treasonable and handed him over to the Spanish. He died in prison at Cádiz, S Spain.

Mishna (Hebrew "repetition") Collection of Jewish legal traditions and moral precepts that form the basis of the Talmud. The Mishna was compiled (*c.*AD 200) under Rabbi Judah ha-Nasi. It is divided into six parts: laws pertaining to agriculture, laws concerning the sabbath, fasts and festivals, family laws, civil and criminal laws, laws regarding sacrifices and laws on ceremonial regulations. *See also* Judaism

missionary societies, Christian Organizations for the promotion of Christianity among non-believers. Christian missionary activities date from *The Acts of the Apostles*. The expansion of European settlement from the 16th century stimulated missions to non-Christian societies, especially by orders such as the Franciscans and Jesuits. Protestant missionary societies only became active in the 18th century. The 19th-century witnessed a great explosion in missionary activity, and the emergence of interdenominational and geographically specialized societies. Missionaries have been attacked for their deleterious effect on other cultures, but missions also often checked imperialist and commercial exploitation. A famous example was David Livingstone, employed in Africa by the London Missionary Society (LMR), who made few converts but fought against the slave-trade and sought to raise living standards. Since the foundation of the International Missionary Council (1921), foreign missionaries have worked increasingly with native churches, while evangelicalism has increased in traditionally Christian countries.

Mississippi State in S central United States; the capital and largest city is Jackson. The state has many sites related to the Mound Builders of the Hopewell and Mississippi cultures. When Hernando de Soto explored the region in 1540, he encountered three major tribes of Native Americans: the Choctaw, Chickasaw and Natchez. In 1673 French explorers Jacques Marquette and Louis Jolliet travelled down the Mississippi River to the mouth of the Arkansas River. In 1682 Sieur de La Salle claimed the region for France, and settlement intensified during the period of John Law's "Mississippi Bubble" (1717–20). The French virtually exterminated the Natchez in the 1730s, but the Chicksaw defeated (1736) Sieur de Bienville and restricted the French to S Mississippi. The region passed to Britain at the end of the Seven Years' War (1756–63), but the Spanish occupied the Natchez area (1781–98) during the American Revolution. In the Yazoo Fraud (1795), most of Natchez was ceded to a land company owned by George Matthews. Mississippi was organized as a US Territory in 1798. The early 19th century was marked by the rise of cotton plantations. In the 1830s, most of the Native American population ceded their land to "King Cotton" and moved to Oklahoma. The plantation-economy was dependent on slavery and Mississippi became the second state to secede from the Union in January 1861. Jefferson Davis, senator from Mississippi, was elected president of the Confederate States of America. The state was a major battleground in the American Civil War (1861–65), notably during the Vickrburg campaign. After the War, Mississippi resisted the process of Reconstruction, implementing the so-called "black codes", but was re-admitted to the Union in 1870. Racial segregation was institutionalized in a new constitution (1890) and African-American sharecroppers remained economically dependent on whites. Economic depression in the 1920s and 1930s was relieved by industrial development and the discovery of oil (1939). Mississippi was a focus for many civil rights campaigns during the 1960s. The Ku Klux Klan resorted to

MISSISIPPI
Statehood :
10 December 1817
Nickname :
Magnolia State
State motto :
By valour and arms

intimidation and even murder to maintain racial segregation. In BROWN V. BOARD OF EDUCATION (1954), racial segregation in schools was declared illegal, but the practice continued until the admission (1962) of an African-American student, James Meredith (1933–), to the University of Mississippi led to race-riots and the intervention of federal troops. In 1991 Republican Kim Fordice became the first non-Democrat to be elected governor of Mississippi for 120 years. Pop. (1990) 2,573,216.

Mississippi Bubble (1717–20) French economic boom, created by speculative share-purchasing in John LAW's Louisiana Company. The Company, which was granted exclusive trading rights in the Mississippi valley of French LOUISIANA, attracted massive investment, based on false expectations of the wealth of French North America. When the Bubble burst in April 1720, France was left burdened with an enormous national debt and was forced to devalue its currency. The Company had meanwhile brought many settlers to French Louisiana and resulted in the founding of New Orleans (1718).

Missouri State in the Midwest United States; the capital is Jefferson City. The Mississippian culture of the MOUND BUILDERS developed in the region from *c*.AD 800. When the first European explorers Jacques MARQUETTE and Louis JOLLIET sailed down the Missouri River in 1673, the region's inhabitants included the Osage and Missouri. In 1682 Sieur de LA SALLE claimed the region for France and the first French settlement, Sainte Genevieve, was established in *c*.1735. St Louis was founded in 1750 and became (1770) the capital of Upper Louisiana. The French ceded the region to the United States as part of the LOUISIANA PURCHASE (1803). Upper Louisiana's location made it an ideal base for the exploration and expansion of the frontier to the West, and Missouri Territory was created in 1815. Missouri became a slave state after the MISSOURI COMPROMISE (1820), but slavery remained a divisive issue within the state, and the DRED SCOTT CASE (1852) and the KANSAS-NEBRASKA ACT (1854) merely intensified differences. Missouri remained in the Union during the American Civil War (1861–65). After the War, Missouri generally prospered with the growth of its mining industries and the arrival of the railroad. Missouri soon recovered from the Great Depression of the 1930s, thanks largely to the increase in military expenditure during World War 2. In 1945 Harry TRUMAN became the first Missourian to serve as president of the United States. Missouri's rapid economic transformation from agriculture to manufacturing led to rural depopulation and poverty, and urban pollution and degeneration. However, improvements in public infrastructure have revitalized remote areas such as the Ozarks. Pop. (1990) 5,117,073.

MISSOURI
Statehood :
10 August 1821
Nickname :
"Show me" State
State motto :
The welfare of the people shall be the supreme law

Missouri Compromise (1820) Effort to end the dispute between slave and free states in the United States. Largely the work of Henry CLAY, it permitted MISSOURI to join the union as a slave state at the same time as MAINE was admitted as a free state, preserving an equal balance between slave and free. It marked the beginnings of the bitter dispute over the extension of SLAVERY that ultimately led to the American CIVIL WAR (1861–65). *See also* DRED SCOTT CASE; KANSAS-NEBRASKA ACT

Mitchell, George John (1933–) US politician. A protégé of Edmund Muskie, he became Democratic majority leader of the Senate (1988–94). In 1995 Mitchell was appointed US economic adviser for NORTHERN IRELAND. He chaired the all-party talks on peace in Northern Ireland and formulated the "Mitchell Principles" that committed all sides to finding a peaceful, democratic solution. Mitchell's skilful diplomacy was largely responsible for the GOOD FRIDAY AGREEMENT (1998).

Mitchell, Sir Thomas Livingstone (1792–1855) Scottish surveyor general (1828–55) of NEW SOUTH WALES, Australia. In the 1830s, Mitchell led three expeditions into the interior of Eastern Australia, exploring the area between the Castlereagh and Gwydir rivers (1831–32), following the River Darling to its junction with the River Murray, and exploring (1835) the land around the River Murray that later became the state of VICTORIA.

Mithradates VI (the Great) (d.63 BC) King of PONTUS (120–63 BC). He succeeded his father, Mithradates V, while still a boy, and his mother ruled as regent until *c*.115 BC. Mithradates VI captured Colchis and Crimea from the SCYTHIANS, but his efforts to restore the empire in Anatolia were opposed by an alliance of Nicomedes III of BITHYNIA and the Romans. At the start of the First Mithradatic War (88–85 BC), Mithradates managed to drive the Romans back to the shores of the Aegean and, after massacring *c*.80,000 inhabitants in the Roman province of Asia Minor, gained most of the Greek cities in Asia Minor. The Romans, led by SULLA, launched a counter-attack and, ignoring Mithradates brutal warnings, the cities surrendered and Mithradates sued for peace. Mithradates defeated a Roman invasion of Pontus in the Second Mithradatic War (83–82 BC), but his army was destroyed by LUCULLUS (73 BC) and Mithradates fled to Armenia. Finally crushed by POMPEY, Mithradates' troops mutinied and he committed suicide. *See also* HELLENISTIC AGE

Mithraism Worship of Mithra, the Iranian god of the sun, contract and war. Mithraism was a mystical religion with rites involving the sacrifice of a bull to symbolize the creation of the world. Women were excluded. Before the advent of ZOROASTRIANISM (*c*.6th century BC), Mithra was the most important god in the Iranian pantheon. MITHRADATES VI of Pontus was named after the god. The Roman worship of Mithras, beginning among veterans of the wars against PARTHIA, became widespread in the empire in the 2nd century AD. A Platonic reinterpretation of Iranian Mithraism, it was suppressed when CONSTANTINE I (THE GREAT) converted to Christianity in AD 312.

Mitterrand, François Maurice Marie (1916–96) French statesman, France's longest-serving president (1981–96). He briefly worked with the Vichy government during World War 2 (1939–45), before joining the French Resistance. Mitterrand served in the governments of the Fourth Republic, and opposed the Fifth Republic of Charles DE GAULLE. Having united the parties of the left in 1965, he narrowly lost the presidential elections of 1966 to De Gaulle. In 1971 Mitterrand became first secretary of the SOCIALIST PARTY (PS). Despite his reorganization of the Party, he failed in his second bid for the presidency in 1974. Mitterrand defeated the incumbent GISCARD D'ESTAING to become France's first socialist president in 1981. He nationalized key industries and the banks, and abolished capital punishment. Soaring inflation and domestic recession, however, forced Mitterrand largely to abandon his socialist policies and cut government spending. Mitterrand moved still further to the right after 1986, when he had to cooperate with a Gaullist (conservative) prime minister, Jacques CHIRAC. Mitterrand was re-elected in 1988. He was a leading supporter of the EUROPEAN UNION (EU) and of closer Franco-German relations, establishing a personal friendship with the German chancellor, Helmut KOHL. He was succeeded as president by Chirac.

Mixtec NATIVE MIDDLE AMERICAN civilization based in Oaxaca, S Mexico. Their city-states can be traced to the 7th century AD. In the 14th century, they gained control of ZAPOTEC territory, becoming the dominant culture in the Oaxaca valley. After 1486 most of their territory fell to the AZTECS, and they were finally defeated by an alliance of their enemies and the Spanish. The estimated population was more than 500,000 in 1519. They were renowned for their expertise in metalwork and stonemasonry.

Mizuno Tadakuni (1794–1851) Japanese statesman, chief adviser (1834–43) to the TOKUGAWA shogun Ieyoshi (r.1837–53). After the death of Ienari (1837), Mizuno exercised almost total control over government. He had to contend with famine, civil unrest and the threat of Western encroachment. Mizuno responded with a programme of reforms that attempted to restore the simple virtues of the early Tokugawa period. His policies, especially a land-redistribution scheme, aroused such protest that the shogun was forced to dismiss him.

Mladić, Ratko (1943–) Bosnian Serb general. As the aggressive and brutal commander of the Bosnian Serb army during the civil war in BOSNIA-HERZEGOVINA, Mladić earned the sobriquet "the butcher of the Balkans". In 1996 he was formally indicted as a war criminal by the United Nations (UN). He has so far evaded arrest.

Moab Ancient kingdom (*c*.14th–6th centuries BC) in Palestine, E of the Dead Sea (now part of Jordan). According to the Bible, the Moabites were related to the Israelites and their language is similar to Hebrew. According to the Book of Samuel, SAUL and DAVID fought against the Moabites in the 13th century BC. The reconquest of Moab by King Omri of Israel (r. *c*.884–*c*.872 BC) and Mesha's subsequent rebellion against Israel is recorded on the Moabite Stone (discovered at Dhiban, Jordan, in AD 1868). Moab began to decline soon after that time.

Mobutu Sese Seko (1930–97) Zaïrean (Congolese) dictator, president (1970–97), b. Joseph-Désiré Mobutu. When Congo gained independence from Belgium in 1960, he was appointed secretary of defence in the coalition government of President Joseph KASAVUBU and Prime Minister Patrice LUMUMBA. Mobutu secretly supported Kasavubu's attempt to depose Lumumba, and took control of government in 1960. Mobutu arrested Lumumba and sent him to his death in KATANGA. In 1965 Mobutu seized power in a military coup. He nationalized the copper mines in Katanga and suppressed a coup in 1967. As part of his "Africanization" programme, Mobutu changed the name of Congo to Zaïre in 1971. His flamboyance and gift for publicity masked the brutal reality of his corrupt regime: Mobutu amassed a huge personal fortune (*c*.US$5 billion) while the population became increasingly impoverished and famished. With the support of Belgium, the US Central Intelligence Agency (CIA) and the brutal tactics of his security forces, Mobotu maintained his grip on power for more than 30 years. In May 1997 he was overthrown in a Tutsi-dominated rebellion, led by Laurent KABILA. Mobutu died in exile.

Mochica (Moche) Ancient NATIVE SOUTH AMERICANS (*c*.200 BC–AD 600) of N Peru. They are named after their capital, Moche, beside the River Moche, where the pyramid Temple of the Sun and the Temple of the Moon are still extant. The monuments suggest that the Mochica acknowledged a priestly ruling class and engaged in blood sacrifices. They expanded into neighbouring coastal areas – the site of Huaca Rajada was discovered by archaeologists in AD 1987. The Mochica are famous for their realistically decorated pottery, textiles and efficient irrigation system. *See also* NAZCA

Model Parliament (1295) English PARLIAMENT summoned by EDWARD I. Members included knights of the shire and burgesses (representing the towns), which 19th-century historians thought was a new development – hence the name "Model Parliament". In fact, commoners were present in earlier parliaments. However, the Model Parliament was unusually large, its total membership of *c*.400 included 73 knights and more than 200 burgesses. *See also* MONTFORT, SIMON DE

modernism In the Roman Catholic Church, movement of the late 19th and early 20th centuries that sought to adapt the Church's beliefs to developments in modern science, philosophy and history. The Modernists favoured the application of the critical method to the Bible and objected to the increasing centralization of Church authority. The movement was initially tolerated by Pope LEO XIII but condemned in 1907 by Pope PIUS X, who later required all suspect clerics to take an anti-Modernist oath.

Mogul Empire *See* MUGHAL EMPIRE

Mohács, Battle of (29 August 1526) Victory of the Ottoman Turks under SULEIMAN I (THE MAGNIFICENT) over Louis II of Hungary. Louis and his entire army of *c*.20,000 men were killed in the Battle, which marked the beginning of Ottoman domination in Hungary. In a later Battle of Mohács (1687), the Turks were defeated.

Mohawk Iroquoian-speaking NATIVE NORTH AMERICANS, formerly inhabiting E central New York.

By tradition, Mohawk chief HIAWATHA was the main instigator of the IROQUOIS CONFEDERACY. The Mohawk supported the British during the French and Indian Wars and the American Revolution. After British defeat in the latter conflict, the Mohawk chief Joseph BRANT led his tribe N into Canada. Disputes over land rights sparked violent clashes with Canadian police in the 1980s.

Mohenjo-daro One of the main cities of the INDUS VALLEY CIVILIZATION (*c*.2300–1750 BC) so far discovered. Remains (in modern s Pakistan) occupy *c*.2.5sq km (1sq mi) and show that the city was laid out in a regular pattern, dominated by a central citadel that acted as the ceremonial centre and granary. The city had a sophisticated sanitation system and many of its inhabitants lived in two-storey brick and mud houses.

Mohican *See* MAHICAN

Moi, Daniel arap (1924–) Kenyan statesman, president (1978–). He was the British-appointed representative to the Kenya Legislative Council from 1958 until independence (1963). Moi succeeded Jomo KENYATTA as president and was re-elected in 1992 and 1997. Moi continued his predecessor's liberal economic policies, but came under increasing criticism for his repressive and corrupt rule. *See also* ODINGA, OGINGA

Moldavia *See* MOLDOVA

Moldova *See* country feature

Mollet, Guy (1905–75) French statesman, premier (1956–57). He was active in the French Resistance during World War 2, and after the War became secretary general (1946–69) of the SOCIALIST PARTY (PS). As premier, Mollet connived with Britain in the invasion of Egypt that led to the SUEZ CRISIS (1956). His failure to quell the rebellion in Algeria led to Charles DE GAULLE's return to power, and Mollet served as minister of state (1958–59) under De Gaulle. *See also* MENDÈS-FRANCE, PIERRE

Molly Maguires Secret terrorist society formed by (predominantly Irish-American) coal miners in Pennsylvania, United States. They acquired their name from a widow, who led a revolt against landlords in Ireland in the 1840s. From *c*.1862 to *c*.1876 the "Molly Maguires" organized a campaign of sabotage and physical intimidation aimed at improving working conditions in the mines. In 1875 they organized a strike that was broken by the mine owners. The organization was infiltrated by Pinkerton detectives and 10 members were convicted of murder and hanged (1877). The Molly Maguires subsequently folded.

Molotov, Vyacheslav Mikhailovich (1890–1986) Soviet statesman, prime minister (1930–41) and foreign minister (1939–49, 1953–56), b. Vyacheslav Mikhailovich Skriabin. He joined the BOLSHEVIKS in 1906 and assumed the name of Molotov ("Hammer"). Although exiled and imprisoned several times under the tsarist regime, Molotov was one of the few Bolshevik leaders present in Russia at the start of the first phase of the RUSSIAN REVOLUTION (March 1917). A loyal ally of Joseph STALIN, Molotov joined the Politburo in 1926 and replaced Maxim LITVINOV as foreign minister in 1939. One of Molotov's first acts as foreign minister was to sign the NAZI-SOVIET PACT (1939) with Joachim von RIBBENTROP. He also signed the Anglo-Soviet Treaty in 1942 and attended the Allies' conferences at TEHRAN (1943), YALTA (1945) and POTSDAM (1945). His frequent use of the veto in the United Nations' (UN) Security Council was a feature of the COLD WAR. Molotov lost influence after his criticism of Nikita KHRUSHCHEV and was expelled from the Communist Party in 1962. He was readmitted to the Party in 1984.

Moltke, Helmuth (Johannes Ludwig), Graf von (1848–1916) German general, chief of the general staff (1906–14), nephew of Helmut Karl Bernhard von MOLTKE. His appointment as successor to Alfred von Schlieffen was based on favouritism rather than merit. Moltke was given the task of modernizing the SCHLIEFFEN PLAN for war on two fronts in Europe. His poor organizational abilities were highlighted at the start of WORLD WAR I (1914–18), when the German offensive was repulsed at the First Battle of the MARNE (1914). Emperor WILLIAM II replaced Moltke with General von Falkenhayn. *See also* LUDENDORFF, ERICH

Moltke, Helmuth Karl Bernhard, Graf von (1800–91) Prussian general, chief of the general staff (1858–88). During the 1830s, he acted as a military adviser to the Ottoman Sultan MAHMUD II. As chief of the Prussian general staff, Moltke realized that the advent of the railway enabled an army to be more highly mobile, and he reorganized the army's command structure to permit swift and decisive offensives. Moltke's strategy produced lightning victories against Denmark (1864), against Austria in the AUSTRO-PRUSSIAN WAR (1866), and against France in the FRANCO-PRUSSIAN WAR (1870). *See also* BISMARCK, OTTO VON; FREDERICK III

Moluccas (Maluku) Island group and province in E INDONESIA; the capital is Ambon. Before the 15th century, the Moluccas formed part of the Javanese kingdom of MAJAPAHIT. The fabled Spice Islands, the objective of European maritime enterprise, were reached first by Portuguese navigator Ferdinand MAGELLAN in 1511. In the 17th century, the Dutch seized the islands and the valuable trade in nutmeg and cloves, expelling English competitors. When Indonesia gained independence in 1949, the islands declared independence but the revolt was quickly suppressed. In 1999–2000, more than 17,000 people died in intercommunal violence between Christians and Muslims. Pop. (1990) 1,857,790.

Mommsen, (Christian Matthais) Theodor (1817–1903) German historian. His masterpiece, the three-volume *History of Rome* (1854–56), challenged many of the prevailing assumptions about the Roman republic. Mommsen codified the Roman legal system in *Roman Constitutional Law* (1871–88) and *Roman Criminal Law* (1899). He championed the creation of a German republic and was briefly exiled from Germany after the failed REVOLUTION OF 1848. Mommsen served in the Reichstag (1863–79). He won the Nobel Prize for literature in 1902.

Monaco Principality in s Europe. The small city-state of Monaco has been ruled by the GRIMALDI family, originally from Genoa, since 1297. Almost surrounded by French territory, it has been closely linked with France in the modern era, and was incorporated (1793–1814) into France by Napoleon. Its independence was guaranteed by the Franco-Monegasque treaty of 1861, which also established a customs union between France and Monaco. Monaco's liberal tax regime made it a haven for the rich. The government bought the famous Monte-Carlo casino in 1967. Tourism is the major source of revenue. Pop. (1990) 29,972.

monasticism Ascetic mode of life followed by men and women who have taken religious vows, belong to a recognized religious order and follow its rule. They generally live in their own, separate community. It is an ancient practise characteristic of many religions, notably BUDDHISM, whose monks in some countries, especially Tibet, at times formed the dominant political class. Christian monasticism originated in the early 4th century with the desert hermits Saint Anthony and Saint Pachomius in Egypt, where the first communities soon arose. The organization of monasticism was effected by Saint BENEDICT in the 6th century, and the BENEDICTINES were practically the only monastic order until the CARTHUSIANS, CISTERCIANS, the mendicant orders of friars (DOMINICANS and FRANCISCANS), and others were

MOLDOVA (FORMERLY MOLDAVIA)

AREA: 33,700sq km (13,010sq mi)
POPULATION: 4,458,000
CAPITAL (POPULATION): Chisinau (700,000)
GOVERNMENT: Multiparty republic
ETHNIC GROUPS: Moldovan 65%, Ukrainian 14%, Russian 13%, Gagauz 4%, Jewish 2%, Bulgarian 1%
LANGUAGES: Moldovan (Romanian) (official)
RELIGIONS: Christianity (Eastern Orthodox)
GDP PER CAPITA (1994): US$322

Republic in E Europe. Under Roman rule, it formed the major part of the province of DACIA. Between the 10th and 12th centuries part of the region was ruled by KIEVAN RUS. It then fell to the TATARS before gaining independence under the Vlach Prince Dragos. At its height, the principality included BESSARABIA and BUKOVINA. It successfully repulsed attacks from Hungary and Poland, before being forced to pay tribute to the OTTOMAN EMPIRE in the early 16th century. From 1711 Moldavia was governed for the Turks by Greek Phanariots. After becoming a Russian protectorate, Moldavia was forced to cede Bukovina to Austria (1775) and Bessarabia to Russia (1812). The Phanariot dysnasty was overthrown in 1821 and Russian influence increased still further after the RUSSO-TURKISH WAR (1828–29). In 1861 the twin principalities of Moldavia and WALLACHIA were united to form ROMANIA and recognized as independent by the Turks.

At the end of World War 1, Bessarabia became part of Romania in the face of Russian opposition. In 1924 the Soviet Union established the tiny Moldavian republic E of the Dneister and in 1940, following the outbreak of World War 2, it occupied Bessarabia. Moldavia, now including Bessarabia, became an autonomous Soviet republic.

Following independence (as Moldova) in 1991, the majority Moldovan population wished to rejoin Romania, but this alienated the Ukrainian and Russian populations E of the Dniester, who declared their independence from Moldova as the Transdniester Republic. War raged between the two, with Transdniester supported by the Russian 14th Army. In August 1992 a cease-fire was declared. The 1994 multiparty elections were won by the former communists of the Agrarian Democratic Party. A referendum rejected reunification with Romania. Parliament voted to join the COMMONWEALTH OF INDEPENDENT STATES (CIS). A new constitution (1994) established a presidential parliamentary republic. In a 1995 referendum, Transdniester voted in favour of independence. In 1996 Russian troops began to withdraw and Petru Lucinschi was elected president.

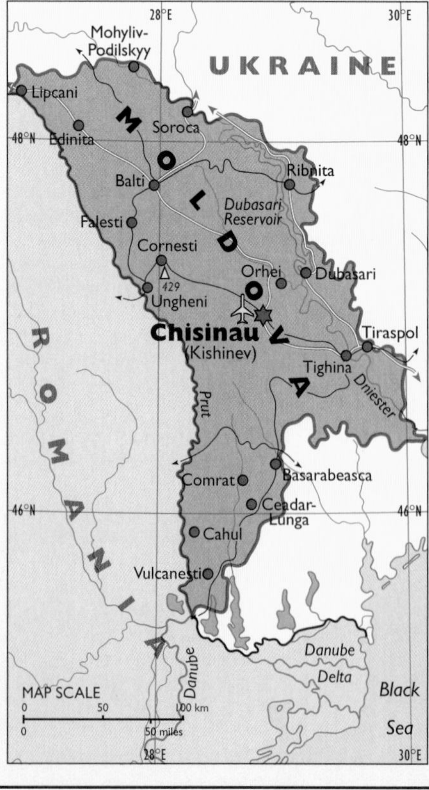

MONACO

AREA: 1.9sq km (0.7sq mi)
POPULATION: 32,000
CAPITAL (POPULATION): Monaco (27,063)
GOVERNMENT: Constitutional monarchy
ETHNIC GROUPS: French 47%, Monégasque 16%, Italian 16%
LANGUAGES: French (official), Monégasque
RELIGIONS: Roman Catholic 95%
GDP PER CAPITA (1994): US$24,693

founded in the 11th–13th centuries. While it continued to feature prominently in the Roman Catholic and Eastern Orthodox churches, monasticism was at first rejected by Protestants. The Anglican Church admitted monastic orders in the 19th century. *See also* Jainism

Monck, George, 1st Duke of Albemarle (1608–70) English general. He helped suppress a rebellion (1642–43) in Ireland, before returning to England to fight for Charles I in the English Civil War (1642–45). In 1644 Monck was captured and imprisoned by the Parliamentarians, but was released (1646) in order to suppress a further Irish revolt for Parliament. In 1650 he helped Oliver Cromwell defeat the Scots at the Battle of Dunbar, and remained as commander in chief in Scotland. Monck won three major victories against the Dutch in the First Dutch War (1652–54). After Oliver Cromwell's death (1658) and the overthrow of the Protectorate in 1659, Monck led his Coldstream Guards to London and reformed the Rump Parliament. Monck was instrumental in persuading Charles II to issue the Declaration of Breda that led to the Restoration of the Stuart monarchy in 1660.

monetarism Economic theory that argues that the quantity of money is the principal cause of changes in the economy, notably inflation. It therefore asserts the importance of controlling the money supply as the means of achieving a non-inflationary, stable economy. The theory is associated particularly with the theories of Milton Friedman (1912–), whose early work in the 1950s and 1960s stimulated the initial debate. Interest in monetarism revived in the 1970s and was especially influential in the United States and Britain in the 1980s.

Mongolia *See* country feature, page 276

Mongols *See* feature article

Monitor and Merrimack Ironclad warships that fought an inconclusive battle (9 March 1862) at Hampton Roads, Virginia, during the American Civil War. It was the first battle between ironclad ships. The *Merrimack*, which had been scuttled by the US navy, was raised by the Confederates and given armour plating. Renamed the *Virginia*, it was designed to break the Union blockade of Southern ports. The *Monitor*, a new ironclad, was designed to destroy it. Neither aim was achieved. The *Virginia* was subsequently destroyed by the retreating Confederates in May 1862, while the *Monitor* foundered in December.

Monmouth, James Scott, Duke of (1649–85) English rebel, illegitimate son of Charles II. He fought in the Third Dutch War (1672–74) and suppressed the Scottish Presbyterians at Bothwell Bridge (1679). Allied with the Earl of Shaftesbury and hopeful of becoming king, Monmouth led opposition to the possible succession of the Catholic Duke of York (later James II), gaining the powerful backing of the 1st Earl of Shaftesbury. The discovery of the Rye House Plot (1683) forced Monmouth into exile in Holland. On James' accession (1685), Monmouth launched a rebellion in the West Country. Monmouth's untrained forces were routed at Sedgemoor, Somerset, and he was executed. *See also* Bloody Assizes

Monmouth, Battle of (28 June 1778) Inconclusive conflict in the American Revolution, fought near Monmouth Court House, New Jersey. George Washington directed General Charles Lee to attack the British under Sir Henry Clinton, who were retreating from Philadelphia towards Sandy Hook. Lee was surprised, however, by the arrival of Lord Cornwallis and beat a hasty retreat, allowing Clinton to regroup in New York.

Monnet, Jean (1888–1979) French economist. In 1947, as head of the National Planning Board, he introduced the Monnet Plan for the revitalization of French industry, including the nationalization of major industries. He proposed and became first president (1952–55) of the European Coal and Steel Community (ECSC), and was a leading proponent of the European Community (EC).

Monophysitism Belief that Jesus Christ had a single, divine nature, whereas the orthodox view is that He was both divine and human in nature. Monophysitism was condemned by the Council of Chalcedon (451). Thereafter, the adherents of Monophysitism became separated from the main body of Christendom, resulting in the consolidation of three great Monophysite churches – the Coptic, Syrian Orthodox and Armenian.

Monroe, James (1758–1831) Fifth president of the United States (1817–25). He fought in the American Revolution and was a personal friend of Thomas Jefferson. Monroe represented Virginia in the Senate (1790–94) and was appointed minister to France (1794–96) by George Washington. He was never committed, however, to securing French approval for Jay's Treaty (1794) and was recalled to the United States, later serving as governor of Virginia (1799–1802, 1811). Monroe and Robert Livingston negotiated the Louisiana Purchase (1803), which almost doubled the size of the United States. As secretary of state (1811–16) under James Madison, Monroe managed foreign affairs during the War of 1812 with Britain, and also served as secretary of war (1814–15). Monroe's presidency is often called the "Era of Good Feeling". His accession was marked by the First Seminole War (1817–18) which, thanks to Secretary of State John Quincy Adams, led to the acquisition of Florida from Spain. The Missouri Compromise (1820) attempted to resolve divisions over the extension of slavery to the new territories, and earned Monroe re-election in 1820. His second term was marked by the promulgation of the Monroe Doctrine (1823), which attempted to end European interference in the affairs of the Western Hemisphere. A treaty with Russia (1824) fixed the border between Alaska and Oregon. Monroe was succeeded as president by John Quincy Adams. *See also* Calhoun, John Caldwell

Monroe Doctrine (2 December 1823) US foreign policy statement by President James Monroe to Congress, made in response to fears of French intervention against Spain's rebellious colonies in Latin America. Passed with the cooperation of Britain, on whom its enforcement initially depended, it asserted that any future European colonization or military intervention in the Western Hemisphere would be regarded as "dangerous to peace and safety" and, correspondingly, that the United States would not become involved in the internal conflicts of Europe. In the 20th century, the Monroe Doctrine was called upon to justify US intervention in the internal affairs of Latin American states.

MONGOLS

Nomadic peoples of E central Asia, descendants of the Huns. The different tribes on the Mongolian Plateau were united (*c.*1206) by Genghis Khan, who built an empire that stretched from the Black Sea to the Pacific Ocean and from Siberia to Tibet. Genghis Khan's possessions were divided among his four sons, with overall command going to Ogodei. Genghis' grandson, Batu, established the Golden Horde in Russia (*c.*1240). Further expansion was achieved under another of Genghis' grandsons, Möngke (r.1251–59), whose brother Hulagu established the Mongol Ilkhanid dynasty in Iran. Möngke was succeeded by another brother, Kublai Khan (r.1260–94), who destroyed the Southern Song and established the Yuan dynasty in China. In the 14th century, the Mongol empire disintegrated: Tamerlane conquered the Ilkhanate and broke up the Golden Horde, and the Ming gained control of China. The Mongol alliance fragmented into individual tribes. By 1691 the Manchu Qing dynasty had conquered S and E Mongolia, which became known as Inner Mongolia, and further attacks led to the dispersal of the Mongol tribes across Central Asia. In 1911 Outer Mongolia (now Mongolia) declared independence.

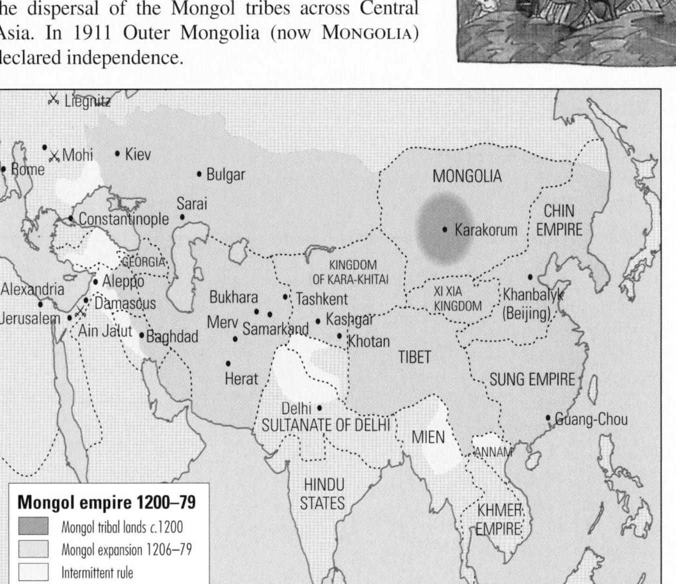

▲ **Battle of Kozelsk** (1240) Illustration from a 16th-century Russian chronicle. In 1237–38, Batu Khan launched a devastating campaign against the Russian principalities. After victory at Kozelsk, the Mongols advanced to Kiev and razed it to the ground.

◄ **The Mongol empire** expanded westwards as the Golden Horde crossed the Russian steppe, seizing Liegnitz (Silesia) and Mohi (Hungary) in 1241. The Mongols were finally defeated by the Mamluks at Ain Jalut (1250).

M

Montagnards (Fr. Mountain Men) Nickname of French deputies of the extreme left, including the JACOBINS, who occupied the upper seats in the NATIONAL CONVENTION during the FRENCH REVOLUTION (1789–99). With the fall of the GIRONDINS (1793), the Montagnards were the dominant political force on the COMMITTEE OF PUBLIC SAFETY during the ascendancy of Maximilien ROBESPIERRE. They were purged during the THERMIDORIAN REACTION (1794–95).

Montagu, Charles *See* HALIFAX, CHARLES MONTAGU, EARL OF

Montagu-Chelmsford Report (1919) Proposals that resulted from consultations (1917) between British Secretary of State Edwin Montagu (1879–1924) and Viceroy of India Lord CHELMSFORD. It was originally prompted by Britain's need for Indian support in World War 1, and by pressure from Indian nationalists. The Report recommended constitutional reforms that were adopted in the Government of India Act (1919), which for the first time gave limited self-government to India. It was regarded as unsatisfactory by Indian nationalists and "Mahatma" GANDHI advocated non-cooperation.

Montana Mountain state in NW United States; the capital is Helena. When the LEWIS AND CLARK EXPEDITION began the white exploration of Montana in 1805, the W region of the Rocky Mountains was populated by the Kootenai, while the Great Plains to the E were inhabited by the ASSINIBOINE, BLACKFOOT, CROW and SALISH. The territory was acquired by the United States as part of the LOUISIANA PURCHASE (1803), and fur-trading posts were quickly established. In 1841 Pierre Jean de SMET established the first permanent settlement, a Roman Catholic mission. The discovery of gold (1858) attracted many settlers, and the Territory of Montana was organized in 1864. Native Americans fought to protect their land and bison from white encroachment, and the SIOUX scored their last major victory over the US army at the Battle of LITTLE BIGHORN (1876). By 1881, however, the Native Americans had been restricted to reservations. Montana was transformed by the discovery of rich deposits of copper at Anaconda in the 1880s, and homesteaders were attracted by the fertile soil. Drought and the Great Depression devastated the farms and mines of Montana, but the economy recovered after World War 2, mainly due to the growth of oil, coal and gas industries. Pop. (1990) 799,065.

Montcalm (de Saint-Véran), Louis Joseph, Marquis de (1712–59) French general, commander in chief (1756–59) of the French army in New France (North America). He first distinguished himself in the War of the AUSTRIAN SUCCESSION (1740–48). Montcalm won several victories over the British in the FRENCH AND INDIAN WARS, most notably at the Battle of Fort TICONDEROGA (1758). In 1759 he held Québec against a British siege for several months, but when the British, under James WOLFE, climbed the cliffs from the St Lawrence River to the Plains of ABRAHAM, he was taken by surprise. Montcalm and Wolfe were both killed in the battle.

Monte Albán Ancient ZAPOTEC site, near present-day Oaxaca, Mexico. Perhaps dating back to the 8th century BC, Monte Albán was built on a level hilltop and dominated the Oaxaca valley. The site includes ziggurats, temples raised on platforms, elaborate tombs, palaces and even an observatory. At the height of its power (AD 300–900), more than 30,000 inhabitants lived on its terraced hillsides. Monte Albán began to decline in the 9th century, although it was adopted by the MIXTEC in the 16th century.

Montesquieu, Charles Louis de Secondat, Baron de la Brède et de (1689–1755) French philosopher, a leading figure of the ENLIGHTENMENT. He first gained attention for *Persian Letters* (1721), an epistolary satire on French society. He is chiefly remembered for his *The Spirit of the Laws* (1748), written after two years in England and influenced by John LOCKE. It compares three forms of government: republic, monarchy and despotism. Montesquieu's advocacy of the SEPARATION OF THE POWERS of government (executive, legislative and judicial) to ensure individual freedom influenced the framers of the CONSTITUTION OF THE UNITED STATES.

Montezuma II (1466–*c*.1520) Ninth Aztec emperor (r.1502–20), nephew and successor of Ahuitzotl. He inherited an empire at the height of its power, but vulnerable to the dissatisfaction of its subjects. The Spanish conquistador Hernán CORTÉS exploited this weakness by fomenting revolt among the subject tribes. In 1519 Montezuma was imprisoned by Cortés, whom he had welcomed into his capital, Tenochtitlán (now MEXICO CITY). He was killed, either by the Spaniards or his own people.

Montfort, Simon de (1165?–1218) French noble, leader of the crusade (1209–18) against the ALBIGENSES in S France. He fought in the Fourth CRUSADE (1202–04) before being sent by Pope INNOCENT III to suppress the heretical Cathari (Albigenses). Montfort captured Béziers and CARCASSONNE and was awarded Toulouse in 1215. Raymond VI, Count of Toulouse, refused to pay tribute to Montfort and occupied the city in 1217. Montfort died attempting to regain Toulouse.

Montfort, Simon de, Earl of Leicester (*c*.1208–65) Anglo-French noble, leader of a revolt against HENRY III, son of Simon de MONTFORT. His marriage to Henry's sister, Eleanor, enraged Richard, Earl of Cornwall, and Montfort was temporarily forced into exile. In 1248 Montfort was sent by Henry to quell a rebellion in GASCONY, SW France, but his brutal tactics led to dismissal. Montfort now turned against Henry, supporting the Provisions of Oxford (1258), which sought to limit royal power. Henry managed to foment division in the baronial ranks and annulled the Provisions. Montfort led a rebellion in the BARONS' WAR (1263) and, after capturing the king at the Battle of LEWES (1264), became military dictator of England. In 1265 Montfort summoned a Parliament, including commoners, but was defeated and killed by the future EDWARD I at the Battle of EVESHAM.

Montenegro (Crna Gora) Constituent republic of the rump state of YUGOSLAVIA; the capital is Podgorica. The region was part of the Serbian empire until the Ottoman Turkish invasion of 1355. SERBIA was decisively defeated by the Ottomans in 1389. Montenegro successfully resisted the sultan, but by 1500 most of its territory had been surrendered to the Turks. In 1799 the Ottoman Empire recognized Montenegro's independence. In 1851 a monarchy was established, and in 1878 the sovereignty of the state was formally recognized. In 1910 NICHOLAS I became king and sought to expel the Turks. In 1914 he declared war on Austria, and Montenegro was quickly overrun by the Austro-German armies. In 1918 Nicholas was deposed and Montenegro was united with Serbia. In 1946 Montenegro became a republic of Yugoslavia. In 1989 the local communist leadership resigned. The communists were returned to power in Montenegro in the 1990 elections, but four of the former six Yugoslav republics voted to secede from the federation. Montenegro supported Serbian President Slobodan MILOŠEVIĆ's creation of a new, Serb-dominated federation. In a 1992 referendum Montenegro voted to remain part of the federation, but there are increasing signs of dissatisfaction with the Milošević regime. Area: 13,812sq km (5331sq mi). Pop. (1991) 615,035.

Montgomery (of Alamein), Bernard Law, 1st Viscount (1887–1976) British field marshal. As commander of the British 8th Army in WORLD WAR 2, he defeated the Germans and Italians under General Erwin ROMMEL at the Battle of El ALAMEIN (1942), North Africa, and pursued the Axis forces to their surrender in Tunisia (1943). Montgomery led the 8th Army in the invasion of Sicily and S Italy, commanded the ground forces in the NORMANDY CAMPAIGN (1944), but miscalculated at ARNHEM. A controversial commander, "Monty" was loved by his men but his cautious approach led to disagreements with US General Dwight EISENHOWER. After the War, Montgomery served as deputy commander of the North Atlantic Treaty Organization (NATO)'s forces in Europe. *See also* AUCHINLECK, SIR CLAUDE JOHN EYRE

MONGOLIA

AREA: 1,566,500sq km (604,826sq mi)
POPULATION: 2,130,000
CAPITAL (POPULATION): Ulan Bator (601,000)
GOVERNMENT: Multiparty republic
ETHNIC GROUPS: Khalkha Mongol 79%, Kazak 6%
LANGUAGES: Khalkha Mongolian (official)
RELIGIONS: Tibetan Buddhism was once the main religion; reliable recent information is unavailable
GDP PER CAPITA (1995): US$1950

Republic in central Asia. Mongolia is the largest landlocked country in the world. In the 13th century, GENGHIS KHAN united the Mongolian peoples and built up a great empire. Under Genghis' grandson, KUBLAI KHAN, the MONGOL empire extended from Korea and China to E Europe and Mesopotamia. The empire broke up in the late 14th century, and in the early 17th century, Inner Mongolia came under Chinese control. By the late 17th century, Outer Mongolia had also become a Chinese province.

In 1911 the Mongolians drove the Chinese out of Outer Mongolia and established a short-lived Buddhist kingdom. In 1919 China re-established control. Revolutionaries then sought the help of the Russian Bolsheviks in driving out the Chinese. A joint Russian-Mongol force captured Urga (now Ulan Bator) in 1921 and the present republic was established (with Inner Mongolia remaining a Chinese province). In 1924 it was proclaimed a People's Republic. The Mongolian Peoples' Revolutionary Party (MPRP) became the sole political party. Traditional nomadic life was disrupted by communism, and under forced COLLECTIVIZATION many nomads were placed in permanent settlements. The revolution in ownership prompted the Lama Rebellion (1932), which saw the migration of thousands of peoples and millions of livestock into Inner Mongolia. In 1939 the Mongols defeated a Japanese invasion and in 1945 they supported the Soviet campaign in Inner Mongolia, where the Japanese had established a puppet government. This was replaced by the Chinese communists. From the 1950s, Mongolia supported Soviet policies, especially in relation to Sino-Soviet disputes. In 1961 Mongolia was admitted to the United Nations (UN).

Popular demonstrations led to multiparty elections in 1990, which were won by the MPRP. In 1992 a new constitution confirmed the process of liberalization, enshrining democratic principles and establishing a mixed economy. In 1993 President Punsalmaagiyn Ochirbat was re-elected, despite the MPRP's refusal to endorse him as a candidate. A treaty of friendship was signed with Russia, which had completed its withdrawal in 1992. A similar treaty was concluded with China in 1994. In 1996 the Democratic Union Coalition formed the first non-communist government for more than 70 years. In 1997 Ochirbat was ousted by Natsagyn Bagabandi, leader of the MPRP.

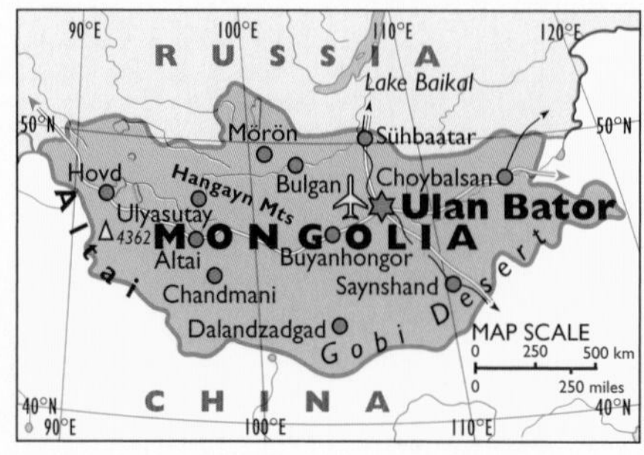

Montmorency, Anne, Duc de (1493–1567) French noble. He was a childhood friend of the future FRANCIS I, who made him marshal of France in 1522. Montmorency fought in the ITALIAN WARS, and was captured with Francis at the Battle of PAVIA (1525), N Italy. After his release, he became Francis' chief minister and helped negotiate the Treaty of CAMBRAI (1529) with Emperor CHARLES V. In 1536 Montmorency forced Charles to withdraw from Italy and was rewarded with an appointment as constable of France (1538). After a series of misjudgements, Montmorency was compelled to retire in 1541, but was restored by HENRY II in 1547 and continued to serve under CHARLES IX. He regained Le Havre from the British in 1563, but was killed fighting the HUGUENOTS during the French Wars of RELIGION.

Montréal City in s Québec province, Canada; second-largest city in Canada and the nation's chief port. Originally a HURON settlement, it was visited (*c*.1535) by the French explorer Jacques CARTIER and the site was settled by the French in 1642. Montréal became the centre of the French FUR-TRADE in North America and remained under French control until 1760, when it was taken by the British. The city's growth accelerated with the opening of the Lachine Canal in 1825, connecting it to the Great Lakes. Montreal served as the capital of Canada from 1844 to 1849. In the 1850s Montréal became Canada's leading port and the hub of Canada's railway network. The city's Métro system was opened to coincide with Expo '67, an international trade fair. Pop. (1990) 1,017,666.

Montrose, James Graham, 5th Earl and Marquess of (1612–50) Scottish general. He signed the Covenant (1638) in support of PRESBYTERIANISM, but fought for CHARLES I in the English CIVIL WAR, partly to combat the ambitions of his enemy, the Earl of ARGYLL. Montrose's men, spearheaded by the Irish MacDonalds, won a series of dramatic victories in the Highlands (1644), but were decisively defeated at Philiphaugh (1645) when the main COVENTANTER army returned from England. Montrose fled abroad, returned in 1650, but was defeated, betrayed and executed.

Moore, Sir John (1761–1809) British general. He served (1784–90) in Parliament before fighting in the French Revolutionary Wars and NAPOLEONIC WARS. Moore acquired a reputation for infantry training and tactics, and was appointed (1808) to command British forces in the PENINSULAR WAR. Realizing that the cause was lost in Spain and that NAPOLEON had blocked his route into Portugal, Moore led his troops in a remarkable retreat across the Cantabrian mountains to La Coruña, NW Spain. He died after successfully defending the city against the French. Although heavily criticized at the time, Moore had saved the British forces and was praised by the Duke of WELLINGTON.

Moors Name, deriving from the Roman province of Mauretania, given by Europeans to the predominantly BERBER people of NW Africa. It usually refers to the Muslims in Spain (711–1492), who established a distinctive, artistically brilliant civilization. GRANADA, the last Moorish stronghold in Spain, was recaptured by the Christian forces of Ferdinand V and Isabella II in 1492. *See also* ALMOHAD

Moravia Region of the CZECH REPUBLIC. In the 9th century Moravia established a large empire and adopted Christianity. It was overrun by the Magyars (Hungarians) in the 10th century, until they were driven out by OTTO I, who subsumed the region into the HOLY ROMAN EMPIRE. From the 11th to 16th century, Moravia formed part of the kingdom of BOHEMIA. It became Austrian HABSBURG territory in 1526, and a process of "Germanification" ensued. The failure of the REVOLUTION OF 1848 led to Moravia becoming Austrian crown land. When the Habsburgs were deposed in 1918, Moravia became a part of Czechoslovakia. In 1938 s Moravia was annexed by Germany, and in 1939 Moravia became a German protectorate. After World War 2, Moravia was restored to Czechoslovakia and the German population expelled.

Moravian Church Reformed (Protestant) church whose origins can be traced to the HUSSITES of Bohemia and Moravia in the 15th century. It was founded (1727) at a time of spiritual reawakening, under the leadership of the German pietist, Count von Zinzendorf. Closely linked with LUTHERANISM, it became a strongly proselytizing church, active in foreign missions, and several Moravian congregations were founded abroad, especially in North America.

MONTANA
Statehood :
8 November 1889
Nickname :
Treasure State
State motto :
Gold and silver

Moray, James Stewart, 1st Earl of (1531–70) Scottish noble, illegitimate son of JAMES V and half-brother of MARY, QUEEN OF SCOTS. After Catholic Mary's return to Scotland (1561), Moray became her adviser. He supported the Calvinist John KNOX, opposed Mary's marriage to Lord DARNLEY and, after an unsuccessful rebellion (1565), fled to England. He was pardoned and allowed to return in Scotland in 1566. Moray was made regent (1567) for James VI (later JAMES I of England), and his forces defeated Mary at Langside (1568). Moray was murdered by James Hamilton, a supporter of Mary. *See also* MORTON, JAMES DOUGLAS, 4TH EARL OF

Morazán, Francisco (1792–1842) Honduran president (1830–39) of the CENTRAL AMERICAN FEDERATION. In 1829 he led the liberal forces of the Federation to victory against Manuel José Arce. As president, Morazán attempted to restrict the power of the Catholic Church, but his reforms were frustrated by conservatives and the Federation disintegrated. In 1840 Morazán was forced into exile by the Guatemalan leader Rafael Carrera. He continued to champion the cause of federalism, launching a successful revolt (1842) against Braulio Carillo, dictator of Costa Rica. Morazán was betrayed, captured and executed.

More, Sir Thomas (1478–1535) English statesman and scholar. He was England's most respected humanist intellectual, now remembered for his *Utopia* (1516), which portrays an ideal state founded on natural reason. More opposed Martin LUTHER and the reformers, and succeeded (1529) Cardinal WOLSEY as lord chancellor to HENRY VIII. In 1532 More resigned after failing to dissuade Henry from divorcing CATHERINE OF ARAGON. In 1534 he declined to swear an oath confirming the king as head of the English church, was charged with treason and executed. He was canonized in 1935.

Morelos (y Pavón), José María (1765–1815) Mexican revolutionary and priest. Of humble birth, he succeeded Miguel HIDALGO Y COSTILLA as leader of the Mexican independence movement in 1811. By the end of 1812 Morelos had gained control of most of s Mexico. After capturing Acapulco, he summoned the Congress of Chilpancingo (1813), which declared Mexico independent and proclaimed Morelos president. He was defeated, captured and shot as a traitor by the royalist forces.

Moreno, Mariano (1778–1811) Argentine revolutionary. He published a pamphlet (1809) that attacked the MERCANTILISM of the Spanish colonial government, and advocated free-trade for Argentina. After the overthrow of the Spanish viceroy in 1810, Moreno became leader of the provisional junta, but his demands for the independence of Argentina proved too radical for the conservative junta, and he was dismissed. He died en route to England.

Morgan, Daniel (1736–1802) American general in the AMERICAN REVOLUTION (1775–83). He was captured by the British during Benedict ARNOLD's assault on Québec (1775), but was released in 1776. Morgan fought alongside General Horatio GATES in the battles of SARATOGA (1777). Morgan achieved one of the most stunning victories of the Revolution, when he defeated Lord CORNWALLIS' superior forces at the Battle of Cowpens (1781). After the Revolution, he helped to suppress the WHISKEY REBELLION in Pennsylvania.

Morgan, Sir Henry (1635–88) Welsh adventurer in the Caribbean. He led a band of buccaneers against Spanish colonies and ships, capturing and looting Panama (1671). In 1672 he was sent back to England charged with piracy, but was greeted as a hero and returned to the West Indies with a knighthood as lieutenant governor of Jamaica.

Morgan, J.P. (John Pierpont) (1837–1913) US financier. Son of a rich banker, he formed (1871) the banking house later known as J.P. Morgan and Co., and was a powerful international money-broker in the late 19th and early 20th centuries. Morgan created vast industrial empires, notably the Northern Securities Company (railroads) and, most famously, the US Steel Corporation (1901).

Morgan, John Hunt (1825–64) Confederate general in the American Civil War (1861–65), who specialized in cavalry raids behind enemy lines. In 1862 he was given command of a cavalry squadron, which launched a number of daring guerrilla attacks on Union supplies in Kentucky and Tennessee. In 1863 Morgan disobeyed orders and embarked on raids in Indiana and Ohio, the furthest N any Confederate forces reached during the War. The campaign was largely ineffective, however, and Morgan lost most of his forces before being captured himself. He escaped, but was later killed fighting in Tennessee.

Morgenthau, Henry, Jr (1891–1967) US statesman, secretary of the treasury (1934–45). He was appointed to the treasury by President Franklin ROOSEVELT, a close friend. Morgenthau managed national finances during the New Deal and World War 2, a period of unprecedented government expenditure. He resigned after his plan to partition Germany and remove its industrial base was rejected by President Harry TRUMAN.

Morison, Samuel Eliot (1887–1976) US historian. He was professor of history (1922–55) at Harvard University. Morison's books on maritime history are noted for their narrative skill and attention to detail. He received Pulitzer prizes for his biographies of Christopher Columbus, *Admiral of the Ocean Sea* (1942), and *John Paul Jones* (1959). Morison also wrote the *History of US Naval Operations in World War 2* (15 vol., 1947–62), the official history of the US Navy in World War 2.

Mormons (formally Church of Jesus Christ of Latter-day Saints) Adventist church, founded (1830) by Joseph SMITH in New York. Smith claimed that the *Book of Mormon* (1830), which recounts the migration (*c*.600 BC) of a group of Hebrews from Jerusalem to the United States, was revealed to him by an angel, Moroni. Smith led his followers to Ohio and Missouri, where their beliefs in polytheism, polygamy and collective ownership led to violent clashes with the local population. When Smith was killed by a mob in Illinois (1844), leadership passed to Brigham YOUNG, who led many of the Mormons to Salt Lake City, UTAH, their present-day headquarters. Polygamy complicated relations with the US government, leading to the Utah War (1857). In 1870 the Supreme Court ruled that freedom of religion did not extend to polygamy, and the Mormons banned it in 1890. The Mormons established a tradition of missionary work, and their belief in retroactive baptism of ancestors led to advances in genealogical studies. Today, there are *c*.10 million Mormons, more than half of whom live in the United States.

Moro, Aldo (1916–78) Italian statesman, premier (1963–64, 1964–66, 1966–68, 1974–76, 1976). In 1959 he became secretary of the Christian Democratic Party (now ITALIAN POPULAR PARTY). In 1963 Moro became premier in an unprecedented coalition between the Christian Democrats and the Italian Socialist Party (PSI), but failed to secure approval of the budget and was forced to resign. His second term ended when the socialists withdrew, but Moro managed to form a new government. In 1974 he led a new coalition with the Republicans. In 1978 Moro was kidnapped and murdered by the terrorist Red Brigades.

Morocco *See* country feature, page 278

Morosini, Francesco (1618–94) Venetian admiral and DOGE. Morosini led a brilliant naval campaign (1684–88) against the Ottoman Turks, conquering Athens and the Peloponnese for the Venetian republic, but destroying the Acropolis in the process. In 1688 he was elected doge.

Morrill, Justin Smith (1810–98) US politician. He represented Vermont in the House of Representatives (1855–67) and in the Senate (1867–98). He sponsored the Morrill Act (1862), which provided federal grants of land

M

to establish agricultural colleges (precursor of the state university system). He also introduced the Tariff Act (1861), which sought to protect US industry via high import duties.

Morris, Gouverneur (1752–1816) US statesman and diplomat. He served (1775–77) in the New York Provincial Congress, ensuring that the first state constitution provided for religious toleration. Morris acted as superintendent of finance (1781–85), proposing the decimal coinage system. In the CONSTITUTIONAL CONVENTION (1787), Morris helped prepare the CONSTITUTION OF THE UNITED STATES. He also served as minister to France (1792–94) but was recalled because of his hostility to the French Revolution.

Morris, Robert (1734–1806) American banker and merchant, b. England. He emigrated to America in 1747. As a member (1775–78) of the CONTINENTAL CONGRESS, Morris signed the Declaration of Independence. He managed the finances of the AMERICAN REVOLUTION (1775–83), borrowing money from France or lending from his own pocket. In 1781 Morris formed the Bank of North America, the oldest financial institution in the United States. He lost his fortune in land speculation and was imprisoned (1798–1801) in a debtors' prison.

Morrison, Herbert Stanley, Baron (1888–1965) British statesman, deputy prime minister (1945–51), foreign minister (1951). He helped found the London LABOUR PARTY in 1914. Morrison was elected to Parliament in 1923 and joined Ramsay MACDONALD's cabinet in 1929. During World War 2, he served as home secretary (1941–45) under Winston CHURCHILL. He planned the Labour Party's winning electoral campaign in 1945. As deputy to Clement ATTLEE, Morrison helped secure many of the pillars of the WELFARE STATE and organized the Festival of Britain (1951). After Attlee retired (1955), Morrison lost the Party leadership election to Hugh GAITSKELL.

Mortimer, Roger, 1st Earl of March (1287?–1330) English nobel, lover of EDWARD II's queen, ISABELLA OF FRANCE. As lieutenant of Ireland, he helped Edward defeat ROBERT I (THE BRUCE) and added to his own personal estates. Mortimer came into conflict with Hugh le DESPENSER in the Welsh Marches and was imprisoned in the Tower of London (1322–23). He escaped to France, where he was joined by Isabella. In 1326 Mortimer and Isabella invaded England, deposed and murdered Edward (1327). Their joint rule proved corrupt and extravagant, and in 1330 the young EDWARD III engineered Mortimer's capture and execution.

Morton, James Douglas, 4th Earl of (*c.*1516–81) Scottish noble, regent (1572–78). Despite his avowed Protestantism, Morton was appointed chancellor by MARY, QUEEN OF SCOTS in 1563. He was implicated in the murders of David RIZZIO (1566) and Lord DARNLEY (1567), Mary's first husband. Morton led the forces that compelled the flight of Mary's second husband, Lord BOTHWELL, and persuaded Mary to abdicate in favour of her son, James VI (later JAMES I of England). Morton helped the Earl of MORAY defeat Mary in the ensuing civil war. He was overthrown as regent after gaining the enmity of the nobility and the Presbyterians, and was later charged with Darnley's murder and executed.

Morton, John (*c.*1420–1500) English prelate, archbishop of Canterbury (1486–1500). He supported the Lancastrian cause during the Wars of the ROSES (1455–85) and was twice forced into exile after the accessions of Edward IV (1461) and Richard III (1483). Morton became a leading adviser to HENRY VII, who appointed him lord chancellor (1487) and persuaded the pope to make him a cardinal (1493). The story of "Morton's Fork", his alleged technique for extracting loans (if rich you can pay, if poor you must be hoarding wealth), may do him injustice.

Mosaddeq, Muhammad (1880–1967) Iranian statesman, prime minister (1951–53). He was forced to retire from the Majles (parliament) after Reza PAHLAVI was

MOROCCO

AREA: 446,550sq km (172,413sq mi)
POPULATION: 26,318,000
CAPITAL (POPULATION): Rabat (518,616)
GOVERNMENT: Constitutional monarchy
ETHNIC GROUPS: Arab 70%, Berber 30%
LANGUAGES: Arabic (official)
RELIGIONS: Islam 99%, Christianity 1%
GDP PER CAPITA (1995): US$3340

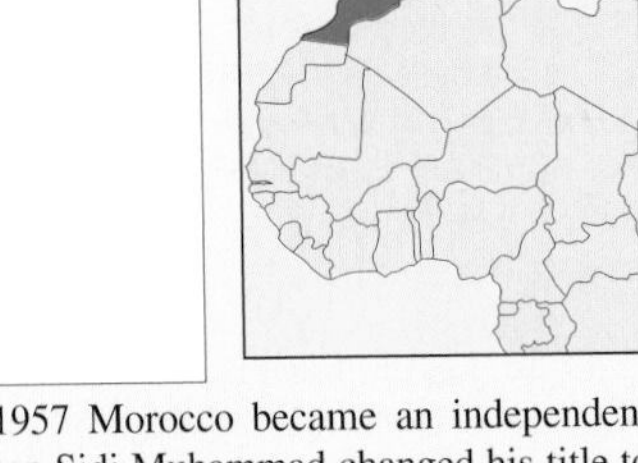

Kingdom in NW Africa. BERBERS settled in the area *c.*3000 years ago. Trading settlements were established by the PHOENICIANS along the Mediterranean coast in the 12th century BC and by CARTHAGE along the Atlantic coast in the 5th century BC. In AD 46 the region was annexed by Rome and became part of the province of Mauretania. Jewish colonies and Christianity were both established in the province.

In *c.*AD 685 Morocco was invaded by Arab armies who introduced Islam and Arabic. In 711 Moroccan Muslims (Moors) invaded Spain. In 788 Berbers and Arabs were united in a Moroccan state that asserted its independence against UMAYYAD and subsequently ABBASID rule. Fez became a major religious and cultural centre. In the mid-11th century the ALMORAVIDS conquered Morocco and established a vast Muslim empire. They were succeeded by the ALMOHADS, who were in turn defeated (1269) by the Marinids. In the 15th century, the Moors were expelled from Spain, and Spain and Portugal made advances into Morocco, which had divided into several independent states. AHMED AL-MANSOUR briefly reunified Morocco after defeating the Portuguese at the Battle of ALCAZARQUIVIR (1578), but civil war ensued after his death (1603).

In 1660 the present ruling dynasty, the Alawite, came to power. Most of the European-held territory was reclaimed. In the mid-19th century Morocco's strategic and economic potential began to attract European imperial interest, especially that of France and Spain. In 1912 Morocco was divided into French Morocco and the smaller protectorate of Spanish Morocco. Nationalist resistance was strong. ABD EL-KRIM led a revolt (1921–26) against European rule. In 1942 Allied forces invaded Morocco and removed the pro-Vichy colonial government. In 1947 Sultan Sidi Muhammad called for the reunification of French and Spanish Morocco, but France refused and exiled the sultan in 1953. In 1955 continuing civil unrest forced the French to accede to the return of the sultan.

In 1956 Morocco gained independence, although Spain retained control of two small enclaves: Ceuta and Melilla. The post-independence exodus of Europeans and Jews from Morocco created an economic vacuum. In 1957 Morocco became an independent monarchy when Sidi Muhammad changed his title to King MUHAMMAD V. In 1961 Muhammad was succeeded by his son, HASSAN II. During the 1960s, Morocco was faced with external territorial disputes (especially with Algeria) and internal political dissent. In 1965 Hassan II declared a state of emergency and assumed extraordinary powers. While the 1972 constitution reduced royal influence, Morocco remains only nominally a constitutional monarchy, and effectively the king wields all political power.

In 1976 Spain finally relinquished its claim to Spanish Sahara, and the region became known as WESTERN SAHARA. Western Sahara was divided between Morocco and MAURITANIA. In 1979 Mauritania withdrew, and Morocco assumed full control of the phosphate-rich region but met with fierce resistance from nationalist movements. In 1993 the collapse of several coalition governments led to Hassan II's appointment of an administration. In 1994 Morocco restored diplomatic links with Israel. Hassan II formed a new government of technocrats and members of the Entente National in 1995. In 1996 a referendum approved the establishment of a bicameral legislature, with a directly elected lower chamber. In 1997 elections a new coalition government was formed. In 1999 Hassan died and was succeeded by his son, Muhammad VI.

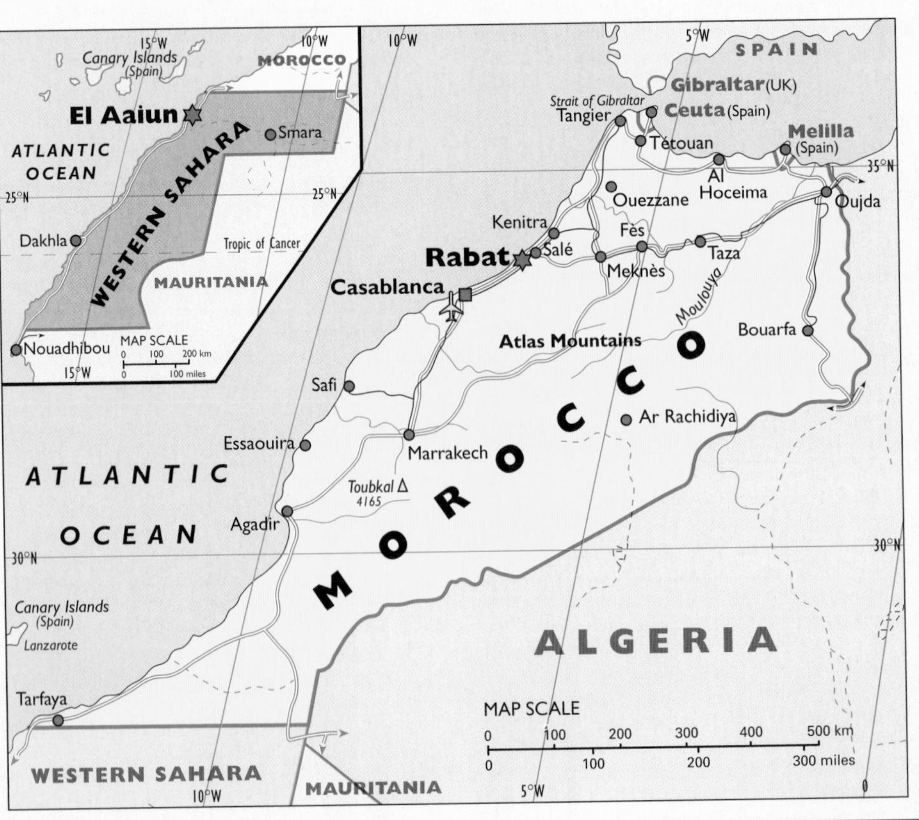

elected shah in 1925, but returned when Reza Shah abdicated in 1941. Mosaddeq led the movement to nationalize the Anglo-Iranian Oil Company in 1951, thereby gaining enough popular support to ensure his appointment as prime minister by Muhammad Reza PAHLAVI. The nationalization resulted in an economic crisis, however, as Britain stopped importing oil from Iran. A power struggle ensued between Mosaddeq and the shah, forcing the latter into brief exile in August 1953. The shah was restored with US support and Mosaddeq was sentenced to three years' imprisonment and, after he was released from prison, remained under house arrest until his death.

Mosby, John Singleton (1833–1916) Confederate guerrilla leader in the American CIVIL WAR (1861–65). His company of *c*.200 rangers, called "Mosby's Confederacy", attacked Union forces, supplies and communications behind the lines in Virginia and Maryland between 1863 and 1865.

Moscow (Muscovy) Capital of RUSSIA. The first recorded reference to Moscow appears in 1147. The KREMLIN was begun in 1156. Despite being sacked by the MONGOLS (1236–40, 1293), Moscow's location ensured its growth as a major trading centre, and it became capital of a principality by 1300 and the headquarters of the Russian ORTHODOX CHURCH in 1326. In the 1330s, it gained control of the principality of Vladimir. In 1382 Moscow was once more plundered by the Mongols. IVAN III (THE GREAT) conquered NOVGOROD in 1478 and established Moscow as the capital of a unified Russian state. From 1547 the grand dukes of Moscow held the title of tsar of Russia. IVAN IV (THE TERRIBLE) conquered the TATAR khanates of Kazan (1552) and Astrakhan (1556), but in 1571 the Crimean Tatars exacted revenge, razing the entire city (except the Kremlin) and killing *c*.170,000 Muscovites. The city witnessed numerous revolts against the ROMANOV dynasty throughout the 17th century. PETER I (THE GREAT) moved the capital to ST PETERSBURG in 1712, but Moscow continued to be the heart of Russian culture and industry. Moscow was practically destroyed during NAPOLEON I's invasion (1812), but was rapidly rebuilt and became the hub of Russia's railway network. In 1922 Moscow formally became the capital of the SOVIET UNION. The city withstood a siege and air bombardment (1941) during the German invasion of WORLD WAR 2. In August 1991 Moscow witnessed a failed coup against the communist regime, but by the end of that year the Soviet Union dissolved. Pop. (1993) 8,881,000. *See also* GODUNOV, BORIS; CRIMEA; FYODOR II; GOLDEN HORDE; KIEV; MICHAEL; RURIK; VASILY I

Moses (active *c*.13th century BC) Biblical hero who, as a prophet and leader of the ancient Hebrew people, was the central figure in their liberation from bondage in Egypt and a formative influence in the founding of their nation-state, Israel. The OLD TESTAMENT books of Exodus and Numbers are the only source for the story of Moses but, disregarding the colourful additions of legend, it is believed to be based on fact. Moses was an abandoned Hebrew child brought up in the Egyptian pharaoh's court. As a man, he sought to lead the Hebrews out of Egypt, and eventually was permitted to lead the exodus. Moses received the Ten Commandments from God (Yahweh) on Mount Sinai, but Yahweh made the Israelites wander in the desert for a further 40 years before they entered the promised land of CANAAN (Palestine). *See also* JUDAISM

Moshoeshoe II (1938–96) First king of LESOTHO (1966–90, 1995–96), paramount chief of Basutoland (1960–66). In 1970 he was briefly forced into exile by Prime Minister Leabua Jonathan, but was restored after agreeing to abstain from politics affairs. In 1986 Moshoeshoe was again forced into exile after Jonathan was overthrown in a military coup, and was replaced as king by his eldest son, Letsie III. A further coup in 1991 led to his return as king in 1995, but Moshoeshoe died the following year in a car crash.

Mosley, Sir Oswald Ernald (1896–1980) British fascist. In 1918, aged only 21, he became the youngest-ever member of Parliament. Mosley left the Conservative Party, briefly acting as an Independent before joining the Labour government of Ramsay MACDONALD in 1929. In

▲ **Mughal Empire** Painting was an integral part of Mughal court life and flourished in the reign (1605–27) of Jahangir, depicted here looking at a portrait of his father, Akbar I.

1931, disillusioned with the political system, Mosley formed the leftist New Party but quickly swung to the right, and in 1932 founded the British Union of Fascists – modelled on German and Italian FASCISM. Mosley's gang of BLACKSHIRTS engaged in confrontational marches, especially targeting the Jewish community in the East End of London. The party failed to win a seat in Parliament and Mosley's outspoken support for Adolf HITLER led to his internment during World War 2.

Mott, Lucretia Coffin (1793–1880) US social reformer. A Quaker, she championed intellectual freedom and opposed slavery, helping to found the American Anti-Slavery Society in 1833. She later concentrated on women's rights and organized (with Elizabeth STANTON) the first women's rights convention at Seneca Falls, New York (1848). *See also* ABOLITIONISTS; FEMINISM

Mound Builders Name given to various Native North Americans, notably the HOPEWELL CULTURE, who, from *c*.1000 BC, built the ancient effigy mounds and other earthworks still visible in the E United States. The richest areas are the Ohio and Mississippi valley regions. Most were either burial mounds or bases for ceremonial buildings, but the purpose of the largest systems in S Ohio is unknown. In some parts, mound-building continued until *c*.AD 1600.

mountain men Fur-trappers and hunters in remote mountain regions of the North American West in the early 19th century. They lived in almost total isolation, although many adopted Native American customs. Some made geographical discoveries, and pioneered the expansion of the Western FRONTIER. In the 1830s, up to 3000 mountain men roamed the West, but their numbers fell in the 1840s with increasing settlement and the decline of the FUR TRADE.

Mountbatten (of Burma), Louis, 1st Earl (1900–79) British admiral and colonial administrator, great-grandson of Queen VICTORIA. During World War 2, he directed commando raids on German-occupied France and Norway and, as supreme allied commander for Southeast Asia (1943–46), masterminded the recapture of Burma from the Japanese. In 1946 Mountbatten was appointed Britain's last viceroy of India, negotiating (with Jawaharlal NEHRU and Muhammad Ali JINNAH) the transition to independence in 1947. As first sea lord (1955–59), he clashed with Anthony EDEN's government over the handling of the SUEZ CRISIS (1956). He was murdered by a bomb planted on his boat by the Irish Republican Army (IRA).

Mousterian culture Palaeolithic culture dating from the period between *c*.125,000 and *c*.30,000 years ago, and named after the first site where it was recognized, Le Moustier, SW France. Mousterian culture is characterized by particular types of finely flaked flint tools, such as hand-axes, and is associated chiefly with NEANDERTHAL man. Mousterian tools have been found in Asia and Africa as well as Europe.

Mozambique *See* country feature, page 280

Muawiya (*c*.602–80) Sixth caliph (661–80), founder of the UMAYYAD caliphate. A former secretary of MUHAMMAD, he conquered Syria and was appointed (640) governor of the territory by the caliph OMAR. Muawiya led the Syrian armies to victory over the Byzantines, capturing Cyprus (649) and Rhodes (654). When the caliph OTHMAN was murdered, Muawiya went to war against his successor ALI. After the capture of Egypt and the assassination of Ali, Muawiya seized the caliphate for himself – the origin of the division in Islam between the SUNNI and SHIITE Muslims. He extended the boundaries of Islam in Asia and North Africa, conquering Khorasan and Tripolitania and establishing a garrison at Kairouan. Muawiya formed *diwans* (government departments) in Damascus to administer his vast empire. By securing the succession of his son, Yazid, Muawiya established the precedent of hereditary rule in Islam.

Mubarak, Hosni (1928–) Egyptian statesman, president (1981–). As commander in chief, he was widely praised for the success of the Egyptian air force at the start of the YOM KIPPUR WAR (1973) against Israel. Mubarak served as vice president (1975–81) under Anwar SADAT, becoming president upon his assassination. Mubarak continued Sadat's policy of rapprochement with the United States and Israel, while securing Egypt's readmission (1989) to the Arab League. He sent Egyptian troops to participate in the US-led coalition against Iraq in the GULF WAR (1991), and acted as a mediator in the ISRAELI-PALESTINIAN ACCORD (1993). Mubarak used strong tactics to suppress the rise of Islamic extremism in Egypt, arresting many leaders of the Muslim Brotherhood.

Muckrakers Nickname for investigative journalists. It was first applied (1906) by President Theodore ROOSEVELT to those US writers, including novelists, who exposed corruption in politics and business. The "Muckrakers" provided powerful evidence to support reform in the Progressive era.

Mugabe, Robert Gabriel (1925–) Zimbabwean statesman, prime minister (1980–), president (1987–). In 1961 he became secretary general of Joshua NKOMO's Zimbabwe African People's Union (ZAPU). In 1963 Mugabe was forced into exile and co-founded the breakaway Zimbabwe African National Union (ZANU). He was imprisoned (1964–74) by Ian SMITH's white minority regime in Rhodesia (now Zimbabwe). After his release, ZAPU and ZANU merged to form the Patriotic Front (PF), and Mugabe continued to wage a guerrilla war against the Smith government from his base in Mozambique. He became leader of Zimbabwe on the attainment of majority rule in 1980, and formed a coalition government with Nkomo. Mugabe initially pursued moderate policies, seeking to retain the skills and wealth of Zimbabwe's white population. He supported FRELIMO in the civil war in Mozambique and was a leading supporter of sanctions against South Africa's apartheid regime. In 1982 Mugabe dismissed Nkomo, provoking conflict between the SHONA and NDEBELE peoples. He crushed domestic opposition, enforcing a new constitution (1987) that established a one-party, ZANU-PF, state. The economy declined, corruption increased and opposition intensified. In 2000 Mugabe was defeated in a referendum to amend the constitution to allow the government to confiscate white farmers' land without compensation. After the referendum, Mugabe attracted international criticism for his support of the illegal occupation of white-owned farms.

Mughal Empire (1526–1857) Indian empire. It was founded by BABUR, a Turkish descendant of Tamerlane, who defeated the Afghans at the Battle of PANIPAT (1526) and thus gained control of DELHI and AGRA. Babur's son and successor, HUMAYUN (r.1530–40, 1555–56), was expelled from India by SHER SHAH in 1540 but later took advantage of a civil war to recapture the Punjab in 1555. Humayun's son and successor, AKBAR I (THE GREAT) (r.1556–1605), consolidated Mughal power by finally vanquishing the Afghans at the Second Battle of Panipat (1556). Akbar secured the support of the powerful Rajputs through a marriage alliance (1562), and by 1569 had conquered almost all of Rajasthan. He continued to extend Mughal power, gaining Gujarat (1573) and Bengal (1576). In the 1590s he subjugated Kabul and Kandahar. In order to administer the vast Mughal Empire, Akbar created central government departments and 15 provincial governors. He diversified the ethnic basis of the Mughal nobility, encouraged religious toleration and established a sophisticated taxation system. Akbar's son and successor, Jahangir (r.1605–27), lost Kandahar to the Iranians (1622), but finally subdued Mewar (now Udaipur) in 1614. He was succeeded by his son, Shah Jahan (r.1627–58), who conquered much of the Deccan but led a disastrous campaign against Samarkand. His illness provoked a war of succession from which Aurangzeb (r.1658–1707) emerged triumphant. The Mughal Empire under Aurangzeb attained its greatest territorial extent, but the priority he attached to Islam helped provoke the rebellions of the Marathas and Pathans, and the Empire began to fracture. It continued to decline under a succession of short-lived emperors. By the time Muhammad Shah came to power (r.1719–48), imperial authority had drained away to the provincial nobility. In 1739 the Iranian leader Nadir Shah captured Delhi, forcing Muhammad Shah to cede Kabul. The Afghans defeated the Marathas at the Third Battle of Panipat (1761), and the last Mughal emperor was deposed by the British in 1805. The Empire formally ended when Victoria became empress of India in 1858.

Mugwumps Mocking name for a group of independent, reform-minded Republicans in the United States who deserted their party's candidate, James Blaine, in the 1884 presidential election and voted instead for the Democratic candidate, Grover Cleveland.

Muhammad (*c*.570–632) Arab prophet, founder of Islam. Born in Mecca, he was orphaned at the age of six and brought up by relatives. At the age of about 25, he began working as a trading agent for Khadijah, a wealthy widow of 40 whom he married. They had several children: a daughter, Fatima, later married Muhammad's cousin, Ali. In *c*.610, while meditating in a cave on Mount Hira outside Mecca, Muhammad experienced the first revelations brought to him, Muslims believe, from Allah (God). The visions continued for the rest of his life and form the text of the Koran. Although Islam incorporated some older traditions, it was a new religion, and Muhammad's teaching, especially his insistence that there is no God but Allah and His followers must submit to Him, aroused hostility in Mecca. In 622 Muhammad and his followers fled to Medina, an event, the Hejira, which marks the beginning of the Muslim calendar. He was well received in Medina and began to organize Islamic society. He also married Aisha, daughter of Abu Bakr and collector of his sayings (Hadith). After a long conflict he conquered Mecca (630), which contained the Kaaba, an ancient shrine vital to Islam. By his death, Muhammad had gained the adherence of many Arab tribes, and Islam was poised for greater expansion. Muhammad was succeeded by Abu Bakr, the first caliph.

MOZAMBIQUE

AREA: 801,590sq km (309,494sq mi)
POPULATION: 14,872,000
CAPITAL (POPULATION): Maputo (2,000,000)
GOVERNMENT: Multiparty republic
ETHNIC GROUPS: Makua 47%, Tsonga 23%, Malawi 12%, Shona 11%, Yao 4%, Swahili 1%, Makonde 1%
LANGUAGES: Portuguese (official)
RELIGIONS: Traditional beliefs 48%, Christianity (Roman Catholic 31%, others 9%), Islam 13%
GDP PER CAPITA (1995): US$810

Republic in SE Africa. Bantu-speakers arrived in the 2nd century AD. Arab traders in gold and ivory settled in coastal regions from the 9th century. Vasco da Gama was the first European to discover Mozambique, in 1498. Portugal established its first settlement in 1505. During the 16th century, Portuguese adventurers built huge, semi-autonomous plantations. In the late-17th century, Portuguese settlers were driven s of the River Zambezi by the Rozuri kingdoms, but they were soon able to return N and in 1752 a colonial governor was appointed. In the late 17th and 18th centuries Mozambique was a major centre of the slave trade.

In 1910 Mozambique formally became a Portuguese colony. Nationalist opposition increased with unfair land rights, forced labour and social inequity. The Front for the Liberation of Mozambique (Frelimo) was founded (1961) to oppose Portuguese rule. In 1964 FRELIMO launched a guerrilla war. Portugal dispatched more than 70,000 troops to re-establish control, but finally to no avail.

In 1975 Mozambique gained independence, and Samora Machel became president. Many Europeans fled the country, taking vital capital and resources. The new FRELIMO government established a one-party Marxist state. FRELIMO's assistance to liberation movements in Rhodesia (now Zimbabwe) and South Africa was countered by these white-minority regimes' support for the Mozambique National Resistance Movement (RENAMO) opposition. Civil war raged for 16 years, claiming tens of thousands of lives. In 1986 Machel died and was succeeded by Joachim Chissano. In 1989 FRELIMO dropped its communist policies and agreed to end one-party rule. In 1992, faced with severe drought and famine, a peace agreement was signed between FRELIMO and RENAMO. In 1994 Chissano was elected president. In 1995 Mozambique became the 53rd member of the Commonwealth of Nations.

In the late 1990s, the government began to make some headway in restoring the country's economy, with an annual growth rate of more than 10% between 1997 and 1999. In 2000 vast areas of Mozambique were submerged by flood waters from the River Limpopo, leaving nearly one million people homeless and shattering the nation's infrastructure.

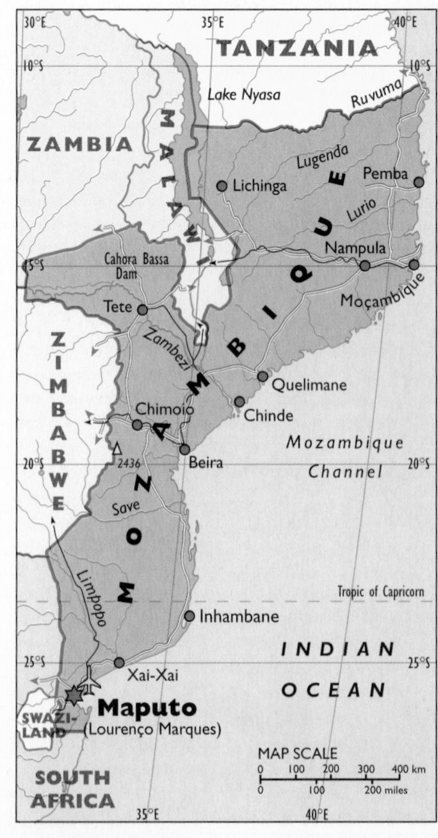

Muhammad I (d.1421) Ottoman sultan (1413–21), son of Bayezid I (the Thundebolt). Tamerlane defeated his father at the Battle of Ankara (1402) and, in the subsequent division of the Ottoman Empire, Muhammad received w Anatolia. In 1405 he captured Bursa from his brother Isa. In 1413, with the assistance of Byzantine Emperor Manuel II (Paleologus), Muhammad defeated another brother (Musa) in Rumelia to emerge as sole ruler. On his death bed, Muhammad ordered news of his death to be withheld until his son, Murad II, could be proclaimed sultan.

Muhammad II (the Conqueror) (1432–81) Ottoman sultan (1444–46, 1451–81). When his father, Murad II, abdicated in his favour (1444), it prompted a crusade against the Ottoman Empire and Murad returned to power. After his second accession, Muhammad devoted his energies to the final destruction of the Byzantine Empire. In 1453 he captured Constantinople (now Istanbul) and immediately converted the Hagia Sophia into a mosque. Muhammad began a major rebuilding project in Istanbul, which grew to become the largest city in Europe by the end of the 15th century. Muhammad extended the Ottoman Empire by conquering Greece, Serbia, Bosnia and Albania. He also codified Ottoman law. Muhammad was succeeded by his son, Bayezid II (the Just).

Muhammad IV (1642–93) Ottoman sultan (1648–87). Power was held by the harem faction at the start of his minority and a series of rebellions broke out across the Empire. In 1656 Muhammad's mother, Turhan, appointed Köprülü Muhammad Pasha as grand vizier (chief minister). Muhammad Pasha and his son, Köprülü Fazil Ahmed pasha, did much to restore the vitality of the Ottoman Empire, while their sultan engaged in his favourite sport of hunting. Muhammad fought in campaigns against Austria (1663) and Poland (1672), but was deposed after a disastrous attempt to capture Vienna.

Muhammad V (1844–1918) Ottoman sultan (1909–18). He became sultan after his elder brother, Abdul Hamid II, was forced to abdicate. Muhammad proved an ineffective ruler and government was dominated by Enver Pasha and the Young Turk movement. During his reign, the Ottomans lost all their European territory in the Balkan Wars (1912–13) and were defeated by the Allies in World War I. He was succeeded by his younger brother, Muhammad VI.

Muhammad VI (1861–1926) Last Ottoman sultan (1918–22), brother and successor of Muhammad V. He followed the example of his brother, Abdul Hamid II, and took personal charge of government. Muhammad agreed to the terms of the Allies at the end of World War I, but failed to suppress the Turkish nationalists led by Mustafa Kemal (later Atatürk), who won the elections in 1919. The punitive provisions of the Treaty of Sèvres (1920) and the extension of Allied occupation in Turkey played further into nationalist hands, and a republican government was established (1920) in Ankara. A new constitution (1922) abolished the sultanate and Muhammad went into exile.

Muhammad V (1909–61) Sultan (1927–57) and king (1957–61) of Morocco, son and successor of Moulay Yusuf. Muhammad became a focus for nationalist aspirations after pressing the French to dissolve the distinct legal systems for Moroccan Arabs and Berbers. He was deported by the French in 1953 but, after a wave of civil unrest, was allowed to return two years' later. In 1956 Muhammad negotiated the treaty that secured Moroccan independence. He was succeeded by his son, Hassan II.

Muhammad I (d.1538) King (1493–1528) of the Songhai empire of West Africa, founder of the Askia dynasty. He came to the throne after overthrowing Sonni Baru, son of Sonni Ali. In 1495 Muhammad went on a pilgrimage to Mecca that attracted international attention

M

for its splendour and ostentation. Upon his return, Muhammad established Islam as the state religion and restored Timbuktu as a centre of Muslim learning. His conquests saw the Songhai empire stretch as far W as the Atlantic Ocean. In order to control this vast empire, Muhammad appointed provincial governors, who were responsible to a central government in Gao (now in E MALI), and created a standing army. The end of his reign was marked by a protracted war of succession among his children, and in 1528 he was overthrown and banished.

Muhammad, Elijah (1897–1975) US leader (1934–75) of the black separatist Nation of Islam (BLACK MUSLIMS), b. Elijah Poole. He succeeded Wallace Fard, the founder of the movement, and moved the organization's headquarters to Chicago, Illinois. Muhammad was jailed (1942–46) for encouraging African-Americans to dodge the draft during World War 2. He gradually moderated his black supremacist rhetoric and established educational, welfare and commercial institutions for African-Americans. The Black Muslims' membership increased partly due to the powerful rhetoric of MALCOLM X, but conflicts with Muhammad led Malcolm to split from the movement. After Muhammad's death, Louis FARRAKHAN became leader of the Nation of Islam.

Muhammad Ali (1769–1849) Ottoman viceroy of Egypt (1805–49). He was appointed viceroy after helping to restore Ottoman sovereignty in Egypt by ending the French occupation (1798–1801) under NAPOLEON Bonaparte. In 1811 Muhammad asserted his control by massacring the MAMLUKS, who had effectively ruled Egypt since the 13th century. He began the process of modernizing Egypt's government and created a regular army. Muhammad's economic and agricultural reforms provided him with a personal fortune with which to pursue his military campaigns. He conquered (1820–22) Sudan, founding the city of KHARTOUM in 1823. Muhammad helped Ottoman Sultan MAHMUD II crush the Greek rebels at the start of the GREEK WAR OF INDEPENDENCE, but the Europeans intervened and his fleet was destroyed at the Battle of NAVARINO (1827). Muhammad rebelled against Mahmud, conquering Syria (1831–33). Muhammad's decisive victory over the sultan at the Battle of Nizip (1839) prompted the European powers to remove him from Syria, although he was granted hereditary rights in Egypt and Sudan. He was succeeded by his son, IBRAHIM PASHA.

Muhammad Reza Pahlavi *See* PAHLAVI, MUHAMMAD REZA

Mujaheddin ("Holy warriors") Muslim guerrillas dedicated to waging a JIHAD (holy war). The term gained wide currency when applied to the armed bands who resisted Soviet forces during the AFGHANISTAN WAR (1979–92).

Mujibur Rahman (1920–75) Bengali statesman, first prime minister (1972–75) of BANGLADESH. Popularly known as Sheikh Mujib, he was a co-founder (1949) of the AWAMI LEAGUE, which sought autonomy for East Pakistan within the new nation of Pakistan. Mujib's arrest in the late 1960s provoked a wave of civil unrest and the Awami League won a majority in the 1970 elections to the National Assembly. Mujib's demands for independence prompted West Pakistan to send troops and a civil war ensued. In 1972, with military assistance from India, East Pakistan emerged victorious and Mujib proclaimed the independent republic of Bangladesh. Faced by continuing civil disorder, Mujib adopted a new constitution (1975) that made him president with increased powers. He was assassinated in a military coup. Mujib's daughter, Hasina Wazed, also served (1996–) as prime minister of Bangladesh.

Mukden Incident (1931) *See* MANCHURIAN INCIDENT

Muldoon, Sir Robert David (1921–92) New Zealand statesman, prime minister (1975–84). He became leader of the National Party in 1974. As prime minister, Muldoon faced economic difficulties due to Britain's abandonment of "imperial preference" and the steepling price of oil. Muldoon's austere prices and incomes policy and authoritarian style contributed to his defeat in the 1984 elections by David LANGE.

Mulroney, (Martin) Brian (1939–) Canadian statesman, prime minister (1984–93). President (1977–83) of the Iron Ore Company of Canada, he was elected leader (1983–93) of the PROGRESSIVE CONSERVATIVE PARTY without ever holding public office. Mulroney's bilingual credentials helped him achieve a landslide victory in the 1984 general election. As prime minister, he introduced the Meech Lake Accord (1987) to ameliorate Québec's objections to the federal constitution (although it was rejected in 1990) and negotiated a controversial free-trade agreement with the United States (1992). After a further attempt to appease Québec was rejected in a referendum (1992), Mulroney resigned. He was succeeded as prime minister and party leader by Kim CAMPBELL.

Mumbai (formerly Bombay) Largest city in India; island capital of Maharashtra state. Occupied since prehistoric times, Bombay formed part of ASHOKA's empire in the 3rd century BC and was ruled by the CHALUKYAS from the 6th to 8th century. The first genuine settlement was built in *c.*1294. Bombay was part of Gujarat from 1348 to 1534, when Sultan Bahadur ceded it to the Portuguese. In 1661 the British gained control of Bombay as part of Catherine of Braganza's dowry to Charles II, and the city became the headquarters (1672–1858) of the English EAST INDIA COMPANY. As the "Gateway of India", Bombay's spectacular waterfront was the first sight of the country for arriving Europeans. The city developed as the power of the MUGHAL EMPIRE and the MARATHAS declined. Its industry prospered with the opening of the Suez Canal in 1869. The original seven islands on which the old town grew were linked, alluvial plains drained, and causeways and the railway built. Bombay was a centre of Indian resistance to British rule and the first session of the Indian National CONGRESS was held in the city in 1885. The population continued to grow rapidly in the 20th century. Pop. (1991) 9,925,891.

Munich (München) City on the River Isar, S Germany; capital of BAVARIA. Its origins date back to the founding (*c.*750) of a Benedictine monastery. A town was established in 1158, and Munich became the home of the WITTELSBACH dukes of Bavaria in 1255. Its early growth was largely due to Emperor LOUIS IV (r.1328–47) and Elector MAXIMILIAN I. During the 19th century, Munich developed rapidly and became a major cultural centre. By 1900 its population was *c.*500,000. From the early 1920s Munich was the centre of support for the NAZI PARTY. It sustained heavy damage from Allied bombing during World War 2. Pop. (1990) 1,241,300.

Munich Agreement (30 September 1938) Pact agreed by Britain, France, Italy and Germany to settle German claims on Czechoslovakia. Hoping to preserve European peace, British Prime Minister Neville CHAMBERLAIN and French Premier Édouard DALADIER compelled Czechoslovakia to surrender the predominantly German-speaking SUDETENLAND to Nazi Germany. In March 1939 Adolf HITLER ignored the stipulation that any future disputes over territory be referred to an international commission and annexed the whole of Czechoslovakia. His invasion of Poland precipitated the start of WORLD WAR 2 in September 1939. *See also* APPEASEMENT; LEBENSRAUM

Munich Putsch (Beer-hall Putsch) (8–9 November 1923) Attempted uprising by Adolf HITLER and his NAZI PARTY against the WEIMAR REPUBLIC in BAVARIA, Germany. The Putsch, supported by General Erich LUDENDORFF, was crushed by the police and Hitler was sentenced to five years in prison, where he wrote *Mein Kampf* (1925). He was released after only eight months.

Munn v. Illinois (1876) Case resulting in a Supreme Court judgment upholding the right of a state to regulate commerce within its own borders, which also clarified the meaning of "due process" of law. Confirming the conviction of a firm found guilty of violating an Illinois law that set maximum rates for grain storage, the Court declared that states could regulate businesses operating in the public sphere. *See also* GRANGER CASES

Muñoz Marín, Luis (1898–1980) Governor of Puerto Rico (1949–64). He initially championed full independence for Puerto Rico, founding the Popular Democratic Party in 1938. As president (1940–48) of the Puerto Rico Senate, Muñoz Marín changed his political stance and worked with the US to improve social and economic conditions in Puerto Rico. In 1948 he became the first elected governor, securing US acknowledgment of the island's status as a commonwealth in 1952. Muñoz served four terms as governor and remained influential after retirement, opposing statehood for Puerto Rico.

Müntzer, Thomas (*c.*1490–1525) German religious revolutionary, leader of the PEASANTS' WAR (1524–25). He was an early supporter of Martin LUTHER, but later developed his own form of REFORMATION theology. Müntzer rejected Luther's emphasis on the Scriptures, regarding the "inner light" of the Holy Spirit, embodied in peasants and workers, as the supreme spiritual authority. In 1522 he was expelled by the Lutherans for preaching open rebellion in Zwickau and Allstedt. In Mühlhausen, Thuringia, Müntzer organized the working classes into the "Eternal Covenant of God" that overthrew the local civil and religious authorities in April 1525. The Peasants' War was crushed by the German princes at the Battle of Frankenhausen (May 1525), and Münzer was tried and executed.

Murad I (1326?–89) Ottoman sultan (1361–89), son and successor of Orhan. He is credited with establishing the JANISSARIES, an élite military force. In 1361 Murad captured the city of Adrianople (now EDIRNE, Turkey) and made it his capital. His victories (1371) in Serbia, Macedonia and Bulgaria extended Ottoman rule into the Balkans and made a vassal out of Byzantine emperor JOHN V (PALAEOLOGUS). In the 1380s Murad made further conquests in Anatolia and the Balkans, including Sofia (1385) and Konya (1386). He was killed in the process of defeating a Serbian-led alliance in the First Battle of KOSOVO (1389). Murad was succeeded by his son, BAYEZID I. *See also* OTTOMAN EMPIRE

Murad II (1404–51) Ottoman sultan (1421–44, 1446–51), son and successor of MUHAMMAD I. He spent the early part of his reign fighting off rivals to the throne, who were supported by Byzantine Emperor MANUEL II (PALAEOLOGUS), and restoring the OTTOMAN EMPIRE in W Anatolia after the ravages of TAMERLANE. In 1530 Murad succeeded in gaining Salonika (now THESSALONÍKI, N Greece) from the Venetians, but was defeated by Władysław III of Poland in 1444 and abdicated in favour

M

MUSSOLINI

Mussolini attempted to revive Italian national pride by creating an Italian empire, comparable to those of Britain and France. His decisive leadership and rhetorical skill secured the support of the Italian people, but his disastrous military decisions ultimately caused his downfall.

MUSSOLINI IN HIS OWN WORDS

"War alone brings up to their highest tensions all human energies and imposes the stamp of nobility upon the peoples who have the courage to make it."
Encyclopedia Italiane (1932)

of his young son, MUHAMMAD II. Murad was persuaded to return to power by the renewed threat from the European powers and he defeated János HUNYADI of Hungary at the Second Battle of KOSOVO (1448).

Murat, Joachim (1767–1815) French marshal, king of NAPLES (1808–15). He fought alongside NAPOLEON in Italy (1796–97) and Egypt (1798–99), and married Napoleon's sister in 1800. During the NAPOLEONIC WARS, Murat's leadership of the cavalry was a decisive factor in the French victories at the battles of MARENGO (1800), AUSTERLITZ (1805) and JENA (1806), and he replaced Joseph BONAPARTE as king of Naples. Murat introduced the CODE NAPOLÉON to the kingdom and established several secret societies that later played a leading role in the RISORGIMENTO. He distinguished himself in the Battle of BORODINO (1812) at the start of Napoleon's invasion of Russia, but later deserted his retreating troops in an attempt to save his his Neapolitan crown. Murat was captured and shot by the Austrians.

Muromachi *See* ASHIKAGA

Murray, Lord George (1694–1760) Scottish JACOBITE general. Prominent in both Jacobite rebellions (1715, 1745), he was the leading military adviser to Prince Charles Edward STUART (the "Young Pretender") and the architect of the victory at PRESTONPANS (1745). Murray advised the withdrawal from England at Derby, central England, and disagreed with the prince's disastrous decision to make a stand at CULLODEN (1746). He died in exile in the Netherlands.

Murray, James Stewart, 1st Earl of *See* MORAY, JAMES STEWART, 1ST EARL OF

Muscovy Company (Russia Company) Joint-stock company of English merchants trading with Russia, founded (1555) by Sebastian CABOT. Their pioneering efforts to find the NORTHEAST PASSAGE earned them a monopoly of Russian trade, chiefly through Arkhangelsk (Archangel), NW Russia, as well as privileges from the tsar. Furs and timber were imported, cloth exported. The monopoly ended in 1698, although by then corporate trading had already ceased.

Museveni, Yoweri Kaguta (1944–) Ugandan statesman, president (1986–). He worked for the government of Milton OBOTE, but was forced into exile when Idi AMIN overthrew Obote in 1971. Museveni organized a guerrilla force, the Front for National Salvation, that succeeded in toppling Amin's regime in 1979. He was defeated by Obote in the 1980 elections, widely held to be fraudulent, and formed the National Resistance Army which overthrew the military junta in 1985. Museveni was hailed as representative of a new generation of African leaders. While imposing one-party rule, he took stringent measures to combat corruption, restore peace and reconstruct Uganda's economy through free-market reforms. In 1996 Museveni won Uganda's first presidential elections since 1980. As part of his aim to achieve regional integration, Museveni supported Laurent KABILA's successful revolt (1997) against MOBUTU SESE SOKO in neighbouring Zaïre and aided Tutsi rebels against the Hutu-minority regime in Rwanda.

Muslim League Political organization founded (1906) to protect the rights of Muslims in British India. The League cooperated with the predominantly Hindu Indian National CONGRESS until the 1930s when, fearing Hindu domination, it turned to independent action under the leadership of Muhammed Ali JINNAH. In 1940 it called for a separate Muslim state. Despite fierce Hindu resistance, Britain supported the principle in the partition that created an independent Pakistan and India in 1947. At first, the League dominated politics in Pakistan but subsequently split into rival factions. *See also* AWAMI LEAGUE

Mussolini, Benito (1883–1945) Italian fascist dictator, prime minister (1922–43). He edited the socialist newspaper *Avanti!*, but resigned and was expelled from the Socialist Party after supporting ITALY's entry into World War 1. In 1919 he turned to revolutionary nationalism and founded the Italian Fascist Party. The weakness of democratic parties, the fear of communism, and the intimidation of the BLACKSHIRTS that culminated in the March on Rome (1922) secured his appointment as prime minister by VICTOR EMMANUEL III. In 1924 Mussolini, a powerful orator, imposed one-party rule, with himself as *Il Duce* (the leader). In order to restore order, his dictatorship imposed strict censorship and violently crushed political opposition. Mussolini's programme of public works began to revive the national economy and his brand of FASCISM served as a model for the German NAZI PARTY of Adolf HITLER, with whom Mussolini formed an alliance (as the AXIS POWERS) in 1936. Mussolini's imperial ambitions led to the conquest of ETHIOPIA (1935–36), and the invasion of Albania (1939). He delayed entering WORLD WAR 2 until June 1940, when a German victory in France seemed inevitable. Mussolini was frustrated by his subordinate status within the Axis and launched a disastrous, unilateral invasion of Greece in October 1940. A succession of defeats led to the Allied invasion of Sicily and Mussolini's dismissal (July 1943). He was sprung from prison by the Germans who briefly restored him as head of a puppet government in N Italy, but in April 1945, fleeing Allied forces, he was captured and killed by Italian partisans. *See* feature, page 281 *See also* CIANO, GALEAZZO; MATTEOTTI, GIACOMO

Mustafa Kemal *See* ATATÜRK, KEMAL

Mutesa I (*c*.1838–84) King of Buganda (1857–84). He brutally asserted his authority over much of UGANDA and began extensive trade in slaves, ivory and guns with the Arabs. He also admitted Christian missionaries in 1877.

Mutesa II (1924–69) Last king of Buganda (1939–53, 1955–66). During the 1940s he was effectively a puppet ruler of the British. However, Mutesa opposed plans to subsume Buganda into the British Protectorate of UGANDA, seeking to create an independent kingdom, and was briefly deported (1953–55). He returned as a constitutional monarch. When Uganda gained independence in 1963, Prime Minister Milton OBOTE secured Mutesa's appointment as president but conflict between the two men escalated and Mutesa was forced into exile in 1966.

Muzorewa, Abel Tendekayi (1925–) Zimbabwean statesman, prime minister (1979). The first black African Methodist bishop of Rhodesia (now Zimbabwe), he formed the United African National Council (UANC), which sought the peaceful overthrow of the white-minority regime of Ian SMITH. Muzorewa agreed to a power-sharing arrangement with Smith and won the 1979 elections after the Patriotic Front, led by Joshua NKOMO and Robert MUGABE, boycotted the polls. The United Kingdom was forced to reassume direct control of its former colony until the 1980 elections, which were won by Mugabe. Muzorewa continued to oppose Mugabe's regime.

Myanmar *See* BURMA

Mycenae Ancient Greek city in the Peloponnese, whose legendary founder was Perseus. The major Late Bronze Age site in mainland Greece, it was at its cultural peak *c*.1400–1100 BC and its rulers included the legendary king, Agamemnon. Taken over by DORIAN invaders in *c*.1100 BC, it was conquered by ARGOS in the 5th century BC. By the 2nd century AD, Mycenae lay in ruins. The massive walls and the Lion Gate remained visible, and when the city was excavated (1874–76) by the German archaeologist Heinrich SCHLIEMANN, he found fabulous gold treasures in the royal shaft tombs that had evaded robbers for a millennium. *See also* KNOSSOS; MINOAN CIVILIZATION; MYCENAEAN CIVILIZATION

Mycenaean civilization *See* feature article

My Lai Massacre (16 March 1968) Slaughter of *c*.500 inhabitants of a South Vietnamese village by US soldiers during the VIETNAM WAR (1955–75). It is believed to be the worst among many similar atrocities perpetrated by frightened and disillusioned US troops who believed their victims were communist sympathizers. The massacre was initially covered up by the army, but when details leaked to the media it increased pressure on President Richard NIXON to end US involvement in the War. In 1970 the platoon leader, Lieutenant William Calley (1943–), was court-martialled, found guilty of the premeditated murder of 22 unarmed civilians, and sentenced to life imprisonment. He was released after only five months. *See also* TET OFFENSIVE

Mysore *See* KARNATAKA

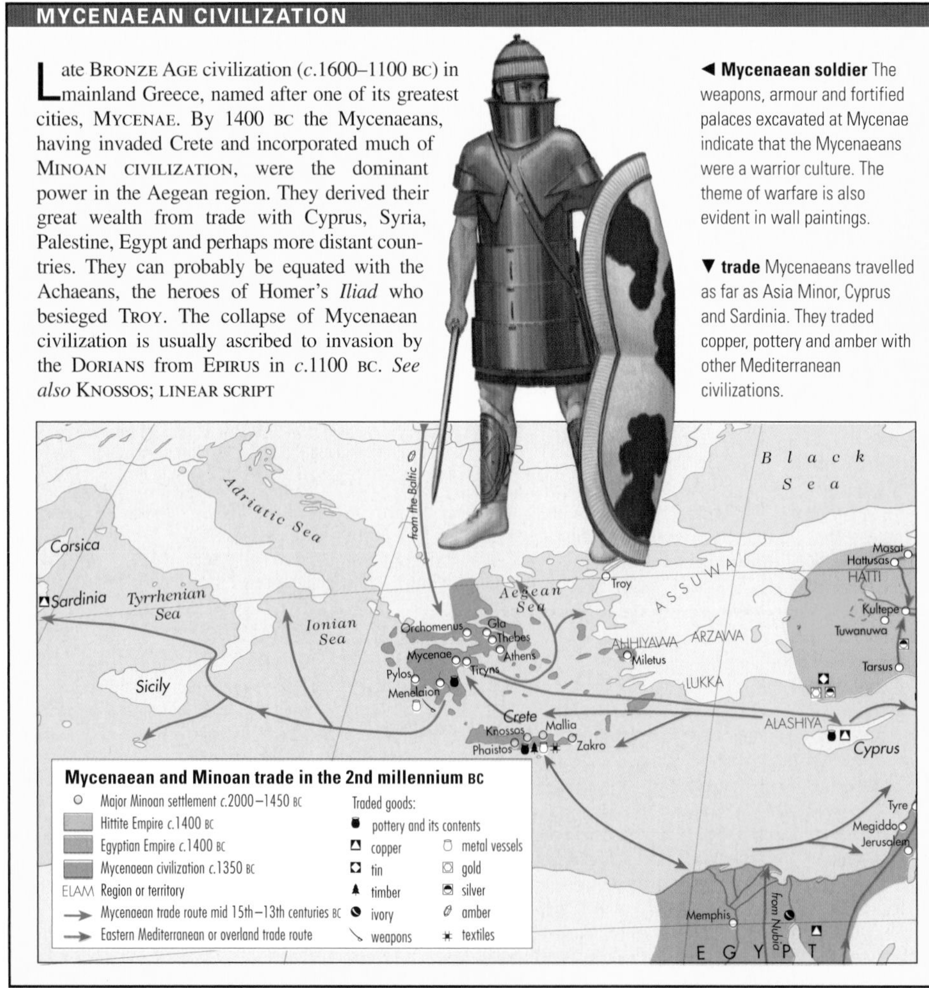

MYCENAEAN CIVILIZATION

Late BRONZE AGE civilization (*c*.1600–1100 BC) in mainland Greece, named after one of its greatest cities, MYCENAE. By 1400 BC the Mycenaeans, having invaded Crete and incorporated much of MINOAN CIVILIZATION, were the dominant power in the Aegean region. They derived their great wealth from trade with Cyprus, Syria, Palestine, Egypt and perhaps more distant countries. They can probably be equated with the Achaeans, the heroes of Homer's *Iliad* who besieged TROY. The collapse of Mycenaean civilization is usually ascribed to invasion by the DORIANS from EPIRUS in *c*.1100 BC. *See also* KNOSSOS; LINEAR SCRIPT

◀ **Mycenaean soldier** The weapons, armour and fortified palaces excavated at Mycenae indicate that the Mycenaeans were a warrior culture. The theme of warfare is also evident in wall paintings.

▼ **trade** Mycenaeans travelled as far as Asia Minor, Cyprus and Sardinia. They traded copper, pottery and amber with other Mediterranean civilizations.

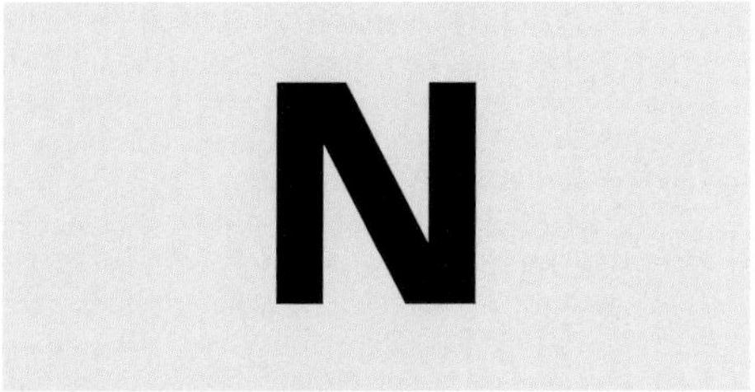

NAACP *See* National Association for the Advancement of Colored People

Nabopolassar (d.*c*.605 BC) Founder and first king (*c*.625–*c*.605 BC) of the Chaldaean (New Babylonian) empire. In *c*.630 BC Nabopolassar became king of Chaldaea. Within five years, he had expelled Assyria from Uruk and crowned himself king of Babylonia. Nabopolassar established his capital at Babylon, where he launched a vast temple-building project. He also restored the Temple of Shamash at Sippar (now Abu Habbah, central Iraq). He was succeeded by his son, Nebuchadnezzar II.

Nadir Shah (1688–1747) Iranian ruler (1736–47), b. Nadir Qoli Beg. During the 1720s, he fought successfully to expel Afghan intruders from Iran and restore power to the Safavid Shah Tahmasp II. Tahmasp, defeated and humiliated by the Ottoman Turks (1732), was deposed by Nadir, who became regent. Nadir then forced the Turks out of Iran and took the throne for himself. He captured Bahrain and Oman before launching an attack on the Mughal Empire of N India. Nadir's victory at the Battle of Karnal (1739) led to the capture and plunder of Delhi, the Mughal capital. He was now ruler of an empire that stretched from the River Indus to the Caucasus Mountains. Nadir was an oppressive and savage ruler, who used torture and execution to crush dissent and impose the Sunni faith on the majority Shiite population. Nadir's ceaseless warring devastated Iran's economy, and his attempts to exact punitive taxation fomented rebellion among his subjects. Nadir was assassinated by his own soldiers.

Nagasaki Port on W Kyushu island, SW Japan. In the 16th century, it was the first Japanese port to receive Western ships and became a centre of Christian influence. During the period of Japanese isolation (1639–1859), Nagasaki was the only port to remain open to foreign trade. On 9 August 1945, the inner city was destroyed by an atomic bomb dropped by the United States' Air Force, and more than 70,000 people were killed. Pop. (1993) 439,000.

Nagorno-Karabakh Autonomous region of Azerbaijan in the mountains of the Lesser Caucasus. The capital is Xankändi (formerly Stepanakert). The region was gained by Russia in the early 19th century. In 1923 it became an autonomous province of the Azerbaijan republic of the Soviet Union, despite the fact that *c*.75% of the population were Armenian. In 1991 Armenia and Azerbaijan gained independence from the collapsing Soviet Union, and the enclave became a source of bitter conflict between the new nations. In December 1991, after Armenia had imposed direct rule, Nagorno-Karabakh declared independence. In 1993 Armenian troops occupied the enclave and a cease-fire was declared in 1994. The bloody civil war claimed *c*.15,000 lives and created *c*.1 million refugees. Area: 4400sq km (1700sq mi). Pop. (1990) 192,400

Nagy, Imre (1896–1958) Hungarian statesman, prime minister (1953–55, 1956). As a founder of the illegal Hungarian Communist Party in 1923, Nagy was forced into exile in Russia. He returned to Hungary during World War 2. He held several government posts before becoming prime minister. His liberal reforms of Hungarian economy and society won popular approval but, under pressure from the Soviet Union, Nagy was dismissed from office and from the Hungarian Communist Party. The Hungarian Uprising (1956) led to his reinstatement as prime minister. Soviet tanks crushed the Uprising and handed power to János Kádár. Nagy was tried and executed for treason.

Naidu, Sarojini (1879–1949) Indian politician and poet. A social reformer, Naidu campaigned for women's rights. She was active in India's struggle for independence and, as a supporter of "Mahatma" Gandhi's tactic of civil disobedience, was imprisoned several times. In 1925 she became the first woman president of the Indian National Congress.

Najibullah, Muhammad (1947–96) Afghan statesman, president (1987–92). He joined the pro-Soviet Parcham faction of the communist People's Democratic Party of Afghanistan (PDPA) in 1965. In 1978 the rival Khalq faction of the PDPA mounted a successful coup. The Soviets invaded Afghanistan (December 1979) and installed a Parcham government. Najibullah served as head of the secret police during the first half of the Afghanistan War (1979–92) and succeeded Babrak Kamal as leader of the PDPA in 1986. In 1987 he was elected president. In 1989 Soviet troops completed their withdrawal, but the War continued until Mujaheddin forces entered the Afghan capital, Kabul, in April 1992. Najibullah took refuge in the United Nations' (UN) mission, from where he was later captured by the Taliban and publicly executed.

Nakasone Yasuhiro (1918–) Japanese statesman, prime minister (1982–87). He served in the Japanese navy during World War 2. Nakasone was first elected to the Diet (parliament) in 1947. A protégé of Tanaka Kakuei, he rose rapidly through the ranks of the Liberal-Democratic Party (LDP) and from 1967 held a succession of leading posts in the cabinet. In 1982 Nakasone succeeded Suzuki Zenko as prime minister and secretary general of the LDP. After the 1983 elections, he formed a coalition government. Nakasone reduced Japan's national debt and lowered import tariffs on goods from the United States. In 1987 he was able to secure the appointment of his nominee, Takeshita Noboru, as prime minister. Nakasone was forced to resign (1989) from the LDP after being implicated in the Lockheed financial scandal. He was allowed to rejoin in 1991.

Nakhichevan Autonomous republic of Azerbaijan in S Caucasia. Nakhichevan was conquered by Persia in the 6th century BC and the capital (also Nakhichevan) developed as a major trading centre on the Silk Road. The region was subsumed into the Russia empire in 1828, and was made an autonomous republic of the Soviet Union in 1924. When the Soviet Union fragmented in 1991, Nakhichevan became part of the republic of Azerbaijan. Its economy was seriously disrupted by the war between Armenia and Azerbaijan over control of Nagorono-Karabakh. Area: 5500sq km (2120sq mi). Pop. (1994) 315,000.

Namibia *See* country feature

Nanak (1469–*c*.1539) Indian spiritual teacher, founder and first guru of Sikhism. Nanak preached a monotheistic religion that combined elements of both Hinduism and Islam. In 1519 he built the first Sikh temple in Kartarpur, Punjab. His teachings are contained in a number of hymns in the Adi Granth.

Nana Sahib (*c*.1820–*c*.1859) Indian nationalist leader, b. Dhondu Pant. Adopted son of the last prince of the Marathas, Nana Sahib was incensed by Lord Dalhousie's refusal to extend him the title and the pension that went along with it (1853). He led the sepoy forces in Kanpur, N India, at the start of the Indian Mutiny (1857–58) and accepted the surrender (27 June 1857) of the British garrison under Sir Hugh Wheeler. His promise of safe passage for the captives was not honoured by the sepoys, and most British soldiers and civilians were murdered. The outcry at the massacre stiffened British resolve and led to widespread revenge killings. In December 1858 Nana Sahib was defeated and fled to Nepal, where he is believed to have died.

Nanjing (Nanking) City on the River Yangtze, E China; capital of Jiangsu province. Founded in the 8th century BC,

NAMIBIA (FORMERLY SOUTH WEST AFRICA)

AREA: 825,414sq km (318,694 sq mi)
POPULATION: 1,562,000
CAPITAL (POPULATION): Windhoek (126,000)
GOVERNMENT: Multiparty republic
ETHNIC GROUPS: Ovambo 50%, Kavango 9%, Herero 7%, Damara 7%, whites 6%, Nama 5%
LANGUAGES: English (official)
RELIGIONS: Christianity 90% (Lutheran 51%)
GDP PER CAPITA (1995): US$4150

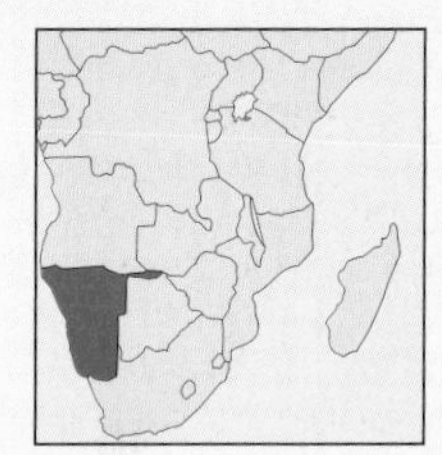

Republic in SW Africa. The nomadic San inhabited the region *c*.2000 years ago. In S Namibia, the San were displaced by the Nama tribe of Khoikhoi, while in N, E and central Namibia they were pushed back by the Bantu-speaking tribes of the Ovambo, Herero and Kavango. Although Portuguese navigator Diogo Cão landed on the Namibian coast in 1486, European colonization did not begin in earnest until after the 1860s. In 1884 Germany claimed the region, except N Namibia, as a protectorate and subsumed it into the territory of South West Africa. A concerted war of resistance (1904–07) was brutally suppressed by the Germans, who massacred most of the Herero and forced the Nama into concentration camps. The discovery (1908) of diamonds increased European settlement.

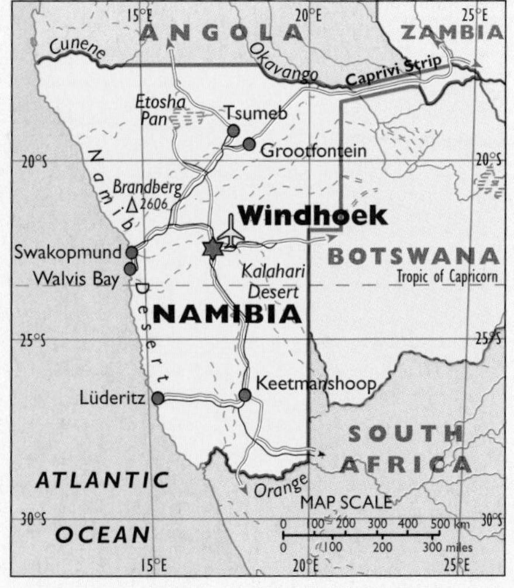

During World War 1, Namibia was occupied (1915) by South African troops, and the De Beers Company gained control of the diamond mines. In 1920 South Africa was granted a mandate by the League of Nations to govern Namibia. After World War 2, South Africa continued to exploit Namibian resources and encourage colonization. The South African system of apartheid was extended to Namibia. In 1966 the South West Africa People's Organization (SWAPO) began a guerrilla war against South Africa. In 1968 the United Nations (UN) called on South Africa to withdraw. In 1971 the International Court of Justice declared that South African rule over Namibia was illegal. South Africa refused to comply and divided Namibia into bantustans (homelands). The raging civil war (1977–89) killed more than 2500 South African soldiers and during the 1980s was costing more than US$1 billion annually.

In 1988 South Africa was forced to withdraw from neighbouring Angola and conceded to UN-supervised elections in Namibia. The resultant ballot (November 1989) was won by SWAPO, led by Sam Nujoma, who began the difficult process of reconciliation. In March 1990 Namibia became an independent republic within the British Commonwealth. In 1994 South Africa ceded control of Walvis Bay to Namibia. Nujoma was re-elected in 1994 and 1999.

it served as capital of the SIX DYNASTIES (AD 229–589) that controlled S China. Nanjing flourished both economically and culturally during the Six Dynasties period, but thereafter was reduced to the status of a prefectural city. In 1368 ZHU YUANZHANG, founder of the MING dynasty, made Nanjing the capital of a united China. In 1421 the capital was transferred to BEIJING and the city became known as Nanjing ("Southern Capital"). The Treaty of NANJING (1842) ended the OPIUM WAR with Britain. The centre of the TAIPING REBELLION, Nanjing was captured by HONG XIUQUAN in 1853 and was devastated when the QING returned in 1864. The city was the seat (1911–12) of the provisional government of the Republic of China after SUN YAT-SEN's revolution. Nanjing served (1928–37) as capital of China under the Nationalist leader CHIANG KAI-SHEK. In the Second SINO-JAPANESE WAR, Nanjing was captured by the Japanese, who massacred more than 100,000 of the population. Nanjing once more served (1946–49) as capital of China until the communists proclaimed the People's Republic of China. Today, the city is a major tourist destination. Sights include the mausoleums of Hong Xiuquan and Sun Yat-sen and the Nanjing Museum. Pop. (1993) 2,430,000.

Nanjing, Treaty of (29 August 1842) Peace settlement that ended the First OPIUM WAR (1839–42) between Britain and China. The treaty, which was supplemented by the Treaty of the Bogue (1843), was the first of a series of UNEQUAL TREATIES in which China was forced to cede many of its territorial rights to Western powers. China agreed to pay Britain an indemnity, ceded HONG KONG to Britain, and opened five "TREATY PORTS" (including GUANGZHOU and SHANGHAI) to British trade.

Nansen, Fridtjof (1861–1930) Norwegian explorer and diplomat. In 1888 he crossed the Greenland ice-cap on foot. In 1893 he set sail aboard the *Fram*, a ship he designed to withstand being frozen in ice so that currents would carry her to the North Pole. In 1895 Nansen and a companion left the *Fram* and set out for the Pole on foot, reaching 86°14'N, the highest latitude then attained. His ship drifted around the Pole to Norway, as he had predicted. After helping to negotiate the separation of Norway and Sweden, he served (1906–08) as Norwegian ambassador in London. In 1922 he was awarded the Nobel Prize for Peace for his humanitarian work with victims of the Russian famine and the repatriation of prisoners of war.

N

Nantes, Edict of (13 April 1598) French decree, proclaimed by HENRY IV, establishing toleration for HUGUENOTS. It granted freedom of worship and legal equality for French Protestants and ended the Wars of RELIGION (1562–98). It also granted the Huguenots political control over *c*.200 towns and cities, as well as financial support for their armies, but these privileges, opposed by cardinals RICHELIEU and MAZARIN, were short-lived. LOUIS XIV renewed the persecution of Protestants (1665) and revoked the Edict in 1685, causing *c*.400,000 Huguenots to emigrate. *See also* LE TELLIER, MICHEL

Naoroji, Dadabhai (1825–1917) Indian nationalist. After 1855 he lived mainly in England, where he worked to improve economic and social conditions in India. In 1892 Naoroji became the first Indian to be elected to the British Parliament. He was a founder (1885) of the Indian National CONGRESS and served as its president (1886, 1893, 1906). His argument that Britain was damaging India's economy through high taxation and exploitation of its natural resources was outlined in *Poverty and Un-British Rule in India* (1901). It was a major influence on the next generation of Indian nationalists, including "Mahatma" GANDHI and Jawaharlal NEHRU.

Napier, Robert Cornelis, 1st Baron (1810–90) British field marshal. He planned (1836–39) the settlement of Darjeeling, E India, and served with distinction in both of the SIKH WARS (1846–48, 1848–49) and during the INDIAN MUTINY (1857–58). In 1868 Napier led a successful Anglo-Indian expedition to release British diplomats being held hostage in MAGDALA, central Ethiopia. He served as commander in chief of India (1870–76) and governor of Gibraltar (1876–82).

Naples (Napoli) City on the Bay of Naples, S central Italy; capital of the province of Campania. Founded *c*.600 BC as the Greek colony of Neapolis ("New City"), Naples was conquered by Rome in the 4th century BC. The eruption of Mount Vesuvius (AD 79) buried the nearby towns of HERCULANEUM and POMPEII for nearly 17 centuries. After the fall of the Roman Empire, Naples was under the control of the Exarchate of Ravenna until the 8th century, when it became an independent duchy. In 1139 Naples was captured by the Normans and was subsequently incorporated into the Kingdom of the Two Sicilies. Emperor FREDERICK II (r.1220–50) fortified the city, and, under the control (1266–1422) of the ANGEVIN dynasty, Naples became the cultural capital of S Italy. Ruled by the Spanish HABSBURGS (1503–1707) and the Spanish BOURBONS (1734–1860), Naples became a major European city. In 1798 the Bourbons fled in fear of the French invasion and a republic was proclaimed. In 1799 the Bourbons returned and, with the help of British admiral Horatio NELSON, brutally crushed the republic. The Bourbons were ousted again in 1805, and the Kingdom of Naples was formed, led by NAPOLEON I's brother Joseph BONAPARTE. In 1815 the Bourbons were once more restored, this time with Austrian assistance. In 1860 Giuseppe GARIBALDI finally overthrew the Bourbons and Naples joined the Kingdom of Italy. Naples was devastated by Allied bombing during World War 2. Pop. (1991) 1,067,365. *See also* RISORGIMENTO

NAPOLEON I

Napoleon I aspired to create a single European empire. After defeat in the Napoleonic Wars and the crushing of his brief return to power at the Battle of Waterloo, Napeolon was exiled to St Helena, where he lived from 1815 until his death. In 1840 Napoleon was accorded a grand state funeral in Paris, France.

NAPOLEON IN HIS OWN WORDS

"I go, but you, my friends, will continue to serve France. Her happiness was my only thought. It will still be the object of my wishes. Do not regret my fate."
Farewell speech to the Old Guard, 29 April 1814

Napoleon I (1769–1821) French general, consul and emperor, b. Corsica as Napoleone Buonaparte. After the outbreak of the FRENCH REVOLUTION (1789–99), Napoleon became president (1792) of the JACOBINS. At the start of the FRENCH REVOLUTIONARY WARS (1792–1802), he was promoted to brigadier general (1793) of the National Convention after driving the British out of Toulon, SE France. In 1794 Maximilien ROBESPIERRE appointed him commander of the artillery in the French Army of Italy. After Robespierre's downfall (July 1794), Napoleon was arrested and relieved of command. He returned to favour when the Vicomte de BARRAS entrusted him with the crushing of a rebellion in Paris. With the establishment of the DIRECTORY (1795–99), Napoleon became commander of the army of the interior. In March 1796, two days after marrying JOSÉPHINE de Beauharnais, Napoleon was given command of the French army in Italy. He went on the offensive against Austria and Sardinia, soon forming the CISALPINE REPUBLIC from occupied territory in N Italy. He then marched on Vienna, forcing Austria to cede the Austrian Netherlands (now Belgium and Netherlands) to France. In 1798 Napoleon launched an invasion of Egypt, where he suffered his first defeat at the hands of Admiral Horatio NELSON at ABOUKIR. In 1799 Napoleon returned to Paris, where he and Emmanuel SIEYÈS planned the coup of 18 Brumaire (9 November), which overthrew the DIRECTORY and set up the CONSULATE. As first consul, Napoleon established a military dictatorship. His "enlightened despotism" brought administrative and judicial reforms, including the issuing of the CODE NAPOLÉON (1804), and gained the recognition of Pope PIUS VII. Napoleon is chiefly remembered, however, as one of the greatest military commanders in history. His victory over the Austrians at the Battle of MARENGO (1800) led to the Treaty of Lunéville (1801), which established the River Rhine as the E border of France. The Treaty of AMIENS (1802) concluded the French Revolutionary Wars, and Napoleon was later proclaimed emperor (1804). Peace was to prove short-lived, however, as the NAPOLEONIC WARS (1803–15) broke out. After Nelson's victory at the Battle of TRAFALGAR (1805), Britain controlled the seas, but Napoleon's Grand Army scored crushing victories against Austro-Russian forces at the battles of AUSTERLITZ and ULM (both 1805). Napoleon reinforced his superiority on land by establishing the CONTINENTAL SYSTEM, which attempted to defeat Britain by a commercial blockade. In 1806 Napoleon captured the kingdom of Naples, S Italy, which he bestowed on his elder brother, Joseph BONAPARTE. Napoleon transformed the United Provinces into the kingdom of HOLLAND for his brother Louis BONAPARTE (r.1806–10), and established the CONFEDERATION OF THE RHINE (most of the German states). Napoleon crushed the Prussian army at the Battle of JENA (1806). He signed the Treaties of TILSIT (1807) with Tsar ALEXANDER I, dividing Europe between France and Russia. In 1807 Napoleon occupied Portugal. His attempt to impose his brother Joseph as king of Spain precipitated the PENINSULAR WAR (1808–14). In 1810 the Napoleonic empire was at its height, with the annexation of the Illyrian Provinces and the German states of Lübeck and Bremen. In 1810, after obtaining a divorce from Joséphine, Napoleon married MARIE LOUISE, who bore him a son, the future NAPOLEON II. In 1812 Napoleon launched his disastrous invasion of Russia. Although he defeated Mikhail KUTUZOV at the Battle of BORODINO (1812) and captured Moscow, the Grand Army was forced to withdraw because of the cold Russian winter. Napoleon was routed by a new European coalition at the Battle of LEIPZIG (1813) and his empire crumbled. In March 1814, Paris was captured and Napoleon was exiled to the Mediterranean island of Elba. In March 1815 he escaped and returned to France, overthrowing the BOURBON king LOUIS XVIII. The HUNDRED DAYS of Napoleon's return to power ended with his defeat by the Duke of WELLINGTON at the Battle of WATERLOO (June 1815). Napoleon was exiled to the remote South Atlantic island of St Helena, where he died. *See also* CAMPO FORMIO, TREATY OF; TALLEYRAND-PÉRIGORD, CHARLES MAURICE DE

Napoleon II (1811–1832) Son of NAPOLEON I and MARIE LOUISE. In 1814 he was taken by his mother to Austria. Although his father abdicated in his favour, he never ruled in France and was forced to remain in Austria, where he died of tuberculosis. He was known as the king of Rome (1811–14) and the prince of Parma (1814–1818), until his grandfather, FRANCIS I of Austria, conferred upon him the title of Duc de Reichstadt.

Napoleon III (1808–73) French president (1849–52) and then emperor (1852–70), son of Louis BONAPARTE and nephew of NAPOLEON I, b. Louis Napoléon. After the fall of his uncle (1815), he was forced into exile in Switzerland. Louis Napoléon led two failed coups against LOUIS PHILIPPE of France (1836, 1840). After the first, he was exiled to the United States; after the second, he was sentenced to life imprisonment, but escaped to Britain in 1846. Louis Napoléon returned from exile after the FEBRUARY REVOLUTION (1848) and, trading largely on the basis of his uncle's legend, won a landslide victory in elections for president of the Second Republic. In December 1851, having failed to change the constitution that restricted him to one term in office, Louis Napoléon carried out a successful coup. In 1852 he established the Second Empire, taking the title Napoleon III. His dictatorship restricted the freedom of the press, but promoted public works and improved social-welfare provision for the poor. In foreign affairs, Napoleon joined the coalition against Russia in the CRIMEAN WAR (1853–56) and defeated the Austrians at the Battle of SOLFERINO (1859), N Italy. He was awarded Nice and Savoy by the Conte di CAVOUR. Napoleon also sought to expand the French empire in Indochina, West Africa and the Middle East, but his attempts to establish a Mexican empire under the Archduke MAXIMILIAN ended in disaster. In 1860 Napoleon signed a a free-trade agreement with Great Britain and began to relax his restrictions on civil liberties in France, granting freedom of assembly in 1868. Napoleon was provoked by Otto von BISMARCK into entering the FRANCO-PRUSSIAN WAR (1870–71) and defeat at the Battle of SEDAN (1870) was swiftly followed by a Republican rising that ended his reign.

Napoleonic Wars *See* feature article

Nara City on s Honshu island, Japan; capital of Nara prefecture. A centre of Japanese BUDDHISM, Nara was founded in 706. From 710 to 784 it acted as Japan's first imperial capital. Todaiji (East Great Temple) houses a 22-m (72-ft) tall bronze statue of Buddha. The 7th-century Horyu Temple is reputedly Japan's oldest building. The tomb of Jimmu, Japan's first emperor, resides here. Pop. (1993) 353,000. *See also* FUJIWARA; HEIAN

Narodnik (Rus. Populist) Member of an underground socialist movement in Russia in the 1860s and 1870s. In place of Karl MARX's emphasis on the role of the industrial proletariat, the Narodniki, consisting largely of students and intellectuals, argued that the Russian peasantry constituted the revolutionary class in Russia and that their communal ownership of land negated the need for the transitional stage of industrial capitalism before the advent of the DICTATORSHIP OF THE PROLETARIAT. The Narodniki were brutally suppressed by the tsarist government and the movement fractured after failing to convince the Russian peasantry. Some members turned to terrorism, including the assassination of Tsar ALEXANDER II (1881).

Narses (*c.*480–574) Byzantine general under JUSTINIAN I. In 532 he helped crush the Nika Revolt of the Greens and Blues in Constantinople (now Istanbul). In 538 Narses was appointed imperial treasurer and sent to assist BELISARIUS in the reconquest of Italy. The generals' mutual antipathy contributed to the loss of Milan, and Narses was recalled to Constantinople. In 552 he led *c.*30,000 troops in a renewed campaign against the OSTROGOTHS in Italy, inflicting a decisive defeat on the Ostrogothic leader Totila.

Narváez, Pánfilo de (1480–1528) Spanish CONQUISTADOR. He was chief lieutenant to Diego de VELÁZQUEZ in his conquest of Cuba (1511). In 1520 Velázquez sent him to Mexico to arrest Hernán CORTÉS. The expedition failed, and Narváez was imprisoned (1520–22) by Cortés. In 1527 he was sent to Florida by Emperor CHARLES V. Narváez landed near Tampa Bay, Florida, and claimed the region for Spain. His march northwards was beset by constant attack from Native Americans. Narváez failed to rendezvous with his ships at St Marks, Florida, and the *c.*250 survivors were forced to construct their own makeshift boats. Narváez and all but four of his men drowned before reaching Mexico. *See* map, page 117

NASA *See* NATIONAL AERONAUTICS AND SPACE ADMINISTRATION

Nasca *See* NAZCA

Naseby, Battle of (14 June 1645) Final battle in the first phase of the English CIVIL WAR, fought near Leicester, central England. The *c.*14,000 troops of the NEW MODEL ARMY, led by Oliver CROMWELL and Thomas FAIRFAX, outnumbered the *c.*10,000 Royalist forces led by Prince RUPERT. Rupert initially forced the retreat of the left wing of the Parliamentary cavalry under Henry IRETON, but the ill-disciplined advance of the Royalists enabled Cromwell to mount a decisive counter-attack. The Parliamentarians routed the Royalist infantry and took *c.*4000 prisoners. *See also* CHARLES I

Nash, Sir Walter (1882–1968) New Zealand statesman, prime minister (1957–60), b. England. In 1909 he emigrated to New Zealand and entered Parliament in 1929. He was instrumental in getting the Labour Party into government for the first time (1935). As finance minister (1935–49) and deputy prime minister (1940–49), Nash helped to introduce wide-ranging reforms of social security and successfully managed the wartime economy. He served (1950–57) as leader of the opposition, becoming prime minister after Labour's narrow election victory in 1957 and implementing additional social reforms.

NAPOLEONIC WARS (1803–15)

Campaigns by a series of European coalitions against French expansion under NAPOLEON I. The Napoleonic Wars were a continuation of the FRENCH REVOLUTIONARY WARS (1792–1802). In 1803 Britain declared war and formed (1804) the **Third Coalition** with Austria, Russia and Sweden. Napoleon used massive, highly mobile armies that struck before the coalition could coordinate their forces. He defeated the Austrians at the Battle of ULM and an Austro-Russian coalition at the Battle of AUSTERLITZ (both 1805), but the British under Admiral Horatio NELSON won a decisive naval victory at the Battle of TRAFALGAR (1805). Prussia joined the **Fourth Coalition** but was decisively defeated at the Battle of JENA (1806). The ensuing Treaties of TILSIT (1807) divided Prussia and created the Grand Duchy of WARSAW. In 1806 Napoleon formed the CONTINENTAL SYSTEM, an economic blockade of Great Britain, and occupied Portugal in an attempt to enforce the sanctions in 1807. Napoleon defeated the Russians at Friedland in June 1807, but temporarily (until 1810) gained Russia as an ally against Britain. Napoleon's appointment of his brother, Joseph BONAPARTE, as king of Spain led to the PENINSULAR WAR (1808–14), which cost *c.*300,000 French lives and contributed to the eventual defeat of Napoleon. French victory at the Battle of WAGRAM (1809) led to the collapse of the **Fifth Coalition** and forced Austria to cede control of Germany to France. In 1812 Napoleon invaded Russia, occupying Moscow after victory at the Battle of BORODINO (September 1812). The Russians razed Moscow and, lacking food and shelter, the Grand Army was forced to withdraw by the onset of a freezing Russian winter. The retreat, dogged by the guerrilla tactics of the Russian forces under Mikhail KUTUZOV, cost more than 400,000 French lives. Against the **Sixth Coalition**, Napoleon was defeated at the Battle of LEIPZIG (October 1813), and Allied forces entered Paris in March 1814. While the Coalition was negotiating at the Congress of VIENNA, Napoleon escaped from exile and overthrew LOUIS XVIII. War was renewed during the HUNDRED DAYS of Napoleon's restoration and ended in his final defeat by the Duke of WELLINGTON and Field Marshal BLÜCHER at the Battle of WATERLOO (16–18 June 1815). *See also* ALEXANDER I; CANNING, GEORGE; CASTLEREAGH, ROBERT STEWART, 2ND VISCOUNT

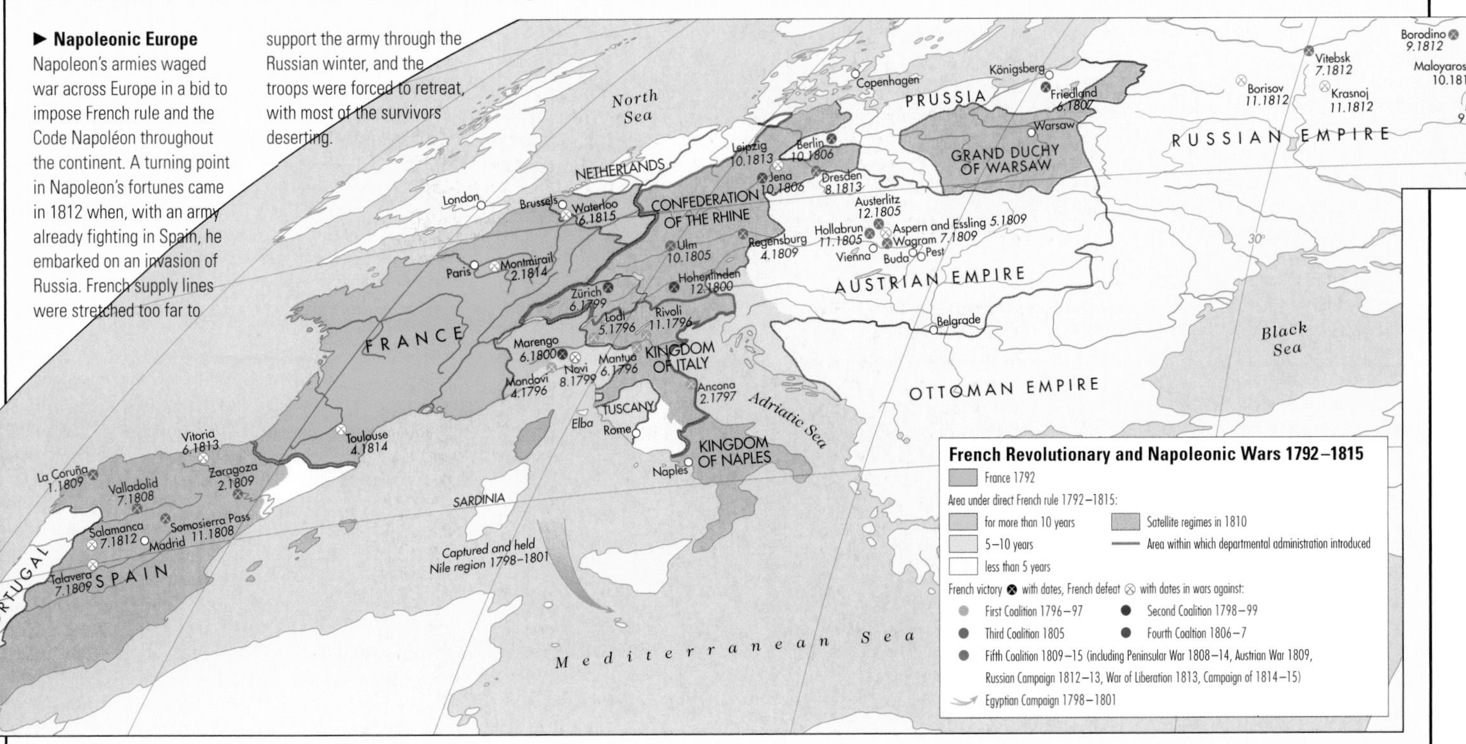

► **Napoleonic Europe** Napoleon's armies waged war across Europe in a bid to impose French rule and the Code Napoléon throughout the continent. A turning point in Napoleon's fortunes came in 1812 when, with an army already fighting in Spain, he embarked on an invasion of Russia. French supply lines were stretched too far to support the army through the Russian winter, and the troops were forced to retreat, with most of the survivors deserting.

Nassau, House of European dynasty. The family descended from a historic region of Germany on the E bank of the River Rhine, where Walram I built a castle and styled himself Count of Nassau. After his death (1198), the region was divided among his sons, Walram II and Otto I. Walram II's son, ADOLF OF NASSAU, was the German king (1292–98). In 1806 Walramian Nassau joined the Napoleonic Confederation of the Rhine and received Ottonian Nassau. In 1866 Nassau was annexed by Prussia. Descendants of Otto I settled in the Netherlands and inherited the principality of Orange in 1544. Since the election of WILLIAM I (THE SILENT) in 1579, members of this house have ruled The Netherlands almost continuously under the name of the House of ORANGE. In 1806 WILLIAM I of The Netherlands lost his German lands to Napoleon, but received LUXEMBOURG in 1815.

Nasser, Gamal Abdel (1918–70) Egyptian soldier and statesman, prime minister (1954–56) and first president of the republic of Egypt (1956–70). In 1942 he joined three other soldiers, including Anwar SADAT, in founding the Society of Free Officers, which secretly campaigned against corruption and for the withdrawal of British troops. In 1952 Nasser led an army coup against King FAROUK, which overthrew the monarchy and established a Revolutionary Command Council under the nominal control of Major General Muhammad Neguib. Nasser soon emerged as the real ruler and assumed presidential powers under the 1956 constitution. He was one of the leading figures in the early days of the NON-ALIGNED MOVEMENT and played a key role in the BANDUNG CONFERENCE (1955). After Britain and the United States cancelled loans to build the Aswan High Dam, Nasser nationalized the SUEZ CANAL (July 1956), with the intention of using the tolls collected to finance the Dam project. This prompted an Anglo-French and Israeli invasion (October 1956). Pressure from the United States, however, forced the withdrawal of European troops, and Israeli forces were removed (March 1957) from the Sinai Peninsula after the establishment of an international peacekeeping force. Nasser had a stated ambition to unite the Arab world, and he won great support from Arabs throughout the Middle East. He formed the UNITED ARAB REPUBLIC (1958–61) with Syria, serving as its president. In Yemen's civil war (1962–67), Nasser sent troops to support the Republican forces against the Royalists, backed by Saudi Arabia. Refusing to recognize the state of ISRAEL, Nasser provoked the SIX-DAY WAR (1967) by demanding the withdrawal of the peacekeeping troops from the Sinai and closing the Gulf of Aqaba to Israel. After Egypt's disastrous defeat in the War, Nasser briefly resigned but returned to office after public demonstrations of support. Domestically Nasser implemented a programme known as Arab socialism. This included economic and land reform as well as a measure of social liberalization. Nasser died in office and was succeeded as president by Anwar Sadat. The Aswan Dam, Nasser's crowning achievement, was completed in 1970 with funding from the Soviet Union. *See also* ARAB-ISRAELI WARS

Natal Former province of South Africa. Portuguese navigator Vasco de Gama sighted the coast of Natal on Christmas Day, 1497, and the Portuguese built a settlement at Delagoa Bay in the 1540s. In the 19th century, the region's interior was forcibly unified by the ZULUS, successively led by DINGISWAYO, SHAKA and DINGAAN. In 1824 the British founded a trading post at Port Natal (now Durban). In 1837 AFRIKANERS arrived in Natal on the GREAT TREK (1835–40) from Cape Colony; Andries PRETORIUS destroyed Dingaan's Zulu army at the Battle of BLOOD RIVER (1838). In 1843 the Afrikaner Republic of Natal was annexed by the British, and many Afrikaners moved on to the TRANSVAAL and Orange FREE STATE. After British victory in the ZULU WAR (1879), Zululand was incorporated into Natal in 1897. During the Second SOUTH AFRICAN WAR (1899–1902), the Afrikaner invasion of Natal was halted at LADYSMITH. In 1910 Natal became a province in the Union of South Africa. South Africa's apartheid regime (1948–94) created the bantustan (black homeland) of KwaZulu for the Zulu population. During the 1980s and early 1990s, KwaZulu and Natal witnessed violent clashes between supporters of the AFRICAN NATIONAL CONGRESS (ANC) and of the INKATHA Freedom Party. In 1994 KwaZulu was joined with Natal to form the province of KWAZULU-NATAL.

Nation, Carry Amelia Moore (1846–1911) US temperance leader. Her alcoholic first husband turned her against liquor and she joined the temperance movement in 1890. Nation, inflamed by the violation of the PROHIBITION laws in Kansas, took up a hatchet which she used to systematically smash the state's saloons and speakeasies. Nation was arrested 30 times for disturbing the peace. Although other temperance organizations rejected her militant methods, Nation carried her crusade to several other states and attracted funds through her speeches and the publicity and merchandise that developed around her use of the hatchet. *See also* ANTI-SALOON LEAGUE

National Aeronautics and Space Administration (NASA) US government agency that organizes civilian aeronautical and space research programmes. NASA was established in 1958 and is the agency behind the many US successes in SPACE EXPLORATION, including the Lunar landings and the space shuttle. It has various departments located throughout the United States. The Lyndon B. Johnson Space Center in Houston, Texas, is responsible for manned space flights. Space rockets, both manned and unmanned, are launched from the John F. Kennedy Space Center at Cape Canaveral, Florida.

National Assembly Name taken (17 June 1789) by the Third Estate of the French STATES-GENERAL at the beginning of the FRENCH REVOLUTION. On 20 June 1789, the members took the TENNIS COURT OATH. The Assembly's most important acts were the abolition of feudal rights and privileges (1789), the DECLARATION OF THE RIGHTS OF MAN AND OF THE CITIZEN (1789) and the Civil Constitution of the Clergy (1790). It dissolved itself on 30 September 1791, after the adoption of the new constitution of 1791, and was replaced by the Legislative Assembly (1791) and later the NATIONAL CONVENTION (1792).

National Association for the Advancement of Colored People (NAACP) US CIVIL-RIGHTS organization. Founded in 1909, its objectives are "to achieve through peaceful and lawful means, equal citizenship rights for all American citizens by eliminating segregation and discrimination in housing, employment, voting, schools, the courts, transportation, and recreation". Early leaders included W.E.B. DU BOIS. In 1939 the NAACP set up the Legal Defense and Educational Fund to finance court battles over discriminatory practices. The NAACP's legal council, led by Thurgood MARSHALL, took the BROWN V. BOARD OF EDUCATION OF TOPEKA (1954) case to the Supreme Court, which rejected segregation in US schools. In 1986 the NAACP moved its headquarters from New York City to Baltimore, Maryland. Its publications include *Crisis*.

▲ **Nasser** liberated Egypt from 60 years of British rule. He survived an assassination attempt in 1954, and thereafter created a police state to crush domestic opposition.

National Convention (September 1792–October 1795) Governing assembly of France during the most critical phase of the FRENCH REVOLUTION. It was the successor to the NATIONAL ASSEMBLY. In September 1792 the National Convention voted to abolish the monarchy and establish the First Republic. It also supported the execution of LOUIS XVI and MARIE ANTOINETTE. In June 1793 the Convention was purged of the GIRONDINS, who were held responsible for early defeats in the FRENCH REVOLUTIONARY WARS (1792–1802), and became dominated by the MONTAGNARDS led by Maximilien ROBESPIERRE. The legislative power of the Convention was transferred to the COMMITTEE OF PUBLIC SAFETY, who initiated the so-called REIGN OF TERROR. Robespierre was overthrown in the THERMIDORIAN REACTION (July 1794) and the Girondins regained the ascendancy. A new constitution (1795) dissolved the Convention and established the DIRECTORY (1795–99).

National Guard Volunteer citizen-militia in the United States. Units are under state jurisdiction in peacetime and in times of war or national emergency may be activated for federal duty. The National Guard are also used during natural disasters and civil unrest. In 1824 the 7th Regiment of the New York State Militia took the title "National Guard", and the term came into general use for state militias after the National Guard Association was formed in 1878. Units are located in all states, and members are trained in the regular armed services.

National Health Service (NHS) In Britain, system of state provision of health care established (1948) by Aneurin BEVAN. The NHS undertook to provide free, comprehensive coverage for most health services, including hospitals, general medical practice and public health facilities. It is administered by the Department of Health. General practitioners (GPs) have registered patients; they may also have private patients and may contract out of the state scheme altogether. They refer patients, when necessary, to specialist consultants in hospitals. Health visitors are the third arm of the service. Hospitals are administered by regional boards, which include governors of teaching hospitals. In 1990 the Conservative government introduced the "internal market" into health care, establishing GP fund-holding practices and NHS Trusts independent of local health authority control. In 1997 the new Labour government replaced the internal market with primary care groups consisting of GPs and community nurses. The NHS is the largest single employer in the United Kingdom.

national insurance (NI) In Britain, state insurance scheme, founded by David LLOYD GEORGE in 1911. In 1946 more comprehensive proposals by Lord BEVERIDGE formed the basis of the National Insurance Act. NI provides sickness, maternity, unemployment and child benefits as well as old-age pensions. It also contributes to the cost of the NATIONAL HEALTH SERVICE (NHS). The scheme is funded by compulsory contributions from employers and employees and is administered by the Department of Social Security.

nationalism Modern ideology according to which all people owe a supreme loyalty to their nation and which holds that each nation should be embodied in a separate state. Nationalist sentiment, drawing upon and extolling a common culture, language and history, can be a powerful unifying force. Before the end of the 18th century, civilization was usually determined by religious allegiance. The AMERICAN REVOLUTION (1775–83) and the FRENCH REVOLUTION (1789–99) can be seen as the first major expressions of nationalist feeling. Nationalism as a historical determinant spread throughout Europe in the 19th century, inspiring the creation of new unified states, such as Italy and Germany. The rise of nationalism in Europe culminated in World War 1, and in its aftermath many new states were created based on the concept of national identity. During the 20th century, nationalism, embodied as a

N

quest for national self-determination and independence, spread through Asia and Africa, hastening the end of COLONIALISM and IMPERIALISM. The increasing influence of supra-national bodies, such as the EUROPEAN UNION (EU), is sometimes construed as a threat to the nation-state. *See also* LEAGUE OF NATIONS; REVOLUTIONS OF 1848; UNITED NATIONS (UN)

nationalization Policy of acquiring for public ownership enterprises that were formerly privately owned. Advocates of nationalization maintain that bringing essential industries under government control enhances social and economic equality. In some cases it is motivated by a socialist or communist ideology, as in the wholesale nationalizations that occurred in the Soviet Union under LENIN after 1918, or in Britain and France in the 1940s and 1950s. Some governments nationalize industries to protect them from foreign domination, as in the nationalizations of oil businesses in Latin America and the Middle East in the 1970s. Industries may also be nationalized, particularly in developing countries, if the private sector is unable to manage and develop them adequately. In the 1980s the trend was towards PRIVATIZATION. *See also* SOCIALISM

National Liberation Front *See* FRONT DE LIBÉRATION NATIONALE (FLN)

National Party Australian political organization, also known as the Country Party (1919–75) and the National Country Party (1975–82). The Party was formed to represent agricultural and rural interests in the federal government. During the 1920s, Country Party leader Earle PAGE formed a coalition government (1923–29) with Stanley BRUCE's Nationalist Party, but thereafter the Party lost a great deal of direct influence and popular support. It has been involved, however, in a coalition with every non-Labor government since 1923, always holding the post of deputy prime minister. Indeed, Country Party leaders Arthur Fadden and John McEwen became prime ministers (1941 and 1967–68 respectively). It has formed coalitions with the United Australia Party (1932–41) and its successor the LIBERAL PARTY (1949–72, 1975–83, 1996–).

National Party (NP) South African political organization, the governing party from 1948 to 1994. It was founded (1914) by James HERTZOG as the party of AFRIKANER nationalism. As prime minister (1924–39), Hertzog enforced greater racial segregation within South Africa and sought more independence from Britain. In 1933 Hertzog formed the United Party with Jan SMUTS, and extremists, led by Daniel MALAN, seized control of the National Party (NP). The NP regained power after the war, and Malan created the system of APARTHEID. The white supremacist ideology of the NP was continued under Malan's successors: Johannes STRIJDOM, Hendrik VERWOERD and John VORSTER. Under the leadership (1978–89) of P.W. BOTHA, South Africa granted (1982) limited political rights to "coloureds" and Asians, although not to Africans. Under the leadership (1989–97) of F.W. DE KLERK, the Party (under pressure from international sanctions) moved towards greater power-sharing with the African population. In South Africa's first multiracial elections in 1994, the NP were defeated by the AFRICAN NATIONAL CONGRESS (ANC) led by Nelson MANDELA, but joined a government of national unity with the ANC. De Klerk stepped down as leader of the NP in 1997. In 1998 the Party was renamed the New National Party (NNP), but lost further support in the 1999 elections.

National Republican Party US political organization that emerged from the split in the DEMOCRATIC-REPUBLICAN PARTY after the presidential election of 1824. The supporters of President John Quincy ADAMS became known as National Republicans, while allies of Andrew JACKSON were referred to as Democratic-Republicans. In the 1828 elections, the Jacksonians led the DEMOCRATIC PARTY to victory. Staunchly opposed to Jackson, the National-Republicans supported the BANK OF THE UNITED STATES and a protective tariff. The National-Republican candidate Henry CLAY was heavily defeated in the 1832 election and by 1836 the organization had become the WHIG PARTY. *See also* WEBSTER, DANIEL

national socialism (Nazism) Doctrine of the German NAZI PARTY (1921–45). It was biologically racist (believing that the so-called Aryan race was superior to others), anti-Semitic, nationalistic, anti-communist, anti-democratic and anti-intellectual. It placed power before justice and the interests of the state before the individual. These beliefs were stated by the Party's leader, Adolf HITLER, in his book *Mein Kampf* (1925). *See also* ANTI-SEMITISM; BORMANN, MARTIN; FASCISM

Nation of Islam *See* BLACK MUSLIMS

Nations, Battle of the *See* LEIPZIG, BATTLE OF

Native Australians (Aboriginals) Indigenous peoples of Australia. Originally from SE Asia, Native Australians started colonizing Australia more than 40,000 years ago. By 30,000 years ago, they had occupied most of the continent. The central feature of Native Australian religion is the concept of "the Dreaming", a never-ending epoch in which nature is continually shaped by mythic beings. These beings may take the form of physiographic features, humans or animals (*see* TOTEMISM), and the sites associated with them are regarded as sacred. At the time of European colonization, all the *c*.500 territorial groups led a nomadic life, hunting and gathering. The groups were essentially egalitarian, but societies were stratified according to age and sex. Before the arrival of the first British settlers (1788) there were probably one million Native Australians, but many thousands soon died from European diseases as well as in violent confrontations with settlers. By 1901 the population had shrunk to less than 95,000. The British colonial government set out to destroy Aboriginal culture by forcibly removing children from the groups and restricting Native Australians to reservations. In 1932 William Cooper founded the Australian Aborigines League, which demanded equal rights for Native Australians, but the enforced assimilation of Aboriginals continued into the 1960s. In 1967, however, they were granted full Australian citizenship. Native Australians were included in the census for the first time in 1971, when their numbers were *c*.140,000. In 1973 the government established a department of aboriginal affairs, which sponsored the Aboriginal Land Rights Act (1976) and the Aboriginal and Torres Islander Heritage Protection Act (1984). Today, there are *c*.300,000 Native Australians.

Native Middle Americans (Mesoamericans) Indigenous peoples of the area between N Mexico and Nicaragua who, like their South American and North American counterparts, are descended from Asians who crossed the Bering Strait. An archaic, hunter-gatherer culture developed in Mexico and Central America after 1400 BC. The first permanent agricultural settlements were established by 2000 BC and the OLMEC had built an impressive civilization in E Mexico by 1400 BC. The theocratic societies of the MAYA (MIXTEC, ZAPOTEC and Nahuatl) had developed in the SE highlands of Mexico by the 1st century AD. The city of TEOTIHUACÁN dominated Mexico for the next six centuries. By AD 1000, the TOLTEC had conquered many Maya cities and begun to build an empire in the Valley of Mexico. The AZTECS gained control over most of Middle America during the 15th century, but their capital, Tenochtitlán (now MEXICO CITY), fell to the Spanish conquistador Hernán CORTÉS in 1519. The Spanish colonizers imposed the ENCOMIENDA system on the native population.

Native North Americans *See* feature, pages 288–289

Native South Americans Indigenous peoples of South America who, like their Middle American and North American counterparts, are descended from Asians who crossed the Bering Strait. The tribes of Native South America are often grouped into four main cultural groups: the irrigation civilizations of the central and southern Andes, the kingdoms of the northern Andes and the Caribbean, the sparse farming settlements in the tropical forests of E South America, and nomadic hunter-gatherers in the narrow S part of the continent. In the **central and southern Andes**, there is evidence of human society from *c*.13,000 BC, and settled agricultural communities were established on the coast of Peru by *c*.2300 BC. From *c*.1000 BC, the CHAVÍN culture developed in the Peruvian Andes. It was eclipsed by the MOCHICA and NAZCA civilizations that grew on the coast of Peru from *c*.200 BC. In the 7th century AD, the powerful state of TIAHUANACO emerged in the southern Andes. After 1000, the coastal state of CHIMÚ flourished around its capital CHAN CHAN. In the 15th century, the mighty QUECHUA state of the INCA conquered almost all of the central and southern Andes, but its entire empire (wracked by civil war) fell to the Spanish conquistador Francisco PIZARRO in 1535. Agricultural settlements were established in the **northern Andes and the Caribbean** in *c*.3000 BC. From *c*.1000 AD the CHIBCHA kingdoms blossomed in N Colombia. The ARAWAK and CARIB tribes of the Caribbean were virtually exterminated by European colonization in the 16th and 17th century. The jungles of the **Amazon basin** have been inhabited by isolated agricultural communities of tribes, such as the YANOMAMI, since 3000 BC. Since the late 20th century, these fragile communities have been threatened by industrial development. ARAUCANIANS in the narrow **S part of South America** successfully resisted Spanish colonization and Chilean expansion until confined to reservations at the end of the 19th century. The nomadic culture of the Tierra del Fuegans of the Pampas remained almost unchanged for more than 9000 years, but was almost extinguished after the arrival of the Spanish in the 16th century.

NATO *See* NORTH ATLANTIC TREATY ORGANIZATION

Nat Turner insurrection *See* TURNER, NAT

Nauru Island republic in the W Pacific Ocean, a coral atoll located almost equidistant from Australia and Hawaii. It is the world's smallest independent state. Nauru was first explored by a British navigator, John Hunter, in 1798. In 1888 the atoll was annexed to Germany. During World War 1, Nauru was occupied by Australian forces. The Japanese occupied (1942–45) Nauru during World War 2 and the island was subject to intensive US bombardment. In 1968 it became an independent republic within the British Commonwealth.

Navajo (Navaho) Athabascan-speaking tribe, the largest group of NATIVE NORTH AMERICANS in the United States. It is thought that the Navajo and APACHE originated in Canada and migrated SW between the 10th and 13th centuries. The Navajo adopted much of the ANASAZI culture after many Pueblo people sought shelter with the tribe following the PUEBLO REVOLT (1680–94) against the Spanish. The Navajo were defeated (1863) by US troops led by Kit CARSON, and *c*.8000 Navajo were captured and forcibly deported (the "Long Walk") to Fort Sumner, New Mexico, where they were imprisoned (1864–68). In 1868 a reservation was created for them in Arizona and New Mexico; it is the largest in the country. Today, the Navajo population is *c*.200,000. *See also* HOPI

Navarino, Battle of (20 October 1827) Naval engagement during the GREEK WAR OF INDEPENDENCE, fought off the SW coast of Greece. A combined British, French and Russian fleet, led by Admiral Edward Codrington (1770–1851), destroyed three-quarters of IBRAHIM PASHA's Turkish-Egyptian fleet anchored in the harbour of Navarino (now Pylos). No Allied ships were lost. The Battle was the last major conflict between wooden warships and helped to ensure Greek independence (1829).

Navarre Autonomous region and ancient kingdom in N Spain. The area was known as the kingdom of PAMPLONA (now the regional capital) until the late 12th century. In the 8th century, the kingdom was occupied by the Moors. Independence was achieved in the 9th century. At the start of the 11th century, Sancho III of Navarre ruled over most of Christian Spain, but upon his death Navarre fell to ARAGÓN. In the 13th and 14th century, Navarre was subject to French rule. FERDINAND V of Spain conquered S

NAURU

AREA: 21sq km (8sq mi)
POPULATION: 12,000
CAPITAL (POPULATION): Yaren District (1000)
GOVERNMENT: Multiparty republic
ETHNIC GROUPS: Nauruan 58%, other Pacific groups 26%
LANGUAGES: Nauruan (official), English
RELIGIONS: Protestant, Roman Catholic
GDP PER CAPITA (1994): US$25,094

N

The many disparate tribes of Native North Americans are often grouped into nine cultural areas, according to similarities of language or culture: Arctic, sub-Arctic, Northwest Coast, Plains, Plateau, Eastern Woodlands, Great Basin, California and Southwest (*see* map, bottom right).

Arctic and sub-Arctic

Unlike many Native North Americans, the peoples of the Arctic and sub-Arctic have largely retained their traditions. The Aleut have lived on the Aleutian Islands, SW of ALASKA, since 6000 BC. The Arctic remained uninhabited until the arrival of the INUIT in *c.*2000 BC, who between AD 900 and 1300 colonized GREENLAND. Peoples of the E sub-Arctic are Algonquian-speakers; they include the OJIBWA and the CREE. Like many other tribes, the Cree was devastated by diseases brought by Europeans. In the W sub-Arctic lived the nomadic ATHABASCANS, who lived by fishing and hunting. The indigenous peoples of modern-day Canada suffered less persecution and displacement than their counterparts in English America. This was due primarily to their role in the FUR TRADE, for example acting as suppliers and guides to the HUDSON'S BAY COMPANY. European powers also employed natives in the FRENCH AND INDIAN WARS (1689–1763).

Northwest Coast and Plateau

The Northwest Coast supported a dense Native American population organized into large villages. Tribes include the TLINGIT, CHINOOK, Haida, Kwakiutl and Nootka. Societies were stratified and slavery was common. Chiefs gained prestige by public displays of wealth, usually in the form of gift-giving (*see* POTLATCH). Expert woodcarvers, these coastal groups fashioned totem poles (*see* TOTEMISM). Northwest culture remained relatively unaffected by European influences until Captain James COOK explored the coast in 1778. In 1793 Sir Alexander MACKENZIE journeyed overland to the Pacific. After 1700 the SALISH and NEZ PERCÉ of the Plateau adopted many Plains customs.

The Plains

The PLAINS CULTURE became the Western stereotype of "Indian" customs. In pre-Columbian times, there were two distinct social systems: nomadic tribes, such as the BLACKFOOT and Kiowa, hunted vast herds of buffalo on foot; sedentary tribes, such as the CROW, Mandan, Pawnee and Wichita, farmed the river valleys. As Europeans colonized the coastal regions, other tribes moved onto the Plains, including the SIOUX (Dakota), COMANCHE and CHEYENNE. In the 18th century, the introduction of the horse saw a vast increase in nomads that, combined with the slaughter of buffalo by white settlers, led to the extermination of the wild herds by the 1880s. The W expansion of the FRONTIER led to conflict between settlers and indigenous peoples. The heaviest fighting of

◄ **Sitting Bull** (1831–90) was one of the principal leaders of Native American resistance to the expansion of the United States. Sitting Bull, Crazy Horse and Gall led the Sioux to victory against the US cavalry under General George Custer at the Battle of Little Bighorn (25 June 1876). In 1885 Sitting Bull appeared in Buffalo Bill's Wild West Show. In 1890 he renewed the Ghost Dance and was killed by native police sent to arrest him.

▲ **buffalo** were a vital source of food, clothing and shelter for the indigenous peoples of the Great Plains. The meat was dried to make pemmican and the hides were pegged out to dry and then cured.

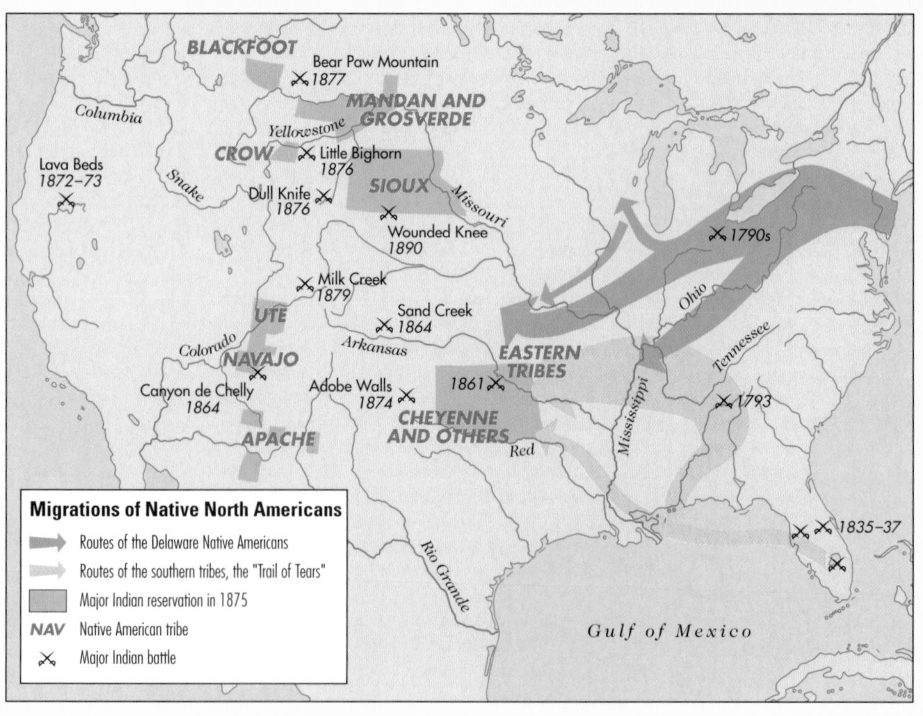

► **In the late 18th century**, Native Americans from Delaware made a slow W migration. The Indian Removal Act (1830) also forced the S tribes to move W. Demands made by white settlers for more land led to the establishment of Indian reservations and a series of bloody conflicts, as Native Americans resisted attempts to confine them.

► **Outside** the SW and SE many different cultures flourished, subsisting on hunting and gathering, fishing and agriculture. The arrival of the Spanish in the 16th century brought horses to North America. Rapidly adopted by the Plains peoples, these animals revolutionized hunting techniques, enabling the wholesale slaughter of the wild buffalo herds and facilitating travel over longer distances. Many people abandoned agriculture in favour of a nomadic life based on horseback.

Mandan earth lodge

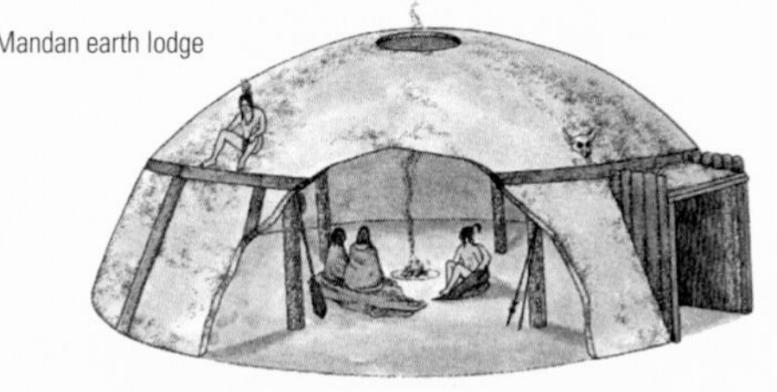

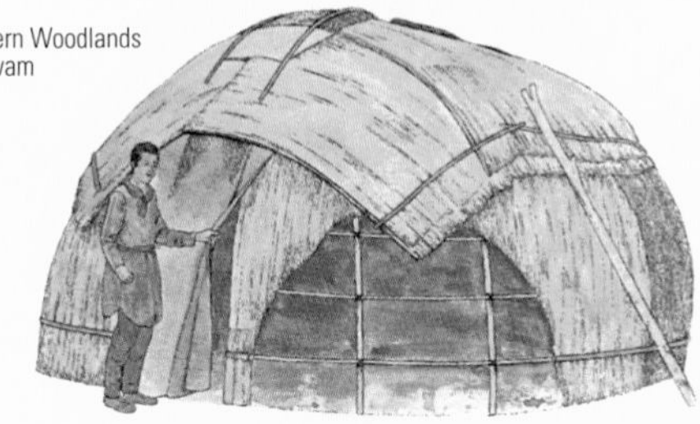

Eastern Woodlands wigwam

Navajo hogan

Apache wickiup

the INDIAN WARS occurred on the Great Plains. The Sioux, led by SITTING BULL and CRAZY HORSE, achieved a famous victory over US General George CUSTER at the Battle of LITTLE BIGHORN (1876). The Sioux were defeated, however, at the Battle of WOUNDED KNEE (1890) and, after the DAWES COMMISSION (1893), Native Americans were confined to reservations.

EASTERN WOODLANDS

By AD 700 the HOPEWELL CULTURE had been supplanted by the MOUND-BUILDERS of the Mississippi culture. In the 1660s, European settlement began and colonization forced many indigenous peoples to move west. The IROQUOIS CONFEDERACY, founded (*c*.1575) by HIAWATHA, resisted NEW FRANCE, while NEW ENGLAND was confronted by KING PHILIP'S WAR (1675–76). After conquering New France, Britain had to deal with PONTIAC'S REBELLION (1763–66), consisting of a coalition that included the OTTAWA, DELAWARE and SHAWNEE. After the creation of the United States, General Anthony WAYNE defeated the Ohio tribes at the Battle of Fallen Timbers (1794) and many tribes agreed to move into INDIANA. Further white expansion led TECUMSEH to form a confederacy of Native forces, and the Shawnee and the CREEK joined the British in the WAR OF 1812. The INDIAN REMOVAL ACT (1830) led to the brutal, forced marches of indigenous peoples, such as the TRAIL OF TEARS (1829–43). The BLACK HAWK WAR (1832) ended with the SAC and FOX forced W of the Mississippi. The attempt to remove the SEMINOLE from Florida led to the Seminole Wars (1817–18, 1835–42, 1855–58).

CALIFORNIA AND THE GREAT BASIN

An archaic, hunter-gatherer culture persisted among the indigenous peoples of California and the Great Basin between 8000 BC and AD 1850. Major tribes include the SHOSHONE, UTE and Yurok. In California, missionaries sought to convert Native Americans and many were forced to build the missions into viable agricultural communities.

SOUTHWEST

An archaic culture also persisted in the Southwest from *c*.8000 BC until *c*.AD 300, when the HOHOKAM (ancestors of the Pima and Papagao) built irrigation systems. By AD 700 adobe houses were common in the ANASAZI region. In the 11th century, Anasazi cliff-dwellers carved out multi-storeyed houses from the faces of the Mesa Verde canyons. In the 1450s APACHE and NAVAJO tribes raided the Pueblo villages: the ZUNI and HOPI cultures date from this period. In 1540 Spanish explorers reached the region and by 1598 had imposed Spanish rule.

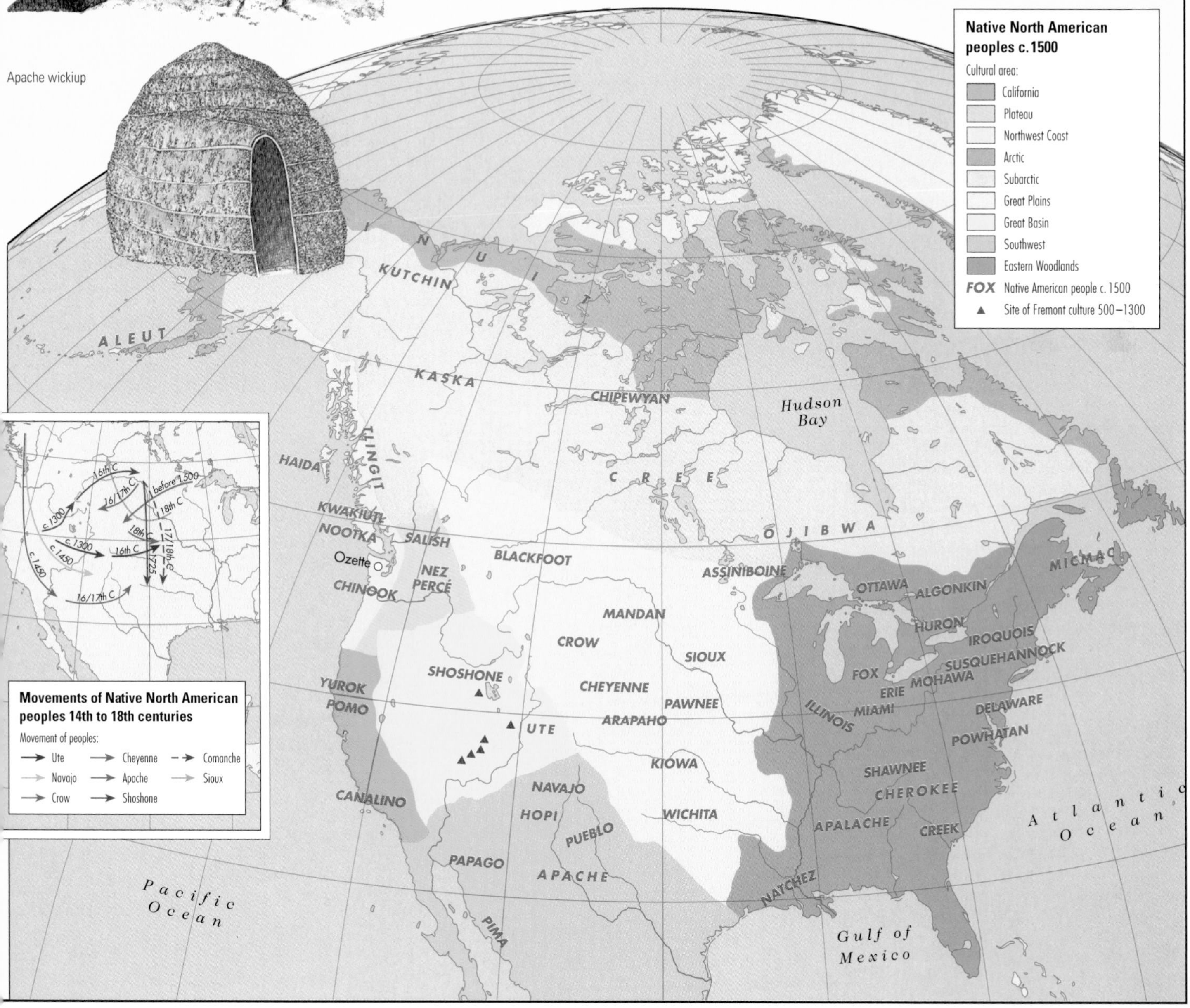

Native North American peoples c.1500

Cultural area: California; Plateau; Northwest Coast; Arctic; Subarctic; Great Plains; Great Basin; Southwest; Eastern Woodlands

FOX Native American people c.1500

▲ Site of Fremont culture 500–1300

Movements of Native North American peoples 14th to 18th centuries

Movement of peoples: Ute; Navajo; Crow; Cheyenne; Apache; Shoshone; Comanche; Sioux

Navarre in 1512, while the N part remained a separate French kingdom until 1589, when it was incorporated into the French crown by Henry III of Navarre (HENRY IV of France). Spanish Navarre retained semi-autonomy until it was united with Spain in 1833. Area: 10,421sq km (4023sq mi). Pop. (1991) 519,227.

Navigation Acts English statutes placing restrictions on foreign trade and shipping. The most important was the Great Navigation Act (1651), which declared that goods imported from outside Europe could only be brought to England in English ships or in ships belonging to an English colony. The Act threatened Dutch maritime interests and precipitated the first of the DUTCH WARS (1652–54). From 1664 certain colonial goods, such as sugar, indigo and tobacco, could only be shipped directly to England or an English colony, while European goods had to be shipped via England. The strict enforcement of the Navigation Acts contributed to the AMERICAN REVOLUTION (1775–83). The Acts were repealed in 1849. *See also* MERCANTILISM

navy Nation's warships and auxiliary vessels and crew, organized for war at sea. The first recorded naval battle was between the Egyptians and the Sea People in *c.*1200 BC. From the 5th century BC Greek city-states, such as Athens and Corinth, relied on galleys to protect their Mediterranean trade routes from PIRATES. The first major naval conflict occurred during the PERSIAN WARS (499–479 BC), when Persian defeat in the Battle of SALAMIS (480 BC) established Greek supremacy in the E Mediterranean. In 331 BC Rome established the first permanent navy, which proved crucial in the PUNIC WARS (264–146 BC). The foundations of the British ROYAL NAVY were established by ALFRED THE GREAT in the 9th century AD, in response to the VIKING invasions. The CINQUE PORTS in S England were built in the 11th century. The early Middle Ages saw the development of specialized armed vessels, deployed to protect trading vessels. Spanish naval supremacy was confirmed by victory over the Byzantine fleet at the Battle of LEPANTO (1571). The Battle of TRAFALGAR (1805) marked a century of British naval superiority. In 1859 France developed the first IRONCLADS. The submarine proved a major weapon in World War 1. In World War 2, naval warfare was conducted largely by aircraft from aircraft carriers. The US NAVY emerged from the War as the world's dominant fleet, rivalled at times by the Soviet Union.

N

Navy, US Naval service of the US armed forces. It consists of more than 500,000 personnel under the president, who is commander in chief of the armed forces, and the general supervision of the secretary of the Navy and his adviser, the chief of naval operations (CNO), who is the Navy's highest ranking officer. It is divided into five operating fleets. The US Navy was formally established by Congress in 1798, although the Continental Navy had fought during the American Revolution (1775–83). It was first employed against pirates off the Barbary Coast in 1801 and fought in the WAR OF 1812 against the British. The Navy played a crucial role in the Union victory in the American Civil War (1861–65) and emerged as a major international force after destroying the Spanish fleet in the Battle of MANILA BAY (1898) in the SPANISH-AMERICAN WAR. It did not engage in any direct conflict during World War 1. The US Navy's aircraft carriers proved a critical weapon against the Japanese in the World War 2 naval battles of the CORAL SEA (1942), MIDWAY (1942) and IWO JIMA (1945). The US Navy launched the world's first nuclear-powered submarine, the *Nautilus* (1954), and the first nuclear-powered aircraft carrier, the *Enterprise* (1961).

Nazarbayev, Nursultan Abishevich (1940–) Kazak statesman, president (1990–). He joined the Communist Party in 1962, becoming chairman of the Kazak Council of Ministers (1984–89) and president of the Kazak Soviet Republic (1990–91). After Kazakstan's independence (1991), Nazarbayev retained the post of president and worked to modernize the economy, inviting Western investment. He sought economic cooperation between other former Soviet republics in Central Asia and worked to expand the COMMONWEALTH OF INDEPENDENT STATES (CIS). Nazarbayev was re-elected in Kazakstan's first multiparty elections (1994) but, after conflict with parliament, ruled by presidential decree until a new election (1995) installed an assembly more favourable to his economic reforms. He won a further term in 1999, although international observers criticized the elections as being rigged.

Nazca (Nasca) Native South American civilization that flourished in coastal valleys of S Peru between 200 BC and AD 600. It is noted for ceramics and fabrics found in graves, but is probably best known for the Nazca Lines – enigmatic markings between the towns of Nazca and Palpa in the desert of S Peru. The Nazca Lines were made *c.*2000 years ago by removing rocks to reveal the lighter sand beneath, and piling them in straight lines several kilometres long. Some lines form geometrical figures, others gigantic animals. The designs resemble those found on Nazca pottery. The purpose of the markings is not fully understood.

Nazi Party (National Socialist German Workers' Party) German political organization. Founded in 1919, with a programme based on NATIONAL SOCIALISM, the Party began to gain support in BAVARIA after Adolf HITLER assumed leadership (1920). It was outlawed after the abortive MUNICH PUTSCH (1923), an attempted coup against the WEIMAR REPUBLIC led by Hitler and 600 armed members of the BROWNSHIRTS. After Hitler was released from prison (1924), he rebuilt the Nazi Party, benefitting from the mass unemployment in GERMANY during the GREAT DEPRESSION. In the July 1932 elections, it became the largest party in the REICHSTAG (German parliament) and Hitler persuaded President Paul von HINDENBURG to appoint him chancellor in January 1933. Hitler wasted little time in banning all other parties and establishing the THIRD REICH. Internal opposition was crushed in the NIGHT OF THE LONG KNIVES (1934). After WORLD WAR 2, the Party was disbanded and outlawed (1945). *See also* BORMANN, MARTIN; FASCISM; GESTAPO; HIMMLER, HEINRICH; HITLER YOUTH; RÖHM, ERNST; ROSENBERG, ALFRED; SS

Nazi-Soviet Pact (23 August 1939) Treaty of mutual non-aggression between the Soviet Union and Germany signed by the foreign ministers Vyacheslav MOLOTOV and Joachim von RIBBENTROP. By ensuring Russian neutrality, the Pact cleared the way for the German invasion of Poland, which took place a week later. Secret clauses provided for the division of Poland and the Baltic countries between Germany and the Soviet Union. The Pact caused international consternation, especially in Britain and France, who were also trying to negotiate a treaty with the Soviet Union, and among communists and Soviet-sympathizers, who regarded Nazi Germany as their greatest enemy. The Pact ended in June 1941 when Germany invaded Russia. *See also* HITLER, ADOLF; LITVINOV, MAXIM MAXIMOVICH; STALIN, JOSEPH; WORLD WAR 2

Ndebele (Matabele) Bantu-speaking people of Matabeleland, Zimbabwe. They were part of the Nguni people of S Africa until the early 19th century, when they were forced to migrate N after a dispute (1823) between their leader, Mzilikazi, and the Zulu king, SHAKA. Conflict with AFRIKANER settlers increased, and the tribe were again forced to migrate N, across the River Limpopo into what is now Zimbabwe, where they established the kingdom of Matabeleland. The Ndebele fought European settlers in the region until their defeat (1893) during the reign of King LOBENGULA. Today, there are *c.*300,000 Ndebele.

Ndongo Southern African kingdom of the Bantu-speaking MBUNDU people, based around modern-day Luanda, Angola. In the early 16th century, it was a client state of the mighty KONGO kingdom, but soon developed independent links with Portuguese slave traders. In 1556 Kongo tried to crush this threat to their own trade with Portugal, but were defeated by Ndongo. In 1575 the Portuguese attempted to conquer Ndongo but, frustrated by effective guerrilla attacks, only managed to claim a 110-km (70-mi) strip of land along the River Kwanza. Peace treaties agreed in 1623 and 1656 were not honoured by the Portuguese, who completed their conquest by 1671.

Neanderthal Middle PALAEOLITHIC variety of human, known from fossils in Europe and Asia. Neanderthals were discovered when a skeleton was unearthed in the Neander Valley, W Germany, in 1856. The skull had a pronounced brow ridge and a larger brain capacity than modern man. Neanderthals used fire and stone tools and conducted burial rites for their dead. They are now considered a separate species of human and not thought to be ancestral to *Homo sapiens sapiens*. Neanderthals predated

► **Nazi Party** The Nazis gained Saarland in 1935 and occupied the Rhineland in 1936. Anschluss with Austria was achieved in March 1938, and Sudetenland and Slovakia fell in March 1939.

modern humans in Europe, but were superseded by them *c.*35,000 years ago. *See also* HUMAN EVOLUTION

Nebraska State in w central United States; the capital is Lincoln. Long inhabited by NATIVE NORTH AMERICANS of the PLAINS CULTURE, the region was acquired by the United States under the LOUISIANA PURCHASE (1803) but was little known to white settlers until the LEWIS AND CLARK EXPEDITION (1804). The Nebraska Territory was created by the KANSAS-NEBRASKA ACT (1854), and white settlement increased rapidly, attracted by land grants under the HOMESTEAD ACT (1862) and the completion (1869) of the Union Pacific Railroad. Area: 199,113sq km (76,878sq mi). Pop. (1990) 1,578,385.

NEBRASKA
Statehood :
1 March 1867
Nickname :
The Cornhusker State
State motto :
Equality before the law

Nebuchadnezzar II (*c.*630–*c.*562 BC) Greatest king of the Chaldaean dynasty of BABYLONIA (r.605 BC–562 BC), son and successor of NABOPOLASSAR. He came to power soon after defeating Egypt at the Battle of CARCHEMISH (605 BC). Nebuchadnezzar subjugated JUDAH in 604 BC, but suffered a heavy defeat by the Egyptians in Palestine (601 BC). In 597 BC he occupied JERUSALEM and installed the puppet king Zedekiah on the throne. After Zedekiah's rebellion, Nebuchadnezzar destroyed the city (586 BC) and the TEMPLE OF JERUSALEM and deported its population to BABYLON. A brilliant military leader, he continued to follow an expansionist strategy. Nebuchadnezzar was responsible for many buildings in Babylon and, according to legend, built the famous Hanging Gardens (one of the SEVEN WONDERS OF THE WORLD) for his Median wife. *See also* BABYLONIAN CAPTIVITY; CHALDAEA

Necker, Jacques (1732–1804) French statesman and banker, director general of finances (1777–81, 1788–89, 1789–90) under LOUIS XVI, b. Switzerland. He acquired a fortune through speculation during the Seven Years' War (1756–63). In his first ministry, Necker made limited reforms to the administration of French finances but was dismissed because of his mishandling of finances needed for French involvement in the American Revolution (1775–83). In 1788 Necker was recalled to deal with the economic crisis and advised calling the STATES-GENERAL. His suggestion of a limited constitutional monarchy was rejected by the royal court and Necker's second dismissal led to riots that culminated in the storming of the BASTILLE. In July 1789 Louis XVI was forced to reappoint Necker, but his moderate stance was unable to prevent the FRENCH REVOLUTION (1789–99) and he resigned.

Nefertiti (active 14th century BC) Queen of Egypt as wife of AKHNATEN. Exceptionally beautiful, she supported her husband's innovative religious ideas. Her best surviving representation is a bust in the Berlin Museum.

Nehru, Jawaharlal (1889–1964) Indian statesman, first prime minister of independent India (1947–64), father of Indira GANDHI. Educated in England, he joined the Indian National CONGRESS in 1919. In 1929 he succeeded his father, Motilal NEHRU, as president of the Congress. During the 1920s and 1930s, Nehru and "Mahatma" GANDHI led nationalist opposition to British rule in India. Between 1921 and 1945 he was imprisoned nine times for non-cooperation with the British. In 1935 India gained provincial autonomy and Nehru rejected the formation of local coalitions between Congress and the MUSLIM LEAGUE, led by Muhammad Ali JINNAH. Towards the end of the 1930s, a rift developed between Nehru and Gandhi, as Nehru came to advocate the importance of industrialization, as opposed to Gandhi's emphasis on rural self-sufficiency. The pair also initially disagreed over India's involvement in World War 2: Nehru argued that India should provide military support for Britain after guarantees of independence, while Gandhi offered unqualified but non-military assistance. Nehru and Gandhi resolved their tactical differences and formed the QUIT INDIA MOVEMENT (1942). Nehru played a leading role in the negotiations with Jinnah and Louis MOUNTBATTEN that led to partition of British India and the creation of the independent states of India and Pakistan (August 1947). The government had to cope with a stream of Hindu refugees from Pakistan, as well as the integration of the semi-autonomous PRINCELY STATES. Although most joined India without incident, Nehru sent troops into the disputed region of KASHMIR and the new nations became embroiled in the first INDIA-PAKISTAN WAR (1948–49). In 1961 Nehru used military force to oust Portugal from Goa – the last remaining colony in India. Nehru's socialist policies sought to promote India's industrial and technological development, while seeking to combat poverty and strengthen the new secular democracy. In foreign affairs, Nehru became a respected leader of the NON-ALIGNED MOVEMENT and a powerful force in the so-called "Third World". Nehru was forced, however, to seek US assistance after a border dispute with China escalated into the brief Sino-Indian War (1962). He died in office, but the "Nehru dynasty" continued to dominate Indian politics for the next three decades.

Nehru, Motilal (1861–1931) Indian nationalist, father of Jawaharlal NEHRU. He was an early member of the Indian National CONGRESS and joined "Mahatma" GANDHI's non-cooperation movement against the British after the AMRITSAR Massacre (1919). He was imprisoned several times. In 1923 Nehru and Chittarangjan Das (1870–1925) founded the Swaraj ("Self-Rule") Party, which sought to disrupt British management of the Indian assembly. He drafted the Nehru Report (1928), which proposed dominion status for India. This was rejected both by the British and by members of the Congress who sought full independence.

Nelson, Horatio, Viscount (1758–1805) British admiral. Joining the navy aged 12, he was a captain at 20. Nelson served under Samuel HOOD at the beginning of the FRENCH REVOLUTIONARY WARS (1792–1802). In 1794 he lost the sight of his right eye in the capture of Calvi, Corsica. Taking action without orders from Admiral John JERVIS, Nelson was largely responsible for Britain's victory over the Spanish fleet at the Battle of Cape St Vincent (1797). Newly promoted to rear admiral, he lost his right arm in battle at Santa Cruz (1797). Nelson's victory at the Battle of ABOUKIR Bay (1798), Egypt, destroyed NAPOLEON's hopes of capturing Britain's eastern empire. Nelson received a hero's welcome at Naples, where he began a love affair with Lady Emma HAMILTON, wife of the British ambassador. In 1799 he helped the Bourbon rulers of Naples escape to Sicily, and later brutally suppressed Naples' republican movement. Nelson crushed the Danish fleet at the First Battle of COPENHAGEN (1801), after ignoring his superior's orders by putting a telescope to his blind eye. At the start of the NAPOLEONIC WARS (1803–15), he was given command of the Mediterranean fleet. In the flagship *Victory*, Nelson led a 22-month siege of Toulon, SE France. He died in the process of securing a brilliant tactical victory over a combined French-Spanish fleet at the Battle of TRAFALGAR (1805).

Nennius (active *c.*800) Welsh historian to whom the *Historia Britonum* ("History of the Britons") is attributed. It contains much on the early history of Britain and the Anglo-Saxon invasions. It also studies early British traditions, especially the legend of King ARTHUR. It is believed that the history is a revision by Nennius of an earlier work.

Nemanja Serbian dynasty (*c.*1168–1371), founded by Stephen Nemanja I. In *c.*1168 Stephen became chief of Raška, sw Serbia, which he expanded to include much of present-day SERBIA. In 1196 he was succeeded by his son, Stephen Nemanja II. I n 1217 Stephen Nemanja II was crowned king of Serbia. In 1219 his brother, Sava, was recognized by the Greek patriarch as archbishop of a national Serbian church. Under STEFAN DUSHAN (r.1331–55), Serbia became the most powerful empire in the Balkans. In 1346 he proclaimed himself emperor of the Serbs, Greeks, Bulgars and Albanians. In 1353 the Serbs captured BELGRADE. Dushan was succeeded by his son, Stephen Urosh V (r.1355–71), last of the Nemanja dynasty. Serbia fell to the Ottoman Empire at the Battle of KOSOVO (1389).

Nenni, Pietro (1891–1980) Italian statesman, vice premier (1946–47, 1963–68). He was editor of the Socialist Party newspaper *Avanti!* before being forced into exile (1926) by Benito MUSSOLINI's fascist regime. Nenni fought for the INTERNATIONAL BRIGADE in the Spanish Civil War (1936–39). During World War 2, he was captured and imprisoned (1943) by the Germans. In 1944 Nenni was released and became secretary general of the Italian Socialist Party (PSI). He served briefly as vice premier under Ferrucio Parri and then as minister of foreign affairs (1946–47) under Alcide DE GASPERI. His decision to serve as vice premier in the centre-left coalition of Aldo MORO led to a split in the PSI.

neoclassicism Late 18th- and early 19th-century movement in art and architecture. Neoclassicism grew out of the Age of ENLIGHTENMENT, whose exponents admired CLASSICAL Greek and Roman art. It was also a reaction to the excesses of the ROCOCO style of the late BAROQUE period. In the 1740s, the archaeological discoveries at HERCULANEUM and POMPEII, Italy, helped to stimulate interest in these ancient civilizations. In sculpture, the style was best exemplified by the elegant work of Antonio Canova (1757–1822). In painting, it was most powerfully visualized by Jacques-Louis David (1748–1825). The most outstanding neoclassical architects were Jacques Germain Soufflot (1713–80) in France, Robert Adam (1728–92) in Britain, and Thomas JEFFERSON (1743–1826) in the United States.

Neolithic (New STONE AGE, 8000 BC–3500 BC) In PREHISTORY, a revolutionary period in human cultural development, following the PALAEOLITHIC era. For millions of years, humans had been hunter-gatherers. In *c.*8000 BC in the Middle East, they began for the first time to cultivate cereal crops and to domesticate animals. The first villages, such as JERICHO, were settled. Between 6000 BC and 2000 BC, Neolithic culture slowly spread to other continents.

NELSON, HORATIO, VISCOUNT

Horatio Nelson broke with rigid tactical and strategic doctrines of his day in favour of imaginative decisions that seized the moment. His "pell-mell" strategy at the Battle of Trafalgar (1805) destroyed Napoleon's plans for an invasion of Britain.

NELSON IN HIS OWN WORDS

"I have only one eye, I have a right to be blind sometimes."
Battle of Copenhagen (1801)
"England expects every man will do his duty."
Battle of Trafalgar (1805)

N

Megalithic monuments, such as Stonehenge, are remnants of Neolithic architecture. By 3500 BC, the villages of the Middle East had developed into cities, ushering in the Bronze Age. *See also* agriculture

Neoplatonism School of philosophy that dominated intellectual thought between *c.*AD 250 and 550, developed by Plotinus. It combined the ideas of Pythagoras, the Stoics, Plato and Aristotle with strains from Judaism, oriental religions and Christianity. Fundamental to Neoplatonism was the concept of "the One", something that transcends knowledge or existence but from which are derived intelligence and the soul. Its influence persisted throughout the Middle Ages and even into the Renaissance.

Nepal *See* country feature

Nerchinsk, Treaty of (1689) Peace agreement between Russia and China. Disputes between the two countries intensified as Russia began to explore the Amur Valley, SE Siberia, in the late-17th century. The Treaty – the first such agreement between China and a Western country – established the border between Russia and China, granting the Amur valley to China, and Transbaikalia (E of Lake Baikal) to Russia. It also created a safe trade route from Russia to Beijing. The Treaty remained the basis of Russo-Chinese relations until 1858.

Neri, Saint Philip (1515–95) Italian priest, mystic and spiritual leader during the Counter-Reformation. In *c.*1533 he settled in Rome, where he studied, taught and dedicated himself to a life of austerity. Neri was ordained in 1551 and joined the religious community at San Girolamo della Carità. The popularity of his sermons prompted the building of an oratory for religious meetings. In 1575 Pope Gregory XIII granted him the Santa Maria, Vallicella, where he founded the Institute of the Oratory (also called Oratorians). Neri persuaded Pope Clement VIII to end (1595) the excommunication of Henry IV of France. He was canonized in 1622. His feast day is 26 May.

Nero (AD 37–68) (Nero Claudius Caesar) Roman emperor (54–68), b. Lucius Domitius Ahenobarbus. In 49 his mother, Agrippina the Younger, married her uncle, Emperor Claudius, and persuaded him to adopt Nero as his successor. In 54 Claudius and his natural son, Britannicus, were murdered. Under the guidance of Seneca, Nero at first pursued moderate policies, and his early reign was heralded as a new golden age. This soon came to an end and Nero became one of the most notorious of rulers, neglecting government in favour of sex, poetry, sport, music and cult practices. He was responsible for the murders of his half-brother, his mother and his first wife. In 64 Nero was widely censured, probably unjustly, for the fire that destroyed half of Rome. He blamed the Christians and began their persecution. A plot to overthrow him (65), the Conspiracy of Piso, was foiled, but later, faced with widespread rebellion and lacking the support of the Praetorian Guard, Nero committed suicide.

Nerva, Marcus Cocceius (AD 30–98) Roman statesman, emperor (96–98). Because of his neutrality, he was chosen by the Senate to succeed Domitian, whose rule had become increasingly despotic. Nerva reformed land laws in favour of the poor, revised taxation and tolerated the Christians, but could not control the Praetorian Guard. He adopted Trajan and assured his smooth accession.

Nestorianism Christian heretical doctrine that stresses the independence of the divine and human natures of Jesus Christ, as opposed to the orthodox belief that Christ is one person who is at once both God and man. The heresy was associated with Nestorius, bishop of Constantinople (d. *c.*451). It was condemned by the councils of Ephesus (431) and Chalcedon (451), and Nestorius was deposed and banished. In 489 Nestorius' supporters migrated to Nisibis, Iran, and Nestorianism flourished in Arabia and spread to India and China. In 1551 a group of Nestorians (Chaldeans) reunited with Rome; the remaining group became the Assyrian Church. *See also* Monophysitism

Netanyahu, Binyamin (1949–) Israeli statesman, prime minister (1996–99). He served as permanent representative (1984–88) to the United Nations (UN) before becoming deputy minister of foreign affairs. In 1993 he became leader of the right-wing Likud. Netanyahu defeated Shimon Peres in the elections that followed the assassination of Yitzhak Rabin. His uncompromising stance over Israeli settlement on the West Bank and Likud's opposition to the Israeli-Palestinian Accord stalled the peace process in the Middle East. Netanyahu and Yasir Arafat signed the Wye Agreement (1998), but the subsequent withdrawal of the religious right from the coalition prompted fresh elections (1999), in which Netanyahu was defeated by Labour Party leader Ehud Barak.

Netherlands, The *See* country feature, page 295

Neto, Agostinho (1922–79) Angolan statesman, poet and doctor, first president of independent Angola (1975–79). He spearheaded a revival of Angolan culture and was imprisoned for his opposition to Portuguese rule (1955–57, 1960–62). In 1962 Neto escaped to Morocco, where he became leader of the Popular Movement for the Liberation of Angola (MPLA). When Angola gained independence, the MPLA, aided by Cuba, emerged as the dominant party and Neto became president. During his presidency, Angola began its transition to a socialist economy.

Neustria Western part of the kingdom of the Franks during the Merovingian period. It was formed (AD 511) when the empire of Clovis I was divided among his four sons, and comprised the area N of the River Seine and W of the River Meuse. Ongoing conflict between Neustria and Austrasia, the E part of the empire, ended in 687 with the victory of the Austrasian leader, Pepin of Herstal, at Tertry.

Neutrality Acts (1935–39) US legislation enacted before World War 2 in an effort to maintain the country's neutrality. The 1935 Act declared an arms embargo against any nations engaged in war. In 1936 the embargo was extended and loans to belligerents were prohibited. The 1937 Act, in response to the outbreak of the Spanish Civil War (1936–39), banned munitions to either side in civil wars. After the outbreak of World War 2, the Acts were gradually relaxed by President Franklin Roosevelt. In 1939 limited arms and munitions sales were allowed, and in 1941 US merchant ships were permitted to be armed and to deliver cargo to belligerent countries. *See also* isolationism

Neva, Battle of the (15 July 1240) Victory of the Novgorod Russians over the invading Swedes on the banks of the River Neva, NW Russia. Alexander Yaroslavich (afterwards known as Alexander Nevski) led the Novgorod forces that destroyed the Swedish army and saved Russia from Swedish conquest.

Nevada Mountain state in W United States; the capital is Carson City. There is archaeological evidence of a Clovis culture in the region more than 10,000 years ago. The Anasazi inhabited Nevada from *c.*300 BC to *c.*AD 1100, when they began to be displaced by the Paiute, Shoshone and Washoe. Spanish missionaries explored the region from 1776. John Frémont was the first white man to properly explore (1843, 1845) the Great Basin, but the Donner Party's attempt to blaze a trail (1846) across the Sierra Nevada ended in tragedy. The United States acquired the region at the end of the Mexican War (1846–48) and it was subsumed into Utah Territory. Fortune hunters flocked to Nevada after the discovery (1859) of rich deposits of gold and silver in the Comstock mines, and Nevada Territory was created in 1861. Nevada's economy was transformed by the legalization of gambling (1931) and the completion (1936) of the Hoover Dam. Area: 286,297sq km (110,539sq mi). Pop. (1990) 1,201,833.

Neville, Richard, Earl of Warwick *See* Warwick, Richard Neville, Earl of

Neville's Cross, Battle of (17 October 1346) English victory over the Scots. A Scottish army under David II, attempting to profit from Edward III's absence in France, invaded N England, but was crushed by English forces near Durham, NE England. David was captured and imprisoned until 1357, leaving the English free to concentrate on the war with France.

Nevski, Alexander *See* Alexander Nevski, Saint

New Amsterdam *See* New York City

New Brunswick Atlantic province in E Canada, on the US-Canadian border; the capital is Fredericton. In 1534 Jacques Cartier became the first European to explore the region and a French settlement was established in 1604. It formed part of the territory of Acadia that was ceded to Britain in 1713. Many Loyalists entered the region from the American colonies during the American Revolution (1775–83). In 1784 New Brunswick was created a separate province from Nova Scotia. In 1867 New Brunswick

N

NEPAL

AREA: 140,800sq km (54,363sq mi)
POPULATION: 21,953,000
CAPITAL (POPULATION): Katmandu (419,073)
GOVERNMENT: Constitutional monarchy
ETHNIC GROUPS: Newar, Indian, Tibetan, Sherpa
LANGUAGES: Nepali
GDP PER CAPITA (1995): US$1170

Independent kingdom in central Asia. Siddhartha Gautama (Buddha) was born (*c.*563 BC) in Lumbini, SW Nepal, and Buddhism and Hinduism co-exist in modern Nepal. In the 4th century AD, the Newar dynasty of Licchavi was established in the Katmandu valley, a vital strategic post on the trade route across the Himalayas. From the 10th to the 18th century, Nepal was ruled by the Malla dynasty. In 1769 the Gurkha ruler, Prithvi Narayan Shah, overthrew the Mallas and established a unified state, based around Katmandu. A Gurkha invasion of Tibet was repulsed by China in 1792. Gurkha expansion into N India led to war (1814–16) with the British. British victory forced Nepal to ratify its present boundaries and accept permanent British representation. From 1846 to 1951 Nepal was ruled by hereditary prime ministers from the Rana family.

In 1923 Britain recognized Nepal as a sovereign state. In 1951 the Rana government was overthrown, and a monarchy re-established. In 1959 the first national constitution was adopted and an ensuing general election was won by B.P. Koirala of the Nepali Congress Party (NCP). In 1960 King Mahendra dissolved parliament and introduced a political system based on village councils (*panchayat*). In 1972 Mahendra was succeeded by his son Birendra (r.1945–). In 1990 *c.*150 protestors were shot by police during mass demonstrations for democracy. A new constitution established a power-sharing arrangement between the king and an elected government. The ensuing elections (1991) were won by G.P. Koirala of the NCP, brother of the previous prime minister. In 1994 fresh elections resulted in a coalition government dominated by communists. Nepal suffered political instability under a succession of minority governments. In 1998 Koirala returned to lead a new coalition.

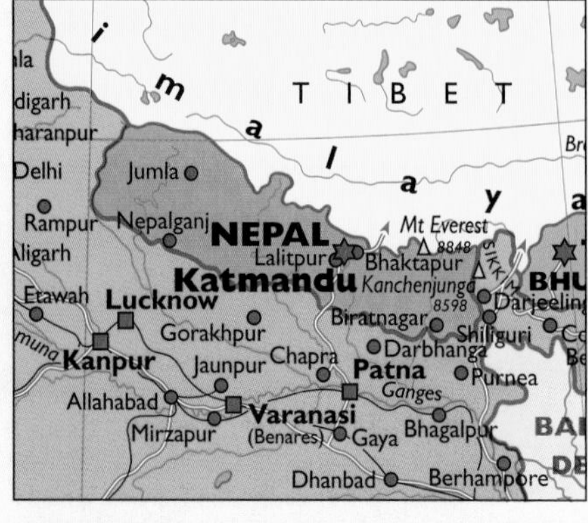

NEVADA
Statehood :
31 October 1864
Nickname :
The Silver State
State motto :
All for our country

joined Nova Scotia, QUÉBEC and ONTARIO to form the Dominion of CANADA. Area: 73,437sq km (28,354sq mi). Pop. (1991) 723,900.

New Caledonia (*Nouvelle Calédonie*) French overseas territory in the SW Pacific Ocean; the capital is Nouméa. Inhabited by Melanesians for more than 3000 years, British Captain James COOK discovered the islands in 1774 and they were annexed by France in 1853. The French brutally suppressed native uprisings against colonial rule and New Caledonia became a French penal colony. In 1946 the archipelago became a French overseas territory. In 1984 the French granted self-government after increased agitation for independence. In a 1998 referendum, voters approved a plan that will grant increasing autonomy to New Caledonia, although France will retain control over the law enforcement and legal systems, and that will delay a further referendum on independence for 15 years. Area: 18,575sq km (7170sq mi). Pop. (1989) 164,182.

Newcastle (under Lyme), Thomas Pelham-Holles, Duke of (1693–1768) British statesman, prime minister (1754–56, 1757–62). A wealthy WHIG landowner, he supported the succession of GEORGE I (r.1714–27). Newcastle was secretary of state (1724–54) first under Robert WALPOLE and then under his brother Henry PELHAM. He succeeded Pelham as prime minister. Newcastle was forced to resign after defeats at the start of the SEVEN YEARS' WAR (1756–63), but returned as prime minister in a coalition with William PITT (THE ELDER). While Pitt managed Britain's war effort, Newcastle concentrated on maintaining support for the ministry by skilful distribution of patronage. He was succeeded as prime minister by the Earl of BUTE, favourite of GEORGE III.

Newcastle (upon Tyne), William Cavendish, 1st Duke of (1592–1676) English Royalist commander during the English CIVIL WAR (1642–45). In 1642 CHARLES I gave him command of Royalist forces in the N of England. In 1643 Newcastle captured most of Yorkshire from Lord FAIRFAX's Parliamentary forces, but was subsequently defeated by Oliver CROMWELL in Lincolnshire. The tactical errors of Prince RUPERT contributed to defeat at the Battle of MARSTON MOOR (1644) and Newcastle fled into exile in the Netherlands. He returned to England after the RESTORATION of CHARLES II in 1660. Newcastle was a great patron of literature, supporting writers such as Ben Jonson (1572–1637) and John Dryden (1631–1700).

New Deal (1933–39) Programme for social and economic reconstruction in the United States launched by President Franklin ROOSEVELT and designed to restore prosperity after the GREAT DEPRESSION. It was based on massive and unprecedented federal intervention in the economy. Much of the New Deal was implemented in the first hundred days of Roosevelt's presidency, and concentrated on relieving unemployment. A number of agencies were created to coordinate relief work and create jobs, including the National Recovery Administration (NRA), the Agricultural Adjustment Agency (AAA), the TENNESSEE VALLEY AUTHORITY (TVA) and the PUBLIC WORKS ADMINISTRATION (PWA). To tighten control over the economy, the Securities and Exchange Commission (SEC) and the Federal Communications Commission (FCC) were founded, and additional legislation, such as the Trade Agreements Act (1934), was passed. During a second phase of activity, the New Deal sought to improve working conditions, strengthen the rights of UNIONS and improve social welfare provision. Between 1935 and 1939 it established the social security system. The SUPREME COURT declared unconstitutional much of the New Deal legislation, but backed down after Roosevelt threatened to reorganize the Court. Industrial expansion, full employment and agricultural prosperity were achieved less by the New Deal than by increases in military expenditure during World War 2. The programme did, however, lay the basis for future federal management of the economy and provision of social welfare. *See also* AGRICULTURAL ADJUSTMENT ACT; FAIR DEAL; WORKS PROGRESS ADMINISTRATION

New Democratic Party (NDP) Canadian political organization. It was founded (1961) when the Co-operative Commonwealth Federation (CCF), a party representing labour and small farmers, reorganized itself and entered into a close relationship with the Canadian trade unions. The Party has a broadly democratic-socialist agenda. Under the leadership (1972–74) of David Lewis, its 31 members sided with the LIBERAL PARTY in a coalition government. The Party has held power intermittently in Manitoba, Ontario, Saskatchewan and British Columbia.

New Economic Policy (NEP) (1921–28) Plan to restore the Soviet economy after the RUSSIAN CIVIL WAR (1918–20). Faced by a peasant rebellion in 1921, LENIN dropped "war communism" and relaxed controls on agriculture and light industry. The NEP replaced the requisition of grain from the peasantry with a fixed tax, and allowed peasants to sell their surplus on the open market. It also permitted the reintroduction of private ownership. The NEP was seen by some as a betrayal of Soviet COMMUNISM and was abandoned by Joseph STALIN in favour of the forcible COLLECTIVIZATION of agriculture instituted by the first FIVE-YEAR PLAN.

New England Region in NE United States, made up of the states of MAINE, NEW HAMPSHIRE, VERMONT, CONNECTICUT, MASSACHUSETTS and RHODE ISLAND. The region was named by English navigator Captain John Smith, who explored its shores in 1614, and settled by English Puritans. New England was the centre of events leading up to the American Revolution (1775–83), and the birthplace of a national culture. It led calls for the abolition of slavery and was a staunch supporter of the Union in the American Civil War (1861–65).

New England Confederation (United Colonies of New England) Alliance of the four Puritan colonies of Massachusetts Bay, Plymouth, Connecticut and New Haven. It was established (1643) primarily for the purposes of defence. The Confederation mounted a successful joint military campaign against Native Americans in S New England in KING PHILIP'S WAR (1675–76), but was dissolved in 1684.

Newfoundland and Labrador Atlantic province in E Canada, consisting of the mainland region of Labrador and the island of Newfoundland; the capital is St John's (on Newfoundland). Norsemen are believed to have landed on the coast of Labrador in *c*.AD 1000. John CABOT reached the island in 1497. The region was disputed by Britain and France until the Treaty of Paris (1763) granted it to Britain. It became a British colony in 1824 but was self-governing until the GREAT DEPRESSION of the 1930s devastated its economy and control reverted to Britain. In 1949 Newfoundland became Canada's tenth province. Area: 404,420sq km (156,185sq mi). Pop. (1991) 568,474.

New France (1534–1765) French colonies in North America. The area was named (1534) by Jacques CARTIER, who explored the St Lawrence River, Newfoundland. In 1604 Samuel de CHAMPLAIN founded Port Royal (now Annapolis Royal, Nova Scotia) – the first French colony in North America. QUÉBEC was founded in 1608 and the Company of New France was created (1627) to govern the colony of New France. In 1663 LOUIS XIV of France incorporated New France as crown land and colonization increased rapidly. Louis JOLLIET added (1673) the Mississippi valley to the territories of New France, and Sieur d'IBERVILLE founded Louisiana in 1699. However, France was forced to cede its North American colonies to Britain at the end of the FRENCH AND INDIAN WARS (1689–1763) and its last territory, Louisiana, was sold to the United States in the LOUISIANA PURCHASE (1803).

New Frontier (1961–63) US legislative programme of President John KENNEDY. It included tax reforms and increased expenditure on social reforms and welfare as well as ambitious new projects, such as the PEACE CORPS and a commitment to SPACE EXPLORATION. Congress opposed much of the package, although significant civil rights and tax reform legislation were pushed through by Lyndon JOHNSON after Kennedy's death.

New Granada, Viceroyalty of Region of colonial SPANISH AMERICA. In 1536 the Spanish conquistador Gonzalo Jiménez de Quesada travelled into the interior of modern-day Colombia, which he called New Granada. In 1543 it became part of the Viceroyalty of PERU. In the 18th century, the Spanish created the separate Viceroyalty of New Granada, which included present-day Colombia, Panama, Ecuador and Venezuela. Its capital was Santa Fé (now Bogotá). In 1810 the Viceroyalty collapsed but Spain regained control and established the United Provinces of New Granada (1814–16). Spanish rule was decisively ended by Simón BOLÍVAR in 1823, and the region became part of Gran Colombia. In 1830 Venezuela and Ecuador seceded from Gran Colombia and the name New Granada was adopted (1830–58) by Colombia.

New Guinea Island of the E Malay archipelago in the W Pacific Ocean. The second-largest island in the world (after Greenland), the first humans arrived *c*.50,000 years ago. New Guinea was discovered by Europeans in 1511, and claimed by the Spanish in the 16th century. In 1828 the Dutch EAST INDIA COMPANY claimed W New Guinea. Germany and Britain annexed the NE and SE of the island respectively in 1884. In 1904 the British-administered part was transferred to Australia, and during World War 1 Australian forces seized German New Guinea. The W half, IRIAN JAYA, became a province of Indonesia in 1969. The E half eventually achieved independence as PAPUA NEW GUINEA in 1975. Area: 885,780sq km (342,000sq mi).

New Hampshire State in NE United States, on the Canadian border; the capital is Concord. The region was inhabited by *c*.12,000 Algonquian-speaking Native Americans when the first English explorer landed on the coast in 1603. The first English settlement was made in 1623 and New Hampshire was administered as part of the Massachusetts Bay Colony until 1679, when it became a separate royal province. New Hampshire was a major battleground of the FRENCH AND INDIAN WARS (1689–1763) as the Native Americans sided with the French against the British. On 12 December 1774, New Hampshire patriots captured Fort William and Mary (now Fort Constitution) in one of the first armed struggles against British colonial rule. In 1776 New Hampshire became the first state to declare independence from Britain. Because it holds the first presidential primary, New Hampshire is regarded as a crucial yardstick for the hopes of candidates. Area: 24,097sq km (9304sq mi). Pop. (1996) 1,162,481.

Ne Win, U (1911–) Burmese statesman and general, prime minister (1958–60), head of state (1962–74) and president (1974–81). He fought alongside AUNG SAN in the Burmese liberation movement and, after independence in 1948, became a commander in chief of the army. Ne Win replaced U NU as leader of a caretaker government, before seizing power in a military coup (1962). He established a military dictatorship and rapidly nationalized Burma's major industries. In 1964 Ne Win created a one-party state, governed by the Burma Socialist Programme Party (BSPP). His corrupt and repressive regime plunged Burma into poverty and famine. In 1988 Ne Win resigned and the BSPP was replaced by the State Law and Order Restoration Council (SLORC).

New Jersey State on the Atlantic coast of the E United States; the capital is Trenton. When the first Europeans landed in 1609, there were *c*.10,000 Delaware living in the region. The Dutch West India Company formed trading posts from the 1620s and established the colony of NEW NETHERLAND. In 1664 the Dutch governor Peter

NEW HAMPSHIRE
Statehood :
21 June 1788
Nickname :
The Granite State
State motto :
Live free or die

N

NEW JERSEY
Statehood :
18 December 1787
Nickname :
The Garden State
State motto :
Liberty and prosperity

Stuyvesant ceded the colony to England. It was divided into the provinces of New Jersey and New York. From 1676 to 1702 New Jersey was subdivided: East Jersey was controlled by Sir George Carteret, while West Jersey went to the Quakers led by William Penn. Queen Anne reunited New Jersey. The region was a major battleground of the American Revolution (1775–83), including the conflicts at Trenton (1776) and Monmouth (1778). New Jersey underwent dramatic industrial expansion during the 19th century. In 1910 Woodrow Wilson was elected governor after promising to restrict the power of trusts. Area: 20,295sq km (7836sq mi). Pop. (1995) 7,987,933.

New Jersey Plan *See* Constitutional Convention

Newman, John Henry (1801–90) English cleric and theologian. As leader (1833–42) of the Oxford Movement, he argued for a reassertion of theology and ritual in the Church of England. In *Tract 90* (1841), Newman claimed that the Thirty-nine Articles, the foundation of the Reformed Church in England, could be reconciled with Roman Catholicism. He resigned from the Anglican Church and converted to Catholicism in 1845. In 1879 Newman became a cardinal. He is perhaps best remembered for his autobiography *Apologia pro vita sua* (1864).

New Mexico State in SW United States, on the border with Mexico; the capital is Santa Fe. The first inhabitants of Mexico were members of the Clovis and Folsom cultures. These nomadic cultures were succeeded by the settled agricultural communities of the Anasazi. In the 15th century, these Pueblo peoples were subject to raids from the Navajo and Apache. In the late 1520s, Spanish explorer Álvar Núñez Cabeza de Vaca became the first European to visit New Mexico. Francisco Vásquez de Coronado was later attracted (1540) by its fabled cities of gold. Spanish colonization began in the 1590s and Santa Fe was established as the capital of the colony in 1610. The colony was destroyed during the Pueblo Revolt (1680) and the Spanish did not return until 1692. Pueblo and Spanish settlements alike were attacked by the Apache and Comanche during the 18th century. In 1821 the region became part of the new Republic of Mexico. During the Mexican War (1846–48), General Stephen Kearny captured New Mexico for the United States in 1846, and further territory was acquired by the Gadsden Purchase (1853). The population swelled after the arrival of the railroad in 1879. In 1943 the US government created a nuclear weapons' laboratory at Los Alamos; the world's first atomic bomb was exploded at Alamogordo in 1945. Area: 314,334sq km (121,335sq mi). Pop. (1996) 1,713,407.

New Model Army Reformed Parliamentary army in the English Civil War (1642–45). Formed in 1645 by Oliver Cromwell and Thomas Fairfax, it was better organized, trained and disciplined than any comparable Royalist force. After a decisive victory at Naseby (1645), the Army emerged as a powerful political force and was responsible for Pride's Purge (1648) of the Long Parliament. The radical Leveller faction within the New Model Army was suppressed by Cromwell. The Army ensured the survival of the Commonwealth with victories in the battles of Dunbar (1650) and Worcester (1651).

New Netherland Dutch colony in North America founded (1624) by the Dutch West India Company. Dutch settlements were established at Fort Nassau (now Albany) and New Amsterdam (now New York City). The last and most able governor, Peter Stuyvesant, annexed New Sweden (1655). The English, basing their claim to the region on the explorations of John Cabot and Henry Hudson, gained control of the colony in 1664 and divided it into two colonies, New York and New Jersey.

New Orleans City and river port in SE Louisiana, United States. The city was founded (1718) by the French explorer Sieur de Bienville. Ceded to Spain in 1763, New Orleans was acquired by the United States in the Louisiana Purchase (1803). The scene of the final battle in the War of 1812, the city flourished as a major cotton port in the early 19th century and became the fourth-largest city in the United States. The Union capture of New Orleans (1862) was a major blow to the Confederacy in the American Civil War (1861–65). It plays host to an annual Mardi Gras festival. Pop. (1994) 484,149.

New Orleans, Battle of (8 January 1815) Final conflict in the War of 1812. It took place two weeks after the Treaty of Ghent was signed because news of the Treaty had not reached New Orleans, Louisiana. The British attempt to capture the city was thwarted by the fortifications erected by General Andrew Jackson. The British suffered more than 2500 casualties to only 71 American wounded.

New Orleans, Battle of (24–25 June 1862) Union victory in the American Civil War (1861–65). A Union naval force, led by David Farragut, broke through Confederate defences and sailed up the Mississippi River to New Orleans, Louisiana. The *c*.3000 Confederate troops withdrew and the city fell to the Union.

New South Wales State in SE Australia; the capital is Sydney. It became the site of the first British colony in Australia, when Captain James Cook landed at Botany Bay in 1770. In 1788 Captain Arthur Phillip established a penal colony at Port Jackson (now Sydney Harbour). The Aboriginal population was devastated by disease and warfare brought by the British. New South Wales prospered under the governorship (1810–21) of Lachlan Macquarie. Victoria and Queensland were separated from New South Wales in the 1850s and European settlement increased rapidly. In 1856 New South Wales achieved self-government. Economic depression in the early 1890s led to industrial unrest and the formation of the Australian Labor Party, which would dominate state politics in the early 20th century. In 1901 New South Wales became a state of the Commonwealth of Australia. Area: 801,430sq km (309,180sq mi). Pop. (1991) 5,730,947.

New Spain, Viceroyalty of One of four viceroyalties in Spanish America. At its height, New Spain included present-day Mexico, Central America, SW United States, Florida and the West Indies. The first viceroy (1535–49), Antonio de Mendoza, sponsored the expeditions of Francisco Coronado. A succession of viceroys sought to exploit the region's resources and convert the natives to Christianity. Spanish colonial rule reduced the native population from 25 million to 1 million. The Viceroyalty was finally conquered by Agustín de Iturbide in 1821. *See also* New Granada, Viceroyalty of

New Testament Second part of the Bible, consisting of 27 books all originally written in Greek after AD 45 and concerning the life and teachings of Jesus Christ. It begins with three Synoptic Gospels (Matthew, Mark and Luke), which present a common narrative of Christ's life and ministry, and a fourth gospel (John), which is more of a theological meditation. The Acts of the Apostles record the early development and spread of Christianity. Next are 21 letters (Epistles) addressed to specific early church communities; the New Testament ends with the Revelation of St John the Divine (otherwise known as the Apocalypse), which is an interpretation of history designed to demonstrate the sovereignty of God.

Newton, Sir Isaac (1642–1727) English scientist. His main works are *Philosophiae Naturalis Principia Mathematica* (1687) and *Opticks* (1704). In the former, Newton outlined his laws of motion and proposed the

NEW MEXICO
Statehood :
16 January 1912
Nickname :
The Land of Enchantment
State motto :
It grows as it goes

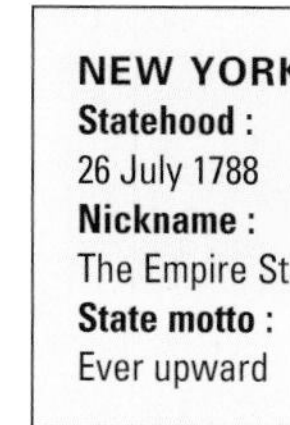

NEW YORK
Statehood :
26 July 1788
Nickname :
The Empire State
State motto :
Ever upward

principle of universal gravitation; in the latter, he showed that white light is made up of colours of the spectrum and proposed a particle theory of light. In the 1660s Newton created the first system of calculus, but did not publish it until Gottfried Leibniz had presented his own system in 1684. In *c*.1671 he built the first reflecting telescope. Newton was president of the Royal Society (1703–27). In 1705 he became the first person to be knighted for scientific work. Newton's theory of celestial mechanics remained unchallenged until Albert Einstein's theory of relativity.

New York State in NE United States; the capital is Albany. New York City is by far the largest city in the state. In 1609, when Henry Hudson sailed up the river that now bears his name, the region was inhabited by the Mahican and the Iroquois Confederacy. The alliance between these two tribes and the British enabled the latter to emerge victorious from the French and Indian Wars (1689–1763). The first European colony, New Netherland, was established by the Dutch in 1624. In 1664 it was claimed by Charles II of England and granted to his son, the Duke of York and Albany (later James II). In 1685 it was subsumed into the Dominion of New England. The dominance of aristocratic landlords and city merchants sparked Leisler's Rebellion (1689–91). New York was a major battleground in the American Revolution (1775–83) and had the largest concentration of Loyalists of any colony. After the War, it became one of the 13 original states of the Union. De Witt Clinton encouraged the opening of the Erie Canal (1825), which proved an enormous stimulus to New York's growth. The political antagonism between upstate New York and New York City was fuelled by the corrupt Tammany Hall organization that dominated municipal government. Four state governors – Martin Van Buren, Grover Cleveland, Theodore and Franklin Roosevelt – have gone on to serve as president of the United States. Area: 127,190sq km (49,108sq mi). Pop. (1996) 18,184,774. *See also* Albany Regency; Anti-Rent War; Conkling, Roscoe; Harriman, William Averell; Hughes, Charles Evans; Rockefeller, Nelson Aldrich; Seward, William Henry; Smith, Alfred Emanuel; Tilden, Samuel Jones; Tweed, William Marcy

New York City City and port at the mouth of the Hudson River, SE New York; the most populous city in the United States. New York City is comprised of five boroughs: the Bronx, Brooklyn, Manhattan, Queens and Staten Island. In 1624 Manhattan Island was settled by the Dutch West India Company and was bought (1626) from Native Americans by Peter Minuit. Governor Peter Stuyvesant founded (1653) the city of New Amsterdam at the S end of Manhattan. In 1664 the British captured the colony and renamed it New York. Held by the British for much of the American Revolution (1775–83), New York City later served as the first capital (1789–90) of the fledgling United States. After the opening of the Erie Canal (1825), it became the commercial, financial and industrial heart of the United States. Tammany Hall, the local Democratic organization, rose to prominence under Aaron Burr and, controlled by William "Boss" Tweed, became a byword for corruption. During the American Civil War (1861–65), New York City was shattered by the Draft Riots (1863), which claimed *c*.2000 lives. In the late-19th century, New York City was transformed by a mass influx of European immigrants, many of whom passed through Ellis Island. The Statue of Liberty was built to celebrate the centenary of US independence in 1876. The completion (1883) of Brooklyn Bridge merged Manhattan and Brooklyn, and the present five boroughs were incorporated as a city in 1898. The election of Fiorello La Guardia as city mayor in 1933 marked the end of Tammany Hall's dominance of municipal politics. Other monuments and sights of interest include the Empire State Building, Rockefeller Center, the Metropolitan Museum of Art, the Museum of Modern Art, the Guggenheim Museum, Lincoln Center, Carnegie Hall, Times Square and the theatre district of Broadway. Pop. (1994) 7,333,253.

New Zealand *See* country feature, page 296

Ney, Michel (1769–1815) French marshal, one of the most brilliant of Napoleon's commanders. He fought bravely during the FRENCH REVOLUTIONARY WARS and the NAPOLEONIC WARS, notably at JENA (1807), Elchingen (1808), BORODINO and the retreat from Moscow (both 1812). It was Ney who informed NAPOLEON I that he had lost the support of his generals, thus forcing the emperor to abdicate in 1814. Ney accepted the BOURBON restoration, but rejoined Napoleon during the HUNDRED DAYS and fought heroically in the defeat at WATERLOO (1815). He was later court-martialled and executed as a traitor. *See also* WELLINGTON, ARTHUR WELLESLEY, DUKE OF

Nez Percé (Fr. Pierced Nose) Largest and most powerful of the Sahaptian NATIVE NORTH AMERICANS. Their Plateau culture was transformed by the acquisition of horses in the early 18th century, enabling them to hunt bison and trade with other native tribes in the Rockies. After contact with the LEWIS AND CLARK EXPEDITION in 1805, the Nez Percé suffered from white settlement in Oregon and were forced onto a reservation by a treaty with the US government in 1855. The discovery of gold (1860) on the reservation led to the tearing up of the agreement and a full-scale war in 1877. Chief JOSEPH and *c.*250 Nez Percé fought a five-month battle against 5000 US soldiers, before being forced to surrender and relocate to Oklahoma. Today, *c.*1500 Nez Percé remain on a reservation in Idaho.

Ngo Dinh Diem *See* DIEM, NGO DINH

Nguyen Last Vietnamese dynasty (1802–1945). The Nguyens came to prominence during the 16th century. Conflict with the equally ambitious and powerful Trinh family led to a *de facto* division of VIETNAM (1673): the Nguyens controlled the S, while the Trinhs held the N. For the next 100 years, the Nguyens consolidated their power base in Vietnam and expanded into Cham and Cambodia. A peasant rebellion (1771) reunited Vietnam, until Nguyen Anh recovered leadership of the country and claimed the throne as GIA LONG. The Nguyen rulers resisted foreign intervention in Vietnam, frustrating French colonial ambitions in Southeast Asia. As a result, the French invaded (1858), completing their conquest by 1885. The Nguyens remained on the throne, although their power was nominal, until the last emperor, BAO DAI, abdicated when Vietnam declared independence (1949). *See also* INDOCHINA

Nguyen Van Thieu (1923–) Vietnamese statesman, president (1967–75) of South Vietnam. He joined the VIET MINH in 1945, but left because of their communist tendencies. He then joined the French forces against the Viet Minh. Nguyen was a leading figure in the coup against Ngo Dinh DIEM in 1963, and acted as head of state (1965–67) before being elected president. As president, Nguyen imposed authoritarian control over South Vietnam and received military and financial support from the United States in order to prosecute the VIETNAM WAR (1955–75) against the VIET CONG. Nguyen continued to wage war even after the withdrawal of US troops in 1973. In 1975, as communist forces advanced on the capital, Saigon (now Ho Chi Minh City), Nguyen resigned and fled into exile.

Nicaea, councils of Two important ECUMENICAL COUNCILS of the Christian church held in Nicaea (now Iznik, Turkey). The **First** Council of Nicaea (325) was convoked by CONSTANTINE I (THE GREAT) to resolve the problems caused by the emergence of ARIANISM. It promulgated the NICENE CREED, affirming belief in the divinity of Christ. The **Second** Council (787) was summoned by the patriarch Tarasius to deal with the ICONOCLASTIC CONTROVERSY.

Nicaea, Empire of (1204–61) Small state centred on the city of Nicaea (now Iznik, Turkey). In 1204 the Fourth CRUSADE overthrew the BYZANTINE EMPIRE and established the Latin Empire of CONSTANTINOPLE under BALDWIN I. Theodore I (Lascaris) founded the rival Empire of Nicaea as a Byzantine state. Nicaea successfully defended itself against the Latin Empire and the SELJUKS and, under the leadership (1222–54) of JOHN III DUKAS VATATZES, captured EPIRUS – another centre of Byzantine resistance – in 1246. In 1259 MICHAEL VIII (PALAEOLOGUS) usurped the throne of Nicaea and, supported by MANFRED of Sicily, regained Constantinople (now ISTANBUL, Turkey) in 1261, establishing the Palaeologus dynasty (the last rulers of the Byzantine Empire).

Nicaragua *See* country feature, page 297

Nicene Creed Statement of Christian faith named after the First Council of NICAEA (325). Its exact origin is, however, uncertain. The Nicene Creed defends the orthodox Christian doctrine of the TRINITY against ARIANISM. It is

NETHERLANDS, THE

AREA: 41,526sq km (16,033sq mi)
POPULATION: 15,178,000
CAPITAL (POPULATION): Amsterdam (724,096)
GOVERNMENT: Constitutional monarchy
ETHNIC GROUPS: Netherlander 95%, Indonesian, Turkish, Moroccan, German
LANGUAGES: Dutch (official)
RELIGIONS: Christianity (Roman Catholic 34%, Dutch Reformed Church 17%, Calvinist 8%), Islam 3%
GDP PER CAPITA (1995): US$19,950

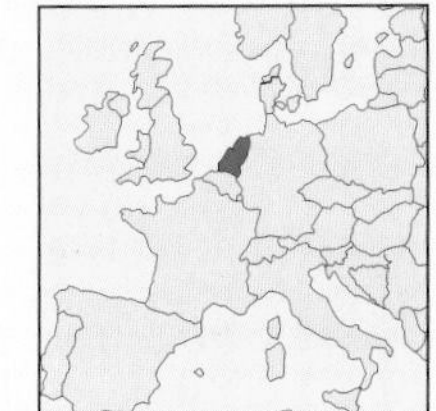

Kingdom in NW Europe. ACHEULIAN, MOUSTERIAN, MAGDALENIAN and MAGLEMOSIAN artefacts have been unearthed in the Netherlands. The BEAKER CULTURE was prevalent in the transition between the NEOLITHIC and BRONZE ages, while the IRON AGE was marked by the Celtic cultures of HALLSTATT and LA TÈNE.

In the 1st century BC, the LOW COUNTRIES were conquered by the Romans, who divided the region into two provinces: Belgica and Germania Inferior. The Romans founded the towns of Nijmegen and Maastricht. In the 5th century AD, the Romans were supplanted by the FRANKS. Under CLOVIS I (r. *c.*481–511), the MEROVINGIAN dynasty gained much of GAUL. The bishopric of UTRECHT was founded in 696 and became the epicentre for the spread of Christianity throughout the N Netherlands. CHARLEMAGNE (r.768–814) conquered the Frankish empire and established the CAROLINGIAN dynasty.

Under the control of the HOLY ROMAN EMPIRE from the 10th century, secular principalities, such as HOLLAND, emerged. In 1477 the Low Countries passed to the HABSBURGS. In the 16th century, towns, such as AMSTERDAM and ANTWERP, became commercial centres and strongholds of CALVINISM. PHILIP II's (r.1556–98) attempt to impose Catholicism led to the REVOLT OF THE NETHERLANDS (1567–79). The Duke of ALBA's brutal attempts to assert Spanish authority merely fuelled the resistance led by WILLIAM I (THE SILENT) and LOUIS OF NASSAU.

The Union of Utrecht (1579) established the UNITED PROVINCES OF THE NETHERLANDS, while the S provinces became known as the Spanish Netherlands (now BELGIUM). In 1581 the United Provinces declared independence. MAURICE OF NASSAU and Johan van OLDENBARNEVELDT insured the survival of the new state. The foundation (1602) of the Dutch EAST INDIA COMPANY marked the beginnings of empire (*see* DUTCH EAST INDIES). Under FREDERICK HENRY (r.1625–49), the House of ORANGE became the dominant force within the United Provinces. The Dutch won a series of victories over the Spanish, who recognized the independence of the United Provinces at the Peace of WESTPHALIA (1648).

The state was governed (1653–72) by Jan de WITT for most of the "first stadtholderless period". The Second DUTCH WAR (1665–67) was concluded by the Treaty of BREDA (1667), in which Britain confirmed Dutch imperial possessions. In 1672 France invaded, de Witt was murdered and William of Orange (later WILLIAM III of England) was appointed stadtholder. William's victory in the Third Dutch War (1672–74) was confirmed by the Treaties of NIJMEGEN (1678–79). William and his wife, MARY II, were confirmed as joint rulers of England after the GLORIOUS REVOLUTION (1688).

A second stadtholderless period (1702–47) ended when the United Provinces was threatened during the War of the AUSTRIAN SUCCESSION (1740–48) and WILLIAM IV was duly elected. In 1795 the United Provinces was invaded by France and renamed the BATAVIAN REPUBLIC. In 1806 NAPOLEON I created the Kingdom of Holland under his brother, LOUIS BONAPARTE.

In 1815 the former United Provinces, Belgium and LUXEMBOURG united to form the kingdom of the Netherlands under WILLIAM I. In 1830 Belgium declared independence. In 1890 Luxembourg seceded, and WILHELMINA began her long reign (1890–1948). The Netherlands remained neutral during World War 1. In May 1940 Germany invaded and most Dutch Jews were deported to Poland, where they were murdered. Queen Wilhelmina was exiled. During World War 2, ARNHEM was a vital bridgehead in the Allied liberation of Europe.

In 1948 Wilhelmina abdicated in favour of her daughter, Juliana. In 1949 the Netherlands joined the North Atlantic Treaty Organization (NATO) and Indonesia was granted independence. Netherlands New Guinea and Surinam gained independence in 1962 and 1975 respectively; it retains the islands of the Netherlands Antilles. The Netherlands was a founding member of the European Community (1957), and in 1958 it joined the BENELUX customs union. In 1980 Queen Juliana abdicated in favour of her daughter, Beatrix. Post-1945, the Netherlands has been ruled by a succession of coalition governments. In 1994 Wim Kok became the first Labour Party leader to be elected prime minister since 1977. He was re-elected in 1998 and led the nation into the European single currency (1999).

subscribed to by all the major Christian churches and in the celebration of the Eucharist. *See also* APOSTLES' CREED; ATHANASIAN CREED

Nicholas I (the Great), Saint (*c.*820–67) Pope (858–67). He attempted to reassert papal authority in the face of CAROLINGIAN domination. Nicholas upheld apostolic succession and opposed LOTHAIR II of Lorraine's attempts to obtain a divorce. He intervened in the affairs of the Eastern Church by supporting the cleric Ignatius of Constantinople in his struggle against PHOTIUS. Nicholas excommunicated Photius in 863. He died before learning of Photius' counter-excommunication (867) and the subsequent SCHISM between the Eastern and Western churches.

Nicholas I (1796–1855) Tsar of Russia (1825–55), son of PAUL I and brother and successor of ALEXANDER I. His marriage (1817) to Princess Charlotte of PRUSSIA cemented the alliance between Prussia and Russia. As tsar, Nicholas was immediately confronted by the DECEMBRIST revolt (1825), in which *c.*3000 troops occupied the central square of the capital, St Petersburg, in support of his elder brother Constantine. In an early indication of the repressive and militaristic nature of his regime, Nicholas brutally crushed the rebellion. Nicholas expanded the Russian empire by defeating Iran (1826–28) and the OTTOMAN EMPIRE (1828–29). He ruthlessly suppressed rebellion in Poland, and assisted Austria against the Hungarian REVOLUTIONS OF 1848. His repeated attacks on the Ottoman Empire led to the CRIMEAN WAR (1853–56). Domestically, Nicholas' rule stressed, in the words of his education minister Sergei Urarov, the principles of "orthodoxy, autocracy and nationality". As a means of imposing his imperial will, Nicholas expanded the chancery, creating the political police to ensure subservience. Other new departments codified Russian law and sought to improve conditions for the Russian peasantry. Nicholas' reign marked a golden age of Russian literature, with writers such as Nikolai Gogol (1809–52) and Alexander Pushkin (1799–1837). He was succeeded by his son, ALEXANDER II.

Nicholas II (1868–1918) Last tsar of Russia (1894–1917), son and successor of ALEXANDER III. He married Alexandra, grand-daughter of Queen Victoria of Britain, in 1894. Nicholas tried unsuccessfully to maintain the autocratic approach of his father. His finance minister Count Sergei WITTE began the rapid industrialization of Russia in the 1890s, but poor working conditions created dissension. Nicholas' attempt to expand Russian power in Asia led to the RUSSO-JAPANESE WAR (1904–05), and Russian defeat prompted the RUSSIAN REVOLUTION OF 1905. Nicholas reluctantly agreed to the creation of an elected national assembly (the DUMA), but kept most of his powers. Prime Minister Peter STOLYPIN dissolved the second Duma in 1907 and gave peasants the opportunity to own their own land. In WORLD WAR I (1914–18), Nicholas took personal command of the army (September 1915), handing control of government to Alexandra and RASPUTIN. Inflation, food shortages and heavy casualties in the War provoked the RUSSIAN REVOLUTION, which began with riots in Petrograd (now ST PETERSBURG) in March 1917. Nicholas was forced to abdicate, and in July 1918 he and his family were executed in Yekaterinburg, E Russia, by local BOLSHEVIKS. *See also* LENIN, VLADIMIR ILYICH

Nicholas I (1841–1921) (Nikola Petrović) Prince (1860–1910) and king (1910–18) of MONTENEGRO. Supported by ALEXANDER II of Russia, Nicholas fought a dazzling campaign against the Turks in 1876 and doubled the size of his principality at the Congress of BERLIN (1878). In 1905 Nicholas was forced to grant a constitution, but proclaimed himself king in 1910. He allied with SERBIA in World War 1 but was forced into exile when Austria occupied Montenegro. He was formally deposed in 1918 after opposing the union of Montenegro and Serbia.

Niemöller, Martin (1892–1984) German Lutheran pastor. He founded the Confessing Church, which led opposition to Adolf HITLER's creation of a "German Christian Church" under the control of the Nazi Party. In 1937 Niemöller was arrested by the Gestapo and interned in a concentration camp (1938–45). As president (1961–68) of the World Council of Churches, Niemöller was a leading critic of the arms race during the Cold War.

Nietzsche, Friedrich Wilhelm (1844–1900) German philosopher who rejected Christianity and emphasized people's freedom to create their own values. In *Thus Spake Zarathustra* (1883–91), Nietzsche presented his notion of the *Übermensch* (Superman), the idealized man, strong, positive, and able to impose his wishes upon the weak. The concept was distorted by the Nazis to justify their notion of Aryan superiority. Other works include *Beyond Good and Evil* (1886) and *On the Genealogy of Morals* (1887). In 1889 Nietzsche was declared insane.

Niger *See* country feature, page 298

Nigeria *See* country feature, page 299

Nightingale, Florence (1820–1910) British nurse, b. Italy. She founded modern nursing and became known as the "lady of the lamp" for her activities in the CRIMEAN WAR (1853–56). In 1854 Nightingale took a unit of 38 nurses to care for wounded British soldiers, greatly improving sanitary conditions and the standard of patient care in military hospitals. In 1860 she founded the Nightingale School and Home for nurse training at St

NEW ZEALAND (AOTEAROA)

AREA: 270,990sq km (104,629sq mi)
POPULATION: 3,414,000
CAPITAL (POPULATION): Wellington (329,000)
GOVERNMENT: Constitutional monarchy
ETHNIC GROUPS: New Zealand European 74%, New Zealand Maori 10%, Polynesian 4%
LANGUAGES: English and Maori (both official)
RELIGIONS: Christianity (Anglican 21%, Presbyterian 16%, Roman Catholic 15%, Methodist 4%)
GDP PER CAPITA (1995): US$16,630

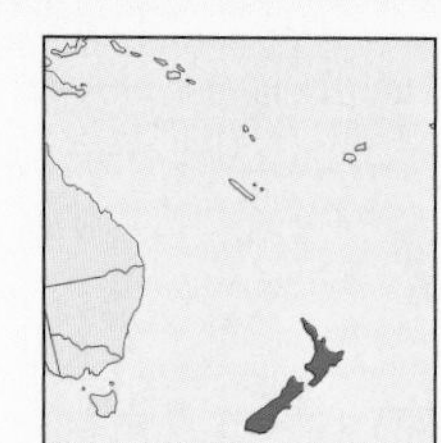

Archipelago state in the South Pacific. MAORI settlers arrived in New Zealand more than 1000 years ago. The first European sighting was made by Dutch navigator Abel TASMAN in 1642. British explorer James COOK completed the circumnavigation of the two major islands in 1769. Trade in fur and whaling brought British settlers in the early 19th century. A series of intertribal wars (1815–40) killed tens of thousands of Maoris.

In 1840 the first British settlement at Wellington was established. The Treaty of WAITANGI (1840) promised to honour Maori land-rights in return for recognition of British sovereignty. In 1841 New Zealand became a separate colony. Increasing colonization led to the first MAORI WAR (1843–48), which was won by the British under Governor George GREY.

Following the Constitution Act (1852), a national assembly was created and New Zealand gained self-government in 1856. In 1857 the Maori in the Waikato formed the so-called KING MOVEMENT, which opposed the colonial drive for land. The British seizure of land in Taranaki led to a second series of Maori Wars (1860–72). Te Kooti Rikirangi led resistance in E North Island and founded the religious cult of Ringatu. New Zealand's economy, badly hit by the wars, was revived by Julius VOGEL. Under Liberal Prime Minister Richard SEDDON (1893–1906), New Zealand enacted a range of progressive social legislation, becoming the first country to give women the vote (1893).

In 1907 New Zealand became a self-governing dominion in the British Commonwealth. After 22 years in office, the Liberal Party, led by Joseph WARD, was defeated in the 1912 elections by the Reformist William Ferguson MASSEY, who served as prime minister until 1925 and committed New Zealand to the Allied cause in WORLD WAR I (1914–18). More than 16,000 New Zealand soldiers were killed in the War. Joseph COATES succeeded Ferguson as prime minister and dominated a United-Reform coalition government (1931–35).

New Zealand's first Labour government (1935–49), led initially by Michael SAVAGE then by Peter FRASER, oversaw a return to economic prosperity after the Great Depression and allied with Britain at the start of WORLD WAR 2 (1939–45). During the War the US Navy provided the greatest protection from Japanese attack and, after the War had been won, New Zealand signed up to the ANZUS PACT (1951) with Australia and the United States.

Sidney HOLLAND's National Party (NP) government (1949–57) relaxed state controls over industry, led New Zealand into the SOUTH EAST ASIA TREATY ORGANZATION (SEATO) in 1954, and committed troops to the Vietnam War (1955–76). Keith HOLYOAKE's spell in office (1960–72) was marked by a protracted balance-of-payments crisis. In 1973 Britain joined the European Economic Community (EEC) and New Zealand's exports to Britain declined. NP Prime Minister (1975–84) Robert MULDOON initially attempted to buy the nation out of economic recession by massive increases in government spending and borrowing but, when that failed, he imposed a strict prices and incomes policy. Muldoon was defeated in the 1984 elections by Labour leader David LANGE, who restructured New Zealand's economy through privatization and adopted an anti-nuclear defence policy. Feuds within the Labour Party and continuing high unemployment aided Jim BOLGER's NP victory in the 1990 elections. A 1993 referendum voted for the introduction of proportional representation (PR). In the 1996 elections, the NP and New Zealand First Party (NZFP) formed a coalition government. In 1997 Bolger was forced to resign as prime minister and leader of the NP, and Jenny SHIPLEY became New Zealand's first woman prime minister. Helen Clark formed a minority Labour administration after the 1999 elections. Maori rights and the preservation of Maori culture remain central political issues.

Thomas' Hospital, London. In 1907 Nightingale became the first woman to be awarded the order of merit.

Night of the Long Knives (30 June 1934) Purge of the Brownshirts (SA) from the German Nazi Party. Adolf Hitler ordered the ss to execute prominent members of the Stormtroopers, including its leader Ernst Röhm. The SS also murdered other opponents of the regime, among them former chancellor Kurt von Schleicher. It is estimated that up to 1000 people were killed in one night.

nihilism (Latin *nihil*, "nothing") Doctrine of certain Russian revolutionaries in the late 19th century. The term was popularized by Ivan Turgenev's novel *Father and Sons* (1862). Nihilists condemned contemporary society as hostile to nature and rejected non-rational beliefs. They sought radical social reform by violent means. A group of nihilists, known as the Narodniks, assassinated Tsar Alexander II after he tried to suppress the movement.

Nijmegen, Treaties of (1678–79) Agreements ending the Dutch Wars (1672–78), signed in modern-day E Netherlands. France negotiated separately with each of its enemies and benefited from substantial peace settlements. With the Dutch, France agreed to cede Maastricht (now in SE Netherlands) and to end the tariff imposed on Dutch goods by Jean Colbert. Spain agreed to grant Franche-Comté, Artois, and several border fortresses to France, in return for control of the Spanish Netherlands. Emperor Leopold I ceded Freiburg and parts of Lorraine to France, as well as rights of passage through some of his territory. These settlements rationalized and strengthened France's borders. *See also* Spanish Succession, War of the

Nikon (1605–81) Russian priest, b. Nikita Minin. In 1652 he became head of the Russian Orthodox Church as patriarch of Moscow. Nikon asserted the independence of church and state. He reformed discipline and introduced a new prayer book. Nikon's reforms created a schism within the Russian Church, and those who opposed him split off to become the *Raskolniki* (Old Believers). In 1657–58 he governed Russia while Tsar Alexei Mikhailovich went to war with Poland. Nikon aroused the enmity of the boyars (Russian aristocracy) with his authoritarian methods and was forced to retire to a monastery in 1658. He was formally deposed in 1666.

Nile, Battle of the *See* Aboukir

Nimeiri, Gaafar Muhammad an- (1930–) Sudanese statesman and general, prime minister (1969–71) and president (1971–85). He assumed power after leading a military coup against the civilian government in 1969. Nimeiri helped resolve the long-running civil war by granting autonomy to S Sudan in 1972 and embarked on ambitious plans to develop Sudanese agriculture. The failure of a Libyan-backed coup (1976) led to a strengthening of ties with Egypt. In 1983 Nimeiri's attempt to apply Sharia law to the whole of Sudan led to renewed unrest in the Christian south and he was later overthrown in a military coup.

Nimitz, Chester William (1885–1966) US admiral. He served on submarines during World War 1. When the bombing of Pearl Harbor (1941) brought the United States into World War 2, Nimitz was appointed commander in chief of the US Pacific Fleet. His victorious operations against Japan include the battles of Midway, Coral Sea, Guadalcanal and Leyte Gulf. The Japanese surrender was signed aboard his flagship, USS *Missouri*, in 1945.

Nineteen Propositions (1 June 1642) Terms put by the Long Parliament to Charles I of England requiring that Parliament be given control over the appointment of royal ministers, the army and the settlement of Church doctrine and organization. Charles rejected the terms and made preparations for the English Civil War. *See also* Grand Remonstrance; Pym, John

Ninety-Five Theses *See* Luther, Martin

Nineveh Oldest and largest city of ancient Assyria, on the River Tigris (opposite modern Mosul, Iraq). In 1931–32 British archaeologists established that the site was first occupied in the 6th millennium BC, and discovered pottery from before 3000 BC that linked Nineveh to cities along the River Euphrates. It became the Assyrian capital under Sennacherib (r.704–681 BC), who built an enormous palace and city walls that stretched for more than 12km (7.5mi). Nineveh received water via a splendid aqueduct and contained gardens irrigated by canals. Ashurbanipal (r.668–627 BC) built the first systematically organized library in the Middle East, *c.*21,000 tablets from which are preserved in the British Museum, London. In 612 BC Nineveh was sacked by Media, but continued to be inhabited until the 13th century AD. *See also* Mesopotamia

nirvana Conception of salvation and liberation from rebirth in the religions of ancient India – Hinduism, Buddhism and Jainism. To Hindus, *nirvana* is extinction in the supreme being, brought about by internal happiness, internal satisfaction and internal illumination. To Buddhists, it is the attainment of a transcendent state of enlightenment through the extinction of all desires. To Jains, *nirvana* is a state of eternal blissful repose.

Nixon, Richard Milhous (1913–94) Thirty-seventh president of the United States (1969–74). He was twice elected as a Republican to the House of Representatives (1947, 1949), gaining national attention with his cross-examination of Alger Hiss for the House Un-American Activities Committee (HUAC). Nixon was elected to the Senate in 1950 and served as vice president (1953–61) under Dwight Eisenhower. He lost the closely fought 1960 presidential election to John Kennedy after the first televised national debates between presidential candidates. In 1968 Nixon received the Republican nomination for a second time and narrowly defeated his Democrat challenger, Hubert Humphrey. As president, Nixon had a number of foreign policy successes: he re-opened US relations with communist China for the first time in 21 years and, on the first visit of a US president to Moscow (1972), concluded the first round of Strategic Arms Limitation Talks (SALT) by signing an arms limitation agreement with the Soviet Union. He began to reduce US military involvement in the Vietnam War (1955–75), withdrawing

NICARAGUA

AREA: 130,000sq km (50,193sq mi)
POPULATION: 4,130,000
CAPITAL (POPULATION): Managua (682,111)
GOVERNMENT: Multiparty republic
ETHNIC GROUPS: Mestizo 77%, White 10%, Black 9%, Native American 4%
LANGUAGES: Spanish (official)
RELIGIONS: Christianity (Roman Catholic 91%, others 9%)
GDP PER CAPITA (1995): US$2000

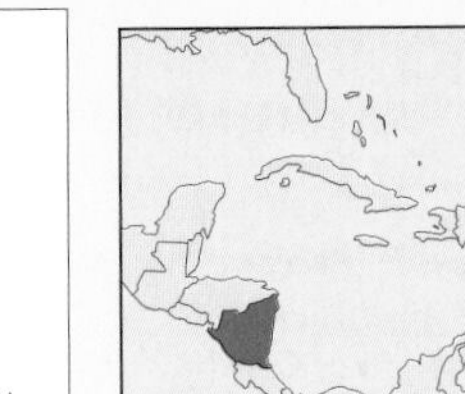

Republic in Central America. Nicaragua is the largest country in Central America. From the 10th century AD peoples from Mexico migrated to the region. Christopher Columbus sighted the coast in 1502 and claimed the region for Spain. Spanish conquistador Gil González Dávila's attempts to conquer the region were repulsed by Native Americans. Permanent settlements were finally established at Granada and León by Francisco Hernández de Córdoba in 1524. Within thirty years of European colonization, more than half of the *c.*200,000 Native Americans had died of Old World diseases and most of the remainder were sold into slavery. Nicaragua was ruled as part of the Spanish Captaincy General of Guatemala. In the 17th and 18th centuries Britain secured control of the Caribbean coast and established a protectorate over an area that became known as the Mosquito Coast after the Miskito, a Native American tribe.

In 1821 Nicaragua gained independence and from 1825 to 1838 it formed part of the Central American Federation. A power struggle developed between the Liberals, based in León, and the Conservatives, based in Granada. US adventurer William Walker, initially invited by the Liberals to restore order, established himself as president of Nicaragua (1856–57). As a compromise between Granada and León, Managua became the capital in 1857.

The Conservatives held power from 1857 until 1893, when General José Santos Zelaya seized power and established a dictatorship. Zelaya improved the economy and infrastructure and gained control of the Mosquito Coast from Britain. In 1909 he was overthrown by a US-backed revolt and US marines were sent in to protect the Conservative regime in 1912. The Marines' withdrawal (1925) led to renewed civil war and *c.*2000 Marines were redeployed in 1927 to support the Conservative government. The US Marines finally left in 1933, after forming the National Guard to help defeat the Liberal guerrilla forces led by Augusto César Sandino.

In 1934 Sandino was assassinated by the National Guard, directed by Anastasio Somoza García. Somoza became president after fraudulent elections in 1936 and rapidly assumed dictatorial powers, building a vast personal fortune by plundering Nicaragua's economy. After Somoza's assassination (1967), control of the country passed to his son **Luis Somoza Debayle** (1922–67). Luis allowed the United States to use Nicaragua as a base for the disastrous Bay of Pigs invasion (1961) of Cuba. Luis was succeeded by his brother **Anastasio Somoza Debayle** (1925–80). Anastasio's personal profiteering from international relief aid, donated after a devastating earthquake in Managua in 1972, and the adoption of a new constitution (1974) to enable his re-election, increased the intensity of opposition to his regime. More than 30,000 Nicaraguans died before Somoza was finally overthrown by the Sandinista National Liberation Front (FSLN) in 1979.

The Sandinista government, led by Daniel Ortega, instigated wide-ranging socialist reforms. US President Ronald Reagan, anxious about the Sandinista's relations with Cuba and the Soviet Union, sought to destabilize the government by organizing and funding the Contra rebels. A ten-year civil war and a US trade embargo destroyed the economy and created dissatisfaction with the Sandinistas.

In the 1990 elections the Sandinistas were defeated by the National Opposition Union (UNO) coalition, led by Violeta Chamorro. Many of Chamorro's reforms were blocked by her coalition partners and the Sandinista-controlled trade unions, but limited economic progress was made. In the 1996 elections Chamorro was defeated by Liberal leader Arnoldo Alemán. In 1998 Hurricane Mitch killed *c.*4000 people and caused extensive damage to Nicaragua. Plans for the deployment of US soldiers to help reconstruction efforts were approved by parliament in March 2000.

troops but continuing to supply the South Vietnamese army and providing air support. He also undertook bombing raids in North Vietnam and, secretly, of North Vietnamese bases in Laos and Cambodia (1969–70). In domestic politics, Nixon was faced by rising inflation and a huge budget deficit. Nonetheless, he won a landslide victory in the 1972 elections. In his second term, Nixon withdrew US troops from the Vietnam War (1973). However, the WATERGATE AFFAIR came to dominate his second term in office, when it was revealed (in his own tape-recordings) that he was implicated in the obstruction of justice following the burglary of Democratic Party headquarters in Washington, D.C. On 8 August 1974, in order to avoid impeachment, Nixon became the first US president to resign from office. He was succeeded by his vice president, Gerald FORD, who issued him a presidential pardon in September 1974. *See also* KISSINGER, HENRY ALFRED

Nkomo, Joshua (1917–99) Zimbabwean statesman, vice president (1990–99). In 1957 he was elected president of the Rhodesian African National Congress (ANC), but founded his own political organization, Zimbabwe African People's Union (ZAPU), in 1961. He was imprisoned (1964–74) by Ian SMITH's white-minority government in Rhodesia (now ZIMBABWE). In 1976 Nkomo and Robert MUGABE's Zimbabwe African National Union (ZANU) joined forces to form the Patriotic Front (PF), which waged a guerrilla war for black-majority rule. When majority government was achieved in 1980, Mugabe became prime minister and Nkomo was given a cabinet post. In 1982, after increasing tension between ZAPU's NDEBELE supporters and ZANU's Shona backers, Nkomo was dismissed from government. The two parties merged in 1988 and Nkomo later became vice president, serving until his death.

Nkrumah, Kwame (1909–72) African statesman, first prime minister (1957–60) and president (1960–66) of GHANA. He was the first black African post-colonial leader. After studying in the United States, Nkrumah returned to the Gold Coast to become general secretary of the United Gold Coast Convention (UGCC), which sought independence through democratic means. In 1949 he founded the Convention People's Party (CPP), a more radical organization that used tactics of non-violent, civil disobedience. He was subsequently imprisoned (1950–52) by the British for calling a series of disruptive strikes and protests, but was released when the CCP won the 1951 elections. Nkrumah led the Gold Coast to independence as Ghana in 1957. In 1960 Ghana became a republic and Nkrumah was made president. A leading proponent of PAN-AFRICANISM, Nkrumah provided support to other African nationalists who were attempting to overthrow European COLONIALISM, forming a loose union with GUINEA and MALI in 1961, and promoting the establishment of the ORGANIZATION OF AFRICAN UNITY (OAU) in 1963. While Nkrumah concentrated on campaigning for the creation of a United States of Africa, Ghana's once-healthy economy plunged into debt with the financing of ambitious and costly development projects. After a general strike (1961) and an attempted assassination (1962), Nkrumah resorted to increasingly authoritarian means to restore order. In 1964 Ghana became a one-party state and Nkrumah encouraged the creation of a personality cult around himself. As Ghana turned to the communist bloc for support, it lost the backing of the West and the economy worsened. While on a visit to China, Nkrumah was deposed in a military coup and spent the rest of his life in exile in Guinea.

Nobel Prize Annual awards for outstanding contributions in the fields of physics, chemistry, physiology or medicine, literature, economics and world peace. Established (1901) by the will of Swedish chemist Alfred Nobel (1833–96), the prizes are awarded annually on 10 December. The winners are selected by committees based in Sweden and Norway.

Nobunaga, Oda (1534–82) Japanese DAIMYO (feudal lord). In 1560, with the aid of Portuguese muskets, he secured control of the province of Owari, Honshu. After forming an alliance with fellow daimyo TOKUGAWA IEYASU in 1562, Nobunaga seized the capital city, KYOTO, in 1568 and overthrew the ASHIKAGA shogunate in 1573. Nobunaga smashed the monastic headquarters of the powerful Tendai sect of Japanese BUDDHISM in 1571, and eventually destroyed (1580) the Ikko sect after ten years of civil war. He further weakened the influence of Buddhism by encouraging Jesuit missionary activities in Japan. Nobunaga secured the support of the SAMURAI by granting them the estates seized from the monastic sects and, by the time of his assassination, had gained control of the whole of central Japan. The unification of Japan was completed by his general and successor HIDEYOSHI.

nomenklatura System in the SOVIET UNION by which the COMMUNIST PARTY OF THE SOVIET UNION (CPSU) controlled government appointments. The nomenklatura was made up of two lists: one of important positions and another of people approved by the CPSU to hold those positions. At its height, the nomenklatura amounted to 10 million people. They were an official élite, who were entitled to special privileges, such as superior consumer goods and housing. Upon coming to power in 1985, Mikhail GORBACHEV attempted to disband the nomenklatura as part of his policy of PERESTROIKA (restructuring). Similar systems were used in communist Poland and Yugoslavia.

non-aligned movement Association of nations that had no allegiance either to the United States or to the Soviet Union during the COLD WAR. Inspired by the BANDUNG CONFERENCE (1955), the movement began in Asia and soon spread internationally. Early leaders included Jawaharlal NEHRU of India, Abdel NASSER of Egypt, Kwame NKRUMAH of Ghana, Fidel CASTRO of Cuba, and Marshal TITO of Yugoslavia. Its first summit was held (1961) in Belgrade, Yugoslavia, and its influence grew so that today there are *c.*110 member states. Although its initial aim was to act as a counterweight to the superpowers and promote the influence of so-called "Third World" countries on international politics, with the end of the Cold War, it broadened its focus to include development issues.

Nonconformism Dissent from or lack of conformity with the religious doctrines or discipline of an established church, especially the CHURCH OF ENGLAND. The term Nonconformist applies to all the sects of British PROTESTANTISM that do not subscribe to the principles of the established Anglican Church or the established CHURCH OF SCOTLAND. It arose in England in reaction to the Act of Uniformity (1662), one of the so-called CLARENDON codes that followed the RESTORATION of the monarchy in 1660. The classic literary text of Nonconformism is *The Pilgrim's Progress* (1684) by English writer John Bunyan (1628–88). Movements such as CONGREGATIONALISM and PRESBYTERIANISM, BAPTISTS and QUAKERS proliferated, and many Nonconformists emigrated to the new North American colonies. In England, Nonconformist churches were eventually granted freedom of worship by the TOLERATION ACT of 1689 and civil and political rights in 1828. Other Nonconformist movements, such as UNITARIANISM, sprang up in the 18th century and were highly influential in the formation of the British LABOUR PARTY. *See also* BAXTER, RICHARD; BROWNE, ROBERT; PILGRIMS; PURITANISM

NIGER

AREA: 1,267,000sq km (489,189sq mi)
POPULATION: 8,252,000
CAPITAL POPULATION: Niamey (392,169)
GOVERNMENT: Multiparty republic
ETHNIC GROUPS: Hausa 53%, Zerma-Songhai 21%, Tuareg 11%, Fulani 10%
LANGUAGES: French (official)
RELIGIONS: Islam 98%
GDP PER CAPITA (1995): US$750

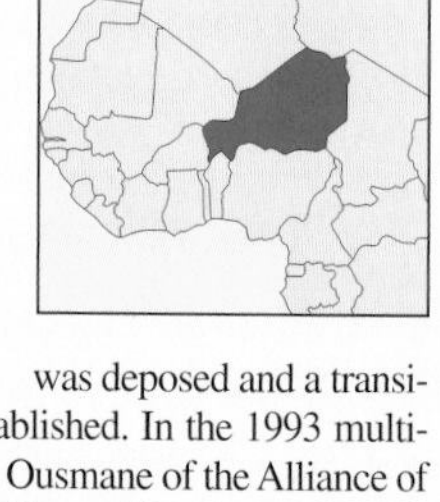

Landlocked republic in W Africa. Neolithic remains have been found in the N desert. A formative influence on much of the history of Niger has been the contact between the nomadic TUAREGS of the N and the HAUSA farmers of the S. In the 14th century the Tuareg kingdom of Takedda developed W of the Aïr Mountains, flourishing on the trans-Saharan trade in copper. Takedda was succeeded by the sultanate of Agadez. The KANEM-BORNU empire dominated E Niger, while the SONGHAI empire commanded W Niger throughout the medieval period but collapsed following defeat by the Moroccans in 1591. The HAUSA STATES ruled in S Niger from the 10th century until 1804, when the FULANI leader USMAN DAN FODIO launched a successful JIHAD (holy war) and established the Muslim empire of SOKOTO.

Scottish explorer Mungo PARK was probably the first European to reach the area (1795), and he was followed by the German pioneer Heinrich BARTH. In 1891 a French expedition arrived. In 1904 the region was declared part of French West Africa, but Tuareg resistance prevented full occupation until 1922, when Niger became a separate French colony.

In 1958 Niger voted to remain an autonomous republic within the French Community, but in 1960 full independence was achieved. Hamani Diori became Niger's first president, and he maintained close ties with France. Beginning in 1968, a succession of droughts in the Sahel resulted in a famine. In 1974 Diori was overthrown in an army coup led by Lieutenant Colonel Seyni Kountché. Kountché established a military dicatatorship. In 1987 Kountché died and was succeeded by his cousin, General Ali Seibou. Seibou introduced a new constitution (1989) that promised a return to civilian rule. Following a wave of strikes and civil unrest, he allowed the formation of opposition parties in 1990.

The same year, the Tuaregs launched a war for the creation of a separate state in N Niger. In 1991 Seibou was deposed and a transitional government was established. In the 1993 multiparty elections, Mahamane Ousmane of the Alliance of the Forces for Change (AFC) coalition became president. In 1995 the collapse of the coalition produced fresh elections, which were won by the opposition National Movement for a Development Society (MNSD). In 1995 a peace accord was signed between the government and the Tuaregs. In 1996 Colonel Ibrahim Bare Mainassara seized power in a military coup, arrested Ousmane and was elected president in a fraudulent election later that year. In April 1999 he was assassinated by his bodyguards and Tanja Mamadou became president. Mamadou was confimed as president in the November 1999 elections.

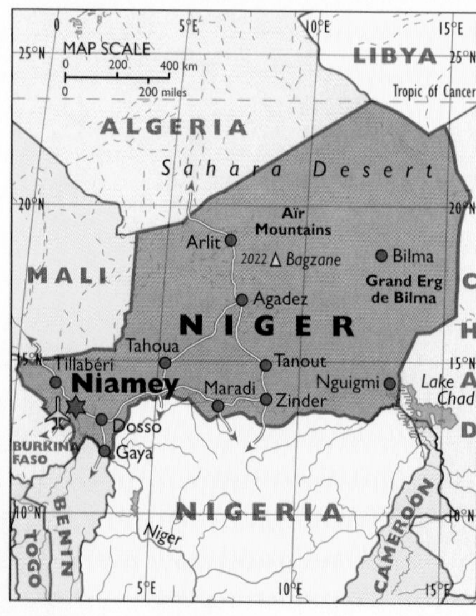

non-cooperation *See* GANDHI, "MAHATMA"

Nonjurors Clergy in England and Scotland who refused to take the oath of allegiance to WILLIAM III and MARY II after the GLORIOUS REVOLUTION (1688), remaining loyal to JAMES II. Anglo-Catholic in sympathy, they included several bishops and *c*.400 priests in England, prominent politicians such as the 2nd Earl of CLARENDON and most of the Scottish episcopal clergy. *See also* JACOBITES

Nordenskjöld, Nils Adolf Erik, Baron (1832–1901) Swedish explorer and scientist, b. Finland. He made several expeditions to Spitsbergen (Svalbard), off the coast of Norway, and led an exploration of Greenland's inland ice-cap in 1870. In 1878–79 Nordenskjöld navigated his ship, the *Vega*, in the first successful voyage through the NORTHEAST PASSAGE. In his later years, he encouraged the explorations of Fridtjof NANSEN.

Norfolk, Thomas Howard, 3rd Duke of (1473–1554) English noble, brother-in-law of HENRY VII. As lord high admiral, he led the English to victory over the Scots at the Battle of FLODDEN (1513). Norfolk led opposition to HENRY VIII's chief minister, Thomas WOLSEY, and succeeded Wolsey as president of the royal council in 1529. He supported Henry's marriage (1533) to his niece Anne BOLEYN and subsequently, when Henry pressed for a divorce from Anne, was eclipsed in the king's favour by Thomas CROMWELL and Thomas CRANMER. In 1536 Howard crushed the PILGRIMAGE OF GRACE and regained favour after the execution of Cromwell and Henry's marriage to another niece, Catherine HOWARD, in 1540. His resurgence proved short-lived, however, when he was condemned to death as an accessory to the treason of his son, Henry Howard, Earl of SURREY, in 1546. Norfolk remained in prison (1546–53) throughout the reign of EDWARD VI, but was released by MARY I.

Noriega, Manuel (Antonio Morena) (1934–) Panamanian statesman and general, head of state (1983–89). In 1963 he became head of Panama's National Defense Forces. Recruited as an operative by the US CENTRAL INTELLIGENCE AGENCY (CIA), Noriega became an important backstage power-broker. For most of the 1980s he was effectively Panama's paramount leader, ruling behind puppet presidents. In 1987 evidence emerged of Noriega's criminal activities, and the United States withdrew its support. In 1988 he was indicted by a US court on drug-connected charges and accused of murder. In December 1989 US troops invaded Panama and installed a civilian government. Noriega surrendered to US forces and was taken to the United States for trial on

NIGERIA

AREA: 923,770sq km (356,668sq mi)
POPULATION: 88,515,000
CAPITAL (POPULATION): Abuja (305,900)
GOVERNMENT: Federal republic
ETHNIC GROUPS: Hausa 21%, Yoruba 21%, Ibo 19%, Fulani 11%, Ibibio 6%
LANGUAGES: English (official)
RELIGIONS: Christianity (Protestant 26%, Roman Catholic 12%, others 11%), Islam 45%
GDP PER CAPITA (1995): US$1220

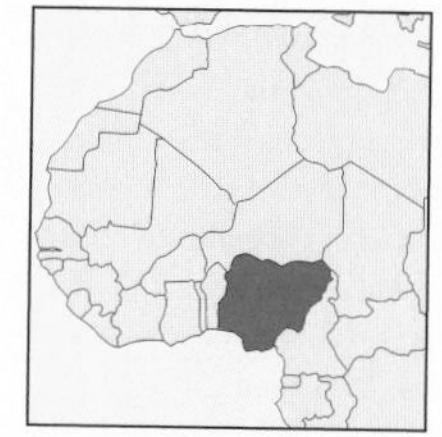

Republic in W Africa. Nigeria is the most populous nation in Africa. The division of Nigeria into 30 states reflects the fact that it contains more than 250 ethnic and language groups and several religious ones. The region has been inhabited by humans since before 9000 BC. Excavations around Nok, N Nigeria, have uncovered some of the oldest and most beautiful examples of African sculpture. The Nok civilization flourished between *c*.500 BC and *c*.AD 200. Sometime before the 9th century AD the kingdom of KANEM emerged E of Lake Chad. The Kanem rulers were converted to Islam in the 11th century. By the 12th century the Kanem had been forced to migrate W to BORNU. The Kanem-Bornu empire was revitalized in the late 16th century, extending its influence to the HAUSA STATES to the west. In the *c*.11th century the YORUBA kingdom of IFE emerged in SW Nigeria. Ife was a formative influence on the kingdoms of BENIN and OYO, which flourished in the 15th century. These states were renowned for their brass, bronze and ivory sculptures. Although the IBO in SE Nigeria had formed complex civilizations by the 10th century, they did not form centralized kingdoms until the growth of the SLAVE TRADE with Europe in the 18th century. The SONGHAI empire dominated N Nigeria in the early 16th century.

The Portuguese were the first Europeans to reach the Nigerian coast; they established trading links with Benin and Oyo in the late 15th century. Nigeria became a centre of the slave trade, with as many as 30 million people sold into slavery. In 1804 the FULANI scholar USMAN DAN FODIO launched a successful JIHAD against the Hausa states and the Oyo state of Ilorin, thus creating the caliphate of SOKOTO. The collapse of Oyo precipitated the Yoruba Wars, which persisted until 1886. In 1807 the slave trade was abolished in the BRITISH EMPIRE and in its place the British encouraged the growth of trade in palm oil. In 1861 Britain seized Lagos, S Nigeria, and, worried about threats to its commerce from other European powers, established the protectorates of Lagos and Oil Rivers (later Niger Coast) in 1887. Britain later conquered Benin (1897) and Sokoto (1903).

The protectorates of Southern Nigeria and Northern Nigeria, created in 1900, were merged in 1914 to form Britain's largest single colony in Africa. The first governor general, Frederick LUGARD, established a system of indirect rule through existing native institutions; major rebellions against colonial rule in Abeokuta (1918) and Aba (1929) were brutally suppressed.

In 1954 Nigeria was federated into three regions (N, E and W) plus the territory of Lagos. In 1960 Nigeria gained independence under Prime Minister Sir Abubakar Tafawa BALEWA. In 1963 it became a republic, led by President Nnamdi AZIKIWE. In January 1966 Ibo army officers staged a successful coup, but the regime was toppled (July 1966) by Lieutenant Colonel Yakubu GOWON and thousands of Ibo were massacred. In 1967 the Ibo formed the independent republic of BIAFRA. For the next three years civil war raged in Nigeria, until Biafra capitulated.

The early 1970s were more peaceful, as Nigeria expanded its oil industry. Nigeria joined the ORGANIZATION OF PETROLEUM EXPORTING COUNTRIES (OPEC) in 1971. Oil revenue created widespread government corruption and increased economic inequality. Drought in the Sahel killed much livestock and led to mass migration to the S. After several military coups, civilian rule was briefly restored in 1979. Following 1983 elections, the military seized power again.

Between 1960 and 1998 Nigeria enjoyed only nine years of civilian government. The 1993 presidential elections, won by Chief Moshood Abiola, were declared invalid by the military government. The army commander in chief, General Sanni Abacha, gained power. In 1994 nationwide demonstrations prompted Abiola to form a rival government, but he was swiftly arrested. In 1995 General Abacha was given an open-ended term in office, vowing to restore civilian rule by 1998. His regime was severely criticized for human rights abuses and the suppression of opposition. In November 1995, after the execution of nine activists, among them the dramatist Ken Saro-Wiwa, Nigeria was suspended from the COMMONWEALTH OF NATIONS. In 1998 Abacha died and was succeeded by General Abubakar. In 1998 the death of Abiola in prison prompted widespread rioting. In the 1999 elections Olusegun Obasanjo, a former military ruler (1976–79), became president and Nigeria was readmitted to the Commonwealth.

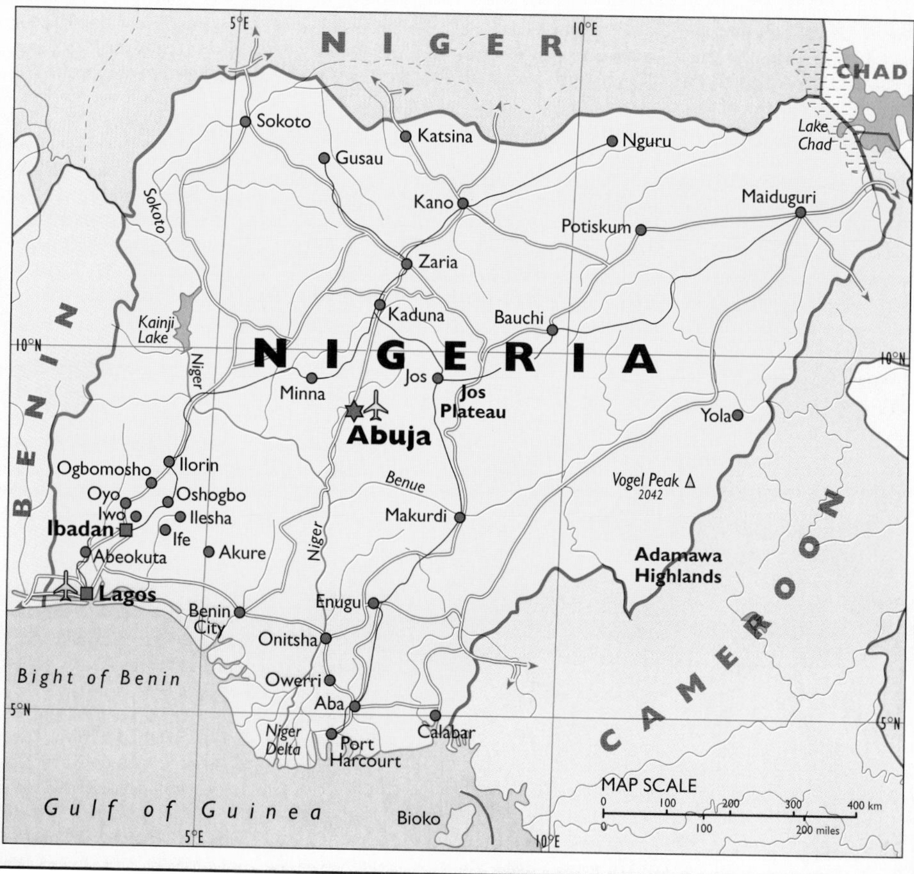

charges of corruption, drug trafficking and money laundering. In 1992 he was sentenced to 40 years in prison.

Norman Conquest (1066) Military subjugation of England by WILLIAM I (THE CONQUEROR), Duke of Normandy. William insisted that EDWARD THE CONFESSOR (d.1066) had recognized him as heir to the throne of England, and thus challenged the succession of HAROLD II. After defeating HARALD III of Norway at the Battle of STAMFORD BRIDGE (September 1066), Harold II was forced to march s to confront William's army. His tired and ill-equipped force of *c*.7000 men was surprised and overwhelmed by William's 5000 knights at the Battle of HASTINGS (1066) and Harold was killed in battle. William advanced on London, where he was crowned king. William suppressed a number of revolts at the start of his reign and built many castles to consolidate his power. The English aristocracy and clergy were gradually replaced by NORMANS, and some Norman legal institutions were imposed. Norman-French became the elite language of court and culture. The cost of Norman government was heavy, obliging William to commission the DOMESDAY BOOK, which provided the Norman regime with a detailed analysis of England's revenue. *See also* ANGLO-SAXON

Normandy Region and former province of NW France. Part of the Roman province of GAUL, it was absorbed into the MEROVINGIAN kingdom of NEUSTRIA by the FRANKS in the 6th century. It was continually devastated by VIKING raiders in the 8th and 9th centuries and was finally ceded to the Viking chief ROLLO by CHARLES III (THE SIMPLE) of France in 911. The Viking settlers became known as NORMANS. Normandy and England were linked by the NORMAN CONQUEST of England by WILLIAM I (THE CONQUEROR), Duke of Normandy, in 1066. But after his death (1087), the union was broken until 1106, when HENRY I of England defeated his brother, ROBERT II of Normandy, and claimed the region for England. In 1144 Geoffrey PLANTAGENET conquered Normandy, which subsequently became part of the ANGEVIN empire of HENRY II of England. It was recovered for the French by the CAPETIAN ruler PHILIP II (AUGUSTUS) in 1204. The region changed hands several times during the HUNDRED YEARS' WAR (1337–1453) between England and France, but was eventually restored to France in 1450 and became French crown land in 1568. It was the site of the NORMANDY LANDINGS (June 1944) of WORLD WAR 2.

Normandy Landings (Operation Overlord) Allied invasion of German-occupied France during WORLD WAR 2, launched on 6 June 1944 (D-Day). General Dwight EISENHOWER was given the task of organizing the largest amphibious operation in military history, involving *c*.156,000 troops (73,000 US, 83,000 British and Canadian), *c*.10,000 aircraft and *c*.5000 ships. The invasion was delayed by 24 hours, due to bad weather in the English Channel. Before daybreak on 6 June 1944, paratroopers from the US 82nd and 101st Airborne divisions landed near the town of Saint-Mère-Église, Normandy, N France, while British commandos knocked out key military installations. Allied forces then landed on five French beaches between Cherbourg and Le Havre, codenamed Gold, Juno, Sword, Utah and Omaha. The first four beaches were captured relatively easily, but the forces on Omaha encountered fierce German resistance before establishing the final beachhead at nightfall. Although the original objective to capture Caen had not been realized, the first step in the liberation of Europe was complete. *See also* BRADLEY, OMAR NELSON; MONTGOMERY (OF ALAMEIN), BERNARD LAW, 1ST VISCOUNT

Normans VIKING warriors who settled in NW France in the 9th and 10th centuries. In 911 the Viking chief ROLLO was ceded the region of NORMANDY by CHARLES III (THE SIMPLE) of France on condition of conversion to Christianity. The Normans forged a powerful state with a strongly centralized feudal society and warlike aristocracy. Normandy and England were linked by the NORMAN CONQUEST of England by WILLIAM I (THE CONQUEROR), Duke of Normandy, in 1066. Robert GUISCARD expelled the Byzantines from s Italy in 1071 and his nephew, ROBERT II, founded the Norman kingdom of SICILY in 1130. Their conquests were consolidated by the building of castles. The Normans quickly assimilated indigenous traditions. *See also* FEUDAL SYSTEM

Norodom Sihanouk (1922–) Cambodian king (1941–55, 1993–) and statesman, prime minister (1955–60) and head of state (1960–70, 1975–76, 1991–93). He was first appointed king by the French, who ruled Cambodia as part of INDOCHINA. Sihanouk negotiated independence for Cambodia in 1953 and later abdicated to become prime minister of a socialist government in Cambodia. Under a new constitution (1960), Sihanouk was elected head of state. He initially pursued a neutral foreign policy during the VIETNAM WAR (1955–75), but broke off diplomatic relations with the United States after they bombed Cambodian villages in 1965. In 1970 Sihanouk was deposed in a US-backed military coup, led by Lon Nol. He returned from exile when the KHMER ROUGE overthrew Lon Nol in 1975, but was placed under house arrest by POL POT in 1976. When Pol Pot was ousted by Vietnamese forces in 1979, Sihanouk formed a government-in-exile in China. In 1991 he returned to Cambodia. In 1993 Sihanouk was reinstated as a constitutional monarch. His son, Prince Ranariddh, became co-premier with HUN SEN. Ranariddh was ousted in 1997.

North, Frederick, Lord (1732–92) British statesman, prime minister (1770–82). He entered Parliament as a Tory in 1754. North was lord of the treasury (1759–65) under the Duke of NEWCASTLE, the Earl of BUTE and then George GRENVILLE, before being appointed chancellor of the exchequer (1767–70) by the Duke of GRAFTON. When North succeeded Grafton as prime minister, GEORGE III had finally defeated the WHIGS under Charles ROCKINGHAM. North restored domestic stability and implemented important financial reforms, including regulating the English EAST INDIA COMPANY. At first he tried to pacify the North American colonies by repealing most of the TOWNSHEND ACTS. However, North's repressive measures against the North American colonies after the BOSTON TEA PARTY, particularly the so-called INTOLERABLE ACTS (1774), have been blamed for precipitating the AMERICAN REVOLUTION (1775–83). British defeat in the Revolution led to North's resignation. In 1783 he formed a short-lived coalition with his Whig opponent Charles James Fox. He then led opposition to the ministry of William PITT (THE YOUNGER) until his retirement in 1786.

North, Oliver Laurence (1943–) US marine lieutenant colonel. North was recruited as an aide to the National Security Council. In 1987 the Congressional committee that investigated the notorious IRAN-CONTRA AFFAIR revealed North as the central figure in the arms-for-hostages scandal and the secret funding of the CONTRAS in Nicaragua. He was subsequently convicted of obstructing justice. North was controversially pardoned by President George Bush in 1992. *See also* REAGAN, RONALD WILSON

▼ **Normans** Norman knights fought on horseback with spears and swords. They wore heavy chain-mail and conical helmets and carried brightly coloured shields.

North Africa campaign Battle for control of North Africa during WORLD WAR 2. After Italy declared war on Britain (June 1940), the British launched attacks against Italian positions in Libya (December 1940). Although the British were heavily outnumbered, they had little trouble taking much of Libya as well as Ethiopia and Italian East Africa by the beginning of 1941. The German Afrika Korps, led by Erwin ROMMEL, was dispatched to support the Italians in February 1941, and within two months Rommel had forced the British back into Egypt. The Axis advance was halted (July 1942) by the British 8th Army under General AUCHINLECK, and his successor, General MONTGOMERY, launched a devastating attack on Rommel at the Battle of El ALAMEIN (October 1942). The British gradually pushed Rommel's forces to the Tunisian border (January 1943). While Montgomery was attacking from the east, *c*.110,000 US troops landed in Morocco and Algeria (Operation Torch, November 1942) under the command of Dwight EISENHOWER. Faced with a pincer movement, Rommel was forced to withdraw and finally surrendered in Tunis (7 May 1943). The Allies took more than 250,000 prisoners as the Axis forces retreated.

North America Continent, including the mainland and offshore islands N of and including PANAMA. North America's first settlers probably arrived *c*.45,000 years ago from Asia by way of ALASKA. When the Viking explorer LEIF ERICSON arrived in *c*.AD 1000, NATIVE NORTH AMERICANS occupied the entire continent. European settlement accelerated after Christopher COLUMBUS' voyage in 1492. The Spaniards settled in MEXICO and the WEST INDIES. The English and French settled farther N; Swedes, Germans and Dutch also formed settlements. Europe's political and economic problems later drove larger numbers to the New World. Descendants of Spanish settlers are predominant in Mexico, Central America and some Caribbean islands. French concentrations exist in QUÉBEC province, CANADA, and parts of the West Indies. In Central America and the Caribbean, European descendants are in the minority. The early 20th century saw mass emigration to the UNITED STATES and Canada. The United States has been the dominant economic force on the continent throughout the 20th century. In the SPANISH-AMERICAN WAR (1898) the United States emerged as a world power. In 1903 US President Theodore ROOSEVELT enforced construction of the PANAMA CANAL, control of which returned to Panama in 1999. The United States emerged from WORLD WAR 2 as a superpower. The ideological battle between CAPITALISM and COMMUNISM led to the COLD WAR and US involvement in the KOREAN WAR (1950–53) and the VIETNAM WAR (1955–75). Since 1994, Canada, the United States and Mexico have been linked through the NORTH AMERICAN FREE TRADE AGREEMENT (NAFTA). As the United States and Canada have developed more service-based economies, some manufacturing has transferred to Mexico. Since World War 2, many Caribbean islands have gained independence. A US trade embargo since Fidel CASTRO's revolution (1959) has crippled CUBA's economy. Central America has also been dominated by US interests and by repressive regimes and economic inequality. *See also* articles on individual countries

North American Free Trade Agreement (NAFTA) (1992) Treaty designed to eliminate all tariffs and other trade barriers between Canada, Mexico and the United States within 15 years. NAFTA forms the world's largest single trading bloc. Inspired by the efforts of the EUROPEAN UNION (EU) to create a single-market, NAFTA had its origins in a free-trade agreement (1988) between Canada and the United States. Signed by US President George BUSH, Canadian Prime Minister Brian MULRONEY and Mexican President Carlos Salinas de Gortari, it came into effect on 1 January 1994. Some Latin American countries have since applied to join.

North Atlantic Treaty Organization (NATO) Military alliance of the United States, Canada and 17 European countries. The North Atlantic Treaty was signed (24 August 1949) in Washington, D.C., by Belgium, Britain, Canada, Denmark, France, Iceland, Italy, Luxembourg, Norway, Portugal, Netherlands and the

NORTH CAROLINA
Statehood :
21 November 1789
Nickname :
The Tar Heel State
State motto :
To be, rather than to seem

United States. Since then, Greece, Turkey (both 1952), Germany (West Germany, 1955) and Spain (1982) have joined. In 1999, despite Russian opposition, the Czech Republic, Hungary and Poland became members. It was initially designed to act as a counterweight to the military dominance of the Soviet Union in Eastern Europe at the end of World War 2. It sought to provide collective security for Western Europe in case of communist invasion. NATO's first supreme commander was US General Dwight Eisenhower. As the Cold War intensified and West Germany joined NATO, the Soviet Union formed the rival Warsaw Pact. The United States and the Soviet Union began to stockpile nuclear weapons in Europe. In 1966 French President Charles De Gaulle condemned US domination of the alliance and withdrew France from the integrated military command of NATO. NATO headquarters were subsequently transferred from Paris to Brussels, Belgium, where they remain. The collapse of communism in Eastern Europe in 1989 and the reunification of Germany in 1990 led to a radical reappraisal of NATO's role in Europe. In 1995 NATO led an international peacekeeping force to implement the Dayton Peace Agreement in Bosnia-Herzegovina. In 1999 NATO launched its first military operation, to protect the ethnic Albanian population in the Serbian province of Kosovo. After 11 weeks of aerial bombardment, Yugoslavia agreed to withdraw its troops from Kosovo.

North Carolina State in SE United States; the capital is Raleigh. After AD 800 Native American Mound Builders established towns in the S and W of the region. When the coast was first explored by Europeans in the 16th century, the Native American population was probably *c*.30,000. The major tribes were the Tuscarora, Cherokee and Catawba. The first English colony in North America was founded by Sir Walter Raleigh on Roanoke Island in 1585, but most of the settlers had to be rescued the following year by Sir Francis Drake and the colony was lost. In 1629 Charles I of England established the colony of Carolina. Carolina became embroiled in the Tuscarora Wars (1711–13), and a separate governor was appointed for the colony of North Carolina in 1712. Its shores proved a haven for pirates such as Blackbeard. George II of Britain took direct control of the colony in 1729. The royal governor was forced to flee at the start of the American Revolution (1775–83). North Carolina was the last state to secede (May 1861) from the Union in the American Civil War (1861–65). After the War, the defeated Confederate states, including North Carolina, enacted the black codes, which perpetuated discrimination against African-Americans and led to the imposition of the tough Reconstruction policies. The Democrats dominated politics in North Carolina for most of the period from 1872 to 1972, and racial segregation persisted in the state until the Civil Rights Acts of the 1960s. The dominant influence of the tobacco industry is slowly waning. The University of North Carolina (founded 1789) was the first state university in the United States. Area: 136,523sq km (52,712sq mi). Pop. (1996) 7,322,870.

Northcliffe, Alfred Charles William Harmsworth, Viscount (1865–1922) British newspaper publisher, b. Ireland. He began his career as a freelance journalist but, with the help of his brother Harold, was soon publishing his own periodicals. In 1896 Harmsworth launched the *Daily Mail*; its concise, readable style of news presentation proved very successful. In 1905 he founded the *Daily Mirror*, the first tabloid newspaper, and in 1908 gained control of *The Times*. Northcliffe was a powerful influence on British politics and society during World War 1.

North Dakota State in W north-central United States; the capital is Bismarck. The original inhabitants of the region were Native North Americans of the Plains culture, such as the Mandan and Hidatsa. The first European to visit the area was the French explorer Sieur de La Vérendrye in 1738. North Dakota was partly mapped by David Thompson of the North West Company in 1797. In 1803 the United States acquired the W half of the present state as part of the Louisiana Purchase and the rest of the territory was acquired from Britain in 1818. In 1804–05 the region was explored by the Lewis and Clark Expedition and white settlement began along the Missouri River. In 1861 President James Buchanan established Dakota Territory. The extension of the railroad across the Red River in 1872, and the rapid increase in white-owned farmland for wheat-production after the Homestead Act (1862), led to war between the US army and the Sioux. The region was divided into North Dakota and South Dakota in 1889 and many ethnic Germans emigrated to the area in the 1880s and 1890s. The state also has a large Native American population (*c*.25,000). Area: 183,022sq km (70,665sq mi). Pop. (1996) 643,539.

Northeast Passage Route from the Atlantic to the Pacific via the Arctic Ocean. Unsuccessful attempts were made to find the Passage by Dutch and English mariners from the 16th century. The complete voyage was first made by Baron Nordenskjöld in 1878–79.

Northern Expedition (July 1926–October 1928) Military campaign in N China by the nationalist Kuomintang. With support from the Soviet Red Army and the Chinese Communist Party (CCP), Chiang Kai-shek launched an expedition against the warlords of N China. Although his National Revolutionary Army was greatly outnumbered, Chiang successfully used propaganda to create division and desertion within the warlords' armies and quickly gained the central provinces of Hunan and Hubei. However, Nationalist control of these provinces was threatened by peasant rebellions and industrial strikes supported by some communists, including Mao Zedong. In March 1927 the Nationalist armies seized the major cities of Shanghai and Nanjing and began a purge of communists. The CCP rose in revolt, capturing Guangzhou, S China, in December 1927. The uprising was crushed and many communists were killed or defected, while the rump forces regrouped in Jiangxi. Meanwhile, the Kuomintang armies renewed their offensive, capturing Beijing (June 1928) and establishing a nationalist government in Nanjing (October 1928).

Northern Ireland *See* Ireland, Northern

Northern Rebellion (1569–70) Revolt against Elizabeth I of England, led by the Earl of Northumberland (1528–72). The rebels sought the restoration of Catholicism and the release of Mary, Queen of Scots. They marched S of York, N England, as far as Selby (November 1569), but dispersed in December when opposed by royalist forces under the Earl of Sussex. A second revolt (January 1570) also failed. About 500 rebels, including Northumberland, were executed.

Northern Territory Territory in N Australia; the capital is Darwin. Ayers Rock (Uluru) lies in the S of the Territory. When the first Europeans (the Dutch) arrived in *c*.1605, the region was home to *c*.35,000 Native Australians. In 1863 it was annexed to South Australia, and the first permanent white settlement, Palmerston (now Darwin), was established in 1869. The discovery of gold encouraged settlers and led to the construction of a railway in 1889. The creation of vast cattle ranches produced conflict with the Aboriginal population and many natives were killed. In 1911 Northern Territory was placed under the control of the federal government, but the Territory remained poor and relatively undeveloped. Darwin was bombed (1941) by Japanese aircraft during World War 2. In 1978 Northern Territory gained self-government. Native Australians own more than 34% of the Territory and that is likely to rise under the terms of the Native Land Title Act (1993). Area: 1,347,525sq km (520,280sq mi). Pop. (1993) 169,298.

NORTH DAKOTA
Statehood :
2 November 1889
Nickname :
The Flickertail State
State motto :
Liberty and union, now and forever, one and inseparable

Northern War, First (1655–60) Conflict between Sweden and Poland. Charles X of Sweden declared war on Poland on the excuse that John II of Poland had not recognized his succession. The real motivation was Sweden's desire to increase its Baltic empire. Sweden, supported by the state of Brandenburg, invaded and occupied Poland, forcing John II into exile. Russia, Denmark and Austria then entered the Northern War in support of Poland, and Brandenburg switched sides. Although the Swedes were eventually expelled from Poland, they gained Skåne from Frederick III of Denmark.

Northern War, Great (1700–21) Conflict in N Europe between Sweden and an alliance of Russia, Denmark-Norway and Poland-Saxony. During the 16th and 17th centuries, Sweden had acquired a powerful Baltic empire. Resentful of Sweden's strength, its neighbours formed an anit-Sweden coalition in 1698. The Great Northern War began when Augustus II (the Strong) of Poland-Saxony invaded Livonia in February 1700. The following month, Frederick IV of Denmark-Norway attacked Schleswig-Holstein, and Peter I (the Great) of Russia besieged the city of Narva (now in Estonia). Charles responded by marching first against Denmark, forcing them to submit in August 1700, and then defeating the Russians (November 1700). He forced Poland-Saxony to retreat and eventually compelled Augustus to abdicate in 1704. In 1708 Charles invaded Russia, but the Russians had taken advantage of the lull in fighting to reorganize its army, and the Swedes suffered a heavy defeat at the Battle of Poltava (1709). Charles was forced to flee to the Ottoman Empire, persuading them to attack Russia in 1711. Meanwhile, the coalition (strengthened by the addition of Prussia and Hanover), had seized the initiative, seizing Swedish territory along the Baltic coast until they threatened the Swedish capital, Stockholm. Expelled by the Ottoman sultan, Charles XI returned to Sweden (1715), whereupon he began to regroup his forces for a fresh offensive. Charles was killed during an attack on Norway (November 1718); his successor, Frederick I, sued for peace. By the Treaties of Stockholm (1719–21), Sweden lost Bremen to Hanover, and Szczecin and part of Swedish Pomerania to Prussia. By the Treaty of Nystad (1721), Russia gained most of Sweden's Baltic possessions, including Estonia, Livonia and part of Finnish Karelia, and emerged as the dominant force in the region.

North German Confederation (1867–71) (*Norddeutscher Bund*) Alliance of 22 German states N of the River Main. After Prussia defeated Austria in the Austro-Prussian War (1866), it annexed a further 17 small German states and declared a federal union. This was the first stage in Otto von Bismarck's plan for German unification. The Confederation encouraged strong ties with the S German states and, after Bismarck had engineered the Franco-Prussian War (1870–71), the North German Confederation combined with the southern German states to create the German Empire.

North Korea *See* Korea, North

Northumberland, John Dudley, Duke of (1502–53) English statesman and soldier, protector of England (1549–53), father of Robert Dudley, Earl of Leicester. He was one of the councillors named by Henry VIII to govern during the minority of Edward VI. Dudley ousted his rival, the Duke of Somerset in 1549, and ordered his execution (1552). In 1551 he appointed himself Duke of Northumberland. Effective ruler of England, Northumberland crushed peasants who resisted enclosure and strictly enforced Protestantism, primarily to accrue wealth for himself and his supporters. In 1553 Northumberland attempted to usurp the succession through his daughter-in-law, Lady Jane Grey, but was thwarted by popular support for the rightful queen, Mary I. He was subsequently executed for treason.

Northumbria, Kingdom of Largest kingdom in ANGLO-SAXON England. It was formed in the early 7th century by Aethelfrith of Bernicia's (r.593–616) union of the kingdoms of Bernicia and Deira. At its military height during the reigns of Edwin (r.616–33), OSWALD (r.633–642) and Oswy (r.641–670), Northumbria encompassed NE England and SE Scotland up to the Firth of Forth and dominated the rival kingdoms of WESSEX and MERCIA. In the early 8th century, Northumbria was the site of the golden age of Anglo-Saxon art and culture. The monasteries in Jarrow and Wearmouth became the leading intellectual institutions of Western Europe, producing scholars such as BEDE. The Lindisfarne Gospels are a supreme example of medieval illumination. Northumbria declined in the face of Viking invasions in the late 8th century and was ultimately conquered by Wessex in the 10th century.

North Vietnam *See* VIETNAM

North West Company Canadian fur-trading organization, founded in 1783. The leading rival of the HUDSON'S BAY COMPANY, its activities in the FUR TRADE were initially confined to E Canada, but it soon began to sponsor expeditions, by men such as Alexander MACKENZIE and David THOMPSON, deep into the interior of Canada. Its traders (Nor'westers) transported furs back to Montréal along the St Lawrence River. The Company's trading domain extended to the Arctic and Pacific oceans, even reaching OREGON. The trading posts of Fort William (founded 1805) and Astoria (founded 1811) were threatened by the RED RIVER SETTLEMENT (1812), leading to violent confrontations with the Hudson's Bay Company. To settle the dispute, the British government merged the two companies in 1821. *See also* ASTOR, JOHN JACOB

Northwest Ordinances (1784, 1785, 1787) Decrees of the CONTINENTAL CONGRESS, establishing the composition of the territory between the Ohio and Mississippi rivers. The **Ordinance of 1794**, drafted by Thomas JEFFERSON, divided Northwest Territory into several self-governing districts. The **Ordinance of 1795** established a policy for federal land sales based on townships. The final (and most important) **Ordinance of 1795** established the criteria by which the districts of Northwest Territory could be included as states of the Union. It outlawed slavery and provided guarantees of basic civil rights. The states of INDIANA, OHIO, ILLINOIS, MICHIGAN, WISCONSIN and part of MINNESOTA were later created from the Northwest Territory. *See also* ARTICLES OF CONFEDERATION

NORWAY

AREA: 323,900sq km (125,050sq mi)
POPULATION: 4,286,000
CAPITAL (POPULATION): Oslo (459,292)
GOVERNMENT: Constitutional monarchy
ETHNIC GROUPS: Norwegian 97%
LANGUAGES: Norwegian (official), Lappish, Finnish
RELIGIONS: Christianity (Lutheran 88%)
GDP PER CAPITA (1995): US$21,940

Kingdom in NW Europe. Norway's seafaring tradition dates back to the VIKINGS, who between the 9th and 11th centuries raided W Europe and established colonies in ICELAND and GREENLAND. OLAF II introduced Christianity in the early 11th century, but was deposed by CANUTE II of DENMARK in 1028. MAGNUS I ruled (1035–46) over Denmark and Norway. The period 1130–1240 was one of civil war between rival claimants to the throne. HAAKON IV (r.1217–63) re-established unity.

In 1319 Magnus II of SWEDEN was elected king of Norway, and in 1397 Norway, Sweden and Denmark were united in the KALMAR UNION. Norway was subject to Danish rule from 1442 to 1814. Lutheranism became the state religion in the mid-16th century. In 1814 Denmark ceded Norway to Sweden. Norway declared independence, but Swedish troops forced Norway to accept union under the Swedish crown. In 1905 an independent monarchy was established. Norway was neutral in World War 1. The 1920s saw economic growth and industrialization, but the country suffered 33% unemployment during the GREAT DEPRESSION. In the 1930s it adopted progressive social welfare provisions.

On the outbreak of World War 2, Norway declared itself neutral. However, between April and June 1940, German troops invaded and conquered the country. During the subsequent resistance, directed by the Norwegian government in London, more than 50% of Norway's merchant fleet was destroyed. In 1942 a Nazi puppet regime was set up under Vidkun QUISLING. Liberation was achieved in May 1945. In 1949 Norway joined the NORTH ATLANTIC TREATY ORGANIZATION (NATO) and was a co-founder (1960) of the EUROPEAN FREE TRADE ASSOCIATION (EFTA). In 1972 and 1994 referenda, Norway voted against joining the EUROPEAN COMMUNITY.

In 1981 Labour leader Gro Harlem BRUNDTLAND became Norway's first woman prime minister. In 1991 King OLAF V was succeeded by his son, Harald V. In 1996 Brundtland was replaced as prime minister by the Conservative Thorbjoern Jagland. In the 1997 elections Jagland was defeated by a centrist coalition led by Kjell Magne Bondevik.

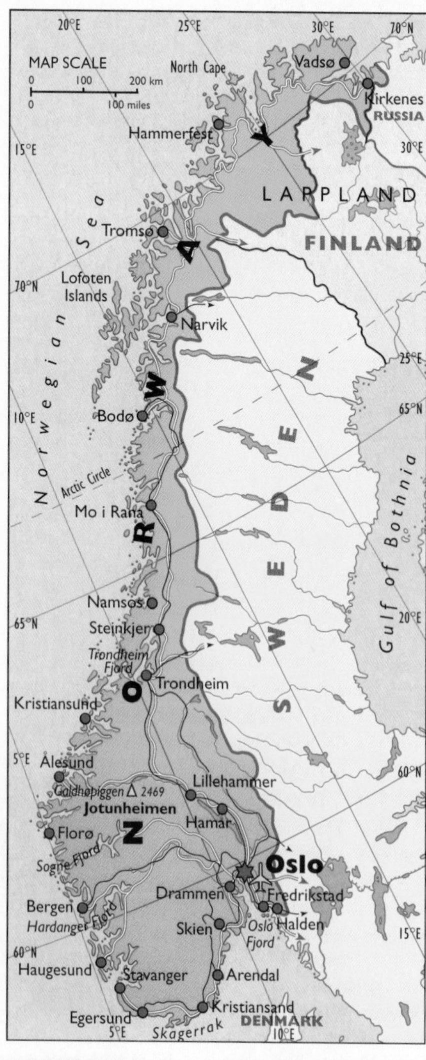

Northwest Passage Treacherous sea route from the Atlantic Ocean to the Pacific Ocean through the Arctic waters of what is now N Canada. The first attempt to find the Passage was made by English explorer Henry CABOT in 1497. Many of the world's greatest explorers followed his example, including (in chronological order): Jacques CARTIER, Martin FROBISHER, Francis DRAKE, Humphrey GILBERT, Henry HUDSON and James COOK. The expedition of Sir John FRANKLIN, which set out in 1845, ended in the tragic loss of all the crew, but during the search for survivors, the route was established (1854) by Robert McClure. Norwegian explorer Roald AMUNDSEN became the first person to sail through the passage, in 1903–06. *See also* EXPLORATION; NORTHEAST PASSAGE

Northwest Territories Region of N Canada, covering more than one-third of the country; the capital is Yellowknife. Much of the N and E of the province is inhabited by the INUIT and other native peoples, who began to arrive in the region *c.*5000 years ago. The first European to reach the area was Samuel HEARNE, who explored the coast for the HUDSON'S BAY COMPANY in 1770–72. Alexander MACKENZIE of the NORTH WEST COMPANY canoed down the river that now bears his name in 1789, founding fur-trading posts along the route. More detailed knowledge of the region was acquired after the tragic disappearance (1847) of Sir John FRANKLIN while on a search for the elusive NORTHWEST PASSAGE. In 1870 the Hudson's Bay Company ceded the territory to Canada. The present boundaries were established in 1912. The discovery of oil in the 1920s led to the development of the region's transport system. In 1999 part of Northwest Territories became the Inuit territory of NUNAVUT. Area: 3.43 million sq km (1.32million sq mi). Pop. (1996) 64,402.

Norway *See* country feature

Nostradamus (1503–66) French seer and astrologer, b. Michel de Nostredame. After practising as a doctor, he began making astrological predictions in 1547. These were published in rhyming quatrains in *Centuries* (1555) and represented one verse for every year from then until the end of the world (in the 1990s). To avoid prosecution as a magician, Nostradamus completely changed the order of the verses so that no time sequence was discernible.

Nova Scotia Maritime province in E Canada; the capital is Halifax. Originally inhabited by the Micmac and Abnaki, the region was claimed for England by John CABOT in 1497. The first settlement was made by the French explorer Samuel de CHAMPLAIN at Port Royal in 1605, and became a base for their colony of ACADIA (which included NEW BRUNSWICK). Contested by France and Britain during the French and Indian Wars (1683–1763), the mainland was awarded to Britain by the Peace of Utrecht (1713). Cape Breton Island was seized from the French in 1758. The region was renamed Nova Scotia and large numbers of French residents were forcibly deported, many settling in Louisiana. In 1848 Nova Scotia became the first British colony to gain the right of self-government. Nova Scotia joined New Brunswick, QUÉBEC and ONTARIO to form the Dominion of CANADA in 1867. Area: 55,490sq km (21,425sq mi). Pop. (1996) 909,282.

Novgorod City on the River Volchov, NW Russia, one of Russia's oldest cities. RURIK became prince of Novgorod in 862, and his successor, Oleg, founded the KIEVAN RUS state in 882. Novgorod declared independence from Kiev in 1136, and subsequently prospered on its trade with the HANSEATIC LEAGUE. Novgorod escaped destruction by the invading TATARS in 1238–40, but was forced to pay tribute to the MONGOLS. Novgorod continued to expand, however, and at its height controlled much of N Russia. After a long struggle for hegemony against Moscow, Novgorod was forced to submit to IVAN III (THE GREAT) in 1478, but resistance to Muscovite rule continued until IVAN IV (THE TERRIBLE) massacred many of the city's inhabitants in 1570. Novgorod declined further after the founding of ST PETERSBURG in 1703. During the German occupation (1941–44) of World War 2, the city was badly damaged but the kremlin and St Sofia Cathedral (1045–50) have subsequently been restored. Pop. (1992) 235,000.

Novotný, Antonin (1904–75) Czechoslovak statesman, first secretary of the Czechoslovak Communist Party

(1953–68), president (1957–68). He joined the Communist Party in 1921. During the World War 2 occupation of Czechoslovakia, Novotný was arrested and spent four years (1941–45) in a concentration camp. In 1948 Novotný played a leading role in the communist seizure of power. As president, Novotný worked closely with the Soviet Union, and this, combined with an economic recession, made him unpopular with reformists. In 1968 he was forced to resign in favour of Alexander DUBČEK. *See also* PRAGUE SPRING

Nu, U (1907–95) Burmese statesman, prime minister (1948–56, 1957–58, 1960–62). A leader of the independence movement with AUNG SAN, he became Burma's first prime minister after it achieved independence from Britain. In foreign affairs, U Nu became a major figure in the NON-ALIGNED MOVEMENT, but was faced with domestic recession and unrest. He was replaced by a caretaker administration in 1958, but returned to power until ousted in a military coup, led by NE WIN. U Nu led opposition to Ne Win from exile, finally being allowed to return to Burma in 1980. He was later (1988–92) placed under house arrest for his leadership of the pro-democracy movement. *See also* AUNG SAN SUU KYI, DAW

Nubia Ancient region in NE Africa (now SUDAN). The region of **Lower Nubia**, between the first and second cataracts of the Nile, saw the birth (before 3000 BC) of one of the first states in the world. Lower Nubia was conquered by ancient EGYPT in *c.*2950 BC, and Pharoah Snefru (r. *c.*2575–*c.*2465 BC) made further inroads into the region. When Egyptian Pharoah Sesostris I (r. *c.*1918–*c.*1875 BC) invaded the region of **Upper Nubia**, based around the city of Kerma, he named it KUSH. Pharoah Sesostris III (r. *c.*1836–*c.*1818 BC) built a network of forts to defend Egyptian territory in Nubia, but a resurgent Kush regained control of Lower Nubia in the 18th century BC. By *c.*1650 BC, the Nubians had advanced as far N as ASWAN and were launching devastating raids on Upper Egypt. In *c.*1492 BC Pharoah THUTMOSE I reconquered Nubia and divided it into two administrative regions: Wawat (Lower Nubia) and Kush (Upper Nubia). In *c.*732 BC King Piye of Kush united the entire Nile Valley, and his successor, Shabaka, founded Egypt's 25th (Kushite) dynasty in *c.*715 BC. Nubian supremacy proved short-lived as ASSYRIA invaded Egypt, forcing the Kushites to retreat to Napata (now Marawi) by *c.*654 BC. In *c.*592 BC the Kushites moved their capital to MEROË, where an increasingly Africanized Nubian culture survived until overrun by AKSUM in *c.*AD 350.

Nuclear Test-Ban Treaty (5 August 1963) Agreement prohibiting the testing of NUCLEAR WEAPONS except in underground explosions, signed by US President John KENNEDY, Soviet Premier Nikita KHRUSHCHEV and British Prime Minister Harold MACMILLAN. The Treaty was ratified by more than 100 other states in 1963, but not China or France. In 1994 China carried out underground nuclear tests and in 1995 France also conducted tests in the South Pacific. A further Test-Ban Treaty was signed by the United States, Britain, Russia, China and France in 1996.

nuclear weapon Device whose enormous explosive force derives from nuclear fission or fusion reactions. To date, nuclear weapons have only be used twice in war: in August 1945 **atomic bombs** were dropped by the United States on the Japanese cities of HIROSHIMA and NAGASAKI. The bombs, each with an explosive force equivalent to 200,000 tonnes of TNT, killed a total of *c.*140,000 people. The **hydrogen bomb** (H-bomb or thermonuclear bomb) was first tested in 1952. The explosive power of the H-bomb can be several million tonnes (megatons) of TNT. Devastation from such bombs covers a wide area: a 15-megaton bomb will cause all flammable material within 20km (12mi) to burst into flame. A third type of weapon, the **neutron bomb** (enhanced radiation bomb) is a small hydrogen bomb that produces a small blast but a very intense burst of high-speed neutrons. The lack of blast means that buildings are not heavily damaged. The neutrons, however, produce intense radiation sickness in people located within a certain range of the explosion, killing those affected within a week. Five nations – the United States, Britain, China, France and Russia – have declared that they have nuclear weapons and have signed both the NUCLEAR TEST-BAN TREATY and the Non-Proliferation Treaty (1968). Belarus, Kazakstan and Ukraine inherited nuclear weapons after the collapse of the Soviet Union (1989) and have since signed the Non-Proliferation Treaty. Other countries that are believed to have nuclear-weapons capability include Israel, India, Pakistan, South Africa, Iran, Brazil and Argentina. *See also* CAMPAIGN FOR NUCLEAR DISARMAMENT (CND); DISARMAMENT; MANHATTAN PROJECT; STRATEGIC ARMS LIMITATION TALKS (SALT)

Nujoma, Sam (1929–) Namibian statesman, first president of NAMIBIA (1990–). Forced into exile by South Africa's occupation of South West Africa (now Namibia), he helped found the SOUTH WEST AFRICA PEOPLE'S ORGANIZATION (SWAPO) and became its president in 1960. In 1966 SWAPO resorted to guerrilla tactics in an effort to remove South African forces from South West Africa. In 1973 SWAPO was recognized by the United Nations (UN) as the legitimate representative of the Namibian people. In 1988 South Africa finally conceded to independence for Namibia. Nujoma returned to Namibia in 1989 and led SWAPO to victory in the ensuing elections. He set about the difficult task of reconstruction. Nujoma was re-elected in 1994 and 1999. *See also* APARTHEID

nullification In US history, the supposed right of a state to declare invalid and not enforce a law passed by the federal government. Nullification was first proposed by Thomas JEFFERSON and James MADISON in their KENTUCKY AND VIRGINIA RESOLUTIONS (1798). Jefferson asserted that supreme sovereignty lay with the states of the Union and that the federal government was their agent with prescribed powers delegated to it by the CONSTITUTION OF THE UNITED STATES. In 1829 John CALHOUN upheld the principle of STATES' RIGHTS in relation to the imposition of the Tariff of 1828 by President Andrew JACKSON. When the Tariff of 1832 proved to be equally harsh, South Carolina adopted the Ordinance of Nullification (1832), which declared both Tariffs null and void and, refusing to enforce them, threatened to secede if the federal government intervened. President Jackson and Congress responded with the Force Bill (1833), authorizing the use of the army to collect the tariffs, but at the same time proposing a compromise Tariff Act. South Carolina accepted the compromise tariff, but remained true to its principles by declaring the Force Bill null and void. Although the Nullification Crisis was defused, the issue of nullification again arose at the time of the Civil War in the debate surrounding the secession of Southern states. *See also* CLAY, HENRY; WEBSTER, DANIEL

Numidia Ancient region of NW Africa, roughly corresponding to modern Algeria. From the 6th century BC it formed part of the Carthaginian empire. In the Second PUNIC WAR (218–201 BC), King MASINISSA of Eastern Numidia deserted CARTHAGE for ROME (206 BC) and, following Rome's victory, gained Western Numidia, which had continued to support HANNIBAL. After Masinissa's death (148 BC), Rome divided Numidia into several chiefdoms. JUGURTHA (r.118–106 BC) forcibly reintegrated the chiefdoms, but Rome regained control in 105 BC. Juba I's efforts to reunify Numidia ended in his defeat by Julius CAESAR at the Battle of Thapsus (46 BC), and Numidia continued to flourish as part of the ROMAN EMPIRE. The region was an early centre of Christianity, but the schismatic DONATISM movement came to dominate the region in the 4th century AD. Roman control was broken by the VANDAL invasion in AD 429, but Numidian culture persisted even after the Arab conquest in the 8th century.

Nunavut Territory in N Canada; the capital is Iqaluit. Formerly part of NORTHWEST TERRITORY, Nunavut was granted self-government in April 1999. Created as a homeland for the INUIT, its first premier was Paul Okalit. Area: *c.*2 million sq km (775,000sq mi).

Núñez, Rafael (1825–94) Colombian statesman, president (1880–82, 1884–94). He helped draft Colombia's first Liberal constitution in 1853. Núñez was elected president with the support of moderates from both the Liberal and Conservative parties,. After a Liberal revolt, he was forced to unite with the Conservatives in order to maintain power. Núñez introduced a new constitution (1886) that created a centralized government and returned powers to the Roman Catholic church. Núñez maintained a dictatorial grip on power until his death.

Nur-ad-Din (1118–74) (Nureddin) Ruler of Syria (1146–74). Under the nominal control of the ABBASID caliphate, Nur-ad-Din united Syrian Muslims against the Christian CRUSADES. He recaptured Edessa from the Crusaders in 1146, and took Damascus from the Seljuk Turks in 1154. He sent one of his generals, SALADIN, to Egypt to assist the FATIMIDS in their struggles against the Crusaders, thus extending his influence into Egypt.

Nuremberg Laws (1935) German legislation promulgated by the Nazi government of Adolf HITLER. They deprived Jews, including all persons who were of Jewish descent, of the rights of citizenship and prohibited marriage of Jews and non-Jews. *See also* HOLOCAUST, THE

Nuremberg Trials (1945–46) Prosecution of leading members of the NAZI PARTY accused of war crimes during WORLD WAR 2, held before a international military tribunal in Nuremberg (Nürnberg), Germany. The tribunal was established in the London Agreement (1945) by the United States, Britain, France and the Soviet Union, and was later ratified by 19 other countries. It was authorized to determine whether any organizations were criminal in nature, and to determine whether any individuals were guilty of war crimes, crimes against peace or crimes against humanity. Twenty-four Nazi leaders stood trial, and a number of groups, including the SS and the GESTAPO, were declared to be criminal. Twelve Nazi leaders were sentenced to death, among them Joachim von RIBBENTROP, Alfred ROSENBERG, Alfred JODL and Arthur SEYSS-INQUART. Hermann GÖRING committed suicide before the death sentence could be carried out and Martin BORMANN was sentenced to death in absentia. Three Nazis were sentenced to life imprisonment: Rudolf HESS, Erich RAEDAR and Walther Funk. Four received lengthy prison sentences, among them Karl DÖNITZ and Albert SPEER. Franz von PAPEN was one of three defendants who were acquitted. *See also* HOLOCAUST, THE

Nurhachi (1559–1626) Juchen chief in MANCHURIA. He suppressed rivals within his own band before defeating the other four Juchen tribes to create a unified MANCHU state. In 1601 Nurhachi established the banner system of political administration and military conscription, control and mobilization. He also introduced a writing system for bureaucratic and literary purposes. In 1616 Nurhachi proclaimed himself khan (emperor) of the Later JIN. He invaded MING China in 1618, capturing Fushun, NE China. In 1625 Nurhachi moved his capital to Mukden, Manchuria, to facilitate further invasions of China, but was defeated and killed by the Chinese. He was succeeded by his son Abahai (d.1643), but it was left to another son, Dorgon (1612–59), to complete the conquest of China and establish the QING dynasty in 1644.

Nyasaland Former name of MALAWI

Nyerere, Julius Kambarage (1922–99) Tanzanian statesman, first president of TANZANIA (1964–85). In 1954 he founded the TANGANYIKA AFRICAN NATIONAL UNION (TANU). Following his victory in the 1960 elections, Nyerere became prime minister of Tanganyika (mainland Tanzania) and led it to independence in 1961. He was the principal architect of the ORGANIZATION OF AFRICAN UNITY (OAU), founded in 1964. Nyerere negotiated the union (1964) between Tanganyika and the island of Zanzibar, which created the Republic of Tanzania. He established a one-party state, governed by the Chama Cha Mapinduzi (CCM) or Revolutionary Party of Tanzania. His ARUSHA DECLARATION (1967) is an important statement of African SOCIALISM. In 1979 Nyerere sent troops into neighbouring Uganda to help topple the regime of Idi AMIN. Under his autocratic but generally benign socialist government, Tanzania made striking progress in social welfare and education, but in the 1980s economic setbacks encouraged demands for greater democracy. Nyerere retired as president in 1985 but continued his work for African unity and for the overthrow of South Africa's APARTHEID regime. *See also* PAN-AFRICANISM

Nystad, Treaty of (1721) Agreement ending the Great NORTHERN WAR (1700–21) between Sweden and Russia. Sweden ceded Ingria, ESTONIA, Livonia, Kexholm, RIGA, and part of Finnish KARELIA to Russia, thus losing its Baltic empire. *See also* PETER I (THE GREAT)

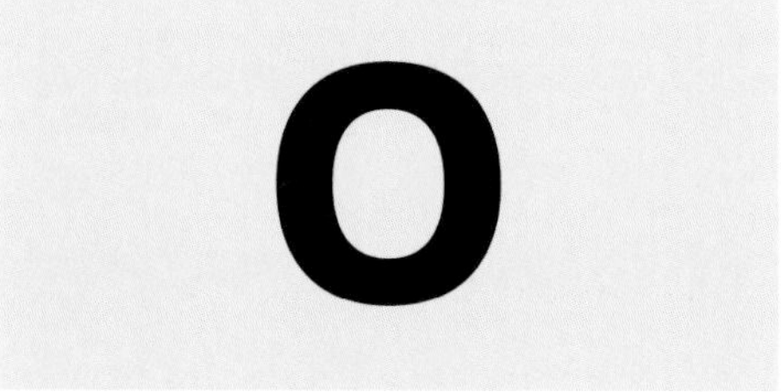

OAS (*Organisation de l'Armée Secrète*) French terrorist group opposed to Algerian independence. It was set up in 1961 by disaffected army officers and French settlers in Algeria, led by Raoul Salan (1899–1984). When it became clear that President DE GAULLE was preparing to come to an agreement with Algerian nationalists, OAS perpetrated acts of terrorism in France and Algeria, including an unsuccessful military coup in Algeria (1962). OAS leaders, including Salan, were arrested, tried and imprisoned, and the organization folded after Algeria gained independence.

OAS *See* ORGANIZATION OF AMERICAN STATES

Oastler, Richard (1789–1861) ("Factory King") British radical reformer. He was a leader of the movement to repeal the POOR LAW Amendment Act of 1834 and an eloquent campaigner against child labour. Imprisoned (1840–44) for debt, he edited the *Fleet Papers*, which explained his social theories. His efforts to gain a maximum ten-hour day in the textile factories eventually came into effect as the Ten Hours Act (1847).

Oates, Titus (1649–1705) English Protestant priest, author of the anti-Catholic POPISH PLOT (1678). Oates and Israel Tonge, a fanatical anti-Jesuit, fabricated a plot to kill CHARLES II, place his Catholic brother, the Duke of York (later JAMES II), on the throne, burn London and massacre Protestants. The supposed Plot terrified England and resulted in the execution of 35 probably blameless citizens. Oates' perjury was later proved, and he was severely flogged, successfully sued by the Duke of York for £100,000 and imprisoned.

OAU *See* ORGANIZATION OF AFRICAN UNITY

O

Obote, (Apollo) Milton (1924–) Ugandan statesman, prime minister (1962–66) and president (1966–71, 1980–85). He became a member of the Uganda National Congress Party in 1957, and when the Party split (1960) he formed the Uganda People's Congress. Obote was the first prime minister of independent Uganda. In 1966 he deposed the president, King MUTESA II of Buganda. In 1971 Obote was ousted by his army chief, Idi AMIN, and went into exile in Tanzania. He returned to power after Amin was overthrown. Obote's second term as president was marked by increased inter-tribal violence. He was deposed in a further coup, led by Yoweri MUSEVENI.

Obregón, Álvaro (1880–1928) Mexican statesman, president (1920–24). Obregón was a supporter of Francisco MADERO. When Madero was overthrown by Victoriano HUERTA, Obregón joined forces with Venustiano CARRANZA, "Pancho" VILLA and Emiliano ZAPATA to defeat Huerta. Obregón then supported Carranza against the rebels. A liberal, Obregón forced Carranza to agree to the restoration of land to the Native Americans. Later, when Carranza attempted to violate the constitution, Obregón raised the revolt that resulted in his becoming president. Widely regarded as a capable president, he enacted some notable land, educational and financial reforms. In 1928 Obregón was re-elected but assassinated before he could take office. *See also* MEXICAN REVOLUTION

Obrenović Ruling dynasty of SERBIA (1817–42, 1858–1903). It was founded by MILOŠ, who led the Serbian revolt against the Turks. In 1839 Miloš was succeeded as prince of Serbia by his son **Michael** (1823–68). In 1842 Michael was deposed by ALEXANDER KARAGEORGEVIĆ and exiled. In 1858 Miloš returned to the throne. On Miloš' death, he was once more succeeded by Michael. Michael proved himself a capable ruler, completing the liberation of Serbia and modernizing the state. Assassinated in 1868, he was succeeded by his cousin **Milan** (1854–1901). In 1876, with support from Russia, Milan declared war on Turkey. At the Congress of BERLIN (1878) he obtained European recognition of Serbian independence. In 1878 Milan declared himself king of Serbia. The failure of the war against Bulgaria (1878) and heavy taxation increased his domestic unpopularity. He abdicated (1889) in favour of his son **Alexander** (1873–1903). Alexander was assassinated in a military coup. He was succeeded by Peter Karageorge as PETER I, thus bringing the Obrenović dynasty to an end.

O'Brien, William (1852–1928) Irish nationalist leader. He edited *United Ireland*, the Irish LAND LEAGUE's newspaper founded by Charles PARNELL, and was a Nationalist member of Parliament (1883–95). In 1898 O'Brien formed the United Irish League to campaign for agrarian reform. He took part in the conference preceding the Irish LAND ACT of 1903, which saw large amounts of land transfer from English to Irish ownership. In 1910 O'Brien formed the All-for-Ireland League, but by 1918 most of his followers had joined SINN FÉIN.

O'Brien, William Smith (1803–64) Irish politician. He was a member (1828–48) of the Westminster Parliament. Although a Protestant, O'Brien was in favour of the Act of CATHOLIC EMANCIPATION (1829). He supported the Act of UNION (1800) until the imprisonment (1843) of Daniel O'CONNELL by the British government. He joined O'Connell's Repeal Association against the Act of Union, but left in 1846 to set up the more militant Repeal League. As a leader of the YOUNG IRELAND movement, O'Brien led an abortive rebellion in Ireland in 1848. He was transported to Australia but subsequently pardoned (1856).

O'Connell, Daniel (1775–1847) Irish nationalist leader, known as "the Liberator". In 1823 he formed the Catholic Association to campaign for an end to discrimination against Roman Catholics. In 1828 his election to Westminster as member of Parliament for County Cork forced the Duke of WELLINGTON's government to pass the Act of CATHOLIC EMANCIPATION (1829). In 1840 O'Connell founded the Repeal Association to overturn the Act of UNION (1800). In 1844 he was arrested and briefly imprisoned for sedition. O'Connell's failure to deliver significant reforms and the IRISH FAMINE (1845–49) led to the formation of the more radical YOUNG IRELAND movement.

O'Connor, Feargus Edward (1794–1855) Irish Chartist leader. He was a member of Parliament (1832–35) for County Cork and a supporter of Daniel O'CONNELL. In 1837 O'Connor founded the *Northern Star*, the most influential newspaper of CHARTISM. In 1840 he founded the National Charter Association (NCA) in an attempt to unify the movement. He became a member of Parliament for Nottingham in 1847, but became insane soon after the folding of the Chartist movement.

O'Connor, Sandra Day (1930–) US Supreme Court justice. A Republican, she won election to two full terms in the Arizona Senate and was elected majority leader in 1973. O'Connor served on the Superior Court in Phoenix (1974–79), until her appointment to the Arizona Court of Appeals. In 1981 she was appointed associate justice of the Supreme Court. The first woman to sit on the Court, she is moderately conservative.

Octavian *See* AUGUSTUS

October Revolution (1917) *See* RUSSIAN REVOLUTION

Oda Nobunaga *See* NOBUNAGA, ODA

Oder-Neisse Line Frontier established between Germany and Poland at the YALTA CONFERENCE (February 1945). It followed the rivers Oder and Neisse from the Baltic Sea to the Czechoslovakian border. Acceptance of the frontier meant that a large amount of previously German territory would be transferred to Poland, compensating Poland for territory being claimed by the Soviet Union in the East. The US and British governments initially opposed the Line because it would make Poland excessively dependent upon the Soviet Union and because it would involve the deportation of large numbers of Germans. No agreement was achieved at Yalta. After disputed areas, including GDAŃSK (Danzig), had been incorporated into Poland, the POTSDAM CONFERENCE (August 1945) recognized the Line, pending a peace treaty with Germany. East Germany and Poland recognized the Line in 1950; the West German government accepted it in 1970, during the OSTPOLITIK period. It was recognized by the reunified Germany in 1990.

Odinga, Oginga (1911–94) Kenyan statesman. Prominent in Kenya's quest for independence from Britain, he served (1960–66) as vice president of the Kenya African National Union (KANU). On independence, he served (1964–66) as vice president in Jomo KENYATTA's government. He then formed the Kenya People's Union (KPU), a more radical party, in opposition to Kenyatta. The KPU was soon banned, and Odinga was imprisoned (1969–71). After his release, he continued to work against government corruption and to campaign for a multiparty system.

Odo (*c*.1036–97) (Odo of Bayeux) Norman warrior-priest, bishop of Bayeux. The son of ROBERT I, Duke of Normandy, Odo received his bishopric from his half-brother, WILLIAM I (THE CONQUEROR), in 1049. He fought at William's side at the Battle of Hastings and was awarded the earldom of Kent (1067). Odo played a major role in Anglo-Norman politics, acting as regent during William's absences abroad. He was later imprisoned (1082–87) by William for raising troops without permission. Odo is thought to have commissioned the BAYEUX TAPESTRY.

Odoacer (*c*.433–93) (Odovacar) Chief of the Germanic Heruli people, conqueror of the Western ROMAN EMPIRE, king of Italy (476–93). The Heruli were Roman mercenaries until 476, when they deposed the last Western Roman emperor, ROMULUS AUGUSTULUS, and declared Odoacer king of Italy. In 489 the OSTROGOTHS invaded Italy, encouraged by the Eastern Roman emperor ZENO. Their leader, THEODERIC, soon captured all Odoacer's territory except his capital, RAVENNA. After Ravenna fell in 493, Odoacer was forced to accept a power-sharing agreement. He was murdered at a banquet given by Theoderic.

OECD Abbreviation of the ORGANIZATION FOR ECONOMIC COOPERATION AND DEVELOPMENT(OECD)

Offa (d.796) King of MERCIA (757–96). He made Mercia the foremost ANGLO-SAXON kingdom of Britain by gaining territory from WESSEX and Wales and controlling the wealthy areas of Kent, Sussex and East Anglia. Offa styled himself *Rex Anglorum* (King of the English). He introduced the first sound and externally valid currency seen in Britain since the Roman period. It is probable that Offa built **Offa's Dyke**, an earthwork fortification in England and Wales, running from the mouth of the River Dee, Clwyd, to Chepstow, Gwent. It was designed to mark the Welsh-Mercian border. Its ditch and high rampart reduced raiding by the Welsh tribes.

Oglethorpe, James Edward (1696–1785) English general and colonist. After military service, he entered Parliament (1722) and became interested in social reform, particularly the problems of debtors. After acquiring a charter (1732), Oglethorpe took a group of settlers to North America and founded (1733) the colony of SAVANNAH in what became the state of Georgia. He encouraged the immigration of unemployed debtors and persecuted Protestants. Oglethorpe's military experience allowed him to defend his territory successfully against Spain (1742). He returned to England in 1743.

Ogodei (1185–1241) Great Khan (1229–41) of the MONGOL empire, son and successor of GENGHIS KHAN. He established his capital at KARAKORUM, on a site previously chosen by Genghis. Ogodei expanded Mongol territory further into China, allying with the Southern SONG to capture Kaifeng from the JIN DYNASTY. Unlike most MONGOL conquests, N China was not destroyed. Instead, Ogodei utilized China's superior technology and administrative systems to improve those of the Mongol empire. The succession crisis caused by Ogodei's death led to the return of BATU KHAN from the W borders of the empire, thus saving Europe from Mongol invasion.

O'Higgins, Bernardo (1778–1842) South American revolutionary leader and ruler of Chile (1817–23). Despite being the illegitimate son of Ambrosio O'Higgins, Spanish governor of Chile and later viceroy of Peru, Bernardo was a champion of Latin-American independence. In 1811 he became a member of Chile's national congress, which had been established while Spain was preoccupied with Napoleon's invasion. O'Higgins commanded the Chilean army against the Spanish. Defeated at Rancagua in 1814, he joined José de SAN MARTÍN in Argentina to defeat the Spanish at CHACABUCO (1817). In

OHIO
Statehood :
1 March 1803
Nickname :
The Buckeye State
State motto :
With God, all things are possible

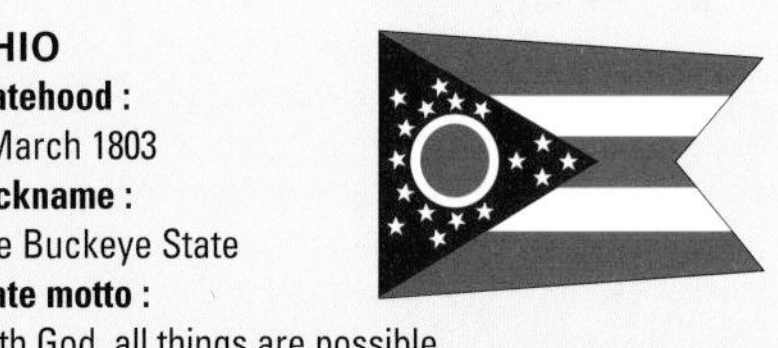

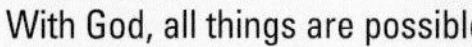

1818 as "supreme director" O'Higgins proclaimed Chile's independence. His reforms met with opposition from the aristocracy and church, and he was forced to resign. O'Higgins spent the rest of his life in exile in Peru.

Ohio State in E central United States, bounded by Lake Erie in the N; the capital is Columbus. The region was largely uninhabited at the time of the first European exploration (*c*.1670). Britain acquired the region at the end of the French and Indian Wars (1756–63). The British were immediately confronted by Pontiac's Rebellion. Ohio was ceded to the United States after the American Revolution. After the Northwest Ordinance (1787), it became part of Northwest Territory. The rapid influx of white settlers led to further conflict with the native population until General Anthony Wayne's victory at the Battle of Fallen Timbers (1794) and the subsequent Treaty of Fort Greenville (1795). Ohio formed a major supply centre for US forces in the War of 1812 against the British. Settlement increased further with the completion of the Erie Canal (1825) and the arrival of the railroads (1830s). In 1870 John D. Rockefeller founded the Standard Oil Company of Ohio, which soon controlled 90% of the nation's oil-refining. Area: 106,764sq km (41,222sq mi). Pop. (1990) 10,847,115.

Ojibwa (Chippewa) Algonquian-speaking Native North Americans of the Eastern Woodlands culture, who used to live by lakes Huron and Superior. Equipped with French guns, the Ojibwa defeated the Sioux in the 1690s and occupied much of present-day N Minnesota. They fought alongside the French in the French and Indian Wars, but sided with the British in the American Revolution and the War of 1812. Today, they number *c*.80,000.

Okinawa Largest island of the Okinawa archipelago, SW of mainland Japan, part of the Ryukyu Islands group in the W Pacific Ocean. In the last major amphibious offensive of World War 2, US troops landed here in April 1945 and met fierce Japanese resistance. In June 1945 Okinawa surrendered at the cost of *c*.50,000 US casualties. The island remained under US administration until 1971. The United States still maintains some bases. Area: 1176sq km (454sq mi). Pop. (1990) 1,222,458.

Oklahoma State in S central United States; the capital is Oklahoma City. Archaeologists have unearthed evidence of the Clovis and Folsom cultures in Oklahoma dating back *c*.15,000 years. Francisco Vázquez de Coronado visisted the region in 1541 and claimed it for Spain. The area was acquired from France by the United States as part of the Louisiana Purchase (1803). During Andrew Jackson's presidency, Congress created (1834) the Indian Territory in the region for the so-called Five Civilized Tribes of Native North Americans, who were forced to move from the settled E. In the 1870s Indian Territory was coveted by the railroads and the cattle industry. In 1889 Congress permitted white settlement in W Indian Territory, renamed the Territory of Oklahoma, resulting in the famous land run (22 April). Those who had settled before this date became known as "Sooners". In 1907 this land was merged with Indian Territory to form the state of Oklahoma. The Democratic Party held the state governorship from statehood until 1962. Oklahoma was devastated by drought during the 1930s, resulting in the so-called Dust Bowl. A terrorist bomb (1995) killed 168 people in Oklahoma City. Area: 181,089sq km (69,918sq mi). Pop. (1990) 3,189,456.

OKLAHOMA
Statehood :
16 November 1907
Nickname :
The Sooner State
State motto :
Labour conquers all things

Okubo Toshimichi (1830–78) Japanese samurai leader. With Saigo Takamori, he was a leader of the revolt that overthrew the Tokugawa shogunate. At the Meiji Restoration (1868), Okubo became an important figure in the imperial government. As minister of home affairs from 1874, he began to modernize Japan's economy, inspired by a visit to the West. He successfully opposed Saigo's plans for war with Korea and Saigo subsequently led a samurai rebellion in Satsuma, their native province. Okubo was assassinated by a disaffected samurai.

Okuma Shigenobu (1838–1922) Japanese statesman, prime minister (1898, 1914–18). He served (1869–81) as a reformist finance minister after the Meiji Restoration. Okuma's proposal that a constitutional government, modelled on the British parliamentary system, be established earned him the enmity of conservative members of the government. Forced to resign (1881), he formed Japan's second political party, the *Kaishinto* (Progressive Party). He returned to government, serving (1888–89, 1896–97) as foreign minister. In 1898 Okuma and Itagaki Taisuke merged their political parties to create the *Kenseito* (Constitutional Party) and formed a short-lived government. In his second term as prime minister, Okuma presided over Japan's entry into World War 1.

Olaf I (*c*.964–*c*.1000) (Olaf Tryggvason) King of Norway (995–*c*.1000), great grandson of Harald I. He spent much of his youth on Viking raids and was converted to Christianity while in the British Isles. On his return to Norway, Olaf overthrew Haakon the Great and attempted to Christianize the country. He sent missionaries to Iceland, Greenland and the Faröe Islands. Olaf founded (997) Nidaros (now Trondheim) as his capital. He was defeated and killed at the Battle of Svolder against the Danes, under Sweyn I, and the Swedes. After Olaf's death, Norway reverted to Danish and Swedish rule.

Olaf II, Saint (*c*.995–1030) (Olaf Haraldsson) Norwegian king (1015–30) and patron saint of Norway. A Viking warrior, he assisted the English king Ethelred II (the Unready) in his struggle against Sweyn I of Denmark. Converted to Christianity, Olaf returned to Norway (1015) and continued Olaf I's efforts to Christianize the country. During his reign, he strengthened and consolidated the Norwegian kingdom but failed to maintain the support of the chieftains. When Canute II of Denmark threatened Norway, a number of chiefs rebelled in his support. In 1028 Olaf was forced into exile and died in battle at Stikelstad. Canute became king of Norway. Following reports of miracles at Olaf's grave, he was canonized in 1164. His feast day is 29 July.

Olaf V (1903–91) King of Norway (1957–91), he succeeded his father, Haakon VII. After the German occupation (1940) of Norway during World War 2, Olaf took an active part in the struggle for liberation, serving (1944–45) as commander in chief of the Norwegian armed forces. His role as monarch was largely ceremonial. He was succeeded by his son, Harald V.

Oldcastle, Sir John (*c*.1377–1417) English leader of the Lollards. He fought in the army under Henry IV and earned the respect and liking of the future Henry V. A fervent supporter of John Wycliffe, Oldcastle was condemned as a heretic in 1413. He escaped to lead an abortive uprising (1414) against Henry V but was later captured and executed. Oldcastle is thought to be the model for the Shakespearian character of Falstaff.

Old Catholics Group of Western Christians who separated from the Roman Catholic Church in 1870 after the First Vatican Council had announced the dogma of papal infallibility. Opposition to the increased centralization of the Roman Catholic Church coalesced in Munich under the leadership of the German historian Johann von Döllinger (1799–1890). With his guidance, Old Catholic Churches were set up in central and N European countries. Döllinger was later excommunicated, although he had not formally joined the Old Catholic Church. In 1873 Joseph Reinkens was elected the first Old Catholic bishop and consecrated by Bishop Heykamp of the Jansenist Church of Holland. Old Catholic Churches later united in the Union of Utrecht (1889) and issued a declaration of their principles. Since then the archbishop of Utrecht has been head of the International Old Catholic Congress. Old Catholics conduct their services in the vernacular and some churches allow priests to marry. They have much affinity with Anglicans. *See also* Jansenism

Oldenbarneveldt, Johan van (1547–1619) Dutch politician in the Revolt of the Netherlands. With William I (the Silent), he was the founder of the United Provinces of the Netherlands. He played an important part in arranging the union of the provinces at Utrecht (1579) and supported Maurice of Nassau as stadtholder after William was assassinated. From 1586 Oldenbarneveldt was the dominant figure in Holland and, with Maurice, practically the ruler of the United Provinces. He was instrumental in securing the truce with Spain (1609), which implied Dutch independence. Oldenbarneveldt fell out with Maurice, largely over religious differences, and after an unjust trial was executed.

Oldowan Type of stone tool dating from the early Pleistocene epoch (*c*.2mya). The name comes from the Olduvai Gorge, N Tanzania, where archaeologists found the first tools of this kind. Probably made by Homo habilis, Oldowan tools were made from quartz or basalt stones. The edges were chipped away to form tools capable of chopping, scraping or cutting; flakes produced by this process were also utilized as tools. Oldowan tools were made for *c*.1.5 million years until gradually superseded by the superior tools of the Acheulian culture.

Old Pretender *See* Stuart, James Francis Edward

Old Testament First and older section of the Bible, originally written in Hebrew or Aramaic, and accepted as religiously inspired and sacred by both Jews and Christians. Among Jews it is known as the Hebrew Bible. It begins with the Creation, but the main theme of the Old Testament is the history of the Hebrews. In addition, there are many examples of prophetic writing, poetry and short narrative tales. It comprises the Pentateuch or Torah (Genesis to Deuteronomy), the Historical Books (Joshua to I and II Kings), the Wisdom Books (Job, Proverbs and Ecclesiastes), the Major Prophets (Isaiah, Jeremiah and Ezekiel), the 12 Minor Prophets (Hosea to Malachi), and the miscellaneous collection of books known as the Writings (including Psalms and the Song of Songs). Sometimes included is a collection of books written in the final three centuries BC, known as the Apocrypha. The number, order and names of the books of the Old Testament

▲ **Olmec** The colossal basalt heads of the Olmec stand up to 3m (9ft) tall. They are depicted wearing helmets for a ritual ball game which was a part of many Mesoamerican cultures.

vary between the Jewish and Christian traditions; texts for both are based mainly on the SEPTUAGINT. Parts of the Hebrew text were found among the DEAD SEA SCROLLS.

Olduvai Gorge Site in N Tanzania, East Africa, where remains of primitive humans have been found. The Kenyan archaeologist Louis Leakey (1903–72) uncovered four layers of remains dating from *c*.2 million years ago to *c*.15,000 years ago. The Gorge, which is 40km (25mi) long and 100m (320ft) deep, runs through the Serengeti Plain. *See also* HOMO HABILIS; OLDOWAN

Olivares, Gaspar de Guzmán, Conde-Duque de (1587–1645) Spanish statesman, chief minister (1623–43) of PHILIP IV of Spain. He supported Spain's continued involvement in the Thirty Years' War and reignited conflict in the Netherlands. Olivares' efforts to centralize power in the hands of the king's ministers contributed to the Portuguese and Catalonian revolts. The heavy taxes he levied to fight wars at home and abroad led to his downfall.

Olmec Early civilization of Central America that flourished between the 12th and 4th centuries BC. Its heartland was the S coast of the Gulf of Mexico, but its influence spread more widely. From the 9th century BC the main Olmec centre was La Venta. Olmec art included high-quality carving of jade and stone, notably giant human heads in basalt. The Olmec heritage can be traced through later civilizations, including the MAYA. *See* picture, page 305

Olympia Area in S Greece, the site of an ancient sanctuary and of the original Olympic Games. The Games were first celebrated in 776 BC, as part of a festival to honour Zeus. They were held every four years until AD 393, when they were abolished by the Roman emperor Theodosius I. The sanctuary dates from *c*.1000 BC. The religious buildings were destroyed under the orders of Emperor Theodosius II in AD 426, and the ruins were buried by earthquakes in the the 6th century. Olympia was not rediscovered until the 18th century. It housed some of the finest works of classical architecture, including the huge temple of Zeus, which contained a giant statue of the god that was numbered among the SEVEN WONDERS OF THE WORLD.

Omaha Siouan-speaking tribe of Native North Americans. In 1854 they sold much of their land to the US government. In the 1880s they participated in a major political action against the government concerning ownership of Native American lands. Today, *c*.2000 Omaha people live in Nebraska and Oklahoma.

Oman *See* country feature

Omar (*c*.581–644) (Umar) Second CALIPH of ISLAM. He was converted to Islam in 618 and became a counsellor of MUHAMMAD. In 632 he chose the first caliph, ABU BAKR, and succeeded him in 634. Under Omar's rule, Islam spread rapidly. The victory of KHALID IBN AL-WALID at the Battle of the Yarmuk Valley (636) led to the Muslim capture of Byzantine Syria and Palestine. Further victories led to the collapse of the Persian empire and the capture of Egypt. Omar's reign saw the secure foundation of the Islamic state. He was murdered by a Persian slave.

Omayyads *See* UMAYYADS

O'Neill, Thomas P. (Philip), Jr ("Tip") (1912–94) US politician, speaker of the House of Representatives (1977–86). In 1952 he was elected to Congress as a Democrat. O'Neill was noted for his behind-the-scenes manipulation of legislative programmes. In the early 1980s he was a constant opponent of Reagan's budget proposals.

Onin War (1467–77) Civil war in Japan. It arose from a dispute over the shogunal succession, with the opposing candidates supported by rival DAIMYOS and their SAMURAI armies. Fighting broke out in the city of KYOTO, which suffered great damage. It soon spread through central Japan, with the small states into which Japan had recently fractured taking the opportunity to fight for more territory. The ASHIKAGA shogunate was greatly weakened by the war, which ushered in a century of unrest known as the *Sengoku* (Warring States) period.

Ontario Province in SE Canada, bounded to the S by four of the Great Lakes (Superior, Huron, Erie and Ontario) and the United States; the capital is Toronto. Trading posts were established in the region during the 17th century by French explorers. The area became part of NEW FRANCE but was ceded to Britain in 1763. Ontario was known as Upper Canada until 1841, when it joined with QUÉBEC to form the province of Canada. In 1867 the Dominion of Canada was created, and the province of Ontario was established. Area: 1,068,587sq km (412,582sq mi). Pop. (1994 est.) 10,900,000.

OPEC Acronym for ORGANIZATION OF PETROLEUM EXPORTING COUNTRIES

open-door policy US strategy designed to preserve its commercial interests in China in the early 20th century. At that time, China was divided into spheres of interest among European powers and Japan. In 1899 US Secretary of State John HAY sent notes to the main powers – Russia, France, Germany, Great Britain, Italy and Japan – requesting that trade and traders from other countries receive equal rights with other foreigners in China. The responses were vague, but Hay considered an agreement to have been reached. In 1900, after the BOXER REBELLION, Hay dispatched a similar note, which was approved by all except Japan. A major violation of the policy occurred when Japan issued its TWENTY-ONE DEMANDS (1915) to China; the Nine-Power Treaty, agreed at the Washington Armament Conference (1921–22), reaffirmed the strategy. The establishment of the People's Republic of China (1949) ended all privileges to foreigners, thus making the open-door policy obsolete.

Opium Wars Two conflicts between Britain and QING China over trading rights. The **First** Opium War (1839–42) arose because Chinese officials prevented the importation of opium and confiscated large quantities from British storage in GUANGZHOU (Canton). The British foreign secretary, Lord PALMERSTON, dispatched several warships to the region. In May 1841 the British attacked Guangzhou. The superiority of the British Royal Navy soon secured victory. The Treaty of NANJING (1842) gave Britain trading rights in five "TREATY PORTS" and the grant of HONG KONG. The **Second** Opium War (1856–60) was fought by the British and French against China. The boarding of the British-registered ship *Arrow* by Guangzhou officials in 1856 served as an excuse to renew hostilities. China was soon defeated but refused to ratify the Treaty of TIANJIN (1858), which granted rights to foreign merchants, diplomats and missionaries and opened more Chinese ports to foreign trade. Anglo-French forces occupied Beijing, N China, forcing China to approve the Treaty at the Beijing Convention (1860). The opium trade was legalized. *See also* UNEQUAL TREATIES

Oppenheimer, (Julius) Robert (1904–67) US theoretical physicist. He was appointed director (1943–45) of the Los Alamos laboratory in New Mexico, where he headed the MANHATTAN PROJECT to develop the atomic bomb. In 1949 Oppenheimer opposed the construction of the hydrogen bomb. In 1953, following investigations by Joseph MCCARTHY, he was suspended by the Atomic Energy Commission. In 1963 he was reinstated.

Opus Dei International Roman Catholic organization of 75,000 laymen and 1000 priests, known for its highly conservative political and religious influence. Its members seek to put into practice Christian values through their chosen professions. Opus Dei was founded (1928) in Spain by Escrivá de Balaguer (1902–75) and approved by the Holy See in 1950. During the rule of General FRANCO, its members had considerable influence in government, presiding over Spain's economic reforms. After Franco's death (1975), Opus Dei's influence lessened. Pope JOHN PAUL II beatified de Balaguer in 1992. Opus Dei has members in more than 80 countries and is noted for its educational establishments.

Orange, House of Royal dynasty of the Netherlands. Orange was a principality in S France, which was inherited by WILLIAM I (THE SILENT) in 1544. He and his son, MAURICE OF NASSAU, led the successful REVOLT OF THE NETHERLANDS against Spain in the late 16th century. WILLIAM III (OF ORANGE) became king of England in 1689. In 1815 the son of William V became WILLIAM I of the Netherlands. *See also* NASSAU, HOUSE OF

Orange Free State Former name of FREE STATE

Orangemen Members of the Orange Society, or Orange Order. It was founded (1795) in County Armagh, N Ireland, in response and opposition to the mainly Roman Catholic, nationalist UNITED IRISHMEN. It aimed to counteract increasing Roman Catholic influence and to ensure Protestant supremacy. It actively opposed Irish HOME RULE. The Order was named after the Protestant

O

OMAN

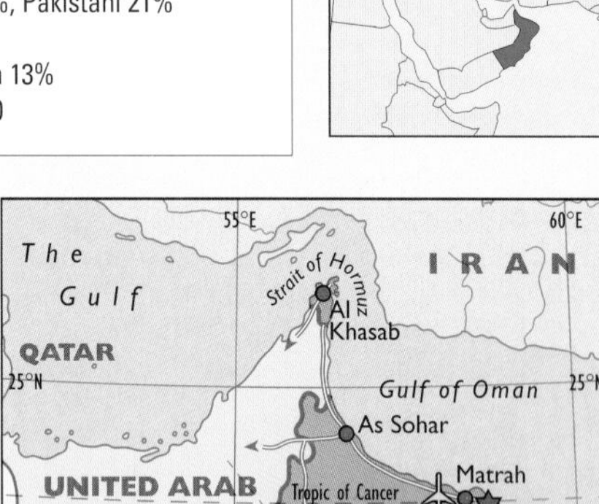

AREA: 212,460sq km (82,278sq mi)
POPULATION: 1,631,000
CAPITAL (POPULATION): Muscat (250,000)
GOVERNMENT: Monarchy with a consultative council
ETHNIC GROUPS: Omani Arab 74%, Pakistani 21%
LANGUAGES: Arabic (official)
RELIGIONS: Islam 86%, Hinduism 13%
GDP PER CAPITA (1995): US$8140

Sultanate on the Arabian Peninsula, SW Asia. It includes the tip of the Musandam Peninsula, separated from the rest of Oman by the United Arab Emirates (UAE). Since ancient times, Oman has flourished on the trade in frankincense between the Gulf and the Indian Ocean. Islam was introduced in the 7th century, and Muslim culture remains a unifying force among Oman's tribes. In 1507 the Portuguese occupied Muscat and subsequently controlled Omani trade until expelled by the Yarubid dynasty in 1650. NADIR SHAH of Iran captued Muscat in 1743, but Omani rule was restored by Ahmad ibn Said in 1749, and the Said dynasty have ruled Oman ever since. SAID IBN SULTAN reasserted Omani control of the East African coast and moved his court to ZANZIBAR in 1840.

During the 20th century, the sultanate was often in conflict with the imams of the Ibadi sect, who pressed for a more theocratic society. British colonial interference and economic inequality led to popular rebellions in the 1950s and 1960s. In 1970 Sultan Said bin Taimur was deposed by his son, QABOOS BIN SAID. Qaboos initiated the modernization of health, education and social welfare. Oman joined the United Nations (UN) and the Arab League in 1971, and was a founder member (1981) of the Gulf Cooperation Council (GCC). Oman allowed coalition forces to use its military bases during the GULF WAR (1991).

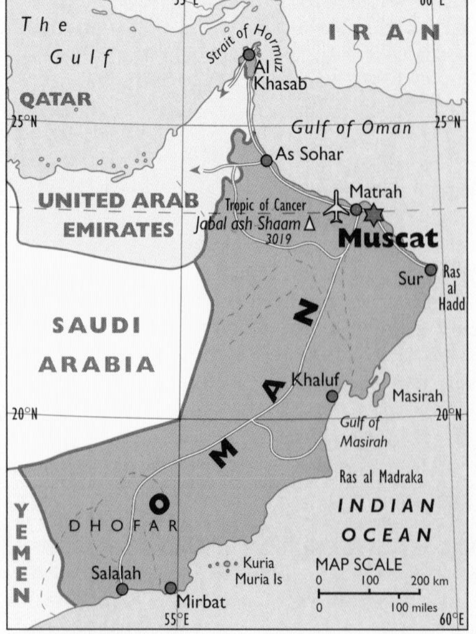

Doric

Ionic

Corinthian

Composite

Tuscan

◀ **orders of architecture** The five main orders of architecture were first presented by Sebastiano Serlio (1475–1554) in Book IV of his treatise on architecture (1537). During the Renaissance, the classical orders formed the basis of a strict set of conventions for architectural design.

hero WILLIAM III (OF ORANGE). William's victory over the Catholic JAMES II at the Battle of the BOYNE (1690) is celebrated on its anniversary, 12 July. The Orange Order remains highly influential in Northern IRELAND.

ordeal Form of trial in early medieval Europe in which the innocence or guilt of the accused, or (in Spain) the truthfulness of a witness, was established by a physical test, commonly involving fire or water. Divine intervention was believed to protect the innocent. Ordeal by water was the usual method for suspected witches. The accused were thrown into water; if they floated they were considered to be guilty. Trial by ordeal gradually disappeared in the 13th century.

orders of architecture In classical architecture, style and decoration of a column, its base, capital and entablature. Of the five orders, the Greeks developed the Doric, Ionic and Corinthian. The Tuscan and Composite orders were Roman adaptations. A typical **Doric** column has no base, a relatively short shaft with surface fluting meeting in a sharp edge and an unornamented capital. The **Ionic** order is characterized by slender columns with 24 flutes and prominent spiral scrolls on the capitals. The **Corinthian** is the most ornate of the classical orders of architecture. A typical Corinthian column has a high base, a slim, fluted column and a bell-shaped capital with acanthus-leaf ornament.

Ordinance of 1787 *See* NORTHWEST ORDINANCE

Ordovician Second-oldest period of the PALAEOZOIC era, *c.*505 to *c.*438 million years ago. All animal life was restricted to the sea. Numerous invertebrates flourished, including trilobites, brachiopods, corals, graptolites, molluscs and echinoderms. Remains of jawless fish from this period are the first record of the vertebrates.

Oregon State on the Pacific coast of NW United States; the capital is Salem. When Francis DRAKE claimed the region for England in 1579, the major Native American tribe was the NEZ PERCÉ. Fur-trading posts were set up in the 1790s, mainly by the NORTH WEST COMPANY. The LEWIS AND CLARK EXPEDITION reached the mouth of the Columbia River in 1805 and the first white settlement, Fort Astoria, was founded here by John Jacob ASTOR of the AMERICAN FUR COMPANY in 1811. After the WAR OF 1812, Oregon was occupied jointly by Britain and the United States. From 1842 the OREGON TRAIL brought more white settlers. The OREGON TREATY (1846) settled the boundary dispute with Britain and Oregon Territory was created in 1848. Chief JOSEPH of the Nez Percé resisted forcible resettlement by the US government. The arrival of the railroad in 1883 spurred further settlement. Area: 251,180sq km (96,981sq mi). Pop. (1993 est.) 3,038,000.

Oregon Trail Main route of US pioneers to the West in the 1840s and 1850s. The Oregon Trail ran 3200km (2000mi) from Independence, Missouri, to Fort Vancouver on the Columbia River, Oregon. It crossed the Rocky Mountains via South Pass. The journey took about six months by wagon.

Oregon Treaty (1846) Compact with Great Britain that settled the Oregon Boundary Dispute. Since 1818 the United States and Britain had jointly occupied the Oregon region. As more and more US settlers arrived along the OREGON TRAIL, pressure mounted on the US government to settle the boundary. The Oregon Treaty established the 49th parallel as the line between the United States and Canada, and gave the United States undisputed claim to the Pacific Northwest. It also gave Britain use of the Columbia River below the 49th parallel.

Orford, Sir Robert Walpole, 1st Earl of *See* WALPOLE, SIR ROBERT, 1ST EARL OF ORFORD

Organisation de l'Armeé Secrète *See* OAS

Organization for Economic Cooperation and Development (OECD) International consultative body set up in 1961 by the major Western trading nations. Its aims are to stimulate economic growth and world trade by raising the standard of living in member countries and by coordinating aid to less developed countries. Its headquarters are in Paris, France, and it has 24 member nations including all the world's major powers.

Organization of African Unity (OAU) Intergovernmental organization. Founded in 1963, the OAU brings together all African states. It aims to safeguard African interests and independence, encourage the continent's development and settle disputes among member states. Its headquarters are in Addis Ababa, Ethiopia.

Organization of American States (OAS) Organization of 35 member states of the Americas that promotes peaceful settlements of disputes, regional cooperation in the limitation of weapons, and economic and cultural development. It was created in 1948 during an international meeting held in Colombia. The successor to the Pan American Union, the OAS works with the UNITED NATIONS (UN). Its headquarters are in Washington, D.C.

Organization of Petroleum Exporting Countries (OPEC) Intergovernmental organization established in 1960 by many of the world's major oil producing states to safeguard their interests. It was able to control oil prices in the 1970s, but its influence has waned since then, largely because of internal differences and the emergence of major oil-producing countries outside OPEC. Its headquarters are in Vienna, Austria.

Orlando, Vittorio Emanuele (1860–1952) Italian statesman, prime minister (1917–19). He entered Parliament in 1897 and held several ministerial posts, notably that of justice (1907–09). Orlando became prime minister during World War 1, after Italy's disastrous defeat at the Battle of Caporetto. He represented Italy at the Treaty of VERSAILLES, where failure to secure expected territorial gains led to the fall of his government. Orlando's early support for Benito MUSSOLINI had turned to opposition by 1925, after the murder of Giacomo MATTEOTTI. After World War 2 Orlando rejoined the Senate and ran unsuccessfully for president (1948).

Orléans, Louis-Philippe, Duc d' (1747–93) French Bourbon prince. Although a representative of the nobility in the STATES-GENERAL, he supported the revolutionary Third Estate, whom he later joined after their proclamation of a NATIONAL ASSEMBLY. A supporter of the FRENCH REVOLUTION and a member of the JACOBIN club, Orléans was elected (1792) to the NATIONAL CONVENTION and voted for the execution of LOUIS XVI. He took the name Philippe Égalité. When his son, the future King LOUIS PHILIPPE, defected to the Austrians (1793), Égalité was arrested. He was executed during the REIGN OF TERROR.

Orléans, Philippe II, Duc de (1674–1723) French noble, regent of France during the minority of LOUIS XV. The nephew of LOUIS XIV, Orléans took office after the king's death in 1715. He persuaded the PARLEMENT to override Louis XIV's will, which had restricted his power as regent. Orléans formed the QUADRUPLE ALLIANCE (1718) in order to counter Spanish claims to the French throne and compelled Philip V of Spain to recognize him as heir to the young Louis XV. In 1717 Orléans appointed the Scottish banker John LAW to put French finances in order, but the bursting of the MISSISSIPPI BUBBLE discredited the regent himself. He died shortly after Louis XV came of age. *See also* SPANISH SUCCESSION, WAR OF THE

OREGON
Statehood :
14 February 1859
Nickname :
The Beaver State
State motto :
She flies with her own wings

STATE OF OREGON
1859

Ormonde, James Butler, 12th Earl and 1st Duke of (1610–88) Irish statesman. He fought with the Earl of STRAFFORD against the Roman Catholic rebellion in Ireland (1641). He was appointed lord lieutenant of Ireland in 1644 and made peace with the rebels in 1649. Following the execution of CHARLES I and Oliver CROMWELL's conquest of Ireland, Ormonde joined CHARLES II in exile in France. After the RESTORATION (1660), Ormonde returned as lord lieutenant of Ireland (1661–69, 1677–84). *See also* PLANTATION OF IRELAND

Ormonde, James Butler, 2nd Duke of (1665–1745) Irish military leader and politician, grandson of the 1st Duke of ORMONDE. He supported WILLIAM III (OF ORANGE) at the Battle of the BOYNE (1690). In 1711 he succeeded the Duke of MARLBOROUGH as commander of British forces in the War of the SPANISH SUCCESSION. After the accession of the Hanoverian GEORGE I to the throne (1714), Ormonde was removed from his post for being a JACOBITE. He lived the rest of his life in exile.

Orsini, Felice (1819–58) Italian revolutionary, a supporter of Giuseppe MAZZINI. During the REVOLUTIONS OF 1848, he participated in the uprisings in Rome. Imprisoned by the Austrians, he escaped (1855) and went into exile. Orsini plotted to assassinate NAPOLEON III, hoping that his death would bring about a revolution that would lead to Italian independence. Napoleon survived the assassination attempt, but seven other people were killed. Orsini was arrested and executed, but the events contributed to Napoleon's willingness to negotiate with the Conte di CAVOUR. *See also* RISORGIMENTO

Ortega (Saavedra), Daniel (1945–) Nicaraguan statesman, president (1984–90). In 1963 he joined the SANDINISTA National Liberation Front (FSLN) and rose to become its leader in 1966. He led their campaign of urban resistance and was imprisoned (1967–74). On his release, he was exiled to Cuba but returned secretly to Nicaragua. In 1979 Ortega led the revolution that toppled the SOMOZA regime. He formed a socialist government, which instigated wide-ranging reforms. In 1984 he was elected president. The Sandinista government was destabilized by the US-backed CONTRA rebels. In 1990 elections Ortega was defeated by Violeta CHAMORRO. In 1996 he again ran for president but was defeated by Arnoldo Alemán.

Orthodox Church, Eastern *See* feature article, page 308

Osborne, Thomas, Earl of Danby *See* DANBY, THOMAS OSBORNE, EARL OF

Osceola (*c.*1800–38) Native American leader of the SEMINOLE in Florida during the Second Seminole War (1835–42). President Andrew JACKSON ordered the Seminoles removed to the West, but Osceola took his people into the Everglades to continue the fight. He was seized while negotiating with General Thomas Jesup under a flag of truce. Osceola was imprisoned in Fort Moultrie, South Carolina, where he died.

Osman I (1258–1326) Founder of the OTTOMAN EMPIRE. As ruler of the small Osmanli, or Ottoman, state in NW Anatolia (Turkey), he declared his independence from the SELJUK sultan in *c.*1290. He expanded his territory in frequent wars against the BYZANTINE EMPIRE.

O

Ostend Manifesto (18 October 1854) In US history, document drawn up in Ostend, Belgium, by US diplomats Pierre Soulé, James Mason and James Buchanan. The Manifesto warned Spain that the United States would take Cuba by force if Spain refused to sell the island. Protests arose both in the United States and Europe, and the Manifesto was finally denounced by the US secretary of state, William Marcy.

Ostpolitik (Ger. eastern policy) Attempt by the former West German government to form better relations with East European communist regimes. The policy was initiated in the late 1960s by Willy Brandt. Relations between East and West Germany were normalized (1972), and West Germany agreed treaties with the Soviet Union and Poland recognizing the Oder-Neisse Line. *Ostpolitik* was continued, though less zealously, by Brandt's successors until the reunification of Germany made it obsolete.

ostracism Practice carried out in Athens and some other ancient Greek cities whereby citizens could vote for the banishment of an individual. At an annual meeting, a vote was taken on whether to have an ostracism. If it was decided to do so, then eligible citizens could write a name on a shard of pottery known as an *ostrakon* (hence ostracism). The device was often used to remove political opponents. Banishment normally lasted for up to ten years. No confiscation of property occurred and the ostracized person kept their Roman citizenship. Aristides (the Just) is thought to have been one of the last people to be ostracized.

Ostrogoths Eastern division of the Goths. After AD 370 the Ostrogoths settled in what is now the Ukraine and Belarus, while the Visigoths moved further west. From *c*.374 to the death of Attila (453) the Ostrogoths were subject to the Huns. In 493 the Ostrogoths, led by Theodoric (the Great), and encouraged by Byzantine Emperor Zeno, assassinated Odoacer and established a kingdom in Italy, based at Ravenna. In 535 the Byzantine general Belisarius was sent by Justinian I (the Great) to reconquer Italy; fighting continued for *c*.20 years, until the Byzantines, under Narses, finally triumphed. The Ostrogoths no longer had a kingdom and were gradually absorbed into other tribes.

Oswald, Lee Harvey (1939–63) Alleged assassin of US President John Kennedy on 22 November 1963 in Dallas, Texas. Before he could stand trial, Oswald was shot and killed in police custody by nightclub owner Jack Ruby. Despite numerous conspiracy theories, the Warren Commission concluded that Oswald had acted alone.

Oswald, Saint (*c*.605–42) King of Northumbria (633–42). During the reign (616–33) of his uncle Edwin, Oswald lived on Iona, where he was converted to Christianity. He came to the throne after defeating King Cadwallon of Gwynedd, who had killed Edwin and invaded Northumbria. Oswald converted his people to Christianity with the help of St Aidan, the first bishop of Lindisfarne. He was killed in battle, defeated by the pagan King Penda of Mercia. His feast day is 5 August.

Othman (Uthman) (574–656) Third caliph (644–56), a son-in-law of Muhammad. He was a member of the Umayyad family, the social élite who had resisted the spread of Islam in its early days. Othman was blamed for revolts and intrigues, ending in his assassination.

Othman I *See* Osman I

Otis, James (1725–83) American colonial leader. He came to notice in 1761 for his opposition to writs of assistance, which allowed merchants' houses to be searched. He argued that the writs were contrary to natural rights and therefore invalid. Otis was elected to the Massachusetts General Court in 1761. He campaigned against the Stamp Act (1765) and the Townshend Acts (1767). Otis received a head injury in an altercation with a British customs officer (1769) and withdrew from public life.

Ottawa Group of Algonquian-speaking Native North Americans. Hunter-farmers, they originally lived north of the Great Lakes. They allied with the French in the French and Indian Wars. Pontiac, an Ottawa chief, led the Ottawa in an uprising against the British known as Pontiac's Rebellion (1763–64). They were broken into five groups by the Iroquois and Anglo-Americans and now live around the Great Lakes, and in Kansas and Oklahoma.

Ottawa Agreements (1932) Economic accords negotiated at the Imperial Economic Conference in Ottawa, Canada, in order to assist the economies of Britain and its dominions during the Great Depression. The Agreements allowed for dominion countries to export most goods to Britain free of duty. Britain imposed new duties on goods imported from non-dominion countries. This policy, known as imperial preference, had been advocated by Joseph Chamberlain at the Colonial Conference of 1897. Trade preferences between the colonies and Britain were gradually removed following the General Agreement on Tariffs and Trade (1948).

Otto I (the Great) (912–73) First Holy Roman emperor (962–73) and king of the Germans (936–73), son of Henry I of Saxony. In 939 he defeated the rebellion of his brother Henry, who was supported by Louis IV of France. Royal power was augmented by Otto's close control of the church and he brought Christianity to Denmark and the Slavic lands. He expanded his territory, conquering Bohemia in 950. In 951 Otto invaded Italy to aid Queen Adelaide of Lombardy, whom he then married, thereby becoming king of Lombardy. Otto returned to Germany to suppress a further revolt and crush the Magyars at the Battle of Lechfeld (955). He was crowned as Roman emperor (the "Holy", meaning "Christian", was added later) by Pope John XII. Otto's negotiations with the Byzantine emperor led to the marriage (972) of his son, Otto II, to the Byzantine princess Theophano.

Otto II (955–83) Holy Roman emperor (967–83) and king of the Germans (961–83), son and successor of Otto I (the Great), with whom he was joint emperor (967–73). Otto suppressed a revolt led by his cousin Duke Henry II of Bavaria in 978 and fought King Lothair of France for possession of Lorraine. Invading Italy in 980, he restored the displaced pope, Benedict VII, but was defeated by Arabs and Byzantines in S Italy. Meanwhile, his father Otto's gains in E Germany were lost. He was succeeded by his infant son, Otto III.

Otto III (980–1002) Holy Roman emperor (996–1002) and king of the Germans (983–1002), son and successor of Otto II. Until 994 he reigned under the regency of his mother, the Byzantine princess Theophano, and his grandmother, Adelaide. In 996 he secured the election of his cousin Bruno as the first German pope, Gregory V. He later made his influential former tutor, Gerbert of Aurillac, pope as Sylvester II. In 998 Otto established his Byzantine-influenced court in Rome.

Otto IV (*c*.1175–*c*.1218) (Otto of Brunswick) Holy Roman emperor (1209–15) and king of the Germans (1198–1215), son of Henry III (the Lion). A grandson of Henry II of England, he was brought up at the English court. In 1198 Otto was elected German king by the Guelphs, and Philip of Swabia was elected king by the Hohenstaufens. For 10 years, they fought for the title, Otto finally triumphing after the death of Philip. Otto antagonized the powerful Pope Innocent III by his invasion of Italy against the Hohenstaufen king Frederick I (later Emperor Frederick II). With Innocent's support, Frederick was elected king by the German princes (1211) and supported by Philip II of France. Otto was defeated by Philip at the Battle of Bouvines (1214) and forced to retire.

Ottoman Empire *See* feature article

Oudenaarde, Battle of (11 July 1708) Allied victory over the French during the War of the Spanish Succession. The Duke of Marlborough and Prince Eugène of Savoy led 80,000 men on a march of 80km (50mi) in 65 hours to relieve the Flemish town of Oudenaarde, which was besieged by 85,000 French troops under the Duc de Vendôme. The Allied forces trapped the French in a pincer movement, killing *c*.6000 men and capturing a further 9000. Allied losses were *c*.4000. The French lost control of the Spanish Netherlands.

Owen, David, Baron (1938–) British statesman, foreign secretary (1977–79). He entered Parliament in 1966. Owen became disillusioned with the shift to the left in the Labour Party and was one of the "Gang of Four" who formed (1981) the breakaway Social Democratic Party (SDP). In 1983 he succeeded Roy Jenkins as party leader. In 1987 Owen led the small faction of SDP who rejected merger with the Liberal Party. In 1992 he retired from the Commons and was appointed as United Nations' chief negotiator in peace talks in the former Yugoslavia.

Owen, Robert (1771–1858) Welsh industrialist and social reformer. He believed that better conditions for workers would lead to greater productivity, and he put these beliefs into practice at his textile mills in New Lanark, Scotland. Owen attempted to establish a self-contained cooperative community in New Harmony, Indiana, United States (1825–27). His ideas provided the basis for the cooperative movement. Owen was also an important influence on Britain's early trade union movement.

Owen Glendower *See* Glyn Dŵr, Owain

Oxenstierna, Count Axel Gustafsson (1583–1654) Swedish statesman. In 1612 he was appointed chancellor of Sweden by Gustavus II. Reconciling the monarchy and the aristocracy, Oxenstierna and Gustavus made a highly effective partnership. Oxenstierna reformed the administrative system and was responsible for Sweden's foreign policy. He supported Gustavus' military interests, negotiating the advantageous Treaty of Altmark with Poland (1629). After Gustavus' death (1632), Oxenstierna directed strategy in the Thirty Years' War. He formed (1633) the League of Heilbronn, an organization of German Protestant princes, through whom Sweden controlled S Germany. Oxenstierna planned the war (1643–45) against Denmark, which resulted in a Swedish victory at Brömsebro. He served (1632–44) as regent of Sweden until Christina's coronation, after which he continued to serve as chancellor. After Christina's abdication (1654), Oxenstierna served her successor, Charles X.

Oxford, Robert Harley, 1st Earl of *See* Harley, Robert, 1st Earl of Oxford

ORTHODOX CHURCH, EASTERN

Community of *c*.130 million Christians living mainly in E and SE Europe, parts of Asia and a significant minority in the United States. The Church is a federation of groups that share forms of worship and episcopal organization, but each group has its own national head. The largest group is the Russian Orthodox Church. Although there is no central authority, member churches recognize the patriarch of Istanbul as titular head. Eastern Orthodox Christians reject the jurisdiction of the Roman pope. When Constantine I (the Great) moved his capital to Byzantium (now Istanbul) in AD 330, a separate non-Roman culture developed. The Eastern Orthodox Christians accepted the Nicene Creed, as modified in 381. Conflicts grew between the Eastern patriarchs and Rome. In the schism (1054), Western and Eastern arms of Christendom excommunicated each other's followers, and the split became irreparable when Crusaders invaded Constantinople (1204). Attempts at reconciliation in 1274 and 1439 failed. In 1962 Orthodox observers attended the Second Vatican Council. In 1963 the Eastern Orthodox churches agreed to open dialogue with Rome.

▲ **Greek Orthodox cross**
The Greek cross depicts a crown of thorns enclosing the letters XP, the first two letters of the Greek word for Christ.

▲ **Russian Orthodox cross**
The slanting arm refers to the thieves crucified either side of Christ.The man to his left went to hell, the other to heaven.

Oxford, University of Oldest university in Britain. It developed from a group of teachers and students who gathered in Oxford in the 12th century. The first colleges, University, Balliol and Merton, were founded between 1249 and 1264. The colleges quickly increased in number and became almost autonomous. Women were finally admitted in 1878.

Oxford Movement (Tractarianism) Attempt by some members of the CHURCH OF ENGLAND to restore the ideals of the pre-REFORMATION Church. The main proponents were John Keble, Edward Pusey and John NEWMAN. An important principle of the movement was the belief that the apostolic succession had not been broken by the Reformation. Leaders of the movement published their views in 90 *Tracts for the Times* (1833–41). Newman caused great controversy with *Tract 90*, in which he discussed the close doctrinal relationship between the THIRTY-NINE ARTICLES of Anglicanism and Roman Catholicism. Newman and many supporters later joined the Roman Catholic Church. The Movement's influence led to an increased interest in ceremony and ritual.

Oyo YORUBA kingdom, situated in what is now SW NIGERIA. It was the dominant state in the region from *c.*1650 to *c.*1750. In the late 16th century the *alafin* (king) Orompoto used the profits gained from trade with the Portuguese to strengthen the army and build up the cavalry. From 1724 to 1748 Oyo extended its influence over the DAHOMEY kingdom, using its superior forces to win several wars. Oyo flourished with the SLAVE TRADE, especially under Abiodun (d. *c.*1789), who maintained a trading route to the coast at Ajase (now Porto Novo) but neglected the army. Civil unrest increased during Abiodun's reign and worsened under his successor, Awole. Oyo was soon split into several smaller states. In the early 19th century, it lost control of Dahomey. Oyo was finally destroyed by a FULANI invasion from Hausaland. *See also* IFE; SOKOTO

OTTOMAN EMPIRE

Former hereditary Islamic state that controlled much of SE Europe, the Middle East and North Africa between the 14th and 20th centuries. It was founded by OSMAN I, a Muslim warrior who declared his independence from the SELJUK sultan in *c.*1290. He ruled a small principality in ANATOLIA, which he greatly enlarged by conquering territory belonging to the Christian BYZANTINE EMPIRE. Osman successfully united his Turkish warriors (*ghazis*) by advancing the cause of Islam against Christianity. Osman's son Orhan (r.1326–62) continued the expansion, capturing Bursa (1326), which subsequently became the Ottoman capital.

In 1354 Orhan gained GALLIPOLI, marking the beginning of Ottoman influence in Europe. Orhan's son and successor, MURAD I (r.1362–89), consolidated territories in Anatolia, extended Ottoman rule into the Balkans and made a vassal out of Byzantine Emperor JOHN V (PALAEOLOGUS). Following a period of expansion, BAYEZID I (r.1389–1402) was defeated by the Turkic warrior TAMERLANE, who returned Ottoman territory to the conquered emirates. Under MUHAMMAD I (r.1413–21), the Ottoman Empire was reunited. A spell of consolidation under MURAD II (r.1421–44, 1446–51), including a resounding victory in Bulgaria (1444), was followed by rapid expansion under MUHAMMAD II (THE CONQUEROR). During his reign (1444–46, 1451–81), the contest with the Byzantines ended with the capture of Constantinople (now ISTANBUL), which became the Ottoman capital in 1453. The reign of Muhammad's son, BAYEZID II (r.1481–1512), saw the rise of the SAFAVID dynasty. The Safavids were defeated by SELIM I (r.1512–20), but remained a continual threat. Selim continued Ottoman expansion, capturing the Islamic holy cities of MECCA and MEDINA.

The Ottoman Empire was at its height under SULEIMAN I (THE MAGNIFICENT) (r.1520–66), when it included the Middle East and North Africa, SE Europe and the E Mediterranean, but it subsequently began to falter. After a brief resurgence under MURAD IV (r.1623–40), who captured Baghdad from the Safavids, the Empire began to fall into decline. The once loyal army showed disaffection over their lack of pay, and along with the widespread corruption and civil unrest, there existed a paucity of adult heirs to the sultanate. However, under the KÖPRÜLÜ grand viziers (1656–76) the Ottoman Empire once again gained territory, even to the point at which, under Kara Mustafa Pasha (r.1676–83), the Ottoman army attempted but failed to take Vienna, Austria. During the 18th century further evidence of decline became apparent. In addition to rising inflation, the Ottomans found it increasingly difficult to recruit keen young warriors, and the once élite JANISSARIES were becoming increasingly corrupt and disloyal. Furthermore, although the first half of the 18th century witnessed some Ottoman military success, the second half saw Russian advances in Romania and NAPOLEON Bonaparte's successful invasion of Egypt. By this time it had become clear to the Ottoman sultans that their army was not keeping pace with Western technological and tactical advances. Both SELIM III (r.1789–1807) and MAHMUD II (r.1808–39) attempted to modernize the military, with Mahmud responsible for the massacre of thousands of Janissaries. Yet Mahmud failed to prevent the secession of Greece (*see* GREEK WAR OF INDEPENDENCE), Serbia (1829) and Egypt, the latter coming under the control of MUHAMMAD ALI.

The 19th century saw attempts to Westernize the Empire (the TANZIMAT REFORMS) and resulted in the formation of provincial assemblies, state courts, new taxation rules, secular schools and the reorganization of the bureaucracy. The RUSSO-TURKISH WARS and the resulting Treaty of SAN STEFANO (1878), although modified in the Congress of BERLIN, greatly reduced Ottoman influence in Europe. In 1876 ABDUL HAMID II (r.1876–1909) granted a Western-style constitution. However, the disaster of the Treaty of San Stefano compelled Abdul Hamid to clamp down on further internal reform and suspend (1878) parliament in the hope that this would give him greater control over a fragmenting Empire. Although much reduced in power, the Empire remained key to the EASTERN QUESTION. In 1908 the YOUNG TURKS forced Abdul Hamid to reinstate the constitution. He was later deposed and exiled for an attempted counter move, and nominally replaced by MUHAMMAD V, although real power lay in the hands of the Young Turks and ENVER PASHA. In the BALKAN WARS (1912–13) the Ottoman Empire lost the majority of its Balkan territory. After WORLD WAR I, which was disastrous for the Empire, Ottoman territory was reduced to roughly the present Turkish borders. Nationalists led by Mustafa Kemal (later ATATÜRK) deposed the last Ottoman sultan, MUHAMMAD VI, so formally ending the Ottoman Empire and creating modern TURKEY (1923).

◄▲ **Ottoman expansion** in Anatolia was accomplished at the expense of Byzantium. They later defeated the Serbs in Kosovo (1389), and expanded W into the Balkans. The Ottoman Empire was founded (*c.*1290) by Osman I, shown here in a portrait by John Young (1755–1825).

O

Paasikivi, Juho Kusti (1870–1956) Finnish statesman, prime minister (1918, 1944–46), president (1946–56). He briefly served as prime minister (1918), after Carl Mannerheim had triumphed in the Finnish Civil War, and headed the delegation that negotiated peace with the Soviet Union. Paasikivi was thus the natural choice to lead further negotiations with the Soviets after the two Russo-Finnish Wars (1939–40, 1941–44). Ater the cease-fire, he headed a coalition government. As president, Paasikivi was instrumental in developing the country's neutral foreign policy, based on friendly relations with the Soviet Union. He was succeeded by Urho Kaleva Kekkonen.

Pacific, War of the (1879–83) Conflict between Chile and an alliance of Peru and Bolivia. It centred around the Bolivian and Chilean dispute over the nitrate-rich Atacama Desert region. An agreement in 1874 allowed Bolivia to control the region, while Chile maintained a controlling interest in the mining industry and had an advantageous tax agreement with Bolivia. In 1878 Bolivia increased taxes and threatened to take over Chilean holdings. Chile sent troops to the Bolivian port of Antofagasta, precipitating the conflict. Peru entered the War because it had an agreement with Bolivia to guarantee their territories. Bolivia and Peru were vanquished by superior Chilean forces, which occupied (1881–83) the Peruvian capital, Lima, forcing the Peruvian government into the highlands. By the end of the conflict, Peru had lost the provinces of Tarapacá, Tacna and Arica, although Chile returned Tacna after international arbitration. Bolivia lost the Atacama province, its only coastal outlet, to Chile. *See also* Tacna-Arica dispute

Pacific Scandal (1873) Canadian political crisis. The Conservative prime minister, Sir John Macdonald, was accused by Liberals of accepting campaign funds from the industrialist Sir Hugh Allan in return for the contract to build the Canadian Pacific Railroad. The scandal forced Macdonald to resign and the contract was withdrawn. The Conservatives were defeated in the next election.

Pacification of Ghent *See* Ghent, Pacification of

pacifism Philosophy opposing the use of war or violence as a means of settling disputes. Elements can be found in ancient Buddhist, Hebrew and early Christian theology and in later Anabaptist and Quaker beliefs. International pacifist groups were organized in the 19th

PAKISTAN

AREA: 796,100sq km (307,374sq mi)
POPULATION: 115,520,000
CAPITAL (POPULATION): Islamabad (201,000)
GOVERNMENT: Federal republic
ETHNIC GROUPS: Punjabi 60%, Sindhi 12%, Pushtun 13%, Baluch, Muhajir
LANGUAGES: Urdu (official)
RELIGIONS: Islam 97%, Christianity, Hinduism
GDP PER CAPITA (1995): US$2230

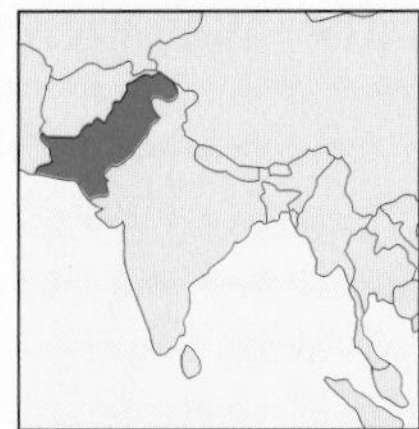

Republic in s Asia. The Indus Valley civilization developed *c.*4500 years ago. Major cities included Mohenjo-daro. The civilization declined (*c.*1800 BC) as Indo-Aryan nomads invaded the region, followed by the Persians and then the Greeks under Alexander III (the Great). Indo-Greek kingdoms dominated the area for much of the period *c.*325–50 BC, until the Kushans began to establish an empire that was to last until the 3rd century AD.

In 712 Arabs conquered Sind and introduced Islam. In 1186 the Ghaznavid capital of Lahore was captured by the Ghurids, who paved the way for the foundation (1211) of the Delhi Sultanate. In 1526 the Sultanate was conquered by Babur, who established the Mughal Empire. Under the Mughals, the Urdu language was introduced and many fine examples of Islamic architecture were built. In the late 18th century Ranjit Singh conquered the Punjab and introduced Sikhism.

The early 19th century saw the emergence of the English East India Company as a dominant force. The British captured Sind (1843) and Punjab (1849). Much of Baluchistan was conquered in the 1850s. Pathans in the NW resisted subjection, and the British created a separate province in 1901. The dominance of Hindus in British India led to the formation of the Muslim League (1906). In the 1940s the League's leader, Muhammad Ali Jinnah, gained popular support for the idea of a separate state of Pakistan (Urdu, "land of the pure") in Muslim-majority areas. In 1947 British India achieved independence and was partitioned into India and Pakistan. The resulting migration of Hindus, Muslims and Sikhs and the associated communal violence claimed more than 500,000 lives.

In 1947 the long-standing war with India over Kashmir began. Jinnah became Pakistan's first governor general. Muslim Pakistan was divided into two parts: East Bengal and West Pakistan, more than 1600km (1000mi) apart. In 1955 East Bengal became East Pakistan, and in 1956 Pakistan became a republic within the Commonwealth of Nations. In 1958 General Muhammad Ayub Khan led a military coup. In 1960 he became president. His dictatorship brought constitutional changes but failed to satisfy East Pakistan's claim for greater autonomy.

In 1971 East Pakistan declared independence as Bangladesh. West Pakistani troops invaded. The ensuing civil war killed hundreds of thousands of people, and millions fled to India. India sent troops to support Bangladesh. West Pakistan was forced to surrender and Zulfikar Ali Bhutto assumed control. In 1977 a military coup, led by General Zia-ul-Haq, deposed Bhutto. In 1978 Zia proclaimed himself president and Bhutto was hanged for murder. During the 1980s Pakistan received US aid for providing a safe haven for Mujaheddin fighters in the war in Afghanistan. In 1988 Zia dismissed Parliament but died shortly after in a mysterious plane crash. The Pakistan People's Party (PPP) won the ensuing elections and Benazir Bhutto, daughter of Zulfikar, became president. Charged with nepotism and corruption, she was removed from office in 1990. The ensuing election was won by the Islamic Democratic Alliance, led by Nawaz Sharif. In 1991 Islamic law (sharia) was given precedence over civil law. Sharif also faced charges of corruption and lost the 1993 elections to Benazir Bhutto. In 1996 Bhutto was again dismissed on corruption charges. Political disenchantment saw a low turnout in 1997 elections and a landslide victory for Nawaz Sharif. In 1998 Pakistan became the world's seventh nuclear power. In 1999 Sharif was ousted in a military coup led by General Pervez Musharraf. There is persistent civil disorder in Sind as insurgents struggle for an autonomous province of Karachi.

century. There are two main forms: **personal** pacifism involves an individual following his or her conviction that violence is wrong, as with conscientious objectors during wartime; advocates of **national** pacifism call for the renunciation of war as a state policy. The doctrine of "Mahatma" GANDHI was based on pacifist philosophy. *See also* CAMPAIGN FOR NUCLEAR DISARMAMENT (CND)

Paderewski, Ignacy Jan (1860–1941) Polish statesman and composer, prime minister (1919). During World War 1 Paderewski was a member of the Polish National Convention. He was largely responsible for Woodrow WILSON's decision to include Polish independence as the thirteenth of his FOURTEEN POINTS (1918). In 1919 Paderewski was asked by Józef PIŁSUDSKI, to become the first prime minister of an independent Poland. He retired after ten months to continue his musical career. During World War 2, he briefly served as president of Poland's government-in-exile.

Padua (Padova) City in Veneto region, NE Italy. The city is first mentioned (as Patavium) early in the 4th century BC. During the Roman period Padua grew to be one of the most powerful and wealthy cities in N Italy. It was destroyed (601) by the LOMBARDS, but recovered during the Middle Ages to become a flourishing artistic centre. Ruled by the Carrara family from 1318, Padua came under Venetian control in 1405. In 1815 it passed to Austria. The city played a major part in the RISORGIMENTO. Padua is renowned for its art treasures. Pop. (1991) 215,137.

Paéz, José Antonio (1790–1873), Venezuelan statesman, president (1831–35, 1839–46) and dictator (1861–63). As the commander of a troop of *llaneros* (horsemen) in the war of independence from Spain, Paéz became one of Simón BOLÍVAR's deputies and won battles at Carabobo (1821) and Puerto Cabello (1823). He led the movement against federation with Gran Colombia (1829) and became the first president of the newly independent VENEZUELA. From 1831 to 1846 Paéz exercised power either directly as president or through puppet rulers, initially encouraging economic and social development but gradually becoming more autocratic. He was exiled in 1850 after leading a revolt against José Tadeo Monagas, whom he had appointed as his successor. Returning to Venezuela in 1861, he became supreme dictator but was again forced into exile.

Pagan Historic Burmese kingdom (AD 849–1287); also capital of the state. Burmans established themselves along the River Irrawaddy in N Myanmar, making Pagan (now in central Burma) their capital in 849. Under King Anawrahta (r.1044–77), they expanded their territory, conquering the Mon capital of Thaton in 1057 and creating a unified Burman kingdom. Over the next 200 years or so, the Pagan kingdom spread THERAVADA Buddhism throughout Southeast Asia, and its renowned artisans built more than 3000 pagoda temples and shrines. Weakened by centuries of donations to the Buddhist monkhood, and by TAI and Mon rebellions, Pagan was conquered by the MONGOLS under KUBLAI KHAN in 1287. *See also* KHMER EMPIRE

Page, Sir Earle Christmas Grafton (1880–1961) Australian statesman, prime minister (1939). He entered Parliament in 1919 and served until his death. Page was a founder and leader (1920–39) of the Country Party (later the NATIONAL PARTY), and he served (1923–29) as treasurer in a coalition government with Stanley BRUCE. Page was made deputy prime minister (1934–39) and was briefly prime minister on the death of Joseph LYONS. He represented Australia in the imperial war cabinet (1941–42). As minister of health (1949–56), Page reformed Australia's health service.

Pahlavi, Muhammad Reza (1919–80) Shah of Iran (1941–79), son of Reza PAHLAVI. After succeeding his father, he eventually overcame opposition by nationalists, led by Muhammad MOSADDEQ, in the early 1950s. His success was mainly due to covert British and US support – both nations keen to retain influence in the oil-rich nation. Pahlavi encouraged rapid economic development and social reforms in a programme (1963) known as the "White Revolution", funding it with the receipts from oil exports. During the 1970s, the increasing Westernization of Iran and the close ties with Britain and the United States aroused strong discontent among religious fundamentalists. Worsening social inequality, economic failure and the increasing use of repressive measures created dissatisfaction among students and the lower classes. After widespread rioting, a theocratic revolution (1979), led by Ayatollah KHOMEINI, forced Pahlavi into exile. He was invited to Egypt by President Anwar SADAT where he died.

Pahlavi, Reza (1878–1944) Iranian shah (1925–41) and army officer. He led the nationalist coup (1921) against the QAJAR DYNASTY and subsequently was appointed minister of war and commander in chief of the armed forces. Pahlavi strengthened the army, which he then used to secure control of the whole of IRAN, and became prime minister (1923–25). In 1925 Pahlavi deposed the absentee monarch, Ahmad Shah, and assumed the crown. He enforced radical social and financial reforms, crushed tribalism and reduced foreign influence over Iran's domestic affairs. In 1941 Britain and the Soviet Union, increasingly concerned with Pahlavi's relationship with the AXIS POWERS, occupied Iran. Pahlavi was forced to abdicate in favour of his son, Muhammad PAHLAVI.

Paine, Thomas (1737–1809) Anglo-American revolutionary political writer. With letters of introduction from Benjamin FRANKLIN, Paine emigrated from England to Pennsylvania in 1774. In 1776 he published his pamphlet *Common Sense*, which demanded independence for the North American colonies and influenced the publication of the DECLARATION OF INDEPENDENCE. Paine returned to England in 1787 and published *The Rights of Man* (1791–92), a defence of the French Revolution. Accused of treason, he fled to France in 1792. Paine became a French citizen and was elected to the National Convention. His opposition to LOUIS XIV's execution led to his imprisonment (1793–94) during the REIGN OF TERROR. While in prison, Paine completed *The Age of Reason* (1795), an attack on Christianity that attracted vehement opposition. He returned to the United States in 1802.

Paisley, Ian (1926–) Northern Irish politician and clergyman. In 1951 he formed the Free Presbyterian Church of Ulster. Paisley was elected to Parliament in 1970. In 1972 he formed the Ulster Democratic Unionist Party (DUP). An outspoken defender of Protestant Unionism, Paisley briefly resigned from Parliament over the ANGLO-IRISH AGREEMENT (1985). In 1979 he was elected to the European Parliament. He is a staunch opponent of the GOOD FRIDAY AGREEMENT (1998). *See also* ULSTER UNIONISTS

Pakistan *See* country feature

Pala Ruling dynasty of Bihar and Bengal, present-day NE India, from the mid-8th to the mid-12th century. The dynasty was founded by **Gopala** (r. *c*.750–70), who gradually gained control of the whole of Bengal. Gopala's son and successor, **Dharmapala** (r.*c*.770–810), occupied Kannauj, N India, initiating a long conflict with the Pratihara and Rastrakuta dynasties. **Devapala** (r.810–50) consolidated the kingdom and even claimed to control the N Deccan. The kingdom fell into decline in the mid-10th century but recovered under **Mahipala I** (r. *c*.988–1038), who captured VARANASI. The Pala dynasty was possibly at its height under **Rampala** (r. *c*.1077–1120), who controlled parts of Orissa (SE) and Assam (N), but subsequently was eclipsed by the Sena dynasty. As Buddhists, the Palas encouraged the building of great monasteries and the spread of BUDDHISM into Tibet. *See also* CHALUKYA

Palacký, František (1798–1876) Czech politician and historian. His most influential work is the five-volume *History of the Bohemian People* (1836–67). An advocate of PAN-SLAVISM, Palacký was chairman of the Prague Slavic Congress (1848) but retired from politics after the collapse of the nationalist uprising (1852). In 1861 he became a deputy in the Austrian Reichsrat (senate). After the creation of the AUSTRO-HUNGARIAN EMPIRE, he promoted Czech independence as a member of the Bohemian parliament and chairman of the Nationalist-Federal Party. He was a major influence on future generations of Czech nationalists, including Tomás MASARYK.

PALAU
AREA: 488sq km (188sq mi)
POPULATION: 15,122
CAPITAL (POPULATION): Koror (10,493)
GOVERNMENT: Multiparty republic
ETHNIC GROUPS: Palauan
LANGUAGES: Palauan, English
RELIGIONS: Catholic 40%, Protestant 25%, Modekngei
GDP PER CAPITA (1995): US$5833

Palaeolithic (Old STONE AGE) Earliest stage of human history, from *c*.2 million years ago until between *c*.40,000 and *c*.10,000 years ago. It was marked by the use of stone tools of growing complexity. During the **Lower** Palaeolithic, the simple chipped stone tools of *Australopithecus* and HOMO HABILIS gave way to the stone-axes of HOMO ERECTUS. NEANDERTHALS, during the **Middle** Palaeolithic (*c*.150,000 years ago), used fire, conducted burial rituals and made fine tools of stone and bone. HOMO SAPIENS arose during the **Upper** Palaeolithic, *c*.50,000 years ago. Tools were carefully worked, and later in the period small stone statuettes and fine cave paintings were created. The Palaeolithic was followed by the MESOLITHIC period. *See also* HUMAN EVOLUTION

Palaeozoic Second era of geological time, after the PRECAMBRIAN era, lasting from 590 million to 248 million years ago. It is sub-divided into six periods: CAMBRIAN, ORDOVICIAN, SILURIAN, DEVONIAN, CARBONIFEROUS and PERMIAN. Invertebrate animals evolved hard skeletons in the Cambrian; fish-like vertebrates appeared in the Ordovician; amphibians emerged in the Devonian; and reptiles in the Carboniferous.

Palatinate Two historic states of the HOLY ROMAN EMPIRE. The **Lower** (Rhenish) Palatinate, with its capital at Heidelberg, occupied a region either side of the River Rhine. The **Upper** Palatinate was in NE BAVARIA. In the 12th century, the lands of the counts palatine (stewards for the Holy Roman emperor) of Lothariniga (Lorraine) were joined to form the (Lower) Palatinate, which later became the property of the WITTELSBACH dynasty. By the Compact of Pavia (1329), Upper Palatinate was separated from the rest of Bavaria and also given to the Wittelsbach dynasty. The GOLDEN BULL (1356) of Emperor CHARLES IV made the count palatine one of the seven ELECTORS of the Holy Roman Empire. Following the introduction of CALVINISM by Elector Frederick III (r.1559–76), the Palatinate became a centre of the REFORMATION. The accession of Elector FREDERICK V as king of Bohemia precipitated the THIRTY YEARS' WAR, which devastated the Palatinate. In 1628 Upper Palatinate was reunited with Bavaria. The Lower Palatinate was further damaged during the War of the GRAND ALLIANCE (1689–97), and lost its land on the W bank of the Rhine to France during the FRENCH REVOLUTIONARY WARS. In the early 19th century, territory on the E bank was split between German *Länder* (states). Today, it forms the present German *Land* of RHINELAND-Palatinate and parts of adjacent *Länder*.

Palau (Belau) Archipelago republic of Micronesia, in the W Pacific Ocean. Settled by migrants from Southeast Asia *c*.3000 years ago, the first Europeans to arrive in the region were the Spanish in 1710. In the 19th century the native population was decimated by contact with Europeans. Germany bought the islands from Spain in 1898, but lost them to Japan in 1914. A large influx of Japanese emigrants aided economic development. During World War 2, Palau was captured (1944) by US marines. In 1947 it became a United Nations' trust territory, administered by the United States. Palau achieved self-government in 1981. It entered into a compact of free association with the United States in 1994.

Pale (Lat. stake) Area of IRELAND under the control of the English following HENRY II's invasion of 1171–72. Its extent varied with English strength but at various times included Louth, Meath, Trim, Dublin, Kilkenny, Wexford, Waterford, Carlow and Tipperary. English control was consolidated in the 14th century by the creation of the Anglo-Norman earldoms of Kildare, Desmond and ORMONDE. The growing independence of the Anglo-Irish nobles was briefly suppressed by Sir Edward POYNINGS

P

at the end of the 15th century and snuffed out by Henry VIII (r.1509–47). The suppression of native rebellions against the Act of Uniformity during Elizabeth I's reign (1558–1603) led to the expansion of English rule and the Plantation of Ireland. The term "Pale" is also applied to areas in 18th- and 19th-century Russia into which Jews were restricted.

Palermo Capital of Sicily, a port on the Tyrrhenian Sea coast, s Italy. The city was founded by the Phoenicians in the 8th century BC. It passed to the Romans in 254 BC and was captured by the Byzantine general Belisarius in AD 535. From the 9th to 11th centuries it prospered under benevolent Arab rule. Captured by the Normans in 1072, it enjoyed a brief period of fame as the capital of the Kingdom of Sicily under Roger II. Its prosperity continued under Hohenstaufen Emperor Frederick II, who established his court here. It fell to the Angevin dynasty in 1266, but they were overthrown by the Sicilian Vespers (1282). Under Spanish rule from 1412, Palermo began a long period of decline. In 1860 the city was captured by Giuseppe Garibaldi. Palermo was badly damaged during World War 2. Pop. (1991) 698,556.

Palestine Region in the Middle East, on the E shore of the Mediterranean Sea; considered a Holy Land by Jews, Christians and Muslims. The Palestinian town of Jericho was one of the earliest sites of human settlement (*c*.9000 BC). The Egyptians conquered the region in the 15th century BC and the Jews began to move into Palestine from ancient Egypt at the end of the 13th century BC. The Israelites were subjects of the Philistines until 1020 BC, when Saul, David and Solomon established Hebrew kingdoms. Solomon completed the Temple of Jerusalem in 957 BC. Following Solomon's death the region split into Israel and Judah, with Israel passing under the control of the Assyrians (722 BC) and Judah falling to Nebuchadnezzar II (*c*.586 BC). With the defeat of Chaldaea by Cyrus II (the Great) of Persia in 539 BC, Jerusalem was rebuilt and Palestine became part of the Achaemenid empire. In 333 BC the Persians were finally overthrown by Alexander III (the Great) and Hellenistic rule was maintained by Ptolemy I (Soter). The Ptolemaic dynasty was defeated by the Seleucids in 200 BC, but Palestine regained its autonomy with the revolt of the Maccabees in 167 BC. Independence proved short-lived, however, as Roman rule was imposed by Pompey (the Great) in 63 BC. In the 4th century AD, Palestine prospered under Constantine I (the Great) and became a focus of Christian pilgrimage. In 640 the region fell to the Arabs, and Islam was consolidated and extended by the Umayyad and Abbasid dynasties. The seizure of Jerusalem by the Fatimids precipitated the start of the Christian Crusades and Jerusalem was captured in 1099. Saladin restored Muslim rule to most of Palestine at the end of the 12th century. His Ayyubid dynasty was supplanted by the Mamluks, who completed the expulsion of the Crusaders in 1291. In 1516 Selim I defeated the Mamluks, and Palestine subsequently formed part of the Ottoman Empire for the next four centuries – apart from Muhammad Ali's brief occupation (1831–40). Zionist colonies multiplied in the early 20th century, and Jewish immigration was encouraged by the Balfour Declaration (1917). General Edmund Allenby led British forces to victory over the Ottoman Turks at the Battle of Megiddo (1918). In 1920 Hussein ibn-Ali's son, later Faisal I of Iraq, was elected king of a united Syria (including Palestine), but the League of Nations divided the Syrian region into three mandated territories: both Syria and Lebanon went to France; Palestine was handed to Britain. Nazi persecution in Europe saw the Jewish population in Palestine rise from 30,000 in 1933 to nearly 400,000 by 1936. The majority Arab population rose in revolt (1936–39) against increased Jewish immigration. The revelations of the horrors of the Holocaust during World War 2 led US President Harry Truman to support unrestricted Jewish emigration to Palestine. In 1947 Britain, unable to satisfy both Jewish and Arab aspirations, consigned the problem to the United Nations (UN). The UN proposed a plan for separate Jewish and Arab states. The Arabs forcibly resisted partition, but the armed Zionist organizations of Haganah and Irgun Zevai Leumi emerged triumphant from the civil war and the state of Israel was proclaimed in May 1948. The first of several Arab-Israeli Wars (1948–49) ended with Israel holding most of ancient Palestine, while the Gaza Strip was controlled by Egypt and the West Bank of the River Jordan held by Transjordan (now Jordan). These two areas were subsequently occupied by Israel in the Six-Day War (1967), creating a large number of Palestinian refugees. From the 1960s, the Palestine Liberation Organization (PLO) led opposition to Israeli rule, which included acts of terrorism and the Intifada in the occupied territories. The Israeli-Palestinian Accord (1993) between Israel and the PLO led to the creation of the Palestine National Authority, which took over nominal administration of the Gaza Strip and West Bank in 1994. In 1996 Yasir Arafat was elected chairman of the Authority. Palestinian police were appointed to maintain security, although the Israeli army retained freedom of movement. Subsequent agreements extended the range of Palestinian self-rule, but progress was slowed by the 1996 election of Binyamin Netanyahu as Israeli prime minister. His successor (1999–), Ehud Barak, stated his commitment to furthering the peace process. *See also* Canaan; Dome of the Rock; Edom; Judaea; Moab; Samaria; Zionism

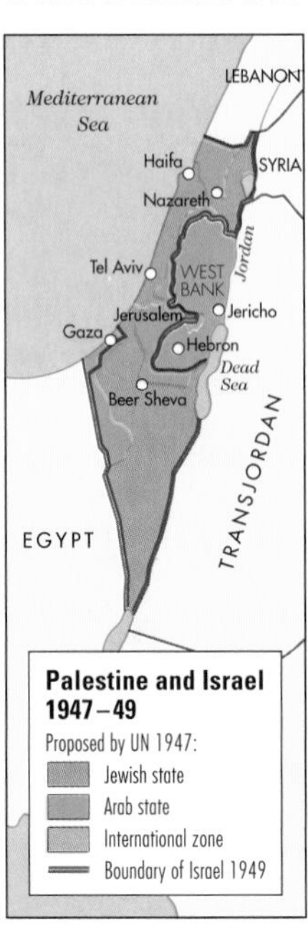

► **Palestine** The United Nations' (UN) proposed (1947) partition of Palestine into Jewish and Arab states with Jerusalem under international control was rejected by the majority Arab population. The Zionist forces won the ensuing civil war and the state of Israel was proclaimed on 14 May 1948. The new state immediately faced attack from the Arab Legion of Transjordan (now Jordan), led by John Bagot Glubb, and forces from Egypt, Iraq, Lebanon and Syria. Israel defeated the Arab armies, and in the armistices (January–July 1949) gained Galilee, the Negev Desert, the entire Palestinian coast except a smaller Gaza Strip (occupied by Egypt), and land between West Jerusalem and the Mediterranean. Jordan received the rest of Jerusalem.

Palestine Liberation Organization (PLO) Organization of Palestinian parties and groups, widely recognized as the main representative of the Palestinian people. It was founded in 1964 with the aim of dissolving the state of Israel and establishing a Palestinian state. Dominated by the al-Fatah group led by Yasir Arafat, many of its component guerrilla groups were involved in political violence against Israel and, in the 1970s, in acts of international terrorism to further their cause. By 1989, due to its renunciation of violence and recognition of the state of Israel, the PLO was recognized as a government-in-exile by the Arab League and the United Nations. In the early 1990s PLO representatives conducted secret negotiations with Israel, culminating in the Israeli-Palestinian Accord (1993). *See also* Black September; Gaza Strip; Palestine; West Bank

Pallava Ruling dynasty of s India from the 4th to the 9th century AD; their capital was at Kanchi (now Kanchipuram). The Pallavas traded with Sri Lanka, SE Asia and China. In the 7th century they were frequently in conflict with the Chalukya and Pandya dynasties. The Pallavas supported Buddhism, Jainism and Brahmanism. The dynasty is celebrated for its architecture, best exemplified by the "Seven Pagodas" at Mahabalipuram, literature and music. They were supplanted by the Chola dynasty.

Palme, (Sven) Olof (1927–86) Swedish statesman, prime minister (1969–76, 1982–86). He entered parliament in 1958 and held a series of cabinet posts before succeeding Tage Erlander as prime minister and leader of the Social Democratic Workers' Party. A committed pacifist, Palme spoke out against superpower interference in the politics of developing nations and was an outspoken opponent of US involvement in the Vietnam War, accepting US Army deserters and draft dodgers. Defeated in the 1976 elections, Palme worked as a United Nations' (UN) mediator in the Iran-Iraq War (1980–88) and chaired the Independent Commission on Disarmament and Security. Re-elected prime minister in 1982, Palme returned to his socialist programme. He was shot dead by an unknown assassin.

Palmerston, Henry John Temple, 3rd Viscount (1784–1865) British statesman, prime minister (1855–58, 1859–65). He entered Parliament as a Tory in 1807 and served as secretary of war (1809–28). In 1830 he resigned from the cabinet of the Duke of Wellington and defected to the Whigs. As foreign secretary (1830–34, 1835–41, 1846–51), Palmerston had his first diplomatic success with the emergence of an independent Belgium (1831). His nationalist foreign policy sought to defend Britain's imperial interests and prevent a coalition of France and Russia. During the 1830s Britain and France allied to support Isabella II of Spain in the Carlist Wars and Maria II of Portugal in the Miguelist Wars. In 1840 the alliance fractured over the so-called Eastern Question, when Palmerston acted to prevent Muhammad Ali of Egypt from conquering the Ottoman Empire. In his last term as foreign secretary, Palmerston acquired a reputation for "gunboat diplomacy" when the Royal Navy bombarded Athens (1850) in support of Don Pacifico, a British resident of Athens, who was seeking compensation from the Greek government after his house was destroyed by rioting. Palmerston was dismissed from office (1851) after approving of Napoleon III's coup in France, but returned to serve as home secretary (1852–53) under Lord Aberdeen. As prime minister, Palmerston vigorously prosecuted the Crimean War (1853–56) and reluctantly made peace with Russia. In 1856 he initiated the Second Opium War against China, and in 1858 he ordered the suppression of the Indian Mutiny. While Palmerston supported the Revolutions of 1848 and the Risorgimento, he was an opponent of political reform at home. Palmerston was forced to resign in 1858, but won the 1859 election to become, at the age of 74, Britain's oldest prime minister and its first Liberal leader. He died in office and was succeeded by John Russell. *See also* Gladstone, William Ewart; Peel, Sir Robert

Palmyra (Tadmur, City of Palms) Ancient oasis city in the Syrian Desert, central Syria. By the 1st century BC it had become a city-state by virtue of its control of the trade route between Mesopotamia and the Mediterranean. In *c*.AD 30 the city-state became a Roman dependency under local rule. By the 2nd century Palmyra's influence had spread as far as Armenia. It reached its apex in the 3rd century under Odenathus (d.267). In 267 his widow, Zenobia, became queen and severed the state's links with Rome, but in 273 the Roman Emperor Aurelian laid waste to the city.

Palo Alto, Battle of (8 May 1846) First battle of the Mexican War, fought near Brownsville, Texas. US General Zachary Taylor defeated a Mexican force under Mariano Arista. US casualties were minimal, but the Mexicans lost several hundred men.

Pamplona Ancient city in N Spain; capital of Navarre province. In 68 BC it was rebuilt by Pompey and in AD 778 conquered by Charlemagne. In the 11th century Pamplona was made capital of the kingdom of Navarre. In 1512 control of Pamplona passed to Ferdinand V (the Catholic), who united Navarre with Castile. During the Peninsular War, Pamplona was captured from the French by the Duke of Wellington (1813). Every July, in the fiesta of San Fermin, bulls are driven through the city streets. Pop. (1991) 179,251.

Pan-Africanism Movement for the unification and independence of African nations (**Continental** Pan-Africanism) and for the promotion of solidarity among all peoples of Africa or of African descent (**Diaspora** Pan-Africanism). Initially an ideological movement, Pan-

Africanism began to assume a more coherent political shape at the Pan-African Congress (1900) in London. It went on to meet on five further occasions between 1900 and 1927, some of which were organized by the US civil rights activist W.E.B. Du Bois. During this time it attracted the attention of African and West Indian politicians, such as Marcus Garvey. Its aim was to bring gradual self-government to African colonial states. In 1945 the Pan-African Federation convened the Sixth Congress, in Manchester, England, which was attended by future leaders of post-colonial Africa, notably Kwame Nkrumah and Jomo Kenyatta. As independence was gained, the movement was eventually replaced (1963) by the Organization of African Unity (OAU).

Pan-Africanist Congress (PAC) Militant black South African political organization. It was formed (1959) as a breakaway group of the African National Congress (ANC), with which the PAC did not share multiracial policies, rather advocating a solely black African government in South Africa. A PAC-organized demonstration against the pass laws, which restricted the movement of non-whites, resulted in the Sharpeville Massacre (March 1960) and the banning of the PAC. It continued to pursue an armed struggle against South Africa's apartheid government from bases in Botswana and Zambia until it was legalized in 1990 as part of the dismantling of apartheid. PAC won 1.2% of the vote in the first multiracial elections (1994) and won five seats in the National Assembly.

Panama *See* country feature

Panama Canal Waterway connecting the Atlantic and Pacific oceans across the Isthmus of Panama. America first became interested in the idea in the late 18th century. In the 19th century, the right to build a canal was disputed between Britain and the United States. A canal, begun in Panama in 1882 by Ferdinand de Lesseps, was subsequently abandoned because of bankruptcy. Although originally favouring a route through Nicaragua, the United States purchased the French rights in Panama and financed the project in order to provide a convenient route for its warships. The Hay-Bunau-Varilla Convention gave the United States control of the canal site. The main construction took about ten years to complete, costing more than US$300 million, and the first ship passed through in 1914. The 82-km (51-mi) waterway reduces the sea voyage between San Francisco and New York by *c.*12,500km (7800mi). Control of the Canal passed from the United States to Panama at the end of 1999. The Canal has given Panama great international importance, and the majority of Panamanians live within 20km (12mi) of it. *See also* Clayton-Bulwer Treaty; Hay-Pauncefote Treaty

Pan-American movement Development of cooperation among the republics of North, Central and South America. Throughout the 19th century, meetings were held (1836, 1847, 1856, 1864) by Latin American states to discuss matters of common concern, such as defence and legal issues. While the United States had stated its commitment to Pan-Americanism in the Monroe Doctrine (1823), the movement did not broaden from its Latin American base until the First International Conference of American States (1889–90), summoned by the United States. This meeting created the Union of American Republics (later known as the Pan-American Union). The Organization of American States (OAS) was formed at the Ninth International Conference of American States (1948). Concern about growing US influence revived interest in Latin American solidarity, with the formation (1960) of the Latin American Free Trade Association (later the Latin American Integration Association) and the Central American Common Market. *See also* North America Free Trade Agreement (NAFTA)

Pan-American Union (PAU) Independent continent-wide organization that was established in 1890 but not officially known as the PAU until 1910. In 1948 the PAU was absorbed by the Organization of American States (OAS). It aimed to promote international cooperation and to improve economic, social and cultural relations among the American nations. PAU was the name given to the secretariat of OAS (1948–70), but after 1970 the name Pan-American Union ceased to be used.

Pan-Arab movement Form of Nationalism that tends towards political unification among Arab nations. While a fairly potent ideology up until World War 1, with the collapse of the Ottoman Empire following the War and the creation of separate Arab countries the movement lost momentum. In the 1930s, in response to increased Jewish emigration to Palestine, the Palestinian Arabs sought political support from other Arab nations. In 1945 the Arab League was formed. It coordinated political, economic and military activities through various treaties. The Arab Bank was formed in 1959. President Nasser of Egypt strengthened the movement and promoted Egypt as its leader. Syria, Egypt and Yemen joined together in the short-lived (1958–61) United Arab Republic. A union between Iraq and Jordan dissolved in 1958. After Arab defeat in the Six-Day War (1967), the Pan-Arab movement declined. In politics, the Ba'ath Party in various Arab states promotes Pan-Arabism. *See also* Arab-Israeli Wars; Faisal I; Hussein ibn-Ali; OPEC

Panchen Lama In Tibetan Buddhism, religious leader who is second in importance to the Dalai Lama. The title was originally bestowed upon the head abbot of the Tashilhunpo monastery, an institution founded by the first Dalai Lama. By the 17th century the Panchen Lama was seen as the reincarnation of the previous one. In 1923 the ninth Panchen Lama fled to China because of disagreements with the Dalai Lama. In 1938 Bskal-bzang Tshebrtan, a boy of Tibetan parentage, was born in China and later hailed by the Chinese government as the 10th Panchen Lama and taken to Tibet. In 1959, when the Dalai Lama fled to India, the Chinese government officially recognized the Panchen Lama as the religious leader of Tibet. In 1964 he was stripped of his power for refusing to denounce the Dalai Lama. He died in 1989. In December 1995 another Tibetan boy, Gyaincain Norbu, was selected by the Chinese government and enthroned in Beijing as the 11th Panchen Lama. He is not recognized as such by the Tibetan government-in-exile nor by the majority of the international community.

Pandit, Vijaya Lakshmi (1900–90) Indian stateswoman, daughter of Motilal Nehru and sister of Jawaharlal Nehru. She was imprisoned several times by the British for her participation in the nationalist movement. After Indian independence, Pandit led (1946–48, 1952–53) the Indian delegation to the United Nations (UN) and was the first woman president (1953–54) of the UN General Assembly. Pandit also served as ambassador to the Soviet Union (1947–49) and the United States (1949–51), and was High Commissioner to Britain (1954–61). She returned to national politics (1962–78) before becoming India's representative to the UN Human Rights Commission (1979).

Pandya Tamil dynasty that ruled s India from the *c.*1st century BC to the 16th century AD; its capital was at Madurai, SE India. From the 1st to the 6th century the Pandya competed for control of regions of s India with the Pallava and Chola dynasties, and by the mid-6th century s India was divided between the Pandya, the Chalukya and the Pallava. In the 9th century the Pandya and the Chola combined to defeat the Pallava dynasty, and by the 13th century the Pandya in turn defeated the Chola to become the major force in s India. It reached the height of its power during the reign of Jatavarman Sundara (r.1251–68). Due to attacks by Turks from the N and the capture of Madurai (1311) by the Delhi Sultanate the Pandya dynasty waned.

Panipat, battles of Three conflicts fought on a strategically located plain in NW India. In the **First** Battle of Panipat (1526), the Lodi dynasty of the Delhi Sultanate was defeated by Babur, who went on to found the Mughal Empire. Akbar defeated the Afghans at the **Second** Battle of Panipat (1556), restoring the Mughal Empire as the major force in India. In the **Third** Battle of Panipat (1761), the Maratha army was crushed by the Afghan chief Ahmad Shah Durrani.

PANAMA

AREA: 77,080sq km (29,761sq mi)
POPULATION: 2,515,000
CAPITAL (POPULATION): Panama City (584,803)
GOVERNMENT: Multiparty republic
ETHNIC GROUPS: Mestizo 60%, Black and Mulatto 20%, White 10%, Native American 8%, Asian 2%
LANGUAGES: Spanish (official)
RELIGIONS: Christianity (Roman Catholic 84%, Protestant 5%), Islam 5%
GDP PER CAPITA (1995): US$5980

Republic on the Isthmus of Panama, connecting Central and South America. The narrowest part of Panama is less than 60km (37mi) wide. Christopher Columbus landed in Panama in 1502. In 1510 Vasco Núñez de Balboa became the first European to cross Panama and see the Pacific Ocean. With the establishment of Spanish control the indigenous population of perhaps 750,000 was soon wiped out.

In 1821 Panama proclaimed its independence from Spain and became a province of Colombia. From the 1830s it made several attempts to secede from Colombia. In 1903, following Colombia's failure to ratify a treaty over the building of a canal across the Isthmus, the United States recognized Panama's declaration of independence. It also concluded the Hay-Bunau-Varilla Treaty (1903), which gave the United States control over the proposed Panama Canal Zone in perpetuity. In 1904 the United States began work on the Canal. Following its opening in 1914, the status of the Canal became a feature of Panamanian politics. US forces intervened in 1908, 1912 and 1918 to protect its interests.

Throughout the 20th century Panama was politically unstable, with a series of dictatorial regimes and military coups. During the 1950s and 1960s civil strife led to negotiations with the United States for the transfer of the Canal Zone. In 1977 a treaty confirmed Panama's sovereignty over the Canal, while providing for US bases in the Canal Zone. The United States agreed to hand over control of the Canal on 31 December 1999. In 1983 General Manuel Noriega took control of the National Guard and ruled Panama through a succession of puppet governments. In 1987 the United States withdrew its support for Noriega after he was accused of murder, electoral fraud and aiding drug smuggling. In December 1989 he made himself president and declared war on the United States. On 20 December 1989, 25,000 US troops invaded Panama. In January 1990 Noriega was captured and taken to the United States for trial. In 1994 Pérez Balladares was elected president. In 1998 he failed in an attempt to amend the constitution in order to serve a second term. He was succeeded in 1999 by Mireya Moscoso, Panama's first woman president.

PANKHURST, EMILY (1858–1928)

English leader of the SUFFRAGETTE MOVEMENT, b. Emmeline Goulden. She helped form the Women's FRANCHISE League in 1889. In 1903 Pankhurst founded the Women's Social and Political Union (WSPU) in Manchester, NW England. The WSPU employed direct action to secure the vote for women, and her eldest daughter, **Christabel** (1880–1958), was arrested (1905) after disrupting a LIBERAL PARTY meeting. Pankhurst resorted to increasingly militant tactics, including arson, to secure her objective and was arrested many times between 1908 and 1913, gaining further publicity through her hunger-strikes while in prison. Pankhurst suspended the campaign during World War 1 and encouraged women to help in the war effort and work in industries normally restricted to men. In 1918 British women over the age of 30 won the right to vote. Pankhurst died shortly after women obtained full equality in voting (1928). See *also* FEMINISM

► **Pankhurst** Emily Pankhurst (centre) and her daughter Christabel (on her right) were the pioneers of the movement to secure for women the right to vote. This photo was taken (1908) just after Emily had been released from prison. Another daughter, Sylvia Pankhurst (1882–1960), shown here on Christabel's right, was also active in the movement but broke with her mother and elder sister after the WSPU began arson attacks in 1912. She also rejected their support for World War 1.

Pankhurst, Emily (Emmeline) *See* feature article

Panmunjom Talks (1951–53) Discussions between the United Nations and North Korea that ended the KOREAN WAR. It took two years to reach an agreement that gave South Korea slightly more territory than it had when the war began in 1950. A demilitarized zone was established between North and South Korea.

Pannonia Province of the ancient ROMAN EMPIRE, SW of the River Danube, encompassing parts of modern Slovenia, Austria and Hungary. The Romans fought the Pannonians from 119 BC to 9 BC, when AUGUSTUS completed their subjugation. The region became part of ILLYRIA. Following a revolt (AD 6) it was organized (AD 9) into the separate province of Pannonia. In *c.*103 the province was split into Upper and Lower Pannonia by TRAJAN and later subdivided again by DIOCLETIAN. Pannonia fell victim to the Barbarian invasions of the 4th century and was abandoned by the Romans in *c.*405.

Pan-Slavism Movement to unite the Slavic peoples. In the early 19th century it aimed to promote the common culture of the SLAVS, and is more accurately termed Slavophilism. It soon took on more political overtones, and meetings of the leaders of Slavic countries were held in 1848, 1867 and 1908. In the late 19th century Russia, the strongest power in Eastern Europe and where the ideology was at it most militant, aspired to the leadership of the Slavs and provoked the RUSSO-TURKISH WAR (1877–78). In the early 20th century the movement concentrated on the liberation of Slavs living under the OTTOMAN and HABSBURG empires. The Balkan Slavic nations united in the Balkan League, which conquered large swathes of the Ottoman Empire in the BALKAN WARS. After World War 1 and the achievement of independence by many Slavic countries, Pan-Slavism ceased to be a political force. Later, however, the Soviet Union applied Pan-Slavism as a justification for its control over Eastern European Communist states.

papacy Office, status or authority of the pope as head of both the ROMAN CATHOLIC CHURCH and the VATICAN CITY. The pope is nominated Bishop of Rome and Christ's spiritual representative on Earth. He is elected by the College of Cardinals. There have been 265 holders of the office of pope from St PETER to JOHN PAUL II (*see* individual popes). The jurisdiction of the pope was not always as far reaching as it is today. In the early centuries of CHRISTIANITY the pope would only intervene in overseas Church matters in times of crises. Over time the papacy extended its jurisdiction, causing a number splits within the Church, most significantly the SCHISM with the Eastern ORTHODOX CHURCH and the formation of PROTESTANTISM during the REFORMATION. *See also* ANTIPOPE; CONCILIAR MOVEMENT; GREAT SCHISM; INDULGENCES; INVESTITURE; PAPAL INFALLIBILITY

papal infallibility Roman Catholic doctrine according to which the pope, under certain conditions, cannot make a mistake in formal statements on issues of faith or morals. It was defined in its present form, amid great controversy, at the First VATICAN COUNCIL (1869–70). *See also* PIUS IX

Papal States Territories of central Italy under the rule of the popes (756–1870). The papacy was first granted land around ROME (the Patrimony of St Peter) in the 4th century. Its holdings were extended with the "Donation of PEPIN" (754), which granted the pope sovereignty over much of N and central Italy. The pope's authority gradually weakened during the early medieval period, with the rise of feudal lords, local communes, and the INVESTITURE controversy with Holy Roman emperors. Under INNOCENT III (r.1198–1216) and Emperor FREDERICK II, however, the papacy greatly increased its territories. In the 15th century the papal government imposed direct control from Rome. The Papal States were lost to NAPOLEON in 1789–99, but restored to the papacy in 1815, and annexed by the Italian nationalists during the RISORGIMENTO. The LATERAN TREATY of 1929 restored the VATICAN CITY in Rome to papal rule.

Papandreou, Andreas (1919–96) Greek statesman, prime minister (1981–89, 1993–96), son of Georgios PAPANDREOU. Imprisoned (1939) by Ioannis METAXAS, he went to the United States on his release. Papandreou returned to GREECE following his father's election victory (1963) and was elected to parliament in 1965. He fled into exile a second time following the military coup in 1967. With the collapse of military rule, Papandreou returned to Greece (1974) and founded the Pan-Hellenic Socialist Movement (PASOK), becoming leader of the opposition in 1977. In 1981 Papandreou became Greece's first socialist prime minister, introducing a number of social reforms. He was re-elected in 1985. The combination of a failing economy, involvement in financial fraud and personal scandal ensured Papandreou was unable to form a government following the 1989 elections and he resigned. Cleared of fraud, Papandreou was re-elected in 1993 and later retired on grounds of ill health. He was succeeded by Costas Simitis.

Papandreou, Georgios (1888–1968) Greek statesman, prime minister (1944, 1963, 1964–65), father of Andreas PAPANDREOU. He served as minister of education (1929–33) in Eleuthérios VENIZÉLOS' government, but broke away to found the Democratic Socialist Party in 1935. Forced into exile during the dictatorship of Ioannis METAXAS, Papandreou was imprisoned by the Germans (1942–44) during World War 2, but managed to escape (April 1944) and form a government-in-exile. He returned to Greece in October 1944, but resigned as prime minister (December 1944) as the country slid into civil war (1946–49). In 1961 he joined with the Liberal Party to form the Centre Union, which was able to form a minority government in 1963. Papandreou secured a majority in the 1964 elections, but struggled with CONSTANTINE II over control of the army and was subsequently dismissed. On course for victory in the 1967 elections, Papandreou was arrested by the army as part of a military coup against Constantine. He died shortly after his release.

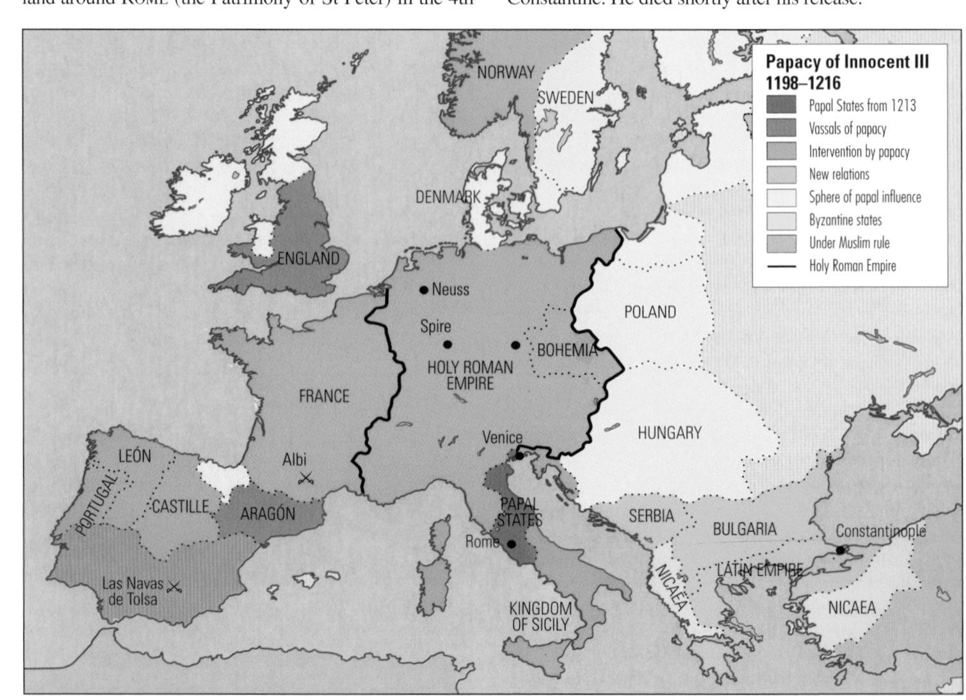

► **papacy** Pope Innocent III (1198–1216) extended the power of the papacy in Europe by suppressing any challenge, temporal or spiritual, to the authority of the Catholic Church.

Papen, Franz von (1879–1969) German statesman, chancellor (1932). A military attaché to the United States, Papen was recalled to Germany in 1915 after the US government accused him of spying. He entered the Reichstag (German parliament) in 1921 as a member of the Catholic Centre Party. As chancellor, Papen passed a range of reactionary policies and lifted the ban on the Nazi BROWNSHIRTS (SA). He was forced to resign after only six months in office, but then persuaded President HINDENBURG to appoint Adolf HITLER. He served (1933–34) as Hitler's vice chancellor, but resigned after the NIGHT OF THE LONG KNIVES. As ambassador to Austria (1936–38), he pressed for ANSCHLUSS. Papen served as ambassador to Turkey (1939–44). He was taken prisoner by the Allies in 1945, but was acquitted (1946) of war crimes at the NUREMBERG TRIALS. *See also* NAZI PARTY

Papineau, Louis Joseph (1786–1871) French-Canadian politician. In 1815 he became speaker of the Legislative Assembly of Lower Canada (QUÉBEC), demanding greater French-Canadian autonomy. Papineau joined with William Lyon MACKENZIE to oppose the unification of Upper and Lower Canada. Although he incited the REBELLION OF 1837, Papineau took no active part in the fighting and escaped arrest by fleeing to the United States, then to France. A further rebellion (1838) resulted in the execution of 12 of Papineau's supporters. Granted an amnesty (1844), he returned to Canada and was a member of the unified legislature (1848–54).

Papua New Guinea *See* country feature

Paraguay *See* country feature, page 317

Paraguayan War *See* TRIPLE ALLIANCE, WAR OF THE

Paris, Matthew (d.1259) English monk and chronicler. He became the historiographer of the monastery of ST ALBANS on the death of Roger of Wendover in 1236. His *Chronica majora* ("Great Chronicle") is one of the best sources for the history of Europe (1235–1259).

Paris Capital of France. When the Romans took Paris in 52 BC, it was a small village on the Île de la Cité on the River Seine. Under Roman rule it became an important administrative centre. Paris was the capital of the MEROVINGIANS (*see also* FRANKS) in the 5th century but subsequently declined. In the 10th century it was re-established as the French capital by the CAPETIAN kings. In the 11th and 12th centuries the city expanded rapidly. During the 14th century Paris rebelled against the Crown and declared itself an independent commune. It suffered further civil disorder during the HUNDRED YEARS' WAR. In the 16th century Paris underwent fresh expansion, its architecture strongly influenced by the Italian Renaissance. In the reign of LOUIS XIII, Cardinal RICHELIEU established Paris as the cultural and political centre of Europe. The FRENCH REVOLUTION began in Paris when the BASTILLE was stormed by crowds in 1789. Under Emperor NAPOLEON I the city began to assume its present-day form. The work of modernization was continued during the reign of NAPOLEON III, when Baron Haussmann (1809–91) was commissioned to plan the boulevards, bridges and parks. Although occupied during the FRANCO-PRUSSIAN WAR (1870–71), Paris was not badly damaged. In 1871 the PARIS COMMUNE resulted in the destruction of the centre of Paris and the death of 20,000 Parisians. During the relatively stable period of the THIRD REPUBLIC, Paris developed into a powerful industrial centre. After the Germans' failure to seize the city in World War 1, it became a cultural centre attracting writers and artists from Europe and the United States. Again occupied during World War 2, Paris escaped relatively unscathed from the conflict. Despite attempts at decentralization, Paris remains the hub of France and retains its importance as a European cultural, commercial and communications centre. Sights include the Eiffel Tower (1889), Arc de Triomphe (1836), the Louvre, and Notre Dame (1163–1250). Pop. (1990, city) 2,152,423; (metropolitan) 9,318,821.

Paris, treaties of Name given to several international agreements made in Paris. The most notable include: the **treaty of 1763**, which ended the SEVEN YEARS' WAR by settling rights to overseas territories in North America, India, Africa and the Caribbean; the **treaty of 1783**, which ended the AMERICAN REVOLUTION when Britain recognized the independence of the United States, establishing its boundaries, and made separate settlements with France, Spain and the Netherlands; the **treaty of 1814**, which settled the affairs of France after the first abdication of NAPOLEON I and called the Congress of VIENNA; the **treaty of 1815**, which imposed harsh terms on France after Napoleon's final defeat; the **treaty of 1856**, which established limits on Russian and Ottoman territories at the end of the the CRIMEAN WAR, and re-enforced the 1841 Straits Convention banning warships in the Black Sea and ensured religious tolerance in the Ottoman empire; the **treaty of 1898**, ending the SPANISH-AMERICAN WAR and giving the Philippines to the United States; and the main international settlement (1919) after World War 1, more often called the Treaty of VERSAILLES. Also signed in Paris was the truce (1973) in the VIETNAM WAR, in which the United States agreed to withdraw its forces.

Paris Commune (18 March–28 May 1871) Revolutionary government in Paris, France. Angry with the provisional national government of Adolphe THIERS, following the humiliating defeat and subsequent armistice with Prussia after the FRANCO-PRUSSIAN WAR, a collection of liberals, socialists and republicans within Paris began to express a desire for independence. To limit tension, Thiers decided to remove the city's cannons. This provoked Paris into open rebellion, and a 92-member independent city government was established. Bombarded for six weeks by the forces of the national government, and following a spirited but ineffective defence during which the archbishop of Paris was murdered, the city fell, and the Commune was violently suppressed. The slaughter of *c.*20,000 COMMUNARDS, and the arrest of *c.*38,000 more, alienated many French workers and encouraged revolutionary doctrines in many regions of France, effectively dividing the country between radicals and reactionaries.

Park, Mungo (1771–1806) Scottish explorer. He was asked by the African Association (forerunner of the Royal Geographical Society) to investigate the course of the River Niger (1795). He explored *c.*450km (280mi) of the Upper Niger, a journey described in his *Travels in the Interior Districts of Africa* (1799). On a second expedition to the Niger (1805) Park and his companions were ambushed and drowned at Bussa, Guinea.

Park Chung Hee (1917–79) South Korean general and statesman, president (1963–79). After fighting for the Japanese during World War 2, Park was an officer in the South Korean army in the KOREAN WAR (1950–53). A major general, Park seized power in a military coup (1961). In 1963 he formed the Democratic Republican Party (DRP) and was elected president in December of that year. Park was re-elected in 1967 and 1971. Park, by astute government planning and investment, presided over great export-led financial growth. He also became increasingly authoritarian, declaring martial law (1972) and enacting emergency measures (1975). Amid rising unrest, much of it brought about by the slowing of the economy, he was assassinated by Kim Jae Kyu, head of the South Korean Central Intelligence Agency.

Parkes, Sir Henry (1815–96) Australian politician, b. England. He emigrated to Australia in 1839. In 1850 he launched the newspaper *Empire*, through which he campaigned for self-government. Between 1872 and 1891 Parkes was five times the premier of NEW SOUTH WALES. Earning the title "Father of Federation", Parkes was a strong advocate of Australian federation, the ending of transportation of convicts and improvements in education. His latter efforts led to the Public Schools Act of 1866, which resulted in compulsory free education.

Parks, Rosa Louise (1913–) African-American CIVIL RIGHTS activist. A member of the NATIONAL ASSOCIATION FOR THE ADVANCEMENT OF COLORED PEOPLE (NAACP), Parks was arrested on a city bus in Montgomery, Alabama, for violating segregation ordinances by refusing to give up her seat in the front row of the "colored" rear section and

PAPUA NEW GUINEA

AREA: 462,840sq km (178,073 sq mi)
POPULATION: 4,056,000
CAPITAL (POPULATION): Port Moresby (193,242)
GOVERNMENT: Constitutional monarchy
ETHNIC GROUPS: Papuan 84%, Melanesian 1%
LANGUAGES: English (official)
RELIGIONS: Christianity (Protestant 58%, Roman Catholic 33%, Anglican 5%), traditional beliefs 3%
GDP PER CAPITA (1995): US$2420

Independent Commonwealth island group in Melanesia, sw Pacific, *c.*160km (100mi) NE of Australia. Papua New Guinea includes the E part of NEW GUINEA, the Bismarck Archipelago, the N SOLOMON ISLANDS, the Trobriand and D'Entrecasteaux Islands and the Louisiade Archipelago. The first European sighting of New Guinea was made by the Portuguese in 1526. In 1828 the Dutch took W New Guinea (now IRIAN JAYA, Indonesia). In 1884 Germany took NE New Guinea as German New Guinea, and Britain formed the protectorate of British New Guinea in SE New Guinea.

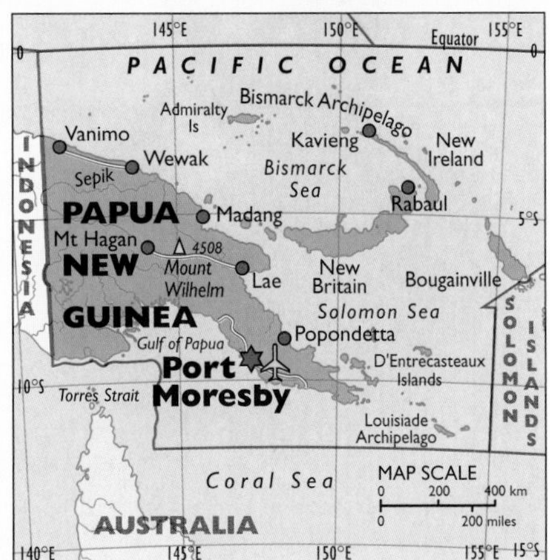

In 1906 British New Guinea passed to Australia as the Territory of Papua. In 1921 German New Guinea became the League of Nations' mandate Territory of New Guinea under Australian administration. In 1942 Japan captured the islands, but the Allies reconquered them in 1944. In 1949 Papua and New Guinea were combined to form the Territory of Papua and New Guinea. The Territory achieved self-government in 1973 as a prelude to full independence as Papua New Guinea in 1975.

Since independence, the government of Papua New Guinea has worked to develop its mineral reserves. One of the most valuable reserves was a copper mine at Panguna, Bougainville. Conflict developed when the people of Bougainville demanded a larger share in mining profits. In 1990, following an insurrection, the Bougainville Revolutionary Army (BRA) proclaimed independence. In 1992 and 1996 Papua New Guinea launched offensives against the BRA. The use of highly paid mercenaries created unrest in the army. In 1997 troops and civilians surrounded Parliament and forced the resignation of the prime minister, Sir Julius Chan. In April 1998 a permanent cease-fire was declared on Bougainville. In July 1998 a tidal wave hit N Papua New Guinea, killing more than 1600 people. Mekere Morauta succeeded Bill Skate as prime minister in 1999.

move further back for a white man who could not find a seat in the "whites-only" front section (1 December 1955). Anger at her treatment triggered the Montgomery bus boycott, led by Martin Luther KING, Jr, the first large-scale, non-violent, civil rights protest in the United States. The boycott continued until the US Supreme Court ordered the buses desegregated (November 1956). After the boycott, Parks moved to Detroit, Michigan, and remained active in the civil rights movement.

Parlement Royal court of law under the ANCIEN RÉGIME in France. The role of the first, the Paris *Parlement* (established in the 12th century), was primarily judicial, acting as a court of appeal and a source of legal rulings. Between the 14th and the 17th centuries provincial *parlements* emerged and, as all royal decrees had to be registered through the *parlements* before becoming law, over time they began to assume political as well as judicial significance. When the position of *parlementaires* was made heriditary in 1604, the nobility was strengthened at the expense of the monarchy. This attack on absolute monarchy was significant in bringing about the FRONDES (1648–53). LOUIS XIV suppressed the *parlements*, but in 1718 they were reinstated by Philippe, Duc d'ORLÉANS. Throughout much of the second half of the 18th century the *parlements* opposed the monarchy, supposedly acting as upholders of liberty in the face of an oppressive monarchy, but in reality defending the rights and privileges of the nobility. LOUIS XV abolished the *parlements* (1771), but in an attempt to appease the nobility they were reinstated on LOUIS XVI's accession (1774). The question of taxation became crucial in the following years. In 1787–88 Louis XVI's finance minister insisted on a new land tax. The *parlements*, made up of landed gentry, insisted on calling the STATES-GENERAL as the only authority high enough to introduce such sweeping new taxes. The calling of the States-General was to precipitate the FRENCH REVOLUTION (1789–99), which abolished the *parlements*.

parliament Legislative assembly that includes elected members and acts as a debating forum for political affairs. Many parliamentary systems are based on the **British Parliament**. The British Parliament emerged in the late 13th century as an extension of the king's council and has been housed at the Palace of Westminster since that time. Advances towards representation were made by Simon de MONTFORT and the MODEL PARLIAMENT of EDWARD I. Throughout the 14th century it became increasingly apparent that Parliament's approval should be secured before the crown could receive taxes, and by the 15th century parliamentary assent was required for the passage of new laws. The REFORMATION resulted in Parliament gaining additional powers, and by the 17th century, parliamentary backing for the king was necessary for the effective rule of the nation. This was demonstrated when CHARLES I was forced to recall Parliament to raise revenue following a period (1629–40) without Parliament. Charles' attempt to arrest five leading opponents (including John PYM and John HAMPDEN) in the HOUSE OF COMMONS precipitated the English CIVIL WAR (1642–46). With Parliament again playing a crucial role in the RESTORATION (1660), the GLORIOUS REVOLUTION (1688–89) and the Act of SETTLEMENT (1701), the Commons emerged as the sovereign power in the land. The party system, first arising in the late 17th century, was firmly established during the early 19th century. Parliament comprises the monarch, in whose name members of the government act but who holds no real power, and two Houses: the HOUSE OF LORDS, an upper chamber of peers, bishops and law lords; and the House of Commons. There are 659 members of the Commons (known as "members of Parliament" or MPs), elected in single-member constituencies by universal adult suffrage. The prime minister and CABINET members are almost always members of the Commons. There is a maximum of five years between elections. In 1999 separate legislative bodies were established for Northern Ireland, Scotland and Wales.

Parma City in N Italy; capital of Parma province. It was founded by the Romans in 183 BC. In the 9th century AD it became a bishopric and in 1513 was incorporated into the PAPAL STATES. In 1545 Pope Paul III established the duchy of Parma, and it was controlled by the FARNESE family until 1731, when it fell to the BOURBONS. In 1802 NAPOLEON conquered Parma and it came under the rule (1816–47) of his second consort, MARIE LOUISE of Austria. It became part of the kingdom of Sardinia in 1860. Despite suffering bombing in World War 2, Parma retains many historic buildings. Pop. (1991) 170,520.

Parnell, Charles Stewart (1846–91) Irish nationalist leader. In 1875 Parnell entered the British Parliament, where he led the parliamentary movement for Irish HOME RULE. His obstructive filibustering tactics made him a popular figure in Ireland and won the support of the FENIAN MOVEMENT in the United States. In 1879 Parnell became president of the National LAND LEAGUE. He organized mass agitation by Irish tenant-farmers, for which he was imprisoned (1881–82) in Kilmainham jail. While in prison he encouraged William O'BRIEN, editor of Parnell's newspaper *United Ireland*, to write a pamphlet against rent payment. Parnell was released on the understanding that in return for a government review of rent arrears he would help to curb violence against landlords. In 1886 he supported William GLADSTONE's introduction of the Home Rule Bill. His career collapsed when he was cited as co-respondent in the divorce of William O'Shea, whose wife, Kitty, he later married. *See also* BUTT, ISAAC

Parr, Catherine (1512–48) Queen consort and sixth wife of HENRY VIII. She was the daughter of Sir Thomas Parr, an official in the royal household. Parr had been twice widowed before marrying Henry (1543). As queen, she was a moderating influence on Henry, and by her intercession the princesses Mary and Elizabeth were reinstated at court. Parr married her fourth husband, Thomas Seymour of Sudeley, after the king's death in 1547. She died after giving birth to a daughter.

Parsi (Parsee) Modern descendant of a small number of ancient Persian followers of ZOROASTRIANISM. To avoid Muslim persecution, they emigrated from Iran to Gujarat in India from the 10th century onwards. Modern Parsis, concentrated mainly in Bombay, follow a mixture of some Indian beliefs and practices and Zoroastrianism, notably their reverence for the natural forces of fire, earth and water. They play a significant role in the economy of Bombay, and their schools have produced a close-knit, educated community that advocates equality for women.

Parthenon Temple to the goddess Athena built (447–432 BC) by PERICLES on the ACROPOLIS, Athens. The finest example of a Doric order temple, it was badly damaged by an explosion in 1687, when the Turks were using it as a munitions dump. Most of the surviving sculptures were removed by Lord Elgin in 1801–03. *See* ELGIN MARBLES

▲ **Parnell** is often called the "uncrowned king of Ireland". He disproved allegations of support for the Phoenix Park murders (1882), but his career was ruined by an adulterous affair.

Parthia Region in ancient Persia, corresponding approximately to the modern Iranian province of Khorasan with part of S Turkmenistan. Originally part of the ACHAEMENID empire, the region came under the control of the SELEUCIDS. In *c*.250 BC, following a successful revolt against the Seleucids, Parthia became the seat of the Parthian empire. Under the ARSACID dynasty, during which time it defeated the Romans at Carrhae (53 BC), the Parthian empire extended, at its peak, from Armenia to Afghanistan and became significant in trade between East and West. In AD 224 the Parthians were defeated by the rising power of the SASANIANS under ARDASHIR I, and the empire rapidly crumbled.

Pašić, Nikolai (1846–1926) Serbian statesman, prime minister of SERBIA (1891–92, 1904–05, 1906–08, 1909–11, 1912–18), founder and prime minister of the Kingdom of Serbs, Croat and Slovenes (1918, 1921–24, 1924–26), later (1929) called YUGOSLAVIA. Pašić entered the Serbian parliament in 1878 and founded the Radical Party in 1881. Pašić came to prominence as he worked to oust Milan OBRENOVIĆ as king of SERBIA, for which he went into exile (1883–89). On his return he became Serbian premier and foreign minister. Again exiled (1899), by Alexander OBRENOVIĆ, he returned to power when PETER I acceded the throne. At the close of World War 1, during which Pašić led Serbia, he argued for the creation of a Slavic union, with Serbia as the dominant partner. Despite his objections, the Kingdom of Serbs, Croat and Slovenes was created (1918) on a power-sharing basis, and he represented it at the Treaty of VERSAILLES (1919). When Pašić was appointed premier of the new kingdom (1921), he issued a new constitution emphasizing centralization of power, limiting autonomy for the traditional national provinces and enforcing Serbian domination. He held on to power by suppressing dissent but was eventually forced to resign (1926).

Passchendaele *See* YPRES

Paston letters Collection of correspondence and legal documents, dating from 1422 to 1509, of four generations of the Paston family, wealthy landowners in Norfolk, E England. The collection also includes letters belonging to their neighbour, Sir John FASTOLF. They were kept by a servant of Fastolf, possibly for use in lawsuits. Some of the letters, which provide invaluable information about life in medieval England, detail legal affairs, others contain gossip.

Pataliputra Ancient capital of the MAURYAN and GUPTA empires, N India. Founded in the 5th century BC on the south bank of the River Ganges, Pataliputra was the capital of MAGADHA (part of modern-day Bihar, N India). During the Mauryan empire (3rd–2nd centuries BC), it became a centre of learning and its reputation survived its sacking by Indo-Greeks (185 BC). From the 4th–6th centuries AD, it was the capital of the Gupta dynasty, and ASHOKA constructed a magnificent palace in the city. Pataliputra was deserted by the 7th century and was later refounded as Patna (1514), returning to prominence under the MUGHAL EMPIRE.

Patel, "Sardar" (Vallabhbhai Jhaverbhai) (1875–1950) Indian statesman. Influenced by "Mahatma" GANDHI, he organized civil disobedience protests during the 1920s, 1930s and 1940s, notably the QUIT INDIA MOVEMENT (1942), and was imprisoned several times. Patel's efforts on behalf of Indian independence earned him the title "Sardar" (Leader) from Gandhi. Patel was president of the Indian National CONGRESS (1931) and held several government posts before becoming deputy prime minister (1947–50) under Jawaharlal NEHRU. He was influential in the negotiations over the partition of India and Pakistan and, with Krishna MENON, in integrating the PRINCELY STATES into the Indian union.

Paterson, William (1658–1719) Scottish financier. He founded the BANK OF ENGLAND in 1694, but resigned as a director the following year following disagreements over policy. Paterson then pursued his DARIEN SCHEME, a project to colonize the Isthmus of Darien, E Panama, and accompanied the 1698 expedition. After the failure of the scheme in 1699, Paterson returned to London, where he became financial adviser to William III.

Pathans (Pashtuns) MUSLIM tribes of SE Afghanistan and NW Pakistan. They speak various dialects of an E Iranian language, Pashto, and are composed of *c*.60 tribes, numbering in total *c*.10 million. Formerly, they were pastoralists inhabiting the mountainous border regions, but they are now mainly farmers and are more widely spread. In their clashes with the British in the late 19th century, particularly over the creation of the international frontier known as the Durand Line which divided the Pathans into British India and Afghanistan, they gained a reputation as formidable warriors. Their resistance forced the British to provide them with the semi-autonomous North-West Frontier Province, which later became part of Pakistan (1947). Pathan calls for an independent homeland continued. Their way of life was disrupted during the AFGHANISTAN WAR (1979–92).

Pathet Lao Laotian left-wing political group. It was founded (1950) by SOUPHANOUVONG and soon joined the VIET MINH in its struggle against French rule in INDOCHINA. LAOS became independent in 1953, but civil war began between the Pathet Lao in the N and Royalist forces in the S. Its political wing, the Lao Patriotic Front (LPF), was formed in 1956 and participated in several coalition governments. During the 1960s, the United States, wary of the communist-leanings of the increasingly popular Pathet Lao, backed the Royal Lao government. The Pathet Lao began armed resistance, and civil war ensued. A secret US bombing campaign followed, which escalated after the start of the VIETNAM WAR. Support for the Pathet Lao increased and by the time the United States withdrew from Vietnam, the Pathet Lao controlled almost the whole of Laos. In 1975 the Pathet Lao, now known as the Lao People's Revolutionary Party, became the governing party of Laos, abolished the monarchy in Vientiane and proclaimed the Lao People's Democratic Republic.

patrician Aristocratic class in the ancient ROMAN REPUBLIC, members of the SENATE. In the early years of the republic, the patricians controlled all aspects of government and society. During the 3rd century BC, the division between patricians and PLEBIANS disappeared, and a mixed nobility became the ruling class.

Patrick, Saint (active 5th century AD) Patron saint of Ireland. Facts about his life are confused by legend. What is known of Patrick comes almost entirely from his autobiography, *Confession*. He was born in Britain into a Romanized Christian family. Abducted by marauders at the age of 16, Patrick was carried off to Ireland and sold to a local chief. After six years as a herdsman, during which period he became increasingly reliant on his Christian faith, he escaped back to Britain. In 432 Patrick returned to Ireland as a missionary of Pope Celestine I. He established an episcopal see at Armagh, N Ireland. Patrick's missionary work was so successful that Christianity was firmly established in Ireland before he died. By tradition he is also said to have banished snakes from Ireland. His feast day is 17 March.

Patten, Christopher Francis (1944–) British politician, last British governor of HONG KONG (1992–97). As chairman of the CONSERVATIVE PARTY (1990–92), he helped engineer a victory in the 1992 election but lost his own seat. As governor of Hong Kong, Patten sought to preserve its political and economic institutions in the handover to China. Returning to Britain, he was appointed chair of the commission on the policing of Northern Ireland.

Patton, George Smith, Jr (1885–1945) US general. In World War 1 he served with the American Expeditionary Force (AEF) in France. A controversial but highly successful officer, Patton commanded a tank corps in North Africa and the 7th Army in Sicily in WORLD WAR 2. Patton lost his command (August 1943) for slapping a soldier suffering from battle fatigue, but was reinstated (August 1944) after making a public apology. After the NORMANDY LANDINGS (1944), he commanded the 3rd Army in its dash across France and into Germany, reaching the German border by the end of January 1945. Patton played a key role in the Battle of the BULGE, before quickly subduing the area N of the Moselle as far as Czechoslovakia. As military governor of Bavaria after the War, Patton was criticized for leniency to Nazis and was removed to command the US 15th Army. He died in a car crash while posted in Germany.

Paul, Saint (active 1st century AD) Apostle of JESUS CHRIST, missionary and early Christian theologian. His missionary journeys among the Gentiles form a large part of the Acts of the Apostles in the NEW TESTAMENT. His many epistles to early Christian communities represent the most important early formulations of Christian theology following the death of JESUS CHRIST. Named Saul at birth, he was both a Jew and a Roman citizen, brought up in the Roman colony of Tarsus, in what is now s Turkey. He saw the teachings of Jesus as a major threat to JUDAISM and became a leading persecutor of early Christians. Travelling to Damascus, Syria, to continue his persecution activities, he suddenly saw a bright light and heard the voice of Jesus addressing him. Having thus undergone his religious conversion, he adopted the name Paul and became a fluent and energetic evangelist and teacher of Christianity. In *c*.AD 60 Paul was arrested after returning to Jerusalem and taken as a prisoner to Rome, where he died sometime between AD 62 and 68, probably suffering a martyr's execution.

Paul III (1468–1549) Pope (1534–49), b. Alessandro Farnese. As pope, he largely initiated the COUNTER-REFORMATION. Paul sponsored reform, established the JESUITS (1540) and summoned the Council of TRENT (1545). He commissioned Michelangelo to paint the ceiling of the Sistine Chapel, Rome.

Paul IV (1476–1559) Pope (1555–59), b. Gian Pietro Carafa. A zealous reformer, he was placed in charge of the Roman INQUISITION (1542). Elected pope (1555) despite the veto of Emperor CHARLES V, he allied with France against Spain, but the approach of Spanish troops on Rome (1557) forced him to make peace. He maintained his hostility to Spain and to the HABSBURGS, refusing to recognize the election of FERDINAND I as Holy Roman emperor (1558) and depriving Cardinal Reginald POLE of his authority, because he had intervened between France and the Habsburgs. Paul's treatment of Pole, combined with his refusal to recognize ELIZABETH I, set back the English COUNTER-REFORMATION. He also denounced the Peace of AUGSBURG.

Paul VI (1897–1978) Pope (1963–78), b. Giovanni Battista Montini. He earned a reputation as a reformer as archbishop of Milan (1954–63). He continued the Second VATICAN COUNCIL, begun by JOHN XXIII, but disappointed liberals by upholding the celibacy of priests and papal primacy, and condemning contraception. Paul travelled widely, becoming the first pope to visit Asia. He promoted Christian unity, meeting with the leaders of other Christian communities, notably the Greek Orthodox patriarch of Constantinople. He was succeeded by JOHN PAUL II.

Paul I (1754–1801) Emperor of Russia (1796–1801), second son of CATHERINE II (THE GREAT) and PETER III. Although Catherine had named Paul's son, Alexander (later ALEXANDER I) her heir, Paul acceded to the throne on Catherine's death (1796). He immediately set about reversing many of Catherine's policies. He re-established the principle of hereditary succession, reintroduced centralized administration and limited the authority of the nobility. Having alienated the nobles, Paul's preference for his personal army offended the military élite. Paul also instituted repressive measures to protect Russia from the influence of the FRENCH REVOLUTION. His increasingly despotic reign and erratic conduct, particularly in foreign affairs, only served to isolate Russia. Having gained approval from Alexander to dispose of his father, a group of nobles and senior military officers assassinated Paul.

Paul I (1901–64) King of Greece (1947–64), youngest son of CONSTANTINE I, and brother and successor to GEORGE II of Greece. He fought against the Turks (1922), but went into exile when a republic was proclaimed (1924). Paul returned as crown prince (1935) but spent most of World War 2 in London and Cairo with the Greek government-in-exile. During his reign, he followed a pro-Western policy and received US aid in the Greek government's successful fight against communist insurgents. In the early 1960s Paul

PARAGUAY

AREA: 406,750sq km (157,046sq mi)
POPULATION: 4,579,000
CAPITAL (POPULATION): Asunción (637,737)
GOVERNMENT: Multiparty republic
ETHNIC GROUPS: Mestizo 90%, Native American 3%
LANGUAGES: Spanish and Guaraní (both official)
RELIGIONS: Christianity (Roman Catholic 96%, Protestant 2%)
GDP PER CAPITA (1995): US$3650

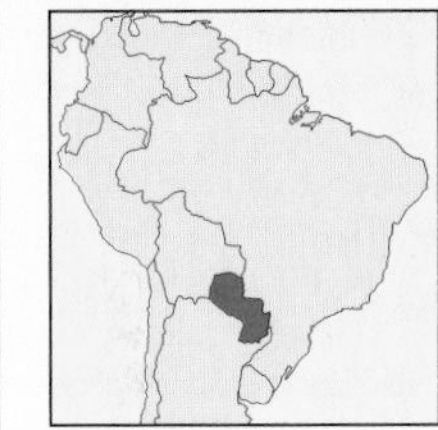

Landlocked republic in central South America. The earliest known inhabitants of Paraguay were the GUARANÍ. Spanish and Portuguese explorers reached the area in the early 16th century. In 1537 a Spanish expedition built a fort at Asunción, which became the capital of Spain's colonies in SE South America. From the late 16th century, Jesuit missionaries worked to protect the Guaraní from colonial exploitation and convert them to Christianity, establishing 30 *reducciones* (Indian missions). In 1767 the Spanish king expelled the Jesuits. In 1776 Paraguay was subsumed into the colony of the viceroyalty of RÍO DE LA PLATA.

Paraguay declared independence in 1811 and José FRANCIA became the first of a series of dictators. In 1864 President Francisco López, alarmed at Brazilian intervention in Uruguay, launched an attack on Brazil. The result was the disastrous War of the TRIPLE ALLIANCE (1865–70) in which Brazil was supported by Argentina and Uruguay. The War killed more than 50% of Paraguay's population and resulted in great loss of territory. A series of border disputes with Bolivia led to the CHACO WAR (1932–35), in which Paraguay regained some land.

In 1954 General Alfredo STROESSNER led a successful military coup. His dictatorial regime suppressed all political opposition. In 1989, shortly after re-election for an eighth successive term, Stroessner was overthrown by General Andrés Rodríguez. In 1993 elections Juan Carlos Wasmosy became Paraguay's first civilian president since 1954. In 1996 General Lino Oviedo was imprisoned for leading an attempted military coup. Raúl Cubas Grau, a supporter of Oviedo, was elected president in 1998, and he released Oviedo the following year. The assassination (1999) of vice president Luis María Argaña led to riots and the killing of four pro-democracy demonstrators. Cubas was forced to resign. He was succeeded by Luis González Macchi.

P

and his wife Frederika clashed with Premier Konstatinos KARAMANLIS, resulting in the latter's resignation (1963). Paul was succeeded by his son, CONSTANTINE II.

Paul Karageorgević (1893–1976) Prince of Yugoslavia, regent (1934–41) for his nephew, PETER II, following the assassination of Peter's father, ALEXANDER I. As regent, Paul failed to solve the problem of increasing pressure from Croatia and Serbia for national autonomy. Paul's personal preference to align with the Allies during World War 2 was swept aside by threatening action from Hitler, and Paul had to pursue a pro-Axis policy, culminating in his making Yugoslavia a signatory to the TRIPARTITE PACT in 1941. This action led to Paul's overthrow in a bloodless coup. He fled to Greece where he was captured by British forces and interned in Kenya. Following his release, Paul settled in France. *See also* TITO

Paulus, Friedrich von (1890–1957) German field marshal in WORLD WAR 2. After serving in World War 1, Paulus became deputy chief of staff at the beginning of World War 2 and helped to plan the German invasion of the Soviet Union. He was commander of the German 6th army, which spearheaded the attack on STALINGRAD. Drained by tenacious Soviet resistance, his troops were unable to withstand a major Soviet counter-offensive. Forbidden by HITLER to retreat, they were surrounded and forced to surrender. In prison, Paulus called for a German surrender, and later testified at the NUREMBURG TRIALS. After his release from prison, he lived in East Germany.

Pavia, Battle of (24 February 1525) Significant conflict in the ITALIAN WARS between the VALOIS King FRANCIS I of France and the HABSBURGS, under Emperor CHARLES V. The Habsburg army arrived at Pavia, 30km (20mi) S of Milan, to lift the French siege of the city. Although the French outnumbered the Habsburg forces by 5000 men, the French army was outmanoeuvred and crushed by the Habsburgs, and Francis I was taken prisoner. In captivity in Spain, Francis I signed the Treaty of Madrid (1526), abandoning his claims on Italy (and Burgundy). He repudiated the treaty after his release later the same year.

Paz Estenssoro, Victor (1907–) Bolivian statesman, president (1952–56, 1960–64, 1985–89). One of the founders of the leftist Nationalist Revolutionary Movement (MNR) in 1941, he became president when the MNR seized power in 1952. During his first term, Paz Estenssoro nationalized the tin mines, introduced electoral and land reforms, and started a number of development projects. His priority for his second term was to confront the economic problems created by government spending, which he achieved by obtaining international investment. After losing support from the miners and the left-wing, Paz Estenssoro was overthrown by the military and went into exile in Peru (1964–71). On his return Paz Estenssoro was made a government adviser, and in 1985 he won congress support to become president for a third time. In his final term, Paz Estenssoro introduced austerity measures to counteract hyperinflation.

PCE (*Partido Comunista Español*) Spanish communist organization. Founded in 1921 as an offshoot of the Spanish Socialist Workers' Party, the PCE enjoyed little support until the outbreak of the Spanish CIVIL WAR (1936–39), when it grew, mainly due to Soviet backing, to become the major political force on the Republican side. Following General FRANCO's victory the PCE was forced underground. It enjoyed a revival from the late 1950s under the leadership of Santiago Carrillo (1915–). An advocate of Eurocommunism (supporting independence from Soviet control for national communist organizations), he positioned the PCE as a moderate party of the left and worked with the government on economic reform. The PCE was legalized in 1977, but membership dwindled and the party split up in 1986.

PCI (*Partito Communista Italiano*) Italian communist organization. Founded by radical members of the Socialist Party (1921), it grew rapidly until Benito MUSSOLINI's abolition of political parties (1926). As an underground movement, it played a key role in the Italian RESISTANCE MOVEMENT. After World War 2, it returned to influence, serving in a coalition government until 1947 and later as an opposition party, consistently remaining the second-largest party in the Italian parliament. Following the collapse of communism in Eastern Europe, the PCI fell into decline and eventually changed its name to the Democratic Party of the Left (*Partito Democratico di Sinistra*) in 1991.

Peabody, George (1795–1869) US financier and philanthropist. He made a fortune from a chain of grocery stores in E United States and then settled in London (1837), where he became a successful international banker. Peabody is chiefly remembered for his philanthropic work, including financing tenement clearance in London and the construction of public housing by the Peabody Trust. In the United States, he endowed the Peabody Education fund, founded the Peabody Institute in Baltimore, Maryland, and the Peabody museums at Yale and Harvard universities.

Peace Corps US government agency that organizes work by volunteers in more than 100 developing countries in Africa, Asia, the Mediterranean, Latin America, the Pacific and the less-developed regions of central and Eastern Europe. The Corps was established (1961) by President John KENNEDY, becoming an independent US government agency in 1981. Peace Corps volunteers usually spend two years overseas and undertake work in areas such as education, agriculture and health, with an emphasis on sustainability and self-sufficiency. More recently, the Peace Corps has also become active in regions with high populations of refugees.

Pearl Harbor US naval base in Hawaii. On 7 December 1941, the base, headquarters of the US Pacific fleet, was attacked by aircraft from a Japanese naval task force, which had approached the islands unobserved. About 300 aircraft and 18 ships were destroyed or severely damaged and *c*.2400 people killed. Although the damage was considerable, the Japanese failed to destroy the prized US aircraft carriers, which were out on manoeuvres. The attack provoked US entry into WORLD WAR 2.

Pearse, Patrick (Pádraic) Henry (1879–1916) Irish politician and writer. He headed the revival of interest in Gaelic culture, writing poems, short stories and plays, and editing the *Gaelic League* journal. Pearse led the insurgents in the EASTER RISING (1916), during which he was made president of the provisional government. Once the rebellion had been contained, Pearse was court-martialled and executed by the British authorities.

Pearson, Lester Bowles (1897–1972) Canadian statesman and diplomat, prime minister (1963–68). A distinguished diplomatic career culminated in his appointment (1945) as head of Canada's delegation to the United Nations (UN). Pearson acted as president (1952–53) of the UN General Assembly. His efforts in resolving the SUEZ CRISIS earned him the 1957 Nobel Prize for Peace.

▲ **Peel** was founder of the modern Conservative Party and of the first British police force, the London Metropolitan Police, whose officers have since been known as "peelers" or "bobbies".

In 1958 Pearson became leader of the LIBERAL PARTY, succeeding John DIEFENBAKER as prime minister. His term was marked by health and social welfare reforms, and the attempted resolution of issues brought about by the growing QUÉBEC separatist movement.

Peary, Robert Edwin (1856–1920) US Arctic explorer. He made several expeditions to Greenland (1886–92) and in 1893 led the first of five expeditions towards the North Pole. Although Peary is widely credited as being the first person to reach the Pole (April 1909), evidence brought to light in the 1980s has revealed that there may have been some navigational misreadings and record-keeping errors, and that Peary was in fact *c*.75km (50mi) short of the North Pole.

Peasants' Revolt (1381) Rebellion in England. Although the immediate provocation was a POLL TAX (1380), there were further underlying, fundamental causes. VILLEINS, SERFS and peasants resented feudal restrictions and wages held down artificially under the Statute of LABOURERS, despite the shortage of labour caused by the BLACK DEATH. Led by Wat TYLER (hence its alternative name "Tyler's Rebellion"), the men of Kent and Essex marched into London, where they murdered a number of merchants, burned houses and prisons, and occupied the Tower of London, killing the archbishop of Canterbury and the treasurer. They were pacified by RICHARD II, who promised, among other reforms, to introduce land reforms and abolish serfdom. However, once the rebellion had been subdued promises to grant their demands were broken. Tyler was killed by the mayor of London in the revolt.

Peasants' War (1524–25) Rebellion of German peasants during the REFORMATION; the largest popular uprising in European history. The German peasantry, living under difficult economic conditions, was inflamed by the teachings of radical preachers, including Martin LUTHER, who were criticizing the established church and calling for the equality of all believers. Sparked by anger over increasing dues demanded by the princes, the uprising began in S and W Germany. The peasants proposed the "Twelve Articles of the Peasantry", calling for economic and social improvements, such as the abolition of serfdom and the return of common lands. The peasants hoped for and needed the support of Luther, but he rejected their charter of liberties and vociferously condemned the violence that ensued from the rebellion. The suppression of the rebellion was exceedingly harsh: *c*.100,000 peasants were killed, largely by the armies of the SWABIAN LEAGUE under the command of PHILIP OF HESSE. *See also* MÜNTZER, THOMAS; SERF

Pedro I (1798–1834) Emperor of Brazil (1822–31). Son of the future JOHN VI of Portugal, he fled with the rest of the royal family to Brazil in 1807 to escape the invasion of NAPOLEON I's army. When his father reclaimed the Portuguese crown (1821), Pedro became prince regent of Brazil and declared it an independent monarchy (1822). His reign was marked by military failure against ARGENTINA (1825–28) and a revolt in Rio de Janeiro (1831), much of it centring around Pedro's continued involvement in Portuguese affairs and republican sentiment. Pedro abdicated in favour of his son, PEDRO II. He returned to Portugal (1832) and secured the succession of his daughter, MARIA II, to the Portuguese throne.

Pedro II (1825–91) Emperor of Brazil (1831–89), son and successor of PEDRO I. He reigned under a regency until 1840. Despite some internal unrest and Brazil's involvement in the War of the TRIPLE ALLIANCE, Pedro's reign was a stable and progressive period. Slavery was abolished (1888), and Pedro's policy was generally reformist, thus antagonizing the army and the influential planters. In 1889 he was forced by the military and republican agitators to abdicate and retire to Europe. Brazil became a republic.

Peel, Sir Robert (1788–1850) British statesman, prime minister (1834–35, 1841–46). He was elected to Parliament as a TORY in 1809. During his first significant post, as secretary for Ireland (1812–18), Peel attracted fierce criticism from Daniel O'CONNELL for his anti-Catholic stance. As home secretary (1822–27, 1828–30) under the Earl of LIVERPOOL and the Duke of WELLINGTON, he reformed the criminal code and created (1829) the first modern POLICE force, the London Metropolitan Police. Although a staunch

P

opponent of Catholic emancipation, he responded to the crisis in IRELAND (1828–29) by supporting the passage of the CATHOLIC EMANCIPATION Act (1829). Although he opposed the REFORM ACT of 1832, Peel offered a commitment to moderate reform in his famous TAMWORTH MANIFESTO (1834), a founding text of the CONSERVATIVE PARTY. As prime minister, Peel took drastic measures to restore the economy, reintroducing income tax but reducing protective duties, having become converted to the doctrine of FREE-TRADE. The onset of the IRISH FAMINE (1846) convinced him of the need to repeal the CORN LAWS, which he had previously supported. The proposal split the Tory Party and Peel briefly resigned (1845), but returned to office to carry through the legislation. *See also* CHARTISM; RUSSELL, JOHN, 1ST EARL

Peelites Section of the TORY PARTY, about one-third, who sided with Robert PEEL when the Party split over the repeal of the CORN LAWS (1846). The Peelites behaved as a separate party for several years but by 1859 their leaders, of whom the most important was William GLADSTONE, had found their way into the LIBERAL PARTY.

Peking man *See* HOMO ERECTUS; HUMAN EVOLUTION

Pelagianism Christian heresy associated with PELAGIUS. In opposition to St AUGUSTINE's belief that humans could attain salvation only through God's grace, the Pelagians saw humans as creatures of inherent spiritual grace and free will. Followers of Pelagius denied original sin and the need of the church for salvation. The church condemned Pelagianism at the Council of EPHESUS (431). The doctrine returned to prominence during the debates between Catholics and Protestants at the time of the REFORMATION.

Pelagius (*c*.360–*c*.420) Monk and theologian, probably born in Britain, who preached the heresy of PELAGIANISM. In *c*.380 Pelagius went to Rome and became the spiritual guide of many clerics and lay persons. After 410 he preached in Africa, where his ideas were denounced by St AUGUSTINE, and later in Palestine. He countered criticisms from Augustine and St JEROME in his book *De Libero Arbitrio* (416). In 417 Pelagius was excommunicated by Pope INNOCENT I.

Pelayo (d.737) Spanish king of Asturias (718–37). When the MOORS conquered Spain from the Christians, beginning in 711, many of the local petty rulers retreated to the Asturian mountains. There they elected one of their members, Pelayo, as leader. His victory over the Moors at Covadonga (*c*.718) is traditionally regarded as the beginning of the long Christian reconquest of Spain.

Pelham, Henry (1696–1754) British statesman, prime minister (1743–54). Pelham entered Parliament as a WHIG in 1717. He became a supporter of Robert WALPOLE, who helped him obtain the post of lord of the treasury (1721–24), secretary for war (1724–30) and finally paymaster general (1730–42). He succeeded Walpole as prime minister. Pelham's government included his brother, Thomas Pelham-Holles, Duke of NEWCASTLE, and John Carteret, 1st Earl of GRANVILLE. Pelham came into conflict with Granville over England's involvement in the War of the AUSTRIAN SUCCESSION. Dismissing Granville (1744), following the latter's leadership challenge, Pelham brought William PITT (THE ELDER) into the government. In 1748 he signed the Treaty of AIX-LA-CHAPELLE, which ended the War and ushered in a period of relative peace and prosperity. Pelham also reorganized and reduced the national debt, before dying in office.

Peloponnesian War (431–404 BC) Conflict in classical GREECE between ATHENS and SPARTA, and their allies. The account of the War by the historian THUCYDIDES is an invaluable source of information. The underlying cause was Sparta's fear of Athenian hegemony, and Athenian hostility toward CORINTH, Sparta's chief ally, provoked the Spartan declaration of war. Having a stronger army, Sparta regularly invaded Attica, the region surrounding and under the control of Athens. PERICLES, the Athenian leader, called on the population to remain within the city walls. He relied on the navy to raid coastal settlements and disrupt Spartan supply routes. Athens was decimated by the plague (430–428 BC), which spread rapidly through the overcrowded city; Pericles was one of its victims and was succeeded by Cleon. Despite the plague, Sparta made little headway against Athens until 425 BC, when military command was assumed by Brasidas. Both Brasidas and Cleon were killed at the Battle of Amphipolis (422 BC), and the new Athenian leader, Nicias, proposed a truce. However, the Peace of Nicias (421 BC) proved temporary. Neither side kept to the agreement, and in 415 BC Athens launched a disastrous attack on SYRACUSE, Sicily, which encouraged Sparta to renew the War. The so-called Sicilian Expedition was the brainchild of ALCIBIADES, Nicias' political rival. Just as the expedition was setting off, Alcibiades was recalled to Athens to answer charges of sacrilege but instead went over to the Spartan side. Informed of the Athenian tactics, the Spartans were able to defeat Athens in Sicily, smashing the Athenian navy. Meanwhile, with help from CYRUS THE YOUNGER of Persia, LYSANDER of Sparta built up a navy, which crushed Athens at AEGOSPOTAMI (405 BC). Besieged and blockaded, Athens surrendered (404 BC).

Pelopónnisos (Peloponnesos) Peninsula in S Greece, connected to the mainland by the Isthmus of CORINTH. The chief cities are Patras, Corinth, Pirgos and SPARTA. It also included the ancient cities of ARGOS and Megalopolis. The peninsula was involved in the PERSIAN WARS (499–479 BC), and it was the site of many battles between Sparta and Athens during the PELOPONNESIAN WAR (431–404 BC). In 146 BC the region fell to the Romans. Held by the Venetians from 1699 to 1718, then becoming part of the OTTOMAN EMPIRE, the peninsula passed to Greece after independence. Area: 21,800sq km (8400sq mi). Pop. (1991) 1,077,002.

penal colony Remote settlement to which convicted criminals were transported for punishment through imprisonment, isolation and hard labour. Britain, France and Russia made the greatest use of penal colonies. British convicts were sent to North America until the AMERICAN REVOLUTION, then to Australia until the mid-19th century, where hard labour was often accompanied by floggings; mutinies were not uncommon. French convicts were transported to New Caledonia and French Guiana. In the Stalinist era, political prisoners in the Soviet Union were transported to GULAGS in Siberia.

Penang (Pinang) Island of MALAYSIA, off the NW coast of the Malay Peninsula, which (together with a coastal strip on the mainland) comprises a state of Malaysia; the capital is Penang. The island's strategic location attracted the attention of the English EAST INDIA COMPANY, becoming Britain's first possession in Malaya (1786). In 1826 it united with Singapore and MALACCA, and in 1826 the group formed the STRAITS SETTLEMENTS colony, becoming a crown colony in 1867. Penang joined the Federation of Malaya in 1948. Area: 1040sq km (400sq mi). Pop. (1993 est.) 1,141,500.

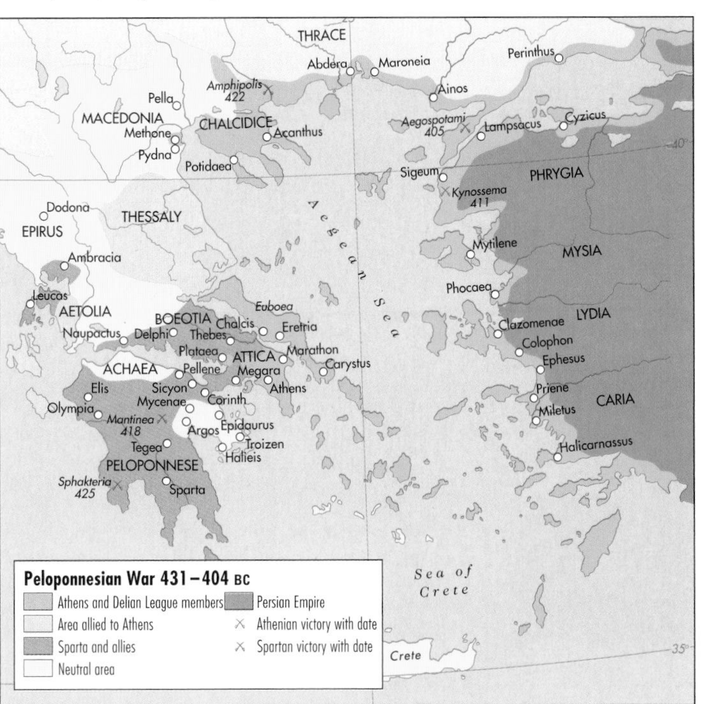

◀ **Peloponnesian War** Thucydides regarded the conflict as the most appalling of all the Greek wars in terms of losses and suffering. Attica's countryside was sacked repeatedly, and Athens' population – withdrawn behind the city's walls – was wracked by famine and a plague which claimed a quarter of its number, including Pericles. The War began with Sparta's invasion of Attica (431 BC). Demosthenes of Athens occupied Pylos, Sphakteria, in 425 BC, but Brasidas routed Cleon at the Athenian colony of Amphipolis (422 BC) and Sparta won a further victory at Mantinea (418 BC). Athens' expedition (415–413 BC) against Sicily was a disaster and they suffered a further loss at Kynossema (411 BC). Lysander of Sparta joined forces with Cyrus the Younger of Persia finally to crush Athens at Aegospotami (405 BC).

Penda (d.654) ANGLO-SAXON king of MERCIA (*c*.632–54). In alliance with King Cadwallon of Gwynedd, Penda increased the power of his kingdom by warring with the kingdom of NORTHUMBRIA. A pagan, he killed the Christian Northumbrian kings Edwin (633) and OSWALD (642), following the latter's invasion of Penda's territory. By defeating Cenwalh of Wessex (645), Penda temporarily ruled England. He was slain by Oswy, king of Northumbria.

Pendleton Act (1883) US reform of the CIVIL SERVICE, designed to curb the SPOILS SYSTEM. In response to James GARFIELD's assassination by a disappointed job-seeker, and named after Senator George Pendleton (1825–89), who sponsored the Act, it aimed to ensure that federal appointments were made on the basis of merit. It re-established the civil service commission, which had first been created in 1871 but had lapsed soon after, to organize examinations for entry to the civil service. The Pendleton Act also provided for appointments of federal officeholders to be apportioned among the states and prohibited the levying of campaign contributions on federal officeholders.

Peninsular Campaign (April–July 1862) Series of battles in the American CIVIL WAR resulting from the attempt by Union forces under George MCCLELLAN to take Richmond, Virginia, by advancing up the peninsula between the York and James rivers. The Confederates, under Joseph JOHNSTON and later General Robert LEE, although losing most of the battles, checked the advance. After the Battle of Malvern Hill, McClellan, not seeing that he had the advantage, ordered his troops to withdraw.

Peninsular War (1808–14) Campaign of the NAPOLEONIC WARS fought on the Iberian Peninsula. It began with NAPOLEON I's invasion of Portugal (1807) to enforce the CONTINENTAL SYSTEM. Napoleon's forces occupied towns in N Spain (an ally of France) and imposed his brother, Joseph BONAPARTE, as king of Spain (1808). The Spanish turned against their former ally and forced a French surrender at Baylen, so beginning what the Spanish term the "War of Independence". In August 1808 British troops, led by Arthur Wellesley (the future Duke of WELLINGTON), landed in Portugal to support Spanish and Portuguese divisions in their expulsion of the French from Portugal. Napoleon personally arrived in Spain to command events, winning a number of battles, taking Burgos, Madrid and Zaragoza, and re-establishing Joseph as king. In January 1809 British forces, under Sir John MOORE, suffered a major setback in their attempt to force the French from Spain and were forced to retreat to La Coruña, NW Spain. Wellesley consolidated British forces at Torres Vedras, near Lisbon, Portugal, and successfully repulsed

Marshal MASSÉNA's offensive (1810–11) – a turning point in the War. Wellesley's forces, supported by Spanish guerrillas, then drove the French from the Peninsula, defeating Masséna and taking Madrid, before defeating Joseph at Vitoria, NE Spain (1813). Having forced the French out of Spain, Wellesley went on to defeat General SOULT at Orthez and Toulouse (1814) in an invasion of S France. Napoleon's abdication (1814) concluded the War and FERDINAND VII of Spain was restored to the throne. The fact that Napoleon was engaged in Russia (1812) at the same time as the Peninsular War was being waged, therefore effectively fighting on two fronts, was a significant factor in his defeat. The War killed *c*.300,000 Frenchmen.

Penn, William (1644–1718) English QUAKER leader and founder of PENNSYLVANIA. Because of his advocacy of religious freedom, he was imprisoned four times. While in the Tower of London, Penn wrote *No Cross, No Crown* (1669), explaining Quaker morality. In 1681 he persuaded CHARLES II to honour an unpaid debt owed to his father, Admrial Sir William Penn (1621–70), by granting him wilderness land in America to be settled by the Quakers and others seeking refuge from religious persecution. He arrived in America (1682) and for the next two years established the colony that came to be named the Commonwealth of Pennsylvania in honour of Penn's father. Penn returned to England in 1684 to assist the Quaker movement's fight for religious tolerance. He was cleared of treason following allegations that he had entered into correspondence with the exiled JAMES II. Penn was summoned to America in 1699 to restore order in the colony. He issued the Charter of Privileges, which guaranteed religious freedom. In 1701 Penn returned to England.

Pennsylvania State in E United States; the capital is Harrisburg. The chief cities are PHILADELPHIA, Pittsburgh and Scranton. Swedish and Dutch settlements were made along the Delaware River in the mid-17th century. By 1664 the area was controlled by the English, and William PENN received a charter from Charles II in 1681 for what is now Pennsylvania. The colony was Penn's "Holy Experiment" and was founded on the principles of equality and religious freedom. A treaty was signed with the Native Americans, ensuring peace that lasted until the FRENCH AND INDIAN WARS. By 1774 Philadelphia was a major commercial, cultural and industrial centre and was one of the original THIRTEEN COLONIES that called for independence. The CONTINENTAL CONGRESSES were held in Philadelphia and the DECLARATION OF INDEPENDENCE was also signed there in 1776. The CONSTITUTIONAL CONVENTION met in Philadelphia and adopted the US CONSTITUTION in 1787. Philadelphia served (1790–1800) as capital of the United States. The Union victory at the Battle of GETTYSBURG (July 1863) was a turning point in the CIVIL WAR. Area: 117,412sq km (45,333sq mi). Pop. (1996) 12,056,112.

Pentagon Papers Documents pertaining to a secret military study of the US role in the VIETNAM WAR, carried out by Robert MCNAMARA during the presidency of Lyndon JOHNSON. It was leaked (1971) to the *New York Times* by Daniel Ellsberg, a former government researcher, to show how the military had been misleading the public about the extent of US involvement in Southeast Asia. Richard NIXON's administration tried to stop publication of the Papers, which led to a court battle which the newspapers eventually won. Ellsberg was indicted for conspiracy, theft and espionage, but the charges were dismissed in 1973. The affair fuelled the anti-war movement and brought about demands for more openness in government.

Pentateuch (Gk. Five scrolls) First five books of the BIBLE, traditionally attributed to MOSES. In JUDAISM they are referred to collectively as the TORAH. The Pentateuch comprises the five OLD TESTAMENT books of Genesis, Exodus, Leviticus, Numbers and Deuteronomy. Composed over a very long period (possibly 1000 years or more), they were probably collected in their present form during the BABYLONIAN CAPTIVITY of the Jews.

PENNSYLVANIA
Statehood :
12 December 1787
Nickname :
The Keystone State
State motto :
Virtue, liberty and independence

Pentecostal Churches Fellowship of revivalist Christian sects, inspired by the belief that all Christians should seek to be baptized with the Holy Spirit and experience events such as speaking in tongues. Pentecostals believe in the literal truth of the Bible, and many abstain from alcohol and tobacco, and disapprove of dancing, theatre and other such pleasures. The Pentecostal movement began in the United States at Topeka, Kansas, in 1901. It became organized in Los Angeles in 1906 and spread rapidly to other countries. Today, there are *c*.22 million Pentecostals worldwide.

peonage (Sp. debt servitude) System based on the indebtedness of the labourer (the *peon*) to his creditor. It replaced the ENCOMIENDA system in Latin America and became prevalent, especially in Mexico and Peru, after independence from Spain in the early 19th century. Labourers in mines and on plantations were encouraged to borrow money from the owners to purchase necessities, such as food and clothing, and were then obliged to work until the debt, usually vastly inflated, was paid off. In Mexico, a decree against *peonage* was issued in 1915. The practice persisted but from that date began to go into decline as areas that once experienced shortage of labour underwent large population growths. *See also* HACIENDA

People's Party *See* POPULIST PARTY

Pepin II (d. *c*.870) King of AQUITAINE, grandson of LOUIS I (THE PIOUS). Pepin became king after defeating CHARLES II (THE BALD) in 844. In 852 Pepin was captured by Charles and imprisoned in a monastery. Although he escaped two years later, Pepin could not rally the support of his people and was again defeated by Charles after attacking Toulouse, having formed an alliance with the Vikings. Pepin was captured and died while imprisoned.

Pepin I (d. *c*.640) (Pepin of Landen, Pepin the Elder) Mayor of the palace of AUSTRASIA, founder of the CAROLINGIAN dynasty. As leader of the nobles under CLOTAIRE II of NEUSTRIA, he overthrew BRUNHILDA, the queen of Austrasia (613). Clotaire assumed the throne of Austrasia, uniting the two territories, but governmental authority rested with Pepin until DAGOBERT I succeeded his father to the throne (629), after which Pepin's political influence waned. With Dagobert's death, however, Pepin resumed political control, and on his death the position of mayor of the palace passed to his son, Grimald I.

Pepin II (d.714) (Pepin of Heristal) Mayor of the palace (680–714) of the Frankish kingdom of AUSTRASIA. His defeat of the Neustrians at the Battle of Tertry (687) extended CAROLINGIAN rule to the other Frankish kingdoms, NEUSTRIA and BURGUNDY. Pepin's reign marked the ascendancy of the Carolingians over the MEROVINGIANS, and witnessed campaigns against the ALEMANNI. Pepin was succeeded by his son, CHARLES MARTEL.

Pepin III (the Short) (*c*.714–68) CAROLINGIAN king of the Franks (750–68), son of CHARLES MARTEL. In 750 he deposed the last MEROVINGIAN king, Childeric III. Defending Rome, Pepin defeated the LOMBARDS in 754 and 756. He ceded the conquered territories (the future PAPAL STATES) to the papacy in what was known as the **Donation of Pepin**. Much of the latter half of Pepin's reign was spent campaigning against SAXONS and SARACENS. Pepin was succeeded by his son, CHARLEMAGNE.

Pepys, Samuel (1633–1703) English diarist and naval administrator. In 1673 Pepys was elected to Parliament and made secretary to the Admiralty Commission in that year. Implicated in the POPISH PLOT, Pepys retired from public life. Cleared of any involvement, he was reinstated and made president of the Royal Society (1684), after which he worked to rebuild the Royal Navy. Pepys' *Diary* (1660–69) describes his private life and contemporary English society. It includes a vivid account of the RESTORATION, the Great Plague and the Great FIRE OF LONDON (1666). Written in a personalized shorthand, the diary was not published until 1815 and was not seen in complete form until 1983.

Pequot War (1637) Conflict between the Pequot NATIVE NORTH AMERICANS and the Connecticut colonists. Following increasing tension over land between the Pequot tribe and the white settlers, notably the British, and reacting to the murder of an English trader, the colonists attacked the tribe. In the process of destroying Pequot settlements, Captain John Mason killed more than 600 Native Americans in a battle on the Mystic River, near Rhode Island. The majority of the survivors became slaves in the West Indies or to the MOHAWK and Mohegan tribes.

Perceval, Spencer (1762–1812) British statesman, prime minister (1809–12). He entered Parliament in 1796, where he was a supporter of William PITT (THE YOUNGER). He served as attorney general (1802–07), before becoming chancellor of the exchequer (1807–09). Perceval succeeded the Duke of PORTLAND as prime minister and pursued the PENINSULAR WAR. Perceval's stable and competent administration came to an abrupt end when he was assassinated in the lobby of the House of Commons by a bankrupt broker. He was succeeded by the Earl of LIVERPOOL.

Percy, Sir Henry (1364–1403) English noble, known as "Hotspur" for his zeal in guarding the Scottish-English border. Son of the Earl of Northumberland, Percy supported the deposition of RICHARD II in 1399 but later quarrelled with the new king, HENRY IV. In 1403 Percy and his father, in alliance with Owain GLYN DŴR, launched a rebellion. They were defeated at Shrewsbury, W England, and Percy was killed.

Peres, Shimon (1923–) Israeli statesman, prime minister (1986–88, 1995–96), b. Poland. He emigrated to Palestine in 1934. In 1947 Peres joined the HAGANAH. There he met David BEN-GURION, who made him head of the navy (1948) of the newly formed state of ISRAEL. In 1953 Peres became director general of the ministry of defence, helping to strengthen Israel's arsenal. Peres was elected to the Knesset (parliament) in 1959 as a member of the MAPAI PARTY. In 1968 Peres helped found the Labour Party. He held various cabinet posts under Golda MEIR and, following her resignation, narrowly lost the Labour Party leadership election to Yitzhak RABIN. Under Rabin, Peres served as minister of defence (1974–77), rebuilding the nation's confidence after the YOM KIPPUR WAR (1973). Peres succeeded Rabin as leader of the Labour Party in 1977, but lost the ensuing elections to LIKUD. In 1984 Peres formed a coalition government with Likud under Yitzhak SHAMIR, becoming prime minister two years later. During his term in office, Peres succeeded in withdrawing Israeli troops from LEBANON and reducing inflation thanks to a loan from the United States. In 1992 Peres was replaced as Party leader by Rabin, who won the ensuing election. As foreign minister (1992–95), Peres played a vital role in the ISRAELI-PALESTINIAN ACCORD (1993) and was jointly awarded, with Rabin and Yasir ARAFAT of the PALESTINIAN LIBERATION ORGANIZATION (PLO), the 1994 Nobel Prize for Peace. On Rabin's assassination (1995), Peres returned as prime minister but was defeated in 1996 elections by Binyamin NETANYAHU.

perestroika (Rus. reconstruction) Adopted by Soviet President Mikhail GORBACHEV in 1986, *perestroika* was linked with GLASNOST. The restructuring included reform of government and the bureaucracy, an attempt at reducing corruption and decentralization, and the abolition of the COMMUNIST PARTY monopoly. Liberalization of the economy included the introduction of limited private enterprise. Although a noble attempt at modernization, *perestroika* only served to highlight the inefficiency and corruption of past regimes, and trying to rectify these only worsened the Soviet economy. Gorbachev found himself attacked by radicals for the slow pace of reform and by conservatives for starting the reform process in the first place.

Pérez de Cuéllar, Javier (1920–) Peruvian diplomat, fifth secretary general of the UNITED NATIONS (1982–91). He emerged as a successful compromise candidate following opposition to the re-election of Kurt WALDHEIM. Pérez earned a reputation for skilful diplomacy in the cease-fire agreements at the end of the FALKLANDS WAR (1982) and the IRAN-IRAQ WAR (1980–88). He was succeeded by Boutros BOUTROS-GHALI. In 1995 Pérez failed in his bid to become president of Peru.

▲ **Peres** was the political disciple of David Ben-Gurion, first prime minister of Israel. As leader of the Labour Party, he lost two elections (1977, 1981) to Menachem Begin.

Pérez Jiménez, Marcos (1914–) Venezuelan dictator, president (1952–58). A leader of the 1948 military coup, Pérez Jiménez was later appointed president by the junta. He began a massive programme of public works. His repressive regime closed the university, censored the press and suppressed the church. Anger at corruption and rampant inflation triggered a popular revolt that forced Pérez Jiménez out of office, and he fled to the United States. Extradited to Venezuela on charges of embezzlement, he was found guilty and sentenced to five years' imprisonment (1963). After his release (1968), Pérez Jiménez lived in exile in Spain. An attempt to re-enter politics in Venezuela (1972) led to riots and he returned to Spain.

Pergamum Ancient city-state on the site of modern Bergama, W Turkey. It was founded by Greek colonists under licence from the Persian emperors in the 4th century BC. At its peak in the 3rd–2nd centuries BC, Pergamum controlled much of W Asia Minor, replacing the SELEUCIDS as the ruling power. One of the great cities of the HELLENISTIC AGE, Pergamum was noted for its fine sculpture and architecture, including its library, where parchment was developed. Long allied with Rome, it was bequeathed to Rome on the death (133 BC) of Attalus III and became a Roman province of Asia. EPHESUS replaced it as the major city of the province.

Pericles (*c*.495–*c*.429 BC) Athenian statesman. He dominated ATHENS from *c*.460 BC to his death, overseeing its golden age. Knowledge of the man stems largely from THUCYDIDES and PLUTARCH. During a period of peace with SPARTA (445–431 BC), Pericles encouraged art and literature and implemented a programme of public works, including the building of the PARTHENON and other constructions on the ACROPOLIS. He strengthened the ATHENIAN EMPIRE, establishing new colonies and consolidating existing ones. Pericles also implemented governmental reforms, opening government positions to all citizens (those men with two Athenian parents) and offering pay for government service and jury duty. By refusing to concede to Sparta, Pericles initiated the PELOPONNESIAN WAR and persuaded the Athenians to strengthen their navy. An outbreak of plague indirectly resulted in his removal from office, but he was reinstated (429 BC) only to die of plague later that year. *See also* CIMON

Perkins, Frances (1882–1965) US social reformer and politician. In New York state, Perkins advocated improved factory conditions and better labour laws, including social security, minimum wages and maximum working hours, while vociferously condemning child labour. In 1923 she became a member of the Industrial Board, later becoming chairwoman (1926–29). Under Franklin ROOSEVELT, Perkins was made secretary of labour (1933–45), the first woman to be a US cabinet member, and she played a significant role in Roosevelt's NEW DEAL programme. Following Roosevelt's death, Perkins resigned from Harry TRUMAN's cabinet and became a member of the Civil Service Commission (1946–52).

Permian Geological period of the PALEOZOIC era, lasting from 286 to 248 million years ago. During this period there was widespread geologic uplift and periods of glaciation in the more southern continents. Many groups of marine invertebrate animals became extinct during the Permian.

Perón, Eva Duarte de (1919–52) Argentine politician, second wife of Juan PERÓN. A former actress, she did not hold an official post, but she administered Argentina's social welfare agencies and was the country's chief labour mediator. Commonly known as "Evita", Perón established many hospitals, schools, orphanages and other social institutions and pushed through a woman's suffrage law. Her popularity contributed to the longevity of the Peronist regime. After her death, Perón's enemies stole her body (1955) in an attempt to weaken her lasting influence, but it was eventually returned (1976).

Perón, Isabel (1931–) Argentine stateswoman, president (1974–76), third wife of Juan PERÓN, b. Maria Estela Martínez Cartas. She became vice president in 1973 and president after Juan Perón died in office. The first woman chief of state in the Americas, she was damaged by the controversy surrounding her chief adviser, José Lopez Rega, who was forced into exile after accusations of corruption and terrorist activities. Unable to remedy Argentina's worsening economy, Perón was overthrown in a miltary coup and held under house arrest for five years (1976–81). In 1981 she was convicted of corruption and subsequently went into exile in Spain.

Perón, Juan Domingo (1895–1974) Argentine statesman, president (1946–55, 1973–74). An army officer, he became the leading figure in the military junta (1943–46). Perón cultivated the trade unions and earned support from the poor by social reforms, greatly assisted by his wife "Evita" PERÓN. He won the 1946 presidential election and was re-elected in 1952. Perón's populist programme was nationalist and totalitarian. Although it benefited the worker and fostered economic growth by means of development projects and the NATIONALIZATION of key industries, it was open to corruption and was achieved by repression of dissent. Changing economic circumstances and the death of his wife reduced Perón's popularity, and he was overthrown by the military in 1955. Péron retired to Spain, but while in exile, the political clout of his supporters, the **Peronists**, grew as successive governments proved ineffective. Péron, despite the army's misgivings, returned in triumph to regain the presidency after political parties were legalized (1972). His second term, marked by violence, was cut short by his death in office. He was succeeded by his third wife, Isabel PERÓN.

Perry, Matthew Calbraith (1794–1858) US naval officer. In 1837 he commanded the first steamship in the US Navy, the *Fulton*. Perry also organized the first naval engineer corps. During the MEXICAN WAR (1846–48), he was made commander of the Gulf squadron, and was a participant in the siege of Veracruz. Perry is best known for leading a naval expedition to Japan (1853–54) with the aim of opening the country to the West. The Japanese, impressed by the US military technology, were pressured into signing the Treaty of KANAGAWA, so ending centuries of isolation.

Perry, Oliver Hazard (1785–1819) US naval officer, brother of Matthew PERRY. He served in the Tripoli campaign (1801–05). In the WAR OF 1812, Perry built and manned a fleet on Lake Erie. In September 1813, his victory over the British fleet near Put-In-Bay, Ohio, gave the United States control of the lake. Perry's message after the battle, "We have met the enemy and they are ours", is often quoted.

Persepolis City of ancient SW Persia (Iran), *c*.60km (35mi) NE of SHIRAZ. The ceremonial capital (539–330 BC) of the ACHAEMENID empire, Persepolis was renowned for its extraordinary wealth and for the splendour of its palaces and tombs, the most elaborate of which were probably built during the reigns of DARIUS I (THE GREAT) and XERXES I. Persepolis was captured, looted and destroyed by the forces of ALEXANDER III (THE GREAT) in 330 BC.

Perseus (*c*.213–*c*.165 BC) Last king of MACEDON (179–168 BC). Following his father PHILIP V's defeat at the hands of the Romans in the Second MACEDONIAN WAR, Perseus set about rebuilding Macedon. By a combination of political guile, which he used to befriend RHODES, and military strength, with which he annexed the regions of THRACE and ILLYRIA, Perseus' Macedon became the envy of the Greek world. When Eumenes II of PERGAMUM complained to its ally, Rome, that Perseus had extensive military intentions, it precipitated the Third Macedonian War. Perseus was defeated at Pydna (168 BC) and taken to Italy, where he died in captivity.

P

◄ **Persian Wars** Darius I of Persia gave Mardonius, his son-in-law, command of a fleet to conquer Athens in 492 BC, but the fleet was lost in a storm off Mount Athos. Undeterred, a further Persian expedition (490 BC) succeeded in gaining Eretria, but Athens united with Sparta and, gaining the element of surprise, defeated the Persians at Marathon (490 BC). In 480 BC Xerxes I, Darius' son and successor, relaunched the conflict, defeating Leonidas at Thermopylae (480 BC) and the Greek navy at Artemisium (480 BC), but sustaining heavy losses. The Greek navy, under Themistocles, recovered to smash the Persians at Salamis (480 BC). The Persian army was finally expelled from mainland Greece after losing the Battle of Plataea (479 BC). The Persian navy scuppered its own ships at Mycale (479 BC).

Pershing, John Joseph (1860–1948) US general. A graduate of West Point military academy (1886), Pershing fought in the SIOUX WARS, served in the Philippines (1899–1903) during the SPANISH-AMERICAN WAR and led a punitive expedition against "Pancho" VILLA in Mexico (1916) before being appointed to command (1917–19) the AMERICAN EXPEDITIONARY FORCE (AEF) in WORLD WAR I. Pershing maintained the separate integrity of the US forces under overall Allied command and won two important victories, at St-Mihiel and Meuse-Argonne, France (1918). On his return, Pershing was made general of the armies of the United States, a rank shared only by George Washington. As army chief of staff (1921–24) he attempted to unite the US Army with the National Guard and the Reserves. Pershing was awarded a Pulitzer Prize for his memoirs *My Experiences in the World War* (1931).

Persia European name for IRAN, SW Asia. The earliest empire in the region was that of MEDIA (*c*.700–549 BC). The Medes were overthrown by the Persian king CYRUS II (THE GREAT), who established the much larger ACHAEMENID dynasty (*c*.550–330 BC), itself destroyed by ALEXANDER III (THE GREAT). Alexander's successors, the SELEUCIDS, were replaced by people from PARTHIA in the 3rd century BC. The Persian SASANIAN dynasty was established by ARDASHIR I in AD 224. Weakened from defeat by the BYZANTINE EMPIRE under HERACLIUS, Persia was overrun by the Arabs in the 7th century. *See also* BABYLONIA; BACTRIA; LYDIA; PERSIAN WARS

Persian Wars (499–479 BC) Series of conflicts between the ancient Greeks and Persians. In 499 BC the IONIAN cities of Asia Minor, dissatisfied with their political and economic treatment, rebelled against Persian rule. Athens sent a fleet to aid them. Having crushed the rebellion, the Persian emperor DARIUS I invaded Greece in retaliation, but lost much of his navy in a storm. Undeterred the Persians returned, sacking Eretria. During their assault on Athens, however, they were defeated at MARATHON (490 BC) by the Greek general MILTIADES THE YOUNGER. In 480 BC Darius' successor, XERXES I, having amassed a vast army (200,000–300,000 men) and navy (700 warships), sacked and burned Athens after a gruelling land battle at THERMOPYLAE, during which the Spartan king LEONIDAS and *c*.300 soldiers heroically defended against the Persians for two days before being overwhelmed and killed. Greek fortunes recovered with THEMISTOCLES' resounding naval victory at SALAMIS (480 BC) and the Persian commander MARDONIUS' defeat at PLATAEA (479 BC), the latter marking the complete failure of the land invasion. Sporadic fighting continued, however, until the Peace of Callias (449 BC), as the Greeks in the DELIAN LEAGUE regained territory in Thrace and Anatolia. The history of the Persian Wars was recounted by HERODOTUS, the first attempt at an impartial historical narrative. *See* map, page 321

Peru *See* country feature

Peru, Viceroyalty of (1543–1824) Southern region of colonial SPANISH AMERICA. The second of the four viceroyalties, the Viceroyalty of PERU initially encompassed all of Spain's South American territories except the coast of modern-day Venezuela. The Viceroyalty was home to vast silver mines, particular those at Potosí (now in S Bolivia), and soon became Spain's most prized South American possession. By the mid-16th century LIMA had become the capital of the Viceroyalty and home to wealthy merchants and mine operators, all enjoying vast wealth created on the backs of the enslaved indigenous population. However, such easily acquired riches, together with inhospitable terrain and the vast distance to Europe, resulted in a chaotic political climate. The viceroyship (1569–81) of Francisco de TOLEDO restored some order, granting the Native Americans some autonomy and improving the mines. Subsequent viceroys also assumed greater responsibility for the region. With the establishment (1739) of the Viceroyalty of NEW GRANADA, which consisted of modern-day Colombia, Panama, Ecuador and Venezuela, and the Viceroyalty of the RÍO DE LA PLATA (1776), which took control of modern-day Argentina, Uruguay, Paraguay and Bolivia, the Viceroyalty of Peru was reduced in area to modern-day Peru and CHILE. By the late 18th century Spain began to lose control of its once-favoured possession. Following the bloody Native American rebellion led by TUPAC AMARU (1780–83) and the declaration of independence from Spain by General José de SAN MARTÍN after his capture of Lima (1821), the viceroy and his generals were defeated at the Battle of Ayacucho (1824) by Antonio José de SUCRE. What remained of the Viceroyalty passed into the control of newly independent Peru and Chile. *See also* ENCOMENIDA

Pétain, Henri Philippe (1856–1951) French general and politician. His defence of VERDUN (1916) during WORLD WAR I made him a national hero. In 1917 Pétain was appointed commander-in-chief of the French army, and he was made a marshal at the end of the War. After the German invasion of France in 1940, Pétain was recalled as vice premier under Paul REYNAUD, and soon succeeded him as leader. Pétain signed the surrender of France and became head of the VICHY regime. At the end of 1940, he replaced his vice premier, Pierre LAVAL, who favoured Franco-German collaboration, with Admiral François DARLAN. His attempt to maintain French neutrality foundered, however, and the Nazis forced him to reappoint Laval in 1942. Thereafter Pétain was only the nominal head of the Vichy government. After the liberation of France by Charles DE GAULLE in 1944, Pétain fled to Germany but was captured by the Allies, convicted of treason and condemned to death. His sentence was commuted to life imprisonment. Pétain died in prison.

Peter, Saint (d. *c*.64) Apostle of JESUS CHRIST. Born Simon, son of Jonas, he was a fisherman from Bethsaida on the Sea of Galilee. Simon and his brother, Andrew, were called by Jesus to be disciples. Jesus gave Simon the name Peter. Peter was one of Jesus' closest and most loyal associates. After Jesus' ascension, Peter was the first publicly to preach Christianity in Jerusalem. He took Christianity to SAMARIA. In his final years, Peter seems to have left Jerusalem and undertaken a missionary journey. Roman Catholic theology accepts him as the first head of the Church and the first bishop of Rome, from whom the popes claim succession. His feast day is 29 June.

Peter I (the Great) (1672–1725) Russian tsar (1682–1721) and emperor (1721–25), son of ALEXEI MIKHAILOVICH. After a revolt by the *streltsi* (musketeers), he was forced to share power (1682–96) with his invalid half-brother Ivan V (1666–96). His half-sister Sophia acted as regent until Peter came of age, whereupon he promptly overthrew her in a coup (1689) and finally crushed the *streltsi* in 1698. Peter inherited a landlocked nation and the gaining of access to the sea became the chief objective of his foreign policy. In 1696 he captured Azov from the TATAR servants of the OTTOMAN EMPIRE, thus securing an

PERU

AREA: 1,285,220sq km (496,223sq mi)
POPULATION: 22,454,000
CAPITAL (POPULATION): Lima (6,386,308)
GOVERNMENT: Transitional republic
ETHNIC GROUPS: Quechua 47%, Mestizo 32%, White 12%, Aymara 5%
LANGUAGES: Spanish and Quechua (both official)
RELIGIONS: Christianity (Roman Catholic 93%, Protestant 6%)
GDP PER CAPITA (1995): US$3770

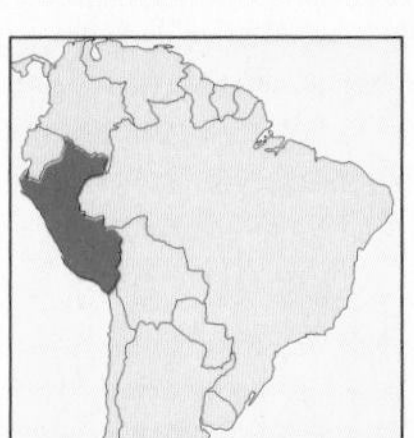

Republic in W South America. Native American civilizations developed from the 2nd millennium BC. By 1200 BC peoples along much of the coast were united by a religious cult centred on CHAVÍN de Huantar. Other cultures then emerged, including those of Paracas (*c*.60–375 BC), NAZCA (375 BC–AD 600) and MOCHICA (*c*.AD 1–650). The CHIMÚ culture dominated a thin coastal strip from the 10th century until 1475, when their emperor was seized by the INCAS. The Incas had begun to conquer their neighbours around the capital of CUZCO in the 14th century, but it was not until *c*.1440 that they started to expand over a vast area. By 1500 their empire extended from Ecuador to Chile.

In 1532 the Spanish conquistador Francisco PIZARRO captured the Inca ruler ATAHUALPA. By 1533 Pizarro had conquered most of Peru; he founded LIMA in 1535. In 1544 LIMA became capital of Spain's South American empire. Spain's rule caused frequent native revolts, such as that of TUPAC AMARU in 1780. In 1820 José de SAN MARTÍN captured coastal Peru and in 1821 Peru declared independence. Spain still held much of the interior, but Simón BOLÍVAR and Antonio Jose de SUCRÉ completed the liberation by 1824. In the War of the PACIFIC (1879–84) Peru lost some of its S provinces to Bolivia.

The early 20th century was characterized by dictatorship and the growing gap between a wealthy oligarchy and the poverty of the native population. From 1968 to 1980 a military junta failed to carry out democratic reforms. Austerity measures, introduced by the civilian government during the 1980s, caused civil unrest. SENDERO LUMINOSO (Shining Path) and the Tupac Amaru Revolutionary Movement (MRTA) waged an insurgency campaign that by 2000 had claimed more than 30,000 lives. In 1990 Alberto FUJIMORI was elected on a platform of tough anti-terrorist policies. In 1992 he suspended the constitution and dismissed parliament. The guerrilla movements' leaders were captured. In 1993 a new constitution was introduced. In 1995 Fujimori was re-elected. In December 1996 MRTA guerrillas captured the Japanese embassy in Lima. The four-month siege ended when the army stormed the complex, killing all the guerrillas. In 1998 Peru and Ecuador signed a peace agreement resolving a protracted border dispute. From 1990 Fujimori's regime instigated a number of free-market reforms that reduced inflation and foreign debt.

PETER I (THE GREAT)

Peter I (the Great) Portrait (1717) by Jean-Marc Nattier (1685–1755). Peter transformed Russia into a major European power. He travelled incognito to Western Europe, working in Dutch and British shipyards. Peter often used brutal methods to Europeanize Russia, such as cutting off the beards of the boyars.

PETER THE GREAT IN HIS OWN WORDS

"Now indeed with God's help the final stone has been laid in the foundation of St Petersburg."
Letter written after his victory at the Battle of Poltava (1709)

outlet to the Black Sea. Turkey regained Azov in a further episode (1710–13) of the RUSSO-TURKISH WARS, but in the interim Peter had become embroiled in the major conflict of his reign, the Great NORTHERN WAR (1700–21) with Sweden. In order to gain access to the Baltic Sea, Peter took a leading part in the conflict, planning the winning strategy against CHARLES XII in the Battle of POLTAVA (1809). By the Treaty of NYSTAD (1721), Russia acquired the E coast of the Baltic and replaced Sweden as the dominant power in N Europe. Peter was subsequently proclaimed emperor. In 1703 he founded the Baltic port of ST PETERSBURG, which succeeded MOSCOW as capital of Russia. After the Northern War, Peter turned his attention to Persia (Iran), gaining the W and S shores of the Caspian Sea. At home, he launched the rapid modernization of Russia, based on knowledge acquired of new industrial methods in Western Europe during his so-called "Grand Embassy" (1697–98) tour. He developed metallurgical and manufacturing industries in order to build a modern army and a powerful Baltic fleet. These industries mainly used SERF labour, and Peter brutally suppressed serf revolts (1705–08). Further revolts against the imposition of a poll tax (1722) led to a nationwide network of army garrisons to enforce the peace. Russian towns, granted powers to elect their own municipalities, became thriving centres of commerce and industry. Peter broke the power of the BOYARS (landed aristocracy) by abolishing the boyar council as the supreme central organization, replacing it with a senate. He also created a meritocratic system of appointment, ending the rule of promotion according to ancestry. Peter placed the Russian ORTHODOX CHURCH under state control and sold off much church land. He also encouraged secular education and introduced a new calendar. He was succeeded by his wife, CATHERINE I.

Peter II (1715–30) Russian tsar (1727–30), grandson of PETER I (THE GREAT) and successor of CATHERINE I. Peter was at first guided by Alexander MENSHIKOV, who had led the ruling council during Catherine's reign. He later came under the influence of Menshikov's rival Vasili Dolgoruki, who exiled Menshikov. Peter died on the day of his wedding and was succeeded by his cousin, ANNA IVANOVNA.

Peter III (1728–62) Russian tsar (1762). During his six-month reign, Peter returned East PRUSSIA voluntarily to FREDERICK II, whom he admired, thus losing all the territory that Russia had gained during the SEVEN YEARS' WAR. Peter was dethroned and murdered in a conspiracy led by the brothers Orlov and probably encouraged by his wife and successor, CATHERINE II (THE GREAT).

Peter I (1844–1921) King of Serbia (1903–21), son of ALEXANDER KARAGEORGEVIĆ. He was brought up in exile and educated in France while the OBRENOVIĆ dynasty ruled Serbia. Peter was elected king by the Serbian parliament after Alexander Obrenović was assassinated (1903). Peter made improvements to the social and military infrastructure and reformed the constitution. During World War 1, Peter was in exile in Greece. Following the War, Peter served (1918–21) as the first king of the new kingdom of Serbs, Croats and Slovenes (later YUGOSLAVIA). He was succeeded by his son, ALEXANDER I.

Peter II (1923–70) King of Yugoslavia (1934–41), son of ALEXANDER I. Peter succeeded to the throne after his father's assassination. His uncle, Prince Paul KARAGEORGEVIĆ, acted as regent until he was removed (1941) by a pro-Allied military coup. Peter ruled for a month until the invasion of the AXIS POWERS, when he fled to London to lead a government-in-exile. After the monarchy was abolished in 1945, he settled in the United States.

Peterloo Massacre (16 August 1819) Violent suppression of a political protest in Manchester, NW England. Magistrates ordered that a large crowd, peacefully demonstrating for reform of Parliament, was dispersed. Ordered only to arrest the speakers, who included Henry HUNT, the local yeomanry were unable to force their way through the crowd. The magistrates responded by sending in cavalry to assist the yeomans. The cavalry, wielding sabres, mounted a charge, in which 11 people were killed and a further 500 injured. The government, under Lord LIVERPOOL, refused to criticize the magistrates' handling of the event, and instead passed the SIX ACTS. This insensitive response led to increased public support for the REFORM ACTS.

Peter the Hermit (1050–1115) French priest who helped to start the First CRUSADE. After Pope URBAN II proclaimed the Crusade in 1095, Peter began preaching in central France in support of war against Islam. In 1096, having made his way to Cologne, W Germany, he set out to Constantinople with a motley army of *c*.20,000 peasants. Most were killed by the Turks, but Peter escaped and succeeded in reaching Jerusalem. He returned to Europe in 1100, becoming prior of a monastery in Belgium.

Petition of Right Means by which an English subject could sue the Crown; in particular, the statement of grievances against the monarchy presented by Parliament to CHARLES I in 1628. It asserted that the Crown had acted illegally in raising taxation without Parliament's consent, imprisoning people without charge, maintaining a standing army, and quartering soldiers on ordinary householders. It led to the dissolution of Parliament and Charles' period of absolute rule.

Petra Ancient city in what is now SW Jordan. It was the capital of the Nabataean kingdom from the 4th century BC. It was captured by the Romans in the 2nd century AD, by the Muslims in the 7th century, and by the Crusaders in the 12th century. The city, which was rediscovered in 1812 and is the scene of extensive excavation, can be reached only through narrow gorges. Many of its remarkable, ruined houses, temples, theatres and tombs were cut from the high, pinkish sandstone cliffs that protected it.

Phalange Party Christian political organization in LEBANON. Founded in 1936 as the *Phalanges Libanaises* by Pierre GEMAYEL, it was initially a youth movement based on the German Nazi Youth, and was established to oppose both French rule and those Muslims who sought to unite Lebanon with Syria. It became the dominant party of the MARONITE Christians after Lebanon gained full independence in 1948. Throughout the 1950s and 1960s the nationalist Phalange Party, backed by Israel, demanded the expulsion of Palestinians from Lebanon. An attempted assassination of Gemayel sparked the Lebanese civil war (1975–76), a conflict that was eventually to lead to the involvement of SYRIA and ISRAEL, and during which the Phalange militia fought running battles with the PALESTINIAN LIBERATION ORGANIZATION (PLO) and Lebanese SHIITE Muslims. In 1982 the assassination of Bashir Gemayel, leader of the Phalange militia, in BEIRUT provoked the revenge killing of *c*.1000 Palestinian refugees. During the 1980s and 1990s the Phalange Party's military wing was at the centre of complex conflicts between Muslim and Christian forces.

Pham Van Dong (1906–2000) *See* DONG, PHAM VAN

Pharisees Members of a conservative Jewish religious group, prominent in ancient PALESTINE from the 2nd century BC to *c*.AD 135. They began as a political party opposed to the pagan influences of their Greek and Roman conquerors, but by New Testament times they were largely non-political. Advocates of strict and unwavering observance of Jewish law, they were the founders of orthodox JUDAISM and were often in conflict with the SADDUCEES.

Pharos Mediterranean island off the coast of N Egypt, connected to the mainland by a causeway built by ALEXANDER III (THE GREAT). A lighthouse was completed by Ptolemy II in *c*.280 BC and was considered one of the SEVEN WONDERS OF THE WORLD. According to writers of the time, it was *c*.135m (450ft) tall and its light could be seen 65km (40mi) away. It was destroyed by an earthquake in 1346. Pharos is now part of the city of ALEXANDRIA.

Pharsalus, Battle of (48 BC) Defeat of POMPEY by Julius CAESAR in Pharsalus, N Greece. Although Caesar's forces were outnumbered two to one by Pompey's, Caesar's tactical genius granted him victory. Pompey sent his cavalry

◄ **Petra** The Ad-Dayr (monastery) shown here is situated on a high plateau above the city of Petra (Gk. Rock), SW Jordan. Originally built as a tomb in the 3rd century BC, it was later used as a church when the city came under Byzantine rule in the 3rd century AD. Petra is renowned for its complex hydrological system built by the Nabataeans, which featured channels and cisterns for water preservation and dams to safeguard against flooding. During the Nabataean era, Petra prospered on the spice trade-route, which linked Rome with India and China. The "oriental" influence is reflected in some buildings' façades. Petra was designated a UNESCO World Heritage Site in 1985.

against Caesar's weaker right flank, unaware that Caesar had reinforced it with 2000 of his best legionnaires. Thrown into disarray by the surprise reinforcement, Pompey's forces were overcome: 24,000 were captured, and *c.*20,000 fled or were killed. Pompey himself survived and fled to Egypt, where he was assassinated.

Phetsarath Ratanavongsa (1890–1959) Lao nationalist leader. He was premier (1941–45) of a cabinet formed by the French to govern both Luang Prabang and Vientiane. Phetsarath joined the Lao Issara (Free LAOS) movement after being dismissed from office by the king, who supported the maintenance of French INDOCHINA. He formed a government-in-exile in Thailand after the French reoccupation (1946). After full independence was achieved in 1953, Phetsarath returned to Laos (1956) to work for an end to the ensuing civil war. His youngest brother, SOUPHANOUVONG, was one of the founders of the PATHET LAO; another brother, SOUVANNA PHOUMA, served as prime minister (1951–54, 1962–75).

Philadelphia City and port at the confluence of the Delaware and Schuylkill rivers, SE PENNSYLVANIA. The site was first settled by Europeans in the early 17th century who found fertile farmland. The city was founded by William PENN in 1681. By 1774 Philadelphia had become a major commercial, cultural and industrial centre of the American colonies. It played an important part in their fight for independence. The CONTINENTAL CONGRESSES were held in the city and the DECLARATION OF INDEPENDENCE was signed here in 1776. The CONSTITUTIONAL CONVENTION met in Philadelphia and adopted the US CONSTITUTION in 1787. Philadelphia served as capital of the United States from 1790 to 1800. Pop. (1994) 1,524,249.

Philip I (1052–1108) King of France (1060–1108), son and successor of HENRY I. His mother and uncle acted as regents during the early years of his reign. One of the CAPETIAN kings, Philip enlarged his kingdom both through diplomacy and combat. He fought with the kings of England, WILLIAM I (THE CONQUEROR) and WILLIAM II, for control of NORMANDY. He supported ROBERT II, son of William I, in his rebellion against his father and later against his brother, William II. Philip aroused the anger of the papacy for practising SIMONY. For his illegal marriage to Bertrada de Montfort (both were already married), Philip was excommunicated by Pope Urban I.

Philip II (Augustus) (1165–1223) King of France (1180–1223), son and successor of LOUIS VII (THE YOUNGER). He was the greatest of the French CAPETIAN kings, increasing the royal domain by marriage, by exploiting his feudal rights, and by war. Against HENRY II of England, Philip allied himself with Henry's son, Richard, Duke of Aquitaine (later RICHARD I), winning territory from Henry. Later he conspired against Richard, and in retaliation Richard fought Philip, reclaiming the land his father had lost (1194–99). Philip also fought Richard's successor, JOHN, winning Normandy, Brittany, Anjou, Maine and Touraine (1202–05), and finally defeating John and his allies, the Holy Roman Empire and FLANDERS, at BOUVINES (1214). Domestically Philip reformed the government bureaucracy and taxation system, and made PARIS the permanent capital of France. Philip limited the power of the nobility by creating a body of local administrators drawn from the middle classes. Philip persecuted Jews and Christian heretics, joined the Third CRUSADE but swiftly withdrew, and opened the crusade against the ALBIGENSES in S France. He was succeeded by his son, LOUIS VIII (THE LION). *See also* ANGEVIN

Philip IV (the Fair) (1268–1314) King of France (1285–1314). Claiming the right to tax the clergy involved him in a long and bitter quarrel with Pope BONIFACE VIII. Philip used assemblies (later called the STATES-GENERAL) to popularize his case. After the death of Boniface VIII (1303), Philip secured the election of a French pope, CLEMENT V, who moved the papacy to AVIGNON. Partly to pay for wars against Flanders and England, Philip expelled the Jews from France (1306) and suppressed the KNIGHTS TEMPLAR, confiscating their property. He failed to gain land from England, but was moderately more successful against FLANDERS, and took Lyons and Viviers from the Holy Roman Empire. He was succeeded by his son, Louis X. *See also* AVIGNON POPES

Philip VI (1293–1350) King of France (1328–50). First ruler of the house of VALOIS, he was chosen to succeed his cousin CHARLES IV, in preference to the rival claimant, EDWARD III of England. Philip's reign was dominated by the HUNDRED YEARS' WAR (from 1337), and many of Philip's vassals supported Edward. The expense of war forced Philip to raise funds through heavy taxation. Philip suffered serious defeats in the naval Battle of SLUYS (1340) and at CRÉCY (1346). Forced to make peace with Edward III, he died soon after.

Philip II (382–336 BC) King of MACEDON (359–336 BC). After seizing the throne when acting as regent for his brother's son, he overcame local and foreign opposition and set about enlarging his kingdom. Throughout Philip's ascent to power, the Athenian orator DEMOSTHENES spoke out in warning against him. Philip conquered neighbouring city-states but was halted in his progress into Greece at THERMOPYLAE (352 BC). After making peace with ATHENS (346 BC), he aided THEBES in its war against Phocis. He was invited to join the Amphictyonic League (346 BC), a confederation of Greek city-states, which gave him a say in Greek affairs. Concern at Philip's growing power led Athens and Thebes to rise against him, but they were defeated at CHAERONEA (338 BC), and Philip gained reluctant acknowledgment as king of Greece. He was preparing to invade the Persian empire when he was assassinated, leaving the task to his son, ALEXANDER III (THE GREAT). *See also* CORINTH; GREECE, CLASSICAL; THESSALY

Philip V (238–179 BC) King of MACEDON (221–179 BC), adopted son and successor of Antigonus III. Hostile to Rome, Philip allied Macedon with HANNIBAL of CARTHAGE (215 BC) during the Second PUNIC WAR. The MACEDONIAN WARS were initiated during Philip's reign. In the **First** (211–205 BC), he fought the AETOLIAN LEAGUE and SPARTA. The War was inconclusive and Philip was able to secure favourable terms from Aetolia and Rome. Philip's attempts to expand Macedonian power in the Aegean provoked Rome into the **Second** Macedonian War (200–196 BC), in which Philip was badly beaten at Cynoscephalae (197 BC). Obliged to pay tribute to Rome and relinquish his conquests, Philip subsequently concentrated on strengthening Macedon internally. He was succeeded by his son PERSEUS.

PHILIPPINES

AREA: 300,000sq km (115,300sq mi)
POPULATION: 64,259,000
CAPITAL (POPULATION): Manila (1,587,000)
GOVERNMENT: Multiparty republic
ETHNIC GROUPS: Tagalog 30%, Cebuano 24%, Ilocano 10%, Hiligaynon Ilongo 9%, Bicol 6%, Samar-Leyte 4%
LANGUAGES: Filipino (Tagalog) and English (both official)
RELIGIONS: Christianity (Roman Catholic 84%, Philippine Independent Church or Aglipayan 6%, Protestant 4%), Islam 4%
GDP PER CAPITA (1995): US$2850

Republic in Southeast Asia, consisting of more than 7000 islands, of which 1000 are inhabited. From *c.*AD 1000 Chinese traders visited the islands but they had little impact on the indigenous population, who practised shifting agriculture, hunting and fishing. Islam was introduced via trade routes in the late 15th century.

In 1521 the Portuguese navigator Ferdinand MAGELLAN landed near Cebu. In 1565 Spain began its conquest of the islands. In 1571 the Spanish founded Manila and named the archipelago *Filipinas*, after PHILIP II. It became a vital trading centre, subject to frequent attack from pirates. In 1896 the Filipinos revolted and declared independence. Two years of armed struggle overwhelmed the Spanish administration, facilitating the intervention of the United States. In the SPANISH-AMERICAN WAR (1898), the United States defeated the Spanish navy in MANILA BAY. Filipinos seized Luzon and captured Manila with US help. In the Treaty of Paris (1898) the islands were ceded to the United States. From 1899 to 1902 Filipinos fought unsuccessfully against US control.

In 1935 the Commonwealth of the Philippines was established. Manuel Luis QUEZON became the first president. In 1941 the Japanese invaded and captured Manila by 1942. General Douglas MACARTHUR was forced to withdraw and US forces were ousted from Bataan. In 1944 the United States began to reclaim the islands. The Philippines became an independent republic in 1946. The United States was granted a 99-year lease on military bases (subsequently reduced to 25 years from 1967).

In 1965 Ferdinand MARCOS became president. Marcos' response to mounting civil unrest was brutal. In 1972 he declared martial law. Marcos was re-elected in 1981, amid charges of electoral fraud. In 1983 the leader of the opposition, Benigno Aquino, was assassinated. His widow, Cory AQUINO, succeeded him. Marcos claimed victory in 1986 elections but faced charges of electoral fraud. Cory Aquino launched a campaign of civil disobedience. The United States withdrew its support for the corrupt regime, and Marcos was forced into exile. Aquino's presidency was marred by attempted military coups. In 1992 Fidel Ramos succeeded Aquino as president. At the end of 1992 the United States closed its military bases. In 1996 an agreement was reached with the Moro National Liberation Front, ending 24 years of rebellion on Mindanao. It allowed the creation of a autonomous Muslim state. In 1998 the fragile cease-fire was broken. In May 1998 Ramos was succeeded by the former vice president, Joseph Estrada.

P

▲ **Philip II** by the Dutch painter Antonio Moro (*c*.1520–*c*.1576). Philip's second marriage, to his second cousin Mary I of England, provoked Wyatt's Rebellion (1554) in England.

Philip I (the Handsome) (1478–1506) King of CASTILE (1504–06), son of Emperor MAXIMILIAN I and MARY OF BURGUNDY. Philip became Duke of Burgundy (1482) upon his mother's death, with his father as regent. He married Joanna the Mad (1479–1555), daughter of FERDINAND V and ISABELLA I. Joanna inherited the crown of Castile from her mother in 1504, but Philip died soon after they both acceded to the throne, and Joanna descended into madness. Through his marriage, Philip established the HABSBURG dynasty in Spain. He was succeeded as Duke of Burgundy by his son, later CHARLES V. Castile was ruled jointly by Ferdinand V (as regent) and Joanna until Charles V claimed the throne after Ferdinand's death (1516).

Philip II (1527–98) King of Spain (1556–98) and king (as Philip I) of Portugal (1580–98), son of Emperor CHARLES V. He married four times: Maria of Portugal (1543–45), who died in childbirth; MARY I of England (1554–58), who bore him no heirs; Elizabeth of France (1559–68), who gave birth to two daughters; and Anne of Austria (1570–80), daughter of Emperor MAXIMILIAN II, who produced the future PHILIP III of Spain. His father bestowed Milan (1540), Naples and Sicily (1554), the Netherlands (1555) and Spain (1556) on Philip, while his uncle became Emperor FERDINAND I and received the HABSBURG lands in Germany. War with France ended in the Treaty of CATEAU-CAMBRÉSIS (1559) and resulted in Philip's third marriage to Anne, so ending the long-running conflict between the Habsburg and VALOIS dynasties. After the war, Philip never again ventured outside the Iberian Peninsula, ruling his vast empire from Madrid, Spain. His reliance on governor generals, such as the Duke of ALBA, JOHN OF AUSTRIA and Alessandro FARNESE, bred suspicion. The champion of the Roman Catholic COUNTER-REFORMATION, Philip oppressed Protestants, and his system of indirect rule precipitated (1567) the REVOLT OF THE NETHERLANDS. He similarly suppressed the Moriscos (Christianized Muslims), in part to limit their support for the OTTOMAN EMPIRE. Philip sent the fleet that destroyed the Ottoman navy at the Battle of LEPANTO (1571) and conquered Portugal (1580). He launched the unsuccessful ARMADA (1588) to crush the English who, as fellow Protestants, aided the Dutch revolt. Towards the end of his reign, Philip renewed war with France, siding with the Catholic HOLY LEAGUE (1590) against the HUGUENOT king HENRY IV. Although Philip ruled during the "golden age" of the Spanish empire, increasing the number of colonies in SPANISH AMERICA and the Philippines, his many military campaigns left Spain in financial ruin.

Philip III (1578–1621) King of Spain (1598–1621), son and successor of PHILIP II. Uninterested in politics, he left government to his favourites, notably the Duque de LERMA. With the exception of a war with SAVOY (1615–17), Philip pursued peace until Spain became involved in the THIRTY YEARS' WAR. The Spanish occupation of Valtellina, a French holding in Lombardy (1620), led eventually to war (1622). The Moriscos (Christianized Muslims) were expelled during Philip's reign, greatly weakening the economy. His tenure marked a golden age for Spanish arts. He was succeeded by his son, PHILIP IV.

Philip IV (1605–65) King of Spain, Naples and Sicily (1621–65), king of Portugal (as Philip III, 1621–40), son and successor of PHILIP III. Economic and social decline in Spain continued during Philip's reign. The THIRTY YEARS' WAR ended disastrously for Spain, with the Peace of WESTPHALIA. While Spain was distracted by ongoing war with France, Portugal threw off Spanish rule (1640) and maintained independence in the ensuing war. Philip supported the arts, and Diego Velázquez (1599–1660) was his court painter. He was succeeded by his son, CHARLES II.

Philip V (1683–1746) King of Spain (1700–46), first ruler of the Spanish BOURBON dynasty. Because Philip was the grandson and possible successor of LOUIS XIV of France, his accession to the Spanish throne, as intended by the will of CHARLES II (THE MAD) and accepted by Louis, provoked the War of the SPANISH SUCCESSION. By the Treaty of UTRECHT (1713), Philip kept the Spanish throne by excluding himself from the succession in France and giving up Sardinia and Sicily to Italy and the Spanish Netherlands. At court Philip was dominated by his wife, Elizabeth Farnese, and her confidant Giulio ALBERONI. Between 1718 and 1720 Philip attempted to regain Sardinia and Sicily but was repulsed by the QUADRUPLE ALLIANCE. Philip also involved Spain in a series of European conflicts, including the War of the AUSTRIAN SUCCESSION and the War of JENKINS' EAR, which increased Bourbon power without substantial Spanish gains. He was succeeded by his son, FERDINAND VI.

Philip, Prince, Duke of Edinburgh (1921–) Prince consort, husband of ELIZABETH II of Britain. The son of Prince Andrew of Greece, he was born in Corfu but educated in Britain. Philip became a naturalized British citizen and took the surname Mountbatten. In 1947 he married Elizabeth after becoming the Duke of Edinburgh. In 1956 he launched the Duke of Edinburgh Award Scheme to encourage the leisure activities of young people.

Philip of Hesse (1504–67) (Philip the Magnanimous) German noble. He introduced the REFORMATION in Hesse, where he established a sovereign state that tolerated all Protestant religions. He formed (1531) the Protestant SCHMALKALDIC LEAGUE to protect LUTHERANISM against the Catholic Emperor CHARLES V. Philip's influence was weakened by a bigamous marriage (1540). Defeat in the Schmalkaldic War (1546–47) was followed by imprisonment (1547–52), although he survived to witness the Peace of AUGSBURG, which ended the conflict between Catholics and Lutherans in Germany.

Philip II (the Bold) (1342–1404) Duke of BURGUNDY (1363–1404), fourth son of JOHN II (THE GOOD), king of France. In 1380 Philip helped to put down a Flemish revolt against his father-in-law, the Count of Flanders. He inherited Flanders on the Count's death in 1384. Philip acted as regent (1380–88) for his nephew, the young king CHARLES VI. When Charles became insane, Philip fought Louis d'Orléans for control of the kingdom. Philip governed his vast territories well and was a notable patron of the arts.

Philip III (the Good) (1396–1467) Duke of BURGUNDY (1419–67). He maintained a long alliance with England, through the Treaty of TROYES (1420), in which HENRY V was recognized as heir to the French throne. In 1430 he captured JOAN OF ARC and handed her over to the English. Philip nonetheless managed friendly relations with France and eventually ended his English alliance with the Treaty of Arras (1435). He greatly enlarged his lands, making Burgundy one of the strongest states in 15th-century Europe. A great patron of the arts, Philip loved pageantry and established the chivalrous Order of the Golden Fleece in honour of his marriage (1429) to Isabella of Portugal. He was succeeded by his son, CHARLES THE BOLD.

Philip Neri, Saint *See* NERI, SAINT PHILIP

Philippi Ancient city of E Macedonia. It was the site of the victory of Mark ANTONY and Octavian (later Emperor AUGUSTUS) over CASSIUS and BRUTUS, the assassins of Julius Caesar, in 42 BC. Philippi became the first European city to receive a Christian mission when visited by St Paul.

Philippines *See* country feature

Philistine Member of a non-Semitic people who lived on the S coast of PALESTINE, known as Philistia, from *c*.1200 BC. A warlike peoples, they prospered through their control of a major trade route between Egypt and Syria. They clashed frequently with the Israelites, defeating Samson and Saul, until decisively defeated by King DAVID.

Phillips, Wendell (1811–84) US social reformer. He became a close associate of ABOLITIONIST William Lloyd GARRISON and was president of the Antislavery Society (1865–70). Unlike many other abolitionists, he campaigned on behalf of former slaves. He also advocated women's and workers' rights, and temperance.

Phnom Penh (Phnum Pénh) Capital of CAMBODIA, in the S of the country, a port at the confluence of the rivers Mekong and Tonle Sap. Founded in the 14th century, the city was the capital of the KHMER EMPIRE after 1434. In 1865 it became the capital of Cambodia. Occupied by the Japanese during World War 2, it was extensively damaged during the Cambodian civil war. After the KHMER ROUGE took power in 1975, the population was drastically reduced when many of its inhabitants were forcibly removed to work in the countryside. Pop. (1994 est.) 920,000.

Phoenicia Greek name for an ancient region bordering the E Mediterranean coast, centred on modern-day LEBANON. The Phoenicians were related to the Canaanites, who arrived in the region *c*.3000 BC. They were dominated by ancient EGYPT until *c*.1200 BC, but with the waning of Egyptian influence, Phoenicia reached the height of its power and prosperity. Its major city-states were at TYRE, SIDON and BYBLOS. Phoenicians were notable traders and navigators, dominating trade in the Mediterranean throughout the BRONZE AGE. There is evidence that they traded for tin in Britain, reached the Iberian Peninsula, and sailed as far as W Africa. Exports included the famed cedar of Lebanon, metalwork, glass (glassblowing was invented in Phoenicia by the 1st century BC), salt, linen and cloth dyed in the traditional Tyrian purple. Phoenicians established colonies along their major trade routes, including CARTHAGE, which came to dominate trade in the W Mediterranean. As early as 1500 BC, Phoenicians developed their own 22-consonant alphabet in place of the CUNEIFORM systems used by their contemporaries, and it is the basis of today's Roman alphabet. After a period of HITTITE control, Phoenicia regained independence but then was forced to pay tribute to SHALMANESER III and TIGLATHPILESER III of ASSYRIA in the 9th and 8th centuries BC. In 573 BC it fell to NEBUCHADNEZZAR II of BABYLONIA. Under the rule of the ACHAEMENID dynasty of PERSIA (538–332 BC), Phoenicia maintained itself as a major naval power. In 332 BC Tyre finally capitulated to ALEXANDER III (THE GREAT) and Phoenicia was absorbed into Hellenistic culture. *See also* CANAAN

Phoenix Park murders (6 May 1882) Assassination in Dublin, SE Ireland, of Lord Frederick CAVENDISH, British

▲ **Phoenicia** This limestone coffin held the body of Hiram of Byblos (active 10th century BC), who expanded the Phoenician empire and, allied with Solomon, built the Temple of Jerusalem.

P

chief secretary for Ireland, and his undersecretary Thomas Burke. Five of the murderers, from a terrorist group known as the Invincibles, an offshoot of the FENIAN MOVEMENT, were hanged; three were imprisoned. Widespread revulsion against terrorism increased support for Charles PARNELL's moderate HOME RULE Party.

Photius (*c*.820–91) Patriarch of Constantinople, who defended the traditions of the Eastern ORTHODOX CHURCH against Rome. In 858 Photius was elected to succeed the deposed patriarch, St Ignatius of Constantinople. In 862 Pope NICHOLAS I declared the election invalid. In 867 Photius summoned the Fourth Council of CONSTANTINOPLE and withdrew from communion with Rome. Deposed in 867 in favour of Ignatius, he was reinstated in 878. He is a saint in the Orthodox Church. His feast day is 6 February.

Phrygia Historic region of W central Anatolia. A prosperous kingdom was established by the Phrygians, immigrants from SE Europe, early in the 1st millennium BC, with its capital at Gordian. Their last king, the legendary MIDAS, was overthrown by the Cimmerians in *c*.700 BC. In the 6th century BC, Phrygia was taken over by LYDIA and subsequently by Persia and later empires.

physiocrats School of 18th-century French economists. Led by François QUESNAY, they argued that agriculture, rather than industry or commerce, was the basis of all wealth. They had some influence in France under LOUIS XV and in Austria under JOSEPH II. The British economist Adam SMITH was strongly influenced by the physiocrats' belief that governments should not interfere in economic affairs. *See also* LAISSEZ-FAIRE

Piast First ruling dynasty of Poland (966–1370), founded in legend by a peasant farmer in the late 9th century. The first known ruler was **Mieszko I** (r. *c*.962–92), who converted to Christianity in 966, a date taken to mark the beginning of the Polish kingdom, and captured POMERANIA and SILESIA. Mieszko's son, BOLESŁAW I (THE BRAVE) (r.992–1025), further expanded the dynastic lands, at the expense of Emperor HENRY II. In 1079 BOLESŁAW II (THE GENEROUS) executed for treason the bishop of Kraków, later Saint STANISLAUS. The authority of the Piast dynasty diminished until the reign (1102–38) of BOLESŁAW III (THE WRY-MOUTHED), who successfully defended the realm from Emperor HENRY V and recaptured Pomerania. WŁADISŁAW I (THE SHORT) (r.1320–33) defeated the Teutonic Knights and Poland was reunited. His son, CASIMIR III (THE GREAT), the last of the dynasty (r.1333–70), was one of Poland's greatest rulers. He codified the law, encouraged commerce and culture, gained GALICIA and admitted Jewish refugees. Casimir was succeeded by his nephew, LOUIS I. *See also* JAGIELLON

Pibul Songgram (1897–1964) Thai field marshal and statesman, prime minister (1938–44, 1948–57). He was a leader of the coup in 1932 that ended the absolute authority of King Prajadhipok. As minister of defence (1934–38), Pibul encouraged the creation of a nationalistic, militaristic society. A year after becoming prime minister, he changed the country's name from Siam to THAILAND. In 1941 Pibul welcomed the Japanese invasion of Thailand and in 1942 joined the Axis forces in World War 2. Thai resistance to Japanese occupation intensified, however, and Pibul was deposed. He returned to power after an army coup and, as part of a wider campaign against communism in Southeast Asia, lent military support to South Korea during the KOREAN WAR (1950–53). He was instrumental in the establishment of the SOUTHEAST ASIA TREATY ORGANIZATION (SEATO). Pibul was deposed by a military coup and fled into exile.

Pichegru, (Jean) Charles (1761–1804) French general in the FRENCH REVOLUTIONARY WARS. Pichegru was regarded as a national hero after conquering the Austrian Netherlands in 1794–95, but soon afterwards he began secret talks with the royalist ÉMIGRÉS. In 1796 Pichegru resigned from the army to take up a seat in parliament, but word of his intrigues leaked out and he was deported. He returned secretly in 1804, but was again arrested after plotting to overthrow Napoleon. He was found dead in his cell.

Pickering, Timothy (1745–1829) American statesman and soldier. During the American Revolution, Pickering was adjutant general (1777–78) and quartermaster general (1780–85). He served as postmaster general (1791–95), secretary of war (1795) and secretary of state (1795–1800) under presidents George WASHINGTON and John ADAMS. As senator (1803–11) and representative (1813–17) from Massachusetts, he led the FEDERALIST PARTY opposition to presidents Thomas JEFFERSON and James MADISON.

Pickett, George Edward (1825–75) Confederate general in the American CIVIL WAR. In the Battle of GETTYSBURG (July 1863), under the command of James LONGSTREET, he led three brigades in "Pickett's Charge", a desperate attempt to break Union lines, in which more than half of his 4300 men were killed or wounded. *See also* LEE, ROBERT EDWARD; MEADE, GEORGE GORDON

Picts (Lat. *picti*, painted) Ancient inhabitants of Scotland north of the River Forth. Their name probably derives from their custom of body-painting. In the 3rd century AD, the Picts launched devastating raids on the Roman colonies to the S of HADRIAN'S WALL.. By the 4th century they had divided into two kingdoms. The northern kingdom adopted Christianity in the 4th century and the southern kingdom converted in the 5th century. The Picts reunited in the 7th century, making their ceremonial capital at Scone. They fought against the Saxons and the Scots. In 843 the Picts were defeated by KENNETH I, the king of the Scots . *See also* CELTS

Pieck, Wilhelm (1876–1960) German statesman, president (1949–60) of the German Democratic Republic (East Germany). He was a member of the SPARTACUS LEAGUE, which mounted an abortive communist coup (1919) in Berlin. He served in the REICHSTAG (German parliament) during the WEIMAR REPUBLIC, but fled to the Soviet Union when Adolf HITLER became chancellor (1933). Pieck returned to Germany at the end of World War 2. He became president of the Soviet zone of East Germany at its creation, but real power lay with Walter ULBRICHT.

Piedmont Region of NW Italy. Almost entirely surrounded by mountains, Piedmont was a prosperous province of the Roman Empire and later formed part of Lombardy. From the 11th century it was held by the dukes of SAVOY, who later took the title prince of Piedmont and made Turin their capital. In 1720 they became kings of SARDINIA. In the early 19th century Piedmont was a centre of the RISORGIMENTO movement for Italian independence, and in 1861 VICTOR EMMANUEL II, the king of Piedmont-Sardinia, became king of Italy. Pop. (1991) 4,302,565.

Pierce, Franklin (1804–69) Fourteenth president of the United States (1853–57). His personal life was plagued by alcoholism and the tragic deaths of his sons. His father was a governor of New Hampshire, and Pierce represented the state as a Democrat in Congress (1833–42). In 1837 he became the youngest member of the Senate. Pierce was a loyal supporter of President Andrew JACKSON and a close associate of Jefferson DAVIS. He left politics to concentrate on family life and his law practice. He later fought in the MEXICAN WAR (1846–48). In 1852, as a pro-slavery Northerner, Pierce became the compromise choice for the Democratic presidential nomination and narrowly defeated General Winfield SCOTT in the ensuing election. As president, he supported the notion of MANIFEST DESTINY, acquiring present-day S Arizona and S New Mexico through the GADSDEN PURCHASE (1853) with Mexico. His attempt to purchase Cuba from Spain led to the disastrous OSTEND MANIFESTO (1854), which was hastily disclaimed by the government. Pierce endorsed the KANSAS-NEBRASKA ACT (1854), which repealed the MISSOURI COMPROMISE (1820), and resulted in near-civil war in KANSAS and the formation of the Republican Party. Pierce was discredited by the government's inept handling of the latter two issues and was not nominated for a second term. In retirement he incurred further hostility in the North by criticising the ABOLITIONISTS and President Abraham LINCOLN's conduct in the CIVIL WAR.

Pietism Influential Christian spiritual movement within PROTESTANTISM, founded in the late 17th century by the German Lutheran minister Philipp Spener (1635–1705). Its aim was to revitalize evangelical Christianity by spiritual devotion and moral purity, emphasizing the heart rather than the head. Through the MORAVIAN CHURCH, Pietism influenced the religious revivals in Europe and North America in the 18th–19th centuries.

Pilate, Pontius *See* PONTIUS PILATE

pilgrimage Religiously motivated journey to a shrine or other holy place in order to gain spiritual help or guidance, or for the purpose of thanksgiving. Pilgrimages are common to most religions. All Muslims are expected, if possible, to make the pilgrimage to MECCA, Saudi Arabia, the *hajj*, at least once. Christians have made pilgrimages to Jerusalem, to Rome, and to Santiago de Compostela in Spain, among other places, since the days of ancient Rome.

Pilgrimage of Grace (1536–37) Popular rebellion in N England against the REFORMATION legislation of Thomas CROMWELL during the reign of HENRY VIII. The rebels called themselves pilgrims and pledged to defend Roman Catholicism against the supremacy of the king. Local discontent was heightened by poor harvests, economic recession and the imposition of new taxes. The uprising was sparked by the arrival of government commissioners to enforce the DISSOLUTION OF THE MONASTERIES. In October 1536 the rebels captured Lincoln, encouraging a larger revolt of *c*.30,000 pilgrims in Yorkshire, led by Robert Aske. The rebels were soon expelled from Lincoln, but Aske's forces continued to hold York until December, when they were persuaded to disperse on the strength of vague promises by the 3rd Duke of NORFOLK. Further riots provided a pretext for the government to renege on its agreement and *c*.230 rebels, including Aske, were executed.

Pilgrims (Pilgrim Fathers) Group of English Separatists (religious dissidents), who migrated to North America in 1620. The core group, from the East Midlands, had previously emigrated to the Netherlands (1608), but sought greater freedom in the New World. Granted land by the LONDON COMPANY of merchants, they sailed from Plymouth, England, on the MAYFLOWER and founded PLYMOUTH COLONY in present-day MASSACHUSETTS.

Piłsudski, Józef (1867–1935) Polish revolutionary and statesman, head of state (1918–22). In 1887 he was banished to Siberia on a trumped-up charge of plotting to assassinate Tsar ALEXANDER III of Russia. Piłsudski returned to Poland in 1892 and soon became leader of the new Polish Socialist Party (PPS). Imprisoned by the Russians in 1900, he escaped in 1901 and began to form an underground resistance army. During World War 1 he led the Polish Legion against Russia, but forsook the Germans (1917) when they refused to commit on the future status of Poland. When Poland gained independence in 1918, Piłsudski became its first chief of state. He led the Polish army to victory over the Red Army in the RUSSO-POLISH WAR (1919–20) and then retired from politics in 1923. Appalled by the subsequent drift of democratic government amid an economic crisis, Piłsudski led a successful coup in 1926, and installed himself as minister of war, from where he controlled government until his death. A socialist campaign against his authoritarian regime was ruthlessly crushed. With Poland unenviably positioned between the military might of Russia and Germany, Foreign Minister Józef BECK attempted to maintain good relations with both powers. *See also* PADEREWSKI, IGNACY JAN

Pinckney, Charles (1757–1824) American politician, cousin of Charles and Thomas PINCKNEY. He was captured by the British during the American Revolution and later served (1784–87) in the Continental Congress. At the CONSTITUTIONAL CONVENTION (1787), Pinckney submitted the so-called "Pinckney Draught", which heavily influenced the framing of the new Constitution. In 1791 he switched from the Federalist Party to the Jeffersonian Republicans. As minister to Spain (1801–05), he secured Spanish acceptance of the LOUISIANA PURCHASE. He was three times governor of South Carolina, and in Congress (1819–21) he led opposition to the MISSOURI COMPROMISE.

Pinckney, Charles Cotesworth (1746–1825) American politician and soldier, brother of Thomas PINCKNEY. During the American Revolution he fought under George Washington at the battles of Brandywine and Germantown (both 1777). He participated in the CONSTITUTIONAL CONVENTION (1787) with his cousin Charles PINCKNEY. As minister to France (1796–97), Pinckney became embroiled in the XYZ AFFAIR. He ran unsuccessfully as the Federalist candidate for president in 1804 and 1808.

Pinckney, Thomas (1750–1828) American diplomat and soldier. An American Revolution veteran, he was South Carolina's governor (1787–89) and US minister to Great Britain (1792–95). As special envoy to Spain, he negotiated the Treaty of San Lorenzo, or "Pinckney's Treaty" (1795), which resolved the borders between US and Spanish territories. Pinckney was the Federalist vice-presidential candidate (1796). He returned to active service during the WAR OF 1812.

Pinkerton, Allan (1819–84) US detective. After emigrating from Scotland in 1842, he became a detective in the Chicago police force, but soon resigned to create his own National Detective Agency (1850). During the American Civil War Pinkerton ran an intelligence service working behind Confederate lines. The Pinkerton Agency revived after the War. It broke up the MOLLY MAGUIRES, and was increasingly employed as an anti-labour force in disputes such as the PULLMAN STRIKE (1894).

Pinochet (Ugarte), Augusto (1915–) Chilean general, military dictator (1973–90). With clandestine US assistance, he led the army coup (September 1973) that overthrew Salvador ALLENDE and established a ruthless dictatorship employing kidnapping, torture and murder against opponents. Pinochet's authoritarian rule did, however, bring economic progress in the late 1970s. Having lost a 1988 referendum, he resigned in 1990 and democracy was restored under Patricio Aylwin. Pinochet remained commander in chief of the army until 1998 and was then made senator for life, gaining immunity from prosecution in Chile. Visiting Britain in 1998, he was arrested after a Spanish judge applied for his extradition to Spain to face charges of human rights violations. Pinochet was held under house arrest until deemed unfit to stand trial and allowed to return to Chile in 2000.

Pinzón, Vicente Yáñez (*c*.1460–*c*.1524) Spanish navigator. He commanded the *Niña* on Christopher Columbus' first voyage to America (1492). His brother Martín Alonso Pinzón (*c*.1441–93) commanded the *Pinta* (another brother, Francisco, was the pilot), which became separated from the main fleet and Martín was accused of treason by Columbus. Vicente later led an expedition (1499–1500) to Brazil, where he discovered the mouth of the River Amazon. In 1505 he was appointed governor of Puerto Rico. Vicente led another voyage to explore the coasts of Brazil and Central America (1508–09).

piracy In international law, robbery on the high seas. Piracy has probably been present since the birth of maritime trade. The VIKINGS wreaked havoc on Western European shipping from the 9th to the 11th century. During the wars in Renaissance Europe, governments commissioned PRIVATEERS to prey on enemy shipping and, after the fighting had ceased, many privateers simply continued their attacks without state authorization, thus becoming pirates. BUCCANEERS, such as Henry MORGAN, proved a major threat to Spanish shipping in the Caribbean in the 16th and 17th century. From the 16th to the 19th century, the BARBARY STATES of North Africa were a notorious haven for Mediterranean pirates. Growing trade, settlement and naval action virtually ended piracy in the Atlantic region in the 18th century.

Pisa City on the River Arno, Tuscany, w central Italy. It was an important Etruscan town, and prospered as a Roman colony after 180 BC. In 1016 Pisa and GENOA combined to expel the SARACENS from Sardinia, and the city also played a major role in the Crusades. In the 12th century Pisa became a powerful maritime republic, primarily through trade with Syria, and many of its landmarks date from this period. A Ghibelline stronghold, Pisa was supported by the German emperors in its battles with FLORENCE and Genoa. Pisa's navy was devastated by Genoa in the Battle of Meloria (1284). In 1406 Pisa was occupied by Florence. The Council of Pisa, which endeavoured to end the GREAT SCHISM in the Catholic Church, met here in 1409. Briefly liberated by France at the start of the Italian Wars (1494–1559), Florence regained control in 1509. Pisa was badly damaged (1944) during World War 2. The city's major sights, a Romanesque cathedral, the baptistry and the famous "Leaning Tower", are all contained in the central Piazza del Duomo. Pop. (1992 est.) 108,000.

Pisistratus (*c*.600–527 BC) (Peisistratus) Tyrant of ATHENS (560–527 BC). He fought with distinction in the war against Megara (*c*.570–565 BC). In 560 BC Pisistratus seized control of Athens, but was overthrown by the aristocratic faction, led by Lycurgus and Megacles, and driven into exile in *c*.555 BC. In 546 BC he inflicted a decisive defeat on the Athenian army and from then on his authority was unchallenged. Pisistratus united Athens through religious reforms, civic rebuilding and the encouragement of Greek culture, all financed by the silver mines of Laurium. He unified Attica through administrative reforms, and established control over the Hellespont (now the DARDANELLES) by recapturing Sigeum. MILTIADES also gained Chersonesus (now Sevastopol) for Athens.

Pitt (the Elder), William (1708–78) British statesman, leading minister (1756–61, 1766–68), father of William PITT (THE YOUNGER). He entered Parliament in 1735, earning the epithet "the Great Commoner" for his ferocious Commons' attacks on the government of Sir Robert WALPOLE. Pitt soon became a leading figure in the Whig opposition gathered around FREDERICK LOUIS, Prince of Wales, and loudly condemned the ministry of the 1st Earl of GRANVILLE for its involvement in the War of the AUSTRIAN SUCCESSION (1740–48). In 1746 GEORGE II was reluctantly persuaded by the Duke of NEWCASTLE and Henry PELHAM to appoint Pitt as paymaster general. Pitt won great popular support by refusing to exploit his post for private profit. Britain's disastrous start to the SEVEN YEARS' WAR (1756–63) compelled George II, in response to popular demand, to invite Pitt to form a government, and in 1757 he formed an alliance with the Duke of Newcastle, who managed Parliament for him. Pitt directed the war effort, concentrating his forces on the conquest of Canada, while supporting Robert CLIVE in India and FREDERICK II (THE GREAT) of Prussia in Europe. Pitt was widely credited for the defeat of the French and the subsequent expansion of the BRITISH EMPIRE. After 1760 the public mood, led by the new king, GEORGE III, was increasingly for peace, and Pitt resigned when the cabinet refused to back his plan to attack Spain. He condemned the Treaty of Paris (1763) and furiously opposed George GRENVILLE's adoption of the STAMP ACT (1765). Pitt was recalled to form a second ministry and, as Earl of Chatham, served as lord privy seal. The government drifted, however, as Pitt fell seriously ill and he was forced to resign. He continued to oppose Lord NORTH's government from the House of Lords, favouring appeasement of the North American colonies at any price short of independence. *See also* FRENCH AND INDIAN WARS

PITT (THE YOUNGER), WILLIAM

William Pitt (the Younger) by John Hoppner (1758–1810). Pitt was born to be a politician. His father was leading minister to George II, while his mother was the sister of George Grenville.

PITT IN HIS OWN WORDS

"Necessity is the plea for every infringement of human freedom. It is the argument of tyrants; it is the creed of slaves."
Speech to the House of Commons (1783)

"England has saved herself by her exertions, and will, as I trust, save Europe by her example."
Speech after the Battle of Trafalgar (1805)

Pitt (the Younger), William (1759–1806) British statesman, prime minister (1783–1801, 1804–06), second son of William PITT (THE ELDER). He entered Parliament in 1781 and became chancellor of the exchequer (1782) under Lord SHELBURNE. Shelburne's ministry soon collapsed, but the succeeding coalition of Lord NORTH and Charles James FOX lacked the backing of GEORGE III, who dismissed it. Pitt, at the age of 24, became Britain's youngest-ever prime minister. Lacking a majority in Parliament, Pitt clung on to power and in the subsequent elections won a comfortable majority. He lacked the backing of a defined party in Parliament, however, and was always dependent on royal patronage. Pitt's immediate task was to deal with the huge burden of national debt (*c*.£250 million) incurred as a result of the AMERICAN REVOLUTION (1775–81). He imposed new taxes, reformed customs and excise duties and created a sinking fund for the purpose of debt repayment. The loss of Britain's North American colonies also entailed a restructuring of Canada, and the CONSTITUTIONAL ACT (1791) divided QUÉBEC into the provinces of Upper Canada and Lower Canada. Pitt assumed greater governmental control of the English EAST INDIA COMPANY (1784), and impeached Warren HASTINGS, the former governor general of BENGAL. Anxious to maintain Britain's tentative economic recovery, Pitt remained neutral at the outbreak of the FRENCH REVOLUTION (1789) and was reluctantly forced into the FRENCH REVOLUTIONARY WARS (1792–1802) in 1793. Faced by a rebellion in Ireland (1798), Pitt passed the Act of UNION (1800), but resigned in favour of Henry ADDINGTON after George III rejected the idea of CATHOLIC EMANCIPATION. Pitt was persuaded to return to power after the resumption of hostilities with France in the NAPOLEONIC WARS (1803–15). He constructed a European coalition against NAPOLEON I. Despite Admiral Horatio NELSON securing British control of the seas with victory at the Battle of TRAFALGAR (1805), the coalition suffered a series of devastating defeats on land. Pitt, worn out by hard work and excessive drinking, died soon after hearing the news of Napoleon's victory at AUSTERLITZ. Pitt had done much to restore national morale and to increase the importance of the position of prime minister, but he had failed to deliver significant social or parliamentary reform. He did not live to see the realization of his ambition to abolish the SLAVE TRADE.

Pius II (1405–64) Pope (1458–64), b. Enea Silvio Piccolomini. He served as a lay member of the Council of BASEL. As secretary to antipope Felix V, he was excommunicated by Eugenius IV. A humanist scholar, he was made imperial poet laureate by Emperor FREDERICK III and, upon being readmitted to the church, acted as a mediator between the German princes and the papacy. Pius succeeded Pope CALIXTUS III. In 1461 he persuaded LOUIS XI of France to repeal the Pragmatic Sanction of Bourges. Pius tried to organize a crusade against the Ottoman Turks, but received little support and led the mission himself. He died en route.

Pius IV (1499–1565) Pope (1559–65), b. Giovanni Angelo Medici. He succeeded PAUL IV, the combative champion of the COUNTER-REFORMATION. In 1562 Pius reconvened the Council of TRENT, achieving considerable success in reconciling the conflicting opinions of Emperor FREDERICK I and PHILIP II of Spain. He began the reform of the catechism and drafted the *Index of Forbidden Books*. He was succeeded by PIUS V.

Pius V, Saint (1504–72) Pope (1566–72), b. Antonio Ghislieri. He served as grand inquisitor of the Roman INQUISITION before succeeding Pope PIUS IV. An austere champion of the COUNTER-REFORMATION, Pius enacted the decrees of the Council of TRENT. He was a strong opponent of nepotism and abuses in the Roman Catholic Church and of immorality in Rome. He increased the per-

P

secution of heretics, expelling Jews from the Papal States and sending troops to aid the crushing of HUGUENOTS in France. He organized the coalition that defeated the Ottoman Turks at the Battle of LEPANTO (1571). His hatred of Protestantism sometimes led to diplomatic error, notably his excommunication of ELIZABETH I of England (1570), which divided the loyalties of English Catholics and made them objects of suspicion. Pius was canonized in 1712.

Pius VI (1717–99) Pope (1775–99), b. Giannangelo Braschi. He succeeded CLEMENT XIV at a time of crisis for the papacy. Pius was unable to prevent Emperor JOSEPH II assuming greater control over the church and granting religious freedoms to non-Catholics in 1781. Faced by French Revolutionary demands for state control over the church, Pius condemned the Revolution. In 1796 French forces under Napoleon invaded the Papal States, and by 1798 they had occupied Rome and established a republic. Pius died in captivity.

Pius VII (1742–1823) Pope (1800–23), b. Barnaba Gregorio Chiaramonti. He was more sympathetic towards the French Revolution than his predecessor, PIUS VI. Pius VII sought a compromise with Napoleon, and in the CONCORDAT OF 1801 secured recognition of Roman Catholicism as France's state religion in return for consecrating Napoleon as emperor (1804). Pius protested when the French added their own provisions to the Concordat and refused to cooperate with Napoleon's CONTINENTAL SYSTEM. The French seized Rome in 1808 and annexed the PAPAL STATES in 1809, whereupon Pius excommunicated Napoleon. He was held captive until the Allied victory (1814) in the Napoleonic Wars and the Congress of Vienna (1814–15) restored most of the Papal States to him. He restored the JESUITS in 1814.

Pius IX (1792–1878) Pope (1846–78), b. Giovanni Maria Mastai-Ferretti. He initially espoused ideas of liberal reform, but popular anti-clericalism changed his views. Pius refused to support the RISORGIMENTO movement of Italian nationalism against Austria and was forced to flee from Rome in the REVOLUTIONS OF 1848. He was restored by NAPOLEON III of France in 1850, and henceforward pursued a conservative agenda. When the PAPAL STATES were seized by the Italian nationalists (1860), Pius refused to acknowledge the new kingdom of ITALY. A French garrison kept him in power in Rome until 1870, when the city was incorporated into Italy. Pius remained a "prisoner" within the VATICAN until he died, after the longest reign in papal history. He defined the doctrine of the Immaculate Conception (1854) and published the Syllabus (1864), which outlined 80 errors – the last of which was the belief that the pope should reconcile himself to "progress, liberalism and modern civilization". In 1869 Pius convened the First VATICAN COUNCIL, which proclaimed the controversial principle of PAPAL INFALLIBILITY. *See also* KULTURKAMPF; ULTRAMONTANISM

Pius X, Saint (1835–1914) Pope (1903–14), b. Giuseppe Melchiorre Sarto. He became cardinal and patriarch of Venice in 1893. Taking his name in memory of Pope PIUS IX, he was a religious conservative who rejected his predecessor Leo XIII's interest in social change and resisted the growing Christian Democracy movement. Pius opposed MODERNISM within the church, placing several modernist texts on the *Index of Forbidden Books*. In 1906 Pius condemned the separation of church and state in France. He was canonized in 1954.

Pius XI (1857–1939) Pope (1922–39), b. Achille Ratti. He succeeded BENEDICT XV. Pius signed the LATERAN TREATY (1929) with Italian dictator Benito MUSSOLINI, in which the sovereignty of the VATICAN CITY was guaranteed in return for official papal recognition of the kingdom of Italy. It also declared Roman Catholicism the official religion of Italy. He formed several international treaties to strengthen the position of Catholicism within Europe and to encourage missionary activity worldwide, especially in Asia. Pius condemned the racist ideology of Mussolini and Hitler and promoted the cause of world peace.

Pius XII (1876–1958) Pope (1939–58), b. Eugenio Pacelli. He served as a papal nuncio in Germany before becoming a cardinal in 1929. As secretary of state under his predecessor PIUS XI, he was responsible for negotiating a concordat (1933) with Nazi Germany. Pius failed to persuade Benito MUSSOLINI to preserve Italy's neutrality at the start of WORLD WAR 2 and remained silent on the persecution of Jews during the Holocaust. He was hostile to the rise of communism in Italy after the War, but was generally supportive of modernism within the church. Seriously ill for much of the last decade of his life, the conservative curia came to dominate the pontificate.

Pizarro, Francisco (*c*.1476–1541) Spanish conqueror of the INCA empire, governor of Peru (1532–41). He was a captain on the expedition (1513), led by Vasco Núñez de BALBOA, that was credited with the European discovery of the Pacific. He subsequently made his fortune in Panama. Pizarro and Diego de ALMAGRO made two voyages (1524–25, 1526–28) down the west coast of South America during which they found evidence of a rich land to the south. Pizarro returned to Spain to gain CHARLES V's approval to conquer the land and set sail with *c*.180 men from Panama in 1531. In November 1532 Pizarro's troops massacred many unarmed Incas at Cajamarca, N Peru, and captured the Inca emperor ATAHUALPA. Pizarro ransomed Atahualpa but, after receiving a massive fortune in gold and silver, broke his pledge and executed the emperor. In 1533 Pizarro occupied the Inca capital, Cuzco, and placed HUASCAR on the throne. Pizarro founded the city of Lima in 1535. A dispute over the divisions of the spoils flared into a war between Pizarro and Almagro. Almagro was captured and executed (1538), and Pizarro was later murdered by supporters of Almagro's son.

Pizarro, Gonzalo (*c*.1502–48) Spanish conqueror, half-brother of Francisco PIZARRO. He fought in the conquest of Peru (1531–33) and became governor of Quito in 1539. Pizarro narrowly escaped death on a disastrous expedition (1541) into the interior of Quito. After the assassination of his half-brother, Pizarro rebelled against the New Laws drafted by Bartolomé de LAS CASAS to protect Native Americans. He killed the Spanish viceroy and proclaimed himself governor of Peru. Pizarro was captured and executed by the new viceroy, Pedro de la Gasca.

Plaatje, Solomon Tshekisho (1877–1932) South African writer and politician, a founder (1912) and first secretary general of what became the AFRICAN NATIONAL CONGRESS (ANC). In 1913 he travelled to Britain to protest against the Natives Land Act, which severely restriced the rights of black South Africans to buy or own land. Plaatje attended the Pan-African Congress (1919) and toured in Europe and North America attempting to raise awareness of the plight of black South Africans. His books include *Sechuana Proverbs....* (1916) and *Mhudi* (1930), one of the first novels by a black African to be published in English.

▲ **Pizarro** Portrait of Francisco Pizarro by Jean Mosnier (1600–56). Pizarro's conquest of the Inca empire was the first stage in the Spanish colonization of South America.

Place, Francis (1771–1854) British radical reformer. A successful tailor, he was active in the early trade UNION clubs and working-class organizations. Place and Joseph HUME led a successful campaign for the repeal (1824) of the COMBINATION ACTS. He was instrumental in securing the passage of the Great REFORM ACT (1832) and the founding of CHARTISM.

plague *See* BLACK DEATH

Plaid Cymru Welsh nationalist political organization, founded 1925. It was originally concerned with furthering the Welsh language and culture, but became political after 1945, embracing the cause of Welsh independence. It won its first parliamentary seat in 1966. A small step towards its ultimate goal was taken with the creation of a Welsh national assembly in 1999.

Plains culture Society of NATIVE NORTH AMERICANS from the grasslands of the Great Plains, between the Mississippi River and the Rocky Mountains. The Plains culture is the Western stereotype of "Indian" society – the teepee, feather head-dresses, the medicine man, elaborate ceremonial rituals (such as the sun dance) and the glorification of the warrior. The majority of the more than 35 tribes of the region were originally nomadic, hunting the huge herds of bison for food, clothes, tools and shelter. The Spanish introduced the horse in the 16th century, and the subsequent increase in hunting by the Plains peoples and European settlers devastated the bison population and destroyed much of the Plains culture. *See also* ARAPAHO; BLACKFOOT; CHEYENNE; COMANCHE; SHOSHONE; SIOUX

Plains of Abraham *See* ABRAHAM, PLAINS OF

Plantagenet English royal dynasty (1154–1485). It encompasses the ANGEVINS, descended from GEOFFREY OF ANJOU and MATILDA, daughter of HENRY I of England. The name derives from Geoffrey of Anjou's habit of wearing a sprig of broom (Lat. *planta genista*) in his hat. The name was first formally adopted (1460) by Richard, Duke of York, the Yorkist claimant in the Wars of the ROSES, to emphasize his descent from EDWARD III. The Plantagenet dynasty ended with RICHARD III's defeat by HENRY VII. *See also* EDWARD I; EDWARD II; HENRY II; HENRY III; HENRY IV; HENRY V; HENRY VI; LANCASTER, HOUSE OF; JOHN; RICHARD I; RICHARD II; YORK, HOUSE OF

Plantation of Ireland Colonization of IRELAND by English and Scottish Protestants in the 16th and 17th centuries. In 1171 HENRY II invaded Ireland, establishing the PALE in E Ireland. MARY I gave formal consent to the colonization of Ireland in 1556, and the increased pace of settlement under ELIZABETH I produced major rebellions (1559, 1568–83, 1594–1603). JAMES I continued Elizabeth's policy and the subsequent exodus of many Gaelic nobles from ULSTER led the City of London to form the plantation of Ulster; the city of Derry was granted (1613) to the citizens of London. Further attacks on Irish nobles by the Earl of STRAFFORD, CHARLES I's lord deputy of Ireland (1633–39), fomented a major rebellion in 1641. During the English Civil War, the Duke of ORMONDE held Dublin for the Royalists until forced to surrender in 1646. Oliver CROMWELL crushed remaining resistance to the Commonwealth by 1652 and veterans of the New Model Army subsequently received substantial Irish estates. The Protestant Ascendancy was established after JAMES II's defeat by WILLIAM III at the Battle of the BOYNE (1690). *See also* LAND LEAGUE

plantation system Form of AGRICULTURE in which a single crop is grown for sale and cultivated on a large scale by a resident workforce. It was characteristic of the colonial West Indies and the American South, where the labour was provided by slaves of African origin. The earliest plantation crop was tobacco. Later, rice and indigo and, by the early 19th century, cotton were important crops. Some plantations covered several square miles and contained all the facilities of a town. After the American Civil War, when SLAVERY was banned, many Southern plantations were broken up.

Plassey, Battle of (23 June 1757) British victory over the forces of Siraj ud Dawlah, nawab of BENGAL, by English EAST INDIA COMPANY troops under Robert CLIVE near Plassey (Palashi) on the River Bhagirthi, West Bengal, E India. The nawab had a unit of French artillery and far larger numbers but was weakened by the suspect loyalty of some of his subordinates, in particular Mir Jafar, who later replaced him. Several thousand Bengalis were killed, but Clive lost only 20 killed and 50 wounded. The victory led to British control of Bengal.

Plataea, Battle of (479 BC) Decisive victory of the Greeks, under the Spartan Pausanias and the Athenian ARISTIDES (THE JUST), in the PERSIAN WARS. Following the withdrawal of the Persian king, XERXES, after his navy's defeat at SALAMIS (180 BC), the Persian army was routed at Plataea, BOEOTIA, and its commander, MARDONIUS, killed. The Battle ended Persian efforts to conquer Greece.

Plate, Battle of the River (13 December 1939) First British naval victory of WORLD WAR 2. The British cruisers *Exeter*, *Ajax* and *Achilles* intercepted the German pocket battleship *Admiral Graf Spee* in the Río de la Plata, South America. Although heavily outgunned, they forced the *Graf Spee* to seek refuge in the neutral harbour of Montevideo, Uruguay. When the time permitted to carry out repairs by international law expired, Captain Langsdorff, erroneously believing heavy British reinforcements had arrived, ordered his ship to be scuttled in the estuary of the Río de la Plata and shot himself.

Plato (*c*.427–347 BC) Ancient Greek philosopher, whose work had enormous influence in ancient times and on Western civilization since the Renaissance. He was a disciple of SOCRATES in Athens and was clearly indebted to him. However, whereas all Plato's work has survived, Socrates is only known through the writings of others, chiefly Plato himself. After the death of Socrates (399 BC), Plato travelled widely, visiting Syracuse, Sicily, during the reigns of the tyrants DIONYSIUS THE ELDER and DIONYSIUS THE YOUNGER. Plato returned to Athens to set up his famous ACADEMY (*c*.387 BC), where his pupils included ARISTOTLE. Most of Plato's 36 works are written in the form of dialogues; they reproduce Socrates' method of teaching by question and answer. Central to Plato's thought is the power of reason to understand and improve the transient, everyday world. Plato's most famous work is the *Republic*, a discussion of justice and government, in which he outlines an ideal state ruled by philosopher-kings.

Platt Amendment (1901) US legislation that provided for the withdrawal of US troops from Cuba after the SPANISH-AMERICAN WAR (1898). Its provisions made Cuba effectively a US protectorate. The Amendment was repealed (1934) by US President Franklin ROOSEVELT as part of his GOOD NEIGHBOR POLICY, although the United States retained the right to maintain its naval base on Guantánamo Bay, SE Cuba.

plebeian Member of the mass of Roman citizens, as distinct from the small PATRICIAN class. In the early years of the Roman Republic, the "plebs" were barred from public office and from marrying patricians. The gulf between the two classes gradually narrowed, however, and by the 3rd century BC there was little legal distinction between them. Under the ROMAN EMPIRE the term lost all legal significance and merely implied lower social CLASS.

Pleistocene Geological epoch of the Quaternary period, which began *c*.2mya and ended with the end of the last Ice Age *c*.10,000 years ago. Human beings and most forms of familiar mammalian life evolved during the Pleistocene.

Plekhanov, Georgi Valentinovich (1856–1918) Russian revolutionary, known as the "father of Russian MARXISM". By 1877 he was a leader of the populist *Zemlya i Volya* (Land and Freedom) party, which had emerged from the NARODNIK movement. Plekhanov was forced to flee by the tsarist regime in 1880. While in exile in Geneva, Switzerland, he wrote *Socialism and Political Struggle* (1883) and *Our Differences* (1885), which attempted to reconcile MARXISM with the economic realities in Russia and highlighted the emergence of an industrial working-class. He outlined a two-stage revolution in Russia: in the first phase, the PROLETARIAT and the BOURGEOISIE would unite to overthrow the tsar; then capitalism would increase the numbers of industrial workers who, organized by a Marxist party of revolutionaries, would produce a second, socialist revolution. In 1898 Plekhanov helped found the Russian Social Democratic Labour Party (RSDLP), but the Party split in 1903: the MENSHEVIKS (minority), led by L. Martov, rejected the BOLSHEVIKS' plan, proposed by Vladimir LENIN, for a highly centralized party of professional revolutionaries. Plekhanov was unable to heal the divisions within the RSDLP. He was a leading figure in the Second INTERNATIONAL, but supported the Allied cause at the start of World War 1. He returned to Russia after the first phase of the RUSSIAN REVOLUTION (February 1917), but opposed the Bolshevik coup in November 1917.

Plessy v. Ferguson (1896) US legal case in which the Supreme Court held that a state law requiring separation of the races on public transportation facilities did not violate the FOURTEENTH AMENDMENT. In effect, the judgment endorsed segregation in state institutions as long as facilities for both races were equal. It was overturned in BROWN V. BOARD OF EDUCATION OF TOPEKA (1954), when the Court held that segregation was inherently unequal. *See also* CIVIL RIGHTS

Plimsoll, Samuel (1824–98) British social reformer. As a Radical member of Parliament (1868–80), he was chiefly responsible for the Merchant Shipping Act (1876), which enforced government inspection of shipping and ended the scandal of "coffin ships", unseaworthy, overloaded vessels that were heavily insured. It also required merchant ships to have marks, subsequently known as the Plimsoll line, painted on their hulls to indicate safe loading limits.

Pliny the Elder (AD 23–79) (Gaius Plinius Secundus) Roman scholar. His one major surviving work is the encyclopedic *Natural History*, which includes anecdote and folklore and is a prime source for ancient scientific knowledge. A keen researcher, Pliny was killed when he ventured too near an eruption of Mount Vesuvius, S Italy.

Pliny the Younger (*c*.AD 62–*c*.113) (Gaius Plinius Caecilius Secundus) Roman writer and administrator. The nephew and adopted son of PLINY THE ELDER, he was a consul (100) and governor of BITHYNIA (*c*.110–113). He is known for his correspondence with the Emperor TRAJAN, which provides a unique insight into life in the ROMAN EMPIRE. *See also* TACITUS

Pliocene Last epoch of the TERTIARY period, which lasted from 5 to 2 mya, preceding the PLEISTOCENE. Forms of animal and plant life were similar to those of today.

PLO *See also* PALESTINE LIBERATION ORGANIZATION

Plotinus (AD 205–70) Ancient philosopher, founder of NEOPLATONISM. In *c*.244 he opened a school in Rome and became a very popular teacher. In essence, Plotinus conceived of the universe as a hierarchy proceeding from matter, through soul and reason, to the One, which imparted a mystical or religious slant to PLATO's theory of forms. His pupil and biographer, Porphyry, compiled and edited Plotinus' writings into 54 books known as the *Enneads*.

Plutarch (*c*. AD 46–120) Greek writer. He practised in many genres, but his best-known work is his *Parallel Lives*, which consists of paired biographies of famous Greeks and Romans. Shakespeare used it as the source for his Roman history plays.

Plymouth Brethren Fundamentalist, evangelical Christian sect that rejects priesthood, founded in Ireland in the late 1820s. It takes its name from the centre established (1831) at Plymouth, Devon, and led by John Nelson Darby. In 1849 they split into two groups, the "Open Brethren"and the stricter "Exclusive Brethren". Further divisions have occurred since.

Plymouth Colony First English colonial settlement in NEW ENGLAND, founded in December 1620. The settlers, mainly separatists from the Church of England known as the PILGRIMS, were sponsored by the LONDON COMPANY of merchants and subsequently granted a patent by the Council of New England (1621). They sailed on the MAYFLOWER and settled on what is now Cape Cod Bay, naming their settlement after their port of departure in S England. They established rudimentary government under the MAYFLOWER COMPACT. During the first winter nearly half the settlers died, but the colony survived independently until 1691, when it merged with the MASSACHUSETTS BAY COLONY.

Pocahontas (*c*.1595–1617) Native American princess, daughter of POWHATAN. According to an account by Captain John SMITH, leader of the JAMESTOWN colonists, she saved his life when he was about to be executed by her father. She was captured by the colonists in 1613, adopted their customs and in 1614 married John ROLFE. In 1616 the Rolfes were received at court in England, but Rebecca, as she was now called, died before returning to Virginia.

Podgorny, Nikolai Viktorovich (1903–83) Soviet statesman, chairman of the presidium (1965–77). A prominent member of the Communist Party in his native Ukraine, he joined the Politburo in 1960 and was promoted to secretary of the Central Committee (1963–65) by Nikita KHRUSHCHEV. After Khrushchev's fall from power (1964), Podgorny was eclipsed by Leonid BREZHNEV and Aleksei KOSYGIN and given the largely ceremonial position of chairman of the presidium, officially head of state. He was replaced in this post by Brezhnev in 1977.

pogrom (Rus. devastation) Mob attack on Jews in Russia and Eastern Europe in the late 19th and early 20th centuries. Pogroms were partly encouraged by tsarist policy and connived at or instigated by local authorities. In 1881 Jews were persecuted in many Russian cities (notably KIEV) after the circulation of false stories of Jewish involvement in the assassination of Nicholas II. Attacks continued in a more sporadic fashion until the period 1903–06. Forty-five Jews were murdered and more than 1500 Jewish residences looted in Kishinev (now Chisinau, Moldova) in 1903 and thousands of Jews were killed in pogroms (notably Odessa) after the failed RUSSIAN REVOLUTION OF 1905. In the RUSSIAN CIVIL WAR (1918–20), hundreds of thousands of Jews were murdered by the White Guard in Ukraine. Pogroms also occurred under Nazi rule in the 1930s, especially in Poland. In the face of such virulent ANTI-SEMITISM many Jews emigrated to Western Europe and the United States. *See also* HOLOCAUST; KRISTALLNACHT

Poincaré, Raymond (1860–1934) French statesman, president (1913–20) and prime minister (1912–13, 1922–24, 1926–29). In his first term as prime minister, Poincaré strengthened France's alliance with Russia and Britain in preparation for what he considered to be the inevitable outbreak of WORLD WAR 1. As president, Poincaré worked to preserve national unity, even accepting his arch-rival Georges CLEMENCEAU as prime minister in 1917. He took a tough stance towards Germany at the VERSAILLES peace conference (1919), and ordered French troops to occupy (1923) the RUHR to force Germany's payment of REPARATIONS. Poincaré's last ministry confronted a major economic crisis, and he managed to save the French currency from collapse.

Point Four Program US foreign policy to share its scientific and technological knowledge with less developed countries, as part of its international defence against communism. The plan received its name after it was first proposed by President Harry TRUMAN as the fourth point in his inaugural address (1949). It was the first of a variety of technical-assistance initiatives. *See also* MARSHALL PLAN; TRUMAN DOCTRINE

Poitiers, Battle of (19 September 1356) Decisive English victory that brought to an end the first phase of the HUNDRED YEARS' WAR. EDWARD THE BLACK PRINCE was leading his *c*.7000 troops on a profitable raid from Bordeaux when they encountered the numerically superior French at Poitiers, W central France. Edward chose a battlefield on marshy ground with a narrow front, thus negating the French numerical superiority and making the French knights easy prey for the English archers. French casualties were *c*.2500. JOHN II of France was captured and forced to accept the humiliating terms of the Treaty of BRÉTIGNY. *See also* CRÉCY, BATTLE OF

Poland *See* country feature, page 330

Poland, Partitions of (1772, 1793, 1795) Dismemberment of POLAND, which was enfeebled through civil war and lack of a strong central government, by Russia, Prussia and Austria. Russia's crushing victories over the OTTOMAN EMPIRE during the RUSSO-TURKISH WARS alarmed Austria, and FREDERICK II (THE GREAT) of Prussia proposed the **First Partition** of Poland in order to preserve the peace. The division reduced the land area of Poland by one-third: Russia gained much of E Poland; Prussia acquired Royal Prussia and Great Poland; and Austria received Little Poland (later known as GALICIA).

Polish resentment resulted in a strong movement for liberal reform, and Russia and Poland intervened (1792) to protect their interests. The **Second Partition** gave Russia most of Lithuanian Belorussia and the w UKRAINE, while Prussia acquired GDAŃSK. Tadeusz KOSCIUSZKO led a national revolt against the Second Partition, resulting in a further Russia-Prussia invasion. The subsequent **Third Partition** entirely eliminated Poland from the world map until 1918. *See also* BAR, CONFEDERATION OF; CATHERINE II (THE GREAT); STANISLAW II AUGUSTUS

Pole, Reginald (1500–58) English prelate, last Roman Catholic archbishop of Canterbury (1556–58). Pole opposed HENRY VIII's divorce from CATHERINE OF ARAGON and in 1532 fled to Padua, N Italy, where he continued to oppose the Henrician Reformation. In 1536 Pope PAUL III made Pole a cardinal, and Pole embarked on several futile diplomatic missions to drum up support for a Catholic war against Henry. Pole returned to England as papal legate after the accession (1553) of the Catholic MARY I. She made him archbishop of Canterbury, but the Catholic restoration was unpopular, and the burning of Protestant heretics did not improve Pole's popularity. He died on the same day as Mary.

police Government organization charged with maintenance of law and order. In AD 6 the Roman Emperor AUGUSTUS created one of the first organized police forces, a military force of three cohorts, each consisting of 1000 freedmen. Other military systems of policing included the SAMURAI in 17th-century Japan. Before the French Revolution (1789), the French police were a political force, controlled by the monarch. The French Ministry of Police was created in 1796, and, under the direction of Joseph FOUCHÉ, its network of agents crushed all potential opposition to the Revolution. In 1826 Tsar NICHOLAS I of Russia formed a political police force, the precursor of Russia's CHEKA and KGB, and Germany's GESTAPO. In Britain, communal policing before the Industrial Revolution depended on a few part-time local officials, such as constables and nightwatches. Serious disorder was dealt with by the militia or army. In the stipendary police system, local communities paid a standard range of fees to private citizens for the arrest and conviction of criminals. This system gave rise to widespread abuse and corruption. The rise of urban crime in the 19th century led to the formation of regular, full-time, uniformed, police forces, one of the earliest

POLAND

AREA: 312,680sq km (120,726sq mi)
POPULATION: 38,356,000
CAPITAL (POPULATION): Warsaw (1,653,300)
GOVERNMENT: Multiparty republic
ETHNIC GROUPS: Polish 98%, Ukrainian 1%
LANGUAGES: Polish (official)
RELIGIONS: Christianity (Roman Catholic 94%, Orthodox 2%)
GDP PER CAPITA (1995): US$5440

Republic in central Europe. Slavs inhabited parts of the area in the 3rd century AD and moved into much of the rest in the 5th century. The first Polish state, Great Poland, was established in the N under Mieskzo I (*c*.963–92), who adopted Christianity. His son, BOLESŁAW I (r.992–1025), established a larger state, which incorporated southern or Little Poland. The kingdom disintegrated in the 12th century, but unity was re-established under the PIAST kings LADISLAS I (r.1305–33) and CASIMIR III (THE GREAT) (r.1333–70). In 1386 the marriage of Jagiello, grand duke of Lithuania, to the Piast crown princess resulted in the creation of Poland-Lithuania under the JAGIELLON dynasty.

In the late 15th and early 16th centuries Poland-Lithuania lost some territory to Russia while gaining other lands, such as Livonia. During the reign (1648–68) of JOHN II it was plundered by both Turks and Russians before being invaded and occupied by the Swedes (1655–58). Greatly weakened, in 1667 Poland lost the E Ukraine and Smolensk to Russia. JOHN III (r.1674–96) restored some prestige, but Poland then became a major theatre of the Great NORTHERN WAR (1700–21). By 1717 PETER I (THE GREAT) of Russia had turned it into a protectorate. In 1733 an international dipute over who should be king of Poland led to the War of the POLISH SUCCESSION (1733–38). In 1772, 1793 and 1795 Poland was divided up between Austria, Prussia and Russia in a series of partitions (*see* POLAND, PARTITIONS OF). Tadeusz KOSCIUSZKO led resistance.

In 1807 NAPOLEON I created the Grand Duchy of WARSAW under the king of SAXONY. The duchy collapsed after the Battle of LEIPZIG (1813), and at the Congress of VIENNA (1814–15) parts were given to Prussia and Austria. The remainder became a semi-independent Polish state based on KRAKÓW, with the Russian tsar as king. Polish uprisings in 1830, 1848 and 1863 against Russian dominance led to further repression. In World War 1 Poland initially fought with Germany against Russia, but Germany occupied Poland. In 1918 Poland regained its independence under Józef PIŁSUDSKI and Ignacy PADEREWSKI. In 1920 Poland recaptured Warsaw from Russia and in 1921 it became a republic.

The 1920s and 1930s were a period of dictatorship and military rule. In September 1939, following the NAZI-SOVIET PACT between Adolf Hitler and Joseph Stalin, Germany invaded and Poland was partitioned between the Soviet Union and Germany. Britain declared war, thus beginning WORLD WAR 2. Following the German invasion of the Soviet Union, all of Poland fell under German rule. The Nazis established concentration camps, such as AUSCHWITZ. More than 6 million Poles perished. Only 100,000 Polish Jews out of a pre-war total of more than 3 million, survived the HOLOCAUST. Polish resistance, led by Władysław SIKORSKI, intensified. In 1944 a provisional government was established. The WARSAW UPRISING (August 1944) was ruthlessly crushed by the Germans. In 1945 Poland regained its independence; land was lost in the E to the Soviet Union, but part of East Prussia (formerly POMERANIA) was gained from Germany.

In 1949 Poland joined the COUNCIL FOR MUTUAL ECONOMIC ASSISTANCE (COMECON). In 1952 Poland became a People's Republic, modelled on the Soviet constitution. In 1955 it was one of the founder members of the WARSAW PACT. Uprisings in 1956 led to the formation of a more liberal administration, led by Władysław GOMUŁKA. The collectivization of agriculture was reversed, and restrictions on religious worship were relaxed. Gomułka was succeeded by Edward GIEREK in 1970. In 1980 striking dockers in GDAŃSK, led by Lech WAŁESA, formed the SOLIDARITY trade union. In 1981 General JARUZELSKI declared martial law – Solidarity was banned and its leaders arrested. In 1983 continuing recession and civil unrest led to the lifting of martial law. Following reforms in the Soviet Union, Solidarity was legalized and won free elections in 1989.

In 1990 the Communist Party was disbanded, and Wałesa became president. In 1995 elections, Wałesa was defeated by the leader of the Democratic Left Alliance, Aleksander Kwaśniewski. Poland faced huge problems in the transition to a market economy. In 1996 it joined the ORGANIZATION FOR ECONOMIC COOPERATION AND DEVELOPMENT (OECD). Elections in 1997 were won by the Solidarity Electoral Alliance (AWS), a centre-right coalition. In 1999 Poland became a member of NATO.

being the Metropolitan Police in London, founded (1829) by Robert PEEL (who had earlier created the more military Irish Constabulary). The Metropolitan Police served as a model for the New York City Police Department (established in 1844). *See also* HUNDRED

Polignac, Auguste Jules Armand Marie de (1780–1847) French statesman, prime minister (1829–30). A fervent royalist, he was imprisoned (1804–13) for conspiracy against Napoleon I. In 1820 he was made a prince by the pope. Impressed by his commitment to the monarchy and ULTRAMONTANISM, CHARLES X appointed Polignac as prime minister. He issued the Four Ordinances that precipitated the JULY REVOLUTION of 1830. Polignac was imprisoned (1830–36) and later exiled (1836–45).

polis *See* CITY-STATE

Polish Corridor Strip of land along the River Vistula, providing landlocked Poland with access to the Baltic Sea and dividing East Prussia from the rest of Germany. It was created by the Treaty of VERSAILLES (1919) after World War 1, when Poland gained independence. The port of Danzig (GDAŃSK) was made a free city but, in practice, was dominated by Germans. Despite the fact that the Corridor was part of Poland before the Partitions of Poland and that it had a majority Polish population, the arrangement caused conflict between Germany and Poland, exploited by Adolf HITLER to justify his invasion of Poland in 1939.

Polish Succession, War of the (1733–38) Conflict between supporters of rival candidates for the elective Polish throne after the death (1733) of AUGUSTUS II (THE STRONG), which involved all the major continental powers and was fought in Italy, Germany, France and Spain. Austria and Russia backed the claim of Augustus II's son, Frederick Augustus II of Saxony, while France and Spain supported STANISLAW I (LESZCZYŃSKI). Stanislaw had previously been king of Poland (1704–09), held a majority of the votes of the Polish nobility, and was the father-in-law of LOUIS XV of France. When Stanislaw refused to abdicate, ANNA IVANOVNA sent 30,000 Russian troops to Poland, forcing Stanislaw to flee to GDAŃSK, where he was besieged by Russian forces and, after an abortive French rescue mission, surrendered in 1734. Meanwhile, in revenge for Emperor CHARLES VI's support of the Russian action, France occupied Lorraine, while Spain captured Naples and Sicily and Don Carlos was crowned CHARLES III. The Italian campaign ground to a halt, however, as the French advance faltered in Lombardy, and Spain and Savoy fell out over the division of spoils. A preliminary settlement at the Treaty of Vienna (1735) was finally ratified in 1738. It confirmed Frederick Augustus as AUGUSTUS III of Poland, while Stanislaw received Lorraine until his death, when it would revert to France; the current Duke of Lorraine, the future Emperor FRANCIS II, was given Tuscany in compensation. The French also recognized the PRAGMATIC SANCTION.

Politburo (political bureau) Chief executive body (1917, 1919–91) of the COMMUNIST PARTY OF THE SOVIET UNION (CPSU). The first Politburo was established (1917) by the BOLSHEVIKS just prior to their coup against the provisional government. Its members included Vladimir LENIN, Leon TROTSKY and Joseph STALIN. Stalin established the supremacy of the general secretary of the CPSU within the Politburo. In 1952 the Politburo was expanded and renamed the **Presidium**. Its increased powers were evident when it dismissed Nikita KHRUSHCHEV as general secretary in 1964. In 1966 its name reverted to the Politburo. The Politburo usually consisted of the minister of defence, the head of the KGB and the leaders of the various republics. The general secretary of the CPSU acted as chairman. In 1991 the Communist Party was banned in Russia. The Chinese Politburo was modelled on the Soviet body.

Polk, James Knox (1795–1849) Eleventh president of the United States (1845–49). He entered politics through the Tennessee legislature and was elected to the House of Representatives (1825–39), serving as Democratic leader in the House (1828–35) under President Andrew JACKSON and speaker of the House (1835–39) under President Matin VAN BUREN. Polk was governor of Tennessee (1839–41) and became the compromise Democratic candidate for president in 1844. He won the ensuing election against the Whig Henry CLAY, thanks largely to James BIRNEY splitting Clay's vote in New York, and became the youngest president up to that time (aged 49). Polk believed wholeheartedly in the MANIFEST DESTINY of the United States, and his presidency was marked by the rapid expansion of the FRONTIER. He also upheld the MONROE DOCTRINE as the linchpin of US foreign policy in the Western Hemisphere. Having helped to provoke the MEXICAN WAR (1846–48), Polk gained California and New Mexico by the Treaty of GUADELOUPE HIDALGO (1848). He also added Oregon to the United States as a result of the OREGON TREATY (1846). His domestic policy aroused strong opposition, but he succeeded in reducing tariffs and reconstructing an independent treasury system. Polk, who died within three months of leaving office, was an unspectacular but extremely successful president. He maintained a neutral stance over the WILMOT PROVISO (1846) to ban SLAVERY in the new territories, but could not prevent the Democrats fracturing over the issue. He was succeeded as president by the Mexican War hero and Whig candidate, Zachary TAYLOR. *See also* FRÉMONT, JOHN CHARLES; KEARNY, STEPHEN WATTS; SCOTT, WINFIELD

poll tax Tax on individuals, usually a fixed sum per head. Such taxes were occasionally levied by medieval governments to raise revenue in emergencies. Unpopular, an English poll tax provoked the PEASANTS' REVOLT (1381). Southern states of the United States after the American Civil War made the right to vote dependent on payment of a poll tax, a device to disenfranchise African-Americans. Its use in federal elections was declared unconstitutional by the 24th Amendment (1964) to the Constitution of the United States. In Britain in 1989 the Community Charge, popularly known as the poll tax, caused violent riots and helped to bring down Margaret THATCHER.

Polo, Marco (*c*.1254–1324) Venetian merchant and traveller. The only details we have of his life come from his classic travelogue, *Il milione* ("The Million"), otherwise known as the *Travels of Marco Polo*. In 1271 he accompanied his father, Niccolò, and uncle, Maffeo, on a trading mission to the court of KUBLAI KHAN, the Mongol emperor of China. The elder Polos had made the journey along the old SILK ROAD before, benefiting from the opening up of Asia after the Mongol conquest, and had acted as Kublai's emissaries to the pope. According to Marco Polo's account, the party arrived at Kublai Khan's summer court at Shangdu in *c*.1275, where they remained for the next *c*.17 years. Marco became the confidant of the emperor, travelling to (among other places) Sichuan and Yunnan, SW China, Hangzhou, SE China, and perhaps even to Burma. In *c*.1292 the Polos were chosen to escort a fleet bearing a Mongol princess to Iran, before returning to Venice in 1295. Captured by the Genoese navy in 1298, Marco recounted his tales to a fellow prisoner, a writer of romances named Rustichello. It was first published in English as *The Description of the World*, probably the most famous travel book ever written. Although highly embellished, many of his descriptions and directions proved accurate and furnished European explorers, such as Christopher Columbus, with valuable geographical information. However, Marco Polo does not appear in Chinese records, and some scholars have suggested that he never went to China at all.

Pol Pot (1928–98) Cambodian ruler. In 1975 he led the communist KHMER ROUGE in the overthrow of the US-backed government of Lon Nol. Pol Pot instigated a reign of terror in CAMBODIA (renamed Kampuchea). Intellectuals were massacred and city-dwellers were driven into the countryside. Estimates suggest that *c*.2 million Cambodians were murdered. In 1979 Pol Pot was overthrown by a Vietnamese invasion, but continued to lead the Khmer Rouge in guerrilla warfare from a refuge in N Cambodia. In 1997, after a rift in the Khmer Rouge, it was reported that Pol Pot had been sentenced to life imprisonment. He died shortly afterwards, perhaps of heart failure. *See also* HUN SEN; NORODOM SIHANOUK

Poltava, Battle of (8 July 1709) Decisive victory of Russia over Sweden in the Great NORTHERN WAR. CHARLES XII and his *c*.17,000 Swedish troops besieged the city of Poltava, Ukraine, but were confronted by *c*.80,000 better-armed Russian soldiers led by PETER I (THE GREAT) and Prince MENSHIKOV. All but *c*.1500 of the Swedish army were killed or captured, and Charles retreated to Poland. Although the War continued for a further twelve years, Poltava marked the end of Swedish supremacy and the beginning of Russia dominance in N Europe.

Polybius (*c*.200–*c*.118 BC) Greek historian. A leader of the ACHAEAN LEAGUE, he was deported as an honoured hostage to Rome in 168 BC. Polybius became a friend of SCIPIO AFRICANUS MINOR and accompanied him to Spain and Africa. He was present at the destruction of CARTHAGE in 146 BC. After the defeat of Achaea by Rome, Polybius successfully intervened to mitigate the terms imposed on Achaea. He is chiefly remembered, however, for his epic *Universal History* (40 vols), a didactic account of Roman history from 264 to 145 BC. The first two books form an introduction, describing events between 264 and 220 BC. Only volumes I to V have survived, but they include his account of HANNIBAL's campaigns in Italy. *See also* PLINY THE ELDER; THUCYDIDES

Pombal, Sebastião José de Carvalho e Mello, Marquês de (1699–1782) Portuguese statesman. He served as the Portuguese ambassador to London (1739–44) and ambassador to Venice (1745–49). Despite his obvious diplomatic skills, Carvalho was overlooked until the death of JOHN V and the subsequent accession of Joseph (r.1750–77). As minister for foreign affairs (1750–56), he sought to expand Portugal's manufacturing industry and established (with variable success) companies for trade with India and Brazil. Carvalho reacted with determination to the earthquake that shook Lisbon in 1755, instigating a major relief effort and a rapid rebuilding project. His adept handling of the crisis led to his appointment as chief minister (1756–77), and from then on Carvalho was virtual dictator of Portugal. He increased royal power at the expense of the old nobility, the Inquisition and the Jesuits, whom he expelled in 1759. His anti-clericalism and other reforms, such as the abolition of slavery in Portugal, led to him being being classed as an "enlightened despot". He brutally dealt with opposition to his rule, torturing members of the Tavora family to death after an attempted assasination of the king (1758). In 1769 the king created him the Marquês de Pombal. After Joseph's death (1777), he was ousted from power by Maria I and banished from Lisbon.

Pomerania (Pol. Pomorze) Region in N Europe, between the Baltic Sea and the River Vistula, on the borders of Poland and Germany. It acquired its name from the Slavic Pomerani who inhabited the region in the 5th century AD. Pomerania was conquered by Mieskzo I of Poland at the end of the 10th century, and his successor, BOLESŁAW I (THE BRAVE), established a diocese at Kolobrzeg in 1000. The region fragmented in 1107, and the western and central areas saw a mass influx of Germans from the end of the 12th century. **Eastern** Pomerania was held by the TEUTONIC KNIGHTS for most of the 14th century and the first half of the 15th century, before being recaptured by Poland. In 1772 it was occupied by PRUSSIA, becoming the province of West Prussia. It was fully restored to Poland in 1945. **Western** Pomerania remained under Polish rule until ceded to Sweden by the Peace of WESTPHALIA (1648). In 1815 western and central Pomerania were merged into the Prussian province of Pommern. After World War 2, Western Pomerania became part of East Germany. It now forms part of a reunified Germany.

Pompadour, Jeanne-Antoinette Poisson, Marquise de (1721–64) Mistress and confidante of LOUIS XV of France (1745–64). Talented, beautiful and intelligent, she had strong influence at court, even on political appointments, but especially on cultural affairs. A great patron of the arts and architecture, she encouraged Denis Diderot and the *philosophes* to produce the *Encyclopédie* (1751–65) and collaborated on the design of the École Militaire and the Place de la Concorde, Paris. Madame de Pompadour was widely blamed for the reverses in the SEVEN YEARS' WAR, a conflict precipitated by the policies of her protégé, the Duc de CHOISEUL.

Pompeii Ancient Roman city on the Gulf of Naples, S Italy. It was founded in the 8th century BC and ruled by Greeks, Etruscans and Samnites before it was conquered

(89 BC) by the Roman General SULLA during the SOCIAL WAR. In AD 79 it was buried by the unexpected eruption of Mount Vesuvius. The swiftness and violence of the eruption killed *c.*2000 people, including PLINY THE ELDER, and left the city covered up to seven metres (23ft) deep in volcanic ash, preserving public and private buildings, objects, even human corpses, intact. The city lay buried and forgotten until rediscovered in the 16th century. Excavation began first at HERCULANEUM (also buried by the eruption), later at Pompeii (1748). To date, about half the site has been unearthed. Insufficient funding and tourist traffic had caused some deterioration of the visible remains. The largest villa, the House of the Faun (late 2nd century BC), includes a mosaic of ALEXANDER III (THE GREAT)'s victory over Darius III at the Battle of Issus (333 BC).

Pompey (the Great) (106–48 BC) (Gnaeus Pompeius) Roman general and statesman. He initially fought for Gaius MARIUS against Lucius SULLA, but later deserted Lucius CINNA to join Sulla, defeating the Marians in Sicily and Africa (82–81 BC). Pompey crushed the revolt (77 BC) of Marcus LEPIDUS and then united with METELLUS Pius in the reconquest of Spain. He helped in the suppression of the slave revolt by SPARTACUS and was appointed (70 BC) joint consul with Marcus Licinius CRASSUS. In 67 BC he replaced Lucius Licinius LUCULLUS as commander in the East, rapidly defeating MITHRADATES VI (THE GREAT), reorganizing the defence of the frontier, expanding the Roman republic to include Colchis and Syria and increasing his own personal fortune. In 59 he secretly formed the so-called First Triumvirate with Crassus and Julius CAESAR, whose daughter he married. The murder of Publius CLODIUS (52 BC) prompted mob warfare on the streets of Rome. Pompey restored order and was appointed sole consul, whereupon he began to organize against Caesar. The Roman Civil War broke out in 49 BC. Pompey, with his command of the seas and dominance in the East, seemed destined to defeat Caesar, but was disastrously defeated at PHARSALUS (48 BC). Pompey fled to Egypt, where he was murdered by PTOLEMY XIII. *See also* CICERO

Pompidou, Georges Jean Raymond (1911–74) French statesman, premier (1962–68) and president (1969–74). He was a close adviser of Charles DE GAULLE from 1944, helping to draw up the constitution of the Fifth Republic. He conducted secret negotiations with the FRONT DE LIBÉRATION NATIONALE (FLN), producing a cease-fire (1961) in the Algerian War of Independence. De Gaulle rewarded him with the post of prime minister. Pompidou persuaded workers to abandon their strike during the student riots in May 1968, and his call for a return to law and order earned the Gaullists a huge majority in the June 1968 elections. De Gaulle surprisingly dismissed Pompidou as prime minister, but after de Gaulle resigned as president in 1969, Pompidou was elected to succeed him. He took a closer and more effective interest in domestic, especially economic, affairs and ended French resistance to British membership of the European Economic Community.

Ponce de León, Juan (1460–1521) Spanish explorer. A veteran of Christopher COLUMBUS' second voyage to the New World, he founded the first Spanish settlement on PUERTO RICO (1508–09), and acted as the island's governor (1510–12). In 1513 Ponce de León led an expedition to explore an island north of Cuba, allegedly in search of the fountain of eternal youth. He reached the land he named FLORIDA, at a point near St Augustine, and explored the Florida Keys. In 1521 Ponce de León returned to Florida, intending to colonize the region, but was wounded in a battle with Seminole Native Americans. He retreated to Havana, Cuba, where he died.

Pontiac's Rebellion (1763–64) Native American uprising against the British during the FRENCH AND INDIAN WAR. Pontiac (*c.*1720–69) was an Ottawa chief who led a loose confederation of allies hostile to the British conquest of Québec (1759). The various tribes mounted a simultaneous attack on 12 British forts in the Great Lakes region, capturing all but four. Pontiac himself led the assault on Detroit but was betrayed and, despite winning a great victory at the Battle of Bloody Run (July 1763), was forced to withdraw. News of the French withdrawal from North America fatally weakened the campaign, which collapsed completely in the face of sustained British attack. The Rebellion influenced the British PROCLAMATION OF 1763, limiting westward expansion by whites. Pontiac formally made peace in 1766.

Pontius Pilate (active 1st century AD) Roman governor (AD 26–36) of JUDAEA under Emperor TIBERIUS. Jewish historian Flavius JOSEPHUS depicts him as an authoritarian ruler, who insulted the Jewish religion and provoked rebellion. The New Testament presents him as a weak governor, who presided over the sentencing of JESUS CHRIST (*c.*AD 30) after the case had been referred to him by the SANHEDRIN. According to the Gospel accounts, Pontius was swayed by the mob into crucifying Jesus. He was recalled to Rome after the massacre of the SAMARITANS.

Pontus Ancient district in NE Anatolia (now part of Turkey). The coastal cities were colonized by Greeks in the 6th–5th centuries BC and retained virtual autonomy under the Persian empire. After the conquests of Alexander III (the Great), Pontus became an independent kingdom at the close of the 4th century BC. The kingdom of Pontus reached its height during the reign (*c.*115–63 BC) of MITHRADATES VI (THE GREAT), who conquered Asia Minor and threatened Rome. After Mithradates' defeat by POMPEY (66 BC), Pontus was divided: the western region joined with BITHYNIA; the eastern portion became part of Galatia.

Pony Express (1860–61) US relay mail service between Saint Joseph, Missouri, and Sacramento, California. About 25 riders changed horses at 190 staging posts on the 3200km (1800mi) journey. The ride took ten days, less than half the time taken by mail coach. The service never made profit and ended after 18 months when the overland telegraph was completed.

poor laws In British history, legislation to relieve poverty. In the Middle Ages, poor relief was undertaken by the parish and funded by a church tax. Deficiencies in the system forced government intervention, and an act of 1563 enforced a levy per household at a rate set by the local justices. The first coherent system was the Elizabethan Poor Law Act of 1601, which placed responsibility on the parishes to look after their own poor, money being raised by a rate on property. In 1795 the Speenhamland system provided levels of poor relief in cash based on the price of bread and the size of families. The Poor Law Amendment Act (1834) stipulated that relief would only be given to those entering a WORKHOUSE, in an effort to encourage the work-shy to seek employment. It was highly unpopular, cited as a cause of the REBECCA RIOTS in Wales and opposed by the CHARTISM movement. It remained the basis of poor relief until 1929, when poor relief was taken over by county councils. In the 1940s the poor laws were replaced by the creation of the WELFARE STATE. *See also* REFORM ACTS

pope *See* PAPACY

Popish Plot (1678) Fictitious conspiracy to assassinate CHARLES II of England and replace him with his Catholic brother James (later JAMES II) with the aid of French troops. The story of a plot was devised by Titus OATES and Israel Tonge. It was carefully prepared and widely believed. In the general hysteria even those who doubted it dared not speak out and 35 people were executed, including nine Jesuit priests. From 1681 doubts increased, and in 1685 Oates was charged with perjury.

▲ **Pompeii** Objects unearthed at Pompeii in the 18th century, such as this bronze magistrate's stool, provided an insight into Roman life and led to a revival of classical designs in Europe.

popular front Political alliance of left-wing parties. In Europe, such alliances were formed in the 1930s, partly in reaction to the growing threat from FASCISM and with the encouragement of the Soviet Union. The 1935 Congress of COMINTERN proclaimed the need for the formation of a popular front of socialists and communists to fight fascism. A popular-front government under Léon BLUM came to power in France (1936–37). In Spain, the election of a Popular Front (1936–37) government, led by Francisco LARGO CABALLERO, provoked a military revolt by General FRANCO and the Spanish CIVIL WAR (1936–39). *See also* COMMUNISM

populism Political term meaning support for the rights of the ordinary individual. In the late 19th century, populism was strong in the agrarian southern and western states of the United States, who distrusted the Eastern industrial establishment, and gave rise to the POPULIST PARTY. In the same era, the Populist movement in Russia, also agrarian in origin, became associated with revolutionary SOCIALISM. *See also* NARODNIK

Populist Party (officially People's Party) US political organization active in the 1890s. The farming boom from 1877 to 1886 was followed by a decade of crop failures and relative drought across the Plains of the Midwest. The economic depression led to agrarian unrest, initially expressed through Farmers' Alliances and the GRANGER MOVEMENT. The agitation caused discomfort to the ruling Republicans, but lacked a coherent national strategy and thus the Populist Party was created in 1891. The Party allied with the KNIGHTS OF LABOR in the (largely forlorn) hope of appealing both to farmers and to the industrial working-class. The Party favoured an increase in the money supply (largely through FREE SILVER), nationalization of the railroads and a graduated income tax. In the 1892 presidential elections, the Populist candidate James WEAVER polled more than one million votes (8.5% of the vote). In the 1896 presidential elections, the Party lost much of its independent identity by supporting the Democratic candidate, William Jennings BRYAN, who had adopted the free-silver policy. Bryan was defeated and the Populist Party virtually disappeared after 1908. *See also* GREENBACK PARTY; PROGRESSIVE PARTY

Portales, Diego José Victor (1793–1837) Chilean dictator. He made a fortune through a monopoly on trade in tobacco and gradually became leader of the Conservative opposition to the Liberal government. In 1829 he joined forces with former dictator Bernardo O'HIGGINS to defeat the Liberal army and, although appointed vice president, was the leading force in the establishment of an autocratic republic in the 1830s. His dictatorship crushed dissent through arbitrary imprisonment and press censorship. Portales drafted a new constitution (1833), which protected the rights of the church and rich landowners. In 1836 he provoked a war with Peru-Bolivia, but was murdered by Chilean soldiers before Chile's victory.

Porteous Riots (1736) Civil disorder in Edinburgh, Scotland, after the city guard fired into a stone-throwing mob angered by the execution of a smuggler, Andrew Wilson. Several people were killed. To defuse mob violence, John Porteous, captain of the guard, was tried and sentenced to death. Queen Caroline, regent for George II, granted a temporary reprieve, but a huge mob stormed the Tolbooth Prison and hanged Captain Porteous. The city was fined £2000 after a parliamentary inquiry (1737). The incident, partly inspired by JACOBITE sentiment, lost Robert WALPOLE's government support in Scotland and contributed to his downfall (1742).

Portland, William Henry Cavendish Bentinck, 3rd Duke of (1738–1809) British statesman, prime minister (1783, 1807–09). He served as lord lieutenant of Ireland (1782) under the Marquess of ROCKINGHAM before succeeding Lord SHELBURNE as prime minister. Portland was only the nominal head of government, however, as effective power resided with Home Secretary Lord NORTH and Foreign Secretary Charles James FOX. The coalition, lacking the support of GEORGE III, soon collapsed and William PITT (THE YOUNGER) became prime minister. As home secretary (1794–1801) under Pitt (the Younger), Portland quelled the Irish Rebellion of 1798. His second term as prime minister was dominated by the discord between his foreign secretary, George CANNING, and his secretary for war and the colonies, Lord CASTLEREAGH. Portland resigned on grounds of poor health and died shortly after. He was succeeded by Spencer PERCEVAL.

Portsmouth, Treaty of (5 September 1905) Agreement ending the RUSSO-JAPANESE WAR, mediated by US President Theodore ROOSEVELT and signed at Portsmouth, New Hampshire, United States. It confirmed Japan's status as a world power, with Russia recognizing Japan's dominant position in KOREA. While both sides agreed to return MANCHURIA to China, Japan retained strategic railway rights and gained Port Arthur and the Liaoding Peninsula from Russia. Japan also acquired s SAKHALIN Island.

Portugal *See* country feature

Potemkin, Grigori Aleksandrovich (1739–91) Russian field marshal and statesman. He was involved in the coup that brought CATHERINE II (THE GREAT) to power in 1762. Potemkin was for a time her lover and remained almost until his death the most powerful man in Russia. One of the architects of Russian expansion, he was largely responsible for Russian gains during the RUSSO-TURKISH WARS (1768–74, 1787–92). He managed developments in the newly conquered territories of UKRAINE and CRIMEA, including the construction of the naval bases at Kherson (1778) and Sevastopol (1784). His ambitious and costly schemes for the colonization of Ukraine were largely unrealized, but Potemkin successfully disguised the ramshackle nature of the project during Catherine's tour of the region in 1787.

Potemkin Russian battleship whose crew mutinied in the RUSSIAN REVOLUTION OF 1905. Some officers were killed and the crew took over. For fear of the mutiny spreading throughout the Black Sea fleet, the *Potemkin* was not fired on and, after bombarding Odessa, Ukraine, the mutineers sought sanctuary in Romania. The events inspired Sergei Eisenstein's silent motion-picture *Potemkin* (1925).

potlatch Ceremonial exchange of gifts and property among NATIVE NORTH AMERICANS of the Northwest Pacific region, especially the Kwakiutl. The ceremonies were held to celebrate births, marriages, the initiation of a new chief, or to mourn the dead. The size of the gatherings and the lavishness of the goods reflected the status of the donor and thus were often highly competitive occasions. The potlatch was outlawed in Canada by the Indian Act (1884), but the ritual covertly continued until the ban was repealed in 1951.

Potsdam Conference (17 July–2 August 1945) Summit meeting of Allied leaders in WORLD WAR 2, held in Potsdam, a suburb of Berlin, NE GERMANY. The main parties at the talks were US President Harry TRUMAN, Soviet leader Joseph STALIN and the British prime minister, at first Winston CHURCHILL, later his successor Clement ATTLEE. It dealt with problems arising from Germany's defeat in the War, including the division of Germany into four zones of military occupation, the NUREMBERG TRIALS of Nazi war criminals and the return of part of East Prussia (formerly POMERANIA) to Poland. President Truman signalled his willingness to use nuclear weapons in order to end the war with Japan. The disagreements between the Allies over the communist control of parts of Eastern Europe prefigured the start of the COLD WAR between the Soviet Union and the West. *See also* YALTA CONFERENCE

POUM (*Partido Obrero de Unificación Marxista*, or Workers' Marxist Unification Party) Spanish political organization. Founded (1935) by a dissident faction of the PCE (Spanish Communist Party), it was led by intellectual anarchists who had considerable influence (though comparatively few active supporters). After the communists gained control of the republican government during the Spanish CIVIL WAR, it was dissolved (June 1937) and its leader, Andreu Nin, was executed. *See also* POPULAR FRONT

Powell, Colin Luther (1937–) US general. He fought in the Vietnam War (1955–75) and rose through the ranks to become national security adviser (1987–89) and chairman of the joint chiefs of staff (1989–93) during the invasion of Panama and the GULF WAR (1991), the first African American to hold the top military post in the United States. Powell retired from the army in 1993 and resisted pressure to seek the Republican nomination for president.

Powell, (John) Enoch (1912–98) British politician. He entered Parliament as a Conservative in 1950 and was minister of health (1960–63). A maverick intellectual, Powell was dismissed from the shadow cabinet after his controversial "river of blood" speech (April 1968), opposing Commonwealth immigration to Britain. He also opposed British entry into the European Economic Community (EEC) and resigned (1974) from the Conservative Party over the issue. Powell later represented (1974–89) the Ulster Unionists in Parliament.

Powhatan (1550?–1618) (Wahunsenacawh) Chief of the POWHATAN CONFEDERACY of Native Americans, father of POCAHONTAS. From his capital at Werowocomoco, Powhatan initially violently resisted the founding (1607) of a British settlement at JAMESTOWN, Virginia. The colonists' leader, John SMITH, reported how Powhatan was about to have him executed, until the intercession of Pocahontas. In 1614 Pocahontas married the colonist John Rolfe, and Powhatan shortly afterwards made peace with the settlers.

Powhatan Confederacy Algonquian-speaking confederacy of Native North Americans who occupied the region from the Potomac River south to Albemarle Sound, Virginia, in the early 17th century. It comprised *c.*9000 people in more than 30 tribal groups under the leadership of POWHATAN. *See also* POCAHONTAS

Poynings, Sir Edward (1459–1521) English lord deputy of Ireland (1494–96). He supported the future HENRY VII during the Wars of the ROSES and was

PORTUGAL

AREA: 92,390sq km (35,670sq mi)
POPULATION: 9,846,000
CAPITAL (POPULATION): Lisbon (2,561,000)
GOVERNMENT: Multiparty republic
ETHNIC GROUPS: Portuguese 99%, Cape Verdean Brazilian, Spanish, British
LANGUAGES: Portuguese (official)
RELIGIONS: Christianity (Roman Catholic 95%, other Christians 2%)
GDP PER CAPITA (1995): US$12,670

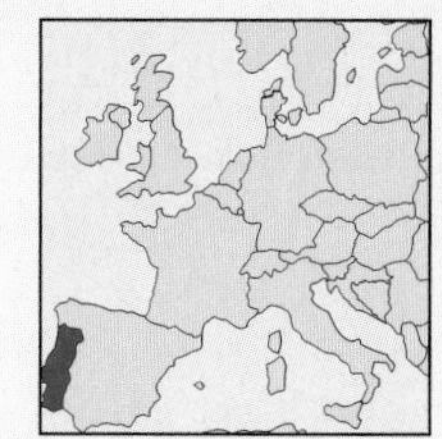

Republic on the w side of the Iberian Peninsula, sw Europe. Portugal also includes the autonomous islands of the AZORES and Madeira. MACAO was returned to China in 1999.

The area came under the control of the Romans in the 2nd century BC. In the 5th century AD it was conquered by the Suebi and then the VISIGOTHS. In 711 all but the N part, known as the County of Portugal, fell to Muslim invaders. In 1139 the County became a kingdom under Alfonso I, who launched a campaign to drive out the Muslim MOORS. The reconquest was completed (1249) when the Moors were removed from the Algarve. In 1385 JOHN I founded the Aviz dynasty and launched Portugal's voyages of EXPLORATION. His son, HENRY THE NAVIGATOR, captured the Azores and Madeira and explored the African coast. During the reign (1481–95) of JOHN II, Bartholomeu DIAS sailed around the Cape of Good Hope. MANUEL I (r.1495–1521) presided over Portugal's golden age when navigators, such as Vasco da GAMA, helped expand Portugal's empire. By 1510 Portugal had established trading settlements on the coasts of Africa, India and Southeast Asia. BRAZIL was claimed for Portugal by Pedro CABRAL in 1500, but settlement was only encouraged by JOHN III (r.1521–57) from 1533.

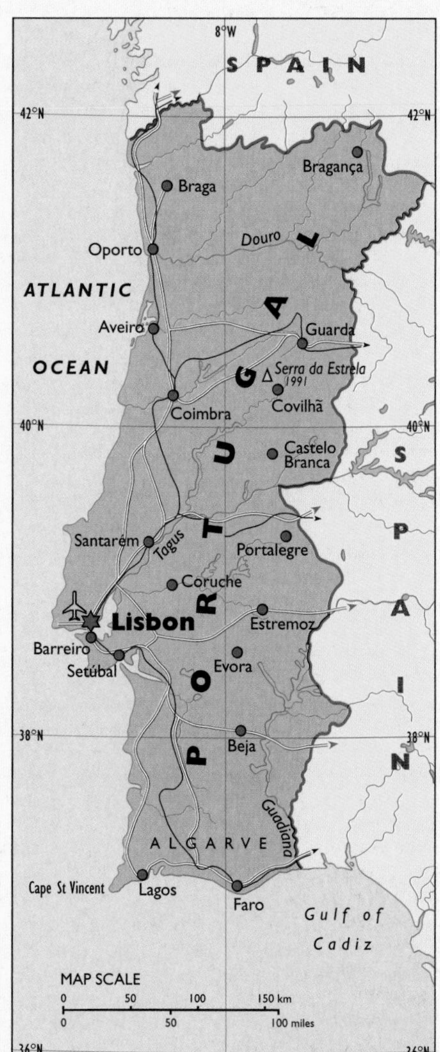

The fall of the Aviz dynasty in 1580 brought PHILIP II of Spain to the throne. For the next 60 years, Portugal was subject to Spanish control. In 1640 PHILIP IV of Spain was overthrown and JOHN IV established the BRAGANZA dynasty, which continued to rule Portugal until 1910. In the 18th century, JOHN V and the Marquês de POMBAL reformed Portugal's institutions and rebuilt LISBON. In 1807 JOHN VI was forced to flee to Brazil to escape the invasion of NAPOLEON I during the PENINSULAR WAR (1808–14). John returned to Portugal in 1821. His son, PEDRO I, declared Brazilian independence in 1822.

In 1828 Portugal was plunged into civil war between the forces of MARIA II and her husband MIGUEL. Republican sentiment continued to grow and in 1908 CHARLES I was assassinated. In 1910 MANUEL II was overthrown and Portugal became a republic. In 1926 a military coup toppled the government. In 1932 António de Oliveira SALAZAR became prime minister. The terms of the 1933 constitution enabled Salazar to become Western Europe's longest-serving dictator. The *Estado Novo* (New State) was repressive and the economy stagnated. In 1968 Salazar was replaced by Marcelo CAETANO. Failure to liberalize the regime and the cost of fighting liberation movements in Portugal's African colonies led to a military coup (1974). In 1975 many Portuguese colonies gained independence. In 1976 a new liberal constitution was adopted under António EANES. In 1986 Portugal joined the European Community, and Mário SOARES became president. Soares was replaced by Jorge Sampaio in 1996. In 1999 Portugal became one of 11 states of the EUROPEAN UNION to adopt the European single currency (the euro).

subsequently sent to Ireland to stamp out possible Yorkist opposition to Henry's rule. He gave his name to **Poynings' Law** (1494), which subordinated the Irish legislature to the English king and PRIVY COUNCIL and made English laws applicable to Ireland. Despite Irish protests, it remained in force until 1782.

praetor Law official in ancient Rome, who dealt with matters of equity and, when the CONSULS were absent, managed the day-to-day affairs of state. Originally restricted to the PATRICIAN class, the post was opened to PLEBIANS in *c.*337 BC. From *c.*242 BC two praetors were elected by the COMITIA: the *praetor urbanus* dealt with all litigation between citizens of Rome; the *praetor peregrinus* handled all civil suits involving foreigners. In the early 1st century BC, the consul Lucius Cornelius SULLA increased the number of praetors to eight. They usually served a one-year term, customarily followed by appointment as provincial governor. The office declined in importance during the Roman Empire.

Praetorian Guard Bodyguard of the Roman emperors. Developed from the force of bodyguards for Roman generals, Emperor AUGUSTUS created (27 BC) a separate Guard of nine cohorts, each consisting of 500 men. It was the only force allowed to be permanently stationed in the environs of Rome itself. Under the command of Lucius SEJANUS from AD 23, the Guard was concentrated at a barracks in Rome. The Praetorian Guard subsequently wielded considerable political power, making and breaking several emperors. In 312 the Guard was abolished by CONSTANTINE I (THE GREAT). *See also* CLAUDIUS I

Pragmatic Sanction (19 April 1713) Decree issued by Holy Roman Emperor CHARLES VI, which sought to prevent the break-up of the HABSBURG empire after his death. Lacking a male heir, Charles settled the succession, hitherto legally confined to males, on his daughter MARIA THERESA. In spite of great diplomatic efforts to gain international acceptance, Charles' death (1740) resulted in the War of the AUSTRIAN SUCCESSION (1740–48), as CHARLES ALBERT of Bavaria and FREDERICK II (THE GREAT) of Prussia disputed the Sanction. *See also* SALIC LAW

Prague (Praha) Capital of the Czech Republic. Founded in the late 9th century, it became a leading centre of trade and culture in central Europe and the national heart of BOHEMIA under the PREMYSLID dynasty. In 929 Saint WENCESLAS capitulated to the Germans and was murdered by his brother, BOLESŁAW I (THE BRAVE). Prague enjoyed a golden period in the late 14th century when the king of Bohemia became the Emperor CHARLES IV. Charles founded (1348) Charles University, the first such institution in central Europe, and began building St Vitus' Cathedral (1344). In the 15th-century REFORMATION, Prague was the centre of the HUSSITE movement. The revolt of the Czech Protestant nobles against Habsburg rule in the DEFENESTRATION OF PRAGUE (1618) started the THIRTY YEARS' WAR. Thereafter, German influence increased and Prague remained largely removed from the tide of European events, with the result that its magnificent late-Gothic and Baroque architecture escaped destruction by war. Prague was the centre of Czech nationalism in the 19th century and became capital of the independent republic of Czechoslovakia in 1919. It languished under German occupation in World War 2 and subsequently under communist domination. The short-lived liberalism of the PRAGUE SPRING (1968) was crushed by Soviet military intervention. The so-called "Velvet Revolution" (1989) brought an end to communist rule, and Prague, as capital of the Czech Republic from 1993, experienced rapid revival and a tourist boom in the 1990s. Pop. (1990) 1,215,000.

Prague Spring (1968) Brief period of liberal reform in CZECHOSLOVAKIA under communism. In January, Alexander DUBČEK came to power and inaugurated what he called "socialism with a human face". Many restrictions on the press were lifted and victims of the Stalinist purges were publicly rehabilitated. After ousting conservatives from the Presidium of the Communist Party, Dubček secured the adoption of the "Action Programme" of democratic reforms in April. The Soviet Union became concerned at the direction and pace of liberalization, but Soviet leader Leonid BREZHNEV gained little reassurance from a meeting with Dubček in July. On 20 August, tanks and troops of the Soviet Union and its Warsaw Pact allies invaded Czechoslovakia and occupied PRAGUE. The continuing presence of Soviet troops on the streets forced Dubček to abandon much of the reform programme and he was replaced by Gustáv HUSÁK in April 1969. The self-immolation (January 1969) of Jan Palach became a symbol of Czechoslovak resistance to Soviet domination.

Prasad, Rajendra (1884–1963) Indian statesman, president (1950–62). In 1920 he joined "Mahatma" GANDHI's Noncooperation movement against British colonial rule and acted as president (1934, 1939, 1947) of the Indian National CONGRESS. Prasad was imprisoned (1942–45) for his opposition to the British war effort during World War 2. After his release, Prasad joined India's first post-colonial government, under Jawaharlal Nehru, and helped draft the constitution. When a republic was declared (1950), Prasad became the first president of India.

Precambrian Oldest and longest era of geological time, from the formation of the Earth *c.*4.6 billion years ago to the beginning of a good fossil record *c.*590 million years ago, comprising *c.*80% of the Earth's lifetime. Precambrian fossils are extremely rare, probably because the earliest life forms did not have hard parts suitable for preservation, and Precambrian rocks have been greatly deformed. Primitive bacteria have been identified in deposits that are more than 3 billion years old.

prehistory Period of human cultural development before the existence of written records. *See also* ARCHAEOLOGY; BRONZE AGE; IRON AGE; STONE AGE

Prempeh I (d.1931) Last king (1888–96) of the ASHANTI empire (now s Ghana) in West Africa. He acceded to the golden stool at a time of crisis for the Ashanti (Asante) people. Prempeh attempted to maintain Ashanti independence from the British, refusing the offer of a protectorate. He was defeated and captured by the British in 1896 and sent into exile on Mahe, Seychelles, in 1900. In 1902 Ashanti became a British colony. Prempeh was permitted to return in 1924, and was later reinstated as chief (1926–31), but with only nominal powers.

Premyslid (*c.*800–1306) Ruling dynasty of medieval BOHEMIA. According to legend, the family was founded by the peasant Premysl, who married Princess Libuse, and was converted to Christianity in the 9th century. Saint WENCESLAS (d.929) capitulated to the Germans and was murdered by his brother, BOLESŁAW I (THE BRAVE), who successfully resisted the German invasion. The reign (967–99) of BOLESŁAW II (THE GENEROUS) saw the establishment of a bishopric in PRAGUE. His death ushered in a period of civil war and Bohemia became a duchy of the HOLY ROMAN EMPIRE. In 1198 **Otakar I** was able to establish a kingdom of Bohemia, and by 1212 he had won almost complete autonomy from the Empire. **Otakar II** (r.1253–78) conquered Carinthia, Carniola, Istria and Styria, thereby establishing Bohemia as the dominant state of the Holy Roman Empire. Otakar's son, Wenceslas II (r.1278–1305), was recognized as king of Poland and made his son, later Wenceslas III, king of Hungary (1301–04). In 1306 Wenceslas III was assassinated and John of Luxembourg became king of Bohemia.

Preparedness Movement (1915–16) Campaign in the United States to ready the nation for entry into WORLD WAR 1. The Movement, led by former president Theodore ROOSEVELT and General Leonard WOOD, put pressure on President Woodrow WILSON to end US neutrality and create a large standing army. Wilson resisted all such calls, until stung into action by German U-boat attacks on shipping, such as the sinking of the LUSITANIA (1915).

Presbyterianism Form of Protestant Christianity that became the national CHURCH OF SCOTLAND in 1689. It was later adopted by other churches, chiefly of British origin, in North America and elsewhere. The original inspiration of Presbyterianism was the teaching of the French Protestant reformer John CALVIN. Brought to Scotland by John KNOX, it eventually evolved into Presbyterianism. Presbyterianism rejected the priestly hierarchy. Ministers and elders are elected by their congregations and local churches are administered by the Presbytery, which in turn elects representatives to the regional synod, from which the General Assembly (the governing body) is selected. Many of the basic principles of Presbyterianism were laid down by the WESTMINSTER ASSEMBLY (1643–49), when the Scottish COVENANTERS (Presbyterians) were allied with the English Parliament against CHARLES I. Oliver CROMWELL purged Presbyterians from Parliament in 1648, creating the so-called RUMP PARLIAMENT, which granted religious privileges to CONGREGATIONALISM. English Presbyterianism subsequently declined in importance. *See also* PURITANS; REFORMED CHURCH

Prescott, John Leslie (1938–) British statesman, deputy prime minister and secretary of state for environment, transport and the regions (1997–). A former merchant seaman, he entered Parliament in 1970. Between 1975 and 1979 he was simultaneously a member of the European and British Parliaments. In 1994 Prescott became deputy leader of the LABOUR PARTY and his "on-the-stump" campaigning helped the Party win a landslide victory in the 1997 general election.

Presidium *See* POLITBURO

Pressburg, Treaty of (26 December 1805) Peace agreement between France and Austria after NAPOLEON I's victories at ULM and AUSTERLITZ, signed at Pressburg (now Bratislava, Slovakia). Emperor FRANCIS II was forced to cede all land gained from Venice by the Treaty of CAMPO FORMIO (1797) to the Napoleonic kingdom of Italy, and to surrender the rest of his Italian territories (Piedmont, Parma and Piacenza) to France. The Treaty also created the German kingdoms of Bavaria and Württemberg, effectively terminating the 1000-year history of the HOLY ROMAN EMPIRE. *See also* NAPOLEONIC WARS

Prester John Legendary Christian ruler of the East in the Middle Ages. Dating from the period of the Christian Crusades against the Muslims in the Middle East, the first record of Prester John occurs in the *Chronicle* (1145) of Otto of Friesling, who tells of the defeat of Persia by Nestorian Christians (in reality, probably the Mongols). Fictitious letters from Prester John circulated among European rulers in the 12th century, describing fabulously rich lands in the Indies. The letters inspired the travels of (among others) MARCO POLO. From the 14th century the kingdom of Prester John was located in Africa (often Ethiopia) and subsequently inspired the Portuguese voyages of exploration.

Preston, Battle of (1648) Decisive conflict of the second phase of the English CIVIL WAR, in which Oliver CROMWELL routed a larger army of Scots, led by the Duke of Hamilton, in Lancashire, NW England. The Battle resulted from the secret intrigues of CHARLES I with the Scots, which convinced his English enemies that he was too untrustworthy to deal with and led to his trial and execution six months later.

Prestonpans, Battle of (1745) Conflict in East Lothian, E Scotland, in which the JACOBITE forces, led by Charles Edward STUART and Lord George MURRAY, inflicted a heavy defeat on the English under Sir John Cope. It was a vital early success for the Young Pretender, encouraging waverers to enlist in the Jacobite cause.

Pretorius, Andries Wilhelmus Jacobus (1798–1853) Afrikaner leader, father of Marthinus Wessel PRETORIUS. He led a reconnaissance party from Cape Colony to NATAL in 1837 took part in the GREAT TREK (1838). Pretorius became the Afrikaners' commander after the ZULUS killed Louis Retief (1838), and he led them to victory over the Zulu chief DINGAAN at the Battle of BLOOD RIVER (1838). He joined forces with Dingaan's brother Mpande to overthrow the chief in 1840. In the same year, Pretorius combined the Afrikaner settlements in TRANSVAAL and Natal to form the republic of Natalia. In 1843 the British annexed Natal. Pretorius initially worked with the British governor to win concessions for Afrikaners in Natal, but when this failed he led another trek to Transvaal (1847). In 1848 the British seized the territory between the Orange and Vaal rivers, proclaiming it the Orange River Sovereignty (now FREE STATE). Pretorius led a successful revolt against British rule, leading to the recognition of the independence of Transvaal as the South African Republic at the Sand River Convention (1852). He died just before the establishment of an independent Orange Free State (1854).

Pretorius, Marthinus Wessel (1819–1901) Afrikaner (Boer) statesman and soldier, first president of the South African Republic (1857–71) and of the Orange FREE STATE (1859–63). He joined his father, Andries PRETORIUS, in the GREAT TREK (1838) to NATAL and in the subsequent battles against the ZULUS. Pretorius also accompanied his father on the march to Transvaal (later the South African Republic). Pretorius failed to unify the two Afrikaner republics, and resigned as president of Orange Free State to concentrate on reforming the South African Republic. He resigned as leader of the Republic after being widely blamed for the loss of the valuable diamond mines in the lower Vaal. Pretorius returned to lead the resistance against the British annexation of TRANSVAAL (1877) and helped negotiate the Treaty of Pretoria (1881), which restored independence. *See also* KRUGER, PAUL (STEPHANUS JOHANNUS PAULUS); SOUTH AFRICAN WARS

Pride's Purge (6 December 1648) Forcible exclusion of 231 members of the English LONG PARLIAMENT, carried out by Colonel Thomas PRIDE (d.1658) on the orders of the army council. The aim was to exclude members prepared to vote for a measure that would have restored the defeated king, CHARLES I. Many of the members arrested or expelled were advocates of PRESBYTERIANISM. The remnant, known as the RUMP PARLIAMENT, brought Charles to trial and execution. *See also* CIVIL WAR, ENGLISH

Primo de Rivera, José Antonio (1903–36) Spanish politician, son of Miguel PRIMO DE RIVERA. He was the founder (1933) of the Spanish FALANGE, a fascist party opposed to the republic. Primo de Rivera was elected to the Cortes (parliament) in 1933, but lost his seat in the 1935 elections that brought the POPULAR FRONT to power. In 1936 the Falange was banned. Primo de Rivera was arrested and, after the outbreak of the Spanish CIVIL WAR (1936–39), executed by the Republicans. He became a martyr for the Nationalist cause and the Falange supporters joined General FRANCO. *See also* FASCISM

Primo de Rivera, Miguel (1870–1930) Spanish general and dictator (1923–30), father of José PRIMO DE RIVERA. He led the military coup that, with the support of ALFONSO XIII, abolished the Cortes (parliament) and established his authoritarian and repressive rule. Modelling himself on Benito MUSSOLINI, Primo de Rivera restored order and ended the revolt (1926) of ABD EL-KRIM in Morocco, but failed to carry out vital social and economic reforms or control expenditure. Having lost the approval of his conservative supporters – landowners, church and royalists – and the backing of the army, he resigned and died shortly afterwards in exile in Paris.

primogeniture Principle of inheritance in which property (and title) passes undivided to the eldest son. It ensured the preservation of large estates, and restricted the aristocracy to a relatively small and powerful CLASS rather than a much larger and poorer number as existed in countries without primogeniture. It had particular advantages in the FEUDAL SYSTEM, when a FIEF carried military obligations that could not be subdivided among several people, and it encouraged a strong monarchy, less subject to succession disputes. The absence of primogeniture virtually ensured the break-up of, for example, the empire of CHARLEMAGNE and prevented the development of a central monarchy in, for instance, Wales.

Prince Edward Island Province in E Canada, in the Gulf of St Lawrence; the capital is Charlottetown. When the island was discovered by Jacques CARTIER in 1534, it was inhabited by groups of the Micmac. Claimed for France in 1603 by Samuel de CHAMPLAIN, it was colonized by French settlers as the Île St Jean from 1720. Ceded to Britain in 1763, it became a separate province (1769) and was renamed after the Duke of York in 1799. In the 19th century it received many Scottish immigrants. Prince Edward Island hosted the Charlottetown Conference (1864), which ultimately led to the creation of the Dominion of Canada. Prince Edward Island joined the confederation in 1873. It is heavily dependent on federal grants. Pop. (1993 est.) 131,600.

princely states Indian principalities that retained internal autonomy under British rule. They numbered more than 500, including several, notably Hyderabad, considerably larger than England. Altogether they made up *c.*40% of India. Their rulers, who generally held despotic powers, were bound to Britain by treaty. When, after the INDIAN MUTINY (1857–58), the government of India passed from the English EAST INDIA COMPANY to the British government, the internal autonomy of the princely states was reconfirmed to ensure their loyalty. After independence (1947), they were compelled to join either India or Pakistan, and the last remaining privileges of the princely families were abolished in 1970.

Princip, Gavrilo (1894–1918) Serbian nationalist. He was a member of a Serbian terrorist group known as the BLACK HAND, who were dedicated to freeing the South Slavs from Austro-Hungarian rule. On 28 June 1914,

PROTESTANTISM

Movement in CHRISTIANITY that began as a demand for reform within the ROMAN CATHOLIC CHURCH and developed into a proliferating number of separate churches. The movement acquired its name from the protest, lodged by supporters of the German preacher Martin LUTHER, against the renewed hostility towards LUTHERANISM at the Diet of Speyer (1529). While figures such as John WYCLIFFE, Jan HUS and Desiderius ERASMUS had previously criticized abuses in the late medieval church, Luther questioned its basic doctrines. In his *Ninety-five Theses* (1517), Luther rejected the doctrine of INDULGENCES, arguing that an individual could only achieve salvation through faith. Furthermore, he maintained that scripture, rather than the pope, was the ultimate religious authority. His denial of the doctrine of TRANSUBSTANTIATION and emphasis on the "priesthood of all believers" further undermined the priestly hierarchy. Luther's ideas inspired more radical reformers: Thomas MÜNTZER led the PEASANTS' WAR (1524–25) in Germany; Ulrich ZWINGLI fought to create a theocratic state in Zürich, Switzerland; and the ANABAPTISTS seized Münster, W Germany (1534). In 1536 John CALVIN published his *Institutes of the Christian Religion*, which became the definitive statement of Reformed theology. Calvin sought to create a kingdom of God in Geneva, Switzerland. The Reformation spread rapidly through N and W Europe.

In England, the separation of the CHURCH OF ENGLAND from Rome in 1534 was prompted by the refusal of Pope CLEMENT VII to grant HENRY VIII a divorce from CATHERINE OF ARAGON. The reign (1547–53) of EDWARD VI brought the Book of COMMON PRAYER, written by Thomas CRANMER. The doctrinal basis of the ANGLICAN COMMUNION was established by the THIRTY-NINE ARTICLES (1563) in the reign (1558–1603) of ELIZABETH I. PURITANS argued, however, that the Elizabethan Settlement retained doctrines and rituals associated with Roman Catholicism, and called for a form of PRESBYTERIANISM in church government, akin to that established by John KNOX in Scotland. The suppression of NONCONFORMISM under JAMES I (r.1603–25) and CHARLES I (r.1625–49) led to the founding of JAMESTOWN, Virginia, and PLYMOUTH COLONY, New England (1607 and 1620 respectively). It was also a major factor in the outbreak of the English Civil War (1642–45). The Puritanism of Oliver Cromwell's COMMONWEALTH (1649–60) was suppressed on the RESTORATION (1660) of the monarchy under CHARLES II. Fear of a return to Roman Catholicism under JAMES II (r.1685–88) sparked off the so-called "GLORIOUS REVOLUTION" (1688) and the accession of the Protestants WILLIAM III and MARY II.

In France, the persecution of the HUGUENOTS sparked off the WARS OF RELIGION (1562–98), which ended in the Edict of NANTES (1598) that gave freedom of worship to Protestants. In 1685 LOUIS XIV revoked the Edict and the resulting mass exodus of Huguenots caused grave damage to the French economy. In the 17th century, the PIETISM movement sought to renew Protestantism through evangelical spirituality and moral rectitude. It later inspired John WESLEY (1703–91), the English founder of METHODISM.

In Massachusetts, North America, Jonathan EDWARDS launched the GREAT AWAKENING movement in the 1730s. In the 19th century, the emigration of many German and Scandinavian Lutherans to the United States helped to preserve the sense of revivalism. In the 19th century, Protestantism expanded rapidly in Africa and Asia, as missions were built in the British and German colonies. *See also* ARMINIUS, JACOBUS; BROWNE, ROBERT; CONGREGATIONALISM; COTTON, JOHN; COUNTER-REFORMATION; DEISM; ECUMENICAL CHURCH; FUNDAMENTALISM; MENNONITES; MISSIONARY SOCIETIES; MORAVIAN CHURCH; MORMONS; OXFORD MOVEMENT; PENTECOSTAL CHURCHES; QUAKERS

◄ **Luther** Portrait by Lucas Cranach the Elder (1472–1553). Cranach was the court painter to Frederick the Wise of Saxony, and the chief propaganda artist of the Protestant Reformation.

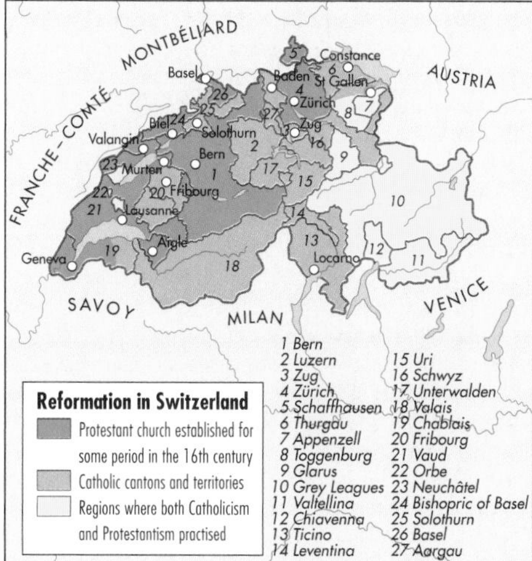

▲ **Switzerland** was a centre of early Protestantism, but was greatly split. After Ulrich Zwingli of Zürich was killed in battle (1531), John Calvin formed a Holy Commonwealth in Geneva.

P

Princip assassinated Archduke FRANZ FERDINAND of Austria and his wife in SARAJEVO, Bosnia-Herzegovina, precipitating the train of events that led to the outbreak of WORLD WAR 1. Princip was sentenced to 20 years' imprisonment but died of tuberculosis in 1918.

printing Technique for making multiple copies of an image on a flat surface, such as paper. The Chinese began to print from images carved in wood blocks in the 8th century, and in the 11th century the first experiments took place with movable type, made initially from wood or pottery, later metal. The first successful European printer appears to have been Johann GUTENBERG of Mainz, Germany, whose first book, a Bible, was printed in 1455. Printing presses spread rapidly, and the invention had revolutionary effects in Europe: the RENAISSANCE would hardly have been possible otherwise. Gutenberg's methods were so effective that the basics of printing hardly changed until the 19th century, and movable metal type remained in use until the late 20th century.

prison Building for the confinement of criminals or people detained by the legal authorities. In most societies before the 18th century, criminals were subject to capital or corporal punishment or exile, and prisons were places of temporary confinement only. Early prisons (often ships) were usually disease-ridden, badly organized and often brutal. The influence of the Enlightenment in the 18th century led to less harsh penalties and the development of prisons as penal institutions. The Eastern State Penitentiary, Philadelphia, Pennsylvania, opened in 1829, and became a model for similar institutions throughout the United States and Europe. The PRISON REFORM movement improved conditions in the 19th century, with emphasis on rehabilitation rather than mere punishment. *See also* PENAL COLONY

prisoner of war (POW) Member of the armed forces captured by the enemy in international warfare. The protected status accorded to POWs has been recognized in international law since the HAGUE PEACE CONFERENCE of 1899 and the Hague Convention of 1907. It was amplified most recently in the Third GENEVA CONVENTION (1949). The Geneva agreement followed the mixed treatment of POWs during WORLD WAR 2: more than 3.5 million Soviet soldiers died in German captivity and *c*.40% of Allied POWs died in Japanese camps. Today, the obligations of the captors (and the captured) are acknowledged by most countries, and the law is enforced by the International RED CROSS and equivalent agencies.

prison reform Movement aimed at improving conditions inside PRISONS and exploring alternative systems of rehabilitation. It developed in Britain at the beginning of the 19th century, when the efforts of prison reformers such as John HOWARD and Elizabeth FRY led to the improvement of conditions by government legislation. Other countries soon followed. In the United States, the National Prison Conference (1870) held in Cincinnati, Ohio, indicated the trend towards rehabilitation rather than punishment. In Europe, the Swedish prison system set new standards of humanitarianism. Rising crime rates in the late 20th century led to some reaction against rehabilitation as the primary aim of prisons, typified by the adoption of mandatory sentences and the reintroduction of capital punishment in many US states.

privateer Privately owned vessel with a government commission to attack enemy shipping. Their government licences (letters of marque) distinguished privateers from PIRATES. Crews were unpaid but were allowed to keep the booty. Privateering was at its height from the 16th to the 18th century, especially in the Caribbean and American coastal waters, but the dividing line between privateer and pirate was a fine one, and was often breached. Due to the small size of its navy, the United States employed many privateers during the WAR OF 1812 with Britain. The practice was abolished by the Hague Convention of 1907. *See also* BUCCANEER; DRAKE, SIR FRANCIS; HAWKINS, SIR JOHN; MORGAN, SIR HENRY

privatization Transfer of state-run enterprises to private ownership, the opposite of NATIONALIZATION. In the 1980s many governments of industrialized nations adopted privatization in the belief that, apart from the profits arising from the sale of nationalized industries, the enterprises concerned would benefit from greater freedom to respond to market forces and would become more efficient through competition. *See also* MONETARISM

Privy Council Advisory body to the British monarch. It was created in the reign (1509–47) of HENRY VIII of England as a smaller (*c*.20 members), more effective group than the large and unwieldy medieval king's council. It was the main engine of government until the late 17th century, when it began to lose power to the developing CABINET. By the reign (1714–27) of George I, the Privy Council had become an entirely formal body. Its membership swelled – today there are *c*.450 privy councillors. It retains a supervisory role in some areas and its judicial committee acts as a final court of appeal for certain British dependencies and Commonwealth countries.

Proclamation of 1763 British government edict designed to restrict white settlement on Native American lands following the FRENCH AND INDIAN WARS and the outbreak of PONTIAC'S REBELLION. It forbade settlement west of the "Proclamation Line", which followed the Appalachian Mountains, designating this land as Indian territory. The Proclamation was strongly resented and soon breached by pioneers.

proconsul In the ROMAN REPUBLIC, a CONSUL whose term of office was extended beyond the usual 12 months so that he could continue in a military command or as governor of a province. This extension became increasingly common as the republic expanded, and after 27 BC the term came to mean a provincial governor. It was applied to British colonial administrators in the 19th century.

Prodi, Romano (1939–) Italian statesman, prime minister (1996–98), president of the EUROPEAN COMMISSION (1999–). He led the centre-left Olive Tree Alliance to a narrow victory in the 1996 elections in Italy. Prodi skilfully managed to preserve the fragile coalition for 18 months, and his austerity measures enabled Italy to qualify for European monetary union in 1999. The Alliance collapsed after hardline communists rejected his proposals for large budget cuts. Prodi was chosen to replace Jacques SANTER as head of the European Commission after the entire Commission had resigned in the midst of a corruption scandal. Prodi sought to restore public confidence in the Commission and to prepare the EUROPEAN UNION (EU) for future enlargement.

Profumo, John Dennis (1915–) British politician. He entered Parliament in 1940 and joined Harold MACMILLAN'S Conservative cabinet as secretary of war (1960). In 1963 he was forced to resign after falsely denying in the House of Commons his affair with a call-girl, Christine Keeler, who was also involved with a Soviet naval attaché. The scandal helped to discredit the government and Macmillan resigned four months later.

Progressive Conservative Party Canadian political organization. In 1854 the Liberal-Conservative Party was founded under the leadership of John MACDONALD. It gradually and informally dropped the Liberal part of its title in order to differentiate itself from the LIBERAL PARTY. Macdonald dominated Canadian politics from the start of the Confederation (1867) until his death in 1891. From 1896 to 1911 the Conservatives remained in opposition, finally regaining power under Sir Robert BORDEN. During World War 1, Borden formed a coalition Unionist government (1917–20). From 1921 to 1957 the Liberals dominated Canadian government, as the Conservatives failed to attract support from French Canadians and its protectionist stance alienated w Canada. In 1942 the Party adopted its present name in an attempt to appeal to reformists. John DIEFENBAKER formed a minority Conservative administration and won a landslide victory in the 1958 elections. After Diefenbaker's defeat in 1963, the Party was out of office almost continuously until Brian MULRONEY'S electoral victory in 1984. In 1993 Mulroney retired and was succeeded by Kim CAMPBELL, Canada's first woman prime minister. The Party suffered a heavy defeat in the 1993 elections, winning only two seats. It recovered in the 1997 elections, but the Reform Party captured many of its traditional voters in w Canada. *See also* CLARK, JOE (CHARLES JOSEPH)

Progressive Party US political organization. The original Progressive, or **Bull Moose**, Party was organized (1912) by Robert LA FOLLETTE to support the presidential campaign of Theodore ROOSEVELT after he had failed to wrest the Republican nomination from William Howard TAFT. It split the Republican vote, thus contributing to the victory of the Democrat Woodrow WILSON. In 1924 La Follette himself ran for president as a Progressive candidate, pledging to root out government corruption and nationalize the railroads. La Follette won only his home state of Wisconsin. Henry WALLACE reformed the Progressive Party in 1947, opposing the foreign policy of President Harry TRUMAN and calling for greater cooperation with the Soviet Union. Wallace polled more than one million votes (2% of the vote) in the 1948 election. *See also* PROGRESSIVISM

progressivism US reform movement. In the early 20th century the Progressives favoured government regulation of big business, child labour laws, women's suffrage, and political reforms, such as the direct primary, the referendum and the power of recall (to remove an unsatisfactory representative). The movement, mostly middle-class and urban, reached its peak in 1912 with the formation of the PROGRESSIVE PARTY, which nominated Theodore ROOSEVELT for president and polled 30% of the popular vote, more than the incumbent, William TAFT. In 1916 Roosevelt's PREPAREDNESS MOVEMENT led to the endorsement of the Republican candidate and broke up the Party.

Prohibition (1919–33) Ban on manufacturing, selling and transporting of alcoholic drinks in the United States. The ANTI-SALOON LEAGUE (founded 1893) led the drive for national prohibition, and the ban was instituted by the 18th Amendment to the CONSTITUTION and enforced by the VOLSTEAD ACT (1919). Smuggling, illicit manufacture and widespread corruption of government officials and police doomed it to failure. Large-scale BOOTLEGGING became the preserve of organized criminals, such as Al CAPONE. The Democratic Party, campaigning for repeal of Prohibition, won the 1932 election and the "noble experiment" was abandoned in the 21st Amendment (1933). *See also* NATION, CARRY; SAINT VALENTINE'S DAY MASSACRE

proletariat Originally, the lowest CLASS in ancient Rome; they paid no taxes and served the state only by producing children. Karl MARX appropriated the term to refer to the class of industrial workers whose major source of income derived from their labour. *See also* DICTATORSHIP OF THE PROLETARIAT; MARXISM

propaganda Dissemination of information to manipulate public opinion. The term derives from the Roman Catholic Church's missionary organization, the *Propaganda Fide*, established in 1622. Political, religious and other organizations have always tried to influence people by selective, if not false, reporting, but propaganda in its most ominous guise has been produced by totalitarian governments in control of mass communications. Nazi Germany is a prime example. *See also* GOEBBELS, (PAUL) JOSEPH

Protectorate (1653–59) Rule of Oliver CROMWELL in England. Cromwell became head of state as lord protector under the "Instrument of Government". Apart from a brief, unsuccessful experiment of rule by a council of major-generals, the rule of law prevailed: Parliament ended the major-generals' rule by refusing funds. In 1657 Parliament presented a programme modestly called the Humble Petition and Advice, which Cromwell accepted (apart from the recommendation that he should become king) in spite of army opposition. Cromwell was succeeded as lord protector by his son, Richard CROMWELL, who lacked prestige and was soon displaced, making way for the RESTORATION of CHARLES II in 1660. *See also* COMMONWEALTH

Protestant ethic Moral code associated with hard work, discipline, enterprise and individualism, alleged to be responsible for the rise of CAPITALISM. The theory connecting PROTESTANTISM (in particular CALVINISM) and capitalist society derives chiefly from Max Weber's *The Protestant Ethic and the Spirit of Capitalism* (1905) and R.H. TAWNEY'S *Religion and the Rise of Capitalism* (1926). It was influential among historians in the mid-20th century, although has now been largely discredited.

Protestantism *See* feature article, page 335

Protocols of the Learned Elders of Zion (1903) Document outlining a plan for Jews to overthrow Christianity and control the world. Alleged to have been written by Theodor HERZL, the leader of ZIONISM, it was first published in Russia. Although clearly fantastic, and proved fraudulent by the British newspaper *The Times* in 1921, it was a powerful piece of ANTI-SEMITIC propaganda.

Proudhon, Pierre Joseph (1809–65) French political philosopher of ANARCHISM. A powerful influence on socialist revolutionary theory in the 19th century, although dismissed by Karl MARX, he is popularly remembered for his statement "property is theft", the opening sentence of *What is Property?* (1840). He took part in the REVOLUTIONS OF 1848 and was imprisoned as a dangerous radical in 1849–52. *See also* BAKUNIN, MIKHAIL ALEXANDROVICH

Provence Region and former province of SE France. The city-port of MARSEILLES was founded by Greek colonists in *c*.600 BC. Provence became part of the Roman province of Gallia Narbonensis in the 2nd century BC. It was later invaded by Visigoths and others, coming under Frankish control in the 6th century AD. It was a separate kingdom from 879 to *c*.934, but was later subsumed into the Holy Roman Empire. In the 12th century, under the nominal control of Spanish CATALONIA, Provence enjoyed a period of cultural brilliance, reflected in its troubadour poetry. It was controlled by the ANGEVINS from *c*.1246 to 1481, but retained its distinctive cultural identity and political autonomy. In 1481 it was acquired by Louis XI of France, but maintained its own assembly until the French Revolution. In 1790 it was divided into several departments.

Prussia *See* feature article

Prynne, William (1600–69) English Puritan pamphleteer. His book *Histrio matrix* (1633) criticized the theatre for promoting immorality. In 1634 Archbishop William LAUD, arguing that the work contained veiled attacks on CHARLES I and HENRIETTA MARIA, sentenced Prynne to life imprisonment. Prynne continued to produce scurrilous tracts against the Anglican church, for which his ears were cropped and his cheeks branded (1637). In 1640 Prynne was released from prison by the LONG PARLIAMENT and hailed as a hero. He was a prime mover in securing the execution of Laud (1645). A tireless pamphleteer, he turned his hostility on the army, and, after being elected to Parliament in 1648, was expelled in PRIDE'S PURGE (1648). From 1650 to 1653 Prynne was imprisoned for his opposition to the Commonwealth. He supported the RESTORATION (1660) of CHARLES II.

Ptolemy I (Soter) (*c*.367–*c*.283 BC) Ruler of Egypt (323–285 BC), founder of the Ptolemaic dynasty. He joined ALEXANDER III (THE GREAT)'s bodyguard in 336 BC and was made a commander of the Macedonian fleet for his successes on the campaign in Persia. On the death of Alexander (323 BC), his empire was divided among his generals and Ptolemy was appointed satrap (governor) of Egypt. Ptolemy expanded his empire by conquering CYRENAICA (322 BC). He gained Cyprus after defeating CASSANDER at the Battle of Gaza (312 BC), but was forced to relinquish the island after defeat by ANTIGONUS I at the Battle of SALAMIS (306 BC). Ptolemy earned the title of Soter (Saviour) for his defence of Rhodes against Antigonus, and the eventual defeat of Antigonus (301 BC) led to a struggle for control of Syria with SELEUCUS I. In the last years of his reign, Ptolemy secured his position in Egypt through a number of marriage alliances. He introduced coinage into Egypt and founded the famous library at his capital, ALEXANDRIA. Ptolemy placated his Egyptian subjects by establishing the cult of Seraphis. He abdicated in favour of his son, PTOLEMY II.

Ptolemy II (Philadelphus) (*c*.308–246 BC) King of Egypt (285–246 BC). He shared power with his father, PTOLEMY I, until the latter's death in *c*.283 BC. Through conquest and skilful diplomacy, Ptolemy made Egypt the dominant power in the E Mediterranean, at the expense of the SELEUCID empire and Macedonia. He brought Egypt's agricultural economy under government management, spending vast sums on building temples to glorify himself, his wife and his sister Arsinoe II. Ptolemy confirmed Alexandria's position as the cultural and commercial centre of the Hellenic world, building (*c*.280 BC) the PHAROS lighthouse, expanding the great library at Alexandria and patronizing poets such as Callimachus. He was succeeded by his son, PTOLEMY III.

Ptolemy III (Euergetes) (d.221 BC) King of Egypt (246–221 BC), son and successor of PTOLEMY II. His marriage to Berenice II, daughter of Magas of Cyrene, reunited CYRENAICA and Egypt. In the Third Syrian War (246–240 BC) against SELEUCUS II, Ptolemy gained ANTIOCH. Thereafter, he avoided direct conflict with Syria or Macedonia, concentrating on consolidating his power within Egypt. At his death, Ptolemaic Egypt was at the height of its power and prosperity. He was succeeded by his son, PTOLEMY IV.

Ptolemy IV (Philopator) (*c*.238–205 BC) King of Egypt (221–205 BC), son and successor of PTOLEMY III. His weak rule saw the loss of much of Ptolemaic Syria to the SELEUCID ruler ANTIOCHUS III. Ptolemy was persuaded by

PRUSSIA (GER. PREUSSEN)

Historic kingdom and state in N GERMANY. The region was conquered by the TEUTONIC KNIGHTS in the mid-13th century. In 1466 the Polish crown gained direct control over the lands W of the River Vistula (**Royal** Prussia), while the Knights retained the E sector (**East** Prussia) in return for acknowledging the suzerainty of POLAND. In 1525 Albert of HOHENZOLLERN made himself Duke of Prussia, and East Prussia became known as **Ducal** Prussia. In 1618 Ducal Prussia passed to John Sigismund, Elector of BRANDENBURG. John's grandson, FREDERICK WILLIAM, gained independence for Ducal Prussia from Poland in 1660. In 1701 Frederick William's son became FREDERICK I, king of Prussia.

FREDERICK WILLIAM I (r.1713–40) made the Prussian army the finest fighting force in Europe. The reign (1740–86) of his son, FREDERICK II (THE GREAT), marked the emergence of Prussia as one of the great powers in Europe. Frederick II's invasion of SILESIA precipitated the War of the AUSTRIAN SUCCESSION, and the province was finally acquired at the end of the SEVEN YEARS' WAR (1756–63). In the First Partition of Poland (1772), Frederick also gained Royal Prussia.

At the start of the NAPOLEONIC WARS, FREDERICK WILLIAM III (r.1797–1840) suffered crushing defeats at Jena and Austerlitz (both 1806), and was forced to cede much of Prussia to NAPOLEON I. The losses spurred the reform of the Prussian state. The army, led by G.L. von BLÜCHER and Graf GNEISENAU, recovered to aid in the defeat of Napoleon at Leipzig (1814) and Waterloo (1815). At the Congress of VIENNA (1814–15), Prussia regained most of the land it held in 1803, and also acquired POMERANIA, parts of SAXONY and land around the River Rhine. During the REVOLUTIONS OF 1848, FREDERICK WILLIAM IV (r.1840–61) initially conceded to liberal reforms, but later revoked them. WILLIAM I (r.1861–88) and his chief minister, Otto von BISMARCK, made Prussia the dominant force in Germany.

In 1864 Prussia conquered SCHLESWIG-HOLSTEIN from Denmark, and the ensuing AUSTRO-PRUSSIAN WAR (1866) saw the acquisition of Hanover, Hesse, Nassau and Frankfurt am Main. Bismarck now engineered the FRANCO-PRUSSIAN WAR (1870–71), in which Helmuth von MOLTKE captured ALSACE and LORRAINE from France. In 1871 Prussian supremacy was confirmed as William I became emperor of Germany. After Germany's defeat at the end of World War 1, Prussia became a state of the WEIMAR REPUBLIC and, after further defeat in World War 2, Prussia was abolished. Northern East Prussia (including Königsberg, now KALININGRAD) was ceded to the Soviet Union, while the rest of East Prussia went to Poland.

◀ **East Prussia** passed to the Elector of Brandenburg, in 1618. At the end of the Thirty Years' War (1618–48), Elector Frederick William gained East Pomerania and Magdeburg. Frederick William's sovereignty over East Prussia was confirmed by the First Northern War (1655–60). In the Great Northern War (1700–21), Frederick William I gained West Pomerania (1720). Frederick II defeated the Austrians at Mollwitz (1741) in the War of the Austrian Succession (1740–48). Prussian control of Silesia was established in the Seven Years' War (1756–63), during which Prussia crushed the French at Rossbach (1757). Frederick II gained West Prussia in 1772.

his chief minister, Sosibius, to murder his mother. The lack of authoritative leadership led to a rebellion by Egyptian natives. He was succeeded by PTOLEMY V.

Ptolemy V (Epiphanes) (*c*.210–180 BC) King of Egypt (205–180 BC), son and successor of PTOLEMY IV. His regency was dominated by his father's chief minister, Sosibius. Capitalizing on Egyptian weakness, ANTIOCHUS III of Syria and PHILIP V of Macedonia partitioned the Ptolemaic lands in Asia and the Aegean between them. In 196 BC Ptolemy issued the decree inscribed on the ROSETTA STONE, which details the attempt to subdue rebellions in Upper Egypt. In 193 BC, as part of a peace treaty with Antiochus, Ptolemy married Cleopatra I. He was succeeded by his son, PTOLEMY VI.

Ptolemy VI (Philometor) (d.145 BC) King of Egypt (180–145 BC), son and successor of PTOLEMY V. His mother, Cleopatra I, served as regent until 176 BC, and from 170 BC he shared the throne with his brother, Ptolemy VIII (Euergetes). The brothers' attempted invasion of Syria resulted in the occupation of Egypt by the Seleucid ruler Antiochus IV. In 164 BC Philometor (mother-loving) was forced into exile by Euergetes (Benefactor). He regained the throne with Roman help, and Euergetes was confined to ruling CYRENAICA. Philometor defeated his brother's attempt to gain Cyprus (154 BC). Philometor died of wounds sustained in his victory over the Syrian pretender, Alexander Balas.

Ptolemy XII (Auletes) (*c*.112–51 BC) King of Egypt (80–51 BC). An illegitimate son of Ptolemy IX (r.116–81 BC), he was heavily dependent on Rome, and gained Caesar's support for his rule with a bribe. Faced by revolt (58 BC) after the Romans took Cyprus, Ptolemy went to Rome to seek military assistance. His eldest daughter, Berenice IV, was popularly acclaimed as ruler. Ptolemy eventually managed to bribe the Roman army into supporting him, and he returned to Egypt in 55 BC. He executed Berenice and later secured the succession upon his son, PTOLEMY XIII, and another daughter, CLEOPATRA VII.

Ptolemy XIII (Theos Philopator) (63–47 BC) King of Egypt (51–47 BC), son and successor of PTOLEMY XII. He ruled jointly with his sister, CLEOPATRA VII. He expelled Cleopatra in 48 BC, but she raised an army against him. Seeking to gain favour with Julius CAESAR, Ptolemy murdered his old ally POMPEY (THE GREAT). Julius Caesar effected a temporary reconciliation between Ptolemy and Cleopatra, but when fighting broke out between Caesar's and Ptolemy's armies, Ptolemy was killed.

Ptolemy (active AD 127–145) (Claudius Ptolemaeus) Greek astronomer, geographer and mathematician. He spent most of his working life in Alexandria, Egypt. His great astronomical book, the *Almagest* (13 vol), drew heavily on the work of Hipparchus. Ptolemy's theory of the Earth as the centre of the universe (the "Ptolemaic system") remained the cornerstone of Western astronomy until overturned by Nicolas COPERNICUS in the 15th century. Ptolemy's *Guide to Geography* gave information on how to construct maps of the known world. It was the basis of European geographical knowledge until the Renaissance, and Ptolemaic maps encouraged Christopher COLUMBUS' belief that he could reach Asia by sailing west.

Public Works Administration (PWA) Former US government agency established (1933) as part of the NEW DEAL of President Franklin ROOSEVELT. It spent *c*.US$4 billion on building schools, courthouses, city halls, sewage plants, hospitals and improving the transport network. The PWA provided employment for thousands of workers, but had little effect in reviving the overall national economy. In 1943 it was superseded by the Federal Works Agency.

Pueblo peoples Native American descendants of the prehistoric ANASAZI culture who live in NW New Mexico and NE Arizona. The Pueblo peoples are divided into two geographic groupings: the **eastern** Pueblo consist of the New Mexico pueblos (Sp. towns) along the Rio Grande, while the **western** Pueblo include the HOPI villages of N Arizona and the ZUNI, Laguna and Acoma villages in W New Mexico. Under Spanish colonial rule, the pueblos lost their political autonomy and many villages disappeared. The PUEBLO REVOLT (1680) was the most concerted Native American uprising against the Spanish.

Pueblo Revolt (1680) Organized uprising against Spanish colonial rule in New Mexico. The Spanish had attempted to destroy Pueblo culture by demolishing their ceremonial centres and ritual objects and forcing them to convert to Christianity. In addition, Spanish law had been enforced through a brutal regime of punishments and enslavery. Several earlier outbreaks had been crushed, but Popé, a medicine man from San Juan Pueblo, united the HOPI, ZUNI and the Pueblo tribes along the Rio Grande in a concerted, full-scale attack on the Spanish. The rebels expelled the Spanish from their capital of Santa Fe, killing *c*.500 colonizers and forcing the rest to flee to El Paso del Norte. The Spanish did not regain New Mexico until 1692.

Puerto Rico Self-governing island commonwealth of the West Indies, freely associated with the United States. When Christopher Columbus landed on W Puerto Rico in 1493, the island was inhabited by *c*.35,000 Taino and other ARAWAK groups. In 1509 Juan PONCE DE LEÓN founded the first Spanish settlement. Native American resistance to Spanish rule was crushed and the majority of the native population was exterminated, replaced by African slave labour. The Spanish built strong fortifications at San Juan. Sugar and coffee plantations, worked by slaves, developed in the 18th century. In 1815 Puerto Rico was opened to foreign trade. After a pro-independence revolt (1868), slavery was abolished in 1873 and the island gained autonomy in 1897. Puerto Rico was captured by the United States during the SPANISH-AMERICAN WAR (1898) and controlled by the US military until 1900, when civil government was restored under the control of the United States. In 1917 Puerto Rico became an "organized but unincorporated" territory of the United States and Puerto Ricans were granted US citizenship. From 1899 to 1930 the island's population nearly doubled due to improvements in medical care and sanitation. In 1948 Luis MUÑOZ MARÍN, campaigning for economic reform, became Puerto Rico's first elected governor (1948–68). In 1952, after a referendum, Puerto Rico became a commonwealth; this arrangement was endorsed by a plebiscite in 1967. Puerto Rico's status remained a contentious political issue and pro-independence extremists shot and wounded five US congressmen in 1952. Further referenda in 1993 and 1998 narrowly voted against US statehood. Pop. (1993 est.) 3,552,039.

Pugachev, Emelian Ivanovich (*c*.1742–75) Russian Cossack rebel. He joined the Russian army in 1759, but was arrested for desertion in 1772. Pugachev escaped and, pretending to be Tsar PETER III, organized a massive popular rebellion against CATHERINE II (THE GREAT). Pugachev gathered support from Cossacks, serfs, peasants and oppressed minorities, promising freedom from serfdom, taxes and military service and the elimination of landlords and government officials. In 1773 he established a court at Breda, SW Siberia. In 1774 the Russian army mounted a counter-offensive against the rebels. Pugachev responded by burning Kazan, capturing Saratov and besieging Tsaritsyn (now Volgograd), where he was betrayed and captured. He was executed in Moscow.

Puglia (Apulia) Region in SE Italy; the capital is Bari. The ancient Apulians (probably originally from Illyria) came under Roman rule in the 4th century BC. It was the scene of Hannibal's great victory (216 BC) in the Second Punic War. The region was held at different times by the Lombards, the Byzantines and others, becoming a duchy under Norman rule in the 11th century. It flourished under the HOHENSTAUFEN dynasty, especially under Emperor Frederick II, who joined Apulia with the Kingdom of the TWO SICILIES. It became part of the kingdom of Italy in 1861. Pop. (1992 est.) 4,049,972.

Pułaski, Kazimierz (*c*.1747–79) Polish patriot and soldier. He fought in the Confederation of BAR (1768) – a revolt against Russian influence in Poland – and became leader of the rebels. The defeat of the revolt led to the First Partition of POLAND and Pułaski fled into exile. In Paris in 1777, Benjamin FRANKLIN encouraged him to join the American Revolution (1775–83) against British rule. Pułaski distinguished himself at the Battle of the Brandywine (1777) and was made a general. In 1778 he formed the so-called Pułaski Legion, a mixed corps of cavalry and light infantry, which he trained in the art of guerrilla warfare. He was fatally wounded in the attack on Savannah, Georgia.

Pulitzer, Joseph (1847–1911) US newspaper publisher, b. Hungary. He emigrated to the United States in 1864 and served in the Union Army in the American Civil War (1861–65). After the War, Pulitzer became a journalist in St Louis, Missouri. In 1878 he bought the St Louis *Dispatch* and the *Post*, merging them to create the *Post-Dispatch*. In 1883 Pulitzer acquired the *New York World*. His combination of sensationalist reporting, feature sections and investigative journalism led to a fierce circulation war with William Randolph HEARST's *New York Morning Journal*. In his will, Pulitzer left endowments to establish Columbia University's school of journalism and the Pulitzer Prizes, awarded annually since 1917.

Pullman Strike (11 May–*c*.20 July 1894) US labour dispute. A *c*.25% cut in workers' wages by the manufacturers of Pullman railroad cars near Chicago, Illinois, led to industrial action by the American Railway Union. The Union president Eugene DEBS called for a nationwide strike, which virtually halted all railroad traffic in the Midwest. The governor of Illinois, John ALTGELD, declined to use the state militia, but US Attorney General Richard Olney, applying the SHERMAN ANTI-TRUST ACT to the UNIONS, obtained a federal court injunction against the strikers. When President Grover CLEVELAND sent in 2500 federal troops to enforce the injunction, violence broke out and several strikers were killed. The strike was broken, and Debs and other union officials were later imprisoned for ignoring the injunction.

Punic Wars (264–146 BC) Three conflicts between ROME and CARTHAGE. The fundamental cause was the growing challenge of Rome to the Carthaginian command of the Mediterranean. The **First** Punic War (264–241 BC) began as a struggle for control of the Sicilian city of Messana (now

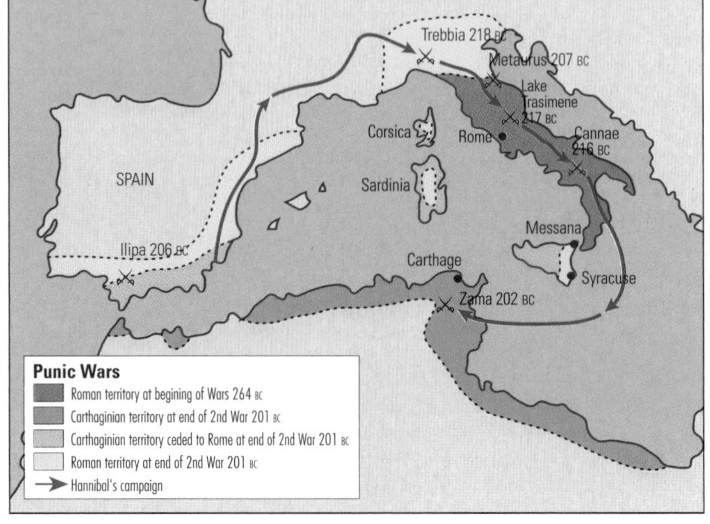

► **Punic Wars** In the First Punic War (264–241 BC), Rome defeated Carthage at Messana (263 BC) and Agrigento (262 BC). Having gained naval supremacy, they conquered Sicily and Corsica. In the Second Punic War (218–201 BC), Hannibal marched across the Alps to crush the Romans at Trebbia (218 BC). He inflicted further heavy defeats on the Roman army at Lake Tresimene (217 BC) and Cannae (216 BC). However, the destruction of Hasdrubal's force at Metaurus (207 BC) ended Carthage's hope of conquering Rome. Hannibal was forced to return to Africa, where he was defeated by Scipio Africanus at Zama (202 BC).

Messina). Rome occupied and held Messana and went on to seize the Carthaginian stronghold of AGRIGENTO (262 BC). Carthage was forced to surrender Corsica (259 BC), but beat off a Roman attack on their African territory. In 241 BC, after a decisive victory for the Roman fleet, Carthage ceded Sicily to Rome. At the start of the **Second** Punic War (218–201 BC), the Carthaginian general HANNIBAL gained the element of surprise by invading Italy via the Alps. He rapidly gained control of N Italy and destroyed the Roman forces at Etruria (217 BC). Quintus FABIUS MAXIMUS prevented Hannibal from moving south, but the Roman army was crushed at the Battle of CANNAE (216 BC). The guerrilla tactics of Fabius and MARCELLUS slowly began to push Hannibal into S Italy, however, and in 207 BC a new Cathaginian force, led by HASDRUBAL BARCA, invaded N Italy. Hasdrubal was prevented from joining forces with his brother and was killed by NERO's army at the Battle of Metaurus (207 BC). Hannibal was eventually forced to withdraw in order to defend Carthage itself, and was defeated by SCIPIO AFRICANUS MAJOR (202 BC) at ZAMA, North Africa. The War ended in complete triumph for the Roman republic: Carthage ceded Spain and its Mediterranean islands, the Carthaginian navy was disbanded, and Rome received an annual tribute of 200 talents. The **Third** Punic War (149–146 BC) was prompted by Carthage's defence of its territory against MASINISSA of NUMIDIA. Rome seized on Carthage's raising of an army as a violation of the treaty ending the Second Punic War. The Third Punic War ended in the burning of Carthage, the enslavement of its citizens and the declaration of the Roman province of Africa. *See also* MACEDONIAN WARS

Punjab Region in NW India and NE Pakistan, a former province of British India, which was divided between India and Pakistan when they became independent in 1947. The capital of the Indian Punjab is Chandigarh; of the Pakistani Punjab, LAHORE. The INDUS VALLEY CIVILIZATION was established by *c*.2500 BC. The Punjab was annexed (*c*.518 BC) by DARIUS I of Persia, before becoming part of the MAURYAN EMPIRE under Chandragupta (*c*.322 BC). Muslim rule over the whole of Punjab was established by MAHMUD OF GHAZNA in the early 11th century and the province thrived under MUGHAL control from the 16th century. In *c*.1800 the Sikhs under RANJIT SINGH established their kingdom in the Punjab with its capital at Lahore, but it fell to the English EAST INDIA COMPANY after the SIKH WARS (1845–49), and the Punjab subsequently became a province of British India. The province was a stronghold of resistance to British rule, and the AMRITSAR Massacre (1919) did much to strengthen support for the liberation movement. When independence was achieved in 1947, Punjab was divided between India and Pakistan, resulting in communal violence and displacement on a vast scale. In 1966 the Indian area was further divided into two states: Punjab (predominantly Sikh and Punjabi-speaking) and Haryana (predominantly Hindu). In the 1980s Sikh militants launched a terrorist campaign to establish an independent Sikh state (Khalistan). The Indian government responded by imposing direct rule. In 1984 the Indian army stormed the Golden Temple in Amritsar, which Sikh militants were using as a stronghold, killing 400 people, including the Sikh leader Jarnail Singh BHINDRANWALE. Indian Punjab pop. (1991) 20,281,969; Pakistani Punjab pop. (1985 est.) 53,840,000.

Purge, Great (1936–38) Elimination of potential opponents of Joseph STALIN in the SOVIET UNION. The murder of Sergei KIROV (1934) was the pretext for mass arrests of suspected opponents of the regime. At the first public "show" trial (August 1936), Grigori ZINOVIEV, Lev KAMENEV and Ivan Smirnov were among those accused of murdering Kirov and conspiring with Leon TROTSKY to overthrow Stalin. Under torture and intimidation, they confessed to treachery and were summarily executed. In a second trial (January 1937), Karl RADEK was among 17 defendants accused of collaborating with Trotsky. A third trial (March 1938) ended with the execution of 18 other leading "Old Bolsheviks", including Nikolai BUKHARIN. These high-profile trials were part of a much more widespread purge of the Communist Party and Soviet society in general. Later, Stalin's suspicion was directed at the Red Army, resulting in the virtual annihilation of the officer class. It is estimated that up to 7 million people died in the Great Purge, many of whom perished in the Siberian GULAGS. *See also* BERIA, LAVRENTI PAVLOVICH; KGB

Puritanism English religious reform movement of the late 16th and early 17th centuries, which believed that the Elizabethan Settlement (1559), a compromise between Roman Catholicism and PROTESTANTISM during the reign of ELIZABETH I, had not sufficiently purified the CHURCH OF ENGLAND of "popery". It was first applied (as a term of abuse) to those who refused the Settlement's demand for uniformity in clerical vestments and the liturgy. A minority of Puritans, including Robert BROWNE, also demanded the adoption of PRESBYTERIANISM in church government. The accession (1583) of John WHITGIFT as archbishop of Canterbury signalled the start of a more sustained suppression of Puritanism. During the reign (1603–25) of JAMES I, some Puritans sought sanctuary in the New World, founding JAMESTOWN, Virginia (1607), and PLYMOUTH COLONY, New England (1620). Later, John WINTHROP and John COTTON established the MASSACHUSETTS BAY COLONY along Puritan lines, and William PENN attempted to create a QUAKER commonwealth in Pennsylvania. Anti-Puritanism became even more acute after CHARLES I (r.1625–49) appointed William LAUD as archbishop of Canterbury in 1633. Laud's attempt to introduce a high-church Anglicanism, derived from Jacobus ARMINIUS, proved highly unpopular, and anti-Catholic sentiment produced a Parliament dominated by the Puritans. The conflict over religion was thus a major factor in causing the English CIVIL WAR. Radical Puritan groups, such as the LEVELLERS, DIGGERS and FIFTH MONARCHY MEN, emerged during Oliver CROMWELL's Commonwealth. The Restoration (1660) of CHARLES II and the subsequent Act of UNIFORMITY (1662) led to widespread persecution of Puritans, but the GLORIOUS REVOLUTION (1688) reinstated religious toleration. *See also* NONCONFORMISM; PIETISM

Putin, Vladimir (1952–) Russian statesman, prime minister (1999–2000), president (2000–). He served for the KGB in East Germany until 1989 and became head of its successor organization in 1998. When Boris Yeltsin resigned in 1999, Putin became acting president. His support for the war in CHECHENIA earned him victory in the ensuing presidential elections. As president, one of his first acts was to grant Yeltsin immunity from prosecution.

Pu Yi (1906–67) (Hsuan Tung) Last emperor (1908–11) of the QING dynasty in China. He was chosen to succeed his uncle, GUANGXU, by the Empress Dowager CIXI. Deposed on the formation of the Chinese republic, Pu Yi was temporarily rescued from obscurity to become president, later "emperor" of the Japanese puppet state of MANCHUKUO in 1932. Captured by Soviet forces in 1945, he was later delivered to the Chinese communist regime and imprisoned (1949–59). He later worked as a gardener in Beijing.

Pym, John (*c*.1584–1643) English leader of the parliamentary opposition to CHARLES I, known as "King Pym". He entered Parliament in 1621, and soon acquired a reputation as a leading opponent of William LAUD's reform of the Church of England. In 1630 Pym became treasurer of the Providence Island Company, which organized resistance to Charles' imposition of SHIP MONEY. Pym dominated the early sessions of the LONG PARLIAMENT (1640), leading calls for the impeachment of the Earl of STRAFFORD, and attempting to persuade Charles to agree to a form of constitutional monarchy. Pym's management of Parliament ensured the issuing of the GRAND REMONSTRANCE (1641) of grievances against the king. Pym was one of the five members whom Charles tried to arrest in the House of Commons (1642), an incident that made the English CIVIL WAR inevitable. Pym used his contacts in the City of London to fund the Parliamentary army during the Civil War and secured parliamentary approval of the SOLEMN LEAGUE AND COVENANT with the Scots.

pyramid Monument on a square base with sloping sides rising to a point. Pyramids are associated particularly with the Old Kingdom of ancient EGYPT, where they were built as burial chambers for pharaohs. The earliest was a step pyramid, or ziggurat, built (*c*.2700 BC) for King Zoser by IMHOTEP. Pyramid building in Egypt reached its peak during the 4th dynasty, the time of the Great Pyramid (*c*.2500 BC) at Giza. Built for CHEOPS, it is the largest known pyramid, at 146m (480ft) high with sides 231m (758ft) square. The labour required to build such a monument gives some indication of the organizational capacity of the Egyptian kingdom. Vast ziggurats were also built in ancient Mesopotamia and in Mesoamerica, where the largest, at TEOTIHUACÁN, Mexico, was built in the 1st century AD.

Pyramids, Battle of the (21 July 1798) French victory over the MAMLUKS in N Egypt. Having invaded Egypt and taken Alexandria, NAPOLEON met the Mamluk army near the pyramids of Giza. He organized his 25,000-strong army into five divisional squares, the mobility of which enabled him to defeat the 40,000-strong Egyptian army. The French lost only *c*.300 men in the destruction of the Mamluks. Napoleon's hold over Egypt was weakened, however, by Horatio NELSON's victory over the French fleet at the Battle of ABOUKIR ten days later.

Pyrenees, Peace of the (7 November 1659) Treaty between France and Spain, completing the Peace of WESTPHALIA (1648) at the end of the THIRTY YEARS' WAR. The Peace reflected the decline of Spain and the ascendancy of France as the dominant power in Europe. It also arranged the marriage between LOUIS XIV and Maria Teresa, daughter of PHILIP IV of Spain.

Pyrrhus (*c*.319–272 BC) King of EPIRUS (307–302 BC, 295–272 BC). He was deposed by an uprising in 302 BC, and later became a hostage of PTOLEMY I, who aided his recovery of the throne. Pyrrhus gained parts of Macedonia from DEMETRIUS I (POLIORCETES). He defeated the Romans in S Italy (280 BC), Apulia (279 BC) and Beneventum (275 BC), but at ruinously high cost, giving rise to the term "pyrrhic victory".

Pythagoras (*c*.580–*c*.500 BC) Greek philosopher, founder of the Pythagorean school. The Pythagoreans were ascetics, bound to their teacher by rigid vows. They believed in the transmigration of souls and that numbers constitute the true nature of things in the universe. Pythagoras is credited with many advances in science and philosophy, but the famous geometrical theorem named after him may have been known earlier. Although much Pythagorean thought seems to have been mystical, it did establish the importance of mathematics as a way of understanding the world.

◀ **pyramid** The three pyramids at Giza, N Egypt, have survived virtually intact to the present-day. The Great Pyramid, shown here in the centre, is the oldest and largest. It was built (*c*.2550 BC) for the pharoah Cheops (Khufu). The other two were built for Chephren (Khafre) and Mycerinus (Menkaure), Khufu's son and grandson respectively. The pyramids were originally cased in white limestone, a small section of which can still be seen on the Chephren (Khafre) Pyramid, shown here on the left.

P

Q

Qaboos bin Said (1940–) Sultan of Oman (1970–), 14th descendant of the Albusaid dynasty. Educated in England at Sandhurst, Qaboos returned to OMAN in 1965 where he was immediately held captive by his father, Said Ibn Taimur (r.1932–70), for his liberal views. With British support, members of the Omani government overthrew Said Ibn Taimur in a bloodless coup and Qaboos was made sultan. While in power Qaboos introduced liberal reforms and a constitution that saw the inception of a second advisory assembly. With Oman's large oil revenue, he improved the transport infrastructure, and built hospitals and schools.

Qaddafi, Muammar al- (1942–) Libyan leader and revolutionary. A devout Muslim and Arab nationalist, Qaddafi rose swiftly through the ranks of the armed forces, and in 1969 he led the coup that toppled King IDRIS I. He was made commander in chief of the armed forces and chairman of the newly formed Revolutionary Command Council (1970–79). As *de facto* head of state, Qaddafi sought to remove all vestiges of Libya's colonial past. He shut down US and British military bases, nationalized all petroleum assets, and encouraged a form of fundamental Islamic socialism. However his attempts to create a North African Arab Federation have so far failed. Although Qaddafi resigned from all official government posts in 1979, he remained the country's ruler. During the 1980s Libya supported a number of revolutionary causes throughout the world including the PALESTINE LIBERATION ORGANIZATION (PLO) and the IRISH REPUBLICAN ARMY (IRA). Within North Africa, Libya attempted to gain territory from neighbouring states, most conspicuously CHAD. In 1986 the United States bombed a number of sites in Libya in an attempt to stop his support of international terrorism. Qaddafi narrowly avoided being killed, but his 16-month old daughter died. Although Libya was neutral during the GULF WAR, Qaddafi remained accused of protecting two Libyans suspected of the bombing of Pan-Am Flight 103 over Lockerbie, Scotland (1988), for which United Nations' sanctions were imposed in 1992. In 1999 he handed over the suspects to Dutch authorities for trial under Scottish law, and the sanctions were automatically revoked.

QING (FORMERLY CH'ING)

Last imperial dynasty of CHINA (1644–1911). It was established (1636) by the MANCHU ruler NURHACHI, who had created a well-organized military movement known as the "Banner system" to protect Qing territory in Manchuria. In 1644 officials of the imperial MING dynasty requested assistance from the Bannermen to expel the bandit leader Li Zicheng from Beijing. Once in control of BEIJING, the Manchu assumed control of imperial China. The Qing retained much of the Ming civil service, gradually replacing the more senior positions with Manchu administrators. Under the Qing emperors, China attained its greatest extent, controlling an area stretching from Siam (Thailand) and Tibet to Mongolia and the River Amur. The two most significant emperors of the dynasty were KANGXI (r.1661–1722) and QIANLONG (r.1736–96).

In the 19th century, the dynasty weakened, and population pressure and corruption increased. Internal struggles, such as the TAIPING REBELLION, together with the SINO-JAPANESE WAR, the OPIUM WARS and the BOXER REBELLION resulted in an unwanted increase of foreign influence. Emperor GUANGXU's support for the HUNDRED DAYS OF REFORM (1898) met with opposition from reactionaries led by Empress Dowager CIXI who mounted a palace coup. The dynasty was ended by the 1911 Republican Revolution and the abdication of the last emperor, PU YI. *See also* LI HONGZHANG; SELF-STRENGTHENING MOVEMENT

◄ **Forbidden City** in Beijing, N China, houses the palaces of the Ming and Qing dynasties. It contains more than 9000 buildings, including audience halls, theatres and libraries. Following the overthrow of the Qing dynasty in 1911, Pu Yi was allowed to remain in the N part of the Forbidden City but separated from the ceremonial halls by a wall.

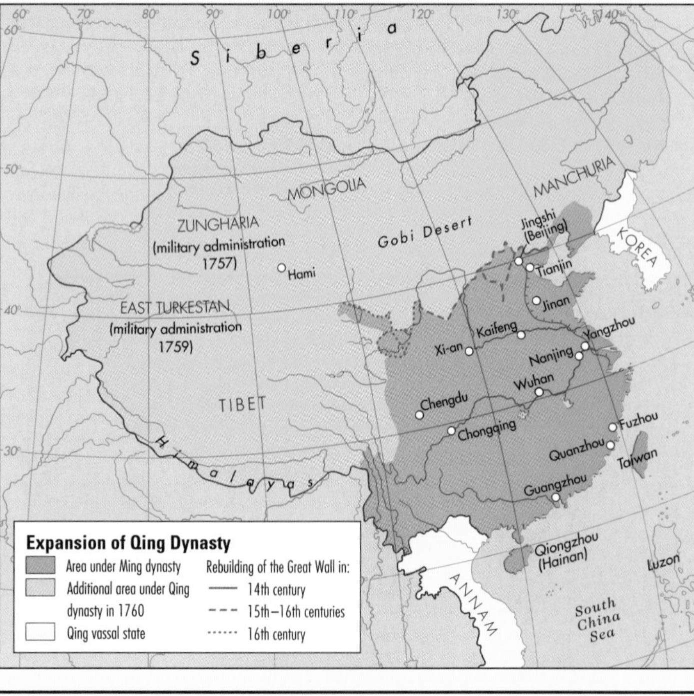

► **Qing dynasty** The Qing empire reached its greatest extent at the end of the 18th century. It expanded S initially, annexing the island of Formosa (Taiwan) in 1683. An agreement was reached with Russia over the N borders in the Treaty of Nerchinsk (1689). During the 17th century, Mongolia, Tibet, Turkistan, Burma, Nepal and Annam (now in Vietnam) were incorporated into the empire. Although much of the territory gained was sparsely populated and not particularly fertile, states like Korea and Annam served as a buffer zone against invasion.

Qajar dynasty Ruling house of Persia (IRAN) from 1794 to 1925. It was established by **Agha Muhammad** (1742–97), a Turkoman eunuch, who gained control of the N of the country, and with the purpose of unifying Persia, defeated the Zand ruler in the S in 1794. Agha was crowned in 1796 and made Tehran his capital. A year later, following Agha Muhammad's assassination, **Fath Ali** acceded to the throne (r.1797–1834). Although Fath Ali Shah improved relations with the West, he lost the Trans-Caucasian territories in two wars against Russia. Fath Ali was succeeded by his grandson **Muhammad** (r.1834–48), who in turn was succeeded by his son **Naser od-Din** (r.1848–96), under whose competent rule Persia underwent a process of modernization. The next shah, **Mozaffar od-Din** (r.1896–1907), was forced to agree to a constitution that curbed the power of the monarchy. His son **Muhammad Ali Shah** (r.1907–09) was deposed when he attempted unsuccessfully to withdraw the constitution. The last Qajar ruler, **Ahmad Shah** (r.1909–25), following a coup in 1921 led by Reza Shah PAHLAVI, effectively lost control of the country and was exiled in 1923. He was formally deposed by the assembly in 1925.

Qatar *See* country feature

Qianlong (Ch'ien-lung) (1711–99) Fourth QING emperor of China (1736–96). His reign saw China grow to its greatest size by taking Tibet and Mongolia, and by receiving tribute from other regions, including Annam and Burma. Although Qianlong encouraged some contact with European traders he severely restricted their operating territory. He rejected the British Macartney mission (1793), the purpose of which was to expand trading and diplomatic ties with China. Despite Qianlong's contemporary success, towards the end of his reign corruption, overpopulation, a weakening of Manchu military power and widespread internal struggles resulted in a China that was unable to withstand the European incursions of the 19th century.

Qin (formerly Ch'in) First imperial dynasty of a unified China (221–206 BC). Originating in NW China, the Qin was just one of many small feudal states that made up China. The Qin's strong central administration, based on strict legal codes, coupled with their superior army enabled them, during the 4th century BC, gradually to subdue the other "Warring States", the remnants of the Eastern ZHOU dynasty. Between 256 and 221 BC, under the leadership of Zheng, the Qin defeated the remaining opposition states, and Zheng was able to unite China, ruling as QIN SHIHUANGDI ("First Sovereign Emperor of Qin"). The first centralized imperial administration was established, and the country was divided into provinces or prefectures, each under a governor. The strict authoritarian attitude of the central administration is reflected in the burning of all non-essential books. Uniformity was encouraged in every sphere, including law, language, coinage, weights and measures, and along with the construction of roads and canals, the GREAT WALL OF CHINA also took permanent shape during this period. Although resentment at the oppressive administration and punishing taxes resulted in the overthrowing of the Qin dynasty four years after Qin Shihuangdi's death, China was to remain a unified country.

QATAR

AREA: 11,000sq km (4247 sq mi)
POPULATION: 551,000
CAPITAL (POPULATION): Doha (217,294)
GOVERNMENT: Constitutional monarchy
ETHNIC GROUPS: Southern Asian 34%, Qatari 20%
LANGUAGES: Arabic (official)
RELIGIONS: Sunni Muslim 92%, Christian, Hindu
GDP PER CAPITA (1995): US$17,690

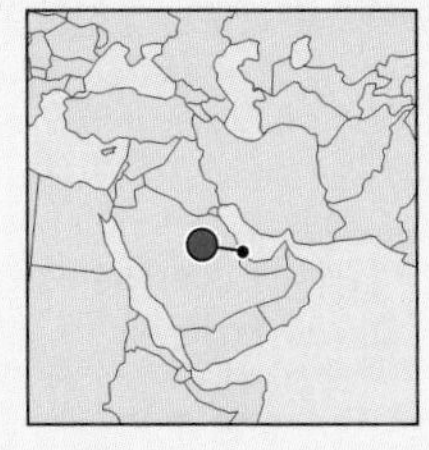

Sheikhdom on the Qatar Peninsula in the Persian Gulf. Inhabited by nomadic tribes, there is very little written history of the region of Qatar until the late 18th century, when the region came under the control of Kuwaiti migrant families, particularly the Al-Khalifa. In the 1780s the Al-Khalifa moved into and took control of BAHRAIN, and Qatar was then ruled by a number of sheiks. From 1872 until 1913 Qatar was part of the OTTOMAN EMPIRE.

Qatar became a British protectorate in 1916, when it signed a treaty with Sheik Abdullah al-Thani in which Britain promised military aid in exchange for control over Qatar's foreign policy. In 1971 Qatar achieved independence and joined the UNITED NATIONS (UN) and the ARAB LEAGUE. Sheikh Khalifa bin Hamad Al-Thani became emir after a coup in 1972. Qatar was a founding member of the GULF COOPERATION COUNCIL (GCC) in 1981. During the 1980s, Qatar's status was threatened by the regional dominance of Iran and Iraq, and a territorial dispute with Bahrain. In the GULF WAR (1991), Allied coalition forces were deployed on Qatar's territory and Palestinian migrant workers expelled because of the pro-Iraqi stance of the PALESTINE LIBERATION ORGANIZATION (PLO). In 1995 the emir was overthrown and replaced by his son, Sheikh Hamad bin Khalifa Al-Thani. A coup attempt failed in 1996.

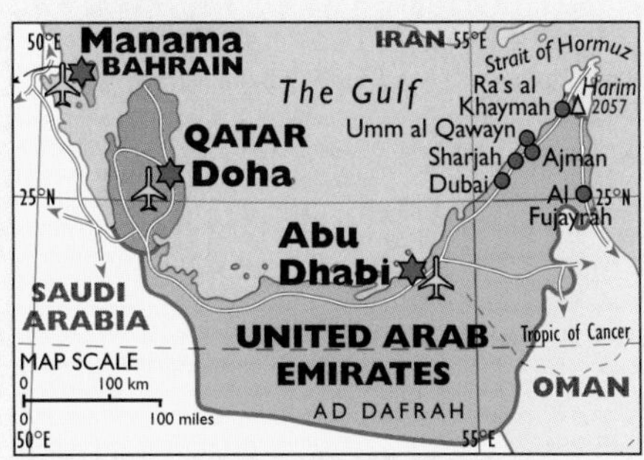

Qing *See* feature article

Qin Shihuangdi (259–210 BC) Emperor of China (221–210 BC), founder of the QIN dynasty. During the period of "Warring States" he extinguished the failing ZHOU dynasty and united neighbouring states under his rule. A powerful, often despotic ruler, he was intolerant of any dissent, even to the point of burning books that were considered inessential or were not significant to the Qin. He created a strong, centralized bureaucracy and administration, dispensed with all feudal power and consolidated his territory by building many roads and fortifications, the most significant of which was the GREAT WALL OF CHINA. Excavations of his tomb on Mount Li (near Xian) during the 1970s revealed, among other treasures, an "army" of *c.*7500 life-size terracotta guardians.

Quadruple Alliance Alliance among four states, in particular three alliances in Europe in the 18th and 19th centuries. The **first** Quadruple Alliance was formed (1718) by Britain, France, the Holy Roman Empire and the Netherlands against PHILIP V of Spain, who, encouraged by Giulio ALBERONI, seized Sicily and Sardinia, so contravening the Treaty of UTRECHT. By 1720 the allies had forced Philip to renounce his claims on Italy. The **second** Quadruple Alliance was formed (1813) by Austria, Britain, Prussia and Russia against NAPOLEON I during the final stages of the NAPOLEONIC WARS. After Napoleon's defeat the four partners met at the Congress of VIENNA (1814–15) to establish the CONGRESS SYSTEM, the purpose of which initially was to deny any further French aggression in Europe, but which in effect became, particularly with the participation of France (1818), a means of suppressing general revolution. The **third** Quadruple Alliance (1834) consisted of Britain and France in support of Portugal and Spain. In Spain the alliance successfully defended ISABELLA II's regent against the reactionary Don CARLOS in the First Carlist War. In Portugal the alliance succeeded in expelling the reactionary Dom MIGUEL. *See also* CARLISM

quaestor (questor) Magistrate of ancient Rome. Originally there were two quaestors, who dealt with judicial matters, but in the late ROMAN REPUBLIC the number was increased and the quaestors became primarily concerned with financial affairs. In the early ROMAN EMPIRE, it was the lowest rank of state official. By the late imperial period, it had become an honorary office for the sons of senators. Military quaestors assisted the commanding generals in the provinces.

Quakers (officially Society of Friends) Christian sect that arose in England in the 1650s, founded by George FOX. The name derived from the injunction given by early Quaker leaders that their followers tremble at the word of the Lord. Quakers rejected the episcopal organization of the CHURCH OF ENGLAND, believing in the priesthood of all believers and a direct relationship between man and the spiritual light of God. Quakers originally worshipped God in meditative silence unless someone was moved by the Holy Spirit to speak. Since the mid-19th century, their meetings have included hymns and readings. The largest national Quaker Church is in the United States, where it began with the founding of a settlement by William PENN in Pennsylvania (1681). Today, there are *c.*200,000 Quakers worldwide.

Quantrill, William Clarke (1837–65) Confederate guerrilla leader during the American CIVIL WAR (1861–65). His guerrilla army terrorized and murdered Union sympathizers in Missouri and Kansas. In 1862 Quantrill was made a captain in the Confederate Army. In 1863 he was responsible for the murder of some 150 citizens of Lawrence, Kansas. He was killed by federal forces in Kentucky.

Quaternary period Most recent period of the CENOZOIC era, beginning *c.*2 million years ago and extending to the present. It is divided into the **Pleistocene epoch**, characterized by a periodic succession of great ice ages, and the **Holocene epoch**, which started *c.*10,000 years ago.

Quatre Bras and Ligny, Battles of (16 June 1815) Twin conflicts fought during the last campaign of the NAPOLEONIC WARS (1803–15). Hoping to prevent the concentration of two Allied armies, Napoleon attacked the Prussians under Field Marshal BLÜCHER at Ligny, while Marshal NEY led forces against the British army under the Duke of WELLINGTON at Quatre Bras. Both allied armies were driven back, but they recombined to defeat Napoleon at WATERLOO on 18 June.

Québec Province in E Canada; the capital is Québec City. In 1535 Jacques CARTIER landed on the Gaspé Peninsula of E CANADA, and in 1536 he sailed up the St Lawrence River. In 1608 Samuel de CHAMPLAIN established the first settlement on the present-day site of Québec City. It served as a headquarters for Catholic missionaries and the fur-traders' exploration of the interior. In 1663 LOUIS XIV of France sent Jean-Baptiste Talon to the region, now called NEW FRANCE, as his royal administrator, the purpose of which was to encourage French immigration. For the next hundred years the region was witness to increasing tension between the British and French, culminating in the FRENCH AND INDIAN WAR (1754–63). Following the decisive battle on the Plains of ABRAHAM (1759), New France was ceded to Britain by the Treaty of PARIS (1763). In an attempt to avoid further unrest, the British passed the QUÉBEC ACT (1774), which broadly allowed the French to retain much of their culture. The CONSTITUTIONAL ACT (1791) separated off the area W of the River Ottawa as the colony of Upper Canada (now ONTARIO), while Québec became the British colony of Lower Canada, gaining an elective assembly in 1791. Continued French unrest resulted in the REBELLION OF 1837 led by Louis PAPINEAU. Although the rebellion was quickly put down, a subsequent report (1839) by the Earl of DURHAM recommended the unification of Upper and Lower Canada (achieved in the 1840 Act of UNION) and led ultimately to the establishment of the Dominion of Canada through the BRITISH NORTH AMERICA ACT (1867). The Québecois remained fiercely independent throughout the early 19th century, and their demands for self-determination and recognition of their cultural heritage intensified in the late 20th century. The 1960s saw bombing campaigns by

◄ **Qin Shihuangdi** The mausoleum of Qin Shihuangdi located at the old Qin capital of Xianyang, N China, covers an area of 50sq km (20sq mi) and took 700,000 conscripted workers 35 years to build. At the centre of the complex is an elaborate underground palace covered by a huge burial mound. Guarding Qin Shihuangdi's tomb is an army of more than 7500 life-size terracotta soldiers. The soldiers stand in battle formation and are accompanied by horses, chariots and weapons. It is thought that the body parts of the figures were made in moulds, then assembled before individual details were added to their faces and clothing. Excavation of the site still continues and in 1987 the tomb was designated a UNESCO World Heritage site.

the poorly supported **Front de Libération du Québec** (FLQ), while in 1976 the constitutional Parti Québecois won power under René LEVESQUE. Defeated in 1989, they regained power in 1995 and called a referendum on "sovereignty-association" (independence) that was defeated by the narrowest of margins. Area: 1,540,687sq km (594,860sq mi). Pop. (1991) 6,895,963. *See also* CARTIER, GEORGES ETIENNE; LESAGE, JEAN; LAURIER, SIR WILFRID; MULRONEY, BRIAN; SAINT LAURENT, LOUIS STEPHEN; TRUDEAU, PIERRE ELLIOTT

Québec Act (1774) British legislation that created a permanent administration (in the form of a governor assisted by a council) to oversee QUÉBEC, E Canada. The Act, largely the work of Sir Guy CARLETON, was passed in an attempt to reconcile the French inhabitants of Québec following Britain's victory in the FRENCH AND INDIAN WAR (1754–63). The act recognized the Roman Catholic Church and the French legal and landholding systems. The fact that Québec's boundary was extended s to the Ohio River coupled with the tolerance of Catholicism caused massive resentment among the Protestant THIRTEEN COLONIES; it was a significant cause of the AMERICAN REVOLUTION.

Québec Conferences Two meetings of the Allied powers held in the city of Québec, E Canada, during World War 2. The first (August 1943) was attended by Franklin ROOSEVELT, Winston CHURCHILL, the Canadian Prime Minister William Mackenzie KING and the Chinese Foreign Minister Song Ziwen, during which it was agreed that Louis MOUNTBATTEN would assume overall command of operations in the war against Japan in Southeast Asia. At the second Conference (September 1944), Roosevelt and Churchill agreed to increase bombing raids on Germany, settled on a general strategy in the war against Japan and discussed approaches to governing Germany once it was defeated.

Queen Anne's War *See* FRENCH AND INDIAN WARS

Queensland State in NE AUSTRALIA; the capital is Brisbane. Thought to have been inhabited by Native Australians for more than 50,000 years, Queensland was first discovered by European explorers in *c.*1606. In 1770 Captain James COOK undertook more detailed surveys of the E coast of Australia and claimed the region for Britain. Queensland, originally the Moreton Bay district of NEW SOUTH WALES, remained unsettled until 1824, at which time it served as a penal colony. In 1840 the penal colony was closed and the first free settlers arrived two years later. In 1859 it separated from New South Wales and was renamed Queensland. The discovery of gold in 1858 saw a large increase in population during the 1860s and early 1870s. The 1870s saw the first railways and the establishment of pastoral farming and sugar and cotton production. In 1901 Queensland was made a state of the Commonwealth of Australia. Area: 1,727,530sq km (667,000sq mi). Pop. (1993 est.) 3,155,400.

Queenston Heights, Battle of (13 October 1812) Decisive battle of the WAR OF 1812. In an attempt to invade Canada, an advance guard of the US Army, comprising *c.*1600 militiamen led by Major General Van Rensselaer, crossed the Niagara River and occupied the heights around Queenston, E Canada. Although initially able to defend their position, the US militiamen were eventually annihilated by the British army, composed chiefly of Canadian volunteers. The British commander, General Isaac BROCK, was killed leading a charge up the Heights.

Quesnay, François (1694–1774) French physician and economist, leader of the PHYSIOCRATS. While attendant physician to LOUIS XV Quesnay developed an interest in economics. In 1758 he devised an economic table (*Tableau économique*), which demonstrated the "natural law" of economic activity. An opponent of MERCANTILISM, Quesnay advocated a LAISSEZ-FAIRE approach, which was later to influence Adam SMITH. Quesnay and his followers were dismissive of industrial and commercial productivity, believing only that land and agriculture could generate sustainable wealth.

Quezon (y Molina), Manuel Luis (1878–1944) Philippine statesman, first president of the Commonwealth of the PHILIPPINES (1935–44). In 1901 he was imprisoned for his part in the revolt, initiated by Emilio AGUINALDO, against US rule. After his release, Quezon became leader of the Nationalist Party and, as commissioner to the United States (1909–16), secured the passage of the Tydings-McDuffie Bill (1934), which paved the way for independence. An autocratic president, Quezon instigated administrative reforms. His strengthening of Philippine defences failed to prevent Japan's invasion. Quezon headed a government-in-exile in the United States until his death.

Quiberon Bay, Battle of (1759) British naval victory over the French fleet in the SEVEN YEARS' WAR. Fought off the coast of Brittany, N France, the British under the command of Lord Edward HAWKE, sunk 11 French ships for the loss of two British. The decisive victory ended any French aspirations of invading Britain.

Quincy, Josiah (1772–1864) US politician. A Federalist, he became a senator (1804) and then represented Boston in the House of Representatives (1805–13), where he became the FEDERALIST PARTY minority leader. Quincy strongly opposed the WAR OF 1812 and was one of the first congressmen to speak out against slavery. He was mayor of Boston in the 1820s.

Quirino, Elpidio (1890–1956) Philippine statesman, second president of the PHILIPPINES (1948–53). He was a member of the Philippine House of Representatives (1919–25) and the Senate (1925–35). He served briefly in Manuel QUEZON's government, before being elected (1946) vice president in the first government of the independent republic, under Manuel Roxas. He succeeded to the presidency on Roxas' death (1948) and won the 1949 elections as a Liberal Party candidate. In 1950 Quirino appointed Ramón MAGSAYSAY to suppress the HUKBALAHAP rebels, who were threatening to overthrow the government. Despite considerable post-war reconstruction and economic improvement during Quirino's presidency, corruption continued and social conditions for many people failed to improve. He was defeated by Magsaysay in the 1953 elections.

Quisling, Vidkun (1887–1945) Norwegian fascist leader. After working in the Soviet Union on humanitarian missions (1922–25), he worked in the Norwegian legation in Moscow (1927–29). On his return to Norway he entered politics on a fervently anti-communist platform and became minister of defence (1931–33). In 1933 he left the government and founded the pro-fascist National Union Party, based on, and partly funded by, the German NAZI PARTY. In 1940 Quisling, having persuaded Hitler to occupy Norway, collaborated with the invading Germans. Once the German envoy had failed to force HAAKON VII to accept Quisling as prime minister they set him up as a puppet ruler (1942) for the duration of their occupation. Quisling, as well as attempting to introduce NATIONAL SOCIALISM to all elements of Norwegian society, was also responsible for the deaths of many hundreds of Norwegian Jews and the brutal suppression of pro-Haakon supporters. After World War 2 he was found guilty of treason by a Norwegian court and executed.

Quit India movement Campaign started in August 1942 by the Indian National CONGRESS. "Mahatma" GANDHI and other Congress leaders urged Indians to undertake massive non-violent demonstrations against British rule in INDIA. The campaign was brought about by Sir Stafford CRIPPS' request to the Congress Party to mobilize India in the war against Japan. Gandhi refused to cooperate with the British, and he and other leaders were arrested. The arrests spurred the movement and the British army had to deploy 57 battalions to suppress the rebellion, resulting in widespread bloodshed. The campaign was a significant factor in the British withdrawal from India at the end of World War 2. *See also* NEHRU, JAWAHARLAL

Quran *See* KORAN

Qutb-ud-Din Aybak (d.1210) Founder of the Muslim DELHI SULTANATE. Sold into slavery as a child, he eventually won the complete trust of his master, Muhammad of Ghur. As Muhamamd's general, Qutb consolidated and increased Muhammad's territory in NW India following Muhammad's return to Khorasan (1192). In 1206 Muhammad was assassinated, and Qutb, by now his natural successor, took control of the NW Indian territories and proclaimed himself the Sultan of Delhi (1206–10), establishing the SLAVE DYNASTY. He obtained his freedom and with judicious marriages was able to ensure the succession of his son, Aram Singh, and then his son-in-law, ILTUTMISH.

Rabat Capital of Morocco, on the Atlantic coast. There was a Roman settlement on the opposite bank of the River Regreg, but Rabat itself was founded when the first ALMOHAD sultan, Abd al-Mumin (d.1163) assembled troops here for his war in Spain. The city was named (Rabat means "camp of victory") by the third Almohad sultan, Abu Yusuf Yaqub al-Mansur (*c*.1160–99), who also built the city walls and the tower of Hassan. In the 17th century Rabat was settled by Muslim refugees from Spain and later became a notorious haunt for Barbary pirates. It became the capital of the French protectorate in 1912, and when the French left (1956), capital of the kingdom. Pop. (1982) 518,616.

Rabin, Yitzhak (1922–95) Israeli statesman, prime minister (1974–77, 1992–95). As chief of staff (1964–68), he directed Israeli operations in the SIX-DAY WAR (1967). Rabin was ambassador to the United States (1968–73) before succeeding Golda MEIR as Israel's first native-born prime minister. His first term in office was marked by the raid on Entebbe airport, Uganda, to rescue Israeli hostages. As minister of defence (1984–90), he directed operations against the Palestinian INTIFADA and, having regained leadership of the Labour Party from his colleague and rival, Shimon PERES, became prime minister for the second time. In 1993 Rabin signed the ISRAELI-PALESTINIAN ACCORD with the PALESTINE LIBERATION ORGANIZATION (PLO), promising progress towards Palestinian autonomy in the occupied territories. Rabin, Peres and the PLO leader Yasser ARAFAT shared the 1994 Nobel Prize for Peace. He also signed a peace treaty (1994) with King Hussein of Jordan. On 4 November 1995, he was assassinated by an Israeli right-wing extremist. *See also* MAPAI

Race Relations Act (1976) British legislation making it unlawful to directly or indirectly discriminate on grounds of race, colour, nationality, or ethnic origin in housing, employment, training, education and the provision of goods and services. It superseded earlier acts (1965, 1968) and set up the Commission for Racial Equality (CRE) to investigate acts of discrimination. In 2000 an Amendment Bill sought to extend the indirect discrimination provisions of the Act to public service functions, such as the police.

racism Belief in the superiority of one group of human beings over others on the basis of racial characteristics, real or imagined. Scientific evidence does not support the concept of biological differences according to race, and racism appears to be merely one of the many notions that people have adopted throughout history as justification for hating their neighbours, rivals, etc. Extreme examples of racist governments in recent times were those of Nazi Germany in 1933–45, with its organized mass murder of Jews (*see* HOLOCAUST), and of South Africa in the APARTHEID era, which aimed at segregation of blacks and whites.

Radek, Karl (1885–1939?) Soviet revolutionary, b. Poland as Karl Sobelsohn. He was imprisoned for a year after participating in the RUSSIAN REVOLUTION OF 1905. Radek accompanied Vladimir LENIN on part of his journey to Russia in 1917 and, after the RUSSIAN REVOLUTION (1917), he was part of the Soviet delegation to Germany that agreed to the Treaty of BREST-LITOVSK. Radek remained in Germany, and was jailed for helping organize the failed rising (1918) by the SPARTACUS LEAGUE. In 1919 Radek was released and returned to Russia, where he became a leading member of the COMINTERN. He was forced to resign after the failure of a second revolt (1923) in Germany. Radek was temporarily expelled (1927–29) from the Communist Party of the Soviet Union (CPSU) for supporting Leon TROTSKY. After being readmitted to the Party, he worked with Nikolai BUKHARIN and edited *Izvestia* (1931–36), but fell victim to Joseph STALIN's Great PURGE in 1937, probably dying in prison.

Radetzky, Joseph, Graf (1766–1858) Austrian general. He served in the French Revolutionary Wars (1792–1802) and the Napoleonic Wars (1803–15). As chief of staff to Fürst zu SCHARWZENBERG, Radetzky helped plan the tactics that won the decisive Battle of LEIPZIG (1813). He served as commander in chief (1831–57) of Austrian forces in N Italy and also governor of Lombardy-Venetia (1849–57). Radetzky crushed the nascent RISORGIMENTO movement, defeating CHARLES ALBERT of Piedmont at the battles of Custoza (1848) and (1849).

Radhakrishnan, Sir Sarvepalli (1888–1975) Indian philosopher and statesman, president (1962–67). As professor of Eastern religions and ethics at Oxford (1936–52), he did much to reconcile classical Hindu philosophy with contemporary social realities. He led the Indian delegation (1946–52) to the United Nations Educational, Scientific and Cultural Organization (UNESCO) and served as ambassador to the Soviet Union (1949–52). Radhakrishnan acted as vice president (1952–62) to Rajendra PRASAD before succeeding him as president. *See also* NEHRU, JAWAHARLAL

Radishchev, Alexander Nikolaievich (1749–1802) Russian writer and would-be liberal reformer. His book *A Journey from St Petersburg to Moscow* (1790) highlighted the prevalence of social injustice in Russia, attacking the treatment of serfs and condemning autocracy and censorship. CATHERINE II (THE GREAT), concerned about the possible spread of the French Revolution, ordered Radishchev's arrest. He was condemned to death, but the sentence was later commuted to exile in Siberia. Radishchev was pardoned (1801) by ALEXANDER I.

Raeder, Erich (1876–1960) German admiral. As chief of staff (1912–18) to Admiral Franz von Hipper, he fought in the battles of Dogger Bank (1915) and Jutland (1916) during World War 1. In 1928 Raeder was appointed commander in chief of the German navy, and as such was responsible for the covert construction of submarines and cruisers – in violation of the Treaty of Versailles (1919). During WORLD WAR 2, he suggested and planned the invasion of Norway and Denmark (1940), but opposed Adolf HITLER's strategy for the invasion of the Soviet Union and Britain. In 1943 he was removed from the supreme command in favour of Karl DÖNITZ. He was sentenced to life imprisonment at the NUREMBERG TRIALS (1946), but released on grounds of poor health in 1955.

▲ **Rabin** Israeli-Palestinian negotiations led by Yitzhak Rabin marked a major breakthrough in the Middle East peace process, but were prematurely halted by his assassination in 1995.

RAF *See* ROYAL AIR FORCE

Raffles, Sir Thomas Stamford (1781–1826) British colonial administrator. He joined the English EAST INDIA COMPANY in 1796 and was sent to PENANG in 1805. Raffles accompanied Lord MINTO on the successful invasion of JAVA (1811), and was subsequently appointed lieutenant governor (1811–16). His liberal reforms and suppression of the slave trade proved too costly for the Company, however, which demoted him to governor of SUMATRA. In 1819 Raffles persuaded Warren HASTINGS that it was necessary to found a settlement on SINGAPORE, then a sparsely inhabited island. Its striking success as a commercial port was immediate. He returned to Britain in 1824.

Rafsanjani, (Ali Akbar) Hashemi (1934–) Iranian statesman and cleric, president (1989–97). He was a student of Ruhollah KHOMEINI, graduating as a *hojatoleslam* in 1958. When Khomeini was exiled for his opposition to Shah Mohammed Reza PAHLAVI (1962), Rafsanjani became his chief fundraiser in Iran and was imprisoned (1975–78) for clandestine political activities. When the shah was overthrown and Khomeini returned from exile in 1979, Rafsanjani helped found the Islamic Republican Party and became speaker (1980–89) of the Majlis (parliament). A leading figure in the new theocracy, he was acting commander of the armed forces in the final stages of the IRAN-IRAQ WAR (1980–88). Rafsanjani attracted criticism in Iran for his secret negotiations with US President Ronald REAGAN's administration to resolve the IRAN HOSTAGE CRISIS. Rafsanjani was elected to succeed Khomeini as president, promising to preserve the Islamic revolution. He proved a political pragmatist, removing ultraconservative clerics from government, modernizing the economy, and improving relations with the West. He supported the election of his reformist successor, Muhammad KHATAMI.

Raglan, Fitzroy James Henry Somerset, 1st Baron (1788–1855) British field marshal. He fought under the Duke of WELLINGTON in the PENINSULAR WAR (1808–14), and lost his right arm at the Battle of WATERLOO (1815). Raglan was commander in chief of British forces in the CRIMEAN WAR (1853–56). He helped the Allies win the Battle of Alma (1854) and repel the Russian advance at the Battle of INKERMAN (1854), but his ambiguous order at the Battle of BALAKLAVA (1854) led to the disastrous CHARGE OF THE LIGHT BRIGADE. Raglan was blamed (perhaps unfairly) for the stalemate in the War and for the wretched conditions for the British troops. He died during the siege of SEVASTOPOL.

Rahman, Tunku Abdul (1903–90) Malaysian statesman, first prime minister of Malaya (1957–63) and then of Malaysia (1963–70), son of the sultan of Kedah. He helped found (1945) the United Malay National Organization (UMNO) and forged an alliance with corresponding Chinese and Indian parties. The Alliance Party won the 1955 elections, and Rahman became chief minister. He successfully led negotiations for independence from Britain, becoming prime minister of the newly sovereign state of Malaya. Rahman was the chief architect of the Federation of Malaysia (1963) and of the alliance that later became the SOUTHEAST ASIA TREATY ORGANIZATION (SEATO). He resigned in 1970 during the discontent that followed riots between Malays and Chinese. Rahman was a leading critic of MAHATHIR BIN MUHAMMAD.

railway (railroad) Form of transport in which carriages or wagons travel on a specially built track. Primitive railways, with carts drawn by horses along wooden rails, were used in mines in 16th-century Europe. The development of an efficient, mobile, steam-engine and reliable iron rails made public railways possible in the early 19th century. Richard Trevithick (1771–1833) demonstrated a self-powered, passenger-carrying railway locomotive in London in 1808, but the greatest of the pioneers was George Stephenson (1781–1848). He was engineer of the first public railway powered (in part) by a steam locomotive, between Stockton and Darlington (1825), and of the first all-locomotive passenger-carrying railway, the Liverpool and Manchester, which opened in 1830. Railways, many British-built in the early years, spread across the world. The first transcontinental railway was completed in the United States in 1869, the first underground railway for commuters in London in

1890. Railways had dramatic effects on the rise of tourism, on military strategy, on the growth of suburbs, and above all on industrial expansion, providing swift, inexpensive transport between producers and markets and giving access to resources in remote regions. The technology, although vastly improved, remained basically unchanged until after World War 2. With the increasing challenge of road and air transport, steam engines were replaced by diesel or electric, and monorails and high-speed trains such as the Japanese "Bullet" train or the French TGV (*Train à Grand Vitesse*), travelling at up to *c.*300km/h (185mph), were introduced. *See also* INDUSTRIAL REVOLUTION

Rajasthan State in NW India; the capital is Jaipur. Archaeologists working on the remains of the INDUS VALLEY CIVILIZATION at Kalibangan discovered evidence of pre-literate and literate culture, indicating a transitional period between the 3rd and 2nd millennium BC. From the 7th century AD Rajasthan was ruled by the RAJPUTS. The crushing defeat of Rana Sanga by the Mughal conqueror BABUR at the Battle of Khanua (1527) signalled the fragmentation of the Rajputs. At the end of the 16th century, AKBAR initiated the tradition of Mughal-Rajput marriage alliances. By the 1800s most of Rajasthan was controlled by the MARATHAS. The British overthrew the Marathas and created the PRINCELY STATES of Rajputana. When India gained independence from Britain, the princely states were combined to form the independent Union of Rajasthan, which joined the Republic of India in 1950. Further territory was added to the state in 1956. Pop. (1991) 44,005,990.

Rajput Warrior caste from NW India. They are traditionally said to be descendants of the HUNS or other tribes from Central Asia. They became divided into four clans, Fire, Snake, Solar and Lunar. Due to their descent and warrior status, the Rajputs were traditionally less strict in matters such as dietary taboos than other high-caste Hindus, and they later included some Muslims. They became powerful in the 7th century AD, gaining control of Rajputana, now RAJASTHAN. The Muslim invaders in the 12th century failed to take their desert strongholds, but AKBAR succeeded in the early 17th century. The Rajput princes still maintained control of their own states under the MUGHAL EMPIRE, but lost it to the MARATHAS in the 18th century. Under the British, they preserved a considerable degree of autonomy. The privileges of the princes disappeared after independence (1947).

Rákóczy Magyar (Hungarian) dynasty, princes of TRANSYLVANIA. **George I** (1591–1648), son of Sigismund (1544–1608), was elected prince of Transylvania in 1630. A strong Protestant, he fought against Austria in 1644–45 in alliance with Hungary and Sweden, and made his capital a Protestant stronghold. His son, **George II** (r.1648–60), allied with the Swedes to invade Poland and was repulsed. He was briefly ejected by the Ottoman Turks, who still held suzerainty, in 1657–58. The most able member of the Rákóczy dynasty was George II's grandson, **Francis II** (1676–1735). He was forcibly removed from his family and brought up in Habsburg Austria, but resisted indoctrination and became the effective leader of the Hungarians. Forced into exile, Francis rejected the Polish crown and returned to lead a Hungarian revolt against Austria in 1703. He was elected prince of Transylvania in 1704. Lacking powerful allies – neither France nor Russia provided hoped-for aid – he was defeated and forced into exile (1711). His son Joseph was recognized as prince of Transylvania by the Ottoman sultan in 1737, but died, the last of the line, in 1738.

Rákosi, Mátyás (1892–1971) Hungarian communist ruler, first secretary of the Hungarian Communist Party (1944–56) and prime minister (1952–53). He was forced into exile in Moscow after taking part in the short-lived government of Béla KUN in 1919. Rákosi later returned to Hungary in order to reorganize the Hungarian Communist Party, but was arrested and imprisoned (1924–40). He remained in the Soviet Union for most of World War 2, returning with the Red Army in 1944. After the War, Rákosi and János KÁDÁR established a Stalinist regime, using the secret police to crush opposition. Following the death of Joseph Stalin (1953), Rákosi was replaced as premier by the more liberal Imre NAGY. Rákosi engineered the dismissal of Nagy in 1955, but was himself forced out of office by Soviet Premier Nikita KHRUSHCHEV in order to placate Marshal TITO of Yugoslavia. Rákosi fled to the Soviet Union after the HUNGARIAN UPRISING (1956).

Raleigh, Sir Walter (1554?–1618) English courtier, adventurer and writer. He became a favourite of ELIZABETH I after helping to suppress an Irish rebellion in Munster, and soon acquired profitable monopolies and large estates. Raleigh was knighted in 1585 and made captain of the queen's guard in 1587, but his friendship with the queen, extravagance, and free-thinking made him many enemies, including the Earl of ESSEX. Raleigh sponsored two ill-fated attempts (1885, 1887) to establish the first English colony in America on ROANOKE ISLAND (now in North Carolina). In 1592 he was briefly imprisoned in the Tower of London after Elizabeth learned of his clandestine marriage. After his release, Raleigh led an expedition to South America in search of the fabled city of EL DORADO, a journey described in *The Discoverie of Guiana* (1596). He served under the Earl of Essex in an unsuccessful attack on CÁDIZ, SW Spain (1597). Soon after the accession of James I (1603), Raleigh was charged with treason and sentenced to death, later commuted to life imprisonment. Back in the Tower (1603–16), Raleigh began his unfinished *History of the World* (1614). He gained release in order to lead another expedition to Guyana in search of gold, but was betrayed to the Spanish authorities, lost his son in a fight, and returned empty-handed. James invoked the death sentence and Raleigh was beheaded.

Rama I (1737–1809) King of Siam (1782–1809), founder of the Chakkri dynasty in THAILAND (1782–). He led the Thai army in the expulsion of Burmese forces from Siam and went on to gain control of Laos, Cambodia and the N Malay states. As king, Rama I transferred the capital from AYUTTHAYA to BANGKOK, codified Thai law (1805) and bolstered the Buddhist sangha (monkhood).

Rama V *See* CHULALONGKORN

Ramillies, Battle of (23 May 1706) Engagement fought near Namur, central Belgium, during the War of the SPANISH SUCCESSION. The Duke of MARLBOROUGH, commanding *c.*62,000 Allied troops, defeated a similarly sized French army under the Duc de Villeroi. Marlborough's victory was achieved through a brilliant, flexible strategy and poor French deployment. The French lost *c.*14000 men, the Allies *c.*3500. The victory enabled the Allies to capture much of the Spanish Netherlands. *See also* LOUIS XIV

Ramses I (active 14th century BC) King of ancient EGYPT, founder of the 19th dynasty of ancient Egypt (r. *c.*1320–18 BC). He was a general under his predecessor HOREMHEB and, acceding to the throne in old age, reigned in tandem with his son, Seti, who succeeded him. Seti fought in Syria and N Palestine, while Ramses concentrated on beginning to build the great hall of the temple at KARNAK.

Ramses II (the Great) (active 13th century BC) Third king of the 19th dynasty of ancient EGYPT (r. *c.*1304–1237 BC), son and successor of Seti I. His reign, the second longest in Egyptian history, was a period of unprecedented prosperity and power. His subdued the warring tribes in S Syria and, although surprised and suffering heavy casualties, won a tactical victory over the HITTITES at the Battle of Kadesh (*c.*1300 BC). The failure to capture Kadesh, however, resulted in a number of rebellions in the ancient Egyptian empire. Ramses embarked on another, more successful invasion of the Hittite empire, concluding a mutually favourable truce (*c.*1258 BC), and later marrying a Hittite princess. His many splendid monuments included the colossal statues at ABU SIMBEL, the temple at KARNAK, and the completion of his father's mortuary temple at Abydos. He was succeeded by his son, Merneptah.

Ramses III (d.1156 BC) Second king of the 20th dynasty of ancient EGYPT (r. *c.*1187–56 BC). He successfully defended Egypt from attacks by the Libyans (*c.*1182 BC, *c.*1178 BC) and the SEA PEOPLES (*c.*1180 BC). His later years were marked by strikes and unrest, including a failed assassination attempt, and Egypt withdrew into political and cultural isolation. Ramses built a vast mortuary temple at Medinet Habu. He was succeeded by Ramses IV.

Randolph, A. (Asa) Philip (1889–1979) US trade unionist and CIVIL RIGHTS activist. He founded the Brotherhood of Sleeping-Car Porters (1925), the first successful predominantly black trade union. In 1938 Randolph pulled his union out of the American Federation of Labor (AFL) in protest over its failure to tackle racial discrimination within its ranks. Randolph became a leading spokesman for the employment rights of African Americans. His threat of a mass march on Washington, D.C., persuaded President Franklin ROOSEVELT's to establish the Fair Employment Practices Committee (1941). A veteran of the civil rights movement, he was one of the leaders of the March on Washington (1963).

Randolph, Edmund Jennings (1753–1813) American statesman. He briefly served as aide-de-camp (1775–76) to George WASHINGTON during the American Revolution. As governor of Virginia (1786–88) and a delegate to the CONSTITUTIONAL CONVENTION (1787), he proposed the Virginia Plan, which favoured representation based on population. The Plan was rejected and Randolph refused to sign the final draft of the CONSTITUTION OF THE UNITED STATES. He served as the first attorney general (1789–94), before replacing Thomas JEFFERSON as secretary of state (1794–95). Randolph helped maintain good relations with the French, while negotiating the JAY TREATY (1794) with the British. He was forced to resign after the British published intercepted dispatches from the French minister to the United States, which implied (falsely) that Randolph was open to bribes in return for influence. Randolph later acted as chief counsel for Aaron BURR at his trial for treason

Ranjit Singh (1780–1839) Indian soldier, founder and maharaja (1801–39) of the PUNJAB, popularly known as "the Lion of the Punjab". He inherited a small kingdom centred on Gujranwala, now in Pakistan. In 1799 Ranjit Singh captured LAHORE from the Afghans, and over the next few years proceeded to absorb neighbouring principalities across the Punjab, including the city of AMRITSAR (1809). The eastwards expansion of his kingdom led to conflict with the British, with whom he signed the Treaty of Amritsar (1809) establishing the River Sutlej as the E border of the Sikh kingdom. Ranjit Singh then turned to the N and W, expelling the Pashtuns (Afghans) from Peshawar (1818) and the Vale of Kashmir (1819). The Sikh army, modernized with European assistance, captured Ladakh (1834) and aided the British invasion of Afghanistan by capturing the Khyber Pass. Less than 10 years after his death, most of the Sikh kingdom fell to the British in the SIKH WARS. *See also* SIKHISM

Ranke, Leopold von (1795–1886) German historian, pioneer of the study of history by objective, scientific examination of primary sources. His historicist approach greatly influenced the subsequent development of Western historiography. As professor of history at Berlin University (1834–71), Ranke inaugurated the seminar method of teaching. Perhaps the major criticism of his work is its concentration on political history to the exclusion of economic and social factors. Important works include *History of the Popes in the 16th and 17th Centuries* (1834–36), *History of the Reformation in Germany* (1839–47) and *Civil Wars and Monarchy in France in the 16th and 17th Centuries* (1852).

Rankin, Jeannette (1880–1973) US feminist and pacifist. She led the campaign for women's suffrage in her native Montana. A Republican, Rankin was the first woman member of the House of Representatives (1917–19), but lost her seat after voting against the declaration of war on Germany. Re-elected in 1940, Rankin cast the only vote in the House against entry into World War 2 (1941). She did not campaign for re-election in 1943. In 1968 Rankin led a protest march of *c.*5000 women in Washington, D.C., against US involvement in the Vietnam War.

Rapallo, Treaties of (1920, 1922) Peace agreements signed in Rapallo, N Italy. The first treaty settled disputes between Italy and the future Yugoslavia, in particular over the status of Fiume (now RIJEKA), which achieved independent status (the city was taken over by Italy in 1924). The second, more significant treaty, between Germany and the Soviet Union, ended financial claims arising out of World War 1, provided for economic co-operation, and included a secret agreement for German military training and weapons development in Russia, in defiance of the Treaty of VERSAILLES.

Rasputin, Grigori Yefimovich (1872?–1916) Russian mystic, b. Grigori Yefimovich Novykh. A Siberian peasant, his libidinous youthful exploits earned him the surname Rasputin (Rus. debauchee). From 1908 Rasputin won great influence at the court of Nicholas II because of his apparent ability to alleviate Crown Prince Alexis' haemophilia. In 1915, with Nicholas II absent on campaign in World War 1, Rasputin and Tsarina Alexandra virtually ruled Russia. His sinister power and advocacy of sexual ecstasy as a means of religious salvation inspired suspicion and hatred. He was poisoned, shot and then drowned by a group of conservative nobles, but this failed to save the autocratic imperial regime which was overthrown in the Russian Revolution (1917). *See also* Stolypin, Peter Arkadievich

Rastafarianism West Indian religious and political movement founded on veneration of Ras Tafari (Haile Selassie I) and the belief that the Ethiopians are the lost tribes of Israel. The movement, which has no churches or priests or formal rituals, started in Jamaica in the 1920s and was influenced by a variety of cultural traditions, African, Caribbean and biblical, and especially by Marcus Garvey and other black activists. Rastafarians advocate a return to Africa.

Rastatt, Treaty of (7 September 1714) Peace agreement between Emperor Charles VI and Louis XIV of France. While Charles renounced his claim to the Spanish throne, he did not recognize the legitimacy of the Bourbon claimant Philip V. It confirmed the arrangements made at the end of the War of the Spanish Succession by Austria's allies in the Peace of Utrecht (1713), which Charles had been unwilling to accept. Charles gained territories in N Italy in return for accepting the loss of Spain.

Rathenau, Walther (1867–1922) German statesman and industrialist. He directed (1914–15) the distribution of raw materials at the start of World War 1, thus ensuring Germany's economic survival amidst a British naval blockade. In 1915 Rathenau succeeded his father, founder of the *Allgemeine Elektrizitäts Gesellschaft* (AEG), as president of the giant corporation. After the War, he served as minister of reconstruction (1921) and foreign minister (1922) in the government of the Weimar Republic under Karl Joseph Wirth, fulfilling Germany's obligations under the Treaty of Versailles to make reparations payments, and signing the Treaty of Rapallo (1922) with the Soviet Union. He was assassinated by extreme, anti-Semitic nationalists. Rathenau wrote *The New Society* (1918), which rejected both laissez-faire capitalism and socialist nationalization in favour of industrial democracy.

Ratsiraka, Didier (1936–) Madagascan statesman, president (1976–93, 1997–). A naval officer, he served in the military government (1972–75) of General Gabriel Ramanantsoa before seizing power as head of a revolutionary council. A referendum (1975) approved a new constitution, which established the Democratic Republic of Madagascar and gave Ratsiraka increased powers. Ratsiraka nationalized major industries and strengthened links with the communist bloc. Although re-elected in 1982 and 1989, he faced growing unrest as the economy slumped and was forced to concede democratic reforms and institute a new constitution (1922). Ratsiraka's defeat by Albert Zafy in the 1993 elections signalled a return to civilian rule. Ratsiraka returned to office after narrowly defeating Zafy in the 1996 elections. He gained greater powers under another new constitution (1998).

Ravenna City in Emilia-Romagna, NE Italy. In the 1st century BC Emperor Augustus made the city the naval base for Rome's Adriatic fleet. From AD 402 to 476 Ravenna was the capital of the Western Roman Empire, and it became an archbishopric in 438. In 476 Ravenna was captured by the Barbarian Odoacer before, after a three-year siege, it fell (493) to Theodoric (the Great) of the Ostrogoths. In 540 Ravenna was occupied by the Byzantine general Belisarius, and thereafter served as the seat of the Byzantine governors of Italy. It was briefly held (751–54) by the Lombards and then Pepin III (the Short), who gifted it to the papacy in 757. Controlled by Venice for the latter half of the 15th century, Ravenna was returned to the Papal States in 1509. In 1861 it became part of the Kingdom of Italy. Sights include the mausoleums of Galla Placidia (*c.*AD 450) and Theodoric (*c.*520), and the Church of San Vitale (*c.*547). Pop. (1991) 135,834.

Rawlings, Jerry John (1947–) Ghanaian statesman and flight lieutenant, president (1981–2000). In 1979 he led a successful military coup, executing three former heads of state before restoring Ghana to civilian rule under Hilla Limann. In 1981 Rawlings, frustrated by continuing government corruption, mounted a second successful coup. He suspended the constitution, banned political opposition, and set up People's Defence Committees (PDC). Faced with continuing recession, Rawlings reversed his economic strategy, and implemented free-market reforms with the blessing of the World Bank. With the revival of the national economy, Rawlings' popularity soared and he drafted a new, democratic constitution (1992). In the 1992 presidential elections, the first since 1979, Rawlings won a landslide victory. He was re-elected in 1996.

Rayburn, Sam (Samuel Taliaferro) (1882–1961) US politician. A Democrat, he served 25 consecutive terms in the House of Representatives (1913–61). In the 1930s Rayburn was instrumental in securing the passage of President Franklin Roosevelt's New Deal legislation. He served as speaker of the House (1940–47, 1949–53, 1966–61) for a record 17 years.

Razin, Stenka (*c.*1630–71) Cossack leader. As head of a Cossack band, he raided towns and ships along the River Volga from 1667. In 1670–71 Razin led a major peasant rebellion against tsarist rule in SE Russia. His 7000-strong Cossack forces captured Tsaritsyn (now Volgograd), Astrakhan and Saratov. Gathering support from the serfs in his advance up the Volga, Razin and his *c.*20,000-strong army threatened Simbirsk (now Ulyanovsk). Tsar Alexei Mikhailovich dispatched a large army under Prince Yuri Baryatinsky, which crushed the rebellion (October 1870). Razin fled to the Don but was later captured, taken to Moscow and executed. He is the subject of legend.

Reagan, Ronald Wilson (1911–) Fortieth president of the United States (1981–89). A well-known movie and television actor, he testified against alleged communists within the industry before the House Committee on Un-American Activities (1947). Reagan won a landslide victory to become Republican governor of California (1966–74). In office, he sought to reduce state welfare and cut taxes. Reagan ran for the Republican presidential nomination in 1968 and 1976, only narrowly losing the latter race to President Gerald Ford. In 1980 he finally gained the nomination. Reagan's genial persuasiveness on television and the on-going Iran Hostage Crisis enabled him to achieve an overwhelming victory over the incumbent president Jimmy Carter, becoming (aged 70) the oldest leader in US history. On 30 March 1981, Reagan was shot and wounded in an attempted assassination by John Hinckley. Reagan launched a bold conservative programme of large income-tax cuts, unparalleled reductions in public spending (except on defence), and a reduction in federal regulation of business. At first, the recession deepened but by 1983 an economic upturn was evident. Reagan's infectious optimism secured him a huge victory (winning 49 states) in the 1984 election against Walter Mondale. However, the Democrats regained control of the Senate in 1986 and, by the end of Reagan's second term, tax cuts had created a huge budget deficit; the national debt exceeded US$2 trillion. Fiercely anti-communist, Reagan took strong measures against opponents abroad, invading Grenada (1983) and undermining the Sandinista regime in Nicaragua. While pursuing his Strategic Defence Initiative (SDI), or "Star Wars", Reagan signed a nuclear disarmament treaty (1987) with Mikhail Gorbachev that signalled an end to the Cold War. He visited Moscow in 1988. The last year of his presidency was overshadowed by the Iran-Contra affair, which suggested that Reagan, at best, was not in full control of his government. His personal popularity remained high, and contributed to the electoral success of his vice president and successor, George Bush.

REAGAN, RONALD

Ronald Reagan, a former actor in movies such as *Knute Rockne* (1940), was known as "the Great Communicator". Fuelled by his anti-communism, the "Star Wars" project was part of the largest military spending programme in US history.

REAGAN IN HIS OWN WORDS

"Some say it will bring war to the heavens but its purpose is to deter war, in the heavens and on earth."
On the Strategic Defense Initiative (February 1985)

"I've often wondered how some people in positions of this kind manage without having had any acting experience"
Television interview (March 1986)

Rebecca Riots (1839–43) Campaign by Welsh tenant farmers increasingly impoverished by rates, rents, tithes and especially turnpike tolls. The tollgates were their main target, and many were destroyed. The rioters took their name from Genesis 24:60 ("the seed of Rebecca shall possess the gates of her enemies"), and were often disguised in women's clothing. An act of 1844 reduced tolls and tightened up regulation of the turnpikes.

Rebellions of 1837 Risings in favour of self-rule in Upper and Lower Canada (Ontario and Québec), where the elected assemblies, including the legislative council, were dominated by government-appointed officials. In Upper Canada, the rising was led by William Lyon MacKenzie and soon fizzled out. The more serious revolt in Lower Canada, led by Louis Papineau, was aggravated by economic depression and by the different nationalities of officials (largely British) and inhabitants (largely French). Some sharp fighting took place between British forces and the rebels before Papineau fled and the rising was suppressed. The outbreaks led to the mission of Lord Durham, whose report recommended the union of Upper and Lower Canada, accomplished in 1841.

Reconstruction (1865–77) Period in United States' history after the Civil War in which the Confederate states were readmitted to the Union and acquired new governments. The process caused fierce argument between those who wanted reconciliation with white Southerners and those who demanded justice for the former slaves. The conciliatory approach of President Andrew Johnson, accepted by most of the Southern whites, eventually provoked an attempt by the Republicans in Congress to impeach him. The first Reconstruction Act was passed over his veto and introduced the programme known as Radical Reconstruction, enshrined in the 14th and 15th Amendments to the Constitution and designed to establish the full political and civil rights of African Americans. It alienated most Southern whites, and federal troops had to be employed in the 1870s to check growing violence. When Rutherford B. Hayes became president (1877), he withdrew the troops, Southern Republican governments collapsed, and Reconstruction was abandoned. *See also* black codes; carpetbaggers; Freedmen's Bureau; scalawags

Red Army Army of the Soviet Union, created by Leon Trotsky to preserve the Bolshevik Russian

REVOLUTION (1917) during the RUSSIAN CIVIL WAR (1918–22). Commanded by former tsarist officers, it was characterized by a high degree of political control through a system of commissars. It was gravely weakened (1937–38) by the removal of many of its officers in Stalin's Great PURGE. During WORLD WAR 2 the strength of the Red Army increased to *c*.5 million, by far the largest army in history, although its total losses in 1941–45 have been estimated at *c*.7 million. The name Red Army, also used in revolutionary China, was dropped in the Soviet Union after World War 2.

Red Brigades Italian terrorist organization. Espousing extreme, if vague, left-wing views, it was founded in 1970 and in *c*.1976–81 directed its animosity particularly towards legal and political figures and businessmen. Its most notorious crime was the abduction and murder (1978) of Aldo MORO. It faded in the early 1980s, when many members were arrested.

Red Cloud (1822–1909) (Makhpiya Luta) Native American chief of the Oglala SIOUX. Based in Wyoming, he fought (1865–67) tenaciously against settlers and the US Army trying to establish the Bozeman Trail across the Continental Divide to the gold fields of sw Montana. After losing 80 men at Fort Kearney, the US government abandoned the Trail (1868) and signed a peace treaty with Red Cloud. Visiting Washington, D.C., he agreed to move to a reservation in South Dakota. *See also* BOZEMAN, JOHN M.

Red Cross International organization that seeks to alleviate human suffering. It was founded (1864) to assist the GENEVA CONVENTION by helping the wounded and prisoners of war, on the basis of the proposals of the Swiss philanthropist Henri DUNANT. Later, it expanded its services, especially in providing relief for victims of natural disasters. National branches were founded in *c*.150 countries, with central headquarters in Geneva, Switzerland. Its workers are mainly volunteers. In Muslim countries it is known as the Red Crescent.

Red Guards Chinese military youth movement, active in the CULTURAL REVOLUTION (1966–68). The Red Guards attacked "revisionists", Westerners and alleged bourgeois influences, including the old communist order, and all manifestations of Chinese culture, launching violent attacks on innocent individuals. Originally encouraged by MAO ZEDONG in the interests of "ongoing revolution", they caused severe social disorder and were suppressed after 1968.

Red Jacket (1758?–1830) (Sagoyewatha) Native American Chief of the SENECA. A colourful but shrewd personality, he had an enigmatic ability to avoid dangerous commitments. He was called Red Jacket from his association with the British during the AMERICAN REVOLUTION. He astutely exploited the differences between rival groups, and in the WAR OF 1812 supported the United States against the British. During his chieftainship, he was a powerful advocate of the preservation of Iroquois traditions.

R

Redmond, John Edward (1856–1918) Irish politician. A supporter of Charles Stewart PARNELL, he led the Parnellite faction of the Irish Nationalist Party in the British Parliament when the Party split over the Parnell divorce scandal (1890). His alliance with the Liberals secured the introduction of a third Irish HOME RULE Bill (1912), but the violent opposition of Ulster Unionists persuaded him to support the exclusion of the NE counties. Redmond offered full support for the British cause in World War 1, the start of which delayed the implementation of the Bill. Redmond's separation from the prevailing mood of Irish nationalism was evident when the EASTER RISING (1916) caught him aback. He resigned from the Nationalist Party and in the elections of 1918 (shortly after his death), the banner of Irish nationalism passed to SINN FÉIN.

Red River Rebellion (1869–70) Popular rebellion in the RED RIVER SETTLEMENT (now MANITOBA), central Canada). The HUDSON'S BAY COMPANY, which controlled the region, agreed to hand over its lands to the newly created Dominion of Canada in 1870. On the eve of the cession, the Métis, people of mixed French and Native American ancestry who formed the majority of the population, plus some others, rose in rebellion, fearing discrimination and the loss of their lands and culture in a wave of Canadian settlement. Led by Louis RIEL, the rebels seized Fort Garry (now Winnipeg) and set up a provisional government. The government in Ottawa agreed to negotiate, and the ensuing Act created the province of Manitoba (1870) and secured, in principle, the land titles and cultural rights of the Métis.

Red River Settlement Colony established (1811–12) in what is now MANITOBA, central Canada, on land granted to the Earl of SELKIRK by the HUDSON'S BAY COMPANY. The Settlement, officially known as Assiniboia and settled by Scots farmers, was resented by the rival NORTH WEST COMPANY. In 1815–16 harassment gave way to full-scale violence: 20 men were killed, including the governor. Selkirk re-established the colony in 1817, and the absorption of the North West Company by its rival in 1821 ended animosities and allowed the settlement to flourish. When it joined (1870) the Dominion of Canada it was renamed Manitoba.

Reeves, William Pember (1857–1932) New Zealand statesman, renowned for his pioneering legislation as minister of labour (1891–96) in New Zealand's first Liberal government under John Ballance. Reeve's progressive and comprehensive reforms regulated wages, working hours and factory conditions, and he initiated the first scheme for compulsory arbitration in industrial disputes (1894). He resigned after disagreements with Ballance's successor Richard SEDDON. Reeves later served as high commissioner in Great Britain (1905–08) and director of the London School of Economics (1908–19).

Reform Acts British statutes reforming Parliament in the 19th and early 20th centuries that led to full democracy. The **Great Reform Act** (1832) extended the FRANCHISE to middle-class property owners and redistributed parliamentary seats to include large industrial cities that were either unrepresented (Birmingham and Manchester) or under-represented in relation to rural areas. The legislation was written by Earl GREY and introduced into the Commons by John RUSSELL. It was blocked by the House of Lords for more than a year. The **Second** Reform Act (1867), largely written by Benjamin DISRAELI, introduced household suffrage, giving the vote to better-off members of the working class. The **Third** Reform Act (1884) gave the vote to most adult males. Women over the age of 30 gained the vote in 1918, and the Representation of the People Act (1928) introduced universal adult suffrage.

Reformation Support for reform of the ROMAN CATHOLIC CHURCH that resulted in the movement known as PROTESTANTISM. Discontent with the church, its clergy, doctrines and practices was widespread, although there was no questioning of CHRISTIANITY. Criticism and heresy were not new: in the 14th and 15th centuries the Church had been challenged by the LOLLARDS and the HUSSITES. The Reformation was a revolt not only against the doctrinal authority of the church, it was also a protest against the interference of the church in secular matters and the questionable activities of the clergy, notably the sale of INDULGENCES and holy relics. The start of the Reformation is traditionally dated from 1517, when Martin LUTHER published his *Ninety-five Theses*. Luther's attack on the corruption of the church and the doctrines of papal supremacy, TRANSUBSTANTIATION and clerical celibacy, his emphasis on the Bible as the true Christian authority and his insistence on justification by faith alone won the support of several German princes, who also saw political advantage in a church not subject to papal or imperial control. Other powerful reformers appeared in Switzerland: Ulrich ZWINGLI in ZÜRICH and, later, the more radical Frenchman John CALVIN in GENEVA. Calvinism was especially influential in France, the Netherlands and Scandinavia. In England, the Reformation began under HENRY VIII with a rejection of papal authority but no change in doctrine. In subsequent reigns, the English church swung between Protestantism and Catholicism before a compromise was reached under ELIZABETH I. In Scotland, the Reformation was led by Calvin's disciple, John KNOX, and by 1560 PRESBYTERIANISM was established as the predominant form. Some of the early gains of Protestantism, for instance in Poland, were reversed by the COUNTER-REFORMATION.

Reformed church Christian denomination outside the Roman Catholic Church, otherwise classed as Protestant. In practice, the term is used of denominations in the Calvinist tradition, such as the various Presbyterian congregations. A World Alliance of Reformed Churches was founded in 1877. The term may also be applied to a modern group that splits from its mother church, such as the Reformed Episcopal Church. *See also* CALVINISM

refugee Person forced to migrate from their native land. Refugees may be expelled or may flee the country to avoid persecution, war or other severe threat, and are usually unable to return, at least in the forseeable future. Refugees have always existed, but their number increased hugely as a result of the high level of political violence in the 20th century, especially the World Wars but also the proliferation of civil wars after 1945. Attempts to deal with the problem at international level began with the appointment of Fridtjof NANSEN as high commissioner for refugees by the League of Nations in 1921. Other international associations have been established since, including the UNITED NATIONS' HIGH COMMISSION FOR REFUGEES (UNHCR). Most countries have legal obligations to admit refugees, although definitions of the term vary.

Regency period (1811–20) Interval in British history when the incapacity of GEORGE III led to the appointment of the Prince of Wales (later GEORGE IV), as prince regent. The term is most often used in the context of art and fashion when it incorporates the actual Regency period and the reign of George IV (r.1820–30).

Rehnquist, William Hubbs (1924–) US jurist, chief justice (1986–) of the Supreme Court. As assistant attorney general (1969–71) under President Richard NIXON, he gained a reputation for his strong support of further powers for the police and opposition to civil-rights legislation. In 1971 Nixon appointed him as associate justice to the Supreme Court (1971). President Ronald Reagan controversially promoted him to chief justice in succession to Warren BURGER.

Rehoboam (active 10th century BC) King of Israel (922–915 BC) and first king of Judah after the division of the Hebrew kingdom. He succeeded his father, SOLOMON, and continued Solomon's authoritarian rule, provoking the northern rebellion (920 BC) that split the kingdom. War followed between Judah and the N kingdom of Israel under Jeroboam, but Rehoboam failed to reunite the kingdom.

Reich (Ger. empire) Name given to three German imperial states. The NAZI PARTY under Adolf HITLER liked to call their state (1933–45) the Third Reich, after the HOLY ROMAN EMPIRE (the first) and the German empire (1871–1918) of WILLLIAM I and WILLIAM II (the second).

Reichstag German "imperial parliament" in Berlin. The Reichstag building was erected (1884–94) as a meeting place for the legislature after the unification of Germany in 1871. Its antecedents lay in the Diet of the HOLY ROMAN EMPIRE and in the representative assembly of the NORTH GERMAN CONFEDERATION. The building was severely damaged in the REICHSTAG FIRE (1933) and parliament ceased to function after Adolf HITLER assumed supreme power a month later. After the reunification of Germany in 1990, the restored Reichstag building again served as the meeting place of Germany's parliament when the government moved from Bonn.

Reichstag fire (27 February 1933) Blaze that destroyed part of the REICHSTAG building in Berlin, Germany. A Dutchman, Marinus van der Lubbe, was convicted of the crime and executed, but Georgi DIMITROV was acquitted. Adolf HITLER, who had become chancellor the previous month, used the incident to suspend civil liberties, eliminate political opponents and establish a dictatorship. The suspicion that the Nazi propaganda minister Joseph GOEBBELS engineered the Reichstag fire is no longer widely held.

Reid, Sir George Houston (1845–1918) Australian statesman, prime minister (1904–05), b. England. As prime minister of New South Wales (1894–99), he introduced a number of financial and civil-service reforms. In the first federal parliament (1901–04), Reid led the free-trade group. He led a coalition government with the Liberal Party. He was leader of the opposition (1905–08), and the first Australian high commissioner in Britain (1910–16), subsequently becoming a member of the British Parliament (1916–18).

Reign of Terror (1793–94) Period of the French Revolution marked by the ascendancy of the Jacobins. It began with the creation of a Revolutionary Tribunal (March 1793) to root out opponents of the regime and of the Committee of Public Safety (April), dominated by the Jacobins. It accelerated with the overthrow of the Girondins (June) and the ascendancy of Maximilien Robespierre, and reached its peak after the execution of Georges Danton (April 1794) and the discovery of a royalist conspiracy (June). Against a background of foreign invasion in the French Revolutionary Wars and the Wars of the Vendée, opponents were ruthlessly persecuted and *c.*17,000 were executed. The Terror ended with the Thermidorian reaction (27 July 1794), when Robespierre and leading Jacobins were arrested and executed. *See also* Hébert, Jacques René; Fouquier-Tinville, Antoine Quentin; Saint-Just, Louis Antoine Léon de

Reith, Sir John Charles Walsham, 1st Baron (1889–1971) British administrator, general manager (1922–27) and first director general (1927–38) of the British Broadcasting Corporation (BBC). He was virtually the creator of public-service broadcasting. Under his control, the BBC, which held a monopoly of public radio-broadcasting, gained a reputation for editorial impartiality and high-quality, broadly educational programmes. He presided over the inauguration of British television in 1936, and initiated overseas' radio broadcasts, later to become the BBC World Service. Lord Reith worked at the admiralty (1943–45) planning the invasion of Europe during World War 2.

religion Code of beliefs and practices formulated in response to a spiritual awareness of human existence. It may involve either faith in a state of existence after earthly death, or a desire for union with an omnipotent spiritual being, or a combination of the two. Polytheistic religions, such as those of ancient Egypt, Greece and Rome, entailed the worship of many distinct gods or personifications of nature. Many cultures classified their deities into hierarchies known as pantheons, as in Hinduism. Other ancient religions, some of which incorporated belief in a state of existence after death, were more a system of ethical philosophy concentrating on metaphysical contemplation; for example, Buddhism and Taoism. The ancient Hebrews were among the first people to worship a single omniscient and omnipotent being, a characteristic of Judaism as well as Christianity and Islam. Common to all monotheistic religions is the idea that God is omnipresent and beyond the physical plane occupied by humans. In many religions, both monotheistic and polytheistic, sacrifice to an individual god or to God is an important element, either in propitiation, to redeem the faithful from some wrongdoing, or in thanksgiving.

Religion, Wars of (1562–98) Series of nine civil wars in France. At stake was freedom of worship for Huguenots (Protestants), but it was also a struggle among aristocratic families for influence over the increasingly embattled Valois dynasty, and it involved interventions by other countries on both sides. The Huguenot leaders were Louis I de Condé, Gaspard de Coligny and Henry of Navarre (later Henry IV). The Catholic faction was led by the House of Guise. The monarchy, represented by Catherine de' Medici and her sons, Charles IX and Henry III, generally attempted to pursue a moderate Catholic line. The **first** war (1562–63) was precipitated by the massacre of Huguenots at Vassy (March 1562). Condé responded by occupying Orléans and marching on Paris, but was defeated and captured at the Battle of Dreux (December 1562). The ensuing Peace of Amboise (March 1563) granted freedom of conscience to Huguenots, but maintained restrictions on freedom of worship. The **second** war (1567–68) was marked by the death of the Catholic Duc de Montmorency at the Battle of of St-Denis (November 1567). In the **third** war (1568–70), Condé was killed at the Battle of Jarnac (1569), but conflict ended with the Treaty of St-Germain (1570), which granted further concessions to the Huguenots. The **fourth** civil war (1572–73) began with the Saint Bartholomew's Day Massacre of *c.*3000 leading Huguenots in Paris. The **fifth** war (1574–76) closed with Henry III securing the Peace of Monsieur, granting Huguenots freedom of worship outside of Paris. The Guise faction responded by forming (1576) the Holy League, which persuaded Henry to revoke the agreement and thus led to the **sixth** war (1577). This conflict ended with the Peace of Bergerac (1577), which removed some of the concessions to Huguenots in the previous Peace. A **seventh** war (1580) was insignificant, but when Henry III recognized Henry of Navarre as heir to the throne (1584), the **War of the Three Henrys** (1585–89) ensued. Henry de Guise and Henry III were assassinated (1588 and 1589 respectively), and Henry IV became the first Bourbon king. He defeated the Holy League's Spanish allies in the **ninth** war (1589–94), converting to Catholicism (1593) and entering Paris in 1594. His Edict of Nantes (1598) extended toleration to the Huguenots and re-established strong royal government.

religious orders Associations of people who join together to follow a life devoted to religious worship through prayer, service or labour. They are generally bound by common vows, for example poverty or chastity. The best-known examples in Christianity are the monastic orders founded in the Middle Ages, including the Benedictines, the oldest monastic order, and the mendicant friars such as the Franciscans and Dominicans. Other, similar Christian institutions may include lay persons committed to specific work, such as the teaching of the Christian Brothers. Since the 19th century, religious orders have also been founded in the Anglican and other Protestant churches. A strong monastic tradition exists also in Buddhism. *See also* monasticism

Remonstrants Dutch followers of the religious reformer, Jacobus Arminius, who reacted against the grim austerity of Calvinism. They took their name from the Remonstrance written by Johannes Uyttenbogaert and presented to the Dutch States-General in 1610. Among other criticisms, it rejected the doctrine of predestination and the concept of of an elect who alone would be saved. The Remonstrants were condemned at the Synod of Dort (1618–19) and suffered severe persecution until 1623, when the ban on their services was removed. A similar group arose in England in the late 16th century. They were called Arminians and came to be regarded by their opponents as crypto-Catholics. Their influence on the Church of England under Archbishop William Laud during the reign of Charles I contributed to the hostility between Crown and Parliament. *See also* Grotius, Hugo

Renaissance (Fr. rebirth) Period in European history and culture supposedly marking the transition from the medieval to the modern world, characterized by dramatic advances in the arts and learning arising from a "rebirth" of knowledge and interest in the ancient civilizations of classical Greece and especially Rome. It began in the 14th century in the small, prosperous, Italian city-states and spread throughout Europe during the 16th century. A so-called Northern Renaissance was centred on the Low Countries and s Germany, another economically advanced region. The Renaissance was traditionally regarded as a unique period, characterized by the rise of the individual, the development of secular values and of a spirit of scientific inquiry, whose fruits included voyages of exploration. More recent scholarship has down-played the uniqueness of the Renaissance and emphasized other, earlier periods of cultural flowering, such as the Carolingian renaissance of the 9th century. Specific conditions for cultural revival in the 15th century included: the existence of wealthy patrons, such as the Medici in Florence; the invention of printing, and the acquisition of classical works via the Arabs and the Byzantines. *See also* Erasmus, Desiderius; humanism; Machiavelli, Niccolò; Renaissance architecture; Renaissance art

Renaissance architecture Architectural style that began in Italy in the 15th century and spread throughout Europe in the 16th century. In essence, it was a revival of the classical style of ancient Rome, and architects such as Filippo Brunelleschi (1377–1446), Leon Battista Alberti (1404–72), and Donato Bramante (1444–1514) studied the Roman ruins. In other European countries, classical forms were often integrated with medieval, Gothic motifs. Most subsequent styles, including baroque which superseded it, had Renaissance affinities.

Renaissance art Style that emerged in Italy in the 15th century, influenced by classical models and by humanism. It covers a long time-span and artists of very different styles, from Masaccio (1401–28) to Titian (1485–1576). It is usually said to have begun in Florence in the 14th century and reached its peak in the early 16th century. The three masters of the High Renaissance were Leonardo da Vinci (1452–1519), Michelangelo (1475–1564) and Raphael (1483–1520). Important, relatively new developments

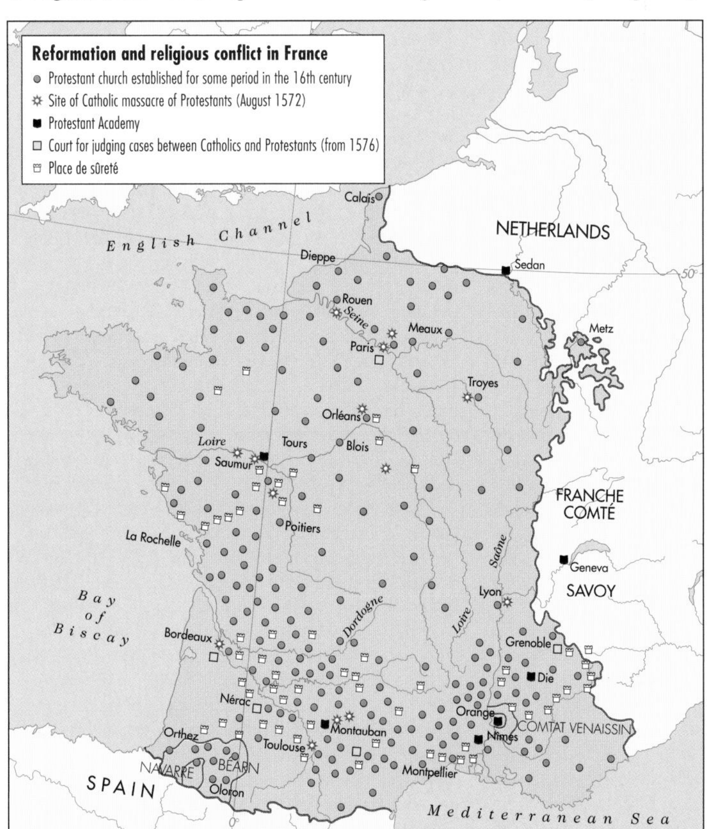

◀ **Religion, Wars of** The threat posed to the monarchy by the growth of Protestantism in France in the mid-15th century led to a prolonged civil war. The first war began in 1562 when Louis I de Condé, a Huguenot (Protestant) leader, captured strategic towns along the River Loire and established his headquarters at Orléans. Royal forces launched a lengthy siege of the occupied towns, eventually defeating the Huguenots in the winter of 1562. Although the Huguenots retained their strongholds in the s during the civil war, life for Protestants in the n became increasingly precarious. Territorial gains made by the Huguenots in the Treaty of St-Germain (1570) and concessions to their freedom to worship were short-lived and later repealed by Henry III, under pressure from the Holy League. The accession of Henry IV brought an end to civil war. His conversion to Catholicism pacified moderate Catholics and the Edict of Nantes (1598) re-established Protestant rights in France.

included: the stature of the artist as creator and the existence of rich and informed patrons, adoption of secular subjects; development of perspective, willingness to experiment, mastery of technique and increasing use of oils.

RENAMO (*Resistência Nacional Moçambicana*) Opposition movement in MOZAMBIQUE, SE Africa. Formed in opposition to the FRELIMO government in 1976, it waged a civil war with support from the white-minority regimes of Rhodesia (now Zimbabwe) and South Africa and from former Portuguese colonials. A non-aggression agreement with South Africa, the Nkomati Accord (1984), failed to stop the civil war, but FRELIMO's abandonment of a one-party state (1989) and the withdrawal of South African troops led to reconciliation. The guerrilla war had claimed *c*.100,000 lives. RENAMO, led by Afonso Dhlakama, accepted the new constitution (1990) and was transformed into a democratic political party (1992). *See also* MACHEL, SAMORA MOISÈS

René, (France) Albert (1935–) Seychelles statesman, prime minister (1976–77), president (1977–). He founded (1964) the Seychelles People's United Party (SPUP) and when the Seychelles achieved independence in 1976, René became its first prime minister. The following year, he overthrew President James Mancham in a coup and instituted a one-party state. René survived a number of coups led by mercenaries in the 1970s and 1980s and, bowing to internal opposition and external pressure, he legalized opposition parties (1991). Under a new constitution (1993), he led his reformed party, the Seychelles People's Progressive Front, to victory over Manacham in the 1993 elections. René was re-elected in 1998.

Reno, Janet (1938–) US lawyer, 78th attorney general (1993–). As state attorney (1978–93) for Dade county, Florida, she acquired a reputation for innovative schemes to deal with drug offenders and strong support of child-support laws. Appointed attorney general by President Bill Clinton, Reno was the first woman to serve as the nation's top law-enforcement official. She ordered the raid on the Branch Dravidian cult headquarters in Waco, Texas, in which 80 members of the cult died.

reparations Compensation for loss and damage caused by war, especially the payments demanded by the victorious Allies from the defeated Central Powers in the Treaty of VERSAILLES (1919) at the end of the WORLD WAR 1. Germany's protest that the reparations were too high was viewed sympathetically by many of their former enemies, and the United States waived some claims. Germany soon defaulted on payments, provoking occupation of the RUHR by French and Belgian troops (1923–24). Reparations were subsequently reduced to more realistic levels by the DAWES PLAN, and all payments ceased with the onset of the GREAT DEPRESSION.

R

Representatives, House of *See* HOUSE OF REPRESENTATIVES

Republican Party US political organization. It was founded in 1854 by opponents of the spread of SLAVERY into the new Western territories, who included WHIGS, Democrats and Free-Soilers. Its first presidential candidate, John FRÉMONT, gained 11 Northern states in the 1856 election. Its second candidate, Abraham LINCOLN, was elected president in 1860. The ensuing American CIVIL WAR (1860–65) dented the Party's support and Lincoln adopted the pro-war Democrat Andrew JOHNSON as his running mate to secure re-election under the banner of the National Union Party in 1864. Lincoln's assassination and the accession of Johnson saw the emergence of a Radical Republican faction that sought to impose RECONSTRUCTION on the defeated South. After the Civil War, the Party enjoyed a long ascendancy: controlling the White House for all but 16 years from 1860 to 1932. The breakaway LIBERAL REPUBLICAN PARTY was formed (1872) in protest against the corrupt Republican administration of President Ulysses S. GRANT. In 1877 Republican President Rutherford B. HAYES ended the period of Radical RECONSTRUCTION. The assassination (1901) of Republican President William MCKINLEY led to the succession of his vice president, Theodore ROOSEVELT, whose progressive policies targeted trusts and embraced labour reform. Roosevelt became discontented with the drift back to conservatism under his Republican presidential successor William Howard TAFT, and formed the PROGRESSIVE PARTY. The subsequent split in the Republican vote handed the 1912 elections to the DEMOCRATIC PARTY. Warren HARDING regained the presidency for the Republicans in 1920, and the booming national economy helped Herbert HOOVER win the 1928 elections. However, Hoover's failure to mitigate the worst effects of the GREAT DEPRESSION produced a landslide victory for the Democrat candidate Franklin D. ROOSEVELT in the 1932 election, marking the start of 20 years of Democratic dominance. After World War 2, there was more of a balance between the two parties, although the Republicans were often the minority in Congress. The Republicans were traditionally strong in New England and the Midwest, but after 1950 they gained strength in the South, traditionally a Democrat stronghold, and West. At the same time, the Party, customarily supported by business interests, became more conservative. The war-hero Dwight EISENHOWER brought the Republicans back into office in 1952. Eisenhower was re-elected in 1956, but his vice president Richard NIXON narrowly lost the 1960 election to the Democrat John F. KENNEDY. Nixon returned to lead the Republicans to victory in 1968 and 1972, but after the WATERGATE SCANDAL was forced to resign and was succeeded in office by his vice president, Gerald FORD. Ford was defeated by Southern Democrat Jimmy Carter in the 1976 elections, but Ronald REAGAN's promise of income-tax cuts and tough anti-communist stance ensured a Republican victory in 1980. Reagan's popular appeal enabled the Republicans to dominate national politics in the 1980s, even controlling the Senate from 1981 to 1987. Reagan was succeeded by his vice president George BUSH in 1988. Economic recession contributed to Bush's defeat by the Southern Democrat Bill Clinton in 1992, but in 1994 the Republicans secured control of both houses of Congress for the first time since 1954. *See also* ARTHUR, CHESTER ALAN; DEMOCRATIC-REPUBLICAN PARTY; FREE-SOIL PARTY; GARFIELD, JAMES ABRAM; GOLDWATER, BARRY MORRIS; HARRISON, BENJAMIN; KANSAS-NEBRASKA ACT; TAFT, ROBERT ALPHONSO; WHIG PARTY

Resistance movement Underground organizations actively opposed to Nazi German occupation during WORLD WAR 2. In some countries, such as Poland, the Soviet Union and Yugoslavia, they were strong enough to mount armed resistance. Elsewhere, as in France, the Low Countries and Scandinavia, their role was confined to sabotage and intelligence. *See also* CHETNIKS; FREE FRENCH; MAQUIS; MIHAILOVIĆ, DRAŽA; TITO; VICHY GOVERNMENT

Restoration In English history, the re-establishment of the monarchy in 1660. The term is often applied to the period from 1660 to *c*.1685. Experiments with republicanism had failed and the death of Oliver CROMWELL (1658) left the country without effective leadership. The RUMP PARLIAMENT was restored by army leaders but it had lost legitimacy. General George MONCK marched south from Scotland and demanded new elections. The resulting assembly invited CHARLES II, already crowned king of Scots, to resume the English throne. In French history, the term refers to the restoration of the BOURBON monarchy in 1814 after the defeat of NAPOLEON I.

Retz, Jean François Paul de Gondi, Cardinal de (1613–79) French statesman. He planned to supersede Cardinal Jules MAZARIN as the dominant force in the government of ANNE OF AUSTRIA. Using his influence with the Parisian bourgeoisie, Retz attempted to exploit the rebellion known as the FRONDE (1648–53) to his advantage. Retz's intrigues gained him a cardinalship (1651) and he was acknowledged as heir to his uncle as archbishop of Paris, but he was later (1652) imprisoned by LOUIS XIV. He escaped abroad in 1654 and was allowed to return to France (1662) after resigning his claim to the office of archbishop in exchange for the rich abbey of St-Denis. His *Memoires* provide a lively if inaccurate account of the period.

Reuter, Paul Julius, Baron von (1816–99) British journalist, b. Germany as Israel Josaphat. In 1849 he tried to open an agency for sending news by telegraph in Paris but, frustrated by government restrictions, moved it to London in 1851. Its early business was mainly private, commercial correspondence and until 1858 British newspapers declined to publish his foreign news telegrams. With the aid of undersea cables, the business soon expanded worldwide.

Revels, Hiram Rhoades (1822–1901) US politician, the first African American to be elected to the Senate (1870–71). In 1845 he was ordained as a minister in the African Methodist Episcopal Church. During the Civil War, Revels helped recruit volunteers for the Union cause and later acted as chaplain to an African-American regiment. He became Republican senator from Mississippi during RECONSTRUCTION and adopted a tolerant attitude towards former Confederates. He was president (1871–74) of Alcorn College, Mississippi.

Revere, Paul (1735–1818) American patriot and silversmith, famous for his ride from Charlestown to Lexington, Massachusetts. Revere, who had taken part in the BOSTON TEA PARTY, made his ride on the night of 18 April 1775 to warn the people of the approach of British troops at the start of the AMERICAN REVOLUTION. It was commemorated (inaccurately) in Henry Longfellow's poem, "Paul Revere's Ride" (1863). After the Revolution he became one of the United States' greatest silversmiths. *See also* LEXINGTON AND CONCORD, BATTLES OF

revisionism Term applied by orthodox communists, especially in the Soviet Union, to describe the policy of socialists who disagree with their principles. It derived from the late 19th-century theories of German Marxist Eduard Bernstein, who asserted, contrary to Karl MARX, that capitalism was not in crisis and that SOCIALISM could be achieved through peaceful evolution. The term is now used more widely, for example of the work of historians who present a view of events contrary to the version generally accepted. *See also* COMMUNISM; MARXISM

revivalism Term given to various movements within certain Christian, especially Protestant, churches characterized by a revitalization of religious activities, with a strong, evangelical emphasis on submission of the individual to faith in Jesus, accompanied by intensive prayer and Bible-reading. Historically, it is particularly associated with movements led by itinerant preachers in North America, beginning with the GREAT AWAKENING (*c*.1730–70). Revivalism is often seen as a reaction against "liberal" trends, most recently over such issues as abortion and homosexuality. The term has also been loosely applied to other movements in favour of a return to earlier, supposedly purer practices in Christianity and other religions. *See also* METHODISM; PROTESTANTISM; PURITANISM

Revolt of the Netherlands (1568–1609) War of independence against Spanish rule in the LOW COUNTRIES. The regency through which PHILIP II of Spain ruled the Low Countries was highly unpopular. Apart from economic restrictions, the crucial provocations were the suspension of the traditional privileges of the provinces and the attempt to enforce Roman Catholicism, which was especially resented in the largely Calvinist N provinces. In 1567, in response to a rising in the S provinces, the Spanish Duke of ALBA was appointed governor of the Netherlands with a remit to quash all opposition. The general revolt began as a reaction against the reign of terror, including the executions (1568) of Graaf van HOORN and Graaf van EGMONT, instituted by Alba. It was led by the Prince of Orange, WILLIAM I (THE SILENT), and his younger brother, LOUIS OF NASSAU. Returning from exile, they invaded the Netherlands in 1568 and after several years of fighting gradually gained control of the N provinces. The PACIFICATION OF GHENT (1576) temporarily united the Netherlands, but the largely Catholic provinces in the south (roughly equivalent to modern BELGIUM) were soon reconquered for Spain by a new governor, Alessandro FARNESE. The Union of UTRECHT (1579) declared a republic, called the UNITED PROVINCES OF THE NETHERLANDS, comprising the seven N provinces led by Holland, with William as stadtholder (president and commander in chief). After William's assassination (1584), the Dutch struggle for independence, aided by England, continued under the leadership of MAURICE OF NASSAU. Spanish forces were driven out of the United Provinces and a 12-year truce, signed in 1609, effectively confirmed Dutch independence, although it was not officially recognized by

Spain until the Peace of Westphalia (1648). *See also* John of Austria; Oldenbarneveldt, Johan von

revolution Fundamental and sudden change in the constitution of a state effected by violence. The French Revolution and the Russian Revolution are obvious examples. The totality of the change distinguishes a revolution from a coup d'état, rebellion, or war of independence, which do not necessarily seek fundamental constitutional change. However, the term is often used more loosely to indicate great changes in other fields, such as the Industrial Revolution or the scientific revolution, which usually occur over a longer time span.

Revolutionary War, American *See* American Revolution

Revolutionary Wars, French *See* French Revolutionary Wars

Revolutions of 1848 Series of republican revolts against monarchies throughout Europe (with the exception of Scandinavia, Russia and Spain). In Britain, it was confined to republican unrest in Ireland and minor demonstrations by the Chartism movement. The general cause was the frustration of liberals and nationalists with conservative governments, against a background of economic depression. The revolutions began with a rising in Sicily (January), which was brutally suppressed by Ferdinand II. The only successful rebellion was the February Revolution against Louis Philippe in France, which resulted in the foundation of the Second Republic. The success of the revolutionaries in France inspired revolts in Vienna, Austria, and among the various national minorities within the Austrian empire. It forced the abdication of Emperor Ferdinand (the Benign) in favour of Franz Joseph, and led to the resignation of Fürst von Metternich. Franz Joseph quickly crushed the revolution in Hungary, led by Sándor Petofi, Lajos Kossuth and Ferenc Deák. In Italy, Charles Albert of Sardinia-Piedmont declared war against Austria, but lack of support from (among others) Pope Pius IX led the Piedmontese forces to crumble. In Rome, a short-lived republic was created (February–July 1849) by Giuseppe Mazzini and Giuseppe Garibaldi, but was crushed by Louis Napoléon (later Napoleon III) of France. In Germany, liberals forced Frederick William IV of Prussia to summon a constitutional assembly, while advocates of German unification hoped to achieve their aim in the Frankfurt Parliament. In general, the Revolutions of 1848 resulted in a reactionary backlash, but they did lead to the Risorgimento in Italy and act as an inspiration for early socialism.

Revolutions of 1989 Popular risings in East European states against communist governments. Long-suppressed opposition to Russian domination erupted spontaneously in most of the Soviet satellite states. However unwelcome to Moscow, the Revolutions encountered little serious resistance from the Soviet government of Mikhail Gorbachev, whose policies of glasnost and perestroika contributed to the general anti-communist climate. In Poland, the Solidarity movement, led by Lech Wałesa, was legalized by Wojciech Jaruzelski in April 1989. In October 1989 Erich Honecker resigned as leader of East Germany, and the Berlin Wall, the most visible symbol of the Cold War, was dismantled in November 1989. In the same month, Todor Zhivkov of Bulgaria resigned. In the so-called "Velvet Revolution" in Czechoslovakia (December 1989), Gustáv Husák was replaced as president by Václav Havel. In most cases, the Revolutions involved comparatively little violence, but the overthrow (December 1989) of Nicolae Ceauşescu in Romania was a notable exception. The Revolutions were followed by the secession from the Soviet Union of its constituent republics. *See also* communism

Reynaud, Paul (1878–1966) French statesman, premier (1940). He was first elected to parliament in 1919 and held various cabinet posts under a succession of short-lived governments between 1930 and 1932. Out of office, he supported Charles de Gaulle's unimplemented plans for military reform. Reynaud returned to government as finance minister under Édouard Daladier (1938–40), criticizing the appeasement of Nazi Germany and preparing the French economy for war. He became premier in March 1940, too late to prevent France's defeat (June). Rejecting Marshal Philippe Pétain's proposal of an armistice with Germany, Reynaud resigned and was imprisoned for the rest of World War 2. He played a prominent part in the immediate post-war reconstruction of French government under de Gaulle, heading the committee that drafted the constitution of the Fifth Republic.

Reynolds, Albert (1933–) Irish statesman, prime minister (1992–94). In 1977 Reynolds entered the Dáil (parliament) and soon joined the Fianna Fáil cabinet. He was dismissed as minister of finance (1988–91) after challenging the compromised party leader and taoiseach (prime minister), Charles Haughey, but succeeded him in 1992. In the ensuing election, Fianna Fáil lost their majority, forcing a coalition with the Labour Party. One of his first acts as taoiseach was to ratify the Maastricht Treaty (1992), which established closer economic relations between members of the European Union (EU). With his British counterpart, John Major, Reynolds issued the Downing Street Declaration (1993), but when Labour withdrew its support for the coalition, Reynolds was forced to resign. He was succeeded by John Bruton.

Reza Khan *See* Pahlavi, Reza

Rhee, Syngman (1875–1965) Korean statesman, first president (1948–60) of South Korea. He was imprisoned (1898–1904) for his opposition to Japanese rule and lived in exile (1904–10, 1912–45) in the United States, becoming leader of a self-proclaimed government-in-exile in 1919. Rhee was leader of US-occupied South Korea after 1945, becoming president when the republic was founded in 1948. The Korean War (1950–53) broke out soon afterwards. Subsequently, Rhee's regime became increasingly authoritarian and corrupt, and a declining economy heightened discontent. After his re-election for a fourth time (1960), accusations of vote-rigging sparked riots, and Rhee was forced into exile. He was succeeded as president by General Park Chung Hee.

Rhineland Region in w Germany, mainly between the River Rhine and the border with the Low Countries and France; Cologne is the major city. From the 6th to 8th century AD, Rhineland formed part of the Merovingian kingdom of Austrasia, but later became divided into many principalities, including Alsace, Lorraine and Brandenburg. In the 19th century, Prussia was the dominant power in the region, which became one of the industrial powerhouses of Europe. After World War 1 the Treaty of Versailles (1919) established Rhineland as a demilitarized zone, initially occupied by Allied forces. It was controlled from Koblenz and a frontier was maintained between it and Germany. The French, with long-standing territorial ambitions in the region, hoped to establish a republic of the Rhineland in the 1930s but met with

▲ **Revolutions of 1848** The unrest in Hungary in 1848–49 was largely an expression of Magyar nationalism and was opposed by minority ethnic groups, in particular the Croats.

RHODE ISLAND
Statehood :
29 May 1790
Nickname :
Ocean State
State motto :
Hope

little encouragement. Allied troops were gradually withdrawn during the 1920s, and Adolf Hitler ordered the German reoccupation of the demilitarized zone in 1936. *See also* Locarno Pact; Nazi Party; Palatinate

Rhode Island State in New England, NE United States, the smallest state in the nation; the capital is Providence. The region was inhabited by various Algonquian-speaking peoples in the 17th century. The first European settlement was made at Providence in 1636 by the separatist minister Roger Williams, after he was driven out of the Massachusetts Bay Colony. In 1638 Anne Hutchinson, another Boston dissident, established the settlement of Portsmouth, but religious disagreements led William Coddington to leave Portsmouth and found Newport in the s of Aquidneck island. In 1644 the settlements were loosely united as Rhode Island under a royal charter. A second charter, issued by Charles II (1663), which granted self-government and religious freedom, remained the basis of government until 1842. Rhode Island was devastated in King Philip's War (1675–76) between Native Americans and the colonies of New England. Rhode Island's commerce with the West Indies, including the slave trade, was hit by the British Parliament's passing of the Sugar Act (1764). Hostility to British commercial restrictions led to the burning (1772) of the *Gaspee*, a British customs' cutter. Rhode Island was the first colony to declare independence (1776), but the last to sign (1790) the US Constitution. Dorr's Rebellion (1842) was an early movement for universal suffrage. As maritime industries slumped in the 19th century, the state became increasingly a textile-manufacturing centre. With the decline of the textile industry in New England from the 1920s, other manufactures took over, especially construction of naval and military equipment. Service industries largely compensated for the drop in US defence contracts after the end of the Cold War. Area: 3144sq km (1214sq mi). Pop. (1996 est.) 990,225.

Rhodes, Cecil John (1853–1902) British imperialist statesman and industrialist. In 1870 Rhodes emigrated to South Africa, where he made a fortune in the diamond mines of Kimberley. In 1888 Rhodes founded the De Beers Consolidated Mines Company, which within five years controlled more than 90% of the world's diamond trade. Rhodes dreamed of building a British Empire in Africa that stretched from the Cape to Cairo. In 1882 he helped to suppress a rebellion in Basutoland (now Lesotho). In 1885 Rhodes persuaded the British government of Lord Salisbury to declare a protectorate over Bechuanaland (now Botswana). He obtained mining concessions (1888) in Matabeleland and Mashonaland (now Zimbabwe) from King Lobengula, which he exploited through the British South Africa Company (founded 1889). In 1890 Rhodes' pioneers occupied Lobengula's kingdom, and in the following year British rule was extended to Northern Rhodesia (now Zambia) and Nyasaland (now Malawi). As prime minister (1890–96) of Cape Colony, Rhodes limited the number of Africans who could vote by imposing financial and literacy restrictions. Only Paul Kruger's Afrikaner republic of Transvaal stood in the way of British domination of s Africa. In 1895 Leander Starr Jameson, Rhodes' administrator in Matabeleland, launched the disastrous Jameson Raid on Transvaal in which Jameson and his entire army were captured, and Rhodes was forced to resign. He bequeathed most of his fortune to the Rhodes scholarships at Oxford University. *See also* Chamberlain, Joseph; Victoria

Rhodes (Ródhos) Greek island in the SE Aegean Sea; Rhodes is also the name of the chief city. After the fall of the Minoan civilization (*c.*1500–1400 BC), Rhodes became an

R

independent kingdom until it was colonized by the DORIANS in *c*.1000 BC. It was conquered by Persia (Iran) in the late 6th century BC and joined (*c*.500 BC) the Ionian revolt that precipitated the PERSIAN WARS. Rhodes joined Athens in the DELIAN LEAGUE, but during the PELOPONNESIAN WAR (431–404 BC) it was the centre of the pro-Sparta Rhodian federation. From the late 4th century BC Rhodes was a major commercial centre of the ancient world until devastated by an earthquake (*c*.224 BC), which toppled the COLOSSUS OF RHODES – one of the SEVEN WONDERS OF THE WORLD. It came under Byzantine rule in AD 395. In 1310 Rhodes was captured by the KNIGHTS HOSPITALLERS, who defended it against the Ottoman Turks until 1522 when, after a memorable siege, the Hospitallers evacuated their fortress and the island. Occupied by Italy in 1912, and subsequently ceded by the Turks, it passed to Greece in 1947. The island has become a popular resort and a major centre of archaeological research. Pop. (1991) 91,300.

Rhodesia Former British territory in S central Africa. It was acquired, in controversial circumstances, by Cecil RHODES' South Africa Company in the 1890s. Northern Rhodesia gained independence as ZAMBIA in 1963, whereupon Southern Rhodesia adopted the name Rhodesia, until it became the republic of ZIMBABWE in 1980.

Ribbentrop, Joachim von (1893–1946) German diplomat, foreign minister (1938–45). He joined the NAZI PARTY in 1932 and became foreign affairs adviser to Adolf HITLER (1933). Ribbentrop was ambassador to Great Britain (1936–38). As foreign minister, his main achievement was to negotiate the NAZI-SOVIET PACT (1939) with Vyacheslav MOLOTOV. He also negotiated the TRIPARTITE PACT (1940) with Japan and Italy. Although never actually dismissed, Ribbentrop steadily lost influence with Hitler during World War 2. At the NUREMBERG TRIALS (1946), he was convicted of war crimes and hanged.

Ricardo, David (1772–1823) English political economist. He entered Parliament in 1819. Ricardo's best-known work, *On Principles of Political Economy and Taxation* (1817), although influenced by Adam SMITH, was highly original across a broad field of economic theory. It outlined a "labour theory of value", that the price of an article reflects the labour involved in its production, a concept that had a profound influence on Karl MARX, among others. It resulted from Ricardo's theory of rent, influenced by Thomas MALTHUS, which maintained that a growing population would result in a squeeze on wages but increased profit for landholders, producing class conflict and economic stagnation. *See also* LAISSEZ-FAIRE; MILL, JOHN STUART

Ricci, Matteo (1552–1610) (Li Madou) Italian Jesuit missionary who founded the first Christian missions in India. In 1578 he travelled to India and thence to Zhaoqing, S China (1583), where he settled with Michele Ruggieri. In 1601 Ricci moved to Beijing, where he remained for the rest of his life, teaching science, translating many Western scientific books into Chinese, and writing several books of his own. Ricci's learning and intellect appealed to the Chinese intelligentsia, and he met the mandarins on their own terms. He adopted Chinese dress and customs, but his efforts to adapt Christian beliefs and rituals to Chinese culture earned him the disapproval of his superiors and, posthumously, the condemnation of the pope.

Richard I (the Lionheart) (*Coeur de Lion*) (1157–99) King of England (1189–99), son of HENRY II and ELEANOR OF AQUITAINE. He inherited the duchy of AQUITAINE in 1168 and was made Duke of Poitiers in 1172. Richard refused to cede Aquitaine to his youngest brother, JOHN, and joined forces with PHILIP II AUGUSTUS of France to force Henry II into exile, where he died in 1189. In 1190 Richard assumed the leadership of the Third CRUSADE (1189–92) against the great Muslim leader SALADIN. Richard displayed remarkable gifts for logistics and strategy, as well as bravery in battle. He regained ACRE (July 1191) and Joppa (September 1191), but failed to achieve his primary objective – the recapture of JERUSALEM. In 1192 Richard's return voyage to England was hit by a storm and he was captured by Leopold V of Austria, who handed him over to Emperor HENRY VI. Richard was released in 1194, after promising to pay a huge ransom of 150,000 marks, the raising of which through increased taxation made him highly unpopular in England. While Richard was in prison, his brother John had conspired against him in England and Philip II had invaded his territories in France. The English revolt was quickly contained, and Philip's encroachments had been largely reversed by the time Richard was killed in battle. He was succeeded by John. Richard was once condemned for supposedly neglecting his English kingdom, but his reputation, always enmeshed in legend and romance, has risen among contemporary historians. *See also* ANGEVINS

Richard II (1367–1400) King of England (1377–99), son of EDWARD THE BLACK PRINCE. Richard succeeded his grandfather, EDWARD III, at the age of 10, and his minority was dominated by his uncle, JOHN OF GAUNT. Gaunt's misrule exacerbated the economic decline, caused by the BLACK DEATH and England's prolonged involvement in the HUNDRED YEARS' WAR (1337–1453), and precipitated the PEASANTS' REVOLT (1381). Richard showed considerable courage and skill in confronting the rebels. When Gaunt left for Castile (1386), Parliament imposed a baronial council. Richard obtained a judgement declaring that this infringed the royal prerogative, but his supporters were defeated at the Battle of Radcot Bridge, Oxfordshire (1387). The "Merciless Parliament" of 1388 accused his allies of treason and some were executed. Richard was forced to submit to the rule of five lords appellants: the Duke of Hereford (son of Gaunt, later HENRY IV), the Duke of Gloucester, the Duke of Norfolk, the Earl of Arundel and the Earl of Warwick. In 1389 John of Gaunt returned to England and gradually restored order. Richard exacted his revenge on the lords appellants in 1397, when Arundel was executed, Gloucester murdered and Warwick exiled. In 1398 Richard banished Norfolk and Hereford, whose Lancastrian estates he confiscated after John of Gaunt's death (1399). When Richard left on a campaign to Ireland in 1399, Hereford invaded. Richard returned to England, but was forced to abdicate in favour of Hereford, and died soon after (probably of natural causes) in Pontefract Castle, N England. *See also* LANCASTER, HOUSE OF

Richard III (1452–85) King of England (1483–85). He was made Duke of Gloucester in 1461 after his eldest brother, Edward of YORK, deposed HENRY VI and assumed the throne as EDWARD IV. In 1470 Richard and Edward were forced into exile by the Earl of WARWICK, who reinstated Henry VI. Richard returned to England, defeating Henry's forces at the battles of BARNET and TEWKESBURY (1471), and thereby securing Edward's restoration. When Edward died, Richard became protector of the realm for the 12-year-old EDWARD V. With the aid of Henry STAFFORD, Richard then manoeuvred against Edward IV's widow, Elizabeth Woodville (1437–92), to gain custody of Edward V and his nine-year old brother. The brothers were subsequently declared illegitimate and Richard became king. Stafford's rebellion in S England was quickly suppressed, and he was executed. Richard's numerous enemies supported the invasion of Henry Tudor (later HENRY VII) in August 1485, and Richard was killed at the Battle of BOSWORTH FIELD, the final battle in the Wars of the ROSES. Controversy surrounds nearly every aspect of Richard's career. Tudor historians and writers blamed him for many crimes, including the murder of Henry VI and of the "princes in the Tower", but some still maintain his innocence. *See also* LANCASTER, HOUSE OF

Richard, Earl of Cornwall (1209–72) King of the Romans (1257–71), second son of King JOHN of England and brother of HENRY III. He skilfully acquired vast estates and titles from his brother by threatening to join a baronial rebellion, and he acted as regent (1253–54) while Henry was in GASCONY, France. Richard secured his election as king of the Romans through bribery, but his dreams of becoming Holy Roman emperor were never realized. Richard fought against the rebels in the BARONS' WAR in England, and was captured at the Battle of LEWES (1264). *See also* MONTFORT, SIMON DE

Richelieu, Armand Jean du Plessis, Duc de (1585–1642) French cardinal and statesman, chief minister to LOUIS XIII of France (1624–42). Known as "the Red Eminence", Richelieu's greatest achievements were the establishment of the basis for royal absolutism in France and the restoration of the prestige of the French kingdom after the lengthy domination of Europe by the Spanish HABSBURGS. He was ordained a priest in 1607 and elected to the States-General in 1614. Richelieu soon became a protégé of MARIE DE' MÉDICIS and was appointed as chaplain to ANNE OF AUSTRIA, wife of Louis XIII. He was dismissed as secretary of state (1616–17) when the regency of Marie was toppled in a palace coup. When Marie regained power in 1619, Richelieu was called upon to act as arbitrator. He became a cardinal in 1622 and was promoted to chief of the royal council in 1624 (first minister from 1628), after expelling the papal forces from the Protestant Swiss canton of Grisons. Richelieu crushed the political and military power of the HUGUENOTS, capturing their stronghold of LA ROCHELLE (1629), but generally abstained from religious persecution. With the French army occupied against the Huguenots, Spain took the opportunity to capture the fortress of Casale, N Italy, precipitating the War of the Mantuan Succession (1628–31) with France. Cardinal Richelieu made powerful enemies, especially among the nobility and devout Catholics, and survived several conspiracies. On the Day of the Dupes (11 November 1630), Marie and her supporters moved against Richelieu, but Louis stood by his first minister and Marie fled into exile. To strike at Habsburg hegemony in Europe, Richelieu subsidized GUSTAVUS II of Sweden's war in Germany, but by 1635 this policy had drawn France into direct involvement against Catholic forces in the THIRTY YEARS' WAR (1618–48). At home, Richelieu reduced the power of the French nobility by creating officials (*intendants*) dependent on crown patronage to govern the provinces. He encouraged industry and foreign trade, but the cost of war against Habsburg Spain drained the royal finances and the use of church revenues led to conflict with Pope URBAN VIII. Richelieu accumulated a huge personal fortune, some of which he used to found (1635) the Académie Française. On his death, he was succeeded as first minister by his own protégé, Cardinal Jules MAZARIN.

Richmond Capital of Virginia, SE United States. Settled in 1637, the city was made state capital in 1779. At the start of the CIVIL WAR, it replaced Montgomery, Alabama, as the capital of the CONFEDERATE STATES. Union General George MCCLELLAN'S attempt to capture Richmond was repelled in the SEVEN DAYS' BATTLES (1862), and the city finally fell to General Ulysses GRANT in 1865. During and after the Reconstruction period, Richmond prospered on its tobacco industry. The State Capitol was designed (1785) by Thomas Jefferson. Pop. (1990) 203,056.

Ridgway, Mathew Bunker (1895–1993) US general. During World War 2, he served in the war department (1939–42) before becoming commander of the 82nd Airborne Division, which he led in the paratroop assault on Sicily. In 1950 Ridgway was given command of the 8th Army in the KOREAN WAR, and the following year replaced Douglas MACARTHUR as Allied commander in the Far East, successfully defending South Korea. In 1952 Ridgway succeeded General Dwight Eisenhower as supreme commander of Allied forces in Europe. He served as US army chief of staff (1953–55) until his retirement.

Ridley, Nicholas (*c*.1500–55) English bishop and Protestant martyr. As chaplain to Thomas CRANMER, he helped to compile the first BOOK OF COMMON PRAYER (1549) and was made bishop of Rochester (1547) and later of London (1550). In 1553 Ridley supported the Protestant Lady Jane GREY against the Catholic MARY I. Convicted of heresy under Mary, he was burned at the stake with Bishop Hugh LATIMER in Oxford, S England.

Ridolfi Plot (1571) Conspiracy to depose ELIZABETH I of England in favour of the Catholic MARY, QUEEN OF SCOTS, then a prisoner in England. It was organized by Roberto Ridolfi (1531–1612), an Italian banker in London, who secured the backing of Pope PIUS V and PHILIP II of Spain, as well as the Catholic Duke of Norfolk, who was intended to marry Mary. English government agents discovered the Plot, Norfolk was executed (1572) and Ridolfi, who was in France, returned to Italy.

Riebeeck, Jan van (1619–77) Dutch founder of Cape Town, the first European settlement in South Africa, and its first governor (1652–62). Van Riebeeck was sent to the Cape to establish a provisions station for Dutch EAST INDIA COMPANY ships en route to the East Indies. His introduction of slaves and granting of freedoms for burghers to establish farms in the interior led to war (1659–60) with the indigenous KHOIKHOI. In 1662 van Riebeeck was transferred to Malacca.

Riel, Louis (1844–85) French-Canadian rebel. He led the *Métis* (people of mixed European and native descent) in the RED RIVER REBELLION (1869–70). Riel seized Fort Garry (now Winnipeg, MANITOBA), forcing the Dominion Parliament to pass the Manitoba Act (1870), which granted concessions to the *Métis*. The subsequent execution of an English-Canadian by Riel's government led to the forcible recapture of Fort Garry, and Riel was forced to flee. In 1871 his supporters repulsed an invasion by US Fenians. Riel was rewarded with election (1873) to the Dominion Parliament, but he never took his seat and was confined to a mental asylum in 1877–78, subsequently moving to Montana, NW United States. In 1885, acting in response to an appeal from the *Métis* in Saskatchewan, Riel led another rebellion against the Canadian government. The revolt was quickly crushed and Riel's execution for treason produced a wave of race riots in Québec and Ontario.

Rienzi, Cola di (1313–54) Italian leader of a popular rebellion, b. Nicola di Lorenzo. In 1347 he mounted a successful revolt in Rome (1347), assuming the title of TRIBUNE (representative of the PLEBEIANS in ancient Rome). Opposed by the Roman nobility and Pope CLEMENT VI, Rienzi was swiftly driven from power and sought refuge in the Abruzzi mountains. In 1350 Rienzi sought the support of Emperor Charles IV, who promptly handed him over to the Inquisition. Rienzi was acquitted of heresy and returned to Rome as senator (1354) with the blessing of Pope Innocent VI. Reinzi's dictatorial rule provoked rioting on the streets of Rome and he was killed by an angry mob.

Riga Capital of LATVIA, on the Gulf of Riga. Founded as a Baltic trading port in 1201, Riga became the headquarters of the LIVONIAN ORDER (later part of the TEUTONIC KNIGHTS) and a member of the HANSEATIC LEAGUE. Captured (1581) by Poland in the LIVONIAN WAR, it later fell (1621) to GUSTAVUS II of Sweden, who granted it self-government. In 1710 CHARLES XII of Sweden was defeated by PETER I (THE GREAT) of Russia, and Russian rule was confirmed at the Treaty of NYSTAD (1721). In 1918 Latvia gained independence and Riga was made capital. In 1940, when Latvia was incorporated into the Soviet Union, thousands of its citizens were deported or executed, and further suffering occurred under German occupation (1941–44). In 1991, following the collapse of the Soviet Union, Riga again became capital of an independent Latvia. Sights include the Doma Cathedral (*c*.1215). Pop. (1991) 910,200.

Rijeka (It. Fiume) Port on the Adriatic Sea, W Croatia. Founded by the Romans in the 3rd century AD, Avars and Slavs settled in the 7th century. From 1471 Rijeka developed into a leading port in the Austro-Hungarian empire. After World War 1, Rijeka was contested by Italy and the Kingdom of the Serbs, Croats and Slovenes (later Yugoslavia). While negotiations over sovereignty continued, the Italian soldier-poet Gabriele D'ANNUNZIO seized the city with a small force of Italian syndicalists. He continued to occupy the city until the Treaty of RAPALLO (1920) made it a free city. In 1922 Italian troops occupied Rijeka and the Treaty of Rome (1924) awarded most of the city to Italy. After World War 2, Rijeka passed to Yugoslavia. Pop. (1991) 167,757.

Rijswijk, Treaty of (1697) Agreement that ended the War of the GRAND ALLIANCE, between France and the opposing coalition of Austria, England, Spain and the United Provinces of the Netherlands. France surrendered much of the territory it had gained during the War, but kept parts of Alsace, including Strasbourg. Trading concessions and the right to garrison border-towns were granted to the Dutch; the independence of SAVOY was recognized; and France acknowledged the Dutch WILLIAM III (OF ORANGE) as king of England. The peace lasted only five years. *See also* AUGSBURG, LEAGUE OF

Rio de Janeiro City on Guanabara Bay, SE Brazil. Among early white settlers were many French Huguenots, who were driven out by the Portuguese in 1567. In the late 17th century, the colony's population rose to *c*.8000, most of whom were slaves employed on the sugar plantations. In the 18th century, Rio developed as the outlet for the gold of Minais Gerais, becoming the colonial capital in 1763. As the residence (1808–21) of JOHN VI of Portugal, after he was forced to flee Napoleonic Europe, Rio acquired many of its fine civic buildings. In 1822 it became the capital of an independent Brazil. The late-19th and early-20th centuries witnessed the development of the city's infrastructure. Between 1920 and 1940 the city's population nearly doubled to 1.75 million. In 1960 the capital was transferred to Brasília. Pop. (1991) 5,336,179.

Río de la Plata, Viceroyalty of the Region of colonial Spanish America, incorporating present-day Argentina, Uruguay, Paraguay and Bolivia. CHARLES III of Spain decided to establish (1776) a fourth viceroyalty in order to protect S Brazil from Portuguese attack and British encroachment. Río de la Plata flourished on the export of silver through the port of BUENOS AIRES and the demand for salt beef, produced on the ranches of the Pampas. In 1810 the Creoles of Buenos Aires overthrew Spanish rule.

Ripley, George (1802–80) US writer and social reformer. A Unitarian minister until 1841, he was associated with Ralph Waldo Emerson and other students of transcendentalism in publishing the *Dial* magazine. In 1841 Ripley established Brook Farm, a utopian community in West Roxbury, Massachusetts, based on a farming and handicraft economy with communal ownership of property. After it failed (1847), he continued his advocacy of social reform as a writer and editor in *The Harbinger*.

Ripon, Frederick John Robinson, 1st Earl of *See* GODERICH, FREDERICK JOHN ROBINSON, VISCOUNT

Risorgimento (It. resurgence) Nationalist movement in 19th-century ITALY that resulted in the establishment of the kingdom of Italy in 1861. It is usually dated from the risings of the CARBONARI in the 1820s, although its antecedents can be traced back to the NAPOLEONIC WARS and beyond. In 1831 Giuseppe MAZZINI founded the influential YOUNG ITALY movement, the aim of which was a single, democratic republic. Mazzini's influence was at its peak in the REVOLUTIONS OF 1848, but thereafter less radical movements took the lead. In SARDINIA-PIEDMONT (the only independent Italian state), the aim of the chief minister, Conte di CAVOUR, the true architect of Italian unity, was a parliamentary monarchy under his king. By securing the support of NAPOLEON III of France in a war against Austria, Cavour acquired much of Austrian-ruled N Italy in 1859. In 1860 Giuseppe GARIBALDI led his 1000-strong band of "Red Shirts" against the Kingdom of the TWO SICILIES. Garibaldi belonged to the republican tradition of Mazzini, but he had no ambition to rule and handed over Sicily and Naples to VICTOR EMMANUEL II. The kingdom of Italy was proclaimed in 1861. Venice was ceded to Italy in 1866 and the pope held out until his French protectors withdrew (1870), whereupon Rome became the capital.

Rivadavia, Bernardino (1780–1845) Argentine statesman, first president (1826–27). He participated in the overthrow of the Spanish Viceroyalty of RÍO DE LA PLATA in 1810, becoming the leading political figure in the tumultuous period of the birth of the Argentine republic. Rivadavia's early reforms included the abolition of the slave trade. In 1814 he went to Europe to secure British support for the fledgling independent state of the United Provinces of La Plata (now ARGENTINA). Returning to Buenos Aires in 1821, he served as minister of state, founding (1821) the University of Buenos Aires, before being elected president. Rivadavia introduced sweeping constitutional, social and economic reforms, such as the extension of the franchise to all men over the age of 19, the ending of press censorship, and the abolition of ecclesiastical courts. His government was hindered, however, by the internal conflict between *unitarios* (centralists) and CAUDILLOS (federalists), and in 1825 war broke out with Brazil over the status of present-day Uruguay. After the rejection of his centralist constitution (1826), Rivadavia resigned and went into exile. In 1834 he returned to face trial and was sentenced to permanent exile.

Rivera, Miguel Primo de *See* PRIMO DE RIVERA, MIGUEL

Rizzio, David (*c*.1533–66) Italian musician at the Scottish court. The cultured young Italian attracted the French-educated MARY, QUEEN OF SCOTS. Their relationship was undoubtedly innocent, but it angered Mary's husband, Lord DARNLEY, resentful because Mary had not granted him regal rank. Rizzio, suspected by some of being a papal agent, was murdered by Protestant lords, including Darnley, in Holyroodhouse, Edinburgh, while the pregnant Mary was held off at the point of a sword.

Roanoke Island Colony Attempted settlement sponsored by Sir Walter RALEIGH on an island now in NORTH CAROLINA, United States. The first settlers, all men and working for pay, arrived in 1585 but opted to leave when visited by Sir Francis DRAKE in 1586. A second attempt, with more than 100 genuine colonists in three ships, arrived in 1587. A child, Virginia Dare, was born soon afterwards. Their leader (and Virginia's grandfather), John White, returned to England for supplies, but on his return (1590), he found the Colony had vanished without trace.

robber barons Aggressive and dishonest businessmen in the United States during the GILDED AGE, whose activities included extensive bribery of judicial and law-enforcement officials. The term was applied to railway entrepreneurs such as Jay GOULD, whose exploits included an attempt to corner the gold-market in 1869. *See also* DREW, DANIEL

Robert II (the Pious) (*c*.970–1031) King of France (996–1031), son and successor of Hugh CAPET. He married (996) as his second wife a cousin, Bertha of Burgundy, and was excommunicated by Pope Gregory V for incest. By a third wife, Constance of Arles, Robert had three sons who, backed by their mother, rebelled against him in his last years.

Robert I (the Bruce) (1274–1329) King of Scots (1306–29). He was descended from a prominent Anglo-Norman family with claims to the Scottish throne: his grandfather had been an unsuccessful claimant against John BALLIOL in 1291. The Bruces remained loyal to EDWARD I of England during the revolt led by Wiliam WALLACE, but in 1306 Robert's rival, John Comyn, was murdered (probably at Robert's instigation) and Robert crowned himself king of Scots. He was quickly defeated by the English at Methven, E Scotland (1306), and forced into hiding. Aided by his brother Edward, nominally high king of Ireland, Robert fought his way back, steadily driving out the English. EDWARD II's attempt to relieve Stirling, the last English stronghold, resulted in Bruce's crushing victory at the Battle of BANNOCKBURN (1314). The victory ensured the independence of SCOTLAND, although the war continued until England acknowledged Scottish independence in the Treaty of Northampton (1328). Robert was able to secure the succession on his son, DAVID II.

Robert II (1316–90) King of Scots (1371–90). Son of Walter the Steward, Robert was the first king of the STUART (Stewart) dynasty. He acted as regent during the spells of exile and imprisonment of his uncle, DAVID II, and led an unsuccessful rebellion in 1362–63. Robert proved a weak king. His reign was marked by conflict between crown and nobility, which became a disruptive force in Scottish government for centuries. From 1384 the kingdom was run by his eldest son, John (later ROBERT III).

Robert III (*c*.1337–1406) King of Scots (1390–1406), son of ROBERT II. He administered the realm for his father from 1384 until 1388, when he was crippled in a riding accident. His injuries prevented him from fulfilling his role as king, virtually abdicating altogether in 1399. The regency was disputed between his son David, Duke of Rothesay, and his brother Robert, Duke of Albany. In 1402 Rothesay was kidnapped and (probably) murdered, leaving Albany supreme. Robert III was succeeded by his 11-year-old son, JAMES I.

Robert II (*c*.1054–1134) (Robert Curthose) Duke of NORMANDY (1087–1106), eldest son of WILLIAM I (THE CONQUEROR). Robert launched two unsuccessful revolts (*c*.1077, *c*.1082) against his father in Normandy before succeeding him as duke. In 1094 his younger brother, WILLIAM II of England, invaded Normandy and forced Robert to cede the duchy to him. Robert left to take part in the First CRUSADE (1096–99), securing victory at the

Battle of Ascalon (1099). After his youngest brother succeeded WILLIAM II as HENRY I of England, Robert led a disastrous invasion. Henry responded by attacking Normandy and capturing Robert at the Battle of Tinchebrai (1106). He spent the rest of his life imprisoned in Cardiff Castle, Wales.

Robert Guiscard *See* GUISCARD, ROBERT

Roberts, Frederick Sleigh, 1st Earl (1832–1914) British field marshal, last commander in chief of the British Army (1901–04). Roberts first distinguished himself in the INDIAN MUTINY (1857–58). His defeat of Ayub Khan at the Battle of KANDAHAR during the Second AFGHAN WAR (1878–80) was rewarded with a barony (raised to an earldom in 1901). He was commander in chief in India (1885–93) and Ireland (1895–99) before taking command (1899–1900) in the Second SOUTH AFRICAN WAR. The British had suffered humiliating defeats; Roberts brought fresh determination and a new strategy, which resulted in the capture of the Afrikaner strongholds of Bloemfontein, Johannesburg and Pretoria. In 1900 he retired in favour of Lord KITCHENER, asserting (incorrectly) that the War was virtually over.

Robespierre, Maximilien François Marie Isidore de (1758–94) French revolutionary, leader of the JACOBINS during the FRENCH REVOLUTION. He was elected to the States-General in 1789 and became a popular member of the subsequent NATIONAL ASSEMBLY. Robespierre called for democratic change, such as universal suffrage, a meritocratic system of public appointment, and an end to racial and religious discrimination. Believing that the people were the only repository of political virtue, he called for full elections to the next assembly and opposed the royal veto over legislation. After LOUIS XVI attempted to flee France, Robespierre demanded the king be tried for treason. He refused to participate in the Legislative Assembly, using the Jacobin Club to speak out against the looming FRENCH REVOLUTIONARY WARS and to attack the Marquis de LAFAYETTE. His opposition to the war with Austria and Prussia was justified by French defeats, and, with the king and the GIRONDINS discredited, the republican revolution of August 1792 resulted in Robespierre being chosen to lead the NATIONAL CONVENTION. He successfully led the prosecution calls for execution (January 1793) at the trial of Louis XVI, and subsequently allied the SANS-CULOTTES with the MONTAGNARDS to purge the Convention of Girondins. The defection of General Charles DUMOURIEZ and the Wars of the VENDÉE convinced Robespierre of the need to create a dictatorship, and he assumed the leadership of the COMMITTEE OF PUBLIC SAFETY (July 1793), which intensified the REIGN OF TERROR. Ex-supporters of Robespierre, such as Jacques René HÉBERT and Georges DANTON, were also victims of this upsurge in state-sponsored violence. Robespierre's poor health and anger over continuing criticism of the dictatorship, despite French victories in the war, saw him retreat into semi-retirement. His opponents, encouraged by this retreat, mounted a coup, and Robespierre was arrested and executed on 10 Thermidor (28 July 1794). *See also* SAINT-JUST, LOUIS ANTOINE LÉON DE; THERMIDORIAN REACTION

Robinson, Mary Bourke (1944–) Irish stateswoman, president (1990–97). A specialist in international law, she was elected to the Irish senate in 1969, but was relatively unknown when she won the election for president on a centre-left platform, with strong advocacy of women's rights. Ireland's first woman president, Robinson was extremely popular, and her humanity and tolerance helped to ameliorate Republican resentment of Unionism in Northern Ireland. She was succeeded as president by another female academic, Mary McAleese. In 1997 Robinson became United Nations' (UN) Commissioner for Human Rights.

Rob Roy (1671–1734) Scottish Highland outlaw, b. Robert MacGregor. He was a son of the 15th chief of the landless MacGregors (the "children of the mist"), and his banditry, a traditional pursuit, seems to have been caused by just grievances against the Duke of Montrose. "Rob Roy" took part in the JACOBITE rising of 1715, capturing Falkland Palace, E Scotland. He made his peace with the authorities, and even with Montrose, in 1722 and thereafter lived a quiet life, enjoying others' admiration of his derring-do, which was later romanticized in Sir Walter Scott's novel *Rob Roy* (1817).

Rockefeller, John Davison (1839–1937) US industrialist and philanthropist. In 1863 he built an oil refinery in Cleveland which was incorporated (1870) into the Standard Oil Company of Ohio, the largest oil corporation in the world. Rockefeller retired (1913) when Standard Oil was broken up under the SHERMAN ANTI-TRUST ACT. He donated half his US$1 billion fortune to charity, founding (1913) the Rockefeller Foundation, a philanthropic institution to promote "the well-being of mankind throughout the world".

Rockefeller, Nelson Aldrich (1908–79) US statesman, 41st vice president (1974–77), grandson of John ROCKEFELLER. He entered government (1940) as coordinator of inter-American affairs and, despite being a liberal Republican, rose to become an assistant secretary of state (1944–45) under Democratic President Franklin ROOSEVELT. Rockefeller also served under President Harry S TRUMAN, and acted as an undersecretary (1953–55) to President Dwight EISENHOWER. As governor of New York (1958–73), Rockefeller greatly expanded the state's administration and education system. He ran for the Republican presidential nomination three times (1960, 1964, 1968), but was defeated by Richard NIXON (twice) and Barry GOLDWATER. In 1974, after Nixon was forced to resign over the WATERGATE AFFAIR, President Gerald FORD picked him to fill the vacant office of vice president.

Rockingham, Charles Watson-Wentworth, 2nd Marquess of (1730–82) British statesman, prime minister (1765–66, 1782). In 1765 GEORGE III appointed him to succeed George GRENVILLE as prime minister. In his first term in office, Rockingham repealed the STAMP ACT and reduced other taxes that had infuriated the American colonists, but he did not surrender the right of the British Parliament to legislate for the colonies. His ministry, riven by factional disputes, collapsed after a year and William PITT (THE ELDER) became prime minister. For the next 16 years Rockingham led the WHIG opposition to British involvement in the AMERICAN REVOLUTION, but frail health and dislike of public speaking meant that his friend Edmund BURKE was the most public critic of British colonial policy. In 1782 Rockingham succeeded Lord NORTH as prime minister and immediately opened peace negotiations with the American colonists. *See also* BUTE, JOHN STUART, 3RD EARL OF; SHELBURNE, WILLIAM PETTY FITZMAURICE

Rodney, George Brydges, 1st Baron (1718–92) British admiral. He joined the Navy in 1732 and, during the War of the Austrian Succession (1740–48), fought under Admiral HAWKE in the victory off Finistère, W France (1747). Appointed to command a squadron in the Leeward Islands during the SEVEN YEARS' WAR, Rodney captured Martinique, St Lucia and Grenada (1762). In 1771 he was promoted to rear admiral. Rodney is mainly remembered for his victories during the AMERICAN REVOLUTION: the defeat of a Spanish fleet off Cape St Vincent (1780) relieved Gibraltar; the victory over the French at the Battle of Les SAINTES (1782) preserved Jamaica. *See also* FRENCH AND INDIAN WARS; NELSON, HORATIO, VISCOUNT

▲ **Robespierre** was one of the most controversial figures of the French Revolution. Revered by some for his democratic ideals, he was despised by others for his supposed dictatorial power.

Roe v. Wade (1973) US legal case in which the Supreme Court ruled against a Texas law declaring abortion illegal except to preserve the mother's life. The judgment established a woman's right to an abortion during the first six months of pregnancy, except under certain conditions, and affected the abortion laws in most states. *See also* BLACKMUN, HARRY ANDREW; BURGER, WARREN EARL

Roger I (1031–1101) Count of SICILY (1072–1101), brother of Robert GUISCARD and father of ROGER II. He fought alongside his brother against the Byzantines in Apulia and Calabria, S Italy, and against the Muslims in Sicily. Guiscard appointed him count of Sicily after the capture of PALERMO (1072). Roger completed the conquest of Sicily with the seizure of Messina (1091) and, after Guiscard's death, headed the NORMAN power in the region. He showed tolerance towards both Arabs and Greeks, employing Muslims in his army.

Roger II (1095–1154) First NORMAN king of SICILY (1130–54), son of ROGER I. In 1105 he succeeded his elder brother, Simon, as count of Sicily. Roger set out to unite the various Norman conquests in S Italy, gaining control of Calabria (1122) and Apulia (1127). In 1130 he overcame opposition from barons and papacy to unite the three duchies as the kingdom of Sicily. By the end of the 1130s Roger had secured his mainland territories from the incursions of Emperor LOTHAIR II, and after the death (1139) of his most determined opponent, Ranulph of Naples, his position was unchallenged. Roger was now master of the Mediterranean and the splendour of his court reflected his position as one of the greatest rulers in Europe. His navy secured control of present-day Tunisia, N Africa, and the Greek island of Corfu, but notably did not participate in the Second CRUSADE (1147). His kingdom was a rich mix of Christian and Muslim cultures. Roger enforced toleration of all religions and languages, and his Assizes of Ariano (1140) codified the kingdom's laws.

Rohan, Louis René Édouard, Cardinal de (1734–1803) French ecclesiastic who became embroiled in the DIAMOND NECKLACE AFFAIR (1785). He was ambassador (1772–74) to the court of MARIA THERESA of Austria. He was appointed a cardinal in 1778, becoming bishop of Strasbourg (1779–1801). Anxious to regain the favour of LOUIS XVI, Rohan was fooled by his mistress, the Countess de la Motte, into arranging the purchase of a necklace supposedly for Queen MARIE ANTOINETTE. The necklace vanished without being paid for and Rohan was tried for fraud. Although acquitted in 1786, he was forced to resign his offices and enter a monastery. Regarded as a martyr by the supporters of the FRENCH REVOLUTION, Rohan was a member of the States-General (1789)

Röhm, Ernst (1887–1934) German army officer, founder of the *Sturmabteilung* (Stormtroopers), or BROWNSHIRTS. He fought in World War I and afterwards helped to found the German NAZI PARTY. Röhm was briefly imprisoned for his involvement in the MUNICH PUTSCH (1923). Röhm subsequently fell out with Adolf HITLER over the scope and role of the Brownshirts and spent five years in Bolivia (1925–30) before returning to reorganize the stormtroopers. Hitler feared his power and had him assassinated in the NIGHT OF THE LONG KNIVES (30 June 1934).

Roh Tae Woo (1932–) South Korean statesman and general, president (1988–93). He fought in the KOREAN WAR (1950–53) and rose to the rank of general in 1979. After the assassination of President PARK CHUNG HEE, Roh lent military support to the coup led by CHUN DOO HWAN, a close friend, and brutally crushed a demonstration (1980) in Kwangju, SW SOUTH KOREA. In 1981 Roh retired from the army and subsequently held a number of cabinet posts under Chun. In 1985 he became chairman of the ruling Democratic Justice Party (DJP). Chun's choice of Roh as his successor prompted a wave of popular protests (1987), forcing Roh to commit to democratic reforms. As president, Roh sought reconciliation with North Korea and gained South Korea's admission (1991) to the United Nations (UN). In 1990 he merged the DJP with two opposition parties to form the Democratic Liberal Party (DLP). Roh supported Kim Young Sam's successful campaign to succeed him as president in the 1992 elections. In 1996 Chun and Roh were convicted of treason and corruption, sentenced to life imprisonment and fined US$3 million. They were both released in 1997.

Rokossovsky, Konstantin Konstantinovich (1896–1968) Soviet general, b. Poland. He served in the Red Army during the Russian Civil War. Rokossovsky was imprisoned (1938–41) during Joseph Stalin's Great Purge, but was released in order to help in the defence of the Soviet Union after the German invasion. During World War 2, Rokossovsky was instrumental in securing a crucial victory over the German 6th Army at the Battle of Stalingrad (1943). He also fought in the defence of Moscow (1941) and Kursk (1943) and led the lightning Soviet advance into Belarus. The Soviet offensive was halted outside Warsaw, enabling the Germans to crush the Warsaw Uprising (1944), but Rokossovsky renewed the attack in 1945, capturing East Prussia and Pomerania. In 1949 he held the position of marshal of Poland until the return of Władysław Gomułka, subsequently serving as Poland's minister of defence (1949–56). In 1956 Rokossovsky led the suppression of striking workers in Poznán, w Poland. He was recalled to Moscow when Nikita Khrushchev decided to accept the return to power of Gomułka, who had been imprisoned (1951–54) on the orders of Stalin.

Roland (de La Platière), Jeanne Marie (1754–93) French revolutionary. Her salon in Paris became the headquarters of the Girondins, and her influence gained the appointment of her husband, Jean-Marie (1734–93), as minister of the interior in 1792. Mme Roland wrote the letter of protest to Louis XVI that led to her husband's dismissal. She also persuaded her husband to attack Maximilien Robespierre and Georges Danton in the National Convention, an event that contributed to the split between the Jacobins and Girondins. Mme Roland was arrested, imprisoned and guillotined during the Reign of Terror. Reputedly, her last words were: "Oh Liberty! What crimes are committed in your name!" Mme Roland's execution prompted the suicide of her husband.

Rollo (*c*.860–*c*.931) (Göngu-Hrólfr) Viking chief, founder of the duchy of Normandy. Acting without orders from Harald I of Norway, he led raids on Scotland and England and in *c*.890 invaded nw France. From his base on the River Seine, Rollo threatened Paris and Chartres until Charles III (the Simple) of France signed a treaty (911), which granted the Vikings land around Rouen, Neustria, in exchange for a commitment to desist from further raids. Rollo converted to Christianity in 912 but is said to have died a pagan. His son and successor, William Longsword, extended the duchy to roughly its present boundaries.

Roman Britain British section of the Roman Empire from AD 43 until *c*.410. Although Julius Caesar had invaded Britain (55 BC, 54 BC) and Augustus had lent military aid to some British tribes, it was Emperor Claudius I who built the first Roman colony, at Colchester (AD 43). The British chief Caractacus was soon defeated, but in *c*.61 Boadicea of the Iceni tribe sacked the Roman settlements at Verulamium (now St Albans) and London before being killed. Governor Agricola (*c*.78–84) extended Roman rule to Wales and a small part of Scotland (Caledonia), and the northern frontier was later roughly indicated by Hadrian's Wall (*see also* Antonine Wall). Only the lowlands were thoroughly Romanized, but here Roman rule brought a period of prosperity not matched for more than 1000 years. The Romans built towns, villas and roads. Roman power disintegrated in the 4th century. By 400, attacks from Ireland, Scotland and the continental mainland were increasing, and Roman troops were withdrawn to deal with enemies nearer home. In 410 Emperor Honorius warned the Britons to expect no further help. Local Romano-British kings held out for more than 100 years before lowland Britain was overrun by the Anglo-Saxons.

Roman Catholic Church Christian denomination that acknowledges the supremacy of the papacy in Rome. Originally the Catholic Church, in which the authority of the pope was largely established by Leo I (r.440–61) and Saint Gregory I (r.590–604), was the only Christian church, but centuries of diverging custom led to the schism with the Orthodox Church in the East in 1054. Gregory VII (r.1073–85) attempted to reform the Roman church and struggled to assert the independence of the papacy from the Holy Roman Empire in the investiture controversy. Pope Innocent III (r.1198–1216) further extended the power of the papacy and convened the Fourth Lateran Council (1215), which established the doctrine of transubstantiation. Also in the 13th century, Saint Thomas Aquinas, the greatest figure of scholasticism, wrote his *Summa Theologiae* (1267–73), which was proclaimed (1879) as the basis of official Catholic philosophy by Pope Leo XIII. The 16th-century Reformation resulted in the foundation of Protestantism in the West, differing in doctrine, ritual and church government, and led to the adoption of the term "Roman Catholic". The Roman Catholic Church responded with the movement of revival and reform known as the Counter-Reformation, which also marked the beginning of Christian missionary societies. In the 18th century, the Roman Catholic Church came under pressure from the growing spirit of scepticism and anti-clericalism associated with the Enlightenment. In the 19th century, reacting against pressures associated with the Industrial Revolution, nationalism and liberalism, the church was seen as oppressively didactic, conservative, and even reactionary. The First Vatican Council (1869), convoked by Pope Pius IX, declared the infallibility of the pope in doctrinal matters. In the 20th century, the modernism movement embraced the need for reform, notably in a Second Vatican Council, summoned by Pope John XXIII in 1962. The abandonment of Latin as the exclusive language of the liturgy, more cooperative relations with other churches, and growing willingness to enter the political arena, reflected a more liberal church. On some issues however, such as homosexuality and abortion, the Vatican proved more conservative, even under a pope as humane as John Paul II. With more than 1000 million members, the Roman Catholic Church remained much the largest Christian denomination at the end of the second millennium. *See* individual popes; *see also* Christianity; conciliar movement; ecumenical council

Roman Empire *See* feature article, page 354

Romania *See* country feature

Roman law Legal system of ancient Rome which became the basis of law in many European countries. Roman law originated in oral custom, and was first codified (*c*.450 BC) in the Twelve Tables. It was much expanded by legislative bodies and authorities such as the praetors, who administered the courts. Their edicts were codified in the reign of the Emperor Hadrian. The edicts of the emperors themselves were another major source. The vast and complex mass of Roman law was codified in the reign (527–65) of Emperor Justinian I (the Great) in the *Corpus Juris Civilis* ("Body of Civil Law"). It was the product of years of work by learned committees under the direction of the quaestor Tribonian, and was

ROMANIA

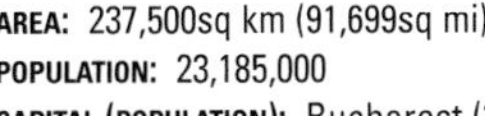

AREA: 237,500sq km (91,699sq mi)
POPULATION: 23,185,000
CAPITAL (POPULATION): Bucharest (2,350,984)
GOVERNMENT: Multiparty republic
ETHNIC GROUPS: Romanian 89%, Hungarian 7%, Romany (Gypsy) 2%
LANGUAGES: Romanian (official)
RELIGIONS: Romanian Orthodox 87%, Roman Catholic 5%, Greek Orthodox 4%)
GDP PER CAPITA (1995): US$4360

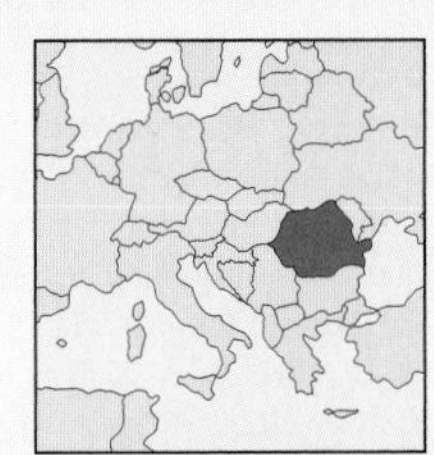

Balkan republic in SE Europe. Modern Romania roughly corresponds to ancient Dacia, which was conquered by the Romans in AD 106. The Dacians assimilated Roman culture and language, and the region became known as Romania. The collapse of the Roman Empire led to the invasions of the Slavs. In the 14th century the principalities of Wallachia (s) and Moldavia (e) were formed. The Ottoman Empire dominated Romania from the 15th to the 19th century.

Russia captured Moldavia and Wallachia in the Russo-Turkish War (1828–29). Romanian nationalism intensified and the two provinces were united in 1861. The Congress of Berlin (1878) ratified Romania as an independent state, and Carol I became king in 1881.

Neutral at the start of World War 1, Romania joined the Allies in 1916 but was occupied by German forces in 1917. The Allied victory led to Romania acquiring large regions, such as Transylvania. In 1927 Michael became king, but surrendered the throne to his father, Carol II, in 1930. Political instability and economic inequality led to the growth of fascism and anti-Semitism. At the start of World War 2, Romania lost territory to Bulgaria, Hungary and the Soviet Union. In 1940 Michael was restored. Ion Antonescu became dictator and, in June 1941, Romania joined the German invasion of the Soviet Union. During World War 2 more than 50% of Romanian Jews were murdered. In 1944 Soviet troops occupied Romania, Antonescu was overthrown and Romania surrendered. In 1945 a communist-dominated coalition assumed power, led by Gheorghe Gheorghiu-Dej. In 1947 Romania became a People's Republic. In 1952 it adopted a Soviet-style constitution. Industry was nationalized and agriculture collectivized.

In 1949 Romania joined the Council of Mutual Economic Assistance (COMECON) and in 1955 became a member of the Warsaw Pact. In 1965 Gheorghiu-Dej was succeeded by Nicolae Ceauşescu. Rapid industrialization and political repression continued. In December 1989 Ceauşescu was executed. Ion Iliescu, a former communist official, formed a provisional government. The National Salvation Front, led by Iliescu, won elections in May 1990. In 1991 a new constitution was introduced. In 1992 Iliescu was re-elected. In 1995 Romania applied to join the European Union (EU). In 1996 elections Iliescu was defeated by Emil Constantinescu and his centre-right coalition. In 1999 and 2000 there was a series of protests and strikes over the pace and direction of economic reform.

R

accompanied by commentaries and a student's handbook. Roman law was rediscovered by Italian scholars in the 11th century, and became a major university subject. It became the basis of the law in all Western European states, except England, and has influenced many other countries' legal systems. *See also* CIVIL LAW

Romanovs Russian imperial dynasty (1613–1917), founded by MICHAEL. Michael's accession ended the Time of Troubles that had followed the death of FYODOR I, last of the RURIK dynasty. His descendants, especially PETER I (THE GREAT) and CATHERINE II (THE GREAT), a Romanov by marriage, transformed RUSSIA into the world's largest empire. The last Romanov emperor, NICHOLAS II, abdicated in 1917 and was later murdered by the BOLSHEVIKS. *See also* ALEXANDER I; ALEXANDER II; ALEXANDER III; ALEXEI MIKHAILOVICH; ANNA IVANOVNA; CATHERINE I; ELIZABETH; FYODOR III; NICHOLAS I; PAUL I; PETER II; PETER III

Roman Republic State centred on the city of ROME, W central Italy, founded in *c.*509 BC when the Latin-speaking Romans threw off the rule of ETRUSCAN kings. The Romans established an independent republic governed by two CONSULS (elected magistrates), who were advised by the SENATE. From 447 BC two QUAESTORS were elected to advise the consuls on financial matters, and in 445 BC military TRIBUNES also acquired consular power. Originally, the Republic was dominated by the PATRICIANS, but by the 3rd century BC the PLEBEIANS had largely gained political equality. ROMAN LAW was first codified in the TWELVE TABLES (*c.*450 BC). The history of the Roman Republic was one of continual expansion. By 338 BC Rome controlled Italy S of the River Po, and by the end of the Pyrrhic War (280–275 BC) it held a broad swathe of central Italy. Victory over CARTHAGE in the PUNIC WARS (264–146 BC) gave Rome dominance of the W Mediterranean region, and success in the MACEDONIAN WARS gave it control of much of the E Mediterranean also. The Romans divided the newly conquered territories into provinces, but central administration was largely absent and taxes were collected by private militias. Military success brought wealth but also social disruption, including impoverishment of the peasantry by cheap, imported food and an influx of slaves. Reforms were attempted by the brothers GRACCHUS in 133–121 BC, but their deaths were followed by a century of anarchy and civil war, culminating in the ruthless dictatorship of SULLA. POMPEY (THE GREAT) emerged as the dominant figure after helping crush a slave revolt (73 BC) led by SPARTACUS. A struggle for power between Pompey and

ROMAN EMPIRE

Lands ruled by ancient ROME from the accession of AUGUSTUS (27 BC) as caesar (emperor) to the deposition of ROMULUS AUGUSTULUS in AD 476. The preceding ROMAN REPUBLIC finally collapsed in the civil war (49–45 BC) between POMPEY (THE GREAT) and Julius CAESAR, who established a dictatorship after his victory. After Caesar's assassination (44 BC), Augustus defeated Mark ANTONY at the Battle of ACTIUM (31 BC) to emerge as sole ruler. Augustus dominated the Roman SENATE and, although he concentrated on the reconstruction of Italy (and Rome in particular), built on the military conquests of Caesar. In Africa, NUMIDIA was annexed and Mauretania created. In Europe, GAUL was organized into provinces and Spain was subjugated. However, Roman expansion was checked in the E in Armenia and in the N by the Germanic tribes across the River Rhine. The more established imperial provinces were controlled by PROCONSULS, while the rest were placed either under the direct control of the emperor or under former senators or PRAETORS appointed to govern in his name. JUDAEA was administered by an equite (*see* PONTIUS PILATE), while ancient EGYPT was unique in being ruled by an equite who commanded legions.

Augustus reorganized the civil service to improve the collection of taxes, expanded trade and greatly increased the number of Roman urban colonies throughout the Empire. Whilst the Roman Empire was ultimately maintained by military hegemony, these urban settlements acted as the engine-rooms for the spread of Roman civilization in terms of technology, ROMAN LAW and the Latin language. Conquered peoples who adopted Roman customs were granted Roman citizenship.

CLAUDIUS I (r.AD 41–54) expanded the Empire, most notably by annexing Britain (*see* ROMAN BRITAIN). NERO (r.54–68), the last of the Julio-Claudian dynasty, had to contend with BOADICEA's revolt in Britain and rebellion in Judaea. TRAJAN (r.98–117) conquered DACIA and PETRA and overran Mesopotamia, marking the greatest extent of the Roman Empire but also beginning the long-running conflict with the PARTHIANS. HADRIAN (r.117–38) halted expansion and consolidated the Empire. The reign (193–211) of Septimius SEVERUS marked the transformation of imperial government into a military monarchy. The collapse (235) of the Severan dynasty brought a crisis of succession, and the Empire began to disintegrate under the threat of BARBARIAN invasions, the rise of the SASANIANS in Persia (Iran), and economic decline. Remarkably, AURELIAN (r.270–75) managed to reunify the Empire. DIOCLETIAN's (r.284–305) reforms and dictatorial rule further arrested the slide into military anarchy, but his division of the Empire into Eastern and Western sectors created rival power bases.

CONSTANTINE I (THE GREAT) established Byzantium as his capital in 330, renaming it Constantinople (now ISTANBUL), and his conversion to CHRISTIANITY ended a sustained period of persecution of Christians. After 375 the Empire was formally divided into the Eastern Roman (later Byzantine) Empire (based in Constantinople) and the Western Roman Empire (Rome). While the BYZANTINE EMPIRE was to last until 1453, the Western empire fared less well. Rome was sacked by the VISIGOTHS in 410, and the last Western emperor was deposed by the Barbarian ODOACER in 476. The Romans set the standards of Western civilization, and Europeans were still trying to restore them, in a new, Christian guise, more than 1000 years after Rome's fall (*see* HOLY ROMAN EMPIRE). *See* individual emperors and provinces. *See also* TACITUS

◄ **Roman legionary** The expansion of the Roman Empire was achieved by the flexibility and discipline of its army. The legions formed the backbone of the Roman army. Each legion consisted of *c.*6000 soldiers divided into ten cohorts. The legionary shown here has short body armour (*cuirass*), braced helmet, short sword (*gladium*) and large shield (*scutum*).

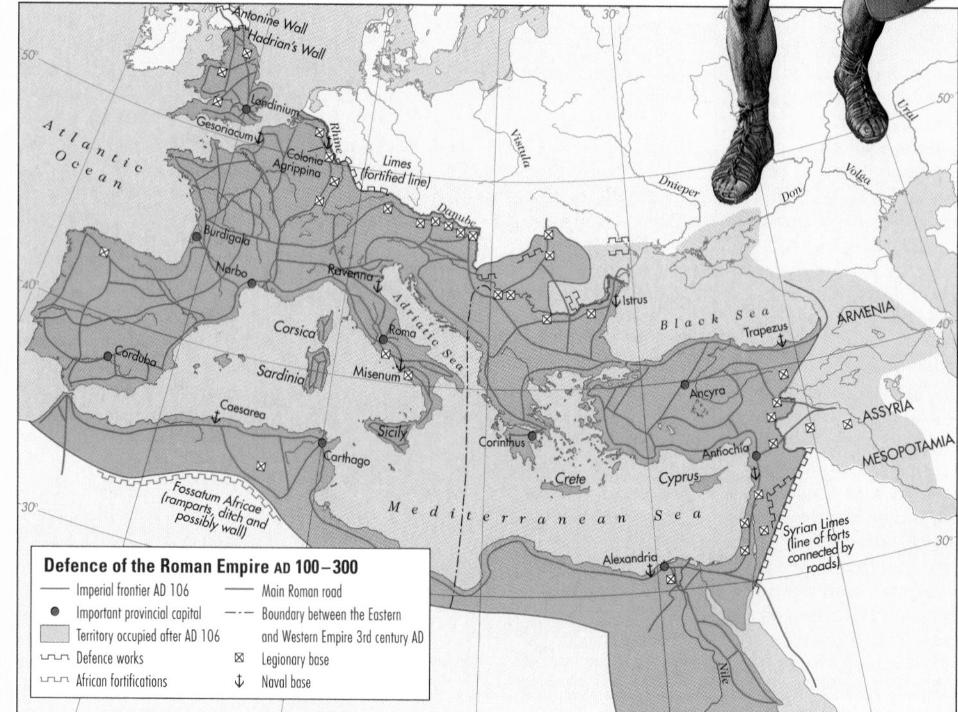

► **Roman Empire** Emperor Hadrian concentrated on reinforcing the previous Roman *limes*, or frontiers. He strengthened the *Agri Decumantes limes* between the Rhine and the Danube with a wooden palisade and numerous forts. He is thought to have started work on a mudbrick wall and ditch which was to become the African frontier, the *fossatum Africae*. He also built Hadrian's Wall, the first stone wall to secure the N British frontier – a second was later constructed by Antoninus (r.138–61) – and reinforced Trajan's work on the Syrian *limes*, a policy later continued by Diocletian.

▲ **In the Roman Empire**, jewellery-making reached a height unsurpassed until the 16th-century Renaissance. The snake motif on the bracelet shown here was very popular.

Julius CAESAR brought further civil war (49–45 BC). After Caesar, who had assumed autocratic powers and conquered GAUL, was assassinated (44 BC), his nephew Octavian emerged as leader of the Republic after defeating Mark ANTONY at the Battle of ACTIUM (31 BC), and was acknowledged as Emperor AUGUSTUS in 27 BC – thus marking the beginnings of the ROMAN EMPIRE. *See also* CATILINE; CICERO, MARCUS TULLIUS; CRASSUS, MARCUS LICINIUS; JUGURTHA; LIVY; MARIUS, GAIUS; PRAETOR; PYRRHUS; SAMNITES; SCIPIO AFRICANUS (THE ELDER); SOCIAL WAR

Romanticism Late 18th- and early 19th-century cultural movement, affecting literature in particular and the arts in general, which had a profound effect on human understanding. The Romantics valued individual experience and imagination, rather than the orderly, concrete universe of classical artists. For this reason, Romantics and classicists are often seen as opposites, but they shared a belief in idealism. Rather, the Romantic movement was a reaction against the rationalism of the ENLIGHTENMENT. Romantics were generally champions of liberal and progressive causes: the English poet Lord Byron (1788–1824), for example, went to fight in the GREEK WAR OF INDEPENDENCE.

Rome (Roma) Capital of Italy, on the River Tiber, central Italy, capital of the ancient ROMAN EMPIRE and spiritual and physical home of the ROMAN CATHOLIC CHURCH. According to legend, the city was founded (753 BC) on the Palatine Hill by Romulus and Remus. It was probably an ETRUSCAN city-kingdom before it became the centre of an independent ROMAN REPUBLIC (*c*.509 BC). In 390 BC Rome was devastated by a Gallic attack, but it was rapidly rebuilt. By the middle of the 3rd century BC, Rome ruled most of Italy and began to expand overseas. Rome survived Hannibal's invasion of the Italian peninsula in the Second PUNIC WAR (218–201 BC), and many peasants sought shelter in the city. The SENATE, preoccupied with the administration of the ROMAN EMPIRE, largely ignored the problems of Rome, which became one of the poorest parts of the Empire. The GRACCHUS brothers tried to deal with high unemployment, overcrowding and increasing food prices by subsidizing grain for the poor. In the 1st century AD, the city was transformed: AUGUSTUS built temples, palaces, public baths and theatres, but did little to improve domestic housing. In AD 64 much of Rome was destroyed in a fire and NERO sought to implement city-planning. The Colosseum, still partly extant, was dedicated by TITUS in AD 80. Emperor TRAJAN erected Trajan's Column (*c*.AD 113) to commemorate his victories across the Danube. Monuments from HADRIAN's reign include the Pantheon (*c*.128) and his tomb (now Castel Sant'Angelo, *c*.134). By the end of the 2nd century Rome was the largest city in the world. CONSTANTINE I (THE GREAT) laid the foundations of papal Rome in the 4th century, but in 410 the city was captured and sacked by the VISIGOTHS, led by ALARIC, and subsequently went into steep decline until the CAROLINGIAN RENAISSANCE of the 9th century. By the end of the 11th century, ST PETER'S had become a focus for Christian pilgrimages. In 1143 Rome became a free COMMUNE. From 1309 to 1400, with Rome plagued by dynastic rivalries such as that between the GUELPHS and GHIBELLINES, the papacy resided in AVIGNON, SE France. Rome was the major centre of the RENAISSANCE, acquiring many splendid new churches and palaces and, although sacked (1527) by Emperor CHARLES V, it flourished throughout the 16th and 17th centuries. From 1809 to 1814 Rome and the Papal States were annexed to France. During the 19th century, the city was the prime object of European gentry taking the "GRAND TOUR" and of artists seeking inspiration. In spite of malaria, it had *c*.250,000 inhabitants by the mid-19th century. In 1861 Pope PIUS IX resisted attempts to incorporate the city into the new Kingdom of Italy and retreated behind the walls of the Vatican when the city was occupied by Italian troops in 1870. In 1921 Benito MUSSOLINI recognized the pope's sovereignty within VATICAN CITY. Mussolini did much to transform Rome into a modern city. Pop. (1991) 2,775,250.

Rome, Treaties of (25 March 1957) Two agreements between France, West Germany, Italy and the BENELUX countries. One treaty established the common-market of the European Economic Community (EEC). Although extensively amended by the Single European Act (1986) and the MAASTRICHT TREATY (1992), which created the EUROPEAN UNION (EU), this treaty forms the legal basis of the EU. The other treaty established the European Atomic Energy Commission (Euratom).

Rommel, Erwin (1891–1944) German field marshal. He joined the German infantry in 1910, fighting as a lieutenant in France during World War 1. As commander of a Panzer tank division at the start of World War 2, Rommel led the lightning advance into France in May 1940. He was subsequently promoted to command the Afrika Korps, which was sent to prevent the collapse of the Italian forces in North Africa. His daring surprise attacks earned him the nickname "the Desert Fox" and the admiration of the Allies. Rommel's victorious campaign ended when his offensive into Egypt was halted by British General AUCHINLECK in the First Battle of El ALAMEIN (July 1942) and defeated by British General MONTGOMERY at the Second Battle of El ALAMEIN, three months later. Rommel negotiated a successful retreat to Tunis and was ordered to return to Europe by Adolf HITLER. In 1944 Rommel reorganized the French coastal defences, but many of his proposals went unheeded and he was unable to repel the Allied NORMANDY LANDINGS (June 1944). He failed to persuade Hitler that the War was now unwinnable and that Germany should sue for peace, and he became the focus of a conspiracy to overthrow Hitler. Rommel was badly wounded in an Allied bombing raid in July 1944, when details of his contacts with those behind a plot to assassinate Hitler also came to light. Rommel accepted the suggestion that he should avoid dishonour by taking poison. The official announcement ascribed his death to war wounds. *See also* NORTH AFRICA CAMPAIGN

Romulus Augustulus (b. *c*.461) Western Roman emperor (r.475–76). He was given the throne by his father, Orestes, who had overthrown Emperor Julius Nepos. The Germanic mercenaries in Italy then mutinied, killed Orestes and forced Romulus to abdicate, whereupon ODOACER, their leader, assumed the title of king, an event that marks the fall of the Western Roman Empire.

ROOSEVELT, FRANKLIN DELANO

Franklin D. Roosevelt harnessed the power of the media to increase his popular support. He used a series of radio broadcasts, known as "Fireside Chats", to explain current issues and policies to the American public.

ROOSEVELT IN HIS OWN WORDS

"Let me assert my firm belief that the only thing we have to fear is fear itself."
First Inaugural Address (4 March 1933)
"More than an end to war, we want an end to the beginning of all wars."
Speech broadcast on the day after his death (13 April 1945)

Roosevelt, (Anna) Eleanor (1884–1962). US reformer and humanitarian, wife (and distant cousin) of Franklin ROOSEVELT and niece of Theodore ROOSEVELT. A determined supporter of social causes, including civil rights for women and African Americans, she was active in politics from the early 1920s, often attending meetings for her incapacitated husband, and converted her position as "first lady" into an effective political office. After her husband's death, Eleanor Roosevelt served as US delegate to the United Nations (1945–52, 1961–62), and chairwoman of the UN Commission on Human Rights (1946–51).

Roosevelt, Franklin Delano (1882–1945) Thirty-second president of the United States (1933–45). In 1905 he married Eleanor ROOSEVELT, niece of President Theodore ROOSEVELT. A powerful campaigner, Franklin Roosevelt was elected as a Democrat for a normally safe Republican seat in the New York Senate (1910) and subsequently gained national attention with his outspoken attacks on the corruption of TAMMANY HALL. His support for Woodrow WILSON won him appointment as assistant secretary of the navy (1913–20), and he was vice presidential candidate in 1920. In 1921 he lost the use of his legs as a result of polio, but made a partial recovery; his vigorous public persona largely concealing the extent of his disability. He was a dynamic governor of New York (1928–32) and, aided by a formidably talented team (the so-called BRAIN TRUST), won the Democratic candidacy for president, and the ensuing election against President Herbert HOOVER, in 1932. At the height of the GREAT DEPRESSION, Roosevelt introduced a radical programme for economic and social regeneration, the NEW DEAL, which involved a striking extension of the powers of the federal government. Much of the New Deal was implemented in the first hundred days of Roosevelt's presidency, and concentrated on providing jobs for some of the nation's 13 million unemployed. A number of agencies were created to coordinate relief work and create jobs, including the TENNESSEE VALLEY AUTHORITY (TVA) and the PUBLIC WORKS ADMINISTRATION (PWA). In addition, the AGRICULTURAL ADJUSTMENT ACT (1933) sought to tackle the crisis in the US farming industry. Although the significance of the New Deal in producing economic recovery has been questioned by historians, Roosevelt by sheer self-confidence won widespread support (and intense hostility in Republican business circles). His most effective opponent was the SUPREME COURT, which ruled many of his innovative measures unconstitutional; his attempt to pack the Court with liberal nominees was defeated in 1937, but in the interim the Court had upheld the WAGNER ACT (1935). Roosevelt's charisma gained him re-election by a huge margin in 1936, and he won a third term in 1940, when he was faced with a second great challenge, posed by the outbreak of WORLD WAR 2. Roosevelt had passed a series of NEUTRALITY ACTS, but after Britain's declaration of war (1939) he gave as much support to Britain as possible for a supposedly neutral government, including securing approval for a LEND-LEASE plan (1941) to aid Britain's war effort and signing the Atlantic Charter (1941) with British Prime Minister Winston CHURCHILL. Japan's attack on PEARL HARBOR (December 1941) finally ended US neutrality. The subsequent massive increase in production for War acted as a vital stimulus to the national economy. During the War, Roosevelt acted in close alliance with Churchill. In 1943 the two men led a series of international summits designed to coordinate Allied plans: the CASABLANCA CONFERENCE, CAIRO CONFERENCE, QUÉBEC CONFERENCES and TEHRAN CONFERENCE. At the YALTA CONFERENCE (1945), Churchill, Roosevelt and Joseph STALIN agreed on the final campaigns of the War and the territorial settlement at the end of the conflict. In 1944 Roosevelt was re-elected for an unprecedented third time, but his health declined rapidly and he died in office. He was succeeded by Vice President Harry TRUMAN. Roosevelt is credited with making the DEMOCRATIC PARTY the vehicle of social and political reform in succeeding decades. *See also* GOOD NEIGHBOR POLICY; WORKS PROGRESS ADMINISTRATION (WPA)

Roosevelt, Theodore (1858–1919) Twenty-sixth president of the United States (1901–09). He served as a Republican in the New York Assembly (1882–84) and later acted as assistant secretary of the navy under President William MCKINLEY (1897–98). In 1898 Roosevelt resigned in order to organize a volunteer cavalry regiment, known as the ROUGH RIDERS, to fight in Cuba during the SPANISH-AMERICAN WAR (1898). Roosevelt's role in the decisive US victory at the Battle of Santiago (1898) made him a national hero. Backed by New York's REPUBLICAN PARTY boss, he was elected governor of New York in 1899 and vice president in 1900. Roosevelt became president after the assassination of McKinley (September 1901). In 1902, as the first step in a "trust-busting" crusade against industrial monopolies, Roosevelt invoked the neglected SHERMAN ANTI-TRUST ACT against the Northern Securities Company. In the same year, he intervened in a mining strike to win a pay rise for the miners. In 1903 Roosevelt announced his "SQUARE DEAL" to balance the interests of capital and labour. Such populist measures won him a landslide victory in the 1904 presidential elections. Now president in his own right, Roosevelt pursued his agenda to regulate large corporations more vigorously. The Hepburn Act (1906), for instance, gave the Interstate Commerce Commission the power to set a maximum interstate railroad rate. He also upheld the cause of nature conservation, greatly increasing the size and number of protected national parks and forests. His foreign policy was equally aggressive. He supported a revolt in Panama to gain US rights over the PANAMA CANAL (1903), and he strongly defended US interests abroad, expanding the MONROE DOCTRINE to justify US intervention in Latin America. In 1906 Roosevelt won the Nobel Prize for Peace for his role in securing the Treaty of PORTSMOUTH (1905), which ended the RUSSO-JAPANESE WAR. He was also largely responsible for making the US Navy a powerful, modern force. In his last years as president, Roosevelt was faced by strong criticism from Republican conservatives who blamed his policies towards big business for the financial crisis of 1907. He was also criticized for his role in the Brownsville Affair (14 August 1906) when he ordered 167 black infantrymen to be discharged without honour for refusing to speak out after the murder of a white man in Texas. When Roosevelt retired (1909), he left the presidency more powerful than at any time since the Civil War, but he left the Republican Party divided between progressives and conservatives. Failing to win the Republican nomination, Roosevelt formed the PROGRESSIVE PARTY (or Bull Moose Party) in order to challenge his Republican successor, President William TAFT, in the 1912 presidential elections. The result was a split in the Republican vote and the election of the Democratic candidate Woodrow WILSON.

R

Root, Elihu (1845–1937) US statesman and lawyer. A well-known New York attorney, Root was secretary of war (1899–1904) under presidents William McKinley and Theodore ROOSEVELT, responsible for handling the territorial readjustments after the SPANISH-AMERICAN WAR. He later served under Roosevelt as secretary of state (1905–09). Combining analytical ability with executive strength, he reformed the consular service, improved US relations with Latin America and raised US diplomatic prestige in Europe. A committed supporter of international arbitration, he was awarded the Nobel Prize for Peace in 1912, and in 1920 took part in drafting the constitution of the INTERNATIONAL COURT OF JUSTICE.

Rosas, Juan Manuel de (1793–1877) Argentine statesman, credited with unifying the country. Son of a wealthy rancher, he led his GAUCHO militia against the *unitarios* (centralists) in the increasingly dominant province of BUENOS AIRES. Rosas was twice governor of Buenos Aires (1829–32, 1835–52), and by his second term the province was his personal fief and he was virtually dictator of Argentina. Although initially supportive of the CAUDILLOS (federalists), Rosas' dictatorship did much to create a strong, central government. His rule was aided by a booming economy, as well as ruthless use of his private police force. He withstood blockades by the British and French resulting from commercial disputes, but was overthrown by a revolt of the interior provinces. He died in exile in Britain.

Rosebery, Archibald Philip Primrose, 5th Earl of (1847–1929) British statesman, prime minister (1894–95). As foreign secretary (1886, 1892–94) under William GLADSTONE, he continued the imperialist policies of Lord SALISBURY, establishing a British protectorate over Uganda (1894). In 1895, despite never being elected to Parliament, Rosebery replaced Gladstone as Liberal prime minister. He inherited, however, an intensely divided LIBERAL PARTY and was unable to secure approval for any legislation except the budget. Rosebery resigned as prime minister and leader of the Liberals, but continued vociferously to defend the BRITISH EMPIRE during the SOUTH AFRICAN WARS and to oppose Irish HOME RULE. *See also* VICTORIA

Rosenberg, Alfred (1893–1946) German Nazi leader, b. Estonia. The ideologist of NATIONAL SOCIALISM, he joined the NAZI PARTY in 1919, edited its newspaper, and wrote *The Myth of the 20th Century* (1934) outlining his doctrine of the racial superiority of Germans and the desirability of conquering "inferior" Slav nations. When Adolf HITLER was imprisoned for his role in the failed MUNICH PUTSCH (1923), Rosenberg acted as caretaker leader of the Nazi Party. During World War 2 Rosenberg was governor of the eastern occupied lands but had little power. He was convicted of war crimes at the NUREMBERG TRIALS and executed.

Rosenberg case (1951–53) US espionage trial. A New York couple, Julius (1918–53) and Ethel Rosenberg (1915–53), were convicted of passing atomic-weapons secrets to Soviet agents in 1944–45. The Rosenberg Case gained international attention because many believed they were victims of anti-communist hysteria. The evidence at the trial was fragile (although later revelations showed that the verdict was correct), and the prevailing "Red Menace" obsession no doubt partly explains the first execution of civilians for spying in the United States.

Roses, Wars of the (1455–85) English dynastic civil wars. They are named after the badges of the rival royal houses of YORK (white rose) and LANCASTER (red rose), although this notion was a later invention. Both houses claimed descent from EDWARD III. The Lancastrian king, HENRY VI, was challenged by Richard, Duke of YORK, who was appointed protector of the realm in 1453. Henry, dominated by his wife, MARGARET OF ANJOU, regained control but was soon defeated at the Battle of St Albans (1455). The Lancastrians recovered in 1456 and three years of peace ensued. The Earl of WARWICK reorganized the Yorkist forces and won a decisive victory at Northampton (July 1460), capturing Henry VI and forcing him to recognize the Duke of York as his successor. Margaret refused to accept the peace terms and her troops killed York at the Battle of Wakefield (December 1460) and defeated Warwick (1461). York's son, Edward (later EDWARD IV), assumed leadership of the Yorkist cause, winning a bloody but decisive victory at TOWTON (1461). In 1469 civil war was resumed. Warwick, allied with Edward IV's younger brother, the Duke of CLARENCE, mounted a revolt and captured Edward. The king regained control and forced the rebels into exile in France, where they joined forces with Margaret and LOUIS XI of France to invade England and restore Henry VI to the throne (1470). Edward quickly regrouped his troops and secured the support of Clarence, defeating Warwick at BARNET (April 1471) and Margaret at TEWKESBURY (May 1471). The final phase in the Wars of the Roses began after the usurpation of the throne by RICHARD III, Edward IV's youngest brother, in 1483. Richard was defeated and killed at the Battle of BOSWORTH FIELD (August 1485) by Henry TUDOR (later HENRY VII). In 1487 Henry defeated the Yorkist rebellion of Lambert SIMNEL.

Rosetta Stone Slab of black basalt inscribed with the same text in Egyptian hieroglyphic, demotic (a simplified form of hieroglyphs) and Greek script. It was found by French soldiers in Egypt in 1799. Only the Greek text was then legible, but it was soon recognised that all three texts were identical. The Rosetta Stone thus offered a clue to the decipherment of the ancient Egyptian language. After 20 years' work, a British doctor, Thomas Young, had made considerable progress, and a full decipherment was finally made (1822) by Jean-François CHAMPOLLION. *See also* EGYPT, ANCIENT

Rosicrucians Esoteric, worldwide society, supposedly dating from the the 14th century, when Christian Rosenkreuz (probably a mythic figure, the elements of his name, rose and cross, being symbols of Christian resurrection and redemption) was supposed to have been initiated into obscure mysteries, including those of ancient Egypt, which Rosicrucianism attempted to link with Christianity. The earliest record, however, comes from the early 17th century, and one early exponent was the English thinker Robert Fludd (1574–1637). Branches of the Rosicrucians, who are organized in a system of lodges and traditionally linked with FREEMASONRY, were founded in many countries, but the name was often used by otherwise unconnected groups. The US Rosicrucian Order, which is active in business activities, is best known. Generally, Rosicrucians are devoted to the promotion of the full potential of human beings, including their psychic powers.

Ross, Sir James Clark (1800–62) British explorer. He accompanied his uncle, John Ross (1777–1856), on a voyage (1829–33) to the Arctic, embarking on a sledge journey to locate the north magnetic pole (1 June 1831). Ross commanded the epic expedition of the *Erebus* and *Terror* to the Antarctic (1839–43). Although he failed to locate the south magnetic pole, Ross discovered many features of Antarctica, including the Erebus volcano, Victoria Land, and the sea named (by Captain Robert SCOTT) after him. The expedition set a farthest-south record that stood for 60 years.

Rothschild, Meyer Amschel (1744–1812) German financier, founder of an international banking dynasty. He and his five sons made a fortune during the French Revolutionary Wars and Napoleonic Wars, and moved their headquarters to London (1804), playing a part in confounding Napoleon's CONTINENTAL SYSTEM. After 1815 his sons established branches in the main financial centres of Europe. The Rothschilds were a significant power in the 19th century, playing an important part in international affairs. A grandson, **Lionel** Rothschild (1808–79), financed Britain's purchase of the SUEZ CANAL Company and was the first Jew to sit in the House of Commons.

Rough Riders Popular name for the 1st Volunteer Cavalry regiment, who fought in Cuba during the SPANISH-AMERICAN WAR (1898). They were largely recruited by Theodore ROOSEVELT (who served as second in command), and included cowboys, miners and college athletes. They gained a flamboyant reputation, especially for their charge up San Juan Hill in the decisive Battle of Santiago (1898), made on foot because their horses had been left behind in Florida.

Roundheads Derisive nickname given to Puritans and Parliamentary soldiers in the English CIVIL WAR by their opponents, the Royalists, or CAVALIERS. Many Puritans had their hair cropped short, unlike the Royalists who generally wore theirs in ringlets.

Rousseau, Jean Jacques (1712–78) French philosopher of the ENLIGHTENMENT, whose ideas had profound effects on 18th-century political thought, especially on the FRENCH REVOLUTION and ROMANTICISM. He was born a Protestant in Geneva, became a Roman Catholic in the 1730s and reconverted in 1754. In 1740 Rousseau moved to Paris and devoted himself to a career as a writer and composer. In the 1740s he contributed articles on music to the *Encyclopédie* of Denis DIDEROT and won fame for his *Discourse on Science and the Arts* (1750). In 1762 he published *The Social Contract*, his chief political work, advocating equality in law and fairer distribution of wealth. He defined the essence of government as a contract between governor and governed, in whom sovereignty resides. He argued that man had been corrupted by civilization, and specifically by the state. Rousseau's ideas on how the individual should be liberated from these corrupting influences were further developed in *Émile* (1762), an equally influential treatise on education, which argued for the unrestricted development of the child in natural surroundings. The Jansenists of Paris called for the book to be burned and Rousseau spent the remainder of his life in flight. *See also* LIBERALISM; SOCIAL CONTRACT

Rowlatt Acts (1919) Legislation passed in British India, drafted by S.A.T. Rowlatt. They sought to continue the suspension of civil liberties that had been imposed during World War I into peacetime, and were fiercely opposed by nationalists. It galvanized "Mahatma" GANDHI into organizing the first national *satyagraha*, a campaign of non-violent civil disobedience. Combined with other sources of popular discontent that had contributed to the passage of the Acts, it resulted in outbreaks of violence leading indirectly to the AMRITSAR MASSACRE (1919). The Acts were never enforced.

Rowntree, Benjamin Seebohm (1871–1954) English sociologist and philanthropist. He conducted a series of surveys into poverty in York, N England. The statistics he arrived at – 10% living in "primary" poverty, 18% in "secondary" poverty – closely coincided with the figures for London established by Charles BOOTH, thus demonstrating that poverty was a national problem. In 1919 he established a five-day working week at his family's chocolate-making business.

Roy, Manabendra Nath (1887–1954) Indian communist leader, b. Narendranath Bhattacharya. He engaged in terrorism against British rule and went abroad in 1915 to obtain arms. In San Francisco, he changed his name to Roy; in Mexico he helped to found the Mexican Communist Party; in Russia he impressed LENIN, who placed him on the governing committee of the COMINTERN. In 1920 Roy founded the COMMUNIST PARTY OF INDIA (CPI). Disillusioned with Joseph STALIN, he returned to India (1929) but was arrested by the British. He later joined the Indian National CONGRESS and, regarding the defeat of fascism as the most vital issue, advocated aiding the British in World War 2. He abandoned communism after India's independence.

Roy, Ram Mohan (1772–1833) Indian religious and social reformer, one of the "fathers" of modern India. He spent his early years attempting to create a monotheistic form of HINDUISM. After 1823 Roy turned towards social and political action, protesting against British censorship of the Indian press and the British administration of India in general, and calling for a modernization of India's education system. He condemned the CASTE system and other practices such as *suttee* (burning of widows). In 1828 Roy founded the BRAHMO SAMAJ, an influential reformist movement within Hinduism. He died in England.

Royal Air Force (RAF) Branch of the British armed services, formed (1918) by the amalgamation of the Royal Naval Air Service and the Royal Flying Corps. Its "finest hour" was the Battle of BRITAIN (1940), when it successfully withstood the efforts of the LUFTWAFFE to drive it from the skies in preparation for a German invasion.

Royal Navy Maritime arm of the British armed services. Traditionally, the first navy in the British Isles is said to have been the fleet built by ALFRED (THE GREAT) as defence against the Vikings. In the 16th century Henry VII built the first specialized warships and established the naval dockyards. From the mid-18th to the early 20th century, the Royal Navy's command of the sea was virtually unchallenged, and it provided for the security of the British empire and protection for Great Britain's commercial supremacy.

Royal Society Earliest surviving scientific body in the world, founded (1660) in London, England. It received its charter (1662) from Charles II for the promotion of knowledge of nature and its journal, *Philosophical Transactions*, still extant, was started in 1665. In the near-absence of science teaching in universities, it provided a valuable centre for scientific discussion (religion and politics were excluded) and an opportunity to publish scientific works. During the 19th century it evolved from a social club for enthusiastic amateurs into an academy of leading professional scientists, which was supported by parliamentary grant and provided the government with scientific advice. In 1768 the Society sponsored James COOK's expedition to the Pacific.

Rozwi empire Southern African empire, centred on GREAT ZIMBABWE. Founded by the Changamire dynasty of the Shona-speaking Karanga in the late 17th century, it succeeded the Mwena Mutapa empire, which had been weakened by Portuguese incursions. In the 1690s the Rozwi expelled the Portuguese from their bases in the Zambezi valley and gained control of the rich gold-producing area. Its influence was felt over much of present-day Zimbabwe until the 1830s, when the *mfecane* (crushing) caused by the expansion of SHAKA's Zulu empire resulted in the migration of the NDEBELE into the region.

Ruanda-Urundi *See* BURUNDI; RWANDA

Rudolf I (1218–91) King of Germany (1273–91), founder of the HABSBURG dynasty. His election as German king in succession to the last HOHENSTAUFFEN, ended a period of anarchy as he set out to restore the position of the monarchy. He regained the duchies of Austria, Styria and Carniola from Ottokar II of Bohemia (1278). Although he failed to persuade the electors to choose his son ALBERT I as his successor, Albert did gain the throne in 1298, and by bestowing land on his family Rudolf established Habsburg power in Germany.

Rudolf II (1552–1612) Holy Roman emperor (1576–1612), son and successor of MAXIMILIAN II. He moved the imperial capital to PRAGUE, which, under his patronage, became a glittering centre of the RENAISSANCE, attracting not only artists and writers but also scientists, such as Tycho Brahe and Johannes Kepler. Melancholic and reclusive, Rudolf was faced by Catholic-Protestant conflicts in Bohemia and Hungary, aggravated by his hostility to Protestantism. A Hungarian revolt was suppressed by his brother and successor, MATTHIAS, to whom he reluctantly ceded Hungary, Austria and Moravia (1608), and Bohemia (1611). Rudolf's religious intolerance did much to precipitate the THIRTY YEARS' WAR (1618–48).

Ruhr River and region in W Germany; the *Ruhrgebiet* (Ruhr valley) is Germany's industrial heartland and major cities include Essen, Dortmund, Duisburg and Mülheim. Watered by the Ruhr and its tributaries, the region contains vast deposits of high-grade coal. The Ruhr region passed to PRUSSIA in the early 19th century, and rapid industrial development after 1815 was aided by the ZOLLVEREIN (customs union), tax advantages, development of railway transport and the establishment of the huge Krupp steelworks at Essen, making armaments. In 1923 France and Belgium occupied the Ruhr when Germany failed to keep up the REPARATIONS called for by the Treaty of VERSAILLES (1919). The altercation was settled by the adoption of the DAWES PLAN (1924) and the occupation ended in 1925. Under the control of Nazi Germany from 1933, large-scale weapons manufacture resumed, and during World War 2 the factories of the Ruhr were a major target of Allied bombers: by 1945 *c.*75% of the region was destroyed. It revived under Allied control after the war, although lighter industries took over from coal and steel.

Rumelia Former state of the OTTOMAN EMPIRE, now divided between Turkey and several Balkan countries. The Ottoman Turks began to gain control of the region in the 14th century. Rumelia was roughly equivalent to the "Greater Bulgaria" proposed in the Treaty of SAN STEFANO (1878), covering more than half the Balkan Peninsula. Under the revised settlement agreed by the Congress of BERLIN (1878), **Eastern** Rumelia became an autonomous state under Turkish protection. Its unauthorized union with the principality of BULGARIA (1885) caused war between SERBIA and Bulgaria (1885–86) and a European crisis, but it remained part of Bulgaria. Most of **Western** Rumelia was also lost by the Turks in the BALKAN WARS. The Treaty of Bucharest (1913) awarded parts to Greece and Serbia, but EDIRNE remained Turkish.

Rump Parliament (1648–53) Period of the LONG PARLIAMENT in England after its numbers were reduced by PRIDE'S PURGE. It enacted the revolution in which England became a COMMONWEALTH, without the monarchy or the House of Lords, but failed to hold new elections and antagonized the leaders of the army. It was dissolved by Oliver CROMWELL. When Parliament was recalled after the collapse of the PROTECTORATE in 1659, the expelled members were reinstated. *See also* CIVIL WAR, ENGLISH

Rum Rebellion (26 January 1808) Revolt in NEW SOUTH WALES, Australia, against Governor William BLIGH. Bligh's efforts to control the rum traffic in the colony irritated officers of the New South Wales Corps, the corrupt clique who controlled the trade. The arrest of Bligh's leading opponent, John Macarthur (1767–1834), precipitated the revolt. Major George Johnston, the Corps' commander, detained Bligh and, with Macarthur, ran the colony for a year until Colonel Lachlan MACQUARIE arrived (1809) as the new governor, wisely bringing his own regiment. The New South Wales Corps was broken up (1818), Macarthur was exiled to England until 1817, Johnston was court-martialled and cashiered (1811), and Bligh was exonerated.

Rundstedt, Gerd von (1875–1953) German field marshal. He fought in World War 1 and helped in the illicit rearmament of Germany after the War. Rundstedt was briefly ousted from the army (1938), but returned as senior field commander at the start of WORLD WAR 2. He commanded an army corps in the attack on Poland (1939), led the decisive advance through the Ardennes into France (1940), and commanded the southern armies in the invasion of the Soviet Union (1941). He was dismissed by Adolf HITLER when the Soviets mounted a counter-offensive, but returned to service (1942) as commander in chief in Western Europe and helped construct France's coastal fortifications in case of Allied invasion. After the Allies' NORMANDY LANDINGS, Rundstedt ably directed German forces in the Battle of the BULGE (September 1944), Germany's last-ditch counter-offensive in the Ardennes. He was captured by the Allies in 1945, but released on grounds of poor health.

Rupert (1352–1410) King of Germany (1400–10) and Elector Palatine (1398–1400). A member of the House of WITTELSBACH, he was elected to succeed WENCESLAS as king of Germany, after the latter had been deposed by SIGISMUND. Rupert travelled to Italy (1401–02), hoping to receive the imperial crown, but became embroiled in an unsuccessful war to recover Milan from Gian Galeazzo VISCONTI. His title was finally recognized by Pope Boniface IX in 1403. Rupert supported the Roman popes during the GREAT SCHISM, in contrast to the majority of German princes, with whom he was continually in conflict.

Rupert, Prince (1619–82) Royalist commander in the English CIVIL WAR (1642–45), son of Elector Palatine FREDERICK V and nephew of CHARLES I of England. He fought against Austria in the THIRTY YEARS' WAR, but was captured and imprisoned (1638–41). After his release, Rupert went to England. On the outbreak of the Civil War, Charles I appointed him commander of the cavalry. Rupert masterminded a series of stunning successes in the early stages of the Civil War, capturing Bristol (July 1943) and gaining most of Lancashire by June 1644. Rupert was heavily defeated, however, by Oliver CROMWELL at the crucial Battle of MARSTON MOOR (1644) and then again at NASEBY (1645). He was dismissed as commander after surrendering Bristol to the Parliamentarians (September 1645). In 1648 Rupert led a Royalist fleet in attacks on English shipping, but was expelled from the Mediterranean by Robert BLAKE. He returned to England at the RESTORATION (1660), and played some part in the DUTCH WARS. In 1670 Rupert became the first governor of the HUDSON'S BAY COMPANY.

Rurik (d. *c.*879) Semi-legendary Prince of NOVGOROD who established his rule in Novgorod in *c.*862. He was said to have been a Swedish Viking (Varangian), and the Swedes were once widely regarded as the founders of the Russian state, a theory now largely discounted. The capital was moved to KIEV under Rurik's apparent successor, Oleg (d.912), and the so-called Rurik dynasty ruled in KIEVAN RUS and later in Moscow until 1598. *See also* ALEXANDER NEVSKI, SAINT; VLADIMIR I (THE GREAT); YAROSLAV I

Rush, Benjamin (1746–1813) American physician and politician. Rush wrote the first American textbooks on chemistry (1770) and psychiatry (1812), but his belief in the unitary origin of disease led him to recommend extensive bloodletting and purges as therapy. As a member of the Continental Congress (1776–77), he signed the Declaration of Independence. Rush served as surgeon general (1777–78) at the start of the American Revolution, but resigned because he thought the military hospitals were mismanaged and later criticized George WASHINGTON's military decisions. He served as treasurer of the US Mint (1797–1813) under President John ADAMS. His son, **Richard** (1780–1859), signed the RUSH-BAGOT CONVENTION (1817) and was secretary of the treasury (1825–29).

Rush-Bagot Convention (1817) Agreement on disarmament of the US-Canadian border, signed by acting US

R

AREA: 17,075,000sq km (6,592,800sq mi)
POPULATION: 149,527,000
CAPITAL (POPULATION): Moscow (8,881,000)
GOVERNMENT: Federal multiparty republic
ETHNIC GROUPS: Russian 82%, Tatar 4%, Ukrainian 3%, Chuvash 1%, more than 100 other nationalities
LANGUAGES: Russian (official)
RELIGIONS: Christianity (mainly Russian Orthodox, with Roman Catholic and Protestant minorities), Islam, Judaism
GDP PER CAPITA (1995): US$4480

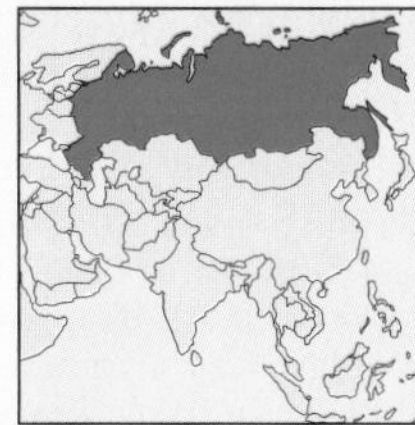

Federation in E Europe and N Asia. By tradition, a Varangian king, RURIK, established the first Russian state in *c*.AD 862. His successor, Oleg, made KIEV his capital and the state became known as KIEVAN RUS. VLADIMIR I adopted Greek ORTHODOX Christianity as the state religion in 988. NOVGOROD and Kiev vied for political supremacy. In 1237–40 the Mongol TATARS conquered Russia and established the GOLDEN HORDE. Saint ALEXANDER NEVSKI submitted to Mongol rule and became grand duke of Kiev.

In the 14th century MOSCOW grew in importance, and the Grand Duchy of Moscow was established in 1380. IVAN III (THE GREAT) extended the power of Moscow, began the construction of the KREMLIN and completed the conquest of the Golden Horde in 1480. In 1547 IVAN IV (THE TERRIBLE) was crowned tsar of all Russia. Ivan conquered the Tatar khanates of KAZAN (1552) and Astrakhan (1556), gaining control of the River Volga, and began the conquest of SIBERIA. Following the death of Boris GODUNOV (1605), Russia was subject to foreign incursions and ruled by a series of usurpers. In 1613 MICHAEL founded the ROMANOV dynasty that ruled Russia until 1917. The reign (1696–1725) of PETER I (THE GREAT) marked the start of the westernization and modernization of Russia: central government institutions were founded, and the church was subordinated to the monarchy. Centralization was achieved at the expense of increasing the number of SERFS. Russia expanded W to the Baltic Sea, and ST PETERSBURG was founded in 1703. Peter made it his capital in 1712.

In 1762 CATHERINE II (THE GREAT) became empress. Under her authoritarian rule, Russia became the greatest power in continental Europe, acquiring much of Poland, BELARUS and UKRAINE. ALEXANDER I's (r.1801–25) territorial gains led him into conflict with the imperial ambitions of NAPOLEON I. In 1812 Napoleon captured Moscow, but his army was devastated by the Russian winter. The DECEMBRIST Conspiracy (1825) failed to prevent the accession of NICHOLAS I. Nicholas' reign (1825–55) was characterized by the struggle against liberalization and Russia's involvement in the CRIMEAN WAR (1853–56). ALEXANDER II (r.1855–81) undertook reforms, such as the emancipation of the serfs, while ALEXANDER III's reign (1881–94) was more reactionary but continued Russia's industrialization, helped by the construction of the TRANS-SIBERIAN RAILWAY. Alexander was succeeded by the last Romanov tsar, NICHOLAS II. In the 1890s drought caused famine in rural areas, and there was discontent in the cities. Defeat in the RUSSO-JAPANESE WAR (1904–05) precipitated the RUSSIAN REVOLUTION OF 1905. Nicholas II was forced to adopt a new constitution and establish an elected DUMA (parliament). The democratic reforms were soon reversed, revolutionary groups were suppressed and POGROMS encouraged. In 1898 the Russian Social Democratic Labour Party (RSDLP) was secretly founded, supported primarily by industrial workers. In 1912 the RSDLP split into BOLSHEVIK and MENSHEVIK factions. Russia's support for a Greater Slavic state contributed to the outbreak of WORLD WAR I, but Russia was ill-prepared for war and suffered great hardship.

The RUSSIAN REVOLUTION (1917) had two main phases. In March, Nicholas II was forced to abdicate (he and his family were executed in July 1918) and a provisional government was formed. In July, Alexander KERENSKY became prime minister, but failed to satisfy the radical hunger of the SOVIETS. In November 1917 the Bolsheviks, led by Vladimir LENIN, seized power and proclaimed Russia a Soviet Federated Socialist Republic. In 1918 the capital was transferred to Moscow. Under the terms of the Treaty of BREST-LITOVSK (1918), Russia withdrew from World War 1 but was forced to cede territory to the Central Powers. For the next five years, the RUSSIAN CIVIL WAR raged between the Reds and Whites, complicated by foreign intervention. The Bolsheviks emerged victorious, but Russia was devastated. In 1922 Russia was united with Ukraine, Belarus and TRANSCAUCASIA (ARMENIA, AZERBAIJAN and GEORGIA) to form the Union of Soviet Socialist Republics (for history 1922–91, *see* SOVIET UNION).

In June 1991 Boris YELTSIN was elected president of the Russian Republic. In August 1991 communist hardliners arrested the Soviet President Mikhail GORBACHEV and attempted to capture the Russian parliament in Moscow. Democratic forces rallied behind Yeltsin, and the coup was defeated. On 25 December 1991, Gorbachev resigned as president of the Soviet Union, and on 31 December the Soviet Union was dissolved. The Russian Federation became a co-founder of the COMMONWEALTH OF INDEPENDENT STATES (CIS), composed of the former Soviet Republics.

In March 1992 a new Federal Treaty was signed between the central government in Moscow and the autonomous republics within the Russian Federation. CHECHENIA refused to sign, and declared independence. Yeltsin's reforms were frustrated by institutional forces, forcing him to dissolve parliament in September 1993. Parliamentary leaders formed a rival government, but the coup failed. In December 1993 a new democratic constitution was adopted. Progress in democratization and economic reform was slow. Many ethnic groups demanded greater autonomy within the federation. In 1992 direct rule was imposed in INGUSHETIA and North Ossetia. From 1994 to 1996, Russia was embroiled in a costly civil war in the secessionist state of Chechenia. In 1996, despite concern about his ill-health, Yeltsin was re-elected. In 1998 the Russian economy was devastated by the financial crisis in Southeast Asia. In 1998 Yeltsin dismissed the entire cabinet, including the prime minister Viktor CHERNOMYRDIN. In August 1998 the stock market collapsed and the rouble was devalued by 50%. In 1999 Yeltsin resigned in favour of Vladimir PUTIN, who relaunched the war in Chechenia and won the 2000 elections

Secretary of State Richard Rush and British Ambassador Charles BAGOT. Besides ensuring an unfortified frontier, it set limits on the number of US and British warships permitted in the Great Lakes. A further convention (1818) confirmed the line of the border east of the Rocky Mountains and provided for joint occupation of OREGON Territory.

Russell, Bertrand Arthur William, 3rd Earl (1872–1970) British philosopher, grandson of Lord John RUSSELL. Russell's most influential work, written in collaboration with A.N. Whitehead, was the monumental *Principia Mathematica* (1910–13), although *History of Western Philosophy* (1950) was his most popular work. Russell's commitment to pacifism led to his imprisonment in 1918, but he supported the anti-fascist aims of World War 2. In 1950 he was awarded the Nobel Prize for literature. A man of great moral stature, Russell was briefly imprisoned for participating in anti-nuclear demonstrations in 1961.

Russell, John, 1st Earl (1792–1878) British statesman, prime minister (1846–52, 1865–66). He entered Parliament as a WHIG in 1813. During the 1820s Russell championed the cause of parliamentary reform and, after the Whigs gained power in 1830, he introduced the Great Reform Bill (1832) and led the fight to secure Parliament's approval of it. As paymaster general (1830–34) under Earl GREY, Russell supported the CATHOLIC EMANCIPATION ACT. He served as home secretary (1835–39) and secretary for war and the colonies (1839–41) under Lord MELBOURNE, reducing capital punishment and introducing state support for public education. From 1841 to 1846 Russell led the Whig opposition to the Tory ministry of Sir Robert PEEL, forcing the prime minister to commit to FREE TRADE. In his first term, Russell was unable to enact many of his liberal reforms because of splits within his own party, but he did introduce a FACTORY ACT (1847) which reduced the working day. His government fell after the resignation of Lord PALMERSTON. He was foreign secretary (1852–55) under the Earl of ABERDEEN, taking Britain into the CRIMEAN WAR against Russia (1853–56), and again (1859–65) under Palmerston, whom he succeeded as prime minister. He kept Britain neutral in the American Civil War, but resisted the US government in the ALABAMA CLAIMS. His second term was curtailed by the defeat of a new Reform Bill (1866), letting in the Tories under Benjamin DISRAELI, who promptly passed a more sweeping REFORM ACT (1867). *See also* CORN LAWS

Russia *See* country feature

Russian Civil War (1918–20) Conflicts between the BOLSHEVIKS and their opponents after the RUSSIAN REVOLUTION. Lenin's signing of the Treaty of BREST-LITOVSK, which ended Russian involvement in WORLD WAR 1 at a high price, led to a coalition of anti-communist and Socialist Revolutionary opposition to the Bolshevik government. The main combatants in the ensuing Civil War were the hastily constructed RED ARMY of Leon TROTSKY and the WHITE RUSSIAN armies, led by General Anton DENIKIN and supported by the Allies, who wished to preserve an E front against Germany. In March 1918 the first British forces landed at Murmansk, NW Russia, and the following month Japanese troops landed at Vladivostok, S Russia. In May 1918 the Czechoslovak Legion, stranded in Russia at the end of World War 1, seized control of part of the Trans-Siberian Railway. These actions encouraged the creation of two anti-Bolshevik authorities: one based in Omsk, W Siberia, and the other at Samara, W Russia. The Bolsheviks responded by ruthlessly suppressing any dissent, expelling the MENSHEVIKS and assassinating Tsar NICHOLAS II and his family (July 1918). By the end of 1918 the Red Army had regained much of E European Russia, while the White Russian coalition in Omsk collapsed when Admiral Alexander KOLCHAK established a dictatorship. In 1919 the Red Army invaded Ukraine, but the final defeat of Germany in World War 1 enabled the Allies to lend greater support to the Whites, and French forces landed in Ukraine as part of the *c.*200,000-strong Allied force. With the exception of the Japanese, the Allied intervention was to be of little consequence. Kolchak's advance in the Urals was halted by April 1919 and his subsequent retreat turned into a rout and Kolchak was captured and shot by the Bolsheviks in February 1920. By September 1919 General Denikin had gained most of Ukraine and advanced towards Moscow. The Red Army counter-offensive was again swift and decisive and the White forces once more collapsed. The Bolsheviks now concentrated their attack on General Piotr WRANGEL's troops in the Crimea, whose defeat in November 1920 signalled the end of the Civil War proper. The last Japanese troops withdrew in 1922 and the crushing of the short-lived Transcaucasian republics of Armenia, Azerbaijan and Georgia enabled the creation of the SOVIET UNION. An estimated 13 million people died in the Civil War and ensuing famine. *See also* RUSSO-POLISH WAR

Russian Orthodox Church *See* ORTHODOX CHURCH, EASTERN

Russian Revolution (1917) Two insurrections, the first of which, in March (February in the old calendar), toppled the tsarist regime and established a republic and the second of which, in November (October), put the BOLSHEVIKS in government. Promises of reforms made after the RUSSIAN REVOLUTION OF 1905 had not been kept and the intense hardships and losses suffered during WORLD WAR 1 aggravated widespread discontent among many classes. Revolutionary outbreaks culminating in strikes and riots in the capital, Petrograd (now ST PETERSBURG), which were supported by the tsar's troops, left NICHOLAS II powerless, and he abdicated on 15 March 1917. A provisional government was formed by liberals in the DUMA (parliament), led by Prince Georgi LVOV. The provisional government's continued commitment to Russian participation in World War 1, and its failure to deal with the issues of food shortages and land reform, did not accord with the popular mood, and the workers' SOVIETS rapidly forming in the cities (most importantly Petrograd) attracted great support. In July 1917 the Socialist Revolutionary Alexander KERENSKY became leader of the provisional government, rapidly defeating a coup by General Lavr KORNILOV. The failure of a new military offensive helped to discredit Kerensky's government and its moderate socialist supporters. Soldiers were deserting in thousands, and peasants took advantage of government weakness to seize land from the gentry. On the night of 6 November (24 October), on the orders of Vladimir LENIN, the Bolsheviks carried out an almost bloodless coup in Petrograd. The Kerensky government collapsed and the soviets took over the cities. An armistice was arranged, a Soviet constitution proclaimed (1918) and the capital moved to MOSCOW. By that time, however, the RUSSIAN CIVIL WAR was in progress.

Russian Revolution of 1905 Rebellion against Tsar NICHOLAS II. There was a long tradition of revolutionary activity in Russia against the absolutist regime of the ROMANOVS, which could be traced back to the DECEMBRISTS (1825) and earlier. The violent strikes and protests that broke out in 1905 were precipitated largely by defeats in the RUSSO-JAPANESE WAR (1904–05) and the hardship caused by heavy wartime taxation. The revolt began on Bloody Sunday (22 January), when troops fired on a peaceful demonstration outside the Winter Palace in ST PETERSBURG, W Russia, killing up to 1000 people. Strikes and peasant risings spread throughout the Russian empire, the crew of the battleship POTEMKIN mutinied, and the first workers' SOVIET was formed (October) in St Petersburg. Under pressure from Count Sergei WITTE, Nicholas II issued the October Manifesto, conceding reforms which included a democratically elected DUMA (parliament) with legislative power. By the time it met in 1906, the government had regained control. Repression followed and the October Manifesto was not implemented.

Russo-Finnish War (November 1939–March 1940) Conflict between Finland and the Soviet Union at the start of WORLD WAR 2, also known as the Winter War. When the Finns rejected the Soviet Union's demands for extensive territorial concessions and demilitarization of the defensive Mannerheim Line, the Red Army invaded Finland, but the Finnish General Carl MANNERHEIM, commanding outnumbered but highly mobile troops, halted the Russians at the Mannerheim Line in January 1940. The Finns' hope for support, particularly from France and Britain, was unrealized, except for some Scandinavian volunteers, and, with

R

the Soviet command reorganized, a sustained artillery bombardment of up to 300,000 shells a day eventually enabled Russian troops to break through the Mannerheim Line (March 1940). In the Treaty of Moscow, Finland was forced to agree to Soviet terms, ceding Western KARELIA and agreeing to the establishment of a Soviet military base on the Hanko Peninsula. Finland temporarily regained its lost territories when the Germans invaded Russia in 1941. The 105-day war claimed *c.*91,000 Soviet lives and *c.*25,000 Finnish. *See also* NAZI-SOVIET PACT

Russo-Japanese War (1904–05) Conflict arising from the rivalry of Russia and Japan for control of MANCHURIA and KOREA. When Russia reneged on a promise to evacuate Manchuria, the Japanese launched a surprise attack (February 1904) on Port Arthur (Lüshun), s Manchuria. Having gained a narrow victory at the Battle of Liaoyang (August 1904) and captured Port Arthur (January 1905), the Japanese also took the Manchurian capital, Mukden, after a ferocious battle (February–March 1905) which claimed *c.*89,000 Russian lives and *c.*71,000 Japanese. Despite the almost-complete Trans-Siberian Railway, the Russians were unable to transport men and supplies to the East in sufficient quantity. Defeats on land were accompanied by the near-annihilation of the Russian Pacific fleet, beginning with the loss of the flagship *Petropavlovsk* with 600 men including Admiral Stepan Makarov. The Russian admiralty then dispatched the Baltic fleet, under Admiral Rodzhdestvenski, on a six-month voyage to the Far East, but when it arrived in the Straits of TSUSHIMA it was annihilated by the more advanced battleships of Admiral TOGO HEIHACHIRO in one of the most decisive battles of history. At the Treaty of PORTSMOUTH (1905), mediated by US President Theodore ROOSEVELT, Russia surrendered Korea, the Liaodong Peninsula and s Sakhalin to Japan. The War demonstrated to the West that Japan had become a major world power, while Russia's humiliating defeat helped provoke the RUSSIAN REVOLUTION OF 1905.

Russo-Polish War (1919–20) Conflict between Soviet Russia and Poland. The War began when the Polish leader Józef PIŁSUDSKI and the Ukrainian nationalist leader Symon Petlyura mounted a joint invasion of Ukraine (April 1920). Within three weeks, Polish-Ukrainian forces had captured KIEV. The RED ARMY mounted a counter-offensive, which not only succeeded in recapturing Ukraine but also advanced to threaten the Polish capital, Warsaw (August 1920). The Poles expelled the Russians from their soil and the ensuing Treaty of Riga (1921) fixed the Russo-Polish border at the so-called Curzon Line until the outbreak of World War 2. *See also* RUSSIAN CIVIL WAR

Russo-Turkish Wars Series of wars between the Russian and Ottoman empires from the 17th to 19th century. The fundamental cause of the conflict was the expansionist aims of the Russian empire and its desire to control economically and strategically valuable areas of SE Europe (the Black Sea, the Caucasus and Ukraine). Additionally, Russia was influenced by its affinity with the Christian and Slav subjects of the Turks in the Balkans, which led to its encouragement of Balkan nationalism in the 19th century. That the growing power of Russia and increasing weakness of the Ottoman Empire did not end in total Russian success in the 19th century was largely ensured by other European powers, who were anxious to limit Russian expansion by preserving the OTTOMAN EMPIRE or who, in the case of Austria, had their own ambitions in the Balkans. The wars of the early 18th century revolved around the struggle for the Black Sea port of Azov, won by Russia in 1739. The **first** major war (1768–74), launched by Catherine II (the Great), ended in the Treaty of KÜÇHÜK KAINARJI, which in the Russian interpretation authorized its intervention in the Turks' Balkan provinces to protect Christians. Russia gained control of CRIMEA after the **war of 1787–92**, and the campaign of Mikhail KUTUZOV forced the Ottoman Turks to cede BESSARABIA after the **war of 1806–12**. The **war of 1828–29** was connected with the GREEK WAR OF INDEPENDENCE and ended with further Russian gains in the Treaty of ADRIANOPLE. In the CRIMEAN WAR (1853–56), France and Great Britain aided the Turks and forced some Russian concessions. The Turks' ruthless suppression of a rising in Bulgaria (1876), denounced in Europe as the "Bulgarian Atrocities", prefaced the **last** Russo-Turkish War (1877–78). Russia, allied with Serbia, advanced through Thrace and captured Adrianople (now EDIRNE). The ensuing Treaty of SAN STEFANO (1878) gave independence to Serbia, Romania and Montenegro and autonomy to Bosnia-Herzegovina. Its creation of a huge autonomous Bulgarian state alarmed Britain and Austria-Hungary who pressured Russia into accepting a more limited settlement at the Congress of BERLIN (1878).

Ruthenia Historic region now in SW Ukraine; the chief city is Uzhgorod. The Ruthenes are closely linked with the Ukrainians. Ruthenia came under Hungarian rule in the 13th century. A movement for autonomy in the 19th century was frustrated. It passed to the new Czechoslovak state in 1920 but was re-occupied by Hungary in 1939. After World War 2 it was ceded to the Soviet Union. A large majority of Ruthenes voted in favour of autonomy from Ukraine in a 1991 referendum, but the result was ignored.

Ruyter, Michiel Adrianszoon de (1607–76) Dutch admiral, the outstanding naval commander of his generation. He fought under Maarten TROMP in the First ANGLO-DUTCH WAR (1652–54) and afterwards worked with Jan de WITT to strengthen the Dutch navy. In the **Second** Anglo-Dutch War (1665–67), Ruyter commanded the Dutch fleet in the Four Days' Battle off Dunkirk (June 1666), which inflicted serious damage on the English. In June 1667, with extraordinary boldness, he sailed up the English River Medway, destroying several English warships at anchor, and towing the flagship, the *Royal Charles*, away to the Netherlands – the greatest humiliation ever suffered by the English navy. In the **Third** Anglo-Dutch War (1672–74), Ruyter surprised the vastly superior Anglo-French fleet in Southwold Bay (1672) and inflicted enough destruction to end all hope of invading the Dutch republic.

Rwanda *See* country feature

Rye House Plot (1683) English conspiracy to capture, perhaps kill, CHARLES II and his brother James (later JAMES II) at Rye House, Hertfordshire, SE England, as they returned from the races at Newmarket. It was organized by Whig extremists determined to prevent the succession of the Catholic James. A change of royal plans frustrated the conspirators, and the plot was revealed. Two prominent politicians, Algernon SIDNEY and Lord William Russell, were later executed after a change in the treason laws. Another conspirator, the Duke of MONMOUTH, was forced into exile in Holland.

Ryswick, Treaty of *See* RIJSWIJK, TREATY OF

Ryzhkov, Nikolai Ivanovich (1929–) Russian statesman, prime minister (1985–91). He joined the Communist Party in 1956 and entered the Central Committee of the Party in 1981, acting as head of its economic department. Ryzhkov served as prime minister under President Mikhail GORBACHEV, and was one of the chief architects of PERESTROIKA. His reforms sought to create a "regulated market" economy with limited decentralization and retention of state control over prices. His leadership was discredited by the slow pace of reform and the failure to deliver tangible improvements in the economy, and he resigned in 1991.

RWANDA

AREA: 26,340sq km (10,170sq mi)
POPULATION: 7,526,000
CAPITAL (POPULATION): Kigali (234,500)
GOVERNMENT: Republic
ETHNIC GROUPS: Hutu 90%, Tutsi 9%, Twa 1%
LANGUAGES: French and Kinyarwanda (both official)
RELIGIONS: Christianity 74% (Roman Catholic 65%), traditional beliefs 17%, Islam 9%
GDP PER CAPITA (1995): US$540

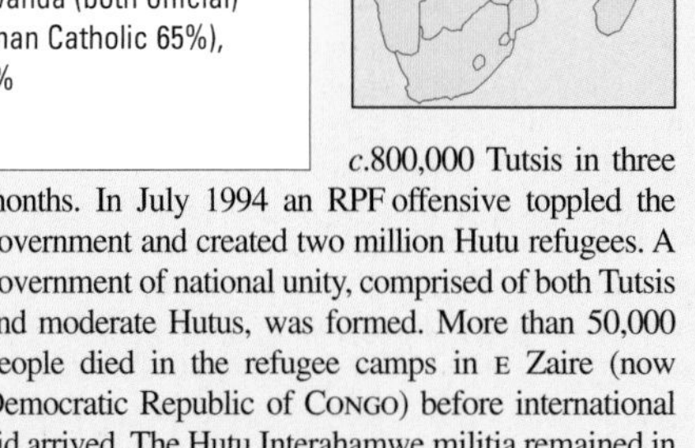

Nation in E central Africa. Rwanda is Africa's most densely populated country. Twa pygmies were the original inhabitants of Rwanda, but Hutu farmers began to settle (*c.*AD 1000), gradually displacing the Twa. In the 15th century Tutsi cattle herders migrated from the N and began to dominate the Hutu. By the late 18th century Rwanda and BURUNDI formed a single Tutsi-dominated state ruled by a king (*mwami*). In 1890 Germany conquered the area and subsumed it into German East Africa. During World War 1, Belgian forces occupied (1916) both Rwanda and Burundi. In 1919 it became part of the Belgian League of Nations' mandated territory of Ruanda-Urundi (which in 1946 became a United Nations' trust territory). The Hutu majority became more vociferous in their demands for political representation.

In 1959 the Tutsi *mwami* died. The ensuing civil war between Hutus and Tutsis claimed more than 150,000 lives. Hutu victory led to a mass exodus of Tutsis. The 1960 elections were won by the Hutu Emancipation Movement, led by Grégoire KAYIBANDA. In 1961 Rwanda declared itself a republic. Belgium formally recognized Rwanda's independence in 1962 and Kayibanda became president. Rwanda was subject to continual Tutsi incursions from Burundi and UGANDA. In 1973 Kayibanda was overthrown in a military coup, led by Major General HABYARIMANA. In 1978 Habyarimana became president. During the 1980s, Rwanda was devastated by drought and more than 50,000 refugees fled to Burundi.

In 1990 Rwanda was invaded by the Tutsi-dominated Rwandan Patriotic Front (RPF), who forced Habyarimana to agree to a multiparty constitution. UN forces were drafted in to oversee the transition. In April 1994 Habyarimana and the Burundi president were killed in a rocket attack on their aircraft. The Hutu army and militia launched a premeditated act of genocide against the Tutsi minority, killing between *c.*800,000 Tutsis in three months. In July 1994 an RPF offensive toppled the government and created two million Hutu refugees. A government of national unity, comprised of both Tutsis and moderate Hutus, was formed. More than 50,000 people died in the refugee camps in E Zaire (now Democratic Republic of CONGO) before international aid arrived. The Hutu Interahamwe militia remained in control of the camps, their leaders facing prosecution for genocide. The sheer number of refugees (1995, one million in Zaïre and 500,000 in Tanzania) destabilized regional politics. In 1996 UN troops left Rwanda. In 1998 former prime minister Jean Kambanda was sentenced to life imprisonment for genocide by the UN International Criminal Tribunal.

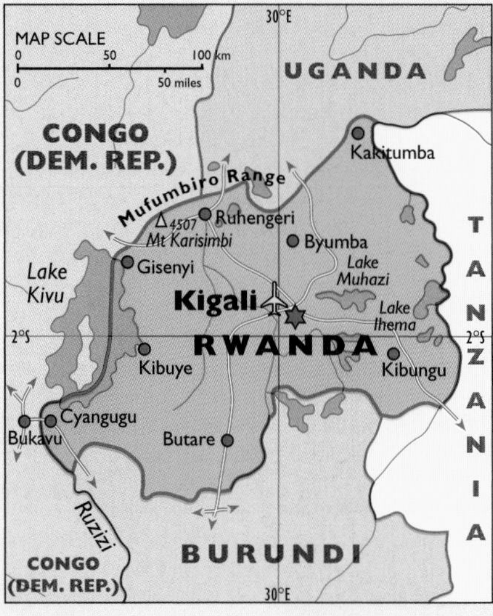

SA (*Sturmabteilung*) *See* BROWNSHIRTS

Saarland State in SW Germany, bordering France and Luxembourg; the capital is Saarbrücken. The FRANKS were among the earliest settlers in the region and subsequently the Saar formed part of the Carolingian empire. It was ruled by the counts of Nassau-Saarbrücken from 1381 to 1793. The French exerted great influence in the region and briefly occupied Saarland (1684–97, 1793–1815). As part of PRUSSIA from 1815, the Saar became a leading coal- and iron-producing region of Europe. After World War 1, its coal mines were awarded to France, while the Saar itself was administered by the League of Nations. In 1935, following a referendum, it returned to Germany. Occupied by France after World War 2, Saarland became the tenth state of West Germany in 1957. Pop. (1991) 1,076,880.

Sabah, Sheikh Jaber al-Ahmad al- (1928–) Emir of KUWAIT (1977–), third son of Ahmad al-Jaber (r.1921–50). He was appointed prime minister (1965) by his brother, Sabah al-Salem al-Sabah (r.1965–77), whom he succeeded as emir. When Iraq invaded Kuwait in 1990, Jaber sought refuge in Saudia Arabia where he set up a government-in-exile. He returned to Kuwait in 1991. Despite the promise of democratic reforms, Jaber and his family continued to dominate the government of Kuwait. *See also* GULF WAR

Sabah (North Borneo) State of MALAYSIA and one of the four political sub-divisions of the island of BORNEO; the capital is Kota Kinabalu. It was settled by Malays in the 14th century. It was the British Protectorate of North Borneo from 1877 to 1963, when it became a state of the Malaysian Federation. Pop. (1990) 1,736,902.

Sabines Ancient people of central Italy. They inhabited the Sabine Hills, NE of Rome. After sporadic fighting, the Sabines were granted Roman citizenship in 290 BC. The presence of so many Sabines and Sabine customs in Rome may have been responsible for the legend of the rape (i.e. abduction) of the Sabine women to provide wives for the early Romans.

Sac (Sauk) Algonquian-speaking Native North Americans. In the 17th century, under threat from Iroquois bands, they moved from the Saginaw Bay region of E Michigan to Wisconsin. From 1733 the Sac were allied with the Fox, and the two tribes settled along the banks of the Mississippi River. In 1804 some of their minor chiefs agreed to cede land E of the Mississippi to the United States' government. The Sac chief Black Hawk denounced the treaty, resulting in the BLACK HAWK WAR (1832). Today, there are *c*.4500 Sac and Fox.

Sacagawea (*c*.1787–*c*.1812) (Sacajawea) SHOSHONE interpreter for the LEWIS AND CLARK EXPEDITION (1804–06). She was sold into slavery as a child and later married her owner, a French-Canadian trapper who was hired by Lewis and Clark in the winter of 1804–05. Sacagawea and her infant son accompanied the Expedition, and she proved to be an invaluable guide and interpreter, helping to negotiate with other Native Americans for supplies and goodwill.

Sacco-Vanzetti Case (1920–27) Controversial murder trial in Massachusetts, United States. Two Italian immigrants and anarchists, Nicola Sacco and Bartolomeo Vanzetti, were convicted (1921) of killing the paymaster and guard of a shoe factory in South Braintree, Massachusetts, and stealing more than US$15,000. The prosecution's case was based on circumstantial evidence and many believed that the conviction was due to prejudice against their status and political beliefs. Despite a confession (1925) to the crime from a convicted murderer, Sacco and Vanzetti were executed in August 1927, the cause of violent demonstrations. On the 50th anniversary of the execution, Massachusetts governor, Michael Dukakis, stated that "disgrace should be...removed from their names."

Sadat, (Muhammad) Anwar (al-) (1918–81) Egyptian statesman, president (1970–81). A leading opponent of the British occupation of Egypt, he joined Gamal NASSER's Free Officers Association in 1950 and took part in the coup against King FAROUK in 1952. Sadat served as vice president (1964–66, 1969–70), before succeeding Nasser as president. Sadat expelled Soviet military advisers, whom he blamed for Egypt's disastrous performance in the SIX-DAY WAR (1967), and launched a surprise invasion of the Sinai Peninsula at the start of the YOM KIPPUR WAR (1973). Israel counter-attacked, quickly re-establishing their 1967 position. Sadat, eager to regain the Sinai and improve Egypt's domestic economy, sought a rapprochement with the United States and Israel. In 1977 he visited Israel, and the CAMP DAVID ACCORDS (1978) led to a peace treaty (1979). Sadat shared the 1978 Nobel Prize for Peace with Israeli Prime Minister Menachem BEGIN. The treaty was condemned throughout the Arab world, and Egypt was suspended from the ARAB LEAGUE. After widespread arrests of political opponents, Sadat was assassinated by Islamic extremists. *See also* ARAB-ISRAELI WARS

Sadducees Jewish sect active in JUDAEA from *c*.200 BC until the destruction of the Second TEMPLE OF JERUSALEM in AD 70. They were a conservative, priestly, social élite, engaged in a fierce dispute with their rivals, the PHARISEES. The principal cause of disagreement was the Sadducees' rejection of the Oral Law in favour of the TORAH as the sole source of authority. Their collaboration with the Roman government aroused the enmity of the general public.

Sadowa, Battle of (3 July 1866) Decisive conflict in the AUSTRO-PRUSSIAN WAR, fought in Sadowa, near Königgrätz (now Hradec Kralové, Czech Republic). Prussian General Helmuth von MOLTKE used the railway to unite his *c*.280,000 forces in Bohemia against the *c*.241,000-strong Austrian army, led by the inexperienced Ludwig von Benedek. The Prussian infantry was also equipped with superior, breech-loading rifles. Benedek was forced to retreat, but the Prussians failed to press home the advantage. The Austrians lost *c*.40,000 men, almost half of whom were captured, while the Prussians lost fewer than 15,000. The Battle confirmed Prussian dominance in Germany.

Safavid Iranian dynasty (1501–1736), founders of the modern SHIITE state. The dynasty descended from Safi od-Din (1253–1334) of Ardabil, leader of the Sufi order of Safaviyeh. Its founder, ISMAIL I, was head of a confederation of Turkmen tribes known as the Kizilbash (Redheads) after the colour of their headdress. In 1501 Ismail was proclaimed shah of Azerbaijan. He spent the next decade creating a unified state in Iran, converting the largely SUNNI population to Shiism. In 1509 Ismail captured BAGHDAD, but was badly defeated by Ottoman Sultan SELIM I at the Battle of Chaldiran (1514). In 1534 SULEIMAN I recaptured Baghdad from Ismail's son and successor, **Tahmasp I** (r.1525–76), and the Safavid capital moved to Tabriz, NW Iran. The dynasty reached its height under ABBAS I (THE GREAT) (r.1588–1629). In 1598 Abbas transferred the capital to ISFAHAN, which subsequently flourished as a major centre of ISLAMIC ART AND ARCHITECTURE. He reorganized his army, enabling the recapture of Baghdad (1623) and the expulsion of the Portuguese from Hormuz. After the reign (1642–66) of **Abbas II**, the Safavid dynasty went into terminal decline. The last Safavid shah was overthrown by the Afghans in 1722 and deposed by NADIR SHAH in 1736.

Said ibn Sultan (1791–1856) Sultan of OMAN and Zanzibar (1806–56). He came to power after the assassination of his cousin Badr, who had usurped the throne in 1804. Said spent the early part of his reign consolidating his rule over Muscat and Oman. In the 1820s, he began to re-establish Omani authority over its East African domains. Said transformed the islands of Zanzibar and Pemba into the largest producers of cloves in the world, crushing (1837) the resistance of the Mazari dynasty in Mombasa. In 1840 he moved the royal court to Zanzibar, which became the major power in East Africa. Its power was based on its control of trade in slaves, ivory and cloves. Treaties (1822, 1845) with Great Britain limited the SLAVE TRADE, but Said took no practical measures against the trade. He died at sea and his Arabian and African territories were divided between two sons.

Saigo Takamori (1827–77) Japanese patriot. Born to a poor SAMURAI family, he rose to become commander of the army of Satsuma. Saigo played a leading role in the overthrow of the TOKUGAWA shogunate and the subsequent MEIJI RESTORATION (1868). After crushing pockets of resistance to Emperor Meiji, he briefly retired but re-emerged as head of the new Imperial Guard in 1871. Anxious to regain support from the samurai after the introduction of conscription, Saigo called for war against Korea, but his plans were rejected by OKUBO TOSHIMICHI and he retired once more. Saigo opened a military school in his native Kagoshima, which soon attracted up to 20,000 disaffected young samurai. Dissatisfaction spilled into the Satsuma Rebellion (January–September 1877), which Saigo reluctantly led. The revolt was crushed by YAMAGATA ARITOMO, and Saigo, badly wounded, arranged to be beheaded by one of his lieutenants.

Sailendra (Shailendra) Dynasty of central JAVA (AD *c*.750–850). It was responsible for the introduction of

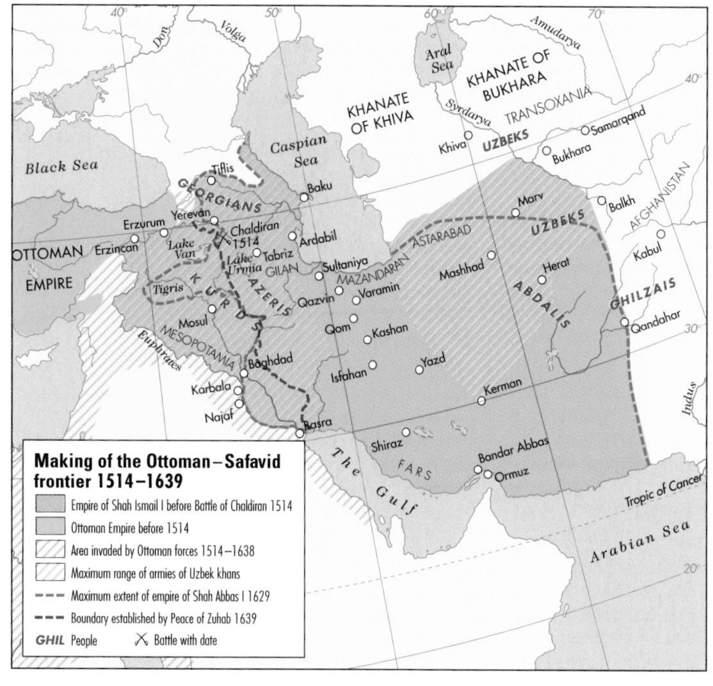

◄ **Safavid** In the early 16th century Shah Ismail and his Kizilbash forces began to infiltrate E Anatolia from Tabriz. Determind to maintain control over the Black Sea, the Ottomans retaliated with force, using their superior military strength to crush the Safavids at Chaldiran (1514). Conflict between the Ottomans and the Safavids continued well into the 17th century with intermittent fighting over land occupied by Azeries, Kurds and Mesopotamian Arabs. Shah Abbas I partially succeeded in restoring the Safavid empire to its former extent, but the border settlement reached in 1639 favoured the Ottomans. The Peace of Zuhab established a border irrespective of linguistic, cultural and ethnic barriers, but it has lasted to the present day as the border between Iran and Iraq.

ST KITTS AND NEVIS, FEDERATION OF

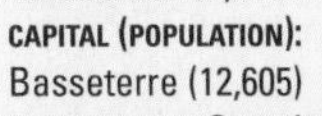

AREA: 261sq km (101sq mi)
POPULATION: 40,618
CAPITAL (POPULATION): Basseterre (12,605)
GOVERNMENT: Constitutional monarchy
ETHNIC GROUPS: Of African descent
LANGUAGES: English (official), Creole
RELIGIONS: Protestant 62%, Catholic 7%
GDP PER CAPITA (1994): US$9410

MAHAYANA Buddhism, which produced a great cultural blossoming, evident in remaining monuments of which the most striking is the huge stupa of BOROBUDUR. Otherwise, little is known of the dynasty, except that it traded with China and Japan and may have extended its rule to the Southeast Asian mainland. The Sailendra dynasty was expelled from Java to Sumatra in the mid-9th century.

St Albans City in Hertfordshire, SE England. The modern city is adjacent to the ruins of the large Roman city of Verulamium, which was destroyed by BOADICEA in the 1st century AD but subsequently rebuilt. The medieval town developed around the abbey built *c.*793 by King OFFA of MERCIA in honour of St Alban, the first English Christian martyr (d.304). The present cathedral, seat of a bishop since 1877, survives from the large Norman abbey. Two battles were fought in or near St Albans in the 15th century. The first, which began the Wars of the ROSES in 1455, was a minor Yorkist victory. The second (1461) was a Lancastrian victory for MARGARET OF ANJOU, who was able to release her husband, HENRY VI, although it allowed the Yorkist king EDWARD IV to reach London first and regain the throne. Pop. (1991) 77,500

Saint Bartholomew's Day Massacre (23–24 August 1572) Slaughter of HUGUENOTS (French Protestants) during the French Wars of RELIGION. The Huguenot leaders had gathered in Paris for the marriage of Henry of Navarre (later HENRY IV) to MARGARET OF VALOIS. The Catholic heads of the house of GUISE persuaded CATHERINE DE' MEDICI to authorize the assassination of Gaspard de COLIGNY, Huguenot adviser to CHARLES IX. Coligny survived and, in order to cover up the plot, a more bloody conspiracy evolved. The murder of Huguenot leaders (including Coligny) incited the Paris mob to attack Protestants at large and *c.*3000 Huguenots died in Paris alone. The killings spread into the provinces and provoked a renewal of religious conflict.

Saintes, Battle of the (12 April 1782) Naval conflict between the French and the British during the American Revolution. The British fleet of 36 ships led by Sir George RODNEY intercepted a French fleet of 35 warships, under the Marquis de Grasse, in the Saintes Passage between the West Indian islands of Dominica and Guadeloupe. Rodney seized advantage of a break in the French line, destroying seven ships and capturing de Grasse. The Battle restored British control of the Caribbean Sea and ended the French threat to its islands in the West Indies.

St-Germain, Treaty of (10 September 1919) Agreement between the Austro-Hungarian Empire and the Allies after WORLD WAR I, signed at St-Germain-en-Laye, N France. It established the new republic of Austria and recognized the independence of Hungary, Poland, Czechoslovakia and the Kingdom of the Serbs, Croats and Slovenes. The Treaty contained the Covenant of the LEAGUE OF NATIONS and outlawed the ANSCHLUSS of Austria and Germany. *See also* SÈVRES, TREATY OF; TRIANON, TREATY OF; VERSAILLES, TREATY OF

St John of Jerusalem, Knights Hospitallers of *See* KNIGHTS HOSPITALLERS

Saint-Just, Louis Antoine Léon de (1767–94) French revolutionary. A leading supporter of Maximilien de ROBESPIERRE, he helped effect the downfall of the GIRONDINS (June 1793) and was a member of the COMMITTEE OF PUBLIC SAFETY. As president (1793–94) of the NATIONAL CONVENTION, Saint-Just passed the Ventôse Decrees, which confiscated property from enemies of the FRENCH REVOLUTION and redistributed it to impoverished patriots. He was the main instigator of the REIGN OF TERROR and was executed in the THERMIDORIAN REACTION.

St Kitts and Nevis, Federation of Self-governing state in the Lesser Antilles, West Indies, formerly a British colony that included Anguilla. The two islands were inhabited by Caribs when sighted (1493) by Christopher Columbus, who named them St Christopher and Nevis. In 1623 St Christopher was settled by the English, who shortened its name. Nevis was settled in 1628. The French contested British rule until the end of the 18th century. The first successful English colony in the West Indies, it was a major sugar producer, and the majority of today's inhabitants are descendants of African slaves. St Kitts, Nevis and Anguilla were federated in 1882 and became a state in association with Britain in 1967. Anguilla soon broke from the federation and became a separate British dependency in 1980. St Kitts and Nevis gained full independence in 1983. In a 1998 referendum Nevis voted in favour of secession, but lacked a sufficient majority. *See* WEST INDIES map

Saint Laurent, Louis Stephen (1882–1973) Canadian statesman, prime minister (1948–57). He entered Parliament in 1942 and became justice minister and attorney general (1941–46) and foreign secretary (1946–48) under W.L. MACKENZIE KING, whom he succeeded as prime minister and head of the LIBERAL PARTY. He was the second French Canadian (after Sir Wilfrid LAURIER) to lead the government. In domestic affairs, he negotiated NEWFOUNDLAND's admission to the Confederation (1949), strengthened Québec's contribution to national interests, and appointed (1952) Vincent MASSEY as the first non-British governor general. Saint Laurent also increased state provision of welfare. In foreign affairs, he sent Canadian troops to fight in the Korean War (1950–53) and played a major role in resolving the SUEZ CRISIS (1956). He was narrowly defeated by the Conservatives under John DIEFENBAKER and resigned as Liberal leader in favour of Lester PEARSON in 1958.

St Lucia Island state in the Lesser Antilles, West Indies. The second largest of the Windward Islands, St Lucia was inhabited by CARIBS when discovered by Europeans in *c.*1502. The first successful European colony was established (1650) by the French, but throughout the 18th century they faced fierce competition from Britain for control of the island. After suppressing a slave revolt, St Lucia was ceded to Britain in 1814, but French influence (still evident in the prevalence of Roman Catholicism and a widely spoken French patois) remained strong. The decline in the sugar industry led to the development of banana and cacao plantations. In 1979 St Lucia gained full independence. *See* WEST INDIES map

St Mark's Basilica in Venice, N Italy. Begun in 829 to enshrine the remains of the city's patron saint, St Mark, it was restored after a fire in 976. It was later demolished and rebuilt in the 11th century in the Byzantine style.

St Paul's Cathedral in London, SE England, rebuilt (1675–1710) on the site of a Gothic cathedral destroyed in the FIRE OF LONDON (1666) to the baroque designs of Sir Christopher WREN.

St Peter's Basilica in Vatican City, N Italy, on the site of an earlier structure over the supposed grave of St Peter. Initiated by Pope JULIUS II, who had the old basilica torn down, it was built between 1506 and 1637. Among the architects were Donato Bramante, Michelangelo (who designed the dome) and Carlo Maderna.

St Petersburg Second-largest city in RUSSIA and a major Baltic seaport on the Gulf of Finland at the mouth of the River Neva. Founded (1703) by PETER I (THE GREAT) as his "window on the West", the city was made capital of Russia in 1712. Peter built the Peter-Paul Fortress, while the Summer Palace was constructed (1710–14) for the city's first governor, Prince MENSHIKOV. A harbour was built at great human cost, and by the 1730s St Petersburg was handling 90% of Russia's foreign trade. It became the cultural capital of Russia and a treasure-house of BAROQUE architecture. The Winter Palace was completed (1762) at the start of the reign of CATHERINE II (THE GREAT). Destroyed by fire in 1837, it was rebuilt (1839) and now houses the Hermitage Museum. The city expanded rapidly

ST LUCIA

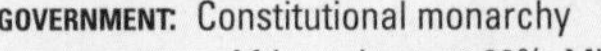

AREA: 622sq km (240sq mi)
POPULATION: 147,000
CAPITAL (POPULATION): Castries (56,000)
GOVERNMENT: Constitutional monarchy
ETHNIC GROUPS: African descent 90%, Mixed 6%, East Indian 3%
LANGUAGES: English (official), French patois
RELIGIONS: Catholic 40%, Protestant 25%, Modekngei
GDP PER CAPITA (1994): US$3014

with the development of the canal and railway systems, and by 1900 it had *c.*1.5 million inhabitants. The growth of large factories and poor conditions for workers made St Petersburg a hotbed of revolutionary activity. It was the scene of the revolt of the DECEMBRISTS (1825) and the massacre of demonstrators (22 January) at the start of the RUSSIAN REVOLUTION OF 1905. Renamed Petrograd in 1914, it was a centre of the political unrest that culminated in the RUSSIAN REVOLUTION of 1917. The BOLSHEVIK government moved the capital back to MOSCOW in 1918, and St Petersburg was renamed Leningrad (1924) after the death of Vladimir LENIN. During World War 2 *c.*660,000 citizens died during the Siege of LENINGRAD (1941–44) and extensive damage was caused by German airplanes and artillery. Massive rebuilding took place after 1945, and in 1991, after the fall of communism and break-up of the Soviet Union, the name St Petersburg was restored. Pop. (1994) 4,883,000.

Saint-Simon, Claude Henry de Rouvroy, Comte de (1760–1825) French social philosopher, one of the founders of CHRISTIAN SOCIALISM. He fought in the American Revolution and was imprisoned in the French Revolution. In *Du Systeme Industriel* (1820–21), he argued for an industrialized state directed by scientist-businessmen. The ideals of egalitarianism and solidarity were presented in *The New Christianity* (1825), in which he combined Catholicism with the ideas of the ENLIGHTENMENT. Saint-Simon influenced later thinkers as varied as Karl MARX and John Stuart MILL.

St Valentine's Day Massacre (14 February 1929) Gangland killings in Chicago, Illinois, United States. The perpetrators were gunmen of Al CAPONE, disguised as policemen, and the seven victims were members of a rival gang of bootleggers during the PROHIBITION era.

St Vincent and the Grenadines Island state in the Lesser Antilles, West Indies. It comprises the volcanic island of St Vincent and five islands of the Grenadine group, including Mustique. St Vincent was probably visited and named by Christopher Columbus in 1498, when it was inhabited by CARIBS who had displaced the earlier ARAWAK. The British established the first successful colony in 1762, and it was ceded to them in 1763. In 1795 the Carib revolted against British rule and most were deported. African slaves were brought in to work on the sugar plantations and their descendants form the majority of the current population. St Vincent was part of the British Windward Islands colony from 1880 to 1958. Self-government was granted in 1969, and full independence achieved in 1979. Besides a persistent trade deficit, volcanic eruptions and hurricanes have caused sporadic but severe economic disruption. *See* WEST INDIES map

Sakhalin (Jap. Karafuto) Island off the E coast of Russia, N of Japan. It was settled by Japanese and Russians in the 18th and 19th centuries. In 1875 Russia gained sole control of Sakhalin in exchange for the Kuril Islands. In the Treaty of PORTSMOUTH (1905), which ended the RUSSO-JAPANESE WAR, Japan regained the south of the island. Sakhalin and the Kuril Islands returned to Russia after World War 2, but Japan continues to claim the S Kuril Islands. Pop. (1994 est.) 681,000.

Sakharov, Andrei Dimitrievich (1921–89) Russian nuclear physicist and human rights activist. He helped develop the Soviet Union's first hydrogen bomb (1953), but later criticized the resumption of nuclear weapons' testing under Nikita KHRUSHCHEV. His treatise "Progress,

ST VINCENT AND THE GRENADINES

AREA: 388sq km (150sq mi)
POPULATION: 111,000
CAPITAL (POPULATION): Kingstown (33,694)
GOVERNMENT: Constitutional monarchy
ETHNIC GROUPS: Of African descent
LANGUAGES: English (official), French patois
RELIGIONS: Protestant 63%, Roman Catholic 12%
GDP PER CAPITA (1994): US$2248

Coexistence and Intellectual Freedom" (1968) called for DÉTENTE with the West and condemned the repression of Soviet dissidents. Sakharov was a founder of the Committee for Human Rights. In 1971 he married fellow activist Yelena Bonner (1923–). Sakharov was awarded the 1975 Nobel Prize for Peace. After denouncing the Soviet invasion of Afghanistan, he was sent into internal exile (1980–86) in Gorky (now Nizhniy Novgorod), w Russia. He was rehabilitated under Mikhail GORBACHEV.

Saladin (1138–93) (Salah ad-din Yusuf ibn Ayyub) Muslim ruler of Egypt, Palestine, Syria and Yemen, founder of the AYYUBID dynasty, b. Iraq. From a leading Kurdish family in the service of NUR-AD-DIN of Syria, he fought in three expeditions to protect the FATIMID dynasty in Egypt from the Crusader states. In 1169 Saladin succeeded his uncle as commander in chief of the Syrian army and was appointed vizier of Egypt. He expelled the Crusaders and overthrew the Shiite Fatimids (1171), returning Egypt to the Sunni ABBASID caliphate. After the death of Nur-ad-din (1171), Saladin sought to unite Egypt, Syria, Yemen and Palestine into a single Muslim empire under his control. After securing Damascus (1174), Aleppo (1183) and Mosul (1186), he proclaimed a JIHAD (holy war) against the Christian Crusaders. He invaded the Kingdom of Jerusalem, crushing the army of GUY OF LUSIGNAN at Hattin and capturing Jerusalem itself in October 1187. In response, Europe launched the Third CRUSADE (1189), led by RICHARD I of England. Richard regained ACRE (1191), but Saladin mounted a brilliant defence and forced the Crusaders to withdraw in 1192, leaving Jerusalem in Muslim hands. Saladin's other great achievement was the restoration of stable government, economic prosperity and Muslim orthodoxy to Egypt which, under his descendants, became the leading power in the Middle East.

Salamis, Battle of (480 BC) First major naval conflict in history, forming part of the PERSIAN WARS (499–479 BC). A Greek fleet of *c.*370 triremes, led by THEMISTOCLES, skilfully lured *c.*800 larger Persian galleys, led by XERXES, into the narrow strait between the island of Salamis and the Greek mainland. Having the advantage of greater manoeuvrability, the Greek fleet sank *c.*300 Persian vessels at the cost of only *c.*40 ships. The Battle deprived Xerxes' army of its sea-borne supplies, and it was defeated the following year at PLATAEA, ending Persia's effort to conquer Greece.

Salazar, António de Oliveira (1889–1970) Portuguese dictator, prime minister (1932–68). He was elected to the Cortes (parliament) in 1921, but resigned to concentrate on teaching at Coimbra University. He returned to politics as finance minister (1928–32) under the military dictatorship of Antonio de Carmona. Given control of the state's finances, Salazar managed to pay off the entire national debt and was promoted to prime minister. He passed a new constitution (1933), which created an authoritarian, corporate "New State". Salazar used the secret police to suppress domestic opposition and employed the army to crush nationalist movements in Portugal's African colonies. Also holding the posts of minister of war (1936–44) and minister of foreign affairs (1936–47), Salazar supported General Francisco FRANCO during the Spanish Civil War (1936–39). Although he presided over moderate economic growth, Salazar left Portugal as one of the poorest nations in Europe. He was replaced by Marcelo CAETANO.

Salem witchcraft trials (1692) Prosecutions of alleged witches in Salem, Massachusetts, United States. A group of young girls claimed to be possessed by the devil after playing at voodoo with a West Indian slave, Tituba. Tituba and three other women were accused of witchcraft and forced into signing confessions. Hysteria took hold of the small town. Many people were arrested and tried by a special court convened by the governor, Sir William Phips. Further accusations followed, 19 people were hanged and hundreds more accused before the hysteria began to dissipate. One of the judges, Samuel Sewall (1652–1730), later admitted he had made erroneous decisions. The episode contributed to the decline of the Puritan ministry in Massachusetts. Arthur Miller's play *The Crucible* (1952) is based on the events in Salem. *See also* MATHER, COTTON; MATHER, INCREASE

Salian Frankish dynasty of the HOLY ROMAN EMPIRE (1024–1125). It was founded by Conrad of Swabia, who was crowned Emperor CONRAD II in 1027, after the death of the last Saxon dynast, HENRY II. Conrad was succeeded by his son, HENRY III (r.1039–56), who created a strong, centralized state. HENRY IV's reign (1056–1106) was marked by the struggle over INVESTITURE with Pope GREGORY VII. HENRY V (r.1106–25) made peace with the papacy before dying childless. *See also* HOHENSTAUFEN

Salic law Law derived from the FRANKS that forbade inheritance of property by or through a female. From the 14th century it was interpreted in France as excluding women from the succession, but it was challenged by Edward III of England, who claimed the French throne through his mother (provoking the HUNDRED YEARS' WAR). It provided support for the adherents of CARLISM in 19th-century Spain, and resulted in the separation of HANOVER, Germany, from Britain in 1837 when Victoria became queen.

Salisbury, Robert Arthur Talbot Gascoyne-Cecil, 3rd Marquess of (1830–1903) British statesman, prime minister (1885–86, 1886–92, 1895–1902). Salisbury entered Parliament as a Conservative in 1853. As Lord Cranborne, he served as secretary of state for India (1866–67) under Lord DERBY. He initially distrusted Derby's successor, Benjamin DISRAELI, but later served under him as secretary of state for India (1874–78) and foreign secretary (1878–80). In the latter post, Salisbury was largely responsible for the diplomatic success at the Congress of BERLIN (1878). After Disraeli's death (1881), Salisbury led Conservative opposition to the government of William GLADSTONE. He headed a caretaker government in 1885 and a minority Conservative administration, dependent on Liberal Unionist support, from 1886. A skilful diplomat, he also held the post of foreign secretary for most of his three terms as prime minister, pursuing a policy of "splendid isolation" that kept Britain out of conflict in Europe. In domestic affairs, his second term witnessed the passage of the Local Government Act (1888) and the establishment of free public education (1891). His main preoccupation, however, was the expansion of the BRITISH EMPIRE in Africa. In 1889 Britain gained possession of what later became the colonies of Northern and Southern Rhodesia (now Zambia and Zimbabwe), and in 1899 Britain seized control of Sudan. The aggressive approach of his colonial secretary, Joseph CHAMBERLAIN, contributed to the outbreak of the Second SOUTH AFRICAN WAR (1899–1902) and an ailing Salisbury relinquished control of the foreign office to Lord LANSDOWNE in 1900. Two years later, Salisbury retired and Arthur BALFOUR became prime minister.

Salisbury, Robert Cecil, 1st Earl of *See* CECIL, ROBERT, 1ST EARL OF SALISBURY

Salish Related groups of Native North Americans of the Pacific Northwest (**Coast** Salish) and the Plateau between the Rocky Mountains and the coastal cordillera (**Interior** Salish). Coast Salish were mainly fishing communities, who lived in permanent wood-built villages in winter and movable lodges during the fishing season. Warfare was frequent and prisoners became slaves. They also held POTLATCH ceremonies. Some Interior Salish lived a similar existence, but the customs of more easterly groups, such as the Flathead, resembled the PLAINS CULTURE.

Sallust (*c.*86–*c.*34 BC) (Gaius Sallustius Crispus) Roman historian. In 52 BC Sallust became tribune of the plebeians, but he was expelled from the Senate in 50 BC. Sallust fought (with mixed success) in the army of Julius CAESAR and became governor of NUMIDIA (roughly modern Algeria). Back in Rome in *c.*44 BC, he was accused of extortion and retired from public life. Sallust's works include *Catiline's War* (43–42 BC), which describes the conspiracy of CATILINE, and *The Jugurthine War* (41–40 BC), a history of the war between the Romans and JUGURTHA of Numidia, in which he ferociously attacked the immorality and incompetence of the Roman ruling class. Although highly subjective accounts of the Roman state, his work greatly influenced LIVY and TACITUS.

Salome (active 1st century AD) Daughter of Herodias and stepdaughter of HEROD ANTIPAS. According to the Gospels of Mark and Matthew, she danced for Herod, who subsequently promised to grant her any wish. Salome asked for the head of JOHN THE BAPTIST, who had condemned her mother's marriage to Herod Antipas, and Herod reluctantly agreed.

SALT *See* STRATEGIC ARMS LIMITATION TALKS

Salvation Army International Christian organization devoted to the propagation of the Gospel and welfare work among urban slums. Its origin was a Methodist mission in Whitechapel, London, England, founded (1865) by William BOOTH. In 1878 it became the Salvation Army, revivalist and pro-temperance in spirit and run on semi-military lines. Its members, themselves mostly working-class, became officers and soldiers, under strict discipline, led by "General" Booth. After Booth's death, leadership of the Army passed first to his son, Bramwell Booth (1856–1929), and then his daughter, Evangeline Booth (1865–1950). From the 1880s it increasingly emphasized social action, such as establishing night shelters and schemes for the jobless. Ultimately, it had branches in nearly 100 countries and its success was reflected in the creation of similar organizations, such as the Church Army and the Volunteers of America. *See also* METHODISM

Samaria (Heb. Shomron) Ancient region and city of central PALESTINE, now part of the WEST BANK. The city was founded (*c.*880 BC) by Omri as the capital of the N kingdom of ISRAEL. The region was conquered (722 BC) by the Assyrians and the city was destroyed. Later rebuilt as Sebaste by HEROD (THE GREAT), the city was a centre of Hellenistic culture. Excavations in the 1900s and 1930s revealed a rich settlement, with traces of the ivory carvings of King AHAB mentioned in the Old Testament.

Samaritans (Kutim) Supposed descendants of the people of SAMARIA who escaped deportation after their kingdom was overrun by the Assyrians in 722 BC. When the JEWS returned from their BABYLONIAN CAPTIVITY, they rejected the Samaritans, who subsequently built their own temple at Nabulus. This enmity forms the basis for Jesus' parable of the good Samaritan. Today, *c.*500 Samaritans remain on the West Bank.

Samarkand (Samarqand) City in the fertile Zeravshan valley, SE Uzbekistan. One of the oldest cities in Asia, it was, as Maracanda, the capital of the Persian province of Sogdiana before it was conquered by ALEXANDER III (THE GREAT) in 329 BC. A vital trading centre on the SILK ROAD, Samarkand flourished under the Arab UMAYYAD caliphs in the 8th century. In 1220 it was destroyed by Genghis Khan, but in 1370 became the capital of the MONGOL empire of TAMERLANE. Ruled by the Uzbeks from the 16th century, it declined along with Central Asian trade. It was captured by the Russians in 1868, and the city flourished as a provincial capital of the Russian empire. Sights include the Gur-e amir mausoleum (*c.*1405) of Tamerlane. Pop. (1990) 370,000.

samizdat (Rus. self-publishing) Underground political writings in the Soviet Union and its satellite states, usually distributed in typewritten form to escape censorship and prosecution. Samizdat began after the death (1953) of Joseph STALIN and increased significantly after the dismissal of Nikita KHRUSHCHEV in 1964. The movement was suppressed by Leonid BREZHNEV in the 1970s, but was resurgent during the 1980s era of GLASNOST under Mikhail GORBACHEV. The collapse of Soviet communism led to greater press freedom and samizdat declined once more.

Samnites Ancient warlike people of Samnium, S Italy, probably descendants of the SABINES. A Samnite confederation fought three wars against Rome between 343 and

SAMOA
AREA: 2831sq km (1093sq mi)
POPULATION: 171,000
CAPITAL (POPULATION): Apia (36,000)
GOVERNMENT: Constitutional monarchy
ETHNIC GROUPS: Samoan (Polynesian) 90%
LANGUAGES: Samoan, English (both official)
RELIGIONS: Christian (Congregationalist 50%, Roman Catholic 20%)
GDP PER CAPITA (1994): US$700

290 BC, which, despite a victory in the Battle of the Claudine Forks (321), ultimately ended in defeat. However, they continued to oppose Rome by assisting its enemies such as PYRRHUS and HANNIBAL. In 82 BC they were finally destroyed by Lucius Cornelius SULLA.

Samoa (formerly Western Samoa) Island republic in the S Pacific Ocean, encompassing the W part of the Samoan archipelago. First settled in *c*.1000, the islands were a cradle of Polynesian culture. Dutch navigator Jacob Roggeveen sighted the islands in 1722, and Louis Antoine de BOUGAINVILLE claimed them for France in 1768. British missionaries arrived in the 1830s, and the population was soon converted to Christianity. The United States, Britain and Germany vied for control of the islands. In 1899 Western Samoa became a German protectorate, while Eastern (American) Samoa was annexed to the United States. In 1914 Western Samoa was seized by New Zealand, who were granted a League of Nations' mandate in 1920. In 1929 several leading nationalists were shot by New Zealand troops during a Mau demonstration. Western Samoa finally gained independence in 1962, although New Zealand continues to handle foreign affairs outside the Pacific zone. In 1997 Western Samoa was renamed Samoa.

Samori Touré (*c*.1830–1900) Mandingo leader, b. Guinea. In 1868 he established an Islamic kingdom in the Kankan region of E Guinea. With military skill and good administration, Samori expanded his kingdom so that by 1882 it encompassed much of the Upper Niger region, stretching from Fouta Djallon, W Guinea, to Bamako, S Mali. This expansion led to conflict with the French, who were keen to build an empire in West Africa. In 1883 the French captured Bamako, and Samori accepted French protection in 1886. Continuing French offensives in the early 1890s forced him to withdraw eastwards, and he established a power base in N Ivory Coast. In 1898 Samori was captured by the French and he died in exile in Gabon.

samurai Member of the élite warrior class in feudal Japan. Beginning as provincial military retainers in the 10th century, the samurai came to form an aristocratic ruling class. During the KAMAKURA (1192–1333) and ASHIKAGA periods (1338–1573), they served the DAIMYO (feudal barons) and conformed to a strict code of conduct, known as BUSHIDO ("the way of the warrior"), bound by honour, loyalty and simple living. In the 16th century HIDEYOSHI restricted the bearing of arms to samurai. Under the TOKUGAWA shogunate, the samurai were transformed into administrators and officials, but maintained their traditional ethic. Samurai were a powerful influence in effecting the MEIJI RESTORATION (1868), but were disappointed by the subsequent direction of the government. Rebellions were suppressed by Japan's new, conscript army, itself an offence to samurai tradition. *See also* OKUBU TOSHIMICHI; SAIGO TAKAMORI

San (Bushmen) Indigenous people of S Africa, related to the KHOIKHOI. They were driven out of most of their traditional hunting grounds by later arrivals, at first Bantu-speakers from the N, then, in the 19th century, Europeans. Some were amalgamated with the Tswana and other Bantu speakers, usually with servile status. Others adapted their hunting-gathering culture to less productive regions, especially the Kalahari Desert where, today, most of the *c*.40,000 surviving San live. At first dismissed as primitives, the San peoples' distinctive cave paintings engaged the attention of Europeans. Further study revealed their highly complex social organization and their possession of abilities hard for more technologically oriented societies to comprehend.

Sana (San'a) Capital and largest city of YEMEN. Situated on a high plateau at *c*.2280m (7500ft), it claims to be the world's oldest city, founded by Shem, eldest son of Noah. It has been the centre of Yemeni culture for *c*.2000 years and its medina is one of the most perfectly preserved in the Arab world. It came under Ottoman Turkish control in the 16th century and remained nominally part of the Ottoman Empire until 1918, when it became independent. The overthrow of the imam in 1962 led to civil war and division, until the united Yemen Arab Republic was created in 1990 with Sana as its capital. Pop. (1990) 500,000.

Sandinista Member of the Sandinista National Liberation Front (FSLN). Founded in 1963, the FSLN took their name from the Nicaraguan revolutionary Augusto César Sandino (1895–1934), murdered by Anastasio SOMOZA. After a long and bloody struggle, the Sandinistas overthrew the Somoza dictatorship in 1979 and Daniel ORTEGA formed a FSLN government. Ortega nationalized Nicaragua's major industries. A right-wing group, the CONTRA, waged a guerrilla war against them, with US support, until free elections were held in 1990. The Contra disbanded and the Sandinistas lost the elections to the National Opposition Union (UNO) coalition, led by Violeta CHAMORRO. They remained politically and militarily influential. *See also* IRAN-CONTRA AFFAIR

San Francisco City and port in W California. In 1776 the Spanish built a presidio (fort) on the N tip of the peninsula between the Pacific and San Francisco Bay, but there was no permanent settlement until 1835. The town (Yerba Buena) was captured (1846) by the United States in the MEXICAN WAR and renamed San Francisco. The GOLD RUSH of 1849–50 rapidly swelled the population, and substanial communities of Chinese, Japanese, Filipinos and other immigrants were established. The centre of the city, close to the San Andreas fault, was virtually destroyed by an earthquake and resulting fire in 1906, but it was quickly rebuilt. Another major earthquake in 1989 did comparatively little damage. The opening of the Panama Canal (1914) brought industrial and commercial expansion. During World War 2, San Francisco was the main port of embarkation for the war in the Pacific and many people migrated to the city to work in war-related industries. During the 1960s the city was the centre of the "flower-power" counter-culture and since the 1970s has been at the heart of the gay-rights movement. San Francisco is a major tourist destination. Pop. (1992) 728,921.

San Francisco Conference (April–June 1945) Meeting of representatives from the United States, Soviet Union, Great Britain, China and the 46 other Allies during WORLD WAR 2, held in California, United States. The Conference, which followed on from proposals for a worldwide organization submitted to the DUMBARTON OAKS CONFERENCE (1944) and the YALTA CONFERENCE (1945), drafted the charter of the UNITED NATIONS (UN) and established the veto powers of the UN Security Council. The charter was signed on 26 June.

San Francisco, Treaty of (8 September 1951) Treaty restoring normal relations between Japan and its enemies in WORLD WAR 2 and ending the post-war occupation of Japan. It was signed by 48 states, including some that had been conquered by Japan and achieved independence since 1945. A Mutual Security Pact authorized the continuing presence of US military bases in Japan.

Sanger, Margaret (1883–1966) US feminist, founder (1916) of the first birth-control clinic in North America, in Brooklyn, New York. Sanger advocated birth control, an expression she coined, to prevent dangerous, illegal abortions, the results of which she had witnessed as a nurse. When her clinic opened, Sanger was arrested, and the ensuing legal wrangles publicized the issue and gained the right of doctors to provide advice on birth control. She also founded (1921) the American Birth Control League and organized the first World Population Conference in 1927.

Sanguinetti, Julio María (1936–) Uruguayan statesman, president (1985–90, 1995–2000). A member of the centre-right Colorado Party, he entered parliament in 1962. As president, Sanguinetti re-established democracy and human and civil rights after a long period of oppression and brutal military autocracy. He took the unpopular step of declaring a general amnesty for the military, eventually approved by a referendum (1989). Sanguinetti failed, however, to deliver economic recovery or to reduce Uruguay's huge burden of debt. In his second term, he introduced electoral reforms to combat political factionalism and took measures to combat unemployment and reduce inflation.

Sanhedrin Ancient Jewish council, the supreme court of justice in Jerusalem during the period of Roman rule in Palestine. It had *c*.70 members, perhaps including both SADDUCEES and PHARISEES, and dealt with religious problems throughout the Jewish world. It also collected taxes and functioned as a civil court. The Sanhedrin probably tried JESUS CHRIST.

San Jacinto, Battle of (21 April 1836) During the TEXAS REVOLUTION, conflict on the San Jacinto River, TEXAS, between *c*.800 Texan forces, led by Samuel HOUSTON, and the Mexican army under Antonio SANTA ANNA. The Battle followed the slaughter of Texans at the ALAMO. The Texan troops defeated the *c*.1500-strong Mexican force and captured Santa Anna. The Battle, which cost *c*.600 Mexican lives and 6 Texans, led to Texas' brief period as an independent republic.

San Juan Hill, Battle of *See* SPANISH-AMERICAN WAR

San Marino World's smallest republic, in the Apennines, NE Italy. According to legend, it was founded in the early 4th century AD. By the 12th century it was a free commune. Its mountainous terrain and the balance of powers in N Italy enabled it to retain independent status, at times under the protection of the papacy or the Duke of Urbino. Under the constitution of 1600, it is governed by an elected council, from which the executive of two captains regent are chosen. It signed a friendship treaty with newly independent Italy in 1862, since regularly renewed.

San Martín, José de (1778–1850) Argentine revolutionary. He fought for Spain in Europe before returning to the Viceroyalty of Río DE LA PLATA (1811) and helping to defeat the Spanish in Argentina (1812). A brilliant strategist, San Martín realized that in order to free Spanish America from colonial rule it was necessary to capture the royalist stronghold of Lima, Peru. San Martín gained the element of surprise by a bold and dramatic crossing of the Andes, capturing Santiago, Chile, in 1817. He refused the governorship of Chile, in favour of Bernardo O'HIGGINS, and continued to pursue his primary objective. With the assistance of Thomas COCHRANE, San Martín built a makeshift Chilean navy, which he used to blockade Lima and transport his army to Pisco. In 1821 Lima fell and Peru declared independence. In 1822 San Martín resigned as protector of Peru in favour of Simón BOLÍVAR and retired to Europe.

San Remo, Conference of (19–26 April 1920) Meeting of WORLD WAR I allies (Belgium, France, Great Britain, Greece, Italy and Japan) at San Remo, NW Italy, to discuss territorial arrangements in the Middle East not settled in the Treaty of VERSAILLES (1919). It discussed the peace terms with Turkey and awarded temporary mandates (later confirmed by the League of Nations) to Britain (Iraq and Palestine) and France (Lebanon and Syria). The Conference resulted in the Treaty of SÈVRES. *See also* LAUSANNE, TREATY OF

sans-culottes (Fr. without knee breeches) Volunteers in the Revolutionary army or, later, extreme democrats during the FRENCH REVOLUTION. The name came from the fashion of the working-classes and petty bourgeoisie,

SAN MARINO
AREA: 61sq km (24sq mi)
POPULATION: 25,000
CAPITAL (POPULATION): San Marino (4251)
GOVERNMENT: Multiparty republic
ETHNIC GROUPS: San Marinese, Italian
LANGUAGES: Italian (official)
RELIGIONS: Roman Catholic 99%
GDP PER CAPITA (1995): US$17,213

S

who wore long trousers rather than the knee breeches of the upper class. They were suppressed after the THERMIDORIAN REACTION (1794). *See also* JACOBINS

San Stefano, Treaty of (3 March 1878) Peace agreement following the defeat of the OTTOMAN EMPIRE in the RUSSO-TURKISH WAR (1877–78). It severely reduced Ottoman power in the Balkans to the advantage of Russia, particularly in creating a large, independent Bulgaria. The Treaty recognized the independence of Romania, Serbia and Montenegro and ceded BESSARABIA to Russia. However, European powers, led by Austria-Hungary and Britain, secured a multilateral treaty at the Congress of BERLIN (1878), which modified the terms and reduced the Bulgarian borders.

Santa Anna, Antonio López de (1794–1876) Mexican general and dictator. He dominated politics in Mexico after helping to overthrow Augustín de ITURBIDE in 1823. Santa Anna became a national hero after helping to defeat Spain's attempt to reconquer Mexico in 1829, and was elected president in 1833. Santa Anna established an autocratic, centralized state. In the TEXAS REVOLUTION (1835–36), he led the Mexican army in a bloody victory at the ALAMO, but was forced into retirement after losing the Battle of SAN JACINTO. Santa Anna regained popularity and power after gallant action against a French raid on Vera Cruz (1838), where he lost a leg. He abandoned the constitution and ruled as a dictator until forced into exile in 1845. Santa Anna regained power at the start of the MEXICAN WAR (1846–48) against the United States, but was defeated by General Winfield SCOTT and once more went into exile. Recalled to power in 1853, he resumed the presidency, but was overthrown in a liberal revolution in 1855. He took refuge in Cuba but was allowed to return to Mexico in 1874, and died in poverty. *See also* JUÁREZ, BENITO PABLO

Santa Fe Trail North American wagon trail from Independence, Missouri, to Santa Fe, New Mexico. It was pioneered (1821) by William Becknell in order to trade silver and furs with newly independent Mexico. The Santa Fe Trail split into three branches west of Dodge City, Kansas, the "Cimmarron Cut-off" being shorter but more exposed to attack from Native Americans. Control of the Trail was one of the factors leading to the United States' seizure of New Mexico in 1848 and, although interrupted by the Civil War, the Trail remained a major route for western settlement and trade until superseded (1880) by the Santa Fe Railroad.

Santander, Francisco de Paula (1792–1840) Colombian statesman, first president (1833–37) of New Granada (now Colombia). He fought alongside Simón BOLÍVAR during the war of independence in Spanish America, and in 1821 he became vice president of the new state of Gran Colombia. Santander served as acting president during Bolívar's absences, but fell out with Bolívar when the latter signalled his intention to keep Venezuela as part of Gran Colombia. Santander was sentenced to death after being accused of complicity in the botched plot (1828) to assassinate Bolívar, but the sentence was commuted to exile due to lack of evidence. He returned after the collapse of Gran Colombia and Bolívar's death (1830). As president, Santander did much to consolidate the new state but dealt harshly with political opponents. His death sparked a civil war.

Santer, Jacques (1937–) Luxembourg statesman, president of the EUROPEAN COMMISSION (1994–99), prime minister (1984–94) of Luxembourg. He was president (1974–82) of the Christian Social People's Party in Luxembourg and served three terms as prime minister. He played a leading role in securing the adoption of the MAASTRICHT TREATY (1992). Santer was a compromise choice to succeed Jacques DELORS as head of the Commission, after British Prime Minister John MAJOR vetoed the selection of Jean-Luc Dehaene. As president, Santer oversaw the creation of a single European currency (the euro), but resigned along with the entire Commission after revelations of nepotism. He was succeeded by Romano PRODI.

Santo Domingo Capital and chief port of the Dominican Republic. Founded in 1496 by Bartholomew Columbus (brother of Christopher COLUMBUS), Santo Domingo is the oldest continuous European settlement in the Americas and the seat of the oldest Roman Catholic archbishopric and university in the Western Hemisphere. It served as capital of Spanish America until the conquest of Mexico and Peru in the 1530s. Santo Domingo has been the capital of the Dominican Republic since independence was first achieved in 1844 and then regained in 1865. The city was renamed Ciudad Trujillo (1936–61) by the Dominican dictator Rafael TRUJILLO. Although vulnerable to hurricanes and earthquakes, it houses more than one-third of the country's population. Pop. (1991) 2,055,000.

Sanusi (Sanusiyah) Islamic Sufi brotherhood, founded (1837) by Muhammad ibn-Ali as-Sanusi (d.1859). It sought a return to the simple and pure faith of early ISLAM and to convert the Bedouin to strict observance of the Koran. Expelled from the Hejaz by the Ottoman Turks, as-Sanusi settled (1843) in CYRENAICA (now NE Libya), which became the stronghold of the Sanusi movement. By 1854 there were *c.*100 *zawiyahs* (religious lodges) scattered throughout North Africa. In the 20th century, the Sanusi became more overtly political, leading resistance to Italian imperialism in Libya and the British occupation of Egypt. When Libya gained independence (1951), as-Sanusi's grandson and head of the Sanusi brotherhood became king as IDRIS I. In 1969 he was overthrown in a military coup led by Colonel QADDAFI. *See also* SUFISM

São Tomé and Príncipe Republic in the Gulf of Guinea, 300km (190mi) off the W coast of Africa. The two small islands of São Tomé and Príncipe were uninhabited when discovered (*c.*1470) by the Portuguese, who established a colony (1485) on São Tomé and brought slaves from the mainland to develop sugar plantations. After the collapse of the sugar industry, Príncipe served as a staging post in the Portuguese SLAVE TRADE to Brazil. Cacao was introduced in 1822, and São Tomé soon became a leading world producer. After a long struggle, the islands gained independence in 1975. The authoritarian presidency (1975–91) of Manuel Pinto da Costa followed a broadly communist agenda. The former prime minister Miguel Trovoada won the country's first democratic elections in 1991. He was briefly deposed by an army coup in 1995.

Saracens Name applied by the ancient Romans to the Arab tribes who threatened their borders. The name later included all Arabs and eventually all Muslims, and was loosely used by medieval Christians to denote their Muslim enemies, especially in the CRUSADES.

Sarajevo Capital of BOSNIA-HERZEGOVINA, on the River Miljacka. It was a flourishing commercial centre under the Ottoman Empire from the late 15th century. The region passed to Austria in 1878, and Sarajevo became a centre of Serb and Bosnian resistance to Austrian rule. On 28 June 1914, the Austrian archduke FRANZ FERDINAND and his wife were assassinated in Sarajevo by a Serb, Gavrilo PRINCIP, an act that led directly to World War 1. In 1991 Bosnia-Herzegovina declared independence from Yugoslavia, and in the ensuing civil war thousands of Bosnian Muslims sought sanctuary in the city from the campaign of "ethnic cleansing" by Bosnian-Serb militias, led by Ratko MLADIĆ. The subsequent siege and bombardment of Sarajevo by Serb forces killed more than 10,500 citizens and almost destroyed the city before the DAYTON PEACE AGREEMENT (1995) brought an end to the conflict. Pop. (1996 est) 350,000.

Saratoga, Battles of (1777) Two decisive conflicts in the AMERICAN REVOLUTION, fought near Saratoga, New York. General John BURGOYNE led *c.*8000 British troops southwards from the St Lawrence River, Canada, capturing Fort TICONDEROGA (6 July), where he left *c.*1000 men to defend the garrison. Burgoyne then crossed the Hudson River, engaging the *c.*12,000-strong American force under Horatio GATES at the **First** Battle of Saratoga (19 September). Burgoyne failed to find a route through the American lines to ALBANY, however, and was forced to camp. In the **Second** Battle of Saratoga (7 October), Burgoyne led *c.*1500 men on a reconnaissance mission, but was forced back by a strong American counter-attack led by Benedict ARNOLD. With supplies exhausted and a depleted force of *c.*5000 men surrounded by an American army numbering more than 17,000, Burgoyne was forced to surrender. The American victory persuaded the French to intervene against Britain.

Sarawak Largest state of MALAYSIA, in NW BORNEO; the capital is Kuching. After the fall of the MAJAPAHIT empire of JAVA in the 15th century, its predominantly Dayak people became subjects of the sultan of BRUNEI. In 1841 Sarawak was ceded to Sir James BROOKE, the first "white raja", after he helped the sultan suppress a rebellion in 1841. It was subsequently recognized as an independent state by the United States and Britain and was ruled by members of the Brooke family until the Japanese occupation (1941–45) in World War 2. In 1946 Sarawak became a British crown colony. Sarawak became part of Malaysia in 1963. Pop. (1990) 1,648,217.

Sardinia Mountainous island of W Italy, 208km (130mi) W of the mainland; the capital is CAGLIARI. Nuraghis (round towers) were built (*c.*1500–1100 BC) by an advanced BRONZE AGE civilization in Sardinia. First settled by Phoenicians in *c.*800 BC, the Carthaginians later built trading towns. Sardinia was seized by the Romans in 238 BC and it remained part of the Roman Empire for the next 700 years. After the fall of the Roman Empire, the island was held by many powers in the Mediterranean region, including the Byzantines and the Saracens. Pisa and Genoa vied for control of Sardinia from the 11th to the 14th century. In 1326 the island was ceded to Aragón, and Spanish hegemony lasted until 1708 when control passed to Austria. In 1720 the Kingdom of SARDINIA came under the rule of the House of SAVOY, who united it with PIEDMONT. In 1861 it became part of the new kingdom of Italy. Pop. (1992) 1,651,902.

Sardinia, Kingdom of (Sardinia-Piedmont) State created (1720) by the House of SAVOY, who joined PIEDMONT with SARDINIA. The kingdom emerged as the strongest of the Italian states and the one least subject to foreign control. Under the leadership of Conte di CAVOUR, it took the lead in the RISORGIMENTO. On the unification of Italy (1861) its king, VICTOR EMMANUEL II, became king of Italy, and the kingdom of Sardinia ceased to exist.

Sardis (Sardes) Ruined capital of ancient LYDIA, close to present-day IZMIR, W Turkey. It was probably the first place where gold and silver coins were minted (*c.*700 BC). Sardis was at its height under CROESUS (r. *c.*560–546 BC), who was overthrown by CYRUS II (THE GREAT) of Persia. As an important entrepôt at the end of the Persian royal road, Sardis subsequently became the W capital of the Persian empire. In 334 BC Sardis was conquered by ALEXANDER III (THE GREAT). After Alexander's death, the empire was divided up and Sardis became part of the SELEUCID kingdom. In 133 BC it was ceded to the Romans. Sardis was the site of one of the Seven Churches of Asia mentioned in the Christian *Book of Revelations*. It was conquered by the Ottoman Turks in the late 14th century and destroyed by TAMERLANE in 1402. The city remained buried until 1958. Archaeological excavations have uncovered remains of the Lydian, Hellenistic and Byzantine city.

Sarekat Islam (Islamic Association) First nationalist political party in Indonesia to gain mass support in the struggle against Dutch colonial rule. It began (1912) as a cooperative organization among traders in batik (traditional Javanese printed cloth), who wished to protect their markets from Chinese competition. Led by Omar Said Tjokroaminoto, Sarekat Islam soon developed into a popular political movement directed towards independence. By 1919 it probably had more than 400,000 members. In 1921 Sarekat Islam split in an ideological battle between

SÃO TOMÉ AND PRÍNCIPE

AREA: 964sq km (372sq mi)
POPULATION: 133,000
CAPITAL (POPULATION): São Tomé (43,420)
GOVERNMENT: Multiparty republic
ETHNIC GROUPS: Mainly descendants of slaves
LANGUAGES: Portuguese (official), Creole
RELIGIONS: Roman Catholic 81%
GDP PER CAPITA (1994): US$120

Islamicists and communists. The communists left to form Sarekat Rakat, which became the mass organization of the Indonesian Communist Party (PKI). *See also* SUKARNO

Sargon I (active 23rd century BC) King of AKKAD (r. *c*.2334–2279 BC), founder of the first Semitic dynasty in MESOPOTAMIA. There is scant historical evidence of Sargon's reign, largely because the capital that he founded, Akkad, was destroyed a century after his death and has yet to be rediscovered. He probably came to the throne after defeating Lugalzaggisi of URUK, who had previously created a unified state in SUMERIA. Sargon conquered all of s Mesopotamia as well as part of N Syria, s Anatolia and ELAM. Trade flourished in his kingdom and commercial links were established with as far-flung places as Crete and the Indus Valley. The earliest known extant map was probably created during his reign. *See also* LAGASH; SUSA

Sargon II (d.705 BC) King of ASSYRIA (721–705 BC), presumed son of TIGLATHPILESER III. He revived and extended the Assyrian empire. Sargon is credited with establishing the first effective imperial administration in history, dividing his kingdom into *c*.70 provinces. He crushed the Aramaean kingdoms, destroying Hamath in 720 BC. Initially defeated in CHALDAEA (720 BC), Assyrian control was restored by 710 BC. In 714 BC Sargon launched a successful campaign against URARTU. Soon after completing his new capital, Dur Sharrukin (now Khorsabad, N Iraq), Sargon was killed in battle against the Cimmerians. He was succeeded by his son SENNACHERIB.

Sarmatians Ancient nomadic people originally from Iran. By the 5th century BC they had migrated to the region between the Urals and the River Don. Skilled equestrians, by the 2nd century BC they had conquered most of the territory of the SCYTHIANS in s Russia. They represented a constant threat to the Roman provinces in the Balkans until the 3rd–4th centuries AD when they were overrun by Goths and Huns. The female Sarmatian infantry may be the source of the Greek legends of the Amazons.

Sarmiento, Domingo Faustino (1811–88) Argentine statesman and writer, president (1868–74). In 1840 he was forced into exile in Chile by the dictatorship of Juan Manuel de ROSAS. His books, such as *Facundo* (1845), criticized the dominance of the GAUCHO in Argentine society. In 1852 Sarmiento returned to Argentina to help overthrow Rosas. As president, he ended the War of the TRIPLE ALLIANCE (1870) with Paraguay in order to concentrate on domestic reforms and strengthen Argentina's liberal and democratic institutions. His major achievement was the creation of primary and secondary state education

Saskatchewan Province of W central Canada; the capital is Regina. Saskatchewan's earliest inhabitants include the Cree, Blackfoot, Assiniboine and Sioux. The first European explorer to visit the region was Henry KELSEY of the HUDSON'S BAY COMPANY in 1691. The first permanent white settlement, a Company fur-trading post, was established in 1774, but development was slow until the completion of the transcontinental Canadian Pacific Railroad in 1885. Louis RIEL led a Métis rebellion (1885) against the encroachment of white settlers. In 1905 Saskatchewan was admitted to the Dominion of Canada and the province flourished as one of the world's leading producers of wheat. It was badly hit by the Great Depression in the early 1930s. Area: 570,110sq km (251,700sq mi). Pop. (1991) 988,928.

S

Sasanian (Sassanid) Ancient Iranian dynasty (AD 224–651). It was founded by ARDASHIR I (r.224–241), who overthrew the PARTHIAN dynasty of the ARSACIDS, and named after his ancestor, Sasan. Ardashir aimed to revive native Iranian traditions, seeking inspiration from the ACHAEMENIDS, and established ZOROASTRIANISM as the state religion. He conquered Armenia and the KUSHAN empire, and gained tribute from the Punjab, India. Ardashir also built a new capital at Gur (now Firuzabad), s Iran. His son and successor, **Shapur I** (r.241–272), further extended the empire in Anatolia and Syria, mainly at the expense of the Roman Empire, and encouraged the growth of MANICHAEISM. The Sasanians placed the various provinces of the empire under Iranian administration. The empire was at its height during the reign (309–79) of SHAPUR II (THE GREAT), who successfully regained MESOPOTAMIA from the Romans. His recapture of Armenia, however, opened up a long and costly conflict with the Romans. Shapur also began the persecution of Christians, but from *c*.485 NESTORIANISM was accepted by the Sasanians. From the end of the 5th century Sasanian rule over Afghanistan was threatened by the White HUNS (Hephthalites). The reign (531–79) of KHUSRAU I (THE JUST) brought much-needed reform of imperial finances and the army. He captured Antioch (now ANTAKYA) from Byzantine Emperor JUSTINIAN I (THE GREAT). KHUSRAU II (THE VICTORIOUS) became king (590–628) with Byzantine assistance but later waged war with them, regaining Antioch (611) and capturing Damascus (613), Jerusalem (614) and Egypt (619). The almost constant conflict with Byzantium and a succession of short-lived kings fatally weakened the Sasanians and facilitated the conquest of the ARABS, who overthrew the last Sasanian king, Yazdegerd III (r.632–51), and established ISLAM as the state religion. Some Zoroastrians subsequently emigrated to India where they are known as PARSIS. The Sasanian palace at CTESIPHON, E central Iraq, dates from the reign of Khusrau I.

Satavahana (Andhra) Hindu dynasty that intermittently commanded the Deccan Plateau between the 1st century and 3rd century AD. It was in almost constant conflict with the rival Ksatrapas dynasty. The Satavahanas first came to prominence under **Satakarni I** (active 1st century AD), but were subsequently forced out of the N Deccan by the Shakas and confined to Andhra Pradesh, SE India. The dynasty was probably at the height of its power under **Gautamiputra Satakarni** (r. *c*.106–130), who not only regained the NW Deccan but also extended the kingdom as far as Rajasthan. The power of the kingdom was based on commerce with Rome. In the 3rd century AD, the kingdom fragmented into local units. The wealth of the Satavahanas is reflected in the Hindu cave temples of the south and the sculptures on the gates to the Buddhist stupas at Sanchi, central India, one of the glories of Indian art.

Sato Eisaku (1901–75) Japanese statesman, prime minister (1964–72). A leading figure in the newly formed Liberal Democratic Party (LDP), he served as minister of finance (1958–60) under his elder brother, KISHI NOBUSUKE. As prime minister, Sato managed the continuing growth of the Japanese economy. In foreign affairs, he restored relations with South Korea (1965) and negotiated (1969) the return of the Ryukyu Islands from the United States. In 1972 the islands were returned to Japan, but Sato was forced to resign after widespread demonstrations against the provision that allowed US bases to remain on Okinawa. He was succeeded by TANAKA KAKUEI. Sato was awarded the 1974 Nobel Prize for Peace for his role in securing the removal of nuclear weapons from the region.

satyagraha *See* GANDHI, "MAHATMA"

Saud, Abdul Aziz ibn (1902–69) King of Saudi Arabia (1953–64), son and successor of IBN SAUD. His fiscal mismanagement and personal extravagance caused a severe financial crisis in 1958 and led to his brother, FAISAL IBN ABDUL AZIZ, taking over all administrative powers. Faisal formally replaced him as king in 1964 and Saud spent the rest of his life in exile. *See also* FAHD IBN ABDUL AZIZ; KHALID

Saudi Arabia *See* country feature

Saul (active 11th century BC) First king of ancient ISRAEL (*c*.1020–*c*.1000 BC). According to the Old Testament of Samuel, he was the son of Kish, a member of the tribe of Benjamin, and was both annointed king by the prophet Samuel and chosen by popular demand after defeating the Ammonites in Gilead. The Israelites decided that they needed to present a united front against their enemies, especially the PHILISTINES, and sought a strong military leader. Saul initially led Israel to a series of victories, but subsequently fell out with Samuel and DAVID. He was killed on Mount Gilboa by the resurgent Philistine forces. Saul was succeeded as king by his arch-rival, David.

Savage, Michael Joseph (1872–1940) New Zealand statesman, prime minister (1935–40), b. Australia. He emigrated to New Zealand in 1907, and became active in the trade union movement. A founder of the Labour Party (1916), Savage became leader in 1933 and led the Party to its first election victory (1935). As prime minister, he was responsible for extensive social and economic reforms, laying the foundations of a welfare state. He died in office and was succeeded as prime minister and Party leader by Peter FRASER.

Savannah City and port on the Savannah River, SE Georgia, United States. It was founded (1733) by James OGLETHORPE. The nation's first orphanage was opened here by George WHITEFIELD in 1738. Savannah served as the colonial capital (1754–82) of British North America and became a major hub for trade, as well as a social and cultural centre. The port flourished on the export of tobacco and cotton. In 1819 the first steamship to cross the Atlantic, the SS *Savannah*, sailed from Savannah to Liverpool, NW England. A vital supply port for the Confederacy during the American CIVIL WAR, Savannah endured a Union blockade for more than two years before falling to General William SHERMAN in December 1864. Pop. (1992) 138,908.

Savimbi, Jonas Malheiro (1934–) Angolan politician, leader of the National Union for the Total Independence of Angola (UNITA). Prominent in the struggle for independence from Portugal, he formed UNITA in 1966. After independence from Portugal (1975), the rival Soviet- and Cuban-backed Popular Movement for the Liberation of Angola (MPLA) emerged as the dominant power. With support from the United States and South Africa, Savimbi launched a guerrilla war against the MPLA from his base in s Angola. In 1991 he signed a peace treaty with President José DOS SANTOS. Savimbi lost the ensuing 1992 elections, and the civil war resumed. In 1993 the US government withdrew its support for Savimbi. The Lusaka Protocol (1994) held out the promise of a permanent cease-fire, but Savimbi refused to participate in the new coalition government and once more civil war raged.

Savonarola, Girolamo (1452–98) Italian religious reformer. A Dominican friar in FLORENCE, his sermons, which included fierce attacks on the corruption and decadence of the clergy and the state of Florence (1485–86), drew large crowds. After the French invasion under CHARLES VIII, which Savonarola prophesied, and the expulsion of the MEDICI from Florence (1494), Savonarola became the spiritual leader of the newly formed republic of Florence. Without holding any specific political office, Savonarola attempted to create a model Christian republic, imposing a strict moral code. The once corrupt Florence became the envy of Italy, and Savonarola's success was eyed with increasing suspicion by Pope ALEXANDER VI and the Duke of Milan, both of whom had joined the HOLY LEAGUE against France. They viewed Savonarola as an obstacle to winning Florence's support. Following continued attacks on the clergy, including references to the corruption in Rome, Alexander suspended Savonarola (1496) and then excommunicated him (1497). Throughout this period the Medici supporters, the Arrabbiati, allied to Alexander, were regaining influence, and a conspiracy to overthrow Savonarola was discovered and three conspirators executed. The Arrabbiati enforced Savonarola's excommunication and in 1498, having ignored the papal bull, he was found guilty of heresy and sedition. Along with two followers, Savonarola was hanged and burned.

Savoy European dynasty, ruling House of SAVOY and PIEDMONT from the 11th century and of Italy, 1861–1946. The dynasty was founded by Humbert the Whitehanded (d. *c*.1047), the first Count of Savoy. His successors, mainly through marriage, enlarged their territory into France, Switzerland and Italy, and were eventually raised to dukes in the 15th century by Emperor SIGISMUND. The House of Savoy fell into decline during the late 15th and early 16th century, and FRANCIS I of France occupied SAVOY in 1536. Emmanuel Philibert (1528–80), 10th Duke of Savoy, regained the duchy in the Treaty of CATEAU-CAMBRÉSIS (1559), and moved the capital to Turin, Piedmont. Although Piedmont was conquered by the French during the War of the SPANISH SUCCESSION (1701–14), ultimately Savoy benefited territorially from the long French-HABSBURG rivalry. Under the Peace of UTRECHT (1713), VICTOR AMADEUS II was elevated to king of SICILY, later exchanging Sicily for SARDINIA in 1720. Having retained its independence and military strength, the House of Savoy was at the forefront of the RISORGIMENTO, after which Italy became a unified kingdom under VICTOR EMMANUEL II

(1861). Victor Emmanuel's successor, UMBERTO I (r.1878–1900), was assassinated and after World War 2 the Italian people voted to abolish the monarchy (1946). VICTOR EMMANUEL III (r.1900–46) abdicated in favour of UMBERTO II, who was forced from the throne in June 1946 after reigning for one month.

Savoy Region of SE France bordering Switzerland and Italy. It was part of the first Burgundian kingdom and the kingdom of Arles and, in the 11th century, became a county, later a duchy, ruled by the House of SAVOY, within the Holy Roman Empire. Its territory enlarged, it became linked with PIEDMONT and, from 1720, SARDINIA. It was occupied by the French (1792–1814) and finally ceded to them by Italy in the Treaty of Turin (1860).

Saxe, Hermann Maurice, Comte de (1696–1750) French marshal, illegitimate son of AUGUSTUS II (THE STRONG) of Poland. He was made Count of Saxony (Fr. Saxe) in 1711. In 1719 his father gave him a German regiment in the French army. A brilliant military strategist, Saxe served with distinction against the Poles in the War of the POLISH SUCCESSION (1733–38). In the War of the AUSTRIAN SUCCESSION (1740–48), he captured Prague (1741) but his invasion of Britain was thwarted by a storm (1744). Saxe won a spectacular victory over the Austrians at the Battle of FONTENOY (1745) and further victories secured French control of the Austrian Netherlands. He wrote a classic study of the art of war, *Mes Rêveries* (1757).

Saxe-Coburg-Gotha German ducal house that became the ruling dynasty of SAXONY. As a result of the marriage of Prince ALBERT, younger son of the Duke of Saxe-Coburg-Gotha, to Queen VICTORIA in 1840, it became the name of the English royal house (1901–17), until changed to Windsor due to anti-German feeling during World War 1.

Saxons Germanic people who inhabited the S Jutland Peninsula of N Germany in the 2nd century AD. During the 3rd and 4th centuries they moved S, coming into conflict with Roman-held territory. By the 5th century, Saxons had settled much of NW Germany, N Gaul and had, with the ANGLES and JUTES, invaded Britain. In Germany they were attacked by PEPIN III (THE SHORT) and eventually subdued by Pepin's son CHARLEMAGNE after a long and brutal conflict (772–804). During the 9th century a Saxon duchy was founded under Frankish rule, out of which emerged, during the 10th century, a dynasty of German kings. In Britain they are popularly known with other Germanic immigrants as ANGLO-SAXONS, or English.

Saxony Federal state and historic kingdom in Germany. Historically, the name applied to different regions within Germany. Originally it was the region between the Rhine and Elbe rivers and between Jutland and Thuringia, roughly equivalent to the present state of **Lower** Saxony (capital: HANOVER). **Upper** Saxony occupied roughly the same area as the current state of Saxony (capital: DRESDEN) plus Saxony-Anhalt (capital: Magdeburg). The original SAXONS were conquered by CHARLEMAGNE (804). When the Frankish empire broke up a duchy of Saxony emerged, ruled by the German kings who, beginning with OTTO I, became Holy Roman emperors. Saxons led the medieval eastward expansion of the Germans, but the duchy was permanently split up in 1180. The new, smaller duchy of Saxony was centred on the River Oder with its capital at WITTENBERG. It was enlarged by the addition of other lands of the ruling Wettin dynasty, but was later divided between two branches of the family to form the electorate and the duchy. Ducal Saxony eventually broke up into small states, but the electorate continued as a considerable

SAUDI ARABIA

AREA: 2,149,690sq km (829,995sq mi)
POPULATION: 15,922,000
CAPITAL (POPULATION): Riyadh (1,500,000)
GOVERNMENT: Absolute monarchy
ETHNIC GROUPS: Arab (Saudi 82%, Yemeni 10%, other Arab 3%)
LANGUAGES: Arabic (official)
RELIGIONS: Islam 99% (almost exclusively Sunni), Christianity 1%
GDP PER CAPITA (1994): US$6977

Arabic kingdom on the Arabian Peninsula, SW Asia. MECCA, situated in the HEJAZ region, is the holiest place in ISLAM. It was the birthplace of the Prophet MUHAMMAD in AD 570 and is the site of the KAABA. In the 18th century, the WAHHABI (a strict Islamic sect) gained the allegiance of the Saud family, who formed an independent state in Nejd. With the support of the Bedouin, the Wahhabi rapidly conquered most of the Arabian Peninsula. In the 1810s the region was conquered by Turkey.

IBN SAUD laid the foundations of the modern state of Saudi Arabia. In 1902 he captured Riyadh and by 1906 had taken the whole of the Nejd. In 1913 the Turkish province of Al Hasa also fell. In 1920 Ibn Saud captured the Asir, and by 1925 he had conquered the Hejaz. In 1932 the territories were combined to form the kingdom of Saudi Arabia. Ibn Saud became king, ruling in accordance with the SHARIA of Wahhabi Islam.

Oil was discovered in 1936 by the US company Arabian Standard Oil, which in 1944 became the Arabian American Oil Company (ARAMCO). Saudi Arabia was recognized as having the largest oil reserves in the world. In 1953 Ibn Saud died and was succeeded by his eldest son, King SAUD, who ruled with the aid of Crown Prince FAISAL. Saud's concern at the growing power of Egypt under General NASSER was heightened by the overthrow of the Yemeni royal family by pro-Nasser republican forces. Saud sent troops to YEMEN to aid the royalists. In 1964 Saud was overthrown, and Faisal became king. In 1970 Saudi troops were withdrawn from Yemen.

Following the withdrawal of British troops from the Gulf in 1971, Faisal supported the creation of the UNITED ARAB EMIRATES (UAE) in the Gulf's southern coastal region. He also sought to increase national ownership of Saudi's oil wealth, and in 1974 Saudi Arabia agreed to a 60% share in ARAMCO. Meanwhile, the minister for petroleum and natural resources, Sheikh Ahmad Yemani, led the ORGANIZATION OF PETROLEUM EXPORTING COUNTRIES (OPEC) in controlling oil prices to the advantage of the oil-producers.

In 1975 Faisal was assassinated by his nephew, and Crown Prince KHALID became king. Khalid's conservativism was challenged by the growth of Islamic fundamentalism, especially in Iran. In 1979 Shiite fundamentalists captured the Great Mosque in Mecca. The rebellion was brutally suppressed. Saudi Arabia's support for Iraq in the IRAN-IRAQ WAR (1980–88) led to Iranian attacks on Saudi shipping. In 1982 Khalid died and was succeeded by Crown Prince FAHD. In 1990 more than 1400 pilgrims died in a stampede during the HAJJ. When Iraq invaded Kuwait in 1990, Fahd invited coalition forces to protect Saudi against possible Iraqi aggression. Saudi air and land forces played a significant role in the Allied victory in the GULF WAR (1991). In 1996 Fahd suffered a stroke and control of government shifted to the crown prince, Fahd's half-brother Abdullah. In the same year, the council's president ruled out elections on Islamic grounds. Saudi Arabia has no formal constitution. It attracts much international criticism for human rights abuses, especially for its state executions and subjugation of women and minorities.

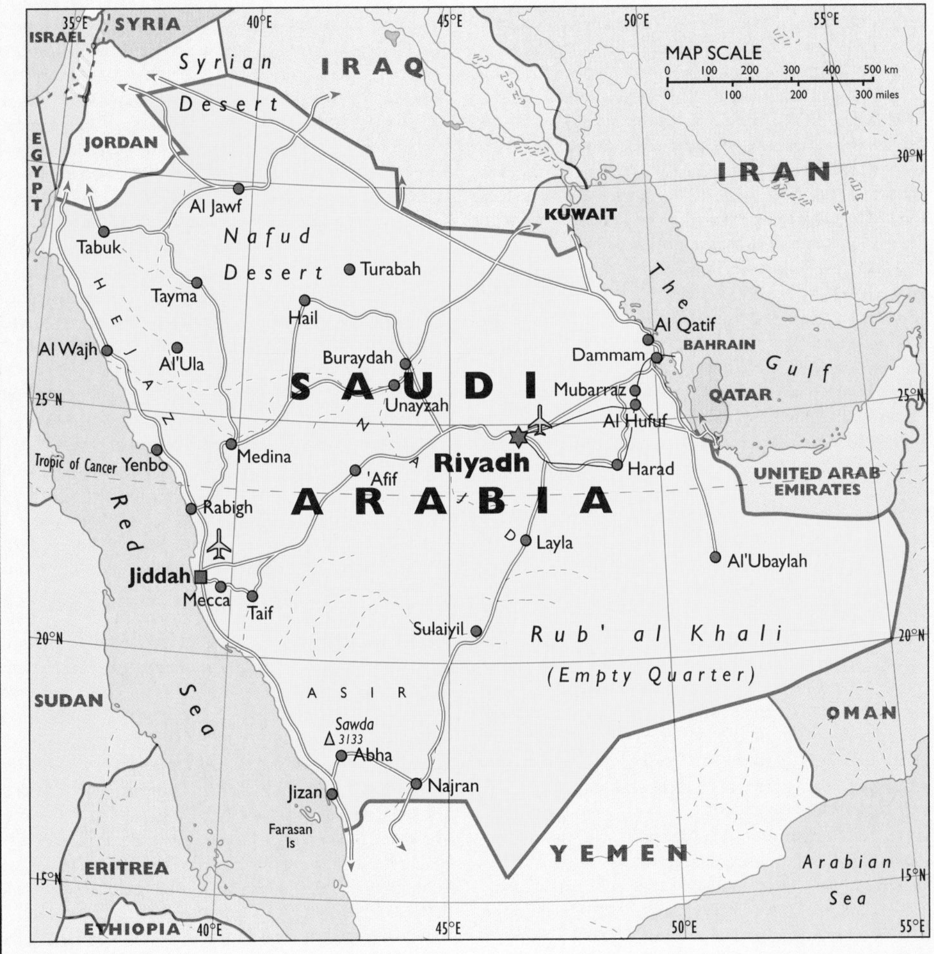

power in Northern Europe, its electors also ruling Poland in the 18th century. It became a kingdom in 1806. In 1815 the N part became a province of PRUSSIA. The entire kingdom was incorporated into the German Empire (1871) and the Weimar Republic (1918). It was included in Soviet-dominated East Germany from 1945 until the reunification of Germany in 1990. Pop. (1993 est.) 4,608,000.

scalawag Abusive name for the white Southerners in the United States who supported RECONSTRUCTION after the American CIVIL WAR. They cooperated, sometimes for selfish reasons, with the CARPETBAGGERS from the North in effecting reforms that were resented by most white Southerners. When the Democratic Party regained dominance in the South, their influence diminished.

Scapa Flow Naval anchorage in the Orkney Islands, off N Scotland. Used as a British naval base in both World Wars, Scapa Flow commands the passage between the North Sea and the Atlantic. The German High Seas fleet was interned here after World War 1, and scuttled (1919) at the order of Admiral von Reuter in protest against disarmament provisions in the Treaty of VERSAILLES. In October 1939 a German U-boat penetrated the harbour undetected and sank the British battleship HMS *Royal Oak*, killing 833 sailors.

Scargill, Arthur (1938–) British UNION leader. Scargill, a miner at the age of 18, was a member (1955–62) of the Young Communist League before joining the Labour Party. He served (1981–) as president of the National Union of Mineworkers (NUM). Scargill's opposition to Margaret THATCHER's programme of pit closures and anti-union legislation led to a bitter miners' strike (1984–85), which ended in victory for the Conservative government and split the miners' movement. In 1996 Scargill broke away from the Labour Party to form the Socialist Labour Party (SLP).

Scharnhorst, Gerhard Johann David von (1755–1813) Prussian general. He fought for the Hanoverian army in Belgium during the early stages of the FRENCH REVOLUTIONARY WARS. Scharnhorst and Gebhard von BLÜCHER were captured by the French at the Battle of JENA (1806). Released in an exchange of prisoners, Scharnhorst and August von GNEISENAU were responsible for the subsequent reform of the Prussian army, which created a highly trained reserve force in order to circumvent the Treaty of TILSIT (1807). He went into retirement when Prussia allied with France (1811–12) against Russia, but re-emerged as chief of staff to Blücher when war with France was renewed. Scharnhorst was fatally wounded at the Battle of LÜTZEN (1813).

Scheer, Reinhard (1863–1928) German admiral. A submarine expert, he was chief of staff to the High Seas fleet from 1910. Appointed commander (1916) during World War 1, he introduced a more aggressive strategy, risking confrontation with the British Grand Fleet at the Battle of JUTLAND (1916). Although Scheer failed in his attempt to divide and destroy the British fleet, he managed to escape, brilliantly saving the High Seas fleet and, on the basis of fewer losses, claiming a victory. Following Jutland, however, Scheer did not go to sea again, and the enforced idleness of his men contributed to the mutiny in the fleet that broke out at Kiel (1918).

Schenck v. United States (1919) Case in the US Supreme Court in which Charles Schenck, general secretary of the Socialist Party of the United States, appealed against conviction for inciting mutiny in the armed forces during World War 1. The defence cited the First Amendment to the Constitution, which protected freedom of speech. Delivering judgment, Justice Oliver Wendell HOLMES formulated the "clear and present danger" test, declaring that speech was not protected if it was likely to result in illegal action.

schism Split or division within a church, sect or other religious organization. It refers in particular to divisions within the medieval Christian Church. The most significant was the split between the Eastern, or ORTHODOX CHURCH, and the Western, or ROMAN CATHOLIC CHURCH, which after a long period of deteriorating relations, became entirely separate in 1054. The period of rival popes in 1378–1417 is called the GREAT SCHISM.

Schleswig-Holstein Federal state in N Germany and historic region on the Jutland Peninsula; the capital is Kiel. The River Eider divides Schleswig and Holstein. Historically, the duchy of Schleswig owed allegiance to the king of Denmark, while the county of Holstein was allied with the Holy Roman Empire, but the two were united under CHRISTIAN I of Denmark in 1460. In 1474 Holstein was promoted to the status of a duchy of the Holy Roman Empire. At the Congress of VIENNA (1814), Holstein was made a duchy of the Austrian-led GERMAN CONFEDERATION, but remained nominally under Danish rule. In 1848, with support from PRUSSIA, the German population of Schleswig-Holstein rebelled. The ensuing war between Denmark and Prussia (1848–50) restored Danish control. In 1863 CHRISTIAN IX subsumed the region into the state of Denmark, precipitating war with Austria and Prussia. The Danes were defeated (1864) and Schleswig passed to Prussia and Holstein to Austria. Otto von BISMARCK then engineered the AUSTRO-PRUSSIAN WAR (1866), which resulted in Prussian annexation of both duchies. They remained German thereafter although, after a referendum in 1920, the mainly Danish part of N Schleswig was returned to Denmark. Pop. (1993 est.) 2,695,000.

Schlieffen Plan German war strategy devised by Alfred von Schlieffen (1833–1913), chief of staff (1891–1905). It was designed for a possible war against France and Russia. An all-out attack in the W would rapidly defeat the French, enabling Germany to transfer its full force to the E against Russia before Russia could mobilize. A modified version was put into effect by Graf von MOLTKE in 1914 and failed. France (supported by Britain) was not defeated, and Russian mobilization was faster than expected.

Schmalkaldic League Alliance of German Protestant states within the HOLY ROMAN EMPIRE, founded (1531) in the town of Schmalkalden, central Germany, to protect LUTHERANISM against the Roman Catholic Emperor CHARLES V. The League's leaders were PHILIP OF HESSE and John Frederick I of Saxony. Initially, Charles was too distracted by events elsewhere to suppress the League, however, war between the Empire and the League eventually broke out in 1546 and the League was decisively defeated by the Duke of ALBA at Mühlberg (1547).

Schmidt, Helmut (1918–) German statesman, chancellor of West Germany (1974–82). He was awarded the Iron Cross during World War 2. Schmidt was elected to the Bundestag in 1953 and became vice chairman of the SOCIAL DEMOCRATIC PARTY (SPD) in 1968. He served as minister of defence (1969–72) and minister of finance (1972–74) under Willy BRANDT, and became chancellor after Brandt resigned. Schmidt continued Brandt's policy of OSTPOLITIK (improving relations with the communist East), while working to strengthen the EUROPEAN COMMUNITY. Re-elected in 1976 and 1980, his failure to implement cuts in public expenditure led the Free Democratic Party (FDP) to withdraw from the coalition in 1982. He was succeeded as chancellor by Helmut KOHL, leader of the CHRISTIAN DEMOCRATIC UNION (CDU).

scholasticism Educational and philosophical method, dominant in medieval European universities in the 12th and 13th centuries. It was a very formal, systematic method of inquiry, which attempted to join faith with reason, Christian theology with classical philosophy. ARISTOTLE, whose works were translated into Latin by BOETHIUS, and Saint AUGUSTINE were powerful influences. Although intellectually formidable in the hands of scholars such as Saint Thomas AQUINAS and ALBERTUS MAGNUS, among lesser scholars the scholastic method tended to degenerate into arid argument over insignificant detail. Towards the end of the Middle Ages, scholasticism became less significant, particularly following the formal logical works of William of OCCAM, some of which argued that faith and reason could not be unified. *See also* ABÉLARD, PIERRE; AVERROËS

Schröder, Gerhard (1944–) German statesman, chancellor (1998–). He entered parliament in 1980 as a member of the SOCIAL DEMOCRATIC PARTY (SPD). As premier (1990–98) of the state of Lower Saxony, Schröder built a reputation for pragmatic and business-friendly politics. In 1998 he defeated party chairman Oskar Lafontaine to gain the SPD nomination for chancellor. Schröder won the ensuing election against the incumbent chancellor, Helmut KOHL, and formed a coalition government with the German GREEN PARTY. As chancellor, Schröder joined Germany to the European single currency (the euro) and presided over a period of economic recovery.

Schuman, Robert (1886–1963) French statesman, premier (1947–48) and foreign minister (1948–52). Schuman was an keen supporter of a federal Europe. His proposal, the **Schuman Plan** (1950), for a single authority to control the production of coal and steel in Europe, was realized with the creation of the European Coal and Steel Community (ECSC) in 1952. The ECSC was the first step in the creation of the European Economic Community (EEC). *See also* EUROPEAN UNION (EU)

Schuschnigg, Kurt von (1897–1977) Austrian statesman, chancellor (1934–38). He served as minister of justice (1932) and minister of education (1933) under Engelbert DOLLFUSS, succeeding Dollfuss as chancellor after his assassination. Schuschnigg tried to resist pressure for ANSCHLUSS (union) with Germany from Adolf HITLER, but conceded to greater powers for Austrian Nazis. His planned referendum on the issue of *Anschluss* was squashed by the German invasion of Austria (March 1938). Schuschnigg was forced to resign in favour of Arthur SEYSS-INQUART and was imprisoned (1938–45) by the Nazis.

Schuyler, Philip John (1733–1804) American Revolutionary soldier. He fought (1755–60) in the FRENCH AND INDIAN WAR and was a delegate to the Second CONTINENTAL CONGRESS (1775–77). As major general of the northern department during the AMERICAN REVOLUTION, Schuyler organized the Québec campaign (1775–76), but after the fall of TICONDEROGA (1777) was replaced by Horatio GATES. He demanded a court-martial, which cleared him of negligence, but he resigned from the army in 1779. He later played an important part in US politics, as an ally of his son-in-law, Alexander HAMILTON, and as US senator from New York (1789–91, 1797–98). *See also* BURR, AARON; WASHINGTON, GEORGE

Schwarzenberg, Felix, Fürst zu (1800–52) Austrian statesman, prime minister (1848–52), nephew of Fürst zu SCHWARZENBERG. He fought under Graf RADETZKY against the REVOLUTION OF 1848 in Italy. Schwarzenberg was chosen as prime minister as revolutionary fervour swept Austria. He immediately persuaded the enfeebled emperor FERDINAND (THE BENIGN) to abdicate in favour of FRANZ JOSEPH. Schwarzenberg dismissed the liberal demands of the constitutional convention and created a centralized, authoritarian state. He defeated a Hungarian rebellion, led by Lajos KOSSUTH, with Russian aid (1849) and restored HABSBURG authority in N Italy. Although Schwarzenberg frustrated PRUSSIA's expansion in Germany, he failed to bring the whole of the Habsburg empire into the German ZOLLVEREIN (customs union).

Schwarzenberg, Karl Philipp, Fürst zu (1771–1820) Austrian field marshal and diplomat. He fought for the Austrian army in the FRENCH REVOLUTIONARY WARS and emerged with credit from the defeat at ULM (1805). Schwarzenberg was given a field command in the ensuing NAPOLEONIC WARS and distinguished himself in a further Austrian defeat at WAGRAM (1809). As ambassador to France (1809–12), he negotiated the marriage between MARIE LOUISE, daughter of Emperor FRANCIS I, and NAPOLEON I. Schwarzenberg led the Austrian troops of Napoleon's army in the fateful invasion of Russia (1812), skilfully arranging their tactical retreat. Schwarzenberg promoted Austria's rejoining of the coalition against France, and was commander in chief of the victorious allied armies at the Battle of LEIPZIG (1813). *See also* BLÜCHER, GEBHARD LEBERECHT VON

Schwarzkopf, H. Norman (1934–) US general. He fought in the Vietnam War and was deputy commander of the US forces that invaded Grenada in 1983. As supreme commander of the Allied forces in the GULF WAR (1991), he liberated KUWAIT from Iraqi occupation. After retiring from the army, he published his memoirs, *It Doesn't Take a Hero* (1992).

scientific revolution Era of rapid scientific advance, particularly in mathematics and cosmology, and the rise of scientific method in early modern Europe. It was at its height in the late 17th century, the age of Isaac NEWTON, although its beginning can be traced to the mid-16th century and, in particular, to the publication of Nicolas COPERNICUS' book *On the Revolutions of the Heavenly Spheres* (1543), which attempted to explain the universe by reason and mathematics. *See also* ENLIGHTENMENT

scientific socialism Phrase used by Karl MARX and Friedrich ENGELS to distinguish their form of SOCIALISM, supposedly founded on objective historical analysis, from the utopian socialism of reformers such as Robert OWEN and Claude SAINT-SIMON. *See also* UTOPIANISM

Scipio Africanus (the Elder) (236–*c*.183 BC) (Publius Cornelius Scipio) Roman general. At the start of the Second PUNIC WAR (218–201 BC), he served as military tribune in the crushing defeat of the Romans by HANNIBAL of CARTHAGE at the Battle of CANNAE (216 BC). In 210 BC Scipio was given the opportunity to avenge his father's death (211 BC) at the hands of the Carthaginians in Spain. He led a brilliant and unconventional campaign, capturing HASDRUBAL's headquarters at Carthago Nova (now Cartagena, SE Spain) in 209 BC, and securing Roman control of Spain with victory at the Battle of Ilipa (206 BC). Elected consul in 205 BC, Scipio invaded Africa (204) with a *c*.35,000-strong army. His defeat of Hannibal at the Battle of ZAMA (202 BC) brought the Second Punic War to an end, and earned Scipio the honorary surname Africanus. Scipio was appointed censor in 199 BC. He helped defeat ANTIOCHUS III of Syria in Greece, but was later accused of corruption by Cato (the Elder) and forced to retire in 184 BC. Scipio was a supporter of Hellenistic culture in Rome. His achievements were noted by POLYBIUS and LIVY.

Scipio Africanus (the Younger) (*c*.185–129 BC) (Publius Cornelius Scipio Aemilianus) Roman general, adopted grandson of SCIPIO AFRICANUS (THE ELDER). He fought in the Third MACEDONIAN WAR (171–168 BC) against PERSEUS and subsequently befriended the historian POLYBIUS. At the start of the Third PUNIC WAR (149–146 BC), Scipio saved the Roman forces from several potentially devastating defeats and organized the division of the lands of MASINISSA of NUMIDIA. In 147 BC he was made consul and given command of the army in Africa. He captured and burned CARTHAGE in 146 BC. He was hailed as the second Africanus and elected as censor (142 BC). In 134 BC Scipio was elected as consul for a second time and appointed commander of the army in Spain. He besieged the Celtiberian capital of NUMANTIA for eight months, starving it into submission (133 BC). During Scipio's absence, his cousin and brother-in-law Tiberius GRACCHUS launched a revolutionary programme of land reforms. Scipio died in mysterious circumstances the night before he was due to make a speech against the agrarian reforms in the Senate.

SCLC *See* SOUTHERN CHRISTIAN LEADERSHIP CONFERENCE

Scopes Trial (10–21 July 1925) US legal case in which John Scopes, a science teacher in Dayton, Tennessee, was arrested for teaching Charles DARWIN's theory of evolution, forbidden under state law. Scopes received support from the AMERICAN CIVIL LIBERTIES UNION (ACLU). The Trial turned into a public contest between Christian Fundamentalists, who believed in the literal interpretation of the Bible, and those who accepted evolution. The prosecution was led by William Jennings BRYAN, a former presidential candidate, and the defence by Clarence DARROW, a famous criminal lawyer. Scopes was convicted and fined US$100. The verdict was overturned on appeal, although the Tennessee Supreme Court upheld the state law against evolution. The law was repealed in 1967.

Scotland Northern part of the main island of Great Britain, and a constituent member of the UNITED KINGDOM of Great Britain and Northern Ireland; the capital is EDINBURGH. The largest city is GLASGOW.

Archaeologists have unearthed evidence of human settlement in W Scotland dating back to 3000 BC. Skara Brae in the Orkneys is one of the best-preserved Stone Age villages in Europe (*c*.2000–1500 BC). From 1800 BC the Beaker culture migrated to E Scotland from Northern Europe. AGRICOLA, Roman governor of Britain (AD 77–84), attempted to subdue the native tribes, but the Romans later built the defensive structures of HADRIAN'S WALL (*c*.136) and the ANTONINE WALL (*c*.142), which marked the N frontier of Roman Britain. From the 3rd century, the Roman colonies were almost constantly beset by raids from the PICTS, who occupied the region N of the River Forth. Also in the 3rd century, the Scots began to migrate from N Ireland, founding settlements in what is now Argyll, W Scotland. In the early 7th century, the Britons, who had built colonies in S Scotland from the 1st century BC, lost control of SE Scotland to the ANGLES, who created the kingdom of NORTHUMBRIA.

Saint Ninian probably introduced Christianity to SW Scotland in the late 4th century, but it was Saint COLUMBA (d.597) who was really responsible for the conversion of Scotland (*see also* CELTS). By the mid-9th century, the northern and western isles of Scotland had been conquered by the VIKINGS. Meanwhile, in AD 843 KENNETH I had united the lands of the Picts and the Scots. In *c*.1016 MALCOLM II gained Lothian, E Scotland, and his son, DUNCAN I, later added the kingdom of Strathclyde. In *c*.1040 Duncan was killed by MACBETH, who was himself overthrown by MALCOLM III in 1057. Malcolm's second marriage, to MARGARET, began a period of SAXON influence in Scotland. The reign (1124–53) of their son, DAVID I, saw the extension of royal power in Scotland and the beginnings of the FEUDAL SYSTEM. In 1174 WILLIAM I (THE LION) was captured by the English and forced to recognize the sovereignty of HENRY II OF England.

In 1189 RICHARD I acknowledged the independence of Scotland. ALEXANDER III (r.1249–86) re-established security and prosperity to the realm. His death prompted EDWARD I of England to claim the throne of Scotland through his intended marriage to MARGARET OF NORWAY, thus beginning a centuries-long enmity between England and Scotland (in alliance with France). Edward defeated John BALLIOL, but William WALLACE launched a Scottish revolt. ROBERT I (THE BRUCE) defeated the English at the Battle of BANNOCKBURN (1314), and forced EDWARD III of England to recognize Scottish independence in 1328. After DAVID II lost the Battle of HALIDON HILL (1333), Berwick remained in English lands, except for the period 1462–82. In the 15th century, the STUART kings were dominated by the nobility, especially the Douglases.

In a disastrous invasion of England, JAMES IV and many Scottish nobles were killed at the Battle of FLODDEN (1513). In 1538 JAMES V cemented the "auld alliance" with France by marrying the Catholic MARY OF GUISE. The Protestant REFORMATION quickly took root in Scotland via the preaching of John KNOX. When MARY, QUEEN OF SCOTS, assumed the throne in 1561, England supported the Scottish Protestants, and France backed the Catholics. In 1567 the Protestant faction forced Mary to abdicate and her son, James VI, assumed the throne. In 1601 he was crowned JAMES I of England, thereby uniting the English and Scottish thrones.

The Scots opposed CHARLES I in the BISHOPS' WARS (1639–40) and at the start of the English CIVIL WAR, but Charles' concessions to PRESBYTERIANISM won the support of the COVENANTERS, who were subsequently defeated by Oliver CROMWELL at the Battle of PRESTON (1648). The GLORIOUS REVOLUTION (1688) led to the re-establishment of Presbyterianism as the CHURCH OF SCOTLAND. The massacre of the Macdonald clan by WILLIAM III at GLENCOE (1692), however, tarnished enthusiasm for his rule, and the JACOBITE agitation prompted the constitutional joining of the two crowns in the Act of UNION (1707). The Jacobite insurgency was finally suppressed with the defeat of the Highlanders, led by Charles Edward STUART, at the Battle of CULLODEN (1746). (*See* UNITED KINGDOM for subsequent history.) A 1979 referendum for a separate Scottish parliament was defeated, but in 1997 a referendum voted in favour of devolution and a Scottish assembly was convened in July 1999. Area: 77,167sq km (29,797sq mi). Pop. (1991) 4,998,567.

Scots Inhabitants of SCOTLAND, originally a Gaelic-speaking, Celtic people from ULSTER. Their raids on the W coast of Roman Britain from the 3rd to the 5th century failed to result in settlement, but in the 5th century they established the kingdom of Dalriada in what is now Argyll, W Scotland, later merging with the PICTS to form a kingdom that included much of modern Scotland.

Scott, James, Duke of Monmouth See MONMOUTH, JAMES SCOTT, DUKE OF

Scott, Robert Falcon (1868–1912) British explorer. A naval officer, Scott was appointed to lead an expedition (1901–04), in the *Discovery*, to the Antarctic. With Ernest SHACKLETON and Edward Wilson (1872–1912), Scott broke the farthest-south record by more than 320km (200mi). Scott's second expedition (1910–12), in the *Terra Nova*, developed into a race for the South Pole against a Norwegian team led by Roald AMUNDSEN. Scott's party reached the Pole (18 January 1912) to find Amundsen had beaten them by a month. Trapped by bad weather and running out of food supplies on the return journey, Captain Oates (1880–1912) sacrificed his own life by crawling out in a blizzard but the three remaining members of the expedition, including Scott, died 12 days later just 11 miles from their base camp.

Scott, Winfield (1786–1866) US general. At the start of the WAR OF 1812, Scott was captured in the Battle of QUEENSTON HEIGHTS (1812) but, after his release, led the US forces to victory at Chippewa and Lundy's Lane (both July 1814) and was hailed as a national hero. He directed the removal of the CHEROKEE from Indian Territory in the so-called "TRAIL OF TEARS" (1838). In 1841 he became general-in-chief of the US Army. When General Zachary TAYLOR seemed to be making little advance in the MEXICAN WAR (1846–48), Scott launched an amphibious invasion of Mexico. He captured Veracruz (March 1847) with almost no casualties, and marched on MEXICO CITY, which fell in September. In 1852 Scott gained the WHIG PARTY nomination for president but, with the Party split over slavery, lost the election to Franklin PIERCE. At the start of the American CIVIL WAR (1861–65), Scott proposed the "Anaconda Plan", which sought to squeeze the Confederacy into submission. Although the Plan was initially derided, it later formed the broad strategy that brought victory for the Union. In 1862 Scott retired in favour of George MCCLELLAN.

Scottish National Party (SNP) Scottish political organization whose major aim is Scottish independence, founded in 1928. The SNP grew out of the Scottish Home Rule Association, formed in 1886, and won its first seat in Parliament in 1945. Its support increased in the 1970s and 1980s, at the expense, chiefly, of the Conservative Party under Margaret THATCHER. It won six seats in the 1997 election under the leadership of Alex Salmond (1954–), and supported the Labour government's proposal for a Scottish assembly, although one with limited powers.

Scythians Nomadic people of Iranian origin, who migrated from the Altai Mountains of central Asia to S Russia from the 8th century BC. Much of our knowledge of the Scythians derives from HERODOTUS. Famed as powerful warriors and skilled equestrians, their expansion in the 7th century BC was achieved largely at the expense of the Cimmerians. In 625 BC the Scythians were expelled from Anatolia by the MEDES. Pressure from the SARMATIANS confined them to Crimea (*c*.300 BC), and their culture disappeared in the 2nd century AD. In Crimea and S Russia, archaeologists have uncovered elaborate underground tombs of Scythian kings, which contain evidence of great wealth.

SDLP Abbreviation of SOCIAL DEMOCRATIC AND LABOUR PARTY

SDP Abbreviation of SOCIAL DEMOCRATIC PARTY

Seaga, Edward (1930–) Jamaican statesman, prime minister (1980–89), b. United States. In 1959 he was nominated to the Legislative Council by Sir Alexander BUSTAMENTE. In 1962 Seaga helped draft Jamaica's constitution and was elected to Parliament. He served as minister of development and social welfare (1962–67) and minister of finance and planning (1967–72). He was elected leader of the Jamaica Labour Party (JLP) in 1974, defeating the incumbent prime minister, Michael MANLEY, in the 1980 elections. He also acted as minister of finance and planning (1980–89). Seaga broke off diplomatic links with Cuba, fostering closer ties with the United States. Re-elected in 1983, his financial reforms failed to boost the

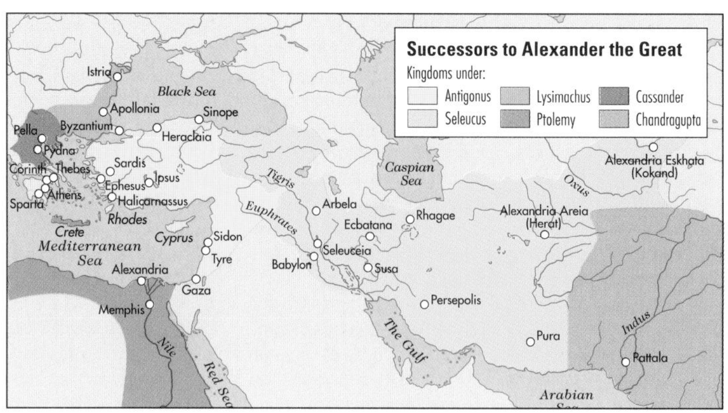

► **Seleucids** Following the death of Alexander the Great (323 BC), a power struggle ensued between his generals: Antigonus of Phrygia, Seleucus of Babylonia, Ptolemy of Egypt and Antipatros (in charge of Macedonia and Greece). Alexander's two sons and heirs were murdered, after which the various successors proclaimed themselves kings. Seleucus gained control of the major cities of Anatolia, providing the foundation for Seleucid domination of the Middle East.

economy, which was badly affected by hurricanes in 1981 and 1988, and he lost the 1989 elections to Manley. Seaga subsequently served as leader of the opposition (1989–).

Sea Peoples Seafaring peoples who raided lands of the E Mediterranean in the 13th and 12th centuries BC. They had probably been driven from their homes in the Aegean by northern invaders. Egyptian records mention several raids of the "sea people", and they were largely responsible for the collapse of the HITTITES. Their exact identity is unknown, but they were of mixed origin and the best-known among them today, thanks largely to the Bible, are the PHILISTINES, who settled on the coast of PALESTINE. The Achaeans (early Greeks) of HOMER may also have been among them.

SEATO *See* SOUTHEAST ASIA TREATY ORGANIZATION

Second World War *See* WORLD WAR 2

Sedan, Battle of (1 September 1870) Decisive conflict in the FRANCO-PRUSSIAN WAR. The French army of *c.*120,000 men under Marshal MACMAHON was encircled by two German armies, more than 200,000-strong and led by Helmuth von MOLTKE, at the fortress of Sedan on the River Meuse, NE France. The desperate French position worsened when MacMahon was wounded, causing a hiatus in the chain of command. After several costly and futile French cavalry charges and intensive German artillery bombardment, Emperor NAPOLEON III of France surrendered along with *c.*83,000 soldiers. The French Second Empire collapsed and the Germans advanced on Paris. The French suffered 17,000 casualties against the Germans' 9000. In WORLD WAR 2 Sedan was the site of the main German breakthrough during the invasion of France (May 1940), which led to the Franco-German armistice in June.

Seddon, Richard John (1845–1906) New Zealand statesman, prime minister (1893–1906), b. England. He emigrated from Britain to Australia (1863) and then New Zealand (1866) to work in the gold mines. He was elected to the New Zealand Parliament for the Liberal Party in 1879. He served as minister of the mines and public works (1891–93) under John Ballance and succeeded him as prime minister. Seddon initiated much progressive social legislation, including the Old-Age Pensions Act (1898). Under his ministry, New Zealand women became the first in the world to gain the right to vote (1893). In foreign affairs, he annexed the Cook Islands (1901), but failed to gain control of FIJI. An advocate of strengthening ties with Britain, Seddon supported the British in the Second SOUTH AFRICAN WAR (1899–1902). His five consecutive election victories and monopoly of cabinet posts after 1899 earned him the nickname "King Dick".

Sedgemoor, Battle of (16 July 1685) Conflict between English rebels, under the Duke of MONMOUTH, and the forces of JAMES II, led by John Churchill (later Duke of MARLBOROUGH), fought in Somerset, SW England. Monmouth's untrained and ill-armed supporters were no match for trained soldiers and were massacred when a surprise, night-time attack foundered in the mud. The survivors appeared before the BLOODY ASSIZES.

Seeckt, Hans von (1866–1936) German general. As chief of staff to August von Mackensen during WORLD WAR 1, he assisted in the Austro-German breakthrough at Gorlice-Tarnów, S Poland (May 1915). After the War, Seeckt served as chief (1920–26) of the *Reichswehr* (army) in the WEIMAR REPUBLIC. Despite the restrictions imposed on German rearmament by the Treaty of VERSAILLES (1919), which he partly evaded by a secret agreement to train troops in Russia, he created an élite combined-arms force that formed the basis for the army of the Nazi THIRD REICH. Forced to resign, Seeckt later acted as a military adviser (1934–35) to Chiang Kai-shek in China.

Sejanus, Lucius Aelius (d.AD 31) Roman administrator. Initially favoured by the Emperor TIBERIUS, he became prefect of the PRAETORIAN GUARD in Rome. After the death of Tiberius' son Drusus (AD 23), Sejanus was denied permission to marry Drusus' widow, with whom he was later accused of murdering Drusus. Sejanus began to intrigue against Drusus' mother, AGRIPPINA THE ELDER, forcing her and NERO into exile in 29. In 31 Sejanus became consul. Tiberius was informed of a supposed plot to overthrow him and executed Sejanus.

Selassie, Haile *See* HAILE SELASSIE

Selden, John (1584–1654) English politician and legal historian. Elected to Parliament in 1623, he was twice imprisoned for opposing CHARLES I's conception of absolute royal government and was one of the authors of the PETITION OF RIGHT (1628). His *History of Tythes* (1618) denied that the Church of England had a divine sanction to collect tithes (taxes), but Selden was later forced to recant. He supported the impeachment (1640) of William LAUD, archbishop of Canterbury. In *Mare clusum* (1635), he rejected Hugo GROTIUS' conception of the freedom of seas.

Seleucids Macedonian dynasty who ruled (312–64 BC) an empire centred on modern-day Syria and Iran. The dynasty was founded by SELEUCUS I, a general of ALEXANDER III (THE GREAT). In 321 BC Seleucus became satrap (governor) of BABYLONIA and, although briefly forced out of the region by ANTIGONUS I, established full control in 312 BC. Seleucus extended his empire eastwards into modern-day Pakistan and westwards to Syria and Anatolia, where he defeated Antigonus at the Battle of Ipsus (301 BC). He established a W capital at Antioch (now ANTAKYA, S Turkey) and an E capital at Seleucia on the Tigris, encouraging Greek colonists to settle in Asia. In 281 BC, after conquering the Thracian peninsula, he was killed by the son of PTOLEMY I of Egypt. Seleucus was succeeded by **Antiochus I** (280–261 BC), who faced rebellions in Syria and incursions by PTOLEMY II. **Antiochus II** (r.261–246 BC) regained much of Anatolia from Ptolemy II, but his marriage to Ptolemy's daughter brought civil war to the Seleucid empire. SELEUCUS II (r.246–225 BC) lost land both to his younger brother Antiochus Hierax and to PTOLEMY III. ANTIOCHUS III (r.223–187 BC) reorganized the imperial administration, creating provincial *strategoi* who were responsible for both military and political affairs. He also rebuilt the empire, seizing territory from PTOLEMY V with the help of PHILIP V of Macedon, but later lost all possessions W of the Taurus Mountains to the Romans (190 BC). The loss of control over the Taurus ended the Seleucid domination of trade in the Middle East. The Seleucid promotion of Hellenistic culture culminated in Antiochus IV's (r.175–163) placing of a statue of Zeus in the TEMPLE OF JERUSALEM, an act that provoked the revolt of the MACCABEES, which resulted in the creation of an independent JUDEA in PALESTINE. The empire finally collapsed when Syria became a Roman province in 63 BC.

Seleucus I (*c.*355–281 BC) Macedonian general, founder of the SELEUCID dynasty, known as Nicator (Gk. "the conqueror"). He fought under ALEXANDER III (THE GREAT) in the conquest of Persia. After Alexander's death, his empire was divided (321 BC) and Seleucus became governor of BABYLONIA. He was ousted from the region by ANTIGONUS I, but joined forces with PTOLEMY I to defeat Antigonus and re-establish control of Babylonia in 312 BC. After being crowned king (305 BC), Seleucus began to expand the E frontier of his kingdom through Iran and into India, where he was finally halted by CHANDRAGUPTA Maurya in 303 BC. Seleucus allied with Ptolemy and Cassander to defeat Antigonus at the Battle of Ipsus (301 BC) and was rewarded with SYRIA and a large part of Asia Minor. Seleucus now commanded an empire that stretched from modern Afghanistan to the Mediterranean Sea. He built a W capital at Antioch (now Antakya, S Turkey) and an E capital at Seleucia on the Tigris. In 285 BC he imprisoned Antigonus' son, DEMETRIUS I, and set about conquering Macedonia. Seleucus appeared to be on the brink of reunifying the whole of Alexander's former empire when he was assassinated by Ptolemy I's son, Ptolemy Ceraunus. He was succeeded by his son, Antiochus I.

Seleucus II (d.225 BC) Fourth ruler of the Seleucid dynasty (246–225 BC), son of Antiochus II. His father was poisoned by his mother, Laodice, and Seleucus' accession was marked by civil war between Laodice and his father's second wife, Berenice. PTOLEMY III of Egypt, Berenice's brother, invaded the Seleucid empire and captured its E provinces. Seleucus later regained N Syria and parts of Iran, but lost the lands beyond the Taurus Mountains in Asia Minor to his brother Antiochus Hierax and allowed BACTRIA and PARTHIA to gain independence. He was succeeded by his son Seleucus III.

Self-Denying Ordinance (April 1645) Parliamentary resolution in the English CIVIL WAR. Steered through Parliament by Lord Saye and Sele (1582–1662), it required all members of Parliament to relinquish any military command they might hold. It was proposed by Oliver CROMWELL in order to unify the army and bring it under central government control, and to get rid of those officers, mainly peers, whose commitment to the total defeat of the king was suspect. An amendment in the House of Lords made it unnecessary for officers of the NEW MODEL ARMY (which included Cromwell himself) to resign.

Self-Strengthening movement In 19th-century China, group of reformers at the QING court, led by Empress Dowager CIXI, ZENG GUOFAN and LI HONGZHANG. The movement developed after the defeat of the TAIPING REBELLION (1850–64). Based on the ideas of the Chinese scholars LIN ZEXU and Feng Kueifen (1809–74), the movement aimed to preserve imperial power by adopting Western technology in industry, especially in armaments, and employing Western models of administration. Among its achievements were the creation of a government department to supervise foreign relations, the construction of a navy and the building of the Kiangnan Arsenal. The reforms had only superficial effects, however, and did not prevent swift defeat in the SINO-JAPANESE WAR (1894–95). *See also* HUNDRED DAYS OF REFORM

Selim I (*c.*1470–1520) Ottoman sultan (1512–20), son and successor of BAYEZID II (THE JUST), whom he forced to abdicate. His brutality to family and enemies alike earned him the nickname Selim the Grim. He expanded the OTTOMAN EMPIRE by defeating the Shiite SAFAVID ruler of Iran, ISMAIL I, at the Battle of Chaldiran (1514). He gained Syria and Egypt by defeating the MAMLUKS (1516–17). Having conquered most of Islam, he revived the title of caliph and made himself the spiritual as well as political leader of Sunni Islam. In spite of his reputation, Selim was a poet and patron of the arts. He was succeeded by his son, SULEIMAN I (THE MAGNIFICENT).

Selim II (1524–74) Ottoman sultan (1566–74), son and successor of SULEIMAN I (THE MAGNIFICENT). He lacked the abilities of his father and grandfather, leaving government largely in the hands of his grand vizier, Mehmed Sokollu, and ceding power to the JANISSARIES. The Ottoman invasion of Cyprus (1570) prompted the formation of a Christian HOLY LEAGUE. The League's navy, led by JOHN OF AUSTRIA, destroyed the Ottoman fleet at the Battle of LEPANTO (1571), but the Ottoman forces quickly regrouped and Venice was forced to recognize Ottoman control of Cyprus in 1573.

Selim III (1761–1808) Ottoman sultan (1789–1807), nephew and successor of ABDUL HAMID. Inspired partly by the French Revolution, he organized extensive reforms of the state and the army, and opened new diplomatic channels to the West. He supported NAPOLEON I during the Napoleonic Wars. Selim's "new order" antagonized religious groups and the military, including the JANISSARIES, and he was deposed and killed in prison by order of his successor, Mustafa IV, who the following year suffered the same fate .

Seljuk (Seljuq) Ruling clan of the nomadic Oguz Turkmen tribes, who converted to Sunni Islam in the 10th century and, led by Seljuk, migrated from Central Asia to the Iranian province of Khorasan in the early 11th century. From 1040 Seljuk's grandsons, Chagri Beg and Togril Beg, conquered most of w Iran and Mesopotamia. In 1055 Togril defeated the Shiite BUYID rulers of BAGHDAD and, as the restorer of the Sunni caliphate, was rewarded with the title of sultan. The Seljuks revived religious and educational institutions, including the *madressas* (Islamic universities), and established their capital at ISFAHAN, central Iran, where they built the Great Mosque. The Seljuks were at their height under ALP ARSLAN, who expanded the empire into Syria and Palestine. His victory over the BYZANTINE EMPIRE at the Battle of MANZIKERT (1071) established Seljuk hegemony in Asia Minor and was a major factor in the launching of the First CRUSADE (1095). After the death of Alp Arslan's son and successor, Malik Shah (r.1072–92), and the murder of Nizim al-Mulk by the ASSASSINS in 1092, the empire fragmented. The last of the Great (Iranian) Seljuks died in battle in 1194, but the Seljuk sultanate of Rum, based in Konya, s central Turkey, survived until made a client state by the Mongols in 1243.

Selkirk, Thomas Douglas, 5th Earl of (1771–1820) Scottish landowner who founded colonies in Canada for dispossessed Highlanders. In 1803 he established settlements in Prince Edward Island and Upper Canada (Ontario). In 1811, having gained a controlling share of the HUDSON'S BAY COMPANY, he acquired a huge tract of land in the valley of the Red River. He was involved in prolonged and costly disputes with the rival NORTH WEST COMPANY but the RED RIVER SETTLEMENT survived to form the basis of the modern city of Winnipeg, MANITOBA.

Seminole NATIVE NORTH AMERICANS, originally linked with the CREEK in Georgia, who migrated to N FLORIDA in the late 18th century. They sheltered many escaped slaves, and their refusal to hand them back was one cause, together with their opposition to increasing white settlement, of the **First** Seminole War (1817–18). on the Georgia-Florida frontier. General Andrew JACKSON crushed native resistance and burned Seminole villages. When Florida joined the United States in 1819, the Seminole were forced to retreat further south. In 1832 some Seminole leaders signed a treaty agreeing to move to Oklahoma. The majority opposed the move, resulting in the **Second** Seminole War (1835–42). The Seminole, led by Chief OSCEOLA, mounted a guerrilla campaign, killing *c*.1500 US troops before Osceola was captured. The majority (*c*.4000) of the remaining Seminole were starved into surrender and forced west into INDIAN TERRITORY (now OKLAHOMA), where they formed one of the so-called FIVE CIVILIZED TRIBES. The **Third** Seminole War (1855–58) was a small-scale conflict between the US Army and the remnants of the Seminoles, who had hidden in the Florida Everglades. Today, there are *c*.13,800 Seminole living in five reservations. *See also* INDIAN REMOVAL ACT

Semites Peoples whose native tongue belongs to the Semitic languages group, including ARABS, JEWS, and others in NE Africa and the Near East. The Semites were pastoral nomads of ARABIA who, roughly three millennia ago, spread into the lands east of the Mediterranean, including Syria, Mesopotamia and Palestine. Besides language, another common element is revealed in the similarities of Islamic and Jewish historical tradition: the Old Testament defines Semites as descendants of Shem, son of NOAH.

Senanayake, Don Stephen (1884–1952) Ceylonese statesman, prime minister (1947–52). He joined the Legislative Council in 1922 and served on the State Council as minister for agriculture (1931–46). As leader of the United National Party (UNP), Senanayake was one of the architects of Ceylonese (now SRI LANKA) independence and became its first prime minister, skilfully managing the transition from British colonial rule. His Gal Oya scheme (1949) to irrigate the Dry Zone of E Sri Lanka encouraged the influx of *c*.250,000 Sinhalese colonizers. The expansion of social welfare projects was achieved through the boom in the price of rubber during the Korean War. He died in office and was succeeded as prime minister (1952–53) by his son, **Dudley Shelton Senanayake** (1911–73). Dudley Senanayake was forced to resign after the collapse of the Korean boom forced him to adopt austerity measures that led to a general strike. Senanayake succeeded Sirimavo BANDARANAIKE as prime minister (1965–70) as the head of a coalition government. He failed to defuse growing Tamil dissatisfaction and further attempts to restrict food subsidies contributed to his defeat by Bandaranaike in the 1970 elections.

Senate, Roman Chief governing body of the ancient ROMAN REPUBLIC. It originated as an advisory council of PATRICIANS to the kings of ancient ROME. When the monarchy was abolished in 509 BC, the Senate became the advisory body to the CONSULS (magistrates). Its 300 members were chosen for life by the consuls and at first were exclusively patricians and mainly former consuls; PLEBEIANS gained entry in the 4th century BC. Although a consul rarely acted against the advice of the Senate, the body initially had no real executive power. In *c*.312 BC the appointment of senators became the prerogative of the CENSOR. By the 2nd century BC, the Senate was the supreme governing body of Rome. It controlled finance, assigned duties and provinces to the consuls and negotiated foreign policy. The authority of the Senate, however, was constantly challenged by generals, such as Gaius MARIUS, and TRIBUNES, such as Tiberius GRACCHUS. In 81 BC Lucius Cornelius SULLA made the Senate an automatically constituted body by stipulating that all former QUAESTORS should become senators. The number of senators thus increased to *c*.550, but the reform failed to prevent the continual attacks on the Senate, and the Republic disintegrated. After the civil war (49–45 BC), Julius CAESAR increased the number of senators to 900, packing it with his supporters. Emperor AUGUSTUS (r.27 BC–AD 14) maintained the Senate, but in a much reduced capacity. The emperor appointed all military and civil officials and guided foreign policy, while the Senate was basically restricted to judicial matters and to the city government of Rome. In the 4th century AD, CONSTANTINE I created two senates, in Rome and Constantinople (now ISTANBUL), each with *c*.2000 members. After AD 580, the Roman Senate disappears from history. *See also* DEMOCRACY; PARLIAMENT

Senate, US Upper house of the United States' legislature which, together with the HOUSE OF REPRESENTATIVES, forms the CONGRESS. It was created by the CONSTITUTION OF THE UNITED STATES and first met in 1789. It is composed of two senators from each state, in contrast to the House of Representatives which is elected on the basis of population. Originally, senators were elected by state legislatures, but since the 17th Amendment (1913) they have been directly elected by the people. Elections are held every other year, with about one-third of the Senate elected each time. A senator serves a six-year term. The Constitution envisaged the House of Representatives as the primary body, but the Senate has come to acquire greater significance, at least in the popular view. It has acquired distinctive traditions, such as the tradition of extended debate that gave rise to the tactic of the FILIBUSTER. The approval of a simple majority of the Senate is necessary for major presidential appointments and a two-thirds majority for treaties. The Senate also adjudicates in impeachment proceedings, a two-thirds majority being necessary for conviction. The Senate can initiate legislation, except on fiscal matters. As in the House of Representatives, the procedure and structure of the Senate is dominated by political parties and the committee system. There are 16 standing committees, which scrutinize major policy areas, and committee chairpersons retain their position for as long as their party commands a majority of the Senate. Each party elects a Senate leader. Officially, the presiding officer of the Senate is the vice president, but the position is often delegated. *See also* DEMOCRACY; PARLIAMENT

Sendero Luminoso (Sp. "Shining Path") Peruvian revolutionary movement, otherwise known as the Communist Party of Peru. Founded (1970) by Abimael Guzmán Reynoso (1934–), Shining Path is a Maoist organization whose models include the Chinese CULTURAL REVOLUTION and the Cambodian KHMER ROUGE. During the 1970s they built up their support among students, Native American peasants and the urban poor, preaching peasant-empowerment and employing tactics of intimidation, violence and fierce discipline. In 1980 Shining Path began a campaign of guerrilla warfare and terrorism in the remote regions of the Andes mountains. The frequent abuses of human rights committed by Peru's army and police in their bid to suppress the movement served to increase support for the Shining Path, whose control of the coca-growing region of the Upper Huallaga Valley financed the extension of the campaign to Peru's cities. By 1991 the war between the government and Shining Path had claimed *c*.25,000 lives. President Alberto FUJIMORI launched a full-scale attack on the movement, and Guzmán was captured and sentenced to life imprisonment in 1992. Between 1992 and 1994, *c*.5500 *Senderistas* surrendered under a government amnesty, but the movement continues to inflict damage on Peru's society and economy. *See also* MAO ZEDONG; TUPAC AMARU

Seneca (the Younger), Lucius Annaeus (*c*.4 BC–AD 65) Roman philosopher, statesman and dramatist, b. Spain. In 41 he was expelled from Rome by Emperor CLAUDIUS on a charge of adultery, but was recalled in 49 on the intercession of AGRIPPINA (THE YOUNGER). A great teacher in the tradition of the STOICS, Seneca become tutor to the young NERO. He was a moderating influence in the early years of Nero's reign, but the emperor's megalomania soon outgrew Seneca's influence and he retired in 62. Accused of plotting to kill Nero in 65, Seneca committed suicide. Besides his nine verse-tragedies, Seneca wrote numerous *Moral Essays* and *Moral Letters*. He had an enormous influence on later European thought and literature, especially in the Renaissance.

Seneca NATIVE NORTH AMERICANS, largest of the five nations of the IROQUOIS CONFEDERACY. They originally inhabited the region W of Lake Seneca in what is now New York state. During the 17th century the Seneca expanded, through wars with neighbouring tribes, down the Allegheny River into Pennsylvania. They supported the British during the American Revolution and produced some notable leaders, such as RED JACKET, who managed to preserve good relations with whites. In 1848 a Seneca Nation was proclaimed by the peoples of reservations in the Seneca homeland.

Seneca Falls Convention (19–20 July 1848) US women's rights convention held at Seneca Falls, New York. Elizabeth Cady STANTON and Lucretia MOTT organized the convention, which established the women's rights movement as a growing organization. Attended by

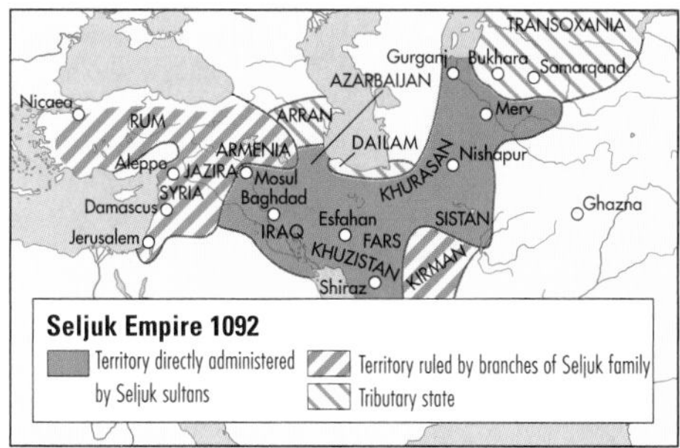

▲ **Seljuk** Under Malik Shah (r.1072–92), the Seljuk empire expanded to include Syria and Palestine. He also asserted direct rule over the former vassal states of Azerbaijan and Mesopotamia.

S

68 women and 32 men, it passed 12 resolutions in favour of women's rights, including the right to vote. *See also* FEMINISM; SUFFRAGETTE MOVEMENT

Senegal *See* country feature

Senghor, Léopold Sédar (1906–) Senegalese statesman and poet, first president (1960–80) of independent SENEGAL. He moved from French West Africa to France in 1928. A writer of international stature, he was one of the originators of the concept of *négritude*, taking pride in the cultural heritage of black Africa. Senghor was interned in a Nazi concentration camp (1940–42) and joined the French Resistance on his release. In 1946 he was elected to represent Senegal in the French National Assembly. A supporter of African socialism and the creation of a united, federal Africa, Senghor was the leading figure behind the creation (1959) of an independent Mali Federation, consisting of Senegal, French Sudan (now MALI), Dahomey (now BENIN) and Upper Volta (now BURKINA FASO). The Federation disintegrated the following year and Senghor was elected president of the republic of Senegal. He survived a coup by Mamadou Dia in 1962 and worked to modernize Senegal's predominantly agricultural economy. In 1975 Senghor led Senegal into the West African Economic Community. He retired as president in favour of Abdou DIOUF in 1980 and subsequently lived in retirement in France, becoming the first African to be elected to the Académie Française (1984).

Sennacherib (d.681 BC) King of ASSYRIA (*c*.705–681 BC), son and successor of SARGON II, whose huge empire he spent most of his reign defending. In 703 BC he defeated a rebellion, supported by ELAM, in CHALDAEA, S BABYLONIA. Sennacherib crushed a revolt in PALESTINE (701 BC), only agreeing to spare JERUSALEM after the payment of a tribute. In *c*.692 the Chaldaeans, again backed by Elam, seized BABYLON. Sennacherib starved the city into submission (689) and then destroyed it. He thereafter devoted himself to rebuilding his magnificent capital, NINEVEH. He was killed by his sons but avenged by another son, Esarhaddon, who succeeded him.

Seoul (Kyongsong) Capital of South KOREA, on the River Han. The development of the modern city dates back to the building of a palace for King Munjong of KORYO in 1068. It was the capital of KOREA under the YI DYNASTY from 1392 until 1910. It began to develop into an industrial city after Korea emerged from isolation in 1876, and development was rapid under Japanese rule (1910–45). Seoul was the headquarters of the US army of occupation (1945–48) and, after partition, capital of South Korea. The city was devastated by the KOREAN WAR (1950–53). Sights include Changdok Palace (begun 1405) and Kyongbok Palace (rebuilt 1867). Pop. (1994) 10,799,000.

separation of powers Constitutional principle designed to prevent despotic rule by balancing power among the three branches of government: executive, legislature and judiciary. It derived from Baron de MONTESQUIEU, who commended such a system in his *The Spirit of the Laws* (1748). It is a basic principle of the CONSTITUTION OF THE UNITED STATES, which precludes a person simultaneously holding office in more than one branch of government and provides for judicial review. *See also* CONGRESS; DEMOCRACY; SUPREME COURT

Sephardim Descendants of the JEWS of medieval Spain and Portugal. Iberian Jews followed the Babylonian rather than the Palestinian Jewish tradition and developed their own language, Ladino. After the expulsion of the Jews from Spain (1492), many eventually settled in more liberal centres in N Europe, such as Amsterdam.

Septuagint Earliest surviving Greek translation of the OLD TESTAMENT in the Bible. It was made from Hebrew for the Greek-speaking Jewish community in Egypt in the 3rd and 2nd centuries BC. It contains the entire Jewish Canon plus the APOCRYPHA. The Septuagint is divided into four sections: the law, history, poetry and prophets. It differs in some respects from the accepted Hebrew Bible, and is still used in the Greek ORTHODOX CHURCH.

Serbia Balkan republic that, combined with the smaller republic of MONTENEGRO, forms the rump federal state of YUGOSLAVIA. It includes the provinces of Vojvodina (N) and KOSOVO (S), formerly autonomous under the Yugoslav federation. The capital is BELGRADE. The area was settled by SERBS in the 7th century AD, and they adopted Orthodox Christianity under BYZANTINE rule in 891. In *c*.1168 Stephen NEMANJA, regarded as the founder of Serbia, became chief of Raška, SW Serbia, which he expanded to include much of the present-day territory. In 1217 his son was crowned king of Serbia by Pope Honorious III.

Under STEPHEN DUŠAN (r.1331–55), Serbia became the leading power in the Balkans, gaining ALBANIA, MACEDONIA, Montenegro and parts of GREECE and Asia Minor. In 1375 a Serbian patriarchate to rival Constantinople was established at Peć, Kosovo. After Stephen Dušan's death (1355), Serbia rapidly declined, and was defeated by Ottoman Sultan MURAD I at the Battle of Kosovo (1389). Serbian resistance continued, however, until 1459 when it was finally subsumed into the OTTOMAN EMPIRE. KARAGEORGE led a revolt (1804–13) against Ottoman rule, but was forced to retreat after ALEXANDER I of Russia withdrew his support. In 1815 MILOŠ OBRENOVIĆ mounted a further rebellion, forcing the Ottomans to grant limited autonomy to Serbia. Full autonomy was achieved in 1830.

Miloš abdicated in favour of his son in 1839, but was recalled after the overthrow of ALEXANDER KARAGEORGEVIĆ in 1858. Milan OBRENOVIĆ entered the RUSSO-TURKISH WAR (1876–77), and the ensuing Congress of BERLIN (1878) confirmed Serbian independence and increased the influence of Russia and Austria-Hungary in the Balkans. In 1885 Milan launched a disastrous war against BULGARIA and was forced to abdicate (1889) in favour of his son, Alexander. Alexander was assassinated in a military coup in 1903, and PETER I became king. In 1908 Austria-Hungary annexed BOSNIA-HERZEGOVINA, prompting Serbia to seek an alternative outlet to the sea. In 1912 the Balkan League (Serbia, Bulgaria, Montenegro and Greece) was formed, which crushed the Ottomans in the First BALKAN WAR (1912), but rapidly fragmented. In 1913 Serbia defeated Bulgaria in the Second BALKAN WAR. It emerged from the conflicts with 80% more land, acquiring Kosovo and most of Macedonia.

The expansion of Serbia caused further tension in its relationship with Austria, and the assassination of Austrian Archduke FRANZ FERDINAND by Gavrilo PRINCIP of the Serbian nationalist group the BLACK HAND precipitated WORLD WAR I. Serbia resisted two Austrian attacks (1914), but collapsed when confronted by a German-Bulgarian advance (1915). Greece joined with Serbia on the Allied side in 1916 and aided in the recapture of Belgrade in 1918. After the War, the Kingdom of the Serbs, Croats and Slovenes was created under Nikolai PAŠIĆ, former prime minister of Serbia. Serbs dominated the new kingdom, creating bitter resentment among Croats. In 1929 ALEXANDER I renamed the kingdom Yugoslavia, creating a dictatorship. In 1934 Alexander was assassinated and PAUL KARAGEORGEVIĆ assumed power.

In 1941 Yugoslavia was occupied and divided by the German army. Resistance was two-fold: TITO led the Yugoslav communist partisans, while Draža MIHAJOVIĆ led the Serbian nationalists (CHETNIKS). In 1946 Serbia became one of six republics in Tito's neo-communist Yugoslavia. In 1987 President Slobodan MILOŠEVIĆ restated nationalist claims for a Greater Serbia, including Vojvodina, Kosovo and Serb-populated areas in CROATIA, Bosnia-Herzegovina and MACEDONIA. In 1989 Serbian

SENEGAL

AREA: 196,720sq km (75,954sq mi)
POPULATION: 7,736,000
CAPITAL (POPULATION): Dakar (1,729,823)
GOVERNMENT: Multiparty republic
ETHNIC GROUPS: Wolof 44%, Fulani-Tukulor 24%, Serer 15%
LANGUAGES: French (official)
RELIGIONS: Islam 94%, Christianity (mainly Roman Catholic) 5%, traditional beliefs and others 1%
GDP PER CAPITA (1995): US$1780

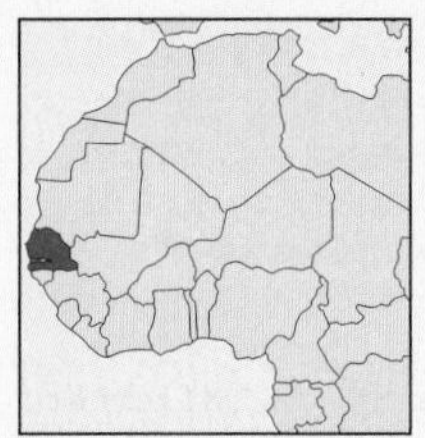

Republic on the NW coast of Africa. It entirely surrounds The GAMBIA. From the 6th to the 10th century Senegal formed part of the empire of ancient GHANA. Between the 10th and 14th centuries, the Tukulor state of Tekrur dominated the Sénégal valley. The ALMORAVID dynasty of Zenega Berbers introduced Islam. Perhaps in response to the growing power of Islam, the Serer and WOLOF peoples colonized southwards from the Sénégal valley, creating a state by the 12th century. In the 14th century the MALI empire conquered Tekrur. However, to the E the new empire of SONGHAI was beginning to expand and in the late 14th century it broke Mali's overlordship.

In 1444 Portuguese sailors became the first Europeans to reach Cape Verde. Trading stations were rapidly established in the area. France gradually gained control of the valuable slave trade and founded St Louis in 1658. By 1763 Britain had expelled the French from Senegal and, in 1765, set up Senegambia, the first British colony in Africa. In 1783 France regained control of the region. In the mid-19th century France battled for control of the interior with, among others, UMAR IBN SAID TAL. In 1857 Dakar was founded.

In 1895 Senegal became a French colony within the federation of French West Africa. In 1902 the capital of this huge empire was transferred from St Louis to Dakar. In 1946 Senegal joined the French Union. In 1959 Senegal joined French Sudan (now MALI) to form the Federation of Mali. In 1960 Senegal withdrew and became an independent republic within the French community. Léopold Sédar SENGHOR was Senegal's first post-colonial president. Following an unsuccessful coup (1962), Senghor gradually assumed wider powers. During the 1960s Senegal's economy deteriorated and a succession of droughts caused starvation and civil unrest. In 1974 Senegal was a founding member of the West African Economic Community. In 1981 Senghor was succeeded by Abdou DIOUF, and Senegalese troops suppressed a coup in The Gambia. In 1982 the two countries were joined in the Confederation of Senegambia, but the union was dissolved in 1989. From 1989 to 1992 Senegal was at war with Mauritania. In 1993 elections Diouf was re-elected for a third term. Internal conflict continued, notably in the S Casamance region where a secessionist movement had gathered strength. In 2000 elections Diouf was defeated by Abdoulaye Wade of the Senegalese Democratic Party, ending 40 years of Socialist Party rule.

S

troops brutally suppressed Albanian nationalism in Kosovo. When Serbia prevented CROATIA from assuming presidency of the federation in 1991, Croatia and SLOVENIA declared independence, prompting invasions by the Serbian-controlled Yugoslav People's Army (YPA). The YPA soon withdrew from Slovenia, but the war in Croatia was more protracted. In a 1992 cease-fire with Croatia, Serbia retained the territory it had captured. Bosnian Serb forces quickly seized nearly 75% of the newly recognized republic of Bosnia-Herzegovina and the United Nations (UN) imposed sanctions on Serbia. In 1995 Bosnian Serb troops captured UN "safe areas", and the NORTH ATLANTIC TREATY ORGANIZATION (NATO) launched air strikes against Serb targets. In 1995 Bosnia-Herzegovina and Croatia began a new offensive against Serbia, reclaiming much territory. Tension in Kosovo was heightened by the influx of Serb refugees from the Croatian province of KRAJINA. The US-brokered DAYTON PEACE AGREEMENT (November 1995) partitioned Bosnia-Herzegovina. In 1997 Milošević resigned the Serbian presidency in order to become president of Yugoslavia. In 1998 he sent the YPA into Kosovo to crush the Kosovo Liberation Army (KLA), forcing *c.*200,000 Kosovar Albanians from their homes. In 1999 NATO forces began a campaign of air strikes against the Yugoslav military. Milošević intensified the assault on the ethnic Albanians, creating a further *c.*860,000 refugees. NATO's intensive bombardment devastated Serbia's economy and the Yugoslav army agreed to withdraw from Kosovo in June 1999, replaced by a United Nations' (UN) peacekeeping force (K-FOR). Area: 88,361sq km (34,107sq mi). Pop. (1991) 9,778,991

Serbs, Croats and Slovenes, Kingdom of *See* YUGOSLAVIA

Serbs SLAVS who settled in the Balkans in the 7th century AD. Under Byzantine rule they became Orthodox Christians in the 9th century, and by the mid-14th century SERBIA was the leading Balkan kingdom.

serf Person legally bound to a lord. In medieval Europe under the FEUDAL SYSTEM, serfs had to provide labour and other services and were usually bound to the land, holding a portion for their own use. Serfdom, which persisted in Russia into the 19th century, was different from SLAVERY in that serfs had certain legal rights. In Western Europe, serfs were largely replaced by a free peasantry by the 14th century. *See also* DEMESNE; VILLEIN

Serra, Saint Junípero (1713–84) Spanish Franciscan missionary, known as the apostle to California. He was a renowned intellectual in Spain before volunteering for mission service in Mexico (1749). Accompanying a military expedition designed to discourage Russian encroachment from Alaska, he founded the first mission in California, near San Diego, in 1769. In suceeding years 20 others were added along the California coast. In 1988 Serra was beatified by Pope John Paul II.

Servetus, Michael (*c.*1511–53) Spanish physician and theologian. His criticism of the doctrine of the Trinity alienated both Catholics and Protestant reformers alike. Having studied medicine in France, he became physician to the archbishop of Vienne (1540). He discovered that blood moves through the lungs. When his views on the Trinity led to his arrest by the INQUISITION (1553), Servetus escaped and unwisely sought sanctuary with John CALVIN in Geneva, Switzerland, where he was condemned as a heretic and burned alive.

Seton, Saint Elizabeth Ann (1774–1821) US teacher and charity organizer, who was converted to Roman Catholicism (1805) after experiencing the kindness of Catholic friends on the early death of her husband in Italy. Seton founded (1809) the first Roman Catholic elementary school in the United States, at Baltimore, Maryland, and created (1813) the first religious society in the United States, the Sisters of Charity. She was the first native-born US citizen to be proclaimed a saint (1975).

Settlement, Act of (12 June 1701) English Act of Parliament designed to prevent the restoration of the Catholic STUART monarchy on the death of WILLIAM III and the future Queen ANNE, both childless. It settled the succession on SOPHIA, Electress of HANOVER, granddaughter of JAMES I, and her heirs, providing they were Protestants. The crown was inherited (1714) by Sophia's son, GEORGE I. The Act also stipulated that all future monarchs must be members of the CHURCH OF ENGLAND. *See also* JACOBITES; JAMES II

Sevastopol (Sebastopol) Black Sea port on the sw Crimean Peninsula, UKRAINE. Site of a Greek colony in ancient times, the modern city was founded (1783) after the Russian conquest of the CRIMEA. Sevastopol became the base of the Russian Black Sea fleet and was the major strategic objective of the CRIMEAN WAR, successfully defended by the Russians during an 11-month siege (1854–55). The ruined city was rebuilt in the 1870s. It was the scene of a naval mutiny during the RUSSIAN REVOLUTION OF 1905 and was the main White Russian base in S Russia during the RUSSIAN CIVIL WAR (1918–20). When the Soviet Union disintegrated in 1991, control of the city and the fleet was disputed between Russia and the Ukraine. Sevastopol passed to Ukraine which, by a compromise agreed in 1995, confirmed the continuance of the Russian base in return for a share in the fleet. Pop. (1993) 366,000.

Seven Days' Battles (25 June–1 July 1862) Engagements in the American CIVIL WAR that ended the PENINSULAR CAMPAIGN. In a series of battles, the Confederate forces under General Robert LEE successfully repulsed a Union attack, led by General George MCCLELLAN, on the Confederate capital of Richmond, Virginia. Lee's attack on the Union right flank at **Mechanicsville** (June 26) was beaten off at great cost, but the following day Lee and General "Stonewall" JACKSON were victorious in a bloody battle at **Gaines' Mill**, and Union forces began to retreat. In the final, ferocious battle at **Malvern Hill** (1 July), McClellan's troops repelled Lee's attempt to block their retreat. Confederate casualties were *c.*20,000, Union casualties *c.*16,000.

Seven Weeks' War *See* AUSTRO-PRUSSIAN WAR

Seven Wonders of the World Greatest man-made structures in the ancient world. The first list was published *c.*130 BC and subsequent lists varied only slightly The Wonders were: the PYRAMIDS of Egypt; the HANGING GARDENS OF BABYLON; the statue of Zeus at OLYMPIA; the temple of Artemis at EPHESUS; the mausoleum at HALICARNASSUS; the Colossus of RHODES; and the Pharos at ALEXANDRIA. Some lists included the walls, as well as the gardens, of Babylon and omitted the Pharos at Alexandria. Only the Pyramids have survived, although models of the others have been reconstructed from archaeological evidence plus a little imagination.

Seven Years' War (1756–63) Major conflict between all the great powers of Europe. While much of the fighting was confined to the German states of Europe, the War also involved the struggle between France (allied with Spain from 1759) and Britain for colonial control of North America (*see* FRENCH AND INDIAN WARS) and India (where Robert CLIVE helped establish British supremacy). The War followed Austria's loss of SILESIA to FREDERICK II (THE GREAT) of PRUSSIA in the War of the AUSTRIAN SUCCESSION (1740–48). MARIA THERESA of Austria, determined to recover Silesia, enlisted the support of Russia, Sweden, SAXONY, Spain and France. Frederick II, who was allied with Britain and HANOVER, seized the initiative by attacking Saxony and forcing its capitulation. Frederick now turned his attention to Bohemia, defeating the Austrians at the Battle of Prague (May 1757). However, a decisive French victory over the Hanoverians, led by the Duke of CUMBERLAND, and Sweden's attack on Eastern POMERANIA put Prussia firmly on the defensive. By August 1757 Russia had occupied large parts of Eastern Prussia. Frederick took a bold gamble and, despite being outnumbered, defeated the Franco-Saxon army at Rossbach (November 1757) and the Austrians at Leuthen (December 1757). The accession of William PITT (THE ELDER) as Britain's leading minister brought greater financial support for Frederick but, after a costly victory over Russia at Zorndorf (1758), Prussia suffered a crushing defeat at Kunersdorf (1759). At the start of 1762, Prussia seemed on the brink of defeat when suddenly Tsarina ELIZABETH died and her successor, PETER III, withdrew Russia from the War. Prussia, now allied with Russia, once more expelled the Austrians from Silesia. At the end of the War, the Treaty of PARIS (1763) confirmed British control of North America and India, while the Peace of HUBERTUSBURG confirmed Prussia's possession of Silesia and its status as a major European power. *See also* CHOISEUL, ETIENNE FRANÇOIS, DUC DE; GEORGE III; KAUNITZ, WENZEL ANTON VON, FÜRST VON; POMPADOUR, JEANNE-ANTOINETTE POISSON, MARQUISE DE; WOLFE, JAMES

Severus, (Lucius) Septimius (146–211) Roman emperor (193–211), b. Tripolitania (now Libya). He became a consul in 190. After the assassination of Emperor COMMODUS (192) and his successor Publius Helvius Pertinax (193), Severus was proclaimed emperor by his troops, who marched on Rome and persuaded the Senate to confirm him. To secure his position, Severus dissolved the PRAETORIAN GUARD, replacing it with his own men, and proclaimed himself posthumously adopted by the Emperor MARCUS AURELIUS. Having defeated his rivals by 197, he enhanced the status of the army, defeated the Parthians (198–199) and divided Britain into two provinces (208). By reducing the power of the Senate and the PATRICIAN class, Severus' reign marks the beginning of the military despotism that characterized the later Roman Empire. His campaign to conquer Caledonia (Scotland) failed, and he died at York, N England. Severus was succeeded by his son, CARACALLA.

Sevier, John (1745–1815) American soldier and politician, first governor of TENNESSEE. He fought against the Native Americans in Lord Dunmore's War (1773–74), and the British in the AMERICAN REVOLUTION (1775–83). In the latter conflict, Sevier was hailed as a national hero for his role in the victory at King's Mountain, North Carolina (1780). After the War, he was governor (1784–88) of the short-lived state of Franklin in what became E Tennessee. When Tennessee was admitted to the Union (1796), Sevier served as governor six times between 1796 and 1809, and represented the state in Congress (1811–15).

Sèvres, Treaty of (10 August 1920) Peace agreement at the end of World War 1 between the defeated OTTOMAN EMPIRE and the Allied powers, signed at Sèvres, N France.

SENGHOR, LÉOPOLD SÉDAR

Léopold Senghor envisaged an African socialism which combined modernization with traditional African culture. He argued for a rejection of excessive materialism in favour of a community-based, humanist approach to government.

SENGHOR IN HIS OWN WORDS

"Négritude is not the defence of a skin or colour. Négritude is the awareness, defence and development of African cultural values, [it] is the awareness by a particular social group or people of its own situation in the world."
Speech to the Ghanian Parliament (1961)

The Treaty abolished the Ottoman Empire and reduced Turkey to the city of Constantinople (now Istanbul) and parts of Asia Minor. Although the pact was agreed by Sultan Muhammad VI, it was rejected by Turkish nationalists led by Mustafa Kemal (later Atatürk), who overthrew the government and established a republic. The Treaty of Sèvres was replaced by the Treaty of Lausanne (1923).

Seward, William Henry (1801–72) US statesman. He served as governor of New York (1838–42). The leader of the anti-slavery wing of the Whig Party, Seward was elected to the Senate in 1849. When the Whig Party disintegrated over the issue of slavery, Seward helped found the Republican Party. He lost the Republican nomination for president (1860) to Abraham Lincoln, who subsequently appointed him secretary of state (1861–69). Seward became Lincoln's most trusted adviser. He succeeded in maintaining good relations with European states during the American Civil War, and prevented wider recognition of the Confederacy, which had many sympathizers in Britain and elsewhere. His adept handling of the Trent Affair (1861) averted a crisis in US-British relations, and he restrained US action against the French occupation of Mexico until after the Civil War. In April 1865 Seward was seriously wounded in a knife-attack by an accomplice of John Wilkes Booth, who had murdered Lincoln the night before, but made a dramatic recovery and continued in office under Andrew Johnson. His support for Reconstruction earned him further enemies, and his successful purchase of Alaska (1867) for US$7.2 million was ridiculed as "Seward's Folly".

Seychelles Republic consisting of more than 100 islands in the Indian Ocean, *c.*970km (600mi) N of Madagascar. In 1502 Vasco da Gama explored the islands and named them the "Seven Sisters". The islands were colonized by the French in 1756, who established spice plantations worked by slaves from Mauritius. In 1794 the archipelago was captured by the British during the Napoleonic Wars and, in 1814, became a dependency of Mauritius. In 1903 the Seychelles became a British crown colony. In 1976 they achieved full independence within the Commonwealth of Nations. A 1977 coup established Albert René as president. In 1981 South African mercenaries failed in an attempt to overthrow the government. Continued civil unrest and another failed coup in 1987 led to the first multiparty elections (1991). In 1998 Albert René was elected for a fifth term.

Seymour, Edward, Duke of Somerset *See* Somerset, Edward Seymour, 1st Duke of

Seymour, Jane (*c.*1509–37) Queen of England, third wife of Henry VIII. A lady-in-waiting to Henry's second wife, Anne Boleyn, Jane married Henry after the execution of Anne in 1536. Henry lavished endowments on her family, and one brother, Edward Seymour, became Duke of Somerset and Protector in the reign of Edward VI. Jane died, much to Henry's distress, shortly after Edward's birth in 1537.

Seyss-Inquart, Arthur (1892–1946) Austrian Nazi leader, chancellor (1938). In 1937 he was brought into government as part of the concessions to Austrian Nazis by Kurt von Schuschnigg. The following year, he was appointed minister of interior and security at the insistence of Adolf Hitler. Seyss-Inquart succeeded Schuschnigg as chancellor, signing the document that brought Anschluss (union) between Austria and Germany. He served as governor (1938–39) of Austria under German rule. As Reich Commissioner (1940–45) in the occupied Netherlands, he sent thousands of Dutch Jews to their deaths. Convicted of war crimes at the Nuremberg Trials, he was hanged. *See also* Nazi Party

Sforza, Carlo, Conte (1873–1952) Italian statesman and diplomat. A former foreign minister (1920–21), he resigned as ambassador to France (1922) and went into exile after Benito Mussolini was appointed prime minister. Returning to Italy after Mussolini's fall (1943), Sforza served in Alcide De Gasperi's cabinet as minister of foreign affairs (1947–51). He secured Italian membership of the North Atlantic Treaty Organization (NATO).

Sforza, Francesco (1401–66) Duke of Milan (1450–66), father of Ludovico Sforza. Like his father, Muzio Attendoli (who was nicknamed *Sforza*, It. "strength"), he was a successful condottiere. In 1434 Sforza entered the service of Cosimo de' Medici, ruler of Florence, for whom he captured Verona from Milan (1438). Sforza married (1441) the daughter of the Duke of Milan, Filippo Maria Visconti, but was overlooked as the duke's successor in favour of Alfonso V of Aragón and Naples in 1447. Under siege from the Venetians, Milan declared itself a republic and called on Sforza to act as captain general. In 1449 Milan signed a truce with Venice without Sforza's knowledge, whereupon he starved the city into surrender. Sforza concluded a peace treaty with Florence and Naples in 1454.

SEYCHELLES

AREA: 455sq km (176sq mi)
POPULATION: 75,000
CAPITAL (POPULATION): Victoria (24,324)
GOVERNMENT: Multiparty republic
ETHNIC GROUPS: Mixture of African, Asian and European
LANGUAGES: Seselwa (official), English, French
RELIGIONS: Roman Catholic 89%, Anglican 9%,
GDP PER CAPITA (1994): US$6798

Sforza, Ludovico (*c.*1451–1508) Duke of Milan (1494–99), known as "the Moor", younger son of Francesco Sforza. Ludovico's elder brother, **Galeazzo Maria** Sforza (1444–76), succeeded their father as duke but was murdered, leaving an infant son, **Gian Galeazzo** (1469–94), for whom Ludovico acted as regent from 1480 and succeeded as duke in 1494. Ludovico united with Lorenzo de' Medici of Florence against Venice, and formed an alliance with Naples by marrying Gian Galeazzo to Ferdinand I's daughter, Isabella. In 1491 Ludovico married the brilliant Beatrice d'Este, and their Renaissance court was the most splendid in Europe, attracting artists and architects such as Leonardo da Vinci (1452–1519) and Donato Bramante (1444–1514). The brilliance of the court cast a shadow over Isabella, who moved (1489) to Pavia and asked her father to intervene on behalf of Gian Galeazzo. The threat from Naples prompted Ludovico to form alliances with Charles VIII of France and Emperor Maximilian I. Ludovico initially supported Charles VIII's attempt to conquer Naples (1494–95), but the success of the French army in Italy led him to change sides and help to expel the French. In 1499 Charles VIII's successor, Louis XII, renewed the Italian Wars, quickly capturing Milan and forcing Ludovico into exile. In 1500 Ludovico returned at the head of a mercenary army, but was captured and imprisoned in France where he died. His son **Massimiliano** (1493–1530) regained the duchy briefly (1513–16) from the French, and another son, **Francesco Maria** (1495–1535), was restored (1522) by Emperor Charles V. On Francesco's death, Milan became part of the Habsburg domains.

Shackleton, Sir Ernest Henry (1874–1922) British Antarctic explorer, b. Ireland. He accompanied Robert Scott on the *Discovery* expedition (1901–04), and led his own *Nimrod* expedition (1907–09), establishing a farthest-south record, 155km (97mi) short of the South Pole. Shackleton's second expedition (1914–16) aimed to cross Antarctica from the Weddell Sea to McMurdo Sound, but his ship, *Endurance*, was crushed by ice and his men marooned. Shackleton's successful rescue mission, which he described in *South* (1919), is one of the great epics of polar exploration. *See also* Amundsen, Roald

Shaftesbury, Anthony Ashley Cooper, 1st Earl of (1621–83) English statesman, lord chancellor (1672–73). He joined the Short Parliament in 1640, but was barred at the start of the Long Parliament. In the English Civil War, Cooper deserted the Royalists for the Parliamentary cause in 1644. He helped secure greater powers for Oliver Cromwell from Barebone's Parliament (1653), and was rewarded with a seat on the Council of State (1653–54). After the Restoration of Charles II (1660), he slowly gained the trust of the king and became one of the members of the so-called Cabal (cabinet council). In 1672 he became Earl of Shaftesbury and, despite lacking any legal training, was appointed lord chancellor. He issued the Declaration of Indulgence (1672), which extended religious tolerance, and supported the Third Dutch War (1672–74). He was sacked by Charles after sponsoring the first Test Act (1673), which was designed to prevent the accession of the Catholic Duke of York (later James II). Shaftesbury subsequently became the most prominent member of the "Whig" opposition and, after Titus Oates' fictitious Popish Plot (1678), organized it into a coherent political force. He supported the claims of Charles' illegitimate son, the Duke of Monmouth, and spearheaded the legislation that led to the Exclusion Crisis. Charles dissolved Parliament and Shaftesbury was arrested for treason. He was acquitted and fled into exile in Holland (1682), where he died.

Shaftesbury, Anthony Ashley Cooper, 7th Earl of (1801–85) British social reformer and philanthropist. He entered Parliament in 1826. Ashley opposed the Reform Bill of 1832 (*see* Reform Acts), but helped secure the repeal of the Corn Laws (1846). He sponsored the Lunacy Act of 1845, which did much to increase understanding and tolerance of madness, but his principal concern was to improve the living and working conditions of the British industrial working-class. Ashley was the driving force behind the Ten Hours Act (1847), which reduced the working day in textile mills, and the Mines Act (1842), which banned employment of women and young children underground. He also headed the Ragged Schools for working-class children, and helped create the Shaftesbury estates that provided low-cost urban housing. He led the evangelical wing in the Church of England, serving as president of the Bible Society. *See also* Factory Acts

Shah Jahan (1592–1666) Fifth Mughal emperor of India (1628–58), third son of Jahangir. In 1622 he rebelled against his father, but was reconciled in 1625. Shah Jahan spent much of his reign fighting against the Deccan states, expanding the Mughal Empire by the acquisition or submission of Ahmadnagar, Golconda and Bijapur. He also fought a costly war against the Persians, briefly holding (1638–49) Kandahar, S Afghanistan. Shah Jahan's reign is mainly remembered, however, for its architectural achievements and the brilliance of his court. In Agra, N central India, he built the Taj Mahal (1632–54) and two magnificent mosques. In 1648 Shah Jahan moved his capital from Agra to Delhi, where he constructed the Great Mosque (Jami Masjid) and began work on the Red Fort. In 1657 he fell ill, prompting a struggle for succession among his sons. Aurangzeb emerged triumphant, imprisoning Shah Jahan in Agra until his death.

Shaka (*c.*1787–1828) Zulu chief (1816–28). His parents' marriage broke Zulu laws and Shaka spent his traumatized childhood in exile. From 1810 to 1816 Shaka fought for Dingiswayo of the Mtetwa, who released him from service on the death of his father, Senzangakona. Shaka reorganized the Zulu state and created a formidable army of *c.*40,000 warriors, formed in *impi* (regiments), armed with short, stabbing spears, and trained to attack in buffalo-horns formation. Within a year of becoming chief, the Zulu nation had quadrupled in number through the forcible assimilation of neighbouring clans. In 1817 Dingiswayo was murdered and Shaka set out to create a mighty Zulu empire in S Africa. Within two years, he had crushed all remaining local resistance. Throughout the 1820s, Shaka waged campaigns against tribal groups to the S. By 1823 the present-day South African province of KwaZulu-Natal was a charred, depopulated plateau. The forced migration of tribes led indirectly to the *Mfecane* (crushing), which killed *c.*2 million people and completely restructured the clan structure from Tanzania to Cape Colony. In 1824 Shaka established good relations with the European colonists at Port Natal (now Durban). Shaka became insane after the death of his mother (1827), killing all pregnant women. He was assassinated by his half brother, Dingaan, who succeeded him.

Shakers (officially United Society of Believers in Christ's Second Appearing) US religious sect. The nickname derived from the trembling fervour of their religious ceremonies. An offshoot of the English QUAKERS in 1747, they remained a tiny group until Ann LEE ("Mother Anne"), who believed she was the female reincarnation of Jesus Christ, emigrated to New York with eight followers in 1774. The movement spread, and by *c*.1850 numbered *c*.6000 in more than 18 communes. A central belief of Shakers is the dual (male and female) nature of the Deity. Among other tenets are sexual equality, pacifism and the sanctity of labour, which is reflected in the simple beauty of their renowned furniture and craftwork.

Shalmaneser III (d.824 BC) King of ASSYRIA (859–824 BC), son and successor of Ashurnasirpal II. He devoted most of his reign to the conquest of N Syria. Shalmaneser captured CILICIA and extracted tribute from TYRE, SIDON and SAMARIA, but failed to gain Damascus. His last years were marked by civil war. Shalmaneser's achievements are recorded on the Black Obelisk that he had erected in his new palace-city of CALAH (now Nimrud, Iraq). It is now in the British Museum, London.

Shamil (*c*.1797–1871) Muslim resistance leader in the Caucasus Mountains. As leader of the Caucasian tribes in Dagestan and Chechenia, he fought a long jihad (holy war) against Russian dominance (1834–59). During the CRIMEAN WAR, Shamil became an unofficial ally of the British and French and gained a reputation in Europe. After the War, when Russia was able to field more troops against him, his movement faded and he was captured (1859).

Shamir, Yitzhak (1915–) Israeli statesman, prime minister (1983–84, 1986–90, 1990–92), b. Poland. He emigrated to PALESTINE in 1935. Shamir joined the Zionist organizations IRGUN ZEVAI LEUMI and the STERN GANG, which resisted the British mandate. He was arrested by the British in 1941 and 1946, escaping to asylum in France. After the creation of the state of ISRAEL in 1948, he joined Mossad (the Israeli secret service). In 1973 Shamir was elected to the Knesset (parliament), becoming chairman of Herut, the largest party in the LIKUD bloc, in 1975. He served as foreign minister (1980–83) under Menachem BEGIN and succeeded him briefly as prime minister. After an inconclusive election in 1984, Shamir entered into a power-sharing arrangement with Shimon PERES, leader of the Labour Party. Shamir served as deputy prime minister and foreign minister until 1986. In 1990 Shamir managed to form a coalition without Labour support. His support for new Jewish settlements on the WEST BANK hindered progress in the Middle East peace process with the PALESTINE LIBERATION ORGANIZATION (PLO). Likud was defeated by Yitzhak RABIN in the 1992 elections, and Shamir was replaced as leader by Binyamin NETANYAHU. *See also* MAPAI; ZIONISM

Shang (Yin) First documented dynasty in China (*c*.1600–*c*.1050 BC) – details of the reputed previous XIA dynasty are found only in Chinese legend. Although no literature has survived, Shang "oracle bones", inscribed with details of their civilization, were discovered (AD 1899) near the modern city of Anyang, Henan, N China. The dynasty possibly had a capital near modern-day Zhengzhou, Henan. In the 14th century BC, the capital was moved to Anyang. At its height, the kingdom covered much of the valley of the Huang He (Yellow River). The Shang mobilized large armies, led by commanders in chariots. The power, wealth, art and technology of the Shang was reflected in their ability to build massive earthworks and timber houses, their crafting of fabulous ritual bronzes, and their jade-carving and pottery. One royal tomb at Anyang, for example, yielded more than 440 bronze vessels and 590 jade objects. The Shang were conquered by the ZHOU dynasty. *See also* BRONZE AGE

Shanghai City and port in SE China. The development of the city dates from the SONG dynasty (AD 960–1279). During the Ming dynasty (1368–1644), Shanghai became a centre of the Chinese cotton industry. The growth of the modern city dates from the Treaty of NANJING (1842), when, as one of the five TREATY PORTS, it was opened to foreign trade, which stimulated industrial development. The United States, Britain, France and Japan held substantial concessions in the city. Their citizens enjoyed immunity from Chinese law, among other privileges, and Shanghai became a cosmopolitan city. By the 1860s Shanghai had overtaken GUANGZHOU as China's busiest port. The Chinese Communist Party was founded (1921) in Shanghai, but soon suppressed by the KUOMINTANG. Between 1937 and 1945 the city was occupied by the Japanese. In the early years of communist rule, Shanghai experienced relative decline, but rapid growth was resumed from the early 1960s. Pop. (1993) 8,760,000.

Shankara (*c*.700–*c*.750) (Sankaracharya) Indian religious thinker, the most famous exponent of the VEDANTA system of Hindu philosophy. According to tradition, he led an austere life, travelling around India to hold discussions with philosophers of various schools. Shankara founded monasteries to help spread his ideas and wrote commentaries on the major Hindu scriptures. He believed in the oneness of all creation, seeing Brahma as the one true reality in the universe and the source of all things. *See also* HINDUISM

Shapur II (the Great) (AD 309–79) Ninth SASANIAN ruler of ancient Iran, son of Hormizd II. According to legend, Shapur's father died before he was born and he ruled under a regency until AD 325. From *c*.339 Shapur enforced uniformity within the empire by vigorously persecuting Christians and forcibly converting them to ZOROASTRIANISM. He crushed the central Asian tribes and annexed their kingdom. Shapur waged a long and bloody conflict against the Romans in N MESOPOTAMIA, capturing Amida (now Diyarbakir) in 359 and finally regaining Nisbis and four other provinces after the death of Emperor JULIAN (THE APOSTATE) at the Battle of Ctesiphon (363). Shapur also won control of most of Armenia from the Romans, marking the peak of the Sasanian empire.

sharia Sacred law of ISLAM, regarded by Muslims as divine revelation, first codified in the 8th century. It is drawn from a number of sources, including the KORAN and the HADITH. It is largely occupied with personal behaviour as well as religious belief. Islamic rulers and governments have generally combined the sharia with secular laws and customs appropriate to particular political circumstances.

Sharon, Ariel (1928–) Israeli general and statesman. He gained a reputation as a bold commander in the first of the ARAB-ISRAELI WARS (1948). Sharon seized the Mitla Pass on the Sinai Peninsula during the SUEZ CRISIS (1956) and regained it during the SIX-DAY WAR (1967). In the YOM KIPPUR WAR (1973), he captured Egypt's 3rd Army. Sharon was a founder (1973) of the right-wing LIKUD coalition and was first elected to the Knesset (parliament) in 1973. As minister of defence (1981–83) under Menachem BEGIN, Sharon was the main architect of Israel's invasion of LEBANON. He was forced to resign after being reprimanded for not taking action to prevent the massacre of Lebanese Christians in two Palestinian refugee camps in Beirut. Sharon served as minister of foreign affairs (1999) under Binyamin NETANYAHU, supporting further Jewish settlement in the Occupied Territories. In 2000 he succeeded Netanyahu as leader of Likud.

Sharpeville Township in Gauteng province, NE South Africa. It was the scene of a massacre (21 March 1960) by South African police of demonstrators engaged in a peaceful protest, organized by the PAN-AFRICANIST CONGESS (PAC), against the introduction of pass laws. A crowd of *c*.20,000 people gathered outside a police station in Sharpeville and the police opened fire, killing 69 protestors (including women and children) and wounding *c*.186 others. The massacre highlighted the brutality of South Africa's APARTHEID regime and prompted its exit from the Commonwealth of Nations (1961). It also led to the founding of UMKHONTE WE SIZWE, the military wing of the AFRICAN NATIONAL CONGRESS (ANC). The South African government banned the ANC and PAC.

Sharpsburg, Battle of *See* ANTIETAM, BATTLE OF

Shawnee Algonquian-speaking NATIVE NORTH AMERICANS who originally inhabited the Ohio River valley. In the 18th century they were expelled by the IROQUOIS and dispersed across a wide area. The majority (Eastern Shawnee) moved initially to present-day Georgia and South Carolina but later further divided, some settling in Pennsylvania and others migrating to the Cumberland Valley, Tennessee. Between 1730 and 1750 the Shawnee reunited in Ohio, where they disrupted the expansion of white settlement. SHAWNEE PROPHET and his brother TECUMSEH failed in their attempts to unite the various tribes in the Ohio Valley and the Shawnee suffered a crushing defeat by US forces under William HARRISON at the Battle of TIPPECANOE (1811). The Shawnee once more fragmented. Some were absorbed by the CHEROKEE, while the largest number, known as the Absentee Shawnee, eventually moved from Kansas to Oklahoma, where most of their descendants remain. Today, there are *c*.2000 Shawnee.

Shawnee Prophet (Tenskwatawa) (*c*.1768–1837) Native North American leader of the SHAWNEE, brother of TECUMSEH. Claiming to have received a divine message urging Native Americans to return to their traditional way of life, he attempted to create a confederacy of Native American nations. He led them to a disastrous defeat at the Battle of TIPPECANOE (1811).

Shays' Rebellion (1786–87) Revolt by debt-ridden US farmers against the state courts in Massachusetts. It was prompted by the failure of the state government to take preventive action against farm closures and seizures of property caused by high state taxes. Daniel Shays (*c*.1747–1825), a destitute farmer, led 1200 insurgents against the state Supreme Court and the federal arsenal in Springfield. The rebels were eventually crushed by a militia raised by private subscription, highlighting the weakness of the state government. Shays and others were condemned to death but later pardoned and some measures for debt relief enacted. The Rebellion strengthened support for a strong central government.

Sheba (Saba') Ancient kingdom in SW Arabia (now part of YEMEN). Its capital was Ma'rib. Its inhabitants, the Semitic Sabaeans, colonized the region at least as early as the 10th century BC when, according to the Old Testament and the Koran, the Queen of Sheba (Bilqis) visited King SOLOMON. According to Ethiopian tradition, Sheba (Makeda) bore Solomon a son, Menelik I, who founded the royal dynasty of Ethiopia. At its height, between the 7th and 5th centuries BC, the kingdom of Sheba prospered from its control of trade on the Red Sea and established colonies along the coast of Africa.

Shelburne, William Petty FitzMaurice, 2nd Earl of (1737–1805) British statesman, prime minister (1782–83). He entered Parliament as a Whig in 1760 and briefly acted as first lord of trade (1763) under George GRENVILLE. Shelburne resigned and allied himself with William PITT (THE ELDER), whom he served as a secretary of state (1766–68). He returned to government as home secretary (1782) to the Marquess of ROCKINGHAM (1782) and, at the insistence of GEORGE III, succeeded him as prime minister. Shelburne drafted the preliminary peace treaty that concluded the AMERICAN REVOLUTION, but the supporters of Charles James Fox and Lord NORTH soon compelled him to resign and he was overlooked by William PITT (THE YOUNGER).

Shenandoah Valley Part of the Great Appalachian Valley between the Blue Ridge and Allegheny mountains, Virginia, United States, *c*.240km (150mi) long. A major route in the westward expansion of the frontier, white settlement in the region began in the 1730s. The Valley was a vital strategic stronghold for the Confederates during the American CIVIL WAR (1861–65). In 1862 the manoeuvres of Confederate General "Stonewall" JACKSON in the Valley tied up Union troops assigned to reinforce George MCCLELLAN during the PENINSULAR CAMPAIGN, thus helping Robert Lee secure victory in the SEVEN DAYS' BATTLES. Jackson then took the offensive, gaining victories at Winchester, Cross Keys and Port Republic. More than 50,000 Northern troops were deployed to counter the threat that Jackson and his *c*.16,000 men posed to the Northern capital of Washington. The Confederates continued to menace the capital until Philip SHERIDAN defeated Jubal EARLY in October 1864.

Shere Ali (1825–79) (Shir 'Ali) Emir of Afghanistan (1863–79), son and successor of DOST MUHAMMAD. In the undeclared war between the British and Russian empires in the region, Shere Ali at first favoured the British. In 1878, however, he received a Russian mission and refused a British one, and pressure by the assertive British viceroy of India, Lord Lytton, led to the outbreak of the Second AFGHAN WAR (1878–81). The British captured the Khyber

Pass and Shere Ali fled. Lord Lytton's policy was reversed by a new British government after 1880.

Sheridan, Philip Henry (1831–88) Union general in the American CIVIL WAR. Sheridan's storming of Missionary Ridge was instrumental in the Federal victory at CHATTANOOGA (1863) and persuaded General Ulysses GRANT to give him command of the cavalry of the Army of the Potomac (1864). Further victories saw him promoted to command the Army of the Shenandoah. In October 1864 Sheridan drove the Confederate forces of Jubal EARLY out of the SHENANDOAH VALLEY, burning the land and farmsteads that fed the Confederate cause. He now turned his attention to cutting off Robert LEE's retreat and helped to force his surrender at APPOMATTOX (1865). His ruthless implementation of RECONSTRUCTION policies as military governor of Louisiana and Texas (1867) caused his dismissal. He later fought in the Indian Wars and crowned his career as general in chief (1883–88).

Sheridan, Richard Brinsley (1751–1816) British dramatist and politician, b. Ireland. He entered Parliament as a Whig in 1780, serving as secretary to the treasury (1783) and treasurer of the navy (1806–07). Sheridan directed the impeachment of Warren HASTINGS, governor general of India, but his brilliant oratory failed to secure conviction. As adviser to the Prince of Wales (later GEORGE IV), Sheridan supported his patron's attempts to become regent for GEORGE III. Although generally a supporter of Charles James Fox, he gave qualified support to the Tory government of Henry ADDINGTON. Sheridan's political ambitions faded after he lost his seat in 1807. He is best remembered as a dramatist, the last and finest exponent of the Restoration comedy of manners. His plays include *The Rivals* (1775) and *The School for Scandal* (1777).

sheriff Government official in Anglo-Saxon England. The name is a shortened form of "shire reeve", and originally the sheriff looked after the royal lands in his shire (county). After the Norman Conquest (1066), the power of the sheriff greatly increased. He became judge of all local civil and criminal cases and leader of local militias. In this period, sheriffs gained a reputation for corruption and exploitation, as typified by the sheriff of Nottingham in the Robin Hood stories. The appointment of other officials, especially justices of the peace, reduced his authority, and by the 16th century the office was largely ceremonial. The name was adopted in the United States for the chief law-enforcement officer of a county.

Sherman, John (1823–1900) US statesman, brother of William SHERMAN. He served in the House of Representatives (1855–61) and the Senate (1861–77, 1881–97). A financial expert, Sherman helped establish a national banking system (1863). As secretary of the treasury (1877–81) under Rutherford HAYES, he was instrumental in returning the nation to the GOLD STANDARD. During the presidency of Benjamin HARRISON, he wrote the Sherman Silver Purchase Act (1890), which increased the government's monthly silver purchases, and the SHERMAN ANTI-TRUST ACT (1890), which placed restrictions on business monopolies. Sherman briefly served as secretary of state (1897–98) under President William MCKINLEY, but resigned on grounds of poor health.

Sherman, Roger (1721–93) US politician. He signed the Declaration of Independence (1776), the Articles of Confederation (1777) and the US Constitution. At the CONSTITUTIONAL CONVENTION (1787), Sherman and Oliver ELLSWORTH proposed the so-called Connecticut Compromise, which called for a bicameral legislature with each house having its own system of representation. The proposal forms the basis of the present CONGRESS OF THE UNITED STATES. Sherman later served in the House of Representatives (1789–91) and the Senate (1791–93).

Sherman, William Tecumseh (1820–91) Union general in the American CIVIL WAR. He graduated from West Point in 1840 and fought against the SEMINOLE in Florida. Sherman did not see active service in the Mexican War and resigned from the US Army in 1853. He joined the Union Army as a colonel at the start of the Civil War (1861–65), fighting in the disastrous defeat at the First Battle of BULL RUN (1861). Sherman was promoted to major general after helping to secure victory for General Ulysses GRANT in the Battle of SHILOH (1862). He commanded the 15th Corps in the successful Siege of VICKSBURG (1863), and led the Army of the Tennessee to victory at the Battle of CHATTANOOGA (1863). In 1864 he became supreme commander in the West. After capturing ATLANTA (September 1864), Sherman led his *c.*60,000-strong army on the "march to the sea" through Georgia, destroying Confederate supplies, communications and morale en route to SAVANNAH. This campaign is often regarded as the first example of "total war". His advance through the Carolinas was perhaps even more destructive. Sherman received the surrender of Joseph JOHNSTON 17 days after Robert LEE had surrendered to Grant (9 April 1865). Sherman succeeded Grant as commanding general of the US army (1869–83), but unlike Grant refused to run for president.

Sherman Anti-Trust Act (1890) US legislation prohibiting any business combination or trust in restraint of trade. Named after Senator John SHERMAN, it was a response to the growth of monopolies and cartels that controlled markets and crushed competitors to their own advantage. The Act's early use was mainly confined to trade UNIONS, and it did not become fully effective until reinforced by other measures, including the creation of the Anti-Trust Division of the Department of Justice (1903), the CLAYTON ANTI-TRUST ACT (1914) and the Federal Trade Commission (1914). It proved an invaluable defence of FREE TRADE.

Sher Shah (*c.*1486–1545) Indian emperor (1540–45), b. Farid Khan. An Afghan solder, he became ruler of Bihar after leading it to victory over Bengal. In 1539 Sher conquered Bengal and defeated the Mughal Emperor HUMAYUN at the Battle of Chausa. He assumed the title Sher Shah after his decisive victory over Humayun at Kannauj (1540). He later extended his rule to most of N India, including the Punjab. Sher Shah centralized the fractured administration of the MUGHAL EMPIRE, creating an equitable taxation system. He died in the siege of Kalinjar and was succeeded by his son, Islam Shah (r.1545–53). The Sur dynasty lasted only until 1556, when Humayun, who had re-established his power in Afghanistan, regained his Indian throne.

Shevardnadze, Eduard Ambrosievich (1928–) Georgian statesman, president (1992–). He rose through the communist hierarchy in GEORGIA and was appointed to the central committee of the Communist Party of the Soviet Union in 1976. A close ally of Mikhail GORBACHEV, Shevardnadze was foreign minister (1985–90). He was influential in the decision to withdraw Soviet troops (1989) from the AFGHANISTAN WAR and worked for good relations with the West. In 1992, after the break-up of the Soviet Union, he was invited to lead the turbulent new state of Georgia. He overcame supporters of the deposed leader, Zviad Gamsakhurdia, with Russian aid, and survived assassination attempts in 1995 and 1998.

Shidehara Kijuro (1872–1951) Japanese statesman and diplomat, foreign minister (1924–27, 1929–31), prime minister (1945–46). He was Japan's chief representative at the Washington Conference (1921–22), which called for naval disarmament in the Pacific. As foreign minister, Shidehara advocated moderation, particularly towards China, and peace through negotiation in international affairs. Such policies became increasingly unpopular with the rise of militarism in Japanese society, and he was driven from office. After Japan's defeat in World War 2, Shidehara acted as prime minister until the completion of demilitarization by the United States. He was succeeded by YOSHIDA SHIGERU.

Shihuangdi *See* QIN SHIHUANGDI

Shiite Follower of Shi'a, smaller of the two main branches of ISLAM. The division between Shiites and majority SUNNITES arose from disagreement over the caliphate succession to MUHAMMAD. Shiites (the party of Ali) believe that only members of the clan of Muhammad were qualified, specifically the descendants of FATIMA, the Prophet's daughter, and ALI, her husband. Although Ali was the fourth caliph, after his murder (661) the caliphate passed to MUAWIYA, founder of the UMAYYAD dynasty. Ali's son Husayn led an insurrection against the Umayyads, but was defeated and killed at the Battle of Karbala (680), central Iraq. Shi'a rejects the *Sunna* (the collection of teachings outside the KORAN) and relies rather on the pronouncements of a succession of imams (religious leaders). The SAFAVID dynasty (1501–1722) in Iran was the first to adopt Shi'a as a state religion. The Iranians belong to the Twelvers, the largest of several subgroups among Shiites, who recognize twelve imams, beginning with Ali, and await the return of the twelfth as the Mahdi. Another significant group are the ISMAILIS, or Seveners, who created the FATIMID dynasty in the 10th century. Today, there are *c.*90 million Shiites. They form the majority in Iran, and large minorities are found in Iraq, Syria, Lebanon, India, Pakistan and parts of Central Asia. *See also* SUFISM

Shiloh, Battle of (6–7 April 1862) Major engagement in the American CIVIL WAR, fought near Pittsburg Landing, SW Tennessee. Confederate General Albert Johnston hoped to defeat the Union Army of the Tennessee, under General Ulysses GRANT, before the arrival of General D.C. Buell with reinforcements. Although the attack took William Sherman, at Shiloh Church, by surprise, Johnston was killed in the advance and the Confederates were unable to exploit their advantage. Buell's arrival during the night enabled Grant to take the offensive. A strong rearguard action held him at bay, however, and the Confederates, now led by P.G.T. BEAUREGARD, withdrew. The Battle ended indecisively, with both sides claiming victory, but it was, in fact, a defeat for the Confederates. Union casualties were more than 13,000, Confederate more than 10,000.

Shimabara Rebellion (1637–38) Revolt of Japanese Roman Catholics in the Shimabara Peninsula, SW Japan. The TOKUGAWA shogunate regarded Japanese Christians as traitors and they were persecuted and exploited. Driven into rebellion, *c.*40,000 Christians were attacked by the shogun's 100,000-strong army with maritime support from the Dutch at Nagasaki. They held out for several months, their numbers augmented by other Christians who came to their aid, but were eventually slaughtered. Only a handful survived. The Rebellion all but extinguished Christianity in Japan and solidified the shogunate's policy of isolation.

Shining Path *See* SENDERO LUMINOSO

Shinto ("way of the divine") Indigenous religion of JAPAN. Its origins lay in ancient custom and belief; uniquely, Shinto has no founder, no scriptural canon and no priestly hierarchy. It includes an incalculable number of holy entities or *kami*, including gods, certain human souls, ancestral spirits, and spirits of nature, including the spirits of specific places, marked by simple shrines and guarded by a sacred gate or arch. During the NARA, HEIAN and KAMAKURA periods it was influenced by BUDDHISM, CONFUCIANISM and TAOISM. There was some mingling with Buddhism, although Shinto retained a separate identity. Under the TOKUGAWA shogunate (1603–1868) Shinto's significance receded, but after the MEIJI RESTORATION, when Buddhism ceased to be the state religion, it was revived and developed into several forms, including a secular form embraced by nationalists and militarists. The emperor was regarded as a divine descendant of the sun goddess Amaterasu Omikami, founder of Japan. This state sect was abolished after World War 2, but the traditional shrines and spirit of Shinto were revived and restored.

Shipley, Jenny (1952–) New Zealand stateswoman, prime minister (1997–99). She joined the National Party in 1975 and was first elected to Parliament in 1987. A strong advocate of women's rights, Shipley served as minister of social welfare (1990–93), minister of women's affairs (1990–96) and minister of health (1993–96). In 1997 she succeeded Jim BOLGER, becoming New Zealand's first woman prime minister and party leader. She lost the 1999 elections to Helen Clark of the Labour Party.

ship money Occasional English tax levied on ports for their protection by the navy. In 1634 CHARLES I, attempting to rule without Parliament and therefore short of money, revived the tax and extended it to the whole country. Resistance grew, returns fell, and in 1638 John HAMPDEN, a country squire, refused to pay on principle. A test case on the legality of taxes not sanctioned by Parliament, including ship money, followed, and the judges found narrowly (7:5) for the king. Ship money was abolished by the LONG PARLIAMENT in 1641.

Shir 'Ali *See* SHERE ALI

Shiraz City in SW Iran, near the ancient citadel of Persepolis. Established as a cultural centre as early as the 4th century, it has long been known for the excellence of its arts and crafts. Birthplace of the Persian poets Sadi and Hafiz, it became a Muslim religious centre and a place of pilgrimage. In 1750 Karim Khan established his capital here, constructing his mausoleum and the Vakil Mosque and Bazaar. Pop. (1991) 965,117.

Shivaji *See* Sivaji

shogun Title of the military ruler of Japan, first conferred upon Yoritomo in 1192. The Kamakura (1192–1333), Ashikaga (1338–1568) and Tokugawa (1603–1868) shogunates ruled feudal Japan, with the emperor retaining only ceremonial and religious duties. The shogunate ended with the Meiji Restoration (1868).

Shona Bantu-speaking people of southern Africa. Comprising a large number of related groups, they are thought to be descended from the builders of Great Zimbabwe. At one time they owed allegiance to a paramount chief, but in the 19th century intruders such as the Ndebele and the British broke up Shona unity.

Short Parliament (13 April–5 May 1640) English Parliament that ended 11 years of personal rule by Charles I. Charles was forced to summon Parliament to raise revenue through taxation for the Bishops' Wars against the Scots. Parliament insisted on redress of its own grievances against royal government, and some members sympathized with the Scots. Charles lost patience and dissolved Parliament in May, but was compelled to summon the Long Parliament a few months later. *See also* Civil War, English; Pym, John; ship money

Shoshone Native North Americans. They were divided into several allied groups distributed through much of the W United States, from SW Nevada to Idaho, Wyoming and E Montana. They were mainly hunter-gatherers and lived in extended-family groups with no formal chiefs. In the 18th century the acquisition of horses changed the habits of the E Shoshone, including the Comanche, to a life resembling the Plains culture. The success of the Lewis and Clark Expedition was largely due to the presence of a young Shoshone woman, Sacagawea, who acted as guide and interpreter.

Shotoku, Taishi (574–622) Japanese prince, regent (593–622) for his aunt Empress Suiko (r.592–628). He aimed to end the endemic feuding of the Japanese clans by strengthening Buddhism, then little known in Japan, and introducing an effective central administration based on Confucianism. He restored Japanese relations with China, which had been broken for many years, encouraged Chinese values, and attracted Chinese craftsmen to Japan. Imperial powers that had slipped away to the feudal chiefs were reclaimed, and Shotoku reputedly wrote the "Seventeen Article Constitution" (604), which called for a centralized state and a court bureaucracy with promotion based on merit. He built many Buddhist temples, including the Horyu Temple (607) at Nara, S Honshu.

Siam *See* Thailand

Siberia (Tatar, Sleeping Land) Asian region of Russia, stretching from the Ural Mountains to the Pacific Ocean. Compromising *c.*14 million sq km (5 million sq mi), the vast distances and cold climate of Siberia resulted in relatively sparse settlement by tribal peoples in the Palaeolithic period. It formed part of the Mongol khanate of the Golden Horde between the 10th and mid-15th century. Tatars from Turkistan founded a khanate before 1500. The Russian conquest of the Tatar khanate, led by Cossacks, was largely accomplished between 1581 and 1644. Furs were the initial attraction, later minerals such as coal and oil, the source of most of the wealth of the Russian empire. Siberia was used as a penal colony under the tsarist regime, and its Soviet successor sent many political opponents to Siberian gulags. Large-scale Russian settlement began after the construction (1881–1905) of the Trans-Siberian Railway and, with rapid industrialization, the population doubled between 1914 and 1946. Pop. (1994) 35,605,000.

Sicilian Vespers (30–31 March 1282) Massacre of French soldiers in Palermo, NW Sicily, which began at vespers (evensong) on Easter Monday. In 1266 Pope Clement IV bestowed Sicily on the Angevin king Charles I, who imposed oppressive rule and onerous taxation. The Sicilians, enraged by Charles' rule, killed *c.*2000 French residents in one night. The massacre initiated a 20-year war for control of Sicily, which ended in the expulsion of the French and the accession of the Aragonese.

Sicily Largest island in the Mediterranean Sea, off the SW tip of the Italian peninsula, comprising (with nearby islands) an autonomous region of Italy. The capital is Palermo. At the centre of the Mediterranean, Sicily has been invaded and settled by many people. The Greeks built colonies on the islands, starting with Naxos (*c.*734 BC) and ending with Agrigento (*c.*580 BC). They were followed (*c.*536 BC) by the Phoenicians, who were for a long time confined to NW Sicily and their conquest of the island was prevented by Dionysius the Elder (r.405–367 BC) of Syracuse. In the 3rd century BC, it was captured by the Romans in the First and Second Punic Wars. The Vandals, the Ostrogoths and the Byzantines held Sicily for varying periods before it was occupied by the Arabs in the 9th century. In 1091 the Norman soldier Robert Guiscard finally drove out the Arabs, and Roger II created the first Kingdom of the Two Sicilies (including Naples), although Islamic cultural influences remained strong. The kingdom passed to the Hohenstaufen dynasty in 1194, and Emperor Frederick II centralized government in 1231. In 1266 Sicily was seized by the Angevin king Charles I, whose unpopular government caused the Sicilian Vespers revolt (1282) and ultimately the division of the Two Kingdoms into Aragonese Sicily and Angevin Naples. They were later reunited under Spanish rule, and the Spanish Bourbon Kingdom of the Two Sicilies was founded in 1735. It was temporarily displaced by Napoleon and subsequently shaken by popular revolts, until conquered (1860) by Giuseppe Garibaldi and incorporated in the kingdom of Italy. Sicily was captured by Anglo-French forces during World War 2. Pop. (1992) 4,997,705.

Siddhartha Gautama *See* Buddha

Sidi Muhammad *See* Muhammad V

Sidmouth, Henry Addington, Viscount *See* Addington, Henry, 1st Viscount Sidmouth

Sidney, Algernon (1622–83) English politician. He fought for Parliament during the English Civil War, but refused to take part in the trial of Charles I and disapproved of Oliver Cromwell's Protectorate. Sidney went into exile with the Restoration (1660) of Charles II, but returned to England in 1677 and joined the Earl of Shaftesbury in opposition to the king. He was charged, perhaps falsely, with involvement in the Rye House Plot and executed. Sidney became a great Whig hero for his opposition to royal absolutism and defence of the sovereignty of the people.

Sidney, Sir Philip (1554–86) English poet and courtier. Handsome, cultured and gallant, he epitomised the ideal of the Renaissance gentleman. Sidney carried out diplomatic missions for Elizabeth I, secretly seeking support from the German princes for the creation of a Protestant League to act as a bulwark against Catholic Spain. He also lent financial support for the English voyages of exploration to the Americas. Sidney joined the Earl of Leicester's army in support of the Revolt of the Netherlands against Spain. He was wounded in battle at Zutphen and later died of gangrene. The story of his heroism on the battlefield – fighting on when wounded and declining water in favour of a dying soldier –is possibly apocryphal. Today, Sidney is chiefly remembered for the pastoral romance *Arcadia* (1590) and the sonnet sequence *Astrophel and Stella* (1591).

Sidon (Saida) Ancient city on the Mediterranean coast of Lebanon. One of the oldest cities in Phoenicia, Sidon was founded in the 3rd millennium BC. With the city of Tyre, it was a centre of Phoenicia's maritime empire from the 13th century BC. It became celebrated for its glassware and purple dye. Captured by virtually every power in the Near East for two millennia, Sidon was destroyed by the Assyrians in 677 BC and sacked again

SIERRA LEONE

AREA: 71,740sq km (27,699sq mi)
POPULATION: 4,376,000
CAPITAL (POPULATION): Freetown (469,776)
GOVERNMENT: Transitional
ETHNIC GROUPS: Mende 35%, Temne 37%, Limba 8%,
LANGUAGES: English (official)
RELIGIONS: Traditional beliefs 51%, Islam 39%, Christianity 9%
GDP PER CAPITA (1995): US$580

Republic on the W coast of Africa. Portuguese sailors reached the coast in 1460. In the 16th century the area became a source of slaves. In 1787 the British Anti-Slavery Society bought some coastal territory from the local ruler and founded Freetown as a home for freed slaves. In 1808 the settlement became a British crown colony. During the 19th century the interior was gradually explored and in 1896 it was made a British protectorate. In 1951 the protectorate and colony were united.

In 1961 Sierra Leone gained independence under Prime Minister Sir Milton Margai. After Margai's death there were two military coups before a civilian government was established in 1978, with the All People's Congress as the sole political party. A 1991 referendum favoured the restoration of multiparty democracy, but in 1992 a military group seized power. A civil war began between the government and the Revolutionary United Front (RUF). The RUF opposed the corrupt Freetown government, which had plundered the wealth from the nation's diamond mines. Following multiparty elections in 1996, a civilian government was installed, led by Ahmed Tejan Kabbah.

In May 1997 Major Johnny Paul Koroma seized power in a military coup. The United Nations (UN) imposed sanctions, and Nigeria led an intervention force that restored Kabbah as president in 1998. A 1999 peace treaty promised an end to a civil war that had claimed *c.*10,000 lives. UN peacekeeping troops were deployed. In 2000 the RUF rebels, led by Foday Sankoh, abducted UN troops and renewed their war of terror. British soldiers were deployed to strengthen the UN force. Sankoh was captured and the government took the offensive.

S

under Persian rule (351 BC). It was destroyed many times during the Crusades and again by the Mongols in 1260. It flourished within the Ottoman Empire from the 16th to 18th century, but was in decline when it was devastated by an earthquake in 1837. Pop. (1998 est.) 38,000.

Siegfried Line Name given by Germany's opponents in 1918 to the defences built on its frontier with France, between Lens and Reims. Before World War 2, the West Wall (the German name), corresponded to the more formidable French Maginot Line. In 1944 it provided a brief respite for the retreating German army and delayed the Allied breakthrough.

Siena City in Tuscany, central Italy. Founded by the Etruscans and ruled in turn by the Romans and Lombards, Siena became a prosperous, independent commune in the 12th century. In the 13th century, it rivalled Florence as a centre of banking and commerce. To their economic rivalry was added involvement on opposite sides in the Guelph and Ghibelline conflict and they fought a series of costly wars. Commercial prosperity encouraged the birth of the Sienese school of painting, which includes such masters as Duccio di Buoninsegna (d. *c.*1318). The ravages of the Black Death (from 1348) and intense factional conflict heralded the end of Siena's golden age, and it fell increasingly under foreign rule. In 1500 Pandolfo Petrucci (*c.*1452–1512) assassinated Niccolò Borghese and established a brutal dictatorship. In 1557, after defeat by the Spanish, it passed to its old rival, Florence. Sights include the Palazzo Pubblico (1297–1310) and the Duomo (12th–13th century), one of the finest Gothic cathedrals in Italy. Pop. (1990) 58,278.

Sierra Leone *See* country feature, page 377

Sieyès, Emmanuel Joseph (1748–1836) French priest and revolutionary, who played an important role in both initiating and ending the French Revolution. His pamphlet *What is the Third Estate?*, proclaiming the sovereignty of the people, was published in January 1789 and had enormous influence. In 1789 Sieyès was elected to the States-General, and it was his motion that led it to transform itself into a National Assembly (June 1789). He guided the Assembly in the early months, ensuring that the bourgeoisie retained control. Sieyès voted for the execution of Louis XVI, but retired from politics during the Reign of Terror. He served on the Council of Five Hundred (1795–99) and the Directory (1799). Sieyès, Napoleon Bonaparte, Joseph Fouché and C.M. de Talleyrand plotted the coup of 18 Brumaire (19 November 1799) that overthrew the Directory. Napoleon gradually assumed supreme power and Sieyès' influence waned. He was forced into exile on the restoration of Louis XVIII (1815), but returned to Paris after the overthrow of Charles X in the July Revolution (1830).

Sigismund (1368–1437) Holy Roman emperor (1433–37), king of Germany (1411–37), Hungary (1387–1437) and Bohemia (1419–37). He inherited Brandenburg (1378) from his father, Emperor Charles IV, and became king of Hungary through marriage (1378) to Maria, daughter of Louis I (the Great). In 1388 Sigismund was forced to sell Brandenburg in order to finance the defence of Hungary. His aggressive foreign policy led to war with his half-brother, Wenceslas, who was king of Germany and Bohemia. After making peace with Wenceslas (1396), Sigismund went to war against the Ottomans, quickly suffering a catastrophic defeat (1396) at the hands of Sultan Bayezid I. In 1400 Wenceslas was deposed as king of Germany and Sigismund attempted to gain Bohemia, imprisoning Wenceslas (1402–03). Sigismund was crowned king of Germany by Pope John XXIII, whom he persuaded to summon the Council of Constance (1414–18), which ended the Great Schism and condemned Jan Hus as a heretic. Sigismund succeeded Wenceslas as king of Bohemia, but the revolt of the Hussites prevented him from securing control. His preoccupation with Bohemia meant that the German princes were able to form a coherent opposition to imperial rule. He was succeeded as king of Germany by his son-in-law, Albert II, the first ruler of the Habsburg dynasty.

Sigismund I (the Old) (1467–1548) King of Poland (1506–48), son of Casimir IV. Before succeeding his brother, Alexander I, as king, Sigismund had gained a reputation as an excellent provincial governor of Silesia. He succeeding in enacting a number of economic reforms, but many of his plans were blocked by the Polish Diet (parliament), which also insisted on his marriage (1512) to the daughter of Stephen Zápolya of Hungary. After her death, Sigismund married Bona Sforza, niece of Emperor Maximilian I. In the 1520s Sigismund gained control of East Prussia from the Teutonic Knights. He was an enlightened patron of the blossoming Renaissance in Poland and was almost unique among Europe's Catholic rulers in (reluctantly) extending tolerance to Protestants and in granting protection to Jews. He was succeeded by his son, Sigismund II. *See also* Jagiellon

Sigismund II Augustus (1520–72) King of Poland (1548–72), son and successor of Sigismund I and his notorious wife Bona Sforza. He served as co-ruler with his father from 1530 and managed the duchy of Lithuania from 1544. As king, Sigismund united Lithuania with Poland by the Union of Lublin (1569). The Livonian Order asked for Sigismund's protection, but his subsequent incorporation of Livonia into Lithuania (1561) resulted in the Livonian War against Ivan IV (the Terrible) of Russia. Sigismund ruled at the height of the Polish Renaissance, heading a brilliant court, but his reign was troubled by war, conflict with the Polish nobility and the battle between Protestantism and Roman Catholicism. Sigismund was the last ruler of the Jagiellon dynasty. His death without an heir meant that the Polish crown, always elective in theory, became so in practice.

Sigismund III (Vasa) (1566–1632) King of Poland (1587–1632) and Sweden (1592–99), son of John III of Sweden and grandson of Sigismund I of Poland. He succeeded his uncle Stephen Báthory as king of Poland, thus uniting the Jagiellon and Vasa dynasties. His power in Poland was limited by the Sejm (parliament), and his rule over Sweden was conditional on the maintenance of Protestantism. Sigismund's hostility to Swedish Lutheranism led to his overthrow by Charles IX and a long and costly series of Polish-Swedish wars. After emerging victorious from a civil war (1606–08) in Poland, Sigismund took advantage of the "Time of Troubles" in Russia to occupy Moscow (1610–12). While Sigismund was battling against the Ottoman Turks in Moldavia (1617–21), Gustavus II of Sweden gained control of Livonia. Sigismund's constant wars and religious bigotry did much to undermine royal authority in Poland. He was succeeded by his son Władysław IV (Vasa).

Sihanouk, Norodom *See* Norodom Sihanouk

Sikhism Indian religion founded in the Punjab in the early 16th century by Guru Nanak. Nanak endeavoured to combine elements of the Bhakti movement of Hinduism with aspects of Islamic Sufism to create a new, monotheistic religion. Sikhism regards all men as brothers and rejects the concept of caste. The centre of the Sikh religion was established at the Golden Temple in Amritsar by Ram Das, the fourth of the nine gurus following Nanak. His successor, Arjun (1536–1606), was responsible for the Adi Granth (Granth Sahib), the Sikh holy book. The tenth guru, Gobind Singh, founded the martial brotherhood *Khalsa* in 1699, a departure from the original pacifism of the Sikhs. Revolts against the Mughal Empire were largely unsuccessful, and in the 18th century the Sikhs were persecuted, until Ranjit Singh established his kingdom in the Punjab. The kingdom fragmented after Ranjit's death (1839), and after the Sikh Wars (1845–49) the Punjab was annexed by the British. When independence brought partition in 1947, the Punjab was divided between Pakistan and India. More than 2 million Sikhs were displaced, and many were killed. The majority settled in the Indian state of Punjab. They grew prosperous, and in the 1980s a movement for greater autonomy gathered support. Militants, led by Jarnail Singh Bhindranwale, advocated the creation of a separate Sikh state, Khalistan. Conflict with the Indian

SINGAPORE

AREA: 618sq km (239 sq mi)
POPULATION: 3,003,000
CAPITAL (POPULATION): Singapore City (2,812,000)
GOVERNMENT: Multiparty republic
ETHNIC GROUPS: Chinese 78%, Malay 14%, Indian 7%
LANGUAGES: Chinese, Malay, Tamil and English (all official)
RELIGIONS: Buddhism, Taoism and other traditional beliefs 54%, Islam 15%, Christianity 13%, Hinduism 4%
GDP PER CAPITA (1995): US$22,770

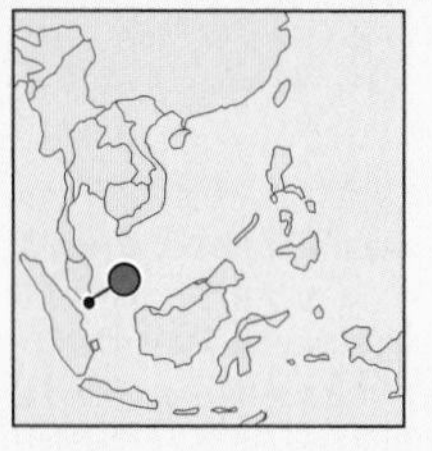

Singapore is a small republic at the s tip of the Malay Peninsula, SE Asia. It consists of the large Singapore Island and 59 small islets, 20 of which are inhabited. According to legend, Singapore was founded in 1299. It was first called Temasak (Sea Town), but was renamed Singapura (City of the Lion). Singapore soon became a busy trading centre within the Sumatran Srivijaya kingdom. Javanese raiders destroyed it in 1377. Subsumed into Johor, Singapore became part of the powerful Malacca sultanate in the 15th century.

In 1526 the Portuguese established a trading post on the island. In the 17th century this came under Dutch control. In 1819 the island was leased from Johor by Sir Thomas Stamford Raffles on behalf of the English East India Company. In 1826 Singapore, Penang and Malacca formed the Straits Settlements. Singapore soon became the most important British trading centre in Southeast Asia, and the Straits Settlement became a crown colony in 1867.

Despite British defensive reinforcements in the early 20th century, Japanese forces seized the island in 1942. British rule was restored in 1945. In 1946 the Straits Settlement was dissolved, and Singapore became a separate colony. In 1959 Singapore achieved self-government. Following a referendum, Singapore merged with Malaya, Sarawak and Sabah to form the Federation of Malaysia (1963). In 1965 Singapore broke away from the Federation to become an independent republic within the Commonwealth of Nations. The People's Action Party (PAP) has ruled Singapore since 1959. Its leader, Lee Kuan Yew, served as prime minister from 1959 until 1990, when he resigned and was succeeded by Goh Chok Tong. Under the PAP, the economy expanded rapidly. The PAP has been criticized by human rights groups for its authoritarian social policies and suppression of political dissent. In 1997 Goh Chok Tong and the PAP were decisively re-elected.

government led to the storming of the Golden Temple (1984), worsening relations between Sikhs and Hindus and perhaps contributing to the assassination of Indira GANDHI.

Sikh Wars (1845–46, 1848–49) Two conflicts fought between the Sikhs and the British in NW India. After the death of RANJIT SINGH in 1839, the Sikh state in the PUNJAB rapidly and violently fragmented and the military seized command. The first war began when a Sikh army, including many non-Sikhs, crossed the River Sutlej into British India. After four bloody battles, the British advanced to LAHORE, where peace was agreed (1846). The conflict was renewed two years later, but superior British artillery led to a Sikh defeat at Gujrat (1849). The Sikhs surrendered, and the Punjab was annexed to British India.

Sikorski, Władysław (1881–1943) Polish general and statesman, prime minister (1922–23). During World War 1, he served in the Polish Legion against Russia and later distinguished himself against the Bolsheviks in the RUSSO-POLISH WAR (1919–20). As prime minister and later minister of military affairs, Sikorski helped modernize the Polish army. Sikorski's opposition to the dictatorship of Józef PIŁSUDSKI drove him into exile (1928). When Germany overran Poland at the start of World War 2 (1939), Sikorski became commander-in-chief of the Free Polish forces and headed the government-in-exile from London, England. His demand (1943) for an international investigation into the KATYN MASSACRE (1940) led to a break in diplomatic relations with the Soviet Union. He was killed in an airplane crash.

Silesia Historic region in E central Europe, now divided between Poland (the major part), the Czech Republic and Germany. Settled by Slavs, in the 10th century AD it was fought over by the Czech PREMYSLID dynasty and the Polish PIASTS, finally falling to the Poles in *c.*992. In 1163 the region was divided into Lower (NW) Silesia and Upper (SE) Silesia. The Piasts encouraged German settlement. In 1335 Silesia became nominally part of the kingdom of Bohemia, and thus part of the Holy Roman Empire. The region was devastated in Emperor SIGISMUND I's battles with the HUSSITES (1425–35) but later, until Austrian Habsburg rule (from 1526), became a centre of the Protestant REFORMATION. Silesia's rich mineral resources and flourishing textile industries encouraged FREDERICK II (THE GREAT) of PRUSSIA to seize it from MARIA THERESA of Austria in the War of the AUSTRIAN SUCCESSION (1740–48). Its loss, bar a small area (known as Austrian Silesia) in SSE Silesia, was bitterly resented, but Austrian efforts to regain it during the SEVEN YEARS' WAR (1756–63) failed. Upper Silesia became a major centre of the Industrial Revolution. After the collapse of the Austrian empire at the end of World War 1, Austrian Silesia was divided between Poland and Czechoslovakia (1919). After a plebiscite (1921), all of Lower Silesia and most of Upper Silesia remained part of Germany, except for the richest mining region in SE Silesia, which became part of Poland. In 1939 Nazi Germany regained SE Silesia, but Poland acquired almost all of Silesia at the end of World War 2.

Silk Road Ancient trade route, 6400-km (4000-mi) long, linking China with the Near East, and thence with the Mediterranean region. It ran from the GREAT WALL OF CHINA through the current province of Xinjiang, NW China, skirted the Taklamakan Desert to Kashgar and then across the Pamir mountains to SAMARKAND and into Iran. More than 2000 years ago, caravans carrying silk and other luxuries travelled along the Road, passing through various hands on the way, to the Roman Empire. The Silk Road, with a branch over the Hindu Kush into India, was also followed by early Buddhist travellers from China. The route, always dangerous, was virtually disused in the early Middle Ages but revived when the Mongols enforced peace in Central Asia in the 13th century. Italian merchants, such as Marco POLO in the 1270s, took the opportunity to travel to China via the Silk Road. He returned by sea, and the speedier and easier sea route became the main highway from Europe to the Far East by the 16th century.

Silla Ancient kingdom in E KOREA. It was one of the states that emerged (*c.*57 BC) in the Period of the Three Kingdoms. It gained ascendancy over its neighbours, Koguryo and Paekche, and unified the Korean Peninsula (AD 668–935). The rich culture was basically Chinese and Buddhist, there was considerable interchange with TANG China, and Silla became the main link between China and Japan, withstanding several Japanese attacks. The monarchy disappeared after 935, when the last king abdicated. Silla was replaced by the kingdom of KORYO, founded by a former Silla general.

Silurian Third-oldest period of the PALAEOZOIC era, *c.*430–*c.*400mya. The name derives from the Silures, early inhabitants of central Wales, where the geological characteristics of the period were first studied. The future North America and Europe were joined and lay in tropical latitudes. The ancient Caledonian Mountains were formed, and the first plants appeared on land.

Sima Qian (*c.*145–*c.*87 BC) (Ssu-ma Ch'ien) Chinese historian. He was the official court historian under the HAN Emperor WUDI. Although Sima fell out of favour, was castrated, and imprisoned for several years, he completed the first history of China, the *Shih Chi* ("Records of History"), which was probably begun by his father and predecessor. It covers *c.*2000 years from the earliest times to his own, and although essentially dynastic, it refers to primary sources and includes notes on economic affairs, as well as crisp biographies.

Simeon I (the Great) (*c.*864–927) Tsar of Bulgaria (893–927), younger son of BORIS I. He spent most of his reign trying to conquer the BYZANTINE EMPIRE. Between 894 and 923 Simeon engaged in a series of wars with the Byzantines, managing to extract tribute from its emperor and expanding his empire by conquering Serbia and defeating the emperor's Magyar allies. In 925 he declared himself tsar of the Romans and Bulgars. Under his son and successor, Peter I, the Bulgar empire declined. Simeon introduced Greek culture to Bulgaria.

Simeon II (1937–) Last tsar of Bulgaria (1943–46), son and successor of BORIS III, who died in suspicious circumstances when Simeon was only six. Bulgaria was ruled by a pro-German regency until the Soviet invasion (1944). Simeon was ousted by plebiscite in September 1946 when Bulgaria became a republic.

Simnel, Lambert (*c.*1475–1535?) English impostor, one of many pretenders to the throne in the reign of HENRY VII. A tradesman's son, Simnel was trained to impersonate the Earl of Warwick, a claimant to the throne then in prison. He was crowned in Dublin, Ireland, and was the titular leader of a force that invaded England in 1487. The rebels were defeated by Henry at the Battle of Stoke (June 1487) and Simnel, an ineffectual pawn, was put to work in the royal kitchens.

simony In the Christian church, the buying or selling of a spiritual office or benefit. The term derives from the biblical figure, Simon Magus, who tried to buy the gifts of the Holy Spirit from St Peter (Acts 8:9–24). The most common form of simony was the purchase of church offices, in expectation of profit. The practice was condemned by the Catholic church as early as the Council of CHALCEDON (451), but it was still the cause of complaints against the clergy in the REFORMATION. *See also* GREGORY VII, SAINT

Sinai Peninsula Region in NE Egypt, linking Africa and Asia. The Sinai is predominantly barren desert but has been of strategic importance from the time of ancient Egypt. After the collapse of the Egyptian empire, the Nabataeans of PETRA prospered on their control of the Sinai trade routes between Egypt and Palestine. An important centre of early Christianity, the monastery of St Catherine on Mount Sinai was begun (AD 530) by Byzantine Emperor Justinian I. The scene of fierce fighting in the ARAB-ISRAELI WARS (1956, 1967, 1973), it was occupied by Israel after the SIX-DAY WAR (1967) but returned to Egypt in 1982. Pop. (1991 est.) 264,000.

Sind Province in S Pakistan; the capital is Karachi. Although much of Sind is desert, it was the site of the ancient INDUS VALLEY CIVILIZATION. In 325 BC it was invaded by ALEXANDER III (THE GREAT) and later included within the MAURYAN EMPIRE. The region was conquered by Arabs in the 8th century and the Mughals in the 16th. It was generally left to local rulers (*mirs*) based in Hyderabad, until it was captured (1843) by the British under Sir Charles Napier (1782–1853). Pop. (1985 est.) 21,682,000.

Singapore *See* country feature

Sinn Féin (Gaelic "Ourselves Alone") Irish republican, nationalist organization founded (*c.*1905) by Arthur GRIFFITH. Sinn Féin became a mass party after the EASTER RISING (1916) against British rule and, led by Eamon DE VALERA, won 75% of the vote in the 1918 elections. Members refused seats in the British Parliament and set up an independent Irish assembly, the DÁIL ÉIREANN. Sinn Féin split over the Anglo-Irish Treaty (1921), which established the Irish Free State (later Republic of IRELAND). While Michael COLLINS supported the agreement, Eamon DE VALERA rejected it. The Irish Free State was engulfed by civil war (1921–23). The pro-treaty wing (later known as FINE GAEL), led by William COSGRAVE, formed a government, while Sinn Féin under De Valera refused to sit in the Dáil Éireann. In 1926 De Valera withdrew from Sinn Féin and formed FIANNA FAIL. In 1938 the remaining republican intransigents joined the outlawed IRISH REPUBLIC ARMY (IRA). In 1969 two groups emerged that mirrored the factions of the Provisional and Official IRA. "Official" Sinn Féin became the Workers' Party (now Democratic Left). The Provisionals continued to refuse to recognize the authority of Dublin or Westminster. Support for Provisional Sinn Féin grew after the hunger strikes by republican prisoners in Northern IRELAND in 1981. In 1983 Gerry ADAMS, president of Sinn Féin, was elected to the British Parliament, but did not take his seat. In the 1997 elections Adams and his deputy Martin McGuinness (1950–) were elected to the British Parliament, and Sinn Féin gained 10% of the vote in Northern Ireland. Sinn Féin signed the GOOD FRIDAY AGREEMENT (1998), which resulted in a devolved assembly for Northern Ireland. In the 1998 elections to the Assembly, Sinn Féin won 18 seats and Martin McGuinness and Bairbre de Brún joined the new power-sharing executive. *See also* ULSTER UNIONISTS; UNITED IRISHMEN, SOCIETY OF

Sino-Japanese Wars Two conflicts between China and Japan, marking the beginning and end of Japanese imperial expansion on the Asian mainland. The **First** Sino-Japanese War (1894–95) arose from rivalry for control of KOREA. A rebellion (1884) by pro-Japanese reformers in Korea was brutally suppressed by Chinese General YUAN SHIKAI and war with Japan was narrowly avoided when both sides agreed to withdraw troops. The assassination of the Korean leader of the 1884 coup by the Chinese provoked the Tonghak Uprising (1894) and Japan took the subsequent deployment of Chinese forces as a declaration of war.

◄ **Sino-Japanese Wars** Woodblock print (1895) of the First Sino-Japanese War (1894–95). In this conflict, the Chinese were easily overcome by the more sophisticated weaponry of the Japanese, and granted significant economic and territorial concessions to Japan in the Treaty of Shimonoseki (1895). Conflict between the two nations continued into the 20th century, culminating in the Second Sino-Japanese War (1937–45).

S

Japan swiftly defeated China, capturing Shandong and Manchuria. China was forced to accept Korean independence and ceded territory, including Taiwan and the Liaodong Peninsula. The latter was retroceded after European pressure. The **Second** Sino-Japanese War (1937–45) arose from Japan's seizure of Manchuria (1931), where it set up the puppet state of Manchukuo. Further Japanese aggression led to war, in which the Japanese swiftly conquered E China, driving Chiang Kai-shek's government out of Beijing. US and British aid was dispatched to China after 1941, and the conflict merged into World War 2, ending with the defeat of Japan in 1945.

Sino-Soviet dispute Period of strained relationships between China and the Soviet Union during the 1960s. The Soviet Union had been the only major ally of China after the communist takeover in 1949 and had provided aid in many forms. Relations cooled from the late 1950s owing to ideological differences, in particular Mao Zedong's dislike of Nikita Khrushchev's more liberal policies in the post-Stalinist era and, in the 1960s, Soviet dislike of Mao's Cultural Revolution. Leonid Brezhnev's formulation of the so-called Brezhnev Doctrine, which asserted the Soviet's right to intervene in any communist state to deal with counter-revolutionary elements further strained the relationship. In 1969 a series of clashes in Xinjiang and Manchuria, led to a massive increase in troops along the Chinese-Soviet border until negotiations resulted in a cooling of tension. Good relations were not fully restored until Mikhail Gorbachev visited China in 1989. *See also* Cold War; communism

Sioux (Dakota) Group of seven Native North American tribes inhabiting Minnesota, Nebraska, North and South Dakota and Montana. In the 18th century they numbered *c*.30,000. The largest of the tribes was the Teton. They opposed US forces in the American Revolution and the War of 1812. The tribes concluded several treaties with the US government (1815, 1825, 1851) and finally agreed in 1867 to settle on a reservation in SW Dakota. The discovery of gold in the Black Hills and the rush of prospectors brought resistance from Sioux chiefs such as Sitting Bull and Crazy Horse. In 1876 they defeated General Custer at the Battle of Little Bighorn. The last confrontation was the Massacre at Wounded Knee (1890), which resulted in the slaughter of *c*.300 Sioux, many of them women and children. Today, the Sioux number more than 50,000.

Sisulu, Walter (1912–) South African civil rights activist, a fierce opponent of apartheid, Sisulu became secretary general of the African National Congress (ANC) in 1949. The ANC was declared illegal in 1961, and Sisulu, Nelson Mandela and six others were sentenced (1964) to life imprisonment. In 1989 Sisulu was released by F.W. de Klerk and, after the legalization of the ANC, became its deputy president (1991–94).

Sitting Bull (1831–90) Native North American leader, chief of the Sioux. An opponent of white settlement during the 1860s and 1870s, Sitting Bull refused to be settled on a reservation. General Custer was sent to enforce the order, resulting in the Sioux victory at the Battle of Little Bighorn (1876). Sitting Bull and his followers fled to Canada, but in 1881 he returned to the United States. Sitting Bull was subsequently imprisoned for two years, after which he was forced onto a reservation. Sitting Bull remained an outspoken critic of white settlement but in 1885 he was allowed to join Buffalo Bill's Wild West Show. In 1890, believed by the US Army to be central to the instigation of a new "ghost dance", Sitting Bull was killed resisting arrest.

Sivaji (*c*.1630–80) Indian ruler, founder of the Maratha kingdom. As a member of the soldierly Bhonsia family, he believed it was his duty to free the Hindus of the Deccan from Muslim rule. Mixing conspiracy with hard fighting, Sivaji defeated the sultan of Bijapur and, after escaping from prison, gained a victory over the Mughal Emperor Aurangzeb. Sivaji made himself ruler, was crowned king in 1674, and proved a good governor as well as an heroic general.

Six Acts (1819) Measures by the British government to suppress radical opposition after the Peterloo Massacre. Collectively, the Acts banned meetings of more than 50 people, prohibited military training for civilians, strengthened the law against seditious libel, and muzzled the radical press by imposing the extension of stamp duty on newspapers and pamphlets. The Acts only served to foment greater radical opposition and Lord Liverpool was eventually forced to assume more liberal policies.

Six-Day War (1967) Third of the Arab-Israeli Wars. Known as the "June War" to Arab participants, the Six-Day War was precipitated by the Egyptian closure of the Strait of Tiran, essential for Israeli shipping, and a combination of the Egyptian President Nasser's insistence on United Nations' (UN) observers withdrawing from the Israeli border in Sinai and the mobilization of a large Egyptian force there. Israel, alarmed at these events and aware of the gradual formation of an Egyptian, Jordan and Syrian alliance, initiated a surprise attack, under the leadership of Moshe Dayan, on the Egyptian airforce, before turning its attention on the Jordanian and Syrian airforces. With almost complete control in the air, Israeli ground forces rapidly defeated the three Arab states. Israel gained control of the old city of Jerusalem, Jordanian territory on the West Bank (of the Jordan River), the Golan Heights and the Sinai Peninsula, including the Gaza Strip.

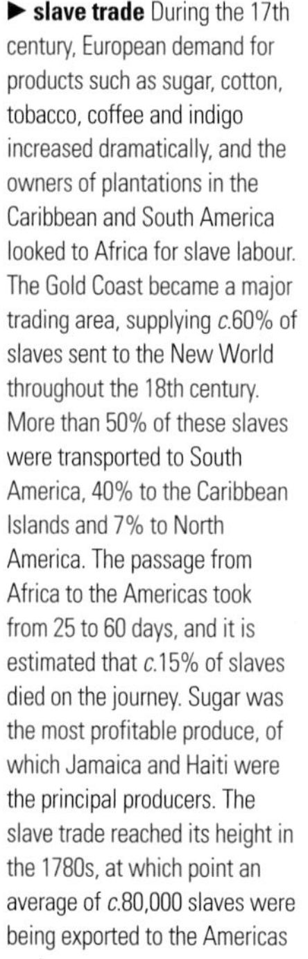

► **slave trade** During the 17th century, European demand for products such as sugar, cotton, tobacco, coffee and indigo increased dramatically, and the owners of plantations in the Caribbean and South America looked to Africa for slave labour. The Gold Coast became a major trading area, supplying *c*.60% of slaves sent to the New World throughout the 18th century. More than 50% of these slaves were transported to South America, 40% to the Caribbean Islands and 7% to North America. The passage from Africa to the Americas took from 25 to 60 days, and it is estimated that *c*.15% of slaves died on the journey. Sugar was the most profitable produce, of which Jamaica and Haiti were the principal producers. The slave trade reached its height in the 1780s, at which point an average of *c*.80,000 slaves were being exported to the Americas each year.

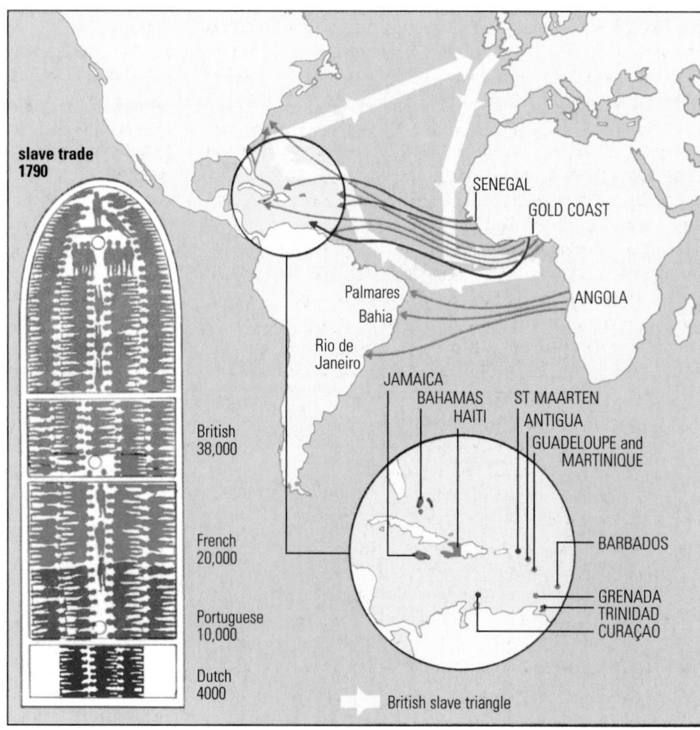

Six Dynasties (220–589) Series of dynasties in S China that had their capital at Nanjing. It covers the period from the end of the Han dynasty to the formation of the Sui. While central Asian invaders were establishing kingdoms in N China, the S kingdoms remained relatively isolated thanks largely to the protective barrier of the River Yangtze. The first of the six dynasties is taken to be the **Wu**, one of the dynasties of the Three Kingdoms period (220–265). A brief interlude without strong central control preceded the **Eastern Jin** (318–420), which was followed by the **Former Song** (420–479), the **Southern Qi** (479–502), the **Southern Liang** (502–557) and the **Southern Chen** (557–589). The Six Dynasties period was a time of great political discord, with much feuding between rival dynasties. Despite this unrest, S China developed new forms of literary expression and a sophisticated court life. Buddhism became widespread, inspiring painters, architects and musicians. The Sui dynasty, which gained control of N China in 581, conquered S China in 589, thus reunifying the country.

Six Nations *See* Iroquois Confederacy

Sixtus IV (1414–84) Pope (1471–84), b. Francesco della Rovere. A Franciscan monk, he became head of the Franciscans (1464) and was made a cardinal (1467). His attempt (1474–76) to unify the Russian Orthodox Church with the Catholic Church failed. Sixtus was involved in a plot (1478) against Giuliano and Lorenzo de' Medici in Florence, and a series of wars between Florence and the Papal States ensued. In 1478 he consented to the Spanish Inquisition, but he disapproved of its methods. A patron of Renaissance art, Sixtus established the Vatican Library and implemented the building of the Sistine Chapel (1472–81). Sixtus will also be remembered for advancing the careers of many of his relatives beyond their abilities, a practice for which he was censured.

Sixtus V (1520–90) Pope (1585–90), b. Felice Peretti. A Franciscan monk, Sixtus was made a cardinal in 1570. He was a keen supporter of the Counter-Reformation (enforcing the Council of Trent) and served (1557–60) in the Inquisition. As pope, Sixtus set in order the Papal States through a combination of force and reform. He undertook a vast building programme in Rome, including the dome of St Peter's Church, which was paid for primarily with increased taxation.

Skanderbeg (1405–68) (George Kastrioti) Albanian hero. Taken hostage by the Ottoman Turks as a child, he was brought up a Muslim. He became a favourite of Sultan Murad II, who gave him his name Iskander and the rank of bey (hence Skanderbeg). When the Turks were defeated in Serbia (1443), Skanderbeg returned to Albania, renounced Islam and devoted himself to defending Albania against the Ottoman Empire. He defeated the Ottoman army on many occasions, maintaining Albanian independence until his death, after which resistance to the Turks collapsed.

Slaughterhouse cases (1873) State Supreme Court trials resulting in a judgment of the US Supreme Court affecting interpretation of the 14th Amendment to the Constitution of the United States. To combat disease, Louisiana passed a law restricting the slaughtering of animals in New Orleans to a single slaughterhouse. The other abbatoirs held that such a monopoly contradicted the 14th Amendment, which restrains states from infringing the rights of individuals. A majority of the Supreme Court upheld the state court's decision on the grounds that the 14th Amendment was designed to protect civil liberties, not to deprive states of jurisdiction over their citizens. The dissenting minority judgment interpreted the 14th Amendment more broadly, and that opinion later gained acceptance.

Slav Largest ethnic and linguistic group of peoples in Europe. Slavs are generally classified in three main divisions: the **East** Slavs, the largest division, include the Ukrainians, Russians and Belorussians; the **South** Slavs include the Serbs, Croats, Macedonians and Slovenes (and frequently also the Bulgarians); the **West** Slavs comprise chiefly the Poles, Czechs, Slovaks and Wends. In the 3rd

S

and 4th centuries the Slavs were confined to the river basins of E Europe. In the 5th–7th centuries they expanded E beyond Kiev, W to the Danube, SW to the Balkans and N to the Baltic Sea. The first Slav states developed in the 10th century and by 1000 ruling Slav dynasties were established in Bohemia, Poland and Russia. *See also* PAN-SLAVISM

Slave dynasty (1206–90) Muizzi rulers of the DELHI SULTANATE in N India, founded by QUTB-UD-DIN AYBAK, Turkish slave-officer and successor of Muhammad of Ghur. In 1210 Qutb died and was succeeded by his son-in-law ILTUTMISH, who moved the dynastic capital from LAHORE to DELHI. Iltutmish's daughter, Raziyya (r.1236–40), tried to assert supreme power after her father's death, but was defeated by the nobility, among whom Ghiyas-ud-Din Balban rose to dominance after 1246 and served as sultan from 1266 to 1287. Balban managed to repel MONGOL and RAJPUT invasions, but the Slave dynasty was overthrown by Jalal-ud-Din Firuz Khalji, founder of the Khalji dynasty.

slavery Social system in which people are the property of their owner and are compelled to work without pay. Slavery of some kind existed in practically all ancient societies, among them ancient Egypt, Rome and Greece, and in most modern societies until the 19th century. An extreme form of slavery also existed in the Americas from the 16th century, where the need for cheap labour in European colonies was not satisfied by enslaving Native Americans or by acquiring poor Europeans as servants. This situation gave rise to the highly organized and profitable Atlantic triangular SLAVE TRADE. In the late 18th and early 19th centuries, slavery was abolished throughout much of Europe. It was abolished in several of the newly independent Latin American republics in the 1820s, and in the British West Indies in 1834, but was not abolished in Brazil until 1888. In the United States, slavery was one cause of the CIVIL WAR and was formally ended when the aims of the EMANCIPATION PROCLAMATION (1863) were incorporated in the 13th Amendment to the Constitution (1865). Isolated cases of slavery were discovered in China and some areas of Africa in the 1990s.

slave trade Organized system by which people were sold for profit into SLAVERY. The most highly organized was the Atlantic triangular slave trade. This began to evolve in the 16th century when slaves were first transported from Africa to the colonies of Spain and Portugal in the Americas and Caribbean. The trade increased in the 17th and 18th centuries when it became dominated by Britain, with France and Portugal playing a subsidiary role. Ships sailed from ports such as LIVERPOOL, NE England, with guns, cotton manufactures and other goods, which were exchanged for slaves in states on West African coasts. The slaves were sold in markets in the Caribbean, Brazil and North America, mainly to work on farms and plantations. On the return journey, the ships carried colonial produce, such as sugar and coffee, from the Americas to Europe. An estimated 15 million Africans were sold into slavery. Millions more died on the the grossly overcrowded and insanitary ships during the journey across the Atlantic. In the early 19th century the trade was abolished in a number of countries (Britain in 1807 and the United States in 1810, for example), but slaves continued to be smuggled out of Africa. Nearly two million were imported to Brazil and the Spanish and French colonies in the Caribbean between 1810 and 1860. The **Arab slave trade** was a much older institution than that of the European-run trade, but was organized in a less regimented way. Slaves were primarily acquired through military conquest and by purchase in regions of Africa, E and S Europe and central Asia. Unlike the slaves that were taken to the European colonies, slaves in the Arab-run trade, due mainly to laws passed down by MUHAMMAD, were given certain rights that were intended to ensure they received humane treatment. Many received vocational and religious training as well as, in the case of the MAMLUKS, military training. Many enslaved women on becoming concubines were legally entitled to the same rights as non-slave wives.

Slidell, John (1793–1871) US politician, senator (1853–61) and diplomat. After serving as a Democrat in the House of Representatives (1843–45), Slidell was appointed (1845) US special envoy to Mexico. Charged with negotiating the purchase of California and New Mexico, the Mexican government refused to receive him. As Louisiana senator (1853–61), he helped secure the election of James BUCHANAN. Following the outbreak of the American CIVIL WAR (1861–65), Slidell and James MASON were sent to France to drum up support for the Confederate cause, but they were intercepted en route, removed from the British steamer *Trent* and imprisoned. They were both released in 1862, but their mission was largely in vain. *See also* TRENT AFFAIR

Slim, William Joseph, 1st Viscount (1891–1970) British field marshal. As commander of the 14th Army during World War 2, he defeated the Japanese in Burma (1943–45). Slim was British commander in chief in SE Asia (1944–45) and chief of the imperial general staff (1948–52). He later served as governor general of Australia (1953–60) and was made a viscount in 1960.

Slovak Republic *See* country feature

Slovenia *See* country feature, page 382

Slovo, Joe (1926–95) South African anti-APARTHEID campaigner and politician, b. Lithuania. A lawyer and member of the South African Communist Party (SACP), he led the defence in many political trials. With his first wife and fellow activist **Ruth First** (1925–82), Slovo was a leader of the Congress of Democrats (founded 1953). When Slovo was accused of treason in 1961, he left South Africa and worked abroad for the AFRICAN NATIONAL CONGRESS (ANC), later taking part in creating its military wing, *Umkhonto we Sizwe*. Between 1984 and 1995 Slovo was either chairman or general secretary of the SACP. He was an important figure in the negotiations leading to democratic government and was appointed minister of housing (1994–95) in Nelson MANDELA's government.

Smet, Pierre Jean de (1801–73) Jesuit missionary in NW United States, b. Belgium. In 1838 he founded his first mission, among the Potawatomi in present-day Iowa, and founded another mission among the SALISH in 1841. Smet's role as peacemaker earned him the epithet "Black Robe". He acted as mediator between the Plains NATIVE NORTH AMERICANS and the government at a peace council in Fort Laramie (1851). In 1868 Smet's diplomatic skills were again called upon in talks with SITTING BULL. His works include *Western Missions and Missionaries* (1859).

Smith, Adam (1723–90) Scottish philosopher, regarded as the founder of modern economics. He was influenced by the French PHYSIOCRATS, notably François QUESNAY. Smith's major work, *An Inquiry into the Nature and Causes of the Wealth of Nations* (1776), proved enormously influential in the development of Western CAPITALISM. It outlined the theory of the division of labour, suggested prices should be based on supply and demand, and that competition was essential for the good of society. In place of MERCANTILISM, Smith proposed the doctrine of LAISSEZ-FAIRE: that governments should not interfere in economic affairs and that free-trade increases wealth.

Smith, Alfred Emanuel (1873–1944) US politician, governor of New York (1919–20, 1923–28). Smith's early political career is closely associated with the Democratic Party organization of TAMMANY HALL, from where he was appointed to the office of the commissioner of jurors (1895). Smith was the unlikely victor in the 1919 gubernatorial election, but once in office he won support for his championing of social welfare legislation, particularly equal rights and suffrage for women, care for the mentally ill, and public works projects. The first Roman Catholic candidate for the Democratic presidential nomination in 1924, Smith's religion, association with Tammany Hall, and opposition to PROHIBITION probably caused his failure. He gained the nomination in 1928, but lost the ensuing election to Herbert HOOVER. Smith remained an important

SLOVAK REPUBLIC (SLOVAKIA)

AREA: 49,035sq km (18,932sq mi)
POPULATION: 5,297,000
CAPITAL (POPULATION): Bratislava (440,421)
GOVERNMENT: Multiparty republic
ETHNIC GROUPS: Slovak, Hungarian, with small groups of Czechs, Germans, Gypsies, Poles, Russians and Ukrainians
LANGUAGES: Slovak (official)
RELIGIONS: Christianity (Roman Catholic 60%, Protestant 6%, Orthodox 3%)
GDP PER CAPITA (1995): US$3610

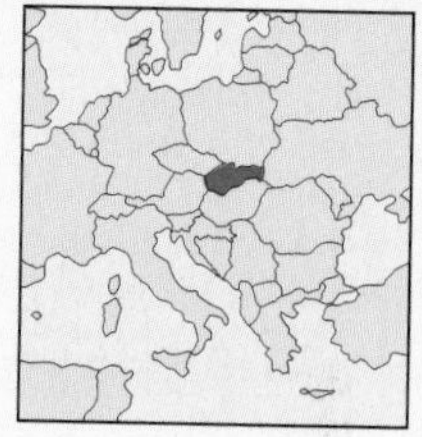

Republic in central Europe. Slavic peoples settled in the region in the 5th and 6th centuries AD. In the 9th century the area formed part of the empire of MORAVIA.

In the 10th century it was conquered by the MAGYARS, and for nearly 900 years the region was dominated by HUNGARY. At the end of the 11th century, it was subsumed into the kingdom of Hungary. In the 16th century the OTTOMAN EMPIRE conquered much of Hungary, and Slovakia was divided between the Turks and the Austrians. From 1541 to 1784 Bratislava served as the Hungarian capital within the HABSBURG empire. In the 18th century the joint rule of MARIA THERESA and JOSEPH II pursued a policy of Magyarization. In 1867 the AUSTRO-HUNGARIAN EMPIRE was formed. It continued the suppression of native culture. Many Slovaks fled to the United States. In World War 1, Slovak patriots fought on the side of the Allies.

After the defeat of Austro-Hungary (1918), Slovakia was incorporated into CZECHOSLOVAKIA as an autonomous region. The Czechs dominated the union, and many Slovaks became dissatisfied. Following the MUNICH AGREEMENT (1938), part of Slovakia became an independent state, while much of S Slovakia (including Košice) was ceded to Hungary. In March 1939 Slovakia gained nominal independence as a German protectorate. In August 1939 Adolf HITLER invaded Czechoslovakia, and Slovakia became a Nazi puppet state. In 1944 Soviet troops liberated Slovakia, and in 1945 it returned to Czechoslovakia. The PRAGUE SPRING (1968) saw the introduction of a federal structure that survived the Soviet invasion. In 1989 the dramatic collapse of Czech communism spurred calls for independence. Elections in 1992 were won by the Movement for a Democratic Slovakia (HZDS), led by Vladimir MEČIAR. In 1993 the federation was dissolved, and the Slovak Republic became a sovereign state, with Mečiar as prime minister. The Slovak Republic has maintained close relations with the Czech Republic.

In 1996 the Slovak Republic and Hungary ratified a treaty enshrining their respective borders and stipulating basic rights for the 560,000 Hungarians in the Slovak Republic. In the republic's first direct presidential elections in 1999, Rudolf Schuster of the Slovak Democratic Coalition defeated Mečiar.

S

figure in the Democratic Party, but his resentment at Franklin ROOSEVELT's victory in 1932 resulted in his support for the Republican Party in the 1936 election.

Smith, Frederick Edwin, 1st Earl of Birkenhead *See* BIRKENHEAD, FREDERICK EDWIN SMITH, 1ST EARL OF

Smith, Ian Douglas (1919–) Rhodesian statesman, prime minister (1964–79). Elected to the Southern Rhodesian assembly (1948), Smith joined the Federal Party on the creation of the Federation of RHODESIA and Nyasaland (1953). In 1961 Smith founded the Rhodesia Front Party in opposition to the Federalist Party's attempt to increase parliamentary representation for black Africans. On a platform of independence from Britain and government based on white-minority rule, Smith won the election in 1962. In 1964 Northern Rhodesia gained independence (as ZAMBIA) and in 1965, following the British government's insistence on increased black-African representation, Smith's white minority regime issued a Unilateral Declaration of Independence (UDI). After 13 years of persistent international sanctions and guerrilla warfare, led by Robert MUGABE and Joshua NKOMO, Smith was forced to extend voting rights to black Africans (1978). Smith resigned as prime minister (1979) and, following Mugabe's Zimbabwe African National Union (ZANU) victory in the first free elections, Rhodesia gained independence as ZIMBABWE in 1980. Smith continued to serve in the Zimbabwean parliament until 1987.

Smith, John (1580–1631) English soldier and colonist. In 1604 he joined the VIRGINIA COMPANY of London's colony council. Smith was instrumental in establishing the first English colony in North America at JAMESTOWN (1607). Exploring Chesapeake Bay, Smith was captured by POWHATAN and possibly saved from death by Powhatan's daughter, POCAHONTAS. In 1608, by obtaining maize from Native Americans, Smith saved the colony from starvation. In 1609 Smith returned to England, but was back in America by 1614, mapping the coast of New England. Another exploration of America failed in 1617.

Smith, John (1938–94) British politician, b. Scotland. He entered Parliament in 1970. In 1978 Smith became trade secretary in James CALLAGHAN's Labour government. During the CONSERVATIVE PARTY's long period in government (1979–97), Smith held a number of shadow cabinet posts. As shadow chancellor (1987–92), Smith proposed increased taxation for high earners to pay for increased pensions and child allowance. After Conservative leader John MAJOR's shock victory in the 1992 elections, Neil KINNOCK resigned as leader of the LABOUR PARTY in favour of John Smith. Smith continued to modernize the Party organization until his sudden death. He was succeeded as Labour leader by Tony BLAIR.

Smith, Joseph (1805–44) US religious leader and founder of the MORMON Church of Jesus Christ of the Latter Day Saints (1830). His *Book of Mormon* (1830) was based on writings he claimed were given to him on golden plates by a heavenly messenger named Moroni. Smith established a community in New York, but he aroused so much opposition that in 1830 he led his followers to found the New Zion, first in Ohio, then in Missouri, and finally at Nauvoo, Illinois. Opposition to the church increased when Smith announced his approval of polygamy. In 1844, following a split in the Mormon church over Smith's leadership abilities and the issue of polygamy, Smith ordered the dissenter's printing press to be destroyed and was jailed on a charge of treason at Carthage, Illinois. Despite assurances from the governor of Illinois that they would be protected, Smith and his brother were murdered by a mob. He was succeeded as leader of the Mormons by Brigham YOUNG.

Smith-Connally Act (1943) US legislation. Passed over President Franklin ROOSEVELT's veto, the Act authorized the president to seize factories where labour disputes would interfere with any war effort and forbade strikes in factories that had been seized. In industries engaged in war production, UNIONS were required to give 30-day notice before striking. The Act was enforced during WORLD WAR 2 in mine and railway disputes and during the KOREAN WAR in the steel industry.

Smolensk City on the upper reaches of the River Dnieper, E Russia. It was an important medieval trading centre on the routes from Byzantium (now ISTANBUL) to the Baltic, and from Moscow to Warsaw. By 1200 it was the capital of a Russian principality. Smolensk was sacked (1238–1240) by the MONGOLS and subsequently incorporated into Lithuania. During the 15th–17th centuries it was fought over by the forces of Poland-Lithuania and Russia before finally being incorporated into Russia. In 1812 NAPOLEON seized the city and burned it in retreat from the Russian army. Occupied by Germans from 1941 to 1943, Smolensk saw some of World War 2's fiercest fighting. Pop. (1994) 353,000.

Smuts, Jan Christiaan (1870–1950) South African statesman, prime minister (1919–24, 1939–48). He joined Paul KRUGER's government in 1898 and championed the AFRIKANER cause against Britain. A highly successful guerrilla commander during the second of the SOUTH AFRICAN WARS (1899–1902), Smuts helped negotiate the subsequent Treaty of VEREENIGING. He then held a number of cabinet posts under Louis BOTHA, working with him to establish the Union of SOUTH AFRICA (1910). During World War 1 Smuts suppressed a pro-German revolt, commanded British forces in East Africa and became a member of the British war cabinet. Upon Botha's death, he succeeded as prime minister. Smuts formed a second administration after James HERTZOG opposed entry into World War 2. He was defeated in the elections of 1948 by the pro-APARTHEID Nationalist Party under Daniel MALAN.

Soares, Mário Alberto Nobre Lopez (1924–) Portuguese statesman, prime minister (1976–78, 1983–85), president (1986–96). A leader of the Portuguese socialist movement during the dictatorship of António SALAZAR, he was imprisoned several times and finally exiled (1968–74). On his return, Soares was elected to parliament for the Social Democratic Party (PSD) and appointed foreign minister (1974–75). Following the elections of 1976 he became prime minister of a PSD-dominated coalition government. Despite grave economic problems, Soares' administration restored confidence in democracy. In 1986 he became Portugal's first civilian president since the military coup of 1926.

Soccer War (1969) Conflict between El Salvador and Honduras following an ill-tempered soccer match between the two countries in a World Cup qualifying competition. Among the underlying causes was a dispute over borders and competition over trade. A more immediate factor was a plan by the Honduran government to repatriate 300,000 Salvadoran migrant workers. El Salvador attacked Honduras on 14 July and, despite a cease-fire four days later, only agreed to stop all hostilities after several thousand lives had been lost and it had been threatened with economic sanctions by the Organization of American States (OAS) on 29 July. A peace treaty was finally signed in 1980.

Social and Liberal Democrats (SLDP) Official name of the LIBERAL DEMOCRATS

social contract Concept that society is based on the surrender of natural freedoms by the individual to the organized group or state in exchange for personal security. The concept was developed by Thomas HOBBES (in *Leviathan*, 1651) and John LOCKE (in *Two Treatises of Government*, 1689), and further explored by Jean-Jacques ROUSSEAU (in *The Social Contract*, 1762). Hobbes argued that individuals would be prepared to give up their rights entirely to ensure stability and security. Locke, however, opposed absolutism and posited that individuals should retain natural rights when accepting state control. Rousseau believed that the will of the collective ("general will") had moral imperative over any individual's will, and that a social contract remains in place only if the government reflects the will of the people. *See also* LIBERALISM

Social Credit Movement Canadian political party, the policies of which were based on the theories of British economist Clifford Douglas (1879–1952). In 1935 William Aberhart (1878–1943) came to power in Alberta on a programme of redistribution of wealth through "social dividends" – cash payments to consumers, the amount being determined by an assessment of the nation's wealth. Aberhart's attempts to tax banks and control the money supply were declared unconstitutional and blocked by federal government. The Social Credit Movement remained in power in Alberta until 1971. It also held power in British Columbia and Ottawa. Its influence waned in the 1980s.

social democracy Political ideology concerning the introduction of SOCIALISM while retaining certain aspects of CAPITALISM and thus avoiding an immediate overhaul of the prevailing political system. Before 1914 parties of central and E Europe that adhered to MARXISM termed themselves social democrats. Contemporary social democracy, however, has been invoked by those wishing to distinguish

SLOVENIA

AREA: 20,251sq km (7817sq mi)
POPULATION: 1,996,000
CAPITAL (POPULATION): Ljubljana (268,000)
GOVERNMENT: Multiparty republic
ETHNIC GROUPS: Slovene 88%, Croat 3%, Serb 2%, Bosnian 1%
LANGUAGES: Slovene
RELIGIONS: Christianity (mainly Roman Catholic)
GDP PER CAPITA (1994): US$7206

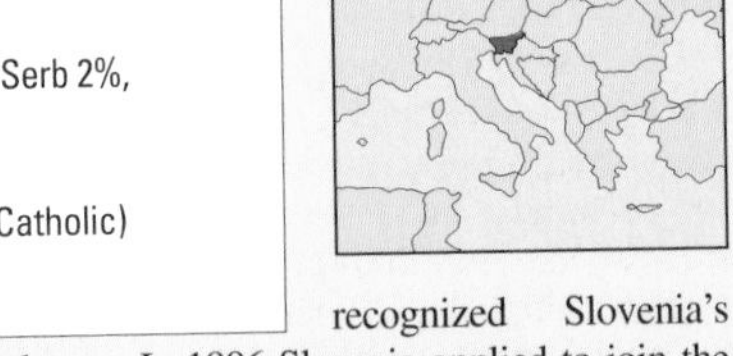

Mountainous republic in SE Europe. The ancestors of the Slovenes, the W branch of the South Slavs, settled in the area *c.*1400 years ago. In the 7th century they established a kingdom, which fell to the FRANKS in 748. From the 10th century they were enserfed by German lords. For most of the period from the 14th century until 1918, the Slovenes were ruled by the Austrian HABSBURGS.

In 1918 Slovenia became part of the Kingdom of the Serbs, Croats and Slovenes, which was renamed YUGOSLAVIA in 1929. During World War 2, Slovenia was invaded and partitioned between Italy, Germany and Hungary, but after the War, Slovenia again became part of Yugoslavia. From the late 1960s, some Slovenes demanded independence, but the central Yugoslav government opposed the breakup of the federation. In 1990 elections were held and a non-communist coalition government was established under Milan Kucan. Slovenia declared itself independent, which led to brief fighting between Slovenes and the federal army. Slovenia did not, however, become a battlefield like other parts of the former Yugoslavia. In 1992 the EUROPEAN COMMUNITY recognized Slovenia's independence. In 1996 Slovenia applied to join the EUROPEAN UNION (EU). In 1997 Kucan was elected for a third term in office.

their socialist beliefs from the dogmas of MARXISM. The term was first coined by Wilhelm LIEBKNECHT on the formation of the German Social Democratic Labour Party (1869). *See also* BOLSHEVIK; CHRISTIAN DEMOCRATS; MENSHEVIK; SOCIAL DEMOCRATIC LABOUR PARTY (SDLP); SOCIAL DEMOCRATIC PARTY (SDP)

Social Democratic and Labour Party (SDLP) Political organization in Northern IRELAND. Founded in 1970, the SDLP favours unification of Northern Ireland with the Republic of IRELAND by gaining the support of the majority of people from both political entities. It advocates the use of non-violent, constitutional means to achieve its goals. When the SDLP did not obtain political and civil rights reforms from the ULSTER UNIONISTS, it withdrew (1971) from the devolved assembly at Stormont. After the British government imposed direct rule (1973), the SDLP advocated a policy of cooperation with the secretary of state for Northern Ireland. The SDLP's pragmatic approach under its leader (1983–) John HUME, including its support of power-sharing between the province's Loyalist and Nationalist communities and its willingness to work with the governments of London and Dublin, enabled it to play a leading role in the peace process. In the 1998 elections, after the GOOD FRIDAY AGREEMENT, the SDLP gained 24 of the 108 seats in the new, devolved Northern Ireland Assembly and its deputy leader, Seamus Mallon (1936–), became deputy first minister under David TRIMBLE. *See also* ADAMS, GERRY; SINN FÉIN

Social Democratic Party (SDP) Political organization in Britain (1981–90), formed by four disaffected members of the LABOUR PARTY – Roy JENKINS, David OWEN, William Rodgers and Shirley Williams. Concerned by the increasing shift to the left by Labour, the "gang of four", as they came to be known, founded the SDP on 26 March, bringing with them 14 members of Parliament (all except one defecting from Labour) and some 20 members from the House of Lords. At the general elections of 1983 and 1987, the SDP joined forces with the LIBERAL PARTY to create the Liberal-SDP Alliance. By the second election, however, the two parties were already in the process of merging to form the LIBERAL DEMOCRATS.

Social Democratic Party (SPD) (*Sozialdemokratische Partei Deutschland*) Political organization in Germany. The German Democratic Labour Party was founded (1869) by Wilhelm LIEBKNECHT and others as a non-revolutionary socialist party. It adopted its present name in 1875. The SPD remained a minority party until 1919, when it became the largest party in the WEIMAR REPUBLIC. When the NAZI PARTY gained power (1933), all other parties, including the SPD, were banned. It re-emerged in West Germany after World War 2 but scarcely challenged the centre-right CHRISTIAN DEMOCRATIC UNION (CDU), because German workers were disillusioned with state bureaucracy after the Nazis. Adoption of a new constitution (1959), which abandoned MARXISM, resulted in the SPD forming a coalition government with the CDU (1966), and later with the smaller Free Democrats. It held power in the 1970s under Willy BRANDT (1969–74) and Helmut SCHMIDT (1974–82), but remained in opposition to CDU chancellor Helmut KOHL for most of the 1980s and 1990s, before returning to power under Gerhard SCHRÖDER in 1998.

socialism System of social and economic organization in which the means of production are owned not by private individuals but by the community, in order that all may share more fairly in the wealth produced. Modern socialism dates from the late 18th–early 19th centuries. Many forms of socialism exist both in theory and in practice, ranging from COMMUNISM to SOCIAL DEMOCRACY, and differing over such questions as the degree of state control and the rights of individuals. With the REVOLUTIONS OF 1848, socialism became a significant political doctrine in Europe. Karl MARX, whose *Communist Manifesto* was published in that year, believed that socialism was to be achieved only through the class struggle. Thereafter, a division appeared between the revolutionary socialism of Marx and his followers, later called communism or MARXISM-Leninism, and more moderate doctrines that held that socialism could be achieved through the democratic process. In Russia, the revolutionary tradition culminated in the RUSSIAN REVOLUTION of 1917. From the moderate wing emerged social-democratic parties such as the British LABOUR PARTY. They were largely instrumental in mitigating the effects of the market economy in Western Europe through support for SOCIAL SECURITY and the WELFARE STATE. *See also* CHRISTIAN SOCIALISM

Socialist Party (PS) (*Parti Socialiste*) Political party in France. It developed from the merger (1905) of two socialist parties, one led by the Marxist Jules Guesde, the other by the more moderate and more influential Jean JAURÈS, and was known officially as the French Section of the Workers' INTERNATIONAL (SFIO). Except during World War 1, it declined to take part in bourgeois ministries, which resulted in the defection of talented and ambitious members. It split again in 1920, into communists and socialists, with the socialists led by Léon BLUM. It emerged as the largest party on the left in 1936, enabling Blum to form the short-lived POPULAR FRONT (1936–38). The Party took part in the governing coalition in 1946–47 but thereafter, weakened by the relative strength of the French Communist Party, was confined to opposition. In 1971 it was re-organized, absorbing several small parties, and renamed the Socialist Party. It won a parliamentary majority in 1981 under the leadership of François MITTERRAND, who was president until 1995, although with a right-wing government from 1986 to 1988. Under a Gaullist president (Jacques CHIRAC), the PS returned to power in 1997, when Lionel JOSPIN became prime minister.

social security Public provision of economic aid to help alleviate poverty and deprivation. In 1883 Germany became the first country to adopt social security legislation, in the form of health insurance. By the end of the 1920s, public social security provisions had been adopted throughout Europe. In 1909 the United Kingdom adopted an old-age pension scheme, and in 1911 David LLOYD GEORGE drafted the NATIONAL INSURANCE Act to provide health and unemployment insurance. In 1941 Winston Churchill asked William BEVERIDGE to examine the issue of social insurance, and the subsequent "Beveridge Report" (1942) was primarily responsible for the National Insurance Act and the National Health Service Act of 1946. In 1948 the National Assistance Act complemented these to create a WELFARE STATE, and the NATIONAL HEALTH SERVICE (NHS) was introduced by Minister of Health Aneurin BEVAN. In the United States, as part of the NEW DEAL, the Social Security Act (1935) was adopted. It provided unemployment compensation, old-age pensions, and federal grants for state welfare programmes, but covered only those in commercial and industrial occupations. This was expanded in 1939. In 1965 Congress enacted the MEDICARE programme, which provided medical benefits for persons more than 65 years of age, and the Medicaid programme for the poor. Such social security programmes have proved costly, with some countries spending up to 25% of their gross domestic product (GDP) to finance them. For this reason, many governments are encouraging private provision.

Social War (91–87 BC) Conflict waged against anicent ROME by her rebellious Italian allies (*socii*), also known as the Marsic Wars. The Marsi and the SAMNITE peoples in the hills of central Italy led the fight to gain Roman citizenship, which had been proposed by Drusus but withheld by the SENATE. In 90 BC the Marsi defeated the Roman army in the N, while in the S the Samnites captured S Campania. In order to quell the revolt, Rome was forced to grant citizenship to Italians S of the River Po. Most of the remaining intransigents in the S were defeated by Lucius Cornelius SULLA in 89 BC, but pockets of Samnite resistance continued until 87 BC.

Society of Friends *See* QUAKERS

Society of Jesus *See* JESUITS

Socrates (*c.*470–399 BC) Greek philosopher. He laid the foundation for an ethical philosophy based on the analysis of human character and motives. Information about his life and philosophy is found in the writings of PLATO, his most gifted pupil, and the historian and military leader XENOPHON, who knew him. According to these accounts, Socrates believed that moral excellence is attained through self-knowledge. For Socrates, knowledge and virtue were synonymous; immorality was founded on ignorance. His criticism of tyranny attracted powerful enemies, and he was charged with impiety and corrupting the young. Condemned to death, he drank the poisonous draft of hemlock required by law.

Soderini, Piero (1452–1522) Italian statesman. He served as ambassador to the French court before being elected (1501) to the highest office in FLORENCE. During Soderini's administration, Florence captured Pisa, bringing to an end a long war, and the city's army of foreign mercenaries was replaced by a national militia. Soderini was ousted from power by the MEDICI family in 1512. He went into exile, never to return to Florence.

Sokoto State and historic sultanate in NW Nigeria. From before the 10th century AD until the start of the 19th century, the region was ruled by a number of HAUSA STATES, and the present state capital, also called Sokoto, was capital of the kingdom of Gobir and one of the seven walled Hausa cities. In 1808 the FULANI Muslim leader USMAN DAN FODIO led a successful *jihad* (holy war) against Gobir. The following year, Usman's son, Muhammad Bello, became emir of Sokoto. After his father's death (1817), Muhammad became sultan. The Sokoto sultanate rapidly expanded to become the largest state in Africa, incorporating most of N Nigeria and parts of Cameroon and Niger. Throughout the latter half of the 19th century, it was threatened by British incursions, finally being subsumed into the British Protectorate of Northern Nigeria in 1903. The assassination (1966) of Sir Ahmadu Bello, the *sardauna* (spiritual leader of the Fulani), in a military coup led by the IBO (Igbo) provoked retaliatory massacres of Ibo and helped precipitate the secession of BIAFRA and the ensuing Nigerian civil war (1967–70). Pop. (1991) 4,392,391.

Solemn League and Covenant (September 1643) Agreement between the LONG PARLIAMENT and the Scottish COVENANTERS during the English CIVIL WAR. In return for Parliament's promise to reorganize the established church on a PRESBYTERIAN basis, the Scots agreed to raise an army in the N of England against CHARLES I. The Scottish help led directly to the Parliamentary victory over the Royalists at the Battle of MARSTON MOOR.

Solferino, Battle of (24 June 1859) Battle between an Austrian army, under the command of FRANZ JOSEPH, and combined Franco-Piedmontese forces. The Piedmontese statesman Conte di CAVOUR enlisted the military support of NAPOLEON III in an attempt to reduce Austrian power in Italy. The Battle ended in stalemate, with both sides suffering more than 14,000 casualties. The Treaty of VILLAFRANCA agreed an armistice: Austria retained Venetia, but gave up Lombardy to France so that it could than be ceded to Italy. Horror at the plight of the wounded during the Battle of Solferino led Henri DUNANT to set up the Red Cross. *See also* MAGENTA, BATTLE OF

Solidarity Polish organization that provided the chief opposition to the communist regime during the 1980s. Led by Lech WAŁESA, the National Committee of Solidarity was founded in 1980 among shipyard workers in GDAŃSK, N Poland, following strikes organized by the Free Union of the Baltic Coast. Solidarity organized further strikes and demanded economic improvements, but soon acquired a political, revolutionary character. Banned in 1981, it re-emerged as a national party, winning the free elections of 1989 and forming the core of the new democratic government headed by Wałesa. Solidarity diversified into a number of political factions, and the name was retained only by a minority party.

Solomon (d.922 BC) King of Israel (*c.*972–922 BC), second son of DAVID and Bathsheba. During his reign, the last of a united ISRAEL, the kingdom prospered, thanks partly to economic relations with the Egyptians and Phoenicians. Solomon divided Israel into discrete administrative centres and implemented a system of enforced labour that enabled him to develop an extensive building programme, which included the construction of the TEMPLE OF JERUSALEM. Solomon's reputation for wisdom, which caused the Queen of SHEBA to visit his court, reflected his interest in literature, although the works attributed to him, including the Old Testament book the Song of Solomon, were probably written by others.

SOLOMON ISLANDS

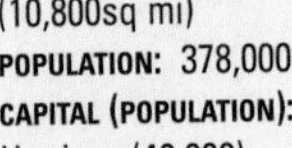

AREA: 27,900sq km (10,800sq mi)
POPULATION: 378,000
CAPITAL (POPULATION): Honiara (40,000)
GOVERNMENT: Constitutional monarchy
ETHNIC GROUPS: Melanesian 94%, Polynesian 4%
LANGUAGES: English (official), Melanesian languages
RELIGIONS: Anglican 34%, Roman Catholic 19%, Evangelical 18%
GDP PER CAPITA (1995): US$2190

Solomon was succeeded in the S by Rehoboam while the N tribes of Israel seceded under Jeroboam I. Solomon is also a significant figure in the Koran, in which, as Sulayman, he is regarded as an apostle and prophet.

Solomonid Ethiopian royal dynasty. According to tradition, commemorated in the 14th-century *Glory of the Kings*, the line originated with Menelik I, the son of Solomon (hence the dynastic name) and the Queen of Sheba. Historical evidence exists only as far back as Yekuno Amlak, who became emperor in 1270. With a brief interruption in the 19th century, the Solomonid line continued until the deposition of Haile Selassie (1974).

Solomon Islands Melanesian archipelago nation in the SW Pacific Ocean, SE of New Guinea. Solomon Islands include several hundred islands spread over 1400km (900mi) of the Pacific Ocean. The vast majority of the population are indigenous Melanesians. The first European discovery of the islands was by the Spanish in 1568. The islands resisted colonization until the late 19th century. In 1893 the S islands became a British protectorate, and the from 1895 the N islands were controlled by the Germans. In 1900 Germany ceded its territory to Britain. During World War 1 Bougainville and Buka (now in Papua New Guinea) were occupied by Australian troops and were mandated to Australia in 1920. In 1942 the S islands were occupied by Japanese troops. After heavy fighting, particularly at the Battle of Guadalcanal (1943), the islands were liberated by US troops in 1944. In 1976 the Solomons became self-governing and in 1978 achieved full independence within the Commonwealth of Nations.

Solon (*c*.639–*c*.599 BC) Athenian statesman, poet and political reformer. In *c*.594 BC, during an economic crisis in classical Greece, Solon was elected archon (chief magistrate) of Athens. In order to boost the economy Solon carried out drastic economic and constitutional reforms, such as the cancellation of many outstanding personal debts, the implementation of financial aid to encourage trade and industry outside of farming, the creation of a class system divided into four categories broadly based on wealth (each of which had specific military and civic duties) and the formation of a new assembly. The last two measures helped to lay the foundations of Athenian democracy. His reforms, however, proved unpopular, in that they devolved power from the existing aristocracy, while at the same time being insufficiently democratic for the citizens.

Solutrean culture European toolmaking culture of upper Palaeolithic times. It is named after Solutré, a site in S France where distinctive, delicately flaked, flint tools have been found. The term Solutrean is now used to define a period of the late Palaeolithic – *c*.21,000–17,000 years ago.

Somalia *See* country feature

Somers, John, 1st Baron (1651–1716) English lawyer and Whig politician. He won a reputation for legal brilliance and was a leader of the powerful group of Whigs called the Junto in the reigns of William III and Anne. Somers was one of those who drafted the Bill of Rights (1689), and held a succession of legal offices, becoming lord chancellor (1697) and William's most trusted minister. His Tory opponents secured his dismissal in 1700 but he continued to play an important role in legislation, including the Act of Union with Scotland (1707).

Somerset, Edward Seymour, 1st Duke of (1500–52) English ruler, regent for Edward VI. His political career began to blossom when his sister Jane Seymour married Henry VIII in 1536. Henry appointed him to a council of regents for the young Edward, and he assumed supreme authority and the title of lord protector on Henry's death. As protector, Somerset defeated the Scots at the Battle of Pinkie (1547), launched an attack on Catholicism, ordering the destruction of all church decoration, and enforced the use of the Book of Common Prayer. In 1549 he was overthrown in a coup led by the Duke of Northumberland. Readmitted to the government in 1550, he was later executed on a flimsy charge of treason.

Somme, Battle of the Major World War I engagement in N France along the River Somme. It was planned by Douglas Haig and Joseph Joffre on 1 July 1916. On the first day, the British suffered 60,000 casualties in an attempt to break through the German lines. A trench war of attrition continued until the offensive was abandoned on 19 November 1916. Total casualties were more than one million, and the British had advanced only 16km (10mi). A second battle around St Quentin (March–April 1918) is sometimes referred to as the **Second Battle of the Somme.** A German offensive, designed to secure victory before the arrival of US troops, was halted by Anglo-French forces.

Somoza García, Anastasio (1896–1956) Nicaraguan dictator, president (1937–47, 1950–56). Son of a wealthy coffee planter, Somoza became head of the National Guard in 1933, a position he exploited to seize power in 1936, ousting President Juan Bautista Sacasa. Over the next 20 years, with support from the United States, Somoza created both a dictatorial government and a political dynasty. Although guilty of misappropriating funds, Somoza also introduced social and economic reforms that benefited Nicaragua. Following his assassination, Somoza was succeeded in office by his two sons, Luis (1922–67) and Anastasio (1925–80), who also increased the family fortune and crushed political opposition. The Somoza dynasty was overthrown by the Sandinistas in 1979.

Sonderbund (Ger. Separatist League) Defensive pact formed (1845) by seven Roman Catholic cantons in Switzerland – Lucerne, Uri, Schwyz, Underwalden, Zug, Fribourg and Valais. They united in opposition to the Radical Party's attempt at centralization and anti-Catholic actions by the Protestant cantons, including the dissolution of several monasteries, an act forbidden by the Federal Pact of 1815. In 1847 *Sonderbund* was declared unconstitutional by the federal Diet. A civil war (the Sonderbund War) followed in which the Catholic cantons were defeated. In 1848 a new constitution was issued, turning Switzerland into one federal state.

SOMALIA

AREA: 637,660sq km (246,201sq mi)
POPULATION: 9,204,000
CAPITAL (POPULATION): Mogadishu (1,200,000)
GOVERNMENT: Single-party republic, military dominated
ETHNIC GROUPS: Somali 98%, Arab 1%
LANGUAGES: Somali and Arabic (both official), English, Italian
RELIGIONS: Islam 99%
GDP PER CAPITA (1994): US$124

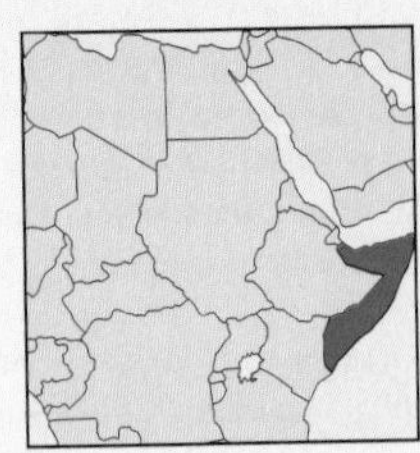

The Republic of Somalia occupies part of the Horn of E Africa. The land of Punt, to which references are found in ancient Egyptian inscriptions dating from the 2nd millennium BC, was probably in this area. Between the 7th and 10th centuries AD, Arab traders established coastal settlements and introduced Islam. Mogadishu was founded *c*.900 as a trading centre. The interest of European imperial powers increased after the opening of the Suez Canal (1869). In 1887 Britain established a protectorate in what is now N Somalia. Italy formed a protectorate in the central region in 1899, and extended its power to the S by 1905. In 1896 France established a colony in modern-day Djibouti. In 1936 Italian Somaliland was united with the Somali regions of Ethiopia to form Italian East Africa. During World War 2, Italy invaded (1940) British Somaliland. In 1941 British forces reconquered the region and captured Italian Somaliland. In 1950 Italian Somaliland returned to Italy as a United Nations trust territory.

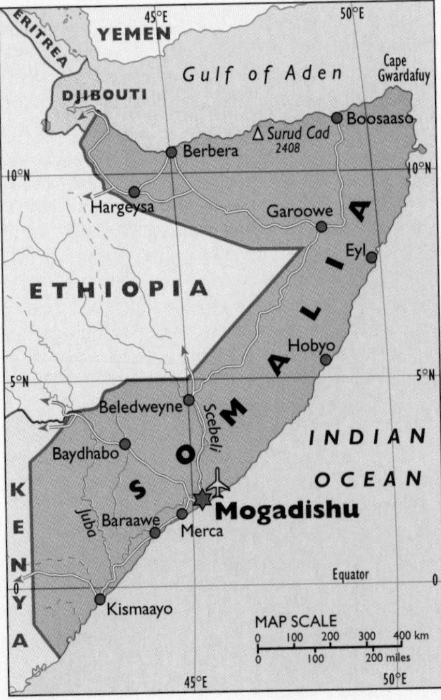

In 1960 both Somalilands gained independence and joined to form the United Republic of Somalia. The new republic was faced with pan-Somali irredentists, calling for the creation of a "Greater Somalia" to include the Somali-majority areas in Ethiopia, Kenya and Djibouti. In 1969 the army, led by Siad Barré, seized power and formed a socialist, Islamic republic. During the 1970s, Somalia and Ethiopia fought for control of the Ogaden Desert, inhabited mainly by Somali nomads. Ethiopia forced Somalia to withdraw (1978), but resistance continued, forcing one million refugees to flee to Somalia. In 1991 Barré was overthrown and the United Somali Congress (USC), led by Ali Mahdi Muhammad, seized power. Somalia disintegrated into civil war between rival clans. The Ethiopia-backed Somali National Movement (SNM) gained control of NW Somalia and seceded as the Somaliland Republic (1991). Mogadishu was devastated by an attack from the Somali National Alliance (SNA), led by General Muhammad Aideed. War and drought resulted in a devastating famine that claimed thousands of lives. The United Nations (UN) was slow to provide relief, and when aid arrived, it was unable to secure distribution. US marines led a taskforce to secure food distribution but became embroiled in conflict with Somali warlords, destroying the headquarters of General Aideed. After the deaths of UN troops, US marines withdrew in 1994. Civil strife continued, and in 1996 Aideed was killed. The Cairo Declaration (December 1997), signed by 26 of the 28 warring factions, including Ali Mahdi Muhammad and Aideed's son Hussein Aideed, held out hope of an end to factional feuding. The installation of a transitional government has been repeatedly postponed, and Djibouti has regularly acted as peace broker. In 2000 Somalia was one of several countries in Africa threatened with serious famine.

S

Song (960–1279) (Sung) Chinese imperial dynasty that was established at the end of the period known as the FIVE DYNASTIES AND TEN KINGDOMS. Responsible for reuniting much of China, the Song dynasty historically is divided into the Northern (960–1126) and, after the N was overrun by Jurchen tribes and subsequently ruled by the JIN dynasty, the Southern (1127–1279) Song. It was notable for a deliberate reduction in military strength, after the initial conquests of Emperor Taizu (r.960–76), and the development of a powerful civil service. There was also a great revival of CONFUCIANISM and a flowering of the arts, indeed Emperor Huizong (r.1100–26) was blamed for the loss of the N because he allowed his interest in the arts to distract him from government. The Song dynasty was also notable for advances in technology. The Southern Song, with its capital at Hangzhou, was overrun (1276) by the Mongols under the leadership of KUBLAI KHAN.

Songhai (Songhay) West African empire that dominated the Niger valley in the 14th–16th centuries. Initially founded by Christian Berbers at the beginning of the 7th century, the Songhai had established its capital at Gao by the start of the 11th century and its rulers converted to Islam. Songhai territory gradually extended along the Niger River for nearly 2000km (1250mi), although it was annexed briefly in 1325 by the MALI empire. The Songhai was at its most powerful between 1464 and 1492 under the rule of SONNI ALI, its wealth increased by the trade of TIMBUKTU. At this time the Songhai had become sufficiently powerful to incorporate the E region of the Mali empire into its territory. Sonni was succeeded by his son Bakari, who proved an ineffectual leader. With the accession of Askia MUHAMMAD I (r.1493–1528), however, the Songhai stranglehold on trade routes was further tightened and the empire became the most powerful in W Africa. There was no stable method of succession, however, and conflict among the royal family and military nobility left the state divided. In 1590 Sultan AHMED AL-MANSOUR of Morocco made a daring assault on Songhai and routed its army. Mansour then withdrew to Timbuktu, allowing a successor Songhai state to survive in the SE of the old empire.

Sonni Ali (d.1492) Ruler (*c*.1464–92) of the SONGHAI EMPIRE in West Africa. His armies steadily took over territories formerly within the imperial remit of MALI, capturing TIMBUKTU (1463) and Jenne (1473). By his death, the Songhai empire was larger than Mali in its prime. He was criticized by Muslim chroniclers as cruel and barbaric and, in particular, irreligious; but the status of Islam was restored under Askia MUHAMMAD I (r.1493–1528).

Sons of Liberty American colonial group of revolutionaries. A secret organization, the Sons of Liberty was founded, initially in Connecticut and New York, to protest against the STAMP ACT (1765). It used assemblies and petitions, and occasional violence, against British officials and loyalists, in a campaign for freedom from British interference in the THIRTEEN COLONIES. The Sons of Liberty spread to other colonies, including Massachusetts, where it was responsible for the BOSTON TEA PARTY (1773). In 1774 the society also assisted in convening the CONTINENTAL CONGRESS. Its leaders included revolutionaries such as Samuel ADAMS and Paul REVERE.

Sophia (1630–1714) Electress of Hanover (1658–1714). She was a granddaughter of JAMES I of England, the daughter of FREDERICK V, Elector of the Palatinate, and the widow of Ernest Augustus, Elector of Hanover. To ensure a Protestant succession and prevent the return of the Catholic STUARTS, Sophia was recognized as ANNE's successor to the English throne by the Act of SETTLEMENT (1701). When she died, her son became king as GEORGE I.

Sophists (Gk. *sophistes*, men of wisdom) Loose collection of itinerant Greek teachers of the 5th–4th centuries BC. Active throughout classical GREECE, its colonies and areas of S Italy, the Sophists were not a formal school, instead they shared a broad philosophy regarding truth and ethics as convenient human inventions with no basis in natural law. To this end they emphasized and taught (for a fee) the intellectual and rhetorical skills needed for young aristocrats to succeed in classical Greece, particularly in public life. Although popular for a time, they were eventually attacked for their lack of belief in absolute truth, and particularly castigated by philosophers such as PLATO and ARISTOTLE, both of whom also disapproved of the Sophists charging fees for their instruction.

Soult, Nicolas Jean de Dieu (1769–1851) French statesman and general in the FRENCH REVOLUTIONARY WARS and the NAPOLEONIC WARS. Created marshal of France by NAPOLEON I in 1804, Soult fought at the victorious battles of AUSTERLITZ (1805) and JENA (1806). He commanded French troops against the Duke of WELLINGTON in the PENINSULAR WAR (1808–14). Soult served as Napoleon's chief of staff in the WATERLOO campaign and was exiled after its failure. Allowed to return to France in 1819, Soult was restored to favour, holding several ministerial appointments under LOUIS PHILIPPE.

Souphanouvong (1902–95) Lao statesman, first president of the Republic of LAOS (1975–86). After World War 2, he opposed the reintroduction of French colonial rule in INDOCHINA and joined the provisional government in Vientiane as defence minister (1947–48). Souphanouvong rejected Lao Issara's (Free Laos) compromise settlement with the French and formed the communist-dominated PATHET LAO in 1950. During the VIETNAM WAR (1955–75), he allied himself with North Vietnam, who aided him in the Laotian civil war. He served (1962–63) in a coalition government with his half-brother, SOUVANNA PHOUMA, but was overthrown in a right-wing coup. After the withdrawal of US troops and the communist victory in Vietnam, Souphanouvong became president.

South Africa *See* country feature, page 386

South African Wars Two wars between the AFRIKANERS (Boers) and the British in SOUTH AFRICA. The **first** (1880–81) arose from the British annexation of the TRANSVAAL in 1877. Under Paul KRUGER, the Transvaal regained autonomy (1881), but further disputes provoked the second, greater conflict (1899–1902), known to Afrikaners as the **Second War of Freedom** and to the British as the **Boer War**. The discovery of gold and diamonds provoked a massive influx of British miners and prospectors, whose presence caused resentment among the mainly agrarian Afrikaner population. The Afrikaners taxed these UITLANDERS (foreigners) heavily and did not extend voting rights to them. The Afrikaner treatment of the British eventually sparked a British revolt in Johannesburg led by Cecil RHODES, who was keen to subsume the South African Republic into the BRITISH EMPIRE. Furthermore, Britain was concerned about a possible alliance between the Afrikaners and the Germans to the W and began to send troops to the border between Cape Colony and Orange FREE STATE. Following the failed JAMESON RAID (1895), a peaceful solution seemed out of the question, and in October 1899 the Afrikaners took pre-emptive action by besieging the British troops and securing some notable victories. However, Robert BADEN-POWELL's heroic defence of MAFEKING (1899–1900) seemed to be a turning point. In 1900 the Afrikaners' main towns of Johannesburg (31 May) and Pretoria (5 June) were captured by the British, and Kruger was forced to escape to Europe. By early 1901 British General Frederick ROBERTS mistakenly believed the war to be over, but the Afrikaners now resorted to guerrilla tactics under the leadership of (among others) Louis BOTHA and Jan SMUTS, and the fighting continued for another year. General Horatio KITCHENER finally defeated the Afrikaners by burning their farmsteads and imprisoning civilians in concentration camps. In the Peace of VEREENIGING (1902), the Afrikaners were forced to accept British rule. The British lost *c*.22000 men, while the Afrikaners lost *c*.14,000 in action and *c*.26,000 in concentration camps. The total number of African dead is unknown; according to low official estimates more than 13,000 died in the camps. *See also* CHAMBERLAIN, JOSEPH; MILNER, ALFRED, 1ST VISCOUNT

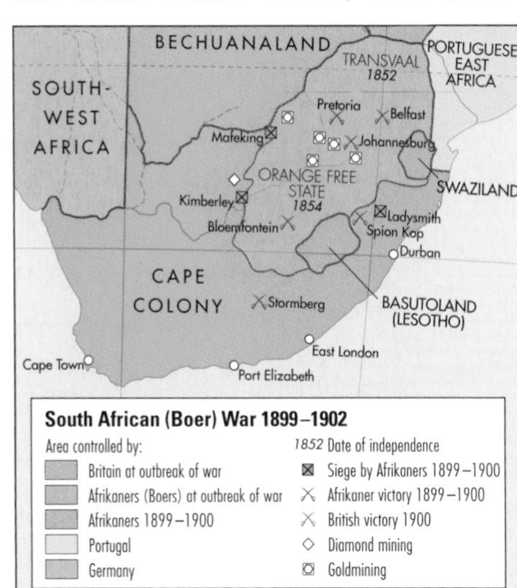

▲ **South African Wars** The Afrikaners' opposition to European domination in South Africa sparked one of the longest and most costly wars prior to World War 1.

SOUTH CAROLINA
Statehood :
23 May 1788
Nickname :
The Palmetto State
State motto :
Prepared in mind and resources

South America Fourth-largest continent, the S of the two continents of America, in the Western Hemisphere, connected to NORTH AMERICA by the isthmus of Panama (*see* CENTRAL AMERICA). First inhabited by hunter-gatherers between *c*.10,000 BC and 9000 BC, more sophisticated cultures, such as the CHAVÍN, had emerged by *c*.1000 BC. By the 15th century AD the INCA was the most advanced empire on the continent. European contact with South America began when Christopher COLOMBUS first sighted the mainland in 1498. Indigenous NATIVE SOUTH AMERICAN peoples were largely conquered by the Spanish, under conquistadors such as Francisco PIZARRO, and the Portuguese in the 16th century. The economies of the Spanish viceroyalties of PERU, NEW GRANADA and RÍO DE LA PLATA, and the Portuguese colony of BRAZIL developed on the basis of agriculture and mining, particularly of silver. In the 1820s these colonies fought for their independence under the leadership of Simón BOLÍVAR, Francisco de MIRANDA and Bernardo O'HIGGINS. By 1826 Spanish colonial rule had been overthrown. Both PERU and BOLIVIA lost territory to CHILE as a result of the War of the PACIFIC in 1879. Border disputes continued in the 20th century, such as the CHACO WAR (1932–35) between Bolivia and PARAGUAY. The 1920s saw the rise of the military, and in 1930 military coups took place in ARGENTINA, Brazil and Peru. Most South American countries declared war on the Axis powers during World War 2, but they only began to have significant influence on international affairs with the foundation of the United Nations (UN) in 1945 and the ORGANIZATION OF AMERICAN STATES (OAS) in 1948.

Since 1945 many countries of South America have swung between military dictatorships and democratic governments, mainly caused by wildly fluctuating economic fortunes. During the 1980s and 1990s, international pressure, particularly from the United States, was brought to bear on those governments, notably Bolivia and COLOMBIA, that were either unwilling or unable to control the production and export of cocaine. During the 1970s and 1980s, the rush for economic growth and industrialization was often at the expense of the continent's rainforests. Worldwide treaties in the 1990s attempted to slow down the deforestation but with little success. *See also* articles on individual countries

South Carolina State on the Atlantic Ocean, in the SE United States; the capital and largest city is Columbia. The main port is CHARLESTON. Once the centre of the Mississippian culture known as the MOUND-BUILDERS, the region was also settled by NATIVE NORTH AMERICANS, most notably the CHEROKEE and CATAWBA. From 1633 the English were the first Europeans to settle the area permanently, founding Charles Town (now Charleston) in 1670. In 1713 the Carolinas were officially divided into North Carolina and South Carolina. Following conflict between the settlers and the Native Americans, particularly the Yamasee War (1715), South Carolina became a royal province (1729), and a plantation society evolved based on rice, indigo and cotton. One of the original Thirteen Colonies that fought against Britain in the American Revolution, the entire state was occupied by British forces following a decisive British victory at the Battle of Camden (1780). British dominance was short-lived, however, and by 1781 revolutionary forces led by General Nathanael Greene had forced the British back to Charles Town. A year later the British were finally expelled from the state. Following the War of 1812, the powerful cotton planters became increasingly irate at the imposition of tariffs by the federal government. Furthermore South Carolina, of which 60% of the population were slaves, was adamantly opposed to the abolitionists, fearful that the uprisings, such as that led by Denmark Vesey, would become commonplace. In December 1860, after Abraham Lincoln had become president, South Carolina became the first state to secede from the Union, claiming a right to nullification. The first shots of the Civil War were fired at Fort Sumter and, although the state did not witness many battles, it was devastated by Union troops in 1865. During the 20th century South Carolina, with its large African-American population, was often the centre of civil rights issues. Area: 80,432sq km (31,055sq mi). Pop. (1996) 3,698,746.

South Dakota State in n central United States, on the Great Plains; the capital is Pierre. Between 12,000 and 10,000 years ago the area was settled by the Clovis culture. By ad 1000 South Dakota was inhabited by Native North Americans of the Sioux federation. French trappers claimed the region for France in the 1740s, after which it passed into Spanish ownership (1762) before being returned to France in 1800. The United States acquired part of the land in the Louisiana Purchase (1803). In 1861 Dakota Territory (now North Dakota and South Dakota, and areas of Wyoming and Montana) was formed. In 1874 the discovery of gold in the Black Hills, which made up part of the Native American reservation, led to a rapid increase in white settlement and heightened tension between prospectors and the Native Americans. The US Army

SOUTH AFRICA

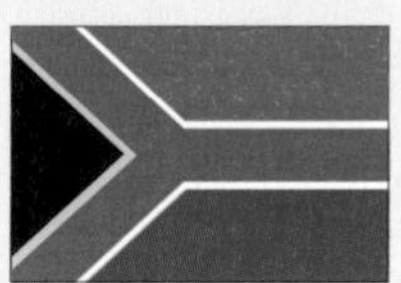

AREA: 1,219,916sq km (470,566sq mi)
POPULATION: 39,790,000
CAPITAL (POPULATION): Cape Town (legislative, 2,350,157); Pretoria (administrative, 1,080,187); Bloemfontein (judicial, 300,150)
GOVERNMENT: Multiparty republic
ETHNIC GROUPS: Black 76%, White 13%, Coloured 9%, Asian 2%
LANGUAGES: Afrikaans, English, Ndebele, North Sotho, South Sotho, Swazi, Tsonga, Tswana, Venda, Xhosa, Zulu (all official)
RELIGIONS: Christianity 68%, Hinduism 1%, Islam 1%
GDP PER CAPITA (1995): US$5030

Republic in s Africa, the southernmost country in Africa. Bantu-speaking peoples occupied much of the area by ad 400. Sotho-Tswana and Nguni-speaking peoples were established by the 12th century and formed numerous small chiefdoms. The first European settlers arrived in 1652, when the Dutch East India Company founded a colony in the sw of the Cape (*see* Cape Province). Dutch Afrikaners (Boers) established farms, employing slaves and using horses and guns to overcome any opposition from the Khoikhoi people who lived in the region. As they moved further inland during the 18th century, the Boers came into conflict with the San and then the Bantu-speaking Xhosa, with whom they fought three wars between 1779 and 1803. In the early 19th century, Britain gained control of the Cape. When Britain abolished slavery in 1833, the Boers began the Great Trek. They met with fierce resistance, particularly from the Zulu kingdom, which had been created from numerous chiefdoms in the 1810s and 1820s. The Boer republics of Transvaal and Orange Free State were established in 1852 and 1854.

The discovery of diamonds and gold in the 1870s and 1880s increased the pace of colonization, and Britain sought to gain control of Boer- and Zulu-held areas. The British defeated the Zulu in the Zulu War (1879), and Zululand was annexed to Natal (1897). In 1890 Cecil Rhodes became governor of Cape Colony. Britain defeated the Boers in the South African Wars (1880–81, 1899–1902).

The Union of South Africa was formed in 1910, with Louis Botha as prime minister. In 1912 the African National Congress (ANC) was founded. During World War 1, South Africa captured Namibia (1915), and after the War it was mandated to the Union. In 1919 Jan Smuts succeeded Botha as prime minister. In 1931 Smuts' successor and National Party founder (1914), James Hertzog, realized Afrikaner ambitions as South Africa achieved full independence within the Commonwealth of Nations. Smuts regained power in 1939, and South Africa joined the Allies in World War 2. This had the effect of destroying Hertzog's government, leaving Smuts in power. There was then a bitter struggle for Afrikaner leadership which was won by Daniel Malan.

The National Party under Malan won the 1948 election, advocating a policy of apartheid. Apartheid placed economic, social and political restrictions on non-whites. It also established "self-governing" but dependent rural homelands or bantustans for the various African "tribes". The ANC began a campaign of passive resistance, but after the Sharpeville massacre (1960), Nelson Mandela formed a military wing. In 1961, faced by international condemnation, Prime Minister Hendrik Verwoerd established South Africa as a republic. In 1964 Mandela was jailed. Verwoerd was assassinated in 1966 and was succeeded by B.J. Vorster. Vorster used South African forces to prevent black-majority rule in South Africa's neighbouring states. The crushing of the Soweto rising (1976) sparked a new wave of opposition. In 1978 P.W. Botha was elected prime minister. During the 1970s, four bantustans gained nominal independence. External economic sanctions forced Botha to adopt a new constitution (1984), which gave Indian and Coloured minorities limited political representation – black Africans were still excluded. From 1985 to 1990 South Africa was in a state of emergency: Archbishop Desmond Tutu pressed for further sanctions.

In 1989 President F.W. de Klerk began the process of dismantling apartheid. In 1990 Mandela was released and resumed leadership of the ANC. Clashes continued between the ANC and Chief Buthelezi's Zulu Inkatha movement. In 1994 the ANC won South Africa's first multi-racial elections, and Mandela became president. The homelands were reintegrated, and South Africa was divided into nine provinces. In 1995 a Truth and Reconciliation Commission, headed by Tutu, was set up to investigate political crimes committed under apartheid. In 1999 Thabo Mbeki, who had replaced Mandela as president of the ANC (1997–), became president of South Africa.

SOUTH DAKOTA
Statehood :
2 November 1889
Nickname :
The Sunshine State
State motto :
Under God the people rule

defeated the Sioux in a number of battles during the 1870s, after which most Sioux returned to the reservations. In 1889 North Dakota and South Dakota became separate states. In 1890 the US Army were sent to arrest SITTING BULL, who was accidently killed. This precipitated the final major battle between the US Army and the Sioux, known as the Massacre of WOUNDED KNEE. In the early 20th century South Dakota suffered from severe drought and many farmers left the region. The state economy recovered with increased industrialization during World War 2. Area: 199,551sq km (77,047sq mi). Pop. (1996) 732,405.

Southeast Asia Treaty Organization (SEATO) Regional defence agreement signed by Australia, New Zealand, France, Pakistan, the Philippines, Thailand, Britain and the United States in Manila in 1954. It was formed in response to communist expansion in Southeast Asia. With administrative headquarters in Bangkok, Thailand, SEATO had no standing forces. Some members were unwilling to support the United States in the VIETNAM WAR, and SEATO was abandoned in 1977. The non-military aspects of the treaty were replaced by the ASSOCIATION OF SOUTHEAST ASIAN NATIONS (ASEAN).

Southern Christian Leadership Conference (SCLC) US CIVIL RIGHTS organization, founded (1957) by Martin Luther KING, Jr. Led by Baptist ministers, the organization employed tactics of non-violent, civil resistance in order to secure full citizenship rights and equality for African Americans. Its foundation followed the bus boycott in Montgomery, Alabama, inspired by the action of Rosa PARKS. The SCLC's first campaign (1961) took place in Albany, Georgia. In 1963 anti-segregation marchers in Birmingham, Alabama, were dispersed by police using dogs and water cannon. National media coverage gained much support for the civil rights movement. Later that year, King led a march on Washington, D.C. The CIVIL RIGHTS ACT (1964) followed. In 1965 the SCLC organized a march in Selma, Alabama, as part of a campaign to expand African American voting rights. State troopers tried to turn the march back, and when the protesters refused they were beaten and tear-gassed. The event, which became known as "Bloody Sunday", again increased support for the SCLC, and the VOTING RIGHTS ACT (1965) was passed by President Lyndon JOHNSON soon afterwards. After King's assassination (1968), Ralph ABERNATHY became leader of the SCLC, organizing the Poor People's March on Washington, D.C. (1968). In the early 1970s, splits within the SCLC led to the resignation of several important leaders, notably Jesse JACKSON. Although weakened, the organization survived to campaign against attempts to limit civil rights legislation in the 1980s. King's son, Martin Luther King III, was appointed leader of the SCLC in 1998.

South Sea Bubble (1720) Speculation in the shares of the English South Sea Company. The Company was founded in 1711 to trade (mainly in slaves) with Spanish America, on the premise that the War of the SPANISH SUCCESSION would end with a treaty favourable to the enterprise. Shares sold so well that in 1720 the Company volunteered to finance the English national debt. The deliberate exaggeration of potential profits, the endorsement of GEORGE I, and payments to politicians to promote the Company resulted in a 900% rise in the price of shares. However, investors became increasingly concerned over false information and the lack of favourable trading rights, and the Bubble burst in September 1720. The value of the Company's shares fell to less than 10% of their peak, bankrupting thousands of investors, closing banks and causing a political scandal. Credit for saving the Company and the government was given to Robert WALPOLE.

South West Africa *See* NAMIBIA

South West Africa People's Organization (SWAPO) Political group formed (1960) in South West Africa (now NAMIBIA). SWAPO was established to achieve independence by halting the South African government's mandate over the region, which was due for renewal in 1966. To this end, SWAPO declared war on South Africa. Soon after ANGOLA gained independence in 1975, SWAPO established guerrilla bases there. In 1978 these bases were attacked by South Africa. Peace talks (1981) in Geneva failed, and SWAPO later refused to cooperate with the rival Multi-Party Conference (MCP) in drawing up a timetable for independence. After independence was achieved, SWAPO won the ensuing 1989 election, gaining 57% of the votes and 75% of the seats in the constituent assembly. In 1990 SWAPO leader Sam NUJOMA became president of Namibia. He was re-elected in 1994 and 1999.

Souvanna Phouma (1901–84) Lao statesman, premier (1951–54, 1956–58, 1960, 1962–75), nephew of King Sisavangvong. After World War 2, he rejected his uncle's support for French colonial rule in INDOCHINA and joined the provisional Lao Issara (Free LAOS) government in Vientiane (1945–46). The Lao Issara split after the French offered concessions: Souvanna supported participation with the French, while his half-brother SOUPHANOUVONG rejected any compromise and formed the communist PATHET LAO. The brothers formed a coalition government (1956–58), which was toppled by a coup. A civil war ensued between the Lao Issara and Pathet Lao. Souvanna unsuccessfully tried to maintain Laos' neutrality during the VIETNAM WAR (1955–75), but became increasingly reliant on US military support. The withdrawal of US forces led to a cease-fire (1973), and Souvanna headed a provisional coalition government until the creation of the People's Democratic Republic of LAOS under Souphanouvong.

soviet (Rus. council) Russian revolutionary workers' council. Soviets first appeared in the RUSSIAN REVOLUTION OF 1905, when striking factory workers in ST PETERSBURG were organized under the Soviet of Workers' Deputies. The BOLSHEVIKS and MENSHEVIKS copied the system, and the Bolshevik Petrograd (St Petersburg) Soviet, led by Leon TROTSKY, was the leading organization in the RUSSIAN REVOLUTION of 1917. Some non-Bolsheviks opposed the Revolution and resigned from the Congress of Soviets, leaving power exclusively in the hands of the Bolsheviks, who established the Council of People's Commissars as the new government. Throughout the SOVIET UNION, soviets were organized at every level from village upwards, becoming the formal unit of local and regional government. At the top was the Supreme Soviet, the chief legislative body.

Soviet Union (officially Union of Soviet Socialist Republics) Former federal republic, successor to the Russian empire and the world's first communist state. The BOLSHEVIK regime, led by Vladimir Ilyich LENIN, came to power in the RUSSIAN REVOLUTION (1917). Lenin's government survived the RUSSIAN CIVIL WAR (1918–20) and famine by instituting a centralized command economy and forming the RED ARMY. However, peasant revolts in the spring of 1921 forced Lenin to introduce the NEW ECONOMIC POLICY (NEP), based on a semi-market economy. On 30 December 1922, a treaty of union was signed by the republics of RUSSIA, UKRAINE, Belorussia (now BELARUS) and TRANSCAUCASIA, thus creating the Soviet Union. In 1923 a new constitution was adopted, establishing the supremacy of the COMMUNIST PARTY OF THE SOVIET UNION (CPSU) and the Supreme Soviet as the highest legislative body.

In 1924 Lenin died and a power struggle ensued between Leon TROTSKY and Joseph STALIN. Stalin emerged the victor and Trotsky was expelled in 1927. In 1928 the first FIVE-YEAR PLAN was adopted. It transformed Soviet agriculture and industry. Collective and state farms were imposed on the peasantry, and industrialization was accelerated. The urban population rapidly doubled. The collectivization schemes directly led to the 1932–34 Ukraine famine, which claimed more than 7 million lives. State control infiltrated all areas of society and was sometimes brutally imposed by the secret police (*see* CHEKA and KGB). The systems of state control led to the creation of a massive bureaucratic administration. The murder (1934) of Sergei KIROV led to the Stalinist PURGES (1936–38). In 1936 Transcaucasia was divided into the republics of GEORGIA, ARMENIA and AZERBAIJAN.

After the NAZI-SOVIET PACT (1939) between Stalin and Adolf HITLER, Germany and the Soviet Union invaded Poland and divided up the country. In 1940 Soviet expansion incorporated the Baltic states of LITHUANIA, LATVIA and ESTONIA into the Union. The costly RUSSO-FINNISH WAR (1939–40) led to the formation of the Karelo-Finnish republic. In 1941 Germany invaded Russia. The failure of the German siege of STALINGRAD (1943) led to the surrender of 330,000 Axis troops, and was a turning-point in WORLD WAR 2. The Red Army launched a counter-offensive that liberated much of Eastern Europe. The War devastated the Soviet Union: *c.*25 million Soviet lives were lost.

The Soviet Union and the United States emerged as the two post-war superpowers. Their antagonistic ideologies and ambitions led to the COLD WAR. The Soviet sphere of influence extended into Albania, Bulgaria, Czechoslovakia, East Germany, Hungary, Poland and Romania. The importance of the military-industrial sector in Soviet politics was greatly enhanced. In 1948 the Soviet army attempted to blockade the W sectors of BERLIN. In 1949 the Soviet Union exploded its first NUCLEAR WEAPON. In March 1953 Stalin died and a collective leadership was installed. In 1955 the WARSAW PACT was established as the communist counterpart to the NORTH ATLANTIC TREATY ORGANIZATION (NATO). In 1956, at the 20th CPSU Congress, Nikita KHRUSHCHEV made his famous secret speech denouncing Stalin as a dictator. In October 1956 the HUNGARIAN UPRISING against Moscow domination was crushed by Soviet troops.

In 1958 Khrushchev won the battle for succession and began a policy of liberalization. Economic decentralization entailed a reduction in the bloated bureaucracy. New alliances were formed with worldwide anti-colonial movements, and Khrushchev formulated a policy of peaceful coexistence with the West. The Cold War shifted into a technological battle to produce more powerful weapons of mass destruction and a "space race". In 1957 the Soviet Union launched *Sputnik 1*, the world's first artificial satellite, and in 1961 Yuri GAGARIN became the first man in space. In the same year, the BERLIN WALL was built to divide East from West Berlin. In 1962 the CUBAN MISSILE CRISIS shattered the Cold War stand-off, and the world stood at the brink of nuclear war. Khrushchev agreed to remove Soviet missiles, and catastrophe was avoided.

In October 1964 Khrushchev was removed from office by a conservative collective leadership, headed by Leonid BREZHNEV and Aleksei KOSYGIN. They were determined to reverse his liberal reforms and improve the Soviet economy. Brezhnev ruled by consensus and brought close political associates, such as Yuri ANDROPOV (KGB chief) and Andrei GROMYKO (foreign minister), into his politburo. He instituted cautious economic reforms and agricultural production increased dramatically. In foreign affairs, the "Brezhnev doctrine" preserved the right of the Soviet Union to intervene in communist states to preserve international communism. On 21 August 1968, Warsaw Pact troops invaded to crush the PRAGUE SPRING in Czechoslovakia. Leading dissidents, such as Andrei SAKHAROV, were sent to prison or forced into exile and the SAMIZDAT movement was suppressed. In 1969 an era of superpower DÉTENTE began with a series of STRATEGIC ARMS LIMITATION TALKS (SALT), resulting in the signing of SALT I by Brezhnev and US President Richard NIXON in 1972. The HELSINKI CONFERENCE (1975) finally ratified the post-war European borders. In 1977 Brezhnev was elected president and a new constitution was formed. In 1979 SALT II was signed, but Soviet involvement (1979–89) in the AFGHANISTAN WAR ended the period of détente, and the treaty was never ratified by the United States. In 1980 the United States led a boycott of the Moscow Olympics and placed new, intermediate range Pershing II missiles on European soil. The Soviet economy stagnated because of the stabilization of oil prices and its outdated manufacturing technology.

In 1982 Brezhnev died, and Yuri Andropov was elected leader. He began a series of far-reaching economic reforms, targeting centralization, corruption, inefficiency and alcoholism. He promoted a series of advisers, including Mikhail Gorbachev, to implement the reforms. His tenure was short; he died after a mere 15 months in office. He was replaced by a hardline Brezhnevite, Konstantin Chernenko. Chernenko died 13 months later and, in March 1985, Gorbachev became general secretary and began a process of economic restructuring (perestroika) and political openness (glasnost). The Chernobyl disaster (1986) provided the first test of glasnost. Dissidents were released, and restraints on emigration were lifted. Gorbachev began a new détente initiative, focusing on nuclear disarmament. A series of meetings with US President Ronald Reagan led to the Intermediate Nuclear Forces (INF) Treaty, which agreed to scrap intermediate-range nuclear missiles. In February 1989 the Soviet Union completed its withdrawal from Afghanistan. Perestroika continued the process begun by Andropov by reducing bureaucracy and allowing a more mixed economy. The restructuring was hampered by opposition from conservatives (anxious to prevent change) and radicals led by Boris Yeltsin, urging more far-reaching policies. In March 1989 the first pluralist elections since 1917 were held, and Gorbachev was elected state president.

The Revolutions of 1989 overthrew every communist leader in the Warsaw Pact and the constituent republics of the Soviet Union began to clamour for secession. In 1989 Gorbachev and US President George Bush declared an end to the Cold War, and the West promised economic support to the Soviet Union. In 1990 the political and economic situation worsened. The Baltic republics, Kazakstan and Georgia, demanded independence, and Armenia and Azerbaijan fought for control of Nagorno-Karabakh. In March 1990 the newly elected Soviet parliament authorized the private ownership of the means of production: the central economic principle of Marxism had been removed and the CPSU fractured. Amid the breakdown in federal government structures, the economy declined by 4%. In December 1990 Gorbachev gained emergency presidential powers, and the conservatives demanded action to prevent the disintegration of the Union of Soviets. Paratroopers were sent to Latvia and Lithuania to prevent secession. Miners went on strike, calling for Gorbachev's resignation. Eduard Shevardnadze resigned as foreign minister and went on to form the Democratic Reform Movement. In June 1991 a new Union Treaty was

SPAIN

AREA: 504,780sq km (194,896sq mi)
POPULATION: 39,085,000
CAPITAL (POPULATION): Madrid (3,121,000)
GOVERNMENT: Constitutional monarchy
ETHNIC GROUPS: Castilian Spanish 72%, Catalan 16%, Galician 8%, Basque 2%
LANGUAGES: Castilian Spanish (official), Catalan, Galician, Basque
RELIGIONS: Christianity (Roman Catholic 97%)
GDP PER CAPITA (1995): US$14.520

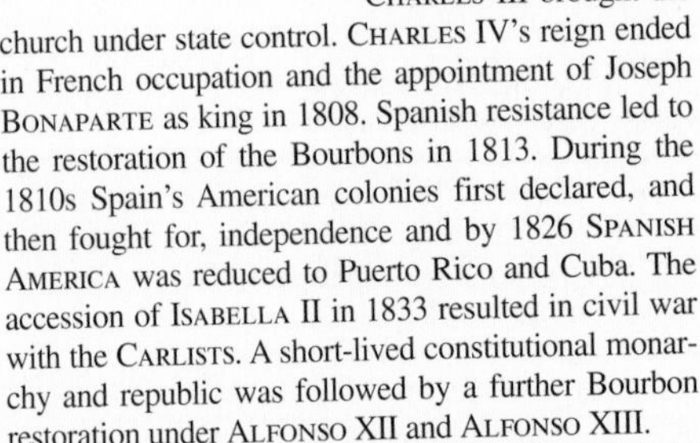

The kingdom of Spain occupies 80% of the Iberian Peninsula. The status of Gibraltar is disputed with Britain. Iberians and Basques were Spain's early inhabitants. In the 9th century BC, the Phoenicians established trading posts on the s coast. In *c.*600 BC Greek merchants set up colonies. In *c.*237 BC the Carthaginian general Hamilcar Barca conquered most of the Peninsula. In the 2nd century BC the Carthaginians were replaced by the Romans, who established two provinces in what is now Portugal and Spain. From *c.*AD 400 Germanic tribes swept into Spain. From the 5th to early 8th centuries, Visigoths controlled s Spain. In 711 the Muslim Moors from Morocco invaded the country. Spain was rapidly conquered (except Asturias and the Basque Country) and an independent Muslim state was founded (756). The Alhambra in the city of Granada is testimony to the splendour of Moorish architecture. The Basques established the independent kingdom of Navarre. In the late 11th, 12th and 13th centuries the counts of Barcelona (from 1137 also kings of Aragón) gradually carved out an empire which by 1300 encompassed Catalonia and Valencia and a number of Mediterranean islands, including Mallorca and Sardinia. In doing so they, together with the kingdom of Castile, reconquered Muslim Spain. Initially they terrorized the successor states (*taifas*) of the once-powerful Umayyads. They then held out against the counter-attack of the Berber Almoravids and Almohads before overrunning the whole of Spain apart from the kingdom of Granada.

In 1479 Castile and Aragón were united by the marriage of Ferdinand V and Isabella I. The reconquest of Granada (1492) saw Ferdinand and Isabella become rulers of all Spain. The Inquisition was used to ensure Catholic supremacy through persecution and conversion. Christopher Columbus' discovery of America (1492) brought vast wealth, and Spain became the leading imperial power, with colonies in South, Central and North America, the Caribbean and Southeast Asia (*see* colonialism). The 16th century was Spain's golden age. In 1519 Charles I became Charles V, Holy Roman emperor. The supremacy of the Habsburgs was established. The extension and centralization of power was continued by Philip II, who gained Portugal (1580). Spanish naval power was dented by the defeat of the Spanish Armada (1588).

During the 17th century, Spain's political and economic power declined. The War of the Spanish Succession (1701–14) resulted in Spain losing many of its lands in Europe as well as the accession of Philip V and the establishment of the Bourbon dynasty. Charles III brought the church under state control. Charles IV's reign ended in French occupation and the appointment of Joseph Bonaparte as king in 1808. Spanish resistance led to the restoration of the Bourbons in 1813. During the 1810s Spain's American colonies first declared, and then fought for, independence and by 1826 Spanish America was reduced to Puerto Rico and Cuba. The accession of Isabella II in 1833 resulted in civil war with the Carlists. A short-lived constitutional monarchy and republic was followed by a further Bourbon restoration under Alfonso XII and Alfonso XIII.

Spain remained neutral during World War 1. In 1923 Primo de Rivera established a dictatorship. He was forced to resign (1930), and a second republic was proclaimed. The Popular Front won the 1936 elections, and conflict between republicans and nationalists, such as the Falange, intensified. With support from the Axis powers, the nationalists led by General Franco emerged victorious from the Spanish Civil War (1936–39), and Franco established a dictatorship. Spain did not participate in World War 2. During the 1960s most of Spain's remaining colonies gained independence.

In 1975 Franco died, and a constitutional monarchy was established under Juan Carlos. Spain began a process of democratization and decentralization. It joined the North Atlantic Treaty Organization (NATO) in 1982, and the European Community (EC) in 1986. There is a historic tension between central government and the regions. From 1959 the militant Basque organization ETA waged a campaign of terror. A cease-fire, announced in 1998, was called off in November 1999. In 1977 the Basque Country, Catalonia and Galicia gained limited autonomy. In 1996 the government was forced to call early elections after allegations of complicity in an illegal anti-terrorist campaign. After 13 years in office, the Spanish Socialist Workers' Party (PSOE) was defeated. José María Aznar formed a minority government. He was re-elected in 2000.

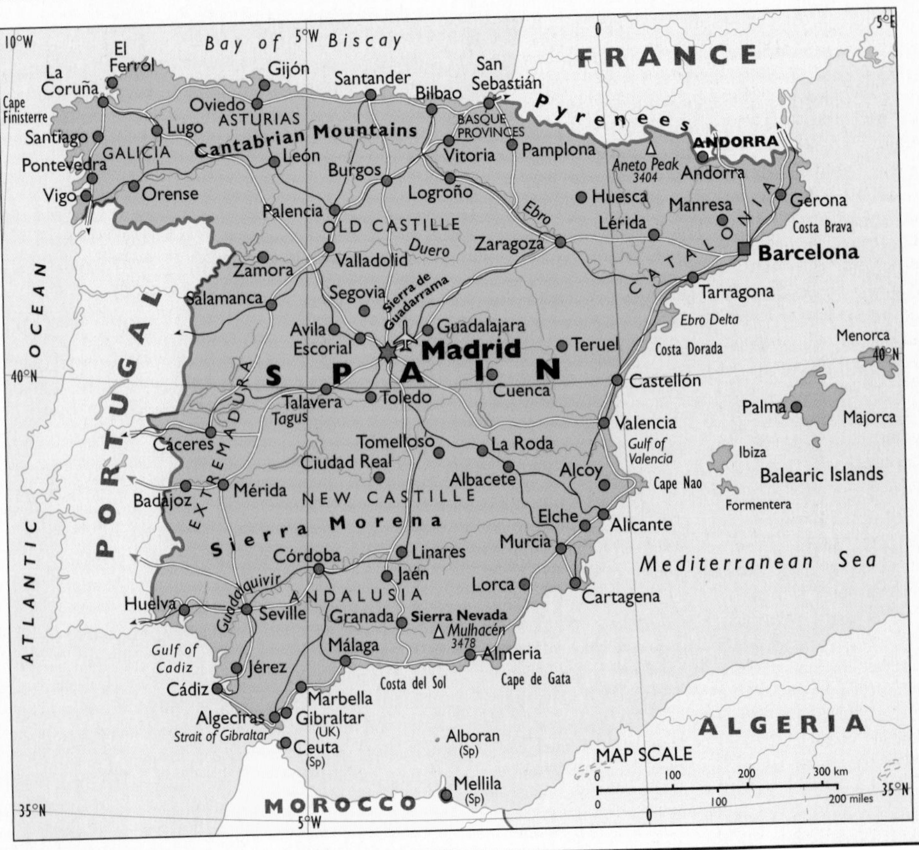

drafted that devolved power to the republics and reconstituted the federal government. It was approved by nine republics, but Armenia, the Baltic states, Georgia and MOLDOVA refused to cooperate. In the same month, Boris Yeltsin was elected president of the Russian republic. In July 1991 Gorbachev attended the Group of Seven (G7) summit and signed the Strategic Arms Reduction Treaty (START), reducing the number of long-range missiles. On 18 August 1991 a coup was launched against Gorbachev by hardliners. Gorbachev was kept under house arrest, while the coup leaders assumed control of the media and sent tanks into Moscow to capture the Russian parliament and Yeltsin. The coup failed, and Gorbachev was reinstated on 22 August 1991. The republics' seized the opportunity to declare independence from federal control.

Yeltsin emerged as the new political power-broker. He banned the CPSU and seized its assets, took control of the Russian armed forces and forced Gorbachev to suspend the Russian Communist Party. Gorbachev resigned as general secretary of the CPSU. In September 1991 the Baltic states of Estonia, Latvia and Lithuania were granted independence. On 8 December 1991 Russia, Ukraine and Belarus formed the COMMONWEALTH OF INDEPENDENT STATES (CIS). By the end of December, the republics of Armenia, Azerbaijan, Kazakstan, KYRGYZSTAN, Moldova, TAJIKISTAN, TURKMENISTAN and UZBEKISTAN had all joined the CIS. On 25 December 1991, Gorbachev resigned as president and, on 31 December the Soviet Union was officially dissolved.

Soweto (South-West Township) Group of black townships of more than a million people on the outskirts of Johannesburg, South Africa. Soweto attracted international attention in January 1976, when a student demonstration against the compulsory teaching of Afrikaans (the official language of AFRIKANERS) in Bantu schools was brutally suppressed by the South African government. This action sparked a series of riots against the APARTHEID regime. The police controlled the disturbances with tear gas and live ammunition, and 618 people, many of them children, had been killed by the end of 1976. The South African government was forced to abandon the enforced implementation of Afrikaans.

Spaak, Paul-Henri (1899–1972) Belgian statesman, prime minister (1938–39, 1946, 1947–1949) and foreign minister (1936–38, 1939–45, 1954–57, 1961–66). He first entered the Belgian parliament in 1932. As well as serving in a number of cabinet posts, Spaak was actively involved in international politics, and in 1946 he became the first president of the UNITED NATIONS' (UN) general assembly. A strong advocate of European unity, he was a founder of the BENELUX (Belgium, Netherlands and Luxembourg) union (1948) and the European Economic Community (1957). He was secretary general of the NORTH ATLANTIC TREATY ORGANIZATION (NATO) (1957–61). *See also* EUROPEAN COMMUNITY (EC)

space exploration Investigation of outer space and heavenly bodies. *Sputnik 1*, launched into Earth orbit by the Soviet Union on 4 October 1957, was the first artificial satellite. Soviet cosmonauts and US astronauts orbited the Earth soon after. Unmanned space probes crash-landed on the Moon, sending back pictures to Earth during the descent. The next development was soft landings, and probes made to orbit the Moon showed its "dark" side for the first time. By 1968 Soviet space scientists had developed techniques for returning a Moon orbiter safely to Earth. In 1969 the US APOLLO 11 mission became the first to place a man on the Moon. By that time, the Soviet Union had sent probes to explore Mars and Venus. **Selective chronology**: first space probe (Explorer 1, launched 31 January 1958); first probe to land on the Moon (Lunik 2, launched 12 September 1959); first manned spaceflight (Yuri GAGARIN, 12 April 1961); first close-up pictures of Mars (Mariner 4, received 14 July 1965); first person to walk on the Moon (Neil ARMSTRONG, 21 July 1969); first pictures from surface of another planet (Venera 9, from Venus on 22 October 1975); first probes to land on Mars (Viking 1 and 2 July 1976); fly-bys of Voyager 2: Jupiter (1979), Saturn (1981), Uranus (1986), Neptune (1989); first space shuttle (Columbia, launched 12 April 1981).

Spain *See* country feature

Spanish America Spanish empire in the Western Hemisphere. The Spanish colonization of the Americas was initiated by the voyages (1492–1504) of Christopher COLUMBUS to the Caribbean and the Gulf of Mexico. The CONQUISTADORS fought to extend Spanish rule to Mexico and Peru. In 1503 ENCOMIENDAS were introduced, but Spanish colonial rule continued to depend largely on the exploitation of NATIVE AMERICANS. The Council of the Indies was established (1524) to directly administer Spain's New World empire and the colonies themselves were later divided into viceroyalties: NEW SPAIN (1535), PERU (1569), NEW GRANADA (1717) and RÍO DE LA PLATA (1776). In the 19th century Spanish rule was overthrown by the liberation movements of Simón BOLÍVAR and José de SAN MARTÍN. *See* individual countries. *See also* EJIDO; HACIENDA; SPANISH-AMERICAN WAR

Spanish-American War (April–July 1898) Conflict fought in the Caribbean and the Pacific between Spain and the United States. The underlying causes were the United States' support for the Cuban movement for independence from Spain and US imperialist ambitions in the Pacific, fuelled by the MANIFEST DESTINY. The immediate cause was the explosion of the US battleship *Maine* at Havana, Cuba. Although the cause of the blast was not clear, Spanish forces were blamed and the United States declared war on Spain. The subsequent conflict lasted ten weeks, during which time the Spanish fleets in the Philippines and Cuba were destroyed by the superior US Navy. Spanish troops in Cuba, although greater in number and better equipped than the US troops (which included Theodore ROOSEVELT's ROUGH RIDERS), without support from the Spanish navy were forced to surrender after defeat at San Juan Hill. Cuba subsequently came under US protection. The occupation of the Philippines, like that of Cuba, was almost totally reliant on the rapid destruction of the Spanish navy, which the US Navy easily achieved on 1 May 1898. However, the commander of the US navy, George DEWEY, had to endure an anxious six weeks before sufficient US soldiers arrived to take Manila. At the Treaty of PARIS (1898), Spain ceded GUAM, Wake Island, PUERTO RICO and the PHILIPPINES to the United States, for which the US government agreed to pay US$20 million to Spain. Cuba became independent. The War effectively ended Spain's colonial aspirations in the Americas, and promoted the United States to a global military power.

Spanish Armada *See* ARMADA, SPANISH

Spanish Civil War *See* CIVIL WAR, SPANISH

Spanish Inquisition *See* INQUISITION

Spanish Sahara Former name of WESTERN SAHARA

Spanish Succession, War of the *See* feature, page 390

Sparta City-state of ancient Greece, near the modern city of Spárti. Founded by DORIANS after *c.*1100 BC, Sparta conquered Laconia (SE Peloponnese) by the 8th century BC and, during the PERSIAN WARS, headed the Peloponnesian League against Persia in 480 BC. In the PELOPONNESIAN WAR (431–404 BC), Sparta defeated its great rival, ATHENS, but was defeated by THEBES in 371 BC and failed to withstand the invasion of PHILIP II of Macedon. In the 3rd century BC Sparta struggled against the ACHAEAN LEAGUE, subsequently joining it but coming under Roman dominance after 146 BC. The ancient city was destroyed by ALARIC I and the GOTHS in AD 395. Sparta was famous for its remarkable social and military organization, which were fully developed by *c.*650 BC. The CITY-STATE was nominally ruled by two leaders, both of whom were hereditary commanders of the army. Together, with an assembly of 28 "elders", they formed a Senate which advised the entire male Spartan population, who ultimately had sovereignty. The massive Spartan HELOT (slave) population performed all the menial tasks and the pure-born Spartan men from the age of seven attended strict military academies that produced the best soldiers in Greece. Spartans were renowned for their austerity and disdain for luxury.

Spartacus (d.71 BC) Thracian gladiator in Rome who led a slave revolt known as the Third Servile (Gladiatorial) War (73–71 BC). His soldiers, who numbered up to 90,000, devastated S Italy and then moved towards Sicily, where they were eventually defeated by CRASSUS with POMPEY's aid. Spartacus died in battle and many of his followers were crucified.

Spartacus League German political party that broke away from the SOCIAL DEMOCRATIC PARTY (SPD) during World War 1. Led by Karl LIEBKNECHT and Rosa LUXEMBOURG, the communist Spartacists refused to support the war effort and rejected participation in the post-Versailles republican government. In 1918 they established the German Communist Party (KPG) with the intention of overthrowing the Berlin government. They instigated a number of uprisings, including one in Berlin in 1919, after which they were brutally repressed. Liebknecht and Luxembourg murdered in police custody.

Speer, Albert (1905–81) German architect and NAZI official, a close associate of Adolf HITLER. Speer drew up the plans for Germany's autobahns and for the Olympic stadium in Berlin. By 1943 his authority over the war economy was second only to that of Hermann GÖRING. Speer pleaded guilty of war crimes at the NUREMBERG TRIALS (1946) and was sentenced to 20 years' in Spandau prison.

Speke, John Hanning (1827–64) British explorer of E Africa. After service in India, he joined Richard BURTON in an expedition to Somalia (1854) and to the E African lakes (1856). In Burton's absence, Speke reached Lake Victoria in 1858, correctly identifiying it as the source of the Nile.

Speranski, Mikhail Mikhailovich, Count (1772–1839) Russian statesman. He became personal assistant to ALEXANDER I in 1807. Commissioned to draft plans for governmental reform, he suggested that the duties of the hereditary nobility be increased and an elected DUMA be established. Speranski also proposed the introduction of examinations to decide promotions within the civil service. Speranski's ideas proved unpopular with the nobility, and he was dismissed in 1812. In 1819 he was appointed governor of Siberia, where he instituted many reforms. Returning to St Petersburg (1821), Speranski served under Tsar NICHOLAS I. He is probably best remembered for his direction of the first comprehensive codification of Russian law (1830).

Spinola, Ambrogio di, Marqués de los Balbases (1569–1630) Genoese soldier. He entered the service of Spain and raised, at his own expense, an army of 9000, which he led to the Netherlands in 1602. Triumphing over the Dutch troops of MAURICE OF NASSAU, Spinola captured Ostend (1604) after a one-year siege. He was rewarded with command of the Spanish armies in the Netherlands. In 1609 he helped negotiate the 12-year truce. Spinola fought with distinction in the early stages of the THIRTY YEARS' WAR (1618–48), before returning to the Spanish Netherlands. In 1625 he achieved his most famous victory, the capture of the Dutch fortress of Breda after a lengthy siege.

Spinoza, Baruch (1632–77) Dutch-Jewish rationalist philosopher. He was the son of Portuguese Jews, who had been forced by the INQUISITION to adopt Christianity and had eventually fled to the relative religious freedom of the Netherlands. Spinoza argued that all mind and matter were modes of the one key substance, which he called either God or Nature. In *Ethics* (1677), he held that free will was an illusion that would be dispelled by man's recognition that every event has a cause.

Split Major port on the Dalmatian coast of the Adriatic Sea, CROATIA. A wealthy medieval city, Split was held either by Venice or Croatia until the 12th century, when it became part of the Hungary-Croatia kingdom. From 1420 to 1797 it was again controlled by Venice, before passing to Austria. Split became part of Kingdom of the Serbs, Croats and Slovenes (later YUGOSLAVIA) in 1918. When Croatia declared independence from Yugoslavia (1991) Split suffered extensive shelling. It is Croatia's second-largest city. Pop. (1991) 189,388.

spoils system Form of US political patronage. The practice of appointing loyal members of the party in power to public offices was first referred to as the spoils system by New York Senator William Marcy in 1832 in response to appointments made by President Andrew JACKSON. It reached its height *c.*1860–80, but declined after the Civil War following the PENDLETON ACT (1883).

Spurs, Battle of the Golden (11 July 1302) Engagement between the Flemish and the French, which ended the plans of PHILIP IV to conquer FLANDERS. It is sometimes called the Battle of Courtrai, the site of the Battle. The victorious Flemish burghers and craftsmen, who fought on foot, commemorated their victory by hanging the spurs of the French knights they had killed in the churches of Bruges.

Squanto (d.1622) NATIVE NORTH AMERICAN of the Pawtuxet tribe of Massachusetts. He may have been taken to England in 1605 before returning with John SMITH in 1614–15. Squanto was then captured by one of Smith's men and taken to Spain, where he was sold into slavery. After escaping to England he returned to Massachusetts in 1619. He acted as an interpreter for the PILGRIMS of PLYMOUTH COLONY, helping them to make a treaty with the Native American chief MASSASOIT. He taught the colonists to plant corn and showed them where to fish.

Square Deal Phrase used by Theodore ROOSEVELT in 1903 to denote his commitment to improving social problems, the rights of the individual and fair play between economic interest groups, such as private businesses and unions. The concept evolved following the settlement of a miners' strike. In reality, the Square Deal included new rules that regulated large corporations more closely and limited their political dominance, and it became part of the reform programme of the PROGRESSIVE PARTY.

Sri Lanka *See* country feature, page 392

Srivijaya (Shrivijaya) Buddhist empire in the Malay archipelago during the 7th–13th centuries. It began on SUMATRA but expanded into the Malay Peninsula, W JAVA and SW BORNEO. It thus gained control of the Strait of MALACCA and trade in the seas of the Indonesian archipelago, establishing commercial relations with China and India. Its capital, Palembang, was famous as a centre of Buddhist learning and culture. In the 11th century Srivijaya was attacked by the CHOLA dynasty of S India. In the 13th century the empire fell apart in the face of the growing power of the MAJAPAHIT.

SS (*Schutzstaffeln*, Ger. guards unit) Chief paramilitary force of Nazi Germany. It was originally Adolf HITLER's bodyguard but expanded under Heinrich HIMMLER to become the NAZI PARTY militia and internal police force. Initially, the SS supported the SA or BROWNSHIRTS, but following the NIGHT OF THE LONG KNIVES (1934) the SS replaced the SA. The SS, with its distinctive black uniform, controlled the GESTAPO and the security organizations. It also ran the CONCENTRATION CAMPS and, from 1936, controlled the police. After the outbreak of World War 2, it formed its own fighting units, the notorious Waffen SS.

SPANISH SUCCESSION, WAR OF THE (1701–14)

Last in a series of wars fought by European coalitions (an alliance of Britain, Austria, the Dutch Republic, Denmark and later Portugal and Savoy, against France, Spain and Bavaria) to contain the expansion of France under LOUIS XIV.

It was precipitated by the death of the last HABSBURG king of Spain, CHARLES II (THE MAD), without an heir. In the First Treaty of Partition (1698) with Louis XIV, WILLIAM III of Britain and the Dutch Republic, Charles II had agreed to nominate Joseph Ferdinand of Bavaria as his successor and to cede control of the Spanish-controlled Italian kingdoms to Austria (Milan) and France (Naples and Sicily). In 1699 Joseph Ferdinand died and a second treaty named Archduke Charles of Austria (later Emperor CHARLES VI), son of Emperor LEOPOLD I, as Charles II's heir. Before his death, Charles II was persuaded against the partition of the Spanish territories and thus changed his will, leaving his kingdom to the BOURBON Philip of Anjou (later PHILIP V of Spain), Louis XIV's grandson. Britain's fear of a radically more powerful French kingdom was realized when France invaded the Spanish Netherlands (roughly modern-day BELGIUM).

The ensuing War of the Spanish Succession marked the emergence of Britain as a maritime and colonial power, with the Duke of MARLBOROUGH, allied with EUGÈNE OF SAVOY, gaining a number of victories, notably at the Battle of BLENHEIM (1704), and driving the French from the German states. Marlborough defeated the French at the Battle of RAMILLIES (1706), and the French were driven out of Italy in 1707. Marlborough's victory at the Battle of OUDENAARDE (1708) forced France from the LOW COUNTRIES, and a further French defeat at the Battle of MALPLAQUET (1709) encouraged Louis to sue for peace. The Allies' terms proved unacceptable, however, and the War continued. When Archduke Charles was named as successor to all Austrian Habsburg possessions (1711), the British and Dutch were loath to allow him also to take control of Spain, and thus recreate the mighty empire of Emperor CHARLES V. The "Grand Alliance" was disbanded and the Spanish succession was settled by a compromise in the Peace of UTRECHT (1713), with Philip attaining the Spanish throne, on condition that he renounce any claim to France, and Britain receiving substantial territorial gains. Archduke Charles refused to sign the treaty as it put an end to his claim on the Spanish throne, and the war with France and Spain continued for another year. A series of defeats finally forced Charles to make peace (Treaty of RASTATT and Baden, 1714) with France, but not Spain, in return for the Spanish Netherlands and some Italian kingdoms. Exhaustion of the participants, especially France, helped ensure general peace in Europe until the outbreak of the War of the AUSTRIAN SUCCESSION in 1740. *See also* ANNE; GRAND ALLIANCE, WAR OF THE; RÁKÓCZY; RYSWICK, TREATY OF

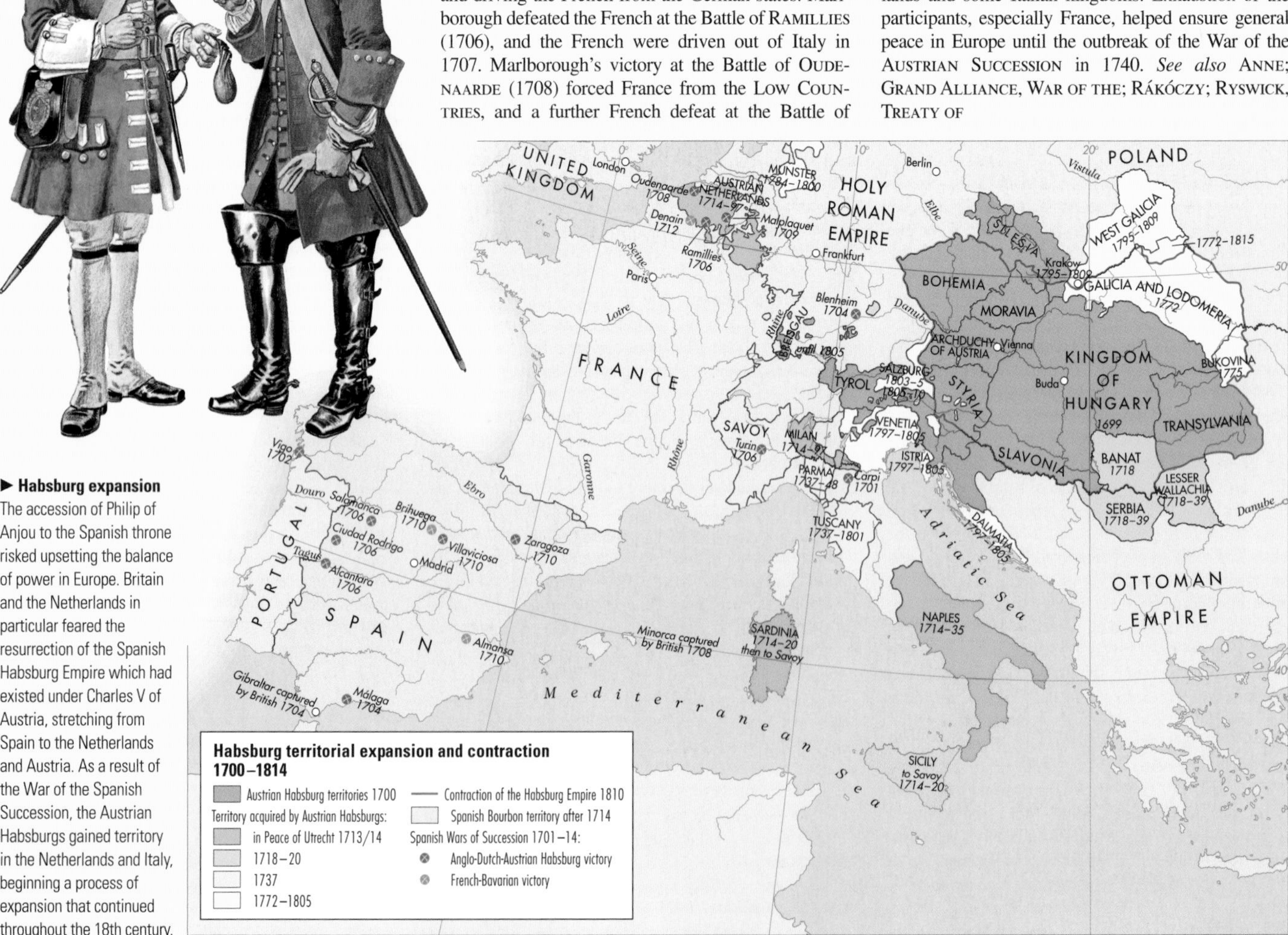

► **Habsburg expansion** The accession of Philip of Anjou to the Spanish throne risked upsetting the balance of power in Europe. Britain and the Netherlands in particular feared the resurrection of the Spanish Habsburg Empire which had existed under Charles V of Austria, stretching from Spain to the Netherlands and Austria. As a result of the War of the Spanish Succession, the Austrian Habsburgs gained territory in the Netherlands and Italy, beginning a process of expansion that continued throughout the 18th century.

Stafford, Henry, 2nd Duke of Buckingham (*c*.1454–83) English noble. In 1466 he married Catherine Woodville, sister-in-law of EDWARD IV. On Edward's death (1483), Stafford supported the Duke of Gloucester's usurpation of the throne as RICHARD III, seizing EDWARD V and his younger brother, and was rewarded with the position of lord high constable. Within two months, Stafford had deserted Richard in favour of the Lancastrian leader, Henry Tudor (later HENRY VII), but perhaps intended to seize the throne for himself. His rebel army failed to capture London, and Stafford was captured and beheaded for treason. *See also* ROSES, WARS OF THE

Stakhanovism Soviet economic policy of the 1930s. It emphasized "socialist competition", the use of incentives to increase productivity in the accelerated industrialization of Joseph STALIN's first FIVE-YEAR PLAN. Stakhanovism was named after Grigoriyevich Stakhanov, a coal miner who, in 1935, was said to have considerably exceeded his quota by mining 102 tonnes of coal.

Stalin, Joseph (1879–1953) Soviet dictator (1924–53), b. Josif Vissarionovich Dzhugashvili. He supported Vladimir LENIN and the BOLSHEVIKS from 1903, adopting the name Stalin ("man of steel") while editing *Pravda*, the party newspaper. Exiled to Siberia (1913–17), he returned to join the RUSSIAN REVOLUTION (1917) and became secretary of the central committee of the COMMUNIST PARTY OF THE SOVIET UNION (CPSU) in 1922. On Lenin's death (1924), Stalin achieved supreme power through his control of the Party organization. He outmanoeuvred rivals such as Leon TROTSKY and Nikolai BUKHARIN, driving them from power and becoming virtual dictator by 1929. In 1928 he launched the first FIVE-YEAR PLAN forcibly to collectivize agriculture and develop heavy industry. Opposition to the changes, which resulted in a catastrophic famine, was suppressed during the Great PURGE (1936–38), with show trials of party leaders and the deportation of million of people to the GULAGS (labour camps). The extent of the terror was not known at the time, and in 1939 the personality cult of Stalin was at its height in Europe. In August 1939 Stalin signed the NAZI-SOVIET PACT with Adolf HITLER and in September, at the beginning of WORLD WAR 2, the Russians joined the Germans in carving up Poland. Stalin was unprepared when, in June 1941, Germany launched a major onslaught on the SOVIET UNION. Taking control of the armed forces, he entered the War on the side of the Allies. Stalin met with Winston CHURCHILL and Franklin ROOSEVELT at the TEHRAN Conference (1943) to discuss tactics and again at YALTA (1945) and POTSDAM (1945) to discuss the post-war division of Europe. After the War, Stalin ensured that Eastern Europe remained under Soviet domination by establishing puppet communist governments. During the early 1950s he reinstated collective farms that had been destroyed during the War, and spared no resources to build an atom bomb (achieved soon after his death), while his increasing sense of paranoia resulted in the deaths and deportations of many former colleagues and prominent Russian figures. After his death, Stalin was denounced (1956) by Nikita KHRUSHCHEV for his tyrannical rule. Under Stalin, the Soviet Union was transformed from a largely agrarian nation into a major industrial nation and one of the two superpowers. However, the millions of people that lost their lives during this remarkable revolution are evidence of the work of one of the most feared dictators the world has ever known. *See also* COLD WAR

Stalingrad, Battle of (1942–43) Decisive conflict in WORLD WAR 2, marking the failure of the German invasion of the SOVIET UNION. During the first half of 1942 the German 6th Army, under the command of General Friedrich von PAULUS, had captured the Soviet cities of Kursk and Kharkov, and occupied the Crimea. In August, following heavy aerial bombardment, Paulus began a siege of Stalingrad (now VOLGOGRAD). During months of bitter fighting, much of it house-to-house, the Russians managed to hold off the Germans. By November 1942, Joseph STALIN had gained sufficient time to assemble six armies, under marshals ZHUKOV, Koniev, Petrov and Malinovsky, and he launched a massive counter-attack. By January 1943 the Germans were surrounded and Paulus was forced to surrender in February. Total casualties at Stalingrad are believed to have exceeded 1.5 million. *See also* ROKOSSOVSKY, KONSTANTIN KONSTANTINOVICH

Stamboliski, Alexander (1879–1923) Bulgarian statesman, prime minister (1919–23). Leader of the Agrarian Party from 1906, he was imprisoned during World War 2 for denouncing the pro-German policy of Ferdinand I, whom he was instrumental in overthrowing (1919). As prime minister, Stamboliski established an authoritarian regime, fiercely anti-communist, prejudiced against the towns and favourable to the peasants. His foreign policy was more conciliatory, but his efforts to improve relations with Yugoslavia further antagonized extremists, especially Macedonian nationalists, and resulted in his overthrow and murder.

Stamford Bridge, Battle of (25 September 1066) Victory for HAROLD II of England over HARALD III of Norway and Harold's exiled brother, Earl TOSTIG, at a village on the River Derwent, NE of York. The Battle was an emphatic victory for the English, and Harald and Tostig were both killed. While Harold was occupied in N England, WILLIAM I (THE CONQUEROR) landed with a Norman army on the S coast. Harold then had to march S to fight the Normans at the Battle of HASTINGS.

Stamp Act (1765) First direct tax levied on the American colonies by the British government, headed by George GRENVILLE. Introduced to raise revenue for the defence of the colonies, it required a special stamp on all printed material, including newspapers and legal documents. It roused widespread opposition, particularly from the SONS OF LIBERTY, who denounced the act as a case of "taxation without representation". The opposition culminated in the **Stamp Act Congress** (1765), at which representatives of nine colonies met in New York City and resolved that only the colonies could tax themselves. The business community agreed to stop the importation of all British goods and a campaign of civil disobedience began. The Act was repealed in 1766 by Charles ROCKINGHAM. The Stamp Act can be seen as one of the contributory factors to the AMERICAN REVOLUTION.

Standish, Miles (*c*.1585–1656) American colonist, b. England. After sailing to America with the PILGRIMS on the *Mayflower*, he organized and led a militia in the PLYMOUTH COLONY, successfully subduing and making peace with the NATIVE NORTH AMERICANS. Although not a PURITAN, he held several leading posts, and on a return trip to England (1625) Standish successfully negotiated the colony's right to purchase its land. Standish was made treasurer (1644–49) of the colony and served on its council.

STALIN, JOSEPH

Joseph Stalin used brutal methods to transform the Soviet economy, creating a powerful industrial nation to rival the United States. His Great Purge (1936–38) claimed up to 7 million lives.

STALIN IN HIS OWN WORDS

"The state is an instrument in the hands of the ruling class for suppressing the resistance of its class enemies."
Stalin's Kampf, 1924

"The Trotsky-Bukharin bunch, that handful of spies, assassins and wreckers..what use that miserable band of venal slaves?"
Report to the 18th Congress, 10 March 1939

Stanislaus, Saint (*c*.1030–79) Patron saint of Poland. As bishop of Kraców (1072–79), he joined a rebellion against the king, BOLESŁAW II (THE GENEROUS), whom he excommunicated for immoral conduct, and was subsequently executed. Stanislaus was canonized in 1253.

Stanislaw I (Leszczyński) (1677–1766) Polish noble, king of Poland (1704–09, 1733). He became king with the support of CHARLES XII of Sweden, replacing AUGUSTUS II, but was later forced to relinquish the throne to Augustus after the Swedish defeat at the Battle of POLTAVA (1709). With French help, Stanislaw regained the throne but was deposed by AUGUSTUS III, who was aided by Russia.

Stanislaw II Augustus (1732–98) (Stanislaw Poniatowski) Last king of POLAND (1764–95). He succeeded to the throne with the support of his lover, CATHERINE II (THE GREAT) of Russia. His reign was spent attempting to reinforce Polish sovereignty in the face of the Partitions of POLAND. The First Partition (1772) saw Polish territory granted to Russia, Austria and Prussia. Following a brief period of renewal, a Second Partition (1793) made Poland almost totally dependent on Russia, and the Third Partition (1795) saw Poland lose its independence. Stanislaw was forced to abdicate and went to live in St Petersburg, W Russia.

Stanley, Edward George Geoffrey Smith, 14th Earl of Derby *See* DERBY, EDWARD GEORGE GEOFFREY SMITH STANLEY, 14TH EARL OF

Stanley, Sir Henry Morton (1841–1904) US journalist and explorer of Africa, b. Wales. An orphan, Stanley emigrated to the United States at the age of 16. During the American Civil War (1861–65), Stanley served in the Confederate army, after which he became a journalist. In 1871 he was commissioned by the *New York Herald* to lead an expedition in search of David LIVINGSTONE in E Africa. Livingstone and Stanley met on 10 November 1871. On a second expedition (1875–77), Stanley led a large party from the E African lakes down the River Congo (Zaire) to the W coast. He returned to the area (1880) as an agent for LEOPOLD II of Belgium and helped to found the CONGO Free State. In 1887–89 Stanley led an expedition supposedly to rescue EMIN PASHA from the Sudan and pressed on, with heavy losses, to the Indian Ocean.

Stanley, Thomas, 1st Earl of Derby *See* DERBY, THOMAS STANLEY, 1ST EARL OF

Stanton, Edwin McMasters (1814–69) US statesman. Attorney general under President James BUCHANAN, he was a firm unionist and was appointed (1862) secretary of war by Abraham LINCOLN. Stanton was persuaded to retain this office under Andrew JOHNSON and attempted to mediate between the president and the Republican Congress over RECONSTRUCTION. Stanton eventually sided with Congress over the issue, and in 1867 Johnson called for his resignation. With Congress in recess Johnson dismissed Stanton, who was reinstated when Congress convened in 1868. Johnson's continued efforts to dismiss Stanton led to his own impeachment; Stanton resigned after Johnson was acquitted in 1868. A year later Stanton was made an associate justice of the Supreme Court but died four days after the appointment.

Stanton, Elizabeth Cady (1815–1902) US social reformer, a lifelong worker for women's rights. She organized the SENECA FALLS CONVENTION (1848), the first public assembly in the United States for female suffrage. In 1851 Stanton met Susan ANTHONY and together they spent the next 50 years campaigning for women's rights, including suffrage and liberalization of the divorce laws. They formed the National Women's Loyal League (1863) and the National Woman Suffrage Association (1890) of which Stanton was president until 1892.

Star Chamber English civil and criminal court of the 15th to 17th centuries, named after its meeting place in Westminster, the ceiling of which was decorated with stars. The Chamber arose as a judicial branch of the royal council, which received petitions from subjects and tried offences against the crown, most commonly public order offences. It proved an honest and speedy source of justice under the early Tudors but was used by Charles I to attack opponents. It was dissolved by the Long Parliament in 1641.

States-General (Estates-General) National assembly composed of separate divisions, or "estates", each historically representing the three major social classes – clergy, nobility and commoners. The States-General served in an advisory capacity to the king particularly over issues of taxation. During the 16th century, the States-General was influential in the Spanish Netherlands' struggle for independence from Spain, and it maintained enormous influence throughout the provinces of the Dutch Republic between 1579 and 1795. In France, the States-General was created (1302) by Philip IV (the Fair) to legitimize his attempt to tax the clergy, but was rarely convoked for the next 100 years. In the 16th century the assembly was used by the House of Guise to attack the Huguenots. Throughout the 17th and most of the 18th century the absolute power of the French monarch ensured the States-General was rarely called. In 1789 Louis XVI summoned the assembly in the hope of resolving France's financial crisis. Through a change in voting procedure (from order – where the nobles and clergy often outvoted the Third Estate – to a count of heads, which gave the Third Estate a distinct advantage) the nobles lost control of the States-General, and the Third Estate precipitated the French Revolution by declaring itself a National Assembly.

states' rights In the United States, political doctrine that restricts the executive privileges of the federal government to those areas specifically cited in the Constitution of the United States, and that ensures individual states have authority in matters not specifically delegated to the federal government. The controversy between federal and state jurisdiction peaked with John Calhoun's interpretation that a state could refuse to obey a federal law it deemed unconstitutional. This led to the nullification crisis (1832) and contributed to the Civil War. It was also an issue during the civil rights movement of the 1950s and 1960s, when many Southern states argued that the federal government was acting unconstitutionally when the Supreme Court ordered states to end racial segregation. Historically, the Republican Party has tended to support strong central government, while the Democratic Party has advocated states' rights.

Stauffenberg, Claus von (1907–44) German colonel, who attempted to assassinate Adolf Hitler in the conspiracy known as the July Plot (1944). An aristocrat and devout Christian, openly critical of the Nazi Party, Stauffenberg had a brilliant career in the cavalry before being disabled by wounds, which restricted him to staff work. Disillusioned with Hitler's prosecution of World War 2, Stauffenberg volunteered to plant the bomb that exploded a few feet from Hitler but only caused superficial injuries. Stauffenberg was arrested and shot the same night.

Steel, Sir David Martin Scott (1938–) British politician, leader of the Liberal Party (1976–88). Steel entered Parliament in 1965, and sponsored the Abortion Act (1967). In 1981 he took the Liberal Party into an electoral alliance with the newly formed Social Democratic Party (SDP). In 1988 the two parties merged to form the Liberal Democrats, and Steel stood down in favour of Paddy Ashdown. Steel resigned from the Westminster Parliament in 1997 and became the Scottish Parliament's first presiding officer (speaker) in 1999.

Stephen Dušan (1308–55) King of Serbia (1331–55). He seized the throne from his father, and embarked on a series of conquests that brought medieval Serbia to the peak of its power, although his conquests did not long survive his death. Having taken much of Macedonia and Albania, Stephen Dušan had himself crowned emperor of the Serbs, Greeks and Albanians (1346). He made further gains at the expense of the Byzantine Empire and was marching on Byzantium itself when he died. He also published a system of laws, the Code of Dušan (1354).

Stein, Karl, Freiherr von und zum (1757–1831) Prussian statesman. Stein became commerce minister in 1804, but his reformist views led to his dismissal by Frederick William III in 1807. Following the Prussian defeat at Jena (1806), Stein returned to power, as chief minister. He transformed the administrative structure of the Prussian government, abolished serfdom and introduced much-needed land reform. Stein's anti-French attitude produced his second dismissal (1808), under pressure from Napoleon I. He entered service with Alexander I of Russia, where he became a leading force in the coalition that eventually destroyed Napoleon.

Stephen, Saint (977–1038) King of Hungary as Stephen I (997–1038), a member of the Árpád dynasty. After the death (997) of his father, Géza, Stephen defeated a pagan uprising. In 1000 he was crowned king of Hungary by Pope Sylvester II, receiving the title of "Apostolic king". Stephen's chief work was to continue the Christianization of Hungary, by endowing abbeys and inviting in foreign prelates. He was canonized in 1083.

Stephen II (d.757) (or Stephen III) Pope (752–57). He succeeded Pope Zacharias, after the first successor, Stephen II, died before being consecrated. In order to defend Rome from the Lombards, Stephen sought the aid of Pepin III (the Short), king of the Franks. He secured a pact with Pepin, resulting in the Donation of Pepin (756), in which territory that had been seized from the Lombards was ceded to the pope. The areas included Ravenna, Venetia and Istria, and they formed the basis of the Papal States.

Stephen (1097–1154) King of England (1135–54), nephew of Henry I. He usurped the throne on Henry's death in spite of an earlier oath of loyalty to Henry's daughter, Matilda. A long civil war (1139–48) began when Matilda's forces invaded. Stephen received support from most of the English barons, many of whom disliked Matilda's husband, Geoffrey of Anjou. Stephen was captured and briefly deposed in 1141 but exchanged for the Duke of Gloucester, Matilda's half-brother. After Stephen's victory at Faringdon (1145), Matilda eventually was forced to leave England (1148). After the death of his son, Eustace, in 1153, Stephen accepted Matilda's son, the future Henry II, as heir to the throne.

Stephen Báthory (1533–86) King of Poland (1575–86), prince of Transylvania (1571–76). He was elected king of Poland by the nobility despite competition from a Habsburg candidate, Maximilian II. Renowned as a soldier, Stephen put down a revolt in Gdańsk (1577). After enlisting Cossacks into the Polish army, he attacked the Russians under Ivan IV (the Terrible) in 1579. The ensuing Livonian War (1558–83) ended with Poland acquiring Polotsk and Livonia. A strong Catholic,

SRI LANKA (FORMERLY CEYLON)

AREA: 65,610sq km (25,332sq mi)
POPULATION: 17,405,000
CAPITAL (POPULATION): Colombo (684,000)
GOVERNMENT: Multiparty republic
ETHNIC GROUPS: Sinhalese 74%, Tamil 18%, Sri Lankan Moor 7%
LANGUAGES: Sinhala and Tamil (both official)
RELIGIONS: Buddhism 69%, Hinduism 16%, Islam 8%, Christianity 7%
GDP PER CAPITA (1995): US$3250

State in the Indian Ocean. The native Veddahs were forced into the mountains *c*.2500 years ago by Sinhalese settlers from N India. Some Veddahs remain in remote regions. The Sinhalese founded Anuradhapura in 437 BC, which acted as their capital. It was also a centre of Theravada Buddhism, which spread through the island after the conversion of the king in the 2nd century BC. The S Indian Chola dynasty conquered the island in the late 10th and 11th centuries. A further invasion from India resulted in the creation of a Tamil Hindu kingdom in the NE part of the island in the 14th century. The area under Sinhalese control gradually divided into several kingdoms.

The Portuguese landed in 1505 and subsequently formed trading settlements on the coast. From the 1630s these settlements were taken over by the Dutch East India Company. In 1796 the British captured the Dutch possessions, and in 1802 the island became a crown colony to which Britain gave the name Ceylon. In 1815 Britain captured the central kingdom of Kandy. Colonial settlers developed tea plantations.

In 1948 Ceylon gained independence and Don Senanayake became prime minister. In the late 1950s, following the declaration of Sinhalese as the official language, communal violence flared between Tamils and Sinhalese. In 1958 Prime Minister Solomon Bandaranaike, leader of the Socialist Freedom Party, was assassinated. His widow, Sirimovo Bandaranaike, became the world's first woman prime minister (1960). Following a brief period in opposition, she was re-elected in 1970.

In 1972 Ceylon became the independent republic of Sri Lanka (Resplendent Island). The new republic was faced with resurgent demands for a separate Tamil state (*Tamil Eelam*) in N and E Sri Lanka. In 1983 secessionist demands spiralled into civil war between government forces and the Tamil Tigers. In 1987 the Sri Lankan government called for Indian military assistance. Unable to enforce a peace settlement, Indian troops withdrew in 1989. In 1993 President Ranasinghe Premadasa was assassinated. In 1994 Prime Minister Chandrika Bandaranaike Kumaratunga was elected president, and her mother, Sirimovo Bandaranaike, became prime minister for the third time. Military offensives against the Tamil Tigers led to the recapture of Jaffna in 1995. The Tamil Tigers refused to accept devolution, and the war, which has claimed more than 40,000 lives, continued. President Kumaratunga was re-elected in 1999.

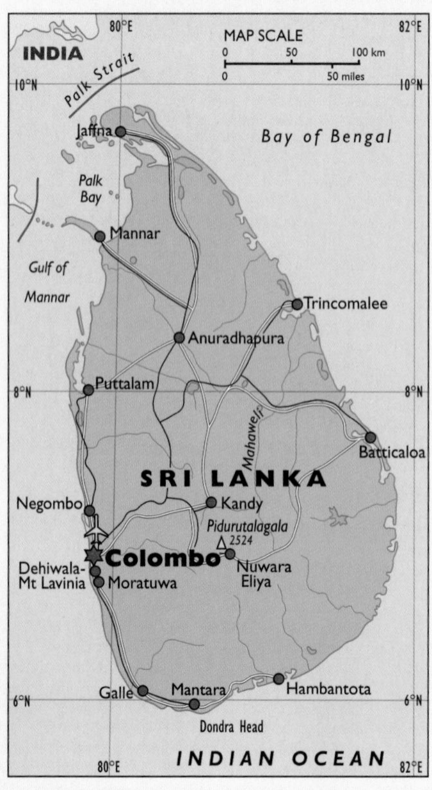

Stephen attempted to promote the COUNTER-REFORMATION in Poland and was planning a crusade against the Ottoman Empire when he died.

Stephens, Alexander Hamilton (1812–83) US statesman, vice president of the CONFEDERATE STATES OF AMERICA during the American CIVIL WAR (1861–65). He represented Georgia in the House of Representatives (1843–59). During the 1850s Stephens was a defender of SLAVERY while opposing the dissolution of the Union, but he accepted Georgia's succession in 1861 and became Confederate vice president. In this position he quarrelled with Jefferson DAVIS over military conscription and other matters, damaging confidence in the government. After the Civil War, he served in the House of Representatives (1873–82) and as governor of Georgia (1882–83).

Stephens, Uriah Smith (1821–82) US UNION leader. In 1869 he founded the KNIGHTS OF LABOR (1869), the first US national labour union, initially established to protect the interests of garment workers in Philadelphia. The Knights of Labor was originally a secret fraternity designed to protect its members from exploitation, and was open to all trades. By 1879, when Stephens retired, it had nearly 10,000 members.

Stern Gang Zionist terrorist group in PALESTINE under the British mandate, so named by the British after its founder, Abraham Stern (1907–42), but known to Zionists as "Fighters for the Freedom of Israel". A splinter group from the IRGUN ZEVAI LEUMI, it had only a few hundred members. The Gang's objective was an independent Jewish state and its predominant weapon was political assassination. Victims included a British minister, Lord Moyne (1944), and the UN mediator in Palestine, Count BERNADOTTE (1948). *See also* ZIONISM

Stevens, Thaddeus (1792–1868) US politician, Congressman (1849–53, 1859–68). Stevens was one of the fiercest opponents of SLAVERY, and was instrumental in persuading Abraham LINCOLN to issue the EMANCIPATION PROCLAMATION (1863). After the CIVIL WAR, Stevens advocated federal intervention in Southern states to ensure they remained democratic. He successfully opposed the lenient policy of Andrew JOHNSON on RECONSTRUCTION, and led calls for Johnson's impeachment.

Stevenson, Adlai Ewing (1835–1914) US statesman, vice president (1893–97). A Democratic Congressman from Illinois (1875–77, 1879–81), he served as assistant paymaster general in the first administration of Grover CLEVELAND. In 1892 he worked hard to secure the renomination of Cleveland for a second term and his efforts were rewarded with the vice presidency.

Stevenson, Adlai Ewing (1900–65) US diplomat and politician, grandson of Adlai STEVENSON. He was instrumental in the founding of the UNITED NATIONS (UN) and acted as the chief US delegate to the UN (1946–47), before being elected governor of Illinois (1948). Stevenson was an unsuccessful Democratic presidential candidate in 1952 and 1956 against Dwight EISENHOWER. John KENNEDY appointed him US ambassador to the UN (1961–65).

Stewart *See* STUART

Stilicho, Flavius (*c*.359–408) Roman general of VANDAL origin. He was a favourite of Emperor THEODOSIUS I, whose niece he married. On the death of Theodosius (395), Stilicho became regent for his young son HONORIUS. A great military leader, Stilicho defeated an invasion of N Italy by the VISIGOTHS under ALARIC I at Pollentia (402) and Verona (403). In 405 he defeated a large force of OSTROGOTHS. When Arcadius, the emperor of the Eastern Roman Empire, died, it was rumoured that Stilicho would put his own son on the throne. Honorius ordered that Stilicho be imprisoned and executed.

Stimson, Henry Lewis (1867–1950) US statesman. Following an unsuccessful bid to become governor of New York, Stimson was secretary of war under President William TAFT (1911–13). After serving in the US Army during World War 1, he was made governor general of the PHILIPPINES (1927–29). As secretary of state under President Herbert HOOVER (1929–33), after the Japanese invasion of MANCHURIA, Stimson tried to secure international disarmament and formulated the "Stimson doctrine": that the United States would not recognize territorial changes brought about by force. He was President Franklin ROOSEVELT's secretary of war throughout World War 2. Stimson supported the dropping of the atom bombs on Japan.

Stockholm Capital of Sweden, port on Lake Mälar's outlet to the Baltic Sea. Founded in the mid-13th century, it became a trade centre dominated by the HANSEATIC LEAGUE. It became the capital of Sweden in 1436. In the 16th century GUSTAVUS I (VASA) ended the privileges of the Hanseatic merchants. In the 17th century Stockholm developed rapidly, as Sweden became a great power. By the 18th century, when many fine buildings were constructed, it was the cultural centre of Sweden. Industrial development began in the mid-19th century. Pop. (1994) 1,708,502.

Stockholm Bloodbath (8–9 November 1520) Mass execution ordered by CHRISTIAN II, king of Denmark and Norway, after he had conquered Sweden. Prior to Christian's conquest, Sten STURE, the Swedish regent, who was opposed to the KALMAR UNION, had imprisoned Archbishop Trolle (1488–1535), who was a supporter of the Union. After the conquest, Christian, encouraged by Trolle, executed 82 people, including nobles, clergy and merchants, in an effort to eliminate the leaders of Sture's party and any other opposition. Christian's brutality sowed the seeds for the successful revolt of GUSTAVUS I (VASA).

Stockton, Robert Field (1795–1866) US naval officer. He served in the WAR OF 1812. In 1821 Stockton travelled to Africa on behalf of the AMERICAN COLONIZATION SOCIETY to negotiate rights to what became LIBERIA. He commanded land and sea forces in the MEXICAN WAR (1846–48), proclaiming California a US territory, and was US senator from New Jersey (1851–53).

Stoics Followers of the ethical school of philosophy called Stoicism, founded by ZENO OF CITIUM in *c*.300 BC. Established on the premise that virtue is attainable only by living in harmony with nature, and that nature is governed by reason, stoicism stressed the importance of self-sufficiency and of equanimity in adversity. The philosophy was first expressed by Chrysippus in the 3rd century BC. It was introduced into Rome in the 2nd century BC, where its principle of equality among men found its greatest adherents: SENECA in the 1st century AD; Epictetus in the 1st and 2nd centuries; and the 2nd-century emperor MARCUS AURELIUS who, in his work *Meditations*, emphasized the Stoic virtues of courage, wisdom, justice and temperance. Other Roman leaders who were influenced by stoicism included BRUTUS, CICERO and CATO (THE YOUNGER).

Stolypin, Peter Arkadievich (1862–1911) Russian statesman. After the RUSSIAN REVOLUTION OF 1905, he became interior minister under NICHOLAS II and then the last prime minister (1906–11) of tsarist Russia. Stolypin introduced agricultural reforms favouring the peasants (KULAKS), but his conservative regime crushed political dissent and enforced changes to reduce the electorate, ensuring a more compliant DUMA. Negotiating between mutually hostile interests, Stolypin eventually antagonized the Duma, fellow ministers and the tsar. He was assassinated.

Stone, Lucy (1818–93) US feminist. She organized a series of women's rights convention in the 1850s. Stone established the American Woman Suffrage Association (1869) and founded (1870) the *Woman's Journal*.

Stone Age Period of HUMAN EVOLUTION defined by the use of stone tools. The Stone Age dates from the earliest identifiable broken-pebble tools made by human ancestors *c*.2.5 million years ago. The period is generally considered to have ended when metal tools first became widespread during the BRONZE AGE. The Stone Age is usually subdivided into the PALAEOLITHIC, MESOLITHIC and NEOLITHIC.

Stonehenge Circular group of prehistoric standing stones within a circular earthwork on Salisbury Plain, S England, 13km (8mi) N of Salisbury. The largest and most precisely constructed MEGALITH in Europe, Stonehenge was built in three stages over about 1000 years. Originally consisting of a circular ditch and bank, between *c*.2100 and 1500 BC a complex arrangement was created using large standing bluestones brought from SW Wales and giant sarsen stones. The significance of Stonehenge is a subject of controversy: it may have been an astronomical observatory, a temple, or a pagan ceremonial centre.

Stowe, Harriet Beecher (1811–96) US writer. Stowe is best known for *Uncle Tom's Cabin* (1851–52), a powerful anti-SLAVERY novel, which was first published in serial form in the abolitionist paper *National Era*. She later published *The Key to Uncle Tom's Cabin* (1953), which contained documents and testimonies supporting the novel. It helped to focus anti-slavery sentiments in northern states in the years preceding the American CIVIL WAR.

Strafford, Thomas Wentworth, 1st Earl of (1593–1641) English statesman, minister of CHARLES I. Strafford first entered Parliament in 1614, and was a leading critic of Charles' foreign policy, particularly the wars against Spain and France. In 1628 he was instrumental in proposing a bill of rights that ultimately led to the PETITION OF RIGHT. Despite Strafford's views, he assumed the role of mediator between Parliament and the king. As lord president of the North (1628–33) and lord deputy of Ireland (1633–39), he successfully introduced agricultural reform, increased revenue to the monarchy and raised an army to combat the rebellious Scots, Strafford unwaveringly implemented Charles' policies and proved an extremely authoritative and capable administrator. Strafford became chief adviser to the king after the death of the Duke of BUCKINGHAM (1628) and, with the onset of the BISHOPS' WARS in 1639, he was summoned to England where Charles made him an earl in 1640. Charles was forced to summon Parliament in a desperate attempt to raise revenue, and Strafford intended to impeach those who opposed. However, John PYM impeached Strafford first and he was subsequently found guilty of subverting the law and sentenced to death. Charles, concerned by outbreaks of civil disobedience, consented to his execution in 1641.

Straits Settlements Former British crown colony on the Malacca Strait. In 1826 MALACCA, PENANG and SINGAPORE, which were possessions of the English EAST INDIA COMPANY in SE Asia, were combined as the Straits Settlements. In 1858 they fell under British Indian control, before, in 1867, passing into British colonial authority. In 1912 Labuan was added. The Settlements were dissolved in 1946, with Singapore becoming a crown colony and the remainder being incorporated in the Malayan Union, which became the Federation of MALAYSIA in 1948.

Strasbourg City on the River Ill, E France, capital of Bas-Rhin department and the commercial capital of the ALSACE region. Known in Roman times as Argentoratum, the city was destroyed by the HUNS in the 5th century. It became part of the HOLY ROMAN EMPIRE in 923 and developed into an important commercial centre, becoming a free imperial city in 1262. Strasbourg was a centre of medieval German literature and of 16th-century Protestantism. It was seized by France in 1681, regained by Germany after the FRANCO-PRUSSIAN WAR, but recovered by France at the end of World War 1. German troops occupied the city during World War 2. Pop. (1990) 252,338.

Strategic Arms Limitation Talks (SALT) Discussions between the United States and the Soviet Union to limit the proliferation of NUCLEAR WEAPONS. The talks began in 1969 between Lyndon JOHNSON and Leonid BREZHNEV. In 1972 Richard NIXON and Brezhnev signed SALT I. This agreement limited anti-ballistic missile systems and produced an interim accord on intercontinental ballistic missiles (ICBMs). In 1973 a second phase began with meetings between Gerald FORD and Brezhnev, and in an interim agreement (1974) they agreed to limit ballistic missile launchers. SALT II, signed in Vienna, Austria, between Jimmy CARTER and Brezhnev in 1979, banned new ICBMs and limited other launchers. The Soviet invasion of Afghanistan in December 1979 meant that the treaty was never ratified by the US Senate. Negotiations resumed in 1982 when SALT was superseded by **START (Strategic Arms Reduction Talks)**. In 1983 the Russians refused to enter into further talks in protest at Ronald REAGAN's approval of the deployment of nuclear missiles in Western Europe. In 1985 START resumed, with the US government focusing the discussions on land-based missiles, while the Soviets were keen to limit the development of the US STRATEGIC DEFENSE INITIATIVE (SDI). In 1987 Reagan and Mikhail GORBACHEV signed the Intermediate Range Nuclear Forces Treaty followed, in 1991, with the signing of START 1 by Gorbachev and Reagan's successor George BUSH. This agreement committed both nations to reducing their nuclear arsenals by 25–30%. With the break up of the Soviet Union later in 1991, former Soviet countries that had inherited nuclear weapons, Belarus, Ukraine, Russia and Kazakstan, signed a supplementary agreement (1992) that upheld START 1, which was finally implemented in 1993–94. While the implementation of START 1 was in progress, Russia, under Boris YELTSIN, and the United States signed START II, which provided for the elimination of 65–75% of the nuclear warheads held by the five countries over nine years. START II remains to be ratified by US Congress and Russia's parliament, which, under Vladimir PUTIN, was reluctant to commit to START II in the light of the US nuclear shield proposals, which, the Russians argue, contravenes the principles of START 1.

Strategic Defense Initiative (SDI) US programme to develop a defence against NUCLEAR WEAPONS. Popularly known as "Star Wars", the programme was initiated after a speech by President Ronald REAGAN in 1983 calling for a defensive system to destroy enemy missiles in space. In theory, satellites would detect the launching of missiles, which would be destroyed in flight by laser weapons, based either on satellites or on the ground. Regarded by some experts as unworkable and exceedingly expensive, SDI may have contributed to the ending of the COLD WAR, since the Soviet Union could not have matched such expenditure. SDI was scaled down, revised, modified and renamed (GPALS) in the 1990s by George BUSH. The new system dispensed with the use of lasers, instead relying on interceptor missiles based in space and around the Earth that effectively provided a protective shield against nuclear attack. GPALS remained a source of international ill feeling, particularly in Russia, whose suggestion for the joint creation of a worldwide system on the lines of SDI/GPALS was regarded as impracticable.

Strauss, Franz Josef (1915–88) German statesman. A founder of the Bavarian Christian Social Union (CSU), he was elected to the Bundestag in 1949. Strauss served as defence minister (1956–62) under Konrad ADENAUER, helping to strengthen Germany's armed forces. In 1962, shortly after becoming chairman of the CSU, Strauss was forced to resign from the West German cabinet after accusations of an abuse of power. He later returned to power as finance minister (1966–69). Strauss was defeated in the 1980 presidential elections by Helmut Schmidt, but continued to be a vociferous critic of Schmidt's policy of OSTPOLITIK (rapprochement with communist East Germany). As prime minister of Bavaria (1978–88), he was credited with increasing the state's prosperity.

Straw, Jack (1946–) British statesman, home secretary (1997–). He entered Parliament in 1979. Straw held several shadow cabinet posts before Labour's victory under Tony BLAIR in the 1997 general election. As home secretary, he dealt with the decision (2000) not to extradite Augusto PINOCHET to Spain.

Stresemann, Gustav (1878–1929) German statesman. He was the outstanding statesman of the WEIMAR REPUBLIC, for which he was foreign minister (1923–29). Stresemann agreed to the DAWES PLAN (1924), which managed German REPARATIONS, and in 1925 he concluded the LOCARNO PACT. Stresemann worked for a practicable post-war settlement with Germany's former enemies under the harsh terms imposed by the Treaty of VERSAILLES. He negotiated Germany's entry into the LEAGUE OF NATIONS (1926), was a signatory to the KELLOGG-BRIAND PACT (1928) and shared the 1926 Nobel Prize for Peace with Aristide BRIAND.

Strijdom, Johannes Gerhardus (1893–1958) South African statesman, prime minister (1954–58). He was elected to the South African National Assembly in 1929 as a member of the NATIONAL PARTY (NP). A fervent advocate of Daniel MALAN's white supremacist ideology, Strijdom became a minister (1948–54) in the NP government. Succeeding Malan as prime minister, Strijdom furthered the APARTHEID system that had been put in place.

Stroessner, Alfredo (1912–) Paraguayan dictator, president (1954–89). He served with distinction in the CHACO WAR (1932–35). As commander in chief (1951–54) of the armed forces, he led the coup that overthrew President Federico Chávez (1954). Stroessner was elected president later that year, after an election in which he was the only candidate. Having altered the constitution, Stroessner was re-elected four times (1958, 1963, 1968, 1973). His rule was totalitarian but, using foreign aid, he improved the nation's infrastructure. Stroessner was ousted in a military coup led by Andrés Rodríguez and fled to Brazil.

Stuart, Charles Edward (1720–88) Scottish prince, known as "Bonnie Prince Charlie" or the "Young Pretender". A grandson of the deposed JAMES II, he led the JACOBITES in the Rebellion of 1745 ("the '45") on behalf of his father, James STUART, the "Old Pretender". Landing in the Scottish Highlands, without the hoped-for backing of France, he gained the support of many clan chiefs, defeated government troops at the Battle of PRESTONPANS (1745), E central Scotland, and marched on London. Lacking widespread support in England, he turned back at Derby. The following year his largely Highland force was decimated in the Battle of CULLODEN. Stuart escaped to the continent and lived in exile until his death.

Stuart, "Jeb" (James Ewell Brown) (1833–64) Confederate general in the American CIVIL WAR. A graduate of West Point, Stuart resigned from the US Army to become a Confederate cavalry commander and one of the most able subordinates of Robert LEE. His reputation was damaged at the Battle of GETTYSBURG (1863), when he undertook an independent operation that prevented him providing Lee with crucial support. Stuart died of wounds sustained at Yellow Tavern, Virginia.

Stuart, James Francis Edward (1688–1766) British claimant to the throne, called the "Old Pretender". He was the only son of JAMES II and was proclaimed king of England by the JACOBITES on the death of his father (1701). He made two attempts to regain the throne (1708 and 1715), landing in Scotland, where support for the STUARTS was greatest. On both occasions the cause was lost before James arrived. His son was Charles STUART.

Stuart, Mary *See* MARY II

Stuart (Stewart) Scottish royal house, which inherited the Scottish crown in 1371 and the English crown in 1603. The Stuarts were descendants of Walter Fitzalan (d.1114), whose grandson Walter (d.1177) was given the hereditary office of steward in the royal household. The sixth steward, Walter (d.1326), married a daughter of ROBERT I (THE BRUCE), and their son, ROBERT II (r.1371–90), became the first Stuart king of Scotland. The crown descended in the direct male line until the death (1542) of JAMES V, who was succeeded by his infant daughter, MARY, QUEEN OF SCOTS. In 1603 her son, James VI, succeeded ELIZABETH I of England as JAMES I. In 1649 James' son, CHARLES I, was executed following the English CIVIL WAR, but the

SUDAN

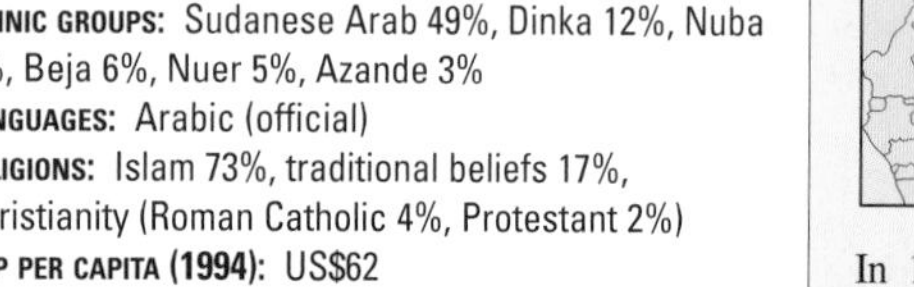

AREA: 2,505,810sq km (967,493 sq mi)
POPULATION: 26,656,000
CAPITAL (POPULATION): Khartoum (476,218)
GOVERNMENT: Military regime
ETHNIC GROUPS: Sudanese Arab 49%, Dinka 12%, Nuba 8%, Beja 6%, Nuer 5%, Azande 3%
LANGUAGES: Arabic (official)
RELIGIONS: Islam 73%, traditional beliefs 17%, Christianity (Roman Catholic 4%, Protestant 2%)
GDP PER CAPITA (1994): US$62

Republic in NE Africa, and Africa's largest country. The ancient state of NUBIA extended into N Sudan. In *c.*2000 BC it became a colony of EGYPT. From the 11th century BC to *c.*350 AD, it was part of the KUSH kingdom. Christianity was introduced in the 6th century. From the 13th to 15th centuries, N Sudan came under Muslim control, and Islam became the dominant religion. By the 19th century the Muslim FUNJ empire was established in the N. This was overthrown between 1820 and 1823 by the Egyptian forces of MUHAMMAD ALI. In 1877 the khedive of Egypt, ISMAIL PASHA, appointed British General Charles GORDON as governor general. Gordon attempted to increase Egypt's influence in the S. In 1881 Muhammad Ahmad declared himself the MAHDI and led an Islamic uprising. British forces invaded from Egypt but the Mahdists resisted until 1898, when they were defeated by General KITCHENER's forces at Omdurman. Following the FASHODA INCIDENT, in 1899 Sudan became Anglo-Egyptian Sudan, governed jointly by Britain and Egypt.

Opposition to colonial rule continued. In 1951 King FAROUK of Egypt proclaimed himself king of Sudan, but in 1952 he was deposed and in 1956 Sudan gained its independence. The S Sudanese, who are predominantly Christians or followers of traditional beliefs, revolted against the dominance of the Muslim N, and civil war broke out. In 1958 the military seized power. Civilian rule was re-established in 1964 but overthrown again in 1969, when Gaafar Muhammad al-NIMEIRI seized control. In 1972 S Sudan was given considerable autonomy, but unrest persisted. In 1983 the imposition of Islamic law sparked off further conflict between the government and the Sudan People's Liberation Army (SPLA) in the S. In 1985 Nimeiri was deposed and a civilian government was installed. In 1989 the military, led by Omar Hassan Ahmed al-Bashir, established a revolutionary command council. Civil war between the SPLA and government forces continued in the S. Peace initiatives foundered as the SPLA split over the nature of independence from the N.

In 1996 Bashir was re-elected, virtually unopposed. The National Islamic Front (NIF) dominated the government and was believed to have links with Iranian terrorist groups. In 1996 the United Nations (UN) imposed sanctions on Sudan. In 1997 an SPLA offensive, led by John Garang, made signficant advances. A South African peace initiative (1997) led to the formation of a Southern States' Coordination Council. In 1997 the United States imposed sanctions on Bashir's regime. In 1999 Bashir declared a state of emergency and dissolved parliament. Sudan's Islamicist leader Hassan al-Turabi was dismissed in 2000.

S

dynasty was restored with the Restoration of Charles II in 1660. His brother, James II, lost the throne in the Glorious Revolution (1685) and was replaced by the joint monarchy of William III and Mary II, James' daughter. When James' second daughter, Anne, died (1714) without an heir the House of Hanover acceded to the throne under George I. The male descendants of James II made several unsuccessful attempts to regain the throne, culminating in the Jacobite rebellion of 1745.

Student Non-Violent Coordinating Committee (SNCC) US civil rights organization. Founded in 1960, it led integration and voter registration drives in the South. After 1966, under the leadership of Stokely Carmichael, the group rejected its white members and became more militant, with black power becoming the theme of SNCC. In 1969 it was renamed Student National Coordinating Committee.

Sture, Sten (the Elder) (*c*.1440–1503) Swedish statesman, regent (1470–97, 1501–03). He fought for independence from Danish rule under the Kalmar Union. Sture helped Charles VIII of Sweden regain the throne (1467), and following Charles' death (1470) became regent of Sweden. He defeated Christian I of Denmark's attempt to regain the Swedish throne at the Battle of Brunkerberg (1471). As regent, Sture increased the power of the monarchy and founded the University of Uppsala (1477). Having successfully delayed the accession of Christian's son John to the Swedish throne, Sture was defeated by a coalition of Russian and Danish troops, and was obliged to accept John as king (1497–1501). He later overthrew John and served as regent until his death.

Sture, Sten (the Younger) (*c*.1492–1520) Swedish statesman, regent (1513–20). He was the son of Svante Nilsson Sture (*c*.1460–1512), who had also been Swedish regent (1503–12). Sture became regent in opposition to a pro-Danish, pro-Kalmar Union faction of nobles. Civil war broke out between the two sets of supporters, and Sture imprisoned Archbishop Trolle (1488–1535), leader of the pro-unionists. In 1520 the Danish king Christian II attacked and defeated Sture, who died from his injuries during the battle. The Stockholm Bloodbath ensued.

Stuyvesant, Peter (1610–72) Dutch colonial administrator. He became governor of the Caribbean islands of Curaçao, Bonaire and Aruba in 1643, and in 1647 he became director general of all the Dutch territories, including New Amsterdam (now New York City). In 1655 he ended Swedish influence in Delaware, and ruled the colony until it was taken over by the English in 1664 and renamed New York. Stuyvesant's often draconian rule, particularly the imposition of heavy taxes and his intolerance to religious dissenters, was partly responsible for the Dutch colonists ready acceptance of English rule. After a brief visit to Holland, Stuyvesant returned to New York where he established a farm, on which he later died.

Suárez González, Adolfo (1933–) Spanish statesman, prime minister (1976–81). He set Spain on the path to democracy after years of dictatorship. In 1975 Suárez became secretary general of the National Movement, General Franco's reformed Falange. The following year, he was appointed prime minister by King Juan Carlos. Suárez legalized the Socialist and Communist parties and, in 1977, announced Spain's first free elections since 1936. His newly formed Democratic Central Union Party triumphed in the elections. As prime minister, Suárez faced growing demands for regional autonomy and a steep increase in acts of terrorism by Basque separatists. In 1981 he resigned as prime minister and leader of his party.

Sucre, Antonio José de (1795–1830) South American revolutionary leader and first president of Bolivia (1826–28). He joined the fight for independence from Spain in 1811 and played a key role in the liberation of Ecuador, Peru and Bolivia, winning the final, decisive Battle at Ayacucho (1824). With Simón Bolívar's support, Sucre became the first elected president of Bolivia, during which time he introduced financial and educational reform. Local opposition and an invasion by Peruvian troops, however, forced his resignation. Sucre was assassinated while trying to preserve the unity of Gran Colombia (Ecuador, Colombia and Venezuela). *See also* San Martín, José de

Sudan *See* country feature

Sudetenland Border region of N Bohemia (Czech Republic), including part of the Sudeten Mountains. It was largely populated by Germans, and in the 1930s Nazi-inspired agitation demanded its inclusion in Germany. Approval for its annexation was given by Britain and France in the Munich Agreement (1938). After World War 2 it was restored to Czechoslovakia, and the German population was expelled.

Suez Canal Waterway in Egypt linking Port Said on the Mediterranean Sea with the Gulf of Suez and the Red Sea. The 169-km (105-mi) canal was planned and built in the period 1859–69 by the Suez Canal Company under the supervision of French canal builder Ferdinand de Lesseps. In 1875 the British government became the major shareholder in the company. In 1955 more than 120 million tonnes of merchandise passed through the Canal, much of it oil. In 1956 Egypt nationalized the Canal and in the ensuing Suez Crisis, Israeli and British forces attacked Egypt. The Canal was closed from 1956 to 1957 while repairs were carried out. It was again closed during the Six-Day War (1967). The Canal reopened in 1975. In the intervening period, many new ships, especially oil tankers, became too large to pass through the Canal. Loss of revenue forced Egypt to clear and widen the waterway.

Suez Crisis (1956) Conflict in the Middle East. When Britain and the United States, concerned by Egypt's approach to Eastern bloc countries for weapons, announced that they would not provide financial assistance for Egypt's Aswan Dam project, President Gamal Abdel Nasser of Egypt nationalized the Suez Canal Company, effectively taking control of the Canal away from Britain and France. He argued that the revenue generated from the nationalization would pay for the Dam project. In a secret pact with France and Britain, Israel, who had been denied use of the Canal and had become increasingly exasperated by guerrilla infringements on Israeli territory from the Egyptian-held Gaza Strip, invaded the Sinai Peninsula and soon took control of the Canal region. As planned, Britain and France demanded the withdrawal of both Israeli and Egyptian troops from the area, but Nasser refused to comply. Britain and France then bombed Egyptian military bases, destroying the majority of the Egyptian airforce. In response, Nasser ordered the sinking of all ships in the canal, effectively blocking it. The United States and the Soviet Union, surprised by the developments, insisted on an immediate cease-fire in the region, and forced France, Britain and Israel to withdraw their forces. A United Nations' (UN) force was sent to enforce the cease-fire thus ending the crisis. Subsequent treaties gave Egypt control of the Canal, and Nasser was hailed an Arab hero.

suffragette movement Women's campaign in Britain in the late 19th and early 20th centuries to win the right to vote. It began in the 1860s and developed until the founding of the National Union of Women's Suffrage Societies in 1897. Emmeline Pankhurst founded the Women's Social and Political Union in 1903. The WSPU promoted their cause by demonstrations and refusing to pay tax. By 1910 the movement had split into several factions, including the Women's Freedom League (founded 1908). Frustrated by parliamentary intransigence, the WSPU employed more radical tactics, including invading the Houses of Parliament, hunger strikes and displays of civil disobedience. In 1913 Sylvia Pankhurst, Emmeline's daughter, founded the East London Federation, which organized mass marches in London. Partly in response to the massive female war effort during World War 1, women of the age of 30 and over were given the vote in 1918. In 1928 the age limit was reduced to 21 and over.

Sufism Mystic philosophical movement within Islam that developed among the Shiite communities in the 10th and 11th centuries. Sufis stress the capability of the soul to attain personal union with God. *See also* dervish

SURINAM (SURINAME)

AREA: 163,270sq km (63,069sq mi)
POPULATION: 438,000
CAPITAL (POPULATION): Paramaribo (200,970)
GOVERNMENT: Multiparty republic
ETHNIC GROUPS: Indian 37%, Creole, 31%, Indonesian 14%, Black 9%, Native American 3%, Chinese 3%, Dutch 1%
LANGUAGES: Dutch (official)
RELIGIONS: Roman Catholic 23%, Protestant 19%, Hinduism 27%, Islam 20%
GDP PER CAPITA (1995): US$2250

Independent nation in NE South America, on the Atlantic Ocean, bordered by Brazil (s), French Guiana (e) and Guyana (w). The first European to reach the area was the Spanish explorer Alfonso de Ojeda, who sailed along the coast in 1499. In the first half of the 17th century the Spanish, British, Dutch and French all attempted to establish settlements but were overwhelmed by the hostility of the indigenous population. The British finally succeeed in founding a colony in 1651. In 1667 it was ceded to Holland in exchange for New Amsterdam (now New York City), and in 1815 the Congress of Vienna gave the Guyana region to Britain and reaffirmed Dutch control of "Dutch Guiana".

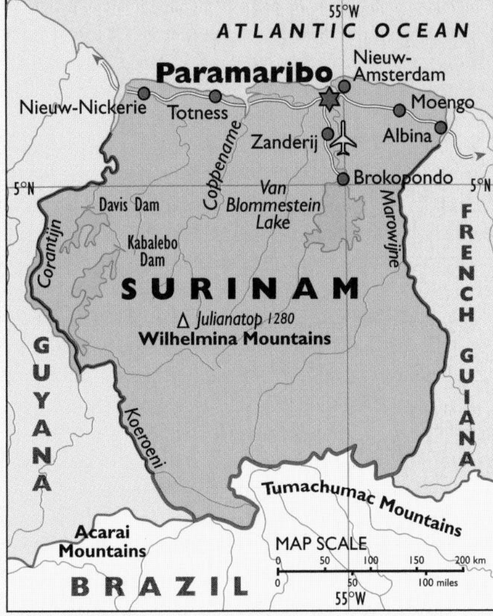

In 1954 the country became officially autonomous, and in 1975, as Surinam, gained full independence from the Netherlands and membership of the United Nations. In 1980 the military seized control, imposing martial law and banning political parties. A guerrilla campaign conducted by the Surinamese Liberation Army (SLA) disrupted the economy. In 1987 a new constitution provided for a 51-member national assembly, with powers to elect the president. Rameswak Shankar was elected president in 1988, but was overthrown by another military coup in 1990. In 1991 the New Front for Democracy and Development won the majority of seats in the national assembly, and their leader, Ronald Venetiaan, became president. The constitution was amended in 1992 to limit the power of the military and a peace agreement was signed with the SLA. The 1996 general election resulted in a coalition government, led by Jules Wijdenbosch of the National Democratic Party.

S

SWAZILAND

AREA: 17,360sq km (6703sq mi)
POPULATION: 792,000
CAPITAL (POPULATION): Mbabane (38,290)
GOVERNMENT: Monarchy
ETHNIC GROUPS: Swazi 84%, Zulu 10%, Tsonga 2%
LANGUAGES: Siswati and English (both official)
RELIGIONS: Protestant 37%, African churches 29%, Roman Catholic 11%, traditional beliefs 21%
GDP PER CAPITA (1995): US$2880

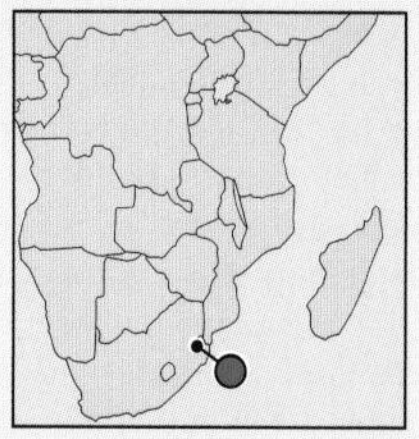

Small, landlocked and mountainous kingdom in s Africa. According to tradition, a group of Bantu-speaking people, under Chief Ngwane II, crossed the Lebombo range and united with local African groups to form the nucleus of the Swazi nation in the 18th century. The Dlamini clan became the most powerful under Sobhuza I in the 1820s and 1830s, and in 1836 his successor, Mswazi II, is thought to have given his name to the people over whom he ruled. Under attack from ZULU armies, the Swazi people were forced to seek British protection in the 1840s. Gold was discovered in the 1880s, and many Europeans sought land concessions from the king, who did not realize that in acceding to their demands he would lose control of his land. In 1894 Britain and the AFRIKANERS (Boers) of South Africa agreed to put Swaziland under the control of the South African Republic (the TRANSVAAL). At the end of the Second SOUTH AFRICAN WAR (1899–1902), Britain took over the administration of Swaziland. It rejected a request made by South Africa in 1949 for control of the country.

In 1963 Swaziland was granted limited self-government. In 1968 it became fully independent as a constitutional monarchy, with Sobhuza II as head of state. During the 1970s it developed strong links with South Africa and joined the South African Customs Union. In 1973 Sobhuza suspended the constitution and assumed supreme power. All political parties were banned in 1978. When Sobhuza died in 1982, his son, Makhosetive, was named as heir. In 1986 he was installed as king, taking the name Mswati III. In the early 1990s pro-democracy demonstrations called for Mswati to reconsider the ban on political parties. In 1993 and 1998 parliamentary elections were held on a non-party basis and were not generally considered to be democratic. Economically, Swaziland continues to be heavily dependent on South Africa.

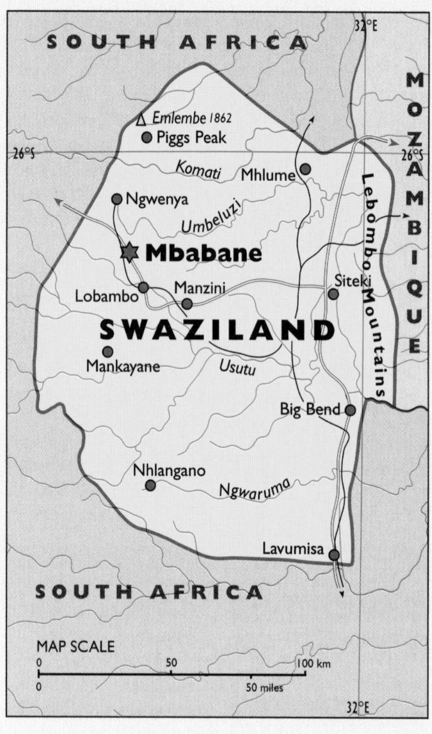

Sugar Act (1764) Legislation imposed by the British government on the American colonies in an attempt to raise revenue for the British government. A variation on the earlier Molasses Act (1733), it required strict customs' enforcement of duties on molasses and refined sugar from the non-British West Indies, thus effectively giving British West Indian sugar producers a monopoly of the American market. The Act was one of the causes of resentment among Americans in the years leading up to the AMERICAN REVOLUTION.

Suger (1081–1151) French abbot. A childhood friend of the future LOUIS VI, Suger acted as Louis' adviser on his accession to the throne, travelling on several diplomatic missions to the court of HENRY I in England. Suger became abbot of the Abbey Church of St Denis in 1122, and presided over its rebuilding in the new GOTHIC style. When LOUIS VII left France on the Second CRUSADE, Suger served (1147–49) as regent, devoting his energies to upholding strong central government.

► **Sumeria** Noted for its pottery and sculpture, Sumerian art relied on trade with other civilizations to obtain materials. Crops were traded for metal, stone, wood and precious stones used to craft religious objects and mosaics. The Sumerians also built musical instruments, like the lyre depicted on this stone tablet. Sumerian culture, in particular cuneiform writing, exerted a strong influence throughout Mesopotamia.

Suharto, Raden (1921–) Indonesian general and statesman, president (1967–98). Having played a significant part in the Indonesian struggle for independence from the Dutch (1945–49), Suharto went on to become head of the army (1965). In 1965 he crushed an Indonesian Communist Party-led coup and started a purge against all communist factions. Support for President SUKARNO, who was involved in the coup, wavered and Suharto effectively seized power in 1966, although Sukarno remained the country's nominal president. Suharto was formally elected president in 1968 and was re-elected (unopposed) five times. In 1976 Suharto ordered the invasion of EAST TIMOR. Under Suharto, INDONESIA experienced rapid economic development and the additional revenue was used to improve the country's infrastructure, finance development and educational programmes. However, his autocratic rule was criticized for frequent abuses of human rights and widespread corruption. In 1997 economic collapse destabilized Suharto's government, and in 1998 he was ousted after widespread student rioting in Jakarta and other major cities. He was succeeded by B.J. Habibie.

Sui (581–618) Chinese dynasty that re-established strong central rule in CHINA after more than 300 years of division and unrest. In 581 Yang Jian seized power from the Northern ZHOU dynasty and established the Sui dynasty. By 589 he had extended his rule to s China, ending the SIX DYNASTIES period and unifying the country. During the reign of Yang Jian's son and successor, Yangdi (r.605–617), the GREAT WALL OF CHINA was refortified, canals were dug (later to form part of the Grand Canal) and towns beautified. Wars were launched in Korea and Vietnam. The human cost in terms of taxation and forced labour was great, and the dissatisfaction that resulted finally produced large-scale revolts in 617, during which Yangdi was murdered. The capital, Changan, was seized by a general, Li Yuan, ushering in the TANG dynasty.

Sukarno (1901–70) Indonesian statesman, first president of independent INDONESIA (1947–67). Founder of the Indonesian Nationalist Party (1927), he led opposition to Dutch rule and was frequently imprisoned or exiled (1933–42). At the end of World War 2 and following the Indonesian struggle for independence from the Dutch (1945–49), Sukarno declared Indonesia's independence and became president of the new republic. In the 1950s his rule became increasingly dictatorial. Sukarno dissolved parliament, declared himself president for life (1963), and aligned himself with the communists. The failure of a communist coup against the leaders of the army in 1965 weakened his position. Sukarno was forced out of power by the generals, led by Raden SUHARTO, who officially replaced him as president (1968).

Sulawesi (formerly Celebes) Large island in E INDONESIA, separated from Borneo by the Makasar Strait, with Ujung Pandang (formerly Makasar) the main port and largest city. In 1512 the Portuguese were the first Europeans to discover the island. The Dutch assumed control in the early 17th century and successfully waged war against the native population in the Makasar War (1666–69). Sulawesi gained its independence in 1949 to became a province of the Indonesian republic. Area: 189,216sq km (73,031sq mi). Pop. (1990) 12,520,711.

Suleiman I (the Magnificent) (1494–1566) Ottoman sultan (1520–66), son and successor of SELIM I. He became renowned among his subjects for the many laws introduced by his government. He captured Rhodes from the KNIGHTS HOSPITALLERS and launched a series of campaigns against the Austrian HABSBURGS, defeating the Hungarians at the Battle of MOHÁCS (1526) and subsequently controlling most of Hungary. Suleiman's troops besieged Vienna (1529), and his admiral, BARBAROSSA, created a navy that dominated the Mediterranean and ensured Ottoman control of much of the North African coastal region. In the E, he won victories against the SAFAVIDS of Persia and conquered MESOPOTAMIA. A patron of the arts and architecture, Suleiman was renowned in Europe for the brilliance of his court. He died during a military campaign against the Austrians.

Sulla, Lucius Cornelius (138–78 BC) Roman general and statesman, dictator (82–79 BC). His early military career was spent under the command of MARIUS, and he

▲ **Sun Yat-sen** led the transition from imperial to republican government in China and implemented a programme of political and industrial modernization.

was instrumental in ending the war (111–106 BC) against Jugurtha. Although Marius was becoming increasingly jealous of the young Sulla, they fought together against Germanic tribes (104–101 BC). Further successes in the Social War resulted in Sulla becoming a consul of the Roman Republic in 88 BC. When Marius, who had by now become Sulla's political enemy, blocked Sulla's command, Sulla marched on Rome and overthrew Marius' party. Sulla then campaigned against Mithradates VI of Pontus before returning to Italy to march on Rome again in 82 BC. Having defeated the Marians, Sulla became dictator and set about restoring the authority of the Senate and reforming the legal system by establishing permanent courts. In 79 BC he suddenly retired.

Sully, Maximilien de Béthune, Duc de (1560–1641) French statesman, minister of finance (1598–1610) under Henry IV. A Huguenot, Sully narrowly escaped the Saint Bartholomew's Day Massacre (1572). In the Wars of Religion, he served the Protestant Henry of Navarre (later Henry IV) in his struggle for the throne. Once crowned, Sully became Henry's most trusted counsellor. In 1600 Sully negotiated Henry's marriage to Marie de' Medicis. As minister of finance, Sully greatly improved France's financial systems and promoted agricultural reform. In 1606 he was rewarded with the title of Duc de Sully, but was forced to retire soon after Henry's assassination.

Sumatra (Sumatera) Island in W Indonesia – the world's sixth-largest island. From the 2nd century BC trade routes linked it to India and China, and this led to Hinduism and Buddhism becoming established in the coastal areas. Between the 7th and 13th centuries the Buddhist trading empire of Srivijaya was based on Sumatra at Palembang, after which it was replaced by the Hindu Majapahit empire. In the late 13th century Islam reached the W tip of the island and the sultanate of Aceh was established, allowing England to set up a trading colony. The Portuguese arrived in the 16th century, and the Dutch followed a century later with the intention of adding Sumatra to the Dutch East Indies. Britain held certain parts of the island briefly in the 18th and 19th centuries. Sumatra gained its independence in 1949 to become part of Indonesia. Area: 425,000sq km (164,000sq mi). Pop. (1990) 36,505,703.

Sumeria World's first civilization, dating from before 3000 BC, in S Mesopotamia. The Sumerians are credited with inventing cuneiform writing, many familiar sociopolitical institutions and a money-based economy. Inscriptions on fragments of pottery and tablets reveal a rich literary culture, comprising epic poems, myths, proverbs, religious works and essays. In technology, the Sumerians developed wheeled vehicles and pottery, and are attributed with inventing the potter's wheel. Over the centuries city-states, such as Ur, Kish and Lagash, developed. In *c.*2340 BC Sumer was subjugated by Sargon I, who had united the lands of Akkadia, to the N of Sumer, under his rule. By 2200 BC his empire had collapsed and Ur was beginning to dominate the region. In 2004 BC Ur was sacked by the Elamites and the Sumerian civilization disintegrated.

Sumner, Charles (1811–74) US politician, senator from Massachusetts (1851–74). A passionate abolitionist, Sumner was one of the leading opponents of slavery, using his skills as an orator to make many fine speeches. In one such speech, he severely criticized Andrew Butler, senator of South Carolina, and two days later, while in the Senate, was physically attacked by Butler's nephew. He sustained injuries sufficiently serious to keep him away from the Senate for three years. Sumner became a leading Radical Republican during Reconstruction, supporting the impeachment of President Andrew Johnson. Sumner attacked President Ulysses Grant over his foreign policy and accusing him of corruption.

Sunderland, Robert Spencer, 2nd Earl of (1641–1702) English statesman. While spending time in Europe as an ambassador (1671–78), Sunderland became a close adviser to Charles II, and was made secretary of state in 1679. Dismissed in 1681 for opposing the succession of Charles' Roman Catholic brother (later James II), he was reinstated in 1683. During James' reign Sunderland was chief minister. Sufficiently flexible to implement James' Catholic policies, he even converted to Roman Catholicism. He went into exile after the Glorious Revolution (1688), but later won the favour of William III (of Orange) by renouncing Catholicism and persuading William that he had been covertly working for him all along. Sunderland was made lord chamberlain (1697) but, distrusted and disliked by Parliament, was soon forced from office. Sunderland remained an influential political "fixer' behind the scenes.

Sung *See* Song

Sunni Traditionalist orthodox branch of Islam, the followers of which are called *Ahl as-Sunnah* ("People of the Path"). It is followed by 85% of Muslims. Sunnis accept the *Hadith*, the body of orthodox teachings based on Muhammad's spoken words outside the Koran. The Sunni differ from the Shiite sect in that they accept the first four caliphs (religious leaders) as the true successors of Muhammad. *See also* Ali; Muawiya

Sun Yat-sen (1866–1925) Chinese nationalist leader, first president of the Chinese Republic (1912). He trained as a doctor in the early 1890s, but then turned his attention to revolutionary activities against the Manchu Qing dynasty. In exile (1896–1911), after instigating an abortive uprising, Sun adopted his "three principles of the people": nationalism, democracy and prosperity. While in Tokyo (1905), he established the revolutionary Tongmenghui, a society that would later form the core of the Kuomintang, the Nationalist Party. After the revolution of 1911 Sun became president (1912), but he soon resigned in favour of the mil-

SWEDEN

AREA: 449,960sq km (173,730sq mi)
POPULATION: 8,678,000
CAPITAL (POPULATION): Stockholm (692,594)
GOVERNMENT: Constitutional monarchy
ETHNIC GROUPS: Swedish 91%, Finnish 3%
LANGUAGES: Swedish (official), Finnish
RELIGIONS: Christianity (Lutheran 89%, Roman Catholic 2%)
GDP PER CAPITA (1995): US$18,540

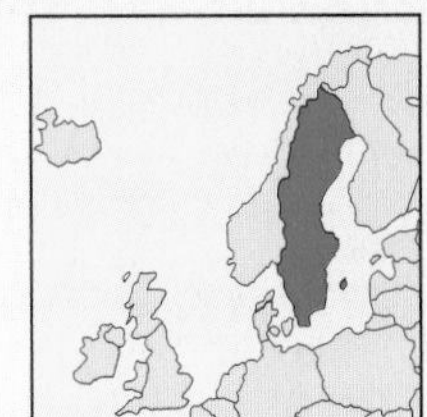

Kingdom on the E half of the Scandinavian Peninsula, N Europe. The earliest inhabitants of the area were the Svear, who merged with the Goths in the 6th century AD. Christianity was introduced in the 9th century. Swedes are thought to have been among the Vikings who plundered areas of S and E Europe between the 9th and 11th centuries. Swedes (Varangians), led by Rurik, also penetrated Russia as far as the Black Sea. In 1319 Sweden and Norway were united under Magnus VII. In 1397 Sweden, Denmark and Norway were united by the Danish Queen Margaret I in the Kalmar Union. Her successors failed to control Sweden, and in 1520 Gustavus Vasa led a successful rebellion. He was crowned king, as Gustavus I, of an independent Sweden in 1523. Southern Sweden, however, remained under Danish control.

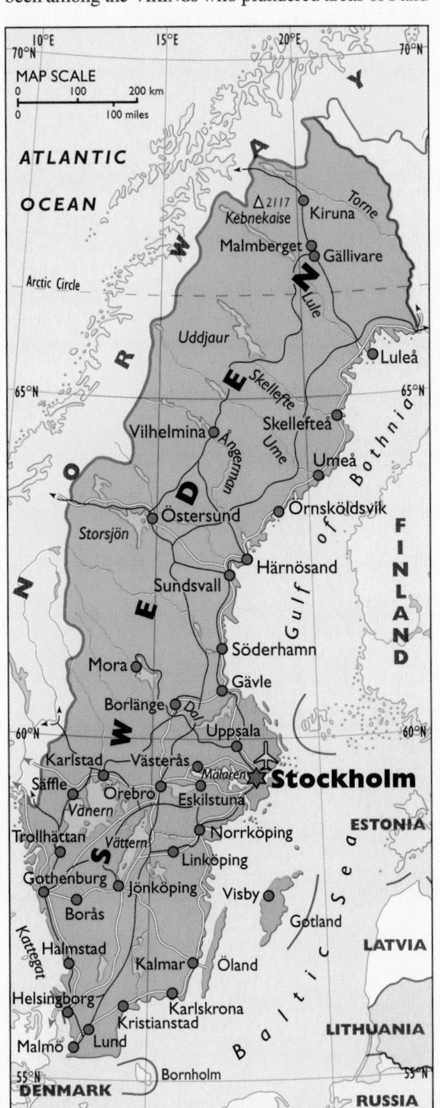

Gustavus made the monarchy hereditary within the Vasa dynasty, and Lutheranism became the state religion. Sweden's power was strengthened by the marriage of John III (r.1568–92) to the king of Poland's sister. Their son, Sigismund III, a Roman Catholic, came to the throne in 1592 but was deposed (because of his religion) by Charles IX in 1599. Charles' son, Gustavus II (r.1611–32), won territory in Russia and Poland, and, in 1626, most of the ports along the Prussian coast. In 1630, when he went to war in Germany against the Habsburgs, Sweden was extremely powerful. Despite setbacks in 1634–36, Sweden emerged as one of the victors of the Thirty Years' War (1630–48). In 1655–58 Charles X invaded and occupied Poland and in 1658 forced Denmark to abandon its provinces on the Swedish mainland. The year 1660 marked in some ways the summit of Swedish imperial power, based on its superior military system. Charles XII fought brilliant campaigns in Denmark, Poland, Saxony and Russia, but his eventual defeat in Russia (1709), during the Great Northern War, seriously weakened Sweden.

The 18th century was marked by internal friction. Gustavus IV brought Sweden into the Napoleonic Wars. Charles XIII lost Finland to Russia in 1809, but the Congress of Vienna granted Norway to Sweden as compensation. Industry grew in the late 19th century. In 1905 the union between Sweden and Norway was dissolved. Under Gustavus V (r.1907–50), Sweden remained neutral in both World Wars. In 1946 it joined the United Nations (UN). The current king, Charles XVI, acceded in 1973. In 1995 Sweden joined the European Union (EU). The Social Democrats have been in government almost continuously since 1932. In 1994 they formed a minority government, led by Ingvar Carlsson. In 1996 Carlsson was replaced by Göran Persson, who was re-elected in 1998. The cost of maintaining Sweden's extensive welfare services has become a major political issue.

S

itarily powerful YUAN SHIKAI. Following the outbreak of civil war in 1917 and the creation of several governing regimes in CHINA, Sun formed a s government in GUANGZHOU. In 1923, with Russian backing, Sun attempted to reorganize the Kuomintang, entering into negotiations with the Chinese COMMUNIST PARTY. In 1924 he went to Beijing to discuss the possible reunification of China, but he died there before an agreement could be concluded.

Supremacy, Acts of Two acts passed by the English Parliament in the 16th century. The first (1534) made the monarch, at that time HENRY VIII, the "supreme head" of the Church of England. It thus made the English Church independent of the papacy and also made it subject to temporal authority. The second act (1559), during the reign of ELIZABETH I, changed the title from supreme head to "supreme governor", but this made no practical difference.

Supreme Court of the United States US court of final appeal, the highest in the nation. It derives its power from the doctrine of "judicial review" and from its ability to pass on the constitutionality of state and federal legislation and of executive acts. It exercises both original jurisdiction ("in all cases affecting ambassadors, other public ministers, consuls, and those in which a State shall be a party") and appellate jurisdiction ("both as to law and fact, with such exceptions and under such regulations as Congress shall make", Sect. 2, Art. III, CONSTITUTION OF THE UNITED STATES). It hears appeals from the courts of appeals, the district courts and the highest state courts where a federal question is involved. Created by the Judiciary Act of 1789, the Supreme Court consists of justices who are appointed by the president with the advice and consent of the Senate. The number of justices has varied, but since 1869 has remained at nine, including a chief justice. Justices are removable only by impeachment. The chief justice presides over all sessions and five judges constitute a quorum to hear a case. There must be a majority vote before a decision is made. If a tie exists, the previous decision is upheld. The Supreme Court has heard several hundred cases since it was established, some of which had controversial effects on the nation's political and social structure.

Surinam *See* country feature, page 395

Surratt, Mary Eugenia (1817–65) Alleged US conspirator. In her boarding house in Washington, D.C., John Wilkes BOOTH and others discussed plans to assassinate President Abraham LINCOLN in 1865. She was convicted as an accessory and hanged.

Surrey, Henry Howard, Earl of (1517–47) English poet, son of Thomas Howard, 3rd Duke of NORFOLK. He served in the English army in campaigns in Scotland (1542) and Flanders (1543–46). Like his cousin Catherine HOWARD, Surrey died on the scaffold, a victim of the bloody power politics of HENRY VIII's court. He wrote some of the earliest English sonnets and, with his translation of two books of the *Aeneid* by Virgil, introduced blank verse into English poetry.

Suryavarman II (d. *c.*1150) Cambodian king (1113–*c.*1150). He reigned when the KHMER EMPIRE was at its height, and is chiefly remembered as a religious reformer and a great temple builder. At the urging of the Brahman Divakarapandita (d. *c.*1120), an adviser to three previous kings, he built the huge temple complex of ANGKOR Wat as a funerary monument for himself. It was completed in the reign of his successor, Yashovarman II.

Susa Ancient city in SW Iran, capital of the ELAMITES in the 3rd millennium BC. It became an important centre under the ACHAEMENID kings of Persia, containing a palace of DARIUS I. After the conquests of ALEXANDER III (THE GREAT), it became the capital of a small Greek state. Among archaeological finds at Susa was the stele (stone slab) of HAMMURABI, inscribed with his code of law.

Sussex Kingdom of ANGLO-SAXON England, settled by the South Saxons under Aelle (*c.*AD 477). It was allegedly the last Anglo-Saxon kingdom to adopt Christianity (*c.*680). A number of kings of Sussex are known from the 7th–8th centuries, but at various times they were under the dominance of MERCIA. Sussex was absorbed by WESSEX in the early 9th century.

Sutton Hoo Archaeological site in Suffolk, SE England. The 1939 excavation of the cenotaph of Raedwald, a Saxon king of East Anglia (d.625), was Britain's richest archaeological find. The digs revealed a Saxon rowing boat 27m (90ft) long. In the centre of the boat lay a wooden funeral chamber, containing silver plate, gold jewellery and coins and bronze armour.

Suvorov, Alexander Vasilyevich (1729–1800) Russian field marshal. One of the most famous commanders of the 18th century and a great Russian military hero, he fought in the SEVEN YEARS' WAR and later won famous victories against the Poles (1768–69, 1794) and the Turks (1773–74). CATHERINE II (THE GREAT) made him a count. In the second RUSSO-TURKISH WAR (1787–92), Suvorov captured the supposedly impregnable fortress of Ismail, its fall followed by a bloody massacre. Given to speaking frankly, he lost favour on the accession of PAUL I, but was recalled in 1799 to command the Russian troops against the French in Italy. Suvorov regained the territory recently conquered by the future NAPOLEON I and was made a prince, but the campaign ended in disaster and the 70-year-old general returned in disgrace.

Suzman, Helen (1917–) South African politician. Suzman was an outspoken opponent of the APARTHEID regime in South Africa for 40 years. Elected to Parliament in 1953, she formed the Progressive Party in 1959 and for the next 12 years was the Party's only representative in Parliament. She retired from parliament in 1989.

Suzuki Zenko (1911–) Japanese statesman, prime minister (1980–82). He entered parliament as a Socialist in 1947, but switched to the conservative Liberal Party in 1949, which later became the Liberal Democratic Party (LDP). In the 1960s and 1970s he held a variety of ministerial posts. A politician who preferred to remain in the back-

SWITZERLAND

AREA: 41,290sq km (15,942sq mi)
POPULATION: 6,905,000
CAPITAL (POPULATION): Bern (135,600)
GOVERNMENT: Federal republic
ETHNIC GROUPS: German 64%, French 19%, Italian 8%, Yugoslav 3%, Spanish 2%, Romansch 1%
LANGUAGES: French, German, Italian and Romansch (all official)
RELIGIONS: Christianity (Roman Catholic 46%, Protestant 40%)
GDP PER CAPITA (1995): US$25,860

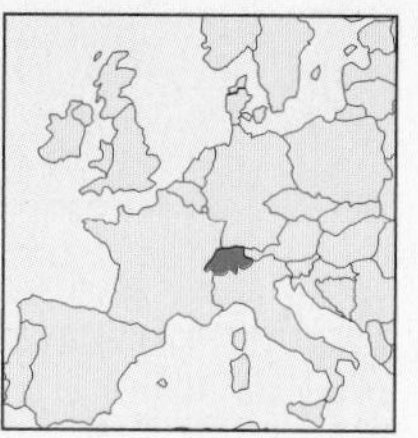

The Swiss Confederation is a small, mountainous, landlocked country in central Europe. Originally occupied by Celtic HELVETII people, the region was taken by Romans in 58 BC. From AD *c.*400 the W part was occupied by Burgundians while the ALEMANNI began to occupy much of the remainder, pushing the CELTS southwards. From the 6th century the area was ruled by the FRANKS. In the 10th century it divided into 12 bishoprics, which were brought together in the 11th century under the HOLY ROMAN EMPIRE, before dividing again into semi-independent states. In 1291 the cantons of Schwyz, Uri and Unterwalden united against their HABSBURG overlords to form an alliance for mutual defence called the Everlasting League. This was the beginning of the Swiss Confederation. Having inflicted defeat on the Habsburgs in 1315, the Confederation expanded in the mid-14th century to include the towns of Lucerne, Bern and ZÜRICH. Another defeat of the Habsburgs in 1386 established the cantons' practical independence. Victory over Burgundy in 1474–76 encouraged further expansion, which was to continue into the 16th century.

The REFORMATION caused religious divisions in Switzerland, but the Confederation survived to achieve formal independence from the Habsburgs in 1648. It then pursued a policy of neutrality until the FRENCH REVOLUTIONARY WARS, when the French occupied much of the country and established the Helvetic Republic (1798–1803). In 1815 the Congress of VIENNA recognized Swiss control over 22 cantons and guaranteed the Confederation's neutrality. A brief civil war, known as the SONDERBUND War, led to the constitution of 1848, turning Switzerland into one federal state. During both World Wars the Swiss succeeded in maintaining their neutrality. A 23rd canton, Jura, was created in 1979. A referendum (1986) rejected Swiss membership of the United Nations (UN) to avoid compromising its neutrality. European Union (EU) membership was similarly rejected (1992). In 1995 the ruling coalition, led by the Christian Democrats, was re-elected. Women did not receive the vote in federal elections until 1971. In 1999 Switzerland's first woman president, Ruth Dreifuss, served in the one-year post.

ground, Suzuki was an unexpected choice as head of the LDP. As prime minister, he failed to revive the economy and was troubled by party factionalism. Suzuki resigned in 1982 and was succeeded by Nakasone Yasuhiro.

Sverrir Sigurdsson (*c.*1149–1202) King of Norway (1177–1202). Believing himself to be the illegitimate son of the former Norwegian king, Sigurd II, Sverrir raised an army against the reigning king, Magnus V. In 1177 he became king of the Birchlegs, who were enemies of Magnus. After he finally defeated and killed Magnus in 1184, Sverrir strengthened the position of the monarchy against fierce opposition from the church and the nobility. His assertion of royal power brought him into bitter conflict with the church, and at one stage he was excommunicated by Pope Innocent III. The last years of Sverrir's reign were marked by civil war brought about by opposition to his ecclesiastical and administrative reforms. He was succeeded by his son Haakon III.

Swabia Historic region of sw Germany, consisting mainly of the s part of the modern states of Baden-Württemberg and sw Bavaria. It is named after its early inhabitants, the Suevi, a Germanic tribe who amalgamated with the Alemanni in the 4th–5th centuries AD. An important duchy in early medieval Germany, Swabia came under the rule of the house of Hohenstaufen from 1079 to 1268. It was then divided into lordships, most of which, by 1313, had become free imperial cities. Several Swabian Leagues were formed in the 14th–16th centuries. At the diet of Regensburg (1801–03) much of Swabia was incorporated into Baden-Württemberg and Bavaria.

Swabian League Association of free imperial cities in the former duchy of Swabia, sw Germany. Leagues were formed in 1331–37, 1376–88 and 1488–1534, and played an important part in the conflicts between the Holy Roman emperor and the German princes. The most important Swabian League was that formed in 1488. It comprised the knights of the League of St George, many s German princes and the 22 imperial cities. With an army of *c.*13,000, the League maintained order, supported Emperor Maximilian I, and suppressed the Peasants' War (1524–25). It disintegrated in 1534 as a result of religious differences brought about by the Reformation.

Swadeshi movement (1905–11) Indian protest against British rule. Swadeshi means "of our own country" and it took the form of a boycott of imported manufactures, especially cloth. Specifically it was a protest against the British government's division of Bengal into two regions for administrative purposes, which Hindus saw as a plan to divide predominantly Muslim East Bengal (now Bangladesh) from predominantly Hindu West Bengal in the interest of continuing British rule. Resistance to the partition persuaded the British to abandon it in 1911.

SWAPO Acronym for South West Africa People's Organization

Swaziland *See* country feature, page 396

Sweden *See* country feature, page 397

Sweyn I (Forkbeard) (d.1014) King of Denmark (987–1014), son of Harald Bluetooth, whom he deposed in order to become king. Sweyn's attack on England in 994 forced Ethelred II (the Unready) to pay tribute. Sweyn allied with the Swedish king and rebellious Norwegian nobles to defeat Olaf I of Norway at the naval Battle of Svolder (*c.*1000), becoming virtual ruler of Norway. In 1013 Sweyn's successful invasion of England forced Ethelred to flee to Normandy. Sweyn became king but died before his coronation. His son Canute II (the Great) eventually succeeded him.

Switzerland *See* country feature

Sydney State capital of New South Wales, se Australia, on Port Jackson, an inlet on the Pacific Ocean. Australia's oldest and largest city, it was founded in 1788 as a British penal colony. With food in short supply, the colony struggled to survive until explorers began in 1813 to cross the Blue Mountains and discover new pasture lands. Under the governorship (1810–21) of Lachlan Macquarie, the number of settlers increased rapidly and Sydney developed into a thriving town. Many buildings dating from this period survive today. The population grew rapidly from 1850, reaching one million soon after 1914. Today, it is the most important financial, industrial and cultural centre, and the principal port in Australia. The city hosted the 2000 summer Olympic Games. Pop. (1994) 3,738,500.

Sykes-Picot Agreement (1916) Secret agreement between Great Britain and France, negotiated by Sir Mark Sykes (1879–1919) and Georges Picot, concerning the status of the Near Eastern provinces of the Ottoman Empire after World War 1. To make up for territorial losses in a previous secret agreement between Britain, France and Russia, in which the Dardanelles and Bosporus passed into Russian control, Britain and France agreed that Syria and Lebanon should comprise a French "sphere of interest", and Transjordan (now Jordan) and Iraq become a British sphere, with most of Palestine an international zone. The agreement was made public by the Bolsheviks after the Russian Revolution (1917) and caused embarrassment to the signatories, since it contradicted promises made to the Arabs as well as the US policy of self-determination for subject peoples as laid down in Woodrow Wilson's Fourteen Points.

Sylvester II (*c.*940–1003) Pope (999–1003), b. Gerbert of Aurillac, the first French pope. He was a former tutor of Emperor Otto III, who made him archbishop of Ravenna in 998 and, after the death of Gregory V, pope. Sylvester aided the Christianization of Hungary and Poland, granting Poland its first archbishop (1000). To strengthen the papacy, he denounced simony and nepotism and insisted upon clerical celibacy. A famous scholar, Sylvester is credited with the introduction of Arabic numerals to w Europe.

syndicalism Late 19th–early 20th-century revolutionary trade unionist movement originating in France but also influential in Spain and Italy, and to a lesser extent in Russia and the United States, where the Industrial Workers of the World (IWW) promoted a similar programme. Influenced by the writings of Pierre Proudhon, it proposed public ownership of the means of production by small worker-groups and called for the elimination of central government. Its advocacy of anarchism differentiated it from mainstream socialism. During the 1920s many adherents of syndicalism swapped allegiance to communism and the movement lost its influence.

Syracuse (Siracusa) Italian city in se Sicily, on the Ionian Sea. Founded by Corinthian Greek colonists in *c.*734 BC, Syracuse prospered and established its own colonies, triumphing over Carthage in 480 BC. Dionysius the Elder acted as tyrant (405–367). It was the most important Hellenic city outside Greece. Pop. (1992) 127,000.

Syria *See* country feature

SYRIA

AREA: 185,180sq km (71,498sq mi)
POPULATION: 12,958,000
CAPITAL (POPULATION): Damascus (1,497,000)
GOVERNMENT: Multiparty republic
ETHNIC GROUPS: Arab 89%, Kurd 6%
LANGUAGES: Arabic (official)
RELIGIONS: Islam 90%, Christianity 9%
GDP PER CAPITA (1995): US$5320

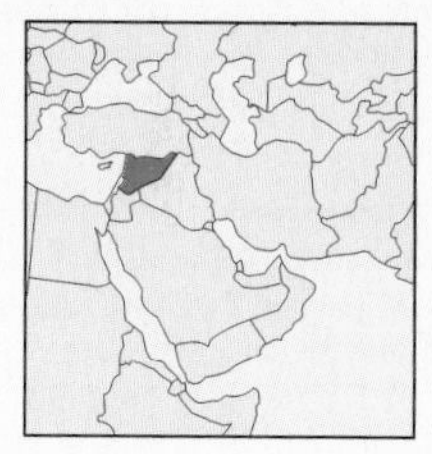

Arab Republic in the Middle East. Syria's location on the trade routes between Europe, Africa and Asia has made it a desired possession of many rulers. The area, including what is now Lebanon and some of modern-day Jordan, Israel, Saudi Arabia and Iraq, was ruled by the Hittites and by Egypt during the 15th–13th centuries BC. Under the Phoenicians (13th–10th centuries BC), trading cities on the Mediterranean coast flourished. From the 10th century BC, Syria suffered invasions by Assyrians and Egyptians. The Achaemenid empire provided stability. From the 3rd century BC, the Seleucids controlled Syria, often challenged by Egypt. Palmyra flourished as a city-state. The Romans conquered the region in AD 63. Christianity was introduced via Palestine. Following the split of the Roman Empire in the 4th century, Syria became part of the Eastern and subsequently the Byzantine Empire.

Arabs invaded in AD 637, and most of the population converted to Islam. Damascus served as the capital of the Umayyad dynasty between 661 and 750. Subsequently Syria became a province ruled by a succession of dynasties, beginning with the Abbasids. In the 11th century, Syria was a target of the Crusades, but at the end of the 12th century, Saladin triumphed. Mongol and Mamluk rule followed Saladin's death. In 1516 the area became part of the Ottoman Empire. European interest in the region grew in the 19th century. During World War 1, Syrian nationalists revolted and helped Britain to defeat the Turks. After the War, Syria, now roughly its present size, became a French mandated territory.

Following the outbreak of World War 2, Syria was occupied by British and Free French forces in 1941. At the same time the Free French proclaimed the country's independence, and elections for the presidency were held in 1943. However, French forces were not finally withdrawn until 1946. Civilian rule did not survive long in Syria, with military coups occurring in 1949, 1951 and 1954. In 1958 Syria joined the United Arab Republic (UAR) with Egypt and North Yemen. Egypt's increasing power led to Syrian withdrawal from the UAR and the formation of a Syrian Arab Republic in 1961. The Ba'ath Party became the ruling party in 1963. In 1970 Hafez al-Assad seized power in a coup and was re-elected in 1971. A new constitution was adopted in 1973, declaring Syria to be a democratic, socialist state. Assad's stable but repressive regime has attracted international criticism.

Since independence Syria has supported the Arab cause in the Middle East and it was involved in the Arab-Israeli Wars. In 1967 it lost the Golan Heights to Israel and in 1973 tried unsuccessfully to reclaim them. A UN-patrolled buffer zone was established in the area. It continues to be a source of considerable tension. In the Gulf War (1991), Syria supported the international coalition against Iraq. In 1994 Syria and Israel held talks over the Golan Heights. These talks, part of an attempt to establish a peace settlement for the entire region, broke down when Binyamin Netanyahu won the 1996 Israeli elections. The election of Ehud Barak in Israel (1999) led to the withdrawal of Israeli troops from s Lebanon and Syria came under pressure to control Hezbollah forces.

S

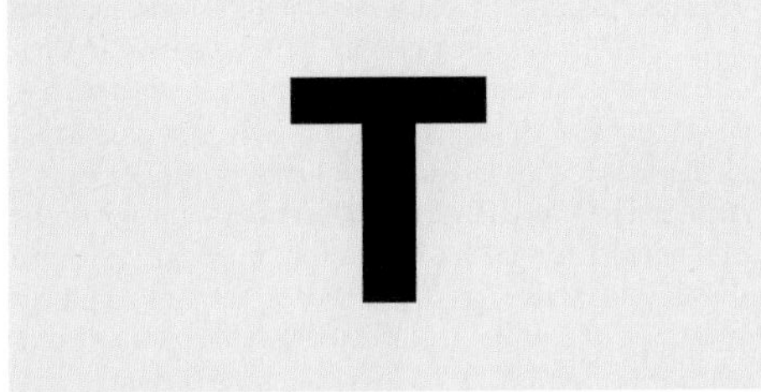

Tacitus, Cornelius (*c.*AD 56–*c.*120) Roman historian. His crisp style and reliability make him one of the greatest of ancient historians. His works include a eulogy for his father-in-law, AGRICOLA, governor of Britain. His major works, the *Annals* and *Histories*, exist only in fragmentary form. *See also* PLINY THE ELDER

Tacna-Arica Dispute (1883–1929) Disagreement between CHILE and PERU over two former Peruvian provinces, Arica and Tacna. At the Treaty of Ancón (1883), which ended the War of the PACIFIC, Chile was ceded Arica and Tacna for a period of 10 years. Sovereignty would then be determined by a plebiscite. Deteriorating relations between the two countries meant that the plebiscite was never held and the provinces remained the territory of Chile. The dispute continued into the 1920s, when both sides agreed to US arbitration. In 1929 a treaty was ratified that returned Tacna to Peru but let Chile keep Arica. Chile also had to pay Peru an indemnity of US$6 million.

Taff Vale Case (1900) British legal dispute following the suing of the Amalgamated Society of Railway Servants (ASRS) by the Taff Vale Railway for damages caused by a strike. Against earlier interpretations of the 1871 Trade Union Act, the House of Lords, on appeal, upheld the judgment that the union was liable. The ASRS paid £23,000. The unions gained redress in the Trade Disputes Act of 1906, which made them not liable for losses suffered by employers in trade disputes. The Case encouraged the unions to reconsider their alliance with the Liberal Party and support the Independent Labour Party.

Taft, Robert Alphonso (1889–1953) US politician, son of William Howard TAFT. He served in the Ohio state legislature before becoming a senator (1938–53). A conservative Republican, he sponsored the TAFT-HARTLEY ACT (1947). Throughout his term in the Senate, he was one of the more outspoken critics of the Democratic administrations of Franklin ROOSEVELT and Harry TRUMAN. Taft failed to gain the Republican presidential nomination in 1940, 1948 and 1952.

Taft, William Howard (1857–1930) Twenty-seventh president of the United States (1909–13) and tenth chief justice of the Supreme Court (1921–30). After a distinguished legal career, Taft gained great credit as an even-handed governor of the Philippines (1901–04), and entered the cabinet of Theodore ROOSEVELT as secretary of war. In 1908 Taft won the Republican nomination for president. His lack of political experience and his surprising tendency to side with the conservatives ("Standpatters") in the REPUBLICAN PARTY against the Progressives, caused increasing dissension. In 1912 Roosevelt, having failed to regain the presidential nomination, set up his own PROGRESSIVE PARTY. With the split in the Republican vote, the Democrat, Woodrow WILSON, won the election. Taft taught at Yale Law School until 1921, when he was appointed chief justice of the Supreme Court. While chief justice, he greatly streamlined the operations of the federal judiciary.

Taft-Hartley Act (1947) US labour legislation that restricted the power of trade UNIONS, sponsored by Robert TAFT. It amended the National Labor Relations Act of 1935 (known as the WAGNER ACT). The Taft-Hartley Act (or Labor-Management Relations Act) outlawed the closed shop, required unions to reveal their financial status, limited union political activity, required union leaders to sign a non-communist affidavit and authorized the government to issue 80-day strike injunctions. Other provisions allowed employers to sue unions and enlarged the National Labor Relations Board. The Act was passed by a Republican-controlled Congress over the veto of President Harry TRUMAN.

Tai (Dai) Peoples of Chinese origin, who inhabit the mainland of SE Asia. They consist of several Tai-speaking groups; the Thai (Siamese), Lao, Shan, Lu, Yunnan Tai and tribal Tai. Agriculturalists, their major crop is rice. Although THERAVADA Buddhism is the principal religion, some animism remains.

Taine, Hippolyte Adolphe (1828–93) French historian. Taine was associated with the school of philosophy known as positivism. His early writings were mainly literary studies, including a four-volume *History of English Literature* (1863–64). Influenced by the disasters of the FRANCO-PRUSSIAN WAR, Taine produced his greatest work, a reappraisal of French history, *The Origins of Contemporary France* (1876–93).

Taiping Rebellion (1850–64) Revolt in China against the Manchurian QING dynasty. Led by HONG XIUQUAN, the Rebellion began in Guangxi and quickly spread through the Yangtze region. In 1853 the rebels captured NANJING, making it the capital of the Heavenly Kingdom of Great Peace. The Taipings' ideology was a mixture of Christianity and radical land reform. After the Taipings failed attempt to seize SHANGHAI, the revolt was eventually crushed by ZENG GUOFAN's Hunan Army and the Ever-Victorious Army led by General Charles GORDON. The fighting had laid 17 provinces to waste and resulted in more than 20 million casualties. The MANCHUS never fully recovered their ability to govern China.

Taira (Heike) Leading SAMURAI (warrior) dynasty in 12th-century Japan, during the late HEIAN period. In 825 Prince Takamune, grandson of Emperor Kammu (r.781–806), was given the name Taira. In 939 Taira **Masakado** (d.940) gained control of the whole district of Kanto, central Japan, and proclaimed himself emperor, but the revolt was quickly suppressed by the KYOTO emperor. In the early 11th century the Taira were subdued by the Minamoto, who helped maintain the supremacy of the FUJIWARA family. The Taira regained influence after Taira **Masamori** suppressed the Minamoto in 1108. In the Hogen Disturbance (1156), Taira **Kiyomori** (1118–81) supported Emperor Go-Shirakawa against the former emperor Sutoku and the Minamoto and emerged victorious, after the defection of Minamoto Yoshitomo. Kiyomori's dominance was confirmed when he crushed the Hogen uprising (1159) by Yoshitomo and subsequently assumed virtually dictatorial powers. After Kiyomori's death, the various samurai clans rallied behind Minamoto YORITOMO, who destroyed the Taira dynasty at the naval Battle of Dannoura (1185).

Taiwan *See* country feature

Taizong (597–649) Chinese emperor (627–49) of the TANG dynasty (618–907). Son of Gaozu, the first Tang emperor, Taizong murdered his brothers in order to ensure his succession. In the early years of his reign, Taizong waged wars against the Eastern Turks, eventually subjugating them in 630. He also gained control of small states along the Silk Road. Taizong's rule is noted for the establishment of central government after the unrest and civil war that marked the final years of the SUI dynasty. His capital, Changan (now XIAN), was visited by merchants and scholars from as far afield as India and Persia and became a noted cultural centre. He was succeeded by his ninth son, Li Chih, as Emperor Gaozong.

Tajikistan *See* country feature

Taj Mahal Muslim mausoleum near AGRA, India, built (1632–54) by the Mughal emperor, SHAH JAHAN, for his favourite wife, Mumtaz Mahal. By far the largest Islamic tomb destined for a woman, it stands in a Persian water garden representing Paradise. With its bulb-shaped dome, inlays of semi-precious stones, and rectangular reflecting pool, it is among the world's most beautiful buildings.

Takeshita Noburo (1924–) Japanese statesman, prime minister (1987–89). Chief cabinet secretary (1971–72) and finance minister (1979–80, 1982–86), he became head of the Liberal Democratic Party in 1987 and succeeded NAKASONE YASUHIRO as prime minister. Takeshita

TAIWAN (OFFICIALLY THE REPUBLIC OF CHINA)

AREA: 35,742sq km (13,800sq mi)
POPULATION: 21,100,000
CAPITAL (POPULATION): Taipei (2,653,000)
GOVERNMENT: Multiparty republic
ETHNIC GROUPS: Taiwanese (Han Chinese) 84%, mainland Chinese 14%
LANGUAGES: Mandarin (official), Min (Fukien), Hakka, Ami
RELIGIONS: Buddhist 43%, Taoist and Confucian 49%, Christian 7%
GDP PER CAPITA (1992): US$12,000

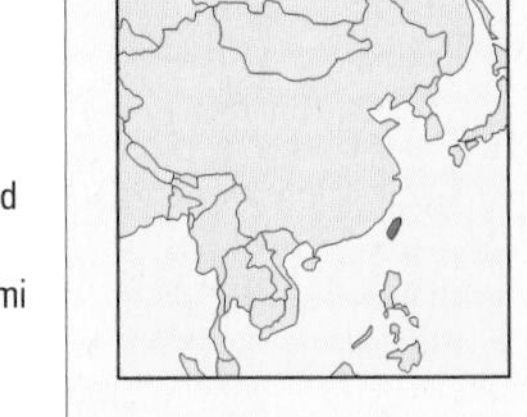

Pacific island, separated from the SE coast of the Chinese mainland by the 160km (100mi) Taiwan Strait. In 1590 the Portuguese visited the island and named it Formosa ("beautiful"); in the 1620s the Dutch and Spaniards established trading posts. In 1642 the Dutch drove out the Spaniards, but in 1661 the Dutch were themselves driven out by opponents of China's Manchu QING dynasty who had been settling the island since 1644. In 1683 the QING dynasty captured Taiwan, making it part of China for the first time. Chinese emigration to the island increased. In 1895 it was ceded to Japan after the first SINO-JAPANESE WAR.

Following the 1949 mainland victory of the Chinese COMMUNIST PARTY, the vanquished Nationalist KUOMINTANG government (led by CHIANG KAI-SHEK) and 500,000 troops fled to Taiwan. MAO ZEDONG's communist regime claimed sovereignty over the island, and in 1950 a Chinese invasion was prevented by the US Navy. The Nationalists, with continued US military and financial support, remained resolute. By 1965 Taiwan's economic success had removed the need for US aid. In 1971 Taiwan lost its seat at the United Nations (UN) to mainland China.

In 1975 Chiang Kai-shek died and was succeeded by his son, CHIANG CHING-KUO. In 1979 the United States switched diplomatic recognition from Taipei to Beijing. In 1987 martial law was lifted. In 1988 LEE TENG-HUI became the first native Taiwanese president. He accelerated the pace of liberalization. Although in the early 1990s contact between China and Taiwan was made at a meeting in Singapore, relations subsequently soured and in 1996 China fired missiles close to the Taiwanese coast, warning the international community of its territorial claims. In 1996 Lee won the first democratic presidential elections, but was defeated in the 2000 elections by Chen Shui-bian of the pro-independence Democratic Progressive Party, thus ending more than fifty years of Kuomintang rule.

passed some tax reforms but resigned after alleged involvement in the Recruit Stock Trading scandal (1988).

Taliban (Perisan, "student') Radical Islamic political movement in AFGHANISTAN. It was formed (1994) by Muhammad Omar, who united various (mainly Pashtun) MUJAHEDDIN factions that had fought the AFGHANISTAN WAR (1980–92) against the communist government and Soviet forces. Trained and armed by Pakistan, by the end of 1994 the Taliban had captured KANDAHAR, S Afghanistan. In 1995 they gained comtrol of Herat and W Afghanistan. In 1996 the Taliban bombarded the capital, Kabul, into submission and executed the Afghan president, Muhammad NAJIBULLAH. Once in power, they strictly enforced SHARIA (Islamic law): banning women from education and paid employment, and executing or amputating certain criminals. In 1997 a rival government was established in Mazar-e Sharif, N Afghanistan, but by 2000 the Taliban controlled 90% of the country.

Talleyrand (-Périgord), Charles Maurice de (1754–1838) French statesman and diplomat. As bishop of Autun (1789–91) he emerged as the leading cleric in the STATES-GENERAL at the start of the FRENCH REVOLUTION. In 1790 Talleyrand was excommunicated by Pope PIUS VI for his support of state control over the church and the appropriation of church property, and he subsequently resigned his bishopric. Throughout 1792 Talleyrand sought to persuade British Prime Minister William PITT (THE YOUNGER) to remain neutral in the FRENCH REVOLUTIONARY WARS, but the execution of LOUIS XVI turned a difficult diplomatic mission into an impossible one. Unwelcome in Britian or France, he sought refuge in the United States (1794–96). Talleyrand returned from exile after the fall of Maximilien ROBESPIERRE and the end of the REIGN OF TERROR and was appointed foreign minister in the DIRECTORY (1797–99). He amassed a vast personal fortune before being forced to resign after the XYZ AFFAIR caused a break in relations with the United States. After only five months, Talleyrand returned as foreign minister when NAPOLEON established the CONSULATE. In 1803 Talleyrand and Joseph FOUCHÉ conspired in the abduction and execution of the BOURBON Duc d'Enghien. Talleyrand gradually lost influence after Napoleon became emperor and he resigned as foreign minister in 1807. At the Congress of Erfurt (1808), Talleyrand held secret talks with ALEXANDER I of Russia imploring him to continue fighting Napoleon in the NAPOLEONIC WARS. In 1814 he negotiated the restoration of the monarchy. As foreign minister to LOUIS XVIII, Talleyrand ably represented France at the Congress of VIENNA (1814–15). He also acted as LOUIS PHILIPPE's chief adviser in the JULY REVOLUTION (1830) and served (1830–34) as his ambassador to Britain.

Talmud Body of Jewish religious and civil laws and learned interpretations of their meanings. Study of the Talmud is central to orthodox JUDAISM. It consists of two elements: the MISHNA and the *Gemara*. The *Mishna* is the written version, completed by *c.*AD 200, of a set of oral laws that were handed down from the time of MOSES (*c.*1200 BC). The *Gemara*, the interpretation and commentary on the *Mishna*, was completed by *c.*AD 500. The Talmud consists of short passages from the *Mishna* followed by the relevant exegesis of the *Gemara*.

Tambo, Oliver (1917–93) South African politician, president of the AFRICAN NATIONAL CONGRESS (ANC) (1969–90). In 1944, together with Nelson MANDELA and other activists, he founded the ANC Youth League. In 1955 Tambo was made secretary general of the ANC, and in 1958 he became the deputy to President Albert LUTHULI. In 1960, after the SHARPEVILLE massacre and the banning of the ANC by the APARTHEID government, Tambo left South Africa to organize the external activities of the ANC. During Mandela's long imprisonment, Tambo served as acting president (1967–69) before succeeding Luthuli as president of the ANC. In 1990, after 30 years in exile, Tambo returned to South Africa where failing health forced him to relinquish the presidency to Mandela.

Tamerlane (1336–1405) (Turkish *Timur Leng*, Timur the Lame) Turkic conqueror. He grew up in Transoxania (West Turkistan, now Uzbekistan), part of the khanate established by GENGHIS KHAN's son, JAGATAI. By 1370 Tamerlane had conquered West Turkistan and proclaimed himself the restorer of the MONGOL empire. From his capital at SAMARKAND, he spent the next decade subduing East Turkistan, finally gaining Kashgar in 1380. Tamerlane now turned towards Persia, taking advantage of the collapse of the ILKHANID dynasty to conquer all of E Persia by 1385. Less than 10 years later, Iraq, Azerbaijan, Armenia, Mesopotamia and Georgia had all fallen to the superior mobility of his nomadic infantrymen and mounted archers. His greatest rival, Tokhtamysh, khan of the GOLDEN HORDE, was finally pacified in 1395. In 1398 Tamerlane invaded India, defeated the DELHI SULTANATE and destroyed the city of Delhi, slaughtering 100,000 of its Hindu citizens. He then concentrated on the MAMLUK empire, capturing Damascus, Syria, in 1401. In 1402 he defeated and took prisoner the Ottoman sultan, BAYEZID I, near Ankara, Asia Minor. Unsurprisingly, given his almost ceaseless campaigning, Tamerlane died on an expedition to China. He was buried in the magnificent Gur-e Amir mausoleum in Samarkand and his vast empire was divided among the TIMURID DYNASTY. One of his descendants, BABUR, founded (1526) the MUGHAL EMPIRE in India.

Tamil Ethnic group, originally of S India. An ancient culture, the Tamils thrived under successive ruling dynasties, particularly the CHOLA. Today, the majority of Tamils live in the S Indian state of Tamil Nadu, making up the largest ethnic group in the state. Tamils can also be found in Malaysia, Singapore and South Africa. There is a significant minority population in SRI LANKA, where a Tamil rebel group, the TAMIL TIGERS, began a guerrilla war in the early 1980s with the aim of establishing a separate Tamil state. There are *c.*35–50 million Tamils worldwide.

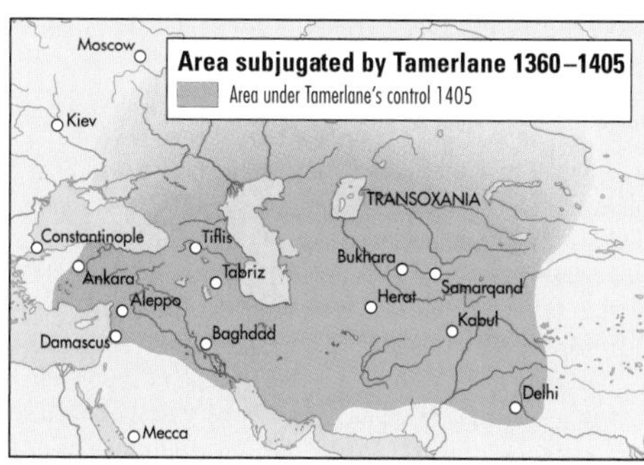

▲ **Tamerlane** The collapse of the Golden Horde (*c.*1400) was partly due to the campaigns of Tamerlane. Smaller hordes arose in its place and were absorbed by the Grand Duchy of Muscow.

Tamil Tigers Militant TAMIL group in SRI LANKA that seeks independence from the Sinhalese majority. Located mainly in the N and E of the island, the 3 million Tamils are Hindus, unlike the Buddhist Sinhalese. In the 1980s the Tamil Tigers embarked on a campaign of civil disobedience and terrorism. In 1986 autonomy for the Tamils was agreed by India and Sri Lanka, but no date was fixed. In 1987 the Indian army was sent to restore order but withdrew in 1990, having failed to stop the violence. It continued throughout the 1990s and by May 2000 a Tamil army was threatening to overwhelm government troops in the Jaffna peninsula.

Tammany Hall DEMOCRATIC PARTY organization in New York City. It evolved from the fraternal and patriotic

TAJIKISTAN

AREA: 143,100sq km (55,520sq mi)
POPULATION: 5,465,000
CAPITAL (POPULATION): Dushanbe (602,000)
GOVERNMENT: Transitional democracy
ETHNIC GROUPS: Tajik 62%, Uzbek 24%, Russian 8%, Tatar, Kyrgyz, Ukrainian, German
LANGUAGES: Tajik (official), Uzbek, Russian
RELIGIONS: Sunni Muslim 83%, Shiite Muslim 5%
GDP PER CAPITA (1995): US$920

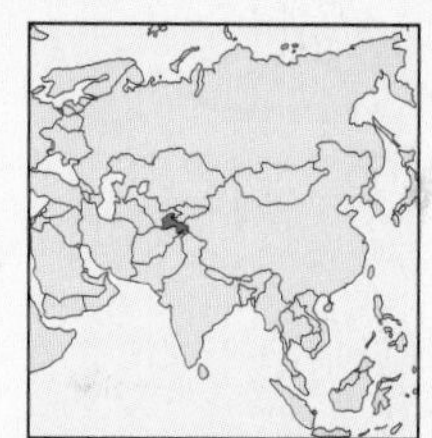

Mountainous republic in SE Central Asia. The Tajiks are descendants of Persians who settled in the area *c.*2500 years ago. ALEXANDER III (THE GREAT) conquered the region in the 4th century BC. In the 7th and 8th centuries AD Tajikistan was conquered by Arabs, who introduced Islam. The Tajik cities of Bukhara and SAMARKAND were vital centres of trade and Islamic learning. In the 13th century Tajikistan was overrun by the MONGOL hordes. TAMERLANE made his capital at Samarkand in the 14th century. From the 16th to the 19th century, UZBEKS ruled the area as the khanate of Bukhara. The fragmentation of the region aided Russian conquest from 1868.

After the RUSSIAN REVOLUTION (1917), Tajikistan rebelled against Russian rule. Although Russian troops annexed N Tajikistan to Turkistan in 1918, the Bukhara emirate held out against the Red Army until 1921. In 1924 Tajikistan became an autonomous part of the republic of UZBEKISTAN. In 1929 Tajikistan achieved full republican status, but Bukhara and Samarkand remained part of Uzbekistan. During the 1930s, vast irrigation schemes greatly increased agricultural land. Many Russians and Uzbeks were settled in Tajikistan. As the pace of reform accelerated in Russia, many Tajiks began to demand independence. In 1989 Tajik replaced Russian as the official language. In 1990 the Tajik parliament declared itself the supreme sovereign body. In 1991 Tajikistan became an independent republic within the COMMONWEALTH OF INDEPENDENT STATES (CIS).

In 1992 tension between the new government (consisting mainly of former communists) and an alliance of Islamic and democratic groups, the United Tajik Opposition (UTO), spiralled into full civil war. The government called for Russian military assistance, and Imamali Rakhmonov was appointed head of state. By 1993 the Islamic-democratic rebels had retreated into Afghanistan. Fighting continued along the Afghan border, and the rebels made frequent incursions into Tajikistan. In 1994 a brief cease-fire enabled elections to take place. Rakhmonov was elected president amid an opposition boycott. In 1995 the civil war resumed, and the Russian air force launched attacks on rebel bases in Afghanistan. Fresh elections in 1995 saw the return of the (former communist) People's Party of Tajikistan, amid charges of ballot-rigging and another opposition boycott. In 1997 a peace agreement was signed, formally ending the five-year civil war and giving the UTO one-third of government and judicial posts. In 1999 Rakhmonov was re-elected and the first multiparty parliamentary elections were held in 2000.

order of St Tammany, founded in 1789, and rapidly became the focal point of resistance to the FEDERALIST PARTY. It gained in significance under Aaron BURR, and by 1865 Tammany Hall, led by William "Boss" TWEED, had become the most important voice of the Democratic Party in the city. During the late 1860s and early 1870s Tammany Hall was synonymous with the organized corruption of urban politics. In the 1930s President Franklin ROOSEVELT and Major Fiorella LA GUARDIA limited its power.

Tamworth Manifesto (18 December 1834) Public statement of the principles of the recently formed Conservative minority government, issued by Prime Minister Robert PEEL prior to a by-election in his constituency of Tamworth, central England. It is widely seen as the founding text of the British CONSERVATIVE PARTY. Peel's reluctant acceptance of the 1832 REFORM ACT put him at odds with those TORIES who continued to oppose parliamentary reform. Although less dogmatic than the Ultra Tories, Peel continued the Tory traditions of support for the royal prerogative, an independent House of Lords, and the link between the state and the Church of England.

Tanaka Kakuei (1918–93) Japanese statesman, prime minister (1972–74). He was elected to the Diet (parliament) in 1947, serving as minister of finance (1962–64) and minister of international trade and industry (1971–72). In 1972 Tanaka succeeded SATO EISAKU as prime minister and leader of the Liberal-Democratic Party (LDP). Tanaka established diplomatic relations with China, but his attempts to revitalize industry in W Japan increased inflation and, faced with allegations of corruption, he resigned. In 1976 Tanaka was charged with accepting US$2 million in bribes from the US Lockheed Aircraft Corporation and he was eventually convicted in 1983. He had continued to dominate the LDP throughout the trial.

Tancred (d.1194) Last Norman king (1190–94) of SICILY. Illegitimate son of Duke Roger of Apulia and grandson of ROGER II of Sicily, he had to fight Emperor HENRY VI (married to Roger of Apulia's sister) for the throne. Although Tancred successfully defended his claim, upon his death Henry deposed Tancred's infant heir, William III, and took Naples, so ending 125 years of Norman rule of Sicily.

Tancred (*c*.1078–1112) Norman prince. A nephew of Robert GUISCARD, Tancred was one of the leaders of the First CRUSADE to the Holy Land. He participated in the siege of Nicaea and in the Battle of Dorylaeum (1097), and helped capture Jerusalem (1099). When GODFREY OF BOUILLON became king of Jerusalem, he was made prince of Galilee. As regent of Antioch (1104–1112), he fought the Turks and Byzantines.

Taney, Roger Brooke (1777–1864) US lawyer, fifth chief justice of the SUPREME COURT (1836–64). As attorney general (1831–33), he supported President Andrew JACKSON in his struggle against the BANK OF THE UNITED STATES. Jackson rewarded Taney by promoting him to secretary of the treasury (1833), but (for the first time) the Senate refused to confirm the appointment, and subsequent attempts to make him associate justice were blocked. In 1836 Taney succeeded John MARSHALL as chief justice. An advocate of STATES' RIGHTS, Taney nonetheless extended the scope and power of the Supreme Court. He is chiefly remembered, however, for the decision in the DRED SCOTT CASE (1856–57), which refused African Americans the right of citizenship and denied Congress power to outlaw SLAVERY in the territories. *See also* KANSAS-NEBRASKA ACT; MISSOURI COMPROMISE

Tang (T'ang) Chinese imperial dynasty (618–907). Established by a SUI general, Li Yuan, the Tang continued the unification of China started by the Sui. The early period under the Tang was a golden age in China's history, when it was by far the largest, richest and culturally most accomplished society in the world. Tang armies carried Chinese authority to Afghanistan, Tibet and Korea, and by the mid-7th century the Chinese empire reached its maximum extent prior to the MANCHU conquests 1000 years later. Towns grew as trade expanded, new ideas and foreign influences were freely admitted, the arts flourished and printing was invented. The expansion of the Tang was finally halted when they were defeated in the Battle of Dali (751) by the kingdom of Nanzhao and in the Battle of Talas River by the Muslim ABBASIDS. The dynasty then became submerged in civil conflict.

Tanganyika *See* TANZANIA

Tanganyika African National Union (TANU) Socialist organization founded (1954) by Julius NYERERE. It was the dominant political party in Tanganyika and later TANZANIA under a one-party political system. In 1977 TANU merged with Zanzibar's Afro-Shirazi Party (ASP) to form the Chama Cha Mapinduzi (CCM) or Revolutionary Party of Tanzania. Although a multiparty system was introduced in 1992, CCM retained control of government in subsequent elections.

Tannenberg, battles of Two conflicts fought at Tannenberg, NE Poland. In the first (15 July 1410), Lithuanian and Polish forces defeated the TEUTONIC KNIGHTS. The second Battle of Tannenberg (August 1914) was an early engagement in WORLD WAR 1. Led by Paul von HINDENBURG and Erich LUDENDORFF, the German army destroyed the Russian 2nd Army, inflicting *c*.30,000 casualties and capturing *c*.92,000 Russian soldiers. The Germans suffered *c*.13,000 casualties.

Tanzania *See* country feature

Tanzimat reforms Number of wide-ranging changes, which resulted in the reorganization of the OTTOMAN EMPIRE (1839–76). They were initiated during the reigns of MAHMUD II, ABDUL MEDJID I and Abdul Aziz, in response both to pressure from the West and the need to strengthen the Empire against foreign intervention and burgeoning nationalist movements. Government was increasingly centralized, new legal codes were introduced resulting in the formation of new state courts that were separate from the Islamic religious courts, the army and taxation systems were restructured, and the public education system was reformed. Despite their successes in modernizing the Empire, by increasing the power of the sultan, the Tanzimat reforms inadvertently opened the way for the despotic rule of later sultanates.

Taoism (Daoism) Philosophy and religion considered as being next to CONFUCIANISM in importance in China. Taoist philosophy is traced to a 6th-century BC classic of LAO TZU, the *Tao Te Ching* (although some question Lao Tzu's involvement in this work). The book's recurrent theme is the *Tao* (way or path). To follow the *Tao* is to follow the path leading to self-realization. *Te* (virtue) and *ch'i* (energy) represent the goal of effortless action. Taoist ethics emphasize patience, simplicity and the harmony of nature, achieved through the proper balance of yin and yang (male and female principles). Many of its philosophical and mystical tenets contrast with the more conservative and austere beliefs of Confucianism. As a structured religion, Taoism dates from the time of Chang

TANZANIA

AREA: 945,090sq km (364,899sq mi)
POPULATION: 27,829,000
CAPITAL (POPULATION): Dodoma (203,833)
GOVERNMENT: Multiparty republic
ETHNIC GROUPS: Nyamwezi and Sukuma 21%, Swahili 9%, Hehet and Bena 7%, Makonde 6%, Haya 6%
LANGUAGES: Swahili and English (both official)
RELIGIONS: Christianity (mostly Roman Catholic) 34%, Islam 33% (99% in Zanzibar), traditional beliefs and others 33%
GDP PER CAPITA (1995): US$640

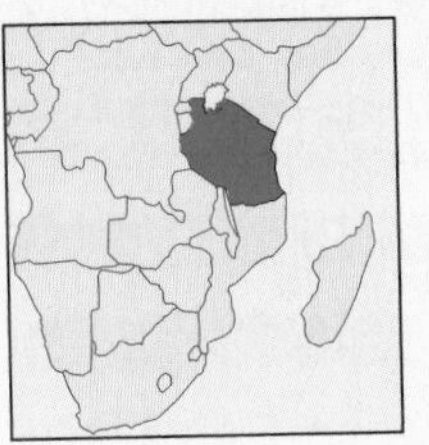

Republic in E Africa. Tanzania consists of the mainland republic of Tanganyika and the island republic of ZANZIBAR. Dr Louis LEAKEY discovered 1.75 million year-old fossils of *Homo habilis* in OLDUVAI GORGE. From *c*.2000 years ago, Arabs, Persians and Chinese traded with coastal settlements, such as Kilwa, which reached their height at the end of the 15th century. In 1498 Vasco da GAMA became the first European to land on the Tanzanian coast. For the next 200 years, the Portuguese controlled coastal trade.

In 1698 the Portuguese were expelled with the help of Omani Arabs. Zanzibar became part of the Omani empire and in the 18th century was the principal centre of the E African ivory and slave trade. In 1840 the sultan of OMAN, SAID IBN SULTAN, moved his capital to Zanzibar. The interior of Tanganyika was opened up by new caravan routes bringing slaves and ivory to the coast for shipment to the Americas. In the European scramble for Africa, Tanganyika was subsumed into GERMAN EAST AFRICA (1887); the sultanate of Zanzibar became a British protectorate (1890). Resistance to German colonial rule was fierce. The Germans established plantations and built railways; missionaries encouraged the spread of Christianity.

During World War 1, British and Belgian troops occupied German East Africa (1916), and in 1919 Tanganyika became a British mandate. The British ruled indirectly, via local leaders. In 1954 Julius NYERERE founded the TANGANYIKA AFRICAN NATIONAL UNION (TANU), and in 1960 elections he became prime minister, leading Tanganyika to independence in 1961. In 1963 Zanzibar gained independence, and in 1964, in an effort by Nyerere to counteract revolutionary forces in Zanzibar, Tanganyika and Zanzibar merged to form the Republic of Tanzania – although Zanzibar retained economic sovereignty – with Nyerere as president. In 1967 Nyerere issued the ARUSHA DECLARATION, an outline of his self-help (*ujamaa*) form of socialism. Over the next 18 years Nyerere introduced social welfare and educational programmes, which resulted in Tanzania having some of the best public health services and primary school systems in Africa. Despite promises of decentralization, however, Tanzania became a one-party state.

In 1977 Tanganyika and Zanzibar's ruling parties merged to form Chama Cha Mapinduzi (CCM) or Revolutionary Party of Tanzania. In 1978 Uganda occupied N Tanzania but in 1979 Tanzanian forces and Ugandan rebels staged a counter-attack and overthrew the Ugandan president, Idi AMIN. In 1985 Nyerere retired as president (although he retained the chairmanship until 1990) and was succeeded by Ali Hassan MWINYI, who in 1992 endorsed the principle of multiparty elections. In 1995 Benjamin Mkapa became the first president to be elected in a multiparty system. In 1997, after a prolonged drought, he declared a state of famine.

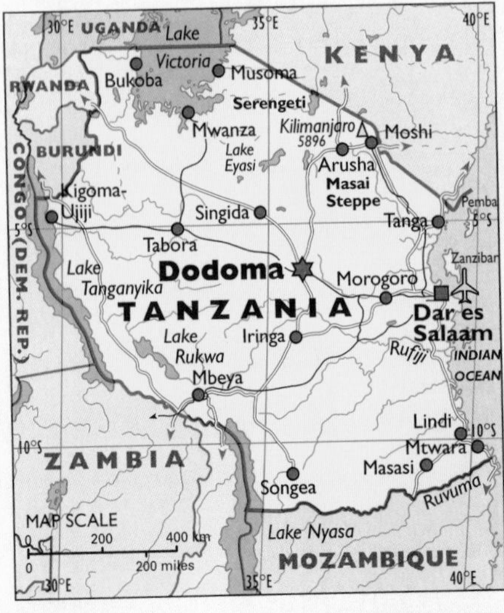

Tao-ling, who organized a group of followers in AD 142. By the 4th century, following a period of competition with MAHAYANA Buddhism, Taoism had assumed similar monastic systems to Buddhism.

Taranaki Wars *See* MAORI WARS

Tariq ibn-Ziyad (d. *c.*720) Muslim soldier who led the Moorish invasion of Spain. He captured GIBRALTAR in 711 with an army of 7000 and then proceeded to conquer Córdoba, Toledo and other parts of Spain. The name "Gibraltar" derives from *Jebel Tariq* (Arabic, Mount Tariq).

Tarquin ETRUSCAN dynasty of ancient ROME. Its best-known members are, according to tradition, the fifth and seventh kings of Rome, **Tarquinius Priscus** (r.616–578 BC), who seized the throne while acting as guardian to the sons of King Ancus Marcius, and **Tarquinius Superbus** (r.534–510 BC), whose cruel and despotic rule ended with a revolt by a number of senators, heralding the foundation of the ROMAN REPUBLIC. There is some doubt, however, as to whether the Tarquins were historical or legendary figures as many of the stories that surround them may have been used to compare the idealism of the newly founded republic with the corruption of the monarchy.

Tartars *See* TATARS

Tasman, Abel Janszoon (*c.*1603–*c.*1659) Dutch maritime explorer who made many discoveries in the Pacific. He joined the DUTCH EAST INDIA COMPANY in 1632, and in 1642 was sent by Anthony van DIEMEN, governor of the DUTCH EAST INDIES, on a voyage, the purpose of which was to find a route to Chile and to prove or not the existence of a semi-legendary continent called Terra Australis. Having sailed around the W coast of Australia, he headed E and discovered TASMANIA, an island he called Van Diemen's Land. Tasman later reached New Zealand but here was attacked by Maori in Golden Bay, North Island. Leaving New Zealand he discovered TONGA and FIJI, before returning to Java. Although he circumnavigated Australia, Tasman never sighted the mainland coast. In 1645, during a second voyage, Tasman charted large stretches of the N Australian coast.

Tasmania Island state of AUSTRALIA, separated from Victoria by the Bass Strait. The state capital is Hobart. The first settlers are believed to have settled the island *c.*35,000 years ago by crossing a land bridge (the Bass Plain) between Tasmania and mainland Australia. In time, rising sea-levels isolated the inhabitants of Tasmania from the Native Australians. The first European discovery was made by Abel TASMAN in 1642, who named it Van Diemen's Land. In 1777 Captain James COOK visited Tasmania and claimed it for the British. In the early 19th century it was colonized largely by British convicts. Further settlement resulted in the near extinction of the indigenous peoples. In 1825 Tasmania became a separate colony, and it was federated as a state of the Commonwealth of Australia in 1901. The early 20th century saw rapid development, but towards the end of the century conservation became the priority for the government. Area: 68,332sq km (26,383sq mi). Pop. (1991) 452,837.

Tatars (Tartars) Turkic-speaking people of central Asia. True Tatars were nomadic peoples who originated in central Siberia. In the 13th century, following the MONGOL ruler GENGHIS KHAN's sweep through much of Asia, Tatars and Mongols were assimilated and were collectively known as Tatars to Europeans. During the 1240s and 1250s the state of the GOLDEN HORDE was established, comprised mainly of Tatars. They ruled most of Russia and were converted to Islam in the 14th century. By the 15th century, however, the Tatars had become divided into two groups, one in S Siberia, who came under Russian rule, the other in the CRIMEA, which was part of the OTTOMAN EMPIRE until annexed by Russia in 1783. Tatar nationalism has its origins in the Crimean Autonomous Socialist Republic, founded in 1921. In 1945 Soviet dictator Joseph Stalin dissolved the republic and deported the entire population as a punishment for their supposed collaboration with the Nazis during World War 2. After the breakup of the Soviet Union in 1991, many of the *c.*350,000 exiled Tatars began to return to Crimea. Today, there are *c.*5–6 million Turkic speakers, most of whom live in the autonomous republic of Tatarstan, with significant populations in W Siberia, Turkmenistan and Uzbekistan. While they are mainly Muslim, some Tatars have converted to the Eastern ORTHODOX CHURCH.

Tawney, Richard Henry (1880–1962) British social historian, writer of *The Acquisitive Society* (1920) and *Religion and the Rise of Capitalism* (1926). One of the most influential social critics of the age, Tawney helped to formulate the social policies of the Labour Party. A self-confessed disciple of Max WEBER, Tawney was president (1928–44) of the Workers' Educational Association and professor of economic history (1931–49) at the London School of Economics. In his books, Tawney argues that CAPITALISM has affected attitudes to work and that the Reformation was a significant movement in the creation of the PROTESTANT ETHIC in N Europe.

Taylor, Zachary (1784–1850) Twelfth president of the United States (1849–50). He joined the army in 1806, seeing action in the WAR OF 1812, the BLACK HAWK WAR (1832) and the Second SEMINOLE War (1835–42). In 1845 Taylor was ordered by President James POLK to occupy the Republic of TEXAS, recently annexed, an action which precipitated the MEXICAN WAR. Taylor won a decisive victory at the Battle of BUENA VISTA (1847) against vastly superior numbers, effectively ending the war in N Mexico, and emerged from the War as a popular hero. Taylor won the Whig nomination for president and defeated Lewis CASS in the ensuing election (1848) but died suddenly after only 16 months in office. Although his tenure was brief, Taylor was steadfast in his belief in the Union and that California had the right to join the Union with its anti-slavery constitution. He was succeeded by Millard FILLMORE.

Tea Act *See* BOSTON TEA PARTY

Teamsters (officially International Brotherhood of Teamsters, Chauffeurs, Warehousemen and Helpers of America) Trade UNION founded in the United States in 1903. Between 1907 and 1952 it was led by Daniel Tobin and increased its membership to more than one million, making it the largest US union. Representing truck drivers and related trades, the Teamsters have been the subject of several government investigations for suspected illegal activities, and three of its presidents were imprisoned in the years 1957–88, including James HOFFA. The Teamsters, having been expelled from the AMERICAN FEDERATION OF LABOR AND CONGRESS OF INDUSTRIAL ORGANIZATIONS (AFL-CIO) in 1957 were permitted to rejoin in 1987. Today, the Teamsters have *c.*1.4 million members.

Teapot Dome Scandal Corruption disgrace involving President Warren HARDING's Republican administration over the fraudulent leasing of government-owned oil reserves without suitable competitive bidding. On entering office (1921), Harding agreed to transfer the administration of the naval oil reserves to the department of the interior. Secretary of the Interior Albert Fall (1861–1944) granted exclusive mining rights to the reserves in Teapot Dome, Wyoming, and Elk Hills and Buena Vista Hills, California, to two private oil companies in return for *c.*US$400,000. Fall was discovered and subsequently convicted of accepting bribes; he served one year in prison.

Tecumseh (1768–1813) NATIVE NORTH AMERICAN leader. A SHAWNEE chief, he worked with his brother Tenskwatawa, known as the SHAWNEE PROPHET, to unite the Native Americans of the West and resist white expansion. With the help of the British in Canada, they established a tribal confederacy to halt white settlements. After the Prophet's defeat at the Battle of TIPPECANOE (1811), Tecumseh joined the British in the WAR OF 1812. He led 2000 braves in several battles and was killed in Upper Canada at the Battle of the Thames (1813).

Tehran Conference (28 November–1 December 1943) Meeting in Tehran, Iran, between the British, Soviet and US leaders (Winston CHURCHILL, Joseph STALIN and Franklin ROOSEVELT) during WORLD WAR 2. It was the first meeting of the "Big Three", during which it was agreed that Stalin would launch an Eastern offensive at the same time as the Allies invaded German-occupied France in 1944. The three leaders also discussed the formation of the UNITED NATIONS.

Telengana Disturbances (1946–51) Number of civil uprisings in the former princely state of Hyderabad, central India, in demand for a united state based on the shared language of Telugu. Although a committee was established (1947) by the All-India Congress to examine the creation of a separate state, little action was taken. The slow progress resulted in civic disturbances and hunger strikes by leaders of the movement. After continued agitation Jawaharlal NEHRU announced (1953) a firm intention to create the first state, Andhra Pradesh, which was to be reorganized on a linguistic basis. It was inaugurated in 1956.

temperance movements Campaigns in a number of countries to end or curtail the consumption of alcoholic beverages. The first temperance societies in the United States appeared in New England in the late 18th century. In 1874 the Women's Christian Temperance Society was formed in Ohio. It attacked the culture of saloons and bars, which often doubled up as brothels. The Society gained in importance and was soon influential in Australia and New Zealand. In the United States the movement reached its peak with the ratification of the 18th Amendment (1919), which brought in the PROHIBITION era. The amendment was later repealed (1933) after enforcement proved impossible. Prominent in the US movement were Benjamin RUSH, Lyman BEECHER, Carry NATION and Frances Willard. In Britain the temperance movement, mainly supported by evangelical and non-conformist Christians, trade unionists and the Church of England, first appeared in Ulster in Northern Ireland and soon spread to Scotland, Wales and England, as well as some areas of Scandinavia. During the early 1900s legislation was passed in Britain restricting the number of public houses, imposing an age restriction of 18 on the consumption of alcohol, and the introduction of specified drinking times. *See also* ANTI-SALOON LEAGUE

Templars *See* KNIGHTS TEMPLAR

Temple, Sir William (1628–99) English diplomat, ambassador to The Hague in 1668. He negotiated the TRIPLE ALLIANCE between England, the United Provinces of the Netherlands and Sweden, and in 1677 arranged the marriage of JAMES II's daughter, Mary (the future MARY II) to WILLIAM OF ORANGE.

Temple of Jerusalem Most significant shrine in JUDAISM, originally located on a hilltop known as Temple Mount in what is now East JERUSALEM. There have been three temples on the site. The first was built in the 10th century BC by order of SOLOMON as a repository for the Ark of the Covenant. In *c.*587 BC it was destroyed by NEBUCHADNEZZAR II of Babylon. In *c.*515 BC a second Temple was completed by Jewish exiles who had returned (*c.*537 BC) from their BABYLONIAN CAPTIVITY. Between 19 and 9 BC, this second Temple was replaced by a more elaborate structure; it was destroyed by the Roman TITUS in AD 70. Some of its ruins, known as the WESTERN WALL, remain as a place of pilgrimage and prayer. Part of the ancient Temple site is occupied by the DOME OF THE ROCK and al-Aqsa Mosque, both built in the late 7th century.

Templer, Sir Gerald Walter Robert (1898–1979) British colonial administrator and field marshal. As British high commissioner in Malaya in the early 1950s, he helped to stem a communist guerrilla campaign, the MALAYAN EMERGENCY, by addressing political and economic grievances. From 1955 to 1958 he was chief of the Imperial general staff.

Tennessee State in SE central United States between the Appalachian Mountains and the Mississippi River; the capital is Nashville. Inhabited by a number of NATIVE NORTH AMERICAN tribes, notably the CHICKASAW and CHEROKEE, the first European discovery was made by Hernando DE SOTO in 1540. Early Spanish settlements were soon abandoned, but many Native Americans subsequently died from European diseases. When the French

TENNESSEE
Statehood :
1 June 1796
Nickname :
The Volunteer State
State motto :
Agriculture and commerce

arrived a century later, the region was sparsely inhabited. With the influx of British fur traders, competition between Britain and France increased, and following the FRENCH AND INDIAN WAR (1754–63), the region was ceded to Britain. In 1769 the first permanent settlement was established, in the Watagua River Valley. Nashville was founded in 1779. North Carolina relinquished its claim to the land in 1784, and dwellers in E Tennessee organized the State of Franklin, which was never recognized by Congress and its government collapsed in 1788. In 1790 Congress created the Southwest Territories, from which the state of Tennessee was later formed. Tennessee's enthusiastic response to the request for volunteers during the MEXICAN WAR (1846–48) earned it the nickname of the Volunteer State. As the CIVIL WAR approached, Union sentiment was strong in Tennessee, but the state seceded in 1861. With Tennesseans fighting on both sides, the state was the site of more than 400 battles; some of them, including SHILOH (1862) and CHATTANOOGA (1863), were extremely bloody. After the Civil War, the vigilante group KU KLUX KLAN was founded in Tennessee forcibly to resist Reconstruction. In 1866 Tennessee became the first Southern state to be readmitted to the Union. For the rest of the 19th century it suffered economic hardship, particularly due to the fall in the price of cotton. Christian fundamentalism has exerted a powerful influence, and the SCOPES TRIAL (1925) highlighted the ban on the teaching of evolution in Tennessee's schools. Industrial development was greatly stimulated by the creation (1933) of the TENNESSEE VALLEY AUTHORITY (TVA). In April 1968 Martin Luther KING, JR, was killed in Memphis. Area: 109,411sq km (42,244sq mi). Pop. (1996) 5,319,654.

Tennessee Valley Authority (TVA) NEW DEAL agency established (1933) as part of a long-range regional planning project. An independent public corporation, it was authorized to build dams (of which there are now 50) and hydroelectric power plants to control flooding in the Tennessee River Valley, to improve the navigability of the river and to produce inexpensive electricity. Many of the lakes created by the dams have become recreational areas, which attract *c.*60 million people each year. The success of the TVA contributed greatly to the wealth of the Tennessee Valley. *See also* ROOSEVELT, FRANKLIN DELANO

Tennis Court Oath (20 June 1789) Defiant vow made by members of the Third ESTATE of the STATES-GENERAL at the start of the FRENCH REVOLUTION. They called themselves the NATIONAL ASSEMBLY and vowed not to disband until a constitution had been established. The name of the oath derives from the indoor tennis court in which they met.

Tenochtitlán *See* AZTECS; MEXICO CITY

Teotihuacán Ancient city of MEXICO, *c.*50km (30mi) N of Mexico City. It flourished between *c.*100 BC and *c.*AD 700. The most important centre of pilgrimage in Mesoamerica, it contained huge and impressive buildings. Teotihuacán was laid out in a grid pattern centred on a thoroughfare named the Street of the Dead – the Pyramid of the Sun and the Temple of Quetzalcóatl dominated the E side, and the Pyramid of the Moon the N area of the city. At its greatest extent, *c.*AD 600, the city was the sixth largest in the world, covering a total area of *c.*21sq km (8sq mi) and supporting a population of *c.*200,000. The centre of a large empire, the peoples of Teotihuacán traded with the MAYA.

Teresa, Mother (1910–97) Roman Catholic missionary, b. Macedonia as Agnes Gonxha Bojaxhiu. She began her missionary work as a teacher in Calcutta, NE India. In 1948 she left her convent in order to tend the homeless, starving and sick in the slums of Calcutta. Her Order of the Missionaries of Charity was established in 1950 and subsequently extended to other countries. She won the first Pope John XXIII Peace Prize in 1971 and the Nobel Prize for Peace in 1979.

Teresa of Ávila, Saint (1515–82) Spanish nun and mystic, b.Teresa de Cepeda y Ahumada. In 1529 she entered the Convent of the Incarnation at Ávila, central Spain. From 1558 she set about reforming the CARMELITE order for women, whose rules had become weakened. Under her influence, Saint JOHN OF THE CROSS introduced a similarly restored Carmelite order for men. She was canonized in 1622. Her feast day is 15 October.

Terror, Reign of *See* REIGN OF TERROR

Tertiary Earlier period of the CENOZOIC era, lasting from 65 million to *c.*2 million years ago. It is divided into five epochs, starting with the Palaeocene, followed by the Eocene, Oligocene, Miocene and Pliocene. Early Tertiary times were marked by great mountain-building activity. Both marsupial and placental mammals diversified greatly. Archaic forms of carnivores and herbivores flourished, along with primitive primates, bats, rodents and whales.

Tertullian (*c.*160–*c.*220) Roman writer and Christian theologian, b. Carthage. He converted to Christianity (197), later joining the Montanists, an ascetic group that was declared heretical. Tertullian used his training in law and rhetoric to develop a systematic approach to theology and the defence of Christian beliefs and practices. He helped to make Latin the official language of Christian theological writing. His works include *Apologeticus* ("Defence") and *De anima* ("Concerning the Soul").

Test Acts (1673, 1678) English laws intended to exclude Protestant dissenters and Roman Catholics from public offices. The Act of 1673 required all holders of military or public office to take communion in an Anglican Church. The Act of 1678 excluded all Catholics, except the Duke of York (later JAMES II), from Parliament. The Acts were not repealed until 1828, although the Indemnity Acts of 1727 mitigated the effects of the 1673 Act by giving protection to anyone not prosecuted within a set period.

Test Ban Treaty (1963) Agreement signed in Moscow by the Soviet Union, United States and Britain to cease most tests of NUCLEAR WEAPONS. Nearly 100 other states eventually signed the treaty, although France and China continued to conduct tests in the atmosphere and underwater.

Tet Offensive (30 January–25 February 1968) Campaign in the VIETNAM WAR (1955–75). Regular North Vietnamese forces and VIET CONG troops launched

TEXAS
Statehood :
29 December 1845
Nickname :
The Lone Star State
State motto :
Friendship

THAILAND

AREA: 513,120sq km (198,116sq mi)
POPULATION: 57,760,000
CAPITAL (POPULATION): Bangkok (5,572,712)
GOVERNMENT: Constitutional monarchy
ETHNIC GROUPS: Thai 80%, Chinese 12%, Malay 4%, Khmer 3%
LANGUAGES: Thai (official)
RELIGIONS: Buddhism 94%, Islam 4%, Christianity 1%
GDP PER CAPITA (1995): US$7540

Kingdom in Southeast Asia. The Mongol capture (1253) of a Thai kingdom in SW China forced the Thai people to move S. A new kingdom was established around Sukhothai in the 13th century, while to the N the state of Lan Na developed around Chiang Mai. To the S the kingdom of AYUTTHAYA was established in the mid-14th century. This kingdom expanded at the expense of the KHMER in CAMBODIA, and in 1438 it took control of Sukhothai.

Thailand's first contact with Europeans came with the arrival of the Portuguese in 1511. They were followed by Dutch, English, Spanish and French traders and missionaries, but at the end of the 1680s the over-zealous efforts of missionaries to convert the Buddhist Thais led to the expulsion of Europeans for over a century. Thailand remained the only Southeast Asian nation to resist European colonization. A more serious threat was posed by BURMA, which in 1767 destroyed the city of Ayutthaya and deported the royal family to Myanmar. The Burmans were finally defeated by the military commander Taksin, who established a new capital at Thonburi, on the opposite side of the river from modern BANGKOK, and created a state that stretched beyond the boundaries of Ayutthaya. In 1782 he was overthrown by another military commander, Chao Phraya Chakri. As RAMA I he established the Chakri dynasty, which has ruled ever since. The country became known as Siam, and Bangkok acted as its capital.

From the mid-19th century, Siam began a gradual process of westernization. In World War 1, Siam supported the Allies. In 1932 Siam became a constitutional monarchy. In 1938 PIBUL SONGGRAM became premier and changed the country's name to Thailand. In 1941 Pibul, despite opposition, invited Japanese forces into Thailand. Military coups and short-lived civilian governments are characteristic of post-war Thai politics. In 1950 Bhumibol Adulyadej acceded to the throne as Rama IX. In 1957 Pibul was overthrown in a military coup.

In 1992 public pressure forced elections that saw the return of civilian rule. In 1997 the prime minister resigned amid criticism of his handling of the economic crisis that had led to the collapse of Thailand's financial sector. A new coalition government, led by Chuan Leekpai, was formed.

attacks on towns and bases in South Vietnam at the time of the annual Tet festival. After early successes the Viet Cong and North Vietnamese troops were forced back, and heavy casualties were sustained on both sides (the North lost *c.*33,000 lives). Although of little strategic value, the Offensive discredited US military reports that victory over North Vietnam was imminent and forced US President Lyndon JOHNSON into opening peace talks with Hanoi and eventually halting bombing raids on North Vietnam.

Teutonic Knights German military and religious order, founded (1190) in Acre, Palestine. Established initially to care for the injured on CRUSADE in Palestine, by 1198 the order had also assumed a military role. Its members, made up of the aristocratic class, priests and lay brothers, and recruited from the Rhineland and other parts of Europe, took monastic vows of poverty and chastity. In the 1220s the Knights moved their focus of operations from Palestine to Eastern Europe, contributing to the defence of Hungary and Poland against non-Christian neighbours in Transylvania and Prussia. In the following decades, closely allied with the LIVONIAN ORDER, they established control over Prussia. After being defeated by ALEXANDER NEVSKI of Novgorod in 1242, the order waged a "Perpetual Crusade" against the Lithuanians. By 1300 it controlled much of central and E Europe, and having been released from its vow of poverty (1263) the order successfully engaged in trade. By 1329 the Knights held the entire Baltic region as a papal fief, but their power was severely curtailed following their defeat by Poles and Lithuanians at the Battle of TANNENBERG (1410). From that time the order's influenced gradually diminished, and when, in 1525, the Grand Master of the time converted to Lutheranism the order was declared secular. *See also* KNIGHTS HOSPITALLERS; KNIGHTS TEMPLAR

Tewkesbury, Battle of (4 May 1471) Conflict during the English Wars of the ROSES. EDWARD IV led the House of YORK to victory over the House of Lancaster thus ensuring that EDWARD IV retained the English throne. The army raised on HENRY VI's behalf by MARGARET OF ANJOU and their son Edward, who was killed in the Battle, was routed.

Texas State in central s United States, separated from MEXICO by the Rio Grande. The state capital is Austin. In the early 16th century, the Spanish became the first Europeans to explore the region and Spain established its first mission in Texas in 1682. In 1685 the French, having sailed down the Mississippi River, built a fort on Matagorda Bay. The 18th century saw the establishment of a number of Spanish missions, and the region became part of the Spanish colony of Mexico. Many of the missions were subsequently abandoned. After the LOUISIANA PURCHASE (1803), Americans began to settle the still thinly inhabited region. By the time Mexico attained independence in 1821, many more Americans, encouraged by Stephen AUSTIN's agreement with the Mexican government for grants of land, had settled the area. As their numbers increased they revolted against Mexican rule and in 1836, following the TEXAS REVOLUTION, they established the **Republic of Texas**. The US annexation of Texas in 1845 led to the MEXICAN WAR (1846–48), which ended with Mexico ceding control of Texas north of the Rio Grande. Although many in the w were pro-Union, Texas seceded in 1861. After the Civil War the population of Texas grew rapidly, creating increased tension between white settlers and Native Americans. To deter the Native Americans, the wholesale slaughter of bison was undertaken, and the Native Americans, without their primary source of food, were eventually forced into reservations. Cattle rearing, which had flourished after the Civil War, was slowly replaced by cotton farming, and by 1890 Texas produced more than 33% of the United States' entire crop. The first major oil discovery was at Spindletop in 1901. As in other states, the NEW DEAL and World War 2 helped to improve the state economy following the GREAT DEPRESSION. By the 1960s oil, the defence industry and agriculture were the major wealth creators. In the 1990s cuts in defence spending and severe droughts affected the defence-related factories and agriculture, but this was offset by increased activity in high-technology and service industries. Area: 692,405sq km (267,338sq mi). Pop. (1996) 19,128,261.

Texas Rangers Mounted law enforcement officers organized in 1835 during the TEXAS REVOLUTION against Mexico. Stephen AUSTIN, founder of the first Texas colony, hired rangers in 1823, before they were formally organized, to defend the colony from Native American attack. The first Rangers were left to protect small Anglo-American settlements from the COMANCHE and APACHE nations, while the main Texas army was fighting the Mexican army in the s. In the MEXICAN WAR (1846–48), the Rangers were effective as guerrilla fighters and scouts. In 1874 they were organized into two battalions, one to control fighting along the frontier, and one to stop banditry and cattle-rustling along the Rio Grande. This was their period of greatest renown. In 1935 they became a division of the Texas Department of Public Safety, serving with the state highway patrol.

Texas Revolution (1835–36) Insurrection against MEXICO by Anglo-American settlers in TEXAS. The Revolution was provoked by the efforts of the Mexican dictator Antonio López de SANTA ANNA to control white settlers in Texas, impose higher taxes and ban the importation of slaves into the state. Initial battles favoured the Texans, who declared independence (1836) and held up Santa Anna's invading army at the ALAMO. After eventual defeat at the Alamo, however, the Texans retreated and one group was massacred after surrendering at Goliad, s Texas. However, under Sam HOUSTON the Texans rallied, and Santa Anna was defeated and captured at the Battle of SAN JACINTO. He was forced to withdraw from Texas, thus paving the way for the creation of the Republic of Texas.

Texas v. White (1869) US Supreme Court decision affirming Abraham LINCOLN's position that the Union was indissoluble and upholding Congress' authority to reconstruct the states. It ruled that, despite secession, Texas had remained a state and that Congress, not the executive, would recognize state governments.

Thailand *See* country feature

Thant, U (1909–74) Burmese diplomat, third secretary general (1962–72) of the UNITED NATIONS (UN).

THATCHER, MARGARET

Margaret Thatcher was the only British prime minister in the 20th century to win three consecutive general elections. Her single-minded determination to transform British society earned her the epithet the "Iron Lady".

THATCHER IN HER OWN WORDS

"In politics, if you want anything said, ask a man; if you want anything done, ask a woman."
In the Changing Anatomy of Britain (1982)

"There is no such thing as society.
There are individual men and women, and there are families."
In Woman's Own (October 1987)

Following BURMA's independence (1948), Thant held several posts in the Burmese government. In 1957 he was made Burma's permanent UN representative, and became acting UN secretary general after the death (1961) of Dag HAMMARSKJÖLD. He was confirmed as secretary general the following year and was re-elected in 1966. Thant helped to settle several major disputes, including the CUBAN MISSILE CRISIS (1962), the civil wars in the Congo (Zaïre) in 1963, and Cyprus in 1964. In 1967 Thant negotiated a settlement to end the SIX-DAY WAR and China's admittance to the UN Security Council (1971).

Thatcher, Margaret Hilda, Baroness (1925–) British stateswoman, prime minister (1979–90). Thatcher was secretary of state for education and science (1970–74) under Edward HEATH, whom she defeated for the leadership of the CONSERVATIVE PARTY in 1975. She led the Conservatives to victory over the LABOUR PARTY under James CALLAGHAN, becoming Britain's first woman prime minister. Her government embarked on a radical free-market programme that became known as "Thatcherism". Her monetarist policies, especially cuts in public spending, provoked criticism and contributed to a recession and high unemployment, but her popularity was restored by victory in the FALKLANDS WAR (1982). Thatcher's determination to curb the power of trade unions provoked a bitter miners' strike (1983–84). Controversial PRIVATIZATION of national utilities boosted government revenue in a period of rapidly rising incomes, except among the poor. In 1987 Thatcher won a third term, but clashed with cabinet colleagues over economic and social policy and her hostile attitude to the EUROPEAN UNION (EU). A POLL TAX (1989) was widely seen as unfair and greatly reduced her popularity. In the ensuing struggle within the Conservative Party, Thatcher was forced to resign as prime minister and party leader in favour of John MAJOR.

Thebes City-state of ancient GREECE, the dominant power in BOEOTIA. It was allied with Persia during the PERSIAN WARS, and during the 5th century BC it was continually in conflict with ATHENS, siding with SPARTA during the PELOPONNESIAN WARS. Thebes, however, dissatisfied with the peace settlement (404 BC) allied itself with Athens, CORINTH and ARGOS in the CORINTHIAN WAR. In the 4th century BC Thebes reached the peak of its power under EPAMINONDAS, defeating Sparta at Leuctra (371 BC) and invading the Peloponnese. Epaminondas, however, was killed in a second conflict with Sparta at Mantinea (362 BC). In 336 BC the city was largely destroyed after a rising against ALEXANDER III (THE GREAT) and never regained its former glory.

Thebes Greek name for the ancient capital of Upper Egypt, roughly corresponding to present-day LUXOR.

thegn (thane) In ANGLO-SAXON England, a man who held land from his lord in return for service. The status was hereditary, and socially and economically varied – because a thegn's importance depended on that of his lord (who might be the king, an earl or even another thegn). All thegns were bound to serve in the king's forces.

theme Military provinces within the BYZANTINE EMPIRE. The first themes were established during the reign (610–641) of HERACLIUS, who created three themes, under the leadership of military governors (*strategoi*) and settled with soldiers who were granted land to farm, thus establishing military administration and a standing citizen army. By the 9th century the system had extended over the entire Empire. The gradual weakening of the theme system during the 11th century was one of the contributing factors in the collapse of the Byzantine Empire.

Themistocles (*c.*528–460 BC) Athenian general and statesman. Aware of the threat of a naval invasion from PERSIA, Themistocles was primarily responsible for persuading ATHENS to build a powerful navy. As commander of the Athenian fleet, he helped secure the crucial victory over the Persian fleet at SALAMIS (480 BC). His arrogance, however, resulted in accusations of conspiracy and his eventual OSTRACISM. Themistocles fled to ARGOS, before travelling to Persia, where he was appointed a governor by Artaxerxes I.

theocracy Government by religious leaders in accordance with divine law. Theocracies were common in non-literate societies and existed in ancient Egypt and the Orient. The term has become less strictly defined and now includes governments that are heavily influenced by religious leaders. Within this looser definition fall countries such as TIBET, until the Chinese occupation (1951), and IRAN, after the establishment of an Islamic republic (1979).

Theodora Name of three empresses of the BYZANTINE EMPIRE. The most famous **Theodora** (*c*.500–48) was the wife of JUSTINIAN I. A courtesan before her marriage, she had such influence that she was virtually joint ruler. The second **Theodora** (d.867) ruled as regent (842–56) for her son Michael III. She expelled the iconoclasts and restored the worship of images. The third **Theodora** (980–1056) was co-ruler from 1042 and was briefly sole empress after the death (1055) of Constantine IX Monomachus.

Theodoric I (d.451) King of the VISIGOTHS (419–51), son of ALARIC. In 439, after a 15-year long war, he was finally defeated by the Romans at Toulouse, SW France. Theodoric then allied himself with Rome to fight the Hun army led by ATTILA, and was killed at the Battle of Châlons-sur-Marne.

Theodoric (the Great) (*c*.454–526) King of the OSTROGOTHS (475–526) and ruler of Italy (493–526). He invaded Italy in 488 and after five years had subdued the whole region, treacherously killing the previous Germanic ruler ODOACER. He made RAVENNA his capital and over the next 32 years attempted to recreate the Western Roman Empire with himself as emperor. Theodoric's reign in Italy was largely peaceful, prosperous and tolerant, and at its height his kingdom included Sicily and parts of Germany as well as Italy. He included Romans among his statesman, notably BOETHIUS, who was, however, later executed for alleged conspiracy. Theodoric was an Arian Christian, and towards the end of his reign religious differences and political rivalries frustrated his empire-building. After his death, the kingdom was destroyed by the anti-Arian Byzantine Emperor JUSTINIAN I (THE GREAT). *See also* ARIANISM

Theodosius I (the Great) (*c*.347–95) Roman emperor (379–95), the last to rule both Eastern (from 379) and Western (from 392) elements of the ROMAN EMPIRE. A champion of orthodox Christianity, he summoned the first ECUMENICAL COUNCIL of Constantinople (381) to solve the religious dispute over the doctrine of ARIANISM. He ended the wars with the VISIGOTHS by an agreement (382) giving them land on the frontiers in return for service in the Roman army. After 392, he briefly reunited the empire after defeating a pretender, but left the two parts separately to his sons.

Theodosius II (401–50) Eastern Roman (Byzantine) emperor (408–50). A scholarly man, he left the running of his government to relatives and ministers. His armies repelled Persian invasions in 422 and 447 but failed to defeat the VANDALS in N Africa. During his reign the fortifications of Constantinople were strengthened and the Theodosian Code, which codified the laws issued since 312, was promulgated (438).

theosophy Religious philosophy that originated in the ancient world but was given impetus in 1875 when the Theosophical Society was founded in New York by the Russian-born mystic Helen Blavatsky (1831–91) and her followers. Modern theosophy continues a mystical tradition in Western thought represented by such thinkers as PYTHAGORAS and PLOTINUS but is most significant in Indian thought. The main aims of the Theosophical Society are to promote a spiritual brotherhood of all humanity; to encourage the comparative study of religions, philosophy and science; and to develop latent spiritual powers. Belief in the transmigration of souls also occupies an important place in theosophical doctrine. *See also* BESANT, ANNIE

Theravada ("Doctrine of the Elders") One of the two major schools of BUDDHISM which arose in the 1st century AD, the other being MAHAYANA Buddhism. Theravada Buddhism stresses that sorrow and suffering can be conquered only by the suppression of desire. Desire can be suppressed only if the individual realizes that everything is always in a state of flux and the only stable condition is NIRVANA, an indefinable state of rest. This type of Buddhism is widespread in Sri Lanka and SE Asia.

Thermidorean reaction Period during the FRENCH REVOLUTION following the coup of 9 Thermidor (27 July 1794), when the NATIONAL CONVENTION ordered the arrest of Maximilien ROBESPIERRE. Robespierre was one of more than 100 leading JACOBINS who were later executed. A new executive was formed known as the DIRECTORY (1795–99).

Thermopylae Strategic mountain pass in E central Greece, site of several battles in ancient times. The most famous was the defence of the pass by LEONIDAS of SPARTA against the Persian invasion of XERXES I in 480 BC during the PERSIAN WARS (499–79 BC). The Spartans, although greatly outnumbered, successfully defended the pass against the Persian frontal attacks. However, a Spartan traitor led part of the Persian force over a mountain track enabling them to attack Leonidas from the rear. Leonidas and 300 Spartans died in the battle.

Thessaly (Gk. Thessalía) Administrative district of N central Greece and region of ancient GREECE. It was the centre of an extensive Neolithic settlement until *c*.2500 BC. Cut off from much of the culture and politics of classical Greece, Thessaly sided with the Persians during the PERSIAN WARS. Due to its isolation Thessaly was captured by PHILIP II of MACEDON in 352 BC and later became part of the province of Macedonia under Roman rule in 148 BC. With the decline of Roman rule, Thessaly became part of the BYZANTINE EMPIRE before passing to the Ottoman Turks in 1393. Thessaly was annexed to Greece in 1881.

Thessaloníki (Salonica) Port on the Gulf of Thessaloníki, Greece, the country's second-largest city and capital of Greek MACEDONIA. Founded *c*.315 BC, it flourished under the Romans after 148 BC as the capital of Macedonia. It was part of the Ottoman Empire until 1913, when it was conquered by Greece. Pop. (1991) 383,967.

Thiers, (Louis) Adolphe (1797–1877) French statesman and historian, first president of the Third Republic (1871–73). He was twice foreign minister under LOUIS PHILIPPE and supported Louis Napoléon (later NAPOLEON III) as president. However he opposed Napoléon's coup (1851) and was banished for several months. On re-entering politics as a deputy in 1863, he led the opposition to Napoleon III. When the Republicans seized power in 1870, Thiers was made head of the provisional government. He negotiated an end to the FRANCO-PRUSSIAN WAR and suppressed the PARIS COMMUNE (1871). In August 1871 Thiers was elected president of France, during which time he completed the peace settlement with Germany. In 1873 he was ousted by monarchist opponents. He wrote a 10-volume *History of the French Revolution* (1823–27) and a 20-volume *History of the Consulate and Empire* (1840–55).

Thieu, Nguyen Van *See* NGUYEN VAN THIEU

Third Reich Official name of NAZI Germany (1933–45). The first *Reich* (Ger. empire) was the HOLY ROMAN EMPIRE, the second the German empire of 1871–1918.

Thirteen Colonies English colonies in North America that jointly declared independence from Britain (1776) in the DECLARATION OF INDEPENDENCE and became the first states of the UNITED STATES. They were: CONNECTICUT, DELAWARE, GEORGIA, MARYLAND, MASSACHUSETTS, NEW HAMPSHIRE, NEW JERSEY, NEW YORK, NORTH CAROLINA, PENNSYLVANIA, RHODE ISLAND, SOUTH CAROLINA and VIRGINIA. Although they disagreed over many issues, most notably SLAVERY, they were very much united in their desire to secede from colonial rule. *See also* AMERICAN REVOLUTION

Thirty-Nine Articles (1563) Set of doctrinal formulations devised by the CHURCH OF ENGLAND during the reign of ELIZABETH I. They developed out of the Forty-Two Articles written (1553) by Thomas CRANMER and became statutary law in 1571. Collectively they do not represent a creed, rather they were a compromise that enabled different interpretations of contentious issues brought about by the REFORMATION, such as TRANSUBSTANTIATION. In such a manner they have, over the years, sought to establish the unity of the ANGLICAN COMMUNION. *See also* COMMON PRAYER, BOOK OF

Thirty Years' War *See* feature article

Thistlewood, Arthur *See* CATO STREET CONSPIRACY

Thomas à Kempis (*c*.1380–1471) German Augustinian monk and spiritual writer. Ordained in 1413, he remained in the monastery of the Brethren of the Common Life, near Zwolle, for most of his life. He wrote or edited numerous treatises on the life of the soul. The most famous work attributed to him is *Imitation of Christ* (*c*.1415–24), which stressed spirituality and denounced materialism, particularly in the church. Other works include *Soliloquium Animae* and *De Tribus Tabernaculis*.

Thomas Aquinas, Saint *See* AQUINAS, SAINT THOMAS

Thompson, David (1770–1857) Canadian fur trader and explorer, b. England. He joined the HUDSON'S BAY COMPANY in 1784, studied surveying and journeyed to Lake Athabasca. In 1797 Thompson left the Hudson's Bay Company and joined the NORTH WEST COMPANY under whom, later that year, he discovered Turtle Lake, the source of the Mississippi River. In 1807, having crossed the Rocky Mountains, he established the first trading post on the Columbia River and later charted the United States-Canada boundary.

Thomson, Joseph (1858–95) Scottish explorer of Africa. A geologist, he explored the East African lakes in 1879–80 for the Royal Geographical Society. A meticulous surveyor, Thomson explored the Rift Valley in a journey through Kenya to Lake Victoria (1883), which opened up the route from the coast to Uganda. He later travelled in N Nigeria and acted as a commercial agent for Cecil RHODES and for Britain in central Africa.

Thorez, Maurice (1900–64) French statesman, secretary general of the French Communist Party (1930–64), deputy premier (1946–47). After joining the Communist Party in the early 1920s, he rose quickly through the ranks to become secretary general. He was elected to the Chamber of Deputies (1932) and served until the outbreak of World War 2, when he was conscripted. Thorez deserted and went into hiding when the Communist Party announced its opposition to the war. When the Party was banned for its anti-war stance, Thorez went to the Soviet Union. Although found guilty of desertion in his absence, he was pardoned (1944) and returned to France, where he was re-elected to the Chamber of Deputies. Having aligned himself closely with Joseph Stalin, Thorez's reputation was discredited with Nikita Khrushchev's denunciation of the former Soviet leader in 1956.

Thothmes *See* THUTMOSE

Thrace (Thráki) Ancient country in SE Europe, now divided between Bulgaria, Greece and European Turkey. From 1300 to 600 BC the Thracian lands extended W to the Adriatic and N to the Danube. In the 7th century BC the Greeks established several colonies on the Thracian coast, among them Byzantium (now ISTANBUL). In the 6th century BC most of the region was incorporated into the Persian ACHAEMENID empire. In 342 BC PHILIP II of MACEDON conquered the country. After 100 BC it became part of the Roman Empire. In the 7th century AD, the N of the region was conquered by the Bulgarians, who by 1300 controlled all Thrace. From 1361 to 1453 the region was disputed between the Bulgarians and the emerging OTTOMAN EMPIRE, eventually falling to the Ottomans. In 1885 N Thrace was annexed to Bulgaria. The regions either side of the River Maritsa became known as Eastern Thrace (Bulgaria) and Western Thrace (Turkey). After World War 1, Bulgaria ceded S and most of E Thrace to Greece. The Treaty of LAUSANNE (1923) restored E Thrace to Turkey, and the region retains these boundaries. A fertile region, its main economic activity is agriculture.

Three Emperors' League (1873–75, 1881–87) Alliance of Germany, Austro-Hungary and Russia. Part of Otto von BISMARCK's network of alliances, the League primarily created stability in the Balkan region, but also served to isolate France. The first, informal agreement (1873–75) expired with growing tension that culminated in the RUSSO-TURKISH WAR. The second agreement, precipitated by the assassination of Tsar ALEXANDER II, was more formal but remained secret. In it the signatories agreed that territories within the Balkans were to remain unchanged unless all parties were in agreement. The League collapsed due to the conflict of interest in the Balkans between Austria-Hungary and Russia. It was supplanted by the TRIPLE ALLIANCE.

Three Henrys, War of *See* RELIGION, WARS OF

Three Mile Island Island on the Susquehanna River near Harrisburg, Pennsylvania. It is the site of a nuclear power-generating plant where a near-disastrous accident took place on 28 March 1979. The accident involved the failure of the feedwater system that absorbs heat from water that has circulated through the reactor core. A series of mechanical failures and human error followed. Radioactive water and gases were released into the environment. Although the ultimate disaster (meltdown of the reactor core) did not take place, the accident demonstrated problems with reactor design, maintenance procedures and operator training.

Thucydides (*c.*460–*c.*400 BC) Greek historian. A commander in the PELOPONNESIAN WAR (431–404 BC) his *History of the Peloponnesian War* is a determined attempt to write objective history, and it displays a profound understanding of human motives. The history finishes in 411 BC. In 424 BC, as a naval commander, he lost territory to Sparta, for which he was exiled. Other episodes covered by Thucydides include the Athenian plague and the failure of Athens to capture Sicily.

THIRTY YEARS' WAR (1618–48)

Complex series of conflicts fought mainly in Germany, arising out of the aspirations of Catholic and Protestant factions and developing into a wider, dynastic struggle for power in Europe.

The **first** (Palatine-Bohemian) phase (1618–25) of the War began with a Protestant revolt in BOHEMIA against the king, the future HABSBURG Emperor FERDINAND II. Bohemian Protestants, who had formed a coalition known as the Evangelical Union, were embittered by their treatment at the hands of the Roman Catholic hierarchy. They appealed to Ferdinand to redress their grievances. Ferdinand, a devout Catholic, ignored their petitions, and following the DEFENESTRATION OF PRAGUE, a Protestant uprising began (1618). After initial Protestant victories Ferdinand was deposed and FREDERICK V, Elector of the PALATINATE, assumed the throne. Frederick, however, was a Calvinist and many elements of the mainly Lutheran Evangelical Union withdrew from the conflict. Emperor Ferdinand II seized the opportunity to defeat the divided Evangelical Union at the Battle of White Mountain (1620), effectively ending the war in Bohemia. The conflict, however, continued in the Palatinate, where Ferdinand, with help from Spain and MAXIMILIAN I of BAVARIA, defeated Frederick.

The **second** (Danish) phase (1625–29) saw the conflict spread into other regions of Europe. The successes of Ferdinand in Bohemia and the Palatinate alarmed other German Protestant states, who sought allies to counteract the Catholic Habsburg threat. CHRISTIAN IV of Denmark and Norway came to their aid, although his motivation was more the prospect of increased territory than a defence of Protestantism. Christian invaded SAXONY (1625) and initially met little resistance. However in 1626 the Habsburg generals, Graf von TILLY and Albrecht WALLENSTEIN, registered victories and drove Christian to the Jutland Peninsula (1627). Imperial victory was assured and Ferdinand issued the Edict of Restitution (1629), which effectively reversed the Peace of AUGSBURG. Throughout the late 1620s the armies of the HOLY ROMAN EMPIRE took control of the whole of N Germany leaving a trail of destruction. Furthermore, Tilly's siege of Madgeburg (1631) ended in the massacre of the city's Protestant population.

These events ushered in the **third** (Swedish) phase (1630–35) of the war. Although England and France were alarmed at the growing power of the Holy Roman Empire neither was able to lend support. However, France's promise of financial support persuaded GUSTAVUS II of Sweden to enter the conflict. Gustavus, spurred on by the thought of gaining control of the Baltic region, waged a series of victorious campaigns, during which Tilly was killed and Swedish forces captured Munich. Wallenstein then assumed command of the imperial forces. At the Battle of LÜTZEN (1632), although Gustavus was killed, Wallenstein was driven back and the Swedish forces under Axel OXENSTIERNA occupied Bavaria. Protestant success was short-lived, however, and in 1633 Wallenstein gained a number of successes against the Swedes. Wallenstein's attempts to broker peace attracted Ferdinand's suspicion and he was removed from his command, and later assassinated. Further imperial successes resulted in the capitulation of the Protestant forces.

The **final** (French) phase (1635–48) was a contest between France and the Habsburgs, and one in which religion was not a significant factor. In 1635 LOUIS XIII of France, fearing Habsburg dominance, declared war on Habsburg Spain. France allied itself with Sweden and a number of Protestant German states. Swedish forces won a series of victories, while Spanish invasions of French-held territory were overcome. By 1645 Swedish forces had occupied Denmark, which had aligned itself with the Empire, and large areas of Germany and Austria, while French forces, under Louis II, Prince de CONDÉ, had defeated a Spanish army at Rocroi (1643), a Bavarian army at Freiburg (1644), and a combined Austro-Bavarian force at Nördlingen (1645). Factions on both sides entered into negotiations in 1645, but the new emperor FERDINAND III was determined to continue the struggle. His intransigence resulted in further failures for the Empire, and following Austrian and Bavarian defeats in 1648, and French and Swedish sieges of Prague and Munich in the same year, Ferdinand was forced to agree to the Peace of WESTPHALIA (1648). War between France and Spain continued until the Peace of the PYRENEES (1659), and other associated conflicts continued for several years. The War claimed *c.*5 million German lives, mainly peasants. Ferdinand and the Habsburgs lost control of Germany. Sweden was established as the dominant state in N Europe, while France replaced Spain as the greatest European power.

◄ **The Thirty Years' War** was a series of wars over religious, dynastic and territorial concerns. It led to the demise of the Holy Roman Empire and established many of the borders of modern Europe.

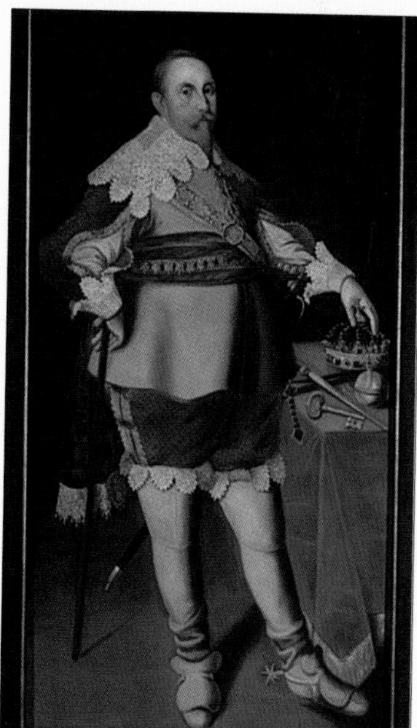

▲ **Gustavus II** (1594–1632) Portrait by G. Ekman. Gustavus led the Swedish invasion of N Germany, crushing the Bavarian army under Graf von Tilly at Breitenfeld (1631) but dying in the victory at Lützen.

Thuringia Historic region and state of central GERMANY. In the 5th century the Thuringians established a large kingdom which was conquered by the FRANKS in the following century. In the 10th century it came under the control of the duke of SAXONY. It was divided up between Saxony and other German states in the 15th century, and at the Congress of VIENNA (1815) part of it was acquired by PRUSSIA. Thuringia was reconstituted as a state under the WEIMAR REPUBLIC in 1920, but it lost its separate identity in 1952. It was recreated as a state shortly before the reunification of East and West Germany in 1990. Area: 16,176sq km (6244sq mi). Pop. (1992) 2,545,808.

Thutmose I (active 2nd millennium BC) Pharoah of ancient EGYPT (r. *c*.1525–*c*.1512 BC), third king of the 18th dynasty, successor of Amenhotep I. Thutmose extended the kingdom S into NUBIA and campaigned successfully in the Near East to reach the River Euphrates. During his reign he added to the temple of Amun at Karnak (now LUXOR). The first king to be buried in the VALLEY OF THE KINGS, he was succeeded by his son, Thutmose II (r. *c*.1512–*c*.1504 BC). His daughter was HATSHEPSUT.

Thutmose III (d.1450 BC) Pharoah of ancient EGYPT (r. *c*.1482–1450 BC), fifth king of the New Kingdom's 18th dynasty. He was the son of Thutmose II, whose wife and half-sister, HATSHETPSUT, acted as regent (*c*.1503–1482 BC). After her death, Thutmose expanded the kingdom to its greatest extent, defeating the HURRIANS on the River Euphrates and pushing the S frontier beyond the fourth cataract of the Nile.

Tiahuanaco Archaeological site on the S shore of Lake Titicaca in the Bolivian highlands. Tiahuanaco, which flourished AD 600–1000, was a ceremonial centre and possibly the capital of a pre-INCA culture. The carvings found on a lava-stone gateway are reminiscent of carvings found as far S as the Atacama Desert in Chile.

Tiananmen Square World's largest public square, covering 40ha (98 acres) in BEIJING, NE CHINA. On the S side of the Square, a marble monument is dedicated to the heroes of the revolution. A huge portrait of MAO ZEDONG adorns the wall of the Mao Zedong Memorial Hall. On 4 May 1919, China's first mass public rally was held in Tiananmen Square, where on 1 October 1949, Mao proclaimed the People's Republic of China. In 1966 Mao made his pronouncements on the CULTURAL REVOLUTION to more than a million RED GUARDS assembled here. In April 1989 hundreds of thousands of citizens joined in pro-democracy demonstrations and student leaders organized hunger-strikes. On 4 June 1989, tanks and troops stormed the Square. Official casualties were put at more than 200 demonstrators and dozens of soldiers. Eyewitness reports suggest thousands of deaths. The government imposed martial law and executed several student leaders.

Tianjin, Treaty of (1858) One of the so-called UNEQUAL TREATIES between China and Western powers. In 1858, during the Second OPIUM WAR, the British and French demanded that the Chinese accept terms under which further ports were opened to Western trade, and European merchants and missionaries were allowed to travel freely in China. When the Chinese emperor refused to ratify the treaty, Britain and France occupied Beijing, forcing him to sign it.

Tiberius (42 BC–AD 37) Second Roman emperor (AD 14–37), adopted son of AUGUSTUS. Tiberius served in Armenia (20 BC) and fought in PANNONIA. In 12 BC Augustus forced Tiberius to divorce Vipsania and marry Augustus' daughter, Julia. Tiberius, having lost his love and wounded by Julia's adulterous behaviour, went into self-imposed exile and seclusion in Rhodes. In 2 BC Tiberius was called back to Rome, where Augustus adopted him as his heir (AD 4) after the deaths of his own grandsons. Tiberius returned to military service, defeating ARMINIUS and thus securing the frontier with Germany. On his return to Rome, Tiberius was awarded the highest military honours. On Augustus' death, Tiberius acceded to the throne unopposed and subdued the SENATE by stationing the PRAETORIAN GUARD outside Rome. As emperor, he consolidated rather than expanded the ROMAN EMPIRE and practised strict economics, bequeathing a huge treasury. After the death of his son Drusus (AD 23), Tiberius left day-to-day affairs of government to SEJANUS, even abandoning Rome for Capri (AD 27). The execution of Sejanus in AD 31 marked the start of a vicious campaign of murder and torture of alleged conspirators. After naming CALIGULA as his successor, Tiberius was murdered.

Tibet (Xizang) Autonomous region in SW CHINA. The capital and largest city is Lhasa. Tibet is the highest region on Earth, with an average altitude of 4875m (16,000ft). The principal religion is TIBETAN BUDDHISM. Until 1959, a large percentage of the urban male population were Buddhist monks (lamas). Tibet flourished as an independent kingdom in the 7th century, and in the 8th century Padmasambhava developed the principles of MAHAYANA Buddhism into its Tibetan form. The spiritual leaders of Tibetan Buddhism (the DALAI LAMA and the PANCHEN LAMA) also acted as the country's temporal rulers. In 1206 GENGHIS KHAN conquered the region, and it remained under nominal Mongol rule until 1720, when the Chinese QING dynasty claimed sovereignty. At the close of the 19th century the Tibetan areas of Ladakh and Sikkim were incorporated into British India, and in 1906 Britain recognized Chinese sovereignty over Tibet. In 1912 the fall of the Qing dynasty prompted the Tibetans to reassert their independence. China, however, maintained its right to govern, and in 1950 the new communist regime invaded. In 1951 Tibet was declared an autonomous region of China, nominally governed by the Dalai Lama. The Chinese government began a series of repressive measures principally targeting the Buddhist monasteries. In March 1959 a full-scale revolt against Chinese rule was suppressed by the Chinese army. The Dalai Lama managed to flee to N India (25 December 1959), where he established a government-in-exile at Dharamsala. In 1965 China formally annexed Tibet as an autonomous region. The CULTURAL REVOLUTION banned religious practice, and 4000 monasteries were destroyed. Many thousands of Tibetans were forced into exile by the brutality of the communist regime. Despite the restoration of some of the desecrated monasteries and the reinstatement of Tibetan as an official language, human-rights violations continued. Pro-independence rallies in 1987–89 were violently suppressed by the Chinese army. Further unrest broke out in 1993, and the Dalai Lama's appeal to the Chinese government for an element of autonomy has been rejected. Area: 1,222,070sq km (471,841sq mi). Pop. (1993) 2,290,000.

Tibetan Buddhism Distinctive blend of MAHAYANA Buddhism and Bonism (a pre-Buddhist SHAMANISM). It mixes meditative monasticism with indigenous folk religion and involves a system of reincarnating lamas (monks). Both spiritual and temporal authority reside in the person and office of the DALAI LAMA. King Srong-tsan-gampo (b.617 or 629) sought to bring Buddhist teachers from China and India to Tibet, but the Bon priests opposed the new teachings and, according to tradition, BUDDHISM was first properly introduced into Tibet by Padmasambhava in the 8th century. Following reforms initiated by the 11th-century Indian master Atisha, four

TOGO

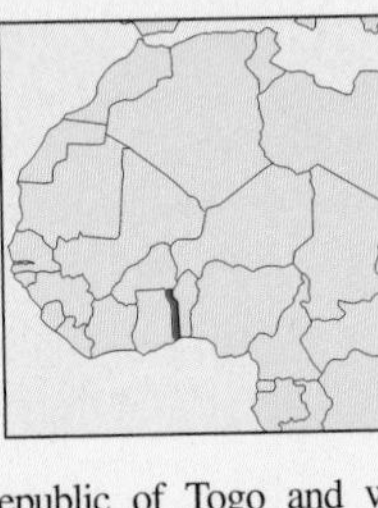

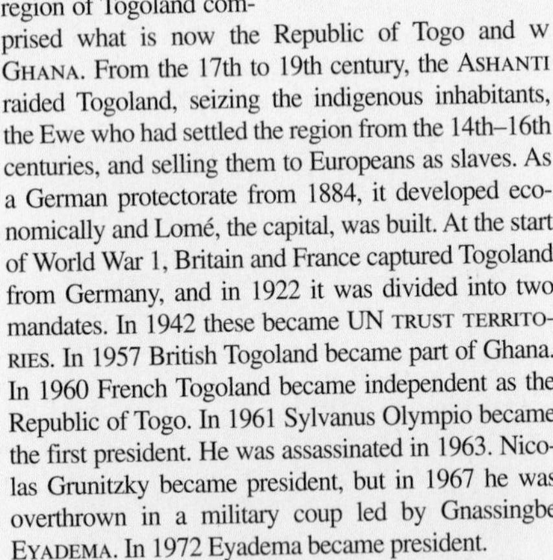

Small republic in W Africa. The historic region of Togoland comprised what is now the Republic of Togo and W GHANA. From the 17th to 19th century, the ASHANTI raided Togoland, seizing the indigenous inhabitants, the Ewe who had settled the region from the 14th–16th centuries, and selling them to Europeans as slaves. As a German protectorate from 1884, it developed economically and Lomé, the capital, was built. At the start of World War 1, Britain and France captured Togoland from Germany, and in 1922 it was divided into two mandates. In 1942 these became UN TRUST TERRITORIES. In 1957 British Togoland became part of Ghana. In 1960 French Togoland became independent as the Republic of Togo. In 1961 Sylvanus Olympio became the first president. He was assassinated in 1963. Nicolas Grunitzky became president, but in 1967 he was overthrown in a military coup led by Gnassingbe EYADEMA. In 1972 Eyadema became president.

In 1979 a new constitution confirmed Togo as a single-party state, the sole legal party being the *Rassemblement du Peuple Togolais* (RPT). Re-elected in 1972 and 1986, Eyadema was forced to resign in 1991 after pro-democracy riots. Kokou Koffigoh led an interim government. Unrest continued with troops loyal to Eyadema attempting to overthrow Koffigoh. In 1992 a new multiparty constitution was introduced and Eyadema regained some power. In 1993 a rigged election, boycotted by opposition parties, was won by Eyadema. In 1994, elections were won by an opposition alliance, but Eyadema formed a coalition government. In 1998 Eyadema was re-elected in suspect elections.

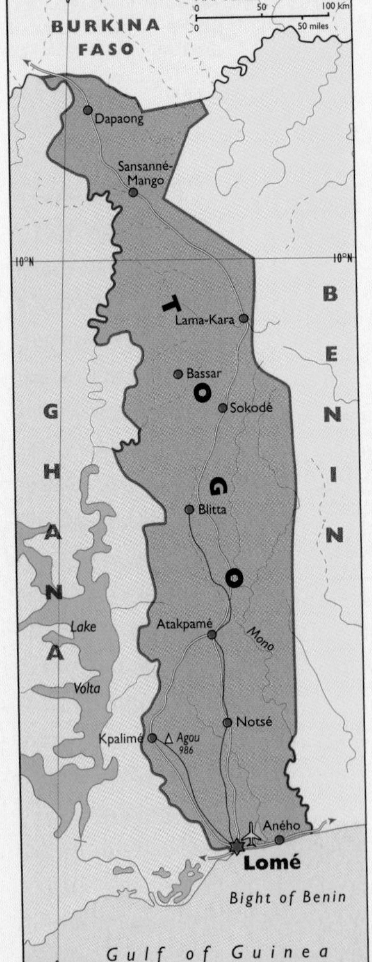

AREA: 56,790sq km (21,927sq mi)
POPULATION: 3,763,000
CAPITAL (POPULATION): Lomé (590,000)
GOVERNMENT: Multiparty republic
ETHNIC GROUPS: Ewe-Adja 43%, Tem-Kabre 26%, Gurma 16%
LANGUAGES: French (official), Ewe, Kabiye
RELIGIONS: Traditional beliefs 50%, Christianity 35%, Islam 15%
GDP PER CAPITA (1995): US$1130

major sects emerged in Tibetan Buddhism. Of these, the Gelugpa order, to which the Dalai and PANCHEN LAMAS belong, was politically dominant from the 17th century. There are now two Gelugpa sects, the Red and Yellow monks. The Dalai Lama, a member of the latter, became revered as the "Living Buddha" and the spiritual and temporal ruler of Tibet. Each new Dalai Lama is believed to be a reincarnation of Avalokitesvara, one of the most distinguished of the Buddhist bodhisattvas (enlightened beings). The Panchen Lama heads the Red monks.

Ticonderoga, Fort (formerly Fort Carillon) Historic military post in NE New York, United States, strategically located near Lake Champlain. Once on a main shipping route between Canada and New York City, it was built by the French (as Fort Carillon). Having survived an attack (July 1758) by General James Abercromby during the FRENCH AND INDIAN WAR, it was captured by Baron Jeffrey AMHERST the following year. During the AMERICAN REVOLUTION, it was taken by Ethan ALLEN (May 1775) and became an American base for Canadian invasion. It was later reoccupied by the British (July 1777) until John BURGOYNE's surrender. In 1820 it was bought by a New York entrepreneur and restored as museum.

Tiglathpileser III (active 8th century BC) King of ASSYRIA (745–727 BC). He came to power in a coup and immediately set about the restoration of imperial administration. Tiglathpileser first regained control of MEDIA and then defeated URARTU in 743 BC, beginning the policy of enforced mass migration and resettlement. He isolated Damascus by conquering surrounding territory in SYRIA and PALESTINE, gaining tribute from EDOM, MOAB and ISRAEL. The culmination of Tiglathpileser's great expansionist policies was realized when he was crowned king of BABYLONIA (*c.*729 BC)

Tikal Mayan city, in N Petén, Guatamala. First settled (*c.*600 BC) as a small village, Tikal grew to become a trading base and an important ceremonial centre (*c.*AD 600–800) before being deserted by the beginning of the 10th century. At its height, it is estimated that Tikal had a population of 10,000, with another 50,000 residing in its environs. Remains include five large pyramid temples as well as three palace-temple complexes, organized around large plazas. *See also* MAYA

Tilak, Bal Gangadhar (1856–1920) Indian scholar and nationalist, active in the campaign for Indian independence. Twice imprisoned by the British for his political activities (1897–99, 1907–14), Tilak led the extreme wing of the Indian National CONGRESS and was the leading spokesman for nationalism before "Mahatma" GANDHI. He came to prominence through his writings in two Maratha newspapers, *Kesari* (the Lion) and the English-language *Mahratta*. Tilak advocated political action to achieve full independence, including passive resistance and a mass boycott of British goods. He was also co-founder (1914) of the Indian Home Rule League, with Annie BESANT, and was one of the signatories to the LUCKNOW PACT.

Tilden, Samuel Jones (1814–86) US politician. He led the campaign against political corruption in New York, speaking out against William Marcy TWEED, and was subsequently elected governor of New York (1875–76). In 1876, as the Democratic Party presidential candidate, Tilden won a majority of the popular votes but controversially lost the election when contested electoral votes were awarded to the Republican candidate Rutherford HAYES by a partisan electoral commission.

Tilly, Jan Tserklaes, Graf von (1559–1632) Bavarian general. He fought for Alessandro FARNESE in his native Spanish Netherlands and for Emperor RUDOLF II against the Turks, before being appointed (1610) by Duke MAXIMILIAN I to reorganize the Bavarian army. At the start of the THIRTY YEARS' WAR (1618–48), Tilly was made commander in chief of the Catholic League forces and won the first decisive battle against FREDERICK V of Bohemia at White Mountain (1620). He went on to conquer the PALATINATE, despite the efforts of Peter von MANSFELD. In the second phase of the War (1625–29), Tilly routed CHRISTIAN IV of Denmark at the Battle of Lutter (1626). At the start of the third phase of the war (1630–35), Tilly replaced General Albrecht von WALLENSTEIN as commander of the imperial forces of FERDINAND II. In 1631, hoping to repel the advance of GUSTAVUS II of Sweden, he laid siege to Magdeburg, E Germany, eventually razing the city and massacring its Protestant population. Tilly was crushed by the Swedes at BREITENFELD (September 1631) and died trying to prevent them crossing the River Lech into Bavaria.

Tilsit, Treaties of (July 1807) Two agreements signed at Tilsit, East PRUSSIA (now in Russia), the first by France and Russia, the second by France and Prussia. The treaties followed NAPOLEON I's victories over Prussia at the Battle of JENA (1806) and over the Russians at the Battle of Friedland (1807). The meetings, which took place on a raft on the River Memel, were between Napoleon and ALEXANDER I of Russia and FREDERICK WILLIAM III of Prussia. Under the terms of the **first** treaty, Russia agreed to a huge reduction in Prussia's territory, the ceding to SAXONY of a new Grand Duchy of WARSAW, and the creation of the kingdom of WESTPHALIA. In return, Napoleon agreed to support Russia in its conflict with the OTTOMAN EMPIRE over European Turkey. Russia also agreed, in principle, to join the CONTINENTAL SYSTEM. In the **second** treaty, Prussia was forced to pay reparations, join the Continental System and reduce the size of its standing army. The Continental System subsequently damaged Russian trade and forced Russia to reopen its ports to all shipping, thereby contributing to the breakdown of the Russo-French alliance and precipitating Napoleon's fateful invasion of Russia in 1812. *See also* NAPOLEONIC WARS

Timbuktu Town in N MALI, W Africa. It was founded by the TUAREG in the 11th century and soon became a centre of Muslim learning. The S terminus of a trans-Saharan caravan route, Timbuktu later became famous throughout Europe as a market for slaves, ivory and gold. Timbuktu was one of the centres of the Mali empire and later the SONGHAI. Sacked by the Moroccans in 1591, it was seized by the French in 1893. Timbuktu's most important trading commodity today is salt. Pop. (1992 est.) 26,000.

Timor *See* EAST TIMOR; INDONESIA

Timur *See* TAMERLANE

Timurid dynasty (1370–1506) Turkicized Mongol family that ruled Transoxiana (West Turkistan, now Uzbekistan). It was founded by TAMERLANE, who became sole ruler in 1369 and made his capital at SAMARKAND. His campaigns extended the empire, which was largely to die with him, into Iraq, Syria, Caucasia and India. In the following century, the Timurid kingdom was twice divided and came to an end when the UZBEKS expelled BABUR, who went on to found the MUGHAL EMPIRE in India.

▲ **Tito** imposed a liberal form of socialism on Yugoslavia. He opposed Yugoslavia's inclusion in the Soviet bloc and encouraged decentralization and worker participation in the economy.

Tippecanoe, Battle of (7 November 1811) Conflict on the Tippecanoe River, Illinois, United States, in which US forces, under William Henry HARRISON, governor of Indiana Territory, were attacked by the British-backed SHAWNEE under TECUMESH and his brother Tenskwata, known as SHAWNEE PROPHET. The Shawnee opposed Harrison's land-grabbing actions, while Harrison wanted to end the Native American threat. Although Harrison's forces sustained many casualties, they repulsed the attack and Harrison was hailed as a hero.

Tipu Sultan (1749–99) Indian ruler, sultan (1782–99) of Mysore (now KARNATAKA). In the service of his father, HYDER ALI, he fought the MARATHA between 1775 and 1779 and the British during the Second Mysore War (1780–84). He concluded peace with the British in 1784, but in 1789 Tipu attacked a British ally, the Raja of Travancore, and the resulting hostilities culminated in Tipu having to cede half his territory to the British (1792). In 1799 the British invaded Mysore after discovering that Tipu was involved in negotiations with the French. The sultan was killed while defending his capital, Seringapatam.

Tirol (Tyrol) Federal state in W Austria. The capital is INNSBRUCK. The Romans conquered the region in 15 BC, and the FRANKS held it during the 8th century. In 1363 the province was taken by the HABSBURGS. In 1805 NAPOLEON I awarded Tirol to Bavaria in return for its support. In 1810 Napoleon gave S Tirol to the Italians, but the Congress of VIENNA (1815) reunited Tirol with Austria. After World War 1, when S Tirol was awarded to Italy, a process of Italianization was resisted by the German-speaking inhabitants. After World War 2, S Tirol was made an autonomous Italian region. Area: 12,647sq km (4882sq mi). Pop. (1994) 654,753.

Tirpitz, Alfred von (1849–1930) German admiral. As secretary of state for the German navy (1897–1916) under WILLIAM II, Tirpitz was chiefly responsible for the build-up of the German navy before WORLD WAR I. The highly ambitious construction programme was an attempt to force Britain, which at that time was the strongest naval power, to reconsider its alliances with France and Russia. The programme proved impossible to implement and Tirpitz, frustrated by government cuts and restrictions on submarine warfare, following the international outcry at the sinking of the LUSITANIA (1915), resigned.

Titanic British passenger liner that sank on her maiden voyage (14–15 April 1912). The largest vessel of her time, she was sailing from Southampton to New York when she struck an iceberg in the N Atlantic. About 1500 people were drowned. The disaster led to international agreements on greater safety precautions at sea. In 1985 the wreck of the *Titanic* was located on the ocean floor.

tithe (Old Eng. tenth) Tax of one-tenth of parishioners' income levied to support a religious institution. Tithes, prescribed in the Old Testament, were enforced by the Hebrew's and were a major source of church income in medieval Europe following the synods of Tours (567) and Mâcon (585). They were generally abandoned in Europe in favour of other sources of income in the 19th century, but remained in England until the early 20th century.

Tito (1892–1980) Yugoslav statesman, prime minister (1945–53) and president (1953–80) b. Croatia as Josip Broz. As a soldier in the Austro-Hungarian army during World War 1, he was captured by the Russians (1915) but became a BOLSHEVIK during the RUSSIAN REVOLUTION (1917) and was subsequently released. He returned to Croatia and helped to organize the then illegal Yugoslav Communist Party. Imprisoned (1928–34), he left Croatia for Moscow under the alias Tito, and there worked for the COMMUNIST INTERNATIONAL. He returned to YUGOSLAVIA (1936) and, following Germany's invasion of Yugoslavia, formed and led the all-Yugoslav Partisans in their effective guerrilla campaign to repulse the Germans during World War 2. Following a brief power struggle between Tito's provisional communist government (established 1942) and the pro-monarchist CHETNIKS, Tito eventually won the support of the Allies and established (1945) a communist government. Soviet efforts to control Yugoslavia led to a split between the two countries in 1948. Tito succeeded in retaining independence for Yugoslavia and sought to balance the interests of the nation's various ethnic and religious groups. He also developed a model of Marxist humanism that embraced "self-management" and minor liberal economic reforms. Abroad, Tito was an influential leader of the NON-ALIGNED MOVEMENT during the COLD WAR. When relationships with the Soviet Union improved, Tito assumed even greater global political significance. An advocate of DÉTENTE, Tito criticized the Soviet Union's invasions of Hungary (1956), Czechoslovakia (1968) and Afghanistan (1979). As later events in the Balkans confirmed, his greatest achievement was to hold the Yugoslav federation together.

Titus (AD 39–81) Roman emperor (79–81), eldest son of VESPASIAN. After serving as a tribune in Germany and Britain, he was sent to PALESTINE where he ended the Jewish revolt with the capture and destruction of JERUSALEM in AD 70. As emperor, Titus stopped persecutions for treason, completed the COLOSSEUM and provided aid for the survivors after the eruption of VESUVIUS (79). His popularity was augmented by splendid and extravagant entertainments. He was succeeded by DOMITIAN.

Tlingit Group of NATIVE NORTH AMERICAN peoples of the SE coast of Alaska. The Tlingit came into conflict with early Russian settlers. Famous for their totem poles (featuring stylized forms of local wildlife), historically they relied economically on fishing, but more recently tourism, logging and government aid have provided their income.

Tobago *See* TRINIDAD AND TOBAGO

Tobruk, Battles of (1941–42) Several conflicts during WORLD WAR 2 for control of the strategic port of Tobruk, NE Libya. An Italian base, Tobruk was captured by the British under General Archibald WAVELL (January 1941), who took 25,000 Italian troops prisoner. As Erwin ROMMEL approached (April 1941), the British withdrew, leaving behind a small Australian garrison. The garrison withstood a long siege, at one point breaking out and capturing Rezegh, before the Germans and Italians finally counter-attacked and took the city (June 1942), capturing large amounts of military supplies and taking 23,000 prisoners. General MONTGOMERY's troops retook the city (November 1942) after the battle of El-ALAMEIN. *See also* NORTH AFRICA CAMPAIGN

Tocqueville, Alexis, Comte de (1805–59) French historian and politician. Sent on a fact-finding tour to the United States by LOUIS PHILIPPE (1831), he produced *Democracy in America* (1835–40), the first in-depth study of the US political system and an extremely influential political critique of authoritarianism. In 1839 he was elected to the chamber of deputies and later briefly served as minister of foreign affairs (1849) after the JULY REVOLUTION (1848). Tocqueville retired from government following NAPOLEON III's coup. His later works include *The Old Regime and the Revolution* (1856).

Togliatti, Palmiro (1893–1964) Italian statesman. One of the founders of the PCI (*Partito Communista Italiano*), Togliatti was in Moscow when Benito MUSSOLINI banned the PCI (1926). He remained in exile until after World War 2, active in the COMMUNIST INTERNATIONAL and in organizing the Italian resistance. After returning to Italy (1944), Togliatti joined the government of Marshal BADOGLIO and then served as vice premier (1944–46) in a coalition government with Alcide DE GASPERI. As leader of the PCI until his death, he made it the largest communist organization in Europe and the second-largest party in Italy. He advocated the independence from Moscow of national communist movements and rejected atheism, promoting polycentrism, a doctrine that allows for a number of differing ideologies within one political system.

Togo *See* country feature, page 408

Togo Heihachiro, Koshaku (1847–1934) Japanese admiral. He was trained at Greenwich Naval Academy, London (1871–78), and served in the SINO-JAPANESE WAR (1894–95) and the RUSSO-JAPANESE WAR (1904–05). In the latter conflict, Togo forced the surrender of the Russian naval base at Port Arthur (1904) and destroyed Russia's Baltic fleet in the Battle of TSUSHIMA (1905).

Tojo Hideki (1885–1948) Japanese statesman and general, prime minister (1941–44). He fought against China in the 1930s before becoming chief of staff (1937–40) in MANCHURIA and minister of war (1940–41). After succeeding KONOE FUMIMARO as prime minister, he advocated alignment with the AXIS POWERS and approved the attack on PEARL HARBOR, Hawaii (1941). Responsible for all aspects of the Japanese war effort during WORLD WAR 2, Tojo granted himself almost dictatorial powers. In July 1944 he resigned after Japan lost Saipan, Northern Marianas. In 1945 Tojo was arrested by the Allies, tried for war crimes at the TOKYO TRIALS, found guilty and hanged.

Tokugawa Japanese hereditary dynasty (1603–1867) that controlled JAPAN through the SHOGUN. The Tokugawa shogunate was established by IEYASU Tokugawa, who completed the unification of Japan. The Tokugawa ruled through the provincial nobility (the DAIMYO) and controlled much of Japan's wealth and farmland as well as the emperor and priests. The SAMURAI were encouraged to take up administrative posts in fortified towns throughout Japan. The Tokugawa banned Christianity and Western trade, reviving CONFUCIANISM, and effectively isolating Japan from the rest of the world. The Genroku period (1688–1704) was a time of rapid economic growth, mainly in agriculture, and a flowering of urban culture. The regime declined, however, during the 19th century as social and economic unrest resulted in an increasing number of revolts, and, from 1853, their isolationist policy began to crack under Western pressure. The last Tokugawa shogun, Tokugawa Yoshinobu, surrendered in 1867, less than a year before the MEIJI RESTORATION.

Tokugawa Ieyasu *See* IEYASU

Tokyo (Jap. Eastern Capital) Capital of Japan, on E central Honshu, at the head of Tokyo Bay. Founded in the 12th century as Edo, it became capital of the TOKUGAWA shogunate in 1603. In 1868 the MEIJI RESTORATION re-established imperial power, and the last SHOGUN surrendered Edo Castle. Emperor Meiji renamed the city Tokyo and it replaced KYOTO as the imperial capital of Japan. The 1923 earthquake and subsequent fire claimed more than 150,000 lives and necessitated the city's reconstruction. In 1944–45 intensive US bombing destroyed more than half of Tokyo, and another modernization and restoration programme began. Pop. (1994) 7,894,000.

Tokyo trials (1946–48) War crimes trials held in Tokyo, Japan, after World War 2. They took place under a charter establishing the International Military Tribunal for the Far East, issued by Douglas MACARTHUR. The 25 Japanese defendants, including the former prime minister TOJO HIDEKI, were accused of crimes ranging from war atrocities to responsibility for prosecuting the War. They were tried in front of an 11-nation court – seven were sentenced to death by hanging, including Tojo, 16 to life imprisonment and two were handed down shorter sentences.

▲ **Tokugawa** This 17th-century Japanese minature is a portrait of Tokugawa Ieyasu (1543–1616), founder of the Tokugawa shogunate which brought stability to Japan.

Toledo, Francisco de (1515–84) Spanish colonial administrator, viceroy of PERU (1569–81). One of the ablest bureaucrats to serve in colonial Spanish America, Toledo maintained order in Peru by drawing up a law code (using many INCA laws) and quelling the revolt (1570–71) of TUPAC AMARU.

Toledo Capital of Toledo province, on the River Tagus, Castilla-La Mancha, central SPAIN. In the 6th century Toledo was the capital of the VISIGOTHS. In 1031 the MOORS made it the capital of an independent kingdom. The city was fortified and acquired its enduring reputation for quality sword-making. Toledo flourished as a multi-denominational city, with Mudéjar-style synagogues, mosques and churches. In the 16th century it became the spiritual capital of Catholic Spain and the headquarters of the Spanish INQUISITION; Jews and Muslims suffered persecution, and the synagogues were converted to churches. During the Spanish CIVIL WAR, Toledo was besieged by Loyalist forces. Pop. (1991) 59,563.

Toleration Act (1689) English legislation permitting freedom of religious practice to Protestant dissenters, subject to their taking oaths of allegiance to the monarch and their acceptance of the THIRTY-NINE ARTICLES. It modified the TEST ACTS, in that it removed the obligation to accept communion in an Anglican Church, but it did not remove the political and social exclusion of dissenters, nor did it extend to Roman Catholics.

Tolpuddle Martyrs Six English farm labourers in Dorset, S England, who were effectively convicted of a crime for forming a trade UNION (1834). Known as the Friendly Society of Agricultural Labourers, it aimed to increase the wage of farm workers. The government was worried by the growth of organized labour, but as unions were not illegal, the Dorset men, led by George and James Loveless, were charged with taking a seditious oath. They were sentenced to seven years' transportation to Australia. After a public outcry involving mass demonstrations in London, they were pardoned by Viscount MELBOURNE's government in 1836. *See also* CHARTISM

Toltec (Nuhuatl, master builder) Ancient Native American civilization, whose capital was Tollán (Tula), N Mexico. The Toltec were the dominant people in central Mexico from AD 900 to 1200, and are believed to have conquered the TEOTIHUACÁN culture. They played a major role in trading networks that stretched as far as the PUEBLO area of SW North America. Their architecture is characterized by PYRAMID building. Although the Toltec is considered a polytheistic culture, images of the god Quetzalcóatl predominate. After the destruction of Tula (*c.*1160) by the CHICHIMECS, the Toltecs probably dispersed to the Valley of Mexico and the MAYA area. In the 15th century the AZTEC emperor was to claim descent from the Toltecs.

Tone, (Theobald) Wolfe (1763–98) Irish revolutionary leader. Tone, who wanted the Irish to sink religious differences and unite for political independence, founded the Society of UNITED IRISHMEN in 1791 and promoted the Catholic Relief Act in 1793. Tone, inspired by the French Revolution, masterminded an abortive French invasion of Ireland in 1796 to overthrow the British. Following the failure of the Irish Rebellion in 1798, he returned with a smaller force and was captured. Sentenced to death, he committed suicide.

Tonga (Friendly Islands) South Pacific island kingdom, *c.*2200km (1370mi) NE of New Zealand. The archipelago consists of nearly 170 islands, only 36 of which are inhabited, in five administrative groups. The largest island is Tongatapu, the seat of the capital, Nukualofa. First inhabited by seafaring Austronesian peoples *c.*1000 BC, by the 10th century AD a distinctive hereditary kingdom had evolved. The N islands were discovered by the Dutch in

1616 and the rest by Abel TASMAN in 1643. Named the Friendly Islands by James COOK, who visited them between 1773 and 1777, by the 19th century, British missionaries had converted the indigenous population to Christianity. In 1845, under George Tupou I (r. 1845–93) the islands became a unified and independent monarchy. In 1900 Tonga became a British protectorate, and the British consul virtually assumed responsibility for Tonga's foreign and economic affairs. In 1970 the country regained full independence within the COMMONWEALTH OF NATIONS. In the 1990s Tupou IV (r.1969–) faced persistent demands for greater political democracy.

Tonkin (Tongking) Historical region of N VIETNAM. It was ruled by the Chinese from 111 BC to AD 939. It subsequently became the kingdom of Dai Viet and a Chinese tributary state. In 1883 it became part of the French protectorate of INDOCHINA. After World War 2 it was again occupied by the Chinese. Although the Chinese withdrew under French pressure, France never fully re-established control.

Tonkin Gulf Resolution (1964) Decision of the US Congress authorizing the president to take military action in Vietnam in response to attacks on US forces. It was passed at the urging of President Lyndon JOHNSON after a US destroyer was allegedly attacked by North Vietnamese torpedo boats in the Gulf of Tonkin. The Tonkin Gulf episode, about which the military intelligence was subsequently shown to be false, gave the United States a cause to enter the VIETNAM WAR.

Tonton Macoutes Personal police force of Haitian dictator François "Papa Doc" DUVALIER, who empowered them to torture, kill and terrorize political dissenters within HAITI. In the service of Duvalier's successor and son, Jean-Claude DUVALIER, their eyes were hidden by dark glasses, presumably to suggest they were zombies, thus invincible. The name is Haitian French for "bogeymen".

Torah (Hebrew, law) Hebrew name for the PENTATEUCH, the first five books of the OLD TESTAMENT. The Torah is the body of written Jewish laws contained within these five books. It also describes the complete Jewish Bible.

Tordesillas, Treaty of (1494) Agreement to divide the newly discovered Atlantic lands, most notably the Americas, into Portuguese and Spanish spheres. In 1493 Pope ALEXANDER VI had defined the line of demarcation between the two spheres as running between two poles *c.*500km (*c.*300mi) W of the CAPE VERDE islands, with the area to the W belonging to Spain and that to the E belonging to Portugal. Portuguese dissatisfaction with this arrangement led to a meeting at Tordesillas, N Spain, at which it was agreed to move the line to *c.*1700 km (1100mi) W of Cape Verde.

Toronto Capital of ONTARIO province and Canada's largest city, on the N shore of Lake Ontario. The region was first inhabited by NATIVE NORTH AMERICAN tribes, including the SENECA. The first European to visit the site was the French explorer Étienne BRULÉ in 1615. In 1787 the British purchased the site from Native North Americans, and the settlement of York was founded in 1793. During the WAR OF 1812 the city was twice captured by US troops. In 1834 it was renamed Toronto (Huron, meeting place), and it became the capital of Ontario province in 1867. Its development as a major distribution centre was spurred by the opening (1959) of the St Lawrence Seaway. Pop. (1991) 635,395 (metropolitan area: 3,893,046).

Torquemada, Tomás de (1420–98) Spanish churchman and grand inquisitor. A DOMINICAN priest and confessor to FERDINAND V and ISABELLA I, he was appointed head of the Spanish INQUISITION (1483). Torquemada was noted for the severity of his judgments and punishments and the introduction of torture as a means of gaining confessions. He was responsible for *c.*2000 burnings and the expulsion of *c.*160,000 Jews from Spain.

Tory British political faction traditionally opposed to the WHIGS. In 1670 the supporters of the Catholic STUART monarchy were called Tories (Irish bandits) by their opponents. Under JAMES II, the Tories represented the interests of landowners and supported the royal prerogative. They maintained close links to the CHURCH OF ENGLAND and favoured an isolationist foreign policy. The Tories, led by Robert HARLEY, were at their most powerful in the reign of Queen ANNE. They were later discredited by association with the JACOBITES and were excluded from power when GEORGE I acceded to the throne. In the late 18th century accusations of Toryism were levelled at independent Whigs, such as William PITT (THE YOUNGER). The Reform Bill of 1832 split the Tories, and the CONSERVATIVE PARTY was formed from its remnants. *See also* PEEL, SIR ROBERT; REFORM ACTS; TAMWORTH MANIFESTO

Tostig (d.1066) Anglo-Saxon noble, son of GODWIN. In 1055 he was made Earl of NORTHUMBRIA, but his rule was unpopular. In 1065 a revolt against him led his brother, HAROLD II, to replace him with Earl Morcar. Tostig went into exile, but returned in 1066 with HARALD III of Norway. Their invasion was defeated and they were both killed at the Battle of STAMFORD BRIDGE.

totalitarianism Form of government in which the state tries to acquire total control of every aspect of social and individual activity or thought, by means of controlling the mass media and suppression of opposition through the use of the police or army, often accompanied by terror tactics and assassination. The term arose in the 1920s to describe Italian FASCISM and has since been applied to the Soviet Union, Germany under the NAZI PARTY, and many other states. *See also* ARENDT, HANNAH; AUTHORITARIANISM

totemism Complex collection of ideas held by certain primitive societies about the relationships between human beings and the animals or plants around them. The natural objects or people with which many tribal societies believe they have a kinship or mystical relationship, are called totems. Members of a totem group are prohibited from marrying others of the same group and from killing or eating their totem. Elaborate, often secret, rituals form an important part of totemistic behaviour.

Touré, Ahmed Sékou (1922–84) African statesman, first president of GUINEA (1958–84). An active trade union leader and nationalist, Touré was first elected to the French National Assembly in 1951. However, he was barred from taking his seat until 1956, having been elected the mayor of Conakry a year earlier. In 1957 Touré became vice president in the Guinean executive council and in the following year advocated independence in a referendum granted by Charles DE GAULLE. As president, Touré had no French support and was forced to seek aid from Russia. Although his rule was often harsh, he was viewed as a moderate Islamic leader. Touré was an influential mediator in the IRAN-IRAQ WAR (1980–88) and a member of the ORGANIZATION FOR AFRICAN UNITY (OAU).

Toussaint L'Ouverture, Pierre Dominique (1744–1803) Haitian revolutionary leader. The son of an educated slave, he was legally freed in 1777. In 1791 Toussaint took part in the slave revolt in HAITI. He briefly joined the British and Spanish when they attacked the French on the island in 1793, persuading Jean Jacques DESSALINES and Henri CHRISTOPHE to join him. In 1794 because the French NATIONAL CONVENTION had recently abolished slavery, he swapped sides and fought with the French in securing the Spanish withdrawal. By 1801 Toussaint had gained control of virtually the whole island of Hispaniola and freed the slaves. In 1802 NAPOLEON sent a military force to restore French control over Haiti. Toussaint was forced to surrender and died a prisoner in France. In 1804 Haiti achieved independence.

Townshend, Charles, 2nd Viscount (1674–1738) British Whig statesman. Robert WALPOLE's brother-in-law, he helped to arrange GEORGE I's accession to the throne in 1714 and, as secretary for the Northern Department, suppressed the JACOBITE rebellion of 1715. Following a disagreement with George I over foreign policy, Townshend was removed from office and Walpole resigned in sympathy. When Walpole came to power in 1721, Townshend was appointed as secretary of state. In this post he pursued an aggressive foreign policy, favouring an alliance with France and Prussia in place of an agreement with Austria and Spain. His heavy handedness resulted in Walpole's frequent intervention and Townshend was forced to resign in 1730. After politics Townshend devoted his retirement to agricultural improvements, thus earning the nickname "Turnip Townshend", and was an influential figure in the AGRICULTURAL REVOLUTION.

Townshend Acts (1767) Four pieces of British legislation that imposed taxes levied on the American colonies and created a powerful American Board of Customs Commissioners responsible for collecting revenue. Proposed by the chancellor of the exchequer, Charles Townshend, grandson of the Whig statesman Charles TOWNSHEND, the taxes were to provide revenue to defray the cost of colonial government. Taxes were imposed on American imports such as paper, lead, glass and tea. The fierce and often violent adverse colonial reaction ("taxation without representation is tyranny") caused the repeal (1770) of all duties except that on tea.

Towton Field Site of a battle (1461) in the Wars of the ROSES in which the House of YORK under EDWARD IV defeated the House of LANCASTER supporters of Queen MARGARET OF ANJOU and HENRY VI. Fought near Tadcaster, N England, in appalling weather conditions, casualties on both sides were heavy, and the Lancastrians lost some of their finest military leaders.

Toyotomi Hideyoshi *See* HIDEYOSHI

Tractarianism *See* OXFORD MOVEMENT

Trades Union Congress (TUC) Permanent association of British trade UNIONS. The TUC was founded in 1868 to promote trade union principles. In 1871 it established a parliamentary committee to lobby members of Parliament, and in 1900 it helped to form the Labour Representation Committee, the future LABOUR PARTY. Influential in organizing unions during the GENERAL STRIKE, by the 1930s and 1940s the TUC had become the mouthpiece for Britain's labour force. During World War 2 the TUC worked closely with the government, planning and mobilizing the industrial war effort, and until Margaret THATCHER came to power it was included in government economic policy-making. During the 1990s the TUC attempted to align itself more closely with the business community, but although a Labour Party came to power in 1997 the TUC did not regain its former level of influence. Each year it holds an annual assembly of delegates who discuss common problems. Today, the TUC has *c.*7 million members.

trade union *See* UNION

Trafalgar, Battle of (21 October 1805) British naval victory over the French and Spanish fleets off Cape Trafalgar, S Spain. The British, under the command of Admiral Cuthbert COLLINGWOOD, were blockading the French-Spanish fleet at CÁDIZ when NAPOLEON I ordered the fleet to sail to Naples to support a campaign in S Italy. The French-Spanish navy slipped harbour hoping to avoid a confrontation, but the English fleet, led by Lord Horatio NELSON and Collingwood, attacked. The victory was secured by the skilful tactics of Nelson. He attacked the French column at right angles with two divisions and engaged in fighting at close quarters, taking 18 French ships with no British losses. Nelson was killed in the Battle. It ended Napoleon's plans for an invasion of England and establish British naval supremacy for the next 100 years.

Trail of Tears (1838–39) Forced migration of CHEROKEE Native North Americans to new reservations W of the Mississippi River in OKLAHOMA territory to make way for white settlement. Under the INDIAN REMOVAL ACT (1830), President Andrew JACKSON enforced the eviction of *c.*15,000 Cherokee from Georgia. US General Winfield SCOTT directed the 116-day forced march in which *c.*4000 Cherokee died from disease, malnutrition, or exhaustion.

Trajan (AD 53–117) Roman emperor (98–117), b. Spain. After serving in the Roman army he was made consul (91)

TONGA

AREA: 747sq km (288sq mi)
POPULATION: 107,000
CAPITAL (POPULATION): Nuku'alofa (29,018)
GOVERNMENT: Constitutional monarchy
ETHNIC GROUPS: Tongan 96%
LANGUAGES: Tongan, English (both official)
RELIGIONS: Wesleyan Methodist 43%, Roman Catholic 15%
GDP PER CAPITA (1994): US$1482

T

by DOMITIAN. He further distinguished himself as a general and administrator and was made junior co-emperor by NERVA in 97. With army support, Trajan became emperor on Nerva's death. Under his rule, the ROMAN EMPIRE grew to its greatest extent. Trajan conducted major campaigns in DACIA (101–102, 105–106) and PARTHIA (*c*.113–117), conquering Upper MESOPOTAMIA and capturing the Parthian capital CTESIPHON. Trajan implemented the construction of many public works, including a new section of the APPIAN WAY. Trajan's Column, built (*c*.106–113) in ROME to commemorate his campaigns in Dacia, is still extant. Much of our knowledge of his reign comes from PLINY THE YOUNGER, whom Trajan appointed as governor of BITHYNIA-Pontus. He was succeeded by HADRIAN.

Transalpine Gaul (Gallia Transalpina) In ancient ROME, the territory bounded by the Alps, the Pyrenees, the Rhine, the English Channel, the Atlantic and the Mediterranean. Transalpine Gaul was distinguished from CISALPINE GAUL, or Gaul "this side of the Alps". After making its first incursions into the region in 121 BC, Rome completed its conquest of Transalpine Gaul after the GALLIC WARS. AUGUSTUS divided the region into four administrative provinces (27 BC), a division that lasted until the 4th century AD. Gallia Narbonensis, in the S; Aquitania from the Cévennes to the River Loire; Gallia Lugdunensis, between the rivers Seine, Loire and Saône; and Gallia Belgica, between the rivers Seine and Rhine and up to the North Sea.

Transcaucasia Former republic of the SOVIET UNION, corresponding to present-day ARMENIA, AZERBAIJAN and GEORGIA. Created in 1918 after the RUSSIAN REVOLUTION, it was re-formed in 1922 and granted full republic status in 1924. Georgia, Azerbaijan and Armenia were re-established as separate republics in 1936 and gained independence on the break-up of the SOVIET UNION in 1990.

Transjordan Region that today coincides with the kingdom of JORDAN. Called Transjordan from the early 1900s, the region officially became the Hashemite Kingdom of Jordan in 1949.

transportation Policy originating in England in the 17th century of sending criminals to the colonies for life, or shorter periods. They were sent to America until the AMERICAN REVOLUTION and then, from 1788, to AUSTRALIA, where the first penal colony was established at Port Jackson (SYDNEY). More than 160,000 convicts of mixed sex were sent to Australia until 1868, when the policy was finally abolished.

Trans-Siberian Railway Russian railway running from MOSCOW round Lake Baikal to Vladivostok. The world's longest railway, the major part, E from Chelyabinsk, was built between 1891 and 1905, giving Russia access to the Pacific via a link with the Chinese Eastern Railroad in Manchuria. Its total length is *c*.9000km (5750mi) and the journey today takes six days to complete.

transubstantiation Belief accepted by the Roman CATHOLIC CHURCH that, during the prayer of consecration at the Mass (the Eucharist), the "substance" of the bread and wine is changed into the "substance" of the body and blood of JESUS CHRIST, while the "accidents" (the outward forms of the bread and wine) remain unchanged. The doctrine was defined at the LATERAN COUNCIL of 1215. The definition involving "substance" and "accidents" was rejected by the architects of the REFORMATION.

Transvaal Former province of SOUTH AFRICA. In the 18th century the indigenous population were the Venda, Sotho and other Bantu-speaking peoples. In the 1820s and 1830s the NDEBELE began to move into the area, as did the European AFRIKANERS (Boers). In the GREAT TREK (1836), the Afrikaners crossed the River Vaal and began to settle, forming the South African Republic in 1857. The republic was annexed by the British in 1877, but after the First SOUTH AFRICAN WAR (1880–81), Transvaal regained internal self-government under the new president, Paul KRUGER. The 1886 discovery of gold in Witwatersrand attracted vast numbers of Britons and Germans (UITLANDERS). The Afrikaners imposed heavy taxation and denied political rights to the newcomers. In 1895 Leander Starr JAMESON launched an incursion into Transvaal. The JAMESON RAID failed to ignite a full-scale rebellion, but the resultant tension between the Afrikaners and the British led to the second of the South African Wars (1899–1902). By the Treaty of VEREENIGING (1902), Transvaal became a British crown colony. In 1907 the region was again allowed self-government under Louis BOTHA, and in 1910 it became a founding province of the Union of South Africa. During the 1960s the APARTHEID government created separate tribal "homelands" (BANTUSTANS). In 1995 Transvaal ceased to exist as a political entity and was split into four of South Africa's nine new provinces: Northern Province, Mpumalanga, Gauteng and North-West Province.

Transylvania (Romanian, Beyond the Forest) High plateau region in central and NW ROMANIA, separated from the rest of Romania by the Carpathian Mountains and the Transylvanian Alps. In AD 107 it became part of the Roman province of DACIA. It was conquered by HUNGARY at the beginning of the 11th century. In 1526 the ruler of Transylvania, John Zápolya, defeated the Hungarian army, and claimed the Hungarian throne as JOHN I. His claim was supported by the Turks who, following Zápolya's death in 1540, occupied Transylvania on the pretext of ensuring his son's succession. For the next two centuries Transylvania retained a semi-independent status as it played off the competing imperial claims of Turkey and Austria. During the 17th century it flourished as Hungary's intellectual and cultural centre, but in 1765 it became an Austrian province. Hungarian supremacy was re-established in 1867. After World War 1 Hungary ceded the territory to Romania, which embarked on a wholesale process of land redistribution and forced assimilation of other nationalities. Hungary annexed part of Transylvania in World War 2, but was forced to return it in 1947.

Traoré, Moussa (1936–) Mali dictator and army lieutenant, president (1969–91). In 1968 Traoré overthrew President Modibo KEITA in an army coup and founded the Military Committee for National Liberation (CMLN). After a number of attempted coups and anti-government demonstrations, he established a single-party civilian state in 1979 and was elected president. He was re-elected in 1985. Despite attempts at liberalizing the economy and introducing political reforms, continued anti-government protests were brutally suppressed by the security forces (1991). Traoré was overthrown by the army and in 1993 was sentenced to death after being convicted for the murder of demonstrators. The sentence was commuted to life imprisonment in 1997, but in 1999 Traoré was again sentenced to death following convictions for fraud.

Trappists Popular name for the CISTERCIANS of the Strict Observance, a religious order of monks and nuns that originated in La Trappe Abbey, France, in 1664, before moving to Citeaux in 1892. Splitting into three congregations as they spread worldwide, Trappists were united by papal decree in 1893. They maintain complete silence and practise vegetarianism.

treaty port Ports, mainly in China but also in Japan, that were established in the 19th century by the so-called UNEQUAL TREATIES, where foreigners had special trading rights. In China, the first treaty ports (Amoy, GUANGZHOU, Fuzhou, Ningpo and SHANGHAI) were opened to the British by the Treaty of NANJING (1842) ending the OPIUM WARS. By 1911 there were 50 treaty ports in China, open to various Western nations. Westerners resided in and conducted business in treaty ports under conditions of extraterritoriality: they remained outside the laws of the country and under the dominion of their home governments. In Japan, the Treaty of KANAGAWA (1858) opened the first treaty ports to the United States. Five treaty ports were established, but special treatment was abolished in 1899. In China foreign rights to conduct business in treaty ports lasted until 1946.

TRINIDAD AND TOBAGO

AREA: 5130sq km (1981sq mi)
POPULATION: 1295,000
CAPITAL (POPULATION): Port of Spain (46,222)
GOVERNMENT: Multiparty republic
ETHNIC GROUPS: Black 40%, East Indian 40%, Mixed 18%, White 1%, Chinese 1%
LANGUAGES: English (official), Creole, Hindi
RELIGIONS: Roman Catholic 29%, Hindu 24%, Anglican 11%, Muslim 6%
GDP PER CAPITA (1995): US$8610

Trebizond empire State established by the Byzantines in the early 13th century. The Black Sea port of Trebizond (Trabzon), NE Turkey, was founded by the ancient Greeks. When the leaders of the Fourth CRUSADE seized Constantinople (now Istanbul) in 1204, refugees established the empire of Trebizond. It prospered on trade and continued an independent existence until conquered by the Ottomans in 1461. *See also* BYZANTINE EMPIRE

Trent, Council of (1545–63) Nineteenth ECUMENICAL COUNCIL of the ROMAN CATHOLIC CHURCH, which provided the main impetus of the COUNTER-REFORMATION in Europe. It met at Trent, N Italy, in three sessions under three popes (PAUL III, Julius III, PIUS IV). It clarified Catholic doctrine and refused concessions to the Protestants, while instituting reform of many of the abuses that had provoked the REFORMATION.

Trent Affair (1861) Diplomatic incident between Britain and the United States during the American CIVIL WAR. When Union Captain Charles WILKES seized Confederate commissioners James MASON and John SLIDELL from the British ship *Trent*, Britain claimed its neutrality had been violated and the government was under pressure to declare war on the Union. Union President Abraham LINCOLN and Secretary of State William SEWARD, wishing to avoid war with Britain, released the two men.

Treurnicht, Andries Petrus (1921–93) South African politician, founder of the Conservative Party. A minister (1946–60) in the Dutch Reformed Church, Treurnicht came to prominence as editor of the Pretoria newspaper *Hoofstad*. He was elected to Parliament (1971), where he was a staunch supporter of APARTHEID. His decision to enforce the teaching of Afrikaans precipitated the SOWETO rising (1976). In 1982 Treurnicht resigned from the NATIONAL PARTY after its proposal to establish separate elective chambers for non-whites, and established the far-right Conservative Party. Treurnicht was re-elected to Parliament in 1983, and after the 1989 election he led the opposition to F.W. DE KLERK's National government.

triad Chinese secret society. Triad societies existed in S China from the earliest days of the QING empire in the 17th century. Founded to restore the MING dynasty, triad societies assumed greater political influence after lending their support to the TAIPING REBELLION. Still influential in some of the larger Chinese cities, today triads are believed to control Chinese organized crime throughout the world. Their chief centre is in Hong Kong.

trial by jury *See* JURY

trial by ordeal *See* ORDEAL

Trianon, Treaty of (1920) Peace agreement between HUNGARY and the ALLIES at the end of WORLD WAR I. Its issuance and acceptance was delayed until the establishment of stable government in Hungary. By its terms, Hungary lost around half its population and two-thirds of its territory, all non-Magyar land, to Czechoslovakia, Austria, Yugoslavia, Romania and Italy. Its army was limited to 35,000 troops and a schedule of reparations was established. Hungary signed the Treaty under protest.

Triassic First period of the MESOZOIC era, lasting from *c*.248 to 13 million years ago. Many new kinds of animals developed. On land, the first dinosaurs roamed. Mammal-like reptiles were common, and by the end of the period the first true mammals existed. In the seas lived the first ichthyosaurs, placodonts and nothosaurs. The first frogs, turtles, crocodilians and lizards also appeared. Plant life consisted mainly of primitive gymnosperms.

tribune Official of ancient ROME. Of the various kinds of tribune, some had military functions, some political. The tribunes of the PLEBEIANS, generally ten in number and elected annually, gained an important role under the ROMAN REPUBLIC by offering a political balance to the PATRICIAN classes. In the 2nd century BC, GRACCHUS used the office to pursue radical social reforms.

Trieste City on the Gulf of Trieste, at the head of the Adriatic Sea, NE Italy. It was an imperial free port from

1719 to 1891, becoming an Austrian crown land in 1867. It was ceded to Italy in 1919, occupied by Yugoslavia in 1945, but returned to Italy in 1954. Pop. (1992) 228,398.

Trimble, David (1944–) Northern Irish statesman, first minister of Northern IRELAND (1998–). He entered the British Parliament in 1990. In 1995 Trimble succeeded James Molyneaux as leader of the Ulster Unionist Party. After the GOOD FRIDAY AGREEMENT (10 April 1998), he became first minister of the Northern Ireland Assembly. In 1998 Trimble and John HUME, leader of the nationalist SOCIAL DEMOCRATIC AND LABOUR PARTY (SDLP), shared the Nobel Prize for Peace for their efforts to find a peaceful solution to the conflict in Northern Ireland. In 2000, following the suspension of the Northern Ireland Assembly, Trimble persuaded the Ulster Unionists to accept continued power-sharing following the IRISH REPUBLICAN ARMY (IRA)'s proposal of putting their weapons beyond use, and the Assembly was reinstated. *See also* ULSTER UNIONISTS

Trinidad and Tobago Republic composed of the two southernmost islands of the Lesser Antilles in the SE Caribbean. Originally inhabited by ARAWAK and CARIB Native Americans, the larger island of **Trinidad** lies only 11km (7mi) off the Venezuelan coast. The Spanish colonized the island in the 16th century, but it was ceded to Britain in 1802. **Tobago** lies 30km (19mi) NE of Trinidad. It was initially settled by the British in 1616. After Spanish, Dutch and French rule, in 1803 it became a British possession. In 1883 Trinidad and Tobago were integrated into a single crown colony, which became an independent state in 1962 and a republic in 1976. In 1990 the prime minister, Arthur Robinson, was captured and later released in an attempted coup. After 1995 elections, a coalition of the United National Congress and the Alliance for Reconstruction came to power, with Basdeo Panday as prime minister. *See* WEST INDIES map

Trinity Central doctrine of CHRISTIANITY, according to which God is three persons: the Father, the Son and the Holy Spirit or Holy Ghost. There is only one God, but he exists as "three in one and one in three". The nature of the Trinity is held to be a mystery that cannot be fully comprehended. The doctrine of the Trinity was stated in early Christian creeds to counter heresies such as GNOSTICISM. *See also* APOSTLES' CREED; ATHANASIAN CREED; JESUS CHRIST; NICENE CREED

Tripartite Pact (27 September 1940) Military and political alliance signed between Germany, Italy and Japan. Known as the AXIS POWERS, the signatories pledged full military and political cooperation.

Triple Alliance Several international alliances involving three states. Among them was the anti-French alliance of Britain, the Netherlands and Sweden (1668), which was formalized by the Treaty of AIX-LA-CHAPELLE. Another was the alliance of Britain, France and the Netherlands (1717), under which all parties agreed to uphold the terms of the Peace of UTRECHT (1714), which had concluded the War of the SPANISH SUCCESSION, and help each other in the event of any internal uprisings. The most recent in Europe was the Triple Alliance of 1882, when Italy joined the Dual Alliance of Austria-Hungary and Germany. It was a secret agreement, instigated by German Chancellor Otto von BISMARCK, and under its terms the three powers agreed to support each other in the event of an attack by France or Russia. In South America, Argentina, Brazil and Uruguay fought the so-called War of the TRIPLE ALLIANCE (1865–70) against Paraguay.

Triple Alliance, War of the (1865–70) Conflict between Paraguay on one side and Argentina, Brazil and Uruguay on the other. Long-standing territorial disputes and Brazilian intervention in the Uruguayan civil war prompted Francisco Solano LÓPEZ of Paraguay to declare war on Brazil in March 1865; by May 1865 the conflict involved all four countries. The war devastated Paraguay; one million Paraguayan lives and 142,450sq km (55,000sq mi) of Paraguayan territory were lost.

Triple Entente Name given to the alliance of Britain, France and Russia before WORLD WAR I. It developed from the Franco-Russian Alliance (1894), a counter-balance to the threat posed by the TRIPLE ALLIANCE of Germany, Austria and Italy. Britain became allied with France in the ENTENTE CORDIALE (1904), and the Anglo-Russian Convention of 1907 completed the Triple Entente. However, Britain did not make a formal pledge of military support for France and Russia in the event of an attack by Germany.

Tripoli Capital and chief port of LIBYA, on the Mediterranean Sea. The city was founded in the 7th century BC by the PHOENICIANS and developed by the Romans. From the 7th century AD the Arabs developed Tripoli as a market centre for the trans-Saharan caravans. In 1551 it was captured by the OTTOMAN Turks. It was made the capital of the Italian colony of Libya in 1911, and during World War 2 it functioned as an important base for Axis forces before its capture by the British in 1943. In 1986 Tripoli was bombed by the US Air Force in retaliation for Libya's support of terrorism. The city is the commercial, industrial, transport and communications centre of Libya. Pop. (1984) 990,697.

Tripoli Mediterranean port and second-largest city in LEBANON. It was an important city of the SELEUCID and Roman empires. Captured in AD 638 by the Arabs, in 1109 Tripoli was conquered by the Crusaders, who developed the city's fortifications. In 1289 it returned to Islamic rule under the Egyptian MAMLUKS. The Turks held the city until the arrival of the British in 1918, and in 1920 it became a Lebanese city. It suffered severe damage during the 1975–76 Lebanese civil war. The city remains an important centre for trade between Syria and Lebanon, and it is the terminus of the oil pipeline from Iraq. Pop. (1991) 203,000.

Tripolitania Historic region in W LIBYA. In the 7th century BC three Phoenician colonies were founded on the N African coast, which developed into an E province of the state of CARTHAGE. Following the collapse of Carthage in 146 BC, the state was ruled first by NUMIDIA and then, from 46 BC, the Romans, who gave it the name of Tripolitania (meaning "Three Cities"). It was subsequently ruled by the VANDALS, Byzantines, Arabs and the KNIGHTS HOSPITALLERS. In 1557 it fell to the OTTOMAN EMPIRE and in the 18th century engaged in piracy as one of the BARBARY STATES. Tripolitania became part of the Italian colony of Libya in 1912, was captured by the British in 1943, and in 1951 became part of the independent state of Libya. *See also* TUNISIA

Tripolitan War (1801–05) Conflict between TRIPOLITANIA and the United States. For several years the United States had made an annual payment to Tripolitania and the other BARBARY STATES in exchange for protection from pirate attacks on its shipping. When, in 1801, the *bey* (governor) of Tripolitania demanded an increase in this payment, the United States sent a naval squadron to Tripolitania. Fighting continued until an American naval blockade and an overland expedition forced the *bey* to sign a treaty (1805) with the United States in which he gave up all rights to levy tributes on US ships. The other Barbary states continued to receive reduced payments until 1815.

TUNISIA

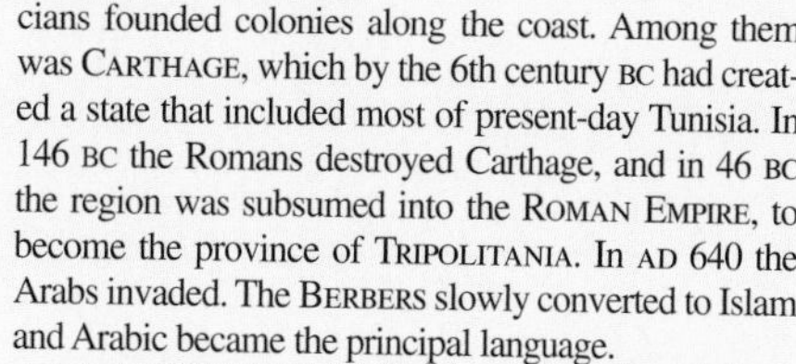

Smallest country in N Africa. From the 12th century BC the Phoenicians founded colonies along the coast. Among them was CARTHAGE, which by the 6th century BC had created a state that included most of present-day Tunisia. In 146 BC the Romans destroyed Carthage, and in 46 BC the region was subsumed into the ROMAN EMPIRE, to become the province of TRIPOLITANIA. In AD 640 the Arabs invaded. The BERBERS slowly converted to Islam and Arabic became the principal language.

In 1159 the ALMOHAD dynasty conquered Tunisia. From 1230 to 1574 Tunisia was ruled by the Hafsids. Spain's capture of ports on Tunisia's coast led to the intervention of the OTTOMAN EMPIRE, and from 1574 to 1881 Tunisia was part of the Ottoman Empire. However, in 1612 a dynasty of *beys* (provincial governors) was established which was to become increasingly independent. In 1801 the *bey* led Tunisia into the TRIPOLITAN WAR with the United States.

In 1881 France invaded and Tunisia became a French protectorate (1883). French rule aroused strong nationalist sentiment, and Habib BOURGUIBA formed the Destour Socialist Party (PSD) in 1934. Tunisia was a major battleground of the North Africa campaigns in World War 2. In 1956 it gained independence. In 1957 the *bey* was deposed and Tunisia became a republic, with Bourguiba as president. In 1975 Bourguiba was proclaimed president-for-life, and in 1981 the first multiparty elections were held.

AREA: 163,610sq km (63,170sq mi)
POPULATION: 8,410,000
CAPITAL (POPULATION): Tunis (674,100)
GOVERNMENT: Multiparty republic
ETHNIC GROUPS: Arab 98%, Berber 1%, French and other 1%
LANGUAGES: Arabic (official), French
RELIGIONS: Islam 99%
GDP PER CAPITA (1995): US$5000

In the 1980s Bourguiba's failing health created a succession crisis, and he was deposed by Zine el Abidine Ben Ali in 1987. The PSD became the Constitutional Democratic Rally (RCD), and Ben Ali won a landslide victory in 1989 elections. He was re-elected in 1994 and 1999. The hegemony of the RCD remains a problem for its fledgling democracy.

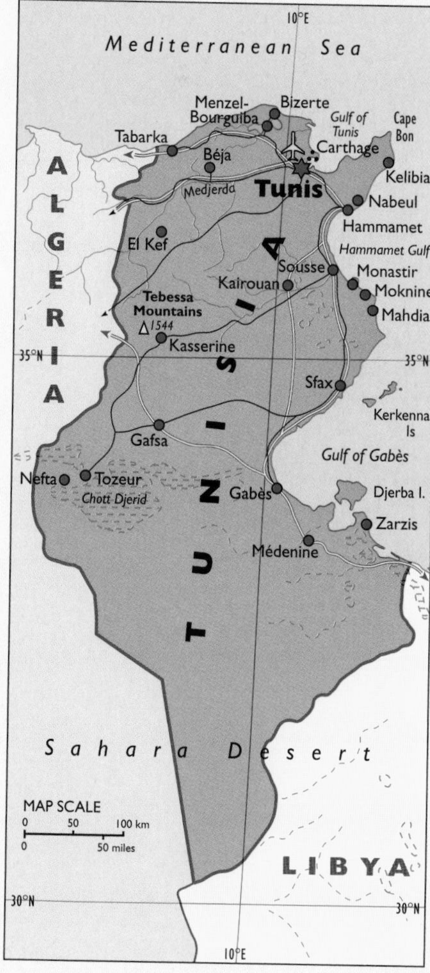

Tromp, Maarten (1598–1653) Dutch admiral, chiefly responsible for the Netherlands' naval victories in the early 17th century. His destruction of a Spanish armada at the Battle of the Downs (1639) effectively ended Spain's naval power. In the First Dutch War (1652–54), Tromp defeated Admiral Robert Blake off Dungeness, SE England, but was later killed while trying to break an English blockade of the Dutch coast.

Trotsky, Leon (1879–1940) Russian revolutionary leader and theoretician, b. Lev Davidovich Bronstein. A Marxist revolutionary from 1897, he headed the workers' soviet in St Petersburg in the Russian Revolution of 1905. Arrested, Trotsky escaped abroad and embarked on the work that made him, with Vladimir Lenin, the leading architect of the Russian Revolution of 1917. He returned to Russia after the Revolution, and joined the Bolsheviks. As chairman of the Petrograd (St Petersburg) Soviet, Trotsky set up the Military Revolutionary Committee to seize power, ostensibly for the Soviet, actually for the Bolsheviks. After the Bolshevik success, he negotiated the Treaty of Brest-Litovsk (1918), withdrawing Russia from World War I. As commissar of war (1918–25), Trotsky created the Red Army, which won the Russian Civil War and made the Bolshevik revolution safe. However, he criticized the growth of bureaucracy in the Communist Party, the lack of democracy and the failure to expand industrialization. Trotsky disapproved of Lenin's dictatorial tendencies in power and fiercely objected to Joseph Stalin's adoption of a policy of "socialism in one country", rather than the worldwide "permanent revolution" in which Trotsky believed. He was driven from power, from the Party, and eventually from the country. In exile, Trotsky continued to write prolifically on many subjects. His ideas, although rejected by the Soviet Union, were extremely influential internationally, especially in Third World countries. In 1936 Trotsky settled in Mexico, where he was assassinated by a Stalinist agent.

Trotskyism Interpretation of Marxism conceived by Leon Trotsky. In contrast to Joseph Stalin, who tried to create "socialism in one country", Trotsky argued that there must be "permanent revolution", not in isolation, but in all the industrialized countries ideally at the same time.

Troy (Ilium) Ancient city at what is now Hissarlik, W Turkey, familiar chiefly through Homer's *Iliad*. The book recounts the tale of the 10-year siege of Troy by the Greeks, under Agamemnon, who finally sacked the city. Archaeological excavation, begun by the German archaeologist Heinrich Schliemann in the 1870s, suggests that the legend of the Trojan War may be based on an actual episode. Nine cities have been detected in the archaeological strata, dating from *c*.3000 BC and reaching a peak in Troy VI (*c*.1800–1300 BC). Troy VI was ruined by an earthquake. Its successor, Troy VIIA, was destroyed, apparently by enemy attack, in *c*.1200 BC, close to the legendary date of the fall of Troy. Further archaeological evidence suggests that by *c*.800 BC the city was rebuilt, eventually ceding to Roman rule.

Troyes, Treaty of (1420) Truce in the Hundred Years' War between Charles VI of France, Henry V of England and Philip III (the Good) of Burgundy. By its terms, Henry married Charles' daughter, Catherine of Valois, and was recognized as the heir to the French crown. He died before he could succeed to the throne.

Trucial States Former name for the United Arab Emirates (UAE), seven emirates on the Persian (Arabian) Gulf: Abu Dhabi, Ajman, Dubai, Fujairah, Ras al-Khaimah, Sharjah and Umm al-Qaiwain. The name "trucial" signifies the truces signed with Britain in 1820 (and a later agreement of 1892), by which the emirates accepted British protection and British control of their defence and foreign policies. They joined together in the UAE when Britain withdrew from the Gulf in 1971.

Trudeau, Pierre Elliott (1919–) French-Canadian statesman, prime minister (1968–79, 1980–84). He was minister of justice before becoming leader of the Liberal Party of Canada and succeeding Lester Pearson as prime minister. Trudeau promoted the economic and diplomatic independence of Canada, helping to reduce US influence. In an attempt to improve relations between French-Canadians and English-Canadians, Trudeau implemented the Bilingual Languages Act (1968), which ensured the French language attained the same status as English. Aided by his French-Canadian origins and his advocacy of federalism, he resisted Québec separatism, imposing martial law to combat separatist terrorism in 1970. Heading a minority government from 1972 Trudeau, primarily due to a failing economy and criticized for not preventing US influence, was defeated in the elections of 1979, but was returned to power with a Liberal Party majority in 1980. Autonomy for Québec was rejected in a referendum (1980), and Trudeau succeeded in winning agreement for a revised constitution (1981).

True Levellers *See* Diggers

Trujillo (Molina), Rafael Leónidas (1891–1961) Dictator of the Dominican Republic from 1930 until his death. He seized power in a military coup against President Horacio Vásquez. Although he only served officially as president from 1930 to 1938 and again from 1942 to 1952, Trujillo maintained a grip on power through his control of the army and a succession of puppet rulers. His authoritarian rule brought stability and prosperity to the Dominican Republic. Despite murdering many of his leading opponents, opposition to his dictatorial rule continued and Trujillo was evenutally assassinated by army leaders.

Truman, Harry S (1884–1972) Thirty-third president of the United States (1945–53). He entered politics in the 1920s and, as a Democrat, won election to the Senate in 1934. In 1944 he was Franklin Roosevelt's running mate and became vice president. Truman automatically became president on Roosevelt's death and was faced with many difficulties abroad. He approved the use of the atom bomb to force Japan's surrender (1945) in World War 2, and by implementing the Truman Doctrine adopted a robust policy towards Soviet and Chinese communism during the Cold War. Truman approved the Marshall Plan (1947) and the creation (1949) of the North Atlantic

TURKEY

AREA: 779,450sq km (300,946sq mi)
POPULATION: 58,775,000
CAPITAL (POPULATION): Ankara (2,541,899)
GOVERNMENT: Multiparty republic
ETHNIC GROUPS: Turkish 86%, Kurdish 11%, Arab 2%
LANGUAGES: Turkish (official)
RELIGIONS: Islam 99%
GDP PER CAPITA (1995): US$5580

Country that straddles SE Europe and Asia, encompassing Thrace and Asia Minor. Settled before 7000 BC, Asia Minor was part of the Hittite empire *c*.1900–1200 BC. Greek colonies were established along its coast from the 8th century BC. It was incorporated into the Persian Achaemenid empire in the 6th century BC, becoming a Hellenes kingdom in the 3rd century BC, and part of the Roman Empire in the 1st century BC. Remains of Greek and Roman buildings can be seen at Ephesus, one of the many ruins of the ancient Anatolian kingdoms of Ionia and Pontus. In AD 330 Byzantium (now Istanbul) became capital of the Eastern Roman Empire; thence capital of the Byzantine Empire (398). In the 11th century, the Seljuks introduced Islam, and the capital moved to Konya. In 1435 Constantinople was captured by Muhammad II, and from this date served as capital of the Ottoman Empire.

Defeat in World War I led to the sultan signing the punitive Treaty of Sèvres (1920). Nationalists, led by Mustafa Kemal (Atatürk), launched a war of independence. In 1923 Turkey became a republic, with Atatürk as its president. Atatürk's 14-year dictatorship created a secular, Westernized state. In 1938 Atatürk died and was succeeded by Ismet Inönü. Turkey remained neutral throughout most of World War 2. In 1950 the first multiparty elections were held. A major post-war recipient of US aid, Turkey joined the North Atlantic Treaty Organization (NATO) in 1952.

In 1960 a military coup led to the creation of a second republic. In 1965 Süleyman Demirel became prime minister. In 1974 Turkey invaded Northern Cyprus and tension with Greece increased. In 1980 a military coup led to martial law. In 1987 martial law was lifted. In 1993 Demirel was elected president, and Tansu Çiller became Turkey's first woman prime minister.

In 1995 Necmettin Erbakan of the Islamist Welfare Party (RP) became prime minister. In 1997 tension between the pro-Islamic government and the military led to Erbakan's resignation. A new secular government was formed, led by Mesut Yilmaz of the Motherland Party (ANAP). In 1998 the RP was declared illegal and Yilmaz resigned after allegations of corruption. He was replaced by Bülent Ecevit of the Democratic Left Party (DSP). Since 1984 Turkey has been fighting the Kurdish Workers Party (PKK), which operates in SE Turkey, Syria and N Iraq, and Turkey has often been accused of violating the human rights of Kurds. In 1999 Turkey captured the PKK leader, Abdullah Öcalan. In the same year, NW Turkey was devastated by a major earthquake.

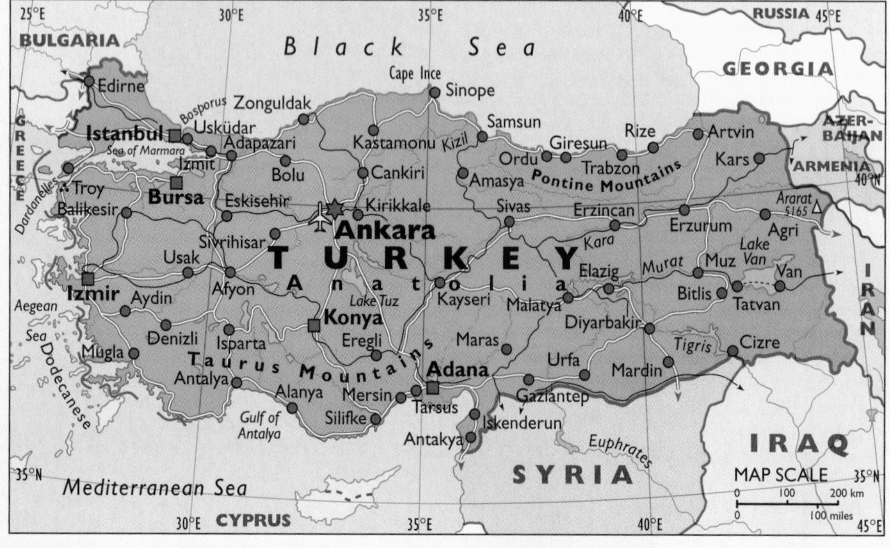

Treaty Organization (NATO). Lacking Roosevelt's charisma, he was expected to lose the election of 1948, but won narrowly. Truman continued Roosevelt's New Deal programme, attempted to implement his own policies in a programme that came to be known as the Fair Deal, and promoted his Point Four Program. Although Congress vetoed many of his proposals, Truman successfully saw through his housing act (1949). In the Korean War (1950–53), he was forced to dismiss US General Douglas MacArthur, who was keen to extend the war into Chinese territory. In 1952 Truman declined renomination. He was succeeded by Dwight Eisenhower.

Truman Doctrine Principle of US foreign policy under President Harry S Truman. Put forward at a time when Greece and Turkey were close to being taken over by communism, it promised military and economic support for any democratic country threatened by foreign domination. In practice, application of the principle was limited. The United States did not act against communist takeovers in Eastern Europe, although it did resist the invasion of South Korea. The policy was given the full support of Congress, but was viewed with hostility by Eastern-bloc countries. *See also* Cold War; Korean War

trust territories Countries administered by the United Nations (UN) as a continuation of the mandate system of the League of Nations. They were former colonial acquisitions of Germany, Italy and Japan that were deemed not to have either the inclination or means to become self-governing. The purpose of the trustee system was to prepare them for self-government. After World War 2 the United Nations established 11 trust territories (British and French Togoland, British and French Cameroons, Somaliland, Ruanda-Urundi, Tanganyika, New Guinea, Nauru, Western Samoa and the Pacific Islands). All have since either become independent or passed to the control of other, newly independent, countries.

Truth, Sojourner (1797–1883) US abolitionist. Born a slave in New York and unable to read or write, she was freed by the New York Emancipation Act (1827). Inspired by a religious calling, she became a leading propagandist for votes for women and abolition of slavery.

Ts'ai Yuan-p'ei *See* Cai Yuanpei

Ts'ao Ts'ao *See* Cao Cao

Tseng Kuo-fan *See* Zeng Guofan

Tshombe, Moise Kapenda (1919–69) Congolese military leader and politician. He participated in the talks that led to the independence of the Belgian Congo (now Democratic Republic of Congo) in 1960 but then declared the secession of the mineral-rich province of Katanga (renamed Shaba). During the ensuing conflict, Tshombe may have been involved in the murder of the former Congolese premier, Patrice Lumumba. After intervention by the United Nations (UN) and the defeat of his troops, he fled to Europe in 1963. He returned as premier of a united Congo in 1964, but he was dismissed in 1965 by President Joseph Kasavubu and went into exile. In 1967 he was kidnapped and taken to Algeria, where he was kept under house arrest until his death in 1969.

Tsushima, Battle of (27–29 May 1905) Major naval engagement in the Russo-Japanese War. The Russian government decided that by combining their Baltic and Pacific fleets they would be able to overcome the Japanese navy. While steaming to the China Sea, however, the Russian commander learned that the Pacific Fleet was being blockaded. He decided to continue with the mission and headed for Vladivostok. Japanese Admiral Togo Heihachiro intercepted the Russian fleet and during the course of the next two days, superior Japanese ships destroyed almost two-thirds of the Russian fleet. Eight Russian battleships, nine cruisers and several other vessels were either sank, disabled or captured.

Tuareg Fiercely independent Berbers of Islamic faith who inhabit the desert regions of n Africa. Their matrilineal, feudal society is based on nomadic pastoralism; it traditionally maintained a class of black, non-Tuareg servants. Tuareg males wear blue veils, while the women are unveiled. About half the population is no longer nomadic, and there have been demands for the Tuareg to have their own homeland.

Tubman, Harriet (1820–1913) US abolitionist. Born a slave in Maryland, she escaped to the North by following the Underground Railroad, a network in which she was later to become highly influential, leading *c*.300 fugitive slaves, including her parents, to freedom during the 1850s. She worked as an agent for the Union during the American Civil War and later became a prominent spokeswoman for abolition and a significant figure in African-American education.

Tubman, William Vacanarat Shadrach (1895–1971) Liberian statesman, president (1944–71). A descendant of US freed slaves who settled in Liberia during the 19th century, Tubman trained and worked as a lawyer before entering politics. A key figure in the Liberian senate from 1923, Tubman was elected president as a member of the True Whig Party. While in office, he preserved Liberia's close connections with the United States, maintained prosperity by attracting foreign investment and showed respect for the customs of the non-Westernized people of the interior.

TUC *See* Trades Union Congress

Tudjman, Franjo (1922–99) Croatian statesman, first president of independent Croatia (1990–99). He fought for Tito's communist Partisans during World War 2, and after the War became the youngest general in the Yugoslav army. Tudjman was twice imprisoned by the Yugoslav government for Croatian nationalist activities during the 1970s and 1980s. In 1989 he founded the right-wing Croatian Democratic Union (HDZ). In January 1990 Croatia seceded from the Federation of Yugoslavia and soon after Tudjman was elected president. Croatia suffered a succession of defeats in the ensuing civil war before Croatian forces seized the initiative and purged central Croatia of Serbs (May 1995). *See also* Dayton Peace Agreement; Izetbeović, Alija; Milošević, Slobodan

Tudors English royal dynasty (1485–1603). Of Welsh origin, they were descended from Owen Tudor (d.1461), who married Catherine of Valois, the widow of Henry V. Their son, Edmund, married the great-granddaughter of John of Gaunt, Margaret Beaufort, (1443–1509), whose son Henry (later Henry VII) thus had a claim to the throne. During the War of the Roses, Henry defeated Richard III at the Battle of Bosworth Field (1485) to win the English throne. A descendant of the House of Lancaster, Henry consolidated the throne by marrying Elizabeth of York, an heiress to the House of York, so ending the long-term rivalry. The Tudor rose symbolically shows the red rose of the Lancastrians superimposed on the white rose of the Yorkists. Henry's eldest son, Arthur, died before attaining the throne, thus he was succeeded by his younger son, Henry VIII. The reign of Henry's only son, Edward VI, was a short-lived minority and he was succeeded by his half-sister Mary I, who died childless, and subsequently by Mary's half-sister Elizabeth I, who never married. When Elizabeth chose the future James I as her successor, the Tudor dynasty was replaced as the ruling royal house by the Stuarts.

Tughluq Muslim dynasty that ruled India (1320–*c*.1412). The dynasty was established when Ghiyas-ud-Din Tughluq (r.1320–25) seized the throne from the last Khalji sultan. Under his son, Muhammad ibn Tughluq (*c*.1290–1351), the Delhi Sultanate achieved its greatest extent, but the empire was ultimately unmanageable. Rebellions broke out throughout Muhammad's territory, and many of the s conquests broke away. Under his successors, the Delhi Sultanate's disintegration was hastened by the invasion of Tamerlane.

Tunisia *See* country feature, page 413

Tupac Amaru (*c*.1742–81) Native South American revolutionary leader in Peru, b. José Gabriel Condorcanqui. Tupac Amaru led (1780–81) an army of more than 10,000 Native Americans in a revolt against Spanish colonial rule. The revolt was ruthlessly quashed and Tupac was executed. A modern Peruvian guerrilla organization, the Tupac Amaru Revolutionary Movement (MRTA), is named after him.

Tupamaros Uruguayan guerrilla organization. Founded (1963) by Raúl Sendic, the Tupamaros (named after Tupac Amaru) began their revolutionary action with bank robberies, distributing the proceeds among the urban poor. From 1968, they turned to more violent means, including arson, kidnapping and assassination, to overturn the government with the aim of establishing a Marxist state. After reaching their peak in the early 1970s, they were crucially weakened by a hardline military and police crackdown that imprisoned 3000 members and killed another 300. After 1985, when democracy was restored, the Tupamaros became a legal political party.

Turenne, Henri de La Tour d'Auvergne (1611–75) French marshal. He distinguished himself against the Bavarians in the Thirty Years' War (1618–48) and in the European wars of Louis XIV. He was involved in the Fronde rebellion (1650–53), briefly joining the anti-royalist faction, but he then switched his support to the young Louis XIV. Given command of an army by Jules Mazarin, he quickly recovered Paris from the forces of Louis II, Prince de Condé.

TURKMENISTAN

AREA: 488,100sq km (188,450sq mi)
POPULATION: 3,714,000
CAPITAL (POPULATION): Ashgabat (or Ashkhabad, 412,200)
GOVERNMENT: Single party republic
ETHNIC GROUPS: Turkmen 72%, Russian 10%, Uzbek 9%, Kazak 3%, Tatar
LANGUAGES: Turkmen (official)
RELIGIONS: Islam
GDP PER CAPITA (1994): US$2023

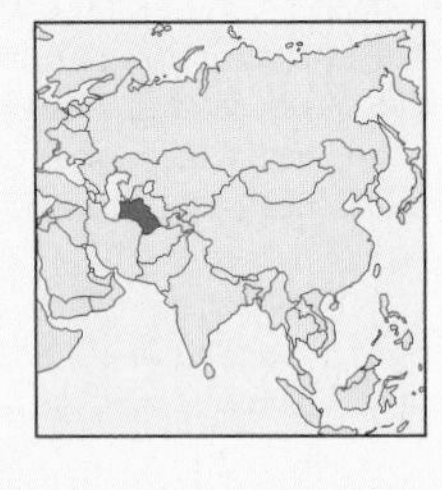

Republic in central Asia. Originally part of the Persian empire, it was overrun by Arabs in the 7th and 8th centuries AD. Genghis Khan invaded in the 13th century, and it became part of Tamerlane's vast empire in the late 14th century. With the break-up of the Timurid dynasty, Turkmenistan came under Uzbek control. In the 19th century Russia became increasingly dominant. In 1899, despite resistance, Turkmenistan became part of Russian Turkistan. In 1925, as part of the Turkistan Autonomous Soviet Socialist Republic, it was absorbed into the Soviet Union.

In 1991 it achieved independence and became a full member of the Commonwealth of Independent States (CIS) in 1993. In 1990 Saparmurad Niyazov (1940–) was elected president. His autocratic government prevented any political opposition to the ruling Democratic Party (formerly Communist Party). In a 1994 referendum, Niyazov's term of presidency was extended to 2002.

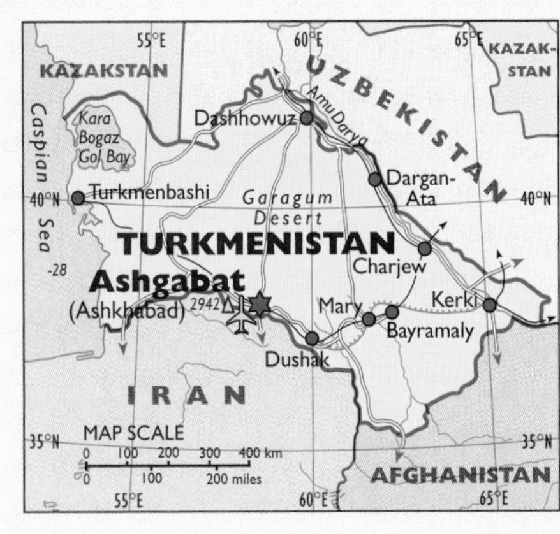

T

Turgot, Anne Robert Jacques (1721–81) French economist. Chief administrator for Limoges (1761–74) under LOUIS XV and comptroller general of finance (1774–76) under LOUIS XVI, Turgot was heavily influenced by the PHYSIOCRATS. His attempts to set France's fiscal house in order by introducing taxation reforms were unsuccessful and his Six Edicts of 1776, in which he advocated the taxation of the nobility, alienated a number of influential factions and led to his downfall.

Turin (Torino) City on the River Po, NW Italy, capital of PIEDMONT region. A Roman town under AUGUSTUS, Turin became part of the LOMBARD kingdom in the 6th century and then part of the empire of the FRANKS. Linked to SAVOY by dynastic marriage from the 11th century, it became the capital of the duchy of Savoy in 1563. From 1720 to 1861 it was capital of the kingdom of SARDINIA and a centre of the RISORGIMENTO. Its Romanesque cathedral (1492–98) houses the Turin Shroud, said by tradition to be the cloth in which the body of Jesus Christ was wrapped after the crucifixion. Pop. (1992) 952,736.

Turkey *See* country feature, page 414

Turkistan (Turkestan) Historic region of central Asia, inhabited by Turkic-speaking peoples. **Western** (Russian) Turkistan now consists of the republics of TURKMENISTAN, UZBEKISTAN, TAJIKISTAN, KYRGYZSTAN and S KAZAKSTAN. It mainly comprises the deserts of Kyzyl Kum and Kara Kum. **Eastern** (Chinese) Turkistan comprises the Chinese region of XINJIANG and includes the Tian Shan mountains. **Southern** Turkistan consists of part of N AFGHANISTAN. For nearly two centuries Turkistan was the geographical bridge for trade between East and West. The first imperial power to control the region was Persia (Iran) in 500 BC, but in *c*.330 BC ALEXANDER III (THE GREAT) defeated the Persians and for the next few centuries the region was disputed between BACTRIA, PARTHIA and China. Market towns developed around the oases, and developed into centres for trade and religion. In the 7th and 8th centuries the Arabs conquered the region, and the local population was converted to Islam. During the 13th century, the region was controlled by the MONGOLS, but then fractured into small, independent khanates. In 1867 the Russian empire imposed military rule over the area. Following the RUSSIAN REVOLUTION (1917), Turkistan became an autonomous region within the SOVIET UNION in 1922. In 1924 the S part of Turkistan was divided into the republics of Uzbekistan and Turkmenistan; in 1929 Tajikistan became a republic and Kyrgyzstan followed in 1936. The N part of Russian Turkistan was incorporated into the Kazak republic, and what remained became known as **Soviet Central Asia**.

Turkmenistan *See* country feature, page 415

Turks and Caicos Islands Two island groups of the British WEST INDIES, including more than 40 islands, eight of them inhabited. The capital is Cockburn Town on Grand Turk Island. Discovered in 1512 by the Spaniard PONCE DE LEÓN, the islands remained uninhabited until 1678, after which the islands were settled by people from Bermuda. The islands were British from 1766, administered via Jamaica from 1873 to 1959, and a separate crown colony from 1973. Area: 430sq km (166sq mi). Pop (1990) 12,350.

T

Turner, Nat (1800–31) US revolutionary. A slave in Southampton County, Virginia, he believed that he was called by God to take violent revenge on whites and to win freedom for African Americans. With *c*.70 followers, he instigated the "Southampton Insurrection" during which he was responsible for the deaths of more than 60 whites before the revolt was crushed. Turner was captured, convicted and hanged.

Tuscan order One of the five ORDERS OF ARCHITECTURE

Tuscany Region in central Italy between the Mediterranean coast and the Apennine mountains; the capital is FLORENCE. Other cities include SIENA and PISA. Settled by an ETRUSCAN tribe *c*.1000 BC (hence its name), Tuscany passed into Roman control in the 3rd century BC, before passing through the hands of the OSTROGOTHS and LOMBARDS. In AD 774 the region was taken over by CHARLEMAGNE and became part of the empire of the FRANKS. By the 11th century Tuscany was the possession of the powerful Attoni family, but when the dynasty collapsed Tuscany fragmented into a number of independent cities. Under the MEDICI, Tuscany became a unified principality and a cultural centre of the RENAISSANCE. During the 16th century its influence waned but was largely restored under Emperor FRANCIS I and his son LEOPOLD II. Annexed to the French empire under NAPOLEON, with Napoleon's defeat the region passed back to the HABSBURG-Lorraine dynasty. After the REVOLUTIONS OF 1848, Tuscany briefly became a republic. In 1861 Tusacny became part of the kingdom of Italy. Area: 22,992sq km (8877sq mi). Pop (1990) 3,528,735.

Tuscarora War (1711–13) Series of expeditions by colonists from North Carolina, South Carolina and Virginia against the Tuscarora, who had attacked North Carolina settlers because of encroachments on NATIVE NORTH AMERICAN lands. Defeated in 1713, the Tuscaroras moved to W Pennsylvania and became the sixth nation of the IROQUOIS CONFEDERACY.

Tutankhamun (*c*.1341–1323 BC) Egyptian pharaoh (r.1333–1323 BC) of the New Kingdom's 18th dynasty (1550–1307 BC). The revolutionary changes made by his predecessor, AKHNATEN, were reversed during his reign. The capital was re-established at Thebes (LUXOR) and worship of the god Amon reinstated. Tutankhamun's fame is due to the discovery of his tomb by Howard CARTER in 1922. The only royal tomb of ancient EGYPT not completely stripped by robbers, it contained magnificent treasures.

Tutu, Desmond Mpilo (1931–) South African Anglican clergyman. A prominent anti-APARTHEID campaigner, he became an Anglican priest in 1960. Appointed bishop of Lesotho in 1976, he advocated civil disobedience as a means of fighting apartheid and was awarded the Nobel Prize for Peace in 1984. Tutu was archbishop of Cape Town (1986–96). From 1995 he chaired the Truth and Reconciliation Committee in Nelson MANDELA's government to investigate allegations of civil-rights abuse during the era of apartheid.

Tuvalu (formerly Ellice Islands) State in the W Pacific Ocean, S of the Equator and W of the International Date Line. None of the cluster of nine low-lying coral islands rises more than 4.6m (15ft) out of the Pacific, making them vulnerable to the rising sea levels that have been predicted. Initially inhabited by Melanesian peoples, they were defeated and overthrown by the Samoans during the 16th century. The first European to discover the islands (1568) was the Spanish navigator Alvaro de Mendaña. In the three decades after 1850 the population was reduced from *c*.20,000 to just 3000 by Europeans abducting workers for plantations on other Pacific islands. The British assumed control in 1892, and the islands were subsequently administered with the nearby Gilbert Islands (now KIRIBATI). In 1978 Tuvalu became a separate self-governing colony within the Commonwealth. In 1979 the United States gave up its sovereignty claim to the four S islands. The first prime minister, Toaripi Lauti, was forced to resign (1981) following allegations of corruption. He was replaced by Tomasi Puapua, under whose leadership the islands voted against becoming an independent republic in a referendum (1986).

Tweed, William Marcy (1823–78) US politician. As leader of TAMMANY HALL, the DEMOCRATIC PARTY's political machine in NEW YORK CITY, he controlled Party nominations. He and his cohorts, known as the Tweed Ring, used fraudulent city contracts and extortion to enrich themselves in the 1860s. Finally arrested in 1871, "Boss" Tweed was sentenced to prison. Released in 1875, he was re-arrested on further charges and convicted, but escaped to Spain. He was extradited and jailed once again.

TUVALU

AREA: 26sq km (10sq mi)
POPULATION: 10,000
CAPITAL (POPULATION): Funafuti (2856)
GOVERNMENT: Constitutional monarchy
ETHNIC GROUPS: Polynesian
LANGUAGES: English (official), Tuvaluan
RELIGIONS: Protestant 90%
GDP PER CAPITA (1994): US$924

Twelve Tables In ancient ROME, laws engraved on wooden or bronze tablets representing the earliest codification of ROMAN LAW and customs, traditionally dated 451–450 BC. They were written by *decemviri* (a committee of 10) in response to the demands of PLEBEIANS for the curbing of PATRICIAN powers.

Twenty-One Demands (1915) Series of orders for special treatment presented to China by Japan. Japan took advantage of its relatively stronger position to demand special status in Chinese affairs. In the agreement, signed reluctantly by China, Japan was granted open access to China's ports and harbours, sole rights to mining in central China, restrictions on further concessions to other nations, and Japanese involvement in Chinese policy-making. Although this last claim was not honoured, Japan's enhanced role inspired great anti-Japanese feeling in China. The terms of the agreement were revoked at the WASHINGTON CONFERENCE (1921).

Two Sicilies, Kingdom of the Historic kingdom of SICILY and S ITALY. Founded by NORMANS in the late 11th century, its court was a brilliant cultural centre in the 13th century. Conquered by Charles of Anjou (1266), from 1282 it was divided between ANGEVIN (French) NAPLES and Aragónese (Spanish) Sicily. In 1443 ALFONSO V of ARAGÓN reunited the two kingdoms, but they were divided again during internal struggles in Italy in the late 15th century between the HABSBURG and VALOIS dynasties. The kingdom of the Two Sicilies was re-established under a Spanish BOURBON dynasty in 1735. In 1861 Naples and Sicily joined the new kingdom of Italy.

Tyler, John (1790–1862) Tenth president of the United States (1841–45). He served in Congress (1811–16) as a Democrat, as governor of Virginia (1825–27), and in the Senate (1827–36). Tyler split with the Democrats over Andrew JACKSON's economic policies and the NULLIFICATION Crisis. The WHIGS chose him as vice-presidential candidate with William HARRISON, and he succeeded to the presidency on Harrison's death (1841). A supporter of STATES' RIGHTS, Tyler came into conflict with the nationalistic Whigs in Congress and repeatedly vetoed legislation to create a national bank. His determination to annex TEXAS bore fruit after he had left office.

Tyler, Wat (d.1381) English leader of the PEASANTS' REVOLT (1381). He was chosen as leader of the rebels in Kent, SE England, and led their march on London. Tyler was eventually killed by the lord mayor of London while negotiating with RICHARD II.

Tyndale, William (*c*.1494–1536) English translator and religious reformer. In 1525 he started printing an English version of the New Testament in Cologne, Germany. Tyndale then began translating the Old Testament. He also wrote numerous Protestant tracts. Tyndale was eventually captured by the church authorities and burned at the stake as a heretic. His translation later provided a basis for the Authorized Version of the English BIBLE.

Tyre Historic city on the coast of modern LEBANON. Built on an island, it was a major commercial port of ancient PHOENICIA. It established colonies, including CARTHAGE in the 9th century, around the E Mediterranean, and having made peace agreements with DAVID and SOLOMON, it supplied both craftsmen and raw materials, especially cedarwood, for the building of the TEMPLE OF JERUSALEM in the 10th century BC. From the 7th century BC Tyre was in almost constant conflict with Assyria, eventually falling to NEBUCHADNEZZAR II in 587 BC. Tyre was besieged by ALEXANDER III (THE GREAT) who built a causeway linking the island to the mainland (332 BC). Ruled by successive empires, including the Romans, by the 2nd century AD it had become a significant Christian settlement, but was captured by the Arabs in AD 638. In 1124 it fell to the Crusaders and became the main town of the kingdom of JERUSALEM. The city was destroyed by the MAMLUKS in 1291 and never regained its former influence. Pop. (1991) 70,000.

Tyrol *See* TIROL

Tz'u Hsi *See* CIXI

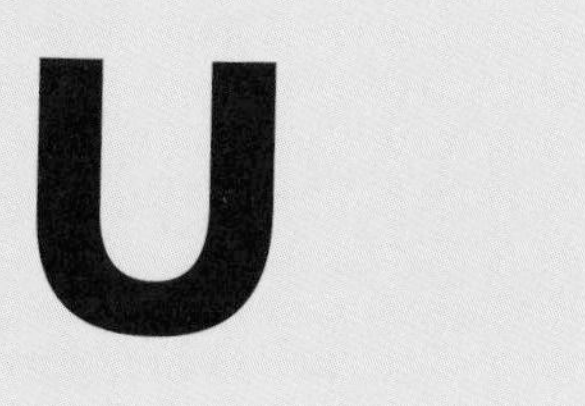

U-2 incident (1960) Cold War confrontation between the United States and the Soviet Union, following the shooting-down of a US spy plane, while on a photographic reconnaissance mission over the Soviet Union. Premier Nikita Khrushchev responded by cancelling a scheduled summit between the Soviet Union, United States, United Kingdom and France. President Dwight Eisenhower denied the existence of such spy missions, but the U-2 pilot, Francis Gary Powers, was produced by the Soviet authorities and confessed to being a spy. Powers was imprisoned but soon released (1962) in a spy exchange.

U-boat (Ger. *Unterseeboot*, "submarine") German submarine. In World War 1, Germany was the first nation to employ submarines for large-scale warfare. The U-boat fleets of World War 2 were initially a great threat to Allied shipping, sinking nearly a million tonnes of British shipping in the first year of the War. After the entry of the United States into the War in 1942, however, more ships and aeroplanes were available for escorting Allied convoys and destroying U-boats, and the struggle to supply Britain (known as the Battle of the Atlantic) was won by the Allies. During the War, 785 of the 1162 U-boats launched were sunk.

Udaipur City on Lake Pichola, Rajasthan, India. In 1586 it was made capital of the Rajput principality of Mewar by Udai Singh, after the Mughal emperor Akbar had sacked the previous capital. Jahangir gained Udaipur for the Mughal Empire in 1614. The walled city has three palaces. Pop. (1991) 309,000.

Uganda *See* country feature

Ugarit Ancient city in NW Syria. Inhabited as early as the 7th millennium BC, it was a great commercial power, trading with Mesopotamia and Egypt. Excavations have revealed a vast palace from the 14th century BC and many large houses filled with treasures and artifacts.

Uitlander (Afrikaans, foreigner) Non-Dutch immigrants to the Transvaal after the discovery of gold (1886). They soon outnumbered the Afrikaners, and Paul Kruger passed laws restricting the Uitlanders' voting and citizenship rights. Tension between the communities led to the Jameson Raid (1895) and to the second of the South African Wars (1899–1902).

Ukraine *See* country feature, page 418

Ulbricht, Walter (1893–1973) East German statesman, general secretary of the communist-dominated Socialist Unity Party (1950–71), head of state (1960–73). A founder member (1919) of the German Communist Party (KPD), Ulbricht served (1928–33) as a communist member of the Reichstag. He was forced into exile in the Soviet Union by the rise of the Nazi Party. In 1945 Ulbricht returned to Soviet-occupied Germany and became head of the KPD. He presided over the merger of the KPD and Social Democratic Party (SPD) to form the Socialist Unity Party (SED). In 1949 Ulbricht became deputy premier of the newly created German Democratic Republic (East Germany). In 1950 he became general secretary of the SED. Ulbricht established close links with the Soviet Union. The repressive nature of his regime led to a rebellion in 1953, and the Berlin Wall was built (1961) to prevent further defections to the West. In 1960, on the death of Wilhelm Pieck, Ulbricht became head of state, as chairman of the Council of State. In 1971 Ulbricht was replaced as general secretary by Erich Honecker, but continued to serve as head of state until his death.

Ulm, Battle of (25 September–20 October 1805) French victory during the Napoleonic Wars (1803–15). An Austrian army under General Karl Mack von Leiberich (1752–1828) was surrounded by Napoleon's Grand Army at the town of Ulm, on the River Danube, SW Germany. Russian forces, under Mikhail Kutuzov, failed to arrive in time to prevent Mack's surrender. French casualties were negligible; *c.*50,000 Austrian troops were taken prisoner. The victory prepared the way for Napoleon's occupation of Vienna and his victory at Austerlitz two months later.

Ulmanis, Karlis (1877–1942) Latvian statesman, prime minister (1918–19, 1919–21, 1925–26, 1931, 1934–40), president (1936–40). In the unrest that followed the Russian Revolution of 1905, Ulmanis began his campaign for Latvian independence. With the failure of the Revolution, Ulmanis fled to the United States. He returned to Latvia in 1913. In 1917 Ulmanis formed the Latvian Farmers' Union to press for independence in the wake of the Russian Revolution. In 1918 he formed a national council, which proclaimed Latvian independence in November of that year. With British, French, Estonian and Lithuanian support, the Latvians finally expelled (1920) the Red Army and the German Army and a peace treaty was concluded with Russia. In 1934 political instability led Ulmanis to suspend the parliament and declare a state of emergency. The Soviet occupation of Latvia (1940) forced Ulmanis' surrender and subsequent arrest. His grand-nephew Guntis Ulmanis (1939–) served as president (1993–99).

Ulster Most northerly of Ireland's four ancient provinces, consisting of nine counties. Since 1922 six of these counties have been in Northern Ireland, while Cavan, Donegal and Monaghan form Ulster province in the Republic of Ireland. The ancient province of Ulster split into three kingdoms in the 4th–5th centuries AD. In the late 12th century Anglo-Normans captured E Ulster and began to settle in the area. The earldom of Ulster was created by King John. By the late 16th century, the nine counties of Ulster were in existence. The strongest families in the area were the Roman Catholic O'Donnells and O'Neills. They rebelled against Elizabeth I's Plantation of Ireland. Negotiations failed and many Catholics fled the area. They were soon replaced by large numbers of Scottish Presbyterians, who flourished in E Ulster. In the early 20th century, the Protestant descendants of these settlers refused to accept Irish Home Rule, leading to the formation of Northern Ireland. Area: 8012sq km (3094sq mi), Pop. (1991) 232,000. *See also* Pale

Ulster Unionists Political parties in Northern Ireland that seek to preserve the union with Britain. Ulster Unionists trace their history to the split (1886) in the British Liberal Party between those who favoured Irish Home Rule and those who opposed it. The opponents, known as Liberal Unionists, allied themselves with the Conservative Party. In 1920, with the establishment of the self-governing province of Northern Ireland, these Unionists formed the majority party, calling themselves the **Ulster Unionist Party (UUP)**. Almost exclusively Protestant, the UUP was the ruling party in Northern Ireland from 1922 until the imposition of direct rule from Westminster in 1972. Prime ministers included James Craig (1921–40), Viscount Brookeborough (1943–63) and Baron O'Neill of the Maine (1963–69). In 1972

UGANDA

AREA: 235,880sq km (91,073sq mi)
POPULATION: 18,592,000
CAPITAL (POPULATION): Kampala (773,463)
GOVERNMENT: Republic in transition
ETHNIC GROUPS: Ganda 18%, Banyoro 14%, Teso 9%, Banyan 8%, Basoga 8%, Bagisu 7%, Bachiga 7%, Lango 6%, Acholi 5%
LANGUAGES: English and Swahili (both official)
RELIGIONS: Christianity (Roman Catholic 40%, Protestant 29%), traditional beliefs 18%, Islam 7%
GDP PER CAPITA (1995): US$1470

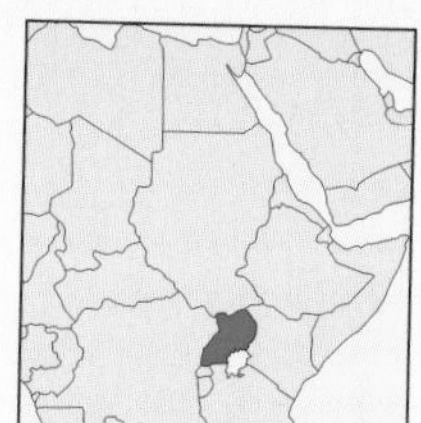

Republic in E central Africa. In *c.*1500 the Nilotic-speaking Lwo people formed various kingdoms in SW Uganda, including Buganda (kingdom of the Ganda) and Bunyoro. During the 18th century, the Buganda kingdom expanded and trade flourished. In 1862 a British explorer, John Speke, became the first European to reach Buganda. He was closely followed (1875) by Sir Henry Stanley. The conversion activities of Christian missionaries led to conflict with Muslims. The *kabaka* (king) Mutesa I came to depend on Christian support. In 1892 Britain dispatched troops to Buganda, and in 1894 Uganda became a British protectorate. Unlike much of Africa, Uganda attracted Asian, rather than European, settlers. African political representation remained minimal until after World War 2.

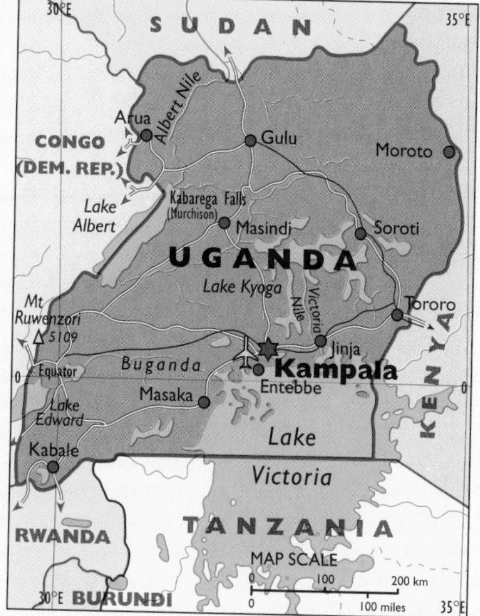

In 1962 Uganda gained independence, with Buganda's *kabaka*, Mutesa II, as president and Milton Obote as prime minister. In 1966 Mutesa II was forced into exile. In 1967 Buganda's traditional autonomy was restricted, and Obote became executive president. In 1971 Obote was deposed in a military coup, led by Major General Idi Amin. Amin quickly established a personal dictatorship and launched a war against foreign interference, which resulted in the mass expulsion of Asians. It is estimated that Amin's regime was responsible for the murder of more than 250,000 Ugandans. Obote loyalists resisted the regime from neighbouring Tanzania. In 1976 Amin declared himself president-for-life, and Israel launched a successful raid on Entebbe airport to end the hijack of one of its passenger planes.

In 1978 Uganda annexed the Kagera region of NW Tanzania. In 1979 Tanzanian troops helped the Uganda National Liberation Front (UNLF) to overthrow Amin and capture Kampala. In 1980 elections Obote was swept back into office. Amid charges of electoral fraud, the National Resistance Army (NRA) began a guerrilla war: more than 200,000 Ugandans sought refuge in Rwanda and Zaïre (now Congo). In 1985 Obote was deposed in another military coup. In 1986 the NRA captured Kampala, and Yoweri Museveni became president. Museveni began to rebuild the domestic economy and improve foreign relations. In 1993 the *kabaka* of Buganda was reinstated as monarch. In 1996 Museveni won Uganda's first direct presidential elections. AIDS is one of the greatest issues facing Uganda; it has the highest number of reported cases in Africa.

differences within the UUP led to its split into the Official Ulster Unionist Party and the Protestant Unionist Party. The latter, led by Ian PAISLEY and renamed the **Ulster Democratic Unionist Party (DUP)**, is the more extreme of the two parties. It is opposed to any weakening of the union with Britain. The UUP, led by David TRIMBLE since 1995, played a key role in the negotiations that led to the GOOD FRIDAY AGREEMENT (1998), as a result of which Trimble became first minister of Northern Ireland.

Ultramontanism (Lat. *ultra montes*, "beyond the mountains") Position taken by Roman Catholics who asserted the supremacy of the papacy over the claims of national churches. It became prominent in the 16th and 17th centuries, particularly in France. Its name refers to the Ultramontanists' practice of looking for guidance beyond the mountains (over the Alps) to Rome. Ultramontanism's greatest success was the definition of PAPAL INFALLIBILITY at the First VATICAN COUNCIL (1869–70).

Umar *See* OMAR

Umar ibn Said Tal (*c*.1797–1864) West African soldier and mystic, founder of a Tukulor empire in W Africa. Educated in the Koran by his scholar father, Umar became a member of the Tijaniyya brotherhood and set out on a pilgrimage to Mecca in *c*.1820. On his return to W Africa, having been designated caliph of black Africa, he launched (1854) a *jihad* (holy war). Umar founded a Muslim empire among the Tukulor people, seizing territory in what is now Guinea, Mali and Senegal. Forced conversions of the population were largely unsuccessful, and Umar continually had to defend his territory. In 1863 he captured TIMBUKTU but was soon beaten by the TUAREGS and FULANI. Umar was killed the following year, but his son, Ahmadu Seku, maintained the empire until 1897.

Umayyads (Omayyads) Muslim CALIPH dynasty (661–750). ALI, the fourth caliph, was assassinated in the struggle for control that followed the death of OTHMAN. MUAWIYA emerged victorious and was proclaimed caliph (661), founding the Umayyad dynasty. Muawiya moved the capital from MEDINA to DAMASCUS. He ensured that his son succeeded him as caliph, thus establishing the Umayyads as a hereditary dynasty. Their empire stretched from Spain to India, incorporating N Africa, the Mediterranean region and much of central Asia. It reached the peak of its power under ABD AL-MALIK. The Umayyads made little effort to convert conquered peoples to Islam, but there was great cultural exchange, and Arabic became established as the language of Islam. The Umayyads' failure to capture Constantinople from the Byzantine emperor LEO III (THE ISAURIAN) in 717 marked the start of the dynasty's decline. Increasing discontent led to the overthrow and murder of the last Umayyad caliph, Marwan II, by the ABBASIDS in 750. ABD AR-RAHMAN I survived the Abbasid massacre and fled to Spain, where he established the Umayyad emirate of CÓRDOBA.

Umberto I (1844–1900) (Humbert I) King of Italy (1878–1900), son and successor of Italy's first king, VICTOR EMMANUEL II. Umberto entered the army in 1858 and fought with distinction against Austria in the wars for Italian unification. As king, he approved the TRIPLE ALLIANCE (1882) with Germany and Austria-Hungary. Umberto's imperialist ambitions were thwarted by Italy's defeat at the Battle of ADWA. He was assassinated by an anarchist at Monza, N Italy.

Umberto II (1904–83) (Humbert II) Prince of Savoy and last king of Italy (1946). The son of VICTOR EMMANUEL III, he became king on his father's abdication in May 1946, having been appointed lieutenant general of the realm by him in 1944. Umberto abdicated in June 1946 after a national vote in favour of a republic. He was banished from Italy.

Umkhonte We Sizwe *See* AFRICAN NATIONAL CONGRESS (ANC)

UN *See* UNITED NATIONS

Un-American Activities Committee, House (HUAC) Committee of the US House of Representatives, established in 1938 to investigate political subversion. Created to combat Nazi propaganda, it began investigating extremist political organizations. After World War 2, encouraged by Senator Joseph MCCARTHY, it attacked alleged communists in Hollywood and in the federal government. It was abolished in 1975.

Underground Railroad Secret network organized by the free black community and other ABOLITIONISTS before the American CIVIL WAR to assist slaves escaping

UKRAINE

AREA: 603,700sq km (233,100sq mi)
POPULATION: 52,140,000
CAPITAL (POPULATION): Kiev (2,600,000)
GOVERNMENT: Multiparty republic
ETHNIC GROUPS: Ukrainian 73%, Russian 22%, Jewish 1%, Belarussian 1%, Moldovan, Bulgarian, Polish
LANGUAGES: Ukrainian (official)
RELIGIONS: Christianity (mostly Ukrainian Orthodox)
GDP PER CAPITA (1995): US$2400

Independent state in E Europe. Ukraine (Borderland) is the second-largest country in Europe (after Russia). In ancient history the area was successively inhabited by Scythians and Sarmatians, before invasions by the Goths, Huns, Avars and Khazars. The first Ukrainian Slavic community originated in the 4th century. In the 9th century, the N regions were united by the Varangians as KIEVAN RUS. The empire disintegrated under the onslaught of the Mongol hordes.

In the late 14th century, Ukraine became part of LITHUANIA. In 1478 the Black Sea region was absorbed into the Ottoman Empire. In 1569 the Lithuanian sector passed to Poland following the Poland-Lithuania union. Polish rule was marked by the enserfment of the peasantry and persecution of the Ukrainian Orthodox Church. In 1648 refugees from Polish rule (COSSACKS) completed Ukraine's liberation. Independence was short-lived due to the emerging power of Russia. A succession of wars resulted (1775) in the division of Ukraine into three Russian provinces. The nationalist movement was barely suppressed and found an outlet in GALICIA. Ukraine's industry was developed from the 1860s.

In 1918, following the Russian Revolution, Ukraine declared independence and was invaded by the Red Army, which was repulsed with the support of the Central Powers. The World War 1 armistice prompted the withdrawal of the Central Powers. A unified, independent Ukraine was once more proclaimed. The Red Army invaded again, this time with greater success. In 1921 W Ukraine was ceded to Poland, and in 1922 E Ukraine became a constituent republic of the SOVIET UNION. In the 1930s Vladimir LENIN's policy of appeasement was replaced by Joseph STALIN's autocratic, agricultural collectivization, which caused 7.5 million Ukrainians to die of famine. The 1939 Nazi-Soviet partition of Poland reunified the Ukraine. In 1940 it also acquired Northern BUKOVINA and part of BESSARABIA from Romania. In 1945 it gained RUTHENIA from Hungary and E Galicia from Poland. After 1945 all Ukrainian land was unified into a single Soviet republic. In 1954 CRIMEA was annexed to the Ukraine. Ukraine became one of the most powerful republics in the Soviet Union, contributing 30% of total Soviet industrial output. In 1986 the CHERNOBYL disaster contaminated large areas of Ukraine.

In 1990 the Ukrainian parliament declared itself a sovereign body. In August 1991 Ukraine proclaimed its independence. In December 1991 Leonid KRAVCHUK, a former Communist leader, was elected president, and Ukraine joined the COMMONWEALTH OF INDEPENDENT STATES (CIS). Tensions with Russia over Crimea, the Black Sea fleet, the control of nuclear weapons, and oil and gas reserves were eased by a 1992 treaty. Crimean independence was refused.

In 1994 elections Leonid Kuchma defeated Kravchuk. Kuchma continued the policy of establishing closer ties with the West and sped up the pace of privatization. In 1995 direct rule was imposed on Crimea for four months. Subsequent elections saw reduced support for pro-Russian parties. Disputes continue over the extent of the powers of the Crimean legislature.

from the South. It was not a railway. Although Quakers were prominent assistants (known as "conductors"), most escapees reached the North by their own efforts. One of the most prominent black conductors was Harriet TUBMAN. The major routes ran through Ohio, Indiana and w Pennsylvania. In the North escaped slaves were guided through a series of safe houses ("stations") to a place of safety, often Canada. The publicity surrounding the Underground Railroad helped increase sympathy for escaped slaves and made the FUGITIVE SLAVE LAWS difficult to enforce.

unequal treaties Series of treaties between QING dynasty China and various imperialist powers, by which China conceded many of its territorial and commercial rights. Following the First OPIUM WAR (1939–42), China was forced to sign the Treaty of NANJING (1842) and its supplement, the Treaty of the Bogue (1843), with Britain. TREATY PORTS were established and opened to foreign trade. After the Second Opium War (1856–60), China signed the Treaty of TIANJIN (1858) with Britain. Other unequal treaties were signed with the United States (the Treaty of Wanghia, 1844) and with France (the Treaty of Whampoa, 1844). The treaties extended the privileges granted to foreigners, not only in trade and commerce but also in all other aspects of life, such that foreigners were exempted from Chinese taxes and not subject to Chinese laws. A greatly weakened Qing dynasty signed the Treaty of SHIMONOSEKI (1895), by which China lost much territory to Japan. The unequal treaties aroused much anti-Western sentiment in China, which led to the BOXER REBELLION (1898–1900). It was not until 1946 that Britain, France and the United States relinquished many of their privileges.

UNESCO Acronym for UNITED NATIONS EDUCATIONAL, SCIENTIFIC AND CULTURAL ORGANIZATION

U Ne Win *See* NE WIN, U

UNHCR Abbreviation of UNITED NATIONS HIGH COMMISSION FOR REFUGEES

UNICEF Acronym for UNITED NATIONS CHILDREN'S FUND

Unification Church International religious movement founded (1954) in South Korea by Sun Myung Moon. Its adherents are popularly known as Moonies. The movement aims to re-establish God's rule on Earth through the restoration of the family. The Unification Church is noted for its mass weddings and has been accused of cult-like practices, such as brainwashing. It has *c.*2 million members.

Uniformity, Act of (1662) English legislation regulating the form of worship in the CHURCH OF ENGLAND after the RESTORATION of the monarchy. It required all clergy to follow the Book of COMMON PRAYER. The Act also obliged the clergy to repudiate the SOLEMN LEAGUE AND COVENANT, to forswear the taking up of arms against the Crown, and to adopt the liturgy of the Church of England. Earlier Acts of Uniformity (1549, 1552, 1559) had required the use of various editions of the Book of Common Prayer.

union Group of workers organized for the purpose of improving wages and conditions of work. In Britain, the first trade unions were founded around the time of the INDUSTRIAL REVOLUTION (from *c.*1760). Although some craft and agricultural unions developed before industrialization, the growth of trade unionism paralleled the growth of industry. The COMBINATION ACTS (1799, 1800) were passed by the British government in an attempt to outlaw trade unions. The Acts were repealed in 1824, although a further Combination Act (1825) restricted union activity. The harsh treatment of the TOLPUDDLE MARTYRS (1834), sentenced to transportation for organizing a union, provoked a public outcry and increased support for unions. The TRADES UNION CONGRESS (TUC) was formed in 1868. It represented only skilled workers until 1889, when the first unions for unskilled workers were admitted. In 1871 the Trades Union Act put the unions on a firm legal basis and gave their funds legal protection. By 1875 peaceful picketing was allowed. The TAFF VALE CASE (1900) temporarily dented the unions' power, making them liable for damages. The Trade Disputes Act of 1906, however, reversed the decision. The Labour Representation Committee, an offshoot from the TUC, was formed in 1900; the modern LABOUR PARTY emerged from it in 1906. Unions cooperated with the government and employers during World War 1, and union membership continued to grow. The GENERAL STRIKE (4–12 May 1926), organized by the TUC, failed to obtain any concessions and led to the passing of the Trade Union Act (1927), which made any secondary strike action illegal. The post-World War 2 Labour government repealed the Trade Union Act in 1946. Union participation at a governmental level increased, and union membership grew in all sectors of the workforce. In 1971 the Conservative government passed the Industrial Relations Act, which regulated the actions of trade unions. Unpopular anti-inflationary measures, such as wage and price controls, led to a series of industrial disputes, culminating in a bitter miners' strike (1973–74). Prime Minister Edward HEATH's campaign for re-election centred on tough policies towards the unions. He was defeated (1974), and the succeeding Labour government repealed the 1971 Act. In the 1980s union rights were progressively curbed by legislation passed by Margaret THATCHER's Conservative government.

In the United States, unlike in Europe, labour unions and their members have generally accepted capitalism. Members of craft unions, organized on a trade or occupational basis in the late 18th century, could be fined or imprisoned when employers, using English common law, accused them of criminal conspiracy. The Supreme Court restricted use of this doctrine in 1842, and thereafter the legality of unions depended on the means they employed to gain better worker conditions. The National Labor Union (formed in 1866) and the KNIGHTS OF LABOR (1869) included trade unions, suffragettes, farmers' organizations and other reform groups with diverse goals; each soon foundered. Samuel GOMPERS, learning from their mistakes, organized the American Federation of Labor (AFL) in 1886; membership was restricted to skilled labourers only, and the AFL had the pragmatic aims of raising wages, improving work conditions, honouring contracts and instigating collective bargaining. The struggle between management and labour often erupted into violence, as when police and labour protesters were killed in the HAYMARKET SQUARE RIOT (1886) in Chicago, Illinois. The federal government did not remain neutral, and troops were deployed against strikers when violence broke out in response to the government's use of the SHERMAN ANTI-TRUST ACT against the American Railroad Union. Opposed by the federally backed employers on one side and the more radical INDUSTRIAL WORKERS OF THE WORLD (IWW) on the other, the AFL nonetheless grew to include four million workers by 1920. Another one million belonged to unaffiliated unions, including the railroad brotherhoods. The influence of the federal government over labour-management relationships enhanced labour's prestige during World War 1, but during the prosperity of the 1920s union membership decreased. Under President Franklin ROOSEVELT's NEW DEAL policies in the 1930s, a series of laws, including the WAGNER ACT (1935), made organizing easier. The right to join a union and the duty of employers to bargain with workers were ensured. This stimulated organization on an industry-wide basis. When the automobile, steel and other mass-production industrial unions were expelled from the AFL, they created the Congress of Industrial Organizations (CIO) in 1938. Rivalry between the CIO and AFL and labour's increased power during World War 2 stimulated union growth until 14 million workers were organized by 1945. George MEANY, president of the AFL, and Walter Reuther, president of the CIO, negotiated a merger in 1955, and by then 17.5 million workers were in unions. Because of apathy at the local union level, power often became concentrated in the hands of a few national leaders. Amid charges of corruption, union power was curbed by the TAFT-HARTLEY ACT of 1947 and the Landrum-Griffin Act of 1959. Membership in the AMERICAN FEDERATION OF LABOR AND CONGRESS OF INDUSTRIAL ORGANIZATIONS (AFL-CIO) declined, partly due to the expulsion of allegedly corrupt unions, such as the International Brotherhood of TEAMSTERS, and partly due to the growing percentage of white collar workers (traditionally difficult to organize) in the workforce. Young workers in the 1960s saw the unions as unsympathetic to their concerns with civil rights, war and pollution. In the 1970s labour unions began to adapt to the needs of white-collar, female, minority and young workers. Unions have shown some success in these areas, and there has been increased unionization among teachers, government employees, and health and farm workers. Economic downturns in the late 1970s and early 1980s weakened the bargaining power of unions.

Union, Acts of Series of laws uniting ENGLAND with WALES (1536) and SCOTLAND (1707), and Britain with IRELAND (1800). In addition, the 1841 Act of Union united French-speaking LOWER CANADA and English-speaking UPPER CANADA and established a parliament for the province. The Welsh acts incorporated Wales within the kingdom of England, provided Welsh parliamentary representation and made English the official language. The Scottish act united the kingdoms of England and Scotland forming Great Britain. Scotland retained its legal system and Presbyterian Church. In accordance with the Irish act, the Irish legislature was abolished and Ireland was given 32 peers and 100 seats in the British Parliament. The established churches of the two countries were united. *See also* HOME RULE; UNITED KINGDOM

Union of Soviet Socialist Republics Official name for the SOVIET UNION

Union Pacific Railroad US company established (1862) by Congress to construct part of the first transcontinental railway line. In 1865 construction commenced westwards from Omaha, Nebraska. The line was completed in 1869, when the Union Pacific joined the Central Pacific near Ogden, Utah. In 1872 a vast profiteering racket was unearthed involving CRÉDIT MOBILIER OF AMERICA. In 1893 the fraud forced Union Pacific into receivership. In 1897 US financier Edward Harriman (1848–1909) acquired the company as part of his vast railroad empire.

Unitarianism Version of CHRISTIANITY that denies the TRINITY, accepts God as the father, and rejects the divinity of JESUS CHRIST. Its theology can be traced back to Michael SERVETUS, whose views forced him to flee the Inquisition. Many religious exiles congregated in Poland during the 16th century, among them Faustus Socinus (1539–1604). Socinus' followers, known as Socinians, published the first Unitarian texts. Their views aroused much opposition, and the Socinians were forced into exile, mainly in Transylvania, where the earliest Unitarian churches were founded. Socian texts reached England, where Theophilus Lindsey founded the first English Unitarian Church in 1774. In America, Congregationalist churches gradually accepted Unitarian views. The movement being particularly strong in New England. Unitarianism in the 20th century has been identified with liberal politics and the movement for world peace and has taken an increasingly humanist point of view.

United Arab Emirates (UAE) *See* country feature, page 420

United Arab Republic (UAR) Political union of EGYPT and SYRIA (1958–61). It was seen as a first step towards Arab union, and other Arab states were invited to join. YEMEN was loosely associated with it (1958–66). The UAR collapsed when Syria withdrew in 1961. Egypt retained the name until 1971, when it became the Arab Republic of Egypt. *See also* NASSER, GAMAL ABDEL

United Democratic Front Multiracial political organization in South Africa. It was founded in 1983 to oppose, without the use of violence, the South African government's plans to give the Coloured and Indian communities a minor role in government, while not giving any role to the black African community. One thousand delegates from 575 various organizations, ranging from women's groups to sporting bodies, opposed the government's proposals, demanding full enfranchisement of all ethnic groups and an end to APARTHEID. By 1985 the UDF had *c.*3 million members; its leaders included Desmond TUTU and Allan Boesak (1946–). Legislation in 1986 restricted the UDF's activities to such an extent that it was effectively banned.

United Irishmen, Society of Irish nationalist society formed (1791) in Ulster by Wolfe TONE, James Napper Tandy and Thomas Russell. Inspired by the French Revolution, it campaigned for parliamentary and religious reform, aiming to establish a representative, independent Irish parliament and religious equality. Its membership included both Protestants and Roman Catholics. Attempts were made to disband the Society in 1793, after which it became an underground, armed organization. It was chiefly responsible for the rebellion of 1798, which began in Wexford. Military support from France failed to arrive in time to assist the rebellion. The leaders, including Tone, were arrested, and the rebellion suppressed. The Society declined thereafter.

United Kingdom *See* country feature

United Nations (UN) International organization set up to enable countries to work together for peace and mutual development. It was established (June 1945) in a charter signed in San Francisco by 50 countries. Today, the UN has 188 members, essentially all the world's sovereign states except for North and South Korea and Switzerland.

United Nations agencies *See* International Labour Organization (ILO); International Monetary Fund (IMF); United Nations Educational, Scientific and Cultural Organization (UNESCO); United Nations High Commission for Refugees (UNHCR); United Nations Children's Fund (UNICEF); World Bank; World Health Organization (WHO); and World Trade Organization (WTO). For administration at its headquarters in New York, United States, the UN has a Secretariat staffed by international personnel.

United Nations Children's Fund (UNICEF) Intergovernmental organization, agency of the United Nations (UN). It was founded in 1946, as the United Nations International Children's Emergency Fund, to help children in countries affected by World War 2. In 1950 its mandate widened to assist children and adolescents worldwide, particularly in war-devastated areas and developing countries. UNICEF was awarded the Nobel Prize for Peace in 1965.

United Nations Educational, Scientific and Cultural Organization (UNESCO) Intergovernmental organization, agency of the United Nations (UN). Founded in 1946, it aims to promote peace by improving the world's standard of education and by bringing together nations in cultural and scientific projects. Concerns about corruption and an alleged anti-Western bias in the organization prompted the withdrawal of the United States (1984) and the United Kingdom (1985). The UK later (1997) rejoined. UNESCO also gives aid to developing countries.

United Nations High Commission for Refugees (UNHCR) Intergovernmental organization, agency of the United Nations (UN). It was founded in 1951 as the successor to the International Refugee Organization. Initially concerned with the care of people in Europe displaced by World War 2, it soon expanded its activities to assist refugees worldwide. UNHCR helps refugees to gain asylum, ensuring that they are not returned to a place in which they are in danger. It also provides practical support, such as food, medicine and shelter. UNHCR was awarded the Nobel Prize for Peace in 1954 and 1981.

United Nations peacekeeping force Military personnel and their equipment placed at the United Nations' (UN) disposal by member states. The function of the force is to keep the peace between warring factions anywhere in the world, as requested by the United Nations Security Council. The first UN peacekeeping forces were deployed (June 1948) in the Sinai Peninsula and Beirut. Large numbers of UN troops were deployed in Bosnia during the mid-1990s. It was awarded the Nobel Prize for Peace in 1988.

United Nations Security Council Council responsible for taking action against any nation or faction considered to represent a threat to the security or continued wellbeing of a member state. It first met in January 1946. Action can be political, economic or, as a last resort, military. The Council also has the power to hold a formal investigation into matters of common concern. There are five permanent member states (the United States, United Kingdom, France, Russia and China) and ten non-permanent member states, which hold two-year terms. All five permanent member states plus four non-permanent members have to agree before any resolution is passed.

United Provinces of the Netherlands (Dutch Republic) Historic state (1579–1795) roughly occupying the area that is now the Netherlands. It was formed out of the Union of Utrecht (1579) during the Revolt of the Netherlands. It comprised the provinces of Friesland, Gelderland, Groningen, Holland, Overijssel, Utrecht and Zeeland. The United Provinces declared independence from Spain in 1581. It became a world power in the 17th century, but declined in the 18th century and was defeated by France in 1795.

United States Air Force (USAF) One of the three major military services established under the Department of Defense in the National Security Act of 1947. It began as the Aeronautical Division of the Army in 1907, became the Aviation Section of the Signal Corps in 1914, the Air Service in 1918, the Army Air Corps in 1926, and the Army Air Forces in 1941. Military aircraft were first used (1916) by the United States in the Mexican Revolution. The Air Corps played a major role in World War 2, culminating in the 20th Air Force's dropping of the atomic bombs on Japan. The development of nuclear weapons delivered by bomber aircraft has ensured a central role for the Air Force in future world conflicts. It is the world's largest air force. In 1996 air force personnel numbered *c.*390,000, of which *c.*60,000 are women.

United States of America *See* country feature, page 422

Universal Declaration of Human Rights International declaration issued by the United Nations Commission on Human Rights in June 1948. It was adopted by the General Assembly on 10 December, a date now marked as Human Rights Day. Its 30 articles detail civil, political, social, economic and cultural rights. The Declaration opens with the statement that "All human beings are born free and equal in dignity and rights" (**Article 1**) and are entitled to such rights "without distinction of any kind, such as race, colour, sex, language, religion, political or other opinion, national or social origin, property, birth or other status" (**Article 2**). Further civil rights include equality before the law (**Article 7**) and entitlement to a fair trial (**Article 10**), the prohibition of slavery (**Article 4**) and torture (**Article 5**). All people should have "the right to freedom of peaceful assembly" (**Article 20**) and "the right to take part in the government of his country" (**Article 21**). Economic rights include "the right to work, to free choice of employment" and to "equal pay for equal work" (**Article 23**). The right to free, elementary education is outlined in **Article 26. Article 27** details "the right freely to participate in the cultural life of the community". The Declaration is not legally binding, but the influence of its contents can be seen in several national constitutions written since 1948. Eleanor Roosevelt chaired the Commission; the principal author of the Declaration was the French jurist René Cassin (1887–1976). *See also* human rights

Unrepresented Nations and Peoples Organization (UNPO) International organization founded (1991) to represent regions and ethnic groups without international recognition. Its members include Abkhazia, Native Australians, Chechenia, Ingushetia, Kurdistan, the Lakota Native North Americans, the Mon people of Burma, and Tibet and Zanzibar. All nations and peoples without adequate international representation may join the UNPO, provided that they adhere to its charter. The charter outlines the UNPO's commitment to a nation's right to self-determination, its acceptance of internationally agreed standards of human rights and democracy, its advocacy of non-violence, and its rejection of terrorism. The UNPO's more than 50 members represent *c.*100 million people.

untouchables (*panchamas*) Lowest *varna* (class) of the Indian class system, making up *c.*20% of India's population. Untouchables lie outside the caste system. The term arises from the belief among high castes, such as Brahmin, that to touch *panchamas* amounts to ritual pollution or defilement. Untouchables perform the most menial and polluting tasks. "Mahatma" Gandhi campaigned for the abolishment of untouchability, renaming the class "*harijans*", meaning "children of God". Although their pariah status and the resultant social injustice were legally abolished in India (1949) and Pakistan (1953), much discrimination remains. *See also* Hinduism

Upanishads (Sanskrit, session) Texts of Hinduism, constituting the final stage of Vedic literature. Written in prose and verse, they take the form of dialogues between teacher and pupil. They are of uncertain authorship and date from *c.*650 BC or earlier. Often referred to as the Vedanta, the *Upanishads* speculate on reality and man's salvation. *See also* Brahmanism; Vedas

Upper Canada British part of British North America from the Constitutional Act (1791) until the union with Lower Canada (Québec) under the 1840 Act of Union. In 1841 the region's name was changed to Canada West. Following the British North America Act (1867), it entered the Dominion of Canada as the province of Ontario.

UNITED ARAB EMIRATES (UAE)

AREA: 83,600sq km (32,278 sq mi)
POPULATION: 2,083,000
CAPITAL (POPULATION): Abu Dhabi (or Abu Zaby, 670,125)
GOVERNMENT: Federal constitutional monarchy
ETHNIC GROUPS: Arab 87%, Indo-Pakistani 9%, Iranian 2%
LANGUAGES: Arabic (official), English
RELIGIONS: Sunni Muslim 80%, Shiite Muslim 16%
GDP PER CAPITA (1995): US$16,470

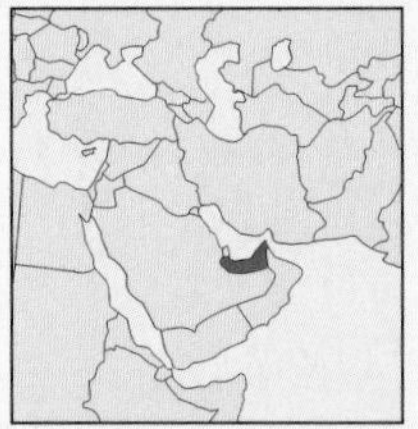

Federation of the seven independent sheikhdoms of Abu Dhabi, Dubai, Ajman, Ras al-Khaimah, Fujairah, Sharja and Umm al-Qaiwain. Abu Dhabi is more than six times the size of the other states put together, has the largest population, is the biggest oil producer and provides the federal capital, the city of Abu Dhabi. The population is almost exclusively Muslim (mostly Sunni), though the great majority of inhabitants are expatriate workers.

Formerly known as the Trucial States, the area was a British protectorate from 1892. After World War 2 the sheikhdoms were granted internal autonomy. In 1971 British troops withdrew from the Persian Gulf, and the United Arab Emirates (UAE) was formed. The economy is dominated by crude oil and natural-gas production, accounting for about half of its GDP. Oil was first discovered in Abu Dhabi in the early 1960s, and the 1973 increase in oil prices transformed a relatively impoverished region into one of the world's wealthiest.

The UAE was part of the coalition against Iraq in the Gulf War (1991) and joined the United Nations (UN) and the Arab League the same year. Disputes over the islands of Abu Musa and Tunbs in the Persian Gulf, occupied by Iraq since 1971, continued throughout the 1990s.

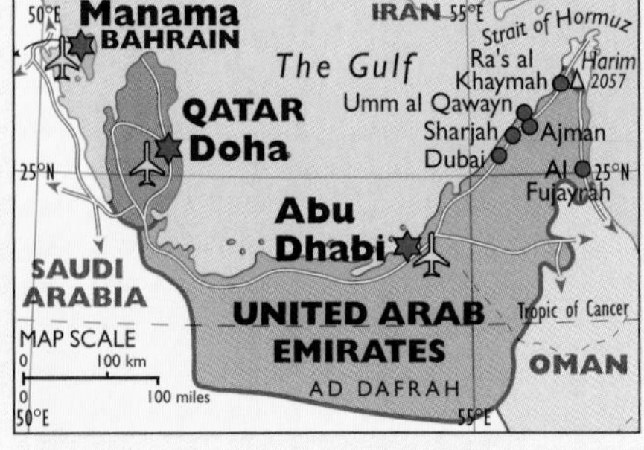

AREA: 243,368sq km (94,202sq mi)
POPULATION: 58,780,000
CAPITAL (POPULATION): London (6,966,800)
GOVERNMENT: Constitutional monarchy
ETHNIC GROUPS: White 94%, Indian 1%, Pakistani 1%, West Indian 1%
LANGUAGES: English (official)
RELIGIONS: Christianity (Anglican 57%, Roman Catholic 13%, Presbyterian 7%, Methodist 4%, Baptist 1%), Islam 1%, Judaism, Hinduism, Sikhism, Buddhism
GDP PER CAPITA (1995): US$19,260

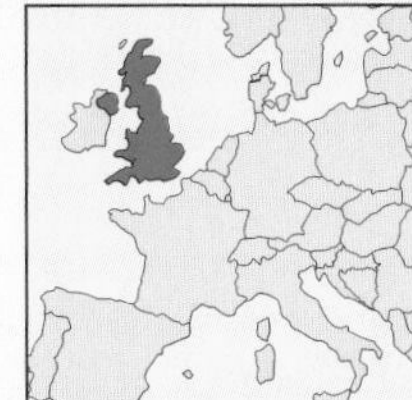

Kingdom on the British Isles, w Europe. The United Kingdom of Great Britain and Northern IRELAND is a union of four countries. Great Britain is composed of ENGLAND, SCOTLAND and WALES. The Isle of Man and the Channel Islands are self-governing UK dependencies. In 1536 England and Wales were formally united. Scotland and England were unified in the Act of UNION (1707).

In the 17th century England's development of empire was combined with a financial revolution, including the founding of the BANK OF ENGLAND (1694). Sir Robert WALPOLE's prime ministership (1721–42) marked the beginnings of CABINET government. Great Britain emerged from the SEVEN YEARS' WAR (1756–63) as the world's leading imperial power. GEORGE III's conception of absolute monarchy and resistance to colonial reform led to conflict with Parliament and contributed to the AMERICAN REVOLUTION (1775–83).

William PITT (THE YOUNGER) oversaw the creation of the United Kingdom of Great Britain and Ireland (1801). The AGRICULTURAL REVOLUTION was both a cause and effect of the doubling of the population between 1801 and 1861. The INDUSTRIAL REVOLUTION brought profound socio-economic changes. The 1820s and 1830s was an era of new reform legislation, including: the Act of CATHOLIC EMANCIPATION (1829), the abolition of SLAVERY (1833), harsh new POOR LAWS (1834), and the extension of the FRANCHISE to the middle class in the REFORM ACTS. Sir Robert PEEL's repeal of the CORN LAWS (1846) marked the beginnings of FREE TRADE and the emergence of the CONSERVATIVE PARTY from the old TORY Party. The LIBERAL PARTY similarly evolved out of the WHIGS. CHARTISM witnessed the beginnings of a working-class movement.

The reign of VICTORIA saw the development of the second BRITISH EMPIRE, spurred on by the imperial ambitions of Lord PALMERSTON. The historic importance of trade to the UK economy was firmly established. Between 1868 and 1880, UK politics was dominated by Benjamin DISRAELI and William GLADSTONE. The defeat of Gladstone's HOME RULE Bill for Ireland (1886) split the Liberal Party. Between 1908 and 1916 Herbert ASQUITH and David LLOYD GEORGE enacted a range of progressive social welfare policies, such as NATIONAL INSURANCE and state pensions. The growing power of Germany led to WORLD WAR I. GEORGE V changed the name of the British royal family from Saxe-Coburg-Gotha to Windsor. The Allied victory cost more than 750,000 British lives. The UK was faced by rebellion in Ireland. The Anglo-Irish Treaty (1921) confirmed the partition of Ireland. The Irish Free State was formed in 1922, and the UK officially became known as the United Kingdom of Great Britain and Northern Ireland. In 1924 Ramsay MACDONALD formed the first LABOUR PARTY government. The COMMONWEALTH OF NATIONS was founded in 1931. In 1936 EDWARD VIII was forced to abdicate in favour of GEORGE VI.

Neville CHAMBERLAIN's policy of APPEASEMENT towards Nazi Germany's growing imperial ambitions ended in failure. On 3 September 1939, following the German invasion of Poland, Britain declared war. From May 1940 Winston CHURCHILL led a coalition government that lasted throughout WORLD WAR 2. In 1941 the United States and the Soviet Union joined the battle against Adolf HITLER. Germany surrendered in May 1945 and Japan in September 1945. Britain had lost more than 420,000 lives, and its economy was devastated. In 1945 elections, the Labour Party was swept back into power, with Clement ATTLEE as prime minister. Attlee began a programme of nationalization and increased welfare provision. The MARSHALL PLAN aided reconstruction. In 1948 the NATIONAL HEALTH SERVICE (NHS) was created. The British Empire was gradually dismantled, beginning with India in 1947. Most newly independent nations joined the Commonwealth. In 1949 the UK joined NATO. In 1951 Churchill returned to power. In 1952 ELIZABETH II succeeded George VI. In 1956 Anthony EDEN led Britain into the SUEZ CANAL CRISIS. Harold MACMILLAN realized the importance of Europe to UK trade, and in 1959 the UK became a founder member of the EUROPEAN FREE TRADE ASSOCIATION (EFTA). In 1964 Harold WILSON narrowly defeated Alec DOUGLAS-HOME. In 1968 the British Army was deployed in Northern Ireland to prevent the violent sectarian conflict that had followed civil-rights marches. In 1971, under Edward HEATH, the UK adopted a decimal currency. In 1972 the British Parliament assumed direct control of Northern Ireland.

In 1973 the UK joined the European Economic Community (EEC). Deep recession led to the introduction of a three-day working week, and a miners' strike forced Heath to resign. The discovery of North Sea oil and natural gas reduced Britain's dependency on coal and fuel imports. James CALLAGHAN's inability to control labour unrest led to his defeat in 1979 elections and Margaret THATCHER became Britain's first woman prime minister. Thatcher introduced MONETARISM and PRIVATIZATION. Unemployment grew as Britain attempted to switch to a more service-centred economy. The FALKLANDS WAR (1982) contributed to Thatcher's re-election in 1983. A miners' strike (1984–85) was followed by further trade-union restrictions. In 1987 Thatcher won an unprecedented third general election. Urban decay, economic inequality and an unpopular POLL TAX forced Thatcher to resign in 1990. John MAJOR signed the MAASTRICHT TREATY and won a surprise victory in the 1992 general election. He was soon forced to remove the pound from the EUROPEAN MONETARY SYSTEM (EMS). Major's administration was dogged by division over Europe and allegations of sleaze.

Tony BLAIR won the 1997 election, forming the first Labour government for 18 years. In September 1997 referenda on devolution saw Scotland and Wales gain their own legislative assemblies. The GOOD FRIDAY AGREEMENT (1998) offered the best chance of peace in Northern Ireland for a generation. In 1999 the UK contributed to NATO's military campaign in KOSOVO.

AREA: 9,372,610sq km (3,618,765sq mi)
POPULATION: 259,681,000
CAPITAL (POPULATION): Washington, D.C. (585,221)
GOVERNMENT: Federal republic
ETHNIC GROUPS: White 80%, African-American 12%, other races 8%
LANGUAGES: English (official), Spanish, more than 30 others
RELIGIONS: Christianity (Protestant 53%, Roman Catholic 26%, other Christian 8%), Islam 2%, Judaism 2%
GDP PER CAPITA (1995): US$26,980

Federal republic in North America, the world's fourth-largest country. The United States of America is made up of a federal district (the capital, WASHINGTON, D.C.) and 50 states (48 of which form a large block of land between Canada and Mexico). The other two states are ALASKA, in NW North America, and the North Pacific archipelago of HAWAII.

NATIVE NORTH AMERICANS arrived perhaps 40,000 years ago from Asia. Vikings, led by LEIF ERICSON, probably reached North America in *c.*AD 1000, but they did not settle. Western European exploration did not begin until the discovery of the New World by Christopher COLUMBUS in 1492. In 1565 the first permanent European settlement was founded by Spain at St Augustine, Florida. The French also formed settlements in LOUISIANA, but the first major colonists were the British, who founded JAMESTOWN, VIRGINIA, in 1607. In 1620 PURITANS landed at Cape Cod, MASSACHUSETTS, and founded the PLYMOUTH COLONY. The economic success of Massachusetts encouraged further colonization along the E coast. In 1681 William PENN founded PENNSYLVANIA. In the southern colonies, SLAVERY was used to develop plantations.

During the 18th century, British MERCANTILISM (especially the NAVIGATION ACTS) restricted commercial growth. The GREAT AWAKENING and the development of higher education promoted greater cultural self-consciousness. British victory in the FRENCH AND INDIAN WARS (1754–63) encouraged independence movements. Benjamin FRANKLIN's failure to win concessions from the British led to the AMERICAN REVOLUTION (1775–83), which ended British rule in the THIRTEEN COLONIES. George WASHINGTON, commander in chief of the Continental Army, became the first president. The ARTICLES OF CONFEDERATION (1777) produced weak central government and were superseded by the CONSTITUTION OF THE UNITED STATES (1787). The BANK OF THE UNITED STATES was created in 1791. US politics became divided between the FEDERALIST PARTY and the DEMOCRATIC-REPUBLICAN PARTY. In 1796 the Federalist president, John ADAMS, passed the ALIEN AND SEDITION ACTS (1798). The XYZ AFFAIR brought conflict with France.

In 1801 the Democratic-Republican Thomas JEFFERSON became president. Jefferson negotiated the LOUISIANA PURCHASE (1803), which nearly doubled the size of the United States. James MADISON led the United States into the WAR OF 1812, which cemented the nation's independence and culminated in the MONROE DOCTRINE (1823), which sought to protect the Western Hemisphere from European interference. The MISSOURI COMPROMISE (1820) papered over the growing conflict between the commercial, industrial North and the cotton plantations of the pro-SLAVERY South. The Democratic-Republican Party became simply the DEMOCRATIC PARTY. Andrew JACKSON's presidency furthered the westward expansion of the FRONTIER. The march to the Pacific became the "MANIFEST DESTINY" of the United States. In 1841 William HARRISON became the first WHIG PARTY president. TEXAS was annexed (1845) and OREGON Territory (1846) was acquired. The MEXICAN WAR (1846–48) confirmed US gains. The 1848 discovery of gold in CALIFORNIA prompted a rush of settlers. Territorial expansion was achieved at the expense of Native Americans, who were forced onto reservations. The addition of states to the Union intensified the conflict between free and slave states. The repeal of the Missouri Compromise led to the founding of the anti-slavery REPUBLICAN PARTY (1854).

In 1861 Abraham LINCOLN became the first Republican president. The southern states seceded as the CONFEDERATE STATES OF AMERICA. The CIVIL WAR (1861–65) claimed more than 600,000 lives and devastated the country. The Union victory resulted in the abolition of slavery. The enforced RECONSTRUCTION of the South was highly unpopular. Ulysses S. GRANT's administration was plagued by corruption. In 1867 the United States bought Alaska from Russia. The late 19th century was the era of the railway, which sped industrialization and urban development. The gleaming, steel skyscrapers symbolized opportunity, and millions of European immigrants were attracted to the United States. The SPANISH-AMERICAN WAR (1898) heralded the emergence of the United States as a major world power. Hawaii was annexed. In 1902 construction started on the PANAMA CANAL.

In 1917 Woodrow WILSON led the United States into WORLD WAR I. The economic boom and PROHIBITION of the roaring 1920s was followed by the GREAT DEPRESSION of the 1930s. Franklin D. ROOSEVELT's NEW DEAL attempted to restore prosperity. The Japanese bombing of

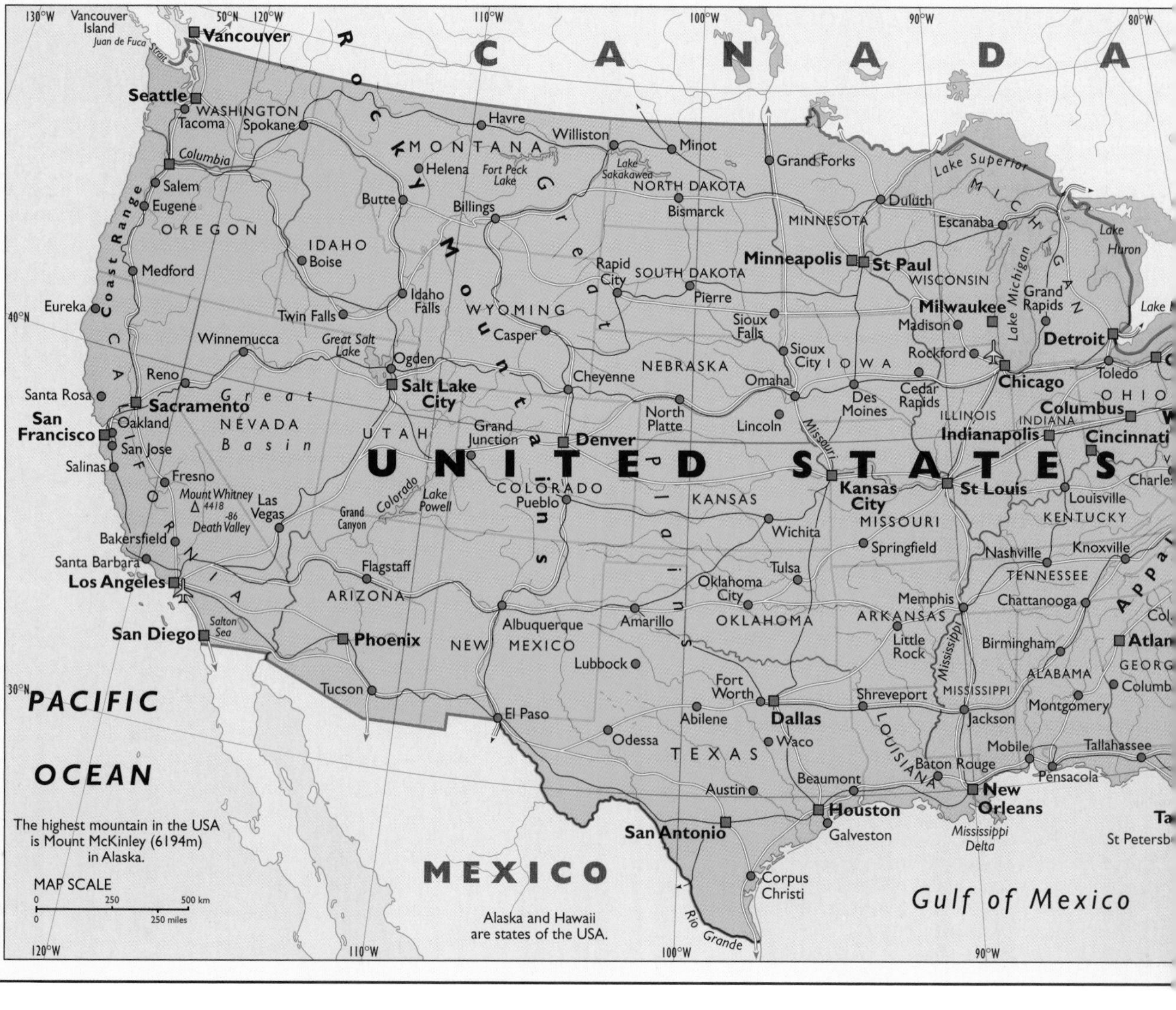

The highest mountain in the USA is Mount McKinley (6194m) in Alaska.

Alaska and Hawaii are states of the USA.

U

PEARL HARBOR (7 December 1941) prompted US entry into WORLD WAR 2. Rearmament aided economic recovery. Harry S TRUMAN became president on Roosevelt's death in 1945. The use of US atom bombs led to Japan's surrender. The United States was a founder member of NATO. Post-war tension with the Soviet Union led to the COLD WAR and spurred the space race. In order to stem the spread of communism, US forces fought in the KOREAN WAR (1950–53).

In 1955 Martin Luther KING, Jr, launched the CIVIL RIGHTS movement. The start of John F. KENNEDY's presidency was marred by the CUBAN MISSILE CRISIS (1962). Kennedy's assassination (22 November 1963) shocked the nation. Lyndon B. JOHNSON led the United States into the VIETNAM WAR (1965–73). Anti-Vietnam protests were coupled with civil unrest. On 20 July 1969 Neil ARMSTRONG became the first man on the Moon. In 1974 Richard NIXON was forced to resign by the WATERGATE AFFAIR. The CAMP DAVID AGREEMENT crowned Jimmy CARTER's foreign policy initiatives. The start of Ronald REAGAN's presidency (1981–89) marked the deepest recession since the Great Depression. Economic recovery brought increases in defence spending. Reagan's loosening grip on power was highlighted by the IRAN-CONTRA AFFAIR (1987–88).

In 1991, after the collapse of Soviet communism, George BUSH proclaimed a "New World Order". Despite the success of the GULF WAR (1991), domestic recession led to Bush's defeat in 1992. Bill CLINTON's reform programme was largely blocked by a Republican-dominated SENATE. Overcoming allegations of financial and personal scandal, economic recovery enabled Clinton's re-election in 1996. In 1999 Clinton survived impeachment charges and authorized the use of force against IRAQ and SERBIA.

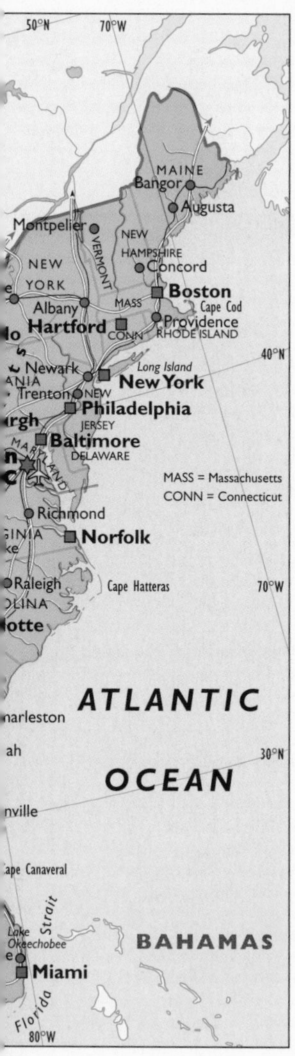

Upper Volta Former name of BURKINA FASO

Ur (Ur of the Chaldees) Ancient city of SUMERIA, S MESOPOTAMIA. Ur flourished in the 3rd millennium BC, but in *c.*2340 BC it was conquered by SARGON I. The Akkadian period witnessed the integration of Semitic and Sumerian cultures. In *c.*2060 BC the great ZIGGURAT was built by Ur-Nammu; during his reign Ur became the wealthiest city in Mesopotamia. In *c.*2000 BC much of the city was destroyed by the invading Elamites. In the 6th century BC NEBUCHADNEZZAR II briefly restored Ur as a centre of Mesopotamian civilization, but by the 5th century BC it had fallen into terminal decline.

Urban II (*c.*1035–99) Pope (1088–99), b. Odo of Châtillon-sur-Marne. He carried on the reforms begun by Pope GREGORY VII. In 1095, at the Council of Clermont, Urban preached the First CRUSADE. His work as a reformer encouraged the development of the CURIA ROMANA and the formation of the College of Cardinals.

Urban V (*c.*1310–70) Pope (1362–70), b. Guillaume de Grimoard. In 1367 he tried to return the papacy from AVIGNON to Rome, but insurrections in Rome and the Papal States forced him back to Avignon in 1370.

Urban VI (1318–89) Pope (1378–89), b. Bartolomeo Prignano. The College of Cardinals declared his election invalid and appointed an ANTIPOPE, CLEMENT VII, beginning the GREAT SCHISM. Urban VI's papacy was marked by confusion and financial losses in the Papal States.

Urban VIII (1568–1644) Pope (1623–44), b. Maffeo Barberini. His reign coincided with much of the THIRTY YEARS' WAR. Fearing possible domination of the papacy by the HABSBURGS, he supported France and gave little help to German Roman Catholics. During Urban's pontificate, GALILEO was forced (1633) to recant his views. In 1643 Urban condemned JANSENISM. An active and knowledgeable patron of the arts, Urban also approved the establishment of new orders.

Urquiza, Justo José de (1801–70) Argentine general and statesman, president (1854–60). As governor of Entre Ríos province from 1841, he enacted progressive fiscal and educational reforms. Discontent with the dictatorial rule of Juan Manuel de ROSAS coalesced in a revolt led by Urquiza, who defeated Rosas at the Battle of Monte Caseros (1852). The following year, Urquiza convened a constitutional conference, which adopted a federal constitution in 1854. All provinces apart from BUENOS AIRES (which held out until 1859) accepted the new Argentine Confederation. As president, Urquiza opened Argentina's ports to international trade. From 1865–68 he was commander of the armed forces in the War of the TRIPLE ALLIANCE against Paraguay. Urquiza was assassinated by followers of a political rival. *See also* CAUDILLO

Ursulines Oldest religious order of women in the Roman Catholic Church. Named after Saint Ursula, it was founded by Angela Merici at Brescia in 1535. The first female teaching order, it soon opened convents in Germany, France and Canada, where the first congregation of women in North America was established in 1639. It again increased in size during the 19th century, and a union of Ursuline convents was created by Pope LEO XIII in 1900.

Uruguay *See* country feature, page 424

Uruk (Erech, now Tall al-Warka, Iraq) Ancient city-state of MESOPOTAMIA, on the River Euphrates, NW of UR. Uruk dates from *c.*5000 BC and was occupied until the PARTHIAN era (247 BC–AD 224). In the third millennium BC the city was surrounded by a wall *c.*10-km (6-mi) long, later said to have been constructed by the legendary GILGAMESH, leader of a rebellion against KISH. During the reign (2112–2095 BC) of Ur-Nammu, Uruk developed into one of the most important cities of SUMERIA. Excavations since 1928 have revealed several ZIGGURATS, one honouring the sky god Anu, indicating that Uruk was an important religious centre. *See also* LAGASH

USA *See* UNITED STATES OF AMERICA

Usman dan Fodio (1754–1817) (Uthman dan Fodio) FULANI cleric who founded the SOKOTO caliphate. A member of an Islamic brotherhood in the HAUSA STATE of Gobir (now NW Nigeria), Usman began preaching in 1775. In 1804, having failed in his repeated attempts to reform the rule of the states in line with Islamic teaching, he launched a *jihad* (holy war). The *jihad* spread into Adamwa (N Cameroon), Nupe and Ilorin (S Nigeria), before being checked by the Kanem-BORNU empire. By 1808 Osman controlled a federation of 30 emirates, with its capital at Sokoto. Muslim culture flourished under the caliphate, which, at its height, ruled over *c.*10 million people. Usman was succeeded by his son, Muhammad Bello.

USSR *See* SOVIET UNION

Ustaša (Ustashe, Croat. uprising) Croatian fascist terrorist organization. It was founded (*c.*1929) by the extreme Croatian nationalist Ante Pavelić (1889–1959) in response to ALEXANDER I's attempt to transform the Kingdom of Serbs, Croats and Slovenes into a united YUGOSLAVIA. Supported by Benito MUSSOLINI, Pavelić set up terrorist training camps in Italy and Hungary. Members of Ustaša were involved in the assassination of Alexander I (1934). During World War 2, Ustaša collaborated with the occupying Italian and German troops and set up a pro-Nazi puppet state in Croatia. They proceeded to fight resistance movements and to massacre many thousands of ethnic minorities, including Serbs, gypsies and Jews, as well as non-Ustaša Croats. With the defeat of the Axis troops, Pavelić and his supporters fled to South America.

Utah Mountain state in W United States. The capital is Salt Lake City. By *c.*10,000 BC the region is thought to have been occupied by a hunter-gatherer culture. In *c.*AD 400 the ANASAZI Native North Americans migrated to the area. Later occupants of the area included the UTE, after whom the state is named. The first Europeans to arrive, in the late 18th century, were Franciscan missionaries. In 1824 Jim BRIDGER became the first white explorer to reach Great Salt Lake. Fur traders, such as the MOUNTAIN MEN, also explored the region, as did John FRÉMONT. The first permanent settlement was made in 1847, when Brigham YOUNG led the MORMONS into the valley of Great Salt Lake. In 1848 the region was ceded to the United States at the end of the MEXICAN WAR. Conflicts arose between federal authorities and the Church of the Latter-Day Saints, leading to the UTAH WAR (1857–58). Settlement increased with the completion (1869) of the UNION PACIFIC RAILROAD, and the late 19th century was marked by conflict between Mormon and non-Mormon settlers. Area: 219,931sq km (84,915sq mi). Pop. (1992) 1,811,215.

Utah War (1857–58) Conflict between the MORMON settlers of UTAH and US federal troops. Some Mormon Church practices, notably polygamy, were incompatible with federal law. Clashes between Mormon settlers and non-Mormon authorities were exaggerated in reports to President James BUCHANAN. Believing a large-scale rebellion to be imminent, Buchanan removed Brigham YOUNG, the Mormon leader, as territorial governor. He dispatched *c.*15,000 US troops to subdue the Mormons. Negotiations produced a peaceful solution to the War, and Young was replaced as governor by a candidate acceptable to both sides. The thousands of Mormons who had fled S to Provo ahead of the arrival of Buchanan's troops returned to Salt Lake City.

Ute Shoshonean-speaking tribe of Native North Americans, who inhabited W Colorado, NW New Mexico and central Utah. First encountered by Europeans in the late 18th century, the Ute had no horses and survived by gathering food. They acquired horses in the early 19th century and were soon organized into bands of hunters. Fierce, nomadic warriors, the Ute engaged in warfare with other Native American tribes and hunted bison. After attacking Mexican settlements in 1855, the Ute were forced to agree a treaty with the United States' government. During the American Civil War, the Ute fought with Kit CARSON in order to attack their traditional enemies, the NAVAJO. By

UTAH
Statehood :
4 January 1896
Nickname :
The Beehive State
State motto :
Industry

URUGUAY

AREA: 177,410sq km (68,498sq mi)
POPULATION: 3,116,802
CAPITAL (POPULATION): Montevideo (1,383,660)
GOVERNMENT: Multiparty republic
ETHNIC GROUPS: White 86%, Mestizo 8%, Mulatto or Black 6%
LANGUAGES: Spanish (official)
RELIGIONS: Christianity (Roman Catholic 66%, Protestant 2%), Judaism 1%
GDP PER CAPITA (1995): US$6630

Republic in South America. The original NATIVE SOUTH AMERICAN inhabitants of Uruguay have largely disappeared. Many were killed by Europeans, others died of European diseases, while some fled into the interior. The first European to arrive in Uruguay was a Spanish navigator in 1516, but few Europeans settled until the late 17th century. In 1726 Spanish settlers founded Montevideo in order to prevent the Portuguese gaining influence in the area.

By the late 18th century, the Spanish had settled most of the country, and Uruguay became part of the Viceroyalty of RÍO DE LA PLATA, which also included Argentina, Paraguay, and parts of Bolivia, Brazil and Chile. José Gervasio ARTIGAS led the fight for independence, but the Spanish were overthrown when Brazil annexed Uruguay in 1820. Uruguayans, supported by Argentina, resisted Brazilian rule, and finally, in 1828, Brazil and Argentina recognized Uruguay as an independent republic. In the 19th century social and economic development was restricted by numerous revolutions and counter-revolutions.

In 1903, following the election of José BATLLE Y ORDÓÑEZ as president, Uruguay became a more democratic and stable country. In 1920 it joined the LEAGUE OF NATIONS and in 1945 it became a member of the UNITED NATIONS (UN). From the 1950s, economic problems caused unrest. Terrorist groups, notably the TUPAMAROS, carried out murders and kidnappings. In 1972 the army crushed the Tupamaros.

In 1973 a military government was established. Repressive military rule continued until 1984, when civilian rule was re-established under Julio María SANGUINETTI of the Colorado Party. Economic difficulties and high foreign debts continued to threaten stability, provoking massive emigration. In 1994 Sanguinetti was again elected president. He was succeeded as president by Jorge Batlle in 2000.

1870 most of the Ute were confined to reservations in Colorado and Utah, where *c*.4000 remain.

Uthman *See* OTHMAN

utilitarianism Branch of ethical philosophy. It holds that actions are to be judged good or bad according to their consequences. An action is deemed to be morally right if it produces good results. Utilitarianism was developed by the English philosophers Jeremy BENTHAM and J.S. MILL.

utopianism (Gk. no place) Projection of ideal states or alternative worlds that are ordered for the benefit of all and where social ills have been eradicated. Sir Thomas MORE's *Utopia* (1516) outlines his notion of an ideal commonwealth based entirely on reason. ENLIGHTENMENT philosophers, such as Jean-Jacques ROUSSEAU, portrayed a vision of a pre-feudal European Golden Age. Writers such as the Comte de SAINT-SIMON, Charles Fourier and Robert OWEN outlined ideal communities based on cooperation and economic self-sufficiency. Karl MARX and Friedrich ENGELS valued the social insights of utopianism, but rejected its unscientific analysis of political and economic realities.

Utrecht City on the River Oude Rijn, central Netherlands. The bishopric of Utrecht was founded in 696, and it soon became a centre for the spread of Christianity. As princes of the Holy Roman Empire, the bishops controlled the region around Utrecht. The city has been a trading centre since medieval times. Participating in the REVOLT OF THE NETHERLANDS, Utrecht was the scene of the Union of UTRECHT, which established the independence of the UNITED PROVINCES OF THE NETHERLANDS. It was the location for several of the treaties comprising the Peace of UTRECHT (1713). The old city includes the 14th-century St Martin's Cathedral. Pop. (1994) 234,106.

Utrecht, Peace of (1713–14) Series of treaties that ended the War of the SPANISH SUCCESSION (1701–14), signed in Utrecht, Netherlands. The treaty between France and Britain (April 1713) confirmed that PHILIP V of Spain, grandson of LOUIS XIV of France, renounced his claim to the throne of France. It ceded French territory in North America, including St Kitts and provinces in E Canada, to Britain. The treaty between France and the Netherlands (April 1713) confirmed that the Spanish Netherlands would pass to Austria, once a treaty had been concluded with Emperor CHARLES VI. SAVOY and Nice were restored to VICTOR AMADEUS II, Duke of Savoy. A treaty between Britain and Spain (July 1713) further dismantled Spain's European empire: Gibraltar and Minorca passed to Britain; Sicily passed to the house of Savoy. Britain also acquired the right to the slave trade with South America. In 1714 Austria agreed to the terms of the treaties of RASTATT and Baden, by which Charles VI gave up his claim to Spain in return for the Spanish Netherlands, Naples and Milan.

Utrecht, Union of (1579) In the Netherlands, agreement among the seven northern provinces (Holland, Zeeland, Utrecht, Gelderland, Groningen, most of Friesland and Overijssel) and the southern cities of Antwerp, Breda, Ghent, Bruges and Ypres to continue the fight against Spanish rule. Negotiated by Johan van OLDENBARNEVELDT, this defence pact ultimately led to a declaration of independence (1581) and the establishment of the UNITED PROVINCES OF THE NETHERLANDS.

Uxmal Ancient city of the MAYA in NW Yucatán, Mexico, *c*.150km (90mi) WSW of CHICHÉN ITZÁ and *c*.40km (25mi) SW of Mayapán. It was an important regional centre in the 9th century AD, during the Postclassic period, when many fine buildings were built in a highly decorative style. The Governor's Palace and the Pyramid of the Magician date from this period. Uxmal declined with the rise of the TOLTEC in the 10th century. The city was abandoned *c*.1450 during a period of civil strife.

Uzbekistan *See* country feature

Uzbeks Turkic-speaking people, originally from Persia, who form two thirds of the population of UZBEKISTAN. They took their name from Uzbeg Khan (d.1340), a chief of the GOLDEN HORDE. By the end of the 16th century, the Uzbeks had extended their rule to parts of Persia, Afghanistan and Chinese TURKISTAN. Their empire was never united, and in the 19th century its various states were absorbed by Russia.

UZBEKISTAN

AREA: 447,400sq km (172,740sq mi)
POPULATION: 21,206,800
CAPITAL (POPULATION): Tashkent (2,094,300)
ETHNIC GROUPS: Uzbek 71%, Russian 8%, Tajik 5%, Kazak 4%, Tatar 2%, Kara-Kalpak 2%, Crimean Tatar, Korean, Kyrgyz, Ukrainian, Turkmen
LANGUAGES: Uzbek (official)
RELIGIONS: Islam
GDP PER CAPITA (1995): US$2370

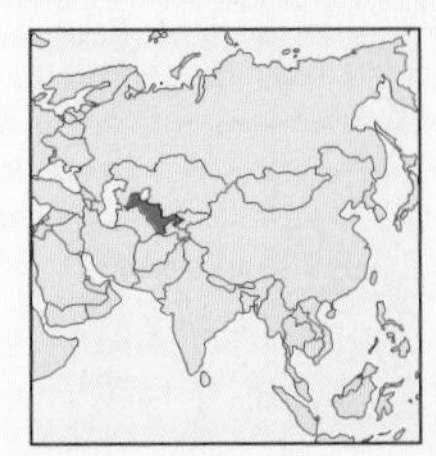

Republic in central Asia. Turkic people first settled in the area that is now Uzbekistan *c*.1500 years ago, and Islam was introduced in the 7th century AD. In the 13th century MONGOLS invaded the land, and in the late 14th century TAMERLANE ruled a great empire from SAMARKAND. Turkic UZBEK people invaded in the 16th century, and gradually the area was divided into states (khanates).

In the 19th century Russia controlled the area, and following the RUSSIAN REVOLUTION of 1917, the communists took over, and the Uzbek Soviet Socialist Republic became part of the SOVIET UNION in 1924. Under Soviet COMMUNISM, all aspects of Uzbek life were controlled; religion was discouraged, but education, health, housing and transport services improved. The Soviets also increased cotton production, but caused great environmental damage in the process.

In the 1980s, when reforms were being introduced in the Soviet Union, the Uzbeks demanded more freedom. In 1990 the government unilaterally declared independence from the Soviet Union. In 1991, following the break-up of the Soviet Union, Uzbekistan became a sovereign nation. It retained its links with Russia, however, through membership of the COMMONWEALTH OF INDEPENDENT STATES (CIS). In December 1991 Islam Karimov, leader of the People's Democratic Party (formerly the Communist Party), was elected president. In 1992 and 1993 many opposition leaders were arrested. In order to avoid internal disruption, Karimov asserted that economic reform would be slow. In 1995 a referendum extended President Karimov's term in office until 2000.

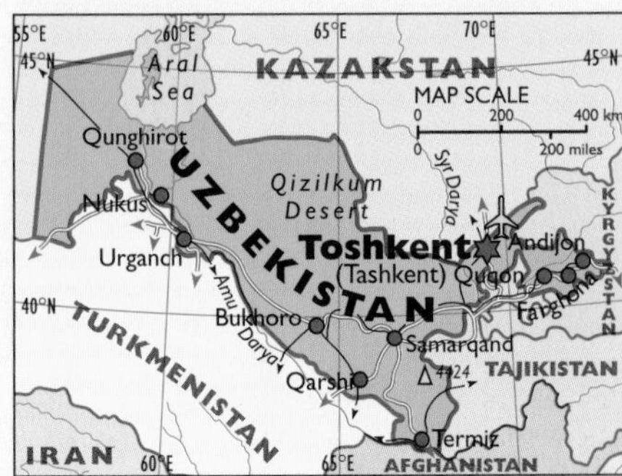

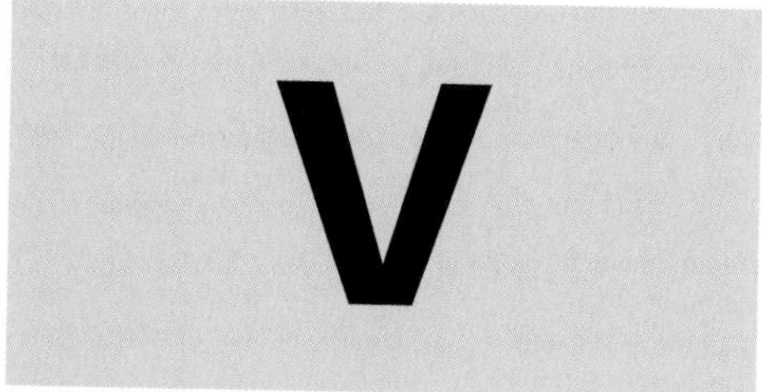

V1, V2 rockets (abbreviation for *Vergeltungswaffen*, Ger. "Vengeance Weapons") German ballistic missiles used in WORLD WAR 2. The **V-1**s, popularly known as **doodlebugs**, **flying bombs** or **buzz bombs**, were pilotless aircraft, powered by a pulse-jet engine. Launched by the LUFTWAFFE against SE England in June 1944, they carried *c.*1 tonne of high explosive. Later in 1944, England was attacked by the **V-2**, a long-range, guided missile carrying a 1-tonne warhead to a range of 320km (200mi), with an altitude of 95–110km (60–70mi). It was powered by a mixture of liquid oxygen and ethyl alcohol. Developed by Wernher von Braun (1912–77), the V2 rockets were the precursors of post-war missiles.

Valdemar IV (*c.*1320–75) (Waldemar Atterday) King of Denmark (1340–75). From 1328 to 1338 Valdemar was based at the court of Emperor LOUIS IV (THE BAVARIAN). By 1340 he had regained sovereignty of Denmark from the counts of Holstein. Valdemar restored the Danish kingdom, after a century of disintegration, by a mixture of force, diplomacy and persuasion. In 1360 he captured Skåne from Sweden; in 1361 he captured the island of Gotland. Valdemar's increasing power threatened that of the HANSEATIC LEAGUE, who, allied with his other enemies, notably Sweden and Holstein, defeated him in 1368. The Treaty of Stralsund (1370) allowed Valdemar to retain the Danish throne, providing that the Hanseatic League were granted trading privileges. The marriage of Valdemar's daughter Margaret (later MARGARET I) to Haakon VI of Norway prepared the way for the KALMAR UNION.

Valdivia, Pedro de (*c.*1498–1554) Spanish CONQUISTADOR. He travelled to South America in 1534 and was important in the conquest of Venezuela. In Peru, he fought with Francisco PIZARRO against Diego de ALMAGRO. In 1541 Valdivia led *c.*150 soldiers across the Atacama Desert to begin the conquest of Chile. He founded the city of Santiago, now capital of Chile, in 1541. Valdivia returned to Peru (1547) to assist in the suppression of Gonzalo PIZARRO's uprising. Returning to Chile (1548), Validivia became governor and began the conquest of the south. He founded the city of Concepción (1550) and Valdivia (1552). Valdivia was killed during a revolt by Araucanian Native Americans.

Valencia City in E Spain, capital of the province of Valencia. Originally settled by the Romans, the city was conquered by the MOORS in the 8th century, eventually becoming capital of the independent Moorish kingdom of Valencia. It was conquered by JAMES I (THE CONQUEROR) in 1238 and became part of the kingdom of ARAGÓN. In the Spanish CIVIL WAR it was the last Republican stronghold to fall to Nationalist forces. Pop. (1991) 752,909.

Valera, Eamon de *See* DE VALERA, EAMON

Valerian (d.260) (Publius Licinius Valerianus) Roman emperor (253–60). He was proclaimed emperor by his troops after the deaths of Emperor Gallus and his rival Aemilianus. Valerian split the ROMAN EMPIRE with his son GALLIENUS, whom he sent to defend territory in the west. In 257 Valerian revived the persecution of Christians, begun under Emperor DECIUS (r.249–51). Christians were required to perform public acts of worship to the state gods, and penalties were ordered for those who refused. The persecution ended when Valerian was captured (260) by the SASANIAN ruler Shapur I while attempting to defend the eastern boundaries of the Roman Empire. He died in captivity and was succeeded by Gallienus.

Valley Forge Site of the winter camp (1777–78) of George WASHINGTON's Continental Army. It was situated 34km (21mi) NW of Philadelphia, which was occupied by British troops. Washington's men were short of food, proper housing and clothes, and *c.*2500 out of 11,000 died. Their ordeal became symbolic of the heroism of the colonial troops in the AMERICAN REVOLUTION.

Valois French dynasty (1328–1589), which provided France with 13 kings. The House of Valois came to power under PHILIP VI, cousin of the last CAPETIAN king, CHARLES IV (THE FAIR). Valois kings survived the HUNDRED YEARS' WAR (1337–1453) and defeated challenges by Burgundian and Armagnac rivals. They consolidated royal strength over feudal lords, establishing the monarch's sole right to raise taxes and to wage war. LOUIS XI (r.1461–83) is considered the founder of French royal absolutism. The direct Valois line ended (1498) with CHARLES VIII. The dynasty was continued by LOUIS XII (Valois-Orléans) and, after his death (1515), by FRANCIS I and the Valois-Angoulême line. Francis embarked on the ultimately disastrous ITALIAN WARS against the HABSBURGS. With the death (1589) of HENRY III, the House of BOURBON, descending from a younger son of LOUIS IX, ascended the throne in the person of HENRY IV. *See also* CHARLES VII (THE WELL-SERVED); CHARLES IX; HENRY II; RELIGION, WARS OF

Van Buren, Martin (1782–1862) Eighth president of the United States (1837–41). He served in the Senate (1821–28), as governor of New York (1828) and as Andrew JACKSON's secretary of state (1829–31). Van Buren's opposition to John CALHOUN's idea of NULLIFICATION earned him the vice-presidency (1832–36) and the DEMOCRATIC PARTY presidential nomination (1836). He was an advocate of STATES' RIGHTS, and his presidency was plunged into crisis by the lack of federal intervention to counteract the economic depression (1837). In foreign affairs, Van Buren sought conciliation with Britain over the AROOSTOOK WAR (1838–39), resulting in the WEBSTER-ASHBURTON TREATY. He was heavily defeated by William HARRISON in the 1840 elections. Van Buren's rejection of the annexation of TEXAS and opposition to the extension of SLAVERY lost him the Democratic nomination in 1844. In 1848 he was the FREE SOIL PARTY's unsuccessful presidential candidate. *See also* ALBANY REGENCY

Vandals Germanic tribe who attacked the ROMAN EMPIRE in the 5th century AD. The Vandals are thought to have originated in the Baltic region. In the 3rd century AD there were Vandals living in the Roman provinces of DACIA and PANNONIA. In the 4th century they were forced west by the HUNS. In the early 5th century they looted Roman Gaul, but were defeated by the Franks. They invaded Spain in 409. Conflict with the Romans and VISIGOTHS forced the Vandals to move south to Andalusia. In 429, under GAISERIC, they invaded North Africa, defeating the forces of the Roman Empire and establishing a kingdom. In 439, following the capture of CARTHAGE, the Vandal kingdom was at the height of its power. Expanding through the Mediterranean region, they sacked Rome in 455. After Gaiseric's death (477), the kingdom declined and was finally destroyed (533–34) when Byzantine general BELISARIUS captured Carthage.

Vanderbilt, Cornelius (1794–1877) US railroad owner and financier. He established a steamboat company (1829) and by 1846 was a millionaire. During the California gold rush (1848–49), Vanderbilt ran a shipping line between New York and San Francisco, providing cheap transport for "Forty-Niners". He then entered the transoceanic transport business (1854). During the American Civil War Vanderbilt built a railroad empire, which, in 1873, connected New York and Chicago by rail.

Vane, Sir Henry (1613–62) English statesman. A Puritan, he served (1636–37) as governor of Massachusetts, but soon returned to English politics. As a member of the LONG PARLIAMENT and an opponent of CHARLES I, Vane was involved in the impeachments of William LAUD and the Earl of STRAFFORD. He was a proponent of the abolition of episcopacy and secured the SOLEMN LEAGUE AND COVENANT (1643) with Scotland. During the English CIVIL WAR, Vane was effectively the civilian head of the Parliamentarians, while Oliver CROMWELL led the Parliamentary army. Vane negotiated with Charles I and was opposed to the king's execution. He objected to PRIDE'S PURGE of the Long Parliament, but served in the resulting RUMP PARLIAMENT, becoming a member (1649–53) of Oliver Cromwell's council of state during the COMMONWEALTH period. Opposed to Cromwell becoming "lord protector", Vane temporarily (1653–59) left politics until after Cromwell's death. After the RESTORATION (1660), Vane was convicted of treason and executed.

VANUATU

AREA: 12,190sq km (4706sq mi)
POPULATION: 181,358
CAPITAL (POPULATION): Vila (31,800)
GOVERNMENT: Parliamentary republic
ETHNIC GROUPS: Melanesian (95%), Micronesian
LANGUAGES: Bislama, English, French
RELIGIONS: Presbyterian 40%, Anglican 20%, Catholic 20%
GDP PER CAPITA (1994): US$2276

Vanuatu Volcanic archipelago in the SW Pacific Ocean, *c.*2300km (1430mi) E of Australia. The main islands are Espiritu Santo, Efate, Malekula, Pentecost, Malo and Tanna. Archaeological evidence suggests that the N islands were inhabited by Melanesians by 1300 BC. The first European discovery was made in 1606 by Pedro Fernandez de Queiros, a Portuguese explorer. Louis de BOUGAINVILLE rediscovered the islands in 1768, and in 1774 James COOK mapped the islands, naming them New Hebrides. The islands were settled by the English and French in the early 1800s. Governed jointly by France and Britain as the New Hebrides from 1906, Vanuatu became an independent republic in 1980.

Varanasi (Benares, Banoras) City on the River Ganges, Uttar Pradesh, N India. By the 2nd millennium BC Varanasi was an Aryan religious centre. In the 6th century BC, Buddha is reputed to have preached his first sermon at nearby Sarnath. The holiest city in HINDUISM, Varanasi suffered under Muslim occupation from the 12th century, when many of its Hindu temples were destroyed. In the 18th century it became an independent kingdom. It remained a religious centre under British rule. After Indian independence (1947) Varanasi became part of Uttar Pradesh. Each year millions of Hindus make the pilgrimage to Varanasi in order to achieve ritual purification by bathing in the Ganges. Pop. (1991) 1,026,000.

Varangians *See* VIKINGS

Vargas, Getúlio Dorneles (1883–1954) Brazilian statesman, president (1930–45, 1951–54). He served as minister of finance (1926–28), before becoming governor of Rio Grande do Sul. In 1930 Vargas stood unsuccessfully as a reformist candidate in presidential elections. After his defeat, he led a revolt, overthrowing the republic. Vargas' autocratic regime was bolstered by the army. In 1937 he abolished the constitutional government and established the totalitarian, pro-fascist *Estado Novo* (New State). A programme of industrialization and nationalization stimulated the economy; educational and social reforms were also introduced. Vargas' refusal to heed calls for greater democracy and to grant elections led to his ousting in a military coup. Vargas was elected to his second term as president as a Labour Party candidate. His administration was tainted by scandal. Opposition from the right wing increased until Vargas, rather than resign, committed suicide.

Vasa dynasty (1523–1818) Ruling family of Sweden. Swedish opposition to the KALMAR UNION had coalesced under the regent Sten STURE (the Younger). CHRISTIAN II of Denmark brutally crushed the rebellion and initiated the STOCKHOLM BLOODBATH (1520). Gustav Ericsson Vasa, a relative of the Stures, escaped from prison in Denmark, launched a successful rebellion (1520) and was elected king, as GUSTAVUS I (VASA), in 1523. He stabilized state finances and confiscated property belonging to the Roman Catholic Church, precipitating the Reformation in Sweden. He was succeeded in turn by his sons ERIC XIV and JOHN III. In 1592 John's son, SIGISMUND III (VASA), united the Polish and Swedish crowns and the JAGIELLON and Vasa dynasties but was overthrown by Gustavus' youngest son, CHARLES IX, thus precipitating a long conflict with Poland.

Charles was succeeded by his son GUSTAVUS II, who took Sweden into the THIRTY YEARS' WAR (1618–48). Gustavus enacted major administrative and constitutional reforms, creating a strong, central government. He was succeeded by his daughter, CHRISTINA, who presided over the end of the Thirty Years' War. Her abdication led to the accession of her cousin, CHARLES X, whose territorial ambitions provoked the First NORTHERN WAR (1655–60). Further territorial expansion took place during the reign (1660–97) of his son, CHARLES XI. The Great NORTHERN WAR erupted during the reign (1697–1718) of CHARLES XII. After his death in the invasion of Norway, Sweden was briefly ruled (1718–20) by his sister, Ulrika Eleonora. She abdicated in favour of her husband, Frederick I, whose reign (1720–51) marked the start of a period of parliamentary government known as the "Age of Freedom". The increasing power of the parliament limited the effectiveness of Frederick's successor, Adolf Frederick (r.1751–71), a distant relative. His son, GUSTAVUS III, imposed a new constitution, restricting the power of the parliament. After Gustavus' assassination (1792), his son, GUSTAVUS IV, acceded to the throne. Gustavus IV led Sweden into the NAPOLEONIC WARS. After a series of defeats, Gustavus was overthrown by the army (1809). He was succeeded by his uncle, CHARLES XIII. Charles died (1818) with no heirs, and one of NAPOLEON'S marshals, Jean Baptiste Bernadotte, became CHARLES XIV.

Vasco da Gama *See* DA GAMA, VASCO

Vasily I (1371–1425) (Vasily Dmitrievich) Grand prince of Moscow (1389–1425), son and successor of Dmitry Donskoy (r.1359–89). In 1383 Vasily travelled to the court of the TATAR khan, Tokhtamysh, in order to obtain permission for his father to rule Vladimir. Vasily was taken hostage by the Tatars but escaped in 1386 and later assisted Tokhtamysh in his campaigns against TAMERLANE. As grand prince of Moscow and Vladimir, Vasily expanded his territory to the Volga region, acquiring Nizhny Novgorod and Murom. Conflict with NOVGOROD continued intermittently for twenty years. Vasily managed to make his principality virtually independent of the Tatars, but towards the end of his reign was again obliged to recognize Tatar suzerainty.

vassal In the FEUDAL SYSTEM, a free man who bound himself to a king or lord by an oath of FEALTY for mutual protection. In exchange for certain obligations, such as military service, the vassal received an area of land known as a FIEF.

VATICAN CITY

AREA: 0.44sq km (0.2sq mi)
POPULATION: 1000
CAPITAL (POPULATION): Vatican City (1000)
GOVERNMENT: Pontificate
ETHNIC GROUPS: Italian, Swiss
LANGUAGES: Latin (official), Italian
RELIGIONS: Roman Catholic
GDP PER CAPITA (1994): US$17,930

Vatican City World's smallest independent state, existing as a walled enclave within the city of ROME, W central Italy. It is the official home of the PAPACY and an independent base for the Holy See (governing body of the ROMAN CATHOLIC CHURCH). The first papal residence was established here in the 5th century, and it has been the papal home ever since, apart from a brief spell at AVIGNON in the 14th century. Vatican City did not achieve full independence until the LATERAN TREATY (1929), by which the papacy surrendered its claim to the PAPAL STATES in return for the establishment of Vatican City as an independent state. The Commission, appointed to administer the Vatican's affairs, has its own radio service, police and railway station, and issues its own stamps and coins. The treasures of the Vatican, notably Michelangelo's frescos in the Sistine Chapel and ST PETER'S, attract huge numbers of tourists and pilgrims.

Vatican Council, First (1869–70) Twentieth ECUMENICAL COUNCIL of the ROMAN CATHOLIC CHURCH. Convened by Pope PIUS IX to rebut various contemporary ideas associated with the rise of liberalism and materialism, it is remembered for the controversial declaration of PAPAL INFALLIBILITY. After the occupation of Rome by Piedmontese troops (1870), Pius was obliged to suspend the Council indefinitely.

Vatican Council, Second (1962–65) Twenty-first ECUMENICAL COUNCIL of the ROMAN CATHOLIC CHURCH. It was convened by Pope JOHN XXIII to revive and renew Christian faith and to put the Church in closer touch with ordinary people. Among the most significant results were the introduction of the Mass in the vernacular, a greater role for lay people and a greater tolerance for other sects and other religions. After the death of John XXIII (1963), Pope PAUL VI continued the Council.

Vauban, Sebastien le Prestre, Marquis de (1633–1707) French military engineer. In 1651 he joined the forces of Louis II, Prince de CONDÉ, during the FRONDE. He was soon persuaded to change sides in support of the royalty. As a royal engineer (1655–1703), Vauban revolutionized siege warfare, participating in *c.*20 successful sieges during the 1670s. He improved and redesigned the fortresses surrounding the French kingdom and introduced the use of ricochet gunfire. Vauban's work was vital to the success of LOUIS XIV's numerous military campaigns, and in 1703 he was rewarded with the title marshal of France.

Vedanta (Sanskrit, conclusion of the VEDAS) Best-known and most popular form of Indian philosophy; it forms the foundation for most modern schools of thought in HINDUISM. One of the most influential Vedanta schools was that expounded by the 8th-century philosopher SHANKARA. This school holds that the natural world is an illusion. There is only one self, Brahman-Atman; ignorance of the oneness of the self with Brahman is the cause of rebirth. The system includes a belief in the transmigration of souls and the desirability of release from the cycle of rebirth. It is based on the writings known as the UPANISHADS.

Vedas Ancient and most sacred writings of HINDUISM. They consist of series of hymns and formulaic chants that constituted a Hindu liturgy. There are four Vedas: *Rig Veda*, containing a priestly tradition originally brought to India by ARYANS; *Yajur Veda*, consisting of prayers and sacred formulas; *Sama Veda*, containing melodies and chants; and *Atharva Veda*, a collection of popular hymns, incantations and magic spells. The Vedas were composed between *c.*1500 and 1200 BC.

Velázquez, Diego de (*c.*1465–1524) Spanish CONQUISTADOR and first governor of Cuba (1514–21, 1523–24). He sailed with Christopher COLUMBUS to Hispaniola in 1493. In 1511 he was sent by Diego Columbus, Christopher COLUMBUS' son, on an expedition to conquer Cuba. By 1514 the whole island had been conquered, and Velázquez became governor. He founded settlements at Baracoa, Bayamo, Santiago de Cuba and Havana. Velázquez commissioned three expeditions to the Mexican coast, placing Hernán CORTÉS in charge of the third venture (1519). When Cortés refused to return, Velázquez sent Pánfilo de NARVÁEZ (1520) and later Cristóbel de Olid (1524) to compel him to return to Cuba; they were both defeated.

Velasco Ibarra, José María (1893–1979) Ecuadorean statesman, president (1934–35, 1944–47, 1952–56, 1960–61, 1968–72). He was deposed from his first two terms in office, going into exile, first in Colombia and later in Argentina. His third term as president was marked by improvements to Ecuador's infrastructure, notably the building of roads and schools. As president for a fourth time, he attempted to reform the economy. His austerity measures were so unpopular that he was forced to resign. Velasco's final term coincided with a period of great

VENEZUELA

AREA: 912,050sq km (352,143sq mi)
POPULATION: 21,378,000
CAPITAL (POPULATION): Caracas (1,824,892)
GOVERNMENT: Federal republic
ETHNIC GROUPS: Mestizo 67%, White 21%, Black 10%, Native American 2%
LANGUAGES: Spanish (official)
RELIGIONS: Christianity (Roman Catholic 94%)
GDP PER CAPITA (1995): US$7900

Republic in N South America. The original inhabitants of Venezuela were the Arawak and Carib Native Americans. The first European discovery was made (1498) by Christopher COLUMBUS. In 1499 Amerigo VESPUCCI explored the coastline and nicknamed the country Venezuela ("little Venice"). Spanish settlements were soon established, and German explorers, notably Nikolaus Federmann, completed the conquest. Venezuela became part of the Spanish Viceroyalty of NEW GRANADA.

In the late 18th century, uprisings against Spanish rule were led by Francisco de MIRANDA. In 1821 Simón BOLÍVAR liberated Venezuela, and it became part of Greater Colombia, a republic that also included Colombia, Ecuador and Panama. In 1830 Venezuela became a separate state. The mid- to late-19th century was marked by political instability and civil war. Venezuela was ruled by a series of dictators: Antonio GUZMÁN BLANCO (r.1870–88) was followed by Joaquín Crespo and then Cipriano Castro, under whom financial corruption reached new heights.

Juan Vicente GÓMEZ's long and autocratic rule (1908–35) provided the stability for Venezuela to pay off its debts, helped by international interest in its rich oil-fields. In 1945 a pro-democracy military junta, led by Rómulo Betancourt, gained control. In 1948 Rómulo Gallegos was elected president, but a military coup the same year re-established a dictatorship. In 1958 popular uprisings brought a return to democracy, with Betancourt as president. Venezuela became increasingly prosperous, but left-wing uprisings, notably two revolts in 1962 (covertly supported by Fidel CASTRO), led to much violence.

In 1976 Venezuela nationalized its oil industry, using the money to raise living standards. In 1989 Carlos Andrés Pérez became president. He introduced free-market reforms, but inflation and unemployment continued to rise. In 1992 there were two failed military coups. In 1993 Pérez resigned after charges of corruption. In 1994 Rafael Caldera became president. His austerity measures provoked civil unrest. In 1999 Hugo Chávez Frías of the Fifth Republic Movement (MVR), leader of one of the failed coups in 1992, became president.

unrest. In 1970 he established a military-backed dictatorship in an attempt to stop the student riots and economic recession. Two years later he was ousted by the army.

Vendée, Wars of the (1793–96) Counter-revolutionary risings by the peasantry of the Vendée district of w France during the FRENCH REVOLUTION. They were provoked by Maximilien ROBESPIERRE's attack on the Roman Catholic Church and by Georges DANTON's introduction of conscription. The uprising began when peasant leaders combined with royalists to raise a force of *c*.30,000 men to rid the district of revolutionary officials. The "Catholic and Royal Army" was initially successful, capturing several towns in the region and spreading to other areas of France. In late 1793 the main army (now *c*.65,000 strong) was defeated at Cholet. A smaller army attempted to maintain the revolt in the Vendée, but was defeated at Le Mans and finally crushed at Savenay. A peace was negotiated by which the region was granted an amnesty and freedom of religion. A brief, and again unsuccessful, rising occurred in 1796. *See also* THERMIDORIAN REACTION

Vendôme, Louis Joseph, Duc de (1654–1712) French soldier. He distinguished himself during the War of the GRAND ALLIANCE (1689–97), when, as the commander in Catalonia, he captured Barcelona (1697). Conflict soon returned to France with the War of the SPANISH SUCCESSION (1701–14). Vendôme commanded the French army in N Italy, fighting Prince EUGÈNE OF SAVOY at Luzzara (1702) and defeating him at Cassano (1705). As commander of the troops in Flanders, however, Vendôme was decisively defeated by Eugène and John Churchill, Duke of MARLBOROUGH, at the Battle of OUDENAARDE (1708). His prestige was restored when, as commander of PHILIP V's troops in Spain, he recaptured Madrid and defeated the British at Brihuega and the Austrians at Villaviciosa (1710).

Venezuela *See* country feature

Venezuelan Boundary Dispute Border controversy between British Guiana (now GUYANA) and VENEZUELA. The boundary between British Guiana and Venezuela had been in dispute ever since the British took control of Guiana from the Dutch (1814). The conflict intensified when gold was discovered in the area. The United States became involved (1895) when Secretary of State Richard Olney (1835–1917) declared that the United States was allowed, by the MONROE DOCTRINE, to intervene in the settling of such conflicts in the Americas. The British agreed to the United States' suggestion that an independent commission determine the border. The boundary was eventually decided in favour of Britain's claims (1899).

Venice (Venezia) City on the Gulf of Venice, at the head of the Adriatic Sea, N Italy, capital of Venetia region. It is built on 118 islands, separated by narrow canals, and joined by a causeway to the mainland. The islands of Venice were settled in the 5th century AD by Veneti fleeing from the Barbarian invasions of Italy. By the late 9th century Venice was an independent republic ruled by an elected DOGE. In 1310 the Council of Ten was established, which, with a senate, controlled the government of the CITY-STATE of Venice. After defeating GENOA at the Battle of Chioggia in 1381, Venice became the most important European seapower, engaging in trade in the Mediterranean and Asia. It was at the height of its powers in the 15th century, when it governed not only many islands in the Mediterranean, but also several mainland Italian towns. In the early 16th century a coalition of European powers established the League of CAMBRAI (1508–10) to reclaim territory from Venice in the ITALIAN WARS. Despite helping to defeat the Ottomans at the Battle of LEPANTO (1571), Venice gradually lost much of its territory to the Turks. In 1797 it was captured by the French; it was ceded to Austria in 1815, and became part of Italy in 1866. Pop. (1992) 305,617.

Venizélos, Eleuthérios (1864–1936) Greek statesman, prime minister (1910–15, 1917–20, 1924, 1928–32, 1933). Active in the anti-Turkish movement in his native Crete, Venizélos participated in the rising that eventually forced the OTTOMAN EMPIRE to leave. During his first term as prime minister, Venizélos presided over a huge increase in Greek territory as a result of the BALKAN WARS (1912–13). In 1917 he forced King CONSTANTINE to abdicate so that Greece could enter WORLD WAR I on the Allied side. He negotiated for Greek interests at the Versailles peace conference, although much of Greece's territorial gains were later lost to Turkey under ATATÜRK. A committed anti-royalist, Venizélos supported an unsuccessful military coup against the monarchy in 1935 and was forced into exile. He died in France.

Ventris, Michael (1922–56) British architect and linguist. In 1952 he deciphered MYCENAEAN CIVILIZATION scripts, written in Linear B, which were found at Knossos, Crete, and other sites. His theory, now universally accepted, that Linear B was an archaic form of the Greek language was published in 1953. *See also* LINEAR SCRIPT

Vercingetorix (d.46 BC) Chieftain of the Gallic Averni tribe during the Roman conquest of GAUL. In 52 BC, towards the end of the GALLIC WARS (58–51 BC), Vercingetorix united the diverse Gallic tribes in a major revolt against Julius CAESAR. A brilliant strategist, Vercingetorix initially achieved a number of victories. He retreated before Caesar's forces, burning towns in order to destroy supplies. Vercingetorix halted at the fortress of Alesia, where Caesar encircled him, destroyed his reinforcements and captured him. He was taken to Rome, displayed in Caesar's triumph (46 BC) and then executed.

Verdun, Battle of (February–December 1916) Campaign of WORLD WAR I. A German offensive in the region of Verdun made initial advances but was checked by the French under General Henri PÉTAIN. After a series of renewed German assaults, the Allied offensive on the SOMME drew off German troops, and the French regained the lost territory. Total casualties were *c*.1 million.

Verdun, Treaty of (August 843) Agreement dividing the Carolingian empire of CHARLEMAGNE among the sons of LOUIS I (THE PIOUS). Louis' attempt to give territory to his son from his second marriage, the future CHARLES II (THE BALD), provoked revolts by his older sons. After Louis' death (840) civil war broke out. LOTHAIR I was defeated at the Battle of Fontenoy (841) and peace negotiations began. The Treaty of Verdun divided the empire into three: Charles II (the Bald) received the W part of the empire (Francia Occidentalis); LOUIS II (THE GERMAN) received the E part of the empire (Francia Orientalis); and Lothair I received Francia Media, the central region from the Low Countries to Italy, as well as confirmation of his imperial title. *See also* CAROLINGIANS; FRANKS

Vereeniging, Treaty of (31 May 1902) Peace treaty negotiated at Vereeniging and signed at Pretoria, SOUTH AFRICA. It ended the second of the SOUTH AFRICAN WARS (1899–1902). The AFRIKANERS were forced to accept British rule, leading to eventual self-government within the BRITISH EMPIRE. Concessions granted to the Afrikaners included: an amnesty to those who had participated in the War; compensation for the destruction of Afrikaner farms; and the postponement of a decision regarding the enfranchisement of black South Africans until the Afrikaners had achieved self-government. *See also* FREE STATE; TRANSVAAL

Vermont State in New England, NE United States, on the Canadian border. The state capital is Montpelier. The earliest inhabitants of the region were the ABNAKI Native North Americans. In 1609 Samuel de CHAMPLAIN discovered the lake that now bears his name, but the region was not settled permanently until a French community was established in 1724. British settlement increased after the last of the FRENCH AND INDIAN WARS (1754–63). Land-grant disputes between New Hampshire and New York persisted for many years; the GREEN MOUNTAIN BOYS militia was formed (1764) to uphold settlers' rights. In 1777 Vermont declared its independence. Area: 24,887sq km (9,609sq mi). Pop. (1996) 588,654.

Versailles City in N France, 16km (10mi) SW of Paris, capital of Yvelines department. It is famous for its former royal palace, now a world heritage site visited by two million tourists a year. Louis XIII built his hunting lodge at Versailles. In 1682 LOUIS XIV made Versailles his royal seat and transformed the lodge into a palace. The architects Louis Le Vau, Jules Hardouin-Mansart and Robert de Cotte built the monumental palace in a French classical style. The interior was designed by Charles Lebrun. The magnificent gardens were landscaped by André Le Nôtre. The palace was a royal residence until the French Revolution (1789–99). It was the scene of the signing of peace treaties after the Franco-Prussian War and World War 1. Pop. (1990) 91,030.

VERMONT
Statehood :
4 March 1791
Nickname :
The Green Mountain State
State motto :
Freedom and unity

Versailles, Treaty of (28 June 1919) Peace agreement concluding WORLD WAR I, signed at VERSAILLES, France. It represented a compromise between US President Woodrow WILSON's FOURTEEN POINTS and the demands of the European allies for heavy penalties against Germany. The major players at the Paris Peace Conference were President Wilson, British Prime Minster David LLOYD GEORGE, French Premier Georges CLEMENCEAU and Italian Prime Minister Vittorio ORLANDO. German territorial concessions included: ALSACE-Lorraine to France; part of the ARDENNES to Belgium; N SCHLESWIG to Denmark; and much territory in the E, including parts of W PRUSSIA and Upper SILESIA, to Poland. Germany lost all its overseas colonies to the various Allied powers. A clause was included in the Treaty by which Germany had to accept "war guilt" and pay extensive REPARATIONS for war damage. The RHINELAND was demilitarized and strict limits were placed on German armed forces. The Treaty also established the LEAGUE OF NATIONS. It was never ratified by the United States, which signed a separate peace with Germany in 1921. The harshness of the Treaty and the resentment that it aroused in Germany is considered by many to have assisted Adolf HITLER in his rise to power in the 1930s. *See also* ST-GERMAIN, TREATY OF; SÈVRES, TREATY OF; TRIANON, TREATY OF

Verwoerd, Hendrik Frensch (1901–66) South African statesman, prime minister (1958–66), b. Holland. A vocal advocate of APARTHEID, he served (1950–58) as minister of native affairs, promoting the policy of "separate development" of the races. On the death of Johannes STRIJDOM, Verwoerd succeeded as prime minister and leader of the NATIONAL PARTY. In 1961 the harshness of Verwoerd's regime was highlighted by the SHARPEVILLE massacre and the banning of the AFRICAN NATIONAL CONGRESS (ANC). In the same year, Verwoerd led South Africa out of the Commonwealth of Nations. He was assassinated in Parliament.

Vesey, Denmark (*c*.1767–1822) African-born slave who led a conspiracy among US slaves in the region of Charleston, South Carolina. In 1800, having won a lottery, Vesey bought his freedom from SLAVERY. Under cover of church meetings, he and his followers planned an uprising in which arsenals would be seized, the city destroyed and slaves freed. The plot was betrayed and *c*.130 people were arrested. Vesey and 35 others were hanged.

Vespasian (AD 9–79) (Titus Flavius Vespasianus) Roman emperor (69–79). A successful general and administrator, he was quelling the Jewish Revolt (66–73) in PALESTINE when he was proclaimed emperor by his soldiers after civil war had erupted following the death of NERO. Vespasian was the founder of the Flavian dynasty. He proved a capable ruler, extending and strengthening the ROMAN EMPIRE, rectifying the budget deficit, widening qualifications for Roman citizenship and adding to the monuments of Rome.

Vespucci, Amerigo (1454–1512) Italian maritime explorer. He was possibly the first to realize that the Americas constituted new continents, which were named after him by the German cartographer Martin Waldseemüller in 1507. Vespucci made at least two transatlantic voyages (1497–1504).

Vichy government (1940–45) Regime established in France during WORLD WAR 2 after its defeat by Germany. Its capital was the town of Vichy, Auvergne, central France. The Franco-German Armistice (22 June 1940)

divided France into two zones, one occupied by Germany and the other, nominally, under French sovereignty. The Vichy regime also held authority over France's overseas possessions. The government was set up in July 1942 under Marshal Henri PÉTAIN, with Pierre LAVAL as his vice premier. France's Third Republic was officially abolished. Laval advocated close cooperation with Germany and was dismissed by Pétain (December 1940). In 1941 Jean DARLAN became vice premier. After German forces occupied Vichy France in November 1942, the Vichy regime became little more than a puppet government. Pétain was forced to reinstate Laval, who actively cooperated with the Nazis. The Allied liberation of France saw the final collapse of the Vichy government.

Vicksburg, Siege of (1863) Culmination of the Union campaign (November 1862–July 1863) to capture Vicksburg, Mississippi, during the American CIVIL WAR. Vicksburg was the Confederates' last stronghold on the Mississippi River. In May–June 1862 an attempt to capture the city by river failed. In November William SHERMAN approached Vicksburg from the north, but was forced to retreat. Ulysses GRANT decided to approach the city from the south. Having crossed the river at Bruinsburg, he led his troops northeast, cutting off Confederate General Joseph JOHNSTON. Grant then marched west towards Vicksburg. He defeated Confederate General John Pemberton, forcing him to retreat to Vicksburg. A six-week siege then ensued before Pemberton and his Confederate troops surrendered. The capture of Vicksburg, on 4 July 1863, gave the Union control of the Mississippi and split the Confederacy in two.

Victor Amadeus II (1666–1732) Duke of SAVOY (1675–1713), king of SICILY (1713–20), king of SARDINIA (1720–30), son and successor of Charles Emmanuel II. In 1690 Victor Amadeus allied Savoy with the coalition opposed to LOUIS XIV in the War of the GRAND ALLIANCE (1689–97). In 1696, however, he agreed a separate peace with France, favourable to the interests of Savoy. In the War of the SPANISH SUCCESSION (1701–14) he initially sided with France, but soon changed to the Habsburg side. At the Peace of UTRECHT, he was awarded the title king of SICILY. In 1720 he was obliged by the QUADRUPLE ALLIANCE to exchange Sicily for Sardinia. He abdicated in favour of his son, CHARLES EMMANUEL III.

Victor Emmanuel II (1820–78) King of Piedmont-Sardinia (1849–61), king of Italy (1861–78). He succeeded his father, CHARLES ALBERT, as king of Piedmont-Sardinia. From 1852, guided by his chief minister, Conte di CAVOUR, Victor Emmanuel strengthened his kingdom. He formed a French alliance to defeat Austria (1859–61), gaining territory from them in N Italy. Further triumphs of the RISORGIMENTO included the conquest (1860) of Sicily and Naples by Giuseppe GARIBALDI. The following year Victor Emmanuel was proclaimed the first king of Italy. Venetia was acquired in 1866, and in 1870 the Papal States were captured. Rome became the new capital after French troops withdrew (1870). He was succeeded by his son, UMBERTO I.

Victor Emmanuel III (1869–1947) King of Italy (1900–46), son and successor of UMBERTO I. He brought Italy into World War 1 on the side of the Allies. In 1922 he appointed Benito MUSSOLINI as his prime minister. With Mussolini's seizure of Ethiopia and Albania, Victor Emmanuel became emperor of the former (1936) and king of the latter (1939). Although Mussolini established a dictatorship, the king retained the power to dismiss him and eventually did so in 1943. He replaced him with Pietro BADOGLIO, who arranged an armistice with the Allies and declared war on Germany. Victor Emmanuel abdicated in 1946 and was succeeded by his son, UMBERTO II.

Victoria *See* feature article

Victoria, Guadalupe (1786–1843) Mexican soldier and statesman, president (1824–29), b. Manuel Félix Fernández. From 1811 he served as a revolutionary soldier in José MORELOS' movement for Mexican independence. On achieving independence, Victoria supported Agustín de ITURBIDE, but when his rule proved dictatorial, Victoria joined Antonio de SANTA ANNA's successful rebellion. As first president of the Mexican Republic, Victoria established diplomatic relations with other countries and abolished slavery.

Victoria State in SE Australia, bounded by the Indian Ocean, the Bass Strait and the Tasman Sea. The capital is Melbourne (home to more than 65% of the state population). The region was part of NEW SOUTH WALES until 1851, when it became a separate colony. The population increased rapidly after 1851, when gold was discovered at Ballarat and Bendigo. The EUREKA STOCKADE (1854) resulted from the government's attempt to profit from the gold rush. Victoria became part of the Commonwealth of Australia in 1901. Area: 227,620sq km (87,813sq mi). Pop. (1991) 4,487,000.

Vienna (Wien) Capital of Austria, on the River Danube. Vienna became an important town under the Romans, but after their withdrawal in the 5th century it fell to a succession of invaders from E Europe. The first HABSBURG ruler was installed in 1276, and the city was the seat of the HOLY ROMAN EMPIRE from 1558 to 1806. Occupied by the French during the NAPOLEONIC WARS, it was later chosen as the site of the Congress of VIENNA. As the capital of the AUSTRO-HUNGARIAN EMPIRE, it was the cultural and social centre of 19th-century Europe under Emperor FRANZ JOSEPH. It suffered an economic and political collapse following the defeat of the Central Powers in World War 1. After World War 2, it was occupied (1945–55) by joint Soviet-Western forces. Pop. (1993) 1,589,052.

Vienna, Congress of (1814–15) European conference that settled international affairs after the NAPOLEONIC WARS (1803–15). It attempted, as far as possible, to restore the Europe of pre-1789, and thus disappointed the nationalists and liberals. Among steps to prevent future European wars, it established the CONGRESS SYSTEM and the GERMAN CONFEDERATION, a loose association for purposes of defence. Austria was represented by Klemens METTERNICH; Britain by Viscount CASTLEREAGH; Prussia by FREDERICK WILLIAM II; Russia by ALEXANDER I; and France by Charles TALLEYRAND. Austria regained most of its pre-war territory and gained Lombardy and Venice. Prussia also regained most of its land, and acquired Pomerania, parts of Saxony and land around the River Rhine. The Kingdom of the Netherlands was formed, comprising the United Provinces and Belgium. Denmark lost Norway to Sweden. The Bourbons returned to power in the Kingdom of the Two Sicilies, and the Papal States were restored to the papacy. Napoleon's Grand Duchy of Warsaw was divided between Prussia and Austria, with the remainder becoming a semi-independent Polish state, with the Russian tsar as king. *See also* PARIS, TREATIES OF

Viet Cong Nickname for the Vietnamese communist guerrillas who fought against the US-supported regime in South Vietnam during the VIETNAM WAR (1955–75). After earlier, isolated revolts against the government of Ngo Dinh DIEM, the movement was unified (1960) as the National Liberation Front (NLF), modelled on the VIET MINH.

Viet Minh Vietnamese organization that fought for independence from the French (1946–54). It resisted the Japanese occupation of French INDOCHINA during World War 2. After the War, when the French refused to recognize it as a provisional government, it began operations against the colonial forces. The French were forced to withdraw after their defeat at DIEN BIEN PHU (1954).

Vietnam *See* country feature

Vietnam War *See* feature article, page 430

Vijayanagar Hindu empire of SE India, centred on the city of Vijayanagar on the River Tungabhadra. In the 14th–16th centuries the empire controlled much of S India. The city itself was an important Hindu cultural centre, and its empire served as a barrier against invasions from Muslim-controlled N India. The empire was ruled by three dynasties: the sons of Sangama founded the empire (1336), and it was ruled by their family until *c.*1485; the Saluva family usurped power in *c.*1485 and ruled until 1503; the Tuluva dynasty (1503–85) presided over Vijayanagar's period of greatest strength. During the reign (1509–29) of Krishna Deva Raya, Vijayanagar's territory was increased by conquest, and several defeats were inflicted on the Muslim sultanates to the north. In 1585, however, Vijayanagar was defeated at the Battle of Talikota by an alliance of its rivals, the Muslim states of Ahmadnagar, Bijapur and Golconda. The city of Vijayanagar was destroyed, and, apart from a brief revival of power in the early 17th century, the empire collapsed.

Vikings Scandinavian, seaborne marauders, traders and settlers, who spread throughout much of Europe and the North Atlantic region between the 9th and 11th centuries. The remarkable Viking expansion seems to have been caused by rapid population growth and consequent scarcity of good farming land, as well as the desire for new sources of wealth. Their advanced maritime technology enabled them to cross N European waters in a period when other sailors feared to venture out of sight of land. They were in many respects more advanced than other European peoples, notably in metalwork. Although they first appeared in their greatly feared "longships" as raiders on the coasts of NW Europe, later groups came to settle. Swedes, known as Varangians, perhaps founded the first Russian state at NOVGOROD and traded via the River Volga in Byzantium and Persia. Danes conquered much of N and E England, an

VICTORIA (1819–1901)

Queen of Great Britain and Ireland (1837–1901) and empress of India (1876–1901). A granddaughter of GEORGE III, she succeeded her uncle, WILLIAM IV. In 1840 Victoria married her first cousin, Prince ALBERT of SAXE-COBURG-GOTHA. During her reign, the longest in English history, the role of the monarchy was established as a ceremonial, symbolic institution with virtually no power but much influence. Victoria learned statecraft from her first prime minister, Lord MELBOURNE, and was greatly influenced by the hard-working Prince Albert. After Albert's death (1861) she went into lengthy seclusion and her neglect of public duties aroused republican sentiments.

Victoria's domestic popularity was restored when she became empress of India and with the golden (1887) and diamond (1897) jubilee celebrations. Among later prime ministers, she maintained excellent terms with Benjamin DISRAELI (who astutely flattered her) but was on frosty terms with William GLADSTONE (who lectured her). Victoria reigned over a BRITISH EMPIRE containing 25% of the world's people and 30% of its land. Britain's trade and industry made it the world's richest country.

► **Victoria** became a symbol of the conservative morality of her era and succeeded in retaining the influence of the British monarchy at a time when its role was in question.

V

area that became known as DANELAW. Norwegians created kingdoms in N Britain and Ireland, founding Dublin (*c.*840) and other cities. Vikings also colonized Iceland, from where ERIC THE RED set out to establish settlements in Greenland. A short-lived settlement, VINLAND, was established in North America by LEIF ERICSON in *c.*1003. In the early 10th century, the Vikings, under ROLLO, settled in NORMANDY. Anarchic conditions in 10th-century Scandinavia resulted in the formation of larger, more powerful kingdoms, and Viking expansion declined. It was renewed in a different form with the conquest of England by King SWEYN I (FORKBEARD) of Denmark in 1013 and the NORMAN CONQUEST of 1066. *See also* RURIK

Villa, "Pancho" (Francisco) (1877–1923) Mexican revolutionary leader. At the start of the MEXICAN REVOLUTION (1910–20), Villa joined the forces of Francisco MADERO and was vital in the overthrow of Porfirio DÍAZ. Villa sided with Venustiano CARRANZA in opposition to Victoriano HUERTA's dictatorship but later supported Emiliano ZAPATA's struggle against Carranza. Angered by US recognition of Carranza's government, Villa murdered (1916) US citizens in N Mexico and New Mexico. US General John PERSHING was dispatched against Villa but failed to capture him. In 1920 Villa was pardoned in return for agreeing to retire from politics. He was assassinated three years later.

Villafranca, Treaty of (1859) Armistice concluded between France and Austria after Franco-Piedmontese victories at the battles of MAGENTA and SOLFERINO in the war to drive Austria out of N Italy. NAPOLEON III and Emperor FRANZ JOSEPH met at Villafranca, Venetia. Austria was allowed to retain Venetia, but Lombardy was given up to France so that it might then be ceded by France to Piedmont-Sardinia. The treaty was broken in 1860 when Piedmont annexed the central duchies of Tuscany and Modena. *See also* CAVOUR, CAMILLO BENSO, CONTE DI

Villehardouin, Geoffroi de (1150–1213) French historian, a leader of the Fourth CRUSADE. Villehardouin's incomplete account of the crusade, *Conquest of Constantinople*, was the first historical chronicle in French.

villein In the MANORIAL SYSTEM of medieval Europe, a peasant who was assigned a share of land in exchange for labour on his lord's DEMESNE as well as providing his lord with a share in what he produced or a sum of money. By the 13th century there was little difference between a villein and a SERF. Both were considered to be the property of the lord and could be bought and sold. The labour shortage caused by the BLACK DEATH (1347–52) resulted in an increase in status and rights for villeins, most of whom became copy holders. Villeinage in England had disappeared by the end of the 15th century. *See also* FEUDAL SYSTEM

VIETNAM

AREA: 331,689sq km (128,065sq mi)
POPULATION: 72,500,000
CAPITAL (POPULATION): Hanoi (1,088,862)
GOVERNMENT: Socialist republic
ETHNIC GROUPS: Vietnamese 87%, Tho (Tay), Chinese (Hoa), Tai, Khmer, Muong, Nung
LANGUAGES: Vietnamese (official)
RELIGIONS: Buddhism 55%, Christianity (Roman Catholic 7%)
GDP PER CAPITA (1994): US$213

Republic occupying an S-shaped strip of land in Southeast Asia. In 111 BC China seized Vietnam, naming it ANNAM. In 939 it became independent. In 1558 it split into two parts: TONKIN in the N, ruled from HANOI, and Annam in the S, ruled from Hué. In 1802, with French support, Vietnam was united as the empire of Vietnam under the NGUYEN emperor GIA LONG. The French took Saigon in 1859 and by 1887 had formed INDOCHINA from the union of Tonkin, Annam and COCHIN CHINA.

Japan conquered Vietnam during World War 2 and established a Vietnamese state under Emperor BAO DAI. After the war, Bao Dai's government collapsed, and the communist VIET MINH, led by HO CHI MINH, set up a Vietnamese republic. In 1946 the French tried to reassert control and war broke out. Despite aid from the United States, the French were defeated at DIEN BIEN PHU (1954) and Vietnam was divided along the 17th parallel: North Vietnam governed by Ho Chi Minh, and South Vietnam led by the French-supported Bao Dai. In 1955 Bao Dai was deposed and Ngo Dinh DIEM was elected president. Despite his authoritarian regime, Diem was recognized as the legal ruler of Vietnam by many Western countries. North Vietnam, supported by China and the Soviet Union, extended its influence into South Vietnam, mainly through the VIET CONG. The United States became increasingly involved in what they perceived to be the fight against communism. The conflict soon escalated into the VIETNAM WAR (1955–75). In 1973 LE DUC THO negotiated a cease-fire with the United States, but South Vietnam's President NGUYEN VAN THIEU continued to wage war until LE DUAN's nationalist forces overran South Vietnam.

In 1976 the reunited Vietnam became a socialist republic under Prime Minister Pham Van DONG. In the late 1970s Vietnam invaded Cambodia, defeating the KHMER ROUGE government. It withdrew its troops in 1989. Vietnam's weak economy was improved in the late 1980s and 1990s with the introduction of free-market economic reforms, known as *Doi Moi*. In 1995 it became a member of ASEAN.

VIRGINIA
Statehood :
25 June 1788
Nickname :
Old Dominion
State motto :
Thus always to tyrants

Villiers, George *See* BUCKINGHAM, GEORGE VILLIERS, 1ST DUKE OF

Vimy Ridge, Battle of (April 1917) Campaign in WORLD WAR I, fought in France. The Allies launched the attack on the German-held position in order to draw German reserves away from the main action on the River Aisne. On the Allied side, the Battle was fought almost entirely by the Canadian Corps under General Julian BYNG. In its finest achievement of the War, the Canadian corps succeeded in capturing the position in four days (14–17 April). Total casualties are estimated at *c.*11,000 killed, of which *c.*5000 were Canadian.

Vinland Region of North America settled by VIKINGS from Greenland led by LEIF ERICSON in *c.*1000. According to sagas, the Icelandic explorer Bjarni Herjulfsson had sighted land W of Greenland in 986. Leif set out on an expedition to discover this land. They settled at a wooded area that they named Vinland because of the grapes growing wild. Leif's party stayed for one season only, but at least two other expeditions, one led by Leif's brother Thorvald, settled there briefly. Vinland was soon abandoned, apparently because of the hostility of local people.

Virginia State in E United States; the capital is RICHMOND. The first permanent British settlement in North America was established at JAMESTOWN (1607) by the VIRGINIA COMPANY of London. After a difficult beginning, survival was assured thanks to colonist John Rolfe's introduction of tobacco cultivation. Virginia flourished during William BERKELEY's first term (1642–52) as governor. An aristocratic plantation society evolved based on vast tobacco holdings worked by slaves. Virginia's leaders, notably George WASHINGTON and Thomas JEFFERSON, were in the forefront of the AMERICAN REVOLUTION. The last major battle of the Revolution was the Siege of YORKTOWN, Virginia. During the CIVIL WAR, Richmond acted as the Confederate capital, and Virginia was the main battleground of the War. In 1865 the Civil War was ended by General Robert LEE's surrender at APPOMATTOX, W Virginia. In 1870 Virginia was readmitted to the Union. Area: 105,710sq km (40,814sq mi). Pop. (1996) 6,675,451.

Virginia companies Two English companies chartered (1606) by JAMES I to establish colonies in America. The **Virginia Company of London** was to found a colony 100 miles inland from the coast between latitudes 34°N and 41°N; the **Virginia Company of Plymouth** was to establish one of the same size between latitudes 38°N and 45°N. The London Company founded the first permanent English colony (JAMESTOWN) in 1607, but lost its charter in 1624. The Plymouth, which was less successful, was reorganized as the Council for New England in 1620.

Virginia Plan *See* CONSTITUTIONAL CONVENTION

Visconti Italian family that ruled Milan from the 13th century until 1447. Ottone Visconti (*c.*1207–95) was appointed archbishop of Milan in 1262 and used his position to become the first Visconti *signore* (lord) of Milan. In 1349 the title of *signore* became hereditary. Supporters of the GHIBELLINES, the Visconti family established control over Lombardy in the 14th century, reaching the height of their powers during the period of Gian Galeazzo VISCONTI's rule. Visconti lordship of Milan ended with the death of Filippo Maria Visconti in 1447. *See also* SFORZA

Visconti, Gian Galeazzo (1351–1402) Duke of Milan, a member of the influential VISCONTI family. He succeeded his father, Galeazzo II Visconti (1320–78). Gian Galeazzo initially ruled jointly with his uncle, Bernabò, but in 1385, worried by Bernabò's influential contacts in France, he had him put to death. He increased Milan's status by forging important alliances with other European powers. In 1395 King WENCESLAS made him a hereditary prince of the Holy Roman Empire, giving him the title Duke of Milan. Gian Galeazzo extended his power to include Pisa, Siena and Bologna. He was planning to attack Florence when he died of the plague. The arts flourished during his reign. The death of Gian Galeazzo's son **Filippo Maria Visconti** (1392–1447) marked the end of Visconti rule of Milan. The duchy of Milan was then contested by the SFORZA family and ALFONSO V of Aragón and Naples.

Visigoths Western division of the GOTHS. In the 2nd century AD the Goths migrated from their original home on the Baltic to the shores of the Black Sea. After AD 370 they separated into two groups, divided by the River Dniester: the Visigoths settled in the West, between the Dniester and Danube rivers; and the OSTROGOTHS settled in what is now the Ukraine and Belarus. In the late 4th century the Visigoths were forced south by the HUNS. They began attacking the frontiers of the ROMAN EMPIRE and inflicted a crushing defeat on the Roman Emperor Valens at the Battle of ADRIANOPLE (378). In 401, under ALARIC I, the Visigoths invaded Italy, capturing Rome in 410. After Alaric's death, the Visigoths left Italy and established themselves on the Iberian Peninsula. LEOVIGILD established a permanent Visigothic capital at Toledo in 584. The Visigoths were eventually defeated by the Moors in 711.

Vittorio Veneto, Battle of (24 October–4 November 1918) Decisive victory of the Italians over the Austro-Hungarian army at the end of WORLD WAR I. The Italians, under General Armando Diaz, shattered the Austrian army to such an extent that they concluded an armistice with the Allies on 3 November 1918.

Vladimir I (the Great) (*c*.956–1015) Grand Duke of Kiev and first Christian ruler of Russia (980–1015). Vladimir raised an army of VIKING mercenaries in 979 and conquered Polotsk and Kiev. Proclaimed prince of all Russia, he extended Russian territories, conquering parts of Poland and Lithuania. He became a Christian and married a Byzantine princess (988). He established the Greek ORTHODOX CHURCH in Russia. *See also* KIEVAN RUS

Vogel, Sir Julius (1835–99) New Zealand statesman and journalist, prime minister (1873–75, 1876), b. England. He entered the New Zealand Parliament in 1863, later serving (1869–72) as colonial treasurer. As prime minister, Vogel sponsored public works, such as the building of roads and railways, and presided over great improvements in the economy. After a period (1876–80) as agent general in London, Vogel returned to New Zealand politics, serving again as treasurer (1884–87).

Volgograd (formerly Stalingrad) Major Russian inland port on the River VOLGA, the E terminus of the Volga-Don Canal. During the Russian Civil War, it was defended (1918–20) by Bolshevik troops under Joseph Stalin and was renamed Stalingrad in his honour (1925). In the winter of 1942–43 it was almost completely destroyed in the Battle of STALINGRAD, which halted the German advance during World War 2. It was renamed Volgograd in 1961. Pop. (1992) 1,031,000.

Volstead Act (1919) During the PROHIBITION era in the United States, legislation that gave Congress and the states power to enforce the 18th Amendment to the CONSTITUTION, which prohibited the manufacture and sale of alcoholic beverages. It was named after Congressman Andrew Volstead and devised by members of the ANTI-SALOON LEAGUE. Poorly enforced and widely flouted, the Volstead Act was overturned by the 21st Amendment. *See also* BOOTLEGGING

Voltaire (1694–1778) French philosopher, historian, dramatist and poet, b. François Marie Arouet. He is the outstanding figure of the French ENLIGHTENMENT. While in the Bastille (1717), Voltaire wrote his first tragedy, *Oedipe* (1718). In 1726 Voltaire was beaten and returned to the Bastille for insulting a nobleman. While in exile in England (1726–29), he was strongly influenced by John LOCKE and Isaac NEWTON and wrote a classic biography of CHARLES XII of Sweden. Back in France, Voltaire wrote several tragedies and the eulogy *Philosophical Letters* (1734), which provoked official censure. Voltaire corresponded for many years with FREDERICK II (THE GREAT) and contributed to Diderot's *Encyclopédie*. His best-known work, the philosophical romance *Candide* (1759), was published anonymously. Other works that express his philosophy of rationalism include *Jeannot et Colin* (1764) and *Essay on Morals* (1756). The *Dictionnaire philosophique* (1764) is a collection of his thoughts on contemporary matters.

Voortrekker *See* GREAT TREK

Voroshilov, Kliment Yefremovich (1881–1969) Soviet statesman, president (1953–60). He joined the BOLSHEVIKS in 1903 and took a military role in the RUSSIAN REVOLUTION (1917). He was a RED ARMY commander in the RUSSIAN CIVIL WAR. As commissar for defence (1925–40), Voroshilov modernized the Red Army. He was appointed to the Politburo in 1926. During World War 2, Voroshilov commanded the Red Army on the NW front but was blamed for failing to prevent the Siege of LENINGRAD and removed from his post. Voroshilov nevertheless remained a member of the Politburo and became president on the death of Joseph STALIN. Implicated in a plot against Nikita KHRUSCHEV, he was forced to resign.

Vorster, Balthazar Johannes (1915–83) South African statesman, prime minister (1966–78). Imprisoned during World War 2 as a Nazi sympathizer, he was a staunch advocate of APARTHEID under Hendrik VERWOERD and succeeded him as prime minister and NATIONAL PARTY leader. Vorster established Transkei as a "bantustan" and suppressed the SOWETO uprising (1976). He invaded Angola to try to prevent Namibian independence. In 1978 Vorster became president, but corruption charges forced his resignation in 1979.

Voting Rights Act (1965) US legislation authorizing federal authorities to check registration and voting procedures in order to protect rights of black voters in nine southern states. Within a year of its passage, the number of African-Americans registered in five Deep South states had increased by almost 50%.

VIETNAM WAR (1955–75)

Conflict between US-backed South VIETNAM and the VIET CONG, who had the support of communist North Vietnam. It followed the defeat of the French at DIEN BIEN PHU (1954). The GENEVA ACCORDS (1954) divided Vietnam along the 17th parallel, pending elections in 1956, which would choose a government for a united Vietnam.

In 1955 a strongly anti-communist government was established in South Vietnam by President Ngo Dinh DIEM. Diem refused to hold democratic elections (1956) and established an autocratic regime. North Vietnamese President HO CHI MINH denounced Diem's cancellation of elections, and the Viet Cong launched an insurgency. Men and arms from North Vietnam began to travel down the Ho Chi Minh trail – in reality a shifting complex of jungle routes – to support the Viet Cong in the South. Diem declared a state of emergency (1961).

Fuelled by fear of the spread of COMMUNISM, the United States gave Diem economic and military support; the number of US "military advisers" in the region increased. The United States received token support from its allies in the Pacific region, and North Vietnam was supplied by China and the Soviet Union. In 1963 Diem was overthrown and executed. In 1964, following the alleged bombing of US destroyers by North Vietnamese torpedo boats, the TONKIN GULF RESOLUTION was proposed by President Lyndon JOHNSON. The following year, the United States began bombing the Ho Chi Minh trail and urban centres in North Vietnam. As fighting intensified, US troops were committed in greater numbers: by 1968 there were more than 500,000.

In early 1968, during celebrations for the lunar new year, the Viet Cong and regular North Vietnamese forces launched the TET OFFENSIVE. Fierce attacks on many South Vietnamese cities produced some successes but failed to dislodge NGUYEN VAN THIEU's regime. Despite US technological superiority and air supremacy, military stalemate ensued. Disquiet at the undemocratic nature of the South Vietnam regime, US involvement in war crimes, such as the MY LAI MASSACRE (1968), combined with heavy casualties and daily TV coverage to make the War highly unpopular in the United States.

US President Richard NIXON announced a ban on the bombing of North Vietnam and peace negotiations between North Vietnam and the United States began. In 1969 some US troops were withdrawn, but the United States continued to supply the South Vietnamese army. In 1970 the United States invaded E CAMBODIA and bombed LAOS with the aim of destroying communist sanctuaries. The North Vietnamese invasion of the DMZ (the demilitarized zone in the centre of Vietnam) precipitated severe US bombing of North Vietnamese cities and the mining of the port of Haiphong.

Peace talks were reopened in Paris, and in 1973 a cease-fire agreement, negotiated by Henry KISSINGER and LE DUC THO, was signed. It allowed for an international force to be deployed until Vietnam could be reunited peacefully. Later in 1973, US troops were withdrawn from Vietnam. The following year was marked by small-scale offensives while North Vietnam prepared for an invasion of the South. In 1975 South Vietnam was overrun by North Vietnamese forces, and the country was united under communist rule. The War had claimed *c*.50,000 American lives, *c*.400,000 South Vietnamese and *c*.1 million Viet Cong and North Vietnamese.

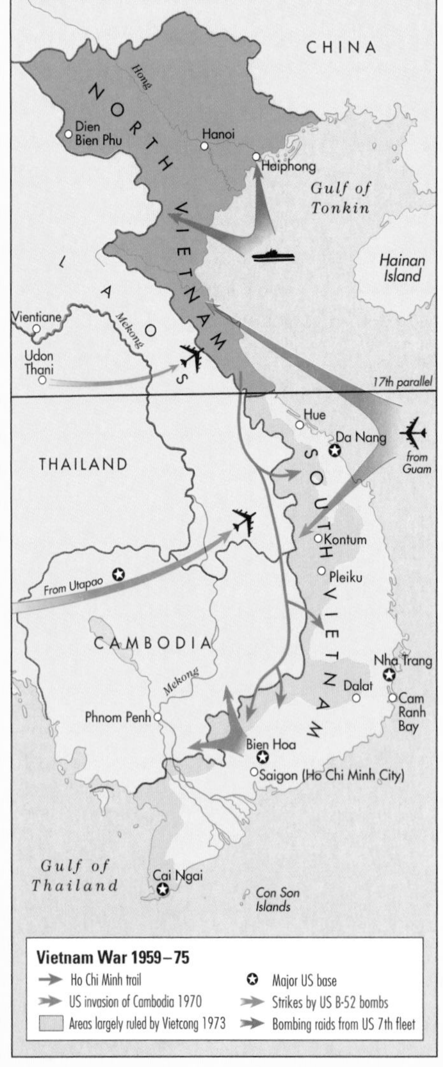

▲ **Vietnam War** The United States repeatedly bombed North Vietnam (1965–73), Cambodia and Laos (1970), but was ultimately defeated by the Viet Cong's guerrilla tactics. In addition, mounting opposition in the United States to the War was a major factor in the withdrawal of troops in 1973.

Wade, Benjamin Franklin (1800–78) US senator and jurist. After a successful career in Ohio as a circuit judge, he became a US senator (1851–69) on the WHIG ticket. A staunch ABOLITIONIST, Wade opposed the FUGITIVE SLAVE LAWS and the KANSAS-NEBRASKA ACT. He denounced Abraham LINCOLN's RECONSTRUCTION plans as too conservative and along with Henry Davis (1817–65) drew up the **Wade-Davis Bill** (1864), which put the Reconstruction plans in the hands of Congress. However, Lincoln vetoed the bill. As president *pro tempore* of the Senate, Wade would have succeeded to the presidency if Andrew JOHNSON had been convicted of impeachment charges (1868). In 1869 he retired to Ohio to practise law.

Wafd (Al-Wafd Al-Misri, Arabic, "Egyptian Delegation") Nationalist political party in EGYPT, founded (1918) by Sa'd ZAGHLUL. Influential in pressing for Egyptian independence, Wafd became an official political party when Britain granted Egypt nominal independence (1922). It advocated Egyptian autonomy, constitutional government and Egyptian control of the SUEZ CANAL. Following elections in 1924 Wafd became the ruling party, often clashing with the Egyptian monarchy and the British ambassador. Under General Gamal NASSER all political parties, including Wafd, were banned. Although the Party was reconstituted in 1978 under Anwar SADAT, Wafd dissolved itself and its assembly members became independent.

Wagner Act (1935) First modern US labour law to be declared constitutional. It represented a positive change in government policy toward labour. The Wagner Act requires that the employer recognize the UNION, bargain collectively with it, and not interfere with employees' rights to join it. The Wagner Act was counterbalanced by the TAFT-HARTLEY ACT (1947). *See also* NEW DEAL

Wagram, Battle of (5–6 July 1809) Military engagement during the NAPOLEONIC WARS, fought on the Marchfeld, a plain NE of Vienna, Austria. NAPOLEON I led his *c*.154,000 French troops to victory over the *c*.158,000-strong Austrian army, led by Archduke Charles (1771–1847). The Battle, dominated by heavy artillery fire, was one of the bloodiest of the entire conflict; Austria lost *c*.40,000 men and France *c*.34,000. After their defeat, the Austrians were compelled to sign the Treaty of Schönbrunn, losing some territory and agreeing to become part of the CONTINENTAL SYSTEM.

Wahhabi Follower of Wahhabism, a puritanical Muslim movement founded in Arabia by Muhammad ibn Abd al-Wahhab (1703–92). The movement, based on SUNNI teachings, stresses the absolute oneness of Allah, literal belief in the KORAN and HADITH, the inseparability of belief from ethical action, belief in predestination, rejection of all nonorthodox views (such as SUFISM), and the need to establish the Muslim state on SHARIA (Islamic law) alone. Under the Saud family, the Wahhabis extended their territory, capturing MECCA (1806). Defeated by the OTTOMAN EMPIRE (1818), Wahhabism re-emerged under IBN SAUD, who founded the militant Ikhwan movement that enforced Wahhabism. The British, alarmed by the fanaticism of the movement, helped to defeat Ibn Saud at the Battle of Sibilla (1929). In the late 20th century Wahhabism gained in significance along with the spread of Islamic fundamentalism.

Wailing Wall *See* WESTERN WALL

Waitangi, Treaty of (February 1840) Pact between Britain and several NEW ZEALAND Maori tribes. The agreement protected and provided rights for MAORI, guaranteeing them possession of certain tracts of land and British citizenship, while permitting Britain formally to annex the islands and purchase other land areas. British sovereignty was declared in May 1840. When the agreement was broken by further white settlement on Maori land, the MAORI WARS broke out resulting in the eventual suppression of the Maori.

Wakefield, Edward Gibbon (1796–1862) British colonial reformer. Concerned that Australian settlement was not succeeding because land could be acquired too cheaply, Wakefield came to prominence with the publication of a *Letter from Sydney* (1829), in which he argued for a rational system of the sale of crown lands in the colonies for a set price. The revenue from the sales could then be used to assist emigration. He organized an association for colonizing NEW SOUTH WALES in 1834 and founded a similar society for New Zealand in 1837.

Waldemar IV *See* VALDEMAR IV

Waldenses Small Christian sect founded in the 12th century. It had its origins in the "Poor Men of Lyon", the followers of Peter Waldo (1140–1218) of Lyon, SE France. The Waldenses renounced private property and led an ascetic life. They repudiated many Roman Catholic doctrines and practices, such as INDULGENCES, purgatory and mass for the dead, and denied the validity of sacraments administered by unworthy priests. The movement flourished briefly in the 13th century, but active persecution extinguished it except in the French and Italian Alps. Persecution continued until the Waldenses received full civil rights in 1848. In the later 19th century, many Waldenses emigrated to the Americas.

Waldheim, Kurt (1918–) Austrian statesman and diplomat, president of Austria (1986–92) and fourth secretary general (1972–81) of the UNITED NATIONS (UN). After serving in the Austrian foreign office, he failed in his bid to win the presidential election of 1971. The following year Waldheim succeeded U THANT as secretary general of the UN. Although Waldheim proved to be a weak appeaser of the major powers, he successfully managed the massive relief operations in Bangladesh, Nicaragua and Guatemala. After failing to be re-elected as general secretary for a third term, Waldheim again stood in the Austrian presidential elections. His candidacy was tainted, however, by revelations of his Nazi war record, allegedly involving the transportation of Jews to concentration camps. Waldheim denied the allegations, and, although he went on the win the election, he became isolated in international politics and decided not to stand for re-election.

Wales Constituent member of the UNITED KINGDOM, occupying a broad peninsula in W Great Britain; the capital is Cardiff. The Celtic-speaking Welsh stoutly resisted Roman invasion in the first centuries AD, and in the 5th century Wales became a refuge to people fleeing from the SAXON invasion. St David introduced Christianity in the 5th century and during the 10th century the many differing and diverse tribes gradually began to unify, forming four major kingdoms – Dyfed, Gwynedd, Deheubarth and Powys. In the 11th century the English conquered the border counties and established the Welsh Marches. Following a number of uprisings against English rule, in 1284 Wales was conquered by the English Norman King EDWARD I, and the last Welsh prince of Wales, LLYWELYN AP GRUFFYDD, was killed. Edward was subsequently accepted as overlord. In 1301 Prince Edward (later EDWARD II) became Prince of Wales. In the early 15th century, Owain GLYN DWR led spirited resistance against English rule. The accession of the Welsh TUDOR dynasty to the English throne paved the way for the Act of UNION (1536) of England and Wales. Wales supported the Royalist cause in the English CIVIL WAR. In the late 19th century Wales became the world's leading producer of coal, but a failing rural economy, which resulted in the REBECCA RIOTS, brought in a period of mass emigration. The burgeoning INDUSTRIAL REVOLUTION caused continued social problems, including unemployment and poverty, particularly in the 20th century during the years of the GREAT DEPRESSION. From the 18th century Wales had been a centre of NONCONFORMISM, and CALVINISM injected new life into Welsh nationalism. In 1996 the Welsh Nationalist Party (PLAID CYMRU) won its first seat in the Westminster Parliament and in 1997 a referendum voted for a devolved Welsh assembly in Cardiff. The maintenance of a distinct Welsh culture has been strengthened by the teaching of Welsh in schools. Area: 20,761sq km (8016sq mi). Pop. (1994) 2,913,000.

Wales, Prince of *See* CHARLES (PRINCE OF WALES)

Wałesa, Lech (1943–) Polish statesman and labour leader, president (1990–95). A former shipyard worker, in August 1980 he organized SOLIDARITY, an independent, self-governing trade union. A general strike took place, and in December 1980 President Wojciech JARUZELSKI agreed to give workers the right to organize freely. In 1981 the government outlawed Solidarity, and Wałesa was interned until late 1982 as part of the government's effort to silence opposition. In 1983 he was awarded the Nobel Prize for Peace. Following reforms in the Soviet Union, Solidarity was legalized and won free elections in 1989. In 1990 the Communist Party was disbanded and Wałesa became president. Wałesa's attempts to implement economic reforms in the hope that they would encourage a free-market economy resulted in a series of strikes and minor civil disturbances. Wałesa found himself increasingly alienated from Solidarity, and in 1995 he lost the presidential election to the former communist Aleksander Kwaśniewski.

Walker, William (1824–60) US adventurer in Central America. He led an armed band in an attempt to seize land in Mexico (1853). Walker made a similar invasion of Nicaragua (1855), with US business support. He set himself up as president (1856) but was expelled (1857). In 1860 he made a sortie into Honduras but was captured and shot.

Wallace, George Corley (1919–98) US governor of Alabama (1963–67, 1971–78, 1982–87). He attempted unsuccessfully to block federal efforts to end racial segregation in Alabama state schools (1962–66). Wallace was the leading spokesman against the CIVIL RIGHTS movement. In 1972, while campaigning for the Democratic presidential nomination, he was shot and paralyzed from the waist down.

Wallace, Henry Agard (1888–1965) US statesman, vice president (1941–45). Wallace was made secretary for agriculture (1933) as a reward from President Franklin ROOSEVELT for his work on the NEW DEAL. As vice president, Wallace worked to promote goodwill in Latin America. In 1945 he was made secretary of commerce under Roosevelt and retained the post under President Harry S TRUMAN. Wallace resigned in 1946, citing dissatisfaction with Truman's COLD WAR policy. Aligning himself further to the political left, in 1948 he was an unsuccessful presidential candidate for the PROGRESSIVE PARTY, which he helped to establish.

Wallace, Sir William (1270–1305) Scottish nationalist leader. He led resistance to EDWARD I of England. Wallace defeated an English army at Stirling Bridge (1297), becoming a national hero. The English were driven from Scotland, and Wallace pursued them over the border. In 1298 he was defeated in a confrontation with a large English army at Falkirk, central Scotland. He went into hiding in France, but was eventually captured (1305), taken to London and executed.

Wallachia (Walachia, Valahia) Historic region in ROMANIA, formerly the principality between the River Danube and the Transylvanian Alps. It is said to have been established in 1290 by Ralph the Black, vassal of the king of Hungary, from whom the region secured temporary independence in 1330. It came gradually, however, under the domination of the Ottoman Turks, whose suzerainty was acknowledged in 1417. Wallachia and MOLDAVIA became protectorates of Russia under the Treaty of Adrianople (1829) and by their union formed the state of Romania in 1859. An important agricultural region, it has been developed industrially since World War 2. Area: 76,599sq km (29,575sq mi).

Wallenstein, Albrecht Eusebius Wenzel von (1583–1634) Bohemian general, Duke of Friedland (1625) and Duke of Mecklenberg (1629). Raised as a Protestant, Wallenstein converted to Catholicism (1606) and married a wealthy widow. Having remained loyal to the HABSBURG Emperor FERDINAND II during a Bohemian revolt against Catholic rule, Wallenstein was richly rewarded. At the outbreak of the THIRTY YEARS' WAR (1618–48) Wallenstein, at his own expense, raised an army and was subsequently made commander of all the armies of the HOLY ROMAN EMPIRE. With Graf von TILLY, Wallenstein won a series of victories over the Protestant forces in Denmark and N Germany in the late 1620s, and was made Duke of Mecklenberg. Thereafter his personal ambition to create a trading empire took precedence over his loyalties to Ferdinand, and he entered into dialogue with Protestant neighbours. Protestant and Catholic German princes, alarmed by the formation of a powerful imperial army, threatened Ferdinand with war unless he dismissed Wallenstein and reduced the size of the army. Ferdinand conceded and Wallenstein was ousted only to be reinstated when GUSTAVUS II of Sweden invaded Germany and defeated Tilly. Wallenstein, who earlier had attempted to reach an agreement with Gustavus, suffered defeat at the hands of the Swedes at the Battle of LÜTZEN (1632). Wallenstein, to preserve his personal army, entered into peace talks with the Protestant leaders. He was convicted of treason by the Habsburgs, dismissed and then assassinated.

Wall Street Centre of the business district of NEW YORK CITY, NE United States, which, together with Broad Street and New Street, houses many US and overseas banks and brokers, as well as the New York Stock Exchange. It has become the international symbol of US finance. The stockmarket crash on Wall Street in October 1929 heralded the GREAT DEPRESSION.

Walpole, Sir Robert, 1st Earl of Orford (1676–1745) British statesman, widely acknowledged as the first prime minister (1721–42). He entered Parliament as a WHIG in 1701 and was quickly elevated to secretary of war (1708) and treasurer of the navy (1710). Following the TORY victory in the general election of 1710, Walpole was impeached for corruption, expelled from Parliament and sent to the Tower of London (1712). A Whig martyr, he was reinstated on the accession of GEORGE I, having supported the Hanoverian succession against JACOBITE resistance. He gained his revenge on the Tories by masterminding the impeachment of their leaders, Robert HARLEY and Vsicount BOLINGBROKE. Walpole was made paymaster general of the armed forces (1714) and chancellor of the exchequer (1715–17). Although he resigned as chancellor, out of sympathy for his brother-in-law Charles TOWNSHEND, he restored order after the SOUTH SEA BUBBLE crisis (1720) and returned as chancellor and first lord of the treasury in 1721. During the course of the next 21 years, Walpole pursued peace abroad and a policy of low taxation at home. In addition, his patronage from George I and GEORGE II, ability to unite the House of Commons, and acute grasp of economic issues ushered in a period of relative peace and prosperity in Britain. In 1739 powerful factions within the Whigs pressured Walpole to declare war on Spain. The War, known as the War of JENKINS' EAR, did not go well for Walpole, and although he won the general election in 1741, he was soon forced to resign in favour of Henry PELHAM. Created the Earl of Orford, Walpole remained active in politics until his death. *See also* GRANVILLE, JOHN CARTERET, 1ST EARL OF

Walsingham, Sir Francis (1532–90) English statesman, a leading minister of ELIZABETH I. A zealous Protestant, he set up an efficient intelligence system, based on bribery, to detect Catholic conspiracies both at home and abroad. Walsingham's network of spies provided useful information on the Spanish ARMADA and produced the evidence that led to the conviction and execution of MARY, QUEEN OF SCOTS.

Walter, Hubert (d.1205) English cleric and statesman. As bishop of Salisbury, he joined RICHARD I on the Third CRUSADE and later negotiated his ransom. Appointed archbishop of Canterbury and chief justiciar (1193), he was virtual ruler of England in Richard's absence. Under his regency, wide-reaching legal and economic reforms were implemented which significantly advanced England's administrative development. In 1195 Walter was made a papal legate, and following John's succession he was appointed chancellor (1199).

Wang Anshih (1021–86) Chinese statesman. As chief councillor in the early SONG period (1069–76), he introduced reforms, known as the "New Policies", intended to encourage economic expansion. They included the reduction of land tax and the cost of borrowing. The policies were largely nullified by conservative opposition, particularly among landowners, once Wang had been dismissed.

Wang Jingwei (1883–1944) Chinese nationalist leader. A close associate of SUN YAT-SEN and one of the founders of the KUOMINTANG, he led the leftist wing of the party in 1925 in opposition to CHIANG KAI-SHEK. Wang was prime minister (1932–35) and headed the puppet government set up by the Japanese in 1940. *See also* SINO-JAPANESE WAR

Wang Mang (45 BC–AD 23) Emperor of China (AD 9–23). In 1 BC Wang became regent for Emperor Pingdi, whose sudden death (AD 6) led to his appointment as acting emperor. Wang then summoned up sufficient support to overthrow the HAN dynasty and proclaim the Xin (New) dynasty. Wang's reign was upset by a natural disaster when the Huang Ho (Yellow River) changed its course (AD 11), flooding one of the most densely populated regions of China. The ensuing famine, pestilence and homelessness led to armed revolts. The rebels eventually reached the capital, Changan (near present-day XIAN), and Wang was killed in battle. The Xin dynasty collapsed two years later and the Later Han dynasty was installed.

Warbeck, Perkin (*c*.1474–99) Flemish pretender to the English throne. In the service of a merchant, Warbeck travelled in Ireland and continental Europe (1491–93), professing to be Richard, Duke of York, son of EDWARD IV. He won support from Scottish, Irish, French and Flemish factions opposed to HENRY VII. He attempted to invade England three times (1495, 1496, 1497) and overthrow Henry. Despite Scottish support, he was finally captured and executed.

war crimes Violations of international laws of war. The modern conception of war crimes followed the atrocities committed in WORLD WAR 2, resulting in the NUREMBERG and TOKYO TRIALS. The laws pertaining to war crimes were formulated at the GENEVA CONVENTION. They cover the torture, killing and enslavement of prisoners, the killing or mass deportations of civilians, and the taking of hostages for use as human shields. In the trials following World War 2 it was established that a defendant, even if following orders from a superior, was still responsible for their actions. Conflicts in the Balkans, parts of Africa and South America have resulted in the convening of the INTERNATIONAL COURT OF JUSTICE, the central legal body of the UNITED NATIONS (UN), to examine allegations of war crimes.

Ward, Sir Joseph George (1856–1930) New Zealand statesman, prime minister (1906–12, 1928–30). Ward's Liberal government introduced a range of social welfare and public health measures, including the National Provident Fund (1910). He shared power (1915–19) with William MASSEY and advocated pro-British policies. In 1928 he was returned to power in the hope that his understanding of the economy would reverse the downturn caused by the GREAT DEPRESSION.

▲ **Walpole** Portrait by Charles Jervas (1675–1739). Robert Walpole was a great patron of the arts. His art collection forms part of the Hermitage Museum, Moscow.

War Hawks Group of DEMOCRATIC-REPUBLICANS in the United States who urged expansionism and nationalism. Mainly from the Western frontier, the War Hawks' continued outcry against British maritime practices helped start the WAR OF 1812 with Britain. Among its leaders were Henry CLAY and John CALHOUN.

War of 1812 (18 June 1812–24 December 1814) Conflict between the UNITED STATES and Britain. The main source of friction was British maritime policy during the NAPOLEONIC WARS, which included the impressment of sailors from US vessels and the interception of US merchant ships. Other factors included: the trade restrictions Britain imposed on the United States in response to NAPOLEON'S CONTINENTAL SYSTEM; increased tension on the border with Canada (*see* Battle of TIPPECANOE); British-US competition in the FUR TRADE; and a US desire for Westward expansion. In 1811 President James MADISON reimposed the Non-Intercourse Act on trade with the British. The United States was ill-prepared for war and, after a failed US invasion of Canada, British General Isaac BROCK advanced to gain DETROIT, Michigan. The United States met with greater success at sea, as the USS CONSTITUTION captured the British frigate *Guerrière*, and Stephen DECATUR seized the *Macedonian*. Victory for US Commander Oliver Hazard PERRY on Lake Erie (September 1813) enabled US forces, led by William HARRISON, to force British troops back across the Canadian border. The possible secession of New England was raised by the HARTFORD CONVENTION, and the end of the Napoleonic Wars (1814) freed more British forces. They imposed a naval blockade and captured Washington, D.C., burning the White House. A US naval victory on Lake Champlain, however, ended the British threat to New York. With the War at stalemate, John Quincy ADAMS and Henry CLAY led US negotiations that resulted in the Treaty of GHENT (1814). Andrew JACKSON'S victory at NEW ORLEANS, Louisiana, occurred after the signing of the Treaty. *See also* EMBARGO ACT; MONROE, JAMES; QUEENSTON HEIGHTS, BATTLE OF; TECUMSEH

Warren, Earl (1891–1974) US politician and jurist. He was governor of California (1943–53) and an unsuccessful Republican candidate for vice president (1953). Appointed as chief justice (1953–69) of the Supreme Court by President Dwight EISENHOWER, he began the "Warren Revolution", which lasted until his retirement. Some of his Court's noteworthy cases include: BROWN V. BOARD OF EDUCATION OF TOPEKA (1954), in which he found separate educational facilities among black and whited populations to be "inherently unequal" and in violation of the Constitution's equal protection clause; *Engel* v. *Vitale* (1962), which prohibited prayers in public schools; and *Miranda* v. *Arizona* (1966), which made it obligatory that a suspect be informed of his rights, be provided with free state counsel, and be given the right to remain silent. *See also* WARREN COMMISSION

Warren Commission (1963–64) US presidential commission that investigated the assassination of President John KENNEDY. It was headed by Earl WARREN. After taking evidence from 552 witnesses, it concluded that the act had been committed by Lee Harvey OSWALD, acting alone. Denial of conspiracy was not universally accepted.

Warsaw Capital and largest city of POLAND, on the River Vistula. Its settlement dates from the 11th century. In 1596 SIGISMUND III (VASA) began to build a palace, and the capital was transferred from KRAKÓW to Warsaw in 1611. It soon developed into the country's main trading market and flourished as the centre of the Polish Enlightenment during the reign (1764–95) of STANISLAW II (AUGUSTUS). It was a focus of Tadeusz KOSCIUSZKO's resistance to the Partitions of POLAND, but in 1795 was reduced to the status of a provincial town in Austrian South Prussia. Briefly revived as capital of the Duchy of Warsaw by Napoleon I of France in 1806, from 1813 to 1915 it was controlled by Russia, and during World War 1 it was occupied by German troops. In 1918 it was liberated by Polish forces and was restored as capital of Poland. The Nazi German invasion and occupation of Warsaw (1939) marked the beginning of World War 2. Warsaw was home to the largest Jewish population of any city in the world (*c*.500,000), but the Nazis forced the Jews into a ghetto from where they were deported, mainly to the Treblinka extermination camp. The Warsaw Ghetto Uprising (1943) marked a last heroic bid to prevent the complete extermination of an entire people and, after the Nazi defeat of the Polish resistance in the Warsaw Uprising (1944), the Soviet Red Army entered a city reduced to rubble and with only 200 surviving Jews. After the War, Warsaw was reinstated as capital of Poland and the old town was reconstructed. Pop. (1993) 1,653,300.

Warsaw Ghetto Uprising (19 April–16 May 1943) Jewish resistance to forced deportation from Warsaw, Poland, to the secret Treblinka extermination camp, established as part of Adolf Hitler's "final solution" for the elimination of European Jews. Following the Nazi occupation of Warsaw, the city's *c*.500,000 Jews were herded (1942) into a small section of the city from where they were sent to the death camp at Treblinka, *c*.100km (60mi) to the NE. Within a year, more than 300,000 had been murdered here. When the remaining Jews in the Ghetto realized the true horror of the deportations they formed the armed resistance movement Jewish Combat Organization (ZOB), which brought a temporary halt to the expulsions at the start of 1943. In April 1943 Heinrich Himmler, head of the SS, ordered the emptying of the Ghetto by force. For 28 days ZOB put up a heroic fight against the vastly superior weaponry of the Nazis before finally succumbing. The Uprising claimed the lives of *c*.60,000 Jews and several hundred Nazi soldiers. *See also* Holocaust, The

Warsaw Pact Agreement creating the Warsaw Treaty Organization (1955), a defensive alliance of the Soviet Union and its communist allies in Eastern Europe, including Albania, Bulgaria, Czechoslovakia, the German Democratic Republic (*see* Germany), Hungary, Poland and Romania. Yugoslavia under Tito refused to join. It was the equivalent of Western Europe's North Atlantic Treaty Organization (NATO), and as such played a significant role in the Cold War. Its headquarters were in Moscow, and it was controlled by the Soviet Union. Attempts to withdraw by Hungary (1956) and Czechoslovakia (1968) were crushed. It was dissolved after the collapse of the Soviet Union (1991).

Warsaw Uprising (August–October 1944) Action during World War 2 in which the Polish underground, led by General Tadeusz Komorowski, attacked the occupying German forces in Warsaw in an attempt to ensure the post-war authority of the government in exile. The breakthrough of Allied armies in France and the rapid approach of the Soviet Red Army to the outskirts of Warsaw encouraged the resistance soldiers, but the Soviet advance under General Konstantin Rokossovsky was halted. The Poles fought valiantly through 63 days of almost constant aerial bombardment before their supplies ran out and they were overwhelmed by a Germany counter-attack. The Germans proceeded to remove the Polish population and raze Warsaw to the ground. The deportation of the Polish population, most of whom were loyal to the Polish government in exile, resulted in the imposition of a communist-backed provisional government in 1945.

Wars of the Roses *See* Roses, Wars of the

Warwick, Richard Neville, 1st Earl of (1428–71) English noble, known as "the kingmaker". Initially an ally of Richard, Duke of York, Warwick secured victories in the Wars of the Roses against Henry VI at St Albans (1455) and Northampton (1460), forcing the king to recognize Richard's son, later Edward IV, as his heir. Margaret of Anjou refused to countenance the deal and her forces killed York and Neville's father at the Battle of Wakefield (December 1460). Warwick and Edward rallied the Yorkist forces and Edward was proclaimed king in 1461. Warwick and Edward fell out after the latter's marriage to Elizabeth Woodville (1437–92), and Warwick allied with Edward's brother, the Duke of Clarence, to mount a rebellion against Edward. The revolts (1469, 1470) failed and both men were forced into exile in France, where Warwick joined forces with Margaret to mount a successful invasion of England and restore Henry VI to the throne. Edward returned with fresh troops, and Warwick was defeated and killed at the Battle of Barnet.

Washington, Booker T. (Taliaferro) (1856–1915) US educator and African-American leader. Born a slave, he gained an education after the Civil War and became a teacher. In 1881 he organized the Tuskegee Industrial Institute in Alabama to train African Americans as farmers and mechanics. Washington advocated self-help, vocational education and economic improvement as precursors to the achievement of equality for African Americans, and he believed in compromise with white segregationists. He had great influence among whites as a spokesman for African-American causes, but was attacked by more militant members of the community, such as W.E.B. Du Bois.

Washington, George (1732–99) US general and statesman, commander in chief of the Continental Army in the American Revolution and first president of the United States (1789–97). In 1752 he inherited Mount Vernon estate in Virginia. Washington fought with distinction under General Edward Braddock in the last of the French and Indian Wars (1754–63) before being elected (1759–74) to the House of Burgesses. He served in the First and Second Continental Congresses (1774, 1775), the latter appointing him commander in chief. At the start of the Revolution, Washington besieged Boston and forced a British withdrawal in March 1776. Next he turned to the defence of New York, narrowly avoiding the complete encirclement of his army at the Battle of Long Island as Sir William Howe failed to take the initiative. Washington recovered to inflict surprise victories over the British at Trenton and Princeton, but losses at Brandywine and Germantown enabled the British to capture Philadelphia (1777). Wintering at Valley Forge, Washington survived a challenge to his leadership by the Conway Cabal. The alliance with France boosted American morale, but Washington was robbed of victory at the Battle of Monmouth (1778) by the treachery of Charles Lee. Washington's defeat of Lord Charles Cornwallis at Yorktown (October 1781) signalled a virtual end to hostilities and, after overseeing Sir Henry Clinton's evacuation of New York, Washington resigned (December 1783). He was recalled from retirement to preside over the Constitutional Convention at Philadelphia (1787); his support secured the adoption of the Constitution of the United States. In 1789 Washington was elected, unopposed, as president of the new republic and was inaugurated on 30 April in New York City. Washington formed a balanced cabinet, including Thomas Jefferson (secretary of state), Alexander Hamilton (secretary of the treasury), Henry Knox (secretary of war) and Edmund Randolph (attorney general). He was unable, however, to heal the divisions between Jefferson and Hamilton that resulted in the creation of the Federalist Party and the Democratic-Republican Party. In 1793 Washington was re-elected. His second administration was dominated by Federalists, and the Jeffersonians criticized John Jay's peace treaty with Britain (1794). In 1796 Washington declined a third term as president. In his *Farewell Address* (17 September 1796), Washington warned against the geographical divisions encouraged by the party system and advised the nation to steer clear of "permanent alliances" with foreign nations. He spent the remainder of his life at Mount Vernon. *See also* Articles of Confederation; Burgoyne, John; Gates, Horatio

WASHINGTON, GEORGE

Washington Portrait (*c*.1796) by Gilbert Stuart (1755–1828). Washington's role in the foundation of the United States and the Constitution earned him the title "Father of His Country".

WASHINGTON IN HIS OWN WORDS

"Liberty, when it begins to take root, is a plant of rapid growth"
Letter, 1788

WASHINGTON
Statehood :
11 November 1889
Nickname :
The Evergreen State
State motto :
Alki (Native American, "by and by")

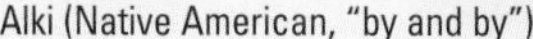

Washington State in the extreme NW United States; the state capital is Olympia. The region was settled by two distinct cultures of Native North American peoples: one group living on the Pacific coast, the other on the Columbia Plateau. The Spanish discovered the mouth of the Columbia River in 1775, and in 1778 Captain James Cook established the area's fur trading links with China. In 1792 George Vancouver mapped Puget Sound and Robert Gray sailed down the Sound to establish the US claim to the region. The claim was strengthened by the Lewis and Clark Expedition (1805) and the establishment (1811) of an American Fur Company trading post at the mouth of the Columbia by John Jacob Astor. From 1821 to 1846 the region was administered by the Hudson's Bay Company. In 1846 a treaty with the British fixed the boundary with Canada, and in 1847 most of present-day Washington state became Oregon Territory. In 1853 Washington Territory was created. Exploitation of its forests, furs and fisheries attracted settlement, and in 1883 the railroad reached the area. Between 1855 and 1859 there was a series of conflicts between white settlers and Native Americans, who were eventually defeated and placed on reservations. By 1886 Seattle had become the supply centre for gold-seekers flocking to Alaska. World War 1 brought a boom to the state, especially in shipbuilding, and before and after World War 2, huge aircraft plants were established. The late 20th century witnessed a growth in high-technology companies, such as Microsoft. Area: 172,431sq km (66,581sq mi). Pop. (1992) 5,142,746.

Washington, D.C. Capital of the United States, on the E bank of the Potomac River, coextensive with the District of Columbia and bordered by Maryland (NE and SE), which gave up land occupied by the District. The site was chosen as the seat of government in 1790, and the city was planned by the French army engineer Pierre Charles L'Enfant. Construction of the White House began in 1793 and of the Capitol the following year. Congress moved from Philadelphia in 1800. During the War of 1812 the city was occupied by the British and many public buildings were burned (1814), including the White House and the Capitol. Washington is the legislative, judicial and administrative centre of the United States. The city has severe social problems, with many of its large African-American population living in slum housing. Pop. (1992) 585,221.

Washington, Treaty of (1871) Agreement settling a number of disputes involving the United States, Britain and Canada. The most serious was the question of the ALABAMA CLAIMS, which was submitted to international arbitration. US-Canadian disputes over fisheries and the border were also resolved.

Watergate affair (1972–74) US political scandal that led to the resignation of President Richard NIXON. It arose from an attempted burglary (17 June 1972) of the Democratic Party's national headquarters in the Watergate building, Washington, D.C., organized by members of Nixon's re-election committee. Evidence of the involvement of the administration to cover-up the affair provoked investigations by the Senate and the Justice Department, which ultimately implicated Nixon. Impeachment proceedings began in 1973, and on 8 August 1974, after being forced by a Supreme Court ruling to relinquish tape recordings that attested to his involvement in the cover-up, Nixon resigned. He was pardoned by his successor, Gerald FORD, but his closest advisers (Halderman, Erlichman, Mitchell and Dean) were convicted.

Waterloo, Battle of (18 June 1815) Final conflict in the NAPOLEONIC WARS, fought *c*.20km (12mi) from Brussels, Belgium. The Allied army of *c*.68,000, commanded by the Duke of WELLINGTON, met NAPOLEON I's *c*.72,000-strong French forces led by Marshal Michel NEY. Napoleon made a crucial mistake in delaying his attack, enabling the Allied army to be augmented by *c*.45,000 Prussians under Marshal Gebhard BLÜCHER. The Prussian attack on the French east flank, drew off several battalions of the Imperial Guard, Napoleon's crack troops. Ney finally managed a joint infantry, cavalry and artillery assault on Wellington, breaking through the Allied centre. Napoleon's delay in sending reinforcements allowed Wellington to regroup and repel the French advance, and the subsequent Allied counter-attack forced the French to beat a hasty retreat. The French lost *c*.25,000 men, the Allies *c*.15,000 and the Prussians *c*.8000. The Battle ended Napoleon's HUNDRED DAYS and resulted in his second, and final, abdication.

Watt, James (1736–1819) Scottish engineer. In 1765 he invented the condensing steam engine. In 1782 Watt invented the double-acting engine, in which steam pressure acted alternately on each side of a piston. With Matthew Boulton, he coined the term "horsepower". *See also* INDUSTRIAL REVOLUTION

Wavell, Archibald Percival, 1st Earl (1883–1950) British field marshal. He was commander of the British forces in Palestine (1937–39). As British commander in chief for the Middle East, he defeated the Italians in N and E Africa (1940–41) but was forced back by the Germans under Field Marshal Erwin ROMMEL in 1941. Dismissed by Winston CHURCHILL, Wavell subsequently commanded forces in Southeast Asia but lost Malaya, Singapore and Burma to the Japanese (1941–42). He was viceroy and governor general of India (1943–47).

Wayne, Anthony (1745–96) American Revolutionary general. He was called "Mad Anthony Wayne" because of his daring tactics. In 1777 he was made brigadier general and joined George WASHINGTON's army. He led a division at the Battle of BRANDYWINE, fought at Germantown, and wintered with Washington at VALLEY FORGE. In 1779 Wayne led the successful night attack on Stony Point, New York. He also fought in the Siege of YORKTOWN and occupied Charleston. In 1792 he became commander in chief in the Northwest Territory and defeated the Ohio tribes in the Battle of Fallen Timbers (1794). Wayne secured the Treaty of Greenville (1795), the first to recognize NATIVE NORTH AMERICAN title to US lands.

Weaver, James Baird (1833–1912) US politician. A Union army hero in the Civil War, he later received the post of federal assessor of internal revenue in Iowa (1867–73). He went on to represent Iowa in the House of Representatives (1879–81) and was the presidential candidate of the GREENBACK PARTY in 1880. Weaver returned to Congress (1885–89) and was a founder of the POPULIST PARTY, gaining more than one million votes as its presidential candidate in 1892.

Webb, Beatrice (née Potter) (1858–1943) and **Sidney** (1859–1947) British social historians and politicians. Sidney Webb was one of the founders of the FABIAN SOCIETY. They founded the London School of Economics (1895) and the *New Statesman* magazine (1913).

Weber, Max (1864–1920) German sociologist. Weber emphasized the plurality and interdependence of causative factors in social action, particularly the role of values, ideologies and individual leaders. He advanced the concept of "ideal types", generalized models of social situations, as a method of analysis, and insisted that the social sciences should be empirical, based on comparative social history, and free of value judgements. In his book *The Protestant Ethic and the Spirit of Capitalism* (1904–05) Weber put forward the idea that CALVINISM was influential in the rise of CAPITALISM. In 1919 Weber helped to draft the constitution of the WEIMAR REPUBLIC.

Webster, Daniel (1782–1852) US statesman. A member of the FEDERALIST PARTY in the House of Representatives (1813–17), he defended the interests of New England and opposed the WAR OF 1812. Webster won fame as a lawyer in the DARTMOUTH COLLEGE CASE (1819). As US senator from Massachusetts (1827–41), he was one of the greatest orators of his generation. Webster supported the tariff of 1828, and opposed the proponents of STATES' RIGHTS and NULLIFICATION. In the **Webster-Hayne Debate** (1830) with Robert Hayne, he defended the union, arguing "Liberty and Union, now and forever, one and inseparable!" He opposed President Andrew JACKSON on the abolition of the BANK OF THE UNITED STATES and was a presidential candidate for the WHIG PARTY (1836). As secretary of state (1841–43) under presidents William Henry HARRISON and John TYLER, he negotiated the WEBSTER-ASHBURTON TREATY (1842), which fixed the boundary between Maine and Canada. In his second term in the Senate (1845–50), Webster opposed the extension of SLAVERY but favoured the COMPROMISE OF 1850. He also served as secretary of state (1850–52) to Millard FILLMORE.

Webster-Ashburton Treaty (1842) Agreement that settled the disputed NE boundary between MAINE and NEW BRUNSWICK, named after US Secretary of State Daniel WEBSTER and Britain's Lord Ashburton. It gave the United States *c*.18,130sq km (7000sq mi) of the territory in dispute. The United States paid US$150,000 to both Maine and Massachusetts to settle their claims, and Britain retained military routes between Québec and New Brunswick. The United States received rights of navigation on the St John River, and free navigation on the St Lawrence, Detroit and St Clair rivers. The New York and Vermont boundaries were also established.

Weimar Republic (1919–33) Popular name for the republic of Germany created after WORLD WAR I. It was named after the city of Weimar, Thuringia, where a constitution was drawn up (1919) that provided for a democratically elected president and a REICHSTAG of deputies. The first president, Friedrich EBERT, was succeeded by Paul von HINDENBERG in 1925. Forced by the Allies to agree to the humiliating demands of the Treaty of VERSAILLES and financially crippled by demands for reparations that could not be met, subsequent Weimar governments, despite gaining some concession from the DAWES PLAN, were convulsed by a succession of economic and political crises. These events facilitated the rise of extremist groups such as Adolf HITLER's NAZI PARTY, which allied itself to the German National Party. In 1933 Hindenberg, faced with massive national unemployment, rampant inflation and a general fear of communist infiltration, was forced to make Hitler chancellor (1933). Following the REICHSTAG FIRE, the Weimar constitution was suspended, and the republic was superseded by the THIRD REICH.

Weizmann, Chaim (1874–1952) Zionist leader and chemist, first president of ISRAEL (1948–52). He was born in Russia and became a British subject in 1910. Weizmann believed ZIONISM must be political, practical

WELLINGTON, ARTHUR WELLESLEY, DUKE OF (1769–1852)

British general and statesman, prime minister (1828–30). Following a campaign in Flanders (1794–95), Wellesley was posted to India, where he fought against TIPU SULTAN of Mysore (now Karnataka) and defeated the MARATHAS (1803). In 1809 he became commander of Allied forces in the PENINSULAR WAR in Portugal and Spain. Although widely criticized for his defensive strategy in the campaign, Wellesley defeated Nicolas SOULT at Oporto and gradually drove the French army of Marshal André MASSÉNA back over the Pyrenees. His victory at the Battle of Toulouse (1814) was preceded by NAPOLEON I's first abdication. In the same year, Wellesley was created the Duke of Wellington.

While representing Britain at the Congress of VIENNA (1814–15), he learned of Napoleon's escape from Elba. Wellington resumed command of Allied troops and, with Prussian General Gebhard BLÜCHER, defeated Napoleon at the Battle of WATERLOO (1815). In 1818 Wellington returned to England and was appointed master general of the ordnance in the Tory cabinet of the Earl of LIVERPOOL. Wellington resigned when George CANNING succeeded Liverpool (1827), but the following year GEORGE IV appointed him as prime minister. Wellington succeeded in passing the Act of CATHOLIC EMANCIPATION (1829), but his opposition to further constitutional reforms proposed by Earl GREY, including the Reform Bill of 1832, made him unpopular and he was forced to resign. WILLIAM IV offered Wellington the prime ministership but he refused, preferring to serve as foreign secretary (1834–35) and minister without portfolio (1841–46) under Sir Robert PEEL. His control of the House of the Lords enabled the repeal of the Corn Laws. In 1848 he was recalled to help organize troops against possible Chartist agitation in London. *See also* CHARTISM; NAPOLEONIC WARS; REFORM ACTS

▶ **Wellington** *The Duke of Wellington at Waterloo* by Robert Hillingford (1825–1904). Following his victory over Napoleon I, Wellington was hailed as a military hero. He remained in France for the next three years as head of the Allied army of occupation, but opposed punitive treatment of the defeated country. His skills as a military leader met with less success in the British Parliament. His uncompromising reactionism left him increasingly isolated within Parliament and resented by the British public.

W

and cultural, and during World War I he was instrumental in securing the Balfour Declaration (1917), which established a Jewish national home in Palestine. He served as president of the World Zionist Organization (1920–31, 1935–46). As president of Israel, he advocated cooperation with Israel's Arab neighbours.

Weld, Theodore Dwight (1803–95) US abolitionist. He and his wife, Angelina Grimké, were leading campaigners for the abolition of slavery. In 1833 he helped to organize the American Anti-Slavery Society. Having trained as a minister, Weld led anti-slavery debates that brought his dismissal from the seminary. Weld was editor (1836–40) of the *Emancipator*, the organ of the antislavery society. He wrote *American Slavery As It Is* (1839).

Welensky, Sir Roy Roland (1907–91) Rhodesian statesman, prime minister of the Federation of Rhodesia and Nyasaland (1956–63). He was a Northern Rhodesian member of parliament (1938–53) and a member of the executive council (1940–53). In 1953 he established the Federal Party, which promoted a policy of "racial partnership". Welensky served (1953–56) as deputy prime minister before becoming prime minister. Following the dissolution of the Central African Federation, which he had helped to create, Welensky lost the support of white Rhodesians to Ian Smith.

welfare state Description of a state that takes responsibility for the health and subsistence of its citizens. Limited forms of welfare were introduced by some countries in the 19th century, including the poor laws of Britain and the provision of free education in Prussia and France. More comprehensive policies evolved, such as the introduction of limited social insurance in Germany by Otto von Bismarck. In the 20th century, some of the legislation of President Franklin Roosevelt's New Deal provided for a number of welfare agencies, while in Britain, following William Beveridge's report, many reforms were implemented and the National Health Service (NHS) was established. The policy of the welfare state is a central tenet of most communist countries. Recently some Western countries, aware of the ever-growing cost of supporting a welfare state, have attempted reforms that create private and public partnerships. *See also* Medicare and Medicaid; social security

Welf *See* Guelph

Wellington, Arthur Wellesley, Duke of *See* feature article

Wells Fargo US transport company. It was founded (1852) by Henry Wells (1805–78) and William Fargo (1818–81) to serve the banking and shipping needs of California miners. The company took over the failing Pony Express, and by 1866 it operated the largest stagecoach network in America. By 1888 Wells Fargo had a transcontinental rail route. In 1918 it merged with the American Railway Express Company. Today, it operates an armoured car service in the E United States.

Wenceslas, Saint (*c.*907–29) Prince of Bohemia and patron saint of the Czechs. In *c.*925 he overthrew his mother who, as regent, persecuted Christians. Wenceslas continued the Christianization of Bohemia but his support of German missionaries aroused opposition. Forced to submit to Henry I (the Fowler) of Germany, Wenceslas was killed by his brother and successor, Bolesław I.

Wenceslas (1361–1419) King of the Germans (1378–1400) and king of Bohemia (1378–1419) as Wenceslas IV. He succeeded his father, Charles IV, as emperor but was never crowned. Wenceslas' neglect of German affairs angered the princes, who deposed him (1400) in favour of Rupert from the House of Wittlesbach. He enabled his half-brother, Sigismund, to become (1387) king of Hungary. Although Wenceslas initially supported the reforms of Jan Hus, he did not oppose his execution (1415).

Wends Name given to the Slavs living between the Oder and Elbe rivers in the early Middle Ages. They were conquered by Charlemagne but not fully Christianized until the 12th century.

Wesley, John (1703–91) English theologian and evangelist, founder of Methodism. With his brother Charles Wesley, he founded (1729) the Holy Club at Oxford, undertaking visits to prisons and aiding the sick. In 1735 the brothers travelled as missionaries to the American colony of Georgia, and while in transit Wesley met and was influenced by members of the German Moravian Church. His trip to the colonies was unsuccessful and Wesley returned in 1737. In 1738, during a meeting of the Moravians, Wesley underwent a personal, religious experience that laid the foundation upon which he built the Methodist movement. In 1739 he joined George Whitefield in Bristol, s England, and began to preach in the open-air, attracting large audiences. After he had split with the Moravians and the Calvinists, Wesley began to lay the foundations of the Methodist Church while advocating social reform. Wesley's *Journal* (1735–90) records the extent of his itinerant preaching.

Wessex Anglo-Saxon kingdom established in Hampshire, sw England. Traditionally founded by Cerdic, by the beginning of the 9th century it had extended its territory to include much of s England. Egbert became overlord of all England, but his successors lost much of the kingdom to the Danes. Alfred (the Great) ensured that Wessex was the only English kingdom to escape Danish conquest. *See also* Danelaw

West Bank Region w of the River Jordan and nw of the Dead Sea. Under the United Nations' (UN) plan for the partition of Palestine (1947), it was designated an Arab district. The West Bank was administered by Jordan after the first Arab-Israeli War (1948) but captured by Israel in the Six-Day War (1967). In 1988 Jordan surrendered its claim to the Israeli-occupied West Bank to the Palestine Liberation Organization (PLO). Under the terms of the Israeli-Palestinian Accord (1993), limited autonomy in the West Bank was conceded to the newly formed Palestinian National Authority (PNA), led by Yasir Arafat. Difficulties created by the growth of Israeli settlements, security disputes, Palestinian terrorism, and the accession of a Likud government (1996–99) in Israel threatened to disrupt progress towards total Israeli withdrawal. In the Wye Agreement (1998), Israel agreed to a partial withdrawal of troops in the West Bank.

Western Australia State in Australia. The capital is Perth. Although Western Australia was first visited by Dirck Hartog in 1616, settlement did not begin until 1826, when a penal colony was founded by the British. The first free settlement was in 1829. By far the largest state in Australia, it was governed by New South Wales until 1831, becoming a state of the Commonwealth of Australia in 1901. Area: 2,525,500sq km (975,095sq mi). Pop. (1991) 1,586,393.

Western European Union (WEU) Defence alliance consisting of most of the European members of the North Atlantic Treaty Organization (NATO). Established in 1955 by Britain, France, Belgium, Luxembourg, the Netherlands, Italy and West Germany, its main purpose was to oversee West German rearmament and integration into NATO. The formation of the WEU ended formal occupation of West Germany and Italy. The founder nations evolved into the Council of Europe, and, following the formation of tactical units within the WEU, by the 1990s it was considered Europe's principal defence force.

Western Jin *See* Jin

Western Sahara (formerly Spanish Sahara) Desert territory on the Atlantic coast of nw Africa. The capital is El Aaiún. The territory comprises two districts: Saguia el Hamra in the n and Río de Oro in the s. The population is composed of Arabs, Berbers and pastoral nomads, most of whom are Sunni Muslims. The first European discovery was in 1434, but the area remained unexploited until the 19th century, and even then Spain controlled only the coastal area. In 1957 a nationalist movement overthrew the Spanish, but in 1958 the Spanish regained control of the region and merged Saguia el Hamra and Río de Oro to form the province of Spanish Sahara. In 1963 large phosphate deposits were discovered. In 1973 the Polisario Front began a guerrilla war that forced Spain to withdraw in 1976. Within a month, Morocco and Mauritania had partitioned the country. Polisario (backed by Algeria) continued to fight for independence, unilaterally renaming the country the Saharawi Arab Democratic Republic. In 1979 Mauritania withdrew, and Morocco assumed full control. In 1982 the Saharawi Republic was granted membership of the Organization of African Unity (OAU) and, by 1988, controlled most of the desert up to the Moroccan defensive line. Fragile cease-fires were agreed in 1988 and 1991. An estimated 200,000 Saharawis live in refugee camps, mostly in Algeria. Area: 266,769sq km (102,680sq mi). Pop. (1993 est.) 214,000.

Western Samoa Former name of Samoa

Western Wall (Wailing Wall) Place in Jerusalem sacred to all Jews. It is a remnant of a wall of the great Temple of Jerusalem destroyed by the Romans in AD 70 and is the focus of many pilgrimages.

West India Company Name of two colonial trading companies, one Dutch, the other French. The **Dutch West India Company** was founded in 1621 and given a monopoly of trade with Dutch colonies in America and Africa and a monopoly of ownership of the American

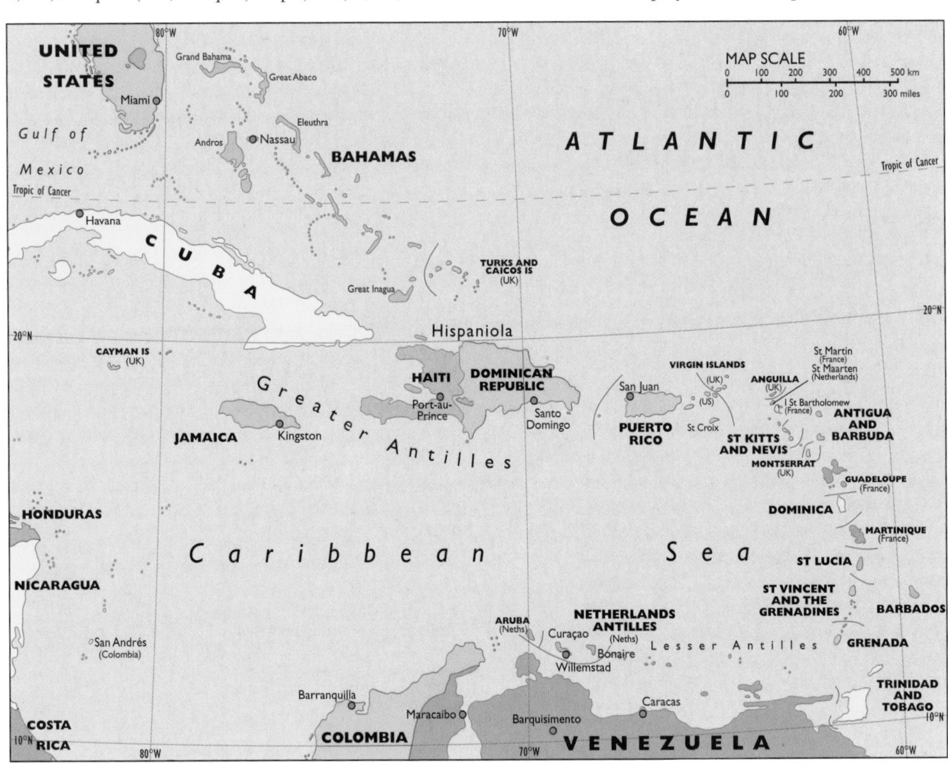

WEST VIRGINIA
Statehood :
20 June 1863
Nickname :
The Mountain State
State motto :
Mountaineers are always free

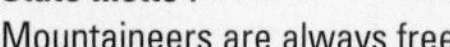

colonies. It was the dominant power in the early days of the SLAVE TRADE. It was dissolved in 1794. The **French West India Company** was incorporated in 1664 and was given a monopoly of trade and ownership in all French colonies in America and West Africa except Newfoundland. The Company was not profitable and its trading rights were revoked in 1674. It was liquidated in 1719.

West Indies Chain of islands encircling the Caribbean Sea and separating it from the Atlantic Ocean. They extend from Florida to Venezuela. Geographically they are divided into three main groups: the BAHAMAS and the Greater and Lesser Antilles. Most islands are now independent, but were formerly British, Spanish, French or Dutch possessions. The indigenous population was killed by the colonial powers, who fought for possession of the islands. The islands were transformed by the introduction of sugarcane in the 17th century, fuelling the SLAVE TRADE from Africa. *See* map, page 435, and individual country articles

West Indies Federation (1958–62) Alliance of Britain's Antillean colonies, with its capital in TRINIDAD. Political rivalries led to the collapse of the Federation.

Westminster, Statutes of English acts of the reign of EDWARD I. The first (1275) and second (1285) statutes enshrined Edward's overhaul of English law. A further statute of 1290 is sometimes called the third statute of Westminster. The Statute of Westminster of 1931 granted autonomy to the dominions, including Canada, New Zealand, Australia and South Africa, within the COMMONWEALTH OF NATIONS.

Westminster Assembly (1643–52) Conference organized by the LONG PARLIAMENT to settle the religion of the CHURCH OF ENGLAND. Most of its 30 lay and 12 clerical members were CALVINISTS, and the Westminster Confession that they drew up has been generally accepted by PRESBYTERIANS. It was rejected in England when the monarchy was restored in 1660.

Westphalia, Peace of (1648) Series of treaties among the states involved in the THIRTY YEARS' WAR. Peace negotiations began in 1642, and meetings were held in cities of Westphalia. In Germany, the peace established the virtual autonomy of the German states, created equality between Protestants and Catholics, and diminished the authority of the HOLY ROMAN EMPIRE. It also established the ascendancy of France, the Netherlands, the power of Sweden in N Europe and the decline of Spain.

West Virginia State in the Appalachian mountains, E central United States; the capital is Charleston. The area was home to the MOUND BUILDERS (*c*.500 BC–AD 100). When the Germans established the first European settlement at New Mecklenburg (Shepherdstown) in 1727, the area was exclusively inhabited by the IROQUOIS CONFEDERACY. Settlers crossing the Appalachian and Allegheny mountains led to the last of the FRENCH AND INDIAN WARS (1754–63). The region was then part of VIRGINIA, but political and economic disagreements, especially regarding SLAVERY, arose between W Virginians and the dominant E. The seizure of Harper's Ferry (1859) by the radical abolitionist John BROWN widened the breach and the Western delegates opposed Virginia's secession from the Union in May 1861. The state of West Virginia was created in the midst of the American Civil War. The state's industrial expansion began in the 1870s. Area: 62,629sq km (24,181sq mi). Pop. (1996) 1,825,754.

Whig Party Major US political organization from 1834 to 1854, formed in opposition to President Andrew JACKSON. It was a coalition party, drawing support from E capitalists, W farmers, S plantation owners, and the remnants of the ANTI-MASONIC PARTY. Fashioned on the policies of Henry CLAY and Daniel WEBSTER, the Party elected two presidents, William Henry HARRISON (1840) and Zachary TAYLOR (1848). The COMPROMISE OF 1850 on the issue of SLAVERY split the Party and the defection of the Southern Whigs to the DEMOCRATIC PARTY destroyed General Winfield SCOTT's chances in the 1852 elections. Most of the Northern Whigs joined the newly formed REPUBLICAN PARTY in 1854. *See also* TYLER, JOHN

Whigs Semi-formal parliamentary grouping in Britain from the late 17th to the mid-19th century. The word Whig was used derisively by the TORY supporters of the Duke of York (later JAMES II) for politicians who wished to exclude him from the throne. The Whig Party thus became those people who promoted the GLORIOUS REVOLUTION of 1688 and who applauded the succession of the House of HANOVER in 1714. Between 1714 and the accession of GEORGE III in 1760, the Tories were so discredited by association with the JACOBITES that most politicians became Hanoverian Whigs, even in opposition to a Whig ministry. In the reign of GEORGE III, Toryism gradually reasserted itself, while Whiggism became the party of religious toleration, parliamentary reform and opposition to slavery. From the appointment of William PITT (THE YOUNGER) as prime minister in 1783 until 1830 the Whigs remained in opposition (with one brief exception). They then returned to office under Earl GREY, passing the Great REFORM ACT of 1832. By the mid-19th century they had come to be replaced by, or were known as, the LIBERAL PARTY.

Whiskey Rebellion (1794) Revolt against the US government in W Pennsylvania. It was provoked by a tax imposed on whiskey by Alexander HAMILTON, and was the first serious challenge to federal authority. Collection of the tax met violent resistance, but when President George WASHINGTON called out the militia, the rebellion collapsed.

White, Walter Francis (1893–1955) US civil rights leader. He was secretary (1931–55) of the NATIONAL ASSOCIATION FOR THE ADVANCEMENT OF COLORED PEOPLE (NAACP). White was a leading campaigner against racial prejudice and violence in the United States. His autobiography is *A Man Called White* (1948).

White Australia Policy Australian legislation to restrict non-European immigration. Following a period when Chinese and Pacific Islanders were brought into the country to make up for the labour shortage, by the mid-1800s there was increasing concern that they were indirectly adding to the problem of European-settler unemployment. Introduced (1901) by Alfred DEAKIN, the policy excluded non-Europeans based on a fabricated language test that would ensure non-Europeans failed. Greatly relaxed by Gough WHITLAM's administration in the 1970s, the number of Asian immigrants has grown considerably.

Whitefield, George (1714–70) English evangelical preacher, an important figure in early METHODISM. A friend of Charles and John WESLEY at Oxford University, in 1738 he joined the Wesley's on their missionary trip to the colony of Georgia. In 1739 Whitefield returned to England to be ordained a priest and, denied access to the pulpits of the Church of England, began to make stirring, open-air sermons. Returning to the American colonies, Whitefield and Jonathan EDWARDS led the revival movement known as the GREAT AWAKENING. He broke away from John Wesley to form the CALVINISTIC METHODIST CHURCH.

Whitlam, (Edward) Gough (1916–) Australian statesman, prime minister (1972–75). In 1967 Whitlam became leader of the Australian LABOR PARTY. His government ended compulsory conscription and relaxed Australia's stringent WHITE AUSTRALIA POLICY. In 1975, following the Loans Affair in which Labor politicians acted independently of the cabinet, Whitlam was dismissed by the British governor general. The action highlighted Australia's constitutional relationship with Britain. In December 1977, after a crushing defeat in the general election, Whitlam resigned as party leader.

WHO *See* WORLD HEALTH ORGANIZATION

Wilberforce, William (1759–1833) English social reformer. In 1780 he was elected to Parliament, and became a close ally of William PITT (THE YOUNGER). In 1785 he was converted to evangelicalism, denouncing the SLAVE TRADE. Wilberforce subsequently led the ABOLITIONIST cause in Parliament for more than 20 years. His campaign led to the abolition of SLAVERY in 1807, but Wilberforce continued to work for abolition throughout the British Empire, and died one month before the adoption of the Emancipation Act (1833). His works include *A Practical View* (1797). *See also* CLAPHAM SECT

Wilderness Campaign (May–June 1864) Series of battles in the American CIVIL WAR, fought in woodland 80km (50mi) NW of RICHMOND, Virginia. In the first battle (5–6 May), Ulysses GRANT's Army of the Potomac was surprised by the advance of the Confederate Army of Northern Virginia led by Robert LEE. In the second battle (8–19 May), Grant's assault on Confederate lines was repulsed with great loss of life. By the beginning of June, both armies were on the outskirts of Richmond. The Battle of COLD HARBOR (3 June 1864) was one of the bloodiest engagements of the War. The Campaign cost *c*.60,000 Union lives and *c*.20,000 Confederate.

Wilderness Road Principal route of Westward migration for US pioneers from 1780 to 1840. Running for *c*.482km (300mi), the trail was blazed (1775) by Daniel BOONE, under the commission of Transylvania Company. It was the only usable road through the Shenandoah Valley and across the Appalachian Mountains to Kentucky.

Wilhelmina (1880–1962) Queen of the Netherlands (1890–1948), daughter and successor of WILLIAM III. She helped keep the country neutral in WORLD WAR 1 and often intervened in political affairs. During WORLD WAR 2, she led the government in exile in England and became a symbol of Dutch independence. In 1948 she abdicated in favour of her daughter, Juliana.

Wilkes, Charles (1798–1877) US naval officer and explorer. In his circumnavigation of the world (1838–42), Wilkes explored the South Seas and proved that ANTARCTICA was a continent. Wilkes Land is named after him. Implicated in the TRENT AFFAIR, he almost brought Britain into the CIVIL WAR on the Confederate side.

Wilkes, John (1725–97) British radical politician and journalist. Elected to Parliament in 1757, he was expelled for his savage criticism of GEORGE III and Lord BUTE's government in the *North Briton*, a political journal (1763). Wilkes' prosecution under a general warrant was condemned in the courts, a landmark in civil liberty. The refusal by Parliament to readmit him as member for Middlesex after he had been elected three times encouraged the movement towards parliamentary reform. Wilkes' public popularity resulted in him regaining his seat (1774–90), but after 1774, having secured a measure of press freedom, he ceased to be politically influential.

Wilkins, Roy (1901–81) US CIVIL RIGHTS leader. He was editor (1934–49) of *The Crisis*, the official magazine of the NATIONAL ASSOCIATION FOR THE ADVANCEMENT OF COLORED PEOPLE (NAACP). As executive secretary (1955–65) and then executive director (1965–77) of the NAACP, Wilkins sought to achieve equal rights through legal redress, such as the BROWN V. BOARD OF EDUCATION OF TOPEKA (1954). He helped Martin Luther KING, Jr, organize a civil rights march on Washington (1963).

Wilkinson, James (1757–1825) American general and adventurer. He served in the AMERICAN REVOLUTION but was forced to resign (1778) over his role in the CONWAY CABAL. In 1784 Wilkinson moved to Kentucky and joined a conspiracy with the Spanish governor of Louisiana to gain trade monopolies for himself and to give Kentucky to Spain. After the LOUISIANA PURCHASE (1803), Wilkinson became governor of Louisiana (1805–06). He probably plotted with Aaron BURR to conquer parts of Mexico, but then betrayed Burr to President Thomas JEFFERSON. Returning to the army at the start of the WAR OF 1812, he was dismissed after failing to capture Montréal (1813).

William I (1797–1888) King of PRUSSIA (1861–88) and emperor of Germany (1871–88), son of FREDERICK WILLIAM III. His role in the suppression of the REVOLUTION OF 1848 in Berlin earned him a reputation as a die-hard reactionary. From 1858 he acted as regent for his sick brother, FREDERICK WILLIAM IV. After Prussia's victory in the AUSTRO-PRUSSIAN WAR (1866), William increasingly relied on the advice of his chancellor, Otto von BISMARCK. Yet, he pursued a more cautious line than Bismarck during the FRANCO-PRUSSIAN WAR (1870), and voiced his disapproval of the policy of KULTURKAMPF. William regarded Bismarck's creation of the German empire with suspicion, fearing a reduction in Prussia's status, and only reluctantly accepted the title of emperor. He was succeeded by his son, FREDERICK III.

William II (1859–1941) Emperor of Germany (1888–1918), son and successor of FREDERICK III and grandson of WILLIAM I of Germany and Queen VICTORIA of Britain. One of his first acts was to force Chancellor Otto von BISMARCK to resign (1890). A succession of chancellors, including Graf von CAPRIVI and Fürst von BÜLOW, failed to enact vital domestic political and social reforms. His telegram (1896) to Paul KRUGER, congratulating him on the defeat of the JAMESON RAID, and his visit (1905) to Tangier, Morocco, alarmed both British and French imperial interests in Africa, and led to the creation of the ENTENTE CORDIALE. The build-up of the German navy under Admiral Alfred von TIRPITZ further worried Britain. In 1908, after receiving poor counsel in making an unwise press statement about anti-British sentiment in Germany, William replaced Bülow with Theobald von BETHMANN-HOLLWEG. William entered WORLD WAR I (1914–18) in an effort to prevent the dissolution of AUSTRO-HUNGARIAN EMPIRE, but he was soon encouraging the imperial aims of his generals, such as Paul von HINDENBURG and Erich LUDENDORFF. William was forced to abdicate after the armistice (November 1918) and went into exile in the Netherlands.

William I (the Conqueror) (1027–87) King of England (1066–87) and Duke of NORMANDY (1035–87). The first NORMAN king of England, William was the illegitimate son of Robert I of Normandy. He was reluctantly accepted as Robert's heir and succeeded to the dukedom. Supported initially by HENRY I of France, William was able to consolidate his position in Normandy against hostile neighbours. In 1051, on a visit to England to see his cousin EDWARD THE CONFESSOR, William was apparently designated the childless Edward's successor to the English throne. In 1054 William married MATILDA, a descendant of ALFRED (THE GREAT), thus underlining his right to be English king. In 1064 Harold, Earl of Essex (later HAROLD II), was captured by William in Normandy, and forced to recognize William's claim before being released. Following Edward's death, William claimed the English throne. When Harold usurped the throne for himself, William invaded England and defeated and killed Harold at the Battle of HASTINGS (1066). Ruthlessly crushing internal resistance, notably in the N and W of England, and defeating the invading Danes, William subsequently enforced his rule over the whole kingdom during a period that would come to be known as the NORMAN CONQUEST. He rewarded his followers by grants of land, eventually replacing almost the entire ANGLO-SAXON feudal ruling class with Normans, and intimidated potential rebels by rapid construction of castles. He invaded Scotland (1072), extracting an oath of loyalty from MALCOLM III (CANMORE), and Wales (1081), although he spent much of his reign in France. He ordered the famous survey known as the DOMESDAY BOOK (1086). William died while campaigning against PHILIP I of France.

William II (Rufus) (1056–1100) King of England (1087–1100), second surviving son and successor of WILLIAM I (THE CONQUEROR) and MATILDA. Soon after his accession, William had to crush revolts by Anglo-Norman barons led by his uncle ODO, who supported his elder brother, ROBERT II, Duke of Normandy. William invaded the duchy twice, and in 1096 Robert mortgaged it to him to raise cash for the First CRUSADE. William invaded Scotland, later killing (1093) MALCOLM III (CANMORE), and subdued Wales (1097). With his brutal, warlike temperament, William's rule in England, although stable, was repressive. He was killed hunting, allegedly (although improbably) by accident. He was succeeded by his younger brother, HENRY I.

William III (of Orange) (1650–1702) King of England, Scotland and Ireland (1689–1702), posthumous son and successor of WILLIAM II, PRINCE OF ORANGE. Although royal authority was limited by Jan de WITT during William's minority, the crisis engendered by a combined French and English assault on the UNITED PROVINCES OF THE NETHERLANDS led to his appointment as stadtholder and captain general in 1672. With aid from Emperor LEOPOLD I, William expelled the French. In 1677 he married Mary (later MARY II), daughter of JAMES II of England. Following the GLORIOUS REVOLUTION (1688), he and Mary, strong Protestants, replaced the Catholic James, finally defeating him in Ireland at the Battle of the BOYNE (1690). William and Mary ruled jointly until her death in 1694. In 1699 William organized the alliance that was to defeat LOUIS XIV of France in the War of the SPANISH SUCCESSION. Never popular in England and beset by constant strife in Scotland following the Massacre of GLENCOE (1692), William approved the BILL OF RIGHTS (1689) and other constitutional reforms. *See also* GRAND ALLIANCE, WAR OF THE; RIJSWIJK, TREATY OF

William IV (1765–1837) King of Great Britain and Ireland and elector of Hanover (1830–37). Third son of GEORGE III, he succeeded, unexpectedly, aged 65 after a long career in the navy. Nicknamed "Silly Billy", he was well-meaning though unkingly. He assisted the Great Reform Bill (1832) by creating new peers to give Earl GREY's government a majority in the House of Lords. He was succeeded by his niece VICTORIA. *See also* REFORM ACTS

William I (1772–1843) First king of the Netherlands and grand duke of Luxembourg (1815–40). He fought in the FRENCH REVOLUTIONARY WARS and the NAPOLEONIC WARS. William's forceful government offended liberals and Roman Catholics, and a revolution in BELGIUM (1830) was followed by Belgian independence (1839). Compelled to accept a constitution restricting his powers, he abdicated in favour of his son, WILLIAM II.

William II (1792–1849) King of the Netherlands and grand duke of Luxembourg (1840–49), son and successor of WILLIAM I. He led the Netherlands troops in the Battle of WATERLOO (1815) against NAPOLEON I. After the Belgian revolution (1830), William commanded the Dutch forces against LEOPOLD I of Belgium. William's reign saw a return to prosperity and, in response to the REVOLUTIONS OF 1848, a new, liberal constitution (1848).

William III (1817–90) King of the Netherlands and grand duke of LUXEMBOURG (1849–90), son and successor of WILLIAM II. He reluctantly appointed Jan Thorbecke to head the government and accepted his liberal reforms, such as the extension of suffrage. William abolished slavery in the Dutch West Indies (1862) and granted Luxembourg independence (1867). He was succeeded by his daughter, WILHELMINA.

▲ William I (the Conqueror) profoundly altered the religious traditions and social structure of England. He is depicted here in the manuscript *Liber Legum Antiquorum Regum* (*c*.1321).

William I (the Lion) (1143–1214) King of Scotland (1165–1214). William succeeded his brother Malcolm IV and forged the "Auld Alliance" with France. Captured by the English during an attempt to regain Northumbria, he was forced to swear fealty to HENRY II (1174). William regained Scotland's independence from RICHARD I in return for a cash payment towards the Third CRUSADE in 1189. He established the independence of the church under the pope and strengthened royal authority in the north.

William I (the Silent) (1533–84) Prince of ORANGE, founder of the UNITED PROVINCES OF THE NETHERLANDS. He gained the support of Emperor CHARLES V, and later PHILIP II of Spain, who made William stadtholder (1555) of the N Dutch provinces. The political and religious persecution of Dutch Protestants turned William against Spain and, with graafs van EGMONT and van HOORN, he began to agitate against regent MARGARET OF PARMA. In response, Philip sent the Duke of ALBA to the Netherlands to crush dissent and William fled to Germany. In 1568, with his younger brother, LOUIS OF NASSAU, William organized an army and invaded the Netherlands, so precipitating the REVOLT OF THE NETHERLANDS. From 1572 to 1576 William led the resistance of the two N maritime provinces of Holland and Zeeland against Spanish forces. A hiatus in Spanish power in the LOW COUNTRIES led to the PACIFICATION OF GHENT (1576), which held out hope of the unification of the N and S provinces. However, when the new Spanish governor general, JOHN OF AUSTRIA, insisted that Roman Catholicism be recognized as the state religion, Holland and Zeeland walked out of the States General. In 1577 John lost support by relaunching the war and William was able to rebuild the union. William's triumph proved short-lived as the S provinces reconciled themselves with the new Spanish governor general, Alessandro FARNESE, in the Union of ARRAS (1579), and the N provinces allied themselves with France in the Union of UTRECHT (1579). William continued as leader of the N provinces until he was assassinated in Delft by a Catholic fanatic. *See also* GRANVELLE, ANTOINE PERRENOT DE

William II, Prince of Orange (1626–50) Prince of ORANGE, stadtholder of several Dutch provinces (1647–50). He married Mary, daughter of CHARLES I of England, in 1650. William's dynastic ambitions were scotched by his early death. He was succeeded by his son, the future WILLIAM III (OF ORANGE) of England.

William of Occam (*c*.1285–*c*.1349) English scholastic philosopher. Contributing to the development of formal logic, he employed the principle of economy known as Occam's razor: a problem should be stated in its most basic terms. As a Franciscan monk, he upheld ideals of poverty against Pope JOHN XXII and was excommunicated. In 1328 he was imprisoned in Avignon, France, but he escaped and fled to Munich, where he later died.

Williams, Eric Eustace (1911–81) West Indian statesman, first prime minister of TRINIDAD AND TOBAGO (1962–81). In 1956 he founded and became leader of the People's National Movement (PNM), the island's first genuinely modern political party. Six years later he led his country to independence. As prime minister, he attracted foreign investment which spurred economic growth.

Williams, Roger (1603–83) English Puritan minister. In 1631 he emigrated to the MASSACHUSETTS BAY COLONY. His radical politics and theology antagonized the Puritan authorities, and he was expelled (1635). In 1636 Williams founded Providence, the first settlement in RHODE ISLAND, on land purchased from the Narragansett. He returned to England and acquired a charter. Williams served (1654–57) as president of Rhode Island colony.

Willkie, Wendell Lewis (1892–1944) US industrialist and politician. He opposed government intervention in business under President Franklin ROOSEVELT's NEW DEAL, objecting in particular to schemes such as the TENNESSEE VALLEY AUTHORITY (TVA). In 1940 Wilkie ran as the Republican candidate against Roosevelt. During World War 2, however, he toured the world in support of Roosevelt's foreign policy. In his book *One World* (1943), he advocated the formation of a post-war world organization.

Wilmot Proviso (1846) US attempt to prohibit slavery in territory acquired from Mexico. It was made in the form

International conflict precipitated by the assassination of the Austrian Archduke FRANZ FERDINAND by Serbs in Sarajevo (28 June 1914). AUSTRIA declared war on SERBIA (28 July), RUSSIA mobilized in support of Serbia (from 29 July), WILLIAM II of GERMANY declared war on Russia (1 August) and FRANCE (3 August), and BRITAIN declared war on Germany (4 August). World War 1 resulted from growing tensions in Europe, exacerbated by the rise of the German Empire since 1871 and the decline of Ottoman power in the BALKAN STATES, resulting in increased nationalist sentiment. The chief contestants were the CENTRAL POWERS (Germany and Austria) and the TRIPLE ENTENTE (Britain, France and Russia). Many other countries were drawn in. Ottoman Turkey joined the Central Powers in 1914, Bulgaria in 1915. Italy joined the Western Allies in 1915, Romania in 1916 and, decisively, the United States in 1917. Russia withdrew following the RUSSIAN REVOLUTION of 1917.

In Europe, fighting was largely static. After the initial German advance through Belgium, according to the revised SCHLIEFFEN PLAN, was checked at the MARNE, the Western Front settled into a war of attrition, with huge casualties but little territory lost or gained on either side. On the Eastern Front, the initial Russian advance was checked by the Germans, who overran Poland before stagnation set in. An Anglo-French effort to relieve the Russians by attacking GALLIPOLI (1916) failed, while Italy and Austria became bogged down on the Isonzo front. Campaigns were also fought outside Europe, against the Turks in the Middle East and the German colonies in Africa and the Pacific. At sea, only one major battle was fought, at JUTLAND (1916). German submarines proved highly effective against Allied merchant ships in the Atlantic, but the naval blockade of Germany caused severe food shortages and helped end the War. An armistice was agreed in November 1918, and peace treaties were signed at Versailles (1919). The War introduced new weapons, such as tanks, poison gas, airplanes and depth charges. Casualties were high, with *c.*10 million people killed. *See also* individual battles and leaders

▲ **The Mark IV tank** was first used by the British in World War 1. Its shape was largely dictated by conflicting requirements: it had to cross wide trenches and also be transported to the front on narrow railway wagons. Mark IV tanks were first used in the Battle of Cambrai, France (20 November 1917), to break through German defences.

► **battlefield** The infantry of the British 15th Brigade, 9 July 1918, in a bomb crater near Morlancourt, Belgium. They were so close to enemy lines that they could hear the Germans talking while the picture was being taken. Conditions in the trenches were horrific; vermin and disease were rife, and soldiers suffered from trauma and shell-shock.

▼ **World War 1** While the outcome of the War was decided on the Western Front, fighting took place in many areas of Europe. On the Eastern Front, the Russians were defeated by the superior weaponry of the German army. The Italians were forced to retreat from NE Italy after the Battle of Caporetto. The troops of the Ottoman Empire fought those of the British Empire in the Tigris valley, while the Arabs assisted the Entente Powers by staging a revolt against the Ottomans, eventually driving them N to Damascus.

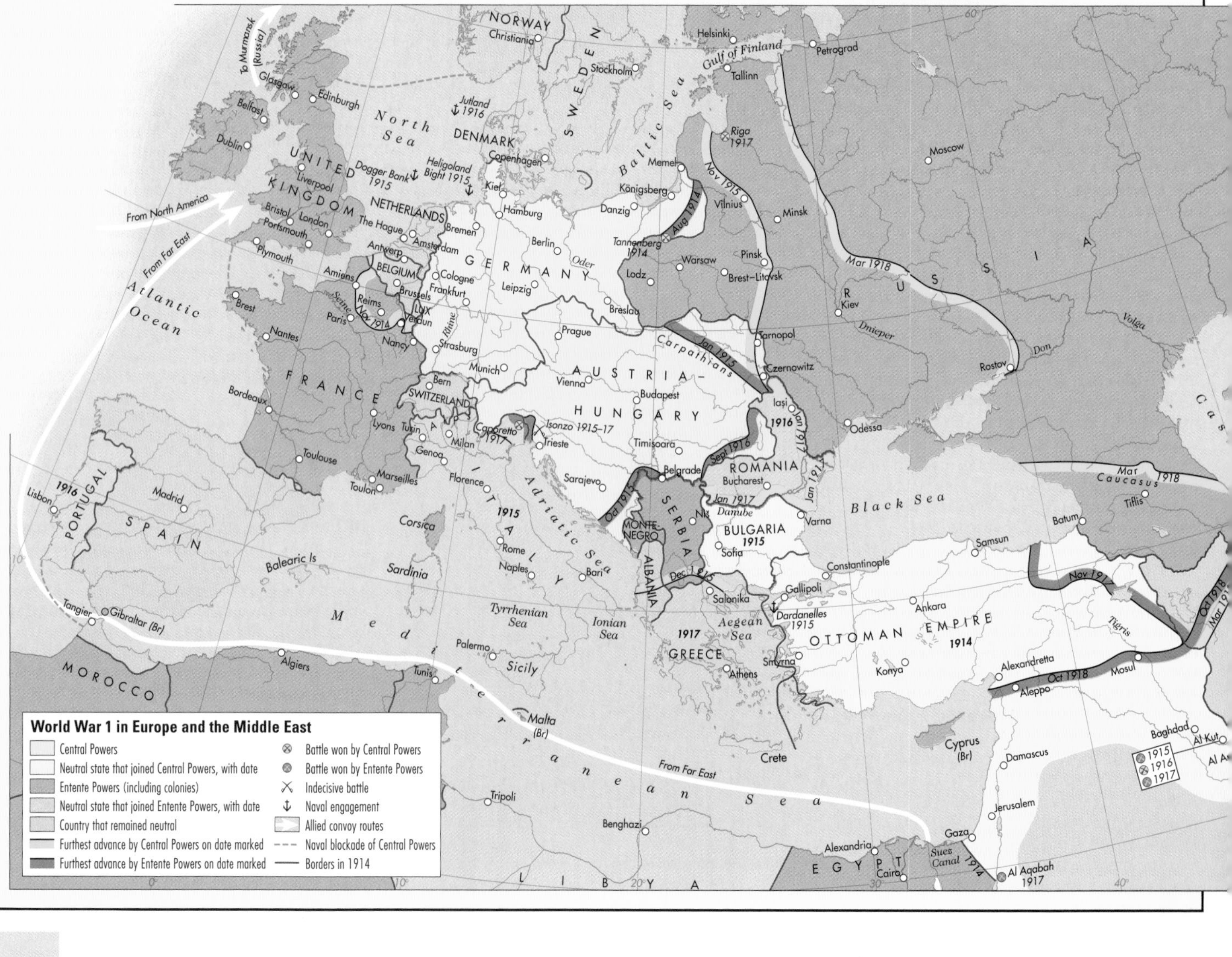

World War 1 in Europe and the Middle East

- Central Powers
- Neutral state that joined Central Powers, with date
- Entente Powers (including colonies)
- Neutral state that joined Entente Powers, with date
- Country that remained neutral
- Furthest advance by Central Powers on date marked
- Furthest advance by Entente Powers on date marked
- Battle won by Central Powers
- Battle won by Entente Powers
- Indecisive battle
- Naval engagement
- Allied convoy routes
- Naval blockade of Central Powers
- Borders in 1914

W

of an amendment to an appropriations bill by Representative David Wilmot of Pennsylvania. The proviso passed the House but was defeated twice in the Senate.

Wilson, Sir (James) Harold (1916–95) British statesman, prime minister (1964–70, 1974–76). He entered Parliament in 1945 and, as president of the board of trade (1947–51) under Clement Attlee, became Britain's youngest cabinet minister since William Pitt (the Younger). In 1951 he resigned over proposals to introduce charges in the National Health Service (NHS) in order to finance British involvement in the Korean War. In 1963 Wilson succeeded Hugh Gaitskell as leader of the Labour Party. In 1964 he won a narrow election victory over Harold Macmillan. His administration was faced by Ian Smith of Rhodesia's (*see* Zimbabwe) Unilateral Declaration of Independence (UDI) and domestic recession. Wilson was forced to impose strict price and income controls and to devalue sterling (1967). His first term in office also saw the introduction of the comprehensive school system and the Open University (OU), and the end of the death penalty. Other reforms included changes in the law on divorce and abortion. Rising unemployment and an increase in labour disputes contributed to his defeat by Conservative leader Edward Heath in the 1970 elections. Conflict between Labour's left and right wing over nationalization and membership of the European Economic Community (*see* European Community) threatened to divide Labour. In 1974, however, Wilson returned to power at the head of a minority government. His second term in office was beset with domestic economic problems, including high inflation. In 1976 he unexpectedly resigned and was succeeded as prime minister and Labour leader by James Callaghan.

Wilson, Sir Henry Hughes (1864–1922) British field marshal, b. Ireland. At the start of World War I, the British forces adopted his strategy of fighting in France, rather than Earl Roberts' tactic of attacking Germany in Belgium. As chief of the imperial general staff (1918), Wilson was the main military adviser to David Lloyd George in the closing stages of the War. Opposed to Lloyd George's granting of Irish Home Rule, in 1922 Wilson was elected as a Conservative member of Parliament for Ulster. He was assassinated by the Irish Republican Army (IRA).

Wilson, (Thomas) Woodrow (1856–1924) Twenty-eighth president of the United States (1913–21). As governor of New Jersey (1910–12), he won a reputation as a progressive Democrat. In 1912 he unexpectedly gained the Democratic Party nomination. The split in the Republican vote between President William Howard Taft's Republican Party and Theodore Roosevelt's Progressive Party handed Wilson the presidency. His "New Freedom" reforms included the establishment of the Federal Reserve System (1913). Several amendments to the US Constitution were introduced, including prohibition (18th, 1919) and the extension of the franchise to women (19th, 1920). The Mexican Revolution brought instability to the s border, and Wilson ordered John Pershing's intervention. Wilson's efforts to maintain US neutrality at the start of World War I aided his re-election in 1916. The failure of diplomacy and continuing attacks on US shipping forced Wilson to declare war (April 1917) on Germany. His Fourteen Points (January 1918) represented US war aims and became the basis of the peace negotiations at the Versailles peace conference (1919). Wilson was forced to compromise in the final settlement but succeeded in securing the establishment of the League of Nations. Domestic opposition to the League was led by Henry Cabot Lodge, and the Republican-dominated Senate rejected it. In October 1919 Wilson suffered a stroke and became an increasingly marginal figure for the remainder of his term.

Windsor Name by which the British royal family has been known since 1917. Queen Victoria's descendants in the male line originally belonged to the German house of Saxe-Coburg-Gotha, the family of her husband, Prince Albert. During World War I, however, this German connection proved embarrassing and George V proclaimed that British subjects descended from Victoria in the male line would henceforth take the surname of "Windsor". In decrees of 1952 and 1960 Elizabeth II modified this decree to the effect that her descendants could also take the name "Mountbatten-Windsor".

Winthrop, John (1588–1649) British Puritan colonist in North America, first governor of the Massachusetts Bay Colony. He led 700 colonists to Salem (1630) and later to Charlestown and Boston. He was governor for 12 years (1630–34, 1637–40, 1642–44, 1646–49), establishing a theocratic government. Winthrop was active in the expulsion of Roger Williams and Anne Hutchinson. Winthrop also served as president of the New England Confederation.

Winthrop (the Younger), John (1606–76) British colonial governor of Connecticut, son of John Winthrop. He settled Ipswich, Massachusetts (1633), and built Fort Saybrook on the Connecticut River (1634), serving as governor (1658–76). Winthrop obtained a liberal charter (1662) that united Connecticut and New Haven and gave the colonists the same rights as Englishmen.

Wisconsin State in N central United States; the state capital is Madison. Initially inhabited by Mound Builders, by the time Jean Nicolet claimed the region for France (1634) it had been settled by Algonquian- and Sioux-speaking Native North Americans. Wisconsin became an important centre in the fur trade and by *c.*1675 Jesuit missions had been established. The 18th century saw increased activity by fur trappers, which brought them into conflict with the Fox tribe. The region was ceded to Britain at the end of the French and Indian Wars (1763). In 1783 it was ceded to the United States. In the 1820s a lead-mining boom encouraged settlement, which increased further after the Black Hawk War (1832) ended Native American resistance and the Territory of Wisconsin was established in 1836. Leading up to the Civil War, Wisconsin opposed the extension of slavery to the Western territories. After the War, wheat farming was replaced by dairy farming as the main agricultural activity and the state became increasingly industrialized. In the 20th century Wisconsin became known for its progressive state governments, which pioneered many political reforms. World War 2 helped Wisconsin out of the economic crisis of the Great Depression and the state's economy grew steadily until the 1970s when dairy farming and manufacturing declined. Area: 145,438sq km (56,154sq mi). Pop. (1992) 4,992,664.

Wishart, George (*c.*1513–46) Scottish religious reformer. He was charged with heresy in 1538 and fled to England, but after studying in Cambridge, he returned to Scotland in 1543. Wishart preached on behalf of Reformed doctrines, and was assisted by John Knox, who became his disciple. He was burned as a heretic at St Andrews.

Witt, Jan de (1625–72) Dutch politician. A republican and opponent of William II, Prince of Orange, he became grand pensionary and effectively head of government in 1653, introducing laws forbidding members of the House of Orange to hold government posts. Witt defeated the English in the Second Dutch War (1665–67), and later signed the Triple Alliance with England and Sweden to stop the French invasion of the Netherlands. In 1672, after the English were persuaded by Louis XIV to abandon the Dutch, the French invaded and William III (of Orange) assumed control. Witt was killed by supporters of William.

▲ **Wilson** held a referendum in 1975 which voted in favour of British membership of the European Economic Community. He avoided British military intervention in the Vietnam War.

WISCONSIN
Statehood : 29 May 1848
Nickname : The Badger State
State motto : Forward

Witte, Count Sergei Yulievich (1849–1915) Russian statesman, prime minister (1905–06). As finance minister (1892–1903), he stimulated industrial growth, encouraging E expansion through construction of the Trans-Siberian Railway. Witte negotiated the treaty ending the Russo-Japanese War (1904–05) and advised Tsar Nicholas II to agree to constitutional government during the Russian Revolution of 1905.

Wittelsbach, House of German dynasty that ruled Bavaria from 1180 to 1918. In 1214 the Rhenish Palatinate was added to the family's holdings by marriage. In 1329 Emperor Louis IV divided the Wittelsbach lands between the dukes of Bavaria at Munich and the counts of the Rhenish Palatinate at Heidelberg. In 1623 the Duchy of Bavaria became an electorate, and in 1806 Maximilian I became the first king of Bavaria.

Władysław I (the Short) (1260–1333) King of Poland (1320–33). He became Duke of Poland as Władysław IV in 1296 and worked to unite Poland. After wars lasting from 1305–12, he united Great and Little Poland. Crowned in 1320, Władysław introduced legal reforms. As an ally of the Teutonic Knights, he saved Gdańsk from Brandenburg, but later warred with the Knights (1327–33).

Władysław II (Jagiello) (1350–1434) Grand duke of Lithuania (1377–86) and king of Poland (1386–1434), founder of the Jagiellon dynasty. As grand duke, he opposed the Teutonic Knights (1377–86) and then married Jadwiga, queen of Poland, which led to his election as king and his acceptance of Roman Catholicism. Władysław's lands stretched from the Baltic to the Black Sea and almost to Moscow. He decisively defeated the Teutonic Knights at Tannenberg (1410), weakened the Tatars, and regained Ruthenia from Hungary (1387).

Władysław IV (Vasa) (1595–1648) King of Poland (1632–48), son of Sigismund III (Vasa). After fighting with Russia, Sweden and the Ottoman Empire, he won favourable settlements from each. He failed, however, to solve internal problems with the Sejm (parliament) and lost part of Ukraine in the Cossack revolt (1648).

Wolfe, James (1727–59) British general. He fought in North America during the French and Indian Wars. Following his successful capture of Louisburg (1758) under Jeffrey Amherst, Wolfe was given command of a force of 5000 men. They captured Québec by scaling the cliffs above the St Lawrence River and defeating the French, under Marquis de Montcalm, on the Plains of Abraham (1759). This victory resulted in Britain's acquisition of Canada. Wolfe's death in action made him a hero.

Wolseley, Garnet Joseph, 1st Viscount (1833–1913) British field marshal, commander in chief of the British Army (1895–1901). He fought in the Crimean War and the Indian Mutiny. Wolseley also suppressed the Red River Rebellion (1870) in Canada. In Africa, he campaigned against the Ashanti, crushed an Egyptian revolt at the Battle of Tell-al-Kebir (1882), and led the attempt to rescue General Gordon from the siege of Khartoum, Sudan. As commander in chief, Wolseley's modernization of the armed forces helped Britain to victory in the Second South African War (1899–1902).

Wolsey, Thomas (*c.*1475–1530) English cardinal and statesman, lord chancellor (1515–29). Initially winning favour with Henry VII, after the accession of Henry VIII (1509) Wolsey was made archbishop of York (1514) and then cardinal and lord chancellor (1515). As chancellor, he controlled virtually all state business. Wolsey's attempts to place England at the centre of European diplomacy ended in failure. Although he became papal legate (1518), his ambition to become pope was never realized. Domestically, he made powerful enemies through his

W

International conflict fought between the AXIS POWERS and the ALLIES. The main causes of the War were disputes provoked by the expansionist policies of GERMANY in Europe and JAPAN in the Far East. During the 1930s, APPEASEMENT failed to check the ambitions of Adolf HITLER'S NAZI PARTY in Germany. Having made the NAZI-SOVIET PACT with the SOVIET UNION (August 1939), Germany invaded Poland, whereupon Britain and France declared war (3 September).

In 1940 Germany rapidly conquered Denmark, Norway, the Low Countries and France (June). Inability to gain command of the air prevented a German invasion of Britain (*see* Battle of BRITAIN), but the BLITZ devastated British cities, and German U-BOATS took a heavy toll on British merchant shipping. Italy, under Benito MUSSOLINI, having annexed Albania (1939) and invaded Greece (1940), joined Germany in 1941. Germany invaded Greece, where the Italians had been checked, and Yugoslavia. In June 1941 the Germans, violating the Pact of 1939, attacked the Soviet Union, advancing to the outskirts of MOSCOW and Leningrad (ST PETERSBURG). Italian defeats by the British in NORTH AFRICA drew in German Field Marshal ROMMEL, who initially repulsed the British. In the Pacific, the Japanese attack on PEARL HARBOR (December 1941) drew the United States into the War. Japan rapidly overran Southeast Asia and Burma, but the Battle of MIDWAY (June 1942) indicated growing US naval and air superiority. From 1942 the tide in Europe turned against Germany. Defeat at STALINGRAD (January 1943) was followed by a Soviet advance that drove the Germans out of the Soviet Union by August 1944. Defeats in North Africa in 1942–43 led to the Allied invasion of Italy, forcing the Italians to make peace (September 1943). German troops then occupied N Italy, where they resisted the Allied advance until 1945.

In June 1944 the Allied NORMANDY LANDINGS resulted first in the liberation of France, and then advanced into Germany, linking up with the Soviets on the River Elbe (April 1945). Germany surrendered in May. Japan continued to resist but surrendered in August after the United States dropped atom bombs on HIROSHIMA and NAGASAKI. Estimates of the numbers killed in the War exceed 50 million. The great majority of the dead were civilians, many murdered in the HOLOCAUST. Politically, two former allies, the United States and the Soviet Union, emerged as conflicting superpowers.

◄ German armed forces Shown here, from left: a lance sergeant, senior private, and regimented sergeant major. World War 2 involved more than three quarters of the world's population, from a total of 61 countries, and was the most deadly conflict in human history. Technological developments led to a new kind of warfare. The battlefield consisted of entire countries, rather than specific areas, making the distinction between civilian and soldier less clear.

▲ Yalta Conference (February 1945) Churchill, Roosevelt and Stalin met at Yalta, Ukraine, to discuss plans for the post-war division of Europe. As the leading superpower, the United States realized that its pre-war isolationist policy was no longer tenable and that it had a major role to play in reconstructing Europe and encouraging democratic regimes.

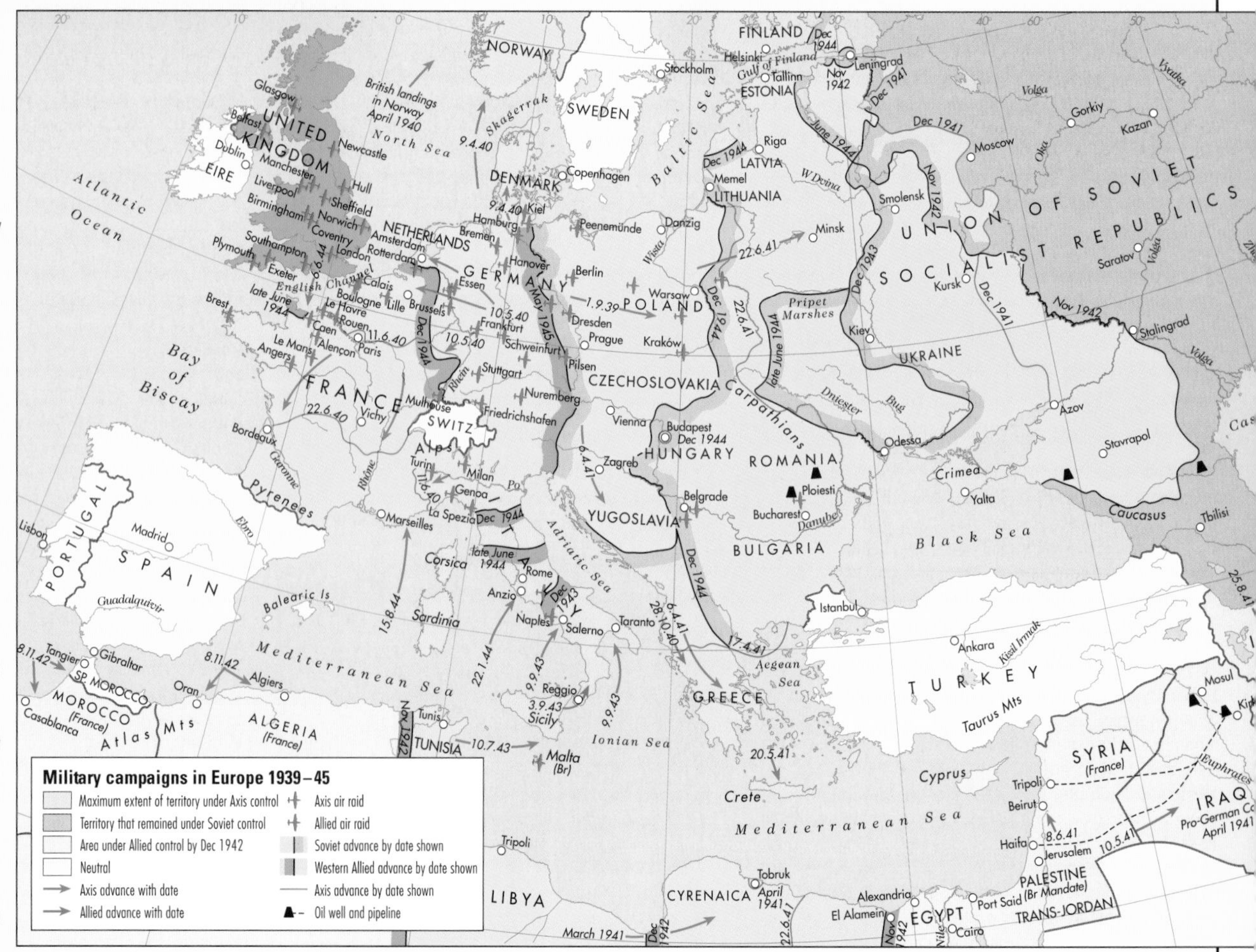

► World War 2 During the War, almost all of Europe came under Axis control. After Germany's invasion of W Europe, and its attempts to bomb Britain into submission, the War was concentrated on the Eastern Front. German forces swept across W Soviet Union, but during 1942, they became bogged down, with losses in the N outweighing gains in the S. The Soviets broke the siege of Stalingrad (February 1943) and the Germans were forced to retreat. Despite the Germans fighting a strong rearguard action in the E, in Italy and in W Europe, the Allied troops eventually met W of Berlin in May 1945.

method of raising taxes through forced loans, his conspicuous wealth and his pluralism. His reform of the STAR CHAMBER (court of the King's Council) gave Henry greater power over the nobility. Wolsey gifted HAMPTON COURT PALACE to Henry, but his failure to obtain the king a divorce from CATHERINE OF ARAGON brought about his downfall. Thomas MORE replaced Wolsey as chancellor. Charged with high treason, he died before his trial.

women's rights movement *See* FEMINISM; SUFFRAGETTE MOVEMENT

Wood, Leonard (1860–1927) US general, physician and administrator. After serving in the army as a surgeon in the APACHE WARS, along with Theodore ROOSEVELT he helped to establish the volunteer force known as the ROUGH RIDERS. Active in the SPANISH-AMERICAN WAR (1898), under Wood's command they helped to defeat the Spanish in Cuba, and Wood was made governor. After serving in the Philippines, Wood returned to the United States and was made army chief of staff (1910–14), advocating rearmament. Following his failure to gain the Republican presidential nomination (1920), Wood was made governor general of the Philippines (1921).

Worcester, Battle of (1651) Last engagement of the English CIVIL WAR. CHARLES II, having raised an army in Scotland, marched S in the hope of regaining the throne. He reached Worcester and on hearing that Oliver CROMWELL's army was nearby decided to make his headquarters in the town. Cromwell's army outnumbered the Royalists, and with a two-pronged attack, the town eventually fell. Charles managed to escape to France.

workhouse Former institution in England for the unemployed. Workhouses originated from the houses of correction provided for vagabonds by the POOR LAW Act of 1601, but officially they date from 1696, when workhouses were established by the Bristol Corporation. In 1723 a general act permitting workhouses to be founded in all parishes was passed. It denied relief to those who refused to enter a workhouse. Workhouses declined in the late 18th and early 19th centuries, but were revived by the Poor Law Act of 1834. With the advent of welfare reforms, workhouses had fallen into disuse by the early 20th century.

Works Progress Administration (WPA) Former US government agency created (1935) under President Franklin ROOSEVELT's "NEW DEAL" to stimulate national economic recovery. Billions of dollars were contributed to the scheme in which work programmes provided jobs for the unemployed. Among its projects were the building of roads, schools, parks, airports, bridges, dams and sewers. It also cleared slums, planted forests and electrified rural areas. About two million people were registered on WPA rolls at any one time between 1935 and 1941. In 1939 it changed its name to the Works Projects Administration.

World Bank Intergovernmental organization based in Washington, D.C., United States. A specialized agency of the UNITED NATIONS (UN), it was established (1945) following the BRETTON WOODS CONFERENCE. Today, the World Bank is divided into two distinct elements: the **International Bank for Reconstruction and Development (IBRD)** (established 1945) and the **International Development Association (IDA)** (established 1960). Working closely with the INTERNATIONAL MONETARY FUND (IMF), the World Bank makes available long-term loans to less-developed countries to aid their economic development. The major part of the Bank's resources is derived from member countries and the world's capital markets. In recent years, following criticism that World Bank funds were being used to aid short-term, industrial-based projects, many of which were harmful to the environment, the Bank began to concentrate on funding programmes based on sustainable rural development, health and education, and family planning.

World Health Organization (WHO) Intergovernmental, specialized agency of the UNITED NATIONS (UN). Founded in 1948, it collects and shares medical and scientific information and promotes international standards for drugs and vaccines. WHO has made major contributions to the prevention of diseases such as malaria, polio, leprosy and tuberculosis, and the eradication of smallpox. Its headquarters are in Geneva, Switzerland.

World Trade Organization (WTO) Body sponsored by the UNITED NATIONS (UN) to regulate international trade. The WTO was established (1 January 1995) to replace the GENERAL AGREEMENT ON TARIFFS AND TRADE (GATT). The WTO took over GATT's rules with increased powers to regulate agriculture, clothing and textiles, intellectual property rights, and services.

World War 1 *See* feature article, page 438

World War 2 *See* feature article

Worms, Concordat of (1122) Agreement made in the city of Worms, W Germany, between Emperor HENRY V and Pope CALIXTUS II settling the INVESTITURE Controversy, a struggle over the control of church offices. The emperor agreed to the free election of bishops and surrendered his claim to appoint them. They were, however, to pay homage to him as feudal overlord for their temporal possessions.

Worms, Diet of (1521) Conference of the HOLY ROMAN EMPIRE presided over by Emperor CHARLES V. Held in the city of Worms, W Germany, Martin LUTHER was summoned to appear before the Diet to retract his teachings. Luther refused to repudiate them, and the **Edict of Worms** (25 May 1521) declared him a heretic and an outlaw. The Diet was one of the most important confrontations of the early REFORMATION. *See also* LEO X; PROTESTANTISM

Wounded Knee, Massacre at (29 December 1890) Last episode in the conflict between the SIOUX and the US Army. During the late 1880s Native North Americans had been increasingly performing a ritual dance, the Ghost Dance, the practice of which they believed would overthrow white settlers. Fearing this would engender a rising by the Sioux, US troops arrested several leaders; one of them, Chief SITTING BULL, was killed in a gunfight that broke out during his arrest. Another group was arrested a few days later and taken by the 7th Cavalry to Wounded Knee Creek, South Dakota. A shot was fired, and the troops opened fire. About 300 people, including women and children, were killed.

Wrangel, Piotr Nikolaievich, Baron (1878–1928) Russian general. He resigned from the Russian army after the arrest of General Lavr KORNILOV. During the RUSSIAN CIVIL WAR (1918–20), Wrangel joined the anti-BOLSHEVIK "White" army of Anton DENIKIN and helped to capture Tsaritsyn (now VOLGOGRAD) from the communists in 1919. In 1920 Wrangel succeeded Denikin as commander in chief and sought an alliance with Poland, but was defeated in Ukraine. Wrangel's army retreated to Crimea from where it was evacuated to Constantinople (now Istanbul, Turkey). Wrangel emigrated to Belgium. His defeat marked the end of "White" Russian resistance.

Wren, Sir Christopher (1632–1723) English architect, mathematician and astronomer. He designed more than 50 new churches in the city of London based on syntheses of CLASSICAL, RENAISSANCE and BAROQUE ideas; the greatest of these is ST PAUL'S Cathedral. Among his many other works are Chelsea and Greenwich hospitals, London, and the Sheldonian Theatre, Oxford.

Wudi (156–87 BC) Chinese emperor (140–87 BC) of the HAN dynasty. He reversed the defensive foreign policy of his predecessors, and by *c*.137 BC had embarked on a number of campaigns to extend Han territory. Wudi defeated the Xiongnu in the N, and incorporated S China and N and central Vietnam into the empire. He regained territory lost to the Koreans and campaigned as far afield as Uzbekistan. To pay for the cost of his expansionist policy, Wudi introduced a number of administrative reforms that centralized bureaucracy and introduced new taxes. These measures were not sufficient, however, and towards the end of his rule, China faced economic crisis. Along with his aggressive foreign policy, Wudi will also be remembered for supporting and encouraging CONFUCIANISM.

Wu Hou (625–705) Chinese empress (r.690–705) of the TANG dynasty. Entering the service of Emperor Gao Zong as a concubine, Wu rapidly established herself as his favourite. By 655 she had become Gao Zong's empress, wielding great influence at court. For the last 23 years of Gao's life, Wu effectively ran state affairs, masterminding the conquest of Korea (675). A combination of ruthlessness and skillful administration resulted in the removal of former aides, and the promotion of those loyal to her. After Gao's death (683), she deposed his successor, Chung Zong, and installed her second son, Rui Zong, as a puppet ruler. Wu Hou suppressed the ensuing Tang uprising and later took the throne for herself, continuing to rule until her death. Her reign reinforced China's unification under the Tang, and she introduced a scholarly bureaucracy in place of military and political elitism. She was forced to abdicate by a palace coup and Chung Zong regained control.

Wyatt's Rebellion (1554) Protestant revolt led by Sir Thomas Wyatt (1521–54) to prevent the marriage of MARY I to PHILIP II of Spain. Fearing the union would make England a vassal of Spain, Wyatt and *c*.3000 followers marched from Maidstone, Kent, to Ludgate, London, where, lacking support, they surrendered to forces loyal to Mary. Wyatt and the other leaders were executed, along with Lady Jane GREY, while Princess Elizabeth (later ELIZABETH I) was imprisoned in the Tower of London.

Wycliffe, John (*c*.1330–84) English religious reformer. Under the patronage of JOHN OF GAUNT, he attacked corrupt practices in the church and the authority of the pope, condemning in particular the church's landed wealth. Wycliffe's criticism became increasingly radical, questioning the authority of the pope and insisting on the primacy of scripture, but he escaped condemnation until after his death. His ideas were continued by the LOLLARDS in England and influenced Jan HUS in Bohemia.

Wye Agreement (October 1998) US-brokered agreement between ISRAEL and PALESTINE. Based at the Wye River resort, United States, Binyamin NETANYAHU and Yasir ARAFAT, with President Bill CLINTON acting as mediator, signed an agreement under which, in exchange for Arafat's implementation of steps aimed at reducing terrorist attacks on Israel, Israel would relinquish territory on the WEST BANK to the Palestinian National Authority. The meeting, which lasted nine days, also outlined a timetable for negotiations leading to an independent Palestinian state. Netanyahu, however, refused to give up the West Bank territories, citing a fresh outbreak of violence as contravening the Agreement.

Wyoming State in the NW United States; the state capital and largest city is Cheyenne. Wyoming is the least populous state in the nation. The N of the state is primarily plain, where bison were hunted by the CROW and then the SIOUX. By 1846 the United States had acquired the entire territory through treaties. Later 19th-century development was linked to the fur trade and W migration along the OREGON TRAIL. The 1860s marked the first major influx of settlers as the BOZEMAN TRAIL was opened (1864), gold was discovered in S Wyoming (1867), and the railroad was completed (1868). By the end of the 1870s, the NATIVE NORTH AMERICAN population had been pacified and placed on reservations. The next 20 years were marked by the rise of vigilante groups and sporadic violence between cattle and sheep farmers. After World War 2, Wyoming profited from exploitation of uranium deposits for nuclear-weapons construction. During the 1970s increased domestic demand for coal and petroleum resulted in the growth of Wyoming's energy-related industries, but when oil prices dropped in the 1980s, the state suffered a lengthy recession. Area: 253,596sq km (97,913sq mi). Pop. (1996) 481,400.

Wyszynski, Stefan (1901–81) Polish Roman Catholic cardinal. As primate of Poland from 1948, he protested against the communist attacks on the church during the trial of Bishop Kaczmarek of Kielce. In 1952 Pope PIUS XII appointed him cardinal. Wyszynski was imprisoned from 1953 to 1956. In 1957 he was allowed to go to Rome to receive the cardinalship. In the early 1980s, he played a mediating role between SOLIDARITY and the government.

WYOMING
Statehood : 10 July 1890
Nickname : The Equality State
State motto : Equal rights

Xavier, Saint Francis *See* FRANCIS XAVIER, SAINT

Xenophon (*c*.430–*c*.354 BC) Greek soldier and historian. He studied with SOCRATES, whose teaching he described in *Memorabilia*. In 401 BC Xenophon joined the 10,000-strong Greek mercenary army of CYRUS THE YOUNGER. After Cyrus' defeat at Cunaxa, Xenophon led the retreat of the Greek troops across Asia Minor. His best-known work, *Anabasis*, is an account of this march. Xenophon later served Agesilaus II of SPARTA in his wars against Persia. His writings include *Hellenica*, a history of Greece from 411 to 362 BC, and treatises on, among other subjects, horsemanship and estate management.

Xerxes I (*c*.519–465 BC) King of Persia (486–465 BC), son and successor of DARIUS I (THE GREAT). He regained Egypt (484 BC) and crushed a rebellion in Babylon. In order to continue the PERSIAN WARS, Xerxes amassed a vast army (200,000–300,000 men) and launched an invasion of Greece (480 BC). Crossing the Dardanelles by means of a bridge of boats, Xerxes marched towards Athens. He defeated the Spartan king LEONIDAS at the Battle of THERMOPYLAE and then burned Athens. Persian fortunes changed, however, with the destruction of the Persian fleet at the Battle of SALAMIS (480). Xerxes retired, leaving MARDONIUS in charge. The decisive defeat of the Persian army at the Battle of PLATAEA (479) ended Xerxes' plans for the conquest of Greece. He was later assassinated by one of his own men.

Xhosa (Xosa) Group of related Bantu tribes. The Xhosa moved from E Africa to the vicinity of the Great Fish River, S Africa, in the 17th and 18th centuries. Between 1779 and 1879 the Xhosa were engaged in conflicts with the European settlers. After the Xhosa were finally defeated, their territories became part of Cape Colony and they came under European rule. In culture the Xhosa are closely related to the ZULU. The 2.5 million Xhosa live in the Transkei and form an important part of South Africa's industrial and mining workforce. Xhosa is the most widely spoken African language in SOUTH AFRICA.

Xia (Hsia) Legendary first dynasty (*c*.22nd century BC–*c*.16th century BC) in Chinese history. By tradition, it is said to have been founded in *c*.2205 BC by Yu the Great. Yu is said to have controlled floods by introducing the use of dykes. The traditional date for the dynasty's end is 1766 BC. The SHANG dynasty, the first documented dynasty of China, came to power in *c*.1600 BC.

Xian (Sian, formerly Changan) Capital of Shaanxi province at the confluence of the rivers Wei and Huang He, NW China. The site has been inhabited since *c*.6000 BC. It was the site of Xianyang, the capital of the QIN dynasty (221–206 BC). The elaborate tomb of the dynastic founder, Emperor QIN SHIHUANGDI, is a world heritage site and major tourist attraction. The city continued as capital of the Former HAN dynasty (206 BC–AD 9). After several centuries of decline, it recovered its power during the SUI (581–618) and TANG (618–907) dynasties, when, as Changan, it once again served as capital. It was the focus for the introduction of Buddhism to China; the Big Wild Goose Pagoda dates from 652. In the following centuries the city became a major centre for other religious missionaries. The Manchus gave it the name Xian ("Western Peace"), which it reverted to in 1943. In 1936 it was the site of the XIAN INCIDENT. Pop. (1993) 2,360,000.

Xian Incident (12–25 December 1936) Kidnapping of CHIANG KAI-SHEK in the city of Xian, China, by Zhang Xueliang, one of Chiang's generals. The action was intended to force cooperation between the nationalist KUOMINTANG and the COMMUNIST PARTY in order to fight the Japanese, who had occupied Manchuria in 1931. With the intervention of ZHOU ENLAI, Chiang was released and an agreement reached in which limited cooperation was agreed. Zhang was arrested and placed under house arrest, initially in China and later in Taiwan. *See also* SINO-JAPANESE WARS

Xinjiang (Mandarin, New Frontier; Sinkiang or Chinese Turkistan) Autonomous region in NW China, bordered by Tajikistan, Kyrgyzstan and Kazakstan (N and W), Mongolia (E) and Kashmir and Tibet (S). The capital is Ürümqi. First conquered by the Chinese in the 1st century BC, the region changed hands many times in the following centuries. It profited from its position on the SILK ROAD. Conquered by GENGHIS KHAN in the 13th century, it came under Mongol control until the 18th century. In 1756 the QING dynasty became the leading power in the region. In the 19th century several uprisings by the largely Muslim population were crushed by the Qing authorities. Xinjiang was made a Chinese province in 1884. Area: 1,647,435sq km (636,075sq mi). Pop. (1990) 15,370,000.

Xuan Zong (685–762) Chinese emperor (712–56), also known as Ming Huang ("The Enlightened Emperor"), grandson of WU HOU. His rule provided the TANG empire with one of its greatest periods of prosperity, grandeur and cultural brilliance. In the early years of his reign, Xuan reformed the bureaucracy and economy and sent Tang armies as far afield as India. In later years, however, political dissatisfaction grew with the rise of powerful opposing factions within his administration. In 755 General An Lushan led a military revolt in NE China. As his troops marched south to the capital, Changan, Emperor Xuan Zong fled and abdicated.

XYZ Affair (1797–98) Diplomatic incident that strained relations between the United States and France. President John ADAMS sent three representatives to renegotiate the French-US alliance of 1778, which had given way to hostility after the signing of JAY'S TREATY (1794) between the United States and Great Britain. Three French agents, known as X, Y and Z, demanded that a bribe be paid to their foreign minister, Charles de TALLEYRAND, and that France be given a large loan before negotiations could begin. Their demands caused an uproar in the United States and the American commissioners were recalled. War was narrowly averted by a settlement negotiated at a convention in 1800.

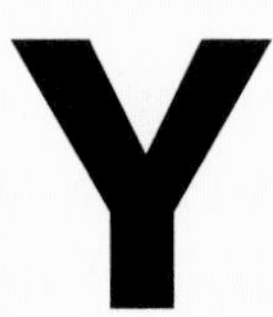

Yahya Khan, Agha Muhammad (1917–80) Pakistani soldier and statesman, president (1969–71). He fought with the British 8th Army in World War 2. As chief of the army general staff (1957–62), he supported the military coup that brought AYUB KHAN to power (1958). In 1966 Yayha Khan became commander in chief of the armed forces. When Ayub Khan resigned, power transferred to Yayha Khan, who declared martial law. He called elections in 1970, at which the rising strength of the East Pakistan (now BANGLADESH) AWAMI LEAGUE under MUJIBUR RAHMAN became clear. The following year saw civil war between East and West Pakistan, leading to the Third INDIA-PAKISTAN WAR. West Pakistan was decisively defeated and Yayha Khan resigned. He was succeeded by Zulfikar Ali BHUTTO, who placed him under house arrest (1972–75).

Yalta Conference (February 1945) Meeting of the main Allied leaders of WORLD WAR 2 at Yalta, Crimea, S Ukraine. With victory over Germany imminent, Franklin ROOSEVELT, Winston CHURCHILL and Joseph STALIN met to discuss the final campaigns of the War and the post-War settlement. Agreements were reached on the foundation of the UNITED NATIONS (UN), the territorial division of Europe into "spheres of interest", the occupation of Germany, and support for democracy in liberated countries. Concessions were made to Stalin in the Far East in order to gain Soviet support against Japan.

▲ **Yeltsin** led Russia through a period of political and economic turmoil. His rapid transformation of the economy saw the emergence of a rich élite and an increase in political corruption.

Yamagata Aritomo, Koshaku (1838–1922) Japanese soldier and statesman, prime minister (1889–91, 1898–1900). Born to a minor SAMURAI family, he was an early and enthusiastic supporter of Emperor MEIJI. In 1871 he was appointed commander of the Imperial Guard. Realizing the necessity of modernizing and westernizing the Japanese army, Yamagata and SAIGO TAKAMORI introduced conscription, and in the subsequent military reorganization Yamagata became minister of the army. In 1877 he led the forces that suppressed Saigo's rebellion and was promoted to chief of the general staff (1878–84). Yamagata issued the "Imperial Precept for the Military" (1882) to ensure the army's absolute loyalty to the emperor. He helped establish a new constitution, drafted by ITO HIROBUMI, and became Japan's first prime minister. Dismayed by political factionalism, Yamagata resigned but retained influence as one of Japan's GENROS (elder statesmen). He served as a commander at the start of the SINO-JAPANESE WAR, but illness forced him to return home. His second term as prime minister brought further Japanese military expansion in Asia, such as involvement in the BOXER REBELLION. Yamagata returned as chief of the general staff in the RUSSO-JAPANESE WAR (1904–05), victory in which illustrated the power of Japan's reorganized army. After 1909 Yamagata held virtually dictatorial powers until 1921, when he was publicly censured for interfering in the marriage arrangements of the Crown Prince.

Yamamoto Isoroku (1884–1943) Japanese admiral. He fought as a junior naval officer in the RUSSO-JAPANESE WAR (1904–05) and later served (1926–27) as naval attaché at the Japanese embassy in Washington, D.C. In 1938 Yamamoto was appointed commander of the first fleet, later becoming admiral (1940) and commander in chief (1941) of the combined fleet. Yamamoto was opposed to Japanese entry into WORLD WAR 2, but planned the attack on PEARL HARBOR (1941) as Japan's only chance of victory. The US defeat of his fleet at the Battle of MIDWAY (1942) marked a turning point in the Pacific War. Yamamoto was killed when his aircraft was shot down over the Solomon Islands.

Yamato Japanese clan from which all Japanese emperors are descended. It gave its name to the formative period of the Japanese state (*c*.AD 400–*c*.800). Originally local rulers in the Yamato region, S of present-day KYOTO, the clan claims its descent from the sun goddess Amaterasu. Huge burial mounds in the area suggest that by the 4th century AD the Yamato were powerful rulers who had mastered advanced agricultural techniques. In the early 5th century contact was established between the Yamato court and Korea, from where many inventions were introduced, notably advanced iron-making techniques and, from China, a writing system. Yamato power began to expand in the 5th century, although local rulers maintained a degree of autonomy. Taishi SHOTOKU, a prince of the Yamato family, did much to increase the influence of China. There was great interchange between the Yamato rulers and the Chinese SUI (581–618) and TANG dynasties (618–907), notably the introduction of CONFUCIANISM. The Taika reforms (645–46) followed the death of Shotoku. The reforms rid the Yamato court of the rival Soga family and established a centralized government headed by an emperor. In 710 the Yamato established their imperial capital at NARA. The influence of Chinese bureaucracy can be seen in the laws governing the new city. Frequent expeditions to China brought new cultural and religious ideas to Japan, notably BUDDHISM. In 794 the imperial capital was moved to KYOTO, where it remained until the MEIJI RESTORATION (1868). The late 8th century also marked the decline in influence of the Yamato clan as the emperor lost many of his powers to the FUJIWARA family and, later, to the SHOGUNS.

Yanomami Native American tribal group living chiefly in the rainforests of N Brazil and S Venezuela. They are traditionally semi-nomadic hunter-gatherers. During the 1980s and 1990s, the Yanomami lost much of their land to road builders, logging companies and gold prospectors, causing the population to fall to *c*.18,000.

Yaroslav I (the Wise) (980–1054) Grand prince of Kiev (1019–54), son of VLADIMIR I (THE GREAT). He used Viking mercenaries to defeat his brother Sviatopolk in order to acquire KIEVAN RUS (1019). Yaroslav codified Russian law and rebuilt KIEV on Byzantine lines. He promoted Christianity, founding (1039) the patriarchate of Kiev. By military conquest, Yaroslav expanded his territory in the Baltic area and regained Galicia from Poland. He developed close relations with the rest of Europe, marrying his daughters to European rulers. Despite Yaroslav's efforts to ensure a peaceful succession, Kievan Rus was fractured by civil war after his death.

Yaroslavl (Jaroslavl') City and river port on the Volga, W central Russia; capital of Yaroslavl region. The oldest town on the Volga, it was founded (1010) by YAROSLAV I. It became the capital of Yaroslavl principality in 1218 and was absorbed by MOSCOW in 1463. From March to July 1612, during the "Time of Troubles", Yaroslavl served as Russia's capital. It still boasts many historic buildings. Pop. (1994) 631,000.

Yazoo Fraud Dispute over land near the Yazoo River, United States. In 1795 the Georgia legislature passed an act selling *c*.14.2 million hectares (*c*.35 million acres) in what is now Alabama and Mississippi to four land companies. It was soon revealed that the legislators had been bribed, and the following year a newly elected legislature rescinded the sale. Much of the land had already been sold on, and disputes over the territory continued until the matter was referred to the Supreme Court (1810). Chief Justice John MARSHALL ruled that the Act of 1795 constituted a legally binding contract; claimants to the territory received financial compensation.

Yeltsin, Boris Nikolaievich (1931–) Russian statesman, first democratically elected president of the Russian Federation (1991–99). In 1961 he joined the COMMUNIST PARTY OF THE SOVIET UNION (CPSU), later becoming (1976) first secretary of the Yekaterinburg (Sverdlovsk) branch. In 1985 he joined the reforming government of Mikhail GORBACHEV and became party chief in Moscow. His blunt criticism of the slow pace of PERESTROIKA led to demotion in 1987, but his immense popularity gained him election as president of the Russian Republic in 1990. Yeltsin's prompt denunciation of the attempted coup against Gorbachev (August 1991) established his ascendancy. Elected president of the Russian Federation, he presided over the dissolution of the SOVIET UNION and the termination of Communist Party rule. Economic disintegration, rising crime and internal conflicts, notably in CHECHENIA, damaged his popularity, and failing health reduced his effectiveness. Nevertheless, he was re-elected in 1996. In 1998–99, in the face of economic crisis in Russia, Yeltsin sacked four prime ministers – Viktor CHERNOMYRDIN, Sergei Kirienko, Yevgeni Primakov and Sergei Stepashin – before appointing Vladimir PUTIN. In late 1999 Yeltsin ordered Russian troops back into Chechenia, after several bombings in Russia were blamed on the Chechens. On 31 December 1999, Yeltsin unexpectedly resigned. He was succeeded by Putin.

Yemen *See* country feature

Yerevan Capital of ARMENIA, on the River Razdan, S Caucasus. One of the world's oldest cities, it was capital of Armenia as early as the 7th century (although under Persian control), and was a crucial crossroads for caravan routes between India and Transcaucasia. From the 15th century Yerevan was disputed between Persia and Turkey. It eventually fell to the Russians in 1827. It is the site of a 16th-century Turkish fortress and is a traditional wine-making centre. Pop. (1994) 1,254,000.

Yi dynasty Korean dynasty (1392–1910). It was founded by Yi Songgye, who established the Yi capital at Hangyang (now SEOUL). Korean culture and bureaucracy in the early Yi period were modelled on MING China, and CONFUCIANISM became the organizing system for politics and ethics. Early in the Yi period, printing with movable metal type was developed and a phonetic alphabet for the Korean language invented. In 1592 Korea was invaded by Japan, under HIDEYOSHI. With the help of China, the invasion was defeated, but the country was devastated and its government severely weakened. In the early 17th century Korea was invaded by the MANCHUS, who, as leaders of QING dynasty China, proceeded to dominate Korea until the late 19th century. Several 18th-century Yi kings, notably Yongjo and Chongjo, brought prosperity to Korea, improving its agricultural productivity and economy. In the late 19th century, Korea was opened up to foreign trade and several wars for control of Korea ensued. The brutal suppression of a rebellion by pro-Japanese reformers led to the First SINO-JAPANESE WAR (1894–95), which resulted in Korea gaining its independence from China. Russian defeat in the RUSSO-JAPANESE WAR (1904–05) brought an end to the Yi dynasty: Korea became a Japanese protectorate and was formally annexed in 1910.

Yin Alternative transliteration of the SHANG dynasty

YEMEN

AREA: 527,970sq km (203,849sq mi)
POPULATION: 11,282,000
CAPITAL (POPULATION): Sana'a (427,502)
GOVERNMENT: Multiparty republic
ETHNIC GROUPS: Arab 96%, Somali 1%
LANGUAGES: Arabic (official)
RELIGIONS: Islam
GDP PER CAPITA (1994): US$1049

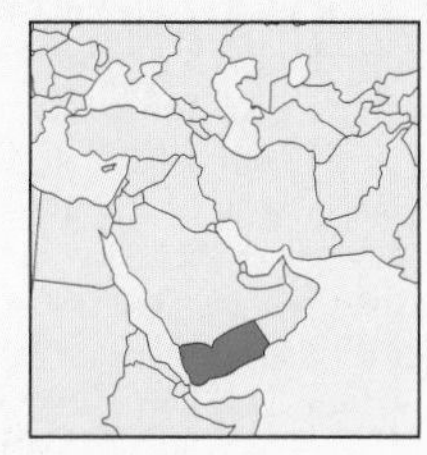

Republic on the SE tip of the Arabian Peninsula. The ancient kingdom of SHEBA (Saba) flourished in present-day S Yemen between *c*.750 BC and 100 BC. The kingdom was renowned for its advanced technology and wealth, gained through its strategic location on important trade routes. The region was invaded by the Romans in the 1st century BC. Islam was introduced in AD 628. The Rassite dynasty of the Zaidi sect established a theocratic state that lasted until 1962.

The FATIMIDS conquered Yemen in *c*.1000. In 1517 the area became part of the OTTOMAN EMPIRE and largely remained under Turkish control until 1918. In the 19th century the Saudi WAHHABI sect ousted the Zaidi imams, but were in turn expelled by IBRAHIM PASHA. In 1839 ADEN was captured by the British. In 1937 Britain formed the Aden Protectorate. Following the defeat of the Ottomans in World War 1, Yemen was ruled by Imam Yahya of the Hamid al-Din dynasty. In 1945 Yemen joined the ARAB LEAGUE. In 1948 Yahya was assassinated. Crown Prince Ahmed became imam. From 1958 to 1961 Yemen formed part of the UNITED ARAB REPUBLIC (with Egypt and Syria).

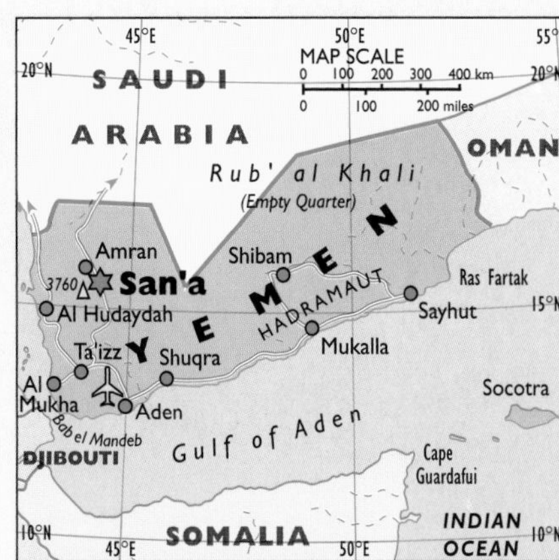

A 1962 army revolution overthrew the monarchy and formed the Yemen Arab Republic. Civil war ensued between republicans (aided by Egypt) and royalists (aided by Saudi Arabia and Jordan). Meanwhile, the Aden Protectorate became part of the British Federation of South Arabia. In 1967 the National Liberation Front forced the British to withdraw from Aden and founded the People's Republic of South Yemen. Marxists won the ensuing civil war in South Yemen and renamed it the People's Democratic Republic of Yemen (1970). Border clashes between the two Yemens were frequent throughout the 1970s and erupted into full-scale war (1979). In 1990, following lengthy negotiations, the two Yemens merged to form a single republic. Ali Abdullah Saleh (1942–), who had been president (1978–90) of the Yemen Arab Republic, became president of the united Yemen. The country's support for Iraq in the GULF WAR (1991) led to the expulsion of 800,000 Yemeni workers from Saudi Arabia. A coalition government emerged from 1993 elections, but increasing tension between North and South led to a further civil war in 1994. The South's brief secession from the union ended with victory for the Northern army. In 1995 agreement was reached with Saudi Arabia and Oman over disputed boundaries. Yemen clashed (1995–96) with Eritrea over the Hanish Islands in the Red Sea but a mutually acceptable agreement had been reached by 1998. President Saleh was decisively re-elected in 1999.

Yogyakarta (Jogjakarta) City in S Java, Indonesia. Founded in 1749, it is the cultural and artistic centre of Java. Capital of a Dutch-controlled sultanate from 1755, it was the scene of a revolt (1825–30) against colonial exploitation. During the 1940s it was the centre of the Indonesian independence movement and, in 1949, acted as the provisional capital of Indonesia. Its many visitors are drawn by the 18th-century palace, the Grand Mosque, the religious and arts festivals, and its proximity to the Borobudur temple. Pop. (1990) 412,392.

Yom Kippur War (1973) Arab-Israeli War that began on the Jewish feast day of Yom Kippur. It is known to its Arab participants as the "October War". On 6 October, the holiest day of the Jewish calendar, Israel was attacked by both Egypt and Syria. Egyptian forces crossed the Suez Canal, and Syrian forces advanced in the Golan Heights. Israeli forces pushed the Egyptian army back across the Suez Canal and, in the N, advanced into Syrian territory. The War lasted 18 days and casualties were heavy. In November a cease-fire was agreed between Israel and Egypt, and a peace agreement was signed the following year. The Israeli army withdrew into the Sinai, Egypt reduced the size of its army on the E bank of the Suez Canal, and a United Nations' (UN) peacekeeping force was deployed between the two armies. Also in 1974, Israel and Syria agreed a cease-fire, and the UN set up a buffer zone in the region. *See also* Sadat, Anwar

Yonglo (1359–1424) (Yung-lo, Yongle) Chinese emperor (1402–24) of the Ming dynasty, son of Zhu Yuanchang, b. Zhu Di. During the reign of his father, he was prince of the Beijing area. On the death of Zhu Yuanchang, the empire was inherited by his grandson, Jianwen (r.1398–1402). Zhu Di led a successful rebellion (1399–1402) against Jianwen, who subsequently disappeared. Becoming Emperor Yonglo, he consolidated dynastic power and set up a strong and stable administration. He dispatched explorers, notably Zheng He, to extract tributes from foreign courts. Yonglo expanded the Ming empire, acquiring Annam (briefly, 1407–28) for China. He led five expeditions (1410–24) against the Mongols in order to secure the N borders of his empire. In 1407 Yonglo transferred the imperial capital from Nanjing to Beijing and started the construction of the Forbidden City. To keep his new capital supplied, Yonglo renovated the Grand Canal. Yonglo died on his way back from a military campaign in Mongolia.

Yoritomo, Minamoto (1147–99) Japanese shogun (1192–99), founder of the Kamakura shogunate (1192–1333). In 1156 the Minamoto family were defeated by their great rivals, the powerful Taira family, and Yoritomo was banished for twenty years. In *c.*1180 he joined his family's new rebellion against the Taira, and in 1185, with the help of his younger half-brothers, defeated the Taira at the Battle of Dannoura. Yoritomo established his government at Kamakura, SE Honshu. By dispatching loyal followers to the provinces, he ensured Kamakura control over much of Japan. His government was largely independent of the imperial court at Kyoto, with whom he managed to maintain stable relations. In 1192 Yoritomo became shogun, formally establishing the Kamakura military dictatorship. On his death, control of the shogunate passed to the Hojo dynasty.

York, Richard, 3rd Duke of (1411–60) English duke. As the grandson of Edmund, 1st Duke of York, and thus the great-grandson of Edward III, Richard was the claimant of the House of York to the Crown. In 1453 the Lancastrian king, Henry VI, suffered a nervous breakdown. The regency of Henry's queen, Margaret of Anjou, proved so unpopular that York was appointed protector of the realm. Fearing for the succession of her son, Margaret arranged York's dismissal, who then took up arms in the Wars of the Roses (1455–85). By 1460 Richard's future succession to the throne had been assured, but Margaret refused to accept the arrangement and fighting continued. In 1460 Richard was killed at the Battle of Wakefield. His son continued the Yorkist campaign, becoming king the following year as Edward IV.

York, archbishop of Second-highest office of the Church of England. The acts of the Council of Arles (314) mention a bishop of York, but the early Christian community in York was destroyed by Saxon invaders. The uninterrupted history of the present see began with the consecration of Wilfrid as bishop of York in 664. York was raised to the dignity of an archbishopric in 735, when Egbert was given the title Primate of the Northern Province. The archbishop is now called Primate of England (the archbishop of Canterbury is Primate of all England).

York, House of English royal house, a branch of the Plantagenets. The House of York was founded by Edmund of Langley (1341–1402), a son of Edward III. Edmund's son, Edward, died childless, and the dukedom passed to his nephew, Richard, 3rd Duke of York. Richard challenged the Lancastrian king, Henry VI, precipitating the Wars of the Roses (1455–85). Richard was killed (1460) at the Battle of Wakefield (1460), but his son gained the crown (1461) as Edward IV. Edward was succeeded (1483) by his young son, Edward V, from whom his brother, Richard III, usurped the crown. The defeat of Richard III by the Tudor king Henry VII at the Battle of Bosworth Field (1485) brought the brief Yorkist line to a close. *See also* Lancaster, House of

Yorktown, Siege of (1781) Last major military campaign of the American Revolution (1775–83). Lord Cornwallis and his 7000 British troops fortified the peninsula of Yorktown, Virginia. American troops under George Washington, supported by French troops, blocked escape routes and besieged Yorktown. A French fleet arrived from the West Indies to prevent any supplies reaching the British by sea. A British fleet was dispatched, but it failed to arrive in time to prevent Cornwallis' surrender (19 October 1781).

YUGOSLAVIA

AREA: 102,173sq km (39,449sq mi)
POPULATION: 10,469,000
CAPITAL (POPULATION): Belgrade (1,168,454)
GOVERNMENT: Federal republic
ETHNIC GROUPS: Serb 62%, Albanian 17%, Montenegrin 5%, Hungarian, Croat
LANGUAGES: Serbo-Croatian (official)
RELIGIONS: Christianity (mainly Serbian Orthodox, with Roman Catholic and Protestant minorities), Islam
GDP PER CAPITA (1994): US$1171

Federal republic, SE Europe, now consisting of Serbia and Montenegro. The rump Yugoslav federation has not gained international recognition as the successor to the Socialist Federal Republic of Yugoslavia created by Tito. In 1991 the federation began to disintegrate when Slovenia, Croatia and Macedonia declared independence. In 1992 Bosnia-Herzegovina followed suit. (*See* individual country/republic articles for pre-1918 history and post-independence events)

Serbian-led demands for the unification of South Slavic lands were a major contributing factor to the outbreak of World War I. In 1918 the "Kingdom of Serbs, Croats and Slovenes" was formed under the Serbian king, Peter I. In 1921 he was succeeded by Alexander I. In 1929 Alexander formed a dictatorship and renamed the country Yugoslavia. Peter II's reign was abruptly halted by German occupation (1941) in World War 2. Yugoslav resistance to the Nazis and fascist puppet regime was stout. The main resistance groups were the communist partisans led by Tito and the royalist Chetniks. In 1945 Tito formed the Federal People's Republic of Yugoslavia. In 1948 Yugoslavia was expelled from the Soviet-dominated Cominform. Tito adopted an independent foreign policy and became a significant force within the Non-Aligned Movement. In domestic affairs, agricultural collectivization was abandoned (1953), economic reforms were introduced and new constitutions (1963, 1974) devolved power to the constituent republics in an effort to quell unrest.

Following Tito's death in 1980, the country's underlying ethnic tensions began to resurface. In 1986 Slobodan Milošević became leader of the Serbian Communist Party. In 1989 he became president of Serbia and called for the creation of a "Greater Serbia". Federal troops were used to suppress demands for autonomy in Albanian-dominated Kosovo. In 1990 elections, non-communist parties won majorities in every republic, except Serbia and Montenegro. Serbian attempts to dominate the federation led to the formal secession of Slovenia and Croatia in June 1991. The Serb-dominated Federal army launched a campaign against Croatia, whose territory included a large Serbian minority. A cease-fire was agreed in January 1992. The European Community (EC) recognized Slovenia and Croatia as separate states. Bosnia-Herzegovina's declaration of independence in March 1992 led to a brutal civil war between Serbs, Croats and Bosnian Muslims. In April 1992 Serbia and Montenegro announced the formation of a new Yugoslav federation and invited Serbs in Croatia and Bosnia-Herzegovina to join. Serbian military and financial aid to the Bosnian Serb campaign of "ethnic cleansing" led the United Nations (UN) to impose economic sanctions on Serbia. The threat of further sanctions prompted Milošević to sever support for the Bosnian Serbs. In 1995 Milošević signed the Dayton Peace Agreement, which ended the Bosnian war.

In 1996 local elections, the Serbian Socialist (formerly Communist) Party was defeated in many areas. In early 1997 public demonstrations in Belgrade forced Milošević to acknowledge the poll results. Later in 1997 Milošević resigned the presidency of Serbia in order to become president of Yugoslavia. In Montenegro, tension remains high between pro- and anti-independence factions. In 1998 fighting erupted in Kosovo between Albanian nationalists and Serbian security forces. In 1999, following the forced expulsion of Albanians from Kosovo, NATO bombed Serbia and Montenegro, and following the withdrawal of the Serbian security forces a UN peacekeeping force was mobilized in an attempt to impose a fragile peace.

Y

Yoruba People of SW NIGERIA of basically Christian or Islamic faith. Most are farmers, growing crops that include yams, maize and cocoa. The Yoruba are thought to have settled in present-day SW Nigeria, Benin and N Togo over a thousand years ago. Many small kingdoms grew up, centred on a town or city where the *oba* (chief) resided. The best known of these kingdoms are the IFE and the OYO. Many Yoruba still live in towns built around the *oba*'s palace and travel daily to their outlying farms. Today, there are *c*.24 million Yoruba.

Yoshida Shigeru (1878–1967) Japanese statesman, prime minister (1946–47, 1949–54). In 1928 he became deputy foreign minister, but his appointment as foreign minister (1936) was blocked by the army. From June to September 1945 he was imprisoned for advocating Japanese surrender. During the Allied occupation of Japan after WORLD WAR 2, Yoshida assumed the leadership of the Liberal Party. As prime minister, he led Japan during a period of economic recovery and the rebuilding of democratic institutions.

Yoshimitsu (1358–1408) Japanese SHOGUN (1368–94) of the ASHIKAGA shogunate. The third ruler of the shogunate, Yoshimitsu, unlike his father and grandfather before him, assumed an active role in civic affairs, becoming minister of state (1394). He succeeded in unifying Japan under one emperor, and reopened trade links with China. Under his reign, Japan underwent a cultural and political renaissance, and many magnificent buildings were constructed.

Young, Brigham (1801–77) US religious leader, founder of Salt Lake City, Utah. An early convert to the Church of Jesus Christ of Latter-Day Saints (MORMONS), Young took over the leadership when Joseph SMITH, the founder, was killed by a mob in 1844. Young held the group together through persecutions and led their W migration (1846–47) to Utah, where he organized the settlement that became Salt Lake City. He was governor of Utah Territory (1850–57), but was replaced when the Mormon practice of polygamy brought them into conflict with the federal government. *See also* UTAH WAR

Young, Whitney, Jr (1921–71) US civil rights leader. He advocated improvement in economic opportunities, housing and welfare for African Americans. He served as the executive director of the National Urban League (1961–71). His books include *To Be Equal* (1964).

Young England Coterie of CONSERVATIVE backbenchers. Its leaders were Benjamin DISRAELI, Lord John Manners and George Smythe. From 1842 to 1845 they were united in their aim to end the political influence of the middle classes and re-establish the aristocracy, allied with the working class, as the agency of social justice. The group provided Disraeli with a platform from which to attack the Conservative prime minister, Robert PEEL. The movement lost direction over disagreements concerning FREE TRADE. Disraeli's novel *Coningsby* (1844) encapsulated many of the beliefs of Young Englanders.

Young Ireland Group of young, chiefly Protestant, Irish nationalists of the 1840s. Its organ was the *Nation* newspaper, and its most important leaders were Charles Gavan Duffy, Smith O'Brien, Thomas Francis Meagher and John Mitchel. Influenced by the YOUNG ITALY movement, Young Ireland worked for an Irish cultural revival as well as independence from Britain. The movement initially aligned itself with Daniel O'CONNELL's policy of reversing the Act of UNION but they later resorted to increasingly radical tactics. Young Ireland declined after an abortive rising in 1848, following which some prominent leaders were sentenced to TRANSPORTATION.

Young Italy (*Giovine Italia*) Republican and nationalist movement in Italy, founded in 1831 and inspired by the exiled radical, Giuseppe MAZZINI. It sought to provoke an Italian revolution against Austrian rule. It failed to become a mass movement, but fostered the growth of national consciousness and Italian unification in the 1830s and 1840s. *See also* CARBONARI; RISORGIMENTO

Young Pretender *See* STUART, CHARLES EDWARD

Young Turks Group of Turks who wished to remodel the OTTOMAN EMPIRE and make it a modern European state with a liberal constitution. Their movement began in the 1880s with unrest in the army and universities. In 1908 a Young Turk rising, led by ENVER PASHA and his chief of staff Mustafa Kemal (later ATATÜRK), deposed Sultan ABDUL HAMID II and replaced him with his brother, MUHAMMAD V. Following a 1913 coup d'etat, Enver Pasha became a virtual dictator. Under Kemal Atatürk, the Young Turks merged into the Turkish Nationalist Party.

Ypres, Battles of Several engagements in WORLD WAR I fought around the Belgian town of Ypres. The **first** (October–November 1914) stopped the German "race to the sea" to capture the Channel ports, but resulted in the near destruction of the BRITISH EXPEDITIONARY FORCE (BEF). The **second** (April–May 1915), the first battle in which poison gas was used, resulted in even greater casualties, without victory to either side. The **third** (summer 1917) was a predominantly British offensive. It culminated in the Passchendaele campaign, the costliest operation in British military history, which continued until November. More than 250,000 British and Allied soldiers lost their lives in the battles of Ypres

Ypres, John Denton Pinkstone French, 1st Earl of *See* FRENCH, JOHN DENTON PINKSTONE, 1ST EARL OF YPRES

Yuan (1246–1368) MONGOL dynasty in CHINA. Continuing the conquests of GENGHIS KHAN, KUBLAI KHAN established his rule over China, eliminating the last Southern SONG claimant in 1279. He returned the capital to BEIJING and promoted construction and commerce. Chinese literature took new forms during the Mongol period. Although native Chinese were excluded from government, and foreign visitors, including merchants such as Marco POLO, were encouraged, the central bureaucracy was organized along lines that reflected a greater Chinese culture than Mongolian. Among the Chinese, resentment of alien rule was aggravated by economic problems, including runaway inflation. The less competent successors of Kublai were increasingly challenged by rebellion, culminating (1368) in the victory of the MING.

Yuan Shikai (1859–1916) Chinese military commander in the last days of the QING dynasty. After successful military campaigns in Korea, on his return to China he was put in charge of modernizing the army. A supporter of Empress CIXI, he retired from public life following her death. Although recalled by the imperial court during periods of civil unrest, he sided with the Republican movement and became the first president of the Chinese Republic in 1913 when SUN YAT-SEN resigned. His suppression of the KUOMINTANG and attempt to start a new dynasty (proclaiming himself emperor in 1916) was thwarted shortly before his death.

Yugoslavia *See* country feature

Yukon Territory Territory in the extreme NW of CANADA, bounded by the Arctic Ocean (N), Northwest Territories (E), British Columbia (S) and Alaska (W). The capital and largest town is Whitehorse. The region, then part of NORTHWEST TERRITORIES, was first explored by fur traders from the HUDSON'S BAY COMPANY after 1840. The KLONDIKE GOLD RUSH brought more than 30,000 prospectors in the 1890s. In 1991 the Canadian government recognized the land claim of the indigenous Yukon (First Nation) Native Americans. Area: 483,450sq km (186,675sq mi). Pop. (1991) 27,797.

Z

Zacharias, Saint (d.752) (Zachary) Pope (741–52). He strengthened the Holy See and achieved a 20-year truce with the LOMBARDS. Along with Saint BONIFACE, Zacharias established cordial relations with the FRANKS by supporting the accession of PEPIN III (THE SHORT) to the Frankish throne.

Zagreb Capital of CROATIA, on the River Sava. Founded in the 11th century, it became capital of the Hungarian province of Croatia and Slavonia during the 14th century. The city was an important centre of the 19th-century Croatian nationalist movement. In 1918 it was the meeting place of the Croatian diet (parliament), which broke all ties with Austria-Hungary. It later joined a new union with Serbia in what was to become YUGOSLAVIA. In World War 2, Zagreb was the capital of the Axis-controlled puppet Croatian state (USTAŠA). Wrested from Axis control in 1945, it became capital of the Croatian Republic of Yugoslavia. It was damaged in 1991 during the Croatian civil war. Following the break-up of Yugoslavia in 1992, Zagreb remained capital of the newly independent state of Croatia. Pop. (1991) 726,770.

Zaghlul, Sa'd (*c*.1857–1927) Egyptian statesman, leader of the WAFD, prime minister (1924). Initially advocating cooperation with the ruling British, by 1913 Zaghlul had aligned himself with more radical nationalists. After World War 1, Zaghlul, formed a delegation (Wafd) in 1918 but was excluded from negotiations with the British and following civil disorder was deported to Malta (1919). After further civil unrest he was released and became the voice of Egyptian nationalism. Zaghlul refused to enter into negotiations with the British for fear of being labelled a collaborator, and when the first semi-independent government failed, Zaghlul rallied his supporters to halt the formation of any further governments. Zaghlul was subsequently exiled to the Seychelles, but was allowed to return to take part in the first independent elections and was swept to power. Unable to contain nationalist extremists, and following a number of political assassinations, including the British commander in chief, Zaghlul resigned. He remained active as president of the assembly. *See also* FUAD I

Zahir Shah, Muhammad (1914–) King of AFGHANISTAN (1933–73). After serving in the cabinet, Zahir acceded to the throne following the assassination of his father. During his reign, a period of relative stability, he implemented a number of foreign-backed building and construction programmes aimed at improving his country's infrastructure. He was deposed in a bloodless coup.

Zahir ud-Din Muhammad *See* BABUR

zaibatsu Large industrial conglomerates in Japan formed after the MEIJI RESTORATION (1868). Headed by powerful families, such as Mitsui and Mitsubishi, they came to dominate the Japanese economy in the early 20th century. Though broken up during the US occupation after 1945, they subsequently reformed and reclaimed their dominant position.

Zaïre *See* CONGO, DEMOCRATIC REPUBLIC OF

Zama Name of one or more ancient towns on the N coast of Africa (in modern Tunisia), traditionally the site of the last battle of the Second PUNIC WAR, in which the Roman general SCIPIO AFRICANUS (THE ELDER) defeated HANNIBAL of Carthage in 202 BC.

Zambia *See* country feature, page 446

Zanzibar Island region of TANZANIA, in the Indian Ocean off the E coast of Africa; the capital is Zanzibar. The first European discovery was by VASCO DA GAMA in 1499, and the Portuguese quickly established colonial rule. In the late 17th century it came under the control of the Omani Arabs. It developed into the major centre of the East African ivory and SLAVE TRADE. In 1840 Sultan SAID IBN SULTAN moved his capital from Oman to Zanzibar. The slave trade was halted in 1873, and in 1890 the sultanate of Zanzibar was made a British protectorate. In 1963 it became an independent state and a member of the COMMONWEALTH of Nations. Tension between the Arab ruling class and the indigenous Africans (who formed the majority of the population) led to the overthrow of the sultanate. In 1964 Zanzibar and Tanganyika merged to form the United Republic of Tanzania, however, Zanzibar retained control over domestic affairs. During the 1980s and 1990s conflict developed between secessionist and mainland centralist forces. In 1993 a regional parliament for Zanzibar was established. The two largest population groups are the indigenous Hadimu and Tumbatu. The major religion is Sunni Muslim, and the main language is Swahili. Area: 1660sq km (641sq mi). Pop. (1988) 375,539.

Zapata, Emiliano (1880–1919) Mexican revolutionary. Of peasant origin, he became leader of the growing peasant movement in 1910. His demands for radical agrarian reform, such as the return of haciendas (great estates) to ejidos (native Mexican communal ownership), led to the Mexican Revolution. Zapata joined forces with Francisco Madero to overthrow the dictator Porfirio Díaz in 1911. He refused to accept a compromise proposal from Madero and waged a guerrilla war in pursuit of "Land and Liberty". When General Victoriano Huerta deposed and killed Madero, Zapata rejected his offer to form a united force and thus enabled Venustiano Carranza to seize power. In 1914 Zapata, allied with "Pancho" Villa, leader of the largest revolutionary army in n Mexico, occupied Mexico City. Carranza's forces regrouped, defeated Villa and forced Zapata to retreat to his stronghold in the s. Led into a trap by forces loyal to Carranza, Zapata was ambushed and shot.

Zápolya, John (1487–1540) *See* John I

Zapotec Native Middle American group that inhabits part of the Mexican state of Oaxaca. Although their subsistence depended on their specific environment, that is mountainous, valley or coastal, generally the Zapotecs lived in agricultural communities centred around villages or towns. The Zapotec also built great pre-Columbian urban centres at Mitla and Monte Albán and fought to preserve their independence from the rival Mixtecs and Aztecs until the arrival of the Spanish.

Zaragoza (Saragossa) City on the River Ebro, ne Spain; capital of Zaragoza province and Aragón region. The city was taken by the Romans in the 1st century bc and by Moors in the 8th century. In 1118 it was captured by Alfonso I of Aragón, who made it his capital. It was the scene of heroic resistance against the French in the Peninsular War (1808–09). Pop. (1991) 586,219

Zarathustra *See* Zoroaster

Zealots Jewish sect, active in opposition to Roman rule at the time of Jesus Christ and after. They refused to agree that Jews could be ruled by pagans, led resistance to the Roman census of ad 6, pursued a terrorist and civil disobedience campaign and played an important role in the Jewish revolt of ad 66–73. Although the revolt in Jerusalem was quashed by Titus (ad 70) and the Temple of Jerusalem destroyed, a contingent of Zealots held out on the fortified hill-town of Masada until ad 73.

Zedekiah Any of several biblical personalities, most notably the last king of Judah (597–586 bc). Placed on the throne as a puppet king by Nebuchadnezzar II, king of Babylon, he could not stave off the Babylonian capture and destruction of Jerusalem. He was captured while trying to escape the city, blinded and deported to Babylon.

▲ **Zapata** became a legendary figure amongst Native North Americans. The agrarian reforms he introduced included a Rural Loan Bank and the establishment of cooperatives.

ZAMBIA

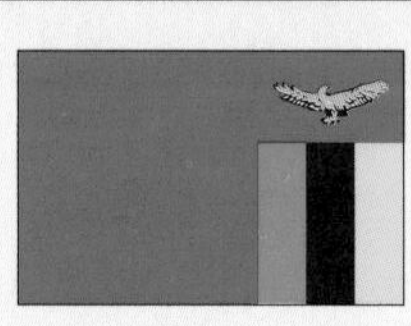

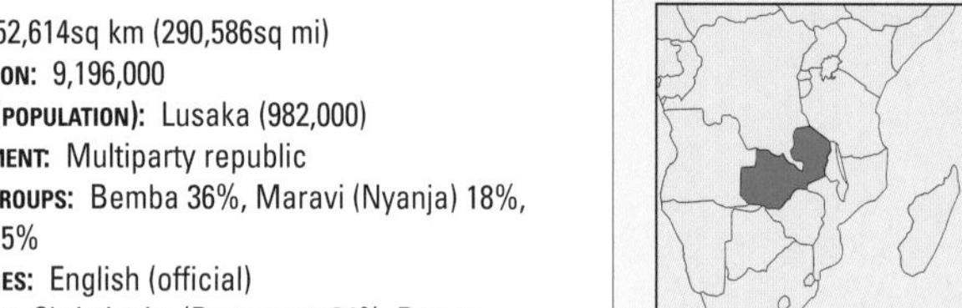

AREA: 752,614sq km (290,586sq mi)
POPULATION: 9,196,000
CAPITAL (POPULATION): Lusaka (982,000)
GOVERNMENT: Multiparty republic
ETHNIC GROUPS: Bemba 36%, Maravi (Nyanja) 18%, Tonga 15%
LANGUAGES: English (official)
RELIGIONS: Christianity (Protestant 34%, Roman Catholic 26%, African Christians 8%), traditional beliefs 27%
GDP PER CAPITA (1995): US$930

Landlocked republic in s central Africa. In *c*.800 ad Bantu-speakers migrated to the area. By the late 18th century Zambia was a significant part of the copper and slave trade. In 1855 the Scottish explorer David Livingstone made the first European discovery of Victoria Falls.

In 1890 the British South Africa Company, managed by Cecil Rhodes, made treaties with local chiefs. The area was administratively divided into nw and ne Rhodesia, and local rebellions against European rule were quickly crushed. Intensive mining of copper and lead saw the development of the railway in the early 1900s. In 1911 the two regions were joined to form Northern Rhodesia. In 1924 Northern Rhodesia became a British crown colony. The discovery of further copper deposits increased European settlement and the migration of African labour. In 1946 mineworkers formed the first national mass movement. In 1953 Britain formed the federation of Rhodesia (including present-day Zambia and Zimbabwe) and Nyasaland (now Malawi). In 1963, following a nationwide campaign of civil disobedience, the federation was dissolved.

In 1964 Northern Rhodesia achieved independence within the Commonwealth of Nations as the Republic of Zambia. Kenneth Kaunda, leader of the United Nationalist Independence Party (UNIP), became its first president. Zambia was faced by problems of national unity, European economic dominance, and tension with the white-minority government in Rhodesia. Following his re-election in 1968, Kaunda established state majority holdings in Zambian companies. Zambia supported the imposition of economic sanctions on Rhodesia. In 1972 Kaunda banned all opposition parties; he won the uncontested 1973 elections. In 1990 a new multiparty constitution was adopted. The Movement for Multiparty Democracy (MMD) won a landslide victory in 1991 elections. The MMD leader, Frederick Chiluba, became president. In 1993 Chiluba declared a state of emergency. Legislation excluded Kaunda from contesting the 1996 presidential elections, and Chiluba was resoundingly re-elected following a UNIP boycott. The government faced charges of electoral fraud. In 1997 a military coup was crushed. Kaunda was arrested and a state of emergency proclaimed. In 1998 Kaunda was freed and the state of emergency lifted. In 2000 there were a number of border skirmishes with Angola.

Zedillo, Ernesto (1951–) Mexican statesman, president (1994–2000). In 1971 he joined the Institutional Revolutionary Party (PRI). As secretary of budget and planning (1988–92) and secratary of education (1992–94), he successfully reduced Mexico's high inflation rate and decentralized the country's education system. In 1994 Zedillo ran for president after the PRI's candidate, Luis Colosio, was assassinated. He was narrowly elected. Zedillo promised to combat unemployment and tackle the failing economy. Within a few months, however, he was forced to devalue the peso and introduce a number of austerity measures in return for US financial aid. In 1996 Zedillo signed a peace deal with the Zapatista revolutionaries in the s state of Chiapas, which gave Native Americans greater political representation. The late 1990s saw strained relations with the United States over the nature and extent of cooperation to end drug trafficking and the involvement of PRI members in the massacre of Native Americans in Chiapas. In 2000 Zedillo signed a free-trade agreement with the European Union (EU).

Zemin, Jiang *See* Jiang Zemin

Zen Japanese school of Buddhism, initially developed in China, where it is known as Ch'an. Instead of doctrines and scriptures, Zen stresses mind-to-mind instruction from master to disciple in order to achieve *satori* (awakening of Buddha-nature). There are two major Zen sects. **Rinzai** (introduced to Japan from China in 1191) emphasizes sudden enlightenment and meditation on paradoxical statements. The **Soto** sect (also brought from China, in 1227) advocates quiet meditation. In its secondary emphasis on mental tranquillity, fearlessness and spontaneity, Zen has had a great influence on Japanese culture. Zen priests inspired art, literature, the tea ceremony and No drama. In recent decades, a number of Zen groups have emerged in Europe and the United States.

Zenger, John Peter (1697–1746) US printer and journalist, b. Germany. Editor of the *New York Weekly Journal* (1733), he attacked Governor William Cosby and was jailed for libel in 1734. He was later tried by a jury and acquitted. His case established truth as a defence for libel and made Zenger a symbol of the freedom of the press. He was public printer of New York (1737) and New Jersey (1738).

Zeng Guofan (1811–72) Chinese soldier and administrator whose Hunan Army crushed the Taiping Rebellion. After producing influential interpretations of

CONFUCIANISM at the prestigious Hanlin Academy for 13 years, he accepted posts in a number of government agencies. In the early 1850s he criticized the emperor and government, but agreed to raise an army to combat the Taiping rebels, who by 1852 constituted a serious threat to the QING dynasty. Zeng's capture of NANJING (1864) ended the Rebellion. He was rewarded with several provinical governorships, including JIANGXI. In 1865 he was called upon to quell another revolt, the Nien Rebellion, in N China, after which he devoted his time to educational reform. He was the tutor of LI HONGZHANG.

Zeno (426–491) Byzantine emperor (474–491), son-in-law of Leo I. In 475 he yielded to the usurper Basilicus for 20 months. Zeno sought unsuccessfully to reconcile heretical MONOPHYSITISM with the orthodox Christians through his *Henotikon* (482). By persuading THEODORIC (THE GREAT) to invade Italy he finally rid the Eastern Roman Empire of the OSTROGOTHS (489).

Zenobia (active 3rd century AD) Queen of PALMYRA (*c*.267–73). She ruled as regent for her young son after the death of her husband. Palmyra was an ally of Rome, but Zenobia, keen for greater autonomy from her overbearing ally, created a powerful army, conquering Egypt in 269 and declaring Palmyra independent from Rome. The Romans, alarmed at Zenobia's rapidly growing military power, resolved to crush her. AURELIAN defeated her in Syria (272) and Zenobia was captured and taken to Rome, where she married a senator. Following further revolts by the Palmyrenes the Romans captured and destroyed Palmyra (273).

Zeno of Citium (*c*.334–*c*.262 BC) Greek philosopher and founder of the STOICS. He attended lectures by various philosophers before formulating his own philosophy. Proceeding from the CYNIC concept of self-sufficiency, Zeno stressed the unity of the universe and the brotherhood of men living in harmony with the cosmos. He claimed virtue to be the only good, and wealth, illness and death to be of no human concern.

Zeno of Elea (*c*.495–*c*.430 BC) Greek philosopher. A disciple of Parmenides, Zeno sought to reveal logical absurdities in theories of motion and change, using paradoxical arguments, a precursor to ARISTOTLE's influential dialectic arguments.

Zeppelin, Ferdinand, Graf von (1838–1917) German army officer and inventor. He fought in the Austro-Prussian War (1866) and the Franco-Prussian War (1870–71). While an observer with the Union army during the American Civil War, Zeppelin made his first balloon ascent. In 1900 he invented the first rigid airship, which was called Zeppelin after him. A fleet of Zeppelins were used during World War 1.

Zhao Kuangyin (927–76) Chinese emperor (960–76), founder of the SONG dynasty (960–1279). He was a scholarly general who eliminated regional military control, established a paid army and laid the basis for three centuries of cultural advance in China. Zhao began the unification of China, a process that was largely completed by his younger brother and successor, TAIZONG.

Zhao Ziyang (1919–) Chinese statesman who played a leading part in China's economic modernization. Zhao joined the Chinese COMMUNIST PARTY in 1938 and during the 1960s acted as party secretary of Guangdong province. He was dismissed by MAO ZEDONG during the CULTURAL REVOLUTION, but rehabilitated and restored to his post in 1971. In 1975 he was appointed party secretary of Sichuan province. Zhao introduced radical economic reforms that vastly improved industrial and agricultural production. In 1980 he was made premier. In 1987 LI PENG replaced him as premier and Zhao became general secretary. With the support of DENG XIAOPING, his liberal economic reforms moved China towards a market economy. In 1989 Zhao was dismissed from office and placed under house arrest for advocating negotiation with the pro-democracy demonstrators in TIANANMEN SQUARE.

Zheng Chenggong (1624–62) (Koxinga) MING pirate who fought against the QING conquest of China. While the Manchu were preoccupied campaigning against Ming forces in SW China, Zheng was able to create a powerful navy on the Fujian coast, around the island of Xiamen (formerly Amoy). By 1659 he had also raised a land army of *c*.100,000 men, with which he sailed up the Yangtze River, reaching the gates of NANJING. In the ensuing battle, however, he was defeated by Qing forces. To escape the encroaching Qing Zheng, who was still unassailable at sea, he defeated the Dutch forces on Taiwan (1661), and settled there with his followers. Plans to invade the Philippines were not realized due to his early death.

Zheng He (*c*.1371–1435) (Cheng Ho) Chinese admiral, explorer and diplomat, known as the "three-jewelled eunuch". Between 1405 and 1433 Zheng He, sponsored by Emperor YONGLO, led seven naval expeditions across the China Sea and the Indian Ocean to gather treasures and unusual tributes for the MING imperial court. Zheng's voyages, the specific purposes of which are still not clear, reached as far W as the Persian Gulf, visiting ports in SE Asia, India, East Africa and Egypt. The expeditions, which underlined the relative sophistication of Chinese navigation and shipbuilding techniques, inadvertently prepared the way for Chinese colonization of SE Asia.

Zhou Chinese dynasty (*c*.1030–221 BC). Widely regarded as the second Chinese dynasty following the overthrow of the SHANG. The Zhou was founded by Wen the Martial who consolidated Zhou territory, but it was his son, Wu, who defeated the Shang, claiming that the oppressive and immoral Shang kings had forfeited the right to the "Mandate of Heaven". The dynasty is divided into two periods. Up until *c*.771 BC the **Western** Zhou controlled vassal states in China's central plain and the Yellow River region. The **Eastern**, or Later, Zhou was less influential than the Western and often struggled for superiority over its vassal states. Although it was a period of upheaval, during the Zhou Chinese civilization spread to most parts of modern China, and with hindsight can be regarded as a golden age, marked by the writings of CONFUCIUS and LAO TZU. It was also a period of rising prosperity. As the provincial states grew in power, the Eastern Zhou dynasty disintegrated.

Zhou Enlai (1898–1976) Chinese statesman. Zhou was a founder of the Chinese COMMUNIST PARTY. As a member of the Communist-KUOMINTANG alliance (1924–27), he directed the general strike (1927) in SHANGHAI, SE China. When CHIANG KAI-SHEK broke the alliance, Zhou joined the LONG MARCH (1934–35) and became one of MAO ZEDONG's most influential advisers. He was the chief negotiator of a renewed peace (1936–46) with Nationalist forces following the XIAN INCIDENT. After the establishment of a communist republic, Zhou became prime minister (1949–76) and foreign minister (1949–58), playing a significant role in the BANDUNG CONFERENCE (1955). Although publicly supportive of the CULTURAL REVOLUTION, he protected many of its intended victims.

Zhu De (1886–1976) Chinese communist military leader. Zhu helped to overthrow (1912) the QING dynasty. In 1922 he met ZHOU ENLAI and joined the Chinese Communist Party. In 1927 Zhu led Communist forces in the Nanchang Rebellion against the Nationalist KUOMINTANG government, an event heralded as marking the foundation of the Chinese Red Army. In 1928 Zhu joined forces with MAO ZEDONG and led his section of the 4th Red Army on the LONG MARCH (1934–35). After serving as commander in

ZIMBABWE

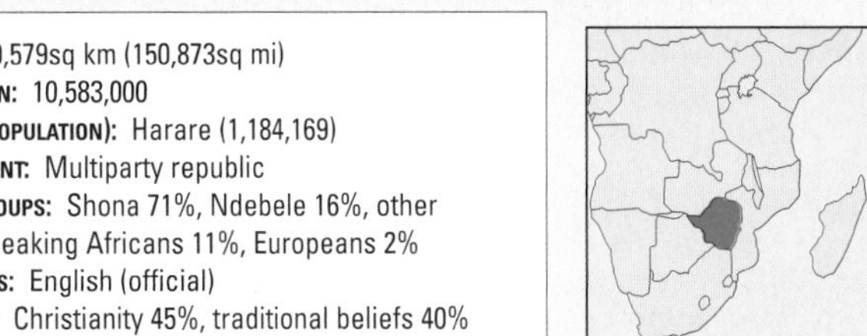

AREA: 390,579sq km (150,873sq mi)
POPULATION: 10,583,000
CAPITAL (POPULATION): Harare (1,184,169)
GOVERNMENT: Multiparty republic
ETHNIC GROUPS: Shona 71%, Ndebele 16%, other Bantu-speaking Africans 11%, Europeans 2%
LANGUAGES: English (official)
RELIGIONS: Christianity 45%, traditional beliefs 40%
GDP PER CAPITA (1995): US$2030

Landlocked republic in S central Africa. Bantu-speakers migrated to the region in AD 300. By 1200 the SHONA had established a kingdom in Mashonaland, E Zimbabwe. GREAT ZIMBABWE was the capital of this advanced culture. Portugal formed trading links in the early 16th century. In 1837 the NDEBELE displaced the Shona from W Zimbabwe and formed MATABELELAND. In 1855 David LIVINGSTONE made the first European discovery of Victoria Falls. In 1888 Matabeleland became a British protectorate.

In 1889 the British South Africa Company, under Cecil RHODES, was granted a charter to exploit the region's mineral wealth. Native revolts were crushed, and the area became Southern RHODESIA (1896). In 1923 it became a British crown colony, and all Africans were excluded from participation in the government. In 1953 Southern Rhodesia, Northern Rhodesia (now ZAMBIA) and Nyasaland (MALAWI) became a federation. In 1961 Joshua NKOMO formed the Zimbabwe African People's Union (ZAPU). In 1963 the federation dissolved and African majority governments were formed in Zambia and Malawi. Southern Rhodesia became simply Rhodesia. Robert MUGABE formed the Zimbabwe African National Union (ZANU). In 1964 the white nationalist leader Ian SMITH became prime minister, and Nkomo and Mugabe were imprisoned. In 1965 Smith made a Unilateral Declaration of Independence (UDI) from Britain. The United Nations' (UN) imposed economic sanctions and in 1969 Rhodesia became a republic. In 1974 Nkomo and Mugabe were released. Smith's refusal to implement democratic reforms intensified the guerrilla war waged by ZAPU and ZANU rebels against the Smith government (aided by SOUTH AFRICA's APARTHEID regime). The 1979 Lancaster House Agreement established a timetable for independence.

ZANU won a decisive victory in 1980 elections, and Robert Mugabe became prime minister. In 1982 Nkomo was dismissed from the cabinet. Mugabe was decisively re-elected in 1985. In 1987 ZANU and ZAPU merged. The post of prime minister was abolished as Mugabe became executive president. In 1988 Nkomo became vice president. Despite the formation of an opposition party, the Zimbabwe Unity Movement, Mugabe was easily re-elected in 1990. In 1991 ZANU-PF abandoned Marxism. Mugabe was elected for a fourth term in 1996. In 1999 there were calls for greater democracy. The government's redistribution of land to the African population via compulsory purchase schemes has been tainted by government corruption. In the run-up to elections in 2000 many white-owned farms were forcibly occupied by supporters of Mugabe.

chief of the Red Army during the Second SINO-JAPANESE WAR (1937–45), his mastery of guerrilla tactics was largely responsible for the defeat of the Nationalists and the subsequent establishment of a communist republic (1949). Zhu held several important party posts before being denounced during the CULTURAL REVOLUTION.

Zhukov, Georgi Konstantinovich (1896–1974) Soviet marshal and statesman. He fought in the Russian Civil War (1918–20) and served as chief of staff in the RUSSO-FINNISH WAR (1939–40). During WORLD WAR 2 he organized the defence of MOSCOW and Leningrad (now ST PETERSBURG) in 1941. In 1942 he was made deputy commander in chief of the Soviet army, becoming the leading military adviser to Joseph STALIN. Zhukov masterminded the defence of STALINGRAD (1942), and his counter-offensive brought an end to the German siege of the city (1943). In 1944 he led the Soviet advance through Belarus and commanded the final assault on Berlin, Germany (1945). After Stalin's death he supported Nikita KHRUSHCHEV against Georgi MALENKOV and was rewarded with the post of minister of defence (1955–57), succeeding Nikolai BULGANIN. Although supportive of Khrushchev's reforms, his attempts to increase the power of the army led to his dismissal in 1957. He was rehabilitated in the 1960s, receiving the Order of Lenin in 1966.

Zhu Yuanzhang (1328–98) First Chinese emperor of the MING dynasty (1368–98). After entering a Buddhist monastery, he left (1352) to become leader of a group of rebels. His band became an increasingly powerful force, and with the decline of the YUAN dynasty, Zhu captured Nanjing. In 1368 he captured Beijing and crowned himself emperor. Over the next 15 years, Zhu fought a number of campaigns and by 1382 he had unified China.

Zia-ul-Haq, Muhammad (1924–88) Pakistani army officer and statesman, president (1978–88). A major general in the PAKISTAN army, he was promoted to chief of staff by Zulfikar ali BHUTTO. In 1977, following a military coup, Zia seized control and Bhutto was found guilty of attempted murder and executed. Zia proclaimed himself president and banned all political parties and labour strikes, and imposed strict press censorship. During his presidency, Pakistan assumed a greater Islamic cultural and political identity. When the Soviet Union became involved in the AFGHANISTAN WAR (1979–92), Zia received US financial aid to help the Muslim refugees pouring into Pakistan and to build up a defence force. Zia was assassinated by a bomb planted on his airplane.

ziggurat Religious monument originating in BABYLON and ASSYRIA. It was constructed as a truncated, stepped PYRAMID, rising in diminishing tiers, usually square or rectangular. The shrine at the top was reached by a series of ramps. Ziggurats date from 3000–600 BC, and the one at UR, S Iraq, still stands.

Zimbabwe *See* country feature, page 447

Zimbabwe, Great *See* GREAT ZIMBABWE

Zimmerman telegram (1917) Cable intercepted by British intelligence from German Foreign Minister Arthur Zimmerman. It stated Germany's intent to wage unrestricted submarine warfare and proposed that Mexico be offered three US states if it allied itself with Germany. Because it violated the Sussex Pledge, President Woodrow WILSON severed diplomatic relations with Germany, which led to the entry of the United States into WORLD WAR I.

Zinoviev, Grigori Evseyevich (1883–1936) Russian revolutionary. A self-educated lawyer, Zinoviev joined the BOLSHEVIKS in 1903, and was active in the RUSSIAN REVOLUTION OF 1905. He was a close collaborator of Vladimir LENIN in exile (1908–17). In the RUSSIAN REVOLUTION (1917), Zinoviev voted against seizing power but remained a powerful figure in ST PETERSBURG and was appointed head of the COMMUNIST INTERNATIONAL in 1919. Although he sided with Joseph STALIN and Lev KAMENEV against Leon TROTSKY in 1924, Zinoviev was arrested at the start of Stalin's GREAT PURGE (1936–38) and tried and executed for complicity in the assassination of Sergei KIROV. *See also* ZINOVIEV LETTER

Zinoviev letter (1924) Document, allegedly signed by the BOLSHEVIK Grigori ZINOVIEV, urging the British Communist Party to launch a revolution. Since proved to be a forgery, the letter was used to discredit the British LABOUR PARTY and was a major factor in the defeat of Ramsay MACDONALD's Labour government in the election of that year.

Zion Hill in E JERUSALEM, Israel. Zion was originally the hill on which a Jebusite fortress was built. It now refers to the hill on which the TEMPLE OF JERUSALEM was built.

Zionism Jewish nationalist movement advocating the return of Jews to the land of Zion (PALESTINE). Though it represents a desire expressed since the Jewish DIASPORA began in the 6th century BC, the modern Zionist movement dates from 1897, when Theodor HERZL established the World Zionist Congress at Basel, Switzerland. In 1917 the Zionist Chaim WEIZMANN secured British approval for its objective in the BALFOUR DECLARATION, and the Jewish population of Palestine more than doubled between 1925 and 1933 and increased even more dramatically after Adolf HITLER came to power in Germany. In 1947 the United Nations (UN) voted to partition Palestine between Jews and Arabs, leading to the foundation of the state of ISRAEL. *See also* DIASPORA; JUDAISM

Zog I (1895–1961) King of ALBANIA (1928–39), b. Ahmed Bey Zogu. Son of a Muslim chieftain, he served in the Austrian army during World War 1. Zog was premier (1922–24) and when Albania was proclaimed a republic in 1925, he was elected president and then proclaimed himself king. His anti-democratic reforms made him a virtual dictator. Zog championed modernization, linguistic and educational reforms, but failed to provide vital land reforms. Moreover, Albania's reliance on Italian financial aid led to Benito MUSSOLINI's gradually assumption of control of the country, and when Italy invaded in 1939, Albania was powerless to resist, and Zog was forced into exile. He was forced to abdicate (1946) after Enver HOXHA established a communist republic.

Zollverein German customs union formed in 1834 by 18 German states under Prussian leadership. By reducing tariffs and improving transport, it promoted economic prosperity amongst the German states. Nearly all other German states had joined the Zollverein by 1867, despite Austrian opposition. Following the AUSTRO-PRUSSIAN WAR (1866), the newly created NORTH GERMAN CONFEDERATION joined the Zollverein, representing the first major step towards the creation (1871) of the German Empire under Otto von BISMARCK.

Zoroaster (*c.*628–*c.*551 BC) (Zarathustra) Ancient Persian (Iranian) religious reformer, founder of ZOROASTRIANISM. At the age of 30, in the first of many visions, he saw the divine being Ahura Mazdah. Unable to convert the petty chieftains of his native region, Zoroaster travelled to E Persia, where in Chorasmia (now Khorasan province, NE Iran) he converted the royal family. By the time of Zoroaster's death (tradition says that he was murdered while at prayer), his new religion had spread to a large part of Persia. Parts of the Avesta, the holy scripture of Zoroastrianism, are believed to have been written by Zoroaster himself.

▲ **Zwingli** Portrait by Hans Asper (1499–1571). Zwingli attracted a large following and broke with church tradition by reading directly from the original Greek and Hebrew scriptures.

Zoroastrianism Religion founded by ZOROASTER in the 6th century BC. It was the state religion of PERSIA (Iran) under the SASANIAN dynasty (AD 224–651). Viewing the world as being divided between the spirits of good and evil, Zoroastrians worship Ahura Mazdah as the supreme deity, who is forever in conflict with Ahriman, the spirit of evil. They also consider fire sacred. The rise of ISLAM in the 7th century led to the decline and near disappearance of Zoroastrianism in Persia. Today, the PARSI comprise most of the adherents of Zoroastrianism, which has its main centre in Mumbai, W India.

Zulu Bantu people of South Africa, most of whom live in KWAZULU-NATAL. They are closely related to the Swazi and the XHOSA. The Zulus have a patriarchal, polygamous society, with a strong militaristic tradition. Traditionally cereal farmers, they possessed large herds of cattle, considered to be status symbols. In the early 19th century, under their leader SHAKA, they joined with the Nguni to create a powerful S African empire. By the end of the 19th century the Zulu had lost most of their land in a series of wars with the British and AFRIKANERS. The predominant religion is now Christianity, although ethnic religions are still common. They are organized politically into the INKATHA movement under Chief Mangusutho BUTHELEZI. Today, there are *c.*9 million Zulu. *See also* CETSHWAYO

Zulu War (1879) Conflict in SOUTH AFRICA between the British colony of NATAL and the ZULU. Fearing a Zulu attack, the AFRIKANERS of the TRANSVAAL requested British protection. The British high commissioner demanded that the Zulu king, CETSHWAYO, disband his army. Cetshwayo refused, and the Zulu made a surprise attack at Isandhlwana, killing 800 British soldiers. Lacking modern weapons, the Zulu were checked at Rorke's Drift and decisively defeated at Ulundi.

Zuni PUEBLO NATIVE NORTH AMERICANS who live on the Zuni reservation in W NEW MEXICO, United States. The present pueblo is on the site of one of the seven Zuni villages discovered by Marcos de Niza in the early 16th century and identified as the mythical Seven Cities of Cibola. In 1540 Francisco de CORONADO sacked the villages, and following a revolt in 1680, the Pueblo abandoned the site for fear of Spanish reprisal.

Zürich City on the River Limmat, at the NW end of Lake Zürich, in the foothills of the Alps, N Switzerland; it is the country's largest city. Conquered by the Romans in 58 BC, the city later came under ALEMANNI and then Frankish rule. It became a free imperial city in 1218 and joined the Swiss Confederation in 1351. In the 16th century it was a focal point of the Swiss REFORMATION. Ulrich ZWINGLI founded Swiss PROTESTANTISM at Zürich's cathedral in 1523. In the 18th and 19th centuries the city developed as a cultural and scientific centre. It has the Swiss National Museum and many old churches. Pop. (1991) 840,000.

Zwingli, Ulrich (1484–1531) Swiss Protestant theologian and reformer. He was ordained as a Roman Catholic priest in 1506, but his studies of the New Testament in ERASMUS' editions led him to become a reformer. By 1522 he was preaching Reformed doctrine in Zürich, a centre for the REFORMATION. More radical than Martin LUTHER, Zwingli saw communion as mainly symbolic and commemorative – an attitude that made it impossible to unite the various sects of PROTESTANTISM. In 1524 he began removing the images and the organ from Zürich's cathedral. Zwingli transformed Zürich into a theocratic state and the city's population were regarded as the elect. The movement quickly spread to the cantons of Basel and Bern. The radical ANABAPTISTS in Zürich were sentenced to death. Zwingli died in battle against the Catholic forest cantons at Kappel. *See also* MÜNTZER, THOMAS; TRANSUBSTANTIATION

HISTORY of the WORLD

Dates are much more than isolated markers of events. Organized into a chronology, dates establish sequence and synchronicity. In creating this particular History of the World, every care has been taken to use accurate and informative dates. However, it is impossible to achieve "definitive" dates when referring to events that occurred many thousands of years ago. Virtually all dates before AD 1 are based on archaeology – the dating of objects dug from the ground. The most useful and widespread method of dating such material is by measuring the decay of the isotope carbon-14 (radiocarbon dating). This method is reliable, but is not strictly precise. Even when correlated with dendrochronology (tree-ring dating) radiocarbon dates are at best accurate to within 50–100 years, and the further back the method is applied, the wider the margin for error. To spare the reader any confusion between correlated and uncorrelated dates, we have often selected a single date, prefixed by the abbreviation *c.* (circa) to indicate a date-range. Broadly speaking, the size of the date-range indicated by *c.* depends on the nature of the date: *c.*5500 BC means 6000 BC–5000 BC; *c.*2500 BC means 2750 BC–2250 BC. In more recent times, *c.* indicates a degree of uncertainty owing to the fact that definitive written records are rare, hence *c.*1500 BC means 1600 BC–1400 BC; *c.*1000 BC means 1050 BC–950 BC; *c.*500 BC means 525 BC–485 BC *c.*250 BC means 255 BC–245 BC. *c.*1281, *c.*1632, or similar, usually means historians are uncertain as to exactly when a particular person was born.

Other complications arise from the use of different dating systems by various peoples at different times in the past. Roman emperors measured their rule in regnal years that straddle our years, which can produce a plethora of unsatisfactory dates, such as 68/69, 138/139, 257/258, and so on, unless a firm hand is applied. Chinese emperors divided their reigns into named periods which could vary in length from 3 to 30 years, and many events are dated accordingly.

Even our present century is beset by chronological problems. The Russian Revolution of 1917, often called the "October Revolution", occurred in November in the Gregorian (New Style) Calendar.

PREHISTORY

15,000 mya (million years ago)
According to the Big Bang theory, the Universe is formed.

4600 mya
The Earth is formed.

3800 mya
Simple single-celled life (bacteria) appears.

1200 mya
Complex single-celled plants and animals appear.

600 mya
Multi-cellular plants and animals appear.

560 mya
Beginning of Cambrian period of geological timescale, during which animals evolve eyes and jointed legs.

400 mya
The first land plants and animals appear.

220 mya
A massive extinction event wipes out 90% of species.

65 mya
An extinction event, probably caused by an asteroid impact, kills the land-living dinosaurs.

***c.*5 mya**
Australopithecines appear in S Africa.

***c.*2 mya**
The most recent ice age starts; *Homo habilis* appears in SE Africa.

***c.*1.7 mya**
Homo erectus appears in E Africa.

***c.*250,000 BC**
Archaic *Homo sapiens* appears in E Africa.

***c.*200,000 BC**
Homo neanderthalensis appears in Europe and Asia.

***c.*150,000 BC**
Modern *Homo sapiens* appears in E Africa.

***c.*55,000 BC**
Modern *Homo sapiens* moves into Europe and Australia.

***c.*35,000 BC**
Neanderthals become extinct in Europe.

ASIA AND AUSTRALASIA

15,000 BC **c.15,000 BC** End of the coldest period of the most recent ice age.

c.10,000 BC Emergence of Natufian culture in the Middle East to the W of the River Euphrates, based on the intensive gathering of wild cereals.

c.10,000 BC Earliest firm evidence of domesticated dogs (from a grave in Palestine).

c.9000 BC Earliest-known permanent human settlements established by Natufian peoples; they build villages with circular houses in parts of the Middle East and Asia Minor.

c.9000 BC Sheep and goats are domesticated in the Middle East.

c.8500 BC Earliest-known rectangular houses are built in Mesopotamia.

c.8500 BC Wheat (einkorn and emmer) and barley are domesticated in the Middle East.

c.8500 BC End of Palaeolithic period (Old Stone Age) in the Middle East.

c.8000 BC Jericho (on the W bank of the River Jordan) has a population of *c.*1000, and is surrounded by a stone wall with a fortified tower.

c.7000 BC Cattle and pigs are domesticated in the Middle East.

c.7000 BC Pigs are domesticated in China.

c.7000 BC Tropical horticulture begins in the highlands of New Guinea.

c. 6500 BC Farming starts in the NE of the Indian subcontinent.

c.6000 BC Domestication of millet and broomcorn in N China and rice in S China; start of Yangshao culture.

c.5400 BC Start of the Early Ubaid period in Mesopotamia; beginnings of urbanization.

5000 BC **c.5000 BC** First permanent settlement is established at Eridu (by tradition the first city) in Mesopotamia.

c.5000 BC Longshan culture emerges on the Shandong peninsula, China.

c.4500 BC Zebu cattle are domesticated in Pakistan.

c. 4500 BC Permanent settlement is established at Ur in S Mesopotamia.

c.4300 BC Start of the Late Ubaid period in Mesopotamia; many cities are established and temples and ziggurats are built.

c.4200 BC Copper mining starts in Oman in SE Arabia.

c.4200 BC Elamites establish the city of Susa in present-day W Iran.

4000 BC **c.3500 BC** Floodplain of the River Indus (present-day Pakistan) is settled by farmers who use some copper tools; start of the Early Indus period (*c.*3500–*c.*2800 BC).

c.3500 BC Start of the Uruk period in S Mesopotamia; development of urban civilization.

c.3300 BC Sumerians (who probably originated in central Asia) settle in S Mesopotamia.

c.3300 BC City-states develop in Syria and Palestine.

c.3200 BC Bronze comes into widespread use for tools in Mesopotamia; start of the Bronze Age in the Middle East.

c.3100 BC End of the Uruk period in S Mesopotamia; start of the Jamdat Nasr period.

3000 BC **c.3000 BC** Agriculture starts at oases in SE Arabia.

c.2900 BC First sizeable town is established on the site of Troy, NW Asia Minor.

c.2900 BC Start of the Early Dynastic period in Sumerian Mesopotamia; the first conflicts between rival city-states occur.

c.2800 BC Akkadians establish a kingdom to the N of Sumeria.

c.2800 BC Indus valley civilization emerges in present-day Pakistan.

c.2700 BC Reign of Gilgamesh, the legendary Sumerian king of Uruk.

c.2600 BC Walled towns are built in N China.

2500 BC **c.2500 BC** Potters wheel is first used in China.

c.2500 BC One-humped dromedary camel in Arabia and two-humped Bactrian camel in central Asia are domesticated.

c.2400 BC City of Ebla in N Syria becomes a major trading centre.

c.2340 BC Akkadians under Sargon I establish empire in Mesopotamia.

c.2300 BC Indus valley civilization starts trade with Mesopotamia and the Arabian Gulf region via the port of Lothal.

2190 BC Akkadian empire collapses under attack from the Guti people.

2119 BC Utuhegal, king of Uruk, defeats the Gutians in battle and re-establishes Sumerian control.

2112 BC King Urnammu takes control of Mesopotamia and founds the Third Dynasty of Ur.

c.2100 BC Amorite nomads move into Mesopotamia from the E.

2004 BC Ur is destroyed by Elamites from present-day SW Iran.

AFRICA

c.15,000 BC End of the coldest period of the most recent ice age.

c.7500 BC Earliest-known African pottery is produced in S Sahara region.

c.6000 BC Wheat, barley, sheep and goats are introduced to Egypt from the N.

c.6000 BC Onset of dryer climatic conditions begins the desertification of the Sahara.

c.5500 BC Bullrush millet is domesticated in the Sahara.

c.5000 BC Badarian culture emerges in central Egypt.

c.4500 BC Start of cattle herding in the Sahara; either with locally domesticated stock or with animals introduced via Egypt.

c.4250 BC Local sorghum and rice are domesticated in Sudan.

c.4000 BC Nagada culture emerges along the River Nile in Egypt.

c.4000 BC Donkeys are domesticated in Egypt.

c.3500 BC First fortified towns are built in Egypt; two distinct centres of urbanization emerge in Upper (S) and Lower (N) Egypt.

c.3100 BC Egypt is unified by King Menes (also known as Narmer) of Upper Egypt, who establishes a capital city at Memphis; start of the First Dynastic (Archaic) Period.

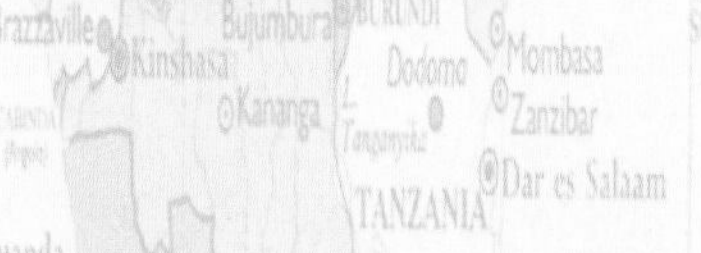

c.2800 BC Egyptian expeditions make first contact with Nubian cultures to the S.

2686 BC First Dynastic (Archaic) Period ends in Egypt; start of the Old Kingdom (2686–2181 BC).

c.2550–c.2525 BC Great Pyramid is built for the Egyptian pharaoh Cheops (Khufu) at Giza.

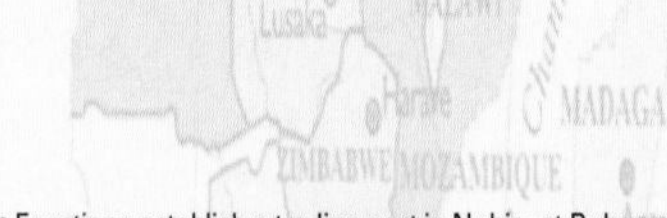

c.2500 BC Egyptians establish a trading post in Nubia, at Buhen near the second cataract of the River Nile.

c.2181 BC End of Old Kingdom in Egypt; collapse of central control; start of the First Intermediate Period.

c.2040 BC Pharaoh Menuhotep re-establishes central control in Egypt; end of the First Intermediate Period; start of Middle Kingdom (2040–1786 BC).

EUROPE

c.15,000 BC End of the coldest period of the most recent ice age.

c.9500 BC Ice sheets start to melt in Europe and North America.

c.8500 BC End of Palaeolithic period in Europe; start of Mesolithic period (Middle Stone Age); bows and arrows come into widespread use.

c.6500 BC Farming (wheat, barley, goats and sheep) starts in Greece and the Balkans.

c.6400 BC Emergence of Karanovo culture in present-day S Bulgaria.

c.5400 BC Start of Vinca culture in present-day Bosnia.

c.5400 BC Farming spreads across the Hungarian Plain to central Europe.

c.5200 BC Farming starts in Spain.

c.4500 BC Earliest megaliths are built in NW Europe to accommodate collective burials.

c.4500 BC Spread of farming reaches the Netherlands.

c.4400–4100 BC Extensive forest clearance takes place in Britain.

c.4400 BC Start of Gumelnita culture in present-day N Bulgaria and S Romania.

c.4250 BC Plough is first used in the Balkans.

c.4200 BC Horses are domesticated (for food) in Ukraine.

c.4000 BC Olives, figs, almonds and pomegranates are domesticated in the E Mediterranean region.

c.3800 BC Rise of TRB (*Trichterbecher*) farming culture in Denmark and N Germany and Poland.

c.3500 BC Copper mining starts near present-day Granada in S Spain.

c.3400 BC Earliest evidence of wheeled vehicles in Europe (from a grave in Poland).

c.3300 BC Megalithic temple is built at Tarxien, Malta.

c.3200 BC "Man in the Ice", equipped with a cast copper axe, dies while crossing the Alps near the present-day Italian–Austrian border.

c.3100 BC First ritual earthworks are constructed at Stonehenge, England.

c.2500 BC Horses are introduced to Ireland.

c.2400 BC People of the Beaker Culture begin migration from Spain to France, Germany and Britain.

c.2300 BC Start of Bronze Age in central Europe.

c.2100 BC Circle of bluestones at Stonehenge, England, is erected.

THE AMERICAS

c.15,000 BC End of the coldest period of the most recent ice age.

c.9500 BC Ice sheets start to melt in Europe and North America.

c.9200–c.8900 BC Clovis period hunters are active in North America.

c.8500 BC Disappearance of the ice-bridge across the Bering Strait ends first period of human migration into the Americas.

c.8900–8400 BC Fulsom period hunters are active in North America.

c.8000 BC Large mammals (including the mammoth and the horse) become extinct in North America.

c.7000 BC Beans and squash are first cultivated in Peru.

7000 BC Start of the Archaic Period in Mesoamerican history.

c.5200 BC Onset of drier climatic conditions on the Great Plains of North America forces people and animals to migrate E.

c.5000 BC Guinea pigs are domesticated in Colombia.

c.4800 BC Peoples from the Central American mainland become the first inhabitants of the Caribbean islands.

c. 4300 BC A variety of cotton is domesticated in Mexico.

c.4000 BC Llamas and alpacas are domesticated in Peru.

c.4000 BC Maize is domesticated in Mexico.

c.3600 BC First American pottery is produced in Guyana on N coast of South America.

c. 3500 BC A variety of cotton is domesticated in lowland Peru.

c.3000 BC Start of Old Copper Culture on S shore of Lake Superior; jewellery and other artifacts are produced from hammered native copper.

c.3000 BC Chillis, avocados, groundnuts and sweet potatoes are domesticated in the coastal region of Peru.

c.2800 BC Several varieties of potato are domesticated in highland Peru.

c.2600 BC First temple mounds are constructed in Peru.

c.2400 BC First Mesoamerican pottery is made.

c.2300 BC Stone temple and ritual centre is built at La Galada in lowland Peru.

c.2200 BC People in present-day SW USA first make pottery.

c.2200 BC Domestication in present-day E USA of sunflowers, sumpweed, goosegrass and a variety of squash.

SCIENCE AND THE ARTS

c.15,000 BC Bow and arrow (the bow consisting of a single piece of wood) is invented towards the end of the Palaeolithic period (Old Stone Age). 15,000 BC

c.15,000–12,000 BC Main period of European cave painting, including the sites of Lascaux in France and Altamira in Spain, although the earliest sites date from *c.*30–25,000 BC.

c.11,000 BC World's earliest-known fired-clay vessels (bag-shaped pots) are made by hunter-gatherers in Japan.

c.10,000 BC Jomon cord-marked pottery is first produced in Japan.

c.8500 BC Earliest-known mudbricks are used to build houses in Mesopotamia.

c.8000 BC Pottery is first made in China.

c.7500 BC Peoples living in Mesopotamia use fermentation to produce the earliest-known beer.

c.7000 BC Shrine at Çatal Hüyük in central Asia Minor is decorated with sculpted bull's heads and goddess figures.

c. 7000 BC Copper (lumps of naturally occurring native copper hammered and cut into shape with stone tools) is first used for jewellery in parts of the Middle East.

c.7000 BC Pottery comes into general use in many parts of the Middle East.

c.6500 BC Earliest-known textile (linen) is woven at Çatal Hüyük.

c.5400 BC Farmers in N central Europe produce distinctive pottery vessels.

c.5500 BC Copper smelting (the extraction of metal from ore) starts in Asia Minor and present-day W Iran. Start of the Chalcolithic (or Copper) Age in the Middle East.

c.5300 BC Earliest-known complex buildings are constructed in Mesopotamia, with upper storeys and numerous internal rooms.

c.5000 BC Earliest-known canals are dug in Mesopotamia; they are used to irrigate crops and to drain marshy ground for settlement and cultivation. 5000 BC

c.5000 BC *Thinker* (also known as the *Sorrowing God*) statue is carved at Cernavoda in present-day E Romania.

c.4800 BC Stamp seals are first used to identify property and goods in Mesopotamia and SE Europe.

c.4500 BC Ox-drawn plough is invented in Mesopotamia; crop farming is extended to soils too difficult to be worked with hand-held sticks.

c.4500 BC Small clay tokens in different shapes are first used for accounting purposes in Mesopotamia.

c.4300 BC Turntable (tournette or slow wheel) for pottery making is invented in N Mesopotamia.

c.4200 BC First deliberate production of bronze (copper alloyed with arsenic or tin) occurs in present-day W Iran.

c.4000 BC A burial at Varna in Bulgaria contains the earliest-known large deposit of gold objects (weighing more than 1.5kg/3.3lb). 4000 BC

c.4000 BC By using the Nilometer (which measures the height of the River Nile's annual flood), the Egyptians calculate that the year is 365 days long.

c.4000 BC First copper axes are produced in present-day W Iran and SE Europe.

c.3800 BC Wheel is invented in Mesopotamia; the first ox-drawn carts are used to transport agricultural produce.

c.3500 BC Start of the Secondary Products Revolution in agriculture; widespread use of animal power, use of wool for textiles, introduction of dairying.

c.3500 BC First systematic use of pictographs for writing occurs in Sumeria (S Mesopotamia).

c.3400 BC Potter's wheel (fast wheel) is invented in Mesopotamia.

c.3200 BC Walls of the so-called Stone Mosaic temple at Uruk are decorated with thousands of small, multicoloured, baked clay cones.

c.3200 BC Food rations for workers in the city of Uruk are distributed in pottery bowls mass-produced in moulds.

c.3200 BC Lost-wax technique (*cire perdue*) for casting metals is developed in Mesopotamia.

c.3000 BC Hieroglyphic writing is first used in Egypt. 3000 BC

c.2850 BC First Cycladic statues are produced on Mediterranean islands to the E of Greece.

c.2800 BC Silkworms and mulberry trees are domesticated in China.

c.2700 BC Earliest examples of Egyptian literature, the Pyramid Texts, are written down on papyrus using a brush and ink.

c.2700 BC Cuneiform writing (wedge-shaped marks made by pressing the end of a reed into clay tablets) is developed in Mesopotamia.

c.2650 BC Egyptian architect Imhotep designs the world's earliest-known pyramid (the so-called stepped pyramid) for the pharaoh Zoser.

c.2600 BC Earliest-known glass is made for jewellery beads in Mesopotamia.

c.2600 BC Earliest-known large-scale use of fired bricks occurs with the construction of the Indus valley cities of Harappa and Mohenjo Daro.

c.2500 BC Earliest-known examples of Sumerian literature are written down at Abu Salabikh in Mesopotamia. 2500 BC

c.2500 BC Reflex bow made from a composite of wood and horn is invented in N Mesopotamia.

c.2500 BC Royal burials at Ur contain lavishly decorated musical instruments.

c.2500 BC Vultures Steele is carved to commemorate the victories of the Sumerian king Eannatum of Lagash in Mesopotamia.

2350 BC Earliest-known law code is compiled for Urukagina, the Sumerian king of Lagash in S Mesopotamia.

c.2300 BC First houses with mains drainage are built in Indus valley cities.

c.2300 BC An as-yet-undeciphered script is developed in the Indus valley.

c.2225 BC Stone victory steele is carved to commemorate the military success of of the Akkadian king Naramsin.

c.2130 BC Stone statues of King Gudea of Lagash mark a brief revival of Sumerian art.

c.2100 BC Mathematicians in Mesopotamia divide a circle into 360 degrees in accordance with their 60-based number system.

ASIA AND AUSTRALASIA

2000 BC **c.2000 BC** Start of the Bronze Age in China and SE Asia.

c.1994–1600 BC Xia dynasty establishes central control over city-states in N China.

c.1900 BC Start of the decline of the Indus valley civilization.

c.1900 BC Having taken over several Mesopotamian cities, the Amorites found a new dynasty in Babylonia.

c.1792–1750 BC King Hammurabi of Babylonia extends Amorite control over all Mesopotamia.

c.1650 BC Hittites settle in Asia Minor and establish a capital at Hattusas.

c.1600 BC Chariots are introduced to China from central Asia.

c.1600 BC Start of Polynesian expansion by boat E from NE New Guinea.

c.1600 BC Aryan peoples begin migrating into the Indus valley region.

c.1600 BC Beginning of the Shang dynasty in China.

c.1595 BC Hittites sack Babylonia and establish temporary control in Mesopotamia.

1530 BC Kassites from present-day NW Iran invade Mesopotamia and take over Hammurabi's empire.

1500 BC **c.1500 BC** Sabaeans establish a state in present-day Yemen, SW Arabia.

c.1480 BC Hurrians in N Syria unite to create the kingdom of Mitanni.

c. 1400 BC Kassites from present-day NW Iran overthrow the Amorites and establish control in Mesopotamia.

c.1350 BC Hittites conquer the Mitanni kingdom; the Hittite empire reaches its greatest extent under King Suppiluliumas (r.c.1375–1335 BC).

c.1300 BC Emergence of the first Assyrian Empire in present-day S Syria.

c.1288 BC Battle of Kadesh in present-day Syria between the Egyptians and Hittites establishes the frontier between their empires.

c.1200 BC Hittite empire collapses under attacks from the Sea Peoples and the Assyrians.

1155 BC Kassites are conquered by the Elamites, who extend their empire into S Mesopotamia.

c.1100 BC Rise of Phoenician city-states in present-day Lebanon, Palestine and Israel.

c.1100 BC Jews establish the kingdom of Israel in Palestine.

1076 BC First Assyrian Empire reaches its greatest extent under King Tiglathpileser I (r.c.1115–1077 BC).

c.1050 BC End of the Shang dynasty in China; start of the Zhou dynasty.

1000 BC **c.1000 BC** Polynesian expansion across the Pacific Ocean reaches Samoa and Tonga.

c.970 BC Solomon (r.c.970–922 BC) succeeds David (r.c.1010–970 BC) as king of Israel.

c.900 BC Kingdom of Urartu is founded in present-day Armenia.

c.883 BC Neo-Assyrian Empire is established by Ashurnasirpal II (r.c.883–859 BC).

771 BC Western capital of the Chinese Zhou emperors is sacked by warrior nomads.

722 BC Collapse of central control in China; Zhou emperors rule in name only; start of the Spring and Autumn period; rival states emerge.

c. 650 BC Scythian peoples begin raiding the Middle East.

627 BC Under Chaldean rulers, the Neo-Babylonian kingdom breaks away from the Assyrian Empire, which goes into decline.

605 BC Medes and Neo-Babylonians under King Nebuchadnezzar II (d.562 BC) defeat the Egyptians at the Battle of Carchemish.

c.600 BC Start of the Iron Age in China and SE Asia.

c.587 BC Neo-Babylonian empire conquers Jerusalem and destroys the Temple.

550 BC Cyrus II (the Great) (c.585–529 BC) of Persia establishes the Persian Achaemenid dynasty.

550 BC Zoroastrianism becomes the state religion of the Persian empire.

546 BC Persians conquer the Greek cities in Asia Minor.

545 BC King Bimbisara of Magadha in the Ganges valley of India initiates a policy of expansion.

538 BC Persians capture Babylonia, which is subsumed into the Achaemenid Empire.

500 BC **499–494 BC** Greek-speaking cities in W Asia Minor revolt against Persian overlordship; Athens and Sparta assist but the revolt is crushed.

c.460 BC State of Qin in W China is partitioned; end of the Spring and Autumn period.

449 BC Peace treaty signed between Athens and Persia.

AFRICA

c.2000 BC Egyptians conquer N Nubia.

c.1900 BC Egyptians establish a series of fortresses around the second cataract of the Nile to protect against raids by Nubians from Kush (present-day Sudan).

c.1786 BC End of the Middle Kingdom; Egypt falls into disarray; start of the Second Intermediate Period (c.1786–1567 BC).

c.1700 BC Hyksos peoples from Palestine introduce horses into Egypt.

c.1674 BC Hyksos peoples establish control of the Nile delta region and dominate the Second Intermediate Period.

c.1567 BC Pharaoh Ahmose unites Egyptians and expels the Hyksos; end of the Second Intermediate Period; start of the New Kingdom (c.1567–1085 BC).

c.1500 BC Egypt regains control of N Nubia.

c.1490 BC Queen Hatshepsut of Egypt (r.c.1503–1482 BC) sends expeditions to Punt (present-day Somalia).

c.1480 BC Following victory at the Battle of Megiddo, Egypt conquers the city-states of present-day Lebanon and Israel; beginning of the Egyptian empire.

c.1450 BC Egyptians establish the fortified town of Napata in central Nubia, near the fourth cataract of the River Nile.

c.1360 BC Pharaoh Akhenaten (r.c.1379–1362 BC) unsuccessfully tries to replace traditional Egyptian religion with sun-worship.

c.1190 BC Sea Peoples attack Egypt, but are defeated by pharaoh Ramses III (r.c.1194–1163 BC).

c.1085 BC End of the New Kingdom in Egypt; end of the Egyptian empire; start of the Third Intermediate Period (c.1085–656 BC).

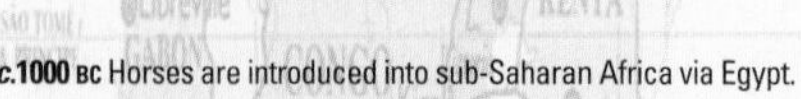

c.1000 BC Horses are introduced into sub-Saharan Africa via Egypt.

c.900 BC Nubian peoples establish Kush (capital Napata) as an independent state in present-day Sudan.

814 BC Traditional date for the founding of the city of Carthage, near present-day Tunis, by Phoenicians from the city of Tyre.

727 BC King Piankhi of Kush completes his conquest of Egypt and establishes the Kushite dynasty.

671 BC Kushite dynasty overthrown by Assyrian conquest of Egypt.

664 BC King Psamtek I establishes a Saite dynasty in N Egypt under Assyrian overlordship.

c.620 BC Greek traders establish the port of Naucratis in the Nile delta.

c.600 BC Beginnings of Nok culture in the River Niger valley.

c.600 BC Phoenician seafarers circumnavigate Africa.

c.600 BC Saite dynasty sacks Napata; shortly afterwards the capital of Kush moves to Meroë.

c.580 BC First African production of iron takes place in Meroë.

c.550 BC Kushite kingdom is extended S to present-day Khartoum.

525 BC Persians conquer Egypt.

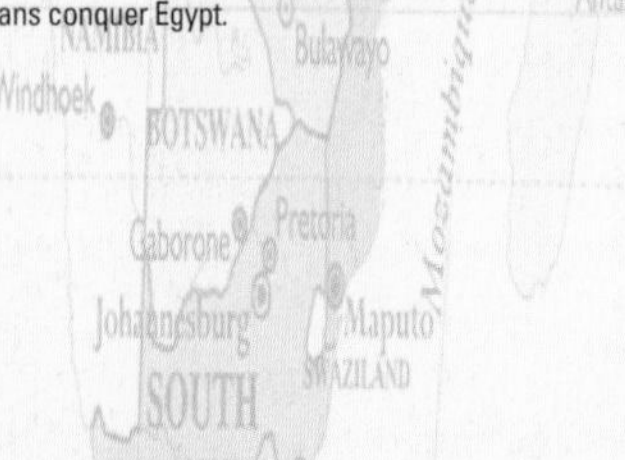

c.500 BC Peoples from SW Arabia settle in Ethiopia.

c.500 BC Iron-working techniques reach W Africa.

480 BC Carthaginians under Hamilcar invade Sicily in support of Phoenician colonies on the island; they are defeated by Greek forces led by Gelon of Syracuse.

EUROPE

c.2000 BC Farming cultures of SE Europe collapse, perhaps because of population movements.

c.2000 BC Rise of Urnfield culture in E central Europe.

c.2000 BC Greek-speakers migrate into Greece from the N.

c.2000 BC Start of Old Palace period of Minoan civilization in Crete.

c.1900 BC Large sarsen stones are added to Stonehenge in England.

c.1650 BC Mycenaean warlords establish control of Greek mainland and engage in long-distance trade with central and N Europe.

c.1620 BC Massive eruption of the Thíra volcano buries the city of Acrotiri on the island of Thíra.

c.1600 BC Cretan palaces are destroyed then rebuilt; start of the New Palace period of Minoan civilization.

c.1500–c.1200 BC Spread of Urnfield culture to Germany and Italy.

c.1450–1375 bc Mycenaeans conquer Crete; Minoan palaces are sacked.

c.1225 BC Legendary Trojan War ends with the capture of Troy by Greeks.

c.1200 BC Citadel at Mycenae is sacked; end of the Mycenaean civilization.

c.1100 BC Iron is first used in SE Europe and Italy.

c.1100 BC Etruscan peoples migrate into N Italy.

c.1050 BC Start of first period of Greek migration to Aegean islands and W coast of Asia Minor.

c.1000 BC Start of the Iron Age in S and central Europe.

c.900 BC Etruscan civilization emerges in N Italy.

c.800 BC Establishment of a town near salt and iron ore mines at Halstatt, Austria.

776 BC Traditional date for the founding of the Olympic Games.

753 BC Traditional date for the founding of Rome by Romulus and Remus.

c.750 BC Rise of city-states in mainland Greece.

734 BC Greek settlers found the city of Syracuse in Sicily.

730–710 BC City-state of Sparta in Greece conquers neighbouring Messenia.

669 BC Defeat by rival city-state Argos and revolt of subjugated Messenians (helots) causes militarization of Spartan society.

c.650 BC Greek colonies are established by the Black Sea.

621 BC Draco introduces a strict (hence draconian) law code in the Greek city-state of Athens.

c.600 BC Rome is conquered by the Etruscans.

600 BC Greek traders establish a colony at Massilia, S France.

594 BC Solon (c.639–c.559 BC) begins reforms in Athens.

c.580 BC Phoenicians establish colonies in W Sicily.

540 BC A Greek fleet is defeated by an alliance of Etruscans and Carthaginians near Corsica.

512 BC Persian armies invade Europe and occupy NE Greece.

510 BC Tarquin Superbus, last of the Etruscan kings of Rome, is expelled; start of Roman Republic.

507 BC Reforms of Cleisthenes mark beginnings of Athenian democracy.

490 BC Persians under Darius I (r.521–486 BC) invade Greece, but are defeated by Athens and Sparta at the Battle of Marathon.

480 BC Persians under Xerxes (r.486–465 BC) invade Greece and sack Athens after the Battle of Thermopylae; they are defeated by a Greek fleet at the Battle of Salamis.

THE AMERICAS

*c.*2000 BC Establishment of irrigated farming villages in coastal Peru, with terracing on mountainsides; start of Initial Period of South American history.

*c.*2000 BC People in present-day E USA first make pottery.

*c.*1800 BC People in Peru first make pottery.

*c.*1700 BC Ritual centre is established at Poverty Point, Louisiana (in present-day USA).

1500 BC Start of the Formative period in Mesoamerican history; beginnings of Olmec civilization on Mexico's Gulf coast.

*c.*1200 BC End of the Initial period in South American history; start of Early Horizon period; beginnings of Chavín culture in Andes region.

*c.*1150 BC Town of San Lorenzo becomes the Olmec political and ritual centre.

*c.*1000 BC Beginning of Adena culture in Ohio valley, present-day USA; it is also known as Early Woodland culture.

*c.*1000 BC Cultivation of maize is introduced to present-day SW USA from Mexico.

*c.*900 BC Olmec capital San Lorenzo, on Gulf coast of Mexico, is destroyed by warfare; the town of La Venta becomes the new political centre of the region.

*c.*850 BC Emergence of Zapotec civilization around the town of San Jose Mogote in the Oaxaca valley region of Mexico.

*c.*850 BC Temple centre at Chavín de Huántar is established in Peru.

*c.*700 BC Abandonment of the ritual centre at Poverty Point, Louisiana, marks the end of the Archaic period in North American history.

*c.*600 BC Mayan people start the construction of the city of Tikal in present-day Guatemala.

*c.*500 BC Emergence of Paracas culture in S Peru.

*c.*500 BC Zapotecs build a new ritual and political centre at Monte Albán.

SCIENCE AND THE ARTS

*c.*2000 BC Egyptian scribes develop their cursive hieratic script. 2000 BC

*c.*2000 BC Minoans in Crete develop a pictographic writing system.

*c.*2000 BC Carved statue menhirs are erected in S France and N Italy.

*c.*1900 BC Earliest-known copy of the Epic of Gilgamesh is written down in Babylon, Mesopotamia.

*c.*1800 BC Horse-drawn, two-wheeled war chariot is invented on the SW fringes of the Eurasian steppes.

*c.*1780 BC Law code of King Hammurabi of Babylon is written down and publicized throughout his empire.

*c.*1700 BC Earliest-known Chinese script is used to pose questions on oracle bones thrown into a fire.

*c.*1600 BC Minoans in Crete begin to use the as-yet-undeciphered Linear A script.

*c.*1600 BC Hittites in Asia Minor develop the first iron-making techniques; the invention remains a Hittite "secret weapon" for several centuries.

*c.*1500 BC Earliest-known alphabet is devised in the city of Ugarit in present-day Syria.

*c.*1500 BC Mycenaeans build beehive tombs in Greece.

*c.*1500 BC Earliest-known glass vessels are buried in an Egyptian pharaoh's tomb.

*c.*1400 BC Mycenaeans in Crete begin to use Linear B script to write the Greek language. 1500 BC

1323 BC Pharaoh Tutankhamun (b.1341 BC) is buried in the Valley of the Kings near Luxor in Egypt.

*c.*1250 BC Rock-cut temple at Abu Simbel is constructed on the orders of pharaoh Ramses II (r.1290–1224 BC).

*c.*1200 BC Egyptian capital Memphis is the world's largest city with a population of up to one million.

*c.*1200 BC The *Vedas*, ancient and most sacred writings of Hinduism, are composed by the Aryan invaders of India.

*c.*1200 BC Start of the Iron Age in the Middle East – the breakup of the Hittite empire ends their monopoly on iron production.

*c.*1100 BC An alphabet is developed by Phoenicians in present-day Lebanon.

*c.*1000 BC Developments in Egyptian writing produce demotic script. 1000 BC

*c.*900 BC First Geometric-style pottery is produced in Athens.

*c.*900 BC Peoples of the Eurasian steppes invent the saddle and develop horse-archer cavalry.

*c.*900 BC *Brahmanas* and *Aranyakas*, ancient writings of Hinduism, are composed in India.

*c.*800 BC Latest date for the introduction of the Phoenician alphabet to Greece.

*c.*750 BC *Illiad* and *Odyssey* are written down in their final form, supposedly by the poet Homer.

*c.*730–*c.*680 BC Orientalizing period of Greek art.

*c.*720 BC First black-figure pottery is produced in Athens.

*c.*700 BC Start of the Halstatt period of Celtic art.

*c.*700 BC Coinage is invented in Greek colonies in SW Asia Minor.

*c.*700 BC Etruscans adopt the Greek alphabet.

*c.*600 BC Development in present-day Mexico of Zapotec pictograph writing.

*c.*600 BC *Upanishads*, texts of Hinduism, are compiled in India.

585 BC Thales of Miletus (636–546 BC) predicts an eclipse of the Sun; this traditionally marks the beginning of Greek philosophy.

*c.*575 BC Etruscan engineers dig the Cloaca Maxima sewer in Rome.

*c.*570 BC Death of the Greek poet Sappho.

*c.*563 BC Birth of Siddhartha Gautama (d.483 BC) – the Buddha.

*c.*560 BC Death of Aesop (b.*c.*620 BC), reputed author of animal fables.

*c.*557 BC Indian teacher Mahavira (*c.*599–527 BC) develops the philosophy of Jainism.

*c.*551 BC Birth of the philosopher Confucius (d.479 BC) in China.

*c.*550 BC Method for mass-producing cast iron is invented in China.

531 BC Death of the Chinese philosopher Lao Tzu (b.604 BC), the founder of Taoism.

*c.*530 BC Red-figure pottery replaces black-figure pottery at Athens.

*c.*500 BC First Chinese coins are manufactured, in the shapes of miniature tools. 500 BC

*c.*430 BC Earliest-known woven wool carpet is buried with a Scythian chief in S Siberia.

*c.*425 BC Greek philosopher Democritus (460–370 BC) theorizes that all matter is made of very small atoms.

423 BC Greek astronomer Meton proposes inserting extra months into a 19-year cycle to align the calendar.

ASIA AND AUSTRALASIA

c.420 BC Nabataeans establish a kingdom with its capital at Petra in present-day Jordan.

c.403 BC Start of Warring States period in China as rival states battle for overall control.

400 BC **c.400 BC** The S Indian kingdoms of the Cholas and the Pandyas are established.

334 BC Alexander III (the Great) (356–323 BC) invades Persian empire, defeats Darius III (380–330 BC) and gains control of Asia Minor.

333 BC Alexander cuts the legendary Gordian knot, and defeats the Persians at the Battle of Issus on the N border of Syria.

331 BC Victory over the Persians at the Battle of Gaugamela gives Alexander control of Mesopotamia.

330 BC Alexander's troops burn the Persian royal palace at Persepolis; Darius is murdered by his bodyguard; end of the Persian empire.

329 BC Alexander invades Bactria and Sogdiana; he founds cities and attempts to establish control over local rulers.

327 BC Alexander crosses Hindu Kush mountains, invades NW India and defeats King Poros at Battle of Hydaspes.

325 BC Alexander leads his army back to Persia.

323 BC Alexander dies in Babylon.

321 BC Chandragupta (d.297 BC) takes over kingdom of Magadha in N India; start of Mauryan empire.

312 BC Seleucus I (d.281 BC) establishes control of Asia Minor, Persia and Alexander's E conquests; start of Seleucid empire.

303 BC Seleucus loses control of Indus valley region and present-day S Afghanistan to Mauryan empire.

300 BC **c.300 BC** Settlers from Korea introduce agriculture into Japan.

c.280 BC King Bindusara (r.298–c.270 BC) extends the Mauryan empire into central India.

c.260 BC King Eumenes (r.263–241 BC) establishes Pergamum in S Asia Minor as an independent kingdom.

256 BC Sickened by the excesses of warfare, King Ashoka (r.c.272–232 BC) declares Buddhism to be the state religion of the Mauryan empire.

256 BC Qin dynasty begins the overthrow of the Zhou dynasty in China.

c.250 BC Diodotus, ruler of Bactria, breaks away from the Seleucid empire.

c.250 BC Emergence of Theravada (Hinayana) Buddhism in S India.

248 BC Parthian leader Arsaces I revolts against Seleucid rule in NE Persia; beginnings of the Parthian empire.

238 BC King Attalus I of Pergamum defeats the Galatian Celts in Asia Minor.

221 BC Qin king Qin Shihuangdi (259–210 BC) completes the conquest of other Chinese states and declares himself emperor of China.

210 BC Death of Chinese emperor leads to collapse of central power and civil wars.

c.210 BC Seleucids make unsuccessful attempt to regain control of Bactria and N India.

c.210 BC Emergence of Mahayana Buddhism in N India.

c.209 BC Nomadic Hun tribes (known to the Chinese as Xiongnu) form a confederation to the N and W of China.

206 BC Liu Bang declares himself emperor of China; start of Han dynasty.

200 BC **190 BC** Artaxiad I establishes the independent Kingdom of Armenia.

187 BC Collapse of the Mauryan empire in India; in the River Ganges valley region the Sunga dynasty seizes control.

171 BC Revolt by Eucratides in Bactria establishes rival Indo-Greek kingdoms in NW India.

AFRICA

c.470 BC Carthaginians under Hanno explore W African coast.

460–454 BC Athens sends an expedition to support an Egyptian revolt against the Persians; the Greek troops are defeated in battle and wiped out.

c.400 BC Start of migration E and S by iron-working Bantu farmers from W Africa.

332 BC Alexander III (the Great) invades Egypt, visits the oracle of Ammon at Siwa and founds the city of Alexandria.

304 BC Ptolemy I (d.283 BC) establishes control over Egypt; start of Ptolemaic period.

295 BC Independent kingdom of Meroë is established in present-day Sudan.

274–217 BC Four wars are fought between Ptolemaic Egypt and Seleucid Persia for control of Palestine.

256 BC Romans invade North Africa and march on Carthage.

255 BC Spartan-trained Carthaginian troops crush the Roman invaders.

c.250 BC Dromedaries (one-humped camels) are introduced into Egypt.

204 BC Roman general Scipio Africanus Major (236–183 BC) invades Africa.

201 BC Scipio defeats the Carthaginians at the Battle of Zama S of Carthage; end of the Second Punic War.

168 BC Seleucid king Antiochus IV (r.175–164 BC) invades Egypt, but retreats after being intimidated by a Roman envoy.

150 BC A Carthaginian army is wiped out in battle against the forces of King Masinissa (238–149 BC) of neighbouring Numidia.

149 BC Romans lay siege to Carthage; start of the Third Punic War.

EUROPE

479 BC Persians are defeated at Plataea and driven from Greece.

477 BC Foundation of Delian League; start of Athenian empire under Cimon's leadership.

461 BC Pericles (490–429 BC) leads democratic revolution in Athens.

461–451 BC War is fought between Athens and Sparta.

445 BC Athens and Sparta sign the Thirty Year Peace agreement.

431 BC Start of Peloponnesian War between Athens and Sparta.

425–424 BC Sparta and its ally Thebes win victories against Athens.

421 BC Peace of Nicias between Athens and Sparta fails to end hostilities.

415–413 BC Athenian naval expedition to capture Sicily ends in defeat.

411 BC Sparta makes an alliance with Persia against Athens.

411 BC Council of Four Hundred takes control in Athens.

405 BC Persia destroys the Athenian fleet at Battle of Aegospotami.

404 BC Athens surrenders to Sparta; end of Peloponnesian War.

396 BC Start of the Corinthian War, in which Sparta fights against Athens and Corinth allied with Persia.

396 BC Romans capture the Etruscan city of Veii.

390 BC Rome is sacked during a Celtic raid into central Italy.

386 BC King's Peace ends the Corinthian War; Persia regains control of the Greek cities in Asia Minor.

371 BC Thebes allied with Athens defeats Sparta at Battle of Leuctra; end of Spartan power; Thebes becomes the dominant city-state in Greece.

359 BC Philip II (382–336 BC) becomes king of Macedon.

355 BC Athenian orator Demosthenes (384–322 BC) denounces the growing power of Philip II of Macedon.

343 BC Rome fights the First Samnite War.

340 BC Athenians declare war on Philip.

338 BC Victory against Athens at the Battle of Chaeronea establishes Philip II of Macedon as sole ruler of Greece; end of independent Greek city-states.

336 BC Philip dies during an attempted invasion of Persia; he is succeeded by his son Alexander III (the Great).

327–304 BC During the Second Samnite War, Roman control expands into central Italy.

323 BC Start of power struggle between various contending successors (the Diadochi) to Alexander III (the Great).

295 BC Romans defeat an Etruscan/Samnite confederation at the Battle of Sentinum.

280 BC King Pyrrhus of Epirus (c.319–272 BC) sends troops to Italy to help the Greek-speaking cities resist Roman expansion.

279 BC Celts pillage the sacred Greek shrine at Delphi.

275 BC Pyrrhus withdraws his support; S Italy falls under Roman control.

264 BC First Punic War (between Rome and Carthage) breaks out over Roman intervention in Sicily.

260 BC First Roman naval battle (against the Carthaginians at Mylae) results in victory.

241 BC Roman naval victory off the Aegates Islands ends the First Punic War; Rome gains Sicily.

238 BC Hamilcar Barca (d.228 BC) revives Carthaginian power in E Spain.

237 BC Rome conquers Sardinia and Corsica from the Carthaginians.

225 BC Romans defeat the Celts at Battle of Telamon in N Italy.

219 BC Romans gain control of E coastline of the Adriatic Sea.

218 BC Carthaginians from Spain under Hannibal (247–183 BC) invade Italy by crossing the Alps; start of the Second Punic War.

217 BC Hannibal defeats the Romans at Battle of Lake Trasimene.

216 BC Massive victory over the Romans at the Battle of Cannae gives Hannibal control of S Italy.

211 BC Hannibal makes unsuccessful attempt to capture city of Rome.

211–206 BC Roman victories bring much of Spain under Roman control.

202 BC Rome gains Spain at the end of the Second Punic War.

197 BC Roman victory at the Battle of Cynoscephalae ends the Second Macedonian War (200–197 BC).

196 BC Seleucid king Antiochus III (r.223–187 BC) occupies NW Greece.

191 BC Roman victory at the Battle of Thermopylae drives the Seleucids from Europe.

THE AMERICAS

c.400 BC Start of Nazca culture in coastal S Peru.

c.400 BC Sack of the Olmec capital La Venta and collapse of Olmec power; start of Late Formative period in Mesoamerican history.

c.300 BC Domestication in present-day E USA of knotweed, maygrass and little barley.

c.300 BC Maya build cities in the lowland region of Peten in Guatemala.

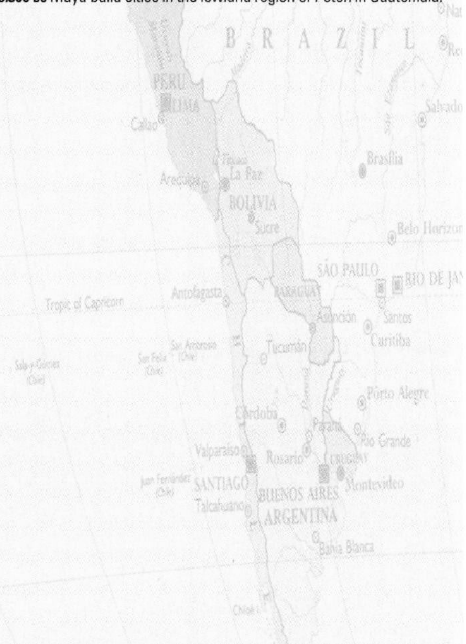

c.200 BC Start of Hopewell culture in the Ohio valley region of present-day USA; it is also known as Middle Woodland culture.

c.200 BC Emergence of the Zapotec state in present-day Mexico.

c.200 BC Decline of the ritual centre at Chavín de Huántar.

SCIENCE AND TECHNOLOGY

c.400 BC Horse-collar is invented in China.

c.400 BC Crossbow is invented in China.

335 BC Greek scientist and philosopher Aristotle (384–322 BC) founds the Lyceum in Athens.

c.325 BC Indian mathematicians add a symbol for zero to their numerals 1–9 to create a decimal positional number system.

c.325–300 BC Influenced by Alexandria, many Greek cities are built (or existing ones rebuilt) on a grid pattern.

c.310 BC First Roman aqueduct, the Aqua Appia, is completed.

c.300 BC Museum and Great Library are founded at Alexandria, Egypt.

c.290 BC Greek mathematician Euclid (*c.*330–260 BC) publishes *The Elements*, which codifies the mathematical knowledge that the Greeks had inherited from the Babylonians and Egyptians.

c.280 BC King Ptolemy II (r.284–246 BC) of Egypt completes a canal between the Mediterranean Sea and the Red Sea and builds a lighthouse at Alexandria.

c.275 BC Greek astronomer Aristarchus (*c.*310–230 BC) of Samos proposes that the Earth orbits the Sun.

c.260 BC Roman naval architects invent the *corvus* – a weighted gangplank for boarding enemy ships in battle.

c.240 BC Greek astronomer Eratosthenes (*c.*276–194 BC) of Cyrene calculates the tilt of the Earth's axis.

238 BC Ptolemy II orders the length of the year in the Egyptian calendar revised from 365 days to 365.25 days.

c.214 BC Chinese emperor Qin Shihuangdi orders existing scattered fortifications to be joined together to make the Great Wall.

212 BC Greek mathematician and engineer Archimedes (b. 287 BC) is killed during the Roman attack on Syracuse in Sicily.

193 BC Newly invented concrete is used to build Porticus Aemilia, Rome.

c.130 BC Greek astronomer Hipparchus (d.127 BC) discovers the precession of the equinoxes.

119 BC Iron-making and salt production become state monopolies in China.

ARTS AND HUMANITIES

500 BC Death of the Greek philosopher Pythagoras (b.*c.*580 BC).

c.490 BC Multicoloured enamelled bricks are used to decorate the palace of Darius I at Susa.

c.490 BC Start of the Classical period of Greek art.

476 BC Greek poet Pindar (522–438 BC) visits Sicily at the invitation of the tyrant Hiero I of Syracuse.

c.475 BC Bronze statue of a *Charioteer* (from Delphi) is cast in Greece.

c.458 BC Greek dramatist Aeschylus (525–456 BC) completes *Oresteia.*

450 BC Greek philosopher Xeno publishes his logical paradoxes.

c.445–438 BC Parthenon in Athens is rebuilt under the direction of the sculptor Phidias (490–430 BC).

430 BC Greek dramatist Sophocles (496–406 BC) writes *Oedipus Rex.*

425 BC Greek historian Herodotus (b. *c.*485 BC) dies at Thurii in S Italy.

415 BC Greek dramatist Euripides (480–406 BC) writes *Trojan Women.*

405 BC Greek dramatist Aristophanes (448–380 BC) writes *Frogs.*

399 BC Greek philosopher Socrates (b.469 BC) is condemned to commit suicide by drinking hemlock having been found guilty of corrupting Athenian youth. 400 BC

395 BC Greek historian Thucydides (460–400 BC) publishes *History of the Peloponnesian War.*

387 BC Greek philosopher Plato (427–347 BC) founds his Academy at Athens.

377 BC Death of Hippocrates of Cos (b.460 BC), who is considered to be the father of western medicine.

c.350 BC Greek theatre at Epidaurus is built.

c.330 BC Start of the Hellenistic period in European and W Asian art.

c. 330 BC Chinese philosopher Mencius (Mengzi) (c.372–289 bc) expands and develops the ideas of Confucius.

c.320 BC Nabataeans construct the first of the monumental rock-cut tombs at Petra.

c.315–c.305 BC Menander (342–292 BC) writes plays in the New Comedy style in Athens.

307 BC Epicurus (341–270 BC) founds a school of philosophy in Athens.

300 BC Zeno of Citium (*c.*334–*c.*262 BC) founds the Stoic school of philosophy, which meets under a stoa (portico) in Athens. 300 BC

c.250 BC Development in present-day Mexico of Mayan hieroglyphs.

241 BC First play in Latin (translated from a Greek original) is performed in Rome.

c.240 BC Ashoka builds the Great Stupa at Sanchi, India.

c.220 BC Roman dramatist Plautus (*c.*254–184 BC) completes his first comedy.

c.220 BC Work starts on the construction of the 7000-strong terracotta army that is to be buried alongside the Qin emperor of China, Qin Shihuangdi.

204 BC Poet Ennius (239–169 BC), author of the *Annals*, is brought to Rome by Cato the Elder (234–149 BC).

202 BC Fabius Pictor publishes the first history of Rome (in Greek).

c.200 BC Greek influence produces the Gandaharan art style in NW India. 200 BC

c.200 BC Earliest of the Dead Sea Scrolls is written.

196 BC Tri-lingual Rosetta Stone is inscribed in Egypt to record the gratitude of the priests of Memphis to King Ptolemy V.

ASIA AND AUSTRALASIA

171 BC Parthian king Mithridates I (r.171–138 BC) establishes complete independence from the Seleucid empire.

170 BC Nomadic warriors Xiongnu (Huns) drive the Yueh-chi confederation from the steppe N of China.

167 BC Led by Judas Maccabaeus (d.161 BC), the Jews revolt against Seleucid rule.

160 BC Wu Di (d.86 BC) becomes emperor of China and begins a series of campaigns against the Huns.

***c.*150 BC** Nomadic Sakas (related to the Scythians) begin settling in parts of present-day Afghanistan.

141 BC Parthians capture the Seleucid capital; end of Seleucid control of Persia and Mesopotamia.

136 BC Confucianism is adopted as the state ideology in China, largely as a result of the work of the philosopher Dong Zongshu (179–104 BC).

133 BC Kingdom of Pergamum is bequeathed to the Romans by its last king, Attalus III (r.138–133 BC).

111 BC Chinese emperor establishes control over SW China and Annam (present-day N Vietnam).

100 BC **92 BC** First official contact between the Parthian and Roman empires takes place in Mesopotamia.

91 BC Huns inflict a crushing defeat on a Chinese army in central Asia.

90 BC Sakas under Maues capture Taxilla in present-day Pakistan and occupy parts of the Indus valley.

89 BC King Mithridates VI (r.120–63 BC) of Pontus in Asia Minor forms an anti-Roman coalition.

73 BC Fall of Sunga dynasty in India. Kanva dynasty takes control of Magadha, the last remnant of the Mauryan empire.

66–63 BC Roman general Pompey (106–48 BC) conquers the remnants of the Seleucid empire in Asia Minor and Syria.

58 BC Azes I becomes Saka ruler in N India; start of the Vikram era.

57 BC Kingdom of Silla is established in S Korea.

***c.*50 BC** Romans begin trade with India for spices and Chinese silk.

***c.*50 BC** Kushans under Kujula Kadphises emerge as the leaders of the Yueh-chi confederation and begin the takeover of Saka India; start of the Kushan empire.

43 BC Huns make peace with the Chinese empire.

37 BC Herod the Great (73–04 BC) is made King of Judaea by the Romans.

***c.*10 BC** Last of the Indo-Greek kingdoms is overthrown by the Sakas.

***c.*10 BC** Satavahana dynasty replaces the Kanvas in India's Magadha kingdom.

***c.*4 BC** Birth of Jesus Christ in Bethlehem.

AD 1 **AD 9** Regent Wang Mang (33 BC–AD 25) appoints himself emperor of China and begins to make radical reforms; end of the Former Han dynasty.

25 Rebels kill Wang Mang; a Han emperor is restored in China; start of Later Han dynasty.

30 Jesus Christ is crucified outside Jerusalem.

53 Tiridates I (d.75) becomes king of Armenia and founds the Arsacid dynasty.

53–63 Roman general Corbulo (d.67) campaigns unsuccessfully against the Parthians over control of Armenia.

70 Roman legions under General Titus (39–81) sack Jerusalem and destroy the temple while crushing a Jewish revolt.

78 Accession of King Kaniska (d.103) marks the highpoint of the Kushan empire in N India and S central Asia.

90 Chinese troops under General Ban Chao curtail Kushan expansion in central Asia.

***c.*95** Nahapana, the Kushan-appointed Saka satrap (governor) of W India forms an independent state.

97 Chinese military expedition attempts to establish control over the Silk Road to the Middle East; an advance party reaches the Black Sea.

100 ***c.*100** Buddhism spreads to China via central Asia.

106 Romans annex the Nabataean kingdom – the Roman province of Arabia is created.

AFRICA

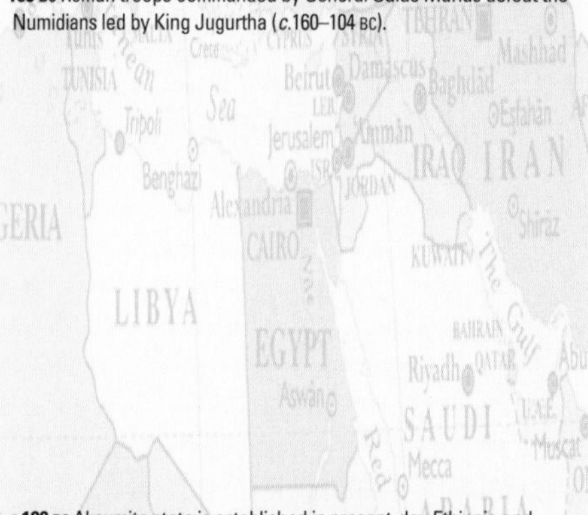

146 BC Carthage falls to the Romans; the city is razed to the ground; end of the Third Punic War.

112 BC War breaks out between Rome and Numidia.

105 BC Roman troops commanded by General Gaius Marius defeat the Numidians led by King Jugurtha (*c.*160–104 BC).

***c.*100 BC** Aksumite state is established in present-day Ethiopia and Eritrea.

***c.*100 BC** Camels are introduced into the Sahara desert.

46 BC Romans found a new city of Carthage on the site of the Phoenician city.

30 BC Following the suicides of Antony and Cleopatra, Egypt becomes a province under Roman control.

***c.*25 BC** Kushites from Meroë invade S Egypt; a Roman reprisal raid sacks Napata.

AD *c.*15 Death of King Natakamani of Meroë (ruled from *c.*15 BC), who built the Lion Temple at Naqa.

40 Roman emperor Caligula annexes Mauretania (present day Algeria and Morocco).

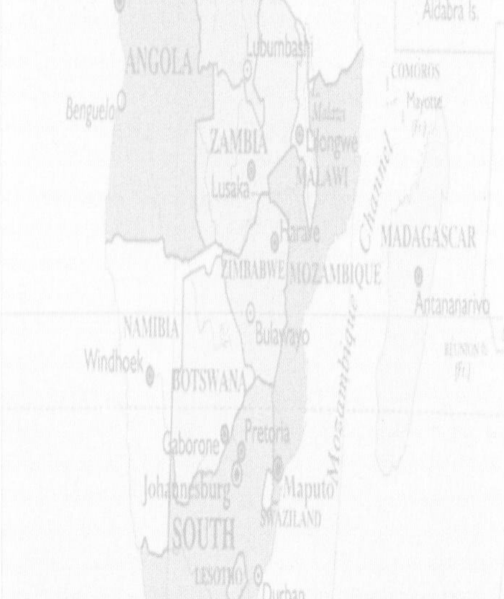

***c.*150** Kingdom of Meroë goes into decline because of trade competition from Aksum.

EUROPE

190 BC Roman victory at Magnesia reduces Seleucid power in Asia Minor.

190–180 BC Roman troops force the Celts out of N Italy.

168 BC Roman victory at the Battle of Pydna ends the Third Macedonian War (171–168 BC).

151 BC While suppressing a revolt in Spain, the Romans massacre 20,000 men in the city of Cauca.

148 BC Macedonia becomes a Roman province.

146 BC Cities in Greece rise against Roman rule; after they are defeated, the city of Corinth is sacked and razed to the ground as punishment.

133 BC Tiberius Gracchus (*c.*163–133 BC) attempts land reforms in Rome.

122 BC Gaius Gracchus (*c.*153–121 BC, brother of Tiberius) makes further attempts at land reform.

121 BC Southern Gaul (France) is incorporated into the Roman Empire.

102–101 BC General Gaius Marius (157–86 BC) defeats the Cimbri and Teutones – Germanic tribes that had invaded S Gaul.

88 BC Mithridates VI of Pontus invades N Greece and liberates Athens from Roman control.

87 BC Gaius Marius declares himself dictator in Rome.

85 BC Roman general Lucius Cornelius Sulla (138–78 BC) makes peace with Mithridates.

82 BC Sulla declares himself dictator; he retires three years later.

73–71 BC Slave uprising in Italy led by Spartacus (d.71 BC).

60 BC Establishment of First Triumvirate – Pompey (106–48 BC), Julius Caesar (100–44 BC) and Crassus (115–53 BC) – to rule Rome.

58–51 BC Roman legions under Caesar conquer Gaul.

55 BC Romans invade Britain, but leave the following year.

53 BC Crassus killed at Battle of Carrhae against the Parthians.

49–47 BC Civil war between Pompey and Caesar results in Pompey's death; Caesar becomes dictator of Rome.

44 BC Caesar is assasinated in Rome.

43 BC Second Triumvirate – Mark Antony (82–30 BC), Lepidus (d. *c.*13 BC) and Octavian (63 BC–14 AD) – established to rule Rome and avenge Caesar's death.

42 BC Caesar's assassins are defeated at Battle of Philippi in Greece.

31 BC Antony and Cleopatra are defeated by Octavian at the sea-battle of Actium; Octavian becomes sole ruler of Rome.

27 BC Octavian takes the name Augustus. This date marks the end of the Roman republic and the beginning of the Principiate (Roman Empire).

AD 14 Roman emperor Augustus dies. His will names his son-in-law Tiberius (42 BC–AD 37) as the next emperor; this establishes the principle of succession for Roman emperors.

37–41 Short reign of Roman emperor Gaius (better known as Caligula, b.12) is marked by extravagance and decadence.

41 Claudius (10–54) becomes Roman emperor.

43 Romans occupy S Britain.

59 Emperor Nero (r.54–68) murders his mother Agrippina (b.15).

60 Boadicea (Boudicca, d.62), queen of the Iceni, leads a short-lived revolt against the Romans in Britain.

64 Great Fire of Rome is blamed on Christians and leads to their first persecution.

68–69 Death of Nero leads to civil war in the Roman Empire. There are four self-proclaimed emperors; Vespasian (9–79) emerges as the victor and founds the Flavian dynasty.

79 Eruption of Mount Vesuvius in S Italy buries the towns of Pompeii and Herculaneum.

79 Titus (39–81) succeeds his father Vespasian as Roman emperor.

81 Domitian (51–96) succeeds his brother Titus as emperor.

82–86 Eastern border of the Roman Empire is established along the rivers Rhine and Danube.

83 Roman control in Britain is extended to S scotland.

96 Domitian is assassinated and Nerva (30–98) is appointed.

98 Trajan (53–117) becomes Roman emperor when Nerva dies.

101 Trajan invades Dacia; he defeats (106) the Dacian king Decebalus; Dacia becomes part of the Roman Empire.

117 Trajan dies and is succeeded as emperor by Hadrian (76–138).

THE AMERICAS

AD *c.*1 Basketmaker culture emerges in present-day SW USA; villages of circular houses are built.

***c.*25** Mochica (Moche) state is established in river valleys along the N coast of Peru.

***c.*50** City of Teotihuacán establishes control of the valley of Mexico; work starts on the construction of the Pyramid of the Sun.

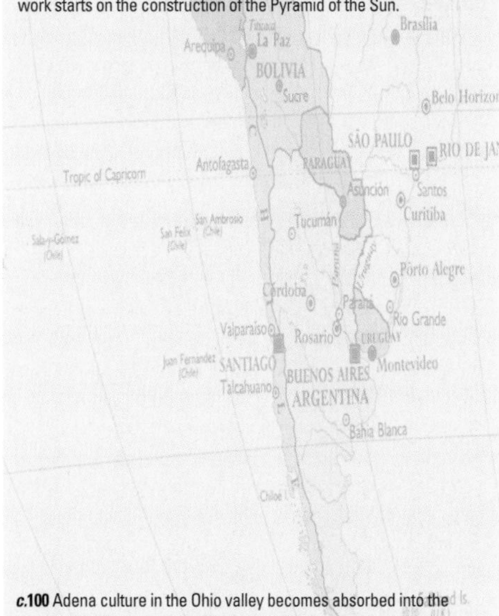

***c.*100** Adena culture in the Ohio valley becomes absorbed into the geographically more extensive Hopewell culture.

***c.*150** End of the Formative period in Mesoamerican history; start of the Classic period.

SCIENCE AND TECHNOLOGY

86 BC Crop rotation is introduced in China.

***c.*50 BC** Roman craftworkers perfect the technique of glass-blowing.

46 BC In Rome, Caesar introduces the Julian calendar, which has 365 days and an extra day every fourth year.

***c.*23 BC** Roman engineer Vitruvius completes *On Architecture*, which later becomes a standard work on construction.

AD *c.*10 Greek geographer Strabo (*c.*63 BC–AD *c.*24) produces a reasonably accurate map of the Roman world.

***c.*39** A wooden ship 71m (233ft) long and 24m (80ft) wide is built on Lake Nemi near Rome for the entertainment of the emperor Gaius (Caligula).

***c.*50** Rome is the world's largest city, with a population of about one million.

***c.*60** Greek engineer Hero of Alexandria (b. *c.*20) experiments with hydraulic machinery and invents a simple steam engine.

***c.*67** Emperor Nero completes the construction of his palace in Rome – the Golden House – on the ruins of the Great Fire.

79 Roman encyclopedist Pliny the Elder (b.23), author of *The Natural History*, dies in the eruption of Mount Vesuvius.

80 Construction of the Colosseum begins in Rome.

***c.*100** Single-wheeled cart or wheelbarrow is invented in China.

***c.*100** Knowledge of the monsoon wind systems of the Indian Ocean becomes widespread, leading to an increase in trade between India and the Arabian Gulf.

ARTS AND HUMANITIES

***c.*190 BC** *Victory of Samothrace* statue is carved in Greece.

***c.*165 BC** Plays of Terence (190–159 BC) become popular in Rome.

124 BC Confucian university is established in China to prepare students for work in the civil service.

***c.*120 BC** *Venus de Milo* statue is carved in Greece.

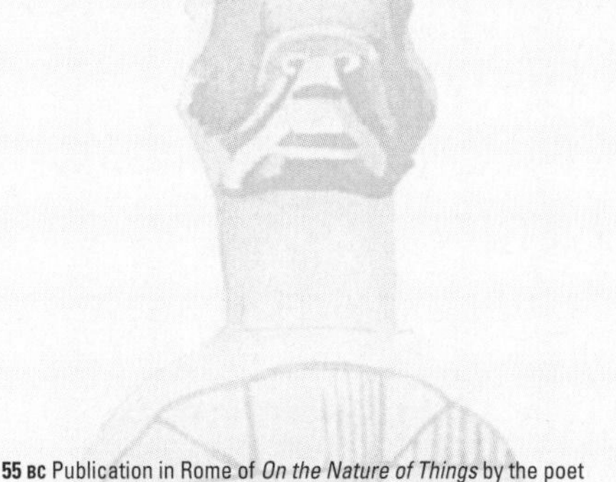

55 BC Publication in Rome of *On the Nature of Things* by the poet and philosopher Lucretius (*c.*95–55 BC). 100 BC

***c.* 50 BC** Great Stupa at Sanchi, India, is enlarged and refurbished by the Sunga dynasty.

43 BC Roman writer and politician Cicero (b.106 BC), author of *On the Republic*, is murdered.

24 BC Roman poet Horace (65–08 BC) publishes the first of his *Odes*.

***c.*25 BC** Pont du Gard aqueduct built at Nîmes, S France.

19 BC Death of the Roman poet Virgil (b.70 BC); *Aeneid* is published posthumously by Emperor Augustus.

AD *c.*3 Roman poet Ovid (43 BC–AD 18) publishes *Metamorphoses*. AD 1

17 Death of the Roman historian Livy (b.59 BC), author of a 142-volume history of Rome entitled *From the Beginning of the City*.

***c.*50** Under Kushan patronage, the Mathura art style develops in N India.

65 Seneca (b.4), the orator, philosopher and tutor of Nero, commits suicide in Rome after being condemned for undue political influence.

66–70 Dead Sea Scrolls are concealed in a cave during the Jewish revolt.

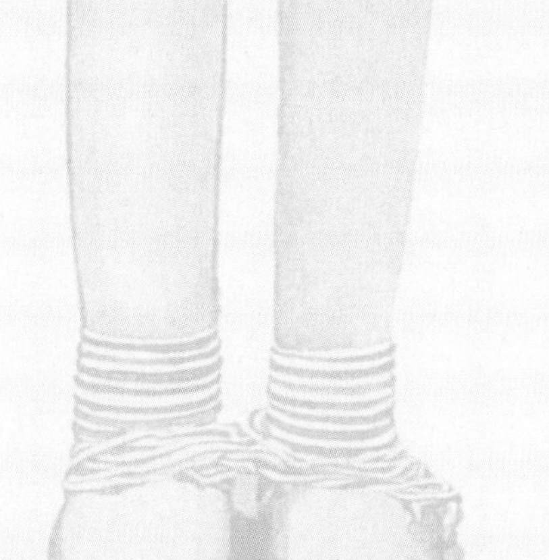

***c.*105** Roman historian Suetonius (*c.*69–140) writes *The Lives of the Caesars*. 100

***c.*110** Roman historian Tacitus (55–120) writes *Annals* and *Histories*.

ASIA AND AUSTRALASIA

114–16 Roman emperor Trajan invades Parthia and occupies Armenia and Mesopotamia – the Roman Empire reaches its greatest extent.

117 Hadrian (76–138) abandons Armenia and Mesopotamia.

***c.*130** Saka state in W India establishes control over Ujain in central India.

132–35 Second Jewish revolt against the Romans takes place.

138 Independent kingdoms of Palmyra in Syria and Elymais in SW Persia attempt a trade alliance to circumvent the Parthian empire.

***c.*150** Huns drive the Chinese out of central Asia.

166 Roman merchants visit China for the first time.

162 Lucius Septimius Severus (146–211) leads a Roman campaign against the Parthians.

184 Yellow Turbans rebellion breaks out in China.

190 Chinese Han emperor is murdered and civil wars ensue.

197–99 Severus invades Parthia and temporarily adds Mesopotamia to the Roman Empire.

200 **220** Civil wars bring the Han dynasty in China to an end; start of the Three Kingdoms (Wei, Wu and Shu) period.

224 King Ardashir (r.*c.*224–41) of Persis, S Persia, takes over the Parthian empire; start of the Sasanian empire.

***c.*235** Sasanians defeat the Kushans near the River Oxus, central Asia.

***c.*240** Kushan empire in India breaks up, local rulers come to power.

244 Sasanians under Shapur I (r.244–72) conquer Armenia.

238 Sasanians conquer Mesopotamia from the Romans.

***c.*250** Chief of the Yamato clan establishes control over central Japan.

253 Sasanians sack the Roman city of Antioch, present-day Syria.

260 Roman emperor Valerian (r.253–60) is captured while campaigning against the Sasanians under Shapur I.

260 Odaenath (d.267) of Palmyra declares his independence from Rome.

267 Zenobia makes herself queen of Palmyra and establishes control over Egypt and much of Asia Minor.

271 Zenobia declares her son to be Roman emperor.

273 Roman legions under Aurelian (*c.*215–75) crush the Palmyrans; Zenobia is taken to Rome in chains.

280 China is reunified under the Western Jin dynasty.

297 Roman legions under Galerius (d.311) defeat the Sasanians; a treaty gives the Sasanians a monopoly over the silk trade with Rome.

300 **311** Huns and other nomad peoples sack the Chinese city of Luoyang.

316 Western Jin emperor is captured by the Huns who occupy N China.

320 Accession of King Chandragupta I at Palipatura (present-day Patna) in India marks the beginning of the Gupta dynasty.

325 Council of Nicaea (in present-day NW Turkey) establishes the basis of Christian belief and denounces the heresy of Arius (*c.*250–336).

***c.*360** King Samudragupta (r.335–76) conquers N and NE India and expands the Gupta empire.

363 Roman emperor Julian is killed in battle against the Sasanians.

369 Japanese empress Jing orders the invasion of Korea.

374 Huns attack the Alans (nomads living on the W bank of the River Volga), who are driven W and in turn attack and defeat the Visigoths.

383 Chinese victory at the Battle of River Fei repulses a Hun invasion of S China.

***c.*395** King Chandragupta II (r. *c.*380–414) conquers W India; the Gupta empire reaches its greatest extent.

400 **420** Fall of the Eastern Jin dynasty (one of the Six Dynasties) in central China; it is replaced by the Former Song dynasty.

***c.*450** Ruan-ruan nomads replace the Huns as the dominant force on the steppes of central Asia.

***c.*450** Steppe nomads the Hepthalites (White Huns) invade N India and occupy the Punjab; they are fought to a standstill by Gupta king Skandagupta.

AFRICA

***c.*200** Bantu peoples reach the E coast of Africa.

249 Bishop Cyprian of Carthage (d.258) leads the Christians during the persecution initiated by the Roman emperor Decius (200–51).

***c.*285** King Aphilas of Aksum invades SW Arabia.

***c.*305** Anthony the Hermit (*c.*250–*c.*355) establishes the tradition of Christian monasticism in Egypt.

343 King Ezana of Aksum is converted to Christianity by missionaries from Egypt.

***c.*350** King Ezana conquers the kingdom of Meroë and sacks the capital city.

***c.*400** Seafaring peoples from Indonesia begin settling on the island of Madagascar off the E coast of Africa.

429 Vandals under Gaeseric cross from Spain to N Africa.

439 Vandals capture the city of Carthage and establish a kingdom.

451 Council of Chalcedon results in the Coptic Christians in Egypt splitting away from the influence of Rome and Constantinople.

EUROPE

121 Hadrian's Wall is built across Britain as the N border of the Roman Empire.

138 Hadrian is succeeded as emperor by Antoninus Pius (86–161), whose reign is regarded as the Golden age of the Roman Empire.

161 Marcus Aurelius (121–80) succeeds Antoninus Pius as Roman emperor.

161 Outbreak of plague devastates the city of Rome.

168 Germanic tribes invade the Roman Empire across the River Danube.

175 Germanic tribes are defeated and expelled from the Empire.

180 Commodus (161–92) becomes emperor on the death of his father Marcus Aurelius.

192 Assassination of Commodus precipitates civil wars between rival emperors for control of the Empire.

197 Severus emerges as sole emperor and founds the Severan dynasty.

211 Severus dies and his sons, Caracalla and Geta, succeed as joint emperors. Caracalla has Geta murdered.

212 Caracalla (118–217) extends Roman citizenship to all free subjects of the Empire.

218–22 Emperor Elagabalus (204–22) introduces sun-worship to Rome, which leads to his assassination.

235 Death of emperor Severus Alexander (b.208) marks the end of the Several dynasty. In the next 50 years there are 36 Roman emperors.

248 Emperor Philip I (r.244–49) holds games to celebrate Rome's 1000th anniversary.

260 Roman emperor Gallienus (r.253–68) defeats the invading Germanic tribe, the Alemanni, near present-day Milan, N Italy.

260–74 Gallic empire (parts of present-day France and Germany) under Postumus and his successors breaks away from Rome.

***c.*260** Goths migrate from Scandinavia to the shores of the Black Sea.

267 Five hundred-ship fleet of Goths and other Germanic tribes raids the coast of Greece and sacks the city of Athens.

274 Aurelian re-establishes Roman control over the Gallic empire.

284 Roman general Diocletian (245–313) makes himself emperor.

293 Diocletian introduces the Tetrarchy, under which the Roman Empire is ruler by two joint emperors (*Augustii*) each assisted by a deputy (*Caesar*).

305 Diocletian's retirement begins a 20-year period of rivalry for control of the Roman Empire.

312 Constantine I (285–337) converts to Christianity and becomes Roman emperor in the W after the Battle of Milvian Bridge near Rome.

313 Edict of Mediolanum (present-day Milan) declares that Christianity is to be tolerated throughout the Roman Empire.

324 Constantine defeats Licinius (*c.*270–325) and becomes sole Roman emperor.

330 Constantine founds Constantinople, on the site of the Greek city of Byzantium, as the E capital of the Roman Empire.

***c.*330** Christianity is proclaimed as the only official religion of the Roman Empire.

337 After the death of Constantine, the Empire is divided between his sons Constans (emperor in the W) and Constantius II (emperor in the E).

350 Constans (b.*c.*323) is killed in battle against the usurper Magnentius in Gaul (present-day France).

353 Constantius II (317–61) re-establishes sole control of the Empire.

360 Emperor Julian (331–63) briefly reintroduces pagan worship.

364 Valentinian I (321–75) and Valens (328–78) become Roman emperors in W and E respectively.

378 Visigoths invade SE Europe and defeat the Romans, led by the emperor Valens, at the Battle of Adrianople.

392 Theodosius (347–95) becomes sole Roman emperor.

395 On the death of Theodosius the Roman Empire is split into W and E parts ruled respectively by his sons Honorius and Arcadius (*c.*377–408).

407 Burgundians establish a kingdom in present-day central and SE France.

409 Vandals and Suevi move into Spain.

410 Goths under Alaric (370–410) sack Rome.

418 Visigoths establish a kingdom in S France.

***c.*420** Angles, Saxons and Jutes begin settling in Britain.

THE AMERICAS

c.200 Warfare breaks out between rival Mayan city-states in the Yucatán region of Mexico.

c.200 City of Teotihuacán establishes an empire than controls most of highland Mexico.

c. 300 City of Teotihuacán establishes control over the highland Mayan cities in present-day Gautemala.

c.300 Lowland Mayan city-state of Tikal conquers neighbouring El Mirador.

c.350 City of Teotihuacán extends its influence over the lowland Mayan cities in the Yucatán region of Mexico.

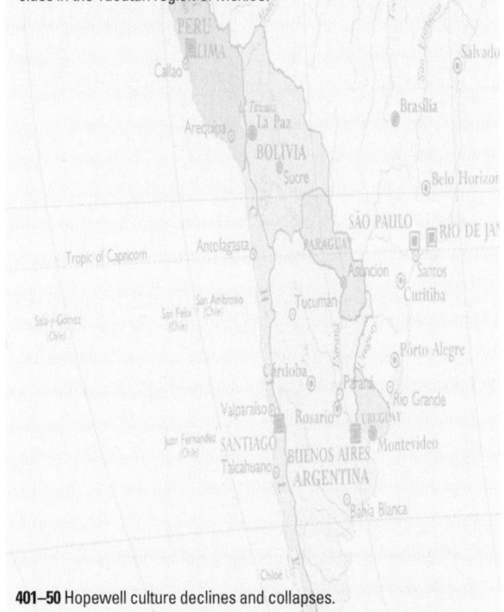

401–50 Hopewell culture declines and collapses.

c.425 Teotihuacán completes its subjugation of the lowland Mayan cities of Tikal, Uaxactun and Becan.

SCIENCE AND TECHNOLOGY

105 Invention of paper is announced to the Chinese court.

c.110 Greek mathematician Menelaus writes *Sphaerica*, a treatise on trigonometry.

c.118 Pantheon is built in Rome with a 43-m (140-ft) concrete dome.

c.150 Roman doctor Galen (129–99) uses dissection and experimentation to establish the function of bodily organs.

c. 160 Greek astronomer Ptolemy (90–168) publishes *The Mathematical Collection* (later known as *The Almagest*).

c.216 Baths of Caracalla in Rome are completed.

c.250 Diophantus of Alexandria establishes algebra as a branch of mathematics and introduces the use of symbols in equations.

c.260 Sasanian royal palace Taq-i-Kisra, containing a 22-m (75-ft) wide arch, is built at Ctesiphon near present-day Baghdad, Iraq.

c.265 Rock-cut reliefs at Bishapur, Persia, celebrate the Sasanian's humiliation of the Roman emperor Valerian.

321 Constantine I introduces the seven-day week into the calendar used throughout the Roman Empire.

c.340 Greek mathematician Pappus of Alexandria explores the geometry of curved surfaces.

c.375 Stirrups are invented in w China, from where they spread to Europe with the AVARS.

c.400 Supposedly rustproof pillar of pure iron is erected in Delhi, India.

415 Philosopher and mathematician Hypatia (b.370) is killed in Alexandria by a Christian mob, who equate her learning with paganism.

c.485 Chinese mathematician Tsu Chung Chi calculates the value of *pi* to an accuracy that is not bettered for a thousand years.

c.499 Indian mathematician Aryabhata (476–550) publishes *Aryabhatiya*, a compendium of scientific knowledge.

ARTS AND HUMANITIES

110 Roman writer Juvenal (55–140) publishes the first of his *Satires*.

112 Trajan's Column is erected in Rome.

114 Death of the historian Ban Zhou (b.45), the leading woman intellectual in China.

120 Death of the Greek writer Plutarch (b.46), author of *The Parallel Lives*.

c.150 Earliest-known inscription in Sanskrit is carved in w India.

c.165 Roman novelist Apuleius (*c.*125–*c.*170) writes the *The Golden Ass*.

172–80 Emperor Marcus Aurelius composes *Meditations*.

c.244 Philosopher Plotinus (205–70) opens a school in Rome where 200
he teaches the ideas of Neoplatonism.

c.250 Prophet Mani (216–76) preaches his new philosophy of Manichaeism in Persia.

341 Ulfilas devises the Gothic alphabet for his translation of the 300
Bible into Gothic.

365 Birth of the Chinese writer and landscape poet Tao Qian (d.427), author of the short story *Peach Tree Spring*.

375 Wall painting in caves at Ajanta, India, mark the flowering of Gupta-period art.

c.380 Ambrose (339–97), bishop of Milan, introduces plainsong into Christian services.

c.385 Jerome (347–420) starts translating the Bible from Greek into Latin (the Vulgate Bible).

c.397 Christian philosopher Augustine of Hippo (354–430) writes *Confessions*.

c.405 Indian poet and dramatist Kalidasa writes *Sakuntala* 400
Recognized at the Gupta court.

413 Traveller monk Faxian returns to China with large numbers of Buddhist texts.

c.425 Galla Placidia (388–450) adorns her mausoleum in Ravenna, Italy, with mosaics.

ASIA AND AUSTRALASIA

479 Former Song dynasty in China is replaced by the Southern Qi dynasty.

484 Hepthalites attack the Sasanian empire, kill King Peroz and occupy parts of E Persia.

***c*.495** Hepthalites invade central India and conquer some Gupta territory.

495 Northern Wei dynasty in N China moves its capital from Datong to Luoyang.

500 ***c*.500** Polynesians settle on Easter Island.

527 Accession of Justinian (483–565) marks the end of the Roman Empire in the E and the start of the Byzantine Empire.

535 Hepthalites invade Gupta territories in India; end of Gupta dynasty.

540 Sasanians under King Khusrau I (the Just) (r.531–79) sack the city of Antioch on the Mediterranean coast in Syria.

***c*.550** Buddhism spreads to Japan.

552 Nomadic Turks under Bumin (r.546–53) win a decisive victory over the Ruan-ruan and establish control across central Asia.

561 Silkworms are smuggled to the Byzantine court from China.

562 Sasanians and Turks in alliance crush the Hepthalites.

***c*.575** Sasanians expel the Aksumites and occupy present-day Yemen.

581 Sui Yang Jian (d.604) becomes emperor in China; start of the Sui dynasty.

589 Through military conquest, the Sui dynasty achieves the reunification of China under a single ruler.

590 Khusrau II(the Victorious) (d.628) becomes Sasanian king with Byzantine military assistance.

600 ***c*.600** Polynesians settle in Hawaii.

604 Prince Shotoku Taishi (574–622) establishes formal principles of government in Japan.

612–15 Sasanians conquer Asia Minor, Syria and Palestine.

618 Tang dynasty is founded by the Sui official Li Yuan.

***c*.620** Ganges valley king Harsha (r.606–47) temporarily unites N India.

622 Muhammad (*c*.570–632) and his followers flee from Mecca to Medina (the Hejira); start of the Islamic calendar.

***c*.625** Srong-brtsan (r.608–50) unifies the Tibetan peoples.

627 Byzantine army sacks the Sasanian capital of Ctesiphon.

630 Chinese establish control over much of central Asia.

630 Muhammad's army marches on Mecca, which surrenders.

632 Death of the prophet Muhammad marks the start of the Arab empire.

636–37 Arab armies under the caliph Omar (r.634–44) conquer Syria and Palestine.

642 Arabs defeat the Sasanians at the Battle of Nihawand and overrun Persia; end of the Sasanian empire.

645 Taika reforms establish central government over all Japan.

656–61 Civil wars are waged for control of the Arab empire during the caliphate of Ali (*c*.600–61); the Umayyad family emerges as the ruling dynasty.

668 Kingdom of Silla unifies most of Korea under its rule.

690 Wu (d.705), the only woman emperor of China, becomes sole ruler.

700 **705** Arab armies carry Islam into Turkistan, central Asia.

710 City of Nara is established as the capital of Japan.

713 Arab expansion to the E reaches the upper Indus valley.

***c*.710** Rise of the city of Srivijaya in Sumatra as an important trade centre.

744 Revolt by the Abbasid family in present-day Iran leads to civil war in the Arab empire.

745 Uighurs establish themselves as the ruling dynasty of the Turks.

AFRICA

468 Combined forces of the E and W Roman Empire make disastrous attempt to invade Vandal kingdom.

***c*.500** Bantu farmers reach Orange River in present-day South Africa.

533 Byzantine armies under General Belisarius (505–65) recapture N Africa from the Vandals.

536 Byzantine authorities close the temple at Philae in Egypt; this marks the end of traditional Egyptian religion.

***c*.543** Ruling warlords of the Ethiopian highlands are converted to Christianity through the efforts of Bishop Frumentius.

***c*.550** Kingdom of Ghana is established in W Africa.

570 Aksumite armies make an unsuccessful attempt to conquer the city of Mecca in W Arabia.

616 Sasanians conquer Egypt.

628 Emperor Heraclius (575–641) restores Byzantine control over Egypt.

639–42 Arab armies conquer Egypt.

648 Byzantine forces temporarily halt Arab expansion in N Africa.

c.650 Traders from Arabia establish the first Islamic settlements on the E coast of Africa.

652 Arab rulers of Egypt agree to respect the existing borders of the Nubian kingdoms.

670 Arab forces move into present-day Tunisia.

697 Arab forces destroy the Byzantine city of Carthage.

702 Aksumites attack the port of Jiddah in present-day Saudi Arabia.

702–11 Arab conquests are extended W along the N African coastline to the Atlantic ocean.

739 Port of Zanzibar on the E coast of Africa is founded by Islamic traders from S Arabia.

***c*.740** Berber peoples in the N Sahara region revolt against Umayyad rule and form independent Islamic kingdoms.

EUROPE

***c*.430** Franks begin settling in N France.

***c*.430** Visigoths take over most of Spain.

434 Attila (406–53) is declared leader of the Huns.

441–48 Huns plunder Balkans until bribed by E Roman emperor to turn W.

451 Huns are defeated at the Battle of Chalons in France.

452 Huns plunder N Italy.

455 Vandals sack Rome.

458 Sicily is captured by the Vandals.

476 Overthrow of Emperor Romulus Augustulus (r.475–76) by Odoacer (433–93) marks end of W Roman Empire.

481 Clovis I (465–511) establishes a Frankish kingdom in France; start of Merovingian dynasty.

491–99 Fiscal and administrative reforms of the emperor Anastasius I (d.518) revive the E Roman Empire.

493 Theodoric (454–526) assassinates Odoacer and establishes an Ostrogoth kingdom in Italy.

498 Clovis I is converted to Christianity.

502 Franks defeat the Alemanni and conquer present-day S Germany.

511 Ostrogoths under Theodoric (454–526) annex Spain.

527 Justinian becomes Roman emperor in Constantinople; start of the Byzantine Empire.

534 Franks under Theudebert I conquer the Burgundian kingdom.

541 Europe's first encounter with smallpox devastates the Mediterranean region.

***c*.540–50** Slav peoples migrate into the Balkans and Greece.

548 Frankish kingdom disintegrates on the death of Theudebert I.

552 Byzantine armies conquer S Spain from the Ostrogoths.

557 Avar nomads invade and settle in Hungary.

558 Clotaire I (497–561) reunites the Frankish kingdom.

568 Lombards invade N Italy and establish a kingdom in the Po valley.

582 Force of Avars and Slavs attacks Athens, Sparta and Corinth.

583 King Leovigild (r.569–86) defeats the Suevi in NW Spain and reunites N and central Spain under Visigoth control.

599 Visigoth king Reccared (r.586–601) converts to Christianity.

626 Combined force of Avars and Sasanians besiege Constantinople.

629 Visigoths drive the Byzantines from S spain.

663 Byzantine emperor Constans II (630–68) leads an army against the Lombards, but retreats to Sicily.

673 Visigoth king Wamba (r.672–81) defeats an Arab fleet near the Straits of Gibraltar.

673–78 Arab armies besiege Constantinople by land and sea.

681 Onogur Huns establish the kingdom of Bulgaria.

687 Victory over dynastic rivals at the Battle of Tertry in N France extends the power of the Frankish king Pepin II (d.714).

711–18 Arab and Berber armies invade and conquer Visigoth Spain.

717–18 Arab armies besiege Constantinople.

732 Frankish armies led by Charles Martel (688–741) defeat the Arabs at the Battle of Tours and confine them S of the Pyrenees mountains.

750 Palace coup makes Pepin III (the Short) (714–68) king of the Franks; end of the Merovingian dynasty.

756 Pepin gives territories in central Italy to the pope; these become the Papal States.

THE AMERICAS

c.500 Settlement is established at Mesa Verde in SE Colorado, present-day USA.

c.500 Mochica state reaches its greatest extent along the lowland coast of Peru.

c.500 Cities of Tiahuanaco and Huari rise to prominence in the Andes highlands of central Peru.

c.600 Mochica state in Peru is absorbed by the city-state of Huari.

c.650 City of Teotihuacán is destroyed by warfare: collapse of the Teotihuacán empire.

682 King Ah-Cacaw becomes ruler of the Mayan city of Tikal.

c.750 Start of the decline of classic Mayan civilization.

c.750 Decline of Huari control in highland Peru.

SCIENCE AND TECHNOLOGY

525 Mathematician Dionysius Exiguus (500–50) begins the practice of dating years using the birth of Jesus Christ as a starting point; beginning of the Christian, Common, or Current Era.

531–37 Church of Hagia Sophia is constructed in Constantinople.

c.600 Earliest-known windmills are used to grind flour in Persia.

c.628 Indian mathematician Brahmagupta (598–665) publishes *The Opening of the Universe.*

c.650 Chinese scholars develop a technique for printing texts from engraved wooden blocks.

c.650 Chinese capital Changan (Xian) is the world's largest city, with a population of about one million.

c.675 Byzantine defenders of Constantinople deploy a new weapon, Greek fire – a type of flamethrower.

685–92 Dome of the Rock mosque (Qubbat al-Sakhrah) is built in Jerusalem.

715 Great Mosque at Damascus is built.

780 Birth of the Islamic mathematician Al-Khwarizmi, who wrote *Calculation with Hindu Numerals* (825), which adopted the Indian 10-digit number system and positional notation.

c.784 First Arab paper factory opens in Baghdad using skills learned from Chinese prisoners taken at the Battle of Talas.

ARTS AND HUMANITIES

438 Law code of Theodosius II (r.408–50) published throughout the Roman Empire; the code is later adopted by many Germanic rulers.

480 Birth of the Italian scholar Boethius (d.524), who translates the works of Aristotle into Latin.

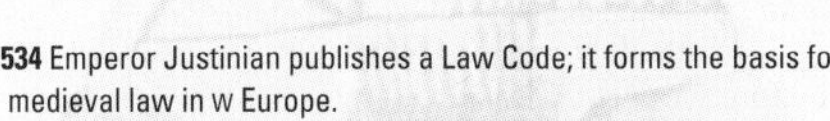

534 Emperor Justinian publishes a Law Code; it forms the basis for medieval law in W Europe. 500

c.550 Byzantine historian Procopius publishes *Secret History.*

c.550 Italian scholar Cassiodorus (490–585) collects and preserves the work of Greek and Latin writers and establishes the practice of monks copying manuscripts.

c.570 Birth of the prophet Muhammad.

c.590 Gregory of Tours (538–94) completes *History of the Franks.*

c.590 Isidore (*c.*560–636), bishop of Seville, begins work on his 20-volume *Etymologies.*

c.600 Pope Gregory (540–604) reforms the use of plainsong in Christian services and is thought to have introduced Gregorian chant.

c.635 Sutras of the Koran are collected and distributed. 600

641 Great Library at Alexandria is destroyed by fire during an Arab attack.

700 Greek language is banned from public documents throughout the Arab empire. 700

726 Iconoclasm movement starts in the Byzantine Empire when emperor Leo III (*c.*750–816) bans the use of figurative images in Christian art.

731 English monk and scholar Bede (673–735) publishes *Ecclesiastical History of the English People.*

c.750 *Book of Kells* illuminated manuscript is produced in Ireland.

ASIA AND AUSTRALASIA

747 Rajputs formally join the Hindu warrior caste.

750 Abbasids defeat the Umayyads at the Battle of Zab and take over as the ruling Islamic dynasty in the Middle East.

c.750 Palla dynasty establishes control over present-day Bangladesh.

751 Combined armies of the Arabs and Turks defeat the Chinese at the Battle of Talas; Tang dynasty control of central Asia is lost.

753 Rashtrakuta dynasty establishes control over W central India.

755–63 Revolt of General An Lushan (703–57) seriously weakens Tang dynasty control of China for the next half century.

762 Abbasids found the city of Baghdad as their new capital.

763 Tibetan power in central Asia reaches its height with the sacking of the Chinese capital of Changan.

794 Capital of Japan moves to Kyoto, start of the Heian period.

800 ***c.*800** Polynesians reach New Zealand.

802 Jayavarman II (*c.*770–850) establishes the kingdom of Angkor in present-day Cambodia.

818 Tang dynasty re-establishes strong central control in China.

823 Arabs conquer Sicily from the Byzantine Empire.

845 Buddhism is banned in China and Confucianism is restored as the state ideology.

849 City-state of Pagan is founded in Burma.

857 Yoshifusa (804–72) establishes the Fujiwara family as the power behind the emperor in Japan.

***c.*880** Tibetan unity dissolves into local rivalries.

900 **907** Rebellion in China leads to the end of the Tang dynasty; disunity and civil wars ensue – the period of the Five Dynasties.

***c.*925** Chola kingdom in S India annexes the neighbouring Pallava kingdom.

945 Buyid dynasty from present-day N Iran captures Baghdad from the Abbasid dynasty.

960 General Zhao Kuang-yin reunifies N China and establishes the Song dynasty.

971 Fatimids conquer Syria and Palestine from the Abbasids.

974 Byzantines establish control over N Syria and N Palestine.

985 Cholas invade the island of Sri Lanka.

999 Warlord Mahmud (969–1030) seizes control in Afghanistan and E Persia and expands the Ghaznavid dynasty.

1000 **1000** Ghaznavid armies begin raiding and pillaging cities in N India.

1022 Chola king Rajendra I (r.1016–44) conquers the E coast of India.

1026 Cholas invade Sumatra and Malaya.

1040 Seljuk Turks defeat the Ghaznavids and invade Persia.

1055 Seljuk Turks under Tughril Bey (*c.*990–1063) capture Baghdad.

1064 Armenia is incorporated into the Byzantine Empire.

1060–67 King Anawrahta (r.1044–77) of Pagan unifies Burma under his rule.

1071 Seljuks led by Alp Arslan (1029–72) defeat the Byzantines at the Battle of Manzikert and occupy most of Asia Minor.

1075–78 Turks occupy Syria and Palestine.

1096 People's Crusade is massacred by Turks in NW Asia Minor.

AFRICA

753 Arab expedition crosses the Sahara desert and makes contact with the kingdom of Ghana.

789 Idrisid dynasty establishes Morocco as an independent Islamic kingdom.

800 Aghlabids establish an independent Islamic dynasty in present-day Tunisia.

***c.*800** Kingdom of Kanem is established around the W shore of Lake Chad.

808 City of Fez becomes the capital of the kingdom of Morocco.

868 Independent Tulunid dynasty is established in Egypt.

905 Ikhshidids replace the Tulunids as the ruling dynasty in Egypt.

909 Fatimid dynasty seizes power in W Tunisia.

960 Falasha warriors under Queen Gudit sack the city of Aksum.

969 Fatimids invade Egypt and establish Cairo as their capital.

1054 Berber chieftain Abu Bakr (d.1087) launches an empire-building campaign in N Africa and establishes the Almoravid dynasty.

1070 Abu Bakr founds the city of Marrakesh in S Morocco.

1075–77 Almoravids conquer N Morocco and W Algeria.

1076 City of Kumbi, capital of Ghana, is sacked by an Almoravid army.

EUROPE

756 Umayyads retain power in Islamic Spain and establish the independent Emirate of Córdoba.

772 New Frankish king Charlemagne (*c.*742–814) campaigns against the Saxons in present-day N Germany.

774 Charlemagne defeats the Lombards and annexes N and central Italy.

781 Charlemagne establishes his capital at Aachen.

793 Danish raiders (Vikings) pillage the island monastery of Lindisfarne off NE England.

795 Charlemagne extends Frankish territory to S of the Pyrenees.

796 Frankish armies defeat and conquer the Avars in present-day Hungary.

800 Charlemagne is crowned emperor of the West in Aachen by Pope Leo III (*c.*750–816); start of the Holy Roman Empire.

804 Charlemagne completes the conquest of present-day N Germany.

812 Byzantines recognize Charlemagne as emperor in the W in return for Venice and present-day N Yugoslavia.

825 Islamic fleet captures the island of Crete.

***c.*830** King Egbert of Wessex (d.839) establishes control over the Anglo-Saxon states in England.

843 Treaty of Verdun divides the Carolingian empire into three kingdoms.

846 Arab army raids Italy and sacks Rome.

***c.*850** Magyars migrate into Hungary, replacing the Avars, and begin raiding W Europe.

858 Swedes establish the state of Kiev in Ukraine.

859–62 Danes raid along the coast of present-day S France.

866 Danes invade SE England.

867 Basil I (*c.*813–86) becomes Byzantine emperor and founds the Macedonian dynasty.

869 Swedish warrior Rurik (d.879) founds the town of Novgorod, Russia.

874 Norwegians begin to settle in Iceland.

878–85 King Alfred of Wessex (Alfred the Great, 849–99) defeats the Danes and confines them to E England (Danelaw).

882 Unification of Novgorod and Kiev under King Oleg creates the first Russian state.

911 Danish warleader Rollo (*c.*860–931) establishes an independent dukedom of Normandy in NW France.

919 Henry I (the Fowler) (*c.*876–936) is elected the first king of Germany.

927 Anglo-Saxon king Athelstan (d.939) expels the Danes from England.

944 Russians from Kiev attack Constantinople.

952 King Otto I (912–73) of Germany declares himself king of the Franks.

955 Magyars are defeated by Otto I at the Battle of Lechfield, Germany.

962 Otto I is crowned Holy Roman emperor in Rome.

***c.*969** Miezko I (d.992) establishes the Christian kingdom of Poland.

973 Christian kingdom of Bohemia is established.

986 Emirate of Córdoba conquers the Christian kingdoms in N Spain.

987 Hugh Capet (938–96) becomes king of France; start of the Capetian dynasty.

988 Russian king Vladimir I (956–1015) converts to Christianity.

996 Byzantines recapture Greece from the Bulgarians.

997 Following their conversion to Christianity, the Magyars establish a kingdom in Hungary under Stephen I (977–1038).

1008–28 Civil wars fragment the Emirate of Córdoba; Christian kingdoms re-emerge in N Spain; end of the Umayyad dynasty.

1013 Danes conquer England.

1014 Emperor Basil II (*c.*958–1025) completes the Byzantine reconquest of Bulgaria and the Balkan region.

1016 Danish prince Canute (*c.*994–1035) is elected king of England.

1028 Danes under King Canute conquer Norway.

1033 German emperor Conrad II (990–1039) adds Burgundy to the Holy Roman Empire.

1037 Christian kingdoms of León and Navarre in N Spain form an alliance and attack the Islamic S.

1040–52 Normans establish control over Byzantine S Italy.

THE AMERICAS

c.800 Metalworking is introduced into Mesoamerica from the S.

c.800 Cultivation of beans and maize is introduced to present-day E USA.

c.800 Huari abandon their capital city in highland Peru.

c.850 Toltecs establish military supremacy in central Mexico.

900 End of the Classic period of Mesoamerican history; start of the Early Postclassic period.

c.900 Chimú people establish the city-state of Chan Chan in N Peru.

c.900 Maya abandon their cities in Guatemala and retreat to the Yucatán region of Mexico.

c.900 Anasazi peoples establish towns around Chaco Canyon in New Mexico, with a ritual centre at Pueblo Bonito.

c.900 Hohokam people establish a town and ritual centre at Snaketown in S Arizona.

c.950 Toltecs build a capital city at Tula in central Mexico.

982–86 Norwegian explorers discover Greenland and establish a colony.

c.987 Toltecs seize control of the Mayan city of Chichén Itzá.

c.1000 Norwegian explorers discover North America and establish temporary settlements on the E coast of Canada.

SCIENCE AND TECHNOLOGY

c.825 Abbasid caliph Al-Mamun (786–833) establishes the House of Wisdom, a library and translation academy at Baghdad.

839 Birth of the Islamic historian Al-Tabri (d.923), who wrote a world history detailing the conquests of the Arabs.

c.850 Gunpowder is invented in China.

c.850 First European windmills are built in Islamic Spain.

870 Birth of the Islamic philosopher Al-Farab (d.950), who studied the works of Plato and Aristotle, and wrote *Views of the Perfect Citizen of the Perfect State.*

925 Death of the Islamic doctor Al-Razi (b.865), author of *Al-Hawi* – a comprehensive survey of Greek, Arab and Indian medical knowledge.

929 Death of the Islamic mathematician Al-Battani (Albategnius) (b.850), author of *On the Motion of Stars.*

953 Arab mathematician Al-Uqlidsi produces the first decimal fractions.

973 Birth of the Islamic scientist Al-Biruni (d.1048), who compiled an analysis of Indian mathematics.

976 Arabic (Indian) numerals are first used in Europe (in N Spain).

1003 Death of the scholar Gerbert of Aurillac (b.946), who translated Arabic texts on the abacus and astrolabe into Latin.

1010 Arab mathematician Ibn al-Haytham (*c.*965–1039), known in Europe as Alhazen, describes the properties of glass lenses.

1037 Death of the Islamic doctor and philosopher Ibn Sina (b.979), known in Europe as Avicenna, who wrote *Canon of Medicine.*

1050 Technique for printing using moveable ceramic type is invented in China.

1054 Chinese astronomers observe the supernova explosion that creates the Crab nebula.

1055–65 Westminster Abbey is built in London, England.

ARTS AND HUMANITIES

c.750 Anglo-Saxon poem *Beowulf* is written down.

c.750 Poets Li Po (701–62) and Tu Fu (712–70) become popular in China.

780 Birth of Sankara (d.820), the Indian philosopher who founded the Advaita Vedanta branch of Hinduism.

804 Death of the Anglo-Saxon monk Alcuin (b.*c.*732), who instigated 800
civil service training and a revival of classical learning at Charlemagne's court.

c.820 Reign of the Abbasid caliph Harun al-Rashid (r.786–809) inspires the writing of the *Thousand and One Nights.*

824 Death in China of Han Yu (b.768), the leading exponent of Neo-Confucianism.

843 End of iconoclasm in the Byzantine Empire; images (icons) are once again permitted in Christian art.

c.860 Cyril (*c.*827–69) and Methodius (*c.*825–84) devise the Cyrillic alphabet to assist their conversion of the Slavs.

868 Earliest-known printed book, the *Diamond Sutra,* is produced in China.

869 Death of the Islamic philosopher and essayist Al-Jahiz (b.776).

965 Death of the Arab poet Al-Mutanabbi (b.915), who worked at the 900
Ikhshidid court in Egypt.

978 Birth of the Japanese woman novelist Murasaki Shikibu (d.1014), author of *The Tale of Genji.*

1020 Death of the Persian Islamic poet Firdausi (b.935) author of the 1000
historical epic *Shah-nameh.*

1033 Birth of the philosopher Anselm of Canterbury (d.1109), who proposed a logical proof for the existence of God.

1048 Birth of the Islamic scientist and poet Omar Khayyám (d.1131).

c.1070–80 Bayeux tapestry is woven to commemorate William of Normandy's invasion of Britain.

1078 Death of the historian Michael Psellus (b.1018), author of *Chronographia,* a history of the reigns of 14 Byzantine emperors.

1088 First officially sanctioned university in Europe is established in Bologna, Italy.

ASIA AND AUSTRALASIA

1099 First Crusade, under Godfrey of Bouillon (1060–1100), captures Jerusalem; independent Christian kingdoms are established along the E coast of the Mediterranean.

1100 **1100** Baldwin (1058–1118) becomes king of Jerusalem.

1118 Order of the Knights Templar is established in Jerusalem.

1127 Jurchen nomads overrun N China; the Song dynasty retreats to S China; start of the Southern Song dynasty.

1149 Second Crusade ends after unsuccessful campaigns against the Turks in Palestine.

1156 Civil war between rival clans breaks out in Japan; end of the Heian period.

1173 Muhammad of Ghur overthrows the Ghaznavid dynasty in Afghanistan.

1187 Victory over Christian forces at the Battle of Hattin allows the Islamic general Saladin to recapture Jerusalem.

1191 Third Crusade captures the island of Cyprus and the town of Acre but fails to recapture Jerusalem.

1192 Yoritomo Minamoto (d.1199) institutes the shogunate in Japan.

1192 Muhammad of Ghur's victory over the Rajputs at the Battle of Thanesar leads to the Islamic conquest of N India.

1200 **1204** Empires of Nicaea (NW Asia Minor) and Trebizond (NE Asia Minor) are created out of remnants of the Byzantine Empire.

1206 Islamic Delhi Sultanate is established in N India.

1206 Mongol warrior Temüjin (*c*.1162–1227) establishes control over the nomads of the Eurasian steppes and adopts the title Genghis Khan (Emperor of the World).

1211 Mongol warriors invade Jurchen-controlled N China.

1215 Mongol advance in China reaches the Yellow River.

1218–25 Mongols conquer E Persia.

1219 Last shogun of the Minamoto family is killed in Japan; after the brief Shokyu War, the Hojo family takes control.

1220 **1222** Mongols conquer Afghanistan and invade N India.

1227 Mongols conquer the Xi-Xai kingdom in NW China. Genghis Khan dies and the Mongol empire is divided between his three sons and a grandson.

1228–29 Sixth Crusade, led by Frederick II of Germany, obtains Jerusalem, Bethlehem and Nazareth by treaty.

1229 Shan people establish the kingdom of Assam in E India.

1229 Genghis Khan's son Ogodei (1185–1241) is elected chief khan of the Mongol empire.

1231 Mongols invade Korea.

1234 Islamic Delhi Sultanate sacks the Hindu city of Ujjain in central India.

1234 Mongols complete their conquest of N China.

AFRICA

1117 City of Lalibela becomes the capital of Christian Ethiopia.

1143–47 Berber Almohad dynasty overthrows the Almoravids in NW Africa.

1171 Turkish general Saladin (1138–93) overthrows the Fatimid dynasty in Egypt and establishes the Ayyubid dynasty.

***c*.1200** Kingdom of Mwenemutapa is established in Zimbabwe.

1203 Samanguru establishes himself as ruler of the remnants of the kingdom of Ghana.

1212 Thousands of children who joined the Children's Crusade are sold into slavery in Alexandria, Egypt.

1219 Fifth Crusade captures the Egyptian port of Damietta, but fails to take Cairo.

1228 Hafsid dynasty takes over from the Almohads in Tunisia.

1230 Sundiata I (d.1255) becomes king of the city-state of Mali.

1239 Ziyanid dynasty overthrows the Almohads in Algeria.

EUROPE

1054 Great Schism divides the Catholic and Orthodox churches.

1054 King Yaroslav (b.980) dies and the Russian state breaks up.

1061–72 Normans under Roger I conquer Sicily from the Arabs.

1066 William of Normandy (1027–87) invades England, wins the Battle of Hastings, and becomes King William I (the Conqueror).

1085 Christian forces capture the city of Toledo in central Spain.

1086 Berber Almoravids under Yusuf (d.1106) are invited to intervene against the Christians in Spain.

1095 Following the Council of Clermont in France, Pope Urban II (*c*.1035–99) proclaims a Crusade to free Palestine from Islamic rule.

1096 First Crusade departs.

1108 Louis VI (1081–1137) becomes king of France and extends the power of the Capetian dynasty.

1138 Conrad III (1093–1152) becomes Holy Roman emperor and establishes the Hohenstaufen dynasty.

1147 Second Crusade departs under the leadership of German emperor Conrad III and King Louis VII (*c*.1120–80) of France.

***c*.1150** Almohad dynasty establishes control over Islamic Spain.

1151 Independent Serbian kingdom is established.

1153 Frederick I (1123–90) becomes Holy Roman emperor.

1154 Dynastic disputes in the Holy Roman Empire erupt into warfare.

1154 Henry II (1133–89) becomes king of England and establishes the Plantagenet dynasty.

1159 Contested papal elections result in both a pope and an antipope being recognized by the warring factions in Italy.

1167 Lombard League is formed against Frederick I in N Italy.

1171–73 Henry II of England establishes formal control over Ireland, Wales and Scotland.

1177 Peace treaty of Venice re-establishes a single papacy.

1186 Independent Bulgarian kingdom is re-established.

1189 Third Crusade departs under the leadership of Frederick I.

1198 Otto IV (1174–1218), a member of the Guelph family, becomes Holy Roman emperor; civil war breaks out in Germany.

1199 John (1167–1216) becomes king of England.

1201 German Crusaders establish the town of Riga in present-day Latvia.

1203 Fourth Crusade captures the Byzantine port of Zara (in present-day Yugoslavia) for Venice.

1204 Danes under King Waldemar II (d.1241) conquer Norway.

1204 At the behest of Venice, the Fourth Crusade captures and sacks Constantinople; the Latin empire of Constantinople is created on former Byzantine territory in Greece and the Balkans; Venice gains Crete.

1209 At the request of Pope Innocent III (1161–1216), an English-led Crusader army invades S France to suppress the Albigensian heretics.

1212 Civil wars in Germany end with Frederick II (1194–1250) becoming the German king.

1212 Christian victory at the Battle of Las Navas de Toloso leads to the downfall of the Islamic Almohad dynasty in Spain.

1214 French king Philip II (1165–1223), supported by Frederick II, defeats the English, supported by Otto IV (1174–1218), at the Battle of Bouvines; he conquers the English-controlled territory N of the River Loire.

1215 King John signs the Magna Carta at Runnymede, England.

***c*.1218** Rivalry between Guelphs (supporters of papal authority) and Ghibellines (supporters of the German emperor) becomes a major factor in Italian politics.

1220 Frederick II becomes Holy Roman emperor and king of S Italy.

1226 Teutonic Knights settle in Riga and NE Poland.

1226 Louis IX (1214–70) becomes king of France, with his mother, Blanche of Castile, as regent.

1227 Della Torre family (Guelphs) gains control of the Italian city-state of Milan.

1228 Italian city-state of Florence adopts a democratic constitution.

1229 At the end of the wars against the Albigensians, the French crown acquires territory in S France.

1231 Teutonic Knights begin the conquest of Prussia.

1232 Frederick II's son, Henry, leads the N Italian cities in a revolt against German control.

1232 Emirate of Granada is established by the Islamic Nasrid dynasty in S Spain.

THE AMERICAS

1156 Last Toltec king, Heumac, flees the destruction of Tula.

1187 Mayan leader Hunac Ceel leads a rebellion that evicts the Toltecs from Chichén Itzá and establishes a new Mayan capital at Mayapan.

***c.*1190** Aztecs establish a small state on the shore of Lake Texcoco in Mexico.

***c.*1200** Manco Capac establishes the Inca ruling dynasty with its capital at Cuzco, Peru.

***c.*1200** Monks Mound is constructed at Cahokia, Illinois, present-day USA.

SCIENCE AND TECHNOLOGY

1104 Construction of the Arsenal begins in Venice, Italy.

1120 Robert of Chester visits Spain and translates Al-Khwarizmi's *Calculation with Hindu Numerals* into Latin.

***c.*1140** Adelard of Bath (*c.*1075–1160) translates Euclid into Latin using both Greek and Arabic texts.

1150 A university is established in Paris, France.

1163 External flying buttresses are used for the first time, in the construction of Notre Dame in Paris.

1167 A university is established in Oxford, England.

1170 Roger of Salerno writes the first European surgery textbook, *Practica chirurgiae.*

1174 Construction work begins on the unintentionally leaning tower in Pisa, Italy.

1187 Death of the Italian scholar Gerard of Cremona (*c.*1114–87), who translated the works of Galen (129–99) from Arabic texts captured at Toledo.

***c.*1200** Sternpost rudders (invented in China) are first used on European ships.

1202 Italian mathematician Leonardo Fibonacci of Pisa (*c.*1170–*c.*1240) publishes *Book of the Abacus* – the first European book to explain Indian numerals.

1215 Syllabus of the university of Paris is revised, with logic replacing Latin literature.

***c.*1230** Explosive bombs and rockets are first used by the defenders of Chinese cities against the Mongols.

ARTS AND HUMANITIES

1111 Death of the Islamic philosopher Al-Ghazali (b.1058), who 1100
wrote *The Revival of the Religious Sciences* to counter the Greek-influenced philosophies of Avicenna and Averröes.

***c.*1120** Scholar Pierre Abélard (1079–1142) revives the teaching of Aristotle in Paris, France.

***c.*1130** Construction of the temples at Angkor Wat in Cambodia begins.

1139 Scholar Geoffrey of Monmouth (1100–54) composes *History of the Kings of Britain.*

1140 Birth of the Japanese philosopher Eisa (d.1215) whose teachings founded Zen Buddhism.

1153 Death of the Byzantine scholar Anna Comnena (b.1083), author of *The Alexiad*, a biography of her father the emperor Alexius (1048–1118).

***c.*1180** Chinese philosopher Zhu Xi (1130–1200) compiles the Confucian Canon.

1198 Death of the Islamic philosopher Ibn Rushd (b.1126), known in Europe as Averröes, who wrote an extended commentary on Aristotelian thought.

***c.*1200** Churches, such as that of St George, are carved out of solid 1200
rock at Lalibela in Ethiopia.

1200 Birth of the Japanese Zen master Dogen (d.1253).

1209 Franciscans, the first order of mendicant friars, are founded by Francis of Assisi (1182–1226).

***c.*1210** German minnesinger Wolfram von Eschenbach (1170–1220) writes the romance *Parzival.*

1210 German poet Gottfried von Strassburg writes his version of *Tristan and Isolde.*

1212 Order of the Poor Clares is founded.

1213 French historian Geoffrey de Villehardouin (1150–1213) writes an account of the Fourth Crusade, *Conquest of Constantinople.*

***c.*1220** In s China the landscape artists Ma Yuan (1190–1224) and Xia 1220
Gui (1180–1230) emphasize mist and clouds.

1220 Building of Amiens cathedral marks the beginning of the Rayonnant Gothic style of architecture, characterized by large circular windows.

1222 Icelandic poet Snorri Sturluson (1179–1241) writes the epic *Prose Edda.*

1225 Qutb Minar tower is built in Delhi, India.

1225 Francis of Assisi (1182–1226) writes *Canticle of Brother Sun.*

***c.*1230** French poet Guillaume de Lorris (1210–37) writes the first part of *Roman de la Rose.*

ASIA AND AUSTRALASIA

1240 **1242** Mongols capture the city of Lahore in present-day Pakistan.

1244 Jerusalem is captured by Islamic armies.

***c*.1250** Turks begin settling in Asia Minor.

1253 Mongols under Hulagu (1217–65) invade W Persia and establish the Ilkhanid dynasty.

1253 Mongols capture the N Burma region; Thai peoples migrate S.

1253 Rivalry between Venetian and Genoese merchants at Acre, Palestine, leads to war between the two Italian city-states.

1255 Mongol khan Mongke (1208–59) bans Taoist books in China.

1256 Mongols exterminate the Assassins in Syria.

1257 Mongol armies conquer present-day N Vietnam.

1258 Mongols launch attacks against the Southern Song dynasty in S China.

1258 Baghdad is destroyed by Mongol armies.

1259 Following the death of Mongke, the division of the Mongol empire into four khanates becomes permanent.

1260 **1260** Mongols are defeated by the Mamluks at the Battle of Ain Jalut in Palestine.

1260 Mongol khan Kublai (1215–94) becomes emperor of N China.

1267 Kublai establishes as his capital the city of Khanbalik, which later becomes Beijing.

1268 Mamluks sack the city of Antioch in Syria.

1268 Mongols invade S China.

1271 Mamluks capture the Christian fortress of Krak des Chevaliers in Syria.

1274 Mongols make an unsuccessful attempt to invade Japan.

1277 Mongol forces capture the city of Guangzhou (Canton) in S China.

1277 Mamluks invade Asia Minor and defeat the Mongols, but later withdraw.

1279 Pandya dynasty completes its conquest of S India; end of the Chola dynasty.

1279 Mongols complete their conquest of S China; end of the Southern Song dynasty, start of the Yuan dynasty.

1280 **1281** Mongols attempt to invade Japan but are repulsed by samurai; the Mongol fleet is destroyed by a storm – the *kamikaze* (divine wind).

1282–88 Mongols make repeated attempts to subdue the kingdom of Champa in present-day S Vietnam.

1287 Mongols conquer and destroy the kingdom of Pagan in Burma.

1291 Mamluks capture the city of Acre, Palestine, the last remnant of the Crusader kingdoms.

1292–93 Mongols attempt a seaborne invasion of Java.

1294 Death of the Mongol Chinese emperor Kublai.

1297 Delhi Sultanate conquers the Hindu kingdom of Gujarat in W India.

1299 Mongol Chaghati khanate of central Asia invades N India.

1300 **1300** Turkish general Osman I (1258–1326) proclaims himself sultan of the Turks in Asia Minor; start of the Ottoman Empire.

1300 Thai peoples under King Rama Kamheng establish a kingdom around the city of Sukhothai in present-day Thailand.

1303 Delhi Sultanate conquers the Rajput fortress of Chitor, the last Hindu stronghold in N India.

1306 Chaghati Mongols are expelled from India by the Delhi Sultanate.

1311 Delhi Sultanate annexes the Pandya kingdom in S India.

1313 Delhi Sultanate conquers central India.

AFRICA

1240 Sundiata, king of Mali, defeats Samanguru, king of Ghana, and establishes the empire of Mali.

1249 Seventh Crusade, led by Louis IX (1214–70) of France, invades Egypt and captures the port of Damietta.

1250 Louis IX is defeated by the Egyptians and is taken prisoner.

1250 Mamluks (Turkish slave bodyguards), led by Baybars, seize power in Egypt; end of the Fatimid dynasty; start of the Bahri Mamluk dynasty.

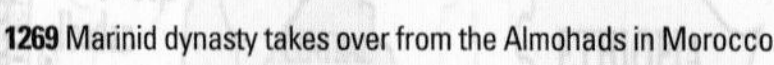

1269 Marinid dynasty takes over from the Almohads in Morocco.

1270 Warlord Yekuno Amlak (r.1270–85) seizes control of Ethiopia and establishes the Solomonid dynasty.

1270 Louis IX of France leads the Eighth Crusade to Tunis, where he dies of fever.

***c*.1300** Kingdom of Benin is established on the W coast of Africa.

1316 Military expedition from Egypt establishes an Islamic ruler in Nubia.

1320 King Amda Seyon (r.1314–44) extends Christian control to S Ethiopia.

EUROPE

1235 Kingdom of Aragón, N Spain, captures the Balearic Islands from Islamic rule.

1236 Ferdinand III (1199–1252) of Castile captures Córdoba and conquers most of S Spain.

1236 Mongols invade Europe.

1237 Armies of Frederick II defeat the N Italian cities at the Battle of Cortenuova.

1237 Mongol khanate of the Golden Horde is established in S Russia.

1240 Mongols destroy Kiev.

1240 Prince of Novgorod, Alexander Nevski (1220–63), defeats a Swedish invasion on the River Neva.

1241 Mongols defeat Polish and German knights at the Battle of Liegnitz.

1241 Mongols defeat the Hungarians at the Battle of Sajo.

1241 Conflicts between Frederick II (1194–1250) and the pope lead to German troops pillaging central Italy.

1242 Teutonic Knights attack Novgorod, but are defeated by Alexander Nevski at the Battle of Lake Peipus.

1242 Mongols withdraw from Europe after the death of Khan Ogodei (1185–1241).

1242 English under King Henry III (1207–72) invade France.

1250 Frederick II dies and is succeeded by his son Conrad IV (1228–54).

1253 Kingdom of Portugal conquers the Algarve region from Islamic rule.

1254 Death of Conrad IV marks the end of the Hohenstaufen dynasty in Germany and the beginning of an interregnum.

1258 English barons rebel against King Henry III.

1259 English are forced to cede territory to the French king, Louis IX (1214–70), at the Peace of Paris.

1259 German ports Lübeck, Hamburg and Rostock form a *Hansa* (union).

1260 City of Siena defeats the ruling Guelph faction of Florence at the Battle of Montaperti.

1261 King Ottokar II (d.1278) of Bohemia captures Austria from Hungary.

1261 Greeks, with Genoese help, seize Constantinople and re-establish the Byzantine Empire; end of the Latin empire of Constantinople.

1264 Venice regains control of Constantinople after defeating Genoa at the Battle of Trepani.

1266 French invade S Italy; Charles (1226–85), brother of French king Louis IX, becomes king of Sicily.

1265 Rebellious English barons are defeated by Prince Edward (later Edward I) at the Battle of Evesham.

1271 Marco Polo (1254–1324) departs for China.

1277 Visconti family (Ghibellines) gains control of Milan.

1277 Genoese merchants establish the first regular Atlantic sea-route between the Mediterranean Sea and N Europe.

1278 After victory over Ottokar II of Bohemia at the Battle of Marchfeld, Rudolf of Habsburg gains control of Austria.

1278–84 Edward I (1239–1307) of England invades and conquers Wales.

1282 French soldiers in Palermo are massacred during the "Sicilian Vespers"; the Sicilians invite Pedro of Aragón to be their king.

1283 Teutonic Knights complete the conquest of Prussia.

1285 Bulgarian kingdom disintegrates under Mongol overlordship.

1291 Three Swiss cantons revolt against Habsburg rule and form a confederation.

1291 Knights of St John move to Cyprus.

1297 William Wallace (1270–1305) leads a rising against English rule in Scotland.

1297 French king Philip IV (1268–1314) occupies Flanders.

1297 English king Edward I invades France in support of Flanders.

1299 Genoa defeats Venice at a naval battle in the Adriatic Sea.

1302 Flanders defeats the French at the Battle of the Golden Spurs at Courtrai.

1305 Flanders submits to French rule.

1305 English execute the Scottish rebel William Wallace.

1307 Knights Templar are disbanded in Paris.

1309 French king Philip IV (1268–1314) compels the pope, Clement V, to move to Avignon in S France; start of the "Babylonian Captivity".

1309 A Bourse (stock exchange) is founded at Bruges, present-day Belgium.

THE AMERICAS

c.1300 Chimú state in Peru expands to rival that of the Incas.

c.1300 Mesa Verde and other Anasazi centres in present-day sw USA are abandoned.

SCIENCE AND TECHNOLOGY

c.1250 Gunpowder is first mentioned in European manuscripts; the secret of its manufacture was learned either from Arabs in Spain or from Mongol prisoners.

1262 Death of the Islamic astronomer Ibn Omar al-Marrakashi, who wrote *Of Beginnings and Ends*.

1264 French scholar Vincent of Beauvais (1190–1264) publishes *Great Mirror*, a combination of encyclopedia and universal history.

1266 English scholar and mathematician Roger Bacon (1220–92) completes *Longer Work*, which advocates the use of scientific experiment.

c.1270 Firearms and cannon (made of reinforced bamboo) are first used in battles between the Mongols and the Chinese.

c.1270 Double-entry book-keeping is developed in the Italian city of Florence.

1275 German scholar and scientist Theodoric of Freiburg describes how a rainbow is formed by reflections within raindrops.

c.1280 Belt-driven spinning wheel is introduced to Europe from India.

1280s Establishment of the Mongol empire across Asia re-opens overland trade routes, such as the Silk Road, between Europe and the Far East.

1291 Venetians move their glass factories to the island of Murano for fire safety.

c.1300 Earliest-known European spectacles are manufactured in Italy.

1311 Pietro Vesaconte makes the earliest-known portolan sea-chart (navigational chart) of the Mediterranean.

1316 Italian doctor Modinus publishes *Anatomy*, a textbook of human anatomy.

c.1320 Cannon are first used on a European battlefield.

ARTS AND HUMANITIES

1248 Construction starts on the Alhambra fortress and palace in 1240
Granada, s Spain.

1248 Building of Cologne cathedral marks the spread of Gothic architecture across N Europe.

c.1250 "Black Pagoda" Temple of the Sun at Konarak in India is built by King Narasimhadeva (r.1238–64).

1259 Death of the English historian and biographer Matthew Paris, author of *Great Chronicle*.

1260 Italian artist Nicola Pisano (1225–84) sculpts a pulpit for the 1260
Baptistry in Pisa.

1262 Death of the philosopher and reformer Shinran (b.1173), who established True Pure Land Buddhism in Japan.

1273 Italian scholar and philosopher Thomas Aquinas (1225–74) completes *Theological Digest*.

1275–80 Tibetan scholar Phags-pa devises a script for writing Mongolian.

1282 Death of the philosopher Nichiren (b.1222), who established 1280
Lotus Sutra Buddhism in Japan.

1283 Italian artist Giovanni Cimabue (*c*.1240–*c*.1302) paints *Sta Croce* crucifix.

1283 Catalan scholar and author Raimon Lull (1235–1315) writes his utopian novel *Blanquerna*.

1285 Italian artist Duccio di Buoninsegna (*c*.1265–1319) paints the *Rucellai Madonna*, which revolutionizes the Byzantine style of Sienese painting.

c.1300 Polynesian settlers on Easter Island begin a period of 1300
intensive statue carving.

1304–09 Italian artist Giotto di Bondone (1266–1337) begins painting his frescos in the Arena chapel, Padua.

1309 French knight Jean, Sire de Joinville (1224–1319) publishes *Life of St Louis* (the French king Louis IX).

1314 Persian statesman Rashid al-Din (1247–1318) publishes his illustrated world history, *Collection of Histories*.

1314 Italian poet Dante Alighieri (1265–1321) begins *Divine Comedy*.

ASIA AND AUSTRALASIA

1320 **1320** Turkish Tughluk dynasty takes over control of the Delhi Sultanate.

1323 Delhi Sultanate conquers the Hindu kingdom of Telingana in India.

1330 Hindu kingdom of Madjapahit in Java begins extending its control over nearby islands.

1333 Emperor Go-daigo tries to re-establish imperial power in Japan.

1335 Mongol Ilkhanid dynasty in Persia is overthrown.

***c.*1335** Epidemic of plague, which later becomes known as the Black Death, breaks out in China.

1336 Revolt establishes the Hindu kingdom of Vijayanagar in S India; start of the Sangama dynasty.

1336 Civil wars break out in Japan, which is split between rival imperial courts.

1337 Ottoman Turks capture Nicaea, the last remaining Byzantine territory in Asia Minor.

1338 Bengal breaks away from the Delhi Sultanate to become an independent Islamic state.

1340 **1341–43** Epidemic of plague – the Black Death – sweeps across China.

1344 Flooding of the Yellow River devastates E China.

1346 Independent Islamic dynasty is founded in Kashmir, N India.

1347 Thai capital is moved to the city of Ayutthaya.

1350 Unrest begins in China among workers repairing the Grand Canal; they are followers of the Buddhist White Lotus cult and wear red turbans.

1353 Kingdom of Laos is established in SE Asia.

1355 Red Turbans, led by former monk Hong-wu (1328–98), foment a popular revolt against Mongol rule in China.

1360 **1367** Victory in battle by the Delhi Sultanate over the Hindu kingdom of Vijayanagar leads to the massacre of 400,000 civilians.

1368 Red Turbans expel the Mongols from China and Hong-wu (1328–98) becomes emperor; start of the Ming dynasty.

1369 Thais sack the Khmer capital of Angkor.

1369 Tamerlane (1336–1405), or Timur, a Turkish soldier, rebels against the Chaghati Mongols and captures their capital, Samarkand.

1377 Islamic empire of Java conquers Hindu Sumatra.

AFRICA

1324 Pilgrimage of Mansa Musa (r.1312–37) to Mecca marks the highpoint of the empire of Mali.

1332 War breaks out between Christian Ethiopia and neighbouring Islamic kingdoms.

1340 Portuguese sailors discover the Canary Islands.

1344 Canary Islands are allocated to Castile by the pope.

1348 Black Death devastates Egypt.

1349 Moroccan traveller Ibn Battutah (1304–68) returns home after a 25-year journey to India and China.

1365 Crusade led by the king of Cyprus sacks the city of Alexandria in Egypt.

1375 Kingdom of Songhai breaks away from the empire of Mali.

EUROPE

1309 Teutonic Knights make Marienburg their capital.

1309 Knights of St John move to the island of Rhodes.

1310 City-state of Venice establishes its Council of Ten.

1314 Scots, led by Robert the Bruce (1274–1329), defeat the English at the Battle of Bannockburn and establish Scottish independence.

1315 Swiss defeat the Austrian army at the Battle of Morgarten.

1319 Sweden and Norway are united under Magnus VII (1316–74).

1325 Ivan I becomes ruler of the Grand Duchy of Moscow under the overlordship of the khanate of the Golden Horde.

1328 Seat of the Russian Church is moved from Vladimir to Moscow.

1328 Death of the French king Charles IV (b.1294) ends the Capetian dynasty; start of the Valois dynasty.

1329 Byzantines capture the island of Chios from Genoa.

1330 After defeating the Greeks and Bulgarians at the Battle of Velbuzdhe, Serbia becomes the dominant power in the Balkans.

1331 Cities in S Germany establish the Swabian League.

1332 Gerhard of Holstein, supported by the Hanseatic League, seizes the Danish crown.

1332 Lucerne is the first city to join the Swiss Confederation.

1337 Edward III (1312–77) of England lays claim to the French throne; beginning of the Hundred Years' War (to 1453).

1339 City of Genoa in Italy adopts a republican constitution.

1339 Island city of Venice conquers the town of Treviso on the Italian mainland.

1340 English defeat the French at a naval battle near the port of Sluys (in present-day Belgium).

1340 Spanish king of Castile, Alfonso XI (1311–50), decisively repels an Islamic attack at the Battle of Rio Salado.

1341–47 Civil war further disrupts the Byzantine Empire.

1344 Hungarian king Louis I (1326–82) expels the Mongols from Transylvania.

1346 Black Death sweeps through S Russia.

1346 Teutonic Knights gain control of Estonia.

1346 English defeat the French at the Battle of Crécy, the first major battle of the Hundred Years' War.

1347 English capture the French port of Calais.

1347 Black Death reaches Constantinople, Italy and S France; in 1348 it reaches Spain, N France and Britain; in 1349 Germany and Scandinavia. This initial outbreak kills *c.*25% of Europe's population.

1348 Danish king Waldemar IV (1320–75) recaptures Jutland from German control.

1351 War breaks out in Italy between Florence and Milan.

1352 Ottoman Turks establish a foothold in Europe at Gallipoli.

1354 Genoese destroy the Venetian fleet at the sea battle of Sapieanza.

1356 English, led by Edward the Black Prince (1330–76), defeat the French at Maupertuis and capture the French king.

1356 Hanseatic League is formally established.

1358 Rising in Paris and peasant revolts weaken France.

1360 By the Peace of Bretigny, Edward III of England gives up his claim to the French throne in return for sovereignty over SW France.

1361 Ottoman Turks capture the city of Adrianople; the Byzantine Empire is reduced to the city of Constantinople.

1361–63 Second outbreak of Black Death devastates parts of Europe.

1361–70 Wars between the Hanseatic League and Denmark leave the League dominant in the Baltic region.

1367 Civil war breaks out between the Swabian League and the German emperor.

1369 French king Charles V (1337–80) attacks English possessions in France.

1370 Teutonic Knights defeat the Lithuanians at the Battle of Rudau.

1371 Robert II (1316–90) becomes king of Scotland; start of the Stuart dynasty.

1372 Swabian League is defeated.

1372 Spanish, allied with the French, defeat the English at the sea battle of La Rochelle.

1375–78 War of the Eight Saints is fought between Florence and the papacy.

THE AMERICAS

c.1325 Aztecs establish the city of Tenochtitlán on an island in Lake Texcoco, Mexico.

c.1350 King Mayta Capa begins expanding Inca control in Peru.

c.1370 Acamapitchtli becomes king of the Aztecs.

c.1370 Chimú complete their conquest of coastal N Peru.

SCIENCE AND TECHNOLOGY

1324 Earliest-known European cannon are manufactured in France.

1340 First European factory for making paper opens in Fabriano, Italy.

1340s Wind-driven pumps are used to drain marshes in Holland.

1343 English philosopher and scholar William of Occam (1285–1349) publishes *Dialogus*, which contains his "razor" of logic.

1363 French doctor Guy de Chauliac (d.1368) completes his textbook of surgery, *Great surgery*.

1364 A university is established in Kraków, Poland.

1370 French king Charles V establishes standard time according to a weight-driven mechanical clock in the royal palace in Paris.

c.1377 French scholar William of Oresme (1320–82) writes his essay on monetary policy, *On money*.

1377 Single arch bridge with a span of 72m (236ft) is completed at Trezzo, N Italy.

1379 Rockets are first used on a European battlefield by the army of Padua in Italy.

ARTS AND HUMANITIES

1315 Italian historian and dramatist Albertino Massato writes his play *Ecerimis* about the political struggles in Padua.

1317 Italian artist Simone Martini (1284–1344) paints *St Louis*.

1324 Italian politician Marciglio of Padua (*c*.1275–1342) writes 1320
Defensor Pacis, an essay on relations between church and state.

c.1325 Beginning of the Renaissance in Italian art is accompanied by a revival of interest in ancient Greece and Rome, and the development of secular thought – humanism.

1332 Birth of the Islamic philosopher Ibn Khaldun (d.1406), author of an *Introduction to History*.

1334 Giotto di Bondone (1266–1337) designs the bell tower of Florence cathedral.

1335 Italian artist Andrea Pisano (d.1348) casts the bronze S doors of the baptistry in Florence.

1335 Mosque of Al-Nasir in Cairo is completed.

1337 Italian artist Ambrogio Lorenzetti paints frescos of *Good and Bad Government* in the town hall in Siena.

1337 Death of the Chinese dramatist Wang Shifu (b.1250), author of *The Romance of the Western Chamber*.

1338 Italian artist Taddeo Gaddi (*c*.1300–*c*.1366) paints frescos in the church of Santa Croce, Florence.

1341 Italian poet Francesco Petrarch (1304–74) publishes *Poems*, a 1340
collection of love poems.

1348 Death from plague of Italian historian Giovanni Villani (b.1276) brings to an end his chronicle of Florentine history.

1352 Palace of the popes at Avignon is completed.

1357 Italian artist Andrea Orcagna (1308–68) creates the altarpiece for the Strozzi family chapel in Florence.

1357 Death of the Italian lawyer Bartolus of Sassoferrato (b.1314), who advocated republican government in *On the government of cities*.

1357 Italian scholar Zanobi da Strada discovers a forgotten manuscript copy of Tacitus' *Annals* in a monastery library.

1358 Italian poet and author Giovanni Boccaccio (1313–75) completes the *Decameron* of tales told during the Black Death.

1360 Italian lawyer Giovanni di Legnano writes *Treatise on War*. 1360

1360 Construction of the Alcázar palace in Seville begins.

c.1362 English priest William Langland (1331–99) writes the poem *Piers Plowman*.

c.1365 Flemish painters establish the Bruges school of painting.

c.1370 Japanese dramatist Kanami Motokiyo (1333–84) establishes the classic form of No drama.

1372 Egyptian scholar and zoologist Al-Damiri (1344–1405) writes *Lives of animals*.

1378 Nun and philosopher Catherine of Siena (1347–80) writes *Dialogo*.

ASIA AND AUSTRALASIA

1380 **1381–87** Tamerlane (Timur, 1336–1405) invades and conquers Persia.

1382 All districts of China are reunited under Ming control.

1389 Islamic empire of Java collapses after the death of king Rajasanagara (b.1334).

1392 Yoshimitsu (1358–1408) becomes ruler of Japan and establishes the Muromachi shogunate.

1392 General Yi Song-gye establishes the Yi (Choson) dynasty in Korea.

1393–94 Tamerlane invades and conquers Mesopotamia.

1394 Islamic kingdom of Jaunpur in N India is established.

1398–99 Tamerlane invades N India and sacks Delhi.

1400 **1400** Tamerlane (Timur, 1336–1405) invades and conquers Syria.

1402 Tamerlane defeats the Ottoman Turks at the Battle of Ankara; collapse of the Ottoman Empire in Asia.

1403 Islamic warlord establishes the city of Malacca in Malaya.

1404–07 Chinese admiral Cheng Ho (1371–1433) subdues Sumatra.

1405 Tamerlane dies and his empire collapses; a Timurid dynasty continues to rule in Persia and Turkistan.

1408–11 Cheng Ho defeats the Ceylonese.

1409 Chinese invade Vietnam.

1413 Sultan Muhammad I (1389–1421) re-establishes Ottoman control over Asia Minor.

1416–19 Chinese fleet sails to Yemen.

1418 Vietnamese leader Le Loi organizes resistance against the Chinese.

1419 Sejong (1397–1450) becomes king of Korea.

1420 **1420** Beijing replaces Nanjing as the the capital of China.

***c.*1420** Coffee, introduced from Ethiopia via Yemen, is domesticated near Mecca, Arabia.

1429 City of Bidur becomes the capital of the much-reduced Delhi Sultanate.

1428 Le Loi declares himself ruler of Annam (N Vietnam).

1431 Annam wins independence from China.

1433 Chinese emperor Xuan-zong prohibits any further long-distance sea voyages.

AFRICA

1382 Burji Mamluks seize control from the Bahris in Egypt.

1415 Portuguese under King John I (1357–1433) capture the town of Ceuta on the Mediterranean coast of Morocco.

1416 Portuguese explorers reach Cape Bojador on the W coast of Africa.

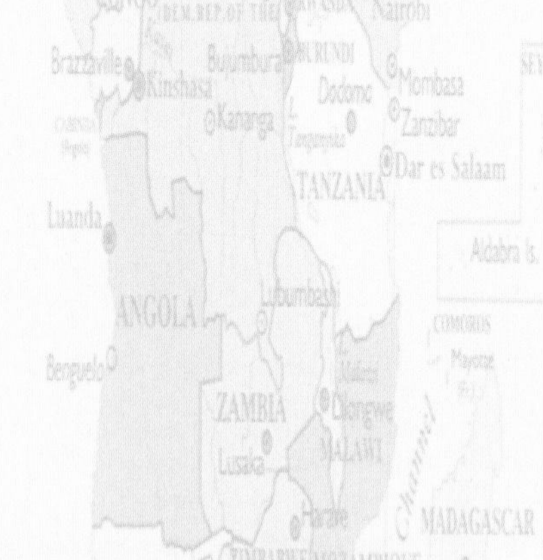

1420 Portuguese occupy the island of Madeira.

1421 Ships from Ming China establish direct contact with the Islamic towns of E Africa.

1424 Chinese ships again visit E Africa.

1425 Portuguese fail to conquer the Canary Islands from Castile.

1430 Portuguese discover the Azores.

1433 Chinese ships make a final visit to E Africa.

1433 Desert nomads capture the city of Timbuktu in the SW Sahara desert.

1434 Zara Yaqob (d.1468) becomes king of Ethiopia.

1437 Portuguese make a disastrous attempt to capture Tangier, Morocco.

EUROPE

1376 Swabian League is revived by the city of Ulm.

1377 Pope returns to Rome; end of the "Babylonian Captivity".

1378–1417 Great Schism occurs in the Roman Catholic Church, with rival popes at Rome and Avignon.

1378 Genoa captures the town of Chioggia, S of Venice.

1378 Flanders revolts against French rule.

1380 Venice recaptures Chioggia and destroys the Genoese fleet.

1381 Peasants' Revolt in England ends with the death of its leader, Wat Tyler.

1382 Flanders revolt is crushed at the Battle of Roosebeke by Philip II (the Bold) (1342–1404), who becomes overlord of the region.

1383 Venice captures Corfu.

1385 Victory at the Battle of Aljubarrota establishes Portuguese independence from Spain.

1386–88 Milan conquers the Italian cities of Verona, Vicenza and Padua.

1386 King Jagiello (1351–1434) of Poland forms a union with the Grand Duchy of Lithuania.

1387 Danish regent Margaret (1363–1412) becomes queen of Sweden and Norway.

1389 Ottoman Turks defeat the Serbs at the Battle of Kosovo.

1388–95 Tamerlane invades and conquers the territory of the Golden Horde but fails to take Moscow.

1396 Bulgaria becomes part of the Ottoman Empire.

1396 Sigismund (1368–1437) of Hungary attempts to break the Turkish encirclement of Constantinople but is defeated at Battle of Nicopolis.

1397 Treaty of Kalmar unites Denmark, Sweden and Norway under Danish control.

1397 Bank of Medici is established in Florence.

1399 Richard II (1367–1400) of England is overthrown by Henry IV (1367–1413); end of Plantagenet dynasty, start of Lancaster dynasty.

1400 Welsh led by Owain Glyn Dŵr (Owen Glendower, *c.*1359–1416) rebel against English rule.

1404 Territory of the Teutonic Knights reaches its greatest extent after acquisition of Brandenburg.

1405 Venetians attack and occupy the city of Padua in NE Italy, initiating their conquest of the *Terrafirma*.

1406 Italian city of Florence gains access to the sea through control of neighbouring Pisa.

1408 Khanate of the Golden Horde unsuccessfully besieges Moscow, but re-establishes its overlordship.

1410 Polish-Lithuanian armies defeat the Teutonic Knights at the Battle of Tannenberg.

1413 Henry V (1387–1422) becomes king of England and renews claims against France.

1414 Attempted rising by Lollards in England is suppressed.

1415 Czech religious reformer Jan Hus (b.1369) is executed.

1415 Henry V of England invades France, wins the Battle of Agincourt, and occupies Paris.

1416 Venetians defeat the Ottoman Turks in a sea battle.

1417 Council of Constance restores a single papacy, ending the Great Schism.

1419 Predominantly Czech supporters of Hus rise against German rule in Bohemia; start of the Hussite Wars.

1420–22 Supporters of Jan Hus in Bohemia defeat a Crusade against them led by Emperor Sigismund of Hungary.

1425 Cities of Florence and Venice ally against Milan.

1427 War breaks out between Denmark and the Hanseatic League.

1427 Venetians conquer the city of Bergamo in NE Italy, and complete their *Terrafirma.*

1429 Joan of Arc (1412–31) leads French forces to relieve the English siege of Orléans; she escorts Charles VII (1403–61) of France to his coronation at Reims.

1429 Florence attacks the nearby city of Lucca.

1430 Ottoman Turks capture the city of Thessaloníki from the Venetians.

1431 Joan of Arc is executed by the English.

1433 Hungarian king Sigismund, also king of Germany and Bohemia, becomes Holy Roman emperor.

1434 Cosimo de' Medici (1389–1464) becomes ruler of Florence.

THE AMERICAS

*c.*1400 Start of the Middle Period of Mississippi mound-building.

1426 Itzcoatl (d.1440) becomes Aztec king and begins a policy of military expansion.

1437 While the Lord Inca is campaigning elsewhere, Cuzco is besieged by the neighbouring Chanca people.

1438 Incas led by Pachacuti conquer the Chancas.

SCIENCE AND TECHNOLOGY

1385 Heidelberg University is established.

1392 Moveable metal type is first used for printing in Korea.

1410 Flagship of the Chinese admiral Cheng Ho is 130m (426ft) long and has five masts and 12 decks; it is the biggest wooden sailing ship ever built.

1419 Portuguese prince Henry (known as Henry the Navigator, 1394–1460) establishes a school of navigation at Sagres.

1420 Italian architect Filippo Brunelleschi (1377–1446) begins designing the dome of Florence cathedral.

1424 Persian mathematician al-Kashi (d.1429) publishes a value for pi (π) that is correct to 16 decimal places.

*c.*1430 Hussite leader Jan Zizka (*c.*1376–1424) invents the cannon-equipped armoured fighting vehicle.

1435 Italian architect Leon Alberti (1404–72) outlines the mathematical laws of perspective in painting in *On painting*.

1437 Islamic astronomers in Samarkand publish the *Tables of Ulugh Beg*, named after the Mongol ruler who established their observatory.

ARTS AND HUMANITIES

1380 English religious reformer John Wycliffe (1330–84) translates the Bible into English. 1380

*c.*1380 English poet Geoffrey Chaucer (1346–1400) begins writing the first of his *Canterbury Tales*.

1386 Construction of Milan cathedral begins.

1391 Byzantine scholar Manuel Chrysolaurus arrives in Italy and begins popularizing the Classical Greek philosophers.

1396 Italian humanist philosopher Coluccio Salutati (1331–1406) publishes *On destiny and fortune*.

1397 Chinese law code *Laws of the Great Ming* is published.

*c.*1399 Greek artist Theophanes (*c.*1330–1405) paints the icon *The Deeds of the Archangel Michael* for the Kremlin cathedral in Moscow.

1400 French scholar Jean Froissart (*c.*1337–1410) completes *Chronicles*, describing events in the Hundred Years' War. 1400

1402 Italian humanist Pietro Paulo Vergerio (1370–1444) writes *Conduct worthy of free men*.

1406 Construction work starts on the Forbidden Palace in Beijing.

1410 French artists the Limbourg brothers produce the illustrated *Les tres riches heures du Duc de Berry*.

1413 Czech philosopher and religious reformer Jan Hus (1369–1415) writes *Exposition of Belief*.

1413 University of St Andrews is founded in Scotland.

1415 French poet Christine de Pisan (1364–1430) writes *The Rights of Women*.

1416 *Hsing Li Ta Ch'uan*, the 120-volume compilation of moral philosophy, is published in China.

1419 Italian sculptor Jacopo della Quercia (1374–1438) creates the *Gaia* fountain in Siena.

1423 Italian artist Gentile da Fabriano (*c.*1370–1427) paints *Adoration of the Magi*. 1420

1424 French poet Alain Chartier (1385–1440) writes *La Belle Dame Sans Merci*, an attack on courtly love.

1425 Italian sculptor Lorenzo Ghiberti (1378–1455) begins work on the bronze N doors of the Baptistry in Florence.

1426 Italian artist Masaccio (1401–28) paints his polyptych panels for the Carmelite Church, Pisa.

1429 Italian humanist Guarino da Verona (1374–1460) becomes professor of classics at Ferrara University.

1434 Flemish artist Jan van Eyck (*c.*1390–1441) paints *Arnolfini Wedding*.

1434 Italian sculptor Donatello (1386–1466) casts his bronze statue of *David* in Florence.

1436 Italian artist Paolo Uccello (1397–1475) paints a frescoed portrait for the tomb of the English mercenary John Hawkwood (d.1394).

ASIA AND AUSTRALASIA

1440 **1448** Trailok (r.1448–88) becomes king of Thailand.

1449 Chinese emperor is captured by a Mongol raiding party.

1460 **1461** Trebizond, the last remnant of the Byzantine Empire, is conquered by the Ottomans.

1467 Onin War starts in Japan between rival feudal warlords.

1469 Last Timurid ruler of Persia is overthrown by Uzun Huzan (*c*.1420–78), leader of the White Sheep Turkmens.

1471 Annam (N Vietnam) conquers Champa (S Vietnam).

1477 At the end of the Onin War in Japan, power lies in the hands of new *daimyo* (territorial rulers).

1479 Vietnam conquers the kingdom of Laos.

1480 **1487** Portuguese explorers sailing from the Red Sea visit India.

1498 Portuguese explorer Vasco da Gama (1469–1524) reaches the port of Calicut in India.

AFRICA

1440 Walled enclosure and tower are built at Great Zimbabwe, capital of the Mwenemutapa kingdom.

1445 Portuguese explorers reach Cape Verde, W Africa.

1448 Portuguese establish a settlement on Arguim Island off the coast of Mauritania.

1455 Portuguese explorers discover the Cape Verde islands.

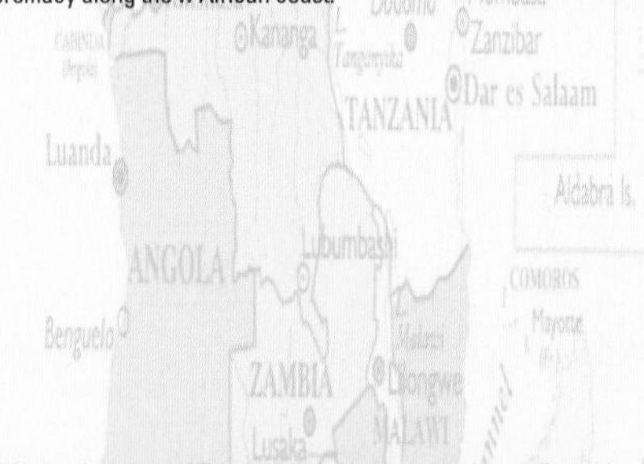

1463 Portuguese capture Casablanca in Morocco.

1464 King of Songhai, Sonni Ali (d.1492), begins campaigns to overthrow Mali; start of Songhai empire.

1468 Songhai empire conquers Timbuktu.

1469 Portuguese explorers cross the Equator.

1471 Portuguese establish a trading post at El Mina on the coast of present-day Ghana.

1471 Portuguese capture the city of Tangier on the N coast of Morocco.

1478 Portuguese ships defeat a fleet sent from Spain and establish supremacy along the W African coast.

1480 Under the treaty of Toledo, Portugal gets exclusive trading rights in Africa in return for agreeing to Spanish control of the Canary Islands.

1482 Portuguese build the fort of São Jorge to protect El Mina in Ghana.

1483 Portuguese explorers make contact with the W African kingdom of Kongo.

1487 Portuguese explorer Bartholomeu Dias (*c*.1450–1500) sails around the S tip of Africa into the Indian Ocean.

1489 Portuguese explorers sailing from the Red Sea visit E Africa.

1490 Nzinga Nkuwu (d.*c*.1506), king of Kongo, converts to Christianity.

1493 Muhammad Askia becomes emperor of Songhai, with the city of Gao as his capital.

1496 Spanish capture the town of Melilla on the N coast of Morocco.

1498 Sailing from Portugal, Vasco da Gama calls at the E African port of Mombasa en route to India.

EUROPE

1434 Defeat by the Holy Roman emperor at the Battle of Lipany leads to civil war between moderate and radical Hussites; it ends in the defeat of the radicals.

1435 Spanish ruler of Sicily, Alfonso V, unites his kingdom with Naples.

1436 French recapture Paris from the English.

1438 Albert of Habsburg (1397–1439) becomes German emperor and king of Hungary and Bohemia as Albert II.

1440 Alliance between Florence and Venice defeats Milan at the Battle of Anghiari.

1444 Ottoman sultan Murad II (1403–51) defeats a Christian army at the Battle of Varna in Bulgaria.

1445 African slaves are auctioned for the first time in Portugal.

1449 Milan defeats Venice and conquers the Lombardy region of N Italy.

1449 French invade the English territory in W France.

1450 Denmark and Norway are united under Danish king Christian I (1426–81).

1450 Sforza family gains control of Milan.

1452 Frederick III (1415–93) becomes the first Habsburg Holy Roman emperor.

1453 Ottoman Turks besiege and capture Constantinople, which is henceforth known as Istanbul.

1453 French victory over the English at the Battle of Castillon near Bordeaux marks the end of the Hundred Years' War.

1454 Peace of Lodi brings to an end the wars in Italy between Milan, Venice and Florence.

1455 Wars of the Roses break out in England between the rival dynasties of Lancaster and York.

1456 Turks capture Athens.

1457 Poland captures Marienberg from the Teutonic Knights who move their capital to Königsberg.

1459 Turks conquer Serbia.

1462 Ivan III (1440–1505) becomes the first ruler of Moscow not to pay tribute to the Golden Horde; end of the "Tartar Yoke".

1466 Teutonic Knights accept Polish overlordship.

1468 Charles the Bold (1433–77), Duke of Burgundy (NE France, Belgium and Holland), allies with England against the French.

1469 Lorenzo "il Magnifico" Medici (1449–92) becomes ruler of Florence.

1470 Louis XI (1423–83) of France allies with the Swiss against Burgundy.

1471 Right to feud is formally abolished in Germany in an attempt to stem rising lawlessness.

1475 Ottoman Turks conquer the Crimean peninsula on the N coast of the Black Sea.

1477 Inquisition is revived in Spain.

1477 Charles the Bold is killed at the Battle of Nancy. France occupies parts of Burgundy; the Low Countries come under Habsburg control by marriage.

1478 Albania is conquered by the Ottomans.

1479 Habsburg heir, Maximilian (1459–1519), defeats French attempts to gain control of the Low Countries.

1479 Ferdinand V (1452–1516) becomes Spanish king, uniting Castile and Aragón.

1483 Tomás Torquemada (1420–98) becomes head of the Spanish Inquisition.

1485 Battle of Bosworth ends the Wars of the Roses in England. Henry VII (1457–1509) becomes king; start of the Tudor dynasty.

1486 Habsburg Maximilian I is elected king of Germany.

1488 Great Swabian League of princes, knights and cities is formed in S Germany.

1492 Spanish, under Ferdinand V (1452–1516) and Isabella I (1451–1504), conquer the Islamic emirate of Granada; the whole of Spain is united under Christian rule.

1493 Maximilian I becomes Holy Roman emperor.

1493 Ottoman Turks invade Croatia.

1493 By the treaty of Senlis, France cedes the rest of Burgundy to Habsburg control.

1494–95 French under Charles VIII (1470–98) invade Italy, capture Florence and Naples, but are then forced to retreat.

1497 Denmark enforces union on Sweden.

THE AMERICAS

1440 Montezuma I (r.1440–69) becomes the Aztec king.

1441 Aztecs conquer Mayapan.

1450 Incas under Pachacuti conquer the Lake Titicaca region.

***c.*1460** Manchancaman becomes Chimú king and attacks the Incas.

1463 Pachacutec becomes the Inca king.

1470 Incas defeat and annex the Chimú kingdom.

1471 Tupac Yupanqui becomes the Inca king.

***c.*1490** Incas expand their empire into parts of Bolivia and Colombia.

1492 Christopher Columbus (1451–1506), a Genoese in the service of Spain, reaches an island he names San Salvador in the Bahamas; he founds the first European settlement, Navidad, on the island of Hispaniola.

1493 On his second voyage, Columbus plants the first sugar cane cuttings in the Caribbean.

1494 Treaty of Tordesillas between Spain and Portugal grants most of the New World to Spain.

1496 Town of Santo Domingo is established on Hispaniola as the Spanish centre of government in the Americas.

1497 John Cabot (*c.*1450–*c.*1498), a Genoese sailing from England, discovers the coast of Newfoundland.

1498 Columbus reaches the American mainland at the mouth of the River Orinoco.

1499 Italian explorer Amerigo Vespucci (1454–1512) discovers the mouth of the River Amazon.

SCIENCE AND TECHNOLOGY

***c.*1445** German goldsmith Johann Gutenberg (1400–68) develops moveable metal type for printing.

1443 Phonetic alphabet is developed in Korea.

1449 Italian artist and inventor Mariano di Jacopo Taccola (1381–1453) completes 10 books of civil and military machines.

1453 Hungarian armourers cast a 7.3m (26ft), 50-tonne cannon to be used by the Ottoman Turks in the siege of Constantinople.

1455 Construction of the Grand Bazaar begins in Istanbul.

1456 German astronomer Johannes Regiomontanus (1436–76) introduces the mathematical symbols for plus and minus in an unpublished manuscript.

***c.*1460** Italian glassmaker Anzolo Barovier perfects the technique of making completely colourless glass by adding manganese.

1462 Pope declares his monopoly over the supply of alum (used in the dyeing industry) to Europe.

1469 Pliny the Elder's *Natural History* is printed for the first time.

1474 Government of Venice issues the world's first patents to protect inventors' rights.

***c.*1475** Italian astronomer and mathematician Paolo Toscanelli (1397–1482) proposes voyaging to China by sailing w across the Atlantic ocean.

1480 Italian artist and inventor Leonardo da Vinci (1452–1519) designs a parachute.

1494 Italian mathematician Luca Pacioli (*c.*1445–1517) introduces algebra to Europe in *Summa de arithmetica, geometrica, proportione et proportionalita.*

ARTS AND HUMANITIES

1439 Cosimo de' Medici founds the Florentine Academy.

1439 Byzantine scholar Gemistus Pletho (1355–1452) publishes his treatise on the differences between the Platonic and Aristotelian philosophies.

***c.*1440** Italian artist Pisanello (*c.*1395–1455) turns the making of bronze portrait medals into an art form. 1440

1444 Italian architect Michelozzi di Bartolommeo (1396–1472) designs the Medici Palace in Florence.

1445 Italian sculptor Bernado Rossellino (1409–64) carves a marble tomb in Florence for the humanist Leonardo Bruni.

1446 Flemish artist Rogier van der Weyden (1400–64) paints *The Last Judgement.*

1449–52 *Gideon Tapestries* are woven in Tournais, present-day Belgium, for Philip III (the Good) (1396–1467), Duke of Burgundy.

1452 Italian artist Fra Filippo Lippi (1406–69) paints his frescos for Prato cathedral.

1455 *Gutenberg Bible* is printed.

1456 French poet François Villon (1430–63) completes *Le petit testament.*

1457 Italian artist Antonio Pollaiuolo (1432–98) completes a silver reliquary of St Giovanni in Florence.

1465 Italian artist Andrea del Verrocchio (1435–88) starts work on his bronze statues of *Christ and St Thomas* in Florence. 1460

1469 Birth of Nanak (d.1539) the Indian philosopher and founder of Sikhism.

1470 Italian artist Piero della Francesca (1415–92) paints portraits of the Duke and Duchess of Urbino.

***c.*1472** Italian artist Giovanni Bellini (*c.*1430–1516) paints his Pesaro altarpiece in Venice.

***c.*1478** Italian artist Sandro Botticelli (1444–1510) paints *Primavera.*

1481 Death of the French artist Jean Fouquet (b.1420), who painted miniature portraits and illustrated manuscripts. 1480

***c.*1482** Italian architect Giuliano da Sangallo (1445–1516) designs the villa Poggio a Caiano in Florence.

1485 William Caxton (1422–91) prints *Le Morte D'Arthur* by Sir Thomas Malory.

1486 Italian humanist Giovanni Pico della Mirandola (1463–94) writes *Oration on the Dignity of Man.*

1486 Italian artist Andrea Mantegna (1431–1506) paints *Triumphs of Caesar* in Mantua.

1489 German scholars publish the *Hammer of Witchcraft.*

1489 German sculptor Viet Stoss (1440–1533) completes his carved limewood altar for the church of St Mary's in Kraków, Poland.

1494 German poet Sebastian Brandt (1458–1521) writes *Ship of Fools.*

1495 Flemish painter Hieronymus Bosch (*c.*1450–1516) paints *The Garden of Earthly Delights.*

1496 Japanese artist-priest Sesshu Toyo (1420–1506) paints *Winter Landscape.*

ASIA AND AUSTRALASIA

1500 **1501** Persian leader Ismail (1486–1524) defeats Turkish tribes at the Battle of Shurur and gains control of Persia.

1502 Portuguese ships commanded by Vasco da Gama (1469–1524) destroy the Indian port of Calicut.

1502 Ismail is proclaimed shah of Persia; start of the Safavid dynasty.

1504 Warlord Babur (1483–1530) captures Kabul, Afghanistan.

1506 Portuguese build a fort at Cochin in India.

1507 Portuguese sack Muscat, near the mouth of the Arabian Gulf.

1508 Turkish fleet destroys Portuguese ships at the port of Chaul, India.

1509 Portuguese destroy a combined Turkish-Indian fleet near the island of Diu.

1510 Portuguese conquer Goa and make it their capital in India.

1511 Portuguese, led by Afonso d'Albuquerque (1453–1515), capture Malacca in Malaya.

1512 Portuguese reach the Spice Islands (the Moluccas).

1514 Ottoman Turks invade Persia and defeat the Safavids at Chaldiran.

1515 Ottoman Turks conquer Kurdistan.

1515 Portuguese capture and fortify Hormuz in Yemen.

1516 Ottoman Turks defeat the Egyptian Mamluks and the Persian Safavids at the Battle of Marj Dabik in Syria.

1516 Portuguese establish a trading post at Guangzhou (Canton) in S China.

1517 Portuguese establish a trading post at Columbo in Ceylon.

1520 **1521** Ferdinand Magellan (1480–1521) discovers and claims the Philippine Islands for Spain.

1521 Portuguese establish a settlement on Amboina, one of the Spice Islands.

1522 Portuguese traders are expelled from China.

1523 Afghan warlord Babur (1483–1530) invades India and captures the city of Lahore.

1526 Babur conquers the W half of the Delhi Sultanate after the Battle of Panipat and establishes the Mughal Empire.

1526 Portuguese explorers reach New Guinea.

1529 Victory at the Battle of the River Gogra completes the Mughal conquest of N India.

1534 Ottomans conquer Mesopotamia.

1537 Portuguese obtain trading concessions at Macao on the coast of S China.

1538 Alliance of Ottoman Turks and Gujaratis fails to evict the Portuguese from Diu in India.

1538 Turkish naval expedition conquers the W coast of Arabia.

1539 Mughal dynasty in India is overthrown by the Afghan warlord Sher Shah (d.1545).

1540 **1543** Portuguese first make contact with Japan.

1546 With Portuguese assistance, Tabin Shwehti (r.1531–50) makes himself king of Burma.

1555 Burmese invade N Thailand.

1555 Peace treaty is signed between the Ottoman Turks and Safavid Persia.

1556 Emperor Akbar I (1542–1605) restores Mughal rule in India and defeats Hindu forces at the second Battle of Panipat.

1557 Portuguese establish a colony at Macao in China.

AFRICA

1501 Portuguese attempt to close the Red Sea to Islamic shipping.

1504 Christian kingdom of Soba in Nubia is conquered by Islamic forces.

1505 Portuguese under Francisco de Almeida (1450–1510) sack the Islamic ports of Kilwa and Mombasa in E Africa.

1506 Portuguese build a fort at Sofala on the E coast of Africa.

1509 Spanish capture the town of Oran on the coast of Algeria.

1510 Spanish capture the town of Tripoli in Libya.

1517 Ottomans under Sultan Selim I (1467–1520) conquer Egypt; end of the Mamluk dynasty.

1517 Hausa states defeat the Songhai empire in W Africa.

1527 Islamic Somalis invade Ethiopia.

1529 Ottoman Turks invade and conquer Algeria.

1535 Charles V campaigns against the Turkish pirate Khayr ad-Din (Barbarossa, 1466–1546) and captures the city of Tunis.

1541 Expedition of Charles V (1500–58) against the Ottoman Turks at Algiers fails.

1543 Ethiopian forces, assisted by Portuguese troops, expel Islamic invaders.

EUROPE

1499 French under Louis XII (1462–1515), allied with Venice, invade Italy and capture Milan.

1499 Switzerland wins political independence from the Habsburg empire in the Swabian War.

1499 Cesare Borgia (1475–1507), son of Pope Alexander IV, begins the conquest of central Italy.

1501 French invade Italy and conquer Naples.

1501 Portuguese establish a direct sea-route to import pepper and spices from India into Europe.

1504 Spain regains control of Naples.

1509 French-led coalition attacks and captures Venetian-controlled towns in N Italy.

1511 Henry VIII (1491–1547) of England joins the Holy League against France in Italy.

1512 Hanseatic League permits Dutch ships to trade in the Baltic Sea.

1513 French are defeated at the Battle of Novara in Italy.

1513 English destroy the Scottish army at the Battle of Flodden.

1515 A marriage alliance gives the Habsburgs control over Spain.

1515 German emperor obtains Bohemia and Hungary from Poland in exchange for Prussia.

1515 After defeat by the French at the Battle of Marignano, Switzerland adopts a policy of neutrality.

1517 Pope Leo X (1475–1521) revives the sale of indulgences to pay for the rebuilding of St Peter's cathedral in Rome.

1517 German priest and reformer Martin Luther (1483–1546) writes his 95 theses against Church corruption; start of the Reformation in Europe.

1518 Swiss religious reformer Ulrich Zwingli (1484–1531) begins preaching in Zurich.

1519 Charles V (1500–58), Habsburg king of Spain and Burgundy, wins election as German emperor over Francis I (1494–1547) of France.

1521 At the diet of Worms, Emperor Charles V condemns Luther's ideas.

1521 Ottoman Turks capture Belgrade and raid S central Europe.

1521–26 First war for control of Italy is fought between France and Spain.

1522 Knights of St John surrender Rhodes to the Turks after a siege.

1523 Gustavus I (1496–1560) establishes the Swedish state; start of the Vasa dynasty.

1524–25 Violent peasant uprisings sweep across Germany.

1525 Spain defeats France at the Battle of Pavia in Italy and captures Francis I (1494–1547).

1526 Louis II (b.1506) of Hungary is killed in the Battle of Mohács against the Ottoman Turks; the Hungarian crown passes to the Habsburgs.

1527 During his second Italian war (1526–29), Spanish king and Habsburg emperor Charles V sacks Rome.

1528 Genoese admiral Andrea Doria (1466–1560) frees Genoa from French rule.

1529 Ottoman Turks unsuccessfully besiege Vienna.

1529 German emperor Charles V ends toleration of Lutheran reforms. Some German princes protest, becoming Protestants.

1531 War breaks out between Protestant and Catholic cantons in Switzerland.

1531 Hungary is partitioned between the Habsburgs and the Ottomans.

1531 Protestant rulers in Germany form the Schmalkaldic League.

1534 Act of Supremacy is passed in England, making Henry VIII (1491–1547) head of the English Church.

1541 French religious reformer John Calvin (1509–64) establishes religious rule in Geneva.

1541 Ottoman Turks capture Budapest and conquer Hungary.

1545 Council of Trent meets to reform the Catholic Church.

1546–47 Charles V defeats the Protestants in the Schmalkaldic War in S and central Germany.

1547 Protestant reformer John Knox (1514–72) is arrested by French soldiers in Scotland.

1547 Ivan IV (1530–84) of Moscow is crowned first tsar of Russia.

1552 Emperor Charles V invades E France.

1553 Following the death of Henry VIII in 1547, and his only son, Edward VI, in 1553, his daughter Mary (1516–58) becomes queen of England as Mary I. She marries the future Philip II (1527–98) of Spain and restores Catholic worship in England; Protestants are persecuted.

THE AMERICAS

1500 Portuguese explorer Pedro Cabral (1467–1520) lands in Brazil and establishes Vera Cruz.

1501 First African slaves are landed in the West Indies.

1502 Montezuma II (r.1502–20) becomes the Aztec king.

1507 German mapmaker Martin Waldseemüller (*c.*1470–*c.*1518) proposes that the New World be named America.

1508–15 Spanish conquer Puerto Rico and Cuba.

1509 Spanish establish a colony on the isthmus of Panama.

1512 Spanish governor of Puerto Rico, Juan Ponce de León (1460–1521), discovers Florida.

1513 Spanish explorer Vasco Núñez de Balboa (1475–1519) crosses the isthmus of Panama and discovers and names the Pacific Ocean.

1516 Bananas are introduced to the Caribbean from the Canary Islands.

1517 Spanish explorer Francisco de Córdoba discovers the Yucatán peninsula in Mexico.

1517 First asiento (agreement) for the supply of African slaves to the American colonies is issued to a Flemish merchant by the Spanish government.

1518 Spanish conquistador Hernán Cortés (1485–1547) lands in Mexico and conquers the Tlaxcalans.

1519 Cortés enters the Aztec capital Tenochtitlan, captures Montezuma II and establishes Spanish control.

1520 Montezuma II dies; the Aztecs force the Spanish from Tenochtitlan.

***c.*1520** Inca king Huyana Capac conquers parts of Ecuador.

1521 Spanish attack and destroy Tenochtitlan.

1522 Viceroyalty of New Spain is created and Mexico City is founded on the ruins of Tenochtitlan.

1521 Sailing in the pay of Spain, the Portuguese navigator Ferdinand Magellan sails around Cape Horn at the S tip of South America.

1522 Spanish expedition from Panama reaches Peru.

1525 Death of Inca king Huyana Capac leads to dispute over throne between sons Huascar (d.1532) and Atahualpa.

1529 Welser family (German bankers) establish a colony in Venezuela.

1530 Portuguese begin the colonization of Brazil.

1531 Inca king Atahualpa invites Spanish soldiers, led by Francisco Pizarro (1471–1541), to join his side in the Inca civil war.

1532 Pizarro captures Atahualpa and holds him to ransom.

1533 Atahualpa is killed by the Spanish, who occupy Cuzco and conquer the Inca empire.

1535 Pizarro founds the city of Lima in Peru.

1537 Spanish establish colonies at Buenos Aires, at the mouth of the River Plate, and Asunción, on the River Paraguay.

1538 Spanish conquistador Gonzalo de Quesada founds the city of Bogotá.

1539 Spanish begin the conquest of the Mayan cities in the Yucatán region of Mexico.

1540–42 Spanish expedition led by Francisco de Coronado (1510–54) discovers the Grand Canyon.

1541 Spanish explorer Hernando De Soto (1500–42) discovers the River Mississippi.

1541 Spanish explorer Francisco de Orellana (*c.*1490–*c.*1546) completes his journey down the River Amazon from the Andes to the Atlantic Ocean.

1541 French explorer Jacques Cartier (1491–1557) makes an unsuccessful attempt to establish a colony at Québec in Canada.

1541 Spanish found the city of Santiago in Chile.

1542 Spanish create the viceroyalty of Peru.

1545 Spanish begin mining silver at Potosi in Peru.

1546 Revolt by the Maya against Spanish rule in Mexico is crushed.

1548 Spanish open silver mines at Zaatecar in Mexico.

SCIENCE AND TECHNOLOGY

1500 Leonardo da Vinci (1452–1519) designs an impractical, but correctly principled, helicopter.

1502 Italian mineralogist Leonardus Camillus publishes *Speculum Lapidum*, which catalogues over 250 minerals.

***c.*1505** Pocket watch is invented by German clockmaker Peter Henlein (1480–1542).

***c.*1510** Polish astronomer and mathematician Nicolas Copernicus (1473–1543) formulates his theory that the Earth orbits the Sun.

***c.*1515** Wheel lock for igniting firearms is invented in Italy.

***c.*1520** Rifling for firearms is invented in central Europe.

1522 Spanish ships returning from Ferdinand Magellan's voyage complete the first circumnavigation of the world.

1525 German mathematician Christoff Rudolff introduces the square root symbol in *Die Coss*.

1533 German surveyor Gemma Frisius (1508–55) discovers the principles of triangulation.

1537 Italian mathematician Niccoló Tartaglia (1449–1557) discusses the trajectory of projectiles in *Nova scientia*.

1540 Italian gunsmith Vannoccio Biringuccio's *Pirotechnia*, a handbook of metal smelting and casting techniques, is published.

1542 French scholar Konrad Gesner (1516–65) publishes *Historia Plantarum*, the first modern work of botany.

1543 Nicolas Copernicus' heliocentric theory is published in *De revolutionibus orbium coelestium*.

1543 Belgian doctor Andreas Vesalius (1514–64) publishes *On the Structure of the Human Body*, an illustrated handbook of human anatomy based on dissection.

1545 Italian scientist Giramolo Cardano (1501–76) introduces negative numbers to European mathematics in his book *Ars magna*.

1551 English mathematician Leonard Digges (*c.*1520–59) invents the theodolite.

1551 German mathematician Georg Rhaeticus (1514–74) publishes the six basic trigonometrical functions in *Canon doctrinae triangulorum*.

ARTS AND HUMANITIES

1498 German artist Albrecht Dürer (1471–1528) publishes his album of woodcuts *The Apocalypse*.

1498 Ottavanio Petrucci (1466–1539) obtains a licence in Venice to become the first commercial music printer.

1502 Italian architect Donato Bramante (1444–1514) reintroduces 1500
the Doric order in his tempietto at San Pietro in Montorio, Rome.

1503 Leonardo da Vinci paints the *Mona Lisa*.

1504 Italian artist Michelangelo Buonarotti (1475–1564) carves his marble sculpture of *David* in Florence.

***c.*1504** Flemish composer Josquin Desprez (1445–1521) writes the mass *Hercules Dux Ferrariae*.

***c.*1505** Italian artist Giorgione (*c.*1478–1510) paints *Tempest*.

1506 Ancient Roman sculpture known as the *Laocoön* is rediscovered in Rome.

1511 Dutch humanist Desiderius Erasmus (1466–1536) publishes *In Praise of Folly*.

1512 Michelangelo finishes painting the Sistine Chapel ceiling in Rome.

1512 Italian artist Raphael Santi (1483–1520) paints a portrait of Pope Julius II.

1513 Italian politician Niccolò Machiavelli (1469–1527) writes *The Prince*.

1515 German artist Mathias Grünewald (1470–1528) paints *The Crucifixion* for the Isenheim altarpiece, Alsace.

1516 English scholar Thomas More (1478–1535) publishes *Utopia*.

1516 Italian poet Lodovico Ariosto (1474–1533) publishes his epic *Orlando Furioso*.

1520 German Christian reformer Martin Luther (1483–1546) writes *The* 1520
Freedom of a Christian Man, which proclaims salvation through faith.

1524 German artist Lucas Cranach (1472–1553) paints *Judgement of Paris*.

1525 Luther writes *Against the Murderous Thieving Hordes of Peasants*.

1525 English religious reformer William Tyndale (*c.*1494–1536) starts printing English versions of the New Testament in Cologne, Germany.

1528 Italian courtier Baldassare Castiglione (1478–1529) publishes *Libro del Cortegiano*.

***c.*1528** German artist Albrecht Altdorfer (1480–1538) paints unpopulated landscapes.

1530 German religious reformer Philip Melanchthon (1497–1560) writes the *Confessions of Augsburg*, a statement of Protestant beliefs.

1530 Italian artist Correggio (*c.*1490–1534) paints *Adoration of the Shepherds*.

1533 German artist Hans Holbein the Younger (1497–1543) paints *The Ambassadors*.

1534 Luther completes his translation of the Bible into German.

1534 French humanist François Rabelais (1494–1553) writes his satire *Gargantua*.

1534 Society of Jesus (Jesuits) is founded by Ignatius Loyola (1491–1556) and Francis Xavier (1506–52).

***c.*1535** Italian artist Parmigiano (1503–40) paints *Madonna with the Long Neck*.

1538 Italian artist Titian (1485–1576) paints *Venus of Urbino*.

1540 Holy Carpet of Ardebil, with an area of 61sq m (72sq yd), is 1540
woven in N Persia.

1541 Spanish priest and protector of Native Americans Bartolomé de Las Casas (1474–1566) writes *Very Brief Account of the Destruction of the Indies*.

1541 Death of the Swiss doctor known as Paracelsus (b.1493).

1545 Indian architect Aliwal Khan designs the octagonal tomb of the Afghan warlord Sher Shah at Sasaram, India.

1545 Italian goldsmith and sculptor Benvenuto Cellini (1500–71) casts his bronze statue of *Perseus* in Florence.

1548 Italian artist Tintoretto (1518–94) paints *The Miracle of the Slave* in Venice.

1549 French poet Joachim du Bellay (1522–60) writes *Defense et Illustration de la Langue Francaise*.

ASIA AND AUSTRALASIA

1560 **1561** Mughals under Emperor Akbar I (1542–1605) conquer Malwa in central India.

1563 Chinese destroy Japanese pirates who have been raiding coastal cities.

1565 Mughals conquer the Hindu kingdom of Vijayanagar in S India.

1568 Oda Nobunaga (1534–82) seizes power in central Japan; start of the Azuchi-Momoyama period.

1570 Port of Nagasaki in Japan is opened to foreign traders.

1571 Spanish found the city of Manila in the Philippines.

1573 Mughals under Akbar I conquer Gujarat in W India.

1576 Mughals conquer Bengal in E India.

1580 **1581** Cossack chieftain Yermak Timofeyevich (d.1584) begins the Russian conquest of Siberia.

1581 Akbar I conquers Afghanistan.

1581 Turkish ships sack the Portuguese fortress at Muscat.

1583 Akbar I proclaims toleration of all religions in India.

1584 General Toyotomi Hideyoshi (1536–98) establishes himself as ruler of central Japan.

1586 Abbas I (1571–1629) becomes shah of Safavid Persia.

1590 Ottoman Turks wrest control of Georgia and Azerbaijan from Persia.

1590 Hideyoshi conquers E and N Japan, reuniting the country under his rule.

1592 Akbar conquers S Pakistan.

1592 Japanese invade Korea, but are forced out by the Chinese.

1597 Japanese again invade Korea, then withdraw.

1597 Persians defeat the nomadic Uzbeks and expel them from W Afghanistan.

1598 Tokugawa Ieyasu (1543–1616) seizes power in Japan on the death of Hideyoshi.

1600 **1600** Victory at the Battle of Sekigahara leaves Tokugawa Ieyasu as sole ruler of Japan; start of the Tokugawa (Edo) period.

1600 English East India Company is formed.

1602 Dutch East India Company is formed.

1603 Persians under Abbas I capture Baghdad from the Ottomans.

1605 Dutch seize the spice island of Amboina from the Portuguese.

1606 Spanish explorer Luis de Torres sights the York peninsula on the N coast of Australia.

1606 Turkey makes peace with Austria.

1609 Dutch conquer Ceylon (present-day Sri Lanka) from the Portuguese.

1609 Persians defeat the Turks at the Battle of Urmia and recapture Baghdad.

AFRICA

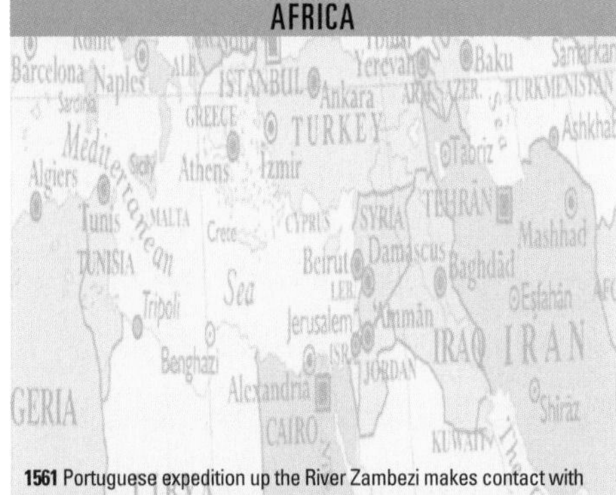

1561 Portuguese expedition up the River Zambezi makes contact with the kingdom of Mwenemutapa.

1571 Idris III (d.1603) becomes king of Kanem and establishes control of the Lake Chad region.

1571–73 Portuguese make a disastrous attempt to conquer Mwenemutapa.

1572 Spanish capture Tunis from the Ottoman Turks.

1574 Portuguese found the city of Luanda in Angola.

1574 Ottoman Turks recapture Tunis.

1578 Portuguese attempt to conquer the interior of Morocco is defeated at the Battle of Alcázar-Kabir.

1581 Morocco begins expanding S into the W Sahara and captures the town of Tuat.

1589 Portuguese defeat the Ottoman Turks at Mombasa, E Africa.

1591 Invading Moroccans crush Songhai forces at the Battle of Tondibi and destroy the city of Gao; end of the Songhai empire.

1595 Dutch establish a trading post in Guinea on the W coast of Africa.

1598 Dutch establish a small colony on the island of Mauritius.

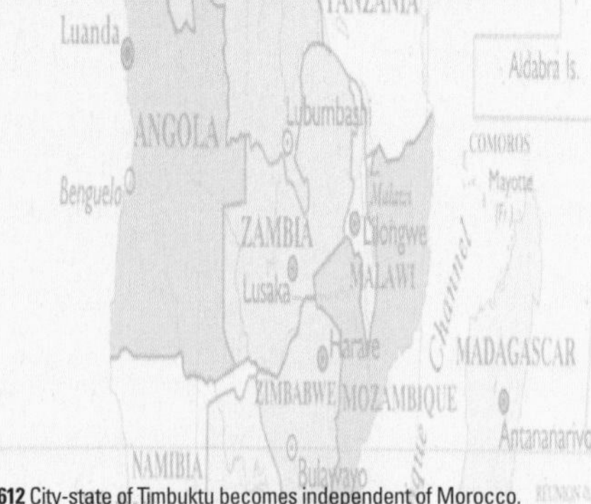

1612 City-state of Timbuktu becomes independent of Morocco.

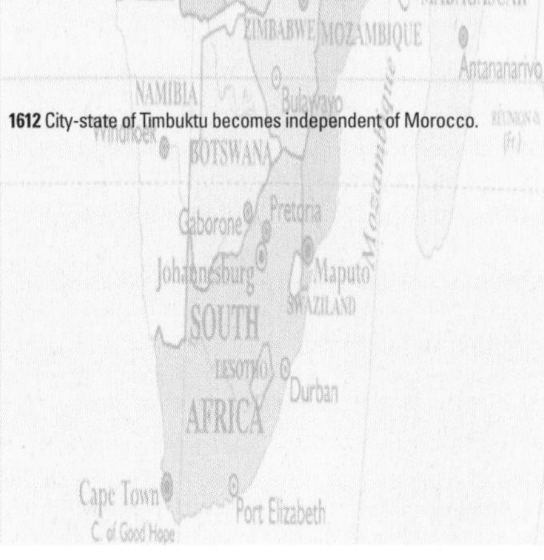

EUROPE

1555 Religious peace of Augsburg establishes freedom of worship in Germany.

1556 Charles V (1500–58) abdicates; his empire is split between Ferdinand I (Austria and Germany) and Philip II (Spain, Low Countries, parts of Italy, America).

1557 Russia invades Livonia, the former territory of the Teutonic Knights.

1558 English, allied to Spain, lose the port of Calais to the French.

1558 Ivan IV (the Terrible) (1530–84) orders the colonization of Siberia.

1558 Elizabeth I (1533–1603) becomes queen of England.

1559 Philip II (1527–98) of Spain defeats France; the Peace of Cateau-Cambrésis restores Naples and the Low Countries to Spanish control.

1560 Scottish Parliament establishes Presbyterianism as the state religion.

1560 Charles IX (1550–74) becomes boy-king of France with his mother Catherine de' Medici (1519–89) as regent.

1562 Massacre of Huguenots (French Protestants) at Vassy in France starts a series of religious civil wars.

1563 Start of the Catholic Counter Reformation in S Germany.

1564 Boyars (Russian aristocrats) revolt against Ivan IV.

1566 Dutch nobles form an anti-Spanish alliance.

1567 Duke of Alba enforces Spanish control in the Low Countries.

1569 Poland and Lithuania unite under Polish control.

1569–71 Revolt by former Muslims is crushed in Spain.

1570 Novgorod is destroyed by armies from Moscow.

1570 Turks attack Cyprus.

1571 Stock Exchange is established in London, England.

1571 Venetian and Spanish fleets defeat the Ottoman Turks at the Mediterranean sea battle of Lepanto.

1572 Thousands of Huguenots are massacred on St Bartholomew's Day.

1573 Venetians abandon Cyprus to the Turks.

1574 Dutch under William I (the Silent), Prince of Orange, open dykes to relieve the Spanish siege of Leyden.

1576 Following the Spanish sack of Antwerp, the Dutch provinces unite under William I (the Silent).

1579 Dutch republic is formed; Belgium remains under Spanish control.

1580 King Philip II of Spain succeeds to the throne of Portugal and the two countries are united under Habsburg rule.

1581 Spain agrees a peace treaty with the Ottoman Turks.

1584 Dutch leader William I of Orange (b.1533) is murdered and is succeeded by Maurice of Nassau (1567–1625).

1585 Elizabeth I of England refuses the Dutch throne but takes the Netherlands under her protection by the treaty of Nonsuch.

1585–89 War of the Three Henrys is fought for the French throne.

1588 Spanish invasion fleet (the Armada) sent against England is defeated at the naval battle of Gravelines.

1589 Russian Church becomes independent of Greek Orthodox Church.

1589 Victorious Henry III (b.1551) of France is assassinated; Henry IV (1553–1610) accedes to the throne; start of the Bourbon dynasty.

1593 War breaks out in Transylvania between Austria and the Ottomans.

1595 After intervening in the Livonian War, Sweden acquires Estonia by the treaty of Teusina.

1598 Boris Godunov (1551–1605) becomes tsar of Russia.

1598 Edict of Nantes grants limited freedom of worship and legal equality for Huguenots (Protestants) in France.

1603 James VI (1566–1625) of Scotland inherits the English throne as James I on the death of Elizabeth I; end of the Tudor dynasty, start of the Stuart dynasty.

1604 Protestant Charles IX (1550–1611) becomes king of Sweden.

1605 Gunpowder Plot fails to blow up the English Parliament; Guy Fawkes (b.1570) is executed the following year.

1608 Protestant Union of German rulers is formed.

1609 Catholic League of German rulers is formed.

1609 Truce ends the fighting in the Netherlands between Philip III (1578–1621) of Spain and the Dutch rebels.

1610 Henry IV of France is assassinated; Louis XIII (1601–43) becomes king with his mother Marie de' Medici (1573–1642) as regent.

THE AMERICAS

1548 Spanish viceroyalty of New Galicia is created in NW Mexico with Guadalajara as its capital.

1549 Spanish viceroyalty of New Granada is created, comprising South America E of the Andes and N of the River Amazon.

1549 Portuguese establish the port of Bahia in Brazil.

1554 Portuguese establish the city of São Paulo in Brazil.

1555 Dutch, English and French sailors form the Guild of Merchant Adventurers to raid Spanish shipping routes from America.

1555 French establish a colony at the bay of Rio de Janeiro on the coast of Brazil.

1561 Following the failure of a settlement at Pensacola, South Carolina, present-day USA, the Spanish king abandons attempts to colonize the E coast of North America.

1561 Spanish treasure fleets are forced to adopt a convoy system as a defence against "pirate" attacks.

1564 French establish a colony at Fort Caroline in Florida, present-day USA.

1565 Spanish destroy Fort Caroline and found the town of St Augustine in Florida.

1567 Portuguese destroy the French colony in Brazil and found the city of Rio de Janeiro.

1568 Spanish destroy the fleet of the English slave-trader John Hawkins (1532–95) at Vera Cruz.

1578 English explorer Francis Drake (1540–96) sails along the W coast of present-day USA and lays claim to California.

1585 Expedition organized by Walter Raleigh (1552–1618) establishes a colony (which immediately fails) on Roanoke Island off the coast of Virginia, present-day USA.

1587 Second, unsuccessful attempt is made to found an English colony on Roanoke Island.

606 London and Plymouth Companies are established in England.

607 London Company establishes a colony at Jamestown, Virginia, under the leadership of John Smith (1580–1631).

608 French explorer Samuel de Champlain (1567–1635) founds Québec as the capital of the colony of New France.

609 English explorer Henry Hudson (d.1611) discovers and sails up the Hudson River; sailing in search of a Northwest Passage to the Far East, he discovers (1610) Hudson Bay.

612 English establish a settlement on the island of Bermuda.

612 Tobacco is first cultivated by English settlers in Virginia.

612 French establish a colony on the island of Maranhão at the mouth of the River Amazon.

613 Dutch set up a trading post on Manhattan Island.

SCIENCE AND TECHNOLOGY

1556 German mineralogist Georg Bauer (1494–1555), also known as Agricola, publishes *De re metallica*, a systematic study of mining and assaying techniques.

1557 English mathematician Robert Recorde (*c*.1510–58) introduces the symbol for equality in his algebra textbook *The Whetstone of Whit*.

1569 Flanders mapmaker Gerardus Mercator (1512–94) publishes a world navigation chart that has meridians and parallels at right-angles.

1572 Italian mathematician Raffaele Bombelli (1526–72) introduces imaginary numbers in *Algebra*.

1576 Danish astronomer Tycho Brahe (1546–1601) builds a royal observatory for King Frederick II (1534–88).

1582 Pope Gregory XIII (1502–85) introduces the New Style (Gregorian) calendar to Catholic countries.

1583 Danish mathematician Thomas Finke (1561–1656) publishes the law of tangents in *Geometriae rotundi*.

1586 Dutch mathematician Simon Stevin (1548–1620) demonstrates that objects fall at an equal rate in a vacuum, irrespective of their weights.

1589 Stocking-frame knitting machine is invented by William Lee (*c*.1550–*c*.1610) in Cambridge, England.

1591 French mathematician François Viete (1540–1603) introduces literal notation to algebra, with the systematic use of letters to represent unknowns and coefficients.

1593 German astronomer Christopher Clavius (1537–1612) invents and uses the decimal point in a table of mathematical sines.

1593 Death of doctor Li Shizen (b.1518) who compiled *The Comprehensive Pharmacopoeia* of traditional Chinese medicine.

1600 English scientist William Gilbert (1544–1603) publishes *Concerning Magnetism*, which discusses the Earth's magnetism.

1602 Italian astronomer and scientist Galileo Galilei (1564–1642) discovers the constancy of a swinging pendulum.

1606 Belgian scholar Justus Lipsius (1547–1606) completes the final revisions and corrections to his edition of Tacitus' *Annals*.

1608 Dutch optician Hans Lippershey (1570–1619) invents a refracting telescope.

1614 Scottish mathematician John Napier (1550–1617) invents logarithms.

1615 Dutch mathematician Ludolp van Ceulen (1540–1610) publishes a value for pi (π) that is correct to 32 decimal places in his posthumous *Arithmetische en Geometishe fondamenten*.

ARTS AND HUMANITIES

1549 English priest Thomas Cranmer (1489–1556) publishes *Book of Common Prayer*.

1555 Italian architect Andrea Palladio (1508–80) publishes a guidebook to Roman antiquities.

1559 *Index of Forbidden Books* is published by the Roman Catholic Church.

1562 Italian artist Paolo Veronese (1528–88) paints *The marriage of Cana*. 1560

1563 Dutch artist Pieter Bruegel the Elder (1525–69) paints *The Tower of Babel*.

1563 English historian John Foxe (1516–87) publishes the book known as *Foxe's Book of Protestant Martyrs*.

1563 Building work starts on the monastery and palace of Escorial near Madrid, Spain, designed by Juan de Herrera (*c*.1530–97).

1568 Italian art critic Giorgio Vasari (1511–74) publishes a revised edition of *Lives of the most excellent Painters, Sculptors and Architects*.

1572 Portuguese poet Luíz vaz de Camões (1524–80) publishes his epic *The Lusiads*.

1575 Italian architect Giacomo della Porta (1537–1602) designs the church of Il Gesù in Rome; this marks the beginning of the Baroque period of European art.

1576 French political philosopher Jean Bodin (1530–96) publishes *Of the Republic*.

1580 French scholar and author Michel Montaigne (1533–92) publishes the first of his *Essays*. 1580

1580 Flemish sculptor Jean de Boulogne (1529–1608) cast his bronze statue of *Mercury*.

1582 Death of the Spanish religious philosopher Teresa of Avila (b.1515).

1586 Greek-born Spanish artist El Greco (1541–1614) paints *Burial of Count Orgasz* in Toledo, Spain.

1589 English poet and dramatist William Shakespeare (1564–1616) writes his first play *Henry VI (part I)*.

1590 English dramatist Christopher Marlowe (1564–93) writes his play *Tamburlaine the Great*.

1595 William Shakespeare writes his play *Romeo and Juliet*.

1596 English poet (1552–99) Edmund Spenser completes *The Faerie Queen*.

1597 Italian composer Giovanni Gabrieli (c.1553–1612) writes *Sonata Pian'e Forte*.

1598 Italian artist Caravaggio (1571–1610) paints *Supper at Emmaus*.

1599 Globe Theatre is built in London.

1600 Italian artist Annibale Carracci (1560–1609) paints *The Virgin mourning Christ*. 1600

1600 William Shakespeare writes *Hamlet*.

1602 Italian philosopher Tommaso Campanella (1568–1639) publishes *City of Sun*.

1604 Confucian Tung-lin Academy is founded in China.

1605 Spanish author Miguel de Cervantes (1547–1616) publishes the first volume of *Don Quixote of the Mancha*.

1605 English dramatist Ben Jonson (1572–1637) writes *Volpone*.

1605 English philosopher Francis Bacon (1561–1626) publishes *Advancement of Learning*.

1611 Flemish artist Peter Paul Rubens (1577–1640) paints *Raising of the Cross*.

ASIA AND AUSTRALASIA

1609 Dutch establish a trading post at Hirado, W Japan.

1610 Russian expansion into Siberia reaches the River Yenisei.

1612 England gains trading rights at Surat in India after defeating the Portuguese in a naval battle.

1615 Nomad tribes of Manchuria form a military coalition under their leader Nurhachi (1559–1626).

1615 Japanese ruler Tokugawa Ieyasu (1543–1616) destroys Osaka castle after a siege.

1619 Dutch establish the fortified port of Batavia (present-day Jakarta) on the island of Java.

1620 **1620** English defeat the Portuguese at the sea battle of Jask off the W coast of India.

1622 English, allied with the Persians, capture Hormuz from the Portuguese.

1623 Dutch massacre English merchants on the island of Amboina.

1624 Spanish traders are expelled from Japan.

1624 Dutch establish a trading post on the island of Formosa.

1625 Janissaries (slave soldiers) revolt against Ottoman rule in Turkey.

1635–37 Manchurian confederation conquers S Mongolia and Korea.

1637 Christian-led Shimabara rebellion is suppressed in Japan.

1638 Japan is closed to foreigners.

1638 Ottoman Turks under Murad IV (1607–1640) recapture Baghdad.

1639 Treaty of Kasr-i-Shirim establishes a permanent border between Turkey and Persia.

1639 English acquire a site for a colony at Madras in India.

1640 **1641** Dutch capture the Malaysian port of Malacca from the Portuguese.

1641 Dutch traders are permitted to operate from an island in Nagasaki harbour in Japan.

1643 Dutch explorer Abel Tasman (1603–59) discovers New Zealand and Tasmania.

1644 Manchurians enter Beijing at the invitation of the last Ming emperor; end of the Ming dynasty in China; start of the Qing dynasty.

1645 Russian explorers in Siberia reach the Sea of Okhotsk.

1648 Janissaries revolt in Turkey and depose Sultan Ibrahim I (1615–48).

1652 Russian colonists found the city of Irkutsk in Siberia.

1656 Ottoman Turks are defeated by the Venetians at a sea battle near the Dardanelles.

1656 Muhammad Köprülü (*c.*1586–1661) becomes Ottoman vizier (chief minister) and stabilizes the Ottoman Empire.

1660 **1661** English establish a colony at Bombay in S India.

1662 Chinese pirate warlord Jeng Cheng-gong (Koxinga, 1624–62) expels the Dutch from Formosa.

1662 Kang-Xi (1654–1722) becomes emperor of China.

1664 Hindu raiders sack the Mughal port of Surat in India.

1664 Russian cossacks raid N Persia.

1669 Hindu religion is prohibited throughout the Mughal Empire in India and Hindu temples are destroyed.

1674 French establish a colony at Pondicherry in E India.

1674 Hindu raider Sivaji (1630–80) becomes independent ruler of Maratha in India.

AFRICA

1621 Dutch capture the W African island slave ports of Arguin and Goree from the Portuguese.

1626 French establish the colony of St Louis at the mouth of the River Senegal.

1626 French settlers and traders establish a colony on the island of Madagascar.

1637 Dutch capture the fortified port of El Mina from the Portuguese.

1650 Ali Bey establishes himself as hereditary ruler of Tunis.

1652 Dutch settlers found the colony of Capetown in South Africa.

1654 French occupy the island of Réunion.

1662 Portugal cedes the city of Tangier in Morocco to England.

1662 English build a fort at the mouth of the River Gambia, W Africa.

1677 French expel the Dutch from Senegal in W Africa.

EUROPE

1610 Poland invades Russia and occupies Moscow in an attempt to gain control of the Russian throne.

1613 Following the expulsion of the Poles, Michael Romanov (d.1645) becomes Russian tsar; start of Romanov dynasty.

1617 Under the peace of Stolbovo with Sweden, Russia loses access to the Baltic Sea.

1618 Protestant revolt in Prague (the Defenestration of Prague) begins the Bohemian War; it marks the start of the Thirty Years' War.

1620 Catholic victory at the Battle of the White Mountain leads to the dissolution of the Protestant Union in Germany.

1621 Gustavus II (1594–1632) of Sweden creates the first modern army and conquers Livonia from Poland.

1621 Warfare between the Dutch and Spanish is renewed.

1625 Huguenots rebel in NW France.

1625 Charles I (1600–49) becomes king of England, Scotland and Ireland.

1625 Christian IV (1577–1648) of Denmark intervenes as leader of the Protestants in Germany; start of the Danish phase of the Thirty Years' War.

1628 French forces under chief minister cardinal Armand Richelieu capture the Huguenot stronghold of La Rochelle.

1629 After defeat by Catholic armies, Denmark withdraws from German politics under the peace of Lübeck.

1630 Gustavus II of Sweden lands in N Germany in support of the Protestants; start of the Swedish phase of the Thirty Years' War.

1631 Swedes defeat the German Catholics at the Battle of Breitenfeld and invade S Germany.

1632 Gustavus II dies following his victory at the Battle of Lutzen.

1635 Catholic victory at the Battle of Nordlingen forces the Swedes out of S Germany; France enters the Thirty Years' War as Sweden's ally.

1640 Portugal and Catalonia revolt against Spanish rule.

1640 Frederick William (1620–88) becomes Great Elector of Prussia.

1642 Civil war breaks out in England between Royalists and Parliamentarians.

1646 French and Swedes invade Bavaria in S Germany.

1648 Spain recognizes Dutch independence.

1648–53 Fronde rebellions erupt in France.

1648 Treaty of Westphalia ends the Thirty Years' War.

1649 Charles I of England is executed; the monarchy is abolished and a Commonwealth is established.

1652 Spain is reunited when Catalonia submits to Spanish rule.

1652–54 England wins a war against the Dutch over shipping rights.

1653 Oliver Cromwell (1599–1658) becomes Lord Protector of England.

1654 Ukrainian Cossacks defect from Poland to Russia, starting a war.

1656 War breaks out between Protestant and Catholic cantons in Switzerland.

1656 English ships capture a Spanish treasure fleet near Cadiz.

1656 Swedes invade Poland and capture Warsaw.

1658 English, allied with the French, capture the Spanish-held port of Dunkirk after the Battle of the Dunes.

1659 Peace of the Pyrenees ends warfare between France and Spain.

1660 Monarchy is re-established in England with the accession of Charles II (1630–85).

1660 By the peace of Olivia, Sweden gains territory from Poland.

1661 On the death of Cardinal Mazarin (b.1602), Louis XIV (1638–1715) becomes sole ruler of France.

1662–63 Spanish invade Portugal in an attempt to re-establish control, but are defeated.

1664 Austria defeats the Ottoman Turks at the Battle of St Gotthard.

1665 War breaks out between the Dutch, supported by France, and England.

1667 By the treaty of Andrussovo, Russia acquires E Ukraine from Poland.

THE AMERICAS

1614 Expedition organized by the Plymouth Company makes an unsuccessful attempt to establish a colony in New England.

1614 Dutch New Netherland Company is established.

1616 Portuguese conquer the French colony at the mouth of the Amazon and found the city of Belém.

1616 Dutch establish the colony of New Netherland on the site of present-day New York, USA.

1616 English explorer William Baffin (1584–1622) discovers Baffin Bay.

1619 First African slaves arrive in Virginia, and the first representative assembly is held.

1620 English Protestant settlers cross the Atlantic in the *Mayflower* and establish a colony in Massachusetts.

1623 English Council for New England establishes colonies at Dover and Plymouth in New Hampshire.

1624 English settlement in Virginia becomes a royal colony.

1624–25 Dutch capture and briefly hold the port of Bahía in Brazil.

1625 English settlers establish a colony on the island of Barbados.

1626 Dutch administrator Peter Minuit (1580–1638) purchases Manhattan Island and establishes the city of New Amsterdam.

1627 French minister Armand Richelieu (1585–1642) organizes the Company of 100 Associates to colonize New France.

1628 John Endicott (*c.*1588–1665) establishes an English colony at Salem.

1630 Dutch capture the port of Recife in Brazil from the Portuguese.

1630 Twelve-year period of intensive migration from England to Massachusetts begins.

1632 English colony of Maryland is established by George Calvert (1580–1632).

1635 French establish colonies on Martinique and Guadeloupe.

1636 Dutch capture the island of Curaçao from the Spanish.

1636 English colonist Roger Williams (1603–83) settles in Providence, Rhode Island.

1638 English colony is established at New Haven on Long Island.

1638 Swedes establish the colony of New Sweden in Delaware.

1641 Body of Liberties law code is established in Massachusetts.

1643 French establish the city of Montreal in Canada.

1643 English colonies form the New England Confederation.

1645 Portuguese settlers revolt against Dutch rule in N Brazil.

1654 Portuguese expel the Dutch from Brazil.

1655 French capture the island of Haiti from Spain.

1655 Under Dutch governor Peter Stuyvesant (1610–72), New Netherland occupies New Sweden.

1656 English ships capture Jamaica from Spain, provoking a war.

1663 English colony of Carolina is established.

1664 Colonies of New Haven and Connecticut unite.

1664 New Amsterdam surrenders to the English; the city becomes known as New York.

1667 Bahamas are added to the colony of Carolina.

1667 Under the treaty of Breda, English occupation of New Netherland is exchanged for the Dutch occupation of Surinam.

1669 English philosopher John Locke (1632–1704) writes the Fundamental Constitutions for Carolina.

1673 French priests Jacques Marquette (1637–75) and Louis Joliet (1646–1700) explore the upper reaches of the River Mississippi.

1673 Dutch briefly recapture New York.

SCIENCE AND TECHNOLOGY

1618 Dutch scientist Snellius (1591–1626) discovers his law of the diffraction of light.

1619 German astronomer Johannes Kepler (1571–1630) outlines the third of his three laws of planetary motion in *Harmonies of the World.*

1628 English doctor William Harvey (1578–1657) explains the circulation of blood pumped around the body by the heart.

1631 French mathematician Pierre Vernier (1580–1637) invents an accurate measuring calliper.

1631 English scientist Thomas Harriot (*c.*1560–1621) introduces the symbols for "greater than" and "less than" in his posthumously published *The Analytical Arts.*

1631 English mathematician William Oughtred (1575–1660) introduces the symbol for multiplication in *The Keys to Mathematics.*

1635 Italian mathematician Bonaventura Cavalieri (1598–1647) publishes the first textbook on integration, *Geometry of Continuous Indivisibles.*

1637 French philosopher and mathematician René Descartes (1596–1650) introduces analytical geometry in *Geometry.*

1639 French mathematician Girard Desargues (1591–1661) introduces the study of projective geometry in *Brouillon project.*

1641 French scientist Blaise Pascal (1623–62) invents a mechanical adding machine.

1643 Italian scientist Evangelista Torricelli (1608–47) invents the mercury barometer.

1644 French mathematician Marin Mersenne (1558–1648) studies prime numbers.

1647 German astronomer Johannes Hevelius (1611–87) draws a map of the Moon's surface.

1650 German scientist Otto von Guericke (1602–86) invents a vacuum pump.

1650 German scientist Athanasius Kircher (1601–80) discovers that sound will not travel in a vacuum.

1655 English mathematician John Wallis (1616–1703) introduces the symbol for infinity in *The Arithmetic of Infinitesimals.*

1657 Academia del Cimento, the first scientific research institute, is established in Florence, Italy.

1657 Dutch scientist Christiaan Huygens (1629–95) constructs a pendulum clock.

1659 Swiss mathematician Johann Rahn (1622–76) introduces the symbol for division in *Teutsche Algebra.*

1659 French mathematician Pierre de Fermat (1601–65), in correspondence with Pascal, develops the theory of probability.

1662 Royal Society of London is established.

1662 Irish scientist Robert Boyle (1627–91) formulates his law of gas expansion.

***c.*1665** English scientist Isaac Newton (1642–1727) formulates the law of gravity.

1666 Italian astronomer Giovanni Cassini (1625–1712) discovers polar ice caps on Mars.

1667 French king Louis XIV founds the Observatoire de Paris.

1668 John Wallis discovers the principle of conservation of momentum.

1669 Isaac Newton creates the first system of calculus.

1672 French astronomer N. Cassegrain invents an improved reflecting telescope.

ARTS AND HUMANITIES

1612 English poet John Donne (1572–1631) writes *Of the Progress of the Soul.*

***c.*1613** Spanish poet and dramatist Felix Lope de Vega Carpio (1562–1635) writes *All Citizens are Soldiers.*

1615 *Bukeshohatto* book of warriors' wisdom is published in Japan.

1619 English architect Inigo Jones (1573–1652) designs the Banqueting House in London.

1623 Death of the Indian poet Tulsi Das (b.1532), author of the Hindu 1620
classic *Tulsi-krit Ramayan.*

1624 Dutch artist Frans Hals (*c.*1580–1666) paints *Laughing Cavalier.*

1625 Dutch lawyer Hugo Grotius (1583–1645) publishes *On the laws of war and peace.*

1632 Dutch artist Rembrandt Harmenszoon van Rijn (1606–69) paints *Anatomy Lesson of Dr Tulp.*

1632 Flemish artist Anthony Van Dyck (1599–1641) becomes court painter to English king Charles I.

1633 Italian architect and sculptor Gianlorenzo Bernini (1598–1680) designs the canopy over the altar at St Peter's in Rome.

1634 Taj Mahal is built in Agra, India, as a tomb for Mumtaz Mahal the wife of Mughal emperor Shah Jahan (1592–1666).

1634 Passion play is inaugurated at Oberammagau, s Germany.

1635 Académie Française is established.

1637 French dramatist Pierre Corneille (1606–84) writes his play *Le Cid.*

1638 Italian architect Francesco Borromini (1599–1667) designs the church of San Carlo alle Quattro Fontane in Rome.

1638 Spanish dramatist Pedro Calderón de la Barca (1600-81) writes his play *Life is a Dream.*

***c.*1637** French artist Nicolas Poussin (1594–1665) paints *The Rape of the Sabine Women.*

1642 Italian composer Claudio Monteverdi (1567–1643) completes 1640
his opera *The Coronation of Poppea.*

1646 Spanish artist Bartolomé Murillo (1617–82) completes his paintings of the lives of Franciscan saints.

1651 English political philosopher Thomas Hobbes (1588–1679) publishes *Leviathan.*

***c.*1652** English religious reformer George Fox (1624–91) founds the Society of Friends, whose adherents become known as Quakers.

1654 Dutch poet and dramatist Joost van den Vondel (1587–1679) writes his play *Lucifer.*

1656 Spanish artist Diego Velázquez (1599–1660) paints *The Maids of Honour.*

1656 Dutch artist Rembrandt Harmenszoon van Rijn (1606–69) paints *Jacob Blessing the Sons of Joseph.*

1662 French landscape gardener André Le Nôtre (1613–1700) 1660
designs the grounds of the palace of Versailles in France.

1664 French dramatist Jean Racine (1639–99) writes *La Thebaïde.*

1667 French dramatist Molière (1622–73) writes his comedy *The Misanthrope.*

1667 English poet John Milton (1608–74) publishes his epic *Paradise Lost.*

1668 Dutch artist Jan Vermeer (1632–75) paints *Astronomer.*

1668 English poet and dramatist John Dryden (1631–1700) writes his essay *Of Dramatick Poesie.*

1669 German author Hans von Grimmelshausen (1621–76) writes his novel *Simplicissimus.*

ASIA AND AUSTRALASIA

1674 Regional rulers rebel against central control in China.

1675–78 Sikhs rebel against their Mughal overlords in India.

1680 **1681** Manchu Qing dynasty re-establishes central control in China.

1683 Qing dynasty conquers the island of Formosa (present-day Taiwan), which comes under direct rule from the Chinese mainland for the first time.

1685 Mughal emperor Aurangzeb (1619–1707) attempts to expel English merchants from Surat.

1689 Russian settlers are forced to withdraw from NW China; the treaty of Nerchinsk establishes the Russian–Chinese border in the Amur region.

1690 English establish a colony at Calcutta, N India.

1691 Mughal Empire in India reaches its greatest extent.

1696 Chinese establish a protectorate in N Mongolia.

1700 **1700** Charles Eyre reorganizes the administration of English Bengal.

1703 The "Forty-seven *ronin*" avenge the execution of their lord in Japan, and are ordered to commit suicide.

1705 Chinese attempt to impose their candidate for Dalai Lama provokes risings and unrest in Tibet.

1707 Death of Emperor Aurangzeb leads to the rapid disintegration of the Mughal Empire in India.

1708 Sikhs establish independent control of the Punjab region of N India.

1709 Mir Vais, Afghan chieftain of Kandahar, rebels against Persian rule and proclaims independence.

1710 **1711** Mir Vais defeats an invading Persian army.

1712 War of succession in India between the sons of the Mughal emperor Bahadur divides India.

1717 Abdali dynasty of Herat establishes another independent Afghan state.

1717 Mongol army seizes control of Lhasa, the Tibetan capital.

1717 English East India Company obtains trading concessions from the Mughal emperor.

1718 Chinese army sent to Tibet is destroyed by Mongol warriors.

AFRICA

1683 Prussians build a fort on the coast of Guinea in W Africa.

1684 England gives Tangier back to Morocco.

1684 French mount naval expeditions to suppress the Islamic pirates at Algiers.

1686 French formally annex Madagascar.

1688 Huguenot refugees from France arrive in S Africa.

1697 French complete the conquest of Senegal.

1698 Portuguese are expelled from most E African ports by Omanis from SE Arabia.

1704 British capture Gibraltar from Spain.

1705 Husseinid dynasty takes control in Tunis and establishes independence from the Turks.

1708 Spanish are expelled from Oran in Algeria.

1709 Dutch cattle farmers in South Africa trek E across the Hottentot Holland Mountains.

1710 French take the island of Mauritius from the Dutch.

1714 Ahmed Bey establishes the Karamanlid dynasty as independent rulers in Tripoli, Libya.

1717 Dutch begin importing slaves to Cape Colony, South Africa.

EUROPE

1667 France occupies Spanish towns in Flanders.

1668 Spain recognizes Portuguese independence.

1669 Ottoman Turks capture Crete from Venice.

1670 Peasants and cossacks revolt in S Russia.

1672 France invades the Netherlands; William III of Orange (1650–1702) becomes Dutch ruler and opens the sluices to save Amsterdam.

1674 German emperor enters the wars against France.

1675 Prussia defeats France's ally Sweden at the Battle of Fehrbellin.

1678 France captures the towns of Ypres and Ghent in Belgium from Spain.

1678 Treaties of Nijmegen end the wars between France and the Dutch, Germans and Spanish; France gains territory from Spain.

1683 Ottoman Turks under Kara Mustafa (1634–83) besiege Vienna and are defeated by a German-Polish army at the Battle of the Kahlenberg.

1683 French under Louis XIV (1638–1715) invade Belgium and occupy Luxembourg and Lorraine.

1684 Venice, Austria and Poland form a Holy Alliance against the Turks.

1685 Louis XIV revokes the Edict of Nantes in France (1598).

1686 German rulers form the League of Augsburg against France.

1688 France invades the Rhineland region of Germany.

1688 Austrian armies liberate Belgrade from the Turks.

1688 Glorious Revolution in England deposes Catholic king James II (1633–1701); the Dutch Protestant ruler William of Orange becomes William III of England.

1689 Peter I (1672–1725) becomes sole ruler of Russia.

1689 England and the Netherlands join the League of Augsburg against France.

1690 William III of England defeats French troops under former king James II at the Battle of the Boyne in Ireland.

1692 English and Dutch ships defeat a French fleet at Cap La Hogue.

1697 Austrians defeat the Turks at the Battle of Zenta.

1697 Peace of Ryswick ends the War of the League of Augsburg against France.

1699 Under the peace of Kalowitz, Turks lose territory to Holy Alliance.

1700 Sweden is attacked by Poland, allied to Denmark and Russia; start of the Great Northern War. Swedes, under Charles XII (1682–1718), defeat the Russians under Peter I at the Battle of Navara.

1700 Charles II (b.1661) of Spain dies childless; the French duke of Anjou is proclaimed King Philip V (1683–1746); end of the Habsburg dynasty in Spain; start of the Bourbon dynasty.

1701 Frederick III (1657–1713) of Brandenburg is crowned Frederick I king of Prussia at Königsburg.

1701 England, Holland and Austria form Grand Alliance against France.

1701 Grand Alliance declares war on France and Spain; the War of the Spanish Succession begins.

1702 William III's daughter Anne (1665–1714) becomes queen of England.

1702 Swedes invade Poland and capture Warsaw and Kraków.

1703 Peter I establishes the city of St Petersburg.

1704 English army led by John Churchill (1650–1722), 1st Duke of Marlborough, defeats the French at the Battle of Blenheim.

1706 Following their defeat at Turin, the French are expelled from Italy.

1706 English defeat the French at the Battle of Ramilles and conquer Belgium.

1707 England and Scotland are united as Great Britain.

1709 British defeat the French at the Battle of Malplaquet.

1709 Swedes in alliance with Ukrainian cossacks invade Russia but are defeated at the Battle of Poltava.

1710 South Sea Company is set up in London.

1711 Following an uprising, Austria grants Hungary self-administration.

1711 Charles XII of Sweden persuades the Turks to attack Russia.

1713 Frederick William I (1688–1740) becomes king of Prussia.

1713 Austrian emperor Charles VI (1685–1740) issues the Pragmatic Sanction, which allows a female to inherit the Habsburg throne.

1714 Treaty of Utrecht between Britain and France ends the War of the Spanish Succession; Britain gains overseas colonies in the Mediterranean and America.

THE AMERICAS

1674 English establish the Hudson's Bay trading post.

1675–76 English colonists fight King Philip's War against Massoit Native North Americans.

1676 Nathaniel Bacon (1647–76) leads a rebellion in Virginia.

1680 Colony of New Hampshire is separated from Massachusetts.

1680 Portuguese establish the colony of Sacramento in w Brazil.

1680 Revolt by Pueblo Native North Americans drives the Spanish from New Mexico.

1682 French explorer Robert de La Salle (1643–87) reaches the mouth of the Mississippi and claims the Louisiana Territory for France.

1683 Portuguese establish the colony of Colonia on the River Plate in Argentina.

1682 English Quaker William Penn (1644–1718) establishes the colony of Pennsylvania.

1684 Charter of Massachusetts is annulled.

1686 English colonies are organized into the Dominion of New England.

1689–97 King William's War, the first of the French and Indian Wars, is fought between English and French colonists and their native allies.

1691 King William III issues a new charter for Massachusetts.

1692 Witchcraft trials are held in Salem, Massachusetts.

1693 College of William and Mary is established in Virginia.

1696 Spanish reconquer New Mexico.

1699 French establish a colony at Biloxi in Louisiana.

1701 French explorer Antoine de Cadillac (1658–1730) founds the town of Detroit between lakes Erie and Huron.

1701 Yale College is founded in Connecticut, present-day USA.

1702 French acquire the asiento to supply African slaves to the Spanish colonies in America.

1702 English attack and burn St Augustine in Florida at the start of Queen Anne's War (the American phase of the War of the Spanish Succession).

1703 English colony of Delaware separates from Pennsylvania.

1704 Native North Americans allied to the French massacre English settlers at Deerfield in Connecticut.

1706 Spanish establish the town Albuquerque in New Mexico.

1707 British troops from New England march into Canada and besiege French settlers at Port Royal, Nova Scotia.

1708–09 Portuguese destroy the power of the Paulistas (slave-raiders) in s Brazil in the War of the Emboabas.

1709 Large numbers of Germans from the Palatinate region begin migrating to the English colonies in North America, especially Pennsylvania.

1710–11 Portuguese defeat Brazilian natives in the War of the Mascates.

1711–12 Tuscarora Native North Americans massacre British colonists in North Carolina and are subsequently defeated.

1711 French capture and ransom Rio de Janeiro in Brazil.

1713 By the treaty of Utrecht, Britain gains Newfoundland and Nova Scotia from the French, and acquires a monopoly on the asiento slave trade with Spanish colonies.

1715 British colonists defeat the Yamasee Native North Americans in South Carolina.

SCIENCE AND TECHNOLOGY

1673 German scientist Gottfried von Leibniz (1646–1716) invents a calculating machine.

1673 French engineer Sebastien de Vauban (1633–1707) introduces his system for attacking fortresses at the siege of Maastricht.

1675 English scientist Isaac Newton (1642–1727) proposes the particle theory of light.

1675 Royal Observatory at Greenwich, near London, is established.

1676 Danish astronomer Ole Romer (1644–1710) discovers that light travels at a finite speed.

1678 Dutch scientist Christiaan Huygens (1629–95) proposes the wave theory of light.

1679 French scientist Denis Papin (1647–*c*.1712) invents the pressure cooker.

1680 Dutch scientist Anton van Leeuwenhoek (1632–1723) discovers bacteria.

1681 Dodo becomes extinct on the island of Mauritius in the Indian Ocean.

1682 English astronomer Edmond Halley (1656–1742) establishes the periodicity of Halley's Comet.

1684 Gottfried von Leibniz publishes his differential calculus and introduces the integral symbol.

1687 Isaac Newton publishes *Mathematical Principles of Natural Philosophy*.

1694 Bank of England is established in London.

1696 French Mathematician Guillaume de L'Hopital (1661–1704) publishes *Analyse des infiniment petits*, the first textbook of infinitesimal calculus.

1698 Swiss mathematician Jakob Bernoulli (1654–1705) studies the properties of the logarithmic spiral.

1698 English engineer Thomas Savery (*c*.1650–1715) invents a practical steam-driven water pump.

1700 German Protestants adopt the Gregorian calendar.

1701 English farmer Jethro Tull (1674–1741) invents the seed drill.

1701 Academy of Sciences is established in Berlin.

1705 English engineer Thomas Newcomen (1663–1729) invents the atmospheric steam engine, which uses a vacuum to drive a piston.

1706 English mathematician William Jones (1675–1749) introduces the symbol for pi (π) in *Synopsis palmariorum matheseos*.

1709 British ironworker Abraham Darby (*c*.1677–1717) perfects a technique for producing iron in a coke-fired blast furnace.

1711 Italian naturalist Luigi Marsigli (1658–1730) shows that corals are animals not plants.

1712 British clockmaker John Rowley constructs the first clockwork orrery.

1714 German scientist Gabriel Fahrenheit (1686–1736) invents the mercury thermometer.

ARTS AND HUMANITIES

1669 English government official Samuel Pepys (1633–1703) completes his 10-year diary of life in London.

1670 English architect Christopher Wren (1632–1723) begins rebuilding London churches destroyed by the Fire of London (1666).

1673 French composer Jean-Baptiste Lully (1632–87) writes his opera *Cadmus and Hermione*.

1677 Dutch philosopher Baruch Spinoza (1632–77) publishes *Ethics*.

1678 English preacher John Bunyan (1628–88) writes *The Pilgrim's Progress*.

1678 French architect Jules Hardouin-Mansart (1646–1708) designs the Hall of Mirrors for the palace of Versailles.

1678 French poet Jean de La Fontaine (1621–95) publishes his second book of *Fables*.

1681 Italian composer Arcangelo Corelli (1653–1713) writes *sonate* 1680
da chiesa.

1689 English composer Henry Purcell (1659–95) writes his opera *Dido and Aeneas*.

1689 English philosopher John Locke (1632–1704) publishes *Two Treatise on Government*.

1694 Death of the Japanese haiku poet Matsuo Basho (b.1644).

1696 German architect Fischer von Erlach (1656–1723) introduces Italian baroque to central Europe with his collegiate church in Salzburg, Austria.

1697 French scholar Pierre Bayle (1647–1706) sets the trend for the Enlightenment with *Historical and Critical Dictionary*.

1690 Italian musical instrument maker Antonio Stradivari (1644–1737) introduces his "long" pattern with his "Tuscan" violin.

1700 English dramatist William Congreve (1670–1729) writes his 1700
comedy *The Way of the World*.

1700 Samuel Sewell (1652–1730) publishes his anti-slavery tract, *The Selling of Joseph*, in Boston, Massachusetts, present-day USA.

1702 World's first daily newspaper, the *Daily Courant*, is published in London.

1705 French writer Bernard de Mandeville (1670–1733) argues that self-interest leads to the general good in his book *The Grumbling Hive*.

1705 German-born English composer George Frideric Handel (1685–1759) writes his opera *Almira*.

1708 Death of Gobind Singh (b.1666), the tenth and last guru of Sikhism, who promoted the warrior ethic.

1709 Italian instrument-maker Bartolommeo Cristofori (1655–1731) invents the piano by substituting hammer action for the plucking action of the harpsichord.

1710 English bishop George Berkeley (1685–1753) introduces 1710
empiricist philosophy in *Treatise concerning the Principles of Human Knowledge*.

1710 Puritan minister Cotton Mather (1663–1728) publishes *Essays to do Good*.

1712 British poet Alexander Pope (1688–1744) publishes *Rape of the Lock*.

1713 School of dance is established at the Paris Opéra.

1714 German philosopher Gottfried Leibniz (1646–1716) outlines his philosophy in *Monadologie*.

ASIA AND AUSTRALASIA

1720 **1720** Japanese shogun Yoshimune (d.1751) permits the importation of non-religious European books.

1722 Dutch explorer Jacob Roggeveen discovers Easter Island and Samoa.

1722 Afghan ruler of Kandahar, Mir Mahmud (d.1725), invades Persia and makes himself shah.

1723 Russians capture Baku on the Caspian Sea from Persia.

1724 Chinese establish a protectorate over Tibet.

1724 Russia and Turkey agree to divide Persia between them.

1724 Persian shah Mahmud goes insane and orders the massacre of the Persian aristocracy.

1726 Ashraf (d.1730), the Afghan shah of Persia, defeats an invading Turkish army.

1727 Kiakhta treaty fixes the borders between Russia and China.

1728 Dutch explorer Vitus Bering (1680–1741), sailing for Russia, discovers the Bering Strait, between Siberia and Alaska.

1730 **1730** Persian chieftain Nadir Kuli (1688–1747) drives the Afghans from Persia and restores the Safavid dynasty.

1731 Trade rivalries in India between Britain and Austria are settled in Britain's favour by the treaty of Vienna.

1733 Turks defeat the Persians at the Battle of Kirkuk.

1735 Russia allies with Persia against the Turks, who are defeated at the Battle of Baghavand.

1736 Nadir becomes shah of Persia on the death of Abbas III; end of the Safavid dynasty.

1737 Persians invade Afghanistan.

1739 Persians invade India, defeat a Mughal army at the Battle of Karnal, and capture Delhi.

1740 **1742** Marathas raid British Bengal in India.

1744 Al-Saud family of central Arabia allies with the new Wahhabi Islamic sect.

1745 Persians under Nadir Shah (1688–1747) defeat the Turks at the Battle of Kars.

1746 French capture Madras from the British.

1747 Nadir Shah is assassinated, leading to a period of anarchy in Persia.

1747 Ahmad Shah (1722–73) establishes the Afghan national state ruled by the Durrani dynasty.

1748 British besiege the French port of Pondicherry in E India.

1748 Madras is returned to the British.

AFRICA

1723 British Africa Company claims the Gambia region of W Africa.

1728–29 Portuguese briefly re-occupy the E African port of Mombasa.

1730 Dutch northward expansion in South Africa reaches the River Olifants.

1732 Spanish recapture Oran in Algeria.

1744 Mazrui the Omani governor of Mombasa declares his independence from the sultan of Oman.

1745 Ashanti warriors armed with muskets defeat Dagomba armoured cavalry in W Africa.

EUROPE

1714 Russia captures Finland from Sweden after the Battle of Storkyro.

1714 Austria makes a separate peace with France and gains territory in Italy and Belgium.

1714 George, Elector of Hanover, becomes King George I (1660–1727) of Britain on the death of Queen Anne (b.1665).

1715 Louis XV (1710–74) becomes king of France with Philip of Orléans as regent.

1715 First Jacobite rebellion in Scotland is defeated by British troops.

1717 Austria liberates Belgrade from the Turks.

1718 Spain conquers Sicily; Britain, Austria, France and Holland form the Quadruple Alliance and defeat Spain at the Battle of Cape Passaro.

1719 Russia invades Sweden.

1720 Defeat in the Great Northern War ends Swedish dominance in the region; Russia gains Livonia and Estonia under the treaty of Nystad.

1720 Savoy gains Sardinia in return for Austrian control of Sicily.

1720 Collapse of Mississippi Company leads to bankruptcies in France.

1720 South Seas Company fails and creates financial panic in London.

1721 Robert Walpole (1676–1745) becomes Britain's first prime minister.

1722 Peter I (1672–1725) makes administrative reforms in Russia and limits the traditional privileges of the aristocracy.

1723 Frederick William I (1688–1740) establishes the General Directory for the centralized administration of Prussia.

1725 French king Louis XV breaks his engagement to a Spanish princess and marries the daughter of the ex-king of Poland; as a result the Spanish make an alliance with Austria.

1725 Following the death of Peter I, his wife Catherine I (1684–1727) becomes the first of a series of weak Russian rulers.

1726 Cardinal Andre Hercule de Fleury (1653–1743) becomes chief minister in France.

1727 George II (1683–1760) accedes to the British throne.

1727 War breaks out between Spain and Britain allied with France.

1729 Treaty of Seville ends the war between Britain and Spain.

1729 Corsica revolts against Genoese rule.

1732 Genoa suppresses the Corsican revolt.

1732 Military conscription is introduced in Prussia.

1733–35 Russia invades Poland after the death of King Augustus II (1670–1733); France allied to Spain fights the War of the Polish Succession against Austria allied to Russia.

1733 Treaty (the first Family Compact) between France and Spain declares the indivisibility of the two branches of the Bourbon dynasty.

1734 Russians capture Danzig in Poland.

1734 Spanish troops conquer Sicily and Naples from Austria.

1735 Charles III (1716–88), son of Philip V (1683–1746) of Spain, becomes king of Sicily and Naples.

1735 French troops occupy Lorraine.

1736–39 War between Austria allied to Russia and the Turks results in Russia regaining Azov and Austria losing Serbia.

1738 Treaty of Vienna settles the War of the Polish Succession; Spain gains Naples and Sicily on condition they are never united with Spain; France gains the promise of Lorraine.

1739 War of Jenkin's Ear breaks out between Britain and Spain.

1740 Frederick William I of Prussia dies and is succeeded by Frederick II (the Great, 1712–86).

1740 Austrian emperor Charles VI (b.1685) dies; under the Pragmatic Sanction his daughter Maria Theresa (1717–80) becomes empress.

1740 War of the Austrian Succession begins when Frederick II (the Great) invades Austrian-controlled Silesia in the first Silesian War.

1741–43 Sweden attacks Russia, but is defeated and forced to cede parts of Finland.

1741 France, Spain and Prussia ally against Austria.

1742 Austrians make a separate peace with Prussia, ceding Silesia under the treaty of Breslau and Berlin.

1743 Holland allies with Britain and Austria against France.

1743 France and Spain strengthen their alliance, with the second Family Compact.

1743 British-led Pragmatic Army defeats the French at the Battle of Dettingen.

1744 Prussians invade Bohemia in the second Silesian War.

THE AMERICAS

1715 Scots-Irish immigrants begin the settlement of the Appalachian foothills.

1716 Governor Alexander Spotswood (1676–1740) of Virginia leads an expedition into the Shenandoah valley.

1717 Mississippi Company, promoted by Scottish economist John Law (1671–1729), is given a monopoly on trade with the French colony of Louisiana.

1717 Portuguese build a fort at Montevideo on the River Plate, Uruguay.

1718 French found the port of New Orleans in Louisiana.

1718 Spanish establish the settlement of Pensacola in Florida.

1718 Warfare breaks out between France and Spain in Florida and Texas.

1720 Spain occupies Texas after hostilities with France.

1720 British establish the colony of Honduras in Central America.

1721 Jose de Antequerra leads the revolt of the communeros against the Spanish in Paraguay.

1726 Spanish capture Montevideo in Uruguay from the Portuguese.

1726 British colonists from New York make a treaty with the Native American Iroquois League against the French.

1729 Natchez Native North Americans massacre French settlers at Fort Rosalie in Louisiana.

1729 British colonies of North and South Carolina are brought under royal control.

1730 Cherokee Native North Americans acknowledge British supremacy.

1731 Paraguayan revolutionary Jose de Antequerra is defeated and executed.

1733 British colony of Georgia is established by James Oglethorpe (1696–1785).

1733 Molasses Act places prohibitive duties on non-British sugar products imported into British North America.

1735 Spanish authorities finally suppress the revolt of the communeros in Paraguay.

1735 Trial in New York of newspaperman John Zenger (1697–1746) establishes the freedom of the press in the British colonies.

1737 William Byrd (1674–1744) founds Richmond, Virginia.

1739 British capture the Spanish settlement of Porto Bello in Panama.

1739 African slaves revolt and kill white settlers at Stono River, South Carolina.

1740 British colonists from Georgia invade Spanish Florida but fail to take St Augustine.

1742 Spanish attack Georgia from Florida.

1743 Hostilities between Britain and Spain become absorbed into King George's War, the American phase of the War of the Austrian Succession.

1745 British colonists from New England besiege and capture the French fortress of Louisburg, Nova Scotia.

1746 Princeton University is founded in New Jersey.

1748 British fleet captures Port Louis in Haiti from the French.

1748 Treaty of Aix-la-Chapelle ends King George's War.

1749 British establish the town of Halifax in Nova Scotia.

1749 British colonists form the Ohio Company to extend British territory W.

1749 French build Fort Rouille on the site of present-day Toronto.

SCIENCE AND TECHNOLOGY

1721 First smallpox inoculations are carried out in Boston.

1725 Academy of Sciences is established at St Petersburg, Russia.

1725 Italian philosophical historian Giambattista Vico (1668–1744) emphasizes the importance of social and cultural history in *New Science*.

1727 British biologist Stephen Hales (1677–1761) publishes *Vegetable Staticks*, which establishes the science of plant physiology.

1728 British astronomer James Bradley (1693–1762) discovers the aberration of light.

1730 British navigator John Hadley (1682–1744) invents the reflecting quadrant.

1730 British politician and farmer Charles Townshend (1674–1738) introduces four-course crop rotation with turnips and clover.

1730 French scientist René Réaumur (1683–1757) invents an alcohol thermometer.

1732 English farmer Jethro Tull (1674–1741) publishes *Horse Hoeing Husbandry*.

1732 Dutch scientist and physician Hermann Boerhaave (1668–1738) publishes his chemistry textbook *Chemical Elements*.

1733 British clothworker John Kay (1704–64) invents the flying shuttle.

1735 Swedish scientist Carolus Linnaeus (1707–78) publishes *Systema naturae*, which classifies all living organisms according to a binomial nomenclature.

1736 Swiss mathematician Leonhard Euler (1707–83) publishes his textbook of mechanics *Mechanica sive mortus analytice exposita*.

1738 Swiss mathematician Daniel Bernoulli (1700–82) demonstrates the relationship between pressure and velocity of fluid flow in *Hydrodynamics*.

***c*.1740** British ironworker Benjamin Huntsman perfects the crucible process for casting steel.

1742 Swedish astronomer Anders Celsius (1701–44) invents the Celsius, or centigrade, temperature scale.

1742 French scientist Paul Malouin invents a process for galvanizing steel.

1743 American Philosophical Society is founded in Philadelphia.

***c*.1745** Leyden jar electrical capacitor is invented in Holland.

1745 French astronomer Pierre Maupertuis (1698–1759) publishes *Venus physique*.

1746 British chemist John Roebuck (1718–94) develops a process for manufacturing sulphuric acid.

1747 German scientist Andreas Marggraf (1709–82) invents a process for extracting sugar from sugar beet.

1749 French naturalist Georges Buffon (1707–88) publishes the first volumes of *Natural History*.

ARTS AND HUMANITIES

1715 Italian composer Alessandro Scarlatti (1660–1725) writes his opera *Il Tigrane*.

1715 French novelist Alain le Sage (1688–1747) publishes *Gil Blas*.

***c*.1715** Japanese dramatist Chikamatsu Mozaemon (1652–1725) writes *Love Suicides*.

1716 French artist Jean Antoine Watteau (1684–1721) paints *The Lesson of Love*.

1717 German-born English composer George Frideric Handel (1685–1759) composes *Water Music*.

1719 British author Daniel Defoe (1660–1731) publishes his novel *Robinson Crusoe*.

1721 German composer Johann Sebastian Bach (1685–1750) 1720
completes *Brandenburg Concertos*.

1721 French philosopher Charles de Montesquieu (1689–1755) publishes *Persian Letters* – the first major work of the Enlightenment.

1725 Italian artist Canaletto (1697–1768) paints *Four Views of Venice*.

1725 Italian composer Antonio Vivaldi (1675–1741) publishes *The Four Seasons*.

1726 British author Jonathan Swift (1667–1745) publishes his satirical *Gulliver's Travels*.

1726 Chinese Academy of Letters publishes its *c*.5000-volume *T'u Shu Chi Ch'eng* encyclopedia.

1728 British poet John Gay (1685–1732) writes *The Beggar's Opera*.

1731 French author Antoine Prévost (1697–1763) publishes his novel 1730
Manon Lescaut.

1732 Italian sculptor Niccolo Salvi (1697–1751) begins work on his Trevi fountain in Rome.

1732 American writer, scientist and politician Benjamin Franklin (1706–90) publishes the first issue of *Poor Richard's Almanac*.

1735 French composer Jean Rameau (1683–1764) writes his ballet *Les Indes Galantes*.

1735 British artist William Hogarth (1697–1764) publishes his engravings of *A Rake's Progress*.

1734 French philosopher and author Voltaire (1694–1778) publishes *English or Philosophical Letters*.

1738 John Wesley (1703–91) lays the foundations of Methodism.

1738 Archaeological excavation starts of the Roman town of Herculaneum in Italy.

1738 Russian Imperial Ballet School is founded in St Petersburg.

1739 Scottish philosopher David Hume (1711–76) publishes *Treatise on Human Nature*.

1740 British novelist Samuel Richardson (1689–1761) publishes *Pamela*. 1740

1741 Italian architect Bartolomeo Rastrelli designs the Summer Palace in St Petersburg.

1741 George Frideric Handel's oratorio *Messiah* is first performed in Dublin.

1742 French artist François Boucher (1703–70) paints *Bath of Diana*.

1745 Italian dramatist Carlo Goldoni (1707–93) publishes his comedy *The Servant of Two Masters*.

1746 French philosopher Denis Diderot (1713–84) publishes *Philosophic Thoughts*.

1746 French philosopher Étienne Condillac (1715–1780) publishes *Essay on the Origin of Human Knowledge*.

1747 French philosopher Julien La Mettrie (1709–51) publishes his aetheist views in his book *Man, A Machine*.

1748 French philosopher Charles de Montesquieu (1689–1755) publishes *The Spirit of Laws*.

1749 British novelist Henry Fielding (1707–54) publishes *Tom Jones*.

ASIA AND AUSTRALASIA

1750 **1750** Tibetans rebel against Chinese overlordship.

1750 French colonial administrator Joseph Dupleix (1697–1763) wins the Battle of Tanjore and gains control of the Carnatic region of S India.

1750 Karim Khan (1705–79) establishes himself as shah of Persia and founds the Zand dynasty.

1751 China invades Tibet.

1751 British colonial administrator Robert Clive (1725–74) captures Arcot and ends French control of the Carnatic.

1752 British troops under Robert Clive capture Trichinpoly in S India from the French.

1752 Afghans capture the city of Lahore in N India from the Mughals.

1753–55 King Alaungpaya (1711–60) reunites Burma, with British assistance, and founds a new capital city at Rangoon.

1755 Afghans conquer the Punjab region of N India and plunder Delhi.

1756 Indian ruler of Bengal captures Calcutta from the British and imprisons British soldiers in the "Black Hole".

1757 Robert Clive recaptures Calcutta and defeats the native ruler of Bengal at the Battle of Plassey.

1758 Marathas occupy the Punjab region of N India.

1758 China occupies E Turkistan.

1759 British defeat a Dutch naval expedition and capture Chinsura.

1760 **1760** British defeat the French at the Battle of Wandiwash in S India.

1760 Chinese emperor declares that all foreign trade shall pass through the port of Canton (Guangzhou).

1761 British capture Pondicherry from the French.

1761 Hyder Ali (1722–82) makes himself ruler of Mysore in S India.

1761 Afghans invade N India and defeat the Marathas at the Battle of Panipat.

1762 Afghans defeat the Sikhs at Lahore.

1762 British bombard Manila and capture the Philippines from Spain.

1763 British establish a trading-post at Bushire in SW Persia.

1764 British return the Philippines to Spain.

1764 British defeat a native coalition at the Battle of Baskar and gain control of the whole of Bengal.

1765–69 Chinese invade Burma and establish overlordship.

1767 Burma invades and conquers Thailand.

1767–69 War between British troops and the Indian state of Mysore ends in a truce.

1768 French explorer Louis de Bougainville (1729–1811) claims Tahiti for France.

1770 **1770** British establish a trading-post at Basra, S Iraq.

1770 British explorer James Cook (1728–79) lands at Botany Bay and claims SE Australia for Britain.

1773 British merchants obtain a monopoly over opium production in Bengal.

1774 British appoint Warren Hastings (1732–1818) as governor of India; he begins a series of economic and administrative reforms.

1774 White Lotus Society foments a rebellion in NE China.

1775 War breaks out between the British and the Marathas in India.

1775 Persians attack and briefly capture Basra from the British.

1778 British forces attack and capture Pondicherry, S India, from the French.

1778 James Cook discovers Hawaii.

1779 British force defeats the Marathas at Surat.

AFRICA

1750 French establish a settlement on the island of Sainte Marie off Madagascar.

1752 Portuguese settlements in SE Africa are placed under a separate government from that of Goa in India.

1755 Death of Emperor Jesus II marks the end of strong government in Ethiopia, which becomes divided between rival claimants to the throne.

1756 City of Tunis is captured by the Algerians.

1757 Muhammad XVI (d.1790) becomes ruler of Morocco and starts economic and military reforms.

1758 British capture Senegal from the French.

1760 Dutch farmers moving N cross the Orange River in South Africa.

1763 Kayambugu (d.1780) becomes king of Buganda in E Africa.

1763 Treaty of Paris confirms British control of Senegal.

1766 Ali Bey (1728–73) establishes himself as ruler of Egypt and declares independence from the Turks.

1774 Abiodun (d.1789) becomes king of Oyo in present-day S Nigeria.

1775 Maritius Benyowski establishes the town of Louisbourg on the coast of Madagascar for the French, who later refuse to support him.

1778 French recapture Senegal.

1778 Dutch settlers moving E cross the Great Fish River in South Africa.

1779 First Suurveld War starts in South Africa when native Khoisan and Xhosa peoples try to stop the E expansion of Dutch Boers (farmers).

EUROPE

1745 French defeat the Pragmatic Army at the Battle of Fontenoy.

1745 Second Jacobite rebellion breaks out in Scotland.

1746 British troops defeat the Jacobite Scots at the Battle of Culloden and the rebellion ends.

1746 French conquer Austrian-controlled Belgium.

1747 Orangists restore the monarchy in Holland.

1748 Treaty of Aix-la-Chapelle ends the War of the Austrian Succession; Prussia emerges as a major European power.

1750 Joseph I (1714–77) becomes king of Portugal, although the real ruler is his chief minister, the future Marquês de Pombal (1699–1782).

1753 Wenzel von Kaunitz (1711–94) becomes chancellor of Austria. His negotiations, through the Marquise de Pompadour (1721–64), the mistress of Louis XV, persuade France to ally with Austria.

1755 Portuguese capital, Lisbon, is destroyed by an earthquake.

1756 French capture the island of Minorca from the British.

1756 Russia and Sweden join Franco-Austrian alliance against Prussia.

1756 Prussia allies with Britain, invades Saxony and starts the Seven Years' War.

1757 Prussia invades Bohemia and defeats the French and Austrians at the Battle of Rossbach in Bohemia.

1757 William Pitt the Elder (1707–78) becomes prime minister of Britain.

1758 Prussians fight the Russians to a standstill at the Battle of Zorndorf in S Germany.

1759 Combined Austrian-Russian army defeats the Prussians at the Battle of Kunersdorf.

1759 British defeat the French at the naval battle of Quiberon Bay.

1759 Prussians defeat the French at the Battle of Minden.

1759 Charles III (1716–88) becomes king of Spain and hands the throne of Sicily and Naples to his son Ferdinand (1751–1825).

1760 George III (1738–1820) becomes king of Britain.

1760 Russian army sacks Berlin.

1761 Third Family Compact strengthens the alliance between France and Spain.

1762 Catherine II (1729–96) seizes power in Russia.

1762 Spain invades Portugal but is repulsed.

1763 Austria makes the peace of Hubertsburg with Prussia, ending the European phase of the Seven Years' War.

1763 "Whiteboys" revolt against British rule in Ireland.

1764 Russia and Prussia form an alliance to control Poland.

1764 Jesuits are expelled from France.

1765 Joseph II (1741–90) is elected Holy Roman emperor and becomes co-ruler, with his mother Maria Theresa (1717–80), of the Austrian empire.

1766 Lorraine formally becomes a part of France.

1767 Jesuits are expelled from Spain.

1767 Catherine II of Russia appoints a commission for the modernization of the Russian state.

1768 Anti-Russian confederation is formed in Poland; its formation leads to a civil war in which Russia intervenes.

1768 Turkey declares war on Russia in defence of Poland.

1768 Genoa cedes Corsica to France.

1770 Louis (1754–93), later Louis XVI, marries Marie Antoinette (1755–93), daughter of Maria Theresa.

1770 Russian fleet defeats the Turks at the Battle of Chesme.

1770 John Struensee (1737–72) attempts radical reforms in Denmark.

1771 Russians conquer the Crimea from the Turks.

1771 Louis XV (1710–74) abolishes the French *parlements*.

1772 John Struensee is executed in Denmark after an aristocratic coup.

1772 Gustavus III (1746–92) restores the power of the monarchy in Sweden.

1772 Following Russian victories against the Turks, Austria and Prussia enforce the first Partition of Poland. Russia, Austria and Prussia annex about 30% of Polish territory.

1773–75 Emelyan Pugachev (1726–75) leads a revolt of cossacks and peasants in SE Russia.

1774 Louis XVI becomes king of France and restores the *parlements*.

THE AMERICAS

1750 By the treaty of Madrid, Spain recognizes Portuguese claims in s and w Brazil.

1752 French capture a British trading-post in the Ohio valley.

1753 French build Fort Duquesne on the River Ohio.

1754 French troops attack the British Fort Necessity in the Ohio valley.

1754 At the Albany Congress, Benjamin Franklin proposes limited union of the British colonies to combat French aggression.

1754 Start of the French and Indian War between French and British settlers, which becomes the American phase of the Seven Years' War.

1755 British expedition against Fort Duquesne is defeated at the Battle of the Wilderness.

1756 Leading Quakers resign from the Pennsylvania Assembly in protest against participation in hostilities.

1756 French under the Marquis de Montcalm (1712–59) drive the British from the Great Lakes region.

1757 French capture Fort William Henry; the British garrison is massacred by Native North Americans.

1758 British forces capture forts Frontenac and Duquesne.

1759 City of Québec in Canada is captured after British general James Wolfe (1727–59) wins the Battle of the Plains of Abraham.

1759 British capture the island of Guadaloupe from the French.

1760 British capture Montreal from the French.

1761 British capture Cuba from the Spanish.

1761 James Otis (1725–83) argues against British writs of assistance in a Massachusetts court.

1763 Peace of Paris ends the French and Indian War; Britain gains Canada, Tobago and Grenada from France and Florida from Spain; France cedes Louisiana to Spain.

1763 Surveyors Charles Mason and Jeremiah Dixon establish the boundary between Pennsylvania and Maryland.

1763–66 Pontiac (1720–69), chief of the Ottawa Native North Americans, wages an unsuccessful war against the British.

1765 Stamp Act places a tax on books and documents in British North America; rioting breaks out in Boston and other cities.

1765 In New York, the Stamp Act Congress adopts a declaration of rights and liberties.

1765 British establish a colony on the Falkland Islands.

1766 Stamp Act is repealed.

1767 New York Assembly is suspended by the British.

1767 Townshend Acts place duties on many goods imported to British North America.

1768 Boston lawyer Samuel Adams (1722–1803) calls for united action against Britain.

1769 Spanish establish a settlement at San Diego in California.

1770 British troops shoot several Massachusetts citizens in what becomes known as the "Boston Massacre".

1773 "Boston Tea Party" occurs when protesters dressed as Native Americans board British ships and dump tea into Boston harbour.

1773–74 Committees of Correspondence are set up throughout the British colonies.

1774 British pass the Coercive Acts restricting American colonial rights.

1774 British fight and win Lord Dunmore's War against the Shawnee Native North Americans.

1774 First Continental Congress meets at Philadelphia and draws up a Declaration of Rights and Grievances to be presented to Britain.

1774 Ann Lee (1736–84) establishes the first Shaker colony.

1775 American Revolution starts with the battles of Lexington and Concord, after which the British retreat to Boston.

1775 American general Ethan Allen (1738–89) captures Fort Ticonderoga from the British.

SCIENCE AND TECHNOLOGY

1750 British astronomer Thomas Wright (1711–1786) suggests that the Milky Way is a huge disc of stars.

1752 Gregorian calendar is adopted in Britain.

1752 American writer, scientist and politician Benjamin Franklin (1706–90) publishes *Experiments and Observations in Electricity.*

1757 British optician John Dollond (1706–61) produces the first achromatic lenses.

1758 French economist François Quesnay (1694–1774) sums up his physiocratic system of political economy in *Tableau economique.*

1758 British optical instrument maker John Bird (1709–76) invents an improved sextant.

1758 British wheelwright Jebediah Strutt (1726–97) invents a ribbing machine for making hosiery.

1759 British clockmaker John Harrison (1693–1776) constructs the first marine chronometer.

1763 First exhibition of industrial arts is held in Paris.

1763 Scottish scientist Joseph Black (1728–99) discovers latent heat.

1764 British engineer James Hargreaves (1722–78) invents the Spinning Jenny.

1765 Scottish engineer James Watt (1736–1819) improves the steam engine by adding a separate condenser.

1766 Benjamin Franklin invents bifocal spectacles.

1766 British chemist Henry Cavendish (1731–1810) discovers hydrogen.

1769 British engineer Richard Arkwright (1732–92) invents a water-powered spinning frame.

1770 Grand Trunk Canal is completed in Britain.

1771 French astronomer Charles Messier (1730–1817) publishes the first volume of his star catalogue.

1771 Italian scientist Luigi Galvani (1737–98) conducts experiments that demonstrate a connection between muscular contractions and electricity.

1772 Imperial library in China begins compiling the *Complete Works of the Four Treasuries,* which contains more than 3000 works of literature.

1774 British chemist Joseph Priestley (1733–1804) discovers oxygen.

1774 British astronomer Nevil Maskelyne (1732–1811) discovers the value of the gravitational constant.

1774 British engineer John Wilkinson (1728–1808) invents a boring machine for making steam-engine cylinders and cannon.

1774 French chemist Antoine Lavoisier (1743–94) demonstrates the conservation of mass in chemical reactions.

1775 Austrian physician Franz Mesmer (1734–1815) claims to be able to heal using "animal magnetism".

ARTS AND HUMANITIES

1751 First volume of the French *Encyclopedia, or Classified* 1750
Dictionary of Sciences, Arts and Trades is published.

1752 Death of the German preacher Johann Bengel (b.1687), who established the evangelical movement Pietism.

1754 British furniture-maker Thomas Chippendale (1718–79) publishes *The Gentleman and Cabinetmaker's Directory.*

1755 British writer Samuel Johnson (1709–84) publishes *Dictionary of the English Language.*

1755 French philosopher Jean Jacques Rousseau (1712–78) writes his essay *A Discourse upon the Origin of Inequality.*

1755 German archaeologist Johann Winckelmann (1717–68) publishes *Thoughts on the Imitation of Greek Painting and Sculpture.*

1756 Italian artist Giambattista Piranesi (1720–78) publishes his book of engravings *The Roman Antiquities.*

1757 Scottish philosopher David Hume (1711–86) publishes *Natural History of Religion.*

1758 French philosopher Claude Helvetius (1715–71) publishes his atheistic book *On the Mind,* which is condemned and burned.

1758 Swedish scientist Emanuel Swedenborg (1688–1772) publishes his religious treatise *The New Jerusalem.*

1759 French philosopher and author Voltaire (1694–1778) publishes his satirical novel *Candide.*

1760 English novelist Laurence Sterne (1713–68) publishes the first 1760
volumes of *Tristram Shandy.*

1760 British artist Joshua Reynolds (1723–92) paints his portrait of *Georgiana, Countess Spencer.*

1762 British artist George Stubbs (1724–1806) paints *Mares and Foals.*

1762 Jean Jacques Rousseau publishes *The Social Contract.*

1762 Scottish poet James Macpherson (1736–96) – "Ossian" – publishes *Fingal.*

1762 German composer Christoph Gluck (1714–87) writes his opera *Orfeo and Euridice.*

1762 Building work starts on the Petit Trianon at Versailles in France.

1764 British author Horace Walpole (1717–97) publishes his Gothic horror novel *Castle of Otranto.*

1766 Irish novelist Oliver Goldsmith (1730–74) publishes *The Vicar of Wakefield.*

1766 German philosopher and critic Gotthold Lessing (1729–81) publishes *Laocoön.*

1766 First purpose-built American theatre opens in Philadelphia.

1766 German poet Heinrich Gerstenberg (1737–1823) publishes the first of his *Letters on the Curiosities of Literature*; this work establishes the *Sturm und Drang* literary movement.

1770 British artist Thomas Gainsborough (1727–88) paints *Blue Boy.* 1770

1770 French philosopher Paul Holbach (1723–89) expounds materialism and determinism in *System of Nature.*

1770 American artist Benjamin West (1738–1820) paints *The Death of General Wolfe.*

1771 Encyclopedia Britannica is first published.

1772 Austrian composer Franz Haydn (1732–1809) writes his Symphony No.45 in F sharp minor, known as "The Farewell Symphony".

1772 French *L'Encyclopédie* is completed with the publication of the *Supplement to Bougainville's Voyage* by French philosopher and writer Denis Diderot (1713–84).

1773 Scottish architects Robert (1728–92) and James Adams publish their *Works of Architecture.*

1774 German poet and author Johann Goethe (1749–1832) publishes his novel *The Sorrows of Young Werther.*

ASIA AND AUSTRALASIA

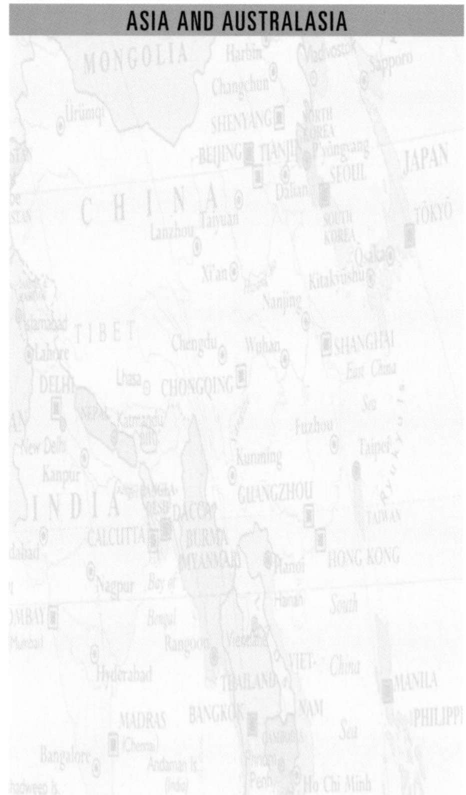

1780 **1781** Assisted by the French, Hyder Ali (1722–82), sultan of Mysore, attacks the British and is defeated at the Battle of Porto Novo.

1781 British conquer the Dutch settlements in Sumatra.

1782 Sultan of Mysore, Hyder Ali, dies during a campaign against the British; his son Tipu Sultan (1747–99) continues the war.

1782 New Thai king Rama I (1737–1809) expels the Burmese and establishes a new capital at Bangkok.

1782 Treaty of Salbai ends the war between the British and the Marathas in India.

1784 India Act places the British colonies in India under government control.

1784 Tipu Sultan is defeated by the British when the French fail to send aid; he signs the treaty of Mangalore.

1784 US merchants start trading with China.

1784 Dutch cede the settlement of Negapatam in SE India to the British.

1786 British establish a settlement at Rangoon in Burma.

1787 Chinese suppress a rebellion in Formosa (present-day Taiwan).

1787 Matsudaira Sadanobu (1759–1829) becomes chief minister to the infant Japanese shogun Ienari (d.1838) and introduces a series of administrative reforms.

1788 Britain transports the first shipment of convicts to Australia.

1789 Crew of the British ship *Bounty* mutiny and cast captain William Bligh (1754–1817) adrift in an open boat.

AFRICA

1781 First Suurveld War in E South Africa ends with Boer (Afrikaner) victory.

1783 Portuguese build a fort at Cabinda in Angola, SW Africa.

1786 United States pays a bribe to Morocco to purchase immunity from pirate attacks.

1786 French expedition attacks Louisbourg in Madagascar and kills Maritius Benyowski.

1787 British establish the colony of Sierra Leone in W Africa.

1789 On the death of Abiodun, Awole becomes king of Oyo in present-day S Nigeria.

1789 Second Suurveld War breaks out when the Xhosa attempt to regain their traditional lands.

EUROPE

1774 Treaty of Kuchuk Kainarji ends the war between Russia and Turkey; Russia gains Crimean ports.

1777 Marquês de Pombal (1699–1782) is dismissed in Portugal and exiled.

1777 French financier Jacques Necker (1732–1804) is appointed finance minister in an attempt to solve the debt crisis.

1778 France declares war on Britain.

1778–79 War of the Bavarian Succession between Prussia and Austria is settled by the treaty of Teschen.

1779 Spain declares war on Britain and besieges Gibraltar.

1780 Britain declares war on Holland.

1780 Anti-Catholic Gordon Riots occur in London.

1781 Jacques Necker is dismissed as French finance minister.

1781 Russia and Austria form an anti-Turkish treaty for control of the Balkans.

1781 Joseph II (1741–90) of Austria abolishes serfdom.

1782 Spanish capture Minorca from the British.

1783 Treaty of Paris ends the war against Britain by France, Spain and the USA.

1783 Russia annexes the Crimea.

1783 William Pitt the Younger (1759–1806) becomes British prime minister.

1784 Treaty of Versailles ends the war between Holland and Britain.

1785 Prussia forms the League of German princes against Austria.

1786 Frederick William II (1744–97) becomes king of Prussia.

1787 Dutch ruler William V (1748–1806) calls in Prussian troops to suppress the pro-French Patriot Party.

1787 Charles III (1716–88) of Spain establishes the *junta*.

1787 French king Louis XVI (1754–93) dismisses an assembly of notables and banishes, then recalls, the Paris *parlement*.

1787 Russia allied to Austria attacks the Turks.

1787 Britain, Holland and Prussia form an alliance against France.

1787 Austria incorporates Belgium as a royal province.

1788 Paris *parlement* presents a list of grievances to Louis XVI, who recalls Necker and summons the States General.

1788 Sweden invades Russian-controlled Finland.

1789 Austrians capture Belgrade from the Turks; the Russian advance reaches the River Danube.

1789 States General meets at Versailles; the third estate declares themselves the National (Constituent) Assembly and takes the "tennis court oath" to establish a constitution.

1789 Louis XVI dismisses Necker again; the Paris mob storms the Bastille and establishes a Commune as a provisional government; Lafayette (1757–1834) becomes commander of the National Guard; peasant risings and urban rioting create the "Great Fear"; National Assembly issues the Declaration of the Rights of Man.

1789 Parisian women march to Versailles and escort Louis XVI to Paris; National Assembly moves to Paris and debates a constitution; church property is confiscated by the state.

1789 Belgians rise against Austrian rule and win the Battle of Turnhout.

THE AMERICAS

1775 Second Continental Congress meets at Philadelphia.

1775 Continental Army is formed outside Boston with George Washington (1732–99) as commander-in-chief.

1775 British win the Battle of Bunker Hill; the Americans besiege Boston.

1775 American troops capture Montreal, but fail to take Québec.

1776 British evacuate Boston.

1776 Congress adopts the Declaration of Independence written by American Statesman Thomas Jefferson (1743–1826).

1776 British win the Battle of Long Island and occupy New York City.

1776 British defeat George Washington at the Battle of White Plains.

1776 Washington crosses the River Delaware and defeats the British at the Battle of Trenton.

1777 Washington defeats the British at the Battle of Princeton.

1777 Following defeat at the Battle of Saratoga, British general John Burgoyne (1722–92) surrenders to the Americans.

1777 British win the Battle of Brandywine and occupy Philadelphia.

1777 British defeat Washington at the Battle of Germanstown.

1777 Congress approves the Articles of Confederation that create the United States.

1778 France makes an alliance with the United States and sends a fleet.

1778 British evacuate Philadelphia.

1778 Washington wins the Battle of Monmouth.

1778 British capture Savannah.

1779 American privateer John Paul Jones (1747–92) captures the British ship *Serapis*.

1779 Britain captures St Lucia from the French.

1780 British capture Charleston.

1780 British defeat the Americans at the Battle of Camden.

1780 American general Benedict Arnold (1741–1801) flees to the British.

1780 American troops drive the Iroquois Native North Americans from the state of New York.

1780 British defeat the Americans at the Battle of King's Mountain.

1780 Tupac Amaru (*c.*1742–81), a descendant of the Inca rulers, leads a short-lived rebellion against the Spanish in Peru.

1780 French general the Marquis de Lafayette (1757–1834) persuades French king Louis XVI (1754–93) to send troops to reinforce the Americans.

1781 Americans win the Battle of the Cowpens.

1781 Combined American and French force besieges the British at Yorktown.

1781 British under General Charles Cornwallis (1738–1805) surrender to the Americans at Yorktown.

1781 Communeros revolt against the Spanish breaks out in Colombia.

1782 British fleet under admiral George Rodney (1718–92) defeats the French at the Battle of the Saints in the Caribbean.

1783 Britain recognizes US independence and cedes Tobago to France and Florida to Spain.

1784 Russia establishes a colony on Kodiak Island, Alaska.

1786 Shays' rebellion is suppressed in Massachusetts.

1787 Northwest Ordinance regulates the creation of new states in the USA.

1787 Constitutional Convention meets in Philadelphia and signs the US constitution.

1788 US constitution comes into effect when New Hampshire becomes the ninth state to ratify it.

1788 New York becomes the capital of the USA.

1789 George Washington is elected the first president of the United States.

1789 Attempted revolution in s Brazil is led by army officer Joaquim de Silva.

1789 US Congress adopts the Bill of Rights, 10 amendments to the constitution.

1789 Spanish challenge British claims to the Nookta Sound region of w Canada.

SCIENCE AND TECHNOLOGY

1779 British engineer Samuel Crompton (1753–1827) invents the spinning mule.

1779 Cast-iron bridge is completed at Coalbrookdale in Britain.

1781 German-born English astronomer William Herschel (1738–1822) discovers the planet Uranus.

1782 Scottish engineer James Watt (1736–1819) perfects the double-acting steam engine producing rotary motion.

1783 Hot-air balloon built by the French Montgolfier brothers, Joseph (1740–1810) and Jacques (1745–99), makes the first crewed flight.

1783 French physicist Jacques Charles (1746–1823) makes the first hydrogen balloon flight.

1783 Swiss scientist Horace de Saussure (1740–99) invents an improved hair hygrometer.

1783 French engineer Claude de Jouffroy d'Abbans (1751–1832) builds a full-sized, paddle-wheel steamboat.

1784 British chemist Henry Cavendish (1731–1810) establishes the chemical composition of water.

1784 British ironworker Henry Cort (1740–1800) devises the puddling process to produce wrought iron.

1785 British clergyman Edmund Cartwright (1743–1823) invents the power loom.

1785 French physicist Charles Coulomb (1736–1806) publishes his law of electrical attraction in *Memoirs on Electricity and Magnetism*.

1785 French chemist Claude Berthollet (1748–1822) invents chlorine bleach.

1785 Steam engine produced by James Watt and Matthew Boulton (1728–1809) is installed in a British factory.

1787 French mathematician Joseph Lagrange (1736–1813) publishes *Analytical Mechanics*.

1788 Scottish engineer Andrew Meikle (1719–1811) patents a threshing machine.

1789 French chemist Antoine Lavoisier (1743–94) expounds his theory of combustion in *Elementary Treatise on Chemistry*.

ARTS AND HUMANITIES

1775 German historian Johann Herder (1744–1803) publishes *Philosophy of History and Culture*.

1776 British historian Edward Gibbon (1737–94) publishes the first volume of *The History of the Decline and Fall of the Roman Empire*.

1776 British economist Adam Smith (1723–90) publishes *An Inquiry into the Nature and Causes of the Wealth of Nations*.

1777 British dramatist Richard Sheridan (1751–1816) writes *School for Scandal*.

1778 La Scala in Milan hosts its first opera.

1779 Italian sculptor Antonio Canova (1757–1822) carves *Daedalus and Icarus*.

1781 German philosopher Immanuel Kant (1724–1804) publishes *Critique of Pure Reason*. 1780

1782 British artist Henry Fuseli (1741–1825) paints *The Nightmare*.

1783 Death of the French philosopher and mathematician Jean d'Alembert (b.1717) who jointly edited *L'Encyclopédie* with French philosopher and writer Denis Diderot (1713–84).

1783 American publisher Noah Webster (1758–1843) produces *The American Spelling Book*.

1785 French artist Jacques David (1748–1825) paints *Oath of the Horatii*.

1786 Austrian composer Wolfgang Amadeus Mozart (1756–91) writes his opera *Marriage of Figaro*.

1786 Scottish poet Robert Burns (1759–96) publishes *Poems, Chiefly in the Scottish Dialect*.

1787 Freed African slave Ottobah Cugoana publishes his book *Thoughts and Sentiments on Slavery*.

1788 Kant publishes *Critique of Practical Reason*.

1788 *Times* newspaper is founded in London.

1789 English social philosopher Jeremy Bentham (1748–1832) expounds his theory of utilitarianism in *Introduction to the Principles of Morals and Legislation*.

1789 British poet William Blake (1757–1827) publishes *Songs of Innocence*.

1789 French revolutionary Camille Desmoulins (1760–94) publishes his republican manifesto *Free France*.

1789 French politician Emmanuel Joseph Sieyes (1748–1836) publishes his pamphlet *What is the Third Estate?*

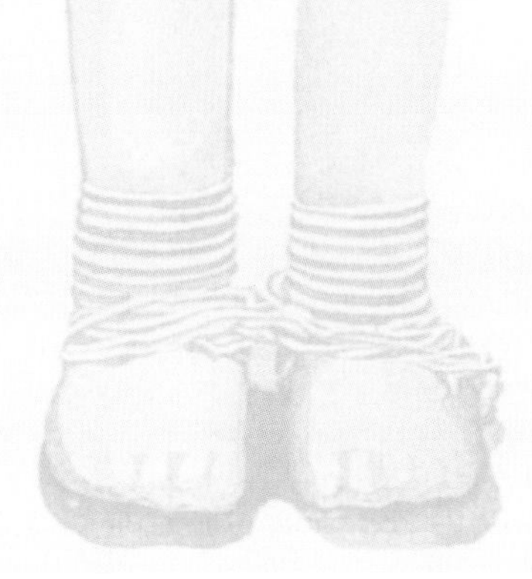

ASIA AND AUSTRALASIA

1790 **1790** Tipu Sultan (1747–99) attacks the pro-British S Indian state of Travancore.

1792 Tipu Sultan is defeated by the British.

1792 Ranjit Singh (1780–1839) becomes king of the Sikhs.

1793 Burma under King Bodawpaya (d.1819) acquires coastal territory Thailand.

1793 French royalists surrender Pondicherry to the British.

1793 Shogun Ienari (d.1838) takes personal control of the Japanese government.

1793 Chinese emperor refuses to lift restrictions on the import of British goods.

1793 First free settlers arrive in Australia.

1794 Last Persian shah of the Zand dynasty is killed and Aga Muhammad (d.1797) founds the Kajar dynasty.

1794 British capture the Seychelles from the French.

1795 British take Dutch Malacca to deny it to the French.

1796 Britain conquers Ceylon (present-day Sri Lanka) from the Dutch.

1796 Jia Qing (d.1820) becomes Chinese emperor and begins campaigns to suppress the White Lotus society.

1798 Persians under Shah Fath Ali (1771–1834) attack Afghanistan.

1799 Tipu Sultan is killed fighting against British forces led by Arthur Wellesley (1769–1852).

1799 French invade Syria and capture Jaffa but withdraw after an outbreak of plague.

1800 **1800** Chinese emperor bans the smoking of opium.

1801 Britain annexes the Carnatic region of S India.

1802 Vietnamese emperor Nguyen Anh (1762–1820) reunites Annam under his control.

1802 British return Malacca to the Dutch.

1802 Ranjit Singh leads the Sikhs into Amristar.

1802 British gain control of central India by the treaty of Bassein.

1803 British navigator Matthew Flinders (1774–1814) circumnavigates Australia.

AFRICA

1791 Fulani scholar and poet Usman dan Fodio (1754–1817) is appointed tutor to the rulers of Gobir in present-day N Nigeria.

1793 Second Suurveld War ends when Dutch magistrates compel the Afrikaners s to concede territory to the Xhosa.

1795 British capture Cape Colony in South Africa from the Dutch.

1797 US government agrees to pay bribes to Algiers and Tripoli to further safeguard US shipping from pirate attacks.

1798 Napoléon Bonaparte lands an army at Alexandria, invades Egypt, and defeats the Mamluks at the Battle of the Pyramids.

1798 British admiral Horatio Nelson (1758–1805) destroys the French fleet at the naval battle of Aboukir.

1798 French settlers on the island of Mauritius overthrow the colonial government.

1799 Bonaparte defeats a Turkish attempt to recapture Egypt at the land battle of Aboukir.

1800 French defeat the Turks and Egyptians outside Cairo.

1801 Yusef Karamanli of Tripoli demands an increased pirate-protection bribe from the USA and declares war; the USA blockades Tripoli; start of the Tripolitanian War.

1801 British defeat the French at Alexandria.

1802 French withdraw from Egypt.

1802 British return Cape Colony to the Dutch.

1803 Tripolitanians capture the US ship *Philadelphia*.

1804 US forces capture the port of Derna near Tripoli.

EUROPE

1790 French revolutionary leader Maximilien Robespierre (1758–94) is elected leader of the Jacobin political club in Paris.

1790 Swedes defeat Russians at the naval battle of Svenksund.

1791 Irish lawyer Wolfe Tone (1763–98) founds the society of United Irishmen.

1791 Louis XVI (1754–93) attempts to flee France but is escorted back to Paris; a constitution is proclaimed and elections held for the new Legislative Assembly.

1791 Polish Diet proclaims the May Constitution, opposed by Russia.

1792 Turks cede the N coast of the Black Sea to the Russians by the treaty of Jassy.

1792 Paris mob storms the Tuileries palace and imprisons the royal family; revolutionary Georges Danton (1759–94) takes control of a provisional government; National Convention is elected; France is proclaimed a republic; Louis XVI is put on trial.

1792 Austria and Prussia form an alliance against France; France declares war on Austria; the Prussian commander issues a manifesto calling for the freeing of Louis XVI.

1792 Austria and Prussia invade France; the French defeat the Prussians at the Battle of Valmy and the Austrians at the Battle of Jemappes; they conquer Belgium and annex Savoy.

1793 Poland loses 60% of its territory to Russia and Prussia in the second partition of Poland.

1793 Louis XVI is guillotined; Jacobins take control of the national convention; revolutionary Jean Marat (b.1743) is murdered by Charlotte Corday (1768–93); a revolutionary tribunal is set up to judge "enemies of the state"; start of the Reign of Terror; General Lazare Carnot (1753–1823) reorganizes the French army; Corsican artillery officer Napoléon Bonaparte (1769–1821) is promoted to general.

1793 Britain, Holland and Spain declare war on France; Austria defeats the French at the Battle of Neerwinden and recaptures Belgium; Britain attempts to invade S France.

1794 French royalists in the Vendée region are exterminated; churches are closed; Robespierre and his followers are condemned by the National Convention and executed; the revolutionary tribunal and political clubs are abolished; end of the Reign of Terror.

1794 French reconquer Belgium and invade Spain.

1794 Thadeus Kósciuszko (1746–1817) leads a popular rising in Poland; it is suppressed by Russian and Prussian troops.

1795 Some French aristocrats return and begin a White Terror in S France; new constitution establishes the Directory in Paris.

1795 France invades Holland and establishes the Batavian Republic; Prussia makes the separate peace of Basle with France.

1795 Polish state is dissolved by the third Partition of Poland between Russia, Austria and Prussia.

1796 France invades S Germany but is repelled; Bonaparte defeats the Austrians at Lodi and captures Milan; Spain makes the treaty of San Ildefonso with France and declares war on Britain; the Spanish fleet is destroyed by the British at Cape St Vincent.

1797 French conquer Venice and N Italy; peace of Campo Formio ends hostilities with Austria; end of War of the First Coalition against France.

1797 Frederick William III (1770–1840) becomes king of Prussia.

1798 French occupy Rome, establish a republic and imprison the pope; French invade Switzerland and annex Geneva; French capture the island of Malta; the Second Coalition against France is formed; French conquer S Italy; Russians capture Corfu and the Ionian Islands.

1798 British troops defeat the United Irishmen at the Battle of Vinegar Hill; an invading French force surrenders.

1799 Austrians and Russians defeat the French at the battles of Zurich, the Trebbia and Novi; they regain control of Italy and drive the French from Switzerland; Russia withdraws from the Coalition.

1799 Bonaparte returns to Paris, seizes power and abolishes the Directory; he establishes the Consulate with himself as First Consul.

1799 Montenegro becomes independent of the Ottoman Empire.

1800 Napoléon Bonaparte defeats the Austrians at the Battle of Marengo; France captures Munich and defeats the Austrians at the Battle of Hohenlinden; France begins the invasion of Austria.

1801 Alexander I (1777–1825) becomes tsar of Russia.

1801 Act of Union joins Ireland to Britain.

1801 Austria makes the peace of Luneville with France.

1801 Russia makes peace with France and joins the Northern Coalition.

1802 Britain makes the peace of Amiens with France; peace is established throughout Europe.

THE AMERICAS

1790 Spain withdraws its claims to Nookta Sound.

1790 Washington D.C. is designated the US capital.

1791 US Bill of Rights is ratified.

1791 Alexander Hamilton (1755–1804) founds the Bank of the United States.

1791 Remaining British possessions in North America are organized into French-speaking Lower Canada and English-speaking Upper Canada.

1791 Slave revolt breaks out on the French island of Haiti in the Caribbean.

1791 Vermont becomes a state of the USA.

1792 New York Stock Exchange is established.

1792 George Washington (1732–99) is re-elected US president.

1792 Kentucky becomes a state of the USA.

1793 Slave rising causes extensive damage in Albany, New York.

1794 Slavery is abolished in French colonies.

1794 Whiskey Insurrection in Pennsylvania is suppressed.

1794 USA signs Jay's treaty regularizing trade with Britain and borders with Canada.

1794 US general Anthony Wayne (1745–96) defeats the Ohio Native North Americans at the Battle of the Fallen Timbers.

1795 USA signs Pinckney's treaty with Spain establishing the border with Florida.

1796 Tennessee becomes a state of the USA.

1796 US settlers found Cleveland in Ohio.

1796 John Adams (1735–1826) is elected US president.

1797 XYZ Affair leads to a naval war between the USA and France.

1798 Slave leader Toussaint L'Ouverture (1744–1803) drives the French from Haiti.

1799 Russian governor of Alaska founds the city of Sitka.

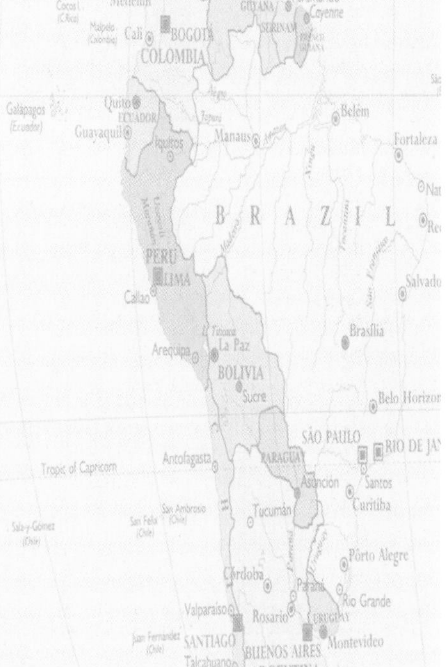

1800 France acquires Louisiana from Spain.

1800 Leaders of an intended slave revolt are hanged in Virginia.

1800 Thomas Jefferson (1743–1826) is elected US president.

1803 Ohio becomes a state of the USA.

1803 USA purchases New Orleans and Louisiana from France.

1803 Russians occupy E Alaska.

1804 Haiti declares independence from France under Emperor Jacques Dessalines (1748–1806).

SCIENCE AND TECHNOLOGY

1790 British engineer Matthew Boulton (1728–1809) patents the steam-powered coining press.

1790 French adopt decimal system of weights and measures.

1791 French military engineer Claude Chappe (1763–1805) invents the semaphore tower for long-distance communication.

1792 French revolutionaries adopt a new calendar starting at Year 1.

1792 Scottish engineer William Murdock (1754–1839) produces coal gas.

1793 US engineer Eli Whitney (1765–1825) invents the cotton gin.

1794 French revolutionary calendar is modified to have three 10-day weeks per month.

1795 Scottish geologist James Hutton (1726–97) publishes *Theory of the Earth.*

1797 French scientist André Garnerin (1769–1823) demonstrates his parachute by jumping from a hot-air balloon.

1798 US engineer Robert Fulton (1765–1815) demonstrates his submarine *Nautilus* to the French navy.

1798 British physician Edward Jenner (1749–1823) inoculates patients against smallpox using cowpox vaccine.

1798 US scientist Benjamin Rumford (1753–1814) publishes *Inquiry Concerning the Heat which is Caused by Friction,* outlining the kinetic theory of heat.

1799 German mathematician Karl Gauss (1777–1855) establishes the fundamental algebraic proof.

1799 French historians in Egypt discover the tri-lingual Rosetta stone.

1800 Italian scientist Alessandro Volta (1745–1827) invents the galvanic cell electrical battery.

1800 Joseph Finlay builds an iron chain suspension bridge in Pennsylvania.

1800 German-born English astronomer William Herschel (1738–1822) discovers infrared light.

1801 German mathematician Karl Gauss (1777–1855) publishes *Arithmetical Investigations.*

1801 Italian astronomer Giuseppe Piazzi (1746–1826) discovers the asteroid Ceres.

ARTS AND HUMANITIES

1790 British author Edmund Burke (1729–97) criticizes liberalism in *Reflections on the Revolution in France.* 1790

1791 British biographer James Boswell (1740–95) publishes *Life of Samuel Johnson.*

1791 French revolutionary Louis de Saint-Just (1767–94) publishes *The Spirit of the Revolution.*

1791 French author Marquis de Sade (1740–1814) publishes *Justine.*

1791 Austrian composer Wolfgang Amadeus Mozart (1756–91) writes his opera *The Magic Flute.*

1792 US writer Thomas Paine (1737–1809) publishes *The Rights of Man.*

1792 British feminist Mary Wollstonecraft (1759–97) publishes *Vindication of the Rights of Women.*

1792 French revolutionary soldier Claude de l'Isle composes the *Marseillaise.*

1794 British poet William Blake (1757–1827) publishes *Songs of Experience.*

1795 Spanish artist Francisco Goya (1746–1828) paints his portrait of *The Duchess of Alba.*

1796 US artist Gilbert Stuart (1755–1828) paints his unfinished portrait of George Washington.

1797 German philosopher Friedrich von Schelling (1775–1854) publishes *Philosophy of Nature.*

1798 British poets William Wordsworth (1770–1850) and Samuel Taylor Coleridge (1772–1834) publish their *Lyrical Ballads.*

1798 British economist Thomas Malthus (1766–1834) publishes the first edition of *Essay on the Principle of Population.*

1798 Austrian composer Franz Haydn (1732–1809) writes his oratorio *The Creation.*

1799 German author and dramatist Friedrich von Schiller (1759–1805) completes his *Wallenstein* trilogy.

1800 German philosopher Johann Fichte (1762–1814) publishes *The Destiny of Man.* 1800

1800 German poet Friedrich von Hardenberg (1772–1801) – Novalis – publishes *Hymns of the Night.*

1802 German composer Ludwig van Beethoven (1770–1827) writes *Moonlight* sonata.

1805 British artist Joseph Turner (1775–1851) paints *Shipwreck.*

1806 German bookseller Johann Palm publishes a pamphlet entitled *Germany in its Deepest Humiliation* and is executed by the French.

ASIA AND AUSTRALASIA

1804 Founding of Hobart marks the beginning of the colonization of Tasmania.

1803 Second Maratha War begins; the British capture Delhi; Arthur Wellesley (1769–1852) wins the Battle of Assaye in S India.

1804 British annex Calcutta.

1804 Chinese emperor finally suppresses the White Lotus society.

1807 Ottoman Janisseries revolt and replace sultan Selim III (1761–1808) with Mustafa IV (1779–1808).

1808 Colonial officers in Australia stage the Rum Rebellion against governor William Bligh (1754–1817).

1808 Dutch conquer the independent state of Bantam in Indonesia.

1808 Mahmud II (1785–1839) becomes Ottoman sultan.

1809 Treaty of Amritsar fixes the boundary between British territory in India and the Sikh kingdom.

1809 British make a defence treaty with the Afghans.

1810 **1811** British recapture Malacca and invade Dutch Java and Sumatra.

1812 Russia defeats the Persians at the Battle of Aslanduz.

1813 Persia cedes Baku and Caucasus territories to Russia under the treaty of Gulistan.

1813 British government abolishes the East India Company's monopoly on trade with India.

1814 Persia signs a defence treaty with Britain.

1814 Border dispute provokes a war between the British and the Gurkhas in Nepal.

1816 Persians invade Afghanistan but are forced to withdraw.

1816 Nepal becomes an independent British protectorate.

1816 Britain returns Java and Sumatra to the Dutch.

1816–18 Egyptian army under General Ibrahim Pasha (1789–1848) suppresses the Wahhabi state in W Arabia.

1817–18 During the third Maratha War Britain gains control of the Rajput states of W central India.

1818 Britain returns Malacca to the Dutch.

1818 Afghanistan disintegrates into small states after a tribal revolt.

1819 Bagyidaw (d.1837) becomes king of Burma and continues the policy of expansion.

1819 Sikhs under Ranjit Singh (1780–1839) conquer Kashmir.

1819 British colonial administrator Stamford Raffles (1781–1826) founds Singapore.

AFRICA

1804 Usman dan Fodio (1754–1817) leads the Fulani people against the Hausa states in Nigeria and establishes the Sokoto caliphate.

1805 Ottoman governor Muhammad Ali (1769–1849) seizes power in Egypt.

1805 Tripolitanian War ends when the bey of Tunis renounces the right to levy pirate-protection bribes on the USA.

1806 British recapture Cape Colony in South Africa.

1807 Slave trade is abolished throughout the British empire; a W African naval patrol is established to enforce the ban.

1807 British, allied to Russia, occupy Alexandria but withdraw after Turkish opposition.

1809 British capture Senegal from the French.

1810 British capture Mauritius and Réunion from the French.

1810 Radama I (1791–1828) becomes king of the Hovas in Madagascar and encourages British influence.

1811 Muhammad Ali secures his position in Egypt by massacring Mamluk generals in Cairo.

1812 British build forts along the Fish River in South Africa.

1815 US navy threatens to bombard Algiers unless piracy against American shipping ends.

1815 France abolishes the slave trade.

1815 Revolt by Afrikaners is suppressed by British troops in South Africa.

1817 Senegal is returned to French control.

1819 Zulu people under King Shaka (1787–1828) establish control of the Natal region of South Africa.

EUROPE

1802 Bonaparte (1769–1821) becomes consul for life and president of the Italian republic; France annexes Piedmont.

1803 Switzerland regains its independence.

1803 Russia annexes Georgia.

1803 France occupies Hanover and prepares to invade Britain.

1804 Bonaparte is crowned Emperor Napoleon I of France by the pope; the Code Napoléon law code is issued.

1804 Kara George (1766–1827) leads a Serbian insurrection against the Turks.

1805 Third Coalition (Britain with Russia, Sweden and Austria) makes war on France; an Austrian army surrenders at Ulm; British under Horatio Nelson (1758–1805) win the naval battle of Trafalgar; French occupy Vienna; Napoleon defeats the Russians and Austrians at the Battle of Austerlitz; Napoleon becomes king of Italy.

1806 Turks, allied to France, attack the Russians.

1806 Napoleon organizes German states into a pro-French Confederation of the Rhine; his brother Joseph Bonaparte (1768–1844) becomes king of Naples; the Holy Roman Empire is dissolved; Prussia attacks the French and is defeated at the battles of Jena and Auerstadt; Napoleon occupies Berlin and proclaims a blockade of Britain (the Continental System).

1807 French defeat the Prussians, capture Danzig and defeat the Russians at the Battle of Friedland; Treaty of Tilsit ends fighting between France and Russia allied to Prussia; grand duchy of Warsaw is created in Poland; British destroy the Danish fleet; French marshal Andache Junot (1771–1813) conquers Portugal.

1808 Russia conquers Finland from Sweden.

1808 French troops invade Spain; Charles IV (1748–1819) abdicates and Joseph Bonaparte becomes king; marshal Joachim Murat (1767–1815) takes the throne of Naples; British troops under Arthur Wellesley (1769–1852) land in Portugal and force a French evacuation; a Spanish revolt is suppressed by Napoleon.

1809 French win the Battle of Coruña, force the British out of Spain, and invade Portugal; an Austrian uprising is defeated by Napoleon at the Battle of Wagram; Austria signs the peace of Schönbrunn.

1810 Napoleon marries Marie Louise (1791–1847), daughter of Austrian emperor Francis I (1768–1835); France annexes Holland; in Spain, Wellesley defeats the French at the Battle of Salamanca.

1811–12 Machine-breaking Luddite riots occur in Britain.

1812 Turks cede Bessarabia (part of present-day Romania) to Russia.

1812 Napoleon invades Russia, wins the battles of Smolensk and Borodino, and occupies Moscow; the Russians burn Moscow and the French withdraw; most of the retreating French army dies.

1812 Liberal constitution is adopted by the Cortes of Spain.

1812 Russia gains control of Poland.

1813 Prussia declares war on France and is joined by Britain, Sweden and Austria; Napoleon is defeated at the Battle of Leipzig; Holland and Italy are freed from French rule; Wellesley wins the Battle of Vittoria and drives the French from Spain; Swedes under French general Jean Bernadotte (1763–1844) invade pro-French Denmark.

1814 Sweden and Norway are united under the Swedish king.

1814 Ferdinand VII (1784–1833) is restored as king of Spain; Prussians under Gebhard Blücher (1742–1819) invade N France; British capture Bordeaux and Paris is occupied; a provisional government under Charles Talleyrand (1754–1838) exiles Napoleon to Elba; Louis XVIII (1755–1824) becomes king of France and issues a liberal constitution; peace of Paris restores the borders of Europe to the status quo of 1792; Austrian foreign minister Klemens Metternich (1773–1859) organizes the congress of Vienna; Wellesley becomes Duke of Wellington.

1815 Napoleon lands in S France and marches to Paris; Louis XVIII flees to Belgium; Austrians defeat Murat at the Battle of Tolentino; Ferdinand I (1751–1825) is restored as king of the Two Sicilies; Napoleon invades Belgium and defeats Blücher at Ligny, but is defeated by the British and Prussians under the Duke of Wellington at the Battle of Waterloo; Napoleon is exiled to St Helena; a second White Terror occurs.

1815 Congress of Vienna establishes the balance of power in Europe. Poland is united with Russia; Holland and Belgium are united as the Kingdom of the Netherlands; German Confederation is formed; perpetual neutrality of Switzerland is declared.

1815 Russia, Austria and Prussia form the anti-liberal Holy Alliance.

1815 British Parliament passes a protectionist Corn Law that restricts the importation of foreign grains.

1817 Liberal German students protest in Wartburg.

1818 Miloš Obrenović (1780–1860) leads a Serbian uprising against the Turks and establishes a degree of self-government.

THE AMERICAS

1804 US vice president Aaron Burr (1756–1836) kills Alexander Hamilton (b.1755) in a duel.

1804 Meriwether Lewis (1774–1809) and William Clark (1770–1838) lead a US expedition across Louisiana.

1806 British occupy Buenos Aires but are evicted by a colonial militia.

1806 Francisco de Miranda (1754–1816) leads an unsuccessful rebellion against the Spanish in Venezuela.

1807 British fleet captures Montevideo but local opposition forces it to leave.

1807 Portuguese royal family flee to Brazil after the French invasion.

1808 Eastern part of Haiti returns to Spanish control.

1808 USA prohibits the importation of slaves.

1808 James Madison (1751–1836) is elected US president.

1809 Shawnee Native American chief Tecumseh (1768–1813) starts a campaign against US westward expansion.

SCIENCE AND TECHNOLOGY

1801 French clothworker Joseph Jacquard (1752–1834) invents a loom to make figured fabric.

1801 German scientist Johann Ritter (1776–1810) discovers ultraviolet light.

1802 British engineer Richard Trevithick (1771–1833) invents a high-pressure steam engine.

1802 French physicist Jacques Charles (1746–1823) formulates his law of gas expansion.

1803 British chemist William Henry (1774–1836) discovers his law of the volume of dissolved gases.

1804 Swiss scientist Nicholas de Saussure (1767–1845) discovers that carbon dioxide and nitrogen are essential for plant growth.

1806 British admiral Francis Beaufort (1774–1857) devises a practical scale for measuring wind speed.

1806 British chemist Humphry Davy (1778–1829) discovers sodium and potassium.

1807 US engineer Robert Fulton (1765–1815) opens the first commercial steamboat service in New York.

1807 British physicist Thomas Young (1773–1829) discovers the modulus of elasticity.

1808 British chemist John Dalton (1766–1844) outlines atomic theory in *New System of Chemical Philosophy.*

1808 French physicist Étienne Malus (1775–1812) announces his discovery of the polarization of light.

1808 French chemist Joseph Gay-Lussac (1778–1850) announces his law of combining gas volumes.

1809 Gas street lighting is installed in Pall Mall, London.

1809 French biologist Jean Baptiste Lamarck (1744–1829) publishes *Zoological Philosophy.*

ARTS AND HUMANITIES

1806 French sculptor Claude Clodion (1738–1814) designs the Arc de Triomphe in Paris.

1807 British poet William Wordsworth (1770–1850) publishes *Ode on Intimations of Immortality.*

1808 French artist Jean Ingres (1780–1867) paints *Bather of Valpinçon.*

1808 French social reformer Charles Fourier (1772–1837) proposes a system of co-operative farms in *Theory of the Four Movements.*

1808 German poet and author Johann Goethe (1749–1832) publishes the first part of his drama *Faust.*

1808 German composer Ludwig van Beethoven (1770–1827) writes Symphony No.5 in C minor.

1810 Provisional junta takes power in Buenos Aires.

1810 USA annexes w Florida.

1810 Mexican priest Miguel Hidalgo (1753–1811) leads a popular revolt against the Spanish.

1811 Paraguay declares independence from Spain.

1811 Venezuelan leader Francisco de Miranda (1750–1816) declares independence from Spain.

1811 US settlers defeat the Shawnee Native North Americans at the Battle of Tippecanoe.

1812 Louisiana becomes a state of the USA.

1812 USA declares war on Britain; British capture Detroit.

1813 Americans recapture Detroit but fail to take Montreal.

1813 Mexican revolutionary Jose Morelos (1765–1815) declares Mexican independence.

1813 Simón Bolívar (1783–1830) takes command of Venezuelan independence forces.

1814 Americans defeat the British at a naval battle on Lake Champlain; British capture and burn Washington, D.C.; treaty of Ghent ends the war between Britain and the USA.

1814 Spanish regain control of Venezuela.

1814 José de Francia (*c.*1766–1840) is declared dictator of Paraguay.

1815 US troops under General Andrew Jackson (1767–1845) defeat the British at the Battle of New Orleans.

1816 Argentines led by José de San Martín (1778–1850) declare their independence from Spain.

1816 Spanish regain control of Mexico.

1816 James Monroe (1758–1831) is elected US president.

1816 Indiana becomes a state of the USA.

1817 Argentina annexes Uruguay.

1817 San Martín invades and liberates Chile.

1817 Mississippi becomes a state of the USA.

1818 Simón Bolívar leads a revolutionary army into Venezuela.

1818 Illinois becomes a state of the USA.

1818 USA and Britain agree on the 49th parallel as the Canadian boundary, with joint occupation of Oregon.

1810 French chef Nicholas Appert (*c.*1750–1840) publishes his method for preserving food in tin cans.

1811 German printer Friedrich König (1774–1833) invents the power-driven, flat-bed, cylinder press.

1811 Italian physicist Amedo Avogadro (1776–1856) discovers that equal volumes of gases have an equal number of molecules.

1812 French zoologist Georges Cuvier (1769–1832) publishes *Researches into the Fossil Bones of Quadrupeds.*

1812 French mathematician Pierre Laplace (1749–1827) refines probability theory in *Analytical Theory.*

1812 British scientist William Wollaston (1766–1828) invents the camera lucida.

1812 German mineralogist Friedrich Mohs (1773–1839) classifies the hardness of materials.

1814 British engineer George Stephenson (1781–1848) builds a steam locomotive, the *Blucher.*

1814 Swedish scientist Jöns Berzelius (1779–1848) introduces modern chemical symbols.

1815 German scientist Joseph von Fraunhofer (1787–1826) discovers black lines in the solar spectrum.

1816 Scottish scientist Robert Stirling (1790–1878) invents a closed-cycle external combustion engine.

1816 French hobbyist Nicéphore Niepce (1765–1833) begins experimenting with photography using a silver chloride solution.

1819 French physician René Laennec (1781–1826) invents the stethoscope.

1810 Scottish poet Walter Scott (1771–1832) publishes *The Lady of* 1810
the Lake.

1810 Spanish artist Francisco Goya (1746–1828) begins his series of engravings *The Disasters of War.*

1810 British architect John Nash (1752–1835) begins designing the Royal Pavilion in Brighton, England.

1811 Swedish poet Esaias Tegner (1782–1846) publishes *Svea.*

1812 British poet George Byron (1788–1824) publishes the first cantos of *Childe Harold's Pilgrimage.*

1812 German language scholars Jakob (1785–1863) and Wilhelm (1786–1859) Grimm publish a collection of folktales and fairy stories.

1813 British novelist Jane Austen (1775–1817) publishes *Pride and Prejudice.*

1813 French novelist Madame de Staël (1766–1817) publishes *On Germany.*

1813 British industrialist Robert Owen (1771–1858) publishes *A New View of Society.*

1814 Kurozumi Munetada (1780–1850) revives popular Shintoism in Japan.

1816 Italian composer Gioacchino Rossini (1792–1868) writes his opera *The Barber of Seville.*

1816 German philosopher Georg Hegel (1770–1831) introduces his dialectical system in *The Science of Logic.*

1817 British artist John Constable (1776–1831) paints *View on the Stour.*

1817 British economist David Ricardo (1772–1823) publishes *Principles of Political Economy and Taxation.*

1818 British novelist Mary Shelley (1797–1851) publishes *Frankenstein.*

1819 German philosopher Arthur Schopenhauer (1788–1860) publishes his pessimistic *The World as Will and Idea.*

1819 Austrian composer Franz Schubert (1797–1828) writes *Trout* quintet.

1819 Walter Scott publishes his novel *Ivanhoe.*

1819 French artist Theodore Géricault (1791–1824) paints *Raft of the Medusa.*

ASIA AND AUSTRALASIA

1820 **1822** Burmese annex Assam.

1824 British declare war on Burma and capture Rangoon.

1824 Dutch cede Malacca to Britain in return for territory in Sumatra.

1825 Persia attempts to recapture Georgia from Russia.

1826 Anti-Sikh jihad is organized by Muslims in N India.

1826 Russians defeat Persians at the Battle of Ganja and gain part of Armenia.

1826 Afghan chieftain Dost Muhammad (1789–1863) captures Kabul.

1826 King Rama III (d.1851) of Thailand signs a trade agreement with Britain.

1826 After defeating the Burmese, Britain gains Assam and part of the Malay peninsula by the treaty of Yandabu.

1826 British unite Penang, Singapore and Malacca into the Straits Settlements.

1826 Sultan Mahmud II (1785–1839) massacres the Janisseries in Turkey.

1826 Dipo Negoro (*c.*1785–1855) leads a Javanese revolt against the Dutch.

1828 Russian forces capture Tehran; Persia cedes territory to Russia by the treaty of Turkmanchai.

1828 Dutch annex W New Guinea.

1829 British claim the whole of Australia.

1830 **1830** Dutch suppress the Javanese revolt.

1831 Muslims defeat the Sikhs at the Battle of Balakot in NW India.

1832 Ottoman governor Muhammad Ali (1769–1849) invades Syria and Asia Minor and defeats the Turks at the Battle of Konya.

1833 Russia sends ships to assist the Turks; France and Britain protest against Russian interference; Muhammad Ali gains control of Syria.

1834 Sikhs capture the Muslim city of Peshawar in present-day Pakistan.

1834 Muhammad Shah becomes ruler of Persia after the death of Fath Ali (b.1771).

1835 Dost Muhammad becomes ruler of all Afghanistan and establishes the Barakzai dynasty.

1838 Ismaili leader Aga Khan I (1800–81) flees to India after his rebellion against the shah of Persia is defeated.

1839 British occupy the port of Aden in Yemen.

1839 Turks invade Syria and are defeated by the Egyptians at the Battle of Nesib.

1839 British invade Afghanistan and overthrow Dost Muhammad.

AFRICA

1820 Egypt invades Sudan.

1820 Several thousand British settlers are sent to South Africa.

1820 Mfecane Wars start in S Africa when Zulu expansion displaces other African peoples; Ngoni raiding parties invade Mozambique.

1821 Sierra Leone, the Gold Coast (present-day Ghana) and Gambia are joined into British West Africa.

1822 Liberia, on the coast of West Africa, is established as a colony for freed American slaves.

1822 Mfecane Wars spread to South Africa.

1823 Egyptians found Khartoum as the capital of Sudan.

1824 British interference in West African affairs angers the Ashanti people, who destroy a British force; start of the first Ashanti War.

1824 Omani governor of Mombasa dies and the British occupy the port.

1825 King Radama I (1791–1828) evicts the French from Madagascar.

1826 Boundary of Cape Colony is extended N to the Orange River.

1827 British defeat an Ashanti invasion of the Gold Coast; end of the first Ashanti War.

1828 British evacuate Mombasa.

1828 Ranavalona I (1800–61) becomes Hova queen in Madagascar.

1828 Zulu leader Shaka (1787–1828) is assassinated by his brothers.

1830 French invade Algeria and occupy the cities of Algiers and Oran.

1831 Britain signs a peace treaty with the Ashanti.

1831 Mfecane Wars spread N to Zimbabwe.

1831 French foreign legion is founded in Algeria.

1832 Abd al-Kadir (1808–83) becomes leader of the Algerian resistance.

1834 Slavery is abolished throughout the British Empire.

1835 Mfecane Wars spread further N to Zambia and Malawi.

1835 Turks overthrow the Karamanli dynasty in Tripoli and impose direct rule.

1835 Afrikaners in South Africa begin the Great Trek to escape British repression.

1836 Abd al-Kadir occupies the inland Algerian city of Mascara.

1837 Afrikaners establish the republic of Natal to the NE of the British Cape Colony.

1838 Afrikaners in Natal inflict a heavy defeat on the Zulus.

EUROPE

1818 France joins the Holy Alliance by the treaty of Aix-la-Chapelle.

1818 Jean Bernadotte (1763–1844) becomes Charles XIV of Sweden.

1819 Carlsbad decrees impose strict censorship and control over university admissions throughout the German Confederation.

1819 Anti-Corn Law protesters are killed by troops at the Peterloo massacre in Britain.

1820 Soldiers join a liberal revolution in S Spain and force Ferdinand VII (1784–1833) to restore the constitution.

1820 Carbonari secret societies foment a liberal revolt in Naples which forces Ferdinand I (1751–1825) to issue a constitution.

1820 Liberal revolution starts in Oporto, Portugal.

1820 George IV (1762–1830) becomes king of Britain.

1821 Liberal unrest spreads to N Italy; the king of Piedmont-Sardinia abdicates; the Congress of Laibach authorizes the Austrians to restore monarchical power in Italy.

1821 Greeks led by Alexander Ypsilante (1792–1828) revolt against Turkish rule and seize Bucharest.

1822 Congress of Verona authorizes the French to intervene in Spain to restore the monarchy.

1822 Greeks declare independence; Turks invade and massacre the inhabitants of Chios, but fail to subdue the rebels.

1822 Egyptians occupy Crete.

1822 Portugal adopts a liberal constitution under John VI (1767–1826).

1823 John VI withdraws the Portuguese constitution; reactionaries led by his son start a civil war.

1823 French occupy Madrid, defeat the revolutionaries at the Battle of the Trocadero, and restore Ferdinand VII.

1824 Greek rebels are divided by civil war.

1824 Charles X (1757–1836) becomes king of France and attempts to restore the power of the monarchy.

1825 Egyptian army invades S Greece.

1825 Alexander I (b.1777) of Russia dies; an attempted military coup (the Decembrists) fails; Nicholas I (1796–1855) becomes tsar.

1826 Infant Maria II (1819–53) becomes queen of Portugal.

1826 Turks capture the Greek stronghold of Missolongi.

1827 Turks capture the Acropolis in Athens.

1828 Force of British, French and Russian ships destroys the Egyptian fleet at the Battle of Navarino; Egyptians evacuate Greece.

1828 Russians declare war on Turkey.

1828 British Corn Law is reformed.

1828 Portuguese regent Dom Miguel (1802–66) proclaims himself king.

1829 German state of Bavaria signs a trade tariff treaty with Prussia.

1829 London protocol establishes Greek independence under a monarchy.

1829 Russia gains the E coast of the Black Sea from the Turks under the treaty of Adrianople.

1829 Catholic Emancipation Act is passed in Britain.

1829 Ultra-conservative Prince de Polignac (1780–1847) becomes prime minister in France.

1830 William IV (1765–1827) becomes king of Britain.

1830 Revolution in Paris overthrows Charles X; Louis Philippe I (1773–1850) becomes king of France with a more liberal constitution.

1830 Revolutionaries in Brussels declare Belgian independence from the Netherlands.

1830 Rising in Warsaw led by Adam Jerzy Czartoryski (1770–1861) establishes a Polish national government.

1830 German revolutionaries force the rulers of Saxony and Brunswick to abdicate.

1831 Russian troops crush the Polish rebels.

1831 Leopold I (1790–1865) becomes king of Belgium with a liberal constitution.

1831 Nationalist risings in the Italian cities of Parma and Modena are suppressed by the Austrians.

1832 Italian nationalist Giuseppe Mazzini (1805–72) founds the Young Italy movement.

1832 Poland is made a province of Russia.

1832 British Parliament is reformed.

THE AMERICAS

1818 Revolutionary leader Bernardo O'Higgins (1778–1842) becomes Supreme Director of Chile.

1819 USA purchases Florida from Spain.

1819 Bolívar defeats the Spanish and becomes president of Gran Colombia (present-day Venezuela, Ecuador and Colombia).

1819 Alabama becomes a state of the USA.

1820 Missouri compromise prohibits slavery in the N part of the Louisiana Purchase territory.

1820 Maine becomes a state of the USA.

1821 Aristocratic revolutionaries declare Mexican independence from Spain.

1821 Brazil incorporates Uruguay.

1821 US farmers begin to settle in Texas.

1821 José de San Martín (1778–1850) and Simón Bolívar (1783–1830) liberate Peru.

1821 Missouri becomes a state of the USA.

1822 Mexican general Agustín de Iturbide (1783–1824) is crowned Emperor Agustín I; Central American states become part of the Mexican Empire.

1822 Brazil under Emperor Pedro I (1798–1834) declares its independence from Portugal.

1823 Revolution overthrows the Mexican emperor.

1823 Guatemala, San Salvador, Nicaragua, Honduras and Costa Rica establish independence from Mexico and form the United Provinces of Central America.

1823 US president James Monroe (1758–1831) issues the Monroe doctrine forbidding European colonialism in the Americas.

1824 Mexico becomes a republic under President Guadalupe Vittoria (1768–1843).

1825 US House of Representatives elects John Quincy Adams (1767–1848) president.

1825 Erie canal is completed, linking New York City with the Great Lakes.

1825 Portugal recognizes the independence of Brazil.

1825 Bolivia under President Antonio de Sucre (1795–1830) gains independence from Peru.

1825 Argentina sends troops to aid Uruguay against Brazil.

1827 Argentines defeat the Brazilians at the Battle of Ituzaingo.

1828 Uruguay obtains independence from Brazil.

1828 General Andrew Jackson (1767–1845) is elected US president.

1829 First US public railway opens.

1829 Peru and Bolivia form a confederation.

1829 Mexican general Antonio de Santa Anna (1794–1876) defeats an attempted Spanish invasion.

1829 Workingmen's party is formed in the USA.

1830 Ecuador under President Juan Flores (1800–64) gains independence from Colombia.

1830 US Indian Removal Act organizes the removal of Native North Americans to W of the River Mississippi.

1830 First American settlers arrive in California having crossed the Rocky Mountains.

1831 Nat Turner (b.1800) is executed after leading a slave revolt in Virginia.

1831 Pedro II (1825–91) becomes emperor of Brazil.

1833 Antonio de Santa Anna is elected president of Mexico.

1833 Britain claims sovereignty over the Falkland Islands.

1835 American settlers declare the independent republic of Texas.

1836 US congressman Davy Crockett (b.1786) and colonel Jim Bowie (b.1796) are killed when Mexican troops defeat Texan rebels at the Alamo mission house; the Mexicans are defeated at the Battle of San Jacinto by Texans under General Sam Houston (1793–1863).

1836 Martin Van Buren (1782–1862) is elected US president.

1836 Arkansas becomes a state of the USA.

SCIENCE AND TECHNOLOGY

1820 French physicians Pierre Pelletier (1788–1842) and Joseph Caventou (1795–1877) discover the anti-malarial drug quinine.

1820 French physicist André Ampère (1775–1836) establishes the science of electromagnetism.

1821 French physicist Augustin Fresnel (1788–1827) finalizes his transverse wave theory of light.

1821 German physicist Thomas Seebeck (1770–1831) invents the thermocouple.

1821 British physicist Michael Faraday (1791–1867) discovers electromagnetic rotation.

1822 French scientist and mathematician Jean Fourier (1768–1830) publishes his theory of heat conduction.

1822 French scholar Jean Champollion (1790–1832) translates Egyptian hieroglyphics.

1823 British mathematician Charles Babbage (1791–1871) begins building a working model of his difference engine calculating machine.

1824 British builder Joseph Aspidin (1779–1855) invents Portland cement.

1824 Scottish chemist Charles Macintosh (1766–1843) devises a method of bonding rubber to fabric for waterproof clothing.

1824 French engineer Sadi Carnot (1796–1832) lays the foundations of thermodynamics in *On the Motive Power of Fire.*

1825 George Stephenson (1781–1848) builds the first public railway between Stockton and Darlington.

1825 Danish physicist Hans Oersted (1777–1851) discovers how to produce aluminium metal.

1825 French engineer Marc Seguin (1786–1875) builds the first wire suspension bridge.

1827 German scientist Georg Ohm (1787–1854) publishes his law of electrical voltage and current.

1827 Scottish scientist Robert Brown (1773–1858) observes the random movements of minute particles (Brownian motion).

1827 British chemist John Walker (*c.*1781–1859) invents friction matches.

1828 German chemist Friedrich Wöhler (1800–82) synthesizes urea.

1829 British chemist Thomas Graham (1805–69) formulates his law of gas diffusion.

1829 French mathematician Gaspard de Coriolis (1792–1843) explains the effect that causes objects moving in the atmosphere to be deflected.

1830 British engineer Joseph Whitworth (1803–87) introduces standardized screw threads.

1830 Michael Faraday discovers electromagnetic induction.

1831 British explorer James Ross (1800–62) reaches the N magnetic pole.

1831 British naturalist Charles Darwin (1809–82) embarks on his round-the-world expedition on HMS *Beagle.*

1831 US physicist Joseph Henry (1797–1878) publishes a description of his electric motor.

1832 French instrument maker Hippolyte Pixii (1808–35) constructs a practical, heteropolar, electrical generator.

1833 Steamship *Royal William* becomes the first to cross the Atlantic Ocean entirely by steam power.

1834 French teacher Louis Braille (1809–52) perfects his system of embossed dots that enable blind people to read.

1834 US farmer Cyrus McCormick (1809–84) invents the horse-drawn reaper-harvester.

1835 US inventor Samuel Colt (1814–62) patents his revolver handgun.

ARTS AND HUMANITIES

1820 Venus de Milo sculpture is discovered. 1820

1820 French poet Alphonse Lamartine (1790–1869) publishes *Poetic Meditations.*

1820 British poet John Keats (1795–1821) publishes *Ode to a Nightingale.*

1820 British poet Percy Shelley (1792–1822) publishes *Prometheus Unbound.*

1821 French social reformer Claude de Saint-Simon (1760–1825) publishes *Of the Industrial System.*

1822 German composer Carl von Weber (1786–1826) writes his opera *Der Freischütz.*

1822 British writer Thomas De Quincey (1785–1859) publishes *Confessions of an English Opium Eater.*

1822 Hungarian composer Franz Liszt (1811–86) makes his debut as a pianist.

1824 French artist Eugène Delacroix (1798–1863) paints *Massacre at Chios.*

1825 Russian poet Alexander Pushkin (1799–1837) publishes *Boris Godunov.*

1826 US novelist James Fenimore Cooper (1789–1851) publishes *The Last of the Mohicans.*

1826 French poet and author Alfred de Vigny (1797–1863) publishes his novel *Cinq-Mars.*

1827 German poet Heinrich Heine (1797–1856) publishes *The Book of Songs.*

1827 Italian poet and author Alessandro Manzoni (1785–1873) publishes his novel *The Betrothed.*

1828 American publisher Noah Webster (1758–1843) publishes the *American Dictionary of the English Language.*

1828 *Memoirs* of Giovanni Casanova (1725–98) are published.

1828 Italian violinist Niccolò Paganini (1782–1840) arrives in Vienna.

1829 French novelist Honore de Balzac (1788–1850) publishes *The Chouans* and begins *The Human Comedy.*

1829 Scottish philosopher James Mill (1773–1836) publishes *An Analysis of the Phenomena of the Human Mind.*

1830 US religious leader Joseph Smith (1805–44) publishes *The Book of Mormon.* 1830

1830 French composer Hector Berlioz (1803–69) writes *Symphonie fantastique.*

1830 French novelist Stendhal (Henry Beyle, 1783–1842) publishes *Scarlet and Black.*

1830 French-born Polish composer Frédéric Chopin (1810–49) writes his first piano concerto.

1831 Barbizon school of landscape painters exhibits at the Paris Salon.

1832 French novelist George Sand (1804–76) publishes *Indiana.*

1832 US artist George Catlin (1796–1872) completes his portfolio of paintings of Native Americans.

1832 Military theories of Prussian general Carl von Clausewitz (1780–1831) are published posthumously as *On War.*

1833 Russian novelist and dramatist Nikolai Gogol (1809–52) publishes his play *The Government Inspector.*

1833 Japanese artist Ando Hiroshige (1797–1858) publishes his woodcuts of the *Fifty-three Stages of the Tokaido.*

ASIA AND AUSTRALASIA

1839 Chinese officials burn British opium in the port of Canton (Guangzhou).

1840 **1840** British colonists land in New Zealand; Maori chiefs cede sovereignty to Britain by the treaty of Waitangi.

1840 British occupy Chinese forts in Canton (Guangzhou).

1841 During the first Opium War, the British navy seizes ports along the Chinese coast.

1841 Afghans rebel against British occupation.

1841 Sultan of Brunei cedes Sarawak to a British merchant.

1841 European powers persuade Egypt to withdraw from Syria.

1842 British are forced to withdraw from Afghanistan; Dost Muhammad (1789–1863) regains power.

1842 Peace of Nanjing ends the first Opium War; Britain obtains Hong Kong.

1842 Tahiti becomes a French protectorate.

1843 British conquer Sind in present-day SW Pakistan.

1843 First Maori War breaks out over a land dispute.

1843 Chinese port of Shanghai is opened to foreign trade.

1843 Chinese emperor repeats his ban on opium smoking.

1844 Cambodia comes under the control of Thailand.

1844 Sayyid Ali Muhammad (*c.*1820–50) proclaims himself Bab and founds Babism in Persia.

1848 Nasir al-Din (1829–96) becomes shah of Persia.

1845 Sikhs invade British territory in N India; start of the Anglo-Sikh War.

1846 British conquer Kashmir from the Sikhs and sell it to a Hindu ruler.

1848 Babists in Persia rebel and declare an independent state.

1849 British annex the Sikh kingdom in the Punjab region of India.

1850 **1850** Babist rebellion in Persia is crushed and the self-proclaimed Bab, Sayyid Ali Muhammad, is executed.

1850 Britain's Australian colonies are granted self-government.

1851 Taiping Rebellion breaks out in SW China led by Hong Xiuquan.

1851 Colonists discover gold in Victoria, Australia.

1852 During the second Burmese War, Britain annexes Pegu (S Burma); Mindon Min (1814–78) becomes king of N Burma.

AFRICA

1840 Sultan of Oman, Sayyid Said (1791–1856), makes Zanzibar his capital.

1841 Algerian leader Abd al-Kadir (1808–83) is driven into Morocco by the French.

1842 French sign trade treaties with chieftains of the Ivory Coast in W Africa.

1843 British conquer Natal from the Afrikaners.

1843 Basutoland in S Africa comes under British protection.

1843 The Gambia is made a separate British colony.

1844 French acquire Gabon in W central Africa.

1844 French bombard Tangier in Morocco and defeat al-Kadir and his Moroccan allies at the Battle of Isly.

1846 British defeat an incursion by the Xhosa people in South Africa.

1847 Liberia becomes an independent republic.

1847 Abd al-Kadir surrenders to the French in Algeria.

1848 Algeria becomes a part of France.

1849 French acquire territory in Guinea, W Africa.

1849 French establish Libreville in Gabon as a refuge for escaped slaves.

1850 Denmark sells its trading posts in W Africa to Britain.

1852 Fulani leader Al-Hadj Umar (*c.*1797–1864) launches a war of expansion against W African states.

1853 Afrikaners establish the independent republic of Transvaal.

1853 Ethiopian chieftain Ras Kasa (*c.*1818–68) reunifies the country and proclaims himself Emperor Tewodros II.

1854 British agree to the Afrikaners establishing an Orange Free State.

EUROPE

1833 German revolutionaries force the ruler of Hanover to issue a constitution.

1833 Maria II (1819–53) is restored to the Portuguese throne.

1833 Infant Isabella II (1830–1904) becomes queen of Spain.

1834 German *Zollverein* (customs union) is formed under Prussian leadership.

1834 Isabella's brother Don Carlos (1788–1845) claims the Spanish throne; start of the Carlist War.

1834 Republican revolts in French cities are repressed.

1835 Ferdinand I (1793–1875) becomes Austrian emperor.

1836 Louis Napoleon (1808–73) attempts to seize power in France and is exiled to America.

1836 Rebellion in Spain forces the regent Maria Christina (1806–78) to grant a new constitution.

1837 Victoria (1819–1901) becomes queen of Britain; Hanover is separated from Britain.

1837 Under Austrian influence, the constitution of Hanover is withdrawn.

1838 British advocates of free trade John Bright (1811–89) and Richard Cobden (1805–65) found the Anti-Corn Law league.

1838 Protestant cantons in Switzerland adopt more liberal constitutions.

1839 First Carlist War in Spain ends when Don Carlos leaves the country.

1839 Radical Chartists cause riots in Britain.

1839 The Netherlands recognizes the independence of Belgium and the grand duchy of Luxembourg by the treaty of London.

1840 Frederick William VI (1795–1861) becomes king of Prussia.

1840 Louis Napoleon attempts a coup in France and is imprisoned.

1840 General Espartero (1793–1879) makes himself dictator in Spain.

1840 Britain, France and Russia agree to aid Turkey and send troops to Palestine.

1841 Straits Convention closes the Dardanelles to non-Turkish warships.

1842 Rising in Barcelona, Spain, declares a republic, which is crushed by Espartero.

1843 Coup overthrows Espartero in Spain; Isabella II is declared of age.

1843 Revolution forces Otto I (1815–67) of Greece to grant a constitution.

1845–46 Potato blight causes famine in Ireland.

1846 British corn laws are repealed.

1846 Polish rising in Kraków is suppressed by Austria.

1847 Protestant Swiss cantons defeat the Catholic Sonderbund.

1847 Unrest in N Italy is suppressed by Austria.

1848 Revolution in France overthrows Louis Philippe I (1773–1850) and forms a provisional government; Paris workers stage a second rising; Louis Napoleon is elected president of the second French republic.

1848 Central and S Italian states receive constitutions; rebels drive Austrians from Milan; Venice declares a republic; Piedmont declares war on Austria.

1848 Switzerland adopts a new federal constitution.

1848 Rising in Berlin leads to a German national assembly meeting in Frankfurt.

1848 Denmark and Prussia go to war over Schleswig-Holstein.

1848 Rising in Vienna causes Klemens Metternich (1773–1859) to flee; a constituent assembly meets; Franz Joseph I (1830–1916) becomes Austrian emperor; Hungarians establish a national government.

1849 Louis Kossuth (1802–94) is elected Hungarian leader; the Russians crush the Hungarian rising.

1849 Ferdinand II (1810–59) restores control in S Italy; Roman republic is suppressed by the French despite resistance of Giuseppe Garibaldi (1807–82); Austrians defeat Piedmontese at the Battle of Novara and crush the Venetian republic.

1849 German national assembly collapses.

1850 German Confederation is restored under Austrian leadership.

1850 British gunboats blockade the Greek port of Piraeus.

1851 Austrian emperor withdraws the constitution.

1851 Louis Napoleon overthrows the French constitution.

1852 Louis Napoleon is declared Emperor Napoleon III.

1852 Camillo di Cavour (1810–61) becomes prime minister of Piedmont-Sardinia.

THE AMERICAS

1836 Settlers in California declare independence from Mexico.

1837 French-speakers in Lower Canada rebel against British administration; a similar revolt occurs in Upper Canada.

1837 Michigan becomes a state of the USA.

1838 British restore order in Canada.

1838 Underground Railroad is organized in the USA to smuggle slaves from the S states.

1838 Britain and France blockade the Argentine coast in a dispute over the Falkland Islands.

1839 Former slave-owners rebel against British rule in Jamaica.

1839 Chilean troops overthrow the Peru–Bolivia confederation.

1840 Confederation of Central American States breaks up.

1840 William Harrison (1773–1841) is elected US president.

1840 Upper and Lower Canada are united and the country is granted self-governing status by the British.

1841 John Tyler (1790–1862) becomes US president.

1841 Peruvian attempt to annex Bolivia is defeated at the Battle of Ingavi.

1842 Treaty between the USA and Britain settles the E stretch of the US–Canadian border.

1844 James Polk (1795–1849) is elected US president.

1844 Dominican Republic becomes independent of Haiti.

1845 British and French ships blockade the River Plate during further disputes with Argentina.

1845 Florida becomes a state of the USA.

1845 Texas is annexed and becomes a state of the USA.

1846 Britain cedes Oregon to the USA; the 49th parallel becomes the W stretch of the US–Canadian border.

1846 USA declares war on Mexico.

1846 Iowa becomes a state of the USA.

1847 US forces make an amphibious landing and capture Vera Cruz in Mexico.

1847 Brigham Young (1801–77) founds Salt Lake City.

1848 Zachary Taylor (1785–1850) is elected US president.

1848 Wisconsin becomes a state of the USA.

1848 California Gold Rush starts.

1848 US troops enter Mexico City; by the peace of Guadaloupe-Hidalgo, Mexico cedes all territory N of Rio Grande to the USA.

1850 USA and Britain agree by treaty the neutrality of a proposed canal construction zone across Panama.

1850 Millard Fillmore (1800–74) becomes US president.

1850 Clay Compromise abolishes the right of the US government to impose anti-slavery polices on new states.

1850 California becomes a state of the USA.

1851 Spanish defeat a nationalist invasion of Cuba.

SCIENCE AND TECHNOLOGY

1836 British electrical engineer William Sturgeon (1783–1850) invents the moving-coil galvanometer.

1836 Belgian scientist Joseph Plateau (1801–83) invents the stroboscope.

1837 British educator Isaac Pitman (1813–97) invents his system of shorthand writing.

1837 US metalworker John Deere (1804–86) invents the steel plough.

1837 British physicists Charles Wheatstone (1802–75) and William Cooke (1806–79) jointly invent an electric telegraph.

1837 US inventor Samuel Morse (1791–1872) devises an electric telegraph and a simple dot-dash message code.

1838 German astronomer Friedrich Bessel (1784–1846) discovers stellar parallax.

1839 German biologist Theodor Schwann (1810–82) publishes his cell theory.

1839 French artist Louis Daguerre (1789–1851) announces his invention of a photographic process for producing images on copper plates.

1839 British scientist William Talbot (1800–77) invents a process for making photographic negatives.

1839 US manufacturer Charles Goodyear (1800–60) discovers the process for vulcanizing rubber.

1839 Scottish engineer James Nasmyth (1808–90) invents the steam hammer.

1839 French physicist Anton Becquerel (1788–1878) invents a photoelectric cell.

1840 German chemist Christian Schönbein (1799–1868) discovers ozone.

1840 Swiss geologist Louis Agassiz (1807–73) proposes his ice ages theory of global glaciation.

1841 German chemist Robert Bunsen (1811–99) invents a zinc-carbon battery.

1841 British palaeontologist Richard Owen (1804–92) introduces the term "dinosaur".

1841 British astronomer John Couch Adams (1819–92) and French astronomer Urbain Leverrier (1811–77) independently predict the existence and position of the planet Neptune.

1842 Austrian physicist Christian Doppler (1805–53) discovers the change in frequency of sound waves from a moving source.

1842 US physician Crawford Long (1815–78) first uses ether as a surgical anaesthetic.

1843 British physicist James Joule (1818–89) establishes the first law of thermodynamics.

1844 US dentist Horace Wells (1815–48) first uses nitrous oxide as an anaesthetic for tooth extraction.

1846 US engineer Elias Howe (1819–67) invents the lockstitch sewing machine.

1846 Italian scientist Ascanio Sobrero (1812–88) invents nitroglycerine.

1846 German astronomer Johann Galle (1812–1910) makes the first sighting of the planet Neptune.

1847 Scottish physician James Simpson (1811–70) first uses chloroform as an anaesthetic for childbirth.

1847 US engineer Richard Hoe (1812–86) invents a rotary printing press.

1848 British mathematician George Boole (1815–64) introduces symbolic logic in *The Mathematical Analysis of Logic.*

1848 British physicist William Kelvin (1824–1907) devises the absolute temperature scale.

1848 French physicist Armand Fizeau (1819–96) applies the Doppler effect to light waves.

1848 French chemist Louis Pasteur (1822–95) introduces the study of stereochemistry.

1849 US inventor Walter Hunt (1796–1859) patents the safety pin.

1849 French army officer and engineer Claude Minié (1814–79) invents a rifle that fires expanding lead bullets.

1850 US scientist Charles Page (1812–68) builds an electric locomotive.

1850 German physicist Rudolph Clausius (1822–88) formulates the second law of thermodynamics.

1850 First submarine telegraph cable is laid, between Britain and France.

1851 US manufacturer Isaac Singer (1811–75) invents the single-thread domestic sewing machine.

1851 Great Exhibition, organized largely by Prince Albert (1819–61), opens in the specially built Crystal Palace in London, England.

ARTS AND HUMANITIES

1835 French historian Alexis de Tocqueville (1805–1859) publishes *Of Democracy in America.*

1836 German composer Felix Mendelssohn (1809–47) writes the *St Paul* oratorio.

1837 British novelist Charles Dickens (1812–70) publishes *Oliver Twist.*

1835 Italian composer Gaetano Donizetti (1797–1848) writes his opera *Lucy of Lammermoor.*

1835 Danish writer Hans Christian Andersen (1805–75) publishes *Tales Told for Children.*

1836 US writer Oliver Wendell Holmes (1809–94) publishes *Poems.*

1836 German theologian David Strauss (1808–74) treats the gospels as myth in *Life of Jesus.*

1836 US philosopher Ralph Waldo Emerson (1803–82) introduces Transcendentalism in his collection of essays *Nature.*

1838 US artist John Audubon (1785–1851) publishes the fourth and final volume of illustrations for *Birds of America.*

1839 French socialist Louis Blanc (1811–82) publishes *The Organization of Labour.*

1839 US poet Henry Longfellow (1807–82) publishes *Voices of the Night.*

1840 French anarchist philosopher Pierre Proudhon (1809–65) 1840
publishes *What is Property?*

1840 German composer Robert Schumann (1810–56) publishes *Women's Love and Life* song-cycle.

1841 German educator Friedrich Froebel (1782–1852) opens the first kindergarten.

1841 German economist Friedrich List (1789–1846) publishes *The National System of Political Economy.*

1841 Scottish historian Thomas Carlyle (1795–1881) publishes *On Heroes and Hero-worship.*

1843 Italian nationalist Vincenzo Gioberti (1801–52) publishes *On the Moral and Civil Primacy of the Italians.*

1844 French writer Alexandre Dumas (1802–70) publishes his novel *The Three Musketeers.*

1844 Danish philosopher Søren Kierkegaard (1813–55) publishes *The Concept of Dread.*

1844 Italian composer Giuseppe Verdi (1813–1901) writes his opera *Ermani.*

1844 Turner paints *Rain, Steam and Speed.*

1845 British politician and author Benjamin Disraeli (1804–81) publishes his novel *Sybil.*

1845 German socialist Friedrich Engels (1820–95) publishes *The Condition of the Working Classes in England.*

1845 US writer Edgar Allan Poe (1809–49) publishes *The Raven and Other Poems.*

1846 Belgian musical instrument maker Adolphe Sax (1814–94) patents the saxophone.

1847 British novelist Charlotte Brontë (1816–55) publishes *Jane Eyre.*

1847 British novelist Emily Brontë (1818–48) publishes *Wuthering Heights.*

1848 British novelist William Thackeray (1811–63) publishes *Vanity Fair.*

1848 British artists form the Pre-Raphaelite Brotherhood.

1848 German socialists Karl Marx (1818–83) and Friedrich Engels issue their *Communist Manifesto.*

1850 US novelist Nathaniel Hawthorne (1804–64) publishes *The* 1850
Scarlet Letter.

1850 German composer Richard Wagner (1813–83) writes the opera *Lohengrin.*

1850 French artist Gustave Courbet (1819–77) paints *The Stone-Breakers.*

1851 US novelist Herman Melville (1819–91) publishes *Moby Dick.*

1852 British artist William Holman Hunt (1827–1910) paints *The Light of the World.*

ASIA AND AUSTRALASIA

1853 French annex the islands of New Caledonia in the S Pacific.

1853 Taiping rebels conquer the city of Nanjing and make it their capital.

1853 Heaven and Earth secret society captures Shanghai in China.

1854 US naval officer Matthew Perry (1794–1858) forces Japan to open to limited foreign trade.

1855 Chinese troops prevent the Taiping rebels from capturing Beijing; imperial troops also recapture Shanghai with French assistance.

1856 Ottoman sultan Abdul Medjid I (1823–61) approves the Hatt-i Humayun reforms, giving religious freedom to Christians.

1856 Britain annexes the Indian state of Oudh.

1856 Persians capture the city of Herat; Britain declares war on Persia.

1856 Chinese authorities arrest the British crew of the *Arrow* for smuggling; start of the second Opium War.

1857 British and French troops capture Canton (Guangzhou), China.

1857 British forces occupy Bushire in Persia.

1857 French occupy Saigon in S Vietnam.

1857 Mandalay becomes the new capital of Burma.

1857 Sepoys (local troops) in India mutiny and massacre British civilians in many cities; British forces recapture Delhi.

1858 Indian Mutiny is suppressed; the English East India company is dissolved and India comes under the control of the British crown.

1858 Treaty of Tianjin opens more Chinese ports to foreign ships and legalizes the opium trade.

1858 China cedes N bank of Amur river to Russia by the treaty of Aigun.

1859 Portuguese and Dutch agree to divide Timor.

1859 US ships assist the British and the French against the Chinese.

1859 Dispute over land sparks the second Maori War in New Zealand.

1860 **1860** Irish explorer Robert Burke (1820–61) and English explorer William Wills (1834–61) lead the first expedition to cross Australia S-N.

1860 In S China, British and French troops defeat the Taiping rebels; in N China they capture the emperor's Dagu forts, occupy Beijing and burn the summer palace; the treaty of Beijing ends the second Opium War.

1860 Russia founds the port of Vladivostok.

1860 French troops land at Beirut (present-day Lebanon) to restore order.

1860 Japanese nationalists murder foreign sailors and officials.

1862 Tongzhi (1856–75) becomes emperor of China, with dowager empress Cixi (1835–1908) as regent.

1862 France annexes SE Vietnam.

1862 Russia annexes parts of Turkistan.

1863 Japanese forts fire at US, French and Dutch merchant ships.

1863 King Norodom (1838–1904) places Cambodia under French protection.

1863 Mercenary Ever-Victorious Army, led by British officer Charles Gordon (1833–85), liberates the city of Suzhou from the Taiping rebels.

1864 Joint French, Dutch, British and US expedition destroys Japanese coastal forts.

1864 Imperial Chinese troops recapture Nanjing: end of the Taiping Rebellion.

1865 Muslim rebels set up an independent state in Chinese Turkistan.

1865 Russians occupy Tashkent in central Asia.

1865 Wellington is established as the capital of New Zealand.

1866 Korean troops defeat a French military expedition marching on Seoul.

1867 Last Japanese shogun abdicates; Emperor Meiji (1852–1912) takes personal control in the Meiji Restoration (1868); Tokyo becomes the new capital.

1867 Turkish radicals form the Young Turks secret society.

1867 Last shipment of British convicts lands in Australia.

1868 Muslim state in Chinese Turkistan is suppressed.

AFRICA

1856 Transvaal becomes the South African Republic, with Pretoria as its capital.

1856 David Livingstone (1813–73) completes the first E–W crossing of Africa by a European, having "discovered" and named the Victoria Falls.

1857 Fulani led by Al-Hadj Umar (*c.*1797–1864) besiege the French fort of Medine in Senegal.

1857 French found Dakar in Senegal.

1857 French forces conquer the Berbers in S Algeria.

1859 Construction of the Suez canal begins under the direction of French engineer Ferdinand de Lesseps (1805–94).

1859 Spanish troops invade Morocco in a dispute over the enclaves of Ceuta and Melila.

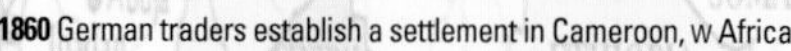

1860 German traders establish a settlement in Cameroon, W Africa.

1861 Zanzibar becomes independent of Oman.

1861 Britain acquires the Lagos coast of Nigeria.

1861 Fulani, under Al-Hadj Umar, conquer the kingdom of Segu.

1862 France purchases the port of Obock on the coast of Somalia, NE Africa.

1863 Ismail Pasha (1830–95) becomes ruler of Egypt.

1863 French establish a protectorate over Dahomey, W Africa.

1863 Madagascan chiefs overthrow pro-European king Radama II.

1864 Tewodros II (*c.*1818–68) of Ethiopia imprisons a British consul and merchants.

1865 Afrikaners from a new Orange Free State defeat Basuto chief Moshoeshoe I (*c.*1786–1870), who cedes territory.

1868 British expedition to Ethiopia defeats Tewodros II at the Battle of Arogee and frees British prisoners.

1868 British annex Basutoland (Lesotho) in South Africa.

1869 Suez canal opens, linking the Mediterranean with the Red Sea and the Indian Ocean.

EUROPE

1852 Schleswig-Holstein comes under Danish protection.

1853 Central and N German states renew the Zollverein agreement from which Austria is excluded.

1853 Russia invades Turkish-occupied Romania.

1854 Britain and France support Turkey against Russia in the Crimean War; British and French forces besiege the Russians at Sebastopol and win the Battle of Balaclava; Florence Nightingale (1820–1910) nurses the British wounded.

1854 British and French ships occupy Piraeus to prevent Greece joining the war against Turkey.

1854 General Leopoldo O'Donnell (1809–67) leads a liberal revolution in Spain.

1855 Alexander II (1818–81) becomes tsar of Russia; Sebastopol falls to British and French troops.

1855 Lord Palmerston (1784–1865) becomes prime minister of Britain.

1856 Peace of Paris ends the Crimean War; Russia loses the Danube delta region; the Black Sea is declared neutral; Britain and France guarantee the Ottoman Empire against further disintegration.

1858 William I (1797–1888) becomes regent of Prussia.

1858 At a secret meeting at Plombiers, Napoleon III (1808–73) and Camillo di Cavour (1810–61) plan the unification of Italy.

1859 During the Italian war of unification, Piedmontese armies defeat the Austrians at the battles of Magenta and Solferino; France captures Lombardy from Austria and cedes it to Piedmont in return for Savoy and Nice.

1860 France and Britain sign a free trade treaty.

1860 Giuseppe Garibaldi (1807–82) and his red shirts liberate Naples.

1861 Victor Emmanuel II (1820–78) of Piedmont becomes king of a united Italy, with its capital at Turin.

1861 William I becomes king of Prussia.

1861 Serfdom is abolished in Russia.

1862 Otto von Bismarck (1815–98) becomes prime minister of Prussia.

1862 Garibaldi marches on Rome but is defeated by Italian troops.

1863 Polish uprising torn by internal disputes is savagely repressed by Russian and Prussian troops.

1863 Christian IX (1818–1906) becomes king of Denmark.

1863 Prince William of Denmark becomes King George I (1845–1913) of Greece.

1864 Prussia makes war on Denmark and gains control of Schleswig-Holstein.

1864 Red Cross is established by the Geneva convention.

1864 Regional elected assemblies (*zemstvos*) are established in Russia.

1864 Britain cedes the Ionian Islands to Greece.

1864 Karl Marx (1818–83) organizes the First International Workingmen's Association in London.

1865 Otto von Bismarck and Napoleon III meet at Biarritz and agree mutual neutrality in the event of war with Austria.

1865 Leopold II (1835–1909) becomes king of Belgium.

1866 Prussia and Italy declare war on Austria; the Austrians defeat the Italians at the Battle of Custozza, but are defeated by the Prussians at the Battle of Sadowa near Königgratz.

1866 Venice joins the kingdom of Italy.

1866 Cretans rise in revolt against the Turks.

1867 North German Confederation is formed under Prussian control.

1867 The Netherlands agrees to sell Luxembourg to France; the treaty of London establishes the independence and neutrality of Luxembourg.

1867 Turkish troops withdraw from Serbia.

1867 Garibaldi again marches on Rome and is defeated by French troops at the Battle of Mentana.

1867 Austria and Hungary become a joint monarchy.

1867 Cretan revolt is crushed.

1868 William Gladstone (1809–98) becomes prime minister of Britain.

1868 Revolution deposes Queen Isabella II (1830–1904) in Spain.

THE AMERICAS

1852 Franklin Pierce (1804–69) is elected US president.

1852 Argentine dictator Juan de Rosas (1793–1877) is overthrown after his defeat at the Battle of Caseros.

1853 New York and Chicago are linked by rail.

1853 Buenos Aires breaks away from Argentina.

1854 US Kansas–Nebraska Act abolishes the Missouri compromise; the "War for Bleeding Kansas" starts between pro- and anti-slavery factions.

1855 Antonio de Santa Anna (1794–1876) is overthrown in Mexico.

1856 US abolitionist John Brown (1800–59) kills pro-slavers in Kansas at the Pottawatomie Creek massacre.

1856 US adventurer William Walker (1824–60) seizes power in Nicaragua.

1856 James Buchanan (1791–1868) is elected US president.

1857 Dredd-Scott decision reinforces the rights of US slave-owners.

1858 Minnesota becomes a state of the USA.

1858 Benito Juárez (1806–72) is elected president of Mexico.

1858 Civil war breaks out in Mexico.

1858 Irish Republican Brotherhood (Fenians) is founded in New York.

1859 John Brown leads a raid on Harper's Ferry; he is caught and executed.

1859 Oregon becomes a state of the USA.

1859 Buenos Aires is compelled to rejoin Argentina.

1860 Abraham Lincoln (1809–65) is elected US president; South Carolina secedes from the Union.

1861 Kansas becomes a state of the USA.

1861 French, British and Spanish troops land in Mexico in a dispute over loan repayments.

1861 Confederate States of America is formed, and Jefferson Davis (1808–89) is elected president; Confederate forces capture Fort Sumter and under Thomas "Stonewall" Jackson (1824–63) defeat a Federal army at the First Battle of Bull Run in Virginia.

1862 Nashville falls to Federal troops under Ulysses S. Grant (1822–85); the Confederates, under commander-in-chief Robert E. Lee (1807–70), invade Maryland, fight the inconclusive Battle of Antietam, and win the Battle of Fredericksburg; Federal troops win the Battle of Shiloh and take Memphis; Lincoln proclaims the emancipation of slaves.

1862 Slavery is abolished in Dutch West indies.

1863 West Virginia is created a state of the USA; the Confederates win the Battle of Chancellorsville in Virginia; Federal troops win the Battle of Gettysburg in Pennsylvania; Grant captures Vicksburg in Mississippi.

1863 French troops enter Mexico City; Maximilian (1832–67) is declared emperor.

1863 US government decides upon the forcible removal of Native North Americans from Kansas.

1864 Nevada is created a US state; Federal troops under William Sherman (1820–91) invade Georgia, destroy Atlanta, and capture Savannah; Lincoln is re-elected US president.

1864 Cheyenne Native North Americans are defeated by US troops in Colorado.

1865 Federal army destroys Richmond, Virginia; Robert E. Lee surrenders at Appomattox court house, ending the Civil War; the 13th amendment to the US constitution prohibits slavery.

1865 Lincoln is assassinated; Andrew Johnson (1808–75) becomes US president.

1865 Paraguay is invaded by the forces of Brazil, Argentina and Uruguay.

1865 Spain fights a naval war against Peru and other South American states.

1865 Klu Klux Klan is founded in Tennessee.

1866 Civil Rights Bill is adopted by the 14th amendment to the US constitution.

1866 France withdraws support for Maximilian in Mexico.

1866 Fenians from the USA attack a British fort on the Canadian border.

1867 Maximilian is overthrown and executed.

1867 Canada becomes an independent dominion of the British Empire.

SCIENCE AND TECHNOLOGY

1852 French physicist Jean Foucault (1819–68) invents the gyroscope.

1853 Swedish physicist Anders Ångström (1814–74) explains the formation of emission and absorption spectra.

1855 British chemist Alexander Parkes (1813–90) discovers celluloid.

1856 German engineer Werner von Siemens (1816–92) designs an improved armature for electrical generators.

1856 Fossil human bones are found in the Neanderthal valley, Germany.

1856 British engineer Henry Bessemer (1813–98) perfects his air-blast method of converting iron to steel.

1856 German anatomist Hermann Helmholtz (1821–94) publishes *Handbook of Physiological Optics.*

1856 Swiss food scientist Henri Nestlé (1814–90) invents condensed milk.

1856 US inventor Elisha Otis (1811–61) installs the first passenger safety elevator.

1856 British chemist William Perkins (1838–1907) produces aniline mauve, the first synthetic dye.

1857 German physicist Gustav Kirchhoff (1824–87) discovers emission spectroscopy.

1858 First transatlantic telegraph cable goes into service.

1858 German chemist Friedrich Kekulé (1829–96) discovers that carbon atoms form chain molecules.

1858 British engineer Isambard Kingdom Brunel (1806–59) builds the *Great Eastern* steamship.

1859 British naturalist Charles Darwin (1809–82) publishes *The Origin of Species by means of Natural Selection,* which proposes his theory of evolution.

1859 British naturalist Alfred Wallace (1823–1913) independently develops a theory of evolution.

1861 French anatomist Pierre Broca (1824–80) discovers the speech-centre of the human brain.

1861 Belgian industrialist Ernest Solvay (1938–1922) invents a process for manufacturing soda ash.

1862 US engineer Richard Gatling (1818–1903) invents a rapid-fire, multi-barrelled, machine gun.

1862 US engineer Joseph Brown (1810–76) builds a universal milling machine.

1862 First engagement between iron-clad ships takes place when the Confederate *Merrimac* and the Federal *Monitor* exchange shots in the US Civil War.

1862 US industrialist John Rockefeller (1839–1937) builds an oil refinery in Cleveland, Ohio.

1863 French engineer Pierre Martin (1824–1915) develops the open-hearth method of steel manufacture in France.

1863 London Underground Railway opens.

1864 Scottish mathematician James Maxwell (1831–79) announces his equations that link light and electricity.

1864 French chemist Louis Pasteur (1822–95) proves the existence of airborne micro-organisms.

1865 German botanist Julius von Sachs (1833–97) discovers chloroplasts in plant cells.

1865 Austrian monk Gregor Mendel (1822–84) describes his experiments cross-breeding plants; the results suggest rules of heredity.

1865 US inventor Thaddeus Lowe (1832–1913) builds a compression ice machine.

1866 French scientist Georges Leclanché (1839–82) invents a zinc-carbon dry cell.

1867 French engineer Pierre Michaux manufactures the velocipede pedalled bicycle.

1867 Swedish industrialist Alfred Nobel (1833–96) invents dynamite.

1867 British physician Joseph Lister (1827–1912) introduces antiseptic surgery when he sprays phenol in an operating theatre.

1867 US engineer Christopher Sholes (1819–90) invents a typewriter with a QWERTY keyboard.

1868 US engineer George Westinghouse (1846–1914) invents the air-brake.

1868 French palaeontologist Édouard Lartet (1801–71) discovers the fossil bones of Cro-Magnon man.

1868 British astronomer William Huggins (1824–1910) measures the radial velocity of a star.

ARTS AND HUMANITIES

1852 French philosopher Auguste Comte (1798–1857) publishes *System of Positive Polity.*

1852 US author Harriet Beecher Stowe (1811–96) publishes *Uncle Tom's Cabin.*

1853 Georges Haussmann (1809–91) begins the rebuilding of Paris.

1853 Heinrich Steinway (1797–1871) opens a piano factory in New York.

1854 British poet Alfred Tennyson (1809–92) publishes *The Charge of the Light Brigade.*

1854 French anthropologist Joseph de Gobineau (1816–82) publishes his racist *Essay on the Inequality of the Human Races.*

1855 British poet Robert Browning (1812–89) publishes *Men and Women.*

1855 US poet Walt Whitman 1819–92) publishes *Leaves of Grass.*

1856 French novelist Gustave Flaubert (1821–80) publishes *Madame Bovary.*

1857 French poet Charles Baudelaire (1821–67) publishes *Les fleurs du mal.*

1857 British novelist Anthony Trollope (1815–82) publishes *Barchester Towers.*

1857 British poet (1806–61) Elizabeth Barrett Browning publishes *Aurora Leigh.*

1859 French composer Jacques Offenbach (1819–80) writes his opera *Orpheus in the Underworld.*

1859 British philosopher John Stuart Mill (1806–73) publishes his essay *On Liberty.*

1859 French artist Édouard Manet (1832–83) paints *The Absinthe Drinker.*

1859 French artist Jean-Baptiste Corot (1796–1875) paints *Dante and Virgil.*

1860 British novelist George Eliot (1819–80) publishes *The Mill on* 1860
the Floss.

1861 French artist Gustave Doré (1832–83) publishes his illustrations for Dante's *Inferno.*

1862 Russian author and dramatist Ivan Turgenev (1818–83) publishes his novel *Fathers and Sons.*

1862 British artist Edward Burne-Jones (1833–98) paints *King Cophetua and the Beggar Maid.*

1862 French author and poet Victor Hugo (1802–85) publishes his novel *Les Miserables.*

1864 British theologian John Newman (1801–90) explains his conversion to catholicism in *Apologia pro vita sua.*

1864 Austrian composer Anton Bruckner (1824–96) writes his Mass No.1 in D minor.

1865 English mathematician Charles Dodgson (pen-name Lewis Carroll, 1832–98) publishes *Alice in Wonderland.*

1866 Russian novelist Fyodor Dostoevsky (1821–81) publishes *Crime and Punishment.*

1867 French artist Edgar Degas (1834–1917) paints *Mlle Fiocre in the Ballet "La Source".*

1867 Norwegian dramatist Henrik Ibsen (1828–1906) writes his play *Peer Gynt.*

1869 Russian novelist Leo Tolstoy (1828–1910) publishes *War and Peace.*

1867 Karl Marx (1818–83) publishes the first volume of *Das Kapital.*

1867 Austrian composer Johann Strauss (1825–99) writes *The Blue Danube* waltz.

1868 German composer Johannnes Brahms (1833–97) writes *German Requiem.*

1868 Norwegian composer Edward Grieg (1843–1907) writes his piano concerto in A minor.

1868 US writer Louisa May Alcott (1832–88) publishes *Little Women.*

1869 French poet Paul Verlaine (1844–96) publishes *Fêtes Galantes.*

1869 French author Jules Verne (1828–1905) publishes *20,000 Leagues under the Sea.*

1869 British poet and social commentator Matthew Arnold (1822–88) publishes *Culture and Anarchy.*

1869 Verdi's opera *Aïda* is premiered.

ASIA AND AUSTRALASIA

1870 **1870** Chinese mob massacres a French consul and missionaries in Tianjin.

1871 US military expedition tries to force Korea to accept foreign trade, but is defeated.

1873 French annex Hanoi and the Red River delta area of Vietnam.

1874 Turkish Ottoman Empire begins to disintegrate rapidly under economic pressure.

1873 Russia annexes Khiva in Uzbekistan.

1874 British annex Fiji in the S Pacific.

1874 Japanese expedition briefly captures Formosa (present-day Taiwan).

1874 Russia conquers Kashgaria in Turkistan.

1875 Infant Zai Tian (1871–1908) becomes Emperor Guangxu of China with the dowager empress Cixi (1835–1908) as regent.

1875 Russia cedes the Kuril Islands to Japan in return for part of Sakhalin Island.

1876 Japan occupies the Ryukyu Islands.

1876 Turkish chief minister Midhat Pasha (1822–84) replaces sultan Murad V (1840–1904) with Abdul Hamid II (1842–1918) and issues a constitution.

1877 Turkish constitution is set aside by Sultan Abdul Hamid II.

1877 Saigo Takamori (1828–77) leads a samurai uprising (the Satsuma rebellion) against modernization in Japan.

1878 During the second Afghan War, the British invade and overthrow Sher Ali (1825–79).

1878 Chinese reconquer part of Turkistan from Islamic rebels.

1879 Abd Al-Rahman (*c.*1830–1901) becomes ruler of Afghanistan; the British gain control of the Khyber pass.

1880 **1880** France annexes Tahiti.

1880 Outlaw Ned Kelly (b.1855) is executed in Australia.

1881 China regains territory in Turkistan from Russia by the treaty of St Petersburg.

1881 Russia annexes the entire Transcaucus region.

1882 Korean nationalists attack Japanese officials in Seoul.

1883 Treaty of Hué establishes a French protectorate over Annam (N Vietnam).

1883 Volcano on the island of Krakatoa erupts violently, causing great destruction.

1884 France and China go to war over control of the Gulf of Tonkin region.

1884 Russians conquer the city of Merv in central Asia.

1884 Chinese Turkistan becomes a province of China.

AFRICA

1870 Arab slave trader Tippu Tip (1837–1905) establishes himself as ruler in present-day Democratic Republic of Congo.

1871 Dutch cede their Gold Coast (present-day Ghana) forts and trading posts to Britain.

1871 US journalist Henry Stanley (1841–1904) finds British explorer David Livingstone (1813–73).

1871 British annex the diamond-producing area of the Orange Free State.

1872 John IV (1831–89) becomes emperor of Ethiopia.

1873 Second Ashanti War begins.

1873 Slave markets in Zanzibar are closed.

1874 British forces destroy the Ashanti capital of Kumasi.

1874 British West Africa is broken up into separate colonies.

1874 British officer Charles Gordon (1833–85) becomes governor of the Egyptian Sudan.

1875 Britain buys Egypt's shares in the Suez canal.

1875 Egypt invades Ethiopia and occupies the coastal region.

1876 Leopold II (1835–1909) of Belgium founds the International Association for the Exploration and Civilization of Africa.

1876 Ethiopian army defeats the Egyptians at the battles of Gura and forces them to withdraw.

1877 British annex the Afrikaner South African republic.

1877 British annex Walvis Bay on the SW coast of Africa.

1879 Ismail Pasha (1830–95) is deposed as Egyptian ruler by the Ottoman sultan and replaced by Tewfik (1852–92).

1879 Zulus under Cetewayo (1825–84) attack the British in South Africa; they win the Battle of Isandhlwana but are defeated at the Battle of Ulundi.

1879 Algeria comes under French civil government.

1880 French found Brazzaville in the Congo region of central Africa.

1880 Afrikaners in Transvaal, South Africa, revolt against British rule and declare a republic.

1881 French invade Tunisia and declare a protectorate.

1881 Nationalist army officers stage a rising in Egypt.

1881 British grant limited independence to the Afrikaner South African republic.

1882 British bombard Alexandria, defeat the Egyptian army at the Battle of Tel-el-Kebir, and occupy Cairo.

1882 Muhammad Ahmed (1840–85) declares himself Mahdi and starts an uprising in Sudan.

1882 Italy acquires the port of Assab in Eritrea.

1883 Britain declares a protectorate over Egypt.

1883 British are defeated by the Mahdists at the Battle of El Obeid.

EUROPE

1869 Spanish Parliament offers the throne to a German prince, provoking French hostility.

1870 An Italian duke becomes King Amadeo I (1845–90) of Spain.

1870 France declares war on Prussia and is disastrously defeated at the Battle of Sedan; Napoleon III (1808–73) is overthrown and the third republic is declared; the Prussians besiege Paris.

1870 International treaty establishes the neutrality of Belgium.

1870 Vatican Council proclaims papal infallibility.

1870 Italian troops occupy the papal states.

1871 Paris surrenders to Prussians; France cedes Alsace-Lorraine to Germany by the peace of Frankfurt; Paris Commune is declared and crushed; Louis Thiers (1797–1877) becomes president of France.

1871 Germany is united into an empire under William I (1797–1888) of Prussia.

1871 Rome becomes the capital of Italy; the Vatican state is established.

1871 Otto von Bismarck (1815–98) begins the *Kulturkamf* struggle with the Roman Catholic Church.

1872 Austria, Prussia and Russia form the league of three emperors against France.

1872 Civil war breaks out in Spain.

1873 Amadeo I abdicates; a Spanish republic is established.

1874 Benjamin Disraeli (1804–81) becomes prime minister of Britain.

1874 Group of Spanish generals declare Alfonso XII (1857–85) king.

1875 Socialist congress at Gotha in Germany founds the Socialist Workingmen's Party.

1875 French third Republic is officially proclaimed with Marshal Patrice McMahon (1808–93) as president.

1875 Kálmán Tisza (1830–92) becomes prime minister of Hungary and begins a programme of Magyarization.

1875 Anti-Turkish revolts break out in Bosnia and Herzegovina; Serbia and Russia support the rebels.

1876 Risings against the Turks in Bulgaria are brutally suppressed; Serbs declare war on Turkey and are defeated at the Battle of Alexinatz.

1876 Mikhail Bakunin (1814–76) organizes the Land and Liberty secret society in Russia.

1877 Russia declares war and invades Turkey; Russian troops reach the walls of Istanbul.

1877 Queen Victoria (1819–1901) of Britain formally becomes Empress of India.

1877 President MacMahon's monarchist policies create a political crisis in France.

1878 Umberto I (1844–1900) becomes king of Italy.

1878 Romania, Serbia and Montenegro become independent states by the treaty of San Stefano between Turkey and Russia.

1878 At the Congress of Berlin, Austria gains control of Bosnia and Herzegovina, Russia gains control of Bulgaria, and Britain gains control of Cyprus.

1878 Anti-socialist laws are passed in Germany.

1879 Germany and Austria sign an alliance against Russia.

1880 Bismarck ends his *Kulturkampf* policy in Germany.

1881 Tsar Alexander II (b.1818) is assassinated; Alexander III (1845–94) becomes ruler of Russia; the *Okhrana* political police are founded.

1881 Serbia places itself under Austrian protection by a secret treaty.

1881 Turks cede Thessaly to Greece but keep Macedonia.

1882 Irish nationalists murder senior British officials in Phoenix Park, Dublin.

1882 Milan Obrenović (1854–1901) declares himself king of Serbia.

1882 Italy, Germany and Austria sign the anti-French Triple Alliance.

1883 Romania signs a secret anti-Russian treaty with Austria.

1883 Georgy Plekhanov (1857–1918) introduces Marxism to Russia.

1884 Carl Peters (1856–1918) founds the society for German colonization.

THE AMERICAS

1867 Basic Reconstruction Act sets conditions for the readmission of Confederate states to the USA.

1867 USA purchases Alaska from Russia.

1867 Nebraska becomes a state of the USA.

1868 Ulysses S. Grant (1822–85) is elected US president.

1869 Red River rebellion in central Canada establishes a short-lived provisional government.

1870 Paraguay loses much territory after defeat by Brazil and Argentina.

1871 British Columbia becomes a part of Canada.

1871 Treaty of Washington settles outstanding differences with Britain over borders, fishing rights and war damage.

1871 US Indian Appropriations Bill abolishes the collective rights of Native American peoples.

1875 Fighting breaks out between Sioux Native North Americans and US prospectors in Dakota.

1876 Colorado becomes a state of the USA.

1876 US troops commanded by George Custer (1839–76) are massacred by Sioux and other Native American tribes led by chief Sitting Bull (1831–90) at the Battle of Little Big Horn in Dakota.

1876 US presidential election produces a disputed result.

1877 Sioux Native American chief Crazy Horse (1842–77) surrenders to US troops.

1877 Electoral commission decides that Rutherford Hayes (1822–93) becomes US president.

1877 Porfirio Díaz (1830–1915) becomes president of Mexico after leading a coup.

1878 Concession to construct a canal across Panama is granted to a French company.

1879 Chile wages war on Peru and Bolivia for control of the nitrate deposits in the Atacama region.

1880 After a brief civil war in Argentina, Buenos Aires becomes the federal capital.

1880 James Garfield (1831–81) is elected US president.

1881 US outlaw William Bonney "Billy the Kid" (b.1859) is shot dead in New Mexico.

1881 US marshal Wyatt Earp (1848–1929) wins a gunfight at the OK Corral in Tombstone, Arizona.

1881 Chester Arthur (1830–86) becomes US president.

1882 Chinese Exclusion Act prohibits Chinese immigration into the USA.

1882 US outlaw Jesse James (b.1847) is shot dead in Missouri.

1883 Northern Pacific Railroad is completed.

1883 Slavery is abolished in the remaining Spanish colonies.

1884 Peru and Bolivia cede nitrate-rich territory to Chile; Bolivia becomes landlocked.

SCIENCE AND TECHNOLOGY

1869 Russian scientist Dmitri Mendeleyev (1834–1907) publishes the periodic table of elements in *Principles of Chemistry*.

1869 French scientist Hippolyte Mege-Mouries invents a process for making margarine.

1869 Irish physicist John Tyndall (1820–93) discovers that the scattering of light by atmospheric particles makes the sky blue.

1870 US inventor Rufus Gilbert (1832–85) patents an elevated railway system.

1870 German mathematician Georg Cantor (1845–1918) founds set theory.

1871 British naturalist Charles Darwin (1809–82) publishes *The Descent of Man*.

1872 US inventor Thomas Edison (1847–1931) patents an electric typewriter.

1873 Dutch physicist Johannes van der Waals (1837–1923) calculates intermolecular forces.

1873 US engineer Joseph Glidden (1813–1906) invents a machine for making barbed wire.

1874 US librarian Melvil Dewey (1851–1931) invents a decimal system for cataloguing books.

1876 British research ship HMS *Challenger* completes a three-year voyage that lays the foundations of oceanography.

1876 German engineer Nikolaus Otto (1832–91) builds a practical internal combustion gas engine.

1876 Scottish engineer Alexander Graham Bell (1847–1922) invents the telephone in the USA.

1876 German engineer Carl von Linde (1842–1934) patents the ammonia compression refrigerator.

1877 First telephone exchanged is installed in New Haven, USA.

1877 Thomas Edison invents the phonograph.

1877 Austrian physicist Ludwig Boltzmann (1844–1906) formulates his equations linking kinetic energy and temperature.

1877 Italian astronomer Giovanni Schiaparelli (1835–1910) announces his observation of "canals" on the surface of Mars.

1878 British scientist Joseph Swan (1828–1914) makes a carbon filament electric light.

1878 German chemist Adolf von Bayer synthesizes indigo dye.

1879 Russian psychologist Ivan Pavlov (1849–1936) discovers how to produce a conditioned reflex in dogs.

1879 Thomas Edison patents an incandescent electric light bulb.

1880 French chemist Louis Pasteur (1822–95) discovers streptococcus bacteria.

1880 British engineer John Milne (1850–1913) invents an accurate seismograph.

1881 German scientist Karl Eberth (1835–1926) discovers the typhoid bacillus.

1881 First commercial electricity generating station is opened in New York, USA.

1882 German bacteriologist Robert Koch (1843–1910) discovers the tuberculosis bacillus.

1882 St Gotthard railway tunnel through the Alps is opened.

1882 German scientist Walther Flemming (1843–1905) observes and describes cell division.

1883 First steel-frame skyscraper is built in Chicago.

ARTS AND HUMANITIES

1871 US artist James Whistler (1834–1903) paints *Arrangement in* 1870
Gray and Black – the Artist's Mother.

1871 British artist John Millais (1829–96) paints *The Boyhood of Raleigh.*

1872 British author Samuel Butler (1835–1902) publishes his novel *Erewhon.*

1872 German philosopher Friedrich Nietzsche (1844–1900) publishes *The Death of Tragedy.*

1873 French poet Arthur Rimbaud (1854–91) publishes *A Season in Hell.*

1874 British novelist Thomas Hardy (1840–1928) publishes *Far from the Madding Crowd.*

1874 First exhibition of Impressionist paintings is held in Paris.

1874 Russian composer Modest Mussorgsky (1839–81) writes *Pictures at an Exhibition.*

1875 French composer Georges Bizet (1838–75) writes his opera *Carmen.*

1875 US founder of the Christian Science movement Mary Baker Eddy (1821–1910) publishes *Science and Health with Key to the Scriptures.*

1875 US author Mark Twain (1835–1910) publishes *The Adventures of Tom Sawyer.*

1876 *The Ring of the Nibelungen* by German composer Richard Wagner (1813–83) is given its first complete performance at the inaugural Bayreuth festival.

1876 French artist Auguste Renoir (1841–1919) paints *Le Moulin de la Galette.*

1876 French symbolist poet Stephane Mallarmé (1842–98) publishes *The Afternoon of a Faun.*

1877 Russian composer Alexander Borodin (1833–87) writes Symphony No.2 in B minor.

1878 British social reformer William Booth (1829–1912) founds the Salvation Army in London.

***c.*1878** French artist Paul Cezanne (1839–1906) paints *Still Life with a Fruit Dish.*

1878 British composers Arthur Sullivan (1842–1900) and William Gilbert (1836–1911) write their comic operetta *HMS Pinafore.*

1878 Russian composer Peter Tchaikovsky (1840–93) composes his ballet *Swan Lake.*

1879 German socialist Albert Bebel (1840–1913) publishes *Women and Socialism.*

1880 US artist John Singer Sargent (1856–1925) paints his portrait of 1880
Mrs Charles Gifford Dyer.

1880 French artist Auguste Rodin (1840–1917) sculpts his statue *The Thinker.*

1880 French novelist Emile Zola (1840–1902) publishes *Nana.*

1880 Swiss author Johanna Spyri (1827–1901) publishes her children's novel *Heidi.*

1881 French author known as Anatole France (1844–1924) publishes his novel *The Crime of Sylvester Bonnard.*

1881 US author Henry James (1843–1916) publishes his novel *The Portrait of a Lady.*

1882 Indian author Bankim Chandra Chatterji (1838–94) publishes his novel *Anandamath.*

1883 Scottish author Robert Stevenson (1850–94) publishes his children's adventure *Treasure Island.*

ASIA AND AUSTRALASIA

1884 Germany acquires Kaiser Wilhelmland in New Guinea; Britain annexes the SE part of island.

1884 Dowager empress Cixi (1835–1908) becomes the sole ruler of China.

1884 Chinese troops defeat a pro-Japanese coup in Korea.

1885 Dispute over the borders of Afghanistan takes Britain and Russia to the brink of war.

1885 Indian National congress is founded.

1885–86 Britain annexes the whole of Burma after the third Burmese War.

1887 French organize their colonies in Vietnam and Cambodia into the Union of Indo-China.

1887 Britain annexes Baluchistan in W Pakistan.

1887 USA gains the use of Pearl Harbor in Hawaii as a naval base.

1888 Britain establishes protectorates over Sarawak and N Borneo.

1888 First railway in China is opened.

1889 Constitution guaranteeing the rights of the emperor is issued in Japan.

1890 **1891** Work starts on the trans-Siberian railway; it is completed in 1903.

1893 Revolution overthrows Queen Lydia Liliuokalani (1838–1917) in Hawaii.

1893 King Chulalongkorn (1853–1910) of Thailand recognizes a French protectorate over Laos by the treaty of Bangkok.

1894 Republic of Hawaii is declared.

1894 Japan defeats China in a war for control of Korea.

1894 Turks massacre thousands of Armenians near the town of Sassun.

1894 Sun Yat-sen (1866–1925) organizes a secret revolutionary society in Guangzhou (Canton), China.

1895 China acknowledges Korean independence under Japanese influence by the treaty of Shimonseki; Japan also gains Formosa (present-day Taiwan) and other islands.

1896 Malay states form a federation under British control.

1896 Japan extends its control of Korea after the murder of Queen Min (b.1851).

1896 Turks again murder thousands of Armenians.

1897 Germans occupy Qingdao, N China.

1898 Russia obtains a lease on Port Arthur on the coast of N China.

1898 France obtains a lease on Leizhou Bandao in China; Britain gains Kowloon.

1898 USA captures Manila from the Spanish and gains the Philippines and Guam.

1898 USA formally annexes Hawaii.

1898 Influenced by reformer Kang Youwei (1858–1927), the Chinese emperor Guangxu (1871–1908) begins the "100-days" reforms; they are withdrawn by dowager empress Cixi and the emperor imprisoned.

1899 George Curzon (1859–1925) becomes British viceroy of India.

1899 Huk insurrection against the USA breaks out in the Philippines.

1899 British sign a treaty with the sheikh of Kuwait.

1899 Concession to build the Berlin to Baghdad railway is granted to a Germany company.

1899 Chinese court begins giving aid to the anti-foreigner society of Harmonious Fists.

1899 USA and Germany partition Samoa.

AFRICA

1883 Paul Kruger (1825–1904) becomes president of the South African republic.

1883 French expand inland from the coast of Dahomey, W Africa.

1883 French go to war with the Hovas of Madagascar.

1884 Germany establishes colonies in Cameroon and Togo in W Africa and in SW Africa.

1884 Britain withdraws from Sudan.

1884 Britain establishes a protectorate over part of the Somali coast; French expand inland from Obock and establish French Somaliland.

1885 Mahdists take Khartoum in Sudan and kill governor Charles Gordon (b.1833).

1885 British colonialist Cecil Rhodes (1853–1902) gains control of Bechuanaland, S Africa.

1885 Spanish establish a protectorate over part of Guinea, W Africa.

1885 Congo Free State is established under the personal control of Leopold II (1835–1909) of Belgium.

1885 French declare a protectorate over parts of the Congo region.

1885 Germans establish a colony in Tanganyika, E Africa.

1885 Italy occupies the port of Massawa and expands into Eritrea.

1886 Gold is discovered in the Transvaal; Johannesburg is established.

1886 Britain acquires Kenya, E Africa.

1887 Henry Stanley (1841–1904) leads an expedition to rescue Emin Pasha (1840–92), an Egyptian governor of Sudan, from the Mahdists.

1887 Ethiopians defeat the Italians at the Battle of Dogali.

1887 Britain establishes a protectorate over Nigeria.

1887 French expand into Djibouti.

1887 Britain annexes Zululand.

1889 With Italian support, Menelik II (1844–1913) overthrows John IV (1831–89) to become emperor of Ethiopia; Italy annexes part of Somalia.

1889 French declare a protectorate over the Ivory Coast.

1889 British grant Rhodes control of a large area of SE Africa.

1890 Britain establishes a protectorate over Zanzibar.

1891 Italians defeat the Mahdists in Ethiopia.

1891 Belgium conquers the Katanga region of Congo.

1892 French defeat the Fulani in W Africa.

1892 Belgium defeats Arab slave-owners in the Congo.

1893 France captures Timbuktu from the Tuaregs.

1893 French establish a colony in Guinea, W Africa.

1894 After victory in the third Ashanti War, Britain establishes a protectorate over Ghana.

1894 Britain establishes a protectorate over Uganda.

1894 British colonialist Leander Starr Jameson (1853–1917) occupies Matabeleland, S Africa.

1894 Italians invade Ethiopia.

1895 British organize and name Rhodesia in SE Africa.

1895 Jameson leads a British raid on the Afrikaner republic in South Africa.

1895 French conquer Madagascar.

1896 British general Horatio Kitchener (1850–1916) captures the Mahdist city of Dongola.

1896 Italians are routed at the Battle of Adowa; the treaty of Addis Ababa secures Ethiopian independence.

1896 British bombard Zanzibar.

1897 Slavery is abolished in Zanzibar.

1898 British defeat the Mahdists decisively at the Battle of Omdurman; British and French troops confront each other at Fashoda; the French are forced to withdraw from Sudan.

1898 Menelik II brings all upland Ethiopia under his control.

1898 British and French agree the division of Nigeria.

1899 British and French reach agreement over joint control of the Sudan.

1899 British lose the early battles of the South African War (Boer War); Afrikaner forces besiege Ladysmith and Mafeking.

1899 Germany takes control of Rwanda, E Africa.

EUROPE

1884 International conference in Berlin decides the future of Africa; Belgian king Leopold II's Congo state is recognized, and the principle of ownership through occupation of coastline is established; start of the "scramble for Africa".

1885 King Alfonso XII (b.1857) of Spain dies; his wife Maria Christina becomes regent for her unborn child, the future Alfonso XIII (1886–1941).

1885 Bulgaria annexes E Roumelia; Serbia declares war on Bulgaria; the Serbs are defeated at the Battle of Slivnitza; Austria intervenes to prevent the invasion of Serbia.

1886 King Ludwig II (1845–86) of Bavaria is declared insane and deposed.

1886 French minister of war General Georges Boulanger (1837–91) becomes a national hero for his anti-German views.

1886 Influenced by Irish politician Charles Parnell (1846–91), the British government attempts to introduce Home Rule in Ireland, but the bill is rejected by Parliament.

1887 Francesco Crispi (1819–1901) becomes Italian prime minister and pursues a policy of colonial expansion.

1888 William II (1859–1941) becomes German emperor.

1889 Having failed to seize power, General Boulanger flees France.

1889 French Panama canal company collapses causing a financial scandal.

1889 International convention declares the Suez canal to be neutral and open to all ships in both peace and war.

1889 Heir to the Austrian throne Archduke Rudolf (b.1858) commits suicide at Mayerling.

1890 Otto von Bismarck (1815–98) is dismissed by the German emperor.

1890 Britain cedes Heligoland to Germany in return for Zanzibar.

1890 Anti-socialist laws are repealed in Germany.

1890 Socialists in Europe initiate May Day celebrations.

1890 Luxembourg becomes independent of the Netherlands.

1890 Wilhelmina (1880–1962) becomes queen of the Netherlands, with her mother, Emma (1858–1934), as regent.

1890 International convention in Brussels agrees on the suppression of the African slave trade.

1891 France and Russia sign a defensive entente.

1891 German Social Democratic party adopts Marxist policies under Karl Kautsky (1854–1938).

1892 Ferdinand De Lesseps (1805–94) goes on trial for his part in the Panama canal company scandal.

1892 German general Alfred von Schlieffen (1833–1913) devises a plan for the eventuality of war on two fronts against France and Russia.

1893 Irish Home Rule bill is passed by the lower house of the British Parliament, but is rejected by the upper house.

1893 Corinth canal opens.

1894 French president Sadi Carnot (b.1837) is stabbed to death by an Italian anarchist.

1894 French army officer Alfred Dreyfus (1859–1935) is court-martialled for treason and sent to Devil's Island in French Guiana.

1894 Nicholas II (1868–1918) becomes tsar of Russia.

1895 Kiel canal opens linking the North and Baltic seas.

1895 French trades unionists form the *Confederation Generale du Travail.*

1896 Olympic Games are revived in Greece.

1896 Cretans revolt against Turkish rule.

1897 Greece declares war on Turkey and is heavily defeated.

1897 Rosa Luxemburg (1871–1919), leader of the Social Democratic Party of Congress in Poland, flees to Germany.

1898 Bread riots occur in Milan and other Italian cities.

1898 German naval law is passed authorizing a larger navy as envisaged by admiral Alfred von Tirpitz (1849–1930).

THE AMERICAS

1884 Grover Cleveland (1837–1908) is elected US president.

1885 Northwest rebellion is suppressed by Canadian troops; leader Louis Riel (b.1844) is executed.

1885 President Justo Barrios (b.1835) of Guatemala leads an invasion of El Salvador but is defeated and killed at the Battle of Chalchuapa.

1886 Colombia adopts a centralized constitution.

1886 American Federation of Labor is formed under the leadership of Samuel Gompers (1850–1924).

1886 Statue of Liberty is erected at the entrance to New York harbour.

1886 Apache Native American leader Geronimo (1829–1908) surrenders to US troops.

1887 Canadian Pacific Railroad is opened.

1888 Slavery is abolished in Brazil.

1888 US Allotment Act allows for the dividing up of Native American reservations.

1888 Benjamin Harrison (1833–1901) is elected US president.

1889 Revolution establishes a republic in Brazil.

1889 North Dakota, South Dakota, Washington and Montana become states of the USA.

1889 US Oklahoma territory is opened for settlement by a "land race".

1889 First Pan-American conference is held in Washington, D.C.

1890 Wyoming and Idaho becomes states of the USA.

1890 US troops massacre Native North Americans at the Battle of Wounded Knee.

1891 United States of Brazil is established.

1891 Civil war establishes parliamentary government in Chile.

1892 US reformer Susan Anthony (1820–1906) becomes president of the National American Women's Suffrage Association.

1892 Immigration facilities are opened at Ellis Island in New York harbour.

1892 Grover Cleveland is again elected US president.

1893 US anarchist Emma Goldman (1869–1940) is arrested in Philadelphia.

1893 Serious rebellions are suppressed in s Brazil.

1895 Nicaragua, El Salvador and Honduras form the Greater Republic of Central America.

1895 Anti-saloon League starts a nationwide anti-alcohol campaign in the USA.

1895 Britain clashes with Venezuela about the borders of British Guiana.

1895 Nationalist revolution occurs in Cuba.

1896 Gold is discovered in the Yukon region of Canada.

1896 Utah becomes a state of the USA.

1896 William McKinley (1843–1901) is elected US president.

1898 USS *Maine* is blown up in Havana harbour; USA declares war on Spain, wins the battles of San Juan Hill and Santiago, and invades Puerto Rico.

1898 Under the peace of Paris, Spain evacuates Cuba and the USA gains Puerto Rico.

1899 US secretary of state John Hay (1838–1905) proposes that the European powers adopt an "open door" policy allowing equal treatment of all foreign goods through treaty ports in China.

SCIENCE AND TECHNOLOGY

1883 US engineer Hiram Maxim (1840–1916) invents the recoil-operated machine gun.

1884 US industrialist George Eastman (1854–1932) invents a roll film for cameras.

1884 British engineer Charles Parsons (1854–1931) patents a steam turbine.

1885 German engineer Gottleib Daimler (1834–1900) patents the internal combustion petrol engine and builds the first motorcycle.

1885 German engineer Karl Benz (1844–1929) builds a prototype car with a four-stroke internal combustion engine.

1889 French engineer Gustave Eiffel (1832–1923) designs and builds a steel tower in Paris.

1886 US scientist Charles Hall (1863–1914) develops a process for obtaining aluminium from bauxite by electrolysis.

1886 Construction starts on a hydroelectric power station at Niagara Falls.

1887 German physicist Heinrich Hertz (1857–94) discovers the propagation of electromagnetic waves produced by electrical discharges.

1888 US engineer Nikola Tesla (1856–1943) invents an electric motor that runs on alternating current.

1888 US engineer William Burroughs (1857–98) patents a recording adding machine.

1888 Scottish inventor John Dunlop (1840–1921) develops the pneumatic tyre.

1888 US industrialist George Eastman (1854–1932) perfects a hand-held (Kodak) camera.

1890 US engineer Emile Berliner (1851–1929) introduces the use of discs for sound recording.

1890 German bacteriologist Emil von Behring (1854–1917) discovers the viruses that cause diphtheria and tetanus.

1890 British mathematician John Venn (1834–1923) devises an overlapping diagram for depicting the relationships between sets.

1892 German engineer Rudolf Diesel (1858–1913) patents his design for an engine that uses compression to ignite fuel oil.

1892 British scientist Charles Cross (1855–1935) invents the viscose method of making artificial fibres.

1892 Scottish chemist James Dewar (1842–1943) invents the silvered vacuum flask.

1892 German engineer Leon Arons (1860–1919) invents the mercury vapour lamp.

1892 French engineer François Hennebique (1842–1921) invents pre-stressed concrete.

1893 British biologist Thomas Huxley (1825–95) publishes *Evolution and Ethics.*

1893 US scientist Theobald Smith (1859–1934) shows that parasites such as ticks can spread disease.

1894 British scientists Lord Rayleigh (1842–1919) and William Ramsay (1852–1916) discover the inert gas argon.

1895 Wilhelm Röntgen (1845–1923) publishes *A New Kind of Radiation,* in which he announces the discovery of X rays.

1895 French inventors Louis (1864–1948) and Auguste (1862–1954) Lumière give the first public cinema presentation in Paris.

1895 French mathematician Henri Poincaré (1854–1912) founds algebraic topology.

1895 Italian physicist Guglielmo Marconi (1874–1937) invents the wireless telegraph.

1895 US industrialist King Gillette (1855–1932) invents the safety razor with disposable blades.

1896 Alfred Nobel (1833–96) endows prizes for achievements in science.

1896 German pioneer of non-powered flight Otto Lilienthal (b.1848) is killed in a glider crash.

1896 French physicist Henri Becquerel (1852–1908) discovers radioactivity in uranium compounds.

ARTS AND HUMANITIES

1883 German philosopher Friedrich Nietzsche (1844–1900) publishes *Thus Spake Zarathustra.*

1883 Spanish architect Antonio Gaudí (1852–1926) begins work on the church of the Holy Family in Barcelona.

1884 French artist Georges Seurat (1859–91) paints *Bathers at Asnières.*

1884 French composer Jules Massenet (1842–1912) writes his opera *Manon.*

1885 French author Guy de Maupassant (1850–93) publishes *Bel Ami.*

1885 British explorer and scholar Richard Burton (1821–90) publishes the first volume of his translation of *The Arabian Nights.*

1885 French composer César Franck (1822–1890) writes *Symphonic Variations.*

1885 US artist Winslow Homer (1836–1910) paints *The Herring Net.*

1886 French composer Camille Saint-Saëns (1835–1921) writes *Carnival of the Animals.*

1887 French poet Stephane Mallarmé (1842–98) publishes *Poésies.*

1888 Dutch artist Vincent Van Gogh (1853–90) paints *Sunflowers.*

1888 Russian composer Nikolai Rimsky-Korsakov (1844–1908) writes *Sheherazade.*

1888 Swedish dramatist August Strindberg (1849–1912) writes *Miss Julie.*

1889 Irish dramatist and critic George Bernard Shaw (1856–1950) edits a collection of *Fabian Essays.*

1889 French composer Gabriel Fauré (1845–1924) writes his song *Clair de lune.*

1889 French philosopher Henri Bergson (1859–1941) publishes *Time and Free Will: an Essay on the Immediate Data of Conscience.*

1889 Italian poet Gabriel D'Annunzio (1863–1938) publishes the first volume of *Romances of the Rose.*

1890 Verse of US poet Emily Dickinson (1830–86) is published 1890
posthumously.

1890 Italian composer Pietro Mascagni (1863–1945) writes his opera *Cavalleria Rusticana.*

1891 French artist Paul Gaugin (1848–1903) arrives in Tahiti.

1891 British writer Arthur Conan Doyle (1859–1930) publishes the first of his *Adventures of Sherlock Holmes.*

1891 Irish dramatist and poet Oscar Wilde (1854–1900) publishes his novel *The Picture of Dorian Gray.*

1891 French artist Henri Rousseau (1844–1910) paints *Surprised! (Tropical Storm with Tiger).*

1892 French artist Henri Toulouse-Lautrec (1864–1901) produces his poster advertising: *The Ambassadors: Aristide Bruant.*

1893 Antonín Dvořák (1841–1904) writes Symphony No.9 in E minor, known as "From the New World".

1893 Norwegian artist Edvard Munch (1863–1944) paints *The Scream.*

1894 French composer Claude Debussy (1862–1918) writes *Prelude to the Afternoon of a Faun.*

1894 British poet and author Rudyard Kipling (1865–1936) publishes his children's stories *The Jungle Book.*

1895 Austrian composer Gustav Mahler (1860–1911) writes Symphony No.2.

1895 US author Stephen Crane (1871–1900) publishes his novel *The Red Badge of Courage.*

1896 Italian composer Giacomo Puccini (1858–1924) writes his opera *La Bohème.*

1896 Hungarian Zionist Theodor Herzl (1860–1904) publishes *The Jewish State.*

1896 Nicaraguan poet Rubén Darío (1867–1916) publishes *Profane Hymns.*

1896 British poet A.E. Housman (1859–1936) publishes *A Shropshire Lad.*

1896 German composer Richard Strauss (1864–1949) writes *Thus Spake Zarathustra.*

1897 French poet Edmond Rostand (1868–1918) writes his verse play *Cyrano de Bergerac.*

1897 French sociologist Emile Durkheim (1858–1917) publishes *Suicide,* in which he outlines his theory of alienation.

ASIA AND AUSTRALASIA

1900 **1900** Foreign legations in Beijing are besieged by the society of Harmonious Fists in the Boxer Rebellion; the empress flees; Russia annexes Manchuria; an international military force restores order.

1900 Turks begin the construction of the Hejaz railway in Arabia.

1901 Boxer protocol imposes a huge fine on China.

1901 Britain grants the Commonwealth of Australia dominion status.

1902 Chinese court returns to Beijing and begins reforms to strengthen the armed forces.

1902 Japan signs an alliance with Britain.

1902 Japanese raid the Russian base at Port Arthur in protest over the continuing occupation of Manchuria.

1903 British declare the Arabian Gulf to be within their sphere of control.

1904 Japanese attack on Port Arthur starts the Russo-Japanese War; the Japanese win the battles of Yalu River and Liaoyang.

1904 British expedition occupies Lhasa, the capital of Tibet.

1905 Japanese capture Port Arthur, defeat the Russians at the Battle of Mukden and annihilate the Russian fleet at Tsushima Straits; the treaty of Portsmouth, New Hampshire, ends the Russo–Japanese War.

1905 Britain partitions the Indian state of Bengal.

1905 Papua New Guinea is joined to Australia.

1906 Revolution in Persia (present-day Iran) compels the shah to issue a constitution.

1906 All-India Muslim league is formed.

1906 China acknowledges British control of Tibet.

1907 Britain and Russia divide Persia into spheres of influence by the treaty of St Petersburg.

1907 Britain grants New Zealand dominion status.

1907 Dutch finally subdue the native revolt in Sumatra.

1907 Japan acquires a protectorate over Korea and disbands the Korean army, provoking rebellion.

1908 Dutch take control of Bali.

1908 Henry Pu Yi (1906–67) becomes child emperor of China, after the death of dowager empress Cixi (b.1835), and grants a draft constitution.

1908 Persian shah Muhammad Ali withdraws the constitution and closes the national assembly; popular opposition causes Russian troops to invade N Persia in support of the shah.

1908 Rising by the Young Turks restores the Turkish constitution.

1908 Oil is discovered in Persia.

1909 Muhammad V (1844–1918) becomes Turkish sultan; a new constitution removes almost all his powers.

1910 **1910** Chinese invade Tibet.

1910 Anti-Turkish revolt in Albania is suppressed.

1910 National assembly meets in China and abolishes slavery.

1910 Japan annexes Korea, which is renamed Chosen.

1911 Military revolution breaks out in S China; the national assembly signs a truce and forms a provisional government.

1911 Russians invade and occupy Persia (present-day Iran).

1911 British reverse the partition of Bengal in India.

1911 Outer Mongolia becomes a Russian protectorate.

1911 Tibet declares independence from China.

1912 Chinese emperor Pu Yi abdicates; end of the Qing dynasty.

1912 Albanian leader Essad Pasha (1864–1920) proclaims independence from Turkey.

1913 Yuan Shikai (1859–1916) is elected president of China and purges the Kuomintang party, led by Sun Yat-sen (1866–1925), from government.

1913 Young Turks, led by Enver Pasha (1881–1922), seize power in Turkey and suppress opposition.

AFRICA

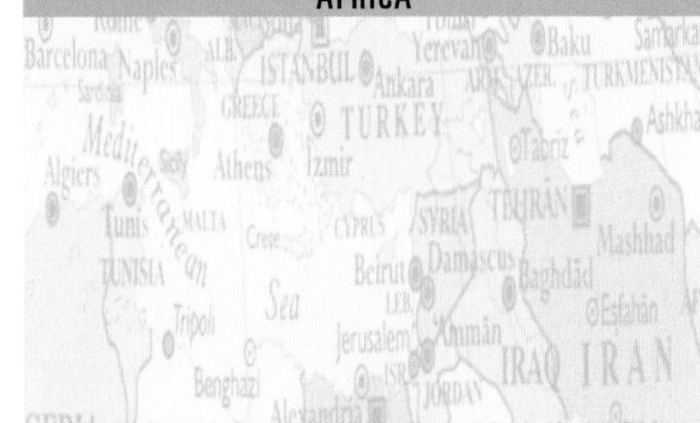

1900 British forces in South Africa under General Frederick Roberts (1832–1914) relieve Ladysmith and Mafeking, invade and annex the Orange Free State and Transvaal and capture Johannesburg and Pretoria; the Afrikaners adopt guerrilla warfare tactics.

1900 British suppress an Ashanti uprising.

1900 France and Italy make a secret agreement giving France control of Morocco and Italy control of Libya.

1900 French defeat the African leader Rabeh Zobeir in the Lake Chad region.

1900 French capture the main Saharan oases S of Morocco and Algeria.

1901 British introduce concentration camps in South Africa for captured Afrikaner civilians.

1901 Britain annexes the Ashanti kingdom.

1902 Portuguese suppress a native rising in Angola.

1902 Peace of Vereeniging ends the South African War (Boer War) and Afrikaner independence.

1902 Dam across the River Nile at Aswan is completed.

1903 Britain captures the cities of Kano and Sokoto, completing the conquest of N Nigeria.

1904 Spain and Morocco sign a treaty agreeing the division of Morocco.

1904 Herero people begin an insurrection in German Southwest Africa.

1905 German emperor visits Tangier and provokes a crisis about French interests in Morocco.

1906 Egypt gains the Sinai peninsula from Turkey.

1906 Conference at Algerciras confirms Moroccan independence with an open door policy.

1906 Lagos is joined to the British colony of S Nigeria.

1906 Britain, France and Italy agree to respect the independence of Ethiopia.

1907 Proclamation of Mulay Hafid as sultan of Morocco leads to unrest; French bombard casablanca and occupy the Atlantic coast region.

1907 Indian lawyer Mohandas Gandhi (1869–1948) leads a campaign of passive resistance against South African immigration policies.

1907 Nairobi becomes the capital of Kenya.

1908 Congo Free State is annexed by Belgium.

1908 Herero rebellion in German Southwest Africa is finally suppressed, with genocidal ferocity.

1909 French complete the conquest of Mauritania.

1909 Spanish enclave of Melilla is attacked by Moroccans from the Rif mountains.

1910 France takes control of the port of Agadir, Morocco.

1910 British grant the Union of South Africa dominion status; Louis Botha (1862–1919) is prime minister.

1910 French Congo is renamed French Equatorial Africa.

1911 French troops occupy Fez; the Germans send the gunboat *Panther* to Agadir; France cedes parts of Congo to Germany in return for freedom of action in Morocco.

1911 Italy invades and annexes Tripoli in Libya, despite fierce Turkish resistance; a naval war develops between Italy and Turkey.

1911 British colony of Northern Rhodesia is created.

1912 Sultan of Morocco is forced to accept a French protectorate.

1912 Italy bombards ports on the Dardanelles and conquers Rhodes and other Turkish islands; the treaty of Lausanne ends hostilities; Italy gains Libya.

1912 Spain and France sign a treaty dividing Morocco between them.

1913 Italians subdue the inland regions of Libya.

1914 British proclaim a protectorate over Egypt.

1914 Arab revolt against the Italians breaks out in Libya.

EUROPE

1898 French nationalists found the *Action Française* movement.

1898 Turks are forced to evacuate Crete, which is occupied by British, French, Italian and Russian troops.

1898 Empress Elizabeth of Austria (b.1837) is assassinated in Switzerland by an Italian anarchist.

1898 Social Democratic party is founded in Russia.

1899 First Hague peace conference outlaws the use of poison gas and dum-dum bullets in warfare.

1899 French president pardons Alfred Dreyfus (1859–1935).

1900 Bernhard von Bülow (1849–1929) becomes chancellor of Germany.

1900 Victor Emmanuel III (1869–1947) becomes king of Italy.

1900 Second German naval law proposes building a fleet to rival Britain's.

1901 Edward VII (1841–1910) becomes king of Britain.

1901 Violent street demostrations are suppressed in St Petersburg, Moscow and Kiev.

1902 Alfonso XIII (1886–1941) becomes king of Spain.

1903 Serbian army officers murder King Alexander Obrenović (b.1876) and set up King Peter I (1844–1921) as a puppet ruler.

1903 Russian Social Democratic party splits into minority Mensheviks and majority Bolsheviks under Vladimir Ilyich Lenin (1870–1924).

1903 Emmeline Pankhurst (1858–1928) founds the Women's Social and Political Union to campaign for female suffrage in Britain.

1905 Emile Combes (1835–1921) introduces a bill that separates church and state in France.

1904 Britain and France sign the Entente Cordiale.

1905 Norway under King Haakon VII (1872–1957) becomes independent of Denmark.

1905 Dissent turns to revolution in Russia; the crew of the battleship *Potemkin* mutiny; Tsar Nicholas II (1868–1918) issues his October manifesto granting a constitution; the suppression of the St Petersburg *soviet* leads to a workers' rising in Moscow.

1905 Popular risings occur in Poland and Finland.

1905 Serbia starts a tariff conflict (the "Pig War") with Austria.

1906 British Labour party is established under the leadership of Ramsay MacDonald (1866–1937).

1906 Georges Clemenceau (1841–1929) becomes prime minister of France.

1906 First Russian *duma* (parliament) meets.

1907 Severe famine devastates Russia.

1907 Sinn Féin league is formed in Ireland.

1908 Ferdinand I (1861–1948) declares himself tsar of an independent Bulgaria; Austria annexes Bosnia and Herzegovina; Serbia, backed by Russia, threatens war against Austria.

1908 Crete proclaims union with Greece.

1909 Serbia is persuaded to back down; Italy and Russia sign the secret treaty of Raconnigi to maintain the status quo in the Balkans.

1909 Spanish priests and monks are massacred during a socialist uprising in Catalonia; the anarchist Francisco Ferrer (b.1849) is executed during the suppression.

1910 George V (1865–1936) becomes king of Britain.

1910 Portuguese king Manuel II (1889–1932) flees after a revolution in Lisbon; a republic is proclaimed.

1911 Serbian army officers form the "Union or Death" (Black Hand) secret society to promote Serbian expansion.

1912 Balkan crisis is provoked by Albanian independence; Serbia and Bulgaria form the Balkan league, with Russian support, and are joined by Greece and Montenegro; the league declares war on Turkey and wins the battles of Kumanovo and Lule Burgas; Italy and Austria oppose Serbian expansion in Albania.

1913 Treaty of London ends the first Balkan War; Bulgaria attacks Serbia, which is supported by Greece, Romania and Turkey; Austria threatens to intervene to aid Bulgaria; the peace of Bucharest ends the war; Bulgaria loses most of Macedonia to Greece and Serbia.

1914 Heir to the Austrian throne, Franz Ferdinand (b.1863), is assassinated in Sarajevo by an agent of the Black Hand; Serbia rejects an Austrian ultimatum and gains Russian support; Austria declares war and Russia mobilizes; Germany declares war on Russia and France and invades Belgium; Britain issues Germany an ultimatum over Belgian neutrality and goes to war; Serbia declares war on Germany; Romania declares its neutrality.

THE AMERICAS

1901 Theodore Roosevelt (1858–1919) becomes US president, following the assassination of William McKinley (b.1843).

1901 New Cuban constitution makes the country virtually a US protectorate.

1902 Argentina obtains the greater part of Patagonia by agreement with Chile.

1902 European powers blockade Venezuela in a dispute over loan repayments.

1903 After a US-inspired coup Panama separates from Colombia.

1903 USA obtains perpetual rights to a canal zone across Panama.

1903 Alaska–Canada border is fixed.

1904 Roosevelt is elected president of the USA.

1904 Roosevelt warns European powers against further intervention in America.

1906 US troops occupy Cuba after political unrest; William Taft (1857–1930) declares himself governor.

1906 Massive earthquake and fire devastates San Francisco, USA.

1907 Nicaragua invades Honduras, installs a puppet ruler and prepares to invade El Salvador; it is forced to withdraw under US pressure.

1907 US army starts work on the construction of the Panama canal.

1907 Oklahoma becomes a state of the USA.

1908 William Taft is elected US president.

1909 Nationalist revolt in Honduras leads to civil war.

1909 US troops are withdrawn from Cuba; José Gómez (1858–1921) becomes president.

1911 National Association for the Advancement of Colored People is founded in the USA.

1911 President Porfirio Díaz (1830–1915) is overthrown by a revolution in Mexico.

1912 Woodrow Wilson (1856–1924) is elected US president.

1912 New Mexico and Arizona become states of the USA.

1912 *Titanic*, a liner, sinks off the coast of Newfoundland.

1913 Victoriano Huerta (1854–1916) seizes power in Mexico.

1914 Huerta is ousted by Venustiano Carranza (1859–1920); civil war breaks out in Mexico.

1914 British warships win the naval battle of the Falklands.

1914 Panama canal opens.

1914 US marines seize Vera Cruz, Mexico.

1915 Klu Klux Klan is revived in the USA.

1915 American nations recognize Venustiano Carranza as president of Mexico.

1915 US troops land in Haiti to restore order after political and financial instability.

SCIENCE AND TECHNOLOGY

1897 British bacteriologist Ronald Ross (1857–1932) discovers the malaria parasite in mosquitoes.

1897 British physicist J.J. Thomson (1856–1940) discovers the electron.

1897 German physicist Ferdinand Braun (1850–1918) invents the cathode-ray tube.

1898 Danish engineer Valdemar Poulsen (1869–1942) invents magnetic sound recording on steel wire.

1898 Scientists Marie (1867–1934) and Pierre (1859–1906) Curie discover the radioactive elements radium and polonium.

1900 German inventor Ferdinand von Zeppelin (1838–1917) builds a rigid airship.

1900 German physicist Max Planck (1858–1947) proposes that energy is radiated in discontinuous quanta and founds quantum theory.

1900 French physicist Paul Villard (1860–1934) discovers gamma rays.

1900 Austrian phsyician Karl Landsteiner (1868–1943) discovers the A, B and O blood groups.

1901 Italian physicist Guglielmo Marconi (1874–1937) transmits a Morse code message across the Atlantic.

1902 British scientist Oliver Heaviside (1850–1925) predicts the existence of an atmospheric layer that will reflect radio waves.

1903 US inventors Orville (1971–1948) and Wilbur (1867–1912) Wright make the first powered aircraft flight at Kitty Hawk in North Carolina, USA.

1903 Russian engineer Konstantin Tsiolkovsky (1857–1935) proposes multi-stage rockets for the exploration of space.

1904 British engineer John Fleming (1849–1945) invents the diode thermionic valve.

1905 French psychologist Alfred Binet (1857–1911) devises a practical intelligence test.

1905 German-born US physicist Albert Einstein (1879–1955) publishes his special theory of relativity and introduces the concept of photons to quantum theory.

1905 German chemist Hermann Nernst (1864–1941) formulates the third law of thermodynamics.

1906 US scientist Lee de Forest (1873–1961) invents the amplifying audion triode valve.

1906 British launch HMS *Dreadnought*, the first big-gun battleship.

1906 US engineer Richard Fessenden (1866–1932) introduces music and speech on AM radio.

1907 German chemist Emil Fischer (1852–1919) discovers that proteins are made up of amino acids.

1908 US industrialist Henry Ford (1863–1947) announces the production of the Model T.

1908 German chemist Fritz Haber (1868–1934) invents a process for synthesizing ammonia.

1909 French aviator Louis Blériot (1872–1936) flies a monoplane across the English Channel.

1909 Belgian-born US chemist Leo Baekeland (1863–1944) invents Bakelite, a thermosetting plastic polymer.

1910 French scientist Georges Claude (1870–1960) invents neon lighting.

1910 US astronomer George Hale (1877–1945) invents the spectroheliograph.

1911 Polish biochemist Casimir Funk (1884–1967) discovers vitamins.

1911 Scottish physicist Charles Wilson (1869–1959) invents the cloud chamber.

1912 German physicist Max von Laue (1879–1960) uses X-ray diffraction to study crystal structure.

1912 Austrian engineer Viktor Kaplan (1876–1934) invents a low-pressure water turbine.

1913 Danish physicist Niels Bohr (1885–1962) proposes a new model of atomic structure.

1913 British chemist Frederick Soddy (1877–1956) discovers isotopes.

1913 US astronomer Henry Russell (1877–1957) devises a diagram of the magnitude and temperature of stars; the diagram was independently conceived by Ejnar Hertzsprung (1873–1967).

1913 British mathematicians Bertrand Russell (1872–1970) and Alfred Whitehead (1861–1947) publish their *Principia Mathematica*.

ARTS AND HUMANITIES

1897 Russian dramatist Anton Chekov (1960–1904) writes *Uncle Vanya*.

1898 Spanish novelist Vicente Blasco Ibáñez (1867–1928) publishes *The Cabin*.

1898 French novelist Emile Zola (1840–1902) writes an open letter about the Dreyfus affair that begins "*J'accuse...*".

1898 British author H.G. Wells (1856–1946) publishes his novel *The War of the Worlds*.

1899 British composer Edward Elgar (1857–1934) writes *Enigma Variations*.

1900 Finnish composer Jean Sibelius (1865–1957) writes *Finlandia*. 1900

1900 Austrian phsyician Sigmund Freud (1856–1939) publishes *The Interpretation of Dreams* and founds psychoanalysis.

1900 British archaeologist Arthur Evans (1851–1941) discovers the ruins of Minoan civilization in Crete.

1900 British novelist Joseph Conrad (1857–1924) publishes *Lord Jim*.

1901 Russian composer Sergei Rachmaninov (1873–1943) writes Piano Concerto No.2.

1902 Russian anarchist Peter Kropotkin (1842–1921) publishes *Mutual Aid*.

1902 US psychologist William James (1842–1910) publishes *Varieties of Religious Experience*.

1902 Russian author Maxim Gorky (1868–1936) writes his play *The Lower Depths*.

1903 US author Jack London (1876–1916) publishes his novel *Call of the Wild*.

1904 German sociologist Max Weber (1864–1920) publishes *The Protestant Ethic and the Spirit of Capitalism*.

1904 Italian philosopher Benedetto Croce (1866–1952) founds the review *La Critica*.

1904 Scottish artist and architect Charles Rennie Mackintosh (1868–1928) designs the Willow Tea Rooms in Glasgow.

1905 German artist Ernst Kirchner (1880–1938) founds *Die Brücke* ("The Bridge") group of expressionist artists.

1905 Spanish artist Pablo Picasso (1881–1973) paints *Acrobat and Young Harlequin*.

1905 French composer Claude Debussy (1862–1918) writes *La Mer*.

1906 British novelist John Galsworthy (1867–1933) publishes *The Man of Property*, the first volume of *The Forsyte Saga*.

1907 Irish dramatist J.M. Synge writes *The Playboy of the Western World*.

1908 Russian artist Marc Chagall (1887–1985) paints *Nu Rouge*.

1908 US writer and educator Helen Keller (1880–1968) publishes *The World I Live In*.

1908 Hungarian composer Béla Bartók (1881–1945) writes String Quartet No.1.

1909 US architect Frank Lloyd Wright (1869–1959) designs the Robie house in Chicago.

1909 Indian poet Rabindranath Tagore (1861–1941) publishes *Gitanjali*.

1909 Italian poet Filippo Marinetti (1876–1944) publishes *First Futurist Manifesto*.

1910 British author Arnold Bennett (1867–1931) publishes his novel 1910
Clayhanger.

1910 French artist Henri Matisse (1869–1954) paints *Dance II*.

1910 British composer Ralph Vaughan Williams (1872–1958) writes *A Sea Symphony*.

1911 US composer Irving Berlin (1888–1989) writes his song "Alexander's Ragtime Band".

1911 Russian impresario Serge Diaghilev (1872–1929) forms the *Ballets Russes* in Paris.

1912 Swiss psychiatrist Carl Jung (1875–1964) publishes *The Psychology of the Unconscious*.

1912 US author Edgar Rice Burroughs (1875–1950) publishes his novel *Tarzan of the Apes*.

1912 British composer Frederick Delius (1862–1934) writes *On Hearing the First Cuckoo in Spring*.

1912 French artist Marcel Duchamp (1887–1968) paints *Nude Descending A Staircase, II*.

1912 Russian dancer Vaslav Nijinsky (1880–1950) creates his ballet *Afternoon of a Faun*.

ASIA AND AUSTRALASIA

1914 Japan declares war on Germany.

1914 Britain, France and Russia declare war on Turkey.

1914 British occupy Basra, present-day Iraq.

1914 New Zealand troops occupy German Samoa.

1914 Australian troops occupy German New Guinea.

1915 China accepts 21 demands made by Japan that undermine Chinese sovereignty.

1915 British and Australian troops land at Gallipoli, Turkey, in an attempt to seize control of the Dardanelles; further landings are made at Suvla.

1915 British capture Kut-el-Amra in Mesopotamia from the Turks; and occupy Bushehr in Persia (present-day Iran).

1916 British troops are evacuated from the Turkish coast.

1916 Indian Hindus and Muslims make the pact of Lucknow, calling for independence.

1916 Russian forces invade Armenia.

1916 Civil wars break out in N China as rival warlords, with foreign support, battle for control of Beijing.

1916 Hussein (1856–1931), the sharif of Mecca, is declared king of the Arabs; a general Arab revolt against the Turks begins.

1916 British troops surrender to the Turks at Kut el-Amra .

1916 British and French reach the Sykes-Picot Agreement over the future partition of the Ottoman Empire.

1917 Arab forces, led by T.E. Lawrence (1888–1935), capture Aqaba.

1917 British forces capture Baghdad and Jerusalem.

1917 Kuomintang forms a S Chinese government in Guangzhou (Canton) and appoints Sun Yat-sen (1866–1925) commander in chief.

1917 China declares war on Germany.

1917 British foreign minister Arthur Balfour (1848–1930) declares his support for the settlement of Jews in Palestine.

1918 British troops capture Damascus; French forces take Beirut.

1918 Britain occupies Persia after Russian troops are withdrawn.

1918 Armenia becomes an independent state.

1919 Britain recognizes the independence of Afghanistan.

1919 Japan acquires from Germany Qingdao in China and the Marshall, Mariana and Caroline islands in the Pacific.

1919 British troops kill hundreds of Indian protestors at Amritsar.

AFRICA

1914 Indian lawyer Mohandas Gandhi (1869–1948) leaves South Africa for India.

1914 British unite N and S Nigeria.

1914 British and French forces invade and occupy Cameroon and Togoland.

1914 British bombard Dar es Salaam, Tanganyika; a landing by British Indian troops is defeated by the Germans at the Battle of Tanga.

1915 South African forces under Louis Botha (1862–1919) defeat the Germans in Southwest Africa.

1916 Afrikaner forces under Jan Smutts (1870–1950) win control of Tanganyika (present-day Tanzania).

1915 Turks attempt to seize the Suez canal.

1916 Zauditu becomes empress of Ethiopia with Ras Tafari Makonnen (1892–1975) as regent.

1916 South African and Portuguese troops capture Dar-es-Salaam, Tanganyika.

1917 Germans invade Portuguese East Africa.

1918 Germans invade Rhodesia.

1919 Belgium acquires Rwanda and Burundi from Germany.

1919 Britain gains Tanganyika from Germany and also shares Cameroon and Togo with France.

1919 South Africa gains a mandate over German Southwest Africa.

1919 International agreement limits the sale of alcohol and arms in Africa.

1919 French create the colony of Upper Volta (present-day Burkina Faso).

EUROPE

1914 Germany signs an alliance with Turkey.

1914 Germany invades Luxembourg and Belgium; British troops first encounter the Germans at the Battle of Mons; British and French forces under General Joseph Joffre (1852–1931) halt the German advance on Paris at the Battle of the Marne; Germans capture Ostend, Belgium, but are prevented from capturing further ports by the first Battle of Ypres; the positions of the opposing armies become fixed, with Germans occupying *c.*10% of French territory; beginning of trench warfare.

1914 German aircraft attack Paris.

1914 St Petersburg is renamed Petrograd.

1914 Britain sinks German ships in a raid on Heligoland Bight; German submarines sink British warships in the North Sea.

1914 Russian armies invade Poland; in N Poland the Germans, under General Paul von Hindenburg (1847–1934), win the battles of Tannenberg and the Masurian Lakes but fail to take Warsaw; an Austrian advance into central Poland fails to dislodge the Russians; two Austrian invasions of Serbia are repulsed; the Germans capture Łódź.

1914 Britain annexes Cyprus.

1915 After signing the treaty of London, Italy quits the Triple Alliance, attacks Austria and fights a series of battles along the Isonzo front.

1915 Bulgaria allies with Germany; German and Austrian forces invade Serbia and Montenegro.

1915 French and British attacks at Champagne and Neuve Chapelle achieve little; the second Battle of Ypres results in slight German gains; French advance slightly at the second Battle of Artois but achieve little at the second Battle of Champagne; British successes at the third Battle of Artois and the Battle of Loos are not exploited; General Douglas Haig (1861–1928) becomes British commander in chief.

1915 Germany orders a submarine blockade of Britain; the liner *Lusitania* with US citizens aboard is sunk off the coast of Ireland.

1915 Russian advance into Hungary is defeated; Germans capture Memel and advance into Lithuania; Austro-German offensive drives the Russians from central Poland and captures Warsaw, Vilna and Brest-Litovsk; Tsar Nicholas II (1868–1918) takes control of the Russian army.

1916 Romania declares war on Austria; German and Austrian forces invade and occupy Bucharest.

1916 Germany and Austria proclaim an independent Poland.

1916 Russian mystic Rasputin (b.1872) is murdered.

1916 Easter Rising by Irish nationalists in Dublin is crushed by British troops.

1916 Austrian emperor dies and martial law is declared.

1916 David Lloyd George (1863–1945) become prime minister of Britain.

1916 Germans capture some of the French fortresses protecting Verdun; British offensive at the Battle of the Somme gains little ground at appalling cost; French recapture the Verdun forts; Hindenburg takes overall control of German forces.

1916 British and German fleets fight the inconclusive Battle of Jutland in the North Sea.

1917 Germans withdraw to the Hindenburg Line; Canadian troops take Vimy Ridge during the Battle of Arras; French capture the Chemin des Dames in the third Battle of Champagne; British take Messines Ridge but fail to make progress in the third Battle of Ypres (Passchendale); US troops under General John Pershing (1860–1948) arrive in France; Austrians and Germans defeat the Italians at the battles of Caporetto.

1917 Germans capture Riga, Lithuania.

1917 Italy declares a protectorate over Albania.

1917 Germans declare unlimited submarine warfare.

1917 February revolution forces Nicholas II to abdicate; a provisional government shares power with the Petrograd *Soviet*; Germans allow Lenin (1870–1924) to return; Alexander Kerensky (1881–1970) becomes prime minister and declares a republic; Bolsheviks establish a politburo which includes Lenin, Leon Trotsky (1879–1940) and Joseph Stalin (1879–1953); Bolsheviks overthrow Kerensky in the October revolution; Congress of Soviets establishes a ruling Council of People's Commissars, takes Russia out of World War 1 and confiscates the estates of landowners; a constituent assembly is elected.

1917 Ukraine, Estonia and Moldavia declare independence from Russia.

1917 Finns under General Carl von Mannerheim (1867–1951) begin a war of independence against Russia.

1918 Ukraine makes a separate peace with Austria and Germany.

1918 By the treaty of Brest-Litovsk, Russia recognizes Finland, Latvia, Lithuania, Estonia and Ukraine as independent states.

1918 "White" Russia declares independence and civil war breaks out; British, French and US troops land in Russia in support of the Whites.

THE AMERICAS

1916 Denmark sells the Virgin Islands to the USA.

1916 Mexican revolutionary Francisco ("Pancho") Villa (1877–1923) raids New Mexico; the USA sends a punitive expedition.

1916 US troops land in Cuba to suppress a liberal revolution.

1916 USA occupies the Dominican Republic and takes over the government.

1917 USA declares war on Germany and Austria.

1918 US president Woodrow Wilson (1856–1924) proposes 14 points for a peace agreement.

1919 Volstead Act is passed in the USA, prohibiting the sale and distribution of alcohol.

1919 Mexican revolutionary Emiliano Zapata (b.1880) is murdered.

SCIENCE AND TECHNOLOGY

1914 US industrialist Henry Ford (1863–1947) introduces conveyor-belt production lines in his car factory.

1915 German-born US physicist Albert Einstein (1879–1955) publishes his general theory of relativity.

1915 German Fokker aircraft revolutionize aerial warfare with a machine gun synchronized to fire through the propeller.

1915 Poison gas (chlorine) is first used in warfare by the Germans, during the first Battle of Ypres.

1915 German geologist Alfred Wegener (1880–1930) proposes his theory of continental drift.

1916 Newly invented tanks are used by the British at the Battle of the Somme.

1916 German scientists develop mustard gas as a weapon.

1917 French scientist Felix d'Herelle (1873–1949) discovers bacteriophages.

1918 US astronomer Harlow Shapley (1885–1972) estimates the size and shape of our Galaxy.

1919 British physicist Ernest Rutherford (1871–1937) transmutes one element into another.

1919 British physicist Arthur Eddington (1882–1944) observes the gravitational bending of light predicted by Einstein's theories.

1919 Austrian zoologist Karl von Frisch (1886–1982) discovers the communication dance of honeybees.

1919 British aviators John Alcock (1892–1919) and Arthur Brown (1886–1948) fly non-stop across the Atlantic Ocean from Newfoundland to Ireland.

ARTS AND HUMANITIES

1912 German author Thomas Mann (1875–1955) publishes his novella *Death in Venice.*

1913 Russian composer Igor Stravinsky (1882–1971) writes his ballet *The Rite of Spring.*

1913 French author Marcel Proust (1871–1922) publishes his novel *Swann's War*, the first volume of *Remembrance of Things Past.*

1913 French writer Henri Alain-Fournier (1886–1914) publishes his novel *Le Grand Meaulnes.*

1913 French artist Maurice Utrillo (1883–1955) paints *Rue Saint-Vincent.*

1913 British architect Edwin Lutyens (1869–1944) designs the Viceroy's House in New Delhi, India.

1913 French poet and dramatist Guillame Apollinaire (1880–1918) attempts to define Cubism in his essay *Cubist Painters.*

1913 Italian artist Umberto Boccioni (1882–1916) creates his sculpture *Unique Forms of Continuity in Space.*

1913 British author D.H. Lawrence (1885–1930) publishes his novel *Sons and Lovers.*

1914 British composer Gustav Holst (1872–1934) writes his orchestral suite *The Planets.*

1914 Scottish author Saki (Hector Munro, 1870–1916) publishes his collection of stories *Beasts and Superbeasts.*

1914 US poet Robert Frost (1874–1963) publishes *North of Boston.*

1914 Irish poet and dramatist William Butler Yeats (1865–1939) publishes his collection of poems *Responsibilities.*

1914 US musician W.C. Handy (1873–1958) writes his "St Louis Blues".

1915 British poet Rupert Brooke (1887–1915) publishes *1914 and Other Poems.*

1915 US poet Ezra Pound (1885–1968) publishes *Cathay.*

1915 British author John Buchan (1875–1940) publishes his novel *The Thirty-Nine Steps.*

1915 Romanian artist Tristan Tzara (1896–1963) and Alsatian sculptor Jean Arp (1887–1966) found the Dada movement in Zurich.

1915 British author W. Somerset Maugham (1874–1965) publishes his novel *Of Human Bondage.*

1916 British poet Edith Sitwell (1887–1964) publishes her experimental anthology *Wheels.*

1916 Mexican artist José Orozco (1883–1949) completes his wash drawings *Mexico in Revolution.*

1916 French artist Claude Monet (1840–1926) paints *Water Lilies* murals at the specially constructed musée d'orangerie in Paris.

1916 US artist Naum Gabo (1890–1977) creates his sculpture *Head No. 2.*

1916 Spanish dramatist Jacinto Benavente y Martínez (1866–1954) writes his play *La cuidad alegre y confiada.*

1917 French poet Paul Valéry (1871–1945) publishes *The Young Fate.*

1917 US novelist Upton Sinclair (1878–1968) publishes *King Coal.*

1917 British author P.G. Wodehouse (1881–1975) publishes the first of his stories about Jeeves and Wooster.

1918 British writer Lytton Strachey (1880–1932) publishes his biographies of *Eminent Victorians.*

1918 British artist Paul Nash (1889–1946) paints *We are Making a New World.*

1918 Swiss artist Paul Klee (1879–1940) paints his *Zoological Garden.*

1918 Italian dramatist Luigi Pirandello (1867–1936) writes his play *Six Characters in Search of an Author.*

1918 Russian composer Sergei Prokofiev (1891–1953) writes Symphony No.1 in D major, known as the "Classical".

1918 US poet Carl Sandberg (1878–1967) publishes *Cornhuskers.*

1918 German historian Oswald Spengler (1880–1936) publishes volume 1 of *The Decline of the West.*

1918 Collected works of British poet Gerard Manley Hopkins (1844–89) are published posthumously.

1919 Swiss theologian Karl Barth (1886–1968) publishes *The Epistle to the Romans.*

1919 German architect and designer Walter Gropius (1883–1969) founds the Bauhaus school of design, building and crafts in Weimar.

ASIA AND AUSTRALASIA

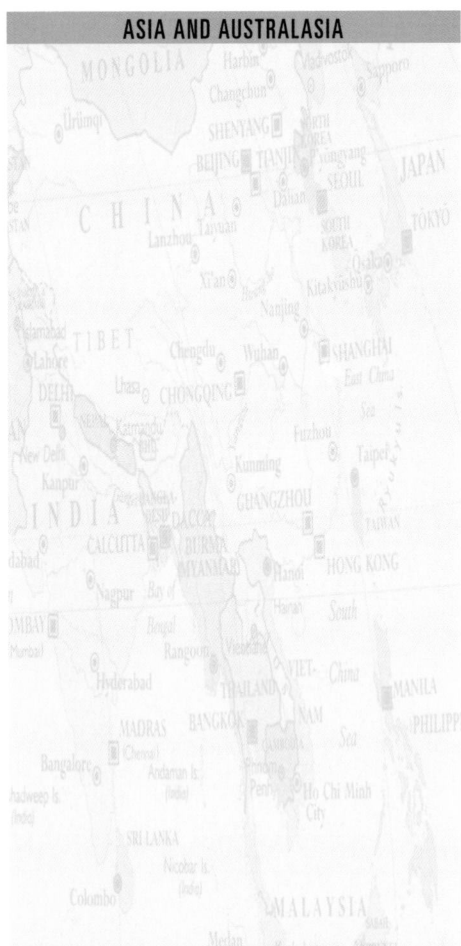

1920 **1920** France acquires a mandate over Syria and Lebanon.

1920 Britain acquires a mandate over Mesopotamia, renaming it Iraq, and Palestine.

1921 Faisal I (1885–1933) is proclaimed king of Iraq.

1921 Sun Yat-sen (1866–1925) is elected president of China.

1921 Cossack officer Reza Pahlavi (1878–1944) stages a coup in Persia (present-day Iran) and becomes minister of war.

1922 Sultanate is abolished in Turkey.

1922 Kurds in Iraq begin an armed campaign for independence.

1922 Mohandas Gandhi (1869–1948) is arrested in India for civil disobedience.

1923 Treaty of Lausanne confirms the dismemberment of the Ottoman Empire and provides for compulsory population exchanges between Greece and Turkey.

1923 Transjordan is separated from Palestine.

1923 Mustafa Kemal (1881–1938) is elected president of Turkey; Ankara becomes the capital.

1923 Earthquake devastates Yokohama and Tokyo.

1924 Chinese communists are admitted to the Kuomintang.

1924 Abdul Aziz Ibn Saud (1880–1953) captures Mecca and Medina from Hussein (1856–1931), sharif of Mecca.

1924 Mongol People's Republic is declared as a satellite of the Soviet Union.

1925 Chiang Kai-shek (1887–1975) becomes head of the Kuomintang nationalist government in China.

1925 Reza Pahlavi (1878–1944) becomes shah of Persia (present-day Iran).

1925–27 Druze rebel against French control in Lebanon and Syria.

1926 Nationalists begin military campaigns to regain control of central and N China.

1926 Abdul Aziz Ibn Saud is proclaimed king of Hejaz and Nejd in Arabia.

1926 Communist-inspired revolt breaks out in the Dutch East Indies.

1926 Lebanon is established as an independent republic.

AFRICA

1920 Britain annexes Kenya.

1921 Spanish are defeated by the peoples of the Rif at the Battle of Anual in Morocco.

1921 Mauritania and Niger are created as French colonies.

1922 Egypt becomes a self-governing monarchy, the sultan becomes King Fuad I (1868–1936).

1922 Italy starts the conquest of S Libya.

1923 Southern Rhodesia becomes a British colony.

1924 Slavery is abolished in Ethiopia.

1924 Rif uprising is revived against Spanish expansion in N Morocco.

1926 International convention gives the League of Nations responsibility for the suppression of slavery.

1926 French and Spanish troops defeat the rebels in N Morocco.

1928 Ethiopian regent Ras Tafari Makonnen (1892–1975) assumes the title Negus.

EUROPE

1918 Bolsheviks order the Red Army to dissolve the constituent assembly; communist Central Committee is given supreme power; Russian Socialist Federative Soviet Republic is established; Moscow becomes the capital; Tsar Nicholas II and his family are executed.

1918 Women get the vote in Britain.

1918 German offensive breaks through British and French lines at the second Battle of the Somme and advances on Paris; Ferdinand Foch (1851–1929) is made French commander; French and US troops halt the Germans at Chateau Thierry and the second Battle of the Marne; allied counter attacks force the Germans to retreat into Belgium; Italians rout the Austrians at the Battle of Vittorio Veneto.

1918 German fleet at Kiel mutinies; revolutions occur in Munich and Berlin; the emperor goes into exile; a German republic is proclaimed.

1918 Revolution in Vienna dissolves the Austrian monarchy and dismantles the empire.

1918 Czechoslovakia and Hungary are proclaimed independent states; independent kingdom of the Serbs, Croats and Slovenes (later named Yugoslavia) is established.

1918 Latvia and Lithuania declare their independence from Russia.

1918 Armistice stops the fighting on the Western Front.

1919 Allied troops withdraw from Russia; Red armies, under minister of war Leon Trotsky (1879–1940), defeat the Whites.

1919 Independent Polish republic is declared, linked to the free city of Danzig by a corridor of territory.

1919 Warfare erupts in Ireland between nationalists and British forces.

1919 Radical Spartacists revolt in Berlin and Rosa Luxemburg (1871–1919) is shot; republics are declared in Bavaria and Rhineland; Weimar constitution is adopted; German national assembly elects Friedrich Ebert (1871–1925) president.

1919 Peace conference in Paris limits the future size of European armies and establishes a league of nations.

1919 Under the treaty of Versailles, Germany has to cede territory overseas and in Europe, accept war guilt and pay financial reparations.

1919 Benito Mussolini (1883–1945) forms fascist gangs in Milan.

1919 Italian nationalist poet Gabriel D'Annunzio (1863–1938) seizes Fiume in Yugoslavia.

1920 Defeated White Russians withdraw from Crimea; end of the Russian civil war.

1920 League of Nations comes into existence.

1920 Poland in alliance with Ukraine invades S Russia and defeats a Russian counter-attack outside Warsaw.

1920 Greece declares war on Turkey.

1921 Lenin introduces the New Economic Policy in Russia.

1921 Peace of Riga fixes the Polish–Russian border.

1921 Adolf Hitler (1889–1945) becomes chairman of the National Socialist German Workers (Nazi) party.

1922 Ireland is partitioned; an independent Irish Free State is proclaimed; civil war breaks out.

1922 Italian fascists march on Rome; Benito Mussolini is asked to form a government.

1921 Hyperinflation begins in Germany.

1922 Union of Soviet Socialist Republics (USSR or Soviet Union) is formally established, joining Russia and Ukraine.

1923 French and Belgian troops occupy Germany's Ruhr region.

1923 Nationalist and socialist risings take place in Germany, including Hitler's attempted putsch in Munich; martial law is declared.

1923 General Primo de Rivera (1870–1930) becomes dictator in Spain.

1923 Alexander Zankoff seizes power in Bulgaria following a coup.

1924 Joseph Stalin (1879–1953) takes control of the Soviet Union on Lenin's death.

1924 Albania and Greece become republics.

1925 At a conference in Locarno, France, Belgium and Germany sign treaties guaranteeing their mutual borders; France also signs treaties with Poland and Czechoslovakia.

1925 Paul von Hindenburg (1847–1934) is elected president of Germany.

1925 President Ahmed Zogu (1895–1961) of Albania declares himself King Zog.

1925 Stalin removes Leon Trotsky from power in Russia.

1926 Josef Pilsudski (1867–1935) seizes power in Poland.

1926 Military coup overthrows the Portuguese government.

THE AMERICAS

1920 Transcontinental air-mail service begins in the USA.

1920 Women get the right to vote in the USA.

1920 US government refuses to join the League of Nations.

1920 Warren Harding (1865–1923) is elected US president.

1921 Washington conference limits the size of Pacific fleets and affirms the independence of China.

1921–22 Costa Rica, Guatemala, Honduras and El Salvador form the short-lived Federation of Central America.

1922 USA restores self-government to the Dominican Republic.

1923 Calvin Coolidge (1872–1933) becomes US president on the death of Warren Harding.

1924 US politician Charles Dawes (1865–1961) chairs a committee that devises a plan to collect German reparations.

1924 Coolidge is elected US president.

1925 US aviator Charles Lindbergh (1902–74) flies solo non-stop from New York to Paris.

1925 Scopes trial confirms the ban on the teaching of evolution in some US schools.

1928 US secretary of state Frank Kellogg (1856–1937) proposes the international renunciation of war.

1928 Herbert Hoover (1874–1964) is elected US president.

1929 New York Stock Exchange slumps in the Wall Street Crash and causes financial collapse and economic depression around the world.

1929 US troops occupy Haiti to restore order after political unrest.

SCIENCE AND TECHNOLOGY

1920 US astronomer Edwin Hubble (1889–1953) discovers that the universe is expanding.

1920 Radio broadcasting begins in Pittsburgh, USA.

1920 US engineer John Thompson (1860–1940) designs a sub-machine gun.

1921 US scientist Albert Hull (1880–1966) invents the magnetron microwave-generating valve.

1921 US engineer Thomas Midgley (1889–1944) discovers the anti-knock properties of tetraethyl lead.

1921 Canadian phsyician Frederick Banting (1891–1941) isolates the hormone insulin.

1922 German engineer Herbert Kalmus invents Technicolour movie film.

1923 Spanish engineer Juan de le Cierva (1896–1936) invents the autogyro.

1924 French physicist Louis Victor de Broglie (1892–1987) proposes that electrons should sometimes behave as waves.

1924 South African anthropologist Raymond Dart (1893–1988) discovers the fossil remains of *Australopithecus*.

1924 US industrialist Clarence Birdseye (1886–1956) puts quick-frozen fish on sale.

1925 US physicist Wolfgang Pauli (1900–1958) formulates his exclusion principle.

1925 Austrian physicist Edwin Schrödinger (1887–1961) establishes the study of quantum wave mechanics.

1925 British physicist Paul Dirac (1902–84) independently formulates wave mechanics.

1926 Scottish engineer John Logie Baird (1888–1946) demonstrates television in London.

1926 US engineer Robert Goddard (1882–1945) launches the first liquid-fuelled rocket.

1926 US aviator Richard Byrd (1888–1957) flies across the North Pole.

1927 French astrophysicist Georges Lemaître (1894–1966) formulates the Big Bang theory of the origin of the universe.

1927 German physicist Werner Heisenberg (1901–76) formulates his uncertainty principle.

ARTS AND HUMANITIES

1919 US poet Amy Lowell (1872–1925) publishes *Pictures of the Floating World.*

1919 US author Sherwood Anderson (1876–1941) publishes his collection of stories *Winesburg, Ohio.*

1921 French artist Georges Braque (1882–1963) paints *Still Life with Guitar.* 1920

1921 US novelist John Dos Passos (1896–1970) publishes *Three Soldiers.*

1922 German philosopher Ludwig Wittgenstein (1889–1951) publishes *Tractatus Logico-Philosophicus.*

1922 US photographer Man Ray (1890–1976) publishes *Delightful Fields.*

1922 British archaeologist Howard Carter (1874–1939) discovers the tomb of Tutankhamun.

1922 British poet T.S. Eliot (1888–1965) publishes *The Waste Land.*

1922 Irish author James Joyce (1882–1941) publishes his novel *Ulysses.*

1923 Spanish artist Jean Miró (1893–1983) paints *Catalan Landscape.*

1924 US composer George Gershwin (1898–1937) writes *Rhapsody in Blue.*

1924 French poet André Breton (1896–1966) writes the *Manifesto of Surrealism.*

1924 German artist Otto Dix (1891–1969) publishes his satirical etchings *The War.*

1924 Mexican artist Diego Rivera (1886–1957) paints murals for the ministry of education in Mexico City.

1925 Austrian composer Alban Berg (1885–1935) writes *Wozzeck.*

1925 Adolf Hitler (1889–1945) publishes the first volume of *Mein Kampf.*

1925 US author F. Scott Fitzgerald (1886–1940) publishes his novel *The Great Gatsby.*

1925 *Exposition des Arts Decoratifs* in Paris popularizes Art Deco style.

1925 US author Theodore Dreiser (1871–1945) publishes his novel *An American Tragedy.*

1925 *The Trial* by German novelist Franz Kafka (1883–1924) is published posthumously.

1925 Russian composer Dmitri Shostakovich (1906–75) writes Symphony No.1 in F minor.

1926 Irish dramatist Sean O'Casey (1880–1964) writes *The Plough and the Stars.*

1927 German philosopher Martin Heidegger (1889–1976) publishes *Being and Time.*

ASIA AND AUSTRALASIA

1927 Communists are liquidated from the Kuomintang, which establishes a new government in Nanjing.

1927 Britain recognizes the independence of Iraq.

1928 Transjordan becomes self-governing under Emir Abdullah ibn Hussein (1882–1951).

1928 Chiang Kai-shek captures Beijing and reunites China under nationalist rule.

1928 Chinese communist Red Army is created in Hunan province by Mao Zedong (1893–1976).

1928 Hirohito (1901–89) is crowned emperor of Japan.

1929 Fighting breaks out between the Chinese and the Russians along the Manchurian border.

1929 Arabs attack Jewish settlements near Jerusalem.

1930 **1930** Kurdish rising erupts on the Turkey–Iran border.

1930 Mohandas Gandhi (1869–1948) organizes and leads the salt march in India and is arrested and imprisoned.

1930 Three-way civil war breaks out in China.

1930 Vietnamese reformer Ho Chi Minh (1880–1969) founds the Indochinese communist party.

1931 Japanese invade Manchuria.

1932 Military coup introduces representative government in Thailand.

1932 Sydney harbour bridge is opened.

1932 Indian National Congress is banned by the British.

1932 Kingdom of Saudi Arabia is formally established.

1932 Japanese declare Manchuria the independent state of Manchukuo.

1934 Saudi capture of Hodeida ends a border war with Yemen.

1934 Turkish president Mustafa Kemal (1881–1938) introduces the use of surnames and himself adopts the surname Atatürk, meaning father of the Turks.

1934 Chinese communist Red Army begins the Long March to evade nationalist forces.

1934 Former emperor of China Henry Pu Yi (1906–67) becomes Japanese puppet emperor of Manchukuo.

1935 New constitution establishes the Philippine Commonwealth as a semi-independent state.

1935 Britain separates Burma and Aden from India and introduces a central legislature in Delhi.

1936 Jawaharlal Nehru (1889–1964) is elected leader of the Indian National Congress.

1936 Britain sends reinforcements to Palestine to impose order on warring Jews and Arabs.

1937 Japanese forces invade NE China and capture Beijing, Shanghai and Nanjing; nationalist and communist Chinese leaders agree on joint defence.

1939 Baron Hiranuma becomes Japanese prime minister.

1939 Faisal II (1935–58) becomes boy-king of Iraq.

1939 Soviet and Mongolian troops defeat the Japanese at the Battle of Nomonhan.

1939 Turkey allies with France and Britain.

AFRICA

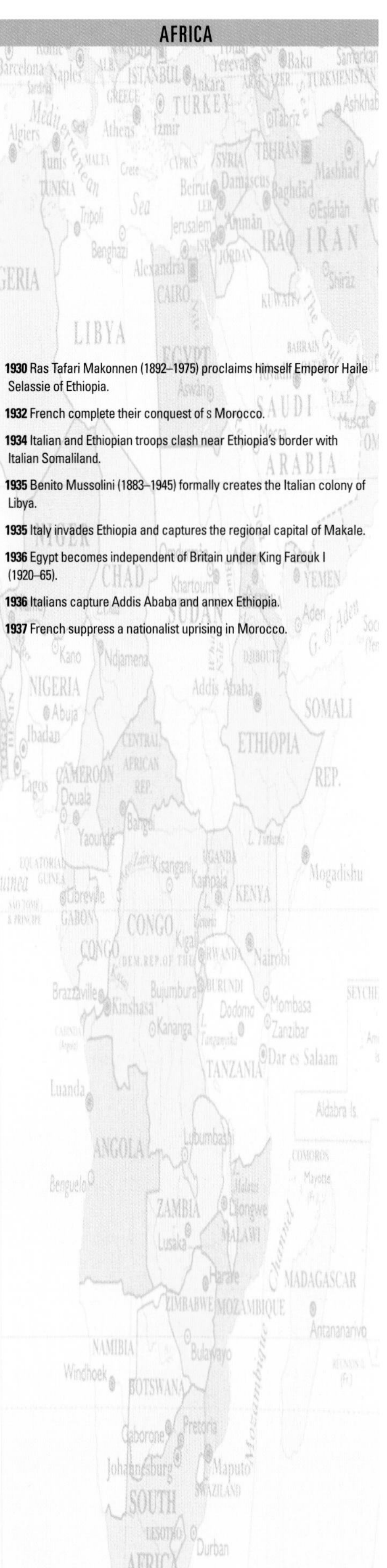

1930 Ras Tafari Makonnen (1892–1975) proclaims himself Emperor Haile Selassie of Ethiopia.

1932 French complete their conquest of S Morocco.

1934 Italian and Ethiopian troops clash near Ethiopia's border with Italian Somaliland.

1935 Benito Mussolini (1883–1945) formally creates the Italian colony of Libya.

1935 Italy invades Ethiopia and captures the regional capital of Makale.

1936 Egypt becomes independent of Britain under King Farouk I (1920–65).

1936 Italians capture Addis Ababa and annex Ethiopia.

1937 French suppress a nationalist uprising in Morocco.

EUROPE

1926 Antanas Smetona (1874–1944) seizes power and makes himself dictator in Lithuania.

1926 General strike afflicts British industry.

1926 Italy establishes a virtual protectorate over Albania.

1928 Kellogg-Briand pact outlaws war and proposes international arbitration in cases of dispute.

1928 Joseph Stalin (1879–1953) ends the New Economic Policy in Russia and introduces the first five-year plan.

1929 Lateran treaties between Italy and the papacy normalize relations and create Vatican City as an independent state.

1929 Alexander I (1888–1934) declares his royal dictatorship over the country he officially renames Yugoslavia.

1929 Trotsky is forced into exile from Russia.

1930 Carol II (1893–1953) returns to Romania and resumes the throne.

1930 Stalin introduces the forced collectivization of farms in Russia.

1931 British Commonwealth of Nations is established.

1931 King Alfonso XIII (1886–1941) flees Spain; a republic is declared.

1931 Bank failure in Austria starts a financial collapse in central Europe.

1932 Eamon De Valera (1882–1975) becomes prime minister of the Irish Free State.

1932 António Salazar (1889–1970) becomes prime minister of Portugal and introduces a new fascist-style constitution.

1932 Catalonia receives a degree of autonomy from Spain.

1933 Adolf Hitler is elected chancellor of Germany; after the Reichstag fire he assumes emergency powers and declares the Third Reich.

1933 Austrian chancellor Engelbert Dollfuss (1892–1934) makes himself dictator.

1933 Nazis establish a concentration camp at Dachau.

1934 Dictatorships are established in Estonia and Latvia.

1934 Hitler purges the Nazi party in the "Night of the Long Knives" and declares himself Führer of Germany.

1934 Dollfuss is murdered during an attempted Nazi coup.

1934 Fascist coup takes power in Bulgaria.

1935 Greek monarchy is restored under King George II (1890–1947).

1935 Saarland region is returned to Germany after a plebiscite.

1935 New constitution ends democratic government in Poland.

1935 Anti-Jewish Nuremberg laws are passed in Germany.

1935 Germany denounces disarmament clauses of the Versailles treaty.

1936 Popular Front under Leon Blum (1872–1950) forms a government in France.

1936 General Joannis Metaxas (1871–1941) becomes dictator in Greece.

1936 German troops occupy the demilitarized Rhineland.

1936 General Francisco Franco (1892–1975) leads a nationalist uprising in Spanish Morocco; he invades Spain and is proclaimed nationalist head of state; start of the Spanish Civil War.

1936 Edward VIII (1894–1972) becomes king of Britain and abdicates; George VI (1895–1952) becomes king.

1936 Germany and Italy form the Rome-Berlin axis alliance.

1937 Italian troops and German aircraft provide military aid to the nationalists in Spain.

1937 Stalin begins to purge the Soviet armed forces.

1937 Irish Free State formally becomes Eire.

1938 German troops occupy Austria; Hitler announces the Anschluss (union) of the two countries.

1938 British prime minister Neville Chamberlain (1869–1940) meets with Hitler to discuss German demands on Czechoslovakia.

1938 Conference of European leaders at Munich decides to appease Germany and to permit the annexation of the Sudetenland region of Czechoslovakia; Poland and Hungary also gain areas of Czech territory.

1938 Jewish shops and businesses are smashed during *Kristallnacht* in Germany.

1939 Nazi-Soviet pact agrees to partition Poland.

1939 Germany occupies the remainder of Czechoslovakia, annexes Memel in Lithuania and demands Danzig from Poland.

1939 Italy invades Albania.

1939 Nationalist forces capture Barcelona and Madrid; end of the Spanish Civil War.

THE AMERICAS

1930 Rafael Trujillo (1891–1961) makes himself president of the Dominican republic.

1930 Army coup makes Getulio Vargas (1883–1954) president of Brazil.

1931 US gangster Al Capone (1899–1947) is imprisoned.

1932 Bolivia and Paraguay go to war over control of the Chaco region.

1932 Franklin Roosevelt (1884–1945) is elected US president.

1933 US government introduces New Deal legislation to promote recovery from economic depression; Federal Emergency Relief Act establishes the Public Works Administration; National Industrial Recovery Act establishes the National Recovery Administration; Tennessee Valley Authority is formed.

1933 Fulgencio Batista (1901–73) leads a military coup in Cuba.

1934 Drought and bad farming techniques combine to form the "Dust Bowl" in the US Midwest.

1934 US troops withdraw from Haiti.

1935 Chaco War ends with Paraguay gaining most of the disputed territory; Bolivia gains access to the sea.

1936 Fascist coup seizes power in Paraguay.

1936 Anastasio Somoza (1896–1956) makes himself dictator in Nicaragua.

1938 Mexico nationalizes US and British oil companies.

1939 German warship *Graf Spee* is scuttled after the Battle of the River Plate.

SCIENCE AND TECHNOLOGY

1927 German geneticist Hermann Muller (1890–1967) induces mutations in fruit flies with X rays.

1927 First talking motion picture, *The Jazz Singer*, is released.

1928 US engineer Vladimir Zworykin (1889–1982) patents a colour television system.

1928 German physicist Hans Geiger (1882–1945) produces an improved version of his radiation counter.

1928 Scottish bacteriologist Alexander Fleming (1881–1955) discovers the antibiotic properties of the penicillin mould.

1930 US astronomer Clyde Tombaugh (1906–97) discovers the planet Pluto.

1930 Acrylic plastics Perspex and Lucite are invented.

1930 US engineer Eugene Houdry (1892–1962) invents the catalytic process of cracking crude oil.

1931 US physicist Ernest Lawrence (1901-58) invents the cyclotron particle accelerator.

1931 US physicist Robert Van de Graaff (1901–67) invents a high-voltage electrostatic generator.

1931 US mathematician Kurt Gödel (1906–78) publishes his proof that any system based on the laws of arithmetic must contain inaccuracies.

1931 Empire State Building is opened in New York.

1932 Swiss physicist Auguste Piccard (1884–1962) and an assistant ascend into the stratosphere in a balloon.

1932 US physicist Carl Anderson (1905–91) discovers positrons.

1932 US engineer Karl Jansky (1905–50) detects cosmic radio waves.

1932 US physicist Edwin Land (1909–91) invents polarized glass.

1932 German chemist Gerhard Domagk (1895–1964) discovers the first of the sulpha drugs.

1932 British physicist James Chadwick (1891–1974) discovers the neutron.

1932 Dutch complete the drainage of the Zuider Zee.

1933 US engineer Edwin Armstrong (1890–1954) invents FM radio transmission.

1935 British engineer Robert Watson-Watt (1892–1973) builds a radar system to detect aircraft.

1935 Fluorescent lighting and sodium vapour lamps are developed.

1935 US geologist Charles Richter (1900–85) devises a scale to measure the intensity of earthquakes.

1936 British mathematician Alan Turing (1912–54) develops the mathematical theory of computing.

1937 British engineer Frank Whittle (1907–96) builds a prototype jet engine.

1937 Nylon, invented by US chemist Wallace Carothers (1896–1937), is patented.

1938 Hungarian engineer Ladislao Biró (1899–1985) invents a ballpoint pen.

1938 US physicist Chester Carlson (1906–68) invents a process for photocopying documents.

1938 Coelacanth "living fossil" fish is caught in the Indian Ocean.

1939 German chemist Otto Hahn (1879–1968) discovers atomic fission.

1939 Helicopter designed by US engineer Igor Sikorsky (1889–1972) goes into production.

1939 Swiss scientist Paul Müller (1899–1965) synthesizes DDT as an insecticide.

1939 British engineers John Randall (1905–84) and Henry Boot (1917–83) invent the cavity magnetron.

ARTS AND HUMANITIES

1927 British author Virginia Woolf (1882–1841) publishes *To The Lighthouse.*

1928 British writer Siegfried Sassoon (1886–1967) publishes his novel *Memoirs of a Fox-hunting Man.*

1929 US author Ernest Hemingway (1898–1961) publishes *A Farewell to Arms.*

1929 Spanish philosopher José Ortega y Gasset (1883–1955) publishes *The Revolt of the Masses.*

1929 French writer Jean Cocteau (1889–1963) publishes his novel *Les Enfants terribles.*

1929 German novelist Erich Remarque (1898–11970) publishes *All Quiet on the Western Front.*

1930 Belgian artist René Magritte (1898–1967) paints *The Key of Dreams.* 1930

1930 British dramatist and composer Noel Coward (1899–1973) writes his play *Private Lives.*

1930 US poet Hart Crane (1899–1932) publishes *The Bridge.*

1931 French novelist Antoine de Saint-Exupéry (1900–44) publishes *Night Flight.*

1931 US dramatist Eugene O'Neill (1888–1953) writes *Mourning Becomes Electra.*

1931 British composer William Walton (1902–83) writes his oratorio *Belshazzar's Feast.*

1931 Spanish artist Salvador Dali (1904–89) paints *The Persistence of Memory.*

1931 French artist Raoul Dufy (1877–1953) paints *Riders in the Wood.*

1932 British novelist Aldous Huxley (1894–1963) publishes *Brave New World.*

1933 French novelist André Malraux (1901–76) writes *La condition humaine.*

1933 Spanish poet and dramatist Federico García Lorca (1898–1936) writes his play *Blood Wedding.*

1933 US author Gertrude Stein (1874–1946) publishes *The Autobiography of Alice B. Toklas.*

1934 US composer Cole Porter (1891–1964) writes his musical *Anything Goes.*

1934 British poet and author Robert Graves (1895–1985) publishes his novel *I, Claudius.*

1934 US author Henry Miller (1891–1980) publishes his novel *Tropic of Cancer.*

1934 Russian novelist Mikhail Sholokhov (1905–84) publishes *And Quiet Flows the Don.*

1935 T.S. Eliot writes his play *Murder in the Cathedral.*

1935 British artist Ben Nicholson (1894–1982) paints *White Relief.*

1936 British economist John Keynes (1883–1946) publishes *General Theory of Employment, Interest and Money.*

1936 Dutch artist Piet Mondrian (1872–1944) paints *Composition in Red and Blue.*

1936 US novelist William Faulkner (1897–1962) publishes *Absalom, Absalom!.*

1937 US sociologist Talcott Parsons (1902–79) publishes *The Structure of Social Action.*

1937 Spanish artist Pablo Picasso (1881–1973) paints *Guernica* in protest at the German air-raid on that Spanish town.

1938 British author Graham Greene (1904–91) publishes his novel *Brighton Rock.*

1938 US actor Orson Welles (1915–85) panics radio audiences with his performance of *War of the Worlds.*

1939 US author John Steinbeck (1902–68) publishes his novel *The Grapes of Wrath.*

1939 Irish author James Joyce (1882–1941) publishes his novel *Finnegan's Wake.*

1939 US novelist Raymond Chandler (1888–1959) writes *The Big Sleep.*

1939 British author Christopher Isherwood (1904–86) publishes his short story *Goodbye to Berlin.*

1939 French philosopher and author Jean-Paul Sartre (1905–80) publishes his novel *Nausea.*

1939 US dramatist and author Lillian Hellman (1907–84) writes her play *Little Foxes.*

ASIA AND AUSTRALASIA

1940 **1940** Japan invades French Indochina and captures Saigon.

1941 British troops capture Damascus from Vichy French forces.

1941 British and Soviet troops occupy Tehran; Muhammad Reza Pahlavi (1919–80) succeeds his father as shah of Iran.

1941 General Hideki Tojo (1885–1948) becomes Japanese prime minister.

1941 Japanese aircraft make a surprise attack on US ships in Pearl Harbor, Hawaii; Japanese troops capture Wake Island and Guam.

1941 Thailand allies with Japan and declares war on Britain and the USA.

1941 Japanese forces invade the Philippines.

1941 Hong kong surrenders to the Japanese.

1942 Japanese take Kuala Lumpar in Malaya and invade Burma and Java; Singapore surrenders; British force the Japanese back from NE India into Burma.

1942 US forces surrender at Bataan and Corregidor fort in the Philippines; the Japanese take Manila.

1942 Allied victory in the naval battle of the Coral Sea prevents the Japanese invasion of Australia.

1942 US fleet defeats the Japanese at the Battle of Midway Island.

1942 US aircraft make a bombing raid on Tokyo.

1942 US troops capture the Henderson Field airstrip on Guadalcanal Island.

1942 Japanese are defeated by the nationalist Chinese at the Battle of Changsha.

1943 At a conference in Tehran, Britain and the USA agree with Russia to open a second front against Germany by invading W Europe.

1943 Syria and Lebanon gain their independence from France.

1944 USA starts a large-scale bombing campaign against Japan.

1944 US forces take the Marshall Islands, Guam and Saipan in the Marianas; landings at Leyte begin the recapture of the Philippines under General Douglas MacArthur (1880–1964).

1944 General Tojo resigns as Japanese prime minister.

1945 Burma is liberated from the Japanese.

1945 US forces capture the islands of Iwo Jima and Okinawa.

1945 USA drops atomic bombs on Hiroshima and Nagasaki; Japan surrenders; US occupation forces land and establish a military government.

1945 Ho Chi Minh (1880–1969) declares the independent republic of Vietnam.

1945 Cambodia declares its independence.

1945 Truce between nationalists and communists in China breaks down with fighting for control of Manchuria.

1945 Independent republics of Syria and Lebanon are established.

1945 Arab league is founded.

1946 War crimes tribunal is set up in Tokyo.

1946 Jewish Irgun terrorists blow up the King David Hotel in Jerusalem.

1946 Jordan becomes an independent kingdom.

1946 French bombard the port of Haiphong while suppressing Vietnamese rebels.

1946 Republic of the Philippines becomes an independent state.

1946 USA tests atomic weapons at Bikini atoll.

1947 Britain grants the status of independent dominions to India and Pakistan (E and W); millions die in factional fighting and there are massive population exchanges.

1947 New constitution is proclaimed in Japan.

1948 Burma becomes independent of Britain.

1948 Ceylon (present-day Sri Lanka) becomes a self governing British dominion.

1948 State of Israel is established and is attacked by the Egyptians and the Jordanian Arab Legion.

1949 Chiang Kai-shek (1887–1975) resigns as Chinese president following communist victories .

AFRICA

1940 British troops repel an Italian invasion of Egypt and advance into Libya.

1940 Italians capture British Somaliland.

1940 British warships destroy part of the French fleet at the Algerian port of Oran.

1940 British and Free French forces attempt to capture Dakar in Senegal.

1941 British capture Torbruk and Benghazi, Libya, from the Italians; German general Erwin Rommel (1891–1944) takes command; German Afrika Korps besieges the British at Torbruk.

1941 Ethiopian troops capture the Italian stronghold of Burye.

1941 British forces capture Mogadishu, in Italian Somaliland, and occupy Addis Ababa, Ethiopia.

1942 German forces capture Torbruk; the British under General Bernard Montgomery (1887–1976) halt the German advance on Cairo at the Battle of El Alamein.

1942 US and British troops land in Morocco and Algeria.

1943 US troops retake the Kasserine Pass and join up with British troops in Tunisia; the German army in North Africa surrenders.

1944 France promises its African colonies independence after the war.

1947 Britain grants Nigeria limited self-government.

1947 All Algerians are granted French citizenship.

1949 South Africa passes legislation enforcing a policy of apartheid.

EUROPE

1939 Adolf Hitler (1889–1945) and Benito Mussolini (1883–1945) sign the "pact of steel".

1939 Germany invades Poland; Britain and France declare war; Russia invades Poland; the Poles surrender; Poland is partitioned; British troops are sent to France.

1939 Russian troops invade Finland and encounter strong resistance.

1940 Russians capture the Karelian isthmus; a treaty ends the Russo–Finnish War.

1940 German troops occupy Denmark and invade Norway; British and French troops are landed in Norway but then withdrawn.

1940 Winston Churchill (1874–1965) becomes British prime minister.

1940 Italy declares war on France and Britain.

1940 Germany conquers the Netherlands, Belgium and Luxembourg, and invades France; British troops are evacuated from Dunkirk; the Germans take Paris; Marshal Henri Pétain (1856–1951) surrenders; France is divided into occupied and unoccupied (Vichy) zones; Alsace and Lorraine become part of Germany; free Polish and French governments are formed in exile in London.

1940 Germany commences a massive bombing campaign that leads to the Battle of Britain; the "Blitz" against London begins.

1940 Ion Antonescu (1882–1946) becomes dictator in Romania.

1940 Estonia, Lithuania and Latvia become part of the Soviet Union.

1940 British occupy Iceland.

1940 German submarines attack neutral shipping in British waters.

1940 Italy invades Greece but is defeated at the Battle of Koritza.

1941 Germans invade Yugoslavia and Greece; German paratroops take Crete and British forces are evacuated.

1941 German troops invade the Soviet Union, capture Kiev, occupy Ukraine, besiege Leningrad, but fail to capture Moscow.

1941 German minister Rudolf Hess (1894–1987) lands in Scotland on a peace mission.

1941 Germany and Italy declare war on the USA.

1942 Nazi Wannassee conference decides upon the "final solution"; Polish, Russian and French Jews are sent to death camps.

1942 Vidkun Quisling (1887–1945) heads a collaborationist government in Norway.

1942 Nazi official Reinhard Heydrich (b.1904) is assassinated by the Czech resistance; the village of Lidice is destroyed in reprisal.

1942 Germans take Sebastopol and surround Stalingrad.

1942 British and Canadian troops raid the French port of Dieppe.

1942 Josip Tito (1892–1980) organizes the Yugoslavian resistance.

1942 Germans occupy Vichy France.

1943 Russian troops break the siege of Leningrad; German general Friedrich von Paulus (1890–1957) surrenders at Stalingrad; the Russians win a Battle at Kursk, retake Kiev, and occupy Romania and Bulgaria.

1943 Jews in the Warsaw ghetto attempt an uprising against the Germans.

1943 British bombers fly the "dambusters" mission.

1943 US and British troops land in Sicily and occupy Messina; Benito Mussolini is overthrown; Allied troops land at Salerno and take Naples; Italy surrenders; German troops occupy Rome; the Allied advance in Italy is halted by the German Gustav line.

1944 Allied troops land at Anzio, break through at Monte Cassino, and enter Rome.

1944 In operation Overlord, Allied forces under General Dwight Eisenhower (1890–1969) invade Normandy, capture Cherbourg and break through German lines near St Lo; Allied troops land in S France; Free French troops enter Paris; General Charles De Gaulle (1890–1970) heads a provisional government; British troops liberate Brussels.

1944 Germans launch V1 and V2 rockets against British and other European cities.

1944 British paratroop assault fails to capture a bridge at Arnhem; Allied troops invade Germany; a German counter attack is defeated in the Battle of the Bulge.

1944 Soviet troops capture Crimea, Minsk and Brest-Litovsk; Polish resistance attempts a rising in Warsaw; Soviet troops invade Czechoslovakia and Hungary.

1944 Attempt by German army officers to assassinate Hitler fails.

1944 Iceland becomes an independent republic.

1944 Greece is liberated from the Germans; civil war starts between monarchists and communists.

THE AMERICAS

1940 Leon Trotsky (b.1879) is assassinated in Mexico City.

1940 Pan-American conference adopts joint trusteeship of European colonies in the western hemisphere.

1941 US government passes the Lend-Lease Act enabling the supply of equipment to Britain.

1941 Franklin Roosevelt (1884–1945) and Winston Churchill (1874–1965) issue the Atlantic charter setting out joint war aims.

1941 USA declares war on Japan after the attack on Pearl harbor.

1941 Manhattan project to build an atomic weapon is started in the USA.

1942 Inter-American conference at Rio de Janeiro agrees a joint position against Germany and Japan.

1942 Japan captures several of the Aleutian Islands.

1942 Japanese-Americans are relocated away from the w coast of the USA.

1944 Conference at Bretton Woods in New Hampshire agrees the postwar establishment of a World Bank and an International Monetary Fund (IMF).

1944 Conference at Dumbarton Oaks agrees the postwar foundation of a United Nations Organization (UN) to replace the League of Nations.

1944 Roosevelt is elected for a fourth term as US president.

1945 Harry S. Truman (1884–1972) becomes US president on Roosevelt's death.

1945 Founding United Nations conference is held in San Francisco; Spain and Portugal are among the countries excluded from membership.

1946 Juan Perón (1895–1974) is elected president of Argentina.

1947 US president Truman pledges a doctrine of support for regimes threatened by communism.

1947 US secretary of state George Marshall (1880–1959) calls for a plan for European economic recovery.

1948 US government pledges massive financial aid to Europe for the implementation of the Marshall plan.

1948 Truman is elected US president.

1948 UN issues a declaration of human rights.

1948 Organization of American States (OAS) is established.

1949 North Atlantic Treaty Organization (NATO) is formed for mutual defence by the USA, Canada and w European states.

1949 Newfoundland becomes a part of Canada.

SCIENCE AND TECHNOLOGY

1940 British scientist Hans Krebs (1900–81) discovers the citric-acid cycle.

1940 Canadian scientist James Hillier (1915–) invents an electron microscope.

1942 French divers Emile Gagnan and Jacques Cousteau (1910–97) devise the scuba aqualung.

1942 German Me 262 flies in combat as the first jet fighter.

1942 US physicist Enrico Fermi (1901–54) builds a nuclear reactor, based on a controlled chain reaction, in Chicago.

1942 Team led by German engineer Werner von Braun (1912–77) designs the A4 (V2) rocket.

1943 German scientist Albert Hoffman discovers the hallucinogenic drug LSD.

1943 Codebreakers at Bletchley Park, England, construct a programmable electronic computer.

1944 US scientist Oswald Avery (1877–1955) discovers that DNA is the agent of inheritance.

1944 US astronomer Walter Baade (1893–1960) classifies stars into young Population I and old Population II.

1945 US scientists and engineers working at Los Alamos, New Mexico, under Robert Oppenheimer (1904–67) design and test an atomic bomb.

1945 US engineer Percy Spencer patents the microwave oven.

1946 US paediatrician Benjamin Spock (1903–98) writes *The Common Sense Book of Baby and Child Care.*

1946 US chemist Willard Libby (1908–80) devises a method of radiocarbon dating.

1946 British engineer Maurice Wilkes (1913–) devises assembler computer-programming language.

1947 Atomic power station opens at Harwell, England.

1947 US aviator Chuck Yeager (1923–) breaks the sound barrier in the Bell X1 rocket-powered aircraft.

1947 US engineers John Bardeen (1908–91), Walter Brattain (1902–87) and William Shockley (1910–89) invent the transistor.

1947 US engineer Buckminster Fuller (1895–1983) designs his geodesic dome.

1948 British physicist Dennis Gabor (1900–79) invents holography.

1948 US physicists Richard Feynman (1918–88) and Julian Schwinger (1918–94) formulate quantum electrodynamics.

ARTS AND HUMANITIES

1940 Russian artist Wassily Kandinsky (1866–1944) paints *Sky Blue.* 1940

1940 US author Ernest Hemingway (1898–1961) publishes his novel *For Whom the Bell Tolls.*

1940 Japanese artist Yasuo Kuniyoshi (1893–1953) paints *Upside Down Table and Mask.*

1940 British author Graham Greene (1904–91) publishes his novel *The Power and the Glory.*

1941 Illinois Institute of Technology, designed by German architect Ludwig Mies van der Rohe (1886–1969), is completed.

1941 German poet and dramatist Berthold Brecht (1898–1956) writes his play *Mother Courage and Her Children.*

1942 French writer Albert Camus (1913–60) publishes his novel *The Outsider.*

1942 French philosopher Maurice Merleau-Ponty (1908–61) publishes *The Structure of Behaviour.*

1942 US artist Edward Hopper (1882–1967) paints *Nighthawks.*

1942 French dramatist Jean Anouilh (1910–87) writes his play *Antigone.*

1943 British artist Barbara Hepworth (1903–75) creates her sculpture *Wave.*

1943 US composers Richard Rodgers (1902–79) and Oscar Hammerstein (1895–1963) write their musical *Oklahoma.*

1944 US dramatist Tennessee Williams (1911–83) writes his play *The Glass Menagerie.*

1944 US musician Glenn Miller (b.1904) is killed in an aircraft accident.

1945 British artist Francis Bacon (1909–92) paints *Three Studies for Figures at the Base of a Crucifixion.*

1945 British philosopher Karl Popper (1902–94) publishes *The Open Society and Its Enemies.*

1945 Italian author Carlo Levi (1902–75) publishes his novel *Christ Stopped at Eboli.*

1945 British novelist Evelyn Waugh (1903–66) publishes *Brideshead Revisited.*

1945 British author J.B. Priestley (1894–1984) writes his play *An Inspector Calls.*

1945 British writer George Orwell (1903–50) publishes his novel *Animal Farm.*

1946 French philosopher and author Jean-Paul Sartre (1905–80) publishes *Existentialism and Humanism.*

1947 Italian writer Primo Levi (1919–87) publishes *If This is a Man.*

1947 Italian artist Marino Marini (1901–80) creates his sculpture *Horseman.*

1947 British poet W.H. Auden (1907–73) publishes *The Age of Anxiety.*

1948 US novelist Norman Mailer (1923–) publishes *The Naked and the Dead.*

1948 US artist Jackson Pollock (1912–56) paints *Composition No.1.*

1949 US dramatist Arthur Miller (1915–) writes his play *Death of a Salesman.*

1949 French anthropologist Claude Lévi-Strauss (1908–90) publishes *The Elementary Structures of Kinship.*

1949 French feminist and novelist Simone de Beauvoir (1908–86) publishes *The Second Sex.*

1949 French author and dramatist Jean Genet (1910–86) publishes his novel *Diary of a Thief.*

ASIA AND AUSTRALASIA

1949 Chinese nationalists evacuate to Formosa (present-day Taiwan); Mao Zedong (1893–1976) declares the People's Republic of China.

1949 Independent republics of North Korea, under President Kim Il Sung (1912–94), and South Korea, under President Syngman Rhee (1875–1965), are established.

1949 Indonesia becomes independent under President Achmad Sukarno (1901–70).

1949 France grants independence to Vietnam but does not recognize the regime of Ho Chi Minh (1880–1969).

1949 Warfare between India and Pakistan over disputed territory in Kashmir is ended by a UN ceasefire.

1949 Israel and Egypt agree an armistice.

1949 Cambodia becomes independent under King Norodom Sihanouk (1922–).

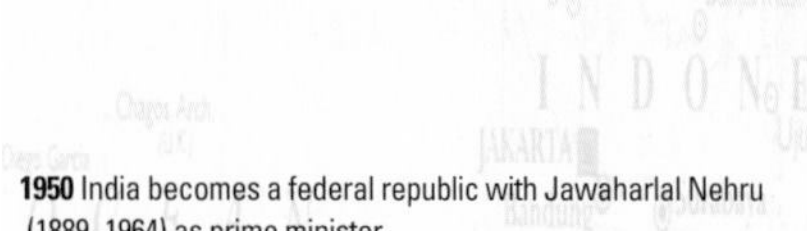

1950 **1950** India becomes a federal republic with Jawaharlal Nehru (1889–1964) as prime minister.

1950 Jordan annexes the West Bank and E Jerusalem.

1950 Soviet Union and China sign a treaty of alliance and co-operation.

1950 North Korean forces invade South Korea and start the Korean War; UN troops land at Ichon, liberate Seoul and invade North Korea; China sends troops to aid North Korea.

1950 Viet Minh forces under Ho Chi Minh defeat the French at the Battle of Cao Bang in Vietnam.

1950 Chinese invade Tibet.

1951 North Korean and Chinese forces take Seoul; UN forces recapture the city and halt a communist offensive at the Battle of Imjin River.

1951 Iran under Prime Minister Muhammad Mossadegh (1880–1967) nationalizes the oil industry and occupies the port of Abadan.

1953 Hussein I (1935–99) becomes king of Jordan.

1953 Laos gains full independence from France.

1953 Shah of Iran dismisses Mossadegh.

1953 Armistice signed at Panmunjom ends the Korean War.

1954 French forces in Vietnam surrender after defeat at the Battle of Dien Bien Phu; Geneva peace treaty splits Vietnam at the 17th parallel.

1954 Manila treaty establishes the South East Asian Treaty Organization.

1955 After a civil war South Vietnam becomes a republic under President Ngo Dinh Diem (1901–63).

1955 Turkey and Iraq sign the Baghdad Pact defence treaty.

1955 Portuguese police kill Indian demonstrators in Goa.

1955 Twenty-nine non-aligned nations meet at Bandung in Indonesia.

1956 Islamic republic of Pakistan is declared.

AFRICA

1951 Libya gains full independence under King Idris I (1890–1983).

1951 British troops occupy the Suez canal zone.

1952 Mau Mau secret society starts a campaign of terrorism against British settlers in Kenya.

1952 King Farouk (1920–65) is overthrown in Egypt; the infant King Fuad II (1952–) becomes a figurehead for Prime Minister Muhammad Naguib.

1952 Eritrea becomes a part of Ethiopia.

1953 Britain establishes the federation of Rhodesia (Northern and Southern) and Nyasaland.

1953 Berber rising overthrows the pro-French sultan.

1953 Kenyan politician Jomo Kenyatta (1893–1978) is jailed by the British for involvement with the Mau Mau.

1954 Nigeria becomes a self-governing federation.

1954 Gamal Nasser (1918–70) becomes prime minister of Egypt.

1954 National Liberation Front (FLN) organizes an anti-French revolt in Algeria.

1956 Sudan and Morocco become independent.

1956 Nasser becomes president of Egypt and nationalizes the Suez canal; Israel invades Egypt; Britain and France send troops but withdraw under international pressure.

1957 British colonies of the Gold Coast and Togoland are joined to form the independent state of Ghana.

1957 Habib Bourguiba (1903–2000) becomes president of the republic of Tunisia.

1957 Morocco becomes a kingdom under Muhammad V (1909–61).

1958 Niger, Upper Volta, Ivory Coast, Dahomey, Senegal, Mauritania, Congo and Gabon gain limited independence from France.

EUROPE

1944 Yugoslav resistance and Russian troops jointly capture Belgrade.

1945 Warsaw and Kraków are liberated by Polish and Soviet troops.

1945 At a conference at Yalta in the Crimea, the USA and Britain tacitly agree to Soviet occupation of postwar Europe.

1945 Benito Mussolini (b.1883) is shot dead by Italian resistance fighters; the German army in Italy surrenders.

1945 Soviet armies take Vienna; US and Soviet forces meet at the River Elbe; Russians under General Georgi Zhukov (1896–1974) take Berlin; Adolf Hitler (b.1889) commits suicide; Admiral Doenitz (1891–1980) surrenders; Germany and Austria are occupied in zones; the Potsdam conference agrees stringent controls on postwar Germany.

1945 Clement Attlee (1883–1967) is elected British prime minister.

1945 Republic of Austria is established under Karl Renner (1870–1950).

1945 Josip Tito (1892–1980) declares the People's Republic of Yugoslavia.

1945 War crimes tribunal is set up at Nuremberg.

1946 Charles De Gaulle (1890–1970) resigns as French president.

1946 Albania becomes an independent republic under Prime Minister Enver Hoxha (1908–85).

1946 Italy becomes a republic.

1946 British government nationalizes coal mines and lays the foundations of a welfare state.

1947 Belgium, the Netherlands and Luxembourg form a customs union.

1947 Italy, Romania and Hungary lose small areas of territory under the Paris peace treaties.

1947 Communist coups seize power in Czechoslovakia, Hungary and Romania.

1948 Brussels treaty agreeing military and economic co-operation is signed by Britain, France, Belgium, the Netherlands and Luxembourg.

1948 Juliana (1909–) becomes queen of the Netherlands.

1948 Russians blockade Berlin; an airlift keeps the city supplied.

1949 Republic of Ireland is declared.

1949 Soviet Union breaks off close relations with Yugoslavia.

1949 Council of Europe and the European Court of Human Rights are established.

1949 Federal Republic of (West) Germany, with its capital in Bonn, and the (East) German Democratic Republic are established.

1949 Greek civil war ends with a monarchist victory.

1949 Soviet Union tests an atomic bomb.

1949 Soviet Union and the communist-controlled countries of E Europe form the Comecon organization for economic co-operation.

1950 French foreign minister Robert Schuman (1886–1963) proposes a plan for the integration of the French and German coal and steel industries.

1950 Gustav VI (1882–1973) becomes king of Sweden.

1951 West Germany is admitted to the Council of Europe.

1951 Leopold III (1901–83) of Belgium abdicates in favour of his son Baudouin (1930–93).

1951 Marshall Plan economic aid to Europe ends.

1951 Winston Churchill (1874–1965) is elected British prime minister.

1952 Swedish diplomat Dag Hammarskjöld (1905–61) is elected secretary general of the United Nations (UN).

1952 European Coal and Steel community is formed.

1952 Elizabeth II (1926–) becomes queen of Britain.

1952 Greece and Turkey join NATO.

1953 Tito is formally appointed president of the Federal People's republic of Yugoslavia.

1953 Konrad Adenauer (1876–1967) is re-elected chancellor of West Germany.

1953 Nikita Khrushchev (1894–1971) becomes first secretary of the Communist Party in the Soviet Union after the death of Stalin (b.1879).

1954 Greek nationalist EOKA movement carries out attacks on British troops in Cyprus.

1954 Italy and Yugoslavia reach agreement over the ownership of Trieste.

1955 Allied occupation troops withdraw from West Germany, which joins Nato.

1955 Communist countries of E Europe form the Warsaw Pact with the Soviet Union.

THE AMERICAS

1951 Twenty-second amendment to the US constitution limits presidents to two terms of office.

1952 Dwight Eisenhower (1890–1969) is elected US president.

1952 Fulgencio Batista (1901–73) makes himself president of Cuba.

1952 "Evita" Perón (b.1919), the wife of the Argentine president, dies.

1954 Anti-communist crusade of Senator Joseph McCarthy (1908–57) reaches a climax with televised hearings of his investigation committee.

1955 US supreme court rules that racial segregation in public schools must soon end.

1955 Juan Perón (1895–1974) is forced into exile from Argentina.

1955 General Alfredo Stroessner (1912–) becomes president of Paraguay after a coup.

1955 US civil rights activist Rosa Parks (1913–) sits in a whites-only seat on a bus in Montgomery, Alabama.

1956 Revolutionary Fidel Castro (1926–) lands in Cuba.

1957 Jamaica becomes self-governing.

1957 François "Papa Doc" Duvalier (1907–71) becomes president of Haiti.

1957 President Eisenhower states his doctrine to oppose communism in the Middle East.

1957 US Civil Rights Act appoints a commission to examine African-American voting rights.

1958 British form the Federation of the West Indies.

1958 Military coup overthrows President Pérez Jiménez (1914–) in Venezuela.

1958 US National Aeronautics and Space Administration (NASA) is established.

SCIENCE AND TECHNOLOGY

1951 US engineers John Eckert (1919–) and John Mauchly (1907–80) build UNIVAC I, the first commercial computer.

1952 USA explodes a hydrogen bomb.

1952 British explode an atom bomb.

1952 US researcher Jonas Salk (1914–95) develops a vaccine against poliomyelitis.

1952 British Comet aircraft makes the first jet passenger flight.

1953 US physicist Charles Townes (1915–) invents the maser.

1953 German chemist Karl Ziegler (1898–1973) invents a process for making high-density polyethene.

1953 British biophysicist Francis Crick (1916–) and US bio physicist James Watson (1928–) discover the helical structure of DNA.

1953 US engineer An Wang (1920–90) invents magnetic core computer memory.

1954 Swiss psychologist Jean Piaget (1896–1980) publishes *The Origin of Intelligence in Children.*

1954 Chinese scientist Min-Chueh Chang (1909–91) and US biologists Gregory Pincus (1903–67) and Frank Colton (1923–) invent the contraceptive pill.

1955 British engineer Christopher Cockerell (1910–99) invents the hovercraft.

1955 US physicists Clyde Cowan (1919–) and Frederick Reines (1918–98) discover the neutrino.

1956 US engineer Alexander Poniatoff (1892–80) invents a video tape recorder.

1956 Implantable heart pacemaker is invented.

1956 US engineer Jack Backus leads a team that devises the FORTRAN computer programming language.

ARTS AND HUMANITIES

1950 Chilean poet Pablo Neruda (1904–73) publishes his epic 1950
General Song.

1950 British novelist Doris Lessing (1919–) publishes *The Grass is Singing.*

1951 US novelist J.D. Salinger (1919–) publishes *Catcher in the Rye.*

1951 British composer Benjamin Britten (1913–76) writes his opera *Billy Budd.*

1951 French artist Fernand Léger (1881–1955) designs stained glass windows for the church of Sacre Coeur at Audicourt in France.

1952 British sculptor Henry Moore (1898–1986) creates *King and Queen.*

1952 US composer John Cage (1912–92) conceives *4'33".*

1952 *Unité d'Habitation* designed by Swiss architect Le Corbusier (1887–1965) is opened in Marseilles, France.

1953 British scholar Michael Ventris (1922–56) deciphers Linear B as the Greek script of the Mycenaeans.

1953 US artist Willem de Kooning (1904–97) paints *Women.*

1954 British author and poet Dylan Thomas (1914–53) writes his verse play *Under Milk Wood.*

1954 British novelist William Golding (1911–93) publishes *Lord of the Flies.*

1954 British novelist J.R.R. Tolkien (1892–1973) publishes the first volume of *Lord of the Rings.*

1955 Irish dramatist and novelist Samuel Beckett (1906–89) writes his play *Waiting for Godot.*

1955 French novelist Alain Robbe-Grillet (1922–) publishes his *nouveau roman Le Voyeur.*

1955 US author James Baldwin (1924–87) publishes his essays *Notes of a Native Son.*

ASIA AND AUSTRALASIA

1956 Solomon Bandaranaike (1899–1959) is elected prime minister of Ceylon (present-day Sri Lanka).

1956 France cedes its colonies on the subcontinent to India.

1957 Malayan Federation gains independence.

1957 Israel evacuates the Gaza strip.

1957 Sihanouk (1922–) again becomes head of state in Cambodia.

1958 Egypt and Syria form the United Arab Republic (UAR).

1958 Iraq and Jordan form a short-lived Arab Federation; the federation is ended by a military coup in Iraq, which then becomes a republic.

1958 Chinese bombard the Quemoy islands off Formosa (Taiwan).

1958 US troops intervene during elections in Beirut, Lebanon.

1958 After a military coup in Pakistan, Muhammad Ayub Khan (1907–74) becomes president.

1959 Singapore becomes an independent state.

1959 Antarctica is safeguarded by international treaty.

1959 Iraq leaves the Baghdad Pact, which becomes the Central Treaty Organization (CENTO).

1959 Chinese troops suppress a rising in Tibet; the Dalai Lama flees.

1960 **1960** Ideological differences split the Soviet–Chinese alliance.

1960 Mrs Sirimavo Bandaranaike (1916–) is elected prime minister of Ceylon (present-day Sri Lanka).

1960 Achmad Sukarno (1901–70) assumes dictatorial powers in Indonesia.

1961 India conquers the Portuguese colony of Goa.

1961 Nazi war criminal Adolf Eichmann (1906–62) is tried and sentenced to death in Israel.

1961 Coup in Syria breaks up the UAR.

1961 Burmese diplomat U Thant (1909–74) is elected secretary general of the United Nations (UN)

1962 Western Samoa becomes independent.

1962 Military coup takes power in Thailand.

1962 Chinese troops invade N India, then withdraw to the disputed border.

1963 Malaya, Northern Borneo, Sarawak and Singapore form the Federation of Malaysia.

1963 Military coup overthrows Ngo Dinh Diem (1901–63) in South Vietnam.

1963 Arrest of Islamic reformer Ruhollah Khomeini (1900–89) sparks riots in Tehran.

1964 Indonesian troops invade Malaysia.

1964 China explodes an atom bomb.

1964 Faisal (1905–75) becomes king of Saudi Arabia.

1965 USA begins a bombing campaign against North Vietnam.

1965 Australian, New Zealand and South Korean troops are sent to Vietnam.

1965 Singapore becomes an independent republic.

1965 War breaks out between India and Pakistan.

1966 Indira Gandhi (1917–84) is elected prime minister of India.

1966 Mao Zedong (1893–1976) launches the Cultural Revolution in China; the Red Guards are formed.

1966 Raden Suharto (1921–) seizes power in Indonesia.

1966 Indonesian-Malay conflict ends.

1967 Israeli defeats its Arab neighbours in a six-day war; it recaptures the West Bank and E Jerusalem and occupies the Golan Heights.

1968 North Vietnam launches the Tet offensive; the US bombing campaign is halted; US troops massacre villagers at My Lai.

1968 Ba'athist officers seize power in Iraq.

1969 Yasir Arafat (1929–) is elected chairman of the Palestine Liberation Organization (PLO).

1969 Military coup seizes power in Pakistan.

1969 US troops begin withdrawing from Vietnam.

1969 Soviet and Chinese troops clash along their border.

1969 Ferdinand Marcos (1917–89) is elected president of the Philippines.

1969 Golda Meir (1898–1978) becomes prime minister of Israel.

1969 Dhofar rebellion starts in S Oman.

AFRICA

1958 Guinea becomes an independent republic.

1958 Mali and Senegal form the Federation of Mali.

1958 FLN rebels declare a provisional government in Algeria.

1959 Pro-independence riots occur in Nyasaland.

1959 Rioting breaks out in Stanleyville in the Belgian Congo.

1959 Hutu people organize an uprising against the Tutsi in Rwanda.

1959 Ceasefire is agreed in the Algerian revolt.

1960 French settlers in Algeria rebel against plans for independence.

1960 Kwame Nkrumah (1909–72) becomes president of the independent republic of Ghana.

1960 South African troops kill demonstrators at Sharpeville.

1960 Nigeria, Upper Volta, Chad, Ivory Coast, Cameroon, Togo, Gabon, Congo, Mauritania, Somalia and the Malagassy republic become fully independent.

1960 Belgian Congo gains independence with Patrice Lumumba (1925–61) as prime minister; the Congo army mutinies; Belgian troops are sent; the province of Katanga declares independence; UN troops replace Belgian forces; Joseph Mobutu (1930–97) seizes power.

1961 South Africa becomes a republic and leaves the British commonwealth.

1962 Algeria becomes independent; the French nationalist OAS organizes a revolt.

1962 Uganda becomes independent.

1963 Organization of African Unity (OAU) is formed in Addis Ababa.

1963 Katanga surrenders to the Congo government.

1964 Tanganyika and Zanzibar unite to form Tanzania with Julius Nyerere (1922–99) as president.

1964 ANC leader Nelson Mandela (1918–) is sentenced to life imprisonment in South Africa.

1964 Zambia becomes independent under President Kenneth Kaunda (1924–).

1964 Kenya becomes independent under President Jomo Kenyatta (1893–1978).

1965 Gambia becomes independent.

1965 White settlers opposed to black majority rule declare Southern Rhodesia independent (UDI).

1965 Houari Boumédienne (1925–78) overthrows President Ahmed Ben Bella (1916–) in Algeria.

1966 Military coup overthrows President Nkrumah in Ghana.

1966 South African prime minister Hendrik Verwoerd (b.1901) is assassinated; Balthazaar Vorster (1915–83) succeeds him.

1966 Colonel Jean Bokassa (1921–96) leads a coup in the Central African Republic.

1966 Milton Obote (1924–) becomes president of Uganda.

1966 Bechuanaland becomes independent as Botswana; Basutoland becomes independent as Lesotho.

1967 State of Biafra declares its independence and secedes from Nigeria; a civil war starts.

1967 Britain evacuates Aden; the People's Democratic Republic of Yemen is established.

1968 Swaziland becomes an independent kingdom.

1968 Equatorial Guinea gains independence from Spain.

1968 Famine conditions develop in Biafra.

1969 Colonel Muammar al-Qaddafi (1942–) overthrows King Idris (1890–1983) in Libya.

1969 Left-wing coup seizes power in Sudan.

EUROPE

1955 Austria, Spain, Italy, Portugal, Ireland, Bulgaria and Hungary are admitted to the UN.

1955 First summit conference of world leaders takes place in Geneva.

1956 British deport Archbishop Makarios (1913–77) from Cyprus.

1956 Hungarian prime minister Imre Nagy (1896–1958) takes charge of an anti-communist uprising that is quickly crushed by Soviet troops.

1957 Harold Macmillan (1894–1986) becomes British prime minister.

1957 Saar region is returned to West Germany.

1957 Olaf V (1903–91) becomes king of Norway.

1957 France, Belgium, the Netherlands, Luxembourg, Italy and West Germany sign the treaty of Rome establishing the European Economic Community (EEC) or Common Market.

1959 Belgium, the Netherlands and Luxembourg become a single economic unit – Benelux.

1958 New constitution establishes the French fifth republic; Charles De Gaulle (1890–1970) is elected president.

1958 Nikita Khrushchev (1894–1971) replaces Nikolai Bulganin (1895–1975) as Soviet premier.

1959 Eamon De Valera (1882–1975) is elected president of Ireland.

1960 Soviets shoot down a US U2 spyplane and capture pilot Gary Powers.

1960 Non-Common Market countries form the European Free Trade Association.

1960 Military coup takes power in Turkey.

1960 Cyprus becomes independent under President Makarios (1913–77).

1960 USA and Canada join W European nations to form the Organization for Economic Co-operation and Development (OECD).

1961 Soviet authorities build a wall across the divided city of Berlin.

1961 Twenty-five countries attend a conference of non-aligned nations in Belgrade.

1962 Disarmament conference starts in Geneva.

1963 France vetoes the British application to join the Common Market.

1963 Britain, the Soviet Union and the USA sign a nuclear-test treaty banning all but underground explosions.

1964 UN troops are sent in response to fighting between Greeks and Turks in Cyprus.

1964 Harold Wilson (1916–95) is elected British prime minister.

1964 Malta gains its independence from Britain.

1964 Khrushchev is deposed in the Soviet Union; Leonid Breznev (1906–82) becomes first secretary and Aleksei Kosygin (1904–80) becomes prime minister.

1964 Constantine II (1940–) becomes king of Greece.

1965 Charles De Gaulle (1890–1970) defeats François Mitterrand (1916–96) in the French presidential elections.

1966 France withdraws from NATO.

1967 Coup by Greek colonels takes power in Athens; King Constantine flees after a failed counter-coup.

1967 Nicolae Ceauşescu (1918–89) becomes head of state in Romania.

1967 Forty-six nations sign the General Agreement on Trade and Tariffs (GATT) in Geneva.

1967 EEC becomes the European Community (EC).

1968 Students and workers build barricades in Paris; student leader Rudi Dutschke is shot in West Germany.

1968 Czech politician Alexander Dubček (1921–92) introduces reforms; a Soviet invasion ends the "Prague Spring".

1968 Albania withdraws from the Warsaw Pact.

1968 Spain closes its frontier with Gibraltar.

1969 Violence flares between Catholics and Protestants in Ulster.

1969 De Gaulle resigns; Georges Pompidou (1911–74) is elected French president.

1969 Willy Brandt (1913–92) becomes chancellor of West Germany.

1969 Spanish dictator Francisco Franco (1892–1975) names Bourbon prince Juan Carlos (1938–) as his successor.

THE AMERICAS

1959 Cuban revolutionaries capture Havana; Batista flees; Castro becomes prime minister.

1959 Alaska and Hawaii become states of the USA.

1959 St Lawrence Seaway opens.

1960 New city of Brasília becomes the capital of Brazil.

1960 US civil rights activist Martin Luther King, Jr (1929–68) organizes a sit-in demonstration in Greesboro, North Carolina.

1960 USA embargoes exports to Cuba and cuts Cuban sugar quotas by 95%.

1960 Israeli agents kidnap Nazi war criminal Adolf Eichmann (1906–62) in Argentina.

1960 John F. Kennedy (1917–63) is elected US president.

1961 President Kennedy announces the formation of the Peace Corps.

1961 Cuban exiles in the USA attempt an invasion of Cuba at the Bay of Pigs.

1961 US civil rights activists organize "freedom rides" on segregated buses.

1962 Jamaica and Trinidad and Tobago become independent.

1962 Soviet Union attempts to install nuclear missiles in Cuba; the USA imposes a naval blockade.

1963 Hot-line is installed between the White House and the Kremlin.

1963 Martin Luther King, Jr, leads a civil rights march to Washington.

1963 Kennedy is assassinated in Dallas, Texas; Lyndon Johnson (1908–73) becomes US president.

1964 Johnson is elected US president.

1964 Free Speech movement starts in US universities.

1964 US government passes the Gulf of Tonkin resolution authorizing military action in Southeast Asia.

1965 African-American activist Malcolm X (b.1925) is assassinated in New York.

1965 Medicare and other welfare legislation is passed in the USA.

1965 Race riots erupt in the Watts district of Los Angeles.

1965 Military coup leads to widespread fighting in the Dominican Republic; US marines land and are then replaced by OAS forces.

1966 British Guyana and Barbados become independent.

1966 African-American activists Bobby Seale (1937–) and Huey Newton (1942–89) form the Black Panthers.

1967 US Court of Appeals orders the desegregation of Southern schools.

1967 Revolutionary Che Guevera (b.1928) is killed by Bolivian troops.

1968 Pierre Trudeau (1919–) becomes Canadian prime minister.

1968 UN approves a nuclear non-proliferation treaty.

1968 Student demonstrations disrupt the start of the Olympic Games in Mexico City.

1968 Martin Luther King, Jr (b.1929) is assassinated in Memphis.

1968 Senator Robert Kennedy (b.1925) is assassinated in Los Angeles.

1968 Anti-war protesters and Yippies demonstrate outside the Democratic party convention in Chicago.

1968 Richard Nixon (1913–94) is elected US president.

1969 War breaks out between Honduras and El Salvador.

SCIENCE AND TECHNOLOGY

1957 Soviet Union launches an artificial satellite – *Sputnik I*.

1957 Soviet satellite *Sputnik II* carries the dog Laika into orbit.

1957 UN forms the International Atomic Energy Commission.

1957 Scottish virologist Alick Isaacs (1921–67) discovers interferon.

1957 International Geophysical Year promotes earth sciences.

1958 Nuclear-powered submarine USS *Nautilus* passes beneath the North Pole.

1958 British industrialist Alistair Pilkington (1920–95) invents the float-glass process for making plate glass.

1958 US satellite *Explorer I* discovers the Van Allen radiation belts around the Earth.

1958 Stereophonic music records go on sale in the USA.

1959 Soviet spaceprobe *Lunik 3* photographs the far side of the Moon.

1960 French explode an atom bomb.

1960 US chemist Robert Woodward (1917–79) synthesizes chlorophyll.

1960 US physicist Theodore Maiman (1927–) invents the laser.

1961 Soviet cosmonaut Yuri Gagarin (1934–68) orbits the Earth.

1961 US astronaut Alan Shepard (1923–98) makes a sub-orbital flight.

1962 US astronaut John Glenn (1921–) orbits the Earth.

1962 US telecommunications satellite *Telstar* is launched.

1963 Soviet cosmonaut Valentina Tereshkova (1937–) orbits the Earth.

1963 US astronomer Maarten Schmidt (1929–) discovers quasars.

1964 US physicist Murray Gell-Mann (1929–) proposes the existence of quarks.

1964 Japanese railways run high-speed "bullet" trains.

1964 US engineer Robert Moog (1934–) invents an electronic music synthesizer.

1965 Soviet cosmonaut Alexei Leonov takes a "space walk" while in orbit.

1965 US spaceprobe *Mariner IV* orbits Mars and transmits photographs back to Earth.

1965 French launch an artificial satellite.

1965 US physicists Arno Penzias (1933–) and Robert Wilson (1936–) discover microwave cosmic background radiation.

1966 Soviet spaceprobe *Luna 9* makes a soft landing on the Moon.

1966 British engineers Charles Kao and George Hockham invent fibre-optic telephone cable.

1967 International treaty bans weapons of mass destruction from space.

1967 South African surgeon Christiaan Barnard (1922–) performs a heart transplant.

1967 Chinese explode a hydrogen bomb.

1967 British astronomer Jocelyn Bell (1943–) discovers pulsars.

1968 US astronauts orbit the Moon in the *Apollo 8* spacecraft.

1969 Anglo-French Concorde supersonic passenger aircraft makes its first flight.

1969 US spacecraft *Apollo 11* lands on the Moon; astronaut Neil Armstrong (1930–) takes the first steps.

1969 US engineer Douglas Engelbart (1925–) invents the "mouse" computer input device.

1969 DDT is banned in the USA.

ARTS AND HUMANITIES

1955 US novelist Vladimir Nabokov (1899–1977) publishes *Lolita*.

1956 British dramatist John Osborne (1929–95) writes his play *Look Back in Anger*.

1956 US singer Elvis Presley (1935–77) releases *Heartbreak Hotel*.

1956 British philosopher A.J. Ayer (1910–89) publishes *The Problem of Knowledge*.

1957 US sculptor Alexander Calder (1898–1976) creates *Mobile* for New York airport.

1957 US writer Jack Kerouac (1922–69) publishes *On the Road*.

1957 Australian novelist Patrick White (1912–90) publishes *Voss*.

1958 US economist J.K. Galbraith (1908–) publishes *The Affluent Society*.

1958 Russian poet and author Boris Pasternak (1890–1960) publishes his novel *Dr Zhivago*.

1959 US novelist William S. Burroughs (1914–97) publishes *The Naked Lunch*.

1959 German poet and author Günter Grass (1927–) publishes his novel *The Tin Drum*.

1959 Irish author Brendan Behan (1923–64) writes his play *The Hostage*.

1960 Guggenheim Museum, designed by US architect Frank Lloyd Wright (1869–1959), opens in New York. 1960

1960 US author John Updike (1932–) publishes his novel *Rabbit Run*.

1960 French dramatist Eugène Ionesco (1912–94) writes his play *The Rhinoceros*.

1960 British author Elias Canetti (1905–94) publishes *Crowds and Power*.

1961 British pop group The Beatles play their first performance at the Cavern Club in Liverpool.

1961 US novelist Joseph Heller (1923–99) publishes *Catch-22*.

1961 US singer-songwriter Bob Dylan (1941–) makes his debut performance in Greenwich Village, New York.

1961 Soviet dancer Rudolf Nureyev (1938–93) defects to the USA.

1962 US economist Milton Friedman (1912–) publishes *Capitalism and Freedom*.

1962 British artist Graham Sutherland (1903–80) creates his *Christ in Glory* tapestry for the rebuilt Coventry cathedral.

1962 Soviet novelist Alexander Solzhenitsyn (1918–) publishes *One Day in the Life of Ivan Denisovich*.

1963 US artist Roy Lichtenstein (1923–97) paints *Whaam!*.

1963 US environmentalist Rachel Carson (1907–64) publishes *Silent Spring*.

1964 Canadian academic Marshall McLuhan (1911–80) publishes *Understanding Media*.

1964 US novelist Saul Bellow (1915–) publishes *Herzog*.

1964 US poet Robert Lowell (1917–77) publishes *For the Union Dead*.

1965 US author Truman Capote (1924–84) publishes his non-fictional *In Cold Blood*.

1965 US dramatist Neil Simon (1927–) writes his play *The Odd Couple*.

1965 US consumer lobbyist Ralph Nader (1934–) publishes his book *Unsafe at Any Speed*.

1966 Vatican abolishes the Inquisition and the index of forbidden books.

1966 Japanese author Yukio Mishima (1925–70) publishes his novel *The Sailor Who fell from Grace with the Sea*.

1966 *Ariel* by US poet Syvia Plath (1932–63) is published posthumously.

1967 US artist Andy Warhol (1928–87) publishes his print of *Marilyn Monroe*.

1967 British artist David Hockney (1937–) paints *A Bigger Splash*.

1967 The Beatles release *Sergeant Pepper's Lonely Hearts Club Band*.

1967 Colombian novelist Gabriel García Márquez (1928–) publishes *One Hundred Years of Solitude*.

1967 British dramatist Tom Stoppard (1937–) writes his play *Rosencrantz and Guildenstern are Dead*.

1968 US psychologist Timothy Leary (1920–96) publishes *The Politics of Ecstasy*.

1969 British novelist John Fowles (1926–) publishes *The French Lieutenant's Woman*.

1969 US novelist Philip Roth (1933–) publishes *Portnoy's Complaint*.

1969 US novelist Kurt Vonnegut Jr (1922–) publishes *Slaughterhouse Five*.

1970

ASIA AND AUSTRALASIA

1970 Norodom Sihanouk (1922–) is overthrown; communist guerrillas threaten Phnom Penh; Cambodia becomes the Khmer Republic.

1970 Sultan Qaboos (1940–) seizes power from his father in Oman.

1970 USA resumes bombing North Vietnam.

1970 Palestinians hijack passenger jets and blow them up in Jordan.

1970 Jordanian forces loyal to King Hussein evict the PLO in a civil war.

1970 Hafez al-Assad (1928–) seizes power, becoming president of Syria.

1971 East Pakistan declares independence; West Pakistan declares war; India intervenes; the republic of Bangladesh is established.

1971 Bahrain and Qatar become independent as does the newly formed United Arab Emirates.

1971 China is admitted to the UN; nationalist Taiwan is expelled.

1972 Ceylon becomes the independent republic of Sri Lanka.

1972 Japanese Red Army terrorists kill passengers at Tel-Aviv airport.

1973 Last US combat troops leave Vietnam.

1973 President Zulfikar Ali Bhutto (1929–79) issues a new constitution in Pakistan.

1973 Arab countries attack Israel; Egyptian forces invade across the Suez canal but are defeated; Israel wins the war.

1973 Afghanistan becomes a republic after a coup.

1973 Arab states cut oil production and cause an energy crisis.

1974 India explodes an atom bomb.

1975 Clashes in Beirut between Palestinians and Christian Falangists start the Lebanese civil war.

1975 Cambodian Khmer Rouge guerrillas under Pol Pot (1928–98) capture Phnom Penh; "year zero" starts the systematic extermination of educated city-dwellers.

1975 Saigon is occupied by North Vietnamese forces; end of the Vietnam War; Vietnam becomes one country with Hanoi as its capital.

1975 Papua New Guinea gains independence from Australia.

1975 Communists take control in Laos.

1976 Deaths of Mao Zedong (b.1893) and Prime Minister Zhou Enlai (b.1898) cause a leadership crisis in China.

1977 Menachem Begin (1913–92) becomes prime minister of Israel.

1977 General Zia al-Huq (1924–88) seizes power in Pakistan.

1977 Chinese "Gang of Four", including Mao's wife, are expelled from power; Deng Xiaoping (1904–97) becomes Chinese premier.

1978 Revolution overthrows the republic in Afghanistan.

1978 Vietnam invades Cambodia.

1979 Vietnamese troops expel Pol Pot from Phnom Penh.

1979 Iranian shah Muhammad Reza Pahlavi (1919–80) flees a revolution in Iran; Ayatollah Khomeini (1900–89) arrives from Paris; students storm the US embassy in Tehran and take the staff hostage.

1979 Soviet Union invades Afghanistan.

1979 Chinese and Vietnamese troops are involved in border clashes.

1979 Saddam Hussein (1937–) seizes power in Iraq.

AFRICA

1970 Biafran War ends with victory for the federal government forces.

1970 Anwar Sadat (1918–81) becomes president of Egypt.

1970 Rhodesia declares itself a republic.

1970 New constitution restores the Moroccan Parliament.

1971 Egypt, Libya and Syria form the federation of Arab republics.

1971 Former Belgian Congo is renamed Zaïre.

1971 Army sergeant Idi Amin (1925–) seizes power and becomes president of Uganda.

1972 Amin expels Asians from Uganda.

1974 Ethiopian emperor Haile Selassie (1892–1975) is deposed and a republic is declared.

1975 Mozambique and Angola gain independence from Portugal.

1975 South Africa establishes Transkei as an "independent" black homeland.

1976 Schoolchildren demonstrating in Soweto are killed by South African security forces.

1976 Israeli commandos raid Entebbe airport in Uganda to free hijacked passengers.

1976 Seychelles becomes independent.

1977 German commandos free hijacked passengers at Mogadishu in Somalia.

1977 South African political activist Steve Biko (b.1956) is murdered in police custody.

1977 Cuban troops assist Ethiopian forces against rebels in Eritrea.

1977 Jean Bokassa (1921–96) proclaims himself emperor of a Central African Empire.

1978 French and Belgian paratroops try to restore order in Kolwezi after a secessionist rebellion in Zaïre.

1979 Tanzanian troops invade Uganda and oust Idi Amin.

1979 Conference in London ends the civil war in Rhodesia between guerrillas and the white minority government, and agrees majority rule.

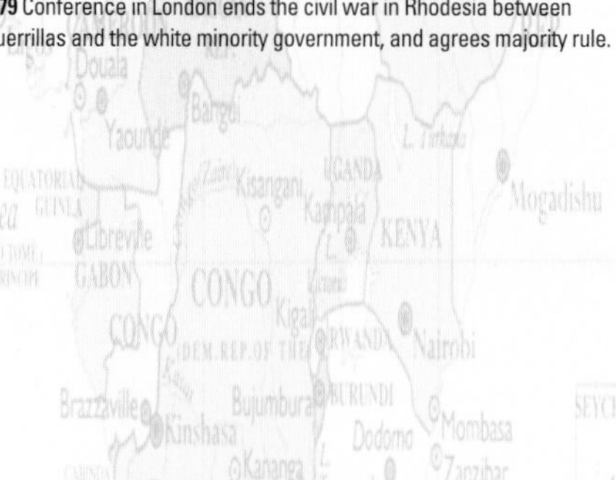

EUROPE

1970 Strategic Arms Limitation Treaty (SALT) talks begin in Helsinki.

1970 Portuguese dictator António Salazar (b.1889) dies.

1971 Angry Brigade terrorists send letter bombs to British politicians.

1971 Austrian diplomat Kurt Waldheim (1918–) becomes UN secretary general.

1972 Britain, Denmark and Ireland join the EC.

1972 Members of the terrorist Baader-Meinhof gang are arrested in West Germany.

1972 British impose direct rule in Ulster.

1972 Palestinian terrorists kidnap and kill Israeli athletes at the Munich Olympics.

1973 "Cod war" breaks out between Iceland and Britain over fishing rights.

1973 Greece officially becomes a republic.

1973 British prime minister Edward Heath (1916–) declares a state of emergency and a three-day working week because of strikes.

1973 Paris peace agreement ends US involvement in Vietnam.

1974 Left-wingers seize power in a bloodless revolution in Portugal.

1974 Valéry Giscard d'Estaing (1926–) becomes president of France.

1974 Greek nationalists stage a coup in Cyprus and declare union with Greece; Turkish troops invade and conquer half the island.

1974 Junta of Greek colonels abdicates power.

1974 Illegal Irish Republican Army (IRA) intensifies its bombing campaign against British targets.

1975 Franco dies (b.1892); Juan Carlos (1938–) becomes king of Spain.

1975 Helsinki accords on peace and human rights mark a major step in the process of détente between NATO and the Warsaw Pact.

1975 Britain becomes an oil-producing nation.

1975 Turkish Federated State of North Cyprus is established; UN forces maintain the border with the Greek sector of the island.

1975 Terrorists led by "Carlos" take hostage members of the Organization of Petroleum Exporting Countries (OPEC) in Vienna.

1977 Czech political reformers form the Charter 77 organization.

1977 Dutch marines rescue hostages on a train hijacked by South Moluccan terrorists.

1977 Adolfo Suarez (1932–) is elected prime minister of Spain.

1978 Italian Red Brigade terrorists kidnap and murder politician Alberto Moro (b.1916).

1978 Group of Seven (G7) industrialized nations meet to discuss economic policy.

1979 Margaret Thatcher (1925–) is elected British prime minister.

1980

1980 Attempt by US special forces to rescue hostages held in Tehran ends in disastrous failure.

1980 Iraq invades Iran in order to gain control of the Shatt al-Arab waterway.

1981 US hostages in Tehran are released.

1981 Chinese "Gang of Four" are convicted of treason.

1981 Israeli aircraft destroy an Iraqi nuclear reactor in a bombing raid.

1982 Israel invades Lebanon and forces the PLO to evacuate to Tunisia and Cyprus; S Lebanon comes under Israeli occupation; an international peacekeeping force arrives in Beirut.

1982 Iranian forces recapture port of Khurramshahr.

1983 US and French troops are killed in bomb attacks in Beirut.

1983 Filipino politician Benigno Aquino (b.1932) is assassinated.

1983 Yitshak Shamir (1915–) becomes prime minister of Israel.

1984 Brunei becomes an independent sultanate.

1984 Indian troops storm Sikh protestors at the Golden Temple in Amritsar; Indira Gandhi (b.1917) is assassinated; Rajiv Gandhi (1944–91) becomes prime minister.

1984 Britain agrees to return Hong Kong to China.

1984 Chinese government introduces liberal economic reforms.

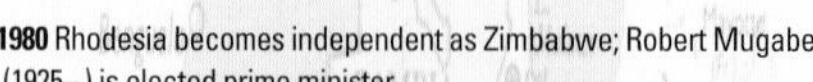

1980 Rhodesia becomes independent as Zimbabwe; Robert Mugabe (1925–) is elected prime minister.

1980 Libya invades and occupies N Chad.

1981 Anwar Sadat (1918–81) is assassinated; Hosni Mubarak (1928–) becomes president of Egypt.

1982 Israel returns the Sinai peninsula to Egypt.

1984 South African president P.W. Botha (1916–) grants limited political rights to Asians and "coloureds".

1985 USA and the EC impose economic sanctions against South Africa.

1985 Famine in Ethiopia is partially alleviated by funds raised by the international Live Aid pop concert.

1986 US warplanes bomb Libya.

1987 Tunisian president Habib Bourguiba (1903–2000) is deposed in a coup led by Ben Ali.

1987 Chadian forces, assisted by the French foreign legion, expel the Libyans from N Chad.

1989 Cuban troops are withdrawn from Angola; a ceasefire is declared in the civil war.

1989 F.W. de Klerk (1936–) becomes president of South Africa.

1980 Following the death of President Tito (b.1892), Yugoslavia comes under collective leadership.

1980 Polish shipyard workers led by Lech Walesa (1943–) form the Solidarity trades union.

1980 Greece joins the European Community (EC).

1981 François Mitterrand (1916–96) is elected president of France.

1981 Andreas Papandreou (1919–96) is elected prime minister of Greece.

1981 Solidarity protests result in martial law being declared in Poland under General Wojciech Jaruzelski (1923–).

1982 Helmut Kohl (1930–) is elected German chancellor.

1983 Yuri Andropov (1914–84) becomes president of the Soviet Union.

1983 Green party wins its first parliamentary seats in West Germany.

1983 Martial law ends in Poland.

1983 US cruise missiles are located at airbases in Britain.

1983 Turkish N Cyprus declares its independence under Rauf Denktas.

1984 Konstantin Chernenko (1911–85) becomes Soviet president.

1985 Spain re-opens its border with Gibraltar.

1985 Mikhail Gorbachev (1931–) becomes general secretary of the Communist Party of the Soviet Union.

THE AMERICAS

1970 US National Guard soldiers kill four protesting students at Kent State University in Ohio.

1970 Weathermen radicals bomb a US Army research centre.

1970 Salvador Allende (1908–73) is elected president of Chile.

1970 French-speaking separatists in Québec kidnap and murder a Canadian official.

1971 Tupamaros guerrillas kidnap foreign businessmen in Uruguay.

1971 US officer William Calley is found guilty of the My Lai massacre.

1972 Burglars are arrested in the Democratic Party election headquarters at the Watergate Hotel in Washington, D.C.

1973 US national security adviser Henry Kissinger (1923–) is appointed secretary of state.

1973 Juan Perón (1895–1974) returns to Argentina and becomes president.

1973 British Honduras is renamed Belize.

1973 General Augusto Pinochet (1915–) leads a military coup that seizes power in Chile.

1974 Isabel Perón (1931–) assumes the presidency of Argentina on her husband's death.

1974 US president Nixon resigns over the Watergate scandal; Gerald Ford (1913–) becomes president.

1975 Dutch Guiana becomes the independent state of Surinam.

1976 Coup overthrows Isabel Perón in Argentina.

1976 Jimmy Carter (1924–) is elected US president.

1977 USA and Panama sign a treaty for the return of the canal zone to Panama.

1978 Anwar Sadat (1918–81) and Menachem Begin (1913–92) meet at Camp David.

1978 Dominica gains independence from Britain.

1979 Israel and Egypt sign a peace treaty in Washington, D.C.

1979 Sandinista guerrillas capture Managua; President Anastasio Somoza (1925–80) flees Nicaragua; Daniel Ortega (1945–) forms a revolutionary government.

1979 Nuclear accident occurs at Three Mile Island power station in Pennsylvania.

1979 Hundreds of US cultists commit mass suicide in the People's Temple at Jonestown, Guyana.

1980 Mount St Helens erupts in Washington state.

1980 Ronald Reagan (1911–) is elected US president.

1980 Ex-Nicaraguan president Somoza is assassinated in Paraguay.

1981 Belize, Antigua and Barbuda gain independence from Britain.

1981 Peruvian diplomat Pérez de Cuéllar (1920–) becomes UN secretary general.

1982 Argentine troops invade the Falkland Islands (Malvinas); British forces invade and recapture the islands.

1983 US president Ronald Reagan announces the development of a Strategic Defence Initiative (SDI) or "Star Wars" defence system; he also announces support for the Nicaraguan Contras.

1983 US marines invade Grenada and overthrow a revolutionary government.

1983 Martin Luther King Day is inaugurated in the USA.

1984 Canadian prime minister Pierre Trudeau (1919–) resigns.

1984 US troops are withdrawn from Lebanon.

1984 Daniel Ortega (1945–) is elected president of Nicaragua.

1985 Earthquake devastates Mexico City.

1986 Space shuttle *Challenger* explodes immediately after launch.

SCIENCE AND TECHNOLOGY

1970 China launches an artificial satellite.

1970 Soviet space probe *Venera VII* soft-lands on Venus and sends information from the surface.

1970 Boeing 747 "Jumbo jet" enters service.

1971 US engineer Ted Hoff (1937–) invents the computer microprocessor ("chip").

1971 Electronic pocket calculator is invented.

1971 Soviet Union launches the *Salyut* space station into orbit.

1971 US palaeontologist Stephen Gould (1941–) proposes his theory of punctuated equilibrium in evolution.

1972 US spaceprobe *Pioneer 10* is launched.

1973 US engineer Nolan Bushnell (1943–) invents the video game Pong.

1973 USA launches the *Skylab* space station.

1973 US biochemists Stanley Cohen (1935–) and Herbert Boyer (1936–) invent recombinant DNA genetic engineering when they use restriction enzymes to "cut and splice" DNA.

1974 US palaeontologist Donald Johanson (1942–) discovers "Lucy" – a partial skeleton of *Australopithecus afarensis* – in Ethiopia.

1974 Bar codes are introduced in US shops.

1975 *Apollo* and *Soyuz* spacecraft link up while in orbit.

1975 Personal computer (PC) in kit form goes on sale in the USA.

1976 Legionnaire's disease is identified in the USA.

1976 US *Viking* probes send back pictures from the surface of Mars.

1977 British biochemist Frederick Sanger (1918–) dicovers the full sequence of bases in DNA.

1977 US engineer Paul MacCready (1925–) designs a human-powered aircraft.

1977 Apple II personal computer is introduced.

1978 World Health Organization (WHO) announces that, apart from some laboratory samples, smallpox has been eradicated.

1978 First in-vitro fertilization baby is born in Britain.

1978 British palaeontologist Mary Leakey (1913–96) discovers 3.5-million-year-old human footprints in Tanzania.

1979 US *Voyager* spaceprobes transmit close-up pictures of Jupiter and its moons.

1979 British scientist James Lovelock (1919–) proposes his Gaia theory.

1979 Liquid crystal display (LCD) television is developed in Japan.

1981 US space shuttle makes its first orbital flight.

1981 French high-speed train (TGV) service enters operation.

1981 IBM launch a PC using the Microsoft MS-DOS operating system.

1981 Disease Acquired Immune Deficiency Syndrome (AIDS) is identified.

1982 Compact music discs (CDs) are introduced.

1982 Genetically engineered insulin is produced for human use.

1983 French phsyician Luc Montagnier (1932–) identifies the human immunodeficiency virus (HIV) as the infective agent that causes AIDS.

1983 *Pioneer 10* leaves the solar system.

1984 Cellphone network is launched in Chicago, USA.

1984 British geneticist Alec Jeffreys (1950–) devises a technique for genetic fingerprinting.

1984 Apple company launches the Macintosh computer featuring windows, icons, a mouse and pull-down menus.

1985 International whaling commission bans commercial whaling.

1986 European spaceprobe *Giotto* intercepts Halley's comet.

1986 *Voyager II* transmits pictures of Uranus.

ARTS AND HUMANITIES

1970 US revolutionary Jerry Rubin publishes his Yippie manifesto *Do It!*. 1970

1970 Australian feminist Germaine Greer (1939–) publishes *The Female Eunuch.*

1970 Complete *New English Bible* is published.

1970 British poet Ted Hughes (1930–98) publishes *Crow.*

1970 US musician Jimi Hendrix (b.1942) dies of a drug overdose.

1970 The Beatles split up to pursue separate careers.

1970 Italian dramatist Dario Fo (1926–) writes *Accidental Death of an Anarchist.*

1971 Death of the US jazz musician Louis Armstrong (b.1900).

1972 Finnish architect Alvar Aalto (1898–1976) designs the North Jutland Museum in Denmark.

1972 US artist Christo Javaceff (1935–) erects his sculpture *Valley Curtain* in Colorado.

1972 British novelist (1917–93) Anthony Burgess writes *A Clockwork Orange.*

1973 US novelist Thomas Pynchon (1937–) publishes *Gravity's Rainbow.*

1973 German economist Ernst Shumacher (1911–77) publishes *Small is Beautiful: A Study of Economics as if People Mattered.*

1974 Terracotta army in China is discovered.

1974 US author Erica Jong (1942–) publishes her novel *Fear of Flying.*

1974 US author Robert Pirsig (1928–) publishes *Zen and the Art of Motorcycle Maintenance.*

1974 US journalists Bob Woodward and Carl Bernstein publish their *All the President's Men.*

1975 Mexican novelist Carlos Fuentes (1928–) publishes *Terra Nostra.*

1975 US novelist E.L. Doctorow (1931–) publishes *Ragtime.*

1975 Argentine writer Jorge Louis Borges (1899–1986) publishes *The Book of Sand.*

1976 US linguist Noam Chomsky (1928–) publishes *Reflections on Language.*

1976 US author Alex Haley (1921–92) publishes *Roots: The Saga of an American Family.*

1976 US novelist Paul Theroux (1941–) publishes *The Family Arsenal.*

1977 Pompidou Centre art gallery, designed by Richard Rogers (1933–) and Italian architect Renzo Piano (1937–), opens in Paris.

1977 British novelist Paul Scott (1930–78) publishes *Staying On.*

1978 US novelist John Irving (1942–) publishes *The World According to Garp.*

1978 British novelist A.S. Byatt (1936–) publishes *The Virgin in the Garden.*

1978 US author Susan Sontag (1933–) publishes *Illness as Metaphor.*

1978 French philosopher Jacques Derrida (1930–) publishes *Truth in Painting.*

1978 US author Armistead Maupin (1944–) publishes *Tales of the City.*

1979 Czech novelist Milan Kundera (1929–) publishes *The Book of Laughter and Forgetting.*

1980 US composer Philip Glass (1937–) writes his opera 1980
Satyagraha.

1980 Former-Beatle John Lennon (b.1940) is murdered in New York.

1981 Italian author Umberto Eco (1932–) publishes his novel *The Name of the Rose.*

1981 US author Toni Morrison (1931–) publishes *Tar Baby.*

1981 Peruvian author Mario Vargas Llosa (1936–) publishes his novel *The War of the End of the World.*

1981 Death of the Jamaican musician Bob Marley (b.1945).

1982 Chilean novelist Isabel Allende (1942–) publishes her novel *The House of the Spirits.*

1982 Australian novelist Thomas Keneally (1935–) publishes *Schindler's Ark.*

1982 US architect Maya Lin (1959–) designs the Vietnam Veterans' Memorial in Washington, D.C.

1983 Italian novelist Italo Calvino (1923–85) publishes *Mr Palomar.*

1983 US poet and author Alice Walker (1944–) publishes her novel *The Color Purple.*

1984 Scottish novelist Iain Banks (1954–) publishes *The Wasp Factory.*

ASIA AND AUSTRALASIA

1985 French secret agents blow up the Greenpeace ship *Rainbow Warrior* in New Zealand.

1986 Ferdinand Marcos (1917–89) flees the Philippines; Corazon Aquino (1933–) becomes president.

1986 Iranian forces capture the Iraqi port of Al Faw.

1987 Indian troops impose a ceasefire in the conflict between the Tamil Tiger guerrillas and Sri Lankan government forces.

1987 Syrian troops enter Beirut to keep the peace.

1988 Soviet republics of Azerbaijan and Armenia clash over the enclave of Nagorno-Karabakh.

1988 Iran-Iraq War ends in stalemate.

1988 General Zia (b.1924) is assassinated; Benazir Bhutto (1953–) becomes prime minister of Pakistan.

1988 Soviet Union begins withdrawing troops from Afghanistan.

1989 Akihito (1933–) becomes emperor of Japan.

1989 Chinese troops kill pro-democracy protestors in Tiananmen Square in Beijing.

1989 Ayatollah Khomeini (b.1900) dies; Hashemi Rafsanjani (1934–) becomes president of Iran.

1990 **1990** North and South Yemen unite to form a single state.

1990 Benazir Bhutto is dismissed as prime minister of Pakistan.

1990 Iraq invades and annexes Kuwait; the USA, EC countries and Arab nations form an opposing coalition.

1991 Warplanes commence the "Desert Storm" bombing campaign against Iraqi military targets; Iraq launches Scud missiles against Israel and Saudi Arabia; a massive land invasion liberates Kuwait.

1991 Risings against Saddam Hussein (1937–) in N and S Iraq fail; UN safe havens are created for the Kurds in the N.

1991 Rajiv Gandhi (b.1944) is assassinated during an election campaign.

1992 Hindu extremists demolish the Ayodhya mosque igniting widespread violence across India.

1992 Afghan Islamic rebels capture Kabul and overthrow the communist government.

1995 Earthquake devastates the Japanese city of Kobe.

1995 Turkish troops invade Iraq to attack Kurdish guerrillas.

1995 Israeli prime minister Yitzhak Rabin (b.1922) is assassinated by a Jewish extremist; in elections the following year Binyamin Netanyahu (1949–) becomes prime minister.

1996 Yasir Arafat (1929–) is elected president of the Palestinians.

1996 Iraqi aircraft enter a no-fly zone to attack Kurds; the USA launches cruise missiles against Iraq.

1996 Afghan Taliban Islamic militia captures Kabul and forms a fundamentalist government.

1997 Rafsanjani is succeeded as president of Iran by liberal reformer Muhammad Khatami (1943–).

1997 Hong Kong is returned to Chinese sovereignty.

1997 Israeli troops withdraw from Hebron in Palestine.

1998 Weakness of the Japanese economy causes other Asian economies to decline.

1998 Iraq refuses access to UN inspectors; the USA launches cruise missiles against Iraqi military targets.

1998 Indonesian president Rahen Suharto (1921–) is ousted from power; he is succeeded by B.J. Habibie (1936–), who is in turn ousted (1999) by Abdurrahman Wahid (1940–).

1999 Hussein I (b.1935) of Jordan dies; he is succeeded by his son Abdullah (1962–).

1999 Ehud Barak (1942–) is elected Israeli prime minister.

1999 In a referendum, Australians vote against becoming a republic.

1999 Pakistani prime minister Nawaz Sharif (1949–) is ousted in a military coup led by General Pervez Musharraf (1943–).

2000 **2000** Israeli troops withdraw from S Lebanon.

AFRICA

1990 Nelson Mandela (1918–) is released from prison in South Africa.

1990 Namibia becomes an independent republic.

1990 Robert Mugabe (1925–) is elected president of Zimbabwe.

1992 US troops arrive in Mogadishu, Somalia, to supervise food distribution.

1992 Algerian president Muhammad Boudiaf (b.1919) is assassinated by an Islamic extremist.

1992 Egyptian statesman Boutros Boutros Ghali (1922–) becomes UN secretary general.

1994 US troops withdraw from Somalia.

1994 Presidents of Burundi and Rwanda are killed in an air crash; inter-tribal violence and civil war erupt in Rwanda.

1994 African National Congress wins the South African elections; Nelson Mandela becomes president.

1994 Palestine National Authority takes control of the Gaza Strip and Jericho.

1994 Terrorist Carlos is arrested in Khartoum and taken to France for trial.

1995 Cameroon and Mozambique join the British Commonwealth.

1996 Renewed violence breaks out between Hutus and Tutsis in Rwanda.

1996 Rebel forces, led by Laurent Kabila, force Zaïrean president Mobutu Sese Seko (1930–97) into exile.

1997 Zaïrean rebels rename the country the Democratic Republic of the Congo.

1997 Ghanaian diplomat Kofi Annan (1938–) becomes UN secretary general.

1998 Border dispute between Eritrea and Ethiopia flares into full-scale war.

1998 Thabo Mbeki (1942–) succeeds Mandela as president of the African National Congress (ANC).

1999 Mbeki is elected president of South Africa.

1999 Moroccan king Hassan II dies (b.1929); he is succeeded by his son, Muhammad VI (1963–).

2000 In Uganda, *c.*1000 members of the cult Movement for the Restoration of the 10 Commandments of God are found dead, probably murdered.

2000 Devastating floods in Mozambique leave *c.*one million people homeless.

2000 Abdoulaye Wade (1926–) is elected president of Senegal; he replaces Abdou Diouf (1935–), who has been president since 1981.

2000 Fighting intensifies between rebel and government forces in Sierra Leone.

EUROPE

1985 Palestinian terrorists hijack the cruise ship *Achille Lauro* and attack Israeli airline desks at Rome and Vienna airports.

1986 Spain and Portugal join the European Community (EC).

1986 Accident at the Chernobyl nuclear reactor in Ukraine releases a radioactive cloud over central and N Europe.

1986 Swedish prime minister Olaf Palme (b.1927) is murdered.

1987 Gorbachev announces policies of *glasnost* and *perestroika*.

1988 USA and the Soviet Union agree to limit the number of missiles in Europe by the Intermediate-range Nuclear Forces (INF) treaty.

1988 US passenger jet is blown up by a terrorist bomb over Lockerbie in Scotland.

1989 Solidarity candidates win a majority in Polish elections.

1989 Hungary adopts a new constitution and opens its borders; popular protests in East Germany lead to the dismantling of the Berlin wall.

1989 Revolution overthrows Nicolae Ceauşescu (1918–89) in Romania.

1989 Vaclav Havel (1936–) forms a democratic government in Czechoslovakia.

1989 Slobodan Milošević (1941–) is elected president of Serbia.

1989 US and Soviet presidents officially declare the end of the Cold War.

1990 Lithuania, Latvia and Estonia declare independence from the Soviet Union; Uzbekistan and Ukraine declare independence; Soviet troops occupy Lithuania and Latvia.

1990 Boris Yeltsin (1931–) is elected president of the Russian federation.

1990 East and West Germany are reunited.

1990 Margaret Thatcher (1925–) resigns; John Major (1943–) becomes British prime minister.

1991 Warsaw Pact is dissolved as a military alliance.

1991 Croatia and Slovenia declare independence from Yugoslavia; the Serb-dominated Yugoslav army invades Croatia and captures Vukovar.

1991 Army officers attempts a coup in Moscow; the Soviet communist party is suspended; Mikhail Gorbachev (1931–) resigns; the Soviet Union ceases to exist; Russia, Belarus and Ukraine form the Commonwealth of Independent States (CIS) under President Yeltsin.

1992 Bosnia-Herzegovina declares independence from Yugoslavia; the Serbs attack Sarajevo.

1993 Czech and Slovak republics are established as separate states.

1993 EC establishes a single market.

1993 Yeltsin orders tanks to attack rebels in the Moscow parliament.

1993 UN declares safe areas in Yugoslavia including Goradze and Srebrenica.

1994 Chechenia declares independence from Russia.

1995 Austria, Finland and Sweden join the European Union (EU).

1995 Russian troops capture the Chechen capital, Grozny.

1995 Renewed fighting in Bosnia leads to NATO airstrikes against the Serbs; a peace agreement is signed in Paris.

1995 Jacques Chirac (1932–) is elected president of France.

1996 Yugoslavian war crimes tribunal opens in the Hague, Netherlands.

1997 Tony Blair (1953–) is elected British prime minister.

1997 Lionel Jospin (1937–) is elected prime minister of France.

1998 Albanian separatists clash with Serb forces in Kosovo; *c.*200,000 Kosovar Albanians are forced to flee from Serbian aggression.

1998 Gerhard Schröder (1944–) is elected chancellor of Germany.

1998 British and Irish prime ministers, together with representatives from eight political parties in Northern Ireland, sign the Good Friday Peace Agreement; David Trimble (1944–) becomes first minister of the Northern Ireland Assembly.

1999 European currency (the "Euro") comes into limited use.

1999 Commissioners of the EU, including the president Jacques Santer (1937–), resign en masse after a corruption scandal; Romano Prodi (1939–) becomes president of the Commission.

1999 Russia launches another offensive against Chechenia.

1999 NATO aircraft bomb Serbia in support of the Kosovar Albanians; a peace agreement is negotiated; a United Nations' (UN) peacekeeping force (K-FOR) is deployed.

1999 Russian president Boris Yeltsin resigns; former prime minister Vladimir Putin (1952–) is elected president in 2000.

2000 European Union imposes diplomatic sanctions against Austria after the far-right Freedom Party joins Austria's coalition government.

THE AMERICAS

1986 Jean Claude "Baby Doc" Duvalier (1951–) flees Haiti to exile in France.

1987 US colonel Oliver North (1943–) is secretly authorized to sell weapons to Iran, the profits to be used to arm the anti-Sandinista Contras in Nicaragua; when revealed, the affair causes a major scandal in the USA.

1987 New York Stock Market crashes triggering a worldwide financial crisis; computerized dealing is blamed for the severity of the collapse.

1988 George Bush (1924–) is elected US president.

1988 Sandinistas and Contras agree an armistice in Nicaragua.

1989 General Manuel Noriega (1934–) proclaims himself president of Panama; US troops invade.

1989 Alfredo Stroessner (1912–) is overthrown by a coup in Paraguay.

1989 San Francisco suffers a major earthquake.

1990 Noriega is captured and taken to the USA to face charges of drug-dealing.

1991 Strategic Arms ReductionTalks (START) limit the size of US and Russian nuclear arsenals.

1991 Peace agreements ends an 11-year civil war in El Salvador.

1992 Bill Clinton (1946–) is elected US president.

1992 Canada, the USA and Mexico form the North American Free Trade Association (NAFTA).

1992 Fernando Collor de Mello (1950–) resigns as president of Brazil.

1992 Abimael Guzman, leader of the Shining Path guerrillas, is arrested in Peru.

1992 UN organizes an environmental Earth Summit in Rio de Janeiro.

1993 World Trade Center, New York City, is damaged by a terrorist bomb; six people are killed and *c.*1000 injured.

1993 US government agents storm the headquarters of the Branch Davidian cult in Waco, Texas.

1993 Israel and the PLO reach a peace agreement in Washington, D.C.

1994 Zapatista National Liberation Army leads a revolt in Chiapas state in Mexico.

1994 US troops invade Haiti.

1995 US government offices in Oklahoma City are blown up by a terrorist bomb.

1995 World Trade Association succeeds GATT.

1995 Louis Farrakhan (1933–) organizes a "million man march" on Washington, D.C.

1998 US president Clinton faces charges of misconduct and of authorizing a cover-up of a sex scandal involving Monica Lewinsky.

1998 Hurrican Mitch kills *c.*5500 in Honduras and *c.*4000 in Nicaragua; millions of people are left homeless.

1998 Former Chilean dictator Augusto Pinochet (1915–) is arrested in London, UK, on charges of human rights violations.

1999 US Senate declines to impeach President Clinton.

1999 Part of the Canadian Northwest Territories becomes the self-governing Inuit territory of Nunavut.

2000 Pinochet, deemed unift to stand trial, is allowed to return to Chile.

2000 More than 500,000 women converge on Washington, D.C., in the "million mom march" to campaign for tougher gun laws.

SCIENCE AND TECHNOLOGY

1986 US aviators Jeana Yeager and Dick Rutan fly the aircraft *Voyager* non-stop around the world without refuelling.

1987 International agreement is reached to limit the amounts of chloroflurocarbons (CFCs) released into the atmosphere.

1987 Work starts on a tunnel between Britain and France.

1987 Supernova SN1987A is visible to the unaided eye.

1988 US scientists start a project to map the human genome.

1988 British mathematician and cosmologist Stephen Hawking (1942–) publishes *A Brief History of Time.*

1989 Convention on the International Trade in Endangered Species (CITES) imposes a worldwide ban on the sale of elephant ivory.

1989 *Voyager II* transmits pictures of Neptune.

1990 US Hubble space telescope is carried into orbit by the space shuttle.

1990 US spaceprobe *Magellan* radar maps Venus.

1991 5000-year-old body is discovered preserved in ice on the Austrian-Italian border.

1991 Energy is experimentally produced by controlled nuclear fusion at the Joint European Torus in Britain.

1992 US COBE satellite discovers ripples in the microwave background that confirm the Big Bang origin of the universe.

1992 Propellerless ship powered by magnetohydrodynamics is launched in Japan.

1994 Fragments of comet Shoemaker-Levi impact on Jupiter.

1994 Rail tunnel opens between Britain and France.

1994 World Wide Web (WWW) is created.

1995 US scientists discover the top quark.

1996 Particles of antimatter are created at CERN (the European Nuclear Research Centre) in Switzerland.

1996 452m-high Petronas Towers in Kuala Lumpur, Malaysia, are constructed.

1997 A sheep ("Dolly") is cloned in Britain.

1997 Deep Blue computer defeats the world chess champion Gary Kasparov (1963–).

1998 Adult sheep Dolly gives birth.

1999 In a flight lasting 19 days, 21 hours and 55 minutes, the first circumnavigation of the Earth by a manned hot-air balloon is achieved by *Breitling Orbiter 3*, piloted by Swiss Bertrand Piccard and Briton Brian Jones.

1999 Scientists at the human genome project announce that human chromosome 22 has been fully decoded; it is the first human chromosome to be decoded.

2000 Scientists at the human genome project announce that human chromosome 21 has been fully decoded; it is the smallest human chromosome, with only 225 genes.

2000 Cosmologists studying the Cosmic Microwave Background conclude that the universe is flat and will continue to expand forever.

ARTS AND HUMANITIES

1984 British novelist J.G. Ballard (1930–) publishes *Empire of the Sun.*

1985 Headquarters of the Hong Kong and Shanghai Bank, designed by British architect Norman Foster (1935–), opens in Hong Kong.

1985 German novelist Patrick Süskind (1949–) publishes *Perfume.*

1986 Japanese novelist Kazuo Ishiguro (1954–) publishes *An Artist of the Floating World.*

1986 British composer Andrew Lloyd Webber (1948–) writes his musical *Phantom of the Opera.*

1987 US author Tom Wolfe (1931–) publishes his novel *Bonfire of the Vanities.*

1988 German composer Karlheinz Stockhausen (1928–) writes *Montag aus Licht.*

1988 British author Salman Rushdie (1947–) publishes *Satanic Verses.*

1988 Australian novelist Peter Carey (1943–) publishes *Oscar and Lucinda.*

1990 US artist Jeff Koons (1955–) creates his sculpture *Jeff and* 1990
Ilona (Made in Heaven).

1990 British novelist Ian McEwan (1948–) publishes *The Innocent.*

1991 British composer Harrison Birtwistle (1934–) writes his opera *Sir Gawain and the Green Knight.*

1991 US composer Stephen Sondheim (1930–) writes *Assassins.*

1991 British novelist Martin Amis (1949–) publishes *Time's Arrow.*

1992 British artist Damien Hirst (1965–) creates his sculpture *The Physical Impossibility of Death in the Mind of Someone Living.*

1992 Chinese novelist Jung Chang (1952–) publishes *Wild Swans.*

1992 Sri Lankan-born Canadian novelist Michael Ondaatje (1943–) publishes *The English Patient.*

1993 Indian novelist Vikram Seth (1952–) publishes *A Suitable Boy.*

1993 Polish composer Witold Lutoslawski (1913–94) writes his fourth symphony.

1995 British novelist Pat Barker (1943–) publishes *The Ghost Road* completing her *Regeneration* trilogy.

1996 Restored Globe Theatre opens in London.

1996 Irish poet Seamus Heaney (1939–) publishes *The Spirit Level.*

1997 US author Carol Shields (1935–) publishes her novel *Larry's Party.*

1997 US scientist Jared Diamond publishes *Guns, Germs, and Steel.*

1997 Branch of the Guggenheim Museum designed by Canadian architect Frank Gehry (1929–) opens in Bilbao, Spain.

1997 British novelist J.K. Rowling publishes *Harry Potter and the Philosopher's Stone.*

1998 British poet Ted Hughes (1930–98) publishes *Birthday Letters.*

1998 US novelist Michael Cunningham (1952–) publishes *The Hours.*

1998 British composer Anthony Payne's completed version of Edward Elgar's incomplete Third Symphony is premiered.

1999 Heaney publishes his translation of *Beowulf.*

2000 Tate Modern art gallery, designed by Swiss architects Herzog 2000
and de Meuron, opens in London, UK, in the former Bankside power station.

OTTOMAN EMPERORS

Years	Emperor
1280-1324	Osman I
1324-62	Orhan
1362-89	Murad I
1389-1402	Bayezid I (the Thunderbolt)*
1402-03	Isa
1402-11	Suleiman
1409-13	Mesa
1413-21	Muhammad I
1421-51	Murad II+
1451-81	Muhammad II (the Conqueror)
1481-1512	Bayezid II (the Just)*
1512-20	Selim I
1520-66	Suleiman I (the Magnificent)
1566-74	Selim II
1574-95	Murad III
1595-1603	Muhammad III
1603-17	Ahmed I
1617-18	Mustafa I*
1618-22	Osman II
1622-23	Mustafa I (restored)*
1623-40	Murad IV
1640-48	Ibrahim*
1648-87	Muhammad IV*
1687-91	Suleiman II
1691-95	Ahmed II
1695-1703	Mustafa II*
1703-30	Ahmed III*
1730-54	Mahmud I
1754-57	Osman III
1757-74	Mustafa III
1774-89	Abdul Hamid I
1789-1807	Selim III*
1807-08	Mustafa IV*
1808-39	Mahmud II
1839-61	Abdul Medjid I
1861-76	Abdul Aziz*
1876	Murad V*
1876-1909	Abdul Hamid II*
1909-18	Muhammad V
1918-22	Muhammad VI*

** Deposed + Abdicated in favour of Muhammad II 1444-46*

JAPANESE EMPERORS

Years	Emperor	Era
1867-1912	Mutsuhito	Meiji
1912-26	Yoshihito	Taisho
1926-89	Hirohito	Showa
1989-	Akihito	Heisei

RUSSIAN TSARS

Years	Tsar
House of Rurik	
1547-84	Ivan IV (the Terrible)
1584-98	Fyodor I
1598	Irina
House of Godunov	
1598-1605	Boris Godunov
1605	Fyodor II
Usurpers*	
1605-06	Dmitri III
1606-10	Basil IV
House of Romanov	
1613-45	Michael Romanov
1645-76	Alexei Mikhailovich
1676-82	Fyodor III
1682-96	Peter I and Ivan V (brothers)
1696-1725	Peter I (the Great)
1725-27	Catherine I
1727-30	Peter II
1730-40	Anna Ivanovna
1740-41	Ivan VI
1741-62	Elizabeth
1762	Peter III
1762-96	Catherine II (the Great)
1796-1801	Paul I
1801-25	Alexander I
1825-55	Nicholas I
1855-81	Alexander II
1881-94	Alexander III
1894-1917	Nicholas II

** Interregnum (no tsar) from 1610-13*

ROMAN EMPERORS

Years	Emperor
27 BC-14 AD	Augustus (Octavian)
14-37	Tiberius I
37-41	Caligula (Gaius Caesar)
41-54	Claudius I
54-68	Nero
68-69	Galba
69	Otho
69	Vitellius
69-79	Vespasian
79-81	Titus
81-96	Domitian
96-98	Nerva
98-117	Trajan
117-138	Hadrian
138-161	Antoninus Pius
161-169	Lucius Verus*
161-180	Marcus Aurelius*
180-192	Commodus
193	Pertinax
193	Didius Julianus
193-211	Septimius Severus
211-217	Caracalla
217-218	Macrinus
218-222	Elagabalus
222-235	Alexander Severus
235-238	Maximinus (the Thracian)
238	Gordian I
238	Gordian II
238	Balbinus
238	Pupienus Maximus
238-244	Gordian III
244-249	Philip I (the Arabian)
249-251	Decius
251	Hostilian
251-253	Trebonianus Gallus
253	Aemilian
253-260	Valerian*
253-268	Gallienus*
268-269	Claudius II
269-270	Quintillus
270-275	Aurelian
275-276	Tacitus
276	Florian
276-282	Probus
282-283	Carus
283-284	Carinus*
283-285	Numerian*
284-305	Diocletian†

** Joint rule † During the reign of Diocletian the empire was divided and then often had both Western and Eastern emperors*

LATER CHINESE EMPERORS

Years	Emperor	Born
Ming dynasty		
1368-98	Hongwu	1328
1398-1402	Jianwen	1377
1402-24	Yongle	1360
1424-25	Hongxi	1378
1425-35	Xuande	1399
1435-49	Zhengtong*	1427
1449-57	Jingtai	1428
1457-64	Tianshun*	1427
1464-87	Chenghua	1447
1487-1505	Hongzhi	1470
1505-21	Zhengde	1491
1521-67	Jiajing	1507
1567-72	Longqing	1563
1620	Taichang	1582
1620-27	Tianji	1605
1627-44	Chongzhen	1611
Manchu Qing dynasty		
1644-61	Shunzhi	1638
1661-1722	Kangxi	1645
1722-36	Yongzheng	1678
1736-96	Qianlong	1711
1796-1820	Jiaqing	1760
1820-50	Daoguang	1782
1850-61	Xianfeng	1831
1861-75	Tongzhi	1856
1875-1908	Guangxu	1871
1908-11	Xuantong (Pu Yi)†	1906

** Zhengtong was deposed by invaders in 1449 and was restored, as Tianshun, in 1457 † Deposed in revolution*

INCA EMPERORS

Years	Emperor
1438-71	Pachacuti*
1471-93	Tupac Yupanqui
1493-1525	Huayna Capac
1525-32	Huáscar†
1532	Atahualpa†

** Abdicated † Deposed*

KINGS OF ITALY

Years	King
1861-78	Victor Emmanuel II
1878-1900	Umberto I
1900-46	Victor Emmanuel III
1946	Umberto II*

** Abdicated*

EMPERORS OF INDIA

Years	Emperor
Mauryan empire	
321-297 BC	Chandragupta Maurya
297-272 BC	Bindusara
272-231 BC	Ashoka
231-224 BC	Dasaratha
224-215 BC	Samprati
215-202 BC	Salisuka
202-195 BC	Devavarman
195-187 BC	Satadhanvan
187-185 BC	Brihadratha
Gupta empire	
320-350	Chandragupta I
350-376	Samudragupta
376-415	Chandragupta II
415-455	Kumaragupta I
455-470	Skandagupta
470-475	Kumaragupta II
475-500	Budagupta
500-515	Vainyagupta
515-530	Narasimhagupta
530-540	Kumaragupta III
540-550	Vishnugupta
Mughal empire (Great Mughals)	
1526-30	Babur
1530-56	Humayun*
1556-1605	Akbar I (the Great)
1605-27	Jahangir
1627	Dawar Baksh
1627-58	Shah Jahan†
1658-1707	Aurangzeb

** Humayun was defeated in 1540 and expelled from India until 1555, a period when northern India fell under the control of usurpers Sher Shah Suri, Islam Shah and Sikander Shah † Deposed*

AZTEC EMPERORS

Years	Emperor
*c.*1372-91	Acamapichtli*
*c.*1391-1416	Huitzilihuitl
*c.*1416-27	Chimalpopoca
1427-40	Itzcóatl
1440-69	Montezuma I
1469-81	Axayacoatl
1481-86	Tizoc
1486-1502	Ahuitzoti
1502-19	Montezuma II
1519-20	Cuitlahuac
1520-21	Cuauhtémoc

** Chieftain at Tenochtitlán and traditional founder of Aztec royal dynasty*

POPES SINCE AD 1000

Years	Pope
999-1003	Sylvester II
1003	John XVII
1004-09	John XVIII
1009-12	Sergius IV
1012-24	Benedict VIII
1024-32	John XIX
1032-44	Benedict IX
1045	Sylvester III
1045	Benedict IX
1045-46	Gregory VI
1046-47	Clement II
1047-48	Benedict IX
1048	Damasus II
1048-54	Leo IX
1055-57	Victor II
1057-58	Stephen IX
1059-61	Nicholas II
1061-73	Alexander II
1073-85	Gregory VII
1086-87	Victor III
1088-99	Urban II
1099-1118	Paschal II
1118-19	Gelasius II
1119-24	Calixtus II
1124-30	Honorius II
1130-43	Innocent II
1143-44	Celestine II
1144-45	Lucius II
1145-53	Eugenius III
1153-54	Anastasius IV
1154-59	Adrian IV
1159-81	Alexander III
1181-85	Lucius III
1185-87	Urban III
1187	Gregory VIII
1187-91	Clement III
1191-98	Celestine III
1198-1216	Innocent III
1216-27	Honorius III
1227-41	Gregory IX
1241	Celestine IV
1243-54	Innocent IV
1254-61	Alexander IV
1261-64	Urban IV
1265-68	Clement IV
1271-76	Gregory X
1276	Innocent V
1276	Adrian V
1276-77	John XXI
1277-80	Nicholas III
1281-85	Martin IV
1285-87	Honorius IV
1288-92	Nicholas IV
1294	Celestine V
1294-1303	Boniface VIII
1303-04	Benedict XI
1305-14	Clement V
1316-34	John XXII
1334-42	Benedict XII
1342-52	Clement VI
1352-62	Innocent VI
1362-70	Urban V
1370-78	Gregory XI
1378-89	Urban VI
1389-1404	Boniface IX
1404-06	Innocent VII
1406-15	Gregory XII
1417-31	Martin V
1431-47	Eugenius IV
1447-55	Nicholas V
1455-58	Calixtus III
1458-64	Pius II
1464-71	Paul II
1471-84	Sixtus IV
1484-92	Innocent VIII
1492-1503	Alexander VI
1503	Pius III
1503-13	Julius II
1513-21	Leo X
1522-23	Adrian VI
1523-34	Clement VII
1534-49	Paul III
1550-55	Julius III
1555	Marcellus II
1555-59	Paul IV
1559-65	Pius IV
1566-72	Pius V
1572-85	Gregory XIII
1585-90	Sixtus V
1590	Urban VII
1590-91	Gregory XIV
1591	Innocent IX
1592-1605	Clement VIII
1605	Leo XI
1605-21	Paul V
1621-23	Gregory XV
1623-44	Urban VIII
1644-55	Innocent X
1655-67	Alexander VII
1667-69	Clement IX
1670-76	Clement X
1676-89	Innocent XI
1689-91	Alexander VIII
1691-1700	Innocent XII
1700-21	Clement XI
1721-24	Innocent XIII
1724-30	Benedict XIII
1730-40	Clement XII
1740-58	Benedict XIV
1758-69	Clement XIII
1769-74	Clement XIV
1775-99	Pius VI
1800-23	Pius VII
1823-29	Leo XII
1829-30	Pius VIII
1831-46	Gregory XVI
1846-78	Pius IX
1878-1903	Leo XIII
1903-14	Pius X
1914-22	Benedict XV
1922-39	Pius XI
1939-58	Pius XII
1958-63	John XXIII
1963-78	Paul VI
1978	John Paul I
1978-	John Paul II

KINGS OF FRANCE

Dates	King
Carolingian dynasty	
750-768	Pepin III (the Short)
768-814	Charlemagne
814-843	Louis I (the Pious)
843-877	Charles II (the Bald)
877-879	Louis II (the Stammerer)
879-882	Louis III
879-884	Carloman
884-888	Charles III (the Fat)
888-893	Eudes
893-922	Charles III (the Simple)
922-923	Robert I
923-936	Rudolf
936-954	Louis IV (from Overseas)
954-986	Lothair
986-987	Louis V (the Sluggard)
Capetian dynasty	
987-996	Hugh Capet
996-1031	Robert II (the Pious)
1031-60	Henry I
1060-1108	Philip I
1108-37	Louis VI (the Fat)
1137-80	Louis VII (the Younger)
1180-1223	Philip II (Augustus)
1223-26	Louis VIII (the Lion)
1226-70	Louis IX
1270-85	Philip III (the Bold)
1285-1314	Philip IV (the Fair)
1314-16	Louis X (the Stubborn)
1316	John I
1316-22	Philip V (the Tall)
1322-28	Charles IV (the Fair)
House of Valois	
1328-50	Philip VI
1350-64	John II
1364-80	Charles V (the Wise)
1380-1422	Charles VI (the Mad)
1422-61	Charles VII (the Well-served)
1461-83	Louis XI
1483-98	Charles VIII
1498-1515	Louis XII
1515-47	Francis I
1547-59	Henry II
1559-60	Francis II
1560-74	Charles IX
1574-89	Henry III
House of Bourbon	
1589-1610	Henry IV
1610-43	Louis XIII (the Just)
1643-1715	Louis XIV
1715-74	Louis XV (the Well-Beloved)
1774-93†	Louis XVI
Restoration	
1814-24	Louis XVIII
1824-30‡	Charles X
1830-48	Louis Philippe§

† Louis XVII, son of Louis XVI, was nominally king while in prison 1793-95 ‡ Louis XIX and Henry V were nominally kings in 1830, for one day and eight days respectively
§ "The Citizen King", he fled to England

KINGS AND QUEENS OF SPAIN

Years	Monarch
House of Habsburg	
1516-56	Charles I (Holy Roman Emperor Charles V)
1556-98	Philip II
1598-1621	Philip III
1621-65	Philip IV
1665-1700	Charles II (the Mad)
House of Bourbon	
1700-46	Philip V
1746-59	Ferdinand VI
1759-88	Charles III
1788-1808	Charles IV
1808	Ferdinand VII*
1808-13	Joseph Bonaparte (House of Bonaparte)
1813-33	Ferdinand VII*
1833-68	Isabella II
1868-70	Provisional government
1870-73	Amadeus I† (House of Savoy)
1873-74	First republic
1874-86	Alfonso XII
1886-1931	Alfonso XIII‡
1931-39	Second republic
1939-75	Fascist government headed by General Francisco Franco
1975-	Juan Carlos I

*restored 1813 † abdicated ‡ deposed

KINGS AND QUEENS OF ENGLAND AND BRITAIN

Years	Monarch	Age*	R'd†
KINGS AND QUEENS OF ENGLAND			
West Saxon Kings (House of Cerdic)			
802-839	Egbert‡	—	37
839-858	Ethelwulf	—	19
858-860	Ethelbald	—	2
860-866	Ethelbert	—	6
866-871	Ethelred I	—	5
871-899	Alfred (the Great)	52	28
899-924	Edward the Elder	55	25
924-939	Athelstan	45	15
939-946	Edmund I	25	6
946-955	Edred	32	9
955-959	Edwy (the Fair)	18	3
959-975	Edgar (the Peaceful)	32	16
975-978	Edward the Martyr	17	3
978-1016	Ethelred II (the Unready)	47	38
1016	Edmund II (Ironside)	2	7m
Danish Kings (House of Denmark)			
1016-35	Canute (Cnut)‡	40	19
1035-40	Harold I	23	4
1040-42	Hardecanute	24	2
West Saxon Kings (restored)			
1042-66	Edward the Confessor	61	23
1066	Harold II	45	10m
House of Normandy			
1066-87	William I (the Conqueror)‡	60	20
1087-1100	William II (Rufus)	41	12
1100-35	Henry I	67	35
1135-54	Stephen§	53	18
House of Anjou (Plantagenets)			
1154-89	Henry II	56	34
1189-99	Richard I (the Lionheart)	42	9
1199-1216	John	48	17
1216-72	Henry III	65	56
1272-1307	Edward I	68	34
1307-27	Edward II	43	19
1327-77	Edward III	64	50
1377-99	Richard II	33	22
House of Lancaster			
1399-1413	Henry IV	47	13
1413-22	Henry V	34	9
1422-61	Henry VI#	49	39
House of York			
1461-83	Edward IV¶	40	21
1483	Edward V	12	2m
1483-85	Richard III	32	2
House of Tudor			
1485-1509	Henry VII	52	23
1509-47	Henry VIII	55	37
1547-53	Edward VI	15	6
1553	Jane (Lady Jane Grey)**	16	9d
1553-58	Mary I (Mary Tudor)	42	5
1558-1603	Elizabeth I	69	44
KINGS AND QUEENS OF BRITAIN			
House of Stuart			
1603-25	James I (VI of Scotland)	58	22
1625-49	Charles I	48	23
1649-60	Commonwealth††		
1660-85	Charles II	54	24
1685-88	James II	67	3
Interregnum 11 December 1688 to 12 February 1689			
1689-1702	William III	51	13
[and to 1694	Mary II	32	5]
1702-14	Anne	49	12
House of Hanover			
1714-27	George I (Elector of Hanover)	67	13
1727-60	George II	76	33
1760-1820	George III	81	59
1820-30	George IV	67	10
1830-37	William IV	71	7
1837-1901	Victoria	81	63
House of Saxe-Coburg-Gotha			
1901-1910	Edward VII	68	9
House of Windsor ‡‡			
1910-36	George V	70	25
1936	Edward VIII§§	77	10m
1936-52	George VI	56	15
1952-	Elizabeth II	—	—

** On death † Duration of reign in years (m = months, d=days) ‡ Became ruler by conquest § Son of William's daughter Adele and Stephen, Count of Blois; sometimes given as the monarch of the House of Blois # Deposed March 1461, restored October 1470, deposed April 1471, and killed in Tower of London May 1471 ¶ Acceded March 1461, deposed October 1470, restored April 1471 ** Edward was forced to name Lady Jane as his successor and a Council of State proclaimed her Queen; Mary, proclaimed Queen by the Council, had Jane beheaded in 1554 †† 1649-53 Council of State; 1653-58 Oliver Cromwell, Lord Protector; 1658-60 Richard Cromwell (son), Lord Protector ‡‡ Name changed from the German Saxe-Coburg-Gotha on 17 July 1917 (during World War 1) §§ Abdicated at the age of 42*

KINGS AND QUEENS OF SCOTLAND

Years	Monarch	Age*	R'd†
1016-1034	Malcolm II	*c.*80	18
1034-40	Duncan I	5	
1040-57	Macbeth	*c.*52	17
1057-58	Lulach	*c.*26	7m
1058-93	Malcom III (Canmore)	*c.*62	35
1093-97	Donald III Ban‡		3
1094	Duncan II	*c.*34	6m
1097-1107	Edgar	*c.*32	9
1107-24	Alexander I (the Fierce)	*c.*47	17
1124-53	David I	*c.*68	29
1153-65	Malcolm IV (the Maiden)	*c.*24	12
1165-1214	William I (the Lion)	*c.*72	49
1214-49	Alexander II	50	34
1249-86	Alexander III	44	36
1286-90	Margaret of Norway	7	3
The House of Balliol			
1292-96	John (Balliol)§	c.63	3
The House of Bruce			
1306-29	Robert I (the Bruce)	54	23
1329-71	David II#	46	41
The House of Stewart			
1371-90	Robert II	74	19
1390-1406	Robert III	*c.*69	16
1406-37	James I	42	30
1437-60	James II	29	23
1460-88	James III	36	27
1488-1513	James IV	40	25
1513-42	James V	30	29
1542-67	Mary, Queen of Scots**	45	24
1567-1625	James VI††	58	57

** On death † Duration of reign in years (m = months) ‡ Deposed May 1094, restored November 1097, deposed October 1097 § abdicated aged 46 # Edward Balliol, son of John, crowned king September 1332, expelled December 1332; restored 1333-36 ** abdicated 1567, prisoner of Elizabeth I from 1568, executed 1587 †† succeeded to the English throne as James I in 1603*

UK PRIME MINISTERS

Years	Prime Minister	Party
1721-42	Sir Robert Walpole	Whig
1742-43	Earl of Wilmington	Whig
1743-54	Henry Pelham	Whig
1754-56	Duke of Newcastle	Whig
1756-57	Duke of Devonshire	Whig
1757-62	Duke of Newcastle	Whig
1762-63	Earl of Bute	Tory
1763-65	George Grenville	Whig
1765-66	Marquis of Rockingham	Whig
1766-67	Earl of Chatham*	Whig
1767-70	Duke of Grafton	Whig
1770-82	Lord North	Tory
1782	Marquis of Rockingham	Whig
1782-83	Earl of Shelburne	Whig
1783	Duke of Portland	Coalition
1783-1801	William Pitt†	Tory
1801-04	Henry Addington	Tory
1804-06	William Pitt†	Tory
1806-07	Lord Grenville	Whig
1807-09	Duke of Portland	Coalition
1809-12	Spencer Perceval	Tory
1812-27	Earl of Liverpool	Tory
1827	George Canning	Tory
1827-28	Viscount Goderich	Tory
1828-30	Duke of Wellington	Tory
1830-34	Earl Grey	Whig
1834	Viscount Melbourne	Whig
1834-35	Sir Robert Peel	Tory
1835-41	Viscount Melbourne	Whig
1841-46	Sir Robert Peel	Conservative
1846-52	Lord John Russell‡	Whig
1852	Earl of Derby	Conservative
1852-55	Earl of Aberdeen	Peelite
1855-58	Viscount Palmerston	Liberal
1858-59	Earl of Derby	Conservative
1859-65	Viscount Palmerston	Liberal
1865-66	Earl Russell‡	Liberal
1866-68	Earl of Derby	Conservative
1868	Benjamin Disraeli	Conservative
1868-74	William Gladstone	Liberal
1874-80	Benjamin Disraeli	Conservative
1880-85	William Gladstone	Liberal
1885-86	Marquis of Salisbury	Conservative
1886	William Gladstone	Liberal
1886-92	Marquis of Salisbury	Conservative
1892-94	William Gladstone	Liberal
1894-95	Earl of Rosebery	Liberal
1895-1902	Marquis of Salisbury	Conservative
1902-05	Arthur Balfour	Conservative
1905-08	Henry Campbell-Bannerman	Liberal
1908-15	Herbert Asquith	Liberal
1915-16	Herbert Asquith	Coalition§
1916-22	David Lloyd George	Coalition§
1922-23	Andrew Bonar Law	Conservative
1923-24	Stanley Baldwin	Conservative
1924	Ramsay MacDonald	Labour
1924-29	Stanley Baldwin	Conservative
1929-31	Ramsay MacDonald	Labour
1931-35	Ramsay MacDonald	National#
1935-37	Stanley Baldwin	National#
1937-40	Neville Chamberlain	National#
1940-45	Winston Churchill	Coalition
1945-51	Clement Attlee	Labour
1951-55	Winston Churchill	Conservative
1955-57	Anthony Eden	Conservative
1957-63	Harold Macmillan	Conservative
1963-64	Alec Douglas-Home	Conservative
1964-70	Harold Wilson	Labour
1970-74	Edward Heath	Conservative
1974-76	Harold Wilson	Labour
1976-79	James Callaghan	Labour
1979-90	Margaret Thatcher	Conservative
1990-97	John Major	Conservative
1997-	Tony Blair	Labour

** William Pitt (the Elder) † William Pitt (the Younger) ‡ Lord John Russell later became the Earl Russell*
§ Coalition governments; Lloyd George was Liberal # National Coalition governments; Chamberlain was a Conservative

US PRESIDENTS

No.	President	Years	Party	Age*
1.	George Washington	1789-97	Federalist	57
2.	John Adams	1797-1801	Federalist	61
3.	Thomas Jefferson	1801-09	Dem-Rep	57
4.	James Madison	1809-17	Dem-Rep	57
5.	James Monroe	1817-25	Dem-Rep	58
6.	John Quincy Adams	1825-29	Dem-Rep	57
7.	Andrew Jackson	1829-37	Democrat	61
8.	Martin Van Buren	1837-41	Democrat	54
9.	William H. Harrison†	1841	Whig	68
10.	John Tyler	1841-45	Whig	51
11.	James K. Polk	1845-49	Democrat	49
12.	Zachary Taylor†	1849-50	Whig	64
13.	Millard Fillmore	1850-53	Whig	50
14.	Franklin Pierce	1853-57	Democrat	48
15.	James Buchanan	1857-61	Democrat	65
16.	Abraham Lincoln‡	1861-65	Republican	52
17.	Andrew Johnson§	1865-69	Nat. Union	56
18.	Ulysses S. Grant#	1869-77	Republican	46
19.	Rutherford B. Hayes	1877-81	Republican	54
20.	James A. Garfield‡	1881	Republican	49
21.	Chester A. Arthur	1881-85	Republican	51
22.	Grover Cleveland	1885-89	Democrat	47
23.	Benjamin Harrison	1889-93	Republican	55
24.	Grover Cleveland	1893-97	Democrat	55
25.	William McKinley‡	1897-1901	Republican	54
26.	Theodore Roosevelt	1901-09	Republican	43
27.	William H. Taft	1909-13	Republican	51
28.	Woodrow Wilson	1913-21	Democrat	56
29.	Warren Harding†	1921-23	Republican	55
30.	Calvin Coolidge	1923-29	Republican	51
31.	Herbert Hoover	1929-33	Republican	54
32.	Franklin D. Roosevelt†	1933-45	Democrat	51
33.	Harry S. Truman	1945-53	Democrat	60
34.	Dwight D. Eisenhower	1953-61	Republican	62
35.	John F. Kennedy‡	1961-63	Democrat	43
36.	Lyndon Johnson	1963-69	Democrat	55
37.	Richard Nixon¶	1969-74	Republican	56
38.	Gerald Ford**	1974-77	Republican	61
39.	Jimmy Carter	1977-81	Democrat	52
40.	Ronald Reagan	1981-89	Republican	69
41.	George Bush	1989-93	Republican	64
42.	Bill Clinton	1993-	Democrat	46

** At inauguration; Kennedy was the youngest, Reagan the oldest † Died in office and succeeded by the vice president ‡ Assassinated in office and succeeded by the vice president § A Democrat, Johnson was nominated vice president by Republicans and elected with Lincoln on a National Union ticket # Born Hiram Grant ¶ Resigned in face of impeachment proceedings following the Watergate affair ** Born Leslie Lynch King*

CANADIAN PRIME MINISTERS

Years	Prime Minister	Party
1867-73	John Macdonald	Conservative*
1873-78	Alexander Mackenzie	Liberal
1878-91	John Macdonald	Conservative
1891-92	John Abbott	Conservative
1892-94	John Thompson	Conservative
1894-96	Mackenzie Bowell	Conservative
1896	Charles Tupper	Conservative
1896-1911	Wilfrid Laurier	Liberal
1911-17	Sir Robert Borden	Conservative
1917-20	Sir Robert Borden	Unionist†
1920-21	Arthur Meighen	Conservative
1921-26	William Lyon Mackenzie King	Liberal
1926	Arthur Meighen	Conservative
1926-30	William Lyon Mackenzie King	Liberal
1930-35	Richard Bennett	Conservative
1935-48	William Lyon Mackenzie King	Liberal
1948-57	Louis Saint Laurent	Liberal
1957-63	John Diefenbaker	Conservative
1963-68	Lester Pearson	Liberal
1968-79	Pierre Trudeau	Liberal
1979-80	Joe Clark	Conservative
1980-84	Pierre Trudeau	Liberal
1984	John Turner	Liberal
1984-93	Brian Mulroney	Conservative
1993	Kim Campbell	Conservative
1993-	Jean Chrétien	Liberal

** Originally called Liberal-Conservative Party; informally became Conservative Party; renamed Progressive Conservative Party in 1942*
† National Liberal and Conservative

UN SECRETARIES GENERAL

Secretary General	Country	Tenure
Trygve Lie	Norway	1946-53
Dag Hammarskjöld	Sweden	1953-61
U Thant	Burma	1962-71
Kurt Waldheim	Austria	1971-81
Javier Pérez de Cuéllar	Peru	1982-92
Boutros Boutros Ghali	Egypt	1992-96
Kofi Annan	Ghana	1997-

FRENCH LEADERS

Years	President	Party
President of the Fifth Republic		
1958-69	Charles De Gaulle	Gaullist
1969-74	Georges Pompidou	Gaullist
1974-81	Valéry Giscard d'Estaing	UDF
1981-95	François Mitterrand	PS
1995-	Jacques Chirac	RPR
Prime Minister of the Fifth Republic		
1962-68	Georges Pompidou	Gaullist
1968-69	Maurice Couve de Murville	Gaullist
1969-72	Jacques Chaban-Delmas	Gaullist
1972-74	Pierre Mesmer	Gaullist
1974-76	Jacques Chirac	Gaullist
1976-81	Raymond Barre	—
1981-84	Pierre Mauroy	PS
1984-86	Laurent Fabius	PS
1986-88	Jacques Chirac	Gaullist
1988-91	Michel Rocard	PS
1991-92	Edith Cresson	PS
1992-93	Pierre Bérégovoy	PS
1993-95	Edouard Balladur	RPR
1995-97	Alain Juppé	RPR
1997-	Lionel Jospin	PS

UDF = Union pour la Démocratie Française
PS = Parti Socialiste
RPR = Reassemblement pour la République

SPANISH PRIME MINISTERS

Years	Prime Minister	Party
1939-73	Francisco Franco*	Falange
1973-76	Carlos Navarro	—
1976-81	Adolfo Suárez	UCD
1981-82	Leopoldo Sotelo	UCD
1982-96	Felipe González	PSOE
1996-	José María Aznar	Popular

UCD = Centre Democrat
PSOE = Socialist Workers' Party

** Franco titled himself "Chairman of the Council of Ministers" from 1936. After his death, the monarchy was restored, in the person of Juan Carlos.*

GERMAN CHANCELLORS

Years	Chancellor	Party
German Empire		
1871-90	Prince Otto von Bismarck	
1890-94	Count Leo von Caprivi	
1894-00	Prince Chlodwig von Hoh.-Schillingsfürst	
1900-09	Prince Bernhard von Bülow	
1909-17	Theobald von Bethmann-Hollweg	
1917	George Michaelis	
1917-18	Count George von Hertling	
1918	Prince Maximilian of Baden	
1918	Friedrich Ebert	
Weimar Republic		
1919	Philipp Scheidemann	SPD
1919-20	Gustav Bauer	SPD
1920	Hermann Müller	SPD
1920-21	Konstantin Fehrenbach	Centre-Catholic
1921-22	Joseph Wirth	Centre
1922-23	Wilhelm Cuno	—
1923	Gustav Stresemann	D. Volk
1923-25	Wilhelm Marx	Centre
1925-26	Hans Luther	—
1926-28	Wilhelm Marx	Centre
1928-30	Hermann Müller	SPD
1930-32	Heinrich Brüning	Centre
1932	Franz von Papen	National
1932-33	Kurt von Schleider	—
1933-45	Adolf Hitler*	Nazi
Federal German Republic		
1949-63	Konrad Adenauer	CDU
1963-66	Ludwig Erhard	CDU
1966-69	Kurt Georg Kiesinger	CDU
1969-74	Willy Brandt†	SPD
1974-82	Helmut Schmidt	SPD
1982-90	Helmut Kohl	CDU
Reunified Germany		
1990-98	Helmut Kohl	CDU
1998-	Gerhard Schröder	SPD

D. Volk = German People's Party
SPD = Social Democratic Party
CDU = Christian Democratic Union
FDP = Free Democratic Party

** Führer from 1934 to 1945 † Born Karl Herbert Frahm*

RUSSIAN AND SOVIET LEADERS

General Secretary of the Communist Party

1922-53	Joseph Stalin (b. Dzhugashvili)
1953	Georgi Malenkov
1953-64	Nikita Khrushchev
1964-82	Leonid Brezhnev
1982-84	Yuri Andropov
1984-85	Konstantin Chernenko
1985-91	Mikhail Gorbachev

President of the Russian Federation

1917	Leo Kamenev
1917-19	Yakov Sverdlov
1919-22	Mikhail Kalinin

President of the Soviet Union

1919-46	Mikhail Kalinin
1946-53	Nikolai Shvernik
1953-60	Kliment Voroshilov
1960-64	Leonid Brezhnev
1964-65	Anastas Mikoyan
1965-77	Nikolai Podgorny
1977-82	Leonid Brezhnev
1982-83	Vassili Kuznetsov
1983-84	Yuri Andropov
1984	Vassili Kuznetsov
1984-85	Konstantin Chernenko
1985	Vassili Kuznetsov
1985-88	Andrei Gromyko
1988-91	Mikhail Gorbachev†

Chairman of the Council of Ministers‡

1917	Georgy Lvov
1917	Alexander Kerensky
1917-24§	Vladimir Ilyich Lenin (b. Ulyanov)
1924-30§	Aleksei Rykov
1930-31§	Genrikh Yagoda
1931-41§	Vyacheslav Molotov
1941-53§	Joseph Stalin (b. Dzhugashvili)
1953-55	Georgi Malenkov
1955-58	Nikolai Bulganin
1958-64	Nikita Khrushchev
1964-80	Alexei Kosygin
1980-85	Nikolai Tikhonov
1985-90	Nikolai Ryzhkov
1990-91	Yuri Maslyukov
1991	Valentin Pavlov

Russian President

1991-99	Boris Yeltsin
2000-	Vladimir Putin

Russian Prime Minister

1991-98	Viktor Chernomyrdin
1998	Sergei Kiriyenko
1998-99	Yevgeni Primakov
1999	Sergei Stepashin
1999-2000	Vladimir Putin
2000-	Mikhail Kasyanov

† Executive President 1990-91 ‡ Equivalent of Prime Minister of the Soviet Union § Between 1917 and 1953 the Council of Ministers was replaced by the Council of People's Commissars

ISRAELI LEADERS

Years	Prime Minister	Party
1948-53	David Ben-Gurion	Mapai
1953-55	Moshe Sharett	Mapai
1955-63	David Ben-Gurion	Mapai
1963-69	Levi Eshkol	Mapai/Labour*
1969	Yigal Allon	Labour
1969-74	Golda Meir	Labour
1974-77	Yitzhak Rabin	Labour
1977-83	Menachem Begin	Likud
1983-84	Yitzhak Shamir	Likud
1984-86	Shimon Peres	Labour
1986-92	Yitzhak Shamir	Likud
1992-95	Yitzhak Rabin†	Labour
1995-96	Shimon Peres	Labour
1996-99	Binyamin Netanyahu	Likud
1999-	Ehud Barak	Labour

** In 1968 Mapai merged with two smaller social-democratic parties to form the Labour Party † Assassinated*

Years	President
1948-52	Chaim Weizmann
1952-63	Itzhak Ben-zvi
1963-73	Zalman Shazar
1973-78	Ephraim Katzir
1978-83	Yitzhak Navon
1983-93	Chaim Herzog
1993-	Ezer Weizman

IRISH LEADERS (REPUBLIC)

Years	Prime Minister	Party
1919-22	Eamon De Valera	Sinn Féin
1922	Arthur Griffith	Sinn Féin
1922	Michael Collins	Sinn Féin
1922-32	William Cosgrave	Fine Gael
1932-48	Eamon De Valera	Fianna Fáil
1948-51	John Costello	Fine Gael
1951-54	Eamon De Valera	Fianna Fáil
1954-57	John Costello	Fine Gael
1957-59	Eamon De Valera	Fianna Fáil
1959-66	Sean Lemass	Fianna Fáil
1966-73	Jack Lynch	Fianna Fáil
1973-79	Liam Cosgrave	Fine Gael
1977-79	Jack Lynch	Fianna Fáil
1979-81	Charles Haughey	Fianna Fáil
1981-82	Garret FitzGerald	Fine Gael
1982	Charles Haughey	Fianna Fáil
1982-87	Garrett FitzGerald	Fine Gael
1987-92	Charles Haughey	Fianna Fáil
1992-94	Albert Reynolds	Fianna Fáil
1994-97	John Bruton	Fine Gael
1997-	Bertie Ahern	Fianna Fáil

Years	President
1938-45	Douglas Hyde
1945-59	Sean O'Kelly
1959-73	Eamon De Valera
1973-74	Erskine Childers
1974-76	Carroll Daly
1976-90	Patrick Hillery
1990-97	Mary Robinson
1997-	Mary McAleese

AUSTRALIAN PRIME MINISTERS

Years	Prime Minister	Party
1900-03	Edmund Barton	Protectionist
1903-04	Alfred Deakin	Protectionist
1904	John Watson	Labor
1904-05	George Reid	Free Trade
1905-08	Alfred Deakin	Protectionist
1908-09	Andrew Fisher	Labor
1909-10	Alfred Deakin	Fusion*
1910-13	Andrew Fisher	Labor
1913-14	Joseph Cook	Liberal
1914-15	Andrew Fisher	Labor
1915-17	William Hughes	National Labor
1917-23	William Hughes	Nationalist
1923-29	Stanley Bruce	Nationalist
1929-32	James Scullin	Labor
1932-39	Joseph Lyons	United Australia†
1939	Earle Page	Country
1939-41	Robert Menzies	United Australia†
1941	Arthur Fadden	Country
1941-45	John Curtin	Labor
1945	Francis Forde	Labor
1945-49	Joseph Chifley	Labor
1949-66	Robert Menzies	Liberal
1966-67	Harold Holt	Liberal
1967-68	John McEwen	Country
1968-71	John Gorton	Liberal
1971-72	William McMahon	Liberal
1972-75	Gough Whitlam	Labor
1975-83	Malcolm Fraser	Liberal
1983-91	Bob Hawke	Labor
1991-96	Paul Keating	Labor
1996-	John Howard	Liberal-National‡

** Protectionist-Free Trade Alliance*
† Became the Liberal Party in 1944 ‡ Coalition

EGYPTIAN PRESIDENTS

Years	President
1954-70	Gamal Abdel Nasser
1970-81	Muhammad Anwar al-Sadat*
1981-	Hosni Mubarak

** Assassinated*

INDONESIAN PRESIDENTS

Years	President
1949-66	Muhammad Ahmed Sukarno*
1966-98	Raden Suharto
1998-1999	B.J. Habibie
1999-	Abdurrahman Wahid

** Sukarno was also president of pre-Republican Indonesia 1945-49, and prime minister (a position abolished in 1966) from 1959 to 1963*

CHINESE LEADERS

Chairman of the Communist Party

1935-76	Mao Zedong (Mao Tse-tung)
1976-81	Hua Guofeng (Huo Kuo-feng)
1981-82	Hu Yaobang (Hu Yao-pang)

General Secretary of the Communist Party

1982-87	Hu Yaobang
1987-89	Zhao Ziyang (Chao Tzu-yang)
1989-	Jiang Zemin (Chiang Tse-min)

President

1949-59	Mao Zedong
1959-68	Liu Shaoqi (Liu Shao-ch'i)
1968-75	Dong Biwu (Tung Pi-wu)
1975-76	Zhu De (Chu Te)
1976-78	Song Qingling (Sung Ch'ing-ling)
1978-83	Ye Jianying (Yeh Chien-ying)
1983-88	Li Xiannian (Li Hsien-nien)
1988-93	Yang Shangkun (Yang Shang-k'un)
1993-	Jiang Zemin

Prime Minister

1949-76	Zhou Enlai (Chou En-lai)
1976-80	Hua Guofeng
1980-87	Zhao Ziyang
1987-98	Li Peng (Li P'eng)
1998-	Zhu Rongji

From 1978 to 1997, effective control of China was in the hands of "paramount leader" Deng Xiaoping (Teng Hsiao-ping). He was succeeded by Jiang Zemin.

SOUTH AFRICAN LEADERS

Until the Republic of South Africa left the Commonwealth in 1961 the governor general performed the role of president, and until 1984, when the prime ministership was abolished, the presidential function remained largely non-political.

Years	Prime Minister	Party
1910-19	Louis Botha	South African Party
1919-24	Jan Christiaan Smuts	South African Party
1924-39	James Hertzog	National
1939-48	Jan Christiaan Smuts	United
1949-54	Daniel Malan	National
1954-58	Johannes Strijdom	National
1958-66	Hendrik Verwoerd	National
1966-78	Johannes Vorster	National
1978-84	P.W. Botha	National

Years	President	
1984-89	P.W. Botha	National
1989-94	F.W. de Klerk	National
1994-99	Nelson Mandela	ANC
1999-	Thabo Mbeki	ANC

ANC = African National Congress

INDIAN PRIME MINISTERS

Years	Prime Minister	Government
1947-64	Jawaharlal Nehru	Congress
1964	Gulzari Lal Nanda	Congress
1964-66	Lal Shastri	Congress
1966	Gulzari Lal Nanda	Congress
1966-77	Indira Gandhi	Congress
1977-79	Morarji Desai	Janata
1979-80	Charan Singh	Coalition
1980-84	Indira Gandhi	Congress (I)
1984-89	Rajiv Gandhi	Congress (I)
1989-90	V.P. Singh	Coalition
1990-91	Chandra Shekhar	Janata
1991-96	P.V. Narasimha Rao	Congress (I)
1996-97	H.D. Deve Gowda	Coalition
1997-98	Inder Kumar Gujral	Coalition
1998-	Atal Bihari Vajpayee	Coalition

EUROPEAN COMMISSION PRESIDENTS

Years	President	Country
1958-66	Walter Hallstein	West Germany
1966-70	Jean Rey	Belgium
1970-72	Franco Malfatti	Italy
1972-73	Sicco Mansholt	Netherlands
1973-77	François Xavier-Ortol	France
1977-81	Roy Jenkins	UK
1981-85	Gaston Thorn	Luxembourg
1985-95	Jacques Delors	France
1995-99	Jacques Santer	Luxembourg
1999-	Romano Prodi	Italy

EUROPEAN UNION MEMBERS

	Area sq km	Area sq mi	Pop'n ('000)	Date of joining	European commissioners (1997)	Members in European Parliament
Austria	83,850	32,374	7,796	1995	1	21
Belgium*	30,510	11,780	10,131	1957	1	25
Denmark†	43,070	16,629	5,216	1973	1	16
Finland	338,130	130,552	5,099	1995	1	16
France*	551,500	212,934	57,800	1957	2	87
Germany*	356,910	137,803	81,338	1957	2	99
Greece	131,990	50,961	10,400	1981	1	25
Ireland	70,280	27,135	3,560	1973	1	15
Italy*	301,270	116,320	56,930	1957	2§	87
Luxembourg*	2,590	1,000	407	1957	1	6
Netherlands*	41,526	16,033	15,424	1957	1	31
Portugal	92,390	35,670	9,902	1986	1	25
Spain	504,780	194,896	39,190	1986	2	64‡
Sweden	449,960	173,730	8,816	1995	1	22
UK	243,368	94,202	58,784	1973	2	87
					20	626

Applications for membership

Turkey (1987), Cyprus, Malta (1990), Switzerland# (1992), Hungary, Poland (1994), Bulgaria, Estonia, Latvia, Lithuania, Romania, Slovakia (1995), Czech Republic, Slovenia (1996)

** Founder member of the European Economic Community (following the Treaty of Rome, signed 25 March 1957) † Greenland exercised its autonomous right granted under the Danish Crown to secede from the Community in 1985 ‡ Includes the president of the European Parliament, José Maria Gil-Delgado § Includes the president of the European Union, Romano Prodi # In a subsequent referendum the people of Switzerland voted against joining the European Economic Area*

NEW ZEALAND PRIME MINISTERS

Years	Prime Minister	Party
1893-1906	Richard Seddon	Liberal
1906-07	William Hall-Jones	Liberal
1906-12	Joseph Ward	Liberal/National
1912	Thomas Mackenzie	National
1912-25	William Massey	Reform
1925	Francis Bell	Reform
1925-28	Joseph Coates	Reform
1928-30	Joseph Ward	Liberal/National
1930-35	George Forbes	United
1935-40	Michael Savage	Labour
1940-49	Peter Fraser	Labour
1949-57	Sidney Holland	National
1957	Keith Holyoake	National
1957-60	Walter Nash	Labour
1960-72	Keith Holyoake	National
1972	John Marshall	National
1972-74	Norman Kirk	Labour
1974	Hugh Watt *	Labour
1974-75	Wallace Rowling	Labour
1975-84	Robert Muldoon	National
1984-89	David Lange	Labour
1989-90	Geoffrey Palmer	Labour
1990	Michael Moore	Labour
1990-96	Jim Bolger	National
1997-99	Jenny Shipley	National
1999-	Helen Clark	Labour

** acting prime minister*

PAKISTANI LEADERS

Years	Prime Minister
1947-51	Liaquat Ali Khan
1951-53	Khawaja Nazimuddin
1953-55	Muhammad Ali
1955-56	Chawdry Muhammad Ali
1956-57	Hussein Shahid Suhrawardi
1957	Ismail Chundrigar
1957-58	Mailk Feroz Khan Noon
1958	Muhammad Ayub Khan
1958-73	no prime minister
1973-77	Zulfikar Ali Bhutto
1977-85	no prime minister
1985-88	Muhammad Khan Junejo
1988	Muhammad Aslam Khan Khattak
1988-90	Benazir Bhutto
1990	Mustafa Jatoi
1990-93	Nawaz Sharif
1993-96	Benazir Bhutto
1996-99	Nawaz Sharif
1999-	Pervez Musharraf

Years	President
1956-58	Iskander Mirza
1958-69	Muhammad Ayub Khan
1969-71	Agha Muhammad Yahya Khan
1971-73	Zulfikar Ali Bhutto
1973-78	Fazal Elahi Chawdry
1978-88	Muhammad Zia-ul-Haq
1988-93	Ghulam Ishaq Khan
1993-97	Farouk Ahmed Leghari
1997-	Muhammad Rafiq Tarar

MAJOR ESTABLISHED RELIGIONS

The figures are estimates, based primarily on UN reports and statistics released by most of the religious bodies. The table does not include the various folk and tribal religions of Africa and Asia, which could total as many as 300 million adherents, including more than 10 million Shamanists.

Religion	Millions	Religion	Millions
Christianity	1780	Confucianism*	350
Roman Catholic	1010	Buddhism *†	320
Protestant	365	Taoism*	25
Orthodox	175	Sikhism	19
Anglican	75	Judaism	18
Islam	1050	Baha'ism	5.9
Sunni	960	Jainism	3.8
Shia (Shiite)	90	Shintoism†	3.5
Hinduism	720		

** The number of practising Confucians, Buddhists and Taoists in China cannot be accurately estimated; there are c.6 million Confucians outside China † Many people in the Far East, notably in Japan, claim to adhere to more than one religion and figures are therefore only approximate at best*

MAJOR LANGUAGES

There are more than 5000 languages in the world, 845 of them in India alone. The tables below give the approximate numbers of native speakers (their "mother tongue") and the populations of countries where the language has official status.

Language	Millions	Language	Millions
Native speakers		Korean	70
Chinese	1070	Tamil	68
English	487	Marathi	67
Hindi	382	Vietnamese	62
Spanish	363		
Bengali	203	**Official populations**	
Arabic	188	English	1420
Portuguese	187	Chinese	1070
Japanese	126	Hindi	800
German	119	Spanish	290
Urdu	96	Russian	275
Punjabi	89	French	220
Javanese	77	Arabic	190
French	73	Portuguese	185
Telugu	72	Malay	165

WORLD POPULATION

Date	Millions	Date	Millions	Date	Millions
2000BC	100	1800	900	1970	3700
1000BC	120	1850	1250	1980	4450
1	180	1900	1620	1990	5245
1000	275	1920	1860	1995	5735
1250	375	1930	2070	2000*	6100
1500	420	1940	2300	2050*	11,000
1650	500	1950	2500		
1700	615	1960	3050		

** United Nations "medium" estimates*

NOBEL PEACE PRIZE

Year	Winner(s)
1901	Henri Dunant (Switzerland) and Frederick Passy (France)
1902	Elie Ducommun and Albert Gobat (Switzerland)
1903	Sir William R. Cremer (UK)
1904	Institut de Droit International (Belgium)*
1905	Bertha von Suttner (Austria)
1906	Theodore Roosevelt (USA)
1907	Ernesto T. Moneta (Italy) and Louis Renault (France)
1908	Klas P. Arnoldson (Sweden) and Frederik Bajer (Denmark)
1909	Auguste M. F. Beernaert (Belgium) and Baron Paul H B B d'Estournelles de Constant de Rebecque (France)
1910	Bureau International Permanent de la Paix (Switzerland)*
1911	Tobias M. C. Asser (Netherlands) and Alfred H Fried (Austria)
1912	Elihu Root (USA)
1913	Henri La Fontaine (Belgium)
1917	International Red Cross*
1919	Woodrow Wilson (USA)
1920	Leon Bourgeois (France)
1921	Karl H. Branting (Sweden) and Christian L. Lange (Norway)
1922	Fridtjof Nansen (Norway)
1925	Sir Austen Chamberlain (UK) and Charles G. Dawes (USA)
1926	Aristide Briand (France) and Gustav Stresemann (Germany)
1927	Ferdinand Buisson (France) and Ludwig Quidde (Germany)
1929	Frank B. Kellogg (USA)
1930	Lars O. J. Soderblom (Sweden)
1931	Jane Addams and Nicholas M. Butler (USA)
1933	Sir Norman Angell (UK)
1934	Arthur Henderson (UK)
1935	Karl von Ossietzky (Germany)
1936	Carlos de S. Lamas (Argentina)
1937	Lord Cecil of Chelwood (UK)
1938	Office International Nansen pour les Refugies (Switzerland)*
1944	International Red Cross*
1945	Cordell Hull (USA)
1946	Emily G. Balch and John R. Mott (USA)
1947	American Friends Service Committee (USA) and British Society of Friends' Service Council (UK)*
1949	Lord John Boyd Orr (Scotland)
1950	Ralph J. Bunche (USA)
1951	Leon Jouhaux (France)
1952	Albert Schweitzer (French Equatorial Africa)
1953	George C. Marshall (USA)
1954	Office of UN High Commissioner for Refugees*
1957	Lester B. Pearson (Canada)
1958	Rev. Dominique Georges Henri Pire (Belgium)
1959	Philip John Noel-Baker (UK)
1960	Albert John Luthuli (South Africa)
1961	Dag Hammarskjöld (Sweden)
1962	Linus Pauling (USA)
1963	International Committee of Red Cross; League of Red Cross Societies (both Geneva)*
1964	Rev. Dr Martin Luther King, Jr (USA)
1965	UNICEF (United Nations Children's Fund)
1968	Rene Cassin (France)
1969	International Labour Organization*
1970	Norman E. Borlaug (USA)
1971	Willy Brandt (West Germany)
1973	Henry A. Kissinger (USA) and Le Duc Tho‡ (North Vietnam)
1974	Eisaku Sato (Japan) and Sean MacBride (Ireland)
1975	Andrei D. Sakharov (Soviet Union)
1975	Andrei Sakharov (Soviet Union)
1976	Mairead Corrigan and Betty Williams (UK)§
1977	Amnesty International*
1978	Menachem Begin (Israel) and Anwar Sadat (Egypt)
1979	Mother Teresa of Calcutta (Macedonia-India)
1980	Adolfo Pérez Esquivel (Argentinia)
1981	Office of UN High Commissioner for Refugees*
1982	Alva Myrdal (Swedish) and Alfonso Robles (Mexico)
1983	Lech Walesa (Poland)
1984	Archbishop Desmond Tutu (South Africa)
1985	International Physicians for the Prevention of Nuclear War*
1986	Elie Wiesel (USA)
1987	Oscar Arias Sánchez (Costa Rica)
1988	United Nations peacekeeping forces*
1989	Dalai Lama (Tibet)
1990	Mikhail Gorbachev (Soviet Union)
1991	Aung San Suu Kyi (Burma)
1992	Rigoberta Menchú (Guatemala)
1993	F.W. de Klerk and Nelson Mandela (South Africa)
1994	Yasser Arafat (Palestine), Shimon Peres and Yitzhak Rabin (Israel)
1995	Joseph Rotblat (UK)
1996	Bishop Belo and José Ramos Horta (East Timor)
1997	International Campaign to Ban Landmines & Jody Williams (USA)*
1998	John Hume and David Trimble (UK)§
1999	Médecins sans Frontières*

** Prize awarded to organization rather than to individual(s) ‡ Le Duc Tho (Vietnam) declined § Northern Ireland*